The Norton Anthology
of English Literature

FIFTH EDITION
VOLUME 1

E. Talbot Donaldson
LATE OF INDIANA UNIVERSITY

Alfred David
PROFESSOR OF ENGLISH, INDIANA UNIVERSITY

Hallett Smith
SENIOR RESEARCH FELLOW, HUNTINGTON LIBRARY

Barbara K. Lewalski
WILLIAM R. KENAN PROFESSOR OF ENGLISH AND OF HISTORY
AND LITERATURE, HARVARD UNIVERSITY

Robert M. Adams
PROFESSOR OF ENGLISH EMERITUS,
UNIVERSITY OF CALIFORNIA AT LOS ANGELES

George M. Logan
PROFESSOR OF ENGLISH, QUEEN'S UNIVERSITY

Samuel Holt Monk
LATE OF THE UNIVERSITY OF MINNESOTA

Lawrence Lipking
PROFESSOR OF ENGLISH AND CHESTER D. TRIPP PROFESSOR OF THE
HUMANITIES, NORTHWESTERN UNIVERSITY

Jack Stillinger
PROFESSOR OF ENGLISH, UNIVERSITY OF ILLINOIS

George H. Ford
JOSEPH H. GILMORE PROFESSOR OF ENGLISH EMERITUS,
UNIVERSITY OF ROCHESTER

Carol T. Christ
PROFESSOR OF ENGLISH, UNIVERSITY OF CALIFORNIA AT BERKELEY

David Daiches
DIRECTOR OF THE INSTITUTE FOR ADVANCED STUDIES,
UNIVERSITY OF EDINBURGH

Jon Stallworthy
PROFESSORIAL FELLOW OF WOLFSON COLLEGE AND
READER IN ENGLISH LITERATURE, OXFORD UNIVERSITY

The Norton Anthology
of English Literature

FIFTH EDITION
VOLUME 1

M. H. Abrams, *General Editor*

CLASS OF 1916 PROFESSOR OF ENGLISH EMERITUS,
CORNELL UNIVERSITY

W · W · NORTON & COMPANY · *New York* · *London*

Published simultaneously in Canada by Penguin Books Canada Ltd, 2801 John
Street, Markham, Ontario L3R 1B4
Printed in the United States of America

The text of this book is composed in Electra, with display type set in Bernhard Modern. Composition by Vail-Ballou. Manufacturing by R. R. Donnelley. Book design
by Antonina Krass.

Since this page cannot legibly accommodate all the copyright notices, pages 2602–
2603 constitute an extension of the copyright page.

Library of Congress Cataloging-in-Publication Data
Main entry under title:
The Norton anthology of English literature.
Includes bibliographies and indexes.
1. English literature.   I. Abrams, M. H. (Meyer
Howard), 1912–
PR1109.N6   1986   820'.8   85-25860

ISBN 0-393-95469-2

ISBN 0-393-95476-5 pbk.

W. W. Norton & Company Inc., 500 Fifth Avenue, New York, N.Y. 10110
W. W. Norton & Company Ltd., 10 Coptic Street, London WC1A 1PU

5 6 7 8 9 0

Contents

The Restoration and the Eighteenth
Century (1660–1798)

Preface
to the Fifth Edition

The aim of this anthology, as in the original edition, is to make available, for the indispensable courses that introduce students to the excellence and variety of English literature, the major works in prose and verse from *Beowulf* to the present, in accurate and readable texts, edited so as to make them readily accessible to students. A vital literary culture, however, never stands still. The policy, therefore, has been to provide periodic revisions designed to take advantage of newly recovered or better edited texts, to stay in touch with scholarly discoveries, new developments in criticism, and the altering interests of readers, and to keep the anthology within the mainstream of contemporary cultural and intellectual concerns.

Two developments have expedited improvements in this fifth edition. First, we have enlarged our staff of editors with a younger generation of men and women who have worked in close collaboration with the earlier editors in devising the present volumes. In addition, the entire anthology has been redesigned and reset in a more readable type, so that it has been much easier than in earlier revisions to introduce extensive changes in the texts and editorial materials. One important result of these developments is that all the introductions, headnotes, and footnotes have been reconsidered and revised, and some of them totally rewritten. The strength of this collection nonetheless remains what it has always been, in that it is designed by editors who have had long experience in teaching an introduction to English literature, many of whom (including the general editor) test each new edition by using it in the classroom. We continue to profit from the steady flow of voluntary suggestions by teachers and students who view the anthology with a loyal yet critical eye. And we have again solicited detailed assessments of the works represented, suggestions for desirable additions, and proposals for improvements in the editorial matter, from close to one hundred critics, most of them teachers who use the book in a course. *The Norton Anthology of English Literature*, in its evolution, has thus been the product of an ongoing collaboration among editors, scholars, teachers, and students.

The changes in this edition are in accord with the criteria announced in the original edition: (1) that the works selected make possible a study in depth of the diverse achievements by the major English writers in prose and verse, in the context of the chief literary types and traditions of each age; (2) that these works be so far as feasible complete, and also abundant enough to allow instructors to choose from the total those that each one prefers to teach; (3) that the student be provided the most reliable texts available, edited so as to expedite understanding, in a format that is easy to the hand and inviting to the eye; (4) that introductions, glosses, and supplementary materials be adequate to free the student from dependence on a reference library, so that the anthology may be read anywhere—in the student's room, in a coffee lounge, on a bus, or under a tree; (5) that each volume, in size and weight, be comfortably portable, for if students won't carry the book to class, lectures are lamed and discussions made profitless.

Some texts which, as our canvass of teachers revealed, are assigned infrequently or not at all have been dropped from this edition, in order to provide space for new selections, or else to allow us to supplement or to complete works hitherto represented by more limited excerpts. Most of the additions are in response to numerous requests; a few of them, as veteran users of the anthology will recognize, are works which had been dropped from preceding editions but are reintroduced here because widespread demand has demonstrated that we made a mistake in doing so. An overview of the more important innovations may help the teacher to appraise the opportunities that this revised edition provides.

The Middle Ages. The prose translation of the complete *Beowulf* by E. Talbot Donaldson, acclaimed for its accuracy and verve, has been supplemented by a translation in verse by Alfred David of the poignant *Last Survivor's Speech*, side by side with the text in Old English, to give the student a sense of the strong beat and emphatic alliteration of the original versification. *Cædmon's Hymn*, in both Old and Modern English, is now presented in its original context, the life of Cædmon as narrated by Bede in his *Ecclesiastical History*, translated from the Latin by our medieval editors. Added to the selections from *The Canterbury Tales* is Chaucer's rollicking parody of the stock romances of his time, *The Tale of Sir Thopas*. *Piers Plowman*, the greatest medieval poem after the works of Chaucer, has been supplemented by the complete Passus 18, *The Harrowing of Hell*, in Donaldson's fine translation. *The York Play of the Crucifixion* now augments *The Second Shepherds' Play* and *Everyman* to provide a broader representation of medieval drama. A new author, the spirited religious visionary Margery Kempe, is included, and there are additional selections, bound to be popular with students, from Malory's *Morte Darthur*.

The Sixteenth Century. On the advice of many users, who preferred to make their own choice of a second Shakespeare play in addition to *1 Henry IV*, *King Lear* has been dropped to make room for many important additions to the writings of other authors in the sixteenth and early seventeenth centuries. Sir Philip Sidney's scope and excellence are now much more adequately represented by nineteen supplementary sonnets from *Astrophil and Stella* (designed to enable the student to trace the structure of a major Elizabethan sonnet sequence), by selections from his prose *Arcadia*, and by a large supplement to *The Defence of Poesy*. There are major increments also to Edmund Spenser: the addition of *Aprill* to *The Shepheardes Calender*, of two sonnets to *Amoretti*, and above all, of copious selections from book 3 (the narrative of the female warrior-knight, Britomart) to supplement the whole of book 1 of *The Faerie Queene*. The representation of each of the other major poets has been improved and extended, and writings by seven new poets have been added to the section of "Songs and Poems": a selection from Arthur Golding's influential translation of Ovid, one of the Countess of Pembroke's translated psalms, part of Sir John Davies's charming and destinctively Elizabethan *Orchestra, or a Poem of Dancing*, and poems by Queen Elizabeth, George Gascoigne, Fulke Greville, and Lady Mary Wroth.

(The selections from Golding and the Countess of Pembroke, conjoined with a newly added passage from the earl of Surrey's *Aeneid*, Hoby's *The Courtier*, and the section *Translating the Bible* now provide an extended opportunity to study the important art of translation in this period.) The section on prose has been greatly strengthened. The selections from More's *Utopia* are in a revised translation from the Latin by Robert M. Adams, and a story is added from More's English work *The History of King Richard III*; the passages from Hoby's translation of *The Courtier* now provide a fuller view of Castiglione's Neoplatonic concept of love; and there are representations of several new writers: Roger Ascham on education, Ralph Lane (from Hakluyt's *Voyages*) on the wonders of the New World, John Lyly writing the elaborately rhetorical prose of *Euphues*, and Aemilia Lanyer uttering sentiments that anticipate the viewpoint of later English feminists.

The Early Seventeenth Century. The writings of John Milton have been substantially augmented: books 1, 2, and 9 of *Paradise Lost* remain complete, while in the selections, almost 900 lines have been added from books 4, 5, and 8 to fill out the narrative of Adam and Eve before and after the Fall; in response to many requests, the early poem *On the Morning of Christ's Nativity* has been added (which may be compared with Crashaw's *On the Holy Nativity of Our Lord God*, also newly included); and Milton's prose is supplemented by autobiographical passages from his *Reason of Church Government* and added passages from *Areopagitica*. The diversity of subject matter and forms in the poetry of Andrew Marvell, George Herbert, and Robert Herrick is more fully represented, and poems by two new writers are included: Henry King's powerful *Exequy* and a selection from John Denham's *Cooper's Hill*, which served as a model both for the "local poem" of description and meditation and for the heroic couplet. Users of the anthology will find that many other writers, from Donne and Jonson through Vaughan, Carew, and Lovelace are more adequately represented by a revised selection of their poems. The prose writers are also better served, by the addition of several essays of Francis Bacon (including, for comparison, *Of Studies* in both the version of 1597 and of 1625); by the choice of more central selections from Burton, Hobbes, and Sir Thomas Browne; and by the representation of four new writers: the historian the earl of Clarendon; the radical Puritan pamphleteer John Lilburne; and the lively writers of memoirs and letters, Lady Anne Halkett and Dorothy Osborne.

The Restoration and the Eighteenth Century. William Congreve's *The Way of the World* is back by popular demand, displacing *Love for Love* which, though simpler in plot, lacks the classic status of Congreve's finest comedy of manners. And we are now able to print the full text of Samuel Johnson's great and eminently teachable *Rasselas*. There are changed selections from Pepys's *Diary* (on the great fire of London) and from Defoe (a passage from his novel *Roxana*). This last selection pairs enlighteningly with one from the "bluestocking" and feminist Mary Astell, who now joins her sister-writers of that era, Lady Mary Wortley Montagu and Anne Finch—the latter in augmented representation. There are also added poems by Matthew Prior, John Gay (songs from *The Beggar's Opera*), and James Thomson.

The Romantic Period. From the questionnaires, it is evident that many users will be pleased by the addition to Blake of his early "prophetic book," *Visions of the Daughters of Albion*, with its radical presentation of the parallels between black slavery and the sexual and social repression of women; there are also new poems from Blake's *Poetical Sketches* and *Songs of Inno-*

cence and of Experience, as well as a fourth of his letters dealing with the difference between ocular sight and imaginative vision. When in 1974 we printed Wordsworth's Two-Part Prelude of 1799, it was not available elsewhere; its ready accessibility now has made it possible to replace it by extensive additions to the final Prelude of 1850 (which, like The Ruined Cottage, is now in the text of The Cornell Wordsworth). Books 1, 2, and 12 of the Prelude are now complete, and the other books have been supplemented, not only to include the supreme passages—readily locatable, for selective assignment, by the subtitles for each excerpt that have been added to the Table of Contents—but also in order to reveal more adequately the complex design of the whole poem. (The first and second books, together with the passage on "spots of time" in book 12, incorporate almost all the material of the original Two-Part Prelude.) We have also added an expanded representation of Mary Wollstonecraft's epochal Vindication of the Rights of Woman; William Hazlitt's essay On Gusto (much requested); Charles Lamb's letter to Wordsworth (proffering his candid judgments on Lyrical Ballads and his equally candid reply, as a city man, to his friend's invitation to visit the Lake Country); Thomas Love Peacock's acerbic Four Ages of Poetry, together with an enlarged selection from Shelley's great reply, A Defence of Poetry; additional passages from Shelley's Prometheus Unbound and Byron's Don Juan; and more of the remarkable letters by Keats which illuminate his life and his intellectual and poetic development.

The Victorian Age. The three major women poets of the period, Elizabeth Barrett Browning, Emily Brontë, and Christina Rossetti, are now fully enough represented to allow them to be studied in depth (many readers will especially pleased by the addition of extensive selections from Elizabeth Browning's Aurora Leigh), and the introductions to all those writers have been newly written so as to do justice to their careers and the range of their work. There are added poems also by Tennyson, Browning, and Dante Gabriel Rossetti, as well as by Gerard Manley Hopkins, who has been moved back to the Victorian Age where chronologically, rather than by his delayed influence on other poets, he belongs.

The Twentieth Century. This section has been especially radically revised, and we feel certain, greatly improved. There are new poems by all the "major" poets and many of the other poets as well. As numerous users have urgently requested, we now include Conrad's Heart of Darkness and Joyce's The Dead. The much-praised section "Poetry of World War I" has been revised by an expert on the subject, Jon Stallworthy, and includes a new poet, May Wedderburn Cannan; there is now in addition a companion section, "Poetry of World War II," which includes four poets new to the anthology who also serve as a bridge between "modernist" and contemporary poetry. The editors have added two recent plays to Pinter's The Dumb Waiter: Samuel Beckett's haunting Happy Days and Tom Stoppard's hilarious parody of Agatha Christie, The Real Inspector Hound. George Orwell is represented by Politics and the English Language, which has achieved the status of a literary classic, and to the selections from Virginia Woolf the editors have added a passage from a posthumously published memoir, Moments of Being, which illuminates both her novels and her writings that are reprinted in the anthology. We represent contemporary short fiction by the Irishwoman Edna O'Brien and by the Englishwoman Susan Hill. The selections of poets who are still writing (including Philip Larkin, Thom Gunn, Ted Hughes, Geoffrey Hill, and especially Seamus Heaney) have been reselected and updated; to them have been added poems by contemporary writers new to the anthology: the Black Caribbean poet Derek Walcott; the working-class poet Tony Harrison; Craig Raine, inventor of the "Martian school" of poems; and the young political poet James Fenton.

It may be useful to review here some of the possibilities for teaching that are afforded by the materials included in this latest edition. It should be noted that the abundance and variety of the included texts make feasible not only a chronological approach to major writers in their literary and social contexts, but also generic or topical ways of organizing either the course as a whole, or else discussion sections and seminars within a course whose primary orientation is the sequence of writers in time.

(1) English poetry, in all its major forms and modes, is of course represented fully, and is supplemented at the end of each volume by a section of "Poems in Process" that presents in precise transcription, from manuscripts, letters, and early printed versions, the very different ways in which poets have worked their initial ideas and drafts into the final text. (A manuscript draft of D. H. Lawrence's *Piano*, startlingly different from the published product, has been added to volume 2.) "Poems in Process" may be used in special sections of a course, or else referred to when teaching any of the poems included in it; to facilitate the latter procedure, a footnote now identifies each poem in the body of the anthology for which earlier versions are made available.

(2) The augmented spectrum of plays in this edition provides an overview of English drama in its diverse forms and their evolution. There are now ten complete dramas in volume 1, ranging from three medieval plays through Marlowe, Shakespeare, Jonson, and Webster to Congreve, and including two masques: Jonson's *Pleasure Reconciled to Virtue* and Dryden's *Secular Masque*. Volume 2 now includes seven plays, from Romantic closet dramas (Byron's *Manfred* and selections from Shelley's *Prometheus Unbound*) through Wilde and Shaw to representative works by three of our contemporaries, Beckett, Pinter, and Stoppard.

(3) A trial in an earlier edition convinced us that almost no users of the anthology wanted an extensive representation of excerpts from novels. It remains possible, however, in this edition to study the development of narrative techniques and style from Sidney's *Arcadia* and Lyly's *Euphues* to the present, as well as the evolution of shorter forms of prose fiction, beginning with *Pilgrim's Progress* and ranging through the narrative papers in *The Spectator*, *Gulliver's Travels*, *Rasselas*, and a great variety of short stories by Mary Shelley, Conrad, Forster, Woolf, Joyce, Lawrence, Mansfield, Lessing, O'Brien, and Hill.

(4) The present edition continues to enlarge the representation of neglected writers who were women, as well as of writings that deal prominently with women in western culture. Literature by men that reveals the diverse social and sexual stereotypes and roles of women may now be studied in a range from "the marriage group" in the *Canterbury Tales*, Spenser's Una, Duessa, and Britomart in *The Faerie Queene*, and the Elizabethan sonneteers and playwrights, through many intervening works (e.g., Donne's poems, *Paradise Lost*, *The Rape of the Lock*, *Rasselas*, and two very different profeminist works, Blake's *Visions of the Daughters of Albion* and Shaw's *Mrs. Warren's Profession*), to a great number of poems and stories in our own century. Social and literary criticism addressed to the situation of women includes

selections from two classic works, Mary Wollstonecraft's *A Vindication of the Rights of Woman* and J. S. Mill's *The Subjection of Women*, documents by George Eliot, Florence Nightingale, and other Victorians in the section "The Woman Question," and the six selections from Virginia Woolf. Above all, the list of women poets and writers of fiction, social and literary criticism, memoirs, and letters has been greatly enlarged, to a total of ten in volume 1, from Margary Kempe to Lady Mary Wortley Montagu, and of fifteen in volume 2, from Wollstonecraft and Dorothy Wordsworth to O'Brien and Hill.

(5) Many other subjects and topics that are prominent in English literature can be profitably studied from materials in the present edition, such as the visionary mode from Chaucer, Langland, Spenser, and Bunyan through Blake, Percy and Mary Shelley, to Yeats and Dylan Thomas; and the variations of the continuing form of spiritual autobiography from Bunyan's *Grace Abounding* through Wordsworth's *Prelude* and Carlyle's *Sartor Resartus* to Eliot's *Little Gidding*. One topic of particular current interest, the imaginative response in various eras to warfare in its changing modes, may be readily surveyed in works such as *Beowulf* and *The Battle of Maldon*, the chivalric warfare in Malory and Spenser, the satiric treatment of war in book 1 of *Guilliver's Travels*, Tennyson's *Charge of the Light Brigade*, and the many poems gathered under the headings "Poetry of World War I" and "Poetry of World War II."

In each literary period the anthology presents, in the order of their birth dates, the writers in prose or verse, and the works of each author in the order of their first publication. The exceptions are instances when it has seemed more useful to group items under headings such as "Songs and Poems of the Sixteenth Century," "Romantic Lyric Poets," or "Victorian Light Verse."

In accord with our policy that students, no less than scholars, deserve the most accurate texts, we continue to introduce, as they become available, new and improved versions of the works included in the anthology. In this edition, for example, we print the revised versions of Wordsworth's *Ruined Cottage* and *Prelude* from The Cornell Wordsworth. To ease a student's access to the texts, we have normalized spelling and capitalization according to modern usage. There are, however, two large-scale exceptions: (1) We leave unaltered texts in which modernizing would change semantic, phonological, or metric qualities, or would cancel distinctive features of the original. Thus the verse of Spenser, Burns, Hopkins, MacDiarmid, and David Jones, as well as the prose of Keats's letters and of the works of Carlyle, Joyce, and Shaw, have been reproduced exactly. Only minor changes in his erratic punctuation have been made in the writings etched by William Blake. The works of Chaucer and other writers in Middle English that are not too difficult for the novice have also been reprinted in the original language; each word, however, has been spelled consistently in that form of its scribal variants which is closest to modern English. (2) We also leave unaltered texts for which we use specially edited versions, or else introduce new standard editions (identified in a headnote or footnote); these include Wollstonecraft's *Vindication*, Wordsworth's *Ruined Cottage* and *Prelude*, Dorothy Wordsworth's *Journals*, the verse and prose of Shelley and Keats, and the selections from Mary Shelley.

The paired editors for each period have reconsidered and revised (in some instances, totally) their introductory essays, headnotes, and footnotes, both in order to take advantage of recent scholarship and to make them as tersely, but adequately and clearly, informative as possible. The editors have made a special effort to minimize commentary that is interpretive rather than, in a very limited sense, explanatory. It has, however, seemed unwise to us (as to many users), in instances of an especially problematic work or passage, to eliminate any help whatever to the student. A standard teaching procedure is to assign many texts which there is no time to discuss adequately—or sometimes, to discuss at all—in the classroom. To avoid leaving the student too much at sea, what we undertake, in especially difficult instances, is to provide an essential modicum of guidance, but in such a way as to invite independent judgment and to provide no more than a point of departure for lectures or dialogue in the classroom.

We continue editorial procedures that have proved their usefulness in prior editions. The introductions to periods and authors, although succinct, are informative enough to eliminate any immediate need for supplementary books on the literary, political, and cultural history of England, or on the lives of individual authors. In most introductions we identify at the beginning a few crucial dates in order to provide a preliminary orientation to the student. After each work we cite (when known) the date of composition on the left and the date of first publication on the right; in some instances the latter is followed by the date of a revised reprinting. Texts that include a large proportion of archaic, dialectal, or unfamiliar words are glossed in the margin, so that readers may assimilate the meaning without constant interruptions to the flow of the reading. In the occasional instances when parts of a work have had to be omitted, that fact is indicated by the word *From* before the title, and the place of the omission is indicated in the text by three asterisks. If the omitted section is important for following the plot or argument, a brief summary is provided either within the text or in a footnote. In order to facilitate a teacher's discovery of what is available we also provide, when the material makes it feasible, invented titles (listed in the Table of Contents and bracketed within the text) to identify the subject matter of the passages that have been included.

The bibliographical guides at the end of each volume have been revised and brought up to date; they have been selected and annotated with the needs of students in view, both to encourage them to pursue writers and topics on their own initiative and to serve as references for assigned essays. Both volumes contain a helpful appendix on "Poetic Forms and Literary Terminology." We draw attention to two illustrations at the end of volume 1 that have proved enlightening to students—a schematic drawing of the Ptolemaic universe, and the exterior and interior of an Elizabethan theater, drawn for the anthology by C. Walter Hodges, author of *The Globe Restored*. We have added to each volume of this new edition brief appendices, prepared by Robert M. Adams, on the complex subjects of the money, the baronage, and the religious sects and church offices of England. In response to numerous requests, the editors are also preparing a Course Guide, intended not only to be helpful to teachers who for the first time undertake a course using this anthology, but also to provide veteran teachers with a medium for the exchange of ideas about diverse possibilities in the design and conduct of such a course.

The editors are deeply grateful to the hundreds of teachers, both in North America and on other continents, who have helped us to improve the fifth edition; we cannot name all of them, but each will recognize changes that he or she proposed. A list of "Acknowledgments" names advisers who prepared detailed critiques of the total anthology or of single periods, or else were of special assistance with respect to some of the editorial materials. Two of the contributing editors would like to thank their assistants, Jacqueline Doyle and Patsy Griffin, while the publishers gratefully acknowledge the valuable help of Nina Bouis, Sue Crooks, Ruth Dworkin, Diane O'Connor, Nancy Palmquist, Antonina Krass, Carol Stiles, and Rachel Teplow. As in every other edition, our greatest debt is to two members of W. W. Norton and Company, Inc.—George P. Brockway, who first conceived this anthology and participated in all stages of its evolution, and John Benedict, an incomparable editor, gadfly, collaborator, and friend. They have helped us solve, or at least mitigate, the dilemmas attendant on representing justly, accurately, and in only two volumes, the scope and variety of the English literary heritage.

M. H. Abrams

Acknowledgments

Among our many critics, advisers, and friends, the following were of especial help in providing critiques of particular periods or of the anthology as a whole, or assisted in preparing texts and editorial matter: Paul Alpers (University of California, Berkeley); Lisa Miller Barnes (Queen's University); W. J. Barnes (Queen's University); Stephen A. Barney (University of California, Irvine); David Bevington (University of Chicago); Mary Carruthers (University of Illinois at Chicago); Paul Christianson (Queen's University); R. W. Crump (Louisiana State University); Eugene R. Cunnar (New Mexico State University); Seamus Deane (University College, Dublin); Hubert English, Jr. (University of Michigan); Robert Essick (University of California, Riverside); Barbara C. Ewell (University of Mississippi); Robert D. Fulk (Indiana University); Paul Gabriner (University of Amsterdam); Nancy M. Goslee (University of Tennessee); Donald J. Gray (Indiana University); A. C. Hamilton (Queen's University); Carolyn G. Heilbrun (Columbia University); James R. Kincaid (University of Colorado, Boulder); Hugh Maclean (State University of New York at Albany); Kevin J. McManus (College of William and Mary); Juliet McMaster (University of Alberta); Phillip L. Marcus (Cornell University); Ruth Perry (Massachusetts Institute of Technology); Jonathan Post (University of California, Los Angeles); Stephen Prickett (The Australian National University); John R. Reed (Wayne State University); David G. Riede (University of Rochester); James Rieger (University of Rochester); Sue Sandera Rummel (State University of New York at Canton); Harry Rusche (Emory University); Peter Sabor (Queen's University); Daniel Schwarz (Cornell University); Ronald A. Sharp (Kenyon College); Elain Showalter (Rutgers University); Sandra Siegel (Cornell University); Pincus Silverman (El Centro College); John Tinkler (University of Sydney); and Joseph Viscomi (University of North Carolina at Chapel Hill).

The Norton Anthology of English Literature

FIFTH EDITION
VOLUME 1

The Middle Ages

to ca. 1485

ca. 450:   Anglo-Saxon Conquest.
597:           St. Augustine arrives in Kent; beginning of Anglo-Saxon conversion to Christianity.
871–899:   Reign of King Alfred.
1066:   Norman Conquest.
ca. 1200:   Beginnings of Middle English literature.
1360–1400:   The summit of Middle English literature: Geoffrey Chaucer; *Piers Plowman; Sir Gawain and the Green Knight*.
1485:   William Caxton's printing of Sir Thomas Malory's *Morte Darthur*, one of the first books printed in England.

The medieval period in English literature extends for more than 800 years, from Cædmon's *Hymn* at the end of the seventh century to *Everyman* at the beginning of the sixteenth. The date 1485 with the accession of Henry VII to the throne of England is an arbitrary but convenient one to mark the "end" of the Middle Ages. Historians used to divide this period into two parts, unfairly calling the earlier centuries the Dark Ages in order to distinguish them from the later centuries, when European culture attained one of the summits of its history. While the term is misleading—for the Dark Ages were only relatively dark—it is nevertheless true that the English Middle Ages embraced two quite different periods of literary history, the Old English (or Anglo-Saxon) and the Middle English, sharply divided from each other by the Norman duke William's conquest of the island in 1066. Both English culture and the English language changed radically in the years following this event, and English literature developed a new spirit.

Because it is impossible to read the Old English language without a great deal of study, Old English texts printed in this book are given in translation. Middle English texts such as Chaucer's, written in a dialect which is the ancestor of Modern Standard English, appear in the original, but have been spelled in a way that it is hoped will aid the reader. Middle English texts written in the more difficult regional dialects are given in translation. Analyses of the sounds and grammar of Middle English, and of Old and Middle English prosody, appear at the end of this introduction.

THE OLD ENGLISH PERIOD

THE ANGLO-SAXONS AND THE HEROIC IDEAL

The Anglo-Saxon invasion of the island of Britain which began in the first half of the fifth century was a phase of a great folk migration that had started some centuries earlier and was to continue for several more—the movement of the Germanic tribes from the northeast of Europe into the areas of the Roman Empire to the west, south, and southeast. The so-called Anglo-Saxon invaders of Britain actually consisted of three tribes, the Angles, the Saxons, and the Jutes. Although each was independent, through their common Germanic heritage these tribes were closely allied with one another and with the many other tribes that already had or would in the future overrun much of the old Roman Empire. They shared the same prehistoric ancestors; even in historical times their individual tongues amounted to little other than variant dialects of a common language, while the customs of one tribe differed little from those of another.

In its earliest period Germanic society had been organized by families: the head of the family was the chief of his close kinsmen, and the family formed an independent political entity. With the passing of time, the unit of society tended to grow larger as a number of families united under a single superior chieftain or "king," to use the word derived from the Old Germanic name for chief. But the unit grew to be very large only rarely, when some particularly successful king attracted others to him in order to perform some specific exploit; and such larger unions rarely endured long after the completion of the venture for which they had been formed. The normal order of society was made up of a number of small bands, which, while they did not always live at peace with one another, still shared a sense of community and kinship, especially in the face of a common enemy such as the people whose lands they were invading; but when they had conquered, their natural political divisiveness reasserted itself. Thus long after the Anglo-Saxons had become settled in Britain, the island was still broken up into a bewildering number of kingdoms, some of them very short-lived, and a coherent union of all England was not achieved until after the Norman conquest.

The same general organization of many kings coexisting within a common culture had been characteristic of that other migratory people, the Greeks (or, more accurately, Achaeans), who centuries earlier had overrun the region of the eastern Mediterranean. And both to the Achaeans and to the Germanic peoples the ideal of kingly behavior was enormously important—indeed, it was perhaps the chief spiritual force behind the civilizations they both developed, the creative power that, in their earliest periods, shaped their history and their literature. It is generally called the heroic ideal; and put most simply, the heroic ideal was excellence. The hero-king strove to do better than anyone else the things that an essentially migratory life demanded: to sail a ship through a storm, to swim a river or a bay, to tame a horse, to choose a campsite and set firm defenses, in times of peace even to plow a field or build a hall, but always and above all, to fight. Skill and courage were the primary qualities of a king who should successfully lead his people in battle and sustain them during peace.

In its oldest form, the ideal was appropriate only to kings, but because society was so closely knit, all the more important male members of the tribe tended to imitate it. (Germanic society was wholly dominated by males: women are rarely mentioned in the surviving records of it, and only if they are the wives or daughters of kings.) In general, of course, the heroic ideal of conduct was aristocratic, restricted to the king and his immediate retainers, though without that quality of unreality and remoteness from daily life that we associate with later medieval aristocracy. The king was the active leader of a small number of fellow warriors who, as members of his household, beheld all that he did. A successful king won from his retainers complete loyalty. It was their duty to defend him in battle, to give up their own lives while defending or avenging his. In return the king gave his retainers gifts from the spoil that had been accumulated in warfare. Royal generosity was one of the most important aspects of heroic behavior, for it symbolized the excellence of the king's rule, implying on the one hand that the retainers deserved what they were given because of their loyalty to him, and, on the other, showing that he himself was worthy of such loyalty. The heroic ideal had a very practical bearing on the life of the people whom the king ruled.

While the heroic ideal would win practical success for a king, it had also another, perhaps more important end—enduring fame. In cultures whose religion, unlike Christianity, offers no promise of an afterlife, a name that will live on after one's death serves as the closest substitute for immortality. From this arises the heroic paradox, still latent in our own civilization, that by dying gloriously one may achieve immortality. The poet who could sing the story of his heroic life was, of course, the agent upon whom the hero depended for his fame, and a good poet—or bard, to use the customary term for the poet of heroic life—was a valued member of a primitive court. Alexander is said to have expressed envy of Achilles because he had had a Homer to celebrate his deeds. The poetic form which primitive bards evolved for their heroic narratives is called "epic"; it is characterized by a solemn dignity of tone and elevation of style. Their poems were not written down, but recited aloud from memory, and hence most of them have been lost: in Greek there have survived Homer's two epics, the *Iliad* and the *Odyssey*, while from Germanic culture the chief survivor is the Old English *Beowulf*. But enough has been preserved to show the enduring popularity of heroic stories throughout the migratory phase of the two peoples, who never tired of hearing the deeds of their folk heroes. Thus the immortality that the old heroes had sought was achieved through poetry, and poetry in turn gave inspiration to later men in leading their own lives.

CHRISTIANITY AND OLD ENGLISH CULTURE

Whatever literary materials the Anglo-Saxons brought with them when they came to Britain existed only in their memories, for the making of written records was something they learned only when they were converted to Christianity. The Celtic inhabitants whose land they were seizing were Christians, as had been the Romans whose forces had occupied the island since the first century and whose withdrawal at the beginning of the fifth had opened the way to the Anglo-Saxons; but for one hundred fifty years after the beginning of the invasion Christianity was maintained only in the remoter regions where the Anglo-Saxons failed to penetrate. In the year 597, however, St. Augustine was sent by Pope Gregory as a missionary to King Ethelbert of Kent, one of the most southerly of the kingdoms into which England was divided, and about the same time missionaries from Ireland began to preach Christianity in the north. Within seventy-five years the island was once more predominantly Christian. Ethelbert himself was one of the first Christian converts, and it is indicative of the relationship between

Christianity and writing that the first written specimen of the Old English (Anglo-Saxon) language is a code of laws promulgated by the first English Christian king.

In the centuries that followed up till the Norman Conquest England produced a large number of distinguished, highly literate churchmen. One of the earliest of these was Bede, whose *Ecclesiastical History of the English People*, written in Latin, was completed in 731; this remains our most important source of knowledge about the Anglo-Saxon period. In the next generation Alcuin, a man of wide culture, became the friend and advisor of the Frankish Emperor Charlemagne, whom he assisted in making the Frankish court a great center of learning: thus by the year 800 English culture had developed so richly that it overflowed its insular boundaries. But the greatest impetus on English culture came from a man who was not of the clergy: Alfred, king of the West Saxons from 871 to 899, who for a time united all the kingdoms of southern England and beat off those new Germanic invaders, the Vikings. This most active king was an enthusiastic patron of literature. He himself translated various works from Latin, the most important of which was Boethius' *Consolation of Philosophy*, the early sixth-century Roman work whose heroic stoicism has proved continuingly congenial to the English temperament. Apparently under Alfred's direction Bede's *History* was also translated into Old English, and the *Anglo-Saxon Chronicle* was begun: this year-by-year record of important events in England was maintained until the middle of the twelfth century. Furthermore, the preservation of many of the surviving earlier English works, including *Beowulf*, is due to the fact that copies of them were made in the West Saxon dialect because, in large part, of the impetus Alfred gave to literary studies. Though the political stability that Alfred achieved was not long-lived, the culture he nourished so lovingly was maintained at a high level until the very end of the Old English period.

OLD ENGLISH POETRY

The genius for heroic poetry the Anglo-Saxons brought with them when they came to Britain, as they probably also brought with them the alliterative form (see the section on "Old and Middle English Prosody" and, for a discussion of poetic style, the end of the introduction to Bede and Cædmon's *Hymn*) in which all the Old English poetry that has survived was composed. Since they wrote nothing down until they had become Christianized, and since in many respects Christian ideals and heroic ideals are difficult to reconcile, it is natural that very little poetry has survived that is surely pre-Christian in composition. But *Beowulf*, the greatest of Germanic epics, contains much evidently pre-Christian material, even though the author of the particular form of the poem that has come down to us was a Christian who refers to events of the Old (but not of the New) Testament. Several other short pieces or fragments also seem to reflect the pagan period without Christian coloring. Yet the vast bulk of Old English poetry is specifically Christian, devoted to religious subjects. Interestingly enough, however, it is almost all in the heroic mode: while the Anglo-Saxons adapted themselves readily to the ideals of Christianity, they did not do so without adapting Christianity to their own heroic ideal. In order to make the alien world of the Bible intelligible to their hearers, Old English poets (almost all of whom are nameless) infused it with many of the values that they had inherited from their own history. Thus Moses and St. Andrew, Christ and God the Father share the attributes of a Beowulf, are represented as heroes who performed famous deeds. In the *Dream of the Rood*, the Cross speaks of Christ as "the young hero, . . . strong and stouthearted," whose crucifixion is less a passion—a suffering—than a heroic action. In Cædmon's *Hymn* the creation of heaven and earth is seen as a mighty deed, an "establishment of wonders" not altogether unlike Hrothgar's building of the hall Heorot in *Beowulf*. The sad consciousness of the transience of all earthly good combined with the compulsion to go on striving—so characteristic of the heroic spirit—appears most poignantly in two Christian laments, the *Wanderer* and the *Seafarer*. That the heroic ideal held its value down to the end of the Old English period is shown by the *Battle of Maldon*, in which the defeat of English defenders by a band of marauding Vikings is described in the highest tradition of Germanic heroism. Against doom, there is only courage.

The world of Old English poetry is a dark one, and to a modern reader it may also seem a narrow one with narrow laws that exclude all but sardonic laughter. Men in the mead-hall are said to be cheerful, but even there they think of struggle in war, of possible triumph but more possible failure. Romantic love—one of the principal topics of later literature—appears hardly at all. Men seem seldom to relax: clothed in their armor, they are always preparing to test their courage against fate. (They are, indeed, so habitually seen as warriors that in the earlier poetry the words for "man" and "warrior" are often interchangeable.) Depressing as this world may seem, it is recreated in Old English poetry with extraordinary intensity, with high spiritual excitement. This excitement is achieved in part by the frequent use of ironic understatement. Actions and things are spoken of as less than they really are because, apparently, the speaker wishes to suggest that they are more—or perhaps other—than they are. "They cared not for battle," says the author of the *Battle of Maldon* about those cowardly Englishmen who fled the fight. Even the "kenning," that highly formalized compound metaphor common to Old Germanic poetry, often seems to suggest potentials ironically—"whale's road" or "swan's path" for a sea so perilous for men lacking the physical equipment of whales and swans. The dignity the Anglo-Saxons assigned to poetry—which was the repository of the ancient traditions by which they lived—apparently prevented the humor latent in ironic understatement from reaching any expression more overt than a grim smile. Yet despite its somberness, Old English poetry goes about its business of depicting harsh reality with an extraordinary subtlety and intensity.

THE MIDDLE ENGLISH PERIOD

THE NORMAN CONQUEST AND ITS EFFECTS

In the year 1066 England was once more invaded and conquered by a Germanic people, though one whose culture was widely different from the Anglo-Saxons. The Normans—the name is actually a form of "Norsemen"—were the descendants of Scandinavian adventurers who at the beginning of the tenth century had seized a wide part of northern France. A highly adaptable nation, they had adopted the language of the land they had settled in and had set up a powerful state; while its ruler was technically a duke subject to the king of France, Normandy was actually an independent political entity. The invasion of England was led by the energetic Duke William. The English were divided and irresolute; at the decisive Battle of Hastings they were defeated by the Normans and their leader Harold was killed. Thereafter William's forces overran much of England, and the Norman duke became its king and insured the succession to his descendants. But, kings of England though they were, he and his followers were not as much interested in the country he had won (though they were constantly fighting the Welsh, the Scots, and their own barons for control of parts or the whole of it) as they were in their continental possessions. The first seven English kings were mostly absentee rulers—and their presence within the kingdom was seldom less troublesome for it than their absence from it. It was not, indeed, until the thirteenth century, with the reign of Henry III (1216–72) that England became the principal concern of its kings. And it was not until the very end of the Middle Ages that English monarchs finally gave up trying to make good their continental claims and became, perforce, purely English.

The immediate effect of the Norman Conquest upon English literature was to remove it from the care of the aristocracy—the spiritual if not actual descendants of the Anglo-Saxon kings and their retainers—and to deprive it of that cohesive spirit that it had previously possessed. The great aristocratic households, which were the centers of pre-Conquest cultural activity, were broken up or parceled out to the Conqueror's Norman barons, and the English aristocracy was either displaced or forced into service with the invaders. For a considerable time, even the English language seems to have fallen into disuse as a vehicle for written literature, for very little survives of English between the Conquest and the year 1200. Initially, educated people who continued to produce literary works wrote either in Latin or in Anglo-Norman, the dialect of French that was spoken by the new rulers of England. While the practical Normans were less preoccupied with culture than the English, the literature in Anglo-Norman contains several works of distinction, but it was not very long enduring, hardly surviving the reign of Edward I (1272–1307). Latin, which had always been and continued to be the language of the international church, produced a fairly rich literature in England during this period—especially in the twelfth century. But throughout the Middle Ages, Latin literature remained essentially conservative and remote, not much dealing with the subjects that are of importance in the development of vernacular literature. Thus for more than a century the twin snobberies—social on the part of Anglo-Norman, intellectual on the part of Latin— probably preempted the energies of educated authors who might at an earlier or a later time have written in English.

But even if the educated were writing literature in other languages, the uneducated were undoubtedly continuing to compose—if not to write—in English. When written English literature begins to reappear at the end of the twelfth century, the larger part of it carries the stamp of popular or at least semipopular origin; indeed, considered in its bulk, Middle English literature is a popular literature. Its origin in the orders of society below the top provides its most striking contrast with Old English literature: most of the latter seems to be uttered by a single aristocratic voice, grave, decorous, responsible, speaking in terms of high communal aspirations. Middle English literature, on the other hand, is uttered by a medley of different voices, dealing with a wide range of topics in a great diversity of styles and tones and genres. Because its writers addressed themselves to a popular audience, they achieved a greater immediacy, a greater recognizability; a modern reader experiences little difficulty in understanding the world they are talking about. The change is perhaps most obvious in the narrative of adventure, where the idealized hero of Old English yields place to the more sympathetic if less admirable protagonist who not only fights and fights again, but also laughs and cries, plays games, and above all, falls in and out of love—the nonaristocrat was the readier to supplant the epic hero because a mature Christianity places as much value on an ordinary human soul as it does on an epic hero's. In dealing with this new kind of hero the imaginative perspective of popular writers was broadened as much, perhaps, as their ability to see deeply was decreased. And the perspective now included women, who became, finally, recognized as half of the human race. True, they appear ordinarily as stereotypes, whether in romance and love lyric or in antifeminist satire— that enormous body of literature that had its foundation in the monastic culture that dominated so much of European thought in the Middle Ages. But woman's place in society was, in any case, recognized in literature, and this recognition undoubtedly reflects a changing attitude in history itself. There are no arch-feminists in literature before Chaucer's Wife of Bath, but she could never have been invented, even by a Chaucer, unless she had had recognizable forebears, with independent minds and incomes, in Bath and elsewhere before Chaucer's time.

While the portrayal of life in Middle English literature is sometimes shallow, it is nevertheless a life in which we find much that evokes our sympathy. Sometimes, when it is portrayed as lively and gay, colorful, full of surprise, its attractiveness earns our active appreciation, and even when some austere moralist reduces human experience to mere wretchedness we may experience amid the overlying gloom the sudden charm of poignancy. Middle English literature gives an accurate presentation of the details of life that is pleasing and sometimes moving. And humor—the chief virtue of Middle English literature—is apt to flash anywhere, even in the most solemn and foreboding of moralizations.

The conventional character of much Middle English literature is partly due to the attempt by many writers, both religious and secular, to make their works reflect the unchanging principles of medieval Christian doctrine. Until almost the end of the fourteenth century Christian teaching was primarily concerned with the issue of personal salvation, putting more emphasis on the moral and spiritual responsibilities of the individual than it did on his ethical or social responsibilities. Medieval religious idealism characteristically looked to the world to come for the only answer to people's troubles and considered the reformation of this world neither possible nor especially desirable. So constant is the attitude that life in this world is only a waiting period before we enter something better (or worse) that the modern reader is apt to get the impression that the Middle Ages was a period of intellectual and social stasis, a period in which time was standing still. And the fact is that not only in specifically moral and doctrinal literature, whose premises are timeless, but also in ephemeral literature designed merely to provide entertainment one senses this unchangingness: a romance written at the beginning of the thirteenth century differs little from one written in the fifteenth (with which it shares its plot), and at the very end of the period Malory is still peopling with his knights a never-never land of chivalry that had its origin in twelfth-century France.

It is clear enough that between 1066 and 1485 England underwent large political and social changes—in the developments in feudalism, the gradual evolution of Parliament, the growth of cities and of the middle class along with the increase in foreign trade, and in many other similar phenomena. But apparently the changes occurred too slowly to produce much intellectual awareness of them on the part of writers. The great exception—to this and to all other generalizations—is Chaucer, whose pages are informed, especially in his handling of the bourgeois, by an excited sense of the novelty of social life in his own times. Langland's *Piers Plowman* also possesses something of this quality—though without Chaucer's tone of approval. But in an age where most people were born in the same village where their grandparents had been born and lived virtually the same lives, doing the same work with the same tools, enjoying the same sports and the same festivals, large slow-moving change is probably bound to be imperceptible to all but the most acute observers—imperceptible and, if perceived, disapproved.

But if in a broad historical sense change was imperceptible, in the daily lives of medieval people it was all too visible. Indeed, the inevitability of change—for the worse, even in the lives of people already apparently wholly wretched—is one of the most insistently repetitive themes of Middle English literature. Nor is this theme to be thought of merely as another expression of the world-hating doctrine. Rather, the theme and the world-hating doctrine itself are both results of the violence of life in the Middle Ages, a violence not matched again in western history until our own times. Famine, war, pestilence, and death—these are the riders who passed through the streets of medieval cities and villages by night and by day. The fact that eight of the eighteen kings who ruled England between 1066 and 1485 died deaths of violence or deaths resulting from violent activity is characteristic of the era. Men hardly less august were also constantly meeting death in battles, or by murder, or by accident, or, not infrequently, on the scaffold before a fascinated populace. The chroniclers who record these events say little of the lower orders of society, but constant warfare against enemies at home and abroad, the depredations of the powerful in supplying themselves from the fruits of the toil of the poor, the fearful severity of the laws combined with the failure to enforce them against the strong, and, especially after the middle of the fourteenth century, recurrent pestilence compounded by famine—all these explain why change for the worse seems to have been the unchanging expectation of medieval people. And, even in the temporary absence of these events, the coldness and darkness of an English winter for people living in badly insulated dwellings with only minimal heat and light might well seem to make life a bleak perpetual twilight.

In view of the violence prevalent during most of the period, it is perhaps extraordinary that so much literature was produced. But even in the worst of times things are not always and everywhere at their worst; spring does come, and some people get through life almost untouched by disasters that seem historically to be omnipresent. And the fact is that, except in its most ruthlessly world-hating forms, Middle English literature is often permeated by a curious normality, and is, indeed, less preoccupied with its age's violence than we are with ours, probably because people then never conceived of a time when violence was not a fact of life. Despite being constantly warned to expect change for the worse, people in the Middle Ages seem, in their daily lives, to have pursued the same pleasures that we pursue today— pursued them with rather more relish because they were rarer: this is clear from the accounts both of those who approved of the pursuit and of those who did not. People took tremendous pleasure in color, in dress, in ritual, in parades, in spectacles, in elaborate food and drink (when they could get them), in all those aspects of life that children especially love, and most adults do not scorn. Medieval people were subject to emotional extremes—

they wept more quickly than we do, went more quickly from weeping to laughter and back again, were headstrong and hasty, quick to sin zestily and to repent heartily and then to sin and repent again. Their life was physically more limited than ours, without our comforts, our mobility, our communications; it was even more precarious, more uncertain; but as it is reflected in the best writers, they lived their life very richly and perhaps with greater awareness and greater savor than we do ours.

MIDDLE ENGLISH LITERATURE

It has been said earlier that from the century and a half after the Conquest very little English literature has survived, and it is probable that in that period very little was written. But that literature was still being composed, if not written down, during the period is suggested by the first considerable Middle English poem to have come down to us: this is Layamon's *Brut*, written about 1205 in an alliterative prosody that is clearly directly descended from the Old English poetic measure, though the subtleties of the older measure have disappeared. Apparently, at least for oral purposes, alliterative poetry never ceased to be composed, as is further suggested by its reappearance later in written form in the so-called alliterative revival of the fourteenth century, which culminated in *Piers Plowman* and *Sir Gawain and the Green Knight*. Layamon's *Brut* is also interesting because it contains the first treatment in English of the Arthurian legend, the story that was to catch the imagination of so many English writers of later times. Layamon's source was a Norman work by the poet Wace, which was in turn based on the Englishman Geoffrey of Monmouth's Latin *History of the Kings of Britain*. According to the old tradition, England had been founded by one Brutus who was a descendant of the Trojan Aeneas, the founder of Rome, and after whom *Brit*ain was named (hence the title *Brut*). Of Brutus' descendants the most distinguished was Arthur, who according to the legend freed Britain from the Roman yoke and successfully defended it from the Anglo-Saxon invaders. It is a double curiosity about the Arthurian legend that not only did the British (Celtic) Arthur become in later centuries the great legendary hero of the English—whose ancestors he was presumably successful in beating off the island—but also that the Arthurian legend itself reached its fullest development in France, whither it may have been brought by Celts crossing the channel to Brittany—some of them perhaps fleeing from the Anglo-Saxons.

Both the poet of *Beowulf* and the creators of the Arthurian saga dealt with legendary materials which they thought of as history. The latter's treatment, however, is different from (and far less impressive than) the epic mode of *Beowulf*: it moves toward the genre, so characteristic of the later Middle Ages, known as "romance." The romance has certain typical features: it generally concerns knights and involves a large amount of fighting as well as a number of miscellaneous adventures; it makes liberal use of the improbable, often of the supernatural; it is often—though not always—involved with romantic love; characterization is standardized, so that heroes, heroines, and wicked stewards could easily move from one romance to another without causing any disturbance in the narrative; the plots generally consist of a great number of events, and the same event is apt to occur several times within the same romance; and the style is apt to be easy and colloquial—not infrequently loose and repetitious.

Although it was enormously popular in medieval England—it makes up a large fraction of the total of preserved Middle English literature—Middle English romance is apt to disappoint the modern reader. Unfortunately, very few accomplished poets—the *Gawain*-poet and Chaucer are two of the principal exceptions—turned their hand to romance; it was apparently left largely to minstrels and other uncultivated versifiers addressing a semiliterate audience, often in dog-trot verse full of windy clichés. The great age of medieval romance had been the twelfth and early thirteenth centuries, and its chief breeding ground had been aristocratic society in France, where such poets as Chrétien de Troyes spun their marvelously sophisticated tales. The Middle English purveyors of romance, functioning before nonaristocratic audiences in the second half of the thirteenth and in the fourteenth century, introduced the French romances into English (the majority of the surviving English romances are either proved or suspected adaptations from the French). The result of the lag in time and change in audience is artistically unfortunate, though often unintentionally amusing. Aristocratic ideals of behavior of a different era and an alien society were replaced by patterns of behavior that could be easily comprehended by bourgeois and lower-class English folk. Heroes who have all the accouterments of the most chivalrous of knights are apt to behave in the crudest fashion, whether they are fighting, eating, or making love: they act as a petty bourgeois might if suddenly given an opportunity to enjoy the high scale of living of chivalric aristocracy with no education in how such a life should be conducted. Nevertheless, it is often agreeable to watch the blunt Englishman who replaced the aristocratic hero react with practical common sense to the extravagant situations in which the poem has placed him. These popular romances tend to be lengthy, rambling, and episodic yarns almost impossible to represent in a brief selection; their essence, however, has been distilled by Chaucer in an inspired parody, the Tale of Sir Thopas, given among the selections from the *Canterbury Tales*.

By far the larger proportion of surviving Middle English literature is religious, though it is not necessarily true that an equal proportion of the literature actually composed in Middle English was religious. The church had a virtual monopoly on literacy during much of the Middle Ages, for the average person who had learned to read and write probably had done so because he had signified his intention (not always fulfilled) of becoming a cleric—that is, an ecclesiast, performing one of the many functions of the church: otherwise, he would probably not have received any but the most elementary kind of education. Furthermore, the church not only had this direct claim upon the services of the majority of literate men but also was itself a large producer of books in the physical sense (books were actually handwritten manuscripts) as well as a maintainer (especially in monasteries) of libraries. Therefore it is quite natural that religious literature should bulk large. But the literature that has been lost probably contained a very large number of secular items. Professional storytellers such as minstrels committed to memory tales that they had heard others recite or had composed themselves and did not trouble to write down—if, indeed, they could write. Their stories depended for survival on some literate hearer who thought them worth recording—and perhaps few clerics would take the trouble. And even secular literature that had been recorded might sometimes be lost because of the low esteem in which it was held by austere churchmen who would enforce St. Paul's precept that everything that is written ought to express specific Christian doctrine: when library shelves became crowded, it was probably the secular works that were removed to make room for books more beneficial to the spirit.

Unfortunately, good doctrine is not necessarily good literature, and the larger part of Middle English religious writing is literature at all only in the broadest sense of that word: sermons, homilies, saints' lives, penitential tracts, manuals for priests, mystical writings, lyric poems, moral allegories, stories of miracles—all the possible genres of religious writing are represented profusely, though not, in quality, richly. An occasional individual work distinguishes itself strikingly from the surrounding drabness—for instance, the very early *Ancrene Riwle*, or "Rule for Anchoresses" (female religious recluses), or a late lyric like *I Sing of a Maiden*. But the brilliant exceptions are few and far between: few minds were able to sustain originality amid the oppressive conventionality of doctrine and response to doctrine. And few educated people before the time of Chaucer seem to have had the temerity to venture into the secular. We are fortunate that the work of one such person, the author of the early *Owl and the Nightingale*, has survived, for this humorous debate between birds is the most original and Chaucer-like poem before Chaucer himself.

During the last quarter of the fourteenth century Middle English literature flowered suddenly in three great poets, writing at almost the same time and giving supreme artistic expression to almost all the characteristic genres of Middle English. The author of *Sir Gawain and the Green Knight* not only produced the best romance of the entire period, but also wrote some of its best religious poetry; his Biblical narrative in alliterative verse, *Patience*, the story of Jonah, is rivaled only by certain Old English poems. In the *Pearl* he combined elegy with theology to produce the most moving religious poem—and the most finely wrought poem—of the English later Middle Ages. William Langland's achievement in *Piers Plowman* is important both in literature and in history, since he faced squarely the great religious and social issues of his day—and these became the great issues of the following century and a half: imitations of *Piers Plowman* which borrow both Piers himself and Langland's anti-ecclesiastical satire played an important part in bringing on the reformation of the church which Langland prophesied but would have deplored. Needless to say, no imitator approaches Langland in the extraordinary originality of his weaving together of all sorts of genres of religious literature, from the most menacing sermon to the most dazzling lyric. Geoffrey Chaucer's achievement was greatest of all. The new perspective which English literature after the Conquest had attained had revealed broader horizons, but they were too broad and too clouded with distractions to enable the average writer to bring everything into clear focus. It takes a powerfully disciplined mind to comprehend infinite variety in a single artistic vision. Such a mind was Chaucer's. While he was entirely rooted in the soil of the Middle Ages and tried his hand at a large number of medieval genres, his art is so fully realized as to carry him out of the Middle Ages and make him one of the two or three greatest poets in English.

This sudden florescence in the *Gawain*-poet, Langland, and Chaucer may have been partly due to patronage of literature by the well-to-do. Chaucer was a "court" poet who seems to have been encouraged not only by John of Gaunt but perhaps also by Gaunt's father, Edward III (died 1377), as well as by his nephew Richard II (deposed 1399), and, in the last year of the poet's life, by Gaunt's son, Henry IV. Within the broad category of the "court," one must also include members of the lower nobility and the middle class who, like Chaucer himself, constituted both a new bureaucracy for the management of England's increasingly complex affairs and a new kind of literary audience. The *Gawain*-poet probably wrote for a provincial aristocratic court, remote from London but no less interested in literary art. Even William Langland seems to have enjoyed patronage, but from what source it is hard to be sure; it is probable that at one time or another he was sheltered by monasteries, and it is not unlikely that he ended his life in one. In any case English literature is fortunate that these three great contemporary poets all found encouragement from one source or another.

But patronage does not assure great poetry. Chaucer's friend, the poet John Gower, also enjoyed royal patronage, but he has not proved much of a threat to Chaucer's reputation. He seems a far more typically medieval writer than Chaucer: he wrote three works which, linguistically at least, summarized the English Middle Ages: one in Latin, one in Norman French, and one, *Confessio Amantis* ("The Lover's Confession"), in English. Were it not for its proximity to Chaucer, this last would probably be rated somewhat higher than it has been, for it is a work of considerable skill and interest. And it is certainly infinitely superior to anything produced by the English poets of the next century, some of whom enjoyed patronage but all of whom seem, after Chaucer, to represent regression into the worst vices of medieval literature. The most Chaucerian of Chaucer's followers are, indeed, Scotsmen, and the best of them, Robert Henryson and William Dunbar, who often reflect Chaucer's satirical spirit and his liveliness, belong not to the medieval period but to the Renaissance.

Yet if the fifteenth century in England lacks great names (Thomas Malory alone enjoys a high reputation as a literary artist), it is nevertheless a period in which popular literature flourished. Some of the best lyrics, religious and secular, date from this time; and this was also the century in which many of the ballads were composed. It was also the period of much activity in drama. The mystery plays, which had probably become established in the previous century, continued to be performed widely, and the cycles of these religious dramas that have been preserved from York, Chester, and Wakefield date from the fifteenth century. The same century saw the development of the morality play, culminating in *Everyman*. The authors of the plays, ballads, and lyrics of the century are nameless; aside from the plays, manuscripts of which were kept only by the towns in which the performances were given, these anonymous works were probably transmitted orally and only haphazardly written down. Fortunately for the future history of English literature, Malory's *Morte Darthur*, written during its author's long sojourn in prison, did not have to depend on the chance survival of a manuscript; it was printed in 1485 by William Caxton, who had introduced printing by movable type to England less than ten years earlier. Malory's is the last great medieval work of literature. Using mostly French sources, Malory put together a history of King Arthur and his knights which, while wholly fictional, has received much the same honor from later centuries that the Anglo-Saxons accorded *Beowulf*.

MEDIEVAL ENGLISH

The medieval works in this book were composed in two different states of our language: Old English, the language which took shape among the Germanic settlers of England and preserved its integrity until the Norman Conquest radically altered English civilization; and Middle English, the earliest records of which date from the early twelfth century and which gave way to Modern English shortly after the introduction of printing at the end of the fifteenth century. Old English is a very heavily inflected language (that is, the words change form to indicate changes in usage, such as person, number, tense, case, mood, etc. Most languages have some inflection—for example, the personal pronouns in Modern English have different forms when used as objects—but a "heavily inflected" language is one in which almost all classes of words undergo elaborate patterns of change). Its vocabulary is almost entirely Germanic. In Middle English, the inflectional system was weakened; and a large number of words were introduced into it from France, so that many of the older native words disappeared. Because of the difficulty of Old English, all selections from it in this book have been given in translation. In order that the reader may see an example of the language, Cædmon's *Hymn* and a passage from *Beowulf* have been printed in the original, together with translations. The present discussion, then, is concerned only with Middle English.

The chief difficulty with Middle English for the modern reader is caused not by its inflections so much as by its spelling, which may be described as a rough-and-ready phonetic system, and by the fact that it is not a single standardized language, but consists of a number of regional dialects each with its own peculiarities of sound and its own systems for representing sounds in writing. The Midland dialect—the dialect of London and of Chaucer, and the ancestor of our own standard speech—differs greatly from the dialect spoken in the west of England (the original dialect of *Piers Plowman*), and from that of the northwest *(Sir Gawain and the Green Knight)*, and from that of the north *(The Second Shepherds' Play)*, and these dialects differ from one another. In this book, the long texts composed in the more difficult dialects have been translated or modernized; and those which, like Chaucer, *Everyman*, the lyrics, and the ballads, appear in the original, have been respelled in a way that it is hoped will aid the reader. The remarks which follow apply chiefly to Chaucer's Midland English, though certain non-Midland dialectal variations are noted if they occur in some of the other selections.

I. THE SOUNDS OF MIDDLE ENGLISH: GENERAL RULES

The following general analysis of the sounds of Middle English will enable the reader who has not time for detailed study to read Middle English aloud so as to preserve some of its most essential characteristics, without, however, giving heed to many important details. Section II, Detailed Analysis, is designed for the reader who wishes to go more deeply into the pronunciation of Middle English.

Middle English differs from Modern English in three principal respects: 1. the pronunciation of the long vowels *a, e, i* (or *y*), *o*, and *u* (spelled *ou, ow*); 2. the fact that Middle English final *e* is often sounded; 3. the fact that all Middle English consonants are sounded.

1. Long Vowels

Middle English vowels are long when they are doubled *(aa, ee, oo)* or when they are terminal *(he, to, holy)*; *a, e,* and *o* are long when followed by a single consonant plus a vowel *(name, mete, note)*. Middle English vowels are short when they are followed by two consonants.

Long *a* is sounded like the *a* in Modern English "father": *maken, maad*.

Long *e* may be sounded like the *a* in Modern English "name" (ignoring the distinction between the close and open vowel): *be, sweete.*

Long *i* (or *y*) is sounded like the *i* in Modern English "machine": *lif, whit; myn, holy.*

Long *o* may be sounded like the *o* in Modern English "note" (again ignoring the distinction between the close and open vowel): *do, soone.*

Long *u* (spelled *ou, ow*) is sounded like the *oo* in Modern English "goose": *hous, flowr.*

Note that in general Middle English long vowels are pronounced like long vowels in modern languages other than English. Short vowels and diphthongs, however, may be pronounced as in Modern English.

2. *Final e*

In Middle English syllabic verse, final *e* is sounded like the *a* in "sofa" to provide a needed unstressed syllable: *Another Nonnë with hire haddë she.* But (cf. *hire* in the example) final *e* is suppressed when not needed for the meter. It is commonly silent before words beginning with a vowel or *h*.

3. *Consonants*

Middle English consonants are pronounced separately in all combinations—*gnat: g-nat; knave: k-nave; write: w-rite; folk: fol-k.* In a simplified system of pronunciation the combination *gh* as in *night* or *thought* may be treated as if it were silent.

II. THE SOUNDS OF MIDDLE ENGLISH: DETAILED ANALYSIS

1. *Simple Vowels*

Sound	Pronunciation	Example
long *a* (spelled *a, aa*)	*a* in "father"	*maken, maad*
short *a*	*o* in "hot"	*cappe*
long *e* close (spelled *e, ee*)	*a* in "name"	*be, sweete*
long *e* open (spelled *e, ee*)	*e* in "there"	*mete, heeth*
short *e*	*e* in "set"	*setten*
final *e*	*a* in "sofa"	*large*
long *i* (spelled *i, y*)	*i* in "machine"	*lif, myn*
short *i*	*i* in "wit"	*wit*
long *o* close (spelled *o, oo*)	*o* in "note"	*do, soone*
long *o* open (spelled *o, oo*)	*oa* in "broad"	*go, goon*
short *o*	*o* in "oft"	*pot*
long *u* when spelled *ou, ow*	*oo* in "goose"	*hous, flowr*
long *u* when spelled *u*	*u* in "pure"	*vertu*
short *u* (spelled *u, o*)	*u* in "full"	*ful, love*

Doubled vowels and terminal vowels are always long, while single vowels before two consonants other than *th, ch* are always short. The vowels *a, e,* and *o* are long before a single consonant followed by a vowel: *nāmë, sēkë* (sick), *hōly.* In general, words that have descended into Modern English reflect their original Middle English quantity: *lĭven* (to live), but *līf* (life).

The close and open sounds of long *e* and long *o* may often be identified by the Modern English spellings of the words in which they appear. Original long close *e* is generally represented in Modern English by *ee*: "sweet," "knee," "teeth," "see" have close *e* in Middle English, but so does "be"; original long open *e* is generally represented in Modern English by *ea*: "meat," "heath," "sea," "great," "breath" have open *e* in Middle English. Similarly, original long close *o* is now generally represented by *oo*: "soon," "food," "good," but also "do," "to"; original long open *o* is represented either by *oa* or by *o*: "coat," "boat," "moan," but also "go," "bone," "foe," "home." Notice that original close *o* is now almost always pronounced like the *oo* in "goose," but that original open *o* is almost never so pronounced; thus it is often possible to identify the Middle English vowels through Modern English sounds.

The nonphonetic Middle English spelling of *o* for short *u* has been preserved in a number of Modern English words ("love," "son," "come"), but in others *u* has been restored: "sun" *(sonne)*, "run" *(ronne)*.

For the treatment of final *e*, see above, General Rules, section 2.

2. *Diphthongs*

Sound	Pronunciation	Example
ai, ay, ei, ay	between *ai* in "aisle" and *ay* in "day"	*saide, day, veine, preye*
au, aw	*ou* in "out"	*chaunge, bawdy*
eu, ew	*ew* in "few"	*newe*
oi, oy	*oy* in "joy"	*joye, point*
ou, ow	*ou* in "thought"	*thought, lowe*

Note that in words with *ou, ow* which in Modern English are sounded with the *ou* of "about," the combination indicates not the diphthong but the simple vowel long *u* (see above, Simple Vowels).

3. *Consonants*

In general, all consonants except *h* were always sounded in Middle English, including consonants that have become silent in Modern English, such as the *g* in *gnaw*, the *k* in *knight*, the *l* in *folk*, and the *w* in *write*. In noninitial *gn*, however, the *g* was silent as in Modern English "sign." Initial *h* was silent in short common English words and in words borrowed from French, and may have been almost silent in all words. The combination *gh* as in *night* or *thought* was sounded like the *ch* of German *ich* or *nach*. Note that Middle English *gg* represents both the hard sound of "dagger" and the soft sound of "bridge."

III. PARTS OF SPEECH AND GRAMMAR

1. *Nouns*

The plural and possessive of nouns end in *es*, formed by adding *s* or *es* to the singular: *knight, knightes; roote, rootes*; a final consonant is frequently doubled before *es: bed, beddes*. A common irregular plural is *yën*, from *yë*, eye.

2. *Pronouns*

The chief differences from Modern English are as follows:

Modern English	Middle English
I	*I, ich (ik* is a northern form)
you (singular)	*thou* (subjective); *thee* (objective)
her	*hir(e), her(e)*
its	*his*
you (plural)	*ye* (subjective); *you* (objective)
their	*hir*
them	*hem*

In formal speech, the second person plural is often used for the singular. The possessive adjectives *my*, *thy* take *n* before a word beginning with a vowel or *h*: *thyn yë*, *myn host*.

3. *Adjectives*

Adjectives ending in a consonant add final *e* when they stand before the noun they modify and after another modifying word such as *the*, *this*, *that*, or nouns or pronouns in the possessive: *a good hors*, but *the (this, my, the kinges) goode hors*. They also generally add *e* when standing before and modifying a plural noun, a noun in the vocative, or any proper noun: *goode men, oh goode man, faire Venus*.

Adjectives are compared by adding *er(e)* for the comparative, *est(e)* for the superlative. Sometimes the stem vowel is shortened or altered in the process: *sweete, swettere, swettest; long, lenger, lengest*.

4. *Adverbs*

Adverbs are formed from adjectives by adding *e*, *ly*, or *liche*; the adjective *fair* thus yields *faire, fairly, fairliche*.

5. *Verbs*

Middle English verbs, like Modern English verbs, are either "weak" or "strong." Weak verbs form their preterites and past participles with a *t* or *d* suffix and preserve the same stem vowel throughout their systems, though it is sometimes shortened in the preterite and past participle: *love, loved; bend, bent; hear, heard; meet, met*. Strong verbs do not use the *t* or *d* suffix, but vary their stem vowel in the preterite and past participle: *take, took, taken; begin, began, begun; find, found, found*.

The inflectional endings are the same for Middle English strong verbs and weak verbs except in the preterite singular and the imperative singular. In the following paradigms, the weak verbs *loven* (to love) and *heeren* (to hear), and the strong verbs *taken* (to take) and *ginnen* (to begin) serve as models.

	Present Indicative	Preterite Indicative
I	love, heere	loved(e), herde
	take, ginne	took, gan
thou	lovest, heerest	lovedest, herdest
	takest, ginnest	tooke, gonne
he, she, it	loveth, heereth	loved(e), herde
	taketh, ginneth	took, gan
we, ye, they	love(n) (th), heere(n) (th)	loved(e) (en), herde(n)
	take(n) (th), ginne(n) (th)	tooke(n), gonne(n)

The present plural ending *eth* is southern, while the *e(n)* ending is Midland and characteristic of Chaucer. In the north, *s* may appear as the ending of all persons of the present. In the weak preterite, when the ending *e* gave a verb three or more syllables, it was frequently dropped. Note that in certain strong verbs like *ginnen* there are two distinct stem vowels in the preterite: even in Chaucer's time, however, one of these had begun to replace the other, and Chaucer occasionally writes *gan* for all persons of the preterite.

	Present Subjunctive	Preterite Subjunctive
Singular	love, heere	lovede, herde
	take, ginne	tooke, gonne
Plural	love(n), heere(n)	lovede(n), herde(n)
	take(n), ginne(n)	tooke(n), gonne(n)

In verbs like *ginnen*, which have two stem vowels in the indicative preterite, it is the vowel of the plural and of the second person singular that is used for the preterite subjunctive.

The imperative singular of most weak verbs is *e: (thou) love*, but of some weak verbs and all strong verbs, the imperative singular is without termination: *(thou) heer, taak, gin*. The imperative plural of all verbs is either *e* or *eth: (ye) love(th), heere(th), take(th), ginne(th)*.

The infinitive of verbs is *e* or *en: love(n), heere(n), take(n), ginne(n)*.

The past participle of weak verbs is the same as the preterite without inflectional ending: *loved, herd*. In strong verbs the ending is either *e* or *en: take(n), gonne(n)*. The prefix *y* often appears on past participles: *yloved, yherd, ytake(n)*.

OLD AND MIDDLE ENGLISH PROSODY

All the poetry of Old English is in the same verse form. The verse unit is the single line, since rhyme was not used to link one line to another, except very occasionally in late Old English. The organizing device of the line is alliteration, the beginning of several words with the same sound ("Foemen fled"). The Old English alliterative line contains four principal stresses, and is divided into two half-lines of two stresses each by a strong medial caesura, or pause. These two half-lines are linked to each other by the alliteration: at least one of the two stressed words in the first half-line, and often both of them, begin with the same sound as the first stressed word of the second half-line (the second stressed word is generally nonalliterative). The fourth line of *Beowulf* is an example *(sc* has the value of modern *sh*; *þ* is a runic symbol with the value of modern *th)*:

Oft Scyld Scefing   sceaþena þreatum.

For further examples, see Cædmon's *Hymn* and the passage from *Beowulf,* printed below. It will be noticed that any vowel alliterates with any other vowel. In addition to the alliteration, the length of the unstressed syllables and their number and pattern is governed by a highly complex set of rules. When sung or intoned—as it was—to the rhythmic strumming of a harp, Old English poetry must have been wonderfully impressive in the dignified, highly formalized way which aptly fits both its subject matter and tone.

The majority of Middle English verse is either in alternately stressed rhyming verse, adapted from French after the Conquest, or in alliterative verse that is descended from Old English. The latter preserves the caesura of Old English and in its purest form the same alliterative system, the two stressed words of the first half-line (or at least one of them) alliterating with the first stressed word in the second half-line. But most of the alliterative poets allowed themselves a number of deviations from the norm. All four stressed words may alliterate, as in the first line of *Piers Plowman:*

In a summer season   when soft was the sun.

Or the line may contain five, six, or even more stressed words, of which all or only the basic minimum may alliterate:

A fair field full of folk   found I therebetween.

There is no rule determining the number of unstressed syllables, and at times some poets seem to ignore alliteration entirely. As in Old English, any vowel may alliterate with any other vowel; furthermore, since initial *h* was silent or lightly pronounced in Middle English, words beginning with *h* are treated as though they began with the following vowel.

There are two general types of stressed verse with rhyme. In the more common, stressed and unstressed syllables alternate regularly: x X x X x X; or, with two unstressed syllables intervening: x x X x x X x x X; or a combination of the two: x x X x X x x X (of the reverse patterns, only X x X x X x is common in English). There is also a line which can only be defined as containing a predetermined number of stressed syllables but an irregular number and pattern of unstressed syllables. Much Middle English verse has to be read without expectation of regularity: some of this was evidently composed in the irregular meter, but some was probably originally composed according to a strict metrical system which has been obliterated by scribes careless of fine points. One receives the impression that many of the lyrics— as well as the *Second Shepherds' Play*—were at least composed with regular syllabic alternation. In the ballads, on the other hand, and in the play *Everyman*, only the number of stresses is predetermined (and perhaps not even this in *Everyman*), but not the number or placement of unstressed syllables.

In pre-Chaucerian verse the number of stresses, whether regularly or irregularly alternated, was most often four, though sometimes the number was three, and rose in some poems to seven. Rhyme in Middle English as in Modern English may be either between adjacent or alternate lines, or may occur in more complex patterns. The *Canterbury Tales* are in rhymed couplets, the line containing five stresses with regular alternation—technically known as iambic pentameter, the standard English poetic line, perhaps introduced into English by Chaucer. In reading Chaucer and much pre-Chaucerian verse one must remember that the final *e*, which is silent in Modern English, was pronounced at any time in order to provide a needed unstressed syllable. Evidence seems to indicate that it was also pronounced at the end of the line, even though it thus produced a line with eleven syllables. Although he was a very regular metricist, Chaucer used various conventional devices which are apt to make the reader stumble until he understands them. Final *e* is often not pronounced before a word beginning with a vowel or *h*, and may be suppressed whenever metrically convenient. The same medial and terminal syllables that are slurred in Modern English are apt to be suppressed in Chaucer's English: *Canterb'ry* for *Canterbury*; *ev'r* (perhaps *e'er*) for *evere*. The plural in *es* may either be syllabic or reduced to *s* as in Modern English. Despite these seeming irregularities, Chaucer's verse is not difficult to read if one constantly bears in mind the basic pattern of the iambic pentameter line.

Old English Literature

BEDE (ca. 673–735) *and* CÆDMON'S HYMN

The Venerable Bede (the title by which he is known to posterity) became a novice at the age of seven and spent the rest of his life at the neighboring monasteries of Wearmouth and Jarrow. Though he never traveled beyond the boundaries of his native district of Northumbria, he achieved an inter-national reputation as one of the greatest scholars of his age. Writing in Latin, the learned language of the era, Bede produced many theological works, as well as books on science and rhetoric, but his most popular and enduring work is the *Ecclesiastical History of the English People* (completed 731). The *History* tells about the Anglo-Saxon conquest and the vicissitudes of the petty kingdoms that comprised Anglo-Saxon England; Bede's main theme, however, is the spread of Christianity and the growth of the English Church. The latter were the great events leading up to Bede's own time, and he regarded them as the unfolding of God's providence. The *History* is, therefore, also a moral work and a hagiography—that is, it contains many stories of saints and miracles meant to testify to the grace and glory of God.

The story we reprint preserves what is probably the earliest extant Old English poem (composed sometime between 658–680) and the only bio-graphical information, outside of what is said in the poems themselves, about any Old English poet. Bede tells how Cædmon, an illiterate cowherd employed by the monastery of Whitby, miraculously received the gift of song, entered the monastery, and became the founder of a school of Christian poetry. Cædmon was clearly an oral-formulaic poet, one who created his work by combining and varying formulas—units of verse developed in a tradition transmitted by one generation of singers to another. In this respect he resem-bles the singers of the Homeric poems and oral-formulaic poets recorded in the twentieth century, especially in the Balkan countries. Although Bede tells us that Cædmon had never learned the art of song, we may suspect that he concealed his skill from his fellow workmen and from the monks because he was ashamed of knowing "vain and idle" songs, the kind Bede says Cædmon never composed. Cædmon's inspiration and the true miracle, then, was to apply the meter and language of such songs, presumably including pagan heroic verse, to Christian themes.

Although most Old English poetry was written by lettered poets, they continued to use the oral-formulaic style. The *Hymn* is, therefore, a good short example of the way Old English verse with its traditional poetic diction and interwoven formulaic expressions is constructed. Eight of the poem's eighteen half-lines contain epithets describing various aspects of God: He is *Weard* (Guardian), *Meatod* (Measurer), *Wuldor-Fæder* (Glory-Father), *Drihten* (Lord), *Scyppend* (Creator), and *Frea* (Master). God is *heofenrices Weard* or *mancynnes Weard* (heaven's or mankind's Guardian), depending on the alliteration required. This formulaic style provides a richness of texture and meaning difficult to convey in translation. As Bede said about his own Latin paraphrase of the *Hymn*, no literal translation of poetry from one language to another is possible without sacrifice of some poetic quality.

Several manuscripts of Bede's *History* contain the Old English text in addition to Bede's Latin version. The poem is given here in a West Saxon form with a literal interlinear translation. In Old English spelling, æ (as in Cædmon's name and line 3) is a vowel symbol that has not survived; it represented both a short *a* sound and a long open *e* sound. þ (line 2) and ð both represented the sound *th*. The large space in the middle of the line indicates the caesura. The alliterating sounds that connect the half-lines have been italicized.

From An Ecclesiastical History of the English People

[*The Story of Cædmon*]

Heavenly grace had especially singled out a certain one of the brothers in the monastery ruled by this abbess,[1] for he used to compose devout and religious songs. Whatever he learned of holy Scripture with the aid of interpreters, he quickly turned into the sweetest and most moving poetry in his own language, that is to say English. It often happened that his songs kindled a contempt for this world and a longing for the life of Heaven in the hearts of many men. Indeed, after him others among the English people tried to compose religious poetry, but no one could equal him because he was not taught the art of song by men or by human agency but received this gift through heavenly grace. Therefore, he was never able to compose any vain and idle songs but only such as dealt with religion and were proper for his religious tongue to utter. As a matter of fact, he had lived in the secular estate until he was well advanced in age without learning any songs. Therefore, at feasts, when it was decided to have a good time by taking turns singing, whenever he would see the harp getting close to his place,[2] he got up in the middle of the meal and went home.

Once when he left the feast like this, he went to the cattle shed, which he had been assigned the duty of guarding that night. And after he had stretched himself out and gone to sleep, he dreamed that someone was standing at his side and greeted him, calling out his name. "Cædmon," he said, "sing me something."

And he replied, "I don't know how to sing; that is why I left the feast to come here—because I cannot sing."

"All the same," said the one who was speaking to him, "you have to sing for me."

1. The Abbess Hilda (614–680), a grand-niece of the first Christian king of Northumbria, founded Whitby, a double house for monks and nuns, in 657 and ruled over it for 22 years.

2. Oral poetry was performed to the accompaniment of a harp; here the harp is being passed from one participant of the feast to another, each being expected to perform in turn.

"What must I sing?" he said.

And he said, "Sing about the Creation."

At this, Cædmon immediately began to sing verses in praise of God the Creator, which he had never heard before and of which the sense is this:

Nu sculon *h*erigean
Now we must praise

*h*eofonrices Weard
heaven-kingdom's Guardian,

*M*eotodes *m*eahte
the Measurer's might

and his *m*odgeþanc
and his mind-plans,

*w*eorc Wuldor-Fæder
the work of the Glory-Father,

swa he *w*undra gehwæs
when he of wonders of every one,

*e*ce Drihten
eternal Lord,

or   onstealde
the beginning established.[3]

He *æ*rest sceop
He first created

*ie*lda[4] bearnum
for men's sons

*h*èofon to hrofe
heaven as a roof,

*h*alig Scyppend
holy Creator;

ða *m*iddangeard
then middle-earth

*m*oncynnes Weard
mankind's Guardian,

*e*ce Drihten
eternal Lord,

*æ*fter teode
afterwards made—

*f*irum *f*oldan
for men earth,

Frea ælmihtig
Master almighty.

This is the general sense but not the exact order of the words that he sang in his sleep; for it is impossible to make a literal translation, no matter how well-written, of poetry into another language without losing some of the beauty and dignity. When he woke up, he remembered everything that he had sung in his sleep, and to this he soon added, in the same poetic measure, more verses praising God.

The next morning he went to the reeve,[5] who was his foreman, and told him about the gift he had received. He was taken to the abbess and ordered to tell his dream and to recite his song to an audience of the most learned men so that they might judge what the nature of that vision was and where it came from. It was evident to all of them that he had been granted the heavenly grace of God. Then they expounded some bit of sacred story or teaching to him, and instructed him to turn it into poetry if he could. He agreed and went away. And when he came back the next morning, he gave back what had been commissioned to him in the finest verse.

Therefore, the abbess, who cherished the grace of God in this man,

---

3. I.e., "established the beginning of every one of wonders."

4. The later manuscript copies read *eorþan*,

"earth," for *ælda* (West Saxon *ielda*), "men's."

5. Superintendent of the farms belonging to the monastery.

instructed him to give up secular life and to take monastic vows. And when she and all those subject to her had received him into the community of brothers, she gave orders that he be taught the whole sequence of sacred history. He remembered everything that he was able to learn by listening, and turning it over in his mind like a clean beast that chews the cud,[6] he converted it into sweetest song, which sounded so delightful that he made his teachers, in their turn, his listeners. He sang about the creation of the world and the origin of the human race and all the history of Genesis; about the exodus of Israel out of Egypt and entrance into the promised land; and about many other stories of sacred Scripture, about the Lord's incarnation, and his passion,[7] resurrection, and ascension into Heaven; about the advent of the Holy Spirit and the teachings of the apostles. He also made many songs about the terror of the coming judgment and the horror of the punishments of hell and the sweetness of the heavenly kingdom; and a great many others besides about divine grace and justice in all of which he sought to draw men away from the love of sin and to inspire them with delight in the practice of good works.[8] * * *

6. In Mosaic law "clean" animals, those that may be eaten, are those that both chew the cud and have a cloven hoof (cf. Leviticus 11.3 and Deuteronomy 14.6).

7. The suffering of Christ on the Cross and during his trial leading up to the Crucifixion.

8. The great majority of extant Old English poems are on religious subjects like those listed here, but they are all thought to be later than Cædmon.

THE DREAM OF THE ROOD

The *Dream of the Rood* (i.e., of the Cross) is the finest of a rather large number of religious poems in Old English. Neither its author nor its date of composition is known. It appears in a late tenth-century manuscript located in Vercelli in northern Italy, a manuscript made up of Old English religious poems and sermons. The poet Cynewulf, about whom nothing is surely known except that he wrote four Old English homiletic poems (two of them found in the Vercelli manuscript), has sometimes been credited with the *Dream*, but on no very convincing evidence. The poem may antedate its manuscript by almost three centuries, for some passages from the Rood's speech were carved, with some variations, in runes on a stone cross early in the eighth century: this is the famous Ruthwell Cross, which is preserved near Dumfries in southern Scotland. The precise relation of the poem to this cross is, however, uncertain.

The homiletic tone of the Dreamer's meditation may seem anticlimactic after the intensity, so terse and exciting, of the Rood's address to him, but the former is nevertheless an admirable frame for the latter. The experience of the Cross—its humiliation at the hands of those who changed it from tree to instrument of punishment for criminals, its humility when the young hero Christ mounts upon it, and its pride as the restored "tree of glory"—has a suggestive relevance to the condition of the sad, lonely, sin-stained Dreamer. In the Cross's experience, hope has replaced torment; when, at the end of the poem, the Dreamer describes Christ's triumphant progress from hell to heaven, the verse recaptures some of the excitement of the Cross's address, reflecting the Dreamer's response to the hope that has been brought him.

The Dream of the Rood[1]

Listen, I will speak of the best of dreams, of what I dreamed at midnight when men and their voices were at rest. It seemed to me that I saw a most rare tree reach high aloft, wound in light, brightest of beams. All that beacon[2] was covered with gold; gems stood fair where it met the ground, five were above about the crosspiece. Many hosts of angels gazed on it, fair in the form created for them. This was surely no felon's gallows, but holy spirits beheld it there, men upon earth, and all this glorious creation. Wonderful was the triumph-tree, and I stained with sins, wounded with wrongdoings. I saw the tree of glory shine splendidly, adorned with garments, decked with gold: jewels had worthily covered the Lord's tree. Yet through that gold I might perceive ancient agony of wretches, for now it began to bleed on the right side.[3] I was all afflicted with sorrows, I was afraid for that fair sight. I saw that bright beacon change in clothing and color: now it was wet with moisture, drenched with flowing of blood, now adorned with treasure. Yet I, lying there a long while troubled, beheld the Saviour's tree until I heard it give voice: the best of trees began to speak words.

"It was long ago—I remember it still—that I was hewn down at the wood's edge, taken from my stump. Strong foes seized me there, hewed me to the shape they wished to see, commanded me to lift their criminals. Men carried me on their shoulders, then set me on a hill; foes enough fastened me there. Then I saw the Lord of mankind hasten with stout heart, for he would climb upon me. I dared not bow or break against God's word when I saw earth's surface tremble. I might have felled all foes, but I stood fast. Then the young Hero stripped himself— that was God Almighty—strong and stouthearted. He climbed on the high gallows, bold in the sight of many, when he would free mankind. I trembled when the Warrior embraced me, yet I dared not bow to earth, fall to the ground's surface; but I must stand fast. I was raised up, a cross; I lifted up the Mighty King, Lord of the Heavens: I dared not bend. They pierced me with dark nails: the wounds are seen on me, open gashes of hatred. Nor did I dare harm any of them. They mocked us both together. I was all wet with blood, drenched from the side of that Man after he had sent forth his spirit. I had endured many bitter happenings on that hill. I saw the God of Hosts cruelly racked. The shades of night had covered the Ruler's body with their mists, the bright splen-

1. This new prose translation, by the senior editor, has been based in general on the edition of the poem by John C. Pope, *Seven Old English Poems* (1966).

2. The Old English word *beacen* means also "token" or "sign" and "battle standard."
3. The wound Christ received on the Cross was supposed to have been on the right side.

dor. Shadow came forth, dark beneath the clouds. All creation wept, bewailed the King's fall; Christ was on Cross.

"Yet from afar some came hastening to the Lord.[4] All that I beheld. I was sore afflicted with griefs, yet I bowed to the men's hands, meekly, eagerly. Then they took Almighy God, lifted him up from his heavy torment. The warriors left me standing, covered with blood. I was all wounded with arrows. They laid him down weary of limb, stood at the body's head, looked there upon Heaven's Lord; and he rested there a while, tired after the great struggle. Then warriors began to build him an earth-house in the sight of his slayer,[5] carved it out of bright stone; they set there the Wielder of Triumphs. Then they began to sing him a song of sorrow, desolate in the evening. Then they wished to turn back, weary, from the great Prince; he remained with small company.[6] Yet we[7] stood in our places a good while, weeping. The voice of the warriors departed. The body grew cold, fair house of the spirit. Then some began to fell us to earth—that was a fearful fate! Some buried us in a deep pit. Yet thanes[8] of the Lord, friends, learned of me there. . . . decked me in gold and silver.[9]

"Now you might understand, my beloved man, that I had endured the work of evildoers, grievous sorrows. Now the time has come that men far and wide upon earth honor me—and all this glorious creation—and pray to this beacon. On me God's Son suffered awhile; therefore I tower now glorious under the heavens, and I may heal every one of those who hold me in awe. Of old I became the hardest of torments, most loathed by men, before I opened the right road of life to those who have voices. Behold, the Lord of Glory honored me over all the trees of the wood, the Ruler of Heaven, just as also he honored his mother Mary, Almighty God for all men's sake, over all woman's kind.

"Now I command you, my beloved man, that you tell men of this vision. Disclose with your words that it is of the tree of glory on which Almighty God suffered for mankind's many sins and the deeds Adam did of old. He tasted death there; yet the Lord arose again to help mankind in his great might. Then he climbed to the heavens. He will come again hither on this earth to seek mankind on Doomsday, the Lord himself, Almighty God, and his angels with him, for then he will judge, he who has power to judge, each one just as in this brief life he has deserved. Nor may any one be unafraid of the word the Ruler will speak. Before his host he will ask where the man is who in the name of the Lord would taste bitter death as he did on the Cross. But then they will be afraid, and will think of little to begin to say to Christ. There need none be afraid who bears on his breast the best of tokens, but through the Cross

---

4. According to John 19.38–39, it was Joseph of Arimathea and Nicodemus who received Christ's body from the Cross.
5. I.e., the Cross.
6. I.e., alone (an understatement).
7. I.e., Christ's Cross and those on which the two thieves were crucified.

8. Members of the king's body of warriors.
9. A number of lines describing the finding of the Cross have apparently been lost here. According to the legend, St. Helen, the mother of Constantine the Great, the first Christian emperor, led a Roman expedition that discovered the true Cross in the 4th century.

shall the kingdom be sought by each soul on this earthly journey that thinks to dwell with the Lord."

Then I prayed to the tree, blithe-hearted, confident, there where I was alone with small company. My heart's thoughts were urged on the way hence. I endured many times of longing. Now is there hope of life for me, that I am permitted to seek the tree of triumph, more often than other men honor it well, alone. For it my heart's desire is great, and my hope of protection is directed to the Cross. I do not possess many powerful friends on earth, but they have gone hence from the delights of the world, sought for themselves the King of Glory. They live now in the heavens with the High Father, dwell in glory. And every day I look forward to when the Lord's Cross that I beheld here on earth will fetch me from this short life and bring me then where joy is great, delight in the heavens, where the Lord's folk are seated at the feast, where bliss is eternal. And then may it place me where thenceforth I may dwell in glory, fully enjoy bliss with the saints. May the Lord be my friend, who once here on earth suffered on the gallows-tree for man's sins: he freed us and granted us life, a heavenly home. Hope was renewed, with joys and with bliss, to those who endured fire.[1] The Son was victorious in that foray, mighty and successful. Then he came with his multitude, a host of spirits, into God's kingdom, the Almighty Ruler; and the angels and all the saints who dwelt then in glory rejoiced when their Ruler, Almighty God, came where his home was.

---

1. This and the following sentences refer to the Harrowing (i.e., pillaging) of Hell: after His death upon the Cross, Christ descended into hell, from which He released the souls of certain of the patriarchs and prophets, conducting them triumphantly to heaven.

BEOWULF

Beowulf, the oldest of the great long poems written in English, may have been composed more than twelve hundred years ago, in the first half of the eighth century, though some scholars would place it as late as the tenth century. Its author may have been a native of what was then West Mercia, the West Midlands of England today, though the late tenth-century manuscript, which alone preserves the poem, originated in the south in the kingdom of the West Saxons. In 1731, before any modern transcription of the text had been made, the manuscript was seriously damaged in the fire that destroyed the building in London which housed the extraordinary collection of medieval English manuscripts made by Sir Robert Bruce Cotton (1571–1631). As a result of the fire and of subsequent deterioration of the manuscript, a number of lines and words have been lost from the poem, but even if the manuscript had not been damaged, the poem would still have been difficult, because the poetic Old English (or Anglo-Saxon) in which it was written is itself hard, the style is allusive, the ideas often seem remote and strange to modern perceptions, and because the text was inevitably corrupted during the transcriptions which must have intervened between the poem's

composition and the copying of the extant manuscript. Yet despite its difficulty, the somber grandeur of *Beowulf* is still capable of stirring the hearts of
readers, and because of its excellence as well as its antiquity, the poem
merits the high position that it is generally assigned in the study of English
poetry.

While the poem itself is English in language and origin, it deals not with
native Englishmen, but with their Germanic forebears, especially with two
south Scandinavian tribes, the Danes and the Geats, who lived on the Danish island of Zealand and in southern Sweden, respectively. Thus, the historical period it concerns—insofar as it may be said to refer to history at all—
is some centuries before the poem was written; that is, it concerns a time
following the initial invasion of England by Germanic tribes in 449, but
before the Anglo-Saxon migration was completed, and perhaps before the
arrival of the ancestors of the audience to whom the poem was sung: this
audience may have considered itself to be of the same Geatish stock as the
hero, Beowulf. The one datable fact of history mentioned in the poem is a
raid on the Franks made by Hygelac, the king of the Geats at the time
Beowulf was a young man, and this raid occurred in the year 520. Yet
despite their antiquity, the poet's materials must have been very much alive
to his audience, for the elliptical way in which he alludes to events not
directly concerned with his plot demands of the listener a wide knowledge
of traditional Germanic history. This knowledge was probably kept alive by
other heroic poetry, of which little has been preserved in English, though
much must once have existed. As it stands, *Beowulf* is not only unique as
an example of the Old English epic, but is also the greatest of the surviving
epics composed by the Germanic peoples.

It is generally agreed that the poet who put the old materials into their
present form was a Christian, and that his poem reflects a Christian tradition: the conversion of the Germanic settlers in England had largely been
completed during the centuries preceding the one in which the poet wrote.
But there is little general agreement as to how clearly *Beowulf* reflects a
Christian tradition or, conversely, the actual nature of the Christian tradition that it is held to reflect. Many specifically Christian references occur,
especially to the Old Testament: God is said to be the Creator of all things
and His will seems recognized (sporadically if not systematically) as being
identical with Fate (*wyrd*); Grendel is described as a descendant of Cain,
and the sword that Beowulf finds in Grendel's mother's lair has engraved on
it the story of the race of giants and their destruction by flood; the dead await
God's judgment, and Hell and the Devil are ready to receive the souls of
Grendel and his mother, while believers will find the Father's embrace;
Hrothgar's speech of advice to Beowulf (p. 57) seems to reflect patristic doctrine in its emphasis on conscience and the Devil's lying in wait for the
unwary. Yet there is no reference to the New Testament—to Christ and His
Sacrifice which are the real bases of Christianity in any intelligible sense of
the term. Furthermore, readers may well feel that the poem achieves rather
little of its emotional power through any direct invocation of Christian values or of values that are consonant with Christian doctrine as we know it.
Perhaps the sense of tragic waste which pervades the Finnsburg episode (pp.
47–49) springs from a Christian perception of the insane futility of the primitive Germanic thirst for vengeance; and the facts that Beowulf's chief adversaries are not men but monsters and that before his death he is able to boast
that as king of the Geats he did not seek wars with neighboring tribes may

reflect a Christian's appreciation for peace among men. But while admitting such values, the poet also invokes many others of a very different order, values that seem to belong to an ancient, pagan, warrior society of the kind described by the Roman historian Tacitus at the end of the first century. It should be noted that even Hrothgar's speech about conscience is directed more toward making Beowulf a good Germanic leader of men than a good Christian. One must, indeed, draw the conclusion from the poem itself that while Christian is a correct term for the religion of the poet and of his audience, it was a Christianity that had not yet by any means succeeded in obliterating an older pagan tradition, which still called forth powerful responses from the hearts of men and women, despite the fact that many aspects of this tradition must be abhorrent to a sophisticated Christian. In this connection it is well to recall that the missionaries from Rome who initiated the conversion of the English proceeded in a conciliatory manner, not so much uprooting paganism in order to plant Christianity as planting Christianity in the faith that it would ultimately choke out the weeds of paganism. And the English clung long to some of their ancient traditions: for instance, the legal principle of the payment of *wergild* (defined below) remained in force until the Norman Conquest, four centuries after the conversion of the English.

In the warrior society whose values the poem constantly invokes, the most important of human relationships was that which existed between the warrior—the thane—and his lord, a relationship based less on subordination of one man's will to another's than on mutual trust and respect. When a warrior vowed loyalty to his lord, he became not so much his servant as his voluntary companion, one who would take pride in defending him and fighting in his wars. In return, the lord was expected to take affectionate care of his thanes and to reward them richly for their valor: a good king, one like Hrothgar or Beowulf, is referred to by such poetic epithets as "protector of warriors" and "dispenser of treasure" or "ring-giver," and the failure of bad kings is ascribed to their ill-temper and avarice, both of which alienate them from their retainers. The material benefit of this arrangement between lord and thane is obvious, yet under a good king the relationship seems to have had a significance more spiritual than material. Thus the treasure that an ideal Germanic king seizes from his enemies and rewards his retainers with is regarded as something more than mere wealth that will serve the well-being of its possessor; rather, it is a kind of visible proof that all parties are realizing themselves to the full in a spiritual sense—that the men of this band are congenially and successfully united with one another. The symbolic importance of treasure is illustrated by the poet's remark that the gift Beowulf gave the Danish coast guard brought the latter honor among his companions, and even more by the fact that although Beowulf dies while obtaining a great treasure for his people, such objects as are removed from the dragon's hoard are actually buried with him as a fitting sign of his ultimate achievement.

The relationship between kinsmen was also of deep significance to this society and provides another emotional value for Old English heroic poetry. If one of his kinsmen had been slain, a man had the special duty of either killing the slayer or exacting from him the payment of *wergild* ("manprice"): each rank of society was evaluated at a definite price, which had to be paid to the dead man's kinsmen by the killer who wished to avoid their vengeance—even if the killing had been accidental. Again, the money itself had less significance as wealth than as a proof that the kinsmen had done what was right. Relatives who failed either to exact *wergild* or to take vengeance could never be happy, having found no practical way of satisfying their grief for their kinsman's death. "It is better for a man to avenge his friend than much mourn," Beowulf says to the old Hrothgar, who is bewailing Aeschere's killing by Grendel's mother. And one of the most poignant passages in the poem describes the sorrow of King Hrethel after one of his sons had accidentally killed another: by the code of kinship Hrethel was forbidden to kill or to exact compensation from a kinsman, yet by the same code he was required to do one or the other in order to avenge the dead. Caught in this curious dilemma, Hrethel became so disconsolate that he could no longer face life.

It is evident that the need to take vengeance would create never-ending feuds, which the practice of marrying royal princesses to the kings or princes of hostile tribes did little to mitigate, though the purpose of such marriages was to replace hostility by alliance. Hrothgar wishes to make peace with the Heatho-Bards by marrying his daughter to their king, Ingeld, whose father was killed by the Danes; but as Beowulf predicts, sooner or later the Heatho-Bards' desire for vengeance on the Danes will erupt, and there will be more bloodshed. And the Danish princess Hildeburh, married to Finn of the Jutes, will see her son and her brother both killed while fighting on opposite sides in a battle at her own home, and ultimately will see her husband killed by the Danes in revenge for her brother's death. Beowulf himself is, for a Germanic hero, curiously free of involvement in feuds of this sort, though he does boast that he avenged the death of his king, Heardred, on his slayer Onela. Yet the potentiality—or inevitability—of sudden attack, sudden change, swift death is omnipresent in *Beowulf*: men seem to be caught in a vast web of reprisals and counterreprisals from which there is little hope of escape. This is the aspect of the poem which is apt to make the most powerful impression on the reader—its strong sense of doom.

Beowulf himself is chiefly concerned not with tribal feuds but with fatal evil both less and more complex. Grendel and the dragon are threats to the security of the lands they infest just as human enemies would be, but they are not part of the social order and presumably have no one to avenge their deaths (that Grendel's mother appeared as an avenger seems to have been a surprise both to Beowulf and to the Danes). On the other hand, because they are outside the normal order of things, they require of their conqueror something greater than normal warfare requires. In each case, it is the clear duty of the king and his companions to put down the evil. But the Danish Hrothgar is old and his companions unenterprising, and excellent though Hrothgar has been in the kingship, he nevertheless lacks the quality that later impels the old Beowulf to fight the dragon that threatens his people. The poem makes no criticism of Hrothgar for this lack; he merely seems not to be the kind of man—one might almost say he was not fated—to develop his human potential to the fullest extent that Fate would permit: that is Beowulf's role. In undertaking to slay Grendel, and later Grendel's mother, Beowulf is testing his relationship with unknowable destiny. At any time, as he is fully aware, his luck may abandon him and he may be killed, as, indeed, he is in the otherwise successful encounter with the dragon. But whether he lives or dies, he will have done all that any man could do to develop his character heroically. It is this consciousness of testing Fate that probably explains the boasting that modern readers of heroic poetry often find offensive. When he boasts, Beowulf is not only demonstrating that he has chosen the heroic way of life, but is also choosing it, for when he invokes his former courage as pledge of his future courage, his boast becomes a vow; the hero has put himself in a position from which he cannot withdraw.

Courage is the instrument by which the hero realizes himself. "Fate often saves an undoomed man when his courage is good," says Beowulf in his account of his swimming match: that is, if Fate has not entirely doomed a man in advance, courage is the quality that can perhaps influence Fate against its natural tendency to doom him now. It is this complex statement (in which it is hard to read the will of God for Fate) that Beowulf's life explores: he will use his great strength in the most courageous way by going alone, even unarmed, against monsters. Doom, of course, ultimately claims him, but not until he has fulfilled to its limits the pagan ideal of a heroic life. And despite the desire he often shows to Christianize pagan virtues, the Christian poet remains true to the older tradition when, at the end of his poem, he leaves us with the impression that Beowulf's chief reward is pagan immortality: the memory in the minds of later generations of a hero's heroic actions. The poem itself is, indeed, a noble expression of that immortality.

TRIBES AND GENEALOGIES

1. The Danes (Bright-, Half-, Ring-, Spear-, North-, East-, South-, West-Danes; Scyldings, Honor-, Victor-, War-Scyldings; Ing's friends).

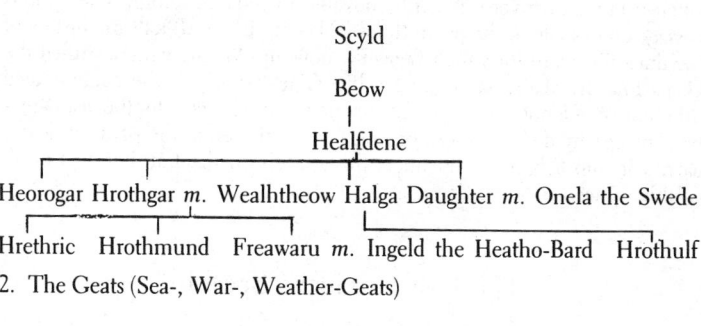

2. The Geats (Sea-, War-, Weather-Geats)

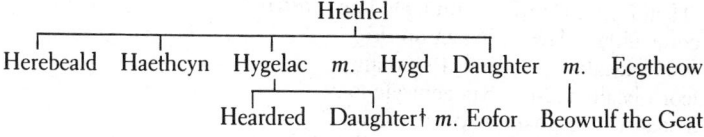

3. The Swedes.

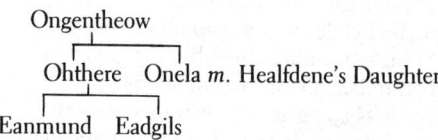

4. Miscellaneous.

A. The Half-Danes (also called Scyldings) involved in the fight at Finnsburg may represent a different tribe from the Danes of paragraph 1, above.

---

†The; daughter of Hygelac who was given to Eofor may have been born to him by a former wife, older than Hygd.

Their king Hoc had a son, Hnaef, who succeeded him, and a daughter
Hildeburh, who married Finn, king of the Jutes.

   B. The Jutes or Frisians are represented as enemies of the Danes in the
fight at Finnsburg and as allies of the Franks or Hugas at the time Hygelac
the Geat made the attack in which he lost his life and from which Beowulf
swam home. Also allied with the Franks at this time were the Hetware.

   C. The Heatho-Bards (i.e., "Battle-Bards") are represented as inveterate
enemies of the Danes. Their king Froda had been killed in an attack on the
Danes, and Hrothgar's attempt to make peace with them by marrying his
daughter Freawaru to Froda's son Ingeld failed when the latter attacked Heorot. The attack was repulsed, though Heorot was burned.

The Last Survivor's Speech in Old English with Verse
Translation   In order to give the reader a sample of the language, style,
and texture of *Beowulf* we print the following passage in the original followed
by a verse translation that attempts to convey the terseness and strong beat
of the alliterative measure, though to observe the strict rules of classical Old
English alliterative verse is hardly possible in modern idiom. The famous
passage comes late in the poem (lines 2247–66, p. 65). It tells the history of
the dragon's hoard for which Beowulf, now an old king who has ruled the
Geats for fifty years, sacrifices his life. The treasure is the accumulated
inheritance of a noble race of warriors, now extinct except for the last nameless "hringa hyrde" (shepherd of rings) who, himself at the point of death,
carries it into a barrow and utters this speech on the transitoriness of all
earthly things.

[The Last Survivor's Speech][1]

"Heald þu nu, hruse,   nu hæleð ne mostan,
eorla æhte!   Hwæt, hyt ær on ðe
gode begeaton.   Guþ-deað fornam,
feorh-bealo frecne   fyra gehwylcne   2250
leoda minra,   þara ðe þis lif ofgeaf,
gesawon sele-dreamas.   Nah hwa sweord wege
oððe feormie   fæted wæge,
drync fæt deore;   duguð ellor scoc.
Sceal se hearda helm   hyrsted golde   2255
fætum befeallen;   feormynd swefað,
þa ðe beado-griman   bywan sceoldon;
ge swylce seo here-pad,   sio æt hilde gebad
ofer borda gebræc   bite irena,
brosnað æfter beorne;   ne mæg byrnan hring   2260
æftrer wig-fruman   wide feran
hæleðum be healfe.   Næs hearpan wyn

---

1. The verse translation is by the junior editor.

gomen gleo-beames,   ne god hafoc
geond sæl swingeð,   ne se swifta mearh
burh-stede beateð.   Bealo-cwealm hafað   2265
fela feorh-cynna   forð onsended!"

"Hold them now, Earth,   now hand of man cannot,
A great tribe's treasures.   Truly, from you
Brave men first got them;   battle-death has taken,
Murderous fighting,   the men, one and all,   2250
Peers of my people: they have passed from this life,
Rest from hall-joys.   None remains with me
To bear the sword,   burnish the rich goblet,
Costly drinking-cup;   the company has gone elsewhere.
Now the hard helmet,   hammered with gold,   2255
Must be stripped of its plating;   the polishers sleep
Who once made bright   those grim battle-masks;
Also the armor,   which endured in battle,
Mid breaking of shields,   the bite of swords,
Rots with the warrior.   The ringed-corslet   2260
May not wander far   on the war-chief's path,
At the soldiers' side.   The harp is silent,
No glad music sounds,   nor any good hawk
Sweeps through the hall,   nor swift hoofbeats
Drum in the courtyard.   Death-qualm has sent   2265
Full many a folk   forth on their way."

Beowulf[1]

[Prologue: The Earlier History of the Danes]

Yes, we have heard of the glory of the Spear-Danes' kings in the old
days—how the princes of that people did brave deeds.

Often Scyld Scefing[2] took mead-benches away from enemy bands,
from many tribes, terrified their nobles—after the time that he was first
found destitute. He lived to find comfort for that, became great under
the skies, prospered in honors until every one of those who lived about
him, across the whale-road, had to obey him, pay him tribute. That was
a good king.

Afterwards a son was born to him, a young boy in his house, whom
God sent to comfort the people: He had seen the sore need they had
suffered during the long time they lacked a king. Therefore the Lord of
Life, the Ruler of Heaven, gave him honor in the world: Beow[3] was
famous, the glory of the son of Scyld spread widely in the Northlands.

---

1. The translation into modern English, by the
senior editor (1966), is based on F. Klaeber's 3rd
ed. of the poem (1950); in general, the emendations suggested by J. C. Pope, The Rhythm of Beowulf, 2nd ed. (1966), have been adopted.

2. The meaning is probably "son of Sceaf,"
although Scyld's origins are mysterious.
3. Although the manuscript reads "Beowulf," most
scholars now agree that it should read "Beow." Beow
was the grandfather of the Danish king Hrothgar.

In this way a young man ought by his good deeds, by giving splendid gifts while still in his father's house, to make sure that later in life beloved companions will stand by him, that people will serve him when war comes. Through deeds that bring praise, a man shall prosper in every country.

Then at the fated time Scyld the courageous went away into the protection of the Lord. His dear companions carried him down to the sea-currents, just as he himself had bidden them do when, as protector of the Scyldings,[4] he had ruled them with his words—long had the beloved prince governed the land. There in the harbor stood the ring-prowed ship, ice-covered and ready to sail, a prince's vessel. Then they laid down the ruler they had loved, the ring-giver, in the hollow of the ship, the glorious man beside the mast. There was brought great store of treasure, wealth from lands far away. I have not heard of a ship more splendidly furnished with war-weapons and battle-dress, swords and mail-shirts. On his breast lay a great many treasures that should voyage with him far out into the sea's possession. They provided him with no lesser gifts, treasure of the people, than those had done who at his beginning first sent him forth on the waves, a child alone.[5] Then also they set a golden standard high over his head, let the water take him, gave him to the sea. Sad was their spirit, mournful their mind. Men cannot truthfully say who received that cargo, neither counsellors in the hall nor warriors under the skies.

Then in the cities was Beow of the Scyldings beloved king of the people, long famous among nations (his father had gone elsewhere, the king from his land), until later great Healfdene was born to him. As long as he lived, old and fierce in battle, he upheld the glorious Scyldings. To him all told were four children born into the world, to the leader of the armies: Heorogar and Hrothgar and the good Halga. I have heard tell that [. . . was On]ela's queen,[6] beloved bed-companion of the Battle-Scylfing.

[Beowulf and Grendel]

[THE HALL HEOROT IS ATTACKED BY GRENDEL]

Then Hrothgar was given success in warfare, glory in battle, so that his retainers gladly obeyed him and their company grew into a great band of warriors. It came to his mind that he would command men to construct a hall, a great mead-building that the children of men should hear of forever, and therein he would give to young and old all that God had given him, except for common land and men's bodies.[7] Then I have heard that the work was laid upon many nations, wide through this

---

4. I.e., the Danes ("descendants of Scyld").

5. In view of the fact that Scyld was said to have arrived destitute, this statement should probably be taken as a kind of curious understatement emphasizing the reversal in Scyld's fortunes.

6. The text is faulty, so that the name of Healf-

dene's daughter has been lost; her husband Onela was a Swedish (Scylfing) king.

7. Or "men's lives." Apparently slaves, along with public land, were not in the king's power to give away.

middle-earth, that they should adorn the folk-hall. In time it came to pass—quickly, as men count it—that it was finished, the largest of hall-dwellings. He gave it the name of Heorot,[8] he who ruled wide with his words. He did not forget his promise: at the feast he gave out rings, treasure. The hall stood tall, high and wide-gabled: it would wait for the fierce flames of vengeful fire;[9] the time was not yet at hand for sword-hate between son-in-law and father-in-law to awaken after murderous rage.

Then the fierce spirit[1] painfully endured hardship for a time, he who dwelt in the darkness, for every day he heard loud mirth in the hall; there was the sound of the harp, the clear song of the scop.[2] There he spoke who could relate the beginning of men far back in time, said that the Almighty made earth, a bright field fair in the water that surrounds it, set up in triumph the lights of the sun and the moon to lighten land-dwellers, and adorned the surfaces of the earth with branches and leaves, created also life for each of the kinds that move and breathe.—Thus these warriors lived in joy, blessed, until one began to do evil deeds, a hellish enemy. The grim spirit was called Grendel, known as a rover of the borders, one who held the moors, fen and fastness. Unhappy creature, he lived for a time in the home of the monsters' race, after God had condemned them as kin of Cain. The Eternal Lord avenged the murder in which he slew Abel. Cain had no pleasure in that feud, but He banished him far from mankind, the Ruler, for that misdeed. From him sprang all bad breeds, trolls and elves and monsters—likewise the giants who for a long time strove with God: He paid them their reward for that.

Then, after night came, Grendel went to survey the tall house—how, after their beer-drinking, the Ring-Danes had disposed themselves in it. Then he found therein a band of nobles asleep after the feast: they felt no sorrow, no misery of men. The creature of evil, grim and fierce, was quickly ready, savage and cruel, and seized from their rest thirty thanes. From there he turned to go back to his home, proud of his plunder, sought his dwelling with that store of slaughter.

Then in the first light of dawning day Grendel's war-strength was revealed to men: then after the feast weeping arose, great cry in the morning. The famous king, hero of old days, sat joyless; the mighty one suffered, felt sorrow for his thanes, when they saw the track of the foe, of the cursed spirit: that hardship was too strong, too loathsome and long-lasting. Nor was there a longer interval, but after one night Grendel again did greater slaughter—and had no remorse for it—vengeful acts and wicked: he was too intent on them. Thereafter it was easy to find the man who sought rest for himself elsewhere, farther away, a bed among

8. I.e., "Hart."
9. The destruction by fire of Heorot occurred at a later time than that of the poem's action, probably during the otherwise unsuccessful attack of the Heatho-Bard Ingeld on his father-in-law, Hroth-

gar, mentioned in the next clause.
1. I.e., Grendel.
2. The "scop" was the Anglo-Saxon minstrel, who recited poetic stories to the accompaniment of a harp.

the outlying buildings—after it was made clear to him, told by clear proof, the hatred of him who now controlled the hall.[3] Whoever escaped the foe held himself afterwards farther off and more safely. Thus Grendel held sway and fought against right, one against all, until the best of houses stood empty. It was a long time, the length of twelve winters, that the lord of the Scyldings suffered grief, all woes, great sorrows. Therefore, sadly in songs, it became well-known to the children of men that Grendel had fought a long time with Hrothgar, for many half-years maintained mortal spite, feud, and enmity—constant war. He wanted no peace with any of the men of the Danish host, would not withdraw his deadly rancor, or pay compensation: no counselor there had any reason to expect splendid repayment at the hands of the slayer.[4] For the monster was relentless, the dark death-shadow, against warriors old and young, lay in wait and ambushed them. In the perpetual darkness he held to the misty moors: men do not know where hell-demons direct their footsteps.

Thus many crimes the enemy of mankind committed, the terrible walker-alone, cruel injuries one after another. In the dark nights he dwelt in Heorot, the richly adorned hall. He might not approach the throne, [receive] treasure, because of the Lord; He had no love for him.[5]

This was great misery to the lord of the Scyldings, a breaking of spirit. Many a noble sat often in council, sought a plan, what would be best for strong-hearted men to do against the awful attacks. At times they vowed sacrifices at heathen temples, with their words prayed that the soul-slayer[6] would give help for the distress of the people. Such was their custom, the hope of heathens; in their spirits they thought of Hell, they knew not the Ruler, the Judge of Deeds, they recognized not the Lord God, nor indeed did they know how to praise the Protector of Heaven, the glorious King. Woe is him who in terrible trouble must thrust his soul into the fire's embrace, hope for no comfort, not expect change. Well is the man who after his death-day may seek the Lord and find peace in the embrace of the Father.

[THE COMING OF BEOWULF TO HEOROT]

So in the cares of his times the son of Healfdene constantly brooded, nor might the wise warrior set aside his woe. Too harsh, hateful and long-lasting was the hardship that had come upon the people, distress dire and inexorable, worst of night-horrors.

A thane of Hygelac,[7] a good man among the Geats, heard in his homeland of Grendel's deeds: of mankind he was the strongest of might

---

3. I.e., Grendel.
4. According to old Germanic law, a slayer could achieve peace with his victim's kinsmen only by paying them *wergild*, i.e., compensation for the life of the slain man.
5. Behind this obscure passage seems to lie the idea that Grendel, unlike Hrothgar's thanes, could

not approach the throne to receive gifts from the king, having been condemned by God as an outlaw.
6. I.e., the Devil. It was believed that pagan deities were actually devils.
7. I.e., Beowulf the Geat, whose king was Hygelac.

in the time of this life, noble and great. He bade that a good ship be made ready for him, said he would seek the war-king over the swan's road, the famous prince, since he had need of men. Very little did wise men blame him for that adventure, though he was dear to them; they urged the brave one on, examined the omens. From the folk of the Geats the good man had chosen warriors of the bravest that he could find; one of fifteen he led the way, the warrior sought the wooden ship, the sea-skilled one the land's edge. The time had come: the ship was on the waves, the boat under the cliff. The warriors eagerly climbed on the prow—the sea-currents eddied, sea against sand; men bore bright weapons into the ship's bosom, splendid armor. Men pushed the well-braced ship from shore, warriors on a well-wished voyage. Then over the sea-waves, blown by the wind, the foam-necked boat traveled, most like a bird, until at good time on the second day the curved prow had come to where the seafarers could see land, the sea-cliffs shine, towering hills, great headlands. Then was the sea crossed, the journey at end. Then quickly the men of the Geats climbed upon the shore, moored the wooden ship; mail-shirts rattled, dress for battle. They thanked God that the wave-way had been easy for them.

Then from the wall the Scyldings' guard who should watch over the sea-cliffs saw bright shields borne over the gangway, armor ready for battle; strong desire stirred him in mind to learn what the men were. He went riding on his horse to the shore, thane of Hrothgar, forcefully brandished a great spear in his hands, with formal words questioned them: "What are you, bearers of armor, dressed in mail-coats, who thus have come bringing a tall ship over the sea-road, over the water to this place? Lo, for a long time I have been guard of the coast, held watch by the sea so that no foe with a force of ships might work harm on the Danes' land: never have shieldbearers more openly undertaken to come ashore here; nor did you know for sure of a word of leave from our warriors, consent from my kinsmen. I have never seen a mightier warrior on earth than is one of you, a man in battle-dress. That is no retainer made to seem good by his weapons—may his appearance, his unequalled form, never belie him. Now I must learn your lineage before you go any farther from here, spies on the Danes' land. Now you far-dwellers, sea-voyagers, hear what I think: you must straightway say where you have come from."

To him replied the leader, the chief of the band unlocked his word-hoard: "We are men of the Geatish nation and Hygelac's hearth-companions. My father was well-known among the tribes, a noble leader named Ecgtheow. He lived many winters before he went on his way, an old man, from men's dwellings. Every wise man wide over the earth readily remembers him. Through friendly heart we have come to seek your lord, the son of Healfdene, protector of the people. Be good to us and tell us what to do: we have a great errand to the famous one, the king of the Danes. And I too do not think that anything ought to be kept secret: you know whether it is so, as we have indeed heard, that among the Scyldings I know not what foe, what dark doer of hateful deeds in the black nights, shows in terrible manner strange malice, injury and slaughter. In openness of heart I may teach Hrothgar remedy for that, how he, wise and good, shall overpower the foe—if change is ever to come to him, relief from evil's distress—and how his surging cares may be made to cool. Or else ever after he will suffer tribulations, constraint, while the best of houses remains there on its high place."

The guard spoke from where he sat on his horse, brave officer: "A sharp-witted shield-warrior who thinks well must be able to judge each of the two things, words and works. I understand this: that here is a troop friendly to the Scyldings' king. Go forward, bearing weapons and war-gear. I will show you the way; I shall also bid my fellow-thanes honorably to hold your boat against all enemies, your new-tarred ship on the sand, until again over the sea-streams it bears its beloved men to the Geatish shore, the wooden vessel with curved prow. May it be granted by fate that one who behaves so bravely pass whole through the battle-storm."

Then they set off. The boat lay fixed, rested on the rope, the deep-bosomed ship, fast at anchor. Boar-images[8] shone over cheek-guards gold-adorned, gleaming and fire-hardened—the war-minded boar held guard over fierce men. The warriors hastened, marched together until they might see the timbered hall, stately and shining with gold; for earth-dwellers under the skies that was the most famous of buildings in which the mighty one waited—its light gleamed over many lands. The battle-brave guide pointed out to them the shining house of the brave ones so that they might go straight to it. Warrior-like he turned his horse, then spoke words: "It is time for me to go back. The All-Wielding Father in His grace keep you safe in your undertakings. I shall go back to the sea to keep watch against hostile hosts."

The road was stone-paved, the path showed the way to the men in ranks. War-corselet shone, hard and hand-wrought, bright iron rings sang on their armor when they first came walking to the hall in their grim gear. Sea-weary they set down their broad shields, marvelously strong protections, against the wall of the building. Then they sat down on the bench—mail-shirts, warrior's clothing, rang out. Spears stood together, seamen's weapons, ash steel-gray at the top. The armed band was worthy of its weapons.

Then a proud-spirited man[9] asked the warriors there about their lineage: "Where do you bring those gold-covered shields from, gray mail-shirts and visored helmets, this multitude of battle-shafts? I am Hrothgar's herald and officer. I have not seen strangers—so many men—more bold. I think that it is for daring—not for refuge, but for greatness of heart—that you have sought Hrothgar." The man known for his courage replied to him; the proud man of the Geats, hardy under helmet, spoke

---

8. Carved images of boars (sometimes represented as clothed like human warriors) were placed on helmets in the belief that they would protect the   wearer in battle.
9. Identified below as Wulfgar.

words in return: "We are Hygelac's table-companions. Beowulf is my name. I will tell my errand to Healfdene's son, the great prince your lord, if, good as he is, he will grant that we might address him." Wulfgar spoke—he was a man of the Wendels, his bold spirit known to many, his valor and wisdom: "I will ask the lord of the Danes about this, the Scyldings' king, the ring-giver, just as you request—will ask the glorious ruler about your voyage, and will quickly make known to you the answer the good man thinks best to give me."

He returned at once to where Hrothgar sat, old and hoary, with his company of earls. The man known for his valor went forward till he stood squarely before the Danes' king: he knew the custom of tried retainers. Wulfgar spoke to his lord and friend: "Here have journeyed men of the Geats, come far over the sea's expanse. The warriors call their chief Beowulf. They ask that they, my prince, might exchange words with you. Do not refuse them your answer, gracious Hrothgar. From their wargear they seem worthy of earls' esteem. Strong indeed is the chief who has led the warriors here."

Hrothgar spoke, protector of the Scyldings: "I knew him when he was a boy. His father was called Ecgtheow: Hrethel of the Geats[1] gave him his only daughter for his home. Now has his hardy offspring come here, sought a fast friend. Then, too, seafarers who took gifts there to please the Geats used to say that he has in his handgrip the strength of thirty men, a man famous in battle. Holy God of His grace has sent him to us West-Danes, as I hope, against the terror of Grendel. I shall offer the good man treasures for his daring. Now make haste, bid them come in together to see my company of kinsmen. In your speech say to them also that they are welcome to the Danish people."

Then Wulfgar went to the hall's door, gave the message from within: "The lord of the East-Danes, my victorious prince, has bidden me say to you that he knows your noble ancestry, and that you brave-hearted men are welcome to him over the sea-swells. Now you may come in your war-dress, under your battle helmets, to see Hrothgar. Let your war-shields, your wooden spears, await here the outcome of the talk."

Then the mighty one rose, many a warrior about him, a company of strong thanes. Some waited there, kept watch over the weapons as the brave one bade them. Together they hastened, as the warrior directed them, under Heorot's roof. The war-leader, hardy under helmet, advanced till he stood on the hearth. Beowulf spoke, his mail-shirt glistened, armor-net woven by the blacksmith's skill: "Hail, Hrothgar! I am kinsman and thane of Hygelac. In my youth I have set about many brave deeds. The affair of Grendel was made known to me on my native soil: sea-travelers say that this hall, best of buildings, stands empty and useless to all warriors after the evening-light becomes hidden beneath the cover of the sky. Therefore my people, the best wise earls, advised me thus, lord

---

1. Hrethel was the father of Hygelac and Beowulf's grandfather and guardian.

Hrothgar, that I should seek you because they know what my strength can accomplish. They themselves looked on when, bloody from my foes, I came from the fight where I had bound five, destroyed a family of giants, and at night in the waves slain water-monsters, suffered great pain, avenged an affliction of the Weather-Geats on those who had asked for trouble—ground enemies to bits. And now alone I shall settle affairs with Grendel, the monster, the demon. Therefore, lord of the Bright-Danes, protector of the Scyldings, I will make a request of you, refuge of warriors, fair friend of nations, that you refuse me not, now that I have come so far, that alone with my company of earls, this band of hardy men, I may cleanse Heorot. I have also heard say that the monster in his recklessness cares not for weapons. Therefore, so that my liege lord Hygelac may be glad of me in his heart, I scorn to bear sword or broad shield, yellow wood, to the battle, but with my grasp I shall grapple with the enemy and fight for life, foe against foe. The one whom death takes can trust the Lord's judgment. I think that if he may accomplish it, unafraid he will feed on the folk of the Geats in the war-hall as he has often done on the flower of men. You will not need to hide my head[2] if death takes me, for he will have me blood-smeared; he will bear away my bloody flesh meaning to savor it, he will eat ruthlessly, the walker alone, will stain his retreat in the moor; no longer will you need trouble yourself to take care of my body. If battle takes me, send to Hygelac the best of war-clothes that protects my breast, finest of mail-shirts. It is a legacy of Hrethel, the work of Weland.[3] Fate always goes as it must."

Hrothgar spoke, protector of the Scyldings: "For deeds done, my friend Beowulf, and for past favors you have sought us. A fight of your father's brought on the greatest of feuds. With his own hands he became the slayer of Heatholaf among the Wylfings. After that the country of the Weather-Geats might not keep him, for fear of war. From there he sought the folk of the South-Danes, the Honor-Scyldings, over the sea-swell. At that time I was first ruling the Danish people and, still in my youth, held the wide kingdom, hoard-city of heroes. Heorogar had died then, gone from life, my older brother, son of Healfdene—he was better than I. Afterwards I paid blood-money to end the feud; over the sea's back I sent to the Wylfings old treasures; he[4] swore oaths to me.

"It is a sorrow to me in spirit to say to any man what Grendel has brought me with his hatred—humiliation in Heorot, terrible violence. My hall-troop, warrior-band, has shrunk; fate has swept them away into Grendel's horror. (God may easily put an end to the wild ravager's deeds!) Full often over the ale-cups warriors made bold with beer have boasted that they would await with grim swords Grendel's attack in the beer-hall. Then in the morning this mead-hall was a hall shining with blood, when the day lightened, all the bench-floor blood-wet, a gore-hall. I

---

2. I.e., "bury my body."
3. The blacksmith of the Norse gods.

4. Ecgtheow, whose feud with the Wylfings Hrothgar had settled.

had fewer faithful men, beloved retainers, for death had destroyed them. Now sit down to the feast and unbind your thoughts, your famous victories, as heart inclines."

[THE FEAST AT HEOROT]

Then was a bench cleared in the beer-hall for the men of the Geats all together. Then the stout-hearted ones went to sit down, proud in their might. A thane did his work who bore in his hands an embellished ale-cup, poured the bright drink. At times a scop sang, clear-voiced in Heorot. There was joy of brave men, no little company of Danes and Weather-Geats.

Unferth spoke, son of Ecglaf, who sat at the feet of the king of the Scyldings, unbound words of contention—to him was Beowulf's undertaking, the brave seafarer, a great vexation, for he would not allow that any other man of middle-earth should ever achieve more glory under the heavens than himself: "Are you that Beowulf who contended with Breca, competed in swimming on the broad sea, where for pride you explored the water, and for foolish boast ventured your lives in the deep? Nor might any man, friend nor enemy, keep you from the perilous venture of swimming in the sea. There you embraced the sea-streams with your arms, measured the sea-ways, flung forward your hands, glided over the ocean; the sea boiled with waves, with winter's swell. Seven nights you toiled in the water's power. He overcame you at swimming, had more strength. Then in the morning the sea bore him up among the Heathoraemas; from there he sought his own home, dear to his people, the land of the Brondings, the fair stronghold, where he had folk, castle, and treasures. All his boast against you the son of Beanstan carried out in deed. Therefore I expect the worse results for you—though you have prevailed everywhere in battles, in grim war—if you dare wait near Grendel a night-long space."

Beowulf spoke, the son of Ecgtheow: "Well, my friend Unferth, drunk with beer you have spoken a great many things about Breca—told about his adventures. I maintain the truth that I had more strength in the sea, hardship on the waves, than any other man. Like boys we agreed together and boasted—we were both in our first youth—that we would risk our lives in the salt sea, and that we did even so. We had naked swords, strong in our hands, when we went swimming; we thought to guard ourselves against whale-fishes. He could not swim at all far from me in the flood-waves, be quicker in the water, nor would I move away from him. Thus we were together on the sea for the time of five nights until the flood drove us apart, the swelling sea, coldest of weathers, darkening night, and the north wind battle-grim turned against us: rough were the waves. The anger of the sea-fishes was roused. Then my body-mail, hard and hand-linked, gave me help against my foes; the woven war-garment, gold-adorned, covered my breast. A fierce cruel attacker dragged me to the bottom, held me grim in his grasp, but it was granted me to reach the monster with my sword-point, my battle-blade. The war-stroke destroyed the mighty sea-beast—through my hand.

"Thus often loathsome assailants pressed me hard. I served them with my good sword, as the right was. They had no joy at all of the feast, the malice-workers, that they should eat me, sit around a banquet near the sea-bottom. But in the morning, sword-wounded they lay on the shore, left behind by the waves, put to sleep by the blade, so that thereafter they would never hinder the passage of sea-voyagers over the deep water. Light came from the east, bright signal of God, the sea became still so that I might see the headlands, the windy walls of the sea. Fate often saves an undoomed man when his courage is good. In any case it befell me that I slew with my sword nine sea-monsters. I have not heard tell of a harder fight by night under heaven's arch, nor of a man more hard-pressed in the sea-streams. Yet I came out of the enemies' grasp alive, weary of my adventure. Then the sea bore me onto the lands of the Finns, the flood with its current, the surging waters.

"I have not heard say of you any such hard matching of might, such sword-terror. Breca never yet in the games of war—neither he nor you—achieved so bold a deed with bright swords (I do not much boast of it), though you became your brothers' slayer, your close kin; for that you will suffer punishment in hell, even though your wit is keen. I tell you truly, son of Ecglaf, that Grendel, awful monster, would never have performed so many terrible deeds against your chief, humiliation in Heorot, if your spirit, your heart, were so fierce in fight as you claim. But he has noticed that he need not much fear the hostility, not much dread the terrible sword-storm of your people, the Victory-Scyldings. He exacts forced levy, shows mercy to none of the Danish people; but he is glad, kills, carves for feasting, expects no fight from the Spear-Danes. But I shall show him soon now the strength and courage of the Geats, their warfare. Afterwards he will walk who may, glad to the mead, when the morning light of another day, the bright-clothed sun, shines from the south on the children of men."

Then was the giver of treasure in gladness, gray-haired and battle-brave. The lord of the Bright-Danes could count on help. The folk's guardian had heard from Beowulf a fast-resolved thought.

There was laughter of warriors, voices rang pleasant, words were cheerful. Wealhtheow came forth, Hrothgar's queen, mindful of customs, gold-adorned, greeted the men in the hall; and the noble woman offered the cup first to the keeper of the land of the East-Danes, bade him be glad at the beer-drinking, beloved of the people. In joy he partook of feast and hall-cup, king famous for victories. Then the woman of the Helmings went about to each one of the retainers, young and old, offered them the costly cup, until the time came that she brought the mead-bowl to Beowulf, the ring-adorned queen, mature of mind. Sure of speech she greeted the man of the Geats, thanked God that her wish was fulfilled, that she might trust in some man for help against deadly deeds. He took the cup, the warrior fierce in battle, from Wealhtheow, and then spoke, one ready for fight—Beowulf spoke, the son of Ecgtheow: "I resolved, when I set out on the sea, sat down in the sea-boat with my band of men, that I should altogether fulfill the will of your people or else fall in slaughter, fast in the foe's grasp. I shall achieve a deed of manly courage or else have lived to see in this mead-hall my ending day." These words were well-pleasing to the woman, the boast of the Geat. Gold-adorned, the noble folk-queen went to sit by her lord.

Then there were again as at first strong words spoken in the hall, the people in gladness, the sound of a victorious folk, until, in a little while, the son of Healfdene wished to seek his evening rest. He knew of the battle in the high hall that had been plotted by the monster, plotted from the time that they might see the light of the sun until the night, growing dark over all things, the shadowy shapes of darkness, should come gliding, black under the clouds. The company all arose. Then they saluted each other, Hrothgar and Beowulf, and Hrothgar wished him good luck, control of the wine-hall, and spoke these words: "Never before, since I could raise hand and shield, have I entrusted to any man the great hall of the Danes, except now to you. Hold now and guard the best of houses: remember your fame, show your great courage, keep watch against the fierce foe. You will not lack what you wish if you survive that deed of valor."

[THE FIGHT WITH GRENDEL]

Then Hrothgar went out of the hall with his company of warriors, the protector of the Scyldings. The war-chief would seek the bed of Wealhtheow the queen. The King of Glory—as men had learned—had appointed a hall-guard against Grendel; he had a special mission to the prince of the Danes: he kept watch against monsters.

And the man of the Geats had sure trust in his great might, the favor of the Ruler. Then he took off his shirt of armor, the helmet from his head, handed his embellished sword, best of irons, to an attendant, bade him keep guard over his war-gear. Then the good warrior spoke some boast-words before he went to his bed, Beowulf of the Geats: "I claim myself no poorer in war-strength, war works, than Grendel claims himself. Therefore I will not put him to sleep with a sword, so take away his life, though surely I might. He knows no good tools with which he might strike against me, cut my shield in pieces, though he is strong in fight. But we shall forgo the sword in the night—if he dare seek war without weapon—and then may wise God, Holy Lord, assign glory on whichever hand seems good to Him."

The battle-brave one laid himself down, the pillow received the earl's head, and about him many a brave seaman lay down to hall-rest. None of them thought that he would ever again seek from there his dear home, people or town where he had been brought up; for they knew that bloody death had carried off far too many men in the wine-hall, folk of the Danes. But the Lord granted to weave for them good fortune in war, for the folk of the Weather-Geats, comfort and help that they should quite overcome their foe through the might of one man, through his sole strength: the truth has been made known that mighty God has always ruled mankind.

There came gliding in the black night the walker in darkness. The warriors slept who should hold the horned house—all but one. It was known to men that when the Ruler did not wish it the hostile creature might not drag them away beneath the shadows. But he, lying awake for the fierce foe, with heart swollen in anger awaited the outcome of the fight.

Then from the moor under the mist-hills Grendel came walking, wearing God's anger. The foul ravager thought to catch some one of mankind there in the high hall. Under the clouds he moved until he could see most clearly the wine-hall, treasure-house of men, shining with gold. That was not the first time that he had sought Hrothgar's home. Never before or since in his life-days did he find harder luck, hardier hall-thanes. The creature deprived of joy came walking to the hall. Quickly the door gave way, fastened with fire-forged bands, when he touched it with his hands. Driven by evil desire, swollen with rage, he tore it open, the hall's mouth. After that the foe at once stepped onto the shining floor, advanced angrily. From his eyes came a light not fair, most like a flame. He saw many men in the hall, a band of kinsmen all asleep together, a company of war-men. Then his heart laughed: dreadful monster, he thought that before the day came he would divide the life from the body of every one of them, for there had come to him a hope of full-feasting. It was not his fate that when that night was over he should feast on more of mankind.

The kinsman of Hygelac, mighty man, watched how the evil-doer would make his quick onslaught. Nor did the monster mean to delay it, but, starting his work, he suddenly seized a sleeping man, tore at him ravenously, bit into his bone-locks, drank the blood from his veins, swallowed huge morsels; quickly he had eaten all of the lifeless one, feet and hands. He stepped closer, then felt with his arm for the brave-hearted man on the bed, reached out towards him, the foe with his hand; at once in fierce response Beowulf seized it and sat up, leaning on his own arm. Straightway the fosterer of crimes knew that he had not encountered on middle-earth, anywhere in this world, a harder hand-grip from another man. In mind he became frightened, in his spirit: not for that might he escape the sooner. His heart was eager to get away, he would flee to his hiding-place, seek his rabble of devils. What he met there was not such as he had ever before met in the days of his life. Then the kinsman of Hygelac, the good man, thought of his evening's speech, stood upright and laid firm hold on him: his fingers cracked. The giant was pulling away, the earl stepped forward. The notorious one thought to move farther away, wherever he could, and flee his way from there to his fen-retreat; he knew his fingers' power to be in a hateful grip. That was a painful journey that the loathsome despoiler had made to Heorot.

The retainers' hall rang with the noise—terrible drink[5] for all the Danes,
the house-dwellers, every brave man, the earls. Both were enraged, fury-
filled, the two who meant to control the hall. The building resounded.
Then was it much wonder that the wine-hall withstood them joined in
fierce fight, that it did not fall to the ground, the fair earth-dwelling; but
it was so firmly made fast with iron bands, both inside and outside,
joined by skillful smith-craft. There started from the floor—as I have
heard say—many a mead-bench, gold-adorned, when the furious ones
fought. No wise men of the Scyldings ever before thought that any men
in any manner might break it down, splendid with bright horns, have
skill to destroy it, unless flame should embrace it, swallow it in fire.
Noise rose up, sound strange enough. Horrible fear came upon the North-
Danes, upon every one of those who heard the weeping from the wall,
God's enemy sing his terrible song, song without triumph—the hell-
slave bewail his pain. There held him fast he who of men was strongest
of might in the days of this life.

   Not for anything would the protector of warriors let the murderous
guest go off alive: he did not consider his life-days of use to any of the
nations. There more than enough of Beowulf's earls drew swords, old
heirlooms, wished to protect the life of their dear lord, famous prince,
however they might. They did not know when they entered the fight,
hardy-spirited warriors, and when they thought to hew him on every
side, to seek his soul, that not any of the best of irons on earth, no war-
sword, would touch the evil-doer: for with a charm he had made victory-
weapons useless, every sword-edge. His departure to death from the time
of this life was to be wretched; and the alien spirit was to travel far off
into the power of fiends. Then he who before had brought trouble of
heart to mankind, committed many crimes—he was at war with God—
found that his body would do him no good, for the great-hearted kinsman of Hygelac had him by the hand. Each was hateful to the other
alive. The awful monster had lived to feel pain in his body, a huge
wound in his shoulder was exposed, his sinews sprang apart, his bone-
locks broke. Glory in battle was given to Beowulf. Grendel must flee
from there, mortally sick, seek his joyless home in the fen-slopes. He
knew the more surely that his life's end had come, the full number of
his days. For all the Danes was their wish fulfilled after the bloody fight.
Thus he who had lately come from far off, wise and stout-hearted, had
purged Heorot, saved Hrothgar's house from affliction. He rejoiced in
his night's work, a deed to make famous his courage. The man of the
Geats had fulfilled his boast to the East-Danes; so too he had remedied
all the grief, the malice-caused sorrow that they had endured before,
and had had to suffer from harsh necessity, no small distress. That was
clearly proved when the battle-brave man set the hand up under the

---

5. The metaphor reflects the idea that the chief purpose of a hall such as Heorot was as a place for men
to feast in.

curved roof—the arm and the shoulder: there all together was Grendel's grasp.

[CELEBRATION AT HEOROT]

Then in the morning, as I have heard, there was many a warrior about the gift-hall. Folk-chiefs came from far and near over the wide-stretching ways to look on the wonder, the footprints of the foe. Nor did his going from life seem sad to any of the men who saw the tracks of the one without glory—how, weary-hearted, overcome with injuries, he moved on his way from there to the mere[6] of the water-monsters with life-failing footsteps, death-doomed and in flight. There the water was boiling with blood, the horrid surge of waves swirling, all mixed with hot gore, sword-blood. Doomed to die he had hidden, then, bereft of joys, had laid down his life in his fen-refuge, his heathen soul: there hell took him.

From there old retainers—and many a young man, too—turned back in their glad journey to ride from the mere, high-spirited on horseback, warriors on steeds. There was Beowulf's fame spoken of; many a man said—and not only once—that, south nor north, between the seas, over the wide earth, no other man under the sky's expanse was better of those who bear shields, more worthy of ruling. Yet they found no fault with their own dear lord, gracious Hrothgar, for he was a good king. At times battle-famed men let their brown horses gallop, let them race where the paths seemed fair, known for their excellence. At times a thane of the king, a man skilled at telling adventures, songs stored in his memory, who could recall many of the stories of the old days, wrought a new tale in well-joined words; this man undertook with his art to recite in turn Beowulf's exploit, and skillfully to tell an apt tale, to lend words to it.

He spoke everything that he had heard tell of Sigemund's valorous deeds, many a strange thing, the strife of Waels's son,[7] his far journeys, feuds and crimes, of which the children of men knew nothing—except for Fitela with him, to whom he would tell everything, the uncle to his nephew, for they were always friends in need in every fight. Many were the tribes of giants that they had laid low with their swords. For Sigemund there sprang up after his death-day no little glory—after he, hardy in war, had killed the dragon, keeper of the treasure-hoard: under the hoary stone the prince's son had ventured alone, a daring deed, nor was Fitela with him. Yet it turned out well for him, so that his sword went through the gleaming worm and stood fixed in the wall, splendid weapon: the dragon lay dead of the murdering stroke. Through his courage the great warrior had brought it about that he might at his own wish enjoy the ring-hoard. He loaded the sea-boat, bore into the ship's bosom the bright treasure, offspring of Waels. The hot dragon melted.

He was adventurer most famous, far and wide through the nations,

---

6. Lake. 7. Waels was Sigemund's father.

for deeds of courage—he had prospered from that before, the protector of warriors—after the war-making of Heremod had come to an end, his strength and his courage.[8] Among the Jutes Heremod came into the power of his enemies, was betrayed, quickly dispatched. Surging sorrows had oppressed him too long: he had become a great care to his people, to all his princes; for many a wise man in former times had bewailed the journey of the fierce-hearted one—people who had counted on him as a relief from affliction—that that king's son should prosper, take the rank of his father, keep guard over the folk, the treasure and stronghold, the kingdom of heroes, the home of the Scyldings. The kinsman of Hygelac became dearer to his friends, to all mankind: crime took possession of Heremod.

Sometimes racing their horses they passed over the sand-covered ways. By then the morning light was far advanced, hastening on. Many a stout-hearted warrior went to the high hall to see the strange wonder. The king himself walked forth from the women's apartment, the guardian of the ring-hoards, secure in his fame, known for his excellence, with much company; and his queen with him passed over the path to the mead-hall with a troop of attendant women.

Hrothgar spoke—he had gone to the hall, taken his stand on the steps, looked at the high roof shining with gold, and at Grendel's hand: "For this sight may thanks be made quickly to the Almighty: I endured much from the foe, many griefs from Grendel: God may always work wonder upon wonder, the Guardian of Heaven. It was not long ago that I did not expect ever to live to see relief from any of my woes—when the best of houses stood shining with blood, stained with slaughter, a far-reaching woe for each of my counselors, for every one, since none thought he could ever defend the people's stronghold from its enemies, from demons and evil spirits. Now through the Lord's might a warrior has accomplished the deed that all of us with our skill could not perform. Yes, she may say, whatever woman brought forth this son among mankind—if she still lives—that the God of Old was kind to her in her childbearing. Now, Beowulf, best of men, in my heart I will love you as a son: keep well this new kinship. To you will there be no lack of the good things of the world that I have in my possession. Full often I have made reward for less, done honor with gifts to a lesser warrior, weaker in fighting. With your deeds you yourself have made sure that your glory will be ever alive. May the Almighty reward you with good—as just now he has done."

Beowulf spoke, the son of Ecgtheow: "With much good will we have achieved this work of courage, that fight, have ventured boldly against the strength of the unknown one. I should have wished rather that you might have seen him, your enemy brought low among your furnishings. I thought quickly to bind him on his deathbed with hard grasp, so that

8. Heremod was an unsuccessful king of the Danes, one who began brilliantly but became cruel and avaricious, ultimately having to take refuge among the Jutes, who put him to death. His reputation was thus overshadowed by that of Sigemund.

because of my hand-grip he should lie struggling for life—unless his body should escape. I could not stop his going, since the Lord did not wish it, nor did I hold him firmly enough for that, my life-enemy: he was too strong, the foe in his going. Yet to save his life he has left his hand behind to show that he was here—his arm and shoulder; nor by that has the wretched creature bought any comfort; none the longer will the loathsome ravager live, hard-pressed by his crimes, for a wound has clutched him hard in its strong grip, in deadly bonds. There, like a man outlawed for guilt, he shall await the great judgment, how the bright Lord will decree for him."

Then was the warrior more silent in boasting speech of warlike deeds, the son of Ecglaf,[9] after the nobles had looked at the hand, now high on the roof through the strength of a man, the foe's fingers. The end of each one, each of the nail-places, was most like steel; the hand-spurs of the heathen warrior were monstrous spikes. Everyone said that no hard thing would hurt him, no iron good from old times would harm the bloody battle-hand of the monster.

Then it was ordered that Heorot be within quickly adorned by hands. Many there were, both men and women, who made ready the wine-hall, the guest-building. The hangings on the walls shone with gold, many a wondrous sight for each man who looks on such things. That bright building was much damaged, though made fast within by iron bonds, and its door-hinges sprung; the roof alone came through unharmed when the monster, outlawed for his crimes, turned in flight, in despair of his life. That is not easy to flee from—let him try it who will—but driven by need one must seek the place prepared for earth-dwellers, soul-bearers, the sons of men, the place where, after its feasting, one's body will sleep fast in its death-bed.

Then had the proper time come that Healfdene's son should go to the hall; the king himself would share in the feast. I have never heard that a people in a larger company bore themselves better about their treasurer-giver. Men who were known for courage sat at the benches, rejoiced in the feast. Their kinsmen, stout-hearted Hrothgar and Hrothulf, partook fairly of many a mead-cup in the high hall. Heorot within was filled with friends: the Scylding-people had not then known treason's web.[1]

Then the son of Healfdene gave Beowulf a golden standard to reward his victory—a decorated battle-banner—a helmet and mail-shirt: many saw the glorious, costly sword borne before the warrior. Beowulf drank of the cup in the mead-hall. He had no need to be ashamed before fighting men of those rich gifts. I have not heard of many men who gave four precious, gold-adorned things to another on the ale-bench in a more friendly way. The rim around the helmet's crown had a head-protection, wound of wire, so that no battle-hard sharp sword might badly hurt him when the shield-warrior should go against his foe. Then

9. I.e., Unferth, who had taunted Beowulf the night before.
1. A reference to the later history of the Danes, when, after Hrothgar's death, his nephew Hrothulf apparently drove his son and successor Hrethric from the throne.

the people's protector commanded eight horses with golden bridles to be led into the hall, within the walls. The saddle of one of them stood shining with hand-ornaments, adorned with jewels: that had been the war-seat of the high king when the son of Healfdene would join sword-play: never did the warfare of the wide-known one fail when men died in battle. And then the prince of Ing's friends[2] yielded possession of both, horses and weapons, to Beowulf: he bade him use them well. So generously the famous prince, guardian of the hoard, repaid the warrior's battle-deeds with horses and treasure that no man will ever find fault with them—not he that will speak truth according to what is right.

Then further the lord gave treasure to each of the men on the mead-bench who had made the sea-voyage with Beowulf, gave heirlooms; and he commanded that gold be paid for the one whom in his malice Grendel had killed—as he would have killed more if wise God and the man's courage had not forestalled that fate. The Lord guided all the race of men then, as he does now. Yet is discernment everywhere best, forethought of mind. Many a thing dear and loath he shall live to see who here in the days of trouble long makes use of the world.

There was song and music together before Healfdene's battle-leader, the wooden harp touched, tale oft told, when Hrothgar's scop should speak hall-pastime among the mead-benches . . . [of] Finn's retainers when the sudden disaster fell upon them. . . .[3]

The hero of the Half-Danes, Hnaef of the Scyldings, was fated to fall on Frisian battlefield. And no need had Hildeburh[4] to praise the good faith of the Jutes: blameless she was deprived of her dear ones at the shield-play, of son and brother; wounded by spears they fell to their fate. That was a mournful woman. Not without cause did Hoc's daughter lament the decree of destiny when morning came and she might see, under the sky, the slaughter of kinsmen—where before she had the greatest of world's joy. The fight took away all Finn's thanes except for only a few, so that he could in no way continue the battle on the field against Hengest, nor protect the survivors by fighting against the prince's thane. But they offered them peace-terms,[5] that they should clear another building for them, hall and high sea, that they might have control of half of it with the sons of the Jutes; and at givings of treasure the son of Folcwalda[6] should honor the Danes each day, should give Hengest's

2. Ing was a Germanic deity, and his "friends" are the Danes.
3. The lines introducing the scop's song seem faulty. The story itself is recounted in a highly allusive way, and many of its details are obscure, though some help is offered by an independent version of the story given in a fragmentary Old English lay called *The Fight at Finnsburg*.
4. Hildeburh, daughter of the former Danish king Hoc and sister of the ruling Danish king Hnaef, was married to Finn, king of the Jutes (Frisians). Hnaef with a party of Danes made what was presumably a friendly visit to Hildeburh and Finn at their home Finnsburg, but during a feast a quarrel broke out between the Jutes and the Danes (since the scop's sympathies are with the Danes, he ascribes the cause to the bad faith of the Jutes), and in the ensuing fight Hnaef and his nephew, the son of Finn and Hildeburh, were killed, along with many other Danes and Jutes.
5. It is not clear who proposed the peace terms, but in view of the teller's Danish sympathies, it was probably the Jutes that sought the uneasy truce from Hengest, who became the Danes' leader after Hnaef's death. The truce imposed upon Hengest and the Danes the intolerable condition of having to dwell in peace with the Jutish king who was responsible for the death of their own king.
6. I.e., Finn.

company rings, such gold-plated treasure as that with which he would cheer the Frisians' kin in the high hall. Then on both sides they confirmed the fast peace-compact. Finn declared to Hengest, with oaths deep-sworn, unfeigned, that he would hold those who were left from the battle in honor in accordance with the judgment of his counselors, so that by words or by works no man should break the treaty nor because of malice should ever mention that, princeless, the Danes followed the slayer of their own ring-giver, since necessity forced them. If with rash speech any of the Frisians should insist upon calling to mind the cause of murderous hate, then the sword's edge should settle it.

The funeral pyre was made ready and gold brought up from the hoard. The best of the warriors of the War-Scyldings[7] was ready on the pyre. At the fire it was easy to see many a blood-stained battle-shirt, boar-image all golden—iron-hard swine—many a noble destroyed by wounds: more than one had died in battle. Then Hildeburh bade give her own son to the flames on Hnaef's pyre, burn his body, put him in the fire at the shoulder of his uncle. The woman mourned, sang her lament. The warrior took his place.[8] The greatest of death-fires wound to the skies, roared before the barrow. Heads melted as blood sprang out—wounds opened wide, hate-bites of the body. Fire swallowed them—greediest of spirits—all of those whom war had taken away from both peoples: their strength had departed.

Then warriors went to seek their dwellings, bereft of friends, to behold Friesland, their homes and high city.[9] Yet Hengest stayed on with Finn for a winter darkened with the thought of slaughter, all desolate. He thought of his land, though he might not drive his ring-prowed ship over the water—the sea boiled with storms, strove with the wind, winter locked the waves in ice-bonds—until another year came to men's dwellings, just as it does still, glorious bright weather always watching for its time. Then winter was gone, earth's lap fair, the exile was eager to go, the guest from the dwelling: [yet] more he thought of revenge for his wrongs than of the sea-journey—if he might bring about a fight where he could take account of the sons of the Jutes with his iron. So he made no refusal of the world's custom when the son of Hunlaf[1] placed on his lap Battle-Bright, best of swords: its edges were known to the Jutes. Thus also to war-minded Finn in his turn cruel sword-evil came in his own home, after Guthlaf and Oslaf complained of the grim attack, the injury after the sea-journey, assigned blame for their lot of woes: breast might not contain the restless heart. Then was the hall reddened from foes' bodies, and thus Finn slain, the king in his company, and the queen taken. The

7. I.e., Hnaef.
8. The line is obscure, but it perhaps means that the body of Hildeburh's son was placed on the pyre.
9. This seems to refer to the few survivors on the Jutish side.
1. The text is open to various interpretations. The one adopted here assumes that the Dane Hunlaf, brother of Guthlaf and Oslaf, had been killed in the fight, and that ultimately Hunlaf's son

demanded vengeance by the symbolical act of placing his father's sword in Hengest's lap, while at the same time Guthlaf and Oslaf reminded Hengest of the Jutes' treachery. It is not clear whether the subsequent fight in which Finn was killed was waged by the Danish survivors alone, or whether the party first went back to Denmark and then returned to Finnsburh with reinforcements.

warriors of the Scyldings bore to ship all the hall-furnishings of the land's king, whatever of necklaces, skillfully wrought treasures, they might find at Finn's home. They brought the noble woman on the sea-journey to the Danes, led her to her people.

The lay was sung to the end, the song of the scop. Joy mounted again, bench-noise brightened, cup-bearers poured wine from wonderful vessels. Then Wealhtheow came forth to walk under gold crown to where all good men sat, nephew and uncle: their friendship was then still unbroken, each true to the other.[2] There too Unferth the spokesman sat at the feet of the prince of the Scyldings: each of them trusted his spirit, that he had much courage, though he was not honorable to his kinsmen at sword-play. Then the woman of the Scyldings spoke:

"Take this cup, my noble lord, giver of treasure. Be glad, gold-friend of warriors, and speak to the Geats with mild words, as a man ought to do. Be gracious to the Geats, mindful of gifts [which][3] you now have from near and far. They have told me that you would have the warrior for your son. Heorot is purged, the bright ring-hall. Enjoy while you may many rewards, and leave to your kinsmen folk and kingdom when you must go forth to look on the Ruler's decree. I know my gracious Hrothulf, that he will hold the young warriors in honor if you, friend of the Scyldings, leave the world before him. I think he will repay our sons with good if he remembers all the favors we did to his pleasure and honor when he was a child."

Then she turned to the bench where her sons were, Hrethric and Hrothmund, and the sons of the warriors, young men together. There sat the good man Beowulf of the Geats beside the two brothers.

The cup was borne to him and welcome offered in friendly words to him, and twisted gold courteously bestowed on him, two arm-ornaments, a mail-shirt and rings, the largest of necklaces of those that I have heard spoken of on earth. I have heard of no better hoard-treasure under the heavens since Hama carried away to his bright city the necklace of the Brosings,[4] chain and rich setting: he fled the treacherous hatred of Eormenric, got eternal favor. This ring Hygelac of the Geats,[5] grandson of Swerting, had on his last venture, when beneath his battle-banner he defended his treasure, protected the spoils of war: fate took him when for pride he sought trouble, feud with the Frisians. Over the cup of the waves the mighty prince wore that treasure, precious stone. He fell beneath his shield; the body of the king came into the grasp of the Franks, his breast-armor and the neck-ring together. Lesser warriors plundered the fallen after the war-harvest: people of the Geats held the place of corpses.

The hall was filled with noise. Wealhtheow spoke, before the com-

---

2. See p. 48, note 1, above.
3. The text seems corrupt.
4. The Brisings' (Brosings') necklace had been worn by the goddess Freya. Nothing more is known of this story of Hama, who seems to have stolen the necklace from the famous Gothic king Eormenric.

5. Beowulf is later said to have presented the necklace to Hygelac's queen, Hygd, though here Hygelac is said to have been wearing it on his ill-fated expedition against the Franks and Frisians, into whose hands it fell at his death.

pany she said to him: "Wear this ring, beloved Beowulf, young man, with good luck, and make use of this mail-shirt from the people's treasure, and prosper well; make yourself known with your might, and be kind of counsel to these boys: I shall remember to reward you for that. You have brought it about that, far and near, for a long time all men shall praise you, as wide as the sea surrounds the shores, home of the winds. While you live, prince, be prosperous. I wish you well of your treasure. Much favored one, be kind of deeds to my son. Here is each earl true to other, mild of heart, loyal to his lord; the thanes are at one, the people obedient, the retainers cheered with drink do as I bid."

Then she walked to her seat. There was the best of feasts, men drank wine. They did not know the fate, the grim decree made long before, as it came to pass to many of the earls after evening had come and Hrothgar had gone to his chambers, the noble one to his rest. A great number of men remained in the hall, just as they had often done before. They cleared the benches from the floor. It was spread over with beds and pillows. One of the beer-drinkers, ripe and fated to die, lay down to his hall-rest. They set at their heads their battle-shields, bright wood; there on the bench it was easy to see above each man his helmet that towered in battle, his ringed mail-shirt, his great spear-wood. It was their custom to be always ready for war whether at home or in the field, in any case at any time that need should befall their liege lord: that was a good nation.

[GRENDEL'S MOTHER'S ATTACK]

Then they sank to sleep. One paid sorely for his evening rest, just as had often befallen them when Grendel guarded the gold-hall, wrought wrong until the end came, death after misdeeds. It came to be seen, wide-known to men, that after the bitter battle an avenger still lived for an evil space: Grendel's mother, woman, monster-wife, was mindful of her misery, she who had to dwell in the terrible water, the cold currents, after Cain became sword-slayer of his only brother, his own father's son. Then Cain went as an outlaw to flee the cheerful life of men, marked for his murder, held to the wasteland. From him sprang many a devil sent by fate. Grendel was one of them, hateful outcast who at Heorot found a waking man waiting his warfare. There the monster had laid hold upon him, but he was mindful of the great strength, the large gift God had given him, and relied on the Almighty for favor, comfort and help. By that he overcame the foe, subdued the hell-spirit. Then he went off wretched, bereft of joy, to seek his dying-place, enemy of mankind. And his mother, still greedy and gallows-grim, would go on a sorrowful venture, avenge her son's death.

Then she came to Heorot where the Ring-Danes slept throughout the hall. Then change came quickly to the earls there, when Grendel's mother made her way in. The attack was the less terrible by just so much as is the strength of women, the war-terror of a wife, less than an armed man's when a hard blade, forge-hammered, a sword shining with blood, good of its edges, cuts the stout boar on a helmet opposite. Then in the hall was hard-edged sword raised from the seat, many a broad shield lifted firmly in hand: none thought of helmet, of wide mail-shirt, when the terror seized him. She was in haste, would be gone out from there, protect her life after she was discovered. Swiftly she had taken fast hold on one of the nobles, then she went to the fen. He was one of the men between the seas most beloved of Hrothgar in the rank of retainer, a noble shield-warrior whom she destroyed at his rest, a man of great repute. Beowulf was not there, for earlier, after the treasure-giving, another lodging had been appointed for the renowned Geat. Outcry arose in Heorot: she had taken, in its gore, the famed hand. Care was renewed, come again on the dwelling. That was not a good bargain, that on both sides they had to pay with the lives of friends.

Then was the old king, the hoary warrior, of bitter mind when he learned that his chief thane was lifeless, his dearest man dead. Quickly Beowulf was fetched to the bed-chamber, man happy in victory. At day-break together with his earls he went, the noble champion himself with his retainers, to where the wise one was, waiting to know whether after tidings of woe the All-Wielder would ever bring about change for him. The worthy warrior walked over the floor with his retainers—hall-wood resounded—that he might address words to the wise prince of Ing's friends, asked if the night had been pleasant according to his desires.

Hrothgar spoke, protector of the Scyldings: "Ask not about pleasure. Sorrow is renewed to the people of the Danes: Aeschere is dead, Yrmen-laf's elder brother, my speaker of wisdom and my bearer of counsel, my shoulder-companion when we used to defend our heads in battle, when troops clashed, beat on boar-images. Whatever an earl should be, a man good from old times, such was Aeschere. Now a wandering mur-derous spirit has slain him with its hands in Heorot. I do not know by what way the awful creature, glorying in its prey, has made its retreat, gladdened by its feast. She has avenged the feud—that last night you killed Grendel with hard hand-grips, savagely, because too long he had diminished and destroyed my people. He fell in the fight, his life for-feited, and now the other has come, a mighty worker of wrong, would avenge her kinsman, and has carried far her revenge—as many a thane may think who weeps in his spirit for his treasure-giver, bitter sorrow in heart. Now the hand lies lifeless that was strong in support of all your desires.

"I have heard landsmen, my people, hall-counselors, say this, that they have seen two such huge walkers in the wasteland holding to the moors, alien spirits. One of them, so far as they could clearly discern, was the likeness of a woman. The other wretched shape trod the tracks of exile in the form of a man, except that he was bigger than any other man. Land-dwellers in the old days named him Grendel. They know of no father, whether in earlier times any was begotten for them among the dark spirits. They hold to the secret land, the wolf-slopes, the windy headlands, the dangerous fen-paths where the mountain stream goes down under the darkness of the hills, the flood under the earth. It is not far from here, measured in miles, that the mere stands; over it hang frost-covered woods, trees fast of root close over the water. There each night may be seen fire on the flood, a fearful wonder. Of the sons of men there lives none, old of wisdom, who knows the bottom. Though the heath-stalker, the strong-horned hart, harassed by hounds makes for the forest after long flight, rather will he give his life, his being, on the bank than save his head by entering. That is no pleasant place. From it the surging waves rise up black to the heavens when the wind stirs up awful storms, until the air becomes gloomy, the skies weep. Now once again is the cure in you alone. You do not yet know the land, the perilous place, where you might find the seldom-seen creature: seek if you dare. I will give you wealth for the feud, old treasure, as I did before, twisted gold—if you come away."

Beowulf spoke, the son of Ecgtheow: "Sorrow not, wise warrior. It is better for a man to avenge his friend than much mourn. Each of us must await his end of the world's life. Let him who may get glory before death: that is best for the warrior after he has gone from life. Arise, guardian of the kingdom, let us go at once to look on the track of Grendel's kin. I promise you this: she will not be lost under cover, not in the earth's bosom nor in the mountain woods nor at the bottom of the sea, go where she will. This day have patience in every woe—as I expect you to."

Then the old man leapt up, thanked God, the mighty Lord, that the man had so spoken. Then was a horse bridled for Hrothgar, a curly-maned mount. The wise king moved in state; the band of shield-bearers marched on foot. The tracks were seen wide over the wood-paths where she had gone on the ground, made her way forward over the dark moor, borne lifeless the best of retainers of those who watched over their home with Hrothgar. The son of noble forebears[6] moved over the steep rocky slopes, narrow paths where only one could go at a time, an unfamiliar trail, steep hills, many a lair of water-monsters. He went before with a few wise men to spy out the country, until suddenly he found mountain trees leaning out over hoary stone, a joyless wood: water lay beneath, bloody and troubled. It was pain of heart for all the Danes to suffer, for the friends of the Scyldings, for many a thane, grief to each earl when on the cliff over the water they came upon Aeschere's head. The flood boiled with blood—the men looked upon it—with hot gore. Again and again the horn sang its urgent war-song. The whole troop sat down to rest. Then they saw on the water many a snake-shape, strong sea-serpents exploring the mere, and water-monsters lying on the slopes of the shore such as those that in the morning often attend a perilous journey on the paths of the sea, serpents and wild beasts.

These fell away from the shore, fierce and rage-swollen: they had

6. I.e. Hrothgar.

heard the bright sound, the war-horn sing. One of them a man of the
Geats with his bow cut off from his life, his water-warring, after the hard
war-arrow stuck in his heart: he was weaker in swimming the lake when
death took him. Straightway he was hard beset on the waves with barbed
boar-spears, strongly surrounded, pulled up on the shore, strange spawn
of the waves. The men looked on the terrible alien thing.

Beowulf put on his warrior's dress, had no fear for his life. His war-
shirt, hand-fashioned, broad and well-worked, was to explore the mere:
it knew how to cover his body-cave so that foe's grip might not harm his
heart, or grasp of angry enemy his life. But the bright helmet guarded
his head, one which was to stir up the lake-bottom, seek out the troubled
water—made rich with gold, surrounded with splendid bands, as the
weapon-smith had made it in far-off days, fashioned it wonderfully, set
it about with boar-images so that thereafter no sword or battle-blade
might bite into it. And of his strong supports that was not the least which
Hrothgar's spokesman[7] lent to his need: Hrunting was the name of the
hilted sword; it was one of the oldest of ancient treasures; its edge was
iron, decorated with poison-stripes, hardened with battle-sweat. Never
had it failed in war any man of those who grasped it in their hands, who
dared enter on dangerous enterprises, onto the common meeting place
of foes: this was not the first time that it should do work of courage.
Surely the son of Ecglaf, great of strength, did not have in mind what,
drunk with wine, he had spoken, when he lent that weapon to a better
swordfighter. He did not himself dare to risk his life under the warring
waves, to engage his courage: there he lost his glory, his name for valor.
It was not so with the other when he had armed himself for battle.

[BEOWULF ATTACKS GRENDEL'S MOTHER]

Beowulf spoke, the son of Ecgtheow: "Think now, renowned son of
Healfdene, wise king, now that I am ready for the venture, gold-friend
of warriors, of what we said before, that, if at your need I should go from
life, you would always be in a father's place for me when I am gone: be
guardian of my young retainers, my companions, if battle should take
me. The treasure you gave me, beloved Hrothgar, send to Hygelac. The
lord of the Geats may know from the gold, the son of Hrethel may see
when he looks on that wealth, that I found a ring-giver good in his gifts,
enjoyed him while I might. And let Unferth have the old heirloom, the
wide-known man my splendid-waved sword, hard-edged: with Hrunting
I shall get glory, or death will take me."

After these words the man of the Weather-Geats turned away boldly,
would wait for no answer: the surging water took the warrior. Then was
it a part of a day before he might see the bottom's floor. Straightway that
which had held the flood's tract a hundred half-years, ravenous for prey,
grim and greedy, saw that some man from above was exploring the

7. I.e., Unferth.

dwelling of monsters. Then she groped toward him, took the warrior in her awful grip. Yet not the more for that did she hurt his hale body within: his ring-armor shielded him about on the outside so that she could not pierce the war-dress, the linked body-mail, with hateful fingers. Then as she came to the bottom the sea-wolf bore the ring-prince to her house so that—no matter how brave he was—he might not wield weapons; but many monsters attacked him in the water, many a sea-beast tore at his mail-shirt with war-tusks, strange creatures afflicted him. Then the earl saw that he was in some hostile hall where no water harmed him at all, and the flood's onrush might not touch him because of the hall-roof. He saw firelight, a clear blaze shine bright.

Then the good man saw the accursed dweller in the deep, the mighty mere-woman. He gave a great thrust to his sword—his hand did not withhold the stroke—so that the etched blade sang at her head a fierce war-song. Then the stranger found that the battle-lightning would not bite, harm her life, but the edge failed the prince in his need: many a hand-battle had it endured before, often sheared helmet, war-coat of man fated to die: this was the first time for the rare treasure that its glory had failed.

But still he was resolute, not slow of his courage, mindful of fame, the kinsman of Hygelac. Then, angry warrior, he threw away the sword, wavy-patterned, bound with ornaments, so that it lay on the ground, hard and steel-edged: he trusted in his strength, his mighty hand-grip. So ought a man to do when he thinks to get long-lasting praise in battle: he cares not for his life. Then he seized by the hair Grendel's mother—the man of the War-Geats did not shrink from the fight. Battle-hardened, now swollen with rage, he pulled his deadly foe so that she fell to the floor. Quickly in her turn she repaid him his gift with her grim claws and clutched at him: then weary-hearted, the strongest of warriors, of foot-soldiers, stumbled so that he fell. Then she sat upon the hall-guest and drew her knife, broad and bright-edged. She would avenge her child, her only son. The woven breast-armor lay on his shoulder: that protected his life, withstood entry of point or of edge. Then the son of Ecgtheow would have fared amiss under the wide ground, the champion of the Geats, if the battle-shirt had not brought help, the hard war-net—and holy God brought about victory in war; the wise Lord, Ruler of the Heavens, decided it with right, easily, when Beowulf had stood up again.

Then he saw among the armor a victory-blessed blade, an old sword made by the giants, strong of its edges, glory of warriors: it was the best of weapons, except that it was larger than any other man might bear to war-sport, good and adorned, the work of giants. He seized the linked hilt, he who fought for the Scyldings, savage and slaughter-bent, drew the patterned-blade; desperate of life, he struck angrily so that it bit her hard on the neck, broke the bone-rings. The blade went through all the doomed body. She fell to the floor, the sword was sweating, the man rejoiced in his work.

The blaze brightened, light shone within, just as from the sky heaven's candle shines clear. He looked about the building; then he moved along the wall, raised his weapon hard by the hilt, Hygelac's thane, angry and resolute: the edge was not useless to the warrior, for he would quickly repay Grendel for the many attacks he had made on the West-Danes—many more than the one time when he slew in their sleep fifteen hearth-companions of Hrothgar, devoured men of the Danish people while they slept, and another such number bore away, a hateful prey. He had paid him his reward for that, the fierce champion, for there he saw Grendel, weary of war, lying at rest, lifeless with the wounds he had got in the fight at Heorot. The body bounded wide when it suffered the blow after death, the hard sword-swing; and thus he cut off his head.

At once the wise men who were watching the water with Hrothgar saw that the surging waves were troubled, the lake stained with blood. Gray-haired, old, they spoke together of the good warrior, that they did not again expect of the chief that he would come victorious to seek their great king; for many agreed on it, that the sea-wolf had destroyed him.

Then came the ninth hour of the day. The brave Scyldings left the hill. The gold-friend of warriors went back to his home. The strangers sat sick at heart and stared at the mere. They wished—and did not expect—that they would see their beloved lord himself.

Then the blade began to waste away from the battle-sweat, the war-sword into battle-icicles. That was a wondrous thing, that it should all melt, most like the ice when the Father loosens the frost's fetters, undoes the water-bonds—He Who has power over seasons and times: He is the true Ruler. Beowulf did not take from the dwelling, the man of the Weather-Geats, more treasures—though he saw many there—but only the head and the hilt, bright with jewels. The sword itself had already melted, its patterned blade burned away: the blood was too hot for it, the spirit that had died there too poisonous. Quickly he was swimming, he who had lived to see the fall of his foes; he plunged up through the water. The currents were all cleansed, the great tracts of the water, when the dire spirit left her life-days and this loaned world.

Then the protector of seafarers came toward the land, swimming stout-hearted; he had joy of his sea-booty, the great burden he had with him. They went to meet him, thanked God, the strong band of thanes, rejoiced in their chief that they might see him again sound. Then the helmet and war-shirt of the mighty one were quickly loosened. The lake drowsed, the water beneath the skies, stained with blood. They went forth on the foot-tracks, glad in their hearts, measured the path back, the known ways, men bold as kings. They bore the head from the mere's cliff, toilsomely for each of the great-hearted ones: four of them had trouble in carrying Grendel's head on spear-shafts to the gold-hall—until at last they came striding to the hall, fourteen bold warriors of the Geats; their lord, high-spirited, walked in their company over the fields to the mead-hall.

Then the chief of the thanes, man daring in deeds, enriched by new glory, warrior dear to battle, came in to greet Hrothgar. Then Grendel's head was dragged by the hair over the floor to where men drank, a terrible thing to the earls and the woman with them, an awful sight: the men looked upon it.

[FURTHER CELEBRATION AT HEOROT]

Beowulf spoke, the son of Ecgtheow: "Yes, we have brought you this sea-booty, son of Healfdene, man of the Scyldings, gladly, as evidence of glory—what you look on here. Not easily did I come through it with my life, the war under water, not without trouble carried out the task. The fight would have been ended straightway if God had not guarded me. With Hrunting I might not do anything in the fight, though that is a good weapon. But the Wielder of Men granted me that I should see hanging on the wall a fair, ancient great-sword—most often He has guided the man without friends—that I should wield the weapon. Then in the fight when the time became right for me I hewed the house-guardians. Then that war-sword, wavy-patterned, burnt away as their blood sprang forth, hottest of battle-sweats. I have brought the hilt away from the foes. I have avenged the evil deeds, the slaughter of Danes, as it was right to do. I promise you that you may sleep in Heorot without care with your band of retainers, and that for none of the thanes of your people, old or young, need you have fear, prince of the Scyldings—for no life-injury to your men on that account, as you did before."

Then the golden hilt was given into the hand of the old man, the hoary war-chief—the ancient work of giants. There came into the possession of the prince of the Danes, after the fall of devils, the work of wonder-smiths. And when the hostile-hearted creature, God's enemy, guilty of murder, gave up this world, and his mother too, it passed into the control of the best of worldly kings between the seas, of those who gave treasure in the Northlands.

Hrothgar spoke—he looked on the hilt, the old heirloom, on which was written the origin of ancient strife, when the flood, rushing water, slew the race of giants—they suffered terribly: that was a people alien to the Everlasting Lord. The Ruler made them a last payment through water's welling. On the sword-guard of bright gold there was also rightly marked through rune-staves, set down and told, for whom that sword, best of irons, had first been made, its hilt twisted and ornamented with snakes. Then the wise man spoke, the son of Healfdene—all were silent: "Lo, this may one say who works truth and right for the folk, recalls all things far distant, an old guardian of the land: that this earl was born the better man. Glory is raised up over the far ways—your glory over every people, Beowulf my friend. All of it, all your strength, you govern steadily in the wisdom of your heart. I shall fulfill my friendship to you, just as we spoke before. You shall become a comfort, whole and long-lasting, to your people, a help to warriors.

"So was not Heremod to the sons of Ecgwela, the Honor-Scyldings. He grew great not for their joy, but for their slaughter, for the destruction of Danish people. With swollen heart he killed his table-companions, shoulder-comrades, until he turned away from the joys of men, alone, notorious king, although mighty God had raised him in power, in the joys of strength, had set him up over all men. Yet in his breast his heart's thought grew blood-thirsty: no rings did he give to the Danes for glory. He lived joyless to suffer the pain of that strife, the long-lasting harm of the people. Teach yourself by him, be mindful of munificence. Old of winters, I tell this tale for you.

"It is a wonder to say how in His great spirit mighty God gives wisdom to mankind, land and earlship—He possesses power over all things. At times He lets the thought of a man of high lineage move in delight, gives him joy of earth in his homeland, a stronghold of men to rule over, makes regions of the world so subject to him, wide kingdoms, that in his unwisdom he may not himself have mind of his end. He lives in plenty; illness and age in no way grieve him, neither does dread care darken his heart, nor does enmity bare sword-hate, for the whole world turns to his will—he knows nothing worse—until his portion of pride increases and flourishes within him; then the watcher sleeps, the soul's guardian; that sleep is too sound, bound in its own cares, and the slayer most near whose bow shoots treacherously. Then is he hit in the heart, beneath his armor, with the bitter arrow—he cannot protect himself— with the crooked dark commands of the accursed spirit. What he has long held seems to him too little, angry-hearted he covets, no plated rings does he give in men's honor, and then he forgets and regards not his destiny because of what God, Wielder of Heaven, has given him before, his portion of glories. In the end it happens in turn that the loaned body weakens, falls doomed; another takes the earl's ancient treasure, one who recklessly gives precious gifts, does not fearfully guard them.

"Keep yourself against that wickedness, beloved Beowulf, best of men, and choose better—eternal gains. Have no care for pride, great warrior. Now for a time there is glory in your might: yet soon it shall be that sickness or sword will diminish your strength, or fire's fangs, or flood's surge, or sword's swing, or spear's flight, or appalling age; brightness of eyes will fail and grow dark; then it shall be that death will overcome you, warrior.

"Thus I ruled the Ring-Danes for a hundred half-years under the skies, and protected them in war with spear and sword against many nations over middle-earth, so that I counted no one as my adversary underneath the sky's expanse. Well, disproof of that came to me in my own land, grief after my joys, when Grendel, ancient adversary, came to invade my home. Great sorrow of heart I have always suffered for his persecution. Thanks be to the Ruler, the Eternal Lord, that after old strife I have come to see in my lifetime, with my own eyes, his blood-stained head. Go now to your seat, have joy of the glad feast, made famous in battle. Many of our treasures will be shared when morning comes."

The Geat was glad at heart, went at once to seek his seat as the wise one bade. Then was a feast fairly served again, for a second time, just as before, for those famed for courage, sitting about the hall.

Night's cover lowered, dark over the warriors. The retainers all arose. The gray-haired one would seek his bed, the old Scylding. It pleased the Geat, the brave shield-warrior, immensely that he should have rest. Straightway a hall-thane led the way on for the weary one, come from far country, and showed every courtesy to the thane's need, such as in those days seafarers might expect as their due.

Then the great-hearted one rested; the hall stood high, vaulted and gold-adorned; the guest slept within until the black raven, blithe-hearted, announced heaven's joy. Then the bright light came passing over the shadows. The warriors hastened, the nobles were eager to set out again for their people. Bold of spirit, the visitor would seek his ship far thence.

Then the hardy one bade that Hrunting be brought to the son of Ecglaf,[8] that he take back his sword, precious iron. He spoke thanks for that loan, said that he accounted it a good war-friend, strong in battle; in his words he found no fault at all with the sword's edge; he was a thoughtful man. And then they were eager to depart, the warriors ready in their armor. The prince who had earned honor of the Danes went to the high seat where the other was: the man dear to war greeted Hrothgar.

[Beowulf Returns Home]

Beowulf spoke, the son of Ecgtheow: "Now we sea-travelers come from afar wish to say that we desire to seek Hygelac. Here we have been entertained splendidly according to our desire: you have dealt well with us. If on earth I might in any way earn more of your heart's love, prince of warriors, than I have done before with warlike deeds, I should be ready at once. If beyond the sea's expanse I hear that men dwelling near threaten you with terrors, as those who hated you did before, I shall bring you a thousand thanes, warriors to your aid. I know of Hygelac, lord of the Geats, though he is young as a guardian of the people, that he will further me with words and works so that I may do you honor and bring spears to help you, strong support where you have need of men. If Hrethric, king's son, decides to come to the court of the Geats, he can find many friends there; far countries are well sought by him who is himself strong."

Hrothgar spoke to him in answer: "The All-Knowing Lord sent those words into your mind: I have not heard a man of so young age speak more wisely. You are great of strength, mature of mind, wise of words. I think it likely if the spear, sword-grim war, takes the son of Hrethel, sickness or weapon your prince, the people's ruler, and you have your life, that the Sea-Geats will not have a better to choose as their king, as guardian of their treasure, if you wish to hold the kingdom of your kins-

8. I.e., Unferth.

men. So well your heart's temper has long pleased me, beloved Beowulf. You have brought it about that peace shall be shared by the peoples, the folk of the Geats and the Spear-Danes, and enmity shall sleep, acts of malice which they practiced before; and there shall be, as long as I rule the wide kingdom, sharing of treasures, many a man shall greet his fellow with good gifts over the sea-bird's baths; the ring-prowed ship will bring gifts and tokens of friendship over the sea. I know your people, blameless in every respect, set firm after the old way both as to foe and to friend."

Then the protector of earls, the kinsman of Healfdene, gave him there in the hall twelve precious things; he bade him with these gifts seek his own dear people in safety, quickly come back. Then the king noble of race, the prince of the Scyldings, kissed the best of thanes and took him by his neck: tears fell from the gray-haired one. He had two thoughts of the future, the old and wise man, one more strongly than the other— that they would not see each other again, bold men at council. The man was so dear to him that he might not restrain his breast's welling, for fixed in his heartstrings a deep-felt longing for the beloved man burned in his blood. Away from him Beowulf, warrior glorious with gold, walked over the grassy ground, proud of his treasure. The sea-goer awaited its owner, riding at anchor. Then on the journey the gift of Hrothgar was oft-praised: that was a king blameless in all things until age took from him the joys of his strength—old age that has often harmed many.

There came to the flood the band of brave-hearted ones, of young men. They wore mail-coats, locked limb-shirts. The guard of the coast saw the coming of the earls, just as he had done before. He did not greet the guests with taunts from the cliff's top, but rode to meet them, said that the return of the warriors in bright armor in their ship would be welcome to the people of the Weather-Geats. There on the sand the broad sea-boat was loaded with armor, the ring-prowed ship with horses and rich things. The mast stood high over Hrothgar's hoard-gifts. He gave the boat-guard a sword wound with gold, so that thereafter on the mead-bench he was held the worthier for the treasure, the heirloom. The boat moved out to furrow the deep water, left the land of the Danes. Then on the mast a sea-cloth, a sail, was made fast by a rope. The boat's beams creaked: wind did not keep the sea-floater from its way over the waves. The sea-goer moved, foamy-necked floated forth over the swell, the ship with bound prow over the sea-currents until they might see the cliffs of the Geats, the well-known headlands. The ship pressed ahead, borne by the wind, stood still at the land. Quickly the harbor-guard was at the sea-side, he who had gazed for a long time far out over the currents, eager to see the beloved men. He[9] moored the deep ship in the sand, fast by its anchor ropes, lest the force of the waves should drive away the fair wooden vessel. Then he bade that the prince's wealth be borne ashore, armor and plated gold. It was not far for them to seek the

9. Beowulf.

giver of treasure, Hygelac son of Hrethel, where he dwelt at home near
the sea-wall, himself with his retainers.

The building was splendid, its king most valiant, set high in the hall,
Hygd[1] most youthful, wise and well-taught, though she had lived within
the castle walls few winters, daughter of Haereth. For she was not niggardly, nor too sparing of gifts to the men of the Geats, of treasures.
Modthryth,[2] good folk-queen, did dreadful deeds [in her youth]: no bold
one among her retainers dared venture—except her great lord—to set
his eyes on her in daylight, but [if he did] he should reckon deadly bonds
prepared for him, arresting hands: that straightway after his seizure the
sword awaited him, that the patterned blade must settle it, make known
its death-evil. Such is no queenly custom for a woman to practice, though
she is peerless—that one who weaves peace[3] should take away the life of
a beloved man after pretended injury. However the kinsman of Hemming stopped that:[4] ale-drinkers gave another account, said that she did
less harm to the people, fewer injuries, after she was given, gold-adorned,
to the young warrior, the beloved noble, when by her father's teaching
she sought Offa's hall in a voyage over the pale sea. There on the throne
she was afterwards famous for generosity, while living made use of her
life, held high love toward the lord of warriors, [who was] of all mankind
the best, as I have heard, between the seas of the races of men. Since
Offa was a man brave of wars and gifts, wide-honored, he held his native
land in wisdom. From him sprang Eomer to the help of warriors, kinsman of Hemming, grandson of Garmund, strong in battle.[5]

Then the hardy one came walking with his troop over the sand on the
sea-plain, the wide shores. The world-candle shone, the sun moved
quickly from the south. They made their way, strode swiftly to where
they heard that the protector of earls, the slayer of Ongentheow,[6] the
good young war-king, was dispensing rings in the stronghold. The coming of Beowulf was straightway made known to Hygelac, that there in
his home the defender of warriors, his comrade in battle, came walking
alive to the court, sound from the battle-play. Quickly the way within
was made clear for the foot-guests, as the mighty one bade.

Then he sat down with him, he who had come safe through the fight,
kinsman with kinsman, after he had greeted his liege lord with formal

1. Hygd is Hygelac's young queen. The suddenness of her introduction here is perhaps due to a
faulty text.

2. A transitional passage introducing the contrast
between Hygd's good behavior and Modthryth's bad
behavior as young women of royal blood seems to
have been lost. Modthryth's practice of having those
who looked into her face put to death may reflect
the folk-motif of the princess whose unsuccessful
suitors are executed, though the text does not say
that Modthryth's victims were suitors. Modthryth's
"great lord" was probably her father.

3. Daughters of kings were frequently given in
marriage to the king of a hostile nation in order to
bring about peace; hence Modthryth may be called
"one who weaves peace."

4. I.e., Offa I, a legendary king of the Angles, and
presumably the ancestor of his namesake Offa II
who ruled Mercia from 757–796; who Hemming
was—besides being Offa's forebear—is not known.

5. Stories about Offa, who provides the only English
connection in this English poem, and the names
of his father Garmund and son Eomer would presumably have been familiar to the poet's audience.
The passage has been seen as a compliment to the
royal house of Mercia.

6. Ongentheow was a Scylfing (Swedish) king,
whose story is fully told below. In fact Hygelac was
not his slayer, but is called so because he led the
attack on the Scylfings in which Ongentheow was
killed.

speech, loyal, with vigorous words. Haereth's daughter moved through the hall-building with mead-cups, cared lovingly for the people, bore the cup of strong drink to the hands of the warriors. Hygelac began fairly to question his companion in the high hall, curiosity pressed him, what the adventures of the Sea-Geats had been. "How did you fare on your journey, beloved Beowulf, when you suddenly resolved to seek distant combat over the salt water, battle in Heorot? Did you at all help the wide-known woes of Hrothgar, the famous prince? Because of you I burned with seething sorrows, care of heart—had no trust in the venture of my beloved man. I entreated you long that you should in no way approach the murderous spirit, should let the South-Danes themselves settle the war with Grendel. I say thanks to God that I may see you sound."

Beowulf spoke, the son of Ecgtheow: "To many among men it is not hidden, lord Hygelac, the great encounter—what a fight we had, Grendel and I, in the place where he made many sorrows for the Victory-Scyldings, constant misery. All that I avenged, so that none of Grendel's kin over the earth need boast of that clash at night—whoever lives longest of the loathsome kind, wrapped in malice. There I went forth to the ring-hall to greet Hrothgar. At once the famous son of Healfdene, when he knew my purpose, gave me a seat with his own sons. The company was in joy: I have not seen in the time of my life under heaven's arch more mead-mirth of hall-sitters. At times the famous queen, peace-pledge of the people, went through all the hall, cheered the young men; often she would give a man a ring-band before she went to her seat. At times Hrothgar's daughter bore the ale-cup to the retainers, to the earls throughout the hall. I heard hall-sitters name her Freawaru when she offered the studded cup to warriors. Young and gold-adorned, she is promised to the fair son of Froda.[7] That has seemed good to the lord of the Scyldings, the guardian of the kingdom, and he believes of this plan that he may, with this woman, settle their portion of deadly feuds, of quarrels.[8] Yet most often after the fall of a prince in any nation the deadly spear rests but a little while, even though the bride is good.

"It may displease the lord of the Heatho-Bards and each thane of that people when he goes in the hall with the woman, [that while] the noble sons of the Danes, her retainers, [are] feasted,[9] the heirlooms of their ancestors will be shining on them[1]—the hard and wave-adorned treasure of the Heatho-Bards, [which was theirs] so long as they might wield those weapons, until they led to the shield-play, to destruction, their dear companions and their own lives. Then at the beer he[2] who sees the treasure, an old ash-warrior who remembers it all, the spear-death of

---

7. I.e., Ingeld, who succeeded his father as king of the Heatho-Bards.
8. I.e., the feud between the Danes and Heatho-Bards.
9. The text is faulty here.
1. I.e., the weapons and armor which had once

belonged to the Heatho-Bards and were captured by the Danes will be worn by the Danish attendants of Hrothgar's daughter Freawaru when she goes to the Heatho-Bards to marry king Ingeld.
2. I.e., some old Heatho-Bard warrior.

warriors—grim is his heart—begins, sad of mind, to tempt a young fighter in the thoughts of his spirit, to awaken war-evil, and speaks this word:

" 'Can you, my friend, recognize that sword, the rare iron-blade, that your father, beloved man, bore to battle his last time in armor, where the Danes slew him, the fierce Scyldings, got possession of the battle-field, when Withergeld[3] lay dead, after the fall of warriors? Now here some son of his murderers walks in the hall, proud of the weapon, boasts of the murder, and wears the treasure that you should rightly possess.' So he will provoke and remind at every chance with wounding words until that moment comes that the woman's thane,[4] forfeiting life, shall lie dead, blood-smeared from the sword-bite, for his father's deeds. The other escapes with his life, knows the land well. Then on both sides the oath of the earls will be broken; then deadly hate will well up in Ingeld, and his wife-love after the surging of sorrows will become cooler. There-fore I do not think the loyalty of the Heatho-Bards, their part in the alliance with the Danes, to be without deceit—do not think their friend-ship fast.

"I shall speak still more of Grendel, that you may readily know, giver of treasure, what the hand-fight of warriors came to in the end. After heaven's jewel had glided over the earth, the angry spirit came, awful in the evening, to visit us where, unharmed, we watched over the hall. There the fight was fatal to Hondscioh, deadly to one who was doomed. He was dead first of all, armed warrior. Grendel came to devour him, good young retainer, swallowed all the body of the beloved man. Yet not for this would the bloody-toothed slayer, bent on destruction, go from the gold-hall empty-handed; but, strong of might, he made trial of me, grasped me with eager hand. His glove[5] hung huge and wonderful, made fast with cunning clasps: it had been made all with craft; with devil's devices and dragon's skins. The fell doer of evils would put me therein, guiltless, one of many. He might not do so after I had stood up in anger. It is too long to tell how I repaid the people's foe his due for every crime. My prince, there with my deeds I did honor to your people. He slipped away, for a little while had use of life's joy. Yet his right hand remained as his spoor in Heorot, and he went from there abject, mourn-ful of heart sank to the mere's bottom.

"The lord of the Scyldings repaid me for that bloody combat with much plated gold, many treasures, after morning came and we sat down to the feast. There was song and mirth. The old Scylding, who has learned many things, spoke of times far-off. At times a brave one in battle touched the glad wood, the harp's joy; at times he told tales, true and sad; at times he related strange stories according to right custom; at times, again, the great-hearted king, bound with age, the old warrior, would begin to speak of his youth, his battle-strength. His heart welled

---

3. Apparently a leader of the Heatho-Bards in their unsuccessful war with the Danes.
4. I.e., the Danish attendant of Freawaru who is wearing the sword of his Heatho-Bard attacker's

father.
5. Apparently a large glove that could be used as a pouch.

within when, old and wise, he thought of his many winters. Thus we took pleasure there the livelong day until another night came to men.

"Then in her turn Grendel's mother swiftly made ready to take revenge for his injuries, made a sorrowful journey. Death had taken her son, war-hate of the Weather-Geats. The direful woman avenged her son, fiercely killed a warrior: there the life of Aeschere departed, a wise old counselor. And when morning came the folk of the Danes might not burn him, death-weary, in the fire, nor place him on the pyre, beloved man: she had borne his body away in fiend's embrace beneath the mountain stream. That was the bitterest of Hrothgar's sorrows, of those that had long come upon the people's prince. Then the king, sore-hearted, implored me by your life[6] that I should do a man's work in the tumult of the waters, venture my life, finish a glorious deed. He promised me reward. Then I found the guardian of the deep pool, the grim horror, as is now known wide. For a time there we were locked hand in hand. Then the flood boiled with blood, and in the war-hall I cut off the head of Grendel's mother with a mighty sword. Not without trouble I came from there with my life. I was not fated to die then, but the protector of earls again gave me many treasures, the son of Healfdene.

"Thus the king of that people lived with good customs. I had lost none of the rewards, the meed of my might, but he gave me treasures, the son of Healfdene, at my own choice. I will bring these to you, great king, show my good will. On your kindnesses all still depends: I have few close kinsmen besides you, Hygelac."

Then he bade bring in the boar-banner—the head-sign—the helmet towering in battle, the gray battle-shirt, the splendid sword—afterwards spoke words: "Hrothgar, wise king, gave me this armor; in his words he bade that I should first tell you about his gift: he said that king Heorogar,[7] lord of the Scyldings, had had it for a long time; not for that would he give it, the breast-armor, to his son, bold Heoroweard, though he was loyal to him. Use it all well!"

I have heard that four horses, swift and alike, followed that treasure, fallow as apples. He gave him the gift of both horses and treasure. So ought kinsmen do, not weave malice-nets for each other with secret craft, prepare death for comrades. To Hygelac his nephew was most true in hard fights, and each one mindful of helping the other. I have heard that he gave Hygd the neck-ring, the wonderfully wrought treasure, that Wealhtheow had given him—gave to the king's daughter as well three horses, supple and saddle-bright. After the gift of the necklace, her breast was adorned with it.

Thus Beowulf showed himself brave, a man known in battles, of good deeds, bore himself according to discretion. Drunk, he slew no hearth-companions. His heart was not savage, but he held the great gift that God had given him, the most strength of all mankind, like one brave in

---

6. I.e., "in your name."
7. Hrothgar's elder brother, whom Hrothgar succeeded as king.

battle. He had long been despised,[8] so that the sons of the Geats did not reckon him brave, nor would the lord of the Weather-Geats do him much gift-honor on the mead-bench. They strongly suspected that he was slack, a young man unbold. Change came to the famous man for each of his troubles.

Then the protector of earls bade fetch in the heirloom of Hrethel,[9] king famed in battle, adorned with gold. There was not then among the Geats a better treasure in sword's kind. He laid that in Beowulf's lap, and gave him seven thousand [hides of land], a hall and a throne. To both of them alike land had been left in the nation, home and native soil: to the other more especially wide was the realm, to him who was higher in rank.

[*Beowulf and the Dragon*]

Afterwards it happened, in later days, in the crashes of battle, when Hygelac lay dead and war-swords came to slay Heardred[1] behind the shield-cover, when the Battle-Scylfings, hard fighters, sought him among his victorious nation, attacked bitterly the nephew of Hereric—then the broad kingdom came into Beowulf's hand. He held it well fifty winters—he was a wise king, an old guardian of the land—until in the dark nights a certain one, a dragon, began to hold sway, which on the high heath kept watch over a hoard, a steep stone-barrow. Beneath lay a path unknown to men. By this there went inside a certain man [who made his way near to the heathen hoard; his hand took a cup, large, a shining treasure. The dragon did not afterwards conceal it though in his sleep he was tricked by the craft of the thief. That the people discovered, the neighboring folk—that he was swollen with rage].[2]

Not of his own accord did he who had sorely harmed him[3] break into the worm's hoard, not by his own desire, but for hard constraint; the slave of some son of men fled hostile blows, lacking a shelter, and came there, a man guilty of wrong-doing. As soon as he saw him,[4] great horror arose in the stranger; [yet the wretched fugitive escaped the terrible worm . . . When the sudden shock came upon him, he carried off a precious cup.][5] There were many such ancient treasures in the earth-house, as in the old days some one of mankind had prudently hidden there the huge legacy of a noble race, rare treasures. Death had taken them all in earlier times, and the only one of the nation of people who still survived, who walked there longest, a guardian mourning his friends, supposed the same of himself as of them—that he might little while enjoy the long-

---

8. Beowulf's poor reputation as a young man is mentioned only here.
9. Hygelac's father.
1. Hygelac's son Heardred, who succeeded Hygelac as king, was killed by the Swedes (Battle-Scylfings) in his own land, as is explained more fully below, p. 67. His uncle Hereric was perhaps Hygd's

brother.
2. This part of the manuscript is badly damaged, and the text within brackets is highly conjectural.
3. The dragon.
4. The dragon.
5. Several lines of the text have been lost.

got treasure. A barrow stood all ready on the shore near the sea-waves, newly placed on the headland, made fast by having its entrances skillfully hidden. The keeper of the rings carried in the part of his riches worthy of hoarding, plated gold; he spoke few words:

"Hold now, you earth, now that men may not, the possession of earls. What, from you good men got it first! War-death has taken each man of my people, evil dreadful and deadly, each of those who has given up this life, the hall-joys of men. I have none who wears sword or cleans the plated cup, rich drinking vessel. The company of retainers has gone elsewhere. The hard helmet must be stripped of its fair-wrought gold, of its plating. The polishers are asleep who should make the war-mask shine. And even so the coat of mail, which withstood the bite of swords after the crashing of the shields, decays like its warrior. Nor may the ring-mail travel wide on the war-chief beside his warriors. There is no harp-delight, no mirth of the singing wood, no good hawk flies through the hall, no swift horse stamps in the castle court. Baleful death has sent away many races of men."

So, sad of mind, he spoke his sorrow, alone of them all, moved joyless through day and night until death's flood reached his heart. The ancient night-ravager found the hoard-joy standing open, he who burning seeks barrows, the smooth hateful dragon who flies at night wrapped in flame. Earth-dwellers much dread him. He it is who must seek a hoard in the earth where he will guard heathen gold, wise for his winters: he is none the better for it.

So for three hundred winters the harmer of folk held in the earth one of its treasure-houses, huge and mighty, until one man angered his heart. He bore to his master a plated cup, asked his lord for a compact of peace: thus was the hoard searched, the store of treasures diminished. His requests were granted the wretched man: the lord for the first time looked on the ancient work of men. Then the worm woke; cause of strife was renewed: for then he moved over the stones, hard-hearted beheld his foe's foot-prints—with secret stealth he had stepped forth too near the dragon's head. (So may an undoomed man who holds favor from the Ruler easily come through his woes and misery.) The hoard-guard sought him eagerly over the ground, would find the man who had done him injury while he slept. Hot and fierce-hearted, often he moved all about the outside of the barrow. No man at all was in the emptiness. Yet he took joy in the thought of war, in the work of fighting. At times he turned back into the barrow, sought his rich cup. Straightway he found that some man had tampered with his gold, his splendid treasure. The hoard-guard waited restless until evening came; then the barrow-keeper was in rage: he would requite that precious drinking cup with vengeful fire. Then the day was gone—to the joy of the worm. He would not wait long on the sea-wall, but set out with fire, ready with flame. The beginning was terrible to the folk on the land, as the ending was soon to be sore to their giver of treasure.

Then the evil spirit began to vomit flames, burn bright dwellings; blaze of fire rose, to the horror of men; there the deadly flying thing would leave nothing alive. The worm's warfare was wide-seen, his cruel malice, near and far—how the destroyer hated and hurt the people of the Geats. He winged back to the hoard, his hidden hall, before the time of day. He had circled the land-dwellers with flame, with fire and burning. He had trust in his barrow, in his war and his wall: his expectation deceived him.

Then the terror was made known to Beowulf, quickly in its truth, that his own home, best of buildings, had melted in surging flames, the throne-seat of the Geats. That was anguish of spirit to the good man, the greatest of heart-sorrows. The wise one supposed that he had bitterly offended the Ruler, the Eternal Lord, against old law. His breast within boiled with dark thoughts—as was not for him customary. The fiery dragon with his flames had destroyed the people's stronghold, the land along the sea, the heart of the country. Because of that the war-king, the lord of the Weather-Geats, devised punishment for him. The protector of fighting men, lord of earls, commanded that a wonderful battle-shield be made all of iron. Well he knew that the wood of the forest might not help him—linden against flame. The prince good from old times was to come to the end of the days that had been lent him, life in the world, and the worm with him, though he had long held the hoarded wealth. Then the ring-prince scorned to seek the far-flier with a troop, a large army. He had no fear for himself of the combat, nor did he think the worm's war-power anything great, his strength and his courage, because he himself had come through many battles before, dared perilous straits, clashes of war, after he had purged Hrothgar's hall, victorious warrior, and in combat crushed to death Grendel's kin, loathsome race.

Nor was that the least of his hand-combats where Hygelac was slain, when the king of the Geats, the noble lord of the people, the son of Hrethel, died of sword-strokes in the war-storm among the Frisians, laid low by the blade. From there Beowulf came away by means of his own strength, performed a feat of swimming; he had on his arm the armor of thirty earls when he turned back to the sea. There was no need for the Hetware[6] to exult in the foot-battle when they bore their shields against him: few came again from that warrior to seek their homes. Then the son of Ecgtheow swam over the water's expanse, forlorn and alone, back to his people. There Hygd offered him hoard and kingdom, rings and a prince's throne. She had no trust in her son, that he could hold his native throne against foreigners now that Hygelac was dead. By no means the sooner might the lordless ones get consent from the noble that he would become lord of Heardred or that he would accept royal power.[7] Yet he held him up among the people by friendly counsel, kindly with honor, until he became older,[8] ruled the Weather-Geats.

---

6. I.e., a tribe, with whom the Frisians were allied.

7. I.e., Beowulf refused to take the throne from the rightful heir Heardred.

8. I.e., Beowulf supported the young Heardred.

Outcasts from over the sea sought him, sons of Ohthere.[9] They had rebelled against the protector of the Scylfings, the best of the sea-kings of those who gave treasure in Sweden, a famous lord. For Heardred that became his life's limit: because of his hospitality there the son of Hygelac got his life's wound from the strokes of a sword. And the son of Ongentheow went back to seek his home after Heardred lay dead, let Beowulf hold the royal throne, rule the Geats: that was a good king.

In later days he was mindful of repaying the prince's fall, became the friend of the destitute Eadgils;[1] with folk he supported the son of Ohthere over the wide sea, with warriors and weapons. Afterwards he got vengeance by forays that brought with them cold care: he took the king's life.

Thus he had survived every combat, every dangerous battle, every deed of courage, the son of Ecgtheow, until that one day when he should fight with the worm. Then, one of twelve, the lord of the Geats, swollen with anger, went to look on the dragon. He had learned then from what the feud arose, the fierce malice to men: the glorious cup had come to his possession from the hand of the finder: he was the thirteenth of that company, the man who had brought on the beginning of the war, the sad-hearted slave—wretched, he must direct them to the place. Against his will he went to where he knew of an earth-hall, a barrow beneath the ground close to the sea-surge, to the struggling waves: within, it was full of ornaments and gold chains. The terrible guardian, ready for combat, held the gold treasure, old under the earth. It was no easy bargain for any man to obtain. Then the king, hardy in fight, sat down on the headland; there he saluted his hearth-companions, gold-friend of the Geats. His mind was mournful, restless and ripe for death: very close was the fate which should come to the old man, seek his soul's hoard, divide life from his body; not for long then was the life of the noble one wound in his flesh.

Beowulf spoke, the son of Ecgtheow: "In youth I lived through many battle-storms; times of war. I remember all that. I was seven winters old when the lord of treasure, the beloved king of the folk, received me from my father: King Hrethel had me and kept me, gave me treasure and feast, mindful of kinship. During his life I was no more hated by him as a man in his castle than any of his own sons, Herebeald and Haethcyn, or my own Hygelac. For the eldest a murder-bed was wrongfully spread through the deed of a kinsman, when Haethcyn struck him down with an arrow from his horned bow—his friend and his lord—missed the mark and shot his kinsman dead, one brother the other, with the bloody arrowhead. That was a fatal fight, without hope of recompense, a deed

9. Ohthere succeeded his father Ongentheow as king of the Scylfings (Swedes), but after his death his brother Onela seized the throne, driving out Ohthere's sons Eanmund and Eadgils. They were given refuge at the Geatish court by Heardred, whom Onela attacked for this act of hospitality. In the fight Eanmund and Heardred were killed, and Onela left the kingdom in Beowulf's charge.

1. The surviving son of Ohthere was befriended by Beowulf, who supported him in his successful attempt to gain the Swedish throne and who killed the usurper Onela.

wrongly done, baffling to the heart; yet it had happened that a prince had to lose life unavenged.

"So it is sad for an old man to endure that his son should ride young on the gallows. Then he may speak a story, a sorrowful song, when his son hangs for the joy of the raven, and, old in years and knowing, he can find no help for him. Always with every morning he is reminded of his son's journey elsewhere. He cares not to wait for another heir in his hall, when the first through death's force has come to the end of his deeds. Sorrowful he sees in his son's dwelling the empty wine-hall, the windy resting place without joy—the riders sleep, the warriors in the grave. There is no sound of the harp, no joy in the dwelling, as there was of old. Then he goes to his couch, sings a song of sorrow, one alone for one gone. To him all too wide has seemed the land and the dwelling.

"So the protector of the Weather-Geats bore in his heart swelling sorrow for Herebeald. In no way could he settle his feud with the life-slayer; not the sooner could he wound the warrior with deeds of hatred, though he was not dear to him. Then for the sorrow that had too bitterly befallen him he gave up the joys of men, chose God's light. To his sons he left—as a happy man does—his land and his town when he went from life.

"Then there was battle and strife of Swedes and Geats, over the wide water a quarrel shared, hatred between hardy ones, after Hrethel died. And the sons of Ongentheow[2] were bold and active in war, wanted to have no peace over the seas, but about Hreosnabeorh often devised awful slaughter. That my friends and kinsmen avenged, both the feud and the crime, as is well-known, though one of them bought it with his life, a hard bargain: the war was mortal to Haethcyn, lord of the Geats.[3] Then in the morning, I have heard, one kinsman avenged the other on his slayer with the sword's edge, when Ongentheow attacked Eofor: the war-helm split, the old Scylfing fell mortally wounded: his hand remembered feuds enough, did not withstand the life-blow.

"I repaid in war the treasures that he[4] gave me—with my bright sword, as was granted me by fate: he had given me land, a pleasant dwelling. There was not any need for him, any reason, that he should have to seek among the Gifthas or the Spear-Danes or in Sweden in order to buy with treasure a worse warrior. I would always go before him in the troop, alone in the front. And so all my life I shall wage battle while this sword endures that has served me early and late ever since I became Daeghrefn's slayer in the press—the warrior of the Hugas.[5] He could not bring armor to the king of the Frisians, breast ornament, but fell in the fight, keeper of the standard, a noble man. Nor was my sword's edge his

2. I.e., the Swedes Onela and Ohthere: the reference is, of course, to a time earlier than that referred to on p. 67, note 9.

3. Haethcyn had succeeded his father Hrethel as king of the Geats after his accidental killing of his brother Herebeald. When Haethcyn was killed while attacking the Swedes, he was succeeded by

Hygelac, who, as the next sentence relates, avenged Haethcyn's death on Ongentheow. The death of Ongentheow is described below.

4. Hygelac.

5. I.e., the Franks. The battle is the one in which Hygelac was slain.

slayer, but my warlike grip broke open his heart-streams, his bone-house. Now shall the sword's edge, the hand and hard blade, fight for the hoard."

[BEOWULF ATTACKS THE DRAGON]

Beowulf spoke, for the last time spoke words in boast: "In my youth I engaged in many wars. Old guardian of the people, I shall still seek battle, perform a deed of fame, if the evil-doer will come to me out of the earth-hall."

Then he saluted each of the warriors, the bold helmet-bearers, for the last time—his own dear companions. "I would not bear sword, weapon, to the worm, if I knew how else according to my boast I might grapple with the monster, as I did of old with Grendel. But I expect here hot battle-fire, steam and poison. Therefore I have on me shield and mail-shirt. I will not flee a foot-step from the barrow-ward, but it shall be with us at the wall as fate allots, the ruler of every man. I am confident in heart, so I forgo help against the war-flier. Wait on the barrow, safe in your mail-shirts, men in armor—which of us two may better bear wounds after our bloody meeting. This is not your venture, nor is it right for any man except me alone that he should spend his strength against the monster, do this man's deed. By my courage I shall get gold, or war will take your king, dire life-evil."

Then the brave warrior arose by his shield; hardy under helmet he went in his mail-shirt beneath the stone-cliffs, had trust in his strength—that of one man: such is not the way of the cowardly. Then he saw by the wall—he who had come through many wars, good in his great-heartedness, many clashes in battle when troops meet together—a stone arch standing, through it a stream bursting out of the barrow: there was welling of a current hot with killing fires, and he might not endure any while unburnt by the dragon's flame the hollow near the hoard. Then the man of the Weather-Geats, enraged as he was, let a word break from his breast. Stout-hearted he shouted; his voice went roaring, clear in battle, in under the gray stone. Hate was stirred up, the hoard's guard knew the voice of a man. No more time was there to ask for peace. First the monster's breath came out of the stone, the hot war-steam. The earth resounded. The man below the barrow, the lord of the Geats, swung his shield against the dreadful visitor. Then the heart of the coiled thing was aroused to seek combat. The good war-king had drawn his sword, the old heirloom, not blunt of edge. To each of them as they threatened destruction there was terror of the other. Firm-hearted he stood with his shield high, the lord of friends, while quickly the worm coiled itself; he waited in his armor. Then, coiling in flames, he came gliding on, hastening to his fate. The good shield protected the life and body of the famous prince, but for a shorter while than his wish was. There for the first time, the first day in his life, he might not prevail, since fate did not assign him such glory in battle. The lord of the Geats raised his hand, struck the shining horror so with his forged blade that the edge failed, bright on the bone, bit less surely than its folk-king had need, hard-pressed in perils. Then because of the battle-stroke the barrow-ward's heart was savage, he exhaled death-fire—the war-flames sprang wide. The gold-friend of the Geats boasted of no great victories: the war blade had failed, naked at need, as it ought not to have done, iron good from old times. That was no pleasant journey, not one on which the famous son of Ecgtheow would wish to leave his land; against his will he must take up a dwelling-place elsewhere—as every man must give up the days that are lent him.

It was not long until they came together again, dreadful foes. The hoard-guard took heart, once more his breast swelled with his breathing. Encircled with flames, he who before had ruled a folk felt harsh pain. Nor did his companions, sons of nobles, take up their stand in a troop about him with the courage of fighting men, but they crept to the wood, protected their lives. In only one of them the heart surged with sorrows: nothing can ever set aside kinship in him who means well.

He was called Wiglaf, son of Weohstan, a rare shield-warrior, a man of the Scylfings,[6] kinsman of Aelfhere. He saw his liege lord under his war-mask suffer the heat. Then he was mindful of the honors he had given him before, the rich dwelling-place of the Waegmundings, every folk-right such as his father possessed. He might not then hold back, his hand seized his shield, the yellow linden-wood; he drew his ancient sword. Among men it was the heirloom of Eanmund, the son of Ohthere:[7] Weohstan had become his slayer in battle with sword's edge—an exile without friends; and he bore off to his kin the bright-shining helmet, the ringed mail-armor, the old sword made by giants that Onela had given him,[8] his kinsman's war-armor, ready battle-gear: he did not speak of the feud, though he had killed his brother's son.[9] He[1] held the armor many half-years, the blade and the battle-dress, until his son might do manly deeds like his old father. Then he gave him among the Geats war-armor of every kind, numberless, when, old, he went forth on the way from life. For the young warrior this was the first time that he should enter the war-storm with his dear lord. His heart's courage did not slacken, nor did the heirloom of his kinsman fail in the battle. That the worm found when they had come together.

Wiglaf spoke, said many fit words to his companions—his mind was

---

6. Though in the next sentence Wiglaf is said to belong to the family of the Waegmundings, the Geatish family to which Beowulf belonged, he is here called a Scylfing (Swede), and immediately below his father Weohstan is represented as having fought for the Swede Onela in his attack on the Geats. But for a man to change his nation was not unusual, and Weohstan, who may have had both Swedish and Geatish blood, had evidently become a Geat long enough before to have brought up his son Wiglaf as one. The identity of Aelfhere is not known.

7. See above, p. 67, note 9. Not only did Weohstan support Onela's attack on the Geat king

Heardred, but actually killed Eanmund whom Heardred was supporting, and it is Eanmund's sword that Wiglaf is now wielding.

8. The spoils of war belonged to the victorious king, who apportioned them among his fighters: thus Onela gave Weohstan the armor of Eanmund, whom Weohstan had killed.

9. This ironic remark points out that Onela did not claim *wergild* or seek vengeance from Weohstan, as in other circumstances he ought to have done inasmuch as Weohstan had killed Onela's close kinsman, his nephew Eanmund: but Onela was himself trying to kill Eanmund.

1. Weohstan.

mournful: "I remember that time we drank mead, when we promised our lord in the beer-hall—him who gave us these rings—that we would repay him for the war-arms if a need like this befell him—the helmets and the hard swords. Of his own will he chose us among the host for this venture, thought us worthy of fame—and gave me these treasures—because he counted us good war-makers, brave helm-bearers, though our lord intended to do this work of courage alone, as keeper of the folk, because among men he had performed the greatest deeds of glory, daring actions. Now the day has come that our liege lord has need of the strength of good fighters. Let us go to him, help our war-chief while the grim terrible fire persists. God knows of me that I should rather that the flame enfold my body with my gold-giver. It does not seem right to me for us to bear our shields home again unless we can first fell the foe, defend the life of the prince of the Weather-Geats. I know well that it would be no recompense for past deeds that he alone of the company of the Geats should suffer pain, fall in the fight. For us both shall there be a part in the work of sword and helmet, of battle-shirt and war-clothing."

Then he waded through the deadly smoke, bore his war-helmet to the aid of his king, spoke in few words: "Beloved Beowulf, do all well, for, long since in your youth, you said that you would not let your glory fail while you lived. Now, great-spirited noble, brave of deeds, you must protect your life with all your might. I shall help you."

After these words, the worm came on, angry, the terrible malice-filled foe, shining with surging flames, to seek for the second time his enemies, hated men. Fire advanced in waves; shield burned to the boss; mail-shirt might give no help to the young spear-warrior; but the young man went quickly under his kinsman's shield when his own was consumed with flames. Then the war-king was again mindful of fame, struck with his war-sword with great strength so that it stuck in the head-bone, driven with force: Naegling broke, the sword of Beowulf failed in the fight, old and steel-gray. It was not ordained for him that iron edges might help in the combat. Too strong was the hand that I have heard strained every sword with its stroke, when he bore wound-hardened weapon to battle: he was none the better for it.

Then for the third time the folk-harmer, the fearful fire-dragon, was mindful of feuds, set upon the brave one when the chance came, hot and battle-grim seized all his neck with his sharp fangs: he was smeared with life-blood, gore welled out in waves.

Then, I have heard, at the need of the folk-king the earl at his side made his courage known, his might and his keenness—as was natural to him. He took no heed for that head,[2] but the hand of the brave man was burned as he helped his kinsman, as the man in armor struck the hateful foe a little lower down, so that the sword sank in, shining and engraved; and then the fire began to subside. The king himself then still controlled his senses, drew the battle-knife, biting and war-sharp, that

2. I.e., the dragon's flame-breathing head.

he wore on his mail-shirt: the protector of the Weather-Geats cut the worm through the middle. They felled the foe, courage drove his life out, and they had destroyed him together, the two noble kinsmen. So ought a man be, a thane at need. To the prince that was the last moment of victory for his own deeds, of work in the world.

Then the wound that the earth-dragon had caused began to burn and to swell; at once he felt dire evil boil in his breast, poison within him. Then the prince, wise of thought, went to where he might sit on a seat near the wall. He looked on the work of giants, how the timeless earth-hall held within it stone-arches fast on pillars. Then with his hands the thane, good without limit, washed him with water, blood-besmeared, the famous prince, his beloved lord, sated with battle; and he unfastened his helmet.

Beowulf spoke—despite his wounds spoke, his mortal hurts. He knew well he had lived out his days' time, joy on earth; all passed was the number of his days, death very near. "Now I would wish to give my son my war-clothing, if any heir after me, part of my flesh, were granted. I held this people fifty winters. There was no folk-king of those dwelling about who dared approach me with swords, threaten me with fears. In my land I awaited what fate brought me, held my own well, sought no treacherous quarrels, nor did I swear many oaths unrightfully. Sick with life-wounds, I may have joy of all this, for the Ruler of Men need not blame me for the slaughter of kinsmen when life goes from my body. Now quickly go to look at the hoard under the gray stone, beloved Wiglaf, now that the worm lies sleeping from sore wounds, bereft of his treasure. Be quick now, so that I may see the ancient wealth, the golden things, may clearly look on the bright curious gems, so that for that, because of the treasure's richness, I may the more easily leave life and nation I have long held."

Then I have heard that the son of Weohstan straightway obeyed his lord, sick with battle-wounds, according to the words he had spoken, went wearing his ring-armor, woven battle-shirt, under the barrow's roof. Then he saw, as he went by the seat, the brave young retainer, triumphant in heart, many precious jewels, glittering gold lying on the ground, wonders on the wall, and the worm's lair, the old night-flier's—cups standing there, vessels of men of old, with none to polish them, stripped of their ornaments. There was many a helmet old and rusty, many an arm-ring skillfully twisted. (Easily may treasure, gold in the ground, betray each one of the race of men, hide it who will.) Also he saw a standard all gold hang high over the hoard, the greatest of hand-wonders, linked with fingers' skill. From it came a light so that he might see the ground, look on the works of craft. There was no trace of the worm, for the blade had taken him. Then I have heard that one man in the mound pillaged the hoard, the old work of giants, loaded in his bosom cups and plates at his own desire. He took also the standard, brightest of banners. The sword of the old lord—its edge was iron—had already wounded the one who for a long time had been guardian of the treasure, waged his fire-terror, hot for the hoard, rising up fiercely at midnight, till he died in the slaughter.

The messenger was in haste, eager to return, urged on by the treasures. Curiosity tormented him, whether eagerly seeking he should find the lord of the Weather-Geats, strength gone, alive in the place where he had left him before. Then with the treasures he found the great prince, his lord, bleeding, at the end of his life. Again he began to sprinkle him with water until this word's point broke through his breast-hoard—he spoke, the king, old man in sorrow, looked on the gold: "I speak with my words thanks to the Lord of All for these treasures, to the King of Glory, Eternal Prince, for what I gaze on here, that I might get such for my people before my death-day. Now that I have bought the hoard of treasures with my old life, you attend to the people's needs hereafter: I can be here no longer. Bid the battle-renowned make a mound, bright after the funeral fire, on the sea's cape. It shall stand high on Hronesness as a reminder to my people, so that sea-travelers later will call it Beowulf's barrow, when they drive their ships far over the darkness of the seas."

He took off his neck the golden necklace, bold-hearted prince, gave it to the thane, to the young spear-warrior—gold-gleaming helmet, ring, and mail-shirt, bade him use them well. "You are the last left of our race, of the Waegmundings. Fate has swept away all my kinsmen, earls in their strength, to destined death. I have to go after." That was the last word of the old man, of the thoughts of his heart, before he should taste the funeral pyre, hot hostile flames. The soul went from his breast to seek the doom of those fast in truth.

[Beowulf's Funeral]

Then sorrow came to the young man that he saw him whom he most loved on the earth, at the end of his life, suffering piteously. His slayer likewise lay dead, the awful earth-dragon bereft of life, overtaken by evil. No longer should the coiled worm rule the ring-hoard, for iron edges had taken him, hard and battle-sharp work of the hammers, so that the wide-flier, stilled by wounds, had fallen on the earth near the treasure-house. He did not go flying through the air at midnight, proud of his property, showing his aspect, but he fell to earth through the work of the chief's hands. Yet I have heard of no man of might on land, though he was bold of every deed, whom it should prosper to rush against the breath of the venomous foe or disturb with hands the ring-hall, if he found the guard awake who lived in the barrow. The share of the rich treasures became Beowulf's, paid for by death: each of the two had journeyed to the end of life's loan.

Then it was not long before the battle-slack ones left the woods, ten weak troth-breakers together, who had not dared fight with their spears in their liege lord's great need. But they bore their shields, ashamed, their war-clothes, to where the old man lay, looked on Wiglaf. He sat wearied, the foot-soldier near the shoulders of his lord, would waken him with water: it gained him nothing. He might not, though he much wished it, hold life in his chieftain on earth nor change anything of the Ruler's: the judgment of God would control the deeds of every man, just as it still does now. Then it was easy to get from the young man a grim answer to him who before had lost courage. Wiglaf spoke, the son of Weohstan, a man sad at heart, looked on the unloved ones:

"Yes, he who will speak truth may say that the liege lord who gave you treasure, the war-gear that you stand in there, when he used often to hand out to hall-sitters on the ale-benches, a prince to his thanes, helmets and war-shirts such as he could find mightiest anywhere, both far and near—that he quite threw away the war-gear, to his distress when war came upon him. The folk-king had no need to boast of his war-comrades. Yet God, Ruler of Victories, granted him that he might avenge himself, alone with his sword, when there was need for his courage. I was able to give him little life-protection in the fight, and yet beyond my power I did begin to help my kinsman. The deadly foe was ever the weaker after I struck him with my sword, fire poured less strongly from his head. Too few defenders thronged about the prince when the hard time came upon him. Now there shall cease for your race the receiving of treasure and the giving of swords, all enjoyment of pleasant homes, comfort. Each man of your kindred must go deprived of his land-right when nobles from afar learn of your flight, your inglorious deed. Death is better for any earl than a life of blame."

Then he bade that the battle-deed be announced in the city, up over the cliff-edge, where the band of warriors sat the whole morning of the day, sad-hearted, shield-bearers in doubt whether it was the beloved man's last day or whether he would come again. Little did he fail to speak of new tidings, he who rode up the hill, but spoke to them all truthfully:

"Now the joy-giver of the people of the Weathers, the lord of the Geats, is fast on his death-bed, lies on his slaughter-couch through deeds of the worm. Beside him lies his life-enemy, struck down with dagger-wounds—with his sword he might not work wounds of any kind on the monster. Wiglaf son of Weohstan sits over Beowulf, one earl by the lifeless other, in weariness of heart holds death-watch over the loved and the hated.

"Now may the people expect a time of war, when the king's fall becomes wide-known to the Franks and the Frisians. A harsh quarrel was begun with the Hugas when Hygelac came traveling with his sea-army to the land of the Frisians, where the Hetware assailed him in battle, quickly, with stronger forces, made the mailed warrior bow; he fell in the ranks: that chief gave no treasure to his retainers. Ever since then the good will of the Merewioing king has been denied us.

"Nor do I expect any peace or trust from the Swedish people, for it is wide-known that Ongentheow took the life of Haethcyn, Hrethel's son, near Ravenswood when in their over-pride the people of the Geats first went against the War-Scylfings. Straightway the wary father of Ohthere,[3] old and terrible, gave a blow in return, cut down the sea-king,[4] rescued his wife, old woman of times past, bereft of her gold, mother of Onela and Ohthere, and then he followed his life-foes until they escaped, lordless, painfully, to Ravenswood. Then with a great army he besieged those whom the sword had left, weary with wounds, often vowed woes to the wretched band the livelong night, said that in the morning he would cut them apart with sword-blades, [hang] some on gallows-trees as sport for birds. Relief came in turn to the sorry-hearted together with dawn when they heard Hygelac's horn and trumpet, his sound as the good man came on their track with a body of retainers. Wide-seen was the bloody track of Swedes and Geats, the slaughter-strife of men, how the peoples stirred up the feud between them. Then the good man went with his kinsmen, old and much-mourning, to seek his stronghold: the earl Ongentheow moved further away. He had heard of the warring of Hygelac, of the war-power of the proud one. He did not trust in resistance, that he might fight off the sea-men, defend his hoard against the war-sailors, his children and wife. Instead he drew back, the old man behind his earth-wall.

"Then pursuit was offered to the people of the Swedes, the standards of Hygelac overran the stronghold as Hrethel's people pressed forward to the citadel. There Ongentheow the gray-haired was brought to bay by sword-blades, and the people's king had to submit to the judgment of Eofor alone. Wulf[5] son of Wonred had struck him angrily with his weapon so that for the blow the blood sprang forth in streams beneath his hair. Yet not for that was he afraid, the old Scylfing, but he quickly repaid the assault with worse exchange, the folk-king, when he turned toward him. The strong son of Wonred could not give the old man a return blow, for Ongentheow had first cut through the helmet of his head so that he had to sink down, smeared with blood—fell on the earth: he was not yet doomed, for he recovered, though the wound hurt him. The hardy thane of Hygelac,[6] when his brother lay low, let his broad sword, old blade made by giants, break the great helmet across the shield-wall; then the king bowed, the keeper of the folk was hit to the quick.

"Then there were many who bound up the brother, quickly raised him up after it was granted them to control the battle-field. Then one warrior stripped the other, took from Ongentheow his iron-mail, hard-hilted sword, and his helmet, too; he bore the arms of the hoary one to Hygelac. He accepted that treasure and fairly promised him rewards among the people, and he stood by it thus: the lord of the Geats, the son of Hrethel, when he came home, repaid Wulf and Eofor for their battle-assault with much treasure, gave each of them a hundred thousand [units]

3. I.e., Ongentheow.
4. I.e., Haethcyn, king of the Geats. Haethcyn's brother Hygelac, who succeeded him, was not present at this battle, but arrived after the death of Haethcyn with reinforcements to relieve the survivors and to pursue Ongentheow in his retreat to

his city.
5. The two sons of Wonred, Wulf and Eofor, attacked Ongentheow in turn. Wulf was struck down but not killed by the old Swedish king, who was then slain by Eofor.
6. I.e., Eofor.

of land and linked rings: there was no need for any man on middle-earth to blame him for the rewards, since they had performed great deeds. And then he gave Eofor his only daughter as a pledge of friendship—a fair thing for his home.

"That is the feud and the enmity, the death-hatred of men, for which I expect that the people of the Swedes, bold shield-warriors after the fall of princes, will set upon us after they learn that our prince has gone from life, he who before held hoard and kingdom against our enemies, did good to the people, and further still, did what a man should. Now haste is best, that we look on the people's king there and bring him who gave us rings on his way to the funeral pyre. Nor shall only a small share melt with the great-hearted one, but there is a hoard of treasure, gold uncounted, grimly purchased, and rings bought at the last now with his own life. These shall the fire devour, flames enfold—no earl to wear ornament in remembrance, nor any bright maiden add to her beauty with neck-ring; but mournful-hearted, stripped of gold, they shall walk, often, not once, in strange countries—now that the army-leader has laid aside laughter, his game and his mirth. Therefore many a spear, cold in the morning, shall be grasped with fingers, raised by hands; no sound of harp shall waken the warriors, but the dark raven, low over the doomed, shall tell many tales, say to the eagle how he fared at the feast when with the wolf he spoiled the slain bodies."

Thus the bold man was a speaker of hateful news, nor did he much lie in his words or his prophecies. The company all arose. Without joy they went below Earnaness[7] to look on the wonder with welling tears. Then they found on the sand, soulless, keeping his bed of rest, him who in former times had given them rings. Then the last day of the good man had come, when the war-king, prince of the Weather-Geats, died a wonderful death. First they saw the stranger creature, the worm lying loathsome, opposite him in the place. The fire-dragon was grimly terrible with his many colors, burned by the flames; he was fifty feet long in the place where he lay. Once he had joy of the air at night, came back down to seek his den. Then he was made fast by death, had made use of the last of his earth-caves. Beside him stood cups and pitchers, plates and rich swords lay eaten through by rust, just as they had been there in the bosom of the earth for a thousand winters. Then that huge heritage, gold of men of old, was wound in a spell, so that no one of men must touch the ring-hall unless God himself, the True King of Victories—He is men's protection—should grant to whom He wished to open the hoard— whatever man seemed fit to Him.

Then it was seen that the act did not profit him who wrongly kept hidden the handiworks under the wall. The keeper had first slain a man like few others, then the feud had been fiercely avenged. It is a wonder where an earl famed for courage may reach the end of his allotted life— then may dwell no longer in the mead-hall, man with his kin. So it was

7. The headland near where Beowulf had fought the dragon.

with Beowulf when he sought quarrels, the barrow's ward: he himself did not then know in what way his parting with the world should come. The great princes who had put it[8] there had laid on it so deep a curse until doomsday that the man who should plunder the place should be guilty of sins, imprisoned in idol-shrines, fixed with hell-bonds, punished with evils—unless the Possessor's favor were first shown the more clearly to him who desired the gold.

Wiglaf spoke, the son of Weohstan: "Often many a man must suffer distress for the will of one man, as has happened to us. We might by no counsel persuade our dear prince, keeper of the kingdom, not to approach the gold-guardian, let him lie where he long was, live in his dwelling to the world's end. He held to his high destiny. The hoard has been made visible, grimly got. What drove the folk-king thither was too powerfully fated. I have been therein and looked at it all, the rare things of the chamber, when it was granted me—not at all friendly was the journey that I was permitted beneath the earth-wall. In haste I seized with my hands a huge burden of hoard-treasures, of great size, bore it out here to my king. He was then still alive, sound-minded and aware. He spoke many things, old man in sorrow, and bade greet you, commanded that for your lord's deeds you make a high barrow in the place of his pyre, large and conspicuous, since he was of men the worthiest warrior through the wide earth, while he might enjoy wealth in his castle.

"Let us now hasten to see and visit for the second time the heap of precious jewels, the wonder under the walls. I shall direct you so that you may look on enough of them from near at hand—rings and broad gold. Let the bier be made ready, speedily prepared, when we come out, and then let us carry our prince, beloved man, where he shall long dwell in the Ruler's protection."

Then the son of Weohstan, man brave in battle, bade command many warriors, men who owned houses, leaders of the people, that they carry wood from afar for the pyre for the good man. "Now shall flame eat the chief of warriors—the fire shall grow dark—who often survived the iron-shower when the storm of arrows driven from bow-strings passed over the shield-wall—the shaft did its task, made eager by feather-gear served the arrowhead."

And then the wise son of Weohstan summoned from the host thanes of the king, seven together, the best; one of eight warriors, he went beneath the evil roof. One who walked before bore a torch in his hands. Then there was no lot to decide who should plunder that hoard, since the men could see that every part of it rested in the hall without guardian, lay wasting. Little did any man mourn that hastily they should bear out the rare treasure. Also they pushed the dragon, the worm, over the cliff-wall, let the wave take him, the flood enfold the keeper of the treasure. Then twisted gold was loaded on a wagon, an uncounted number of things, and the prince, hoary warrior, borne to Hronesness.

8. The treasure.

Then the people of the Geats made ready for him a funeral pyre on the earth, no small one, hung with helmets, battle-shields, bright mail-shirts, just as he had asked. Then in the midst they laid the great prince, lamenting their hero, their beloved lord. Then warriors began to awaken on the barrow the greatest of funeral-fires; the wood-smoke climbed, black over the fire; the roaring flame mixed with weeping—the wind-surge died down—until it had broken the bone-house, hot at its heart. Sad in spirit they lamented their heart-care, the death of their liege lord. [And the Geatish woman, wavy-haired, sang a sorrowful song about Beowulf, said][9] again and again that she sorely feared for herself invasions of armies, many slaughters, terror of troops, humiliation, and captivity. Heaven swallowed the smoke.

Then the people of the Weather-Geats built a mound on the promontory, one that was high and broad, wide-seen by seafarers, and in ten days completed a monument for the bold in battle, surrounded the remains of the fire with a wall, the most splendid that men most skilled might devise. In the barrow they placed rings and jewels, all such ornaments as troubled men had earlier taken from the hoard. They let the earth hold the wealth of earls, gold in the ground, where now it still dwells, as useless to men as it was before. Then the brave in battle rode round the mound, children of nobles, twelve in all, would bewail their sorrow and mourn their king, recite dirges and speak of the man. They praised his great deeds and his acts of courage, judged well of his prowess. So it is fitting that man honor his liege lord with words, love him in heart when he must be led forth from the body. Thus the people of the Geats, his hearth-companions, lamented the death of their lord. They said that he was of world-kings the mildest of men and the gentlest, kindest to his people, and most eager for fame.

9. The manuscript is badly damaged and the interpretation conjectural.

THE WANDERER

The lament of *The Wanderer* is an excellent example of the elegiac mood so common in Old English poetry. The loss of a lord, of companions in arms, of a mead-hall (in which Anglo-Saxon life realized itself to the full) are themes that enhance the melancholy tone of *Beowulf* as they are the emotional basis for such a poem as the present one. But nowhere more poignantly expressed than in *The Wanderer* is the loneliness of the exile in search of a new lord and hall: this is what Beowulf's father, Ecgtheow, would have suffered, had it not been for Hrothgar's hospitality. To the wretched seeker all weather is wintry, for nature seems to conspire to match a man's mood as he moves over the water from one land to another, yearning for a home and kin to replace those vanished ones that still fill his thoughts.

As is true of most Old English elegiac laments, both the language and the structure of *The Wanderer* are difficult. At the beginning the speaker (whom the poet identifies as an "earth-walker") voices hope of finding comfort after his many tribulations. After the poet's interruption, the wanderer continues to speak—to himself—of his long search for a new home, describing how he must keep his thoughts locked within him while he makes his search. But these thoughts form the most vivid and moving part of his soliloquy—how, floating upon the sea, dazed with sorrow and fatigue, he imagines that he sees his old companions, and how, as he wakens to reality, they vanish over the water like sea-birds. The second part of the poem, beginning with the seventh paragraph ("Therefore I cannot think why . . ."), expands the theme from one man to all human beings in a world wasted by war and time, and the speaker draws philosophical implications from his harsh experiences (presumably now in the past). He derives such cold comfort as he can from asking the old question, *Ubi sunt?*—where are they who were once so glad to be alive? And he concludes with the thought that "all this earthly habitation shall be emptied" of humankind. The narrator, "wise in heart," sits apart at the council, apparently as an indication of his detachment from life. The poem concludes with a characteristic Old English injunction to practice restraint on earth, place hope only in heaven.

The Wanderer is preserved only in the Exeter Book, a manuscript copied about 975, which contains the largest surviving collection of Old English poetry.

The Wanderer[1]

"He who is alone often lives to find favor, mildness of the Lord, even though he has long had to stir with his arms the frost-cold sea, troubled in heart over the water-way had to tread the tracks of exile. Fully-fixed is his fate."

So spoke the earth-walker, remembering hardships, fierce war-slaughters—the fall of dear kinsmen.

"Often before the day dawned I have had to speak of my cares, alone: there is now none among the living to whom I dare clearly express the thought of my heart. I know indeed that it is a fine custom for a man to lock tight his heart's coffer, keep closed the hoard-case of his mind, whatever his thoughts may be. Words of a weary heart may not withstand fate, nor those of an angry spirit bring help. Therefore men eager for fame shut sorrowful thought up fast in their breast's coffer.

"Thus I, wretched with care, removed from my homeland, far from dear kinsmen, have had to fasten with fetters the thoughts of my heart—ever since the time, many years ago, that I covered my gold-friend in the darkness of the earth; and from there I crossed the woven waves, winter-sad, downcast for want of a hall, sought a giver of treasure—a place, far or near, where I might find one in a mead-hall who should know of my people, or would comfort me friendless, receive me with

1. This new translation by the senior editor is based on the text as edited by John C. Pope in *Seven Old English Poems* (1966).

gladness. He who has experienced it knows how cruel a companion sorrow is to the man who has no beloved protectors. Exile's path awaits him, not twisted gold—frozen thoughts in his heart-case, no joy of earth. He recalls the hall-warriors and the taking of treasure, how in youth his gold-friend made him accustomed to feasting. All delight has gone.

"He who has had long to forgo the counsel of a beloved lord knows indeed how, when sorrow and sleep together bind the poor dweller-alone, it will seem to him in his mind that he is embracing and kissing his liege lord and laying his hands and his head on his knee, as it some times was in the old days when he took part in the gift-giving. Then he wakens again, the man with no lord, sees the yellow waves before him, the sea-birds bathe, spread their feathers, frost and snow fall, mingled with hail.

"Then the wounds are deeper in his heart, sore for want of his dear one. His sorrow renews as the memory of his kinsmen moves through his mind: he greets them with glad words, eagerly looks at them, a company of warriors. Again they fade, moving off over the water; the spirit of these fleeting ones brings to him no familiar voices. Care renews in him who must again and again send his weary heart out over the woven waves.

"Therefore I cannot think why the thoughts of my heart should not grow dark when I consider all the life of men through this world—with what terrible swiftness they forgo the hall-floor, bold young retainers. So this middle-earth each day fails and falls. No man may indeed become wise before he has had his share of winters in this world's kingdom. The wise man must be patient, must never be too hot-hearted, nor too hasty of speech, nor too fearful, nor too glad, nor too greedy for wealth, nor ever too eager to boast before he has thought clearly. A man must wait, when he speaks in boast, until he knows clearly, sure-minded, where the thoughts of his heart may turn.

"The wise warrior must consider how ghostly it will be when all the wealth of this world stands waste, just as now here and there through this middle-earth wind-blown walls stand covered with frost-fall, storm-beaten dwellings. Wine-halls totter, the lord lies bereft of joy, all the company has fallen, bold men beside the wall. War took away some, bore them forth on their way; a bird carried one away over the deep sea; a wolf shared one with Death; another a man sad of face hid in an earth-pit.

"So the Maker of mankind laid waste this dwelling-place until the old works of giants[2] stood idle, devoid of the noise of the stronghold's keepers. Therefore the man wise in his heart considers carefully this wall-place and this dark life, remembers the multitude of deadly combats long ago, and speaks these words: 'Where has the horse gone? Where the young warrior? Where is the giver of treasure? What has become of the feasting seats? Where are the joys of the hall? Alas, the bright cup!

___

2. Probably a reference to Roman ruins.

Alas, the mailed warrior! Alas, the prince's glory! How that time has gone, vanished beneath night's cover, just as if it never had been! The wall, wondrous high, decorated with snake-likenesses, stands now over traces of the beloved company. The ash-spears' might has borne the earls away—weapons greedy for slaughter, Fate the mighty; and storms beat on the stone walls, snow, the herald of winter, falling thick binds the earth when darkness comes and the night-shadow falls, sends harsh hailstones from the north in hatred of men. All earth's kingdom is wretched, the world beneath the skies is changed by the work of the fates. Here wealth is fleeting, here friend is fleeting, here man is fleeting, here woman is fleeting—all this earthly habitation shall be emptied.' "

So spoke the man wise in heart, sat apart at the council. He is good who keeps his word; a man must never utter too quickly his breast's passion, unless he knows first how to achieve remedy, as a leader with his courage. It will be well with him who seeks favor, comfort from the Father in heaven, where for us all stability resides.

THE BATTLE OF MALDON

The *Battle of Maldon* celebrates an event of the year 991, when a large party of Scandinavian raiders met the English defense forces on the estuary of the Blackwater River (the Pant of the poem), near Maldon in Essex. The Vikings had made a number of successful raids on seaports in the vicinity, after which they had encamped on an island near the mouth of the river. The island, since it was accessible from the mainland by a causeway that might be used only at low tide, provided a natural base from which the Vikings could continue their hit-and-run depredations on the countryside. Birhtnoth, the Earl of Essex, who was leader of the English militia, took up his position at the end of the causeway and from there was able to prevent the enemy from crossing to the mainland. As the poem relates, however, in his "overconfidence" he allowed them free passage so that a battle might take place. As a result, he was himself killed, and many of the defenders took to their heels; but the earl's retinue—his close associates and retainers—continued to fight bravely until they were overwhelmed. In the incomplete form in which the poem has come down to us we do not hear of the ultimate defeat of the English, though the grim tone and in particular the famous speech of Birhtwold prepare us for the disaster.

The unknown poet of late Anglo-Saxon times was apparently well versed in heroic English poetry of the type of *Beowulf*, and he does a brilliant job of adapting traditional epic mannerisms to his description of a local battle of no particular historical importance, which involved people with whom he was acquainted. The defense forces were actually no more than a home guard: inexperienced farmers and laborers conscripted for the local defense, together with a small group of aristocrats who were acquainted with heroic martial tradition but had not before had the opportunity to behave heroically. Since the defeat of the Scandinavians at Brunanburg in 937, the kingdom had enjoyed a long, peaceful respite from attack; the present Viking raid was, indeed, the beginning of a new and bloody era during which the realm that Alfred had consolidated weakened badly under Ethelred "the Unready." Godric and his brothers, who, according to the poem, fled from the battle, are representative of those Englishmen who preferred to pay tribute rather than to fight. But Birhtnoth and his retinue are of the traditional tough fiber, and it is especially in their speeches and single combats that the poet uses the epic style, contenting himself elsewhere with a forceful but generally realistic narrative of what occurred. Birhtnoth's decision to let the Vikings cross the river is treated in the epic manner as an instance of heroic overconfidence, like Beowulf's refusal to use his sword against the unarmed Grendel—but in this case it is a gesture that leads to tragic doom. Probably Birhtnoth had a practical motive for his rashness: if the Vikings were prevented from raiding here, they would simply sail along the coast to a less well-defended spot in order to continue their depredations. Only their destruction would insure general peace; but from the local point of view, Birhtnoth's permitting the enemy to come where he could fight with them might well appear as the rashly noble act of a traditional hero.

The poem was written down in a manuscript that was reduced to charred fragments in the same fire that damaged the *Beowulf* manuscript. Fortunately, a transcript had been made of it before the fire, and on this modern editions depend. Even before the manuscript was burned the poem must have lacked a number of lines at its beginning and end, though most scholars feel that nothing very substantial has been lost.

The Battle of Maldon[1]

Then he[2] commanded each of his warriors to leave his horse, drive it far away, and walk forward, trusting in his hands and in his good courage. When Offa's kinsman[3] understood that the earl would not put up with cowardice, he let his beloved hawk fly from his hand toward the woods and advanced to the battle: by this men might know that the youth would not weaken in the fight once he had taken up his weapons. Eadric wished also to serve his lord the earl in the battle; he carried his spear forward to the conflict. He was of good heart as long as he might hold shield and broadsword in his hands; he carried out the vow that he had made, now that he was to fight before his lord.

Then Birhtnoth began to place his men at their stations; he rode about and advised them, taught the troops how they should stand and hold the place and bade them grasp their shields aright, firm in their hands, and have no fear. When he had arranged his folk properly, he alighted among them where it seemed best to him, where he knew his retainers to be most loyal.

Then the Vikings' herald stood on the river bank, cried out loudly,

---

1. In this prose translation by the senior editor, a few liberties have been taken with the text in order to make clear the references of some of the loosely used Old English terms for "warrior." The translation is in general based on the text in J. C. Pope's *Seven Old English Poems* (1966).

2. Earl Birhtnoth, commander of the English defense forces.
3. Offa is mentioned later in the poem as one of Birhtnoth's principal retainers; his young kinsman is not otherwise identified.

spoke words, boastfully proclaimed the seafarers' message to the earl where he stood on the shore: "Bold seamen have sent me to you, have commanded me to say to you that you must quickly send treasure in order to protect yourself; and it is better for you to buy off this spear-assault with tribute than to have us give you harsh war. There is no need for us to destroy one another, if you are rich enough to pay. With the gold we will confirm truce. If you that are highest here decide upon this, that you will ransom your people, and in return for peace give the seamen money in the amount they request, and receive peace from us, we will go to ship with the tribute, set sail on the sea, and keep peace with you."

Birhtnoth spoke, raised his shield, his slender ash-spear, uttered words, angry and resolute gave him answer: "Do you hear, seafarer, what this folk says? They will give you spears for tribute, poisoned point and old sword, heriot[4] that avails you not in battle. Sea-wanderers' herald, take back our answer, speak to your people a message far more hateful, that here stands with his host an undisgraced earl who will defend this country, my lord Æthelred's[5] homeland, folk and land. Heathen shall fall in the battle. It seems to me too shameful that you should go unfought to ship with our tribute, now that you have come thus far into our land. Not so easily shall you get treasure: point and edge shall first reconcile us, grim battle-play, before we give tribute."

Then he ordered the men to bear their shields, go forward so that they all stood on the river bank. Because of the water neither band could come to the other: after the ebb, the floodtide came flowing in; currents met and crossed. It seemed to them too long a time before they might bear their spears together. On the river Pant they stood in proud array, the battle-line of the East Saxons and the men from the ash-ships. Nor might any of them injure another, unless one should receive death from the flight of an arrow.

The tide went out. The seamen stood ready, many Vikings eager for war. The earl, protector of men, bade a war-hard warrior—he was named Wulfstan, of bold lineage—to hold the bridge:[6] he was Ceola's son, who with his spear pierced the first man bold enough to step upon the bridge. There stood with Wulfstan fearless fighters, Ælfhere and Maccus, bold men both who would not take flight from the ford, but defended themselves stoutly against the enemy as long as they might wield weapons.

When the loathed strangers saw that, and understood clearly that they would face bitter bridge-defenders there, they began to prefer words to deeds,[7] prayed that they might have access to the bank, pass over the ford and lead their forces across. Then in his overconfidence the earl began to yield ground—too much ground—to the hateful people: Birhthelm's son began to call over the cold water while warriors listened:

---

4. The weapons a tenant received from his lord; they were returned to the lord upon the tenant's death.

5. King Ethelred "the Unready," who reigned from 978 to 1016.

6. Not a bridge in the modern sense, but probably a stone causeway, under water even at low tide; immediately below, it is called a ford.

7. Literally, "to practice deception"—an overstatement due to the poet's scorn for fighters who refused to do things the hard heroic way.

"Now the way is laid open for you. Come straightway to us, as men to battle. God alone knows which of us may be master of the field."

The slaughter-wolves advanced, minded not the water, a host of Vikings westward over the Pant, over the bright water bore their shields: sailors to land brought shields of linden. Opposite stood Birhtnoth with his warriors, ready for the fierce invaders. He ordered his men to form a war-hedge[8] with their shields and to hold the formation fast against the enemy. Now was combat near, glory in battle. The time had come when doomed men should fall. Shouts were raised; ravens circled, the eagle eager for food. On earth there was uproar.

They let the file-hard spears fly from their hands, grim-ground javelins. Bows were busy, shield felt point. Bitter was the battle-rush. On either side warriors fell, young men lay dead. Wulfmær was wounded, chose the slaughter-bed: kinsman of Birhtnoth—his sister's son—he was cruelly hewn down with swords. Then requital was made to the Vikings: I have heard that Eadweard struck one fiercely with his sword, withheld not the stroke, so that the warrior fell doomed at his feet; for this his lord gave the chamberlain[9] thanks when he had opportunity. Thus men stood firm in the battle, stern of purpose. Eagerly all these armed fighters contended with one another to see who could be the first with his weapon's point to take life from doomed man. The slain fell, carrion, to the earth. The defenders stood fast; Birhtnoth urged them on, bade each man who would win glory from the Danes to give his whole heart to the battle.

A war-hard Viking advanced, raised up his weapon, his shield to defend himself, moved against Birhtnoth. As resolute as the churl,[1] the earl advanced toward him. Each of them meant harm to the other. Then the seaman threw his southern-made[2] spear so that the fighters' chief was wounded. But he thrust the spear with his shield so that the shaft split and the spearhead broke off and sprang away.[3] The war-chief was maddened; with his spear he stabbed the proud Viking that had given him the wound. Wise in war was the host's leader: he let his spear go through the man's neck, guided his hand so that he mortally wounded the raider. Then he quickly stabbed another, breaking through the mail-shirt: in the breast, quite through the corselet, was this one wounded; at his heart stood the deadly point. The earl was the blither; the bold man laughed, gave thanks to God that the Lord had given him this day's work.

One of the Vikings loosed a javelin from his hand, let it fly from his fist, and it sped its way through Æthelred's noble thane. By the earl's side stood a lad not yet grown, a boy in the battle, son of Wulfstan, Wulfmær the young, who plucked full boldly the bloody spear from the

---

8. A wall of shields (a common defensive formation).
9. I.e., Eadweard.
1. Here "churl" means something like "villain."
2. Apparently the Vikings preferred weapons made in England or France—the "south."
3. The maneuver described frees the spear from the wounded man's body and enables him to take retaliatory action.

warrior. He sent the hard spear flying back again: its point went in, and on the earth lay the man who had sorely wounded his lord. Then an armed Viking stepped toward the earl. He wished to seize the earl's war-gear, make booty of rings and ornamented sword. Then Birhtnoth took his sword from its sheath, broad and bright-edged, and struck at his assailant's coat of mail. Too soon one of the seafarers hindered him, wounded the earl in his arm. Then the gold-hilted sword fell to the earth: he might not hold the hard blade, wield his weapon. Yet he spoke words, the hoar battle-leader, encouraged his men, bade them go forward stoutly together. He might no longer stand firm on his feet. He looked toward Heaven and spoke: "I thank thee, Ruler of Nations, for all the joys that I have had in the world. Now, gentle Lord, I have most need that thou grant my spirit grace, that my soul may travel to thee—under thy protection, Prince of Angels, depart in peace. I beseech thee that fiends of hell harm it not." Then the heathen warriors slew him and both the men who stood by him; Ælfnoth and Wulfmær both were laid low; close by their lord they gave up their lives.

Then there retired from the battle those who did not wish to be there. The son of Odda was the first to flee: Godric went from the fight and left the good man that had given him many a steed. He leaped upon the horse that his lord had owned, upon trappings that he had no right to, and both his brothers galloped with him, Godwine and Godwig cared not for battle, but went from the war and sought the wood, fled to its fastness and saved their lives—and more men than was in any way right, if they remembered all the favors he had done for their benefit. So Offa had said to him that day at the meeting he had held in the place, that many there spoke boldly who would not remain firm at need.

The folk's leader had fallen, Æthelred's earl: all his hearth-companions saw that their lord lay dead. Then the proud thanes advanced; men without fear pressed eagerly on. They all desired either of two things, to leave life or avenge the man they loved. Thus Ælfric's son urged them on; the warrior young of winters spoke words; Ælfwine it was who spoke, and spoke boldly: "Remember the speeches we have spoken so often over our mead,[4] when we raised boast on the bench, heroes in the hall, about hard fighting. Now may the man who is bold prove that he is. I will make my noble birth known to all, that I was of great kin in Mercia. My grandfather was named Ealhelm, a wise earl, worldly-prosperous. Thanes among that people shall not have reason to reproach me that I would go from this band of defenders, seek my home, now that my lord lies hewn down in battle. To me that is greatest of griefs: he was both my kinsman and my lord." Then he went forward, bent on revenge, and with the point of his spear pierced one of the pirate band, so that he lay on the earth, destroyed by the weapon. Then Ælfwine began to encourage his comrades, friends and companions, to go forward.

4. Boasting of prowess while drinking is a common element in Old English poetry.

Offa spoke, shook his ash-spear: "Lo, you, Ælfwine, have encouraged us all, thanes in need. Now that our lord the earl lies on the earth, there is need for us all that each one of us encourage the other, warriors to battle, as long as he may have and hold weapon, hard sword, spear and good blade. The coward son of Odda, Godric, has betrayed us all; when he rode off on that horse, on that proud steed, many a man thought that he was our lord. Therefore here on the field folk were dispersed, the shield-wall broken. Curses on his action, by which he caused so many men here to flee."

Leofsunu spoke, raised the linden buckler, his shield to defend himself; he answered the warrior: "I promise that I will not flee a footstep hence, but I will go forward, avenge my dear lord in the fight. Steadfast warriors about Sturmer[5] need not reproach me with their words that now that my patron is dead I would go lordless home, abandon the battle. But weapon, point and iron, shall take me." Full wrathful he went forward, fought fiercely; flight he despised.

Then Dunnere spoke, shook his spear; humble churl,[6] he cried over all, bade each warrior avenge Birhtnoth: "He who intends to avenge his lord on the folk may not hesitate nor care for life." Then they advanced: they cared not for life. The retainers began to fight hardily, fierce spear-bearers, and prayed God that they might avenge their patron and bring destruction to their enemies.

The hostage[7] began to help them eagerly. He was of bold kin among the Northumbrians, the son of Ecglaf: his name was Æscferth. He did not flinch at the war-play, but threw spears without pause. Now he hit shield, now he pierced man: each moment he caused some wound, as long as he might wield weapons.

Eadweard the Long still stood in the line, ready and eager, spoke boasting words, how he would not flee a footstep nor turn back, now that his chief lay dead. He broke the shield-wall and fought against the foe until he had worthily avenged his treasure-giver on the seamen— before he himself lay on the slaughter-bed.

So also did Æthelric, noble companion, eager and impetuous; he fought most resolutely, this brother of Sibirht, as did many another: they split the hollow shield and defended themselves boldly[8] . . . The shield's rim broke and the mail-shirt sang one of horror's songs. Then in the battle Offa struck the seafarer so that he fell on the earth, and there Gadd's kinsman himself sought the ground: Offa was quickly hewn down in the fight. He had, however, performed what he had promised his lord, what he had vowed before to his ring-giver, that they should either both ride to the town, hale to their home, or fall among the host, die of wounds in the slaughter-place. He lay as a thane should, near his lord.

Then there was a crash of shields. The seamen advanced, enraged by

5. The Essex village where the speaker lived.
6. I.e., freeman of the lowest rank.
7. Among Germanic peoples, hostages of high rank generally fought on the side of the warriors who held them in hostage.
8. Apparently a description of a Viking's attack on Offa has been lost.

the fight. Spear oft pierced life-house of doomed man. Then Wistan advanced: Thurstan's son fought against the men. He was the slayer of three of them in the throng before the son of Wigelm[9] lay dead in the carnage. There was stubborn conflict. Warriors stood fast in the fight. Fighting men fell, worn out with wounds: slain fell among slain.

All the while Oswold and Eadwold, brothers both, encouraged the men, with their words bade their dear kinsmen that they should stand firm at need, wield their weapons without weakness.

Birhtwold spoke, raised his shield—he was an old retainer—shook his ash-spear; full boldly he exhorted the men: "Purpose shall be the firmer, heart the keener, courage shall be the more, as our might lessens.[1] Here lies our lord all hewn down, good man on ground. Ever may he lament who now thinks to turn from war-play. I am old of life; from here I will not turn, but by my lord's side, by the man I loved, I intend to lie."

So also the son of Æthelgar encouraged them all to the battle: this Godric oft let spear go, slaughter-shaft fly on the Vikings; thus he advanced foremost among the folk, hewed and laid low until he died in the fighting: he was not that Godric who fled the battle.

9. Identification uncertain: perhaps Offa was the son of Wigelm.
1. These famous lines appear thus in the original: "Hige sceal þe heardra, heorte þe cenre, / mod sceal þe mare, þe ure mægen lytlaþ."

GEOFFREY CHAUCER

ca. 1343–1400

1372:   First Italian journey: contact with Italian literature.
1385:   *Troilus and Criseide*.
1386:   *Canterbury Tales* begun.

Social thought in the Middle Ages lagged far behind social realities. Medieval England did not recognize the existence of any class between the aristocracy, a relatively small group that attained its position by birth alone, and the commons, which included everyone not of high birth. There was, theoretically, no way by which one might advance from the commons to the aristocracy. But in actual fact there existed a large and increasingly important middle class that was constantly infiltrating the aristocracy, and it was into this middle class that Chaucer was born. He was the son of a well-to-do wine merchant, and probably spent his boyhood in the down-to-earth atmosphere of London's Vintry, the wine merchandising area; here, despite the privileges, especially in the way of education, that his father's wealth secured for him, he must have mixed daily with other commoners of all sorts. He might well have passed his whole life there, counting casks and money; but in his early teens he was sent to serve as a page in one of the great aristocratic households of England, that of Lionel of Antwerp, a son of the reigning monarch, Edward III. The rest of his life Chaucer spent in close association with the ruling nobility of the kingdom, not only with Lionel, but with his more powerful brother, John of Gaunt; with their father King Edward; with their nephew, Richard II, who succeeded to the throne in 1377; and finally with John's son, Henry IV, who deposed his cousin and became king in 1399. Chaucer's wife, Philippa, was a member of the households of Edward's queen and of John of Gaunt's second wife, Constance of Castile, and she was doubtless of higher birth than the poet. A Thomas Chaucer, who was probably their son, was an eminent man in the next generation, and an Alice Chaucer, quite possibly Chaucer's granddaughter, was sufficiently important in her day to have been married successively to the Earl of Salisbury and the Duke of Norfolk. The theoretically unbridgeable gap between the commons and the aristocracy was thus ably bridged by the poet.

In order to accomplish this, Chaucer must have been able in other ways than as a poet, though doubtless his extraordinary poetic ability was of great service to his advancement. Yet if one were to rely merely on the preserved historical records, one would have little reason to suspect that the Geoffrey Chaucer they keep mentioning ever wrote a line of verse. We catch glimpses of him serving as a page in Lionel's household (1357); as a soldier getting himself captured by the French in one of Edward III's many sallies to the continent (1359); of his being the well-beloved *vallectus* of Edward III (1367)—despite the term, which means "valet," Chaucer's duties were hardly menial—and the well-beloved servant of John of Gaunt (1374), and of receiving substantial rewards for his services; of his being sent to Italy to assist in arranging a trade agreement with the Genoese (1372), and to France, perhaps to assist in getting a royal bride for young Prince Richard (1377); of his receiving a rent-free house on the city wall of London (1374); of his keeping, "in his own hand," the accounts for which he was responsible as Controller of the Customs and Subsidies on Wool for the port of London (1374–86)—and the wool trade was England's largest trade; of other trips abroad on official business; of his becoming Justice of the Peace and Knight of the Shire (Member of Parliament) for the county of Kent (1385–86); of his erecting grandstands, inventorying pots and pans, and getting himself robbed as Clerk of the King's Works (1389–91); of his being appointed deputy forester of one of the royal preserves in Somerset (1391); and—throughout his life—of his receiving grants and annuities, or having them confirmed by royal act when a new king took the throne, or asking that butts of wine given him by the crown be transformed into cash, or merely asking for money or more money. We last glimpse him, in the final months of his life, renting a house in the garden of Westminster Abbey, within a stone's throw of Westminster Hall, the ancient seat of English government.

It might seem that a man so busy would have had little time to write poetry, but Chaucer seems to have been an assiduous versifier all his adult life. Unfortunately, few of his poems can be precisely dated, and some have not been preserved. Probably among his earliest works was a translation of the *Roman de la Rose*, a thirteenth-century French poem that exercised a profound influence on Chaucer's work. The first part of the *Roman* is an allegory, written by Guillaume de Lorris, which tells, in the form of a dream, the progress of a youthful love affair. Guillaume left the poem unfinished, but an enormous sequel was added to it after Guillaume's death by Jean de Meun: in this sequel the young courtier finally wins his lady (the rose), but not until Jean has discussed at great length many of the issues considered important by medieval intellectuals. The poem is a mixture of highly diverse elements, and it is characteristic of Chaucer's love of variety that he was able to assimilate into his own work both the courtly emotionalism of Guillaume and the philosophical, often satiric, detachment of Jean. Of a fourteenth-century English translation of the French poem only a fragment has come down to us, and that without any mention of the translator's name; scholars are generally agreed that the first 1700 lines of this fragment are Chaucer's.

Chaucer's work on the *Roman* is thought to have been done during the sixties. During this decade he probably made other translations from the French, and kept on sharpening his rhetorical tools. At the end of the decade he produced his first major work (and the only one of his poems that can be accurately dated): the *Book of the Duchess*, probably completed in early 1369, an elegy for John of Gaunt's first wife, the lovely Blanche of Lancaster, who died in 1368. This is at once one of Chaucer's most derivative and most original poems: many of its octosyllabic lines are translated directly from various works by Jean Froissart, a French poet contemporary with Chaucer, and from his countryman Guillaume de Machaut as well as from other Frenchmen; yet the plan of the work is imaginative and daring, and as a whole the elegy is on a level of excellence never attained by the poets from whom Chaucer is borrowing. It is also interesting to observe how that tact which was later to earn Chaucer his status as a minor diplomat controls the direction of the poem and gives it artistic form.

In the first period of his literary activity Chaucer's specific poetic models were French, but a knowledge of writings in Latin lies behind virtually everything he wrote—although the Latin writers Chaucer read were not the same as those whom we should study today. He probably had a more than adequate knowledge of the *Aeneid* and of Ovid in the original, but it is likely that he knew the other classical authors mostly through French translations and paraphrases. He was directly familiar with a number of (to us) cumbersome medieval Latin poems. Certainly his favorite Latin writer was Boethius, the sixth-century Roman whose *Consolation of Philosophy*, written while its author was in prison awaiting his execution, became one of the most valued of books for the whole Middle Ages, which never failed to find inspiration and comfort in its nobly stoic doctrine. Chaucer's own philosophical attitude, that of living wholeheartedly in the world while remaining spiritually detached from it, is at least partially a legacy from Boethius. His wooden but painstaking prose translation of the *Consolation*, probably made during the seventies, is only one of innumerable indications of Chaucer's reverence for the Roman writer.

The journey that Chaucer made to Italy in 1372 was in all likelihood a milestone in his literary development. Hitherto the influences upon him had been largely French and Latin, and while he may have read Italian before, it is likely that it was his Italian journey that immersed him in the works of Dante, Petrarch, and Boccaccio—the last two still alive at the time of Chaucer's visit, though he probably did not meet them. Between Chaucer and the greatest of the Italian writers, Dante, there was a large dissimilarity of temperament; yet if Chaucer could not assimilate *The Divine Comedy*, he nevertheless appreciated its austere moral grandeur, and his work shows its influences in subtle, oblique ways. Moreover, one of his funniest poems, the *House of Fame*, written sometime while he was in the customs (1374–86), may be read as a lighthearted imitation of the *Comedy*, though not a wholly successful one. From the works of Petrarch, also a writer of alien temperament, Chaucer obtained less, though he accords him respect on the several occasions when he mentions him. It was Boccaccio, whose cast of mind was far more congenial to Chaucer than the more sober Dante and Petrarch, who was to provide the source for some of Chaucer's finest poems—though his name is never mentioned in Chaucer's works. Many of the *Canterbury Tales* are indebted to one or another of Boccaccio's works, as is his lovely, cryptic love vision, the *Parliament of Fowls* (between 1375 and 1385). And his longest poem, *Troilus and Criseide*, probably completed about 1385, is an adaptation of Boccaccio's *Il Filostrato* ("The Love-Stricken"). The Italian work is one of considerable stature, which Chaucer reworked into one of the greatest love poems in any language. Even if he had never written the *Canterbury Tales*, *Troilus* would have secured Chaucer a place among the great English poets.

Chaucer probably began work on the *Canterbury Tales* in 1386, and this was his chief literary interest until his death. The old tripartite division of Chaucer's literary career which assigns him a French period (to 1372), and an Italian period (1372–85), calls this last period of his life "English." But it was not English in the same sense as the earlier periods were French and Italian (i.e., dominated by French and Italian models), for the fact is that Chaucer from the beginning to the end stands apart from the mainstream of English literature. In the Tale of Sir Thopas, which he assigns himself in the *Canterbury Tales*, the wonderful fun he makes of popular Middle English romances shows his intimate knowledge of them; and undoubtedly he had read much English writing of all kinds. Yet his notion of literary art seems to have excluded many of the common characteristics—and the characteristic vices—of what had been and was being written in English, so that it is difficult to relate his work to that of his fellow English writers. His friend John Gower is a case in point: like Chaucer, he wrote a collection of English narrative poems in his *Confessio Amantis* ("The Lover's Confession"), and Chaucer tells some of the same stories in the *Canterbury Tales* and in the *Legend of Good Women*. The last, which may have interrupted Chaucer's work on the *Canterbury Tales* in the late 1380s, was apparently assigned him by some eminent person; in order to make amends for his portrait of the unfaithful Criseide, he had to write a series of short poems celebrating famous faithful women. To make each story prove exactly the same point and nothing more is something that the conventional Gower had no trouble in doing. Yet Chaucer was able to complete the tales of only nine solemnly steadfast ladies before giving up in something like despair, and the most amusing thing about his narratives is his evident exasperation with having to make everything accord to a single formula. He could not bring himself to use the simple moralistic technique of conventional English poetry, and what Gower treats seriously appears in Chaucer often to be bordering on burlesque. Every comparison between Chaucer and run-of-the-mill English poetry either so exalts him as to make the act of comparison ludicrous or else, when Chaucer is trying to behave conventionally, shows him writing with his left hand. Chaucer had no really "English" period; English poetry had little to teach the first great English poet.

The extraordinary variety of the *Canterbury Tales* as well as their number might well have demanded their author's full energy and attention during the last fourteen years of his life, but while he was at work on them he continued, almost to the end, to perform what seem to have been full-time jobs having nothing to do with literature. Doubtless this practical business prevented him from achieving more than the twenty-two tales he finished; and it probably made him search his old papers for tales that he could work in without substantial revision. Yet if it reduced his literary output—which, even so, is enormous—this lifelong involvement with the practical is one of the chief reasons for his greatness as a poet. From his birth to his death he dealt continually with all sorts of people, the highest and the lowest, and his wonderfully observant mind made the most of this ever-present opportunity. His wide reading gave him plots and ideas, but his experience gave him people. As a commoner himself he had a sympathy with and understanding of the lower classes that few people who attained his ultimate station might boast of—and the lower classes must have accepted him. Similarly, he seems to have won full acceptance from the proud and important personages with whom he associated at court, and this he could not have won if he had not understood them perfectly. He understands both the high and the low, but he remains curiously detached from both, and it is detachment, perfectly balanced in his poetry by sympathy, which distinguishes Chaucer's art. Although he was born a commoner, he did not live as a commoner; and although he was accepted by the aristocracy, he must always have been conscious of the fact that he did not really belong to that society of which birth alone could make one a true member. Medieval aristocratic society arrogated to itself all idealism, and Chaucer characteristically regards life in terms of aristocratic ideals; but he never lost the ability, which for the poorer class was also a positive necessity, of regarding life as a purely practical matter. The art of being at once involved in and detached from a given situation is peculiarly Chaucer's.

In the physical realm, double vision results in a blurred image, but not so in Chaucer's poetic world, where images have often an extraordinary clarity, as if reality itself were made more real. His Prioress in the *Canterbury Tales* is an example of the basic human paradox which places what people are in opposition to what they think they are or pretend to be: Chaucer shows us clearly her inability to be what she professes to be, a nun; shows also the inadequacy of what she thinks a nun ought to be, a lady; and shows the great human charm of what she is, a woman. The elements of the portrait are divided between the critical and the admiring: a heavily satiric poet might well enhance the critical comment, so that our ultimate impression would be of the Prioress' weakness, while a sentimental one might enhance her amiable side so as to make that the aspect which we should remember. But in Chaucer's handling the reality comprehends both sides of the Prioress, expresses the paradox without attempting to resolve it. He appears to have been a man who had no illusions about the world or its inhabitants, but was nevertheless deeply fond of them both, and thought it worth while to keep the world spinning as well as possible, either by telling stories of high artistic truth or by counting pots and pans.

The text given here is from the senior editor's *Chaucer's Poetry: An Anthology for the Modern Reader* (1958, 1975). For the *Canterbury Tales* the Hengwrt Manuscript has provided the textual basis. The spelling has been altered to improve consistency and has been modernized in so far as is possible without distorting the phonological values of the Middle English. Discussions of Middle English pronunciation, grammar, and prosody will be found in the introduction to the period.

The Canterbury Tales   Chaucer's original plan for the *Canterbury Tales* projected about one hundred twenty stories, two for each pilgrim to tell on the way to Canterbury and two more on the way back. Chaucer actually completed only twenty-two, though two more exist in fragments; a modification of the original plan is seen in the assignment of one of the completed tales to a pilgrim who was not a member of the group that assembled at Southwark. The work was probably first conceived in 1386, when Chaucer was living in Greenwich, some miles east of London. From his house he might have been able to see the pilgrim road that led toward the shrine of the famous English saint, Thomas à Becket, the Archbishop of Canterbury who was murdered in his cathedral in 1170. Medieval pilgrims were notorious tale tellers (liars, according to the austere Langland), and the sight and sound of the bands riding toward Canterbury may well have suggested to Chaucer the idea of using a fictitious pilgrimage as a "framing" device for a number of stories. Collections of stories linked by such a device were common in the later Middle Ages. Chaucer's contemporary John Gower had used one in his *Confessio Amantis;* earlier in the century Boccaccio had placed the hundred tales of his *Decameron* in the mouths of ten characters, each of whom told a tale a day for ten days; and another Italian, Giovanni Sercambi, had placed a series of stories in the mouth of the leader of a group of persons journeying on horseback. Even if, as seems likely, Chaucer was unaware of the Italian precedents, the device of the framing fiction was in the air.

Chaucer's artistic exploitation of the device is, however, altogether his own. In Gower and Sercambi, one speaker relates all the stories; and in Boccaccio, the relationship between any one of the ten speakers and the stories they tell is haphazard, so that reassignment of all the stories to different speakers would not materially change the effect. But in the best of the *Canterbury Tales* there is a fascinating accord between the narrators and their stories, so that the story takes on rich overtones from what we have learned of its teller in the General Prologue and elsewhere, and the character itself grows and is revealed by the story. Chaucer conducts two fictions simultaneously—that of the individual tale and that of the pilgrim to whom he has assigned it. He develops the second fiction not only through the General Prologue but also through the "links," the interchanges among the pilgrims between stories. These interchanges sometimes lead to animosities. Thus the Miller's Tale offends the Reeve, who, formerly a carpenter, sees himself slandered in the figure of the Miller's silly, cuckolded carpenter; and the Reeve replies with a story that scores a miller who seems very like the pilgrim Miller. Similarly the Friar and the Summoner quarrel at the end of the Wife of Bath's Prologue, so that when the Friar is called upon he tells a tale most offensive to the Summoner, who in turn retaliates with an even more offensive story about a friar. The effect of each of these tales is enhanced by the animus of its teller, while the description of the animus in the links is exciting in itself: we are given at once a story and a drama. Furthermore, the Wife of Bath's aggressive feminism sets up resonances that are felt through all the succeeding tales. Indeed, so powerful are these resonances that some see in them a thematic unifying device: the question of marriage that the Wife introduces is further treated from two opposing points of view by the Clerk and the Merchant, and is finally settled by the common sense of the Franklin. In addition to such artistic stratagems as these, the personality and mind of the reporter—a half-burlesque version of Chaucer himself—permeate the poem and enrich its meaning.

The composition of none of the tales can be accurately dated; most of them were written during the last fourteen years of Chaucer's life, though some that fail to fit their tellers may be much earlier. The popularity of the poem in late medieval England is attested by the number of surviving manuscripts: more than eighty, none from Chaucer's lifetime. It was also twice printed by Caxton, and often reprinted by Caxton's early successors. The manuscripts reflect the unfinished state of the poem—the fact that when he died Chaucer had not made up his mind about a number of details, and hence left many inconsistencies. The poem appears in the manuscripts as nine or ten "fragments" or blocks of tales; the order of the poems within each fragment is generally the same, but the order of the fragments themselves varies widely. The fragment containing the General Prologue, the Knight's, Miller's and Reeve's Tales, and the Cook's unfinished tale, always comes first, and the fragment consisting of the Parson's Tale and the Retraction always comes last; but the others, such as that containing the Wife of Bath, the Friar, and the Summoner, or that consisting of the Physician and Pardoner, or the longest fragment consisting of six tales concluding with the Nun's Priest's, are by no means stable in relation to one another. The order followed here is one of the two that seem most nearly satisfactory.

THE GENERAL PROLOGUE

Chaucer did not need to make a pilgrimage himself in order to meet the types of people that his fictitious pilgrimage includes, for most of them had long inhabited literature as well as life: the ideal Knight, who had fought against the pagans in all the great battles of the last half-century; his son the Squire, a lover out of any love poem; the Prioress without a vocation but with the dogs and jewelry that satirical literature was always condemning nuns for; the hunting Monk and flattering Friar, chief butts of medieval satirists; the too-busy and too-rich Sergeant of the Law; the prosperous Franklin; the fraudulent Doctor; the Wife—or Archwife—of Bath; the austere Parson; and so on down through the lower orders to that flamboyant hypocrite, the Pardoner, a living vice. One meets all these types in medieval literature, and, since literature imitates life, one might have met them also in medieval society, as Chaucer, with his wide experience, undoubtedly did. Indeed, it has been argued that in some of his portraits he is drawing real people; but the appearance of doing so is actually a function of his art, which is able to endow types with a reality we generally associate only with people we know. Chaucer achieves this effect largely by persuading us that his own interest lies only in the visible, in what actually met his eye on the pilgrimage. He pretends to let the salient features of each pilgrim leap out directly at the reader, and does not seem to mind if some of his descriptions are from top to toe, others all toe and no top. This imitation of the way our minds actually perceive reality may make us fail to notice the care with which Chaucer has selected his details in order to give an integrated sketch of the person being described. While they are generally not full-blown literary symbols, most of these details give something more than mere verisimilitude to the description; actually, they mediate between the world of types and the world of real people. Independent bourgeois women of the time were often makers of cloth, so that the Wife of Bath's proficiency at the trade is, in one way, merely part of her historical reality; yet the first weaver of cloth was the unparadised Eve, and her descendant is an unregenerate member of her sex. The Franklin's red face and white beard are in the same way merely individualizing factors in the portrait; yet the red face and white beard seem always to associate themselves with a man of good will who likes good living, and since Chaucer's time they have become the distinguishing marks of a kind of mythic Franklin, Santa Claus.

The rich suggestiveness of the details is what makes the portraits worth reading again and again. One may begin by enjoying the bright if flat photographic image of reality that the reporter creates, but one will find that the initial appearance of flatness is deceptive, and that the more one rereads the more complex and significant the portraits become. Here, as elsewhere in his work, Chaucer shows himself to be a rival to Shakespeare in the art of providing entertainment on the most primitive level, and at the same time, of significantly increasing the reader's ability to comprehend reality.

From THE CANTERBURY TALES

The General Prologue

Whan that April with his° showres soote°	*its / sweet*
The droughte of March hath perced to the roote,	
And bathed every veine[1] in swich° licour,°	*such / liquid*
Of which vertu[2] engendred is the flowr;	
5 Whan Zephyrus[3] eek° with his sweete breeth	*also*
Inspired hath in every holt° and heeth°	*grove / field*
The tendre croppes,° and the yonge sonne[4]	*shoots*
Hath in the Ram his halve cours yronne,	
And smale fowles maken melodye	
10 That sleepen al the night with open yë°—	*eye*
So priketh hem° Nature in hir corages[5]—	*them*
Thanne longen folk to goon° on pilgrimages,	*go*
And palmeres[6] for to seeken straunge strondes	
To ferne halwes, couthe° in sondry londes;	*known*
15 And specially from every shires ende	
Of Engelond to Canterbury they wende,	
The holy blisful martyr[7] for to seeke	
That hem hath holpen° whan that they were seke.°	*helped / sick*
Bifel that in that seson on a day,	
20 In Southwerk[8] at the Tabard as I lay,	
Redy to wenden on my pilgrimage	
To Canterbury with ful° devout corage,	*very*
At night was come into that hostelrye	
Wel nine and twenty in a compaignye	
25 Of sondry folk, by aventure° yfalle	*chance*
In felaweshipe, and pilgrimes were they alle	
That toward Canterbury wolden° ride.	*would*
The chambres and the stables weren wide,	
And wel we weren esed° at the beste.[9]	*accommodated*
30 And shortly, whan the sonne was to reste,[1]	
So hadde I spoken with hem everichoon°	*every one*
That I was of hir felaweshipe anoon,°	*at once*
And made forward[2] erly for to rise,	
To take oure way ther as[3] I you devise.°	*describe*
35 But nathelees,° whil I have time and space,[4]	*nevertheless*
Er° that I ferther in this tale pace,°	*before / pass*

---

1. I.e., in plants.
2. By the power of which.
3. The west wind.
4. The sun is young because it has run only half-way through its course in Aries, the Ram—the first sign of the zodiac in the solar year.
5. Their hearts.
6. Palmers, wide-ranging pilgrims—especially those who sought out the "straunge strondes" (foreign shores) of the Holy Land. "Ferne halwes": far-off

shrines.
7. St. Thomas à Becket, murdered in Canterbury Cathedral in 1170.
8. Southwark, site of the Tabard Inn, was then a suburb of London, south of the Thames River.
9. In the best possible way.
1. Had set.
2. I.e., (we) made an agreement.
3. "Ther as": where.
4. I.e., opportunity.

Me thinketh it accordant to resoun[5]
To telle you al the condicioun
Of eech of hem, so as it seemed me,
40 And whiche they were, and of what degree,
And eek in what array that they were inne:
And at a knight thanne° wol I first biginne.   *then*
      A Knight ther was, and that a worthy man,
That fro the time that he first bigan
45 To riden out, he loved chivalrye,
Trouthe[6] and honour, freedom and curteisye.
Ful worthy was he in his lordes werre,°   *war*
And therto hadde he riden, no man ferre,°   *further*
As wel in Cristendom as hethenesse,°   *heathen lands*
50 And[7] evere honoured for his worthinesse.
      At Alisandre[8] he was whan it was wonne;
Ful ofte time he hadde the boord bigonne[9]
Aboven alle nacions in Pruce;
In Lettou had he reised,° and in Ruce,   *campaigned*
55 No Cristen man so ofte of his degree;
In Gernade at the sege eek hadde he be
Of Algezir, and riden in Belmarye;
At Lyeis was he, and at Satalye,
Whan they were wonne; and in the Grete See[1]
60 At many a noble arivee° hadde he be.   *military landing*
      At mortal batailes[2] hadde he been fifteene,
And foughten for oure faith at Tramissene
In listes[3] thries,° and ay° slain his fo.   *thrice / always*
      This ilke° worthy Knight hadde been also   *same*
65 Sometime with the lord of Palatye[4]
Again° another hethen in Turkye;   *against*
And everemore he hadde a soverein pris.°   *reputation*
And though that he were worthy,[5] he was wis,
And of his port° as meeke as is a maide.   *demeanor*
70 He nevere yit no vilainye° ne saide   *rudeness*
In al his lif unto no manere wight:[6]
He was a verray,° parfit,° gentil knight.   *true / perfect*
But for to tellen you of his array,
His hors° were goode, but he was nat gay.   *horses*
75 Of fustian° he wered° a gipoun[7]   *thick cloth / wore*

5. It seems to me according to reason.
6. Integrity. "Freedom" is here generosity of spirit, while "curteisye" is courtesy.
7. I.e., and he was.
8. The Knight has taken part in campaigns fought against all three groups who threatened Europe during the 14th century: the Moslems in the Near East, from whom Alexandria was seized after a famous siege; the northern barbarians in Prussia, Lithuania, and Russia; and the Moors in North Africa. The place names in the following lines refer to battlegrounds in these continuing wars.
9. Sat in the seat of honor at military feasts.

1. The Mediterranean.
2. Tournaments fought to the death.
3. Lists, tournament grounds.
4. "The lord of Palatye" was a pagan: alliances of convenience were often made during the Crusades between Christians and pagans.
5. I.e., a valiant knight.
6. "No manere wight": any sort of person. In Middle English, negatives are multiplied for emphasis: as in these two lines: "nevere," "no," "ne," "no."
7. Tunic worn underneath the coat of mail.

Al bismotered with his haubergeoun,[8]
For he was late° come from his viage,°   *lately / expedition*
And wente for to doon his pilgrimage.
    With him ther was his sone, a yong Squier,[9]
80 A lovere and a lusty bacheler,
With lokkes crulle° as° they were laid in presse.   *curly / as if*
Of twenty yeer of age he was, I gesse.
Of his stature he was of evene° lengthe,   *moderate*
And wonderly delivere,° and of greet° strengthe.   *agile / great*
85 And he hadde been som time in chivachye[1]
In Flandres, in Artois, and Picardye,
And born him wel as of so litel space,[2]
In hope to stonden in his lady° grace.   *lady's*
    Embrouded° was he as it were a mede,[3]   *embroidered*
90 Al ful of fresshe flowres, white and rede;°   *red*
Singing he was, or floiting,° al the day: *whistling*
He was as fressh as is the month of May.
Short was his gowne, with sleeves longe and wide.
Wel coude he sitte on hors, and faire ride;
95 He coude songes make, and wel endite,°   *compose verse*
Juste[4] and eek daunce, and wel portraye° and write.   *sketch*
So hote° he loved that by nightertale[5]   *hotly*
He slepte namore than dooth a nightingale.
Curteis he was, lowely,° and servisable,   *humble*
100 And carf biforn his fader at the table.[6]
    A Yeman[7] hadde he and servants namo°   *no more*
At that time, for him liste[8] ride so;
And he[9] was clad in cote and hood of greene.
A sheef of pecok arwes,° bright and keene,   *arrows*
105 Under his belt he bar° ful thriftily;°   *bore / properly*
Wel coude he dresse° his takel° yemanly:[1]   *tend to / gear*
His arwes drouped nought with fetheres lowe.
And in his hand he bar a mighty bowe.
A not-heed° hadde he with a brown visage.   *close-cut head*
110 Of wodecraft wel coude° he al the usage.   *knew*
Upon his arm he bar a gay bracer,[2]
And by his side a swerd° and a bokeler,[3]   *sword*
And on that other side a gay daggere,
Harneised° wel and sharp as point of spere;   *mounted*
115 A Cristophre[4] on his brest of silver sheene;°   *bright*

8. All rust-stained from his hauberk (coat of mail).
9. The vague term "Squier" (Squire) here seems to be the equivalent of "bacheler," a young knight still in the service of an older one.
1. On cavalry expeditions. The places in the next line are sites of skirmishes in the constant warfare between the English and the French.
2. I.e., considering the little time he had been in service.
3. Mead, meadow.
4. Joust, fight in a tournament.

5. At night.
6. It was a squire's duty to carve his lord's meat.
7. The "Yeman" (Yeoman) is an independent commoner who acts as the Knight's military servant; "he" is the Knight.
8. "Him liste": it pleased him to.
9. I.e., the Yeoman.
1. In a workmanlike way.
2. Wristguard for archers.
3. Buckler (a small shield).
4. St. Christopher medal.

An horn he bar, the baudrik[5] was of greene.
A forster° was he soothly,° as I gesse.   *forester / truly*
   Ther was also a Nonne, a Prioresse,[6]
That of hir smiling was ful simple and coy.
120 Hir gretteste ooth was but by sainte Loy!°   *Eloi*
And she was cleped° Madame Eglantine.   *named*
Ful wel she soong° the service divine,   *sang*
Entuned° in hir nose ful semely;[7]   *chanted*
And Frenssh she spak ful faire and fetisly,°   *elegantly*
125 After the scole° of Stratford at the Bowe[8]—   *school*
For Frenssh of Paris was to hire unknowe.
At mete° wel ytaught was she withalle:°   *meals / besides*
She leet° no morsel from hir lippes falle,   *let*
Ne wette hir fingres in hir sauce deepe;
130 Wel coude she carye a morsel, and wel keepe°   *take care*
That no drope ne fille° upon hir brest.   *should fall*
In curteisye was set ful muchel hir lest.[9]
Hir over-lippe wiped she so clene
That in hir coppe° ther was no ferthing° seene   *cup / bit*
135 Of grece,° whan she dronken hadde hir draughte;   *grease*
Ful semely after hir mete she raughte.°   *reached*
And sikerly° she was of greet disport,[1]   *certainly*
And ful plesant, and amiable of port,°   *mien*
And pained hire to countrefete cheere[2]
140 Of court, and to been statlich° of manere,   *dignified*
And to been holden digne[3] of reverence.
But, for to speken of hir conscience,
She was so charitable and so pitous°   *merciful*
She wolde weepe if that she saw a mous
145 Caught in a trappe, if it were deed° or bledde.   *dead*
Of[4] smale houndes hadde she that she fedde
With rosted flessh, or milk and wastelbreed;°   *fine white bread*
But sore wepte she if oon of hem were deed,
Or if men smoot it with a yerde smerte;[5]
150 And al was conscience and tendre herte.
Ful semely hir wimpel° pinched° was,   *headdress / pleated*
Hir nose tretis,° hir yën° greye as glas,   *well-formed / eyes*
Hir mouth ful smal, and therto° softe and reed,°   *moreover / red*
But sikerly° she hadde a fair forheed: *certainly*
155 It was almost a spanne brood,[6] I trowe,°   *believe*
For hardily,° she was nat undergrowe.   *assuredly*
Ful fetis° was hir cloke, as I was war;°   *becoming / aware*
Of smal° coral aboute hir arm she bar   *dainty*

---

5. Baldric (a supporting strap).
6. The Prioress is the mother superior of her nunnery. "Simple and coy": sincere and mild.
7. In a seemly manner.
8. The French learned in a convent school in Stratford-at-the-Bow, a suburb of London, was evidently not up to the Parisian standard.

9. I.e., her chief delight lay in good manners.
1. Of great good cheer.
2. And took pains to imitate the behavior.
3. And to be considered worthy.
4. I.e., some.
5. If someone struck it with a rod sharply.
6. A handsbreadth wide.

A paire[7] of bedes, gauded all with greene,
160 And theron heeng° a brooch of gold ful sheene,°   *hung / bright*
On which ther was first writen a crowned A,[8]
And after, *Amor vincit omnia.*[9]
Another Nonne with hire hadde she
That was hir chapelaine,° and preestes three.[1]   *secretary*
165 A Monk ther was, a fair for the maistrye,[2]
An outridere[3] that loved venerye,°   *hunting*
A manly man, to been an abbot able.°   *worthy*
Ful many a daintee° hors hadde he in stable,   *fine*
And whan he rood,° men mighte his bridel heere   *rode*
170 Ginglen° in a whistling wind as clere   *jingle*
And eek as loude as dooth the chapel belle
Ther as this lord was kepere of the celle.[4]
The rule of Saint Maure or of Saint Beneit,[5]
By cause that it was old and somdeel strait—
175 This ilke Monk leet olde thinges pace,°   *pass away*
And heeld° after the newe world the space.[6]   *held*
He yaf nought of that text a pulled hen[7]
That saith that hunteres been° nought holy men,   *are*
Ne that a monk, whan he is recchelees,[8]
180 Is likned til° a fissh that is waterlees—   *to*
This is to sayn, a monk out of his cloistre;
But thilke° text heeld he nat worth an oystre.   *that same*
And I saide his opinion was good:
What° sholde he studye and make himselven wood° *why / crazy*
185 Upon a book in cloistre alway to poure,
Or swinke° with his handes and laboure,   *work*
As Austin bit?[9] How shal the world be served?
Lat Austin have his swink to him reserved!
Therefore he was a prikasour° aright.   *hard rider*
190 Grehoundes he hadde as swift as fowl in flight.
Of priking° and of hunting for the hare   *riding*
Was al his lust,° for no cost wolde he spare.   *pleasure*
I sawgh his sleeves purfiled° at the hand   *fur-lined*
With gris,° and that the fineste of a land;   *gray fur*
195 And for to festne his hood under his chin
He hadde of gold wrought a ful curious[1] pin:
A love-knotte in the grettere° ende ther was.   *greater*
His heed was balled,° that shoon as any glas,   *bald*
And eek his face, as he hadde been anoint:

7. String (i.e., a rosary). "Gauded al with greene":
provided with green beads to mark certain prayers.
8. An A with an ornamental crown on it.
9. A Latin motto meaning "Love conquers all."
1. Although he here awards this charming lady
three priests, Chaucer later reduces the number to
one.
2. I.e., a superlatively fine one.
3. A monk charged with supervising property distant from the monastery.

4. Keeper of an outlying cell (branch) of the monastery.
5. St. Maurus and St. Benedict, authors of
monastic rules. "Somdeel strait": somewhat strict.
6. I.e., in his own lifetime (?).
7. He didn't give a plucked hen for that text.
8. Reckless, careless of rule.
9. I.e., as St. Augustine bids. St. Augustine had
written that monks should perform manual labor.
1. Of careful workmanship.

200   He was a lord ful fat and in good point;[2]
      His yën steepe,° and rolling in his heed,   *protruding*
      That stemed as a furnais of a leed,[3]
      His bootes souple,° his hors in greet estat°—   *supple / condition*
      Now certainly he was a fair prelat.[4]
205   He was nat pale as a forpined° gost: *wasted away*
      A fat swan loved he best of any rost.
      His palfrey° was as brown as is a berye.   *saddle horse*
         A Frere[5] ther was, a wantoune and a merye,
      A limitour, a ful solempne° man.   *pompous*
210   In alle the ordres foure is noon that can°   *knows*
      So muche of daliaunce° and fair langage: *flirtation*
      He hadde maad ful many a mariage
      Of yonge wommen at his owene cost;
      Unto his ordre he was a noble post.[6]
215   Ful wel biloved and familier was he
      With frankelains over al[7] in his contree,
      And with worthy wommen of the town—
      For he hadde power of confessioun,
      As saide himself, more than a curat,°   *parish priest*
220   For of° his ordre he was licenciat.[8]   *by*
      Ful swetely herde he confessioun,
      And plesant was his absolucioun.
      He was an esy man to yive penaunce
      Ther as he wiste to have[9] a good pitaunce;°   *donation*
225   For unto a poore ordre for to yive
      Is signe that a man is wel yshrive,[1]
      For if he yaf, he dorste make avaunt°   *boast*
      He wiste that a man was repentaunt;
      For many a man so hard is of his herte
230   He may nat weepe though him sore smerte:[2]
      Therfore, in stede of weeping and prayeres,
      Men mote° yive silver to the poore freres.[3]   *may*
         His tipet° was ay farsed° ful of knives   *scarf / packed*
      And pinnes, for to yiven faire wives;
235   And certainly he hadde a merye note;
      Wel coude he singe and playen on a rote;°   *fiddle*
      Of yeddinges he bar outrely the pris.[4]
      His nekke whit was as the flowr-de-lis;°   *lily*
      Therto he strong was as a champioun.

---

2. In good shape, plump.
3. That glowed like a furnace with a pot in it.
4. Prelate (an important churchman).
5. The "Frere" (Friar) is a member of one of the four religious orders whose members live by begging; as a "limitour" (line 209) he has been granted by his order exclusive begging rights within a certain limited area.
6. I.e., pillar.
7. I.e., with franklins everywhere. Franklins were well-to-do country men.

8. I.e., licensed to hear confessions.
9. Where he knew he would have.
1. Shriven, absolved.
2. Though he is sorely grieved.
3. Before granting absolution, the confessor must be sure the sinner is contrite; moreover, the absolution is contingent upon the sinner's performance of an act of satisfaction. In the case of Chaucer's Friar, a liberal contribution served both as proof of contrition and as satisfaction.
4. He absolutely took the prize for ballads.

240 He knew the tavernes wel in every town,
    And every hostiler° and tappestere,°   *innkeeper / barmaid*
    Bet° than a lazar[5] or a beggestere.   *better*
    For unto swich a worthy man as he
    Accorded nat, as by his facultee,[6]
245 To have with sike° lazars aquaintaunce: *sick*
    It is nat honeste,° it may nought avaunce,°   *dignified / profit*
    For to delen with no swich poraile,[7]
    But al with riche, and selleres of vitaile;°   *foodstuffs*
    And over al ther as profit sholde arise,
250 Curteis he was, and lowely of servise.
    Ther was no man nowher so vertuous:°   *efficient*
    He was the beste beggere in his hous.°   *friary*
    And yaf a certain ferme for the graunt:[8]
    Noon of his bretheren cam ther in his haunt.[9]
255 For though a widwe° hadde nought a sho,°   *widow / shoe*
    So plesant was his *In principio*[1]
    Yit wolde he have a ferthing° er he wente;   *small coin*
    His purchas was wel bettre than his rente.[2]
    And rage he coude as it were right a whelpe;[3]
260 In love-dayes[4] ther coude he muchel° helpe,   *much*
    For ther he was nat lik a cloisterer,
    With a thredbare cope, as is a poore scoler,
    But he was lik a maister[5] or a pope.
    Of double worstede was his semicope,°   *short robe*
265 And rounded as a belle out of the presse.°   *bell-mold*
    Somwhat he lipsed° for his wantounesse°   *lisped / affectation*
    To make his Englissh sweete upon his tonge;
    And in his harping, whan he hadde songe,°   *sung*
    His yën twinkled in his heed aright
270 As doon the sterres° in the frosty night.   *stars*
    This worthy limitour was cleped Huberd.
        A Marchant was ther with a forked beerd,
    In motelee,[6] and hye on hors he sat,
    Upon his heed a Flandrissh° bevere hat,   *Flemish*
275 His bootes clasped faire and fetisly.°   *elegantly*
    His resons° he spak ful solempnely,   *opinions*
    Souning° alway th' encrees of his winning.   *sounding*
    He wolde the see were kept for any thing[7]

---

5. Leper. "Beggestere": female beggar.
6. It was not suitable because of his position.
7. I.e., poor people. The oldest order of friars had been founded by St. Francis to administer to the spiritual needs of precisely those classes the Friar avoids.
8. And he paid a certain rent for the privilege of begging.
9. Assigned territory.
1. A friar's usual salutation: "In the beginning [was the Word]" (John 1.1).
2. I.e., the money he got through such activity

was more than his regular income.
3. And he could flirt wantonly, as if he were a puppy.
4. Days appointed for the settlement of lawsuits out of court.
5. A man of recognized learning.
6. Motley, a cloth of mixed color.
7. I.e., he wished the sea to be guarded at all costs. The sea route between Middelburgh (in the Netherlands) and Orwell (in Suffolk) was vital to the Merchant's export and import of wool—the basis of England's chief trade at the time.

Bitwixen Middelburgh and Orewelle.
280 Wel coude he in eschaunge sheeldes[8] selle.
This worthy man ful wel his wit bisette:°   employed
Ther wiste° no wight that he was in dette,   knew
So statly° was he of his governaunce,[9]   dignified
With his bargaines,[1] and with his chevissaunce.
285 Forsoothe he was a worthy man withalle;
But, sooth to sayn, I noot° how men him calle.   don't know
     A Clerk[2] ther was of Oxenforde also
That unto logik hadde longe ygo.[3]
As lene was his hors as is a rake,
290 And he was nought right fat, I undertake,
But looked holwe,° and therto sobrely.   hollow
Ful thredbare was his overeste courtepy,[4]
For he hadde geten him yit no benefice,
Ne was so worldly for to have office.°   secular employment
295 For him was levere[5] have at his beddes heed
Twenty bookes, clad in blak or reed,
Of Aristotle and his philosophye,
Than robes riche, or fithele,° or gay sautrye.[6]   fiddle
But al be that he was a philosophre[7]
300 Yit hadde he but litel gold in cofre;°   coffer
But al that he mighte of his freendes hente,°   take
On bookes and on lerning he it spente,
And bisily gan for the soules praye
Of hem that yaf him wherwith to scoleye.°   study
305 Of studye took he most cure° and most heede.   care
Nought oo° word spak he more than was neede,   one
And that was said in forme[8] and reverence,
And short and quik,° and ful of heigh sentence:[9]   lively
Souning° in moral vertu was his speeche,   resounding
310 And gladly wolde he lerne, and gladly teche.
     A Sergeant of the Lawe,[1] war and wis,
That often hadde been at the Parvis[2]
Ther was also, ful riche of excellence.
Discreet he was, and of greet reverence—
315 He seemed swich, his wordes weren so wise.
Justice he was ful often in assise°   circuit courts
By patente[3] and by plein° commissioun.   full

---

8. Shields, *ecus* (French coins): he made a profit trading on international credit and exchange rates.
9. The management of his affairs.
1. Bargainings. "Chevissaunce": borrowing.
2. The Clerk is a student at Oxford; in order to become a student, he would have had to signify his intention of becoming a cleric, but he was not bound to proceed to a position of responsibility in the church.
3. Who had long since matriculated in philosophy.
4. Outer cloak. "Benefice": ecclesiastical living,

such as the income a parish priest receives.
5. He would rather.
6. Psaltery (a kind of harp).
7. The word may also mean "alchemist."
8. With decorum.
9. Elevated thought.
1. The Sergeant is not only a practicing lawyer, but one of the high justices of the nation. "War and wis": wary and wise.
2. The "Paradise," a meeting place for lawyers and their clients.
3. Royal warrant.

For his science° and for his heigh renown   *knowledge*
Of fees and robes hadde he many oon.
320 So greet a purchasour° was nowher noon;   *speculator in land*
Al was fee simple[4] to him in effect—
His purchasing mighte nat been infect.[5]
Nowher so bisy a man as he ther nas;°   *was not*
And yit he seemed bisier than he was.
325 In termes[6] hadde he caas and doomes alle
That from the time of King William[7] were falle.
Therto he coude endite and make a thing,[8]
Ther coude no wight pinchen° at his writing;   *cavil*
And every statut coude° he plein° by rote.[9]   *knew / entire*
330 He rood but hoomly° in a medlee cote,[1]   *unpretentiously*
Girt with a ceint of silk, with barres smale.
Of his array telle I no lenger tale.
     A Frankelain[2] was in his compaignye:
Whit was his beerd as is the dayesye;°   *daisy*
335 Of his complexion he was sanguin.[3]
Wel loved he by the morwe a sop in win.[4]
To liven in delit° was evere his wone,°   *sensual delight / wont*
For he was Epicurus[5] owene sone,
That heeld opinion that plein° delit   *full*
340 Was verray felicitee parfit.
An housholdere and that a greet was he:
Saint Julian[6] he was in his contree.
His breed, his ale, was always after oon;[7]
A bettre envined° man was nevere noon.   *wine-stocked*
345 Withouten bake mete was nevere his hous,
Of fissh and flessh, and that so plentevous°   *plenteous*
It snewed° in his hous of mete and drinke,   *snowed*
Of alle daintees that men coude thinke.
After° the sondry sesons of the yeer   *according to*
350 So chaunged he his mete[8] and his soper.
Ful many a fat partrich hadde he in mewe,°   *cage*
And many a breem,° and many a luce° in stewe.[9]   *carp / pike*
Wo was his cook but if his sauce were
Poinant° and sharp, and redy all his gere.   *pungent*
355 His table dormant in his halle alway

---

4. "Fee simple": owned outright without legal
impediments.
5. Invalidated on a legal technicality.
6. I.e., by heart. "Caas and doomes": lawcases and
decisions.
7. I.e., the Conqueror (reigned 1066–87).
8. Compose and draw up a deed.
9. By heart.
1. A coat of mixed color. "Ceint": belt. "Barres":
transverse stripes.
2. The "Frankelain" (Franklin) is a prosperous
country man, whose lower-class ancestry is no
impediment to the importance he has attained in

his county.
3. A reference to the fact that the Franklin's temperament is dominated by blood as well as to his
red face.
4. I.e., in the morning he was very fond of a piece
of bread soaked in wine.
5. The Greek philosopher whose teaching is popularly believed to make pleasure the chief goal of
life.
6. The patron saint of hospitality.
7. Always of the same high quality.
8. Dinner. "Soper": supper.
9. Fishpond.

Stood redy covered all the longe day.[1]
At sessions[2] ther was he lord and sire.
Ful ofte time he was Knight of the Shire.
An anlaas° and a gipser° al of silk   dagger / purse
360 Heeng at his girdel,[3] whit as morne° milk.   morning
A shirreve° hadde he been, and countour.[4]   sheriff
Was nowhere swich a worthy vavasour.[5]

An Haberdasshere and a Carpenter,
A Webbe,° a Dyere, and a Tapicer°—   weaver / tapestry-maker
365 And they were clothed alle in oo liveree[6]
Of a solempne and greet fraternitee.
Ful fresshe and newe hir gere apiked° was;   polished
Hir knives were chaped° nought with bras,   mounted
But al with silver; wrought ful clene and weel
370 Hir girdles and hir pouches everydeel.°   altogether
Wel seemed eech of hem a fair burgeis°   burgher
To sitten in a yeldehalle° on a dais.   guildhall
Everich, for the wisdom that he can,[7]
Was shaply° for to been an alderman.   suitable
375 For catel° hadde they ynough and rente,°   property / income
And eek hir wives wolde it wel assente—
And elles certain were they to blame:
It is ful fair to been ycleped "Madame,"
And goon to vigilies[8] all bifore,
380 And have a mantel royalliche ybore.[9]

A Cook they hadde with hem for the nones,[1]
To boile the chiknes with the marybones,°   marrowbones
And powdre-marchant tart and galingale.[2]
Wel coude he knowe° a draughte of London ale.   recognize
385 He coude roste, and seethe,° and broile, and frye,   boil
Maken mortreux,° and wel bake a pie.   stews
But greet harm was it, as it thoughte° me,   seemed to
That on his shine a mormal° hadde he,   ulcer
For blankmanger,[3] that made he with the beste.
390 A Shipman was ther, woning° fer by weste—   dwelling
For ought I woot,° he was of Dertemouthe.[4]   know
He rood upon a rouncy° as he couthe,[5]   large nag
In a gowne of falding° to the knee.   heavy wool
A daggere hanging on a laas° hadde he   strap
395 Aboute his nekke, under his arm adown.

---

1. Tables were usually dismounted when not in use, but the Franklin kept his mounted and set ("covered"), hence "dormant."
2. I.e., sessions of the justices of the peace. "Knight of the Shire": county representative in Parliament.
3. Hung at his belt.
4. Auditor of county finances.
5. Member of an upper, but not an aristocratic, feudal class.
6. In one livery, i.e., the uniform of their "fraternitee" or guild, a partly religious, partly social organization.
7. Was capable of.
8. Feasts held on the eve of saints' days. "Al bifore": i.e., at the head of the procession.
9. Royally carried.
1. For the occasion.
2. "Powdre-marchant" and "galingale" are flavoring materials.
3. An elaborate stew.
4. Dartmouth, a port in the southwest of England.
5. As best he could.

The hote somer hadde maad his hewe° al brown;   *color*
And certainly he was a good felawe.
Ful many a draughte of win hadde he drawe[6]
Fro Burdeuxward,[7] whil that the chapman sleep:
400 Of nice° conscience took he no keep;°   *fastidious / heed*
If that he faught and hadde the hyer hand,
By water he sente hem hoom to every land.[8]
But of his craft, to rekene wel his tides,
His stremes° and his daungers° him bisides,[9]   *currents / hazards*
405 His herberwe° and his moone, his lodemenage,[1]   *anchorage*
There was noon swich from Hulle to Cartage.[2]
Hardy he was and wis to undertake;
With many a tempest hadde his beerd been shake;
He knew alle the havenes° as they were   *harbors*
410 Fro Gotlond to the Cape of Finistere,[3]
And every crike° in Britaine° and in Spaine.   *inlet / Brittany*
His barge ycleped was the Maudelaine.°   *Magdalene*
        With us ther was a Doctour of Physik:°   *medicine*
In al this world ne was ther noon him lik
415 To speken of physik and of surgerye.
For° he was grounded in astronomye,°   *because / astrology*
He kepte° his pacient a ful greet deel[4]   *tended to*
In houres[5] by his magik naturel.
Wel coude he fortunen the ascendent
420 Of his images[6] for his pacient.
He knew the cause of every maladye,
Were it of hoot or cold or moiste or drye,
And where engendred and of what humour:[7]
He was a verray parfit praktisour.[8]
425 The cause yknowe,° and of his harm the roote,   *known*
Anoon he yaf the sike man his boote.°   *remedy*
        Ful redy hadde he his apothecaries
To senden him drogges° and his letuaries,°   *drugs / medicines*
For eech of hem made other for to winne:
430 Hir frendshipe was nought newe to biginne.

---

6. Drawn, i.e., stolen.
7. From Bordeaux; i.e., while carrying wine from Bordeaux (the wine center of France). "Chapman sleep": merchant slept.
8. He drowned his prisoners.
9. Around him.
1. Pilotage.
2. From Hull (in northern England) to Cartagena (in Spain).
3. From Gotland (an island in the Baltic) to Finisterre (the westernmost point in Spain).
4. Closely.
5. I.e., the astrologically important hours (when conjunctions of the planets might help his recovery). "Magik naturel": natural—as opposed to black—magic.

6. Assign the propitious time, according to the position of stars, for using talismanic images. Such images, representing either the patient himself or points in the zodiac, were thought to be influential on the course of the disease.
7. Diseases were thought to be caused by a disturbance of one or another of the four bodily "humors," each of which, like the four elements, was a compound of two of the elementary qualities mentioned in line 422: the melancholy humor, seated in the black bile, was cold and dry (like earth); the sanguine, seated in the blood, hot and moist (like air); the choleric, seated in the yellow bile, hot and dry (like fire); the phlegmatic, seated in the phlegm, cold and moist (like water).
8. True perfect practitioner.

Wel knew he the olde Esculapius,[9]
And Deiscorides and eek Rufus,
Olde Ipocras, Hali, and Galien,
Serapion, Razis, and Avicen,
435 Averrois, Damascien, and Constantin,
Bernard, and Gatesden, and Gilbertin.
Of his diete mesurable° was he,   *moderate*
For it was of no superfluitee,
But of greet norissing° and digestible.   *nourishment*
440 His studye was but litel on the Bible.
In sanguin° and in pers° he clad was al,   *blood-red / blue*
Lined with taffata and with sendal;°   *silk*
And yit he was but esy of dispence;°   *expenditure*
He kepte that he wan in pestilence.[1]
445 For° gold in physik is a cordial,[2]   *because*
Therfore he loved gold in special.

   A good Wif was ther of biside Bathe,
But she was somdeel deef, and that was scathe.°   *a pity*
Of cloth-making she hadde swich an haunt,°   *practice*
450 She passed° hem of Ypres and of Gaunt.[3]   *surpassed*
In al the parissh wif ne was ther noon
That to the offring[4] bifore hire sholde goon,
And if ther dide, certain so wroth° was she   *angry*
That she was out of alle charitee.
455 Hir coverchiefs ful fine were of ground°—   *texture*
I dorste° swere they weyeden° ten pound   *dare / weighed*
That on a Sonday weren° upon hir heed.   *were*
Hir hosen weren of fin scarlet reed,°   *red*
Ful straite yteyd,[5] and shoes ful moiste° and newe.   *unworn*
460 Bold was hir face and fair and reed of hewe.
She was a worthy womman al hir live:
Housbondes at chirche dore[6] she hadde five,
Withouten other compaignye in youthe—
But therof needeth nought to speke as nouthe.°   *now*
465 And thries hadde she been at Jerusalem;
She hadde passed many a straunge° streem;   *foreign*
At Rome she hadde been, and at Boloigne,
In Galice at Saint Jame, and at Coloigne:[7]

---

9. The Doctor is familiar with the treatises that the Middle Ages attributed to the "great names" of medical history, whom Chaucer names in lines 431–36: the purely legendary Greek demigod Aesculapius; the Greeks Dioscorides, Rufus, Hippocrates, Galen, and Serapion; the Persians Hali and Rhazes; the Arabians Avicenna and Averroës; the early Christians John (?) of Damascus and Constantine Afer; the Scotsman Bernard Gordon; the Englishmen John of Gatesden and Gilbert, the former an early contemporary of Chaucer.
1. He saved the money he made during the plague time.

2. A stimulant. Gold was thought to have some medicinal properties.
3. Ypres and Ghent ("Gaunt") were Flemish cloth-making centers.
4. The offering in church, when the congregation brought its gifts forward.
5. Tightly laced.
6. In medieval times, weddings were performed at the church door.
7. Rome; Boulogne (in France); St. James (of Compostella) in Galicia (Spain); Cologne (in Germany): all sites of shrines much visited by pilgrims.

She coude° muchel of wandring by the waye: *knew*
470 Gat-toothed[8] was she, soothly for to saye.
Upon an amblere[9] esily she sat,
Ywimpled° wel, and on hir heed an hat   *veiled*
As brood as is a bokeler or a targe,[1]
A foot-mantel° aboute hir hipes large,   *riding skirt*
475 And on hir feet a paire of spores° sharpe.   *spurs*
In felaweshipe wel coude she laughe and carpe:°   *talk*
Of remedies of love she knew parchaunce,°   *as it happened*
For she coude of that art the olde daunce.[2]
     A good man was ther of religioun,
480 And was a poore Person° of a town,   *parson*
But riche he was of holy thought and werk.
He was also a lerned man, a clerk,
That Cristes gospel trewely° wolde preche;   *faithfully*
His parisshens° devoutly wolde he teche.   *parishioners*
485 Benigne he was, and wonder° diligent,   *wonderfully*
And in adversitee ful pacient,
And swich he was preved° ofte sithes.°   *proved / times*
Ful loth were him to cursen for his tithes,[3]
But rather wolde he yiven, out of doute,[4]
490 Unto his poore parisshens aboute
Of his offring[5] and eek of his substaunce:°   *property*
He coude in litel thing have suffisaunce.°   *sufficiency*
Wid was his parissh, and houses fer asonder,
But he ne lafte° nought for rain ne thonder,   *neglected*
495 In siknesse nor in meschief,° to visite   *misfortune*
The ferreste° in his parissh, muche and lite,[6]   *farthest*
Upon his feet, and in his hand a staf.
This noble ensample° to his sheep he yaf   *example*
That first he wroughte,[7] and afterward he taughte.
500 Out of the Gospel he tho° wordes caughte,°   *those / took*
And this figure he added eek therto:
That if gold ruste, what shal iren do?
For if a preest be foul, on whom we truste,
No wonder is a lewed° man to ruste.   *uneducated*
505 And shame it is, if a preest take keep,°   *heed*
A shiten° shepherde and a clene sheep.   *befouled*
Wel oughte a preest ensample for to yive
By his clennesse how that his sheep sholde live.
He sette nought his benefice[8] to hire
510 And leet° his sheep encombred in the mire   *left*

---

8. Gap-toothed, considered to be a sign of amorousness.
9. Horse with an easy gait.
1. "Bokeler" and "targe": small shields.
2. I.e., she knew all the tricks of that trade.
3. He would be most reluctant to invoke excommunication in order to collect his tithes.
4. Without doubt.

5. The offering made by the congregation of his church was at the Parson's disposal.
6. Great and small.
7. I.e., he practiced what he preached.
8. I.e., his parish. A priest might rent his parish to another and take a more profitable position. "Leet": i.e., he did not leave.

And ran to London, unto Sainte Poules,[9]
To seeken him a chaunterye[1] for soules,
Or with a bretherhede to been withholde,[2]
But dwelte at hoom and kepte wel his folde,
515 So that the wolf ne made it nought miscarye:
He was a shepherde and nought a mercenarye.
And though he holy were and vertuous,
He was to sinful men nought despitous,°   *scornful*
Ne of his speeche daungerous° ne digne,°   *disdainful / haughty*
520 But in his teching discreet and benigne,
To drawen folk to hevene by fairnesse
By good ensample—this was his bisinesse.
But it° were any persone obstinat,   *if there*
What so he were, of heigh or lowe estat,
525 Him wolde he snibben° sharply for the nones:[3]   *scold*
A bettre preest I trowe° ther nowher noon is.   *believe*
He waited after[4] no pompe and reverence,
Ne maked him a spiced conscience,[5]
But Cristes lore° and his Apostles twelve   *teaching*
530 He taughte, but first he folwed it himselve.
    With him ther was a Plowman, was his brother,
That hadde ylad° of dong° ful many a fother.[6]   *carried / dung*
A trewe swinkere° and a good was he,   *worker*
Living in pees° and parfit charitee.   *peace*
535 God loved he best with al his hoole° herte   *whole*
At alle times, though him gamed or smerte,[7]
And thanne his neighebor right as himselve.
He wolde thresshe, and therto dike° and delve,   *dig ditches*
For Cristes sake, for every poore wight,
540 Withouten hire, if it laye in his might.
His tithes payed he ful faire and wel,
Bothe of his propre swink[8] and his catel.°   *property*
In a tabard° he rood upon a mere.°   *short coat / mare*
    Ther was also a Reeve° and a Millere,   *estate manager*
545 A Somnour, and a Pardoner[9] also,
A Manciple,° and myself—ther were namo.   *steward*
    The Millere was a stout carl° for the nones.   *fellow*
Ful big he was of brawn° and eek of bones—   *muscle*
That preved[1] wel, for overal ther he cam
550 At wrastling he wolde have alway the ram.[2]

---

9. St. Paul's Cathedral.
1. Chantry, i.e., a foundation that employed priests for the sole duty of saying masses for the souls of certain persons. St. Paul's had many of them.
2. Or to be employed by a brotherhood; i.e., to take a lucrative and fairly easy position as chaplain with a parish guild.
3. On any occasion.
4. I.e., expected.
5. Nor did he assume an overfastidious conscience.

6. Load.
7. Whether he was pleased or grieved.
8. His own work.
9. "Somnour" (Summoner): server of summonses to the ecclesiastical court; Pardoner: dispenser of papal pardons. See lines 625 and 671, and notes, below.
1. Proved, i.e., was evident.
2. A ram was frequently offered as the prize in wrestling.

He was short-shuldred, brood,[3] a thikke knarre.
Ther was no dore that he nolde heve of harre,[4]
Or breke it at a renning° with his heed.°   *running / head*
His beerd as any sowe or fox was reed,°   *red*
555 And therto brood, as though it were a spade;
Upon the cop right[5] of his nose he hade
A werte,° and theron stood a tuft of heres,   *wart*
Rede as the bristles of a sowes eres;
His nosethirles° blake were and wide.   *nostrils*
560 A swerd and a bokeler° bar° he by his side.   *shield / bore*
His mouth as greet was as a greet furnais.°   *furnace*
He was a janglere° and a Goliardais,[6]   *chatterer*
And that was most of sinne and harlotries.°   *obscenities*
Wel coude he stelen corn and tollen thries[7]—
565 And yit he hadde a thombe[8] of gold, pardee.°   *by heaven*
A whit cote and a blew hood wered° he.   *wore*
A baggepipe wel coude he blowe and soune,°   *sound*
And therwithal° he broughte us out of towne.   *therewith*
     A gentil Manciple[9] was ther of a temple,
570 Of which achatours° mighte take exemple   *buyers of food*
For to been wise in bying of vitaile;°   *victuals*
For wheither that he paide or took by taile,[1]
Algate he waited so in his achat[2]
That he was ay biforn[3] and in good stat.
575   Now is nat that of God a ful fair grace
That swich a lewed° mannes wit shal pace°   *ignorant / surpass*
The wisdom of an heep of lerned men?
Of maistres° hadde he mo than thries ten   *masters*
That weren of lawe expert and curious,°   *cunning*
580 Of whiche ther were a dozeine in that hous
Worthy to been stiwardes of rente° and lond   *income*
Of any lord that is in Engelond,
To make him live by his propre good[4]
In honour dettelees but if[5] he were wood,°   *insane*
585 Or live as scarsly° as him list° desire,   *sparely / it pleases*
And able for to helpen al a shire
In any caas° that mighte falle° or happe,   *event / befall*
And yit this Manciple sette hir aller cappe![6]
     The Reeve[7] was a sclendre° colerik man;   *slender*
590 His beerd was shave as neigh° as evere he can;   *close*

---

3. Broad. "Knarre": sturdy fellow.
4. He would not heave off (its) hinge.
5. Right on the tip.
6. Goliard, teller of ribald stories.
7. Take toll thrice—i.e., deduct from the grain far more than the lawful percentage.
8. Thumb. The narrator seems to be questioning the validity of the adage that (only) an honest miller has a golden thumb.
9. The Manciple is the steward of a community of lawyers in London (a "temple").

1. By talley, i.e., on credit.
2. Always he was on the watch in his purchasing.
3. I.e., ahead of the game. "Stat": financial condition.
4. His own money.
5. Out of debt unless.
6. This Manciple made fools of them all.
7. The Reeve is the superintendent of a large farming estate; "colerik" (choleric) describes a man whose dominant humor is yellow bile (choler)—i.e., a hot-tempered man.

His heer was by his eres ful round yshorn;
His top was dokked[8] lik a preest biforn;
Ful longe were his legges and ful lene,
Ylik a staf, ther was no calf yseene.°   *visible*
595 Wel coude he keepe° a gerner° and a binne—   *guard / granary*
Ther was noon auditour coude on him winne.[9]
Wel wiste° he by the droughte and by the rain   *knew*
The yeelding of his seed and of his grain.
His lordes sheep, his neet,° his dayerye,   *cattle*
600 His swin, his hors, his stoor,° and his pultrye   *stock*
Was hoolly° in this Reeves governinge,   *wholly*
And by his covenant yaf[1] the rekeninge,
Sin° that his lord was twenty-yeer of age.   *since*
There coude no man bringe him in arrerage.[2]
605 Ther nas baillif, hierde, nor other hine,
That he ne knew his sleighte and his covine[3]—
They were adrad° of him as of the deeth.°   *afraid / plague*
His woning° was ful faire upon an heeth;°   *dwelling / meadow*
With greene trees shadwed was his place.
610 He coude bettre than his lord purchace.°   *acquire goods*
Ful riche he was astored° prively.°   *stocked / secretly*
His lord wel coude he plesen subtilly,
To yive and lene° him of his owene good,°   *lend / property*
And have a thank, and yit a cote and hood.
615 In youthe he hadde lerned a good mister:°   *occupation*
He was a wel good wrighte, a carpenter.
This Reeve sat upon a ful good stot°   *stallion*
That was a pomely° grey and highte° Scot.   *dapple / was named*
A long surcote° of pers° upon he hade,[4]   *overcoat / blue*
620 And by his side he bar° a rusty blade.   *bore*
Of Northfolk was this Reeve of which I telle,
Biside a town men clepen Baldeswelle.°   *Bawdswell*
Tukked[5] he was as is a frere aboute,
And evere he rood the hindreste of oure route.[6]
625   A Somnour[7] was ther with us in that place
That hadde a fir-reed° cherubinnes[8] face,   *fire-red*
For saucefleem° he was, with yën narwe,   *pimply*
And hoot° he was, and lecherous as a sparwe,°   *hot / sparrow*
With scaled° browes blake and piled[9] beerd: *scabby*
630 Of his visage children were aferd.°   *afraid*

8. Cut short: the clergy wore the head partially shaved.
9. I.e., find him in default.
1. And according to his contract he gave.
2. Convict him of being in arrears financially.
3. There was no bailiff (i.e., foreman), shepherd, nor other farm laborer whose craftiness and plots he didn't know.
4. "Upon he hade": he had on.
5. With clothing tucked up.
6. Hindmost of our group.

7. The "Somnour" (Summoner) is an employee of the ecclesiastical court, whose defined duty is to bring to court persons whom the archdeacon—the justice of the court—suspects of offenses against canon law. By this time, however, summoners had generally transformed themselves into corrupt detectives who spied out offenders and black-mailed them by threats of summonses.
8. Cherub's, often depicted in art with a red face.
9. Uneven, partly hairless.

Ther nas quiksilver, litarge, ne brimstoon,
Boras, ceruce, ne oile of tartre noon,[1]
Ne oinement that wolde clense and bite,
That him mighte helpen of his whelkes° white,   *blotches*
635 Nor of the knobbes° sitting on his cheekes.   *lumps*
Wel loved he garlek, oinons, and eek leekes,
And for to drinke strong win reed as blood.
Thanne wolde he speke and crye as he were wood;°   *mad*
And whan that he wel dronken hadde the win,
640 Thanne wolde he speke no word but Latin:
A fewe termes hadde he, two or three,
That he hadde lerned out of som decree;
No wonder is—he herde it al the day,
And eek ye knowe wel how that a jay°   *parrot*
645 Can clepen "Watte"[2] as wel as can the Pope—
But whoso coude in other thing him grope,°   *examine*
Thanne hadde he spent all his philosophye;[3]
Ay *Questio quid juris*[4] wolde he crye.
         He was a gentil harlot° and a kinde;   *rascal*
650 A bettre felawe sholde men nought finde:
He wolde suffre,° for a quart of win,   *permit*
A good felawe to have his concubin
A twelfmonth, and excusen him at the fulle;[5]
Ful prively a finch eek coude he pulle.[6]
655 And if he foond° owher° a good felawe   *found / anywhere*
He wolde techen him to have noon awe
In swich caas of the Ercedekenes curs,[7]
But if[8] a mannes soule were in his purs,
For in his purs he sholde ypunisshed be.
660 "Purs is the Ercedekenes helle," saide he.
         But wel I woot he lied right in deede:
Of cursing° oughte eech gilty man him drede,   *excommunication*
For curs wol slee° right as assoiling° savith—   *slay / absolution*
And also war him of a *significavit*.[9]
665   In daunger[1] hadde he at his owene gise°   *disposal*
The yonge girles of the diocise,
And knew hir conseil,° and was al hir reed.[2]   *secrets*
A gerland hadde he set upon his heed
As greet as it were for an ale-stake,[3]

1. These are all ointments for diseases affecting
the skin, probably diseases of venereal origin.
2. Call out: "Walter"—like modern parrots'
"Polly."
3. I.e., learning.
4. "What point of law does this investigation
involve?": a phrase frequently used in ecclesiastical courts.
5. "At the fulle": fully. Ecclesiastical courts had
jurisdiction over many offenses which today would
come under civil law, including sexual offenses.
6. "To pull a finch" is to have carnal dealings with
a woman.
7. Archdeacon's sentence of excommunication.
8. "But if": unless.
9. And also one should be careful of a *significavit*
(the writ which transferred the guilty offender from
the ecclesiastical to the civil arm for punishment).
1. Under his domination.
2. Was their chief source of advice.
3. A tavern was signalized by a pole ("ale-stake"),
rather like a modern flagpole, projecting from its
front wall; on this hung a garland, or "bush."

670   A bokeler hadde he maad him of a cake.
       With him ther rood a gentil Pardoner[4]
       Of Rouncival, his freend and his compeer,°   *comrade*
       That straight was comen fro the Court of Rome.
       Ful loude he soong,° "Com hider, love, to me."   *sang*
675   This Somnour bar to him a stif burdoun:[5]
       Was nevere trompe° of half so greet a soun.   *trumpet*
       This Pardoner hadde heer as yelow as wex,
       But smoothe it heeng° as dooth a strike° of flex;° *hung / hank / flax*
       By ounces[6] heenge his lokkes that he hadde,
680   And therwith he his shuldres overspradde,°   *overspread*
       But thinne it lay, by colpons,° oon by oon;   *strands*
       But hood for jolitee° wered° he noon,   *nonchalance / wore*
       For it was trussed up in his walet:°   *pack*
       Him thoughte he rood al of the newe jet.°   *fashion*
685   Dischevelee° save his cappe he rood al bare. *with hair down*
       Swiche glaring yën hadde he as an hare.
       A vernicle[7] hadde he sowed upon his cappe,
       His walet biforn him in his lappe,
       Bretful° of pardon, come from Rome al hoot.° *brimful / hot*
690   A vois he hadde as smal° as hath a goot;°   *fine / goat*
       No beerd hadde he, ne nevere sholde have;
       As smoothe it was as it were late yshave:
       I trowe° he were a gelding or a mare.   *believe*
       But of his craft, fro Berwik into Ware,[8]
695   Ne was ther swich another pardoner;
       For in his male° he hadde a pilwe-beer° *bag / pillowcase*
       Which that he saide was Oure Lady veil;
       He saide he hadde a gobet° of the sail   *piece*
       That Sainte Peter hadde whan that he wente
700   Upon the see, til Jesu Crist him hente.°   *seized*
       He hadde a crois° of laton,° ful of stones, *cross / brassy metal*
       And in a glas he hadde pigges bones,
       But with thise relikes[9] whan that he foond°   *found*
       A poore person° dwelling upon lond,[1]   *parson*
705   Upon° a day he gat° him more moneye   *in / got*
       Than that the person gat in monthes twaye;
       And thus with feined° flaterye and japes° *false / tricks*
       He made the person and the peple his apes.° *dupes*
       But trewely to tellen at the laste,
710   He was in chirche a noble ecclesiaste;
       Wel coude he rede a lesson and a storye,° *liturgical narrative*

---

4. A Pardoner dispensed papal pardon for sins to those who contributed to the charitable institution that he was licensed to represent; this Pardoner purported to be collecting for the hospital of Roncesvalles ("Rouncival") in Spain, which had a London branch.
5. I.e., provided him with a strong vocal accompaniment.

6. I.e., thin strands.
7. Portrait of Christ's face as it was said to have been impressed on St. Veronica's handkerchief.
8. Probably towns south and north of London.
9. Relics—i.e., the pigs' bones which the Pardoner represented as saints' bones.
1. "Upon lond": upcountry.

But alderbest° he soong an offertorye,   *best of all*
For wel he wiste° whan that song was songe,   *knew*
He moste° preche and wel affile° his tonge   *must / sharpen*
715   To winne silver, as he ful wel coude—
Therefore he soong the merierly° and loude.   *more merrily*
    Now have I told you soothly in a clause[2]
Th'estaat, th'array, the nombre, and eek the cause
Why that assembled was this compaignye
720   In Southwerk at this gentil hostelrye
That highte the Tabard, faste° by the Belle;[3]   *close*
But now is time to you for to telle
How that we baren us[4] that ilke° night   *same*
Whan we were in that hostelrye alight;
725   And after wol I telle of oure viage,°   *trip*
And al the remenant of oure pilgrimage.
But first I praye you of youre curteisye
That ye n'arette it nought my vilainye[5]
Though that I plainly speke in this matere
730   To telle you hir wordes and hir cheere,°   *behavior*
Ne though I speke hir wordes proprely;°   *accurately*
For this ye knowen also wel as I:
Who so shal telle a tale after a man
He moot° reherce,° as neigh as evere he can,   *must / repeat*
735   Everich a word, if it be in his charge,°   *responsibility*
Al speke he[6] nevere so rudeliche and large,°   *broadly*
Or elles he moot telle his tale untrewe,
Or feine° thing, or finde° wordes newe;   *falsify / devise*
He may nought spare[7] although he were his brother:
740   He moot as wel saye oo word as another.
Crist spak himself ful brode° in Holy Writ,   *broadly*
And wel ye woot no vilainye is it;
Eek Plato saith, who so can him rede,
The wordes mote be cosin to the deede.
745   Also I praye you to foryive it me
Al° have I nat set folk in hir degree   *although*
Here in this tale as that they sholde stonde:
My wit is short, ye may wel understonde.
    Greet cheere made oure Host[8] us everichoon,
750   And to the soper sette he us anoon.°   *at once*
He served us with vitaile° at the beste.   *food*
Strong was the win, and wel to drinke us leste.°   *it pleased*
A semely man oure Hoste was withalle
For to been a marchal[9] in an halle;
755   A large man he was, with yën steepe,°   *prominent*
A fairer burgeis° was ther noon in Chepe[1]—   *burgher*

2. I.e., in a short space.
3. Another tavern in Southwark.
4. Bore ourselves.
5. That you do not charge it to my lack of decorum.
6. Although he speak.
7. I.e., spare anyone.
8. The Host is the landlord of the Tabard Inn.
9. Marshal, one who was in charge of feasts.
1. Cheapside, bourgeois center of London.

Bold of his speeche, and wis, and wel ytaught,
And of manhood him lakkede right naught.
Eek therto he was right a merye man,

760 And after soper playen he bigan,
And spak of mirthe amonges othere thinges—
Whan that we hadde maad oure rekeninges[2]—
And saide thus, "Now, lordinges, trewely,
Ye been to me right welcome, hertely.°   *heartily*

765 For by my trouthe, if that I shal nat lie,
I sawgh nat this yeer so merye a compaignye
At ones in this herberwe° as is now.   *inn*
Fain° wolde I doon you mirthe, wiste I[3] how.   *gladly*
And of a mirthe I am right now bithought,

770 To doon you ese, and it shal coste nought.
"Ye goon to Canterbury—God you speede;
The blisful martyr quite you youre meede.[4]
And wel I woot as ye goon by the waye
Ye shapen you[5] to talen° and to playe,   *converse*

775 For trewely, confort ne mirthe is noon
To ride by the waye domb as stoon;°   *stone*
And therefore wol I maken you disport
As I saide erst,° and doon you som confort;   *before*
And if you liketh alle, by oon assent,

780 For to stonden at[6] my juggement,
And for to werken as I shall you saye,
Tomorwe whan ye riden by the waye—
Now by my fader° soule that is deed,   *father's*
But° ye be merye I wol yive you myn heed!°   *unless / head*

785 Holde up youre handes withouten more speeche."
Oure counseil was nat longe for to seeche;°   *seek*
Us thought it was not worth to make it wis,[7]
And graunted him withouten more avis,°   *deliberation*
And bade him saye his voirdit° as him leste.[8]   *verdict*

790 "Lordinges," quod he, "now herkneth for the beste;
But taketh it nought, I praye you, in desdain.
This is the point, to speken short and plain,
That eech of you, to shorte with oure waye
In this viage, shal tellen tales twaye°—   *two*

795 To Canterburyward, I mene it so,
And hoomward he shal tellen othere two,
Of aventures that whilom° have bifalle;   *once upon a time*
And which of you that bereth him best of alle—
That is to sayn, that telleth in this cas

800 Tales of best sentence° and most solas°—   *purport / delight*
Shal have a soper at oure aller cost,[9]

---

2. Had paid our bills.
3. If I knew.
4. Pay you your reward.
5. "Shapen you": intend.
6. Abide by.

7. We didn't think it worthwhile to make an issue of it.
8. It pleased.
9. At the cost of us all.

Here in this place, sitting by this post,
Whan that we come again fro Canterbury.
And for to make you the more mury°   *merry*
805 I wol myself goodly° with you ride—
Right at myn owene cost—and be youre gide.
And who so wol my juggement withsaye°   *contradict*
Shal paye al that we spende by the waye.
And if ye vouche sauf that it be so,
810 Telle me anoon, withouten wordes mo,°   *more*
And I wol erly shape me¹ therefore."
        This thing was graunted and oure othes swore
With ful glad herte, and prayden² him also
That he wolde vouche sauf for to do so,
815 And that he wolde been oure governour,
And of oure tales juge and reportour,°   *accountant*
And sette a soper at a certain pris,°   *price*
And we wol ruled been at his devis,°   *disposal*
In heigh and lowe; and thus by oon assent
820 We been accorded to his juggement.
And therupon the win was fet° anoon;   *fetched*
We dronken and to reste wente eechoon
Withouten any lenger° taryinge.   *longer*
        Amorwe° whan that day bigan to springe   *in the morning*
825 Up roos oure Host and was oure aller cok,³
And gadred us togidres in a flok,
And forth we riden, a litel more than pas,°   *a step*
Unto the watering of Saint Thomas;⁴
And ther oure Host bigan his hors arreste,°   *halt*
830 And saide, "Lordes, herkneth if you leste:°   *it please*
        Ye woot youre forward° and it you recorde:⁵   *agreement*
If evensong and morwesong° accorde,°   *morningsong / agree*
Lat see now who shal telle the firste tale.
As evere mote I drinken win or ale,
835 Who so be rebel to my juggement
Shal paye for al that by the way is spent.
Now draweth cut⁶ er that we ferrer twinne:
He which that hath the shorteste shal biginne.
        "Sire Knight," quod he, "my maister and my lord,
840 Now draweth cut, for that is myn accord.°   *will*
Cometh neer," quod he, "my lady Prioresse,
And ye, sire Clerk, lat be youre shamefastnesse°—   *modesty*
Ne studieth nought. Lay hand to, every man!"
        Anoon to drawen every wight bigan,
845 And shortly for to tellen as it was
Were it by aventure, or sort, or cas,⁷

1. Prepare myself.
2. I.e., we prayed.
3. Was rooster for us all.
4. A watering place near Southwark.

5. You recall it.
6. I.e., draw straws. "Ferrer twinne": go farther.
7. Whether it was luck, fate, or chance.

The soothe° is this, the cut fil° to the Knight;   *truth / fell*
Of which ful blithe and glad was every wight,
And telle he moste° his tale, as was resoun,   *must*
850   By forward and by composicioun,[8]
As ye han herd. What needeth wordes mo?
And whan this goode man sawgh that it was so,
As he that wis was and obedient
To keepe his forward by his free assent,
855   He saide, "Sin I shal biginne the game,
What, welcome be the cut, in Goddes name!
Now lat us ride, and herkneth what I saye."
And with that word we riden forth oure waye,
And he bigan with right a merye cheere°   *countenance*
860   His tale anoon, and saide as ye may heere.

The Miller's Tale[1]

The Introduction

Whan that the Knight hadde thus his tale ytold,[2]
In al the route° nas ther yong ne old   *group*
That he ne saide it was a noble storye,
And worthy for to drawen° to memorye,   *recall*
5   And namely° the gentils everichoon.   *especially*
Oure Hoste lough° and swoor, "So mote I goon,[3]   *laughed*
This gooth aright: unbokeled is the male.°   *pouch*
Lat see now who shal telle another tale.
For trewely the game is wel bigonne.
10   Now telleth ye, sire Monk, if that ye conne,°   *can*
Somwhat to quite° with the Knightes tale."   *repay*
The Millere, that for dronken[4] was al pale,
So that unnethe° upon his hors he sat,   *with difficulty*
He nolde avalen° neither hood ne hat,   *doff*
15   Ne abiden no man for his curteisye,
But in Pilates vois[5] he gan to crye,
And swoor, "By armes[6] and by blood and bones,
I can° a noble tale for the nones,   *know*
With which I wol now quite the Knightes tale."
20   Oure Hoste sawgh that he was dronke of ale,
And saide, "Abide, Robin, leve° brother,   *dear*

8. By agreement and compact.
1. The Miller's Tale belongs to the literary genre known as the "fabliau," a short story in verse that generally involves bourgeois or lower-class characters in an outrageous, often obscene plot, which is, however, realistically handled by the narrator. The fabliau is peculiarly French, and aside from the three or four examples in Chaucer there are few representatives of it in English. Yet Chaucer was supreme in this kind of tale as in many others, and the Miller's Tale is generally considered the best-told fabliau in any language.
2. The Knight's Tale is actually the first one told on the Canterbury pilgrimage, immediately following the General Prologue.
3. So might I walk, an oath
4. I.e., drunkenness.
5. The harsh voice usually associated with the character of Pontius Pilate in the mystery plays.
6. I.e., by God's arms, a blasphemous oath.

Som bettre man shal telle us first another.
Abide, and lat us werken thriftily."°   *with propriety*
    "By Goddes soule," quod he, "that wol nat I,
25 For I wol speke or elles go my way."
    Oure Host answerde, "Tel on, a devele way![7]
Thou art a fool; thy wit is overcome."
    "Now herkneth," quod the Millere, "alle and some.[8]
But first I make a protestacioun°   *public affirmation*
30 That I am dronke: I knowe it by my soun.°   *tone of voice*
And therfore if that I mis° speke or saye,   *amiss*
Wite it[9] the ale of Southwerk, I you praye;
For I wol telle a legende and a lif
Bothe of a carpenter and of his wif,
35 How that a clerk hath set the wrightes cappe."[1]
    The Reeve answerde and saide, "Stint thy clappe![2]
Lat be thy lewed° dronken harlotrye.°   *ignorant / obscenity*
It is a sinne and eek° a greet folye   *also*
To apairen° any man or him defame,   *injure*
40 And eek to bringen wives in swich fame.°   *report*
Thou maist ynough of othere thinges sayn."
    This dronken Millere spak ful soone again,
And saide, "Leve° brother Osewold,   *dear*
Who hath no wif, he is no cokewold.°   *cuckold*
45 But I saye nat therfore that thou art oon.
Ther ben ful goode wives many oon,°   *a one*
And evere a thousand goode ayains oon badde.
That knowestou wel thyself but if thou madde.°   *rave*
Why artou angry with my tale now?
50 I have a wif, pardee, as wel as thou,
Yit nolde° I, for the oxen in my plough,   *would not*
Take upon me more than ynough
As deemen of myself that I were oon:
I wol bileve wel that I am noon.
55 An housbonde shal nought been inquisitif
Of Goddes privetee,° nor of his wif.   *secrets*
So[3] he may finde Goddes foison° there,   *plenty*
Of the remenant° needeth nought enquere."°   *rest / inquire*
    What sholde I more sayn but this Millere
60 He nolde his wordes for no man forbere,
But tolde his cherles tale in his manere.
M'athinketh° that I shal reherce° it here,   *I regret / repeat*
And therefore every gentil wight I praye,
Deemeth nought, for Goddes love, that I saye
65 Of yvel entente, but for ° I moot reherse   *because*
Hir tales alle, be they bet° or werse,   *better*
Or elles falsen° som of my matere.   *falsify*

---

7. I.e., in the devil's name.
8. Each and every one.
9. Blame it on.

1. I.e., how a clerk made a fool of a carpenter.
2. Stop your chatter.
3. Provided that.

And therfore, whoso list it nought yheere
Turne over the leef, and chese° another tale,   *choose*
70   For he shal finde ynowe,° grete and smale,   *enough*
Of storial⁴ thing that toucheth gentilesse,°   *gentility*
And eek moralitee and holinesse:
Blameth nought me if that ye chese amis.
The Millere is a cherl, ye knowe wel this,
75   So was the Reeve eek, and othere mo,
And harlotrye° they tolden bothe two.   *ribaldry*
Aviseth you,⁵ and putte me out of blame:
And eek men shal nought maken ernest of game.

The Tale

Whilom° ther was dwelling at Oxenforde   *once upon a time*
80   A riche gnof° that gestes heeld to boorde,⁶   *boor*
And of his craft he was a carpenter.
With him ther was dwelling a poore scoler,
Hadde lerned art,⁷ but al his fantasye°   *interest*
Was turned for to lere° astrologye,   *learn*
85   And coude a certain of conclusiouns,
To deemen by interrogaciouns,⁸
If that men axed° him in certain houres   *asked*
Whan that men sholde have droughte or elles showres,
Or if men axed him what shal bifalle
90   Of every thing—I may nat rekene hem alle.
This clerk was cleped° hende⁹ Nicholas.   *called*
Of derne love he coude, and of solas,¹
And therto he was sly and ful privee,°   *secretive*
And lik a maide meeke for to see.
95   A chambre hadde he in that hostelrye
Allone, withouten any compaignye,
Ful fetisly ydight² with herbes swoote,°   *sweet*
And he himself as sweete as is the roote
Of licoris or any setewale.³
100 His *Almageste*⁴ and bookes grete and smale,
His astrelabye,⁵ longing for his art,
His augrim stones,⁶ layen faire apart
On shelves couched° at his beddes heed;   *set*
His presse° ycovered with a falding reed;⁷   *storage chest*
105 And al above ther lay a gay sautrye,°   *psaltery*

---

4. Historical, i.e., true.
5. Take heed.
6. I.e., took in boarders.
7. Who had completed the first stage of university education (the trivium).
8. I.e., and he knew a number of propositions on which to base astrological analyses (which would reveal the matters in lines 87–90).
9. Handy, sly, attractive.
1. I.e., he knew about secret love and pleasurable

practices.
2. Elegantly furnished.
3. Setwall, a spice.
4. The 2nd-century treatise by Ptolemy, still the standard astronomy textbook.
5. Astrolabe, an astronomical instrument. "Longing for": belonging to.
6. Counters used in arithmetic.
7. Red coarse wool.

On which he made a-nightes melodye
So swetely that al the chambre roong,°   *rang*
And *Angelus ad Virginem*[8] he soong,
And after that he soong the *Kinges Note*:
110 Ful often blessed was his merye throte.
And thus this sweete clerk his time spente
After his freendes finding and his rente.[9]
       This carpenter hadde wedded newe° a wif   *lately*
Which that he loved more than his lif.
115 Of eighteteene yeer she was of age;
Jalous he was, and heeld hire narwe in cage,
For she was wilde and yong, and he was old,
And deemed himself been lik a cokewold.[1]
He knew nat Caton,[2] for his wit was rude,
120 That bad men sholde wedde his similitude:[3]
Men sholde wedden after hir estat,[4]
For youthe and elde° is often at debat.   *age*
But sith that he was fallen in the snare,
He moste endure, as other folk, his care.
125   Fair was this yonge wif, and therwithal
As any wesele° hir body gent and smal.[5]   *weasel*
A ceint she wered, barred[6] al of silk;
A barmcloth° as whit as morne milk   *apron*
Upon hir lendes,° ful of many a gore;°   *loins / strip of cloth*
130 Whit was hir smok,° and broiden[7] al bifore   *undergarment*
And eek bihinde, on hir coler° aboute,   *collar*
Of° col-blak silk, withinne and eek withoute;   *with*
The tapes° of hir white voluper°   *ribbons / cap*
Were of the same suite of[8] hir coler;
135 Hir filet° brood° of silk and set ful hye;   *headband / broad*
And sikerly° she hadde a likerous° yë;   *certainly / wanton*
Ful smale ypulled[9] were hir browes two,
And tho were bent,° and blake as any slo.°   *arching / sloeberry*
She was ful more blisful on to see
140 Than is the newe perejonette° tree,   *pear*
And softer than the wolle° is of a wether;°   *wool / ram*
And by hir girdel° heeng° a purs of lether,   *belt / hung*
Tasseled with silk and perled with latoun.[1]
In al this world, to seeken up and down,
145 Ther nis no man so wis that coude thenche°   *imagine*
So gay a popelote° or swich° a wenche.   *doll / such*

---

8. "The Angel's Address to the Virgin," a hymn;
"*Kinges Note*": probably a popular song of the time.
9. In accordance with his friends' provision and
his own income.
1. I.e., suspected of himself that he was like a
cuckold.
2. Dionysius Cato, the supposed author of a book
of maxims used in elementary education.
3. Commanded that one should wed his equal.

4. Men should marry according to their condition.
5. Slender and delicate.
6. A belt she wore, with transverse stripes.
7. Embroidered.
8. I.e., the same pattern as.
9. Delicately plucked.
1. I.e., with brassy spangles on it.

Ful brighter was the shining of hir hewe
Than in the Towr[2] the noble° yforged newe.   *gold coin*
But of hir song, it was as loud and yerne°   *lively*
150 As any swalwe sitting on a berne.°   *barn*
Therto she coude skippe and make game[3]
As any kide or calf folwing his dame.°   *mother*
Hir mouth was sweete as bragot or the meeth,[4]
Or hoord of apples laid in hay or heeth.°   *heather*
155 Winsing° she was as is a joly° colt,   *skittish / high-spirited*
Long as a mast, and upright° as a bolt.°   *straight / arrow*
A brooch she bar upon hir lowe coler
As brood as is the boos° of a bokeler;°   *boss / shield*
Hir shoes were laced on hir legges hye.
160 She was a primerole,° a piggesnye,[5]   *cowslip*
For any lord to leggen° in his bedde,   *lay*
Or yit for any good yeman to wedde.
     Now sire, and eft° sire, so bifel the cas   *again*
That on a day this hende Nicholas
165 Fil° with this yonge wif to rage° and playe,   *happened / flirt*
Whil that hir housbonde was at Oseneye[6]
(As clerkes been ful subtil and ful quainte),°   *clever*
And prively he caughte hire by the queinte,°   *pudendum*
And saide, "Ywis, but if ich° have my wille,   *I*
170 For derne° love of thee, lemman, I spille,"°   *secret / die*
And heeld hire harde by the haunche-bones,
And saide, "Lemman,° love me al atones,[7]   *mistress*
Or I wol dien, also° God me save."   *so*
And she sproong° as a colt dooth in a trave,[8]   *sprang*
175 And with hir heed she wried° faste away;   *twisted*
She saide, "I wol nat kisse thee, by my fay.°   *faith*
Why, lat be," quod she, "lat be, Nicholas!
Or I wol crye 'Out, harrow,° and allas!'   *help*
Do way youre handes, for your curteisye!"
180 This Nicholas gan mercy for to crye,
And spak so faire, and profred him so faste,[9]
That she hir love him graunted atte laste,
And swoor hir ooth by Saint Thomas of Kent[1]
That she wolde been at his comandement,
185 Whan that she may hir leiser[2] wel espye.
"Myn housbonde is so ful of jalousye
That but ye waite° wel and been privee   *be on guard*
I woot right wel I nam but deed," quod she.
"Ye moste been ful derne as in this cas."
190   "Nay, therof care thee nought," quod Nicholas.

---

2. The Tower of London, the Mint.
3. Play.
4. "Bragot" and "meeth" are honey drinks.
5. A pig's eye, a name for a common flower.
6. A town near Oxford.

7. Right now.
8. Frame for a restive horse.
9. I.e., pushed himself so vigorously.
1. Thomas à Becket.
2. I.e., opportunity.

"A clerk hadde litherly biset his while,[3]
But if he coude a carpenter bigile."
And thus they been accorded and ysworn
To waite° a time, as I have told biforn.   *watch for*
195 Whan Nicholas hadde doon this everydeel,
And thakked° hire upon the lendes° weel,   *patted / loins*
He kiste hire sweete, and taketh his sautrye,
And playeth faste, and maketh melodye.
       Thanne fil° it thus, that to the parissh chirche,   *befell*
200 Cristes owene werkes for to wirche,°   *perform*
This goode wif wente on an haliday:°   *holy day*
Hir forheed shoon as bright as any day,
So was it wasshen whan she leet° hir werk.   *left*
       Now was ther of that chirche a parissh clerk,
205 The which that was ycleped° Absolon: *called*
Crul° was his heer, and as the gold it shoon,   *curly*
And strouted° as a fanne[4] large and brode;   *spread out*
Ful straight and evene lay his joly shode.[5]
His rode° was reed, his yën greye as goos.°   *complexion / goose*
210 With Poules window corven[6] on his shoos,
In hoses° rede he wente fetisly.°   *stockings / elegantly*
Yclad he was ful smale° and propely,   *finely*
Al in a kirtel° of a light waget°—   *tunic / blue*
Ful faire and thikke been the pointes[7] set—
215 And therupon he hadde a gay surplis,°   *surplice*
As whit as is the blosme upon the ris.°   *bough*
A merye child° he was, so God me save.   *lad*
Wel coude he laten° blood, and clippe, and shave,   *let*
And maken a chartre of land, or acquitaunce;[8]
220 In twenty manere° coude he trippe and daunce   *ways*
After the scole of Oxenforde tho,
And with his legges casten° to and fro,   *prance*
And playen songes on smal rubible;°   *fiddle*
Therto he soong somtime a loud quinible,[9]
225 And as wel coude he playe on a giterne:°   *guitar*
In al the town nas brewhous ne taverne
That he ne visited with his solas,°   *entertainment*
Ther any gailard tappestere[1] was.
But sooth to sayn, he was somdeel squaimous°   *squeamish*
230 Of farting, and of speeche daungerous.°   *fastidious*
       This Absolon, that joly° was and gay,   *pretty, amorous*
Gooth with a cencer° on the haliday,   *incense-burner*
Cencing the wives of the parissh faste,
And many a lovely look on hem he caste,

---

3. Poorly employed his time.
4. Wide-mouthed basket for separating grain from chaff.
5. Parting of the hair.
6. Carved with intricate designs, like the tracery in the windows of St. Paul's.

7. Laces for fastening the tunic and holding up the hose.
8. Legal release.
9. Part requiring a very high voice.
1. Gay barmaid.

235 And namely° on this carpenteres wif: *especially*
     To looke on hire him thoughte a merye lif.
     She was so propre° and sweete and likerous,²   *neat*
     I dar wel sayn, if she hadde been a mous,
     And he a cat, he wolde hire hente° anoon.   *pounce on*
240 This parissh clerk, this joly Absolon,
     Hath in his herte swich a love-longinge°   *lovesickness*
     That of no wif ne took he noon offringe—
     For curteisye he saide he wolde noon.
     The moone, whan it was night, ful brighte shoon,°   *shone*
245 And Absolon his giterne° hath ytake—   *guitar*
     For paramours° he thoughte for to wake—   *love*
     And forth he gooth, jolif° and amorous,   *pretty*
     Til he cam to the carpenteres hous,
     A litel after cokkes hadde ycrowe,
250 And dressed him up by a shot-windowe³
     That was upon the carpenteres wal.
     He singeth in his vois gentil and smal,°   *dainty*
     "Now dere lady, if thy wille be,
     I praye you that ye wol rewe° on me,"   *have pity*
255 Ful wel accordant to his giterninge.⁴
     This carpenter awook and herde him singe,
     And spak unto his wif, and saide anoon,
     "What, Alison, heerestou nought Absolon
     That chaunteth thus under oure bowres° wal?"   *bedroom's*
260 And she answerde hir housbonde therwithal,
     "Yis, God woot, John, I heere it everydeel."
        This passeth forth. What wol ye bet than weel?⁵
     Fro day to day this joly Absolon
     So woweth° hire that him is wo-bigoon: *woos*
265 He waketh° al the night and al the day;   *stays awake*
     He kembed° his lokkes brode⁶ and made him gay;   *combed*
     He woweth hire by menes and brocage,⁷
     And swoor he wolde been hir owene page°   *personal servant*
     He singeth, brokking° as a nightingale;   *trilling*
270 He sente hire piment,⁸ meeth, and spiced ale,
     And wafres° piping hoot out of the gleede;°   *pastries / coals*
     And for she was of towne,⁹ he profred meede°—   *bribe*
     For som folk wol be wonnen for richesse,
     And som for strokes,° and som for gentilesse.   *blows*
275 Somtime to shewe his lightnesse and maistrye,¹
     He playeth Herodes² upon a scaffold° hye.   *platform, stage*
     But what availeth him as in this cas?
     She loveth so this hende Nicholas

---

2. Wanton, appetizing.   8. Spiced wine. "Meeth": mead.
3. Took his position by a hinged window.   9. Since she was a town woman.
4. In harmony with his guitar playing.   1. Facility and virtuosity.
5. Better than well.   2. Herod, a role traditionally played as a bully in
6. I.e., wide-spreading.   the mystery plays.
7. By intermediaries and mediation.

That Absolon may blowe the bukkes horn;[3]
280   He ne hadde for his labour but a scorn.
And thus she maketh Absolon hir ape,[4]
And al his ernest turneth til a jape.°   *joke*
Ful sooth is this proverbe, it is no lie;
Men saith right thus: "Alway the nye slye
285   Maketh the ferre leve to be loth."[5]
For though that Absolon be wood° or wroth,   *furious*
By cause that he fer was from hir sighte,
This nye° Nicholas stood in his lighte.   *nearby*
Now beer° thee wel, thou hende Nicholas,   *bear*
290   For Absolon may waile and singe allas.
And so bifel it on a Saterday
This carpenter was goon til Oseney,
And hende Nicholas and Alisoun
Accorded been to this conclusioun,
295   That Nicholas shal shapen° hem a wile°   *arrange / trick*
This sely[6] jalous housbonde to bigile,
And if so be this game wente aright,
She sholden sleepen in his arm al night—
For this was his desir and hire° also.   *hers*
300   And right anoon, withouten wordes mo,
This Nicholas no lenger wolde tarye,
But dooth ful softe unto his chambre carye
Bothe mete and drinke for a day or twaye,
And to hir housbonde bad hire for to saye,
305   If that he axed after Nicholas,
She sholde saye she niste° wher he was—   *didn't know*
Of al that day she sawgh him nought with yë:
She trowed° that he was in maladye,   *believed*
For for no cry hir maide coude him calle,
310   He nolde answere for no thing that mighte falle.°   *happen*
This passeth forth al thilke° Saterday   *this*
That Nicholas stille in his chambre lay,
And eet,° and sleep,° or dide what him leste,[7]   *ate / slept*
Til Sonday that the sonne gooth to reste.
315   This sely carpenter hath greet mervaile
Of Nicholas, or what thing mighte him aile,
And saide, "I am adrad,° by Saint Thomas,   *afraid*
It stondeth nat aright with Nicholas.
God shilde° that he deide sodeinly!   *forbid*
320   This world is now ful tikel,° sikerly: *changeable*
I sawgh today a corps yborn to chirche
That now a° Monday last I sawgh him wirche.°   *on / work*
Go up," quod he unto his knave° anoon,   *manservant*
"Clepe° at his dore or knokke with a stoon.°   *call / stone*

---

3. Blow the buck's horn, i.e., go without reward.   dear one hated.
4. I.e., thus she makes a fool of Absolon.   6. "Poor innocent."
5. Always the sly man at hand makes the distant   7. He wanted.

325 Looke how it is and tel me boldely."
    This knave gooth him up ful sturdily,
And at the chambre dore whil that he stood
He cride and knokked as that he were wood,°   *mad*
"What? How? What do ye, maister Nicholay?
330 How may ye sleepen al the longe day?"
But al for nought: he herde nat a word.
An hole he foond ful lowe upon a boord,
Ther as the cat was wont in for to creepe,
And at that hole he looked in ful deepe,
335 And atte laste he hadde of him a sighte.
    This Nicholas sat evere caping° uprighte   *gaping*
As he hadde kiked° on the newe moone.   *gazed*
Adown he gooth and tolde his maister soone
In what array° he saw this ilke° man.   *condition / same*
340   This carpenter to blessen him[8] bigan,
And saide, "Help us, Sainte Frideswide!
A man woot litel what him shal bitide.
This man is falle, with his astromye,[9]
In som woodnesse° or in som agonye.   *madness*
345 I thoughte ay° wel how that it sholde be: *always*
Men sholde nought knowe of Goddes privetee.
Ye, blessed be alway a lewed° man   *ignorant*
That nought but only his bileve° can.°   *creed / knows*
So ferde° another clerk with astromye: *fared*
350 He walked in the feeldes for to prye
Upon the sterres,° what ther sholde bifalle,   *stars*
Til he was in a marle-pit[1] yfalle—
He saw nat that. But yit, by Saint Thomas,
Me reweth sore[2] for hende Nicholas.
355 He shal be rated of[3] his studying,
If that I may, by Jesus, hevene king!
Get me a staf that I may underspore,°   *pry up*
Whil that thou, Robin, hevest° up the dore.   *heave*
He shal[4] out of his studying, as I gesse."
360 And to the chambre dore he gan him dresse.[5]
His knave was a strong carl° for the nones,° *fellow / purpose*
And by the haspe he haaf° it up atones: *heaved*
Into° the floor the dore fil° anoon.   *on / fell*
This Nicholas sat ay as stille as stoon,
365 And evere caped up into the air.
    This carpenter wende° he were in despair,   *thought*
And hente° him by the shuldres mightily,   *seized*
And shook him harde, and cride spitously,°   *roughly*
"What, Nicholay, what, how! What! Looke adown!

---

8. Cross himself.   3. Scolded for.
9. Illiterate form of "astronomye."   4. I.e., shall come.
1. Pit from which a fertilizing clay is dug.   5. Took his stand.
2. I sorely pity.

370 Awaak and thenk on Cristes passioun![6]
     I crouche[7] thee from elves and fro wightes."
     Therwith the nightspel saide he anoonrightes[8]
     On foure halves° of the hous aboute,   sides
     And on the thresshfold° on the dore withoute: threshold
375 "Jesu Crist and Sainte Benedight,°   Benedict
     Blesse this hous from every wikked wight!
     For nightes nerye the White Pater Noster.[9]
     Where wentestou, thou Sainte Petres soster?°   sister
     And at the laste this hende Nicholas
380 Gan for to sike° sore, and saide, "Allas,   sigh
     Shal al the world be lost eftsoones° now?"   again
          This carpenter answerde, "What saistou?
     What, thenk on God as we doon, men that swinke."[1]
          This Nicholas answerde, "Fecche me drinke,
385 And after wol I speke in privetee
     Of certain thing that toucheth me and thee.
     I wol telle it noon other man, certain."
          This carpenter gooth down and comth again,
     And broughte of mighty ale a large quart,
390 And when that eech of hem hadde dronke his part,
     This Nicholas his dore faste shette,°   shut
     And down the carpenter by him he sette,
     And saide, "John, myn hoste lief° and dere,   beloved
     Thou shalt upon thy trouthe° swere me here   word of honor
395 That to no wight thou shalt this conseil° wraye;°   secret / disclose
     For it is Cristes conseil that I saye,
     And if thou telle it man,[2] thou art forlore,°   lost
     For this vengeance thou shalt have therfore,
     That if thou wraye me, thou shalt be wood."[3]
400   "Nay, Crist forbede it, for his holy blood,"
     Quod tho this sely° man. "I nam no labbe,[4]   innocent
     And though I saye, I nam nat lief to gabbe.[5]
     Say what thou wilt, I shal it nevere telle
     To child ne wif, by him that harwed helle."[6]
405   "Now John," quod Nicholas, "I wol nought lie.
     I have yfounde in myn astrologye,
     As I have looked in the moone bright,
     That now a Monday next, at quarter night,[7]
     Shal falle a rain, and that so wilde and wood,°   furious
410 That half so greet was nevere Noees° flood.   Noah's
     This world," he saide, "in lasse° than an hour   less

6. I.e., the Crucifixion.
7. Make the sign of the cross on. "Wightes": wicked
creatures.
8. The night-charm he said right away.
9. I.e., the White Lord's Prayer defend (us). This
personification was considered a powerful beneficent spirit.
1. Work.

2. To anyone.
3. Go mad.
4. Blabbermouth.
5. And though I say it myself, I don't like to gossip.
6. By Him that despoiled hell—i.e., Christ.
7. I.e., shortly before dawn.

Shal al be dreint,° so hidous is the showr.   *drowned*
Thus shal mankinde drenche° and lese° hir lif."   *drown / lose*
   This carpenter answerde, "Allas, my wif!
415 And shal she drenche? Allas, myn Alisoun!"
For sorwe of this he fil almost[8] adown,
And saide, "Is there no remedye in this cas?"
   "Why yis, for[9] Gode," quod hende Nicholas,
"If thou wolt werken after lore and reed[1]—
420 Thou maist nought werken after thyn owene heed;°   *head*
For thus saith Salomon that was ful trewe,
'Werk al by conseil and thou shalt nought rewe.'°   *be sorry*
And if thou werken wolt by good conseil,
I undertake, withouten mast or sail,
425 Yit shal I save hire and thee and me.
Hastou nat herd how saved was Noee
Whan that oure Lord hadde warned him biforn
That al the world with water sholde be lorn?"°   *lost*
   "Yis," quod this carpenter, "ful yore ago."
430   "Hastou nat herd," quod Nicholas, "also
The sorwe of Noee with his felaweshipe?
Er that he mighte gete his wif to shipe,
Him hadde levere,[2] I dar wel undertake,
At thilke time than alle his wetheres blake
435 That she hadde had a ship hirself allone.[3]
And therfore woostou° what is best to doone?   *do you know*
This axeth° haste, and of an hastif° thing   *requires / urgent*
Men may nought preche or maken tarying.
Anoon go gete us faste into this in°   *lodging*
440 A kneeding trough or elles a kimelin°   *brewing tub*
For eech of us, but looke that they be large,°   *wide*
In whiche we mowen swimme as in a barge,[4]
And han therinne vitaile suffisaunt[5]
But for a day—fy° on the remenaunt!   *fie*
445 The water shal aslake° and goon away   *diminish*
Aboute prime[6] upon the nexte day.
But Robin may nat wite° of this, thy knave,   *know*
Ne eek thy maide Gille I may nat save.
Axe nought why, for though thou axe me,
450 I wol nought tellen Goddes privetee.°   *secrets*
Suffiseth thee, but if thy wittes madde,°   *go mad*
To han° as greet a grace as Noee hadde.   *have*
Thy wif shal I wel saven, out of doute.
Go now thy way, and speed thee heraboute.
455 But whan thou hast for hire° and thee and me   *her*

---

8. Almost fell.
9. I.e., by.
1. Act according to learning and advice.
2. He had rather. "Wetheres": rams. I.e., he'd have
given all the rams he had.

3. The reluctance of Noah's wife to board the ark
is a traditional comic theme in the mystery plays.
4. In which we can float as in a vessel.
5. Sufficient food.
6. 9 A.M.

Ygeten us thise kneeding-tubbes three,
Thanne shaltou hangen hem in the roof ful hye,
That no man of oure purveyance° espye.   *foresight*
And whan thou thus hast doon as I have said,
460 And hast oure vitaile faire in hem ylaid,
And eek an ax to smite the corde atwo,
Whan that the water comth that we may go,
And broke an hole an heigh[7] upon the gable
Unto the gardinward,[8] over the stable,
465 That we may freely passen forth oure way,
Whan that the grete showr is goon away,
Thanne shaltou swimme as merye, I undertake,
As dooth the white doke° after hir drake.   *duck*
Thanne wol I clepe,° 'How, Alison? How, John?   *call*
470 Be merye, for the flood wol passe anoon.'
And thou wolt sayn, 'Hail, maister Nicholay!
Good morwe, I see thee wel, for it is day!'
And thanne shal we be lordes al oure lif
Of al the world, as Noee and his wif.
475 But of oo thing I warne thee ful right:
Be wel avised on that ilke night
That we been entred into shippes boord
That noon of us ne speke nought a word,
Ne clepe, ne crye, but been in his prayere,
480 For it is Goddes owene heeste dere.[9]
Thy wif and thou mote hange fer atwinne,[1]
For that bitwixe you shal be no sinne—
Namore in looking than ther shal in deede.
This ordinance is said: go, God thee speede.
485 Tomorwe at night whan men been alle asleepe,
Into oure kneeding-tubbes wol we creepe,
And sitten there, abiding Goddes grace.
Go now thy way, I have no lenger space°   *time*
To make of this no lenger sermoning.
490 Men sayn thus: 'Send the wise and say no thing.'
Thou art so wis it needeth thee nat teche:
Go save oure lif, and that I thee biseeche."
      This sely carpenter gooth forth his way:
Ful ofte he saide allas and wailaway,
495 And to his wif he tolde his privetee,
And she was war,° and knew it bet° than he,   *aware / better*
What al this quainte cast° was for to saye.°   *trick / mean*
But nathelees she ferde° as she wolde deye,   *acted*
And saide, "Allas, go forth thy way anoon.
500 Help us to scape,° or we been dede eechoon.   *escape*
I am thy trewe verray wedded wif:

7. On high.   9. Precious commandment.
8. Toward the garden.   1. Far apart.

Go, dere spouse, and help to save oure lif."
    Lo, which a greet thing is affeccioun!°   *emotion*
Men may dien of imaginacioun,
505 So deepe° may impression be take.   *deeply*
This sely carpenter biginneth quake;
Him thinketh verrailiche° that he may see   *truly*
Noees flood come walwing° as the see   *rolling*
To drenchen° Alison, his hony dere.   *drown*
510 He weepeth, waileth, maketh sory cheere;
He siketh° with ful many a sory swough,°   *sighs / breath*
And gooth and geteth him a kneeding-trough,
And after a tubbe and a kimelin,
And prively he sente hem to his in,°   *dwelling*
515 And heeng° hem in the roof in privetee;   *hung*
His° owene hand he made laddres three,   *with his*
To climben by the ronges° and the stalkes° *rungs / uprights*
Unto the tubbes hanging in the balkes,°   *rafters*
And hem vitailed,° bothe trough and tubbe, *victualed*
520 With breed and cheese and good ale in a jubbe,° *jug*
Suffising right ynough as for a day.
But er that he hadde maad al this array,
He sente his knave, and eek his wenche also,
Upon his neede[2] to London for to go.
525 And on the Monday whan it drow to[3] nighte,
He shette° his dore withouten candel-lighte,   *shut*
And dressed° alle thing as it sholde be,   *arranged*
And shortly up they clomben° alle three.   *climbed*
They seten° stille wel a furlong way.[4]   *sat*
530   "Now, Pater Noster, clum,"[5] saide Nicholay,
And "Clum" quod John, and "Clum" saide Alisoun.
This carpenter saide his devocioun,
And stille he sit° and biddeth his prayere,   *sits*
Awaiting on the rain, if he it heere.°   *might hear*
535   The dede sleep, for wery bisinesse,
Fil° on this carpenter right as I gesse   *fell*
Aboute corfew time,[6] or litel more.
For travailing of his gost[7] he groneth sore,
And eft° he routeth,° for his heed mislay.[8] *then / snores*
540   Down of the laddre stalketh Nicholay,
And Alison ful softe adown she spedde:
Withouten wordes mo they goon to bedde
Ther as the carpenter is wont to lie.
Ther was the revel and the melodye,
545 And thus lith° Alison and Nicholas   *lies*
In bisinesse of mirthe and of solas,°   *pleasure*

---

2. On an errand for him.   5. Hush (?).
3. Drew toward.   6. Probably about 8 P.M.
4. The time it takes to go a furlong (i.e., a few   7. Affliction of his spirit.
minutes).   8. Lay in the wrong position.

Til that the belle of Laudes[9] gan to ringe,
And freres in the chauncel° gonne singe.   *chancel*
   This parissh clerk, this amorous Absolon,
550 That is for love alway so wo-bigoon,
Upon the Monday was at Oseneye,
With compaignye him to disporte and playe,
And axed upon caas[1] a cloisterer
Ful prively after John the carpenter;
555 And he drow him apart out of the chirche,
And saide, "I noot:[2] I sawgh him here nought wirche
Sith Saterday. I trowe that he be went
For timber ther oure abbot hath him sent.
For he is wont for timber for to go,
560 And dwellen atte grange[3] a day or two.
Or elles he is at his hous, certain.
Where that he be I can nought soothly sayn."
   This Absolon ful jolif was and light,[4]
And thoughte, "Now is time to wake al night,
565 For sikerly,° I sawgh him nought stiringe   *certainly*
Aboute his dore sin day bigan to springe.
So mote° I thrive, I shal at cokkes crowe   *may*
Ful prively knokken at his windowe
That stant° ful lowe upon his bowres[5] wal.   *stands*
570 To Alison now wol I tellen al
My love-longing,° for yet I shal nat misse   *lovesickness*
That at the leeste way[6] I shal hire kisse.
Som manere confort shal I have, parfay.°   *in faith*
My mouth hath icched al this longe day:
575 That is a signe of kissing at the leeste.
Al night me mette[7] eek I was at a feeste.
Therfore I wol go sleepe an hour or twaye,
And al the night thanne wol I wake and playe."
   Whan that the firste cok hath crowe, anoon
580 Up rist° this joly lovere Absolon,   *rises*
And him arrayeth gay at point devis.[8]
But first he cheweth grain[9] and licoris,
To smellen sweete, er he hadde kembd° his heer.   *combed*
Under his tonge a trewe-love[1] he beer,°   *bore*
585 For therby wende° he to be gracious.°   *supposed / pleasing*
He rometh° to the carpenteres hous,   *strolls*
And stille he stant° under the shot-windowe—   *stands*
Unto his brest it raughte,° it was so lowe—   *reached*
And ofte he cougheth with a semisoun.°   *small sound*
590 "What do ye, hony-comb, sweete Alisoun,

---

9. The first church service of the day.   5. Bower's, bedroom's.
1. By chance. "Cloisterer": here, a member of the 6. I.e., at least.
religious order of Osney Abbey.   7. I dreamed.
2. Don't know. "Wirche": work.   8. To perfection.
3. The outlying farm belonging to the abbey.   9. Grain of paradise (a spice).
4. Was very amorous and gay.   1. Sprig of a clover-like plant.

My faire brid,[2] my sweete cinamome?
Awaketh, lemman° myn, and speketh to me.   *mistress*
Wel litel thinken ye upon my wo
That for your love I swete° ther I go.   *sweat*
595 No wonder is though that I swelte° and swete: *melt*
I moorne as doth a lamb after the tete.°   *teat*
Ywis, lemman, I have swich love-longinge,
That lik a turtle° trewe is my moorninge: *dove*
I may nat ete namore than a maide."
600   "Go fro the windowe, Jakke fool," she saide.
"As help me God, it wol nat be com-pa-me.°   *come-kiss-me*
I love another, and elles I were to blame,
Wel bet° than thee, by Jesu, Absolon.   *better*
Go forth thy way or I wol caste a stoon,
605 And lat me sleepe, a twenty devele way."[3]
    "Allas," quod Absolon, "and wailaway,
That trewe love was evere so yvele biset.[4]
Thanne kis me, sin that it may be no bet,
For Jesus love and for the love of me."
610   "Woltou thanne go thy way therwith?" quod she.
    "Ye, certes, lemman," quod this Absolon.
    "Thanne maak thee redy," quod she. "I come anoon."
And unto Nicholas she saide stille,°   *quietly*
"Now hust,° and thou shalt laughen al thy fille."   *hush*
615 This Absolon down sette him on his knees,
And said, "I am a lord at alle degrees,[5]
For after this I hope ther cometh more.
Lemman, thy grace, and sweete brid, thyn ore!"°   *mercy*
    The windowe she undooth, and that in haste.
620 "Have do," quod she, "come of and speed thee faste,
Lest that oure neighebores thee espye."
    This Absolon gan wipe his mouth ful drye:
Derk was the night as pich or as the cole,
And at the windowe out she putte hir hole,
625 And Absolon, him fil no bet ne wers,[6]
But with his mouth he kiste hir naked ers,
Ful savoury,° er he were war of this.   *with relish*
Abak he sterte,° and thoughte it was amis,   *started*
For wel he wiste a womman hath no beerd.
630 He felte a thing al rough and longe yherd,°   *haired*
And saide, "Fy, allas, what have I do?"
    "Teehee," quod she, and clapte the windowe to.
And Absolon gooth forth a sory pas.[7]
    "A beerd, a beerd!" quod hende Nicholas,
635 "By Goddes corpus,° this gooth faire and weel."   *body*
    This sely Absolon herde everydeel,

---

2. Bird or bride.   5. In every way.
3. In the name of twenty devils.   6. It befell him neither better nor worse.
4. Ill-used.   7. I.e., walking sadly.

And on his lippe he gan for anger bite,
And to himself he saide, "I shal thee quite."°   *repay*
   Who rubbeth now, who froteth° now his lippes   *wipes*
640 With dust, with sond,[8] with straw, with cloth, with chippes,
But Absolon, that saith ful ofte allas?
"My soule bitake° I unto Satanas,°   *commit / Satan*
But me were levere[9] than all this town," quod he,
"Of this despit° awroken° for to be.   *insult / avenged*
645 Allas," quod he, "allas I ne hadde ybleint!"°   *turned aside*
His hote love was cold and al yqueint,°   *quenched*
For fro that time that he hadde kist hir ers
Of paramours he sette nought a kers,[1]
For he was heled° of his maladye.   *cured*
650 Ful ofte paramours he gan defye,°   *renounce*
And weep° as dooth a child that is ybete.   *wept*
A softe paas[2] he wente over the streete
Until° a smith men clepen daun Gervais,[3]   *to*
That in his forge smithed plough harneis:°   *equipment*
655 He sharpeth shaar and cultour[4] bisily.
This Absolon knokketh al esily,°   *quietly*
And saide, "Undo, Gervais, and that anoon."°   *at once*
   "What, who artou?" "It am I, Absolon."
"What, Absolon? What, Cristes sweete tree!
660 Why rise ye so rathe?° Ey, benedicite,°   *early / bless me*
What aileth you? Som gay girl, God it woot,
Hath brought you thus upon the viritoot.[5]
By Sainte Note, ye woot wel what I mene."
   This Absolon ne roughte nat a bene[6]
665 Of al his play. No word again he yaf:
He hadde more tow on his distaf[7]
Than Gervais knew, and saide, "Freend so dere,
This hote cultour in the chimenee° here,   *fireplace*
As lene[8] it me: I have therwith to doone.
670 I wol bringe it thee again ful soone."
   Gervais answerde, "Certes, were it gold,
Or in a poke nobles alle untold,[9]
Thou sholdest have, as I am trewe smith.
Ey, Cristes fo,[1] what wol ye do therwith?"
675   "Therof," quod Absolon, "be as be may.
I shal wel telle it thee another day."
And caughte the cultour by the colde stele.°   *handle*
Ful softe out at the dore he gan to stele,
And wente unto the carpenteres wal:

8. Sand.
9. I had rather.
1. He didn't care a piece of cress for woman's love.
2. I.e., quiet walk.
3. Master Gervais.
4. He sharpens plowshare and coulter (the turf-cutter on a plow).

5. I.e., on the prowl.
6. Didn't care a bean.
7. I.e., more on his mind.
8. I.e., please lend.
9. Or gold coins all uncounted in a bag.
1. Foe, i.e., Satan.

680 He cougheth first and knokketh therwithal
    Upon the windowe, right as he dide er.°   *before*
        This Alison answerde, "Who is ther
    That knokketh so? I warante² it a thief."
    "Why, nay," quod he, "God woot, my sweete lief,°   *dear*
685 I am thyn Absolon, my dereling.
    Of gold," quod he, "I have thee brought a ring—
    My moder yaf it me, so God me save;
    Ful fin it is and therto wel ygrave:°   *engraved*
    This wol I yiven thee if thou me kisse."
690   This Nicholas was risen for to pisse,
    And thoughte he wolde amenden³ al the jape:°   *joke*
    He sholde kisse his ers er that he scape.
    And up the windowe dide he hastily,
    And out his ers he putteth prively,
695 Over the buttok to the haunche-boon.
        And therwith spak this clerk, this Absolon,
    "Speek, sweete brid, I noot nought wher thou art."
    This Nicholas anoon leet flee⁴ a fart
    As greet as it hadde been a thonder-dent°   *thunderbolt*
700 That with the strook he was almost yblent,°   *blinded*
    And he was redy with his iren hoot,°   *hot*
    And Nicholas amidde the ers he smoot:°   *smote*
    Of gooth the skin an hande-brede° aboute;   *handsbreadth*
    The hote cultour brende so his toute°   *buttocks*
705 That for the smert he wende for to⁵ die;
    As he were wood° for wo he gan to crye,   *crazy*
    "Help! Water! Water! Help, for Goddes herte!"
        This carpenter out of his slomber sterte,
    And herde oon cryen "Water!" as he were wood,
710 And thoughte, "Allas, now cometh Noweles⁶ flood!"
    He sette him up withoute wordes mo,
    And with his ax he smoot the corde atwo,
    And down gooth al: he foond neither to selle
    Ne breed ne ale til he cam to the celle,⁷
715 Upon the floor, and ther aswoune° he lay.   *in a faint*
        Up sterte hire⁸ Alison and Nicholay,
    And criden "Out" and "Harrow" in the streete.
    The neighebores, bothe smale and grete,
    In ronnen for to gauren° on this man   *gape*
720 That aswoune lay bothe pale and wan,
    For with the fal he brosten° hadde his arm;   *broken*
    But stonde he moste° unto his owene harm,   *must*
    For whan he spak he was anoon bore down⁹
    With° hende Nicholas and Alisoun: *by*

2. I.e., wager.   (Christmas).
3. Improve on.   7. He found time to sell neither bread nor ale until
4. Let fly.   he arrived at the foundation.
5. Thought he would.   8. Started.
6. The carpenter is confusing Noah and Noel   9. Refuted.

725   They tolden every man that he was wood—
      He was agast so of Noweles flood,
      Thurgh fantasye, that of his vanitee°   *folly*
      He hadde ybought him kneeding-tubbes three,
      And hadde hem hanged in the roof above,
730   And that he prayed hem, for Goddes love,
      To sitten in the roof, *par compaignye.*[1]
        The folk gan laughen at his fantasye.
      Into the roof they kiken° and they cape,°   *peer / gape*
      And turned al his harm unto a jape,°   *joke*
735   For what so that this carpenter answerde,
      It was for nought: no man his reson° herde;   *argument*
      With othes grete he was so sworn adown,
      That he was holden° wood in al the town,   *considered*
      For every clerk anoonright heeld with other:
740   They saide, "The man was wood, my leve brother,"
      And every wight gan laughen at this strif.°   *fuss*
      Thus swived° was the carpenteres wif   *slept with*
      For al his keeping° and his jalousye,   *guarding*
      And Absolon hath kist hir nether° yë,   *lower*
745   And Nicholas is scalded in the toute:
      This tale is doon, and God save al the route!°   *company*

The Wife of Bath's Prologue and Tale

The Prologue[1]

    Experience, though noon auctoritee
    Were in this world, is right ynough for me
    To speke of wo that is in mariage:
    For lordinges,° sith I twelf yeer was of age—   *gentlemen*

---

1. For company's sake.

1. The Wife of Bath is the remarkable culmination of many centuries of an antifeminism that was particularly nurtured by the medieval church. In their eagerness to exalt the spiritual ideal of chastity, certain theologians developed an idea of womankind that was nothing less than monstrous. According to these, insatiable lecherousness and indomitable shrewishness (plus a host of attendant vices) were characteristic of women. This notion was given most eloquent expression by St. Jerome in his attack (written about A.D. 400) on the monk Jovinian, who had uttered some good words for matrimony, and it is Jerome that the Wife of Bath comes forward not, curiously enough, to refute, but to confirm. The first part of her Prologue is a mass of quotations from that part of Jerome's tract where he is appealing to St. Paul's Epistle (1 Corinthians 7) for antimatrimonial authority. On the narrow issue of her right to remarry, to be sure,

the Wife finds fault—rather mildly—with Jerome, but on the more central issue of why she wishes to marry and remarry she expresses no disagreement with him. Yet in the failure to defend herself and refute the saint, she somehow manages to make the latter's point of view look a good deal sillier than she looks herself; and instead of embodying the satire on womanhood that one would expect because of her origins in antifeminist literature, she becomes instead a satirist of the grotesquely woman-hating men who had first defined her personality.

More important, because of the extraordinary vitality that Chaucer has imparted to her, the Wife of Bath by the end of her Prologue comes to bear a less significant relation to satire than she does to reality itself. Making the best of the world in which they have arbitrarily been placed is the occupation of both the Wife of Bath and the reader, and it is in doing this that the Wife ceases to be a monstros-

5   Thanked be God that is eterne on live—
    Housbondes at chirche dore² I have had five
    (If I so ofte mighte han wedded be),
    And alle were worthy men in hir degree.
    But me was told, certain, nat longe agoon is,
10   That sith that Crist ne wente nevere but ones
    To wedding in the Cane³ of Galilee,
    That by the same ensample° taughte he me   *example*
    That I ne sholde wedded be but ones.
    Herke eek,° lo, which° a sharp word for the nones,[4]   *also / what*
15   Biside a welle, Jesus, God and man,
    Spak in repreve° of the Samaritan: *reproof*
    "Thou hast yhad five housbondes," quod he,
    "And that ilke° man that now hath thee   *same*
    Is nat thyn housbonde." Thus saide he certain.
20   What that he mente therby I can nat sayn,
    But that I axe° why the fifthe man   *ask*
    Was noon housbonde to the Samaritan?[5]
    How manye mighte she han in mariage?
    Yit herde I nevere tellen in myn age
25   Upon this nombre diffinicioun.°   *definition*
    Men may divine° and glosen° up and down,   *guess / interpret*
    But wel I woot,° expres,° withouten lie,   *know / expressly*
    God bad us for to wexe[6] and multiplye:
    That gentil text can I wel understonde.
30   Eek wel I woot° he saide that myn housbonde   *know*
    Sholde lete° fader and moder and take to me,[7]   *leave*
    But of no nombre mencion made he—
    Of bigamye or of octogamye:[8]
    Why sholde men thanne speke of it vilainye?
35   Lo, here the wise king daun° Salomon: *master*
    I trowe° he hadde wives many oon,[9]   *believe*
    As wolde God it leveful° were to me   *permissible*
    To be refreshed half so ofte as he.
    Which yifte[1] of God hadde he for alle his wives!
40   No man hath swich that in this world alive is.
    God woot this noble king, as to my wit,°   *knowledge*

---

ity of fiction and becomes alive—wonderfully alive, both to the potentialities of which she and her world are capable and to the limitations that even in her world time and age place upon her. It is especially in the attitude with which she regards these limitations that her fiction becomes most true to life, since they are also the limitations imposed by the real world. Despite the loss of youth and beauty, her best weapons, she faces her future not only with a woman's ability to endure and enjoy what she cannot reshape, but also with a zest for life on its own terms that is almost more than human.

2. The actual wedding ceremony was celebrated at the church door, not in the chancel. .

3. Cana (see John 2.1).
4. To the purpose.
5. Christ was actually referring to a sixth man who was not married to the Samaritan woman (cf. John 4.6 ff.).
6. I.e., increase. See Genesis 1.28.
7. See Matthew 19.5.
8. I.e., of two or even eight marriages. The Wife is referring to successive, rather than simultaneous marriages.
9. Solomon had 700 wives and 300 concubines (1 Kings 11.3).
1. What a gift.

The firste night hadde many a merye fit°   *bout*
With eech of hem, so wel was him on live.[2]
Blessed be God that I have wedded five,
45   Of whiche I have piked out the beste,[3]
Bothe of hir nether° purs and of hir cheste.°   *lower / moneybox*
Diverse scoles maken parfit° clerkes,   *perfect*
And diverse practikes[4] in sondry werkes
Maken the werkman parfit sikerly:°   *certainly*
50   Of five housbondes scoleying° am I.   *schooling*
Welcome the sixte whan that evere he shal![5]
For sith I wol nat kepe me chast in al,
Whan my housbonde is fro the world agoon,
Som Cristen man shal wedde me anoon.°   *right away*
55   For thanne th'Apostle[6] saith that I am free
To wedde, a Goddes half,[7] where it liketh me.
He saide that to be wedded is no sinne:
Bet° is to be wedded than to brinne.°   *better / burn*
What rekketh me[8] though folk saye vilainye
60   Of shrewed° Lamech[9] and his bigamye?   *cursed*
I woot wel Abraham was an holy man,
And Jacob eek, as fer as evere I can,°   *know*
And eech of hem hadde wives mo than two,
And many another holy man also.
65   Where can ye saye in any manere age
That hye God defended° mariage   *prohibited*
By expres word? I praye you, telleth me.
Or where comanded he virginitee?
I woot as wel as ye, it is no drede,°   *doubt*
70   Th'Apostle, whan he speketh of maidenhede,°   *maidenhood*
He saide that precept therof hadde he noon:
Men may conseile a womman to be oon,°   *single*
But conseiling nis no comandement.
He putte it in oure owene juggement.
75   For hadde God comanded maidenhede,
Thanne hadde he dampned° wedding with the   *condemned*
        deede;[1]
And certes, if there were no seed ysowe,
Virginitee, thanne wherof sholde it growe?
Paul dorste nat comanden at the leeste
80   A thing of which his maister yaf° no heeste.°   *gave / command*
The dart[2] is set up for virginitee:
Cacche whoso may, who renneth° best lat see.   *runs*
But this word is nought take of[3] every wight,

---

2. I.e., so pleasant a life he had.
3. Whom I have cleaned out of everything worthwhile.
4. Practical experiences.
5. I.e., shall come along.
6. St. Paul.
7. On God's behalf. "It liketh me": I please.

8. What do I care.
9. The first man whom the Bible mentions as
having two wives (Genesis 4.19–24).
1. I.e., at the same time.
2. I.e., prize in a race.
3. Understood for, i.e., applicable to.

But ther as[4] God list° yive it of his might.   *it pleases*
85 I woot wel that th'Apostle was a maide,°   *virgin*
But nathelees, though that he wroot and saide
He wolde that every wight were swich° as he,   *such*
Al nis but conseil to virginitee;
And for to been a wif he yaf me leve
90 Of indulgence; so nis it no repreve°   *disgrace*
To wedde me[5] if that my make° die,   *mate*
Withouten excepcion of bigamye[6]—
Al° were it good no womman for to touche   *although*
(He mente as in his bed or in his couche,
95 For peril is bothe fir° and tow° t'assemble—   *fire / flax*
Ye knowe what this ensample may resemble).[7]
This al and som,[8] he heeld virginitee
More parfit than wedding in freletee.°   *frailty*
(Freletee clepe I but if[9] that he and she
100 Wolde leden al hir lif in chastitee.)
I graunte it wel, I have noon envye
Though maidenhede preferre° bigamye:°   *excel / remarriage*
It liketh hem to be clene in body and gost.°   *spirit*
Of myn estaat ne wol I make no boost;
105 For wel ye knowe, a lord in his houshold
Ne hath nat every vessel al of gold:
Some been of tree,° and doon hir lord servise.   *wood*
God clepeth folk to him in sondry wise,
And everich hath of God a propre[1] yifte,
110 Som this, som that, as him liketh shifte.°   *ordain*
Virginitee is greet perfeccioun,
And continence eek with devocioun,
But Crist, that of perfeccion is welle,°   *source*
Bad nat every wight he sholde go selle
115 Al that he hadde and yive it to the poore,
And in swich wise folwe him and his fore:[2]
He spak to hem that wolde live parfitly°—   *perfectly*
And lordinges, by youre leve, that am nat I.
I wol bistowe the flour of al myn age
120 In th'actes and in fruit of mariage.
     Telle me also, to what conclusioun°   *end*
Were membres maad of generacioun
And of so parfit wis a wrighte ywrought?[3]
Trusteth right wel, they were nat maad for nought.
125 Glose° whoso wol, and saye bothe up and down   *interpret*
That they were maked for purgacioun
Of urine, and oure bothe thinges smale

---

4. Where.
5. For me to marry.
6. I.e., without there being any legal objection on the score of remarriage.
7. I.e., what this metaphor may apply to.
8. This is all there is to it.
9. Frailty I call it unless.
1. I.e., his own.
2. Matthew 19.21. "Fore": footsteps.
3. And wrought by so perfectly wise a maker.

Was eek to knowe a female from a male,
And for noon other cause—saye ye no?
130   Th'experience woot it is nought so.
So that the clerkes be nat with me wrothe,
I saye this, that they been maad for bothe—
That is to sayn, for office° and for ese   excretion
Of engendrure, ther we nat God displese.
135   Why sholde men elles in hir bookes sette
That man shal yeelde[4] to his wif hir dette?
Now wherwith sholde he make his payement
If he ne used his sely° instrument?   innocent
Thanne were they maad upon a creature
140   To purge urine, and eek for engendrure.
      But I saye nought that every wight is holde,°   bound
That hath swich harneis° as I to you tolde,   equipment
To goon and usen hem in engendrure:
Thanne sholde men take of chastitee no cure.°   heed
145   Crist was a maide° and shapen as a man,   virgin
And many a saint sith that the world bigan,
Yit lived they evere in parfit chastitee.
I nil envye no virginitee:
Lat hem be breed° of pured° whete seed,   bread / refined
150   And lat us wives hote° barly breed—   be called
And yit with barly breed, Mark telle can,
Oure Lord Jesu refresshed many a man.[5]
In swich estaat as God hath cleped us
I wol persevere: I nam nat precious.°   fastidious
155   In wifhood wol I use myn instrument
As freely° as my Makere hath it sent.   generously
If I be daungerous,° God yive me sorwe: stand-offish
Myn housbonde shal it han both eve and morwe,°   morning
Whan that him list[6] come forth and paye his dette.
160   An housbonde wol I have, I wol nat lette,[7]
Which shal be bothe my dettour° and my thral,°   debtor / slave
And have his tribulacion withal
Upon his flessh whil that I am his wif.
I have the power during al my lif
165   Upon his propre° body, and nat he: own
Right thus th'Apostle tolde it unto me,
And bad oure housbondes for to love us weel.
Al this sentence° me liketh everydeel.°   purport / entirely

[AN INTERLUDE]

      Up sterte° the Pardoner and that anoon: started
170   "Now dame," quod he, "by God and by Saint John,

---

4. I.e., pay.
5. In the descriptions of the miracle of the loaves
and fishes, it is actually John, not Mark, who
mentions barley bread (6.9).
6. When he wishes to.
7. I will make no difficulty.

Ye been a noble prechour in this cas.
I was aboute to wedde a wif: allas,
What° sholde I bye° it on my flessh so dere?　　　*why / purchase*
Yit hadde I levere wedde no wif toyere."°　　　*this year*
175　　"Abid," quod she, "my tale is nat bigonne.
Nay, thou shalt drinken of another tonne,°　　　*tun*
Er that I go, shal savoure wors than ale.
And whan that I have told thee forth my tale
Of tribulacion in mariage,
180　　Of which I am expert in al myn age—
This is to saye, myself hath been the whippe—
Thanne maistou chese° wheither thou wolt sippe　　　*choose*
Of thilke° tonne that I shal abroche;°　　　*this same / broach*
Be war of it, er thou too neigh approche,
185　　For I shal telle ensamples mo than ten.
'Whoso that nile° be war by othere men,　　　*will not*
By him shal othere men corrected be.'
Thise same wordes writeth Ptolomee:
Rede in his *Almageste* and take it there."[8]
190　　"Dame, I wolde praye you if youre wil it were,"
Saide this Pardoner, "as ye bigan,
Telle forth youre tale; spareth for no man,
And teche us yonge men of youre practike."°　　　*mode of operation*
　　"Gladly," quod she, "sith it may you like;°　　　*please*
195　　But that I praye to al this compaignye,
If that I speke after my fantasye,[9]
As taketh nat agrief° of that I saye,　　　*amiss*
For myn entente nis but for to playe."

[THE WIFE CONTINUES]

Now sire, thanne wol I telle you forth my tale.
200　　As evere mote I drinke win or ale,
I shal saye sooth: tho° housbondes that I hadde,　　　*those*
As three of hem were goode, and two were badde.
The three men were goode, and riche, and olde;
Unnethe° mighte they the statut holde　　　*with difficulty*
205　　In which they were bounden unto me—
Ye woot wel what I mene of this, pardee.
As help me God, I laughe whan I thinke
How pitously anight I made hem swinke;°　　　*work*
And by my fay,° I tolde of it no stoor:[1]　　　*faith*
210　　They hadde me yiven hir land and hir tresor;
Me needed nat do lenger diligence

8. The *Almagest*, an astronomical work by the Greek astronomer and mathematician Ptolemy (2nd century A.D.), contains no such aphorism. The aphorism does, however, appear in a collection ascribed to him.
9. If I speak according to my whim.
1. I set no store by it.

To winne hir love or doon hem reverence.
They loved me so wel, by God above,
That I ne tolde no daintee of[2] hir love.
215   A wis womman wol bisye hire evere in oon[3]
To gete hire love, ye, ther as she hath noon.
But sith I hadde hem hoolly in myn hand,
And sith that they hadde yiven me al hir land,
What° sholde I take keep° hem for to plese,   why / care
220   But it were for my profit and myn ese?
I sette hem so awerke,° by my fay,   awork
That many a night they songen° wailaway.   sang
The bacon was nat fet° for hem, I trowe,   brought back
That some men han in Essexe at Dunmowe.[4]
225   I governed hem so wel after° my lawe   according to
That eech of hem ful blisful was and fawe°   glad
To bringe me gaye thinges fro the faire;
They were ful glade whan I spak hem faire,
For God it woot, I chidde° hem spitously.°   chided / cruelly
230   Now herkneth how I bar me[5] proprely:
Ye wise wives, that conne understonde,
Thus sholde ye speke and bere him wrong on honde[6]—
For half so boldely can ther no man
Swere and lie as a woman can.
235   I saye nat this by wives that been wise,
But if it be whan they hem misavise.[7]
A wis wif, if that she can hir good,[8]
Shal bere him on hande the cow is wood,[9]
And take witnesse of hir owene maide
240   Of hir assent.[1] But herkneth how I saide:
    "Sire olde cainard,° is this thyn array?[2]   sluggard
Why is my neighebores wif so gay?
She is honoured overal ther she gooth:
I sitte at hoom; I have no thrifty° cloth.   decent
245   What doostou at my neighebores hous?
Is she so fair? Artou so amorous?
What roune° ye with oure maide, benedicite?[3]   whisper
Sire olde lechour, lat thy japes° be.   tricks, intrigues
And if I have a gossib° or a freend,   confidant
250   Withouten gilt ye chiden as a feend,
If that I walke or playe unto his hous.
Thou comest hoom as dronken as a mous,

2. Set no value on.
3. Busy herself constantly.
4. The Dunmow flitch was awarded to the couple who after a year of marriage could claim no quarrels, no regrets, and the desire, if freed, to remarry one another.
5. Bore myself, behaved.
6. Accuse him falsely.
7. When they make a mistake.
8. If she knows what's good for her.
9. Shall persuade him the chough has gone crazy. The chough, or jackdaw, was popularly supposed to tell husbands of their wives' infidelity.
1. And call as a witness her maid, who is on her side.
2. I.e., is this how you behave?
3. Bless me.

And prechest on thy bench, with yvel preef.[4]
Thou saist to me, it is a greet meschief°   *misfortune*
255   To wedde a poore womman for costage.[5]
And if that she be riche, of heigh parage,°   *descent*
Thanne saistou that it is a tormentrye
To suffre hir pride and hir malencolye.
And if that she be fair, thou verray knave,
260   Thou saist that every holour° wol hire have: *whoremonger*
She may no while in chastitee abide
That is assailed upon eech a side.
      "Thou saist som folk desiren us for richesse,
Som[6] for oure shap, and som for oure fairnesse,
265   And som for she can outher° singe or daunce,   *either*
And som for gentilesse and daliaunce,°   *flirtatiousness*
Som for hir handes and hir armes smale°—   *slender*
Thus gooth al to the devel by thy tale![7]
Thou saist men may nat keepe[8] a castel wal,
270   It may so longe assailed been overal.°   *everywhere*
And if that she be foul, thou saist that she
Coveiteth° every man that she may see;   *desires*
For as a spaniel she wol on him lepe,
Til that she finde som man hire to chepe.°   *buy*
275   Ne noon so grey goos gooth ther in the lake,
As, saistou, wol be withoute make;°   *mate*
And saist it is an hard thing for to weelde°   *possess*
A thing that no man wol, his thankes, heelde.[9]
Thus saistou, lorel,° whan thou goost to bedde,   *loafer*
280   And that no wis man needeth for to wedde,
Ne no man that entendeth° unto hevene—   *aims*
With wilde thonder-dint[1] and firy levene
Mote thy welked nekke be tobroke![2]
Thou saist that dropping° houses and eek smoke   *leaking*
285   And chiding wives maken men to flee
Out of hir owene hous: a, benedicite,
What aileth swich an old man for to chide?
Thou saist we wives wil oure vices hide
Til we be fast,[3] and thanne we wol hem shewe—
290   Wel may that be a proverbe of a shrewe!°   *villain*
Thou saist that oxen, asses, hors,° and houndes,   *horses*
They been assayed at diverse stoundes;°   *times*
Bacins, lavours,° er that men hem bye,   *washbowls*
Spoones, stooles, and al swich housbondrye,°   *household goods*
295   And so be° pottes, clothes, and array°—   *are / clothing*
But folk of wives maken noon assay

---

4. I.e., (may you have) bad luck.
5. Because of the expense.
6. "Som," in this and the following lines, means "one."
7. I.e., according to your story.
8. I.e., keep safe.
9. No man would willingly hold.
1. Thunderbolt. "Levene": lightning.
2. May thy withered neck be broken!
3. I.e., married.

Til they be wedded—olde dotard shrewe!
And thanne, saistou, we wil oure vices shewe.
Thou saist also that it displeseth me
300 But if that thou wolt praise my beautee,
And but thou poure alway upon my face,
And clepe me 'Faire Dame' in every place,
And but thou make a feeste on thilke day
That I was born, and make me fressh and gay,
305 And but thou do to my norice° honour,   *nurse*
And to my chamberere within my bowr,[4]
And to my fadres folk, and his allies[5]—
Thus saistou, olde barel-ful of lies.
And yit of our apprentice Janekin,
310 For his crispe° heer, shining as gold so fin,   *curly*
And for he squiereth me bothe up and down,
Yit hastou caught a fals suspecioun;
I wil° him nat though thou were deed° tomorwe.   *want / dead*
   "But tel me this, why hidestou with sorwe[6]
315 The keyes of thy cheste away fro me?
It is my good° as wel as thyn, pardee.   *property*
What, weenestou° make an idiot of oure dame?   *do you think to*
Now by that lord that called is Saint Jame,
Thou shalt nought bothe, though thou were wood,°   *furious*
320 Be maister of my body and of my good:
That oon thou shalt forgo, maugree thine yën.[7]
   "What helpeth it of me enquere° and spyen?   *inquire*
I trowe thou woldest loke° me in thy cheste.   *lock*
Thou sholdest saye, 'Wif, go wher thee leste.°   *it may please*
325 Taak youre disport. I nil leve° no tales: *believe*
I knowe you for a trewe wif, dame Alis.'
We love no man that taketh keep or charge[8]
Wher that we goon: we wol been at oure large.[9]
Of alle men yblessed mote he be
330 The wise astrologen° daun Ptolomee,   *astronomer*
That saith this proverbe in his *Almageste*:
'Of alle men his wisdom is the hyeste
That rekketh° nat who hath the world in honde.'   *cares*
By this proverbe thou shalt understonde,
335 Have thou[1] ynough, what thar° thee rekke or care   *need*
How merily that othere folkes fare?
For certes, olde dotard, by youre leve,
Ye shal han queinte° right ynough at eve: *pudendum*
He is too greet a nigard that wil werne°   *refuse*
340 A man to lighte a candle at his lanterne;
He shal han nevere the lasse° lighte, pardee.   *less*

---

4. And to my chambermaid within my bedroom.
5. Relatives by marriage.
6. I.e., with sorrow to you.
7. Despite your eyes—i.e., despite anything you
can do about it.
8. Notice or interest.
9. I.e., liberty.
1. If you have.

Have thou ynough, thee thar nat plaine thee.[2]
　　"Thou saist also that if we make us gay
With clothing and with precious array,
345　That it is peril of oure chastitee,
And yit with sorwe thou moste enforce thee,[3]
And saye thise wordes in th' Apostles name:
'In habit° maad with chastitee and shame　　　　　　　*clothing*
Ye wommen shal apparaile you,' quod he,
350　'And nat in tressed heer[4] and gay perree,°　　　　　　*jewelry*
As perles ne with gold ne clothes riche.'[5]
After thy text, ne after thy rubriche,[6]
I wol nat werke as muchel as a gnat.
Thou saidest this, that I was lik a cat:
355　For whoso wolde senge° a cattes skin,　　　　　　　　*singe*
Thanne wolde the cat wel dwellen in his in;°　　　　　*lodging*
And if the cattes skin be slik° and gay,　　　　　　　*sleek*
She wol nat dwelle in house half a day,
But forth she wol, er any day be dawed,[7]
360　To shewe her skin and goon a-caterwawed.°　　　　*caterwauling*
This is to saye, if I be gay, sire shrewe,
I wol renne° out, my borel° for to shewe.　　　　　*run / clothing*
Sir olde fool, what helpeth[8] thee t'espyen?
Though thou praye Argus with his hundred yën
365　To be my wardecors,° as he can best,　　　　　　　*bodyguard*
In faith, he shal nat keepe° me but me lest:[9]　　　　　*guard*
Yit coude I make his beerd,[1] so mote I thee.°　　　　*thrive*
　　"Thou saidest eek that ther been thinges three,
The whiche thinges troublen al this erthe,
370　And that no wight may endure the ferthe.°　　　　　*fourth*
O leve° sire shrewe, Jesu shorte° thy lif!　　　*dear / shorten*
Yit prechestou and saist an hateful wif
Yrekened is for oon of thise meschaunces.
Been ther nat none othere resemblaunces
375　That ye may likne youre parables to,[2]
But if[3] a sely° wif be oon of tho?　　　　　　　　　*innocent*
　　"Thou liknest eek wommanes love to helle,
To bareine° land ther water may nat dwelle;　　　　　*barren*
Thou liknest it also to wilde fir—
380　The more it brenneth,° the more it hath desir　　　　*burns*
To consumen every thing that brent° wol be;　　　　　*burned*
Thou saist right° as wormes shende° a tree,　　*just / destroy*
Right so a wif destroyeth hir housbonde—
This knowen they that been to wives bonde."°　　　　　*bound*

2. I.e., you need not complain.
3. Strengthen your position.
4. I.e., elaborate hairdo.
5. See 1. Timothy 2.9.
6. Rubric, i.e., direction.
7. Has dawned.

8. What does it help.
9. Unless I please.
1. I.e., deceive him.
2. Isn't there something else appropriate to which you can apply your metaphors?
3. Unless.

385   Lordinges, right thus, as ye han understonde,
    Bar I stifly mine olde housbondes on honde[4]
    That thus they saiden in hir dronkenesse—
    And al was fals, but that I took witnesse
    On Janekin and on my nece also.
390   O Lord, the paine I dide hem and the wo,
    Ful giltelees, by Goddes sweete pine!°   *suffering*
    For as an hors I coude bite and whine;°   *whinny*
    I coude plaine° and° I was in the gilt,   *complain / if*
    Or elles often time I hadde been spilt.°   *ruined*
395   Whoso that first to mille comth first grint.°   *grinds*
    I plained first: so was oure werre stint.[5]
    They were ful glade to excusen hem ful blive° *quickly*
    Of thing of which they nevere agilte hir live.[6]
    Of wenches wolde I beren hem on honde,
400   Whan that for sik[7] they mighte unnethe° stonde, *scarcely*
    Yit tikled I his herte for that he
    Wende° I hadde had of him so greet cheertee.[8] *thought*
    I swoor that al my walking out by nighte
    Was for to espye wenches that he dighte.[9]
405   Under that colour[1] hadde I many a mirthe.
    For al swich wit is yiven us in oure birthe:
    Deceite, weeping, spinning God hath yive
    To wommen kindely° whil they may live.   *naturally*
    And thus of oo thing I avaunte me:[2]
410   At ende I hadde the bet° in eech degree,   *better*
    By sleighte or force, or by som manere thing,
    As by continuel murmur° or grucching;° *complaint / grumbling*
    Namely° abedde hadden they meschaunce: *especially*
    Ther wolde I chide and do hem no plesaunce;[3]
415   I wolde no lenger in the bed abide
    If that I felte his arm over my side,
    Til he hadde maad his raunson° unto me; *ransom*
    Thanne wolde I suffre him do his nicetee.° *lust*
    And therfore every man this tale I telle:
420   Winne whoso may, for al is for to selle;
    With empty hand men may no hawkes lure.
    For winning° wolde I al his lust endure,   *profit*
    And make me a feined appetit—
    And yit in bacon[4] hadde I nevere delit.
425   That made me that evere I wolde hem chide;
    For though the Pope hadde seten° hem biside, *sat*
    I wolde nought spare hem at hir owene boord.

4. I rigorously accused my old husbands.
5. Our war brought to an end.
6. Of a thing in which they never offended in their lives.
7. I.e., sickness.
8. Affection.
9. Had intercourse with.
1. I.e., excuse.
2. Boast.
3. Show them no affection.
4. I.e., old meat.

For by my trouthe, I quitte° hem word for word.   *repaid*
As help me verray God omnipotent,
430   Though I right now sholde make my testament,
I ne owe hem nat a word that it nis quit.
I broughte it so aboute by my wit
That they moste yive it up as for the beste,
Or elles hadde we nevere been in reste;
435   For though he looked as a wood° leoun,   *furious*
Yit sholde he faile of his conclusioun.°   *object*
     Thanne wolde I saye, "Goodelief, taak keep,[5]
How mekely looketh Wilekin, oure sheep!
Com neer my spouse, lat me ba° thy cheeke—   *kiss*
440   Ye sholden be al pacient and meeke,
And han a sweete-spiced[6] conscience,
Sith ye so preche of Jobes pacience;
Suffreth alway, sin ye so wel can preche;
And but ye do, certain, we shal you teche
445   That it is fair to han a wif in pees.
Oon of us two moste bowen, doutelees,
And sith a man is more resonable
Than womman is, ye mosten been suffrable.°   *patient*
What aileth you to grucche° thus and grone?   *grumble*
450   Is it for ye wolde have my queinte° allone?   *pudendum*
Why, taak it al—lo, have it everydeel.°   *altogether*
Peter, I shrewe° you but ye love it weel.   *curse*
For if I wolde selle my bele chose,[7]
I coude walke as fressh as is a rose;
455   But I wol keepe it for youre owene tooth.°   *taste*
Ye be to blame. By God, I saye you sooth!"
Swiche manere° wordes hadde we on honde.   *kind of*
Now wol I speke of my ferthe° housbonde.   *fourth*
     My ferthe housbonde was a revelour—
460   This is to sayn, he hadde a paramour°—   *mistress*
And I was yong and ful of ragerye,°   *wantonness*
Stibourne° and strong and joly as a pie:°   *untamable / magpie*
How coude I daunce to an harpe smale,°   *gracefully*
And singe, ywis,° as any nightingale,   *indeed*
465   Whan I hadde dronke a draughte of sweete win.
Metellius, the foule cherl, the swin,
That with a staf birafte° his wif hir lif   *deprived*
For° she drank win, though I hadde been his wif,   *because*
Ne sholde nat han daunted me fro drinke;
470   And after win on Venus moste° I thinke,   *must*
For also siker° as cold engendreth hail,   *sure*
A likerous° mouth moste han a likerous° tail: *greedy / lecherous*
In womman vinolent° is no defence—   *bibulous*

---

5. Good friend, take notice.   7. Fair thing.
6. I.e., delicate.

This knowen lechours by experience.
475   But Lord Crist, whan that it remembreth me[8]
Upon my youthe and on my jolitee,
It tikleth me aboute myn herte roote—
Unto this day it dooth myn herte boote°   good
That I have had my world as in my time.
480   But age, allas, that al wol envenime,°   poison
Hath me biraft[9] my beautee and my pith—
Lat go, farewel, the devel go therwith!
The flour is goon, ther is namore to telle:
The bren° as I best can now moste I selle;   bran
485   But yit to be right merye wol I fonde.°   strive
Now wol I tellen of my ferthe housbonde.
      I saye I hadde in herte greet despit
That he of any other hadde delit,
But he was quit,° by God and by Saint Joce: paid back
490   I made him of the same wode a croce[1]—
Nat of my body in no foul manere—
But, certainly, I made folk swich cheere
That in his owene grece I made him frye,
For angre and for verray jalousye.
495   By God, in erthe I was his purgatorye,
For which I hope his soule be in glorye.
For God it woot, he sat ful ofte and soong°   sang
Whan that his sho ful bitterly him wroong.°   pinched
Ther was no wight save God and he that wiste°   knew
500   In many wise how sore I him twiste.
He deide whan I cam fro Jerusalem,
And lith ygrave under the roode-beem,[2]
Al° is his tombe nought so curious[3]   although
As was the sepulcre of him Darius,
505   Which that Apelles wroughte subtilly:[4]
It nis but wast to burye him preciously.°   expensively
Lat him fare wel, God yive his soule reste;
He is now in his grave and in his cheste.
      Now of my fifthe housbonde wol I telle—
510   God lete his soule nevere come in helle—
And yit he was to me the moste shrewe:[5]
That feele I on my ribbes al by rewe,[6]
And evere shal unto myn ending day.
But in oure bed he was so fressh and gay,
515   And therwithal so wel coulde he me glose°   wheedle
Whan that he wolde han my bele chose,

---

8. When I look back.
9. Has taken away from me.
1. I made him a cross of the same wood. The proverb has much the same sense as the one quoted in line 493.
2. And lies buried under the rood beam (the crucifix beam running between nave and chancel).

3. Carefully wrought.
4. Accordingly to medieval legend, the artist Apelles decorated the tomb of Darius, king of the Persians.
5. Worst rascal.
6. In a row.

That though he hadde me bet° on every boon,°   *beaten / bone*
He coude winne again my love anoon.°   *immediately*
I trowe I loved him best for that he
520 Was of his love daungerous[7] to me.
We wommen han, if that I shal nat lie,
In this matere a quaint fantasye:
Waite what[8] thing we may nat lightly° have,   *easily*
Therafter wol we crye al day and crave;
525 Forbede us thing, and that desiren we;
Preesse on us faste, and thanne wol we flee.
With daunger oute we al oure chaffare:[9]
Greet prees° at market maketh dere° ware,   *crowd / expensive*
And too greet chepe is holden at litel pris.[1]
530 This knoweth every womman that is wis.
    My fifthe housbonde—God his soule blesse!—
Which that I took for love and no richesse,
He somtime was a clerk at Oxenforde,
And hadde laft° scole and wente at hoom to boorde   *left*
535 With my gossib,° dwelling in oure town—   *confidante*
God have hir soule!—hir name was Alisoun;
She knew myn herte and eek my privetee°   *secrets*
Bet° than oure parissh preest, as mote I thee.°   *better / thrive*
To hire biwrayed° I my conseil° al,   *disclosed / secrets*
540 For hadde myn housbonde pissed on a wal,
Or doon a thing that sholde han cost his lif,
To hire,° and to another worthy wif,   *her*
And to my nece which I loved weel,
I wolde han told his conseil everydeel;°   *entirely*
545 And so I dide ful often, God it woot,
That made his face often reed° and hoot°   *red / hot*
For verray shame, and blamed himself for he
Hadde told to me so greet a privetee.
    And so bifel that ones in a Lente—
550 So often times I to my gossib wente,
For evere yit I loved to be gay,
And for to walke in March, Averil, and May,
From hous to hous, to heere sondry tales—
That Janekin clerk and my gossib dame Alis
555 And I myself into the feeldes wente.
Myn housbonde was at London al that Lente:
I hadde the better leiser for to playe,
And for to see, and eek for to be seye°   *seen*
Of lusty folk—what wiste I wher my grace°   *luck*
560 Was shapen° for to be, or in what place?   *destined*
Therfore I made my visitaciouns
To vigilies[2] and to processiouns,

---

7. I.e., he played hard to get.   1. Too good a bargain is held at little value.
8. "Waite what": whatever.   2. Feasts preceding a saint's day.
9. With coyness, we spread out our merchandise.

To preching eek, and to thise pilgrimages,
To playes of miracles and to mariages,
565　And wered upon[3] my gaye scarlet gites°—   *dress*
Thise wormes ne thise motthes ne thise mites,
Upon my peril, frete° hem neveradeel: *ate*
And woostou why? For they were used weel.
　　Now wol I tellen forth what happed me.
570　I saye that in the feeldes walked we,
Til trewely we hadde swich daliaunce,°   *flirtation*
This clerk and I, that of my purveyaunce°   *foresight*
I spak to him and saide him how that he,
If I were widwe, sholde wedde me.
575　For certainly, I saye for no bobaunce,°   *boast*
Yit was I nevere withouten purveyaunce
Of mariage n'of othere thinges eek:
I holde a mouses herte nought worth a leek
That hath but oon hole for to sterte° to,   *run*
580　And if that faile thanne is al ydo.[4]
I bar him on hand[5] he hadde enchaunted me
(My dame taughte me that subtiltee);
And eek I saide I mette° of him al night: *dreamed*
He wolde han slain me as I lay upright,°   *supine*
585　And al my bed was ful of verray blood—
"But yit I hope that ye shul do me good;
For blood bitokeneth gold, as me was taught."
And al was fals, I dremed of it right naught,
But as I folwed ay my dames° lore°   *mother's / teaching*
590　As wel of that as othere thinges more.
But now sire—lat me see, what shal I sayn?
Aha, by God, I have my tale again.
　　Whan that my ferthe housbonde was on beere,°   *bier*
I weep,° algate,° and made sory cheere,   *wept / anyhow*
595　As wives moten,° for it is usage,°   *must / custom*
And with my coverchief covered my visage;
But for I was purveyed° of a make.°   *provided / mate*
I wepte but smale, and that I undertake.°   *guarantee*
　　To chirche was myn housbonde born amorwe[6]
600　With neighebores that for him maden sorwe,
And Janekin oure clerk was oon of tho.
As help me God, whan that I saw him go
After the beere, me thoughte he hadde a paire
Of legges and of feet so clene[7] and faire,
605　That al myn herte I yaf unto his hold.°   *possession*
He was, I trowe,° twenty winter old,   *believe*
And I was fourty, if I shal saye sooth—

3. Wore.
4. I.e., the game is up.
5. I pretended to him.

6. In the morning.
7. I.e., neat.

But yit I hadde alway a coltes tooth:[8]
Gat-toothed was I, and that bicam me weel;
610 I hadde the prente[9] of Sainte Venus seel.
As help me God, I was a lusty oon,
And fair and riche and yong and wel-bigoon,°   *well-situated*
And trewely, as mine housbondes tolde me,
I hadde the beste quoniam° mighte be.   *pudendum*
615 For certes I am al Venerien[1]
In feeling, and myn herte is Marcien:
Venus me yaf my lust, my likerousnesse,°   *lecherousness*
And Mars yaf me my sturdy hardinesse.
Myn ascendent was Taur[2] and Mars therinne—
620 Allas, allas, that evere love was sinne!
I folwed ay° my inclinacioun   *ever*
By vertu of my constellacioun;[3]
That made me I coude nought withdrawe
My chambre of Venus from a good felawe.
625 Yit have I Martes° merk upon my face,   *Mars'*
And also in another privee place.
For God so wis° be my savacioun,°   *surely / salvation*
I loved nevere by no discrecioun,
But evere folwede myn appetit,
630 Al were he short or long or blak or whit;
I took no keep,° so that he liked° me,   *heed / pleased*
How poore he was, ne eek of what degree.
    What sholde I saye but at the monthes ende
This joly clerk Janekin that was so hende°   *nice*
635 Hath wedded me with greet solempnitee,°   *splendor*
And to him yaf I al the land and fee°   *property*
That evere was me yiven therbifore—
But afterward repented me ful sore:
He nolde suffre no thing of my list.°   *pleasure*
640 By God, he smoot° me ones on the list°   *struck / ear*
For that I rente° out of his book a leef,   *tore*
That of the strook° myn ere weex° al deef.   *blow / grew*
Stibourne° I was as is a leonesse,   *stubborn*
And of my tonge a verray jangleresse,°   *blabbermouth*
645 And walke I wolde, as I hadde doon biforn,
From hous to hous, although he hadde it[4] sworn;
For which he often times wolde preche,
And me of olde Romain geestes° teche,   *stories*
How he Simplicius Gallus lafte° his wif,   *left*
650 And hire forsook for terme of al his lif,
Nought but for open-heveded he hire sey[5]

---

8. I.e., youthful appetites. "Gat-toothed": gap-toothed women were considered to be amorous.
9. Print, i.e., a birthmark. "Seel": seal.
1. Astrologically influenced by Venus. "Marcien": influenced by Mars.
2. My birth sign was the constellation Taurus.
3. I.e., horoscope.
4. I.e., the contrary.
5. Just because he saw her bareheaded.

Looking out at his dore upon a day.
 Another Romain tolde he me by name
That, for his wif was at a someres° game   *summer's*
655 Withouten his witing,° he forsook hire eke;   *knowledge*
And thanne wolde he upon his Bible seeke
That ilke proverbe of Ecclesiaste[6]
Where he comandeth and forbedeth faste°   *strictly*
Man shal nat suffre his wif go roule° aboute;   *roam*
660 Thanne wolde he saye right thus withouten doute:
"Whoso that buildeth his hous al of salwes,°   *willow sticks*
And priketh° his blinde hors over the falwes,[7]   *rides*
And suffreth his wif to go seeken halwes,°   *shrines*
Is worthy to be hanged on the galwes."°   *gallows*
665 But al for nought—I sette nought an hawe[8]
Of his proverbes n'of his olde sawe;
N' I wolde nat of him corrected be:
I hate him that my vices telleth me,
And so doon mo, God woot, of us than I.
670 This made him with me wood al outrely:[9]
I nolde nought forbere° him in no cas.   *submit to*
 Now wol I saye you sooth, by Saint Thomas,
Why that I rente° out of his book a leef,   *tore*
For which he smoot me so that I was deef.
675 He hadde a book that gladly night and day
For his disport he wolde rede alway.
He cleped it *Valerie*[1] *and Theofraste,*
At which book he lough° alway ful faste;   *laughed*
And eek ther was somtime a clerk at Rome,
680 A cardinal, that highte Saint Jerome,
That made a book[2] again Jovinian;
In which book eek ther was Tertulan,[3]
Crysippus, Trotula, and Helouis,
That was abbesse nat fer fro Paris;
685 And eek the Parables of Salomon,[4]
Ovides *Art,* and bookes many oon—
And alle thise were bounden in oo volume.
And every night and day was his custume,
Whan he hadde leiser and vacacioun
690 From other worldly occupacioun,
To reden in this book of wikked wives.

---

6. Ecclesiasticus (25.25).
7. Plowed land.
8. I did not rate at the value of a hawthorn berry.
9. Entirely.
1. I.e., the *Letter of Valerius Concerning Not Marrying,* by Walter Map; "*Theofraste*": Theophrastus's *Book Concerning Marriage.* Medieval manuscripts often contained a number of different works, sometimes, as here, dealing with the same subject.

2. St. Jerome's antifeminist *Reply to Jovinian.* "Again": against.
3. Tertullian, author of treatises on sexual modesty. Crysippus (or Chrysippus), in the next line, is mentioned by Jerome as an antifeminist; Trotula was a female doctor whose presence here is unexplained; "Helouis" is Eloise, whose love affair with the great scholar Abelard was a medieval scandal.
4. The Biblical Book of Proverbs. "Ovides *Art*": Ovid's *Art of Love.*

He knew of hem mo legendes and lives
Than been of goode wives in the Bible.
For trusteth wel, it is an impossible°   *impossibility*
695   That any clerk wol speke good of wives,
But if it be of holy saintes lives,
N'of noon other womman nevere the mo—
Who painted the leon, tel me who?[5]
By God, if wommen hadden writen stories,
700   As clerkes han within hir oratories,
They wolde han writen of men more wikkednesse
Than al the merk[6] of Adam may redresse.
The children of Mercurye and Venus[7]
Been in hir werking° ful contrarious:°   *operation / opposed*
705   Mercurye loveth wisdom and science,
And Venus loveth riot° and dispence;°   *parties / expenditures*
And for hir diverse disposicioun
Each falleth in otheres exaltacioun,[8]
And thus, God woot, Mercurye is desolat
710   In Pisces wher Venus is exaltat,[9]
And Venus falleth ther Mercurye is raised:
Therfore no womman of no clerk is praised.
The clerk, whan he is old and may nought do
Of Venus werkes worth his olde sho,°   *shoe*
715   Thanne sit° he down and writ° in his dotage   *sits / writes*
That wommen can nat keepe hir mariage.
    But now to purpose why I tolde thee
That I was beten for a book, pardee:
Upon a night Janekin, that was our sire,[1]
720   Redde on his book as he sat by the fire
Of Eva first, that for hir wikkednesse
Was al mankinde brought to wrecchednesse,
For which that Jesu Crist himself was slain
That boughte° us with his herte blood again—   *redeemed*
725   Lo, heer expres of wommen may ye finde
That womman was the los° of al mankinde.[2]   *ruin*
    Tho° redde he me how Sampson loste his heres: *then*
Sleeping his lemman° kitte° it with hir sheres,   *mistress / cut*
Thurgh which treson loste he both his yën.
730   Tho redde he me, if that I shal nat lien,
Of Ercules and of his Dianire,[3]

---

5. In one of Aesop's fables, the lion, shown a picture of a man killing a lion, asked who painted the
picture. Had a lion been the artist, of course, the
roles would have been reversed.
6. Mark, sex.
7. I.e., clerks and women, astrologically ruled by
Mercury and Venus respectively.
8. Because of their contrary positions (as planets),
each one descends (in the belt of the zodiac) as the
other rises; hence one loses its power as the other

becomes dominant.
9. I.e., Mercury is deprived of power in Pisces (the
sign of the Fish), where Venus is most powerful.
1. My husband.
2. The stories of wicked women Chaucer drew
mainly from St. Jerome and Walter Map.
3. Dejanira unwittingly gave Hercules a poisoned
shirt, which hurt him so much that he committed
suicide by fire.

That caused him to sette himself afire.
No thing forgat he the sorwe and wo
That Socrates hadde with his wives two—
735 How Xantippa caste pisse upon his heed:
This sely° man sat stille as he were deed;   *silly*
He wiped his heed, namore dorste he sayn
But "Er that thonder stinte,° comth a rain."   *stops*
Of Pasipha[4] that was the queene of Crete—
740 For shrewednesse° him thoughte the tale sweete—   *malice*
Fy, speek namore, it is a grisly thing
Of hir horrible lust and hir liking.°   *pleasure*
Of Clytermistra[5] for hir lecherye
That falsly made hir housbonde for to die,
745 He redde it with ful good devocioun.
He tolde me eek for what occasioun
Amphiorax[6] at Thebes loste his lif:
Myn housbonde hadde a legende of his wif
Eriphylem, that for an ouche° of gold   *trinket*
750 Hath prively unto the Greekes told
Wher that hir housbonde hidde him in a place,
For which he hadde at Thebes sory grace.
Of Livia[7] tolde he me and of Lucie:
They bothe made hir housbondes for to die,
755 That oon for love, that other was for hate;
Livia hir housbonde on an even late
Empoisoned hath for that she was his fo;
Lucia likerous° loved hir housbonde so   *lecherous*
That for° he sholde alway upon hire thinke,   *in order that*
760 She yaf him swich a manere love-drinke
That he was deed er it were by the morwe.[8]
And thus algates° housbondes han sorwe.   *constantly*
Thanne tolde he me how oon Latumius
Complained unto his felawe Arrius
765 That in his garden growed swich a tree,
On which he saide how that his wives three
Hanged hemself for herte despitous.[9]
"O leve° brother," quod this Arrius,   *dear*
"Yif me a plante of thilke blessed tree,
770 And in my gardin planted shal it be."
Of latter date of wives hath he red
That some han slain hir housbondes in hir bed
And lete hir lechour dighte[1] hire al the night,
Whan that the cors° lay in the floor upright;°   *corpse / supine*

---

4. Pasiphaë, who fell in love with a bull.
5. Clytemnestra, who, with her lover Aegisthus, slew her husband Agamemnon.
6. Amphiaraus, betrayed by his wife Eriphyle and forced to go to the war against Thebes.
7. Livia murdered her husband in behalf of her lover Sejanus. "Lucie": Lucilla, who was said to have poisoned her husband, the poet Lucretius, with a potion designed to keep him faithful.
8. He was dead before it was near morning.
9. For malice of heart.
1. Have intercourse with.

775 And some han driven nailes in hir brain
Whil that they sleepe, and thus they han hem slain;
Some han hem yiven poison in hir drinke.
He spak more harm than herte may bithinke,°   *imagine*
And therwithal he knew of mo proverbes
780 Than in this world ther growen gras or herbes:
"Bet is," quod he, "thyn habitacioun
Be with a leon or a foul dragoun
Than with a womman using° for to chide."   *accustomed*
"Bet is," quod he, "hye in the roof abide
785 Than with an angry wif down in the hous:
They been so wikked° and contrarious,   *perverse*
They haten that hir housbondes loveth ay."
He saide, "A womman cast° hir shame away   *casts*
When she cast of° hir smok,"[2] and ferthermo,   *off*
790 "A fair womman, but she be chast also,
Is like a gold ring in a sowes nose."
Who wolde weene,° or who wolde suppose   *think*
The wo that in myn herte was and pine?°   *suffering*
    And whan I sawgh he wolde nevere fine°   *end*
795 To reden on this cursed book al night,
Al sodeinly three leves have I plight°   *snatched*
Out of his book right as he redde, and eke
I with my fist so took[3] him on the cheeke
That in oure fir he fil° bakward adown.   *fell*
800 And up he sterte as dooth a wood° leoun,   *raging*
And with his fist he smoot me on the heed°   *head*
That in the floor I lay as I were deed.
And whan he sawgh how stille that I lay,
He was agast, and wolde have fled his way,
805 Til atte laste out of my swough° I braide:°   *swoon / started*
"O hastou slain me, false thief?" I saide,
"And for my land thus hastou mordred° me?   *murdered*
Er I be deed° yit wol I kisse thee."   *dead*
And neer he cam and kneeled faire adown,
810 And saide, "Dere suster Alisoun,
As help me God, I shal thee nevere smite.
That I have doon, it is thyself to wite.°   *blame*
Foryif it me, and that I thee biseeke."
And yit eftsoones° I hitte him on the cheeke,   *again*
815 And saide, "Thief, thus muchel am I wreke.°   *avenged*
Now wol I die: I may no lenger speke."
    But at the laste with muchel care and wo
We fille[4] accorded by us selven two.
He yaf me al the bridel° in myn hand,   *bridle*
820 To han the governance of hous and land,

---

2. Undergarment.
3. I.e., hit.
4. I.e., became.

And of his tonge and his hand also;
And made[5] him brenne° his book anoonright tho.   *burn*
And whan that I hadde geten unto me
By maistrye° al the sovereinetee,°   *skill / dominion*

825   And that he saide, "Myn owene trewe wif,
Do as thee lust° the terme of al thy lif;   *it pleases*
Keep thyn honour, and keep eek myn estat,"
After that day we hadde nevere debat.
God help me so, I was to him as kinde

830   As any wif from Denmark unto Inde,
And also trewe, and so was he to me.
I praye to God that sit° in majestee,   *sits*
So blesse his soule for his mercy dere.
Now wol I saye my tale if ye wol heere.

[ANOTHER INTERRUPTION]

835   The Frere lough° whan he hadde herd all this: *laughed*
"Now dame," quod he, "so have I joye or blis,
This is a long preamble of a tale."
And whan the Somnour herde the Frere gale,°   *exclaim*
"Lo," quod the Somnour, "Goddes armes two,

840   A frere wol entremette him[6] everemo!
Lo, goode men, a flye and eek a frere
Wol falle in every dissh and eek matere.
What spekestou of preambulacioun?
What, amble or trotte or pisse or go sitte down!

845   Thou lettest° oure disport in this manere."   *hinder*
    "Ye, woltou so, sire Somnour?" quod the Frere.
"Now by my faith, I shal er that I go
Telle of a somnour swich a tale or two
That al the folk shal laughen in this place."

850   "Now elles, Frere, I wol bishrewe° thy face,"   *curse*
Quod this Somnour, "and I bishrewe me,
But if I telle tales two or three
Of freres, er I come to Sidingborne,[7]
That I shal make thyn herte for to moorne—

855   For wel I woot thy pacience is goon."
    Oure Hoste cride, "Pees, and that anoon!"
And saide, "Lat the womman telle hir tale:
Ye fare as folk that dronken been of ale.
Do, dame, tel forth youre tale, and that is best."

860   "Al redy, sire," quod she, "right as you lest°—   *it pleases*
If I have licence of this worthy Frere."
"Yis, dame," quod he, "tel forth and I wol heere."

5. I.e., I made.   7. Sittingbourne (a town 40 miles from London).
6. Intrude himself.

The Tale[1]

In th'olde dayes of the King Arthour,
Of which that Britouns° speken greet honour,   *Bretons*
865 Al was this land fulfild of faïrye:[2]
The elf-queene with hir joly compaignye
Daunced ful ofte in many a greene mede°—   *meadow*
This was the olde opinion as I rede;
I speke of many hundred yeres ago.
870 But now can no man see none elves mo,
For now the grete charitee and prayeres
Of limitours,[3] and othere holy freres,
That serchen every land and every streem,
As thikke as motes in the sonne-beem,
875 Blessing halles, chambres, kichenes, bowres,
Citees, burghes,° castels, hye towres,   *townships*
Thropes, bernes, shipnes,[4] dayeries—
This maketh that ther been no faïries.
For ther as wont to walken was an elf
880 Ther walketh now the limitour himself,
In undermeles° and in morweninges,°   *afternoons / mornings*
And saith his Matins and his holy thinges,
As he gooth in his limitacioun.[5]
Wommen may go saufly° up and down: *safely*
885 In every bussh or under every tree
Ther is noon other incubus[6] but he,
And he ne wol doon hem but dishonour.
And so bifel it that this King Arthour
Hadde in his hous a lusty bacheler,
890 That on a day cam riding fro river,[7]
And happed° that, allone as he was born,   *it happened*
He sawgh a maide walking him biforn;

---

1. The story of the knight who fully realizes what women most desire only after having been told it in a number of ways was popular in Chaucer's time and a natural one for him to assign to the Wife of Bath, whose well-loved fifth husband had also been slow to learn. But Chaucer reshaped the tale in such a way as to make it fit the Wife and her thesis even more closely. In the other medieval versions of the story the knight is guiltless of any offense to womanhood, and in several of them he is Sir Gawain, traditional model of chivalric courtesy, who weds the hideous hag to save not his own life but that of his lord, King Arthur. Chaucer has made the knight a most ill-behaved and ill-mannered man who needs to learn what women most desire as much in order to redeem his disagreeably virile character as to save his neck. Because within her story he is the sole male in a world of women, Dame Alice is able not only to prove conclusively the value of woman's sovereignty, but also to pay her respects to a world of men that had preached antifeminism, a world here represented by a single rapist.

The story is suited to the Wife's own character psychologically as well as dramatically, for she, like the old hag, had wedded a young man—though unlike the hag she could not restore her former beauty. But if there is a touch of melancholy in the incompleteness of this similarity, it is sharply dispelled by the Wife's final comments, which reassert the sturdy fighting spirit that permeates her Prologue.

2. I.e., filled full of supernatural creatures.
3. Friars licensed to beg in a certain territory.
4. Thorps (villages), barns, stables.
5. I.e., the friar's assigned area. His "holy thinges" are prayers.
6. A spirit that lies with mortal women. "Ne . . . but" in the next line means "only."
7. Hawking, usually carried out on the banks of a stream.

Of which maide anoon, maugree hir heed,[8]

By verray force he rafte° hir maidenheed;   *deprived her of*

895   For which oppression° was swich clamour,   *rape*

And swich pursuite° unto the King Arthour,   *petitioning*

That dampned was this knight for to be deed[9]

By cours of lawe, and sholde han lost his heed—

Paraventure° swich was the statut tho—   *perchance*

900   But that the queene and othere ladies mo

So longe prayeden the king of grace,

Til he his lif him graunted in the place,

And yaf him to the queene, al at hir wille,

To chese° wheither she wolde him save or spille.[1]   *choose*

905   The queene thanked the king with al hir might,

And after this thus spak she to the knight,

Whan that she saw hir time upon a day:

"Thou standest yit," quod she, "in swich array°   *condition*

That of thy lif yit hastou no suretee.°   *guarantee*

910   I graunte thee lif if thou canst tellen me

What thing it is that wommen most desiren:

Be war and keep thy nekke boon° from iren.   *bone*

And if thou canst nat tellen me anoon,

Yit wol I yive thee leve for to goon

915   A twelfmonth and a day to seeche° and lere°   *search / learn*

An answere suffisant° in this matere,   *satisfactory*

And suretee wol I han er that thou pace,°   *pass*

Thy body for to yeelden in this place."

        Wo was this knight, and sorwefully he siketh.°   *sighs*

920   But what, he may nat doon al as him liketh,

And atte laste he chees° him for to wende,   *chose*

And come again right at the yeres ende,

With swich answere as God wolde him purveye,°   *provide*

And taketh his leve and wendeth forth his waye.

925   He seeketh every hous and every place

Wher as he hopeth for to finde grace,

To lerne what thing wommen love most.

But he ne coude arriven in no coost[2]

Wher as he mighte finde in this matere

930   Two creatures according in fere.[3]

        Some saiden wommen loven best richesse;

Some saide honour, some saide jolinesse;°   *wantonness*

Some riche array, some saiden lust° abedde,   *pleasure*

And ofte time to be widwe and wedde.

935   Some saide that oure herte is most esed

Whan that we been yflatered and yplesed—

He gooth ful neigh the soothe, I wol nat lie:

A man shal winne us best with flaterye,

---

8. Despite her head, i.e., despite anything she could do.

9. This knight was condemned to death.

1. Put to death.

2. I.e., country.

3. Agreeing together.

And with attendance and with bisinesse°   *assiduousness*
940   Been we ylimed,° bothe more and lesse.   *ensnared*
     And some sayen that we loven best
     For to be free, and do right as us lest,°   *it pleases*
     And that no man repreve° us of oure vice,   *reprove*
     But saye that we be wise and no thing nice.°   *foolish*
945   For trewely, ther is noon of us alle,
     If any wight wol clawe us on the galle,°   *sore spot*
     That we nil kike° for° he saith us sooth: *kick / because*
     Assaye and he shal finde it that so dooth.
     For be we nevere so vicious withinne,
950   We wol be holden° wise and clene of sinne.   *considered*
     And some sayn that greet delit han we
     For to be holden stable and eek secree,[4]
     And in oo purpos stedefastly to dwelle,
     And nat biwraye° thing that men us telle—   *disclose*
955   But that tale is nat worth a rake-stele.°   *rake handle*
     Pardee, we wommen conne no thing hele:°   *conceal*
     Witnesse on Mida.° Wol ye heere the tale?   *Midas*
     Ovide, amonges othere thinges smale,
     Saide Mida hadde under his longe heres,
960   Growing upon his heed, two asses eres,
     The whiche vice° he hidde as he best mighte   *defect*
     Ful subtilly from every mannes sighte,
     That save his wif ther wiste° of it namo.   *knew*
     He loved hire most and trusted hire also.
965   He prayed hire that to no creature
     She sholde tellen of his disfigure.°   *deformity*
     She swoor him nay, for al this world to winne,
     She nolde do that vilainye or sinne
     To make hir housbonde han so foul a name:
970   She nolde nat telle it for hir owene shame.
     But nathelees, hir thoughte that she dyde°   *would die*
     That she so longe sholde a conseil° hide;   *secret*
     Hire thoughte it swal° so sore about hir herte   *swelled*
     That nedely som word hire moste asterte,[5]
975   And sith she dorste nat telle it to no man,
     Down to a mareis° faste° by she ran—   *marsh / close*
     Til she cam there hir herte was afire—
     And as a bitore[6] bombleth in the mire,
     She laide hir mouth unto the water down:
980   "Biwray° me nat, thou water, with thy soun,"°   *betray / sound*
     Quod she. "To thee I telle it and namo:°   *to no one else*
     Myn housbonde hath longe asses eres two.
     Now is myn herte al hool,[7] now is it oute.

---

4. Reliable and also close-mouthed.
5. Of necessity some word must escape her.
6. Bittern, a heron. "Bombleth": makes a boom-ing noise.
7. I.e., sound.

I mighte no lenger keep it, out of doute."
985 Here may ye see, though we a time abide,
Yit oute it moot:° we can no conseil hide.   *must*
The remenant of the tale if ye wol heere,
Redeth Ovide, and ther ye may it lere.[8]
    This knight of which my tale is specially,
990 Whan that he sawgh he mighte nat come thereby—
This is to saye what wommen loven most—
Within his brest ful sorweful was his gost,°   *spirit*
But hoom he gooth, he mighte nat sojourne:°   *delay*
The day was come that hoomward moste° he turne.   *must*
995 And in his way it happed him to ride
In al this care under a forest side,
Wher as he sawgh upon a daunce go
Of ladies foure and twenty and yit mo;
Toward the whiche daunce he drow ful yerne,[9]
1000 In hope that som wisdom sholde he lerne.
But certainly, er he cam fully there,
Vanisshed was this daunce, he niste° where.   *knew not*
No creature sawgh he that bar° lif,   *bore*
Save on the greene he sawgh sitting a wif—
1005 A fouler wight ther may no man devise.°   *imagine*
Again[1] the knight this olde wif gan rise,
And saide, "Sire knight, heer forth lith° no way.°   *lies / road*
Telle me what ye seeken, by youre fay.°   *faith*
Paraventure it may the better be:
1010 Thise olde folk conne° muchel thing," quod she.   *know*
    "My leve moder,"° quod this knight, "certain,   *mother*
I nam but deed but if that I can sayn
What thing it is that wommen most desire.
Coude ye me wisse,° I wolde wel quite youre hire."[2]   *teach*
1015 "Plight me thy trouthe here in myn hand," quod she,
"The nexte thing that I requere° thee,   *require of*
Thou shalt it do, if it lie in thy might,
And I wol telle it you er it be night."
    "Have heer my trouthe," quod the knight. "I graunte."
1020 "Thanne," quod she, "I dar me wel avaunte°   *boast*
Thy lif is sauf,° for I wol stande therby.   *safe*
Upon my lif the queene wol saye as I.
Lat see which is the pruddeste° of hem alle   *proudest*
That wereth on[3] a coverchief or a calle°   *headdress*
1025 That dar saye nay of that I shal thee teche.
Lat us go forth withouten lenger speeche."
Tho rouned° she a pistel° in his ere,   *whispered / sentence*
And bad him to be glad and have no fere.

---

8. Learn. The reeds disclosed the secret by whispering "*aures aselli*" (ass's ears).
9. Drew very quickly.

1. I.e., to meet.
2. Repay your trouble.
3. That wears.

Whan they be comen to the court, this knight
1030 Saide he hadde holde his day as he hadde hight,°   *promised*
And redy was his answere, as he saide.
Ful many a noble wif, and many a maide,
And many a widwe—for that they been wise—
The queene hirself sitting as justise,
1035 Assembled been this answere for to heere,
And afterward this knight was bode° appere.   *bidden to*
To every wight comanded was silence,
And that the knight sholde telle in audience°   *open hearing*
What thing that worldly wommen loven best.
1040 This knight ne stood nat stille as dooth a best,°   *beast*
But to his question anoon answerde
With manly vois that al the court it herde.
"My lige° lady, generally," quod he,   *liege*
"Wommen desire to have sovereinetee°   *dominion*
1045 As wel over hir housbonde as hir love,
And for to been in maistrye him above.
This is youre moste desir though ye me kille.
Dooth as you list:° I am here at youre wille."   *please*
In al the court ne was ther wif ne maide
1050 Ne widwe that contraried° that he saide,   *contradicted*
But saiden he was worthy han° his lif.   *to have*
And with that word up sterte° that olde wif,   *started*
Which that the knight sawgh sitting on the greene;
"Mercy," quod she, "my soverein lady queene,
1055 Er that youre court departe, do me right.
I taughte this answere unto the knight,
For which he plighte me his trouthe there
The firste thing I wolde him requere°   *require*
He wolde it do, if it laye in his might.
1060 Bifore the court thanne praye I thee, sire knight,"
Quod she, "that thou me take unto thy wif,
For wel thou woost that I have kept° thy lif.   *saved*
If I saye fals, say nay, upon thy fay."
This knight answerde, "Allas and wailaway,
1065 I woot right wel that swich was my biheeste.°   *promise*
For Goddes love, as chees° a newe requeste: *choose*
Taak al my good and lat my body go."
"Nay thanne," quod she, "I shrewe° us bothe two.   *curse*
For though that I be foul and old and poore,
1070 I nolde for al the metal ne for ore
That under erthe is grave° or lith° above,   *buried / lies*
But if thy wif I were and eek thy love."
"My love," quod he. "Nay, my dampnacioun!°   *damnation*
Allas, that any of my nacioun[4]
1075 Sholde evere so foule disparaged° be."   *disgraced*

4. I.e., family.

But al for nought, th'ende is this, that he
Constrained was: he needes moste hire wedde,
And taketh his olde wif and gooth to bedde.
    Now wolden some men saye, paraventure,
1080 That for my necligence I do no cure[5]
To tellen you the joye and al th'array
That at the feeste was that ilke day.
To which thing shortly answere I shal:
I saye ther nas no joye ne feeste at al;
1085 Ther nas but hevinesse and muche sorwe.
For prively he wedded hire on morwe,[6]
And al day after hidde him as an owle,
So wo was him, his wif looked so foule.
    Greet was the wo the knight hadde in his thought,
1090 Whan he was with his wif abedde brought,
He walweth° and he turneth to and fro.   *tosses*
His olde wif lay smiling everemo,
And saide, "O dere housbonde, benedicite,°   *bless me*
Fareth° every knight thus with his wif as ye?   *behaves*
1095 Is this the lawe of King Arthures hous?
Is every knight of his thus daungerous?°   *stand-offish*
I am youre owene love and youre wif;
I am she which that saved hath youre lif;
And certes yit ne dide I you nevere unright.
1100 Why fare ye thus with me this firste night?
Ye faren like a man hadde lost his wit.
What is my gilt? For Goddes love, telle it,
And it shal been amended if I may."
    "Amended!" quod this knight. "Allas, nay, nay,
1105 It wol nat been amended neveremo.
Thou art so lothly° and so old also,   *loathsome*
And therto comen of so lowe a kinde,°   *race*
That litel wonder is though I walwe and winde.°   *turn*
So wolde God myn herte wolde breste!"°   *break*
1110 "Is this," quod she, "the cause of youre unreste?"
"Ye, certainly," quod he. "No wonder is."
"Now sire," quod she, "I coude amende al this,
If that me liste, er it were dayes three,
So° wel ye mighte bere you[7] unto me.   *provided that*
1115 "But for ye speken of swich gentilesse
As is descended out of old richesse—
That therfore sholden ye be gentilmen—
Swich arrogance is nat worth an hen.
Looke who that is most vertuous alway,
1120 Privee and apert,[8] and most entendeth ay
To do the gentil deedes that he can,

5. I do not take the trouble.   7. Behave.
6. In the morning.   8. Privately and publicly.

Taak him for the gretteste° gentilman.   *greatest*
Crist wol° we claime of him oure gentilesse,   *desires that*
Nat of oure eldres for hir 'old richesse.'⁹

1125 For though they yive us al hir heritage,
For which we claime to been of heigh parage,°   *descent*
Yit may they nat biquethe for no thing
To noon of us hir vertuous living,
That made hem gentilmen ycalled be,
1130 And bad¹ us folwen hem in swich degree.
    "Wel can the wise poete of Florence,
That highte Dant,² speken in this sentence;°   *topic*
Lo, in swich manere rym is Dantes tale:
'Ful selde° up riseth by his braunches³ smale   *seldom*
1135 Prowesse° of man, for God of his prowesse   *excellence*
Wol that of him we claime oure gentilesse.'
For of oure eldres may we no thing claime
But temporel thing that man may hurte and maime.
Eek every wight woot this as wel as I,
1140 If gentilesse were planted natureelly
Unto a certain linage down the line,
Privee and apert, thanne wolde they nevere fine°   *cease*
To doon of gentilesse the faire office°—   *function*
They mighte do no vilainye or vice.
1145   "Taak fir and beer° it in the derkeste hous   *bear*
Bitwixe this and the Mount of Caucasus,
And lat men shette° the dores and go thenne,°   *shut / thence*
Yit wol the fir as faire lie⁴ and brenne°   *burn*
As twenty thousand men mighte it biholde:
1150 His° office natureel ay wol it holde,   *its*
Up° peril of my lif, til that it die.   *upon*
Heer may ye see wel how that genterye°   *gentility*
Is nat annexed° to possessioun,⁵   *related*
Sith folk ne doon hir operacioun
1155 Alway, as dooth the fir, lo, in his kinde.°   *nature*
For God it woot, men may wel often finde
A lordes sone do shame and vilainye;
And he that wol han pris of his gentrye,⁶
For he was boren° of a gentil hous,   *born*
1160 And hadde his eldres noble and vertuous,
And nil himselven do no gentil deedes,
Ne folwen his gentil auncestre that deed° is,   *dead*
He nis nat gentil, be he duc or erl—
For vilaines sinful deedes maken a cherl.
1165 Thy gentilesse⁷ nis but renomee°   *renown*
Of thine auncestres for hir heigh bountee,°   *magnanimity*

9. See Chaucer's *Gentilesse*, line 16.   4. I.e., remain.
1. I.e., they bade.   5. I.e., inheritable property.
2. Dante; see his *Convivio*.   6. Have credit for his noble birth.
3. I.e., by its own efforts.   7. I.e., the gentility you claim.

Which is a straunge° thing for thy persone.   *alien*
For gentilesse[8] cometh fro God allone.
Thanne comth oure verray gentilesse of grace:
1170 It was no thing biquethe us with oure place.
Thenketh how noble, as saith Valerius,[9]
Was thilke Tullius Hostilius
That out of poverte° roos to heigh noblesse.   *poverty*
Redeth Senek° and redeth eek Boece:°   *Seneca / Boethius*
1175 Ther shul ye seen expres that no drede° is   *doubt*
That he is gentil that dooth gentil deedes.
And therfore, leve housbonde, I thus conclude:
Al were it that mine auncestres weren rude,[1]
Yit may the hye God—and so hope I—
1180 Graunte me grace to liven vertuously.
Thanne am I gentil whan that I biginne
To liven vertuously and waive° sinne.   *avoid*
    "And ther as ye of poverte me repreve,°   *reprove*
The hye God, on whom that we bileve,
1185 In wilful° poverte chees° to live his lif;   *voluntary / chose*
And certes every man, maiden, or wif
May understonde that Jesus, hevene king,
Ne wolde nat chese° a vicious living.   *choose*
Glad poverte is an honeste° thing, certain;   *honorable*
1190 This wol Senek and othere clerkes sayn.
Whoso that halt him paid of[2] his poverte,
I holde him riche al hadde he nat a sherte.°   *shirt*
He that coveiteth[3] is a poore wight,
For he wolde han that is nat in his might;
1195 But he that nought hath, ne coveiteth° have,   *desires to*
Is riche, although we holde him but a knave.
Verray poverte it singeth proprely.°   *appropriately*
Juvenal saith of poverte, 'Merily
The poore man, whan he gooth by the waye,
1200 Biforn the theves he may singe and playe.'
Poverte is hateful good, and as I gesse,
A ful greet bringere out of bisinesse;[4]
A greet amendere eek of sapience
To him that taketh it in pacience;
1205 Poverte is thing, although it seeme elenge,°   *wretched*
Possession that no wight wol chalenge;[5]
Poverte ful often, whan a man is lowe,
Maketh[6] his God and eek himself to knowe;
Poverte a spectacle° is, as thinketh me,   *pair of spectacles*
1210 Thurgh which he may his verray freendes see.
And therfore, sire, sin that I nought you greve,

---

8. I.e., true gentility.
9. A Roman historian.
1. I.e., low born.
2. Considers himself satisfied with.

3. I.e., suffers desires.
4. I.e., cares.
5. Claim as his property.
6. I.e., makes him.

Of my poverte namore ye me repreve.°   reproach
     "Now sire, of elde° ye repreve me: old age
And certes sire, though noon auctoritee
1215 Were in no book, ye gentils of honour
Sayn that men sholde an old wight doon favour,
And clepe him fader for youre gentilesse—
And auctours[7] shal I finde, as I gesse.
     "Now ther ye saye that I am foul and old:
1220 Thanne drede you nought to been a cokewold,°   cuckold
For filthe and elde, also mote I thee,[8]
Been grete wardeins° upon chastitee.   guardians
But nathelees, sin I knowe your delit,
I shal fulfille youre worldly appetit.
1225   "Chees now," quod she, "oon of thise thinges twaye:
To han me foul and old til that I deye
And be to you a trewe humble wif,
And nevere you displese in al my lif,
Or elles ye wol han me yong and fair,
1230 And take youre aventure° of the repair[9]   chance
That shal be to youre hous by cause of me—
Or in some other place, wel may be.
Now chees youreselven wheither° that you liketh."   whichever
     This knight aviseth him[1] and sore siketh;°   sighs
1235 But atte laste he saide in this manere:
"My lady and my love, and wif so dere,
I putte me in youre wise governaunce:
Cheseth° youreself which may be most plesaunce[2]   choose
And most honour to you and me also.
1240 I do no fors the wheither[3] of the two,
For as you liketh it suffiseth° me."   satisfies
     "Thanne have I gete° of you maistrye," quod she,   got
"Sin I may chese and governe as me lest?"°   it pleases
     "Ye, certes, wif," quod he. "I holde it best."
1245   "Kisse me," quod she. "We be no lenger wrothe.
For by my trouthe, I wol be to you bothe—
This is to sayn, ye, bothe fair and good.
I praye to God that I mote sterven wood,[4]
But° I to you be al so good and trewe   unless
1250 As evere was wif sin that the world was newe.
And but I be tomorn° as fair to seene   tomorrow morning
As any lady, emperisse, or queene,
That is bitwixe the eest and eek the west,
Do with my lif and deeth right as you lest:
1255 Caste up the curtin,[5] looke how that it is."
     And whan the knight sawgh verraily al this,

---

7. I.e., authorities.   2. Pleasure.
8. So may I thrive.   3. I do not care whichever.
9. I.e., visits.   4. Die mad.
1. Considers.   5. The curtain around the bed.

That she so fair was and so yong therto,
For joye he hente° hire in his armes two;   *took*
His herte bathed in a bath of blisse;
1260   A thousand time arewe° he gan hire kisse,   *in a row*
And she obeyed him in every thing
That mighte do him plesance or liking.°   *pleasure*
And thus they live unto hir lives ende
In parfit° joye. And Jesu Crist us sende   *perfect*
1265   Housbondes meeke, yonge, and fresshe abedde—
And grace t'overbide° hem that we wedde.   *outlive*
And eek I praye Jesu shorte° hir lives   *shorten*
That nought wol be governed by hir wives,
And olde and angry nigardes of dispence°—   *expenditure*
1270   God sende hem soone a verray° pestilence!   *veritable*

The Franklin's Tale[1]

The Introduction[2]

"In faith, Squier, thou hast thee wel yquit°   *acquitted*
And gentilly. I praise wel thy wit,"
Quod the Frankelain. "Considering thy youthe,
So feelingly thou spekest, sire, I allowe° thee: *praise*
5   As to my doom° ther is noon that is heer   *judgment*
Of eloquence that shal be thy peer,
If that thou live. God yive thee good chaunce,
And in vertu sende thee continuaunce,
For of thy speeche I have greet daintee.°   *delight*
10   I have a sone, and by the Trinitee,
I hadde levere° than twenty pound worth land,   *rather*
Though it right now were fallen[3] in myn hand,

---

1. The Franklin says that his tale is a Breton lay, a subgenre of romance, but his source is probably not a lost Breton lay but an old story told by, among others, Boccaccio. But in any case, features found in Breton lays also occur in the Franklin's Tale: a rash promise that must be kept; a supernatural intervention in a plot containing a love situation; stylistic simplicity; and a generally optimistic spirit.

The Franklin is a fine type of the man of humble origins who has risen to the middle class and has adopted the aspirations of the aristocracy while accumulating wealth. His tale shows a nice blend of unselfconscious interest in the value of money and a self-conscious one in *gentilesse*, the gentle behavior which should distinguish not only the nobly born but (as the Wife of Bath's old hag tells her husband) any free-born man. In this tale *gentilesse* embraces the virtues of patience (which Dorigen has to learn the hard way) and, more significantly, of *trouthe* and *freedom*, "integrity" and "generosity." Though the Franklin shows no awareness of the Biblical text, "Ye shall know the truth and the truth shall make you free" (John 8.32),

his tale exemplifies it almost in the manner of a parable. The characters concerned resolve to maintain their *trouthe*—their pledged word—and this sets up a chain reaction of *freedom* which releases them from the dire consequences that keeping their word would entail: when the old law of the covenant is honored, it brings into being the new law of forgiveness. The word *franklin* means "freeman," a meaning Chaucer seems to be playing on when in the last lines of the tale he has the Franklin ask about the three men in the story, "Which was the most free?"

2. The Squire has been speaking for more than 650 lines but has not made much narrative progress in his enormously over-plotted Oriental tale of Cambyuskan and his three children when the Franklin speaks, apparently interrupting the story. It is uncertain, however, whether the Franklin's words represent an intentional interruption or whether they were written to be spoken at the end of the Squire's Tale, which Chaucer intended sometime to complete.

3. I.e., delivered.

He were a man of swich discrecioun
As that ye been. Fy on possessioun
15 But if[4] a man be vertuous withal!
I have my sone snibbed° and yit shal   *scolded*
For he to vertu listeth nat entende,°   *attend*
But for to playe at dees° and to dispende,[5]   *dice*
And lese° al that he hath is his usage.   *lose*
20 And he hath levere talken with a page°   *servant*
Than to commune with any gentil wight,
Where he mighte lerne gentilesse° aright."   *gentility*
    "Straw for thy gentilesse!" quod oure Host.
"What, Frankelain, pardee sire, wel thou woost°   *know*
25 That eech of you moot° tellen atte leeste   *must*
A tale or two, or breken his biheeste."°   *promise*
    "That knowe I wel, sire," quod the Frankelain.
"I praye you, haveth me nat in desdain,
Though to this man I speke a word or two."
30 "Tel on thy tale withouten wordes mo."
    "Gladly, sire Host," quod he, "I wol obeye
Unto youre wil. Now herkneth what I saye.
I wol you nat contrarien[6] in no wise
As fer as that my wittes wol suffise.
35 I praye to God that it may plesen you:
Thanne woot I wel that it is good ynow."°   *enough*

The Prologue

    Thise olde gentil Britons° in hir dayes   *Bretons*
Of diverse aventures maden layes,
Rymeyed[7] in hir firste Briton tonge;
40 Whiche layes with hir instruments they songe,°   *sung*
Or elles redden° hem for hir plesaunce;   *read*
And oon of hem have I in remembraunce,
Which I shal sayn with good wil as I can.
    But sires, by cause I am a burel° man,   *ignorant*
45 At my biginning first I you biseeche
Have me excused of my rude speeche.
I lerned nevere retorike,° certain: *rhetoric*
Thing that I speke it moot° be bare and plain;   *must*
I sleep° nevere in the Mount of Parnaso,[8]   *slept*
50 Ne lerned Marcus Tullius Scithero;°   *Cicero*
Colours[9] ne knowe I noon, withouten drede,°   *doubt*
But swiche colours as growen in the mede,°   *meadow*
Or elles swiche as men dye or painte;
Colours of retorike been too quainte:°   *unfamiliar*

---

4. Unless.
5. Spend money.
6. Act contrary to.

7. Composed in rhyme.
8. Parnassus, home of the Muses.
9. I.e., rhetorical figures.

55   My spirit feeleth nat of swich matere.
     But if you list, my tale shul ye heere.

The Tale

         In Armorik,° that called is Britaine,°   *Armorica / Brittany*
     Ther was a knight that loved and dide his paine[1]
     To serve a lady in his beste wise;
60   And many a labour, many a greet emprise°   *enterprise*
     He for his lady wroughte er she were wonne,
     For she was oon[2] the faireste under sonne,
     And eek therto come of so heigh kinrede°   *kindred*
     That wel unnethes[3] dorste this knight for drede
65   Telle hire his wo, his paine, and his distresse.
     But atte laste she for his worthinesse,
     And namely° for his meeke obeisaunce,°   *especially / obedience*
     Hath swich a pitee caught of his penaunce°   *suffering*
     That prively she fil of[4] his accord
70   To taken him for hir housbonde and hir lord,
     Of swich lordshipe as men han over hir wives.
     And for to lede the more in blisse hir lives,
     Of his free wil he swoor hire as a knight
     That nevere in al his lif he day ne night
75   Ne sholde upon him take no maistrye°   *dominion*
     Again hir wil, ne kithe° hire jalousye,   *show*
     But hire obeye and folwe hir wil in al,
     As any lovere to his lady shal°—   *ought*
     Save that the name of sovereinete,°   *sovereignty*
80   That wolde he have, for shame of[5] his degree.
         She thanked him, and with ful greet humblesse
     She saide, "Sire, sith° of youre gentilesse   *since*
     Ye profre me to have so large[6] a reine,
     Ne wolde nevere God bitwixe us twaine,
85   As in[7] my gilt, were outher° werre° or strif.   *either / war*
     Sire, I wol be your humble, trewe wif—
     Have heer my trouthe[8]—til that myn herte breste."°   *break*
     Thus been they bothe in quiete and in reste.
         For oo thing, sires, saufly° dar I saye: *safely*
90   That freendes° everich° other moot° obeye,   *lovers / each / must*
     If they wol longe holden compaignye.
     Love wol nat be constrained by maistrye:°   *force*
     Whan maistrye comth, the God of Love anoon
     Beteth his winges and farewel, he is goon!
95   Love is a thing as any spirit free;

1. I.e., made every effort.   5. Out of respect for.
2. I.e., one of.   6. I.e., free.
3. With difficulty.   7. As a result of.
4. I.e., fell in.   8. Troth, word of honor.

Wommen of kinde[9] desiren libertee,
And nat to been constrained as a thral°—　　　　　　slave
And so doon men, if I sooth sayen shal.
Looke who that is most pacient in love,
100　He is at his avantage al above.
Pacience is an heigh vertu, certain,
For it venquissheth,° as thise clerkes sayn,　　　vanquishes
Thinges that rigour sholde nevere attaine.[1]
For° every word men may nat chide or plaine:°　　at / complain
105　Lerneth to suffre, or elles, so mote I goon,[2]
Ye shul it lerne, wherso° ye wol or noon.　　　　　whether
For in this world, certain, ther no wight is
That he ne dooth or saith somtime amis:
Ire, siknesse, or constellacioun,[3]
110　Win, wo, or chaunging of complexioun[4]
Causeth ful ofte to doon amis or speken.
On every wrong a man may nat be wreken:°　　　avenged
After the time moste° be temperaunce　　　　　　must
To every wight that can on governaunce.[5]
115　And therfore hath this wise worthy knight
To live in ese suffrance° hire bihight,°　　toleration / promised
And she to him ful wisly° gan to swere　　　　　surely
That nevere sholde ther be defaute° in here.　　defect
　　　Here may men seen an humble wis accord:
120　Thus hath she take hir servant and hir lord—
Servant in love and lord in mariage.
Thanne was he bothe in lordshipe and servage.[6]
Servage? Nay, but in lordshipe above,
Sith° he hath bothe his lady and his love;　　　since
125　His lady, certes, and his wif also,
The which that[7] lawe of love accordeth to.
And whan he was in this prosperitee,
Hoom with his wif he gooth to his contree,
Nat fer fro Pedmark[8] ther his dwelling was,
130　Wher as he liveth in blisse and in solas.°　　　delight
　　　Who coude telle but he hadde wedded be
The joye, the ese, and the prosperitee
That is bitwixe an housbonde and his wif?
A yeer and more lasted this blisful lif,
135　Til that the knight of which I speke of thus,
That of Kairrud[9] was cleped° Arveragus,　　　called
Shoop him[1] to goon and dwelle a yeer or twaine
In Engelond, that cleped was eek° Britaine,　　　also

9. By nature.　　　　　　　　　　　6. Position of a servant.
1. I.e., overcome.　　　　　　　　　7. As.
2. So may I walk, an oath.　　　　　8. Penmarch, in Brittany.
3. I.e., planetary influences.　　　　9. Kerru, a town in Brittany.
4. The balance of humors in the body.　1. Prepared.
5. Is capable of self-control.

To seeke in armes worshipe and honour—
140 For al his lust° he sette in swich labour—   *pleasure*
And dwelled ther two yeer, the book saith thus.
      Now wol I stinte° of this Arveragus,   *cease*
And speke I wol of Dorigen his wif,
That loveth hir housbonde as hir hertes lif.
145 For his absence weepeth she and siketh,°   *sighs*
As doon thise noble wives whan hem liketh.[2]
She moorneth, waketh, waileth, fasteth, plaineth;°   *complains*
Desir of his presence hire so distraineth°   *afflicts*
That al this wide world she sette[3] at nought.
150 Hir freendes, whiche that knewe hir hevy thought,
Conforten hire in al that evere they may:
They prechen hire, they telle hire night and day
That causeless she sleeth° hirself, allas;   *slays*
And every confort possible in this cas
155 They doon to hire with al hir bisinesse,°   *assiduousness*
Al for to make hire leve° hir hevinesse.   *abandon*
      By proces,[4] as ye knowen everichoon,
Men may so longe graven° in a stoon   *engrave*
Til som figure therinne emprinted be:
160 So longe han they conforted hire til she
Received hath, by hope and by resoun,
The emprinting of hir consolacioun,
Thurgh which hir grete sorwe gan assuage:
She may nat alway duren° in swich rage.°   *remain / passion*
165   And eek Arveragus in al this care
Hath sent hir lettres hoom of his welfare,
And that he wol come hastily again—
Or elles hadde this sorwe hir herte slain.
Hir freendes sawe hir sorwe gan to slake,°   *diminish*
170 And prayed hire on knees, for Goddes sake,
To come and romen hire in compaignye,
Away to drive hir derke fantasye,
And finally she graunted that requeste:
For wel she saw that it was for the beste.
175   Now stood hir castel faste by the see,
And often with hir freendes walketh she,
Hire to disporte upon the bank an heigh,
Wher as she many a ship and barge° seigh,°   *vessel / saw*
Sailing hir cours wher as hem liste go—
180 But thanne was that a parcel° of hir wo,   *component*
For of hirself ful ofte, "Allas!" saith she,
"Is ther no ship of so manye as I see
Wol bringen hoom my lord? Thanne were myn herte
Al warisshed° of his bittre paines smerte."   *recovered*

2. It pleases.   4. Course of time.
3. I.e., valued.

185   Another time ther wolde she sitte and thinke,
And caste hir yën downward fro the brinke;
But whan she sawgh the grisly rokkes blake,
For verray° fere so wolde hir herte quake   *real*
That on hir feet she mighte hire nat sustene:°   *sustain*
190   Thanne wolde she sitte adown upon the greene
And pitously into the see biholde,
And sayn right thus, with sorweful sikes° colde:[5]   *sighs*
     "Eterne God that thurgh thy purveyaunce°   *providence*
Ledest the world by certain governaunce,
195   In idel,[6] as men sayn, ye nothing make:
But Lord, thise grisly feendly° rokkes blake,   *hostile*
That seemen rather a foul confusioun
Of werk, than any fair creacioun
Of swich a parfit° wis God and a stable,   *perfect*
200   Why han ye wrought this werk unresonable?
For by this werk south, north, ne west ne eest,
Ther nis yfostred man ne brid[7] ne beest:
It dooth no good, to my wit, but anoyeth.
See ye nat, Lord, how mankinde it destroyeth?
205   An hundred thousand bodies of mankinde
Han rokkes slain, al° be they nat in minde: *although*
Which mankinde is so fair part of thy werk
That thou it madest lik to thyn owene merk:[8]
Thanne seemed it ye hadde a greet cheertee°   *affection*
210   Toward mankinde. But how thanne may it be
That ye swiche menes° make it to destroyen?—   *means*
Whiche menes do no good, but evere anoyen.
I woot wel clerkes wol sayn as hem leste,[9]
By arguments, that al is for the beste,
215   Though I ne can the causes nat yknowe.
But thilke° God that made wind to blowe,   *that*
As keepe my lord! This[1] my conclusioun.
To clerkes lete° I al disputisoun,°   *leave / disputation*
But wolde God that alle thise rokkes blake
220   Were sonken° into helle for his sake!   *sunken*
Thise rokkes slain myn herte for the fere."
Thus wolde she sayn with many a pitous tere.
     Hir freendes sawe that it was no disport
To romen by the see, but disconfort,
225   And shopen° for to playen somwher elles: *arranged*
They leden hire by rivers and by welles,°   *springs*
And eek in othere places delitables;°   *delightful*
They dauncen and they playen at ches and tables.°   *backgammon*
So on a day, right in the morwetide,°   *morning*

---

5. I.e., grievous.   8. Mark, i.e., image.
6. I.e., without purpose.   9. May please.
7. Bird. "Yfostred": fed.   1. I.e., this is.

230 Unto a gardin that was ther biside,
In which that they hadde maad hir ordinaunce° *arrangements*
Of vitaile° and of other purveyaunce,° *food / provisions*
They goon and playe hem al the longe day.
And this was on the sixte morwe° of May, *morning*
235 Which May had painted with his softe showres
This gardin ful of leves and of flowres;
And craft of mannes hand so curiously° *skillfully*
Arrayed hadde this gardin trewely
That nevere was ther gardin of swich pris,° *excellence*
240 But if² it were the verray Paradis.
The odour of flowres and the fresshe sighte
Wolde han maked any herte lighte
That evere was born, but if too greet siknesse,
Or too greet sorwe heeld it in distresse,
245 So ful it was of beautee with plesaunce.
At after-diner gonne they to daunce,
And singe also, save Dorigen allone,
Which made alway hir complainte and hir mone,° *moan*
For she ne sawgh him on the daunce go
250 That was hir housbonde and hir love also.
But nathelees she moste° a time abide, *must*
And with good hope lete° hir sorwe slide. *make*
    Upon this daunce, amonges othere men,
Daunced a squier bifore Dorigen
255 That fressher was and jolier° of array, *gayer*
As to my doom,° than is the month of May. *judgment*
He singeth, daunceth, passing° any man *surpassing*
That is or was sith° that the world bigan. *since*
Therwith he was, if men him sholde descrive,° *describe*
260 Oon of the beste-faring° man on live: *handsomest*
Yong, strong, right vertuous, and riche and wis,
And wel-biloved, and holden in greet pris.° *repute*
And shortly, if the soothe I tellen shal,
Unwiting of³ this Dorigen at al,
265 This lusty squier, servant to Venus,
Which that ycleped° was Aurelius, *called*
Hadde loved hire best of any creature
Two yeer and more, as was his aventure.
But nevere dorste he tellen hire his grevaunce:
270 Withouten coppe° he drank al his penaunce.⁴ *cup*
He was despaired, no thing dorste he saye—
Save in his songes somwhat wolde he wraye° *disclose*
His wo, as in a general complaining:
He saide he loved and was biloved no thing;⁵
275 Of which matere made he manye layes,

---

2. Unless.
3. Unknown to.

4. Suffering; i.e., he suffered in silence.
5. Not at all.

Songes, complaintes, roundels, virelayes,[6]
How that he dorste nat his sorwe telle,
But languissheth as a furye dooth in helle;
And die he moste° he saide, as dide Ekko   *must*
280 For Narcius that dorste nat telle hir wo.[7]
In other manere than ye heere me saye
Ne dorste he nat to hire his wo biwraye,°   *disclose*
Save that paraventure° som time at daunces,   *perchance*
Ther yonge folk keepen hir observaunces,[8]
285 It may wel be he looked on hir face
In swich a wise as man that asketh grace;
But no thing wiste° she of his entente.   *knew*
Nathelees° it happed, er they thennes° wente, *nevertheless / thence*
By cause that he was hir neighebour,
290 And was a man of worshipe and honour,
And hadde[9] yknowen him of time yore,[1]
They fille° in speeche, and forth more and more   *fell*
Unto his purpos drow° Aurelius,   *drew*
And whan he sawgh his time, he saide thus:
295   "Madame," quod he, "by God that this world made,
So that I wiste° it mighte youre herte glade,°   *knew / gladden*
I wolde that day that youre Arveragus
Wente over the see that I, Aurelius,
Hadde went ther nevere I sholde have come again.
300 For wel I woot my service is in vain:
My gerdon° is but bresting° of myn herte.   *reward / breaking*
Madame, reweth[2] upon my paines smerte,
For with a word ye may me slee° or save.   *slay*
Here at youre feet God wolde that I were grave!°   *buried*
305 I ne have as now no leiser more to saye:
Have mercy, sweete, or ye wol do° me deye."   *make*
        She gan to looke upon Aurelius:
"Is this youre wil?" quod she, "and saye ye thus?
Nevere erst,"° quod she, "ne wiste I what ye mente.   *before*
310 But now, Aurelie, I knowe youre entente,
By thilke° God that yaf me soule and lif,   *that*
Ne shal I nevere been untrewe wif,
In word ne werk, as fer as I have wit.
I wol be his to whom that I am knit:°   *joined*
315 Take this for final answere as of me."
But after that in play thus saide she:
        "Aurelie," quod she, "by hye God above,
Yit wolde I graunte you to been youre love,
Sin° I you see so pitously complaine,   *since*

---

6. The lover unable to declare his love conventionally expressed his frustration by writing verse:
Aurelius produced five kinds of verse, but only
rondels and virelays are strictly defined forms.
7. Echo was unable to communicate her love for

Narcissus and eventually died in despair.
8. Carry on their rituals.
9. I.e., she had.
1. Long past.
2. Have pity on.

320 Looke what day that endelong° Britaine   *along*
  Ye remeve° alle the rokkes, stoon by stoon,   *remove*
  That they ne lette° ship ne boot° to goon. *hinder / boat*
  I saye, whan ye han maad the coost° so clene *coast*
  Of rokkes that there nis no stoon yseene,
325 Thanne wol I love you best of any man—
  Have heer my trouthe°—in al that evere I can. *word*
  For wel I woot that it shal nevere bitide.
  Lat swiche folies out of youre herte slide!
  What daintee° sholde a man han by his lif   *delight*
330 For to love another mannes wif,
  That hath hir body whan so that him liketh?"[3]
    Aurelius ful ofte sore siketh:°   *sighs*
  "Is ther noon other grace in you?" quod he.
   "No, by that Lord," quod she, "that maked me."
335 Wo was Aurelie whan that he this herde,
  And with a sorweful herte he thus answerde.
    "Madame," quod he, "this were an impossible.
  Thanne moot° I die of sodein deeth horrible." *must*
  And with that word he turned him anoon.
340 Tho° come hir othere freendes many oon,   *then*
  And in the aleyes° romeden up and down,   *paths*
  And no thing wiste of this conclusioun,
  But sodeinly bigonne revel newe,
  Til that the brighte sonne loste his hewe,
345 For th' orisonte° hath reft[4] the sonne his light— *horizon*
  This is as muche to saye as it was night.
  And hoom they goon in joye and in solas,°   *delight*
  Save only wrecche° Aurelius, allas.   *wretched*
  He to his hous is goon with sorweful herte;
350 He seeth he may nat from his deeth asterte;° *escape*
  Him seemed that he felte his herte colde;
  Up to the hevene his handes he gan holde,
  And on his knees bare he sette him down,
  And in his raving saide his orisoun.
355 For verray wo out of his wit he braide;°   *went*
  He niste[5] what he spak, but thus he saide;
  With pitous herte his plainte° hath he bigonne *lament*
  Unto the goddes, and first unto the sonne:
    He saide, "Apollo, god and governour
360 Of every plaunte, herbe, tree and flowr,
  That yivest after thy declinacioun[6]
  To eech of hem his time and his sesoun,
  As thyn herberwe[7] chaungeth, lowe or hye;
  Lord Phebus, cast thy merciable° yë   *merciful*

---

3. It pleases.
4. Deprived of.
5. Knew not.
6. Who give, according to your position in the

sky.
7. Lodging, i.e., one of the astrological houses in which the planets reside in alternation.

365   On wrecche Aurelie which that am but lorn.°   *lost*
      Lo, lord, my lady hath my deeth ysworn
      Withouten gilt, but° thy benignitee   *unless*
      Upon my deedly herte have som pitee;
      For wel I woot, lord Phebus, if you lest,[8]
370   Ye may me helpen, save my lady, best.[9]
      Now voucheth sauf that I may you devise°   *describe*
      How that I may been holpe,° and in what wise: *helped*
         Youre blisful suster, Lucina[1] the sheene,°   *bright*
      That of the see is chief goddesse and queene—
375   Though Neptunus have deitee in the see,
      Yit emperisse° aboven him is she—   *empress*
      Ye knowen wel, lord, that right as hir desir
      Is to be quiked° and lighted of youre fir,   *quickened*
      For which she folweth you ful bisily,°   *constantly*
380   Right so the see desireth naturelly
      To folwen hire, as she that is goddesse
      Bothe in the see and rivers more and lesse;
      Wherfore, lord Phebus, this is my requeste:
      Do this miracle—or do° myn herte breste°—   *make / break*
385   That now next at this opposicioun,[2]
      Which in the signe shal be of the Leoun,
      As prayeth hire so greet a flood to bringe
      That five fadme° at the leeste it overspringe° *fathoms / overrun*
      The hyeste rok in Armorik Britaine;
390   And lat this flood endure yeres twaine:
      Thanne certes to my lady may I saye,
      'Holdeth youre heeste,° the rokkes been awaye.'   *promise*
         Lord Phebus, dooth this miracle for me!
      Praye hire she go no faster cours than ye—
395   I saye this, prayeth youre suster that she go
      No faster cours than ye thise yeres two:
      Thanne shal she been evene at the fulle alway,
      And spring-flood lasten bothe night and day.
      And but° she vouche sauf in swich manere   *unless*
400   To graunte me my soverein lady dere,
      Praye hire[3] to sinken every rok adown
      Into hir owene derke regioun
      Under the ground ther Pluto dwelleth inne,
      Or nevere mo° shal I my lady winne.   *more*
405   Thy temple in Delphos° wol I barefoot seeke.   *Delphi*
      Lord Phebus, see the teres on my cheeke,
      And of my paine have som compassioun."
      And with that word in swoune° he fil° adown,   *swoon / fell*
      And longe time he lay forth in a traunce.

---

8. It pleases.
9. Except for my lady, you may help me best.
1. I.e., Diana, the Moon.
2. The position of the sun and moon when they
are at a 180-degree angle from one another as seen
from the earth.
3. I.e., Diana in her capacity as goddess of the
underworld.

410 His brother, which that knew of his penaunce,°   *pain*
Up caughte him, and to bedde he hath him brought.
Despaired in this torment and this thought
Lete° I this woful creature lie—   *leave*
Chese[4] he for me wher° he wol live or die.   *whether*
415 Arveragus with hele° and greet honour,   *prosperity*
As he that was of chivalrye the flowr,
Is comen hoom, and othere worthy men:
O, blisful artou now, thou Dorigen,
That hast thy lusty housbonde in thine armes,
420 The fresshe knight, the worthy man of armes,
That loveth thee as his owene hertes lif.
No thing list[5] him to been imaginatif
If any wight hadde spoke whil he was oute
To hire of love; he ne hadde of it no doute:
425 He nought entendeth[6] to no swich matere,
But daunceth, justeth,° maketh hire good cheere.   *jousts*
And thus in joye and blisse I lete hem dwelle,
And of the sike Aurelius wol I telle.
    In langour and in torment furious
430 Two yeer and more lay wrecche Aurelius,
Er any foot he mighte on erthe goon,
Ne confort in this time hadde he noon,
Save of his brother, which that was a clerk:
He knew of al this wo and al this werk,
435 For to noon other creature, certain,
Of this matere he dorste no word sayn.
Under his brest he bar it more secree°   *secret*
Than evere dide Pamphilus for Galathee.[7]
His brest was hool° withoute° for to seene,   *whole / outwardly*
440 But in his herte ay° was the arwe keene;   *ever*
And wel ye knowe that of a sursanure[8]
In surgerye is perilous the cure,
But° men mighte touche the arwe or come therby.   *unless*
His brother weep° and wailed prively,   *wept*
445 Til at the laste him fil in remembrance[9]
That whiles he was at Orliens° in France,   *Orleans*
As yonge clerkes that been likerous°   *desirous*
To reden artes[1] that been curious,°   *occult*
Seeken in every halke and every herne[2]
450 Particuler[3] sciences for to lerne,
He him remembred that, upon a day,
At Orliens in studye a book he sey°   *saw*
Of magik naturel,[4] which his felawe,

4. Let him choose.
5. It pleases.
6. Pays attention.
7. Pamphilus and Galataea are the lovers in the medieval Latin *Pamphilus de Amore*.
8. Superficially healed wound.

9. I.e., he happened to remember.
1. Study subjects.
2. Every nook and cranny.
3. Out of the way.
4. Natural magic employs astrological knowledge rather than spirits.

That was that time a bacheler of lawe—
455 Al were he[5] ther to lerne another craft—
     Hadde prively upon his desk ylaft:°   *left*
     Which book spak muchel of the operaciouns
     Touching the eighte and twenty mansiouns[6]
     That longen° to the moone—and swich folye   *belong*
460 As in oure dayes is nat worth a flye,
     For holy chirches faith in oure bileve°   *creed*
     Ne suffreth noon illusion us to greve.
     And whan this book was in his remembraunce,
     Anoon for joye his herte gan to daunce,
465 And to himself he saide prively,
     "My brother shal be warisshed° hastily,   *cured*
     For I am siker° that ther be sciences   *sure*
     By whiche men make diverse apparences,°   *apparitions*
     Swiche as thise subtile tregettoures° playe;   *magicians*
470 For ofte at feestes have I wel herd saye
     That tregettours withinne an halle large
     Have maad come in a water and a barge,°   *ship*
     And in the halle rowen up and down;
     Som time hath seemed come a grim leoun;
475 Som time flowres springe° as in a mede;   *grow*
     Som time a vine and grapes white and rede;
     Som time a castel al of lim° and stoon—   *lime*
     And whan hem liked voided[7] it anoon:
     Thus seemed it to every mannes sighte.
480   Now thanne conclude I thus: that if I mighte
     At Orliens som old felawe yfinde
     That hadde thise moones mansions in minde,
     Or other magik naturel above,
     He sholde wel make my brother han his love.
485 For with an apparence a clerk may make
     To mannes sighte that alle the rokkes blake
     Of Britaine were yvoided everichoon,
     And shippes by the brinke comen and goon,
     And in swich forme enduren a day or two:
490 Thanne were my brother warisshed° of his wo;   *cured*
     Thanne moste° she needes holden hir biheeste,°   *must / promise*
     Or elles he shal shame hire at the leeste."
        What sholde I make a lenger° tale of this?   *longer*
     Unto his brothers bed he comen is,
495 And swich confort he yaf him for to goon
     To Orliens, that up he sterte° anoon,   *started*
     And on his way forthward thanne is he fare,
     In hope for to been lissed° of his care.   *assuaged*
        Whan they were come almost to that citee,

5. Although he was.   7. Caused to disappear.
6. I.e., daily positions.

500	But if it were a two furlong or three,	
	A yong clerk roming by himself they mette,	
	Which that in Latin thriftily° hem grette,°	*properly / greeted*
	And after that he saide a wonder thing:	
	"I knowe," quod he, "the cause of your coming."	
505	And er they ferther any foote wente,	
	He tolde hem al that was in hir entente.	
	This Briton clerk him axed° of felawes,	*asked*
	The whiche that he hadde knowe in olde dawes,°	*days*
	And he answered him that they dede° were;	*dead*
510	For which he weep° ful ofte many a tere.	*wept*
	Down of his hors Aurelius lighte anoon,	
	And with this magicien forth is he goon	
	Hoom to his hous, and maden hem wel at ese:	
	Hem lakked no vitaile that mighte hem plese;	
515	So wel arrayed hous as ther was oon	
	Aurelius in his lif saw nevere noon.	
	He shewed him er he wente to soper°	*supper*
	Forestes, parkes ful of wilde deer:	
	Ther saw he hertes° with hir hornes hye,	*harts*
520	The gretteste° that evere were seen with yë;	*greatest*
	He sawgh of hem an hundred slain with houndes,	
	And some with arwes bledde of bittre woundes.	
	He saw, when voided[8] were thise wilde deer,	
	Thise fauconers° upon a fair river,	*falconers*
525	That with hir hawkes han the heron slain.	
	Tho sawgh he knightes justing° in a plain.	*jousting*
	And after this he dide him this plesaunce,	
	That he him shewed his lady on a daunce—	
	On which himself he daunced, as him thoughte.	
530	And whan this maister that this magik wroughte	
	Sawgh it was time, he clapte his handes two,	
	And farewel, al oure revel was ago.	
	And yit remeved° they nevere out of the hous	*moved*
	While they sawe al this sighte merveilous,	
535	But in his studye, ther as his bookes be,	
	They sitten stille, and no wight but they three.	
	To him this maister called his squier	
	And saide him thus, "Is redy oure soper?	
	Almost an houre it is, I undertake,	
540	Sith I you bad oure soper for to make,	
	Whan that thise worthy men wenten with me	
	Into my studye, ther as my bookes be."	
	"Sire," quod this squier, "whan it liketh you,	
	It is al redy, though ye wol right now."	
545	"Go we thanne soupe," quod he, "as for the beste:	
	This amorous folk som time mote° han hir reste."	*must*

8. Made to disappear.

At after-soper fille° they in tretee°   *fell / negotiation*
What somme° sholde this maistres gerdon° be *sum / reward*
To remeven° alle the rokkes of Britaine,   *remove*
550 And eek from Gerounde[9] to the mouth of Seine:
He made it straunge,[1] and swoor, so God him save,
Lasse° than a thousand pound he wolde nat have, *less*
Ne gladly for that somme he wolde nat goon.
 Aurelius with blisful herte anoon
555 Answerde thus, "Fy on a thousand pound!
This wide world, which that men saye is round,
I wolde it yive, if I were lord of it.
This bargain is ful drive, for we been knit.[2]
Ye shal be payed trewely, by my trouthe.
560 But looketh now, for no necligence or slouthe,° *sloth*
Ye tarye us heer no lenger than tomorwe."
 "Nay," quod this clerk, "have heer my faith to
  borwe."[3]
 To bedde is goon Aurelius whan him leste,° *pleased*
And wel neigh al that night he hadde his reste:
565 What for his labour and his hope of blisse,
His woful herte of penance° hadde a lisse.° *suffering / alleviation*
 Upon the morwe, whan that it was day,
To Britaine tooke they the righte° way,   *direct*
Aurelius and this magicien biside,
570 And been descended ther they wolde abide;
And this was, as thise bookes me remembre,[4]
The colde frosty seson of Decembre.
 Phebus wax° old, and hewed° lik   *grew / colored*
  latoun,°   *brass*
That in his hote declinacioun[5]
575 Shoon as the burned° gold with stremes° *burnished / beams*
  brighte;
But now in Capricorn[6] adown he lighte,
Wher as he shoon ful pale, I dar wel sayn:
The bittre frostes with the sleet and rain
Destroyed hath the greene in every yeerd.° *yard*
580 Janus[7] sit° by the fir with double beerd, *sits*
And drinketh of his bugle horn[8] the win;
Biforn him stant° brawn° of the tusked swin, *stands / flesh*
And "Nowel!" crieth every lusty man.
 Aurelius in al that evere he can
585 Dooth to this maister cheere and reverence,
And prayeth him to doon his diligence
To bringen him out of his paines smerte,
Or with a swerd that he wolde slitte his herte.[9]

---

9. The Gironde River.
1. I.e., difficulties.
2. I.e., this bargain is fully made, for we are in accord.
3. As a pledge.
4. Recall to me.

5. I.e., celestial position.
6. The House of the Goat.
7. The god with two faces who knew both past and future, perpetuated in the name "January."
8. Wild ox horn.
9. I.e., stab his own heart.

This subtil clerk swich routhe° hadde of this man   *pity*

590 That night and day he spedde him[1] that he can

To waiten a time of his conclusioun[2]—

This is to sayn, to make illusioun

By swich an apparence° or jogelrye[3]   *apparition*

(I ne can° no termes of astrologye)   *know*

595 That she and every wight sholde weene° and saye   *think*

That of Britaine the rokkes were awaye,

Or elles they were sonken° under grounde.   *sunk*

So at the laste he hath his time yfounde

To maken his japes° and his wrecchednesse[4]   *tricks*

600 Of swich a supersticious cursednesse.°   *wickedness*

His tables tolletanes[5] forth hath he brought,

Ful wel corrected; ne ther lakked nought,

Neither his collect ne his expans yeres,[6]

Ne his rootes,[7] ne his othere geres,°   *paraphernalia*

605 As been his centres and his arguments,[8]

And his proporcionels conveniens,[9]

For his equacions in every thing;

And by his eighte spere[1] in his werking°   *operation*

He knew ful wel how fer Alnath was shove[2]

610 Fro the heed of thilke fixe Aries above

That in the ninte spere considered is:[3]

Ful subtilly he calculed° al this.   *calculated*

When he hadde founde his firste mansioun,[4]

He knew the remenant by proporcioun,[5]

615 And knew the arising of his moone weel,

And in whos face and terme[6] and every deel,°   *part*

And knew ful wel the moones mansioun

Accordant[7] to his operacioun,

And knew also his othere observaunces°   *rules*

620 For swiche illusions and swiche meschaunces

As hethen folk useden in thilke° dayes;   *those*

For which no lenger maked he delayes,

But, thurgh his magik, for a wike° or twaye   *week*

It seemed that alle the rokkes were awaye.

625 Aurelius, which that yit despaired is

---

1. Hurried.
2. To watch for a time for his astrological operation.
3. Optical illusion.
4. Miserable performance.
5. Astronomical tables based on the latitude of Toledo, in Spain.
6. Neither his table of collect years nor his table of expanse years: the former recorded planetary movements for long periods such as twenty years, the latter for short periods of a year.
7. Tables for making astrological propositions concerning planetary position, degrees of influence, etc.
8. Centers and arguments are astronomical instruments for determining the positions of planets in relation to fixed stars.
9. Fitting proportionals, i.e., special tables for scaling down more general planetary motions to the most particular.
1. Sphere: i.e., the sphere of the fixed stars.
2. He knew full well how far Alnath (the star Aries) had moved.
3. From the head of that fixed star Aries which is considered to be above, in the ninth sphere.
4. I.e., the first position of the moon.
5. He knew the remnant (rest of the positions) by the use of proportion.
6. Face and term are sectors of the signs of the zodiac.
7. I.e., to be comfortable.

Wher° he shall han his love or fare amis,   *whether*
Awaiteth night and day on this miracle;
And whan he knew that there was noon obstacle,
That voided were thise rokkes everichoon,
630 Down to his maistres feet he fil° anoon,   *fell*
And saide, "I, woful wrecche Aurelius,
Thanke you, lord, and lady myn Venus,
That me han holpen° from my cares colde."   *helped*
And to the temple his way forth hath he holde,
635 Wher as he knew he sholde his lady see.
And whan he saw his time, anoon right he,
With dredful° herte and with ful humble cheere,   *fear-struck*
Salued° hath his soverein lady dere.   *greeted*
      "My righte⁸ lady," quod this woful man,
640 "Whom I most drede and love as best I can,
And lothest were of al this world displese,
Nere it⁹ that I for you have swich disese
That I moste° dien heer at youre foot anoon,   *must*
Nought wolde I telle how me is wo-bigoon.
645 But certes, outher° moste I die or plaine:°   *either / complain*
Ye sleen° me giltelees for verray paine;   *slay*
But of my deeth though that ye have no routhe,°   *pity*
Aviseth you¹ er that ye breke youre trouthe.
Repenteth you, for thilke God above,
650 Er ye me sleen° by cause that I you love.   *slay*
For Madame, wel ye woot what ye han hight°—   *promised*
Not that I chalenge any thing of right
Of you, my soverein lady, but youre grace:
But in a gardin yond at swich a place,
655 Ye woot right wel what ye bihighten° me,   *promised*
And in myn hand youre trouthe plighten ye
To love me best. God woot ye saiden so,
Al° be that I unworthy am therto.   *although*
Madame, I speke it for the honour of you
660 More than to save myn hertes lif right now.
I have do so as ye comanded me,
And if ye vouche sauf, ye may go see.
Dooth as you list, have youre biheeste° in minde,   *promise*
For quik° or deed° right ther ye shal me finde.   *living / dead*
665 In you lith° al to do° me live or deye: *lies / cause*
But wel I woot the rokkes been away."
      He taketh his leve and she astoned° stood: *astonished*
In al hir face nas a drope of blood;
She wende° nevere have come in swich a trappe.   *thought*
670 "Allas," quod she, "that evere this sholde happe!
For wende I nevere by possibilitee
That swich a monstre° or merveile mighte be;   *wonder*
It is agains the proces² of nature."

8. Own true.   1. Consider.
9. Were it not.   2. Due course.

And hoom she gooth a sorweful creature.
675 For verray fere unnethe° may she go.°   *scarcely / walk*
     She weepeth, waileth al a day or two,
     And swouneth° that it routhe° was to see.   *swoons / pity*
     But why it was to no wight tolde she,
     For out of town was goon Arveragus.
680 But to hirself she spak and saide thus,
     With face pale and with ful sorweful cheere,°   *countenance*
     In hir complainte, as ye shal after heere:
        "Allas," quod she, "on thee, Fortune, I plaine,°   *complain*
     That unwar° wrapped hast me in thy chaine,   *unawares*
685 For which t' escape woot I no socour°—   *help*
     Save only deeth or elles dishonour:
     Oon of thise two bihoveth me to chese.°   *choose*
     But nathelees yit have I levere to lese°   *lose*
     My lif, than of my body to have a shame,
690 Or knowen myselven fals or lese my name,
     And with my deeth I may be quit[3] ywis.
     Hath ther nat many a noble wif er this,
     And many a maide, yslain hirself, allas,
     Rather than with hir body doon trespas?°   *sin*
695   Yis, certes, lo, thise stories beren witnesse:
     Whan thritty tyrants ful of cursednesse°   *wickedness*
     Hadde slain Phidon[4] in Atthenes atte feeste,
     They comanded his doughtren for t'arreste,
     And bringen hem biforn hem in despit°   *scorn*
700 Al naked, to fulfille hir foule delit,
     And in hir fadres blood they made hem daunce
     Upon the pavement—God yive hem meschaunce!
     For which thise woful maidens, ful of drede,
     Rather than they wolde lese° hir maidenhede,   *lose*
705 They prively been stert[5] into a welle,
     And dreinte° hemselven, as the bookes telle.   *drowned*
       They of Messene lete enquere and seeke[6]
     Of Lacedomye° fifty maidens eke,   *Lacedaemonia*
     On whiche they wolden doon hir lecherye;
710 But ther was noon of al that compaignye
     That she nas slain, and with a good entente
     Chees° rather for to die than assente   *chose*
     To been oppressed° of hir maidenhede: *ravished*
     Why sholde I thanne to die been in drede?
715   Lo, eek, the tyrant Aristoclides
     That loved a maiden highte Stymphalides,°   *Stymphalis*
     Whan that hir fader slain was on a night,
     Unto Dianes temple gooth she aright,
     And hente° the image in hir handes two;   *seized*

---

3. Freed from dilemma.
4. The story of Phidon's daughters and the thirty
tyrants, as well as all the following stories about
virtuous women, are from St. Jerome's tract against

Jovinian.
5. Have jumped.
6. Had inquiries and searches made.

720   Fro which image wolde she nevere go:
      No wight ne mighte hir handes of it arace,°   *tear*
      Til she was slain right in the selve° place.   *same*
      Now sith° that maidens hadden swich despit°   *since / indignation*
      To been defouled with mannes foul delit,
725   Wel ought a wif rather hirselven slee°   *slay*
      Than be defouled, as it thinketh me.
         What shal I sayn of Hasdrubales wif
      That at Cartage birafte[7] hirself hir lif?
      For whan she saw that Romains wan° the town,   *won*
730   She took hir children alle and skipte adown
      Into the fir, and chees rather to die
      Than any Romain dide hire vilainye.
         Hath nat Lucrece yslain hirself, allas,
      At Rome whan that she oppressed° was   *raped*
735   Of° Tarquin, for hire thoughte it was a shame   *by*
      To liven whan that she hadde lost hir name?
         The sevene maidens of Milesie° also   *Miletus*
      Han slain hemself for verray drede and wo
      Rather than folk of Gaule hem sholde oppresse:
740   Mo° than a thousand stories, as I gesse,   *more*
      Coude I now telle as touching this matere.
         Whan Habradate° was slain, his wif so dere   *Abradates*
      Hirselven slow,° and leet hir blood to glide   *slew*
      In Habradates woundes deepe and wide,
745   And saide, 'My body at the leeste way
      Ther shal no wight defoulen, if I may.'[8]
         What sholde I mo ensamples° herof sayn?   *examples*
      Sith° that so manye han hemselven slain   *since*
      Wel rather than they wolde defouled be,
750   I wol conclude that it is bet° for me   *better*
      To sleen° myself than been defouled thus: *slay*
      I wol be trewe unto Arveragus,
      Or rather slee myself in som manere—
      As dide Demociones° doughter dere,   *Demotion's*
755   By cause that she wolde nat defouled be.
         O Cedasus,° it is ful greet pitee   *Scedasus*
      To reden how thy doughtren deide, allas,
      That slowe hemself for[9] swich manere cas.
         As greet a pitee was it, or wel moor,
760   The Theban maiden that for Nichanor°   *Nicanor*
      Hirselven slow right for swich manere wo.
      Another Theban maiden dide right so:
      For oon of Macedonie hadde hire oppressed,
      She with hir deeth hir maidenhede redressed.[1]
765   What shal I sayn of Nicerates wif

---

7. Deprived; Hasdrubal was King of Carthage when   9. I.e., for fear of.
it was destroyed by the Romans.   1. Made amends for.
8. If I can help it.

That for swich caas birafte hirself hir lif?
   How trewe eek was to Alcebiades[2]
His love, that rather for to dien chees°   *chose*
Than for to suffre his body unburied be.
770   Lo, which a wif was Alceste,"[3] quod she.
   "What saith Omer[4] of goode Penolopee?
Al Greece knoweth of hir chastitee.
   Pardee, of Laodomia[5] is writen thus,
That whan at Troye was slain Protheselaus,
775   No lenger wolde she live after his day.
   The same of noble Porcia[6] telle I may:
Withoute Brutus coude she nat live,
To whom she hadde al hool° hir herte yive.   *whole*
   The parfit wifhood of Arthemesie[7]
780   Honoured is thurgh al the Barbarye.
   O Teuta[8] queen, thy wifly chastitee
To alle wives may a mirour be!
   The same thing I saye of Biliea,
Of Rodogone and eek Valeria."[9]
785   Thus plained° Dorigen a day or twaye,   *lamented*
Purposing evere that she wolde deye.
   But nathelees upon the thridde night
Hoom cam Arveragus, this worthy knight,
And axed° hire why that she weep° so sore,   *asked / wept*
790   And she gan weepen evere lenger the more.[1]
   "Allas," quod she, "that evere I was born:
Thus have I said," quod she; "thus have I sworn—".
And tolde him al as ye han herd bifore:
It needeth nat reherce it you namore.
795   This housbonde with glad cheer° in freendly wise   *manner*
Answerde and saide as I shal you devise:
   "Is there ought elles, Dorigen, but this?"
   "Nay, nay," quod she, "God help me so as wis,° *surely*
This is too muche, and° it were Goddes wille."   *if*
800   "Ye, wif," quod he, "lat sleepen that° is stille.   *what*
It may be wel paraunter° yit today.   *perhaps*
Ye shul youre trouthe[2] holden, by my fay,°   *faith*
For God so wisly° have mercy upon me,   *surely*
I hadde wel levere ystiked° for to be,   *stabbed*

---

2. Alcibiades' mistress risked death by burying his body after he had been decapitated by the Spartan Lysander; she did not, however, lose her life as a result.
3. Alcestis, the proposed heroine of Chaucer's *Legend of Good Women*, died in her husband's place.
4. Homer relates Odysseus' return from Troy to his faithful wife Penelope.
5. Laodamia followed her dead husband Protesilaus to the underworld.
6. Portia swallowed burning coals on learning of Brutus' death at the battle of Philippi.

7. Artemesia built for her husband King Mausolus the famed tomb called the Mausoleum.
8. Teuta, Queen of Illyria, was unmarried: Dorigen seems to be stretching a point.
9. Bilia's prowess seems to have consisted in enduring her husband's bad breath in uncomplaining silence; Rhodogune slew her nurse, who suggested that she remarry; Valeria refused to marry again.
1. Always more and more.
2. Pledged word.

805 For verray love which that I to you have,
But if³ ye sholde youre trouthe keepe and save:
Trouthe is the hyeste thing⁴ that man may keepe."
But with that word he brast° anoon to weepe,   *burst*
And saide, "I you forbede, up° paine of deeth,   *upon*
810 That nevere whil thee lasteth lif ne breeth,
To no wight tel thou of this aventure.
As I may best I wol my wo endure,
Ne make no countenance° of hevinesse,   *appearance*
That folk of you may deemen° harm or gesse."   *suspect*
815   And forth he cleped° a squier and a maide: *called*
"Go forth anoon with Dorigen," he saide,
"And bringeth hire to swich a place anoon."
They tooke hir leve and on hir way they goon,
But they ne wiste° why they thider wente: *knew*
820 He nolde no wight tellen his entente.
Paraventure an heep of you, ywis,°   *indeed*
Wol holden him a lewed° man in this,   *stupid*
That he wol putte his wif in jupartye.°   *jeopardy*
Herkneth the tale er ye upon hire crye:
825 She may have better fortune than you seemeth,⁵
And whan that ye han herd the tale, deemeth.°   *judge*
This squier which that highte Aurelius,
On Dorigen that was so amorous,
Of aventure⁶ happed° hire to meete   *happened*
830 Amidde the town, right in the quikkest° streete,   *busiest*
As she was boun° to goon the way forth right°   *prepared / direct*
Toward the gardin ther as she hadde hight;°   *promised*
And he was to the gardinward also,
For wel he spied whan she wolde go
835 Out of hir hous to any manere place.
But thus they meete of aventure or grace,
And he salueth° hire with glad entente,   *greets*
And axed° of hire whiderward she wente.   *asked*
And she answerde half as she were mad,
840 "Unto the gardin as myn housbonde bad,°   *bade*
My trouthe for to holde, allas, allas!"
Aurelius gan wondren on this cas,
And in his herte hadde greet compassioun
Of hire and of hir lamentacioun,
845 And of Arveragus, the worthy knight,
That bad hire holden al that she hadde hight,
So loth him was his wif sholde breke hir trouthe;
And in his herte he caughte of this greet routhe,°   *pity*
Considering the beste on every side
850 That fro his lust° yit were him levere abide⁷   *pleasure*
Than doon so heigh a cherlissh wrecchednesse⁸

3. Unless.   6. By chance.
4. Legal bond.   7. I.e., abstain.
5. It seems.   8. I.e., low-born, miserable act.

Agains franchise° and alle gentilesse;   *generosity*
For which in fewe wordes saide he thus:
   "Madame, sayeth to youre lord Arveragus
855 That sith° I see his grete gentilesse   *since*
To you, and eek I see wel youre distresse,
That him were levere han shame—and that were
    routhe—
Than ye to me sholde breke thus youre trouthe,
I have wel levere⁹ evere to suffre wo
860 Than I departe° the love bitwixe you two.   *divide*
I you releesse, Madame, into youre hond,
Quit every serement° and every bond   *oath*
That ye han maad to me as herbiforn,
Sith° thilke time which that ye were born.   *since*
865 My trouthe I plighte, I shal you nevere repreve°   *reproach*
Of no biheeste.° And here I take my leve,   *promise*
As of the treweste and the beste wif
That evere yit I knew in al my lif.
But every wif be war of hir biheeste:
870 On Dorigen remembreth at the leeste.
Thus can a squier doon a gentil deede
As wel as can a knight, withouten drede."°   *doubt*
She thanketh him upon hir knees al bare,
And hoom unto hir housbonde is she fare,
875 And tolde him al as ye han herd me said.
And be ye siker,° he was so wel apaid°   *sure / pleased*
That it were impossible me to write.
What sholde I lenger of this caas endite?
   Arveragus and Dorigen his wif
880 In soverein blisse leden forth hir lif.
Never eft° ne was ther angre hem bitweene: *again*
He cherisseth hire as though she were a queene,
And she was to him trewe for evermore.
Of thise two folk ye gete of me namore.
885   Aurelius, that his cost hath al forlorn,°   *lost*
Curseth the time that evere he was born.
"Allas," quod he, "allas that I bihighte°   *promised*
Of pured° gold a thousand pound of wighte°   *refined / weight*
Unto this philosophre. How shall I do?
890 I see namore but that I am fordo.°   *ruined*
Myn heritage moot° I needes selle   *must*
And been a beggere. Here may I nat dwelle,
And shamen al my kinrede° in this place,   *kindred*
But° I of him may gete bettre grace.   *unless*
895 But nathelees I wol of him assaye
At certain dayes yeer by yere to paye,
And thanke him of his grete curteisye:
My trouthe wol I keepe, I nil nat lie."

9. Had much rather.

With herte soor he gooth unto his cofre,
900 And broughte gold unto this philosophre
The value of five hundred pound, I gesse,
And him biseecheth of his gentilesse
To graunten him dayes[1] of the remenaunt,°   *remainder*
And saide, "Maister, I dar wel make avaunt°   *boast*
905 I failed nevere of my trouthe as yit,
For sikerly° my dette shal be quit   *surely*
Towardes you, how evere that I fare,
To goon abegged° in my kirtel° bare.   *abegging / undergarment*
But wolde ye vouche sauf upon suretee°   *security*
910 Two yeer or three for to respiten[2] me,
Thanne were I wel, for elles moot° I selle   *must*
Myn heritage: ther is namore to telle."
      This philosophre sobrely answerde,
And saide thus, whan he thise wordes herde,
915 "Have I nat holden covenant unto thee?"
      "Yis, certes, wel and trewely," quod he.
      "Hastou nat had thy lady as thee liketh?"[3]
      "No, no," quod he and sorwefully he siketh.°   *sighs*
      "What was the cause? Tel me if thou can."
920   Aurelius his tale anoon bigan,
And tolde him al as ye han herd bifore:
It needeth nat to you reherce it more.
      He saide, "Arveragus, of gentilesse,
Hadde levere die in sorwe and in distresse
925 Than that his wif were of hir trouthe fals."
The sorwe of Dorigen he tolde him als,°   *also*
How loth hire was to been a wikked wif,
And that she levere hadde lost that day hir lif,
And that hir trouthe she swoor thurgh innocence:
930 She nevere erst° hadde herd speke of apparence.°   *before / illusion*
"That made me han of hire so greet pitee;
And right as freely° as he sente hire me,   *generously*
As freely sente I hire to him again:
This al and som,[4] ther is namore to sayn."
935   This philosophre answerde, "Leve° brother,   *dear*
Everich of you dide gentilly to other.
Thou art a squier, and he is a knight:
But God forbede, for his blisful might,
But if a clerk coude doon a gentil deede
940 As wel as any of you, it is no drede.°   *doubt*
      Sire, I releesse thee thy thousand pound,
As thou right now were cropen[5] out of the ground,
Ne nevere er° now ne haddest knowen me.   *before*
For sire, I wol nat take a peny of thee,

1. I.e., extended terms.   4. This is all there is to it.
2. Give respite.   5. Had crept.
3. It pleases.

945 For al my craft° ne nought for my travaile.°   art / labor
     Thou hast ypayed wel for my vitaile:°   food
     It is ynough. And farewel, have good day."
     And took his hors and forth he gooth his way.
         Lordinges, this question thanne wol I axe now:
950 Which was the moste free,° as thinketh you?   generous
     Now telleth me, er that ye ferther wende.
     I can namore: my tale is at an ende.

The Pardoner's Prologue and Tale[1]

The Introduction

Oure Hoste gan to swere as he were wood;°   insane
"Harrow,"° quod he, "by nailes[2] and by blood,   help

1. The Pardoner is the chief actor in a grim comedy which shows how a clever hypocrite exploits Christian principles in order to enrich himself—and which, in the Epilogue, suggests that the exploiter of Christian principles is not immune to their operation. The medieval pardoner's function was to collect money for charitable enterprises supported by branches of the church and to act as the Pope's agent in rewarding donors with some temporal remission of their sins. According to theological doctrine, St. Peter—and through him his papal successors—received from Christ the power to make a gift of mercy from God's infinite treasury to those of the faithful that had earned special favor, such as contributors to charity. The charitable enterprises themselves—generally hospitals—hired pardoners to raise money, but the pardoners had also to be licensed by the Pope to pass on to contributors the papal indulgence. By canon law pardoners were permitted to work only in a prescribed area; within that area they might visit churches during Sunday service, briefly explain their mission, receive contributions, and, in the Pope's name, issue indulgence, which was considered not a sale, but a free gift made in return for a free gift. In actual fact pardoners seem seldom to have behaved as the law required them. Since a parish priest was forbidden to exclude properly licensed pardoners, they made their way into churches at will, and once there did not confine themselves to a mere statement of their business, but rather, in order to make the congregation free of its gifts, preached highly emotive sermons and boasted of the extraordinary efficacy of their own particular pardon, claiming for it powers that not even the Pope could have invested it with. An honest pardoner, if such existed, was entitled to a percentage of his collections; dishonest pardoners took more than their share, and some took everything; indeed, some were complete frauds, bearing forged credentials which, in an age when even clerical illiteracy was common, were no less impressive than if they had been real.

While Chaucer's Pardoner belongs, as he boastfully tells us, to the most dishonest class of fund-gatherers, he is an extremely able one. His text is always the same: *Radix malorum est cupiditas*, "The love of money is the root of all evil," and he uses it most effectively in order to frighten his hearers into a generosity that will fulfill his own cupidity. The Pardoner's audacious description of his behavior in a parish church is followed by a sample sermon on his invariable text. Aware that his audience is more interested in narrative than in the moralization one expects of a sermon he first introduces the three dissolute young men of his *exemplum*, that is, of the story which is to illustrate concretely the sermon's point. Having titillated his hearers with the promise of a lurid story, he proceeds to the moralization; curiously enough, this does not concern the sin of avarice, but drunkenness, gluttony, lechery, gambling, and cursing. Yet the apparent lack of logic serves the Pardoner's deeper purpose, for these are the sins people find it exciting to hear about. When his audience has thus been emotionally prepared by a discussion of the debauchees' more flamboyant sins, the Pardoner tells his *exemplum* of the destructiveness of avarice, shutting it off at the moment of highest interest, and concluding with a demand to the congregation for money in return for his pardon.

The story of the young men who seek Death only to find him in a treasure that had made them forget him is a masterpiece of irony, and indeed the Pardoner is in all ways a master ironist. So highly developed is his own sense of irony that it enables him to feel superior not only to other men but to God, for he dares to exempt himself from the effect of his Christian text. Yet the brief Epilogue seems to show that God's irony, like His other attributes, is supreme. The one fact that the Pardoner's candid confession has concealed—that it was perhaps spoken in order to conceal—is that he is a eunuch. When in the Epilogue his proud avarice leads him to see if he can get money from the pilgrims to whom he has revealed his hypocrisy, the Pardoner's secret is revealed by the Host's coarse response, and the verbal facility by which he maintains his superiority fails him.

2. I.e., God's nails.

  This was a fals cherl and a fals justise.[3]
  As shameful deeth as herte may devise
5 Come to thise juges and hir advocats.
  Algate° this sely° maide is slain, allas!   *at any rate / innocent*
  Allas, too dere boughte she beautee!
  Wherfore I saye alday° that men may see   *always*
  The yiftes of Fortune and of Nature
10 Been cause of deeth to many a creature.
  As bothe yiftes that I speke of now,
  Men han ful ofte more for harm than prow.°   *benefit*
   "But trewely, myn owene maister dere,
  This is a pitous tale for to heere.
15 But nathelees, passe over, is no fors:[4]
  I praye to God to save thy gentil cors,°   *body*
  And eek thine urinals and thy jurdones,[5]
  Thyn ipocras[6] and eek thy galiones,
  And every boiste° ful of thy letuarye°—   *box / medicine*
20 God blesse hem, and oure lady Sainte Marye.
  So mote I theen,[7] thou art a propre man,
  And lik a prelat, by Saint Ronian![8]
  Saide I nat wel? I can nat speke in terme.[9]
  But wel I woot, thou doost° myn herte to erme°   *make / grieve*
25 That I almost have caught a cardinacle.[1]
  By corpus bones,[2] but if I have triacle,°   *medicine*
  Or elles a draughte of moiste° and corny° ale,   *fresh / malty*
  Or but I here anoon° a merye tale,   *at once*
  Myn herte is lost for pitee of this maide.
30 "Thou bel ami,[3] thou Pardoner," he saide,
  "Tel us som mirthe or japes° right anoon."   *joke*
   "It shal be doon," quod he, "by Saint Ronion.
  But first," quod he, "here at this ale-stake[4]
  I wol bothe drinke and eten of a cake."
35 And right anoon thise gentils gan to crye,
  "Nay, lat him telle us of no ribaudye.°   *ribaldry*
  Tel us som moral thing that we may lere,°   *learn*
  Som wit,[5] and thanne wol we gladly heere."
   "I graunte, ywis," quod he, "but I moot thinke
40 Upon som honeste° thing whil that I drinke."   *decent*

---

3. The Host has been affected by the Physician's sad tale of the Roman maiden Virginia, whose great beauty caused a judge to attempt to obtain her person by means of a trumped-up lawsuit in which he connived with a "churl" who claimed her as his slave; in order to preserve her chastity, her father killed her.
4. I.e., never mind.
5. Jordans (chamber pots): the Host is somewhat confused in his endeavor to use technical medical terms.
6. A medicinal drink named after Hippocrates. "Galiones": a medicine, probably invented on the

spot by the Host, named after Galen.
7. So might I thrive.
8. St. Ronan or St. Ninian, with a possible play on "runnion" (sexual organ).
9. Speak in technical idiom.
1. Apparently a cardiac condition, confused in the Host's mind with a cardinal.
2. An illiterate oath, mixing "God's bones" with *corpus dei.* "But if": unless.
3. Fair friend.
4. Sign of a tavern.
5. I.e., something with significance.

The Prologue

Lordinges—quod he—in chirches whan I preche,
I paine me[6] to han an hautein° speeche,   *loud*
And ringe it out as round as gooth a belle,
For I can al by rote[7] that I telle.
45 My theme is alway oon,[8] and evere was:
Radix malorum est cupiditas.[9]
First I pronounce whennes° that I come,   *whence*
And thanne my bulles[1] shewe I alle and some:
Oure lige lordes seel on my patente,[2]
50 That shewe I first, my body to warente,°   *keep safe*
That no man be so bold, ne preest ne clerk,
Me to destourbe of Cristes holy werk.
And after that thanne telle I forth my tales[3]—
Bulles of popes and of cardinales,
55 Of patriarkes and bisshopes I shewe,
And in Latin I speke a wordes fewe,
To saffron with[4] my predicacioun,°   *preaching*
And for to stire hem to devocioun.
Thanne shewe I forth my longe crystal stones,°   *jars*
60 Ycrammed ful of cloutes° and of bones—   *rags*
Relikes been they, as weenen° they eechoon.   *suppose*
Thanne have I in laton° a shulder-boon   *zinc*
Which that was of an holy Jewes sheep.
"Goode men," I saye, "take of my wordes keep:°   *notice*
65 If that this boon be wasshe in any welle,
If cow, or calf, or sheep, or oxe swelle,
That any worm hath ete or worm ystonge,[5]
Take water of that welle and wassh his tonge,
And it is hool[6] anoon. And ferthermoor,
70 Of pokkes° and of scabbe and every soor°   *pox / sore*
Shal every sheep be hool that of this welle
Drinketh a draughte. Take keep eek° that I telle: *also*
If that the goode man that the beestes oweth°   *owns*
Wol every wike,° er that the cok him croweth,   *week*
75 Fasting drinken of this welle a draughte—
As thilke° holy Jew oure eldres taughte—   *that same*
His beestes and his stoor° shal multiplye.   *stock*
"And sire, also it heleth jalousye:
For though a man be falle in jalous rage,
80 Lat maken with this water his potage,°   *soup*
And nevere shal he more his wif mistriste,°   *mistrust*

---

6. Take pains.
7. I know all by heart.
8. I.e., the same.
9. Avarice is the root of evil (1 Timothy 6.10).
1. Episcopal mandates. "Alle and some": each and every one.

2. I.e., the Pope's seal on my papal license.
3. I go on with my yarn.
4. To add spice to.
5. That has eaten any worm or been bitten by any snake.
6. I.e., sound.

Though he the soothe of hir defaute wiste,[7]
Al hadde she[8] taken preestes two or three.
   "Here is a mitein° eek that ye may see: *mitten*
85 He that his hand wol putte in this mitein
He shal have multiplying of his grain,
Whan he hath sowen, be it whete or otes—
So that he offre pens or elles grotes.[9]
   "Goode men and wommen, oo thing warne I you:
90 If any wight be in this chirche now
That hath doon sinne horrible, that he
Dar nat for shame of it yshriven° be,   *absolved*
Or any womman, be she yong or old,
That hath ymaked hir housbonde cokewold,°   *cuckold*
95 Swich folk shal have no power ne no grace
To offren to[1] my relikes in this place;
And whoso findeth him out of swich blame,
He wol come up and offre in Goddes name,
And I assoile° him by the auctoritee   *absolve*
100 Which that by bulle ygraunted was to me."
   By this gaude° have I wonne, yeer by yeer,   *trick*
An hundred mark[2] sith° I was pardoner.   *since*
I stonde lik a clerk in my pulpet,
And whan the lewed° peple is down yset,   *ignorant*
105 I preche so as ye han herd bifore,
And telle an hundred false japes° more.   *tricks*
Thanne paine I me[3] to strecche forth the nekke,
And eest and west upon the peple I bekke[4]
As dooth a douve,° sitting on a berne;°   *dove / barn*
110 Mine handes and my tonge goon so yerne°   *fast*
That it is joye to see my bisinesse.
Of avarice and of swich cursednesse°   *sin*
Is al my preching, for to make hem free°   *generous*
To yiven hir pens, and namely° unto me,   *especially*
115 For myn entente is nat but for to winne,[5]
And no thing for correccion of sinne:
I rekke° nevere whan that they been beried°   *care / buried*
Though that hir soules goon a-blakeberied.[6]
For certes, many a predicacioun°   *sermon*
120 Comth ofte time of yvel entencioun:
Som for plesance of folk and flaterye,
To been avaunced° by ypocrisye,   *promoted*
And som for vaine glorye, and som for hate;
For whan I dar noon otherways debate,°   *fight*
125 Thanne wol I stinge him with my tonge smerte

---

7. Knew the truth of her infidelity.   3. I take pains.
8. Even if she had.   4. I.e., I shake my head.
9. Pennies, groats, coins.   5. Only to gain.
1. To make gifts in reverence of.   6. Go blackberrying, i.e., go to hell.
2. Marks (pecuniary units).

In preching, so that he shal nat asterte°   *escape*
To been defamed falsly, if that he
Hath trespassed to my bretheren[7] or to me.
For though I telle nought his propre name,
130 Men shal wel knowe that it is the same
By signes and by othere circumstaunces.
Thus quite° I folk that doon us displesaunces;[8]   *pay back*
Thus spete° I out my venim under hewe°—   *spit / color*
Of holinesse, to seeme holy and trewe.
135 But shortly myn entente I wol devise:°   *describe*
I preche of no thing but for coveitise;
Therfore my theme is yit and evere was
Radix malorum est cupiditas.
       Thus can I preche again that same vice
140 Which that I use, and that is avarice.
But though myself be gilty in that sinne,
Yit can I make other folk to twinne°   *separate*
From avarice, and sore to repente—
But that is nat my principal entente:
145 I preche no thing but for coveitise.
Of this matere it oughte ynough suffise.
       Thanne telle I hem ensamples[9] many oon
Of olde stories longe time agoon,
For lewed° peple loven tales olde—   *ignorant*
150 Swiche thinges can they wel reporte and holde.[1]
What, trowe° ye that whiles I may preche,   *believe*
And winne gold and silver for° I teche,   *because*
That I wol live in poverte wilfully?
Nay, nay, I thoughte° it nevere, trewely,   *intended*
155 For I wol preche and begge in sondry landes;
I wol nat do no labour with mine handes,
Ne make baskettes and live therby,
By cause I wol nat beggen idelly.[2]
I wol none of the Apostles countrefete:°   *imitate*
160 I wol have moneye, wolle,° cheese, and whete,   *wool*
Al were it[3] yiven of the pooreste page,
Or of the pooreste widwe in a village—
Al sholde hir children sterve[4] for famine.
Nay, I wol drinke licour of the vine
165 And have a joly wenche in every town.
But herkneth, lordinges, in conclusioun,
Youre liking° is that I shal telle a tale: *pleasure*
Now have I dronke a draughte of corny ale,
By God, I hope I shal you telle a thing
170 That shal by reson been at youre liking;

---

7. Injured my fellow-pardoners.
8. Do us discourtesies.
9. *Exempla* (stories illustrating moral principles).
1. Repeat and remember.

2. I.e., without profit.
3. Even though it were.
4. Even though her children should die.

For though myself be a ful vicious man,
A moral tale yit I you telle can,
Which I am wont to preche for to winne.
Now holde youre pees, my tale I wol biginne.

The Tale

175 In Flandres whilom° was a compaignye   *once*
 Of yonge folk that haunteden° folye—   *practiced*
 As riot, hasard, stewes,[5] and tavernes,
 Wher as with harpes, lutes, and giternes°   *guitars*
 They daunce and playen at dees° bothe day and night, *dice*
180 And ete also and drinke over hir might,[6]
 Thurgh which they doon the devel sacrifise
 Within that develes temple in cursed wise
 By superfluitee° abhominable.   *overindulgence*
 Hir othes been so grete and so dampnable
185 That it is grisly for to heere hem swere:
 Oure blessed Lordes body they totere[7]—
 Hem thoughte that Jewes rente° him nought ynough. *tore*
 And eech of hem at otheres sinne lough.°   *laughed*
 And right anoon thanne comen tombesteres,° *dancing girls*
190 Fetis° and smale,° and yonge frutesteres,[8] *shapely / neat*
 Singeres with harpes, bawdes,° wafereres[9]— *pimps*
 Whiche been the verray develes officeres,
 To kindle and blowe the fir of lecherye
 That is annexed unto glotonye:[1]
195 The Holy Writ take I to my witnesse
 That luxure° is in win and dronkenesse.   *lechery*
 Lo, how that dronken Lot[2] unkindely°   *unnaturally*
 Lay by his doughtres two unwitingly:
 So dronke he was he niste° what he wroughte. *didn't know*
200 Herodes, who so wel the stories soughte,[3]
 Whan he of win was repleet at his feeste,
 Right at his owene table he yaf his heeste° *command*
 To sleen° the Baptist John, ful giltelees.   *slay*
 Senek[4] saith a good word douteless:
205 He saith he can no difference finde
 Bitwixe a man that is out of his minde
 And a man which that is dronkelewe,°   *drunken*
 But that woodnesse, yfallen in a shrewe,[5]
 Persevereth lenger than dooth dronkenesse.
210 O glotonye, ful of cursednesse!°   *wickedness*

---

5. Wild parties, gambling, brothels.
6. Beyond their capacity.
7. Tear apart (a reference to oaths sworn by parts of His body, such as "God's bones!" or "God's teeth!").
8. Fruit-selling girls.
9. Girl cake-vendors.

1. I.e., closely related to gluttony.
2. For Lot, see Genesis 19.30–36.
3. For the story of Herod and St. John the Baptist, see Mark 6.17–29. "Who so . . . soughte": i.e., whoever looked it up in the Gospel would find.
4. Seneca, the Roman Stoic philosopher.
5. But that madness, occurring in a wicked man.

O cause first of oure confusioun!°   downfall
O original of oure dampnacioun,°   damnation
Til Crist hadde bought° us with his blood again!   redeemed
Lo, how dere, shortly for to sayn,
215 Abought° was thilke° cursed vilainye;   paid for / that same
Corrupt was al this world for glotonye:
Adam oure fader and his wif also
Fro Paradis to labour and to wo
Were driven for that vice, it is no drede.°   doubt
220 For whil that Adam fasted, as I rede,
He was in Paradis; and whan that he
Eet° of the fruit defended° on a tree,   ate / forbidden
Anoon he was out cast to wo and paine.
O glotonye, on thee wel oughte us plaine!°   complain
225   O, wiste a man[6] how manye maladies
Folwen of excesse and of glotonies,
He wolde been the more mesurable°   moderate
Of his diete, sitting at his table.
Allas, the shorte throte, the tendre mouth,
230 Maketh that eest and west and north and south,
In erthe, in air, in water, men to swinke,°   work
To gete a gloton daintee mete and drinke.
Of this matere, O Paul, wel canstou trete:
"Mete unto wombe,° and wombe eek unto mete,   belly
235 Shal God destroyen bothe," as Paulus saith.[7]
Allas, a foul thing is it, by my faith,
To saye this word, and fouler is the deede
Whan man so drinketh of the white and rede[8]
That of his throte he maketh his privee°   privy
240 Thurgh thilke cursed superfluitee.°   overindulgence
    The Apostle[9] weeping saith ful pitously,
"Ther walken manye of which you told have I—
I saye it now weeping with pitous vois—
They been enemies of Cristes crois,°   cross
245 Of whiche the ende is deeth—wombe is hir god!"[1]
O wombe, O bely, O stinking cod,°   bag
Fulfilled° of dong° and of corrupcioun!   filled full / dung
At either ende of thee foul is the soun.°   sound
How greet labour and cost is thee to finde!°   provide for
250 Thise cookes, how they stampe[2] and straine and grinde,
And turnen substance into accident[3]
To fulfillen al thy likerous° talent!°   dainty / appetite
Out of the harde bones knokke they
The mary,° for they caste nought away   marrow

6. If a man knew.
7. See 1 Corinthians 6.13.
8. I.e., white and red wines.
9. I.e., St. Paul.
1. See Philippians 3.18.

2. Pound.
3. A philosophic joke, depending on the distinction between inner reality (substance) and outward appearance (accident).

255 That may go thurgh the golet[4] softe and soote.°   *sweetly*
    Of spicerye° of leef and bark and roote   *spices*
    Shal been his sauce ymaked by delit,
    To make him yit a newer appetit.
    But certes, he that haunteth swiche delices°   *pleasures*
260 Is deed° whil that he liveth in tho° vices.   *dead / those*
        A lecherous thing is win, and dronkenesse
    Is ful of striving° and of wrecchednesse.   *quarreling*
    O dronke man, disfigured is thy face!
    Sour is thy breeth, foul artou to embrace!
265 And thurgh thy dronke nose seemeth the soun
    As though thou saidest ay,° "Sampsoun, Sampsoun."   *always*
    And yit, God woot,° Sampson drank nevere win.[5]   *knows*
    Thou fallest as it were a stiked swin;[6]
    Thy tonge is lost, and al thyn honeste cure,
270 For dronkenesse is verray sepulture°   *burial*
    Of mannes wit° and his discrecioun.   *intelligence*
    In whom that drinke hath dominacioun
    He can no conseil° keepe, it is no drede.°   *secrets / doubt*
    Now keepe you fro the white and fro the rede—
275 And namely° fro the white win of Lepe[7]   *particularly*
    That is to selle in Fisshstreete or in Chepe:[8]
    The win of Spaine creepeth subtilly
    In othere wines growing faste° by,   *close*
    Of which ther riseth swich fumositee°   *heady fumes*
280 That whan a man hath dronken draughtes three
    And weeneth° that he be at hoom in Chepe,   *supposes*
    He is in Spaine, right at the town of Lepe,
    Nat at The Rochele ne at Burdeux town;[9]
    And thanne wol he sayn, "Sampsoun, Sampsoun."
285   But herkneth, lordinges, oo° word I you praye,   *one*
    That alle the soverein actes,[1] dar I saye,
    Of victories in the Olde Testament,
    Thurgh verray God that is omnipotent,
    Were doon in abstinence and in prayere:
290 Looketh° the Bible and ther ye may it lere.°   *behold / learn*
        Looke Attila, the grete conquerour,[2]
    Deide° in his sleep with shame and dishonour,   *died*
    Bleeding at his nose in dronkenesse:
    A capitain sholde live in sobrenesse.
295   And overal this, aviseth you[3] right wel
    What was comanded unto Lamuel[4]—

---

4. Through the gullet.
5. Before Samson's birth an angel told his mother
that he would be a Nazarite throughout his life;
members of this sect took no strong drink.
6. Stuck pig. "Honeste cure": care for self-respect.
7. A town in Spain.
8. Fishstreet and Cheapside in the London market district.
9. The Pardoner is joking about the illegal custom

of adulterating fine wines of Bordeaux and La
Rochelle with strong Spanish wine.
1. Distinguished deeds.
2. Attila was the leader of the Huns who captured
Rome in the 5th century.
3. Consider.
4. Lemuel's mother told him that kings should not
drink (Proverbs 31.4–5).

Nat Samuel, but Lamuel, saye I—
Redeth the Bible and finde it expresly,
Of win-yiving° to hem that han⁵ justise: *wine-serving*
300 Namore of this, for it may wel suffise.
 And now that I have spoken of glotonye,
Now wol I you defende° hasardrye:°   *prohibit / gambling*
Hasard is verray moder° of lesinges,°   *mother / lies*
And of deceite and cursed forsweringes,
305 Blaspheme of Crist, manslaughtre, and wast° also   *waste*
Of catel° and of time; and ferthermo,   *property*
It is repreve° and contrarye of honour   *disgrace*
For to been holden a commune hasardour,°   *gambler*
And evere the hyer he is of estat
310 The more is he holden desolat.⁶
If that a prince useth hasardrye,
In alle governance and policye
He is, as by commune opinioun,
Yholde the lasse° in reputacioun.   *less*
315 Stilbon, that was a wis embassadour,
Was sent to Corinthe in ful greet honour
Fro Lacedomye° to make hir alliaunce,   *Sparta*
And whan he cam him happede° parchaunce   *it happened*
That alle the gretteste° that were of that lond   *greatest*
320 Playing at the hasard he hem foond,°   *found*
For which as soone as it mighte be
He stal him⁷ hoom again to his contree,
And saide, "Ther wol I nat lese° my name,   *lose*
N'I wol nat take on me so greet defame°   *dishonor*
325 You to allye unto none hasardours:
Sendeth othere wise embassadours,
For by my trouthe, me were levere⁸ die
Than I you sholde to hasardours allye.
For ye that been so glorious in honours
330 Shal nat allye you with hasardours
As by my wil, ne as by my tretee."°   *treaty*
This wise philosophre, thus saide he.
 Looke eek that to the king Demetrius
The King of Parthes,° as the book⁹ saith us,   *Parthians*
335 Sente him a paire of dees° of gold in scorn,   *dice*
For he hadde used hasard therbiforn,
For which he heeld his glorye or his renown
At no value or reputacioun.
Lordes may finden other manere play
340 Honeste° ynough to drive the day away.   *honorable*
 Now wol I speke of othes false and grete

---

5. I.e., administer.
6. I.e., dissolute.
7. He stole away.
8. I had rather.

9. The book that relates this and the previous incident is the *Policraticus* of the 12th-century Latin writer, John of Salisbury.

A word or two, as olde bookes trete:
   Greet swering is a thing abhominable,
And fals swering is yit more reprevable.°   *reprehensible*
345 The hye God forbad swering at al—
Witnesse on Mathew.[1] But in special
Of swering saith the holy Jeremie,[2]
"Thou shalt swere sooth thine othes and nat lie,
And swere in doom[3] and eek in rightwisnesse,
350 But idel swering is a cursednesse."°   *wickedness*
   Biholde and see that in the firste Table[4]
Of hye Goddes heestes° honorable   *commandments*
How that the seconde heeste of him is this:
"Take nat my name in idel or amis."
355 Lo, rather° he forbedeth swich swering   *sooner*
Than homicide, or many a cursed thing.
I saye that as by ordre thus it stondeth—
This knoweth that[5] his heestes understondeth
How that the seconde heeste of God is that.
360 And fertherover,° I wol thee telle al plat°   *moreover / flat*
That vengeance shal nat parten° from his hous   *depart*
That of his othes is too outrageous.
"By Goddes precious herte!" and "By his nailes!"°   *fingernails*
And "By the blood of Crist that is in Hailes,[6]
365 Sevene is my chaunce, and thyn is cink and traye!"[7]
"By Goddes armes, if thou falsly playe
This daggere shal thurghout thyn herte go!"
This fruit cometh of the bicche bones[8] two—
Forswering, ire, falsnesse, homicide.
370 Now for the love of Crist that for us dyde,
Lete° youre othes bothe grete and smale.   *leave*
But sires, now wol I telle forth my tale.
   Thise riotoures° three of whiche I telle,   *revelers*
Longe erst er prime[9] ronge of any belle,
375 Were set hem in a taverne to drinke,
And as they sat they herde a belle clinke
Biforn a cors° was caried to his grave.   *corpse*
That oon of hem gan callen to his knave:°   *servant*
Go bet,"[1] quod he, "and axe° redily°   *ask / promptly*
380 What cors is this that passeth heer forby,
And looke° that thou reporte his name weel."°   *be sure / well*
   "Sire," quod this boy, "it needeth neveradeel:[2]
It was me told er ye cam heer two houres.
He was, pardee, an old felawe of youres,

---

1. "But I say unto you, Swear not at all" (Matthew 5.34).
2. Jeremiah 4.2.
3. Equity. "Rightwisnesse": righteousness.
4. I.e., the first 4 of the Ten Commandments.
5. I.e., he that.
6. An abbey in Gloucestershire supposed to possess some of Christ's blood.
7. Five and three.
8. I.e., damned dice.
9. Long before 9 A.M.
1. Better, i.e., quick.
2. It isn't a bit necessary.

385 And sodeinly he was yslain tonight,°   *last night*
     Fordronke° as he sat on his bench upright;   *very drunk*
     Ther cam a privee° thief men clepeth° Deeth,   *stealthy / call*
     That in this contree al the peple sleeth,°   *slays*
     And with his spere he smoot his herte atwo,
390 And wente his way withouten wordes mo.
     He hath a thousand slain this° pestilence.   *during this*
     And maister, er ye come in his presence,
     Me thinketh that it were necessarye
     For to be war of swich an adversarye;
395 Beeth redy for to meete him everemore:
     Thus taughte me my dame.° I saye namore."   *mother*
          "By Sainte Marye," saide this taverner,
     "The child saith sooth, for he hath slain this yeer,
     Henne° over a mile, within a greet village,   *hence*
400 Bothe man and womman, child and hine[3] and page.
     I trowe° his habitacion be there.   *believe*
     To been avised° greet wisdom it were   *wary*
     Er that he dide a man a dishonour."
          "Ye, Goddes armes," quod this riotour,
405 "Is it swich peril with him for to meete?
     I shal him seeke by way and eek by streete,[4]
     I make avow to Goddes digne° bones.   *worthy*
     Herkneth, felawes, we three been alle ones:°   *of one mind*
     Lat eech of us holde up his hand to other
410 And eech of us bicome otheres brother,
     And we wol sleen this false traitour Deeth.
     He shal be slain, he that so manye sleeth,
     By Goddes dignitee, er it be night."
          Togidres han thise three hir trouthes plight[5]
415 To live and dien eech of hem with other,
     As though he were his owene ybore° brother.   *born*
     And up they sterte,° al dronken in this rage,   *started*
     And forth they goon towardes that village
     Of which the taverner hadde spoke biforn,.
420 And many a grisly ooth thanne han they sworn,
     And Cristes blessed body they torente:°   *tore apart*
     Deeth shal be deed° if that they may him hente.°   *dead / catch*
          Whan they han goon nat fully half a mile,
     Right as they wolde han treden° over a stile,   *stepped*
425 An old man and a poore with hem mette;
     This olde man ful mekely hem grette,°   *greeted*
     And saide thus, "Now lordes, God you see."[6]
          The pruddeste° of thise riotoures three   *proudest*
     Answerde again, "What, carl° with sory grace,   *churl*
430 Why artou al forwrapped save thy face?

---

3. Farm laborer.   5. Pledged their words of honor.
4. By highway and byway.   6. May God protect you.

Why livestou so longe in so greet age?"
   This olde man gan looke in his visage,
And saide thus, "For° I ne can nat finde   *because*
A man, though that I walked into Inde,
435 Neither in citee ne in no village,
That wolde chaunge his youthe for myn age;
And therefore moot I han myn age stille,
As longe time as it is Goddes wille.
   "Ne Deeth, allas, ne wol nat have my lif.
440 Thus walke I lik a restelees caitif,°   *captive*
And on the ground which is my modres° gate   *mother's*
I knokke with my staf bothe erly and late,
And saye, 'Leve° moder, leet me in: *dear*
Lo, how I vanisshe, flessh and blood and skin.
445 Allas, whan shal my bones been at reste?
Moder, with you wolde I chaunge° my cheste[7]   *exchange*
That in my chambre longe time hath be,
Ye, for an haire-clout[8] to wrappe me.'
But yit to me she wol nat do that grace,
450 For which ful pale and welked° is my face.   *withered*
But sires, to you it is no curteisye
To speken to an old man vilainye,°   *rudeness*
But° he trespasse° in word or elles in deede.   *unless / offend*
In Holy Writ ye may yourself wel rede,
455 'Agains[9] an old man, hoor° upon his heed,   *hoar*
Ye shall arise.'[1] Wherfore I yive you reed,°   *advice*
Ne dooth unto an old man noon harm now,
Namore than that ye wolde men dide to you
In age, if that ye so longe abide.
460 And God be with you wher ye go° or ride: *walk*
I moot go thider as I have to go."
   "Nay, olde cherl, by God thou shalt nat so,"
Saide this other hasardour anoon.
"Thou partest nat so lightly,° by Saint John!   *easily*
465 Thou speke° right now of thilke traitour Deeth,   *spoke*
That in this contree alle oure freendes sleeth:
Have here my trouthe, as thou art his espye,°   *spy*
Tel wher he is, or thou shalt it abye,°   *pay for*
By God and by the holy sacrament!
470 For soothly thou art oon of his assent[2]
To sleen us yonge folk, thou false thief."
   "Now sires," quod he, "if that ye be so lief°   *anxious*
To finde Deeth, turne up this crooked way,
For in that grove I lafte° him, by my fay,°   *left / faith*
475 Under a tree, and ther he wol abide:
Nat for youre boost° he wol him no thing hide.   *boast*

---

7. Chest for one's belongings, used here as the symbol for life—or perhaps a coffin.
8. Haircloth, for a winding sheet.
9. In the presence of.
1. Cf. Leviticus 19.32.
2. I.e., one of his party.

See ye that ook?° Right ther ye shal him finde.   oak
God save you, that boughte again[3] mankinde,
And you amende." Thus saide this olde man.
480   And everich of thise riotoures ran
Til he cam to that tree, and ther they founde
Of florins° fine of gold ycoined rounde   coins
Wel neigh an eighte busshels as hem thoughte—
Ne lenger thanne after Deeth they soughte,
485   But eech of hem so glad was of the sighte,
For that the florins been so faire and brighte,
That down they sette hem by this precious hoord.
The worste of hem he spak the firste word:
      "Bretheren," quod he, "take keep° what that I saye: heed
490   My wit is greet though that I bourde° and playe.   joke
This tresor hath Fortune unto us yiven
In mirthe and jolitee oure lif to liven,
And lightly° as it cometh so wol we spende.   easily
Ey, Goddes precious dignitee, who wende[4]
495   Today that we sholde han so fair a grace?
But mighte this gold be caried fro this place
Hoom to myn hous—or elles unto youres—
For wel ye woot that al this gold is oures—
Thanne were we in heigh felicitee.
500   But trewely, by daye it mighte nat be:
Men wolde sayn that we were theves stronge,°   flagrant
And for oure owene tresor doon us honge.[5]
This tresor moste ycaried be by nighte,
As wisely and as slyly as it mighte.
505   Therefore I rede° that cut° amonges us alle   advise / lots
Be drawe, and lat see wher the cut wol falle;
And he that hath the cut with herte blithe
Shal renne° to the town, and that ful swithe,°   run / quickly
And bringe us breed and win ful prively;
510   And two of us shal keepen° subtilly   guard
This tresor wel, and if he wol nat tarye,
Whan it is night we wol this tresor carye
By oon assent wher as us thinketh best."
That oon of hem the cut broughte in his fest°   fist
515   And bad hem drawe and looke wher it wol falle;
And it fil° on the yongeste of hem alle,   fell
And forth toward the town he wente anoon.
And also° soone as that he was agoon,°   as / gone away
That oon of hem spak thus unto that other:
520   "Thou knowest wel thou art my sworen brother;
Thy profit wol I telle thee anoon:
Thou woost wel that oure felawe is agoon,

3. Redeemed.   5. Have us hanged.
4. Who would have supposed.

And here is gold, and that ful greet plentee,
That shall departed° been among us three.   *divided*
525 But nathelees, if I can shape° it so   *arrange*
That it departed were among us two,
Hadde I nat doon a freendes turn to thee?"
    That other answerde, "I noot[6] how that may be:
He woot that the gold is with us twaye.
530 What shal we doon? What shal we to him saye?"
    "Shal it be conseil?"[7] saide the firste shrewe.°   *villain*
"And I shal telle in a wordes fewe
What we shul doon, and bringe it wel aboute."
    "I graunte," quod that other, "out of doute,
535 That by my trouthe I wol thee nat biwraye."°   *expose*
    "Now," quod the firste, "thou woost wel we be twaye,
And two of us shal strenger° be than oon: *stronger*
Looke whan that he is set that right anoon
Aris as though thou woldest with him playe,
540 And I shal rive° him thurgh the sides twaye,   *pierce*
Whil that thou strugelest with him as in game,
And with thy daggere looke thou do the same;
And thanne shal al this gold departed be,
My dere freend, bitwixe thee and me.
545 Thanne we may bothe oure lustes° al fulfille,   *desires*
And playe at dees° right at oure owene wille."   *dice*
And thus accorded been thise shrewes twaye
To sleen the thridde, as ye han herd me saye.
    This yongeste, which that wente to the town,
550 Ful ofte in herte he rolleth up and down
The beautee of thise florins newe and brighte.
"O Lord," quod he, "if so were that I mighte
Have al this tresor to myself allone,
Ther is no man that liveth under the trone°   *throne*
555 Of God that sholde live so merye as I."
And at the laste the feend oure enemy
Putte in his thought that he sholde poison beye,°   *buy*
With which he mighte sleen his felawes twaye—
Forwhy° the feend foond him in swich livinge   *because*
560 That he hadde leve° him to sorwe bringe:[8]   *permission*
For this was outrely° his fulle entente,   *plainly*
To sleen hem bothe, and nevere to repente.
    And forth he gooth—no lenger wolde he tarye—
Into the town unto a pothecarye,°   *apothecary*
565 And prayed him that he him wolde selle
Som poison that he mighte his rattes quelle,°   *kill*
And eek ther was a polcat[9] in his hawe°   *yard*
That, as he saide, his capons hadde yslawe,°   *slain*
And fain he wolde wreke him[1] if he mighte

6. Don't know.
7. A secret.
8. Christian doctrine teaches that the devil may

not tempt men except with God's permission.
9. A weasellike animal.
1. He would gladly avenge himself.

570 On vermin that destroyed him[2] by nighte.
    The pothecarye answerde, "And thou shalt have
A thing that, also° God my soule save,   *as*
In al this world there is no creature
That ete or dronke hath of this confiture°—   *mixture*
575 Nat but the mountance° of a corn° of whete— *amount / grain*
That he ne shal his lif anoon forlete.°   *lose*
Ye, sterve° he shal, and that in lasse° while   *die / less*
Than thou wolt goon a paas[3] nat but a mile,
The poison is so strong and violent."
580 This cursed man hath in his hand yhent°   *taken*
This poison in a box and sith° he ran   *then*
Into the nexte streete unto a man
And borwed of him large botels three,
And in the two his poison poured he—
585 The thridde he kepte clene for his drinke,
For al the night he shoop him[4] for to swinke° *work*
In carying of the gold out of that place.
And whan this riotour with sory grace
Hadde filled with win his grete botels three,
590 To his felawes again repaireth he.
    What needeth it to sermone of it more?
For right as they had cast° his deeth bifore, *plotted*
Right so they han him slain, and that anoon.
And whan that this was doon, thus spak that oon:
595 "Now lat us sitte and drinke and make us merye,
And afterward we wol his body berye."°   *bury*
And with that word it happed him par cas[5]
To take the botel ther the poison was,
And drank, and yaf his felawe drinke also,
600 For which anoon they storven° bothe two.   *died*
    But certes I suppose that Avicen
Wroot nevere in no canon ne in no *fen*[6]
Mo wonder signes[7] of empoisoning
Than hadde thise wrecches two er hir ending:
605 Thus ended been thise homicides two,
And eek the false empoisonere also.
    O cursed sinne of alle cursednesse!
O traitours homicide, O wikkednesse!
O glotonye, luxure,° and hasardrye!   *lechery*
610 Thou blasphemour of Crist with vilainye
And othes grete of usage° and of pride!   *habit*
Allas, mankinde, how may it bitide
That to thy Creatour which that thee wroughte,
And with his precious herte blood thee boughte,° *redeemed*
615 Thou art so fals and so unkinde,° allas?   *unnatural*

---

2. I.e., were ruining his farming.
3. Take a walk.
4. He was preparing.
5. By chance.

6. The *Canon of Medicine*, by Avicenna, an 11th-century Arabic philosopher, was divided into sections called "fens."
7. More wonderful symptoms.

Now goode men, God foryive you youre trespas,
And ware° you fro the sinne of avarice: *guard*
Myn holy pardon may you alle warice°—   *save*
So that ye offre nobles or sterlinges,[8]
620   Or elles silver brooches, spoones, ringes.
Boweth your heed under this holy bulle!
Cometh up, ye wives, offreth of youre wolle!°   *wool*
Youre name I entre here in my rolle: anoon
Into the blisse of hevene shul ye goon.
625   I you assoile° by myn heigh power—   *absolve*
Ye that wol offre—as clene and eek as cleer
As ye were born.—And lo, sires, thus I preche.
And Jesu Crist that is oure soules leeche°   *physician*
So graunte you his pardon to receive,
630   For that is best—I wol you nat deceive.

The Epilogue

"But sires, oo word forgat I in my tale:
I have relikes and pardon in my male°   *bag*
As faire as any man in Engelond,
Whiche were me yiven by the Popes hond.
635   If any of you wol of devocioun
Offren and han myn absolucioun,
Come forth anoon, and kneeleth here adown,
And mekely receiveth my pardoun,
Or elles taketh pardon as ye wende,
640   Al newe and fressh at every miles ende—
So that ye offre alway newe and newe[9]
Nobles or pens whiche that be goode and trewe.
It is an honour to everich that is heer
That ye have a suffisant° pardoner   *competent*
645   T'assoile you in contrees as ye ride,
For aventures whiche that may bitide:
Paraventure ther may falle oon or two
Down of his hors and breke his nekke atwo;
Looke which a suretee° is it to you alle   *safeguard*
650   That I am in youre felaweshipe yfalle
That may assoile you, bothe more and lasse,[1]
Whan that the soule shal fro the body passe.
I rede° that oure Hoste shal biginne,   *advise*
For he is most envoluped° in sinne.   *involved*
655   Com forth, sire Host, and offre first anoon,
And thou shalt kisse the relikes everichoon,°   *each one*
Ye, for a grote: unbokele° anoon thy purs."   *unbuckle*
     "Nay, nay," quod he, "thanne have I Cristes curs!
Lat be," quod he, "it shal nat be, so theech!°   *may I thrive*
660   Thou woldest make me kisse thyn olde breech°   *breeches*

8. "Nobles" and "sterlinges" were valuable coins.   1. Both high and low (i.e., everybody).
9. Over and over.

And swere it were a relik of a saint,
Though it were with thy fundament depeint.°   *stained*
But, by the crois which that Sainte Elaine foond,[2]
I wolde I hadde thy coilons° in myn hond,   *testicles*
665   In stede of relikes or of saintuarye.°   *relic-box*
Lat cutte hem of: I wol thee helpe hem carye.
They shal be shrined in an hogges tord."°   *turd*
      This Pardoner answerde nat a word:
So wroth he was no word ne wolde he saye.
670   "Now," quod oure Host, "I wol no lenger playe
With thee, ne with noon other angry man."
      But right anoon the worthy Knight bigan,
Whan that he sawgh that al the peple lough,°   *laughed*
"Namore of this, for it is right ynough.
675   Sire Pardoner, be glad and merye of cheere,
And ye, sire Host that been to me so dere,
I praye you that ye kisse the Pardoner,
And Pardoner, I praye thee, draw thee neer,
And as we diden lat us laughe and playe."
680   Anoon they kiste and riden forth hir waye.

The Tale of Sir Thopas[1]

The Introduction

Whan said was al this miracle,[2] every man
As sobre was that wonder was to see,

2. I.e., by the cross that St. Helena found. Helena, mother of Constantine the Great, was reputed to have found the True Cross.

1. The Tale of Sir Thopas is a burlesque of popular romances. These were stripped-down, cliché-ridden versions of French chivalric romances, composed and recited by minstrels for unsophisticated English audiences with little or no French and no taste for the stylistic refinements and psychological subtleties that appealed to more courtly audiences in both France and England. The emphasis was on plenty of action—love and adventure; the slaying of giants, dragons, and wicked knights; the rescue of fair maidens. Chaucer doubtless enjoyed such medieval horse operas for their very absurdities, and his satire shows a connoisseur's eye for hackneyed and inane detail. His hero Sir Thopas, in ancestry, personal appearance, costume, sports, love-longing, horsemanship, oaths, and encounter with a three-headed giant, lampoons such popular derring-do heroes as Bevis of Hampton and Guy of Warwick. Sir Thopas's birthplace in Flanders would mark him to the English as ultra-bourgeois; his exaggeratedly white complexion and rosy lips link him to the heroines of the romances.

Chaucer burlesques not only the plot but also the style of such performances. Oral delivery demanded first of all a dogtrot rhythm, and, secondly, a handy store of formulas to fit all occasions,

especially those occasions when the poet was stuck for a rhyme. Chaucer's imitation is an exercise in brilliant monotony and witty banality.

But within the frame story of the *Canterbury Tales*, Chaucer's parody turns into a truly Olympian jest about the nature of art and artists. The Introduction to the tale brings onstage again the narrator who described his fellow pilgrims with such wide-eyed enthusiasm in the General Prologue and apologized for the fact that a strict adherence to truth obliged him to relate every word spoken on the pilgrimage, no matter how vulgar and offensive. Here the Host draws a portrait of this pilgrim, inviting him to tell a tale, and the pilgrim apologizes once again—the only story he knows is a rhyme he learned long ago. Thus on the literal level of the frame story the creator of the entire pilgrimage knows only one tale, and that one so wretched that he is not allowed to finish it. The supreme irony of the Tale of Sir Thopas may be the author's humble acknowledgment, within the frame of his fiction, that he, too, is a member of the tribe of versifiers who strove according to their greatly varying talents to provide the best rhymes and entertainment that they could.

2. The Prioress has just completed a moving tale of a child martyr. The verse form of the Introduction, the only link between tales not in couplets, is the rhyme royal stanza of the Prioress's Tale and other religious stories in the *Canterbury Tales*.

Til that oure Hoste japen° he bigan,   *joke*
And thanne at erst° he looked upon me,   *for the first time*
5   And saide thus, "What man artou?"° quod he.   *art thou*
"Thou lookest as thou woldest finde an hare,
For evere upon the ground I see thee stare.

Approche neer and looke up merily.
Now ware you, sires, and lat this man have place:
10 He in the wast is shape as wel as I—
This were a popet° in an arm t' enbrace,   *doll*
For any womman, smal and fair of face;
He seemeth elvissh° by his countenaunce,   *elfin*
For unto no wight dooth he daliaunce.°   *makes conversation*

15 Say now somwhat, sin° other folk han said.   *since*
Tel us a tale of mirthe, and that anoon."
"Hoste," quod I, "ne beeth nat yvele apaid,³
For other tale, certes, can° I noon,   *know*
But of a rym I lerned longe agoon."
20 "Ye, that is good," quod he. "Now shul we heere
Som daintee° thing, me thinketh by his   *delightful*
        cheere."°   *face*

The Tale

Listeth,° lordes, in good entent,   *listen*
And I wil telle verrayment°   *truly*
        Of mirthe and of solas:°   *delight*
25 Al of a knight was fair and gent°   *noble, pretty*
In bataile and in tournament—
        His name was Sir Thopas.

Yborn he was in fer° contree,   *far*
In Flandres al biyonde the see—
30   At Popering in the place.⁴
His fader was a man ful free,°   *noble*
And lord he was of that contree,
        As it was Goddes grace.

Sir Thopas wax° a doughty swain:°   *grew into / youth*
35 Whit was his face as paindemain,°   *fine white bread*
        His lippes rede as rose;
His rode° is lik scarlet in grain,°   *complexion / deep-dyed*
And I you telle in good certain⁵
        He hadde a semely nose.

---

3. Ill-pleased.
4. Poperinghe, a Flemish town. "In the place":
formula used for the sake of rhyme.

5. For sure. Another example of line-filling formulas to make a rhyme.

40 His heer, his beerd, was lik saffroun,[6]	
That to his girdel raughte adown,	
His shoon of cordewane;[7]	
Of Brugges were his hosen brown,[8]	
His robe was of siklatoun,°	*cloth of gold*
45 That coste many a jane.°	*small coin, cent*
He coude hunte at wilde deer,	
And ride an-hawking for river,[9]	
With grey goshawk on honde.	
Therto he was a good archer,	
50 Of wrastling was ther noon his peer,°	*peer, equal*
Ther any ram shal stonde.[1]	
Ful many a maide bright in bowr[2]	
They moorne° for him paramour,°	*mourn / in love*
Whan hem were bet° to sleepe.	*better*
55 But he was chast, and no lechour,	
And sweete as is the brambel flowr	
That bereth the rede hepe.°	*roseberry*
And so bifel upon a day—	
Forsoothe as I you telle may—	
60 Sir Thopas wolde out ride:	
He worth° upon his steede grey,	*mounted*
And in his hand a launcegay,°	*lance*
A long swerd by his side.	
He priketh° thurgh a fair forest—	*rides*
65 Therinne is many a wilde beest:	
Ye, bothe bukke and hare;	
And as he priketh north and eest,	
I telle it you, him hadde almeest°	*almost*
Bitid a sory care.	
70 There springen herbes grete and smale—	
The licoris and setewale,[3]	
And many a clowe-gilofre.°	*clove*
And notemuge° to putte in ale,	*nutmeg*
Wheither it be moiste or stale,	
75 Or for to laye in cofre.°	*chest*

6. Saffron, an orange-red spice.
7. His shoes of Cordovan leather. "To his girdel raughte": reached to his belt.
8. His stockings came from Bruges, a town in Flanders.
9. Hawking was generally practiced near a river where game birds were plentiful.

1. Where a ram was put up as prize. See General Prologue, line 550. Both archery and wrestling were "lower-class" sports.
2. Bright in bower, i.e. "pretty in chamber." Such alliterative formulas abound in the romances.
3. Setwall, a spice. Here follow catalogues of spices and of songbirds found in chivalric romances.

The briddes singe, it is no nay,
The sperhawk° and the popinjay,°   *sparrowhawk / parrot*
     That joye it was to heere;
The thrustelcok° made eek his lay,°   *male thrush / song*
80   The wodedouve° upon the spray,   *wooddove*
     She soong ful loude and clere.

Sir Thopas fil in love-longinge,
Al whan he herde the thrustel singe,
     And priked° as he were wood.°   *spurred / insane*
85   His faire steede in his prikinge
So swatte° that men mighte him wringe—   *sweated*
     His sides were al blood.

Sir Thopas eek so wery was
For priking on the softe gras—
90   So fiers was his corage°—   *spirit*
That down he laide him in the plas,°   *place*
To make his steede som solas,°   *rest*
     And yaf him good forage.

"O Sainte Marye, bencite,°   *bless me*
95   What aileth this love at me[4]
     To binde me so sore?
Me dremed al this night, pardee,°   *by God*
An elf-queene shal my lemman be,[5]
     And sleepe under my gore.°   *skirt*

100   And elf-queene wol I have, ywis,
For in this world no womman is
     Worthy to be my make°   *mate*
         In towne:[6]
Alle othere wommen I forsake,
105   And to an elf-queene I me take,[7]
     By dale and eek by downe."

Into his sadel he clomb° anoon,   *climbed*
And priketh over stile and stoon,[8]
     And elf-queene for t'espye;
110   Til he so longe hath riden and goon,
That he foond in a privee woon[9]
     The contree of fairye,°   *Fairyland*
         So wild-e:
For in that contree was ther noon

---

4. What cause of dissatisfaction has love with me?
5. The queen of the fairies shall be my mistress. Elf-queens seek out knights in romance (as in the Wife of Bath's Tale), but it would be futile and presumptuous for a knight to seek an elf-queen as his mistress.
6. An example of tail-rhyme, a phrase stuck on strictly for the sake of rhyme.
7. Devote myself.
8. Alliterative formula. A stile is a set of steps over a fence or wall.
9. Found in a secret abode.

115   That to him dorste ride or goon—
          Neither wif ne child-e.

      Til that ther cam a greet geaunt—
          His name was sire Oliphaunt,°   *Elephant*
          A perilous° man of deede.   *dangerous*
120   He saide, "Child, by Termagaunt,[1]
          But if thou prike out of myn haunt,[2]
          Anoon I slee° thy steede   *slay*
                          With mace.
      Here is the Queene of Fairye,
125   With harpe and pipe and symphonye,°   *orchestral music*
          Dwelling in this place."

      The child saide, "Also mote I thee,[3]
          Tomorwe wil I meete thee,
          Whan I have myn armoure.
130   And yit I hope, par ma fay,[4]
          That thou shalt with this launcegay
          Abyen it° ful sowre:[5]
                          Thy mawe°   *belly*
          Shal I percen if I may,
135   Er it be fully prime° of day,   9 A.M.
          For here shaltou been slawe."°   *slain*

      Sire Thopas drow° abak ful faste—   *drew*
      This geaunt at him stones caste
          Out of a fel staf-slinge.[6]
140   But faire escapeth child Thopas,
      And al it was thurgh Goddes gras,°   *grace*
          And thurgh his fair beringe.°   *conduct*

      Yit listeth, lordes, to my tale,
      Merier than the nightingale,
145   For now I wol you roune°   *whisper, inform*
      How Sire Thopas with sides smale,[7]
      Priking over hil and dale,
          Is come again to towne.

      His merye men comanded he
150   To make him bothe game and glee,[8]
          For needes moste he fighte
      With a geaunt with hevedes° three—   *heads*

---

1. Oath by a heathen idol such as frequently sworn by romance villains. "Child" was a common appellation for a knight.
2. Unless you spur out of my territory.
3. So may I thrive.
4. By my faith.
5. Pay for it very bitterly.
6. Dreadful slingshot.
7. Dainty waist, a feature of romance heroines.
8. Entertainment and music—a formula.

For paramour° and jolitee°   *true love / pleasure*
   Of oon that shoon ful brighte.

155 "Do come," he saide, "my minstrales[9]
And geestours° for to tellen tales,   *tale-tellers*
   Anoon in myn arminge,
Of romances that been royales—
Of popes and of cardinales,
160   And eek of love-likinge."°   *love pleasures*

They fette° him first the sweete win,   *fetched*
And meede eek in a maselin,°   *wooden bowl*
   And royal spicerye,°   *variety of spices*
And gingebreed that was ful fin,
165 And licoris and eek comin,°   *cumin, a spice*
   With sugre that is trye.°   *good*

He dide° next his white leer,°   *donned / flanks*
Of cloth of lake° fin and cleer,°   *linen / bright*
   A breech° and eek a sherte;°   *pair of pants / shirt*
170 And next his sherte an aketoun,°   *undertunic*
And over that an haubergeoun,°   *shirt of mail*
   For° percing of his herte;   *to prevent*

And over that a fin hauberk°—   *coat of mail*
Was al ywrought of Jewes werk—[1]
175   Ful strong it was of plate;
And over that his cote-armour,[2]
   As whit as is a lilye flowr,
In which he wol debate.°   *fight*

His sheeld was al of gold so reed,
180 And therinne was a bores heed,
   A charbocle by his side.
And there he swoor° on ale and breed   *swore*
How that the geaunt shal be deed°—   *dead*
   Bitide what bitide.

185 His jambeaux° were of quirboily,°   *leg-armor / shaped leather*
His swerdes sheethe of ivory,
   His helm of laton° bright;   *brassy metal*
His sadel was of rewel boon,[3]
His bridel as the sonne shoon—
190   Or as the moone light.

---

9. "Have my minstrels come," he said.
1. Jews had a reputation as makers of fine armor.
2. Coat of arms, i.e., the cloth jacket on which
the knight's heraldic bearings were usually woven:

Sir Thopas's was on his shield only: a boar's head
and a "charbocle," carbuncle, a ruby shooting forth
large rays.
3. Ivory.

His spere was of fin cypres,
That bodeth werre and nothing pees[4]—
   The heed ful sharpe ygrounde;
His steede was al dappel grey—
195 It gooth an ambel° in the way,   *amble, easy pace*
   Ful softely and rounde,°   *in a circle*
         In londe.
Lo, lordes mine, here is a fit:°   *division of a poem*
If ye wol any more of it,
200   To telle it wol I fonde.°   *try*

THE SECOND FIT

Now holde youre mouth, par charitee,
Bothe knight and lady free,°   *noble*
   And herkneth to my spelle:°   *song, tale*
Of bataile, and of chivalry,
205 And of ladies love-drury,°   *love-making*
   Anoon I wol you telle.

Men speken of romances of pris,°   *reputation*
Of Horn Child and of Ypotis,
   Of Beves and Sir Gy,
210 Of Sir Libeux and Pleindamour—[5]
But sire Thopas, he bereth the flowr
   Of royal chivalry.

His goode steede al he bistrood,
And forth upon his way he glood,°   *glided*
215 As sparcle out of the bronde.[6]
Upon his creest° he bar° a towr—   *crest / bore*
And therinne stiked a lilye flowr—
   God shilde his cors fro shonde![7]

And for° he was a knight auntrous,° *because / adventurous*
220 He nolde sleepen in noon hous,
   But liggen° in his hoode;   *lie*
His brighte helm was his wonger,°   *pillow*
And by him baiteth his dextrer,[8]
   Of herbes fine and goode.

225 Himself drank water of the wel,
As dide the knight Sire Percivel,[9]

4. Which bodes war and peace not at all.
5. *Horn Child, Bevis of Southampton, Guy of Warwick,* and *The Fair Unknown* (*Li Beux Desconus*), as well as *Sir Percival of Wales* (line 226) were romances popular in Chaucer's time; *Pleindamour* (the "love-filled") has not survived if it ever existed, and the only known *Ypotis* is a theological debate.
6. Like a spark from a brand.
7. God defend his body from harm.
8. And beside him grazes his horse.
9. Percival lived by a spring in the woods.

So worly under weede;[1]
Til on a day—

[THE HOST INTERRUPTS]

    "Namore of this, for Goddes dignitee!"
230 Quod oure Hoste, "for thou makest me
So wery of thy verray lewednesse,°   *ignorance*
That also wisly God my soule blesse,[2]
Mine eres° aken of thy drasty° speeche.   *ears / rubbishy*
Now swich a rym the devel I biteche!°   *commit to*
235 This may wel be rym dogerel," quod he.
    "Why so?" quod I. "Why wiltou lette° me   *hinder*
More of my tale than another man,
Sin that it is the beste rym I can?"
    "By God," quod he, "for plainly, at oo° word,   *one*
240 Thy drasty ryming is nat worth a tord!°   *turd*
Thou doost nought elles but dispendest time:
Sire, at oo word, thou shalt no lenger ryme.
Lat see wher thou canst tellen ought in geeste,[3]
Or tel in prose somwhat at the leeste,
245 In which ther be som mirthe or som doctrine."
    "Gladly," quod I, "by Goddes sweete pine,°   *suffering*
I wol you telle a litel thing in prose,
That oughte like° you, as I suppose;   *please*
Or elles, certes, ye be too daungerous:°   *hard to please*
250 It is a moral tale vertuous,
Al be it told sometime in sondry wise,
Of sondry folk, as I shal you devise.[4]

---

1. Worthy under clothing—a formula.
2. As surely as God bless my soul.
3. Perhaps "in couplets as opposed to tail rhyme" or "in alliterative verse."

4. Chaucer's second effort is the Tale of Melibee, a long prose moral allegory, which draws a much more favorable response from the Host.

The Nun's Priest's Tale[1]

	A poore widwe somdeel stape° in age	*advanced*
	Was whilom° dwelling in a narwe[2] cotage,	*once upon a time*
	Biside a grove, stonding in a dale:	
	This widwe of which I telle you my tale,	
5	Sin thilke° day that she was last a wif,	*that same*
	In pacience ladde° a ful simple lif.	*led*
	For litel was hir catel° and hir rente,°	*property / income*
	By housbondrye° of swich as God hire sente	*economy*
	She foond° hirself and eek hir doughtren two.	*provided for*
10	Three large sowes hadde she and namo,	
	Three kin,° and eek a sheep that highte° Malle.	*cows / was called*
	Ful sooty was hir bowr° and eek hir halle,	*bedroom*
	In which she eet ful many a sclendre° meel;	*scanty*
	Of poinant° sauce hire needed neveradeel:	*pungent*
15	No daintee morsel passed thurgh hir throte—	
	Hir diete was accordant to hir cote.°	*cottage*
	Repleccioun° ne made hire nevere sik:	*overeating*
	Attempre° diete was al hir physik,°	*moderate / medicine*
	And exercise and hertes suffisaunce.°	*contentment*
20	The goute lette hire nothing for to daunce,[3]	
	N'apoplexye shente° nat hir heed.°	*hurt / head*
	No win ne drank she, neither whit ne reed:°	*red*
	Hir boord° was served most with whit and blak,[4]	*table*
	Milk and brown breed, in which she foond no lak;[5]	
25	Seind bacon, and somtime an ey° or twaye,	*egg*
	For she was as it were a manere daye.[6]	
	A yeerd° she hadde, enclosed al withoute	*yard*

1. The Nun's Priest's Tale is an example of the literary genre known as the "beast fable," in which animals behave like human beings. The beast fable is inevitably injurious to man's dignity, since to pretend that animals behave like men is to suggest that men behave like animals, for a pig cannot look like a man unless a man in some way looks like a pig. In the Nun's Priest's tale, as in its French source, the history of Reynard the Fox, the beast fable is combined with the mock heroic, and the result is doubly injurious to man's dignity. The elevated language of true heroic poetry means to enhance the splendid deeds of men of great stature, while the elevated language of mock heroic, by treating the trivial as if it were sublime, reveals man's lack of dignity in the awful gulf that separates the idealized language from the petty action it describes; and when the petty action is carried on not even by men, but by animals masquerading as men (that is, by men reduced to the status of animals), the loss of human dignity is even greater.

The nominal hero of the Tale is Chauntecleer, a fowl of courtly bearing, profound learning, and superior crowing. This rooster is, like Achilles or Aeneas, made the center of a "great" action— which, however, takes up a relatively small portion of the total number of lines in the poem. The hero of the larger portion, and the real hero of the poem, is rhetoric, which is responsible for all Chauntecleer's importance, though it almost drowns his story in its vast tumid flow. Rhetoric as employed by the Nun's Priest includes not only elevated speech, but proverbs, saws, conventional similes—all the clichés of formal language and thought. Epic mannerisms abound; proverbs fly thick and fast and contradict one another with impunity; sententious generalizations about the tragic inevitability of certain events, the bad counsel given by women, and the folly of heeding flattery are successively used to account for Chauntecleer's near-fall; and throughout the tale learned pedantry invokes rhetorical tradition to footnote the least original of ideas. All rhetoric's ordering devices achieve a fine disorder.
2. I.e., small.
3. The gout didn't hinder her at all from dancing.
4. I.e., milk and bread.
5. Found no fault. "Seind": scorched (i.e., broiled).
6. I.e., a kind of dairymaid.

With stikkes, and a drye dich aboute,
In which she hadde a cok heet° Chauntecleer: *named*
30   In al the land of crowing nas° his peer.   *was not*
His vois was merier than the merye orgon
On massedayes that in the chirche goon;[7]
Wel sikerer[8] was his crowing in his logge°   *dwelling*
Than is a clok or an abbeye orlogge;°   *timepiece*
35   By nature he knew eech ascensioun
Of th'equinoxial[9] in thilke town:
For whan degrees fifteene were ascended,
Thanne crew[1] he that it mighte nat been amended.
His comb was redder than the fin coral,
40   And batailed° as it were a castel wal;   *battlemented*
His bile° was blak, and as the jeet° it shoon;   *bill / jet*
Like asure[2] were his legges and his toon;°   *toes*
His nailes whitter° than the lilye flowr,   *whiter*
And lik the burned° gold was his colour.   *burnished*
45   This gentil cok hadde in his governaunce
Sevene hennes for to doon al his plesaunce,°   *pleasure*
Whiche were his sustres and his paramours,[3]
And wonder like to him as of colours;
Of whiche the faireste hewed° on hir throte   *colored*
50. Was cleped faire damoisele Pertelote:
Curteis she was, discreet, and debonaire,°   *meek*
And compaignable,[4] and bar° hirself so faire,   *bore*
Sin thilke day that she was seven night old,
That trewely she hath the herte in hold
55   Of Chauntecleer, loken° in every lith.°   *locked / limb*
He loved hire so that wel was him therwith.[5]
But swich a joye was it to heere hem singe,
Whan that the brighte sonne gan to springe,
In sweete accord *My Lief is Faren in Londe*[6]—
60   For thilke time, as I have understonde,
Beestes and briddes couden speke and singe.
     And so bifel that in a daweninge,
As Chauntecleer among his wives alle
Sat on his perche that was in the halle,
65   And next him sat this faire Pertelote,
This Chauntecleer gan gronen in his throte,
As man that in his dreem is drecched° sore.   *troubled*
     And whan that Pertelote thus herde him rore,
She was agast, and saide, "Herte dere,
70   What aileth you to grone in this manere?

7. I.e., is played.
8. More reliable.
9. I.e., he knew by instinct each step in the progression of the celestial equator. The celestial equator was thought to make a 360-degree rotation around the earth every 24 hours; therefore a progression of 15 degrees would be equal to the passage of an hour (line 37).
1. Crowed. "Amended": improved.
2. Lapis lazuli.
3. His sisters and his mistresses.
4. Companionable.
5. That he was well contented.
6. A popular song of the time.

Ye been a verray slepere,[7] fy, for shame!"
    And he answerde and saide thus, "Madame,
I praye you that ye take it nat agrief.°   *amiss*
By God, me mette I was in swich meschief[8]
75 Right now, that yit myn herte is sore afright.
Now God," quod he, "my swevene recche aright,[9]
And keepe my body out of foul prisoun!
Me mette how that I romed up and down
Within oure yeerd, wher as I sawgh a beest,
80 Was lik an hound and wolde han maad arrest[1]
Upon my body, and han had me deed.[2]
His colour was bitwixe yelow and reed,
And tipped was his tail and bothe his eres
With blak, unlik the remenant° of his heres;°   *rest / hairs*
85 His snoute smal, with glowing yën twaye.
Yit of his look for fere almost I deye:°   *die*
This caused me my groning, doutelees."
    "Avoi,"° quod she, "fy on you, hertelees!°   *fie / coward*
Allas," quod she, "for by that God above,
90 Now han ye lost myn herte and al my love!
I can nat love a coward, by my faith.
For certes, what so any womman saith,
We alle desiren, if it mighte be,
To han housbondes hardy, wise, and free,°   *generous*
95 And secree,° and no nigard, ne no fool,   *discreet*
Ne him that is agast of every tool,°   *weapon*
Ne noon avauntour.° By that God above,   *boaster*
How dorste ye sayn for shame unto youre love
That any thing mighte make you aferd?
100 Have ye no mannes herte and han a beerd?
Allas, and conne° ye been agast of swevenes?°   *can / dreams*
No thing, God woot, but vanitee[3] in swevene is!
Swevenes engendren of replexiouns,[4]
And ofte of fume° and of complexiouns,°   *gas / bodily humors*
105 Whan humours been too habundant in a wight.[5]
Certes, this dreem which ye han met° tonight   *dreamed*
Comth of the grete superfluitee
Of youre rede colera,[6] pardee,
Which causeth folk to dreden° in hir dremes   *fear*
110 Of arwes,° and of fir with rede lemes,°   *arrows / flames*
Of rede beestes, that they wol hem bite,
Of contek,° and of whelpes grete and lite[7]—   *strife*

---

7. Sound sleeper.
8. I dreamed that I was in such misfortune.
9. Interpret my dream correctly (i.e., in an auspicious manner).
1. Would have laid hold.
2. I.e., killed me.
3. I.e., empty illusion.

4. Dreams have their origin in overeating.
5. I.e., when humors are too abundant in a person. Pertelote's diagnosis is based on the familiar concept that an overabundance of one of the bodily humors in a person affected his temperament.
6. Red bile.
7. And of big and little dogs.

Right° as the humour of malencolye[8]   *just*
Causeth ful many a man in sleep to crye
115   For fere of blake beres° or boles° blake,   *bears / bulls*
Or elles blake develes wol hem take.
Of othere humours coude I tell also
That werken many a man in sleep ful wo,
But I wol passe as lightly° as I can.   *quickly*
120   Lo, Caton,[9] which that was so wis a man,
Saide he nat thus? 'Ne do no fors of[1] dremes.'
Now, sire," quod she, "whan we flee fro the bemes,[2]
For Goddes love, as take som laxatif.
Up° peril of my soule and of my lif,   *upon*
125   I conseile you the beste, I wol nat lie,
That bothe of colere and of malencolye
Ye purge you; and for° ye shal nat tarye,   *in order that*
Though in this town is noon apothecarye,
I shal myself to herbes techen you,
130   That shal been for youre hele[3] and for youre prow,
And in oure yeerd tho herbes shal I finde,
The whiche han of hir propretee by kinde°   *nature*
To purge you binethe and eek above.
Foryet° nat this, for Goddes owene love.   *forget*
135   Ye been ful colerik° of complexioun;   *bilious*
Ware° the sonne in his ascencioun   *beware that*
Ne finde you nat repleet° of humours hote;°   *filled / hot*
And if it do, I dar wel laye° a grote   *bet*
That ye shul have a fevere terciane,[4]
140   Or an agu that may be youre bane.°   *death*
A day or two ye shul han digestives
Of wormes, er ye take youre laxatives
Of lauriol, centaure, and fumetere,[5]
Or elles of ellebor° that groweth there,   *hellebore*
145   Of catapuce, or of gaitres beries,[6]
Of herb-ive° growing in oure yeerd ther merye is[7]   *herb ivy*
Pekke hem right up as they growe and ete hem in.
Be merye, housbonde, for youre fader kin!
Dredeth no dreem: I can saye you namore."
150   "Madame," quod he, "graunt mercy of youre lore,[8]
But nathelees, as touching daun° Catoun,   *master*
That hath of wisdom swich a greet renown,
Though that he bad no dremes for to drede,
By God, men may in olde bookes rede
155   Of many a man more of auctoritee°   *authority*

---

8. I.e., black bile.
9. Dionysius Cato, supposed author of a book of maxims used in elementary education.
1. Pay no attention to.
2. Fly down from the rafters.
3. Health. "Prow": benefit.
4. Tertian (recurring every other day).

5. Of laureole, centaury, and fumitory. These, and the herbs mentioned in the next lines, were all common medieval medicines used as cathartics.
6. Of caper berry or of gaiter berry.
7. Where it is pleasant.
8. Many thanks for your instruction.

Than evere Caton was, so mote I thee,°   *thrive*
That al the revers sayn of his sentence,°   *opinion*
And han wel founden by experience
That dremes been significaciouns
160 As wel of joye as tribulaciouns
That folk enduren in this lif present.
Ther needeth make of this noon argument:
The verray preve[9] sheweth it in deede.
    "Oon of the gretteste auctour[1] that men rede
165 Saith thus, that whilom two felawes wente
On pilgrimage in a ful good entente,
And happed so they comen in a town,
Wher as ther was swich congregacioun
Of peple, and eek so strait of herbergage,[2]
170 That they ne founde as muche as oo cotage
In which they bothe mighte ylogged° be;   *lodged*
Wherfore they mosten° of necessitee   *must*
As for that night departe° compaignye.   *part*
And eech of hem gooth to his hostelrye,
175 And took his logging as it wolde falle.°   *befall*
That oon of hem was logged in a stalle,
Fer° in a yeerd, with oxen of the plough;   *far away*
That other man was logged wel ynough,
As was his aventure° or his fortune,   *lot*
180 That us governeth alle as in commune.
And so bifel that longe er it were day,
This man mette° in his bed, ther as he lay,   *dreamed*
How that his felawe gan upon him calle,
And saide, 'Allas, for in an oxes stalle
185 This night I shal be mordred° ther I lie!   *murdered*
Now help me, dere brother, or I die!
In alle haste com to me,' he saide.
    "This man out of his sleep for fere abraide,°   *started up*
But whan that he was wakened of his sleep,
190 He turned him and took of this no keep:°   *heed*
Him thoughte his dreem nas but a vanitee.
Thus twies in his sleeping dremed he,
And atte thridde time yit his felawe
Cam, as him thoughte, and saide, 'I am now slawe:°   *slain*
195 Bihold my bloody woundes deepe and wide.
Aris up erly in the morwe tide[3]
And atte west gate of the town,' quod he,
'A carte ful of dong° ther shaltou see,   *dung*
In which my body is hid ful prively:
200 Do thilke carte arresten boldely.[4]

---

9. Actual experience.
1. I.e., one of the greatest authors (perhaps Cicero or Valerius Maximus).
2. And also such a shortage of lodging.
3. In the morning.
4. Boldly have this same cart stopped.

My gold caused my mordre, sooth to sayn'
—And tolde him every point how he was slain,
With a ful pitous face, pale of hewe.
And truste wel, his dreem he foond° ful trewe,   *found*
205 For on the morwe° as soone as it was day,   *morning*
To his felawes in° he took the way,   *lodging*
And whan that he cam to this oxes stalle,
After his felawe he bigan to calle.
     "The hostiler° answerde him anoon,   *innkeeper*
210 And saide, 'Sire, youre felawe is agoon:°   *gone away*
As soone as day he wente out of the town.'
     "This man gan fallen in suspecioun,
Remembring on his dremes that he mette;°   *dreamed*
And forth he gooth, no lenger wolde he lette,°   *tarry*
215 Unto the west gate of the town, and foond
A dong carte, wente as it were to donge° lond,   *put manure on*
That was arrayed in that same wise
As ye han herd the dede° man devise;   *dead*
And with an hardy herte he gan to crye,
220 'Vengeance and justice of this felonye!
My felawe mordred is this same night,
And in this carte he lith° gaping upright!°   *lies / supine*
I crye out on the ministres,' quod he,
'That sholde keepe and rulen this citee.
225 Harrow,° allas, here lith my felawe slain!'   *help*
What sholde I more unto this tale sayn?
The peple up sterte° and caste the carte to grounde,   *started*
And in the middel of the dong they founde
The dede man that mordred was al newe.[5]
230   "O blisful God that art so just and trewe,
Lo, how that thou biwrayest° mordre alway!   *disclose*
Mordre wol out, that see we day by day:
Mordre is so wlatsom° and abhominable   *loathsome*
To God that is so just and resonable,
235 That he ne wol nat suffre it heled° be,   *concealed*
Though it abide a yeer or two or three.
Mordre wol out: this my conclusioun.
And right anoon ministres of that town
Han hent° the cartere and so sore him pined,[6]   *seized*
240 And eek the hostiler so sore engined,°   *racked*
That they biknewe° hir wikkednesse anoon,   *confessed*
And were anhanged° by the nekke boon.   *hanged*
Here may men seen that dremes been to drede.[7]
     "And certes, in the same book I rede—
245 Right in the nexte chapitre after this—
I gabbe° nat, so have I joye or blis—   *lie*

Two men that wolde han passed over see
For certain cause into a fer contree,
If that the wind ne hadde been contrarye
250   That made hem in a citee for to tarye,
That stood ful merye upon an haven° side—   *harbor's*
But on a day again° the even tide   *toward*
The wind gan chaunge, and blewe right as hem leste:[8]
Jolif° and glad they wenten unto reste,   *merry*
255   And casten[9] hem ful erly for to saile.
    "But to that oo man fil° a greet mervaile;   *befell*
That oon of hem, in sleeping as he lay,
Him mette[1] a wonder dreem again the day:
Him thoughte a man stood by his beddes side,
260   And him comanded that he sholde abide,
And saide him thus, 'If thou tomorwe wende,
Thou shalt be dreint:° my tale is at an ende.'   *drowned*
    "He wook and tolde his felawe what he mette,
And prayed him his viage° to lette;°   *voyage / delay*
265   As for that day he prayed him to bide.
    "His felawe that lay by his beddes side
Gan for to laughe, and scorned him ful faste.°   *hard*
'No dreem,' quod he, 'may so myn herte agaste°   *terrify*
That I wol lette° for to do my thinges.°   *delay / business*
270   I sette nat a straw by thy dreminges,[2]
For swevenes been but vanitees and japes:[3]
Men dreme alday° of owles or of apes,[4]   *constantly*
And of many a maze° therwithal—   *delusion*
Men dreme of thing that nevere was ne shal.[5]
275   But sith I see that thou wolt here abide,
And thus forsleuthen° wilfully thy tide,°   *waste / time*
Good woot, it reweth me;[6] and have good day.'
And thus he took his leve and wente his way.
But er that he hadde half his cours ysailed—
280   Noot I nat why ne what meschaunce it ailed—
But casuelly the shippes botme rente,[7]
And ship and man under the water wente,
In sighte of othere shippes it biside,
That with hem sailed at the same tide.
285   And therfore, faire Pertelote so dere,
By swiche ensamples olde maistou lere°   *learn*
That no man sholde been too recchelees°   *careless*
Of dremes, for I saye thee doutelees
That many a dreem ful sore is for to drede.
290   "Lo, in the lif of Saint Kenelm[8] I rede—

8. Just as they wished.
9. Determined.
1. He dreamed.
2. I don't care a straw for your dreamings.
3. Dreams are but illusions and frauds.
4. I.e., of absurdities.

5. I.e., shall be.
6. I'm sorry.
7. I don't know why nor what was the trouble with it—but accidentally the ship's bottom split.
8. Kenelm succeeded his father as king of Mercia at the age of 7, but was slain by his aunt (in 821).

That was Kenulphus sone, the noble king
Or Mercenrike°—how Kenelm mette a thing   *Mercia*
A lite° er he was mordred on a day.   *little*
His mordre in his avision° he sey.°   *dream / saw*
295   His norice° him expounded everydeel°   *nurse / entirely*
His swevene, and bad him for to keepe him[9] weel
For traison, but he nas but seven yeer old,
And therfore litel tale hath he told
Of any dreem,[1] so holy was his herte.
300   By God, I hadde levere than my sherte[2]
That ye hadde rad° his legende as have I.   *read*
      "Dame Pertelote, I saye you trewely,
Macrobeus,[3] that writ the *Avisioun*
In Affrike of the worthy Scipioun,
305   Affermeth° dremes, and saith that they been   *confirms*
Warning of thinges that men after seen.
      "And ferthermore, I praye you looketh wel
In the Olde Testament of Daniel,
If he heeld° dremes any vanitee.[4]   *considered*
310   "Rede eek of Joseph[5] and ther shul ye see
Wher° dremes be somtime—I saye nat alle—   *whether*
Warning of thinges that shul after falle.
      "Looke of Egypte the king daun Pharao,
His bakere and his botelere° also,   *butler*
315   Wher they ne felte noon effect in dremes.[6]
Whoso wol seeke actes of sondry remes°   *realms*
May rede of dremes many a wonder thing.
      "Lo Cresus, which that was of Lyde° king,   *Lydia*
Mette° he nat that he sat upon a tree,   *dreamed*
320   Which signified he sholde anhanged° be?   *hanged*
      "Lo here Andromacha, Ectores° wif,   *Hector's*
That day that Ector sholde lese° his lif,   *lose*
She dremed on the same night biforn
How that the lif of Ector sholde be lorn,°   *lost*
325   If thilke° day he wente into bataile;   *that same*
She warned him, but it mighte nat availe:°   *do any good*
He wente for to fighte nathelees,
But he was slain anoon° of Achilles.   *right away*
But thilke tale is al too long to telle,
330   And eek it is neigh day, I may nat dwelle.
Shortly I saye, as for conclusioun,
That I shal han of this avisioun[7]
Adversitee, and I saye ferthermoor

---

9. Guard himself.
1. Therefore he has set little store by any dream.
2. I.e., I'd give my shirt.
3. Macrobius wrote a famous commentary on Cicero's account in *De Republica* of the dream of Scipio Africanus Minor; the commentary came to be regarded as a standard authority on dream lore.
4. See Daniel 7.
5. See Genesis 37.
6. See Genesis 39–41.
7. Divinely inspired dream (as opposed to the more ordinary "swevene" or "dreem").

That I ne telle of[8] laxatives no stoor,
335 For they been venimes,° I woot it weel: *poisons*
I hem defye, I love hem neveradeel.°   *not a bit*
    "Now lat us speke of mirthe and stinte° al this.   *stop*
Madame Pertelote, so have I blis,
Of oo thing God hath sente me large grace:
340 For whan I see the beautee of youre face—
Ye been so scarlet reed° aboute youre yën—   *red*
It maketh al my drede for to dien.
For also siker° as *In principio*,[9]   *certain*
Mulier est hominis confusio.[1]
345 Madame, the sentence° of this Latin is,   *meaning*
'Womman is mannes joye and al his blis.'
For whan I feele anight youre softe side—
Al be it that I may nat on you ride,
For that oure perche is maad so narwe, allas—
350 I am so ful of joye and of solas°   *delight*
That I defye bothe swevene and dreem."
And with that word he fleigh° down fro the beem,   *flew*
For it was day, and eek his hennes alle,
And with a "chuk" he gan hem for to calle,
355 For he hadde founde a corn lay in the yeerd.
Real° he was, he was namore aferd:°   *regal / afraid*
He fethered[2] Pertelote twenty time,
And trad[3] hire as ofte er it was prime.
He looketh as it were a grim leoun,
360 And on his toes he rometh up and down:
Him deined[4] nat to sette his foot to grounde.
He chukketh whan he hath a corn yfounde,
And to him rennen° thanne his wives alle.   *run*
Thus royal, as a prince is in his halle,
365 Leve I this Chauntecleer in his pasture,
And after wol I telle his aventure.
    Whan that the month in which the world bigan,
That highte March, whan God first maked man,
Was compleet, and passed were also,
370 Sin March biran, thritty dayes and two,[5]
Bifel that Chauntecleer in al his pride,
His sevene wives walking him biside,
Caste up his yën to the brighte sonne,
That in the signe of Taurus hadde yronne
375 Twenty degrees and oon and somwhat more,
And knew by kinde,° and by noon other lore,   *nature*
That it was prime, and crew with blisful stevene.°   *voice*

---

8. Set by.
9. A tag from the Gospel of St. John which gives
the essential premises of Christianity: "In the
beginning was the Word."
1. Woman is man's ruination.

2. I.e., embraced.
3. Trod, copulated with. "Prime": 9 A.M.
4. He deigned.
5. The rhetorical time telling yields the date
May 3. "Biran": passed by.

"The sonne," he saide, "is clomben[6] up on hevene
Fourty degrees and oon and more, ywis.
380 Madame Pertelote, my worldes blis,
Herkneth thise blisful briddes° how they singe,   birds
And see the fresshe flowers how they springe:
Ful is myn herte of revel and solas."
But sodeinly him fil° a sorweful cas,°   befell / chance
385 For evere the latter ende of joye is wo—
God woot that worldly joye is soone ago,
And if a rethor° coude faire endite,   rhetorician
He in a cronicle saufly° mighte it write,   safely
As for a soverein notabilitee.[7]
390 Now every wis man lat him herkne me:
This storye is also° trewe, I undertake,   as
As is the book of *Launcelot de Lake*,[8]
That wommen holde in ful greet reverence.
Now wol I turne again to my sentence.°   main point
395   A colfox[9] ful of sly iniquitee,
That in the grove hadde woned° yeres three,   dwelled
By heigh imaginacion forncast,[1]
The same night thurghout the hegges° brast°   hedges / burst
Into the yeerd ther Chauntecleer the faire
400 Was wont, and eek his wives, to repaire;
And in a bed of wortes° stille he lay   cabbages
Til it was passed undren° of the day,   midmorning
Waiting his time on Chauntecleer to falle,
As gladly doon thise homicides alle,
405 That in await liggen to mordre[2] men.
O false mordrour, lurking in thy den!
O newe Scariot![3] Newe Geniloun!
False dissimilour!° O Greek Sinoun,[4]   dissembler
That broughtest Troye al outrely° to sorwe!   utterly
410 O Chauntecleer, accursed be that morwe°   morning
That thou into the yeerd flaugh° fro the bemes!   flew
Thou were ful wel ywarned by thy dremes
That thilke day was perilous to thee;
But what that God forwoot° moot° needes be,   foreknows / must
415 After° the opinion of certain clerkes: according to
Witnesse on him that any parfit° clerk is   perfect
That in scole is greet altercacioun
In this matere, and greet disputisoun,°   disputation
And hath been of an hundred thousand men.
420 But I ne can nat bulte° it to the bren,°   sift / husks

6. Has climbed.
7. Indisputable fact.
8. Romances of the courteous knight Lancelot of
the Lake were very popular.
9. Fox with black markings.
1. Predestined by divine planning.
2. That lie in ambush to murder.

3. Judas Iscariot. "Geniloun" is Ganelon, who
betrayed Roland to the Saracens (in the medieval
French epic *The Song of Roland*).
4. Sinon, who persuaded the Trojans to take the
Greeks' wooden horse into their city—with, of
course, the result that the city was destroyed.

As can the holy doctour Augustin,
Or Boece, or the bisshop Bradwardin[5]—
Wheither that Goddes worthy forwiting°   *foreknowledge*
Straineth me nedely[6] for to doon a thing
425   ("Nedely" clepe I simple necessitee),
Or elles if free chois be graunted me
To do that same thing or do it naught,
Though God forwoot° it er that I was wrought;   *foreknew*
Or if his witing° straineth neveradeel,   *knowledge*
430   But by necessitee condicionel[7]—
I wol nat han to do of swich matere:
My tale is of a cok, as ye may heere,
That took his conseil of his wif with sorwe,
To walken in the yeerd upon that morwe
435   That he hadde met° the dreem that I you tolde.   *dreamed*
Wommenes conseils been ful ofte colde,[8]
Wommanes conseil broughte us first to wo,
And made Adam fro Paradis to go,
Ther as he was ful merye and wel at ese.
440   But for I noot° to whom it mighte displese   *don't know*
If I conseil of wommen wolde blame,
Passe over, for I saide it in my game°—   *sport*
Rede auctours where they trete of swich matere,
And what they sayn of wommen ye may heere—
445   Thise been the cokkes wordes and nat mine:
I can noon harm of no womman divine.°   *guess*
        Faire in the sond° to bathe hire merily   *sand*
Lith° Pertelote, and alle hir sustres by,   *lies*
Again° the sonne, and Chauntecleer so free°   *in / noble*
450   Soong° merier than the mermaide in the see—   *sang*
For Physiologus[9] saith sikerly
How that they singen wel and merily.
        And so bifel that as he caste his yë
Among the wortes on a boterflye,°   *butterfly*
455   He was war of this fox that lay ful lowe.
No thing ne liste him[1] thanne for to crowe,
But cride anoon "Cok cok!" and up he sterte,°   *started*
As man that[2] was affrayed in his herte—
For naturelly a beest desireth flee
460   Fro his contrarye[3] if he may it see,
Though he nevere erst° hadde seen it with his yë.   *before*
This Chauntecleer, whan he gan him espye,

---

5. St. Augustine, Boethius (6th-century Roman philosopher, whose *Consolation of Philosophy* was translated by Chaucer), and Thomas Bradwardine (archbishop of Canterbury, d. 1349) were all concerned with the interrelationship between man's free will and God's foreknowledge.
6. Constrains me necessarily.
7. Boethius' "conditional necessity" permitted a large measure of free will.
8. I.e., baneful.
9. Supposed author of a bestiary, a book of moralized zoology describing both natural and supernatural animals (including mermaids).
1. He wished.
2. Like one who.
3. I.e., his natural enemy.

He wolde han fled, but that the fox anoon
Saide, "Gentil sire, allas, wher wol ye goon?
465 Be ye afraid of me that am youre freend?
Now certes, I were worse than a feend
If I to you wolde° harm or vilainye.   *meant*
I am nat come youre conseil° for t'espye,   *secrets*
But trewely the cause of my cominge
470 Was only for to herkne how ye singe:
For trewely, ye han as merye a stevene°   *voice*
As any angel hath that is in hevene.
Therwith ye han in musik more feelinge
Than hadde Boece,[4] or any that can singe.
475 My lord your fader—God his soule blesse!—
And eek youre moder, of hir gentilesse,°   *gentility*
Han in myn hous ybeen, to my grete ese.
And certes sire, ful fain° wolde I you plese.   *gladly*
    "But for men speke of singing, I wol saye,
480 So mote I brouke[5] wel mine yën twaye,
Save ye, I herde nevere man to singe
As dide youre fader in the morweninge.
Certes, it was of herte[6] al that he soong.°   *sang*
And for to make his vois the more strong,
485 He wolde so paine him[7] that with bothe his yën
He moste winke,[8] so loude wolde he cryen;
And stonden on his tiptoon therwithal,
And strecche forth his nekke long and smal;
And eek he was of swich discrecioun
490 That ther nas no man in no regioun
That him in song or wisdom mighte passe.
I have wel rad° in *Daun Burnel the Asse*[9]   *read*
Among his vers how that ther was a cok,
For a preestes sone yaf him a knok[1]
495 Upon his leg whil he was yong and nice,°   *foolish*
He made him for to lese° his benefice.[2]   *lose*
But certain, ther nis no comparisoun
Bitwixe the wisdom and discrecioun
Of youre fader and of his subtiltee.
500 Now singeth, sire, for sainte° charitee!   *holy*
Lat see, conne° ye youre fader countrefete?"°   *can / imitate*
    This Chauntecleer his winges gan to bete,
As man that coude his traison nat espye,
So was he ravisshed with his flaterye.
505 Allas, ye lordes, many a fals flatour°   *flatterer*

4. Boethius also wrote a treatise on music.
5. So might I enjoy the use of.
6. Heartfelt.
7. Take pains.
8. He had to shut his eyes.
9. Master Brunellus, a discontented donkey, was
the hero of a 12th-century satirical poem by Nigel
Wireker.
1. Because a priest's son gave him a knock.
2. The offended cock neglected to crow so that his
master, now grown to manhood, overslept, missing his ordination and losing his benefice.

Is in youre court, and many a losengeour°   *deceiver*
That plesen you wel more, by my faith,
Than he that soothfastnesse° unto you saith!   *truth*
Redeth Ecclesiaste³ of flaterye.
510   Beeth war, ye lordes, of hir trecherye.
         This Chauntecleer stood hye upon his toos,
Strecching his nekke, and heeld his yën cloos,
And gan to crowe loude for the nones;°   *occasion*
And daun Russel the fox sterte° up atones,   *jumped*
515   And by the gargat° hente° Chauntecleer,   *throat / seized*
And on his bak toward the wode him beer,°   *bore*
For yit ne was ther no man that him sued.°   *followed*
         O destinee that maist nat been eschued!°   *eschewed*
Allas that Chauntecleer fleigh° fro the bemes!   *flew*
520   Allas his wif ne roughte nat of⁴ dremes!
And on a Friday fil° al this meschaunce!   *befell*
         O Venus that art goddesse of plesaunce,
Sin that thy servant was this Chauntecleer,
And in thy service dide al his power—
525   More for delit than world⁵ to multiplye—
Why woldestou suffre him on thy day⁶ to die?
         O Gaufred,⁷ dere maister soverein,
That, whan thy worthy king Richard was slain
With shot,⁸ complainedest his deeth so sore,
530   Why ne hadde I now thy sentence and thy lore,⁹
The Friday for to chide as diden ye?
For on a Friday soothly slain was he.
Thanne wolde I shewe you how that I coude plaine¹
For Chauntecleres drede and for his paine.
535   Certes, swich cry ne lamentacioun
Was nevere of ladies maad when Ilioun°   *Ilium, Troy*
Was wonne, and Pyrrus² with his straite swerd,
Whan he hadde hent° King Priam by the beerd   *seized*
And slain him, as saith us *Eneidos,*³
540   As maden alle the hennes in the cloos,°   *yard*
Whan they hadde seen of Chauntecleer the sighte.
But sovereinly⁴ Dame Pertelote shrighte°   *shrieked*
Ful louder than dide Hasdrubales⁵ wif
Whan that hir housbonde hadde lost his lif,
545   And that the Romains hadden brend° Cartage: *burned*
She was so ful of torment and of rage°   *madness*

---

3. The Book of Ecclesiasticus, in the Apocrypha.
4. Didn't care for.
5. I.e., population.
6. Friday is Venus's day.
7. Geoffrey of Vinsauf, a famous medieval rhetorician, who wrote a lament on the death of Richard I in which he scolded Friday, the day on which the king died.
8. I.e., a missile.

9. Thy wisdom and thy learning.
1. Lament.
2. Pyrrhus was the Greek who slew Priam, king of Troy. "Straite": rigorous, unsparing.
3. As the *Aeneid* tells us.
4. Splendidly.
5. Hasdrubal was king of Carthage when it was destroyed by the Romans.

That wilfully unto the fir she sterte,°   *jumped*
And brende hirselven with a stedefast herte.
    O woful hennes, right so criden ye
550 As, whan that Nero brende the citee
Of Rome, criden senatoures wives
For that hir housbondes losten alle hir lives:[6]
Withouten gilt this Nero hath hem slain.
Now wol I turne to my tale again.
555   The sely° widwe and eek hir doughtres two   *innocent*
Herden thise hennes crye and maken wo,
And out at dores sterten° they anoon,   *leaped*
And sien° the fox toward the grove goon,   *saw*
And bar upon his bak the cok away,
560 And criden, "Out, harrow,° and wailaway,   *help*
Ha, ha, the fox," and after him they ran,
And eek with staves many another man;
Ran Colle oure dogge, and Talbot and Gerland,[7]
And Malkin with a distaf in hir hand,
565 Ran cow and calf, and eek the verray hogges,
Sore aferd° for berking of the dogges   *frightened*
And shouting of the men and wommen eke.
They ronne° so hem thoughte hir herte breke;[8]   *ran*
They yelleden as feendes doon in helle;
570 The dokes° criden as men wolde hem quelle;°   *ducks / kill*
The gees for fere flowen° over the trees;   *flew*
Out of the hive cam the swarm of bees;
So hidous was the noise, a, benedicite,°   *bless me*
Certes, he Jakke Straw[9] and his meinee°   *company*
575 Ne made nevere shoutes half so shrille
Whan that they wolden any Fleming kille,
As thilke day was maad upon the fox:
Of bras they broughten bemes° and of box,°   *trumpets / boxwood*
Of horn, of boon,° in whiche they blewe and pouped,[1]   *bone*
580 And therwithal they skriked[2] and they houped—
It seemed as that hevene sholde falle.
    Now goode men, I praye you herkneth alle:
Lo, how Fortune turneth° sodeinly   *reverses, overturns*
The hope and pride eek of hir enemy.
585 This cok that lay upon the foxes bak,
In al his drede unto the fox he spak,
And saide, "Sire, if that I were as ye,
Yit sholde I sayn, as wis° God helpe me,   *surely*
'Turneth ayain, ye proude cherles alle!
590 A verray pestilence upon you falle!*

---

6. According to the legend, Nero not only set fire to Rome (in A.D 64) but also put many senators to death.
7. Two other dogs.
8. Would break.

9. One of the leaders of the Peasants' Revolt in 1381, which was partially directed against the Flemings living in London.
1. Tooted.
2. Shrieked. "Houped": whooped.

Now am I come unto this wodes side,
Maugree your heed,[3] the cok shal here abide.
I wol him ete, in faith, and that anoon.' "
    The fox answerde, "In faith, it shal be doon."
595 And as he spak that word, al sodeinly
The cok brak from his mouth deliverly,°   *nimbly*
And hye upon a tree he fleigh° anoon.   *flew*
    And whan the fox sawgh that he was agoon,
"Allas," quod he, "O Chauntecleer, allas!
600 I have to you," quod he, "ydoon trespas,
In as muche as I maked you aferd
Whan I you hente° and broughte out of the yeerd.   *seized*
But sire, I dide it in no wikke° entente: *wicked*
Come down, and I shal telle you what I mente.
605 I shal saye sooth to you, God help me so."
    "Nay thanne," quod he, "I shrewe° us bothe two: *curse*
But first I shrewe myself, bothe blood and bones,
If thou bigile me ofter than ones;
Thou shalt namore thurgh thy flaterye
610 Do° me to singe and winken with myn yë.   *cause*
For he that winketh whan he sholde see,
Al wilfully, God lat him nevere thee."°   *thrive*
    "Nay," quod the fox, "but God yive him meschaunce
That is so undiscreet of governaunce°   *self-control*
615 That jangleth° whan he sholde holde his pees."   *chatters*
    Lo, swich it is for to be reccheless°   *careless*
And necligent and truste on flaterye.
But ye that holden this tale a folye
As of a fox, or of a cok and hen,
620 Taketh the moralitee, goode men.
For Saint Paul saith that al that writen is
To oure doctrine it is ywrit, ywis:[4]
Taketh the fruit, and lat the chaf be stille.
Now goode God, if that it be thy wille,
625 As saith my lord, so make us alle goode men,
And bringe us to his hye blisse. Amen.

---

3. Despite your head—i.e., despite anything you can do.
4. See Romans 15.4.

From The Parson's Tale[1]

The Introduction

By that[2] the Manciple hadde his tale al ended,
The sonne fro the south line[3] was descended
So lowe, that he has nat to my sighte
Degrees nine and twenty as in highte.
5   Four of the clokke it was, so as I gesse,
For elevene foot, or litel more or lesse,
My shadwe was at thilke time as there,
Of swich feet as° my lengthe parted° were   *as if / divided*
In sixe feet equal of proporcioun.[4]
10   Therwith the moones exaltacioun[5]—
I mene Libra—always gan ascende,
As we were entring at a thropes° ende.   *village's*
For which oure Host, as he was wont to gie°   *lead*
As in this caas oure joly compaignye,
15   Saide in this wise, "Lordinges everichoon,
Now lakketh us no tales mo than oon:
Fulfild is my sentence° and my decree;   *purpose*
I trowe° that we han herd of ech degree;   *believe*
Almost fulfild is al myn ordinaunce.
20   I praye to God, so yive him right good chaunce
That telleth this tale to us lustily.

1. Among the moral writers of the later Middle Ages the pilgrimage was so commonly treated as an allegory of man's life that Chaucer's audience must have been surprised to find the *Canterbury Tales* so little allegorical. At the end of his life, however, and at the end of his work, Chaucer seems to have been caught up in the venerable allegory. Some 10 months before his death he rented a house in the garden of Westminster Abbey, and it is possible that during these months—perhaps when he felt his death approaching—he fell under the influence of the monks of Westminster. In any case, in the Parson's Tale, and in its short Introduction and in the Retraction that follows it, Chaucer seems to be making an end for two pilgrimages that had become one, that of his fiction and that of his life.

In the Introduction to the tale we find the 29 pilgrims moving through a nameless little village as the sun sinks to within 29 degrees of the horizon. The atmosphere contains something of both the chill and the urgency of a late autumn afternoon, and we are surprised to find that the pilgrimage is almost over, that there is need for haste in order to make that "good end" that every medieval Christian hoped for. This delicately suggestive passage, rich with allegorical overtones, introduces an extremely long sermon on penitence and the deadly sins, probably translated by Chaucer from French or Latin some years earlier, before he had begun the *Canterbury Tales*.

The sermon is at times not without animation, but in general Chaucer provides no exception to the statement that Middle English prose is inferior to Middle English verse. But then the intent of the sermon is didactic, not artistic, and according to the more rigorous theologians of the time, didactic intent is infinitely more important than artistic expression.

It is to this doctrine that Chaucer yielded at the end of his life. The Retraction which follows and concludes the Parson's Tale offers Chaucer's apology for having written all the works on which his reputation as a great poet depends, not only such stories as the Miller's Tale, but also his loveliest and seemingly most harmless poems. Yet a readiness to deny his own reality before the reality of his God is implicit in many of Chaucer's works, and the placement of the Retraction within the artistic structure of the *Canterbury Tales* suggests that while Chaucer denied his art, he seems to have recognized that he and it were inseparable.

2. By the time that.
3. I.e., the line that runs some 28 degrees to the south of the celestial equator and parallel to it.
4. This detailed analysis merely says that the shadows are lengthening.
5. I.e., the astrological sign in which the moon's influence was dominant. "Libra": the constellation of the Scales.

Sire preest," quod he, "artou a vicary,°   *vicar*
Or arte a Person? Say sooth, by thy fay.°   *faith*
Be what thou be, ne breek° thou nat oure play,   *break*
25 For every man save thou hath told his tale.
Unbokele and shew us what is in thy male!°   *bag*
For trewely, me thinketh by thy cheere°   *expression*
Thou sholdest knitte up wel a greet matere.
Tel us a fable anoon, for cokkes bones!"
30   This Person answerde al atones,[6]
"Thou getest fable noon ytold for me,
For Paul, that writeth unto Timothee,
Repreveth° hem that waiven soothfastnesse,[7]   *reproves*
And tellen fables and swich wrecchednesse.
35 Why sholde I sowen draf° out of my fest,°   *chaff / fist*
Whan I may sowen whete if that me lest?[8]
For which I saye that if you list to heere
Moralitee and vertuous matere,
And thanne that ye wol yive me audience,
40 I wol ful fain,° at Cristes reverence,   *gladly*
Do you plesance leveful° as I can.   *lawful*
But trusteth wel, I am a southren man:
I can nat geeste Rum-Ram-Ruf by lettre[9]—
Ne, God woot, rym holde° I but litel bettre.   *consider*
45 And therfore, if you list, I wol nat glose;[1]
I wol you telle a merye tale in prose,
To knitte up al this feeste and make an ende.
And Jesu for his grace wit me sende
To shewe you the way in this viage°   *journey*
50 Of thilke parfit glorious pilgrimage
That highte Jerusalem celestial.
And if ye vouche sauf, anoon I shal
Biginne upon my tale, for which I praye
Telle youre avis:° I can no bettre saye.   *opinion*
55 But nathelees, this meditacioun
I putte it ay under correccioun
Of clerkes, for I am nat textuel:[2]
I take but the sentence,° trusteth wel.   *meaning*
Therefore I make protestacioun°   *public acknowledgment*
60 That I wol stonde to correccioun."
   Upon this word we han assented soone,
For, as it seemed, it was for to doone
To enden in som vertuous sentence,°   *doctrine*
And for to yive him space and audience;
65 And bede[3] oure Host he sholde to him saye

---

6. Immediately.
7. Depart from truth. See 1 Timothy 1.4.
8. It pleases me.
9. I.e., I cannot tell stories in the alliterative measure (without rhyme): this form of poetry was not

common in southeastern England.
1. I.e., speak in order to please.
2. Literal, faithful to the letter.
3. I.e., we bade.

That alle we to telle his tale him praye.
　　Oure Hoste hadde the wordes for us alle:
"Sire preest," quod he, "now faire you bifalle:
Telleth," quod he, "youre meditacioun.
70　But hasteth you; the sonne wol adown.
Beeth fructuous,° and that in litel space,°   *fruitful / time*
And to do wel God sende you his grace.
Saye what you list, and we wol gladly heere."
And with that word he saide in this manere.

Chaucer's Retraction

Now praye I to hem alle that herkne this litel tretis[1] or rede, that if
ther be any thing in it that liketh[2] hem, that therof they thanken oure
Lord Jesu Crist, of whom proceedeth al wit[3] and al goodnesse. And if
ther be any thing that displese hem, I praye hem also that they arrette it
to the defaute of myn unconning,[4] and nat to my wil, that wolde ful
fain have said bettre if I hadde had conning. For oure book saith, "Al
that is writen is writen for oure doctrine,"[5] and that is myn entente.
Wherfore I biseeke[6] you mekely, for the mercy of God, that ye praye for
me that Crist have mercy on me and foryive me my giltes, and namely[7]
of my translacions and enditinges of worldly vanitees, the whiche I revoke
in my retraccions: as is the *Book of Troilus*; the Book also of *Fame*; the
Book of the Five and Twenty Ladies;[8] the *Book of the Duchesse*; the *Book
of Saint Valentines Day of the Parlement of Briddes*; the *Tales of Canterbury*, thilke that sounen into[9] sinne; the *Book of the Leon*;[1] and many
another book, if they were in my remembrance, and many a song and
many a leccherous lay: that Crist for his grete mercy foryive me the
sinne. But of the translacion of Boece[2] *De Consolatione*, and othere
bookes of legendes of saintes, and omelies,[3] and moralitee, and devo-
cion, that thanke I oure Lord Jesu Crist and his blisful Moder and alle
the saintes of hevene, biseeking hem that they from hennes[4] forth unto
my lives ende sende me grace to biwaile my giltes and to studye to the
salvacion of my soule, and graunte me grace of verray penitence, confession, and satisfaccion to doon in this present lif, thurgh the benigne
grace of him that is king of kinges and preest over alle preestes, that
boughte[5] us with the precious blood of his herte, so that I may been oon
of hem at the day of doom that shulle be saved. *Qui cum patre et Spiritu
Sancto vivis et regnas Deus per omnia saecula.*[6] Amen.

1386–1400

---

1. Hear this little treatise.
2. Pleases.
3. Understanding.
4. Ascribe it to the defect of my lack of skill.
5. Romans 15.4.
6. Beseech.
7. Especially. "Enditinges": compositions.
8. I.e., the *Legend of Good Women*.

9. Those that tend toward.
1. The *Book of the Lion* has not been preserved.
2. Boethius.
3. Homilies.
4. Hence.
5. Redeemed.
6. Who with the Father and the Holy Spirit livest
and reignest God forever.

LYRICS AND OCCASIONAL VERSE[1]

Merciless Beauty[2]

1

Youre yën two wol slee° me sodeinly:		*slay*
I may the beautee of hem nat sustene,°		*withstand*
So woundeth it thurghout myn herte keene.°		*keenly*

And but° youre word wol helen hastily   *unless*
5 Myn hertes wounde, whil that it is greene,[3]
    Youre yën two wol slee me sodeinly:
    I may the beautee of hem nat sustene.

Upon my trouthe, I saye you faithfully
That ye been of my lif and deeth the queene,
10 For with my deeth the trouthe shal be seene.
    Youre yën two wol slee me sodeinly:
    I may the beautee of hem nat sustene,
    So woundeth it thurghout myn herte keene.

2

So hath youre beautee fro youre herte chaced		
15 Pitee, that me ne availeth nought to plaine:°		*complain*
For Daunger halt[4] youre mercy in his chaine.		

Giltelees my deeth thus han ye me purchaced;°		*procured*
I saye you sooth, me needeth nought to feine:°		*dissemble*
So hath youre beautee fro youre herte chaced		
20 Pitee, that me ne availeth nought to plaine.		

Allas, that nature hath in you compaced°		*enclosed*
So greet beautee that no man may attaine		
To mercy, though he sterve° for the paine.		*die*
So hath youre beautee fro youre herte chaced		
25 Pitee, that me ne availeth nought to plaine:		
For Daunger halt youre mercy in his chaine.		

1. As a man of accomplishments who was often at court, Chaucer must, like other courtiers, have been called upon to write both occasional verse and lyrics. Of the handful of these shorter poems that have survived, several of the best are included here: they reveal the ways in which Chaucer handled some of the poetic modes and attitudes of his time. These modes include courtly lyrics like the stereotyped lover's complaint to a cruel mistress; but the extreme convention of this form also aroused Chaucer's sense of parody in what might well be termed "antilyrics"—poems in which the courtly-love framework brings Chaucer's irony and indirection into play. He sometimes addressed particular per-

sons in a manner that could be light and teasing. But he could also be quite serious in a few homiletic poems dispensing political, social, and moral wisdom.
2. The first two sections of this poem employ the typical imagery and extravagant emotion of courtly-love lyrics—the power of the lady's eyes to slay the lover, for instance, and the struggle between her native pity and her "daunger" (haughtiness). But it ends where a real lyric could never end: the poet's self-congratulation, at the failure of his affair, on his unimpaired health.
3. I.e., fresh.
4. Haughtiness holds.

3

Sin° I fro Love escaped am so fat,   *since*
I nevere thenke° to been in his prison lene: *intend*
Sin I am free, I counte him nat a bene.[5]

30   He may answere and saye right this and that;
I do no fors,[6] I speke right as I mene:
Sin I fro Love escaped am so fat,
I nevere thenke to been in his prison lene.

Love hath my name ystrike° out of his sclat,°   *struck / slate*
35   And he is strike out of my bookes clene
For everemo; ther is noon other mene.°   *solution*
Sin I fro Love escaped am so fat,
I nevere thenke to been in his prison lene:
Sin I am free, I counte him nat a bene.

To His Scribe Adam[1]

Adam scrivain,° if evere it thee bifalle   *scribe*
Boece[2] or *Troilus* for to writen newe,
Under thy longe lokkes thou moste[3] have the scalle,°   *scurf*
But after my making thou write more trewe,[4]
5   So ofte a day I moot° thy werk renewe,   *must*
It to correcte, and eek to rubbe and scrape:
And al is thurgh thy necligence and rape.°   *haste*

Complaint to His Purse[1]

To you, my purs, and to noon other wight,
Complaine I, for ye be my lady dere.
I am so sory, now that ye be light,
For certes, but if[2] ye make me hevy cheere,
5   Me were as lief[3] be laid upon my beere;°   *bier*
For which unto youre mercy thus I crye:
Beeth hevy again, or elles moot° I die.   *must*

---

5. I don't consider him worth a bean.
6. I don't care.
1. This *jeu d'esprit*, called forth by the ineffi-
ciency of his amanuensis, is written in the verse
form of Chaucer's great poem *Troilus and Criseide.*
2. I.e., Chaucer's translation of Boethius's *De
Consolatione.* "*Troilus*": *Troilus and Criseide.*
3. I.e., may you.
4. Unless you write more accurately what I've
composed.
1. In this variation on the courtly-love lyric the

conventional language of love is both used and
misused to express love of cash. Ladies, like coins,
should be golden, and like purses they should not
be "light" (i.e., fickle). On the other hand, they
should not be heavy, as purses should be. The poem
is in the characteristic three-stanza *ballade* form,
with the usual "envoy" addressed to a friend or
noble patron. The patron in this case was the
recently crowned Henry IV, who is being indirectly petitioned to refill Chaucer's empty purse.
2. Unless.
3. I'd just as soon.

Now voucheth sauf this day er it be night
That I of you the blisful soun may heere,
10 Or see youre colour, lik the sonne bright,
That of yelownesse hadde nevere peere.
Ye be my life, ye be myn hertes steere,°   *rudder, guide*
Queene of confort and of good compaignye:
Beeth hevy again, or elles moot I die.

15 Ye purs, that been to me my lives light
And saviour, as in this world down here,
Out of this tonne[4] helpe me thurgh your might,
Sith that ye wol nat be my tresorere;°   *disburser*
For I am shave as neigh° as any frere.°   *close / friar*
20 But yit I praye unto youre curteisye:
Beeth hevy again, or elles moot I die.

Envoy to Henry IV

O conquerour of Brutus Albioun,[5]
Which that by line° and free eleccioun   *lineage*
Been verray king, this song to you I sende:
25 And ye, that mowen° alle oure harmes amende, *may*
Have minde upon my supplicacioun.

Gentilesse[1]

The firste fader and findere° of gentilesse,   *founder*
What° man desireth gentil for to be   *whatever*
Moste folwe his traas,° and alle his wittes dresse[2] *path*
Vertu to sue,° and vices for to flee: *follow*
5 For unto vertu longeth° dignitee,   *belongs*
And nought the revers, saufly° dar I deeme,   *safely*
Al were he[3] mitre, crowne, or diademe.

This firste stok was ground of rightwisnesse,° *righteousness*
Trewe of his word, sobre, pietous,[4] and free,
10 Clene of his gost,° and loved bisinesse   *spirit*
Against the vice of slouthe,° in honestee;   *sloth*
And but his heir love vertu as dide he,
He is nat gentil, though he riche° seeme,   *noble*
Al were he mitre, crowne, or diademe.

---

4. Tun, meaning "predicament."
5. Britain (Albion) was supposed to have been
founded by Brutus, the grandson of Aeneas, the
founder of Rome.
1. The virtue of "gentilesse" combined a courtesy
of manner with a courtesy of mind. That it is not
the inevitable adjunct of aristocratic birth (though
most appropriate to it) was a medieval commonplace, to which Chaucer here gives succinct—if

conventional—expression. It is important to
observe, however, that the moral democracy
implied by this doctrine was never transferred by
the Middle Ages to the political or even the social
realm.
2. I.e., must follow his (the first father's) path and
dispose all his (own) wits.
3. Even if he wear.
4. Merciful. "Free": generous.

15 Vice may wel be heir to old richesse,
But ther may no man, as ye may wel see,
Biquethe his heir his vertuous noblesse:
That is appropred° unto no degree   *exclusively assigned*
But to the firste fader in majestee,
20 That maketh his heir him that wol him queme,°   *please*
Al were he mitre, crowne, or diademe.

Truth[1]

Flee fro the prees° and dwelle with soothfastnesse;   *crowd*
Suffise unto° thy thing, though it be smal;   *be content with*
For hoord hath[2] hate, and climbing tikelnesse;°   *insecurity*
Prees hath envye, and wele° blent° overal.   *prosperity / blinds*
5 Savoure° no more than thee bihoove shal;   *relish*
Rule wel thyself that other folk canst rede:°   *advise*
And Trouthe shal delivere,[3] it is no drede.°   *doubt*

Tempest thee nought al crooked to redresse[4]
In trust of hire[5] that turneth as a bal;
10 Muche wele stant in litel bisinesse;[6]
Be war therfore to spurne ayains an al.[7]
Strive nat as dooth the crokke° with the wal.   *pot*
Daunte° thyself that dauntest otheres deede: *master*
And Trouthe shal delivere, it is no drede.

15 That thee is sent, receive in buxomnesse;°   *obedience*
The wrastling for the world axeth° a fal;   *asks for*
Here is noon hoom, here nis° but wildernesse: *is not*
Forth, pilgrim, forth! Forth, beest, out of thy stal!
Know thy countree, looke up, thank God of al.
20 Hold the heigh way and lat thy gost° thee lede: *spirit*
And Trouthe shal delivere, it is no drede.

Envoy

Therfore, thou Vache,[8] leve thyn olde wrecchednesse
Unto the world; leve[9] now to be thral.
Crye him mercy that of his heigh goodnesse
25 Made thee of nought, and in especial

---

1. Taking as his theme Christ's words to his disciples (in John 8.32), "And ye shall know the truth,
and the truth shall make you free," Chaucer plays
upon the triple meaning that the Middle English
word "trouthe" seems to have had for him: the
religious truth of Christianity, the moral virtue of
integrity, and the philosophical idea of reality. By
maintaining one's faith and one's integrity, one rises
superior to the vicissitudes of this world and comes
eventually to know reality—which is not, however, of this world.

2. Hoarding causes.
3. I.e., truth shall make you free.
4. Do not disturb yourself to straighten all that's
crooked.
5. Fortune, who turns like a ball in that she is
always presenting a different aspect to men.
6. Peace of mind stands in little anxiety.
7. I.e., to kick against the pricks.
8. Probably Sir Philip de la Vache, with a pun on
the French for "cow."
9. I.e., cease.

Draw unto him, and pray in general,
For thee and eek for othere, hevenelich meede:[1]
And Trouthe shal delivere, it is no drede.

1. "Reward," with a pun on "meadow."

SIR GAWAIN AND THE GREEN KNIGHT

ca. 1375–1400

Nothing is known about the author of *Sir Gawain and the Green Knight* except that he probably wrote the three religious poems—*Pearl, Patience,* and *Purity*—that are preserved in the same manuscript as *Sir Gawain* (no other copies of any of the poems have come to light); and he may also have written a fifth poem, which, like the others, is alliterative, but is preserved in a different manuscript—a charming legend of St. Erkenwald. The dialect of *Sir Gawain* points to an origin in provincial England, about 150 miles northwest of the capital: thus of the three great poets of late medieval England, two, the authors of *Sir Gawain* and *Piers Plowman,* were representatives of cultural centers remote from the royal court at London where Chaucer spent his life. We know almost nothing about these provincial centers, but the works that emanated from them demonstrate a high level of culture. The poet of *Sir Gawain,* indeed, was a most sophisticated and urbane writer, and even though his language (a dialect most difficult for us today and probably difficult for Londoners in his own time) and his alliterative measure would have been considered barbaric by Chaucer's London audience, the subtlety of his perceptions and the delicacy with which he handles his narrative is not unworthy of Chaucer himself. And although it is impossible to date the poem with any accuracy, its author must have been an almost exact contemporary of Chaucer.

Sir Gawain ingeniously combines two plots, common in folklore and romance, though not found together elsewhere: the beheading contest, in which two parties agree to an exchange of blows with a sword or ax, and the temptation, an attempted seduction of the hero by a lady. The motif of the green man's decapitation originates in very ancient folklore, probably in a vegetation myth in which the beheading would have been a ritual death that insured the return of spring to the earth and the regrowth of the crops. But this primitive theme has been entirely rationalized by the late medieval poet, who sees in his inherited plot an opportunity to study how successfully Gawain, as a man wholly dedicated to Christian ideals, maintains those ideals when he is subjected to unusual pressures. The poem is a rare combination: at once a comedy—even a satire—of manners and a profoundly Christian view of character and its destiny. The court of King Arthur is presented, in the most grandiose and laudatory of language, as the place where the ideal of chivalry has reached its zenith, where all is courtesy and martial prowess in defense of the right. The praise bestowed by the poet upon this court may seem excessive, and indeed the sequel suggests that the author made it so intentionally. For when the court is invaded by the Green Knight, arrogant, monstrous, and yet exasperatingly reasonable, it suddenly seems to become slightly unreal, as if, the Green Knight insultingly implies, its reputation were founded more on fiction than on fact—as if the poets that celebrated it had been working harder to enhance its glory than the knights themselves. In any case, the court is to receive a testing, which is naturally entrusted to the most courteous and valiant knight of the Round Table (in this most English of Arthurian romances Gawain has not been replaced as the best of knights by the continental-born Lancelot).

Sir Gawain's coat of arms, displayed on his shield, is the five-pointed star called the pentangle, which the poet tells us is a symbol of truth—the first of the chivalric virtues also loved by Chaucer's Knight. Truth is the quality, even more than martial courage, that is put to the test in Gawain's quest to seek out the Green Chapel where he will presumably die under the Green Knight's return blow. It is also tested, however, in the bedroom of a magical castle in the wilderness in ways that are by no means obvious to the hero—or to the reader—until the final encounter with the Green Knight.

Sir Gawain is one of the latest and certainly the best of the Middle English romances; yet its greatness lies in the fact that, without ever ceasing to be a romance, a fiction full of the most exquisite comic touches, it is something much larger, one of the really significant literary achievements of the Middle Ages.

Sir Gawain belongs to the so-called Alliterative Revival, a sudden emergence of a body of poems in the alliterative meter of Old English verse. Actually the alliterative tradition must have continued almost without interruption, but only a handful of alliterative poems survives to testify to it from the eleventh century until the Revival in the latter half of the fourteenth. Although the Middle English alliterative line preserves the essential feature of Old English verse—the binding of the two halves of the line together through alliteration—it is longer and does not observe all the rules governing alliteration and stress in Old English. For details, see the section on Old and Middle English Prosody in the general introduction. *Sir Gawain* is written in a unique stanza combining alliteration and rhyme. A group of long alliterative lines (the number of lines varies) concludes with a word or phrase of two syllables—the "bob"—followed by a quatrain—the "wheel"—rhyming *ababa* with the bob. The opening stanza is given below in Middle English with a literal interlinear translation. The alliterating sounds, which should be stressed in reading, have been italicized.

Sithen the *sege* and the *assaut* was *sesed* at Troye,
After the siege and the assault was ceased at Troy,

The *borgh* *brittened* and *brent* to *brondes* and askes,
The city crumbled and burned to brands and ashes,

The *tulk* that the *trammes* of *tresoun* ther wroght
The man who the plots of treason there wrought

Was *tried* for his *tricherie*, the *trewest* on erthe.
Was tried for his treachery, the truest on earth.

Hit was *Ennias* the *athel* and his *highe* kynde,
It was Aeneas the noble and his high race,

That sithen *depreced* *provinces*, and *patrounes* bicome
Who after subjugated provinces, and lords became

Welneghe of al the wele in the west iles.
Wellnigh of all the wealth in the west isles.

Fro riche Romulus to Rome ricchis hym swythe,
Then noble Romulus to Rome proceeds quickly,

With gret bobbaunce that burghe he biges upon fyrst
With great pride that city he builds at first

And nevenes hit his aune nome, as hit now hat;
And names it his own name, as it now is called;

Ticius to Tuskan and teldes bigynnes,
Ticius (goes) to Tuscany and houses begins,

Langaberde in Lumbardie lyftes up homes,
Longbeard in Lombardy raises up homes,

And fer over the French flod, Felix Brutus
And far over the English Channel, Felix Brutus

On mony bonkkes ful brode Bretayn he settes
On many banks very broad Brittain he sets

Wyth wynne,
With joy,

Where werre and wrake and wonder
Where war and revenge and wondrous happenings

Bi sythes has wont therinne,
On occasions have dwelled therein

And oft bothe blysse and blunder
And often both joy and strife

Ful skete has skyfted synne.
Very swiftly have alternated since.

Sir Gawain and the Green Knight[1]

Part 1

Since the siege and the assault was ceased at Troy,
The walls breached and burnt down to brands and ashes,
The knight that had knotted the nets of deceit
Was impeached for his perfidy, proven most true,[2]
It was high-born Aeneas and his haughty race   5
That since prevailed over provinces, and proudly reigned
Over well-nigh all the wealth of the West Isles.[3]

---

1. The Modern English translation is by Marie Borroff (1967), who has reproduced the alliterative meter of the original as well as the "bob and wheel," the five-line rhyming group that concludes each of the long irregular stanzas.
2. The treacherous knight is Aeneas who was a traitor to his city, Troy, according to medieval tradition, but Aeneas was actually tried ("impeached") by the Greeks for his refusal to hand over to them his sister Polyxena.
3. Perhaps western Europe.

Great Romulus[4] to Rome repairs in haste;
With boast and with bravery builds he that city
And names it with his own name, that it now bears.   10
Ticius[5] to Tuscany, and towers raises,
Langobard in Lombardy lays out homes,
And far over the French Sea, Felix Brutus[6]
On many broad hills and high Britain he sets,
            most fair.   15
       Where war and wrack and wonder
       By shifts have sojourned there,
       And bliss by turns with blunder
       In that land's lot had share.

And since this Britain was built by this baron great,   20
Bold boys bred there, in broils delighting,
That did in their day many a deed most dire.
More marvels have happened in this merry land
Than in any other I know, since that olden time,
But of those that here built, of British kings,   25
King Arthur was counted most courteous of all,
Wherefore an adventure I aim to unfold,
That a marvel of might some men think it,
And one unmatched among Arthur's wonders.
If you will listen to my lay but a little while,   30
As I heard it in hall, I shall hasten to tell
            anew.
       As it was fashioned featly
       In tale of derring-do,
       And linked in measures meetly   35
       By letters tried and true.

This king lay at Camelot[7] at Christmastide;
Many good knights and gay his guests were there,
Arrayed of the Round Table[8] rightful brothers,
With feasting and fellowship and carefree mirth.   40
There true men contended in tournaments many,
Joined there in jousting these gentle knights,
Then came to the court for carol-dancing,
For the feast was in force full fifteen days,
With all the meat and the mirth that men could devise,   45
Such gaiety and glee, glorious to hear,
Brave din by day, dancing by night.
High were their hearts in halls and chambers,

---

4. The legendary founder of Rome is here given Trojan ancestry, like Aeneas.
5. Not otherwise known. "Langobard" was the reputed founder of Lombardy.
6. Great-grandson of Aeneas and legendary founder of Britain; not elsewhere given the name Felix (Latin "happy").

7. Capital of Arthur's kingdom, presumably located in southwest England or southern Wales.
8. According to legend, Merlin made the Round Table after a dispute broke out among Arthur's knights about precedence: it seated 100 knights. The table described in the poem is not round.

These lords and these ladies, for life was sweet.
In peerless pleasures passed they their days,   50
The most noble knights known under Christ,
And the loveliest ladies that lived on earth ever,
And he the comeliest king, that that court holds,
For all this fair folk in their first age
                were still.   55
      Happiest of mortal kind,
      King noblest famed of will;
      You would now go far to find
      So hardy a host on hill.

While the New Year was new, but yesternight come,   60
This fair folk at feast two-fold was served,
When the king and his company were come in together,
The chanting in chapel achieved and ended.
Clerics and all the court acclaimed the glad season,
Cried Noel anew, good news to men;   65
Then gallants gather gaily, hand-gifts to make,
Called them out clearly, claimed them by hand,
Bickered long and busily about those gifts.
Ladies laughed aloud, though losers they were,
And he that won was not angered, as well you will know.[9]   70
All this mirth they made until meat was served;
When they had washed them worthily, they went to their seats,
The best seated above, as best it beseemed,
Guenevere the goodly queen gay in the midst
On a dais well-decked and duly arrayed   75
With costly silk curtains, a canopy over,
Of Toulouse and Turkestan tapestries rich,
All broidered and bordered with the best gems
Ever brought into Britain, with bright pennies
                to pay.   80
      Fair queen, without a flaw,
      She glanced with eyes of grey.
      A seemlier that once he saw,
      In truth, no man could say.

But Arthur would not eat till all were served;   85
So light was his lordly heart, and a little boyish;
His life he liked lively—the less he cared
To be lying for long, or long to sit,
So busy his young blood, his brain so wild.
And also a point of pride pricked him in heart,   90
For he nobly had willed, he would never eat
On so high a holiday, till he had heard first
Of some fair feat or fray some far-borne tale,

---

9. The dispensing of New Year's gifts seems to have involved kissing.

Of some marvel of might, that he might trust,
By champions of chivalry achieved in arms,   95
Or some suppliant came seeking some single knight
To join with him in jousting, in jeopardy each
To lay life for life, and leave it to fortune
To afford him on field fair hap or other.
Such is the king's custom, when his court he holds   100
At each far-famed feast amid his fair host
                              so dear.
              The stout king stands in state
              Till a wonder shall appear;
              He leads, with heart elate,   105
              High mirth in the New Year.

So he stands there in state, the stout young king,
Talking before the high table[1] of trifles fair.
There Gawain the good knight by Guenevere sits,
With Agravain à la dure main on her other side,   110
Both knights of renown, and nephews of the king.
Bishop Baldwin above begins the table,
And Yvain, son of Urien, ate with him there.
These few with the fair queen were fittingly served;
At the side-tables sat many stalwart knights.   115
Then the first course comes, with clamor of trumpets
That were bravely bedecked with bannerets bright,
With noise of new drums and the noble pipes.
Wild were the warbles that wakened that day
In strains that stirred many strong men's hearts.   120
There dainties were dealt out, dishes rare,
Choice fare to choose, on chargers so many
That scarce was there space to set before the people
The service of silver, with sundry meats,
                              on cloth.   125
              Each fair guest freely there
              Partakes, and nothing loth;
              Twelve dishes before each pair;
              Good beer and bright wine both.

Of the service itself I need say no more,   130
For well you will know no tittle was wanting.
Another noise and a new was well-nigh at hand,
That the lord might have leave his life to nourish;
For scarce were the sweet strains still in the hall,
And the first course come to that company fair,   135
There hurtles in at the hall-door an unknown rider,
One the greatest on ground in growth of his frame:
From broad neck to buttocks so bulky and thick,

1. The high table is on a dais; the side tables (line 115) are on the main floor and run along the walls at a right angle with the high table.

And his loins and his legs so long and so great,
Half a giant on earth I hold him to be,   140
But believe him no less than the largest of men,
And that the seemliest in his stature to see, as he rides,
For in back and in breast though his body was grim,
His waist in its width was worthily small,
And formed with every feature in fair accord   145
               was he.
        Great wonder grew in hall
        At his hue most strange to see,
        For man and gear and all
        Were green as green could be.   150

And in guise all of green, the gear and the man:
A coat cut close, that clung to his sides,
And a mantle to match, made with a lining
Of furs cut and fitted—the fabric was noble,
Embellished all with ermine, and his hood beside,   155
That was loosed from his locks, and laid on his shoulders.
With trim hose and tight, the same tint of green,
His great calves were girt, and gold spurs under
He bore on silk bands that embellished his heels,
And footgear well-fashioned, for riding most fit.   160
And all his vesture verily was verdant green;
Both the bosses on his belt and other bright gems
That were richly ranged on his raiment noble
About himself and his saddle, set upon silk,
That to tell half the trifles would tax my wits,   165
The butterflies and birds embroidered thereon
In green of the gayest, with many a gold thread.
The pendants of the breast-band, the princely crupper,
And the bars of the bit were brightly enameled;
The stout stirrups were green, that steadied his feet,   170
And the bows of the saddle and the side-panels both,
That gleamed all and glinted with green gems about.
The steed he bestrides of that same green
              so bright.
        A green horse great and thick;   175
        A headstrong steed of might;
        In broidered bridle quick,
        Mount matched man aright.

Gay was this goodly man in guise all of green,
And the hair of his head to his horse suited;   180
Fair flowing tresses enfold his shoulders;
A beard big as a bush on his breast hangs,
That with his heavy hair, that from his head falls,
Was evened all about above both his elbows,
That half his arms thereunder were hid in the fashion   185

Of a king's cap-à-dos,[2] that covers his throat.
The mane of that mighty horse much to it like,
Well curled and becombed, and cunningly knotted
With filaments of fine gold amid the fair green,
Here a strand of the hair, here one of gold;   190
His tail and his foretop twin in their hue,
And bound both with a band of a bright green
That was decked adown the dock with dazzling stones
And tied tight at the top with a triple knot
Where many bells well burnished rang bright and clear.   195
Such a mount in his might, nor man on him riding,
None had seen, I dare swear, with sight in that hall
                              so grand.
                    As lightning quick and light
                    He looked to all at hand;   200
                    It seemed that no man might
                    His deadly dints withstand.

Yet had he no helm, nor hauberk neither,
Nor plate, nor appurtenance appending to arms,
Nor shaft pointed sharp, nor shield for defense,   205
But in his one hand he had a holly bob
That is goodliest in green when groves are bare,
And an ax in his other, a huge and immense,
A wicked piece of work in words to expound:
The head on its haft was an ell long;   210
The spike of green steel, resplendent with gold;
The blade burnished bright, with a broad edge,
As well shaped to shear as a sharp razor;
Stout was the stave in the strong man's gripe,
That was wound all with iron to the weapon's end,   215
With engravings in green of goodliest work.
A lace lightly about, that led to a knot,
Was looped in by lengths along the fair haft,
And tassels thereto attached in a row,
With buttons of bright green, brave to behold.   220
This horseman hurtles in, and the hall enters;
Riding to the high dais, recked he no danger;
Not a greeting he gave as the guests he o'erlooked,
Nor wasted his words, but "Where is," he said,
"The captain of this crowd? Keenly I wish   225
To see that sire with sight, and to himself say
                              my say."
                    He swaggered all about
                    To scan the host so gay;

2. The word *capados* occurs in this form in Middle English only in *Gawain*, here and in line 572. The translator has interpreted it, as the poet apparently did also, as *cap-à-dos*—i.e., a garment covering its wearer "from head to back," on the model of *cap-à-pie*, "from head to foot," referring to armor.

He halted, as if in doubt   230
Who in that hall held sway.

There were stares on all sides as the stranger spoke,
For much did they marvel what it might mean
That a horseman and a horse should have such a hue,
Grow green as the grass, and greener, it seemed,   235
Than green fused on gold more glorious by far.
All the onlookers eyed him, and edged nearer,
And awaited in wonder what he would do,
For many sights had they seen, but such a one never,
So that phantom and faerie the folk there deemed it,   240
Therefore chary of answer was many a champion bold,
And stunned at his strong words stone-still they sat
In a swooning silence in the stately hall.
As all were slipped into sleep, so slackened their speech
                                                        apace.   245
                    Not all, I think, for dread,
                    But some of courteous grace
                    Let him who was their head
                    Be spokesman in that place.

Then Arthur before the high dais that entrance beholds,   250
And hailed him, as behooved, for he had no fear,
And said "Fellow, in faith you have found fair welcome;
The head of this hostelry Arthur am I;
Leap lightly down, and linger, I pray,
And the tale of your intent you shall tell us after."   255
"Nay, so help me," said the other, "He that on high sits,
To tarry here any time, 'twas not mine errand;
But as the praise of you, prince, is puffed up so high,
And your court and your company are counted the best,
Stoutest under steel-gear on steeds to ride,   260
Worthiest of their works the wide world over,
And peerless to prove in passages of arms,
And courtesy here is carried to its height,
And so at this season I have sought you out.
You may be certain by the branch that I bear in hand   265
That I pass here in peace, and would part friends,
For had I come to this court on combat bent,
I have a hauberk at home, and a helm beside,
A shield and a sharp spear, shining bright,
And other weapons to wield, I ween well, to boot,   270
But as I willed no war, I wore no metal.
But if you be so bold as all men believe,
You will graciously grant the game that I ask
                                        by right."
                    Arthur answer gave   275
                    And said, "Sir courteous knight,

> If contest bare you crave,
> You shall not fail to fight."

"Nay, to fight, in good faith, is far from my thought;
There are about on these benches but beardless children,   280
Were I here in full arms on a haughty steed,
For measured against mine, their might is puny.
And so I call in this court for a Christmas game,
For 'tis Yule and New Year, and many young bloods about;
If any in this house such hardihood claims,   285
Be so bold in his blood, his brain so wild,
As stoutly to strike one stroke for another,
I shall give him as my gift this gisarme noble,
This ax, that is heavy enough, to handle as he likes,
And I shall bide the first blow, as bare as I sit.   290
If there be one so wilful my words to assay,
Let him leap hither lightly, lay hold of this weapon;
I quitclaim it forever, keep it as his own,
And I shall stand him a stroke, steady on this floor,
So you grant me the guerdon to give him another,   295
> sans blame.
>> In a twelvemonth and a day
>> He shall have of me the same;
>> Now be it seen straightway
>> Who dares take up the game."   300

If he astonished them at first, stiller were then
All that household in hall, the high and the low;
The stranger on his green steed stirred in the saddle,
And roisterously his red eyes he rolled all about,
Bent his bristling brows, that were bright green,   305
Wagged his beard as he watched who would arise.
When the court kept its counsel he coughed aloud,
And cleared his throat coolly, the clearer to speak:
"What, is this Arthur's house," said that horseman then,
"Whose fame is so fair in far realms and wide?   310
Where is now your arrogance and your awesome deeds,
Your valor and your victories and your vaunting words?
Now are the revel and renown of the Round Table
Overwhelmed with a word of one man's speech,
For all cower and quake, and no cut felt!"   315
With this he laughs so loud that the lord grieved;
The blood for sheer shame shot to his face,
> and pride.
>> With rage his face flushed red,
>> And so did all beside.   320
>> Then the king as bold man bred
>> Toward the stranger took a stride.

And said "Sir, now we see you will say but folly,
Which whoso has sought, it suits that he find.
No guest here is aghast of your great words.   325
Give to me your gisarme, in God's own name,
And the boon you have begged shall straight be granted."
He leaps to him lightly, lays hold of his weapon;
The green fellow on foot fiercely alights.
Now has Arthur his ax, and the haft grips,   330
And sternly stirs it about, on striking bent.
The stranger before him stood there erect,
Higher than any in the house by a head and more;
With stern look as he stood, he stroked his beard,
And with undaunted countenance drew down his coat,   335
No more moved nor dismayed for his mighty dints
Than any bold man on bench had brought him a drink
                         of wine.
              Gawain by Guenevere
              Toward the king doth now incline: 340
              "I beseech, before all here,
              That this melee may be mine."

"Would you grant me the grace," said Gawain to the king,
"To be gone from this bench and stand by you there,
If I without discourtesy might quit this board,   345
And if my liege lady misliked it not,
I would come to your counsel before your court noble.
For I find it not fit, as in faith it is known,
When such a boon is begged before all these knights,
Though you be tempted thereto, to take it on yourself   350
While so bold men about upon benches sit,
That no host under heaven is hardier of will,
Nor better brothers-in-arms where battle is joined;
I am the weakest, well I know, and of wit feeblest;
And the loss of my life would be least of any;   355
That I have you for uncle is my only praise;
My body, but for your blood, is barren of worth;
And for that this folly befits not a king,
And 'tis I that have asked it, it ought to be mine,
And if my claim be not comely let all this court judge,   360
                         in sight."
              The court assays the claim,
              And in counsel all unite
              To give Gawain the game
              And release the king outright.   365

Then the king called the knight to come to his side,
And he rose up readily, and reached him with speed,
Bows low to his lord, lays hold of the weapon,
And he releases it lightly, and lifts up his hand,

And gives him God's blessing, and graciously prays 370
That his heart and his hand may be hardy both.
"Keep, cousin," said the king, "what you cut with this day,
And if you rule it aright, then readily, I know,
You shall stand the stroke it will strike after."
Gawain goes to the guest with gisarme in hand, 375
And boldly he bides there, abashed not a whit.
Then hails he Sir Gawain, the horseman in green:
"Recount we our contract, ere you come further.
First I ask and adjure you, how you are called
That you tell me true, so that trust it I may." 380
"In good faith," said the good knight, "Gawain am I
Whose buffet befalls you, what'er betide after,
And at this time twelvemonth take from you another
With what weapon you will, and with no man else
                         alive." 385
               The other nods assent:
               "Sir Gawain, as I may thrive,
               I am wondrous well content
               That you this dint shall drive."

"Sir Gawain," said the Green Knight, "By God, I rejoice 390
That your fist shall fetch this favor I seek,
And you have readily rehearsed, and in right terms,
Each clause of my covenant with the king your lord,
Save that you shall assure me, sir, upon oath,
That you shall seek me yourself, wheresoever you deem 395
My lodgings may lie, and look for such wages
As you have offered me here before all this host."
"What is the way there?" said Gawain. "Where do you dwell?
I heard never of your house, by him that made me,
Nor I know you not, knight, your name nor your court. 400
But tell me truly thereof, and teach me your name,
And I shall fare forth to find you, so far as I may,
And this I say in good certain, and swear upon oath."
"That is enough in New Year, you need say no more,"
Said the knight in the green to Gawain the noble, 405
"If I tell you true, when I have taken your knock,
And if you handily have hit, you shall hear straightway
Of my house and my home and my own name;
Then follow in my footsteps by faithful accord.
And if I spend no speech, you shall speed the better: 410
You can feast with your friends, nor further trace
                   my tracks.
               Now hold your grim tool steady
               And show us how it hacks."
               "Gladly, sir; all ready," 415
               Says Gawain; he strokes the ax.

The Green Knight upon ground girds him with care:
Bows a bit with his head, and bares his flesh:
His long lovely locks he laid over his crown,
Let the naked nape for the need be shown.   420
Gawain grips to his ax and gathers it aloft—
The left foot on the floor before him he set—
Brought it down deftly upon the bare neck,
That the shock of the sharp blow shivered the bones
And cut the flesh cleanly and clove it in twain,   425
That the blade of bright steel bit into the ground.
The head was hewn off and fell to the floor;
Many found it at their feet, as forth it rolled;
The blood gushed from the body, bright on the green,
Yet fell not the fellow, nor faltered a whit,   430
But stoutly he starts forth upon stiff shanks,
And as all stood staring he stretched forth his hand,
Laid hold of his head and heaved it aloft,
Then goes to the green steed, grasps the bridle,
Steps into the stirrup, bestrides his mount,   435
And his head by the hair in his hand holds,
And as steady he sits in the stately saddle
As he had met with no mishap, nor missing were
        his head.
        His bulk about he haled,   440
        That fearsome body that bled;
        There were many in the court that quailed
        Before all his say was said.

For the head in his hand he holds right up;
Toward the first on the dais directs he the face,   445
And it lifted up its lids, and looked with wide eyes,
And said as much with its mouth as now you may hear:
"Sir Gawain, forget not to go as agreed,
And cease not to seek till me, sir, you find,
As you promised in the presence of these proud knights.   450
To the Green Chapel come, I charge you, to take
Such a dint as you have dealt—you have well deserved
That your neck should have a knock on New Year's morn.
The Knight of the Green Chapel I am well-known to many,
Wherefore you cannot fail to find me at last;   455
Therefore come, or be counted a recreant knight."
With a roisterous rush he flings round the reins,
Hurtles out at the hall-door, his head in his hand,
That the flint-fire flew from the flashing hooves.
Which way he went, not one of them knew   460
Nor whence he was come in the wide world
        so fair.
        The king and Gawain gay
        Make game of the Green Knight there,

Yet all who saw it say   465
'Twas a wonder past compare.

Though high-born Arthur at heart had wonder,
He let no sign be seen, but said aloud
To the comely queen, with courteous speech,
"Dear dame, on this day dismay you no whit;   470
Such crafts are becoming at Christmastide,
Laughing at interludes, light songs and mirth,
Amid dancing of damsels with doughty knights.
Nevertheless of my meat now let me partake,
For I have met with a marvel, I may not deny."   475
He glanced at Sir Gawain, and gaily he said,
"Now, sir, hang up your ax,[3] that has hewn enough,"
And over the high dais it was hung on the wall
That men in amazement might on it look,
And tell in true terms the tale of the wonder.   480
Then they turned toward the table, these two together,
The good king and Gawain, and made great feast,
With all dainties double, dishes rare,
With all manner of meat and minstrelsy both,
Such happiness wholly had they that day   485
                    in hold.
          Now take care, Sir Gawain,
          That your courage wax not cold
          When you must turn again
          To your enterprise foretold.   490

Part 2

This adventure had Arthur of handsels[4] first
When young was the year, for he yearned to hear tales;
Though they wanted for words when they went to sup,
Now are fierce deeds to follow, their fists stuffed full.
Gawain was glad to begin those games in hall,   495
But if the end be harsher, hold it no wonder,
For though men are merry in mind after much drink,
A year passes apace, and proves ever new:
First things and final conform but seldom.
And so this Yule to the young year yielded place,   500
And each season ensued at its set time;
After Christmas there came the cold cheer of Lent,
When with fish and plainer fare our flesh we reprove;
But then the world's weather with winter contends:
The keen cold lessens, the low clouds lift;   505
Fresh falls the rain in fostering showers

---

3. A colloquial expression equivalent to "bury the   also.
hatchet," but here with an appropriate literal sense   4. New Year's presents.

On the face of the fields; flowers appear.
The ground and the groves wear gowns of green;
Birds build their nests, and blithely sing
That solace of all sorrow with summer comes   510
                ere long.
        And blossoms day by day
        Bloom rich and rife in throng;
        Then every grove so gay
        Of the greenwood rings with song.   515

And then the season of summer with the soft winds,
When Zephyr sighs low over seeds and shoots;
Glad is the green plant growing abroad,
When the dew at dawn drops from the leaves,
To get a gracious glance from the golden sun.   520
But harvest with harsher winds follows hard after,
Warns him to ripen well ere winter comes;
Drives forth the dust in the droughty season,
From the face of the fields to fly high in air.
Wroth winds in the welkin wrestle with the sun,   525
The leaves launch from the linden and light on the ground,
And the grass turns to gray, that once grew green.
Then all ripens and rots that rose up at first,
And so the year moves on in yesterdays many,
And winter once more, by the world's law,   530
                draws nigh.
        At Michaelmas[5] the moon
        Hangs wintry pale in sky;
        Sir Gawain girds him soon
        For travails yet to try.   535

Till All-Hallows' Day[6] with Arthur he dwells,
And he held a high feast to honor that knight
With great revels and rich, of the Round Table.
Then ladies lovely and lords debonair
With sorrow for Sir Gawain were sore at heart;   540
Yet they covered their care with countenance glad:
Many a mournful man made mirth for his sake.
So after supper soberly he speaks to his uncle
Of the hard hour at hand, and openly says,
"Now, liege lord of my life, my leave I take;   545
The terms of this task too well you know—
To count the cost over concerns me nothing.
But I am bound forth betimes to bear a stroke
From the grim man in green, as God may direct."
Then the first and foremost came forth in throng: 550
Yvain and Eric and others of note,

5. September 29.   6. All Saints' Day, November 1.

Sir Dodinal le Sauvage, the Duke of Clarence,
Lionel and Lancelot and Lucan the good,
Sir Bors and Sir Bedivere, big men both,
And many manly knights more, with Mador de la Porte.   555
All this courtly company comes to the king
To counsel their comrade, with care in their hearts;
There was much secret sorrow suffered that day
That one so good as Gawain must go in such wise
To bear a bitter blow, and his bright sword   560
                         lay by.
                 He said, "Why should I tarry?"
                 And smiled with tranquil eye;
                 "In destinies sad or merry,
                 True men can but try."   565

He dwelt there all that day, and dressed in the morning;
Asked early for his arms, and all were brought.
First a carpet of rare cost was cast on the floor
Where much goodly gear gleamed golden bright;
He takes his place promptly and picks up the steel,   570
Attired in a tight coat of Turkestan silk
And a kingly cap-à-dos, closed at the throat,
That was lavishly lined with a lustrous fur.
Then they set the steel shoes on his sturdy feet
And clad his calves about with comely greaves,   575
And plate well-polished protected his knees,
Affixed with fastenings of the finest gold.
Fair cuisses enclosed, that were cunningly wrought,
His thick-thewed thighs, with thongs bound fast,
And massy chain-mail of many a steel ring   580
He bore on his body, above the best cloth,
With brace burnished bright upon both his arms,
Good couters and gay, and gloves of plate,
And all the goodly gear to grace him well
                         that tide.   585
                 His surcoat blazoned bold;
                 Sharp spurs to prick with pride;
                 And a brave silk band to hold
                 The broadsword at his side.

When he had on his arms, his harness was rich,   590
The least latchet or loop laden with gold;
So armored as he was, he heard a mass,
Honored God humbly at the high altar.
Then he comes to the king and his comrades-in-arms,
Takes his leave at last of lords and ladies,   595
And they clasped and kissed him, commending him to Christ.
By then Gringolet was girt with a great saddle
That was gaily agleam with fine gilt fringe,

New-furbished for the need with nail-heads bright;
The bridle and the bars bedecked all with gold;   600
The breast-plate, the saddlebow, the side-panels both,
The caparison and the crupper accorded in hue,
And all ranged on the red the resplendent studs
That glittered and glowed like the glorious sun.
His helm now he holds up and hastily kisses,   605
Well-closed with iron clinches, and cushioned within;
It was high on his head, with a hasp behind,
And a covering of cloth to encase the visor,
All bound and embroidered with the best gems
On broad bands of silk, and bordered with birds,   610
Parrots and popinjays preening their wings,
Lovebirds and love-knots as lavishly wrought
As many women had worked seven winters thereon,
                         entire.
            The diadem costlier yet   615
            That crowned that comely sire,
            With diamonds richly set,
            That flashed as if on fire.

Then they showed forth the shield, that shone all red,
With the pentangle[7] portrayed in purest gold.   620
About his broad neck by the baldric he casts it,
That was meet for the man, and matched him well.
And why the pentangle is proper to that peerless prince
I intend now to tell, though detain me it must.
It is a sign by Solomon sagely devised   625
To be a token of truth, by its title of old,
For it is a figure formed of five points,
And each line is linked and locked with the next
For ever and ever, and hence it is called
In all England, as I hear, the endless knot.   630
And well may he wear it on his worthy arms,
For ever faithful five-fold in five-fold fashion
Was Gawain in good works, as gold unalloyed,
Devoid of all villainy, with virtues adorned
                         in sight.   635
            On shield and coat in view
            He bore that emblem bright,
            As to his word most true
            And in speech most courteous knight.

And first, he was faultless in his five senses,   640
Nor found ever to fail in his five fingers,
And all his fealty was fixed upon the five wounds

---

7. A five-pointed star, formed by five lines which
are drawn without lifting the pencil from the paper,
supposed to have mystical significance; as Solomon's sign (line 625) it was enclosed in a circle.

That Christ got on the cross, as the creed tells;
And wherever this man in melee took part,
His one thought was of this, past all things else,   645
That all his force was founded on the five joys[8]
That the high Queen of heaven had in her child.
And therefore, as I find, he fittingly had
On the inner part of his shield her image portrayed,
That when his look on it lighted, he never lost heart.   650
The fifth of the five fives followed by this knight
Were beneficence boundless and brotherly love
And pure mind and manners, that none might impeach,
And compassion most precious—these peerless five
Were forged and made fast in him, foremost of men.   655
Now all these five fives were confirmed in this knight,
And each linked in other, that end there was none,
And fixed to five points, whose force never failed,
Nor assembled all on a side, nor asunder either,
Nor anywhere at an end, but whole and entire   660
However the pattern proceeded or played out its course.
And so on his shining shield shaped was the knot
Royally in red gold against red gules,
That is the peerless pentangle, prized of old
                       in lore.   665
           Now armed is Gawain gay,
           And bears his lance before,
           And soberly said good day,
           He thought forevermore.

He struck his steed with the spurs and sped on his way   670
So fast that the flint-fire flashed from the stones.
When they saw him set forth they were sore aggrieved,
And all sighed softly, and said to each other,
Fearing for their fellow, "Ill fortune it is
That you, man, must be marred, that most are worthy!   675
His equal on this earth can hardly be found;
To have dealt more discreetly had done less harm,
And have dubbed him a duke, with all due honor.
A great leader of lords he was like to become,
And better so to have been than battered to bits,   680
Beheaded by an elf-man,[9] for empty pride!
Who would credit that a king could be counseled so,
And caught in a cavil in a Christmas game?"
Many were the warm tears they wept from their eyes
When goodly Sir Gawain was gone from the court   685
                      that day.
           No longer he abode,

---

8. The Annunciation, Nativity, Resurrection, Ascension, and Assumption.
9. Supernatural being.

But speedily went his way
Over many a wandering road,
As I heard my author say.   690

Now he rides in his array through the realm of Logres,[1]
Sir Gawain, God knows, though it gave him small joy!
All alone must he lodge through many a long night
Where the food that he fancied was far from his plate;
He had no mate but his mount, over mountain and plain,   695
Nor man to say his mind to but almighty God,
Till he had wandered well-nigh into North Wales.
All the islands of Anglesey he holds on his left,
And follows, as he fares, the fords by the coast,
Comes over at Holy Head, and enters next   700
The Wilderness of Wirral[2]—few were within
That had great good will toward God or man.
And earnestly he asked of each mortal he met
If he had ever heard aught of a knight all green,
Or of a Green Chapel, on ground thereabouts,   705
And all said the same, and solemnly swore
They saw no such knight all solely green
                         in hue.
          Over country wild and strange
          The knight sets off anew;   710
          Often his course must change
          Ere the Chapel comes in view.

Many a cliff must he climb in country wild;
Far off from all his friends, forlorn must he ride;
At each strand or stream where the stalwart passed   715
'Twere a marvel if he met not some monstrous foe,
And that so fierce and forbidding that fight he must.
So many were the wonders he wandered among
That to tell but the tenth part would tax my wits.
Now with serpents he wars, now with savage wolves,   720
Now with wild men of the woods, that watched from the rocks,
Both with bulls and with bears, and with boars besides,
And giants that came gibbering from the jagged steeps.
Had he not borne himself bravely, and been on God's side,
He had met with many mishaps and mortal harms.   725
And if the wars were unwelcome, the winter was worse,
When the cold clear rains rushed from the clouds
And froze before they could fall to the frosty earth.
Near slain by the sleet he sleeps in his irons
More nights than enough, among naked rocks,   730
Where clattering from the crest the cold stream ran

1. One of the names for Arthur's kingdom.
2. Gawain went from Camelot north to the northern coast of Wales, opposite the islands of Anglesey; there he turned east across the Dee to the forest of Wirral in Cheshire.

And hung in hard icicles high overhead.
Thus in peril and pain and predicaments dire
He rides across country till Christmas Eve,
                              our knight.   735
                    And at that holy tide
                    He prays with all his might
                    That Mary may be his guide
                    Till a dwelling comes in sight.

By a mountain next morning he makes his way   740
Into a forest fastness, fearsome and wild;
High hills on either hand, with hoar woods below,
Oaks old and huge by the hundred together.
The hazel and the hawthorn were all intertwined
With rough raveled moss, that raggedly hung,   745
With many birds unblithe upon bare twigs
That peeped most piteously for pain of the cold.
The good knight on Gringolet glides thereunder
Through many a marsh and mire, a man all alone;
He feared for his default, should he fail to see   750
The service of that Sire that on that same night
Was born of a bright maid, to bring us his peace.
And therefore sighing he said, "I beseech of Thee, Lord,
And Mary, thou mildest mother so dear,
Some harborage where haply I might hear mass   755
And Thy matins tomorrow—meekly I ask it,
And thereto proffer and pray my pater and ave
                              and creed."
                    He said his prayer with sighs,
                    Lamenting his misdeed;   760
                    He crosses himself, and cries
                    On Christ in his great need.

No sooner had Sir Gawain signed himself thrice
Than he was ware, in the wood, of a wondrous dwelling,
Within a moat, on a mound, bright amid boughs   765
Of many a tree great of girth that grew by the water—
A castle as comely as a knight could own,
On grounds fair and green, in a goodly park
With a palisade of palings planted about
For two miles and more, round many a fair tree.   770
The stout knight stared at that stronghold great
As it shimmered and shone amid shining leaves,
Then with helmet in hand he offers his thanks
To Jesus and Saint Julian,[3] that are gentle both,
That in courteous accord had inclined to his prayer;   775
"Now fair harbor," said he, "I humbly beseech!"

---

3. Patron saint of hospitality.

Then he pricks his proud steed with the plated spurs,
And by chance he has chosen the chief path
That brought the bold knight to the bridge's end
                      in haste.   780
          The bridge hung high in air;
          The gates were bolted fast;
          The walls well-framed to bear
          The fury of the blast.

The man on his mount remained on the bank   785
Of the deep double moat that defended the place.
The wall went in the water wondrous deep,
And a long way aloft it loomed overhead.
It was built of stone blocks to the battlements' height,
With corbels under cornices in comeliest style;   790
Watch-towers trusty protected the gate,
With many a lean loophole, to look from within:
A better-made barbican the knight beheld never.
And behind it there hoved a great hall and fair:
Turrets rising in tiers, with tines[4] at their tops,   795
Spires set beside them, splendidly long,
With finials[5] well-fashioned, as filigree fine.
Chalk-white chimneys over chambers high
Gleamed in gay array upon gables and roofs;
The pinnacles in panoply, pointing in air,   800
So vied there for his view that verily it seemed
A castle cut of paper for a king's feast.[6]
The good knight on Gringolet thought it great luck
If he could but contrive to come there within
To keep the Christmas feast in that castle fair   805
                      and bright.
          There answered to his call
          A porter most polite;
          From his station on the wall
          He greets the errant knight.   810

"Good sir," said Gawain, "Wouldst go to inquire
If your lord would allow me to lodge here a space?"
"Peter!" said the porter, "For my part, I think
So noble a knight will not want for a welcome!"
Then he bustles off briskly, and comes back straight,   815
And many servants beside, to receive him the better.
They let down the drawbridge and duly went forth
And kneeled down on their knees on the naked earth
To welcome this warrior as best they were able.
They proffered him passage—the portals stood wide—   820

---

4. Spikes.
5. Gable ornaments.

6. A common table decoration at feasts.

And he beckoned them to rise, and rode over the bridge.
Men steadied his saddle as he stepped to the ground,
And there stabled his steed many stalwart folk.
Now come the knights and the noble squires
To bring him with bliss into the bright hall.   825
When his high helm was off, there hied forth a throng
Of attendants to take it, and see to its care;
They bore away his brand[7] and his blazoned shield;
Then graciously he greeted those gallants each one,
And many a noble drew near, to do the knight honor.   830
All in his armor into hall he was led,
Where fire on a fair hearth fiercely blazed.
And soon the lord himself descends from his chamber
To meet with good manners the man on his floor.
He said, "To this house you are heartily welcome: 835
What is here is wholly yours, to have in your power
                        and sway."
            "Many thanks," said Sir Gawain;
            "May Christ your pains repay!"
            The two embrace amain   840
            As men well met that day.

Gawain gazed on the host that greeted him there,
And a lusty fellow he looked, the lord of that place:
A man of massive mold, and of middle age;
Broad, bright was his beard, of a beaver's hue,   845
Strong, steady his stance, upon stalwart shanks,
His face fierce as fire, fair-spoken withal,
And well-suited he seemed in Sir Gawain's sight
To be a master of men in a mighty keep.
They pass into a parlor, where promptly the host   850
Has a servant assigned him to see to his needs,
And there came upon his call many courteous folk
That brought him to a bower where bedding was noble,
With heavy silk hangings hemmed all in gold,
Coverlets and counterpanes curiously wrought,   855
A canopy over the couch, clad all with fur,
Curtains running on cords, caught to gold rings,
Woven rugs on the walls of eastern work,
And the floor, under foot, well-furnished with the same.
Amid light talk and laughter they loosed from him then   860
His war-dress of weight and his worthy clothes.
Robes richly wrought they brought him right soon,
To change there in chamber and choose what he would.
When he had found one he fancied, and flung it about,
Well-fashioned for his frame, with flowing skirts,   865
His face fair and fresh as the flowers of spring,

7. Sword.

All the good folk agreed, that gazed on him then,
His limbs arrayed royally in radiant hues,
That so comely a mortal never Christ made
                                        as he.   870
                Whatever his place of birth,
                It seemed he well might be
                Without a peer on earth
                In martial rivalry.

A couch before the fire, where fresh coals burned,   875
They spread for Sir Gawain splendidly now
With quilts quaintly stitched, and cushions beside,
And then a costly cloak they cast on his shoulders
Of bright silk, embroidered on borders and hems,
With furs of the finest well-furnished within,   880
And bound about with ermine, both mantle and hood;
And he sat at that fireside in sumptuous estate
And warmed himself well, and soon he waxed merry.
Then attendants set a table upon trestles broad,
And lustrous white linen they laid thereupon,   885
A saltcellar of silver, spoons of the same.
He washed himself well and went to his place,
Men set his fare before him in fashion most fit.
There were soups of all sorts, seasoned with skill,
Double-sized servings, and sundry fish,   890
Some baked, some breaded, some broiled on the coals,
Some simmered, some in stews, steaming with spice,
And with sauces to sup that suited his taste.
He confesses it a feast with free words and fair;
They requite him as kindly with courteous jests,   895
                                well-sped.
                "Tonight you fast[8] and pray;
                Tomorrow we'll see you fed."
                The knight grows wondrous gay
                As the wine goes to his head.   900

Then at times and by turns, as at table he sat,
They questioned him quietly, with queries discreet,
And he courteously confessed that he comes from the court,
And owns him of the brotherhood of high-famed Arthur,
The right royal ruler of the Round Table,   905
And the guest by their fireside is Gawain himself,
Who has happened on their house at that holy feast.
When the name of the knight was made known to the lord,
Then loudly he laughed, so elated he was,
And the men in that household made haste with joy   910
To appear in his presence promptly that day,

---

8. Gawain is said to be "fasting" because the meal, though elaborate, consisted only of fish dishes, appropriate to a fasting day.

That of courage ever-constant, and customs pure,
Is pattern and paragon, and praised without end:
Of all knights on earth most honored is he.
Each said solemnly aside to his brother,   915
"Now displays of deportment shall dazzle our eyes
And the polished pearls of impeccable speech;
The high art of eloquence is ours to pursue
Since the father of fine manners is found in our midst.
Great is God's grace, and goodly indeed,   920
That a guest such as Gawain he guides to us here
When men sit and sing of their Savior's birth
                                        in view.
                         With command of manners pure
                         He shall each heart imbue;   925
                         Who shares his converse, sure,
                         Shall learn love's language true."

When the knight had done dining and duly arose,
The dark was drawing on; the day nigh ended.
Chaplains in chapels and churches about   930
Rang the bells aright, reminding all men
Of the holy evensong of the high feast.
The lord attends alone: his fair lady sits
In a comely closet, secluded from sight.
Gawain in gay attire goes thither soon;   935
The lord catches his coat, and calls him by name,
And has him sit beside him, and says in good faith
No guest on God's earth would he gladlier greet.
For that Gawain thanked him; the two then embraced
And sat together soberly the service through.   940
Then the lady, that longed to look on the knight,
Came forth from her closet with her comely maids.
The fair hues of her flesh, her face and her hair
And her body and her bearing were beyond praise,
And excelled the queen herself, as Sir Gawain thought.   945
He goes forth to greet her with gracious intent;
Another lady led her by the left hand
That was older than she—an ancient, it seemed,
And held in high honor by all men about.
But unlike to look upon, those ladies were,   950
For if the one was fresh, the other was faded:
Bedecked in bright red was the body of one;
Flesh hung in folds on the face of the other;
On one a high headdress, hung all with pearls;
Her bright throat and bosom fair to behold,   955
Fresh as the first snow fallen upon hills;
A wimple the other one wore round her throat;
Her swart chin well swaddled, swathed all in white;
Her forehead enfolded in flounces of silk

That framed a fair fillet, of fashion ornate,   960
And nothing bare beneath save the black brows,
The two eyes and the nose, the naked lips,
And they unsightly to see, and sorrily bleared.
A beldame, by God, she may well be deemed,
                              of pride!   965
              She was short and thick of waist,
              Her buttocks round and wide;
              More toothsome, to his taste,
              Was the beauty by her side.

When Gawain had gazed on that gay lady,   970
With leave of her lord, he politely approached;
To the elder in homage he humbly bows;
The lovelier he salutes with a light embrace.
He claims a comely kiss, and courteously he speaks;
They welcome him warmly, and straightway he asks   975
To be received as their servant, if they so desire.
They take him between them; with talking they bring him
Beside a bright fire; bade then that spices
Be freely fetched forth, to refresh them the better,
And the good wine therewith, to warm their hearts.   980
The lord leaps about in light-hearted mood;
Contrives entertainments and timely sports;
Takes his hood from his head and hangs it on a spear,
And offers him openly the honor thereof
Who should promote the most mirth at that Christmas feast;   985
"And I shall try for it, trust me—contend with the best,
Ere I go without my headgear by grace of my friends!"
Thus with light talk and laughter the lord makes merry
To gladden the guest he had greeted in hall
                              that day.   990
              At the last he called for light
              The company to convey;
              Gawain says goodnight
              And retires to bed straightway.

On the morn when each man is mindful in heart   995
That God's son was sent down to suffer our death,
No household but is blithe for his blessed sake;
So was it there on that day, with many delights.
Both at larger meals and less they were lavishly served
By doughty lads on dais, with delicate fare;   1000
The old ancient lady, highest she sits;
The lord at her left hand leaned, as I hear;
Sir Gawain in the center, beside the gay lady,
Where the food was brought first to that festive board,
And thence throughout the hall, as they held most fit,   1005
To each man was offered in order of rank.

There was meat, there was mirth, there was much joy,
That to tell all the tale would tax my wits,
Though I pained me, perchance, to paint it with care;
But yet I know that our knight and the noble lady   1010
Were accorded so closely in company there,
With the seemly solace of their secret words,
With speeches well-sped, spotless and pure,
That each prince's pastime their pleasures far
                              outshone.   1015
        Sweet pipes beguile their cares,
        And the trumpet of martial tone;
        Each tends his affairs
        And those two tend their own.

That day and all the next, their disport was noble,   1020
And the third day, I think, pleased them no less;
The joys of St. John's Day[9] were justly praised,
And were the last of their like for those lords and ladies;
Then guests were to go in the gray morning,
Wherefore they whiled the night away with wine and with mirth,   1025
Moved to the measures of many a blithe carol;
At last, when it was late, took leave of each other,
Each one of those worthies, to wend his way.
Gawain bids goodbye to his goodly host
Who brings him to his chamber, the chimney beside,   1030
And detains him in talk, and tenders his thanks
And holds it an honor to him and his people
That he has harbored in his house at that holy time
And embellished his abode with his inborn grace.
"As long as I may live, my luck is the better   1035
That Gawain was my guest at God's own feast!"
"Noble sir," said the knight, "I cannot but think
All the honor is your own—may heaven requite it!
And your man to command I account myself here
As I am bound and beholden, and shall be, come   1040
                              what may."
        The lord with all his might
        Entreats his guest to stay;
        Brief answer makes the knight:
        Next morning he must away.   1045

Then the lord of that land politely inquired
What dire affair had forced him, at that festive time,
So far from the king's court to fare forth alone
Ere the holidays wholly had ended in hall.
"In good faith," said Gawain, "you have guessed the truth: 1050
On a high errand and urgent I hastened away,

---

9. December 27.

For I am summoned by myself to seek for a place—
I would I knew whither, or where it might be!
Far rather would I find it before the New Year
Than own the land of Logres, so help me our Lord!   1055
Wherefore, sir, in friendship this favor I ask,
That you say in sober earnest, if something you know
Of the Green Chapel, on ground far or near,
Or the lone knight that lives there, of like hue of green.
A certain day was set by assent of us both   1060
To meet at that landmark, if I might last,
And from now to the New Year is nothing too long,
And I would greet the Green Knight there, would God but allow,
More gladly, by God's Son, than gain the world's wealth!
And I must set forth to search, as soon as I may;   1065
To be about the business I have but three days
And would as soon sink down dead as desist from my errand."
Then smiling said the lord, "Your search, sir, is done,
For we shall see you to that site by the set time.
Let Gawain grieve no more over the Green Chapel;   1070
You shall be in your own bed, in blissful ease,
All the forenoon, and fare forth the first of the year,
And make the goal by midmorn, to mind your affairs,
                              no fear!
                    Tarry till the fourth day   1075
                    And ride on the first of the year.
                    We shall set you on your way;
                    It is not two miles from here."

The Gawain was glad, and gleefully he laughed:
"Now I thank you for this, past all things else!   1080
Now my goal is here at hand! With a glad heart I shall
Both tarry, and undertake any task you devise."
Then the host seized his arm and seated him there;
Let the ladies be brought, to delight them the better,
And in fellowship fair by the fireside they sit;   1085
So gay waxed the good host, so giddy his words,
All waited in wonder what next he would say.
Then he stares on the stout knight, and sternly he speaks:
"You have bound yourself boldly my bidding to do—
Will you stand by that boast, and obey me this once?"   1090
"I shall do so indeed," said the doughty knight;
"While I lie in your lodging, your laws will I follow."
"As you have had," said the host, "many hardships abroad
And little sleep of late, you are lacking, I judge,
Both in nourishment needful and nightly rest;   1095
You shall lie abed late in your lofty chamber
Tomorrow until mass, and meet then to dine
When you will, with my wife, who will sit by your side

And talk with you at table, the better to cheer
                              our guest.   1100
                    A-hunting I will go
                    While you lie late and rest."
                    The knight, inclining low,
                    Assents to each behest.

"And Gawain," said the good host, "agree now to this: 1105
Whatever I win in the woods I will give you at eve,
And all you have earned you must offer to me;
Swear now, sweet friend, to swap as I say,
Whether hands, in the end, be empty or better."
"By God," said Sir Gawain, "I grant it forthwith!   1110
If you find the game good, I shall gladly take part."
"Let the bright wine be brought, and our bargain is done,"
Said the lord of that land—the two laughed together.
Then they drank and they dallied and doffed all constraint,
These lords and these ladies, as late as they chose,   1115
And then with gaiety and gallantries and graceful adieux
They talked in low tones, and tarried at parting.
With compliments comely they kiss at the last;
There were brisk lads about with blazing torches
To see them safe to bed, for soft repose   1120
                              long due.
                    Their covenants, yet awhile,
                    They repeat, and pledge anew;
                    That lord could well beguile
                    Men's hearts, with mirth in view.   1125

Part 3

Long before daylight they left their beds;
Guests that wished to go gave word to their grooms,
And they set about briskly to bind on saddles,
Tend to their tackle, tie up trunks.
The proud lords appear, appareled to ride,   1130
Leap lightly astride, lay hold of their bridles,
Each one on his way to his worthy house.
The liege lord of the land was not the last
Arrayed there to ride, with retainers many;
He had a bite to eat when he had heard mass;   1135
With horn to the hills he hastens amain.
By the dawn of that day over the dim earth,
Master and men were mounted and ready.
Then they harnessed in couples the keen-scented hounds,
Cast wide the kennel-door and called them forth,   1140
Blew upon their bugles bold blasts three;
The dogs began to bay with a deafening din,
And they quieted them quickly and called them to heel,

A hundred brave huntsmen, as I have heard tell,
                              together.   1145
          Men at stations meet;
          From the hounds they slip the tether;
          The echoing horns repeat,
          Clear in the merry weather.

At the clamor of the quest, the quarry trembled;   1150
Deer dashed through the dale, dazed with dread;
Hastened to the high ground, only to be
Turned back by the beaters, who boldly shouted.
They harmed not the harts, with their high heads,
Let the bucks go by, with their broad antlers,   1155
For it was counted a crime, in the close season,
If a man of that demesne should molest the male deer.
The hinds were headed up, with "Hey!" and "Ware!"
The does with great din were driven to the valleys.
Then you were ware, as they went, of the whistling of arrows;   1160
At each bend under boughs the bright shafts flew
That tore the tawny hide with their tapered heads.
Ah! they bray and they bleed, on banks they die,
And ever the pack pell-mell comes panting behind;
Hunters with shrill horns hot on their heels—   1165
Like the cracking of cliffs their cries resounded.
What game got away from the gallant archers
Was promptly picked off at the posts below
When they were harried on the heights and herded to the streams:
The watchers were so wary at the waiting-stations,   1170
And the greyhounds so huge, that eagerly snatched,
And finished them off as fast as folk could see
                              with sight.
          The lord, now here, now there,
          Spurs forth in sheer delight.   1175
          And drives, with pleasures rare,
          The day to the dark night.

So the lord in the linden-wood leads the hunt
And Gawain the good knight in gay bed lies,
Lingered late alone, till daylight gleamed,   1180
Under coverlet costly, curtained about.
And as he slips into slumber, slyly there comes
A little din at his door, and the latch lifted,
And he holds up his heavy head out of the clothes;
A corner of the curtain he caught back a little   1185
And waited there warily, to see what befell.
Lo! it was the lady, loveliest to behold,
That drew the door behind her deftly and still
And was bound for his bed—abashed was the knight,
And laid his head low again in likeness of sleep;   1190

And she stepped stealthily, and stole to his bed,
Cast aside the curtain and came within,
And set herself softly on the bedside there,
And lingered at her leisure, to look on his waking.
The fair knight lay feigning for a long while,   1195
Conning in his conscience what his case might
Mean or amount to—a marvel he thought it.
But yet he said within himself, "More seemly it were
To try her intent by talking a little."
So he started and stretched, as startled from sleep,   1200
Lifts wide his lids in likeness of wonder,
And signs himself swiftly, as safer to be,
                              with art.
                    Sweetly does she speak
                    And kindling glances dart,   1205
                    Blent white and red on cheek
                    And laughing lips apart.

"Good morning, Sir Gawain," said that gay lady,
"A slack sleeper you are, to let one slip in!
Now you are taken in a trice—a truce we must make,   1210
Or I shall bind you in your bed, of that be assured."
Thus laughing lightly that lady jested.
"Good morning, good lady," said Gawain the blithe,
"Be it with me as you will; I am well content!
For I surrender myself, and sue for your grace,   1215
And that is best, I believe, and behooves me now."
Thus jested in answer that gentle knight.
"But if, lovely lady, you misliked it not,
And were pleased to permit your prisoner to rise,
I should quit this couch and accoutre me better,   1220
And be clad in more comfort for converse here."
"Nay, not so, sweet sir," said the smiling lady;
"You shall not rise from your bed; I direct you better:
I shall hem and hold you on either hand,
And keep company awhile with my captive knight.   1225
For as certain as I sit here, Sir Gawain you are,
Whom all the world worships, whereso you ride;
Your honor, your courtesy are highest acclaimed
By lords and by ladies, by all living men;
And lo! we are alone here, and left to ourselves: 1230
My lord and his liegemen are long departed,
The household asleep, my handmaids too,
The door drawn, and held by a well-driven bolt,
And since I have in this house him whom all love,
I shall while the time away with mirthful speech   1235
                              at will.
                    My body is here at hand,
                    Your each wish to fulfill;

Your servant to command
I am, and shall be still." 1240

"In good faith," said Gawain, "my gain is the greater,
Though I am not he of whom you have heard;
To arrive at such reverence as you recount here
I am one all unworthy, and well do I know it.
By heaven, I would hold me the happiest of men 1245
If by word or by work I once might aspire
To the prize of your praise—'twere a pure joy!"
"In good faith, Sir Gawain," said that gay lady,
"The well-proven prowess that pleases all others,
Did I scant or scout it, 'twere scarce becoming. 1250
But there are ladies, believe me, that had liefer far
Have thee here in their hold, as I have today,
To pass an hour in pastime with pleasant words,
Assuage all their sorrows and solace their hearts,
Than much of the goodly gems and gold they possess. 1255
But laud be to the Lord of the lofty skies,
For here in my hands all hearts' desire
                              doth lie."
            Great welcome got he there
            From the lady who sat him by; 1260
            With fitting speech and fair
            The good knight makes reply.

"Madame," said the merry man, "Mary reward you!
For in good faith, I find your beneficence noble.
And the fame of fair deeds runs far and wide, 1265
But the praise you report pertains not to me,
But comes of your courtesy and kindness of heart."
"By the high Queen of heaven" (said she) "I count it not so,
For were I worth all the women in this world alive,
And all wealth and all worship were in my hands, 1270
And I should hunt high and low, a husband to take,
For the nurture I have noted in thee, knight, here,
The comeliness and courtesies and courtly mirth—
And so I had ever heard, and now hold it true—
No other on this earth should have me for wife." 1275
"You are bound to a better man," the bold knight said,
"Yet I prize the praise you have proffered me here,
And soberly your servant, my sovereign I hold you,
And acknowledge me your knight, in the name of Christ."
So they talked of this and that until 'twas nigh noon, 1280
And ever the lady languishing in likeness of love.
With feat words and fair he framed his defense,
For were she never so winsome, the warrior had
The less will to woo, for the wound that his bane
                              must be. 1285

He must bear the blinding blow,
For such is fate's decree:
The lady asks leave to go;
He grants it full and free.

Then she gaily said goodbye, and glanced at him, laughing,   1290
And as she stood, she astonished him with a stern speech:
"Now may the Giver of all good words these glad hours repay!
But our guest is not Gawain—forgot is that thought."
"How so?" said the other, and asks in some haste,
For he feared he had been at fault in the forms of his speech.   1295
But she held up her hand, and made answer thus:
"So good a knight as Gawain is given out to be,
And the model of fair demeanor and manners pure,
Had he lain so long at a lady's side,
Would have claimed a kiss, by his courtesy,   1300
Through some touch or trick of phrase at some tale's end."
Said Gawain, "Good lady, I grant it at once!
I shall kiss at your command, as becomes a knight,
And more, lest you mislike, so let be, I pray."
With that she turns toward him, takes him in her arms,   1305
Leans down her lovely head, and lo! he is kissed.
They commend each other to Christ with comely words,
He sees her forth safely, in silence they part,
And then he lies no later in his lofty bed,
But calls to his chamberlain, chooses his clothes,   1310
Goes in those garments gladly to mass,
Then takes his way to table, where attendants wait,
And made merry all day, till the moon rose
                         in view
              Was never knight beset   1315
              'Twixt worthier ladies two:
              The crone and the coquette;
              Fair pastimes they pursue.

And the lord of the land rides late and long,
Hunting the barren hind over the broad heath.   1320
He had slain such a sum, when the sun sank low,
Of does and other deer, as would dizzy one's wits.
Then they trooped in together in triumph at last,
And the count of the quarry quickly they take.
The lords lent a hand with their liegemen many,   1325
Picked out the plumpest and put them together
And duly dressed the deer, as the deed requires.
Some were assigned the assay of the fat:
Two fingers' width fully they found on the leanest.
Then they slit the slot open and searched out the paunch,   1330
Trimmed it with trencher-knives and tied it up tight.
They flayed the fair hide from the legs and trunk,

Then broke open the belly and laid bare the bowels,
Deftly detaching and drawing them forth.
And next at the neck they neatly parted   1335
The weasand[1] from the windpipe, and cast away the guts.
At the shoulders with sharp blades they showed their skill,
Boning them from beneath, lest the sides be marred;
They breached the broad breast and broke it in twain,
And again at the gullet they begin with their knives,   1340
Cleave down the carcass clear to the breach;
Two tender morsels they take from the throat,
Then round the inner ribs they rid off a layer
And carve out the kidney-fat, close to the spine,
Hewing down to the haunch, that all hung together,   1345
And held it up whole, and hacked it free,
And this they named the numbles,[2] that knew such terms
                       of art.
        They divide the crotch in two,
        And straightway then they start   1350
        To cut the backbone through
        And cleave the trunk apart.

With hard strokes they hewed off the head and the neck,
Then swiftly from the sides they severed the chine,
And the corbie's bone[3] they cast on a branch.   1355
Then they pierced the plump sides, impaled either one
With the hock of the hind foot, and hung it aloft,
To each person his portion most proper and fit.
On a hide of a hind the hounds they fed
With the liver and the lights,[4] the leathery paunches,   1360
And bread soaked in blood well blended therewith.
High horns and shrill set hounds a-baying,
Then merrily with their meat they make their way home,
Blowing on their bugles many a brave blast.
Ere dark had descended, that doughty band   1365
Was come within the walls where Gawain waits
                    at leisure.
        Bliss and hearth-fire bright
        Await the master's pleasure;
        When the two men met that night,   1370
        Joy surpassed all measure.

Then the host in the hall his household assembles,
With the dames of high degree and their damsels fair.
In the presence of the people, a party he sends
To convey him his venison in view of the knight.   1375

1. Esophagus.
2. The other internal organs.
3. A bit of gristle assigned to the ravens ("cor-
bies").
4. Lungs.

And in high good-humor he hails him then,
Counts over the kill, the cuts on the tallies,
Holds high the hewn ribs, heavy with fat.
"What think you, sir, of this? Have I thriven well?
Have I won with my woodcraft a worthy prize?"   1380
"In good earnest," said Gawain, "this game is the finest
I have seen in seven years in the season of winter."
"And I give it to you, Gawain," said the goodly host,
"For according to our convenant, you claim it as your own."
"That is so," said Sir Gawain, "the same say I: 1385
What I worthily have won within these fair walls,
Herewith I as willingly award it to you."
He embraces his broad neck with both his arms,
And confers on him a kiss in the comeliest style.
"Have here my profit, it proved no better;   1390
Ungrudging do I grant it, were it greater far."
"Such a gift," said the good host, "I gladly accept—
Yet it might be all the better, would you but say
Where you won this same award, by your wits alone."
"That was no part of the pact; press me no further,   1395
For you have had what behooves; all other claims
                    forbear."
          With jest and compliment
          They conversed, and cast off care;
          To the table soon they went;
          Fresh dainties wait them there.   1400

And then by the chimney-side they chat at their ease;
The best wine was brought them, and bounteously served;
And after in their jesting they jointly accord
To do on the second day the deeds of the first: 1405
That the two men should trade, betide as it may,
What each had taken in, at eve when they met.
They seal the pact solemnly in sight of the court;
Their cups were filled afresh to confirm the jest;
Then at last they took their leave, for late was the hour,   1410
Each to his own bed hastening away.
Before the barnyard cock had crowed but thrice
The lord had leapt from his rest, his liegemen as well.
Both of mass and their meal they made short work:
By the dim light of dawn they were deep in the woods   1415
                    away.
          With huntsmen and with horns
          Over plains they pass that day;
          They release, amid the thorns,
          Swift hounds that run and bay.   1420

Soon some were on a scent by the side of a marsh;
When the hounds opened cry, the head of the hunt

Rallied them with rough words, raised a great noise.
The hounds that had heard it came hurrying straight
And followed along with their fellows, forty together.   1425
Then such a clamor and cry of coursing hounds
Arose, that the rocks resounded again.
Hunters exhorted them with horn and with voice;
Then all in a body bore off together
Between a mere in the marsh and a menacing crag,   1430
To a rise where the rock stood rugged and steep,
And boulders lay about, that blocked their approach.
Then the company in consort closed on their prey:
They surrounded the rise and the rocks both,
For well they were aware that it waited within,   1435
The beast that the bloodhounds boldly proclaimed.
Then they beat on the bushes and bade him appear,
And he made a murderous rush in the midst of them all;
The best of all boars broke from his cover,
That had ranged long unrivaled, a renegade old,   1440
For of tough-brawned boars he was biggest far,
Most grim when he grunted—then grieved were many,
For three at the first thrust he threw to the earth,
And dashed away at once without more damage.
With "Hi!" "Hi!" and "Hey!" "Hey!" the others followed,   1445
Had horns at their lips, blew high and clear.
Merry was the music of men and of hounds
That were bound after this boar, his bloodthirsty heart
                                    to quell.
            Often he stands at bay,   1450
            Then scatters the pack pell-mell;
            He hurts the hounds, and they
            Most dolefully yowl and yell.

Men then with mighty bows moved in to shoot,
Aimed at him with their arrows and often hit,   1455
But the points had no power to pierce through his hide,
And the barbs were brushed aside by his bristly brow;
Though the shank of the shaft shivered in pieces,
The head hopped away, wheresoever it struck.
But when their stubborn strokes had stung him at last,   1460
Then, foaming in his frenzy, fiercely he charges,
Hies at them headlong that hindered his flight,
And many feared for their lives, and fell back a little.
But the lord on a lively horse leads the chase;
As a high-mettled huntsman his horn he blows;   1465
He sounds the assembly and sweeps through the brush,
Pursuing this wild swine till the sunlight slanted.
All day with this deed they drive forth the time
While our lone knight so lovesome lies in his bed,

Sir Gawain safe at home, in silken bower   1470
                so gay.
        The lady, with guile in heart,
        Came early where he lay;
        She was at him with all her art
        To turn his mind her way.   1475

She comes to the curtain and coyly peeps in;
Gawain thought it good to greet her at once,
And she richly repays him with her ready words,
Settles softly at his side, and suddenly she laughs,
And with a gracious glance, she begins on him thus: 1480
"Sir, if you be Gawain, it seems a great wonder—
A man so well-meaning, and mannerly disposed,
And cannot act in company as courtesy bids,
And if one takes the trouble to teach him, 'tis all in vain.
That lesson learned lately is lightly forgot,   1485
Though I painted it as plain as my poor wit allowed."
"What lesson, dear lady?" he asked all alarmed;
"I have been much to blame, if your story be true."
"Yet my counsel was of kissing," came her answer then,
"Where favor has been found, freely to claim   1490
As accords with the conduct of courteous knights."
"My dear," said the doughty man, "dismiss that thought;
Such freedom, I fear, might offend you much;
It were rude to request if the right were denied."
"But none can deny you," said the noble dame,   1495
"You are stout enough to constrain with strength, if you choose,
Were any so ungracious as to grudge you aught."
"By heaven," said he, "you have answered well,
But threats never throve among those of my land,
Nor any gift not freely given, good though it be.   1500
I am yours to command, to kiss when you please;
You may lay on as you like, and leave off at will."
              With this,
        The lady lightly bends
        And graciously gives him a kiss;   1505
        The two converse as friends
        Of true love's trials and bliss.

"I should like, by your leave," said the lovely lady,
"If it did not annoy you, to know for what cause
So brisk and so bold a young blood as you,   1510
And acclaimed for all courtesies becoming a knight—
And name what knight you will, they are noblest esteemed
For loyal faith in love, in life as in story;
For to tell the tribulations of these true hearts,
Why, 'tis the very title and text of their deeds,   1515
How bold knights for beauty have braved many a foe,

Suffered heavy sorrows out of secret love,
And then valorously avenged them on villainous churls
And made happy ever after the hearts of their ladies.
And you are the noblest knight known in your time;   1520
No household under heaven but has heard of your fame,
And here by your side I have sat for two days
Yet never has a fair phrase fallen from your lips
Of the language of love, not one little word!
And you, that with sweet vows sway women's hearts,   1525
Should show your winsome ways, and woo a young thing,
And teach by some tokens the craft of true love.
How! are you artless, whom all men praise?
Or do you deem me so dull, or deaf to such words?
                    Fie! Fie!   1530
          In hope of pastimes new
          I have come where none can spy;
          Instruct me a little, do,
          While my husband is not nearby."

"God love you, gracious lady!" said Gawain then;   1535
"It is a pleasure surpassing, and a peerless joy,
That one so worthy as you would willingly come
And take the time and trouble to talk with your knight
And content you with his company—it comforts my heart.
But to take to myself the task of telling of love,   1540
And touch upon its texts, and treat of its themes
To one that, I know well, wields more power
In that art, by a half, than a hundred such
As I am where I live, or am like to become,
It were folly, fair dame, in the first degree!   1545
In all that I am able, my aim is to please,
As in honor behooves me, and am evermore
Your servant heart and soul, so save me our Lord!"
Thus she tested his temper and tried many a time,
Whatever her true intent, to entice him to sin,   1550
But so fair was his defense that no fault appeared,
Nor evil on either hand, but only bliss
                    they knew.
          They linger and laugh awhile;
          She kisses the knight so true,   1555
          Takes leave in comeliest style
          And departs without more ado.

Then he rose from his rest and made ready for mass,
And then a meal was set and served, in sumptuous style;
He dallied at home all day with the dear ladies,   1560
But the lord lingered late at his lusty sport;
Pursued his sorry swine, that swerved as he fled,
And bit asunder the backs of the best of his hounds

When they brought him to bay, till the bowmen appeared
And soon forced him forth, though he fought for dear life,   1565
So sharp were the shafts they shot at him there.
But yet the boldest drew back from his battering head,
Till at last he was so tired he could travel no more,
But in as much haste as he might, he makes his retreat
To a rise on rocky ground, by a rushing stream.   1570
With the bank at his back he scrapes the bare earth,
The froth foams at his jaws, frightful to see.
He whets his white tusks—then weary were all
Those hunters so hardy that hoved round about
Of aiming from afar, but ever they mistrust   1575
                    his mood.
            He had hurt so many by then
            That none had hardihood
            To be torn by his tusks again,
            That was brainsick, and out for blood.   1580

Till the lord came at last on his lofty steed,
Beheld him there at bay before all his folk;
Lightly he leaps down, leaves his courser,
Bares his bright sword, and boldly advances;
Straight into the stream he strides towards his foe.   1585
The wild thing was wary of weapon and man;
His hackles rose high; so hotly he snorts
That many watched with alarm, lest the worst befall.
The boar makes for the man with a mighty bound
So that he and his hunter came headlong together   1590
Where the water ran wildest—the worse for the beast,
For the man, when they first met, marked him with care,
Sights well the slot, slips in the blade,
Shoves it home to the hilt, and the heart shattered,
And he falls in his fury and floats down the water,   1595
                    ill-sped.
            Hounds hasten by the score
            To maul him, hide and head;
            Men drag him in to shore
            And dogs pronounce him dead.   1600

With many a brave blast they boast of their prize,
All hallooed in high glee, that had their wind;
The hounds bayed their best, as the bold men bade
That were charged with chief rank in that chase of renown.
Then one wise in woodcraft, and worthily skilled,   1605
Began to dress the boar in becoming style:
He severs the savage head and sets it aloft,
Then rends the body roughly right down the spine;
Takes the bowels from the belly, broils them on coals,
Blends them well with bread to bestow on the hounds.   1610

Then he breaks out the brawn in fair broad flitches,
And the innards to be eaten in order he takes.
The two sides, attached to each other all whole,
He suspended from a spar that was springy and tough;
And so with this swine they set out for home;   1615
The boar's head was borne before the same man
That had stabbed him in the stream with his strong arm,
                          right through.
                 He thought it long indeed
                 Till he had the knight in view;   1620
                 At his call, he comes with speed
                 To claim his payment due.

The lord laughed aloud, with many a light word,
When he greeted Sir Gawain—with good cheer he speaks.
They fetch the fair dames and the folk of the house;   1625
He brings forth the brawn, and begins the tale
Of the great length and girth, the grim rage as well,
Of the battle of the boar they beset in the wood.
The other man meetly commended his deeds
And praised well the prize of his princely sport,   1630
For the brawn of that boar, the bold knight said,
And the sides of that swine surpassed all others.
Then they handled the huge head; he owns it a wonder,
And eyes it with abhorrence, to heighten his praise.
"Now, Gawain," said the good man, "this game becomes yours   1635
By those fair terms we fixed, as you know full well."
"That is true," returned the knight, "and trust me, fair friend,
All my gains, as agreed, I shall give you forthwith."
He clasps him and kisses him in courteous style,
Then serves him with the same fare a second time.   1640
"Now we are even," said he, "at this evening feast,
And clear is every claim incurred here to date,
                          and debt."
                 "By Saint Giles!" the host replies,
                 "You're the best I ever met!   1645
                 If your profits are all this size,
                 We'll see you wealthy yet!"

Then attendants set tables on trestles about,
And laid them with linen; light shone forth,
Wakened along the walls in waxen torches.   1650
The service was set and the supper brought;
Royal were the revels that rose then in hall
At that feast by the fire, with many fair sports:
Amid the meal and after, melody sweet,
Carol-dances comely and Christmas songs,   1655
With all the mannerly mirth my tongue may describe.
And ever our gallant knight beside the gay lady;

So uncommonly kind and complaisant was she,
With sweet stolen glances, that stirred his stout heart,
That he was at his wits' end, and wondrous vexed;   1660
But he could not rebuff her, for courtesy forbade,
Yet took pains to please her, though the plan might
                              go wrong.
                    When they to heart's delight
                    Had reveled there in throng,   1665
                    To his chamber he calls the knight,
                    And thither they go along.

And there they dallied and drank, and deemed it good sport
To enact their play anew on New Year's Eve,
But Gawain asked again to go on the morrow,   1670
For the time until his tryst was not two days.
The host hindered that, and urged him to stay,
And said, "On my honor, my oath here I take
That you shall get to the Green Chapel to begin your chores
By dawn on New Year's Day, if you so desire.   1675
Wherefore lie at your leisure in your lofty bed,
And I shall hunt hereabouts, and hold to our terms,
And we shall trade winnings when once more we meet,
For I have tested you twice, and true have I found you;
Now think this tomorrow: the third pays for all;   1680
Be we merry while we may, and mindful of joy,
For heaviness of heart can be had for the asking."
This is gravely agreed on and Gawain will stay.
They drink a last draught and with torches depart
                              to rest.   1685
                    To bed Sir Gawain went:
                    His sleep was of the best;
                    The lord, on his craft intent,
                    Was early up and dressed.

After mass, with his men, a morsel he takes;   1690
Clear and crisp the morning; he calls for his mount;
The folk that were to follow him afield that day
Were high astride their horses before the hall gates.
Wondrous fair were the fields, for the frost was light;
The sun rises red amid radiant clouds,   1695
Sails into the sky, and sends forth his beams.
They let loose the hounds by a leafy wood;
The rocks all around re-echo to their horns;
Soon some have set off in pursuit of the fox,
Cast about with craft for a clearer scent;   1700
A young dog yaps, and is yelled at in turn;
His fellows fall to sniffing, and follow his lead,
Running in a rabble on the right track,
And he scampers all before; they discover him soon,

And when they see him with sight they pursue him the faster,   1705
Railing at him rudely with a wrathful din.
Often he reverses over rough terrain,
Or loops back to listen in the lee of a hedge;
At last, by a little ditch, he leaps over the brush,
Comes into a clearing at a cautious pace,   1710
Then he thought through his wiles to have thrown off the hounds
Till he was ware, as he went, of a waiting-station
Where three athwart his path threatened him at once,
      all gray.
     Quick as a flash he wheels   1715
     And darts off in dismay;
     With hard luck at his heels
     He is off to the wood away.

Then it was heaven on earth to hark to the hounds
When they had come on their quarry, coursing together!   1720
Such harsh cries and howls they hurled at his head
As all the cliffs with a crash had come down at once.
Here he was hailed, when huntsmen met him;
Yonder they yelled at him, yapping and snarling;
There they cried "Thief!" and threatened his life,   1725
And ever the harriers at his heels, that he had no rest.
Often he was menaced when he made for the open,
And often rushed in again, for Reynard was wily;
And so he leads them a merry chase, the lord and his men,
In this manner on the mountains, till midday or near,   1730
While our hero lies at home in wholesome sleep
Within the comely curtains on the cold morning.
But the lady, as love would allow her no rest,
And pursuing ever the purpose that pricked her heart,
Was awake with the dawn, and went to his chamber   1735
In a fair flowing mantle that fell to the earth,
All edged and embellished with ermines fine;
No hood on her head, but heavy with gems
Were her fillet and the fret[5] that confined her tresses;
Her face and her fair throat freely displayed;   1740
Her bosom all but bare, and her back as well.
She comes in at the chamber-door, and closes it with care,
Throws wide a window—then waits no longer,
But hails him thus airily with her artful words,
      with cheer: 1745
     "Ah, man, how can you sleep?
     The morning is so clear!"
     Though dreams have drowned him deep,
     He cannot choose but hear.

5. Ornamental net.

Deep in his dreams he darkly mutters   1750
As a man may that mourns, with many grim thoughts
Of that day when destiny shall deal him his doom
When he greets his grim host at the Green Chapel
And must bow to his buffet, bating all strife.
But when he sees her at his side he summons his wits,   1755
Breaks from the black dreams, and blithely answers.
That lovely lady comes laughing sweet,
Sinks down at his side, and salutes him with a kiss.
He accords her fair welcome in courtliest style;
He sees her so glorious, so gaily attired,   1760
So faultless her features, so fair and so bright,
His heart swelled swiftly with surging joys.
They melt into mirth with many a fond smile,
Nor was fair language lacking, to further that hour's
                                    delight.   1765
        Good were their words of greeting;
        Each joyed in other's sight;
        Great peril attends that meeting
        Should Mary forget her knight.

For that high-born beauty so hemmed him about,   1770
Made so plain her meaning, the man must needs
Either take her tendered love or distastefully refuse.
His courtesy concerned him, lest crass he appear,
But more his soul's mischief, should he commit sin
And belie his loyal oath to the lord of that house.   1775
"God forbid!" said the bold knight, "That shall not befall!"
With a little fond laughter he lightly let pass
All the words of special weight that were sped his way;
"I find you much at fault," the fair one said,
"Who can be cold toward a creature so close by your side,   1780
Of all women in this world most wounded in heart,
Unless you have a sweetheart, one you hold dearer,
And allegiance to that lady so loyally knit
That you will never love another, as now I believe.
And, sir, if it be so, then say it, I beg you;   1785
By all your heart holds dear, hide it no longer
                                    with guile."
        "Lady, by Saint John,"
        He answers with a smile,
        "Lover have I none,   1790
        Nor will have, yet awhile."

"Those words," said the woman, "are the worst of all,
But I have had my answer, and hard do I find it!
Kiss me now kindly: I can but go hence
To lament my life long like a maid lovelorn."   1795
She inclines her head quickly and kisses the knight,

Then straightens with a sigh, and says as she stands,
"Now, dear, ere I depart, do me this pleasure:
Give me some little gift, your glove or the like,
That I may think on you, man, and mourn the less."   1800
"Now by heavens," said he, "I wish I had here
My most precious possession, to put it in your hands,
For your deeds, beyond doubt, have often deserved
A repayment far passing my power to bestow.
But a love-token, lady, were of little avail;   1805
It is not to your honor to have at this time
A glove as a guerdon from Gawain's hand,
And I am here on an errand in unknown realms
And have no bearers with baggage with becoming gifts,
Which distresses me, madame, for your dear sake.   1810
A man must keep within his compass: account it neither grief
                              nor slight."
                    "Nay, noblest knight alive,"
                    Said that beauty of body white,
                    "Though you be loath to give,   1815
                    Yet you shall take, by right."

She reached out a rich ring, wrought all of gold,
With a splendid stone displayed on the band
That flashed before his eyes like a fiery sun;
It was worth a king's wealth, you may well believe.   1820
But he waved it away with these ready words:
"Before God, good lady, I forgo all gifts;
None have I to offer, nor any will I take."
And she urged it on him eagerly, and ever he refused,
And vowed in very earnest, prevail she would not.   1825
And she sad to find it so, and said to him then,
"If my ring is refused for its rich cost—
You would not be my debtor for so dear a thing—
I shall give you my girdle; you gain less thereby."
She released a knot lightly, and loosened a belt   1830
That was caught about her kirtle, the bright cloak beneath,
Of a gay green silk, with gold overwrought,
And the borders all bound with embroidery fine,
And this she presses upon him, and pleads with a smile,
Unworthy though it were, that it would not be scorned.   1835
But the man still maintains that he means to accept
Neither gold nor any gift, till by God's grace
The fate that lay before him was fully achieved.
"And be not offended, fair lady, I beg,
And give over your offer, for ever I must   1840
                              decline.
                    I am grateful for favor shown
                    Past all deserts of mine,

      And ever shall be your own
      True servant, rain or shine."   1845

"Now does my present displease you," she promptly inquired,
"Because it seems in your sight so simple a thing?
And belike, as it is little, it is less to praise,
But if the virtue that invests it were verily known,
It would be held, I hope, in higher esteem.   1850
For the man that possesses this piece of silk,
If he bore it on his body, belted about,
There is no hand under heaven that could hew him down,
For he could not be killed by any craft on earth."
Then the man began to muse, and mainly he thought   1855
It was a pearl for his plight, the peril to come
When he gains the Green Chapel to get his reward:
Could he escape unscathed, the scheme were noble!
Then he bore with her words and withstood them no more,
And she repeated her petition and pleaded anew,   1860
And he granted it, and gladly she gave him the belt,
And besought him for her sake to conceal it well,
Lest the noble lord should know—and, the knight agrees
That not a soul save themselves shall see it thenceforth
                  with sight.   1865
      He thanked her with fervent heart,
      As often as ever he might;
      Three times, before they part,
      She has kissed the stalwart knight.

Then the lady took her leave, and left him there,   1870
For more mirth with that man she might not have.
When she was gone, Sir Gawain got from his bed,
Arose and arrayed him in his rich attire;
Tucked away the token the temptress had left,
Laid it reliably where he looked for it after.   1875
And then with good cheer to the chapel he goes,
Approached a priest in private, and prayed to be taught
To lead a better life and lift up his mind,
Lest he be among the lost when he must leave this world.
And shamefaced at shrift he showed his misdeeds   1880
From the largest to the least, and asked the Lord's mercy,
And called on his confessor to cleanse his soul,
And he absolved him of his sins as safe and as clean
As if the dread Day of Doom were to dawn on the morrow.
And then he made merry amid the fine ladies   1885
With deft-footed dances and dalliance light,
As never until now, while the afternoon wore
              away.
      He delighted all around him,
      And all agreed, that day,   1890

> They never before had found him
> So gracious and so gay.

Now peaceful be his pasture, and love play him fair!
The host is on horseback, hunting afield;
He has finished off this fox that he followed so long: 1895
As he leapt a low hedge to look for the villain
Where he heard all the hounds in hot pursuit,
Reynard comes racing out of a rough thicket,
And all the rabble in a rush, right at his heels.
The man beholds the beast, and bides his time,   1900
And bares his bright sword, and brings it down hard,
And he blenches from the blade, and backward he starts;
A hound hurries up and hinders that move,
And before the horse's feet they fell on him at once
And ripped the rascal's throat with a wrathful din.   1905
The lord soon alighted and lifted him free,
Swiftly snatched him up from the snapping jaws,
Holds him over his head, halloos with a will,
And the dogs bayed the dirge, that had done him to death.
Hunters hastened thither with horns at their lips,   1910
Sounding the assembly till they saw him at last.
When that comely company was come in together,
All that bore bugles blew them at once,
And the others all hallooed, that had no horns.
It was the merriest medley that ever a man heard,   1915
The racket that they raised for Sir Reynard's soul
> > that died.
> > Their hounds they praised and fed,
> > Fondling their heads with pride,
> > And they took Reynard the Red   1920
> > And stripped away his hide.

And then they headed homeward, for evening had come,
Blowing many a blast on their bugles bright.
The lord at long last alights at his house,
Finds fire on the hearth where the fair knight waits,   1925
Sir Gawain the good, that was glad in heart.
With the ladies, that loved him, he lingered at ease;
He wore a rich robe of blue, that reached to the earth
And a surcoat lined softly with sumptuous furs;
A hood of the same hue hung on his shoulders;   1930
With bands of bright ermine embellished were both.
He comes to meet the man amid all the folk,
And greets him good-humoredly, and gaily he says,
"I shall follow forthwith the form of our pledge
That we framed to good effect amid fresh-filled cups."   1935
He clasps him accordingly and kisses him thrice,
As amiably and as earnestly as ever he could.

"By heaven," said the host, "you have had some luck
Since you took up this trade, if the terms were good."
"Never trouble about the terms," he returned at once,   1940
"Since all that I owe here is openly paid."
"Marry!" said the other man, "mine is much less,
For I have hunted all day, and nought have I got
But this foul fox pelt, the fiend take the goods!
Which but poorly repays such precious things   1945
That you have cordially conferred, such kisses three
                              so good."
                    "Enough!" said Sir Gawain;
                    "I thank you, by the rood!"
                    And how the fox was slain   1950
                    He told him, as they stood.

With minstrelsy and mirth, with all manner of meats,
They made as much merriment as any men might
(Amid laughing of ladies and light hearted girls;
So gay grew Sir Gawain and the goodly host)   1955
Unless they had been besotted, or brainless fools.
The knight joined in jesting with that joyous folk,
Until at last it was late; ere long they must part,
And be off to their beds, as behooved them each one.
Then politely his leave of the lord of the house   1960
Our noble knight takes, and renews his thanks:
"The courtesies countless accorded me here,
Your kindness at this Christmas, may heaven's King repay!
Henceforth, if you will have me, I hold you my liege,
And so, as I have said, I must set forth tomorrow,   1965
If I may take some trusty man to teach, as you promised,
The way to the Green Chapel, that as God allows
I shall see my fate fulfilled on the first of the year."
"In good faith," said the good man, "with a good will
Every promise on my part shall be fully performed."   1970
He assigns him a servant to set him on the path,
To see him safe and sound over the snowy hills,
To follow the fastest way through forest green
                              and grove.
                    Gawain thanks him again,   1975
                    So kind his favors prove,
                    And of the ladies then
                    He takes his leave, with love.

Courteously he kissed them, with care in his heart,
And often wished them well, with warmest thanks,   1980
Which they for their part were prompt to repay.
They commend him to Christ with disconsolate sighs;
And then in that hall with the household he parts—
Each man that he met, he remembered to thank

For his deeds of devotion and diligent pains,   1985
And the trouble he had taken to tend to his needs;
And each one as woeful, that watched him depart,
As he had lived with him loyally all his life long.
By lads bearing lights he was led to his chamber
And blithely brought to his bed, to be at his rest.   1990
How soundly he slept, I presume not to say,
For there were matters of moment his thoughts might well
                     pursue.
           Let him lie and wait;
           He has little more to do,   1995
           Then listen, while I relate
           How they kept their rendezvous.

Part 4

Now the New Year draws near, and the night passes,
The day dispels the dark, by the Lord's decree;
But wild weather awoke in the world without: 2000
The clouds in the cold sky cast down their snow
With great gusts from the north, grievous to bear.
Sleet showered aslant upon shivering beasts;
The wind warbled wild as it whipped from aloft,
And drove the drifts deep in the dales below.   2005
Long and well he listens, that lies in his bed;
Though he lifts not his eyelids, little he sleeps;
Each crow of the cock he counts without fail.
Readily from his rest he rose before dawn,
For a lamp had been left him, that lighted his chamber.   2010
He called to his chamberlain, who quickly appeared,
And bade him get him his gear, and gird his good steed,
And he sets about briskly to bring in his arms,
And makes ready his master in manner most fit.
First he clad him in his clothes, to keep out the cold,   2015
And then his other harness, made handsome anew,
His plate-armor of proof, polished with pains,
The rings of his rich mail rid of their rust,
And all was fresh as at first, and for this he gave thanks
                     indeed.   2020
           With pride he wears each piece,
           New-furbished for his need:
           No gayer from here to Greece;
           He bids them bring his steed.

In his richest raiment he robed himself then: 2025
His crested coat-armor, close-stitched with craft,
With stones of strange virtue on silk velvet set;
All bound with embroidery on borders and seams
And lined warmly and well with furs of the best.

Yet he left not his love-gift, the lady's girdle;   2030
Gawain, for his own good, forgot not that:
When the bright sword was belted and bound on his haunches,
Then twice with that token he twined him about.
Sweetly did he swathe him in that swatch of silk,
That girdle of green so goodly to see,   2035
That against the gay red showed gorgeous bright.
Yet he wore not for its wealth that wondrous girdle,
Nor pride in its pendants, though polished they were,
Though glittering gold gleamed at the tips,
But to keep himself safe when consent he must   2040
To endure a deadly dint, and all defense
                    denied.
           And now the bold knight came
           Into the courtyard wide;
           That folk of worthy fame   2045
           He thanks on every side.

Then was Gringolet girt, that was great and huge,
And had sojourned safe and sound, and savored his fare;
He pawed the earth in his pride, that princely steed.
The good knight draws near him and notes well his look,   2050
And says sagely to himself, and soberly swears,
"Here is a household in hall that upholds the right!
The man that maintains it, may happiness be his!
Likewise the dear lady, may love betide her!
If thus they in charity cherish a guest   2055
That are honored here on earth, may they have his reward
That reigns high in heaven—and also you all;
And might I live in this land but a little while,
I should willingly reward you, and well, if I might."
Then he steps into the stirrup and bestrides his mount;   2060
His shield is shown forth; on his shoulder he casts it;
Strikes the side of his steed with his steel spurs,
And he starts across the stones, nor stands any longer
                   to prance.
           On horseback was the swain   2065
           That bore his spear and lance;
           "May Christ this house maintain
           And guard it from mischance!"

The bridge was brought down, and the road gates
Unbarred and carried back upon both sides;   2070
He commended him to Christ, and crossed over the planks;
Praised the noble porter, who prayed on his knees
That God save Sir Gawain, and bade him good day,
And went on his way alone with the man
That was to lead him ere long to that luckless place   2075
Where the dolorous dint must be dealt him at last.

Under bare boughs they ride, where steep banks rise,
Over high cliffs they climb, where cold snow clings;
The heavens held aloof, but heavy thereunder
Mist mantled the moors, moved on the slopes.   2080
Each hill had a hat, a huge cape of cloud;
Brooks bubbled and broke over broken rocks,
Flashing in freshets that waterfalls fed.
Roundabout was the road that ran through the wood
Till the sun at that season was soon to rise,   2085
                that day.
          They were on a hilltop high;
          The white snow round them lay;
          The man that rode nearby
          Now bade his master stay.   2090

"For I have seen you here safe at the set time,
And now you are not far from that notable place
That you have sought for so long with such special pains.
But this I say for certain, since I know you, sir knight,
And have your good at heart, and hold you dear—   2095
Would you heed well my words, it were worth your while—
You are rushing into risks that you reck not of:
There is a villain in yon valley, the veriest on earth,
For he is rugged and rude, and ready with his fists,
And most immense in his mold of mortals alive,   2100
And his body bigger than the best four
That are in Arthur's house, Hector[6] or any.
He gets his grim way at the Green Chapel;
None passes by that place so proud in his arms
That he does not dash him down with his deadly blows,   2105
For he is heartless wholly, and heedless of right,
For be it chaplain or churl that by the Chapel rides,
Monk or mass-priest or any man else,
He would as soon strike him dead as stand on two feet.
Wherefore I say, just as certain as you sit there astride,   2110
You cannot but be killed, if his counsel holds,
For he would trounce you in a trice, had you twenty lives
                for sale.
          He has lived long in this land
          And dealt out deadly bale;   2115
          Against his heavy hand
          Your power cannot prevail.

"And so, good Sir Gawain, let the grim man be;
Go off by some other road, in God's own name!
Leave by some other land, for the love of Christ,   2120

---

6. Either the Trojan hero or one of Arthur's knights.

And I shall get me home again, and give you my word.
That I shall swear by God's self and the saints above,
By heaven and by my halidom[7] and other oaths more,
To conceal this day's deed, nor say to a soul
That ever you fled for fear from any that I knew."   2125
"Many thanks!" said the other man—and demurring he speaks—
"Fair fortune befall you for your friendly words!
And conceal this day's deed I doubt not you would,
But though you never told the tale, if I turned back now,
Forsook this place for fear, and fled, as you say,   2130
I were a caitiff coward; I could not be excused.
But I must to the Chapel to chance my luck
And say to that same man such words as I please,
Befall what may befall through Fortune's will
                              or whim.   2135
            Though he be a quarrelsome knave
            With a cudgel great and grim,
            The Lord is strong to save:
            His servants trust in him."

"Marry," said the man, "since you tell me so much,   2140
And I see you are set to seek your own harm,
If you crave a quick death, let me keep you no longer!
Put your helm on your head, your hand on your lance,
And ride the narrow road down yon rocky slope
Till it brings you to the bottom of the broad valley.   2145
Then look a little ahead, on your left hand,
And you will soon see before you that self-same Chapel,
And the man of great might that is master there.
Now goodbye in God's name, Gawain the noble!
For all the world's wealth I would not stay here,   2150
Or go with you in this wood one footstep further!"
He tarried no more to talk, but turned his bridle,
Hit his horse with his heels as hard as he might,
Leaves the knight alone, and off like the wind
                              goes leaping.   2155
            "By God," said Gawain then,
            "I shall not give way to weeping;
            God's will be done, amen!
            I commend me to his keeping."

He puts his heels to his horse, and picks up the path;   2160
Goes in beside a grove where the ground is steep,
Rides down the rough slope right to the valley;
And then he looked a little about him—the landscape was wild,
And not a soul to be seen, nor sign of a dwelling,

---

7. Holiness or, more likely, patron saints.

But high banks on either hand hemmed it about,   2165
With many a ragged rock and rough-hewn crag;
The skies seemed scored by the scowling peaks.
Then he halted his horse, and hoved there a space,
And sought on every side for a sight of the Chapel,
But no such place appeared, which puzzled him sore,   2170
Yet he saw some way off what seemed like a mound,
A hillock high and broad, hard by the water,
Where the stream fell in foam down the face of the steep
And bubbled as if it boiled on its bed below.
The knight urges his horse, and heads for the knoll;   2175
Leaps lightly to earth; loops well the rein
Of his steed to a stout branch, and stations him there.
He strides straight to the mound, and strolls all about,
Much wondering what it was, but no whit the wiser;
It had a hole at one end, and on either side,   2180
And was covered with coarse grass in clumps all without,
And hollow all within, like some old cave,
Or a crevice of an old crag—he could not discern
                          aright.
           "Can this be the Chapel Green?   2185
           Alack!" said the man, "here might
           The devil himself be seen
           Saying matins at black midnight!"

"Now by heaven," said he, "it is bleak hereabouts;
This prayer-house is hideous, half-covered with grass!   2190
Well may the grim man mantled in green
Hold here his orisons, in hell's own style!
Now I feel it is the Fiend, in my five wits,
That has tempted me to this tryst, to take my life;
This is a Chapel of mischance, may the mischief take it!   2195
As accursed a country church as I came upon ever!"
With his helm on his head, his lance in his hand,
He stalks toward the steep wall of that strange house.
Then he heard, on the hill, behind a hard rock,
Beyond the brook, from the bank, a most barbarous din: 2200
Lord! it clattered in the cliff fit to cleave it in two,
As one upon a grindstone ground a great scythe!
Lord! it whirred like a mill-wheel whirling about!
Lord! it echoed loud and long, lamentable to hear!
Then "By heaven," said the bold knight, "that business
           up there   2205
Is arranged for my arrival, or else I am much
                          misled.
           Let God work! Ah me!
           All hope of help has fled!
           Forfeit my life may be   2210
           But noise I do not dread."

Then he listened no longer, but loudly he called,
"Who has power in this place, high parley to hold?
For none greets Sir Gawain, or gives him good day;
If any would a word with him, let him walk forth   2215
And speak now or never, to speed his affairs."
"Abide," said one on the bank above over his head,
"And what I promised you once shall straightway be given."
Yet he stayed not his grindstone, nor stinted its noise,
But worked awhile at his whetting before he would rest,   2220
And then he comes around a crag, from a cave in the rocks,
Hurtling out of hiding with a hateful weapon,
A Danish[8] ax devised for that day's deed,
With a broad blade and bright, bent in a curve,
Filed to a fine edge—four feet it measured   2225
By the length of the lace that was looped round the haft.
And in form as at first, the fellow all green,
His lordly face and his legs, his locks and his beard,
Save that firm upon two feet forward he strides,
Sets a hand on the ax-head, the haft to the earth;   2230
When he came to the cold stream, and cared not to wade,
He vaults over on his ax, and advances amain
On a broad bank of snow, overbearing and brisk
                    of mood.
            Little did the knight incline   2235
            When face to face they stood;
            Said the other man, "Friend mine,
            It seems your word holds good!"

"God love you, Sir Gawain!" said the Green Knight then,
"And well met this morning, man, at my place!   2240
And you have followed me faithfully and found me betimes,
And on the business between us we both are agreed:
Twelve months ago today you took what was yours,
And you at this New Year must yield me the same.
And we have met in these mountains, remote from all eyes: 2245
There is none here to halt us or hinder our sport;
Unhasp your high helm, and have here your wages;
Make no more demur than I did myself
When you hacked off my head with one hard blow."
"No, by God," said Sir Gawain, "that granted me life,   2250
I shall grudge not the guerdon, grim though it prove;
Bestow but one stroke, and I shall stand still,
And you may lay on as you like till the last of my part
                    be paid."
            He proffered, with good grace,   2255
            His bare neck to the blade,

8. I.e., long-bladed.

                    And feigned a cheerful face:
                    He scorned to seem afraid.

Then the grim man in green gathers his strength,
Heaves high the heavy ax to hit him the blow.   2260
With all the force in his frame he fetches it aloft,
With a grimace as grim as he would grind him to bits;
Had the blow he bestowed been as big as he threatened,
A good knight and gallant had gone to his grave.
But Gawain at the great ax glanced up aside.   2265
As down it descended with death-dealing force,
And his shoulders shrank a little from the sharp iron.
Abruptly the brawny man breaks off the stroke,
And then reproved with proud words that prince among knights.
"You are not Gawain the glorious," the green man said,   2270
"That never fell back on field in the face of the foe,
And now you flee for fear, and have felt no harm:
Such news of that knight I never heard yet!
I moved not a muscle when you made to strike,
Nor caviled at the cut in King Arthur's house;   2275
My head fell to my feet, yet steadfast I stood,
And you, all unharmed, are wholly dismayed—
Wherefore the better man I, by all odds,
                              must be."
                    Said Gawain, "Strike once more;   2280
                    I shall neither flinch nor flee;
                    But if my head falls to the floor
                    There is no mending me!"

"But go on, man, in God's name, and get to the point!
Deliver me my destiny, and do it out of hand,   2285
For I shall stand to the stroke and stir not an inch
Till your ax has hit home—on my honor I swear it!"
"Have at thee then!" said the other, and heaves it aloft,
And glares down as grimly as he had gone mad.
He made a mighty feint, but marred not his hide;   2290
Withdrew the ax adroitly before it did damage.
Gawain gave no ground, nor glanced up aside,
But stood still as a stone, or else a stout stump
That is held in hard earth by a hundred roots.
Then merrily does he mock him, the man all in green: 2295
"So now you have your nerve again, I needs must strike;
Uphold the high knighthood that Arthur bestowed,
And keep your neck-bone clear, if this cut allows!"
Then was Gawain gripped with rage, and grimly he said,
"Why, thrash away, tyrant, I tire of your threats;   2300
You make such a scene, you must frighten yourself."
Said the green fellow, "In faith, so fiercely you speak

That I shall finish this affair, nor further grace
                              allow."
                    He stands prepared to strike   2305
                    And scowls with both lip and brow;
                    No marvel if the man mislike
                    Who can hope no rescue now.

He gathered up the grim ax and guided it well:
Let the barb at the blade's end brush the bare throat;   2310
He hammered down hard, yet harmed him no whit
Save a scratch on one side, that severed the skin;
The end of the hooked edge entered the flesh,
And a little blood lightly leapt to the earth.
And when the man beheld his own blood bright on the snow,   2315
He sprang a spear's length with feet spread wide,
Seized his high helm, and set it on his head,
Shoved before his shoulders the shield at his back,
Bares his trusty blade, and boldly he speaks—
Not since he was a babe born of his mother   2320
Was he once in this world one-half so blithe—
"Have done with your hacking—harry me no more!
I have borne, as behooved, one blow in this place;
If you make another move I shall meet it midway
And promptly, I promise you, pay back each blow   2325
                              with brand.
                    One stroke acquits me here;
                    So did our covenant stand
                    In Arthur's court last year—
                    Wherefore, sir, hold your hand!"   2330

He lowers the long ax and leans on it there,
Sets his arms on the head, the haft on the earth,
And beholds the bold knight that bides there afoot,
How he faces him fearless, fierce in full arms,
And plies him with proud words—it pleases him well.   2335
Then once again gaily to Gawain he calls,
And in a loud voice and lusty, delivers these words:
"Bold fellow, on this field your anger forbear!
No man has made demands here in manner uncouth,
Nor done, save as duly determined at court.   2340
I owed you a hit and you have it; be happy therewith!
The rest of my rights here I freely resign.
Had I been a bit busier, a buffet, perhaps,
I could have dealt more directly, and done you some harm.
First I flourished with a feint, in frolicsome mood,   2345
And left your hide unhurt—and here I did well
By the fair terms we fixed on the first night;
And fully and faithfully you followed accord:
Gave over all your gains as a good man should.

A second feint, sir, I assigned for the morning   2350
You kissed my comely wife—each kiss you restored.
For both of these there behooved two feigned blows
                              by right.
                    True men pay what they owe;
                    No danger then in sight.   2355
                    You failed at the third throw,
                    So take my tap, sir knight.

"For that is my belt about you, that same braided girdle,
My wife it was that wore it; I know well the tale,
And the count of your kisses and your conduct too,   2360
And the wooing of my wife—it was all my scheme!
She made trial of a man most faultless by far
Of all that ever walked over the wide earth;
As pearls to white peas, more precious and prized,
So is Gawain, in good faith, to other gay knights.   2365
Yet you lacked, sir, a little in loyalty there,
But the cause was not cunning, nor courtship either,
But that you loved your own life; the less, then, to blame."
The other stout knight in a study stood a long while,
So gripped with grim rage that his great heart shook.   2370
All the blood of his body burned in his face
As he shrank back in shame from the man's sharp speech.
The first words that fell from the fair knight's lips:
"Accursed be a cowardly and covetous heart!
In you is villainy and vice, and virtue laid low!"   2375
Then he grasps the green girdle and lets go the knot,
Hands it over in haste, and hotly he says:
"Behold there my falsehood, ill hap betide it!
Your cut taught me cowardice, care for my life,
And coveting came after, contrary both   2380
To largesse and loyalty belonging to knights.
Now am I faulty and false, that fearful was ever
Of disloyalty and lies, bad luck to them both!
                              and greed.
                    I confess, knight, in this place,   2385
                    Most dire is my misdeed;
                    Let me gain back your good grace,
                    And thereafter I shall take heed."

Then the other laughed aloud, and lightly he said,
"Such harm as I have had, I hold it quite healed.   2390
You are so fully confessed, your failings made known,
And bear the plain penance of the point of my blade,
I hold you polished as a pearl, as pure and as bright
As you had lived free of fault since first you were born.
And I give you, sir, this girdle that is gold-hemmed   2395
And green as my garments, that, Gawain, you may

Be mindful of this meeting when you mingle in throng
With nobles of renown—and known by this token
How it chanced at the Green Chapel, to chivalrous knights.
And you shall in this New Year come yet again   2400
And we shall finish out our feast in my fair hall,
with cheer."
He urged the knight to stay,
And said, "With my wife so dear
We shall see you friends this day,   2405
Whose enmity touched you near."

"Indeed," said the doughty knight, and doffed his high helm,
And held it in his hands as he offered his thanks,
"I have lingered long enough—may good luck be yours,
And he reward you well that all worship bestows!   2410
And commend me to that comely one, your courteous wife,
Both herself and that other, my honoured ladies,
That have trapped their true knight in their trammels so quaint.
But if a dullard should dote, deem it no wonder,
And through the wiles of a woman be wooed into sorrow,   2415
For so was Adam by one, when the world began,
And Solomon by many more, and Samson the mighty—
Delilah was his doom, and David thereafter
Was beguiled by Bathsheba, and bore much distress;
Now these were vexed by their devices—'twere a very joy   2420
Could one but learn to love, and believe them not.
For these were proud princes, most prosperous of old,
Past all lovers lucky, that languished under heaven,
bemused.
And one and all fell prey   2425
To women that they had used;
If I be led astray,
Methinks I may be excused.

"But your girdle. God love you! I gladly shall take
And be pleased to possess, not for the pure gold,   2430
Nor the bright belt itself, nor the beauteous pendants,
Nor for wealth, nor worldly state, nor workmanship fine,
But a sign of excess it shall seem oftentimes
When I ride in renown, and remember with shame
The faults and the frailty of the flesh perverse,   2435
How its tenderness entices the foul taint of sin;
And so when praise and high prowess have pleased my heart,
A look at this love-lace will lower my pride.
But one thing would I learn, if you were not loath,
Since you are lord of yonder land where I have long sojourned   2440
With honor in your house—may you have His reward
That upholds all the heavens, highest on throne!
How runs your right name?—and let the rest go."
"That shall I give you gladly," said the Green Knight then;

"Bercilak de Hautdesert this barony I hold,   2445
Through the might of Morgan le Faye,[9] that lodges at my house,
By subtleties of science and sorcerers' arts,
The mistress of Merlin,[1] she has caught many a man,
For sweet love in secret she shared sometime
With that wizard, that knows well each one of your knights   2450
          and you.
        Morgan the Goddess, she,
        So styled by title true;
        None holds so high degree
        That her arts cannot subdue.   2455

"She guided me in this guise to your glorious hall,
To assay, if such it were, the surfeit of pride
That is rumored of the retinue of the Round Table.
She put this shape upon me to puzzle your wits,
To afflict the fair queen, and frighten her to death   2460
With awe of that elvish man that eerily spoke
With his head in his hand before the high table.
She was with my wife at home, that old withered lady,
Your own aunt[2] is she, Arthur's half-sister,
The Duchess' daughter of Tintagel, that dear King Uther   2465
Got Arthur on after, that honored is now.
And therefore, good friend, come feast with your aunt;
Make merry in my house; my men hold you dear,
And I wish you as well, sir, with all my heart,
As any man God ever made, for your great good faith."   2470
But the knight said him nay, that he might by no means.
They clasped then and kissed, and commended each other
To the Prince of Paradise, and parted with one
          assent.
        Gawain sets out anew;   2475
        Toward the court his course is bent;
        And the knight all green in hue,
        Wheresoever he wished, he went.

Wild ways in the world our worthy knight rides
On Gringolet, that by grace had been granted his life.   2480
He harbored often in houses, and often abroad,
And with many valiant adventures verily he met
That I shall not take time to tell in this story.
The hurt was whole that he had had in his neck,
And the bright green belt on his body he bore,   2485
Oblique, like a baldric, bound at his side,
Below his left shoulder, laced in a knot,

9. Arthur's half-sister, an enchantress who sometimes abetted him, sometimes made trouble for
him.
1. The wise magician who had helped Arthur
become king.

2. Morgan was the daughter of Igraine, Duchess
of Tintagel, and her husband the Duke; Igraine
conceived Arthur when his father Uther lay with
her through one of Merlin's trickeries.

In betokening of the blame he had borne for his fault;
And so to court in due course he comes safe and sound.
Bliss abounded in hall when the high-born heard   2490
That good Gawain was come; glad tidings they thought it.
The king kisses the knight, and the queen as well,
And many a comrade came to clasp him in arms,
And eagerly they asked, and awesomely he told,
Confessed all his cares and discomfitures many,   2495
How it chanced at the Chapel, what cheer made the knight,
The love of the lady, the green lace at last.
The nick on his neck he naked displayed
That he got in his disgrace at the Green Knight's hands,
                                        alone.   2500
            With rage in heart he speaks,
            And grieves with many a groan;
            The blood burns in his cheeks
            For shame at what must be shown.

"Behold, sir," said he, and handles the belt,   2505
"This is the blazon of the blemish that I bear on my neck;
This is the sign of sore loss that I have suffered there
For the cowardice and coveting that I came to there;
This is the badge of false faith that I was found in there,
And I must bear it on my body till I breathe my last.   2510
For one may keep a deed dark, but undo it no whit,
For where a fault is made fast, it is fixed evermore."
The king comforts the knight, and the court all together
Agree with gay laughter and gracious intent
That the lords and the ladies belonging to the Table,   2515
Each brother of that band, a baldric should have,
A belt borne oblique, of a bright green,
To be worn with one accord for that worthy's sake.
So that was taken as a token by the Table Round,
And he honored that had it, evermore after,   2520
As the best book of knighthood bids it be known.
In the old days of Arthur this happening befell;
The books of Brutus' deeds bear witness thereto
Since Brutus, the bold knight, embarked for this land
After the siege ceased at Troy and the city fared   2525
                                        amiss.
            Many such, ere we were born,
            Have befallen here, ere this.
            May He that was crowned with thorn
            Bring all men to His bliss! Amen.   2530

Hony Soyt Qui Mal Pense[3]

---

3. "Shame be to the man who has evil in his mind." This is the motto of the Order of the Garter, founded ca. 1350: apparently a copyist of the poem associated this order with the one founded to honor Gawain.

PIERS PLOWMAN
ca. 1372–1389

The large number of manuscripts in which the *Vision of Piers Plowman* has been preserved indicates its wide popularity from the end of the fourteenth century up to the reign of Elizabeth I. Yet celebrated as the poem was, we know little about its origin. It exists in three versions, which scholars refer to as the A, B, and C texts. The first, about 2,400 lines long, stops at a rather inconclusive point in the action; the second (generally agreed to be the best form of the poem) is a revision of the first plus an extension of more than 4,000 lines; and the third is a revision of the second. The name frequently associated with the poem is William Langland, but who he was and whether he wrote all three versions is not known. The little that can be inferred about him suggests that he came from the west of England and was probably a native of the Malvern Hills area in which the poem is set and where many of the surviving manuscripts were copied. If he wrote all three versions, then his interests and opinions must have changed while he was at work, for the versions differ from one another in many respects; but if more than one poet was involved, then it is extraordinary that all three versions share the same highly individual style and reflect the same curious and interesting poetic personality. Whatever its origin, the poem was avidly read and studied by a great many people. Within four years of the writing of the second version—which scholars have good evidence to date 1377, the year of Edward III's death and Richard II's accession to the throne—it had become so well known that the leaders of the Peasants' Revolt of 1381 used phrases borrowed from it as part of the rhetoric of the rebellion. The poem must therefore have managed to catch the imagination of a number of readers.

Piers Plowman has the form of a dream vision, a common medieval type in which the author presents his story under the guise of having dreamed it. Most dream visions concern romantic love; *Piers Plowman* also concerns love, but in this instance the love is theological. The dream vision generally involves allegory, not only because one expects from a dream the unrealistic, the fanciful, but also because people have always suspected that dreams relate the truth in a disguised form—that they are natural allegories. *Piers Plowman* is perhaps the greatest of English allegories, though the reader who expects to find in it the kind of definite and clear statement that allegory makes in the morality *Everyman* will be disappointed; allegory here is used not so much in order to define the known, as the character "Good Deeds" does in that play, as to explore the unknown, in particular the great spiritual mysteries of Christianity. When handling these the poet's imagination (for convenience let us assume a single poet, Langland) is apt to soar into a mode of expression that stimulates and excites readers' imaginations while, perhaps, bewildering their intellects. Langland's theme is nothing less than the history of Christianity as it unfolds both in the world of the Old and New Testaments and in the life and heart of an individual fourteenth-century Christian—two seemingly distinct realms between which the poet's allegory moves with dizzying rapidity.

Expanding the genre of dream-vision, *Piers Plowman* takes the form of a whole series of visions, separated by brief intervals when the narrator is awake.

The first passage presented here—the Prologue to the poem—introduces the famous first vision of the Field of Folk. The poet thought of Christianity as properly informing—and reforming—society, and he describes fourteenth-century English society in terms of its failure to represent an ideal society living in accord with Christian principles: hence the satirical poetry for which Langland is generally noted. Society's failure, of course, is attributable in part to the corruption of the church and churchmen, and whenever he considers clerical and ecclesiastical corruption, he pours out savagely indignant satire. But he is equally angry with the failure of the wealthy laity—untaught by the church to practice charity—to alleviate the sufferings of the poor, and it was probably his preoccupation with the poor that made his poem popular with the rebels of 1381; these, though confused in their motives, were eager to obtain correction of certain social abuses that Langland touches upon. This use of his poem must have horrified him, for despite his interest in social reform, he remains a fundamentally conservative and orthodox thinker: yet his passionate sympathy for the common man—idealized in his titular hero Piers the Plowman—made him seem a radical who felt that true religion was best represented not by the church but by the humblest orders of society. Many persons reading his poem more than a century and a half after it was written (it was first printed in 1550) saw in its Prologue strong historical reasons for the reformation of the church that had been carried out in the intervening years.

After his vision of the Field of Folk in the Prologue, Will the Dreamer is in Passus 1 ("Passus" is Latin for step, and the word the poet uses for the sections of his poem) approached by Lady Holy Church, who explains to him the fundamental principles of Christianity—with which, presumably, he has been familiar since childhood. But mere knowledge is not enough for him: he must learn by experience and feel in his heart what he learns. Having heard about truth, he asks to be shown the false, and Holy Church leaves him to witness the marriage of the compliant and wealthy Lady Meed to a conveniently personified figure named False. Meed, unlike False, is an ambiguous allegorical figure: most people, including her rascally followers, recognize her as bribery, but others, including Theology, think she is the reward that God has promised to just men. Theology therefore objects to the marriage with False, and the wedding party then goes up to London to the King's court to get a legal opinion on the propriety of the marriage. For several *passūs* Langland's lively satire dwells on the corruption that Meed and her train sow wherever they go. Even the King has to be persuaded by Conscience and Reason that she is evil. The incident ends inconclusively, with the King resolving to rule with Conscience and Reason but with Lady Meed still busily corrupting whomever she can.

Here the Dreamer awakes for the first time, but after a very short interval he falls asleep again and dreams that Reason preaches a sermon to the whole kingdom, causing the people to confess their sins. Langland describes the confession by personifying the seven deadly sins and having each one relate to the personified figure Repentance how badly he behaves in society. The confessions of two of these, Envy and Gluttony, constitute the second selection below: they display most clearly Langland's social realism.

The third selection represents a wholly different side of Langland's art. It is a description of the central event of Christianity, Christ's crucifixion, followed by an account of the descent into Hell. In this passage Langland's titular hero, Piers, who first appears in the poem as a simple, honest farmer but who later assumes aspects of Adam and Moses, is now partially identified with Christ. With this development his farm produce is no longer simple foodstuffs, but becomes the souls of the patriarchs and prophets, and of all mankind, which must be redeemed from the Devil's power by Christ's sacrifice on the cross. In lines 20 and 33 these souls are referred to as the "fruit" of Piers Plowman, which Christ, having assumed Pier's human nature, will win back from Hell, where it has been since Adam's sin. Langland describes the crucifixion as a literal, historical event—yet at the same time he speaks of it as if it were a medieval joust between the Christ-knight and an adversary. After Christ dies on the cross, the Dreamer descends to the lower world, where he hears an argument among the Four Daughters of God about the efficacy of Christ's sacrifice: Righteousness and Truth maintain that the Old Law condemns mankind irredeemably, while Mercy and Peace prophesy that by Christ's New Law man will be saved. Christ appears before Hell's gates as a great light, the devils are thrown into confusion, and the souls of the righteous are released from Hell's power. The Four Daughters of God are reconciled as the New Law fulfills the Old, and the Dreamer wakes to celebrate Easter.

From The Vision of Piers Plowman[1]

From *The Prologue*

[THE FIELD OF FOLK]

In a summer season when the sun was mild
I got myself up in garb as though I'd grown into a sheep;
In the habit of a hermit, unholy of works,[2]
I went wide in the world, watching for wonders.
And on a May morning on Malvern Hills   5
A marvel befell me—magic it seemed.
I was wearied from wandering and went to rest
At the bottom of a broad bank by a brook's side,
And as I lay lazily looking in the water
I slid into a slumber, it sounded so soothing.   10
Then there came to me reclining there a most curious dream,
That I was in a wilderness—where, I'd no idea.
But as I looked into the east, up high toward the sun,
I saw a tower on a hill-top, trimly constructed,
A deep dale beneath, a dungeon-tower in it,   15
With deep dark ditches, dreadful to see.
A fair field full of folk I found between the towers,
Of people of all positions, the poor and the rich,
Working and wandering as the world requires.
Some applied themselves to plowing, played very seldom,   20
Sowing seeds and setting plants worked very hard;

---

1. The translations by the senior editor are based on *Piers Plowman: The B Version*, edited by George Kane and E. T. Donaldson (1975).

2. For Langland's opinion of hermits see lines 28–30 immediately below.

Won what wasters destroy with their gluttony.
And some applied themselves to pride, wore proud garments,
Came all costumed in costly clothes.
To prayers and to penance many put themselves,   25
All for love of our Lord lived hard lives
In hope to have afterwards heaven's bliss—
Such as anchorites and hermits that hold to their cells
And don't care to go cantering about the countryside,
With some lush livelihood delighting their bodies.   30
And some made themselves merchants—they managed better,
As it seems to our sight that such men prosper.
And some make mirths as minstrels can,
And get gold with their glee,[3] guiltless, I think.
But word-jugglers and jokers, Judas' children,[4]   35
Invent fantasies to speak of and make fools of themselves,
Yet they have whatever wit they need to work if they wanted.
What Paul preaches of them I don't dare repeat it here:
Qui loquitur turpiloquim[5] is Lucifer's servant.
Beggars and beadsmen[6] went about fast   40
Till both their bellies and their bags were crammed to the brim;
Staged flytings[7] for their food, fought over ale.
In gluttony, God knows, they go to bed
And rise up with ribaldry, those Robert's boys;[8]
Sleep and sloth always pursue them.   45
Pilgrims and palmers[9] made pacts with each other
To seek Saint James[1] and saints at Rome.
They went along the way with many wise tales,
And had leave to tell lies all their lives after.
I saw some that said they'd sought after saints: 50
In every tale they told their tongues tended to lie
More than to tell the truth, their talk was such.
A heap of hermits carrying hooked staffs
Went off to Walsingham,[2] with their wenches behind.
Great long lubbers that don't like to work   55
Clothed themselves in copes[3] to keep distinct from other men,
And behaved like hermits to have their ease.
Friars I found there, all the four orders,[4]
Preaching to the populace for their own paunches' profit,
Explaining Holy Scripture as seemed best for themselves,   60

3. I.e., music.
4. Minstrels who entertain with jokes and fantas-tic stories are regarded as descendants of Christ's betrayer, Judas.
5. "Who speaks slander": the text is not St. Paul's but expresses the poet's reason for not quoting St. Paul in such a way as to speak maliciously about the minstrels under discussion.
6. Prayer-sayers, i.e., people who offered to pray for the souls of those who gave them alms.
7. Contests in which the participants took turns insulting each other, preferably in verse.

8. I.e., robbers.
9. Virtually professional pilgrims, who took advantage of the hospitality offered pilgrims in order to go on traveling year after year.
1. I.e., his shrine at Compostella, Spain.
2. English town, site of a famous shrine to the Virgin Mary.
3. Monks', friars', and hermits' capes.
4. In Langland's day there were four orders of friars in England: Franciscans, Dominicans, Carme-lites, and Augustinians.

In hope to acquire copes[5] construed it as they pleased.
Many of these Masters[6] may clothe themselves gaily
For their money and their merchandise march hand in hand.[7]
Since Charity[8] has proved a peddler and principally shrives lords
Many marvels have been meted out within a few years.   65
Unless Holy Church and friars' orders hold together better
The worst trouble in the world will well up soon.
A pardoner[9] preached there as if he'd a priest's rights,
Brought out a bull with bishop's seals,
And said he himself could absolve them all   70
Of failure to fast, of vows they'd broken.
Unlearnèd men believed him and liked his words,
Came crowding up on knees to kiss his bulls.
He banged them with his brevet[1] and bleared their eyes,
And raked in with his parchment-roll rings and brooches.   75
Thus you give your gold for gluttons' profit,
And squander it on scoundrels who're schooled as lechers.
If the bishop were blessed and worth both his ears
His seal should not be sent out to deceive the people.
It's not by the bishop's leave that the blackguard preaches;   80
What's more, the parish priest and the pardoner split the money
That the poor people of the parish should otherwise have.
Parsons and parish priests complained to the bishop
That their parishes were poor since the pestilence-time,[2]
Asked for license and leave to live in London,   85
And sing masses there for simony, for silver is sweet.[3]

*   *   *

Yet there stood scores of men in scarves of silk,[4]
Law-sergeants[5] they seemed to be who served at the bar,
Pleaded cases for pennies[6] and impounded the law,
And for love of our Lord not once unloosed their lips:
You might better measure mist on Malvern Hills   215
Than get a "mum" from their mouths till money is produced.
Barons and burgesses and bondmen also
I saw in this assemblage, as you shall hear later;
Bakers and brewers and butchers aplenty.
Woolen-weavers and weavers of linen.   220

---

5. I.e., new garments.
6. I.e., Masters of Divinity.
7. The "merchandise" sold by the friars for money is shrift, which by canon law may not be sold.
8. The ideal of the friars, as stated by St. Francis, founder of the Franciscans, was simply love.
9. An official empowered to pass on from the pope temporal indulgence for the sins of people who contributed to charitable enterprises—a function frequently abused (see Chaucer's Pardoner, General Prologue to the *Canterbury Tales*, lines 671 ff.). "Bull": papal license.
1. Pardoner's license.
2. Since 1349, England had suffered a number of

epidemics of the plague, which had caused famine and depopulated the countryside.
3. Wealthy persons, especially in London, set up foundations to pay priests to sing masses for their souls and those of their relatives. "Simony": abuse of ecclesiastical office; a priest who had charge of a parish was forbidden to exercise any other salaried function in the church.
4. A silk scarf was a lawyer's badge of office.
5. Important lawyers (see the General Prologue to the *Canterbury Tales*, lines 311 ff.).
6. Pennies were fairly valuable coins in medieval England. "Impounded": detained in legal custody.

Tailors, tinkers, tax-collectors in markets,
Masons, miners, many other craftsmen.
Of all kinds of living laborers there leapt forth some,
Such as diggers of ditches that do their jobs badly
And dawdle away the long day with *"Dieu save dame Emma."*[7]   225
Cooks and their kitchen-boys cried, "Hot pies, hot!
Good goose and pork! Let's go and dine!"
Taverners told the same tale to them:
"White wine of Alsace and wine of Gascony,
Of the Rhine and of La Rochelle, to wash the roast down."   230
All this I saw sleeping and seven times more.

From *Passus 5*

[THE CONFESSION OF ENVY]

Envy with heavy heart asked for shrift   75
And, grieving for his guilt, began his confession.
He was pale as a sheep's pelt, appeared to have the palsy;
He was clothed in a coarse cloth—I couldn't describe it—
A tabard[1] and a tunic, a knife attached to his side,
Like those of a friar's frock were the foresleeves.   80
Like a leek that had lain long in the sun
So he looked with lean cheeks, louring foully.
His body was so blown up for wrath that he bit his lips
And shook his fist fiercely—he wanted to avenge himself
With deeds or with words when he saw his chance.   85
Every syllable he spat out was of a serpent's tongue;
From chiding and bringing charges was his chief livelihood,
With backbiting and bitter scorn and bearing false witness.
This was all his courtesy wherever he showed himself.
"I'd like to be shriven," said this scoundrel,
        "if shame would let me.   90
By God, I'd be gladder that Gib had bad luck
Than if I'd won this week a wey[2] of Essex cheese.
I have a near neighbor, I've nettled him often
And blamed him behind his back to blacken his name:
I've done my best to damage him day after day,   95
And lied to lords about him to make him lose money,
And turned his friends into his foes with my false tongue.
His good luck and glad lot grieve me greatly.
Between one household and another I often start disputes
So that both life and limb are lost for my speech.   100
When I met in the market the man I most hated
I fondled him affectionately as if I was a friend of his:
He's stronger than I am—I don't dare harm him.
But if I had might and mastery I'd murder him once for all.

---

7. "God save Dame Emma": apparently a popular
song.

1. A loose sleeveless jacket, worn over the tunic.
2. A very large measure.

When I come to kirk[3] and kneel before Christ's cross   105
And ought to pray for the people as the priest teaches,
For pilgrims, for palmers, for all the people after,
Then crouching there I call on Christ to give him sorrow
That took away my tankard and my torn sheet.[4]
Away from the altar I turn my eyes   110
And see how Heinie has a new coat;
Then I wish it were mine, and all the web[5] it came from.
And when he loses I laugh—that lightens my heart;
But when he wins I weep and wail the time.
I condemn men when they do evil, yet I do much worse: 115
Whoever upbraids me for that, I hate him deadly after.
I wish that everyone were my servant,
And if any man has more than I, that angers my heart.
So I live loveless like a loathsome dog
So that all my breast is blown up for bitterness of spirit.   120
For many years I might not eat as a man ought,
For envy and ill will are hard to digest.
Is there any sugar or sweet thing to assuage my swelling,
Or any *diapenidion*[6] that will drive it from my heart,
Or any shrift or shame, unless I have my stomach scraped?"   125
"Yes, readily," said Repentance, directing him to live better;
"Sorrow for sins is salvation for souls."
"I am sorry," said Envy. "I'm seldom otherwise,
And that makes me so miserable, since I may not avenge myself.
I've been among burgesses[7] buying at London   130
And made Backbiting a broker to blame men's wares.
When he sold and I didn't, then I was ready
To lie and to lour at my neighbor and belittle his merchandise.
I will amend this if I may, by might of God almighty."

[THE CONFESSION OF GLUTTONY]

Now Glutton begins to go to shrift
And takes his way toward the church to tell his sins.
But Betty the brewer bade him good morning
And she asked him where he was going.
"To Holy Church," he said, "to hear mass,   300
And then I shall be shriven and sin no more."
"I've good ale, good friend," said she. "Glutton, will you try it?"
"Have you," he asked, "any hot spices?"
"I have pepper and peony[8] and a pound of garlic,
A farthing-worth of fennel seed[9] for fasting days."   305
Then Glutton goes in, and great oaths after.

---

3. Church.
4. The loss of Envy's tankard and torn sheet, and
his fury at it, have not been explained.
5. I.e., bolt.
6. A twist of medicinal sugar.

7. City people.
8. In the Middle Ages, a spice.
9. This herb was apparently considered salubrious
to one drinking on an empty stomach.

Cissy the seamstress was sitting on the bench,
Wat the warren-keeper and his wife both,
Tim the tinker and two of his servants,
Hick the hackneyman and Hugh the needle-seller,   310
Clarice of Cock's Lane[1] and the clerk of the church,
Sir Piers of Pridie and Parnel of Flanders,
Dave the ditch-digger and a dozen others,
A rebeck-player,[2] a rat-catcher, a street-raker of Cheapside,
A rope-maker, a redingking, and Rose the dish-vendor,   315
Godfrey of Garlickhithe and Griffin the Welshman,
A heap of old clothesmen early in the morning
Gladly treated Glutton to drinks of good ale.
Clement the cobbler took the coat off his back
And put it up as a prize for whoever would play "New Fair,"[3]   320
Then Hick the ostler[4] took off his hood
And bade Bette the butcher to be on his side.
Then peddlers were appointed to appraise the goods:
Clement for his coat should get the hood plus compensation.
They went to work quickly and whispered together   325
And appraised these prizes apart by themselves.
There were heaps of oaths for anyone to hear.
They couldn't in conscience come to an agreement
Till Robin the roper was requested to arise
And named as an umpire so no quarrel should break out.   330
Then Hick the ostler had the cloak
In covenant that Clement should have his cup filled
And have Hick the ostler's hood, and call it a deal;
The first to regret the agreement should get up at once
And greet Sir Glutton with a gallon of ale.   335
There was laughing and louring and "Let go the cup!"
They began to make bets and bought more rounds,
And sat so till evensong and sang sometimes,
Till Glutton had gulped down a gallon and a gill.[5]
His guts began to grumble like two greedy sows;   340
He pissed four pints in a Paternoster's length,[6]
And on the bugle of his backside he blew a fanfare
So that all that heard that horn held their noses after
And wished it had been waxed[7] with a wisp of gorse.

---

1. Clarice (and Parnel of the next line) are prostitutes.
2. Fiddle-player. "Street-raker": a scavenger—
hence street-cleaner—of Cheapside, a section of
London. What a "redingking" was is not known.
3. "New Fair" was a game in which two participants exchanged items in their possession which
were not of equal value and hence involved a cash
payment by the player who put up the least valuable object. Clement puts up his cloak, Hick his
hood; each chooses an agent to represent him in
the evaluation of the objects, which is carried on
by peddlers. Hick is represented by Bette, but since

the evaluators are unable to agree, Robin is named
as an umpire. It is decided that Hick should have
Clement's cloak and Clement Hick's hood, but that
Clement should receive a cup of ale as well, or
perhaps the money for a cup of ale which he would
then share with all the participants. A fine of further ale would be placed on either of the men who
grumbled at the exchange.
4. I.e., a stableman.
5. I.e., a quarter pint.
6. I.e., the time it takes to say the Lord's Prayer.
7. I.e., sealed. "Gorse" is a spiny shrub.

He had no strength to stand before he had his staff in hand,   345
And then he made off, moving like a minstrel's bitch,[8]
Sometimes sidewards and sometimes backwards,
Like some one laying lines to lime[9] birds with.
But as he started stepping to the door his sight grew dim;
He felt for the threshold and fell on the ground.   350
Clement the cobbler caught him by the waist
To lift him aloft, and laid him on his knees.
But Glutton was a large lout and a load to lift.
And he coughed up a custard in Clement's lap.
There's no hound so hungry in Hertfordshire   355
That would dare lap up that leaving, so unlovely the taste.
With all the woe of this world his wife and his maid
Brought him to his bed and bundled him in it,
And after all this excess he had a fit of sloth
So that he slept Saturday and Sunday till the sun set.   360
When he was awake and had wiped his eyes,
The first word he spoke was, "Where is the bowl?"
His spouse scolded him for his sin and wickedness,
And right so Repentance rebuked him at that time.
"As with words and with deeds you've worked evil in your life   365
Shrive yourself and be ashamed, and show it with your mouth."
"I, Glutton," he began, "admit I'm guilty of this:
That I've trespassed with my tongue, I can't tell how often;
Sworn by God's soul and his sides and 'so God help me!'
When there was no need for it, nine hundred times;   370
And overstuffed myself at supper and sometimes at midday
So that I, Glutton, got rid of it before I'd gone a mile;
And swilled what might have been saved and dispensed to the
     hungry;
Overindulgently on feast days I've drunk and eaten both;
And sometimes sat so long there that I slept and ate at once;   375
To hear tales in taverns I've taken more drink;
Fed myself before noon on fasting days."
"This full confession," said Repentance, "will procure favor for you."
Then Glutton began to groan and to make great woe
For his life that he had lived in so loathsome a way,   380
And vowed he would fast, what for hunger or for thirst:
"Never shall fish on Friday be fed to my belly
Till Abstinence my aunt has given me leave,
And yet I have hated her all my lifetime."

Passus 18 [The Harrowing of Hell]

Wool-chafed[1] and wet-shoed I went forth after
Like a careless creature unconscious of woe,

---

8. I.e., a trained dog.
9. Birds were caught by smearing a sticky substance ("lime") on strings laid out on the ground.

1. The hairy side of a hide was worn next to the
body as an act of penance.

And trudged forth like a tramp, time of all my life,
Till I grew weary of the world and wished again to sleep,
And lay down till Lent, and slept a long time,   5
Rested there, snoring roundly, till *Ramis-Palmarum.*[2]
I dreamed chiefly of children and cheers of *Gloria, laus!*
And how old folk to an organ sang "Hosanna!"
And of Christ's passion and pain for the people he had reached for.
One resembling the Samaritan[3] and somewhat Piers the
       Plowman   10
Barefoot on an ass's back bootless came riding
Without spurs or spear: sprightly was his look,
As is the nature of a knight that draws near to be dubbed,
To get himself gilt spurs and engraved jousting shoes.
Then was Faith watching from a window and cried,
       "A, *fili David!*"   15
As does a herald of arms when armed men come to joust.
Old Jews of Jerusalem joyfully sang,
       "*Blessed is he who cometh in the name of the Lord.*"[4]
And I asked Faith to reveal what all this affair meant,
And who should joust in Jerusalem. "Jesus," he said,
"And fetch what the Fiend claims, the fruit of Piers the
       Plowman."   20
"Is Piers in this place?" said I; and he pierced me with his look:
"This Jesus for his gentleness will joust in Piers's arms,
In his helmet and in his hauberk, *humana natura,*[5]
So that Christ be not disclosed here as *consummatus Deus.*[6]
In the plate armor of Piers the Plowman this jouster will ride,   25
For no dint will do him injury as *in deitate Patris.*"[7]
"Who shall joust with Jesus," said I, "Jews or scribes?"[8]
"No," said Faith, "but the Fiend and False-Doom-to-Die.[9]
Death says he will undo and drag down low
All that live or look upon land or water.   30
Life says that he lies, and lays his life in pledge
That for all that Death can do, in three days he'll walk
And fetch from the Fiend the fruit of Piers the Plowman,

---

2. Palm Sunday (literally, "branches of palms"):
the background of this part of the poem is the biblical account of Christ's entry into Jerusalem on
this day, when the crowds greeted him crying,
"Hosanna [line 8] to the son of David [line 15]:
Blessed is he that cometh in the name of the Lord
[line 17a]; Hosanna in the highest": see Matthew
21.9. *Gloria, laus* [line 7] are the first words of an
anthem, "Glory, praise, and honor," which was
sung by children in medieval religious processions
on Palm Sunday.
3. In the previous vision, the Dreamer has
encountered Abraham, or Faith (mentioned in lines
15, 18, 28, and 92), Moses, or Hope, and the Good
Samaritan, or Charity, who was riding toward a
"jousting in Jerusalem" and who now appears as
an aspect of Christ. For Piers Plowman, see the
introductory note.

4. The line numbering is that of the edition upon
which the translation is based: the indented lines
printed in italics are translated from the Latin of
the original, and are generally quotations from the
Bible, the liturgy, or the Fathers of the Church,
and hence are given the status of "a–lines" since
they are not composed by Langland. This line is
therefore numbered 17a.
5. Human nature, which Christ assumed in order
to redeem humanity. "Hauberk": coat of mail.
6. The perfect (three-personed) God.
7. In the godhead of the Father: as God Christ
could not suffer, but as man he could.
8. "Scribes" were persons who made a very strict,
literal interpretation of the Old Law and hence
rejected Christ's teaching of the New.
9. "Doom": sentence.

And place it where he pleases, and put Lucifer in bonds,
And beat and bring down burning death forever.
    O death, I will be thy death."[1]   35
Then Pilate came with many people, *Sedens pro tribunali,*[2]
To see how doughtily Death should do, and judge the rights of both.
The Jews and the justice were joined against Jesus,
And all the court cried "*Crucifige!*"[3] loud.
Then a plaintiff appeared before Pilate and said,   40
"This Jesus made jokes about Jerusalem's temple,
To have it down in one day and in three days after
Put it up again all new—here he stands who said it—
And yet build it every bit as big in all dimensions,
As long and as broad both, above and below."   45
"*Crucifige!*" said a sergeant, "he knows sorcerers' tricks."
"*Tolle! tolle!*"[4] said another, and took some sharp thorns
And began to make a garland out of green thorns,
And set it sorely on his head and said in hatred,
"*Ave, Rabbi,*" said that wretch, and shot reeds at him;[5]   50
They nailed him with three nails naked on a cross,
And with a pole put a potion up to his lips
And bade him drink to delay his death and lengthen his days,
And said, "If you're subtle, let's see you now help yourself.
If you are Christ and a king's son, come down from the cross!   55
Then we'll believe that Life loves you and will not let you die."
"*Consummatum est,*"[6] said Christ and started to swoon,
Piteously and pale like a prisoner dying.
The Lord of Life and of Light then laid his eyes together.
The day withdrew for dread and darkness covered the sun;   60
The wall wavered and split and the whole world quaked.
Dead men for that din came out of deep graves
And spoke of why that storm lasted so long:
"For a bitter battle," the dead body said;
"Life and Death in this darkness, one destroys the other.   65
No one will know surely which shall have the victory
Before Sunday about sunrise"; and sank with that to earth.
Some said that he was God's son that died so fairly:
    Truly this was the Son of God.[7]
And some said he was a sorcerer: "We should see first
Whether he is dead or not dead before we dare take him down."   70
Two thieves were there that suffered death that time
Upon crosses beside Christ; such was the common law.
A constable came forth and cracked both their legs
And the arms afterwards of each of those thieves.

---

1. Cf. Hosea 13.14.
2. "Sitting as a judge" (cf. Matthew 27.19).
3. "Crucify him!" (John 19.6).
4. "Away with him, away with him!" (John 19.15).
5. "Hail, master" (Matthew 26.49): these are actually Judas's words when he kissed Christ in order to identify him to the arresting officers. "Reeds": arrows, probably small ones intended to hurt rather than to kill.
6. "It is finished" (John 19.30).
7. Matthew 27.54.

But was no bastard so bold to touch God's body there;   75
Because he was a knight and a king's son, Nature decreed that time
That no knave should have the hardiness to lay hand on him.
But a knight with a sharp spear was sent forth there
Named Longeus[8] as the legend tells, who had long since lost his sight;
Before Pilate and the other people in that place he waited on
    horse.   80
For all that he might demur, he was made that time
To joust with Jesus, this blind Jew Longeus.
For all that watched there were unwilling, whether mounted or afoot,
To touch him or tamper with him or take him down from the cross,
Except this blind bachelor[9] that bore him through the heart.   85
The blood sprang down the spear and unsparred[1] his eyes.
The knight knelt down on his knees and begged Jesu for mercy.
"It was against my will, Lord, to wound you so sorely."
He sighed and said, "Sorely I repent it.
For what I here have done, I ask only your grace.   90
Have mercy on me, rightful Jesu!" and thus lamenting wept.
Then Faith began fiercely to scorn the false Jews,[2]
Called them cowards, accursed forever.
"For this foul villainy, may vengeance fall on you!
To make the blind beat the dead, it was a bully's thought.   95
Cursed cowards, no kind of knighthood was it
To beat a dead body with any bright weapon.
Yet he's won the victory in the fight, for all his vast wound,
For your champion jouster, the chief knight of you all,
Weeping admits himself worsted at the will of Jesus.   100
For when this darkness is done, Death will be vanquished,
And you louts have lost, for Life shall have the victory."

                              *   *   *

What for fear of this adventure and of those false Jews   110
I withdrew in that darkness to *Descendit-ad-Inferna*,[3]
And *Secundum Scripturas*[4] I saw there clearly
Where out of the west a wench,[5] as I thought,
Came walking on the way—she looked toward hell.
Mercy was that maid's name, a meek thing withal,   115
A most gracious girl, and goodly of speech.

---

8. Longeus (usually Longinus) appears in the apocryphal Gospel of Nicodemus, which provided Langland with the material for much of his account of Christ's despoiling of Hell.
9. Knight.
1. Opened; in the original there is a play on words with "spear."
2. The reference here and in line 110 below appears to reflect a blind anti-Semitism all too prevalent in late-medieval art and literature, brought out especially in portrayals of the Passion: the two passages omitted below (lines 103–09 and 258–60) are of the same tenor. Elsewhere Langland exhibits a more enlightened attitude—for instance, in a passage

where he holds up Jewish charity as an example to Christians. In the present passage he may intend a distinction between those who betrayed and condemned Jesus and the "old Jews of Jerusalem" who welcomed him in the Palm Sunday procession, lines 7–17 above.
3. "He descended into Hell" (from the Creed).
4. According to the Scriptures.
5. The word is Langland's and had much the same connotations in his time as it has in ours: his use of it is characteristic of his tendency to be irreverent to even the most august of his allegorical figures.

Her sister as it seemed came softly walking
Out of the east, opposite, and she looked westward,
A comely creature and cleanly: Truth was her name.
Because of the virtue that followed her, she was afraid of
    nothing.   120
When these maidens met, Mercy and Truth,
Each of them asked the other about this great wonder,
Of the din and of the darkness, and how the day lowered,
And what a gleam and a glint glowed before hell.
"I marvel at this matter, by my faith," said Truth,   125
"And am coming to discover what this queer affair means."
"Do not marvel," said Mercy, "it means only mirth.
A maiden named Mary, and mother without touching
By any kind of creature, conceived through speech
And grace of the Holy Ghost; grew great with child;   130
With no blemish to her woman's body brought him into this world.
And that my tale is true, I take God to witness,
Since this baby was born it has been thirty winters,
Who died and suffered death this day about midday.
And that is the cause of this eclipse that is closing off the sun,   135
In meaning that man shall be removed from darkness
While this gleam and this glow go to blind Lucifer.
For patriarchs and prophets have preached of this often
That man shall save man through a maiden's help,
And what a tree took away a tree shall restore.[6]   140
And what Death brought down a death shall raise up."
"What you're telling," said Truth, "is just a tale of nonsense.
For Adam and Eve and Abraham and the rest,
Patriarchs and prophets imprisoned in pain,
Never believe that yonder light will lift them up,   145
Or have them out of hell—hold your tongue, Mercy!
Your talk is mere trifling. I, Truth, know the truth,
For whatever is once in hell, it comes out never.
Job the perfect patriarch disproves what you say:
    Since in hell there is no redemption."[7]
Then Mercy most mildly uttered these words: 150
"From observation," she said, "I suppose they shall be saved,
Because venom destroys venom, and in that I find evidence
That Adam and Eve shall have relief.
For of all venoms the foulest is the scorpion's:
No medicine may amend the place where it stings   155
Till it's dead and placed upon it—the poison is destroyed,
The first effect of the venom, through the virtue it possesses.
So shall this death destroy—I dare bet my life—
All that Death did first through the Devil's tempting.
And just as through guile the beguiler beguiled man first,   160

6. The first tree bore the fruit which Adam and   redeeming mankind.
Eve ate, thereby damning mankind; the second tree   7. Cf. Job 7.9.
is the cross on which Christ was crucified, thereby

So shall grace that began everything make a good end,
And beguile the beguiler—and that's a good trick:
   A *trick by which to trick trickery.*[8]
"Now let's be silent," said Truth. "It seems to me I see
Out of the nip[9] of the north, not far from here,
Righteousness come running—let's wait right here,   165
For she knows far more than we—she was here before us both."
"That is so," said Mercy, "and I see here to the south
Where Peace clothed in patience comes sportively this way.
Love has desired her long: I believe surely
That Love has sent her some letter, what this light means   170
That hangs over hell thus: she will tell us what it means."
When Peace clothed in patience[1] approached near them both,
Righteousness did her reverence for her rich clothing
And prayed Peace to tell her to what place she was going,
And whom she was going to greet in her gay garments.   175
"My wish is to make my way," said she, "and welcome them all
That many a day I might not see for murk of sin.
Adam and Eve and the others in hell,
Moses and many more will merrily sing,
And I shall dance to their song: sister, do the same.   180
Because Jesus jousted well, joy begins to dawn.
   Weeping may endure for a night, but joy cometh in the
      morning.[2]
Love who is my lover sent letters to tell me
That Mercy, my sister, and I shall save mankind,
And that God has forgiven and granted me, Peace, and Mercy,
To make bail for mankind for evermore after.   185
Look, here's the patent," said Peace: "*In pace in idipsum.*
And that this deed shall endure *dormiam et requiescam.*"[3]
"What? You rave," said Righteousness. "You must be really drunk.
Do you believe that yonder light might unlock hell
And save man's soul? Sister, don't suppose it.   190
At the beginning God gave the judgment himself
That Adam and Eve and all that followed them
Should die downright and dwell in torment after
If they touched a tree and ate the tree's fruit.
Adam afterwards against his forbidding   195
Fed on that fruit and forsook, as it were,
The love of our Lord and his lore too,
And followed what the Fiend taught, and his flesh's will.
Against Reason. I, Righteousness, record this with Truth,

---

8. A line from a medieval Latin hymn.
9. The word is Langland's and the sense obscure;
it probably meant "coldness" to him, though an
Old English word similar to "nip" meant "gloom."
1. What Langland envisioned clothes of patience
to look like—aside from their "richness" (line 123)—
it is impossible to say: to him any abstraction could
become a concrete allegory without visual identi-

fication.
2. Psalm 30.5.
3. The "patent" or "deed" is a document conferring authority: this one consists of phrases from
Psalm 4.8: "I will both lay me down in peace and
sleep: for thou, Lord, only makest me dwell in
safety."

That their pain is perpetual, and no prayer helps them.   200
Therefore let them chew as they chose, and let us not chide, sisters,
For it's misery without amends, the morsel they ate."
"And I shall prove," said Peace, "that their pain must end,
And in time trouble must turn into well-being.
For had they known no woe, they'd not have known well-being;   205
For no one knows what well-being is that was never in woe,
Nor what is hot hunger who has never lacked food.
If there were no night, no man, I believe,
Should be well aware of what day means.
Never would a really rich man who lives in rest and ease   210
Know what woe is if it weren't for natural death.
So God, who began everything, of his good will
Became man by a maid for mankind's salvation
And allowed himself to be sold to see the sorrow of dying.
And that cures all care and is the first cause of rest,   215
For until we meet *modicum*,[4] I may well avow it,
No man knows, I suppose, what 'enough' means.
Therefore God of his goodness gave the first man Adam
A place of supreme ease and of perfect joy,
And then he suffered him to sin so that he might know sorrow,   220
And thus know what well-being is—to be naturally aware of it.
And afterward God offered himself, and took Adam's nature,
To see what he has suffered in three sundry places.
Both in heaven and on earth, and now he heads for hell,
To learn what all woe is like who has learned of all joy.   225
So it shall fare with these folk: their folly and their sin
Shall show them what sickness is—and succor from all pain.
No one knows what war is where peace prevails,
Nor what is true well-being till 'Woe, alas!' teaches him."
Then was there a wight with two broad eyes: 230
Book was that beaupere's[5] name, a bold man of speech.
"By God's body," said this Book, "I will bear witness
That when this baby was born there blazed a star
That all the wise men in the world agreed in one opinion
That such a baby was born in Bethlehem city   235
That should save man's soul and destroy sin.
And all the elements," said the Book, "hereof bore witness.
The sky first revealed that he was God who formed all things:
The hosts in heaven took *stella comata*[6]
And tended her like a torch to reverence his birth.   240
The light followed the Lord into the low earth.
The water witnesses that he was God for he walked on it;
Peter the Apostle perceived his walking
And as he went on the water knew him well and said,
    'Lord, bid me come unto thee on the water.'[7]

4. A small quantity.
5. Fine fellow; Book's two broad eyes suggest the
Old and New Testaments.

6. Hairy star, i.e., comet.
7. Matthew 14.28.

And lo, how the sun locked her light in herself   245
When she saw him suffer that made sun and sea.
The earth for heavy heart because he would suffer
Quaked like a quick thing and the rock all crashed to pieces.
Lo, hell might not hold, but opened when God suffered,
And let out Simeon's sons[8] to see him hang on cross.   250
And now shall Lucifer believe it, loath though he is,
For Jesus like a giant with an engine[9] comes yonder
To break and beat down all that may be against him,
And to have out of hell every one he pleases.
And I, Book, will be burnt unless Jesus rises to life   255
In all the mights of a man, and brings his mother joy,
And comforts all his kin, and takes their cares away."

*   *   *

"Let's be silent," said Truth, "I hear and see both
A spirit speaks to hell and bids the gates spring open:"
       Lift up your gates.[1]
A voice loud in that light cried to Lucifer.
"Princes of this place, unpin and unlock,
For he comes here with crown who is King of Glory."   265
Then Satan[2] sighed and said to hell,
"Without our leave such a light fetched Lazarus away:[3]
Care and concern have come to us all.
If this king comes in he will carry off mankind
And lead it to where Lazarus is, and with small labor bind me.   270
Patriarchs and prophets have long prated of this,
That such a lord and a light should lead them all hence."
"Listen," said Lucifer, "for this lord is one I know;
Both this lord and this light, it's long ago I knew him.
No death may do this lord harm, nor any devil's trickery,   275
And his way is where he wishes—but let him beware of the perils.
If he bereaves me of my right, he robs me by force.
For by right and by reason the race that is here
Body and soul belongs to me, both good and evil.
For he himself said it who is Sire of heaven,   280
If Adam ate the apple, all should die
And dwell with us devils: that threat the Lord laid down.

---

8. Simeon, who was present at the presentation of the infant Jesus in the temple, had been told by the Holy Ghost that "he should not see death" before he had seen "the Lord's Christ" (Luke 2.26). The apocryphal Gospel of Nicodemus echoes the incident in reporting that Simeon's sons were raised from death at the time of Jesus's crucifixion.

9. A device, probably thought of as a gigantic slingshot, though of course Christ needs nothing to break down his enemies but his own authority.

1. The first words of Psalm 24.9, which reads in the Latin version, "Lift up your gates, O princes, and be ye lift up, ye everlasting doors, and the King of Glory shall come in."

2. Langland, following a tradition also reflected in Milton's *Paradise Lost*, pictures hell as populated by a number of devils: Satan; Lucifer (line 273 ff.), who began the war in heaven and tempted Eve; Goblin (line 293); Belial (line 321); and Ashtoreth (line 404). Lucifer the rebel angel naturally became identified with Satan, a word which in the Old Testament had originally meant an evil adversary; many of the other devils are displaced gods of pagan religions.

3. For Christ's raising of Lazarus from the dead cf. John 11.

And since he who is truth himself said these words,
And since I've possessed them seven thousand winters,
I believe that law will not allow him the least of them."   285
"That is so," said Satan, "but I'm sore afraid
Because you took them by trickery and trespassed in his garden,
And in the semblance of a serpent sat upon the appletree
And egged them to eat, Eve by herself,
And told her a tale with treasonous words;   290
And so you had them out, and hither at the last."
"It's an ill-gotten gain where guile is at the root,
For God will not be beguiled," said Goblin, "nor tricked.
We have no true title to them, for treason made them damned."
"Certainly I fear," said the Fiend,[4] "lest Truth fetch them out.   295
These thirty winters, as I think, he's gone here and there and preached.
I have assailed him with sin, and sometimes asked
Whether he was God or God's son: he gave me short answer.
And thus he has traveled about like a true man these two and thirty
     winters.
And when I saw it was so, while she slept I went   300
To warn Pilate's wife what sort of man was Jesus,[5]
For some hated him and have put him to death.
I would have lengthened his life, for I believed if he died
That his soul would suffer no sin in his sight.
For the body, while it walked on its bones, was busy always   305
To save men from sin if they themselves wished.
And now I see where a soul comes slipping hitherward
With glory and with great light; God it is, I'm sure.
My advice is we all flee," said the Fiend, "fast away from here,
For we had better not be at all than abide in his sight.   310
For your lies, Lucifer, we've lost all our prey.
Through you we fell first from heaven so high:
Because we believed your lies we all leapt out.
And now for your latest lie we have lost Adam,
And all our lordship, I believe, on land and in hell."   315
     Now shall the prince of this world be cast out.[6]
Again the light bade them unlock, and Lucifer answered,
     Who is that?[7]
"What lord are you?" said Lucifer. The light at once replied,
     The King of Glory.
"The Lord of might and of main and of all manner of powers,
     The Lord of Powers.

4. Here and in line 309 "the Fiend" is presumably
Lucifer's most articulate critic, Satan, whom Christ
names as his tempter in Luke 4.8 and Matthew
4.10.
5. In Matthew 27.19 Pilate's wife warns Pilate to
"have nothing to do with that just man [Jesus],"
for she has been troubled by a dream about him:
Langland has the Fiend admit to having caused
the dream in order that Pilate's wife should per-

suade her husband not to harm Jesus and thus keep
him safe on earth and not come to visit Hell and
despoil it.
6. John 12.31. "Prince of this world" is a title for
the Devil.
7. This and the next two phrases translated from
the Latin are from Psalm 24.8, following immediately on the words quoted at line 262a.

Dukes of this dim place, at once undo these gates
That Christ may come in, the Heaven-King's son."   320
And with that breath hell broke along with Belial's bars;
For any warrior or watchman the gates wide opened.
Patriarchs and prophets, *populus in tenebris*,[8]
Sang Saint John's song, *Ecce Agnus Dei*.[9]
Lucifer could not look, the light so blinded him.   325
And those that the Lord loved his light caught away,
And he said to Satan, "Lo, here's my soul in payment
For all sinful souls, to save those that are worthy.
Mine they are, and of me—I may the better claim them.
Although Reason records, and right of myself,   330
That if they ate the apple, all should die,
I did not hold out to them hell here forever.
For the deed that they did, your deceit caused it;
You got them with guile against all reason.
For in my palace Paradise, in the person of an adder,   335
You stole by stealth something I loved.
Thus like a lizard with a lady's face[1]
Falsely you filched from me; the Old Law confirms
That beguilers be beguiled, and that is good logic:
    A tooth for a tooth and an eye for an eye.[2]
Ergo[3] soul shall requite soul and sin revert to sin,   340
And all that man has done amiss, I, man, will amend.
Member for member was amends in the Old Law,
And life for life also, and by that law I claim
Adam and all his issue at my will hereafter.
And what Death destroyed in them, my death shall restore   345
And both quicken[4] and requite what was quenched through sin.
And that grace destroy guile is what good faith requires.
So don't believe it, Lucifer, against the law I fetch them,
But by right and by reason here ransom my liegemen.
    I have not come to destroy the law but to fulfill it.[5]
You fetched mine in my place unmindful of all reason   350
Falsely and feloniously; good faith taught me
To recover them by reason and rely on nothing else.
So what you got with guile through grace is won back.
You, Lucifer, in likeness of a loathsome adder
Got by guile those that God loved;   355
And I, in likeness of a mortal man, who am master of heaven,
Have graciously requited your guile: let guile go against guile!
And as Adam and all died through a tree

---

8. "People in the shades": the phrase is from Matthew 4.16, citing Isaiah 9.2, "The people that
walked in darkness have seen a great light."
9. "Behold the Lamb of God" (John 1.36).
1. In medieval art the Devil tempting Eve was
sometimes represented as a snake (see the "serpent" of line 288) and sometimes as a lizard with

a female human face, standing upright.
2. See Matthew 5.38 citing Exodus 21.24.
3. "Therefore": the Latin conjunction was used in
formal debate to introduce the conclusion derived
from a number of propositions.
4. Revitalize.
5. See Matthew 5.17.

Adam and all through a tree return to life,
And guile is beguiled and grief has come to his guile: 360
    And [he] is fallen into the ditch which he made.[6]
And now your guile begins to turn against you,
And my grace to grow ever greater and wider.
The bitterness that you have brewed, imbibe it yourself
Who are doctor[7] of death, the drink you made.
For I who am Lord of Life, love is my drink   365
And for that drink today I died upon earth.
I struggled so I'm thirsty still for man's soul's sake.
No drink may moisten me or slake my thirst
Till vintage time befall in the Vale of Jehoshaphat,[8]
When I shall drink really ripe wine, *Resurrectio mortuorum.*[9]   370
And then I shall come as a king crowned with angels
And have out of hell all men's souls.
Fiends and fiendkins shall stand before me,
And be at my bidding, where best it pleases me.
But to be merciful to man then my nature requires it.   375
For we are brothers of one blood, but not in baptism all.
And all that may be my whole brothers in blood and in baptism
Shall not be damned to the death that endures without end.
    Against thee only have I sinned.[1]
It is not the use on earth to hang a felon
Oftener than once, even though he were a traitor.   380
And if the king of that kingdom comes at that time
When a felon should suffer death or other such punishment,
Law would that he give him life if he looked upon him.
And I that am King of Kings shall come in such a time
Where doom to death damns all wicked,   385
And if law wills I look on them, it lies in my grace
Whether they die or not die because they did evil.
If it be any bit paid for the boldness of their sins,
I may grant mercy through my righteousness and all my true words;
And though Holy Writ will that I wreak vengeance on those that wrought
    evil,   390
    No evil unpunished, etc.[2]
They shall be cleansed and made clear and cured of their sins,
In my prison purgatory till *Parce!*[3] says 'Stop!'
And my mercy shall be shown to many of my half-brothers,
For blood-kin may see blood-kin both hungry and cold,
But blood-kin may not see blood-kin bleed without his pity: 395

---

6. Psalm 7.15.
7. The ironical use of the word carries both the sense of "physician" and of "one learned in a discipline."
8. On the evidence of Joel 3.2, 12, the site of the Last Judgment was thought to be the Vale of Jehoshaphat.
9. "The resurrection of the dead" (from the Creed).

1. Psalm 51.4. The psalm is understood to assign the sole power of judging the sinner to God, since it is only against God that the sinner has acted.
2. "[He is a just judge who leaves] no evil unpunished [and no good unrewarded]": not from the Bible, but from Pope Innocent III's tract, *Of Contempt for the World* (1195).
3. "Spare!"

I heard unspeakable words which it is not lawful for a man to utter.[4]
But my righteousness and right shall rule all hell,
And mercy rule all mankind before me in heaven.
For I'd be an unkind king unless I gave my kin help,
And particularly at such a time when help was truly needed.
    Enter not into judgment with thy servant.[5]
Thus by law," said our Lord, "I will lead from here   400
Those I looked on with love who believed in my coming;
And for your lie, Lucifer, that you lied to Eve
You shall buy it back in bitterness"—and bound him with chains.
Ashtoreth and all the gang hid themselves in corners;
They dared not look at our Lord, the least of them all,   405
But let him lead away what he liked and leave what he wished.
Many hundreds of angels harped and sang,
    Flesh sins, flesh redeems, flesh reigns as God of God.[6]
Then Peace piped a note of poetry:
    As a rule the sun is brighter after the biggest clouds;
    After hostilities brighter is love.
"After sharp showers," said Peace, "the sun shines brightest;
No weather is warmer than after watery clouds;   410
Nor any love lovelier, or more loving friends,
Then after war and woe when Love and Peace are masters.
There was never war in this world or wickedness so sharp
That Love, if he liked, might make a laughing matter.
And Peace through patience puts an end to all perils."   415
"Truce!" said Truth, "you tell the truth, by Jesus!
Let's kiss in covenant, and each of us clasp other."
"And let no people," said Peace, "perceive that we argued;
For nothing is impossible to him that is almighty."
"You speak the truth," said Righteousness, and reverently
    kissed her,   420
Peace, and Peace her, *per saecula saeculorum:*[7]
    Mercy and Truth have met together; Righteousness and Peace have
    kissed each other.[8]
Truth sounded a trumpet then and sang *Te Deum Laudamus,*[9]
And then Love strummed a lute with a loud note:
    Behold how good and how pleasant, etc.[1]
Till the day dawned these damsels caroled.
When bells rang for the Resurrection, and right then I awoke   425
And called Kit my wife and Calote my daughter:

4. In 2 Corinthians 12.4, St. Paul tells how in a vision he was snatched up to heaven where he heard things that may not be repeated among men. Langland is apparently invoking a similar mystic experience when he puts into Christ's mouth a promise to spare many of his half-brothers, the unbaptized. The orthodox theology of the time taught that all the unbaptized were irredeemably damned, a proposition Langland refused to accept: in his vision he has heard words to the contrary that might not be repeated among men since they would be held heretical.
5. Psalm 143.2.
6. From a medieval Latin hymn. The source of the two Latin verses immediately below is Alain of Lisle, a late 12th-century poet and philosopher.
7. "For ever and ever" (the liturgical formula).
8. Psalm 85.10.
9. "We praise thee, O Lord."
1. Psalm 133.1. The verse continues, "it is for brothers to dwell together in unity."

"Arise and go reverence God's resurrection,
And creep to the cross on knees, and kiss it as a jewel,
For God's blessed body it bore for our good,
And it frightens the Fiend, for such is its power   430
That no grisly ghost may glide in its shadow."

MIDDLE ENGLISH LYRICS

The best of the Middle English lyrics, both religious and secular, seem remarkably fresh despite the fact that in both theme and form they are extremely conventional—at times almost stylized. The song of spring (the French *reverdie*), the love lyric and love complaint, the celebration of the Virgin Mary, the witty satire of women, the meditation upon Calvary—even the rollicking verse in praise of good food, good drink, and good living—are members of ancient genres, most of which had developed in France (some of the poems here printed closely parallel French lyrics). The poet's love in *Alison* is conventional even in her name, which is that of the Wife of Bath and of the heroine of the Miller's Tale, and the poet could have written her praise without ever having loved anything more feminine than books, which contained hundreds of ladies with Alison's charms. The fact that most of them would have been blue-eyed blondes might make love for a black-eyed brunette seem daringly realistic, but conventions set up anticonventions which become as rigid as their older antitheses. Yet those who feel that such a lyric as *Alison* is the genuine complaint of a thirteenth-century English lad are right in their reactions as readers if wrong in fact, for the poem re-creates excellently the excitement of young love—and the time must have been full of young men yearning for black-eyed Alisons.

It is the same with the spring songs. Spring returns in much the same literary terms in poem after poem, year after year, century after century, but the best medieval spring songs also vigorously reproduce the actual excitement of its natural return every March and April. For while all good poets bring something of their own observing to the tradition they are following, the writers of medieval lyrics are especially distinguished for their unselfconsciousness and immediacy. Just as there was no consciousness on the part of medieval people of anachronism—historical differences in time or place—there seems to have been no self-consciousness about their attempts to express themselves in poetic terms: convention apparently liberated them, instead of oppressing them, in the way it is often supposed to do. It is with perfect naturalness that the poet of *Sunset on Calvary* relives the scene, standing with the mother Mary beside the cross on which her Son hangs; or the poet of *I Sing of a Maiden* visualizes the mystery of the Virgin Birth in terms of the most natural of mysteries, the falling dew; or the poet of *Adam Lay Bound* cheerfully regards Adam's sin and its dire consequences as a kind of childish naughtiness and punishment that had the tremendous effect of bringing Christ to earth. The very simplicity of the poet's attitude achieves the most striking artistic results.

Several of the poems printed here depend on traditions that are no longer alive. The *Corpus Christi Carol* relies upon the ancient fertility myth of the

Fisher King that had been caught up and Christianized in Arthurian legend. *I Have a Young Sister* is a riddling poem whose highly suggestive sexual symbols are of a fully developed sophistication. It still survives in the folk song *I Gave My Love a Cherry*.

It is impossible to date the individual lyrics with any certainty. Perhaps the oldest is the *Cuckoo Song*, which is probably of the twelfth century, and one may guess that the other spring songs are of the late thirteenth or early fourteenth; but some of the best of the lyrics (*I Sing of a Maiden, Adam Lay Bound*) may be of the fifteenth century. In general, we know only that the poems must be earlier than the manuscripts in which they appear, but because of the fact that an early lyric might have been reworded by a late scribe in such a way as to make it appear late, we can rarely tell by how many years any given lyric preceded the manuscript that records it. The sources of the texts printed here are too diverse to be listed. Spelling has been normalized as in the selections from Chaucer.

Fowls in the Frith

	Fowles° in the frith,°	birds / woods
	The fisshes in the flood,	
	And I mon waxe wood:[1]	
	Much sorwe° I walke with	sorrow
5	For beste[2] of boon° and blood.	bone

Alison

	Bitweene° Merch and Averil,	in the seasons of
	When spray biginneth to springe,	
	The litel fowl hath hire wil°	pleasure
	On hire leod[1] to singe.	
5	Ich° libbe° in love-longinge	I / live
	For semlokest° of alle thinge.	seemliest, fairest
	Heo° may me blisse bringe:	she
	Ich am in hire baundoun.°	power
	An hendy hap ich habbe yhent,[2]	
10	Ichoot° from hevene it is me sent:	I know
	From alle[3] wommen my love is lent,°	removed
	And light° on Alisoun.	alights
	On hew° hire heer° is fair ynough,	hue / hair
	Hire browe browne, hire yë"° blake;	eye
15	With lossum cheere heo on me lough;[4]	
	With middel smal and wel ymake.	
	But° heo me wolle to hire take	Unless

1. Must go mad.
2. Probably "the best," i.e., his lady. The meaning "beast" is, however, not impossible.
1. In her language.

2. A gracious chance I have received.
3. I.e., all other.
4. With lovely face she on me smiled.

For to been hire owen make,°   *mate*
Longe to liven ichulle° forsake,   *I will*
20   And feye° fallen adown.   *dead*
            An hendy hap, etc.

Nightes when I wende° and wake,   *turn*
Forthy° mine wonges° waxeth wan: *therefore / cheeks*
Levedy,° al for thine sake   *lady*
25   Longinge is ylent me on.[5]
In world nis noon so witer° man   *clever*
That al hire bountee° telle can;   *excellence*
Hire swire° is whittere° than the swan,   *neck / whiter*
            And fairest may° in town.   *maid*
30   An hendy, etc.

Ich am for wowing° al forwake,°   *wooing / worn out from waking*
Wery so water in wore.[6]
Lest any reve me[7] my make
Ich habbe y-yerned yore.[8]
35   Bettere is tholien° while° sore   *endure / for a time*
Than mournen evermore.
Geinest under gore,[9]
            Herkne to my roun:°   *song*
            An hendy, etc.

My Lief Is Faren in Londe

My lief is faren in londe[1]—
Allas, why is she so?
And I am so sore bonde°   *bound*
I may nat come her to.
5   She hath myn herte in holde
Wherever she ride or go°—   *walk*
With trewe love a thousand folde.

Western Wind

Westron wind, when will thou blow?
The small rain down can rain.
Christ, that my love were in my arms,
And I in my bed again.

---

5. Longing has come upon me.   8. I have been worrying long since.
6. Perhaps "millpond."   9. Fairest beneath clothing.
7. Deprive me.   1. My beloved has gone away.

I Have a Young Sister

I have a yong suster
  Fer° biyonde the see;   *far*
Manye be the druries°   *gifts*
  That she sente me.

5 She sente me the cherye
    Withouten any stoon,°   *stone*
And so she dide the dove
    Withouten any boon.°   *bone*

She sene me the brere°   *briar*
10   Withouten any rinde;°   *bark*
She bad me love my lemman°   *mistress*
    Withoute longinge.

How sholde any cherye
  Be withoute stoon?
15 And how sholde any dove
    Be withoute boon?

How sholde any brere
  Be withoute rinde?
How sholde I love my lemman
20   Withoute longinge?

Whan the cherye was a flowr,
  Thanne hadde it no stoon;
Whan the dove was an ey,°   *egg*
  Thanne hadde it no boon.

25 Whan the brere was unbred,°   *ungrown*
    Thanne hadde it no rinde;
Whan the maiden hath that° she loveth,   *what*
    She is withoute longinge.

The Cuckoo Song

Sumer is ycomen in,
Loude sing cuckou!
Groweth seed and bloweth meed,[1]
And springth the wode° now.   *wood*
5 Sing cuckou!

1. The meadow blossoms.

Ewe bleteth after lamb,
Loweth after calve cow,
Bulloc sterteth,° bucke verteth,°   *leaps / farts*
Merye sing cuckou!
10 Cuckou, cuckou,
Wel singest thou cuckou:
Ne swik° thou never now!   *cease*

Tell Me, Wight in the Broom

"Say me, wight° in the broom,°   *creature / shrub*
What is me for to doon?
Ich° have the werste bonde°   *I / husband*
That is in any londe."

5   "If thy bonde is ille,°   *bad*
Hold thy tonge stille."

I Am of Ireland

Ich am of Irlonde,
And of the holy londe
   Of Irlonde.
Goode sire, praye ich thee,
5 For of° sainte charitee,   *sake of*
Com and dance with me
   In Irlonde.

Sunset on Calvary

Now gooth sunne under wode:[1]
Me reweth,[2] Marye, thy faire rode.°   *face*
Now gooth sunne under tree:
Me reweth, Marye, thy sone and thee.

I Sing of a Maiden

I sing of a maiden
   That is makelees:[1]
King of alle kinges
   To° her sone she chees.°   *as / chose*

---

1. Wood, i.e., the Cross.
2. I pity.

1. Spotless, matchless, and mateless—a triple pun.

5   He cam also° stille   *as*
    Ther° his moder° was   *where / mother*
 As dewe in Aprille
    That falleth on the gras.

 He cam also stille
10   To his modres bowr
 As dewe in Aprille
    That falleth on the flowr.

 He cam also stille
    Ther his moder lay
15 As dewe in Aprille
    That falleth on the spray.

 Moder and maiden
    Was nevere noon but she:
 Wel may swich° a lady   *such*
20   Godes moder be.

Adam Lay Bound

Adam lay ybounden, bounden in a bond,
Four thousand winter thoughte he not too long;
And al was for an apple, an apple that he took,
As clerkes finden writen, writen in hire book.
5   Ne hadde[1] the apple taken been, the apple taken been,
Ne hadde nevere Oure Lady ybeen hevene Queen.
Blessed be the time that apple taken was:
Therfore we mown° singen *Deo Gratias*.[2]   *may*

The Corpus Christi Carol

Lully, lullay, lully, lullay,
The faucon° hath borne my make° away.   *falcon / mate*

He bare him up, he bare him down,
He bare him into an orchard brown.

5   In that orchard ther was an hall
That was hanged with purple and pall.°   *black velvet*

And in that hall ther was a bed:
It was hanged with gold so red.

---

1. Had not.   2. Thanks be to God.

And in that bed ther lith° a knight,   *lies*
10 His woundes bleeding by day and night.

By that beddes side ther kneeleth a may,°   *maid*
And she weepeth both night and day.

And by that beddes side ther standeth a stoon:°   *stone*
Corpus Christi[1] writen thereon.

1. Body of Christ.

THE SECOND SHEPHERDS' PLAY

ca. 1425

The *Second Shepherds' Play* is the finest example in English of a medieval mystery play. The word "mystery" in this context refers to the spiritual mystery of Christ's redemption of mankind, and mystery plays are dramatizations of incidents of the Old Testament, which foretells that redemption, and of the New, which recounts it. In England the mysteries were generally composed in cycles containing as many as forty-eight individual plays; a typical cycle would begin with the Creation, continue with the Fall of Man, and proceed through the most significant events of the Old Testament, such as the Flood, to the New Testament, which provided plays on the Nativity, the chief events of Christ's life, the Crucifixion, the Harrowing of Hell (based on sources now deemed apocryphal), and the Last Judgment.

The Church had its own drama in Latin, dating back to the tenth century, which developed through the dramatization and elaboration of the liturgy— the regular service—for certain holidays, the Easter morning service in particular. The vernacular drama was once thought to have evolved from the liturgical, passing by stages from the church into the streets of the town. However, even though the vernacular plays at times echo their Latin counterparts and though their authors may have been clerics, the mysteries represent an old and largely independent tradition of vernacular religious drama. As early as the twelfth century a *Play of Adam* in Anglo-Norman French was performed in England, a dramatization of the Fall with highly sophisticated dialogue, characterization, and stagecraft. During the late fourteenth and the fifteenth centuries the great English mystery cycles, four of which have survived complete, were formed in the towns which, in spite of war and plague, became increasingly prosperous and independent. Most of our knowledge of the plays, apart from the texts themselves, comes through municipal records pertaining to their production by the guilds.

Every trade in urban society had its guild, an organization combining the functions of a modern club, trade union, and religious society, and each of these guilds had its traditional play to perform on the days when the cycles were presented. In certain of the towns each company had a wagon that served as a stage. The wagon would proceed from one strategic point in the town to another, and the play would be performed a number of times on the same day: the spectators gathered at any one strategic point would never be without a play before them, and might see the whole cycle without moving. In other towns, however, the plays were probably acted out in sequence on a platform erected at a single location such as the main city square.

The plays were performed every year at the time of one of two great early summer festivals—Whitsuntide, the week following the seventh Sunday after Easter, or Corpus Christi, a week later. They served as both religious instruction and entertainment for a wide audience, including unlearned folk like the Carpenter in the Miller's Tale, who recalls from them the trouble Noah had getting his wife aboard the ark, but also educated laypeople and clerics, who besides enjoying the sometimes boisterous comedy would find the plays acting out traditional interpretations of Scripture such as the ark as a type, or prefiguration, of the Church.

The mystery plays, then, were a festive celebration of the bonds of medieval society, and they were also a mirror of that society. For in putting on the stage biblical shepherds and soldiers, the playwrights inevitably and often quite deliberately gave them the appearance and characters of contemporary men and women. No play better illustrates this aspect of the drama than the *Second Shepherds' Play*, so called because it is the second of two Nativity plays that are part of the cycle believed to have been performed at Wakefield in Yorkshire. As the play opens, the shepherds complain about the cold, the taxes, and the high-handed treatment they get from the gentry—evils closer to shepherds on the Yorkshire moors than to those keeping their flocks near Bethlehem. The sophisticated dramatic intelligence at work in this and several other of the Wakefield plays belonged undoubtedly to one individual, who probably revised older, more traditional plays. His identity is not known, but because of his achievement scholars refer to him as the Wakefield Master. He was probably a highly educated cleric stationed in the vicinity of Wakefield, perhaps a friar of a nearby priory. The Wakefield Master had a genius for combining comedy, including broad farce, with religion in ways that make them enhance one another. In the *Second Shepherds' Play*, by linking the comic subplot of Mak and Gill with the solemn story of Christ's nativity, the Wakefield Master has produced a dramatic parable of what the Nativity means in Christian history and in Christian hearts. No one will fail to observe the parallelism between the stolen sheep, ludicrously disguised as Mak's latest heir, lying in the cradle, and the real Lamb of God, born in the stable among beasts. A complex of relationships based upon this relationship suggests itself. But perhaps the most important point is that the charity twice shown by the shepherds—in the first instance to the supposed son of Mak and in the second instance to Mak and Gill when they decide to let them off with only the mildest of punishments—is rewarded when they are invited to visit the Christ Child, the embodiment of charity. The bleak beginning of the play, with its series of individual complaints, is ultimately balanced by the optimistic ending, which sees the shepherds once again singing together in harmony.

The *Second Shepherds' Play* is exceptional among the mystery plays in its development of plot and character. There is no parallel to its elaboration of the comic subplot and no character quite like Mak, who has doubtless been imported into religious drama from popular farce. Mak is perhaps the best humorous character outside of Chaucer's works in this period. A braggart of the worst kind, he has something of Falstaff's charm; and he resembles Falstaff also in his grotesque attempts to maintain the last shreds of his dignity

when he is caught in a lie. Most readers will be glad that the shepherds do
not carry out their threat to have the death penalty invoked for his crime.

The Second Shepherds' Play[1]

Cast of Characters

COLL	GILL
GIB	ANGEL
DAW	MARY
MAK	

[*A moor.*]

[*Enter* COLL]

COLL.   Lord, what[2] these weathers are cold, and I am ill
        happed;
   I am nearhand dold,° so long have I napped;   *numb*
   My legs they fold,° my fingers are chapped.   *give way*
   It is not as I would, for I am all lapped°   *wrapped*
5   In sorrow:
      In storms and tempest,
      Now in the east, now in the west,
      Woe is him has never rest
        Midday nor morrow.

10   But we silly° husbands° that walks on the
        moor,   *poor / farmers*
   In faith we are nearhands out of the door.[3]
   No wonder, as it stands, if we be poor,
   For the tilth° of our lands lies fallow as the
        floor,   *arable part*
      As ye ken.°   *know*
15   We are so hammed,
      Fortaxed, and rammed,
      We are made hand-tamed
        With these gentlery-men.[4]

   Thus they reave us[5] our rest—Our Lady them
        wary!°   *curse*
20   These men that are lord-fest,[6] they cause the plow tarry.
   That men say is for the best, we find it contrary.

---

1. The text is based on that given by A. W. Pollard in *The Towneley Plays* (1897), but has been
freely edited. Spelling has been normalized except
where rhyme makes changes impossible. Since the
original text has no indications of scenes and only
four stage directions, written in Latin, appropriate
scenes of action and additional stage directions have
been added; the four original stage directions are
identified in the footnotes.

2. How. "Ill happed": badly covered.
3. I.e., homeless.
4. We are so hamstrung, overtaxed, and beaten
down (that) we are made slaves by these highborn
men. Coll is complaining of the peasant's hard lot,
at the mercy of the agents of the Crown and of the
wealthy landholders.
5. Deprive us of.
6. Attached to lords.

Thus are husbands oppressed in point to miscarry.[7]
> On live
> Thus hold they us under,
25 > Thus they bring us in blunder,°   *trouble*
> It were a great wonder
> > And° ever should we thrive.   *if*

There shall come a swain as proud as a po:°   *peacock*
He must borrow my wain,° my plow also;   *wagon*
30 Then I am full fain° to grant ere he go.   *glad*
Thus live we in pain, anger, and woe,
> By night and by day.
> He must have if he lang° it,   *wants*
> If I should forgang it:[8]
35 > I were better be hanged
> > Than once say him nay.[9]

For may he get a paint-sleeve[1] or a brooch nowadays,
Woe is him that him grieve or once again-says.°   *gainsays*
Dare no man him reprieve, what mastery he maes.[2]
40 And yet may no man lieve° one word that he   *believe*
> > says,
> > No letter.
> He can make purveyance[3]
> With boast and bragance,°   *bragging*
> And all is through maintenance°   *protection*
45 > > Of men that are greater.

It does me good, as I walk thus by mine one,°   *self*
Of this world for to talk in manner of moan.
To my sheep will I stalk, and hearken anon,
There abide on a balk,° or sit on a stone,   *grassy mound*
50 > Full soon;
> For I trow,° pardie,°   *think / by God*
> True men if they be,
> We get more company
> > Ere it be noon.

[*Enter* GIB, *who at first does not see* COLL.]

55 GIB.   Benste and Dominus,[4] what may this bemean?°   *mean*
Why fares this world thus? Such have we not seen.
Lord, these winds are spiteous° and the weathers full *cruel*
> > keen
And the frosts so hideous they water mine een,°   *eyes*
> No lie.
60 > Now in dry, now in wet,
> Now in snow, now in sleet,

---

7. To the point of ruin. "On live": in life. | 2. No one dares to reprove him, no matter what
8. Even if I have to do without it. | force he uses.
9. In the manuscript, this stanza follows the next. | 3. Requisition (of private property).
1. Embroidered sleeve (i.e., sign of authority). | 4. Bless us and Lord.

When my shoon° freeze to my feet   *shoes*
   It is not all easy.

But as far as I ken,° or yet as I go,°   *see / walk*
65 We silly wedmen dree mickle woe;[5]
We have sorrow then and then[6]—it falls oft so.
Silly Capple,[7] our hen, both to and fro
   She cackles;
  But begin she to croak,
70   To groan or to cluck,
  Woe is him our cock,
   For he is in the shackles.

These men that are wed have not all their will:
When they are full hard stead[8] they sigh full still;
75 God wot° they are led full hard and full ill;   *knows*
In bower nor in bed they say nought theretill.°   *thereagainst*
   This tide°   *time*
  My part have I fun;°   *found, learned*
  I know my lesson:
80 Woe is him that is bun,°   *bound*
   For he must abide.

But now late in our lives—a marvel to me,
That I think my heart rives° such wonders to see; *splits*
What that destiny drives it should so be[9]—
85 Some men will have two wives, and some men three
   In store.
  Some are woe[1] that has any,
  But so far can° I,   *know*
  Woe is him that has many,
90   For he feels sore.

But young men a-wooing, for God that you
   bought,°   *redeemed*
Be well ware of wedding and think in your thought:
"Had I wist"° is a thing, it serves of nought.   *known*
Mickle° still° mourning has wedding home   *much / continual*
   brought,
95   And griefs
  With many a sharp shower,°   *fight*
  For thou may catch in an hour
  That° shall savor° full sour   *what / taste*
   As long as thou lives.

100 For as ever read I 'pistle,° I have one to my fere[2] *Epistle*
As sharp as a thistle, as rough as a brere;°   *briar*

---

5. We poor married men suffer much woe.
6. Constantly.
7. I.e., one's wife.
8. Beset. "Still": constantly.

9. What destiny causes must occur.
1. I.e., wretched.
2. As my mate.

She is browed like a bristle, with a sour-loten cheer;[3]
Had she once wet her whistle she could sing full clear
  Her Pater Noster.

105   She is great as a whale;
  She has a gallon of gall:
  By Him that died for us all,
   I would I had run to° I had lost her.   *until*

COLL. Gib, look over the raw!° Full deafly ye stand!   *hedge*
110 GIB. Yea, the devil in thy maw, so tariand![4]
  Saw thou awhere° of Daw?   *anywhere*

COLL.   Yea, on a
  lea-land°   *pasture land*
Heard I him blaw.[5] He comes here at hand,
  Not far.
  Stand still.

GIB.   Why?
115 COLL. For he comes, hope° I.   *think*
GIB. He will make us both a lie
  But if[6] we be ware.

[*Enter* DAW, *who does not see the others.*]

DAW. Christ's cross me speed, and Saint Nicholas!
  Thereof had I need: it is worse than it was.
120   Whoso could take heed and let the world pass,
  It is ever in dread° and brickle° as glass,   *doubt / brittle*
   And slithes.°   *slips away*
  This world foor° never so,   *behaved*
  With marvels mo° and mo,   *more*
125   Now in weal, now in woe,
   And all thing writhes.°   *changes*

  Was never sin° Noah's flood such floods seen, *since*
  Winds and rains so rude and storms so keen:
  Some stammered, some stood in doubt,[7] as I
   ween.°   *suppose*
130   Now God turn all to good! I say as I mean.
   For ponder:
  These floods so they drown
  Both in fields and in town,
  And bears all down,
135   And that is a wonder.

  We that walk on the nights, our cattle to keep,
  We see sudden° sights when other men sleep. *unexpected*
  Yet methink my heart lights: I see shrews peep.[8]

[*He sees the others, but does not hail them.*]

---

3. She has brows like pig's bristles and a sour-looking face.
4. Yes, the devil take thy guts for being so late.
5. Blow (his horn).
6. Unless.
7. The line apparently refers to men's behavior at the time of Noah's flood.
8. I see rascals are watching.

Ye are two tall wights.° I will give my sheep   *creatures*
140   A turn.
    But full ill have I meant:[9]
    As I walk on this bent°   *field*
    I may lightly° repent,   *quickly*
        My toes if I spurn.°   *stub*

145   Ah, sir, God you save, and master mine!
    A drink fain would I have, and somewhat to dine.
COLL.   Christ's curse, my knave, thou art a lither hine![1]
GIB.   What, the boy list° rave! Abide unto sine.[2]   *wants to*
        We have made it.[3]
150   Ill thrift on thy pate!
    Though the shrew° came late   *rascal*
    Yet is he in state
        To dine, if he had it.

DAW.   Such servants as I, that sweats and swinks,°   *toil*
155   Eats our bread full dry, and that me forthinks.°   *angers*
    We are oft wet and weary when master-men winks,°   *sleep*
    Yet comes full lately° both dinners and drinks.   *tardily*
        But nately°   *profitably*
    Both our dame and our sire,
160   When we have run in the mire,
    They can nip at our hire,[4]
        And pay us full lately.

    But here my troth, master, for the fare° that ye   *food /*
        make°   *provide*
    I shall do thereafter: work as I take.[5]
165   I shall do a little, sir, and among° ever   *meanwhile /*
        lake,°   *play*
    For yet lay my supper never on my stomach
        In fields.
        Whereto should I threap?°   *haggle*
    With my staff can I leap,[6]
170   And men say, "Light cheap
        Litherly foryields."[7]

COLL.   Thou were an ill lad to ride a-wooing
    With a man that had but little of spending.[8]
GIB.   Peace, boy, I bade—no more jangling,
175   Or I shall make thee full rad,° by the heaven's   *frightened*
        King,
        With thy gauds.°   *tricks*
    Where are our sheep, boy? We scorn.[9]

---

9. But that is a poor idea.
1. Thou art a worthless servant.
2. Wait till later.
3. I.e., had dinner.
4. They can deduct from our wages.
5. I.e., work in the same way as I am paid.

6. I.e., run away.
7. A cheap bargain repays badly (a proverb).
8. You would be a bad servant for a poor man to take wooing with him.
9. I.e., waste time.

DAW.   Sir, this same day at morn
        I them left in the corn
180   When they rang Lauds.[1]

        They have pasture good, they cannot go wrong.

COLL.   That is right. By the rood,° these nights are long!   *cross*
        Yet I would, ere we yode,° one gave us a song.   *went*

GIB.   So I thought as I stood, to mirth° us   *cheer*
        among.°   *meanwhile*

185 DAW.   I grant.

COLL.   Let me sing the tenory.°   *tenor*

GIB.   And I the treble so hee.°   *high*

DAW.   Then the mean° falls to me.   *middle part*
        Let see how you chant.

[*They sing.—Enter* MAK *with a cloak over his clothes.*[2]]

190 MAK.   Now, Lord, for thy names seven, that made both moon
        and starns[3]
        Well mo than I can neven, thy will, Lord, of me
        tharns.[4]
        I am all uneven°—that moves oft my harns.[5]   *at odds*
        Now would God I were in heaven, for there weep no
        barns.°   *children*
        So still.°   *continually*

195 COLL.   Who is that pipes so poor?

MAK.   [*aside*] Would God ye wist° how I foor!°   *knew / fared*
        [*aloud*] Lo, a man that walks on the moor
        And has not all his will.

GIB.   Mak, where has thou gane?° Tell us tiding.   *gone*

200 DAW.   Is he come? Then ilkane[6] take heed to his thing.

[*Snatches a cloak from him.*]

MAK.   What! Ich[7] be a yeoman, I tell you, of the king,
        The self and the same, sond° from a great   *messenger*
        lording   *suchlike*
        And sich.°
        Fie on you! Goth hence
205   Out of my presence:
        I must have reverence.
        Why, who be ich?

COLL.   Why make ye it so quaint? Mak, ye do wrang.[8]

GIB.   But, Mak, list ye saint? I trow that ye lang.[9]

---

1. Rang the bells for the church service held at dawn.
2. Mak's entrance is a stage direction in the original MS.
3. Stars.
4. Well more than I can name, thy will, Lord, falls short in regard to me.
5. That often disturbs my brains.
6. Each one. "Thing": possessions. The stage direction here is in the MS.
7. I (the southern form): Mak is pretending to be an important person from the south.
8. Why do you behave in such an unfriendly manner? Mak, you do wrong.
9. But, Mak, do you want to act as if you were a saint? I guess you do.

210	DAW.	I trow the shrew can paint[1]—the devil might him hang!
MAK.	Ich shall make complaint and make you all to
	thwang°	*be flogged*
	At a word,
	And tell even° how ye doth.	*exactly*
COLL.	But Mak, is that sooth?
215		Now take out that southern tooth,[2]
	And set in a turd!

GIB.	Mak, the devil in your ee![3] A stroke would I lean you!
DAW.	Mak, know ye not me? By God, I could teen° you.	*vex*
MAK.	God look° you all three: Methought I had seen	*guard*
	you.
220		Yè are a fair company.
COLL.	Can ye now mean you?[4]
GIB.	Shrew, peep![5]
	Thus late as thou goes,
	What will men suppose?
	Thou has an ill nose[6]
225 | | Of stealing of sheep. |

MAK.	And I am true as steel, all men wate.°	*know*
	But a sickness I feel that holds me full hate:°	*hot, feverish*
	My belly fares not weel, it is out of estate.
DAW.	Seldom lies the devil dead by the gate.[7]
230	MAK.	Therefore
	Full sore am I and ill
	If I stand stone-still:
	I eat not a needill[8]
	This month and more.

235	COLL.	How fares thy wife? By my hood, how fares sho?°	*she*
MAK.	Lies waltering,° by the rood, by the fire, lo!	*lounging*
	And a house full of brood.° She drinks well, too:	*children*
	Ill speed other good that she will do![9]
	But sho
240		Eats as fast as she can;
	And ilk° year that comes to man	*every*
	She brings forth a lakan,°	*baby*
	And some years two.

	But were I now more gracious° and richer by	*prosperous*
	far,
245		I were eaten out of house and of harbar.°	*home*
	Yet is she a foul douce,° if ye come nar:[1]	*sweetheart*
	There is none that trows° nor knows a war°	*imagines / worse*

---

1. I think the shrew can play tricks.
2. Now stop speaking like a southerner.
3. Eye. "Lean": lend.
4. Remember.
5. Rascal, watch out.
6. Noise, i.e., reputation.
7. Road, i.e., the devil is always on the move.
8. Needle, i.e., a little bit.
9. I.e., that's the only good thing she does.
1. I.e., near the truth.

	Than ken° I.	*know*
250	Now will ye see what I proffer:	
	To give all in my coffer	
	Tomorn at next² to offer	
	Her head-masspenny.³	

GIB. I wot° so forwaked° is none in this shire. *know / sleepless*
   I would sleep if° I taked less to my hire. *even if*

255 DAW. I am cold and naked and would have a fire.
   I am weary forraked° and run in the mire. *from walking*
    Wake thou.⁴

GIB. Nay, I will lie down by,
   For I must sleep, truly.

260 DAW. As good a man's son was I
    As any of you.

   But Mak, come hither, between shall thou lie down.

MAK. Then might I let you bedeen of that ye would rown,⁵
    No dread.° *doubt*
265 From my top to my toe,

[*Saying his prayers.*]

  Manus tuas commendo
  *Pontio Pilato.*⁶
   Christ's cross me speed!

[*He gets up as the others sleep and speaks.*]⁷

  Now were time for a man that lacks what he would
270 To stalk privily than° unto a fold, *then*
  And nimbly to work than, and be not too bold,
  For he might abuy° the bargain if it were told *pay for*
   At the ending.
   Now were time for to reel:° *move spryly*
275 But he needs good counseel
   That fain would fare weel° *well*
   And has but little spending.

[*He casts a spell.*]

  But about you a circill,° as round as a moon, *circle*
  To° I have done that° I will, till that it be *until / what*
   noon,
280 That ye lie stone-still to that I have done;
  And I shall say theretill° of good words a *moreover*
   foon:° *few*
   "On height,
   Over your heads my hand I lift.
   Out go your eyes! Fordo your sight!"⁸

---

2. "Tomorn at next": tomorrow.
3. The penny paid for a mass for her departed spirit.
4. You stay awake.
5. Then I might hinder you if you wanted to whisper together.

6. Mak's prayer means, "Thy hands I commend to Pontius Pilate."
7. One of the original stage directions.
8. May your sight be rendered powerless.

285   But yet I must make better shift
                  And it be right.[9]

          Lord, what° they sleep hard—that may ye all hear.   *how*
          Was I never a shephard, but now will I lear.°   *learn*
          If the flock be scar'd, yet shall I nip near.
290   How! Draws hitherward! Now mends our cheer
              From sorrow.
            A fat sheep, I dare say!
            A good fleece, dare I lay!°   *bet*
295   Eft-quit° when I may,   *repay*
             But this will I borrow.
         [*Exit with sheep.*]

        [MAK'S *house.* MAK *speaks outside the door.*]

MAK.   How, Gill, art thou in? Get us some light.
GILL.   [*within*] Who makes such a din this time of the night?
          I am set for to spin; I hope not I might[1]
          Rise a penny to win—I shrew° them on height!   *curse*
300   So fares
            A housewife that has been
            To be raised thus between:[2]
            Here may no note° be seen   *completed work*
              For such small chares.°   *chores*

305 MAK.   Good wife, open the hek!° Sees thou not what I   *door*
           bring?
GILL.   I may thole thee draw the sneck.[3] Ah, come in, my
           sweeting.
MAK.   Yea, thou thar not reck of[4] my long standing.

        [*She opens the door.*]

GILL.   By the naked neck art thou like for to hing.°   *hang*
MAK.   Do way!
310   I am worthy° my meat,   *worthy of*
          For in a strait° can I get   *pinch*
          More than they that swink° and sweat   *work*
            All the long day.

         Thus it fell to my lot, Gill, I had such grace.
315 GILL. It were a foul blot to be hanged for the case.
MAK.   I have 'scaped,° Jelot,[5] oft as hard a glase.°   *escaped / blow*
GILL.   But "So long goes the pot to the water," men says,
           "At last
          Comes it home broken."
320 MAK. Well know I the token,
          But let it never be spoken!
          But come and help fast.

9. If it is to be all right.
1. I don't think I could.
2. This is what happens to anyone who's been a housewife—to be got up all the time.
3. I may let you draw the latch.
4. You need not care about.
5. I.e., Gill.

	I would he were flain,° I list° well eat:	*skinned / wish*
	This twelvemonth was I not so fain of one sheep-meat.	
325 GILL.	Come they ere he be slain, and hear the sheep bleat—	
MAK.	Then might I be taen°—that were a cold sweat!	*taken*
	Go spar°	*fasten*
	The gate° door.	*street*
GIL.	Yes, Mak,	
	For and° they come at thy back—	*if*
330 MAK.	Then might I buy,° for all the pack,	*have to pay*
	The devil of the war.°	*worse*

GILL.	A good bourd have I spied, sin thou can none:[6]	
	Here shall we him hide, to° they be gone,	*until*
	In my cradle. Abide, let me alone,	
335	And I shall lie beside in childbed and groan.	
MAK.	Thou red,°	*get ready*
	And I shall say thou was light°	*delivered*
	Of a knave-child° this night.	*boy child*
GILL.	Now well is me day bright	
340	That ever was I bred.[7]	

	This is a good guise° and a fair cast:°	*method / trick*
	Yet a woman's advice helps at the last.	
	I wot° never who spies: again go thou fast.	*know*
MAK.	But° I come ere they rise, else blows a cold blast.	*unless*
345	I will go sleep.	
	Yet sleeps all this meny,°	*company*
	And I shall go stalk privily,	
	As it had never been I	
	That carried their sheep.	

[*The moor. The shepherds are waking.*]

350 COLL.	*Resurrex a mortruus!*[8] Have hold my hand!	
	Judas carnas dominus![9] I may not well stand.	
	My foot sleeps, by Jesus, and I walter°	*lie*
	fastand.°	*fasting*
	I thought that we laid us full near England.	
GIB.	Ah, yea?	
355	Lord, what° I have slept weel!°	*how / well*
	As fresh as an eel,	
	As light I me feel	
	As leaf on a tree.	

DAW.	Benste° be herein! So my body quakes,	*blessing*
360	My heart is out of skin, what-so° it	*whatever*
	makes.°	*causes*
	Who makes all this din? So my brows blakes,[1]	

---

6. A good trick have I found, since you know none.
7. Now it was a good day that I was born.
8. An illiterate oath referring, apparently, to Christ's Resurrection from the dead.

9. Judas, (in?)carnate lord.
1. The meaning is probably "my eyes are dim." Daw's head may be under a blanket.

<table>
<tr><td></td><td></td><td>To the door will I win. Hark, fellows, wakes!</td><td></td></tr>
<tr><td></td><td></td><td>We were four:</td><td></td></tr>
<tr><td></td><td></td><td>See ye awhere of Mak now?</td><td></td></tr>
<tr><td>365</td><td>COLL.</td><td>We were up ere thou.</td><td></td></tr>
<tr><td></td><td>GIB.</td><td>Man, I give God avow</td><td></td></tr>
<tr><td></td><td></td><td>Yet yede he naw're.[2]</td><td></td></tr>
</table>

	DAW.	Methought he was lapped° in a wolfskin.	*covered*
	COLL.	So are many happed° now, namely° within.	*clad / especially*
370	DAW.	When we had long napped, methought with a gin°	*snare*
		A fat sheep he trapped, but he made no din.	
	GIB.	Be still:	
		Thy dream makes thee wood.°	*mad*
		It is but phantom, by the rood.°	*cross*
375	COLL.	Now God turn all to good,	
		If it be his will.	

	GIB.	Rise, Mak, for shame! Thou lies right lang.°	*long*
	MAK.	Now Christ's holy name be us amang!°	*among*
		What is this? For Saint Jame, I may not well gang.°	*walk*
380		I trow° I be the same. Ah, my neck has lain	*think*
		wrang.°	*wrong*
		[*One of them twists his neck.*]	
		Enough!	
		Mickle thank! Sin yestereven	
		Now, by Saint Strephen,[3]	
		I was flayed with a sweven[4]—	
385		My heart out of slough.°	*skin*

		I thought Gill began to croak and travail full sad,°	*hard*
		Well-near at the first cock, of a young lad,	
		For to mend° our flock—then be I never glad:	*increase*
		I have tow on my rock[5] more than ever I had.	
390		Ah, my head!	
		A house full of young tharms!°	*guts*
		The devil knock out their harns!°	*brains*
		Woe is him has many barns,°	*children*
		And thereto little bread.	

		I must go home, by your leave, to Gill, as I thought.	
		I pray you look° my sleeve, that I steal nought.	*examine*
		I am loath you to grieve or from you take aught.	
	DAW.	Go forth! Ill might thou chieve!° Now would I we	*prosper*
		sought[6]	
		This morn	
400		That we had all our store.	
	COLL.	But I will go before.	
		Let us meet.	

---

2. He's gone nowhere yet.
3. Probably St. Stephen.
4. I was terrified by a dream.

5. Flax on my distaff (i.e., trouble).
6. I want us to seek.

GIB.	Whore?°	*where*
DAW.	At the crooked thorn.	

[MAK'S *house.* MAK *at the door.*]

MAK.	Undo this door! Who is here? How long shall I stand?	
405 GILL.	Who makes such a bere?° Now walk in the[7]	*clamor*
	weniand![7]	
MAK.	Ah, Gill, what cheer? It is I, Mak, your husband.	
GILL.	Then may we see here the devil in a band,[8]	
	Sir Guile!	
	Lo, he comes with a lote°	*noise*
410	As he were holden in the throat:	
	I may not sit at my note°	*work*
	A hand-long° while.	*short*

MAK.	Will ye here what fare[9] she makes to get her a glose?	
	And does nought but lakes° and claws her toes?	*plays*
415 GILL.	Why, who wanders? Who wakes? Who comes? Who	
	goes?	
	Who brews? Who bakes? What makes me thus	
	hose?°	*hoarse*
	And than°	*then*
	It is ruth° to behold,	*pity*
	Now in hot, now in cold,	
420	Full woeful is the household	
	That wants° a woman.	*lacks*

	But what end has thou made with the herds,°	*shepherds*
	Mak?	
MAK.	The last word that they said when I turned my back,	
	They would look that they had their sheep all the pack.	
425	I hope[1] they will not be well paid when they their sheep	
	lack.	
	Pardie!°	*by God*
	But how-so the game goes,	
	To me they will suppose,°	*suspect*
	And make a foul nose,°	*noise*
430	And cry out upon me.	

	But thou must do as thou hight.°	*promised*
GILL.	I accord me theretill.[2]	
	I shall swaddle him right in my cradill.	
	If it were a greater sleight, yet could I help till.[3]	
	I will lie down straight.° Come, hap°	*straightway / cover*
	me.	
MAK.	I will.	
435 GILL.	Behind	
	Come Coll and his marrow;°	*mate*

7. Waning of the moon (an unlucky time).   1. Expect. "Paid": pleased.
8. On a leash.   2. I agree to it.
9. Fuss. "Glose": excuse.   3. I.e., with it.

	They will nip us full narrow.	
MAK.	But I may cry "Out, harrow,"°	*help*
	The sheep if they find.	

440 GILL.   Hearken ay when they call—they will come anon.
Come and make ready all, and sing by thine one.°   *self*
Sing "lullay"° thou shall, for I must groan   *lullaby*
And cry out by the wall on Mary and John
    For sore.°   *pain*
445   Sing "lullay" on fast
    When thou hears at the last,
    And but I play a false cast,[4]
      Trust me no more.

[*The moor.*]

DAW.   Ah, Coll, good morn. Why sleeps thou not?
450 COLL.   Alas that ever I was born! We have a foul blot:
A fat wether° have we lorn.°   *ram / lost*
DAW.   Marry, God's forbot![5]
GIB.   Who should do us that scorn? That were a foul spot!
COLL.   Some shrew.°   *rascal*
     I have sought with my dogs
455   All Horbury shrogs,°   *thickets*
     And of fifteen hogs
      Found I but one ewe.[6]

DAW.   Now trow me,° if ye will, by Saint Thomas of   *believe*
     Kent,
Either Mak or Gill was at that assent.°   *conspiracy*
460 COLL.   Peace, man, be still! I saw when he went.
Thou slanders him ill, thou ought to repent
    Good speed.
GIB.   Now as ever might I thee,°   *thrive*
     If I should even here dee,°   *die*
465   I would say it were he
      That did that same deed.

DAW.   Go we thither, I read,° and run on our feet.   *advise*
Shall I never eat bread the sooth to I weet.[7]
COLL.   Nor drink in my head, with him till I meet.
470 GIB.   I will rest in no stead° till that I him greet,   *place*
    My brother.
    One I will hight:[8]
    Till I see him in sight
    Shall I never sleep one night
475   There° I do another.   *where*

---

4. Unless I play a false trick.   (i.e., the wether was missing).
5. God forbid.   7. Until I know the truth.
6. And with 15 young sheep I found only a ewe   8. One thing will I promise.

[MAK'S *house.* MAK *and* GILL *within, she in bed, groaning,*
        he singing a lullaby; the shepherds enter outside the
        door.]

DAW.	Will ye hear how they hack?[9] Our sire list croon.	
COLL.	Heard I never none crack° so clear out of tune.	*song*
	Call on him.	
GIB.	Mak, undo your door soon!°	*at once*
MAK.	Who is that spake, as° it were noon,	*as if*
480	On loft?[1]	
	Who is that, I say?	
DAW.	Good fellows, were it day.[2]	
MAK.	As far as ye may,	
	[*opening*] Good,° speaks soft	*good men*

485   Over a sick woman's head, that is at malease.[3]

	I had liefer° be dead ere she had any	*rather*
	disease.°	*distress*
GILL.	Go to another stead, I may not well wheeze:°	*breathe*
	Each foot that ye tread goes through my nese.°	*nose*
	So, hee!°	*scat*
490 COLL.	Tell us, Mak, if you may,	
	How fare ye, I say?	
MAK.	But are ye in this town today?	
	Now how fare ye?	

Ye have run in the mire and are wet yit.
495   I shall make you a fire if you will sit.

	A nurse would I hire—Think ye one[4] yit?	
	Well quit is my hire—my dream, this is it	
	A season.[5]	
	I have barns,° if ye knew,	*children*
500	Wel mo° than enew:°	*more / enough*
	But we must drink as we brew,	
	And that is but reason.	

	I would ye dined ere ye yode.° Methink that ye	*went*
	sweat.	
GIB.	Nay, neither mends our mood[6] drink nor meat.	
505 MAK.	Why, sir, ails you aught but good?[7]	
DAW.	Yea, our sheep that we get	
	Are stolen as they yode:° our loss is great.	*walked*
MAK.	Sirs, drinks!	
	Had I been thore°	*there*
	Some should have bought° it full sore.	*paid for*
510 COLL.	Marry, some men trows° that ye wore,°	*think / were*
	And that us forthinks.°	*disturbs*

---

9. Bellow. "List": wants to.
1. Loudly.
2. Good companions, if it were daytime.
3. That feels badly.

4. Can you think of one?
5. Right on time.
6. Appeases our anger.
7. Is there anything wrong with you? "Get": tend.

GIB.	Mak, some men trows that it should be ye.	
DAW.	Either ye or your spouse, so say we.	
MAK.	Now if you have suspouse° to Gill or to me,	*suspicion*
515		Come and ripe° the house, and then may ye see	*search*
	Who had her[8]—	
	If I any sheep fot,°	*fetched*
	Either cow or stot[9]—	
	And Gill my wife rose not	
520 | | Here sin she laid her. | |

	As I am true and leal,° to God here I pray	*just*
	That this be the first meal that I shall eat this day.	
COLL.	Mak, as I have sele,[1] advise thee, I say:	
	[*They begin the search.*]	
	He learned timely to steal that could not say nay.	
525 GILL.	I swelt!°	*die*
	Out, thieves, from my wones!°	*dwelling*
	Ye come to rob us for the nones.[2]	
MAK.	Hear ye not how she groans?	
	Your hearts should melt.	

530 GILL.	Out, thieves, from my barn!° Nigh him not thore![3]	*child*
MAK.	Wist ye how she had farn,[4] your hearts would be sore.	
	You do wrong, I you warn, that thus comes before	
	To a womman that has farn°—but I say no	*been in labor*
	more.	
GILL.	Ah, my middill!	
535		I pray to God so mild,	
	If ever I you beguiled,	
	That I eat this child	
	That lies in this cradill.	

MAK.	Peace, woman, for God's pain, and cry not so!	
540		Thou spills° thy brain and makes me full woe.	*spoil*
GIB.	I trow our sheep be slain. What find ye two?	
DAW.	All work we in vain; as well may we go.	
	But hatters,[5]	
	I can find no flesh,	
545		Hard nor nesh,°	*soft*
	Salt nor fresh,	
	But two tome° platters.	*empty*

	Quick cattle[6] but this, tame nor wild,
	None, as have I bliss, as ioud as he smiled.[7]

[*Approaches the cradle.*]

---

8. I.e., the sheep.
9. Either female or male.
1 Happiness. "Advise thee": take thought.
2. You come for the purpose of robbing us.
3. Approach him not there.

4. If you knew how she had fared.
5. Except for clothing.
6. Livestock.
7. Smelled as badly as he (the baby).

550	GILL.	No, so God me bliss,° and give me joy of my child!	*bless*
	COLL.	We have marked° amiss—I hold us beguiled.	*aimed*
	GIB.	Sir, don!°	*thoroughly*
		Sir—Our Lady him save—	
		Is your child a knave?[8]	
555	MAK.	Any lord might him have,	
		This child, to his son.	
		When he wakens he kips,° that joy is to see.	*kicks*
	DAW.	In good time to his hips, and in sely.[9]	
		But who were his gossips,° so soon ready?	*godparents*
560	MAK.	So fair fall their lips—	
	COLL.	Hark, now, a lee,°	*lie*
	MAK.	So God them thank,	
		Perkin, and Gibbon Waller, I say,	
		And gentle John Horne, in good fay°—	*faith*
		He made all the garray	
565		With the great shank.[1]	
	GIB.	Mak, friends will we be, for we are all one.°	*in accord*
	MAK.	We? Now I hold for me, for mends get I none.[2]	
		Farewell all three, all glad[3] were ye gone.	
	DAW.	Fair words may there be, but love is there none	
570		This year.	
		[They go out the door.]	
	COLL.	Gave ye the child anything?	
	GIB.	I trow not one farthing.	
	DAW.	Fast again will I fling.°	*dash*
		Abide ye me there.	
575		Mak, take it to no grief if I come to thy barn.°	*child*
	MAK.	Nay, thou does me great reprief,[4] and foul has thou farn.	
	DAW.	Thy child it will not grief, that little day-starn.°	*day star*
		Mak, with your leaf,° let me give your barn	*leave*
		But sixpence.	
580	MAK.	Nay, do way, he sleeps.	
	DAW.	Methinks he peeps.°	*opens his eyes*
	MAK.	When he wakens he weeps.	
		I pray you go hence.	
	DAW.	Give me leave him to kiss, and lift up the clout.[5]	
		[Lifts the cover.]	
585		What the devil is this? He has a long snout.	
		[The others re-enter.]	
	COLL.	He is marked[6] amiss. We wot ill about.	

8. Boy (although Mak takes the word in its alternate meaning of "rascal").
9. Perhaps "that's the best thing for him."
1. He made all the trouble with his long legs (the reference is obscure).
2. Now I'll remain apart, for I get no apology.
3. I.e., I would be glad.
4. Shame. "Farn": behaved.
5. Cover.
6. Fashioned. "We wot ill about": we know mischief has been at work.

GIB.	Ill-spun weft, ywis, ay comes foul out.[7]	
	Aye, so!	
	He is like to our sheep.	
590 DAW.	How, Gib, may I peep?	
COLL.	I trow kind will creep	
	Where it may not go.[8]	

GIB.	This was quaint gaud and a fair cast.[9]	
	It was a high fraud.	
DAW.	Yea, sirs, was 't.	
595	Let burn this bawd and bind her fast.	
	A false scaud° hang at the last:	scold
	So shall thou.	
	Will you see how they swaddle	
	His four feet in the middle?	
600	Saw I never in cradle	
	A horned lad ere now.	

MAK.	Peace bid I! What, let be your fare!°	fuss
	I am he that him gat,° and yond woman him bare.	begot
COLL.	What devil shall he hat?° Mak? Lo, Gib, Mak's	be named
	heir!	
605 GIB.	Let be all that: now God give him care°—	sorrow
	I sawgh.[1]	
GILL.	A pretty child is he	
	As sits on a woman's knee,	
	A dillydown, pardie,	
610	To gar° a man laugh.	make

DAW.	I know him by the earmark—that is a good token.	
MAK.	I tell you, sirs, hark, his nose was broken.	
	Sithen° told me a clark that he was	later
	forspoken.°	bewitched
COLL.	This is a false wark.° I would fain be	work
	wroken.°	avenged
615	Get wapen.°	weapon
GILL.	He was taken with° an elf—	by
	I saw it myself—	
	When the clock struck twelf	
	He was forshapen.°	transformed

620 GIB.	Ye two are well feft sam in a stead.[2]	
DAW.	Sin[3] they maintain their theft, let do them to dead.	
MAK.	If I trespass eft,° gird° off my head.	again / cut
	With you will I be left.[4]	
COLL.	Sirs, do my read:°	advice
	For this trespass	

---

7. An ill-spun web, indeed, always comes out badly.
8. I think kinship will creep where it can't walk (i.e., only a parent could love this child).
9. This was a strange trick and a fine dodge.

1. Probably "I saw it."
2. I.e., you two birds of a feather properly flock together.
3. Since. "Dead": death.
4. I put myself in your mercy.

625   We will neither ban° ne flite,°   curse / wrangle
      Fight nor chite,°   chide
      But have done as tite,°   quickly
            And cast him in canvas.

      [*They toss* MAK *in a blanket.*]

            [*The moor.*]

COLL. Lord, what° I am sore, in point for to brist!°   how / burst
630   In faith, I may no more—therefore will I rist.°   rest
GIB.   As a sheep of seven score⁵ he weighed in my fist:
      For to sleep aywhore° methink that I list.°   anywhere / want
DAW.   Now I pray you
            Lie down on this green.
635 COLL. On these thieves yit I mean.°   think
DAW.   Whereto should ye teen?°   worry
            Do as I say you.

      [*An* ANGEL *sings* Gloria in Excelsis *and then speaks.*]⁶

ANGEL. Rise, herdmen hend,° for now is he born   gentle
      That shall take fro the fiend that Adam had lorn;⁷
640   That warlock° to shend,° this night is he   devil
            born.   confound
      God is made your friend now at this morn
            He beheests.°   promises
      At Bedlem° go see: Bethlehem
      There lies that free,°   noble one
645   In a crib full poorly,
            Betwixt two beasts.

      [*Exit.*]

COLL. This was a quaint steven⁸ that ever yet I hard.°   heard
      It is a marvel to neven° thus to be scar'd.°   tell of / scared
GIB.   Of God's Son of heaven he spake upward.°   on high
650   All the wood on a leven methought that he gard
            Appear.⁹
DAW.   He spake of a barn°   child
            In Bedlem, I you warn.
COLL. That betokens yond starn.¹
655   Let us seek him there.

GIB.   Say, what was his song? Heard ye not how he cracked
            it,²
      Three breves³ to a long?
DAW.   Yea, marry, he hacked it.
      Was no crochet° wrong, nor nothing that lacked it.⁴   note

---

5. 140 pounds.   of light.
6. One of the original stage directions.   1. That's what yonder star means.
7. What Adam had brought to ruin.   2. Sang it out.
8. Fine voice.   3. Short notes. "Hacked": sang loud.
9. I thought he made the whole wood seem full   4. It lacked.

	COLL.	For to sing us among, right as he knacked° it,	*trilled*
660		I can.°	*know how*
	GIB.	Let see how ye croon!	
		Can ye bark at the moon?	
	DAW.	Hold your tongues! Have done!	
	COLL.	Hark after, than!	

665	GIB.	To Bedlem he bade that we should gang:°	*go*
		I am full rad° that we tarry too lang.°	*afraid / long*
	DAW.	Be merry and not sad; of mirth is our sang:	
		Everlasting glad to meed may we fang.[5]	
	COLL.	Without nose°	*noise*
670		Hie we thither forthy°	*therefore*
		To that child and that lady;	
		If° we be wet and weary,	*though*
		We have it not to lose.[6]	

	GIB.	We find by the prophecy—let be your din!—	
675		Of David and Isay, and mo than I min,[7]	
		That prophesied by clergy° that in a virgin	*learning*
		Should he light° and lie, to sloken° our sin	*alight / quench*
		And slake° it,	*relieve*
		Our kind,[8] from woe,	
680		For Isay said so:	
		Ecce virgo	
		Concipiet[9] a child that is naked.	

	DAW.	Full glad may we be and° we abide that day	*if*
		That lovely to see, that all mights may.[1]	
685		Lord, well were me for once and for ay	
		Might I kneel on my knee, some word for to say	
		To that child.	
		But the angel said	
		In a crib was he laid,	
690		He was poorly arrayed,	
		Both mean° and mild.	*lowly*

	COLL.	Patriarchs that has been, and prophets beforn,	
		That desired to have seen this child that is born,	
		They are gone full clean—that have they lorn.[2]	
695		We shall see him, I ween,° ere it be morn,	*think*
		To token.[3]	
		When I see him and feel,	
		Then wot I full weel[4]	
		It is true as steel	
700		That prophets have spoken:	

5. Eternal joy as our reward may we receive.
6. We must not neglect it.
7. Of David and Isaiah and more than I remember.
8. I.e., mankind.
9. Behold, a virgin shall conceive (Isaiah 7.14).

1. I.e., when we see that lovely one who is all-powerful.
2. That (sight) have they lost.
3. As a sign.
4. Then know I full well.

		To so poor as we are that he would appear,	
		First find, and declare by his messenger.	
	GIB.	Go we now, let us fare, the place is us near.	
	DAW.	I am ready and yare,° go we in fere[5]	*prepared*
705		To that bright.°	*glorious one*
		Lord, if thy wills be—	
		We are lewd° all three—	*ignorant*
		Thou grant us some kins glee[6]	
		To comfort thy wight.°	*creature*

[*A stable in Bethlehem.*]

710	COLL.	Hail, comely and clean! Hail, young child!	
		Hail Maker, as I mean, of° a maiden so mild!	*born of*
		Thou has waried,° I ween, the warlock°	*put a curse on / devil*
		so wild.	
		The false guiler of teen,[7] now goes he beguiled.	
		Lo, he merries!	
715		Lo, he laughs, my sweeting!	
		A well fair meeting!	
		I have holden my heting:°	*promise*
		Have a bob° of cherries.	*bunch*

	GIB.	Hail, sovereign Saviour, for thou has us sought!	
720		Hail freely food[8] and flower, that all thing has wrought!	
		Hail, full of favor, that made all of nought!	
		Hail! I kneel and I cower.° A bird have I brought	*crouch*
		To my barn.°	*child*
		Hail, little tiny mop!°	*baby*
725		Of our creed thou art crop.°	*head*
		I would drink on thy cup,	
		Little day-starn.	

	DAW.	Hail, darling dear, full of Godhead!	
		I pray thee be near when that I have need.	
		Hail, sweet is thy cheer°—my heart would bleed	*face*
		To see thee sit here in so poor weed,°	*clothing*
		With no pennies.	
		Hail! Put forth thy dall!°	*hand*
		I bring thee but a ball:	
735		Have and play thee withal,	
		And go to the tennis.	

	MARY.	The Father of heaven, God omnipotent,	
		That set all on seven,[9] his Son has he sent.	
		My name could he neven, and light ere he went.[1]	
740		I conceived him full even through might as he meant.[2]	
		And now is he born.	

---

5. Together.
6. Some kind of cheer.
7. The false grievous deceiver.
8. Noble child.
9. Who created everything perfectly.

1. My name did he name, and alighted ere he went.
2. I conceived him through his power, just as he intended.

He[3] keep you from woe!
I shall pray him so.
Tell forth as ye go,
745   And min on[4] this morn.

COLL.   Farewell, lady, so fair to behold,
         With thy child on thy knee.
GIB.   But he lies full cold.
         Lord, well is me. Now we go, thou behold.
DAW.   Forsooth, already it seems to be told
750   Full oft.
COLL.   What grace we have fun!°   *received*
GIB.   Come forth, now are we won!°   *redeemed*
DAW.   To sing are we bun:°   *bound*
         Let take on loft.[5]
         [*They sing.*]

3. May he.   5. Let's raise our voices.
4. Remember.

THE YORK PLAY OF THE CRUCIFIXION
ca. 1425

The climax of the mystery cycles (on the cycles see the introduction to the *Second Shepherds' Play*) is reached with a sequence of plays about the passion of Christ. Everything in the cycle leads up to the Crucifixion, the turning point in human history, when the original sin of Adam and Eve is paid for by the blood of Christ. And no cycle has a more dramatic series of passion plays than that performed at York, the longest of the four extant English cycles. Records of the York mystery plays begin to appear in the last quarter of the fourteenth century when York was, next to London, England's most populous and prosperous city. Richard II came to see the cycle in 1397. Sometime after 1415 the plays of the passion sequence were extensively revised by a gifted playwright referred to by scholars as the York Realist. *The Crucifixion of Christ*, although not written in that author's distinctive alliterative style, has sometimes been attributed to him, and is, in any case, a powerful example of late medieval dramatic art.

Earlier medieval literature and art had treated the Crucifixion in a more abstract style, emphasizing the majesty of Christ and the theological significance of his sacrifice. The Old English *Dream of the Rood*, for example, represents Christ as a young hero fighting a great battle. Late medieval treatments of the Crucifixion in painting, sculpture, poetry, and drama, however, emphasize the agony of the passion, although there are notable exceptions like *Piers Plowman;* and, of course, Christ's ultimate triumph in the Harrowing of Hell and the Resurrection lends dramatic irony to the taunts of his judges and executioners. The York plays leading up to the *Crucifixion* are especially cruel: a silent Jesus is vilified, scourged, crowned with thorns, and battered and mocked in a cruel game of blind man's bluff. Much of the

York *Crucifixion* revolves around the mechanical difficulties the soldiers encounter in nailing Jesus to the Cross. The play focuses on the soldiers; they are villains, to be sure, but ordinary men, not monsters. Their boasting and jeering thinly veil their nervousness and apprehension. They think Christ is a sorcerer—in an earlier play the soldiers' banners have magically bowed down to him—and they are not all sure that some sort of lightning is not about to strike them.

The gory details, part of the play's "realism," create a shudder, but they also fulfill a larger aim of the drama, which is to bring the audience to participate imaginatively in Christ's suffering, to stir them to true compassion, and to make them aware of the personal application of the play to themselves. When the Cross is finally raised and the actor-Christ speaks to "All men that walk by way or street," he addresses the spectators in the streets of York as though *they* were representing the crowd around the Cross on Calvary, directly involving and implicating them in the drama and its theme of salvation. But the meaning of those words is lost on the soldiers who truly "know not what they do" and proceed to quarrel about Christ's cloak, which, in a switch from the dicing described in the Bible, the soldier in command preempts as his property.

The York Play of The Crucifixion

Cast of Characters

JESUS   FOUR SOLDIERS

[Calvary]

1ST SOLDIER.	Sir knights, take heed hither in hie,°	*haste*
	This deed on dergh we may not draw:[1]	
	Ye woot° yourself as well as I	*know*
	How lords and leaders of our law	
5	Has given doom that this dote° shall die.	*fool*
2ND SOLDIER.	Sir, all their counsel well we know.	
	Sen° we are comen to Calvary,	*since*
	Let ilk° man help now as him awe.°	*each / ought*
3RD SOLDIER.	We are all ready, lo,	
10	This forward° to fulfill.	*agreement*
4TH SOLDIER.	Let hear how we shall do,	
	And go we tite theretill.[2]	
1ST SOLDIER.	It may not help here for to hone,°	*delay*
	If we shall any worship° win.	*honor*
15 2ND SOLDIER.	He must be dead needlings° by noon.	*of necessity*
3RD SOLDIER.	Then is good time that we begin.	
4TH SOLDIER.	Let ding° him down, then is he done:	*strike*
	He shall not dere° us with his din.	*annoy*

---

1. We may not delay the time of this deed.   2. And let's get to it quickly.

1ST SOLDIER.	He shall be set and learned soon[3]	
20	With care° to him and all his kin.	sorrow
2ND SOLDIER.	The foulest dead° of all	death
	Shall he die for his deeds.	
3RD SOLDIER.	That means cross° him we shall.	crucify
4TH SOLDIER.	Behold, so right he reads.°	speaks
25 1ST SOLDIER.	Then to this work us must take heed,	
	So that our working be not wrang.°	wrong
2ND SOLDIER.	None other note to neven is need,[4]	
	But let us haste him for to hang.	
3RD SOLDIER.	And I have gone for gear good speed,[5]	
30	Both hammers and nails large and lang.°	long
4TH SOLDIER.	Then may we boldly do this deed.	
	Come on, let kill this traitor strong.°	flagrant
1ST SOLDIER.	Fair might ye fall in fere[6]	
	That has wrought on this wise.	
35 2ND SOLDIER.	Us needs not for to lear°	learn
	Such faitours° to chastise.	fakers
3RD SOLDIER.	Sen ilk a thing is right arrayed,	
	The wiselier° now work may we.	more skillfully
4TH SOLDIER.	The cross on ground is goodly graid,°	prepared
40	And bored[7] even as it ought to be.	
1ST SOLDIER.	Look that the lad on length be laid,	
	And made be fest° unto this tree.[8]	fastened
2ND SOLDIER.	For all his fare he shall be flayed:°	beaten
	That on assay[9] soon shall ye see.	
45 3RD SOLDIER.	Come forth, thou cursed knave,	
	Thy comfort soon shall keel.°	grow cold
4TH SOLDIER.	Thine hire here shall thou have.	
1ST SOLDIER.	Walk on, now work we weel.°	well
JESUS	Almighty God, my Father free,°	noble
50	Let these matters be made in mind:	
	Thou bade that I should buxom° be,	obedient
	For Adam° plight for to be pined.°	Adam's / tortured
	Here to dead° I oblige me[1]	death
	Fro° that sin for to save mankind,	from
55	And sovereignly beseek I thee,[2]	
	That they for me may favor find.	
	And from the Fiend them fend,°	defend
	So that their souls be safe,	
	In wealth° withouten end.	welfare
60	I keep° nought else to crave.	care

---

3. He'll be put in his place and taught quickly.
4. There is no need to mention any other business.
5. Quickly.
6. May you all have good luck together.
7. I.e., bored with holes for the nails, which were probably wooden.
8. I.e., the cross. "Fare": behavior.
9. I.e., in actual experience.
1. Render myself liable.
2. And above all I beseech thee.

1ST SOLDIER.	We,[3] hark, sir knights, for Mahound's blood.	
	Of Adam-kind° is all his thought!	mankind
2ND SOLDIER.	The warlock waxes worse than wood.[4]	
	This doleful dead° ne dreadeth he nought.	death
65 3RD SOLDIER.	Thou should have mind, with main and mood,[5]	
	Of wicked works that thou hast wrought.	
4TH SOLDIER.	I hope° that he had been as good°	think / well off
	Have ceased of saws that he up sought.[6]	
1ST SOLDIER.	Those saws° shall rue° him	sayings
	sore	repent
70	For all his sauntering[7] soon.	
2ND SOLDIER.	Ill speed them that him spare[8]	
	Till he to dead° be done.	death
3RD SOLDIER.	Have done belive,° boy, and make thee	at once
	boun,°	ready
	And bend thy back unto this tree.	
	[*Jesus lies down.*]	
75 4TH SOLDIER.	Behold, himself has laid him down,	
	In length and breadth as he should be.	
1ST SOLDIER.	This traitor here tainted° of treasoun,	convicted
	Go fast and fetch him then, ye three.	
	And sen he claimeth kingdom with crown,	
80	Even as a king here hang shall he.	
2ND SOLDIER.	Now certes I shall not fine°	stop
	Ere his right hand be fest.°	fastened
3RD SOLDIER.	The left hand then is mine:	
	Let see who bears him[9] best.	
85 4TH SOLDIER.	His limbs on length then shall I lead,°	stretch
	And even unto the bore° them bring.	hole
1ST SOLDIER.	Unto his head I shall take heed,	
	And with my hand help him to hing.°	hang
2ND SOLDIER.	Now sen we four shall do this deed,	
90	And meddle° with this unthrifty° thing,	deal / unrewarding
	Let no man spare for special speed,[1]	
	Till that we have made ending.	
3RD SOLDIER.	This forward° may not fail,	agreement
	Now are we right arrayed.°	set up
95 4TH SOLDIER.	This boy here in our bail°	control
	Shall bide° full bitter braid.°	abide / treatment
1ST SOLDIER.	Sir knights, say, how work we now?	
2ND SOLDIER.	Yes, certes, I hope° I hold this hand.	think
	And to the bore I have it brought,	

3. "We": an exclamation of surprise or displeasure. "Mahound's": Mohammed's; the sacred figures of other religions were considered devil by Christians in the Middle Ages; the soldier is swearing by the Devil.
4. This devil grows worse than crazy.
5. You should think, with all your strength and wits.
6. I.e., to have ceased of the sayings that he thought up.
7. ? Behaving like a saint.
8. Bad luck to them that spare him.
9. Handles himself.
1. Let nobody slacken because of his own welfare.

100		Full buxomly° withouten band.° *effortlessly / cord*
	1ST SOLDIER.	Strike on then hard, for him thee bought.[2]
	2ND SOLDIER.	Yes, here is a stub° will safely stand: *nail*
		Through bones and sinews it shall be
		sought.° *driven*
		This work is well, I will warrand.° *warrant*
105	1ST SOLDIER.	Say, sir, how do we thore?° *there*
		This bargain may not blin.[3]
	3RD SOLDIER.	It fails° a foot and more, *falls short*
		The sinews are so gone in.° *shrunken*
	4TH SOLDIER.	I hope that mark° amiss be bored. *hole*
110	2ND SOLDIER.	Then must he bide° in bitter bale.° *wait / woe*
	3RD SOLDIER.	In faith, it was over-scantly scored:[4]
		That makes it foully° for to fail. *badly*
	1ST SOLDIER.	Why carp° ye so? Fast° on a cord *complain / fasten*
		And tug him to, by top and tail.[5]
115	3RD SOLDIER.	Yea, thou commands lightly° as a lord: *readily*
		Come help to haul, with ill hail.[6]
	1ST SOLDIER.	Now certes° that shall I do *certainly*
		Full snelly° as a snail. *quickly*
	3RD SOLDIER.	And I shall tach° him to *attach*
120		Full nimbly with a nail.
		This work will hold, that dare I heet,° *promise*
		For now are fest° fast both his *fastened*
		hend.° *hands*
	4TH SOLDIER.	Go we all four then to his feet:
		So shall our space° be speedly° spend. *time / well*
125	2ND SOLDIER.	Let see, what bourd his bale might beet:[7]
		Thereto my back now will I bend.
	4TH SOLDIER.	Ow! this work is all unmeet:° *wrongly done*
		This boring must be all amend.
	1ST SOLDIER.	Ah, peace, man, for Mahound,° *Mohammed*
130		Let no man woot° that wonder. *know*
		A rope shall rug° him down, *jerk*
		If all his sinews go asunder.
	2ND SOLDIER.	That cord full kindly can I knit,° *knot*
		The comfort of this carl° to keel.° *knave / cool*
135	1ST SOLDIER.	Fest on then fast that all be fit.
		It is no force° how fell° he feel. *matter / badly*
	2ND SOLDIER.	Lug on, ye both, a little yit,° *yet.*
	3RD SOLDIER.	I shall not cease, as I have seel.[8]
	4TH SOLDIER.	And I shall fond° him for to hit. *try*
	2ND SOLDIER.	Ow, hail!° *pull*

2. Drive the nail in hard, for him who redeemed thee: a splendidly anachronistic oath.

3. This arrangement may not fail: the arrangement is of the four soldiers at the four ends of the cross.

4. It was overcarelessly bored.

5. And stretch him to it, head and toe.

6. With bad luck to you.

7. Let's see, what trick could increase his suffering.

8. As I may have good luck.

140	4TH SOLDIER.	Ho, now I hold° it weel.°	*think / well*
	1ST SOLDIER.	Have done, drive in that nail	
		So that no fault be found.	
	4TH SOLDIER.	This working would not fail	
		If four bulls here were bound.	

145	1ST SOLDIER.	These cords have evil° increased his pains	*badly*
		Ere° he were till° the borings brought.	*before / to*
	2ND SOLDIER.	Yea, asunder are both sinews and veins	
		On ilk a side, so have we sought.°	*afflicted*
	3RD SOLDIER.	Now all his gauds° nothing him gains:	*tricks*
150		His sauntering shall with bale be bought.[9]	
	4TH SOLDIER.	I will go say to our sovereigns	
		Of all these works how we have wrought.	
	1ST SOLDIER.	Nay, sirs, another thing	
		Falls first to you and me:[1]	
155		They bade we should him hing°	*hang*
		On height that men might see.	

	2ND SOLDIER.	We woot well so their words were,	
		But sir, that deed will do us dere.°	*harm*
	1ST SOLDIER.	It may nought mend° for to	*improve*
		moot° more:	*argue*
160		This harlot° must be hanged here.	*rascal*
	2ND SOLDIER.	The mortise[2] is made fit° therefore.	*ready*
	3RD SOLDIER.	Fast on your fingers then, in fere.[3]	
	4TH SOLDIER.	I ween° it will never come there.	*think*
		We four raise it not right to°-year.	*this*
165	1ST SOLDIER.	Say, man, why carps thou so?	
		Thy lifting was but light.°	*easy*
	2ND SOLDIER.	He means there must be mo°	*more*
		To heave him up on height.	

	3RD SOLDIER.	Now certes I hope it shall not need	
170		To call to us more company.	
		Methink we four should do this deed,	
		And bear him to yon hill on high.	
	1ST SOLDIER.	It must be done withouten dread:°	*doubt*
		No more, but look ye be ready,	
175		And this part shall I lift and lead.°	*carry*
		On length he shall no longer lie.	
		Therefore now make you boun:°	*ready*
		Let bear him to yon hill.	
	4TH SOLDIER.	Then will I bear here down,	
180		And tent his toes untill.[4]	

---

9. His acting like a saint (?) shall be paid for with pain.
1. You and I must do first.
2. A hole in the ground shaped to receive the cross.

3. Fasten your fingers on it, all together.
4. Then I'll carry the part down here and attend to his toes.

2ND SOLDIER.	We two shall see till either side,	
	For else this work will wry° all	*turn out*
	wrang.°	*wrong*
3RD SOLDIER.	We are ready.	
4TH SOLDIER.	Good sirs, abide,	
	And let me first his feet up fang.°	*take*
2ND SOLDIER.	Why tent ye so to tales this tide?[5]	
1ST SOLDIER.	Lift up!	

[All lift the cross together.]

4TH SOLDIER.	Let see!	
2ND SOLDIER.	Ow! Lift along!	
3RD SOLDIER.	From all this harm he should him hide°	*protect*
	And° he were God.	*if*
4TH SOLDIER.	The Devil him hang!	
1ST SOLDIER.	For great harm° I have hent:°	*injury / received*
	My shoulder is in sunder.	
2ND SOLDIER.	And certes I am near shent,°	*ruined*
	So long have I born under.[6]	

3RD SOLDIER.	This cross and I in two must twin°—	*separate*
	Else breaks my back in sunder soon.	
4TH SOLDIER.	Lay down again and leave° your din.	*cease*
	This deed for us will never be done.	

[They lay it down.]

1ST SOLDIER.	Assay,° sirs, let see if any gin°	*try / trick*
	May help him up, withouten hone.°	*delay*
	For here should wight° men worship win,	*strong*
	And not with gauds° all day to gone.	*pranks*
2ND SOLDIER.	More wighter° men than we	*stronger*
	Full few I hope° ye find.	*think*
3RD SOLDIER.	This bargain° will not be,°	*arrangement / work*
	For certes me wants wind.	

4TH SOLDIER.	So will° of work never we wore.°	*at a loss / were*
	I hope this carl some cautels cast.[7]	
2ND SOLDIER.	My burden sat° me wonder sore:	*vexed*
	Unto the hill I might not last.	
1ST SOLDIER.	Lift up and soon he shall be thore.°	*there*
	Therefore fest° on your fingers fast.	*fasten*
3RD SOLDIER.	Ow, lift!	
1ST SOLDIER.	We, lo!	
4TH SOLDIER.	A little more!	
2ND SOLDIER.	Hold then!	
1ST SOLDIER.	How now?	
2ND SOLDIER.	The worst is past.	
3RD SOLDIER.	He weighs a wicked weight.	
2ND SOLDIER.	So may we all four say,	
	Ere he was heaved on height	
	And raised on this array.°	*way*

---

5. Why are you so intent on talking at a time like this?

6. So long have I borne it up.

7. I think this knave cast some spells.

4TH SOLDIER.	He made us stand as any stones,		
	So boistous° was he for to bear.		*bulky*
1ST SOLDIER.	Now raise him nimbly for the nonce,[8]		
220	And set him by this mortise here;		
	And let him fall in all at once,		
	For certes that pain shall have no peer.°		*equal*
3RD SOLDIER.	Heave up!		
4TH SOLDIER.	Let down, so all his bones		
	Are asunder now on sides sere.[9]		
	[The cross is raised.]		
225 1ST SOLDIER.	That falling was more fell°		*cruel*
	Than all the harms he had.		
	Now may a man well tell°		*count*
	The least lith° of this lad.		*joint*

3RD SOLDIER.	Methinketh this cross will not abide		
230	Nor stand still in this mortise yit.°		*yet*
4TH SOLDIER.	At the first was it made overwide:		
	That makes it wave, thou may well wit.°		*learn*
1ST SOLDIER.	It shall be set on ilk a side,		
	So that it shall no further flit.°		*move*
235	Good wedges shall we take this tide,°		*time*
	And fast° the foot, then is all fit.		*fasten*
2ND SOLDIER.	Here are wedges arrayed°		*prepared*
	For that, both great and small.		
3RD SOLDIER.	Where are our hammers laid		
240	That we should work withal?		

4TH SOLDIER.	We have them here even at our hand.		
2ND SOLDIER.	Give me this wedge, I shall it in drive.		
4TH SOLDIER.	Here is another yit ordand.°		*ready*
3RD SOLDIER.	Do take° it me hither belive.°		*give / quickly*
245 1ST SOLDIER.	Lay on then fast.		
3RD SOLDIER.	Yes. I warrand.°		*guarantee*
	I thring them sam, so mote I thrive.[1]		
	Now will this cross ful stably stand:		
	All if he rave they will not rive.[2]		
1ST SOLDIER.	Say, sir, how likes thou now		
250	The work that we have wrought?		
4TH SOLDIER.	We pray you, say us how		
	Ye feel, or faint ye aught?[3]		

JESUS	All men that walk by way or street,		
	Take tent—ye shall no travail tine[4]—		
255	Behold mine head, mine hands, my feet,		
	And fully feel now ere ye fine°		*cease*
	If any mourning may be meet		
	Or mischief° measured unto mine.		*injury*

---

8. For the purpose.
9. Are pulled apart on every side.
1. I press them together, so may I thrive.

2. Even if he struggles, they will not budge.
3. Or do you feel somewhat faint?
4. Take heed, you shall not lose your labor.

260	My Father, that all bales may bete,[5]	
	Forgive these men that do me pine.°	torment
	What they work woot° they nought:	know
	Therefore my Father I crave	
	Let never their sins be sought,°	searched
	But see their souls to save.	

265	1ST SOLDIER.	We, hark! he jangles like a jay.
	2ND SOLDIER.	Methink he patters like a pie.°

magpie

	3RD SOLDIER.	He has been doand° all this day,

doing so

And made great mening° of mercy. — *talk*

	4TH SOLDIER.	Is this the same that gun° us say

did

270 That he was God's son almighty?[6]

	1ST SOLDIER.	Therefore he feels full fell affray,[7]

And doomed this day was for to die.

	2ND SOLDIER.	Vath! *qui destruis templum!*[8]
	3RD SOLDIER.	His saws° were so, certain.

sayings

275	4TH SOLDIER.	And, sirs, he said to some

He might raise it again.

	1ST SOLDIER.	To muster° that he had no might,

exhibit

For all the cautels° that he could cast; — *charms*

All if he were in word so wight,[9]

280 For all his force now is he fast.

All Pilate deemed is done and dight:° — *accomplished*

Therefore I read° that we go rest. — *advise*

	2ND SOLDIER.	This race must be rehearsed right[1]

Through the world both east and west.

285	2ND SOLDIER.	Yea, let him hang here still

And make mows on the moon.[2]

	4TH SOLDIER.	Then may we wend° at will.

go away.

	1ST SOLDIER.	Nay, good sirs, not so soon.

For certes us needs another note:[3]

290 This kirtle would I of you crave.

	2ND SOLDIER.	Nay, nay, sir, we will look° by lot

see

Which of us four falls° it to have. — *chances*

	3RD SOLDIER.	I read° we draw cut° for this coat.

advise / lots

Lo, see now soon, all sides to save.[4]

295	4TH SOLDIER.	The short cut° shall win, that well ye woot,

straw

Whether it fall to knight or knave.

	1ST SOLDIER.	Fellows, ye thar not flite,[5]

For this mantle is mine.

	2ND SOLDIER.	Go we then hence tite,°

quickly

300 This travail here we tine.[6]

5. My father, who may remedy all evils.
6. That he was the son of almighty God.
7. For that he suffers a full cruel assault.
8. In Faith thou who destroys the temple (cf. Mark 14.58, John 2.19).
9. Even though he was so clever in words.
1. This course of action must be repeated cor-

rectly.
2. And make faces at the moon.
3. For surely we have another piece of business to settle.
4. See now straightway, to protect all parties.
5. Fellows, you don't need to quarrel.
6. We're wasting our time here.

EVERYMAN
after 1485

Everyman is the best surviving example of that kind of medieval drama which is known as the morality play. Moralities apparently evolved side by side with the mysteries and in England were, like them, acted by trade guilds, though they were composed individually and not in cycles. They too have a primarily religious purpose, though their method of attaining it is different. The mysteries endeavored to make the Christian religion more real to the unlearned by dramatizing significant events in Biblical history and by showing what these events meant in terms of human experience. The moralities, on the other hand, employed allegory to dramatize the moral struggle that Christianity envisions as present in every man: the actors are every man and the qualities within him, good or bad, and the plot consists of his various reactions to these qualities as they push and pull him one way or another—that is, in Christian terms, toward heaven or toward hell. The intent of the morality is more overtly didactic than the mystery, but most of the moralities share with the mysteries a good deal of rough humor. This is perhaps more evident in other plays of the genre than in *Everyman*, where the chief humor lies in the undue haste with which the hero's friends abandon him when he calls on them for help.

Everyman inculcates its austere lesson by the simplicity and directness of its language and of its approach. A fine sense of inevitability is built up as Everyman is stripped, one by one, of those apparent goods on which he had relied. First he is deserted by his patently false friends: his casual companions, his kinsmen, and his wealth. Receiving some comfort from his enfeebled good deeds, he falls back on them and on his other resources—his strength, his beauty, his intelligence, and his knowledge—qualities which, when properly used, help to make an integrated man. These assist him through the crisis in which he must make up his book of accounts, but at the end, when he must go to the grave, all desert him save his good deeds alone. While the play contains rather too much direct sermonizing, it makes most effectively its grim point that we can take along from this world nothing that we have received, only what we have given.

In *Everyman* allegory appears in its most meticulously worked-out form. Each actor has his allegorical significance defined by his name and behaves entirely within the limits of that definition. The onlooker takes a good deal of intellectual satisfaction in watching the nice operation of the allegorical equations. On the other hand, one might object that allegory, when so neatly handled, sacrifices for a kind of mathematical regularity the suggestiveness that inheres in the far looser allegory of such a work as *Piers Plowman*, which stimulates the imagination more than it satisfies the intellect. Nevertheless, when it is well staged and well acted, *Everyman*, despite its uncompromising didacticism, is a powerful drama.

The play was written near the end of the fifteenth century. It is probably a translation of a Flemish play, though it is not impossible that the Flemish play is the translation and the English *Everyman* the original.

Everyman[1]

Cast of Characters

MESSENGER	KNOWLEDGE
GOD	CONFESSION
DEATH	BEAUTY
EVERYMAN	STRENGTH
FELLOWSHIP	DISCRETION
KINDRED	FIVE-WITS
COUSIN	ANGEL
GOODS	DOCTOR
GOOD DEEDS	

HERE BEGINNETH A TREATISE HOW THE HIGH FATHER OF
HEAVEN SENDETH DEATH TO SUMMON EVERY CREATURE TO COME
AND GIVE ACCOUNT OF THEIR LIVES IN THIS WORLD, AND IS IN
MANNER OF A MORAL PLAY

[*Enter* MESSENGER.]

MESSENGER. I pray you all give your audience,
    And hear this matter with reverence,
    By figure[2] a moral play.
    The Summoning of Everyman called it is,
5   That of our lives and ending shows
    How transitory we be all day.[3]
    The matter is wonder precious,
    But the intent of it is more gracious
    And sweet to bear away.
10   The story saith: Man, in the beginning
    Look well, and take good heed to the ending,
    Be you never so gay.
    You think sin in the beginning full sweet,
    Which in the end causeth the soul to weep,
15   When the body lieth in clay.
    Here shall you see how fellowship and jollity,
    Both strength, pleasure, and beauty,
    Will fade from thee as flower in May.
    For ye shall hear how our Heaven-King
20   Calleth Everyman to a general reckoning.
    Give audience and hear what he doth say.

[*Exit* MESSENGER.—*Enter* GOD.]

GOD. I perceive, here in my majesty,
    How that all creatures be to me unkind,°   *thoughtless*

---

1. The text is based upon the earliest printing of the play (no manuscript is known) by John Skot about 1530, as reproduced by W. W. Greg (Louvain, 1904). The spelling has been modernized except where modernization would spoil the rhyme, and modern punctuation has been added. The stage directions have been amplified.
2. In form.
3. Always.

Living without dread in worldly prosperity.
25 Of ghostly° sight the people be so blind,   *spiritual*
Drowned in sin, they know me not for their God.
In worldly riches is all their mind:
They fear not of my righteousness the sharp rod;
30 My law that I showed when I for them died
They forget clean, and shedding of my blood red.
I hanged between two,[4] it cannot be denied:
To get them life I suffered to be dead.
I healed their feet, with thorns hurt was my head.
I could do no more than I did, truly—
35 And now I see the people do clean forsake me.
They use the seven deadly sins damnable,
As pride, coveitise,° wrath, and lechery[5]   *avarice*
Now in the world be made commendable.
And thus they leave of angels the heavenly company.
40 Every man liveth so after his own pleasure,
And yet of their life they be nothing sure.
I see the more that I them forbear,
The worse they be from year to year:
All that liveth appaireth° fast.   *degenerates*
45 Therefore I will, in all the haste,
Have a reckoning of every man's person.
For, and° I leave the people thus alone   *if*
In their life and wicked tempests,
Verily they will become much worse than beasts;
50 For now one would by envy another up eat.
Charity do they all clean forgeet.
I hoped well that every man
In my glory should make his mansion,
And thereto I had them all elect.°   *chosen*
55 But now I see, like traitors deject,°   *abased*
They thank me not for the pleasure that I to° them   *for*
                                          meant,
Nor yet for their being that I them have lent.
I proffered the people great multitude of mercy,
And few there be that asketh it heartily.°   *sincerely*
60 They be so cumbered° with worldly riches   *encumbered*
That needs on them I must do justice—
On every man living without fear.
Where art thou, Death, thou mighty messenger?

    [*Enter* DEATH.]

DEATH. Almighty God, I am here at your will,
65   Your commandment to fulfill.
GOD. Go thou to Everyman,
And show him, in my name,
A pilgrimage he must on him take,
Which he in no wise may escape;

---

4. I.e., the 2 thieves between whom Christ was crucified.

5. The other 3 deadly sins are envy, gluttony, and sloth.

70   And that he bring with him a sure reckoning
     Without delay or any tarrying.
DEATH. Lord, I will in the world go run over all,[6]
     And cruelly out-search both great and small.

     [*Exit* GOD.]

     Everyman will I beset that liveth beastly
75   Out of God's laws, and dreadeth not folly.
     He that loveth riches I will strike with my dart,
     His sight to blind, and from heaven to depart°—   *separate*
     Except that Almsdeeds be his good friend—
     In hell for to dwell, world without end.
80   Lo, yonder I see Everyman walking:
     Full little he thinketh on my coming;
     His mind is on fleshly lusts and his treasure,
     And great pain it shall cause him to endure
     Before the Lord, Heaven-King.

     [*Enter* EVERYMAN.]

85   Everyman, stand still! Whither art thou going
     Thus gaily? Hast thou thy Maker forgeet?°   *forgotten*
EVERYMAN. Why askest thou?
     Why wouldest thou weet?°   *know*
DEATH. Yea, sir, I will show you:
90   In great haste I am sent to thee
     From God out of his majesty.
EVERYMAN. What! sent to me?
DEATH. Yea, certainly.
     Though thou have forgot him here,
95   He thinketh on thee in the heavenly sphere,
     As, ere we depart, thou shalt know.
EVERYMAN. What desireth God of me?
DEATH. That shall I show thee:
     A reckoning he will needs have
100 Without any longer respite.
EVERYMAN. To give a reckoning longer leisure I crave.
     This blind° matter troubleth my wit.   *unexpected*
DEATH. On thee thou must take a long journay:
     Therefore thy book of count° with thee thou bring,   *accounts*
105 For turn again thou cannot by no way.
     And look thou be sure of thy reckoning,
     For before God thou shalt answer and shew
     Thy many bad deeds and good but a few—
     How thou hast spent thy life and in what wise,
110 Before the Chief Lord of Paradise.
     Have ado that we were in that way,[7]
     For weet thou well thou shalt make none attornay.[8]
EVERYMAN. Full unready I am such reckoning to give.
     I know thee not. What messenger art thou?

---

6. Everywhere.   8. I.e., none to appear in your stead.
7. I.e., let's get started at once.

115 DEATH. I am Death that no man dreadeth,[9]
         For every man I 'rest,° and no man spareth;   *arrest*
         For it is God's commandment
         That all to me should be obedient.
     EVERYMAN. O Death, thou comest when I had thee least in
         mind.
120   In thy power it lieth me to save:
         Yet of my good° will I give thee, if thou will be kind,   *goods*
         Yea, a thousand pound shalt thou have—
         And defer this matter till another day.
     DEATH. Everyman, it may not be, by no way.
125   I set nought by[1] gold, silver, nor riches,
         Nor by pope, emperor, king, duke, nor princes,
         For, and° I would receive gifts great,   *if*
         All the world I might get.
         But my custom is clean contrary:
130   I give thee no respite. Come hence and not tarry!
     EVERYMAN. Alas, shall I have no longer respite?
         I may say Death giveth no warning.
         To think on thee it maketh my heart sick,
         For all unready is my book of reckoning.
135   But twelve year and I might have a biding,[2]
         My counting-book I would make so clear
         That my reckoning I should not need to fear.
         Wherefore, Death, I pray thee, for God's mercy,
         Spare me till I be provided of remedy.
140 DEATH. Thee availeth not to cry, weep, and pray;
         But haste thee lightly° that thou were gone that   *quickly*
             journay,
         And prove° thy friends, if thou can.   *test*
         For weet° thou well the tide° abideth no man,   *know / time*
         And in the world each living creature
145   For Adam's sin must die of nature.[3]
     EVERYMAN. Death, if I should this pilgrimage take
         And my reckoning surely make,
         Show me, for saint° charity,   *holy*
         Should I not come again shortly?
150 DEATH. No, Everyman. And thou be once there,
         Thou mayst never more come here,
         Trust me verily.
     EVERYMAN. O gracious God in the high seat celestial,
         Have mercy on me in this most need!
155   Shall I have company from this vale terrestrial
         Of mine acquaintance that way me to lead?
     DEATH. Yea, if any be so hardy
         That would go with thee and bear thee company.
         Hie° thee that thou were gone to God's magnificence,   *hasten*
160   Thy reckoning to give before his presence.

---

9. That fears nobody.   2. If I might have a delay for just 12 years.
1. I care nothing for.   3. Naturally.

What, weenest° thou thy life is given thee,   *suppose*
And thy worldly goods also?
EVERYMAN. I had weened so, verily.
DEATH. Nay, nay, it was but lent thee.
165   For as soon as thou art go,
Another a while shall have it and then go therefro,
Even as thou hast done.
Everyman, thou art mad! Thou hast thy wits° five,   *senses*
And here on earth will not amend thy live![4]
170   For suddenly I do come.
EVERYMAN. O wretched caitiff! Whither shall I flee
That I might 'scape this endless sorrow?
Now, gentle Death, spare me till tomorrow,
That I may amend me
175   With good advisement.°   *preparation*
DEATH. Nay, thereto I will not consent,
Nor no man will I respite,
But to the heart suddenly I shall smite,
Without any advisement.
180   And now out of thy sight I will me hie:
See thou make thee ready shortly,
For thou mayst say this is the day
That no man living may 'scape away.

            [*Exit* DEATH.]

EVERYMAN. Alas, I may well weep with sighs deep:
185   Now have I no manner of company
To help me in my journey and me to keep.°   *guard*
And also my writing[5] is full unready—
How shall I do now for to excuse me?
I would to God I had never be geet![6]
190   To my soul a full great profit it had be.
For now I fear pains huge and great.
The time passeth: Lord, help, that all wrought!
For though I mourn, it availeth nought.
The day passeth and is almost ago:°   *gone by*
195   I wot° not well what for to do.   *know*
To whom were I best my complaint to make?
What and I to Fellowship thereof spake,
And showed him of this sudden chance?
For in him is all mine affiance,°   *trust*
200   We have in the world so many a day
Be good friends in sport and play.
I see him yonder, certainly.
I trust that he will bear me company.
Therefore to him will I speak to ease my sorrow.

            [*Enter* FELLOWSHIP.]

4. In thy life.   6. Been begotten.
5. I.e., ledger.

205 Well met, good Fellowship, and good morrow!
 FELLOWSHIP. Everyman, good morrow, by this day!
  Sir, why lookest thou so piteously?
  If anything be amiss, I pray thee me say,
  That I may help to remedy.
210 EVERYMAN. Yea, good Fellowship, yea:
  I am in great jeopardy.
 FELLOWSHIP. My true friend, show to me your mind.
  I will not forsake thee to my life's end
  In the way of good company.
215 EVERYMAN. That was well spoken, and lovingly!
 FELLOWSHIP. Sir, I must needs know your heaviness.°   *sorrow*
  I have pity to see you in any distress.
  If any have you wronged, ye shall revenged be,
  Though I on the ground be slain for thee,
220 Though that I know before that I should die.
 EVERYMAN. Verily, Fellowship, gramercy.°   *many thanks*
 FELLOWSHIP. Tush! by thy thanks I set not a stree.° *straw*
  Show me your grief and say no more.
 EVERYMAN. If I my heart should to you break,°   *disclose*
225 And then you to turn your mind fro me,
  And would not me comfort when ye hear me speak,
  Then should I ten times sorrier be.
 FELLOWSHIP. Sir, I say as I will do, indeed.
 EVERYMAN. Then be you a good friend at need.
230 I have found you true herebefore.
 FELLOWSHIP. And so ye shall evermore.
  For, in faith, and thou go to hell,
  I will not forsake thee by the way.
 EVERYMAN. Ye speak like a good friend. I believe you well.
235 I shall deserve° it, and ° I may.   *repay / if*
 FELLOWSHIP. I speak of no deserving, by this day!
  For he that will say and nothing do
  Is not worthy with good company to go.
  Therefore show me the grief of your mind,
240 As to your friend most loving and kind.
 EVERYMAN. I shall show you how it is:
  Commanded I am to go a journey,
  A long way, hard and dangerous,
  And give a strait° count,° without delay, *strict / accounting*
245 Before the high judge Adonai.[7]
  Wherefore I pray you bear me company,
  As ye have promised, in this journay.
 FELLOWSHIP. This is matter indeed! Promise is duty—
  But, and I should take such a voyage on me,
250 I know it well, it should be to my pain.
  Also it maketh me afeard, certain.
  But let us take counsel here, as well as we can—

---

7. I.e., God.

For your words would fear° a strong man.   *frighten*
EVERYMAN. Why, ye said if I had need,
255   Ye would me never forsake, quick ne dead,
         Though it were to hell, truly.
FELLOWSHIP. So I said, certainly,
         But such pleasures° be set aside, the sooth to say.   *jokes*
         And also, if we took such a journay,
260   When should we again come?
EVERYMAN. Nay, never again, till the day of doom.
FELLOWSHIP. In faith, then will not I come there!
         Who hath you these tidings brought?
EVERYMAN. Indeed, Death was with me here.
265 FELLOWSHIP. Now by God that all hath bought,°   *redeemed*
         If Death were the messenger,
         For no man that is living today
         I will not go that loath° journay—   *loathsome*
         Not for the father that begat me!
270 EVERYMAN. Ye promised otherwise, pardie.°   *by God*
FELLOWSHIP. I wot well I said so, truly.
         And yet, if thou wilt eat and drink and make good cheer,
         Or haunt to women the lusty company,[8]
         I would not forsake you while the day is clear,
275   Trust me verily!
EVERYMAN. Yea, thereto ye would be ready—
         To go to mirth, solace,° and play: *pleasure*
         Your mind to folly will sooner apply°   *attend*
         Than to bear me company in my long journay.
280 FELLOWSHIP. Now in good faith, I will not that way.
         But, and thou will murder or any man kill,
         In that I will help thee with a good will.
EVERYMAN. O that is simple° advice, indeed!   *foolish*
         Gentle fellow, help me in my necessity:
285   We have loved long, and now I need—
         And now, gentle Fellowship, remember me!
FELLOWSHIP. Whether ye have loved me or no,
         By Saint John, I will not with thee go!
EVERYMAN. Yet I pray thee take the labor and do so much for
              me,
290   To bring me forward,[9] for saint charity,
         And comfort me till I come without the town.
FELLOWSHIP. Nay, and° thou would give me a new gown,   *if*
         I will not a foot with thee go.
         But, and thou had tarried, I would not have left thee so.
295   And as now, God speed thee in thy journay!
         For from thee I will depart as fast as I may.
EVERYMAN. Whither away, Fellowship? Will thou forsake me?

---

8. Or frequent the lusty company of women.   9. Escort me.

FELLOWSHIP. Yea, by my fay!° To God I betake°   *faith* / *commend*
     thee.
EVERYMAN. Farewell, good Fellowship! For thee my heart is sore.
300   Adieu forever—I shall see thee no more.
FELLOWSHIP. In faith, Everyman, farewell now at the ending:
     For you I will remember that parting is mourning.

     [*Exit* FELLOWSHIP.]

EVERYMAN. Alack, shall we thus depart° indeed—   *part*
     Ah, Lady, help!—without any more comfort?
305   Lo, Fellowship forsaketh me in my most need!
     For help in this world whither shall I resort?
     Fellowship herebefore with me would merry make,
     And now little sorrow for me doth he take.
     It is said, "In prosperity men friends may find
310   Which in adversity, be full unkind."
     Now whither for succor shall I flee,
     Sith° that Fellowship hath forsaken me?   *since*
     To my kinsmen I will, truly,
     Praying them to help me in my necessity.
315   I believe that they will do so,
     For kind will creep where it may not go.[1]
     I will go 'say°—for yonder I see them—   *assay*
     Where° be ye now my friends and kinsmen.   *whether*

     [*Enter* KINDRED *and* COUSIN.]

KINDRED. Here be we now at your commandment:
320   Cousin, I pray you show us your intent
     In any wise, and not spare.
COUSIN. Yea, Everyman, and to us declare
     If ye be disposed to go anywhither.
     For, weet° you well, we will live and die togither.   *know*
325 KINDRED. In wealth and woe we will with you hold,
     For over his kin a man may be bold.[2]
EVERYMAN. Gramercy,° my friends and kinsmen kind.   *much thanks*
     Now shall I show you the grief of my mind.
     I was commanded by a messenger
330   That is a high king's chief officer:
     He bade me go a pilgrimage, to my pain—
     And I know well I shall never come again.
     Also I must give a reckoning strait,°   *strict*
     For I have a great enemy that hath me in wait,[3]
335   Which intendeth me to hinder.
KINDRED. What account is that which ye must render?
     That would I know.
EVERYMAN. Of all my works I must show
     How I have lived and my days spent;
340   Also of ill deeds that I have used

---

1. For kinship will creep where it cannot walk (i.e., kinsmen will suffer hardship for one another).
2. I.e., for a man may make demands of his kins-   men.
3. I.e., Satan lies in ambush for me.

In my time sith life was me lent,
And of all virtues that I have refused.
Therefore I pray you go thither with me
To help me make mine account, for saint charity.

345 COUSIN. What, to go thither? Is that the matter?
Nay, Everyman, I had liefer fast[4] bread and water
All this five year and more!

EVERYMAN. Alas, that ever I was bore!°   *born*
For now shall I never be merry
350 If that you forsake me.

KINDRED. Ah, sir, what? Ye be a merry man:
Take good heart to you and make no moan.
But one thing I warn you, by Saint Anne,
As for me, ye shall go alone.

355 EVERYMAN. My Cousin, will you not with me go?

COUSIN. No, by Our Lady! I have the cramp in my toe:
Trust not to me. For, so God me speed,
I will deceive you in your most need.

KINDRED. It availeth you not us to 'tice.°   *entice*
360 Ye shall have my maid with all my heart:
She loveth to go to feasts, there to be nice,°   *wanton*
And to dance, and abroad to start.[5]
I will give her leave to help you in that journey,
If that you and she may agree.

365 EVERYMAN. Now show me the very effect° of your mind: *bent*
Will you go with me or abide behind?

KINDRED. Abide behind? Yea, that will I and I may!
Therefore farewell till another day.

[*Exit* KINDRED.]

EVERYMAN. How should I be merry or glad?
370 For fair promises men to me make,
But when I have most need they me forsake.
I am deceived. That maketh me sad.

COUSIN. Cousin Everyman, farewell now,
For verily I will not go with you;
375 Also of mine own an unready reckoning
I have to account—therefore I make tarrying.
Now God keep thee, for now I go.

[*Exit* COUSIN.]

EVERYMAN. Ah, Jesus, is all come hereto?°   *to this*
Lo, fair words maketh fools fain:°   *glad*
380 They promise and nothing will do, certain.
My kinsmen promised me faithfully
For to abide with me steadfastly,
And now fast away do they flee.
Even so Fellowship promised me.
385 What friend were best me of to provide?

---

4. I.e., rather fast on.   5. To go gadding about.

I lose my time here longer to abide.
Yet in my mind a thing there is:
All my life I have loved riches;
If that my Good° now help me might,   Goods
390   He would make my heart full light.
I will speak to him in this distress.
Where art thou, my Goods and riches?
GOODS. [*within*] Who calleth me? Everyman? What, hast thou
    haste?
I lie here in corners, trussed and piled so high,
395   And in chests I am locked so fast—
Also sacked in bags—thou mayst see with thine eye
I cannot stir, in packs low where I lie.
What would ye have? Lightly° me say.   quickly
EVERYMAN. Come hither, Good, in all the haste thou may,
400   For of counsel I must desire thee.

    [*Enter* GOODS.]

GOODS. Sir, and° ye in the world have sorrow or adversity,   if
That can I help you to remedy shortly.
EVERYMAN. It is another disease° that grieveth me: distress
In this world it is not, I tell thee so.
405   I am sent for another way to go,
To give a strait count general
Before the highest Jupiter[6] of all.
And all my life I have had joy and pleasure in thee:
Therefore I pray thee go with me,
410   For, peradventure, thou mayst before God Almighty
My reckoning help to clean and purify.
For it is said ever among[7]
That money maketh all right that is wrong.
GOODS. Nay, Everyman, I sing another song:
415   I follow no man in such voyages.
For, and° I went with thee,   if
Thou shouldest fare much the worse for me;
For because on me thou did set thy mind,
Thy reckoning I have made blotted and blind,°   illegible
420   That thine account thou cannot make truly—
And that hast thou for the love of me.
EVERYMAN. That would grieve me full sore
When I should come to that fearful answer.
Up, let us go thither together.
425   GOODS. Nay, not so, I am too brittle, I may not endure.
I will follow no man one foot, be ye sure.
EVERYMAN. Alas, I have thee loved and had great pleasure
All my life-days on good and treasure.
GOODS. That is to thy damnation, without leasing,°   lie
430   For my love is contrary to the love everlasting.
But if thou had me loved moderately during,°   in the meanwhile

---

6. I.e., God.   7. Now and then.

As to the poor to give part of me,
Then shouldest thou not in this dolor be,
Nor in this great sorrow and care.
435 EVERYMAN. Lo, now was I deceived ere I was ware,
And all I may wite° misspending of time.   *blame on*
GOODS. What, weenest° thou that I am thine?   *suppose*
EVERYMAN. I had weened so.
GOODS. Nay, Everyman, I say no.
440 As for a while I was lent thee;
A season thou hast had me in prosperity.
My condition° is man's soul to kill;   *disposition*
If I save one, a thousand I do spill.°   *ruin*
Weenest thou that I will follow thee?
445 Nay, from this world, not verily.
EVERYMAN. I had weened otherwise.
GOODS. Therefore to thy soul Good is a thief;
For when thou art dead, this is my guise°—   *custom*
Another to deceive in the same wise
450 As I have done thee, and all to his soul's repreef.°   *shame*
EVERYMAN. O false Good, cursed thou be,
Thou traitor to God, that hast deceived me
And caught me in thy snare!
GOODS. Marry, thou brought thyself in care,°   *sorrow*
455 Whereof I am glad;
I must needs laugh, I cannot be sad.
EVERYMAN. Ah, Good, thou hast had long my heartly°   *sincere*
love;
I gave thee that which should be the Lord's above.
But wilt thou not go with me, indeed?
460 I pray thee truth to say.
GOODS. No, so God me speed!
Therefore farewell and have good day.

[*Exit* GOODS.]

EVERYMAN. Oh, to whom shall I make my moan
For to go with me in that heavy° journay?   *sorrowful*
465 First Fellowship said he would with me gone:°   *go*
His words were very pleasant and gay,
But afterward he left me alone.
Then spake I to my kinsmen, all in despair,
And also they gave me words fair—
470 They lacked no fair speaking,
But all forsake me in the ending.
Then went I to my Goods that I loved best,
In hope to have comfort; but there had I least,
For my Goods sharply did me tell
475 That he bringeth many into hell.
Then of myself I was ashamed,
And so I am worthy to be blamed;
Thus may I well myself hate.
Of whom shall I now counsel take?

480 I think that I shall never speed
     Till that I go to my Good Deed.
     But alas, she is so weak
     That she can neither go° nor speak.   *walk*
     Yet will I venture° on her now.   *gamble*
485 My Good Deeds, where be you?
     GOOD DEEDS. [*speaking from the ground*] Here I lie, cold in the
           ground:
     Thy sins hath me sore bound
     That I cannot stear.°   *stir*
     EVERYMAN. O Good Deeds, I stand in fear:
490 I must you pray of counsel,
     For help now should come right well.
     GOOD DEEDS. Everyman, I have understanding
     That ye be summoned, account to make,
     Before Messiah of Jer'salem King.
495 And you do by me,[8] that journey with you will I take.
     EVERYMAN. Therefore I come to you my moan to make:
     I pray you that ye will go with me.
     GOOD DEEDS. I would full fain, but I cannot stand, verily.
     EVERYMAN. Why, is there anything on you fall?°   *fallen*
500 GOOD DEEDS. Yea, sir, I may thank you of all:
     If ye had perfectly cheered me,
     Your book of count full ready had be.

          [GOOD DEEDS *shows him the account book.*]

     Look, the books of your works and deeds eke,°   *also*
     As how they lie under the feet,
505 To your soul's heaviness.°   *distress*
     EVERYMAN. Our Lord Jesus help me!
     For one letter here I cannot see.
     GOOD DEEDS. There is a blind° reckoning in time of   *illegible*
           distress!
     EVERYMAN. Good Deeds, I pray you help me in this need,
510 Or else I am forever damned indeed.
     Therefore help me to make reckoning
     Before the Redeemer of all thing
     That King is and was and ever shall.
     GOOD DEEDS. Everyman, I am sorry of° your fall   *for*
515 And fain would help you and° I were able.   *if*
     EVERYMAN. Good Deeds, your counsel I pray you give me.
     GOOD DEEDS. That shall I do verily,
     Though that on my feet I may not go;
     I have a sister that shall with you also,
520 Called Knowledge, which shall with you abide
     To help you to make that dreadful reckoning.

          [*Enter* KNOWLEDGE.]

     KNOWLEDGE. Everyman, I will go with thee and be thy guide,
     In thy most need to go by thy side.

8. I.e., if you do what I say.

EVERYMAN. In good condition I am now in everything,
525   And am whole content with this good thing,
        Thanked be God my Creator.
GOOD DEEDS. And when she hath brought you there
        Where thou shalt heal thee of thy smart,°   *pain*
        Then go you with your reckoning and your Good Deeds
            together
530   For to make you joyful at heart
        Before the blessed Trinity.
EVERYMAN. My Good Deeds, gramercy!
        I am well content, certainly,
        With your words sweet.
535 KNOWLEDGE. Now go we together lovingly
        To Confession, that cleansing river.
EVERYMAN. For joy I weep—I would we were there!
        But I pray you give me cognition,°   *knowledge*
        Where dwelleth that holy man Confession?
540 KNOWLEDGE. In the House of Salvation:
        We shall us comfort, by God's grace.

            [KNOWLEDGE *leads* EVERYMAN *to* CONFESSION.]

        Lo, this is Confession: kneel down and ask mercy,
        For he is in good conceit° with God Almighty.   *esteem*
545 EVERYMAN. [*kneeling*] O glorious fountain that all uncleanness
            doth clarify,[9]
        Wash from me the spots of vice unclean,
        That on me no sin may be seen.
        I come with Knowledge for my redemption,
        Redempt° with heart and full contrition,   *redeemed*
550   For I am commanded a pilgrimage to take
        And great accounts before God to make.
        Now I pray you, Shrift, mother of Salvation,
        Help my Good Deeds for my piteous exclamation.
CONFESSION. I know your sorrow well, Everyman:
555   Because with Knowledge ye come to me,
        I will you comfort as well as I can,
        And a precious jewel I will give thee,
        Called Penance, voider° of adversity.   *expeller*
        Therewith shall your body chastised be—
560   With abstinence and perseverance in God's service.
        Here shall you receive that scourge of me,
        Which is penance strong° that ye must endure,   *harsh*
        To remember thy Saviour was scourged for thee
        With sharp scourges, and suffered it patiently.
565   So must thou ere thou 'scape that painful pilgrimage.
        Knowledge, keep° him in this voyage,   *guard*
        And by that time Good Deeds will be with thee.
        But in any wise be secure° of mercy—   *certain*

9. Purify.

For your time draweth fast—and ye will saved be.
570   Ask God mercy and he will grant, truly.
When with the scourge of penance man doth him°   *himself*
    bind,
The oil of forgiveness then shall he find.
EVERYMAN. Thanked be God for his gracious work,
For now I will my penance begin.
575   This hath rejoiced and lighted my heart,
Though the knots[1] be painful and hard within.
KNOWLEDGE. Everyman, look your penance that ye fulfill,
What pain that ever it to you be;
And Knowledge shall give you counsel at will
580   How your account ye shall make clearly.
EVERYMAN. O eternal God, O heavenly figure,
O way of righteousness, O goodly vision,
Which descended down in a virgin pure
Because he would every man redeem,
585   Which Adam forfeited by his disobedience;
O blessed Godhead, elect and high Divine,°   *divinity*
Forgive my grievous offense!
Here I cry thee mercy in this presence:
O ghostly Treasure, O Ransomer and Redeemer,
590   Of all the world Hope and Conduiter,°   *guide*
Mirror of joy, Foundator° of mercy,   *Founder*
Which enlumineth° heaven and earth thereby,   *lights up*
Hear my clamorous complaint, though it late be;
Receive my prayers, of thy benignity.
595   Though I be a sinner most abominable,
Yet let my name be written in Moses' table.[2]
O Mary, pray to the Maker of all thing
Me for to help at my ending,
And save me from the power of my enemy,
600   For Death assaileth me strongly.
And Lady, that I may by mean of thy prayer
Of your Son's glory to be partner—
By the means of his passion I it crave.
I beseech you help my soul to save.
605   Knowledge, give me the scourge of penance:
My flesh therewith shall give acquittance.°   *satisfaction for sins*
I will now begin, if God give me grace.
KNOWLEDGE. Everyman, God give you time and
    space!°   *opportunity*
Thus I bequeath you in the hands of our Saviour:
610   Now may you make your reckoning sure.
EVERYMAN. In the name of the Holy Trinity
My body sore punished shall be:

---

1. I.e., the knots on the scourge (whip) of penance.   recorded those who have been baptized and have
"Within": i.e., to my senses.   done penance.
2. "Moses' table" is here the tablet on which are

Take this, body, for the sin of the flesh!
Also° thou delightest to go gay and fresh,   *as*
615   And in the way of damnation thou did me bring,
Therefore suffer now strokes of punishing!
Now of penance I will wade the water clear,
To save me from purgatory, that sharp fire.
GOOD DEEDS. I thank God, now can I walk and go,
620   And am delivered of my sickness and woe.
Therefore with Everyman I will go, and not spare:
His good works I will help him to declare.
KNOWLEDGE. Now, Everyman, be merry and glad:
Your Good Deeds cometh now, ye may not be sad.
625   Now is your Good Deeds whole and sound,
Going° upright upon the ground.   *walking*
EVERYMAN. My heart is light, and shall be evermore.
Now will I smite faster than I did before.
GOOD DEEDS. Everyman, pilgrim, my special friend,
630   Blessed be thou without end!
For thee is preparate° the eternal glory.   *prepared*
Ye have me made whole and sound
Therefore I will bide by thee in every stound.°   *trial*
EVERYMAN. Welcome, my Good Deeds! Now I hear thy voice,
635   I weep for very sweetness of love.
KNOWLEDGE. Be no more sad, but ever rejoice:
God seeth thy living in his throne above.
Put on this garment to thy behove,°   *advantage*
Which is wet with your tears—
640   Or else before God you may it miss
When ye to your journey's end come shall.
EVERYMAN. Gentle Knowledge, what do ye it call?
KNOWLEDGE. It is a garment of sorrow;
From pain it will you borrow:°   *redeem*
645   Contrition it is
That getteth forgiveness;
It pleaseth God passing° well.   *surpassingly*
GOOD DEEDS. Everyman, will you wear it for your heal?°   *welfare*
EVERYMAN. Now blessed be Jesu, Mary's son,
650   For now have I on true contrition.
And let us go now without tarrying.
Good Deeds, have we clear our reckoning?
GOOD DEEDS. Yea, indeed, I have it here.
EVERYMAN. Then I trust we need not fear.
655   Now friends, let us not part in twain.
KNOWLEDGE. Nay, Everyman, that will we not, certain.
GOOD DEEDS. Yet must thou lead with thee
Three persons of great might.
EVERYMAN. Who should they be?
660   GOOD DEEDS. Discretion and Strength they hight,°   *are called*
And thy Beauty may not abide behind.

KNOWLEDGE. Also ye must call to mind
   Your Five-Wits° as for your counselors.   *senses*
GOOD DEEDS. You must have them ready at all hours.
665 EVERYMAN. How shall I get them hither?
KNOWLEDGE. You must call them all togither,
   And they will be here incontinent.°   *at once*
EVERYMAN. My friends, come hither and be present,
   Discretion, Strength, my Five-Wits, and Beauty!

   [*They enter.*]

670 BEAUTY. Here at your will we be all ready.
   What will ye that we should do?
GOOD DEEDS. That ye would with Everyman go
   And help him in his pilgrimage.
   Advise you:[3] will ye with him or not in that voyage?
675 STRENGTH. We will bring him all thither,
   To his help and comfort, ye may believe me.
DISCRETION. So will we go with him all togither.
EVERYMAN. Almighty God, loved° might thou be!   *praised*
   I give thee laud that I have hither brought
680   Strength, Discretion, Beauty, and Five-Wits—lack I nought—
   And my Good Deeds, with Knowledge clear,
   All be in my company at my will here:
   I desire no more to my business.
STRENGTH. And I, Strength, will by you stand in distress,
685   Though thou would in battle fight on the ground.
FIVE-WITS. And though it were through the world round,
   We will not depart for sweet ne sour.
BEAUTY. No more will I, until death's hour,
   Whatsoever thereof befall.
690 DISCRETION. Everyman, advise you first of all:
   Go with a good advisement° and deliberation.   *preparation*
   We all give you virtuous° monition°   *confident / prediction*
   That all shall be well.
EVERYMAN. My friends, hearken what I will tell;
695   I pray God reward you in his heaven-sphere;
   Now hearken all that be here,
   For I will make my testament,
   Here before you all present:
   In alms half my good° I will give with my hands twain,   *goods*
700   In the way of charity with good intent;
   And the other half, still[4] shall remain,
   I 'queath° to be returned there it ought to be.   *bequeath*
   This I do in despite of the fiend of hell,
   To go quit out of his perel,[5]
705   Ever after and this day.
KNOWLEDGE. Everyman, hearken what I say:
   Go to Priesthood, I you advise,
   And receive of him, in any wise,[6]

---

3. Take thought.
4. I.e., which still.
5. In order to go free of danger from him.
6. At all costs.

The holy sacrament and ointment° togither;   *extreme unction*
710   Then shortly see ye turn again hither:
        We will all abide you here.
     FIVE-WITS. Yea, Everyman, hie you that ye ready were.
        There is no emperor, king, duke, ne baron,
        That of God hath commission
715   As hath the least priest in the world being:
        For of the blessed sacraments pure and bening°   *benign*
        He beareth the keys, and thereof hath the cure°   *care*
        For man's redemption—it is ever sure—
        Which God for our souls' medicine
720   Gave us out of his heart with great pine,°   *torment*
        Here in this transitory life for thee and me.
        The blessed sacraments seven there be:
        Baptism, confirmation, with priesthood° good,   *ordination*
        And the sacrament of God's precious flesh and blood,
725   Marriage, the holy extreme unction, and penance:
        These seven be good to have in remembrance,
        Gracious sacraments of high divinity.
     EVERYMAN. Fain° would I receive that holy body,   *gladly*
        And meekly to my ghostly° father I will go.   *spiritual*
730 FIVE-WITS. Everyman, that is the best that ye can do:
        God will you to salvation bring.
        For priesthood exceedeth all other thing:
        To us Holy Scripture they do teach,
        And converteth man from sin, heaven to reach;
735   God hath to them more power given
        Than to any angel that is in heaven.
        With five words[7] he may consecrate
        God's body in flesh and blood to make,
        And handleth his Maker between his hands.
740   The priest bindeth and unbindeth all bands,[8]
        Both in earth and in heaven.
        Thou ministers° all the sacraments seven;   *administer*
        Though we kiss thy feet, thou were worthy;
        Thou art surgeon that cureth sin deadly;
745   No remedy we find under God
        But all only priesthood.[9]
        Everyman, God gave priests that dignity
        And setteth them in his stead among us to be.
        Thus be they above angels in degree.

            [*Exit* EVERYMAN.]

750 KNOWLEDGE. If priests be good, it is so, surely.
        But when Jesu hanged on the cross with great smart,°   *pain*
        There he gave out of his blessed heart
        The same sacrament in great torment,

---

7. The 5 words ("For this is my body") spoken by the priest when he offers the wafer at communion.
8. A reference to the power of the keys, inherited by the priesthood from St. Peter, who received it from Christ (Matthew 16.19) with the promise that whatever St. Peter bound or loosed on earth would be bound or loosed in heaven.
9. Except from priesthood alone.

He sold them not to us, that Lord omnipotent:
755   Therefore Saint Peter the Apostle doth say
       That Jesu's curse hath all they
       Which God their Saviour do buy or sell,[1]
       Or they for any money do take or tell.[2]
       Sinful priests giveth the sinners example bad:
760   Their children sitteth by other men's fires, I have heard;
       And some haunteth women's company
       With unclean life, as lusts of lechery.
       These be with sin made blind.
    FIVE-WITS. I trust to God no such may we find.
765   Therefore let us priesthood honor,
       And follow their doctrine for our souls' succor.
       We be their sheep and they shepherds be
       By whom we all be kept in surety.
       Peace, for yonder I see Everyman come,
770   Which hath made true satisfaction.
    GOOD DEEDS. Methink it is he indeed.

       [*Re-enter* EVERYMAN.]

    EVERYMAN. Now Jesu be your alder speed![3]
       I have received the sacrament for my redemption,
       And then mine extreme unction.
775   Blessed be all they that counseled me to take it!
       And now, friends, let us go without longer respite.
       I thank God that ye have tarried so long.
       Now set each of you on this rood° your hond   *cross*
       And shortly follow me:
780   I go before there° I would be. God be our guide!   *where*
    STRENGTH. Everyman, we will not from you go
       Till ye have done this voyage long.
    DISCRETION. I, Discretion, will bide by you also.
    KNOWLEDGE. And though this pilgrimage be never so
                  strong,°   *harsh*
785   I will never part you fro.
    STRENGTH. Everyman, I will be as sure by thee
       As ever I did by Judas Maccabee.[4]
    EVERYMAN. Alas, I am so faint I may not stand—
       My limbs under me doth fold!
790   Friends, let us not turn again to this land,
       Not for all the world's gold.
       For into this cave must I creep
       And turn to earth, and there to sleep.
    BEAUTY. What, into this grave, alas?
795   EVERYMAN. Yea, there shall ye consume,° more and lass.[5]   *decay*
    BEAUTY. And what, should I smother here?

1. To give or receive money for the sacraments is
simony, named after Simon, who wished to buy
the gift of the Holy Ghost and was cursed by St.
Peter.
2. Or who, for any sacrament, take or count out
money.

3. The prosperer of you all.
4. Judas Maccabaeus was an enormously powerful warrior in the defense of Israel against the Syr-
ians in late Old Testament times.
5. More and less (i.e., all of you).

EVERYMAN. Yea, by my faith, and nevermore appear.
   In this world live no more we shall,
   But in heaven before the highest Lord of all.
800 BEAUTY. I cross out all this! Adieu, by Saint John—
   I take my tape in my lap and am gone.[6]
EVERYMAN. What, Beauty, whither will ye?
BEAUTY. Peace, I am deaf—I look not behind me,
   Not and thou wouldest give me all the gold in thy chest.

     [*Exit* BEAUTY.]

805 EVERYMAN. Alas, whereto may I trust?
   Beauty goeth fast away fro me—
   She promised with me to live and die!
STRENGTH. Everyman, I will thee also forsake and deny.
   Thy game liketh° me not at all.   *pleases*
810 EVERYMAN. Why then, ye will forsake me all?
   Sweet Strength, tarry a little space.
STRENGTH. Nay, sir, by the rood of grace,
   I will hie me from thee fast,
   Though thou weep till thy heart tobrast.°   *break*
815 EVERYMAN. Ye would ever bide by me, ye said.
STRENGTH. Yea, I have you far enough conveyed!°   *escorted*
   Ye be old enough, I understand,
   Your pilgrimage to take on hand:
   I repent me that I hither came.
820 EVERYMAN. Strength, you to displease I am to blame,[7]
   Yet promise is debt, this ye well wot.°   *know*
STRENGTH. In faith, I care not:
   Thou art but a fool to complain;
   You spend your speech and waste your brain.
825   Go, thrust thee into the ground.

     [*Exit* STRENGTH.]

EVERYMAN. I had weened° surer I should you have   *supposed*
     found.
   He that trusteth in his Strength
   She him deceiveth at the length.
   Both Strength and Beauty forsaketh me—
830   Yet they promised me fair and lovingly.
DISCRETION. Everyman, I will after Strength be gone:
   As for me, I will leave you alone.
EVERYMAN. Why Discretion, will ye forsake me?
DISCRETION. Yea, in faith, I will go from thee.
835   For when Strength goeth before,
   I follow after evermore.
EVERYMAN. Yet I pray thee, for the love of the Trinity,
   Look in my grave once piteously.
DISCRETION. Nay, so nigh will I not come.
840   Farewell everyone!

6. I tuck my skirts in my belt and am off.   7. I'm to blame for displeasing you.

[*Exit* DISCRETION.]

EVERYMAN. O all thing faileth save God alone—
  Beauty, Strength, and Discretion.
  For when Death bloweth his blast
  They all run fro me full fast.
845 FIVE-WITS. Everyman, my leave now of thee I take.
  I will follow the other, for here I thee forsake.
EVERYMAN. Alas, then may I wail and weep,
  For I took you for my best friend.
FIVE-WITS. I will no longer thee keep.°   *watch over*
850   Now farewell, and there an end!

      [*Exit* FIVE-WITS.]

EVERYMAN. O Jesu, help, all hath forsaken me!
GOOD DEEDS. Nay, Everyman, I will bide with thee:
  I will not forsake thee indeed;
  Thou shalt find me a good friend at need.
855 EVERYMAN. Gramercy, Good Deeds! Now may I true friends
          see.
  They have forsaken me every one—
  I loved them better than my Good Deeds alone.
  Knowledge, will ye forsake me also?
KNOWLEDGE. Yea, Everyman, when ye to Death shall go,
860   But not yet, for no manner of danger.
EVERYMAN. Gramercy, Knowledge, with all my heart!
KNOWLEDGE. Nay, yet will I not from hence depart
  Till I see where ye shall become.[8]
EVERYMAN. Methink, alas, that I must be gone
865   To make my reckoning and my debts pay,
  For I see my time is nigh spent away.
  Take example, all ye that this do hear or see,
  How they that I best loved do forsake me,
  Except my Good Deeds that bideth truly.
870 GOOD DEEDS. All earthly things is but vanity.
  Beauty, Strength, and Discretion do man forsake,
  Foolish friends and kinsmen that fair spake—
  All fleeth save Good Deeds, and that am I.
EVERYMAN. Have mercy on me, God most mighty,
875   And stand by me, thou mother and maid, holy Mary!
GOOD DEEDS. Fear not: I will speak for thee.
EVERYMAN. Here I cry God mercy!
GOOD DEEDS. Short our end, and 'minish our pain.[9]
  Let us go, and never come again.
880 EVERYMAN. Into thy hands, Lord, my soul I commend:
  Receive it, Lord, that it be not lost.
  As thou me boughtest,° so me defend,   *redeemed*
  And save me from the fiend's boast,
  That I may appear with that blessed host

8. Till I see what shall become of you.
9. I.e., make our dying quick and diminish our pain.

885   That shall be saved at the day of doom.
       In manus tuas, of mights most,
       Forever *commendo spiritum meum.*[1]

         [EVERYMAN *and* GOOD DEEDS *descend into the grave.*]

     KNOWLEDGE. Now hath he suffered that we all shall endure,
       The Good Deeds shall make all sure.
890   Now hath he made ending,
       Methinketh that I hear angels sing
       And make great joy and melody
       Where Everyman's soul received shall be.
     ANGEL. [*within*] Come, excellent elect° spouse to Jesu![2]   *chosen*
895   Here above thou shalt go
       Because of thy singular virtue.
       Now the soul is taken the body fro,
       Thy reckoning is crystal clear:
       Now shalt thou into the heavenly sphere—
900   Unto the which all ye shall come
       That liveth well before the day of doom.

         [*Enter* DOCTOR.[3]]

     DOCTOR. This memorial° men may have in mind: *reminder*
       Ye hearers, take it of worth,[4] old and young,
       And forsake Pride, for he deceiveth you in the end.
905   And remember Beauty, Five-Wits, Strength, and Discretion,
       They all at the last do Everyman forsake,
       Save his Good Deeds there doth he take—
       But beware, for and they be small,
       Before God he hath no help at all—
910   None excuse may be there for Everyman.
       Alas, how shall he do than?°   *then*
       For after death amends may no man make,
       For then mercy and pity doth him forsake.
       If his reckoning be not clear when he doth come,
915   God will say, "*Ite, maledicti, in ignem eternum!*"[5]
       And he that hath his account whole and sound,
       High in heaven he shall be crowned,
       Unto which place God bring us all thither,
       That we may live body and soul together.
920   Thereto help, the Trinity!
       Amen, say ye, for saint charity.

---

1. "Into thy hands, O greatest of powers, I commend my spirit forever."
2. Man's soul is often referred to as the bride of Jesus.
3. The Doctor is the learned theologian who explains the meaning of the play.
4. Prize it.
5. "Depart, ye cursed, into everlasting fire."

MARGERY KEMPE
ca. 1373—1438

The Book of Margery Kempe is the spiritual autobiography of a medieval housewife, telling of her struggles to carry out instructions for a holy life that she claimed to have received in personal visions from Christ and the Virgin Mary. The assertion of such a mission by a married woman, the mother of fourteen children, was in itself sufficient grounds for controversy; in addition, Margery Kempe's outspoken defense of her visions as well as her highly emotional style of religious expression embroiled her with fellow citizens and pilgrims and with the Church, though she also won both lay and clerical supporters. Ordered by the archbishop of York to swear not to teach in his diocese, she courageously stood up for her freedom to speak her conscience.

Margery Kempe was the daughter of John Burnham, five-time mayor of King's Lynn, a thriving commercial town in Norfolk. At about the age of twenty she married John Kempe, a well-to-do fellow townsman. After the traumatic delivery of her first child—the rate of maternal mortality in childbirth was high—she sought to confess to a priest whose harsh, censorious response precipitated a mental breakdown, from which she eventually recovered through the first of her visions. Her subsequent conversion and strict religious observances generated a good deal of domestic strife, but she continued to share her husband's bed until, around the age of forty, she negotiated a vow of celibacy with him, which was confirmed before the bishop and left her free to undertake a pilgrimage to the Holy Land. There she experienced visions of Christ's passion and of the sufferings of the Virgin. These visions recurred during the rest of her life, and her noisy weeping at such times made her the object of much scorn and hostility. Her orthodoxy was several times examined, as in her famous encounter with the archbishop of York, but her unquestioning acceptance of the Church's doctrines and authority, and perhaps also her status as a former mayor's daughter, shielded her against charges of heresy.

Like the Wife of Bath in the *Canterbury Tales*, Margery Kempe was illiterate and acquired her command of Scripture and theology from sermons and other oral sources. Late in her life, she dictated her story in two parts to two different scribes; the latter of these was a priest who revised the whole text. Nevertheless, it seems certain that the work retains the characteristic form and expression of its author.

Margery Kempe was an exceptional woman and was regarded by many of her contemporaries as an eccentric and even a heretic. The generally accepted way for a woman to follow a religious vocation was for her to enter a convent or to become a recluse like Julian of Norwich, author of a profound mystical treatise, *The Revelations of Divine Love*. Margery tells of her visit to the famous anchoress; the two women talked, and Julian seems to have understood and approved of Kempe's way of life. Modern scholars have linked that way of life to patterns of late-medieval religious experience. In particular, she exemplifies the affective piety advocated by the Franciscans, which emphasized the importance of love through a direct experiential knowledge of Christ by every Christian. *The Book of Margery Kempe* is a remarkable record of the powerful and potentially liberating effect this doctrine exercised upon the fifteenth-century laity, and on women in particular.

From The Book of Margery Kempe[1]

[*The Birth of Her First Child and Her First Vision*]

When this creature[2] was twenty year of age or somedeal more, she was married to a worshipful burgess and was with child within short time, as kind[3] would. And after that she had conceived, she was labored with great accesses[4] till the child was born, and then, what for labor she had in childing and for sickness going before, she despaired of her life, weening[5] she might not live. And then she sent for her ghostly father,[6] for she had a thing in conscience which she had never showed before that time in all her life. For she was ever letted[7] by her enemy, the Devil, evermore saying to her while she was in good heal[8] her needed no confession but [to] do penance by herself alone, and all should be forgiven, for God is merciful enow. And therefore this creature oftentimes did great penance in fasting bread and water and other deeds of alms with devout prayers, save she would not show it in confession. And when she was any time sick or diseased, the Devil said in her mind that she should be damned for she was not shriven of that default.[9] Wherefore after that her child was born she, not trusting her life, sent for her ghostly father, as said before, in full will to be shriven of all her lifetime as near as she could. And, when she came to the point for to say that thing which she had so long concealed, her confessor was a little too hasty and gan sharply to undernim[1] her ere that she had fully said her intent, and so she would no more say for nought he might do.

And anon for dread she had of damnation on that one side and his sharp reproving on that other side, this creature went out of her mind and was wonderly vexed and labored with spirits half year eight weeks and odd days. And in this time she saw, as her thought, devils open their mouths all inflamed with burning lows[2] of fire as they should 'a swallowed her in, sometime ramping[3] at her, sometime threating her, sometime pulling her and hauling her both night and day during the foresaid time. And also the devils cried upon her with great threatings and bade her she should forsake her Christendom, her faith, and deny her God, his Mother, and all the saints in Heaven, her good works and all good virtues, her father, her mother, and all her friends. And so she did. She

1. The text is based on the unique manuscript, first discovered in 1934, edited by Sanford B. Meech and Hope Emily Allen, but has been freely edited. Spelling has been modernized. The selections here given are from chaps. 1, 2, 11, 28, and 52.
2. Throughout the book Margery refers to herself in the third person as "this creature," a standard way of saying "this person, a being created by God."
3. Nature.

4. Fits of pain.
5. Supposing.
6. Spiritual father, i.e., a priest.
7. Prevented.
8. Health.
9. Sin.
1. Rebuke. "Gan": began.
2. Blazes.
3. Raising their arms.

slandered her husband, her friends, and her own self; she spoke many a reprevous word and many a shrewd[4] word; she knew no virtue nor goodness; she desired all wickedness; like as the spirits tempted her to say and do so she said and did. She would 'a fordone[5] herself many a time at their steering[6] and 'a been damned with them in Hell, and into witness thereof she bit her own hand so violently that it was seen all her life after. And also she rived[7] her skin on her body again her heart with her nails spiteously,[8] for she had none other instruments, and worse she would 'a done save she was bound and kept with strength both day and night that she might not have her will.

And when she had long been labored in this and many other temptations that men weened she should never 'a scaped[9] or lived, then on a time as she lay alone and her keepers were from her, our merciful Lord Christ Jesu, ever to be trusted (worshiped be his name) never forsaking his servant in time of need, appeared to his creature, which had forsaken him, in likeness of a man, most seemly, most beauteous, and most amiable that ever might be seen with man's eye, clad in a mantle of purple silk, sitting upon her bed's side, looking upon her with so blessed a cheer[1] that she was strengthened in all her spirits, said to her these words: "Daughter, why hast thou forsaken me, and I forsook never thee?" And anon as he had said these words she saw verily how the air opened as bright as any levin,[2] and he sty[3] up into the air, not right hastily and quickly, but fair and easily that she might well behold him in the air till it was closed again. And anon the creature was stabled[4] in her wits and in her reason as well as ever she was before, and prayed her husband as so soon as he came to her that she might have the keys of the buttery[5] to take her meat and drink as she had done before.

[Her Pride and Attempts To Start a Business]

And when this creature was thus graciously come again to her mind, she thought she was bound to God and that she would be his servant. Nevertheless, she would not leave her pride nor her pompous array that she had used beforetime, neither for her husband nor for none other man's counsel. And yet she wist full well that men said her full much villainy, for she wore gold pipes on her head and her hoods with the tippets were dagged.[6] Her cloaks also were dagged and laid with divers colors between the dags that it should be the more staring[7] to men's sight and herself the more be worshiped. And when her husband would speak to her for to leave her pride she answered shrewdly and shortly and said

---

4. Wicked. "Reprevous": reproachful.
5. Destroyed.
6. Direction.
7. Tore.
8. Cruelly.
9. Escaped.
1. Expression.
2. Flash of lightning.

3. Ascended.
4. Made stable.
5. Pantry.
6. I.e., her hoods were ornamented with loose bands of cloth ("tippets") and slashed according to high fashion of the time. "Pipes": tubular head ornaments.
7. Obtrusive.

that she was come of worthy kindred—him seemed never for to 'a wedded her[8]—for her father was sometime mayor of the town N and sithen[9]
he was alderman of the high Gild of the Trinity in N.[1] And therefore
she would save[2] the worship of her kindred whatsoever any man said.
She had full great envy at her neighbors that they should be arrayed as
well as she. All her desire was for to be worshiped of the people. She
would not beware by one's chastening nor be content with the good that
God had sent her, as her husband was, but ever desired more and more.

And then, for pure covetise[3] and for to maintain her pride, she gan to
brew and was one of the greatest brewers in the town N a three year or
four till she lost much good,[4] for she had never ure[5] thereto. For though
she had never so good servants and cunning[6] in brewing, yet it would
never prove[7] with them. For when the ale was as fair standing under
barm[8] as any man might see, suddenly the barm would fall down[9] that
all the ale was lost every brewing after other, that her servants were
ashamed and would not dwell with her. Then this creature thought how
God had punished her beforetime and she could not beware, and now
eftsoons[1] by losing of her goods, and then she left and brewed no more.
And then she asked her husband mercy for she would not follow his
counsel aforetime, and she said that her pride was cause of all her punishing and she would amend that she had trespassed with good will.

[Margery and Her Husband Reach a Settlement][2]

It befell upon a Friday on Midsummer Even in right hot weather, as
this creature was coming from York-ward[3] bearing a bottle with beer in
her hand and her husband a cake in his bosom, he asked his wife this
question: "Margery, if there came a man with a sword and would smite
off my head unless that I should commune kindly[4] with you as I have
done before, say me truth of your conscience—for ye say ye will not
lie—whether would ye suffer my head to be smit off or else suffer me to
meddle with you again as I did sometime?" "Alas, sir," she said, "why
move[5] ye this matter and have we been chaste this eight weeks?" "For I
will wit[6] the truth of your heart." And then she said with great sorrow,
"Forsooth, I had liefer[7] see you be slain than we should turn again to
our uncleanness." And he said again, "Ye are no good wife."

And then she asked her husband what was the cause that he had not

---

8. It never became him to have married her.
9. Afterward.
1. The merchant guild of Lynn was the Guild of
the Holy Trinity.
2. Maintain.
3. Avarice.
4. Wealth.
5. Experience [in brewing].
6. Skill.
7. Turn out well.
8. The froth or head.
9. I.e., go flat.

1. Again.
2. Despite her resolution, Margery Kempe made
one more attempt to run a profitable business: she
set up a horse mill to grind grain, but the horses
refused to draw, and the enterprise was as disastrous as her brewing had been. After that she did
indeed reform.
3. The direction of York.
4. In the way of nature.
5. Bring up.
6. Learn.
7. Rather.

meddled with her eight weeks before, sithen[8] she lay with him every night in his bed. And he said he was so made afeared when he would 'a touched her that he durst no more do. "Now, good sir, amend you and ask God mercy, for I told you near three year sithen that ye should be slain suddenly, and now is this the third year, and yet I hope I shall have my desire. Good sir, I pray you grant me that I shall ask, and I shall pray for you that ye shall be saved through the mercy of our Lord Jesu Christ, and ye shall have more meed[9] in Heaven than if ye wore a hair or a habergeon.[1] I pray you, suffer me to make a vow of chastity in what bishop's hand that God will." "Nay," he said, "that will I not grant you, for now I may use you without deadly sin and then might I not so." Then she said again, "If it be the will of the Holy Ghost to fulfill that I have said, I pray God ye might consent thereto; and if it be not the will of the Holy Ghost, I pray God ye never consent thereto."

Then went they forth to-Bridlington-ward[2] in right hot weather, the foresaid creature having great sorrow and great dread for her chastity. And as they came by a cross, her husband set him down under the cross, cleping[3] his wife unto him and saying these words unto her, "Margery, grant me my desire, and I shall grant you your desire. My first desire is that we shall lie still together in one bed as we have done before; the second that ye shall pay my debts ere ye go to Jerusalem; and the third that ye shall eat and drink with me on the Friday as ye were wont to do."[4] "Nay, sir," she said, "to break the Friday I will never grant you while I live." "Well," he said, "then shall I meddle with you again."

She prayed him that he would give her leave to make her prayers, and he granted it goodly. Then she knelt down beside a cross in the field and prayed in this manner with great abundance of tears, "Lord God, thou knowest all thing; thou knowest what sorrow I have had to be chaste in my body to thee all this three year, and now might I have my will and I dare not for love of thee. For if I would break that manner of fasting which thou commandest me to keep on the Friday without meat[5] or drink, I should now have my desire. But, blessed Lord, thou knowest I will not contrary thy will, and mickle[6] now is my sorrow unless that I find comfort in thee. Now, blessed Jesu, make thy will known to me unworthy that I may follow thereafter and fulfil it with all my might." And then our Lord Jesu Christ with great sweetness spoke to this creature, commanding her to go again to her husband and pray him to grant her that she desired, "And he shall have that he desireth. For, my dear-worthy daughter, this was the cause that I bade thee fast for thou should-est the sooner obtain and get thy desire, and now it is granted thee. I will no longer thou fast, therefore I bid thee in the name of Jesu eat and drink as thy husband doth."

---

8. Since.
9. Reward.
1. Hairshirt or mailshirt.
2. In the direction of Bridlington.
3. Calling.

4. Christ had told her that keeping a strict Friday fast would allow her to have her wish to end further sexual relations with her husband.
5. Food.
6. Much.

Then this creature thanked our Lord Jesu Christ of his grace and his goodness, sithen[7] rose up and went to her husband, saying unto him, "Sir, if it like[8] you, ye shall grant me my desire and ye shall have your desire. Granteth me that ye shall not come in my bed, and I grant you to quit your debts ere I go to Jerusalem. And maketh my body free to God so that ye never make no challenging in me[9] to ask no debt of matrimony after this day while ye live, and I shall eat and drink on the Friday at your bidding." Then said her husband again to her, "As free may your body be to God as it hath been to me." This creature thanked God greatly, enjoying that she had her desire, praying her husband that they should say three Pater Noster[1] in the worship of the Trinity for the great grace that he had granted them. And so they did, kneeling under a cross, and sithen they ate and drank together in great gladness of spirit. This was on a Friday on Midsummer Even.

[Pilgrimage to Jerusalem]

* * * And so they[2] went forth into the Holy Land till they might see Jerusalem. And when this creature saw Jerusalem, riding on an ass, she thanked God with all her heart, praying him for his mercy that like as he had brought her to see this earthly city Jerusalem, he would grant her grace to see the blissful city Jerusalem above, the city of Heaven. Our Lord Jesu Christ, answering to her thought, granted her to have her desire. Then for joy that she had and the sweetness that she felt in the dalliance[3] of our Lord, she was in point to 'a fallen off her ass, for she might not bear the sweetness and grace that God wrought in her soul. Then twain[4] pilgrims of Dutchmen went to her and kept her from falling, of which the one was a priest. And he put spices in her mouth to comfort her, weening[5] she had been sick. And so they helped her forth to Jerusalem. And when she came there, she said, "Sirs, I pray you be not displeased though I weep sore in this holy place where our Lord Jesu Christ was quick[6] and dead."

Then went they to the Temple in Jerusalem, and they were let in that one day at evensong time and they abide there till the next day at evensong time. Then the friars lifted up a cross and led the pilgrims about from one place to another where our Lord had suffered his pains and his passions, every man and woman bearing a wax candle in their hand. And the friars always as they went about told them what our Lord suffered in every place.[7] And the foresaid creature wept and sobbed so plentivously[8] as though she had seen our Lord with her bodily eye suffering his Passion at that time. Before her in her soul she saw him verily by contemplation, and that caused her to have compassion. And when

7. Afterward.
8. Please.
9. Make my body free to [be possessed by] God so that you never call me to account. Margery uses legal terminology.
1. "Our Father's."
2. The company of pilgrims.

3. Conversation.
4. Two.
5. Thinking.
6. Living.
7. I.e., in Jerusalem.
8. Plenteously.

they came up onto the Mount of Calvary she fell down that she might not stand nor kneel but wallowed and wrested[9] with her body, spreading her arms abroad, and cried with a loud voice as though her heart should 'a burst asunder, for in the city of her soul she saw verily and freshly how our Lord was crucified. Before her face she heard and saw in her ghostly sight the mourning of our Lady, of St. John and of Mary Magdalene,[1] and of many other that loved our Lord. And she had so great compassion and so great pain to see our Lord's pain that she might not keep herself from crying and roaring though she should 'a been dead therefore.

And this was the first cry that ever she cried in any contemplation. And this manner of crying endured many years after this time for aught that any man might do, and therefore suffered she much despite and much reproof. The crying was so loud and so wonderful that it made the people astoned[2] unless that they had heard it before or else that they knew the cause of the crying. And she had them so oftentimes that they made her right[3] weak in her bodily mights, and namely if she heard of our Lord's Passion. And sometime when she saw the Crucifix, or if she saw a man had a wound or a beast, whether[4] it were, or if a man beat a child before her or smote a horse or another beast with a whip, if she might see it or hear it, her thought she saw our Lord be beaten or wounded like as she saw in the man or in the beast, as well in the field as in the town, and by herself alone as well as among the people. First when she had her cryings at Jerusalem, she had them oftentimes, and in Rome also. And when she came home into England, first at her coming home it came but seldom as it were once in a month, sithen[5] once in the week, afterward quotidianly,[6] and once she had fourteen on one day, and another day she had seven, and so as God would visit her, sometime in the church, sometime in the street, sometime in the chamber, sometime in the field when God would send them, for she knew never time nor hour when they should come. And they came never without passing[7] great sweetness of devotion and high contemplation. And as soon as she perceived that she should cry, she would keep it in as much as she might that the people should not 'a heard it for noying[8] of them. For some said it was a wicked spirit vexed her; some said it was a sickness; some said she had drunken too much wine; some banned[9] her; some wished she had been in the haven;[1] some would she had been in the sea in a bottomless boat; and so each man as him thought. Other ghostly[2] men loved her and favored her the more. Some great clerks[3] said our Lady cried never so, nor no saint in Heaven, but they knew full little what

---

9. Twisted and turned.
1. Mary, St. John, and Mary Magdalene are traditionally portrayed at the foot of the cross in medieval art. See John 19.25.
2. Astonished.
3. Especially.
4. Whichever.
5. After.

6. Daily.
7. Surpassing.
8. Annoying.
9. Cursed.
1. Harbor.
2. Spiritual.
3. Clerics.

she felt, nor they would not believe but that she might 'a abstained her from crying if she had wished.

[Examination before the Archbishop]

There was a monk should preach in York, the which had heard much slander and much evil language of the said creature. And when he should preach, there was much multitude of people to hear him, and she present with them. And so when he was in his sermon, he rehearsed[4] many matters so openly that the people conceived well that it was for cause of her, wherefore her friends that loved her well were full sorry and heavy thereof, and she was much the more merry, for she had matter to prove her patience and her charity wherethrough she trusted to please our Lord Christ Jesu. When the sermon was done, a doctor of divinity which loved her well with many other also came to her and said, "Margery, how have ye done this day?" "Sir," she said, "right well, blessed be God. I have cause to be right merry and glad in my soul that I may anything suffer for his love, for he suffered much more for me."

Anon after came a man which loved her right well of good will with his wife and other more and led her seven mile thence to the Archbishop of York,[5] and brought her into a fair chamber, where came a good clerk, saying to the good man which had brought her thither, "Sir, why have ye and your wife brought this woman hither? She shall steal away from you, and then shall ye have a villainy[6] of her." The good man said, "I dare well say she will abide and be at her answer[7] with good will."

On the next day she was brought into the Archbishop's Chapel, and there came many of the Archbishop's meinie, despising her, calling her "loller"[8] and "heretic," and swore many an horrible oath that she should be burnt. And she through the strength of Jesu said again to them, "Sirs, I dread me ye shall be burnt in hell without end, unless that ye amend you of your oaths-swearing, for ye keep not the commandments of God. I would not swear as ye do for all the good[9] of this world." Then they went away as they had been ashamed. She then, making her prayer in her mind, asked grace so to be demeaned[1] that day as was most pleasance[2] to God and profit to her own soul and good example to her even-Christians.[3] Our Lord, answering her, said it should be right well.

At the last the said Archbishop came into the Chapel with his clerks and sharply he said to her, "Why goest thou in white? Art thou a maiden?" She, kneeling on her knees before him, said, "Nay, sir, I am no maiden; I am a wife." He commanded his men to fetch a pair of fetters and said she should be fettered, for she was a false heretic. And then she said, "I am none heretic, nor ye shall none prove me." The Archbishop went

4. Repeated.
5. The archbishop was at this time residing not in York but at his palace in Cawood.
6. Slander.
7. Answer charges against her.
8. Lollard: a follower of the reformer John Wycliffe.

"Meinie": household.
9. Property.
1. Treated.
2. Pleasing.
3. Fellow Christians.

away and let her stand alone. Then she made her prayers to our Lord God almighty for to help her and succor her against all her enemies, ghostly and bodily, a long while, and her flesh trembled and quaked wonderly that she was fain[4] to put her hands under her clothes that it should not be espied.

Sithen[5] the Archbishop came again into the Chapel with many worthy clerks, amongst which was the same doctor[6] which had examined her before and the monk that had preached again her a little time before in York. Some of the people asked whether she were a Christian woman or a Jew; some said she was a good woman, and some said nay. Then the Archbishop took his see,[7] and his clerks also, each of them in his degree, much people being present. And in the time while the people was gathering together and the Archbishop taking his see, the said creature stood all behind, making her prayers for help and succor against her enemies with high devotion so long that she melted all into tears. And at the last she cried loud therewith that the Archbishop and his clerks and much people had great wonder of her, for they had not heard such crying before.

When her crying was passed, she came before the Archbishop and fell down on her knees, the Archbishop saying full boistously[8] unto her, "Why weepest thou so, woman?" She answering said, "Sir, ye shall will some day that ye had wept as sore as I." And then anon after the Archbishop put to her the Articles of our Faith,[9] to the which God gave her grace to answer well and truly and readily without any great study so that he might not blame her, then he said to the clerks, "She knoweth her Faith well enough. What shall I do with her?" The clerks said, "We know well that she can[1] the Articles of the Faith, but we will not suffer her to dwell among us, for the people hath great faith in her dalliance, and peradventure[2] she might pervert some of them." Then the Archbishop said unto her, "I am evil informed of thee; I hear say thou art a right wicked woman." And she said again, "Sir, so I hear say that ye are a wicked man. And if ye be as wicked as men say, ye shall never come in Heaven unless that ye amend you while ye be here." Then said he full boistously, "Why, thou wretch, what say men of me?" She answered, "Other men, sir, can tell you well enow." Then said a great clerk with a furred hood, "Peace, thou speak of thyself and let him be."

Sithen said the Archbishop to her, "Lay thine hand on the book here before me and swear that thou shalt go out of my diocese as soon as thou may." "Nay, sir," she said, "I pray you, give me leave to go again into York to take my leave of my friends." Then he gave her leave for one day or two. She thought it was too short a time, wherefore she said again, "Sir, I may not go out of this diocese so hastily, for I must tarry

---

4. Glad.
5. Then.
6. Doctor of theology.
7. Throne.
8. Coarsely.

9. The 12 separate statements of the Apostles' Creed.
1. Knows.
2. Perhaps. "Dalliance": conversation.

and speak with good men ere I go, and I must, sir, with your leave, go to Bridlington and speak with my confessor, a good man, the which was the good Prior's confessor that is now canonized."[3] Then said the Archbishop to her, "Thou shalt swear that thou shalt not teach nor challenge the people in my diocese." "Nay, sir, I shall not swear," she said, "for I shall speak of God and undernim[4] them that swear great oaths wheresoever I go unto the time that the Pope and Holy Church hath ordained that no man shall be so hardy to speak of God, for God almighty forbids not, sir, that we shall speak of him. And also the Gospel maketh mention that when the woman had heard our Lord preach, she came before him with a loud voice and said, 'Blessed be the womb that thee bore and the teats that gave thee suck.' Then our Lord said again to her, 'Forsooth so are they blessed that hear the word of God and keep it.' And therefore, sir, me thinketh that the Gospel giveth me leave to speak of God." "Ah, sir," said the clerks, "here woot[5] we well that she hath a devil within her, for she speaks of the Gospel." As swithe[6] a great clerk brought forth a book and laid Saint Paul for his party[7] against her that no woman should preach. She answering thereto said, "I preach not, sir, I come in no pulpit. I use but communication and good words, and that will I do while I live." Then said a doctor which had examined her beforetime, "Sir, she told me the worst tales of priests that ever I heard." The Bishop commanded her to tell that tale. "Sir, with your reverence, I spoke but of one priest by the manner of example."[8] * * *

Then the Archbishop liked well the tale and commended it, saying it was a good tale. And the clerk which had examined her beforetime in the absence of the Archbishop said, "Sir, this tale smiteth me to the heart." The foresaid creature said to the clerk, "Ah, worshipful doctor, sir, in place where my dwelling is most is a worthy clerk, a good preacher, which boldly speaketh again the misgovernance[9] of the people and will flatter no man. He sayeth many times in the pulpit, 'If any man be evil-pleased with my preaching, note him well, for he is guilty.' And right so, sir," said she to the clerk, "fare ye by me,[1] God forgive it you." The clerk wist not well what he might say to her. Afterward the same clerk came to her and prayed her of forgiveness that he had so been again her. Also he prayed her specially to pray for him.

And then anon[2] after the Archbishop said, "Where shall I have a man that might lead this woman from me?" As swithe there started up many young men, and every man said of them, "My Lord, I will go with her." The Archbishop answered, "Ye be too young; I will not have you." Then a good sad[3] man of the Archbishop's meinie asked his Lord what he would give him and[4] he should lead her. The Archbishop proffered

---

3. St. John of Bridlington, recently canonized.
4. Reprove.
5. Know.
6. At once.
7. Side of the argument.
8. Here she tells an exemplary story of a priest who learns the depths of his own wickedness when a

dream of his is interpreted to him.
9. Against the misconduct.
1. You behave with me.
2. Straightway.
3. Sober.
4. If.

him five shillings, and the man asked a noble.[5] The Archbishop answering said, "I will not ware[6] so much on her body." "Yes, good sir," said the said creature, "our Lord shall reward you right well again." Then the Archbishop said to the man, "See, here is five shillings, and lead her fast out of this country." She kneeling down on her knees asked his blessing. He, praying her to pray for him, blessed her and let her go. Then she going again to York was received of much people and of full worthy clerks, which enjoyed[7] in our Lord that had given her, not lettered, wit and wisdom to answer so many learned men without villainy or blame, thanking be to God.

1436–38

5. A coin worth 6 shillings and 8 pence.   7. Rejoiced.
6. Spend.

POPULAR BALLADS

Ballads are anonymous narrative songs that have been preserved by oral transmission. Although any stage of a given culture may produce ballads, they are most characteristic of primitive societies such as that of the American frontier in the eighteenth and nineteenth centuries or that of the English-Scottish border region in the later Middle Ages. These northern English songs, even divorced from the tunes to which they were once sung, are narrative poems of great literary interest.

The origins of the popular (or folk) ballad are much disputed. The theory that they were first composed by communal effort, taking shape as the songs with which primitive people accompanied ritual dances, no longer seems plausible. On the other hand, the forms in which the ballads have come down to us show that they have been subjected to a continuing process of revision, both conscious and unconscious, by those through whose lips and memories they passed. Though the English ballads were probably composed during the five-hundred-year period from 1200 to 1700, few of them were printed before the eighteenth century and some not until the nineteenth. Bishop Thomas Percy (1729–1811) was among the first to take a literary interest in ballads, stimulated by his chance discovery of a seventeenth-century manuscript in which a number of them had been copied down among a great welter of Middle English verse. Percy's publication of this material in his *Reliques of Ancient English Poetry* inspired others, notably Sir Walter Scott, to go to the living source of the ballads and to set them down on paper at the dictation of the border people among whom the old songs were still being sung. These collectors often found that one ballad was remembered differently by different people: for instance, when one speaks of *Sir Patrick Spens* one is actually speaking of a number of poems that tell the same story in slightly or widely different words. If a single original form by a single author lies behind this diversity, it is too far back in the mists of time to be recovered.

A work that is the product of a consciously artistic mind will not ordinarily be improved by the revision that most ballads have been subjected to, but some of the ballads are probably better in their revised form than they were in their original form. The distinctive quality that popular ballads share is spareness: they are apt to deal only with the culminating incident or climax of a plot, to describe that event with intense compression, to put the burden of narration on allusive monologue or dialogue, and to avoid editorial comment. This concentration upon the bare essential is precisely the quality that the fallible human memory is likely not only to preserve but also to enhance, for the effort of remembering causes a sloughing-off of what is not strictly relevant. Some of the best of the ballads may have thus been refined in their transmission through people's minds, gaining rather than losing artistic stature.

The fact that ballads were originally songs is important to their development. The simplicity of the tunes to which they were sung not only influenced the distinctive verse form—normally a quatrain with four stresses per line—but also encouraged a corresponding simplicity in the narrative itself, and made individualizing flourishes impossible. Furthermore, the choral practice of using refrains and other kinds of repetitions probably lent the ballad one of its most impressive qualities, for while the actual narratives are tightly compressed, ballads rarely develop in an unbroken line. The reader— originally, the hearer—is constantly made to pause by a repeated phrase, or even by nonsense syllables, which provide suspense in a very primitive and effective form. The progress to a foreknown, foredoomed conclusion is paradoxically made to seem more inevitable, more urgent, by such relaxations of narrative tension. The use of repetition and refrain also imparts to the ballads something of the quality of incantation, of ritual, of liturgy—all of which are, of course, themselves closely allied with music.

Most of the best ballads have as their subject a tragic incident, often a murder or accidental death, generally involving supernatural elements. These motifs are a part of the common legacy of European folklore, and many of the English ballads have counterparts in other languages. To this class belong, among the selections chosen for inclusion here, *Lord Randall*, *Edward*, *Barbara Allan*, *The Wife of Usher's Well*, *The Three Ravens*, and—though not in its present form—*Sir Patrick Spens*.

Some ballads go back to actual historical incidents. A late song, the *Bonny Earl of Murray*, laments the political murder of a popular sixteenth-century Scots noble. The presumably much older ballad *Sir Patrick Spens* may be based on a historical incident of the end of the thirteenth century. Yet both of these achieve that mood of sadness that is characteristic of the best of the tragic stories derived from ancient folklore. The quasi-historical Robin Hood ballads, which form a large class by themselves, are less impressive. Most of them seem to have been composed relatively late and hence not to have gone through many stages of oral transmission; they lack the better ballads' intensity, often exhibiting an expansive development that is not free from chattiness. They are probably the work of minstrels who exploited the old folklore figure of Robin Hood by making him a symbol of that rebellion against authority that their own hearers perhaps longed for but did not dare to undertake. In the ballads Robin Hood is placed in a kind of never-never land of English history, where he can strike down tyrants with impunity, but often with far too much gloating: the attractive folklore figure of a natural, freedom-loving man has been burdened with too many political and social implications.

The great collection of English ballads is that of F. J. Child, *The English and Scottish Popular Ballads*, first published in 1882. The numbers under which Child lists the various versions of each of the ballads printed here are given in footnotes to the individual titles. The versions chosen for this anthology are those which the editor considers the most effective as poetry. Spelling has been modernized; the majority of the northernisms in the originals have been retained.

Lord Randall[1]

"Oh where ha'e ye been, Lord Randall my son?
O where ha'e ye been, my handsome young man?"
　"I ha'e been to the wild wood: mother, make my bed soon,
　For I'm weary wi' hunting, and fain° wald° lie
　　down."　　　　　　　　　　　　　　　　　　*gladly / would*

5　"Where gat ye your dinner, Lord Randall my son?
　　Where gat ye your dinner, my handsome young man?"
　　"I dined wi' my true love: mother, make my bed soon,
　　For I'm weary wi' hunting, and fain wald lie down."

"What gat ye to your dinner, Lord Randall my son?
10　What gat ye to your dinner, my handsome young man?"
　　"I gat eels boiled in broo:° mother, make my bed
　　　soon,　　　　　　　　　　　　　　　　　　　　　*broth*
　　For I'm weary wi' hunting and fain wald lie down."

"What became of your bloodhounds, Lord Randall my son?
What became of your bloodhounds, my handsome young man?"
15　"O they swelled and they died: mother, make my bed soon,
　　For I'm weary wi' hunting and fain wald lie down."

"O I fear ye are poisoned, Lord Randall my son!
O I fear ye are poisoned, my handsome young man!"
　"Oh yes, I am poisoned: mother, make my bed soon,
20　For I'm sick at the heart, and I fain wald lie down."

Edward[1]

"Why does your brand sae drap wi' bluid,[2]
　Edward, Edward?
Why does your brand sae drap wi' bluid,
　And why sae sad gang° ye, O?"　　　　　　　　　　　*go*
5　"O I ha'e killed my hawk sae guid,
　Mither, mither,

---

1. Child, no. 12.　　　　　　　　2. I.e., why does your sword so drip with blood?
1. Child, no. 13.

O I ha'e killed my hawk sae guid,
  And I had nae mair° but he, O."   *more*

"Your hawkes bluid was never sae reid,°   *red*
10   Edward, Edward.
Your hawkes bluid was never sae reid,
  My dear son I tell thee, O."
"O I ha'e killed my reid-roan° steed,   *chestnut*
   Mither, mither,
15 O I ha'e killed my reid-roan° steed,
  That erst° was sae fair and free, O."   *before*

"Your steed was auld° and ye ha'e gat mair,   *old*
   Edward, Edward.
Your steed was auld and ye ha'e gat mair:
20 Som other dule° ye dree,° O."   *grief / suffer*
"O I ha'e killed my fader dear,
   Mither, mither,
"O I ha'e killed my fader dear,
  Alas and wae° is me, O!"   *woe*

25 "And whatten° penance wul ye dree for that, *what sort of*
   Edward, Edward?
And whatten penance wul ye dree for that,
  My dear son, now tell me, O?"
"I'll set my feet in yonder boat,
30   Mither, Mither,
I'll set my feet in yonder boat,
  And I'll fare over the sea, O."

"And what wul ye do wi' your towers and your ha',
   Edward, Edward,?
35 And what wul ye do wi' your towers and your ha',
  That were sae fair to see, O?"
"I'll let thame stand til they down fa',
   Mither, mither,
I'll let thame stand til they down fa',
40 For here never mair maun° I be, O."   *must*

"And what wul ye leave to your bairns° and your wife, *children*
   Edward, Edward,
And what wul ye leave to your bairns and your wife,
  Whan ye gang over the sea, O?"
45 "The warldes room[3] late° them beg thrae° life, *let / through*
   Mither, mither,
The warldes room late them beg thrae life,
  For thame never mair wul I see, O."

3. The world's space.

"And what wul ye leave to your ain° mither dear,   *own*
50   Edward, Edward?
    And what wul ye leave to your ain mither dear,
          My dear son, now tell me, O?"
    "The curse of hell frae° me sal° ye bear,   *from / shall*
          Mither, mither,
55 The curse of hell frae me sal ye bear,
          Sic° counseils ye gave to me, O."   *such*

Barbara Allan[1]

    It was in and about the Martinmas[2] time,
          When the green leaves were a-fallin';
    That Sir John Graeme in the West Country
          Fell in love with Barbara Allan.

5   He sent his man down through the town
          To the place where she was dwellin':
    "O haste and come to my master dear,
          Gin° ye be Barbara Allan."   *if*

    O slowly, slowly rase° she up,   *rose*
10   To the place where he was lyin',
    And when she drew the curtain by:
          "Young man, I think you're dyin'."

    "O it's I'm sick, and very, very sick,
          And 'tis a' for Barbara Allan."
15 "O the better for me ye sal° never be,   *shall*
          Though your heart's blood were a-spillin'.

    "O dinna ye mind,[3] young man," said she,
          "When ye the cups were fillin',
    That ye made the healths gae° round and round,   *go*
20   And slighted Barbara Allan?"

    He turned his face unto the wall,
          And death with him was dealin':
    "Adieu, adieu, my dear friends all,
          And be kind to Barbara Allan."

25 And slowly, slowly, rase she up,
          And slowly, slowly left him;
    And sighing said she could not stay,
          Since death of life had reft° him.   *deprived*

---

1. Child, no. 84.   3. Don't you remember.
2. November 11.

She had not gane° a mile but twa,°   *gone / two*
30 When she heard the dead-bell knellin',
And every jow° that the dead-bell ga'ed[4]   *stroke*
It cried, "Woe to Barbara Allan!"

"O mother, mother, make my bed,
O make it soft and narrow:
35 Since my love died for me today,
I'll die for him tomorrow."

The Wife of Usher's Well[1]

There lived a wife at Usher's Well,
And a wealthy wife was she;
She had three stout and stalwart sons,
And sent them o'er the sea.

5   They hadna' been a week from her,
A week but barely ane,°   *one*
When word came to the carlin° wife   *old*
That her three sons were gane.°   *gone*

They hadna' been a week from her,
10 A week but barely three,
When word came to the carlin wife
That her sons she'd never see.

"I wish the wind may never cease
Nor fashes° in the flood,   *disturbances*
15 Till my three sons come hame° to me,   *home*
In earthly flesh and blood."

It fell about the Martinmas,[2]
When nights are long and mirk,°   *dark*
The carlin wife's three sons came hame,
20 And their hats were o' the birk.[3]

It neither grew in sike° nor ditch,   *field*
Nor yet in ony sheugh,°   *furrow*
But at the gates o' Paradise
That birk grew fair eneugh.

25 "Blow up the fire, my maidens,
Bring water from the well:

---

4. I.e., made.
1. Child, no. 79.
2. November 11.

3. Birch: those returning from the dead were
thought to wear vegetation on their heads.

For a' my house shall feast this night,
 Since my three sons are well."

And she has made to them a bed,
30 She's made it large and wide,
And she's ta'en her mantle her about,
 Sat down at the bedside.

Up then crew the red, red cock,
 And up and crew the gray.
35 The eldest to the youngest said,
 " 'Tis time we were away."[4]

The cock he hadna' crawed but once,
 And clapped his wings at a',
When the youngest to the eldest said,
40 "Brother, we must awa'.°   *away*

"The cock doth craw, the day doth daw,°   *dawn*
 The channerin'° worm doth chide: *fretting*
Gin° we be missed out o' our place,   *if*
 A sair pain we maun bide.[5]

45 "Fare ye weel,° my mother dear,   *well*
 Fareweel to barn and byre.°   *cow house*
And fare ye weel, the bonny lass
 That kindles my mother's fire."

The Three Ravens[1]

There were three ravens sat on a tree,
 Down a down, hay down, hay down,
There were three ravens sat on a tree,
 With a down,

5 There were three ravens sat on a tree,
They were as black as they might be,
 With a down, derry, derry, derry, down, down.

The one of them said to his mate,
"Where shall we our breakfast take?

10 "Down in yonder green field
There lies a knight slain under his shield.

---

4. Dead men must return to their graves at cock-
crow.

5. A sore pain we must abide.
1. Child, no. 26.

"His hounds they lie down at his feet,
So well they can their master keep.

"His hawks they fly so eagerly,°   *fiercely*
15 There's no fowl° dare him come nigh."   *bird*

Down there comes a fallow° doe,   *red-brown*
As great with young as she might go.°   *walk*

She lifted up his bloody head,
And kissed his wounds that were so red.

20 She got him up upon her back,
And carried him to earthen lake.°   *pit*

She buried him before the prime;[2]
She was dead herself ere evensong time.

God send every gentleman
25 Such hawks, such hounds, and such a lemman.°   *mistress*

Sir Patrick Spens[1]

The king sits in Dumferline town,
    Drinking the blude-reid° wine: *blood-red*
"O whar will I get a guid sailor
    To sail this ship of mine?"

5 Up and spak an eldern° knicht,   *ancient*
    Sat at the king's richt knee:
"Sir Patrick Spens is the best sailor
    That sails upon the sea."

The king has written a braid° letter   *broad*
10   And signed it wi' his hand,
And sent it to Sir Patrick Spens,
    Was walking on the sand.

The first line that Sir Patrick read,
    A loud lauch° lauched he;   *laugh*
15 The next line that Sir Patrick read,
    The tear blinded his ee.°   *eye*

"O wha° is this has done this deed,   *who*
    This ill deed done to me,

---

2. The first hour of the morning.   1. Child, no. 58.

To send me out this time o' the year,
20 To sail upon the sea?

"Make haste, make haste, my mirry men all,
  Our guid ship sails the morn."
"O say na° sae,° my master dear,   *not / so*
  For I fear a deadly storm.

25 "Late late yestre'en I saw the new moon
  Wi' the auld° moon in her arm,   *old*
And I fear, I fear, my dear master,
  That we will come to harm."

O our Scots nobles were richt laith°   *loath*
30 To weet° their cork-heeled shoon,°   *wet / shoes*
But lang owre° a' the play were played   *ere*
  Their hats they swam aboon.°   *above*

O lang, lang may their ladies sit,
  Wi' their fans into their hand,
35 Or e'er they see Sir Patrick Spens
  Come sailing to the land.

O lang, lang may the ladies stand,
  Wi' their gold kembs° in their hair,   *combs*
Waiting for their ain° dear lords,   *own*
40 For they'll see thame na mair.°   *more*

Half o'er,[2] half o'er to Aberdour
  It's fifty fadom° deep,   *fathoms*
And there lies guid Sir Patrick Spens,
  Wi' the Scots lords at his feet.

The Bonny Earl of Murray[1]

Ye Highlands and ye Lawlands,°   *Lowlands*
  O where have you been?
They have slain the Earl of Murray,
  And they laid him on the green.

5 "Now wae° be to thee, Huntly,[2]   *woe*
  And wherefore did you sae?°   *so*
I bade you bring him wi' you,
  But forbade you him to slay."

---

2. Halfway over.
1. Child, no. 181.
2. Huntly, who slew Murray in 1592, had been

ordered by King James VI of Scotland (the speaker
of this stanza) to arrest the earl.

He was a braw° gallant,   *brave*
10   And he rid[3] at the ring;
And the bonny Earl of Murray,
    O he might have been a king.

He was a braw gallant,
    And he played at the ba';°   *ball*
15 And the Bonny Earl of Murray
    Was the flower amang them a'.

He was a braw gallant,
    And he played at the glove;[4]
And the bonny Earl of Murray,
20 O he was the queen's love.

O lang will his lady
    Look o'er the Castle Down,
Ere she see the Earl of Murray
    Come sounding[5] through the town.

Robin Hood and the Three Squires[1]

There are twelve months in all the year,
    As I hear many men say,
But the merriest month in all the year
    Is the merry month of May.

5 Now Robin Hood is to Nottingham gone,
    With a link-a-down and a-day,
And there he met a silly° old woman,   *poor, innocent*
    Was weeping on the way.

"What news? what news, thou silly old woman?
10 What news hast thou for me?"
Said she, "There's three squires in Nottingham town,
    Today is condemned to dee."°   *die*

"O have they parishes burnt?" he said,
    "Or have they ministers slain?
15 Or have they robbed any virgin,
    Or with other men's wives have lain?"

"They have no parishes burnt, good sir,
    Nor yet have ministers slain,

---

3. Rode. "The ring" was a hanging ring which   5. Blowing horns.
mounted knights tried to impale on their spears.   1. Child, no. 140.
4. Either the goal in a race or else a lady's favor.

Nor have they robbed any virgin,
20   Nor with other men's wives have lain."

"O what have they done?" said bold Robin Hood,
    "I pray thee tell to me."
"It's for slaying of the king's fallow° deer,   *brown-red*
    Bearing their longbows with thee."

25   "Dost thou not mind,° old woman," he said,   *remember*
    "Since thou made me sup and dine?
By the truth of my body," quoth bold Robin Hood,
    "You could not tell it in better time."

Now Robin Hood is to Nottingham gone,
30   *With a link-a-down and a-day,*
And there he met with a silly old palmer,[2]
    Was walking along the highway.

"What news? what news, thou silly old man?
    What news, I do thee pray?"
35   Said he, "Three squires in Nottingham town
    Are condemned to die this day."

"Come change thine apparel with me, old man,
    Come change thine apparel for mine.
Here is forty shillings in good silver,
40   Go drink it in beer or wine."

"O thine apparel is good," he said,
    "And mine is ragged and torn.
Wherever you go, wherever you ride,
    Laugh ne'er an old man to scorn."

45   "Come change thine apparel with me, old churl,
    Come change thine apparel with mine:
Here are twenty pieces of good broad gold,
    Go feast thy brethren with wine."

Then he put on the old man's hat,
50   It stood full high on the crown:
"The first bold bargain that I come at,
    It shall make thee come down."

Then he put on the old man's cloak,
    Was patched black, blue, and red:
55   He thought it no shame all the day long
    To wear the bags of bread.

---

2. A poor old palmer: a palmer was one who had made the pilgrimage to the Holy Land.

Then he put on the old man's breeks,°   *underbreeches*
    Was patched from ballup[3] to side:
"By the truth of my body," bold Robin can° say,   *did*
60   "This man loved little pride."

Then he put on the old man's hose,°   *tights*
    Were patched from knee to wrist:
"By the truth of my body," said bold Robin Hood,
    "I'd laugh if I had any list."°   *desire*

65 Then he put on the old man's shoes,
    Were patched both beneath and aboon:°   *above*
Then Robin Hood swore a solemn oath,
    "It's good habit° that makes a man."   *clothing*

Now Robin Hood is to Nottingham gone,
70   *With a link-a-down and a-down,*
And there he met with the proud sheriff,
    Was walking along the town.

"O Christ you save, O sheriff," he said,
    "O Christ you save and see:
75 And what will you give to a silly old man
    Today will your hangman be?"

"Some suits, some suits," the sheriff he said,
    "Some suits I'll give to thee;
Some suits, some suits, and pence thirteen,
80   Today's a hangman's fee."

Then Robin he turns him round about,
    And jumps from stock° to stone: *stump*
"By the truth of my body," the sheriff he said,
    "That's well jumped, thou nimble old man."

85 "I was ne'er a hangman in all my life,
    Nor yet intends to trade.
But cursed be he," said bold Robin,
    "That first a hangman was made.

"I've a bag for meal, and a bag for malt,
90   And a bag for barley and corn,
A bag for bread, and a bag for beef,
    And a bag for my little small horn.

"I have a horn in my pocket:
    I got it from Robin Hood;

---

3. I.e., center.

95 And still when I set it to my mouth,
    For thee it blows little good."

"O wind° thy horn, thou proud fellow: *blow*
    Of thee I have no doubt;°   *fear*
I wish that thou give such a blast
100   Till both thy eyes fall out."

The first loud blast that he did blow,
    He blew both loud and shrill,
A hundred and fifty of Robin Hood's men
    Came riding over the hill.

105 The next loud blast that he did give,
    He blew both loud and amain,
And quickly sixty of Robin Hood's men
    Came shining[4] over the plain.

"O who are those," the sheriff he said,
110   "Come tripping over the lea?"°   *meadow*
"They're my attendants," brave Robin did say,
    "They'll pay a visit to thee."

They took the gallows from the slack,°   *hollow*
    They set it in the glen;
115 They hanged the proud sheriff on that,
    Released their own three men.

4. I.e., making a brave show.

SIR THOMAS MALORY

ca. 1405–1471

1451:   First of a long series of arrests and imprisonments.
ca. 1469–70:   *Morte Darthur* completed in prison.
1485:   *Morte Darthur* printed by William Caxton.

The little that we know of Malory (and that the Malory discussed here was indeed the Malory who wrote the *Morte Darthur* is an assumption that has been challenged severely though by no means fatally) suggests a man of violent temperament much given to lawless action. He seems to have been a respectable enough person in his youth, but in 1451 he got into difficulties with the law that lasted the rest of his life. In that year he was arrested in order to prevent his doing injury—presumably further injury—to a priory in Lincolnshire, and shortly thereafter he was accused of a number of criminal acts. These included escaping from prison after his first arrest, twice breaking into and plundering the Abbey of Coombe, extorting money from various persons, and committing rape. Malory pleaded innocent of all charges, and it is indeed possible that he was less guilty of (or had more provocation for) the crimes than the records make it appear. The years of the Wars of the Roses were violent ones, when a supporter of the party out of power was apt to be subjected to much persecution by the ruling group; such a man might at times feel himself justified in taking the law into his own hands in order to recover what had wrongfully been taken from him. But one suspects that Malory took the law into his own hands with unnecessary enthusiasm.

How much time Malory passed in prison is not known, but he was surely a prisoner in 1468 after he had supported an unsuccessful Lancastrian revolt against the Yorkist king, Edward IV, who specifically excluded Malory from two amnesties granted to the Lancastrians. It was probably in prison that he became engaged on the *Morte Darthur*; he was still in prison when he completed it, and may have died there. The book was printed (and edited) in 1485 by William Caxton, the first English printer. A manuscript of it discovered in 1934 helps us to a better text than Caxton's.

Arthurian romance, of which Malory's book is a compilation, is a body of highly diverse narrative materials which originated at various times among various peoples and which only gradually became associated with the name of Arthur. Arthur himself was probably a British or Roman-British king who resisted the Anglo-Saxon invasions of England in the sixth century, but his historical reality is less important than the legendary role he played as the great figure around whom the medieval ideal of chivalry flourished. At its simplest, chivalry is the code that governs the actions of the knight-adventurer who rides out in search of wrongs that he may right—typically in search of ladies whom he may rescue from monsters, churls, and wicked (non-Arthurian) knights. The ideal was invented and given a local habitation in the brilliantly imaginative and idealistic twelfth century. History had, of course, never witnessed such knights, such ladies, nor such a landscape as that on which their adventures took place, and when chivalry was first invented it was already placed in the past. The human urge to devise an idealized past seems to be recurrent, for the Camelot of Arthur has its counterpart in the Sherwood Forest of Robin Hood and in the American West. All three of these fictions have the same ideal: that of maintaining order in an essentially lawless land by the efforts of the individual, who fights for the right against seemingly overwhelming odds. Naïve as the practice of this ideal may seem in the Arthurian fiction, the ideal itself has made an important contribution to civilization—though if one imitates literally the Arthurian practice of enforcing the right by violence, as Malory's life suggests that he did, one will find oneself not maintaining order, but disrupting it.

The Arthurian milieu attracted to itself all sorts of diverse motifs, such as the remnants of primitive pagan religious rites, heavily moralized Christianity, an elaborate and in general flagrantly immoral code of romantic love, and others equally miscellaneous. In thirteenth-century France the amorphous Arthurian material was given a kind of order in a series of prose narratives. Long and often rather vaguely told, these formed the chief material which Malory further edited and ordered while translating it into English.

His book is attractive, however, not only because it is the best and most complete treatment of the story of Arthur and his knights, but also because it is one of the greatest pieces of prose in English. Malory was the first

English writer to make prose as sensitive an instrument of narrative as English poetry had always been. One has only to turn from a page of Chaucer's prose to a page of Malory's to be struck by the naturalness and lack of self-consciousness of the later writer. Indeed, Malory achieves in his prose that wonderful impression of simplicity that Chaucer achieves only in his poetry. No matter how extravagant the adventure Malory is recounting, he always manages to give it a hard base of realism. He is in particular a master of naturalistic dialogue, with which he keeps his narrative close to earth. And both he and the majority of his characters are masters of understatement who express themselves, in moments of great emotional tension, with a bare minimum of words. The result is highly provocative to the reader's imagination, which is made, in a sense, to do the writer's work for him. This appeal to the reader's creative imagination probably explains why the *Morte Darthur* brings forth such widely differing responses from its readers, who agree, perhaps, only in their affection for the work.

Although Malory considerably abridged the immensely long French romances he was adapting, the *Morte Darthur* remains a work of imposing length. Its title, "The Death of Arthur" (which was given to it by its first editor, Caxton), although it rightly emphasizes the tragic nature of the ending, is misleading; for the bulk of the work is taken up with the separate adventures of the knights of the Round Table. Preeminent among these is Sir Lancelot, the "head of all Christian knights," as he is called in a great eulogy by his brother, Sir Ector. But Lancelot is compromised by his fatal liaison with Arthur's queen and torn between the incompatible loyalties that bind him as an honorable knight, on the one hand, to his lord Arthur, and on the other, to his lady Guinevere. Malory loves his character Lancelot even to the point of indulging in the fleeting speculation, after Lancelot has been admitted to the Queen's chamber, that their activities might have been innocent, "for love that time was not as love is nowadays." But when the jealousy and malice of two wicked knights forces the affair into the open, nothing can avert the breaking up of the fellowship of the Round Table and the death of Arthur himself, which Malory relates with somber magnificence in one of his finest passages, the one on which Tennyson based a famous *Idyll*. This catastrophic chain of events is the subject of the last of eight romances into which the unique manuscript of Malory's work is divided (a division suppressed in Caxton's edition). All the selections, starting with the opening, are taken from this final one of Malory's tales.

From Morte Darthur[1]

[*The Conspiracy against Lancelot and Guinevere*]

In May, when every lusty[2] heart flourisheth and burgeoneth, for as the season is lusty to behold and comfortable,[3] so man and woman rejoiceth and gladdeth of summer coming with his fresh flowers, for winter

---

1. The selections here given are from the section that Caxton called book 20, chaps. 1–4, 8–10, and book 21, chaps. 3–7, 10–12, with omissions. In the Winchester MS this section is entitled "The Most Piteous Tale of the Morte Arthur Saunz Guerdon" (i.e., the death of Arthur without reward

or compensation). The text has been based on Winchester, with some readings introduced from the Caxton edition; spelling has been modernized and modern punctuation added.
2. Merry.
3. Pleasant.

with his rough winds and blasts causeth lusty men and women to cower and to sit fast by the fire—so this season it befell in the month of May a great anger and unhap that stinted not[4] till the flower of chivalry of all the world was destroyed and slain. And all was long upon two unhappy[5] knights which were named Sir Agravain and Sir Mordred that were brethren unto Sir Gawain.[6] For this Sir Agravain and Sir Mordred had ever a privy[7] hate unto the Queen, Dame Guinevere, and to Sir Lancelot, and daily and nightly they ever watched upon Sir Lancelot.

So it misfortuned Sir Gawain and all his brethren were in King Arthur's chamber, and then Sir Agravain said thus openly, and not in no counsel,[8] that many knights might hear: "I marvel that we all be not ashamed both to see and to know how Sir Lancelot lieth daily and nightly by the Queen. And all we know well that it is so, and it is shamefully suffered of us all[9] that we should suffer so noble a king as King Arthur is to be shamed."

Then spoke Sir Gawain and said, "Brother, Sir Agravain, I pray you and charge you, move no such matters no more afore[1] me, for wit you well, I will not be of your counsel."[2]

"So God me help," said Sir Gaheris and Sir Gareth,[3] "we will not be known of your deeds."[4]

"Then will I!" said Sir Mordred.

"I lieve[5] you well," said Sir Gawain, "for ever unto all unhappiness, sir, ye will grant.[6] And I would that ye left all this and make you not so busy, for I know," said Sir Gawain, "what will fall of it."[7]

"Fall whatsoever fall may," said Sir Agravain, "I will disclose it to the King."

"Not by my counsel," said Sir Gawain, "for and[8] there arise war and wrack betwixt[9] Sir Lancelot and us, wit you well, brother, there will many kings and great lords hold with Sir Lancelot. Also, brother, Sir Agravain," said Sir Gawain, "ye must remember how often times Sir Lancelot hath rescued the King and the Queen. And the best of us all had been full cold at the heart-root[1] had not Sir Lancelot been better than we, and that has he proved himself full oft. And as for my part," said Sir Gawain, "I will never be against Sir Lancelot for[2] one day's deed, when he rescued me from King Carados of the Dolorous Tower and slew him and saved my life. Also, brother, Sir Agravain and Sir Mordred, in like wise Sir Lancelot rescued you both and three score and

---

4. Misfortune that ceased not.
5. On account of two ill-fated.
6. Gawain and Agravain are sons of King Lot of Orkney and his wife, Arthur's half-sister Morgause. Mordred is the illegitimate son of Arthur and Morgause.
7. Secret.
8. Secret manner.
9. Put up with by all of us.
1. Before. "Move": propose.
2. On your side. "Wit you well": know well, i.e.,

I give you to understand.
3. Sons of King Lot and Gawain's brothers.
4. A party to your doings.
5. Believe.
6. You will consent to all mischief.
7. Come of it.
8. If.
9. Strife between.
1. Would have been dead.
2. On account of.

two[3] from Sir Tarquin. And therefore, brother, methinks such noble deeds and kindness should be remembered."

"Do as ye list,"[4] said Sir Agravain, "for I will layne[5] it no longer."

So with these words came in Sir Arthur.

"Now, brother," said Sir Gawain, "stint your noise."[6]

"That will I not," said Sir Agravain and Sir Mordred.

"Well, will ye so?" said Sir Gawain. "Then God speed you, for I will not hear of your tales, neither be of your counsel."

"No more will I," said Sir Gaheris.

"Neither I," said Sir Gareth, "for I shall never say evil by[7] that man that made me knight." And therewithal they three departed making great dole.[8]

"Alas!" said Sir Gawain and Sir Gareth, "now is this realm wholly destroyed and mischieved,[9] and the noble fellowship of the Round Table shall be disparbeled."[1]

So they departed, and then King Arthur asked them what noise they made. "My lord," said Sir Agravain, "I shall tell you, for I may keep[2] it no longer. Here is I and my brother Sir Mordred broke[3] unto my brother Sir Gawain, Sir Gaheris, and to Sir Gareth—for this is all, to make it short—how that we know all that Sir Lancelot holdeth your queen, and hath done long; and we be your sister[4] sons, we may suffer it no longer. And all we woot[5] that ye should be above Sir Lancelot, and ye are the king that made him knight, and therefore we will prove it that he is a traitor to your person."

"If it be so," said the King, "wit[6] you well, he is none other. But I would be loath to begin such a thing but[7] I might have proofs of it, for Sir Lancelot is an hardy knight, and all ye know that he is the best knight among us all. And but if he be taken with the deed,[8] he will fight with him that bringeth up the noise, and I know no knight that is able to match him. Therefore, and[9] it be sooth as ye say, I would that he were taken with the deed."

For, as the French book saith, the King was full loath that such a noise should be upon Sir Lancelot and his queen. For the King had a deeming[1] of it, but he would not hear of it, for Sir Lancelot had done so much for him and for the Queen so many times that, wit you well, the King loved him passingly[2] well.

"My lord," said Sir Agravain, "ye shall ride tomorn[3] on hunting, and doubt ye not, Sir Lancelot will not go with you. And so when it draweth toward night, ye may send the Queen word that ye will lie out

---

3. 62.
4. You please.
5. Conceal.
6. Stop making scandal.
7. About.
8. Lamentation.
9. Put to shame.
1. Dispersed.
2. Conceal.
3. Revealed.

4. Sister's.
5. Know.
6. Know.
7. Unless.
8. Unless he is caught in the act.
9. If.
1. Suspicion.
2. Exceedingly.
3. Tomorrow.

all that night, and so may ye send for your cooks. And then, upon pain of death, that night we shall take him with the Queen, and we shall bring him unto you, quick[4] or dead."

"I will well,"[5] said the King. "Then I counsel you to take with you sure fellowship."

"Sir," said Sir Agravain, "my brother, Sir Mordred, and I will take with us twelve knights of the Round Table."

"Beware," said King Arthur, "for I warn you, ye shall find him wight."[6]

"Let us deal!"[7] said Sir Agravain and Sir Mordred.

So on the morn King Arthur rode on hunting and sent word to the Queen that he would be out all that night. Then Sir Agravain and Sir Mordred got to them[8] twelve knights and hid themself in a chamber in the castle of Carlisle. And these were their names: Sir Colgrevance, Sir Mador de la Porte, Sir Guingalen, Sir Meliot de Logres, Sir Petipace of Winchelsea, Sir Galeron of Galway, Sir Melion de la Mountain, Sir Ascamore, Sir Gromore Somyr Jour, Sir Curselayne, Sir Florence, and Sir Lovell. So these twelve knights were with Sir Mordred and Sir Agravain, and all they were of Scotland, or else of Sir Gawain's kin, or well-willers[9] to his brother.

So when the night came, Sir Lancelot told Sir Bors[1] how he would go that night and speak with the Queen.

"Sir," said Sir Bors, "ye shall not go this night by my counsel."

"Why?" said Sir Lancelot.

"Sir," said Sir Bors, "I dread me[2] ever of Sir Agravain that waiteth upon[3] you daily to do you shame and us all. And never gave my heart against no going that ever ye went[4] to the queen so much as now, for I mistrust[5] that the King is out this night from the Queen because peradventure he hath lain[6] some watch for you and the Queen. Therefore, I dread me sore of some treason."

"Have ye no dread," said Sir Lancelot, "for I shall go and come again and make no tarrying."

"Sir," said Sir Bors, "that me repents,[7] for I dread me sore that your going this night shall wrath[8] us all."

"Fair nephew," said Sir Lancelot, "I marvel me much why ye say thus, sithen[9] the Queen hath sent for me. And wit you well, I will not be so much a coward, but she shall understand I will[1] see her good grace."

"God speed you well," said Sir Bors, "and send you sound and safe again!"

---

4. Alive.
5. Readily agree.
6. Strong.
7. Leave it to us.
8. Gathered to themselves.
9. Partisans.
1. Nephew and confidant of Sir Lancelot.
2. I am afraid.
3. Lies in wait.

4. Never misgave my heart against any visit you made.
5. Suspect.
6. Perhaps he has set.
7. I regret.
8. Cause injury to.
9. Since.
1. Wish to.

So Sir Lancelot departed and took his sword under his arm, and so he walked in his mantel,[2] that noble knight, and put himself in great jeopardy. And so he passed on till he came to the Queen's chamber, and so lightly he was had[3] into the chamber. And then, as the French book saith, the Queen and Sir Lancelot were together. And whether they were abed or at other manner of disports, me list[4] not thereof make no mention, for love that time[5] was not as love is nowadays.

But thus as they were together there came Sir Agravain and Sir Mordred with twelve knights with them of the Round Table, and they said with great crying and scaring[6] voice: "Thou traitor, Sir Lancelot, now are thou taken!" And thus they cried with a loud voice that all the court might hear it. And these fourteen knights all were armed at all points, as[7] they should fight in a battle.

"Alas!" said Queen Guinevere, "now are we mischieved[8] both!"

"Madam," said Sir Lancelot, "is there here any armor within your chamber that I might cover my body withal? And if there be any, give it me, and I shall soon stint[9] their malice, by the grace of God!"

"Now, truly," said the Queen, "I have none armor neither helm, shield, sword, neither spear, wherefore I dread me sore our long love is come to a mischievous end. For I hear by their noise there be many noble knights, and well I woot they be surely[1] armed, and against them ye may make no resistance. Wherefore ye are likely to be slain, and then shall I be burned! For and[2] ye might escape them," said the Queen, "I would not doubt but that ye would rescue me in what danger that ever I stood in."

"Alas!" said Sir Lancelot, "in all my life thus was I never bestead[3] that I should be thus shamefully slain for lack of mine armor."

But ever in one[4] Sir Agravain and Sir Mordred cried: "Traitor knight, come out of the Queen's chamber! For wit thou well thou art beset so that thou shalt not escape."

"Ah, Jesu mercy!" said Sir Lancelot, "this shameful cry and noise I may not suffer, for better were death at once than thus to endure this pain." Then he took the Queen in his arms and kissed her and said, "Most noblest Christian queen, I beseech you, as ye have been ever my special good lady, and I at all times your poor knight and true unto[5] my power, and as I never failed you in right nor in wrong sithen the first day King Arthur made me knight, that ye will pray for my soul if that I be slain. For well I am assured that Sir Bors, my nephew, and all the remnant of my kin, with Sir Lavain and Sir Urry,[6] that they will not fail you to rescue you from the fire. And therefore, mine own lady, recom-

---

2. Cloak. Lancelot goes unarmed.
3. Quickly he was received.
4. I care. "Disports": pastimes.
5. At that time.
6. Terrifying.
7. Completely, as if.
8. Come to grief.
9. Stop.

1. Securely.
2. If.
3. Beset.
4. In unison.
5. To the utmost of.
6. The brother of Elaine, the Fair Maid of Astolat, and a knight miraculously healed of his wound by Sir Lancelot. "Remnant": rest.

fort yourself,[7] whatsoever come of me, that ye go with Sir Bors, my nephew, and Sir Urry and they all will do you all the pleasure that they may, and ye shall live like a queen upon my lands."

"Nay, Sir Lancelot, nay!" said the Queen. "Wit thou well that I will not live long after thy days. But and[8] ye be slain I will take my death as meekly as ever did martyr take his death for Jesu Christ's sake."

"Well, Madam," said Sir Lancelot, "sith it is so that the day is come that our love must depart,[9] wit you well I shall sell my life as dear as I may. And a thousandfold," said Sir Lancelot, "I am more heavier[1] for you than for myself! And now I had liefer[2] than to be lord of all Christendom that I had sure armor upon me, that men might speak of my deeds ere ever I were slain."

"Truly," said the Queen, "and[3] it might please God, I would that they would take me and slay me and suffer[4] you to escape."

"That shall never be," said Sir Lancelot. "God defend me from such a shame! But, Jesu Christ, be Thou my shield and mine armor!" And therewith Sir Lancelot wrapped his mantel about his arm well and surely; and by then they had gotten a great form[5] out of the hall, and therewith they all rushed at the door. "Now, fair lords," said Sir Lancelot, "leave[6] your noise and your rushing, and I shall set open this door, and then may ye do with me what it liketh you."[7]

"Come off,[8] then," said they all, "and do it, for it availeth thee not to strive against us all. And therefore let us into this chamber, and we shall save thy life until thou come to King Arthur."

Then Sir Lancelot unbarred the door, and with his left hand he held it open a little, that but one man might come in at once. And so there came striding a good knight, a much[9] man and a large, and his name was called Sir Colgrevance of Gore. And he with a sword struck at Sir Lancelot mightily. And he put aside[1] the stroke and gave him such a buffet[2] upon the helmet that he fell groveling dead within the chamber door. Then Sir Lancelot with great might drew the knight within[3] the chamber door. And then Sir Lancelot, with help of the Queen and her ladies, he was lightly[4] armed in Colgrevance's armor. And ever stood Sir Agravain and Sir Mordred, crying, "Traitor knight! Come forth out of the Queen's chamber!"

"Sirs, leave[5] your noise," said Sir Lancelot, "for wit you well, Sir Agravain, ye shall not prison me this night. And therefore, and [6] ye do by my counsel, go ye all from this chamber door and make you no such crying and such manner of slander as ye do. For I promise you by my knighthood, and ye will depart and make no more noise, I shall as tomorn

---

7. Take heart again.
8. If.
9. Come to an end.
1. More grieved.
2. Rather.
3. If.
4. Allow.
5. Bench.
6. Stop.

7. Pleases you.
8. Go ahead.
9. Big.
1. Fended off.
2. Blow.
3. Inside.
4. Quickly.
5. Stop.
6. If.

appear afore you all and before the King, and then let it be seen which of you all, other else ye all,[7] that will deprove[8] me of treason. And there shall I answer you, as a knight should, that hither I came to the Queen for no manner of mal engine,[9] and that will I prove and make it good upon you with my hands."

"Fie upon thee, traitor," said Sir Agravain and Sir Mordred, "for we will have thee malgré thine head[1] and slay thee, and we list. For we let thee wit we have the choice of [2] King Arthur to save thee other slay thee."

"Ah, sirs," said Sir Lancelot, "is there none other grace with you? Then keep[3] yourself!" And then Sir Lancelot set all open the chamber door and mightily and knightly he strode in among them. And anon[4] at the first stroke he slew Sir Agravain, and after twelve of his fellows. Within a little while he had laid them down cold to the earth, for there was none of the twelve knights might stand Sir Lancelot one buffet.[5] And also he wounded Sir Mordred, and therewithal he fled with all his might.

And then Sir Lancelot returned again unto the Queen and said, "Madam, now wit you well, all our true love is brought to an end, for now will King Arthur ever be my foe. And therefore, Madam, and it like you[6] that I may have you with me, I shall save you from all manner adventurous[7] dangers."

"Sir, that is not best," said the Queen, "me seemeth, for[8] now ye have done so much harm, it will be best that ye hold you still with this. And if ye see that as tomorn they will put me unto death, then may ye rescue me as ye think best."

"I will well,"[9] said Sir Lancelot, "for have ye no doubt, while I am a man living I shall rescue you." And then he kissed her, and either of them gave other a ring, and so there he left the Queen and went until[1] his lodging.

[War Breaks Out between Arthur and Lancelot][2]

Then said King Arthur unto Sir Gawain, "Dear nephew, I pray you make ready in your best armor with your brethren, Sir Gaheris and Sir Gareth, to bring my Queen to the fire, there to have her judgment and receive the death."

"Nay, my most noble king," said Sir Gawain, "that will I never do,

7. Or else all of you.
8. Accuse.
9. Evil design.
1. In spite of you.
2. From.
3. Defend.
4. Right away.
5. Withstand Sir Lancelot one blow.
6. If it please you.
7. Perilous.
8. Because.

9. Agree.
1. To.
2. Lancelot and Sir Bors mobilize their friends for the rescue of Guinevere. In the morning Mordred reports the events of the night to Arthur who, against Gawain's strong opposition, condemns the queen to be burned, for "the law was such in those days that whatsoever they were, of what estate or degree, if they were found guilty of treason there should be none other remedy but death."

for wit you well I will never be in that place where so noble a queen as is my lady Dame Guinevere shall take such a shameful end. For wit you well," said Sir Gawain, "my heart will not serve me for to see her die, and it shall never be said that ever I was of your counsel for her death."

"Then," said the King unto Sir Gawain, "suffer[3] your brethren Sir Gaheris and Sir Gareth to be there."

"My lord," said Sir Gawain, "wit you well they will be loath to be there present because of many adventures[4] that is like to fall, but they are young and full unable to say you nay."

Then spake Sir Gaheris and the good knight Sir Gareth unto King Arthur: "Sir, ye may well command us to be there, but wit you well it shall be sore against our will. But and[5] we be there by your straight commandment, ye shall plainly[6] hold us there excused—we will be there in peaceable wise and bear none harness of war upon us."

"In the name of God," said the King, "then make you ready, for she shall have soon[7] her judgment."

"Alas," said Sir Gawain, "that ever I should endure[8] to see this woeful day." So Sir Gawain turned him and wept heartily, and so he went into his chamber.

And then the Queen was led forth without[9] Carlisle, and anon she was dispoiled into[1] her smock. And then her ghostly father[2] was brought to her to be shriven of her misdeeds.[3] Then was there weeping and wailing and wringing of hands of many lords and ladies, but there were but few in comparison that would bear any armor for to strengthen[4] the death of the Queen.

Then was there one that Sir Lancelot had sent unto that place, which went to espy what time the Queen should go unto her death. And anon as[5] he saw the Queen dispoiled into her smock and shriven, then he gave Sir Lancelot warning. Then was there but spurring and plucking up[6] of horses, and right so they came unto the fire. And who[7] that stood against them, there were they slain—there might none withstand Sir Lancelot. So all that bore arms and withstood them, there were they slain, full many a noble knight. * * * And so in this rushing and hurling, as Sir Lancelot thrang[8] here and there, it misfortuned him[9] to slay Sir Gaheris and Sir Gareth, the noble knight, for they were unarmed and unwares.[1] As the French book saith, Sir Lancelot smote Sir Gaheris and Sir Gareth upon the brain-pans, wherethrough[2] that they were slain in the field, howbeit[3] Sir Lancelot saw them not. And so were they found dead among the thickest of the press.

---

3. Allow.
4. Chance occurrences.
5. If.
6. Openly. "Straight": strict.
7. Right away.
8. Live.
9. Outside.
1. Undressed down to.
2. Spiritual father, i.e. her priest.
3. For her to be confessed of her sins.

4. Secure.
5. As soon as.
6. Urging forward.
7. Whoever.
8. Pressed. "Hurling": turmoil.
9. He had the misfortune.
1. Unaware.
2. Through which.
3. Although.

Then when Sir Lancelot had thus done, and slain and put to flight all that would withstand him, then he rode straight unto Queen Guinevere and made a kirtle[4] and a gown to be cast upon her, and then he made her to be set behind him and prayed her to be of good cheer. Now wit you well the Queen was glad that she was escaped from death, and then she thanked God and Sir Lancelot.

And so he rode his way with the Queen, as the French book saith, unto Joyous Garde,[5] and there he kept her as a noble knight should. And many great lords and many good knights were sent him, and many full noble knights drew unto him. When they heard that King Arthur and Sir Lancelot were at debate,[6] many knights were glad, and many were sorry of their debate.

Now turn we again unto King Arthur, that when it was told him how and in what manner the Queen was taken away from the fire, and when he heard of the death of his noble knights, and in especial Sir Gaheris and Sir Gareth, then he swooned for very pure[7] sorrow. And when he awoke of his swoon, then he said: "Alas, that ever I bore crown upon my head! For now have I lost the fairest fellowship of noble knights that ever held Christian king[8] together. Alas, my good knights be slain and gone away from me. Now within these two days I have lost nigh forty knights and also the noble fellowship of Sir Lancelot and his blood,[9] for now I may nevermore hold them together with my worship.[1] Alas, that ever this war began!

"Now, fair fellows," said the King, "I charge you that no man tell Sir Gawain of the death of his two brethren, for I am sure," said the King, "when he heareth tell that Sir Gareth is dead, he will go nigh out of his mind. Mercy Jesu," said the King, "why slew he Sir Gaheris and Sir Gareth? For I dare say, as for Sir Gareth, he loved Sir Lancelot above all men earthly."[2]

"That is truth," said some knights, "but they were slain in the hurling,[3] as Sir Lancelot thrang in the thickest of the press. And as they were unarmed, he smote them and wist[4] not whom that he smote, and so unhappily[5] they were slain."

"Well," said Arthur, "the death of them will cause the greatest mortal war that ever was, for I am sure that when Sir Gawain knoweth hereof that Sir Gareth is slain, I shall never have rest of him[6] till I have destroyed Sir Lancelot's kin and himself both, other else he to destroy me. And therefore," said the King, "wit you well, my heart was never so heavy as it is now. And much more I am sorrier for my good knights' loss[7] than for the loss of my fair queen; for queens I might have enough, but such a fellowship of good knights shall never be together in no company. And

4. Petticoat.
5. Lancelot's castle in England.
6. Strife.
7. Sheer.
8. That Christian king ever held.
9. Kin.
1. Glory.

2. Earthly men.
3. Turmoil.
4. Knew.
5. Unluckily.
6. He will never give me any peace.
7. The loss of my good knights.

now I dare say," said King Arthur, "there was never Christian king that ever held such a fellowship together. And alas, that ever Sir Lancelot and I should be at debate. Ah, Agravain, Agravain!" said the King, "Jesu forgive it thy soul, for thine evil will that thou and thy brother Sir Mordred haddest unto Sir Lancelot hath caused all this sorrow." And ever among these complaints the King wept and swooned.

Then came there one to Sir Gawain and told him how the Queen was led away with[8] Sir Lancelot, and nigh a four-and-twenty knights slain. "Ah, Jesu, save me my two brethren!" said Sir Gawain. "For full well wist I," said Sir Gawain, "that Sir Lancelot would rescue her, other else he would die in that field. And to say the truth he were not of worship but if he had[9] rescued the Queen, insomuch as she should have been burned for his sake. And as in that," said Sir Gawain, "he hath done but knightly, and as I would have done myself and I had stood in like case. But where are my brethren?" said Sir Gawain. "I marvel that I hear not of them."

Then said that man, "Truly, Sir Gaheris and Sir Gareth be slain."

"Jesu defend!"[1] said Sir Gawain. "For all this world I would not that they were slain, and in especial my good brother Sir Gareth."

"Sir," said the man, "he is slain, and that is great pity."

"Who slew him?" said Sir Gawain.

"Sir Lancelot," said the man, "slew them both."

"That may I not believe," said Sir Gawain, "that ever he slew my good brother Sir Gareth, for I dare say my brother loved him better than me and all his brethren and the King both. Also I dare say, an[2] Sir Lancelot had desired my brother Sir Gareth with him, he would have been with him against the King and us all. And therefore I may never believe that Sir Lancelot slew my brethren."

"Verily, sir," said the man, "it is noised[3] that he slew him."

"Alas," said Sir Gawain, "now is my joy gone." And then he fell down and swooned, and long he lay there as he had been dead. And when he arose out of his swoon, he cried out sorrowfully and said, "Alas!" And forthwith he ran unto the King, crying and weeping, and said, "Ah, mine uncle King Arthur! My good brother Sir Gareth is slain, and so is my brother Sir Gaheris, which were two noble knights."

Then the King wept and he both, and so they fell on swooning. And when they were revived, then spake Sir Gawain and said, "Sir, I will go and see my brother Sir Gareth."

"Sir, ye may not see him," said the King, "for I caused him to be interred and Sir Gaheris both, for I well understood that ye would make overmuch sorrow, and the sight of Sir Gareth should have caused your double sorrow."

"Alas, my lord," said Sir Gawain, "how slew he my brother Sir Gareth? Mine own good lord, I pray you tell me."

8. By.
9. Of honor if he had not.
1. Forbid.

2. If.
3. Reported.

"Truly," said the King, "I shall tell you as it hath been told me—Sir Lancelot slew him and Sir Gaheris both."

"Alas," said Sir Gawain, "they bore none arms against him, neither of them both."

"I woot not how it was," said the King, "but as it is said, Sir Lancelot slew them in the thickest of the press and knew them not. And therefore let us shape a remedy for to revenge their deaths."

"My king, my lord, and mine uncle," said Sir Gawain, "wit you well, now I shall make you a promise which I shall hold by my knighthood, that from this day forward I shall never fail[4] Sir Lancelot until that one of us have slain the other. And therefore I require you, my lord and king, dress[5] you unto the wars, for wit you well, I will be revenged upon Sir Lancelot; and therefore, as ye will have my service and my love, now haste you thereto and assay[6] your friends. For I promise unto God," said Sir Gawain, "for the death of my brother Sir Gareth I shall seek Sir Lancelot throughout seven kings' realms, but I shall slay him, other else he shall slay me."

"Sir, ye shall not need to seek him so far," said the King, "for as I hear say, Sir Lancelot will abide me and us all within the castle of Joyous Garde. And much people draweth unto him, as I hear say."

"That may I right well believe," said Sir Gawain, "but my lord," he said, "assay your friends and I will assay mine."

"It shall be done," said the King, "and as I suppose I shall be big[7] enough to drive him out of the biggest tower of his castle."

So then the King sent letters and writs throughout all England, both the length and the breadth, for to summon all his knights. And so unto King Arthur drew many knights, dukes, and earls, that he had a great host, and when they were assembled the King informed them how Sir Lancelot had bereft him his Queen. Then the King and all his host made them ready to lay siege about Sir Lancelot where he lay within Joyous Garde.

[The Death of Arthur][8]

So upon Trinity Sunday at night King Arthur dreamed a wonderful dream, and in his dream him seemed[9] that he saw upon a chafflet a chair, and the chair was fast to a wheel, and thereupon sat King Arthur in the richest cloth of gold that might be made. And the King thought there was under him, far from him, an hideous deep black water, and

4. Give up the pursuit of.
5. Prepare.
6. Appeal to.
7. Strong.
8. The Pope arranges a truce, Guinevere is returned to Arthur, and Lancelot and his kin leave England to become rulers of France. At Gawain's instigation Arthur invades France to resume the war against Lancelot. Word comes to the king that

Mordred has seized the kingdom, and Arthur leads his forces back to England. Mordred attacks them upon their landing, and Gawain is mortally wounded and dies, though not before he has repented for having insisted that Arthur fight Lancelot and has written Lancelot to come to the aid of his former lord.
9. It seemed to him. "Chafflet": scaffold.

therein was all manner of serpents, and worms, and wild beasts, foul and horrible. And suddenly the King thought that the wheel turned upside down, and he fell among the serpents, and every beast took him by a limb. And then the King cried as he lay in his bed, "Help, help!"

And then knights, squires, and yeomen awaked the King, and then he was so amazed that he wist[1] not where he was. And then so he awaked[2] until it was nigh day, and then he fell on slumbering again, not sleeping nor thoroughly waking. So the King seemed[3] verily that there came Sir Gawain unto him with a number of fair ladies with him. So when King Arthur saw him, he said, "Welcome, my sister's son. I weened ye had been dead. And now I see thee on-live, much am I beholden unto Almighty Jesu. Ah, fair nephew and my sister's son, what been these ladies that hither be come with you?"

"Sir," said Sir Gawain, "all these be ladies for whom I have foughten for when I was man living. And all these are tho[4] that I did battle for in righteous quarrels, and God hath given them that grace, at their great prayer, because I did battle for them for their right, that they should bring me hither unto you. Thus much hath given me leave God, for to warn you of your death. For and ye fight as tomorn[5] with Sir Mordred, as ye both have assigned,[6] doubt ye not ye must be slain, and the most party of your people on both parties. And for the great grace and goodness that Almighty Jesu hath unto you, and for pity of you and many mo[7] other good men there shall be slain, God hath sent me to you of his special grace to give you warning that in no wise ye do battle as tomorn, but that ye take a treatise[8] for a month-day. And proffer you largely,[9] so that tomorn ye put in a delay. For within a month shall come Sir Lancelot with all his noble knights and rescue you worshipfully and slay Sir Mordred and all that ever will hold with him."

Then Sir Gawain and all the ladies vanished. And anon the King called upon his knights, squires, and yeomen, and charged them wightly[1] to fetch his noble lords and wise bishops unto him. And when they were come the King told them of his avision,[2] that Sir Gawain had told him and warned him that, and he fought on the morn, he should be slain. Then the King commanded Sir Lucan the Butler[3] and his brother Sir Bedivere the Bold, with two bishops with them, and charged them in any wise to take a treatise for a month-day with Sir Mordred. "And spare not: proffer him lands and goods as much as ye think reasonable."

So then they departed and came to Sir Mordred where he had a grim host of an hundred thousand, and there they entreated[4] Sir Mordred long time. And at the last Sir Mordred was agreed for to have Cornwall

1. Knew.
2. Lay awake.
3. It seemed to the King.
4. Those.
5. If you fight tomorrow.
6. Decided.
7. More. "There": i.e., who there.
8. Treaty, truce. "For a month-day": for a month from today.
9. Make generous offers.
1. Quickly.
2. Dream.
3. "Butler" here is probably only a title of high rank, although it was originally used to designate the officer who had charge of wine for the king's table.
4. Dealt with.

and Kent by King Arthur's days,[5] and after that, all England, after the
days of King Arthur.

Then were they condescended[6] that King Arthur and Sir Mordred
should meet betwixt both their hosts, and everich[7] of them should bring
fourteen persons. And so they came with this word unto Arthur. Then
said he, "I am glad that this is done," and so he went into the field.

And when King Arthur should depart, he warned all his host that,
and they see any sword drawn, "Look ye come on fiercely and slay that
traitor Sir Mordred, for I in no wise trust him." In like wise Sir Mordred
warned his host that "And ye see any manner of sword drawn, look that
ye come on fiercely, and so slay all that ever before you standeth, for in
no wise I will not trust for this treatise." And in the same wise said Sir
Mordred unto his host, "For I know well my father will be avenged upon
me."

And so they met as their pointment[8] was and were agreed and accorded
thoroughly. And wine was fetched and they drank together. Right so
came an adder out of a little heath-bush, and it stung a knight in the
foot. And so when the knight felt him so stung, he looked down and saw
the adder. And anon he drew his sword to slay the adder, and thought[9]
none other harm. And when the host on both parties saw that sword
drawn, then they blew beams,[1] trumpets, and horns, and shouted grimly.
And so both hosts dressed them[2] together. And King Arthur took his
horse and said, "Alas, this unhappy day!" and so rode to his party, and
Sir Mordred in like wise.

And never since was there never seen a more dolefuller battle in no
Christian land, for there was but rushing and riding, foining[3] and striking; and many a grim word was there spoken of either to other, and
many a deadly stroke. But ever King Arthur rode throughout the battle[4]
of Sir Mordred many times and did full nobly, as a noble king should
do, and at all times he fainted never. And Sir Mordred did his devoir[5]
that day and put himself in great peril.

And thus they fought all the long day, and never stinted[6] till the noble
knights were laid to the cold earth. And ever they fought still till it was
near night, and by then was there an hundred thousand laid dead upon
the down. Then was King Arthur wood-wroth[7] out of measure when he
saw his people so slain from him. And so he looked about him and could
see no mo[8] of all his host, and good knights left no mo on-live, but two
knights: the t'one[9] was Sir Lucan the Butler and [the other] his brother
Sir Bedivere. And yet they were full sore wounded.

"Jesu, mercy," said the King, "where are all my noble knights become?[1]

---

5. During King Arthur's lifetime.
6. Agreed.
7. Each.
8. Arrangement.
9. Meant.
1. A kind of trumpet.
2. Prepared to come.
3. Lunging.

4. Battalion.
5. Knightly duty.
6. Stopped.
7. Mad with rage.
8. Others.
9. That one, i.e., the first.
1. What has become of all my noble knights?

Alas that ever I should see this doleful day! For now," said King Arthur, "I am come to mine end. But would to God," said he, "that I wist[2] now where were that traitor Sir Mordred that has caused all this mischief."

Then King Arthur looked about and was ware where stood Sir Mordred leaning upon his sword among a great heap of dead men.

"Now give me my spear," said King Arthur unto Sir Lucan, "for yonder I have espied the traitor that all this woe hath wrought."

"Sir, let him be," said Sir Lucan, "for he is unhappy.[3] And if ye pass this unhappy day ye shall be right well revenged upon him. And, good lord, remember ye of your night's dream, and what the spirit of Sir Gawain told you tonight, and yet God of his great goodness hath preserved you hitherto. And for God's sake, my lord, leave off by this,[4] for, blessed be God, ye have won the field: for yet we been here three onlive, and with Sir Mordred is not one on-live. And therefore if ye leave off now, this wicked day of destiny is past."

"Now, tide[5] me death, tide me life," said the King, "now I see him yonder alone, he shall never escape mine hands. For at a better avail[6] shall I never have him."

"God speed you well!" said Sir Bedivere.

Then the King got his spear in both his hands and ran toward Sir Mordred, crying and saying, "Traitor, now is thy deathday come!"

And when Sir Mordred saw King Arthur he ran until him with his sword drawn in his hand, and there King Arthur smote Sir Mordred under the shield, with a foin[7] of his spear, throughout the body more than a fathom.[8] And when Sir Mordred felt that he had his death's wound, he thrust himself with the might that he had up to the burr[9] of King Arthur's spear, and right so he smote his father King Arthur with his sword holden in both his hands, upon the side of the head, that the sword pierced the helmet and the tay[1] of the brain. And therewith Sir Mordred dashed down stark dead to the earth.

And noble King Arthur fell in a swough[2] to the earth, and there he swooned oftentimes, and Sir Lucan and Sir Bedivere ofttimes heaved him up. And so, weakly betwixt them, they led him to a little chapel not far from the seaside, and when the King was there, him thought him reasonably eased. Then heard they people cry in the field. "Now go thou, Sir Lucan," said the King, "and do me to wit[3] what betokens that noise in the field."

So Sir Lucan departed, for he was grievously wounded in many places. And so as he yede[4] he saw and harkened by the moonlight how that pillers[5] and robbers were come into the field to pill and to rob many a full noble knight of brooches and bees[6] and of many a good ring and

2. Knew.
3. I.e., unlucky for you.
4. I.e., with this much accomplished.
5. Betide.
6. Advantage.
7. Thrust.
8. Six feet.

9. Hand guard.
1. Edge.
2. Swoon.
3. Let me know.
4. Walked.
5. Plunderers.
6. Bracelets.

many a rich jewel. And who that were not dead all out[7] there they slew them for their harness and their riches. When Sir Lucan understood this work, he came to the King as soon as he might and told him all what he had heard and seen. "Therefore by my read,"[8] said Sir Lucan, "it is best that we bring you to some town."

"I would it were so," said the King, "but I may not stand, my head works[9] so. Ah, Sir Lancelot," said King Arthur, "this day have I sore missed thee. And alas that ever I was against thee, for now have I my death, whereof Sir Gawain me warned in my dream."

Then Sir Lucan took up the King the t'one party[1] and Sir Bedivere the other party; and in the lifting up the King swooned and in the lifting Sir Lucan fell in a swoon that part of his guts fell out of his body, and therewith the noble knight's heart burst. And when the King awoke he beheld Sir Lucan how he lay foaming at the mouth and part of his guts lay at his feet.

"Alas," said the King, "this is to me a full heavy[2] sight to see this noble duke so die for my sake, for he would have holpen[3] me that had more need of help than I. Alas that he would not complain him for[4] his heart was so set to help me. Now Jesu have mercy upon his soul."

Then Sir Bedivere wept for the death of his brother.

"Now leave this mourning and weeping, gentle knight," said the King, "for all this will not avail me. For wit thou well, and[5] I might live myself, the death of Sir Lucan would grieve me evermore. But my time passeth on fast," said the King. "Therefore," said King Arthur unto Sir Bedivere, "take thou here Excalibur[6] my good sword and go with it to yonder water's side; and when thou comest there I charge thee throw my sword in that water and come again and tell me what thou sawest there."

"My lord," said Sir Bedivere, "your commandment shall be done, and [I shall] lightly[7] bring you word again."

So Sir Bedivere departed. And by the way he beheld that noble sword, that the pommel and the haft[8] was all precious stones. And then he said to himself, "If I throw this rich sword in the water, thereof shall never come good, but harm and loss." And then Sir Bedivere hid Excalibur under a tree. And so, as soon as he might, he came again unto the King and said he had been at the water and had thrown the sword into the water.

"What saw thou there?" said the King.

"Sir," he said, "I saw nothing but waves and winds."

"That is untruly said of thee," said the King. "And therefore go thou lightly again and do my commandment; as thou art to me lief[9] and dear, spare not, but throw it in."

---

7. Entirely. "Harness": armor.
8. Advice.
9. Aches.
1. On one side.
2. Sorrowful.
3. Helped.
4. Because.
5. If.

6. The sword which Arthur had received as a young man from the Lady of the Lake; it is presumably she who catches it when Bedivere finally throws it into the water.
7. Quickly.
8. Handle. "Pommel": rounded knob on the hilt.
9. Beloved.

Then Sir Bedivere returned again and took the sword in his hand. And yet him thought[1] sin and shame to throw away that noble sword. And so eft[2] he hid the sword and returned again and told the King that he had been at the water and done his commandment.

"What sawest thou there?" said the King.

"Sir," he said, "I saw nothing but waters wap and waves wan."[3]

"Ah, traitor unto me and untrue," said King Arthur, "now hast thou betrayed me twice. Who would have weened that thou that has been to me so lief and dear, and thou art named a noble knight, and would betray me for the riches of this sword. But now go again lightly, for thy long tarrying putteth me in great jeopardy of my life, for I have taken cold. And but if thou do now as I bid thee, if ever I may see thee I shall slay thee mine[4] own hands, for thou wouldest for my rich sword see me dead."

Then Sir Bedivere departed and went to the sword and lightly took it up, and so he went to the water's side; and there he bound the girdle[5] about the hilts, and threw the sword as far into the water as he might. And there came an arm and an hand above the water and took it and clutched it, and shook it thrice and brandished; and then vanished away the hand with the sword into the water. So Sir Bedivere came again to the King and told him what he saw.

"Alas," said the King, "help me hence, for I dread me I have tarried overlong."

Then Sir Bedivere took the King upon his back and so went with him to that water's side. And when they were at the water's side, even fast[6] by the bank hoved[7] a little barge with many fair ladies in it; and among them all was a queen; and all they had black hoods, and all they wept and shrieked when they saw King Arthur.

"Now put me into that barge," said the King; and so he did softly. And there received him three ladies with great mourning, and so they set them[8] down. And in one of their laps King Arthur laid his head, and then the queen said, "Ah, my dear brother, why have ye tarried so long from me? Alas, this wound on your head hath caught overmuch cold." And anon they rowed fromward the land, and Sir Bedivere beheld all tho ladies go froward him.

Then Sir Bedivere cried and said, "Ah, my lord Arthur, what shall become of me, now ye go from me and leave me here alone among mine enemies?"

"Comfort thyself," said the King, "and do as well as thou mayest, for in me is no trust for to trust in. For I must into the vale of Avilion[9] to heal me of my grievous wound. And if thou hear nevermore of me, pray for my soul."

---

1. It seemed to him.
2. Again.
3. The phrase seems to mean "waters wash the shore and waves grow dark."
4. I.e., with mine.
5. Sword belt.
6. Close.
7. Waited.
8. I.e., they sat.
9. A legendary island, sometimes identified with the earthly paradise.

But ever the queen and ladies wept and shrieked that it was pity to hear. And as soon as Sir Bedivere had lost the sight of the barge he wept and wailed and so took[1] the forest, and went all that night. And in the morning he was ware betwixt two holts hoar[2] of a chapel and an hermitage.[3]

*   *   *

Thus of Arthur I find no more written in books that been authorized,[4] neither more of the very certainty of his death heard I never read,[5] but thus was he led away in a ship wherein were three queens: that one was King Arthur's sister, Queen Morgan la Fée, the t'other[6] was the Queen of North Wales, and the third was the Queen of the Waste Lands. *   *   *

Now more of the death of King Arthur could I never find but that these ladies brought him to his burials,[7] and such one was buried there that the hermit bore witness that sometime was Bishop of Canterbury.[8] But yet the hermit knew not in certain that he was verily the body of King Arthur, for this tale Sir Bedivere, a Knight of the Table Round, made it to be written. Yet some men say in many parts of England that King Arthur is not dead, but had by the will of our Lord Jesu into another place. And men say that he shall come again and he shall win the Holy Cross. Yet I will not say that it shall be so, but rather I will say, Here in this world he changed his life. And many men say that there is written upon his tomb this verse: *Hic iacet Arthurus, rex quondam, rexque futurus.*[9]

[*The Deaths of Lancelot and Guinevere*][1]

And thus upon a night there came a vision to Sir Lancelot and charged him, in remission[2] of his sins, to haste him unto Amesbury: "And by then[3] thou come there, thou shalt find Queen Guinevere dead. And therefore take thy fellows with thee, and purvey them of an horse-bier,[4] and fetch thou the corse[5] of her, and bury her by her husband, the noble King Arthur. So this avision[6] came to Lancelot thrice in one night. Then Sir Lancelot rose up ere day and told the hermit.

"It were well done," said the hermit, "that ye made you ready and that ye disobey not the avision."

1. Took to. "Went": walked.
2. Ancient copses.
3. In the passage here omitted, Sir Bedivere meets the former bishop of Canterbury, now a hermit, who describes how on the previous night a company of ladies had brought to the chapel a dead body, asking that it be buried. Sir Bedivere exclaims that the dead man must have been King Arthur, and vows to spend the rest of his life there in the chapel as a hermit.
4. That have authority.
5. Tell.
6. The second.
7. Grave.
8. Of whom the hermit, who was formerly Bishop of Canterbury, bore witness.
9. "Here lies Arthur, who was once king and king will be again."
1. Guinevere enters a convent at Amesbury where Lancelot, returned with his companions to England, visits her, but she commands him never to see her again. Emulating her example, Lancelot joins the bishop of Canterbury and Bedivere in their hermitage where he takes holy orders and is joined in turn by seven of his fellow-knights.
2. For the remission.
3. By the time.
4. Provide them with a horse-drawn hearse.
5. Body.
6. Dream.

Then Sir Lancelot took his eight fellows with him, and on foot they yede[7] from Glastonbury to Amesbury, the which is little more than thirty mile, and thither they came within two days, for they were weak and feeble to go. And when Sir Lancelot was come to Amesbury within the nunnery, Queen Guinevere died but half an hour afore. And the ladies told Sir Lancelot that Queen Guinevere told them all ere she passed that Sir Lancelot had been priest near a twelve-month:[8] "and hither he cometh as fast as he may to fetch my corse, and beside my lord King Arthur he shall bury me." Wherefore the Queen said in hearing of them all, "I beseech Almighty God that I may never have power to see Sir Lancelot with my worldly eyes."

"And thus," said all the ladies, "was ever her prayer these two days till she was dead."

Then Sir Lancelot saw her visage, but he wept not greatly, but sighed. And so he did all the observance of the service himself, both the *dirige*[9] and on the morn he sang mass. And there was ordained[1] an horse-bier, and so with an hundred torches ever burning about the corse of the Queen, and ever Sir Lancelot with his eight fellows went about[2] the horse-bier, singing and reading many an holy orison,[3] and frankincense upon the corse incensed.[4]

Thus Sir Lancelot and his eight fellows went on foot from Amesbury unto Glastonbury, and when they were come to the chapel and the hermitage, there she had a *dirige* with great devotion.[5] And on the morn the hermit that sometime[6] was Bishop of Canterbury sang the mass of requiem with great devotion, and Sir Lancelot was the first that offered, and then als[7] his eight fellows. And then she was wrapped in cered cloth of Rennes,[8] from the top to the toe, in thirtyfold, and after she was put in a web[9] of lead, and then in a coffin of marble.

And when she was put in the earth Sir Lancelot swooned and lay long still, while[1] the hermit came and awaked him, and said, "Ye be to blame, for ye displease God with such manner of sorrow-making."

"Truly," said Sir Lancelot, "I trust I do not displease God, for He knoweth mine intent—for my sorrow was not, nor is not, for any rejoicing of sin, but my sorrow may never have end. For when I remember of her beaulté and of her noblesse[2] that was both with her king and with her,[3] so when I saw his corse and her corse so lie together, truly mine heart would not serve to sustain my careful[4] body. Also when I remember me how by my defaute and mine orgule[5] and my pride that they were both laid full low, that were peerless that ever was living of Christian people, wit you well," said Sir Lancelot, "this remembered, of their

---

7. Went.
8. Nearly 12 months.
9. Funeral service.
1. Prepared.
2. Around.
3. Reciting many a prayer.
4. Burned frankincense over the body.
5. Solemnity.
6. Once.

7. Also. "Offered": made his donation.
8. A shroud made of fine linen smeared with wax, produced at Rennes. "Top": head.
9. Afterwards she was put in a sheet.
1. Until.
2. Her beauty and nobility.
3. That she and her king both had.
4. Sorrowful.
5. My fault and my haughtiness.

kindness and mine unkindness, sank so to mine heart that I might not sustain myself." So the French book maketh mention.

Then Sir Lancelot never after ate but little meat,[6] nor drank, till he was dead, for then he sickened more and more and dried and dwined[7] away. For the Bishop nor none of his fellows might not make him to eat, and little he drank, that he was waxen by a kibbet[8] shorter than he was, that the people could not know him. For evermore, day and night, he prayed, but sometime he slumbered a broken sleep. Ever he was lying groveling on the tomb of King Arthur and Queen Guinevere, and there was no comfort that the Bishop nor Sir Bors, nor none of his fellows could make him—it availed not.

So within six weeks after, Sir Lancelot fell sick and lay in his bed. And then he sent for the Bishop that there was hermit, and all his true fellows. Then Sir Lancelot said with dreary steven,[9] "Sir Bishop, I pray you give to me all my rights that longeth[1] to a Christian man."

"It shall not need you,"[2] said the hermit and all his fellows. "It is but heaviness of your blood. Ye shall be well mended by the grace of God tomorn."

"My fair lords," said Sir Lancelot, "wit you well my careful body will into the earth; I have warning more than now I will say. Therefore give me my rights."

So when he was houseled and annealed[3] and had all that a Christian man ought to have, he prayed the Bishop that his fellows might bear his body to Joyous Garde. (Some men say it was Alnwick, and some men say it was Bamborough.) "Howbeit," said Sir Lancelot, "me repenteth[4] sore, but I made mine avow sometime that in Joyous Garde I would be buried. And because of breaking[5] of mine avow, I pray you all, lead me thither." Then there was weeping and wringing of hands among his fellows.

So at a season of the night they all went to their beds, for they all lay in one chamber. And so after midnight, against[6] day, the Bishop that was hermit, as he lay in his bed asleep, he fell upon a great laughter. And therewith all the fellowship awoke and came to the Bishop and asked him what he ailed.[7]

"Ah, Jesu mercy," said the Bishop, "why did ye awake me? I was never in all my life so merry and so well at ease."

"Wherefore?" said Sir Bors.

"Truly," said the Bishop, "here was Sir Lancelot with me, with mo[8] angels than ever I saw men in one day. And I saw the angels heave[9] up Sir Lancelot unto heaven, and the gates of heaven opened against him."

---

6. Food.
7. Wasted.
8. Grown by a cubit.
9. Sad voice.
1. Pertains. "Rights": last sacrament.
2. You shall not need it.
3. Given communion and extreme unction.

4. I am sorry.
5. In order not to break.
6. Toward.
7. Ailed him.
8. More.
9. Lift.

"It is but dretching of swevens,"[1] said Sir Bors, "for I doubt not Sir Lancelot aileth nothing but good."[2]

"It may well be," said the Bishop. "Go ye to his bed and then shall ye prove the sooth."

So when Sir Bors and his fellows came to his bed, they found him stark dead. And he lay as he had smiled, and the sweetest savor[3] about him that ever they felt. Then was there weeping and wringing of hands, and the greatest dole they made that ever made men. And on the morn the Bishop did his mass of Requiem, and after the Bishop and all the nine knights put Sir Lancelot in the same horse-bier that Queen Guinevere was laid in tofore that she was buried. And so the Bishop and they all together went with the body of Sir Lancelot daily, till they came to Joyous Garde. And ever they had an hundred torches burning about him.

And so within fifteen days they came to Joyous Garde. And there they laid his corse in the body of the choir,[4] and sang and read many psalters[5] and prayers over him and about him. And ever his visage was laid open and naked, that all folks might behold him; for such was the custom in tho[6] days that all men of worship should so lie with open visage till that they were buried.

And right thus as they were at their service, there came Sir Ector de Maris that had seven year sought all England, Scotland, and Wales, seeking his brother, Sir Lancelot. And when Sir Ector heard such noise and light in the choir of Joyous Garde, he alight and put his horse from him and came into the choir. And there he saw men sing and weep, and all they knew Sir Ector, but he knew not them. Then went Sir Bors unto Sir Ector and told him how there lay his brother, Sir Lancelot, dead. And then Sir Ector threw his shield, sword, and helm from him, and when he beheld Sir Lancelot's visage, he fell down in a swoon. And when he waked, it were hard any tongue to tell the doleful complaints that he made for his brother.

"Ah, Lancelot!" he said, "thou were head of all Christian knights. And now I dare say," said Sir Ector, "thou Sir Lancelot, there thou liest, that thou were never matched of earthly knight's hand. And thou were the courteoust[7] knight that ever bore shield. And thou were the truest friend to thy lover that ever bestrode horse, and thou were the truest lover, of a sinful man,[8] that ever loved woman, and thou were the kindest man that ever struck with sword. And thou were the goodliest person that ever came among press of knights, and thou was the meekest man and the gentlest that ever ate in hall among ladies, and thou were the sternest knight to thy mortal foe that ever put spear in the rest."[9]

Then there was weeping and dolor out of measure.

---

1. Illusion of dreams.
2. Has nothing wrong with him.
3. Odor. A sweet scent is a conventional sign in saints' lives of a sanctified death.
4. The center of the chancel, the place of honor.
5. Psalms.
6. Those.
7. Most courteous.
8. Of any man born in original sin.
9. Support for the butt of the lance.

Thus they kept Sir Lancelot's corse aloft fifteen days, and then they buried it with great devotion. And then at leisure they went all with the Bishop of Canterbury to his hermitage, and there they were together more than a month.

Then Sir Constantine that was Sir Cador's son of Cornwall was chosen king of England, and he was a full noble knight, and worshipfully he ruled this realm. And then this King Constantine sent for the Bishop of Canterbury, for he heard say where he was. And so he was restored unto his bishopric and left that hermitage, and Sir Bedivere was there ever still hermit to his life's end.

Then Sir Bors de Ganis, Sir Ector de Maris, Sir Gahalantine, Sir Galihud, Sir Galihodin, Sir Blamour, Sir Bleoberis, Sir Villiars le Valiant, Sir Clarrus of Clermount, all these knights drew them to their countries. Howbeit[1] King Constantine would have had them with him, but they would not abide in this realm. And there they all lived in their countries as holy men.

And some English books make mention that they went never out of England after the death of Sir Lancelot—but that was but favor of makers.[2] For the French book maketh mention—and is authorized—that Sir Bors, Sir Ector, Sir Blamour, and Sir Bleoberis went into the Holy Land, thereas Jesu Christ was quick[3] and dead, and anon as they had stablished their lands;[4] for the book saith so Sir Lancelot commanded them for to do ere ever he passed out of this world. There these four knights did many battles upon the miscreaunts,[5] or Turks, and there they died upon a Good Friday for God's sake.

Here is the end of the whole book of King Arthur and of his noble knights of the Round Table, that when they were whole together there was ever an hundred and forty. And here is the end of *The Death of Arthur*.[6]

I pray you all gentlemen and gentlewomen that readeth this book of Arthur and his knights from the beginning to the ending, pray for me while I am alive that God send me good deliverance. And when I am dead, I pray you all pray for my soul.

For this book was ended the ninth year of the reign of King Edward the Fourth, by Sir Thomas Malory, knight, as Jesu help him for His great might, as he is the servant of Jesu both day and night.

1469–70   1485

---

1. However.
2. The authors' bias.
3. Living. "Thereas": where.
4. As soon as they had put their lands in order.
5. Infidels.

6. By the "whole book" Malory refers to the entire work; *The Death of Arthur*, which Caxton made the title of the entire work, refers to the last part of Malory's book.

The Sixteenth Century
1485-1603

1485: Accession of Henry VII, inaugurates age of the Tudor sovereigns.
1509: Accession of Henry VIII.
1517: Martin Luther's Wittenberg Theses; beginning of the Reformation.
1534: Henry VIII acknowledged "Supreme Head on Earth" of the English church.
1557: Publication of *Tottel's Miscellany*, containing poems by Sir Thomas Wyatt, Henry Howard Earl of Surrey, and others.
1558: Accession of Queen Elizabeth I.
1576: Building of The Theatre, the first permanent structure in England for the presentation of plays.
1588: Defeat of the Spanish Armada.
1603: Death of Elizabeth I; accession of James I, the first Stuart king.

ENGLAND UNDER HENRY VII

The sixteenth century in England is the age of the Tudor sovereigns. Three generations of Tudors ruled England from 1485 to 1603. The earl of Richmond became Henry VII, the first Tudor monarch: he won his crown by defeating Richard III at Bosworth field, ending the dynastic strife that had raged for more than thirty years between the noble houses of York and Lancaster. Henry VII was Lancastrian, but he married Elizabeth of the house of York, niece of the Yorkist king Richard III. The barons, impoverished and divided by the dynastic wars, could not effectively oppose the power of the crown, and the church also generally supported the royal power. So Henry VII was able to counter the multiple and competing power structures characteristic of feudal society and to impose a much stronger central authority and order upon the nation.

Seven years after Henry VII became king, Columbus discovered America, and a few years later Vasco da Gama reached India by sailing around the Cape of Good Hope. The English were not pioneers in the discovery and exploration of the western hemisphere, but the discoveries affected their place in the world profoundly, for in the next century they became great colonizers and merchant adventurers.

Significant changes in trade and in the arts of war also marked the early years of the Tudor regime. Henry VII made commercial treaties with European countries; England, which had always been a sheep-raising country, was by now manufacturing and exporting significant amounts of cloth. As lands were enclosed to permit grazing on a larger scale, people were driven off the land to the cities, and London grew into a metropolitan market, with sophisticated commercial institutions. At the same time the feudal order continued its decline, partly because the introduction of firearms made armored knights on horseback obsolete, as well as the English bowmen who had won famous victories in France under King Henry V. The "new men" who supported the Tudors and profited from their favor could adapt themselves more easily to a changed society than could the descendants of the great families of the feudal fifteenth century.

About a decade before Henry VII won his throne, the art of printing from movable type, a German invention, was introduced into England by William Caxton (ca. 1422–1491), who had learned and practiced it in the Low Countries. Literacy increased during the fifteenth century, so that many more people could read than in Chaucer's time; it is estimated that some 30 percent of the people could read English in the early fifteenth century and some 60 percent by 1530. Printing made books cheaper and more plentiful, providing more opportunity to read, and more incentive to learn.

Yet it would be a mistake to imagine these changes as sudden and dramatic. Although Caxton introduced printed books, and was an author and translator as well as a printer, his publications consisted of long prose romances translated from the French, collections of moral sayings, and other works—such as Malory's *Morte Darthur*—that were medieval rather than modern. Also, jousts and tournaments continued at court for a century, and the approved code of behavior was the traditional code of chivalry. As often in an age of spectacular novelty, people dreamed of an idealized past instead of looking forward to an uncertain future. The best writers of the time of Henry VII were imitators of Chaucer, who had died about a century before. They were Scottish rather than English: William Dunbar (ca. 1460–1530), Gavin Douglas (1475–1522), and Sir David Lindsay (1485–1555). English writers also looked back, for example, Stephen Hawes (1474–1523), who imitated not Chaucer but John Lydgate, monk of Bury.

HUMANISM

During the fifteenth century a few English clerics and government officials had journeyed to Italy and had seen something of the extraordinary cultural and intellectual movement flourishing in the city-states there. That movement, generally known as the Renaissance, involved a rebirth of letters and arts stimulated by the recovery and study of texts from classical antiquity, and the development of new aesthetic norms based on classical models. It also unleashed new ideas and new social, political, and economic forces that displaced the otherworldly and communal values of the Middle Ages, emphasizing instead the dignity and potential of the individual and the worth of life in this world. These Renaissance ideals were variously reflected in the poetry of Petrarch, the philosophy of Pico della Mirandola, the art of Leonardo da Vinci, and the statecraft of Lorenzo di Medici. But it was not until Henry VII's reign brought some measure of political stability to England that the Renaissance could take root there, and it was not until the accession of Henry VIII that it began to flower.

Humanism was a fundamental intellectual current in the Renaissance, whose first major exponents in England were Sir Thomas More and Desiderius Erasmus of Rotterdam. More rose to become lord chancellor to Henry

VIII: his masterpiece, *Utopia*, written in Latin, was a critique of European social, political, and religious institutions and practices, from the vantage point of an imaginary society based on reason. His English writings were chiefly controversial tracts against Luther and the Protestants, but he also wrote a vivid and impressive history of Richard III. More's friend Erasmus spent some time in England, but his influence was spread also through his scripture translations and commentaries, and his writings on rhetoric and education.

Education—of the Christian prince, of the courtier, of the Christian gentleman—was a prime concern of the English humanists. John Colet (founder of St. Paul's School), Roger Ascham (tutor to Princess Elizabeth), and Sir Thomas Elyot, among others, wrote treatises on education to promote the kind of learning they regarded as the most suitable preparation for public service. That education—conducted by tutors in the great families or in grammar schools—was ordered according to the subjects of the medieval *trivium* (grammar, logic, and rhetoric) and the *quadrivium* (arithmetic, geometry, astronomy, and music), but with new emphasis on rhetoric and classical texts. The grammar studied was Latin grammar, and the rhetoric was a rigorous discipline in all the stylistic devices used by classical authors. The purpose was to train the sons of the nobility and gentry to speak and write good Latin, the language of diplomacy, of the professions, and of all higher learning. (Their sisters were always educated at home, in modern languages, religion, music, and art, but most often they did not receive the firm grounding in Latin and classical literature so central to Renaissance culture.) Elizabethan schoolmasters might use the system of double translation, from English into Latin and then from Latin back into English, to develop facility and rhetorical elegance. But the books read and studied rhetorically were not considered mere exhibitions of literary style: from the *Sententiae Pueriles* (Childish Maxims) for beginners, on up through the dramatist Terence, the poets Virgil and Horace, and the orator Cicero, the classics were also studied for the moral, political, and philosophical truth they contained, and as a means to inculcate moral values.

From the outset, English Humanism was vitally concerned with Christianity as well as with classical learning. The second generation of humanists—men like Roger Ascham (1515–1568), Sir John Cheke (1514–1557), professor of Greek at Cambridge, and Thomas Wilson (1525–1581), rhetorician and translator—combined an earnest Protestantism with their classical learning, and Ascham vigorously opposed the more secular, pagan humanism that was coming out of Italy. These men had a profound influence on the University of Cambridge, and Cambridge, in turn, educated many of the greatest writers of the age—including Spenser and Milton, who are also in this special English sense, Christian humanists.

For humanists committed to classical learning, the question of whether to write one's own works in Latin or in English became an issue of great seriousness. Sir Thomas More turned naturally to Latin in writing his *Utopia*. And to many other learned men, influenced both by the Humanist exaltation of the classical languages and by the characteristic Renaissance desire for eternal fame, the vernacular languages seemed relatively new and unstable. But at the same time, a revolt was being mounted in Italy, France, and England against the slavish imitation, in Latin, of Cicero and other classical writers. In his *Défense et Illustration de la Langue Française* (1549), Joachim Du Bellay argued that the value of a language is dependent upon the great works written in it, and urged scholars and poets to refine and improve the native tongue by writing ambitious works in it, thereby promoting a sense of national identity. In his book on archery, *Toxophilus*, dedicated to Henry VIII, Roger Ascham defended using the vernacular, though he said he found it easier to write in Latin or Greek. Later, Richard Mulcaster (ca. 1530–1611), principal of the Merchant Taylors' School and teacher of Edmund Spenser, waxed much more eloquent in praise of English:

> Is it not indeed a marvelous bondage, to become servants to one tongue for learning's sake the most of our time, with loss of most time, whereas we may have the very same treasure in our own tongue, with the gain of more time? our own bearing the joyful title of our liberty and freedom, the Latin tongue remembering us of our thralldom and bondage? I love Rome, but London better; I favor Italy, but England more; I honor the Latin, but I worship the English.

These two impulses—Humanist reverence for the classics and English pride in the vernacular language—gave rise to many distinguished translations throughout the century: Virgil's *Aeneid* by the Earl of Surrey; Homer's *Iliad* and *Odyssey* by George Chapman; Plutarch's *Lives of the Noble Grecians and Romans* by Sir Thomas North; and Ovid's *Metamorphoses* by Arthur Golding. Translators also sought to make available in English the most notable literary works in the modern languages: Castiglione's *Il Cortegiano* ("The Courtier") by Sir Thomas Hoby, Ariosto's *Orlando Furioso* ("Orlando Mad") by Sir John Harington, Tasso's *Gerusalemme Liberata* ("Jerusalem Delivered") by Edward Fairfax. At the midcentury, Ralph Robynson put into English the Latin *Utopia* of that notable English humanist, Sir Thomas More.

THE REFORMATION

Humanists like Erasmus advocated and engaged in a scholarly and critical study of the Scriptures; Humanists like More satirized the corrupt and ignorant clergy, and such abuses as the sale of papal indulgences and pardons. But neither Erasmus nor More followed the course which led to the Protestant Reformation: for both, the unity of Christendom was an overriding value. Nor did Martin Luther at first intend schism: when he nailed his famous ninety-five theses to the church door in Wittenberg on the first of November 1517, he thought he was simply opening up some topics for academic discussion. But his ideas soon sparked a mass revolution.

What was the Reformation? From the point of view of those who supported it, it was a return to pure Christianity—cleansing the church of all the corruption and idolatry that had accumulated over the centuries. From the point of view of the Catholic Church it was, of course, damnable heresy. From the perspective of later ages, it can be recognized as a major factor in the break-up of Western Christendom, the secularization of society, the establishment of princely ascendancy over the church and, consequently, the identification of religion and nationalism.

For medieval people, the Roman Catholic Church was a universal, infallible, omnicompetent guide to the conduct of life from cradle to grave. They walked hand in hand with it, instructed by its teachings, corrected by its discipline, sustained by its sacraments, comforted by its promises. A vast system of confession, pardons, penance, absolution, indulgences, sacred relics, and ceremonies gave the hierarchy great power over their largely illiterate flock. The Bible, the order of the Mass, and most of the theological discussions were in Latin, which lay people could not understand; however, religious doctrine and spirituality were mediated to them by priests and hierarchy, by church art and music, and by the liturgical ceremonies of daily life—festivals, holy days, baptisms, marriages, funerals.

When Luther revolted against the ancient church, was cast out by it, and founded his own church, he did so in the name of individual conscience enlightened by a personal reading of the Scriptures. The common watchwords of the Reformation were these: only the Scriptures (not the Church or Tradition) have authority in matters of religion; only God's grace and personal faith (not good works or religious practices) can effect a Christian's salvation; and only the enlightened individual conscience (not priests or ministers or hierarchies) can determine what an individual must believe and do. Despite differences in many matters of doctrine and church order, these principles were common to Lutherans in Germany, Calvinists at Geneva, and other Protestant groups throughout Europe.

In England, however, the Reformation did not begin with ideological controversy. In the time of Chaucer, John Wycliffe and the Lollard movement had mounted a grass-roots challenge to some practices and doctrines of the church, elements of which lasted into the sixteenth century. But the split with the Church of Rome was caused by a man who considered himself a Catholic champion against Luther and his opinions: Henry VIII, who received from Pope Leo X the title "Defender of the Faith" for writing a book against Luther. Henry's motives for the break with Rome were dynastic, not religious: he needed a legitimate son; his queen, Catherine of Aragon, could not give him one; and he was unable after long negotiations to obtain permission from Rome to divorce her. He then declared himself Supreme Head of the English church and required oaths of allegiance affirming his right to that role. His lord chancellor, Sir Thomas More, resigned and was at length executed for refusing to sign that oath. Thomas Cromwell, Henry's powerful secretary of state, dissolved the monasteries and distributed their property to his courtiers, thereby binding them firmly to his cause. In his earlier role as Defender of the (Roman Catholic) Faith, Henry had caused the great English translator of the Bible, William Tyndale, to be persecuted, driven out of England, and finally martyred in 1536. But after his break with Rome, Henry authorized a vernacular translation (The Great Bible), making the Bible available in English to anyone who could read.

Henry's son (by his third wife, Lady Jane Seymour) was the boy king Edward VI (1537–1553). In his brief reign (1547–53) the English Reformation acquired a strong doctrinal basis and spiritual energy, as Lutheran and Calvinist theologians from the continent swarmed into England. The Book of Common Prayer was published in 1549 and 1552, and by 1553 the beliefs of the English Church were officially defined in forty-two articles, thoroughly Protestant in formulation.

The successor to the young Protestant king was his older sister, Mary Tudor, the half-Spanish and devoutly Catholic daughter of Henry and Catherine of Aragon, who married her cousin Philip II of Spain. In her reign the leading Protestants either fled to the Continent or were burned at the stake as heretics. Mary tried to reverse the doctrinal changes of the Reformation, but some of its practical consequences, like the distribution of monastery lands, were irreversible. A Spaniard on the throne of England was not popular, and Mary dared not press her people too far: her accession had been opposed by the Privy Council, which proclaimed Lady Jane Grey queen, and she was also challenged by a rebellion led by Sir Thomas Wyatt the Younger, son of the poet. She maintained her Roman allegiance, she burned many Protestants at the stake, but she could not undo the work of her father and brother. Had she been able to produce an heir she might have done so, but failing that, her death in 1558 brought the Protestants back to power. The Protestant exiles returned from the continent to become a potent force in English society during the long reign of Mary's half sister, Elizabeth Tudor, daughter of Henry's second wife, Anne Boleyn.

Queen Elizabeth established the English Church in terms acceptable to the vast majority of her subjects. She imposed a form of service (retaining much of the old Roman ritual), and while she compelled her subjects to attend it she left their consciences to themselves. The Elizabethan manifesto of faith, the Thirty-Nine Articles, formulated the chief matters of doctrinal controversy in somewhat ambiguous terms; and Elizabeth made every effort to eliminate controversial preaching from the pulpits. That compromise satisfied neither Roman Catholics, who sought to return to Rome, nor the Puritans, who pressed for more radical reform. But it accommodated most of the populace, who now looked neither to Rome nor Geneva as the prime source of authority in religion, but to their own sovereign.

NATIONALISM—ELIZABETH I

Queen Elizabeth I, who ascended the throne in 1558 and ruled until 1603, was one of the most remarkable political geniuses England has ever produced. Vain, difficult, and headstrong, she nevertheless had a very shrewd instinct about her country's strengths and weaknesses, and she identified herself with England as no previous ruler had done. Although she was susceptible to the flattery of courtiers and favorites, she entrusted the power of state to solid men such as William Cecil (Lord Burleigh) and Francis Walsingham. Cecil (1520–1598) was her chief and most trusted secretary. With unswerving loyalty he devoted his great talents to the service of the queen in domestic affairs, as well as in the complex relations with the governments of Europe. He sought also, with limited success, to raise money from Parliament to pay for the increasing cost of government. Walsingham (ca. 1530–1590) was a radical Protestant, who tried to promote a more ideologically committed foreign policy than the queen and Cecil were prepared to support.

England's strength lay in its power to sway the balance of power in Europe: it could throw its weight either way in the ongoing power struggle between Spain and France; and it could support or fail to support the Protestant uprisings against Spain in the Low Countries. Moreover, Elizabeth made adroit use of her situation as an unmarried monarch generally expected to marry so as to provide a legitimate heir to the throne. She kept all Europe guessing as to her intentions, skillfully playing her several suitors off against one another—and at length insisted that England alone was her spouse. By the time it was too late for her to marry and bear children, England was strong and united.

Ironically, the papal bull (decree) of 1570, excommunicating Elizabeth and relieving her subjects of their loyalty to her, contributed greatly to that unity. This bull was intended to bring to the throne Mary Stuart, Queen of Scots, who was Catholic by faith and French by culture—an insupportable thought. The English rallied to their queen, and she became a symbol of Englishness and nationalism. The adulation of her, in the face of trouble on the Scottish border, near-chaos in Ireland, and continued threats from the Continent, took on religious intensity. Her reputation for beauty (which was exaggerated) and for wisdom (which was not) became articles of faith. In 1588 God himself seemed to testify to her divine mission to guide England: Philip II of Spain sent out the mightiest invasion fleet ever mounted against England, but that Spanish Armada was almost wholly destroyed by a violent storm, which seemed an act of God.

Despite the Elizabethan settlement of the English Church, Elizabeth's reign continued to be plagued by politico-religious unrest. Catholics who adhered to the pro-Spanish faction of the previous reign continued their plots to put Mary Stuart on the throne (causing Elizabeth at length to concur in her execution). And the Protestant exiles whose sojourn on the Continent had sharpened their zeal for more radical reforms coalesced into a strong and vocal Puritan movement. But most English people, remembering the civil conflicts of the previous century, placed a high value on order in church and state; and for them Elizabeth became, in her person and her policy, a symbol of national unity.

The desire for commercial profit also strengthened nationalistic feelings. In 1493 the Pope had divided the new world between the Spanish and the Portuguese by drawing a line from pole to pole (hence Brazil speaks Portuguese today, and the rest of Latin America speaks Spanish): the English were not in the picture. But by the end of Edward VI's reign the Company of Merchant Adventurers was founded, and Englishmen began to explore Asia and North America. Some of these adventurers turned to piracy, preying on Spanish ships which were returning laden with wealth from the New World. This business soon became a private undeclared war, with the queen and her courtiers investing in these raids privately but accepting no responsibility for them. The greatest of many dazzling exploits was the voyage of Francis Drake in 1577–80: he sailed through the Straits of Magellan, pillaged Spanish towns on the Pacific, reached as far north as San Francisco, crossed to the Philippines, and returned around the Cape of Good Hope; he came back with one million pounds in treasure, and his investors earned a dividend of 5,000 percent. Queen Elizabeth knighted him on the deck of his ship, *The Golden Hind*.

The mere survival of Elizabeth for so long provided the opportunity for nationalistic consciousness to become firmly established. When she came to the throne in 1558 she was only twenty-five years old, and she remained queen for almost forty-five years. It is wholly appropriate therefore that the second half of the sixteenth century bear her name, the Elizabethan Age.

PATRONS, WRITERS, AND PUBLISHERS

During Elizabeth's reign patronage was a social institution of the first importance, a major force in transforming the great nobles and gentry from independently powerful local magnates into courtiers dependent upon the monarch. The queen's chief ministers and favorites (Cecil, Leicester, Essex) were the primary channels through which patronage was dispensed to courtiers who wanted offices in the court, the government bureaucracies, the royal household, the army, the Church, the universities, or who sought titles, grants of land, leases, or similar favors. In their turn, successful courtiers could dispense benefits to their petitioners. Men like Sir Christopher

Hatton and Sir Walter Ralegh leapt from obscurity to great power and prominence as a result of their success as courtiers, which owed as much to their gallantry and their dancing as to their more solid abilities. And some noble women also wielded considerable power and influence as patrons, notably Mary Herbert, Countess of Pembroke, Margaret Clifford, Countess of Cumberland, Anne Dudley, Countess of Warwick, and Lucy (Harington) Russell, Countess of Bedford.

The great guide and conduct book for the courtier was Castiglione's *Il Cortegiano* (1528, translated into English by Sir Thomas Hoby in 1561). That book declared that the chief function of the courtier is to give good and honest advice to the prince, but courtiers who followed that honorable course were very likely to provoke a monarch's resentment, as Sir Philip Sidney found out when he tried to advise Queen Elizabeth against a proposed French marriage. Literary men of lower rank who were not in a position to be real courtiers might still look to the court for livelihood, notice, and encouragement, but that prospect was often discouraging. "A thousand hopes, but all nothing," wailed John Lyly, alluding to his long wait for the office of Master of the Revels; "a hundred promises, but yet nothing." Spenser's bitter disappointment in failing to win court patronage (reflected in *Mother Hubberds Tale* and *Colin Clouts Come Home Againe*) was dispelled only toward the end of his life when Queen Elizabeth awarded him a pension of fifty pounds. Indeed, a pervasive sense of court life as precarious, superficial, and hypocritical gave rise to works in the vein of the poems of Horace praising the retired country life far from corruptions of the court: early examples are Sir Thomas Wyatt's verse epistles to Sir Francis Bryan and John Poins, and the motif remained prominent to the time of Ralegh—and beyond.

Literary patronage was part of the interlocking patronage system whereby grants, offices, and honors were exchanged for service and praise. We must recognize that the career of a professional man or woman of letters did not exist: literature was regarded as an adjunct activity, not a primary occupation, and there were comparatively few readers, purchasers, and publishers of books. Elizabethan writers of higher rank, like Sir Philip Sidney, thought of themselves as courtiers, statesmen, landowners; they considered poetry a social grace and a courtly pastime. Writers of lower rank like Samuel Daniel or Michael Drayton sought careers as civil servants, secretaries, tutors, and divines; they might take up more or less permanent residence in a noble household, or, more casually, they might offer their literary work to actual or prospective patrons, amid lavish praises, in the hope of support, career advancement, or financial reward. Even Ben Jonson, who more than most of his contemporaries claimed the role of poet and managed to live tolerably well by it, summed up the situation in these words:

> Poetry in this latter age hath proved but a mean mistress to such as have wholly addicted themselves to her, or given their names up to her family. Those who have but saluted her on the way, and now and then tendered their visits, she hath done much for, and advanced in the way of their own professions (both the law and the gospel) beyond all they could have hoped or done for themselves without her favor.

Financial rewards for writing prose or poetry came mostly in the form of gifts from patrons, who sought to enhance their status and flatter their vanity through the service and lavish praises of many clients. But we hear constant complaints about patrons who do not reward authors for dedications (the usual reward was two or three pounds for a pamphlet or small volume of verse). Shakespeare's relations with his patron, the Earl of Southampton, little as we know about them, were apparently satisfactory, as the dedication to *The Rape of Lucrece* (1594) attests. But the experience of Robert Greene is perhaps more typical: the fact that he had sixteen different patrons for seventeen books suggests that he did not find much favor or support from any one of them. Indeed, a fraudulent practice grew up of printing off several dedications to be inserted into particular copies of a book, so that an impecunious author could deceive several patrons each into thinking that he was the one to be honored by the volume. However, some Elizabethan patrons were well-educated humanists motivated by genuine literary interests, and with them, patronage extended beyond financial support to the creation of literary and intellectual circles. Several writers (among them Samuel Daniel, Fulke Greville, Spenser) enjoyed long- or short-term hospitality and stimulation as members of the circles of the Sidneys at Penshurst or the Pembrokes at Wilton.

In addition to the court and the great families as dispensers of patronage, the two universities and the City of London were also major influences on the literary production of this period. Before Elizabeth's time, the universities were mainly devoted to educating the clergy, and that remained an important part of their function. But in the second half of the century the sons of the gentry and the aristocracy were going in increasing numbers to the universities and the Inns of Court (law schools), though often they did not take degrees or get called to the bar. Their residence in these places was simply an educational preparation for public service or managing their estates. A group of graduates, the so-called "university wits," associated themselves with the literary scene in London; these men (among them Thomas Nashe, Christopher Marlowe, Robert Greene, and George Peele) gave to the Elizabethan drama some of the classical form it needed and contributed to the great outpouring of literature in the 1590s. But their lives testify to the difficulties they found trying to sustain themselves by writing. The diary of Philip Henslowe, a leading theatrical manager, has entry after entry showing university graduates in prison or in debt, or at best eking out a miserable existence patching plays.

The City of London itself had a major impact on the literature of Elizabeth's reign. In Chaucer's time London had a population of about 50,000; in 1563 it had around 93,250, and nearly 225,000 in 1605. It was by far the most important city in the realm, and the political history of the seventeenth century is incomprehensible unless one recognizes the great power the City had, even as against the Crown. The printing presses were located in London, the printers and booksellers were in London, and the mass of the middle-class population that set the style for literature written for ordinary people was also in London. And although Thomas Nashe scornfully rejected the claim of the bourgeoisie to have any literary taste at all, or any ability to produce literature, that class had its own writers, like Thomas Deloney, and it knew what it liked—books of instruction, romances, religious tracts, conduct books for men and women, and sensational ballads. The London populace also found among the university men some writers who catered to them: Thomas Heywood is a good example. Whether the aristocrats admitted it or not, the standards and tastes of the middle class affected all publishing and literary success. The customers who frequented the stalls of St. Pauls

Churchyard—the center of the book trade—were more often members of the middle class than of the court circle. Louis B. Wright has shown (in his *Middle-Class Culture in Elizabethan England*) how extensive and profound was the influence of the citizenry upon the writing and publication of books, and how bourgeois standards of edification and utility dictated to most of the authors of the time.

The sixteenth century was the first century of the printed book, and the Elizabethan age was an extremely prolific one in writing and publishing. The *Short Title Catalogue* of the Bibliographical Society, which lists works and editions published in England between 1475 and 1640, includes over 26,000 items, and that is an incomplete list. But the rewards for having books published were nothing like they are today. There was no such thing as copyright, and no such thing, in the ordinary way, as royalties paid to an author according to the sale of the book. Authors sold their manuscripts to the printer or bookseller outright, for what now seems like a ridiculously low price—for a pamphlet or small book of poetry, usually forty shillings.

Nor did the author's troubles end with that sale. Writers as well as their publishers had to abide by stringent regulations governing the publication of books, and might be punished for failure to do so by several political and ecclesiastical authorities. The regulations provided that the number of printers (not booksellers) be strictly limited; that nothing could be printed except in the City of London and at the universities of Oxford and Cambridge; that everything printed must receive the imprimatur of the archbishop of Canterbury and the bishop of London or their representatives; and that everything published in London must be entered on the registers of the Stationers' Company—a regulation that protected the property rights of the publisher and printer rather than the author. The enforcing authorities included the Privy Council, the highest political authority in the realm below the queen; the Court of Star Chamber, which punished breaches of censorship; the Court of High Commission, the supreme ecclesiastical authority; and the Stationers' Company.

An extreme example of the dangers besetting authors is provided by the history of John Stubbs, who protested against Elizabeth's projected French marriage in a pamphlet called *The Discovery of a Gaping Gulf* (1579). For writing this pamphlet, Stubbs had his right hand cut off with one stroke of a butcher's cleaver—after which he took up his hat with his left hand and cried, "God save the queen." Indeed, almost every writer of the period got into some sort of trouble for publishing a book. It might be prison, it might be merely a reprimand, it might be an investigation by the Star Chamber. It was dangerous to put pen to paper and so unprofitable that it is a wonder any original writing was published at all.

However, to suppose that poetry, or even prose, circulated only in printed form would be a mistake. The older way of passing works around in manuscript lingered on into the seventeenth century, and was especially the practice of poets of gentle or noble rank. Sidney is the most prominent example. Sir John Harington, in his translation of Ariosto's *Orlando Furioso* in 1591, mentions a sonnet of Sidney's "which many I am sure have read;" but that sonnet was not published until seven years later. This was certainly the practice of some noblewomen: we have a few manuscript poems by Queen Elizabeth and the Countess of Pembroke, but those of other women reputed to have written poetry have been lost. Many people kept commonplace books in which they copied down poems from borrowed manuscript copies.

Professional scribes made a living by copying manuscripts for authors and for readers. There were even complaints by printers that literary manuscripts were being hoarded by "their grand possessors." Difference of audience clearly affected the kinds of literature produced—on the one hand by professional writers intending to publish, and on the other, by gentle or noble poets who passed their work about among their cultivated friends.

ART AND NATURE: ELIZABETHAN AESTHETICS

We can read Elizabethan literature with more comprehension if we recognize the differences between the aesthetic principles of the sixteenth century and those of our own day. At the root of the matter is a different conception of art, and of the relation between art and nature. The Romantic movement (which still profoundly affects our aesthetics) glorified nature and valued art that seems "natural," personal, sincere, uncontrived; it also valued the artist for originality, and often ascribed that quality to a special, mysterious inspiration. Such views would have seemed strange indeed to the Elizabethans. They recognized of course that nature is the basis of art, but had no uneasiness about a possible conflict between art and nature. The term "artificial" had for them good rather than dubious meanings, referring to the proper use of human ingenuity to enhance nature, to enable it to outdo itself. The point is underscored in Shakespeare's *Winter's Tale*, in an amusing exchange about horticulture. Perdita exclaims that she will have no streaked carnations or gillyflowers in her garden because the art that produces them seems to challenge "great creating nature," but Polixenes replies that such art is itself a part of nature:

> Yet Nature is made better by no mean
> But Nature makes that mean; so over that art
> Which you say adds to Nature, is an art
> That Nature makes. You see, sweet maid, we marry
> A gentler scion to the wildest stock,
> And make conceive a bark of baser kind
> By bud of nobler race. This is an art
> Which does mend Nature—change it rather; but
> The art itself is Nature.

Such concern with the improvement by device, by arrangement, by human ingenuity, by art of something naturally beautiful extended to all aspects of life, so that there was no great gulf between the art or craft of writing and the techniques of other crafts—hawking, archery, building, cookery, managing a great horse in a tournament, sailing, planting a garden. And intricacy of design, elaborateness of pattern were especially valued. The Elizabethan garden was designed as a square, filled with elaborate and intricate, but perfectly regular, design. Some Elizabethans had their houses built in the shape of an E, out of honor to the queen, and one man, John Thorpe, designed his house in the form of his own initials. The several Elizabethan dances—pavans, galliards, almains, sarabands—also presented elaborate, highly patterned designs. Contrapuntal music (composed of several independent melodies joined together) was very intricate, with its elaborate patterns and complex harmonies. The composer Thomas Morley (ca. 1557–1603) praises the madrigal for displaying just such qualities:

> As for the music it is, next unto the motet, the most artificial and to men of understanding most delightful. If therefore you will compose in this kind . . . you must in your music be wavering like the wind, some-time wanton, sometime grave and staid, otherwise effeminate; you may maintain points and revert them, use triplaes [triplets] and show the very uttermost of your variety, and the more variety you show the better shall you please.

But a rigid form was to control all of this extravagance, and the fusion of such complexity with such order was often seen, as in Sir John Davies's poem, *Orchestra, or, a Poem on Dancing*, as an emblem of concord and harmony in the universe.

Another vital principal of Elizabethan aesthetics was the concern with models, with conventions, with the literary tradition as the very vehicle for artistic expression. Renaissance writers were in their own way profoundly original, but they did not think of originality as involving opposition to or revolt against literary traditions or artistic conventions. But neither were they slavish imitators. Rather, they looked to classical (and continental) works as models to learn from, emulate, transform, and if possible surpass. The chief models were Homer and Virgil for epic, Theocritus and Virgil for pastoral, Cicero for rhetoric and prose style, Plautus and Terence for comedy, Seneca for tragedy, Petrarch for the sonnet, Ariosto and Tasso for the romantic epic, Ovid for love poetry and erotic mythological narratives.

Sidney's *Defence of Poesy* is the only major work of literary criticism in sixteenth-century England, a period during which Italy and France pro-duced large numbers of critical treatises, heavily influenced by Aristotle's *Poetics*. By contrast, Sidney's engaging tract is highly eclectic, drawing together aesthetic precepts from several traditions and underscoring those which are of primary importance to the Elizabethans: ideal imitation, moral teaching, decorum. Looking back to Aristotle, Sidney defines poetry as an imitation of nature, but links that imitation to his view of the poet as maker, whose activity reflects that of the Divine Creator. The poet imitates not the real, fallen nature we see, but "lifted up with the vigor of his own invention" he imitates an ideal nature: "her world is brazen, the Poets only deliver a golden." Sidney also makes large claims for the didactic role of poetry: he invokes Horace's formula that poetry teaches by delighting, but (staunch Protestant that he is) he emphasizes even more its rhetorical power to move us to be virtuous. He also highlights the importance of suiting subject to genre and style—the idea of literary decorum that Milton was later to term "the grand masterpiece to observe."

From Sidney, from Puttenham's *Art of English Poesy*, and from numer-ous Elizabethan treatises on rhetoric that define and illustrate literally hundreds of rhetorical and poetic figures of speech, we can infer some other aesthetic principles: the delight in *copia* or "abundance" of words, poetic figures, ornament; the close relation of poetry and rhetoric; the concern with levels of style (high, middle, and low); and the continuing importance of allegory as a means to teach moral truths, and also to suggest the mysterious analo-gies and symbolic relationships that permeate and order God's universe. Among such symbolic relationships are those suggested by the pervasive macrocosm–microcosm analogy, according to which everything in the vast universe may be found, replicated in little, in the human body; and also those suggested by the image of the Great Chain of Being, according to which all orders of being, from speck of dust to highest angel, are ranged hierarchically in their divinely ordered stations.

POETIC CONVENTIONS, MODES, AND GENRES

Literary conventions are patterns that have become habitual, and arouse certain expectations in the reader. They are by no means stale and lifeless, but are charged with values and associations: for example, we all recognize the conventions in a patriotic song or a religious hymn pertaining to subject, topics, tone, and expected responses. Literary conventions challenged Elizabethan poets to find fit forms for their experiences, to show their learning and virtuosity by the ingenious elaboration of these well-known patterns, and to create from these patterns something fresh and new. Because such conventions are shared cultural codes, they enable poets to elicit particular responses from readers and to relate both poets and readers to other times, other languages, other cultures.

Clusters of such literary conventions—pertaining to subject matter, attitude, tone, values, and some set topics—identify several important literary modes (or "kinds" as Sidney terms them) in the period, including pastoral, heroic, lyric, satiric, elegiac, tragic, and comic. Other conventions—pertaining not only to subject matter and attitude but also to formal structure, meter, style, size, occasion, and the like—identify such important Elizabethan genres or particular literary forms as epic, tragedy, sonnet, verse epistle, epigram, hymn, masque, funeral elegy, and many more. Though Aristotle considered tragedy the noblest form, Elizabethans commonly placed epic at the pinnacle of their genre system, and pastoral poems at the base. Accordingly, Renaissance poets of lofty ambition, like Spenser and Milton, consciously followed the course of poetic development set by Virgil, beginning with pastoral and rising to epic. It is important to remember, however, that such genres and modes are not simply a cluster of conventions and patterns: they carry with them a whole range of culturally defined assumptions and values relating to man and woman, nature, language, heroism, virtue, pleasure, work, and love.

The conventions of the pastoral mode (or kind) present a simple and idealized world inhabited by shepherds and shepherdesses who are chiefly concerned to tend their flocks, fall in love, engage in friendly poetry contests. The values of this mode are defined by *otium* (leisure and humble contentment)—which is at the opposite pole from pride, ambition, the pursuit of fame and fortune. Pastoral exalts the simple country life over the city and its business, the military camp and its warfare, the court and its burdens of rule. The conventions of the pastoral mode could be assimilated to several different genres. Pastoral songs commonly expressed the joys of the shepherd's life, or disappointment in love. Pastoral eclogues were dialogues between shepherds, which might stage a simple poetry contest or might conceal serious, satiric comment on abuses in the great world under the guise of homely, local concerns. There were also pastoral funeral elegies, pastoral dramas, pastoral romances (prose fiction), and even pastoral episodes within epics.

Poems in the satirical mode were also placed among the "low" kinds, plain in matter and style. The genres for satire were less well fixed in the sixteenth century than they were later, but there is a good deal of satirical verse. Some early examples belong to a medieval tradition coming down from *Piers Plowman*, while others, notably Wyatt's epistolary satires, are related to the classical satirists Horace and Juvenal. In the 1590s verse sat-

ires, chiefly in rhymed iambic pentameter couplets and closely modeled
upon Horace, Juvenal, and Persius, were published by Joseph Hall and John
Marston; at the same time, the young John Donne was circulating satires in
manuscript that were published only after his death (in 1631). These satires
hold up to ridicule and scorn a society (usually a city society) peopled by
fops and fools, venal lawyers, toadying courtiers, money-grubbing merchants, self-deluded lovers, and all their ilk. The brief, pointed epigram in
the tradition of Martial (often with a surprise ending or "sting" in the tail)
was probably the most important of the Elizabethan satiric genres, but
throughout the sixteenth and seventeenth centuries epigrams were still often
written in Latin. The most notable English achievement in this kind is Ben
Jonson's *Epigrams*, first published in 1616. (It is worth noting, however,
that some epigrams were lyric in mode, sometimes in the form of words for
a madrigal: *The Silver Swan* is an example.)

Poems in the lyric mode were comparatively brief, and usually concerned
with praises of various kinds, with love in its various moods, or with celebrations of nature, the good life, or other such matters. The noblest lyric genres
were thought to be hymns (praises of God or the gods) and odes (celebrating
worthy men and women, and notable occasions); such poems were conventionally exalted in tone, elevated in language, charged with feeling; they
often had complex stanzaic patterns and frequent apostrophes. An important
variety of ode in the sixteenth century was the epithalamium, a poem in
praise of marriage, conventionally following the course of the wedding day—
and night. The most famous example is Spenser's *Epithalamion*, whose long
stanzas (varying from 17 to 19 lines) display an astonishing metrical complexity, fairly illustrating the height of Elizabethan craft in verse. Notable
classical models were Horace, Catullus, Pindar, and Callimachus, and notable biblical models were the Book of Psalms and the Song of Songs.

Often, Elizabethan lyrics retained something of the original association
of this mode with song (the lyre). There were dance songs with their definite
rhythms and refrains, and many well-known tunes provided the formula by
which poet after poet composed new words. There were also many varieties
of song, written to fixed formal specifications: the popular ballad with its
simple four-line stanza, of anonymous or perhaps composite authorship; the
polyphonic madrigal for two or more voices in counterpoint, which had to
be short and simple both in language and ideas; the stanzaic "air" for single
voice and lute, its more complex thought carried by the recurrent melody.

A most important lyric genre in the sixteenth century was the sonnet,
which reached the height of its vogue in the 1590s. Its conventions were
established by Petrarch (1304–1374), carried on by his numerous imitators
in Italy and France, and introduced into England by Wyatt and Surrey in
the reign of Henry VIII. The Petrarchan sonnet sequence is a series of fourteen-line sonnets (with songs interspersed) exploring the contrary states of
feeling a lover experiences as he desires and idolizes an unattainable lady:
some conventional themes concern the lady's great beauty, her power over
him, her cruelty to him, his sleeplessness, the fire of his love and the ice of
her chastity, the pain of absence, the renunciation of love, the eternity and
originality of his poems. One late sequence by Lady Mary Wroth (*Pamphilia
to Amphilanthus*, 1621) reverses the conventional situation, presenting a
female speaker who explores her various emotions, conflicts, and experiences in love. The purposes of the love sonneteers differed, of course, but

they chiefly sought to celebrate the dignity and power of love by the elaborate rhetorical and stylistic devices available in the Petrarchan tradition.

All love sonnets were not Petrarchan, nor were all sonnets, or sonnet sequences, devoted to love: some sequences treated religious devotion, and occasional sonnets might address a wide variety of topics. More than most genres the sonnet has come to be identified by its formal structure, a fourteen-line poem in iambic pentameter, in three principal rhyming patterns. The most common Italian form, which Wyatt, Sidney, and others imitated, was divided structurally into an octave (first eight lines, rhymed *abba abba*) and a sestet (last six, typically rhymed *cdecde* or some variant thereof). The so-called English sonnet, introduced by Surrey and practiced by Shakespeare, is divided structurally into three quatrains and a couplet, rhymed *abab cdcd efef gg*. Spenser, the most experimental and gifted prosodist of the century, preferred a form that is harder to write and richer in rhymes: *abab bcbc cdcd ee*. Yet sonnets were not so rigidly defined in the sixteenth century: Elizabethans often called them "quatorzains," and often used the term "sonnet" quite loosely, to refer to any short poem.

There were also poems (as well as dramas) in the tragic mode. A principal genre was the complaint, developed especially by the Italian Boccaccio and his English imitators, Lydgate and the authors of *The Mirror for Magistrates*. The chief convention of the complaint is that the ghost of someone who fell from high place bemoans his fate and warns others; the warning carries a moral lesson. If the ghost is a woman like Daniel's Rosamond, her fall was caused by the frailty of her sex. A related kind of poem is the heroical epistle, in which the complaint is written as a letter, usually by a wronged woman to the man who abandoned or betrayed her. Drayton was the chief Elizabethan writer in this kind, which harks back to Ovid.

Another set of conventions defined a mythological-erotic mode, derived mainly from the *Metamorphoses* of Ovid but influenced also by his Italian imitators. The medieval disposition to allegorize and moralize Ovid's poetry continued into the seventeenth century (as did the habit of allegorizing the erotic love songs in the Song of Solomon in the Old Testament). But in the late sixteenth century the Ovidian erotic mode was revived: its values and conventions of lush and elaborate descriptions of physical beauty, of delight in the pleasures of the senses, and of frank eroticism appealed to a courtly taste. In this vein were several poems in the genre of the epyllion, or short mythological narrative, among them Shakespeare's *Venus and Adonis* and Marlowe's *Hero and Leander*.

Finally of course, there was the heroic mode, with its values of honor, battle courage, loyalty, leadership, endurance, glorification of nation or people. The chief genre was the epic, conventionally a long, exalted poem in the high style, based on a heroic story from the nation's distant history and imitating Homer and Virgil in structure and specific topics. Renaissance poets throughout Europe undertook to honor their nations and their vernacular languages by writing this highest kind of poetry. In sixteenth-century England the only real success in epic is Spenser's *Faerie Queene*, which is, properly speaking, a romantic epic, in that it draws more heavily upon the conventions of the romantic Italian epics of Ariosto and Tasso (with their interwoven plots, their exotic adventures and marvels, and their fundamental concern with love as well as war) than upon the classical epics. Spenser points to that genre explicitly when he declares, "Fierce warres and faithfull loves shall moralize my song." By convention, epics had to achieve an elevated, high style, and Spenser devised an elaborate nine-line stanza (called after him the "Spenserian stanza") to serve his special narrative and descriptive needs. It consisted of eight lines of iambic pentameter (rhymed *ababbcbc*), concluding with a line of twelve syllables, an Alexandrine, which rhymes with the preceding line and provides firm closure for each stanza.

We should remember that genres and modes were often mixed in Renaissance England, and that large poems like *The Faerie Queene* contained elements of many kinds. Some new, mixed kinds—like tragicomedy—attracted considerable criticism, but flourished nonetheless. Some others, like Sidney's *Arcadia*, are obviously experimental—a prose romance incorporating both pastoral and heroic elements. The Elizabethans did not approach genre with the rigidity and purism of the Italian or French neoclassicists, but in the spirit of Sidney's inclusivism: "if severed they be good, the conjunction cannot be hurtful."

Also worth noting are some distinctive verse patterns that came to be associated, conventionally, with certain kinds of poems. Henry Howard, earl of Surrey, introduced blank verse (unrhymed iambic pentameter) into England, in his translation of Virgil; this became the conventional meter for Elizabethan tragedy (and later for Milton's epics.) The most common verse form in the 1560s and 1570s was an iambic couplet in which the first line had twelve syllables and the second fourteen, called "poulter's measure" (because a poultryman typically gave twelve eggs in the first dozen and fourteen in the second). An example is:

> The young man eke that feels his bones with pains oppressed,
> How he would be a rich old man, to live and lie at rest.

The dreary monotony of this meter is matched only by the "fourteener" couplet of fourteen syllables to a line. But both were taken into the Elizabethan hymnbooks and survive there: when each line of poulter's measure is printed as two lines it is called "short meter"; when fourteeners are so divided it is called "common meter." Also, some Chaucerian verse forms survive, to be used by Shakespeare in his narrative poems: the six-line pentameter stanza (a quatrain and a couplet, rhymed *ababcc*) in *Venus and Adonis*; and the rhyme royal stanza (seven iambic pentameter lines, rhymed *ababbcc*) in *The Rape of Lucrece*.

DRAMATIC LITERATURE AND THE THEATER

If the morality play *Everyman* at the end of the fifteenth century marks the end of medieval drama, some new beginnings are in evidence at the same time in the household of John Morton, archbishop of Canterbury and chancellor of England under Henry VII, where young Thomas More served as a page. There at Christmastime, plays or revels were put on, and the story goes that young More would sometimes improvise a part and step in with the players. Cardinal Morton even maintained a chaplain on his staff, Henry Medwall, to write plays for his entertainment; two of them survive, called *Nature* and *Fulgens and Lucrece*. These plays were short, given in the great hall at Lambeth Palace, and were called "interludes." Some interludes, especially those by John Heywood, are heavily dependent upon French farce.

Interludes and morality plays continued to be popular down to Shakespeare's lifetime, but the development of drama into a sophisticated art form required another influence, the classics. In the middle of the century a schoolmaster, Nicholas Udall, wrote a classical comedy in English, based upon the Latin comedies his students had been reading; he called it *Ralph Roister Doister*. At about the same time another comedy, putting vivid, native English material into classical form, was amusing the students at Cambridge. It was called *Gammar Gurton's Needle*. In the development of comedy as a genre the great classical models were the Latin comic playwrights Plautus and Terence, from whom English dramatists derived some elements of structure and content: intrigue plots, a structure of acts and scenes, and type characters such as the rascally servant and the *miles gloriosus* (cowardly braggart soldier). The latter type appears in *Ralph Roister Doister* and is a remote ancestor of Shakespeare's Sir John Falstaff in *1 Henry IV*. Comedy was generally taken to be a lower genre than tragedy, and the style often mixed prose and verse: middle and lower class characters especially tended to speak prose.

Many varieties of comedy developed during the Elizabethan and Jacobean age, influenced by classical models and also Italian and French examples. The conventions of romantic comedy call for noble characters and a central love plot (as in Shakespeare's *As You Like It* and *Twelfth Night*). Domestic comedy, as the name implies, has a domestic situation at the center of the plot (as in Thomas Dekker's *Shoemaker's Holiday*). City comedy typically has bourgeois characters, a London setting, and much satire (as in Thomas Middleton's *A Chaste Maid in Cheapside*). Humor comedy (such as Ben Jonson's *Every Man in his Humour*) has type characters created on the theory that the predominance of a particular fluid, or humor, in the body creates a specific temperament (melancholic, choleric, splenetic, phlegmatic). Jonson also wrote classical intrigue comedy in *The Alchemist* and *Volpone*, with their complex, fast-paced plots and discoveries, their characters based on classical types, their witty dialogue. Tragicomedy was a mixed kind, in which evils and problems which seem destined to end tragically are brought to sudden, happy resolution (as in Shakespeare's *Measure for Measure* and, in different mood, *The Winter's Tale*.)

Elizabethan tragedy also began with a fusion of medieval and classical elements. The precarious position of men in high estate formed the basis for medieval notions of tragedy; it owed much to the Latin tragedies of Seneca (known throughout the Middle Ages) which portray the Roman Goddess Fortuna turning her wheel, and thereby bringing low those that were high. This is the tragic vision of the narrative tales in Boccaccio's *Falls of Illustrious Men*, in Chaucer's *Monk's Tale*, and Lydgate's *Falls of Princes*; it is also the conception of tragedy in the collection of tales and complaints about the falls of princes called *The Mirror for Magistrates*, first published in 1559 and reprinted with additions in 1563, 1587, and 1610). A "mirror" in this sense is a warning, something to see oneself in and learn from; a "magistrate" is anyone in a position of power or authority.

When tragedies began to be dramatized, they took over very different elements from Seneca: violent and bloody plots, resounding rhetorical speeches, the frequent use of ghosts among the cast of characters, and sometimes the five-act structure. The first regular English tragedy using some of these elements was called *Gorboduc or Ferrex and Porrex*; it was written by two lawyers, Thomas Sackville and Thomas Norton, was first produced at the Inner Temple (a law school) in 1561, and was later acted before the queen. Significantly, *Gorboduc* was written in blank verse rather than in one of the awkward verse forms characteristic of much midcentury writing; its use here begins the establishment of blank verse as the accepted medium for English tragedy. In due course it evolved into "Marlowe's mighty line" and Shakespeare's wonderfully flexible and expressive poetry.

While Aristotle's *Poetics* did not provide rigid norms for tragedy in England as it did on the continent, it did influence the conception of the genre. Particularly important were the Aristotelian principles that the tragic fall should be caused by some error or moral weakness in the protagonist; that the plot should involve a fall from eminent success into misery, marked by reversals and discoveries; that the characters should be persons of high estate, "better than we"; and that the tragedy should evoke pity and fear in the viewers, working at last to achieve a purgation (catharsis) of those emotions. Some of Shakespeare's great tragedies (e.g., *Othello, King Lear*) can be analyzed in such terms, though, like most other Elizabethan tragedies, they are far from classical in their use of subplots and comic relief, their violations of the unities of time and place, their sheer expansiveness.

Several distinct varieties of tragedy developed during the Elizabethan period. The Senecan influence remained pervasive, giving rise to a subgenre of revenge tragedy, in which a wronged protagonist plots and executes revenge, destroying himself (or herself) in the process. An early, highly influential example is Thomas Kyd's *Spanish Tragedy* (1592); and for all its psychological complexity Shakespeare's *Hamlet* is also of this kind. A related but distinct kind (which Aristotle considered untragic) is the villain tragedy in which the protagonist is blatantly evil, as in Shakespeare's *Richard III* and *Macbeth*. Still another sort is the heroic tragedy, in which the hero is larger than life, continually challenging the limits of human possibility: Marlowe's "overreaching" heroes (Tamberlaine and Dr. Faustus) are of this kind, as are the two protagonists of Shakespeare's *Antony and Cleopatra*.

This exuberant era also gave rise to dramatic kinds that fall quite outside the generic boundaries of comedy and tragedy. The festival beginnings of drama in entertainments presented by the servants of a lord in the hall of his castle (often at winter and midsummer holidays and festivals) find some continuity in the several dramatic entertainments provided for Queen Elizabeth when she made progresses through her realm, visiting her nobles in their great houses. Another offshoot was the masque, an entertainment at court combining dance, song, dialogue, and spectacle; there were masques at the courts of Henry VIII and Queen Elizabeth, but the form was especially fostered by the Stuart monarchs in the next century—at which time it took on its characteristic qualities of extravagant display in costume and scenery. Yet another Elizabethan kind is the history play: taking its subjects from English history, it was especially suited to reflect the nationalistic sentiment, the sense of epic destiny, and the moral complexities of gaining and holding on to sovereign power. Shakespeare offers the prime example in his two cycles of history plays. His *1 Henry IV* is perhaps his supreme achievement in that kind.

This flowering of English drama depended centrally upon professional actors, a theater, and an audience. The earliest English drama had been acted by members of the clergy in the church; and medieval miracle and mystery plays had been acted by amateurs—members of the local trade guilds—ordinarily on wagons in the streets of the towns. Moralities and interludes were produced by the servants of a lord in the hall of his castle, or by semi-professional groups who traveled about, giving their performances wherever they could. Such actors did not have respectable status; they tended to be classified with jugglers, acrobats, mountebanks, and other persons of dubious character. In 1545 they were classified by statute as idle rogues and vagabonds, and as such were subject to arrest.

Some noblemen, however, maintained a company of actors as personal servants; since they wore the livery and badge of their master they were exempt from the statute and could travel when not needed by their master and practice their craft where they would. This practice explains why the professional acting companies of Shakespeare's time, including Shakespeare's own, attached themselves to a nobleman and were technically his servants (the Lord Chamberlain's men, the Lord Admiral's men), even though virtually all their time was devoted to, and their income came from, the public. The rise in social status of actors during Shakespeare's lifetime is illustrated by the fact that he and his fellows were made officers of the royal household when James came to the throne and became known as the King's Men. However, the earliest successful acting companies, if success is measured by acceptance at court, were companies of boys. Richard Edwards, master of the children of the Chapel Royal in the 1560s, wrote plays for them, and for almost twenty years the rival company, the Children of Paul's (the choir school of St. Paul's cathedral) regularly presented plays at court.

At first, the adult companies played in various places—great houses, the hall of an Inn of Court, on makeshift stages, or in London inn-yards. In 1576 James Burbage, one of the earl of Leicester's players, built a structure to house their performances and called it The Theatre. It was in Shoreditch, outside the limits of the City of London, and accordingly beyond the jurisdiction of the city authorities who were generally hostile to dramatic spectacles. Soon, other public theaters were erected, which could accommodate some 2,000 spectators: they were usually oval in shape, with an unroofed yard in the center where the groundlings (apprentices, servants, men of the lower classes) stood, and covered seats in three rising tiers around the yard for the spectators of higher social status. A large platform stage jutted out into the yard, surrounded on three sides by spectators—who sometimes also sat on the stage. (See the drawing of a typical London Playhouse on p. 2599).

Plays were acted at high speed, without the act-and-scene breaks we are used to; there was no scenery and few props, but costumes were usually sumptuous and elaborate. Performances were given in the afternoon, and were subject to cancelation by bad weather or by epidemics of plague that periodically ravaged the city. Before long there were also enclosed private theaters, secured under conditions that would also allow them freedom from municipal control; they were indoors, artificially lighted, and patronized by a more select audience. After 1608 Shakespeare's company had its regular public theater, the Globe, and a private theater, the Blackfriars.

The companies of players were what would now be called "repertory companies"—that is, they filled the roles of each play from members of their own group, not employing outsiders. They performed a number of different plays on consecutive days, and the principal actors were shareholders in the profits of the company. Boys were apprenticed to actors just as they had been apprenticed to master craftsmen in the guilds; they took the women's parts in plays until their voices changed. The plays might be bought for the company from hack writers, or as in Shakespeare's company, the group might include an actor-playwright who could supply it with some (but by no means all) of its plays. The text remained the property of the company, but a popular play was eagerly sought by the printers, and the company sometimes had trouble achieving effective control over its rights to the play. The editors of the first collected edition of Shakespeare's plays, the First Folio (1623) alluded to the prior publication of "divers stolen and surreptitious copies" of his plays, "maimed and deformed by the frauds and stealths of injurious imposters."

ELIZABETHAN ATTITUDES

The English Renaissance made no sharp break with the past. Attitudes characteristic of the fourteenth or fifteenth centuries persisted well into the era of Humanism and Reformation. George Gascoigne, the leading poet of the 1570s, has in many ways a medieval point of view, as well as a notably plain style, and that flamboyant and "modern" Elizabethan Sir Walter Ralegh also dwells on the vanity and transitoriness of all earthly ambitions and achievements. The Dance of Death and related images were still living symbols to the Elizabethans, as Shakespeare's *Richard II* (3.2.155–70) indicates:

> For God's sake let us sit upon the ground
> And tell sad stories of the death of kings:
> How some have been depos'd; some slain in war,
> Some haunted by the ghosts they have deposed,
> Some poisoned by their wives, some sleeping killed,
> All murthered—for within the hollow crown
> That rounds the mortal temples of a king
> Keeps Death his court, and there the antic sits,
> Scoffing his state and grinning at his pomp,
> Allowing him a breath, a little scene,
> To monarchize, be feared, and kill with looks,
> Infusing him with self and vain conceit,
> As if this flesh which walls about our life
> Were brass impregnable, and humor'd thus,
> Comes at the last and with a little pin
> Bores through the castle wall, and farewell king!

Yet there was at the same time a spirit of joy and gaity, of innocence and lightheartedness, which welds the love of the English for their countryside to the mood of pastoral—quiet contentment and reflective leisure. Marlowe's *Passionate Shepherd to His Love* embodies this spirit, as do also many songs from Shakespeare's plays:

> When daisies pied, and violets blue,
> And lady-smocks all silver-white,
> And cookoo-buds of yellow hue
> Do paint the meadows with delight.

But the Elizabethans also manifest the opposite mood: the burning desire for conquest, for achievement, for surmounting all obstacles. The great poet of this "aspiring mind" is Christopher Marlowe, whose several heroes fling themselves into the lust for gold—"Infinite riches in a little room"; or into the pursuit of power—"Is it not passing brave to be a king / And ride in triumph through Persepolis?"; or into the search for knowledge—"All things that move between the quiet poles / Shall be at my command. . . . / [For]

. . . his dominion that excels in this / Stretches as far as doth the mind of man." Marlowe's heroes are defeated finally, all of them, but their fiery striving spirit endures long after they are gone.

The Elizabethan spirit has been described as "sensuous, comprehensive, extravagant, disorderly, thirsty for beauty, abounding in the zest for life." But we need also to remember Ben Jonson, with his classical principles of structure and decorum, his ideal of the centered self and the balanced moral life, his emphasis upon learning, and his reconciliation of classical and native English elements in his poetry and drama. Even more centrally, there is Sidney, the very embodiment of the Elizabethan Renaissance man—courtier, soldier, humanist scholar, Petrarchan sonneteer, literary critic, and earnest supporter of Protestant reform at home and abroad.

If the beginning of the Tudor era showed more links with the past than with the future, the end of Elizabeth's reign prefigured the conflict and uncertainty of the next age. In 1599, the year of Spenser's death, the headstrong Earl of Essex returned from Ireland, and at length mounted a rebellion that led to his execution in 1601. Elizabeth was old, a peaceful succession was by no means assured, and the rifts (religious and social, and political) which were to lead to civil war in the mid-seventeenth century were already in evidence. An outbreak of satire and epigrams in the 1590s was thought to be dangerous and was repressed by the authorities. Some of the cynical undercurrents in Shakespeare's *Hamlet* and *Troilus and Cressida* reflect the general disenchantment and disillusionment. In 1603, Elizabeth, the last of the Tudors, died, and, to the immense relief of anxious Englishmen, the succession that brought in the Stuart kings took place peacefully. The new monarch was the Protestant James VI of Scotland, who became James I of England.

SIR THOMAS MORE

1478–1535

1499:	Meets Erasmus.
1516:	*Utopia* published.
1529–32:	Lord Chancellor.

Sir Thomas More was one of the most versatile and most enigmatic figures of the English Renaissance. He was born in London, the son of a prominent lawyer. As a boy he served as a page in the household of Archbishop Morton; it is reported that sometimes when a play was being presented at the palace young More would step into it and improvise a part for himself. In a sense he continued to do that all his life.

He studied at Oxford and at the Inns of Court, but he did not automatically follow in his father's footsteps. He was deeply torn between the appeal of a life of ascetic devotion and an active role in public affairs. His literary interests appeared early. One of his first works was a translation of a biography of Pico della Mirandola (1463–1494); he became a close friend of Erasmus (ca. 1466–1536) and he, like them, became a great Humanist. The first of this trio was Italian, the second Dutch, and the third English. Humanism was international in scope.

Emphasis upon classical learning was at the heart of the Humanist movement, but the Latin and Greek classics were not monuments to dead cultures for More and his friends. He was profoundly influenced by Plato's *Republic* when he wrote his *Utopia* (in Latin), but he was also fascinated by accounts of the recent explorations of Amerigo Vespucci (1507). Newly discovered countries with their strange customs provided a fresh perspective from which to view the older societies of Europe, burdened by wars, fierce economic rivalry, and feudal hierarchies.

Book 2 of *Utopia*, a description of the laws and customs of an imagined society, was written first. When he came to write the introduction to it, book 1, More's dramatic instincts led him to make it a dialogue, an argument between a character named More and a returned traveler named Raphael Hythloday. Their debate focuses on a subject that so troubled the real More personally: should the scholar participate in government or should he confine himself to the ivory tower?

Any reader of More should be warned that he is a very ironic and witty writer. In this he resembles his friend Erasmus, who dedicated his *Praise of Folly* to More. Erasmus's title, in the original Latin, is *Moriae Encomium* ("Praise of More" as well as "Praise of Folly," since the Greek word for a fool is *moros*). Central to the constitution of Utopia is community of property, for which More had a precedent in Plato and in the rules of the monastic orders of More's own time. No fundamental reform in society is possible, the reader is led to believe, until private property is abolished. Yet a standard defense of private property is put into the mouth of the character named More, against the position of the main speaker, Hythloday.

Utopia was written and published in Latin; it was designed for the educated readers of all Europe. About the same time that he wrote *Utopia* More undertook his major work in English, the *History of King Richard III*. Though it was never finished, it has had tremendous influence. An eminent historian of the Tudor period, A. F. Pollard, has declared that More's *Richard III* is the first "history" in English that has any claim to be English literature. More's characterization of the last Yorkist king was adopted by the chroniclers Hardyng (1543), Halle (1548), and Grafton (1568–69) and so came down to Shakespeare, whose *Richard III* (1597) fixed the portrait of Richard as a deformed, malicious, hypocritical villain.

Richard's usurpation of the throne and his deposition by the first Tudor monarch, Henry VII, took place when More was a small boy. When he wrote his history, however, one of the prominent figures of Richard's reign was still alive. She was Jane Shore, the mistress of Edward IV, and a victim of Richard's cruelty. More's handling of her story has been well described by A. N. Kincaid:

> In the episode of Jane Shore's penance, More, conscious of the difficulty of winning sympathy for a harlot, instead of giving an objective description, addresses the reader directly and makes him share in estimating her beauty. . . . In connection with Mistress Shore, More preaches a lesson in charity, telling us that now she is poor and friendless she is much more worthy of remembrance.

More's sense of obligation to active citizenship and statesmanship finally won out over his monastic inclinations, and his rise to high office under Henry VIII was spectacular: master of requests, privy councillor, speaker of the House of Commons, and finally, lord chancellor, the highest office under the crown. He resigned this post when the king married Anne Boleyn; when he was required to take the oath for the act of Succession and Supremacy he refused. He could not, in conscience, admit that Henry was supreme head of that spiritual body, the church. From the point of view of the government, his refusal was treason and in 1535 he was beheaded. He was of course certain that he was not dying for treason, but in and for the faith of the Catholic Church. Four hundred years later he was canonized by that church as St. Thomas More.

From Utopia[1]

From *Book 1*

[MORE MEETS A RETURNED TRAVELER]

The most invincible King of England, Henry the Eighth of that name, a prince adorned with the royal virtues beyond any other, had recently some differences of no slight import with Charles, the most serene Prince

---

1. Our selections are taken from Thomas More, *Utopia*: text and translation by Robert M. Adams, introduction and commentary by George M. Logan (in preparation).

The marginal comments are not by More. Since he had to be in England while *Utopia* was being printed on the Continent, the details of publication were handled by several of his friends, including Peter Giles, who figures as a character in book 1. Giles added these marginal notes; but the printer, who naturally wanted to attach a better-known name to the book, gave out that they were by Erasmus. They may even have been a joint production, since Giles had been Erasmus's pupil. In later life he became town clerk of Antwerp, as he is when he appears in *Utopia*.

of Castille,[2] and sent me into Flanders as his spokesman to discuss and settle them. I was companion and associate to that incomparable man Cuthbert Tunstall,[3] *Cuthbert Tunstall* whom the king has recently created Master of the Rolls, to everyone's great satisfaction. I will say nothing in praise of this man, not because I fear the judgment *Adages* of a friend might be questioned, but because his learning and integrity are greater than I can describe—unless I would, according to the proverb, "Show the sun with a lantern."

Those appointed by the prince to deal with us, all excellent men, met us at Bruges by prearrangement. Their head man and leader was the Margrave of Bruges, a most distinguished person. But their main speaker and guiding spirit was Georges de Themsecke, the Provost of Cassel, a man eloquent by nature as well as by training, very learned in the law, and most skillful in diplomatic affairs through his ability and long practice. After we had met several times, certain points remained on which we could not come to agreement; so they adjourned the meeting and went to Brussels for some days to consult their prince in person.

Meanwhile, since my business required it, I went to Antwerp. Of those who visited me while I was there, Peter Giles was more welcome to me than any of *Peter Giles* the others. He was a native of Antwerp, a man of high reputation, already appointed to a good position and worthy of the very best: I hardly know a young man of more learning or better character. Apart from being cultured, virtuous, and courteous to all, with his intimates he is so open, trustworthy, loyal, and affectionate that it would be hard to find another friend like him anywhere. No man is more modest or more frank; none better combines simplicity with wisdom. His conversation is so pleasant, and so witty without malice, that the ardent desire I felt to see my native country, my wife, and my children (from whom I had been separated more than four months) was much eased by his agreeable company and pleasant talk.

One day after I had heard mass at Nôtre Dame, the most beautiful and most popular church in Antwerp, I was about to return to my quarters when I happened to see him talking with a stranger, a man of quite advanced years. The stranger had a sunburned face, a long beard, and a cloak hanging loosely from his shoulders; from his face and dress, I took him to be a ship's captain. When Peter saw me, he approached and greeted me. As I was about to return his greeting, he drew me aside and, indicating the stranger, said, "Do you see that man? I was just on the point of bringing him to you."

"He would have been very welcome on your behalf," I answered.

"And on his own too, if you knew him," said Peter, "for there is no man alive today can tell you so much about strange peoples and unex-

---

2. Later Charles V (1500–1558), King of Spain and Holy Roman Emperor. The differences had to do with the wool trade.

3. Later bishop of London and of Durham, one of More's closest friends (1474–1559).

plored lands; and I know that you're always greedy for such information."

"In that case," said I, "my guess wasn't a bad one, for at first glance I supposed he was a skipper."

"Then you're off the mark," he replied, "for his sailing has not been like that of Palinurus, but more that of Ulysses, or rather of Plato.[4] This man, who is named Raphael—his family name is Hythloday—knows a good deal of Latin and is particularly learned in Greek. He studied Greek more than Latin because his main interest is philosophy, and in that field he found that the Romans have left us nothing very valuable except certain works of Seneca and Cicero. Being eager to see the world, he bestowed on his brothers the patrimony to which he is entitled at home (for he is Portuguese by birth), and took service with Amerigo Vespucci.[5] He accompanied Vespucci on the last three of his four voyages, accounts of which are now common reading everywhere; but on the last voyage, he did not return home with the commander. After much persuasion and expostulation he got Amerigo's permission to be one of the twenty-four men who were left in a garrison at the farthest point of the last voyage. Being marooned in this way was altogether agreeable to him, as he was more eager to pursue his travels than afraid of death. He would often say, 'The man who has no grave is covered by the sky,' and 'The road to heaven is   *Aphorism*
equally short from all places.' Yet this frame of mind would have cost him dear, if God had not been gracious to him. After Vespucci's departure he traveled through many countries with five companions from the garrison. At last, by strange good fortune, he got via Ceylon to Calicut, where by good luck he found some Portuguese ships; and so, beyond anyone's expectation, he returned to his own country."

When Peter had told me this, I thanked him for his kindness in introducing me to a man whose conversation he hoped I would enjoy, and then I turned toward Raphael. After greeting one another and exchanging the usual civilities of strangers upon their first meeting, we all went to my house. There in the garden we sat down on a bench covered with grassy turf to talk together.

He told us that when Vespucci sailed away, he and his companions who had stayed behind in the garrison often met with the people of the countryside, and by ingratiating speeches gradually won their friendship. Before long they came to dwell with them safely and even affectionately. The prince also gave them his favor (I have forgotten his name and that of his country), furnishing Raphael and his five companions not only with ample provisions, but with means for traveling—rafts when they went by water, wagons when they went by land. In addition, he sent

4. Palinurus, Aeneas' pilot, fell asleep, fell overboard and drowned. Ulysses, by contrast, was a wily, alert traveler. Plato is cited as the profound philosopher; his *Republic* strongly influenced *Utopia*. Raphael Hythloday is an invented character. His last name is coined from Greek words meaning "a skilled conveyor of nonsense."

5. Vespucci's last two voyages were made for the king of Portgual (hence Hythloday's birthplace). His account of his voyages, published in 1507, made him more famous than Columbus.

with them a most trusty guide who was to introduce and recommend
them to such other princes as they wanted to visit. After many days'
journey, he said, they came to towns and cities, and to commonwealths
that were both populous and not badly governed.

To be sure, under the equator and as far on both sides of the line as
the sun moves, there lie vast empty deserts, scorched with the perpetual
heat. The whole region is desolate and squalid, grim and uncultivated,
inhabited by wild beasts, serpents, and men no less wild and dangerous
than the beasts themselves. But as they went on, conditions gradually
grew milder. The heat was less fierce, the earth greener, the creatures
less savage. At last they reached people, cities, and towns which not only
traded among themselves and with their neighbors, but even carried on
commerce by sea and land with remote countries. After that, he said,
they were able to visit different lands in every direction, for he and his
companions were welcome as passengers aboard any ship about to make
a journey.

The first vessels they saw were flat-bottomed, he said, with sails made
of papyrus-reeds and wicker, occasionally of leather. Farther on they
found ships with pointed keels and canvas sails, much like our own.
The seamen were skilled in managing wind and water; but they were
most grateful to him, Raphael said, for showing them the use of the
compass, of which they had been ignorant. For that reason they had
formerly sailed with great timidity, and only in summer. Now they have
such trust in the compass that they no longer fear winter at all, and tend
to be rash rather than cautious. There is some danger that through their
imprudence this discovery, which they thought would be so advantageous to them, may become the cause of much mischief.

It would take too long to repeat all that Raphael told us he had observed
in various places, nor would it make altogether for our present purpose.
Perhaps on another occasion we shall tell more about the things that are
most profitable, especially the wise and sensible institutions that he
observed among the civilized nations. We asked him many eager questions about such things, and he answered us willingly enough. We made
no inquiries, however, about monsters, which are the routine of travelers' tales. Scyllas, ravenous Celaenos, man-eating Lestrygonians,[6] and
that sort of monstrosity you can hardly avoid, but to find governments
wisely established and sensibly ruled is not so easy. While he told us of
many ill-considered usages in these new-found nations, he also described
quite a few other customs from which our own cities, nations, races,
and kingdoms might take lessons in order to correct their errors. These
I shall discuss in another place, as I said. Now I intend to relate only
what he told us about the manners and institutions of the Utopians, first
explaining the occasion that led him to speak of that commonwealth.
Raphael had been discoursing very wisely on the many errors and also

---

6. "Scyllas" were fabulous monsters, like the one
who lived in a cave in the rock Scylla in the *Odyssey*; Celaeno was leader of the harpies in the *Aeneid*,
large birds with the faces of women, pale with
hunger, and provided with long, sharp talons. Lestrygonians were cannibals in the *Odyssey*.

the wise institutions found both in that hemisphere and in this (as many of both sorts in one place as in the other), speaking as shrewdly about the manners and governments of each place he had visited briefly as though he had lived there all his life. Peter was amazed.

"My dear Raphael," he said, "I'm surprised that you don't enter some king's service; for I don't know of a single prince who wouldn't be glad to have you. Your learning and your knowledge of various countries and men would entertain him while your advice and and supply of examples would be helpful at the counsel board. Thus you might advance your own interest and be useful at the same time to all your relatives and friends."

"About my relatives and friends," he replied, "I'm not much concerned, because I consider I've already done my duty by them. While still young and healthy, I distributed among my relatives and friends the possessions that most men do not part with till they're old and sick (and then only reluctantly, when they can no longer keep them). I think they should be content with this gift of mine, and not expect, even insist, that for their sake I should enslave myself to any king whatever."

"Well said," Peter replied; "but I do not mean that you should be in servitude to any king, only in his service."

"The difference is only a matter of one syllable," Raphael replied.[7]

"All right," said Peter, "but whatever you call it, I do not see any other way in which you can be so useful to your friends or to the general public, apart from making yourself happier."

"Happier indeed!" exclaimed Raphael. "Would a way of life so absolutely repellent to my spirit make my life happier? As it is now, I live as I please, and I fancy very few courtiers, however splendid, can say that. As a matter of fact, there are so many men soliciting favors from the great that it will be no great loss if they have to do without me and a couple of others like me."

Then I said, "It is clear, my dear Raphael, that you seek neither wealth nor power, and indeed I prize and revere a man of your disposition no less than I do the greatest persons in the world. Yet I think if you would devote your time and energy to public affairs, you would be doing something worthy of a generous and philosophical nature, even if you did not much like it. You could best perform such a service by joining the council of some great prince, whom you would incite to just and noble actions. I'm sure you would do this if you held such an office, and your influence would be felt, because a people's welfare or misery flows in a stream from their prince as from a never-failing spring. Your learning is so full, even if it weren't combined with experience, and your experience is so great, even apart from the learning, that you would be an extraordinary counsellor to any king in the world."

"You are twice mistaken, my dear More," he replied, "first in me and then in the situation itself. I don't have the capacity you ascribe to me,

---

7. The play on words here depends on the Latin original: *servias* and *inservias*.

and if I had it in the highest degree, the public would not be any better off for my bending my neck to some prince's beck. In the first place, most princes apply themselves to the arts of war, in which I have neither interest nor ability, instead of to the good arts of peace. They are generally more set on acquiring new kingdoms by hook or crook than on governing well those they already have. Moreover, the counsellors of kings are so wise already that they need no further knowledge—or else they have that opinion of themselves. At the same time they endorse and flatter the most absurd statements of special favorites through whose influence they hope to stand well with the prince. It's only natural, of course, that each man should think his own opinions best: the old crow loves his fledgling and the ape his cub.

"Now in a court composed of people who envy everyone else and admire only themselves, if a man should suggest something he had read of in other ages or seen in practice elsewhere, the other counsellors would think their reputation for wisdom was endangered, and henceforth they would look like simpletons, unless they could find fault with his proposal. If all else failed, they would take refuge in some remark like this: 'The way we're doing it is the way we've always done it, this custom was good enough for our fathers, and I only hope we're as wise as they were.' And with this deep thought they would take their seats, as though they had said the last word on the subject—implying, forsooth, that it would be a very dangerous matter if a man were found to be wiser on any point than his forefathers were. As a matter of fact, we quietly neglect the best examples they have left us; but if something better is proposed, we seize the excuse of reverence for times past and cling to it desperately. Such proud, obstinate, ridiculous judgments I have encountered many times, and once even in England."

From *Book 2*

[THE GEOGRAPHY OF UTOPIA]

The island of Utopia is two hundred miles across in the middle part where it is widest, and is nowhere much narrower than this except toward the two ends. These ends, drawn toward one another in a five-hundred-mile circle, make the island crescent-shaped, like a new moon. Between the horns of the crescent, which are about eleven miles apart, *Site and shape of Utopia the new island* the sea enters and spreads into a broad bay. Being sheltered from the wind by the surrounding land, the bay is never rough, but quiet and smooth instead, like a big lake. Thus, nearly the whole inner coast is one great harbor, across which ships pass in every direction, to the great advantage of the people. What with shallows on one side, and rocks on the other, entrance into the bay is very dangerous. Near midchannel, there is one rock that rises above *Being naturally safe, the entry is defended by a single fort* the water, and so presents no danger in itself; on top of it a tower has been built, and there a garrison is kept. Since the other rocks lie under water, they are very dangerous to navigation. The channels are known only to the Utopians, so hardly any strangers enter the bay without one of their pilots; and even they themselves could not enter safely if they did not direct their course by some landmarks on the coast. Should *The trick of shifting landmarks* these landmarks be shifted about, the Utopians could lure to destruction an enemy fleet coming against them, however big it was.

On the outer side of the island, occasional harbors are to be found; but the coast is rugged by nature, and so well fortified that a few defenders could beat off the attack of a strong force. They say (and the appearance of the place confirms this) that their land was not always an island. But Utopus, who conquered the country and gave it his name (for it had previously been called Abraxa),[8] brought its rude, uncouth inhabitants *Utopia named for king Utopus* to such a high level of culture and humanity that they now excel in that regard almost every other people. After subduing them at his first landing, he cut a channel fifteen miles wide where their land joined the continent, and caused the sea to *This was a bigger job than digging across the Isthmus (of Corinth)* flow around the country. He put not only the natives to work at this task, but all his own soldiers too, so that the vanquished would not think the labor a disgrace. With the work divided among so many hands, the project was finished quickly, and the neighboring *Many hands make light work* peoples, who at first had laughed at his folly, were struck with wonder and terror at his success.

There are fifty-four cities on the island, all spacious and magnificent, identical in language, customs, institutions, and laws. So far as the location permits, all of them are built on the same plan, and have the same appearance. The nearest are at least twenty-four miles apart, *The towns of Utopia Likeness breeds sympathy* and the farthest are not so remote that a man cannot go on foot from one to the other in a day.

Once a year each city sends three of its old and experienced citizens to Amaurot[9] to consider affairs of common interest to the island. Amaurot lies near the omphalos[1] of the land, so to speak, and *A short distance between towns* convenient to every other district, so it acts as a capital. Every city has enough ground assigned to it so that at least ten miles of farm land are available in every direction, though where the cities are *Distribution of land* farther apart, their territories are more extensive. No city wants to

8. From Greek, "not small" or "insignificant."
9. Coined from a Greek adjective meaning "dark, obscure"—a suitable name for the capital of a country whose name means "Nowhere."
1. Navel, umbilicus—the spiritual as well as physical center of a nation.

enlarge its boundaries, for the inhabitants *But today this is the curse* consider themselves good cultivators rather *of all countries* than landlords. At proper intervals all over the countryside they have built houses and furnished them with farm equipment. These houses are inhabited by *Farming is the* citizens who come to the country by turns *prime occupation* to occupy them. No rural house has fewer than forty men and women in it, besides two slaves.[2] A master and mistress, serious and mature persons, are in charge of each household, and over every thirty households is placed a single phylarch.[3] Each year twenty persons from each rural household move back to the city after completing a two-year stint in the country. In their place, twenty others are sent out from town, to learn farm work from those who have already been in the country for a year, and who are better skilled in farming. They, in turn, will teach those who come the following year. If all were equally untrained in farm work and new to it, they might harm the crops out of ignorance. This custom of alternating farm workers is solemnly established so that no one will have to perform such heavy labor for more than two years; but many of them who take a natural pleasure in farm life ask to stay longer.

The farm workers till the soil, hew wood, *Farmers' jobs* and take their produce to the city by land or water, as is most convenient. They breed an enormous number of chickens by a most marvelous method. Men, not hens, hatch the eggs by keeping them in a warm place at an even *A notable way of* temperature. As soon as they come out of *hatching eggs* the shell, the chicks recognize the men, follow them around, and are devoted to them instead of to their real mothers.

They raise very few horses, and these full of *Uses of the horse* mettle, which they keep only to exercise the young men in the art of horsemanship. For the heavy work of plowing and hauling they use oxen, which they agree *Uses of oxen* are inferior to horses over the short haul, but which can hold out longer under heavy burdens, are less subject to disease (as they suppose), and so can be kept with less cost and trouble. Moreover, when oxen are too old for work, they can be used for meat.

Grain they use only to make bread. They drink wine made of grapes, apple or pear cider, or simple water, which they sometimes mix with honey or licorice, of which they have plenty. *Food and drink* Although they know very well, down to the last detail, how much food each city and its surrounding district will consume, they produce much more grain and *Planned planting* cattle than they need for themselves, and share

2. More provides for a few bondmen or slaves in Utopia, to perform tasks unfit for citizens, such as   slaughtering.
3. From Greek words meaning "head of a tribe."

the surplus with their neighbors. Whatever goods the folk in the country need which cannot be produced there, they request of the town magistrates, and since there is nothing to be paid or exchanged, they get what they want at once without any haggling. They generally go to town once a month in any case, to observe the holy days.

When harvest time approaches, the phylarchs in the country notify the town-magistrates how

The value of collective labor

many hands will be needed. Crews of harvesters come just when they're wanted, and in one day of good weather they can usually get in the whole crop.

[THEIR GOLD AND SILVER]

For these reasons,[4] therefore, they have accumulated a vast treasure, but they do not keep it like a treasure. I'm really quite ashamed to tell you how they do keep it, because you probably won't believe me. I would not have believed

O crafty fellow!

it myself if someone had just told me about it; but I was there, and saw it with my own eyes. As a general rule, the more different anything is from what people are used to, the harder it is to accept. But considering that all their other customs are so unlike ours, a sensible man will not be surprised that they treat gold and silver quite differently than we do. After all, they never do use money among themselves, but keep it only for a contingency that may or may not actually arise. So in the meanwhile they take care that no one shall overvalue gold and silver, of which money is made, beyond what the metals themselves deserve. Anyone can see, for example, that iron is far superior to either;

As far as utility goes, gold is inferior to iron

men could not live without iron, by heaven, any more than without fire or water. But gold and silver have, by nature, no function with which we cannot easily dispense. Human folly has made them precious because they are rare. But in fact nature, like a most indulgent mother, has placed her best gifts out in the open, like air, water, and the earth itself; vain and unprofitable things she has hidden away in remote places.

If in Utopia gold and silver were kept locked up in some tower, foolish heads among the common people might concoct a story that the prince and senate[5] were out to cheat ordinary folk and get some advantage for themselves. The gold and silver might indeed be put into beautiful plateware and rich handiwork, but then in case of necessity the people would not want to give up such articles, on which they had begun to fix their hearts, only to melt them down for soldiers' pay. To avoid these problems they thought of a plan which conforms with their institutions as clearly as it contrasts with our own. Unless one has actually seen it

---

4. More has explained, in a section here omitted, that the Utopians hire mercenary soldiers in time of war and pay them very highly; enemy soldiers often desert to them.

5. The prince, as More has earlier explained, is chosen for life by the senate, whose members are selected by an assembly, whose members are in turn selected from households.

working, their plan may seem incredible, because we prize gold so highly and are so careful about guarding it. With them it's just the other way. While they eat from china dishes and drink from glass cups, well made but inexpensive, their chamber pots and toilet bowls—all their *O magnificent scorn for gold!* humblest vessels, for use in common halls and even in private homes— are made of gold and silver. The chains and heavy fetters of slaves are also made of these metals. Finally, criminals who are to bear through life the mark of some disgraceful act are forced to wear golden ornaments on their ears, golden rings on their fingers, golden chains around their necks, even gold crowns on their heads. Thus they hold up gold and silver to scorn in every conceivable way. As a result, when they have to part with these *Gold the mark of infamy* metals, which other nations give up with as much agony as if they were being disemboweled, the Utopians feel it no more than the loss of a penny.

They pick up pearls by the seashore, diamonds and garnets in certain cliffs, but never go out of set purpose to look for them. If they happen to find some, they polish them and give them to the children who, when they are small, feel *Gems the playthings of children* proud and pleased with such gaudy decorations. But after, when they grow a bit older and notice that only babies like such toys, they lay them aside. The parents don't have to say anything, they simply put these trifles away out of a shamefaced sense that they're no longer suitable, just as our children, when they grow up, put away their rattles, marbles, and dolls.

Different customs, different feelings: I never saw the adage better illustrated than in the *A most elegant story* case of the Anemolian[6] ambassadors, who came to Amaurot while I was there. Because they came to discuss important business, the senate had assembled ahead of time, three citizens from each city. The ambassadors from nearby nations, who had visited Utopia before and knew the local customs, realized that fine clothing was not much respected in that land, silk was despised, and gold a badge of contempt; therefore they came in the very plainest of their clothes. But the Anemolians, who lived farther off and had had fewer dealings with the Utopians, had heard only that they all dressed alike and very simply; so they took for granted that their hosts had nothing to wear that they didn't put on. Being themselves rather more proud than wise, they decided to dress as splendidly as the very gods, and dazzle the eyes of the poor Utopians with their gaudy garb.

Consequently the three ambassadors made a grand entry with a suite of a hundred attendants, all in clothing of many colors, and most in silk. Being noblemen at home, the ambassadors were arrayed in cloth of gold, with heavy gold chains on their necks, gold jewels at their ears and on

6. From Greek, "windy people."

their fingers, and sparkling strings of pearls and gems on their caps. In fact, they were decked out in all the articles which in Utopia are used to punish slaves, shame wrongdoers, or pacify infants. It was a sight to see how they strutted when they compared their finery with the dress of the Utopians who had poured out into the street to see them pass. But it was just as funny to see how wide they fell of the mark, and how far they were from getting the consideration they expected. Except for a very few Utopians who for some special reason had visited foreign countries, all the onlookers considered this splendid pomp a mark of disgrace. They therefore bowed to the humblest servants as lords, and took the ambassadors, because of their golden chains, *The rascal!* to be slaves, passing them by without any reverence at all. You might have seen children, who had themselves thrown away their pearls and gems, nudge their mothers when they saw the ambassadors' jeweled caps, and say:

"Look at that big lummox, mother, who's still wearing pearls and jewels as if he were a little kid!"

But the mother, in all seriousness, would answer:

"Hush, my boy, I think he is one of the ambassador's fools."

Others found fault with the golden chains as useless because they were so flimsy any slave could break them, and so loose that he could easily shake them off and run away whenever he wanted.

But after the ambassadors had spent a couple of days among the Utopians, they learned of the immense amounts of gold which were as thoroughly despised there as they were prized at home. They saw too that more gold and silver went into making chains and fetters for a single runaway slave than into costuming all three of them. Somewhat crestfallen, then, they put away all the finery in which they had strutted so arrogantly; but they saw the wisdom of doing so after they had talked with the Utopians enough to learn their customs and opinions.

[MARRIAGE CUSTOMS]

Women do not marry till they are eighteen, nor men till they are twenty-two. Clandestine premarital intercourse, if discovered and proved, brings severe *Marriages* punishment on both man and woman; and the guilty parties are forbidden to marry for their whole lives, unless the prince by his pardon mitigates the sentence. Also both the father and mother of the household where the offense occurred suffer public disgrace for having been remiss in their duty. The reason they punish this offense so severely is that they suppose few people would join in married love—with confinement to a single partner and all the petty annoyances that married life involves—unless they were strictly restrained from promiscuity.

In choosing marriage partners they solemnly and seriously follow a custom which seemed to us foolish and absurd in the extreme. Whether

she be widow or virgin, the bride-to-be is shown *Not very modest, but not* naked to the groom by a responsible and re- *so impractical either* spectable matron; and similarly, some respect-
able man presents the groom naked to his future bride. We laughed at this custom, and called it absurd; but they were just as amazed at the folly of all other peoples. When men go to buy a colt, where they are risking only a little money, they are so cautious that, though the animal is almost bare, they won't close the deal until saddle and blanket have been taken off, lest there be a hidden sore underneath. Yet in the choice of a mate, which may cause either delight or disgust for the rest of their lives, men are so careless that they leave all the rest of the woman's body covered up with clothes and estimate her attractiveness from a mere handsbreadth of her person, the face, which is all they can see. And so they marry, running great risk of bitter discord, if something in either's person should offend the other. Not all people are so wise as to concern themselves solely with character; even the wise appreciate physical beauty as a supplement to a good disposition. There's no doubt that a deformity may lurk under clothing, serious enough to make a man hate his wife when it's too late to be separated from her. When deformities are discovered after marriage, each person must bear his own fate, so the Utopians think everyone should be legally protected from deception beforehand.

There is extra reason for them to be careful, because in that part of the world, they are the only people who practice monogamy. Their marriages are seldom terminated except by death, *Divorce* though they do allow divorce for adultery or for
intolerably offensive behavior. A husband or wife who is an aggrieved party to such a divorce is granted leave by the senate to take a new mate, but the guilty party suffers disgrace and is permanently forbidden to remarry. They absolutely forbid a husband to put away his wife against her will and without any fault on her part, just because of some bodily misfortune; they think it cruel that a person should be abandoned when most in need of comfort; and they add that old age, since it not only entails disease but is a disease itself, needs more than a precarious fidelity.

It happens occasionally that a married couple cannot get along, and have both found other persons with whom they hope to live more harmoniously. After getting approval of the senate, they may then separate by mutual consent and contract new marriages. But such divorces are allowed only after the senators and their wives have carefully investigated the case. Divorce is deliberately made difficult because they know that couples will have a hard time settling down if each has in mind that another new relation is easily available.

They punish adulterers with the strictest form of slavery. If both parties were married, both are divorced, and the injured parties may marry one another if they want, or someone else. But if one of the injured parties continues to love such an undeserving spouse, the marriage may go on, provided the innocent person chooses to share in the labor to which every slave is condemned. And sometimes it happens that the repentance of the guilty and the devotion of the innocent party so move the prince to pity that he restores both to freedom. But a second conviction of adultery is punished by death.

[RELIGIONS]

There are different forms of religion throughout the island, and in the different cities as well. Some worship as a god the sun, others the moon, still others one of the planets. There are some who worship a man of past ages, conspicuous either for virtue or glory; they consider him not only a god, but the supreme god. Most Utopians, however, and among these all the wisest, believe nothing of the sort: they believe in a single power, unknown, eternal, infinite, inexplicable, far beyond the grasp of the human mind, and diffused throughout the universe, not physically, but in influence. Him they call father, and to him alone they attribute the origin, increase, progress, change, and end of all visible things; they do not offer divine honors to any other.

Though the other sects differ from this group in various particular doctrines, they all agree in a single main head, that there is one supreme power, the maker and ruler of the universe; in their native tongue they all call him Mithra.[7] Different people define him differently, and each supposes the object of his worship is the special vessel of that great force which all people agree in worshipping. But gradually they are coming to forsake this mixture of superstitions and unite in that one religion which seems more reasonable than any of the others. And there is no doubt that the other religions would have disappeared long ago, had not various unlucky accidents, befalling certain Utopians who were thinking of changing their religion, been interpreted as a sign of divine anger, not chance—as if the deity who was being abandoned were avenging an insult against himself.

But after they heard from us the name of Christ, and learned of his teachings, his life, his miracles, and the no less marvelous devotion of the many martyrs who shed their blood to draw nations far and near into the Christian fellowship, you would not believe how they were impressed. Either through the secret inspiration of God, or because Christianity is very like the opinion prevailing and influential among them, they were well disposed toward it from the start. But I think they were also much influenced by the fact that Christ encouraged his disciples to practice community of goods, and that among the truest groups of Christians, the practice still prevails.[8] *Monasteries*
Whatever the reason, no small number of them chose to join our communion, and received the holy water of baptism. By that time, two

---

7. The spirit of light in ancient Persian religion, which More could have learned about from reading Pico della Mirandola.

8. Many monastic orders of More's time abolished private property for their members.

of our group had died, and among us four survivors there was, I am sorry to say, no priest. So, though they received instruction in other matters, they still lack those sacraments which in our religion can be administered only by priests. They do, however, understand what these are, and eagerly desire them. In fact, they dispute warmly whether a man chosen from among themselves could be considered a priest without ordination by a Christian bishop. Though they seemed about to select such a person, they had not yet done so when I left.

Those who have not accepted Christianity make no effort to restrain others from it, nor do they criticize new converts to it. While I was there, only one of the Christians got into trouble with the law. As soon as he was baptized, he took on himself to preach the Christian religion publicly, with more zeal than discretion. We warned him not to do so, but he soon worked himself up to a pitch where he not only preferred our religion, but condemned all others as profane, leading *Men must be drawn to religion by its merits* their impious and sacrilegious followers to the hell-fires they richly deserved. After he had been going on in this style for a long time, they arrested him. He was tried, not on a charge of despising their religion, but of creating a public disorder, convicted, and sentenced to exile. For it is one of their oldest rules that no man's religion shall be held against him.

Even before he came to the island, King Utopus had heard that the natives were continually squabbling over religious matters. Actually, he found it easy to conquer the country because the different sects were too busy fighting one another to oppose him. As soon as he had gained the victory, therefore, he decreed that every man might cultivate the religion of his choice, and proselytize for it too, provided he did so quietly, modestly, rationally, and without bitterness toward others. If persuasions failed, no man might resort to abuse or violence, under penalty of exile or slavery.

Utopus laid down these rules, not simply for the sake of peace, which he saw was in danger of being destroyed by constant quarrels and implacable hatreds, but also for the sake of religion itself. In such matters he was not at all quick to dogmatize, because he suspected that God perhaps likes various forms of worship and has therefore deliberately inspired different men with different views. On the other hand, he was quite sure that it was arrogant folly for anyone to enforce conformity with his own beliefs by threats or violence. He supposed that if one religion is really true and the rest false, the true one will prevail by its own natural strength, if men will only consider the matter reasonably and moderately. But if they try to decide things by fighting and rioting, since the worst men are always most headstrong, the best and holiest religion in the world will be crowded out by foolish superstitions, like grain choked out of a field by thorns and briars. So he left the whole matter open, allowing each person to choose what he would believe. The only exception was a positive and strict law against anyone who should sink so far below the dignity of human nature as to think that the soul perishes with the body, or that the universe is ruled by blind chance, not divine providence.

Thus they believe that after this life vices are to be punished and virtue rewarded. Anyone who denies this proposition they consider less than a man, since he has degraded the sublimity of his own soul to the base level of a beast's wretched body. They will not even count him as one of their citizens, since he would openly despise all the laws and customs of society, if not prevented by fear. Who can doubt that a man who has nothing to fear but the law, and no hope of life beyond the grave, will do anything he can to evade his country's laws by craft or to break them by violence, in order to gratify his own personal greed? Therefore a man who holds such views is offered no honors, entrusted with no offices, and given no public responsibility; he is universally regarded as a low and sordid fellow. Yet they do not punish him, because they are persuaded that no man can choose to believe by a mere act of the will. They do not compel him by threats to dissemble his views, nor do they tolerate in the matter any deceit or lying, which they detest as next door to deliberate malice. The man may not argue with common people in behalf of his opinion; but in the presence of priests and other important persons, they not only permit but encourage it. For they are confident that in the end his madness will yield to reason.

There are some others, in fact no small number of them, who err the other way in supposing that animals too have immortal souls, though not comparable to ours in excellence nor destined to equal felicity. *A strange opinion on the souls of animals* These men are not thought to be evil, their opinion is not considered wholly unreasonable, and so they are not interfered with.

Almost all the Utopians are absolutely convinced that man's bliss after death will be enormous and eternal; thus they lament every man's sickness, but mourn over a death only if the man was torn from life wretchedly and against his will. Such behavior they take to be a very bad sign, as if the soul, despairing and conscious of guilt, dreaded death through a secret premonition of punishments to come. Besides, they suppose God can hardly be well pleased with the coming of one who, when he is summoned, does not come gladly, but is dragged off reluctantly and against his will. Such a death fills the onlookers with horror, and they carry off the corpse to the cemetery in melancholy silence. There, after begging God to have mercy on his spirit and to pardon his infirmities, they bury the unhappy man. But when someone dies blithely and full of good hope, they do not mourn for him, but carry the body cheerfully away, singing and commending the dead man's soul to God. They cremate him in a spirit of reverence more than of grief, and erect a tombstone on which the dead man's honors are inscribed. As they go home, they talk of his character and deeds, and no part of his life is mentioned more frequently or more gladly than his joyful death.

They think that recollecting the good qualities of a man helps the living to behave virtuously and is the most acceptable form of honor to the dead. For they think that dead persons are actually present among us, and hear what we say about them, though through the dullness of human sight they remain invisible. Given their state of bliss, the dead must be able to travel freely when they please, and it would be unkind of them to cast off every desire of seeing those friends to whom in life they had been joined by mutual affection and charity. Like other good qualities they think that after death charity is increased rather than diminished in all good men; and thus they believe the dead come frequently among the living, to observe their words and acts. Hence they go about their business the more confidently because of their trust in such protectors; and the belief that their forefathers are physically present keeps men from any secret dishonorable deed.

Fortune-telling and other vain, superstitious divinations, such as other peoples take very seriously, they consider ridiculous and contemptible. But they venerate miracles which occur without the help of nature, considering them direct and visible manifestations of the divinity. Indeed, they report that miracles have often occurred in their country. Sometimes in great and dangerous crises they pray publicly for a miracle, which they then anticipate with great confidence, and obtain.

They think the investigation of nature and the reverence rising from it are most acceptable to God. There are some people, however, and quite a few of them, who from religious motives reject learning, pursue no studies, and refuse all *The active life* leisure, but devote their full time to good works. Constant dedication to the offices of charity, these people think, will increase their chances of happiness after death; and so they are always busy. Some tend the sick; others repair roads, clean ditches, rebuild bridges, dig turf, gravel or stones; still others fell trees and cut them up, and transport wood, grain, or other commodities into the cities by wagon. They work for private citizens as well as for the public, and work even harder than slaves. With cheery good will they undertake any task that is so rough, hard, and dirty that most people refuse to tackle it because of the toil, boredom, and frustration involved. While constantly engaged in heavy labor themselves, they procure leisure for others, yet claim no credit for it. They neither criticize the way others live, nor boast of their own doings. The more they put themselves in the position of slaves, the more highly they are honored by everyone.

These people are of two opinions. The first are celibates who abstain not only from sex, but also from eating meat, and some from any sort of animal food whatever. They reject all the pleasures of this life as harmful, and look forward only to the joys of the life to come, which they hope to merit by hard labor and all-night vigils. As they hope to attain it soon, they are cheerful and active in the here and now. The other kind are just as fond of hard work, but prefer to marry. They don't despise the comforts of marriage, but think as they owe nature their labor, so they owe children to their country. Unless it interferes with their labor, they avoid no pleasure, and gladly eat meat, precisely because they think it makes them stronger for any sort of heavy work. The Utopians regard the second sort as more sensible, but the first sort as the holier men. If anyone chose celibacy before marriage and a hard life before a comfortable one on grounds of reason alone, they would laugh at him; but as these men say they are motivated by religion, the Utopians respect and revere them. On no subject are they more careful of jumping to conclusions than in this matter of religion. These then are the men who in their own language they call Buthrescas, a term which can be translated as "specially religious."

[CONCLUSION]

Now I have described to you as accurately as I could the structure of that commonwealth which I consider not only the best but the only one that can rightfully claim that name. In other places men talk very liberally of the commonwealth, but what they mean is simply their own wealth; in Utopia, where there is no private business, every man zealously pursues the public business. And in both places men are right to act as they do. For among us, even though the commonwealth may flourish, each man knows that unless he makes separate provision for himself, he may perfectly well die of hunger. Bitter necessity, then, forces men to look out for themselves rather than for the people, that is, for other people. But in Utopia, where everything belongs to everybody, no man need fear that, so long as the public warehouses are filled, he will ever lack for anything he needs. Distribution is not one of their problems; in Utopia no men are poor, no men are beggars, and though no man owns anything, everyone is rich.

For what can be greater riches than for a man to live joyfully and peacefully, free from all anxieties, and without worries about making a living? No man is bothered by his wife's querulous complaints about money, no man fears poverty for his son, or struggles to scrape up a dowry for his daughter. Each man can feel secure of his own livelihood and happiness, and of his whole family's as well: wife, sons, grandsons, great-grandsons, great-great-grandsons, and that whole long line of descendants that the gentry are so fond of contemplating. Indeed, even those who once worked but can no longer do so are cared for just as well as if they were still productive.

Let me now make bold to compare this justice of the Utopians with the so-called justice that prevails among other nations—among whom let me perish if I can discover the slightest scrap of justice or fairness. What kind of justice is it when a nobleman, a goldsmith,[9] a moneylender, or someone else who makes his living by doing either nothing at all or something completely useless to the commonwealth, gets to live a life of luxury and grandeur? while in the meantime, a laborer, a carter, a

9. Banker.

carpenter, or a farmer works so hard and so constantly that even a beast of burden would perish under the load; and this work of theirs is so necessary that no commonwealth could survive for a year without it. Yet they earn so meager a living and lead such miserable lives that a beast would really be better off. Beasts do not have to work every minute and their food is not much worse; in fact they like it better, and besides, they do not have to worry about their future. But workingmen must not only sweat and suffer without present reward, but agonize over the prospect of a penniless old age. Their daily wage is inadequate even for present needs, so there is no possible chance of their saving for their declining years.

Now isn't this an unjust and ungrateful commonwealth? It lavishes rich rewards on so-called gentry, bankers, yellow-money dealers, and the rest of that crew, who don't work at all or are mere parasites, purveyors of empty pleasures. And yet it makes no provision whatever for the welfare of farmers and colliers,[1] laborers, carters, and carpenters, without whom the commonwealth would simply cease to exist. After society has taken the labor of their best years, when they are worn out by age, sickness, and utter destitution, then the thankless commonwealth, forgetting all their pains and services, throws them out to die a miserable death. What is worse, the rich constantly try to grind out of the poor part of their meager pittance, not only by private swindling but by public tax-laws. It is basically unjust that people who deserve most from the commonwealth should receive least. But now they have distorted and debased the right even further by giving their extortion the form of law; and thus they have palmed injustice off as legal.

Reader, note well!

When I run over in my mind the various commonwealths flourishing today, so help me God, I can see in them nothing but a conspiracy of the rich, who are fattening up their own interests under the name and title of the commonwealth. They invent ways and means to hang onto whatever they have acquired by sharp practice, and then they scheme to oppress the poor by buying up their toil and labor as cheaply as possible. These devices become law as soon as the rich, speaking through the commonwealth—which, of course, includes the poor as well—say they must be observed.

And yet when these insatiably greedy and evil men have divided among themselves goods which would have sufficed for the entire people, how far they remain from the happiness of the Utopian Republic, which has abolished not only money but with it greed! What a mass of trouble was cut away by that one step! What a thicket of crimes was uprooted! Everyone knows that if money were abolished, fraud, theft, robbery, quarrels, brawls, seditions, murders, treasons, poisonings, and a whole set of crimes which are avenged but not prevented by the hangman would at once die out. If money disappeared, so would fear, anxiety, worry, toil, and sleep-

1. Miners.

less nights. Even poverty, which seems to need money more than anything else, would vanish if money were entirely done away with.

Consider if you will this example. Take a barren year of failed harvests, when many thousands of men have been carried off by hunger. If at the end of the famine the barns of the rich were searched, I dare say positively enough grain would be found in them to have kept all those who died of starvation and disease from even realizing that a shortage ever existed—if only it had been divided equally among them. So easily might men get the necessities of life if that cursed money, which is supposed to provide access to them, were not in fact the chief barrier to our getting what we need to live. Even the rich, I'm sure, understand this. They must know that it's better to have enough of what we really need than an abundance of superfluities, much better to escape from our many present troubles than to be burdened with great masses of wealth. And in fact I have no doubt that every man's perception of where his true interest lies, along with the authority of Christ our Savior (whose wisdom could not fail to recognize the best, and whose goodness would not fail to counsel it), *A striking phrase* would long ago have brought the whole world to adopt Utopian laws, were it not for one single monster, the prime plague and begetter of all others—I mean Pride.

Pride measures her advantages not by what she has but by what other people lack. Pride would not deign even to be made a goddess if there were no wretches for her to sneer at and domineer over. Her good fortune is dazzling only by contrast with the miseries of others, her riches valuable only as they torment and tantalize the poverty of others. Pride is a serpent from hell that twines itself around the hearts of men, acting like a suckfish[2] to hold them back from choosing a better way of life.

Pride is too deeply fixed in the hearts of men to be easily plucked out. So I am glad that the Utopians at least have been lucky enough to achieve this Republic which I wish all mankind would imitate. The institutions they have adopted have made their community most happy, and as far as anyone can tell, capable of lasting forever. Now that they have rooted up the seeds of ambition and faction at home, along with most other vices, they are in no danger from internal strife, which alone has been the ruin of many other states that seemed secure. As long as they preserve harmony at home, and keep their institutions healthy, the Utopians can never be overcome or even shaken by their envious neighbors, who have often attempted their ruin, but always in vain.

When Raphael had finished his story, it seemed to me that quite a few of the laws and customs he had described as existing among the Utopians were really absurd. Their methods of waging war, their religious ceremonies, and their social customs were some of these but my

2. The remora, which attaches itself by a suction cup to larger fish or ships. It was fabled to be strong enough to hold back a ship under sail.

chief objection was to the basis of their whole system, that is, their communal living and their moneyless economy. This one thing alone takes
away all the nobility, magnificence, splendor, and majesty which (in the
popular view) are considered the true ornaments of any commonwealth.
But I saw Raphael was tired with talking, and I was not sure he could
take contradiction in these matters, particularly when I recalled what he
had said about certain counsellors who were afraid they might not appear
knowing enough unless they found something to criticize in other men's
ideas. So with praise for the Utopian way of life and his account of it, I
took him by the hand and led him in to supper. But first I said that we
would find some other time for thinking of these matters more deeply,
and for talking them over in more detail. And I still hope such an opportunity will present itself some day.

Meantime, while I can hardly agree with everything he said (though
he is a man of unquestionable learning and enormous experience of
human affairs), yet I freely confess that in the republic of the Utopians
there are many features that in our own societies I would like rather than
expect to see.

1514–16   1516

From The History of King Richard III

[A *King's Mistress*[1]]

Now then, bye and bye, as it were for anger not for covetise,[2] the
Protector sent into the house of Shore's wife (for her husband dwelled
not with her) and spoiled her of all that ever she had, above the value of
two or three thousand marks,[3] and sent her body to prison. And when
he had a while laid unto her for the manner' sake,[4] that she went about
to bewitch him, and that she was of counsel with the Lord Chamberlain[5]
to destroy him; in conclusion when that no color[6] could fasten upon
these matters, then he laid heinously to her charge that thing that herself
could not deny, that all the world wist was true, and that natheles[7] every
man laughed at to hear it then so suddenly so highly taken, that she was
naught of her body.[8] And for this cause (as a goodly continent prince
clean and faultless of himself, sent out of heaven into this vicious world
for the amendment of men's manners) he caused the Bishop of London
to put her to open penance, going before the cross in procession upon a
Sunday with a taper in her hand.[9] In which she went in countenance
and pace demure, so womanly, and albeit she were out of all array save

---

1. Jane Shore, wife of a London merchant and
mistress of the late king, Edward IV, persecuted by
Richard Duke of Gloucester, "the Protector" during the minority of Edward's sons. After their mysterious death in the Tower of London he ascended
the throne as Richard III.
2. Greed.

3. A mark equals ⅔ of a pound.
4. Accused her, to justify arrest.
5. Lord Hastings, beheaded by Richard.
6. Plausibility.
7. Nevertheless.
8. Unchaste.
9. The standard punishment for a harlot.

her kirtle only,[1] yet went she so fair and lovely, namely while the wondering of the people cast a comely rud in her checks (of which she before had most miss)[2] that her great shame won her much praise among those that were more amorous of her body than curious of[3] her soul. And many good folk also that hated her living and glad were to see sin corrected, yet pitied they more her penance than rejoiced therein when they considered that the Protector procured it, more of a corrupt intent than any virtuous affection.[4]

This woman was born in London, worshipfully friended, honestly brought up, and very well married, saving somewhat too soon, her husband an honest citizen, young and goodly and of good substance. But forasmuch as they were coupled ere she were well ripe, she not very fervently loved for whom she never longed. Which was haply[5] the thing that the more easily made her incline unto the King's appetite when he required[6] her. Howbeit that respect of his royalty, the hope of gay apparel, ease, pleasure and other wanton wealth was able soon to pierce a soft tender heart. But when the king had abused her, anon[7] her husband (as he was an honest man and one that could his good,[8] not presuming to touch a King's concubine) left her up to him altogether. When the king died, the Lord Chamberlain took her, which in the King's days, albeit he was sore[9] enamored upon her, yet he forbare her, either for reverence or for a certain friendly faithfulness. Proper[1] she was, and fair: nothing in her body that you would have changed, but if you would have wished her somewhat higher. Thus say they that knew her in her youth. Albeit some that now see her (for yet she liveth) deem her never to have been well visaged. Whose judgment seemeth me somewhat like as though men should guess the beauty of one long before departed by her scalp taken out of the charnel house;[2] for now she is old, lean, withered and dried up, nothing left but rivelled[3] skin and hard bone. And yet being even such, whoso well advise[4] her visage might guess and devise which parts how filled might make it a fair face. Yet delighted men not so much in her beauty as in her pleasant behavior. For a proper wit had she, and could both read well and write, merry in company, ready and quick of answer, neither mute nor full of babble, sometime taunting without displeasure and not without disport.[5] The King would say that he had three concubines, which in three divers[6] properties diversly excelled: one the merriest, one the wiliest, and one the holiest harlot in his realm, as one whom no man could get out of the church lightly[7] to any place but it were to his bed. The other two were somewhat greater personages, and natheles[8] of their humility content to be nameless and

1. Dressed only in a loose gown.
2. Lack.
3. Concerned about.
4. Motive.
5. Perhaps.
6. Attempted to seduce.
7. Immediately.
8. Knew what was good for him.
9. Very.

1. Handsome.
2. Common burial place.
3. Shrivelled.
4. Would like to reconstruct.
5. Playfulness.
6. Different.
7. Easily.
8. Nevertheless.

to forbear the praise of those properties. But the merriest was this Shore's wife, in whom the King therefore took special pleasure. For many he had, but her he loved, whose favor,[9] to say the truth, (for sin it were to belie the devil) she never abused to any man's hurt, but to many a man's comfort and relief. Where the King took displeasure, she would mitigate and appease his mind. Where men were out of favor, she would bring them in his grace. For many that had highly offended, she attained pardon. Of great forfeitures she gat men remission.[1] And finally in many weighty suits, she stood many men in great stead, either for none or very small rewards, and those rather gay than rich, either for that she was content with the deed'[2] self well done, or for that she delighted to be sued unto and to show what she was able to do with the king, or for that wanton women and wealthy be not always covetous.

I doubt not some shall think this woman so slight a thing to be written of and set among the remembrances of great matters, which they shall specially think that haply shall esteem her only by that[3] they now see her. But me seemeth[4] the chance so much the more worthy to be remembered, in how much she is now in the more beggarly condition, unfriended and worn out of acquaintance,[5] after good substance, after as great favor with the prince, after as great suit[6] and seeking to with all those that those days had business to speed, as many other men were in their times, which be now famous only by the infamy of their ill deeds. Her doings were not much less, albeit they be much less remembered, because they were not so evil. For men use if they have an evil turn to write it in marble; and whoso doth us a good turn, we write it in dust, which is not worst proved[7] by her; for at this day she beggeth of many at this day living, that at this day had begged if she had not been.

1557

9. Influence.
1. I. e., got cancellation of orders to forfeit property.
2. Deed's.
3. That which.

4. I think.
5. Without friends.
6. Influence at court.
7. I. e., is a good example.

JOHN SKELTON
ca. 1460–1529

According to one of the jest-book tales, John Skelton suddenly interrupted one of his sermons to ask the members of his congregation why they had complained that he kept a fair wench in the rectory. To be sure, he said, he did keep a fair wench; she was fairer than his parishioners' wives and had given him a son. Holding the child up naked before the congregation, he exclaimed, "How say you, neighbors all? Is not this child as fair as is the best of all yours? It hath nose, eyes, hands, and feet, as well as any of yours. It is not like a pig, nor a calf, nor like no foul nor no monstrous beast. If I had brought forth this child without arms or legs, or that it were deformed being a monstrous thing, I would never have blamed you to have complained to the Bishop of me, but to complain without a cause! I say as I said before, in my antetheme, *vos estis*, you be, and have been, and will and shall be knaves to complain of me without a cause reasonable."

Many and colorful were the stories circulated about the mad wag Skelton—who was also the major poet of the first quarter of the century, with the title of Poet Laureate from both Oxford and Cambridge. He was famous as a rhetorician and a translator, and he was also, for a time, tutor to the young Henry VIII. He took orders and, after writing *The Bowge of Court* (1498), a satire on courtiers and court life, retired about 1503, became rector of the parish church at Diss, in Norfolk. By 1512 he had returned to the court, appointed King's Orator. He moved to a house in the sanctuary of Westminister in 1518, and shortly thereafter began his vituperous attacks upon Cardinal Wolsey, the great prelate-statesman, including *Speak, Parrot, Colin Clout*, and *Why Come Yet Not to Court?* (1521–22). Wolsey had him imprisoned for a time but later released him.

While in retirement at Diss, he began to write poetry in a "plain style" that rejected ornate rhetorical devices and aureate language. His satires gain some of their most startling effects by mixing high and low styles. These "open satires," as they are called, are written in short rhymed lines that to the modern ear resemble doggerel, although something like this form was probably familiar enough to readers of medieval satire. A Skeltonic line may have from two to five beats, and the lines can keep on rhyming until the resources of the language give out. To many of his poems, particularly the satires, this strange meter is singularly appropriate. *The Tunning of Elinour Rumming* is, for example, a wonderfully disordered, clattering portrait of an alewife that reminds one of Brueghel's paintings in its realism, and the Skeltonics do much to contribute to the effect of disorder. The lines give the voice of the narrator of the satires a breathless urgency much admired by Robert Graves and W. H. Auden, among other modern poets. Skelton's satires draw upon a long tradition of medieval anti-clerical satire but he brings a fresh voice to the genre.

Skelton's lyrics also partake of traditional medieval modes which the poet makes his own. To the three-part song *Mannerly Margery*, a traditional ballad of the clerk and the serving maid, he gives an ironic ending. His rather salacious *Lullay, Lullay* is a parody on traditional lullabies in which the Virgin Mary rocks the Christ child in her lap. In an entirely different mood is the pleasant lyric in praise of Mistress Margaret Hussey. It is one of several that Skelton published in 1523 in *The Garland of Laurel*; in that work the poet is crowned with a laurel wreath by the countess of Surrey and her ladies, and in gratitude he writes a poem to each of them. In his lyrics as well as his satires we hear a genuine music and find, as always, the impress of the distinctive character of their author.

Mannerly Margery Milk and Ale[1]

Aye, beshrew you, by my fay,[2]
These wanton clerks be nice° alway,   *foolish*

---

1. The clerk's lines are in quotation marks; Margery sings the rest, except the chorus lines, which

are sung by a bass.

2. "Beshrew": curse (not used seriously); "fay": faith.

Avaunt, avaunt, my popinjay!
"What, will you do nothing but play?"
5   Tilly vally straw, let be I say!
Gup,[3] Christian Clout, gup, Jack of the Vale!
With Mannerly Margery milk and ale.

"By God, ye be a pretty pode,°   *toad*
And I love you an whole cartload."
10   Straw, James Foder, ye play the fode,°   *deceiver, seducer*
I am no hackney for your rod:°   *riding*
Go watch a bull, your back is broad!
Gup, Christian Clout, gup, Jack of the Vale!
With Mannerly Margery milk and ale.

15   Ywis° ye deal uncourteously;   *certainly*
What, would ye frumple° me? now fie!   *rumple, tumble*
"What, and ye shall not be my pigsny?"°   *darling*
By Christ, ye shall not, no hardily:
I will not be japped° bodily!   *tricked, deceived*
20   Gup, Christian Clout, gup, Jack of the Vale!
With Mannerly Margery milk and ale.

"Walk forth your way, ye cost me naught;
Now have I found that I have sought:
The best cheap flesh that ever I bought."
25   Yet, for his love that hath all wrought,
Wed me, or else I die for thought.
Gup, Christian Clout, your breath is stale!
Go, Mannerly Margery milk and ale!
Gup, Christian Clout, gup, Jack of the Vale!
30   With Mannerly Margery milk and ale.

c. 1495   1523

To Mistress Margaret Hussey

Merry Margaret,
    As midsummer flower,
Gentle as falcon
Or hawk of the tower;[1]
With solace and gladness,   5
Much mirth and no madness,
All good and no badness;
    So joyously,
    So maidenly,
    So womanly   10

3. Contracted from "go up."
1. "Falcon-gentle" was the term applied to the female and young of the goshawk; a "hawk of the tower" was one that towered aloft, sailing high in the air before swooping on its prey.

Her demeaning
In every thing,
Far, far passing
That I can endite,[2]
Or suffice to write   15
Of merry Margaret
As midsummer flower,
Gentle as falcon
Or hawk of the tower.
As patient and as still   20
And as full of good will
As fair Isaphill;[3]
Colyander,
Sweet pomander,[4]
Good Cassander;[5]   25
Steadfast of thought,
Well made, well wrought,
Far may be sought
Ere that ye can find
So courteous, so kind   30
As merry Margaret,
This midsummer flower,
Gentle as falcon
Or hawk of the tower.

1495, 1522   1523

Lullay, Lullay, Like a Child

With lullay, lullay, like a child,
Thou sleepest too long, thou art beguiled.°   *deceived*

"My darling dear, my daisy flower,
Let me," quod° he, "lie in your lap."   *quoth*
5   "Lie still," quod she, "my paramour,
Lie still, hardily,° and take a nap."   *confidently*
His head was heavy, such was his hap,
All drowsy dreaming, drowned in sleep,
That of his love he took no keep.
10   With hey, lullay, lullay, like a child,
Thou sleepest too long, thou art beguiled.

With ba, ba, ba![1] and bas, bas, bas!
She cherished him, both cheek and chin,

2. I.e., surpassing anything that I can compose.
3. Hypsipyle, queen of Lemnos, famous for her
devotion to her father and to her children.
4. Colyander or coriander was an herb supposed
to soothe pain; like sweet pomander, it had a pleasant odor.

5. The beautiful daughter of Priam of Troy; she
could prophesy accurately but no one believed her
prophecies. This did not discourage her; she is
preeminently "steadfast of thought" (line 26).
1. The "by" of *lullaby*; "bas, bas, bas": kiss, kiss,
kiss.

That he wist never where he was,
15   He had forgotten all deadly sin.
He wanted wit her love to win,
He trusted her payment and lost all his pay;
She left him sleeping and stale° away,   *stole*
With hey, lullay, lullay, like a child,
20   Thou sleepest too long, thou art beguiled.

The rivers rough, the waters wan,
She sparèd not to wet her feet;
She waded over, she found a man
That halsèd° her heartily and kissed her sweet—   *embraced*
25   Thus after her cold she caught a heat.
"My lief," she said, "routeth[2] in his bed;
Ywis° he hath an heavy head."   *certainly*
With hey, lullay, lullay, like a child,
Thou sleepest too long, thou are beguiled.

30   What dreamest thou, drunkard, drowsy pate?
Thy lust and liking is from thee gone.
Thou blinkard blowboll,[3] thou wakest too late.
Behold thou liest, luggard,° alone!   *sluggard*
Well may thou sigh, well may thou groan,
35   To deal with her so cowardly.
Ywis, pole-hatchet,[4] she bleared thine eye.

1495–1500   1527

From Colin Clout[1]

[*The Spirituality vs. the Temporality*]

And if ye stand in doubt
Who brought this rhyme about,
My name is Colin Clout.
50   I purpose to shake out
All my conning° bag,   *learning*
Like a clerkly hag.[2]
For though my rhyme be ragged,
Tattered and jagged,
55   Rudely rain-beaten,
Rusty and moth-eaten,
If ye take well therewith,
It hath in it some pith.
For, as far as I can see,

---

2. My lover snores.
3. Blink-eyed drunkard.
4. A soldier who carried a pole-axe.
1. In these lines, comprising part of the introduc-

tory matter, Colin Clout, the narrator, introduces the theme of the whole long poem, in the characteristically jagged Skeltonic line.
2. Old scholar.

60　It is wrong with each degree.
　　For the temporality°　　　　　　　　　　*laymen*
　　Accuseth the spirituality;
　　The spirituality again
　　Doth grudge and complain
65　Upon the temporal men;
　　Thus, each of other blother°　　　　　　*babble*
　　The one against the other.
　　Alas, they make me shudder!
　　For in hugger-mugger°　　　　　　　　　*haste*
70　The Church is put in fault;
　　The prelates been so haut,°　　　　　　　*haughty*
　　They say, and look so high
　　As though they wouldè fly
　　Above the starry sky.

c. 1523　　　　　　　　　　　　　　　　　　　　1530

SIR THOMAS WYATT THE ELDER
1503–1542

Wyatt was born at Allington Castle in Kent, and educated at St. John's College, Cambridge. He spent most of his life as a courtier and diplomat, serving King Henry VIII as Clerk of the King's Jewels and as ambassador to Spain and to Emperor Charles V. He was also a member of various missions to France and Italy. He spent much of his adult life abroad; his interest in foreign literature, especially Italian, is evident from his translations and imitations of poems by the Italian sonneteers Petrarch, Sannazaro, Alamanni, and others. The life of a courtier under Henry VIII was not a calm life: Wyatt was twice arrested and imprisoned, once in 1536, after a quarrel with the duke of Suffolk, and again in 1541, when he was charged with treason, lodged in the Tower of London, and stripped of all his property. On both occasions he was fortunate enough to regain the king's favor and receive a pardon. His praise of quiet retired life in the country and the cynical comments about foreign courts in his verse epistle to John Poins derive from his own experience.

For all his travel abroad, Wyatt remained essentially an Englishman. His poetry includes not only the sonnets, based upon Italian models, but also many delightful lyrics with short stanzas and refrains in the manner of the native English "ballet" (pronounced to rhyme with *mallet*) or dance-song. Wyatt's own temperament and disposition show more clearly in these English poems than in the sonnets. The lover in the Petrarchan sonnet is usually in a mood of doleful despair; the typical poem is essentially a complaint, though the interest lies in following the elaborately worked out "conceits" or comparisons. The lover is abject, he is the lady's slave; her coldness is a perpetual torture to him. In the ballets, however, a rather gay, manly independence is the characteristic note.

The sonnet, a fourteen-line poem with a complicated rhyme scheme, was introduced into English by Wyatt. He took his subject matter from Petrarch's sonnets, for the most part, but his rhyme schemes came from other Italian models. The most common rhyme scheme in Wyatt's sonnets is *abba abba cddc ee*; the usual Italian structure of an octave (first eight lines) followed after a turn in the sense by a sestet (last six lines) was already beginning to break down into the "English" structure for the sonnet, three quatrains and a couplet.

Although Wyatt intended to publish a collection of his poems, he never did so. In fact, very little of his verse was published until after his death. In aristocratic circles poems circulated in manuscript and were copied by hand; the general public usually saw courtiers' poems only when some enterprising publisher acquired manuscripts, perhaps already formed into a collection, and printed them as a miscellany. An early volume of this sort, called *The Court of Venus*, published a few Wyatt poems before 1540. A dozen such collections were published during the second half of the sixteenth century, with titles like A *Paradise of Dainty Devices*, A *Handful of Pleasant Delights*, and A *Gorgeous Gallery of Gallant Inventions*. By far the most important of these miscellanies was issued by the printer Richard Tottel in 1557 (fifteen years after Wyatt's death) with the title *Songs and Sonnets written by the Right Honorable Lord Henry Howard late Earl of Surrey and other*. Until modern times it was always called simply *Songs and Sonnets* (Shakespeare has his Master Slender in *The Merry Wives of Windsor* say "I had rather than forty shillings I had my book of Songs and Sonnets here"); but now it is always referred to as *Tottel's Miscellany*. The printer, Richard Tottel, addressed the reader in an interesting epistle:

> That to have well written in verse, yea and in small parcels, deserveth great praise, the works of divers Latins, Italians and other do prove sufficiently. That our tongue is able in that kind to do as praiseworthy as the rest, the honorable style of the noble Earl of Surrey and the weightiness of the deep-witted Sir Thomas Wyatt the Elder's verse, with several graces in sundry good English writers, do show abundantly. It resteth now, gentle reader, that thou think it not ill done to publish, to the honor of the English tongue, and for profit of the studious of English eloquence, those works which the ungentle hoarders up of such treasure have heretofore envied thee. And for this point, good reader, thine own profit and pleasure in these presently, and moe hereafter, shall answer for my defence. If perhaps some mislike the stateliness of style, removed from the rude skill of common ears, I ask help of the learned to defend their learned friends, the authors of this work. And I exhort the unlearned, by reading to be more skilfull, and to purge that swine-like grossness that maketh the sweet marjoram not to smell to their delight.

The anthology includes 271 poems—97 attributed to Wyatt, 40 to Surrey, 40 to Nicholas Grimald, and 94 to "Uncertain Authors." It is surely one of the most important books in the history of English literature, for it was the channel through which the main currents of European Renaissance poetry flowed into the British Isles. In it the sonnet, blank verse, *terza rima*, ottava rima, rondeau, and other forms were naturalized into English, and suddenly the ragged, undisciplined, pedestrian verse of the first part of the century became antiquated. When Wyatt was a boy it was possible for Alexander

Barclay, an ambitious and by no means uneducated poet, to write verse like this:

> The famous poets with the muses nine
> With wit inspired, fresh, pregnant and divine,
> Say boldly endite in style substantial;
> Some in poems high and historical,
> Some them delight in heavy tragedies
> And some in wanton or merry comedies.

Wyatt was not primarily concerned with regularity of accent and smoothness of rhythm. By the time *Tottel's Miscellany* was published, Wyatt's rather rough and vigorous metrical practice was felt to be crude, and Tottel's editor smoothed out the versification. We reprint *They Flee from Me* in the versions of the Egerton manuscript and of Tottel. The Egerton manuscript (E. MS.) contains poems in Wyatt's own hand and corrections in his hand of scribal texts. The Devonshire manuscript (D. MS.) was not apparently in the poet's possession, but some of its texts seem earlier than Egerton's and it furnishes additional poems.

The Long Love That in My Thought Doth Harbor[1]

> The long love that in my thought doth harbor,
> And in mine heart doth keep his residence,
> Into my face presseth with bold pretense
> And therein campeth, spreading his banner.[2]
> She that me learneth to love and suffer   5
> And will that my trust and lust's negligence[3]
> Be reined by reason, shame, and reverence
> With his hardiness taketh displeasure.
> Wherewithal unto the heart's forest he fleeth,
> Leaving his enterprise with pain and cry,   10
> And there him hideth, and not appeareth.
> What may I do, when my master feareth,
> But in the field with him to live and die?
> For good is the life ending faithfully.

E. MS.

Farewell, Love

> Farewell, Love, and all thy laws forever,
> Thy baited hooks shall tangle me no more;

1. Wyatt's version of Petrarch's *Sonnetto in Vita* 91; his younger friend, the earl of Surrey, also translated it (see *Love, That Doth Reign and Live Within My Thought*).
2. I.e., the poet's blush. The first 4 lines of this sonnet contain the "conceit" (or elaborately sustained metaphor) of love as a kind of warrior who "harbors" in the speaker's thought, lives in his heart,

and occasionally invades his face "with bold pretense" (i.e., making bold claim). He flaunts his warlike presence by means of the "banner." Elaborate metaphors of this kind are found often in Elizabethan love poetry; sometimes an entire sonnet will turn on one conceit. "Learns": teaches.
3. I.e., my open and careless revelation of my love. "Shame": modesty, shamefastness.

Senec and Plato call me from thy lore,
To perfect wealth my wit for to endeavor. [1]
In blind error when I did persever,   5
Thy sharp repulse, that pricketh aye so sore,
Hath taught me to set in trifles no store
And 'scape forth since liberty is lever. [2]
Therefore farewell, go trouble younger hearts,
And in me claim no more authority;   10
With idle youth go use thy property,
And thereon spend thy many brittle darts.
For hitherto though I have lost all my time,
Me lusteth[3] no longer rotten boughs to climb.

E. MS.

My Galley[1]

My galley chargèd with forgetfulness
Thorough[2] sharp seas, in winter nights doth pass
'Tween rock and rock; and eke[3] mine enemy, alas,
That is my lord, steereth with cruelness,
And every oar a thought in readiness,   5
As though that death were light in such a case. [4]
An endless wind doth tear the sail apace
Of forcèd sighs and trusty fearfulness. [5]
A rain of tears, a cloud of dark disdain,
Hath done the wearied cords great hinderance;   10
Wreathèd with error and eke with ignorance.
The stars be hid that led me to this pain.
Drownèd is reason that should me consort,[6]
And I remain despairing of the port.

E. MS.

Madam, Withouten Many Words

Madam, withouten many words,
Once[1] I am sure ye will or no,
And if ye will, then leave your bordes,[2]
And use your wit and show it so.

---

1. I.e., "Senec" (Seneca, the Roman moral philosopher and tragedian) and Plato call him to educate his mind to perfect well-being ("wealth").
2. More pleasing, dearer.
3. I care.
1. Translated from Petrarch, *Sonnetto in Vita* 137.
2. Through.

3. Also.
4. As though my destruction wouldn't matter much.
5. Fear to trust.
6. Accompany.
1. Sometime.
2. Jests.

And with a beck ye shall me call,   5
And if of one that burneth alway
Ye have any pity at all,
Answer him fair with yea or nay.

If it be yea I shall be fain,
If it be nay, friends as before;   10
Ye shall another man obtain
And I mine own and yours no more.

E. MS.

Whoso List to Hunt[1]

Whoso list[2] to hunt, I know where is an hind,
But as for me, alas, I may no more.
The vain travail hath wearied me so sore
I am of them that farthest cometh behind.
Yet may I, by no means, my wearied mind   5
Draw from the deer, but as she fleeth afore,
Fainting I follow. I leave off therefore,
Since in a net I seek to hold the wind.
Who list her hunt, I put him out of doubt,
As well as I, may spend his time in vain.   10
And graven with diamonds in letters plain
There is written, her fair neck round about,
"*Noli me tangere,* for Caesar's I am,
And wild for to hold, though I seem tame."

E. MS.

My Lute, Awake!

My lute, awake! Perform the last
Labor that thou and I shall waste,
And end that I have now begun;
For when this song is sung and past,
My lute, be still, for I have done.   5

As to be heard where ear is none,
As lead to grave in marble stone[1]

1. An adaptation of Petrarch, *Rime* 190, perhaps influenced by commentators on Petrarch, who said that *Noli me tangere quia Caesaris sum* ("Touch me not, for I am Caesar's") was inscribed on the collars of Caesar's hinds which were then set free and were presumably safe from hunters. Wyatt's sonnet is usually supposed to refer to Anne Bol-

eyn, in whom Henry VIII became interested in 1526.
2. Cares.
1. I.e., when sound may be heard with no ear to hear it, or when soft lead is able to carve ("grave") hard marble.

My song may pierce her heart as soon.
Should we then sigh or sing or moan?
No, no, my lute, for I have done.　　10

The rocks do not so cruelly
Repulse the waves continually
As she my suit and affection.
So that I am past remedy,
Whereby my lute and I have done.　　15

Proud of the spoil that thou hast got
Of simple hearts, thorough love's shot;
By whom, unkind, thou hast them won,
Think not he hath his bow forgot,
Although my lute and I have done.　　20

Vengeance shall fall on thy disdain
That makest but game on earnest pain.
Think not alone under the sun
Unquit[2] to cause thy lovers plain,
Although my lute and I have done.　　25

Perchance thee lie withered and old
The winter nights that are so cold,
Plaining in vain unto the moon.
Thy wishes then dare not be told.
Care then who list,[3] for I have done.　　30

And then may chance thee to repent
The time that thou hast lost and spent
To cause thy lovers sigh and swoon.
Then shalt thou know beauty but lent,
And wish and want as I have done.　　35

Now cease, my lute. This is the last
Labor that thou and I shall waste,
And ended is that we begun.
Now is this song both sung and past;
My lute, be still, for I have done.　　40

E. MS.

They Flee from Me

They flee from me, that sometime did me seek,
With naked foot stalking in my chamber.
I have seen them, gentle, tame, and meek,

---

2. Unrevenged. "Plain": to complain.　　　3. Likes.

That now are wild, and do not remember
That sometime they put themselves in danger   5
To take bread at my hand; and now they range,
Busily seeking with a continual change.

Thankèd be fortune it hath been otherwise,
Twenty times better; but once in special,
In thin array, after a pleasant guise,   10
When her loose gown from her shoulders did fall,
And she me caught in her arms long and small,[1]
Therewithall sweetly did me kiss
And softly said, "Dear heart, how like you this?"

It was no dream, I lay broad waking.   15
But all is turned, thorough my gentleness,
Into a strange fashion of forsaking;
And I have leave to go, of her goodness,
And she also to use newfangleness.[2]
But since that I so kindely[3] am servèd,   20
I fain would know what she hath deservèd.

E. MS.

The Lover Showeth How He Is Forsaken of Such as
He Sometime Enjoyed

[*They Flee from Me*]

They flee from me, that sometime did me seek
With naked foot stalking within my chamber.
Once have I seen them gentle, tame, and meek
That now are wild, and do not once remember
That sometime they have put themselves in danger   5
To take bread at my hand, and now they range,
Busily seeking in continual change.

Thankèd be fortune, it hath been otherwise,
Twenty times better; but once especial,
In thin array, after a pleasant guise,   10
When her loose gown did from her shoulders fall,
And she me caught in her arms long and small,
And therewithal, so sweetly did me kiss
And softly said, "Dear heart, how like you this?"

It was no dream, for I lay broad awaking.   15
But all is turned now, through my gentleness,

---

1. Slender.
2. Fickleness.

3. Naturally, but with an ironic suggestion of the modern meaning of "kindly."

Into a bitter fashion of forsaking.
And I have leave to go, of her goodness,
And she also to use newfangleness.
But since that I unkindly so am servèd,   20
How like you this, what hath she now deservèd?

Tottel, 1557

Divers Doth Use

Divers doth use, as I have heard and know,
When that to change their ladies do begin,
To mourne and wail, and never for to lin,[1]
Hoping thereby to pease[2] their painful woe.
And some there be, that when it chanceth so   5
That women change and hate where love hath been,
They call them false and think with words to win
The hearts of them which otherwhere doth grow.
But as for me, though that by chance indeed
Change hath outworn the favor that I had,   10
I will not wail, lament, nor yet be sad,
Nor call her false that falsely did me feed,
But let it pass, and think it is of kind[3]
That often change doth please a woman's mind.

D. MS.

And Wilt Thou Leave Me Thus?

And wilt thou leave me thus?
Say nay, say nay, for shame,
To save thee from the blame
Of all my grief and grame![1]
And wilt thou leave me thus?   5
    Say nay, say nay!

And wilt thou leave me thus,
That hath loved thee so long
In wealth[2] and woe among?
And is thy heart so strong   10
As for to leave me thus?
    Say nay, say nay!

And wilt thou leave me thus,
That hath given thee my heart

---

1. Cease.   1. Sorrow.
2. Appease, relieve.   2. Welfare (not specifically riches).
3. Nature.

Never for to depart,   15
Neither for pain nor smart?
And wilt thou leave me thus?
    Say nay, say nay!

And wilt thou leave me thus,
And have no more pity   20
Of him that loveth thee?
Alas thy cruelty!
And wilt thou leave me thus?
    Say nay, say nay!

D. MS.

Blame Not My Lute

Blame not my lute, for he must sound
Of this or that as liketh[1] me:
For lack of wit[2] the lute is bound
To give such tunes as pleaseth me.
Then though my songs be somewhat strange   5
And speaks such words as touch thy change,[3]
    Blame not my lute.

My lute alas doth not offend,
Though that perforce he must agree
To sound such tunes as I intend   10
To sing to them that heareth me.
Then though my songs be somewhat plain
And toucheth some that use to feign,[4]
    Blame not my lute.

My lute and strings may not deny,   15
But as I strike they must obey:
Break not them then so wrongfully,
But wreak thyself some wiser way.
And though the songs which I indite
Do quit thy change[5] with rightful spite,   20
    Blame not my lute.

Spite asketh spite, and changing change,
And falsèd faith must needs be known;
The fault so great, the case so strange,
Of right it must abroad be blown.   25
Then since that by thine own desert

1. Pleases.
2. Intelligence.
3. Unfaithfulness.
4. And comment on some false ones.
5. Requite your unfaithfulness.

My songs do tell how true thou art,
    Blame not my lute.

Blame but thyself, that hast misdone
And well deservèd to have blame,   30
Change thou thy way so evil begun,
And then my lute shall sound that same.
But if till then my fingers play
By thy desert their wonted[6] way,
    Blame not my lute.   35

D. MS.

Forget Not Yet

Forget not yet the tried intent
Of such a truth as I have meant,
My great travail[1] so gladly spent
    Forget not yet.

Forget not yet when first began   5
The weary life ye know since when,
The suit, the service[2] none tell can,
    Forget not yet.

Forget not yet the great essays,
The cruel wrong, the scornful ways,   10
The painful patience in denays,[3]
    Forget not yet.

Forget not yet, forget not this,
How long ago hath been and is
The mind that never meant amiss,   15
    Forget not yet.

Forget not then thine own approved,
The which so long hath thee so loved,
Whose steadfast faith yet never moved,
    Forget not this.   20

D. MS.

---

6. Accustomed.
1. Laborious efforts.
2. Actions of a lover, often called the lady's "ser-

vant."
3. Denials, refusals.

Mine Own John Poins[1]

Mine own John Poins, since ye delight to know
The cause why that homeward I me draw,
And flee the press of courts, whereso they go,
Rather than to live thrall, under the awe
Of lordly looks, wrapped within my cloak,   5
To will and lust[2] learning to set a law;
It is not for because I scorn and mock
The power of them to whom Fortune hath lent
Charge over us, of right to strike the stroke.[3]
But true it is that I have always meant   10
Less to esteem them than the common sort,
Of outward things that judge in their intent
Without regard what doth inward resort.
I grant sometime that of glory the fire
Doth touch my heart; me list not to report   15
Blame by honor, and honor to desire.[4]
But how may I this honor now attain
That cannot dye the color black a liar?
My Poins, I cannot frame me tune to feign,
To cloak the truth, for praise without desert,   20
Of them that list all vice for to retain.
I cannot honor them that sets their part
With Venus and Bacchus all their life long.[5]
Nor hold my peace of them, although I smart.
I cannot crouch nor kneel to do so great a wrong,   25
To worship them like God on earth alone,
That are as wolves these sely[6] lambs among.
I cannot with my words complain and moan
Nor suffer naught, nor smart without complaint,
Nor turn the word that from my mouth is gone;   30
I cannot speak and look like a saint,
Use wiles for wit, or make deceit a pleasure;
And call craft counsel, for profit still to paint;
I cannot wrest the law to fill the coffer,
With innocent blood to feed myself fat,   35
And do most hurt where most help I offer.
I am not he that can allow the state

---

1. A friend of Wyatt's. This verse epistle of informal satire is based upon the tenth satire of the Italian Luigi Alamanni, but personalized and
Anglicized in detail by Wyatt. It was apparently
written during Wyatt's banishment from court in
1536. Lines 1–51 of the poem are from the Devonshire manuscript, lines 52–103 from the Egerton manuscript.
2. Pleasure.
3. I.e., my retirement from court is not because I

scorn great and powerful princes. But (lines 10–
13) I esteem them less than do the "common sort"
of people, who judge by externals only.
4. I.e., I do not wish to attack honor, nor to call
dishonorable desire honorable.
5. I.e., I cannot honor those who devote themselves to Venus (goddess of love-making) and Bacchus (god of drinking).
6. Innocent.

Of high Caesar, and damn Cato[7] to die,
That with his death did 'scape out of the gate
From Caesar's hands, if Livy[8] do not lie,   40
And would not live where liberty was lost,
So did his heart the common weal[9] apply.
I am not he, such eloquence to boast
To make the crow in singing as the swan,
Nor call the lion of coward beasts the most,   45
That cannot take a mouse as the cat can;
And he that dieth of hunger of the gold,
Call him Alexander,[1] and say that Pan
Passeth Apollo in music manifold,[2]
Praise Sir Thopas for a noble tale,   50
And scorn the story that the Knight told,[3]
Praise him for counsel that is drunk of ale;
Grin when he laugheth that beareth all the sway,
Frown when he frowneth, and groan when he is pale;
On others' lust to hang both night and day—   55
None of these points would ever frame in me;
My wit is naught: I cannot learn the way;
And much the less of things that greater be
That asken help of colors of device[4]
To join the mean with each extremity.   60
With nearest virtue to cloak alway the vice,
And as to purpose, likewise it shall fall
To press the virtue that it may not rise;
As drunkenness, good fellowship to call;
The friendly foe, with his double face,   65
Say he is gentle and courteous therewithal;
And say that favel[5] hath a goodly grace
In eloquence; and cruelty to name
Zeal of justice, and change in time and place;
And he that suff'reth offense without blame,   70
Call him pitiful, and him true and plain
That raileth reckless to every man's shame,
Say he is rude that cannot lie and feign,
The lecher a lover, and tyranny
To be the right of a prince's reign.   75
I cannot, I: no, no, it will not be.
This is the cause that I could never yet
Hang on their sleeves, that weigh, as thou mayst see,
A chip of chance more than a pound of wit.
This maketh me at home to hunt and hawk,   80

---

7. Cato the Younger, the famous Roman patriot
who committed suicide rather than submit to Caesar.
8. Titus Livius (59 B.C.–A.D. 17), the great Roman
historian.
9. The common good, or the state.
1. Alexander yearned for more worlds to conquer.
2. Pan's music was simple and rustic, played on

"Pan's pipes."
3. The silly tale of Sir Thopas, in Chaucer's *Canterbury Tales*, is told by Chaucer himself, until the
Host forces him to stop. The Knight's Tale is the
most courtly and dignified of the tales.
4. Tricks of rhetoric.
5. Flattery.

And in foul weather at my book to sit,
In frost and snow then with my bow to stalk.
No man doth mark whereso I ride or go.
In lusty leas[6] at liberty I walk,
And of these news I feel nor weal nor woe,   85
Save that a clog doth hang yet at my heel.[7]
No force for that, for it is ordered so
That I may leap both hedge and dike full well;
I am not now in France, to judge the wine,
With sav'ry sauce those delicates[8] to feel;   90
Nor yet in Spain, where one must him incline,
Rather than to be, outwardly to seem.
I meddle not with wits that be so fine;
Nor Flanders' cheer[9] letteth not my sight to deem
Of black and white, nor taketh my wit away   95
With beastliness, they beasts do so esteem.
Nor am I not where Christ is given in prey
For money, poison, and treason—at Rome[1]
A common practice, usèd night and day.
But here I am in Kent and Christendom,   100
Among the Muses, where I read and rhyme;
Where, if thou list, my Poins, for to come,
Thou shalt be judge how I do spend my time.

                                                              E. MS.

6. Pleasant fields.
7. "I feel neither happiness nor unhappiness about current political affairs, except that a 'clog' (i.e., his confinement on parole to his estate) keeps me from traveling far." Note that "news" is a plural in Elizabethan English. "No force": no matter.
8. Delicacies.

9. I.e., the drinking for which Flemings were notorious in the 16th century; "letteth": hinders, prevents.
1. In *Tottel's Miscellany*, published in the reign of the Catholic Queen Mary, these lines were altered as follows: "where *truth* is given in prey / For money, poison and treason; *of some.*"

HENRY HOWARD, EARL OF SURREY
1517–1547

Surrey was the eldest son of the duke of Norfolk, who was the premier English nobleman and the chief bulwark of the old aristocracy against the rising tide of "new men" and the Reformed religion. Surrey was descended from kings on both sides of his family; he was brought up with Henry VIII's illegitimate son, the duke of Richmond, who married Surrey's sister. Some stories indicate that Surrey was a proud, high-spirited youth, not above wandering about the streets at night, in the company of Sir Thomas Wyatt's son, using stone-bows to break the windows of sober sleeping citizens. Surrey, like his father and grandfather, was an able soldier, and the Howards were called upon whenever military brilliance was needed. But their fortunes at court depended upon Henry's queens; the Howards were in high favor when Surrey's cousin, Catherine Howard, was queen, but they were low on Fortune's wheel when the queen was Jane Seymour, the mother of the future king.

Surrey's importance and interest as a poet depend upon his continuing the practice of the sonnet in English as instituted by Wyatt and establishing a form for it which was used by Shakespeare and has become known as the "English" sonnet form: three quatrains and a couplet, rhyming *abab cdcd efef gg*. Even more significantly, he was the first English poet to publish in blank verse—unrhymed iambic pentameter—a verse form that has so flourished in the succeeding four centuries that it seems almost indigenous to the language. The work in which he used this "strange meter," as the publisher called it, was a translation of part of Virgil's *Aeneid*. Book 4 was published in 1554 and book 2 in 1557.

Surrey was a courtier poet, interested in circulating his poems in manuscript in aristocratic court circles. His friends would have read with interest his poem about being imprisoned in Windsor Castle, where he had spent his boyhood under happier circumstances. He did publish his *Epitaph on Wyatt*, but the bulk of his poetry first appeared in *Tottel's Miscellany*, ten years after his death.

Surrey shows a more regular maintenance of normal accent than Wyatt, and he is often more fluent and musical. His poetic diction is clear and consistent, and in many ways Surrey indicates the direction in which the main stream of English verse will flow. Yet he often seems less vivid and vigorous than Wyatt, and he perhaps takes the figurative language he uses less seriously.

Love, That Doth Reign and Live Within My Thought[1]

> Love, that doth reign and live within my thought,
> And built his seat within my captive breast,
> Clad in the arms wherein with me he fought,
> Oft in my face he doth his banner rest.
> But she that taught me love and suffer pain,   5
> My doubtful hope and eke[2] my hot desire
> With shamefast look to shadow and refrain,
> Her smiling grace converteth straight to ire.
> And coward Love, then, to the heart apace
> Taketh his flight, where he doth lurk and plain,[3]   10
> His purpose lost, and dare not show his face.
> For my lord's guilt thus faultless bide I pain,
> Yet from my lord shall not my foot remove:
> Sweet is the death that taketh end by love.

1557

1. Compare this version of Petrarch's *Sonnetto in Vita* 91 with Wyatt's translation of the same original (*The Long Love That in My Thought Doth Harbor*, above).
2. Also; "shamefast": modest.
3. Complain.

The Soote Season[1]

The soote season, that bud and bloom forth brings,
With green hath clad the hill and eke the vale;
The nightingale with feathers new she sings;
The turtle to her make[2] hath told her tale.
Summer is come, for every spray now springs;   5
The hart hath hung his old head on the pale;
The buck in brake his winter coat he flings,
The fishes float with new repairèd scale;
The adder all her slough away she slings,
The swift swallow pursueth the fliès small;   10
The busy bee her honey now she mings.[3]
Winter is worn, that was the flowers' bale.[4]
And thus I see among these pleasant things,
Each care decays, and yet my sorrow springs.

1557

Alas! So All Things Now Do Hold Their Peace[1]

Alas! so all things now do hold their peace,
Heaven and earth disturbèd in no thing;
The beasts, the air, the birds their song do cease,
The nightès chare[2] the stars about doth bring.
Calm is the sea, the waves work less and less;   5
So am not I, whom love, alas, doth wring,
Bringing before my face the great increase
Of my desires, whereat I weep and sing,
In joy and woe, as in a doubtful ease.
For my sweet thoughts sometime do pleasure bring,   10
But by and by the cause of my disease[3]
Gives me a pang that inwardly doth sting,
When that I think what grief it is again
To live and lack the thing should rid my pain.

1557

O Happy Dames, That May Embrace[1]

O happy dames, that may embrace
The fruit of your delight,

---

1. In this adaptation from Petrarch's *Sonnetto in Morte* 42, Surrey has changed the details of nature from Italian to English. Note that the sonnet has only two rhymes. "Soote": sweet, fragrant.
2. Turtledove to her mate.
3. Mingles.
4. Harm.

1. Translated from Petrarch's *Sonnetto in Vita* 113.
2. From Italian *carro* (the Great Bear).
3. Dis-ease, i.e., discomfort.
1. The speaker is a lady. An extant manuscript copy is in the handwriting of Mary Shelton, the sweetheart of Thomas Clere, who was with Surrey in France.

Help to bewail the woeful case
And eke[2] the heavy plight
Of me, that wonted[3] to rejoice   5
The fortune of my pleasant choice:
Good ladies, help to fill my mourning voice.

In ship, freight[4] with rememberance
Of thoughts and pleasures past,
He sails, that hath in governance   10
My life, while it will last;
With scalding sighs, for lack of gale,
Furdering[5] his hope, that is his sail,
Toward me, the sweet port of his avail.[6]

Alas, how oft in dreams I see   15
Those eyes, that were my food,
Which sometime so delighted me,
That yet they do me good;
Wherewith I wake with his return,
Whose ancient flame did make me burn,   20
But when I find the lack, Lord how I mourn!

When other lovers, in arms across,[7]
Rejoice their chief delight,
Drowned in tears to mourn my love,
I stand the bitter night,   25
In my window, where I may see
Before the winds, how the clouds flee,
Lo, what a mariner love hath made me!

And in green waves when the salt flood
Doth rise by rage of wind,   30
A thousand fancies in that mood
Assail my restless mind,
Alas, now drencheth my sweet foe,[8]
That with the spoil of my heart did go
And left me; but, alas, why did he so?   35

And when the sea was calm again,
To chase from me annoy,
My doubtful hope doth cause me plain,[9]
So dread cuts off my joy.

2. Also.
3. Was accustomed.
4. Loaded.
5. Pushing forward.
6. Destination.

7. Embracing.
8. A conventional expression for a loved one, going
back as far as Chaucer. "Drencheth": drowns.
9. To complain.

Thus is my wealth[1] mingled with woe,   40
And of each thought a doubt doth grow;
Now he comes, will he come? alas, no, no!

1557

My Friend, the Things That Do Attain[1]

My friend, the things that do attain
The happy life be these, I find:
The riches left, not got with pain;
The fruitful ground; the quiet mind;

The equal friend; no grudge, no strife;   5
No charge of rule, nor governance;
Without disease, the healthy life;
The household of continuance;

The mean diet, no dainty fare;
Wisdom joined with simpleness;   10
The night dischargèd of all care,
Where wine the wit may not oppress;

The faithful wife, without debate;
Such sleeps as may beguile the night;
Content thyself with thine estate,   15
Neither wish death, nor fear his might.

1547

Epitaph on Sir Thomas Wyatt

Wyatt resteth here, that quick[1] could never rest,
Whose heavenly gifts, increasèd by disdain[2]
And virtue, sank the deeper in his breast:
Such profit he of envy could obtain.

A head where wisdom mysteries[3] did frame,   5
Whose hammers beat still in that lively brain
As on a stithy,[4] where some work of fame
Was daily wrought to turn to Britain's gain.

---

1. Happiness, the opposite of woe.
1. A translation of an epigram by the Latin poet
Martial (10.47). The theme, a glorification of "the
mean estate," is very common in Elizabethan literature.
1. Alive.
2. Hostility (equivalent to "envy" in line 4). I.e.,

he could turn hostility toward him to his advantage.
3. Subtle meanings.
4. Forge or anvil (a conventional image from
Horace; see Ben Jonson's poem on Shakespeare,
lines 58–64).

A visage stern and mild, where both did grow
Vice to condemn, in virtues to rejoice;   10
Amid great storms whom grace assuréd so
To live upright and smile at fortune's choice.

A hand that taught what may be said in rhyme,
That reft[5] Chaucer the glory of his wit—
A mark the which, unperfected for time,   15
Some may approach but never none shall hit.

A tongue that served in foreign realms his king,
Whose courteous talk to virtue did inflame
Each noble heart: a worthy guide to bring
Our English youth by travail unto fame.   20

An eye whose judgment no affect[6] could blind,
Friends to allure and foes to reconcile,
Whose piercing look did represent a mind
With virtue fraught, reposéd, void of guile.

A heart where dread yet never so impressed   25
To hide the thought that might the truth advance;
In neither fortune lift[7] nor yet repressed
To swell in wealth or yield unto mischance.

A valiant corpse[8] where force and beauty met,
Happy—alas, too happy, but for foes,   30
Lived and ran the race that Nature set,
Of manhood's shape, where she the mold did lose.[9]

But to the heavens that simple[1] soul is fled,
Which left with such as covet Christ to know
Witness of faith[2] that never shall be dead,   35
Sent for our health, but not receivéd so.

Thus, for our guilt, this jewel have we lost;
The earth his bones, the heaven possess his ghost.[3]
AMEN.

1542

---

5. Bereft, robbed.
6. Passion or prejudice.
7. Elevated.
8. Body (not, as now, a dead body).
9. Another conventional idea, that Nature, in creating someone, made a masterpiece and lost the pattern.
1. Innocent. The soul is referred to as "simple" by Plato and Dante.
2. I.e., which left with Christians ("such as covet Christ to know") a testimony.
3. Spirit.

Prisoned in Windsor, He Recounteth His Pleasure There Passed[1]

So cruel prison how could betide,[2] alas,
As proud Windsor, where I in lust[3] and joy,
With a king's son, my childish[4] years did pass
In greater feast than Priam's sons of Troy?[5]

Where each sweet place returns a taste full sour: 5
The large green courts, where we were wont to hove,[6]
With eyes cast up unto the Maidens' Tower,
And easy sighs, such as folk draw in love.

The stately seats, the ladies bright of hue;
The dances short, long tales of great delight,   10
With words and looks that tigers could but rue,[7]
Where each of us did plead the other's right.

The palm play[8] where, dispoilèd for the game,
With dazed eyes oft we by gleams of love
Have missed the ball and got sight of our dame   15
To bait[9] her eyes, which kept the leads above.

The gravel ground, with sleeves tied on the helm,
On foaming horse, with swords and friendly hearts,
With cheer[1] as though one should another whelm,
Where we have fought and chasèd oft with darts.   20

With silver drops the mead[2] yet spread for ruth,
In active games of nimbleness and strength,
Where we did strain, trainèd with[3] swarms of youth,
Our tender limbs that yet shot up in length.

The secret groves, which oft we made resound   25
Of pleasant plaint and of our ladies' praise,
Recording oft what grace each one had found,
What hope of speed, what dread of long delays.

The wild forest, the clothèd holts[4] with green,
With reins availed[5] and swift ybreathed horse,   30
With cry of hounds and merry blasts between,
Where we did chase the fearful hart of force.[6]

---

1. In the summer of 1537 Surrey was imprisoned at Windsor Castle for striking a courtier. In the poem he recalls his boyhood stay there (1530–32) with Henry Fitzroy, illegitimate son of Henry VIII.
2. I.e., how could there happen to be.
3. Pleasure.
4. Youthful.
5. Priam, ancient King of Troy, had 50 sons whom he feasted, according to Homer.
6. Linger.
7. Sympathize with, despite tigers' legendary fierceness.
8. Handball.
9. Attract, as in fishing.
1. Appearance.
2. The dewy meadow.
3. Accompanied by.
4. I.e., wooded hills.
5. Slackened.
6. Perforce.

The wide vales eke that harbored us each night
Wherewith, alas, reviveth in my breast
The sweet accord; such sleeps as yet delight,   35
The pleasant dreams, the quiet bed of rest.

The secret thoughts imparted with such trust;
The wanton talk, the divers change of play;
The friendship sworn, each promise kept so just,
Wherewith we pass the winter nights away.   40

And with this thought, the blood forsakes my face,
The tears berain my cheeks of deadly hue,
The which, as soon as sobbing sighs, alas,
Upsuppèd have, thus I my plaint renew:

"Oh place of bliss, renewer of my woe,   45
Give me accompt, where is my noble fere,[7]
Whom in thy walls thou didst each night enclose,
To other lief,[8] but unto me most dear."

Each stone, alas, that doth my sorrow rue,
Returns thereto a hollow sound of plaint.   50
Thus I alone, where all my freedom grew,
In prison pine with bondage and restraint.

And with remembrance of the greater grief
To banish the less I find my chief relief.

                                                     1557

From The Second Book of Virgil

[Hector Warns Aeneas To Flee Troy][1]

It was the time when, granted from the gods,   120
The first sleep creeps most sweet in weary folk.
Lo, in my dream before mine eyes, methought,
With rueful cheer[2] I saw where Hector stood:
Out of whose eyes there gushed streams of tears,
Drawn at a cart as he of late had be,   125
Distained[3] with bloody dust, whose feet were bowln[4]
With the straight cords wherewith they haled him.
Ay me, what one! that Hector how unlike,
Which erst[5] returnèd clad with Achilles' spoils,
Or when he threw into the Greekish ships   130

7. Companion. The reference is to Henry Fitzroy, who had died the year before, aged 17; he was married to Surrey's sister.
8. Dear.
1. Our selection consists of lines 1020–60. Hector was chief Trojan warrior; Aeneas, his brother,

founder of Rome; Achilles, chief Greek warrior, slayer of Hector.
2. Countenance, expression.
3. Stained, discolored.
4. Swollen.
5. Formerly.

The Troyan flame! So was his beard defiled,
His crisped[6] locks all clustered with his blood,
With all such wounds as many he received
About the walls of that his native town.
Whom frankly thus, methought, I spake unto,   135
With bitter tears and doleful deadly voice:
'O Troyan light! O only hope of thine!
What lets[7] so long thee staid? or from what coasts,
Our most desired Hector, dost thou come?
Whom, after slaughter of thy many friends,   140
And travail of thy people and thy town,
All-wearied, lord, how gladly we behold!
What sorry chance hath stained thy lively face?
Or why see I these wounds, alas so wide?'
He answered nought, nor in my vain demands   145
Abode, but from the bottom of his breast
Sighing he said: 'Flee, flee, O goddess' son,
And save thee from the fury of this flame.
Our en'mies now are masters of the walls,
And Troyë town now falleth from the top.   150
Sufficeth that is done for Priam's reign.
If force might serve to succor Troyë town,
This right hand well mought[8] have been her defense.
But Troyë now commendeth to thy charge
Her holy reliques and her privy gods.   155
Them join to thee, as fellows of thy fate.
Large walls rear thou for them: for so thou shalt,
After time spent in th' overwandered flood.'
This said, he brought forth Vesta[9] in his hands,
Her fillets eke,[1] and everlasting flame.   160

1554

6. Curled.
7. Hindrances.
8. Might.
9. Roman goddess of the hearth. Aeneas brought

her "everlasting flame" from Troy to Rome.
1. Also. The fillets were headbands worn by her
priestesses, the Vestal Virgins.

SIR PHILIP SIDNEY
1554–1586

Sir Philip Sidney—courtier, soldier, poet, friend, and patron—seemed to
the Elizabethans to embody all the traits of character and personality they

admired: he was Castiglione's perfect courtier come to life. When he was killed in battle in the Low Countries at the age of thirty-two, all England mourned.

He was the son of Sir Henry Sidney, thrice lord deputy (governor) of Ireland, and of a sister of Robert Dudley, earl of Leicester, the most spectacular and powerful of all the queen's subjects. He entered Shrewsbury School in 1564, at the age of ten, on the same day as Fulke Greville, who became his lifelong friend and biographer. Greville said of Sidney, "though I lived with him and knew him from a child, yet I never knew him other than a man—with such staidness of mind, lovely and familiar gravity, as carried grace and reverence above greater years." He attended Oxford but left without taking a degree and completed his education by extended travels on the Continent. There he met the most important people of the time and witnessed such crucial events as the Massacre of St. Bartholomew's Day, which began in Paris on August 24, 1572, and raged through France for more than a month, as Catholic mobs incited by Queen Catherine de Medici slaughtered perhaps 50,000 Protestant Huguenots. This experience undoubtedly strengthened Sidney's Protestant sympathies, which had been inculcated by his family background and education and reinforced by his friendship with the Protestant scholar-diplomat Hubert Languet.

When Sidney returned to England he lived the life of a prominent courtier, serving occasionally on diplomatic missions and actively encouraging authors such as Edward Dyer, Fulke Greville, and, most importantly, the young Edmund Spenser, who dedicated *The Shepheardes Calender* to him as "the president [chief exemplar] of noblesse and chevalree." So strong were Sidney's Protestant convictions that in 1580 he incurred the queen's displeasure by opposing her projected marriage to the Duke of Anjou—a circumstance that led to his dismissal from court for a time.

He retired to Wilton, the estate of his beloved sister Mary Herbert, Countess of Pembroke, and there he wrote for her entertainment a long pastoral romance in prose called *Arcadia*, which exists in an original version, and a partially revised new version. As William Ringler says, "The *Arcadia*, in both its old and new forms, is the most important original work of English prose fiction produced before the eighteenth century." Our selection is from the "New Arcadia," which represents Sidney's latest conception and style.

In 1579 Spenser wrote to his friend Gabriel Harvey, "New books I hear of none but only of one that writing a certain book called *The School of Abuse*, and dedicating it to Master Sidney, was for his labor scorned, if at least it be in the goodness of that nature to scorn." The book referred to was by Stephen Gosson; it was an attack upon poets and players from a narrowly Puritan point of view. Sidney did not specifically answer Gosson's attack, but he must have had it in mind when he composed, at some uncertain date, a major piece of critical prose that was published after his death under two titles, *The Defence of Poesy* and *An Apology for Poetry*. In this long essay Sidney systematically defends poetry (his term for all imaginative literature) against its attackers, and in the process, greatly exalts the role of the poet and the moral value of poetry. This is the only major work of literary criticism produced in the English Renaissance.

Sidney's *Astrophil and Stella* ("Starlover and Star") is the first of the great Elizabethan sonnet cycles, which relied heavily upon the conventions established by Petrarch. Sidney's collection has 108 sonnets and eleven songs. It was probably begun in 1576, when Sidney's ambiguous relationship with Penelope Devereux (the supposed original of Stella) began; for four years there was talk of an engagement, but in 1581 she married Lord Robert Rich, and two years later Sidney also married. Some of the sonnets contain puns on the name "Rich." However, Penelope Devereux was hardly a woman of icy virtue, like the Stella of the sonnets whose favors to Astrophil were limited to a single kiss; she was known as a coquette, and after her marriage lived openly as another man's mistress. There is little profit in speculating about the autobiographical elements behind an Elizabethan sequence, since they are subsumed into the created fiction and its Petrarchan conventions.

Sidney's strong devotion to the cause of Protestantism at home and abroad took him to the Low Countries in 1585, where as volunteer and knight-errant he engaged in several battles in the war against Spain. He was badly wounded at Zutphen on September 13, 1586, leading a charge against great odds; a famous story records that despite his own parching thirst he proffered his bottle of water to a dying man with the words, "Thy necessity is yet greater than mine." He died after lingering for twenty-six days.

Sidney called poetry his "unelected vocation," and he did not publish it himself. He probably saw himself as more of a patron than an artist. Yet he was the author of the most important work of prose fiction, the most important piece of literary criticism, and the most important sonnet cycle of the Elizabethan age.

Astrophil and Stella   Sidney's sonnet sequence, like most of the Elizabethan sequences, imitates Petrarch and his French imitators, and employs well-understood conventions. Sonnet cycles have a loose framework of plot, marking the stages of a love relationship from its starting point in the lover's attraction to the lady's beauty, through various trials, sufferings, conflicts, and occasional encouragements, to a conclusion in which nothing is resolved. The poet undertook to display all the contrary feelings of a lover—hope and despair, tenderness and bitterness, exultation and modesty—by the use of "conceits" or ingenious comparisons. Many of these became traditional, and eventually, stale: the poet who complained that in love he both burned and froze, or that his sighs were the winds driving his ship on a tossing sea, was echoing many an earlier poet. So Sidney protests, in the role of Astrophil, that he uses no standard conventional phrases, that his verse is original and comes from the heart—though this pretense is itself conventional. But what gives Sidney's sonnets their extraordinary vigor and freshness is his ability to dramatize Astrophil's state of mind through the use of dialogue, colloquial speech, and probing self-analysis. Stella's voice is heard in dialogic exchange with Astrophil in some of the songs—including the two included here.

From Astrophil and Stella

1[1]

Loving in truth, and fain[2] in verse my love to show,
    That the dear she might take some pleasure of my pain,

1. One of 6 sonnets in the sequence written in hexameters.   2. Desirous.

Pleasure might cause her read, reading might make her know,
Knowledge might pity win, and pity grace obtain,
   I sought fit words to paint the blackest face of woe: 5
Studying inventions fine, her wits to entertain,
Oft turning others' leaves, to see if thence would flow
Some fresh and fruitful showers upon my sunburned brain.
   But words came halting forth, wanting Invention's stay;[3]
Invention, Nature's child, fled step-dame Study's blows,   10
And others' feet still seemed but strangers in my way.
Thus great with child to speak, and helpless in my throes,
   Biting my trewand[4] pen, beating myself for spite,
   "Fool," said my Muse to me, "look in thy heart and write."

2

Not at first sight, nor with a dribbèd[5] shot
   Love gave the wound, which while I breathe will bleed,
   But known worth did in mine[6] of time proceed,
Till by degrees it had full conquest got.
I saw and liked, I liked but lovèd not,   5
   I loved, but straight did not what *Love* decreed;
   At length to Love's decrees, I, forced, agreed,
Yet with repining at so partial[7] lot.
   Now even that footstep of lost liberty
Is gone, and now like slave-borne Muscovite,[8]   10
I call it praise to suffer tyranny;
And now employ the remnant of my wit,[9]
   To make myself believe, that all is well,
   While with a feeling skill I paint my hell.

5

It is most true that eyes are formed to serve
The inward light,[1] and that the heavenly part
Ought to be king, from whose rules who do swerve,
Rebels to nature, strive for their own smart.
   It is most true, what we call Cupid's dart   5
An image is, which for ourselves we carve;
And, fools, adore in temple of our heart,
Till that good god make church and churchman starve.[2]
   True, that true beauty virtue is indeed,

---

3. Prop.
4. Truant.
5. Ineffectual or at random.
6. Tunnel dug to undermine a beseiged fortress.
7. Unfair.
8. Inhabitant of Muscovy, an important Russian principality ruled from Moscow; 16th-century travel books describe Muscovites as contented slaves.

9. Intelligence.
1. Reason
2. The concessions made in the argument are to Neoplatonic and Christian doctrines opposed to romantic love. Neoplatonic theory held that physical beauty is only a shadow of inner virtue, which is at one with the true, transcendent and immortal Idea of Beauty.

Whereof this beauty can be but a shade,   10
Which elements with mortal mixture breed;[3]
True, that on earth we are but pilgrims made,
     And should in soul up to our country move;
     True, and yet true that I must Stella love.

6

Some lovers speak, when they their muses entertain,
Of hopes begot by fear, of wot[4] not what desires,
Of force of heavenly beams, infusing hellish pain,
Of living deaths, dear wounds, fair storms and freezing fires;[5]
     Someone his song in Jove, and Jove's strange tales attires,   5
Broidered with bulls and swans, powdered with golden rain;[6]
Another humbler wit to shepherd's pipe retires,
Yet hiding royal blood full oft in rural vein.[7]
To some a sweetest plaint a sweetest style affords,[8]
     While tears pour out his ink, and sighs breathe out his words,
His paper pale dispair, and pain his pen doth move.   10
     I can speak what I feel, and feel as much as they,
     But think that all the map of my state I display,
When trembling voice brings forth that I do Stella love.

7

When Nature made her chief work, Stella's eyes,
In colour black, why wrapped she beams so bright?
Would she in beamy[9] black, like painter wise,
Frame daintiest lustre, mixed of shades and light?
     Or did she else that sober hue devise,   5
In object best to knit and strength[1] our sight,
Least if no veil those brave gleams did disguise,
They sun-like should more dazzle then delight?
     Or would she her miraculous power show,
That whereas black seems beauty's contrary,   10
She even in black doth make all beauties flow?
Both so and thus, she, minding[2] Love should be
     Placed ever there, gave him this mourning weed,[3]
     To honor all their deaths, who for her bleed.

---

3. Physical beauty is a mixture of the 4 elements (earth, air, water, fire) and so is mortal.
4. Know.
5. Conventional Petrarchan oxymorons (see p. 2591).
6. I.e., embroidered with mythological figures. Jove courted Europa in the shape of a bull, Leda as a swan, Danae as a golden shower.
7. Pastoral allegory. By convention, the pastoral poet pipes his songs on an oaten or reed pipe.
8. Overuse of the word "sweet" in love complaints, with allusion to the very musical *dolce stil nuovo* (sweet new style) associated with Dante and his Italian contemporaries.
9. Radiant.
1. Strengthen.
2. Remembering.
3. Funeral garb.

9

Queen Virtue's court, which some call Stella's face,
    Prepared by Nature's chiefest furniture,[4]
    Hath his front[5] built of alablaster pure;
Gold is the covering of that stately place.
The door, by which sometimes comes forth her Grace,   5
    Red porphir[6] is, which lock of pearl makes sure;
    Whose porches rich, which name of cheeks endure,
Marble mixed red and white do interlace.
    The windows now through which this heavenly guest
Looks over the world, and can find nothing such,   10
Which dare claim from those lights the name of best,
Of touch[7] they are that without touch doth touch,
    Which Cupid's self from Beauty's mine did draw;
    Of touch they are, and poor I am their straw.

10

Reason, in faith thou art well served, that still
Wouldst brabling[8] be with sense and love in me;
I rather wished thee climb the Muses' hill,[9]
Or reach the fruit of Nature's choicest tree;[1]
    Or seek heaven's course, or heaven's inside to see.   5
Why shouldst thou toil our thorny soil to till?
Leave sense, and those which sense's objects be:
Deal thou with powers of thoughts, leave love to will.
    But thou wouldst needs fight both with love and sense,
With sword of wit, giving wounds of dispraise,   10
Till down-right blows did foil thy cunning fence;[2]
For soon as they strake[3] thee with Stella's rays,
    Reason thou kneel'dst, and offeredst straight to prove
    By reason good, good reason her to love.

15

You that do search for every purling[4] spring
    Which from the ribs of old Parnassus[5] flows,
    And every flower,[6] not sweet perhaps, which grows
Near therabout, into your poesy[7] wring;
You that do dictionary's method bring   5
    Into your rhymes, running in rattling rows;

---

4. The best materials Nature furnishes.
5. Also, forehead. "Alablaster": alabaster.
6. Porphyry, an ornamental red or purple stone.
7. Glossy black stone (lignite or jet) able to attract light bodies such as straw by static electricity.
8. Quarreling.
9. Mt. Helicon in Greece, sacred to the 9 Muses—a symbol of poetic inspiration.

1. The tree of knowledge.
2. Swordplay.
3. Struck.
4. Murmuring.
5. Mountain near Delphos in Greece, sacred to the Muses, who foster poetry and other arts.
6. Also poetic figures (flowers of rhetoric).
7. Also a nosegay of flowers.

You that poor Petrarch's long-deceasèd woes,
With new-born sighs and denizened wit[8] do sing;
   You take wrong ways, those far-fet[9] helps be such,
    As do bewray a want of inward touch,[1]   10
And sure at length stolen goods do come to light
   But if (both for your love and skill) your name
   You seek to nurse at fullest breasts of Fame,
Stella behold, and then begin to endite.[2]

16

In nature apt to like when I did see
   Beauties, which were of many carats fine,
   My boiling sprites[3] did thither soon incline,
And, Love, I thought that I was full of thee;
But finding not those restless flames in me,   5
   Which others said did make their souls to pine,
   I thought those babes of some pin's hurt did whine,
By my love judging what love's pain might be.
   But while I thus with this young lion[4] played,
Mine eyes (shall I say cursed or blessed) beheld   10
Stella; now she is named, need more be said?
In her sight I a lesson new have spelled,
   I now have learned love right, and learned even so,
   As who by being poisoned doth poison know.

18

With what sharp checks I in myself am shent,[5]
   When into Reason's audit I do go,
   And by just counts myself a banckrout[6] know
Of all those goods, which heaven to me hath lent;
Unable quite to pay even Nature's rent,   5
   Which unto it by birthright I do owe;
   And which is worse, no good excuse can show,
But that my wealth I have most idly spent.
   My youth doth waste, my knowledge brings forth toys,[7]
My wit doth strive those passions to defend,   10
Which for reward spoil it with vain annoys.
I see my course to lose myself doth bend:
   I see and yet no greater sorrow take,
   Then that I lose no more for Stella's sake.

---

8. Naturalized ingenuity.
9. Far-fetched.
1. Reveal a lack of innate talent.
2. Write.
3. Spirits.
4. In a popular fable, a shepherd raised a lion cub

which, while young, was a pet for his children,
but when grown destroyed all his flocks.
5. Shamed. "Checks": rebukes.
6. Bankrupt.
7. Trifles, i.e., these poems.

21

Your words, my friend, right healthful caustics,[8] blame
  My young mind marred, whom Love doth windlass[9] so,
  That mine own writings like bad servants show
My wits, quick in vain thoughts, in virtue lame;
That Plato I read for nought, but if[1] he tame   5
  Such coltish gyres,[2] that to my birth I owe
  Nobler desires, least else that friendly foe,
Great expectation, wear a train of shame.
    For since mad March great promise made of me,
If now the May of my years much decline,   10
What can be hoped my harvest time will be?
Sure you say well; your wisdom's golden mine
  Dig deep with learning's spade; now tell me this,
  Hath this world ought so fair as Stella is?

31

With how sad steps, O Moon, thou climb'st the skies,
  How silently, and with how wan a face!
  What, may it be that even in heavenly place
That busy archer[3] his sharp arrows tries?
Sure, if that long-with-love-acquainted eyes   5
  Can judge of Love, thou feel'st a Lover's case;
  I read it in thy looks: thy languished grace,
To me that feel the like, thy state descries.
    Then even of fellowship, O Moon, tell me
Is constant *love* deemed there but want of wit?   10
Are beauties there as proud as here they be?
Do they above love to be loved, and yet
  Those lovers scorn whom that *love* doth possess?
  Do they call *virtue* there ungratefulness?[4]

37

My mouth doth water, and my breast doth swell,
  My tongue doth itch, my thoughts in labour be;
  Listen then, lordings, with good ear to me,
For of my life I must a riddle tell.
Towards Aurora's court, a nymph doth dwell,[5]   5

---

8. Caustic substances for burning away diseased
tissue.
9. Ensnare.
1. Unless.
2. Wild circles, like those of a young horse; there
is a probable reference to Plato's story of the char-
ioteer Reason reining in the horses of Passion
(*Phaedrus* 254).
3. Cupid.

4. I.e., is the lady's ingratitude considered virtue
in heaven (as here)? Also, is the lover's virtue
(fidelity) considered distasteful in heaven (as here)?
5. Aurora (the dawn) has her court in the East;
Penelope Devereux Rich, the original of Stella,
dwells in Essex, one of the eastern counties. Sidney puns on her married name throughout this
sonnet.

Rich in all beauties which man's eye can see,
  Beauties so far from reach of words, that we
Abase her praise, saying she doth excell:
  Rich in the treasure of deserved renown,
Rich in the riches of a royal heart,   10
Rich in those gifts which give the eternal crown;
Who though most rich in these and every part,
  Which make the patents[6] of true worldly bliss,
  Hath no misfortune, but that Rich she is.

39

Come sleep! O sleep the certain knot of peace,
The baiting place[7] of wit, the balm of woe,
The poor man's wealth, the prisoner's release,
Th' indifferent[8] judge between the high and low;
  With shield of proof shield me from out the prease[9]   5
Of those fierce darts, Despair at me doth throw;
O make in me those civil wars to cease;
I will good tribute pay if thou do so.
  Take thou of me smooth pillows, sweetest bed,
A chamber deaf to noise and blind to light,   10
A rosy garland, and a weary head;[1]
And if these things, as being thine by right,
  Move not thy heavy grace, thou shalt in me,
  Livelier then elsewhere, Stella's image see.

41

Having this day my horse, my hand, my lance
  Guided so well that I obtained the prize,
  Both by the judgement of the English eyes,
And of some sent from that sweet enemy France;[2]
Horsemen my skill in horsemanship advance;   5
  Townfolks my strength; a daintier[3] judge applies
  His praise to sleight, which from good use doth rise;[4]
Some lucky wits impute it but to chance;
  Others, because of both sides I do take
My blood from them, who did excel in this,[5]   10
Think Nature me a man of arms did make.
How far they shoot awry! the true cause is,
  Stella looked on, and from her heavenly face
  Sent forth the beams which made so fair my race.

---

6. Grants, titles to possession.
7. Resting place on a journey.
8. Impartial.
9. Throng. "Proof": proven strength.
1. The offer of gifts to Morpheus, god of sleep, is a poetic convention. A likely source is Chaucer's *Book of the Duchess*, lines 240–69.
2. Sidney took part in several tournaments between

1579 and 1585 with French spectators present, but the one in May 1581 was devised specifically to entertain French commissioners.
3. More precise.
4. Experience. "Sleight": art.
5. Sidney's father and grandfather and his maternal uncles, the earls of Leicester and Warwick, were frequent participants in tournaments.

45

Stella oft sees the very face of woe
    Painted in my beclouded stormy face,
    But cannot skill to pity my disgrace,[6]
Not though thereof the cause herself she know;[7]
Yet hearing late a fable which did show   5
    Of lovers never known, a grievous case,
    Pity thereof gate[8] in her breast such place
That, from that sea derived, tears' spring did flow.
    Alas, if fancy,[9] drawn by imaged things,
Though false, yet with free scope more grace doth breed   10
Than servant's wrack, where new doubts honor brings,[1]
Then think, my dear, that you in me do read
    Of lover's ruin some sad tragedy.
    I am not I; pity the tale of me.

47

What, have I thus betrayed my liberty?
    Can those black beams such burning marks[2] engrave
    In my free side? or am I born a slave,
Whose neck becomes[3] such yoke of tyranny?
Or want I sense to feel my misery?   5
    Or sprite,[4] disdain of such disdain to have?
    Who for long faith, though daily help I crave,
May get no alms but scorn of beggary.[5]
    Virtue awake! Beauty but beauty is;
I may, I must, I can, I will, I do   10
Leave following that which it is gain to miss.
Let her go. Soft, but here she comes. Go to,
    Unkind, I love you not. O me, that eye
    Doth make my heart give to my tongue the lie.

49

I on my horse, and Love on me doth try
    Our horsemanships, while by strange work I prove
    A horseman to my horse, a horse to *Love*;
And now man's wrongs in me, poor beast, descry.[6]
The reins wherewith my rider doth me tie   5
    Are humbled thoughts, which bit of reverence move,

6. The state of being out of favor. "Cannot skill": is unable to.
7. I.e., even though she knows she herself is the cause of it.
8. Got.
9. Fantasy.
1. I.e., than the ruin of her lover ("servant"), caused by the new scruples ("doubts") her honor brings up.
2. Brands of slavery.
3. Is suited to.
4. Spirit.
5. I.e., scorn for (my) begging.
6. Discover.

Curbed in with fear, but with gilt bosse[7] above
Of hope, which makes it seem fair to the eye.
   The wand is will; thou, fancy, saddle art,[8]
Girt fast by memory; and while I spur   10
My horse, he spurs with sharp desire my heart;
He sits me fast, however I do stir,
   And now hath made me to his hand so right
   That in the manage[9] myself takes delight.

52

A strife is grown between Virtue and Love,
   While each pretends[1] that Stella must be his:
   Her eyes, her lips, her all, saith Love, do this,
Since they do wear his badge,[2] most firmly prove.
But Virtue thus that title doth disprove,   5
   That Stella (O dear name) that Stella is
   That virtuous soul, sure heir of heavenly bliss;
Not this fair outside, which our hearts doth move.
   And therefore, though her beauty and her grace
Be *Love's* indeed, in Stella's self he may   10
   By no pretence claim any manner[3] place.
Well, Love, since this demur[4] our suit doth stay,
   Let Virtue have that Stella's self; yet thus,
   That Virtue but that body grant to us.

53

In martial sports I had my cunning tried,
   And yet to break more staves[5] did me address;
   While with the people's shouts I must confess,
Youth, luck and praise even filled my veins with pride.
When Cupid, having me his slave descried[6]   5
   In Mars's livery, prancing in the press,[7]
   "What now, sir fool," said he, "I would no less;
Look here, I say," I looked, and Stella spied,
   Who hard by made a window send forth light.
My heart then quaked, then dazzled were mine eyes,   10
One hand forgot to rule,[8] th' other to fight.
Nor trumpets' sound I heard, nor friendly cries;
   My foe came on, and beat the air for me,[9]
   Till that her blush taught me my shame to see.

---

7. Gold studs.
8. I.e., you, Fancy (imagination) are the saddle.
"Wand": whip.
9. Training or handling of a horse.
1. Claims.
2. Device or livery worn to identify someone's
(here, Cupid's) servants.

3. Kind of.
4. Objection.
5. Lances.
6. Discerned.
7. Throng. "Marse's": Mars's—the god of war.
8. Govern the horse.
9. Struck the empty air instead of me.

56

Fie, school of Patience, fie, your lesson is
   Far far too long to learn it without book;[1]
   What, a whole week without one piece of look,[2]
And think I should not your large precepts miss?[3]
When I might read those letters fair of bliss,   5
   Which in her face teach virtue, I could brook
   Somewhat thy leaden counsels, which I took
As of a friend that meant not much amiss.
   But now that I, alas, do want[4] her sight,
What, dost thou think that I can ever take   10
In thy cold stuff a phlegmatic delight?
No, Patience, if thou wilt my good, then make
   Her come, and hear with patience my desire,
   And then with patience bid me bear my fire.

61

Oft with true sighs, oft with uncallèd tears,
Now with slow words, now with dumb eloquence
I Stella's eyes assail, invade her ears;
But this at last is her sweet-breathed defence:
   That who indeed infelt affection bears,   5
So captives to his saint both soul and sense,
That, wholly hers, all selfness[5] he forbears;
Thence his desires he learns, his life's course thence.
   Now since her chaste mind hates this love in me,
   With chastened mind I straight must shew that she   10
Shall quickly me from what she hates remove.
   O Doctor[6] Cupid, thou for me reply,
   Driven else to grant by angel's sophistry,
That I love not, without I leave to love.[7]

69

O joy, too high for my low style to show,
   O bliss, fit for a nobler state than me!
   Envy, put out thine eyes, lest thou do see
What oceans of delight in me do flow.
My friend, that oft saw through all masks my woe,   5
   Come, come, and let me pour myself on thee:
   Gone is the winter of my misery;
My spring appears; O see what here doth grow.
   For Stella hath, with words where faith doth shine,
Of her high heart given me the monarchy;   10

1. By memory.   5. Concern with self.
2. Without the briefest glimpse of her.   6. Eminently learned scholar.
3. Forget.   7. Unless I stop loving.
4. Lack.

I, I, O I may say, that she is mine.
And though she give but thus conditionly
   This realm of bliss, while virtuous course I take,
   No kings be crowned but they some covenants[8] make.

71

Who will in fairest book of Nature know
   How Virtue may best lodged in beauty be,
   Let him but learn of *Love* to read in thee,
Stella, those fair lines, which true goodness show.
There shall he find all vices' overthrow,   5
   Not by rude force, but sweetest sovereignty
   Of reason, from whose light those night-birds[9] fly;
That inward sun in thine eyes shineth so.
   And not content to be Perfection's heir
Thyself, dost strive all minds that way to move,   10
Who mark in thee what is in thee most fair.
So while thy beauty draws the heart to love,
   As fast thy Virtue bends that love to good;
   "But, ah," Desire still cries, "give me some food."

72

Desire, though thou my old companion art
   And oft so clings to my pure love, that I
   One from the other scarcely can descry,[1]
While each doth blow the fire of my heart,
Now from thy fellowship I needs must part.   5
   Venus is taught with Dian's wings to fly;[2]
   I must no more in thy sweet passions lie;
Virtue's gold now must head my Cupid's dart.
   Service and honor, wonder with delight,
Fear to offend, will worthy to appear,   10
Care shining in mine eyes, faith in my sprite:[3]
These things are left me by my only dear;
   But thou, Desire, because thou wouldst have all,
   Now banished art, but yet alas how shall?

74

I never drank of Aganippe well,
Nor ever did in shade of Tempe[4] sit;

---

8. Solemn coronation oaths taken by English monarchs, promising to protect the laws and the people.
9. The owl, for example, was an emblem of various vices.
1. Discern.
2. Venus: goddess of beauty and love, mother of Cupid. Diana: goddess of the moon and patron of chastity.
3. Spirit.
4. Aganippe: well at the foot of Mt. Helicon in Greece, sacred to the muses. Tempe: valley beside Mt. Olympus, sacred to Apollo, the god of song.

And Muses scorn with vulgar brains to dwell;
Poor layman I, for sacred rites unfit.
　　Some do I hear of Poets' fury[5] tell,   5
But God wot,[6] wot not what they mean by it;[7]
And this I swear by blackest brook of hell,
I am no pick-purse of another's wit.
　　How falls it then that with so smooth an ease
My thoughts I speak, and what I speak doth flow   10
In verse, and that my verse best wits doth please?
Guess we the cause. "What, is it thus?" Fie no.
　　"Or so?" Much less. "How then?" Sure thus it is:
My lips are sweet, inspired with Stella's kiss.

81

O kiss, which dost those ruddy gems impart,
Or gems, or fruits of new-found *Paradise*,
Breathing all bliss and sweetening to the heart,
Teaching dumb lips a nobler exercise!
　　O kiss, which souls, even souls together, ties   5
By links of love, and only nature's art,
How fain[8] would I paint thee to all men's eyes,
Or of thy gifts at least shade out some part.
　　But she forbids, with blushing words, she says
　　She builds her fame on higher seated praise.   10
But my heart burns, I cannot silent be.
　　Then since, dear life, you fain would have me peace,[9]
　　And I, mad with delight, want wit[1] to cease,
Stop you my mouth with still still kissing me.

Fourth Song[2]

Only joy, now here you are,
Fit to hear and ease my care;
Let my whispering voice obtain
Sweet reward for sharpest pain:
Take me to thee, and thee to me.   5
"No, no, no, no, my dear, let be."

Night hath closed all in her cloak,
Twinkling stars love-thoughts provoke,
Danger hence good care doth keep,
Jealousy itself doth sleep: 10

5. Inspiration.
6. Knows.
7. The most binding of all oaths were those sworn
by the River Styx.
8. Gladly.
9. You want me to be silent.

1. Lack the mental faculties.
2. Like Petrarch, Sidney intersperses songs (11 of
them) in his sequence, thereby extending its emotional range. Some of them incorporate Stella's
voice. This song appears between sonnets 85 and
86.

Take me to thee, and thee to me.
"No, no, no, no, my dear, let be."

Better place no wit can find
Cupid's yoke to loose or bind;
These sweet flowers on fine bed, too,   15
Us in their best language woo:
Take me to thee, and thee to me.
"No, no, no, no, my dear, let be."

This small light the moon bestows
Serves thy beams but to disclose,   20
So to raise my hap more high;
Fear not else, none can us spy:
Take me to thee, and thee to me.
"No, no, no, no, my dear, let be."

That you heard was but a mouse;   25
Dumb sleep holdeth all the house;
Yet asleep methinks they say,
"Young folks, take time while you may."
Take me to thee, and thee to me.
"No, no, no, no, my dear, let be."   30

Niggard Time threats, if we miss
This large offer of our bliss,
Long stay ere he grant the same;
Sweet, then, while each thing doth frame,[3]
Take me to thee, and thee to me.   35
"No, no, no, no, my dear, let be."

Your fair mother is abed,
Candles out, and curtains spread;
She thinks you do letters write.
Write, but first let me indite: 40
Take me to thee, and thee to me.
"No, no, no, no, my dear, let be."

Sweet, alas, why strive you thus?
Concord better fitteth us.
Leave to Mars[4] the force of hands,   45
Your power in your beauty stands:
Take me to thee, and thee to me.
"No, no, no, no, my dear, let be."

Woe to me, and do you swear
Me to hate? But I forbear.   50

---

3. Serve.   4. God of war.

Cursèd be my destines[5] all
That brought me so high to fall:
Soon with my death I will please thee.
"No, no, no, no, my dear, let be."

87

When I was forced from Stella ever dear,
Stella, food of my thoughts, heart of my heart,
Stella, whose eyes make all my tempests clear,
By iron laws of duty to depart,
Alas, I found that she with me did smart;   5
I saw that tears did in her eyes appear;
I saw that sighs her sweetest lips did part,
And her sad words my sadded sense did hear.
For me, I wept to see pearls scattered so,
I sighed her sighs, and wailèd for her woe,   10
Yet swam in joy, such love in her was seen.
Thus while th' effect most bitter was to me,
And nothing than the cause more sweet could be,
I had been vexed, if vexed I had not been.

89[6]

Now that of absence the most irksome night
With darkest shade doth overcome my day,
Since Stella's eyes, wont to give me my day,
Leaving my hemisphere, leave me in night,
Each day seems long, and longs for long-stayed night;   5
The night, as tedious, woos th' approach of day.
Tired with the dusty toils of busy day,
Languished with horrors of the silent night,
Suffering the evils both of the day and night
(While no night is more dark than is my day,   10
Nor no day hath less quiet than my night),
With such bad mixture of my night and day
That, living thus in blackest winter night,
I feel the flames of hottest summer day.

91

Stella, while now by honour's cruel might,
I am from[7] you, light of my life, mis-led,
And that fair you, my Sun, thus overspread
With absence' veil, I live in Sorrow's night.
If this dark place yet shew, like candle light,   5

---

5. Fates.
6. A sonnet with only 2 rhyme words, night and   day.
7. Away from.

Some beauty piece,[8] as amber-coloured head,
　Milk hands, rose cheeks, or lips more sweet, more red,
Or seeing jets,[9] black, but in blackness bright,
　They please I do confess, they please mine eyes;
But why? because of you they models be;   10
Models such be wood-globes of glistering skies.[1]
Dear, therefore be not jealous over me,
　If you hear that they seem my heart to move,
　Not them, O no, but you in them I love.

Eleventh Song[2]

"Who is it that this dark night
Underneath my window plaineth?"[3]
It is one who from thy sight
Being (ah) exiled, disdaineth
Every other vulgar light.   5

"Why, alas, and are you he?
Be not yet those fancies changèd?"
Dear, when you find change in me,
Though from me you be estrangèd,
Let my change to ruin be.   10

"Well, in absence this will die;
Leave to see, and leave to wonder."
Absence sure will help, if I
Can learn how myself to sunder
From what in my heart doth lie.   15

"But time will these thoughts remove:
Time doth work what no man knoweth."
Time doth as the subject prove;[4]
With time still th' affection groweth
In the faithful turtle dove.   20

"What if you new beauties see;
Will not they stir new affection?"
I will think they pictures be,
Imagelike of saints' perfection,
Poorly counterfeiting thee.   25

"But your reason's purest light,
Bids you leave such minds to nourish."[5]
Dear, do reason no such spite;

---

8. Some beauties in other women.
9. Black eyes.
1. Wooden globes of the heavens, with painted constellations and planets.
2. This last song, a dialogue between Astrophil and Stella, is located between sonnets 104 and 105.
3. Complains (in song) of his love woes.
4. Things change in time according to their natures.
5. Stop indulging such thoughts.

Never doth thy beauty flourish
More than in my reason's sight.   30

"But the wrongs love bears will make
Love at length leave undertaking."
No, the more fools it do shake,
In a ground of so firm making,
Deeper still they drive the stake.   35

"Peace, I think that some give ear:
Come no more, least I get anger."
Bliss, I will my bliss forbear,
Fearing, sweet, you to endanger,
But my soul shall harbour there.   40

"Well, begone, begone I say,
Lest that Argus[6] eyes perceive you."
O unjustest fortune's sway,
Which can make me thus to leave you,
And from louts to run away.   45

108[7]

When sorrow (using mine own fire's might)
    Melts down his lead into my boiling breast,
    Through that dark furnace to my heart oppressed
There shines a joy from thee, my only light;
But soon as thought of thee breeds my delight,   5
    And my young soul flutters to thee, his nest,
    Most rude Despair, my daily unbidden guest,
Clips straight my wings, straight wraps me in his night,
    And makes me then bow down my head, and say,
"Ah, what doth Phoebus'[8] gold that wretch avail,   10
Whom iron doors do keep from use of day?"
So strangely (alas) thy works in me prevail
    That in my woes for thee thou art my joy,
    And in my joys for thee my only annoy.

1582   1591, 1598

The Countess of Pembroke's Arcadia   Sidney's romance exists
in two forms, called the "Old Arcadia" and the "New Arcadia." When the
"Old Arcadia" was completed, Sidney began to recast and expand it, but left
the revision unfinished. This revised fragment, almost three books, is known
as the "New Arcadia;" it was published in 1590. In 1593 the Countess of
Pembroke republished it with slight changes and added the last two books of

6. The 100-eyed monster set by Juno to guard Io,   7. In many sequences, as here, the final sonnet
a mistress of Jupiter whom Juno had transformed   brings no resolution.
into a cow.   8. God of the sun.

the "Old Arcadia." (The complete "Old Arcadia" was not published until the twentieth century.) Both versions are full of oracles, disguisings, mistaken identity, melodramatic incidents and tangled love situations, but the "New Arcadia" has a much more complex and interwoven plot, as well as a more consistently heroic tone, than the "Old Arcadia." Some episodes are of political interest, and Sidney clearly put more of his serious thought on statecraft (the responsibilities of a king or queen, the evils of rebellion, the duties of ministers and advisers of state) into it than he pretends when he describes the book as mere entertainment. The *Arcadia* also contains many poems—eclogues and songs—that are interspersed throughout the narrative; they represent Sidney's experiments with lyric kinds and verse forms. A good example is the double sestina, *Ye Goatherd Gods.*

From The Countess of Pembroke's Arcadia[1]

[*The Country of Arcadia*]

* * * The third day after, in the time that the morning did strew roses and violets in the heavenly floor against the coming of the sun, the nightingales (striving one with the other which could in most dainty variety recount their wrong-caused sorrow)[2] made them put off their sleep, and rising from under a tree (which that night had been their pavilion) they went on their journey, which by and by welcomed Musidorus' eyes, wearied with the wasted soil of Laconia,[3] with delightful prospects.

There were hills which garnished their proud heights with stately trees; humble valleys whose base estate seemed comforted with refreshing of silver rivers; meadows enamelled[4] with all sorts of eye-pleasing flowers; thickets, which, being lined with most pleasant shade, were witnessed so to by the cheerful deposition[5] of many well-tuned birds; each pasture stored with sheep feeding with sober security, while the pretty lambs with bleating oratory craved the dams' comfort; here a shepherd's boy piping as though he should never be old; there a young shepherdess knitting and withal singing, and it seemed that her voice comforted her hands to work and her hands kept time to her voice's music. As for the houses of the country—for many houses came under their eye—they were all scattered, no two being one by the other, and yet not so far off as that it barred mutual succour: a show, as it were, of an accompanable solitariness and of a civil wildness.[6]

"I pray you," said Musidorus, then first unsealing his long silent lips,

1. These sections, from chapters 2 and 3 of the *New Arcadia*, present one of the two young heroes, the shipwrecked Musidorus, being led into the land of Arcadia by the shepherds Klaius and Strephon (who are also the singers of the song, *Ye Goat-herd Gods*, p. 502). They lead him to the house of the wise and noble Kalander, who introduces the central plot of Sidney's romance in the curious situation of King Basilius and his family.
2. Sorrows caused by wrongs. See the story of the nightingale, note 1, p. 526.
3. The ancient name of the southeastern district of the Greek Peloponnese, which includes Sparta. Much of it is hilly, rugged, and barren.
4. Adorned with varied colors, like enamel work.
5. Testimony.
6. "Accompanable (sociable) solitariness" and "civil (civilized) wildness" are oxymorons, figures of flat contradiction.

"what countries be these we pass through which are so divers in show, the one wanting no store, the other having no store but of want?"

"The country," answered Claius, "where you were cast ashore and now are passed through is Laconia, not so poor by the barrenness of the soil (though in itself not passing fertile) as by a civil war, which being these two years within the bowels of that estate between the gentlemen and the peasants (by them named Helots)[7] hath in this sort as it were disfigured the face of nature, and made it so unhospital[8] as now you have found it: the towns neither of the one side nor the other willingly opening their gates to strangers, nor strangers willingly entering for fear of being mistaken.

"But this country where now you set your foot is Arcadia;[9] and even hard by is the house of Kalander whither we lead you: this country being thus decked with peace and (the child of peace) good husbandry. These houses you see so scattered are of men as we two are that live upon the commodity of their sheep, and therefore in the division of the Arcadian estate are termed shepherds: a happy people, wanting little because they desire not much."

"What cause then," said Musidorus, "made you venture to leave this sweet life and put yourself in yonder unpleasant and dangerous realm?"

"Guarded with poverty," answered Strephon, "and guided with love."

[Kalander tells about Basilius]

Which Kalander perceiving, "Well," said he, "my dear guest, I know your mind and I will satisfy it. Neither will I do it like a niggardly answerer, going no further than the bounds of the question; but I will discover[1] unto you as well that wherein my knowledge is common with others as that which by extraordinary means is delivered unto me, knowing so much in you (though not long acquainted) that I shall find your ears faithful treasurers." So then sitting down in two chairs and sometimes casting his eye to the picture, he thus spake:

"This country Arcadia among all the provinces of Greece hath ever been had in singular reputation; partly for the sweetness of the air and other natural benefits, but principally for the well-tempered minds of the people who (finding that the shining title of glory, so much affected by other nations, doth indeed help little to the happiness of life) are the only people which, as by their justice and providence give neither cause nor hope to their neighbours to annoy them, so are they not stirred with false praise to trouble others' quiet, thinking it a small reward for the wasting of their own lives in ravening[2] that their posterity should long after say they had done so. Even the Muses[3] seem to approve their good

---

7. The original inhabitants of Laconia, enslaved by the Spartans.
8. Inhospitable.
9. A country in the middle of the Peloponnese, surrounded by mountains and very fertile; the Arcadians were regarded as the most ancient peo-

ple of Greece.
1. Disclose, reveal.
2. Plundering.
3. The 9 divinities who preside over the different kinds of poetry, and the several arts and sciences.

determination by choosing this country for their chief repairing place, and by bestowing their perfections so largely here that the very shepherds have their fancies lifted to so high conceits that the learned of other nations are content both to borrow their names and imitate their cunning.

"Here dwelleth and reigneth this prince (whose picture you see) by name Basilius;[4] a prince of sufficient skill to govern so quiet a country, where the good minds of the former princes had set down good laws, and the well-bringing up of the people did serve as a most sure bond to hold them. But to be plain with you, he excels in nothing so much as in the zealous love of his people, wherein he doth not only pass all his own foregoers but, as I think, all the princes living. Whereof the cause is that though he exceed not in the virtues which get admiration, as depth of wisdom, height of courage and largeness of magnificence, yet is he notable in those which stir affection, as truth of word, meekness, courtesy, mercifulness and liberality.

"He, being already well stricken in years, married a young princess named Gynecia, daughter to the king of Cyprus, of notable beauty as by her picture you see: a woman of great wit, and in truth of more princely virtues than her husband; of most unspotted chastity, but of so working a mind and so vehement spirits as a man may say it was happy she took a good course, for otherwise it would have been terrible.

"Of these two are brought into the world two daughters, so beyond measure excellent in all the gifts allotted to reasonable creatures that we may think they were born to show that nature is no stepmother to that sex, how much soever some men, sharp-witted only in evil speaking, have sought to disgrace them. The elder is named Pamela, by many men not deemed inferior to her sister. For my part, when I marked them both, methought there was (if at least such perfections may receive the word of more) more sweetness in Philoclea but more majesty in Pamela: methought love played in Philoclea's eyes and threatened in Pamela's; methought Philoclea's beauty only persuaded, but so persuaded as all hearts must yield; Pamela's beauty used violence, and such violence as no heart could resist. And it seems that such proportion is between their minds: Philoclea so bashful, as though her excellencies had stolen into her before she was aware; so humble, that she will put all pride out of countenance; in sum, such proceeding as will stir hope but teach hope good manners. Pamela of high thoughts, who avoids not pride with not knowing her excellencies, but by making that one of her excellencies to be void of pride; her mother's wisdom, greatness, nobility, but—if I can guess aright—knit with a more constant temper. Now then, our Basilius—being so publicly happy as to be a prince, and so happy in that happiness as to be a beloved prince, and so in his private blessed as to have so excellent a wife and so over-excellent children—hath of late taken a course which yet makes him more spoken of than all these bless-

4. The Greek word for king.

ings. For, having made a journey to Delphos[5] and safely returned, within short space he brake up his court and retired himself, his wife and children, into a certain forest hereby which he calleth his desert; wherein, besides a house appointed for stables and lodgings for certain persons of mean calling who do all household services, he hath built two fine lodges. In the one of them himself remains with his younger daughter Philoclea—which was the cause they three were matched together in this picture—without having any other creature living in that lodge with him.

"Which though it be strange, yet not strange as the course he hath taken with the princess Pamela whom he hath placed in the other lodge; but how think you accompanied? Truly with none other but one Dametas, the most arrant doltish clown that I think ever was without the privilege of a bauble,[6] with his wife Miso and daughter Mopsa, in whom no wit can devise anything wherein they may pleasure her but to exercise her patience and to serve for a foil of her perfections."

Ye Goat-herd Gods[1]

Strephon. Ye Goat-herd gods, that love the grassy mountains,
    Ye nymphs which haunt the springs in pleasant valleys,
    Ye satyrs joyed with free and quiet forests,
    Vouchsafe your silent ears to plaining music,
    Which to my woes gives still an early morning,   5
    And draws the dolor on till weary evening.

Klaius. O Mercury,[2] foregoer to the evening,
    O heavenly huntress of the savage mountains,
    O lovely star, entitled of the morning,
    While that my voice doth fill these woeful valleys,   10
    Vouchsafe your silent ears to plaining music,
    Which oft hath *Echo* tired in secret forests.

Strephon. I that was once free burgess[3] of the forests,
    Where shade from Sun, and sport I sought in evening,
    I, that was once esteemed for pleasant music,   ·15
    Am banished now among the monstrous mountains
    Of huge despair, and foul affliction's valleys,
    Am grown a screech-owl to myself each morning.

Klaius. I that was once delighted every morning,
    Hunting the wild inhabiters of forests,   20

5. To consult the famous oracle of Apollo there.
6. Jester's baton (which would explain and excuse his folly.)
1. One of 78 interpolated poems in the *Old Arcadia*, many of which are ingenious metrical experiments. It is a dialogue between Strephon and Klaius, idealized shepherds who are both in love with the absent Urania, and is in the form of a double sestina (12 stanzas rather than the usual 6, with concluding triplet). The terminal words of each stanza are the same, but rearranged according to a progressive sequence, and all 6 terminal words must appear in the final 3 lines.
2. The evening star. He then addresses the moon (Diana, the "huntress"), and the morning star.
3. Citizen.

I, that was once the music of these valleys,
So darkened am, that all my day is evening,
Heart-broken so, that molehills seem high mountains,
And fill the vales with cries instead of music.

Strephon. Long since alas, my deadly swannish music[4]   25
Hath made itself a crier of the morning,
And hath with wailing strength climbed highest mountains;
Long since my thoughts more desert be than forests,
Long since I see my joys come to their evening,
And state[5] thrown down to over-trodden valleys.   30

Klaius. Long since the happy dwellers of these valleys
Have prayed me leave my strange exclaiming music,
Which troubles their day's work, and joys of evening;
Long since I hate the night, more hate the morning;
Long since my thoughts chase me like beasts in forests,   35
And make me wish myself laid under mountains.

Strephon. Meseems I see the high and stately mountains
Transform themselves to low dejected valleys;
Meseems I hear in these ill-changèd forests
The nightingales do learn of owls their music;   40
Meseems I feel the comfort of the morning
Turned to the mortal serene[6] of an evening.

Klaius. Meseems I see a filthy cloudy evening
As soon as sun begins to climb the mountains;
Meseems I feel a noisome scent, the morning[7]   45
When I do smell the flowers of these valleys;
Meseems I hear, when I do hear sweet music,
The dreadful cries of murdered men in forests.

Strephon. I wish to fire the trees of all these forests;
I give the sun a last farewell each evening;   50
I curse the fiddling finders-out of music;
With envy I do hate the lofty mountains
And with despite despise the humble valleys;
I do detest night, evening, day, and morning.

Klaius. Curse to myself my prayer is, the morning;   55
My fire is more than can be made with forests,
My state more base than are the basest valleys;
I wish no evenings more to see, each evening;
Shamèd, I hate myself in sight of mountains
And stop mine ears, lest I grow mad with music.   60

4. Doleful, like the song supposedly sung by the
swan as it dies.
5. High position.
6. Deadly dew.
7. Stinking scent, (in) the morning.

Strephon. For she, whose parts maintained a perfect music,
  Whose beauties shined more than the blushing morning,
  Who much did pass[8] in state the stately mountains,
  In straightness passed the cedars of the forests,
  Hath cast me, wretch, into eternal evening   65
  By taking her two suns from these dark valleys.

Klaius. For she, with whom compared, the Alps are valleys,
  She, whose least word brings from the spheres their music,
  At whose approach the sun rase in the evening,
  Who, where she went, bare[9] in her forehead morning,   70
  Is gone, is gone from these our spoilèd forests,
  Turning to deserts our best pastured mountains.

Stephon. These mountains witness shall, so shall these valleys,
Klaius. These forests eke, made wretched by our music,
  Our morning hymn this is, and song at evening.   75

1577–80   1593

The Defence of Poesy

The *Defence of Poesy* is a graceful but closely argued tract intended to establish the high nobility and the great social and moral value of poetry, thereby defending it against Puritan attacks. Sidney points out the antiquity of poetry, its prestige in the ancient world, its universality; and he cites the names given to poets—*vates*, or prophet by the Romans, *poietes*, or maker by the Greeks—as evidence of their ancient dignity. But he bases his defense essentially upon what the poet does. While all arts depend upon works of nature, the poet, supreme among artists, can make another nature, new and more beautiful: "Nature never set forth the earth in so rich tapestry as divers poets have done, neither with pleasant rivers, fruitful trees, sweet-smelling flowers, nor whatsoever else may make the too much loved earth more lovely."

Moreover, the poet presents virtues and vices in a more lively and affecting way than nature does, teaching, delighting, and moving the reader at the same time. The poet is superior to both the philosopher and the historian, because he is more concrete than the one and more universal than the other. Sidney also refutes Plato's charge that poets are liars by stating that "the poet nothing affirmeth," and he denies as well the Platonic claim that poetry arouses base desires. Surveying the English literary scene up to his time, Sidney finds little to praise except for Surrey's lyrics, the *Mirror for Magistrates*, Spenser's *Shepheardes Calender;* the drama he found generally bad. Despite his seriousness and logical rigor, Sidney's manner in this tract is graceful and easy, a manifestation of that *sprezzatura*, or casualness in doing something difficult perfectly, which Castiglione held up as an ideal in *The Courtier*.

8. Surpass.   9. Bore. "Rase": rose.

From The Defence of Poesy

[*The Poet, Poetry*]

* * * Since the authors of most of our sciences were the Romans, and before them the Greeks, let us a little stand upon their authorities, but even so far as to see what names they have given unto this now scorned skill.[1]

Among the Romans a poet was called *vates*, which is as much as a diviner, foreseer, or prophet, as by his conjoined words *vaticinium* and *vaticinari*[2] is manifest: so heavenly a title did that excellent people bestow upon this heart-ravishing knowledge. And so far were they carried into the admiration thereof, that they thought in the chanceable hitting upon any such verses great foretokens of their following fortunes were placed. Whereupon grew the word of *Sortes Virgilianae*,[3] when by sudden opening Virgil's book they lighted upon any verse of his making, whereof the histories of the emperors' lives are full: as of Albinus,[4] the governor of our island, who in his childhood met with this verse

Arma amens capio nec sat rationis in armis[5]

and in his age performed it. Which, although it were a very vain and godless superstition, as also it was to think spirits were commanded by such verses—whereupon this word charms, derived of *carmina*,[6] cometh—so yet serveth it to show the great reverence those wits were held in; and altogether not without ground, since both the oracles of Delphos and Sibylla's prophecies[7] were wholly delivered in verses. For that same exquisite observing of number and measure in the words, and that high flying liberty of conceit[8] proper to the poet, did seem to have some divine force in it.

And may not I presume a little further, to show the reasonableness of this word *vates*, and say that the holy David's[9] Psalms are a divine poem? If I do, I shall not do it without the testimony of great learned men, both ancient and modern. But even the name of Psalms will speak for me, which being interpreted, is nothing but songs; then that it is fully written in metre, as all learned hebricians agree, although the rules be not yet fully found;[1] lastly and principally, his handling his prophecy, which is merely[2] poetical: for what else is the awaking his musical instruments,

1. I.e., poetry.
2. *Vates*: poet-prophet; *vaticinium*: a prophecy; *vaticinari*: to prophesy.
3. Casting of lots out of Virgil, i.e., accepting as prophecy a line of Virgil chosen by random opening of the *Aeneid*.
4. Roman governor of Britain, declared emperor by his troops in 193 A.D., but defeated 4 years later.
5. "Frantic, I take up arms, yet there is little purpose in arms," (*Aeneid* 2.314).
6. Songs, poems.
7. The Pythia (priestesses) at Delphi in Greece

proclaimed Apollo's oracles; the Sibyls were thought to be prophetesses from the East. The Cumaean Sibyl directed Aeneas to the underworld and brought the famous Sibylline Books to Rome.
8. Imaginative conception.
9. The biblical King David, commonly identified in the Renaissance as author of the Book of Psalms.
1. Many Renaissance scholars who knew some Hebrew ("hebricians") thought the psalms were written in verse forms approximating classical meters.
2. Entirely.

the often and free changing of persons, his notable *prosopopoeias*,[3] when he maketh you, as it were, see God coming in His majesty, his telling of the beasts' joyfulness and hills leaping, but a heavenly poesy, wherein almost[4] he showeth himself a passionate lover of that unspeakable and everlasting beauty to be seen by the eyes of the mind, only cleared by faith? But truly now having named him, I fear me I seem to profane that holy name, applying it to poetry, which is among us thrown down to so ridiculous an estimation. But they that with quiet judgements will look a little deeper into it, shall find the end and working of it such as, being rightly applied, deserveth not to be scourged out of the Church of God.

But now let us see how the Greeks named it, and how they deemed of it. The Greeks called him a "poet," which name hath, as the most excellent, gone through other languages. It cometh of this word *poiein*, which is, to make: wherein, I know not whether by luck or wisdom, we Englishmen have met with[5] the Greeks in calling him a maker: which name, how high and incomparable a title it is, I had rather were known by marking the scope of other sciences than by any partial[6] allegation.

There is no art delivered to mankind that hath not the works of nature for his principal object, without which they[7] could not consist, and on which they so depend, as they become actors and players, as it were, of what nature will have set forth. So doth the astronomer look upon the stars, and, by that he seeth, set down what order nature hath taken therein. So doth the geometrician and arithmetician in their diverse sorts of quantities. So doth the musicians in time tell you which by nature agree,[8] which not. The natural philosopher thereon[9] hath his name, and the moral philosopher standeth upon[1] the natural virtues, vices, or passions of man; and follow nature (saith he) therein, and thou shalt not err. The lawyer saith what men have determined; the historian what men have done. The grammarian speaketh only of the rules of speech; and the rhetorician and logician, considering what in nature will soonest prove and persuade, thereon give artificial rules, which still are compassed within the circle of a question according to the proposed matter.[2] The physician weigheth the nature of man's body, and the nature of things helpful or hurtful unto it. And the metaphysic, though it be in the second and abstract notions, and therefore be counted supernatural, yet doth he indeed build upon the depth of nature. Only the poet, disdaining to be tied to any such subjection, lifted up with the vigour of his own invention, doth grow in effect another nature, in making things either better than nature bringeth forth, or, quite anew, forms such as never were in nature, as the Heroes, Demigods, Cyclops, Chimeras,

3. Personifications.
4. Indeed.
5. Agree with.
6. Biased.
7. The several arts.
8. Which rhythmic measures agree with nature.

9. I.e., from studying nature. A "natural philosopher" is a scientist.
1. Takes as subject matter.
2. The rules of those arts ("artificial rules") are always bound by the specific proposed issue. "Weigheth": studies.

Furies,[3] and such like: so as he goeth hand in hand with nature, not enclosed within the narrow warrant of her gifts, but freely ranging only within the zodiac of his own wit. Nature never set forth the earth in so rich tapestry as divers poets have done; neither with so pleasant rivers, fruitful trees, sweet-smelling flowers, nor whatsoever else may make the too much loved earth more lovely. Her[4] world is brazen, the poets only deliver a golden.

But let those things alone, and go to man—for whom as the other things are, so it seemeth in him her uttermost cunning is employed—and know whether she have brought forth so true a lover as Theagenes, so constant a friend as Pylades, so valiant a man as Orlando, so right a prince as Xenophon's Cyrus,[5] so excellent a man every way as Virgil's Aeneas. Neither let this be jestingly conceived, because the works of the one be essential, the other in imitation or fiction,[6] for any understanding knoweth the skill of each artificer standeth in that *idea* or fore-conceit[7] of the work, and not in the work itself. And that the poet hath that *idea* is manifest, by delivering them forth in such excellency as he had imagined them. Which delivering forth also is not wholly imaginative,[8] as we are wont to say by them that build castles in the air; but so far substantially it worketh, not only to make a Cyrus, which had been but a particular excellency as nature might have done, but to bestow a Cyrus upon the world to make many Cyruses, if they will learn aright why and how that maker made him.

Neither let it be deemed too saucy a comparison to balance the highest point of man's wit with the efficacy of nature; but rather give right honour to the heavenly Maker of that maker, who having made man to His own likeness, set him beyond and over all the works of that second nature:[9] which in nothing he showeth so much as in poetry, when with the force of a divine breath[1] he bringeth things forth surpassing her doings—with no small arguments to the incredulous of that first accursed fall of Adam, since our erected wit maketh us know what perfection is, and yet our infected will[2] keepeth us from reaching unto it. But these arguments will by few be understood, and by fewer granted. This much (I hope) will be given me, that the Greeks with some probability of reason gave him the name above all names of learning.

Now let us go to a more ordinary opening[3] of him, that the truth may

---

3. Heroes: in the Greek sense, part human, part divine. Cyclops: one-eyed giants in Homer's *Odyssey*. Chimeras: fire-breathing monsters with lion's head, goat's body, and serpent's tail. Furies: avenging deities who punish crimes both in this world and after death.
4. I.e., Nature's. A reference to the Four Ages of Man (see p. 969), the idea that the world has declined from the first and perfect Golden Age, through the Silver, Bronze, and Iron ages.
5. Theagenes: hero of Heliodorus' Greek romance, *Aethiopica* (3rd century A.D.). Pylades: friend of the Greek hero Orestes. Orlando: hero of Ariosto's

Orlando Furioso (1516). Cyrus: Cyrus the Great of Persia, exemplary hero of Xenophon's prose romance, the *Cyropaedia* (4th century B.C.).
6. The works of nature are real ("essential"); those of the poet are fiction.
7. Imaginative plan, conception.
8. Fanciful.
9. Physical nature.
1. Literally, inspiration.
2. Will corrupted in the Fall by Original Sin. "Erected wit": sound intelligence.
3. Analysis or explanation.

bé the more palpable: and so I hope, though we get not so unmatched a praise as the etymology of his names will grant, yet his very description, which no man will deny, shall not justly be barred from a principal commendation.

Poesy therefore is an art of imitation, for so Aristotle termeth it in the word *mimesis*[4]—that is to say, a representing, counterfeiting, or figuring forth—to speak metaphorically, a speaking picture—with this end, to teach and delight.

[Three Kinds of Mimetic Poets]

Of this have been three general kinds. The chief, both in antiquity and excellency, were they that did imitate the unconceivable excellencies of God. Such were David in his Psalms; Solomon in his Song of Songs, in his Ecclesiastes, and Proverbs; Moses and Deborah in their Hymns; and the writer of Job: which, beside other, the learned Emanuel Tremellius and Franciscus Junius[5] do entitle the poetical part of the Scripture. Against these none will speak that hath the Holy Ghost in due holy reverence. (In this kind, though in a full wrong divinity, were Orpheus, Amphion, Homer in his Hymns, and many other, both Greeks and Romans.) And this poesy must be used by whosoever will follow St. James's counsel in singing psalms when they are merry,[6] and I know is used with the fruit of comfort by some, when, in sorrowful pangs of their death-bringing sins, they find the consolation of the never-leaving goodness.

The second kind is of them that deal with matters philosophical, either moral, as Tyrtaeus, Phocylides, Cato,[7] or natural, as Lucretius and Virgil's *Georgics*;[8] or astronomical, as Manilius and Pontanus; or historical, as Lucan:[9] which who mislike, the fault is in their judgement quite out of taste, and not in the sweet food of sweetly uttered knowledge.

But because this second sort is wrapped within the fold of the proposed subject, and takes not the course of his own invention, whether they properly be poets or no let grammarians dispute, and go to the third, indeed right poets, of whom chiefly this question ariseth: betwixt whom and these second is such a kind of difference as betwixt the meaner sort of painters, who counterfeit only such faces as are set before them, and the more excellent, who having no law but wit,[1] bestow that in colours upon you which is fittest for the eye to see: as the constant though lamenting look of Lucretia, when she punished in herself another's fault,[2]

4. *Poetics*, 1.2.

5. Two scholars who produced a Protestant Latin translation of the Bible in 1575–80.

6. "Is any merry? Let him sing psalms" (James 5.13).

7. Dionysus Cato was the reputed author of the *Disticha de moribus*, 4 books of epigrammatic moral precepts in Latin hexameters, used as a textbook in Elizabethan schools.

8. Lucretius wrote a philosophical epic *De rerum natura (On the Nature of Things)*. Virgil's *Georg-*

ics exalts the life and work of the farmer.

9. Lucan wrote *De Bello Civili (Pharsalia)*, a heroic poem on the struggle between Caesar and Pompey.

1. Imagination, governed by sound understanding.

2. A notable exemplar of chastity and honor, the Roman matron Lucretia committed suicide after being raped by the son of King Tarquinius Superbus.

wherein he painteth not Lucretia whom he never saw, but painteth the outward beauty of such a virtue. For these third[3] be they which most properly do imitate to teach and delight, and to imitate borrow nothing of what is, hath been, or shall be; but range, only reined with learned discretion, into the divine consideration of what may be and should be. These be they that, as the first and most noble sort may justly be termed *vates*, so these are waited on in the excellentest languages and best understandings with the fore-described name of poets. For these indeed do merely[4] make to imitate, and imitate both to delight and teach; and delight, to move men to take that goodness in hand, which without delight they would fly as from a stranger; and teach, to make them know that goodness whereunto they are moved—which being the noblest scope to which ever any learning was directed, yet want there not idle tongues to bark at them.

These be subdivided into sundry more special denominations. The most notable be the heroic, lyric, tragic, comic, satiric, iambic, elegiac, pastoral, and certain others, some of these being termed according to the matter they deal with, some by the sorts of verses they liked best to write in; for indeed the greatest part of poets have apparelled their poetical inventions in that numbrous[5] kind of writing which is called verse— indeed but apparelled, verse being but an ornament and no cause to poetry, since there have been many most excellent poets that never versified, and now swarm many versifiers that need never answer to the name of poets. For Xenophon, who did imitate so excellently as to give us *effigiem iusti imperii*, the portraiture of a just empire, under the name of Cyrus, (as Cicero saith of him) made therein an absolute heroical poem. So did Heliodorus in his sugared invention of that picture of love in Theagenes and Chariclea; and yet both these wrote in prose: which I speak to show that it is not rhyming and versing that maketh a poet—no more than a long gown maketh an advocate, who though he pleaded in armour should be an advocate and no soldier. But it is that feigning notable images of virtues, vices, or what else, with that delightful teaching, which must be the right describing note to know a poet by; although indeed the senate of poets hath chosen verse as their fittest raiment, meaning, as in matter they passed all in all,[6] so in manner to go beyond them: not speaking (table-talk fashion or like men in a dream) words as they chanceably fall from the mouth, but peising[7] each syllable of each word by just proportion according to the dignity of the subject.

[Poetry, Philosophy, History]

Now therefore it shall not be amiss first to weigh this latter sort of poetry by his works, and then by his parts; and if in neither of these anatomies[8] he be condemnable, I hope we shall obtain a more favourable sentence.

3. I.e., the "right" poets.
4. Only.
5. I.e., in "numbers," poetic meters.

6. All others, in all respects.
7. Weighing.
8. Analyses.

This purifying of wit—this enriching of memory, enabling of judgement, and enlarging of conceit—which commonly we call learning, under what name soever it come forth, or to what immediate end soever it be directed, the final end is to lead and draw us to as high a perfection as our degenerate souls, made worse by their clayey lodgings, can be capable of.

This, according to the inclination of the man, bred many-formed impressions. For some that thought this felicity principally to be gotten by knowledge, and no knowledge to be so high or heavenly as acquaintance with the stars, gave themselves to astronomy; others, persuading themselves to be demigods if they knew the causes of things, became natural and supernatural philosophers; some an admirable delight drew to music; and some the certainty of demonstration to the mathematics. But all, one and other, having this scope: to know, and by knowledge to lift up the mind from the dungeon of the body to the enjoying his own divine essence.

But when by the balance of experience it was found that the astronomer, looking to the stars, might fall in a ditch, that the inquiring philosopher might be blind in himself, and the mathematician might draw forth a straight line with a crooked heart, then lo, did proof, the overruler of opinions, make manifest that all these are but serving sciences, which, as they have each a private end in themselves, so yet are they all directed to the highest end of the mistress-knowledge, by the Greeks called *architectonike*[9] which stands (as I think) in the knowledge of a man's self, in the ethic and politic consideration, with the end of well-doing and not of well-knowing only—even as the saddler's next[1] end is to make a good saddle, but his further end to serve a nobler faculty, which is horsemanship, so the horseman's to soldiery, and the soldier not only to have the skill, but to perform the practice of a soldier. So that, the ending end of all earthly learning being virtuous action, those skills that most serve to bring forth that have a most just title to be princes over all the rest.

Wherein, if we can, show we the poet's nobleness, by setting him before his other competitors. Among whom as principal challengers step forth the moral philosophers, whom, me thinketh, I see coming towards me with a sullen gravity, as though they could not abide vice by daylight, rudely clothed for to witness outwardly their contempt of outward things, with books in their hands against glory, whereto they set their names, sophistically[2] speaking against subtlety, and angry with any man in whom they see the foul fault of anger. These men casting largess as they go, of definitions, divisions, and distinctions,[3] with a scornful interrogative do soberly ask whether it be possible to find any path so ready to lead a man to virtue as that which teacheth what virtue is; and teach it not only by delivering forth his very being, his causes and effects, but

9. The science which orders or systematizes knowledge.
1. Nearest.

2. With deceptive subtlety.
3. Bountiful gifts of scholastic terms and arguments.

also by making known his enemy, vice, which must be destroyed, and his cumbersome servant, passion, which must be mastered; by showing the generalities that containeth it, and the specialities that are derived from it; lastly, by plain setting down how it extendeth itself out of the limits of a man's own little world to the government of families and maintaining of public societies.

The historian scarcely giveth leisure to the moralist to say so much, but that he, laden with old mouse-eaten records, authorizing himself[4] (for the most part) upon other histories, whose greatest authorities are built upon the notable foundation of hearsay; having much ado to accord differing writers and to pick truth out of their partiality;[5] better acquainted with a thousand years ago than with the present age, and yet better knowing how this world goeth than how his own wit runneth; curious for antiquities and inquisitive of novelties; a wonder to young folks and a tyrant in table talk, denieth, in a great chafe, that any man for teaching of virtue, and virtuous actions is comparable to him. "I am *testis temporum, lux veritatis, vita memoriae, magistra vitae, nuntia vetustatis.*[6] The philosopher," saith he, "teacheth a disputative virtue, but I do an active. His virtue is excellent in the dangerless Academy of Plato, but mine showeth forth her honourable face in the battles of Marathon, Pharsalia, Poitiers, and Agincourt.[7] He teacheth virtue by certain abstract considerations, but I only bid you follow the footing of them that have gone before you. Old-aged experience goeth beyond the fine-witted philosopher, but I give the experience of many ages. Lastly, if he make the songbook, I put the learner's hand to the lute; and if he be the guide, I am the light." Then would he allege you innumerable examples, confirming story by stories, how much the wisest senators and princes have been directed by the credit of history, as Brutus, Alphonsus of Aragon,[8] and who not, if need be? At length the long line of their disputation maketh a point in this, that the one giveth the precept, and the other the example.[9]

*   *   *

Now, to that which commonly is attributed to the praise of history, in respect of the notable learning is got by marking the success,[1] as though therein a man should see virtue exalted and vice punished—truly that commendation is particular to poetry, and far off from history. For indeed poetry ever sets virtue so out in her best colours, making Fortune her well-waiting handmaid, that one must needs be enamoured of her. Well may you see Ulysses in a storm,[2] and in other hard plights; but they are

4. Basing his authority.
5. Bias.
6. "I am the witness of the times, the light of truth, the life of memory, the teacher of life, and the messenger of antiquity" (Cicero, *De Oratore,* 2.9.36).
7. At Marathon the Greeks defeated the Persians (490 B.C.); at Pharsalia Caesar defeated Pompey (48 B.C.); at Poitiers (1356) and Agincourt (1415) the

English defeated the French.
8. Marcus Brutus was inspired to rise up against Caesar by the history of his great republican ancestor, Junius Brutus, who expelled the Tarquin kings. Alphonsus V of Aragon (1396–1458) carried the histories of Livy and Caesar into battle with him.
9. "The one": philosophy; "the other": history.
1. The outcome.
2. In *Odyssey* 5:291ff.

but exercises of patience and magnanimity, to make them shine the more in the near-following prosperity. And of the contrary part, if evil men come to the stage, they ever go out (as the tragedy writer[3] answered to one that misliked the show of such persons) so manacled as they little animate folks to follow them. But the history, being captived to the truth of a foolish world, is many times a terror from well-doing, and an encouragement to unbridled wickedness. For see we not valiant Miltiades rot in his fetters? The just Phocion and the accomplished Socrates put to death like traitors? The cruel Severus live prosperously? The excellent Severus miserably murdered? Sulla and Marius dying in their beds? Pompey and Cicero slain then when they would have thought exile a happiness? See we not virtuous Cato driven to kill himself, and rebel Caesar so advanced that his name yet, after 1600 years, lasteth in the highest honour?[4] And mark but even Caesar's own words of the aforenamed Sulla (who in that only did honestly, to put down his dishonest tyranny), *literas nescivit*, as if want of learning caused him to do well.[5] He meant it not by[6] poetry, which, not content with earthly plagues, deviseth new punishments in hell for tyrants, nor yet by philosophy, which teacheth *occidendos esse;*[7] but no doubt by skill in history, for that indeed can afford you Cypselus, Periander, Phalaris, Dionysius,[8] and I know not how many more of the same kennel, that speed well enough in their abominable injustice of usurpation.

I conclude, therefore, that he[9] excelleth history, not only in furnishing the mind with knowledge, but in setting it forward to that which deserveth to be called and accounted good: which setting forward, and moving to well-doing, indeed setteth the laurel crown upon the poets as victorious, not only of the historian, but over the philosopher, howsoever in teaching it may be questionable.[1]

For suppose it be granted (that which I suppose with great reason may be denied) that the philosopher, in respect of his methodical proceeding, doth teach more perfectly than the poet, yet do I think that no man is so much *philophilosophos*[2] as to compare the philosopher in moving with the poet. And that moving is of a higher degree than teaching, it may by this appear, that it is well nigh both the cause and effect of teaching. For who will be taught, if he be not moved with desire to be taught?

3. Euripides (as reported by Plutarch).
4. Miltiades: Athenian general and victor at Marathon, later imprisoned by the Athenians. Phocion: Athenian general and statesman executed for treason because he opposed an unjust war. "Cruel Severus": Emperor Lucius Septimus Severus, a plunderer of cities. "Excellent Severus": Emperor Alexander Severus, a reformer slain by his troops. Sulla and Marius: political rivals who brought unrest and destruction to Rome for more than 20 years. Pompey: Pompey the Great, defeated by Caesar at Pharsalia and slain in Egypt. Cicero: great statesman and orator killed at Antony's command trying to escape from Rome. Cato: Cato the Younger

committed suicide after his party failed to defeat Caesar.
5. Caesar did well only in putting down Sulla's dishonest tyranny, and it was the fact that Sulla did not know (historical) literature *(literas nescivit)* that enabled Caesar to defeat him.
6. With reference to.
7. They (tyrants) must be killed.
8. Four famous tyrants of the classical world: the first 2 of Corinth, Phalaris of Agrigentum, Dionysus the Elder of Syracuse.
9. The poet.
1. Arguable.
2. A lover of philosophers.

And what so much good doth that teaching bring forth (I speak still of moral doctrine) as that it moveth one to do that which it doth teach? For, as Aristotle saith, it is not *gnosis* but *praxis*[3] must be the fruit. And how *praxis* can be, without being moved to practise, it is no hard matter to consider.

The philosopher showeth you the way, he informeth you of the particularities, as well of the tediousness of the way, as of the pleasant lodging you shall have when your journey is ended, as of the many by-turnings that may divert you from your way. But this is to no man but to him that will read him, and read him with attentive studious painfulness;[4] which constant desire whosoever hath in him, hath already passed half the hardness of the way, and therefore is beholding to the philosopher but for the other half. Nay truly, learned men have learnedly thought that where once reason hath so much overmastered passion as that the mind hath a free desire to do well, the inward light each mind hath in itself is as good as a philosopher's book; since in nature[5] we know it is well to do well, and what is well, and what is evil, although not in the words of art which philosophers bestow upon us; for out of natural conceit[6] the philosophers drew it. But to be moved to do that which we know, or to be moved with desire to know, *hoc opus, hic labor est*.[7]

Now therein of all sciences (I speak still of human, and according to the human conceit) is our poet the monarch. For he doth not only show the way, but giveth so sweet a prospect into the way, as will entice any man to enter into it. Nay, he doth, as if your journey should lie through a fair vineyard, at the first give you a cluster of grapes, that full of that taste, you may long to pass further. He beginneth not with obscure definitions, which must blur the margin with interpretations, and load the memory with doubtfulness; but he cometh to you with words set in delightful proportion, either accompanied with, or prepared for, the well enchanting skill of music; and with a tale forsooth he cometh unto you, with a tale which holdeth children from play, and old men from the chimney corner. And, pretending no more, doth intend the winning of the mind from wickedness to virtue—even as the child is often brought to take most wholesome things by hiding them in such other as have a pleasant taste, which, if one should begin to tell them the nature of *aloes* or *rhabarbarum*[8] they should receive, would sooner take their physic at their ears than at their mouth. So is it in men (most of which are childish in the best things, till they be cradled in their graves): glad will they be to hear the tales of Hercules, Achilles, Cyrus, Aeneas; and, hearing them, must needs hear the right description of wisdom, valour, and justice; which, if they had been barely, that is to say philosophically, set out, they would swear they be brought to school again.

---

3. Doing; *gnosis:* knowing (*Ethics* 1.1).
4. Carefully.
5. Considering that by nature.
6. Natural understanding, as opposed to the philosophers' special vocabulary ("words of art").
7. "This is the task, this is the work to be done" (*Aeneid*, 6.129).
8. Two bitter purgatives.

[*"Parts" or Kinds of Poetry*]

But I am content not only to decipher him[9] by his works (although works, in commendation or dispraise, must ever hold a high authority), but more narrowly will examine his parts; so that (as in a man) though all together may carry a presence full of majesty and beauty, perchance in some one defectuous piece[1] we may find blemish.

Now in his parts, kinds, or species (as you list to term them), it is to be noted that some poesies have coupled together two or three kinds, as the tragical and comical, whereupon is risen the tragi-comical. Some, in the manner, have mingled prose and verse, as Sannazzaro and Boethius.[2] Some have mingled matters heroical and pastoral. But that cometh all to one in this question, for, if severed they be good, the conjunction cannot be hurtful. Therefore, perchance forgetting some and leaving some as needless to be remembered, it shall not be amiss in a word to cite the special kinds, to see what faults may be found in the right use of them.

Is it then the Pastoral poem which is misliked? (For perchance where the hedge is lowest[3] they will soonest leap over.) Is the poor pipe[4] disdained, which sometime out of Meliboeus' mouth can show the misery of people under hard lords or ravening soldiers, and again, by Tityrus, what blessedness is derived to them that lie lowest from the goodness of them that sit highest;[5] sometimes, under the pretty tales of wolves and sheep, can include the whole considerations of wrong-doing and patience; sometimes show that contentions for trifles can get but a trifling victory: where perchance a man may see that even Alexander and Darius, when they strave who should be cock of this world's dunghill, the benefit they got was that the after-livers may say

Haec memini et victum frustra contendere Thyrsin:
Ex illo Corydon, Corydon est tempore nobis.[6]

Or is it the lamenting Elegiac; which in a kind heart would move rather pity than blame; who bewails with the great philosopher Heraclitus,[7] the weakness of mankind and the wretchedness of the world; who surely is to be praised, either for compassionate accompanying just causes of lamentations, or for rightly painting out how weak be the passions of woefulness?[8] Is it the bitter but wholesome Iambic,[9] who rubs the galled

9. I.e., the poet.
1. Defective part.
2. Jacopo Sannazaro's pastoral romance *Arcadia* (1502) influenced Sidney's own *Arcadia*; Boethius' *Consolation of Philosophy* (524 A.D.).
3. Pastoral was considered the humblest kind of poetry, written in the lowest style.
4. The shepherd's oaten flute, symbol of pastoral poetry.
5. In Virgil's first eclogue, Meliboeus laments the seizure of his land while Tityrus rejoices that his lands were protected by the emperor.
6. Virgil, Eclogue 7.69–70: "This I remember,

and how Thyrsis vanquished, strove in vain. / From that day it is Corydon, Corydon with us." I.e., the great victory of Alexander the Great over Darius of Persia comes to the same thing as Corydon's victory over Thyrsis in a singing contest.
7. Ancient Greek philosopher who believed that everything will be consumed by mutability.
8. Sidney restricts the elegiac to lamentations; classical poets used elegiac meter for funeral poems but also poems treating love and other topics.
9. Iambic trimeter was first used by Greek poets for direct attacks—whereas satiric verse used irony and ridicule.

mind, in making shame the trumpet of villainy, with bold and open crying out against naughtiness? Or the Satiric, who

> Omne vafer vitium ridenti tangit amico;[1]

who sportingly never leaveth till he make a man laugh at folly, and at length ashamed, to laugh at himself, which he cannot avoid without avoiding the folly; who, while

> circum praecordia ludit,[2]

giveth us to feel how many headaches a passionate life bringeth us to; how, when all is done,

> Est Ulubris, animus si nos non deficit aequus?[3]

No, perchance it is the Comic, whom naughty play-makers and stage-keepers have justly made odious. To the arguments of abuse I will answer after. Only this much now is to be said, that the comedy is an imitation of the common errors of our life, which he representeth in the most ridiculous and scornful sort that may be, so as it is impossible that any beholder can be content to be such a one. Now, as in geometry the oblique must be known as well as the right, and in arithmetic the odd as well as the even, so in the actions of our life who seeth not the filthiness of evil wanteth a great foil to perceive the beauty of virtue. This doth the comedy handle so in our private and domestical matters as with hearing it we get as it were an experience what is to be looked for of a niggardly Demea, of a crafty Davus, of a flattering Gnatho, of a vainglorious Thraso;[4] and not only to know what effects are to be expected, but to know who be such, by the signifying badge given them by the comedian.[5] And little reason hath any man to say that men learn the evil by seeing it so set out, since, as I said before, there is no man living but, by the force truth hath in nature, no sooner seeth these men play their parts, but wisheth them *in pistrinum*;[6] although perchance the sack of his own faults lie so hidden behind his back that he seeth not himself dance the same measure;[7] whereto yet nothing can more open his eyes than to find his own actions contemptibly set forth.

So that the right use of comedy will (I think) by nobody be blamed; and much less of the high and excellent Tragedy, that openeth the greatest wounds, and showeth forth the ulcers that are covered with tissue; that maketh kings fear to be tyrants, and tyrants manifest their tyrannical humours; that, with stirring the affects[8] of admiration and commisera-

1. Persius (*Satires* 1.116) on the satire of Horace, who "probes every fault while making his friends laugh."
2. "He plays around the innermost feelings" (Persius, 1.117)
3. "It is at Ulubrae, if a well-balanced mind does not fail us"—an adaptation of Horace, *Epistle* 1.11.30. Ulubrae was a proverbially uninspiring town surrounded by marshes.
4. Type characters in the Roman comedies of Terence (195–159 B.C.), respectively, the heavy

father, clever servant, parasite, and braggart. Terence and Plautus (251–184 B.C.) were the chief classical models for comedy for the Renaissance.
5. Writer of comedies.
6. Mill used for punishment of Roman slaves.
7. In a fable of Aesop, a sack filled with one's own faults is carried (out of sight) on the back, while one filled with the faults of others is carried in front.
8. Feelings. "Humours": natures or dispositions, as influenced by the balance of 4 chief bodily fluids, or humors—blood, phlegm, choler, bile.

tion, teacheth the uncertainty of this world, and upon how weak foundations gilden roofs are builded; that maketh us know

> Qui sceptra saevus duro imperio regit
> Timet timentes; metus in auctorem redit.[9]

But how much it can move, Plutarch yieldeth a notable testimony of the abominable tyrant Alexander Phaeraeus,[1] from whose eyes a tragedy, well made and represented, drew abundance of tears, who without all pity had murdered infinite numbers, and some of his own blood: so as he, that was not ashamed to make matters for tragedies, yet could not resist the sweet violence of a tragedy. And if it wrought no further good in him, it was that he, in despite of himself, withdrew himself from hearkening to that which might mollify his hardened heart. But it is not the tragedy they do mislike; for it were too absurd to cast out so excellent a representation of whatsoever is most worthy to be learned.

Is it the Lyric[2] that most displeaseth, who with his tuned lyre and well-accorded voice, giveth praise, the reward of virtue, to virtuous acts; who gives moral precepts, and natural problems; who sometimes raiseth up his voice to the height of the heavens, in singing the lauds of the immortal God? Certainly, I must confess my own barbarousness, I never heard the old song of Percy and Douglas[3] that I found not my heart moved more than with a trumpet; and yet is it sung but by some blind crowder,[4] with no rougher voice than rude style; which, being so evil apparelled in the dust and cobwebs of that uncivil age, what would it work trimmed in the gorgeous eloquence of Pindar?[5] In Hungary I have seen it the manner at all feasts, and other such meetings, to have songs of their ancestors' valour, which that right soldierlike nation think one of the chiefest kindlers of brave courage. The incomparable Lacedemonians[6] did not only carry that kind of music ever with them to the field, but even at home, as such songs were made, so were they all content to be singers of them—when the lusty men were to tell what they did, the old men what they had done, and the young what they would do. And where a man may say that Pindar many times praiseth highly victories of small moment, matters rather of sport than virtue; as it may be answered, it was the fault of the poet, and not of the poetry, so indeed the chief fault was in the time and custom of the Greeks, who set those toys at so high a price that Philip of Macedon reckoned a horserace won at Olympus among his three fearful felicities.[7] But as the unimitable Pindar often did, so is that kind most capable and most fit to

9. "He who rules his people with a harsh government / Fears those who fear him; the fear returns upon its author." Seneca, *Oedipus*, 705.
1. Plutarch records that this cruel tyrant wept at the sufferings of Hecuba and Andromache in Euripides' *Troades*.
2. Here defined as poetry concerned chiefly with praise, and sung (originally) to musical accompaniment.
3. Ballad of Chevy Chase.

4. Fiddler.
5. Pindar's odes, the most exalted lyric poetry of Greece, celebrated victors in athletic games. "That uncivil age": the Middle Ages.
6. Spartans.
7. Plutarch records that Philip received 3 awesome tidings in one day: that his general was victorious in battle, that his wife had borne a son, and that his horse won a race at Olympia.

awake the thoughts from the sleep of idleness to embrace honourable enterprises.

There rests the Heroical—whose very name (I think) should daunt all backbiters: for by what conceit[8] can a tongue be directed to speak evil of that which draweth with him no less champions than Achilles, Cyrus, Aeneas, Turnus, Tydeus, and Rinaldo?[9]—who doth not only teach and move to a truth, but teacheth and moveth to the most high and excellent truth; who maketh magnanimity and justice shine through all misty fearfulness and foggy desires; who, if the saying of Plato and Tully[1] be true, that who could see virtue would be wonderfully ravished with the love of her beauty—this man sets her out to make her more lovely in her holiday apparel, to the eye of any that will deign not to disdain until they understand. But if anything be already said in the defence of sweet poetry, all concurreth to the maintaining the heroical, which is not only a kind, but the best and most accomplished kind of poetry. For, as the image of each action stirreth and instructeth the mind, so the lofty image of such worthies most inflameth the mind with desire to be worthy, and informs with counsel how to be worthy. Only let Aeneas be worn in the tablet of your memory, how he governeth himself in the ruin of his country; in the preserving his old father, and carrying away his religious ceremonies;[2] in obeying God's commandment to leave Dido, though not only all passionate kindness, but even the human consideration of virtuous gratefulness, would have craved other of him; how in storms, how in sports, how in war, how in peace, how a fugitive, how victorious, how besieged, how besieging, how to strangers, how to allies, how to enemies, how to his own; lastly, how in his inward self, and how in his outward government—and I think, in a mind not prejudiced with a prejudicating humour, he will be found in excellency fruitful, yea, even as Horace saith,

melius Chrysippo et Crantore.[3]

But truly I imagine it falleth out with these poet-whippers, as with some good women, who often are sick, but in faith they cannot tell where; so the name of poetry is odious to them, but neither his cause nor effects, neither the sum that contains him, nor the particularities descending from him, give any fast[4] handle to their carping dispraise.

Since then poetry is of all human learning the most ancient and of most fatherly antiquity, as from whence other learnings have taken their beginnings; since it is so universal that no learned nation doth despise it, nor barbarous nation is without it; since both Roman and Greek gave such divine names unto it, the one of prophesying, the other of making,

---

8. Conception.
9. Tydeus: in Statius' epic, *Thebaid*. Rinaldo: in Ariosto's *Orlando Furioso* and Tasso's *Gerusalemme Liberata*.
1. Marcus Tullius Cicero.
2. Sacred objects, household gods. After fleeing Troy, Aeneas and his Trojans stayed for a time in Carthage, whose queen, Dido, became Aeneas'

lover. She killed herself when Aeneas (at the gods' command) sailed away to accomplish his fate, the founding of the Roman Empire.
3. In *Epistle* 1.2.4, Horace praises Homer as a "better [teacher] than Chrysippus [a great Stoic philosopher] and Crantor" (a commentator on Plato).
4. Firm.

and that indeed that name of making is fit for him, considering that
where all other arts retain themselves within their subject, and receive,
as it were, their being from it, the poet only bringeth his own stuff, and
doth not learn a conceit out of a matter, but maketh matter for a conceit;
since neither his description nor end containing any evil, the thing
described cannot be evil; since his effects be so good as to teach goodness
and to delight the learners; since therein (namely in moral doctrine, the
chief of all knowledges) he doth not only far pass the historian, but, for
instructing, is well nigh comparable to the philosopher, for moving leaves
him behind him; since the Holy Scripture (wherein there is no uncleanness) hath whole parts in it poetical, and that even our Saviour Christ
vouchsafed to use the flowers of it; since all his kinds are not only in
their united forms but in their severed dissections fully commendable; I
think (and think I think rightly) the laurel crown appointed for triumphant captains doth worthily (of all other learnings) honour the poet's
triumph.

[Answers to Charges against Poetry]

Now then go we to the most important imputations laid to the poor
poets. For aught I can yet learn, they are these. First, that there being
many other more fruitful knowledges, a man might better spend his time
in them than in this. Secondly, that it is the mother of lies. Thirdly,
that it is the nurse of abuse, infecting us with many pestilent desires;
with a siren's sweetness drawing the mind to the serpent's tail of sinful
fancies (and herein, especially, comedies give the largest field to ear[5] as
Chaucer saith); how, both in other nations and in ours, before poets did
soften us, we were full of courage, given to martial exercises, the pillars
of manlike liberty, and not lulled asleep in shady idleness with poets'
pastimes. And lastly, and chiefly, they cry out with open mouth as if
they had overshot Robin Hood, that Plato banished them out of his
commonwealth.[6] Truly, this is much, if there be much truth in it.

First, to the first.[7] That a man might better spend his time, is a reason
indeed; but it doth (as they say) but *petere principium*.[8] For if it be as I
affirm, that no learning is so good as that which teacheth and moveth to
virtue; and that none can both teach and move thereto so much as poetry:
then is the conclusion manifest that ink and paper cannot be to a more
profitable purpose employed. And certainly, though a man should grant
their first assumption, it should follow (methinks) very unwillingly, that
good is not good, because better is better. But I still and utterly deny that
there is sprung out of earth a more fruitful knowledge.

To the second, therefore, that they should be the principal liars, I will
answer paradoxically, but truly, I think truly, that of all writers under
the sun the poet is the least liar, and, though he would, as a poet can

5. To plough (*Knight's Tale*, 28).
6. Plato proposed (*Republic*, 10.595–608c) that
most sorts of poets be banished from his ideal commonwealth, because they stir up unworthy emotions and because their imitations are far removed
from truth.
7. First objection.
8. Beg the question.

scarcely be a liar. The astronomer, with his cousin the geometrician, can hardly escape, when they take upon them to measure the height of the stars. How often, think you, do the physicians lie, when they aver things good for sicknesses, which afterwards send Charon[9] a great number of souls drowned in a potion before they come to his ferry? And no less of the rest, which take upon them to affirm. Now, for the poet, he nothing affirms, and therefore never lieth. For, as I take it, to lie is to affirm that to be true which is false. So as the other artists,[1] and especially the historian, affirming many things, can, in the cloudy knowledge of mankind, hardly escape from many lies. But the poet (as I said before) never affirmeth. The poet never maketh any circles[2] about your imagination, to conjure you to believe for true what he writes. He citeth not authorities of other histories, but even for his entry[3] calleth the sweet Muses to inspire into him a good invention; in truth, not labouring to tell you what is or is not, but what should or should not be. And therefore, though he recount things not true, yet because he telleth them not for true, he lieth not—without we will say that Nathan lied in his speech before-alleged to David;[4] which as a wicked man durst scarce say, so think I none so simple would say that Aesop lied in the tales of his beasts; for who thinks that Aesop wrote it for actually true were well worthy to have his name chronicled among the beasts he writeth of. What child is there, that, coming to a play, and seeing *Thebes* written in great letters upon an old door, doth believe that it is Thebes? If then a man can arrive to that child's age to know that the poets' persons and doings are but pictures what should be, and not stories what have been, they will never give the lie to[5] things not affirmatively but allegorically and figuratively written.

* * *

So that, since the excellencies of it may be so easily and so justly confirmed, and the low-creeping objections so soon trodden down: it not being an art of lies, but of true doctrine; not of effeminateness, but of notable stirring of courage; not of abusing man's wit, but of strengthening man's wit; not banished, but honoured by Plato: let us rather plant more laurels for to engarland the poets' heads (which honour of being laureate, whereas besides them only triumphant captains were, is a sufficient authority too show the price they ought to be held in) than suffer the ill-favoured breath of such wrong-speakers once to blow upon the clear springs of poesy.

[Poetry in England]

But since I have run so long a career[6] in this matter, methinks, before I give my pen a full stop, it shall be but a little more lost time to inquire

9. In classical myth, the ferryman who takes the souls of the dead over the river Styx.
1. Practitioners of the liberal arts.
2. As a magician does in conjuring.
3. In his opening lines.

4. Nathan's parable (2 Samuel 12.1–15) of a man robbed of his one ewe lamb by a rich man.
5. Accuse of lying.
6. Course.

why England, the mother of excellent minds, should be grown so hard
a stepmother to poets, who certainly in wit ought to pass all other, since
all only proceedeth from their wit, being indeed makers of themselves,
not takers of others.

*   *   *

But I that, before ever I durst aspire unto the dignity, am admitted
into the company of the paper-blurrers, do find the very true cause of
our wanting estimation is want of desert—taking upon us to be poets in
despite of Pallas.[7]

Now, wherein we want desert were a thankworthy labour to express;
but if I knew, I should have mended myself. But I, as I never desired
the title, so have I neglected the means to come by it. Only, overmastered by some thoughts, I yielded an inky tribute unto them. Marry,
they that delight in poesy itself should seek to know what they do, and
how they do; and especially look themselves in an unflattering glass of
reason, if they be inclinable unto it. For poesy must not be drawn by
the ears; it must be gently led, or rather it must lead—which was partly
the cause that made the ancient-learned affirm it was a divine gift, and
no human skill: since all other knowledges lie ready for any that hath
strength of wit. A poet no industry can make, if his own genius be not
carried into it; and therefore it is an old proverb, *orator fit, poeta nasci-
tur.*[8]

Yet confess I always that as the fertilest ground must be manured, so
must the highest-flying wit have a Daedalus[9] to guide him. That Daedalus, they say, both in this and in other, hath three wings to bear itself
up into the air of due commendation: that is, art, imitation, and exercise. But these, neither artificial rules nor imitative patterns, we much
cumber ourselves withal. Exercise indeed we do, but that very foreback-
wardly: for where we should exercise to know, we exercise as having
known; and so is our brain delivered of much matter which never was
begotten by knowledge. For there being two principal parts, matter to be
expressed by words and words to express the matter, in neither we use
art or imitation rightly. Our matter is *quodlibet* indeed, though wrongly
performing Ovid's verse,

Quicquid conabor dicere, versus erit;[1]

never marshalling it into any assured rank, that almost the readers cannot tell where to find themselves.

Chaucer, undoubtedly, did excellently in his *Troilus and Criseyde*: of
whom, truly, I know not whether to marvel more, either that he in that
misty time could see so clearly, or that we in this clear age go so stum-
blingly after him. Yet had he great wants, fit to be forgiven in so reverent

---

7. I.e., scorning the dictates of Wisdom.
8. "An orator is made; a poet is born."
9. The legendary craftsman who invented wings
of wax for himself and his son Icarus. Ignoring his

father's instructions, Icarus flew too close to the
sun, melted his wings, and fell into the sea.
1. "Whatever I try to say will turn to verse" (Ovid,
Tristia, 4.10.26). "Quodlibet": what you will.

an antiquity. I account the *Mirror of Magistrates*[2] meetly furnished of beautiful parts, and in the Earl of Surrey's lyrics many things tasting of a noble birth, and worthy of a noble mind. The *Shepherds' Calendar* hath much poetry in his eclogues, indeed worthy the reading, if I be not deceived. (That same framing of his style to an old rustic language I dare not allow, since neither Theocritus in Greek, Virgil in Latin, nor Sannazzaro in Italian did affect it.)[3] Besides these I do not remember to have seen but few (to speak boldly) printed that have poetical sinews in them; for proof whereof, let but most of the verses be put in prose, and then ask the meaning, and it will be found that one verse did but beget another, without ordering at the first what should be at the last; which becomes a confused mass of words, with a tingling sound of rhyme, barely accompanied with reason.

Our tragedies and comedies (not without cause cried out against), observing rules neither of honest civility nor skilful poetry—excepting *Gorboduc*[4] (again, I say, of those that I have seen), which notwithstanding as it is full of stately speeches and well-sounding phrases, climbing to the height of Seneca's style, and as full of notable morality, which it doth most delightfully teach, and so obtain the very end of poesy, yet in truth it is very defectious in the circumstances, which grieveth me, because it might not remain as an exact model of all tragedies. For it is faulty both in place and time, the two necessary companions of all corporal actions. For where the stage should always represent but one place, and the uttermost time presupposed in it should be, both by Aristotle's precept and common reason, but one day, there is both many days, and many places, inartificially[5] imagined.

But if it be so in *Gorboduc*, how much more in all the rest, where you shall have Asia of the one side, and Afric of the other, and so many other under-kingdoms, that the player, when he cometh in, must ever begin with telling where he is, or else the tale will not be conceived? Now you shall have three ladies walk to gather flowers: and then we must believe the stage to be a garden. By and by we hear news of shipwreck in the same place: and then we are to blame if we accept it not for a rock. Upon the back of that comes out a hideous monster with fire and smoke: and then the miserable beholders are bound to take it for a cave. While in the meantime two armies fly in, represented with four swords and bucklers:[6] and then what hard heart will not receive it for a pitched field?

Now, of time they are much more liberal: for ordinary it is that two young princes fall in love; after many traverses,[7] she is got with child, delivered of a fair boy; he is lost, groweth a man, falls in love, and is

2. A large collection of Elizabethan poems on the downfall of princes and great men.
3. Models for pastoral poetry in the Renaissance.
4. Senecan blank verse tragedy by Thomas Sackville and Thomas Norton (1565), called the first regular English tragedy. The highly rhetorical and declamatory Roman tragedies of Seneca (5 B.C.– 65 A.D.) were models of the grand tragic style in the Renaissance.

5. Unskillfully. Sidney here voices the Renaissance commonplace (erroneously derived from Aristotle) that tragedies should observe the 3 unities: time (one day), place (one locale), and action (one plot). Aristotle insisted only on unity of action.
6. Shields.
7. Difficulties, mishaps.

ready to get another child; and all this in two hours' space: which, how absurd it is in sense, even sense may imagine, and art hath taught, and all ancient examples justified—and at this day, the ordinary players in Italy will not err in. Yet will some bring in an example of *Eunuchus* in Terence, that containeth matter of two days, yet far short of twenty years. True it is, and so was it to be played in two days, and so fitted to the time it set forth. And though Plautus have in one place done amiss, let us hit with him, and not miss with him.

But they will say: How then shall we set forth a story which containeth both many places and many times? And do they not know that a tragedy is tied to the laws of poesy, and not of history; not bound to follow the story, but having liberty either to feign a quite new matter or to frame the history to the most tragical conveniency? Again, many things may be told which cannot be showed, if they know the difference betwixt reporting and representing. As, for example, I may speak (though I am here) of Peru, and in speech digress from that to the description of Calicut; but in action I cannot represent it without Pacolet's horse;[8] and so was the manner the ancients took, by some *Nuntius*[9] to recount things done in former time or other place. Lastly, if they will represent a history, they must not (as Horace saith) begin *ab ovo*;[1] but they must come to the principal point of that one action which they will represent.

By example this will be best expressed. I have a story of young Polydorus,[2] delivered for safety's sake, with great riches, by his father Priam to Polymnestor, king of Thrace, in the Trojan war time; he, after some years, hearing the overthrow of Priam, for to make the treasure his own, murdereth the child; the body of the child is taken up by Hecuba; she, the same day, findeth a sleight to be revenged most cruelly of the tyrant. Where now would one of our tragedy writers begin, but with the delivery of the child? Then should he sail over into Thrace, and so spend I know not how many years, and travel numbers of places. But where doth Euripides? Even with the finding of the body, leaving the rest to be told by the spirit of Polydorus. This need no further to be enlarged; the dullest wit may conceive it.

But besides these gross absurdities, how all their plays be neither right tragedies, nor right comedies, mingling kings and clowns, not because the matter so carrieth it, but thrust in the clown by head and shoulders to play a part in majestical matters with neither decency nor discretion,[3] so as neither the admiration and commiseration, nor the right sportfulness,[4] is by their mongrel tragi-comedy obtained. I know Apuleius[5] did somewhat so, but that is a thing recounted with space of time, not represented in one moment; and I know the ancients have one or two exam-

8. A flying horse in the French romance *Valentine and Orson* (1489). Calicut: Calcutta.
9. Messenger.
1. From the beginning, literally, from the egg (*Ars Poetica*, 147).
2. In Euripides' *Hecuba*.

3. Mingling of social levels (kings and clowns) was thought to violate the principle of decorum.
4. Effect proper to comedy, as "admiration and commiseration" are proper to tragedy.
5. Roman author of *The Golden Ass*, a satirical romance (2nd century A.D.).

ples of tragi-comedies, as Plautus hath *Amphitryo*;[6] but, if we mark them well, we shall find that they never, or very daintily, match hornpipes[7] and funerals. So falleth it out that, having indeed no right comedy, in that comical part of our tragedy, we have nothing but scurrility, unworthy of any chaste ears, or some extreme show of doltishness, indeed fit to lift up a loud laughter, and nothing else: where the whole tract of a comedy should be full of delight, as the tragedy should be still maintained in a well-raised admiration.

But our comedians think there is no delight without laughter; which is very wrong, for though laughter may come with delight, yet cometh it not of delight, as though delight should be the cause of laughter; but well may one thing breed both together. Nay, rather in themselves they have, as it were, a kind of contrariety: for delight we scarcely do but in things that have a conveniency to ourselves or to the general nature; laughter almost ever cometh of things most disproportioned to ourselves and nature. Delight hath a joy in it, either permanent or present. Laughter hath only a scornful tickling.

For example, we are ravished with delight to see a fair woman, and yet are far from being moved to laughter; we laugh at deformed creatures, wherein certainly we cannot delight. We delight in good chances, we laugh at mischances: we delight to hear the happiness of our friends, or country, at which he were worthy to be laughed at that would laugh; we shall, contrarily, laugh sometimes to find a matter quite mistaken and go down the hill against the bias[8] in the mouth of some such men—as for the respect of them one shall be heartily sorry, he cannot choose but laugh, and so is rather pained than delighted with laughter.

Yet deny I not but that they may go well together. For as in Alexander's picture well set out we delight without laughter, and in twenty mad antics we laugh without delight; so in Hercules, painted with his great beard and furious countenance, in a woman's attire, spinning at Omphale's commandment,[9] it breedeth both delight and laughter: for the representing of so strange a power in love procureth delight, and the scornfulness of the action stirreth laughter. But I speak to this purpose, that all the end of the comical part be not upon such scornful matters as stir laughter only, but, mixed with it, that delightful teaching which is the end of poesy. And the great fault even in that point of laughter, and forbidden plainly by Aristotle, is that they stir laughter in sinful things, which are rather execrable than ridiculous, or in miserable, which are rather to be pitied than scorned. For what is it to make folks gape at a wretched beggar and a beggarly clown; or, against law of hospitality, to jest at strangers, because they speak not English so well as we do? What do we learn, since it is certain

---

6. *Amphitruo* is tragicomic only in that it contains gods and heroes; otherwise it is pure comedy.
7. Merry tunes for country dances.
8. End in unexpected disaster, as when in the game of bowls a hill deflects the ball from its course or "bias."

9. Hercules, infatuated with Omphale, Queen of Lydia, submitted to be dressed as her female slave and to spin wool.

> Nil habet infelix paupertas durius in se,
> Quam quod ridiculos homines facit?[1]

But rather, a busy loving courtier and a heartless threatening Thraso; a self-wise-seeming schoolmaster; an awry-transformed traveller. These, if we saw walk in stage names, which we play naturally, therein were delightful laughter, and teaching delightfulness—as in the other, the tragedies of Buchanan[2] do justly bring forth a divine admiration.

But I have lavished out too many words of this play matter. I do it because, as they are excelling parts of poesy, so is there none so much used in England, and none can be more pitifully abused; which, like an unmannerly daughter showing a bad education, causeth her mother Poesy's honesty to be called in question.

Other sort of poetry almost have we none, but that lyrical kind of songs and sonnets: which, Lord, if He gave us so good minds, how well it might be employed, and with how heavenly fruit, both private and public, in singing the praises of the immortal beauty: the immortal goodness of that God who giveth us hands to write and wits to conceive; of which we might well want words, but never matter; of which we could turn our eyes to nothing, but we should ever have new-budding occasions. But truly many of such writings as come under the banner of unresistible love, if I were a mistress, would never persuade me they were in love: so coldly they apply fiery speeches, as men that had rather read lovers' writings—and so caught up certain swelling phrases which hang together like a man that once told my father that the wind was at northwest and by south, because he would be sure to name winds enough—than that in truth they feel those passions, which easily (as I think) may be bewrayed by that same forcibleness or *energia* (as the Greeks call it) of the writer. But let this be a sufficient though short note, that we miss the right use of the material point of poesy.

*   *   *

Now of versifying there are two sorts, the one ancient, the other modern: the ancient marked the quantity of each syllable, and according to that framed his verse; the modern, observing only number[3] (with some regard of the accent), the chief life of it standeth in that like sounding of the words, which we call rhyme. Whether of these be the more excellent, would bear many speeches: the ancient (no doubt) more fit for music, both words and time observing quantity, and more fit lively to express diverse passions, by the low or lofty sound of the well-weighed syllable; the latter likewise, with his rhyme, striketh a certain music to the ear, and, in fine, since it doth delight, though by another way, it obtains the same purpose: there being in either sweetness, and wanting

---

1. "Unfortunate poverty has in itself nothing harder to bear than that it makes men ridiculous" (Juvenal, *Satires* 3.152–3).
2. George Buchanan (1506–1582), influential

Scotch humanist and poet.
3. Classical "quantity" meant the length or duration of syllables. Moderns simply count the "number" of syllables.

in neither majesty. Truly the English, before any vulgar[4] language I
know, is fit for both sorts. For, for the ancient, the Italian is so full of
vowels that it must ever be cumbered with elisions; the Dutch[5] so, of
the other side, with consonants, that they cannot yield the sweet sliding,
fit for a verse; the French in his whole language hath not one word that
hath his accent in the last syllable saving two, called *antepenultima*; and
little more hath the Spanish, and therefore very gracelessly may they use
dactyls.[6] The English is subject to none of these defects. Now for the
rhyme, though we do not observe quantity, yet we observe the accent
very precisely, which other languages either cannot do, or will not do so
absolutely. That *caesura*,[7] or breathing place in the midst of the verse,
neither Italian nor Spanish have, the French and we never almost fail
of. Lastly, even the very rhyme itself, the Italian cannot put it in the last
syllable, by the French named the masculine rhyme, but still in the
next to the last, which the French call the female, or the next before
that, which the Italian term *sdrucciola*. The example of the former is
buono: suono, of the *sdrucciola* is *femina: semina*. The French, of the
other side, hath both the male, as *bon: son*, and the female, as *plaise:
taise*, but the *sdrucciola* he hath not: where the English hath all three,
as *due: true, father: rather, motion: potion*[8]—with much more which
might be said, but that already I find the triflingness of this discourse is
much too much enlarged.

[Conclusion]

So that since the ever-praiseworthy Poesy is full of virtue-breeding
delightfulness, and void of no gift that ought to be in the noble name of
learning; since the blames laid against it are either false or feeble; since
the cause why it is not esteemed in England is the fault of poet-apes, not
poets; since, lastly, our tongue is most fit to honour poesy, and to be
honoured by poesy; I conjure you all that have had the evil luck to read
this ink-wasting toy of mine, even in the name of the nine Muses, no
more to scorn the sacred mysteries of poesy; no more to laugh at the
name of poets, as though they were next inheritors to fools; no more to
jest at the reverent title of a rhymer; but to believe, with Aristotle, that
they were the ancient treasurers of the Grecians' divinity; to believe, with
Bembus, that they were first bringers-in of all civility; to believe, with
Scaliger, that no philosopher's precepts can sooner make you an honest
man than the reading of Virgil; to believe, with Clauserus,[9] the transla-

---

4. The common or "vulgar" people spoke the vernacular languages, while the learned could speak
and write in Latin.
5. German.
6. For dactyls, see p. 2584. Because of the accent
patterns in French and Spanish, those languages
cannot make good use of this poetic foot.
7. In its use of caesuras (see p. 2586) as well as the
several kinds of metrical feet, English poetry
achieves greater variety and flexibility than poetry
in the other vernacular languages.
8. Pronounced with three syllables, accented on

the first.
9. Bembus: Cardinal Pietro Bembo, Italian poet,
Platonist philosopher, and character in Castiglione's *Courtier*, see p. 1006. Julius-Caesar Scaliger: Italian scholar and author of a highly influential
treatise on poetry, *Poetices* (1561). Conrad Clau-
ser: German scholar (ca. 1520–1611) who translated a Greek treatise by Cornutus, a Stoic
pedagogue of Nero's time. Hesiod: early Greek poet
whose *Theogony* recounts myths of the birth and
warfare of the Gods and the origin of the world.

tor of Cornutus, that it pleased the heavenly Deity, by Hesiod and Homer, under the veil of fables, to give us all knowledge, logic, rhetoric, philosophy natural and moral, and *quid non?*;[1] to believe, with me, that there are many mysteries contained in poetry, which of purpose were written darkly, lest by profane wits it should be abused; to believe, with Landino,[2] that they are so beloved of the gods that whatsoever they write proceeds of a divine fury; lastly, to believe themselves, when they tell you they will make you immortal by their verses. Thus doing, your name shall flourish in the printers' shops; thus doing, you shall be of kin to many a poetical preface; thus doing, you shall be most fair, most rich, most wise, most all, you shall dwell upon superlatives; thus doing, though you be *libertino patre natus*, you shall suddenly grow *Herculea proles*,[3]

Si quid mea carmina possunt;[4]

thus doing, your soul shall be placed with Dante's Beatrice, or Virgil's Anchises. But if (fie of such a but) you be born so near the dull-making cataract of Nilus[5] that you cannot hear the planet-like music of poetry; if you have so earth-creeping a mind that it cannot lift itself up to look to the sky of poetry, or rather, by a certain rustical disdain, will become such a mome as to be a Momus[6] of poetry; then, though I will not wish unto you the ass's ears of Midas,[7] nor to be driven by a poet's verses, as Bubonax[8] was, to hang himself, nor to be rhymed to death, as is said to be done in Ireland;[9] yet thus much curse I must send you, in the behalf of all poets, that while you live, you live in love, and never get favour for lacking skill of a sonnet; and, when you die, your memory die from the earth for want of an epitaph.

1595

The Nightingale

The nightingale, as soon as April bringeth[1]
Unto her rested sense a perfect waking
(While late bare earth, proud of new clothing, springeth),
Sings out her woes, a thorn her song-book making,
   And mournfully bewailing,   5

1. What not?
2. Christoforo Landino, Florentine humanist, who developed this argument in his edition of Dante's *Divine Comedy* (1481).
3. "Born of a freed slave father"; "a descendent of Hercules" (Horace, *Satires* 1.6.45).
4. "If my songs are of any avail" (*Aeneid* 9.446).
5. According to Cicero, the noise of the Nile's cataracts deafened those who lived nearby. "Planet-like": resembling the music of the spheres, most beautiful of all music.
6. Mome: a stupid person. Momus: God of ridicule, son of Night and Sleep, hence, a critic.
7. He was given ass's ears because he preferred Pan's

music to Apollo's (Ovid, *Metamorphoses* 11.146–79).
8. Buphalus, a sculptor who hanged himself when his works were satirized by the poet Hipponax. Sidney fuses the two names.
9. Irish bards were thought to be able to cause death with their rhymed charms.
1. In England, the nightingale's song is heard only in the spring. According to myth, the nightingale was once Philomela, who was raped and had her tongue cut out by her brother-in-law, King Tereus; she presses her breast against a thorn while singing to remind her of that pain.

Her throat in tunes expresseth
What grief her breast oppresseth,
For Thereus' force on her chaste will prevailing.
   O Philomela fair, O take some gladness,
   That here is juster cause of plaintful sadness: 10
   Thine earth now springs, mine fadeth;
   Thy thorn without, my thorn my heart invadeth.

Alas, she hath no other cause of anguish
But Thereus' love, on her by strong hand wroken,[2]
Wherein she suffering, all her spirits languish;   15
Full womanlike complains her will was broken.
   But I who daily craving,
   Cannot have to content me,
   Have more cause to lament me,
Since wanting is more woe then too much having.   20
   O Philomela fair, O take some gladness,
   That here is juster cause of plaintful sadness:
   Thine earth now springs, mine fadeth;
   Thy thorn without, my thorn my heart invadeth.

1581   1598

Thou Blind Man's Mark[1]

Thou blind man's mark,[2] thou fool's self-chosen snare,
Fond fancy's scum, and dregs of scattered thought,
Band[3] of all evils, cradle of causeless care,
Thou web of will, whose end is never wrought—

Desire, desire! I have too dearly bought,   5
With price of mangled mind, thy worthless ware;
Too long, too long asleep thou hast me brought,
Who should my mind to higher things prepare.

But yet in vain thou hast my ruin sought;
In vain thou madest me to vain things aspire;   10
In vain thou kindlest all thy smoky fire;

For virtue hath this better lesson taught—
Within myself to seek my only hire,
Desiring nought but how to kill desire.

1581   1598

2. Inflicted.
1. This and the sonnet following are the final poems (numbers 31 and 32) in the miscellany of his early poems that Sidney collected under the title *Certain Sonnets*.
2. Target.
3. Swaddling band.

Leave Me, O Love

Leave me, O Love which reachest but to dust,
And thou my mind aspire to higher things;
Grow rich in that which never taketh rust;
Whatever fades but fading pleasure brings.

Draw in thy beams, and humble all thy might 5
To that sweet yoke where lasting freedoms be;
Which breaks the clouds and opens forth the light,
That doth both shine and give us sight to see.

O take fast hold; let that light be thy guide
In this small course which birth draws out to death, 10
And think how evil becometh him to slide,
Who seeketh heaven, and comes of heavenly breath.[1]
Then farewell world; thy uttermost I see;
Eternal Love, maintain thy life in me.

1581   1598

1. I.e., it ill becomes one who has a soul and seeks heaven to "slide" to earthly things.

EDMUND SPENSER

1552–1599

1579: Publication of *The Shepheardes Calender*.
1580: In Ireland, where he remains for the rest of his life.
1590: Publication of *The Faerie Queene*, books 1–3; 1596, books 1–6.

The greatest nondramatic poet of the English Renaissance, Edmund Spenser, was born in London, probably in 1552, and attended the Merchant Taylors' School under its famous headmaster Richard Mulcaster. In 1569 he went to Cambridge as a "sizar" or poor scholar. In the Puritan environment of Cambridge, where the popular preacher Thomas Cartwright was beginning to make the authorities uneasy, Spenser began as a poet by translating some poems for a volume of anti-Catholic propaganda. He also began his friendship with Gabriel Harvey, an eccentric Cambridge don, humanist, and pamphleteer. Their correspondence shows that both men were interested in theories of poetry and in experiments in quantitative versification in English; it also shows that Spenser had ambitious plans as a poet.

After receiving the degree of A. B. in 1573 and A. M. in 1576, Spenser served as personal secretary and aide to several prominent men, including Dr. John Young, bishop of Rochester, and the earl of Leicester, the queen's favorite. During his employment in Leicester's household he came to know

Sir Philip Sidney and his friend Sir Edward Dyer, courtiers who sought to promote a new English poetry. Spenser's contribution to the movement is *The Shepheardes Calender*, published in 1579 and dedicated to Sidney.

In the *Shepheardes Calender* Spenser used a deliberately archaic language, partly out of homage to Chaucer, whom he identified as Tityrus, "Who taught me homely, as I can, to make"; but Spenser also used this language to achieve a rustic effect. Sidney did not approve; in his *Defence of Poesy* he wrote, "*The Shepheardes Calender* hath much poetry in his Eclogues, indeed worthy the reading, if I be not deceived. That same framing of his style to an old rustic language I dare not allow, since neither Theocritus in Greek, Virgil in Latin, nor Sannazaro in Italian did affect it." Another classical purist, Ben Jonson, growled that Spenser "writ no language," but that he would have him read nevertheless for his matter. Now, however, we can recognize that Spenser's skillful use of many verse forms and his extraordinary musical effects did much to inaugurate the "new poetry" of the Elizabethan age.

There are thirteen different meters in *The Shepheardes Calender*. Some of these Spenser invented, some he adapted, but most of them were novel; only three or four were at all common in 1579. Spenser was a prolific experimenter who went on to make further innovations in his later poems: the special rhyme scheme of the Spenserian sonnet, the remarkably beautiful adaptation of the Italian *canzone* forms for the *Epithalamion* and *Prothalamion*, and the nine-line stanza of *The Faerie Queene*, with its extraordinary six-foot line at the end, are the best known. Spenser is sometimes called the "poet's poet" because so many later English poets learned the art of versification from him. In the nineteenth century alone his influence may be seen in Shelley's *Revolt of Islam*, Byron's *Childe Harold's Pilgrimage*, Keats's *Eve of St. Agnes*, and Tennyson's *The Lotos-Eaters*.

The year after the publication of *The Shepheardes Calender* Spenser went to Ireland as secretary and aide to Lord Grey of Wilton, Lord Deputy of Ireland. He spent the rest of his life there holding various minor government posts, except for two visits to England. He was at work on his great romantic epic, *The Faerie Queene*, when Sir Walter Ralegh visited him at Kilcolman Castle; the result was a trip to England and the publication, in 1590, of the first three books of *The Faerie Queene*. Soon after, he published a volume of poems called *Complaints*; a pastoral called *Colin Clouts Come Home Againe* (1595), commenting on the courtiers and ladies at the center of English court life at the time of his visit in 1590; the sonnet cycle *Amoretti*; and two marriage poems, *Epithalamion* and *Prothalamion*. But he completed only six of his projected twelve books of *The Faerie Queene*. The six-book *Faerie Queene* was published in 1596, with some revisions in the first part and a changed ending to book 3, to provide a bridge to the added books; the so-called "Mutability Cantos" first appeared in the edition of 1609.

In the second half of the decade, Ireland was torn by revolt and civil war; Spenser's castle was destroyed, and the poet was sent to England with messages from the besieged garrison in Ireland. He died in Westminster on January 13, 1599, and was buried near his beloved Chaucer in what is now called the Poets' Corner of Westminster Abbey.

Spenser is a complex genius who cannot be put into neatly labeled categories. He was strongly influenced by Renaissance Neoplatonism, but was also earthy and practical. He is a lover and celebrator of physical beauty yet also sternly moral. His is not a repressive morality, however, but an attitude based upon his understanding of right action and of the temptations that entrap people as they try to achieve such action. Spenser was strongly influenced by Puritanism in his early days, remained a thoroughgoing Protestant all his life, and portrayed the Roman Catholic Church as a villain in *The Faerie Queene*; yet his understanding of faith and of sin owes much to the great Catholic thinkers. He is profoundly English and patriotic; in him nationality and religion were inextricably joined. He is in some ways a backward-looking poet who paid homage to Chaucer, used archaic language, and compared his own age unfavorably to the antique world. Yet as Christian humanist, British epic poet, and poet-prophet he points to the future directions of poetry, especially the poetry of Milton—who himself paid homage to Spenser as "a better teacher than Scotus or Aquinas."

Since it was a deliberate choice on Spenser's part that his language should seem antique, Spenser's poetry is here printed in the original spelling and punctuation; a few of the most confusing punctuation marks have however been altered in the present text, Spenser also spells words in such a way as to suggest rhymes to the eye, or to suggest etymologies (often incorrect ones). This inconsistency in his spelling is typical of his time; in the sixteenth century people even, from time to time, varied the spelling of their own names.

The Shepheardes Calender

The twelve eclogues of the *Shepheardes Calender* are titled for the months of the year. Each is prefaced by an illustrative woodcut representing the characters or theme of the poem and picturing the appropriate sign of the zodiac for that month in the clouds above. The eclogue was a classical form practiced by Virgil and others; it presents, usually in dialogue between shepherds, the moods and feelings and attitudes of the simple, rural life. But often the eclogue criticizes the world as it is by measuring it against the idealized pastoral world, so that, in Spenser as in other Renaissance poets, the eclogue at times becomes a didactic or satirical comment on contemporary affairs. The eclogues of the *Calender* are divided by its commentator, "E. K.," into three groups—plaintive, recreative, and moral. *Aprill* is the finest of the recreative eclogues: it includes Hobbinol's rendering of Colin's elegantly artful pastoral song praising Elisa, Queen of Shepherds (Queen Elizabeth). Of the moral eclogues, the final and climactic one is *October*, which deals with the problem of poetry and the responsibility of the poet in the modern world—an important theme of the whole *Calender*, and one which Milton later explores in *Lycidas*.

From The Shepheardes Calender

To His Booke

Goe little booke:[1] thy selfe present,
As child whose parent is unkent:°   *unknown*
To him that is the president°   *pattern*

1. A deliberate echo of Chaucer's line, "Go, litel bok, go litel myn tragedye" (*Troilus and Criseyde* 5.1786).

Of noblesse and of chevalree,
5   And if that Envie barke at thee,
    As sure it will, for succoure flee
      Under the shadow of his wing,[2]
    And askèd, who thee forth did bring,
    A shepheards swaine saye did thee sing,
10 All as his straying flocke he fedde:
    And when his honor has thee redde,°   *seen*
    Crave pardon for my hardyhedde.°   *boldness*
      But if that any aske thy name,
    Say thou wert base° begot with blame: *lowly*
15 For thy[3] thereof thou takest shame.
    And when thou art past jeopardee,
    Come tell me, what was sayd of mee:
    And I will send more after thee.
              IMMERITO.[4]

Aprill[1]

Aegloga Quarta[2]

ARGUMENT

    This Aeglogue is purposely intended to the honor and prayse of our most gracious sovereigne, Queene Elizabeth. The speakers herein be

2. I.e., the protective sponsorship of Sir Philip Sidney.
3. Therefore.
4. Unworthy.
1. When *The Shepheardes Calender* was published in 1579, each of the 12 eclogues was followed by a "Glosse," which contained explications of difficult or archaic words, together with learned discussions of—and disagreements with—Spenser's ideas, imagery, and poetics. The glosses are by one "E. K.," whom some scholars identify with one of Spenser's friends, others with Spenser himself. E. K.'s editorial apparatus is usually published along with the poems. In these notes, the editors have incorporated the glosses that are especially useful to the modern reader; they are marked [E. K.]. The original spelling is retained.
2. Fourth Eclogue. An eclogue ("aeglogue") is a short pastoral poem in the form of a dialogue or soliloquy. Spenser's spelling is based on a false etymology (*aix*-goat + *logos*-speech), signifying, according to E. K., "Goteheards tales." The illustration portrays Colin Clout (the Shepherd persona assumed by Spenser) piping a song of Elizabeth, shown with the ladies of her court. The shepherds Thenot and Hobbinol are in the background, and the astrological sign for April, Taurus the bull, is at the top of the picture.

Hobbinoll and Thenot, two shepheardes: the which Hobbinoll being
before mentioned, greatly to have loved Colin, is here set forth more
largely, complayning him of that boyes great misadventure in Love,
whereby his mynd was alienate and with drawen not onely from him,
who moste loved him, but also from all former delightes and studies,
aswell in pleasaunt pyping, as conning[3] ryming and singing, and other
his laudable exercises. Whereby he taketh occasion, for proofe of his
more excellencie and skill in poetrie, to recorde a songe, which the sayd
Colin sometime made in honor of her Majestie, whom abruptely[4] he
termeth Elysa.

THENOT   HOBBINOLL

Tell me good Hobbinoll, what garres thee greete?[5]
What? hath some Wolfe thy tender Lambes ytorne?
Or is thy Bagpype broke, that soundes so sweete?
Or art thou of thy lovèd lasse forlorne°?   *forsaken*

5 Or bene thine eyes attempred to the yeare,[6]
Quenching the gasping furrowes thirst with rayne?
Like April shoure, so stremes the trickling teares
Adowne thy cheeke, to quenche thy thirstye° payne.   *thirsty*

HOBBINOLL

Nor thys, nor that, so muche doeth make me mourne,
10 But for the ladde,[7] whome long I lovd so deare,
Nowe loves a lasse,[8] that all his love doth scorne:
He plongd in payne, his tressèd° locks dooth teare.   *curled*

Shepheards delights he dooth them all forsweare,
Hys pleasaunt Pipe, whych made us meriment,
15 He wylfully hath broke, and doth forbeare
His wonted songs, wherein he all outwent.[9]

THENOT

What is he for a Ladde,[1] you so lament?
Ys love such pinching payne to them, that prove?
And hath he skill to make[2] so excellent,
20 Yet hath so little skill to brydle love?

HOBBINOLL

Colin thou kenst,° the Southerne shepheardes boye: *knowest*
Him Love hath wounded with a deadly darte.

---

3. Learning.
4. With a sudden change.
5. "Causeth thee weepe and complain" [E. K.]
6. "Agreeable to the season of the yeare, that is
Aprill, which moneth is most bent to shoures and
seasonable rayne: to quench . . . the drought" [E.
K.]. "Bene": are.

7. "Colin Clout" [E. K.]; "for": that.
8. "Rosalinda" [E. K.].
9. His usual songs, which surpassed those of all
others.
1. "What maner of Ladde is he?" [E. K.].
2. "To rime and versifye" [E. K.]. "Maker" is the
Greek word for "poet."

Whilome° on him was all my care and joye,   *once*
Forcing° with gyfts to winne his wanton heart.   *striving*

25   But now from me hys madding° mynd is   *foolish*
         starte,°   *broken away*
     And woes the Widdowes daughter of the glenne:[3]
     So nowe fayre Rosalind hath bredde° hys smart,   *caused*
     So now his frend is chaungèd for a frenne.°   *stranger*

THENOT

     But if hys ditties bene so trimly dight,[4]
30   I pray thee Hobbinoll, recorde° some one: *sing*
     The whiles our flockes doe graze about in sight,
     And we close shrowded in thys shade alone.

HOBBINOLL

     Contented I: then will I singe his laye°   *song*
     Of fayre Elisa, Queene of shepheardes all:[5]
35   Which once he made, as by a spring he laye,
     And tunèd it unto the Waters fall.

     "Ye dayntye Nymphs, that in this blessèd Brooke
         doe bathe your brest,
     For sake your watry bowres, and hether looke,
40   at my request:
     And eke you Virgins, that on Parnasse dwell,
     Whence floweth Helicon the learnèd well,[6]
         Helpe me to blaze[7]
         Her worthy praise,
45   Which in her sexe doth all excell.

     "Of fayre Elisa be your silver song,
         that blessèd wight:°   *being*
     The flowre of Virgins, may shee florish long,
         In princely plight.°   *condition*
50   For shee is Syrinx daughter without spotte,
     Which *Pan* the shepheards God of her begot:[8]

---

3. "He calleth Rosalind the Widowes daughter of the glenne, that is, of a country Hamlet or borough, which I thinke is rather sayde to concele the person, then simply spoken. For it is well knowne . . . that shee is a Gentle woman of no meane house" [E. K.]. "Woes": woos.
4. "Adorned" [E. K.].
5. "In all this songe is not to be respected, what the worthinesse of her Majestie deserveth, nor what to the highnes of a Prince is agreeable, but what is moste comely for the meanesse of a shepheards witte, or to conceive, or to utter" [E. K.].
6. "The nine Muses, daughters of Apollo and Memorie, whose abode the Poets faine to be on

Parnassus, a hill in Grece" [E. K.]. According to Spenser and E. K., Helicon is a well or spring at the foot of Parnassus, but in fact it is a mountain itself sacred to the Muses.
7. A blason was a poem cataloguing and praising a lady's various physical features.
8. "Syrinx is the name of a Nymphe of Arcadie, whom when Pan being in love pursued. . . . By Pan is here meant the most famous and victorious King, her highnesse Father, late of worthy memorye K. Henry the eyght" [E. K.]. "Without spotte" qualifies Syrinx, not daughter, a covert repudiation of the scandals surrounding Anne Boleyn.

So sprong° her grace   *sprung*
    Of heavenly race,
No mortall blemishe may her blotte.

55 "See, where she sits upon the grassie greene,
    (O seemely° sight)   *pleasing*
Yclad in Scarlot like a mayden Queene,
    And Ermines white.
Upon her head a Cremosin° coronet,   *crimson*
60 With Damaske roses and Daffadillies set:
    Bayleaves betweene,
    And Primroses greene
Embellish[9] the sweete Violet.

"Tell me, have ye seene her angelick face,
65   Like Phoebe fayre?[1]
Her heavenly haveour,° her princely grace   *bearing*
    can you well compare?
The Redde rose medled with the White yfere,[2]
In either cheeke depeincten° lively chere.   *depict*
70   Her modest eye,
    Her Majestie,
Where have you seene the like, but there?

"I sawe Phoebus thrust out his golden hedde,
    upon her to gaze:
75 But when he sawe, how broade her beames did spredde,
    it did him amaze.
He blusht to see another Sunne belowe,
Ne durst againe his fyrye face out showe:[3]
    Let him, if he dare,
80   His brightnesse compare
With hers, to have the overthrowe.[4]

"Shewe thy selfe Cynthia[5] with thy silver rayes,
    and be not abasht:
When shee the beames of her beauty displayes,
85   O how art thou dasht?
But I will not match her with *Latonaes* seede,
Such follie great sorow to Niobe did breede.[6]
    Now she is a stone,

9. "Beautifye and set out" [E. K.], i.e., by contrast of colors.
1. "The Moone, whom the Poets faine to be sister
unto Phoebus, that is the Sunne" [E. K.].
2. "Together" [E. K.]. "Medled": mingled. Elizabeth, like her father Henry VIII, descends from
both the houses of Lancaster and of York (symbolized, respectively, by the red and the white rose),
whose conflicting claims to the throne caused the

Hundred Years' War.
3. Show abroad.
4. Be overthrown.
5. "The Moone" [E. K.].
6. When Niobe vaunted herself above Latona by
reason of her seven sons and seven daughters, the
goddess caused her two children, Apollo and Diana,
to slay Niobe's entire progeny, after which her sorrow transformed her to stone.

And makes dayly mone,
90   Warning all other to take heede.

"Pan may be proud, that ever he begot
     such a Bellibone,[7]
And Syrinx rejoyse, that ever was her lot
     to beare such an one.
95   Soone as my younglings cryen for the dam,
To her will I offer a milkwhite Lamb:
     Shee is my goddesse plaine,°   *absolute*
     And I her shepherds swayne,°   *servant*
Albee forswonck and forswatt I am.[8]

100 "I see Calliope[9] speede her to the place,
     where my Goddesse shines:
And after her the other Muses trace,°   *step*
     with their Violines.
Bene° they not Bay braunches,[1] which they doe beare,   *are*
105 All for Elisa in her hand to weare?
     So sweetely they play,
     And sing all the way,
That it a heaven is to heare.

"Lo how finely the graces[2] can it foote
110   to the Instrument:
They dauncen deffly,° and singen soote,°   *nimbly/sweet*
     in their meriment.
Wants not a fourth grace, to make the daunce even?
Let that rowme° to my Lady be yeven:°   *place/given*
115   She shalbe a grace,
          To fyll the fourth place,
And reigne with the rest in heaven.

"And whither rennes° this bevie° of Ladies bright,   *runs/company*
     raungèd in a rowe?
120 They bene all Ladyes of the lake[3] behight,
     that unto her goe.
Chloris,[4] that is the chiefest Nymph of al,
Of Olive braunches beares a Coronall:°   *crown*
     Olives bene° for peace,   *are*
125   When wars doe surcease:
Such for a Princesse bene principall.°   *princely*

---

7. A *belle bonne*: "homely spoken for a fayre mayde or Bonilasse" [E. K.].
8. "Overlaboured and sunneburnt" [E. K.].
9. The muse of epic poetry.
1. "Be the signe of honor and victory . . . and eke [also] of famous Poets" [E. K.].
2. "Be three sisters, the daughters of Jupiter, whose names are Aglaia, Thalia, Euphrosyne . . . whom

the Poetes feyned to be Goddesses of al bountie and comelines" [E. K.]. "Foote": dance.
3. Nymphs. E. K. records the ancient view that every spring and fountain had a goddess as its soveraign. "Behight": called.
4. According to E. K., the nymph of flowers and green herbs; her name signifies greenness.

"Ye shepheards daughters, that dwell on the greene,
    hye° you there apace:°   *come/quickly*
Let none come there, but that Virgins bene,
130   to adorne her grace.
And when you come, whereas shee is in place,
See, that your rudenesse doe not you disgrace:
    Binde your fillets° faste,   *hair ribbons*
    And gird in your waste,°   *waist*
135 For more finesse, with a tawdrie lace.[5]

"Bring hether the Pincke and purple Cullambine,
    With Gelliflowres:
Bring Coronations, and Sops in wine,
    worne of Paramoures.°   *lovers*
140 Strowe me the ground with Daffadowndillies,
And Cowslips, and Kingcups, and lovèd Lillies:
    The pretie° Pawnce,   *pretty*
    And the Chevisaunce,[6]
Shall match with the fayre flowre Delice.

145 "Now ryse up Elisa,[7] deckèd as thou art,
    in royall aray:
And now ye daintie Damsells may depart
    echeone° her way.   *each one*
I feare, I have troubled your troupes to° longe: *too*
150 Let dame Eliza thanke you for her song.
    And if you come hether,
    When Damsines° I gether,   *plums*
I will part them all you among."[8]

THENOT

And was thilk° same song of Colins owne making?   *this*
155 Ah foolish boy, that is with love yblent:°   *blinded*
Great pittie is, he be in such taking,°   *plight*
For naught caren, that bene so lewdly bent.[9]

HOBBINOLL

Sicker° I hold him, for a greater fon,°   *surely/fool*
That loves the thing, he cannot purchase.
160 But let us homeward: for night draweth on,
And twincling starres the daylight hence chase.

---

5. I.e., to present a finer appearance, with a band of lace bought at the fair of St. Audrey (Etheldreda).
6. All these are names of flowers common in pastoral poetry. "Coronations" are carnations; "sops in wine" are clove pinks; "paunce," the pansy; "daffadowndillies," daffodils; "flowre Delice (fleur de lis)," a kind of iris; "chevisaunce" may be a species of wallflower.
7. "Is the conclusion. For having so decked her with prayses and comparisons, he returneth all the thanck of hys laboure to the excellencie of her Majestie" [E. K.].
8. Among you all.
9. I.e., for they that are so foolishly inclined are heedless of everything.

Thenots Embleme[1]
O quam te memorem virgo?
Hobbinolls Embleme
O dea certe.

October

Aegloga decima[1]

ARGUMENT

In Cuddie[2] is set out the perfecte paterne of a Poete, which finding no maintenaunce of his state and studies, complayneth of the comtempte of Poetrie, and the causes thereof: Specially having bene in all ages, and even amongst the most barbarous alwayes of singular accounpt[3] and honor, and being indede so worthy and commendable an arte: or rather no arte, but a divine gift and heavenly instinct not to bee gotten by laboure and learning, but adorned with both: and poured into the witte by a certaine *enthousiasmòs*[4] and celestiall inspiration, as the Author hereof els where at large discourseth, in his booke called the English Poete, which booke being lately come to my hands, I mynde[5] also by Gods grace upon further advisement to publish.

1. An "embleme" is a motto or relevant quotation. Both emblems are from *Aeneid* 1.327–8, in which Aeneas is overwhelmed by the appearance of Venus in the guise of one of Diana's maidens and cries out: "By what name should I call thee, O maiden? . . . O goddess surely." E. K. notes that Hobbinoll and Thenot are similarly struck with amazement by the "divine" Elizabeth.

1. Tenth Eclogue. E. K. identifies as sources Theocritus' *Idyl 16*, which reproves the tyrant Hiero of Syracuse for his neglect of poets, and also Baptista Spagnuoli, called Mantuan [the fifth eclogue]. The illustration portrays Cuddie (left) holding a pipe and crowned with a laurel wreath (emblems of a poet). He talks with his fellow shepherd, Piers, in a pastoral landscape, with the court in the background. The astrological sign for October, Scorpio (the scorpion) is at the top of the picture.

2. E. K. queries "whether by Cuddie be specified the authour selfe, or some other," noting that in *August* he was introduced as singing a song of Colin's making. It may be that Cuddie and Piers present different aspects of Spenser the poet.

3. Esteem.

4. Inspiration. The Greek word originally meant "possessed by a god." The *English Poete* is evidently a lost work by Spenser.

5. Intend.

PIERCE   CUDDIE

Cuddie, for shame hold up thy heavye head,
    And let us cast with what delight to chace,
    And weary thys long lingring Phoebus race.[6]
Whilome° thou wont the shepheards laddes to leade,   *once*
5   In rymes, in ridles, and in bydding base:[7]
Now they in thee, and thou in sleepe art dead.

CUDDIE

Piers, I have pypèd erst° so long with payne,°   *up to now/care*
That all mine Oten reedes[8] bene rent and wore:
And my poore Muse hath spent her sparèd store,
10   Yet little good hath got, and much lesse gayne.
Such pleasaunce makes the Grashopper so poore,
And ligge so layd,[9] when Winter doth her straine.

The dapper° ditties, that I wont devise,   *pretty*
To feede youthes fancie, and the flocking fry,[1]
15   Delighten much: what I the bett for thy?[2]
They han° the pleasure, I a sclender prise.   *have*
I beate the bush, the byrds to them doe flye:
What good thereof to Cuddie can arise?

PIERS

Cuddie, the prayse is better, then the price,
20   The glory eke° much greater then the gayne: *also*
O what an honor is it, to restraine
    The lust of lawlesse youth with good advice:[3]
Or pricke° them forth with pleasaunce of   *spur*
        thy vaine,°   *poetic vein*
Whereto thou list their traynèd° willes entice.   *ensnared*

25   Soone as thou gynst to sette thy notes in frame,
O how the rurall routes° to thee doe cleave: *crowds*
Seemeth thou dost their soule of sence bereave,[4]
All as the shepheard, that did fetch his dame

---

6. I.e., let us see how we may pass this long day
pleasantly.
7. A popular game, here, probably a poetry contest.
8. The shepherd's pipe, symbol of pastoral poetry.
9. I.e., lie so subdued. The reference is to the fable
of the industrious ant who laid up supplies for winter, and the carefree grasshopper who did not.
"Straine": constrain.
1. Newly-spawned fish. E. K. terms this a "bold

metaphor."
2. I.e., How am I the better for that?
3. E. K. compares these lines with *De Legibus*,
book 1, in which Plato declares "that the first
invention of Poetry, was of very vertuous intent."
4. I.e., hypnotize them. E. K. cites Plato and
Pythagoras for the theory that the mind is made of
"a certaine harmonie and musicall nombers" and
gives several examples of music's irresistable power
over the emotions.

From Plutoes balefull bowre withouten leave:
His musicks might the hellish hound did tame.[5]

30

CUDDIE

So praysen babes the Peacoks spotted traine,
And wondren at bright Argus blazing eye:[6]
But who rewards him ere the more for thy?
Or feedes him once the fuller by a graine?
Sike° prayse is smoke, that sheddeth° in the   *such/is dispersed*
    skye,
Sike words bene wynd, and wasten soone in vayne.

35

PIERS

Abandon then the base and viler clowne,°   *rustic*
Lyft up thy selfe out of the lowly dust:
And sing of bloody Mars, of wars, of giusts.°   *jousts*
Turne thee to those, that weld° the awful crowne,   *bear*
To doubted Knights, whose woundlesse[7] armour rusts,
And helmes unbruzed wexen dayly browne.

40

There may thy Muse display her fluttryng wing,
And stretch her selfe at large from East to West:[8]
Whither thou list in fayre Elisa rest,
Or if thee please in bigger notes to sing,
Advaunce° the worthy whome shee loveth best,   *extol*
That first the white beare to the stake did bring.[9]

45

And when the stubborne stroke of stronger stounds,°   *efforts*
Has somewhat slackt[1] the tenor of thy string:
Of love and lustihead° tho mayst thou sing,   *pleasure*
And carrol lowde, and leade the Myllers rownde,[2]
All were Elisa one of thilke same ring.
So mought our Cuddies name to Heaven sownde.

50

---

5. "Orpheus: of whom is sayd, that by his excellent skil in Musick and Poetry, he recovered his wife Eurydice from hell" [E. K.], that is, from "Plutoes balefull bowre."
6. E. K. recounts the myth of Argus of the 100 eyes, set by Juno to guard Io, Jupiter's paramour, but lulled asleep by Mercury's music and then killed. Juno placed his eyes in the tail of her bird, the peacock, whose splendor elicits the praises even of "babes." "For thy": therefore.
7. "Unwounded in warre, doe rust through long peace" [E. K.]. "Doubted": dreaded.
8. E. K. explains this "poeticall metaphore" as indicating the heroic subjects available to Cuddie

if he wishes to "showe his skill in matter of more dignitie, then is the homely Aeglogue." These include "our most gratious soveraign whom (as before) he calleth Elisa" and also the "noble and valiaunt men" who deserve his praise and have been his patrons.
9. "He meaneth (as I guesse) the most honorable and renowmed the Erle of Leycester" [E. K.]. Leicester's device was the bear and ragged staff.
1. "That is when thou chaungest thy verse from stately discourse, to matter of more pleasaunce and delight" [E. K.].
2. "A kind of daunce" [E. K.]. "Ring": a "company of dauncers" [E. K.]. "All": although.

CUDDIE

55   Indeede the Romish Tityrus,[3] I heare,
  Through his Mecaenas left his Oaten reede,
  Whereon he earst° had taught his flocks to feede,   *before*
  And laboured lands to yield the timely eare,
  And eft° did sing of warres and deadly drede,°   *after/danger*
60   So as the Heavens did quake his verse to here.[4]

  But ah Mecaenas is yclad in claye,
  And great Augustus long ygoe is dead:
  And all the worthies liggen° wrapt in leade,   *lie*
  That matter made for Poets on to play:
65   For ever, who in derring doe were dreade,°   *held in awe*
  The loftie verse of hem was lovèd aye.[5]

  But after vertue gan for age to stoupe,
  And mighty manhode brought a bedde of ease:[6]
  The vaunting Poets found nought worth a pease,°   *pea*
70   To put in preace[7] among the learnèd troupe.
  Tho° gan the streames of flowing wittes to cease,   *then*
  And sonnebright honour pend in shamefull coupe.°   *cage*

  And if that any buddes of Poesie,
  Yet of the old stocke gan to shoote agayne:
75   Or° it mens follies mote° be forst to fayne,   *either/must*
  And rolle with rest in rymes of rybaudrye:°   *ribaldry*
  Or as it sprong, it wither must agayne:
  Tom Piper makes us better melodie.[8]

PIERS

  O pierlesse Poesye, where is then thy place?
80   If nor in Princes pallace thou doe sitt:
  (And yet is Princes pallace the most fitt)
  Ne brest of baser birth[9] doth thee embrace.
  Then make thee winges of thine aspyring wit,
  And, whence thou camst, flye backe to heaven apace.

3. "Well knowen to be Virgile, who by Mecaenas means was brought into the favour of the Emperor Augustus, and by him moved to write in loftier kinde, then he erst had doen." [E. K.]. Maecenas ("Mecaenas") was Virgil's patron.
4. "In these three verses are the three severall workes of Virgile intended. For in teaching his flocks to feede, is meant his Aeglogues. In labouring of lands, is hys Georgiques. In singing of wars and deadly dreade, is his divine Aeneis figured" [E. K.].
5. "He sheweth the cause, why Poetes were wont be had in such honor of noble men; that is, that by them their worthines and valor shold through

theyr famous Posies be commended to al posterities" [E. K.]. "Derring-doe": "In manhoode and chevalrie" [E. K.].
6. "He sheweth the cause of contempt of Poetry to be idlenesse and basenesse of mynd" [E. K.].
7. Put in practice, exercise. I.e., poets found nothing worthy to write of, and the spirit of heroic achievement (sun-bright honor) found expression neither in deeds nor in song.
8. "An Ironicall Sarcasmus, spoken in derision of these rude wits, whych make more account of a ryming rybaud, then of skill grounded upon learning and judgment" [E. K.].
9. "The meaner sort of men" [E. K.].

CUDDIE

85 Ah Percy it is all to weake and wanne,
    So high to sore,° and make so large a flight: *soar*
    Her peecèd pyneons bene not so in plight,
    For Colin fittes such famous flight to scanne:[1]
    He, were he not with love so ill bedight,°   *furnished*
90 Would mount as high, and sing as soote as Swanne.[2]

PIERS

    Ah fon,° for love does teach him climbe so hie,   *fool*
    And lyftes him up out of the loathsome myre:
    Such immortall mirrhor,[3] as he doth admire,
    Would rayse ones mynd above the starry skie.
95 And cause a caytive corage[4] to aspire,
    For lofty love doth loath a lowly eye.

CUDDIE

    All otherwise the state of Poet stands,
    For lordly love is such a Tyranne fell:°   *fierce*
    That where he rules, all power he doth expell.
100 The vaunted verse a vacant head demaundes,
    Ne wont with crabbèd care the Muses dwell:
    Unwisely weaves, that takes two webbes in hand.[5]

    Who ever casts° to compasse° weightye prise,   *tries/attain*
    And thinks to throwe out thondring words of threate:
105 Let powre in lavish cups and thriftie bitts of meate,
    For Bacchus fruite is frend to Phoebus wise.[6]
    And when with Wine the braine begins to sweate,
    The nombers flowe as fast as spring doth ryse.

    Thou kenst° not Percie howe the ryme should rage.   *knowest*
110 O if my temples were distaind° with wine,   *stained*
    And girt in girlonds of wild Yvie twine,[7]
    How I could reare the Muse on stately stage,
    And teache her tread aloft in buskin[8] fine,
    With queint Bellona in her equipage.°   *retinue*

1. Cuddie explains that the imperfect, patched wings ("peeced pyneons") of his own poetic powers are not in condition, but that it is proper for ("fittes") Colin to attempt ("scanne") such a high poetic flight.
2. "It is sayd of the learned that the swan a little before hir death, singeth most pleasantly" [E. K.]. "Soote": sweet.
3. "Beauty, which is an excellent object of Poeticall spirites" [E. K.].
4. "A base and abject minde" [E. K.].
5. I.e., the Muses are not accustomed ("wont") to dwell with those afflicted by love ("crabbed care"); he is an unwise weaver who takes two pieces of cloth ("webbes") in hand at once.
6. I.e., let him pour lavish drink and nourishing ("thriftie") food, for wine ("Bacchus fruit") promotes poetry ("Phoebus wise" is god of poetry.)
7. "He seemeth here to be ravished with a Poetical furie. For (if one rightly mark) the numbers rise so ful, and the verse groweth so big, that it seemeth he hath forgot the meanenesse of shepheards state and stile." "Wild Yvie": worn by followers of Bacchus.
8. A boot worn by the actors in tragedies, hence, a symbol for tragedy. "Queint *Bellona*": "strange Bellona; the goddesse of battaile, that is Pallas" [E. K.].

115   But ah my corage cooles ere it be warme,
        For thy, content us in thys humble shade:
        Where no such troublous tydes° han us   *seasons/assaulted*
              assayde,°
        Here we our slender pipes may safely charme.[9]

                              PIERS

        And when my Gates shall han their bellies layd:[1]
120   *Cuddie* shall have a Kidde to store his farme.

                         Cuddies Embleme

                   Agitante calescimus illo &c.[2]

                                                              1579

The Faerie Queene
Spenser's exuberant, multifaceted poem is peculiarly characteristic of its age. In some respects it is a "courtesy book," like Castiglione's *Courtier*, intended to "fashion a gentleman or noble person" by exhibiting the qualities such a person should have. The six books which Spenser completed (of the projected twelve) exhibit the virtues of Holiness, Temperance, Chastity, Friendship, Justice, and Courtesy. A fragment of another book, the cantos on Mutability (the principle of constant change in nature), also survives.

In other respects *The Faerie Queene* is a romantic epic, like Ariosto's *Orlando Furioso* ("Orlando Mad," 1516), full of adventures and marvels, dragons, witches, enchanted trees, giants, jousting knights, and castles. As such it fulfills the expectation that a romance will produce wonder, that it will enthrall us with its intricate plots, amazing episodes, heroic characters, elaborate descriptions. It also fulfills the common Elizabethan expectation that poetry should teach by delighting.

The poem is also an allegory like Tasso's *Gerusalemme Liberata* ("Jerusalem Delivered," 1575), as Spenser's preliminary letter to Sir Walter Ralegh indicates. That letter invites us to interpret the characters and adventures in the several books in terms of particular virtues and vices: e.g., the Redcrosse Knight in book 1 is the knight of Holiness (and also St. George, the patron saint of England); Sir Guyon in book 2 is the knight of Temperance; and the female knight Britomart in book 3 is the knight of Chastity (in her, chaste love leading toward marriage). However, far from being static embodiments of their respective virtues, each advances in the understanding and practice of the virtue in question in the course of his or her book. By the same token the meaning of the various characters, episodes, and places is dense and complex, and is revealed to us only by degrees as we read and interpret the poem. In addition, persistent allusions to many personages and

9. "Temper and order" [E. K.].
1. I.e., when my goats bear their young.
2. The Latin line, of which Spenser gives the first three words here, is from Ovid, *Fasti* 6.5: "There is a god within us; it is from his stirring that we feel warm." E. K. comments, "Hereby is meant, as

also in the whole course of this Aeglogue, that Poetry is a divine instinct and unnatural rage passing the reache of comen reason. Whom Piers answereth Epiphonematicos [by way of summary] as admiring the excellencye of the skyll whereof in Cuddie hee hadde alreadye hadde a taste."

events in Spenser's own England lead us to recognize that the poem incorporates historical allegory. The poem may be enjoyed as a fascinating story with multiple meanings. It works on several levels at once, inviting the reader to move as the story moves, taking the meaning at whatever level seems most viable at the moment.

The introductory lines of the poem are intended to remind the reader of Virgil, who began his poetic career with pastoral poetry and moved on to the epic, as Spenser did in moving from the *Shepheardes Calender* to the *Faerie Queene*. The organization of each book into twelve cantos also imitates the twelve books of Virgil's *Aeneid*. But Spenser replaces Virgil's theme of epic heroism, "Arms and the man," with something more romantic— "Fierce warres and faithfull loves." The scenery too is romantic: plains and forests and caves and castles and magical trees and springs, where one meets dwarfs and giants and lions and pilgrims and magicians and Saracens or "paynims" (with French names). In Spenser's Faerie Land, if you are going somewhere you just start out, and after many adventures, get there. A clear, pleasant stream may be dangerous to drink because it produces loss of strength. Any stranger you meet may well be a villain and may be in disguise. Houses, castles, and gardens are often places of education or of especially dense allegorical significance, affording special keys to the meaning of the books in which they appear.

The Faerie Queene's subjects in Faeryland are called Faeries or Elves. They are human beings, and undergo the trials and tribulations people undergo in the ordinary world. But Faerie Land is also inhabited by knights who are not Faeries but Britons—Redcrosse, Britomart, and Prince Arthur (who loves and seeks for the Faerie Queene throughout the poem). The bad creatures, people and monsters, represent various vices, evils, and temptations. Spenser's characters, both good and evil, may be initially identified to the reader by their names or by the short verse summaries at the beginning of each canto, but their natures are revealed progressively, in the course of the narrative. Some of Spenser's characters are identified by conventional symbols and attributes which would be obvious to every reader of his time. For example, such a reader would know immediately that a woman who wears a miter and scarlet clothes, and who dwells near the river Tiber, represents (in one sense at least) the Roman Catholic Church, which had often been identified by Protestant preachers with the Whore of Babylon in the Book of Revelation.

The various books are composed on different structural principles. Book 1 is almost entirely self-contained: it has been called a miniature epic in itself, centering upon the adventures of one principal hero, Redcrosse, who at length achieves the quest he undertakes at Una's behest—killing the dragon who has imprisoned her parents, and winning her as his bride. The spiritual allegory is similarly self-contained: it presents the Christian struggling heroically against many evils—error, hypocrisy, the seven deadly sins, despair— but succumbing to some of them, shows him separated from the one true faith and, aided by many interventions of divine grace, at length reunited with it once more; and treats his purgation from sin, his education in the House of Holiness, and his final salvation. By contrast, the structure of book 3 is romance-like, with its many heroines and heroes (who present, allegorically, several varieties of chaste and unchaste love); its interwoven stories (Amoret and Scudamore, Belphoebe and Timias, Florimell and Marinell as well as Britomart and Arthegall); and its lack of closure—for the adventures of all these characters extend into books 4 and 5.

The Faerie Queene draws constantly upon the riches of literary and pictorial traditions. Entire episodes are adopted from the Italian romantic epics of Ariosto and Tasso, and either through them or independently, from Homer, Virgil, or Ovid. (In the Renaissance, borrowing from and reworking older materials was praiseworthy in a poet.) Places, such as Lucifera's castle or the Garden of Adonis; individual attributes such as Una's lamb or Speranza's anchor or Britomart's spear; and even certain names or colors come to Spenser from the classics, from theologians, from liturgical tradition, from folk tales and pageants, from tapestries, paintings, and emblem books. Our notes point to some of these sources—but more important is the understanding that these were living traditions for Spenser and his readers. They flow together, separate, and recombine to produce the uniquely Spenserian delights of the Faerie Queene.

From THE FAERIE QUEENE

A Letter of the Authors

EXPOUNDING HIS WHOLE INTENTION IN THE COURSE OF THIS WORKE: WHICH FOR THAT IT GIVETH GREAT LIGHT TO THE READER, FOR THE BETTER UNDERSTANDING IS HEREUNTO ANNEXED

To the Right noble, and Valorous, Sir Walter Raleigh knight, Lo. Wardein of the Stanneryes, and her Majesties liefetenaunt of the County of Cornewayll

Sir knowing how doubtfully all Allegories may be construed, and this booke of mine, which I have entituled the *Faery Queene*, being a continued Allegory, or darke conceit,[1] I have thought good as well for avoyding of gealous opinions and misconstructions, as also for your better light in reading thereof, (being so by you commanded,) to discover unto you the general intention and meaning, which in the whole course thereof I have fashioned, without expressing of any particular purposes or by-accidents[2] therein occasioned. The generall end therefore of all the booke is to fashion[3] a gentleman or noble person in vertuous and gentle[4] discipline: Which for that I conceived shoulde be most plausible and pleasing, being coloured with an historicall fiction, the which the most part of men delight to read, rather for variety of matter, then for profite of the ensample:[5] I chose the historye of King Arthure, as most fitte for the excellency of his person, being made famous by many mens former workes, and also furthest from the daunger of envy, and suspition of present time.[6] In which I have followed all the antique Poets historicall, first Homere, who in the Persons of Agamemnon and Ulysses hath

1. Poetic figure.
2. Secondary matters.
3. I.e., to represent, to educate.
4. Pertaining to a gentleman.
5. Example.
6. I.e., free from current political controversy.

ensampled a good governour and a vertuous man, the one in his *Ilias*, the other in his *Odysseis*: then Virgil, whose like intention was to doe in the person of Aeneas: after him Ariosto comprised them both in his Orlando: and lately Tasso dissevered them againe, and formed both parts in two persons, namely that part which they in Philosophy call Ethice, or vertues of a private man, coloured in his Rinaldo: The other named Politice in his Godfredo.[7] By ensample of which excellente Poets, I labour to pourtraict in Arthure, before he was king, the image of a brave knight, perfected in the twelve private morall vertues, as Aristotle hath devised,[8] the which is the purpose of these first twelve bookes: which if I finde to be well accepted, I may be perhaps encouraged, to frame the other part of polliticke vertues in his person, after that hee came to be king. To some I know this Methode will seeme displeasaunt, which had rather have good discipline delivered plainly in way of precepts, or sermoned at large, as they use, then thus clowdily enwrapped in Allegoricall devises. But such, me seeme, should be satisfide with the use of these dayes, seeing all things accounted by their showes,[9] and nothing esteemed of, that is not delightfull and pleasing to commune sence.[1] For this cause is Xenophon preferred before Plato, for that the one in the exquisite depth of his judgment, formed a Commune welth[2] such as it should be, but the other in the person of Cyrus and the Persians fashioned a governement such as might best be: So much more profitable and gratious is doctrine by ensample, then by rule. So have I laboured to doe in the person of Arthure: whome I conceive after his long education by Timon, to whom he was by Merlin delivered to be brought up, so soone as he was borne of the Lady Igrayne, to have seene in a dream or vision the Faery Queen, with whose excellent beauty ravished, he awaking resolved to seeke her out, and so being by Merlin armed, and by Timon throughly instructed, he went to seeke her forth in Faerye land. In that Faery Queene I meane glory in my generall intention, but in my particular I conceive the most excellent and glorious person of our soveraine the Queene, and her kingdome in Faery land. And yet in some places els, I doe otherwise shadow[3] her. For considering she beareth two persons, the one of a most royall Queene or Empresse, the other of a most vertuous and beautifull Lady, this latter part in some places I doe express in Belphoebe, fashioning her name according to your owne excellent conceipt of Cynthia,[4] (Phoebe and Cynthia being both names of Diana.) So in the person of Prince Arthure I sette forth magnificence in particular, which vertue for that (according to Aristotle and the rest) it is the

---

7. Lodovico Ariosto (1474–1533) was author of the epic-romance *Orlando Furioso*, first published in complete form in 1532. Torquato Tasso (1544–1595) published his chivalric romance *Rinaldo* in 1562 and the epic *Gerusalemme Liberata* (centered on the heroic figure of Count Godfredo) in 1581.

8. Aristotle did not devise 12 private moral virtues: Spenser was in fact relying upon more modern philosophers—his friend Lodowick Bryskett and the Italian Piccolomini. That Spenser actually planned a poem 4 times as long as the 6 books we now have rather staggers the imagination.

9. Appearances.

1. The notions of the many.

2. The allusion is to Plato's *Republic* and Xenophon's *Cyropaedia*.

3. Picture, portray.

4. Ralegh's poem *Cynthia* praised Queen Elizabeth.

perfection of all the rest, and conteineth in it them all, therefore in the
whole course I mention the deedes of Arthure applyable to that vertue,
which I write of in that booke. But of the xii. other vertues, I make xii.
other knights the patrones, for the more variety of the history. Of which
these three bookes contayn three, The first of the knight of the Redcrosse, in whome I expresse Holynes: The seconde of Sir Guyon, in
whome I sette forth Temperaunce: The third of Britomartis a Lady knight,
in whome I picture Chastity. But because the beginning of the whole
worke seemeth abrupte and as depending upon other antecedents, it
needs that ye know the occasion of these three knights severall adventures. For the Methode of a Poet historical is not such, as of an Historiographer.[5] For an Historiographer discourseth of affayres orderly as
they were donne, accounting as well the times as the actions, but a Poet
thrusteth into the middest, even where it most concerneth him, and
there recoursing to the thinges forepaste,[6] and divining of thinges to
come, maketh a pleasing Analysis of all. The beginning therefore of my
history, if it were to be told by an Historiographer, should be the twelfth
booke, which is the last, where I devise that the Faery Queene kept her
Annuall feaste xii. dayes, uppon which xii. severall dayes, the occasions
of the xii. severall adventures hapned, which being undertaken by xii.
severall knights, are in these xii books severally handled and discoursed.
The first was this. In the beginning of the feaste, there presented him
selfe a tall clownishe[7] younge man, who falling before the Queen of
Faeries desired a boone (as the manner then was) which during that feast
she might not refuse: which was that hee might have the atchievement
of any adventure, which during that feaste should happen, that being
graunted, he rested him on the floore, unfitte through his rusticity for a
better place. Soone after entred a faire Ladye in mourning weedes, riding on a white Asse, with a dwarfe behind her leading a warlike steed,
that bore the Armes of a knight, and his speare in the dwarfes hand.
Shee falling before the Queene of Faeries, complayned that her father
and mother an ancient King and Queene, had bene by an huge dragon
many years shut up in a brasen Castle, who thence suffred them not to
yssew:[8] and therefore besought the Faery Queene to assygne her some
one of her knights to take on him that exployt. Presently that clownish
person upstarting, desired that adventure: whereat the Queene much
wondering, and the Lady much gainesaying, yet he earnestly importuned his desire. In the end the Lady told him that unlesse that armour
which she brought, would serve him (that is the armour of a Christian
man specified by Saint Paul v. Ephes.[9]) that he could not succeed in
that enterprise, which being forthwith put upon him with dewe furnitures[1]
thereunto, he seemed the goodliest man in al that company, and was

5. Historian.
6. Past.
7. Rustic-looking.
8. Come forth.
9. Ephesians 6.13–17 itemizes the "whole armor
of God" as follows: loins girt about with truth;

breastplate of righteousness; feet shod with the gospel of peace; shield of faith "wherewith ye shall be
able to quench all the fiery darts of the wicked";
helmet of salvation; and "sword of the Spirit, which
is the word of God."
1. Suitable equipment.

well liked of the Lady. And eftesoones taking on him knighthood, and mounting on that straunge Courser, he went forth with her on that adventure: where beginneth the first booke, vz.

> A gentle knight was pricking on the playne. &c.

The second day ther came in a Palmer bearing an Infant with bloody hands, whose Parents he complained to have bene slayn by an Enchaunteresse called Acrasia: and therfore craved of the Faery Queene, to appoint him some knight, to performe that adventure, which being assigned to Sir Guyon, he presently went forth with that same Palmer: which is the beginning of the second booke and the whole subject thereof. The third day there came in, a Groome who complained before the Faery Queene, that a vile Enchaunter called Busirane had in hand a most faire Lady called Amoretta, whom he kept in most grievous torment, because she would not yield him the pleasure of her body. Whereupon Sir Scudamour the lover of that Lady presently tooke on him that adventure. But being unable to performe it by reason of the hard Enchauntments, after long sorrow, in the end met with Britomartis, who succoured him, and reskewed his love.

But by occasion hereof, many other adventures are intermedled, but rather as Accidents, then intendments.[2] As the love of Britomart, the overthrow of Marinell, the misery of Florimell, the vertuousnes of Belphoebe, the lasciviousnes of Hellenora, and many the like.

Thus much Sir, I have briefly overronne to direct your understanding to the wel-head of the History, that from thence gathering the whole intention of the conceit,[3] ye may as in a handfull gripe al the discourse, which otherwise may happily[4] seeme tedious and confused. So humbly craving the continuaunce of your honorable favour towards me, and th' eternall establishment of your happines, I humbly take leave.

23. January, 1589
Yours most humbly affectionate.
ED. SPENSER.

The First Booke of the Faerie Queene

Contayning
The Legende of the
Knight of the Red Crosse,
or
of Holinesse

1

Lo I the man, whose Muse whilome did maske,
    As time her taught, in lowly Shepheards weeds,[1]

---

2. I.e., there are episodes that are not part of these principal stories.
3. Conception.
4. By chance.
1. I.e., behold me, the poet who appropriately appeared before ("whilome") as a writer of humble pastoral (i.e., *The Shepheardes Calender*). These lines are imitated from the verses prefixed to Renaissance editions of Virgil's *Aeneid*. "Weeds:" garb.

Am now enforst a far unfitter taske,
For trumpets sterne to chaunge mine Oaten reeds,[2]
5   And sing of Knights and Ladies gentle° deeds;   *noble*
Whose prayses having slept in silence long,[3]
Me, all too meane, the sacred Muse areeds°   *appoints*
To blazon° broad emongst her learned throng: *proclaim*
Fierce warres and faithfull loves shall moralize my song.

                                      2
10   Helpe then, O holy Virgin chiefe of nine,[4]
Thy weaker Novice to performe thy will,
Lay forth out of thine everlasting scryne[5]
The antique rolles, which there lye hidden still,
Of Faerie knights and fairest Tanaquill,[6]
15   Whom that most noble Briton Prince[7] so long
Sought through the world, and suffered so much ill,
That I must rue his undeservèd wrong:
O helpe thou my weake wit, and sharpen my dull tong.

                                      3
And thou most dreaded impe[8] of highest Jove,
20   Faire Venus sonne, that with thy cruell dart
At that good knight so cunningly didst rove,°   *shoot*
That glorious fire it kindled in his hart,
Lay now thy deadly Heben° bow apart,   *ebony*
And with thy mother milde come to mine ayde:
25   Come both, and with you bring triumphant Mart,[9]
In loves and gentle jollities arrayd,
After his murdrous spoiles and bloudy rage allayd.

                                      4
And with them eke,° O Goddesse heavenly bright,   *also*
Mirrour of grace and Majestie divine,
30   Great Lady of the greatest Isle, whose light
Like Phoebus lampe throughout the world doth shine,
Shed thy faire beames into my feeble eyne,
And raise my thoughts too humble and too vile,°   *lowly*
To thinke of that true glorious type[1] of thine,
35   The argument of mine afflicted stile:
The which to heare, vouchsafe, O dearest dred[2] a-while.

Canto 1

The Patron of true Holinesse,
Foule Errour doth defeate:
Hypocrisie him to entrappe,
Doth to his home entreate.

2. To write heroic poetry, of which the trumpet is
a symbol, instead of pastoral poetry symbolized by
the humble shepherd's pipe ("Oaten reeds").
3. Lines 5 and 6 are imitated from the opening
lines of Ariosto's *Orlando Furioso.*
4. Clio, the muse of history. "Weaker": too weak.
5. A chest for papers.

6. I.e., Gloriana.
7. I.e., Arthur, named in canto 9, line 50.
8. Child, i.e., Cupid.
9. Mars, god of war and lover of Venus.
1. I.e., Gloriana is the "type" (foreshadowing) of
Queen Elizabeth.
2. Object of awe.

1

A Gentle Knight was pricking° on the plaine,   *cantering*
   Ycladd in mightie armes and silver shielde,
   Wherein old dints of deepe wounds did remaine,
   The cruell markes of many a bloudy fielde;
5   Yet armes till that time did he never wield:[3]
   His angry steede did chide his foming bitt,
   As much disdayning to the curbe to yield:
   Full jolly° knight he seemd, and faire did sitt,   *gallant*
As one for knightly giusts° and fierce encounters   *tourneys, jousts*
   fitt.

2

10 But on his brest a bloudie Crosse he bore,
   The deare remembrance of his dying Lord,
   For whose sweete sake that glorious badge he wore,
   And dead as living ever him adored:
   Upon his shield the like was also scored,
15 For soveraine[4] hope, which in his helpe he had:
   Right faithfull true[5] he was in deede and word,
   But of his cheere[6] did seeme too solemne sad;°   *grave*
Yet nothing did he dread, but ever was ydrad.°   *dreaded, feared*

3

Upon a great adventure he was bond,
20   That greatest Gloriana to him gave,
   That greatest Glorious Queene of Faerie Lond,
   To winne him worship,° and her grace to have,   *honor*
   Which of all earthly things he most did crave;
   And ever as he rode, his hart did earne°   *yearn*
25 To prove his puissance in battell brave
   Upon his foe, and his new force to learne;
Upon his foe, a Dragon horrible and stearne.

4

A lovely Ladie rode him faire beside,
   Upon a lowly Asse more white then snow,
30 Yet she much whiter, but the same did hide
   Under a vele, that wimpled° was full low,   *lying in folds*
   And over all a blacke stole she did throw,
   As one that inly mournd: so was she sad,
   And heavie sat upon her palfrey slow:
35 Seemèd in heart some hidden care she had,
And by her in a line a milke white lambe she lad.

5

So pure an innocent, as that same lambe,
   She was in life and every vertuous lore,

---

3. Redcrosse wears the armor of the Christian man, as Spenser explained in the letter to Ralegh: "put on the whole armor of God, that ye may be able to stand against the wiles of the devil" (Ephesians 6.10–22). The armor bears the dents of every Christian's fight against evil; Redcrosse himself is as yet untried.

4. Having greatest power (often applied to medical remedies).

5. An echo of Revelation 19.11: "And I saw heaven opened; and behold a white horse; and he that sat upon him was called Faithful and True. . . ."

6. Facial expression, mood.

And by descent from Royall lynage came
40   Of ancient Kings and Queenes, that had of yore
    Their scepters stretcht from East to Westerne shore,
    And all the world in their subjection held;
    Till that infernall feend with foule uprore
    Forwasted° all their land, and them expeld: *laid waste*
45 Whom to avenge, she had this Knight from far compeld.°   *summoned*

6

Behind her farre away a Dwarfe did lag,
    That lasie seemd in being ever last,
    Or wearied with bearing of her bag
    Of needments at his backe. Thus as they past,
50   The day with cloudes was suddeine overcast,
    And angry Jove an hideous storme of raine
    Did poure into his Lemans[7] lap so fast,
    That every wight° to shrowd° it did constrain,   *creature/cover*
And this faire couple eke° to shroud themselves were fain.° *also/forced*

7

55 Enforst to seeke some covert nigh at hand,
    A shadie grove not far away they spide,
    That promist ayde the tempest to withstand:
    Whose loftie trees yclad with sommers pride,
    Did spred so broad, that heavens light did hide,
60   Not perceable° with power of any starre: *penetrable*
    And all within were pathes and alleies wide,
    With footing worne, and leading inward farre:
Faire harbour that them seemes; so in they entred arre.

8

And foorth they passe, with pleasure forward led,
65   Joying to heare the birdes sweete harmony,
    Which therein shrouded from the tempest dred,°   *fearful*
    Seemd in their song to scorne the cruell sky.
    Much can° they prayse the trees, so straight and hy,   *did*
    The sayling Pine, the Cedar proud and tall,
70   The vine-prop Elme, the Poplar never dry,
    The builder Oake, sole king of forrests all,
The Aspine good for staves, the Cypresse funerall.

9

The Laurell, meed° of mightie Conquerours   *reward*
    And Poets sage, the Firre that weepeth still,
75   The Willow worne of forlorne Paramours,
    The Eugh° obedient to the benders will,   *yew*
    The Birch for shaftes, the Sallow° for the mill,   *willow*
    The Mirrhe sweete bleeding in the bitter wound,
    The warlike Beech, the Ash for nothing ill,
80   The fruitfull Olive, and the Platane° round,   *plane-tree*
The carver Holme, the Maple seeldom inward sound.[8]

---

7. His lover, i.e., the earth.
8. In these lines, Spenser has been imitating Chaucer's catalogue of trees in the *Parliament of*

Fowls; the convention goes back to Ovid. The oak is used in building; the cypress is used to dress graves; the holly ("holm") is suitable for carving.

10

Led with delight, they thus beguile the way,
 Untill the blustring storme is overblowne;
 When weening° to returne, whence they did stray,   *supposing*
85 They cannot finde that path, which first was showne,
 But wander too and fro in wayes unknowne,
 Furthest from end then, when they neerest weene,
 That makes them doubt, their wits be not their owne:
 So many pathes, so many turnings seene,
90 That which of them to take, in diverse doubt they been.

11

At last resolving forward still to fare,
 Till that some end they finde or° in or out,   *either*
 That path they take, that beaten seemed most bare,
 Which when by tract[9] they hunted had throughout,
95 And like to lead the labyrinth about;°   *out of*
 At length it brought them to a hollow cave,
 Amid the thickest woods. The Champion stout
 Eftsoones° dismounted from his courser brave,   *forthwith*
And to the Dwarfe a while his needlesse spere[1] he gave.

12

100 "Be well aware,"° quoth then that Ladie milde,   *watchful*
 "Least suddaine mischiefe° ye too rash provoke: *misfortune*
 The danger hid, the place unknowne and wilde,
 Breedes dreadfull doubts: Oft fire is without smoke,
 And perill without show: therefore your stroke
105 Sir knight with-hold, till further triall made."
 "Ah Ladie," said he, "shame were to revoke°   *draw back*
 The forward footing for° an hidden shade: *because of*
Vertue gives her selfe light, through darkenesse for to wade."

13

"Yea but," quoth she, "the perill of this place
110 I better wot then[2] you, though now too late
 To wish you backe returne with foule disgrace,
 Yet wisedome warnes, whilest foot is in the gate,
 To stay the stepe, ere forcèd to retrate.
 This is the wandring wood, this Errours den,
115 A monster vile, whom God and man does hate:
 Therefore I read° beware." "Fly fly," quoth then   *advise*
The fearefull Dwarfe: "this is no place for living men."

14

But full of fire and greedy hardiment,°   *boldness*
 The youthfull knight could not for ought° be staide,   *anything*
120 But forth unto the darksome hole he went,
 And lookèd in: his glistring° armor made   *shining*
 A litle glooming light, much like a shade,
 By which he saw the ugly monster plaine,

9. By following the track.
1. "Needlesse" because the spear is used only on

horseback.
2. Know than.

Halfe like a serpent horribly displaide,[3]
125 But th' other halfe did womans shape retaine,
Most lothsom, filthie, foule, and full of vile
    disdaine.°   *loathsomeness*

15

And as she lay upon the durtie ground,
Her huge long taile her den all overspred,
Yet was in knots and many boughtes° upwound,   *coils*
130 Pointed with mortall sting. Of her there bred
A thousand yong ones, which she dayly fed,
Sucking upon her poisonous dugs, eachone
Of sundry shapes, yet all ill favorèd:
Soone as that uncouth° light upon them shone,   *unfamiliar*
135 Into her mouth they crept, and suddain all were gone.

16

Their dam upstart, out of her den effraide,°   *alarmed*
And rushèd forth, hurling her hideous taile
About her cursèd head, whose folds displaid°   *extended*
Were stretcht now forth at length without
140   entraile.°   *winding, coiling*
She lookt about, and seeing one in mayle
Armèd to point,[4] sought backe to turne againe;
For light she hated as the deadly bale,°   *evil*
Ay wont in desert darknesse to remain,
145 Where plaine none might her see, nor she see any plaine.

17

Which when the valiant Elfe[5] perceived, he lept
As Lyon fierce upon the flying pray,
And with his trenchand° blade her boldly kept   *cutting*
From turning backe, and forcèd her to stay:
150 Therewith enraged she loudly gan to bray,
And turning fierce, her speckled taile advaunst,
Threatning her angry sting, him to dismay:°   *defeat*
Who nough° aghast, his mightie hand enhaunst:°   *now/lifted up*
The stroke down from her head unto her shoulder glaunst.

18

Much daunted with that dint,° her sence was dazd,   *blow*
155 Yet kindling rage, her selfe she gathered round,
And all attonce her beastly body raizd
With doubled forces high above the ground:
Tho° wrapping up her wrethèd sterne arownd,   *then*
Lept fierce upon his shield, and her huge traine°   *tail*
160 All suddenly about his body wound,
That hand or foot to stirre he strove in vaine:
God helpe the man so wrapt in Errours endlesse traine.

---

3. That Error (or doctrinal heresy) is half serpent
reminds us of the primal error in Eden, which the
serpent instigated. The description echoes both
classical and biblical monsters (cf. Revelation 9.7–

10).
4. I.e., completely.
5. Knight of Faerie Land.

19

His Lady sad to see his sore constraint,°   *fettered state*
 Cride out, "Now now Sir knight, shew what ye bee,
165 Add faith unto your force, and be not faint:
 Strangle her, else she sure will strangle thee."
 That when he heard, in great perplexitie,° *entangled state*
 His gall did grate for griefe° and high disdaine, *wrath*
 And knitting all his force got one hand free,
170 Wherewith he grypt her gorge° with so great paine, *neck*
That soone to loose her wicked bands did her constraine.

20

Therewith she spewd out of her filthy maw
 A floud of poyson horrible and blacke,
 Full of great lumpes of flesh and gobbets raw,
175 Which stunck so vildly, that it forst him slacke
 His grasping hold, and from her turne him backe:
 Her vomit full of bookes and papers was,[6]
 With loathly frogs and toades, which eyes did lacke,
 And creeping sought way in the weedy gras:
180 Her filthy parbreake° all the place defilèd has.[7] *vomit*

21

As when old father Nilus gins to swell
 With timely° pride above the Aegyptian vale, *in season*
 His fattie° waves do fertile slime outwell,   *rich*
 And overflow each plaine and lowly dale:
185 But when his later spring gins to avale,°   *subside*
 Huge heapes of mudd he leaves, wherein there breed
 Ten thousand kindes of creatures, partly male
 And partly female of his fruitfull seed;
Such ugly monstrous shapes elswhere may no man reed.° *see*

22

190 The same so sore annoyèd has the knight,
 That welnigh chokèd with the deadly stinke,
 His forces faile, ne can no longer fight.
 Whose corage when the feend perceived to shrinke,
 She pourèd forth out of her hellish sinke
195 Her fruitfull cursèd spawne of serpents small,
 Deformèd monsters, fowle, and blacke as inke,
 Which swarming all about his legs did crall,
And him encombred sore, but could not hurt at all.

23

As gentle Shepheard in sweete even-tide,
200 When ruddy Phoebus gins to welke° in west, *sink*
 High on an hill, his flocke to vewen wide,

6. This alludes to books and pamphlets of Catholic propaganda, notably attacks on Queen Elizabeth in 1588.
7. Revelation 16.13: "And I saw three unclean spirits like frogs come out of the mouth of the dragon, and out of the mouth of the beast, and out of the mouth of the false prophet."

Markes° which do byte their hasty supper best;   *observes*
A cloud of combrous° gnattes do him molest,   *encumbering*
All striving to infixe their feeble stings,
205   That from their noyance he no where can rest,
But with his clownish° hands their tender wings   *rustic*
He brusheth oft, and oft doth mar their murmurings.

24

Thus ill bestedd,° and fearful more of shame,   *situated*
Then of the certaine perill he stood in,
210   Halfe furious unto his foe he came,
Resolved in minde all suddenly to win,
Or soone to lose, before he once would lin;°   *cease, stop*
And strooke at her with more then manly force,
That from her body full of filthie sin
215   He raft° her hatefull head without remorse;   *cut away*
A streame of cole black bloud forth gushèd from her corse.

25

Her scattred brood, soone as their Parent deare
They saw so rudely° falling to the ground,   *with great force*
Groning full deadly, all with troublous feare,
220   Gathred themselves about her body round,
Weening° their wonted entrance to have found   *thinking*
At her wide mouth: but being there withstood
They flockèd all about her bleeding wound,
And suckèd up their dying mothers blood,
225 Making her death their life, and eke her hurt their good.   *also*

26

That detestable sight him much amazde,°   *stunned*
To see th' unkindly Impes[8] of heaven accurst,
Devoure their dam; on whom while so he gazd,
Having all satisfide their bloudy thurst,
230   Their bellies swolne he saw with fulnesse burst,
And bowels gushing forth: well worthy end
Of such as drunke her life, the which them nurst;
Now needeth him no lenger labour spend,
His foes have slaine themselves, with whom he should contend.

27

235 His Ladie seeing all, that chaunst, from farre
Approcht in hast to greet° his victorie,   *congratulate*
And said, "Faire knight, borne under happy starre,
Who see your vanquisht foes before you lye;
Well worthy be you of that Armorie,[9]
240   Wherein ye have great glory wonne this day,
And prooved your strength on a strong enimie,
Your first adventure: many such I pray,
And henceforth ever wish, that like succeed it may."

---

8. Unnatural offspring.   9. I.e., Christian armor.

28

Then mounted he upon his Steede againe,
245   And with the Lady backward sought to wend;°   *go*
       That path he kept, which beaten was most plaine,
       Ne ever would to any by-way bend,
       But still did follow one unto the end,
       The which at last out of the wood them brought.
250   So forward on his way (with God to frend[1])
       He passèd forth, and new adventure sought;
Long way he travelèd, before he heard of ought.

29

At length they chaunst to meet upon the way
       An aged Sire, in long blacke weedes yclad,[2]
255   His feete all bare, his beard all hoarie gray,
       And by his belt his booke he hanging had;
       Sober he seemde, and very sagely sad,°   *pensive*
       And to the ground his eyes were lowly bent,
       Simple in shew, and voyde of malice bad,
260   And all the way he prayèd, as he went,
And often knockt his brest, as one that did repent.

30

He faire the knight saluted, louting° low,   *bowing*
       Who faire him quited,° as that courteous was: *answered*
       And after askèd him, if he did know
265   Of straunge adventures, which abroad did pas.
       "Ah my deare Sonne," quoth he, "how should, alas,
       Silly° old man, that lives in hidden cell,   *simple*
       Bidding° his beades all day for his trespas,   *telling*
       Tydings of warre and worldly trouble tell?
270 With holy father sits not with such things to mell.[3]

31

       "But if of daunger which hereby doth dwell,
       And homebred evill ye desire to heare,
       Of a straunge man I can you tidings tell,
       That wasteth all this countrey farre and neare."
275   "Of such," said he, "I chiefly do inquere,
       And shall you well reward to shew the place,
       In which that wicked wight his dayes doth weare.°   *spend*
       For to all knighthood it is foule disgrace,
That such a cursed creature lives so long a space."

32

280 "Far hence," quoth he, "in wastfull° wildernesse   *desolate*
       His dwelling is, by which no living wight
       May ever passe, but thorough great distresse."
       "Now," sayd the Lady, "draweth toward night,
       And well I wote, that of your later° fight   *recent*

1. With God as friend.   3. I.e., it is not fitting for a holy hermit to meddle
2. Dressed in long black garments.   ("mell") with such things.

285   Ye all forwearied be: for what so strong,
        But wanting rest will also want of might?
        The Sunne that measures heaven all day long,
        At night doth baite° his steedes the Ocean waves emong.   *feed, refresh*

                              33

        "Then with the Sunne take Sir, your timely rest,
290   And with new day new worke at once begin:
        Untroubled night they say gives counsell best."
        "Right well Sir knight ye have advisèd bin,"
        Quoth then that aged man; "the way to win
        Is wisely to advise:° now day is spent;   *take thought*
295   Therefore with me ye may take up your In°   *lodging*
        For this same night." The knight was well content.
        So with that godly father to his home they went.

                              34

        A little lowly Hermitage it was,
        Downe in a dale, hard by a forests side,
300   Far from resort of people, that did pas
        In travell to and froe: a little wyde°   *apart*
        There was an holy Chappell edifyde,°   *built*
        Wherein the Hermite dewly wont° to say   *was wont*
        His holy things° each morne and eventyde: *prayers*
305   Thereby a Christall streame did gently play,
        Which from a sacred fountaine wellèd forth alway.

                              35

        Arrivèd there, the little house they fill,
        Ne looke for entertainement, where none was:
        Rest is their feast, and all things at their will;
310   The noblest mind the best contentment has.
        With faire discourse the evening so they pas:
        For that old man of pleasing wordes had store,
        And well could file° his tongue as smooth as glas;   *polish*
        He told of Saintes and Popes, and evermore
315   He strowd an *Ave-Mary* after and before.

                              36

        The drouping Night thus creepeth on them fast,
        And the sad humour[4] loading their eye liddes,
        As messenger of Morpheus[5] on them cast
        Sweet slombring deaw, the which to sleepe them biddes.
320   Unto their lodgings then his guestes he riddes:°   *leads*
        Where when all drownd in deadly sleepe[6] he findes,
        He to his study goes, and there amiddes
        His Magick bookes and artes of sundry kindes,
        He seekes out mighty charmes, to trouble sleepy mindes.

                              37

325   Then choosing out few wordes most horrible
        (Let none them read), thereof did verses frame,

---

4. Heavy moisture.   6. Sleep like death.
5. The god of sleep.

With which and other spelles like terrible,
He bade awake blacke Plutoes griesly Dame,[7]
And cursèd heaven, and spake reprochfull shame
330   Of highest God, the Lord of life and light;
A bold bad man, that dared to call by name
Great Gorgon[8], Prince of darknesse and dead night,
At which Cocytus quakes, and Styx is put to flight.

38

And forth he cald out of deepe darknesse dred
335   Legions of Sprights, the which like little flyes[9]
Fluttring about his ever damnèd hed,
A-waite whereto their service he applyes,
To aide his friends, or fray° his enimies: *frighten*
Of those he chose out two, the falsest twoo,
340   And fittest for to forge true-seeming lyes;
The one of them he gave a message too,
The other by him selfe staide other worke to doo.

39

He making speedy way through spersèd° ayre,   *dispersed*
And through the world of waters wide and deepe,
345   To Morpheus house doth hastily repaire.
Amid the bowels of the earth full steepe,
And low, where dawning day doth never peepe,
His dwelling is; there Tethys[1] his wet bed
Doth ever wash, and Cynthia[2] still doth steepe
350   In silver deaw his ever-drouping hed,
Whiles sad° Night over him her mantle black doth spred.   *sober*

40

Whose double gates he findeth lockèd fast,
The one faire framed of burnisht Yvory,
The other all with silver overcast;
355   And wakefull dogges before them farre do lye,
Watching to banish Care their enimy,
Who oft is wont° to trouble gentle Sleepe.   *accustomed to*
By them the Sprite doth passe in quietly,
And unto Morpheus comes, whom drownèd deepe
360 In drowsie fit he findes: of nothing he takes keepe.°   *notice*

41

And more, to lulle him in his slumber soft,
A trickling streame from high rocke tumbling downe
And ever-drizling raine upon the loft,
Mixt with a murmuring winde, much like the sowne°   *sound*
365   Of swarming Bees, did cast him in a swowne:°   *faint*
No other noyse, nor peoples troublous cryes,
As still° are wont t'annoy the wallèd towne,   *always*

---

7. I.e., Proserpine, as patron of witchcraft.
8. Demogorgon, in some myths the progenitor of
all the gods, so powerful that the mention of his
name causes hell's rivers (Styx and Cocytus) to
tremble.

9. The simile associates him with Beelzebub (Lord
of Flies).
1. The wife of Ocean.
2. I.e., Diana, the goddess of the moon. "Still":
continually.

Might there be heard: but carelesse° Quiet lyes,   *free from care*
Wrapt in eternall silence farre from enemyes.[3]

42

370 The messenger approching to him spake,
    But his wast° wordes returnd to him in vaine: *wasted*
    So sound he slept, that nought mought° him awake.   *might*
    Then rudely he him thrust, and pusht with paine,°   *effort*
    Whereat he gan to stretch: but he againe
375   Shooke him so hard, that forced him to speake.
    As one then in a dreame, whose dryer braine[4]
    Is tost with troubled sights and fancies° weake,   *fantasies*
He mumbled soft, but would not all his silence breake.

43

The Sprite then gan more boldly him to wake,
380   And threatned unto him the dreaded name
    Of Hecate:[5] whereat he gan to quake,
    And lifting up his lumpish head, with blame
    Halfe angry askèd him, for what[6] he came.
    "Hither," quoth he, "me Archimago[7] sent,
385   He that the stubborne Sprites can wisely tame,
    He bids thee to him send for his intent
A fit false dreame, that can delude the sleepers sent."°   *senses*

44

The God obayde, and calling forth straight way
    A diverse° dreame out of his prison darke,   *misleading*
390   Delivered it to him, and downe did lay
    His heavie head, devoide of carefull carke,[8]
    Whose sences all were straight benumbd and starke.
    He backe returning by the Yvorie dore,[9]
    Remounted up as light as chearefull Larke,
395   And on his litle winges the dreame he bore
In hast unto his Lord, where he him left afore.

45

Who all this while with charmes and hidden artes,
    Had made a Lady of that other Spright,
    And framed of liquid ayre her tender partes
400   So lively,° and so like in all mens sight,   *lifelike*
    That weaker° sence it could have ravisht quight   *too weak*
    The maker selfe for all his wondrous witt,
    Was nigh beguilèd with so goodly sight:
    Her all in white he clad, and over it
405 Cast a blacke stole, most like to seeme for Una[1] fit.

---

3. Spenser is imitating descriptions of the house of Morpheus in Chaucer, Ovid, and other ancient writers.
4. According to the old physiology, old people and other light sleepers had too little moisture in the brain.
5. Queen of Hades.
6. Why.
7. Archmagician or chief deceiver; also, *archimago*, architect of images.

8. Anxious concerns.
9. False dreams came through the ivory door, true dreams through the gate of horn (Homer, *Odyssey* 19.562–67; Virgil, *Aeneid* 6.893–96).
1. Her name means "one, unity." Elizabethan readers would know the Latin *Una Vera Fides* (one true faith) and also the proverb, "Truth is one." She is named now, when her false double is introduced.

46

Now when that ydle dreame was to him brought
    Unto that Elfin knight he bad him fly,
    Where he slept soundly void of evill thought
    And with false shewes abuse his fantasy,°   *imagination*
410   In sort as[2] he him schoolèd privily:
    And that new creature borne without her dew[3]
    Full of the makers guile, with usage sly
    He taught to imitate that Lady trew,
Whose semblance she did carrie under feignèd hew.°   *form*

47

415 Thus well instructed, to their worke they hast
    And comming where the knight in slomber lay
    The one upon his hardy head him plast,°   *placed*
    And made him dreame of loves and lustfull play
    That nigh his manly hart did melt away,
420   Bathèd in wanton blis and wicked joy:
    Then seemèd him his Lady by him lay,
    And to him playnd,° how that false wingèd boy[4]   *complained*
Her chast hart had subdewd, to learne Dame pleasures toy.

48

And she her selfe of beautie soveraigne Queene
425   Faire Venus seemde unto his bed to bring
    Her, whom he waking evermore did weene°   *think*
    To be the chastest flowre, that ay° did spring   *ever*
    On earthly braunch, the daughter of a king,
    Now a loose Leman° to vile service bound: *paramour*
430   And eke the Graces seemèd all to sing,
    Hymen iô Hymen, dauncing all around,
Whilst freshest Flora her with Yvie girlond crownd.[5]

49

In this great passion of unwonted° lust,   *unaccustomed*
    Or wonted feare of doing ought amis,
435   He started up, as seeming to mistrust°   *suspect*
    Some secret ill, or hidden foe of his:
    Lo there before his face his Lady is,
    Under blake stole hyding her bayted hooke,
    And as halfe blushing offred him to kis,
440   With gentle blandishment and lovely° looke,   *loving*
Most like that virgin true, which for her knight him took.

50

All cleane dismayd to see so uncouth° sight,   *unseemly*
    And halfe enragèd at her shamelesse guise,
    He thought have slaine her in his fierce despight:°   *indignation*
445   But hasty heat tempring with sufferance wise,

---

2. In the way.
3. Unnaturally.
4. Cupid.
5. The three graces of classical mythology were personifications of grace and beauty; here they sing a call to the pleasures of the marriage bed (Hymen was god of marriage). On Flora, cf. E. K.'s gloss to the March eclogue: "the Goddesse of flowres, but indede (as saith Tacitus) a famous harlot."

He stayde his hand, and gan himselfe advise
To prove his sense, and tempt° her faignèd truth.   test
Wringing her hands in wemens pitteous wise,
Tho can she[6] weepe, to stirre up gentle ruth,°   pity
450   Both for her noble bloud, and for her tender youth.

51

And said, "Ah Sir, my liege Lord and my love,
Shall I accuse the hidden cruell fate,
And mightie causes wrought in heaven above,
Or the blind God, that doth me thus amate,°   dismay
455   For° hopèd love to winne me certaine hate?   instead of
Yet thus perforce° he bids me do, or die.   forcibly
Die is my dew[7]: yet rew my wretched state
You, whom my hard avenging destinie
Hath made judge of my life or death indifferently.

52

460   "Your owne deare sake forst me at first to leave
My Fathers kingdome," There she stopt with teares;
Her swollen hart her speach seemd to bereave,
And then againe begun, "My weaker yeares
Captived to fortune and frayle worldly feares,
465   Fly to your faith for succour and sure ayde:
Let me not dye in languor° and long teares.   sorrow
"Why Dame," quoth he, "what hath ye thus dismayd?
What frayes° ye, that were wont to comfort me affrayd?"   frightens

53

"Love of your selfe," she said, "and deare° constraint   dire
470   Lets me not sleepe, but wast the wearie night
In secret anguish and unpittied plaint,
Whiles you in carelesse sleepe are drownèd quight."
Her doubtfull words made that redoubted[8] knight
Suspect her truth: yet since no untruth he knew,
475   Her fawning love with foule disdainefull spight
He would not shend,° but said, "Deare dame I rew,°   reject/pity
That for my sake unknowne such griefe unto you grew.

54

"Assure your selfe, it fell not all to ground;
For all so deare as life is to my hart,
480   I deeme your love, and hold me to you bound;
Ne let vaine feares procure your needlesse smart,
Where cause is none, but to your rest depart."
Not all content, yet seemd she to appease°   cease
Her mournefull plaintes, beguiléd° of her art,   foiled
485   And fed with words, that could not chuse but please,
So slyding softly forth, she turnd° as to her ease.   returned

6. Then she began to.   8. Dreaded, also, doubting again. "Doubtfull":
7. I.e., I deserve to die.   fearful, also questionable.

55

Long after lay he musing at her mood,
    Much grieved to thinke that gentle Dame so light,
    For whose defence he was to shed his blood.
490   At last dull wearinesse of former fight
    Having yrockt a sleepe his irkesome spright,°   *spirit*
    That troublous dreame gan freshly tosse his braine,
    With bowres and beds, and Ladies deare delight:
    But when he[9] saw his labour all was vaine,
495 With that misformèd spright he backe returnd againe.

Canto 2

The guilefull great Enchaunter parts
The Redcrosse Knight from Truth:
Into whose stead faire falshood steps,
And workes him wofull ruth.

1

By this the Northerne wagoner had set
    His seven fold teame behind the stedfast starre,[1]
    That was in Ocean waves yet never wet,
    But firme is fixt, and sendeth light from farre
5   To all, that in the wide deepe wandring arre.
    And chearefull Chaunticlere with his note shrill
    Had warnèd once, that Phoebus fiery carre[2]
    In hast was climbing up the Easterne hill,
Full envious that night so long his roome did fill.

2

10 When those accursèd messengers of hell,
    That feigning dreame, and that faire-forgèd Spright
    Came to their wicked maister, and gan tell
    Their bootelesse° paines, and ill succeeding night: *useless*
    Who all in rage to see his skilfull might
15   Deluded so, gan threaten hellish paine
    And sad Prosèrpines wrath, them to affright.
    But when he saw his threatning was but vaine,
He cast about, and searcht his balefull° of bookes againe.   *deadly*

3

Eftsoones° he tooke that miscreated faire,   *soon after*
20   And that false other Spright, on whom he spred
    A seeming body of the subtile° aire,   *rarefied*
    Like a young Squire, in loves and lusty-hed
    His wanton dayes that ever loosely led,
    Without regard of armes and dreaded fight:
25   Those two he tooke, and in a secret bed,

9. I.e., Archimago.
1. I.e., by this time the Big Dipper had set behind

the North Star.
2. The chariot of the sun.

Covered with darknesse and misdeeming° night,   *misleading*
Them both together laid, to joy in vaine delight.

                              4

Forthwith he runnes with feignèd faithfull hast
    Unto his guest, who after troublous sights
30 And dreames, gan now to take more sound repast,°   *rest*
    Whom suddenly he wakes with fearefull frights,
    As one aghast with feends or damnèd sprights,
    And to him cals, "Rise rise unhappy Swaine,
    That here wex° old in sleepe, whiles wicked wights   *grows*
35 Have knit themselves in Venus shamefull chaine;
Come see, where your false Lady doth her honour staine."

                              5

All in amaze he suddenly up start
    With sword in hand, and with the old man went;
    Who soone him brought into a secret part,
40 Where that false couple were full closely ment°   *mingled*
    In wanton lust and lewd embracèment:
    Which when he saw, he burnt with gealous fire,
    The eye of reason was with rage yblent,°   *blinded*
    And would have slaine them in his furious ire,
45 But hardly° was restreinèd of that aged sire.   *with difficulty*

                              6

Returning to his bed in torment great,
    And bitter anguish of his guiltie sight,
    He could not rest, but did his stout heart eat,
    And wast his inward gall with deepe despight,°   *malice*
50 Yrkesome° of life, and too long lingring night.   *tired*
    At last faire Hesperus[3] in highest skie
    Had spent his lampe, and brought forth dawning light
    Then up he rose, and clad him hastily;
The Dwarfe him brought his steed: so both away do fly.

                              7

55 Now when the rosy-fingred Morning faire,
    Weary of aged Tithones[4] saffron bed,
    Had spred her purple robe through deawy aire,
    And the high hils Titan° discoverèd,°   *the sun/revealed*
    The royall virgin shooke off drowsy-hed,
60 And rising forth out of her baser° bowre,   *humbler*
    Lookt for her knight, who far away was fled,
    And for her Dwarfe, that wont to wait each houre:
Then gan she waile and weepe, to see that woefull stowre.° *affliction*

                              8

And after him she rode with so much speede
65 As her slow beast could make; but all in vaine:
    For him so far had borne his light-foot steede,
    Prickéd with wrath and fiery fierce disdaine,°   *indignation*
    That him to follow was but fruitlesse paine;

3. The evening star.   4. The husband of Aurora, goddess of the dawn.

Yet she her weary limbes would never rest,
70 But every hill and dale, each wood and plaine
Did search, sore grievèd in her gentle brest,
He so ungently left her, whom she lovèd best.

9

But subtill° Archimago, when his guests   *cunning*
He saw divided into double parts,
75 And Una wandring in woods and forrests,
Th' end of his drift,° he praisd his divelish arts   *plot*
That had such might over true meaning harts;
Yet rests not so, but other meanes doth make,
How he may worke unto her further smarts:
80 For her he hated as the hissing snake,
And in her many troubles did most pleasure take.

10

He then devisde himselfe how to disguise;
For by his mightie science° he could take   *knowledge*
As many formes and shapes in seeming wise,°   *in appearance*
85 As ever Proteus to himselfe could make:
Sometime a fowle, sometime a fish in lake,
Now like a foxe, now like a dragon fell,°   *fierce*
That of himselfe he oft for feare would quake,
And oft would flie away. O who can tell
90 The hidden power of herbes, and might of Magicke spell?

11

But now seemde best, the person to put on
Of that good knight, his late beguilèd guest:
In mighty armes he was yclad anon,
And silver shield: upon his coward brest
95 A bloudy crosse, and on his craven crest
A bounch of haires discolourd diversly:°   *variously colored*
Full jolly° knight he seemde, and well addrest,°   *gallant/armed*
And when he sate upon his courser free,
Saint George himself ye would have deemèd him to be.

12

100 But he the knight, whose semblaunt° he did beare,   *likeness*
The true Saint George was wandred far away,
Still flying from° his thoughts and gealous feare;   *because of*
Will was his guide,[5] and griefe led him astray.
At last him chaunst to meete upon the way
105 A faithlesse Sarazin° all armed to point,   *Saracen*
In whose great shield was writ with letters gay
Sans foy:[6] full large of limbe and every joint
He was, and carèd not for God or man a point.[7]

13

He had a faire companion of his way,
110 A goodly Lady clad in scarlot red,

---

5. Will should not be the guide, but should itself   6. Literally, without faith, faithless.
be under the guidance of intelligence or truth.   7. At all.

Purfled with gold and pearle of rich assay,[8]
And like a Persian mitre on her hed
She wore, with crownes and owches° garnishèd,   *brooches*
The which her lavish lovers to her gave;[9]
115   Her wanton° palfrey all was overspred   *unruly*
With tinsell trappings, woven like a wave,
Whose bridle rung with golden bels and bosses brave.[1]

14

With faire disport° and courting dalliaunce   *diversion*
She intertainde her lover all the way:
120   But when she saw the knight his speare advaunce,
She soone left off her mirth and wanton play,
And bad her knight addresse him to the fray:
His foe was nigh at hand. He prickt° with pride   *pranced*
And hope to winne his Ladies heart that day,
125   Forth spurrèd fast: adowne his coursers side
The red bloud trickling staind the way, as he did ride.

15

The knight of the Redcrosse when him he spide,
Spurring so hote with rage dispiteous,°   *cruel*
Gan fairely couch° his speare, and towards ride: *lower*
130   Soone meete they both, both fell and furious,
That daunted with their forces hideous,
Their steeds do stagger, and amazèd stand,
And eke° themselves too rudely rigorous,°   *also/violent*
Astonied° with the stroke of their owne hand,   *stunned*
135   Do backe rebut,° and each to other yeeldeth land.   *recoil*

16

As when two rams stird with ambitious pride,
Fight for the rule of the rich fleecèd flocke,
Their hornèd fronts so fierce on either side
Do meete, that with the terrour of the shocke
140   Astonied both, stand sencelesse as a blocke,°   *inanimate object*
Forgetfull of the hanging[2] victory:
So stood these twaine, unmovèd as a rocke,
Both staring fierce, and holding idely
The broken reliques of their former cruelty.

17

145   The Sarazin sore daunted with the buffe
Snatcheth his sword, and fiercely to him flies;
Who well it wards, and quyteth° cuff with cuff: *requites*
Each others equall puissaunce envies,
And through their iron sides with cruell spies°   *looks*

8. Proven valuable by analysis. "Purfled": decorated.
9. The lady's garb associates her with the Whore of Babylon (Revelation 17.3–4): "And I saw a woman sit upon a scarlet colored beast, full of names of blasphemy, having seven heads and ten horns. And the woman was arrayed in purple and scarlet color, and decked with gold and precious stones and pearls, having a golden cup in her hand full of abominations and filthiness of her fornication."
1. Handsome metal knobs.
2. In the balance.

150 Does seeke to perce: repining courage yields
  No foote to foe. The flashing fier flies
  As from a forge out of their burning shields,
And streames of purple bloud new dies the verdant fields.

18

 "Curse on that Crosse," quoth then the Sarazin,
155 "That keepes thy body from the bitter fit;°   *stroke*
  Dead long ygoe I wote° thou haddest bin,   *thought*
  Had not that charme from thee forwarnéd° it: *prevented*
  But yet I warne thee now assuréd° sitt,   *securely*
  And hide thy head." Therewith upon his crest
160 With rigour° so outrageous he smitt,   *violence*
  That a large share it hewd out of the rest,
And glauncing downe his shield, from blame him fairely blest.[3]

19

 Who thereat wondrous wroth, the sleeping spark
  Of native vertue° gan eftsoones revive,   *strength*
165 And at his haughtie helmet making mark,
  So hugely° stroke, that it the steele did rive, *mightily*
  And cleft his head. He tumbling downe alive,
  With bloudy mouth his mother earth did kis
  Greeting his grave: his grudging° ghost did strive *complaining*
170 With the fraile flesh; at last it flitted is,
Whither the soules do fly of men, that live amis.

20

 The Lady when she saw her champion fall,
  Like the old ruines of a broken towre,
  Staid not to waile his woefull funerall,°   *death*
175 But from him fled away with all her powre;
  Who after her as hastily gan scowre,°   *scurry*
  Bidding the Dwarfe with him to bring away
  The Sarazins shield, signe of the conqueroure.
  Her soone he overtooke, and bad to stay,
180 For present cause was none of dread her to dismay.

21

 She turning backe with ruefull countenaunce,
  Cride, "Mercy mercy Sir vouchsafe to show
  On silly° Dame, subject to hard mischaunce, *helpless*
  And to your mighty will." Her humblesse low
185 In so ritch weedes and seeming glorious show,
  Did much emmove his stout heroicke heart,
  And said, "Deare dame, your suddein overthrow
  Much rueth° me; but now put feare apart,   *grieves*
And tell, both who ye be, and who that tooke your part."

22

190 Melting in teares, then gan she thus lament;
  "The wretched woman, whom unhappy howre
  Hath now made thrall° to your commandèment, *slave*

3. Preserved him from harm.

Before that angry heavens list to lowre,°   *frown*
And fortune false betraide me to your powre
195   Was (O what now availeth that I was!)
Borne the sole daughter of an Emperour,
He that the wide West under his rule has,
And high hath set his throne, where Tiberis doth pas.[4]

23

"He in the first flowre of my freshest age,
200   Betrothèd me unto the onely haire°   *heir*
Of a most mighty king, most rich and sage;
Was never Prince so faithfull and so faire,
Was never Prince so meeke and debonaire;°   *gracious*
But ere my hopèd day of spousall shone,
205   My dearest Lord fell from high honours staire,
Into the hands of his accursed fone,°   *foes*
And cruelly was slaine, that shall I ever mone.[5]

24

'His blessed body spoild of lively breath,
Was afterward, I know not how, convaid°   *carried away*
210   And fro me hid: of whose most innocent death
When tidings came to me unhappy maid,
O how great sorrow my sad soule assaid.°   *afflicted*
Then forth I went his woefull corse to find,
And many yeares throughout the world I straid,
215   A virgin widow, whose deepe wounded mind
With love, long time did languish as the striken hind.°   *deer*

25

"At last it chauncèd this proud Sarazin
To meete me wandring, who perforce° me led   *by violence*
With him away, but yet could never win
220   The fort, that Ladies hold in soveraigne dread.
There lies he now with foule dishonour dead,
Who whiles he livde, was callèd proud Sans foy,
The eldest of three brethren, all three bred
Of one bad sire, whose youngest is Sans joy,
225   And twixt them both was borne the bloudy bold Sans loy.[6]

26

"In this sad plight, friendlesse, unfortunate,
Now miserable I Fidessa[7] dwell,
Craving of you in pitty of my state,
To do none° ill, if please ye not do well."   *no*
230   He in great passion all this while did dwell,°   *continue*
More busying his quicke eyes, her face to view,

---

4. The Tiber River runs through Rome. The lady is the daughter of Rome (and hence is associated with the Roman Catholic Church). Her father, she says, is ruler of the West—but Una's father had the rule of both East *and* West (canto 1, line 41): on the historical plane, the true church once embraced east and west whereas the false rules only the west.

5. The lady claims to be betrothed to Christ, bridegroom of the Church.

6. Literally, "without law." Sans joy means "without joy."

7. Faith.

Then his dull eares, to heare what she did tell;
And said, "Faire Lady hart of flint would rew
The undeservèd woes and sorrowes, which ye shew.

27

235 "Henceforth in safe assuraunce may ye rest,
Having both found a new friend you to aid,
And lost an old foe, that did you molest:
Better new friend than an old foe is[8] said."
With chaunge of cheare the seeming simple maid
240 Let fall her eyen, as shamefast[9] to the earth,
And yeelding soft, in that she nought gain-said,
So forth they rode, he feining° seemely merth,   *simulating*
And she coy lookes: so dainty they say maketh derth.[1]

28

Long time they thus together traveilèd,
245 Till weary of their way, they came at last,
Where grew two goodly trees, that faire did spred
Their armes abroad, with gray mosse overcast,
And their greene leaves trembling with every blast,°   *breeze*
Made a calme shadow far in compasse round:
250 The fearefull Shepheard often there aghast
Under them never sat, ne wont[2] there sound
His mery oaten pipe, but shund th' unlucky ground.

29

But this good knight soone as he them can° spie,   *did*
For the coole shade him thither hastly got:
255 For golden Phoebus now ymounted hie,
From fiery wheeles of his faire chariot
Hurlèd his beame so scorching cruell hot,
That living creature mote° it not abide;   *might*
And his new Lady it endurèd not.
260 There they alight, in hope themselves to hide
From the fierce heat, and rest their weary limbs a tide.° *time*

30

Faire seemely pleasaunce° each to other makes,   *courtesy*
With goodly purposes there as they sit:
And in his falsèd° fancy he her takes   *deceived*
265 To be the fairest wight that livèd yit;
Which to expresse, he bends his gentle wit,
And thinking of those braunches greene to frame
A girlond for her dainty forehead fit,
He pluckt a bough; out of whose rift there came
270 Small drops of gory bloud, that trickled downe the same.

31

Therewith a piteous yelling voyce was heard,
Crying, "O spare with guilty hands to teare

---

8. I.e., it is.
9. As if modestly.
1. Proverbial: "what's dear is rare." Here, "coy-

ness creates unsatisfied desire."
2. Nor was accustomed to.

My tender sides in this rough rynd embard,°   *imprisoned*
But fly, ah fly far hence away, for feare
275   Least to you hap, that happened to me heare,
And to this wretched Lady, my deare love,
O too deare love, love bought with death too deare."
Astond he stood, and up his haire did hove°   *heave, raise*
And with that suddein horror could no member move.

32

280   At last whenas the dreadfull passion
Was overpast, and manhood well awake,
Yet musing at the straunge occasion,
And doubting much his sence, he thus bespake;
"What voyce of damnèd Ghost from Limbo³ lake,
285   Or guilefull spright wandring in empty aire,
Both which fraile men do oftentimes mistake,°   *mislead*
Sends to my doubtfull eares these speaches rare,
And ruefull plaints, me bidding guiltlesse bloud to spare?"

33

Then groning deepe, "Nor damned Ghost," quoth he,
290   "Nor guilefull sprite to thee these wordes doth speake,
But once a man Fradubio,⁴ now a tree,
Wretched man, wretched tree; whose nature weake,
A cruell witch her cursèd will to wreake,
Hath thus transformed, and plast in open plaines,
295   Where Boreas° doth blow full bitter bleake,   *the North Wind*
And scorching Sunne does dry my secret vaines:
For though a tree I seeme, yet cold and heat me paines."

34

"Say on Fradubio then, or° man, or tree,"   *whether*
Quoth then the knight, "by whose mischievous arts
300   Art thou misshapèd thus, as now I see?
He oft finds med'cine, who his griefe imparts;
But double griefs afflict concealing harts,
As raging flames who striveth to suppresse."
"The author then," said he, "of all my smarts,
Is one Duessa⁵ a false sorceresse,
That many errant° knights hath brought to wretchednesse.   *wandering*

35

"In prime of youthly yeares, when corage hot
The fire of love and joy of chevalree
First kindled in my brest, it was my lot
310   To love this gentle Lady, whom ye see,
Now not a Lady, but a seeming tree;
With whom as once I rode accompanyde,
Me chauncèd of a knight encountred bee,

---

3. A region of Hell, traditionally the abode of the unbaptized.
4. *Fra* (Italian in, or brother) + *dubbio* (doubt). The motif of a man imprisoned in a tree derives from Virgil (*Aeneid* 3.27–42) and is used by Ariosto (*Orlando Furioso* 6.26–53).
5. Duessa means "double being." *Due* (Italian two) + *esse* (Latin, being).

That had a like faire Lady by his syde,
315　Like a faire Lady, but did fowle Duessa hyde.

36

"Whose forgèd beauty he did take in hand,[6]
　　All other Dames to have exceeded farre,
　　I in defence of mine did likewise stand,
　　Mine, that did then shine as the Morning starre:
320　So both to battell fierce arraungèd arre,
　　In which his harder fortune was to fall
　　Under my speare: such is the dye° of warre:　　　　*hazard*
　　His Lady left as a prise martiall,[7]
Did yield her comely person, to be at my call.

37

325　"So doubly loved of Ladies unlike° faire,　　　　*diversely*
　　Th' one seeming such, the other such indeede,
　　One day in doubt I cast° for to compare,　　　　*determined*
　　Whether° in beauties glorie did exceede;　　*which one (of two)*
　　A Rosy girlond was the victors meede:°　　　　*reward*
330　Both seemde to win, and both seemde won to bee,
　　So hard the discord was to be agreede.
　　Fraelissa[8] was as faire, as faire mote bee,
And ever false Duessa seemde as faire as shee.

38

"The wicked witch now seeing all this while
335　The doubtfull ballaunce equally to sway,
　　What not by right, she cast to win by guile,
　　And by her hellish science° raisd streight way　　　　*magic*
　　A foggy mist, that overcast the day,
　　And a dull blast, that breathing on her face,
340　Dimmed her former beauties shining ray,
　　And with foule ugly forme did her disgrace:
Then was she[9] faire alone, when none was faire in place.

39

"Then cride she out, 'Fye, fye, deformèd wight,
　　Whose borrowed beautie now appeareth plaine
345　To have before bewitchèd all mens sight;
　　O leave her soone, or let her soone be slaine.'
　　Her lothly visage viewing with disdaine,
　　Eftsoones° I thought her such, as she me told,　　　　*before*
　　And would have kild her; but with faignèd paine,
350　The false witch did my wrathfull hand withhold;
So left her, where she now is turnd to trëen mould.[1]

40

"Thens forth I tooke Duessa for my Dame,
　　And in the witch unweeting° joyd long time,　　　　*unknowingly*
　　Ne ever wist, but that she was the same,

---

6. He maintained.
7. Spoil of battle.
8. Frailty (Italian *Fralezza*).

9. Duessa. "In place": when nobody else was fair.
1. The form of a tree.

355 Till on a day (that day is every Prime,[2]
 When Witches wont do penance for their crime)
 I chaunst to see her in her proper hew,[3]
 Bathing her selfe in origane and thyme:[4]
360 A filthy foule old woman I did vew,
That ever to have toucht her, I did deadly rew.°   *regret*

41

"Her neather partes misshapen, monstruous,
 Were hidd in water, that I could not see,
 But they did seeme more foule and hideous,
 Then womans shape man would beleeve to bee.
365 Thens forth from her most beastly companie
 I gan refraine, in minde to slip away,
 Soone as appeard safe opportunitie:
 For danger great, if not assured decay°   *destruction*
I saw before mine eyes, if I were knowne to stray.

42

370 "The divelish hag by chaunges of my cheare°   *countenance*
 Perceived my thought, and drownd in sleepie night,
 With wicked herbes and ointments did besmeare
 My bodie all, through charmes and magicke might,
 That all my senses were bereavèd quight:°   *quite*
375 Then brought she me into this desert waste,
 And by my wretched lovers side me pight,°   *planted*
 Where now enclosd in wooden wals full faste,[5]
Banisht from living wights,° our wearie dayes we waste."   *persons*

43

"But how long time," said then the Elfin knight,
380 "Are you in this misformèd house to dwell?"
 "We may not chaunge," quoth he, "this evil plight,
 Till we be bathèd in a living well;[6]
 That is the terme prescribèd by the spell."
 "O how," said he, "mote° I that well out find,   *might*
385 That may restore you to your wonted well?"°   *well-being*
 "Time and suffisèd fates to former kynd
Shall us restore,[7] none else from hence may us unbynd."

44

The false Duessa, now Fidessa hight,°   *called*
 Heard how in vaine Fradubio did lament,
390 And knew well all was true. But the good knight
 Full of sad feare and ghastly dreriment,°   *gloom*
 When all this speech the living tree had spent,
 The bleeding bough did thrust into the ground,
 That from the bloud he might be innocent,

---

2. The first appearance of the new moon.
3. In her own shape.
4. Oregano and thyme were used to cure scabs and itching.
5. I.e., imprisoned within the trees.

6. With allusion to 1 John 4.14, the "well of water, springing up into eternal life."
7. I.e., time and the satisfaction of the fates alone can restore us to our former human nature.

395   And with fresh clay did close the wooden wound:
          Then turning to his Lady, dead with feare her found.

45

       Her seeming dead he found with feignèd feare,
          As all unweeting of that well she knew,[8]
          And paynd himselfe with busie care to reare
400   Her out of carelesse° swowne. Her eylids blew   *unconscious*
          And dimmèd sight with pale and deadly hew[9]
          At last she up gan lift: with trembling cheare°   *demeanor*
          Her up he tooke, too simple and too trew,
          And oft her kist. At length all passèd feare,[1]
405 He set her on her steede, and forward forth did beare.

Canto 3

Forsaken Truth long seekes her love,
   And makes the Lyon mylde,
  Marres° blind Devotions mart,° and fals   *spoils/business*
    In hand of leachour° vylde.   *lecher*

1

       Nought is there under heav'ns wide hollownesse,°   *concavity*
          That moves more deare compassion of mind,
          Then beautie brought t' unworthy° wretchednesse   *undeserved*
          Through envies snares or fortunes freakes° unkind: *sudden changes*
5   I, whether lately through her brightnesse blind,
          Or through alleageance and fast fealtie,
          Which I do owe unto all woman kind,
          Feele my heart perst° with so great agonie,   *pierced*
      When such I see, that all for pittie I could die.

2

10 And now it is empassionèd° so deepe,   *moved*
          For fairest Unas sake, of whom I sing,
          That my fraile eyes these lines with teares do steepe,
          To thinke how she through guilefull handeling,°   *treatment*
          Though true as touch,° though daughter of a king, *touchstone*
15   Though faire as ever living wight was faire,
          Though nor in word nor deede ill meriting,
          Is from her knight divorcèd° in despaire   *separated*
      And her due loves derived° to that vile witches share. *diverted*

3

       Yet she most faithfull Ladie all this while
20   Forsaken, wofull, solitarie mayd
          Farre from all peoples prease,° as in exile,   *press, crowd*
          In wildernesse and wastfull° deserts strayd,   *desolate*
          To seeke her knight; who subtilly betrayd
          Through that late vision, which th' Enchaunter wrought,
25   Had her abandond. She of nought affrayd,

---

8. I.e., pretending ignorance of what she knew   9. Deathlike appearance.
well.   1. I.e., having overcome all fear.

Through woods and wastnesse° wide him daily sought;   *wilderness*
     Yet wishèd tydings more of him unto her brought.

4

One day nigh wearie of the yrkesome way,
     From her unhastie° beast she did alight,   *slow*
30   And on the grasse her daintie limbes did lay
     In secret shadow,° farre from all mens sight: *shade*
     From her faire head her fillet she undight,[1]
     And laid her stole aside. Her angels face
     As the great eye of heaven shynèd bright,
35   And made a sunshine in the shadie place;
Did never mortall eye behold such a heavenly grace.

5

It fortunèd out of the thickest wood   *chanced*
     A ramping° Lyon rushèd suddainly,   *raging*
     Hunting full greedie after salvage blood;[2]
40   Soone as the royall virgin he did spy,
     With gaping mouth at her ran greedily,
     To have attonce devoured her tender corse;°   *body*
     But to the pray when as he drew more ny,
     His bloudie rage asswagèd with remorse,
45   And with the sight amazd, forgat his furious forse.

6

In stead thereof he kist her wearie feet,
     And lickt her lilly hands with fawning tong,
     As he her wrongèd innocence did weet.[3]
     O how can beautie maister the most strong,
50   And simple truth subdue avenging wrong?
     Whose yeelded pride and proud submission,
     Still dreading death, when she had markèd long,
     Her hart gan melt in great compassion,
And drizling teares did shed for pure affection.

7

55   "The Lyon Lord of everie beast in field,"
     Ouoth she, "his princely puissance° doth abate   *power*
     And mightie proud to humble weake does yield,
     Forgetfull of the hungry rage, which late
     Him prickt, in pittie of my sad estate:°   *condition*
60   But he my Lyon, and my noble Lord,
     How does he find in cruell hart to hate
     Her that him loved, and ever most adord,
As the God of my life? why hath he me abhord?"

8

Redounding° teares did choke th' end of her plaint,   *overflowing*
65   Which softly ecchoed from the neighbour wood;
     And sad to see her sorrowfull constraint°   *affliction*

1. She took off her headband.
2. Wild game.

3. As though he understood ("did weet") her
innocence.

The kingly beast upon her gazing stood;
With pittie calmd, downe fell his angry mood.
At last in close hart shutting up her paine,
70   Arose the virgin borne of heavenly brood,°   *parentage*
And to her snowy Palfrey got againe,
To seeke her strayèd Champion, if she might attaine.°   *overtake*

9

The Lyon would not leave her desolate,
But with her went along, as a strong gard
75   Of her chast person, and a faithfull mate
Of her sad troubles and misfortunes hard:
Still° when she slept, he kept both watch and ward,   *always*
And when she wakt, he waited diligent,
With humble service to her will prepard:
80   From her faire eyes he tooke commaundement,
And ever by her lookes conceivèd her intent.[4]

10

Long she thus traveilèd through deserts wyde,
By which she thought her wandring knight shold pas,
Yet never shew of living wight espyde;
85   Till that at length she found the troden gras,
In which the tract° of peoples footing was,   *track*
Under the steepe foot of a mountaine hore;°   *gray*
The same she followes, till at last she has
A damzell spyde slow footing her before,[5]
90   That on her shoulders sad° a pot of water bore.   *heavy*

11

To whom approching she to her gan call,
To weet, if dwelling place were nigh at hand;
But the rude° wench her answered nought at all,   *ignorant*
She could not heare, nor speake, nor understand;[6]
95   Till seeing by her side the Lyon stand,
With suddaine feare her pitcher downe she threw,
And fled away: for never in that land
Face of faire Ladie she before did vew,
And that dread Lyons looke her cast in deadly° hew.   *deathlike*

12

100   Full fast she fled, ne ever lookt behynd,
As if her life upon the wager lay,[7]
And home she came, whereas her mother blynd
Sate in eternall night: nought could she say,
But suddaine catching hold, did her dismay
105   With quaking hands, and other signes of feare:
Who full of ghastly fright and cold affray,°   *terror*

---

4. Lions have long been associated with the British crown.
5. I.e., walking slowly in front of her.
6. Cf. Mark 4.11–12: ". . . unto them that are without, all these things are done in parables: / That seeing they may see, and not perceive; and hearing they may hear, and not understand."
7. Were at stake.

Gan shut the dore. By this arrivèd there
Dame Una, wearie Dame, and entrance did requere.°   *request*

13

Which when none yeelded, her unruly Page
110   With his rude° clawes the wicket° open rent,   *rough/door*
And let her in; where of his cruell rage
Nigh dead with feare, and faint astonishment,[8]
She found them both in darkesome corner pent;°   *huddled*
Where that old woman day and night did pray
115   Upon her beades° devoutly penitent;   *rosary*
Nine hundred *Pater nosters* every day,
And thrise nine hundred *Aves* she was wont to say.[9]

14

And to augment her painefull pennance more,
Thrise every weeke in ashes she did sit,
120   And next her wrinkled skin rough sackcloth wore,[1]
And thrise three times did fast from any bit:°   *food*
But now for feare her beads she did forget.
Whose needlesse dread for to remove away,
Faire Una framèd words and count'nance fit:
125   Which hardly° doen, at length she gan them pray,   *with difficulty*
That in their cotage small, that night she rest her may.[2]

15

The day is spent, and commeth drowsie night,
When every creature shrowded is in sleepe;
Sad Una downe her laies in wearie plight,
130   And at her feet the Lyon watch doth keepe:
In stead of rest, she does lament, and weepe
For the late° losse of her deare lovèd knight,   *recent*
And sighes, and grones, and evermore does steepe
Her tender brest in bitter teares all night,
135   All night she thinks too long, and often lookes for light.

16

Now when Aldeboran was mounted hie
Above the shynie Cassiopeias chaire,[3]
And all in deadly sleepe did drownèd lie,
One knockèd at the dore, and in would fare;°   *come*
140   He knockèd fast,° and often curst, and sware,   *insistently*
That readie entrance was not at his call:
For on his backe a heavy load he bare
Of nightly stelths and pillage severall,[4]
Which he had got abroad by purchase° criminall.   *acquisition*

---

8. I.e., fainting with amazement.
9. Her prayers are the Lord's Prayer ("Our Father") and the "Hail Mary."
1. Sackcloth and ashes are symbols of penitence.
2. I.e., that she might rest herself.

3. The star Aldebaran, in the constellation Taurus, mounts over the constellation Cassiopeia.
4. I.e., he carried the booty gained from nightly thefts and various kinds of pillage.

17

145   He was to weete[5] a stout and sturdie thiefe,
      Wont to robbe Churches of their ornaments,
      And poore mens boxes[6] of their due reliefe,
      Which given was to them for good intents;
      The holy Saints of their rich vestiments
150   He did disrobe, when all men carelesse slept,
      And spoild the Priests of their habiliments,°   *vestments*
      Whiles none the holy things in safety kept;
  Then he by cunning sleights in at the window crept.

18

  And all that he by right or wrong could find,
155   Unto this house he brought, and did bestow
      Upon the daughter of this woman blind,
      Abessa daughter of Corceca[7] slow,
      With whom he whoredome usd, that few did know,
      And fed her fat with feast of offerings,
160   And plentie, which in all the land did grow;
      Ne sparèd he to give her gold and rings:
  And now he to her brought part of his stolen things.

19

  Thus long the dore with rage and threats he bet,°   *beat*
      Yet of those fearefull women none durst rize,
165   The Lyon frayèd them, him in to let:[8]
      He would no longer stay him to advize,°   *consider*
      But open breakes the dore in furious wize,
      And entring is; when that disdainfull° beast   *indignant*
      Encountring fierce, him suddaine doth surprize,
170   And seizing° cruell clawes on trembling brest,   *fastening*
  Under his Lordly foot him proudly hath supprest.

20

  Him booteth not resist,[9] nor succour call,
      His bleeding hart is in the vengers hand,
      Who streight him rent in thousand peeces small,
175   And quite dismembred hath: the thirstie land
      Drunke up his life; his corse left on the strand.°   *ground*
      His fearefull friends weare out the wofull night,
      Ne dare to weepe, nor seeme to understand
      The heavie hap,° which on them is alight,°   *lot/fallen*
180 Affraid, least to themselves the like mishappen might.[1]

21

  Now when broad day the world discovered° has,   *revealed*
      Up Una rose, up rose the Lyon eke,

---

5. In fact.
6. A box for alms for the poor.
7. Corceca means "blind heart"; her daughter Abessa's name comes from "abbess." Also *ab* + *esse* (Latin), away from being.

8. I.e., neither of the women dared rise to let him in because the lion terrified ("frayed") them.
9. It does no good to resist.
1. I.e., lest the same thing might happen amiss ("mishappen") to them.

And on their former journey forward pas,
In wayes unknowne, her wandring knight to seeke,
185 With paines farre passing that long wandring Greeke,
That for his love refusèd deitie;[2]
Such were the labours of this Lady meeke,
Still seeking him, that from her still did flie,
Then furthest from her hope, when most she weenèd nie.[3]

                              22

190 Soone as she parted thence, the fearefull twaine,
That blind old woman and her daughter deare
Came forth, and finding Kirkrapine° there slaine,   church robber
For anguish great they gan to rend their heare,
And beat their brests, and naked flesh to teare.
195 And when they both had wept and wayld their fill,
Then forth they ranne like two amazèd deare,
Halfe mad through malice, and revenging will,[4]
To follow her, that was the causer of their ill.

                              23

Whom overtaking, they gan loudly bray,
200 With hollow howling, and lamenting cry,
Shamefully at her rayling all the way,
And her accusing of dishonesty,°   unchastity
That was the flowre of faith and chastity;
And still amidst her rayling, she[5] did pray,
That plagues, and mischiefs, and long misery
Might fall on her, and follow all the way,
And that in endlesse error° she might ever stray.   wandering

                              24

But when she saw her prayers nought prevaile,
She backe returnèd with some labour lost;
210 And in the way as she did weepe and waile
A knight her met in mighty armes embost,°   encased
Yet knight was not for all his bragging bost,°   boast
But subtill Archimag, that Una sought
By traynes° into new troubles to have tost: tricks
215 Of that old woman tydings he besought,
If that of such a Ladie she could tellen ought.[6]

                              25

Therewith she gan her passion to renew,
And cry, and curse, and raile, and rend her heare,°   hair
Saying, that harlot she too lately knew,
220 That causd her shed so many a bitter teare,
And so forth told the story of her feare:
Much seemèd he to mone her haplesse chaunce,
And after for that Ladie did inquere;

2. Odysseus, who renounced immortality and the
love of the nymph Calypso for his wife Penelope.
3. Believed near.
4. Desire of revenge.

5. I.e., Corceca.
6. I.e., if she could tell anything ("ought") about
such a lady.

Which being taught, he forward gan advaunce
225 His fair enchaunted steed, and eke his charmèd launce.

26

Ere long he came, where Una traveild slow,
  And that wilde Champion wayting° her besyde: *attending*
  Whom seeing such, for dread he durst not show
  Himselfe too nigh at hand, but turnèd wyde
230 Unto an hill; from whence when she him spyde,
  By his like seeming shield, her knight by name
  She weend it was, and towards him gan ryde:
  Approching nigh, she wist° it was the same,   *believed*
And with faire fearefull humblesse° towards him shee   *humility*
    came.

27

235 And weeping said, "Ah my long lackèd Lord,
  Where have ye bene thus long out of my sight?
  Much fearèd I to have bene quite abhord,
  Or ought° have done, that ye displeasen might,   *aught*
  That should as death unto my deare hart light:[7]
240 For since mine eye your joyous sight did mis,
  My chearefull day is turnd to chearelesse night,
  And eke my night of death the shadow is;
But welcome now my light, and shining lampe of blis."

28

He thereto meeting[8] said, "My dearest Dame,
245 Farre be it from your thought, and fro my will,
  To thinke that knighthood I so much should shame,
  As you to leave, that have me lovèd still.
  And chose in Faery court of meere° goodwill,   *pure*
  Where noblest knights were to be found on earth:
250 The earth shall sooner leave her kindly° skill   *natural*
  To bring forth fruit, and make eternall derth,°   *desert*
Then I leave you, my liefe,° yborne of heavenly berth.   *beloved*

29

"And sooth to say, why I left you so long,
255 Was for to seeke adventure in strange place,
  Where Archimago said a felon strong
  To many knights did daily worke disgrace;
  But knight he now shall never more deface:°   *discredit*
  Good cause of mine excuse; that mote° ye please   *may*
  Well to accept, and evermore embrace
260 My faithfull service, that by land and seas
Have vowd you to defend, now then your plaint appease."° *cease*

30

His lovely° words her seemd due recompence   *loving*
  Of all her passèd paines: one loving howre

---

7. I.e., be as a death blow to my sad heart.   8. Answering in like manner.

For many yeares of sorrow can dispence:°   *make amends*
265   A dram of sweet is worth a pound of sowre:
       She has forgot, how many a wofull stowre°   *trouble*
       For him she late endured; she speakes no more
       Of past: true is, that true love hath no powre
       To looken backe; his eyes be fixt before.
270 Before her stands her knight, for whom she toyld so sore.

                                  31

       Much like, as when the beaten marinere,
          That long hath wandred in the Ocean wide,
          Oft soust° in swelling Tethys⁹ saltish teare,   *soaked*
          And long time having tand his tawney hide
275   With blustring breath of heaven, that none can bide,
          And scorching flames of fierce Orions hound,¹
          Soone as the port from farre he has espide,
          His chearefull whistle merrily doth sound,
       And Nereus crownes with cups;² his mates him
                pledg° around.   *toast*

                                  32

280 Such joy made Una, when her knight she found;
          And eke th' enchaunter joyous seemd no lesse,
          Then the glad marchant, that does vew from ground
          His ship farre come from watrie wildernesse,
          He hurles out vowes, and Neptune oft doth blesse:
285   So forth they past, and all the way they spent
          Discoursing of her dreadfull late distresse,
          In which he askt her, what the Lyon ment:
       Who told her all that fell° in journey as she went.³   *befell*

                                  33

       They had not ridden farre, when they might see
290   One pricking° towards them with hastie heat,   *riding*
          Full strongly armd, and on a courser free,
          That through his fiercenesse fomed all with sweat,
          And the sharpe yron° did for anger eat,   *bit*
          When his hot ryder spurd his chauffèd° side;   *heated*
295   His looke was sterne, and seemèd still to threat
          Cruell revenge, which he in hart did hyde,
       And on his shield Sans loy in bloudie lines was dyde.

                                  34

       When nigh he drew unto this gentle payre
          And saw the Red-crosse, which the knight did beare,
300   He burnt in fire, and gan eftsoones prepare
          Himselfe to battell with his couchèd speare.
          Loth was that other, and did faint through feare,
          To taste th' untryed dint° of deadly steele;   *blow*

---

9. The wife of Ocean; here, the Ocean.
1. Sirius, the dog star, symbolizing hot weather
(the "dog days").

2. Nereus is god of the Mediterranean, to whom
the mariner in gratitude makes libations.
3. I.e., she told all that befell ("fell") her.

But yet his Lady did so well him cheare,
305   That hope of new good hap he gan to feele;
So bent° his speare, and spurnd his horse with yron heele.   *lowered*

35

But that proud Paynim° forward came so fierce,   *pagan*
    And full of wrath, that with his sharp-head speare
    Through vainely crossèd shield[4] he quite did pierce,
310   And had his staggering steede not shrunke for feare,
    Through shield and bodie eke° he should him beare:°   *also/thrust*
    Yet so great was the puissance of his push,
    That from his saddle quite he did him beare:
    He tombling rudely° downe to ground did rush,   *violently*
315 And from his gorèd wound a well of bloud did gush.

36

Dismounting lightly from his loftie steed,
    He to him lept, in mind to reave° his life,   *take*
    And proudly said, "Lo there the worthie meed°   *recompense*
    Of him, that slew Sans foy with bloudie knife;
320   Henceforth his ghost freed from repining strife,
    In peace may passen over Lethe[5] lake,
    When mourning altars purgd° with enemies life,   *cleansed*
    The blacke infernall Furies[6] doen aslake:
Life from Sans foy thou tookst, Sans loy shall from thee take."

37

325 Therewith in haste his helmet gan unlace,
    Till Una cride, "O hold that heavie hand,
    Deare Sir, what ever that thou be in place:[7]
    Enough is, that thy foe doth vanquisht stand
330   Now at thy mercy: Mercie not withstand:
    For he is one the truest knight alive,[8]
    Though conquered now he lie on lowly land,[9]
    And whilest him fortune favourd, faire did thrive
In bloudie field: therefore of life him not deprive."

38

Her piteous words might not abate his rage,
335   But rudely rending up his helmet, would
    Have slaine him straight: but when he sees his age,
    And hoarie head of Archimago old,
    His hastie hand he doth amazèd hold,
    And halfe ashamèd, wondred at the sight:
340   For the old man well knew he, though untold,
    In charmes and magicke to have wondrous might,
Ne ever wont in field, ne in round lists[1] to fight.

---

4. The cross on Archimago's shield was false and
did not give him the protection the Redcrosse knight
received in his fight with Sans Foy; see 1.2.18.
5. The river of forgetfulness in Hades.
6. Spirits of discord and revenge. "Aslake": appease.

7. Whoever you are.
8. I.e., do not withhold mercy, for he is the one
truest knight.
9. I.e., low on the ground.
1. Enclosures for fighting tournaments.

39

And said, "Why Archimago, lucklesse syre,
   What doe I see? what hard mishap is this,
345   That hath thee hither brought to taste mine yre?
   Or thine the fault, or mine the error is,
   In stead of foe to wound my friend amis?"
   He answered nought, but in a traunce still lay,
   And on those guilefull dazèd eyes of his
350   The cloud of death did sit. Which doen away,[2]
He left him lying so, ne would no lenger stay.

40

But to the virgin comes, who all this while
   Amasèd stands, her selfe so mockt° to see   *deceived*
   By him, who has the guerdon° of his guile,   *reward*
355   For so misfeigning her true knight to bee:
   Yet is she now in more perplexitie,°   *trouble*
   Left in the hand of that same Paynim bold,
   From whom her booteth not[3] at all to flie;
   Who by her cleanly° garment catching hold,   *pure*
360 Her from her Palfrey pluckt, her visage to behold.

41

But her fierce servant full of kingly awe
   And high disdaine,° whenas his soveraine Dame   *indignation*
   So rudely handled by her foe he sawe,
   With gaping jawes full greedy at him came,
365   And ramping on his shield, did weene° the same   *intend*
   Have reft away with his sharpe rending clawes
   But he was stout, and lust did now inflame
   His corage more, that from his griping pawes
He hath his shield redeemed,° and foorth his swerd he *recovered*
   drawes.

42

370 O then too weake and feeble was the forse
   Of salvage beast, his puissance to withstand:
   For he was strong, and of so mightie corse,
   As ever wielded speare in warlike hand,
   And feates of armes did wisely° understand.   *skilfully*
375   Eftsoones he percèd through his chaufèd chest
   With thrilling point of deadly yron brand,[4]
   And launcht° his Lordly hart: with death opprest   *pierced*
He roared aloud, whiles life forsooke his stubborne brest.

43

Who now is left to keepe the forlorne maid
380   From raging spoile of lawlesse victors will?
   Her faithfull gard removed, her hope dismaid,
   Her selfe a yeelded pray to save or spill.°   *destroy*

2. When the swoon passed.
3. Was of no use.
4. I.e., afterwards he pierced through the lion's
angry ("chaufed") chest with the penetrating
("thrilling") point of his sword.

He now Lord of the field, his pride to fill,
With foule reproches, and disdainfull spight
385   Her vildly entertaines, and will or nill,
Beares her away upon his courser light:[5]
Her prayers nought prevaile; his rage is more of might.

44

And all the way, with great lamenting paine,
And piteous plaints she filleth his dull° eares,   *deaf*
390   That stony hart could riven have in twaine,
And all the way she wets with flowing teares:
But he enraged with rancor, nothing heares.
Her servile beast yet would not leave her so,
But followes her farre off, ne ought he feares,
395   To be partaker of her wandring woe,
More mild in beastly kind,° then that her beastly foe.   *nature*

Canto 4

To sinfull house of Pride, Duessa
guides the faithfull knight,
Where brothers death to wreak° Sansjoy   *avenge*
doth chalenge him to fight.

1

Young knight, what ever that dost armes professe,
And through long labours huntest after fame,
Beware of fraud, beware of ficklenesse,
In choice, and change of thy deare lovèd Dame,
5   Least thou of her beleeve too lightly blame,
And rash misweening° doe thy hart remove: *misjudgment*
For unto knight there is no greater shame,
Then lightnesse and inconstancie in love;
That doth this Redcrosse knights ensample° plainly prove.   *example*

2

10 Who after that he had faire Una lorne,°   *forsaken*
Through light misdeeming° of her loialtie,   *misjudging*
And false Duessa in her sted had borne,[1]
Called Fidess', and so supposd to bee;
Long with her traveild, till at last they see
15   A goodly building, bravely garnishèd,°   *adorned*
The house of mightie Prince it seemd to bee:
And towards it a broad high way[2] that led,
All bare through peoples feet, which thither travailèd.

3

Great troupes of people traveild thitherward
20   Both day and night, of each degree and place,°   *rank*
But few returnèd, having scapèd hard,°   *with difficulty*

---

5. I.e., he treats her basely ("vildly") and willingly
or not bears her away quickly ("light") upon his
horse.

1. Taken as companion.
2. "Broad is the way that leadeth to destruction"
(Matthew 7.13).

With balefull° beggerie, or foule disgrace,　　　　*wretched*
Which ever after in most wretched case,
Like loathsome lazars,° by the hedges lay.　　　　*lepers*
25　Thither Duessa bad him bend his pace:[3]
For she is wearie of the toilesome way,
And also nigh consumèd is the lingring day.

4

A stately Pallace built of squarèd bricke,
Which cunningly was without morter laid,
30　Whose wals were high, but nothing strong, nor thick,
And golden foile[4] all over them displaid,
That purest skye with brightnesse they dismaid°:　　　　*outdid*
High lifted up were many loftie towres,
And goodly galleries farre over laid,[5]
35　Full of faire windowes, and delightfull bowres;
And on the top a Diall told the timely howres.[6]

5

It was a goodly heape° for to behould,　　　　*building*
And spake the praises of the workmans wit;°　　　　*skill*
But full great pittie, that so faire a mould°　　　　*structure*
40　Did on so weake foundation ever sit:
For on a sandie hill,[7] that still did flit,
And fall away, it mounted was full hie,
That every breath of heaven shakèd it:
And all the hinder parts, that few could spie,
45　Were ruinous and old, but painted cunningly.

6

Arrivèd there they passèd in forth right;
For still to all the gates stood open wide,
Yet charge of them was to a Porter hight°　　　　*committed*
Cald Malvenù,[8] who entrance none denide:
50　Thence to the hall, which was on every side
With rich array and costly arras dight:[9]
Infinite sorts of people did abide
There waiting long, to win the wishèd sight
Of her, that was the Lady of that Pallace bright.

7

55　By them they passe, all gazing on them round,
And to the Presence[1] mount; whose glorious vew
Their frayle amazèd senses did confound:
In living Princes court none ever knew
Such endlesse richesse, and so sumptuous shew;

3. Direct his steps.
4. Thin layer of gold.
5. Placed above.
6. A sundial measured the hours of the day.
7. Matthew 7.26–7: "A foolish man . . . built his house upon the sand: / And the rain descended, and the floods came, and the winds blew, and beat upon that house; and it fell; and great was the fall

of it." "Flit": shift.
8. The name means "unwelcome." In courtly love allegories, the porter is often called "Bienvenu" or "Bel-accueil" ("welcome").
9. Decorated with costly wall hangings.
1. Presence chamber, where a sovereign receives guests.

60   Ne Persia selfe, the nourse of pompous pride
        Like ever saw. And there a noble crew
        Of Lordes and Ladies stood on every side,
    Which with their presence faire, the place much beautifide.

                            8

        High above all a cloth of State² was spred,
65   And a rich throne, as bright as sunny day,
        On which there sate most brave embellishèd³
        With royall robes and gorgeous array,
        A mayden Queene, that shone as Titans° ray,   *the sun's*
        In glistring gold, and peerelesse pretious stone:
70   Yet her bright blazing beautie did assay°   *attempt*
        To dim the brightnesse of her glorious throne,
    As envying her selfe, that too exceeding shone.

                            9

        Exceeding shone, like Phoebus fairest childe,
        That did presume his fathers firie wayne,°   *chariot*
75   And flaming mouthes of steedes unwonted° wilde   *unusually*
        Through highest heaven with weaker° hand to rayne; *too weak*
        Proud of such glory and advancement vaine,
        While flashing beames do daze his feeble eyen,
        He leaves the welkin° way most beaten plaine,   *skyey*
80   And rapt° with whirling wheeles, inflames the skyen, *carried away*
    With fire not made to burne, but fairely for to shyne.⁴

                            10

        So proud she shynèd in her Princely state,°   *throne*
        Looking to heaven; for earth she did disdayne,
        And sitting high; for lowly° she did hate: *lowliness*
85   Lo underneath her scornefull feete, was layne
        A dreadfull Dragon with an hideous trayne,°   *tail*
        And in her hand she held a mirrhour bright,⁵
        Wherein her face she often vewèd fayne,°   *with pleasure*
        And in her selfe-loved semblance tooke delight;
90 For she was wondrous faire, as any living wight.

                            11

        Of griesly° Pluto she the daughter was,   *horrid*
        And sad Proserpina the Queene of hell;
        Yet did she thinke her pearelesse worth to pas°   *surpass*
        That parentage, with pride so did she swell,
95   And thundring Jove, that high in heaven doth dwell,
        And wield° the world, she claymèd for her syre,   *govern*
        Or if that any else did Jove excell:
        For to the highest she did still aspyre,
    Or if ought° higher were then that, did it desyre.   *anything*

---

2. Canopy.
3. Handsomely clad.
4. Phaëthon tried to drive the chariot of Phoebus, his father, but set the skies on fire and fell.

5. Pride, and figures associated with her in Renaissance literature and art, often hold a mirror, emblematic of self-love.

12

100 And proud Lucifera men did her call,
        That made her selfe a Queene, and crownd to be,
        Yet rightfull kingdome she had none at all,
        Ne heritage of native soveraintie,
        But did usurpe with wrong and tyrannie
105   Upon the scepter, which she now did hold:
        Ne ruld her Realmes with lawes, but pollicie,°   *political cunning*
        And strong advizement of six wisards old,
     That with their counsels bad her kingdome did uphold.

13

     Soone as the Elfin knight in presence came,
110   And false Duessa seeming Lady faire,
        A gentle Husher,° Vanitie by name   *usher*
        Made rowme, and passage for them did prepaire:
        So goodly° brought them to the lowest staire   *graciously*
        Of her high throne, where they on humble knee
115   Making obeyssance,° did the cause declare,   *submission*
        Why they were come, her royall state to see,
     To prove° the wide report of her great Majestee.   *verify*

14

     With loftie eyes, halfe loth to looke so low,
        She thankèd them in her disdainefull wise,
120   Ne other grace vouchsafèd them to show
        Of Princesse worthy, scarse them bad arise.
        Her Lordes and Ladies all this while devise°   *make ready*
        Themselves to setten forth to straungers sight:
        Some frounce° their curlèd haire in courtly guise,   *frizzle*
125   Some prancke° their ruffes, and others trimly dight° *pleat/arrange*
     Their gay attire: each others greater pride does spight.

15

     Goodly they all that knight do entertaine,
        Right glad with him to have increast their crew:
        But to Duess' each one himselfe did paine
130   All kindnesse and faire courtesie to shew;
        For in that court whylome° her well they knew: *formerly*
        Yet the stout Faerie mongst the middest° crowd   *thickest*
        Thought all their glorie vaine in knightly vew,
        And that great Princesse too exceeding prowd,
135   That to strange° knight no better countenance° allowd. *stranger / favor*

16

     Suddein upriseth from her stately place
        The royall Dame, and for her coche doth call:
        All hurtlen° forth and she with Princely pace,   *rush*
        As faire Aurora in her purple pall,[6]
140   Out of the East the dawning day doth call:

6. Goddess of dawn, in her crimson robe ("purple pall").

> So forth she comes: her brightnesse brode° doth blaze;   abroad
> The heapes of people thronging in the hall,
> Do ride° each other, upon her to gaze: climb up
> Her glorious glitterand° light doth all mens eyes amaze.   glittering

17

145 So forth she comes, and to her coche does clyme,
> Adornèd all with gold, and girlonds gay,
> That seemd as fresh as Flora in her prime,
> And strove to match, in royall rich array,
> Great Junos golden chaire,° the which they say   chariot
150 The Gods stand gazing on, when she does ride
> To Joves high house through heavens bras-pavèd way
> Drawne of by faire Pecocks, that excell in pride,
> And full of Argus eyes their tailes dispredden wide.[7]

18

> But this was drawne of six unequall beasts,
155 On which her six sage Counsellours did ryde,
> Taught to obay their bestiall beheasts,
> With like conditions to their kinds applyde:[8]
> Of which the first, that all the rest did guyde,
> Was sluggish Idlenesse the nourse of sin;
160 Upon a slouthfull Asse he chose to ryde,
> Arayd in habit blacke, and amis thin,[9]
> Like to an holy Monck, the service to begin.

19

> And in his hand his Portesse° still he bare,   breviary
> That much was worne, but therein little red,
165 For of devotion he had little care,
> Still drownd in sleepe, and most of his dayes ded;
> Scarse could he once uphold his heavie hed,
> To looken, whether it were night or day:
> May seeme the wayne° was very evill led,   chariot
170 When such an one had guiding of the way,
> That knew not, whether right he went, or else astray.

20

> From worldly cares himselfe he did esloyne,°   withdraw
> And greatly shunnèd manly exercise,
> From every worke he chalengèd essoyne,[1]
175 For contemplation sake: yet otherwise,
> His life he led in lawlesse riotise;°   riotous conduct
> By which he grew to grievous malady;

7. Peacocks, with their tails outspread ("dispred-den wide") are a symbol of pride. The hundred-eyed monster Argus was set by Juno to watch Io, Jupiter's love. When Mercury killed Argus, his eyes were put in the peacock's tail feathers.
8. It is not clear whether the "sage Counsellors" command their beasts or are guided by them; since riders and their mounts are alike bestial, the same conditions pertain (are "applyed") to both natures

("kinds"). This procession of the seven deadly sins—of which Pride is queen—had a long tradition in medieval art and literature. See also Marlowe's *Doctor Faustus* (2.2.111–164).
9. Idleness wears the garb ("habit") and hood or amice ("amis") of a monk. Traditionally, Idleness led the procession of the deadly sins.
1. Claimed exemption.

For in his lustlesse° limbs through evill guise°   *feeble/living*
A shaking fever raignd continually:
180   Such one was Idlenesse, first of this company

21

And by his side rode loathsome Gluttony,
    Deformèd creature, on a filthie swyne,
    His belly was up-blowne with luxury.[2]
    And eke with fatnesse swollen were his eyne,
185   And like a Crane his necke was long and fyne,[3]
    With which he swallowd up excessive feast,
    For want whereof poore people oft did pyne;°   *starve*
    And all the way, most like a brutish beast,
He spuèd up his gorge,[4] that all did him deteast.

22

190   In greene vine leaves he was right fitly clad;
    For other clothes he could not weare for heat,
    And on his head an yvie girland had,[5]
    From under which fast trickled downe the sweat:
    Still as he rode, he somewhat° still did eat,   *something*
195   And in his hand did beare a bouzing° can,   *drinking*
    Of which he supt so oft, that on his seat
    His dronken corse° he scarse upholden can,   *body*
In shape and life more like a monster, then a man.

23

Unfit he was for any worldly thing,
200   And eke unhable once° to stirre or go,°   *at all/walk*
    Not meet to be of counsell to a king,
    Whose mind in meat and drinke was drownèd so,
    That from his friend he seldome knew his fo:
    Full of diseases was his carcas blew,
205   And a dry dropsie through his flesh did flow:
    Which by misdiet daily greater grew:
Such one was Gluttony, the second of that crew.

24

And next° to him rode lustfull Lechery,   *just after*
    Upon a bearded Goat,[6] whose rugged haire,
210   And whally° eyes (the signe of gelosy,)   *glaring*
    Was like the person selfe, whom he did beare:
    Who rough, and blacke, and filthy did appeare,
    Unseemely man to please faire Ladies eye;
    Yet he of Ladies oft was lovèd deare,
215   When fairer faces were bid standen by:°   *away*
O who does know the bent of womens fantasy?

---

2. Indulgence (in rich food).
3. The crane is a common symbol of gluttony because its long and thin ("fyne") neck allows more pleasure in swallowing.
4. Vomited.

5. He resembles the drunken satyr Silenus, foster father of Bacchus, god of wine; ivy is sacred to Bacchus.
6. Traditional symbol of Lust.

25

In a greene gowne he clothèd was full faire,
    Which underneath did hide his filthinesse,
    And in his hand a burning hart he bare,
220   Full of vaine follies, and new fangleness:°   *fickleness*
    For he was false, and fraught with ficklenesse,
    And learnèd had to love with secret lookes,
    And well could daunce, and sing with ruefulnesse,°   *pity*
    And fortunes tell, and read in loving° bookes,   *erotic*
225 And thousand other wayes, to bait his fleshly hookes.

26

Inconstant man, that lovèd all he saw,
    And lusted after all, that he did love,
    Ne would his looser life be tide to law,
    But joyd weake wemens hearts to tempt and prove°   *try*
230   If from their loyall loves he might them move;
    Which lewdnesse fild him with reprochfull paine
    Of that fowle evill, which all men reprove,
    That rots the marrow, and consumes the braine:[7]
Such one was Lecherie, the third of all this traine.

27

235 And greedy Avarice by him did ride,
    Upon a Camell loaden all with gold;[8]
    Two iron coffers hong on either side,
    With precious mettall full, as they might hold,
    And in his lap an heape of coine he told;°   *counted*
240   For of his wicked pelfe° his God he made,   *money*
    And unto hell him selfe for money sold;
    Accursèd usurie was all his trade,
And right and wrong ylike in equall ballaunce waide.[9]

28

His life was nigh unto deaths doore yplast,
245   And thread-bare cote, and cobled shoes he ware,
    Ne scarse good morsell all his life did tast,
    But both from backe and belly still did spare,
    To fill his bags, and richesse to compare;°   *acquire*
    Yet chylde ne kinsman living had he none
250   To leave them to; but thorough daily care
    To get, and nightly feare to lose his owne,
He led a wretched life unto him selfe unknowne.

29

Most wretched wight, whom nothing might suffise,
    Whose greedy lust did lacke in greatest store,°   *plenty*
255   Whose need had end, but no end covetise,

---

7. I.e., syphilis.
8. The camel as a symbol of avarice is based on Matthew 19.24: "It is easier for a camel to go through the eye of a needle, than for a rich man to enter into the kingdom of God."
9. I.e., he made no distinction between right and wrong.

Whose wealth was want, whose plenty made him pore,
Who had enough, yet wishèd ever more;
A vile disease, and eke in foote and hand
A grievous gout tormented him full sore,
260   That well he could not touch, not go,° nor stand: *walk*
Such one was Avarice, the fourth of this faire band.

30

And next to him malicious Envie rode,
  Upon a ravenous wolfe,[1] and still did chaw
Betweene his cankred° teeth a venemous tode,   *ulcerated*
265   That all the poison ran about his chaw;°   *jaw*
But inwardly he chawèd his owne maw°   *entrails*
At neighbours wealth, that made him ever sad;
  For death it was, when any good he saw,
  And wept, that cause of weeping none he had,
270 But when he heard of harme, he wexèd wondrous glad.

31

All in a kirtle of discolourd say[2]
  He clothèd was, ypainted full of eyes;
And in his bosome secretly there lay
An hatefull Snake,[3] the which his taile uptyes
275   In many folds, and mortall sting implyes.°   *enfolds*
Still as he rode, he gnasht his teeth, to see
  Those heapes of gold with griple° Covetyse,   *grasping*
And grudgèd at the great felicitie
Of proud Lucifera, and his owne companie.

32

280 He hated all good workes and vertuous deeds,
  And him no lesse, that any like did use,°   *perform*
And who with gracious bread the hungry feeds,
  His almes for want of faith he doth accuse;
So every good to bad he doth abuse:°   *twist*
285   And eke° the verse of famous Poets witt
He does backebite, and spightfull poison spues
  From leprous mouth on all, that ever writt:
Such one vile Envie was, that fifte in row did sitt.

33

And him beside rides fierce revenging Wrath,
290   Upon a Lion,[4] loth for to be led;
And in his hand a burning brond° he hath,   *sword*
  The which he brandisheth about his hed;
His eyes did hurle forth sparkles fiery red,
  And starèd sterne on all, that him beheld,
295 As ashes pale of hew and seeming ded;
  And on his dagger still his hand he held,
Trembling through hasty rage, when choler° in him sweld.   *anger*

---

1. Traditional attribute of Envy. "Still": contin-   3. The traditional attribute of Envy.
ually.   4. The lion is the symbol of Wrath.
2. Jacket of many-colored wool.

34

His ruffin° raiment all was staind with blood,   *disorderly*
  Which he had spilt, and all to rags yrent,°   *torn*
300 Through unadvisèd rashnesse woxen wood,[5]
  For of his hands he had no governement,°   *control*
  He cared for bloud in his avengement:
  But when the furious fit was overpast,
  His cruell facts° he often would repent;   *actions*
305 Yet wilfull man he never would forecast,
How many mischieves should ensue his heedlesse hast.[6]

35

Full many mischiefes follow cruell Wrath;
  Abhorrèd bloudshed, and tumultuous strife,
  Unmanly murder, and unthrifty scath,[7]
310 Bitter despight,° with rancours rusty knife,   *malice*
  And fretting griefe the enemy of life;
  All these, and many evils moe° haunt ire,°   *more/anger*
  The swelling Splene,[8] and Frenzy raging rife,
  The shaking Palsey, and Saint Fraunces fire:[9]
315 Such one was Wrath, the last of this ungoldly tire.°   *train*

36

And after all, upon the wagon beame
  Rode Sathan, with a smarting whip in hand,
  With which he forward lasht the laesie teme,
  So oft as Slowth[1] still in the mire did stand.
320 Huge routs° of people did about them band,   *crowds*
  Showting for joy, and still before their way
  A foggy mist had covered all the land;
  And underneath their feet, all scattered lay
Dead sculs and bones of men, whose life had gone astray.

37

325 So forth they marchen in this goodly sort,
  To take the solace° of the open aire,   *recreation*
  And in fresh flowring fields themselves to sport;
  Emongst the rest rode that false Lady faire,
  The fowle Duessa, next unto the chaire
330 Of proud Lucifera, as one of the traine:
  But that good knight would not so nigh repaire,°   *approach*
  Him selfe estraunging from their joyaunce° vaine,   *festivity*
Whose fellowship seemd far unfit for warlike swaine.

38

So having solacèd themselves a space
335 With pleasaunce of the breathing° fields yfed,   *emitting fragrance*
  They backe returnèd to the Princely Place;
  Whereas an errant knight in armes ycled,°   *clad*

5. Grown insane.
6. I.e., he never would foresee ("forecast") the calamities his "heedless haste" caused.
7. I.e., inhuman murder and destructive harm ("unthrifty scath").

8. Organ associated with anger in Renaissance physiology.
9. St. Anthony's fire, erysipelas, or the flaming itch; appropriate to Wrath.
1. I.e., Idleness (stanzas 18–20).

And heathnish shield, wherein with letters red
Was writ Sans joy,[2] they new arrivèd find:
340 Enflamed with fury and fiers hardy-hed,°   *boldness*
He seemd in hart to harbour thoughts unkind,
And nourish bloudy vengeaunce in his bitter mind.

39

Who when the shamèd shield[3] of slaine Sans foy
He spied with that same Faery champions page,
345 Bewraying° him, that did of late destroy   *revealing*
His eldest brother, burning all with rage
He to him leapt, and that same envious gage[4]
Of victors glory from him snatcht away:
But th 'Elfin knight, which ought that warlike wage,[5]
350 Disdaind to loose the meed he wonne in fray,°   *battle*
And him rencountring fierce, reskewd the noble pray.

40

Therewith they gan to hurtlen° greedily,   *rush together*
Redoubted battaile ready to darrayne,°   *contest*
And clash their shields, and shake their swords on hy,
355 That with their sturre° they troubled all the traine;   *tumult*
Till that great Queene upon eternall paine
Of high displeasure, that ensewen° might,   *ensue*
Commaunded them their fury to refraine,
And if that either to that shield had right,
360 In equall lists[6] they should the morrow next it fight.

41

"Ah dearest Dame," quoth then the Paynim bold,
"Pardon the errour of enragèd wight,
Whom great griefe made forget the raines to hold
Of reasons rule, to see this recreant° knight,   *cowardly*
365 No knight, but treachour° full of false despight°   *deceiver/disdain*
And shamefull treason, who through guile hath slayn
The prowest° knight, that ever field did fight,   *bravest*
Even stout Sans foy (O who can then refrayn?)
Whose shield he beares renverst, the more to heape disdayn.

42

370 "And to augment the glorie of his guile,
His dearest love[7] the faire Fidessa loe
Is there possessed of° the traytour vile,   *by*
Who reapes the harvest sowen by his foe,
Sowen in bloudy field, and bought with woe:
375 That[8] brothers hand shall dearely well requight
So be, O Queene, you equall favour showe."[9]

---

2. Sans Joy ("without joy"), darkness of spirit.
3. Carrying a shield upside down, with the heraldic arms reversed, was a great insult. See below, line 369.
4. Envied prize.
5. The knight (Redcrosse) who owned ("ought")

that spoil of war ("warlike wage").
6. Impartial formal combat.
7. I.e., Sans Foy's.
8. I.e., that act.
9. I.e., if, O Queen, you show impartiality ("equall favour").

Him litle answerd th 'angry Elfin knight:
He never meant with words, but swords to plead his right.

43

But threw his gauntlet as a sacred pledge,
His cause in combat the next day to try:
So been they parted both, with harts on edge,
To be avenged each on his enimy.
That night they pas in joy and jollity,
Feasting and courting both in bowre and hall;
For Steward was excessive Gluttonie,
That of his plenty pourèd forth to all;
Which doen, the Chamberlain[1] Slowth did to rest them call.

44

Now whenas darkesome night had all displayd
Her coleblacke curtein over brightest skye,
The warlike youthes on dayntie° couches layd,   *fine*
Did chace away sweet sleepe from sluggish eye,
To muse on meanes of hopèd victory.
But whenas Morpheus[2] had with leaden mace
Arrested all that courtly company,
Up-rose Duessa from her resting place,
And to the Paynims° lodging comes with silent pace.   *pagan*

45

Whom broad awake she finds, in troublous fit,[3]
Forecasting, how his foe he might annoy,°   *injure*
And him amoves° with speaches seeming fit: *arouses*
"Ah deare Sans joy, next dearest to Sans foy,
Cause of my new griefe, cause of my new joy,
Joyous, to see his ymage in mine eye,
And greeved, to thinke how foe did him destroy,
That was the flowre of grace and chevalrye;
Lo his Fidessa to thy secret faith I flye."

46

With gentle wordes he can° her fairely° greet,   *did/courteously*
And bad say on the secret of her hart.
Then sighing soft, "I learne that litle sweet
Oft tempred is," quoth she, "with muchell° smart: *much*
For since my brest was launcht with lovely dart[4]
Of deare Sans foy, I never joyèd howre,
But in eternall woes my weaker hart
Have wasted, loving him with all my powre,
And for his sake have felt full many an heavie stowre.° *grief*

47

"At last when perils all I weenèd past,
And hoped to reape the crop of all my care,

---

1. The court attendant in charge of the bedchambers. "Doen": done.
2. The god of sleep.

3. Troubled mood.
4. I.e., since my breast was pierced with the dart of love.

Into new woes unweeting° I was cast,   *unknowing*
By this false faytor,° who unworthy ware°   *deceiver/wore*
His worthy shield, whom he with guilefull snare
420 Entrappèd slew, and brought to shamefull grave.
Me silly° maid away with him he bare,   *helpless*
And ever since hath kept in darksome cave,
For that I would not yeeld, that° to Sans foy I gave.   *what*

48

"But since faire Sunne hath sperst° that lowring clowd,   *dispersed*
425 And to my loathèd life now shewes some light,
Under your beames I will me safely shrowd,°   *take shelter*
From dreaded storme of his disdainfull spight:
To you th' inheritance belongs by right
Of brothers prayse, to you eke longs° his love.   *belongs*
430 Let not his love, let not his restlesse spright°   *ghost*
Be unrevenged, that calles to you above
From wandring Stygian[5] shores, where it doth endlesse move."

49

Thereto said he, "Faire Dame be nought dismaid
For sorrowes past; their griefe is with them gone:
435 Ne yet of present perill be affraid;
For needlesse feare did never vantage° none,   *aid*
And helplesse hap it booteth not to mone.[6]
Dead is Sans-foy, his vitall° paines are past,   *living*
Though greevèd ghost for vengeance deepe do grone:
440 He lives, that shall him pay his dewties° last,   *rites*
And guiltie Elfin bloud shall sacrifice in hast."

50

"O but I feare the fickle freakes,"[7] quoth shee,
"Of fortune false, and oddes of armes[8] in field."
"Why dame," quoth he, "what oddes can ever bee,
445 Where both do fight alike, to win or yield?"
"Yea but," quoth she, "he beares a charmèd shield,
And eke enchaunted armes, that none can perce,
Ne none can wound the man, that does them wield."
"Charmd or enchaunted," answerd he then ferce,°   *fiercely*
450 "I no whit reck,[9] ne you the like need to reherce.°   *recount*

51

"But faire Fidessa, sithens° fortunes guile,   *since*
Or enimies powre hath now captivèd you,
Returne from whence ye came, and rest a while
Till morrow next, that I the Elfe subdew,
455 And with Sans foyes dead dowry you endew."[1]
"Ay me, that is a double death," she said,
"With proud foes sight my sorrow to renew:

5. I.e., from wandering on the banks of the Styx
river, in Hades.
6. I.e., it does not help to moan over that which
is beyond help ("helplesse hap").
7. Unpredictable tricks.

8. Advantage of superior arms.
9. I do not care at all. "Reherce": recount.
1. I.e., endow you with the legacy of the dead
Sans Joy.

Where ever yet I be, my secrete aid
Shall follow you." So passing forth she him obaid.

Canto 5

*The faithfull knight in equall field
subdewes his faithlesse foe,
Whom false Duessa saves, and for
his cure to hell does goe.*

1

The noble hart, that harbours vertuous thought,
   And is with child of glorious great intent,
   Can never rest, untill it forth have brought
   Th 'eternall brood of glorie excellent:[1]
5   Such restlesse passion did all night torment
   The flaming corage of that Faery knight,
   Devizing, how that doughtie° turnament   *worthy*
   With greatest honour he atchieven might;
Still did he wake, and still did watch for dawning light.

2

10 At last the golden Orientall gate
   Of greatest heaven gan to open faire,
   And Phoebus[2] fresh, as bridegrome to his mate,
   Came dauncing forth, shaking his deawie haire:
   And hurld his glistring beames through gloomy aire.
15   Which when the wakeful Elfe perceived, streight way
   He started up, and did him selfe prepaire,
   In sun-bright armes, and battailous° array: *warlike*
For with that Pagan proud he combat will that day.

3

And forth he comes into the commune hall,
20   Where earely waite him many a gazing eye,
   To weet what end to straunger knights may fall.
   There many Minstrales maken melody,
   To drive away the dull melancholy,
   And many Bardes, that to the trembling chord
25   Can tune their timely° voyces cunningly,   *measured*
   And many Chroniclers, that can record
Old loves, and warres for ladies doen by many a Lord.[3]

4

Soone after comes the cruell Sarazin,
   In woven maile all armèd warily,
30   And sternly lookes at him, who not a pin
   Does care for looke of living creatures eye.
   They bring them wines of Greece and Araby,

1. That good is manifested only in action, not in mere intent, is an important Renaissance commonplace.
2. The sun. Cf. Psalm 19.4–5: "In them hath he sat a Tabernacle for the sun, / Which is as a bridegroom coming out of his chamber."
3. Minstrels play the music on their instruments, Bards sing the words, Chroniclers—historians, epic poets—write of love and war.

And daintie spices fetcht from furthest Ynd,°   *India*
     To kindle heat of courage privily:°   *within*
35   And in the wine a solemne oth they bynd
     T'observe the sacred lawes of armes, that are assynd.

5

At last forth comes that far renowmèd Queene,
     With royall pomp and Princely majestie;
     She is ybrought unto a palèd° greene,   *fenced*
40   And placèd under stately canapee,°   *canopy*
     The warlike feates of both those knights to see.
     On th' other side in all mens open vew
     Duessa placèd is, and on a tree
     Sans-foy his shield is hangd with bloudy hew:
45   Both those the lawrell girlonds[4] to the victor dew.

6

A shrilling trompet sownded from on hye,
     And unto battaill bad them selves addresse:
     Their shining shieldes about their wrestes° they tye,   *wrists*
     And burning blades about their heads do blesse,°   *brandish*
50   The instruments of wrath and heavinesse:°   *rage*
     With greedy force each other doth assayle,
     And strike so fiercely, that they do impresse
     Deepe dinted furrowes in the battred mayle;
     The yron walles to ward their blowes are weake and fraile.[5]

7

55   The Sarazin was stout,° and wondrous strong,   *fierce*
     And heapèd blowes like yron hammers great:
     For after bloud and vengeance he did long.
     The knight was fiers,° and full of youthly heat: *high-spirited*
     And doubled strokes, like dreaded thunders threat:
60   For all for prayse and honour he did fight.
     Both stricken strike, and beaten both do beat,
     That from their shields forth flyeth firie light,
     And helmets hewen deepe, shew marks of eithers might.

8

So th' one for wrong, the other strives for right:
65   As when a Gryfon[6] seizèd of his pray,
     A Dragon fiers encountreth in his flight,
     Through widest ayre making his ydle° way,   *casual*
     That would his rightfull ravine° rend away;   *plunder*
     With hideous horrour both together smight,
70   And souce° so sore, that they the heavens affray: *strike*
     The wise Southsayer° seeing so sad sight,   *soothsayer*
     Th' amazèd vulgar tels of warres and mortall fight.

---

4. Garlands of victory.
5. I.e., their armor is too frail to withstand such blows.

6. A legendary monster, half eagle, half lion. "Seized": in possession.

9

So th' one for wrong, the other strives for right,
   And each to deadly shame would drive his foe:
75 The cruell steele so greedily doth bight
   In tender flesh, that streames of bloud down flow,
   With which the armes, that earst so bright did show,
   Into a pure vermillion now are dyde:
   Great ruth° in all the gazers harts did grow,   *pity*
80 Seeing the gorèd woundes to gape so wyde,
That victory they dare not wish to either side.

10

At last the Paynim chaunst to cast his eye,
   His suddein° eye, flaming with wrathfull fyre,   *darting*
   Upon his brothers shield, which hong thereby:
85 Therewith redoubled was his raging yre,°   *anger*
   And said, "Ah wretched sonne of wofull syre,
   Doest thou sit wayling by black Stygian lake
   Whilest here thy shield is hangd for victors hyre,°   *reward*
   And sluggish german[7] doest thy forces slake,
90 To after-send his foe, that him may overtake?

11

"Goe caytive° Elfe, him quickly overtake,   *miserable*
   And soone redeeme from his long wandring woe;
   Goe guiltie ghost, to him my message make,
   That I his shield have quit° from dying foe."   *rescued*
95 Therewith upon his crest he stroke him so,
   That twise he reelèd, readie twise to fall;
   End of the doubtfull battell deemèd tho
   The lookers on,[8] and lowd to him gan call
The false Duessa, "Thine the shield, and I, and all."[9]

12

100 Soone as the Faerie heard his Ladie speake,
   Out of his swowning dreame he gan awake,
   And quickning° faith, that earst was woxen weake,   *life-restoring*
   The creeping deadly cold away did shake:
   Tho moved with wrath, and shame, and Ladies sake,°   *cause*
105 Of all attonce he cast° avengd to bee,   *determined*
   And with so'exceeding furie at him strake,
   That forcèd him to stoupe upon his knee;
Had he not stoupèd so, he should have cloven bee,

13

And to him said, "Goe now proud Miscreant,°   *misbeliever*
110 Thy selfe thy message doe° to german deare,   *give*
   Alone he wandring thee too long doth want:
   Goe say, his foe thy shield with his doth beare."

---

7. Kinsman, here, brother. "Slake": slacken.
8. I.e., the onlookers then ("tho") thought this would end the battle, heretofore in doubt ("doubtfull").
9. Duessa is, of course, calling to Sans Joy, but Redcrosse (lines 100 ff.) hears her as "Fidessa."

Therewith his heavie hand he high gan reare,
Him to have slaine; when loe a darkesome clowd
115   Upon him fell: he no where doth appeare,
But vanisht is. The Elfe him cals alowd,
But answer none receives: the darknes him does shrowd.[1]

14

In haste Duessa from her place arose,
And to him running said, "O prowest° knight,   *bravest*
120   That ever Ladie to her love did chose,
Let now abate the terror of your might,
And quench the flame of furious despight,°   *anger*
And bloudie vengeance; lo th' infernall powres
Covering your foe with cloud of deadly night,
125   Have borne him hence to Plutoes balefull bowres.[2]
The conquest yours, I yours, the shield, and glory yours."

15

Not all so satisfide, with greedie eye
He sought all round about, his thirstie blade
To bath in bloud of faithlesse enemy;
130   Who all that while lay hid in secret shade:
He standes amazèd, how he thence should fade.
At last the trumpets Triumph sound on hie,
And running Heralds humble homage made,
Greeting him goodly with new victorie,
135   And to him brought the shield, the cause of enmitie.

16

Wherewith he goeth to that soveraine Queene,
And falling her before on lowly knee,
To her makes present of his service seene;°   *proved*
Which she accepts, with thankes, and goodly gree,°   *favor*
140   Greatly advauncing° his gay chevalree.   *extolling*
So marcheth home, and by her takes the knight,
Whom all the people follow with great glee,
Shouting, and clapping all their hands on hight,[3]
That all the aire it fils, and flyes to heaven bright.

17

145   Home is he brought, and laid in sumptuous bed:
Where many skilfull leaches° him abide,°   *doctors / attend*
To salve° his hurts, that yet still freshly bled.   *annoint*
In wine and oyle they wash his woundes wide,
And softly can embalme[4] on every side.
150   And all the while, most heavenly melody
About the bed sweet musicke did divide,[5]
Him to beguile of griefe and agony:
And all the while Duessa wept full bitterly.

---

1. The device of a god rescuing a hero in danger
by hiding him in a cloud has parallels in *Iliad* 3.380,
Aeneid 5.810–12, and *Gerusalemme Liberata* 7.44–
45.

2. I.e., Hades.
3. Aloud.
4. Carefully did anoint.
5. Played variations.

18

As when a wearie traveller that strayes
155   By muddy shore of broad seven-mouthèd Nile,
          Unweeting of the perillous wandring wayes,
          Doth meet a cruell craftie Crocodile,
          Which in false griefe hyding his harmefull guile,
          Doth weepe full sore, and sheddeth tender teares:
160   The foolish man, that pitties all this while
          His mournefull plight, is swallowed up unwares,°   unexpectedly
Forgetfull of his owne, that mindes anothers cares.

19

So wept Duessa untill eventide,
          That shyning lampes in Joves high house were light:[6]
165   Then forth she rose, ne lenger would abide,
          But comes unto the place, where th' Hethen knight
          In slombring swownd nigh voyd of vitall spright,[7]
          Lay covered with inchaunted cloud all day:
          Whom when she found, as she him left in plight,[8]
170   To wayle his woefull case she would not stay,
But to the easterne coast of heaven makes speedy way.

20

Where griesly° Night, with visage deadly sad,   grim, horrible
          That Phoebus chearefull face durst never vew,
          And in a foule blacke pitchie mantle clad,
175   She findes forth comming from her darkesome mew,°   den
          Where she all day did hide her hated hew.°   shape, color
          Before the dore her yron charet stood,
          Alreadie harnessèd for journey new;
          And cole blacke steedes yborne of hellish brood,
180   That on their rustie bits did champ, as they were wood.°   mad

21

Who when she saw Duessa sunny bright,
          Adorned with gold and jewels shining cleare,°   brightly
          She greatly grew amazèd at the sight,
          And th' unacquainted° light began to feare: unfamiliar
185   For never did such brightnesse there appeare,
          And would have backe retyred to her cave,
          Untill the witches speech she gan to heare,
          Saying, "Yet O thou dreaded Dame, I crave
Abide,° till I have told the message, which I have."   stay

22

190   She stayd, and foorth Duessa gan proceede,
          "O thou most auncient Grandmother of all,[9]
          More old then Jove, whom thou at first didst breede,
          Or that great house of Gods caelestiall,
          Which wast begot in Daemogorgons hall,

6. I.e., when ("that") the stars came out.
7. Nearly ("nigh") devoid of life.
8. I.e., in the same desperate state she left him.
9. By tradition Night was eldest of the gods, existing before the world was formed and the Olympian
gods were begotten in the hall of Demogorgon
(Chaos).

195   And sawst the secrets of the world unmade,[1]
      Why suffredst thou thy Nephewes° deare to rall   *grandsons*
      With Elfin sword, most shamefully betrade?
  Lo where the stout Sans joy doth sleepe in deadly shade.

23

    "And him before, I saw with bitter eyes
200   The bold Sans foy shrinke underneath his speare;
      And now the pray of fowles in field he lyes,
      Nor wayld of friends, nor laid on groning beare,[2]
      That whylome was to me too dearely deare.
      O what of Gods then boots it[3] to be borne,
205   If old Aveugles sonnes so evill heare?[4]
      Or who shall not great Nightes children scorne,
  When two of three her Nephews are so fowle forlorne.[5]

24

    "Up then, up dreary Dame, of darknesse Queene,
      Go gather up the reliques of thy race,
210   Or else goe them avenge, and let be seene,
      That dreaded Night in brightest day hath place,
      And can the children of faire light deface."°   *destroy*
      Her feeling speeches some compassion moved
      In hart, and chaunge in that great mothers face:
215   Yet pittie in her hart was never proved°   *known*
  Till then: for evermore she hated, never loved.

25

  And said, "Deare daughter rightly may I rew
      The fall of famous children borne of mee,
      And good successes, which their foes ensew:°   *attend*
220   But who can turne the streame of destinee,
      Or breake the chayne of strong necessitee,
      Which fast is tyde to Joves eternall seat?[6]
      The sonnes of Day he favoureth, I see,
      And by my ruines thinkes to make them great:
225 To make one great by others losse, is bad excheat.°   *exchange*

26

    "Yet shall they not escape so freely all;
      For some shall pay the price of others guilt:
      And he the man that made Sans foy to fall,
      Shall with his owne bloud price that[7] he hath spilt.
230   But what art thou, that telst of Nephews kilt?"
      "I that do seeme not I, Duessa am,"
      Quoth she, "how ever now in garments gilt,
      And gorgeous gold arayd I to thee came:
  Duessa I, the daughter of Deceipt and Shame."

---

1. Before it was made.
2. Bier attended by mourners ("groning").
3. What is it worth ("boots it").
4. I.e., are so badly thought of. "Aveugle" means "blind"; he is the son of Night and father of Sans Foy, Sans Joy, and Sans Loy.
5. Wretchedly lost.
6. The golden chain that binds the entire universe; the image goes back as far as Homer (*Iliad* 8.18–27).
7. I.e., pay for what.

27

235 Then bowing downe her agèd backe, she kist
        The wicked witch, saying; "In that faire face
        The false resemblance of Deceipt, I wist
        Did closely° lurke; yet so true-seeming grace   *secretly*
        It carried, that I scarse in darkesome place
240   Could it discerne, though I the mother bee
        Of falshood, and root of Duessaes race.
        O welcome child, whom I have longd to see,
    And now have seene unwares.° Lo now I go with thee." *unexpectedly*

28

        Then to her yron wagon she betakes,
245   And with her beares the fowle welfavour'd witch:
        Through mirkesome° aire her readie way she makes. *murky, dense*
        Her twyfold° Teme, of which two blacke as pitch,   *twofold*
        And two were browne, yet each to each unlich,°   *unlike*
        Did softly swim away, ne ever stampe,
250   Unlesse she chaunst their stubborne mouths to twitch;
        Then forming tarre,⁸ their bridles they would champe,
    And trampling the fine element,⁹ would fiercely rampe.

29

        So well they sped, that they be come at length
        Unto the place, whereas the Paynim lay,
255   Devoid of outward sense, and native strength,
        Coverd with charmèd cloud from vew of day,
        And sight of men, since his late luckelesse fray.
        His cruell wounds with cruddy° bloud congealed,   *clotted*
        They binden up so wisely,° as they may,   *skillfully*
260   And handle softly, till they can be healed:
    So lay him in her charet, close in night concealed.

30

        And all the while she stood upon the ground,
        The wakefull dogs did never cease to bay,
        As giving warning of th' unwonted° sound,   *unusual*
265   With which her yron wheeles did them affray,
        And her darke griesly° looke them much dismay;   *horrid*
        The messenger of death, the ghastly Owle
        With drearie shriekes did also her bewray;°   *reveal*
        And hungry Wolves continually did howle,
270   At her abhorrèd face, so filthy and so fowle.

31

        Thence turning backe in silence soft they stole,
        And brought the heavie corse with easie pace
        To yawning gulfe of deepe Avernus hole.¹
        By that same hole an entrance darke and bace
275   With smoake and sulphure hiding all the place,

8. Black froth.
9. The air. "Rampe": rear up.
1. In classical mythology, Avernus is Hell, where
Pluto reigns (line 282). Acheron (line 289) and

Phlegeton (line 291) are rivers in Hell. Cerberus
(line 298), the three-headed dog, is guardian there.
Stanzas 31–35 recall Aeneas's descent into Hell
(Virgil, *Aeneid* 6.200, 239–40).

Descends to hell: there creature never past,
That backe returnèd without heavenly grace;
But dreadfull Furies, which their chaines have brast,°   burst
And damnèd sprights sent forth to make ill° men aghast.   evil

32

280 By that same way the direfull dames doe drive
Their mournefull charet, fild° with rusty blood,   defiled
And downe to Plutoes house are come bilive:°   quickly, alive
Which passing through, on every side them stood
The trembling ghosts with sad amazèd mood,
285 Chattring their yron teeth, and staring wide
With stonie eyes; and all the hellish brood
Of feends infernall flockt on every side,
To gaze on earthly wight, that with the Night durst ride.

33

They pas the bitter waves of Acheron,
290 Where many soules sit wailing woefully,
And come to fiery flood of Phlegeton,
Whereas the damnèd ghosts in torments fry,
And with sharpe shrilling shriekes doe bootlesse° cry,   without avail
Cursing high Jove, the which them thither sent.
295 The house of endlesse paine is built thereby,
In which ten thousand sorts of punishment
The cursèd creatures doe eternally torment.

34

Before the threshold dreadfull Cerberus
His three deformèd heads did lay along,°   at full length
300 Curled with thousands adders venemous,
And lillèd° forth his bloudie flaming tong: lolled
At them he gan to reare his bristles strong,
And felly gnarre,[2] untill dayes enemy
Did him appease; then downe his taile he hong
305 And suffered them to passen quietly:
For she in hell and heaven had power equally.

35

There was Ixion turnèd on a wheele,
For daring tempt the Queene of heaven to sin;
And Sisyphus an huge round stone did reele°   roll
310 Against an hill, ne° might from labour lin;°   nor/cease
There thirstie Tantalus hong by the chin;
And Tityus fed a vulture on his maw;°   liver
Typhoeus joynts were stretchèd on a gin,°   rack
Theseus condemned to endlesse slouth° by law,   sloth
315 And fifty sisters water in leake vessels draw.[3]

---

2. Savagely snarl.
3. Ixion was being punished for attempting to seduce Juno; Sisyphus for refusing to pray to the gods; Tantalus for stealing the gods' nectar; Tityus for having tried to seduce Apollo's mother; the monster Typhoeus for creating destructive winds;

Theseus for stealing Persephone from Hades; and the daughters of King Danaus for having killed their husbands on their wedding night. Tantalus stood chin-deep in water which receded whenever he tried to drink—hence he is "thirstie." Ovid, Virgil, and Homer are Spenser's sources here.

36

They all beholding worldly° wights in place,°   *mortal/there*
  Leave off their worke, unmindfull of their smart,
  To gaze on them; who forth by them doe pace,
  Till they be come unto the furthest part:
320   Where was a Cave ywrought by wondrous art,
  Deepe, darke, uneasie,° dolefull, comfortlesse,   *lacking ease*
  In which sad Aesculapius farre a part
  Emprisond was in chaines remedilesse,°   *beyond any remedy*
For that Hippolytus rent corse he did redresse.[4]

37

325 Hippolytus a jolly° huntsman was,   *gallant*
  That wont° in charet chace the foming Bore;   *used to*
  He all his Peeres in beautie did surpas,
  But Ladies love as losse of time forbore:
  His wanton stepdame[5] lovèd him the more,
330   But when she saw her offred sweets refused
  Her love she turnd to hate, and him before
  His father fierce of treason false accused,
And with her gealous° termes his open eares
    abused.   *arousing jealousy*

38

Who all in rage his Sea-god syre[6] besought,
335   Some cursèd vengeance on his sonne to cast:
  From surging gulf two monsters straight were brought,
  With dread whereof his chasing steedes aghast,
  Both charet swift and huntsman overcast.
  His goodly corps on ragged cliffs yrent,
340   Was quite dismembred, and his members chast
  Scattered on every mountaine, as he went,
That of Hippolytus was left no moniment.[7]

39

His cruell stepdame seeing what was donne,
  Her wicked dayes with wretched knife did end,
345   In death avowing th' innocence of her sonne.
  Which hearing his rash Syre, began to rend
  His haire, and hastie tongue, that did offend:
  Tho gathering up the relicks of his smart[8]
  By Dianes meanes, who was Hippolyts frend,
350   Them brought to Aesculape, that by his art
Did heale them all againe, and joynèd every part.

40

Such wondrous science in mans wit to raine
  When Jove avizd,° that could the dead revive,   *discovered*
  And fates expirèd[9] could renew againe,
355   Of endlesse life he might him not deprive,

4. Aesculapius was god of medicine. "Redresse":
cure.
5. Phaedra, the wife of his father, Theseus.
6. Poseidon (Neptune).

7. I.e., no trace of identity.
8. I.e., his son's remains, that caused his grief.
"Tho": then.
9. The completed term of life as fixed by the Fates.

But unto hell did thrust him downe alive,
With flashing thunderbolt ywounded sore:
Where long remaining, he did alwaies strive
Himselfe with salves to health for to restore,
360   And slake the heavenly fire, that raged evermore.

41

There auncient Night arriving, did alight
    From her nigh wearie waine,[1] and in her armes
    To Aesculapius brought the wounded knight:
    Whom having softly disarayd of armes,
365   Tho gan to him discover all his harmes,
    Beseeching him with prayer, and with praise,
    If either salves, or oyles, or herbes, or charmes
    A fordonne° wight from dore of death mote raise,   undone
He would at her request prolong her nephews daies.

42

370   "Ah Dame," quoth he, "thou temptest me in vaine,
    To dare the thing, which daily yet I rew,
    And the old cause of my continued paine
    With like attempt to like end to renew.
    Is not enough, that thrust from heaven dew[2]
375   Here endlesse penance for one fault I pay,
    But that redoubled crime with vengeance new
    Thou biddest me to eeke?° Can Night defray°   increase/appease
The wrath of thundring Jove, that rules both night and day?"

43

"Not so," quoth she; "but sith that heavens king
380   From hope of heaven hath thee excluded quight,
    Why fearest thou, that canst not hope for thing,°   anything
    And fearest not, that more thee hurten might,
    Now in the powre of everlasting Night?
    Goe to them, O thou farre renowmèd sonne
385   Of great Apollo, shew thy famous might
    In medicine, that else° hath to thee wonne   already
Great paines, and greater praise, both never to be donne."°   ended

44

Her words prevaild: And then the learnèd leach°   doctor
    His cunning hand gan to his wounds to lay,
390   And all things else, the which his art did teach:
    Which having seene, from thence arose away
    The mother of dread darknesse, and let stay
    Aveugles sonne there in the leaches cure,°   care
    And backe returning tooke her wonted way,
395   To runne her timely race,[3] whilst Phoebus pure
In westerne waves his wearie wagon did recure.°   refresh

---

1. I.e., the horses of Night's chariot are nearly   2. The proper ("due") place for a god.
exhausted.   3. Her nightly journey.

45

The false Duessa leaving noyous° Night,   *harmful*
   Returnd to stately pallace of dame Pride;
   Where when she came, she found the Faery knight
400   Departed thence, albe° his woundes wide   *although*
   Not throughly heald, unreadie were to ride.
   Good cause he had to hasten thence away;
   For on a day his wary Dwarfe had spide,
   Where in a dongeon deepe huge numbers lay
405 Of caytive° wretched thrals,° that waylèd night   *captive/slaves*
   and day.

46

A ruefull sight, as could be seene with eie;
   Of whom he learnèd had in secret wise
   The hidden cause of their captivitie,
   How mortgaging their lives to Covetise,
410   Through wastfull° Pride, and wanton Riotise,   *causing desolation*
   They were by law of that proud Tyrannesse[4]
   Provokt with Wrath, and Envies false surmise,
   Condemnèd to that Dongeon mercilesse,
   Where they should live in woe, and die in wretchednesse.

47

415 There was that great proud king of Babylon[5]
   That would compell all nations to adore,
   And him as onely God to call upon,
   Till through celestiall doome° throwne out of dore,   *judgment*
   Into an Oxe he was transformed of yore:
420   There also was king Croesus,[6] that enhaunst°   *exalted*
   His heart too high through his great riches store;
   And proud Antiochus,[7] the which advaunst
   His cursèd hand gainst God, and on his altars daunst.°   *danced*

48

And them long time before, great Nimrod[8] was,
425   That first the world with sword and fire warrayd;°   *ravaged*
   And after him old Ninus farre did pas°   *surpass*
   In princely pompe, of all the world obayd;
   There also was that mightie Monarch layd
   Low under all, yet above all in pride,
430   That name of native° syre did fowle upbrayd,   *natural*
   And would as Ammons sonne[9] be magnifide,
   Till scornd of God and man a shamefull death he dide.

---

4. Lucifera. The noble sinners named in stanzas 47–50 exemplify a theme common in Renaissance morality, the fall of princes.
5. Nebuchadnezzar (Daniel 3–4).
6. King of Lydia, famous for his riches.
7. King of Syria, who desecrated the Jewish temple of Jerusalem (1 Maccabees 1.20–24).

8. Nimrod, identified as the first tyrant, caused the Tower of Babel to be built in defiance of God (Genesis 10.9). Ninus was founder of Ninevah, archetype of the wicked city (See the Book of Jonah).
9. Alexander the Great, occasionally worshiped as the son of Jupiter Ammon.

49

All these together in one heape were throwne,
    Like carkases of beasts in butchers stall.
435   And in another corner wide were strowne
    The antique ruines of the Romaines fall:
    Great Romulus[1] the Grandsyre of them all,
    Proud Tarquin, and too lordly Lentulus,
    Stout Scipio, and stubborne Hanniball,
440   Ambitious Sylla, and sterne Marius,
High Caesar, great Pompey, and fierce Antonius.

50

Amongst these mighty men were wemen mixt,
    Proud wemen, vaine, forgetfull of their yoke:°   *duty*
    The bold Semiramis,[2] whose sides transfixt
445   With sonnes owne blade, her fowle reproches spoke;
    Faire Sthenoboea,[3] that her selfe did choke
    With wilfull cord, for wanting° of her will;   *lacking*
    High minded Cleopatra, that with stroke
    Of Aspes sting her selfe did stoutly kill:
450 And thousands moe the like, that did that dongeon fill.

51

Besides the endlesse routs° of wretched thralles,   *crowds*
    Which thither were assembled day by day,
    From all the world after their wofull falles,
    Through wicked pride, and wasted wealthes decay.
455   But most of all, which in that Dongeon lay
    Fell from high Princes courts, or Ladies bowres,
    Where they in idle pompe, or wanton play,
    Consuměd had their goods, and thriftlesse howres,
And lastly throwne themselves into these heavy stowres.°   *disasters*

52

460 Whose case wheneas the carefull° Dwarfe had tould,   *anxious*
    And made ensample of their mournefull sight
    Unto his maister, he no lenger would
    There dwell in perill of like painefull plight,
    But early rose, and ere that dawning light
465   Discovered had the world to heaven wyde,
    He by a privie Posterne° tooke his flight,   *gate*
    That of no envious eyes he mote be spyde:
For doubtlesse death ensewd, if any him descryde.

53

Scarse could he footing find in that fowle way,
470   For many corses, like a great Lay-stall°   *rubbish heap*
    Of murdred men which therein strowěd lay,
    Without remorse, or decent funerall:

1. Romulus, founder of Rome; Tarquin, Roman tyrant; Lentulus, a conspirator with Catiline; Scipio, Roman general, conqueror of Carthage; Hannibal, Carthaginian general; Sulla, Roman civil war general; Marius, Sulla's rival; Julius Caesar; Pompey the Great; and Mark Anthony. All are memorialized in Plutarch's *Lives*.
2. Wife of Ninus.
3. Queen of King Proteus of Argos, who lusted after her brother-in-law Bellerophon.

Which all through that great Princesse pride did fall
And came to shamefull end. And them beside
475 Forth ryding underneath the castell wall,
A donghill of dead carkases he spide,
The dreadfull spectacle of that sad house of Pride.[4]

Canto 6

From lawlesse lust by wondrous grace
fayre Una is releast:
Whom salvage° nation does adore,   wild, of the woods
and learnes her wise beheast.°   bidding

1

As when a ship, that flyes faire under saile,
   An hidden rocke escapèd hath unwares,°   unexpectedly
   That lay in waite her wrack for to bewaile,[1]
   The Marriner yet halfe amazèd stares
5   At perill past, and yet in doubt ne dares
   To joy at his foole-happie oversight:[2]
   So doubly is distrest twixt joy and cares
   The dreadlesse° courage of this Elfin knight,   fearless
Having escapt so sad ensamples in his sight.

2

10 Yet sad he was that his too hastie speed
   The faire Duess' had forst him leave behind;
   And yet more sad, that Una his deare dreed°   object of reverence
   Her truth had staind with treason so unkind;
   Yet crime in her could never creature find,
15   But for his love, and for her owne selfe sake,
   She wandred had from one to other Ynd,[3]
   Him for to seeke, ne ever would forsake,
Till her unwares the fierce Sansloy did overtake.

3

Who after Archimagoes fowle defeat,
20   Led her away into a forrest wilde,
   And turning wrathfull fire to lustfull heat,
   With beastly sin thought her to have defilde,
   And made the vassall of his pleasures vilde.°   vile
   Yet first he cast by treatie,° and by traynes,°   persuasion/tricks
25   Her to perswade, that stubborne fort to yilde:
   For greater conquest of hard love he gaynes,
That workes it to his will, then he that it constraines.°   forces

4

With fawning wordes he courted her a while,
   And looking lovely,° and oft sighing sore,   lovingly

---

4. Named now, after we have been shown what the name means. "Spectacle": example.
1. I.e., cause the shipwreck and thereby cause it to be bewailed.

2. Lucky ignorance.
3. I.e., she would have wandered from the East to the West Indies.

30   Her constant hart did tempt with diverse guile:
        But wordes, and lookes, and sighes she did abhore,
        As rocke of Diamond stedfast evermore.[4]
        Yet for to feed his fyrie lustfull eye,
        He snatcht the vele, that hong her face before;
35   Then gan her beautie shine, as brightest skye,
        And burnt his beastly hart t' efforce° her chastitye.   *violate*

                                5

        So when he saw his flatt'ring arts to fayle,
        And subtile engines bet from batteree,[5]
        With greedy force he gan the fort assayle,
40   Whereof he weend° possessèd soone to bee,   *thought*
        And win rich spoile of ransackt chastetee.
        Ah heavens, that do this hideous act behold,
        And heavenly virgin thus outragèd see,
        How can ye vengeance just so long withhold,
45   And hurle not flashing flames upon that Paynim bold?

                                6

        The pitteous maden carefull° comfortlesse,   *full of cares*
        Does throw out thrilling° shriekes, and shrieking cryes,   *piercing*
        The last vaine helpe of womens great distresse,
        And with loud plaints importuneth the skyes,
50   That molten starres do drop like weeping eyes;
        And Phoebus flying so most shamefull sight,
        His blushing face in foggy cloud implyes,[6]
        And hides for shame. What wit of mortall wight
        Can now devise to quit a thrall[7] from such a plight?

                                7

55   Eternall providence exceeding° thought,   *transcending*
        Where none appeares can make her selfe a way:
        A wondrous way it for this Lady wrought,
        From Lyons clawes to pluck the gripèd pray.
        Her shrill outcryes and shriekes so loud did bray,
60   That all the woodes and forestes did resownd;
        A troupe of Faunes and Satyres[8] far away
        Within the wood were dauncing in a rownd,
        Whiles old Sylvanus slept in shady arber sownd.

                                8

        Who when they heard that pitteous strainèd voice,
65   In hast forsooke their rurall meriment,
        And ran towards the far rebownded° noyce,   *re-echoed*
        To weet, what wight so loudly did lament.
        Unto the place they come incontinent:°   *immediately*
        Whom when the raging Sarazin espide,

---

4. The diamond, because of its hardness, was an emblem of fidelity.
5. I.e., beaten ("bet") from their fruitless assault ("batteree") upon her unmovable virtue.
6. The sun is overcast by clouds. "Implyes": buries.
7. Release a victim.
8. Woodland deities with men's bodies above the waist and goats' bodies below, noted for their sensuality. Sylvanus, Roman god of the woods, is traditionally associated with fauns.

70 A rude, misshapen, monstrous rablement,
   Whose like he never saw, he durst not bide,
  But got his ready steed, and fast away gan ride.

9

  The wyld woodgods arrivèd in the place,
   There find the virgin dolefull desolate,
75 With ruffled rayments, and faire blubbred° face, *flooded with tears*
   As her outrageous foe had left her late,
  And trembling yet through feare of former hate;
   All stand amazèd at so uncouth° sight, *strange*
  And gin to pittie her unhappie state,
80 All stand astonied° at her beautie bright, *stupified*
  In their rude° eyes unworthie° of so wofull plight. *rustic/undeserving*

10

  She more amazed, in double dread doth dwell;
   And every tender part for feare does shake:
  As when a greedie Wolfe through hunger fell
85 A seely° Lambe farre from the flocke does take, *innocent*
   Of whom he meanes his bloudie feast to make,
  A Lyon spyes fast running towards him,
   The innocent pray in hast he does forsake,
  Which quit from death yet quakes in every lim
90 With chaunge of feare, to see the Lyon looke so grim.° *savage*

11

  Such fearefull fit assaid° her trembling hart, *assailed*
   Ne word to speake, ne joynt to move she had:
  The salvage nation feele her secret smart,
   And read her sorrow in her count'nance sad;
95 Their frowning forheads with rough hornes yclad,
   And rusticke horror° all a side doe lay, *roughness*
  And gently grenning, shew a semblance glad
   To comfort her, and feare to put away,
  Their backward bent knees teach her humbly to obay.[9]

12

100 The doubtfull Damzell dare not yet commit
   Her single person to their barbarous truth,[1]
  But still twixt feare and hope amazd does sit,
   Late learnd° what harme to hastie trust ensu'th, *taught*
  They in compassion of her tender youth,
105 And wonder of her beautie soveraine,
   Are wonne with pitty and unwonted ruth,° *pity*
  And all prostrate upon the lowly plaine,
  Do kisse her feete, and fawne on her with count'nance faine.° *glad*

13

  Their harts she ghesseth by their humble guise,° *appearance*
110 And yieldes her to extremitie of time;[2]

9. I.e., teach their knees, bent backwards like a ("barbarous truth").
goat's, to obey her.   2. I.e., necessity of the time.
1. I.e., her solitary self to their wild allegiance

So from the ground she fearelesse doth arise,
And walketh forth without suspect° of crime: *suspicion*
They all as glad, as birdes of joyous Prime,°   *springtime*
Thence lead her forth, about her dauncing round,
115   Shouting, and singing all a shepheards ryme,
And with greene braunches strowing all the ground,
Do worship her, as Queene, with olive girlond cround.

14

And all the way their merry pipes they sound,
That all the woods with doubled Eccho ring,
120   And with their hornèd feet do weare the ground,
Leaping like wanton kids in pleasant Spring.
So towards old Sylvanus they her bring;
Who with the noyse awakèd, commeth out,
To weet° the cause, his weake steps governing   *learn*
125   And agèd limbs on Cypresse stadle° stout,   *staff*
And with an yvie twyne his wast is girt about.

15

Far off he wonders, what them makes so glad,
Or Bacchus merry fruit they did invent,[3]
Or Cybeles franticke rites[4] have made them mad;
130   They drawing nigh, unto their God present
That flowre of faith and beautie excellent.
The God himselfe vewing that mirrhour rare,
Stood long amazd, and burnt in his intent;[5]
His owne faire Dryope now he thinkes not faire,
135   And Pholoe fowle, when her to this he doth compaire.[6]

16

The woodborne people fall before her flat,
And worship her as Goddesse of the wood;
And old Sylvanus selfe bethinkes not,[7] what
To thinke of wight so faire, but gazing stood,
140   In doubt to deeme her borne of earthly brood;
Sometimes Dame Venus selfe he seemes to see,
But Venus never had so sober mood;
Sometimes Diana he her takes to bee,
But misseth bow, and shaftes, and buskins° to her knee.   *soft boots*

17

145   By vew of her he ginneth to revive
His ancient love, and dearest Cyparisse,[8]
And calles to mind his pourtraiture alive,[9]
How faire he was, and yet not faire to this,
And how he slew with glauncing dart amisse

---

3. I.e., whether ("or") they did find ("invent") wine grapes.
4. Orgiastic dances in worship of Cybele, goddess of the powers of Nature.
5. Glowed with intense concentration. Una is a "mirrhour rare" in that she reflects heavenly beauty.
6. Dryope and Pholoe were nymphs loved by Faunus and Pan; for Spenser, the names "Faunus," "Pan," and "Sylvanus" were apparently interchangeable.
7. Cannot decide.
8. A fair youth, beloved of Sylvanus, turned into a cypress tree.
9. I.e., his appearance when alive.

150   A gentle Hynd, the which the lovely boy
        Did love as life, above all worldly blisse;
        For griefe whereof the lad n'ould° after joy,   *would not*
    But pynd away in anguish and selfe-wild annoy.°   *suffering*

18

    The wooddy Nymphes, faire Hamadryades[1]
155   Her to behold do thither runne apace,
        And all the troupe of light-foot Naiades,[2]
        Flocke all about to see her lovely face:
        But when they vewèd have her heavenly grace,
        They envie her in their malitious mind,
160   And fly away for feare of fowle disgrace:
        But all the Satyres scorne their woody kind,[3]
    And henceforth nothing faire, but her on earth they find.

19

    Glad of such lucke, the luckelesse lucky maid,
        Did her content to please their feeble eyes,
165   And long time with that salvage people staid,
        To gather breath in many miseries.
        During which time her gentle wit she plyes,
        To teach them truth, which worshipt her in vaine,
        And made her th' Image of Idolatryes;[4]
170   But when their bootlesse zeale she did restraine
    From her own worship, they her Asse would worship fayn.°   *willingly*

20

    It fortunèd a noble warlike knight
        By just occasion to that forrest came,
        To seeke his kindred, and the lignage right,°   *true*
175   From whence he tooke his well deservèd name:
        He had in armes abroad wonne muchell° fame,   *great*
        And fild far landes with glorie of his might,
        Plaine, faithfull, true, and enimy of shame,
        And ever loved to fight for Ladies right,
180   But in vaine glorious frayes he litle did delight.

21

    A Satyres sonne yborne in forrest wyld,
        By straunge adventure as it did betyde,°   *happen*
        And there begotten of a Lady myld,
        Faire Thyamis the daughter of Labryde,
185   That was in sacred bands of wedlocke tyde
        To Therion, a loose unruly swayne;[5]
        Who had more joy to raunge the forrest wyde,
        And chase the salvage beast with busie payne,[6]
    Then serve his Ladies love, and wast° in pleasures vayne.   *live idly*

---

1. Spirits of trees whose lives ended when the tree they inhabited died.
2. Water nymphs.
3. Forest inhabitants.
4. The idol of their idolatries.
5. "Thyamis" means passion; "Labryde," turbulent; "Therion," wild beast.
6. Painstaking care.

22

190 The forlorne mayd did with loves longing burne,
        And could not lacke° her lovers company,   be without
        But to the wood she goes, to serve her turne,
        And seeke her spouse, that from her still does fly,
        And followes other game and venery:[7]
195 A Satyre chaunst her wandring for to find,
        And kindling coles of lust in brutish eye,
        The loyall links of wedlocke did unbind,
    And made her person thrall unto his beastly kind.

23

    So long in secret cabin there he held
200   Her captive to his sensuall desire,
        Till that with timely fruit her belly sweld,
        And bore a boy unto that salvage sire:
        Then home he suffred her for to retire,°   return
        For ransome leaving him the late borne childe;
205   Whom till to ryper yeares he gan aspire,°   grow up
        He noursled° up in life and manners wilde,   reared
    Emongst wild beasts and woods, from lawes of men exilde.

24

    For all he taught the tender ymp,° was but   child
        To banish cowardize and bastard° feare;   base
210   His trembling hand he would him force to put
        Upon the Lyon and the rugged Beare,
        And from the she Beares teats her whelps to teare;
        And eke wyld roring Buls he would him make
        To tame, and ryde their backes not made to beare;
215   And the Robuckes[8] in flight to overtake,
    That every beast for feare of him did fly and quake.

25

    Thereby so fearelesse, and so fell° he grew,   fierce
        That his owne sire and maister of his guise[9]
        Did often tremble at his horrid vew,[1]
220   And oft for dread of hurt would him advise,
        The angry beasts not rashly to despise,
        Nor too much to provoke; for he would learne°   teach
        The Lyon stoup to him in lowly wise,
        (A lesson hard) and make the Libbard° sterne   leopard
225 Leave roaring, when in rage he for revenge did earne.°   yearn

26

    And for to make his powre approvèd° more,   demonstrated
        Wyld beasts in yron yokes he would compell;
        The spotted Panther, and the tuskèd Bore,
        The Pardale° swift, and the Tigre cruell;   female leopard
230   The Antelope, and Wolfe both fierce and fell;°   savage

7. The word means both "hunting" and "sexual   9. Teacher of his behavior.
play."   1. Rough appearance.
8. Deer, especially noted for their speed.

And them constraine in equall teme² to draw.
    Such joy he had, their stubborne harts to quell,
    And sturdie courage tame with dreadfull aw,
That his beheast they fearèd, as a tyrans law.

27

235 His loving mother came upon a day
    Unto the woods, to see her little sonne;
    And chaunst unwares° to meet him in the way,   *unexpectedly*
    After his sportes, and cruell pastime donne,
    When after him a Lyonesse did runne,
240   That roaring all with rage, did lowd requere°   *demand*
    Her children deare, whom he away had wonne:°   *seized*
    The Lyon whelpes she saw how he did beare,
And lull in rugged armes, withouten childish feare.

28

The fearefull Dame all quakèd at the sight,
245   And turning backe, gan fast to fly away,
    Untill with love revokt° from vaine affright,   *recalled*
    She hardly° yet perswaded was to stay,   *with difficulty*
    And then to him these womanish words gan say;
    "Ah Satyrane, my dearling, and my joy,
250   For love of me leave off this dreadfull play;
    To dally thus with death, is no fit toy,
Go find some other play-fellowes, mine own sweet boy."

29

In these and like delights of bloudy game
    He traynèd was, till ryper yeares he raught,°   *reached*
255   And there abode, whilst any beast of name
    Walkt in that forest, whom he had not taught
    To feare his force: and then his courage haught°   *high*
    Desird of forreine foemen to be knowne;
    And far abroad for straunge adventures sought:
260   In which his might was never overthrowne,
But through all Faery lond his famous worth was blown.°   *spread*

30

Yet evermore it was his manner faire,
    After long labours and adventures spent,
    Unto those native woods for to repaire,°   *return*
265   To see his sire and ofspring° auncient.   *origin*
    And now he thither came for like intent;
    Where he unwares the fairest Una found,
    Straunge Lady, in so straunge habiliment,°   *attire*
    Teaching the Satyres, which her sat around,
270 Trew sacred lore, which from her sweet lips did redound.°   *flow*

31

He wondred at her wisedome heavenly rare,
    Whose like in womens wit he never knew;
    And when her curteous deeds he did compare,

2. Side by side, yoked together in a team.

Gan her admire, and her sad sorrowes rew,°   *pity*
275   Blaming of Fortune, which such troubles threw,
And joyd to make proofe of her crueltie
On gentle Dame, so hurtlesse,° and so trew: *harmless*
Thenceforth he kept her goodly company,
And learnd her discipline° of faith and veritie.   *teachings*

32

280   But she all vowd³ unto the Redcrosse knight,
His wandring perill closely° did lament,   *secretly*
Ne in this new acquaintaunce could delight,
But her deare° heart with anguish did torment,   *loving*
And all her wit in secret counsels spent,
285   How to escape. At last in privie wise⁴
To Satyrane she shewèd her intent;
Who glad to gain such favour, gan devise,
How with that pensive Maid he best might thence arise.°   *depart*

33

So on a day when Satyres all were gone,
290   To do their service to Sylvanus old,
The gentle virgin left behind alone
He led away with courage stout and bold.
Too late it was, to Satyres to be told,
Or ever hope recover her againe:
295   In vaine he seekes that having cannot hold.
So fast he carried her with carefull paine,⁵
That they the woods are past, and come now to the plaine.

34

The better part now of the lingring day,
They traveild had, when as they farre espide
300   A wearie wight forwandring° by the way,   *wandering far and wide*
And towards him they gan in hast to ride,
To weet of newes, that did abroad betide,
Or tydings of her knight of the Redcrosse.
But he them spying, gan to turne aside,
305   For feare as seemid, or for some fieignèd losse;⁶
More greedy they of newes, fast towards him do crosse.

35

A silly° man, in simple weedes forworne,°   *simple/worn out*
And soild with dust of the long dried way;
His sandales were with toilesome travell torne,
310   And face all tand with scorching sunny ray,
As he had traveild many a sommers day,
Through boyling sands of Arabie and Ynde;°   *India*
And in his hand a Jacobs staffe,⁷ to stay
His wearie limbes upon: and eke behind,
315   His scrip° did hang, in which his needments he did bind.   *bag*

3. Entirely promised.   6. Pretended harm.
4. Privately.   7. I.e., pilgrim's staff.
5. Painstaking care.

36

The knight approching nigh, of him inquerd
   Tydings of warre, and of adventures new;
   But warres, nor new adventures none he herd.
   Then Una gan to aske, if ought he knew,
320 Or heard abroad of that her champion trew,
   That in his armour bare a croslet° red.   *small cross*
   "Aye me, Deare dame," quoth he, "well may I rew
   To tell the sad sight, which mine eies have red:°   *beheld*
These eyes did see that knight both living and eke ded."

37

325 That cruell word her tender hart so thrild,°   *pierced*
   That suddein cold did runne through every vaine,
   And stony horrour all her sences fild
   With dying fit,[8] that downe she fell for paine.
   The knight her lightly° reard up againe,   *quickly*
330 And comforted with curteous kind reliefe:
   Then wonne from death, she bad him tellen plaine
   The further processe° of her hidden griefe;   *account*
The lesser pangs can beare, who hath endured the chiefe.

38

Then gan the Pilgrim thus, "I chaunst this day,
335 This fatall day, that shall I ever rew,
   To see two knights in travell on my way
   (A sory° sight) arraunged in battell new,   *grievous*
   Both breathing vengeaunce, both of wrathfull hew:
   My fearefull flesh did tremble at their strife,
340 To see their blades so greedily imbrew,[9]
   That drunke with bloud, yet thristed after life:
What more? the Redcrosse knight was slaine with Paynim knife."

39

"Ah dearest Lord," quoth she, "how might that bee,
   And he the stoutest knight, that ever wonne?"°   *lived*
345 "Ah dearest dame," quoth he, "how might I see
   The thing, that might not be, and yet was donne?"
   "Where is," said Satyrane, "that Paynims sonne,
   That him of life, and us of joy hath reft?"
   "Not far away," quoth he, "he hence doth wonne°   *stay*
350 Foreby° a fountaine, where I late him left   *close by*
Washing his bloudy wounds, that through° the steele were cleft." *by*

40

Therewith the knight thence marchèd forth in hast,
   Whiles Una with huge heavinesse° opprest,   *grief*
   Could not for sorrow follow him so fast;
355 And soone he came, as he the place had ghest,
   Whereas that Pagan proud him selfe did rest,
   In secret shadow by a fountaine side:
   Even he it was, that earst would have supprest°   *violated*

8. Deathlike swoon.   9. Soak themselves in blood.

Faire Una: whom when Satyrane espide,
360 With fowle reprochfull words he boldly him defide.

41

And said, "Arise thou cursèd Miscreaunt,°   *infidel*
   That hast with knightlesse° guile and trecherous   *unknightly*
     train°   *deceit*
   Faire knighthood fowly shamed, and doest vaunt
   That good knight of the Redcrosse to have slain:
365 Arise, and with like treason now maintain°   *defend*
   Thy guilty wrong, or else thee guilty yield."
   The Sarazin this hearing, rose amain,°   *at once*
   And catching up in hast his three square[1] shield,
And shining helmet, soone him buckled to the field.

42

370 And drawing nigh him said, "Ah misborne Elfe,[2]
   In evill houre thy foes thee hither sent,
   Anothers wrongs to wreake upon thy selfe:
   Yet ill thou blamest me, for having blent°   *stained*
   My name with guile and traiterous intent;
375 That Redcrosse knight, perdie, I never slew,
   But had he beene, where earst° his armes were lent,   *before*
   Th' enchaunter vaine his errour should not rew:
But thou his errour shalt, I hope now proven trew."[3]

43

Therewith they gan, both furious and fell,°   *fierce*
380 To thunder blowes, and fiersly to assaile
   Each other bent° his enimy to quell,°   *determined/kill*
   That with their force they perst° both plate and maile, *pierced*
   And made wide furrowes in their fleshes fraile,
   That it would pitty° any living eie.   *bring pity to*
385 Large floods of bloud adowne their sides did raile:°   *flow*
   But floods of bloud could not them satisfie:
Both hungred after death: both chose to win, or die.

44

So long they fight, and fell revenge pursue,
   That fainting each, themselves to breathen let,
390 And oft refreshèd, battell oft renue:
   As when two Bores with rancling malice met,
   Their gory sides fresh bleeding fiercely fret,°   *tear*
   Til breathlesse both them selves aside retire,
   Where foming wrath, their cruell tuskes they whet,
395 And trample th' earth, the whiles they may respire
Then backe to fight againe, new breathèd and entire.°   *fresh*

45

So fiersly, when these knights had breathèd once,
   They gan to fight returne, increasing more

---

1. Triangular.
2. Base-born knight of Faerie Land ("Elfe").
3. I.e., had Redcrosse been wearing his arms the
enchanter Archimago would not have to regret his
error in fighting me. But you will now repeat his
error in fighting me and demonstrate what an error
it is.

Their puissant force, and cruell rage attonce,
400 With heapèd strokes more hugely, then before,
That with their drerie° wounds and bloudy gore   *gory*
They both deformèd,° scarsely could be known.   *disfigured*
By this sad Una fraught with anguish sore,
Led with their noise, which through the aire was thrown,
405 Arrived, where they in erth their fruitles bloud had sown.

46

Whom all so soone as that proud Sarazin
Espide, he gan revive the memory
Of his lewd lusts, and late attempted sin,
And left the doubtfull° battell hastily,   *undecided*
410 To catch her, newly offred to his eie:
But Satyrane with strokes him turning, staid,
And sternely bad him other businesse plie,
Then hunt the steps of pure unspotted Maid:
Wherewith he all enraged, these bitter speaches said.

47

415 "O foolish faeries sonne, what furie mad
Hath thee incenst, to hast thy dolefull fate?
Were it not better, I that Lady had,
Then that thou hadst repented it too late?
Most sencelesse man he, that himselfe doth hate,
420 To love another. Lo then for thine ayd
Here take thy lovers token on thy pate."
So they to fight; the whiles the royall Mayd
Fled farre away, of that proud Paynim sore afrayd.

48

But that false Pilgrim, which that leasing° told,   *lie*
425 Being in deed old Archimage, did stay
In secret shadow, all this to behold,
And much rejoycèd in their bloudy fray:
But when he saw the Damsell passe away
He left his stond,° and her pursewd apace,   *place*
430 In hope to bring her to her last decay.°   *death*
But for to tell her lamentable cace,
And eke this battels end, will need another place.

Canto 7

The Redcrosse knight is captive made
By Gyaunt proud opprest,°   *overwhelmed*
Prince Arthur meets with Una great-
ly with those newes distrest.

1

What man so wise, what earthly wit so ware,°   *wary*
As to descry° the crafty cunning traine,°   *perceive/guile*

By which deceipt doth maske in visour° faire,   *a mask*
And cast her colours dyèd deepe in graine,[1]
5 To seeme like Truth, whose shape she well can faine,
And fitting gestures to her purpose frame,
The guiltlesse man with guile to entertaine?°   *receive*
Great maistresse of her art was that false Dame,
The false Duessa, clokèd with Fidessaes name.

2

10 Who when returning from the drery° Night,   *dismal*
She fownd not in that perilous house of Pryde,
Where she had left, the noble Redcrosse knight,
Her hopèd pray, she would no lenger bide,
But forth she went, to seeke him far and wide.
15 Ere long she fownd, whereas° he wearie sate,   *where*
To rest him selfe, foreby° a fountaine side,   *beside*
Disarmèd all of yron-coted Plate,
And by his side his steed the grassy forage ate.

3

He feedes upon the cooling shade, and bayes[2]
20 His sweatie forehead in the breathing wind,
Which through the trembling leaves full gently playes
Wherein the cherefull birds of sundry kind
Do chaunt sweet musick, to delight his mind:
The Witch approaching gan him fairely° greet,   *courteously*
25 And with reproch of carelesnesse unkind
Upbrayd, for leaving her in place unmeet,°   *unfitting*
With fowle words tempring faire, soure gall with hony sweet.

4

Unkindnesse past, they gan of solace treat,°   *speak*
And bathe in pleasaunce of the joyous shade,
30 Which shielded them against the boyling heat,
And with greene boughes decking a gloomy glade,
About the fountaine like a girlond made;
Whose bubbling wave did ever freshly well,
Ne ever would through fervent° sommer fade:°   *hot/dry up*
35 The sacred Nymph, which therein wont to dwell,
Was out of Dianes favour, as it then befell.

5

The cause was this: one day when Phoebe[3] fayre
With all her band was following the chace,
This Nymph, quite tyred with heat of scorching ayre
40 Sat downe to rest in middest of the race:
The goddesse wroth gan fowly her disgrace,
And bad the waters, which from her did flow,
Be such as she her selfe was then in place.[4]

---

1. I.e., Deceit disposes her colors, thoroughly dyed, so as to seem like Truth.
2. Bathes. "Feedes upon": enjoys.
3. I.e., Diana, goddess of the moon and of chastity.
4. I.e., in that place.

Thenceforth her waters waxèd dull and slow,
45 And all that drunke thereof, did faint and feeble grow.

6

Hereof this gentle knight unweeting° was,   *ignorant*
    And lying downe upon the sandie graile,°   *gravel*
    Drunke of the streame, as cleare as cristall glas;
    Eftsoones his manly forces gan to faile,
50   And mightie strong was turnd to feeble fraile.
    His chaunged powres at first themselves not felt,
    Till crudled° cold his corage° gan assaile,   *congealing/vigor*
    And chearefull° bloud in faintnesse chill did melt,   *lively*
Which like a fever fit through all his body swelt.°   *raged*

7

55 Yet goodly court he made still to his Dame,
    Pourd out in loosnesse[5] on the grassy grownd,
    Both carelesse of his health, and of his fame:
    Till at the last he heard a dreadfull sownd,
    Which through the wood loud bellowing, did rebownd,
60   That all the earth for terrour seemed to shake,
    And trees did tremble. Th' Elfe therewith astownd,°   *amazed*
    Upstarted lightly from his looser make,[6]
And his unready weapons gan in hand to take.

8

But ere he could his armour on him dight,
65   Or get his shield, his monstrous enimy
    With sturdie steps came stalking in his sight,
    An hideous Geant horrible and hye,
    That with his talnesse seemd to threat the skye,
    The ground eke groned under him for dreed;
70   His living like saw never living eye,
    Ne durst behold: his stature did exceed
The hight of three the tallest sonnes of mortall seed.

9

The greatest Earth his uncouth mother was,
    And blustring Aeolus his boasted sire,[7]
75 Who with his breath, which through the world doth pas,
    Her hollow womb did secretly inspire,°   *breathe into*
    And fild her hidden caves with stormie yre,
    That she conceived; and trebling the dew time,
    In which the wombes of women do expire,°   *bring forth*
80   Brought forth this monstrous masse of earthly slime,
Puft up with emptie wind, and fild with sinfull crime.

10

So growen great through arrogant delight
    Of th' high descent, whereof he was yborne,

---

5. Stretched out and indulging in amorous play ("loosnesse").
6. More licentious ("looser") companion. "Lightly": quickly.

7. Aeolus was keeper of the winds. The giant's descent from Earth and Wind links him to earthquakes.

And through presumption of his matchlesse might,
85   All other powres and knighthood he did scorne.
    Such now he marcheth to this man forlorne,°   *abandoned*
    And left to losse:° his stalking steps are stayde   *destruction*
    Upon a snaggy Oke,[8] which he had torne
    Out of his mothers bowelles, and it made
90 His mortall mace, wherewith his foemen he dismayde.[9]

11

That when the knight he spide, he gan advance
    With huge force and insupportable mayne,[1]
    And towardes him with dreadfull fury praunce;
    Who haplesse, and eke hopelesse, all in vaine
95   Did to him pace, sad battaile to darrayne,°   *engage*
    Disarmd, disgrast, and inwardly dismayde,
    And eke so faint in every joynt and vaine,
    Through that fraile° fountaine, which him feeble made,   *enfeebling*
That scarsely could he weeld his bootlesse° single blade.   *useless*

12

100 The Geaunt strooke so maynly° mercilesse,   *mightily*
    That could have overthrowne a stony towre,
    And were not heavenly grace, that him did blesse,
    He had beene pouldred° all, as thin as flowre: *powdered*
    But he was wary of that deadly stowre,°   *peril*
105 And lightly° lept from underneath the blow: *quickly*
    Yet so exceeding was the villeins powre,
    That with the wind it did him overthrow,
And all his sences stound,° that still he lay full low.   *stunned*

13

As when that divelish yron Engin[2] wrought
110 In deepest Hell, and framd by Furies skill,
    With windy Nitre and quick Sulphur fraught,[3]
    And ramd with bullet round, ordaind to kill,
    Conceiveth fire, the heavens it doth fill
    With thundring noyse, and all the ayre doth choke,
115 That none can breath, nor see, nor heare at will,
    Through smouldry cloud of duskish stincking smoke,
That th' onely breath[4] him daunts, who hath escapt the stroke.

14

So daunted when the Geaunt saw the knight,
    His heavie hand he heavèd up on hye,
120 And him to dust thought to have battred quight,
    Untill Duessa loud to him gan crye;
    "O great Orgoglio,[5] greatest under skye,
    O hold thy mortall hand for Ladies sake,

---

8. I.e., he uses as walking stick a knotty ("snaggy") oak tree.
9. Dis-made, dissolved (also in line 96). "Mortall": death-dealing.
1. Irresistible power.
2. I.e., cannon.

3. Filled ("fraught") with gunpowder ("Nitre" and "Sulphur").
4. I.e., the blast or smell alone ("onely") overcomes him.
5. Orgoglio is Italian for "pride," haughtiness, disdain.

Hold for my sake, and do him not to dye,[6]

125 But vanquisht thine eternall bondslave make,

And me thy worthy meed unto thy Leman take."[7]

15

He hearkned, and did stay° from further harmes,   *refrain*

   To gayne so goodly guerdon,° as she spake: *reward*

   So willingly she came into his armes,

130 Who her as willingly to grace° did take,   *favor*

   And was possessèd of his new found make.°   *mate*

   Then up he tooke the slombred° sencelesse corse,   *unconscious*

   And ere he could out of his swowne awake,

   Him to his castle brought with hastie forse,

135 And in a Dungeon deepe him threw without remorse.

16

From that day forth Duessa was his deare,

   And highly honourd in his haughtie eye,

   He gave her gold and purple pall[8] to weare,

   And triple crowne set on her head full hye,[9]

140 And her endowd with royall majestye:

   Then for to make her dreaded more of men,

   And peoples harts with awfull terrour tye,°   *enthrall*

   A monstrous beast ybred in filthy fen

He chose, which he had kept long time in darksome den.

17

145 Such one it was, as that renowmèd Snake

   Which great Alcides in Stremona slew,

   Long fostred in the filth of Lerna lake,

   Whose many heads out budding ever new,

   Did breed° him endlesse labour to subdew: *cause*

150 But this same Monster much more ugly was;[1]

   For seven great heads out of his body grew,

   An yron brest, and backe of scaly bras,

And all embrewd° in bloud, his eyes did shine as glas.   *stained*

18

His tayle was stretchèd out in wondrous length,

155 That to the house of heavenly gods it raught,°   *reached*

   And with extorted powre, and borrowed strength,

   The ever-burning lamps° from thence it brought,   *stars*

   And prowdly threw to ground, as things of nought;

   And underneath his filthy feet did tread

160 The sacred things, and holy heasts foretaught.[2]

---

6. Do not cause him to die.

7. I.e., take me, your worthy reward, as your mistress.

8. Crimson robe of royalty.

9. Duessa is attired like the Whore of Babylon in Revelation 17.3–4; the triple crown is that of the papacy. See canto 2, stanzas 13 and 22, and notes.

1. The nine-headed Lernean hydra slain by Hercules (Alcides). The seven-headed monster is the red dragon of Revelation: "behold a great red dragon, having seven heads and ten horns, and seven crowns upon his heads . . . [whose] tail drew the third part of the stars of heaven, and did cast them to the earth . . . [he is] that old serpent, called the Devil, and Satan, which deceiveth the whole world" (12.3–4,9). Many Protestants associated the Beast with the Roman church.

2. Doctrines ("holy heasts") previously taught.

Upon this dreadfull Beast with sevenfold head
He set the false Duessa, for more aw and dread.

19

The wofull Dwarfe, which saw his maisters fall,
    Whiles he had keeping of his grasing steed,
165   And valiant knight become a caytive° thrall,   *captive*
    When all was past, tooke up his forlorne weed,[3]
    His mightie armour, missing most at need;
    His silver shield, now idle maisterlesse;
    His poynant° speare, that many made to bleed,   *sharp*
170   The ruefull moniments° of heavinesse,°   *memorials/grief*
And with them all departes, to tell his great distresse.

20

He had not travaild long, when on the way
    He wofull Ladie, wofull Una met,
    Fast flying from the Paynims greedy pray,°   *clutch*
175   Whilest Satyrane him from pursuit did let:°   *prevent*
    Who when her eyes she on the Dwarfe had set,
    And saw the signes, that deadly tydings spake,
    She fell to ground for sorrowfull regret,°   *grief*
    And lively breath her sad brest did forsake,
180   Yet might her pitteous hart be seene to pant and quake.

21

The messenger of so unhappie newes
    Would faine have dyde: dead was his hart within,
    Yet outwardly some little comfort shewes:
    At last recovering hart, he does begin
185   To rub her temples, and to chaufe her chin,
    And every tender part does tosse and turne:
    So hardly he the flitted life does win,
    Unto her native prison to retourne:[4]
Then gins her grievèd ghost° thus to lament and mourne.   *spirit*

22

190 "Ye dreary instruments of dolefull sight,
    That doe this deadly spectacle behold,
    Why do ye lenger feed on loathèd light,
    Or liking find to gaze on earthly mould,[5]
    Sith cruell fates the carefull° threeds unfould,   *sad*
195   The which my life and love together tyde?
    Now let the stony dart of senselesse cold[6]
    Perce to my hart, and pas through every side,
And let eternall night so sad sight fro me hide.

23

"O lightsome day, the lampe of highest Jove,
200   First made by him,[7] mens wandring wayes to guyde,

---

3. Abandoned garment.
4. I.e., with such difficulty ("so hardly") he persuades ("does win") the life back to her body ("native prison").
5. I.e., or find it pleasure to gaze on earthly forms ("mould").
6. I.e., death.
7. An allusion to Genesis 1.3: "And God said, Let there be light: and there was light."

When darknesse he in deepest dongeon drove,
Henceforth thy hated face for ever hyde,
And shut up heavens windowes shyning wyde:
For earthly sight can nought but sorrow breed,
205   And late° repentance, which shall long abyde.   *too late*
Mine eyes no more on vanitie shall feed,
But seelèd up with death, shall have their deadly meed."[8]

24

Then downe againe she fell unto the ground;
But he her quickly rearèd up againe:
210   Thrise did she sinke adowne in deadly swownd,
And thrise he her revived with busie paine:°   *care*
At last when life recovered had the raine,°   *rein*
And over-wrestled his strong enemie,
With foltring° tong, and trembling every vaine,   *faltering*
215   "Tell on," quoth she, "the wofull Tragedie,
The which these reliques sad present unto mine eie.

25

"Tempestuous fortune hath spent all her spight,
And thrilling° sorrow throwne his utmost dart;   *piercing*
Thy sad tongue cannot tell more heavy plight,
220   Then that I feele, and harbour in mine hart:
Who hath endured the whole, can beare each part.
If death it be, it is not the first wound,
That launchèd° hath my brest with bleeding smart.   *pierced*
Begin, and end the bitter balefull stound;°   *blow*
225   If lesse, then that I feare, more favour I have found."

26

Then gan the Dwarfe the whole discourse° declare,   *story*
The subtill traines° of Archimago old;   *wiles*
The wanton loves of false Fidessa faire,
Bought with the bloud of vanquisht Paynim bold:
230   The wretched payre transformed to treen mould;[9]
The house of Pride, and perils round about;
The combat, which he with Sans joy did hould;
The lucklesse conflict with the Gyant stout,
Wherein captived, of life or death he stood in doubt.

27

235   She heard with patience all unto the end,
And strove to maister sorrowfull assay,°   *affliction*
Which greater grew, the more she did contend,
And almost rent her tender hart in tway°   *two*
And love fresh coles unto her fire did lay:
240   For greater love, the greater is the losse.
Was never Ladie lovèd dearer day,[1]
Then she did love the knight of the Redcrosse;
For whose deare sake so many troubles her did tosse.

---

8. Reward of death.
9. Shape of a tree.

1. I.e., there was never a lady who loved life ("day")
more dearly than she loved Redcrosse.

28

At last when fervent sorrow slakèd was,
245   She up arose, resolving him to find
      Alive or dead: and forward forth doth pas,
      All° as the Dwarfe the way to her assynd:°   *just/showed*
      And evermore in constant carefull mind
      She fed her wound with fresh renewèd bale;°   *anguish*
250   Long tost with stormes, and bet° with bitter wind,   *beaten*
      High over hils, and low adowne the dale,
   She wandred many a wood, and measurd many a vale.

29

At last she chauncèd by good hap to meet
   A goodly knight, faire marching by the way
255   Together with his Squire, arayèd meet:°   *properly*
      His glitterand° armour shinéd farre away,   *glittering*
      Like glauncing° light of Phoebus brightest ray;   *flashing*
      From top to toe no place appearèd bare,
      That deadly dint° of steele endanger may: *stroke*
260   Athwart his brest a bauldrick² brave he ware,
   That shynd, like twinkling stars, with stons most pretious rare.

30

And in the midst thereof one pretious stone
   Of wondrous worth, and eke of wondrous mights,°   *powers*
   Shapt like a Ladies head, exceeding shone,
265   Like Hesperus° emongst the lesser lights,°   *evening star/stars*
      And strove for to amaze the weaker sights;
      Thereby his mortall blade full comely hong
      In yvory sheath, ycarved with curious slights;°   *designs*
      Whose hilts were burnisht gold, and handle strong
270   Of mother pearle, and buckled with a golden tong.°   *pin*

31

His haughtie helmet, horrid° all with gold,   *bristling*
   Both glorious brightnesse, and great terrour bred;
   For all the crest a Dragon did enfold
   With greedie pawes, and over all did spred
275   His golden wings: his dreadfull hideous hed
      Close couchèd on the bever,° seemed to throw   *visor*
      From flaming mouth bright sparkles fierie red,
      That suddeine horror to faint harts did show;
   And scaly tayle was stretcht adowne his backe full low.

32

280   Upon the top of all his loftie crest,°   *top of helmet*
      A bunch of haires discolourd° diversly,   *dyed*
      With sprincled pearle, and gold full richly drest,
      Did shake, and seemed to daunce for jollity,
      Like to an Almond tree ymounted hye
285   On top of greene Selinis³ all alone,

---

2. Sash worn over the shoulder to support the   3. Town associated with the palm awarded to vic-
sword.   tors (Virgil, *Aeneid* 3.705).

With blossomes brave bedeckèd daintily;
Whose tender locks do tremble every one
At every little breath, that under heaven is blowne.

33

His warlike shield all closely covered was,
290   Ne might of mortall eye be ever seene;
Not made of steele, nor of enduring bras,
Such earthly mettals soone consumèd bene:
But all of Diamond perfect pure and cleene°   clear
It framèd was, one massie entire mould,[4]
295   Hewen out of Adamant rocke with engines keene,
That point of speare it never percen could,
Ne dint of direfull sword divide the substance would.

34

The same to wight° he never wont disclose,   creature
But° when as monsters huge he would dismay,   except
300   Or daunt unequall armies of his foes,
Or when the flying heavens he would affray;[5]
For so exceeding shone his glistring ray,
That Phoebus golden face it did attaint,°   make dim
As when a cloud his beames doth over-lay;
305   And silver Cynthia° wexèd pale and faint,   the moon
As when her face is staynd with magicke arts constraint.[6]

35

No magicke arts hereof had any might,
Nor bloudie wordes of bold Enchaunters call,
But all that was not such, as seemd in sight,
310   Before that shield did fade, and suddeine fall:
And when him list the raskall routes[7] appall,
Men into stones therewith he could transmew,°   change
And stones to dust, and dust to nought at all;
And when him list the prouder lookes subdew,
315   He would them gazing blind, or turne to other hew.°   form

36

Ne let it seeme, that credence this exceedes,
For he that made the same, was knowne right well
To have done much more admirable° deedes.   marvelous
It Merlin was, which whylome° did excell   formerly
320   All living wightes in might of magicke spell:
Both shield, and sword, and armour all he wrought
For this young Prince, when first to armes he fell;°   came
But when he dyde, the Faerie Queene it brought
To Faerie lond, where yet it may be seene, if sought.[8]

4. The shield was made of one solid piece of Diamond, whose qualities—unflawed, unpierceable,
translucent—point to this knight's significance and
role.
5. I.e., when he would frighten ("affray") the
revolving constellations.
6. Magicians were believed to be able to cause an
eclipse of the moon.
7. Unruly mobs.

8. I.e., Arthur's virtues may be seen still in Queen
Elizabeth's England. By the references to Merlin
and the Faerie Queene, we now know that this
knight is Arthur, identified in the Letter to Ralegh
with "magnificence," understood as the perfection
of all the virtues and containing them all. The Letter
also states that in each book the deeds of Arthur
are applicable to the particular virtue treated in that
book.

37

325 A gentle youth, his dearely lovèd Squire
  His speare of heben° wood behind him bare,   *ebony*
  Whose harmefull head, thrice heated in the fire,
  Had riven many a brest with pikehead square;
  A goodly person, and could menage° faire   *control*
330   His stubborne steed with curbèd canon bit,[9]
  Who under him did trample as the aire,
  And chauft,° that any on his backe should sit;   *fretted*
The yron rowels° into frothy fome he bit.   *ends of the bit*

38

When as this knight nigh to the Ladie drew,
335   With lovely° court he gan her entertaine;   *kind*
  But when he heard her answers loth, he knew
  Some secret sorrow did her heart distraine:°   *afflict*
  Which to allay, and calme her storming paine,
  Faire feeling words he wisely gan display,°   *pour forth*
340   And for her humour fitting purpose faine,[1]
  To tempt the cause it selfe for to bewray;°   *reveal*
Wherewith emmoved, these bleeding words she gan to say.

39

"What worlds delight, or joy of living speach
  Can heart, so plunged in sea of sorrowes deepe,
345   And heapèd with so huge misfortunes, reach?
  The carefull° cold beginneth for to creepe,   *afflicting*
  And in my heart his yron arrow steepe,
  Soone as I thinke upon my bitter bale:°   *grief*
  Such helplesse harmes yts better hidden keepe,
350   Then rip up griefe, where it may not availe,
My last left comfort is, my woes to weepe and waile."

40

"Ah Ladie deare," quoth then the gentle knight,
  "Well may I weene, your griefe is wondrous great;
  For wondrous great griefe groneth in my spright,° *spirit*
355   Whiles thus I heare you of your sorrowes treat.
  But wofull Ladie let me you intrete,
  For to unfold the anguish of your hart:
  Mishaps are maistred by advice discrete,
  And counsell mittigates the greatest smart;
360 Found never helpe, who never would his hurts impart."[2]

41

"O but," quoth she, "great griefe will not be tould,
  And can more easily be thought, then said."
  "Right so"; quoth he, "but he, that never would,
  Could never: will to might gives greatest aid."[3]
365   "But grief," quoth she, "does greater grow displaid,

---

9. Cannon-bit; a smooth, round bit.
1. I.e., suited his manner to her mood.
2. I.e., he never found help who would not tell
his sorrows.

3. I.e., he that fails to will something cannot do
it: willing gives the greatest help to one's power
("might").

If then it find not helpe, and breedes despaire."
"Despaire breedes not," quoth he, "where faith is staid."°   *firm*
"No faith so fast," quoth she, "but flesh does paire."°   *impair*
"Flesh may empaire," quoth he, "but reason can repaire."

42

370 His goodly reason, and well guided speach
    So deepe did settle in her gratious thought,
    That her perswaded to disclose the breach,
    Which love and fortune in her heart had wrought,
    And said; "Faire Sir, I hope good hap hath brought
375 You to inquire the secrets of my griefe,
    Or° that your wisedome will direct my thought,   *either*
    Or that your prowesse can me yield reliefe:
Then heare the storie sad, which I shall tell you briefe.

43

"The forlorne° Maiden, whom your eyes have seene   *forsaken*
380   The laughing stocke of fortunes mockeries,
    Am th' only daughter of a King and Queene,
    Whose parents deare, whilest equall destinies
    Did runne about,[4] and their felicities
    The favourable heavens did not envy,
385   Did spread their rule through all the territories,
    Which Phison and Euphrates floweth by,
And Gehons golden waves doe wash continually.[5]

44

"Till that their cruell cursèd enemy,
    An huge great Dragon horrible in sight,
390   Bred in the loathly lakes of Tartary,°   *Tartarus (Hell)*
    With murdrous ravine,° and devouring might   *destruction*
    Their kingdome spoild, and countrey wasted quight:
    Themselves, for feare into his jawes to fall,
    He forst to castle strong to take their flight,
395   Where fast embard° in mightie brasen wall,   *imprisoned*
He has them now foure yeres besiegd to make them thrall.

45

"Full many knights adventurous and stout
    Have enterprizd that Monster to subdew;
    From every coast° that heaven walks about,   *land*
400   Have thither come the noble Martiall crew,
    That famous hard atchievements still pursew,
    Yet never any could that girlond win,
    But all still shronke,° and still he greater grew: *quailed*
    All they for want of faith, or guilt of sin,
405 The pitteous pray of his fierce crueltie have bin.

46

"At last yledd° with farre reported praise,   *led*
    Which flying fame throughout the world had spread,

4. I.e., while the impartial fates ran their course.
5. Since these three rivers flow in the Garden of

Eden (Genesis 2.11–14), we know that Eden is
the country of Una's parents.

    Of doughtie° knights, whom Faery land did raise,   *brave*
    That noble order hight of Maidenhed,[6]
410 Forthwith to court of Gloriane I sped,
    Of Gloriane great Queene of glory bright,
    Whose kingdomes seat Cleopolis is red,[7]
    There to obtaine some such redoubted knight,
That Parents deare from tyrants powre deliver might.

47

415 "It was my chance (my chance was faire and good)
    There for to find a fresh unprovèd° knight,   *untried*
    Whose manly hands imbrewed in guiltie blood
    Had never bene,[8] ne ever by his might
    Had throwne to ground the unregarded° right: *unrespected*
420 Yet of his prowesse proofe he since hath made
    (I witnesse am) in many a cruell fight;
    The groning ghosts of many one dismaide°   *defeated*
Have felt the bitter dint of his avenging blade.

48

  "And ye the forlorne reliques of his powre,
425 His byting sword, and his devouring speare,
    Which have endurèd many a dreadfull stowre,°   *conflict*
    Can speake his prowesse, that did earst° you beare,   *before*
    And well could rule: now he hath left you heare,
    To be the record of his ruefull losse,
430 And of my dolefull disaventurous deare:[9]
    O heavie record of the good Redcrosse,
Where have you left your Lord, that could so well you tosse?°*handle*

49

  "Well hopèd I, and faire beginnings had,
    That he my captive langour should redeeme,[1]
435 Till all unweeting,° an Enchaunter bad   *unknowing*
    His sence abusd, and made him to misdeeme°   *misjudge*
    My loyalty, not such as it did seeme;
    That rather death desire, then such despight.[2]
    Be judge ye heavens, that all things right esteeme,
440 How I him loved, and love with all my might,
So thought I eke of him, and thinke I thought aright.

50

  "Thenceforth me desolate he quite forsooke,
    To wander, where wilde fortune would me lead,
    And other bywaies he himselfe betooke,
445 Where never foot of living wight did tread,
    That brought not backe the balefull body dead;[3]
    In which him chauncèd false Duessa meete,

---

6. The type or analogue of the Order of the Garter. Its emblem shows St. George killing the dragon and its star is the Red Cross. "Hight": called.
7. Named. "Cleopolis" means "famous city."
8. I.e., his strong hands had never been guiltily stained ("imbrewed") with blood.

9. Sad unfortunate dear one.
1. I.e., relieve my state, captive to sadness.
2. I.e., I, who prefer death to such treachery ("despight").
3. I.e., who returned alive.

Mine onely foe, mine onely deadly dread,[4]
Who with her witchcraft and misseeming° sweete, *false appearance*
450 Inveigled him to follow her desires unmeete.°   *improper*

51

"At last by subtill sleights she him betraid
Unto his foe, a Gyant huge and tall,
Who him disarmèd, dissolute,° dismaid,   *enfeebled*
Unwares surprisèd and with mightie mall°   *club*
455 The monster mercilesse him made to fall,
Whose fall did never foe before behold;
And now in darkesome dungeon, wretched thrall,
Remedilesse, for aie[5] he doth him hold;
This is my cause of griefe, more great, then may be told."

52

460 Ere she had ended all, she gan to faint:
But he her comforted and faire bespake,
"Certes, Madame, ye have great cause of plaint,
That stoutest heart, I weene, could cause to quake.
But be of cheare, and comfort to you take:
465 For till I have acquit° your captive knight,   *freed*
Assure your selfe, I will you not forsake."
His chearefull words revived her chearelesse spright,
So forth they went, the Dwarfe them guiding ever right.

Canto 8

Faire virgin to redeeme her deare
brings Arthur to the fight:
Who slayes the Gyant, wounds the beast,
and strips Duessa quight.

1

Ay me, how many perils doe enfold
The righteous man, to make him daily fall?
Were not, that heavenly grace doth him uphold,
And stedfast truth acquite° him out of all.   *deliver*
5 Her love is firme, her care continuall,
So oft as he through his owne foolish pride,
Or weaknesse is to sinfull bands° made thrall: *bonds*
Else should this Redcrosse knight in bands have dyde,
For whose deliverance she this Prince doth thither guide.

2

10 They sadly traveild thus, untill they came
Nigh to a castle builded strong and hie:
Then cryde the Dwarfe, "lo yonder is the same;
In which my Lord my liege doth lucklesse lie,
Thrall to that Gyants hatefull tyrannie:
15 Therefore, deare Sir, your mightie powres assay."°   *put to trial*

4. I.e., the only object of my mortal fear.
5. I.e., forever ("for aie") without hope of rescue ("remedilesse").

The noble knight alighted by and by[1]
From loftie steede, and bad the Ladie stay,
To see what end of fight should him befall that day.

3

So with the Squire, th' admirer of his might,
20 He marchèd forth towards that castle wall;
   Whose gates he found fast shut, ne living wight
   To ward° the same, nor answere commers call.   guard
   Then tooke that Squire an horne of bugle small,[2]
   Which hong adowne his side in twisted gold,
25 And tassels gay. Wyde wonders over all[3]
   Of that same hornes great vertues weren told,
Which had approvèd° bene in uses manifold.   demonstrated

4

Was never wight, that heard that shrilling sound,
   But trembling feare did feele in every vaine;°   vein
30 Three miles it might be easie heard around,
   And Ecchoes three answered it selfe againe:
   No false enchauntment, nor deceiptfull traine°   snare
   Might once abide the terror of that blast,
   But presently° was voide and wholly vaine: at once
35 No gate so strong, no locke so firme and fast,
But with that percing noise flew open quite, or brast.° burst

5

The same before the Geants gate he blew,
   That all the castle quakèd from the ground,
   And every dore of freewill open flew.
40 The Gyant selfe dismaièd with that sownd,
   Where he with his Duessa dalliance° fownd,   amorous play
   In hast came rushing forth from inner bowre,
   With staring° countenance sterne, as one astownd,   glaring
   And staggering steps, to weet, what suddein stowre° disturbance
45 Had wrought that horror strange, and dared his dreaded powre.

6

And after him the proud Duessa came,
   High mounted on her manyheaded beast,
   And every head with fyrie tongue did flame,
   And every head was crownèd on his creast,
50 And bloudie mouthèd with late cruell feast.
   That when the knight beheld, his mightie shild
   Upon his manly arme he soone addrest,°   made ready
   And at him fiercely flew, with courage fild,
And eger greedinesse[4] through every member thrild.

---

1. Immediately.
2. A "bugle" is a wild ox; the "wide wonders" (marvelous tales) told of the horn connect it with the horn of Roland and the ram's horn of Joshua, with which he razed the walls of Jericho (Joshua

6.5). See also Romans 10.18, referring to the word of God as the horn of salvation.
3. Everywhere.
4. Intense eagerness for battle.

7

55 Therewith the Gyant buckled him to fight,
　　Inflamed with scornefull wrath and high disdaine,°　　*indignation*
　　And lifting up his dreadfull club on hight,
　　All armed with ragged snubbes° and knottie graine,　　*snags*
　　Him thought at first encounter to have slaine.
60　But wise and warie was that noble Pere,°　　*peer*
　　And lightly leaping from so monstrous maine,°　　*force*
　　Did faire° avoide the violence him nere;　　*quite*
It booted nought, to thinke, such thunderbolts to beare.[5]

8

Ne shame he thought to shunne so hideous might:
65　The idle° stroke, enforcing furious way,　　*useless*
　　Missing the marke of his misaymèd sight
　　Did fall to ground, and with his° heavie sway°　　*its/force*
　　So deepely dinted in the driven clay,
　　That three yardes deepe a furrow up did throw:
70　The sad earth wounded with so sore assay,°　　*assault*
　　Did grone full grievous underneath the blow,
And trembling with strange feare, did like an earthquake show.

9

As when almightie Jove in wrathfull mood,
　　To wreake° the guilt of mortall sins is bent,　　*punish*
75　Hurles forth his thundring dart with deadly food,[6]
　　Enrold in flames, and smouldring dreriment,°　　*horror*
　　Through riven cloudes and molten firmament;
　　The fierce threeforkèd engin° making way,　　*weapon*
　　Both loftie towres and highest trees hath rent,
80　And all that might his angrie passage stay,
And shooting in the earth, casts up a mount of clay.

10

His boystrous° club, so buried in the ground,　　*massive*
　　He could not rearen up againe so light,°　　*easily*
　　But that the knight him at avantage found,
85　And whiles he strove his combred° clubbe to　　*encumbered*
　　　quight°　　*release*
　　Out of the earth, with blade all burning bright
　　He smote off his left arme, which like a blocke
　　Did fall to ground, deprived of native might;
　　Large streames of bloud out of the trunckèd stocke
90　Forth gushèd, like fresh water streame from riven rocke.[7]

11

Dismaièd with so desperate deadly wound,
　　And eke impatient of unwonted paine,[8]

---

5. I.e., it is useless to think to withstand such blows.
This battle alludes to the struggle of the Protestant
against the Roman church, as well as to the struggle of divine grace against evil, the Antichrist.
6. Hatred (feud).

7. Cf. Exodus 17.6, where Moses smites the rock
and water flows forth.
8. I.e., unable to bear ("impatient of") this unfamiliar ("unwonted") pain.

He loudly brayd with beastly yelling sound,
That all the fields rebellowèd againe;
95   As great a noyse, as when in Cymbrian[9] plaine
An heard of Bulles, whom kindly° rage doth sting,   *natural*
Do for the milkie mothers want complaine,[1]
And fill the fields with troublous bellowing,
The neighbour woods around with hollow murmur ring.

12

100 That when his deare Duessa heard, and saw
The evill stownd, that daungerd her estate,[2]
Unto his aide she hastily did draw
Her dreadfull beast, who swolne with bloud of late
Came ramping° forth with proud presumpteous gate,°   *rearing/gait*
105 And threatned all his heads like flaming brands.°   *torches*
But him the Squire made quickly to retrate,
Encountring fierce with single° sword in hand,   *only*
And twixt him and his Lord did like a bulwarke stand,

13

The proud Duessa full of wrathfull spight,
110 And fierce disdaine, to be affronted so,
Enforst her purple beast with all her might
That stop° out of the way to overthroe,   *obstacle*
Scorning the let° of so unequall foe: *hindrance*
But nathemore° would that courageous swayne   *never the more*
115 To her yeeld passage, gainst his Lord to goe,
But with outrageous° strokes did him restraine,   *exceedingly fierce*
And with his bodie bard the way atwixt them twaine.

14

Then tooke the angrie witch her golden cup,
Which still she bore, replete with magick artes;[3]
120 Death and despeyre did many thereof sup,
And secret poyson through their inner parts,
Th' eternall bale° of heavie wounded harts;   *woe*
Which after charmes and some enchauntments said,
She lightly sprinkled on his weaker° parts;   *too weak*
125 Therewith his sturdie courage soone was quayd,°   *quelled*
And all his senses were with suddeine dread dismayd.

15

So downe he fell before the cruell beast,
Who on his necke his bloudie clawes did seize,
That life nigh crusht out of his panting brest:
130 No powre he had to stirre, nor will to rize.
That when the carefull° knight gan well avise,°   *watchful/observe*
He lightly° left the foe, with whom he fought,   *quickly*
And to the beast gan turne his enterprise;

---

9. Probably Wales.
1. I.e., mourn the cows' absence.
2. I.e., the peril ("stownd") that endangered her state.
3. Cf. the golden cup of the woman in Revela-

tion, which is "full of abominations and filthiness of her fornications" (17.4), the chalice of the Roman church, and the cup of Circe, the sorceress who turned men into beasts (in *Odyssey* 10).

For wondrous anguish in his hart it wrought,
135 To see his lovèd Squire into such thraldome° brought.   *slavery*

16

And high advauncing° his bloud-thirstie blade,   *lifting up*
Stroke one of those deformèd heads so sore,[4]
That of his puissance proud ensample made;
His monstrous scalpe° downe to his teeth it tore   *skull*
140 And that misformèd shape mis-shapèd more:
A sea of bloud gusht from the gaping wound,
That her gay garments staynd with filthy gore,
And overflowèd all the field around;
That over shoes in bloud he waded on the ground.

17

145 Thereat he roarèd for exceeding paine,
That to have heard, great horror would have bred,°   *produced*
And scourging th' emptie ayre with his long traine,°   *tail*
Through great impatience of his grievèd hed[5]
His gorgeous ryder from her loftie sted°   *place*
150 Would have cast downe, and trod in durtie myre,
Had not the Gyant soone her succourèd;
Who all enraged with smart° and franticke yre,°   *pain/anger*
Came hurtling in full fierce, and forst the knight retyre.

18

The force, which wont in two to be disperst,
155 In one alone left hand[6] he now unites,
Which is through rage more strong then both were erst;°   *before*
With which his hideous club aloft he dites,°   *raises*
And at his foe with furious rigour° smites,   *violence*
That strongest Oake might seeme to overthrow:
160 The stroke upon his shield so heavie lites,
That to the ground it doubleth him full low:
What mortall wight could ever beare so monstrous blow?

19

And in his fall his shield, that covered was,
Did loose his vele[7] by chaunce, and open flew:
165 The light whereof, that heavens light did pas,°   *surpass*
Such blazing brightnesse through the aier threw,
That eye mote not the same endure to vew.
Which when the Gyaunt spyde with staring° eye,   *awed*
He downe let fall his arme, and soft withdrew
170 His weapon huge, that heavèd was on hye
For to have slaine the man, that on the ground did lye.

20

And eke the fruitfull-headed° beast, amazed   *many-headed*
At flashing beames of that sunshiny shield,
Became starke blind, and all his senses dazed,

4. "I saw one of [the beast's] heads as it were
wounded to death" (Revelation 13.3).
5. I.e., through inability to endure ("impatience")
his afflicted ("grieved") head.
6. I.e., in the one hand left to him.
7. Its covering.

175 That downe he tumbled on the durtie field,
    And seemed himselfe as conquerèd to yield.
    Whom when his maistresse proud perceived to fall,
    Whiles yet his feeble feet for faintnesse reeld,
    Unto the Gyant loudly she gan call,
180 "O helpe Orgoglio, helpe, or else we perish all."

21

At her so pitteous cry was much amooved
    Her champion stout, and for to ayde his frend,°   *lover*
    Againe his wonted angry weapon prooved:°   *tried*
    But all in vaine: for he has read his end
185 In that bright shield, and all their forces spend
    Themselves in vaine: for since that glauncing° sight,   *flashing*
    He hath no powre to hurt, nor to defend;
    As where th' Almighties lightning brond does light,
It dimmes the dazèd eyen, and daunts the senses quight.

22

190 Whom when the Prince, to battell new addrest,
    And threatning high his dreadfull stroke did see,
    His sparkling blade about his head he blest,°   *brandished*
    And smote off quite his right leg by the knee,
    That downe he tombled; as an aged tree,
195 High growing on the top of rocky clift,
    Whose hartstrings with keene steele nigh hewen be,
    The mightie trunck halfe rent, with ragged rift°   *split*
Doth roll adowne the rocks, and fall with fearefull drift.°   *impact*

23

Or as a Castle rearèd high and round,
200 By subtile engins and malitious slight[8]
    Is underminèd from the lowest ground,
    And her foundation forst,° and feebled quight,   *shattered*
    At last downe falles, and with her heapèd hight
    Her hastie ruine does more heavie make,
205 And yields it selfe unto the victours might;
    Such was this Gyaunts fall, that seemed to shake
The stedfast globe of earth, as it for feare did quake.

24

The knight then lightly° leaping to the pray,   *quickly*
    With mortall steele him smot againe so sore,
210 That headlesse his unweldy bodie lay,
    All wallowd in his owne fowle bloudy gore,
    Which flowèd from his wounds in wondrous store.
    But soone as breath out of his breast did pas,
    That huge great body, which the Gyaunt bore,
215 Was vanisht quite, and of that monstrous mas
Was nothing left, but like an emptie bladder was.

---

8. Clever machines of war ("engins") and evil strategy.

25

Whose grievous fall, when false Duessa spide,
　　Her golden cup she cast unto the ground,
　　And crownèd mitre⁹ rudely threw aside;
220　Such percing griefe her stubborne hart did wound,
　　That she could not endure that dolefull stound,°   *sorrow*
　　But leaving all behind her, fled away:
　　The light-foot Squire her quickly turned around,
　　And by hard meanes enforcing her to stay,
225 So brought unto his Lord, as his deservèd pray.

26

The royall Virgin, which beheld from farre,
　　In pensive° plight, and sad perplexitie,   *anxious*
　　The whole atchievement of this doubtfull warre,¹
　　Came running fast to greet his victorie,
230　With sober gladnesse, and myld modestie,
　　And with sweet joyous cheare him thus bespake;
　　"Faire braunch of noblesse, flowre of chevalrie,
　　That with your worth the world amazèd make,
How shall I quite° the paines, ye suffer for my sake?   *requite*

27

235 "And you² fresh bud of vertue springing fast,
　　Whom these sad eyes saw nigh unto deaths dore,
　　What hath poore Virgin for such perill past,
　　Wherewith you to reward? Accept therefore
　　My simple selfe, and service evermore;
240　And he that high does sit, and all things see
　　With equall° eyes, their merites to restore,°   *impartial/reward*
　　Behold what ye this day have done for mee,
And what I cannot quite, requite with usuree.°   *interest*

28

"But sith the heavens, and your faire handeling°   *conduct*
245　Have made you maister of the field this day,
　　Your fortune maister eke with governing,³
　　And well begun end all so well, I pray,
　　Ne let that wicked woman scape away;
　　For she it is, that did my Lord bethrall,
250　My dearest Lord, and deepe in dongeon lay,
　　Where he his better dayes hath wasted all.⁴
O heare, how piteous he to you for ayd does call."

29

Forthwith he gave in charge unto his Squire,
　　That scarlot whore to keepen carefully;
255　Whiles he himselfe with greedie° great desire   *eager*

9. An allusion to the pope's triple tiara. "Rudely": violently.
1. I.e., the final outcome, long in doubt ("doubt-full") of this battle.
2. I.e., the Squire.

3. Secure your good fortune also by prudent management.
4. I.e., he has consumed ("wasted") here his best days.

Into the Castle entred forcibly,
Where living creature none he did espye;
Then gan he lowdly through the house to call:
But no man cared to answere to his crye.
260 There raignd a solemne silence over all,
Nor voice was heard, nor wight was seene in bowre or hall.

30

At last with creeping crooked pace forth came
An old old man, with beard as white as snow,
That on a staffe his feeble steps did frame,°   support
265 And guide his wearie gate° both too and fro: gait
For his eye sight him failèd long ygo,
And on his arme a bounch of keyes he bore,
The which unusèd rust did overgrow:
Those were the keyes of every inner dore,
270 But he could not them use, but kept them still in store.

31

But very uncouth° sight was to behold,   strange
How he did fashion his untoward° pace,   awkward
For as he forward mooved his footing old,
So backward still was turned his wrincled face,
275 Unlike to men, who ever as they trace,°   walk
Both feet and face one way are wont to lead.
This was the auncient keeper of that place,
And foster father of the Gyant dead;
His name Ignaro did his nature right aread.[5]

32

280 His reverend haires and holy gravitie
The knight much honord, as beseemèd well,[6]
And gently askt, where all the people bee,
Which in that stately building wont to dwell.
Who answerd him full soft, he could not tell.
285 Againe he askt, where that same knight was layd,
Whom great Orgoglio with his puissaunce fell
Had made his caytive° thrall; againe he sayde,   captive
He could not tell: ne ever other answere made.

33

Then askèd he, which way he in might pas:
290 He could not tell, againe he answerèd.
Thereat the curteous knight displeasèd was,
And said, "Old sire, it seemes thou hast not red°   recognized
How ill it sits with[7] that same silver hed
In vaine to mocke, or mockt in vaine to bee:
295 But if thou be, as thou art pourtrahèd
With natures pen, in ages grave degree,[8]
Aread° in graver wise, what I demaund of thee."   answer

5. His name Ignaro makes clear ("did aread") that
his nature is Ignorance, fit servant for Pride and
the false church.

6. Seemed proper.
7. I.e., suits.
8. I.e., dignity.

34

His answere likewise was, he could not tell.
   Whose sencelesse speach, and doted° ignorance   *foolish*
300 When as the noble Prince had markèd well,
   He ghest his nature by his countenance,
   And calmd his wrath with goodly temperance.
   Then to him stepping, from his arme did reach
   Those keyes, and made himselfe free enterance.
305 Each dore he openèd without any breach;°   *forcing*
There was no barre to stop, nor foe him to empeach.°   *hinder*

35

There all within full rich arayd he found,
   With royal arras° and resplendent gold.   *tapestry*
   And did with store of every thing abound,
310 That greatest Princes presence° might behold.   *person*
   But all the floore (too filthy to be told)
   With bloud of guiltlesse babes, and innocents trew,[9]
   Which there were slaine, as sheepe out of the fold,
   Defilèd was, that dreadfull was to vew,
315 And sacred ashes over it was strowèd new.

36

And there beside of marble stone was built
   An Altare, carved with cunning imagery,°   *images*
   On which true Christians bloud was often spilt,
   And holy Martyrs often doen to dye,[1]
320 With cruell malice and strong tyranny:
   Whose blessed sprites from underneath the stone
   To God for vengeance cryde continually,[2]
   And with great griefe were often heard to grone,
That hardest heart would bleede, to heare their piteous mone.

37

325 Through every rowme he sought, and every bowr,
   But no where could he find that wofull thrall:
   At last he came unto an yron doore,
   That fast was lockt, but key found not at all
   Emongst that bounch, to open it withall;
330 But in the same a little grate was pight,°   *placed*
   Through which he sent his voyce, and lowd did call
   With all his powre, to weet, if living wight
Were housèd therewithin, whom he enlargen° might.   *set free*

38

Therewith an hollow, dreary, murmuring voyce
335 These piteous plaints and dolours° did resound;   *laments*
   "O who is that, which brings me happy choyce°   *chance*

9. Probably a reference to Herod's massacre of the Innocents (Matthew 2.16), traditionally viewed as the first martyrs for Christ.
1. Put to death.
2. "And when he had opened the fifth seal, I saw under the altar the souls of them that were slain for the word of God, and for the testimony which they held: And they cried with a loud voice, saying, How long, O Lord, holy and true, dost thou not judge and avenge our blood on them that dwell on the earth?" (Revelation 6.9.10).

Of death, that here lye dying every stound,°   *moment*
Yet live perforce in balefull° darkenesse bound?   *evil*
For now three Moones have changèd thrice their hew,°   *shape*
340   And have beene thrice hid underneath the ground,
Since I the heavens chearefull face did vew,
O welcome thou, that doest of death bring tydings trew."

39

Which when that Champion heard, with percing point
Of pitty deare° his hart was thrillèd sore,   *extreme*
345   And trembling horrour ran through every joynt,
For ruth of gentle knight so fowle forlore:[3]
Which shaking off, he rent that yron dore,
With furious force, and indignation fell;°   *fierce*
Where entred in, his foot could find no flore,
350   But all a deepe descent, as darke as hell,
That breathèd ever forth a filthie banefull smell.

40

But neither darkenesse fowle, nor filthy bands,
Nor noyous° smell his purpose could withhold,   *noxious*
(Entire affection hateth nicer° hands)   *too fastidious*
355   But that with constant zeale, and courage bold,
After long paines and labours manifold,
He found the meanes that Prisoner up to reare;
Whose feeble thighes, unhable to uphold
His pinèd° corse, him scarse to light could beare,   *wasted*
360   A ruefull spectacle of deathe and ghastly drere.°   *wretchedness*

41

His sad dull eyes deepe sunck in hollow pits,
Could not endure th' unwonted sunne to view;
His bare thin cheekes for want of better bits,°   *food*
And empty sides deceivèd° of their dew,   *cheated*
365   Could make a stony hart his hap to rew;
His rawbone armes, whose mighty brawnèd bowrs[4]
Were wont to rive steele plates, and helmets hew,
Were cleane consumed, and all his vitall powres
Decayd, and all his flesh shronk up like withered flowres.

42

370   Whom when his Lady saw, to him she ran
With hasty joy: to see him made her glad,
And sad to view his visage pale and wan,
Who earst in flowres of freshest youth was clad.
Tho when her well of teares she wasted had,
375   She said, "Ah dearest Lord, what evill starre
On you hath fround, and pourd his influence bad,
That of your selfe ye thus berobbèd arre,
And this misseeming hew[5] your manly looks doth marre?

---

3. Foully forsaken.   5. Unseemly shape.
4. Brawny muscles.

43

"But welcome now my Lord, in wele or woe,
380   Whose presence I have lackt to long a day;
       And fie on Fortune mine avowèd foe,
       Whose wrathfull wreakes° them selves do now alay.   *punishments*
       And for these wrongs shall treble penaunce pay
       Of treble good: good growes of evils priefe."[6]
385   The chearelesse man, whom sorrow did dismay,°   *unnerve*
       Had no delight to treaten° of his griefe;   *speak*
His long endurèd famine needed more reliefe.

44

"Faire Lady," then said that victorious knight,[7]
       "The things, that grievous were to do, or beare,
390   Them to renew,° I wote,° breeds no delight;   *recall/know*
       Best musicke breeds delight in loathing eare
       But th' onely good, that growes of passèd feare,
       Is to be wise, and ware° of like agein.   *wary*
       This dayes ensample hath this lesson deare
395   Deepe written in my heart with yron pen,
That blisse may not abide in state of mortall men.

45

"Henceforth sir knight, take to you wonted strength,
       And maister these mishaps with patient might;
       Loe where your foe lyes stretcht in monstrous length,
400   And loe that wicked woman in your sight,
       The roote of all your care, and wretched plight,
       Now in your powre, to let her live, or dye."
       "To do her dye," quoth Una, "were despight,[8]
       And shame t' avenge so weake an enimy;
405 But spoile° her of her scarlot robe, and let her fly."   *despoil*

46

So as she bad, that witch they disaraid,
       And robd of royall robes, and purple pall,°   *cloak*
       And ornaments that richly were displaid;
       Ne sparèd they to strip her naked all.
410   Then when they had despoild her tire° and call,°   *robe/headdress*
       Such as she was, their eyes might her behold,
       That her misshapèd parts did them appall,
       A loathly, wrinckled hag, ill favoured, old,
Whose secret filth good manners biddeth not be told.

47

415 Her craftie head was altogether bald,
       And as in hate of honorable eld,°   *age*
       Was overgrowne with scurfe and filthy scald;[9]
       Her teeth out of her rotten gummes were feld,°   *fallen*

6. I.e., Fortune will now make amends for his   7. I.e., Arthur.
wrongs with triple benefits, as good comes from   8. I.e., to cause her to die would be despicable.
evils endured ("priefe").   9. A scabby disease of the scalp. "Scurfe": scabs.

And her sowre breath abhominably smeld;
420   Her dried dugs, like bladders lacking wind,
      Hong downe, and filthy matter from them weld;°   welled
      Her wrizled° skin as rough, as maple rind,   wrinkled
   So scabby was, that would have loathd all womankind.

                          48
   Her neather parts, the shame of all her kind,[1]
425   My chaster Muse for shame doth blush to write;
      But at her rompe she growing had behind
      A foxes taile, with dong all fowly dight;°   covered
      And eke her feete most monstrous were in sight;
      For one of them was like an Eagles claw,
430   With griping talaunts armd to greedy fight,
      The other like a Beares uneven° paw: rough
   More ugly shape yet never living creature saw.[2]

                          49
   Which when the knights beheld, amazd they were,
      And wondred at so fowle deformèd wight.
435   "Such their," said Una, "as she seemeth here,
      Such is the face of falshood, such the sight
      Of fowle Duessa, when her borrowed light
      Is laid away, and counterfesaunce° knowne."   deceit
      Thus when they had the witch disrobèd quight,
440   And all her filthy feature° open showne,   form
   They let her goe at will, and wander wayes unknowne.

                          50
   She flying fast from heavens hated face,
      And from the world that her discovered wide,
      Fled to the wastfull° wildernesse apace,   desolate
445   From living eyes her open shame to hide,
      And lurkt in rocks and caves long unespide.
      But that faire crew° of knights, and Una faire   company
      Did in that castle afterwards abide,
      To rest them selves, and weary powres repaire,
450   Where store they found of all, that dainty° was and rare. precious

                       Canto 9

              His loves and lignage Arthur tells:
                 The knights knit friendly bands:°   bonds
              Sir Trevisan flies from Despayre,
                 Whom Redcrosse knight withstands.

                          1
   O goodly golden chaine,[1] wherewith yfere°   together
      The vertues linkèd are in lovely wize:

---

1. I.e., womankind.
2. An allusion to Revelation 17.16: "these shall
hate the whore, and shall make her desolate and
naked." Foxes (cf. line 427) were emblems of cunning; eagles and bears (lines 429, 431) of rapacity,
of cruelty, and brutality.
1. The golden chain of love or concord which binds
the world and the human race together (cf. canto
5, stanza 25, and note).

And noble minds of yore allyèd were,
In brave poursuit of chevalrous emprize,°   *adventure*
5   That none did others safety despize,°   *disregard*
Nor aid envy° to him, in need that stands,   *begrudge*
But friendly each did others prayse devize
How to advaunce with favourable hands,
As this good Prince redeemd the Redcrosse knight from bands.

2

10   Who when their powres, empaird through labour long,
With dew repast they had recurèd° well,   *restored*
And that weake captive wight now wexèd strong,
Them list no lenger there at leasure dwell,
But forward fare, as their adventures fell,
15   But ere they parted, Una faire besought
That straunger knight his name and nation tell;
Least so great good, as he for her had wrought,
Should die unknown, and buried be in thanklesse thought.

3

"Faire virgin," said the Prince, "ye me require
20   A thing without the compas² of my wit:
For both the lignage and the certain Sire,
From which I sprong, from me are hidden yit.
For all so soone as life did me admit
Into this world, and shewèd heavens light,
25   From mothers pap I taken was unfit:³
And streight delivered to a Faery knight,
To be upbrought in gentle thewes° and martiall might.   *manners*

4

"Unto old Timon⁴ he me brought bylive,
Old Timon, who in youthly yeares hath beene
30   In warlike feates th' expertest man alive,
And is the wisest now on earth I weene;
His dwelling is low in a valley greene,
Under the foot of Rauran mossy hore,°   *gray*
From whence the river Dee as silver cleene°   *pure*
35   His tombling billowes rolls with gentle rore:⁵
There all my dayes he traind me up in vertuous lore.

5

"Thither the great Magicien Merlin came,
As was his use, ofttimes to visit me:
For he had charge my discipline° to frame,   *education*
40   And Tutours nouriture° to oversee.   *upbringing*
Him oft and oft I askt in privitie,
Of what loines and what lignage I did spring:
Whose aunswere bad me still assurèd bee,

2. I.e., beyond the reach of.
3. I.e., not yet weened.
4. The name means "Honor." "Bylive": immediately.
5. The hill Rauran is in Wales; the river Dee also

flows in, and forms part of, the boundary of Wales.
The Tudors (Queen Elizabeth's family) were
orginally Welsh, and the legends of Arthur had
their beginnings in the Celtic mythology of early
Wales.

     That I was sonne and heire unto a king,
45   As time in her just terme[6] the truth to light should bring."

6

     "Well worthy impe,"° said then the Lady gent,°   *offspring/gentle*
       "And Pupill fit for such a Tutours hand.
       But what adventure, or what high intent
       Hath brought you hither into Faery land,
50   Aread Prince Arthur,[7] crowne of Martiall band?"
       "Full hard it is," quoth he, "to read° aright   *discern*
       The course of heavenly cause, or understand
       The secret meaning of th' eternall might,
That rules mens wayes, and rules the thoughts of living wight.

7

55   "For whither he through fatall deepe foresight[8]
       Me hither sent, for cause to me unghest,
       Or that fresh bleeding wound, which day and night
       Whilome° doth rancle in my riven brest,   *all the while*
       With forcèd fury following his° behest,   *its*
60   Me hither brought by wayes yet never found,
       You to have helpt I hold my selfe yet blest."
       "Ah curteous knight," quoth she, "what secret wound
Could ever find,° to grieve the gentlest hart on ground?"   *succeed*

8

     "Deare Dame," quoth he, "you sleeping sparkes awake,
65   Which trubled once, into huge flames will grow,
       Ne ever will their fervent fury slake
       Till living moysture into smoke do flow,
       And wasted° life do lye in ashes low.   *consumed*
       Yet sithens° silence lesseneth not my fire,   *since*
70   But told it flames, and hidden it does glow,
       I will revele, what ye so much desire:
Ah Love, lay downe thy bow, the whiles I may respire.°   *breathe*

9

     "It was in freshest flowre of youthly yeares,
       When courage first does creepe in manly chest,
75   Then first the coale of kindly° heat appeares   *natural*
       To kindle love in every living brest;
       But me had warnd old Timons wise behest,
       Those creeping flames by reason to subdew,
       Before their rage grew to so great unrest,
80   As miserable lovers use to rew,
Which still wex° old in woe, whiles woe still wexeth new.   *grow*

10

     "That idle name of love, and lovers life,
       As losse of time, and vertues enimy
       I ever scornd, and joyd to stirre up strife,

---

6. Due course.
7. Arthur is named here for the first time. "Aread": declare.

8. I.e., whether he (God—"eternal might") sent me here through foresight ordained by fate ("fatall").

85   In middest of their mournfull Tragedy,
        Ay wont to laugh, when them I heard to cry,
        And blow the fire, which them to ashes brent:°   *burned*
        Their God himselfe, grieved at my libertie,
        Shot many a dart at me with fiers intent,
90   But I them warded all with wary government.[9]

                            11
     "But all in vaine: no fort can be so strong,
        Ne fleshly brest can armèd be so sound,
        But will at last be wonne with battrie° long,   *siege*
        Or unawares at disavantage found;
95   Nothing is sure, that growes on earthly ground:
        And who most trustes in arme of fleshly might,
        And boasts, in beauties chaine not to be bound,
        Doth soonest fall in disaventrous° fight.   *disastrous*
     And yeeldes his caytive neck to victours most° despight.   *greatest*

                            12
100 "Ensample make of him your haplesse joy,
        And of my selfe now mated,° as ye see;   *overcome*
        Whose prouder° vaunt that proud avenging boy   *too proud*
        Did soone pluck downe, and curbd my libertie.
        For on a day prickt° forth with jollitie   *spurred*
105   Of looser life, and heat of hardiment,°   *boldness*
        Raunging the forest wide on courser free,
        The fields, the floods, the heavens with one consent
     Did seeme to laugh° on me, and favour mine intent.   *smile*

                            13
     "For-wearied° with my sports, I did alight   *utterly wearied*
110   From loftie steed, and downe to sleepe me layd;
        The verdant° gras my couch did goodly dight,°   *green/make*
        And pillow was my helmet faire displayd:
        Whiles every sence the humour sweet embayd,[1]
        And slombring soft my hart did steale away,
115   Me seemèd, by my side a royall Mayd
        Her daintie limbes full softly down did lay:
     So faire a creature yet saw never sunny day.

                            14
     "Most goodly glee° and lovely blandishment°   *entertainment/compli-*
        She to me made, and bad me love here deare,   *ment*
120   For dearely sure her love was to me bent,
        As when just time expirèd[2] should appeare.
        But whether dreames delude, or true it were,
        Was never hart so ravisht with delight,
        Ne living man like words did ever heare,

---

9. I.e., self-control. The descriptions here of
Cupid's archery and of the siege of the castle of
chastity (in the next stanza) have many echoes from
the courtly-love traditions.

1. I.e., While the dew of sleep ("humour") per-
vaded ("embayd") every sense.
2. A fitting length of time having passed.

125 As she to me delivered all that night;
    And at her parting said, She Queene of Faeries hight.[3]

15

"When I awoke, and found her place devoyd,°   empty
    And nought but pressèd gras, where she had lyen,
    I sorrowed all so much, as earst I joyd,
130 And washèd all her place with watry eyen.
    From that day forth I loved that face divine;
    From that day forth I cast in carefull° mind,   care-filled
    To seeke her out with labour, and long tyne,°   hardship
    And never vow to rest, till her I find,
135 Nine monethes I seeke in vaine yet ni'll° that vow unbind." will not

16

Thus as he spake, his visage wexèd pale,
    And chaunge of hew great passion did bewray;°   reveal
    Yet still he strove to cloke his inward bale,°   grief
    And hide the smoke, that did his fire display,
140 Till gentle Una thus to him gan say;
    "Oh happy Queene of Faeries, that hast found
    Mongst many, one that with his prowesse may
    Defend thine honour, and thy foes confound:
True Loves are often sown, but seldom grow on ground."

17

145 "Thine, O then," said the gentle Redcrosse knight,
    "Next to that Ladies love, shalbe the place,
    O fairest virgin, full of heavenly light,
    Whose wondrous faith, exceeding earthly race,
    Was firmest fixt in mine extremest case.°   plight
150 And you, my Lord, the Patrone° of my life,   protector
    Of that great Queene may well gaine worthy grace:
    For onely worthy you through prowes priefe[4]
Yf living man mote° worthy be, to be her liefe."°   may/love

18

So diversly discoursing of their loves,
155 The golden Sunne his glistring head gan shew,
    And sad remembraunce now the Prince amoves,
    With fresh desire his voyage to pursew:
    Als° Una earnd° her traveill to renew.   so/yearned
    Then those two knights, fast friendship for to bynd,
160 And love establish each to other trew,
    Gave goodly gifts, the signes of gratefull mynd,
And eke as pledges firme, right hands together joynd.

19

Prince Arthur gave a boxe of Diamond sure,°   true
    Embowd° with gold and gorgeous ornament,   bound
165 Wherein were closd few drops of liquor pure,

3. Was called. This is one of the passages where the "faery" nature of *The Faerie Queene* makes itself strongly felt. In the background are many folktales and ballads of a hero bewitched by the Queene of Faery. Spenser's *Letter to Ralegh* identifies Gloriana allegorically with glory and with Queene Elizabeth.
4. Demonstration of prowess.

Of wondrous worth, and vertue excellent,
That any wound could heale incontinent:°   *immediately*
Which to requite, the Redcrosse knight him gave
A booke, wherein his Saveours testament
170 Was writ with golden letters rich and brave;°   *splendid*
A worke of wondrous grace, and able soules to save.[5]

20

Thus beene they parted, Arthur on his way
To seeke his love, and th' other for to fight
With Unas foe, that all her realme did pray.°   *prey upon*
175 But she now weighing the decayèd plight,
And shrunken synewes of her chosen knight,
Would not a while her forward course pursew,
Ne bring him forth in face of dreadfull fight,
Till he recovered had his former hew:°   *appearance*
180 For him to be yet weake and wearie well she knew.

21

So as they traveild, lo they gan espy
An armèd knight towards them gallop fast,
That seemèd from some fearèd foe to fly,
Or other griesly thing, that him agast.°   *terrified*
185 Still as he fled, his eye was backward cast,
As if his feare still followed him behind;
Als flew his steed, as he his bands had brast,°   *broken*
And with his wingèd heeles did tread the wind,
As he had beene a fole of Pegasus his kind.[6]

22

190 Nigh as he drew, they might perceive his head
To be unarmd, and curld uncombèd heares
Upstaring° stiffe, dismayd with uncouth° dread;   *bristling/unknown*
Nor drop of bloud in all his face appeares
Nor life in limbe: and to increase his feares,
195 In fowle reproch° of knighthoods faire degree,°   *disgrace/condition*
About his neck an hempen rope he weares,
That with his glistring armes does ill agree;
But he of rope or armes has now no memoree.

23

The Redcrosse knight toward him crossèd fast,
200 To weet, what mister° wight was so dismayd: *kind of*
There him he finds all sencelesse and aghast,
That of him selfe he seemd to be afrayd;
Whom hardly he from flying forward stayd,
Till he these wordes to him deliver might;
205 "Sir knight, aread° who hath ye thus arayd,   *declare*
And eke° from whom make ye this hasty flight: *also*
For never knight I saw in such misseeming° plight."   *unseemly*

5. Medieval romances mention such healing balms, but here the "drops of liquor pure" represent grace, perhaps in the Eucharist; Redcrosse gives Arthur the New Testament.
6. I.e., as if he had been a foal of a horse like Pegasus (a flying horse).

24

He answerd nought at all, but adding new
   Feare to his first amazment, staring wide
210   With stony eyes, and hartlesse hollow hew,[7]
   Astonisht stood, as one that had aspide
   Infernall furies, with their chaines untide.
   Him yet againe, and yet againe bespake
   The gentle knight; who nought to him replide,
215   But trembling every joynt did inly quake,
And foltring tongue at last these words seemd forth to shake.

25

"For Gods deare love, Sir knight, do me not stay;
   For loe he comes, he comes fast after mee."
   Eft° looking backe would faine have runne away;   *again*
220   But he him forst to stay, and tellen free
   The secret cause of his perplexitie:°   *distress*
   Yet nathemore° by his bold hartie speach,   *not at all*
   Could his bloud-frosen hart emboldned bee,
   But through his boldnesse rather feare did reach,
225 Yet forst, at last he made through silence suddein breach.

26

"And am I now in safetie sure," quoth he,
   "From him, that would have forcèd me to dye?
   And is the point of death now turnd fro mee,
   That I may tell this haplesse history?"
230   "Feare nought:" quoth he, "no daunger now is nye."
   "Then shall I you recount a ruefull cace,"°   *event*
   Said he, "the which with this unlucky eye
   I late beheld, and had not greater grace
Me reft from it, had bene partaker of the place.[8]

27

235 "I lately chaunst (Would I had never chaunst)
   With a faire knight to keepen companee,
   Sir Terwin hight, that well himselfe advaunst
   In all affaires, and was both bold and free,
   But not so happie as mote happie bee:
240   He loved, as was his lot, a Ladie gent,°   *noble*
   That him againe° loved in the least degree: *in return*
   For she was proud, and of too high intent,°   *spirit*
And joyd to see her lover languish and lament.

28

"From whom returning sad and comfortlesse,°   *desolate*
245   As on the way together we did fare,
   We met that villen (God from him me blesse°)   *defend*
   That cursèd wight, from whom I scapt why leare,[9]

---

7. I.e., with blanched, bloodless countenance.   9. A while before.
8. I.e., shared the same fate; "reft": carried from.

A man of hell, that cals himselfe Despaire;[1]
Who first us greets, and after faire areedes°   *tells*
250   Of tydings strange, and of adventures rare:
So creeping close, as Snake in hidden weedes,
Inquireth of our states, and of our knightly deedes.

29

"Which when he knew, and felt our feeble harts
Embost° with bale,° and bitter byting griefe,   *exhausted/sorrow*
255   Which love had launchèd° with his deadly darts,   *pierced*
With wounding words and termes of foule repriefe°   *insult*
He pluckt from us all hope of due reliefe,
That earst us held in love of lingring life;
Then hopelesse hartlesse, gan the cunning thiefe
260   Perswade us die, to stint° all further strife: *end*
To me he lent this rope, to him a rustie knife.

30

"With which sad instrument of hastie death,
That wofull lover, loathing lenger° light,   *longer*
A wide way made to let forth living breath.
265   But I more fearefull, or more luckie wight,
Dismayd with that deformèd dismall sight,
Fled fast away, halfe dead with dying feare:[2]
Ne yet assured of life by you, Sir knight,
Whose like infirmitie like chaunce may beare:
270   But God you never let his charmèd speeches heare."[3]

31

"How may a man," said he, "with idle speach
Be wonne, to spoyle° the Castle of his health?"   *destroy*
"I wote," quoth he, "whom triall° late did teach,   *experience*
That like would not[4] for all this worldes wealth:
275   His subtill tongue, like dropping honny, mealt'th°   *melts*
Into the hart, and searcheth every vaine,
That ere one be aware, by secret stealth
His powre is reft, and weaknesse doth remaine.
O never Sir desire to try° his guilefull traine."°   *test/treachery*

32

280   "Certes,"° said he, "hence shall I never rest,   *surely*
Till I that treachours art have heard and tride;
And you Sir knight, whose name mote° I request,   *might*
Of grace° do me unto his cabin° guide."   *favor/cave*
"I that hight Trevisan,"[5] quoth he, "will ride
285   Against my liking backe, to doe you grace:
But nor for gold nor glee[6] will I abide

---

1. Despair is the ultimate Christian sin, denying the possibility of Divine mercy and grace. Dr. Faustus at the end of Marlowe's play is in a state of despair (see pp. 863–64).
2. Fear of death.
3. I.e., may God never let you hear his mesmer-

izing ("charmed") speeches.
4. I.e., would not do the like again.
5. His name may connote weariness, fatigue ("terwyn"); "hight": am called.
6. Song; i.e., anything you can say to me.

By you, when ye arrive in that same place;
For lever° had I die, then see his deadly face."   *rather*

33

Ere long they come, where that same wicked wight
290   His dwelling has, low in an hollow cave,
   Farre underneath a craggie clift ypight,°   *placed*
   Darke, dolefull, drearie, like a greedie grave,
   That still for carrion carcases doth crave:
   On top whereof aye dwelt the ghastly Owle,[7]
295   Shrieking his balefull note, which ever drave
   Farre from that haunt all other chearefull fowle;
And all about it wandring ghostes did waile and howle.

34

And all about old stockes° and stubs of trees,   *stumps*
   Whereon nor fruit, nor leafe was ever seene,
300   Did hang upon the ragged rocky knees;°   *crags*
   On which had many wretches hangèd beene,
   Whose carcases were scattered on the greene,
   And throwne about the cliffs. Arrivèd there,
   That bare-head knight for dread and dolefull teene,°   *grief*
305   Would faine° have fled, ne durst approachen neare,   *gladly*
But th' other forst him stay, and comforted in feare.

35

That darkesome cave they enter, where they find
   That cursèd man, low sitting on the ground,
   Musing full sadly in his sullein° mind;   *morose*
310   His griesie° lockes, long growen, and unbound,   *gray*
   Disordred hong about his shoulders round,
   And hid his face; through which his hollow eyne
   Lookt deadly dull, and starèd as astound;
   His raw-bone cheekes through penurie and pine,°   *starvation*
315 Were shronke into his jawes, as° he did never dine.   *as if*

36

His garment nought but many ragged clouts,°   *rags*
   With thornes together pind and patchèd was,
   The which his naked sides he wrapt abouts;
   And him beside there lay upon the gras
320   A drearie° corse, whose life away did pas,   *bloody*
   All wallowd in his owne yet luke-warme blood,
   That from his wound yet wellèd fresh alas;
   In which a rustie° knife fast fixèd stood,   *bloodstained*
And made an open passage for the gushing flood.

37

325 Which piteous spectacle, approving° trew   *confirming*
   The wofull tale that Trevisan had told,
   When as the gentle Redcrosse knight did vew,
   With firie zeale he burnt in courage bold,

7. Traditionally a messenger of death.

Him to avenge, before his bloud were cold,
330   And to the villein said, "Thou damnèd wight,
The author of this fact,° we here behold,   *deed*
What justice can but judge against thee right,
With thine owne bloud to price° his bloud, here   *pay for*
    shed in sight?"

38

"What franticke fit," quoth he,[8] "hath thus distraught
335   Thee, foolish man, so rash a doome° to give?   *judgment*
What justice ever other judgement taught,
But he should die, who merites not to live?
None else to death this man despayring drive,°   *drove*
But his owne guiltie mind deserving death.
340   Is then unjust to each his due to give?
Or let him die, that loatheth living breath?
Or let him die at ease, that liveth here uneath°?   *in unease*

39

"Who travels by the wearie wandring way,
    To come unto his wishèd home in haste,
345   And meetes a flood, that doth his passage stay,
Is not great grace to helpe him over past,
Or free his feet, that in the myre sticke fast?
Most envious man, that grieves at neighbours good,
And fond,° that joyest in the woe thou hast,   *foolish*
350   Why wilt not let him passe, that long hath stood
Upon the banke, yet wilt thy selfe not passe the flood?

40

"He there does now enjoy eternall rest
    And happie ease, which thou doest want and crave,
    And further from it daily wanderest:
355   What if some litle paine the passage have,
That makes fraile flesh to feare the bitter wave?
Is not short paine well borne, that brings long ease,
And layes the soule to sleepe in quiet grave?
Sleepe after toyle, port after stormie seas,
360   Ease after warre, death after life does greatly please."[9]

41

The knight much wondred at his suddeine wit,[1]
    And said, "The terme of life is limited,
    Ne may a man prolong, nor shorten it;
    The souldier may not move from watchfull sted,[2]
365   Nor leave his stand, untill his Captaine bed."°   *commands*
"Who life did limit by almightie doome,"
Quoth he,[3] "knowes best the termes establishèd;

---

8. I.e., Despaire.
9. Despaire's arguments on behalf of suicide as against a painful life are derived, like those of Hamlet in his third soliloquy (*Hamlet* 3.1.56–88), principally from Seneca, Marcus Aurelius, and the ancient Stoics, and from Old Testament utterings

on divine justice. His speech is devised according to classical rules of rhetoric.
1. Quick intelligence.
2. The sentry post assigned him.
3. I.e., Despaire.

And he, that points the Centonell his roome,°   *station*
Doth license him depart at sound of morning droome.[4]

42

370 "Is not his deed, what ever thing is donne,
    In heaven and earth? did not he all create
    To die againe? all ends that was begonne.
    Their times in his eternall booke of fate
    Are written sure, and have their certaine° date.   *fixed*
375 Who then can strive with strong necessitie,
    That holds the world in his still chaunging state,
    Or shunne the death ordaynd by destinie?
When houre of death is come, let none aske whence, nor why.

43

"The lenger life, I wote° the greater sin,   *know*
380 The greater sin, the greater punishment:
    All those great battels, which thou boasts to win,
    Through strife, and bloud-shed, and avengement,
    Now praysd, hereafter deare° thou shalt repent: *bitterly*
    For life must life, and bloud must bloud repay.[5]
385 Is not enough thy evill life forespent?
    For he, that once hath missèd the right way,
The further he doth goe, the further he doth stray.

44

"Then do no further goe, no further stray,
    But here lie downe, and to thy rest betake,
390 Th' ill to prevent, that life ensewen may.[6]
    For what hath life, that may it lovèd make,
    And gives not rather cause it to forsake?
    Feare, sicknesse, age, losse, labour, sorrow, strife,
    Paine, hunger, cold, that makes the hart to quake;
395 And ever fickle fortune rageth rife,
All which, and thousands mo° do make a loathsome life.   *more*

45

"Thou wretched man, of death hast greatest need,
    If in true ballance thou wilt weigh thy state:
    For never knight, that darèd warlike deede,
400 More lucklesse disaventures° did amate:°   *misfortunes/appall*
    Witnesse the dongeon deepe, wherein of late
    Thy life shut up, for death so oft did call;
    And though good lucke prolongèd hath thy date,°   *span of life*
    Yet death then, would the like mishaps forestall,
405 Into the which hereafter thou maiest happen fall.[7]

46

"Why then doest thou, O man of sin, desire
    To draw thy dayes forth to their last degree?

---

4. Drum, with a pun on doom.
5. An echo of Genesis 9.6: "Whoso sheddeth man's blood, by man shall his blood be shed."
6. I.e., to prevent the evil that will ensue in the rest of your life.
7. Happen to fall.

Is not the measure of thy sinfull hire[8]
High heapèd up with huge iniquitie,
410 Against the day of wrath,[9] to burden thee?
Is not enough that to this Ladie milde
Thou falsèd° hast thy faith with perjurie,   *betrayed*
And sold thy selfe to serve Duessa vilde,°   *vile*
With whom in all abuse thou hast thy selfe defilde?

47

415 "Is not he just, that all this doth behold
From highest heaven, and beares an equall° eye?   *impartial*
Shall he thy sins up in his knowledge fold,
And guiltie be of thine impietie?
Is not his law, Let every sinner die:[1]
420 Die shall all flesh? what then must needs be donne,
Is it not better to doe willinglie,
Then linger, till the glasse° be all out ronne?   *hourglass*
Death is the end of woes: die soone, O faeries sonne."

48

The knight was much enmovèd with his speach,
425 That as a swords point through his hart did perse,
And in his conscience made a secret breach,
Well knowing true all, that he did reherse°   *recount*
And to his fresh remembrance did reverse°   *bring back*
The ugly vew of his deformèd crimes,
430 That all his manly powres it did disperse,
As he were charmèd with inchaunted rimes,
That oftentimes he quakt, and fainted oftentimes.

49

In which amazement, when the Miscreant°   *wretch*
Perceivèd him to waver weake and fraile,
435 Whiles trembling horror did his conscience dant,° *daunt*
And hellish anguish[2] did his soule assaile,
To drive him to despaire, and quite to quaile,°   *be dismayed*
He shewed him painted in a table° plaine,   *picture*
The damnèd ghosts, that doe in torments waile,
440 And thousand feends that doe them endlesse paine
With fire and brimstone, which for ever shall remaine.

50

The sight whereof so throughly him dismaid,
That nought but death before his eyes he saw,
And ever burning wrath before him laid,
445 By righteous sentence of th' Almighties law:
Then gan the villein him to overcraw,°   *exult over*
And brought unto him swords, ropes, poison, fire,

---

8. Service to sin.
9. Judgment Day.
1. Despaire cites only half of the scripture verse: "The wages of sin is death; but the gift of God is eternal life through Jesus Christ our Lord" (Romans 6.23).
2. I.e., fear of hell.

And all that might him to perdition draw;
And bad him choose, what death he would desire:
450   For death was due to him, that had provokt Gods ire.

51

But when as none of them he saw him take,
  He to him raught° a dagger sharpe and keene,   *reached*
  And gave it him in hand: his hand did quake,
  And tremble like a leafe of Aspin greene,
455   And troubled bloud through his pale face was seene
  To come, and goe with tydings from the hart,
  As it a running messenger had beene.
At last resolved to worke his finall smart,
He lifted up his hand, that backe againe did start.

52

460 Which when as Una saw, through every vaine
   The crudled° cold ran to her well of life,°   *congealing/heart*
  As in a swowne: but soone relived° againe,   *revived*
  Out of his hand she snatcht the cursèd knife,
  And threw it to the ground, enragèd rife,°   *deeply*
465   And to him said, "Fie, fie, faint harted knight,
  What meanest thou by this reprochfull° strife? *deserving reproach*
  Is this the battell, which thou vauntst to fight
With the fire-mouthèd Dragon, horrible and bright?

53

"Come, come away, fraile, feeble, fleshly wight,
470   Ne let vaine words bewitch thy manly hart,
  Ne divelish thoughts dismay thy constant spright.
  In heavenly mercies hast thou not a part?
  Why shouldst thou then despeire, that chosen art?
  Where justice growes, there grows eke° greater grace, *also*
475   The which doth quench the brond of hellish smart,
  And that accurst hand-writing[3] doth deface.°   *blot out*
Arise, Sir knight arise, and leave this cursèd place."

54

So up he rose, and thence amounted[4] streight.
  Which when the carle° beheld, and saw his guest   *churl*
480   Would safe depart, for° all his subtill sleight,   *in spite of*
  He chose an halter from among the rest,
  And with it hung himselfe, unbid° unblest.   *unprayed for*
  But death he could not worke himselfe thereby;
  For thousand times he so himselfe had drest,°   *made ready*
485   Yet nathelesse it could not doe him die,
Till he should die his last, that is eternally.

---

3. An echo of Colossians 2.14: "Blotting out the handwriting that was against us, which was contrary to us [The Old Testament Law], and took it out of the way, nailing it to his cross."
4. Mounted his horse.

Canto 10

> Her faithfull knight faire Una brings
> to house of Holinesse,
> Where he is taught repentance, and
> the way to heavenly blesse.°   bliss

1

What man is he, that boasts of fleshly might,
  And vaine assurance of mortality,°   mortal life
  Which all so soone, as it doth come to fight,
  Against spirituall foes, yeelds by and by,[1]
5 Or from the field most cowardly doth fly?
  Ne let the man ascribe it to his skill,
  That thorough grace hath gainèd victory.
  If any strength we have, it is to ill,
But all the good is Gods, both power and eke will.[2]

2

10 By that, which lately hapned, Una saw,
  That this her knight was feeble, and too faint;
  And all his sinews woxen weake and raw,°   unready
  Through long enprisonment, and hard constraint,°   affliction
  Which he endurèd in his late restraint,
15 That yet he was unfit for bloudie fight:
  Therefore to cherish him with diets daint,°   choice
  She cast to bring him, where he chearen° might,   be cheered
Till he recovered had his[3] late decayèd plight.

3

There was an auntient house not farre away,
20 Renowmd throughout the world for sacred lore,
  And pure unspotted life: so well they say
  It governd was, and guided evermore,
  Through wisedome of a matrone grave and hore;°   venerable
  Whose onely joy was to relieve the needes
25 Of wretched soules, and helpe the helpelesse pore:
  All night she spent in bidding of her bedes,[4]
And all the day in doing good and godly deedes.

4

Dame Caelia[5] men did her call, as thought
  From heaven to come, or thither to arise,
30 The mother of three daughters, well upbrought
  In goodly thewes,° and godly exercise: habits
  The eldest two most sober, chast, and wise,
  Fidelia and Speranza virgins were,
  Though spousd,° yet wanting wedlocks solemnize;   bethrothed

---

1. Immediately.
2. "For by grace are ye saved through faith; and that not of yourselves: it is the gift of God: Not of works, lest any men should boast" (Ephesians 2.8–9). "Eke": also.
3. I.e., from his.
4. Saying prayers.
5. The name means "heavenly."

35   But faire Charissa to a lovely fere[6]
    Was linckèd, and by him had many pledges dere.[7]

5

    Arrivèd there, the dore they find fast lockt;
      For it was warely watchèd night and day,
      For feare of many foes: but when they knockt,
40   The Porter opened unto them streight way:
      He was an agèd syre, all hory gray,
      With lookes full lowly cast, and gate full slow,
      Wont on a staffe his feeble steps to stay,
      Hight° Humilta.° They passe in stouping low;   *called/humility*
45   For streight and narrow was the way, which he did show.[8]

6

    Each goodly thing is hardest to begin,
      But entred in a spacious court they see,
      Both plaine, and pleasant to be walkèd in,
      Where them does meete a francklin° faire and free,   *freeholder*
50   And entertaines with comely courteous glee,
      His name was Zele,° that him right well became,   *zeal*
      For in his speeches and behaviour hee
      Did labour lively to expresse the same,
    And gladly did them guide, till to the Hall they came.

7

55   There fairely them receives a gentle Squire,
      Of milde demeanure, and rare courtesie,
      Right cleanly clad in comely sad° attire;   *sober*
      In word and deede that shewed great modestie,
      And knew his good° to all of each degree,   *proper respect*
60   Hight Reverence. He them with speeches meet
      Does faire entreat; no courting nicetie,[9]
      But simple true, and eke° unfainèd sweet,   *also*
    As might become a Squire so great persons to greet.

8

    And afterwards them to his Dame he leades,
65   That agèd Dame, the Ladie of the place:
      Who all this while was busie at her beades:
      Which doen, she up arose with seemely grace,
      And toward them full matronely[1] did pace.
      Where when that farest Una she beheld,
70   Whom well she knew to spring from heavenly race,
      Her hart with joy unwonted inly sweld,°   *swelled*
    As feeling wondrous comfort in her weaker eld.°   *older age*

---

6. Loving mate.
7. I.e., many children. The daughters' names mean "faith," "hope," and "charity." Cf. with them the three Saracens, Sans Foy, Sans Joy, and Sans Loy. This canto draws heavily on scriptural references, especially 1 Corinthians 13.13. "And now abideth faith, hope, charity, these three; but the greatest of these is charity." Many aspects of the

House of Holiness oppose their counterparts in the House of Pride (canto 4).
8. See fn. 3, p. 653.
9. He treats them courteously ("faire"); no courtly affectation ("nicetie").
1. Like a matron, i.e., a woman in charge of an establishment.

9

And her embracing said, "O happie earth,
    Whereon thy innocent feet doe ever tread,
75   Most vertuous virgin borne of heavenly berth,
    That to redeeme thy woefull parents head,
    From tyrans rage, and ever-dying dread,[2]
    Hast wandred through the world now long a day;
    Yet ceasest not thy wearie soles to lead,
80   What grace hath thee now hither brought this way?
Or doen thy feeble feet unweeting° hither stray?   *unknowing*

10

"Strange thing it is an errant° knight to see   *wandering*
    Here in this place, or any other wight,
    That hither turnes his steps. So few there bee,
85   That chose the narrow path, or seeke the right:
    All keepe the broad high way, and take delight
    With many rather for to go astray,
    And be partakers of their evill plight,
    Then with a few to walke the rightest way;[3]
90   O foolish men, why haste ye to your owne decay?"

11

"Thy selfe to see, and tyred limbs to rest,
    O matrone sage," quoth she, "I hither came,
    And this good knight his way with me addrest,°   *directed*
    Led with thy prayses and broad-blazèd fame,
95   That up to heaven is blowne."[4] The auncient Dame
    Him goodly greeted in her modest guise,
    And entertaynd them both, as best became,
    With all the court'sies,° that she could devise,   *courtesies*
Ne wanted ought, to shew her bounteous or wise.

12

100 Thus as they gan of sundry things devise,°   *talk*
    Loe two most goodly virgins came in place,
    Ylinkèd arme in arme in lovely° wise,   *loving*
    With countenance demure, and modest grace,
    They numbred even steps and equall pace:
105   Of which the eldest, that Fidelia hight,
    Like sunny beames threw from her Christall face,
    That could have dazd° the rash beholders sight,   *dazzled*
And round about her head did shine like heavens light.

13

She was araièd° all in lilly white,   *arrayed*
110   And in her right hand bore a cup of gold,
    With wine and water fild up to the hight,
    In which a Serpent did himselfe enfold,

2. Continuing fear of death; "long a day": many a long day.
3. An echo of Matthew 7.13–4: "Broad is the way that leadeth to destruction, and many there be which go in thereat: / . . . strait is the gate and nar-row is the way, which leadeth unto life, and few there be that find it."
4. I.e., your praises and fame are widely cele-brated ("blazed"), reaching ("blowne") up to heaven.

That horrour made to all, that did behold;
But she no whit did chaunge her constant mood:[5]
115 And in her other hand she fast did hold
A booke, that was both signd and seald with blood,
Wherein darke things were writ, hard to be understood.[6]

14

Her younger sister, that Speranza hight,
Was clad in blew, that her beseemèd well;
120 Not all so chearefull seemèd she of sight,[7]
As was her sister; whether dread° did dwell,   fear
Or anguish in her hart, is hard to tell:
Upon her arme a silver anchor[8] lay,
Whereon she leanèd ever, as befell:
125 And ever up to heaven, as she did pray,
Her stedfast eyes were bent, ne swarvèd other way.

15

They seeing Una, towards her gan wend,°   walk
Who them encounters° with like courtesie;   meets
Many kind speeches they betwene them spend,
130 And greatly joy each other well to see:
Then to the knight with shamefast° modestie   humble
They turne themselves, at Unas meeke request,
And him salute with well beseeming glee;[9]
Who faire them quites,° as him beseeméd best,   returns the salute
135 And goodly gan discourse of many a noble gest.°   deed

16

Then Una thus; "But she your sister deare;
The deare Charissa where is she become?°   gone to
Or wants she health, or busie is elsewhere?"
"Ah no," said they, "but forth she may not come:
140 For she of late is lightned of her wombe,
And hath encreast the world with one sonne more,[1]
That her to see should be but troublesome."
"Indeede," quoth she, "that should her trouble sore,
But thankt be God, that her encrease so evermore."[2]

17

145 Then said the aged Caelia, "Deare dame,
And you good Sir, I wote that of your toyle,
And labours long, through which ye hither came,
Ye both forwearied° be: therefore a whyle   utterly weary
I read you rest, and to your bowres recoyle."[3]
150 Then callèd she a Groome, that forth him led
Into a goodly lodge, and gan despoile°   disrobe

---

5. Expression. The cup of wine and water signifies the sacrament of Communion: the serpent is a symbol of the crucified Christ (of whom the serpent lifted up by Moses, Numbers 21.9, is a recognized type).
6. The New Testament. See 2 Peter 3.16: "in which are some things hard to be understood."
7. In appearance.
8. The iconographic symbol of hope.
9. Appropriate joy.
1. Charity, the fruitful virtue, is often depicted pictorially as a mother with many children.
2. I.e., God be thanked, who continually increases her thus.
3. Retire to your rooms. "Read": counsel.

Of puissant armes, and laid in easie bed;

His name was meeke Obedience rightfully aréd.°   *understood*

18

Now when their wearie limbes with kindly° rest,   *natural*

155 And bodies were refresht with due repast,

Faire Una gan Fidelia faire request,

To have her knight into her schoolehouse plaste,

That of her heavenly learning he might taste,

And heare the wisedome of her words divine.

160 She graunted, and that knight so much agraste,°   *favored*

That she him taught celestiall discipline,

And opened his dull eyes, that light mote in them shine.

19

And that her sacred Booke, with bloud[4] ywrit,

That none could read, except she did them teach,

165 She unto him disclosèd every whit,

And heavenly documents° thereout did preach,   *doctrines*

That weaker wit of man could never reach,

Of God, of grace, of justice, of free will,

That wonder was to heare her goodly speach:

170 For she was able, with her words to kill,

And raise againe to life the hart, that she did thrill.°   *pierce*

20

And when she list poure out her larger spright,[5]

She would commaund the hastie Sunne to stay,

Or backward turne his course from heavens hight;

175 Sometimes great hostes of men she could dismay,

Dry-shod to passe, she parts the flouds in tway;

And eke huge mountaines from their native seat

She would commaund, themselves to beare away,

And throw in raging sea with roaring threat.

180 Almightie God her gave such powre, and puissance great.[6]

21

The faithfull knight now grew in litle space,°   *time*

By hearing her, and by her sisters lore,

To such perfection of all heavenly grace,

That wretched world he gan for to abhore,[7]

185 And mortall life gan loath, as thing forelore,°   *doomed*

Greeved with remembrance of his wicked wayes,

And prickt with anguish of his sinnes so sore,

That he desirde to end his wretched dayes:

So much the dart of sinfull guilt the soule dismayes.

22

190 But wise Speranza gave him comfort sweet,

And taught him how to take assurèd hold

4. I.e., the blood of Christ.

5. Full spiritual power.

6. Joshua made the sun stand still (Joshua 10.12); Hezekiah made it turn backwards (2 Kings 20.10); Gideon was victorious over the Midianite hosts (Judges 7.7); Moses led the Israelites through the parted waters of the Red Sea (Exodus 14.21–31); faith, said Christ, can move mountains (Matthew 21.21). All these are miracles of faith.

7. I.e., he began to abhor the world.

Upon her silver anchor, as was meet;
Else had his sinnes so great, and manifold
Made him forget all that Fidelia told.
195   In this distressèd doubtfull° agonie,   *fearful*
When him his dearest Una did behold,
Disdeining life, desiring leave to die,
She found her selfe assayld with great perplexitie.°   *distress*

                          23

And came to Caelia to declare her smart,
200   Who well acquainted with that commune° plight,   *common*
Which sinfull horror[8] workes in wounded hart,
Her wisely comforted all that she might,
With goodly counsell and advisement right;
And streightway sent with carefull diligence,
205   To fetch a Leach,° the which had great insight   *doctor*
In that disease of grievèd° conscience,   *distressed*
And well could cure the same; His name was Patience.

                          24

Who comming to that soule-diseasèd knight,
Could hardly° him intreat, to tell his griefe: *with difficulty*
210   Which knowne, and all that noyd° his heavie spright   *troubled*
Well searcht,° eftsoones° he gan apply reliefe   *probed/soon after*
Of salves and med'cines, which had passing priefe,[9]
And thereto added words of wondrous might:
By which to ease he him recurèd briefe,[1]
215   And much asswaged the passion° of his plight,   *suffering*
That he his paine endured, as seeming now more light.

                          25

But yet the cause and root of all his ill,
Inward corruption, and infected sin,[2]
Not purged nor heald, behind remainéd still,
220   And festring sore did rankle yet within,
Close° creeping twixt the marrow and the skin.   *secretly*
Which to extirpe,° he laid him privily   *extirpate*
Downe in a darkesome lowly place farre in,
Whereas he meant his corrosives to apply,
225   And with streight° diet tame his stubborne malady.   *strict*

                          26

In ashes and sackcloth he did array
His daintie corse, proud humors[3] to abate,
And dieted with fasting every day,
The swelling of his wounds to mitigate,
230   And made him pray both earely and eke late:
And ever as superfluous flesh did rot
Amendment readie still at hand did wayt,

---

8. Horror of sin.   grace).
9. Which had extraordinary power.   2. I.e., the effects of original sin.
1. I.e., he spoke words of spiritual consolation to   3. Whatever is conducive to pride.
ease the knight he had quickly cured of sin (by

To pluck it out with pincers firie whot,°   *hot*
That soone in him was left no one corrupted jot.

27

235 And bitter Penance with an yron whip,
Was wont him once to disple° every day: *discipline*
And sharpe Remorse his hart did pricke and nip,
That drops of bloud thence like a well did play;
And sad Repentance usèd to embay°   *bathe*
240 His bodie in salt water smarting sore,
The filthy blots of sinne to wash away.[4]
So in short space they did to health restore
The man that would not live, but earst° lay at deathes dore. *formerly*

28

In which his torment often was so great,
245 That like a Lyon he would cry and rore,
And rend his flesh, and his owne synewes eat.
His own deare Una hearing evermore
His ruefull shriekes and gronings, often tore
Her guiltlesse garments, and her golden heare,
250 For pitty of his paine and anguish sore;
Yet all with patience wisely she did beare;
For well she wist, his crime could else be never cleare.°   *cleansed*

29

Whom thus recovered by wise Patience,
And trew Repentance they to Una brought:
255 Who joyous of his curèd conscience,
Him dearely kist, and fairely° eke besought   *courteously*
Himselfe to chearish,° and consuming thought   *cheer, cherish*
To put away out of his carefull° brest.   *care-full*
By this[5] Charissa, late in child-bed brought,
260 Was woxen strong, and left her fruitfull nest;
To her faire Una brought this unacquainted guest.

30

She was a woman in her freshest age,
Of wondrous beauty, and of bountie° rare,   *goodness*
With goodly grace and comely personage,°   *appearance*
265 That was on earth not easie to compare;°   *rival*
Full of great love, but Cupids wanton snare
As hell she hated, chast in worke and will;
Her necke and breasts were ever open bare,
That ay thereof her babes might sucke their fill;
270 The rest was all in yellow robes arayèd still.[6]

31

A multitude of babes about her hong,
Playing their sports, that joyd her to behold,

4. "Wash me throughly from mine iniquity, and
cleanse me from my sin" (Psalms 51.2).
5. By this time.
6. Her yellow (saffron) robe is the color of marriage, fertility, and maternity. Her chaste, fruitful
love (Christian *agape*) is opposed to "Cupid's wanton snare" (*eros*).

Whom still she fed, whiles they were weake and young,
But thrust them forth still, as they wexèd old:
275 And on her head she wore a tyre° of gold,   *headdress*
Adornd with gemmes and owches° wondrous faire,   *jewels*
Whose passing° price uneath° was to be told;   *surpassing/scarcely*
And by her side there sate a gentle paire
Of turtle doves,[7] she sitting in an yvorie chaire.

32

280 The knight and Una entring, faire her greet,
And bid her joy of that her happie brood;
Who them requites with court'sies seeming meet,°   *appropriate*
And entertaines with friendly chearefull mood.
Then Una her besought, to be so good,
285 As in her vertuous rules to schoole her knight,
Now after all his torment well withstood,
In that sad° house of Penaunce, where his spright   *solemn*
Had past° the paines of hell, and long enduring night. *passed through*

33

She was right joyous of her just request,
290 And taking by the hand that Faeries sonne,
Gan him instruct in every good behest,°   *command*
Of love, and righteousness, and well to donne,[8]
And wrath, and hatred warely° to shonne,   *warily*
That drew on men Gods hatred, and his wrath,
295 And many soules in dolours° had fordonne:°   *misery/destroyed*
In which when him she well instructed hath,
From thence to heaven she teacheth him the ready° path.   *direct*

34

Wherein his weaker° wandring steps to guide,   *too weak*
An aunchient matrone she to her does call,
300 Whose sober lookes her wisedome well describe:°   *made known*
Her name was Mercie, well knowne over all,
To be both gratious, and eke° liberall: *also*
To whom the carefull charge of him she gave,
To lead aright, that he should never fall
305 In all his wayes through this wide worldès wave,°   *expanse*
That Mercy in the end his righteous soule might save.

35

The godly Matrone by the hand him beares°   *leads*
Forth from her[9] presence, by a narrow way,
Scattred with bushy thornes, and ragged breares,°   *briers*
310 Which still before him she removed away,
That nothing might his ready passage stay:
And ever when his feet encombred were,
Or gan to shrinke, or from the right to stray,
She held him fast, and firmely did upbeare,
315 As carefull Nourse her child from falling oft does reare.

---

7. Emblem of true love and faithful marriage.   9. I.e., Charissa's.
8. I.e., right action.

36

Eftsoones unto an holy Hospitall,[1]
   That was fore° by the way, she did him bring,   *close*
   In which seven Bead-men[2] that had vowèd all
   Their life to service of high heavens king
320   Did spend their dayes in doing godly thing:
   Their gates to all were open evermore,
   That by the wearie way were traveiling,
   And one sate wayting ever them before,
To call in commers-by, that needy were and pore.[3]

37

325 The first of them that eldest was, and best,°   *chief*
   Of all the house had charge and governement,
   As Guardian and Steward of the rest:
   His office was to give entertainement
   And lodging, unto all that came, and went:
330   Not unto such, as could him feast againe,°   *in return*
   And double quite,° for that he on them spent,   *repay*
   But such, as want of harbour° did constraine:°   *shelter/afflict*
Those for Gods sake his dewty was to entertaine.

38

The second was as Almner[4] of the place,
335   His office was, the hungry for to feed,
   And thristy give to drinke, a worke of grace:
   He feard not once him selfe to be in need,
   Ne cared to hoord for those, whom he did breede:[5]
   The grace of God he layd up still in store,
340   Which as a stocke° he left unto his seede;°   *resource/children*
   He had enough, what need him care for more?
And had he lesse, yet some he would give to the pore.

39

The third had of their wardrobe custodie,
   In which were not rich tyres,° nor garments gay,   *robes*
345   The plumes of pride, and wings of vanitie,
   But clothes meet to keepe keene could° away,   *cold*
   And naked nature seemely° to aray;   *decently*
   With which bare wretched wights he dayly clad,
   The images of God in earthly clay;
350   And if that no spare clothes to give he had,
His owne coate he would cut, and it distribute glad.

40

The fourth appointed by his office was,
   Poore prisoners to relieve with gratious ayd,
   And captives to redeeme with price of bras,[6]
355   From Turkes and Sarazins, which them had stayd;°   *held captive*

---

1. House of rest for pilgrims and travelers.
2. Men of prayer.
3. I.e., one beadsman sat in front of the gates, to call in needy wayfarers.
4. An almoner distributed charity to the poor.
5. I.e., his children.
6. Payment of money.

And though they faultie were, yet well he wayd,
That God to us forgiveth every howre
Much more then that, why° they in bands were layd,   *for which*
And he that harrowd hell[7] with heavie stowre,
360 The faultie° soules from thence brought to his heavenly   *sinful*
     bowre.

41

The fift had charge sicke persons to attend,
    And comfort those, in point of death which lay;
    For them most needeth comfort in the end,
    When sin, and hell, and death do most dismay
365   The feeble soule departing hence away.
    All is but lost, that living we bestow,°   *store up*
    If not well ended at our dying day.
    O man have mind of that last bitter throw;°   *throes of death*
For as the tree does fall, so lyes it ever low.

42

370 The sixt had charge of them now being dead,
    In seemely sort their courses to engrave,[8]
    And deck with dainty flowres their bridall bed,
    That to their heavenly spouse both sweet and brave°   *fair*
    They might appeare, when he their soules shall save.
375   The wondrous workemanship of Gods owne mould,[9]
    Whose face he made, all beasts to feare, and gave
    All in his hand, even dead we honour should.
Ah dearest God me graunt, I dead be not defould.°   *defiled*

43

The seventh now after death and buriall done,
380   Had charge the tender Orphans of the dead
    And widowes ayd, least they should be undone:
    In face of judgement[1] he their right would plead,
    Ne ought[2] the powre of mighty men did dread
    In their defence, nor would for gold or fee°   *bribe*
385   Be wonne their rightfull causes downe to tread:
    And when they stood in most necessitee,
He did supply their want, and gave them ever free.[3]

44

There when the Elfin knight arrivèd was,
    The first and chiefest of the seven, whose care
390   Was guests to welcome, towardes him did pas:
    Where seeing Mercie, that his steps up bare,[4]

---

7. I.e., Christ, who journeyed to hell to deliver those good people who lived before his time, according to a popular story in the Middle Ages. It originated in the apocryphal gospel of Nicodemus. See *Piers Plowman*, Passus 18, above, p. 297. "Stowre": assault.
8. Bodies ("courses," i.e., corpses) to bury.
9. The human body is God's own image ("mould") and a "mould" of God's making. See Genesis 1.26–30, 2.7.

1. I.e., in court.
2. Neither at all.
3. Always freely. The seven beadsmen here correspond to, and perform, the seven works of charity, or corporal mercy: lodging the homeless, feeding the hungry, clothing the naked, redeeming the captive, comforting the sick, burying the dead, and succoring the orphan.
4. Supported.

And alwayes led, to her with reverence rare
    He humbly louted° in meeke lowlinesse,   *bowed*
    And seemely welcome for her did prepare:
395   For of their order she was Patronesse,
Albe° Charissa were their chiefest founderesse.   *although*

45

There she awhile him stayes, him selfe to rest,
    That to the rest more able he might bee:
    During which time, in every good behest°   *command*
400   And godly worke of Almes and charitee
    She him instructed with great industree;
    Shortly therein so perfect he became,
    That from the first unto the last degree,
    His mortall life he learnèd had to frame
405 In holy righteousnesse, without rebuke or blame.

46

Thence forward by that painfull way they pas,
    Forth to an hill, that was both steepe and hy;
    On top whereof a sacred chappell was,
    And eke° a litle Hermitage thereby,   *also*
410   Wherein an agèd holy man did lye,°   *live*
    That day and night said his devotion,
    Ne other worldly busines did apply;[5]
    His name was heavenly Contemplation;
Of God and goodnesse was his meditation.

47

415 Great grace that old man to him given had;
    For God he often saw from heavens hight,
    All° were his earthly eyen both blunt° and bad,   *although/dim*
    And through great age had lost their kindly° sight,   *natural*
    Yet wondrous quick and persant° was his spright,°   *piercing/spirit*
420   As Eagles eye, that can behold the Sunne:
    That hill they scale with all their powre and might,
    That his frayle thighes nigh wearie and fordonne°   *exhausted*
Gan faile, but by her helpe the top at last he wonne.

48

There they do finde that godly agèd Sire,
425   With snowy lockes adowne his shoulders shed,
    As hoarie frost with spangles doth attire
    The mossy braunches of an Oke halfe ded.
    Each bone might through his body well be red,°   *observed*
    And every sinew seene through° his long fast: *because of*
430   For nought he cared his carcas long unfed;
    His mind was full of spirituall repast,
And pynèd° his flesh, to keepe his body low° and chast.   *starved / thin*

49

Who when these two approching he aspide,
    At their first presence grew agrievèd sore,[6]

---

5. I.e., he did not attend to any worldly activities.   6. I.e., he was at first sorely grieved at their arrival.

435   That forst him lay his heavenly thoughts aside;
        And had he not that Dame respected more,°   *greatly*
        Whom highly he did reverence and adore,
        He would not once have movèd for the knight.
        They him saluted standing far afore;°   *away*
440   Who well them greeting, humbly did requight,°   *respond*
        And asked, to what end they clomb° that tedious height.   *had climbed*

                                        50
        "What end," quoth she, "should cause us take such paine,
        But that same end, which every living wight
        Should make his marke,° high heaven to attaine?   *goal*
445   Is not from hence the way, that leadeth right
        To that most glorious house, that glistreth bright
        With burning starres, and everliving fire,
        Whereof the keyes are to thy hand behight°   *entrusted*
        By wise Fidelia? she doth thee require,
450   To shew it to this knight, according his desire."

                                        51
        "Thrise happy man," said then the father grave,
        "Whose staggering steps thy[7] steady hand doth lead,
        And shewes the way, his sinfull soule to save.
        Who better can the way to heaven aread°   *direct*
455   Then thou thy selfe, that was both borne and bred
        In heavenly throne, where thousand Angels shine?
        Thou doest the prayers of the righteous sead°   *seed*
        Present before the majestie divine,
        And his avenging wrath to clemencie incline.

                                        52
460   "Yet since thou bidst, thy pleasure shalbe donne.
        Then come thou man of earth,[8] and see the way,
        That never yet was seene of Faeries sonne,
        That never leads the traveiler astray,
        But after labours long, and sad delay,
465   Brings them to joyous rest and endlesse blis.
        But first thou must a season fast and pray,
        Till from her bands the spright assoilèd° is,   *released*
        And have her strength recured° from fraile infirmitis."   *recovered*

                                        53
        That done, he leads him to the highest Mount;
470   Such one, as that same mighty man of God,
        That bloud-red billowes like a wallèd front
        On either side disparted° with his rod,   *parted asunder*
        Till that his army dry-foot through them yod,°   *went*
        Dwelt fortie dayes upon; where writ in stone
475   With bloudy letters by the hand of God,

---

7. I.e., Mercy's.
8. An allusion to humankind's formation from the

dust of the earth (Genesis 2.7) and also to the
knight's name. See 66.5–6 and note.

The bitter doome of death and balefull mone[9]
He did receive, whiles flashing fire about him shone.

54

Or like that sacred hill, whose head full hie,
  Adornd with fruitfull Olives all arownd,
480 Is, as it were for endlesse memory
  Of that deare Lord, who oft thereon was fownd,
  For ever with a flowring girlond crownd:
  Or like that pleasaunt Mount, that is for ay
  Through famous Poets verse each where° renownd,   *everywhere*
485 On which the thrise three learned Ladies play
Their heavenly notes, and make full many a lovely lay.[1]

55

From thence, far off he unto him did shew
  A litle path, that was both steepe and long,
  Which to a goodly Citie led his vew;
490 Whose wals and towres were builded high and strong
  Of perle and precious stone, that earthly tong
  Cannot describe, nor wit of man can tell;
  Too high a ditty° for my simple song;   *subject*
  The Citie of the great king hight it well,
495 Wherein eternall peace and happinesse doth dwell.

56

As he thereon stood gazing, he might see
  The blessed Angels to and fro descend
  From highest heaven, in gladsome companee,
  And with great joy into that Citie wend,
500 As commonly as friend does with his frend.[2]
  Whereat he wondred much, and gan enquere,
  What stately building durst so high extend
  Her loftie towres unto the starry sphere,
And what unknowen nation there empeopled were.

57

505 "Faire knight," quoth he, "Hierusalem that is,
  The new Hierusalem, that God has built
  For those to dwell in, that are chosen his,
  His chosen people purged from sinfull guilt,
  With pretious bloud, which cruelly was spilt
510 On cursèd tree, of that unspotted lam,[3]
  That for the sinnes of all the world was kilt:

---

9. I.e., the ten commandments ("bloudy letters") carried with them the judgment ("doome") of death and pain (causing sorrowful moans—"balefull mone").
1. Song. The mountain is successively compared to Mt. Sinai (lines 469–77), where Moses, after parting the "bloud-red billowes" of the Red Sea, received the tablets of the ten commandments; to the Mount of Olives (lines 478–82), associated with

Christ; and to Mount Parnassus (lines 483–86), where dwelled the nine muses of art and poetry.
2. Cf. Jacob's ladder, which "reached to heaven; and behold the angels of God ascending and descending on it" (Genesis 28.12). "Commonly": familiarly.
3. Lamb; a reference to Christ (the lamb of God) whose death on the cross ("cursed tree") purged the guilt of sin from those "chosen his."

Now are they Saints all in that Citie sam,°   together
More deare unto their God, then younglings to their dam."[4]

58

"Till now," said then the knight, "I weenèd well,
515 That great Cleopolis,[5] where I have beene,
In which that fairest Faerie Queene doth dwell,
The fairest Citie was, that might be seene;
And that bright towre all built of christall cleene,°   clear
Panthea,[6] seemd the brightest thing, that was:
520 But now by proofe all otherwise I weene;
For this great Citie[7] that does far surpas,
And this bright Angels towre quite dims that towre of glas."

59

"Most trew," then said the holy aged man;
"Yet is Cleopolis for earthly frame,°   structure
525 The fairest peece,° that eye beholden can: masterpiece
And well beseemes° all knights of noble name,   becomes
That covet in th' immortall booke of fame
To be eternizèd, that same to haunt,°   frequent
And doen their service to that soveraigne Dame,
530 That glorie does to them for guerdon° graunt: reward
For she is heavenly borne, and heaven may justly vaunt.°   claim

60

"And thou faire ymp,° sprong out from English race,   youth
How ever now accompted° Elfins sonne,   accounted
Well worthy doest thy service for her grace,°   favor
535 To aide a virgin desolate foredonne.°   undone
But when thou famous victorie hast wonne,
And high emongst all knights has hong thy shield,
Thenceforth the suit° of earthly conquest shonne,   pursuit
And wash thy hands from guilt of bloudy field:
540 For bloud can nought but sin, and wars but sorrowes yield.

61

"Then seeke this path, that I to thee presage,°   point out prophetically
Which after all to heaven shall thee send;
Then peaceably thy painefull° pilgrimage   laborious
To yonder same Hierusalem do bend,
545 Where is for thee ordaind a blessed end:
For thou emongst those Saints, whom thou doest see,
Shalt be a Saint, and thine owne nations frend
And Patrone: thou Saint George shalt callèd bee,
Saint George of mery England, the signe of victoree."[8]

4. The New Jerusalem is described in Revelation 21–22; "the nations of them which are saved shall walk in the light of it" (21.24).
5. London, Camelot—the earthly counterpart of the Heavenly Kingdom.
6. Reminiscent of the temple of glass in Chaucer's *Hous of Fame*; perhaps intended to represent Richmond Palace or Westminster Abbey.
7. I.e., The New Jerusalem far surpasses Cleopolis ("that").
8. Spenser's conception of St. George, patron saint of England, draws on the *Legenda Aurea* (translated by Caxton in 1487); on pictures, tapestries, pageants, and folklore.

62

550   "Unworthy wretch," quoth he, "of so great grace,
      How dare I thinke such glory to attaine?"
      "These that have it attaind, were in like cace,"
      Quoth he, "as wretched, and lived in like paine."
      "But deeds of armes must I at last be faine,°   *content to leave*
555   And Ladies love to leave so dearely bought?"
      "What need of armes, where peace doth ay remaine,"
      Said he, "and battailes none are to be fought?
  As for loose loves are⁹ vaine, and vanish into nought."

63

  "O let me not," quoth he, "then turne againe
560   Backe to the world, whose joyes so fruitlesse are;
      But let me here for aye in peace remaine,
      Or streight way on that last long voyage fare,
      That nothing may my present hope empare."°   *impair*
      "That may not be," said he, "ne maist thou yit
565   Forgo that royall maides bequeathèd care,°   *charge*
      Who did her cause into thy hand commit,
  Till from her cursèd foe thou have her freely quit."°   *released*

64

  "Then shall I soone," quoth he, "so God me grace,
      Abet° that virgins cause disconsolate,   *maintain*
570   And shortly backe returne unto this place
      To walke this way in Pilgrims poore estate.
      But now aread,° old father, why of late   *declare*
      Didst thou behight° me borne of English blood,   *call*
      Whom all a Faeries sonne doen nominate?"°   *name*
575   "That word shall I," said he, "avouchen° good,   *prove*
  Sith to thee is unknowne the cradle of thy brood.

65

  "For well I wote,° thou springst from ancient race   *know*
      Of Saxon kings, that have with mightie hand
      And many bloudie battailes fought in place°   *there*
580   High reard their royall throne in Britane land,
      And vanquisht them, unable to withstand:
      From thence a Faerie thee unweeting reft,¹
      There as thou slepst in tender swadling band,
      And her base Elfin brood there for thee left.
585   Such men do Chaungelings call, so chaungd by Faeries theft.

66

  "Thence she thee brought into this Faerie lond,
      And in an heapèd furrow did thee hyde,
      Where thee a Ploughman all unweeting° fond,   *unknowing*
      As he his toylesome teme° that way did guyde,   *team of oxen*
590   And brought thee up in ploughmans state to byde,

---

9. I.e., they are.   1. Secretly stole.

Whereof Georgos he thee gave to name;[2]
Till prickt° with courage, and thy forces pryde,   spurred
To Faery court thou cam'st to seeke for fame,
And prove thy puissaunt armes, as seemes thee best became."[3]

67

595 "O holy Sire," quoth he, "how shall I quight°   repay
The many favours I with thee have found,
That has my name and nation red aright,
And taught the way that does to heaven bound?"°   go
This said, adowne he lookèd to the ground,
600 To have returnd, but dazèd° were his eyne,   dazzled
Through passing° brightnesse, which did   surpassing
   quite confound
His feeble sence, and too exceeding shyne.
So darke are earthly things compard to things divine.

68

At last whenas himselfe he gan to find,°   recover
605 To Una back he cast him to retire;
Who him awaited still with pensive° mind.   anxious
Great thankes and goodly meed° to that good syre,   gift
He thence departing gave for his paines hyre.°   reward
So came to Una, who him joyd to see,
610 And after litle rest, gan him desire,
Of her adventure mindfull for to bee.
So leave they take of Caelia, and her daughters three.

Canto 11

The knight with that old Dragon fights
two dayes incessantly:
The third him overthrowes, and gayns
most glorious victory.

1

High time now gan it wex° for Una faire,   grow
To thinke of those her captive Parents deare,
And their forwasted kingdome to repaire:[1]
Whereto whenas they now approachèd neare,
5 With hartie° words her knight she gan to cheare,   bold
And in her modest manner thus bespake;
"Deare knight, as deare, as ever knight was deare,
That all these sorrowes suffer for my sake,
High heaven behold the tedious toyle, ye for me take.

2

10 "Now are we come unto my native soyle,
And to the place, where all our perils dwell;
Here haunts that feend, and does his dayly spoyle,

---

2. I.e., as a name. *Georgos* is Greek for "farmer"
(cf. Virgil's *Georgics*, on farming).
3. As best suited you.

1. I.e., to restore their kingdom, laid waste (by the
dragon).

Therefore henceforth be at your keeping well,[2]
And ever ready for your foeman fell.

15   The sparke of noble courage now awake,
     And strive your excellent selfe to excell;
     That shall ye evermore renowmèd make,
Above all knights on earth, that batteill undertake."

3

And pointing forth, "lo yonder is," said she,
20   "The brasen towre in which my parents deare
     For dread of that huge feend emprisond be,
     Whom I from far see on the walles appeare,
     Whose sight my feeble° soule doth greatly cheare: *doleful*
     And on the top of all I do espye
25   The watchman wayting tydings glad to heare,
     That O my parents might I happily
Unto you bring, to ease you of your misery."

4

With that they heard a roaring hideous sound,
     That all the ayre with terrour fillèd wide,
30   And seemd uneath° to shake the stedfast ground.   *almost*
     Eftsoones° that dreadfull Dragon they espide,   *soon after*
     Where stretcht he lay upon the sunny side
     Of a great hill, himselfe like a great hill.
     But all so soone, as he from far descride
35   Those glistring armes, that heaven with light díd fill,
He rousd himselfe full blith,° and hastned them   *joyfully*
     untill.°   *toward*

5

Then bad the knight his Lady yede° aloofe,   *step*
     And to an hill her selfe withdraw aside,
     From whence she might behold that battailles proof°   *outcome*
40   And eke be safe from daunger far descryde:
     She him obayd, and turnd a little wyde.°   *aside*
     Now O thou sacred Muse,[3] most learned Dame,
     Faire ympe of Phoebus, and his aged bride,[4]
     The Nourse of time, and everlasting fame,
45   That warlike hands ennoblest with immortall name;

6

O gently come into my feeble brest,
     Come gently, but not with that mighty rage,
     Wherewith the martiall troupes thou doest infest,°   *arouse*
     And harts of great Heroës doest enrage,
50   That nought their kindled courage may aswage,
     Soone as thy dreadfull trompe° begins to sownd;   *trumpet*
     The God of warre with his fiers equipage
     Thou doest awake, sleepe never he so sownd,°   *sound*
And scarèd nations doest with horrour sterne astown.°   *appall*

---

2. I.e., be well on your guard.   of history.
3. Calliope, muse of epic poetry, or Clio, muse   4. I.e., Mnemosyne (memory). "Impe": child.

7

55 Faire Goddesse lay that furious fit° aside,   strain
        Till I of warres and bloudy Mars do sing[5]
        And Briton fields with Sarazin bloud bedyde,
        Twixt that great faery Queene and Paynim king,
        That with their horrour heaven and earth did ring,
60   A worke of labour long, and endlesse prayse:
        But now a while let downe that haughtie string,
        And to my tunes thy second tenor rayse,[6]
    That I this man of God his godly armes may blaze.°   describe

8

    By this the dreadfull Beast drew nigh to hand,
65   Halfe flying, and halfe footing° in his hast,   walking
        That with his largenesse measurèd much land,
        And made wide shadow under his huge wast;°   girth
        As mountaine doth the valley overcast.
        Approching nigh, he rearèd high afore
70   His body monstrous, horrible, and vast,
        Which to increase his wondrous greatnesse more,
    Was swolne with wrath, and poyson, and with bloudy gore.

9

    And over, all with brasen scales was armd,
        Like plated coate of steele, so couchèd neare,[7]
75   That nought mote perce,[8] ne might his corse be harmd
        With dint of sword, nor push of pointed speare;
        Which as an Eagle, seeing pray appeare,
        His acry Plumes doth rouze, full rudely dight,[9]
        So shakèd he, that horrour was to heare,
80   For as the clashing of an Armour bright,
    Such noyse his rouzèd scales did send unto the knight.

10

    His flaggy° wings when forth he did display,   drooping
        Were like two sayles, in which the hollow wynd
        Is gathered full, and worketh speedy way:
85   And eke the pennes,° that did his pineons bynd,   quills
        Were like mayne-yards, with flying canvas lynd,
        With which whenas him list the ayre to beat,
        And there by force unwonted° passage find,   unaccustomed
        The cloudes before him fled for terrour great,
90 And all the heavens stood still amazèd with his threat.

11

    His huge long tayle wound up in hundred foldes,
        Does overspred his long bras-scaly backe,
        Whose wreathèd boughts° when ever he unfoldes,   coils
        And thicke entangled knots adown does slacke,
95   Bespotted as with shields° of red and blacke,   scales

5. Apparently a reference to a projected but unwritten book of *The Faerie Queene*.
6. The "haughtie" (high-pitched) mode would be appropriate to a large-scale epic war; the "second tenor" (lower in pitch) to this present battle.
7. Closely overlaid.
8. Nothing might pierce ("perce"). "Corse": body.
9. Ruggedly arrayed. "Rouze": shake.

It sweepeth all the land behind him farre,
And of three furlongs does but litle lacke;
And at the point two stings in-fixèd arre,
Both deadly sharpe, that sharpest steele exceeden farre.

12

100   But stings and sharpest steele did far exceed[1]
The sharpnesse of his cruell rending clawes;
Dead was it sure, as sure as death in deed,[2]
What ever thing does touch his ravenous pawes,
Or what within his reach he ever drawes.
105   But his most hideous head my toung to tell
Does tremble: for his deepe devouring jawes
Wide gapèd, like the griesly° mouth of hell,   *horrid*
Through which into his darke abisse all ravin° fell.   *prey, booty*

13

And that° more wondrous was, in either jaw   *what*
110   Threeranckes of yron teeth enraungèd were,
In which yet trickling bloud and gobbets raw[3]
Of late devourèd bodies did appeare,
That sight thereof bred cold congealèd feare:
Which to increase, and all at once to kill,
115   A cloud of smoothering smoke and sulphur seare°   *burning*
Out of his stinking gorge° forth steemèd still,   *maw*
That all the ayre about with smoke and stench did fill.

14

His blazing eyes, like two bright shining shields,
Did burne with wrath, and sparkled living fyre;
120   As two broad Beacons, set in open fields,
Send forth their flames farre off to every shyre,°   *shire*
And warning give, that enemies conspyre,
With fire and sword the region to invade;
So flamed his eyne° with rage and rancorous yre:°   *eyes/anger*
125   But farre within, as in a hollow glade,
Those glaring lampes were set, that made a dreadfull shade.

15

So dreadfully he towards him did pas,
Forelifting up aloft his speckled brest,
And often bounding on the brusèd gras,
130   As for great joyance of his newcome guest.
Eftsoones he gan advance his haughtie crest,
As chauffèd° Bore his bristles doth upreare,   *vexed*
And shoke his scales to battell readie drest;°   *prepared*
That made the Redcrosse knight nigh quake for feare,
135   As bidding bold defiance to his foeman neare.

16

The knight gan fairely couch° his steadie speare,   *rest, aim*
And fiercely ran at him with rigorous° might: *violent*

1. I.e., were far exceeded by.   3. Chunks of undigested food.
2. In its effect.

The pointed steele arriving rudely° theare,　　　　　　　*roughly*
His harder hide would neither perce, nor bight,
140　But glauncing by forth passèd forward right;
Yet sore amovèd with so puissant push,
The wrathfull beast about him turnèd light,°　　　　　*quickly*
And him so rudely passing by, did brush
With his long tayle, that horse and man to ground did rush.

17

145　Both horse and man up lightly rose againe,
And fresh encounter towards him addrest:
But th' idle stroke yet backe recoyld in vaine,
And found no place his° deadly point to rest.　　　　　　*its*
Exceeding rage enflamed the furious beast,
150　To be avengèd of so great despight;°　　　　　　　　*outrage*
For never felt his imperceable brest
So wondrous force, from hand of living wight;
Yet had he provèd° the powre of many a puissant knight.　　*tested*

18

Then with his waving wings displayèd wyde,
155　Himselfe up high he lifted from the ground,
And with strong flight did forcibly divide
The yielding aire, which nigh too feeble found
Her flitting° partes, and element unsound,°　　　　*moving/weak*
To beare so great a weight: he cutting way
160　With his broad sayles, about him soarèd round:
At last low stouping with unweldie sway,[4]
Snatcht up both horse and man, to beare them quite away.

19

Long he them bore above the subject plaine,[5]
So farre as Ewghen[6] bow a shaft may send,
165　Till struggling strong did him at last constraine,
To let them downe before his flightès end:
As hagard° hauke presuming to contend　　　　　　　　*untamed*
With hardie fowle, above his hable might,[7]
His wearie pounces° all in vaine doth spend,　　　　　　　*claws*
170　To trusse° the pray too heavie for his flight;　　　　　　　*seize*
Which comming downe to ground, does free it selfe by fight.

20

He so disseizèd of his gryping grosse,[8]
The knight his thrilant° speare againe assayd　　　　　*piercing*
In his bras-plated body to embosse,°　　　　　　　　　*plunge*
175　And three mens strength unto the stroke he layd;
Wherewith the stiffe beame quakèd, as affrayd,
And glauncing from his scaly necke, did glyde
Close under his left wing, then broad displayd.

4. Ponderous force.　　　　　　　　　7. Able power.
5. I.e., the ground below.　　　　　　　8. Freed from his formidable grip.
6. Yewen, of yew.

    The percing steele there wrought a wound full wyde,
180 That with the uncouth° smart the Monster lowdly cryde.   *unusual*

21

He cryde, as raging seas are wont to rore,
    When wintry storme his wrathfull wreck does threat,
    The rolling billowes beat the ragged shore,
    As they the earth would shoulder from her seat,
185   And greedie gulfe[9] does gape, as he would eat
    His neighbour element[1] in his revenge:
    Then gin the blustring brethren[2] boldly threat,
    To move the world from off his stedfast henge,°   *axis*
And boystrous battell make, each other to avenge.

22

190 The steely head stucke fast still in his flesh,
    Till with his cruell clawes he snatcht the wood,
    And quite a sunder broke. Forth flowèd fresh
    A gushing river of blacke goarie° blood,   *clotted*
    That drownèd all the land, whereon he stood;
195   The stream thereof would drive a water-mill.
    Trebly augmented was his furious mood
    With bitter sense of his deepe rooted ill,°   *injury*
That flames of fire he threw forth from his large noséthrill.

23

His hideous tayle then hurlèd he about,
200   And therewith all enwrapt the nimble thyes°   *thighs*
    Of his froth-fomy steed, whose courage stout
    Striving to loose the knot, that fast him tyes,
    Himselfe in streighter bandes too rash implyes,[3]
    That to the ground he is perforce constraynd
205   To throw his rider: who can° quickly ryse   *began to*
    From off the earth, with durty bloud distaynd,°   *defiled*
For that reprochfull fall right fowly he disdaynd.

24

And fiercely tooke his trenchand° blade in hand,   *sharp*
    With which he stroke so furious and so fell,
210 That nothing seemd the puissance could withstand:
    Upon his crest the hardned yron fell,
    But his more hardned crest was armd so well,
    That deeper dint therein it would not make;[4]
    Yet so extremely did the buffe° him quell,°   *blow/dismay*
215 That from thenceforth he shund the like to take,
But when he saw them come, he did them still forsake.°   *avoid*

25

The knight was wrath to see his stroke beguyld,°   *foiled*
    And smote againe with more outrageous might;

9. I.e., the sea.   3. I.e., too suddenly entangles. "Streighter": tigh-
1. I.e., earth.   ter.
2. I.e., the winds.   4. I.e., it could not make a deep gash there.

But backe againe the sparckling steele recoyld,
220   And left not any marke, where it did light;
       As if in Adamant rocke it had bene pight.°   struck against
       The beast impatient of his smarting wound,
       And of so fierce and forcible despight,[5]
       Thought with his wings to stye° above the ground;   mount
225   But his late wounded wing unserviceable found.

                                 26
       Then full of griefe and anguish vehement,
       He lowdly brayd, that like was never heard,
       And from his wide devouring oven sent
       A flake° of fire, that flashing in his beard,   flash
230   Him all amazd, and almost made affeard;
       The scorching flame sore swingèd° all his face,   singed
       And through his armour all his bodie seard,
       That he could not endure so cruell cace,°   plight
       But thought his armes to leave, and helmet to unlace.

                                 27
235   Not that great Champion of the antique world,
       Whom famous Poetes verse so much doth vaunt,
       And hath for twelve huge labours high extold,
       So many furies and sharpe fits did haunt,
       When him the poysoned garment did enchaunt
240   With Centaures bloud, and bloudie verses charmed,
       As did this knight twelve thousand dolours° daunt,   sufferings
       Whom fyrie steele now burnt, that earst° him armed,   formerly
       That erst him goodly armed, now most of all him harmed.[6]

                                 28
       Faint, wearie, sore, emboylèd, grievèd, brent°   burned
245   With heat, toyle, wounds, armes, smart, and inward fire
       That never man such mischiefes° did torment;   misfortunes
       Death better were, death did he oft desire,
       But death will never come, when needes require.
       Whom so dismayd when that his foe beheld,
250   He cast to suffer him no more respire,°   rest
       But gan his sturdie sterne° about to weld,°   tail/lash
       And him so strongly stroke, that to the ground him feld.

                                 29
       It fortunèd (as faire it then befell)
       Behind his backe unweeting,° where he stood,   unnoticed
255   Of auncient time there was a springing well,
       From which fast trickled forth a silver flood,
       Full of great vertues, and for med'cine good.
       Whylome,° before that cursèd Dragon got   formerly
       That happie land, and all with innocent blood

---

5. Powerful injury.
6. Redcrosse's fire-baptism is compared to the burning shirt of Nessus, which killed Hercules, "that great Champion of the antique world" (line 235). His "twelve huge labours" are replicated in the knight's "twelve thousand dolours."

260 Defyld those sacred waves, it rightly hot°   *was called*
  The Well of Life,[7] ne yet his vertues had forgot.

      30

  For unto life the dead it could restore,
   And guilt of sinfull crimes cleane wash away,
   Those that with sicknesse were infected sore,
265 It could recure, and aged long decay
   Renew, as one were borne that very day.
   Both Silo this, and Jordan did excell,
   And th' English Bath, and eke the german Spau,
  Ne can Cephise, nor Hebrus match this well:
270 Into the same the knight backe overthrowen, fell.[8]

      31

  Now gan the golden Phoebus for to steepe
   His fierie face in billowes of the west,
   And his faint steedes watred in Ocean deepe,
   Whiles from their journall° labours they did rest, *daily*
275 When that infernall Monster, having kest°   *cast*
   His wearie foe into that living well,
   Can° high advaunce his broad discoloured brest, *did*
   Above his wonted pitch,° with countenance fell,° *height/sinister*
  And clapt his yron wings, as victor he did dwell.° *remain*

      32

280 Which when his pensive Ladie saw from farre,
   Great woe and sorrow did her soule assay,°   *attack*
   As weening that the sad end of the warre,
   And gan to highest God entirely° pray,   *earnestly*
   That fearèd chaunce° from her to turne away; *fate*
285 With folded hands and knees full lowly bent
   All night she watcht, ne once adowne would lay
   Her daintie limbs in her sad dreriment,[9]
  But praying still did wake, and waking did lament.

      33

  The morrow next gan early to appeare,
290 That Titan[1] rose to runne his daily race;
   But early ere the morrow next gan reare
   Out of the sea faire Titans deawy face,
   Up rose the gentle virgin from her place,
   And lookèd all about, if she might spy
295 Her loved knight to move his manly pace:

7. An allusion to Revelation 22.1–2: "And he showed me a pure river of water of life, clear as crystal, proceeding out of the throne of God, and of the Lamb. In the midst of the street of it, and on either side of the river, was the tree of life which bore twelve manner of fruits and gave fruit every month, and the leaves of the tree served to heal the nation with."

8. The Well of Life, with its powers of renewal, is successively compared to waters of the Bible, of England and Europe, and of classical antiquity. In Siloam (Silo) a blind man was cured by Christ (John 9.7); the crossing of the river Jordan saved the Jews (Deuteronomy 27.2–9), and Christ was baptized therein (Matthew 3.16); "Bath" and "Spau" (Spa) were famed for their medicinal waters; "Cephise" and "Hebrus" in Greece were noted for purifying and healing powers.

9. Dismal condition.

1. When the sun.

For she had great doubt of his safety,
Since late she saw him fall before his enemy.

34

At last she saw, where he upstarted brave
    Out of the well, wherein he drenchèd lay;
300 As Eagle fresh out of the Ocean wave,
    Where he hath left his plumes all hoary gray,
    And deckt himselfe with feathers youthly gay,
    Like Eyas° hauke up mounts unto the skies,   *young*
    His newly budded pineons to assay,
305 And marveiles at himselfe, still as he flies:
So new this new-borne knight to battell new did rise.[2]

35

Whom when the damnèd feend so fresh did spy,
    No wonder if he wondred at the sight,
    And doubted, whether his late enemy
310 It were, or other new supplièd knight.
    He, now to prove his late renewèd might,
    High brandishing his bright deaw-burning blade,
    Upon his crested scalpe so sore did smite,
    That to the scull a yawning wound it made:
315 The deadly dint° his dullèd senses all dismaid.   *blow*

36

I wote° not, whether the revenging steele   *know*
    Were hardnèd with that holy water dew,
    Wherein he fell, or sharper edge did feele,
    Or his baptizèd hands now greater° grew;   *stronger*
320 Or other secret vertue did ensew;
    Else never could the force of fleshly arme,
    Ne molten mettall in his bloud embrew:°   *plunge*
    For till that stownd° could never wight him harme, *stunning blow*
By subtilty, nor slight,° nor might, nor mighty charme.   *trickery*

37

325 The cruell wound enragèd him so sore,
    That loud he yellèd for exceeding paine;
    As hundred ramping Lyons seemed to rore,
    Whom ravenous hunger did there to constraine:
    Then gan he tosse aloft his stretchèd traine,°   *tail*
330 And therewith scourge the buxome° aire so sore,   *yielding*
    That to his force to yeelden it was faine;°   *obliged*
    Ne ought his sturdie strokes might stand afore,[3]
That high trees overthrew, and rocks in peeces tore.

38

The same advauncing high above his head,
335 With sharpe intended° sting so rude° him smot, *extended/roughly*
    That to the earth him drove, as stricken dead,

---

2. Legend had it that the eagle could renew its
youth by bathing in a spring.

3. I.e., neither could anything ("ought") stand
before his violent ("sturdie") strokes.

Ne living wight would have him life behot:[4]
  The mortall sting his angry needle shot
  Quite through his shield, and in his shoulder seasd,
340 Where fast it stucke, ne would there out be got:
  The griefe° thereof him wondrous sore diseasd,°   *pain/afflicted*
Ne might his ranckling paine with patience be appeasd.

39

But yet more mindfull of his honour deare,
  Then of the grievous smart, which him did wring,°   *torment*
345 From loathèd soile he can° him lightly reare,   *began to*
  And strove to loose the farre infixèd sting:
  Which when in vaine he tryde with struggeling,
  Inflamed with wrath, his raging blade he heft,°   *heaved*
  And strooke so strongly, that the knotty string
350 Of his huge taile he quite a sunder cleft,
Five joynts thereof he hewd, and but the stump him left.

40

Hart cannot thinke, what outrage,° and what cryes,   *violent clamor*
  With foule enfouldred[5] smoake and flashing fire,
  The hell-bred beast threw forth unto the skyes,
355 That all was coverèd with darknesse dire:
  Then fraught with rancour, and engorgèd° ire,   *choking*
  He cast at once him to avenge for all,
  And gathering up himselfe out of the mire,
  With his uneven wings did fiercely fall
360 Upon his sunne-bright shield, and gript it fast withall.

41

Much was the man encombred with his hold,
  In feare to lose his weapon in his paw,
  Ne wist yet, how his talents° to unfold;   *talons*
  Nor harder was from Cerberus[6] greedie jaw
365 To plucke a bone, then from his cruell claw
  To reave° by strength the gripéd gage° away: *seize/prize*
  Thrise he assayd it from his foot to draw,
  And thrise in vaine to draw it did assay,
It booted nought to thinke, to robbe him of his pray.

42

370 Tho° when he saw no power might prevaile,   *then*
  His trustie sword he cald to his last aid,
  Wherewith he fiercely did his foe assaile,
  And double blowes about him stoutly laid,
  That glauncing fire out of the yron plaid;
375 As sparckles from the Andvile° use to fly,   *anvil*
  When heavie hammers on the wedge are swaid;°   *struck*
  Therewith at last he forst him to unty°   *loosen*
One of his grasping feete, him to defend thereby.

---

4. I.e., no one would have thought ("behot"—
called) him alive.

5. Black as a thunderbolt.
6. The dog that guards the mouth of Hell.

43

The other foot, fast fixèd on his shield,
380   Whenas no strength, nor stroks mote° him constraine   *might*
      To loose, ne yet the warlike pledge to yield,
      He smot thereat with all his might and maine,
      That nought so wondrous puissance might sustaine;
      Upon the joynt the lucky steele did light,
385   And made such way, that hewd it quite in twaine;
      The paw yet missèd not his minisht° might,   *lessened*
But hong still on the shield, as it at first was pight.°   *placed*

44

For griefe thereof, and divelish despight,
      From his infernall fournace forth he threw
390   Huge flames, that dimmèd all the heavens light,
      Enrold in duskish smoke and brimstone blew;
      As burning Aetna from his boyling stew°   *cauldron*
      Doth belch out flames, and rockes in peeces broke,
      And ragged ribs of mountaines molten new
395   Enwrapt in coleblacke clouds and filthy smoke,
That all the land with stench, and heaven with horror choke.

45

The heate whereof, and harmefull pestilence
      So sore him noyd,° that forst him to retire   *troubled*
      A little backward for his best defence,
400   To save his bodie from the scorching fire,
      Which he from hellish entrailes did expire.°   *breathe out*
      It chaunst (eternall God that chaunce did guide)
      As he recoylèd backward, in the mire
      His nigh forwearied feeble feet did slide,
405   And downe he fell, with dread of shame sore terrifide.

46

There grew a goodly tree him faire beside,
      Loaden with fruit and apples rosie red,
      As they in pure vermilion had beene dide,
      Whereof great vertues over all were red:°   *declared*
410   For happie life to all, which thereon fed,
      And life eke everlasting did befall:
      Great God it planted in that blessed sted°   *place*
      With his almightie hand, and did it call
The Tree of Life, the crime of our first fathers fall.[7]

47

415   In all the world like was not to be found,
      Save in that soile, where all good things did grow,
      And freely sprong out of the fruitfull ground,
      As incorrupted Nature did them sow,

7. Genesis 2.9 describes the Tree of Life and also the Tree of Knowledge of Good and Evil, both of which God planted in the Garden of Eden. The "crime of our first fathers fall" is that Adam, in eating of the second and being banished from Eden, separated himself—and us—from the first. The Tree of Life appears again in the New Jerusalem (Revelation 22.2).

Till that dread Dragon all did overthrow.
420   Another like faire tree eke grew thereby,
     Whereof who so did eat, eftsoones did know
     Both good and ill: O mornefull memory:
That tree through one mans fault hath doen us all to dy.[8]

48

From that first tree forth flowd, as from a well,
425   A trickling streame of Balme, most soveraine°   *powerful for cures*
     And daintie deare,[9] which on the ground still fell,
     And overflowèd all the fertill plaine,
     As it had deawèd bene with timely° raine: *seasonable*
     Life and long health that gratious° ointment gave,   *full of grace*
430   And deadly woundes could heale, and reare° againe   *raise*
     The senselesse corse appointed° for the grave.   *made ready*
Into that same he fell: which did from death him save.[1]

49

For nigh thereto the ever damnèd beast
     Durst not approch, for he was deadly made,[2]
435   And all that life preservèd, did detest:
     Yet he it oft adventured° to invade.   *attempted*
     By this the drouping day-light gan to fade,
     And yeeld his roome to sad succeeding night,
     Who with her sable mantle gan to shade
440   The face of earth, and wayes of living wight,
And high her burning torch set up in heaven bright.

50

When gentle Una saw the second fall
     Of her deare knight, who wearie of long fight,
     And faint through losse of bloud, moved not at all,
445   But lay as in a dreame of deepe delight,
     Besmeard with pretious Balme, whose vertuous might
     Did heale his wounds, and scorching heat alay,[3]
     Againe she stricken was with sore affright,
     And for his safetie gan devoutly pray;
450   And watch the noyous° night, and wait for joyous day.   *afflicting*

51

The joyous day gan early to appeare,
     And faire Aurora from the deawy bed
     Of aged Tithone gan her selfe to reare,[4]
     With rosie cheekes, for shame as blushing red;
455   Her golden lockes for haste were loosely shed
     About her eares, when Una her did marke
     Clymbe to her charet, all with flowers spred,

---

8. I.e., killed us.
9. Precious.
1. The healing balm flowing from the Tree of Life is understood to be Christ's blood, shed to redeem mankind from eternal damnation.
2. I.e., a child of death.

3. Cf. Revelation 2.7,11: "To him that overcometh will I give to eat of the tree of life;" "He that overcometh shall not be hurt of the second death."
4. Aurora is goddess of the dawn, Tithones her husband ("aged" because he was granted everlasting life without everlasting youth).

From heaven high to chase the chearelesse darke;
With merry note her loud salutes the mounting larke.

52

460 Then freshly up arose the doughtie knight,
    All healèd of his hurts and woundès wide,
    And did himselfe to battell readie dight;°   *prepare*
    Whose early foe awaiting him beside
    To have devourd, so soone as day he spyde,
465 When now he saw himselfe so freshly reare,
    As if late fight had nought him damnifyde,°   *injured*
    He woxe° dismayd, and garr his fate to feare;   *grew*
  Nathlesse° with wonted rage he him advauncèd neare. *nevertheless*

53

And in his first encounter, gaping wide,
470 He thought attonce him to have swallowed quight,
    And rusht upon him with outragious pride;
    Who him r'encountring fierce, as hauke in flight,
    Perforce rebutted° backe. The weapon bright   *drove*
    Taking advantage of his open jaw,
475 Ran through his mouth with so importune° might, *violent*
    That deepe emperst his darksome hollow maw,
And back retyrd,[5] his life bloud forth with all did draw.

54

So downe he fell, and forth his life did breath,
    That vanisht into smoke and cloudès swift;
480 So downe he fell, that th' earth him underneath
    Did grone, as feeble so great load to lift;
    So downe he fell, as an huge rockie clift,
    Whose false° foundation waves have washt away, *insecure*
    With dreadfull poyse° is from the mayneland *falling weight*
    rift,°   *split*
485 And rolling downe, great Neptune doth dismay;
  So downe he fell, and like an heapèd mountaine lay.

55

The knight himselfe even trembled at his fall,
    So huge and horrible a masse it seemed;
    And his deare Ladie, that beheld it all,
490 Durst not approch for dread, which she misdeemed,° *misjudged*
    But yet at last, when as the direfull feend
    She saw not stirre, off-shaking vaine affright,
    She nigher drew, and saw that joyous end:
    Then God she praysd, and thankt her faithfull knight,
495 That had atchieved so great a conquest by his might.

---

5. On being drawn back.

Canto 12

Faire Una to the Redcrosse knight
betrouthéd is with joy:
Though false Duessa it to barre
her false sleights doe imploy.

1

Behold I see the haven nigh at hand,
  To which I meane my wearie course to bend;
  Vere the maine shete, and beare up with the land,[1]
  The which afore is fairely to be kend,°   *recognized*
5 And seemeth safe from stormes, that may offend;
  There this faire virgin wearie of her way
  Must landed be, now at her journeyes end:
  There eke my feeble barke° a while may stay,   *ship*
Till merry° wind and weather call her thence away. *favorable*

2

10 Scarsely had Phoebus in the glooming East[2]
  Yet harnessèd his firie-footed teeme,
  Ne reard above the earth his flaming creast,°   *crest*
  When the last deadly smoke aloft did steeme,
  That signe of last outbreathèd life did seeme
15 Unto the watchman on the castle wall;
  Who thereby dead that balefull° Beast did deeme,   *evil*
  And to his Lord and Ladie lowd gan call,
To tell, how he had seene the Dragons fatall fall.

3

Uprose with hastie joy, and feeble speed
20 That aged Sire, the Lord of all that land,
  And lookèd forth, to weet, if true indeede
  Those tydings were, as he did understand,
  Which whenas true by tryall he out fond,
  He bad to open wyde his brazen gate,
25 Which long time had bene shut, and out of hond[3]
  Proclaymèd joy and peace through all his state;
For dead now was their foe, which them forrayèd late.[4]

4

Then gan triumphant Trompets sound on hie,
  That sent to heaven the ecchoèd report
30 Of their new joy, and happie victorie
  Gainst him, that had them long opprest with tort,°   *wrong*
  And fast imprisonèd in siegèd fort.
  Then all the people, as in solemne feast,
To him assembled with one full consort,[5]

---

1. Release the mainsail line and sail toward the land. The nautical metaphor echoes many classical authors and Chaucer's *Troilus and Criseyde* (2.1–7).
2. I.e., dawn.
3. Straightway.
4. Had recently ravaged.
5. All together.

35   Rejoycing at the fall of that great beast,
       From whose eternall bondage now they were releast.

                                        5

       Forth came that auncient Lord and aged Queene,
           Arayd in antique robes downe to the ground,
           And sad habiliments right well beseene;[6]
40   A noble crew about them waited round
           Of sage and sober Peres,° all gravely gownd;   *peers*
           Whom farre before did march a goodly band
           Of tall young men, all hable armes to sownd,[7]
           But now they laurell braunches bore in hand;
45   Glad signe of victorie and peace in all their land.

                                        6

       Unto that doughtie Conquerour they came,
           And him before themselves prostrating low,
           Their Lord and Patrone° loud did him proclaime,   *defender*
           And at his feet their laurell boughes did throw.
50   Soone after them all dauncing on a row
           The comely virgins came, with girlands dight,°   *adorned*
           As fresh as flowres in medow greene do grow,
           When morning deaw upon their leaves doth light:
       And in their hands sweet Timbrels° all upheld   *tambourines*
           on hight.

                                        7

55   And them before, the fry° of children young   *crowd*
           Their wanton° sports and childish mirth did play,   *playful*
           And to the Maydens sounding tymbrels sung
           In well attunèd notes, a joyous lay,
           And made delightfull musicke all the way,
60   Untill they came, where that faire virgin stood;
           As faire Diana[8] in fresh sommers day
           Beholds her Nymphes, enraunged° in shadie wood,   *ranged*
       Some wrestle, some do run, some bathe in christall flood.

                                        8

       So she beheld those maydens meriment
65   With chearefull vew; who when to her they came,
           Themselves to ground with gratious humblesse° bent,   *humility*
           And her adored by honorable name,[9]
           Lifting to heaven her everlasting fame:
           Then on her head they set a girland greene,
70   And crownèd her twixt earnest and twixt game:[1]
           Who in her selfe-resemblance well beseene,[2]
       Did seeme such, as she was, a goodly maiden Queene.

---

6. I.e., their sober, appropriate ("right well   9. With titles of honor.
beseene") attire.   1. I.e., half in fun.
7. Able to fight with weapons.   2. I.e., looking appropriately like herself.
8. Goddess of the hunt.

9

    And after all, the raskall many ran,
       Heapèd together in rude rablement,[3]   *confusion*
75   To see the face of that victorious man:
       Whom all admired,° as from heaven sent,   *wondered at*
       And gazd upon with gaping wonderment.
       But when they came, where that dead Dragon lay,
       Stretcht on the ground in monstrous large extent,
80   The sight with idle° feare did them dismay,   *baseless*
  Ne durst approch him nigh, to touch, or once assay.

10

    Some feard, and fled; some feard and well it faynd;°   *concealed*
       One that would wiser seeme, then all the rest,
       Warnd him not touch, for yet perhaps remaynd
85   Some lingring life within his hollow brest,
       Or in his wombe might lurke some hidden nest
       Of many Dragonets,° his fruitfull seed;   *young dragons*
       Another said, that in his eyes did rest
       Yet sparckling fire, and bad thereof take heed;
90 Another said, he saw him move his eyes indeed.

11

    One mother, when as her foolehardie chyld
       Did come too neare, and with his talants° play,   *talons*
       Halfe dead through feare, her litle babe revyld,°   *scolded*
       And to her gossips° gan in counsell° say;   *women friends/private*
95   "How can I tell, but that his talants may
       Yet scratch my sonne, or rend his tender hand?"
       So diversly themselves in vaine they fray;°   *scare*
       Whiles some more bold, to measure him nigh stand,
  To prove° how many acres he did spread of land.   *determine*

12

100 Thus flockèd all the folke him round about,
       The whiles that hoarie° king, with all his traine,   *gray-haired*
       Being arrivèd, where that champion stout
       After his foes defeasance° did remaine,   *defeat*
       Him goodly greetes, and faire does entertaine,
105 With princely gifts of yvorie and gold,
       And thousand thankes him yeelds for all his paine.
       Then when his daughter deare he does behold,
  Her dearely doth imbrace, and kisseth manifold.°   *many times*

13

    And after to his Pallace he them brings,
110 With shaumes,[4] and trompets, and with Clarions sweet;
       And all the way the joyous people sings,
       And with their garments strowes the pavèd street:
       Whence mounting up, they find purveyance° meet   *provisions*

3. Discordant confusion. "Raskall many": rabble   4. Ancient wind instrument like an oboe.
throng.

Of all, that royall Princes court became,°   *suited*
115   And all the floore was underneath their feet
Bespred with costly scarlot of great name,[5]
On which they lowly sit, and fitting purpose frame.

                              14

What needs me tell their feast and goodly guize,°   *behavior*
In which was nothing riotous nor vaine?
120   What needs of daintie dishes to devize,°   *talk*
Of comely services, or courtly trayne?
My narrow leaves cannot in them containe
The large discourse[6] of royall Princes state.
Yet was their manner then but bare and plaine:
125   For th' antique world excesse and pride did hate,
Such proud luxurious pompe is swollen up but late.[7]

                              15

Then when with meates and drinkes of every kinde
Their fervent appetites they quenchèd had,
That auncient Lord gan fit occasion finde,
130   Of straunge adventures, and of perils sad,°   *grave*
Which in his travell him befallen had,
For to demaund of his renowmèd guest:
Who then with utt'rance grave, and count'nance sad,
From point to point, as is before exprest,
135   Discourst his voyage long, according° his request.   *granting*

                              16

Great pleasure mixt with pittifull° regard,   *sympathetic*
That godly King and Queene did passionate,[8]
Whiles they his pittifull° adventures heard,   *deserving pity*
That oft they did lament his lucklesse state,
140   And often blame the too importune° fate,   *severe*
That heapd on him so many wrathfull wreakes:[9]
For never gentle knight, as he of late,
So tossèd was in fortunes cruell freakes,°   *whims*
And all the while salt teares bedeawd the hearers cheaks.

                              17

145   Then said that royall Pere in sober wise:
"Deare Sonne, great beene the evils, which ye bore
From first to last in your late enterprise,
That I note,° whether prayse, or pitty more: *know not*
For never living man, I weene, so sore
150   In sea of deadly daungers was distrest;
But since now safe ye seisèd° have the shore,   *reached*
And well arrivèd are (high God be blest),
Let us devize° of ease and everlasting rest."   *think*

                              18

"Ah dearest Lord," said then that doughty knight,
155   "Of ease or rest I may not yet devize;

---

5. I.e., famous scarlet cloth.   8. I.e., did feel and express.
6. I.e., full description.   9. Vengeful injuries.
7. Just recently.

For by the faith, which I to armes have plight,°   *pledged*
I bounden am streight after this emprize,°   *enterprise*
As that your daughter can ye well advize,
Backe to returne to that great Faerie Queene,
160   And her to serve six yeares in warlike wize,
Gainst that proud Paynim king, that workes her teene:°   *sorrow*
Therefore I ought crave pardon, till I there have beene."[1]

19

"Unhappie falles that hard necessitie,"
Quoth he, "the troubler of my happie peace,
165   And vowèd foe of my felicitie;
Ne° I against the same can justly preace:°   *Neither/press*
But since that band° ye cannot now release,   *obligation*
Nor doen undo (for vowes may not be vaine),[2]
Soone as the terme of those six yeares shall cease,
170   Ye then shall hither backe returne againe,
The marriage to accomplish vowd betwixt you twain.

20

"Which for my part I covet to performe,
In sort as through the world I did proclame,
That who so kild that monster most deforme,
175   And him in hardy battaile overcame,
Should have mine onely daughter to his Dame,°   *wife*
And of my kingdome heire apparaunt bee:
Therefore since now to thee perteines° the same,   *belongs*
By dew desert of noble chevalree,
180 Both daughter and eke° kingdome, lo I yield to thee."   *also*

21

Then forth he callèd that his daughter faire,
The fairest Un' his onely daughter deare,
His onely daughter, and his onely heyre;
Who forth proceeding with sad° sober cheare,°   *grave/countenance*
185   As bright as doth the morning starre appeare
Out of the East, with flaming lockes bedight,°   *bedecked*
To tell that dawning day is drawing neare,
And to the world does bring long wishèd light;
So faire and fresh that Lady shewd her selfe in sight.

22

190 So faire and fresh, as freshest flowre in May;
For she had layd her mournefull stole aside,
And widow-like sad wimple° throwne away,   *veil*
Wherewith her heavenly beautie she did hide,
Whiles on her wearie journey she did ride;
195   And on her now a garment she did weare,
All lilly white, withoutten spot, or pride,°   *ornament*

---

1. The final Christian triumph, the marriage of
Christ and the true church, will be achieved only
at the end of time, the Day of Judgment. Meanwhile, the struggle against evil (and the Roman
Church) continues. "Ought": must.
2. I.e., you cannot undo what is done ("doen"),
for vows may not be (made) vain.

That seemed like silke and silver woven neare,°   *tightly*
But neither silke nor silver therein did appeare.[3]

23

The blazing brightnesse of her beauties beame,
200   And glorious light of her sunshyny face[4]
To tell, were as to strive against the streame.
My ragged rimes are all too rude and bace,
Her heavenly lineaments for to enchace.°   *adorn*
Ne wonder; for her owne deare lovèd knight,
205   All° were she dayly with himselfe in place,   *although*
Did wonder much at her celestiall sight:
Oft had he seene her faire, but never so faire dight.

24

So fairely dight, when she in presence came,
She to her Sire made humble reverence,
210   And bowèd low, that her right well became,
And added grace unto her excellence:
Who with great wisdome, and grave eloquence
Thus gan to say. But eare° he thus had said,   *ere*
With flying speede, and seeming great pretence,°   *purpose*
215   Came running in, much like a man dismaid,
A Messenger with letters, which his message said.

25

All in the open hall amazèd stood,
At suddeinnesse of that unwarie° sight,   *unexpected*
And wondred at his breathlesse hastie mood.
220   But he for nought would stay his passage right°   *direct*
Till fast° before the king he did alight;   *close*
Where falling flat, great humblesse he did make,
And kist the ground, whereon his foot was pight;°   *placed*
Then to his hands that writ° he did betake,°   *document/deliver*
225   Which he disclosing, red thus, as the paper spake.

26

"To thee, most mighty king of Eden faire,
Her greeting sends in these sad lines addrest,
The wofull daughter, and forsaken heire
Of that great Emperour of all the West;
230   And bids thee be advizèd for the best,
Ere thou thy daughter linck in holy band
Of wedlocke to that new unknowen guest:
For he already plighted his right hand
Unto another love, and to another land.

27

235   "To me sad mayd, or rather widow sad,
He was affiauncèd long time before,

---

3. "The marriage of the Lamb is come, and his
wife hath made herself ready. And to her was
granted that she should be arrayed in fine linen,
clean and white: for the fine linen is the righteousness of saints" (Revelation 19.7–8).
4. Revelation 21.9,11 describes the New Jerusalem as "the bride, the Lamb's wife . . . her light
was like unto a stone most precious."

And sacred pledges he both gave, and had,
  False erraunt knight, infamous, and forswore:
  Witnesse the burning Altars, which° he swore,   *by which*
240 And guiltie heavens of⁵ his bold perjury,
  Which though he hath polluted oft of yore,
  Yet I to them for judgement just do fly,
And them conjure° t' avenge this shamefull injury.   *implore*

28

"Therefore since mine he is, or° free or bond,°   *whether/bound*
245 Or false or trew, or living or else dead,
  Withhold, O soveraine Prince, your hasty hond
  From knitting league with him, I you aread;°   *advise*
  Ne wene° my right with strength adowne to tread,   *think*
  Through weakenesse of my widowhed, or woe:
250 For truth is strong, her rightfull cause to plead,
  And shall find friends, if need requireth soe,
So bids thee well to fare, Thy neither friend, nor foe, Fidessa."

29

When he these bitter byting words had red,
  The tydings straunge did him abashèd make,
255 That still he sate long time astonishèd
  As in great muse,° ne word to creature spake.   *amazement*
  At last his solemne silence thus he brake,
  With doubtfull eyes fast fixèd on his guest:
  "Redoubted knight, that for mine onely sake⁶
260 Thy life and honour late adventurest,
Let nought be hid from me, that ought to be exprest.

30

"What meane these bloudy vowes, and idle threats,
  Throwne out from womanish impatient mind?
  What heavens? what altars? what enragèd heates
265 Here heapèd up with termes of love unkind,°   *unnatural*
  My conscience cleare with guilty bands⁷ would bind?
  High God be witnesse, that I guiltlesse ame.
  But if your selfe, Sir knight, ye faultie° find,   *guilty*
  Or wrappèd be in loves of former Dame,
270 With crime do not it cover, but disclose the same."

31

To whom the Redcrosse knight this answere sent,
  "My Lord, my King, be nought hereat dismayd,
  Till well ye wote by grave intendiment,⁸
  What woman, and wherefore doth me upbrayd
275 With breach of love, and loyalty betrayd.
  It was in my mishaps, as hitherward
  I lately traveild, that unwares I strayd
  Out of my way, through perils straunge and hard;
That day should faile me, ere I had them all declard.

---

5. I.e., and heavens polluted by.   7. I.e., bonds of guilt.
6. For my sake alone. "Redoubted": honored.   8. I.e., serious investigation.

32

280 "There did I find, or rather I was found
         Of this false woman, that Fidessa hight,
         Fidessa hight the falsest Dame on ground,
         Most false Duessa, royall richly dight,
         That easie was t' invegle° weaker sight: *deceive*
285   Who by her wicked arts, and wylie skill,
         Too false and strong for earthly skill or might,
         Unwares me wrought unto her wicked will,
And to my foe betrayd, when least I fearèd ill."

33

Then steppèd forth the goodly royall Mayd,
290   And on the ground her selfe prostrating low,
         With sober countenaunce thus to him sayd:
         "O pardon me, my soveraigne Lord, to show
         The secret treasons, which of late I know
         To have bene wroght by that false sorceresse.
295   She onely she it is, that earst did throw
         This gentle knight into so great distresse,
That death him did awaite in dayly wretchednesse.

34

"And now it seemes, that she subornèd hath
         This craftie messenger with letters vaine,
300   To worke new woe and improvided scath,[9]
         By breaking of the band betwixt us twaine;
         Wherein she usèd hath the practicke paine[1]
         Of this false footman, clokt with simplenesse,
         Whom if ye please for to discover plaine,
305   Ye shall him Archimago find, I ghesse,
The falsest man alive; who tries shall find no lesse."

35

The king was greatly movèd at her speach,
         And all with suddein indignation fraight,°   *filled*
         Bad° on that Messenger rude hands to reach.   *bade*
310   Eftsoones° the Gard, which on his state did wait,
         Attacht that faitor° false, and bound him strait: *impostor*
         Who seeming sorely chauffèd° at his band,   *angered*
         As chainèd Beare, whom cruell dogs do bait,
         With idle force did faine them to withstand,
315   And often semblaunce made to scape out of their hand.

36

But they him layd full low in dungeon deepe,
         And bound him hand and foote with yron chains.
         And with continuall watch did warely° keepe;   *vigilantly*
         Who then would thinke, that by his subtile trains
320   He could escape fowle death or deadly paines?[2]

9. Unexpected harm.
1. Treacherous skill.
2. "And he laid hold on the dragon, that old serpent, which is the Devil, and Satan, and bound
him a thousand years, And cast him into the bottomless pit, and shut him up, and set a seal upon
him, that he should deceive the nations no more,
till the thousand years should be fulfilled: and after

Thus when that Princes wrath was pacifide,
He gan renew the late forbidden banes,[3]
And to the knight his daughter deare he tyde,
With sacred rites and vowes for ever to abyde.

37

325 His owne two hands the holy knots did knit,
That none but death for ever can devide;
His owne two hands, for such a turne° most fit,   *act*
The housling° fire did kindle and provide,   *sacramental*
And holy water thereon sprinckled wide;[4]
330 At which the bushy Teade° a groome did light,   *marriage torch*
And sacred lampe in secret chamber hide,
Where it should not be quenchèd day nor night,
For feare of evill fates, but burnen ever bright.

38

Then gan they sprinckle all the posts with wine,
335 And made great feast to solemnize that day;
They all perfumde with frankencense divine,
And precious odours fetcht from far away,
That all the house did sweat with great aray:
And all the while sweete Musicke did apply
340 Her curious° skill, the warbling notes to play,   *intricate*
To drive away the dull Melancholy;
The whiles one sung a song of love and jollity.

39

During the which there was an heavenly noise
Heard sound through all the Pallace pleasantly,
345 Like as it had bene many an Angels voice,
Singing before th' eternall majesty,
In their trinall triplicities[5] on hye;
Yet wist no creature, whence that heavenly sweet°   *delight*
Proceeded, yet each one felt secretly°   *inwardly*
350 Himselfe thereby reft of his sences meet,°   *proper*
And ravishèd with rare impression in his sprite.[6]

40

Great joy was made that day of young and old,
And solemne feast proclaimd throughout the land,
That their exceeding merth may not be told:
355 Suffice it heare by signes to understand
The usuall joyes at knitting of loves band.
Thrise happy man the knight himselfe did hold,
Possessèd of his Ladies hart and hand,

---

that he must be loosed a little season" (Revelation 20.2–3).

3. Banns, i.e., announcements of marriage.

4. Marriages in ancient times were solemnized with sacramental fire and water.

5. The "trinall triplicities" are the 9 angelic orders, divided into 3 groups of 3, the whole hierarchy corresponding to the 9 spheres of the universe. The

music heard in this stanza is the music of the spheres, not audible on earth since the Fall.

6. Spirit. "Let us be glad and rejoice, and give honor to him: for the marriage of the Lamb is come" (Revelation 9.6). In Revelation, the marriage of Christ and the New Jerusalem signals the general redemption.

And ever, when his eye did her behold,
360   His heart did seeme to melt in pleasures manifold.

41

Her joyous presence and sweet company
    In full content he there did long enjoy,
    Ne wicked envie, ne vile gealosy
    His deare delights were able to annoy:
365   Yet swimming in that sea of blisfull joy,
    He nought forgot, how he whilome had sworne,
    In case he could that monstrous beast destroy,
    Unto his Faerie Queene backe to returne:
The which he shortly did, and Una left to mourne.

42

370   Now strike your sailes ye jolly Mariners,
    For we be come unto a quiet rode,°   *harbor*
    Where we must land some of our passengers,
    And light this wearie vessell of her lode.
    Here she a while may make her safe abode,
375   Till she repairèd have her tackles spent,°   *worn out*
    And wants supplide. And then againe abroad
    On the long voyage whereto she is bent:
Well may she speede and fairely finish her intent.

From The Third Booke of the Faerie Queene

Contayning
The Legend of Britomartis,[1]
or
Of Chastitie

1

It falles° me here to write of Chastity,   *falls to*
    That fairest vertue, farre above the rest;
    For which what needs me fetch from Faery
    Forreine ensamples, it to have exprest?
5   Sith it is shrinèd in my Soveraines brest,[2]
    And formed so lively° in each perfect part,   *lifelike*
    That to all Ladies, which have it profest,
    Need but behold the pourtraict° of her hart,   *picture*
If pourtrayd it might be by any living art.

2

10   But living art may not least part expresse,°   *portray*
    Nor life-resembling pencill it can paint,[3]

---

1. The heroine's name is taken from Virgil's Britomartis (*Ciris*, 295–305) a goddess associated with Diana, chaste goddess of the moon. Spenser intends the etymology, Brito (Britain), Mart (Mars—god of war).
2. Elizabeth, the Virgin Queen. "Sith": since.

3. I.e., nor can any artist, however lifelike his representation, paint her heart. "Pencill": brush. Zeuxis and Praxiteles were a Greek painter and sculptor, respectively, famed for lifelike representations.

All were it Zeuxis or Praxiteles:
His daedale[4] hand would faile, and greatly faint,
And her perfections with his error taint:
15   Ne Poets wit, that passeth Painter farre
In picturing the parts of beautie daint,°   *choice*
So hard a workmanship adventure darre,[5]
For fear through want of words her excellence to marre.

3

How then shall I, Apprentice of the skill,
20   That whylome° in divinest wits did raine,°   *formerly/reign*
Presume so high to stretch mine humble quill?
Yet now my lucklesse lot doth me constraine
Hereto perforce. But O dred° Soveraine   *revered*
Thus farre forth pardon, sith that choicest wit
25   Cannot your glorious pourtraict figure plaine
That I in colour showes may shadow it,[6]
And antique° praises unto present persons fit.   *ancient*

4

But if in living colours, and right hew,
Your selfe you covet to see picturèd,
30   Who can it doe more lively, or more trew,
Then that sweet verse, with Nectar sprinckelèd,
In which a gracious servant[7] picturèd
His Cynthia, his heavens fairest light?
That with his melting sweetnesse ravishèd,
35   And with the wonder of her beamès bright,
My senses lullèd are in slomber of delight.

5

But let that same delitious° Poet lend   *sweet*
A little leave unto a rusticke Muse[8]
To sing his mistresse prayse, and let him mend,
40   If ought° amis her liking may abuse: *anything*
Ne let his fairest Cynthia refuse,
In mirrours more then one her selfe to see,
But either Gloriana let her chuse,
Or in Belphoebe fashionèd to bee:
45   In th' one her rule, in th' other her rare chastitee.

---

4. Skillful, like the hand of Daedalus, the Greek artificer who devised wings for himself and his son Icarus, to escape from a labyrinth.
5. I.e., nor can a poet's ingenuity, which far surpasses ("passeth") that of a painter, dare to undertake such a difficult task.
6. I.e., since none can portray you as you truly are ("plaine"), may I do so by artful but imperfect images, "colour showes." In Platonic terms, everything in the material world is but a shadow of

the true reality in the world of Ideas. Britomart also foreshadows her descendant, Queen Elizabeth.
7. Sir Walter Ralegh, who, in his poetic fragment, *The Ocean's Love to Cynthia*, uses the names Belphoebe and Cynthia for Elizabeth. Diana, Phoebe, and Cynthia are all names for the goddess of the moon and of chastity. Hence Spenser's name, Bel (beautiful) + Phoebe.
8. Spenser, in his shepherd persona, Colin Clout.

Canto 1

Guyon encountreth Britomart,
faire Florimell is chaced:
Duessaes traines and Malecastaes
champions are defaced.°   defeated

1

The famous Briton Prince and Faerie knight,[1]
    After long wayes and perilous paines endured,
    Having their wearie limbes to perfect plight°   condition
    Restord, and sory° wounds right well recured,°   painful/healed
5 Of the faire Alma greatly were procured,[2]
    To make there lenger sojourne and abode;
    But when thereto they might not be allured,
    From seeking praise, and deeds of armes abrode,
They courteous congè° tooke, and forth together   farewell
    yode.°   went

2

10 But the captived Acrasia he[3] sent,
    Because of travell° long, a nigher° way,   travail/nearer
    With a strong gard, all reskew to prevent,
    And her to Faerie court safe to convay,
    That her for witnesse of his hard assay,°   trial
15 Unto his Faerie Queene he might present:
    But he himselfe betooke another way,
    To make more triall of his hardiment,°   daring
And seeke adventures, as he with Prince Arthur went.

3

Long so they travellèd through wastefull° wayes,   desolate
20   Where daungers dwelt, and perils most did wonne,°   inhabit
    To hunt for glorie and renowmèd praise;
    Full many Countries they did overronne,°   pass through
    From the uprising to the setting Sunne,
    And many hard adventures did atchieve;
25 Of all the which they honour ever wonne,
    Seeking the weake oppressèd to relieve,
And to recover right for such, as wrong did grieve.[4]

4

At last as through an open plaine they yode,°   went
    They spide a knight, that towards prickèd faire,[5]
30 And him beside an agèd Squire there rode,
    That seemed to couch under his shield three-square,[6]
    As if that age bad him that burden spare,
    And yield it those, that stouter could it wield:

---

1. Guyon (Knight of Temperance), the hero of book 2, here rides with the "Briton Prince" Arthur.
2. Urged; Alma and Acrasia (below) are characters in book 2.
3. Guyon.

4. I.e., to restore their rights to those grieved by wrongs.
5. Rode in their direction.
6. With three equal sides. "Couch": stoop.

He them espying, gan himselfe prepare,[7]
35   And on his arme addresse° his goodly shield   *make ready*
That bore a Lion passant in a golden field.[8]

5

Which seeing good Sir Guyon, deare besought
The Prince of grace,[9] to let him runne that turne.
He graunted: then the Faery quickly raught°   *seized*
40   His poinant° speare, and sharpely gan to spurne°   *sharp/spur*
His fomy° steed, whose fierie feete did burne *covered with foam*
The verdant° grasse, as he thereon did tread;   *green*
Ne did the other backe his foot returne,
But fiercely forward came withouten dread,
45 And bent° his dreadfull speare against the others head. *aimed*

6

They bene ymet, and both their points arrived,[1]
But Guyon drove so furious and fell,°   *fierce*
That seemed both shield and plate° it would have *armor*
    rived°   *torn*
Nathelesse it bore his foe not from his sell,°   *seat*
50   But made him stagger, as he were not well:
But Guyon selfe, ere well he was aware,
Nigh a speares length behind his crouper[2] fell,
Yet in his fall so well him selfe he bare,   *bore*
That mischievous mischance his life and limbes did spare.

7

55 Great shame and sorrow of that fall he tooke;
For never yet, sith warlike armes he bore,
And shivering[3] speare in bloudie field first shooke,
He found himselfe dishonorèd so sore.
Ah gentlest knight, that ever armour bore,
60   Let not thee grieve dismounted to have beene,
And brought to ground, that never wast before;
For not thy fault, but secret powre unseene,
That speare enchaunted was, which layd thee on the greene.

8

But weenedst thou what wight thee overthrew,[4]
65   Much greater griefe and shamefuller regret
For thy hard fortune then thou wouldst renew,
That of a single damzell thou wert met
On equall plaine, and there so hard beset;
Even the famous Britomart it was,
70   Whom straunge adventure° did from Britaine fet,° *chance/fetch*
To seeke her lover (love farre sought alas,)
Whose image she had seene in Venus looking glas.

---

7. Began to prepare himself.
8. Heraldic description of a walking lion, against a golden background—the arms of Brute (ancestor of Britomart) who, according to legend, founded Britain.
9. As a matter of favor (perhaps with a pun on Arthur's symbolic significance.)

1. I.e., they came together, with each spear hitting on the other's shield.
2. The back of the saddle; i.e., he fell behind the horse a spear's length.
3. Capable of splitting, quivering at the ready. "Shooke": wielded.
4. Did you know what person overthrew you?

9

Full of disdainefull° wrath, he fierce uprose,   *indignant*
   For to revenge that foule reprochfull shame,
75 And snatching his bright sword began to close
   With her on foot, and stoutly forward came;
   Die rather would he, then endure that same.
   Which when his Palmer[5] saw, he gan to feare
   His toward perill and untoward blame,[6]
80 Which by that new rencounter he should reare:°   *bring about*
For death sate on the point of that enchaunted speare.

10

And hasting towards him gan faire perswade,
   Not to provoke misfortune, nor to weene°   *think*
   His speares default to mend with cruell blade;
85 For by his mightie Science he had seene
   The secret vertue of that weapon keene,[7]
   That mortall puissance mote° not withstond: *might*
   Nothing on earth mote alwaies happie° beene.   *fortunate*
   Great hazard were it, and adventure fond,°   *foolish*
90 To loose long gotten honour with one evill hond.°   *action*

11

By such good meanes he him discounsellèd,°   *dissuaded*
   From prosecuting his revenging rage;
   And eke° the Prince like treaty° handelèd,   *also/entreaty*
   His wrathfull will with reason to asswage,
95 And laid the blame, not to his carriage,°   *conduct*
   But to his starting steed, that swarved asyde,
   And to the ill purveyance° of his page,   *preparation*
   That had his furnitures[8] not firmely tyde:
So is his angry courage° fairely° pacifyde.   *spirit/entirely*

12

100 Thus reconcilement was betweene them knit,
   Through goodly temperance, and affection chaste,[9]
   And either vowd with all their power and wit,°   *skill*
   To let not others honour be defaste,
   Of friend or foe, who ever it embaste,[1]
105 Ne armes to beare against the others syde:
   In which accord the Prince was also plaste,°   *placed*
   And with that golden chaine of concord tyde.
So goodly all agreed, they forth yfere° did ryde.   *together*

13

O goodly usage of those antique times,
110 In which the sword was servant unto right;

5. The Palmer (signifying reason) was Guyon's guide in book 2. Pilgrims to the Holy Land were called palmers, in token of the palm leaves they often brought back.
6. Imminent shame. "Toward": approaching.
7. "Science:" knowledge; the Palmer has seen the secret power ("virtue") of Britomart's spear, which symbolizes the power of the virtue associated with her, chastity.
8. The horse's equipment and harness.
9. The special moral qualities of the two knights signify the ground of their accord.
1. I.e., neither would let the other's honor be defaced by friend or foe who might seek to degrade it.

When not for malice and contentious crimes,
    But all for praise, and proofe of manly might,
    The martiall brood accustomèd to fight:
    Then honour was the meed° of victorie,   *reward*
115   And yet the vanquishèd had no despight:
    Let later age that noble use envie,°   *emulate*
Vile rancour to avoid, and cruell surquedrie.[2]

14

Long they thus travellèd in friendly wise,
    Through countries waste, and eke well edifyde,°   *built up*
120   Seeking adventures hard, to exercise
    Their puissance, whylome full dernely tryde:[3]
    At length they came into a forrest wyde,
    Whose hideous horror and sad trembling sound
    Full griesly° seemed: Therein they long did ryde,   *horrible*
125   Yet tract° of living creatures none they found,   *trace*
Save Beares, Lions, and Buls, which romèd them around.

15

All suddenly out of the thickest brush,
    Upon a milk-white Palfrey all alone,
    A goodly Ladie did foreby° them rush,   *close by*
130   Whose face did seeme as cleare° as Christall stone,   *shining*
    And eke through feare as white as whalès bone:
    Her garments all were wrought of beaten gold,
    And all her steed with tinsell° trappings shone,   *glittering*
    Which fled so fast, that nothing mote° him hold,   *might*
135 And scarse them leasure gave, her passing to behold.

16

Still as she fled, her eye she backward threw,
    As fearing evill, that pursewd her fast;
    And her faire yellow locks behind her flew,
    Loosely disperst with puffe of every blast:
140   All as a blazing starre doth farre outcast
    His hearie beames, and flaming lockes dispred,[4]
    At sight whereof the people stand aghast:
    But the sage wisard telles, as he has red,°   *interpreted*
That it importunes death and dolefull drerihed.°   *disaster*

17

145 So as they gazèd after her a while,
    Lo where a griesly Foster[5] forth did rush,
    Breathing out beastly lust her to defile:
    His tyreling jade[6] he fiercely forth did push,
    Through thicke and thin, both over banke and bush
150   In hope her to attaine by hooke or crooke,
    That from his gorie sides the bloud did gush:

2. The arrogance of the victor; "rancour": the enmity felt by the vanquished.
3. I.e., their power ("puissance") at times ("why-lome") sorely ("dernely") tried.
4. The comparison with the comet suggests the

awe aroused by the beauty of this lady, identified in the argument as Florimell; her name combines flower and honey. "Hearie": hairy.
5. Horrible forester.
6. Tired nag.

Large were his limbes, and terrible his looke,
And in his clownish hand a sharp bore speare[7] he shooke.

18

Which outrage when those gentle knights did see,
Full of great envie and fell gealosy,
They stayd not to avise,° who first should bee,   *consider*
But all spurd after fast, as they mote° fly,   *might*
To reskew her from shamefull villany
The Prince and Guyon equally bylive[8]
Her selfe pursewd, in hope to win thereby
Most goodly meede,° the fairest Dame alive: *reward*
But after the foule foster Timias[9] did strive.

19

The whiles faire Britomart, whose constant mind,
Would not so lightly follow beauties chace,[1]
Ne reckt of Ladies Love, did stay behind,
And them awayted there a certaine space,
To weet° if they would turne backe to that place: *know*
But when she saw them gone, she forward went,
As lay her journey, through that perlous Pace,[2]
With stedfast courage and stout hardiment;
Ne evill thing she feared, ne evill thing she ment.°   *intended*

20

At last as nigh out of the wood she came,
A stately Castle farre away she spyde,
To which her steps directly she did frame.°   *direct*
That Castle was most goodly edifyde,°   *built*
And plaste for pleasure nigh that forrest syde:
But faire before the gate a spatious plaine,
Mantled with greene, it selfe did spredden wyde,
On which she saw six knights, that did darraine°   *wage*
Fierce battell against one, with cruell might and maine.

21

Mainly° they all attonce upon him laid,   *mightily*
And sore beset on every side around,
That nigh he breathlesse grew, yet nought dismaid,
Ne ever to them yielded foot of ground
All° had he lost much bloud through many a wound,   *although*
But stoutly dealt his blowes, and every way
To which he turnèd in his wrathfull stound,[3]
Made them recoile, and fly from dred decay,°   *death*
That none of all the sixe before, him durst assay.[4]

Line numbers: 155, 160, 165, 170, 175, 180, 185

---

7. Associated with the boar that wounded Adonis.
"Clownish": rough, rustic.
8. With equal speed.
9. Arthur's squire, a character also in book 2. His name means "honored."
1. Florimell is here identified with Beauty; the pun,

chased / chaste is probably intended.
2. Perilous passage.
3. Storm, here his violent wrath.
4. I.e., none of the six knights in front of him dared to assail him.

22

190 Like dastard Curres, that having at a bay[5]
     The salvage beast embost° in wearie chace,   *exhausted*
     Dare not adventure on the stubborne pray,
     Ne byte before, but rome from place to place,
     To get a snatch, when turnèd is his face.
195 In such distresse and doubtfull° jeopardy,   *fearful*
     When Britomart him saw, she ran a pace
     Unto his reskew, and with earnest cry,
Bad those same sixe forbeare that single enimy.

23

But to her cry they list not lenden eare,
200 Ne ought the more their mightie strokes surceasse,[6]
     But gathering him round about more neare,
     Their direfull rancour rather did encrease;
     Till that she rushing through the thickest preasse,°   *crush*
     Perforce disparted their compacted gyre,[7]
205 And soone compeld to hearken unto peace:
     Tho° gan she myldly of them to inquyre   *then*
     The cause of their dissention and outrageous yre.°   *ire*

24

Whereto that single knight did answere frame;
     These sixe would me enforce by oddes of might,
210 To chaunge my liefe,° and love another Dame,   *beloved*
     That death me liefer were, then such despight,
     So unto wrong to yield my wrested right:[8]
     For I love one, the truest one on ground,
     Ne list me chaunge; she th' Errant Damzell[9] hight,°   *called*
215 For whose deare sake full many a bitter stownd,°   *peril*
I have endured, and tasted many a bloudy wound.

25

"Certes," said she, "then bene° ye sixe to blame,   *are*
     To weene° your wrong by force to justifie: *think*
     For knight to leave his Ladie were great shame,
220 That faithfull is, and better were to die.
     All losse is lesse,[1] and lesse the infamie,
     Then losse of love to him, that loves but one;
     Ne may love be compeld by maisterie;°   *superior force*
     For soone as maisterie comes, sweet love anone°   *immediately*
225 Taketh his nimble wings, and soone away is gone."

26

Then spake one of those sixe, "There dwelleth here
     Within this castle wall a Ladie faire,

5. At close quarters, when a hunted animal turns to confront its pursuers.
6. They did not wish to lend an ear, nor did they at all stop their mighty blows.
7. Forcibly broke up their circling about the knight.
8. I.e., Death is preferable to such dishonor as to yield my own right love of my lady under duress

to (their) wrong.
9. This epithet indicates that the lady is Una (Truth), the heroine of book 1; in book 2 that epithet is specifically assigned to Una. By this identification we also know the knight to be Redcrosse.
1. I.e., any loss (even death) is less than such a loss of a faithful lover.

Whose soveraine beautie hath no living pere,
Thereto so bounteous and so debonaire,°   *gracious*
230 That never any mote° with her compaire.   *might*
She hath ordaind this law, which we approve,°   *uphold*
That every knight, which doth this way repaire,
In case he have no Ladie, nor no love,
Shall doe unto her service never to remove.°   *leave*

27

235 "But if he have a Ladie or a Love,
Then must he her forgoe with foule defame,°   *dishonor*
Or else with us by dint of sword approve,°   *prove*
That she is fairer, then our fairest Dame,
As did this knight, before ye hither came."
240 "Perdie,"° said Britomart, "the choise is hard: *truly (by God)*
But what reward had he, that overcame?"
"He should advauncèd be to high regard,"
Said they, "and have our Ladies love for his reward."

28

"Therefore aread° Sir, if thou have a love."   *tell*
245 "Love have I sure," quoth she, "but Lady none;
Yet will I not fro mine owne love remove,
Ne to your Lady will I service done,°   *do*
But wreake your wrongs wrought to this knight alone,[2]
And prove his cause." With that her mortall speare
250 She mightily aventred° towards one,   *cast*
And downe him smot, ere well aware° he weare,   *on guard*
Then to the next she rode, and downe the next did beare.

29

Ne did she stay, till three on ground she layd,
That none of them himselfe could reare° againe;   *rise*
255 The fourth was by that other knight dismayd,°   *defeated*
All were he wearie of his former paine,
That now there do but two of six remaine;
Which two did yield, before she did them smight.
"Ah," said she then, "now may ye all see plaine,
260 That truth is strong, and trew love most of might,
That for his trusty servaunts doth so strongly fight."

30

"Too well we see," said they, "and prove too well
Our faulty weaknesse,[3] and your matchlesse might:
For thy, faire Sir, yours be the Damozell,
265 Which by her owne law to your lot doth light,
And we your liege men faith unto you plight."
So underneath her feet their swords they mard,°   *debased*
And after her besought, well as they might,
To enter in, and reape the dew reward:
270 She graunted, and then in they all together fared.

2. I.e., visit upon you the wrongs you visited upon   3. I.e., weakness because they are at fault.
this single knight.

31

Long were it to describe the goodly frame,
   And stately port of Castle Joyeous,
   (For so that Castle hight by commune name)
   Where they were entertaind with curteous
275   And comely glee° of many gracious   *entertainment*
   Faire Ladies, and of many a gentle knight,
   Who through a Chamber long and spacious,
   Eftsoones° them brought unto their Ladies sight,   *soon after*
That of them cleeped° was the Lady of delight.   *named*

32

280 But for to tell the sumptuous aray
   Of that great chamber, should be labour lost:
   For living wit, I weene,° cannot display   *think*
   The royall riches and exceeding cost,
   Of every pillour and of every post;
285   Which all of purest bullion° framèd were,   *gold*
   And with great pearles and pretious stones embost,
   That the bright glister of their beames cleare
Did sparckle forth great light, and glorious did appeare.

33

These straunger knights through passing, forth were led
290   Into an inner rowme,° whose royaltee   *room*
   And rich purveyance might uneath be red;
   Mote Princes place beseeme so deckt to bee.[4]
   Which stately manner when as they did see,
   The image of superfluous riotize,[5]
295   Exceeding much the state of meane° degree,   *moderate*
   They greatly wondred, whence so sumptuous guize° *fashion*
Might be maintaynd, and each gan° diversely devize.° *began/guess*

34

The wals were round about apparellèd
   With costly clothes of Arras and of Toure,[6]
300   In which with cunning hand was pourtrahèd°   *portrayed*
   The love of Venus and her Paramoure
   The faire Adonis, turned to a flowre,[7]
   A worke of rare device,° and wondrous wit.°   *design/skill*
   First did it shew the bitter balefull stowre,°   *turmoil*
305 Which her assayd with many a fervent fit,
When first her tender hart was with his beautie smit.

35

Then with what sleights and sweet allurements she
   Entyst the Boy, as well that art she knew,

---

4. I.e., whose rich furnishings can hardly be told;
it would become a prince's palace to be so ornamented.
5. Immoderate extravagance.
6. Arras and Tours (France) were famous for their
tapestries.
7. The tapestries depict the myth of Venus and

Adonis—Venus' first love passion, her wooing of
Adonis, their lovemaking, his wounding and death
from the boar (signifying lust), his metamorphosis
to a flower (the anemone). The myth provides a
reference point for the love stories that follow in
book 3.

And wooèd him her Paramoure to be;
310   Now making girlonds of each flowre that grew,
    To crowne his golden lockes with honour dew;
    Now leading him into a secret shade
    From his Beauperes,° and from bright heavens vew,   *companions*
    Where him to sleepe she gently would perswade,
315 Or bathe him in a fountaine by some covert glade.

36

    And whilst he slept, she over him would spred
    Her mantle, coloured like the starry skyes,
    And her soft arme lay underneath his hed,
    And with ambrosiall kisses bathe his eyes;
320   And whilest he bathed, with her two crafty spyes,
    She secretly would search each daintie lim,
    And throw into the well sweet Rosemaryes,[8]
    And fragrant violets, and Pances trim,
And ever with sweet Nectar she did sprinkle him.

37

325 So did she steale his heedelesse hart away,
    And joyed his love in secret unespyde.
    But for she saw him bent to cruell play,
    To hunt the salvage beast in forrest wyde,
    Dreadfull° of daunger, that mote him betyde,   *fearful*
330   She oft and oft advized him to refraine
    From chase of greater beasts, whose brutish pryde
    Mote breede him scath unwares:[9] but all in vaine;
For who can shun the chaunce, that dest'ny doth ordaine?

38

    Lo, where beyond he lyeth languishing,°   *growing weak*
335   Deadly° engorèd of a great wild Bore,   *fatally*
    And by his side the Goddesse groveling°   *lying prostrate*
    Makes for him endlesse mone, and evermore
    With her soft garment wipes away the gore,
    Which staines his snowy skin with hatefull hew:
340   But when she saw no helpe might him restore,
    Him to a daintie flowre she did transmew,°   *transmute*
Which in that cloth was wrought, as if it lively° grew.   *living*

39

    So was that chamber clad in goodly wize,
    And round about it many beds° were dight,°   *couches/arranged*
345   As whilome was the antique worldes guize,°   *custom*
    Some for untimely ease, some for delight,
    As pleased them to use, that use it might:
    And all was full of Damzels, and of Squires,
    Dauncing and reveling both day and night,
350   And swimming deepe in sensuall desires,
And Cupid still emongst them kindled lustfull fires.

8. Associated with remembrance; violets and pansies ("Pances") also have erotic associations.

9. I.e., might cause him harm when he is unwary.

40

And all the while sweet Musicke did divide
　　Her looser notes with Lydian[1] harmony;
　　And all the while sweet birdes thereto applide
355　　Their daintie layes and dulcet melody,
　　　Ay° caroling of love and jollity,　　　　　　　　　　*always*
　　That wonder was to heare their trim consort.[2]
　　Which when those knights beheld, with scornefull eye,
　　They sdeignèd° such lascivious disport,　　　　　　*disdained*
360 And loathed the loose demeanure of that wanton sort.°　*company*

41

Thence they were brought to that great Ladies vew,
　　Whom they found sitting on a sumptuous bed,
　　That glistred all with gold and glorious shew,
　　As the proud Persian Queenes accustomèd:
365　　She seemd a woman of great bountihed,°　　　　　*generosity*
　　And of rare beautie, saving that askaunce°　　　　　*aside*
　　Her wanton eyes, ill signes of womanhed,
　　Did roll too lightly, and too often glaunce,
Without regard of grace,[3] or comely amenaunce.

42

370 Long worke it were, and needlesse to devize°　　　　*describe*
　　Their goodly entertainement and great glee:
　　She causèd them be led in curteous wize
　　Into a bowre, disarmèd for to bee,
　　And chearèd well with wine and spiceree:°　　　　　*spiced wine*
375　　The Redcrosse Knight was soone disarmèd there,
　　But the brave Mayd would not disarmèd bee,
　　But onely vented up her umbriere,[4]
And so did let her goodly visage to appere.

43

As when faire Cynthia, in darkesome night,
380　　Is in a noyous° cloud envelopèd,　　　　　　　　*troublesome*
　　Where she may find the substaunce thin and light,
　　Breakes forth her silver beames, and her bright hed
　　Discovers to the world discomfited;[5]
　　Of the poore traveller, that went astray,
385　　With thousand blessings she is herièd;°　　　　　*praised*
　　Such was the beautie and the shining ray,
With which faire Britomart gave light unto the day.

44

And eke those six, which lately with her fought,
　　Now were disarmd, and did them selves present
390　　Unto her vew, and company unsoght;
　　For they all seemèd curteous and gent,°　　　　　　*noble*

---

1. The mode of Greek music associated with soft, sensuous qualities and emotions.
2. Well-balanced ensemble, pleasing harmony.
3. Echoing 2 Peter 2.14: "Having eyes full of adultery, and that cannot cease from sin, beguiling unstable souls." "Amenaunce": conduct.
4. Raised the face guard of her helmet.
5. I.e., as when the moon, after being hidden by a cloud, breaks forth in splendor upon a world troubled by the loss of her light.

And all sixe brethren, borne of one parent,
Which had them traynd in all civilitee,°   *courtly graces*
And goodly taught to tilt and turnament;
395   Now were they liegemen to this Lady free,
And her knights service ought, to hold of her in fee.[6]

45

The first of them by name Gardante hight,
A jolly person, and of comely vew;
The second was Parlante, a bold knight,
400   And next to him Jocante did ensew;
Basciante did him selfe most curteous shew;
But fierce Bacchante seemd too fell and keene;
And yet in armes Noctante greater grew:[7]
All were faire knights, and goodly well beseene,
405   But to faire Britomart they all but shadowes beene.

46

For she was full of amiable grace,
And manly terrour mixèd therewithall,
That as the one stird up affections bace,
So th' other did mens rash desires apall,
410   And hold them backe, that would in errour fall;
As he, that hath espide a vermeill° Rose,   *vermilion*
To which sharpe thornes and breres° the way forstall,   *briars*
Dare not for dread his hardy hand expose,
But wishing it far off, his idle wish doth lose.

47

415   Whom when the Lady saw so faire a wight,
All ignoraunt of her contrary sex,
(For she her weend a fresh and lusty knight)
She greatly gan enamourèd to wex,[8]
And with vaine thoughts her falsèd° fancy vex: *deceived*
420   Her fickle hart conceivèd hasty fire,
Like sparkes of fire, which fall in sclender flex,°   *flakes*
That shortly brent° into extreme desire,   *burned*
And ransackt all her veines with passion entire.

48

Eftsoones she grew to great impatience
425   And into terms of open outrage brust,
That plaine discovered her incontinence,[9]
Ne reckt° she, who her meaning did mistrust;°   *cared/suspect*
For she was given all to fleshly lust,
And pourèd forth in sensuall delight,

---

6. They were feudal vassals ("liegemen") of the lady, holding all their goods and privileges from her grant, and owing all knightly service to her.
7. The names of these knights denote the rungs of the ladder of lechery: gazing [Gardante], conversing [Parlante], joking [Jocante], kissing [Basciante], drunken reveling [Bacchante—from Bacchus, god of wine], and consummation of love at night [Noctante]. "Goodly well beseene": of good appearance.
8. I.e., she began to grow greatly enamored.
9. I.e., she soon burst forth in language so sexually explicit as to make very clear her intemperance.

430   That all regard of shame she had discust,°   discarded
        And meet respect of honour put to flight:
        So shamelesse beauty soone becomes a loathly° sight.   loathsome

                            49

        Faire Ladies, that to love captivèd arre,
            And chaste desires to nourish in your mind,
435   Let not her fault your sweet affections marre,
            Ne° blot the bounty of all womankind;   nor
            'Mongst thousands good one wanton Dame to find:
            Emongst the Roses grow some wicked weeds;
            For this was not to love, but lust inclind;
440   For love does alwayes bring forth bounteous deeds,
        And in each gentle hart desire of honour breeds.

                            50

        Nought so of love this looser Dame did skill,[1]
            But as a coale to kindle fleshly flame,
            Giving the bridle to her wanton will,
445   And treading under foote her honest name:
            Such love is hate, and such desire is shame.
            Still did she rove[2] at her with crafty glaunce
            Of her false eyes, that at her hart did ayme,
            And told her meaning in her countenaunce;
450   But Britomart dissembled it with ignoraunce.[3]

                            51

        Supper was shortly dight° and downe they sat,   prepared
            Where they were servèd with all sumptuous fare,
            Whiles fruitfull Ceres, and Lyaeus fat[4]
            Pourd out their plenty, without spight° or spare: grudging
455   Nought wanted there, that dainty° was and rare;   precious
            And aye the cups their bancks did overflow,
            And aye betweene the cups, she did prepare
            Way to her love, and secret darts did throw;
        But Britomart would not such guilfull message know.

                            52

460   So when they slakèd had the fervent heat
            Of appetite with meates of every sort,
            The Lady did faire Britomart entreat,
            Her to disarme, and with delightfull sport
            To loose her warlike limbs and strong effort,[5]
465   But when she mote not thereunto be wonne,
            (For she her sexe under that straunge purport
            Did use to hide, and plaine apparaunce shonne:)[6]
        In plainer wise to tell her grievaunce begonne.

---

1. I.e., this too loose lady did not understand love
in that way.
2. Shoot an arrow at a mark chosen at will.
3. I.e., pretended not to know her meaning.
4. Ceres is goddess of crops, Lyaeus (Bacchus) is
god of wine.

5. I.e., the Lady entreated Britomart to unloose
her "warlike limbs" from their armor and relax her
martial force in delightful sport.
6. I.e., Britomart refused to disarm because she
used that disguise ("strange purport") to hide her
female sex.

53

And all attonce discovered° her desire   *revealed*
470   With sighes, and sobs, and plaints, and piteous griefe,
         The outward sparkes of her in° burning fire;   *inner*
         Which spent in vaine, at last she told her briefe,
         That but if° she did lend her short reliefe,   *unless*
         And do her comfort, she mote algates[7] dye.
475   But the chaste damzell, that had never priefe°   *experience*
         Of such malengine° and fine forgerie,   *deceit*
Did easily beleeve her strong extremitie.

54

Full easie was for her to have beliefe,
         Who by self-feeling of her feeble sexe,
480   And by long triall of the inward griefe,
         Wherewith imperious love her hart did vexe,
         Could judge what paines do loving harts perplexe.°   *torment*
         Who meanes no guile, beguilèd soonest shall,
         And to faire semblaunce doth light faith annexe;[8]
485   The bird, that knowes not the false fowlers call,
Into his hidden net full easily doth fall.

55

For thy[9] she would not in discourteise wise,
         Scorne the faire offer of good will profest;
         For great rebuke° it is, love to despise,   *shame*
490   Or rudely sdeigne a gentle harts request;
         But with faire countenaunce, as beseemed best,
         Her entertaynd; nath'lesse she inly deemd
         Her love too light, to wooe a wandring guest:
         Which she[1] misconstruing, thereby esteemd
495   That from like inward fire that outward smoke had steemd.

56

Therewith a while she her flit° fancy fed,   *flitting*
         Till she mote winne fit time for her desire,
         But yet her wound still inward freshly bled,
         And through her bones the false instillèd fire
500   Did spred it selfe, and venime close° inspire.   *secret*
         Tho° were the tables taken all away,   *then*
         And every knight, and every gentle Squire
         Gan choose his dame with *Basciomani*[2] gay,
With whom he meant to make his sport and courtly play.

57

505   Some fell to daunce, some fell to hazardry,°   *gambling*
         Some to make love,[3] some to make meriment,
         As diverse wits to divers things apply;
         And all the while faire Malecasta[4] bent

---

7. Must otherwise.
8. I.e., one who means no guile is easily beguiled, and gives ready ("light") faith to false appearances.
9. Therefore.
1. The Lady.

2. Italian, "I kiss your hand."
3. Court, woo.
4. Now that her nature is fully revealed by her actions, she is named: Malecasta, unchaste (*malus*—bad; *castus*—chaste).

Her crafty engins° to her close intent.   *wiles*
510 By this th' eternall lampes, wherewith high Jove
Doth light the lower world, were halfe yspent,
And the moist daughters of huge Atlas⁵ strove
Into the *Ocean* deepe to drive their weary drove.

58

High time it seemèd then for every wight
515 Them to betake unto their kindly° rest;   *natural*
Eftsoones long waxen torches weren light,
Unto their bowres to guiden every guest:
Tho when the Britonesse saw all the rest
Avoided° quite, she gan her selfe despoile,°   *retired/undress*
520 And safe commit to her soft fethered nest,
Where through long watch, and late dayes weary toile,
She soundly slept, and carefull thoughts did quite assoile.°   *dispel*

59

Now whenas all the world in silence deepe
Yshrowded was, and every mortall wight
525 Was drownèd in the depth of deadly° sleepe,   *deathlike*
Faire Malecasta, whose engrievèd spright°   *spirit*
Could find no rest in such perplexèd plight,
Lightly arose out of her wearie bed,
And under the blacke vele of guilty Night,
530 Her with a scarlot mantle coverèd,
That was with gold and Ermines faire envelopèd.

60

Then panting soft, and trembling everie joynt,
Her fearfull feete towards the bowre she moved;
Where she for secret purpose did appoynt
535 To lodge the warlike mayd unwisely loved,
And to her bed approching, first she prooved,°   *tested*
Whether she slept or wakt, with her soft hand
She softly felt, if any member mooved,
And lent her wary eare to understand,
540 If any puffe of breath, or signe of sence she fond.

61

Which whenas none she fond, with easie shift,
For feare least her unwares she should abrayd,°   *startle*
Th' embroderd quilt she lightly up did lift,
And by her side her selfe she softly layd,
545 Of every finest fingers touch affrayd;
Ne any noise she made, ne word she spake,
But inly sighed. At last the royall Mayd
Out of her quiet slomber did awake,
And chaungd her weary side, the better ease to take.

62

550 Where feeling one close couched by her side,
She lightly° lept out of her filèd° bed,   *quickly/defiled*

5. Seven stars in the constellation Taurus, called the daughters of Atlas. Their setting locates this episode at midnight.

And to her weapon ran, in minde to gride°   *pierce*
The loathèd leachour. But the Dame halfe ded
Through suddein feare and ghastly drerihed,°   *terror*
555   Did shrieke alowd, that through the house it rong,
And the whole family therewith adred,
Rashly° out of their rouzèd couches sprong,   *hastily*
And to the troubled chamber all in armes did throng.

63

And those six Knights that Ladies Champions,
560   And eke the *Redcrosse* knight ran to the stownd,°   *uproar*
Halfe armd and halfe unarmd, with them attons:°   *together*
Where when confusedly they came, they fownd
Their Lady lying on the sencelesse grownd;
On th' other side, they saw the warlike Mayd
565   All in her snow-white smocke, with locks unbownd,
Threatning the point of her avenging blade,
That with so troublous terrour they were all dismayde.

64

About their Lady first they flockt arownd,
Whom having laid in comfortable couch,
570   Shortly they reard out of her frosen swownd;[6]
And afterwards they gan with fowle reproch
To stirre up strife, and troublous contecke° broch: *descord*
But by ensample of the last dayes losse,
None of them rashly durst to her approch,
575   Ne in so glorious spoile themselves embosse;[7]
Her succourd eke the Champion of the bloudy Crosse.

65

But one of those sixe knights, Gardante hight,°   *named*
Drew out a deadly bow and arrow keene,
Which forth he sent with felonous despight,[8]
580   And fell intent against the virgin sheene:°   *shining*
The mortall steele stayd not, till it was seene
To gore her side, yet was the wound not deepe,
But lightly rasèd° her soft silken skin,   *grazed*
That drops of purple bloud thereout did weepe,
585   Which did her lilly smock with staines of vermeil° steepe. *vermilion*

66

Wherewith enraged she fiercely at them flew,
And with her flaming sword about her layd,
That none of them foule mischiefe° could eschew,°   *harm/escape*
But with her dreadfull strokes were all dismayd:
590   Here, there, and every where about her swayd
Her wrathfull steele, that none mote it abide;
And eke the *Redcrosse* knight gave her good aid,
Ay joyning foot to foot, and side to side,
That in short space their foes they have quite terrifide.

6. Cold faint, swoon.   taking her as his spoil or booty.
7. I.e., none tries to cover himself with glory by   8. Fierce spite.

67

595 Tho whenas all were put to shamefull flight,
　　The noble Britomartis her arayd,
　　And her bright armes about her body dight:°　　　　　　*drew*
　　For nothing would she lenger there be stayd,
　　Where so loose life, and so ungentle trade
600 Was usd of Knights and Ladies seeming gent:[9]
　　So earely ere the grosse Earthes gryesy° shade,　　　*gray*
　　Was all disperst out of the firmament,
They tooke their steeds, and forth upon their journey went.

Canto 2

The Redcrosse knight to Britomart
describeth Artegall:
The wondrous myrrhour, by which she
in love with him did fall.

1

Here have I cause, in men just blame to find,
　　That in their proper° prayse too partiall bee,　　　　*own*
　　And not indifferent° to woman kind,　　　　　　　　*just*
　　To whom no share in armes and chevalrie
5　　They do impart, ne maken memorie
　　Of their brave gestes° and prowesse martiall;　　　　*deeds*
　　Scarse do they spare to one or two or three,
　　Rowme in their writs; yet the same writing small
Does all their deeds deface, and dims their glories all.[1]

2

10 But by record of antique° times I find,　　　　　　　*ancient*
　　That women wont° in warres to beare most sway,　*were accustomed*
　　And to all great exploits them selves inclind:
　　Of which they still the girlond bore away,[2]
　　Till envious Men fearing their rules decay,
15　　Gan coyne streight° lawes to curb their liberty;　　*strict*
　　Yet sith they warlike armes have layd away,
　　They have exceld in artes and pollicy,
That now we foolish men that prayse gin eke t' enuy.[3]

3

Of warlike puissaunce in ages spent,
20　　Be thou faire Britomart, whose prayse I write,
　　But of all wisedome be thou precedent,°　　　　　　*pattern*
　　O soveraigne Queene, whose prayse I would endite,°　*write*
　　Endite I would as dewtie doth excite;
　　But ah my rimes too rude and rugged arre,

9. I.e., she would not stay where such discour-
teous and ignoble conduct ("ungentle trade") was
used by knights and ladies seemingly of gentle birth.
1. I.e., men scarcely spare room in their writings
to 1 or 2 or 3 women, yet those brief accounts
outshine all the mens' deeds and glory.

2. I.e., they always won the greatest praise ("bore
the garland away") in these exploits.
3. I.e., now we foolish men begin also to envy
women that praise (of excelling in arts and statesmanship).

25   When in so high an object they do lite,
            And striving, fit to make,[4] I feare do marre:
        Thy selfe thy prayses tell, and make them knowen farre.

                                6

        She travelling with Guyon[5] by the way,
            Of sundry things faire purpose° gan to find,   *conversation*
30   T' abridg their journey long, and lingring day;
            Mongst which it fell into that Faeries mind,
            To aske this Briton Mayd, what uncouth° wind,   *strange*
            Brought her into those parts, and what inquest°   *quest*
            Made her dissemble her disguised kind:°   *nature*
35   Faire Lady she him seemd, like Lady drest,
        But fairest knight alive, when armèd was her brest.

                                7

        Thereat she sighing softly, had no powre
            To speake a while, ne ready answere make,
            But with hart-thrilling throbs and bitter stowre,°   *turmoil*
40   As if she had a fever fit, did quake,
            And every daintie limbe with horrour shake;
            And ever and anone the rosy red,
            Flasht through her face, as it had been a flake°   *flash*
            Of lightning, through bright heaven fulminèd;°   *thundered*
45   At last the passion past she thus him answerèd.

                                8

        "Faire Sir, I let you weete,° that from the howre   *know*
            I taken was from nourses tender pap,°   *breast*
            I have beene trainèd up in warlike stowre,°   *struggle*
            To tossen speare and shield, and to affrap°   *hit*
50   The warlike ryder to his most mishap;
            Sithence° I loathèd have my life to lead,   *ever since*
            As Ladies wont, in pleasures wanton lap,
            To finger the fine needle and nyce° thread;   *slender*
        Me lever were[6] with point of foemans speare be dead.

                                9

55   "All my delight on deedes of armes is set,
            To hunt out perils and adventures hard,
            By sea, by land, where so they may be met,
            Onely for honour and for high regard,
            Without respect of richesse or reward.
60   For such intent into these parts I came,
            Withouten compasse, or withouten card,°   *map*
            Far fro my native soyle, that is by name
        The greater Britaine,[7] here to seeke for prayse and fame.

                                10

        "Fame blazed hath, that here in Faery lond
65   Do many famous Knightes and Ladies wonne,°   *dwell*

And many straunge adventures to be fond,
Of which great worth and worship° may be wonne;   renown
Which I to prove, this voyage have begonne.
But mote° I weet° of you, right curteous knight,   might/know
70 Tydings of one, that hath unto me donne
Late foule dishonour and reprochfull spight
The which I seeke to wreake, and Arthegall[8] he hight."

9

The word gone out, she backe againe would call,
As her repenting so to have missayd,
75 But that he it up-taking ere the fall,[9]
Her shortly answered; "Faire martiall Mayd
Certes ye misavised° beene, t' upbrayd   misinformed
A gentle knight with so unknightly blame:
For weet° ye well of all, that ever playd   know
80 At tilt or tourney, or like warlike game,
The noble Arthegall hath ever borne the name.[1]

10

"For thy[2] great wonder were it, if such shame
Should ever enter in his bounteous thought,
Or ever do, that mote deserven blame:[3]
85 The noble courage° never weeneth° ought,   nature/thinks
That may unworthy of it selfe be thought.
Therefore, faire Damzell, be ye well aware,
Least that too farre ye have your sorrow sought:
You and your countrey both I wish welfare,°   to fare well
90 And honour both; for each of other worthy are."

11

The royall Mayd woxe° inly wondrous glad,   grew
To heare her Love so highly magnifide,°   extolled
And joyd that ever she affixèd had,
Her hart on knight so goodly glorifide,
95 How ever finely° she it faind° to hide: cunningly/pretended
The loving mother, that nine monethes did beare,
In the deare closet of her painefull side,
Her tender babe, it seeing safe appeare,
Doth not so much rejoyce, as she rejoycèd theare.

12

100 But to occasion him to further talke,
To feed her humour with his pleasing stile,
Her list in strifull termes with him to balke,[4]
And thus replide, "How ever, Sir, ye file
Your curteous tongue, his prayses to compile,[5]
105 It ill beseemes a knight of gentle sort,
Such as ye have him boasted, to beguile

---

8. The name suggests "equal to Arthur" (Arthegall).
9. I.e., before she finished speaking.
1. Won the title.
2. Therefore.

3. I.e., it would be a great wonder if he would think or do anything shameful or blameworthy.
4. It pleased her ("her list") to oppose him with hostile words.
5. I.e., speak falsely in praise of his virtues.

A simple mayd, and worke so haynous tort,°   *wrong*
In shame of knighthood, as I largely can report.

13

"Let be[6] therefore my vengeaunce to disswade,
110   And read,° where I that faytour° false may find."   *tell/deceiver*
"Ah, but if reason faire might you perswade,
To slake your wrath, and mollifie your mind,"
Said he, "perhaps ye should it better find:
For hardy thing it is, to weene° by might,   *think*
115   That man to hard conditions to bind,
Or ever hope to match in equall fight,
Whose prowesse paragon saw never living wight.[7]

14

"Ne soothlich° is it easie for to read,   *truly*
Where now on earth, or how he may be found;
120   For he ne wonneth° one certaine stead,   *dwells*
But restlesse walketh all the world around,
Ay doing things, that to his fame redound,
Defending Ladies cause, and Orphans right,
Where so he heares, that any doth confound°   *overthrow*
125   Them comfortlesse, through tyranny or might;
So is his soveraine honour raisde to heavens hight."

15

His feeling words her feeble sence much pleased,
And softly sunck into her molten hart;
Hart that is inly hurt, is greatly eased
130   With hope of thing, that may allegge° his smart;   *allay*
For pleasing words are like to Magick art,
That doth the charmèd Snake in slomber lay:
Such secret ease felt gentle Britomart,
Yet list the same efforce with faind gainesay;[8]
135   So dischord oft in Musick makes the sweeter lay.°   *song*

16

And said, "Sir knight, these idle termes forbeare,
And sith it is uneath° to find his haunt,   *difficult*
Tell me some markes, by which he may appeare,
If chaunce I him encounter paravaunt;°   *by chance*
140   For perdie° one shall other slay, or daunt:°   *surely/subdue*
What shape, what shield, what armes, what steed, what sted,°   *mark*
And what so else his person most may vaunt?"°   *display*
All which the Redcrosse knight to point ared,[9]
And him in every part before her fashionèd.

17

145   Yet him in every part before she knew,
How ever list her now her knowledge faine,°   *disguise*
Sith him whilome° in Britaine she did vew,   *formerly*

---

6. Cease.
7. I.e., no living person ever saw the equal of his prowess.
8. I.e., she chose to reinforce the pleasure by pretending to disagree with him.
9. Exactly declared.

To her revealèd in a mirrhour plaine,
    Whereof did grow her first engraffèd° paine;   *engrafted*
150   Whose root and stalke so bitter yet did tast,
    That but the fruit more sweetnesse did containe,
    Her wretched dayes in dolour she mote° wast,   *must*
And yield the pray[1] of love to lothsome death at last.

18

By strange occasion she did him behold,
155   And much more strangely gan to love his sight,
    As it in bookes hath written bene of old.
    In Deheubarth that now South-wales is hight,
    What time king Ryence[2] raigned, and dealèd right,
    The great Magitian Merlin had devized,
160   By his deepe science,° and hell-dreadèd might,   *wizardry*
    A looking glasse,[3] right wondrously aguized,
Whose vertues through the wyde world soone were
    solemnized.°   *celebrated*

19

It vertue° had, to shew in perfect sight,   *power*
    What ever thing was in the world contaynd,
165   Betwixt the lowest earth and heavens hight,
    So that it to the looker appertaynd;[4]
    What ever foe had wrought,° or frend had faynd,°   *done/pretended*
    Therein discovered was, ne ought° mote pas,   *anything*
    Ne ought in secret from the same remaynd;
170   For thy° it round and hollow shapèd was,   *therefore*
Like to the world it selfe, and seemed a world of glas.

20

Who wonders not, that reades° so wonderous worke?   *sees*
    But who does wonder, that has red the Towre,
    Wherein th' Aegyptian Phao[5] long did lurke
175   From all mens vew, that none might her discoure,°   *discover*
    Yet she might all men vew out of her bowre?
    Great Ptolomaee it for his lemans° sake   *lover's*
    Ybuilded all of glasse, by Magicke powre,
    And also it impregnable did make;[6]
180   Yet when his love was false, he with a peaze° it brake.   *blow*

21

Such was the glassie globe that Merlin made,
    And gave unto king Ryence for his gard,[7]
    That never foes his kingdome might invade,
    But he it knew at home before he hard°   *heard*
185   Tydings thereof, and so them still debared.

---

1. I.e., yield (herself) the prey of love.
2. In Sir Thomas Malory's medieval romance, *Morte Darthur*, Ryence is a king of North Wales and enemy of Arthur.
3. A glass globe (like that of a fortune teller). "Aguized": fashioned.
4. I.e., provided that it pertained to the viewer.

5. Spenser's source for this myth has not been found.
6. Ptolemy II, confused with the astronomer Ptolemy who built the lighthouse and library at Alexandria, and who was considered in the Renaissance to be a magician and esoteric philosopher.
7. To protect him.

It was a famous Present for a Prince,
And worthy worke of infinite reward,
That treasons could bewray,° and foes convince;°   *reveal/vanquish*
Happie this Realme, had it remained ever since.

22

190 One day it fortunèd, faire Britomart
Into her fathers closet to repayre;
For nothing he from her reserved apart,
Being his onely daughter and his hayre:°   *heir*
Where when she had espyde that mirrhour fayre,
195 Her selfe a while therein she vewd in vaine;[8]
Tho° her avizing° of the vertues rare,   *then/remembering*
Which thereof spoken were, she gan againe
Her to bethinke of, that mote to her selfe pertaine.[9]

23

But as it falleth, in the gentlest harts
200 Imperious Love hath highest set his throne,
And tyrannizeth in the bitter smarts
Of them, that to him buxome° are and prone:°   *yielding/abject*
So thought this Mayd (as maydens use to done)
Whom fortune for her husband would allot,
205 Not that she lusted after any one;
For she was pure from blame of sinfull blot,
Yet wist° her life at last must lincke in that same knot.   *knew*

24

Eftsoones° there was presented to her eye   *soon after*
A comely knight, all armed in complet wize,
210 Through whose bright ventayle[1] lifted up on hye
His manly face, that did his foes agrize,°   *terrify*
And friends to termes of gentle truce entize,
Lookt foorth, as Phoebus face[2] out of the east,
Betwixt two shadie mountaines doth arize;
215 Portly° his person was, and much increast   *dignified*
Through his Heroicke grace, and honorable gest.°   *countenance*

25

His crest was covrerd with a couchant Hound,[3]
And all his armour seemed of antique mould,
But wondrous massie° and assurèd sound,   *heavy*
220 And round about yfretted° all with gold,   *decorated*
In which there written was with cyphers° old,   *letters*
Achilles armes, which Arthegall did win.[4]
And on his shield enveloped sevenfold

---

8. To no purpose.
9. I.e., she began to think of those things that might pertain to herself.
1. Lower moveable part of a helmet.
2. The sun.
3. The emblem of a hound lying in crouched position, ready to spring.
4. It is traditional for heroes of Romance to inherit the arms (and thereby the qualities) of Homeric and Virgilian heroes. Achilles was the greatest of the Greeks in martial prowess.

He bore a crownèd litle Ermilin,[5]
225 That deckt the azure field with her faire pouldred° skin.   *spotted*

26

The Damzell well did vew his personage,
   And likèd well, ne further fastned not,[6]
   But went her way; ne her unguilty age
   Did weene, unwares, that her unlucky lot
230 Lay hidden in the bottome of the pot;[7]
   Of hurt unwist° most daunger doth redound: *unknown*
   But the false Archer, which that arrow shot
   So slyly, that she did not feele the wound,
Did smyle full smoothly at her weetlesse wofull stound.[8]

27

235 Thenceforth the feather in her loftie crest,
   Ruffed of love, gan lowly to availe,[9]
   And her proud portance,° and her princely gest,   *bearing*
   With which she earst° tryumphèd, now did quaile:°   *first/decline*
   Sad, solemne, sowre, and full of fancies fraile
240 She woxe,° yet wist° she neither how, nor why,   *grew/knew*
   She wist not, silly° Mayd, what she did aile,   *innocent*
   Yet wist, she was not well at ease perdy,
Yet thought it was not love, but some melancholy.

28

So soone as Night had with her pallid° hew   *pale*
245 Defast° the beautie of the shining sky,   *defaced*
   And reft from men the worlds desirèd vew,
   She with her Nourse adowne to sleepe did lye;
   But sleepe full farre away from her did fly:
   In stead thereof sad sighes, and sorrowes deepe
250 Kept watch and ward about her warily,
   That nought she did but wayle, and often steepe
Her daintie couch with teares, which closely° she did   *secretly*
   weepe.

29

And if that any drop of slombring rest
   Did chaunce to still° into her wearie spright,   *distill*
255 When feeble nature felt her selfe opprest,
   Streight way with dreames, and with fantasticke sight
   Of dreadfull things the same[1] was put to flight,
   That oft out of her bed she did astart,°   *start up*
   As one with vew of ghastly feends affright:°   *terrified*
260 Tho gan she to renew her former smart,°   *pain*
And thinke of that faire visage, written in her hart.

---

5. Achilles' shield was made of 7 layers of skins. Arthegall's heraldic arms are a crowned ermine (associated with Elizabeth the virgin queen) on a blue field.
6. I.e., gave no further thought to him.
7. I.e., she did not suppose that her lot would remain hidden (until revealed by Merlin).

8. I.e., Cupid wounded her (all unawares) with his arrow of love and smiled at what was to her inexplicable pain.
9. I.e., the feather in her helmet's crest, ruffled by love, began to droop.
1. The drop of sleep.

30

One night, when she was tost with such unrest,
    Her agèd Nurse, whose name was Glauce[2] hight,
    Feeling her leape out of her loathèd nest,
265   Betwixt her feeble armes her quickly keight,°   *caught*
    And downe againe in her warme bed her dight;°   *placed*
    "Ah my deare daughter, ah my dearest dread,°   *object of anxiety*
    What uncouth° fit," said she, "what evill plight   *strange*
    Hath thee opprest, and with sad drearyhead°   *sorrow*
270 Chaunged thy lively cheare°, and living made thee dead? *expression*

31

"For not of nought these suddeine ghastly feares
    All night afflict thy naturall repose,
    And all the day, when as thine equall peares°   *peers*
    Their fit° disports with faire delight doe chose,   *appropriate*
275   Thou in dull corners doest thy selfe inclose,
    Ne tastest Princes pleasures, ne doest spred
    Abroad thy fresh youthes fairest flowre, but lose
    Both leafe and fruit, both too untimely shed,
As one in wilfull bale° for ever burièd.   *misery*

32

280 "The time, that mortall men their weary cares
    Do lay away, and all wilde beastes do rest,
    And every river eke his course forbeares,
    Then doth this wicked evill thee infest,°   *infect*
    And rive° with thousand throbs thy thrillèd brest; *pierce*
285   Like an huge Aetn'[3] of deepe engulfèd griefe,
    Sorrow is heapèd in thy hollow chest,
    Whence forth it breakes in sighes and anguish rife,
As smoke and sulphure mingled with confused strife.

33

"Aye me, how much I feare, least love it bee;
290   But if that love it be, as sure I read°   *discern*
    By knowen signes and passions, which I see,
    Be it worthy of thy race and royall sead,
    Then I avow by this most sacred head
    Of my deare foster child, to ease thy griefe,
295   And win thy will: Therefore away doe dread;[4]
    For death nor daunger from thy dew reliefe
Shall me debarre, tell me therefore my liefest liefe."[5]

34

So having said, her twixt her armès twaine
    She straightly straynd, and collèd tenderly,[6]
300   And every trembling joynt, and every vaine°   *vein*
    She softly felt, and rubbèd busily,

---

2. Her name associates her with the mother of
Diana, and with the owl, companion of Minerva.
3. Aetna, a volcanic mountain in Sicily.
4. I.e., to gain your wish. Therefore, do away with

fear.
5. Dearest love.
6. I.e., she tightly clasped, and embraced tenderly.

To doe° the frosen cold away to fly;   *make*
And her faire deawy eies with kisses deare
She oft did bath, and oft againe did dry;
305   And ever her importund, not to feare
To let the secret of her hart to her appeare.

35

The Damzell pauzd, and then thus fearefully;
"Ah Nurse, what needeth thee to eke° my paine?   *increase*
Is not enough, that I alone doe dye,
310   But it must doubled be with death of twaine?
For nought for me but death there doth remaine."
"O daughter deare," said she, "despaire no whit;
For never sore, but might a salve obtaine:
That blinded God, which hath ye blindly smit,
315 Another arrow hath your lovers hart to hit."[7]

36

"But mine is not," quoth she, "like others wound;
For which[8] no reason can find remedy.
Was never such, but mote the like be found,"
Said she, "and though no reason may apply
320   Salve to your sore, yet love can higher stye,°   *fly*
Then reasons reach, and oft hath wonders donne.
But neither God of love, nor God of sky
Can doe," said she, "that, which cannot be donne."
"Things oft impossible," quoth she, "seeme, ere begonne."

37

325 "These idle words," said she, "doe nought asswage
My stubborne smart, but more annoyance breed,
For no no usuall fire, no usuall rage
It is, O Nurse, which on my life doth feed,
And suckes the bloud, which from my hart doth bleed.
330   But since thy faithfull zeale lets me not hyde
My crime, (if crime it be) I will it reed.°   *tell*
Nor Prince, nor pere[9] it is, whose love hath gryde
My feeble brest of late, and launchèd° this wound wyde.   *cut*

38

"Nor man it is, nor other living wight;
335   For then some hope I might unto me draw,
But th' only shade and semblant[1] of a knight,
Whose shape or person yet I never saw,
Hath me subjected to loves cruell law:
The same one day, as me misfortune led,
340   I in my fathers wondrous mirrhour saw,
And pleasèd with that seeming goodly-hed,°   *goodly appearance*
Unwares the hidden hooke with baite I swallowèd.

---

7. I.e., blind Cupid who has blindly smitten you,
has another arrow to smite your beloved's heart
with love.

8. I.e., my wound.
9. Peer, nobleman. "Gryde": pierced.
1. I.e., but only the illusion and image of a knight.

39

"Sithens° it hath infixèd faster hold   *since then*
　　Within my bleeding bowels,[2] and so sore
345　Now ranckleth in this same fraile fleshly mould,°   *body*
　　That all mine entrailes flow with poysnous gore,
　　And th' ulcer groweth daily more and more;
　　Ne can my running sore find remedie,
　　Other then my hard fortune to deplore,
350　And languish as the leafe falne from the tree,
Till death make one end of my dayes and miserie.

40

"Daughter," said she, "what need ye be dismayd,
　　Or why make ye such Monster of your mind?
　　Of much more uncouth° thing I was affrayd;   *stranger*
355　Of filthy lust, contrarie unto kind:
　　But this affection nothing straunge I find;
　　For who with reason can you aye reprove,
　　To love the semblant° pleasing most your mind,   *image*
　　And yield your heart, whence ye cannot remove?
360　No guilt in you, but in the tyranny of love.

41

"Not so th' Arabian Myrrhe did set her mind;
　　Nor so did Biblis spend her pining hart,
　　But loved their native flesh against all kind,
　　And to their purpose usèd wicked art:[3]
365　Yet playd Pasiphaë a more monstrous part,
　　That loved a Bull, and learnd a beast to bee;[4]
　　Such shamefull lusts who loaths not, which depart
　　From course of nature and of modestie?
Sweet love such lewdnes bands° from his faire companie.   *bans*

42

370　"But thine my Deare (welfare thy heart my deare)[5]
　　Though strange beginning had, yet fixèd is
　　On one, that worthy may perhaps appeare;
　　And certes seemes bestowèd not amis:
　　Joy thereof have thou and eternall blis."
375　With that upleaning on her elbow weake,
　　Her alablaster brest she soft did kis,
　　Which all that while she felt to pant and quake,
As it an Earth-quake were; at last she thus bespake.

43

"Beldame,° your words doe worke me litle ease;   *good mother*
380　For though my love be not so lewdly bent,
　　As those ye blame, yet may it nought appease
　　My raging smart, ne ought my flame relent,°   *abate*

2. Internal organs, seat of the tender passions.
3. Myrrha tricked her father into committing incest
with her; Biblis lusted after her brother.
4. Pasiphae placed herself inside the statue of a

cow to enjoy the love of a bull, to whom she bore
the Minotaur.
5. I.e., may thy heart fare well (in this love adventure).

But rather doth my helpelesse griefe augment.
    For they, how ever shamefull and unkind,°   *unnatural*
385   Yet did possesse their horrible intent:
    Short end of sorrowes they thereby did find;
So was their fortune good, though wicked were their mind.

44

But wicked fortune mine, though mind be good,
    Can have no end, nor hope of my desire,
390   But feed on shadowes, whiles I die for food,
    And like a shadow wexe,° whiles with entire   *grow*
    Affection, I doe languish and expire.
    I fonder, then Cephisus foolish child,
    Who having vewèd in a fountaine shere°   *clear*
395   His face, was with the love thereof beguild;[6]
I fonder° love a shade, the bodie farre exild."   *more foolish*

45

"Nought like," quoth she, "for that same wretched boy
    Was of himselfe the idle Paramoure;
    Both love and lover, without hope of joy,
400   For which he faded to a watry flowre.
    But better fortune thine, and better howre,
    Which lov'st the shadow of a warlike knight;
    No shadow, but a bodie hath in powre:[7]
    That bodie, wheresoever that it light,
405 May learned be by cyphers,° or by Magicke might.   *signs*

46

"But if thou may with reason yet represse
    The growing evill, ere it strength have got,
    And thee abandond wholly doe possesse,
    Against it strongly strive, and yield thee not,
410   Till thou in open field adowne be smot.[8]
    But if the passion mayster thy fraile might,
    So that needs love or death must be thy lot,
    Then I avow to thee, by wrong or right
To compasse thy desire, and find that lovèd knight."

47

415 Her chearefull words much cheard the feeble spright°   *spirit*
    Of the sicke virgin, that her downe she layd
    In her warme bed to sleepe, if that she might;
    And the old-woman carefully displayd
    The clothes about her round with busie ayd;
420   So that at last a little creeping sleepe
    Surprisd her sense: She therewith well apayd,°   *satisfied*
    The drunken lampe downe in the oyle did steepe,[9]
And set her by to watch, and set her by to weepe.

---

6. Narcissus, who drowned in a pool trying to kiss his own reflection; he was then transformed into the flower of that name.

7. I.e., this is not really a shadow, but has a body producing it.

8. I.e., till you be struck down in battle.

9. I.e., drowned the lamplight in its own oil.

48

Earely the morrow next, before that day
425   His joyous face did to the world reveale,
        They both uprose and tooke their readie° way   *direct*
        Unto the Church, their prayers to appeale,°   *offer*
        With great devotion, and with litle zeale:
        For the faire Damzell from the holy herse°   *ceremony*
430   Her love-sicke hart to other thoughts did steale;
        And that old Dame said many an idle verse,
Out of her daughters hart fond fancies to reverse.°   *turn away*

49

Returnèd home, the royall Infant° fell   *Princess*
        Into her former fit; for why,[1] no powre
435   Nor guidance of her selfe in her did dwell.
        But th' agèd Nurse her calling to her bowre,
        Had gathered Rew, and Savine, and the flowre
        Of Camphora, and Calamint, and Dill,[2]
        All which she in a earthen Pot did poure,
440   And to the brim with Colt wood did it fill,
And many drops of milke and bloud through it did spill.

50

Then taking thrise three haires from off her head,
        Them trebly breaded° in a threefold lace,   *braided*
        And round about the pots mouth, bound the thread,
445   And after having whisperèd a space
        Certaine sad° words, with hollow voice and bace,°   *solemn/base*
        She to the virgin said, thrise said she it;
        "Come daughter come, come; spit upon my face,
        Spit thrise upon me, thrise upon me spit;
450 Th' uneven number for this businesse is most fit."

51

That sayd, her round about she from her turnd,
        She turnèd her contrarie to the Sunne,
        Thrise she her turnd contrary, and returnd,
        All contrary, for she the right did shunne,
455   And ever what she did, was streight undonne.
        So thought she to undoe her daughters love:
        But love, that is in gentle brest begonne,
        No idle charmes so lightly may remove,
That well can witnesse, who by triall° it does prove.   *experience*

52

460 Ne ought it mote the noble Mayd avayle,[3]
        Ne slake the furie of her cruell flame,
        But that she still did waste, and still did wayle,
        That through long languour,° and hart-burning   *affliction*
            brame°   *desire*

1. Because.
2. All these medicinal herbs were thought to damp down the fires of love. Glauce here attempts to
cast a spell or charm to undo Britomart's love melancholy.
3. I.e., neither could it help the noble maid.

She shortly like a pynèd ghost became,
465   Which long hath waited by the Stygian strond.[4]
That when old Glauce saw, for feare least blame
Of her miscarriage° should in her be fond,   *overthrow*
She wist not how t' amend, nor how it to withstond.

From *Canto 3*

[THE VISIT TO MERLIN]

Merlin bewrayes° to Britomart,   reveals
*   the state of Artegall.*
And shewes the famous Progeny
*   which from them springen shall.*

1

Most sacred fire, that burnest mightily
   In living brests, ykindled first above,
   Emongst th' eternall spheres and lamping° sky,   *star-lit*
   And thence pourd into men, which men call Love;
5   Not that same, which doth base affections° move   *passions*
   In brutish minds, and filthy lust inflame,
   But that sweet fit, that doth true beautie love,
   And choseth vertue for his dearest Dame,[1]
Whence spring all noble deeds and never dying fame:

2

10   Well did Antiquitie a God thee deeme,
   That over mortall minds hast so great might,
   To order them, as best to thee doth seeme,
   And all their actions to direct aright;
   The fatall° purpose of divine foresight,   *fated*
15   Thou doest effect in destinèd descents,°   *dynasties*
   Through deepe impression of thy secret might,
   And stirrèdst up th' Heroes high intents,
Which the late° world admyres for wondrous moniments.   *ancient*

3

But thy dread darts in none doe triumph more,
20   Ne braver proofe in any, of thy powre
   Shewedst thou, then in this royall Maid of yore,
   Making her seeke an unknowne Paramoure,°   *lover*
   From the worlds end, through many a bitter stowre:°   *trial*
   From whose two loynes thou afterwards did rayse
25   Most famous fruits of matrimoniall bowre,
   Which through the earth have spred their living prayse,
That fame in trompe of gold[2] eternally displayes.

---

4. I.e., like one of the dead, who had to wait by the River Styx in hell until ferried to the underworld by Charon.

1. Spenser invokes the Neoplatonic doctrines that love is the desire for beauty, and that virtue is true beauty. See Castiglione, *The Courtier*, pp. 1013–14.

2. I.e., the golden trumpet, emblem of good fame.

4

Begin then, O my dearest sacred Dame,
   Daughter of Phoebus and of Memorie,
30   That doest ennoble with immortall name
     The warlike Worthies, from antiquitie,
     In thy great volume of Eternitie:
   Begin, O Clio,[3] and recount from hence
   My glorious Soveraines goodly auncestrie,
35   Till that by dew degrees and long protense,°   *duration*
Thou have it lastly brought unto her Excellence.[4]

5

Full many wayes within her troubled mind,
   Old Glauce cast,° to cure this Ladies griefe: *considered*
   Full many waies she sought, but none could find,
40   Nor herbes, nor charmes, nor counsell that is chiefe
     And choisest med'cine for sicke harts reliefe:
     For thy great care she tooke, and greater feare,
   Least that it should her turne to foule repriefe,°   *reproof*
   And sore reproch, when so her father deare
45 Should of his dearest daughters hard misfortune heare.

6

At last she her avisd,° that he, which made   *recalled*
   That mirrhour, wherein the sicke Damosell
   So straungely vewèd her straunge lovers shade,
   To weet, the learned Merlin, well could tell,
50   Under what coast° of heaven the man did dwell,   *region*
     And by what meanes his love might best be wrought:°   *gained*
     For though beyond the Africk Ismaell,[5]
   Or th' Indian Peru he were, she thought
Him forth through infinite endevour to have sought.

7

55 Forthwith themselves disguising both in straunge
   And base attyre, that none might them bewray,°   *discover*
   To Maridunum, that is now by chaunge
   Of name Cayr-Merdin[6] cald, they tooke their way:
     There the wise Merlin whylome wont (they say)
60   To make his wonne,[7] low underneath the ground,
     In a deepe delve,° farre from the vew of day,   *cave*
   That of no living wight he mote° be found,   *might*
When so he counseld with his sprights encompast round.[8]

8

And if thou ever happen that same way
65   To travell, goe to see that dreadfull place:
   It is an hideous hollow cave (they say)

---

3. Clio, muse of history, is invoked (instead of Calliope, muse of epic poetry) because this book incorporates a chronicle history of Britain.
4. I.e., Queen Elizabeth. "Lastly": at last.
5. Africa was supposedly inhabited by the descendants of the biblical Ishmael.

6. Carmarthen, in Wales.
7. I.e., Merlin was formerly accustomed ("whylome wont") to make his dwelling place ("wonne") there.
8. I.e., when he conjured with his spirits gathered around him.

Under a rocke that lyes a litle space
From the swift Barry, tombling downe apace,
Emongst the woodie hilles of Dynevowre:[9]
70   But dare thou not, I charge, in any cace,
To enter into that same balefull Bowre,
For feare the cruell Feends should thee unwares devowre.

9

But standing high aloft, low lay thine eare,
And there such ghastly noise of yron chaines,
75   And brasen Caudrons thou shalt rombling heare,
Which thousand sprights with long enduring paines
Doe tosse, that it will stonne° thy feeble braines,   *stun*
And oftentimes great grones, and grievous stounds,°   *roars*
80   When too huge toile and labour them constraines:°   *afflicts*
And oftentimes loud strokes, and ringing sounds
From under that deepe Rocke most horribly rebounds.

10

The cause some say is this: A litle while
Before that Merlin dyde, he did intend,
85   A brasen wall in compas to compile
About Cairmardin,[1] and did it commend
Unto these Sprights, to bring to perfect end.
During which worke the Ladie of the Lake,
Whom long he loved, for him in hast did send,
90   Who thereby forst his workemen to forsake,
Them bound till his returne, their labour not to slake.°   *slacken*

11

In the meane time through that false Ladies traine,°   *treachery*
He was surprisd, and buried under beare,°   *bier*
Ne ever to his worke returnd againe:
95   Nath'lesse those feends may not their worke forbeare,
So greatly his commaundèment they feare,
But there doe toyle and travell° day and night,   *travail*
Untill that brasen wall they up doe reare:
For Merlin had in Magicke more insight,
100   Then ever him before or after living wight.[2]

12

For he by words could call out of the sky
Both Sunne and Moone, and make them him obay:
The land to sea, and sea to maineland dry,
And darkesome night he eke° could turne to day: *also*
105   Huge hostes of men he could alone dismay,°   *defeat*
And hostes of men of meanest things could frame,
When so him list° his enimies to fray:°   *he wished/terrify*
That to this day for terror of his fame,
The feends do quake, when any him to them does name.

9. Dynevor castle, seat of the princes of South Wales; "*Barry*": The river Cadoxton in Wales.
1. I.e., Merlin intended to build ("compile") a wall of brass to encompass ("in compas") Cairmardin.
2. I.e., Merlin had more understanding of magic than any person before or after him.

13

110   And sooth, men say that he was not the sonne
          Of mortall Syre, or other living wight,
          But wondrously begotten, and begonne
          By false illusion of a guilefull Spright,
          On a faire Ladie Nonne, that whilome hight
115   Matilda, daughter to Pubidius,
          Who was the Lord of Mathravall by right,
          And coosen unto king Ambrosius:[3]
     Whence he indued was with skill so marvellous.

14

     They here ariving, staid a while without,
120   Ne durst adventure rashly in to wend,°   go
          But of their first intent gan make new dout°   scruple
          For dread of daunger, which it might portend:
          Untill the hardie Mayd (with love to frend)[4]
          First entering, the dreadfull Mage there found
125   Deepe busièd bout worke of wondrous end,
          And writing strange characters in the ground,
     With which the stubborn feends he to his service bound.

15

     He nought was movèd° at their entrance bold: surprised
          For of their comming well he wist° afore,   knew
130   Yet list them bid their businesse to unfold,
          As if ought in this world in secret store
          Were from him hidden, or unknowne of yore.
          Then Glauce thus, "Let not it thee offend,
          That we thus rashly through thy darkesome dore,
135   Unwares have prest: for either fatall end,[5]
     Or other mightie cause us two did hither send."

16

     He bad tell on; And then she thus began.
          "Now have three Moones with borrowed brothers light,
          Thrice shinèd faire, and thrice seemed dim and wan,[6]
140   Sith a sore evill, which this virgin bright
          Tormenteth, and doth plonge in dolefull plight,
          First rooting tooke; but what thing it mote° bee,   might
          Or whence it sprong, I cannot read aright:
          But this I read,[7] that but if remedee
145   Thou her afford, full shortly I her dead shall see."

17

     Therewith th' Enchaunter softly gan to smyle
          At her smooth speeches, weeting° inly well,   knowing

---

3. Spenser here elaborates upon the account in
Geoffrey of Monmouth's *History of the Kings of
Britain* (12th century); Mathravall was one of the
three divisions of Wales; Ambrosius was king just
before his brother, Uther Pendragon (father of King
Arthur). "Coosen": kinsman.
4. I.e., with her love acting as a friend, encouraging her. "Hardie": bold. "Dreadful Mage": awe-

some magician.
5. Fated purpose.
6. The moon, borrowing its light from the sun
(Apollo, god of the sun, is brother of Diana, goddess of the moon), has gone through three cycles
of waxing and waning.
7. Know. "But if": unless.

That she to him dissembled womanish guyle,[8]
And to her said, "Beldame,° by that ye tell,   *good mother*
150 More need of leach-craft° hath your Damozell,   *doctor's skill*
Then of my skill: who helpe may have elsewhere,
In vaine seekes wonders out of Magicke spell."
Th' old woman wox half blanck,° those words to   *bewildered*
         heare;
And yet was loth to let her purpose plaine appeare.

                              18
155 And to him said, "If any leaches skill,
Or other learnèd meanes could have redrest°   *healed*
This my deare daughters deepe engraffèd° ill,   *engrafted*
Certes I should be loth thee to molest:
But this sad evill, which doth her infest,°   *infect*
160 Doth course of naturall cause farre exceed,
And housèd is within her hollow brest,
That either seemes some cursèd witches deed,
Or evill spright, that in her doth such torment breed."

                              19
The wisard could no lenger beare her bord,°   *idle talk*
165 But brusting forth in laughter, to her sayd;
"Glauce, what needs this colourable° word,   *deceiving*
To cloke the cause, that hath it selfe bewrayd?
Ne ye faire Britomartis, thus arayd,
More hidden are, then Sunne in cloudy vele;
170 Whom thy good fortune, having fate obayd,
Hath hither brought, for succour to appele:
The which the powres to thee are pleasèd to revele."

                              20
The doubtfull° Mayd, seeing her selfe   *apprehensive*
         descryde,°   *discovered*
Was all abasht, and her pure yvory
175 Into a cleare Carnation suddeine dyde;
As faire Aurora rising hastily,
Doth by her blushing tell, that she did lye
All night in old Tithonus frosen bed,
Whereof she seemes ashamèd inwardly.[9]
180 But her old Nourse was nought dishartenèd,
But vauntage° made of that, which Merlin had   *opportunity*
         ared.°   *disclosed*

                              21
And sayd, "Sith then thou knowest all our griefe,
(For what doest not thou know?) of grace° I pray,   *by your favor*
Pitty our plaint, and yield us meet° reliefe."   *fitting*
185 With that the Prophet still awhile did stay,
And then his spirite thus gan forth display;°   *declare*

---

8. He knows that Glauce does understand what ails Britomart.
9. Aurora, goddess of dawn, won for her mortal husband Tithonus the boon of immortality, but since he grows ever older she rises "hastily" from his "frosen bed."

"Most noble Virgin, that by fatall lore[1]
Hast learned to love, let no whit thee dismay
The hard begin,° that meets thee in the dore,   *beginning*
190 And with sharpe fits° thy tender hart oppresseth sore.   *pains*

22

"For so must all things excellent begin,
And eke enrooted deepe must be that Tree,
Whose big embodied braunches shall not lin,°   *cease*
Till they to heavens hight forth stretchèd bee.
195 For from thy wombe a famous Progenie
Shall spring, out of the auncient Trojan blood,
Which shall revive the sleeping memorie
Of those same antique Peres, the heavens brood,
Which Greeke and Asian rivers stainèd with their blood.[2]

23

200 "Renowmèd kings, and sacred Emperours,
Thy fruitfull Ofspring, shall from thee descend,
Brave Captaines, and most mighty warriours,
That shall their conquests through all lands extend,
205 And their decayèd kingdomes shall amend:°   *restore*
The feeble Britons, broken with long warre,
They shall upreare,° and mightily defend   *raise up*
Against their forrein foe, that comes from farre,
Till universall peace compound all civill iarre.[3]

24

210 "It was not, Britomart, thy wandring eye,
Glauncing unwares° in charmèd looking glas,   *by chance*
But the streight° course of heavenly destiny,   *strict*
Led with eternall providence, that has
Guided thy glaunce, to bring his will to pas:
215 Ne is thy fate, ne is thy fortune ill,
To love the prowest° knight, that ever was.   *strongest*
Therefore submit thy wayes unto his will,
And do by all dew meanes thy destiny fulfill."

25

"But read,"° said Glauce, "thou Magitian   *tell*
220 What meanes shall she out seeke, or what wayes take?
How shall she know, how shall she find the man?
Or what needs her to toyle, sith fates can make
Way for themselves, their purpose to partake?°"   *fulfill*
Then Merlin thus; "Indeed the fates are firme,
225 And may not shrinck, though all the world do shake:
Yet ought mens good endevours them confirme,
And guide the heavenly causes to their constant terme.[4]

---

1. I.e., the teaching of fate.
2. The chroniclers usually traced the origins of the British people to Brute, great-grandson of Aeneas; the Britons are thereby descendants of the Trojan heroes ("those same antique Peres"), who were descended from the gods.
3. A brief forecasting of the long history of Britomart's descendants, concluding with the universal peace of Elizabeth's reign. "Compound": settle.
4. Fixed ends.

26

"The man whom heavens have ordaynd to bee
  The spouse of Britomart, is Arthegall:
230   He wonneth in the land of Fayeree,
  Yet is no Fary borne, ne sib° at all   *kin*
  To Elfes, but sprong of seed terrestriall,
  And whilome° by false Faries stolne away,   *formerly*
  Whiles yet in infant cradle he did crall;
235   Ne other to himselfe is knowne this day,
  But that he by an Elfe was gotten of a Fay."[5]

Summary   In stanzas 27–61 Merlin recounts a chronicle history of
Britain, deriving the British kings from the union of Britomart and Arthegall
(half-brother to Arthur). He narrates the struggles of Britons and Saxons, the
succession of Saxon and then Norman kings, and the return of Briton rule
with the Tudor monarchs, concluding with a prophecy of Elizabeth's glorious reign. Inspired to fulfill the prophecy, Britomart takes on the role and
arms of a knight, with her nurse Glauce as her squire.

Canto 4. Summary   This canto treats the story of Marinell, a figure
of the sea and its riches, and Florimell, whose name suggests the rich products of the land, flowers and honey. Florimell also represents Beauty itself,
which attracts all men and makes female chastity vulnerable to all. Florimell
loves Marinell but he, warned that a woman will do him deadly harm, has
repudiated all women. However, the prophecy is fulfilled when he accosts
Britomart (not knowing she is a woman) and she wounds him almost to the
death—suggesting the opposition between Britomart's chaste love and the
fear-inspired renunciations of Marinell. Seeing Florimell in flight from a
lecherous forester, Arthur pursues them, but is forced to abandon his quest
at nightfall.

From *Canto 5*

Summary   In stanzas 1–26, Arthur learns from Florimell's dwarf about
her love of Marinell, Marinell's repudiation of her and its cause, and Florimell's flight from the court at the report of Marinell's supposed death.
Meanwhile, Arthur's squire Timias fights and kills the forester and his two
brothers, but the desperate fight leaves him near death himself.

[BELPHOEBE AND TIMIAS]

27

Providence heavenly passeth° living thought,   *surpasses*
  And doth for wretchèd mens reliefe make way;

5. He is a Briton knight kidnapped in his cradle
by Fairies, and so he thinks himself a fairy knight.
"Elf" and "Fay" refer to male and female inhabitants of Faerie Land, without connotations of the
supernatural or the diminutive.

230   For loe great grace or fortune thither brought
          Comfort° to him, that comfortlesse now lay.   *help*
       In those same woods, ye well remember may,
       How that a noble hunteresse did wonne,°   *dwell*
       She, that base Braggadochio did affray,°   *frighten*
235   And made him fast out of the forrest runne;[1]
       Belphoebe was her name, as faire as Phoebus sunne.[2]

                                    28

       She on a day, as she pursewd the chace
          Of some wild beast, which with her arrowes keene
       She wounded had, the same along did trace
240   By tract° of bloud, which she had freshly seene,   *track*
       To have besprinckled all the grassy greene;
       By the great persue,° which she there perceaved,   *track of blood*
       Well hopèd she the beast engored had beene,
       And made more hast, the life to have bereaved:[3]
245   But ah, her expectation greatly was deceaved.

                                    29

       Shortly she came, whereas that woefull Squire
          With bloud deformèd, lay in deadly swownd:[4]
       In whose faire eyes, like lamps of quenchèd fire,
       The Christall humour° stood congealèd rownd;   *fluid*
250   His locks, like faded leaves fallen to grownd,
       Knotted with bloud, in bounches rudely° ran,   *coarsely*
       And his sweete lips, on which before that stownd°   *violent attack*
       The bud of youth to blossome faire began,
       Spoild of their rosie red, were woxen° pale and wan.   *grown*

                                    30

255   Saw never living eye more heavy sight,
          That could have made a rocke of stone to rew,°   *pity*
       Or rive° in twaine: which when that Lady bright   *split*
       Besides all hope with melting eyes did vew,
       All suddeinly abasht she chaungèd hew,
260   And with sterne horrour backward gan to start:
       But when she better him beheld, she grew
       Full of soft passion and unwonted smart:[5]
       The point of pitty percèd through her tender hart.[6]

                                    31

       Meekely she bowèd downe, to weete° if life   *know*
265   Yet in his frosen members did remaine,
       And feeling by his pulses beating rife,°   *strongly*
       That the weake soule her seat did yet retaine,

1. In book 2, canto 3, the braggart but cowardly
knight fitly named Braggadochio sought to force
his love on Belphoebe and was put to ignominious
flight.
2. Her name relates her to Phoebe (Diana), goddess of the moon, of the hunt, and of chastity, but
also to the sun god Phoebus for her bright beauty.
3. She hoped the beast had been wounded and

hastened to finish the kill.
4. Arthur's squire, Timias, sorely wounded from
his battle with the forester pursuing Florimell, and
the forester's two brothers. "Deformed": disfigured.
5. Unfamiliar pain.
6. An echo of Chaucer's *Knight's Tale*: "For pitee
renneth soone in gentil herte" (1.1761).

She cast to comfort him with busie paine:°   *care*
His double folded necke she reard upright,
270   And rubd his temples, and each trembling vaine;
His maylèd haberjeon° she did undight,°   *coat of mail/undo*
And from his head his heavy burganet° did light.°   *helmet/remove*

32

Into the woods thenceforth in hast she went,
To seeke for hearbes, that mote° him remedy;   *might*
275   For she of hearbes had great intendiment,°   *understanding*
Taught of the Nymphe, which from her infancy
Her nourcèd had in trew Nobility:
There, whether it divine Tobacco were,
Or Panachaea, or Polygony,[7]
280   She found, and brought it to her patient deare
Who al this while lay bleeding out his hart-bloud neare.

33

The soveraigne[8] weede betwixt two marbles plaine
She pownded small, and did in peeces bruze,°   *crush*
And then atweene her lilly handès twaine,
285   Into his wound the juyce thereof did scruze,°   *squeeze*
And round about, as she could well it uze,
The flesh therewith she suppled° and did steepe,   *massaged*
T' abate all spasme, and soke the swelling bruze,
And after having searcht° the intuse° deepe,   *probed/wound*
290   She with her scarfe did bind the wound from cold to keepe.

34

By this he had sweete life recured° againe,   *recovered*
And groning inly deepe, at last his eyes,
His watry eyes, drizling like deawy raine,
He up gan lift toward the azure skies,
295   From whence descend all hopelesse° remedies: *beyond hope*
Therewith he sighed, and turning him aside,
The goodly Mayd full of divinities,[9]
And gifts of heavenly grace he by him spide,
Her bow and gilden° quiver lying him beside.   *golden*

35

300   "Mercy deare Lord," said he, "what grace is this,
That thou hast shewèd to me sinfull wight,
To send thine Angell from her bowre of blis,
To comfort me in my distressèd plight?
Angell, or Goddesse do I call thee right?
305   What service may I do unto thee meete,°   *fitting*
That hast from darkenesse me returnd to light,[1]
And with thy heavenly salves and med'cines sweete,
Hast drest my sinfull wounds? I kisse thy blessèd feete."

7. All these herbs were thought to have curative properties. This is the first reference in English literature to tobacco, introduced to England in 1584.
8. Supremely effective for cures.
9. Divine qualities.
1. A biblical echo: "who hath called you out of darkness into his marvelous light" (1 Peter 2.9).

36

Thereat she blushing said, "Ah gentle Squire,
310   Nor Goddesse I, nor Angell, but the Mayd,
    And daughter of a woody Nymphe,[2] desire
    No service, but thy safety and ayd;
    Which if thou gaine, I shalbe well apayd.°   *repayed*
    We mortall wights, whose lives and fortunes bee
315   To commun accidents still open layd,
    Are bound with commun bond of frailtee,
To succour wretched wights, whom we captivèd see."

37

By this her Damzels, which the former chace
    Had undertaken after her, arrived,
320   As did Belphoebe, in the bloudy place,
    And thereby deemd the beast had bene deprived
    Of life, whom late their Ladies arrow ryved:°   *pierced*
    For thy° the bloudy tract° they followd fast,   *therefore/track*
    And every one to runne the swiftest stryved;
325   But two of them the rest far overpast,
And where their Lady was, arrivèd at the last.

38

Where when they saw that goodly boy, with blood
    Defowlèd, and their Lady dresse his wownd,
    They wondred much, and shortly understood,
330   How him in deadly case their Lady fownd,
    And reskewed out of the heavy stownd.°   *trouble*
    Eftsoones° his warlike courser, which was strayd   *soon after*
    Farre in the woods, whiles that he lay in swownd,°   *a faint*
    She made those Damzels search, which being stayd,
335   They did him set thereon, and forth with them convayd.

39

Into that forest farre they thence him led,
    Where was their dwelling, in a pleasant glade,
    With mountaines round about environed,
    And mighty woods, which did the valley shade,
340   And like a stately Theatre[3] it made,
    Spreading it selfe into a spatious plaine.
    And in the midst a little river plaide°   *played*
    Emongst the pumy° stones, which seemd to plaine   *pumice*
With gentle murmure, that his course they did restraine.

40

345   Beside the same a dainty place there lay,
    Planted with mirtle trees[4] and laurels greene,
    In which the birds song many a lovely lay
    Of gods high prayse, and of their loves sweet teene,°   *grief*
    As it an earthly Paradize had beene:
350   In whose enclosèd shadow there was pight

---

2. I.e., the woodland nymph who raised her.   nature.
3. I.e., an amphitheater formed by elements of   4. Sacred to Venus.

A faire Pavilion, scarcely to be seene,
   The which was all within most richly dight,°   ornamented
That greatest Princes living it mote° well delight.   might

41

Thither they brought that wounded Squire, and layd
355   In easie couch his feeble limbes to rest.
   He rested him a while, and then the Mayd
   His ready° wound with better salves new drest;   prepared
   Dayly she dressèd him, and did the best
   His grievous hurt to garish,° that she might,   cure
360   That shortly she his dolour° hath redrest,°   pain / relieved
   And his foule sore reducèd to faire plight:°   condition
It she reducèd, but himselfe destroyèd quight.

42

O foolish Physick, and unfruitfull paine,°   labor
   That heales up one and makes another wound:
365   She his hurt thigh to him recured againe,
   But hurt his hart, the which before was sound,
   Through an unwary° dart, which did rebound   unexpected
   From her faire eyes and gracious countenaunce.
   What bootes it him from death to be unbound,
370   To be captivèd in endlesse duraunce°   prison
Of sorrow and despaire without aleggeaunce?°   relief

43

Still as his wound did gather,[5] and grow hole,
   So still his hart woxe° sore, and health decayd: grew
   Madnesse to save a part, and lose the whole.
375   Still whenas he beheld the heavenly Mayd,
   Whiles dayly plaisters to his wound she layd,
   So still his Malady the more increast,
   The whiles her matchlesse beautie him dismayd.°   conquered
   Ah God, what other could he do at least,
380   But love so faire a Lady, that his life releast?°   saved

44

Long while he strove in his courageous brest,
   With reason dew° the passion to subdew,   proper
   And love for to dislodge out of his nest:
   Still when her excellencies he did vew,
385   Her soveraigne bounty, and celestiall hew,
   The same to love he strongly was constrain:
   But when his meane estate he did revew,°   review
   He from such hardy boldnesse was restrain,
And of his lucklesse lot and cruell love thus plaind.

45

390   "Unthankfull wretch," said he, "is this the meed,°   recompense
   With which her soveraigne mercy thou doest quight?°   requite
   Thy life she savèd by her gracious deed,

___

5. I.e., permitting the infection to be drawn out.

But thou doest weene° with villeinous
    despight,°   *think/wickedness*
To blot her honour, and her heavenly light.
395 Dye rather, dye, then so disloyally
Deeme of her high desert, or seeme so light:
Faire death it is to shonne more shame, to dye:[6]
Dye rather, dye, then ever love disloyally.

46

"But if to love disloyalty it bee,
400 Shall I then hate her, that from deathès dore
Me brought? ah farre be such reproch fro mee.
What can I lesse do, then her love therefore,
Sith I her dew reward cannot restore:
Dye rather, dye, and dying do her serve,
405 Dying her serve, and living her adore;
Thy life she gave, thy life she doth deserve:°   *deserve*
Dye rather, dye, then ever from her service swerve.

47

"But foolish boy, what bootes thy service bace
To her, to whom the heavens do serve and sew?°   *pay homage*
410 Thou a meane Squire, of meeke and lowly place,
She heavenly borne, and of celestiall hew.
How then? of all love taketh equall vew:
And doth not highest God vouchsafe to take
The love and service of the basest crew?
415 If she will not, dye meekly for her sake;
Dye rather, dye, then ever so faire love forsake."

48

Thus warreid° he long time against his will,   *waged war*
Till that through weaknesse he was forst at last,
To yield himselfe unto the mighty ill:
420 Which as a victour proud, gan ransack fast
His inward parts, and all his entrayles wast,
That neither bloud in face, nor life in hart
It left, but both did quite drye up, and blast;
As percing levin, which the inner part
425 Of every thing consumes, and calcineth by art.[7]

49

Which seeing faire Belphoebe, gan to feare,
Least that his wound were inly well not healed,
Or that the wicked steele empoysned were:
Litle she weend,° that love he close concealed;   *thought*
430 Yet still he wasted, as the snow congealed,
When the bright sunne his beams thereon doth beat,
Yet never he his hart to her revealed,

---

6. I.e., it is a worthy death to die in order to avoid shame.
7. I.e., piercing lightning ("levin") disintegrates the body's inward parts, and by its action ("art") reduces everything to dust ("calcineth").

But rather chose to dye for sorrow great,
Then with dishonorable termes her to entreat.

50

435 She gracious Lady, yet no paines did spare,
        To do him ease, or do him remedy:
        Many Restoratives of vertues rare,
        And costly Cordialles° she did apply,   *medicines*
        To mitigate his stubborne mallady:
440   But that sweet Cordiall, which can restore
        A love-sick hart, she did to him envy;°   *refuse*
        To him, and to all th' unworthy world forlore°   *forsaken*
    She did envy that soveraigne salve, in secret store.

51

That dainty Rose, the daughter of her Morne,
445   More deare then life she tenderèd,° whose flowre   *cherished*
        The girlond of her honour did adorne:[8]
        Ne suffred she the Middayes scorching powre,
        Ne the sharp Northerne wind thereon to showre,
        But lappèd up her silken leaves most chaire,
450   When so the froward skye began to lowre:[9]
        But soone as calmèd was the Christall aire,
    She did it faire dispred, and let to florish faire.

52

Eternall God in his almighty powre,
        To make ensample of his heavenly grace,
455   In Paradize whilome° did plant this flowre;   *formerly*
        Whence he it fetcht out of her native place,
        And did in stocke of earthly flesh enrace,°   *implant*
        That mortall men her glory should admire:
        In gentle Ladies brest, and bounteous race
460   Of woman kind it fairest flowre doth spire,°   *put forth*
    And beareth fruit of honour and all chast desire.

53

Faire ympes° of beautie, whose bright shining beames   *offspring*
        Adorne the world with like to heavenly light,
        And to your willes both royalties and Realmes
465   Subdew, through conquest of your wondrous might,
        With this faire flowre your goodly girlonds dight,°   *adorned*
        Of chastity and vertue virginall,
        That shall embellish more your beautie bright,
        And crowne your heades with heavenly coronall,
470   Such as the Angels weare before Gods tribunall.

54

To youre faire selves a faire ensample frame,
        Of this faire virgin, this Belphoebe faire,

8. The rose is a long-enduring symbol of female
virginity.
9. I.e., she folded up ("lapped") the rose's leaves

most carefully ("chaire"), when the angry sky began
to threaten.

To whom in perfect love, and spotlesse fame
Of chastitie, none living may compaire:
475 Ne poysnous Envy justly can empaire
The prayse of her fresh flowring Maidenhead;
For thy[1] she standeth on the highest staire
Of th' honorable stage of womanhead,
That Ladies all may follow her ensample dead.[2]

55

480 In so great prayse° of stedfast chastity,   *worth*
Nathlesse she was so curteous and kind,
Tempred° with grace, and goodly modesty,   *mixed, balanced*
That seemed those two vertues strove to find
The higher place in her Heroick mind:
485 So striving each did other more augment,
And both encreast the prayse of woman kind,
And both encreast her beautie excellent;
So all did make in her a perfect complement.°   *completeness*

Canto 6

*The birth of faire Belphoebe and
Of Amoret is told.
The Gardins of Adonis fraught
With pleasures manifold.*

1

Well may I weene, faire Ladies, all this while
Ye wonder, how this noble Damozell
So great perfections did in her compile,°   *gather together*
Sith that in salvage° forests she did dwell,   *wild*
5   So farre from court and royall Citadell,
The great schoolmistresse of all curtesy:
Seemeth that such wild woods should far expell
All civill° usage and gentility,   *polite*
And gentle sprite deforme with rude rusticity.

2

10   But to this faire Belphoebe in her berth
The heavens so favourable were and free,°   *generous*
Looking with myld aspect upon the earth,
In th' Horoscope of her nativitee,
That all the gifts of grace and chastitee
15   On her they pourèd forth of plenteous horne;[1]
Jove laught on Venus from his soveraigne see,°   *throne*
And Phoebus with faire beames did her adorne,
And all the Graces rockt her cradle being borne.

---

1. Therefore.
2. I.e., when she is dead.
1. The planets were in favorable relationship ("myld aspect") at her birth; the combination of Jupiter ("Jove") and Venus was thought to be especially fortunate.

3

Her berth was of the wombe of Morning dew,[2]
20   And her conception of the joyous Prime,°   *springtime*
     And all her whole creation did her shew
     Pure and unspotted from all loathly crime,
     That is ingenerate in fleshly slime.[3]
     So was this virgin borne, so was she bred,[4]
25   So was she traynèd up from time to time,
     In all chast vertue, and true bounti-hed°   *goodness*
Till to her dew perfection she was ripenèd.

4

Her mother was the faire Chrysogonee,[5]
     The daughter of Amphisa, who by race
30   A Faerie was, yborne of high degree,
     She bore Belphoebe, she bore in like cace
     Faire Amoretta in the second place:
     These two were twinnes, and twixt them two did share
     The heritage of all celestiall grace.
35   That all the rest it seemed they robbèd bare
Of bountie,° and of beautie, and all vertues rare.   *goodness*

5

It were a goodly storie, to declare,
     By what straunge accident° faire Chrysogone   *happening*
     Conceived these infants, and how them she bare,
40   In this wild forrest wandring all alone,
     After she had nine moneths fulfild and gone:
     For not as other wemens commune brood,
     They were enwombèd in the sacred throne
     Of her chaste bodie, nor with commune food,
45   As other wemens babes, they suckèd vitall blood.

6

But wondrously they were begot, and bred
     Through influence of th' heavens fruitfull ray,[6]
     As it in antique bookes is mentionèd.
     It was upon a Sommers shynie day,
50   When Titan[7] faire his beamès did display,
     In a fresh fountaine, farre from all mens vew,
     She bathed her brest, the boyling heat t' allay;
     She bathed with roses red, and violets blew,
And all the sweetest flowres, that in the forrest grew.

---

2. An echo of Psalm 110.3 (Book of Common Prayer): "The dew of thy birth is of the womb of the morning," taken to refer to the conception and birth of Christ.
3. Like Christ or the Virgin, she is said to be free of original sin, which is innate ("ingenerate") in human flesh.
4. I.e., nourished in the womb. "From time to time": at all times.

5. Golden-born (Greek), alluding to Danaë who conceived when Jove visited her in a golden shower. *Amphisa:* of double nature (Greek).
6. I.e., an emanation from the heavens—continuing the analogue to the Virgin's miraculous conception of Christ.
7. The sun; the first Greek sun god, Helios, was descended from the Titans.

7

55　Till faint through irkesome° wearinesse, adowne　　　*burdensome*
　　　　Upon the grassie ground her selfe she layd
　　　　To sleepe, the whiles a gentle slombring swowne°　　*deep sleep*
　　　　Upon her fell all naked bare displayd;
　　　　The sunne-beames bright upon her body playd,
60　Being through former bathing mollifide,°　　　　*softened*
　　And pierst into her wombe, where they embayd°　　*steeped*
　　With so sweet sence° and secret power unspide,　　*sensation*
　　That in her pregnant flesh they shortly fructifide.

8

　　Miraculous may seeme to him, that reades
65　So straunge ensample of conception;
　　But reason teacheth that the fruitfull seades
　　Of all things living, through impression
　　Of the sunbeames in moyst complexion,
　　Doe life conceive and quickned are by kynd:°　　　*nature*
70　So after Nilus° inundation,　　　　　　　　*the Nile*
　　Infinite shapes of creatures men do fynd,
　　Informèd in the mud, on which the Sunne hath shynd.[8]

9

　　Great father he of generation
　　Is rightly cald, th' author of life and light;[9]
75　And his faire sister for creation
　　Ministreth matter fit, which tempred right
　　With heate and humour, breedes the living wight.
　　So sprong these twinnes in wombe of Chrysogone,
　　Yet wist° she nought thereof, but sore affright,　　*knew*
80　Wondred to see her belly so upblone,
　　Which still increast, till she her terme had full outgone.

10

　　Whereof conceiving shame and foule disgrace,
　　Albe her guiltlesse conscience her cleard,
　　She fled into the wildernesse a space,
85　Till that unweeldy burden she had reard,°　　　*brought forth*
　　And shund dishonor, which as death she feard:
　　Where wearie of long travell, downe to rest
　　Her selfe she set, and comfortably cheard;[1]
　　There a sad° cloud of sleepe her overkest,°　　*heavy/overcast*
90　And seized every sense with sorrow sore opprest.

11

　　It fortunèd,° faire Venus having lost　　　　*chanced*
　　Her little sonne, the wingèd god of love,
　　Who for some light displeasure, which him crost,

---

8. The theory that life was spontaneously generated by the sun's influence on the moist earth, is
drawn from Ovid and Lucretius. "Informed":
formed within.
9. The sun; his sister (the moon) is said to be propitious to generation in that it stimulates the moist
fluids ("humour") of the body.
1. I.e., weary of her long travels (and of the travail
of childbirth) she sat down to rest, and was cheered
by that comfort.

Was from her fled, as flit as ayerie Dove,[2]
95   And left her blisfull bowre of joy above,
    (So from her often he had fled away,
    When she for ought him sharpely did reprove,
    And wandred in the world in strange aray,
   Disguized in thousand shapes, that none might him
      bewray.)°   *reveal*

12

100 Him for to seeke, she left her heavenly hous,
    The house of goodly formes and faire aspects,[3]
    Whence all the world derives the glorious
    Features of beautie, and all shapes select,°   *choice*
    With which high God his workmanship hath deckt;°   *adorned*
105   And searchèd every way, through which his wings
    Had borne him, or his tract° she mote° detect: *track/might*
    She promist kisses sweet, and sweeter things
   Unto the man, that of him tydings to her brings.

13

   First she him sought in Court, where most he used
110   Whylome° to haunt, but there she found him not;   *formerly*
    But many there she found, which sore accused
    His falsehood, and with foule infamous blot
    His cruell deedes and wicked wyles did spot:°   *vilify*
    Ladies and Lords she every where mote heare
115   Complayning, how with his empoysned shot
    Their wofull harts he wounded had whyleare,°   *a while before*
   And so had left them languishing twixt hope and feare.

14

   She then the Citties sought from gate to gate,
    And every one did aske, did he him see;
120   And every one her answerd, that too late
    He had him seene, and felt the crueltie
    Of his sharpe darts and whot artillerie;[4]
    And every one threw forth reproches rife
    Of his mischievous deedes, and said, That hee
125   Was the disturber of all civill life,
   The enimy of peace, and author of all strife.

15

   Then in the countrey she abroad him sought,
    And in the rurall cottages inquired,
    Where also many plaints to her were brought,
130   How he their heedlesse harts with love had fyred,
    And his false venim through their veines inspyred;
    And eke° the gentle shepheard swaynes,° which sat   *also/lovers*
    Keeping their fleecie flockes, as they were hyred,
    She sweetly heard complaine, both how and what
135 Her sonne had to them doen; yet she did smile thereat.

2. Venus' bird; Venus' search for the lost Cupid is based on a Greek poem by Moschus, often imitated in the Renaissance.

3. Astrological aspects of the planet Venus.
4. Hot gunfire.

16

But when in none of all these she him got,
    She gan avize,° where else he mote him hyde: *consider*
    At last she her bethought, that she had not
    Yet sought the salvage° woods and forrests wyde,   *wild*
140   In which full many lovely Nymphes abyde,
    Mongst whom might be, that he did closely lye,
    Or that the love of some of them him tyde:[5]
    For thy she thither cast her course t' apply,
To search the secret haunts of Dianes company.

17

145 Shortly unto the wastefull° woods she came,   *desolate*
    Whereas she found the Goddesse with her crew,
    After late chace of their embrewèd° game,   *blood-stained*
    Sitting beside a fountaine in a rew,°   *row*
    Some of them washing with the liquid dew
150   From off their dainty limbes the dustie sweat,
    And soyle which did deforme their lively hew;
    Others lay shaded from the scorching heat;
The rest upon her person gave attendance great.[6]

18

She having hong upon a bough on high
155   Her bow and painted quiver, had unlaste°   *unlaced*
    Her silver buskins° from her nimble thigh,   *boots*
    And her lancke loynes[7] ungirt, and brests unbraste,
    After her heat the breathing cold to taste;
    Her golden lockes, that late in tresses bright
160   Embreaded were for hindring of her haste,[8]
    Now loose about her shoulders hong undight,
And were with sweet Ambrosia° all besprinckled light.   *perfume*

19

Soone as she Venus saw behind her backe,
    She was ashamed to be so loose surprized,
165   And woxe halfe wroth against her damzels slacke,
    That had not her thereof before avized,[9]
    But suffred her so carelesly disguized°   *undressed*
    Be overtaken. Soone her garments loose
    Upgath'ring, in her bosome she comprized,°   *drew together*
170   Well as she might, and to the Goddesse rose,
Whiles all her Nymphes did like a girlond her enclose.

20

Goodly she gan faire Cytherea[1] greet,
    And shortly askèd her, what cause her brought

---

5. I.e., bound him to them. "For thy": therefore.
6. This episode alludes to the myth of Actaeon who angered Diana by surprising her in her bath; she transformed him into a stag and he was torn apart by his own hounds.
7. Slender hips.
8. I.e., her golden locks were braided ("embreaded"), lest they should hinder her swift-

ness. "Undight": unbound.
9. I.e., she was half-angered at her nymphs who were remiss in not warning her (of Venus' presence).
1. Venus, so named in allusion to her emergence from the sea on the island of Cythera. "Goodly": courteously.

Into that wildernesse for her unmeet,
175 From her sweete bowres, and beds with pleasures fraught:
That suddein change she strange adventure° thought.   *chance*
To whom halfe weeping, she thus answerèd,
That she her dearest sonne Cupido sought,
Who in his frowardnesse° from her was fled;   *stubbornness*
180 That she repented sore, to have him angerèd.

21

Thereat Diana gan to smile, in scorne
 Of her vaine plaint, and to her scoffing sayd;
 "Great pittie sure, that ye be so forlorne°   *bereft*
 Of your gay sonne, that gives ye so good ayd
185 To your disports: ill mote ye bene apayd."[2]
 But she was more engrieved, and replide;
 "Faire sister, ill beseemes it to upbrayd
 A dolefull heart with so disdainfull pride;
The like that mine, may be your paine another tide.°   *time*

22

190 "As you in woods and wanton wildernesse
 Your glory set, to chace the salvage beasts,
 So my delight is all in joyfulnesse,
 In beds, in bowres, in banckets,° and in feasts: *banquets*
 And ill becomes you with your loftie creasts,°   *helmets*
195 To scorne the joy, that Jove is glad to seeke;
 We both are bound to follow heavens beheasts,
 And tend our charges with obeisance meeke:
Spare, gentle sister, with reproch my paine to eeke.°   *augment*

23

"And tell me, if that ye my sonne have heard,
200 To lurk emongst your Nymphes in secret wize;
 Or keepe their cabins:° much I am affeard,   *caves*
 Least he like one of them him selfe disguize,
 And turne his arrowes to their exercize:[3]
 So may he long himselfe full easie hide:
205 For he is faire and fresh in face and guize,
 As any Nymph (let not it be envyde.°)"   *begrudged*
So saying every Nymph full narrowly she eyde.

24

But Phoebe[4] therewith sore was angerèd,
 And sharply said; "Goe Dame, goe seeke your boy,
210 Where you him lately left, in Mars his bed;[5]
 He comes not here, we scorne his foolish joy,
 Ne lend we leisure to his idle toy:°   *game*
 But if I catch him in this company,
By Stygian lake I vow, whose sad annoy

---

2. I.e., your son aids you in your bad sports; may
you be repaid in kind by this ill trick he plays on
you.
3. I.e., he may shoot his arrows disguised as one
of Diana's hunting nymphs (also, he may shoot at
them, causing them to fall in love).
4. Another name for Diana.
5. Referring to Venus' love affair with Mars.

215   The Gods doe dread,[6] he dearely shall abye:°   *suffer*
     Ile clip his wanton wings, that he no more shall fly."

25

     Whom when as Venus saw so sore displeased,
       She inly sory was, and gan relent,°   *soften*
       What she had said: so her she soone appeased,
220   With sugred words and gentle blandishment,[7]
       Which as a fountaine from her sweet lips went,
       And wellèd goodly forth, that in short space
       She was well pleasd, and forth her damzels sent,
       Through all the woods, to search from place to place,
225   If any tract° of him or tydings they mote trace.   *track*

26

     To search the God of love, her Nymphes she sent
       Throughout the wandring forrest every where:
       And after them her selfe eke° with her went   *also*
       To seeke the fugitive, both farre and nere.
230   So long they sought, till they arrivèd were
       In that same shadie covert, whereas lay
       Faire Crysogone in slombry traunce whilere:°   *a while before*
       Who in her sleepe (a wondrous thing to say)
     Unwares had borne two babes, as faire as springing° day.   *dawning*

27

235   Unwares she them conceived, unwares she bore:
       She bore withouten paine, that she conceived
       Withouten pleasure: ne her need implore
       Lucinaes aide:[8] which when they both perceived,
       They were through wonder nigh of sense bereaved,
240   And gazing each on other, nought bespake:
       At last they both agreed, her seeming grieved° *oppressed (with sleep)*
       Out of her heavy swowne not to awake,
     But from her loving side the tender babes to take.

28

     Up they them tooke, each one a babe uptooke,
245   And with them carried, to be fosterèd;
       Dame Phoebe to a Nymph her babe betooke,°   *gave in charge*
       To be upbrought in perfect Maydenhed,°   *virginity*
       And of her selfe her name Belphoebe red:°   *named*
       But Venus hers thence farre away convayd,
250   To be upbrought in goodly womanhed,
       And in her litle loves stead, which was strayd,
     Her Amoretta cald, to comfort her dismayd.[9]

29

     She brought her to her joyous Paradize,
       Where most she wonnes,° when she on earth does dwel.   *dwells*

---

6. An oath sworn on the river Styx even the gods feared to break.
7. In making peace with her opposite, Venus here enacts one of her traditional roles, Concord.
8. Another name for Juno as goddess of childbirth.
9. Since she takes the place of Cupid (Amor), she is named Amoretta—a little love.

255   So faire a place, as Nature can devize:
       Whether in Paphos, or Cytheron hill,
       Or it in Gnidus be, I wote not well;[1]
       But well I wote° by tryall,° that this same   *know/experience*
       All other pleasant places doth excell,
260   And called is by her lost lovers name,
       The Gardin of Adonis, farre renowmd by fame.

                              30

       In that same Gardin all the goodly flowres,
       Wherewith dame Nature doth her beautifie,
       And decks the girlonds° of her paramoures,   *garlands*
265   Are fetcht: there is the first seminarie°   *seedbed*
       Of all things, that are borne to live and die,
       According to their kindes. Long worke it were,
       Here to account° the endlesse progenie   *recount*
       Of all the weedes,° that bud and blossome there;   *plants*
270   But so much as doth need, must needs be counted° here.   *recounted*

                              31

       It sited° was in fruitfull soyle of old,   *placed*
       And girt in with two walles on either side;
       The one of yron, the other of bright gold,
       That none might thorough breake, nor over-stride:
275   And double gates it had, which opened wide,
       By which both in and out men moten pas;
       Th' one faire and fresh, the other old and dride:
       Old Genius[2] the porter of them was,
       Old Genius, the which a double nature has.

                              32

280   He letteth in, he letteth out to wend,
       All that to come into the world desire;
       A thousand thousand naked babes attend
       About him day and night, which doe require,
       That he with fleshly weedes would them attire:[3]
285   Such as him list, such as eternall fate
       Ordained hath, he clothes with sinfull mire,°   *earth*
       And sendeth forth to live in mortall state,
       Till they againe returne backe by the hinder gate.

                              33

       After that they againe returnèd beene,
290   They in that Gardin planted be againe;
       And grow afresh, as they had never seene
       Fleshly corruption, nor mortall paine.
       Some thousand yeares so doen they there remaine;
       And then of him are clad with other hew,°   *form*
295   Or sent into the chaungefull world againe,

1. These are all shrines of Venus.
2. God of generation and so of the natural processes, birth and death. The Garden of Adonis is
a myth of Spenser's devising. See canto 1, stanzas
34–38, for the account of the traditional myth of

Venus and Adonis, as portrayed in Malacasta's
tapestries.
3. I.e., the souls in their preexistent state ("naked
babes") request to be clothed with flesh.

Till thither they returne, where first they grew:
So like a wheele around they runne from old to new.[4]

34

Ne° needs there Gardiner to set, or sow,   *neither*
   To plant or prune: for of their owne accord
300 All things, as they created were, doe grow,
   And yet remember well the mightie word,
   Which first was spoken by th' Almightie lord,
   That bad them to increase and multiply:[5]
   Ne° doe they need with water of the ford,°   *nor/stream*
305 Or of the clouds to moysten their roots dry;
   For in themselves eternall moisture they imply.°   *contain*

35

Infinite shapes of creatures there are bred,
   And uncouth° formes, which none yet ever knew,   *strange*
   And every sort is in a sundry° bed   *separate*
310 Set by it selfe, andranckt in comely rew:°   *row*
   Some fit for reasonable soules t' indew,[6]
   Some made for beasts, some made for birds to weare,
   And all the fruitfull spawne of fishes hew°   *shape*
   In endlesse rancks along enraungèd were,
315 That seemed the Ocean could not containe them there.

36

Daily they grow, and daily forth are sent
   Into the world, it to replenish more;
   Yet is the stocke° not lessenèd, nor spent,   *matter*
   But still remaines in everlasting store,
320 As it at first created was of yore.
   For in the wide wombe of the world there lyes,
   In hatefull darkenesse and in deepe horrore,
   An huge eternall Chaos, which supplyes
The substances of natures fruitfull progenyes.

37

325 All things from thence doe their first being fetch,
   And borrow matter, whereof they are made,
   Which when as forme and feature it does ketch,°   *take*
   Becomes a bodie, and doth then invade°   *enter*
   The state of life, out of the griesly° shade.   *gray*
330 That substance° is eterne, and bideth so,   *matter*
   Ne when the life decayes, and forme does fade,
   Doth it consume,[7] and into nothing go,
But chaungèd is, and often altred to and fro.

---

4. The original source for Spenser's myth of cyclic
generation and re-incarnation is Plato's *Republic*,
book 10 (the myth of Er).
5. "And God said unto them, Be fruitful, and
multiply, and replenish the earth" (Genesis 1.28).
6. I.e., some of these shapes are fit for humans to
assume. An echo of 1 Corinthians 15.39: "All flesh
is not the same flesh: but there is one kind of flesh
of men, another flesh of beasts, another of fishes,
and another of birds."
7. Is it destroyed.

38

The substance is not chaunged, nor alterèd,
335   But th' only forme[8] and outward fashion;
       For every substance is conditionèd
       To change her hew, and sundry formes to don,
       Meet° for her temper and complexion: suited
       For formes are variable and decay,
340   By course of kind,° and by occasion;   nature
       And that faire flowre of beautie fades away,
As doth the lilly fresh before the sunny ray.

39

Great enimy to it, and to all the rest,
       That in the Gardin of Adonis springs,
345   Is wicked Time, who with his scyth addrest,°   armed
       Does mow the flowring herbes and goodly things,
       And all their glory to the ground downe flings,
       Where they doe wither, and are fowly mard:°   marred
       He flyes about, and with his flaggy° wings   drooping
350   Beates downe both leaves and buds without regard,
Ne ever pittie may relent° his malice hard.   soften

40

Yet pittie often did the gods relent,
       To see so faire things mard, and spoylèd quight:°   quite
       And their great mother Venus did lament
355   The losse of her deare brood, her deare delight;
       Her hart was pierst with pittie at the sight,
       When walking through the Gardin, them she spyde,
       Yet no'te° she find redresse for such despight.°   could not/wrong
       For all that lives, is subject to that law:
360 All things decay in time, and to their end do draw.

41

But were it not, that Time their troubler is,
       All that in this delightfull Gardin growes,
       Should happie be, and have immortall blis:
       For here all plentie, and all pleasure flowes,
365   And sweet love gentle fits[9] emongst them throwes,
       Without fell rancor, or fond° gealosie;   foolish
       Franckly each paramour his leman knowes,[1]
       Each bird his mate, ne any does envie
Their goodly meriment, and gay felicitie.

42

370 There is continuall spring, and harvest there[2]
       Continuall, both meeting at one time:
       For both the boughes doe laughing blossomes beare,

8. Except only the form.
9. I.e., fits of passion.
1. Openly each lover has intercourse with ("knowes")
his mistress.

2. The coincidence of spring and autumn is characteristic of unfallen nature in Eden; other features of this description are drawn from a common
literary topic, the *locus amoenus* (pleasant place).

And with fresh colours decke the wanton Prime,°   *spring*
And eke attonce the heavy trees they clime,
375   Which seeme to labour under their fruits lode:
The whiles the joyous birdes make their pastime
Emongst the shadie leaves, their sweet abode,
And their true loves without suspition tell abrode.

43

Right in the middest of that Paradise,
380   There stood a stately Mount,[3] on whose round top
A gloomy grove of mirtle trees did rise,
Whose shadie boughes sharpe steele did never lop,
Nor wicked beasts their tender buds did crop,
But like a girlond compassèd the hight,
385   And from their fruitfull sides sweet gum did drop,
That all the ground with precious deaw bedight,
Threw forth most dainty odours, and most sweet delight.

44

And in the thickest covert of that shade,
There was a pleasant arbour, not by art,
390   But of the trees owne inclination° made,   *inclining*
Which knitting their rancke° braunches part to part,   *dense*
With wanton yvie twyne entrayld athwart,[4]
And Eglantine, and Caprifole° emong,   *honeysuckle*
Fashiond above within their inmost part,
395   That nether Phoebus beams could through them throng,°   *press*
Nor Aeolus[5] sharp blast could worke them any wrong.

45

And all about grew every sort° of flowre,   *species*
To which sad lovers were transformd of yore;
Fresh Hyacinthus, Phoebus paramoure,
400   And dearest love,
Foolish Narcisse, that likes the watry shore,
Sad Amaranthus, made a flowre but late,
Sad Amaranthus, in whose purple gore
Me seemes I see Amintas wretched fate,
405   To whom sweet Poets verse hath given endlesse date.[6]

46

There wont faire Venus often to enjoy
Her deare Adonis joyous company,
And reape sweet pleasure of the wanton boy;
There yet, some say, in secret he does ly,
410   Lappèd in flowres and pretious spycery,°   *spices*
By her hid from the world, and from the skill°   *knowledge*
Of Stygian Gods,[7] which doe her love envy;

---

3. With sexual allusion to the *mons veneris*; myrtle ("mirtle") trees were sacred to Venus.
4. I.e., with luxuriant ivy entwined among them.
5. God of winds.
6. The purple Amaranthus is a symbol of immortality; the Greek name means "unfading." By one poetic account, Amintas died for the love of Phillis and was transformed into the Amaranthus. Hyacinth and Narcissus were also transformed into flowers and thereby eternized.
7. Gods of the underworld—e.g., Pluto, Hecate, the furies, Charon—who have a claim upon Adonis in that in the usual formulation of the myth he was killed by the boar.

But she her selfe, when ever that she will,
Possesseth him, and of his sweetnesse takes her fill.[8]

47

415 And sooth° it seemes they say: for he may not   truth
  For ever die, and ever buried bee
  In balefull night, where all things are forgot;
  All° be he subject to mortalitie,   although
  Yet is eterne in mutabilitie,
420 And by succession made perpetuall,
  Transformèd oft, and chaungèd diverslie:
  For him the Father of all formes they call;[9]
Therefore needs mote he live, that living gives to all.

48

There now he liveth in eternall blis,
425 Joying° his goddesse, and of her enjoyd: enjoying
  Ne feareth he henceforth that foe of his,
  Which with his cruell tuske him deadly cloyd:°   gored
  For that wilde Bore, the which him once annoyd,[1]
  She firmely hath emprisonèd for ay,
430 That her sweet love his malice mote avoyd,
  In a strong rocky Cave, which is they say,
Hewen underneath that Mount, that none him losen may.

49

There now he lives in everlasting joy,
  With many of the Gods in company,
435 Which thither haunt, and with the wingèd boy
  Sporting himselfe in safe felicity:
  Who when he[2] hath with spoiles and cruelty
  Ransackt the world, and in the wofull harts
  Of many wretches set his triumphes hye,
440 Thither resorts, and laying his sad darts
Aside, with faire Adonis playes his wanton parts.

50

And his true love faire Psyche with him playes,[3]
  Faire Psyche to him lately reconcyld,
  After long troubles and unmeet upbrayes,°   upbraidings
445 With which his mother Venus her revyld,°   reviled
  And eke himselfe her cruelly exyld:
  But now in stedfast love and happy state
  She with him lives, and hath him borne a chyld,
  Pleasure, that doth both gods and men aggrate,°   gratify
450 Pleasure, the daughter of Cupid and Psyche late.°   recently born

---

8. In the erotic sense.
9. Adonis imposes successive forms on enduring substance, and thereby brings living creatures into being.
1. In the original myth, Adonis died from the boar's wound (see 3.1.34–38).
2. Cupid, now restored to Venus.

3. Suggests, as well, sexual play. Cupid abandoned Psyche when she disobeyed his command not to look upon his face; she became his bride, and immortal, after enduring many severe trials imposed by Venus. The myth was often read as an allegory of the soul's trials in this life before it gains heaven.

51

Hither great Venus brought this infant faire,
  The younger daughter of Chrysogonee,
  And unto Psyche with great trust and care
  Committed her, yfosterèd to bee,
455 And trainèd up in true feminitee:°   *womanliness*
  Who no lesse carefully her tenderèd,°   *cared for*
  Then her owne daughter Pleasure, to whom shee
  Made her companion, and her lessonèd
In all the lore of love, and goodly womanhead.

52

460 In which when she to perfect ripenesse grew,
  Of grace and beautie noble Paragone,
  She brought her forth into the worldès vew,
  To be th' ensample of true love alone,
  And Lodestarre[4] of all chaste affectione,
  To all faire Ladies, that doe live on ground.
465 To Faery court she came, where many one
  Admyrd her goodly haveour,° and found   *demeanor*
  His feeble hart wide launchèd° with loves cruell wound. *pierced*

53

But she to none of them her love did cast,
  Save to the noble knight Sir Scudamore,
470 To whom her loving hart she linkèd fast
  In faithfull love, t' abide for evermore,
  And for his dearest sake endurèd sore,
  Sore trouble of an hainous enimy;
  Who her would forced have to have forlore°   *forsaken*
475 Her former love, and stedfast loyalty,
As ye may elsewhere read that ruefull history.

54

But well I weene, ye first desire to learne,
  What end unto that fearefull Damozell,
  Which fled so fast from that same foster stearne,[5]
480 Whom with his brethren Timias slew, befell:
  That was to weet, the goodly Florimell;
  Who wandring for to seeke her lover deare,
  Her lover deare, her dearest Marinell,
  Into misfortune fell, as ye did heare,
485 And from Prince Arthur fled with wings of idle feare.

Cantos 7–8. Summary   These cantos treat the adventures of the
true and false Florimells. Always in flight, Florimell narrowly escapes a
series of disasters. The son of a witch in whose cottage she takes refuge is
smitten with passion for her; when she escapes in the night the witch sends

4. Guiding star.   1).
5. I.e., the cruel forester pursuing Florimell (canto

a hyena "that feeds on womens flesh" to capture or kill her. To escape him
she leaps into the boat of an aged fisherman who promptly tries to rape her;
she is saved by the god Proteus, who carries her off to his bower in the sea
and presses his suit to her continually, in every shape and guise. Meantime,
to save her pining son from death the Witch creates for him a false Florimell
made of snow, but he loses her quickly to the braggart knight Braggadochio,
who himself loses her to a stranger knight. Meanwhile, Sir Satyrane (see
book 1, canto 6) tames the hyena and rescues the Squire of Dames (a knight
whose name reflects his promiscuity) from the giantess Argante, figure of
unnatural lust in female form. These two knights meet up with a third,
Paridell, and all seek shelter from a sudden thunderstorm in Malbecco's
castle.

Cantos 9–10. Summary   The cantos tell the story of Paridell,
Hellenore, and Malbecco. Malbecco, miser and aged husband of a young
wife, Hellenore, at first refuses entrance to the three knights and to Britomart, who also seeks shelter from the storm. But at length he gives way
before their show of force. At dinner Paridell woos Hellenore with all manner of courtly address. He also tells the story of Troy, identifying himself as
the descendant of Paris; at Britomart's behest he carries the tale forward to
the founding of Troynovant (Britain) by Aeneas' descendant, Brute. Soon
after, Paridell enacts a version of Paris' rape of Helen from Menelaus: he
entices Hellenore to flee with him, setting fire to the castle. The miser saves
his money first and then goes after his wife (whom Paridell quickly abandons); he finds her serving as sexual partner to a band of Satyrs, but she flatly
refuses to leave them to return to him. He is also tricked out of his money
by Braggadochio. Desperate, he wastes away and is transformed into the very
allegorical essence of jealousy: "he has quight / Forgot he was a man, and
Gealosie is hight."

Canto 11

Britomart chaceth Ollyphant,
findes Scudamour distrest:
Assayes° the house of Busyrane,   assails
where Loves spoyles are exprest.°   displayed

1

O Hatefull hellish Snake, what furie furst
    Brought thee from balefull house of Proserpine, [1]
    Where in her bosome she thee long had nurst,
    And fostred up with bitter milke of time,°   anguish
5   Fowle Gealosie, [2] that turnest love divine
    To joylesse dread, and mak'st the loving hart
    With hatefull thoughts to languish and to pine,
    And feed it selfe with selfe-consuming smart?
Of all the passions in the mind thou vilest art.

1. Queen of Hades and consort of Pluto.
2. The snake is an attribute of Envy, to which

Jealousy is related; also, the hair of the vengeful
deities, the Furies, is made up of snakes.

2

10 O let him far be banishèd away,
        And in his stead let Love for ever dwell,
        Sweet Love, that doth his golden wings embay°   *steep*
        In blessèd Nectar,[3] and pure Pleasures well,
        Untroubled of vile feare, or bitter fell.°   *gall, rancor*
15   And ye faire Ladies, that your kingdomes make
        In th' harts of men, them governe wisely well,
        And of faire Britomart ensample take,
    That was as trew in love, as Turtle to her make.[4]

3

    Who with Sir Satyrane, as earst ye red,[5]
20   Forth ryding from Malbeccoes hostlesse° hous,   *inhospitable*
        Far off aspyde a young man, the which fled
        From an huge Geaunt, that with hideous
        And hatefull outrage long him chacèd thus;
        It was that Ollyphant, the brother deare
25   Of that Argante vile and vitious,
        From whom the Squire of Dames was reft whylere;°   *formerly*
    This all as bad as she, and worse, if worse ought were.[6]

4

    For as the sister did in feminine
        And filthy lust exceed all woman kind,
30   So he surpassèd his sex masculine,
        In beastly use that I did ever find;
        Whom when as Britomart beheld behind
        The fearefull boy so greedily pursew,
        She was emmovèd in her noble mind,
35   T' employ her puissaunce° to his reskew,   *power*
    And prickèd° fiercely forward, where she him did vew.   *rode*

5

    Ne was Sir Satyrane her far behinde,
        But with like fiercenesse did ensew° the chace: *follow*
        Whom when the Gyaunt saw, he soone resinde°   *resigned*
40   His former suit, and from them fled apace;
        They after both, and boldly bad him bace,[7]
        And each did strive the other to out-goe,
        But he them both outran a wondrous space,
        For he was long, and swift as any Roe,°   *female deer*
45 And now made better speed, t' escape his fearèd foe.

6

    It was not Satyrane, whom he did feare,
        But Britomart the flowre of chastity;
        For he the powre of chast hands might not beare,
        But alwayes did their dread encounter fly:

---

3. The drink of the gods.
4. The turtledove was a common symbol of matrimonial love and fidelity.
5. As you saw before (in Canto 10.1).

6. Ollyphant and Argante, brother and sister giants,
lived in incest and practiced many other sexual evils.
"Ought": anything.
7. Challenged him.

50   And now so fast his feet he did apply,°   direct
        That he has gotten to a forrest neare,
        Where he is shrowded in security.
        The wood they enter, and search every where,
     They searched diversely,° so both divided were.   in different directions

7

55   Faire Britomart so long him followèd,
        That she at last came to a fountaine sheare,°   clear
        By which there lay a knight all wallowèd°   lying prostrate
        Upon the grassy ground, and by him neare
        His haberjeon,° his helmet, and his speare;   armor
60   A little off, his shield was rudely throwne,
        On which the wingèd boy in colours cleare
        Depeincted° was, full easie to be knowne,   depicted
     And he thereby, where ever it in field was showne.[8]

8

     His face upon the ground did groveling° ly,   prone
65   As if he had bene slombring in the shade,
        That the brave Mayd would not for courtesy,
        Out of his quiet slomber him abrade,°   arouse
        Nor seeme too suddeinly him to invade:°   intrude upon
        Still as she stood, she heard with grievous throb
70   Him grone, as if his hart were peeces made,
        And with most painefull pangs to sigh and sob,
     That pitty did the Virgins hart of patience rob.

9

     At last forth breaking into bitter plaintes
        He said, "O soveraigne Lord that sit'st on hye,
75   And raignst in blis emongst thy blessèd Saintes,
        How suffrest thou such shamefull cruelty,
        So long unwreakèd° of thine enimy?   unrevenged
        Or hast thou, Lord, of good mens cause no heed?
        Or doth thy justice sleepe, and silent ly?
80   What booteth then[9] the good and righteous deed,
     If goodnesse find no grace, nor righteousnesse no meed?°   reward

10

     "If good find grace, and righteousnesse reward,
        Why then is Amoret in caytive° band,   captive
        Sith that more bounteous° creature never fared   virtuous
85   On foot, upon the face of living land?
        Or if that heavenly justice may withstand
        The wrongfull outrage of unrighteous men,
        Why then is Busirane[1] with wickèd hand
        Suffred, these seven monethes day[2] in secret den
90   My Lady and my love so cruelly to pen?

8. The knight, soon identified as Scudamour, takes
his name from his shield upon which the figure of
Cupid is painted (Italian *scudo* + *amore*). That
shield indicates both his identity and his nature.
9. I.e., what is the use.

1. His name associates him with Busiris, an Egyptian king famous for his cruelty and identified with
the Pharoah of Exodus; hence, he is a symbol of
tyranny.
2. A period of seven months.

11

"My Lady and my love is cruelly pend
  In dolefull darkenesse from the vew of day,
  Whilest deadly torments do her chast brest rend,
  And the sharpe steele doth rive° her hart in tway,°   *cut/two*
95 All for she Scudamore will not denay.
  Yet thou vile man, vile Scudamore art sound,
  Ne° canst her ayde, ne° canst her foe dismay;°   *neither/nor/defeat*
  Unworthy wretch to tread upon the ground,
For whom so faire a Lady feeles so sore a wound."

12

100 There an huge heape of singulfes° did oppresse   *sobs*
  His strugling soule, and swelling throbs empeach°   *hinder*
  His foltring toung with pangs of drerinesse,°   *anguish*
  Choking the remnant of his plaintife speach,
  As if his dayes were come to their last reach.
105 Which when she heard, and saw the ghastly fit,
  Threatning into his life to make a breach,
  Both with great ruth° and terrour she was smit,   *pity*
Fearing least from her cage the wearie soule would flit.

13

Tho stooping downe she him amovèd° light;   *touched*
110 Who therewith somewhat starting, up gan looke,
  And seeing him behind a straunger knight,
  Whereas no living creature he mistooke,°   *supposed*
  With great indignaunce he that sight forsooke,
  And downe againe himselfe disdainefully
115 Abjecting, th' earth with his faire forhead strooke:[3]
  Which the bold Virgin seeing, gan apply
Fit medcine to his griefe, and spake thus courtesly.

14

"Ah gentle knight, whose deepe conceivèd griefe
  Well seemes t' exceede the powre of patience,
120 Yet if that heavenly grace some good reliefe
  You send, submit you to high providence,
  And ever in your noble hart prepense,°   *consider before*
  That all the sorrow in the world is lesse,
  Then vertues might, and values° confidence,   *valor's*
125 For who nill° bide the burden of distresse,   *will not*
Must not here thinke to live: for life is wretchednesse.

15

"Therefore, faire Sir, do comfort to you take,
  And freely read,° what wicked felon so   *tell*
  Hath outraged you, and thrald° your gentle make.°   *enslaved/lover*
130 Perhaps this hand may helpe to ease your woe,
  And wreake° your sorrow on your cruell foe,   *revenge*

---

3. Taking her to be a goddess, he turns away with a profound sense of unworthiness ("indignaunce") and self-abnegation ("himselfe disdainefully / Abjecting").

At least it faire endevour will apply."
Those feeling wordes so neare the quicke° did goe,   *heart*
That up his head he rearèd easily,
135 And leaning on his elbow, these few wordes let fly.

16

"What boots it plaine, that cannot be redrest,[4]
And sow vaine sorrow in a fruitlesse eare,
Sith powre of hand, nor skill of learnèd brest,
Ne worldly price cannot redeeme my deare,
140 Out of her thraldome° and continuall feare?   *slavery*
For he the tyraunt, which her hath in ward°   *in his power*
By strong enchauntments and blacke Magicke leare,°   *lore*
Hath in a dungeon deepe her close embard,
And many dreadfull feends hath pointed° to her gard.   *appointed*

17

145 "There he tormenteth her most terribly,
And day and night afflicts with mortall paine,
Because to yield him love she doth deny,
Once to me yold,[5] not to be yold againe:
But yet by torture he would her constraine
150 Love to conceive in her disdainfull brest;
Till so she do, she must in doole° remaine,   *pain*
Ne may by living meanes be thence relest:
What boots it then to plaine, that cannot be redrest?"

18

With this sad hersall° of his heavy stresse,°   *tale/affliction*
155 The warlike Damzell was empassiond sore,
And said, "Sir knight, your cause is nothing lesse,
Then is your sorrow, certes if not more;[6]
For nothing so much pitty doth implore,
As gentle Ladies helplesse misery.
160 But yet, if please ye listen to my lore,°   *teaching*
I will with proofe of last extremity,[7]
Deliver her fro thence, or with her for you dy."

19

"Ah gentlest° knight alive," said Scudamore,   *noblest*
"What huge heroicke magnanimity[8]
165 Dwels in thy bounteous brest? what couldst thou more,
If she were thine, and thou as now am I?
O spare thy happy dayes, and them apply
To better boot,° but let me dye, that ought;   *use*
More is more losse: one is enough to dy."
170 "Life is not lost," said she, "for which is bought
Endlesse renowm, that more then death is to be sought."

---

4. What is the use of complaining for what cannot be helped.
5. Yielded. Scudamore's courtship and winning of Amoret as his love is described in book 4, canto 10.

6. I.e., your cause is worthy of your great sorrow, or even more.
7. I.e., at the extreme peril of my life.
8. Nobility of mind, which produces the highest virtues and the greatest deeds.

20

Thus she at length perswaded him to rise,
   And with her wend,° to see what new successe   go
   Mote° him befall upon new enterprise;   might
175   His armes, which he had vowèd to disprofesse,°   renounce
   She gathered up and did about him dresse,
   And his forwandred° steed unto him got: wandered away
   So forth they both yfere° make their progresse,   together
   And march not past the mountenaunce of a shot,
180 Till they arrived, whereas their purpose they did plot.[9]

21

There they dismounting, drew their weapons bold
   And stoutly° came unto the Castle gate;   bravely
   Whereas no gate they found, them to withhold,
   Nor ward° to wait at morne and evening late,   guard
185   But in the Porch, that did them sore amate,°   dismay
   A flaming fire, ymixt with smouldry smoke,
   And stinking Sulphure, that with griesly° hate   horrid
   And dreadfull horrour did all entraunce choke,
   Enforced them their forward footing to revoke.°   draw back

22

190 Greatly thereat was Britomart dismayd,
   Ne in that stownd wist, how her selfe to beare;[1]
   For daunger vaine it were, to have assayd°   attempted
   That cruell element, which all things feare,
   Ne none can suffer to approchen neare:
195   And turning backe to Scudamour, thus sayd;
   "What monstrous enmity provoke° we heare,   challenge
   Foolhardy as th' Earthes children, the which made
   Battell against the Gods?[2] so we a God invade.

23

"Daunger without discretion to attempt,
200   Inglorious and beastlike is: therefore Sir knight,
   Aread° what course of you is safest dempt,°   declare/deemed
   And how we with our foe may come to fight."
   "This is," quoth he, "the dolorous despight,°   evil
   Which earst° to you I playnd:° for neither may earlier/complained
205   This fire be quencht by any wit or might,
   Ne yet by any meanes removed away,
   So mighty be th' enchauntments, which the same do stay.° maintain

24

"What is there else, but cease these fruitlesse paines,
   And leave me to my former languishing?
210   Faire Amoret must dwell in wicked chaines,
   And Scudamore here dye with sorrowing."
   "Perdy° not so," said she, "for shamefull thing   truly

9. I.e., they went no further than the distance of
a bow-shot when they arrived to the place they
purposed to go.
1. I.e., nor in that trouble ("stownd") did she know

("wist") what to do.
2. I.e., we are like the Titans who dared to do
battle against the Olympian gods.

It were t' abandon noble chevisaunce,[3]
For shew of perill, without venturing:
215   Rather let try extremities of chaunce,
Then enterprisèd prayse for dread to disavaunce."[4]

25

Therewith resolved to prove her utmost might,
Her ample shield she threw before her face,
And her swords point directing forward right,
220   Assayld° the flame, the which eftsoones° gave place,   *assaulted/soon*
And did it selfe divide with equall space,[5]
That through she passèd; as a thunder bolt
Perceth the yielding ayre, and doth displace
The soring clouds into sad showres ymolt;°   *melted*
225 So to her yold the flames, and did their force revolt.°   *turn back*

26

Whom whenas Scudamour saw past the fire,
Safe and untoucht, he likewise gan assay,
With greedy will, and envious desire,
And bad the stubborne flames to yield him way:
230   But cruell Mulciber[6] would not obay
His threatfull pride, but did the more augment
His mighty rage, and with imperious sway
Him forst (maulgre)° his fiercenesse to relent,°   *despite/give way*
And backe retire, all scorcht and pitifully brent.

27

235 With huge impatience he inly swelt,°   *burned*
More for great sorrow, that he could not pas,
Then for the burning torment, which he felt,
That with fell woodnesse he effiercèd was,[7]
And wilfully him throwing on the gras,
240   Did beat and bounse° his head and brest full sore;   *thump*
The whiles the Championesse now entred has
The utmost rowme,[8] and past the formest dore,
The utmost rowme, abounding with all precious store.

28

For round about, the wals yclothed were
245   With goodly arras° of great majesty,   *tapestries*
Woven with gold and silke so close and nere,°   *tight*
That the rich metall lurkèd privily,°   *secretly*
As faining to be hid from envious eye;
Yet here, and there, and every where unwares°   *unexpectedly*
250 It shewd it selfe, and shone unwillingly;
Like a discolourd° Snake, whose hidden snares   *multicolored*
Through the greene gras his long bright burnisht backe declares.

---

3. Chivalric enterprise.
4. I.e., it is better to chance extreme danger than retreat because of fear from praiseworthy enterprises.
5. Equally on both sides.

6. God of fire. The manner of Scudamore's assault on the flames suggests why he is unsuccessful.
7. I.e., he was maddened with fierce fury.
8. Outermost room.

29

And in those Tapets° weren fashionèd   *tapestries*
    Many faire pourtraicts, and many a faire feate,
255 And all of love, and all of lusty-hed,
    As seemèd by their semblaunt did entreat;[9]
    And eke° all Cupids warres they did repeate,°   *also/recount*
    And cruell battels, which he whilome° fought   *formerly*
    Gainst all the Gods, to make his empire great;
260 Besides the huge massacres, which he wrought
On mighty kings and kesars,° into thraldome brought.   *caesars*

30

Therein was writ,° how often thundring Jove   *woven*
    Had felt the point of his hart-percing dart,
    And leaving heavens kingdome, here did rove
265 In straunge disguize, to slake his scalding smart;
    Now like a Ram, faire Helle to pervart,
    Now like a Bull, Europa to withdraw:[1]
    Ah, how the fearefull Ladies tender hart
    Did lively° seeme to tremble, when she saw   *lifelike*
270 The huge seas under her t' obay her servaunts° law.   *lovers*

31

Soone after that into a golden showre
    Him selfe he chaunged faire Danaë to vew,
    And through the roofe of her strong brasen towre
    Did raine into her lap an hony dew,[2]
275 The whiles her foolish garde, that little knew
    Of such deceipt, kept th' yron dore fast bard,
    And watcht, that none should enter nor issew;°   *go out*
    Vaine was the watch, and bootlesse° all the ward,   *useless*
    Whenas the God to golden hew° him selfe   *shape*
      transfard.°   *transformed*

32

280 Then was he turnd into a snowy Swan,
    To win faire Leda to his lovely trade:[3]
    O wondrous skill, and sweet wit° of the man,   *ingenuity*
    That her in daffadillies sleeping made,
    From scorching heat her daintie limbes to shade:
285 Whiles the proud Bird ruffing° his fethers wyde,   *ruffling*
    And brushing° his faire brest, did her invade;   *preening*
    She slept, yet twixt her eyelids closely spyde,
How towards her he rusht, and smilèd at his pryde.

---

9. I.e., the pictures ("semblaunt") seemed to treat entirely of deeds of love and merriment ("lusty-hed").

1. A golden ram (not specifically identified in legend as Jove) came to carry away ("pervert") Helle from the fury of Ino; Jove assumed the shape of a bull to seduce Europa, and carried her over the seas.

2. In another part of the tapestry ("soone after") Jove is shown as a shower of gold, impregnating Danaë.

3. Jove became a swan to seduce Leda, who gave birth to Castor and Pollux and (some said) Helen of Troy. See Yeats, *Leda and the Swan*, vol. 2, p. 1952. "Trade": practice.

33

Then shewd it, how the Thebane Semelee
290   Deceived of gealous Juno, did require
To see him in his soveraigne majestee,
Armd with his thunderbolts and lightning fire,
Whence dearely she with death bought her desire.[4]
But faire Alcmena better match did make,
295   Joying his love in likenesse more entire;[5]
Three nights in one, they say, that for her sake
He then did put, her pleasures lenger° to partake.   *longer*

34

Twise was he seene in soaring Eagles shape,
And with wide wings to beat the buxome° ayre,   *yielding*
300   Once, when he with Asterie did scape,
Againe, when as the Trojane boy so faire
He snatcht from Ida hill, and with him bare:[6]
Wondrous delight it was, there to behould,
How the rude Shepheards after him did stare,
305   Trembling through feare, least down he fallen should,
And often to him calling, to take surer hould.

35

In Satyres shape Antiopa he snatcht:
And like a fire, when he Aegin' assayd:
A shepheard, when Mnemosyne he catcht:
310   And like a Serpent to the Thracian mayd.[7]
Whiles thus on earth great Jove these pageaunts playd,
The wingèd boy did thrust into his throne,
And scoffing, thus unto his mother sayd,
"Lo now the heavens obey to me alone,
315 And take me for their Jove, while Jove to earth is gone."

36

And thou, faire Phoebus, in thy colours bright
Wast there enwoven, and the sad distresse,
In which that boy thee plongèd, for despight,
That thou bewrayedst his mothers wantonnesse,
320   When she with Mars was meynt° in joyfulnesse: *mingled*
For thy he thrild thee with a leaden dart,
To love faire Daphne, which thee lovèd lesse:[8]
Lesse she thee loved, then was thy just desart,
Yet was thy love her death, and her death was thy smart.°   *pain*

4. Juno tricked Semele into having Jove visit her
in all his power; she was burned to death by lightning and thunderbolts.
5. Jove visited Alcmena in the likeness of her husband Amphitryon, and made that one night the
length of three.
6. Asterie changed herself into a quail to avoid
Jove's advances, but he captured her as an eagle;
in that form he also snatched Ganymede, who
became cup-bearer to the gods.
7. Jove came as a satyr to Antiope; in fire to Aegina;

as a shepherd to Mnemosyne, goddess of memory
(who bore the 9 muses); as a serpent to Proserpina
"the Thracian maid."
8. Two stories are combined: Apollo's punishment for revealing Venus' adultery with Mars was
"the sad distresse" of doting upon Leucothoe; later
he chased Daphne who escaped by metamorphosis
into a laurel tree. Cupid's leaden dart produces
unhappiness in love. "For thy": therefore. "Thrild":
pierced. "Lesse": too little.

37

325 So lovedst thou the lusty° Hyacinct,   *handsome*
    So lovedst thou the faire Coronis deare:
    Yet both are of thy haplesse hand extinct,
    Yet both in flowres do live, and love thee beare,
    The one a Paunce, the other a sweet breare:[9]
330 For griefe whereof, ye mote have lively° seene   *lifelike*
    The God himselfe rending his golden heare,
    And breaking quite his gyrlond° ever greene,   *garland*
With other signes of sorrow and impatient teene.°   *grief*

38

Both for those two, and for his owne deare sonne,
    The sonne of Climene he did repent,
335 Who bold to guide the charet of the Sunne,
    Himselfe in thousand peeces fondly rent,[1]
    And all the world with flashing fier brent;
    So like, that all the walles did seeme to flame.
    Yet cruell Cupid, not herewith content,
340 Forst him eftsoones° to follow other game,   *soon after*
And love a Shepheards daughter for his dearest Dame.

39

He lovèd Isse for his dearest Dame,
    And for her sake her cattell fed a while,
    And for her sake a cowheard vile became,
345 The servant of Admetùs cowheard vile,
    Whiles that from heaven he suffered exile.[2]
    Long were to tell each other lovely fit,[3]
    Now like a Lyon, hunting after spoile,
    Now like a Stag, now like a faulcon flit:°   *fleet*
350 All which in that faire arras was most lively writ.

40

Next unto him was Neptune[4] picturèd,
    In his divine resemblance wondrous lyke:
    His face was rugged, and his hoarie hed
    Droppèd with brackish° deaw; his three-forkt Pyke   *salty*
355 He stearnly shooke, and therewith fierce did stryke
    The raging billowes, that on every syde
    They trembling stood, and made a long broad dyke,
    That his swift charet might have passage wyde,
Which foure great Hippodames did draw in temewise tyde.

41

360 His sea-horses did seeme to snort amayne,°   *violently*
    And from their nosethrilles° blow the brynie streame,   *nostrils*

9. Apollo accidentally killed his lover Hyacinth at a game of quoits, and transformed him into a flower ("paunce"—pansy); he killed Coronis out of jealousy, but her transformation to a sweetbriar seems to be Spenser's invention.
1. Foolishly tore apart. Phaëthon, son of Apollo and Climene, extracted permission to drive the chariot of the Sun through the heavens; unable to control the horses, he killed himself and almost destroyed the world.
2. Two stories are combined: Apollo disguising himself as a shepherd to gain Isse, and serving Admetus as a cowherd.
3. Amorous passion.
4. God of the sea, here portrayed with his trident ("three forkt Pyke"), riding in a chariot ("charet") drawn by a team of 4 sea-horses ("Hippodames").

That made the sparckling waves to smoke agayne,
And flame with gold, but the white fomy creame,
Did shine with silver, and shoot forth his beame.
365 The God himselfe did pensive seeme and sad,
And hong adowne his head, as he did dreame:
For privy° love his brest empiercèd had,   *secret*
Ne ought but deare Bisaltis[5] ay could make him glad.

42

He loved eke Iphimedia deare,
370 And Aeolus faire daughter Arne hight,
For whom he turnd him selfe into a Steare,°   *steer*
And fed on fodder, to beguile her sight.
Also to win Deucalions daughter bright,
He turnd him selfe into a Dolphin fayre;[6]
375 And like a wingèd horse he tooke his flight,
To snaky-locke Medusa to repayre,
On whom he got faire Pegasus, that flitteth in the ayre.[7]

43

Next Saturne was, (but who would ever weene,°   *think*
That sullein Saturne ever weend° to love?   *was minded*
380 Yet love is sullein,° and Saturnlike seene,   *melancholy*
As he did for Erigone it prove,)
That to a Centaure did him selfe transmove.[8]
So prooved it eke that gracious° God of wine,   *graceful*
When for to compasse Philliras hard love,
385 He turnd himselfe into a fruitfull vine,
And into her faire bosome made his grapes decline.°   *hang down*

44

Long were to tell the amorous assayes,°   *assaults*
And gentle pangues, with which he[9] makèd meeke
The mighty Mars, to learne his wanton playes:
390 How oft for Venus, and how often eek
For many other Nymphes he sore did shreek,
With womanish teares, and with unwarlike smarts,°   *pains*
Privily° moystening his horrid° cheek.   *secretly/bristly*
There was he painted full of burning darts,
395 And many wide woundes launchèd° through his inner parts.   *torn*

45

Ne did he spare (so cruell was the Elfe)
His owne deare mother, (ah why should he so?)
Ne did he spare sometime to pricke himselfe,
That he might tast the sweet consuming woe,
400 Which he had wrought to many others moe.°   *more*

5. Neptune made love to Theophane, daughter of
Bisaltes, in the form of a ram.
6. Neptune came to Iphimedia as a flowing river,
to Arne as a steer, to Deucalion's daughter Melan-
tho as a dolphin.
7. Neptune ravished Medusa in Minerva's temple, for which cause her hair was turned to snakes;
she gave birth to the winged horse, Pegasus.

8. Saturn, associated with melancholy, is not
usually portrayed as a lover. Spenser here trans-
poses two myths: Saturn loved Philyra ("Phillaras")
not Erigone, from which union came the Centaur; Bacchus ("God of wine") tricked Erigone with
a false bunch of grapes.
9. I.e., Cupid, god of love.

But to declare the mournfull Tragedyes,
And spoiles, wherewith he all the ground did strow,
More eath° to number, with how many eyes   *easy*
High heaven beholds sad lovers nightly theeveryes.[1]

46

405 Kings Queenes, Lords Ladies, Knights and Damzels gent°   *gentle*
    Were heaped together with the vulgar sort,
    And mingled with the raskall rablement,°   *rabble, masses*
    Without respect of person or of port,°   *position*
    To shew Dan° Cupids powre and great effort:°   *Master/effort*
410   And round about a border was entrayld,°   *woven*
    Of broken bowes and arrowes shivered short,
    And a long bloudy river through them rayld,°   *flowed*
So lively and so like, that living sence it fayld.[2]

47

And at the upper end of that faire rowme,
415   There was an Altar built of pretious stone,
    Of passing° valew, and of great renowme,   *surpassing*
    On which there stood an Image all alone,
    Of massy° gold, which with his owne light shone;   *solid*
    And wings it had with sundry colours dight,°   *adorned*
420   More sundry colours, then the proud Pavone°   *peacock*
    Beares in his boasted fan, or Iris[3] bright,
When her discolourd° bow she spreds through heaven
    bright.   *multicolored*

48

Blindfold he was, and in his cruell fist
    A mortall° bow and arrowes keene did hold,   *deadly*
425 With which he shot at randon, when him list,
    Some headed with sad lead, some with pure gold;[4]
    (Ah man beware, how thou those darts behold)
    A wounded Dragon[5] under him did ly,
    Whose hideous tayle his left foot did enfold,
430   And with a shaft was shot through either eye,
That no man forth might draw, ne no man remedye.

49

And underneath his feet was written thus,
    Unto the Victor of the Gods this bee:
    And all the people in that ample hous
435 Did to that image bow their humble knee,
    And oft committed fowle Idolatree.
    That wondrous sight faire Britomart amazed,
    Ne seeing could her wonder satisfie,

---

1. I.e., it would be easier to number the stars ("eyes") that watch lovers' nightly exploits (thieveries) than the tragedies caused by love.
2. I.e., so animated and so lifelike, that it deceived ("fayled") the senses of those looking on.
3. Goddess of the rainbow.

4. Cupid, by tradition blindfolded, shoots at random ("randon"): his leaden arrows cause unhappiness in love, his golden arrows happiness.
5. The dragon is traditionally a guard, symbolic of vigilance.

But ever more and more upon it gazed,
440 The whiles the passing brightnes her fraile sences dazed.

50

Tho as she backward[6] cast her busie eye,
  To search each secret of that goodly sted,°   *place*
  Over the dore thus written she did spye
  Be bold: she oft and oft it over-red,
445   Yet could not find what sence it figurèd:
  But what so were therein or writ or ment,
  She was no whit thereby discouragèd
  From prosecuting of her first intent,
But forward with bold steps into the next roome went.

51

450 Much fairer, then the former, was that roome,
  And richlier by many partes arayd:[7]
  For not with arras made in painefull° loome,   *painstaking*
  But with pure gold it all was overlayd,
  Wrought with wilde Antickes,[8] which their follies playd,
455   In the rich metall, as° they living were: *as if*
  A thousand monstrous formes therein were made,
  Such as false love doth oft upon him weare,
For love in thousand monstrous formes doth oft appeare.

52

And all about, the glistring walles were hong
460   With warlike spoiles, and with victorious prayes,°   *prizes*
  Of mighty Conquerours and Captaines strong,
  Which were whilome° captivèd in their dayes   *formerly*
  To cruell love, and wrought their owne decayes:
  Their swerds° and speres were broke, and   *swords*
    hauberques° rent;   *coats of mail*
465   And their proud girlonds of tryumphant bayes[9]
  Troden in dust with fury insolent,
To shew the victors might and mercilesse intent.

53

The warlike Mayde beholding earnestly
  The goodly ordinance° of this rich place,   *order*
470   Did greatly wonder, ne could satisfie
  Her greedy eyes with gazing a long space,
  But more she mervaild that no footings trace,[1]
  Nor wight appeared, but wastefull° emptinesse,   *uninhabited*
  And solemne silence over all that place:
475   Straunge thing it seemed, that none was to possesse
So rich purveyance,° ne them keepe with carefulnesse.   *furnishings*

---

6. I.e., behind the statue.
7. I.e., much ("by many parts") more richly decorated ("arayd").
8. Grotesque statues.

9. Wreaths of laurel ("bays") were traditionally
awarded to great military conquerors.
1. I.e., trace of footprints.

54

And as she lookt about, she did behold,
   How over that same dore was likewise writ,
   Be bold, be bold, and every where *Be bold,*
480   That much she muzed, yet could not construe it
   By any ridling skill, or commune wit.[2]
   At last she spyde at that roomes upper end,
   Another yron dore, on which was writ,
   Be not too bold; whereto though she did bend
485 Her earnest mind, yet wist not what it might intend.°   *mean*

55

Thus she there waited untill eventyde,
   Yet living creature none she saw appeare:
   And now sad° shadowes gan the world to hyde,   *somber*
   From mortall vew, and wrap in darkenesse dreare;
490   Yet nould° she d' off her weary armes, for feare   *could not*
   Of secret daunger, ne let sleepe oppresse
   Her heavy eyes with natures burdein deare,
   But drew her selfe aside in sickernesse,°   *safety*
And her welpointed weapons did about her dresse.[3]

Canto 12

The maske[1] of Cupid, and th' enchaunted
      Chamber are displayd,
   Whence Britomart redeemes faire
      Amoret, through charmes decayd.°   *wasted away*

1

Tho when as chearelesse Night ycovered had
   Faire heaven with an universall cloud,
   That every wight dismayd with darknesse sad,°   *sober*
   In silence and in sleepe themselves did shroud,
5   She heard a shrilling Trompet sound aloud,
   Signe of nigh° battell, or got° victory;   *approaching/achieved*
   Nought therewith daunted was her courage proud,
   But rather stird to cruell° enmity,   *fierce*
Expecting° ever, when some foe she might descry.   *waiting*

2

10 With that, an hideous storme of winde arose,
   With dreadfull thunder and lightning atwixt,
   And an earth-quake, as if it streight would lose
   The worlds foundations from his centre fixt;
   A direfull stench of smoke and sulphure mixt

2. Common sense.
3. Her well-appointed (and / or sharp) weapons she
drew ("did dresse") about her.
1. This episode resembles a court masque with
allegorical personages and emblematic clothing and
properties—possibly the masque for the wedding
of Amoret and Scudamore. It is also a "Triumph"
of Cupid who is preceded and followed by the allegorical qualities that attend upon his reign, and
who displays Amoret as the spoils of his victory,
the victim of the attitudes toward love which he
promotes.

15   Ensewd, whose noyance° fild the fearefull   *annoyance*
            sted,°   *place*
        From the fourth houre of night untill the sixt;[2]
        Yet the bold Britonesse was nought ydred,
        Though much emmoved, but stedfast still perseverèd.

                                            3
        All suddenly a stormy whirlwind blew
20   Throughout the house, that clappèd° every dore,   *slammed*
        With which that yron wicket open flew,
        As it with mightie levers had bene tore:
        And forth issewd, as on the ready flore
        Of some Theatre, a grave personage,
25   That in his hand a branch of laurell bore,
        With comely haveour° and count'nance sage,   *bearing*
        Yclad in costly garments, fit for tragicke Stage.

                                            4
        Proceeding to the midst, he still did stand,
        As if in mind he somewhat had to say,
30   And to the vulgar° beckning with his hand,   *groundlings*
        In signe of silence, as to heare a play,
        By lively actions he gan bewray
        Some argument of matter passioned;[3]
        Which doen, he backe retyrèd soft away,
35   And passing by, his name discoverèd,
        Ease, on his robe in golden letters cypherèd.

                                            5
        The noble Mayd, still standing all this vewd,
        And merveild at his strange intendiment;°   *purpose*
        With that a joyous fellowship issewd
40   Of Minstrals, making goodly meriment,
        With wanton Bardes, and Rymers impudent,
        All which together sung full chearefully
        A lay° of loves delight, with sweet concent:°   *song/harmony*
        After whom marcht a jolly company,
45 In manner of a maske, enrangèd orderly.[4]

                                            6
        The whiles a most delitious harmony,
        In full straunge notes was sweetly heard to sound,
        That the rare sweetnesse of the melody
        The feeble senses wholly did confound,
50   And the fraile soule in deepe delight nigh dround:
        And when it ceast, shrill trompets loud did bray,
        That their report° did farre away rebound,   *echo*

---

2. Night begins at 6 P.M., so these effects take place from 10 P.M. to midnight, when the masque begins.
3. I.e., by pantomime he indicates that the subject ("argument") of the masque concerns passion. The part of presenter is taken by Ease—suggesting that it predisposes to lechery. Similarly, Idleness

leads the procession of the 7 deadly sins in *Faerie Queene* 1.4.18–20.
4. As here, most masques had 12 masquers, forming 6 couples. The love song at the processional is performed by musicians ("minstrals") and poets of varying quality ("Bardes" and "Rymers").

And when they ceast, it gan againe to play,
The whiles the maskers marched forth in trim aray.

7

55   The first was Fancy,[5] like a lovely boy,
     Of rare aspect, and beautie without peare;
     Matchable either to that ympe of Troy,[6]
     Whom Jove did love, and chose his cup to beare,
     Or that same daintie lad, which was so deare
60   To great Alcides,[7] that when as he dyde,
     He wailed womanlike with many a teare,
     And every wood, and every valley wyde
He fild with Hylas name; the Nymphes eke Hylas cryde.

8

His garment neither was of silke nor say,°   *fine wool*
65   But painted plumes, in goodly order dight,
     Like as the sunburnt Indians[8] do aray
     Their tawney bodies, in their proudest plight:°   *attire*
     As those same plumes, so seemd he vaine and light,
     That by his gate might easily appeare;
70   For still he fared as dauncing in delight,
     And in his hand a windy° fan did beare,   *causing wind*
That in the idle aire he moved still here and there.

9

And him beside marcht amorous Desyre,
     Who seemd of riper yeares, then th' other Swaine,°   *lover*
75   Yet was that other swayne this elders syre,[9]
     And gave him being, commune to them twaine:
     His garment was disguisèd very vaine,
     And his embrodered Bonet sat awry;
     Twixt both his hands few sparkes he close did straine,°   *clasp*
80   Which still he blew, and kindled busily,
That soone they life conceived, and forth in flames did fly.

10

Next after him went Doubt, who was yclad
     In a discoloured° cote, of straunge disguyse,   *multicolored*
     That at his backe a brode Capuccio had,
85   And sleeves dependant Albanese-wyse:[1]
     He lookt askew with his mistrustfull eyes,
     And nicely trode, as thornes lay in his way,
     Or that the flore to shrinke he did avyse,
     And on a broken reed he still did stay
90   His feeble steps, which shrunke, when hard theron he lay.[2]

---

5. The mind's power to produce images which are often misleading or false.
6. Ganymede, as in Canto 11.34.4–9.
7. Hercules, whose beloved Hylas was drowned.
8. Of North America.
9. I.e., Desire seems older than Fancy, but Fancy is in fact his father; he was dressed fantastically ("disguised very vaine").
1. "Doubt": a state of apprehension or uncertainty. His hood ("Capucchio") resembles that of a Capuchin monk, and his sleeves hang down "dependant Albanese-wyse"—perhaps like those of an alb, a priest's long tunic.
2. I.e., he trod with great precision and care ("nicely") as if thorns lay in his path, or as if he supposed ("did avyse") the floor to give way ("shrinke"). His cane was a broken reed which collapsed ("shrunke") when he leaned heavily on it.

11

With him went Daunger, clothed in ragged weed,°   garment
    Made of Beares skin, that him more dreadfull made,
    Yet his owne face was dreadfull, ne did need
    Straunge horrour, to deforme his griesly shade;[3]
95   A net in th' one hand, and a rustie blade
    In th' other was, this Mischiefe, that Mishap;
    With th' one his foes he threatned to invade,°   attack
    With th' other he his friends ment to enwrap:
For whom he could not kill, he practizd° to entrap.   plotted

12

100 Next him was Feare, all armed from top to toe,
    Yet thought himselfe not safe enough thereby,
    But feard each shadow moving to and fro,
    And his owne armes when glittering he did spy,
    Or clashing heard, he fast away did fly,
105   As ashes pale of hew, and wingyheeld;[4]
    And evermore on Daunger fixt his eye,
    Gainst whom he alwaies bent° a brasen shield,   turned
Which his right hand unarmèd fearefully did wield.

13

With him went Hope in rancke, a handsome Mayd,
110   Of chearefull looke and lovely to behold;
    In silken samite° she was light arayd,   a rich silk
    And her faire lockes were woven up in gold;
    She alway smyld, and in her hand did hold
    An holy water Sprinckle,[5] dipt in deowe,
115   With which she sprinckled favours manifold,
    On whom she list, and did great liking sheowe,
Great liking unto many, but true love to feowe.°   few

14

And after them Dissemblance, and Suspect[6]
    Marcht in one rancke, yet an unequall paire:
120   For she was gentle, and of milde aspect,
    Courteous to all, and seeming debonaire,°   gracious
    Goodly adornèd, and exceeding faire:
    Yet was that all but painted, and purloynd,°   stolen
    And her bright browes were deckt with borrowed haire:
125   Her deedes were forgèd, and her words false coynd,
And alwaies in her hand two clewes° of silke she   balls of thread
    twynd.

15

But he was foule, ill favourèd, and grim,
    Under his eyebrowes looking still askaunce;
    And ever as Dissemblance laught on him,

---

3. Danger's face was terrifying, needing nothing external ("strange") to further deform his horrid ("griesly") appearance. His net and bloodstained ("rustie") knife indicate the kinds of perils he signifies.

4. I.e., he was pale as ashes, and fled as if his heels had wings.

5. Aspergillum, a brush to sprinkle holy water. "Deowe": water (dew).

6. Dissimulation and Suspicion.

130   He lowrd° on her with daungerous°   *scowled/threatening*
      eyeglaunce;
    Shewing his nature in his countenance;
    His rolling eyes did never rest in place,
    But walkt° each where, for feare of hid mischaunce,   *moved*
    Holding a lattice° still before his face,   *screen*
135 Through which he still did peepe, as forward he did pace.

16

    Next him went Griefe, and Fury matcht yfere;°   *together*
    Griefe all in sable sorrowfully clad,
    Downe hanging his dull head, with heavy chere,
    Yet inly being more, then seeming sad:
140   A paire of Pincers in his hand he had,
    With which he pinchèd people to the hart,
    That from thenceforth a wretchèd life they lad,°   *lead*
    In wilfull languor° and consuming smart,°   *pining/pain*
    Dying each day with inward wounds of dolours dart.

17

145 But Fury was full ill appareilèd
    In rags, that naked nigh° she did appeare,   *nearly*
    With ghastly lookes and dreadfull drerihed;°   *wretchedness*
    For from her backe her garments she did teare,
    And from her head oft rent her snarled heare:
150   In her right hand a firebrand she did tosse°   *brandish*
    About her head, still roming here and there;
    As a dismayèd° Deare in chace embost,° *panic-stricken/exhausted*
    Forgetfull of his safety, hath his right way lost.

18

    After them went Displeasure and Pleasance,
155   He looking lompish and full sullein sad,[7]
    And hanging downe his heavy countenance;
    She chearefull fresh and full of joyance glad,
    As if no sorrow she ne felt ne drad;°   *feared*
    That evill matchèd paire they seemd to bee:
160   An angry Waspe th' one in a viall had,
    Th' other in hers an hony-lady Bee;
    Thus marchèd these six couples forth in faire degree.°   *order*

19

    After all these there marcht a most faire Dame,
    Led of two grysie° villeins, th' one Despight,   *grim*
165   The other clepèd Cruelty by name:[8]
    She dolefull Lady, like a dreary Spright,
    Cald by strong charmes out of eternall night,
    Had deathes owne image figurd in her face,
    Full of sad signes, fearefull to living sight;

---

7. Morose; "lompish": dejected.
8. Typical attributes of the lady in the world of courtly love and the love sonnets: her "cruelty" causes her to reject her lover with scorn ("despight"). "Cleped": called.

170   Yet in that horror shewd a seemely grace,
      And with her feeble feet did move a comely pace.

20

    Her brest all naked, as net° ivory,   *pure*
      Without adorne° of gold or silver bright,   *adornment*
      Wherewith the Craftesman wonts it beautify,[9]
175   Of her dew honour was despoylèd quight,
      And a wide wound therein (O ruefull sight)
      Entrenched deepe with knife accursèd keene,
      Yet freshly bleeding forth her fainting spright,°   *spirit*
      (The worke of cruell hand) was to be seene,
180 That dyde in sanguine° red her skin all snowy cleene.   *bloody*

21

    At that wide orifice her trembling hart
      Was drawne forth, and in silver basin layd,
      Quite through transfixèd with a deadly dart,
      And in her bloud yet steeming fresh embayd:°   *steeped*
185   And those two villeins, which her steps upstayd,
      When her weake feete could scarcely her sustaine,
      And fading vitall powers gan to fade,
    Her forward still with torture did constraine,
    And evermore encreasèd her consuming paine.

22

190 Next after her the wingèd God himselfe[1]
      Came riding on a Lion ravenous,
      Taught to obay the menage° of that Elfe,   *horsemanship*
      That man and beast with powre imperious
      Subdeweth to his kingdome tyrannous:
195   His blindfold eyes he bad a while unbind,
      That his proud spoyle of that same dolorous
      Faire Dame he might behold in perfect kind;°   *clearly*
    Which seene, he much rejoycèd in his cruell mind.

23

    Of which full proud, himselfe up rearing hye,
200   He lookèd round about with sterne disdaine;
      And did survay his goodly company:
      And marshalling the evill ordered traine,
      With that the darts which his right hand did straine,°   *clasp*
      Full dreadfully he shooke that all did quake,
205   And clapt on hie his coulourd winges twaine,
      That all his many° it affraide did make: *company*
    Tho blinding° him againe, his way he forth did take.   *blindfolding*

24

    Behinde him was Reproch, Repentance, Shame;
      Reproch the first, Shame next, Repent behind:
210   Repentance feeble, sorrowfull, and lame:

9. I.e., without the jewels which usually beautify her breast.
1. I.e., Cupid

Reproch despightfull, carelesse, and unkind;[2]
Shame most ill favour, bestiall, and blind:
Shame lowrd,° Repentance sighed, Reproch did scould; *scowled*
Reproch sharpe stings, Repentance whips entwind,
215   Shame burning brond-yrons in her hand did hold:
All three to each unlike, yet all made in one mould.

25

And after them a rude confusèd rout
Of persons flockt, whose names is hard to read:° *interpret*
Emongst them was sterne Strife, and Anger stout,° *fierce*
220   Unquiet Care, and fond° Unthriftihead, *foolish*
Lewd° Losse of Time, and Sorrow seeming dead, *base*
Inconstant Chaunge, and false Disloyaltie,
Consuming Riotise,° and guilty Dread *debauchery*
Of heavenly vengeance, faint Infirmitie,
225   Vile Povertie, and lastly Death with infamie.

26

There were full many moe° like maladies, *more*
Whose names and natures I note readen well;[3]
So many moe, as there be phantasies
In wavering wemens wit, that none can tell,° *count*
230   Or paines in love, or punishments in hell;
All which disguized marcht in masking wise,
About the chamber with that Damozell,
And then returnèd, having marchèd thrise,
Into the inner roome, from whence they first did rise.

27

235   So soone as they were in, the dore streight way
Fast lockèd, driven with that stormy blast,
Which first it openèd; and bore all away.
Then the brave Maid, which all this while was plast° *placed*
In secret shade, and saw both first and last,
240   Issewèd° forth, and went unto the dore, *came*
To enter in, but found it lockèd fast:
It vaine she thought with rigorous uprore[4]
For to efforce, when charmes had closèd it afore.

28

Where force might not availe, there sleights and art
245   She cast° to use, both fit for hard emprize;° *resolved/enterprise*
For thy° from that same roome not to depart *therefore*
Till morrow next, she did her selfe avize,° *counsel*
When that same Maske againe should forth arize.
The morrow next appeard with joyous cheare,
250   Calling men to their daily exercize,
Then she, as morrow fresh, her selfe did reare
Out of her secret stand,° that day for to out weare. *standing place*

---

2. I.e., full of scorn, careless of where his attacks   3. I cannot well interpret.
fall, unnatural.   4. Violent force.

29

All that day she outwore in wandering,
   And gazing on that Chambers ornament,
255 Till that againe the second evening
   Her covered with her sable vestiment,
   Wherewith the worlds faire beautie she hath blent:°   *obscured*
   Then when the second watch⁵ was almost past,
   That brasen dore flew open, and in went
260 Bold Britomart, as she had late forecast,°   *planned*
   Neither of idle shewes, nor of false charmes aghast.°   *terrified*

30

So soone as she was entred, round about
   She cast her eies, to see what was become
   Of all those persons, which she saw without:
265 But lo, they streight° were vanisht all and some,   *immediately*
   Ne living wight she saw in all that roome,
   Save that same woefull Ladie, both whose hands
   Were bounden fast, that did her ill become,
   And her small wast girt round with yron bands,
270 Unto a brasen pillour, by the which she stands.

31

And her before the vile Enchaunter sate,
   Figuring straunge characters of his art,
   With living bloud he those characters wrate,°   *wrote*
   Dreadfully dropping from her dying hart,
275 Seeming transfixed with a cruell dart,
   And all perforce° to make her him to love.   *by force*
   Ah who can love the worker of her smart?
   A thousand charmes he formerly did prove;°   *try*
   Yet thousand charmes could not her stedfast heart remove.

32

280 Soone as that virgin knight he saw in place,
   His wicked bookes in hast he overthrew,
   Not caring his long labours to deface,⁶
   And fiercely ronning to that Lady trew,
   A murdrous knife out of his pocket drew,
285 The which he thought, for villeinous despight,°   *cruelty*
   In her tormented bodie to embrew:°   *plunge*
   But the stout° Damzell to him leaping light,   *fierce*
   His cursèd hand withheld, and maisterèd his might.

33

From her, to whom his fury first he ment,°   *directed*
290 The wicked weapon rashly he did wrest,
   And turning to her selfe his fell intent,
   Unwares° it strooke into her snowie chest,   *suddenly*
   That little drops empurpled her faire brest.

5. From 9 P.M. to midnight.
6. I.e., he did not care if he ruined the spells he has labored over.

Exceeding wroth therewith the virgin grew,
295   Albe° the wound were nothing deepe imprest,   *although*
   And fiercely forth her mortall blade she drew,
To give him the reward for such vile outrage dew.

34

So mightily she smote him, that to ground
   He fell halfe dead; next stroke him should have slaine,
300   Had not the Lady, which by him stood bound,
   Dernely° unto her callèd to abstaine,   *dismally*
   From doing him to dy. For else her paine
   Should be remedilesse, sith none but hee,
   Which wrought it, could the same recure° againe.   *heal*
305 Therewith she stayd her hand, loth stayd to bee;
For life she him envyde,° and longed revenge to see.   *begrudged*

35

And to him said, "Thou wicked man, whose meed°   *reward*
   For so huge mischiefe, and vile villany
   Is death, or if that ought do death exceed,
310   Be sure, that nought may save thee from to dy,
   But if that thou this Dame doe presently
   Restore unto her health, and former state;[7]
   This doe and live, else die undoubtedly."
   He glad of life, that lookt for death but late,°   *just recently*
315 Did yield himselfe right willing to prolong his date.°   *term of life*

36

And rising up, gan streight to overlooke°   *look over*
   Those cursèd leaves, his charmes backe to reverse;
   Full dreadfull things out of that balefull booke
   He red, and measured many a sad verse,[8]
320   That horror gan the virgins hart to perse,°   *pierce*
   And her faire locks up starèd° stiffe on end,   *stood*
   Hearing him those same bloudy lines reherse;[9]
   And all the while he red, she did extend
Her sword high over him if ought he did offend.

37

325 Anon she gan perceive the house to quake,
   And all the dores to rattel round about;
   Yet all that did not her dismaièd make,
   Nor slacke her threatfull hand for daungers dout,[1]
   But still with stedfast eye and courage stout
330 Abode,° to weet° what end would come of all.   *waited/learn*
   At last that mightie chaine, which round about
   Her tender waste was wound, adowne gan fall,
And that great brasen pillour broke in peeces small.

---

7. I.e., you deserve death, or if possible something worse than death, and nothing will save you
from death ("to dy") unless ("But if") you immediately ("presently") restore this lady.
8. I.e., he pronounced in proper meter many distressing verses (incantations).
9. I.e., say over again.
1. I.e., nor relax her threatening hand for fear of
dangers.

38

The cruell steele, which thrild° her dying hart,   *pierced*
335   Fell softly forth, as of his owne accord,
    And the wyde wound, which lately did dispart°   *divide*
    Her bleeding brest, and riven bowels° gored,   *intestines*
    Was closèd up, as it had not bene bored,
    And every part to safety full sound,
340   As she were never hurt, was soone° restored: *immediately*
    Tho° when she felt her selfe to be unbound,   *then*
And perfect hole, prostrate she fell unto the ground.

39

Before Faire Britomart, she fell prostrate,
    Saying, "Ah noble knight, what worthy meed
345   Can wretched Lady, quit from wofull state,
    Yield you in liew² of this your gratious deed?
    Your vertue selfe her owne reward shall breed,
    Even immortall praise, and glory wyde,
    Which I your vassall, by your prowesse freed,
350   Shall through the world make to be notifyde,
And goodly well advance, that goodly well was tryde."³

40

But *Britomart* uprearing her from ground,
    Said, "Gentle Dame, reward enough I weene°   *think*
    For many labours more, then I have found,
355   This, that in safety now I have you seene,
    And meane° of your deliverance have beene: *means*
    Henceforth faire Lady comfort to you take,
    And put away remembrance of late teene;°   *pain*
    In stead thereof know, that your loving Make,°   *mate*
360   Hath no lesse griefe endurèd for your gentle sake."

41

She much was cheard to heare him mentiond,
    Whom of all living wights she loved best.
    Then laid the noble Championesse strong hond
    Upon th' enchaunter, which had her distrest
365   So sore, and with foule outrages opprest:
    With that great chaine, wherewith not long ygo
    He bound that pitteous Lady prisoner, now relest,°   *released*
    Himselfe she bound, more worthy to be so,
And captive with her led to wretchednesse and wo.

42

370   Returning backe, those goodly roomes, which erst°   *before*
    She saw so rich and royally arayd,
    Now vanisht utterly, and cleane subverst°   *overturned*
    She found, and all their glory quite decayd,°   *destroyed*
    That sight of such a chaunge her much dismayd.
375   Thence forth descending to that perlous° Porch,   *perilous*

2. As reward.
3. I.e., as your vassal I will make known ("noti-   fyed") throughout the world and extol ("advaunce")
your virtue, that was so fully tested ("tryde").

Those dreadfull flames she also found delayd,°   *allayed*
And quenchèd quite, like a consumèd torch,
That erst° all entrers wont so cruelly to scorch.   *before*

43

More easie issew now, then entrance late
380   She found: for now that fainèd° dreadfull flame,   *imagined*
Which chokt the porch of that enchaunted gate,
And passage bard to all, that thither came,
Was vanisht quite, as it were not the same,
And gave her leave at pleasure forth to passe.
385   Th' Enchaunter selfe, which all that fraud did frame,
To have efforst° the love of that faire lasse,   *enforced*
Seeing his worke now wasted deepe engrievèd was.

44

But when the victoresse arrivèd there,
Where late she left the pensife Scudamore,
390   With her owne trusty Squire,[4] both full of feare,
Neither of them she found where she them lore:°   *left*
Thereat her noble hart was stonisht sore;
But most faire Amoret, whose gentle spright
Now gan to feede on hope, which she before
395   Conceivèd had, to see her owne deare knight,
Being thereof beguyld was fild with new affright.

45

But he sad° man, when he had long in drede   *sorrowful*
Awayted there for Britomarts returne,
Yet saw her not nor signe of her good speed,°   *success*
400   His expectation to despaire did turne,
Misdeeming° sure that her those flames did   *mistakenly thinking*
burne;
And therefore gan advize° with her old Squire,   *consult*
Who her deare nourslings losse no lesse did mourne,
Thence to depart for further aide t' enquire:
405   Where let them wend at will, whilest here I doe respire.[5]

From Amoretti[1]

Sonnet 1

Happy ye leaves when as those lilly hands,
Which hold my life in their dead doing[2] might,

---

4. Her nurse Glauce was her squire.
5. Take a breath, rest from my labors. In the 1590 edition this book, and the poem, ended with the happy reunion of Scudamore and Amoret. But in the 1596 edition Spenser made a bridge to his 3 added books by replacing the earlier ending with stanzas 43–45, as given here.
1. I.e., "little loves" or "little love poems." They are sonnets to a woman named Elizabeth—probably Elizabeth Boyle, who became Spenser's sec-
ond wife. The sequence, or cycle, tells of a courtship (*Epithalamion*, with which they were published, is a song for a wedding). The *Amoretti* draws, like other sonnet cycles, upon characteristic and conventional themes and conceits; what is characteristically Spenserian about them is his yoking of the spirit and the flesh. The rhyme scheme is *abab bcbc cdcd ee*, a difficult pattern requiring 4 words for 2 of the rhymes.
2. I.e., killing.

Shall handle you and hold in loves soft bands,
Lyke captives trembling at the victors sight.
5   And happy lines, on which with starry light,
Those lamping° eyes will deigne sometimes to look   *flashing*
And reade the sorrowes of my dying spright,°   *spirit*
Written with teares in harts close° bleeding book.   *secret*
And happy rymes bathed in the sacred brooke,
10 Of Helicon³ whence she derivèd is,
When ye behold that Angels blessed looke,
My soules long lackèd foode, my heavens blis.
Leaves, lines, and rymes, seeke her to please alone,
Whom if ye please, I care for other none.

Sonnet 34

Lyke as a ship that through the ocean wyde,
By conduct of some star doth make her way,
Whenas a storme hath dimd her trusty guyde,
Out of her course doth wander far astray.
5   So I whose star, that wont with her bright ray,
Me to direct, with cloudes is overcast,
Doe wander now in darknesse and dismay,
Through hidden perils round about me plast.°   *placed*
Yet hope I well, that when this storme is past
10 My Helice⁴ the lodestar of my lyfe
Will shine again, and looke on me at last,
With lovely light to cleare my cloudy grief.
Till then I wander carefull° comfortlesse,   *full of cares*
In secret sorow and sad pensivenesse.

Sonnet 37

What guyle is this, that those her golden tresses,
She doth attyre under a net of gold:
And with sly° skill so cunningly them dresses,   *clever*
That which is gold or heare,° may scarse be told?   *hair*
5   Is it that mens frayle eyes, which gaze too bold,
She may entangle in that golden snare:
And being caught may craftily enfold,
Theyr weaker harts, which are not wel aware?
Take heed therefore, myne eyes, how ye doe stare
10 Henceforth too rashly on that guilefull net,
In which if ever ye entrappèd are,
Out of her bands ye by no means shall get.
Fondnesse° it were for any being free,   *foolishness*
To covet fetters, though they golden bee.

---

3. The "sacred brooke" is the Hippocrene, which   to the Muses.
flows from Mount Helicon, the mountain sacred   4. The Big Dipper or North Star.

Sonnet 54

Of this worlds theatre in which we stay,
My love like the spectator ydly sits
Beholding me that all the pageants° play,　　　*roles*
Disguysing diversly my troubled wits.
5　Sometimes I joy when glad occasion fits,
And mask in myrth lyke to a comedy:
Soone after when my joy to sorrow flits,
I waile and make my woes a tragedy.
Yet she, beholding me with constant eye,
10　Delights not in my merth nor rues my smart:
But when I laugh she mocks, and when I cry
She laughs and hardens evermore her heart.
What then can move her? if nor merth nor mone,°　　　*moan*
She is no woman, but a sencelesse stone.

Sonnet 64[5]

Comming to kisse her lyps (such grace I found)
Me seemd I smelt a gardin of sweet flowres
That dainty odours from them threw around
For damzels fit to decke their lovers bowres.
5　Her lips did smell lyke unto gillyflowers,°　　　*carnations*
Her ruddy cheeks like unto roses red;
Her snowy browes lyke budded bellamoures,°　　　*bellflowers*
Her lovely eyes like pincks but newly spred,
Her goodly bosome lyke a strawberry bed,
10　Her neck lyke to a bounch of cullambynes;
Her brest lyke lillyes ere theyr leaves be shed,
Her nipples lyke yong blossomd jessemynes.°　　　*jasmines*
Such fragrant flowres doe give most odorous smell,
But her sweet odour did them all excell.

Sonnet 65

The doubt which ye misdeeme, fayre love, is vaine,
That fondly feare to loose your liberty,
When loosing one, two liberties ye gayne,
And make him bond that bondage earst° dyd fly.　　　*formerly*
5　Sweet be the bands, the which true love doth tye,
Without constraynt or dread of any ill:
The gentle birde feels no captivity
Within her cage, but singes and feeds her fill.
There pride dare not approch, nor discord spill°　　　*destroy*
10　The league twixt them, that loyal love hath bound;
But simple truth and mutuall good will,

5. Much of the imagery of this sonnet is imitated from the Song of Solomon 4.10–16.

Seekes with sweet peace to salve each others wound.
There fayth doth fearlesse dwell in brasen towre,
And spotlesse pleasure builds her sacred bowre.

Sonnet 67[6]

Lyke as a huntsman after weary chace,
Seeing the game from him escapt away,
Sits downe to rest him in some shady place,
With panting hounds beguiled of their pray,
So after long pursuit and vaine assay,
When I all weary had the chace forsooke,
The gentle deare returnd the selfe-same way,
Thinking to quench her thirst at the next brooke.
There she beholding me with mylder looke,
Sought not to fly, but fearelesse still did bide,
Till I in hand her yet halfe trembling tooke,
And with her owne goodwill hir fyrmely tyde.
Strange thing me seemd to see a beast so wyld,
So goodly wonne with her owne will beguyld.°   entangled

Sonnet 68

Most glorious Lord of lyfe, that on this day,[7]
Didst make thy triumph over death and sin:
And having harrowed hell,[8] didst bring away
Captivity thence captive us to win:
5   This joyous day, deare Lord, with joy begin,
And grant that we for whom thou diddest dye
Being with thy deare blood clene washt from sin,
May live for ever in felicity.
And that thy love we weighing worthily,
10 May likewise love thee for the same againe:
And for thy sake that all lyke deare didst buy,
With love may one another entertayne.
So let us love, deare love, lyke as we ought,
Love is the lesson which the Lord us taught.[9]

Sonnet 74

Most happy letters framed by skilfull trade,°   practice
With which that happy name was first desynd:
The which three times thrise happy hath me made,
With guifts of body, fortune and of mind.
5   The first my being to me gave by kind,°   nature

6. An imitation of Petrarch's sonnet 190, *Una candida cerva*, but with a very different ending.
7. Easter Day.
8. In the apocryphal gospels, Christ descended into hell and led out those who had lived before his time that deserved to be saved. "Captivity thence captive" is a biblical phrase, as in Judges 5.12 and Ephesians 4.8.
9. Cf. John 15.12: "This is my commandment, That ye love one another, as I have loved you."

From mothers womb derived by dew descent,
The second is my sovereigne Queene most kind,
That honour and large richesse to me lent.
The third my love, my lives last ornament,
10   By whom my spirit out of dust was raysed:
To speake her prayse and glory excellent,
Of all alive most worthy to be praysed.
Ye three Elizabeths for ever live,
That three such graces did unto me give.

Sonnet 75

One day I wrote her name upon the strand,°   *beach*
But came the waves and washèd it away:
Agayne I wrote it with a second hand,
But came the tyde, and made my paynes his pray.°   *prey*
5   "Vayne man," sayd she, "that doest in vaine assay,°   *attempt*
A mortall thing so to immortalize,
For I my selve shall lyke to this decay,
And eek° my name bee wypèd out lykewize."   *also*
"Not so," quod° I, "let baser things devize,°   *quoth/contrive*
10   To dy in dust, but you shall live by fame:
My verse your vertues rare shall eternize,
And in the heavens wryte your glorious name.
Where whenas death shall all the world subdew,
Our love shall live, and later life renew."

Sonnet 79

Men call you fayre, and you doe credit° it,   *believe*
For that your selfe ye dayly such doe see:
But the trew fayre,° that is the gentle wit,   *beauty*
And vertuous mind, is much more praysd of me.
5   For all the rest, how ever fayre it be,
Shall turne to nought and loose that glorious hew:°   *form*
But onely that is permanent and free
From frayle corruption, that doth flesh ensew.°   *outlast*
That is true beautie: that doth argue you
10   To be divine and borne of heavenly seed:
Derived from that fayre Spirit,[1] from whom al true
And perfect beauty did at first proceed.
He onely fayre, and what he fayre hath made:
All other fayre, lyke flowres, untymely fade.

                                    1595

---

1. I.e., God.

Epithalamion   An epithalamion is a wedding song or poem; its Greek
name conveys that it was sung on the threshold of the bridal chamber. The
genre was widely practiced by the Latin poets, particularly Catullus. Common elements are the invocation to the Muses, the bringing home of the
bride, the singing and dancing at the wedding party, and the preparations
for the wedding night. The poem's merit is not in its "originality" but in its
evocative commingling of the conventions, with which Spenser blends his
own Irish setting and native folklore.

The *Epithalamion* has a complex structure. First there is an introductory
stanza, then two 10-stanza sections on each side of the two central stanzas
about the church ceremony itself. Each of the 10-stanza sections is divided
into units of 3-4-3. As A. Kent Hieatt has pointed out in his book, *Short
Time's Endless Monument* (1960), the poem also has a numerical structure
that reinforces the motif of the passage of time. For example, the poem has
exactly 365 long lines (composed of 5 or more metrical feet) matching the
number of days in the year. There are 24 stanzas, counting the envoy,
matching the hours of one day and night. Of these stanzas, the first 16
describe the course of the day, in which the woods echo the various sounds;
the last 8 describe the night, a time of silence in which the woods no longer
echo. At the summer solstice (cf. line 266 and note) in the latitude of Ireland, night falls after 16 hours of daylight.

The subtle time structure serves to reinforce the idea implicit throughout
the poem that this marriage has reference to all marriages. It emphasizes the
endless cycle of time, measured by the passing of the hours and the years—
as against which marriage, as a Christian sacrament, stands firm, "eterne in
mutabilitie."

Epithalamion

Ye learned sisters which have oftentimes
Beene to me ayding, others to adorne:[1]
Whom ye thought worthy of your gracefull rymes,
That even the greatest did not greatly scorne

5   To heare theyr names sung in your simple layes,
But joyèd in theyr prayse.
And when ye list your owne mishaps to mourne,
Which death, or love, or fortunes wreck did rayse,
Your string could soone to sadder tenor° turne,   *mood*

10   And teach the woods and waters to lament
Your dolefull dreriment.°   *sorrow*
Now lay those sorrowfull complaints aside,
And having all your heads with girland crownd,
Helpe me mine owne loves prayses to resound,

15   Ne let the same of° any be envide: *by*
So Orpheus did for his owne bride,[2]

1. I.e., to write poems in praise of others. The
"learned sisters" are the Muses.
2. Orpheus, archetype of the poet in classical

antiquity, was equally famous for his love for his
wife Eurydice.

So I unto my selfe alone will sing,
The woods shall to me answer and my Eccho ring.

Early before the worlds light giving lampe,
His golden beame upon the hils doth spred,
Having disperst the nights unchearefull dampe,
Doe ye awake, and with fresh lustyhed°   *vigor*
Go to the bowre° of my belovèd love,   *bedchamber*
My truest turtle dove,
Bid her awake; for Hymen[3] is awake,
And long since ready forth his maske to move,
With his bright Tead[4] that flames with many a flake,°   *spark*
And many a bachelor to waite on him,
In theyr fresh garments trim.
Bid her awake therefore and soone her dight,°   *dress*
For lo the wishèd day is come at last,
That shall for al the paynes and sorrowes past,
Pay to her usury° of long delight: *interest*
And whylest she doth her dight,
Doe ye to her of joy and solace sing,
That all the woods may answer and your Eccho ring.

Bring with you all the Nymphes that you can heare[5]
Both of the rivers and the forrests greene:
And of the sea that neighbours to her neare,
Al with gay girlands goodly wel beseene.[6]
And let them also with them bring in hand,
Another gay girland
For my fayre love of lillyes and of roses,
Bound truelove wize[7] with a blew silke riband.
And let them make great store of bridale poses,°   *posies*
And let them eeke° bring store of other flowers   *also*
To deck the bridale bowers.
And let the ground whereas her foot shall tread,
For feare the stones her tender foot should wrong
Be strewed with fragrant flowers all along,
And diapred lyke the discolored mead.[8]
Which done, doe at her chamber dore awayt,
For she will waken strayt,°   *straightway*
The whiles doe ye this song unto her sing,
The woods shall to you answer and your Eccho ring.

Ye Nymphes of Mulla[9] which with careful heed,
The silver scaly trouts doe tend full well,

---

3. The god of marriage, who leads a "maske" or procession at weddings.
4. A ceremonial torch, associated with marriages since classical times.
5. I.e., that can hear you.
6. I.e., beautified.

7. I.e., in a love knot.
8. I.e., ornamented like the many-colored meadow.
9. The vale of Mulla, near Spenser's home in Ireland.

And greedy pikes which use therein to feed,
(Those trouts and pikes all others doo excell)
60   And ye likewise, which keepe the rushy lake,
Where none doo fishes take,
Bynd up the locks the which hang scatterd light,
And in his waters which your mirror make,
Behold your faces as the christall bright,
65   That when you come whereas° my love doth lie,   *where*
No blemish she may spie.
And eke ye lightfoot mayds which keepe the deere,[1]
That on the hoary mountayne use to towre,
And the wylde wolves which seeke them to devoure,
70   With your steele darts doo chace from comming neer
Be also present heere,
To helpe to decke her and to help to sing,
That all the woods may answer and your Eccho ring.

Wake, now my love, awake; for it is time,
75   The Rosy Morne long since left Tithones bed,[2]
All ready to her silver coche° to clyme,   *coach*
And Phoebus gins to shew his glorious hed.
Hark how the cheerefull birds do chaunt theyr laies
And carroll of loves praise.
80   The merry Larke hir mattins° sings aloft,   *morning prayers*
The thrush replyes, the Mavis descant[3] playes,
The Ouzell shrills, the Ruddock warbles soft,
So goodly all agree with sweet consent,
To this dayes merriment.
85   Ah my deere love why doe ye sleepe thus long,
When meeter° were that ye should now awake,   *more fitting*
T' awayt the comming of your joyous make,°   *mate*
And hearken to the birds lovelearnèd song,
The deawy leaves among.
90   For they of joy and pleasance to you sing,
That all the woods them answer and theyr Eccho ring.

My love is now awake out of her dreame,
And her fayre eyes like stars that dimmèd were
With darksome cloud, now shew theyr goodly beams
95   More bright then Hesperus° his head doth rere.   *evening star*
Come now ye damzels, daughters of delight,
Helpe quickly her to dight,°   *adorn*
But first come ye fayre houres which were begot

---

1. I.e., all wild animals, kept by the forest nymphs.
To "towre" (a falconry term) is to occupy heights.
2. See Song of Songs 2.10–13: "Rise up, my love,
my fair one, and come away. For, lo, the winter
is past, the rain is over and gone; the flowers appear
on the earth; the time of the singing of birds is
come. . . ." In myth, Tithones is the aged husband of Aurora, the dawn.
3. A melody or counterpoint written above a
musical theme—a soprano obbligato. The "Mavis"
is the thrush. The "Ouzell" is the blackbird (which
sings in England); the "Ruddock," the European
robin. The birds' concert is a convention of medieval love poetry.

In Joves sweet paradice, of Day and Night,
100   Which doe the seasons of the yeare allot,
And al that ever in this world is fayre
Doe make and still repayre.°   *continuously*
And ye three handmayds of the Cyprian Queene,[4]
The which doe still adorne her beauties pride,
105   Helpe to addorne my beautifullest bride:
And as ye her array, still throw betweene°   *now and then*
Some graces to be seene,
And as ye use to Venus, to her sing,
The whiles the woods shal answer and your Eccho ring.

110   Now is my love all ready forth to come,
Let all the virgins therefore well awayt,
And ye fresh boyes that tend upon her groome
Prepare your selves; for he is comming strayt.
Set all your things in seemely good aray°   *order*
115   Fit for so joyfull day,
The joyfulst day that ever sunne did see.
Faire Sun, shew forth thy favourable ray,
And let thy lifull° heat not fervent be   *lifegiving*
For feare of burning her sunshyny face,
120   Her beauty to disgrace.
O fayrest Phoebus, father of the Muse,[5]
If ever I did honour thee aright,
Or sing the thing, that mote° thy mind delight,   *might*
Doe not thy servants simple boone° refuse,   *request*
125   But let this day let this one day be myne,
Let all the rest be thine.
Then I thy soverayne prayses loud wil sing,
That all the woods shal answer and theyr Eccho ring.

Harke how the Minstrels gin° to shrill aloud   *begin*
130   Their merry Musick that resounds from far,
The pipe, the tabor, and the trembling Croud,[6]
That well agree withouten breach or jar.°   *discord*
But most of all the Damzels doe delite,
When they their tymbrels° smyte,   *tambourines*
135   And thereunto doe daunce and carrol sweet,
That all the sences they doe ravish quite,
The whyles the boyes run up and downe the street,
Crying aloud with strong confusèd noyce,
As if it were one voyce.
140   *Hymen iô Hymen, Hymen*[7] they do shout,

---

4. The Graces attending on Venus ("Cyprian Queene"), representing brightness, joy, and bloom.
5. Phoebus (Apollo), god of the sun, was also father of the 9 muses.
6. Primitive fiddle; the "tabor" is a small drum.

Spenser here designates Irish, not classical, instruments and music for the classical masque or ballet.
7. The name of the god of marriage, used as a conventional exclamation at weddings.

That even to the heavens theyr shouting shrill
Doth reach, and all the firmament doth fill,
To which the people standing all about,
As in approvance doe thereto applaud
145   And loud advaunce her laud,°   praise
And evermore they *Hymen Hymen* sing,
That all the woods them answer and theyr Eccho ring.

Loe where she comes along with portly° pace   stately
Lyke Phoebe from her chamber of the East,
150   Arysing forth to run her mighty race,[8]
Clad all in white, that seemes° a virgin best.   suits
So well it her beseems that ye would weene
Some angell she had beene.
Her long loose yellow locks lyke golden wyre,
155   Sprinckled with perle, and perling° flowres a tweene,   winding
Doe lyke a golden mantle her attyre,
And being crownèd with a girland greene,
Seeme lyke some mayden Queene.
Her modest eyes abashèd to behold
160   So many gazers, as on her do stare,
Upon the lowly ground affixèd are.
Ne dare lift up her countenance too bold,
But blush to heare her prayses sung so loud,
So farre from being proud.
165   Nathlesse doe ye still loud her prayses sing.
That all the woods may answer and your Eccho ring.

Tell me ye merchants daughters did ye see
So fayre a creature in your towne before,
So sweet, so lovely, and so mild as she,
170   Adornd with beautyes grace and vertues store,
Her goodly eyes lyke Saphyres shining bright,
Her forehead yvory white,
Her cheekes lyke apples which the sun hath rudded,°   made red
Her lips lyke cherryes charming men to byte,
175   Her brest like to a bowle of creame uncrudded,°   uncurdled
Her paps lyke lyllies budded,
Her snowie necke lyke to a marble towre,
And all her body like a pallace fayre,
Ascending uppe with many a stately stayre,
180   To honors seat and chastities sweet bowre.[9]
Why stand ye still ye virgins in amaze,
Upon her so to gaze,
Whiles ye forget your former lay to sing,
To which the woods did answer and your Eccho ring.

---

8. Phoebe is the moon, a virgin like the bride; the reference to her anticipates the night.
9. The head, where the higher faculties are. The catalogue of qualities is a convention in love poetry. Cf. also The Song of Solomon 4–8.

185　But if ye saw that which no eyes can see,
　　The inward beauty of her lively spright,°　　　　　　soul
　　Garnisht with heavenly guifts of high degree,
　　Much more then would ye wonder at that sight,
　　And stand astonisht lyke to those which red°　　　　saw
190　Medusaes mazeful hed.[1]
　　There dwels sweet love and constant chastity,
　　Unspotted fayth and comely womanhood,
　　Regard of honour and mild modesty,
　　There vertue raynes as Queene in royal throne,
195　And giveth lawes alone.
　　The which the base° affections doe obay,　　　　　lower
　　And yeeld theyr services unto her will,
　　Ne thought of thing uncomely ever may
　　Thereto approch to tempt her mind to ill.
200　Had ye once seene these her celestial threasures,
　　And unrevealèd pleasures,
　　Then would ye wonder and her prayses sing,
　　That all the woods should answer and your Eccho ring.

　　Open the temple gates unto my love,
205　Open them wide that she may enter in,[2]
　　And all the postes adorne as doth behove,[3]
　　And all the pillours deck with girlands trim,
　　For to recyve this Saynt with honour dew,
　　That commeth in to you.
210　With trembling steps and humble reverence,
　　She commeth in, before th' almighties vew,
　　Of her ye virgins learne obedience,
　　When so ye come into those holy places,
　　To humble your proud faces:
215　Bring her up to th' high altar, that she may
　　The sacred ceremonies there partake,
　　The which do endless matrimony make,
　　And let the roring Organs loudly play
　　The praises of the Lord in lively notes,
220　The whiles with hollow throates
　　The Choristers the joyous Antheme sing,
　　That all the woods may answere and theyr Eccho ring.

　　Behold whiles she before the altar stands
　　Hearing the holy priest that to her speakes
225　And blesseth her with his two happy hands,
　　How the red roses flush up in her cheekes,
　　And the pure snow with goodly vermill° stayne,　　vermilion

1. Medusa, one of the Gorgons, had serpents instead of hair (hence a "mazeful hed"): the effect on a beholder was to turn him to stone.
2. Cf. Psalm 24.7: "Lift up your heads, O ye gates; and be ye lift up, ye everlasting doors; and the King of glory shall come in."
3. As is proper. The doorposts were trimmed for weddings in classical times, and the custom was often referred to in classical and medieval love poetry.

Like crimsin dyde in grayne,°   *fast color*
That even th' Angels which continually,
230 About the sacred Altare doe remaine,
Forget their service and about her fly,
Ofte peeping in her face that seemes more fayre,
The more they on it stare.
But her sad° eyes still fastened on the ground,   *modest*
235 Are governèd with goodly modesty,
That suffers not one looke to glaunce awry,
Which may let in a little thought unsownd.
Why blush ye love to give to me your hand,
The pledge of all our band?°   *bond, tie*
240 Sing ye sweet Angels, Alleluya sing,
That all the woods may answere and your Eccho ring.

Now al is done; bring home the bride againe,
Bring home the triumph of our victory,
Bring home with you the glory of her gaine,[4]
245 With joyance bring her and with jollity.
Never had man more joyfull day then this,
Whom heaven would heape with blis.
Make feast therefore now all this live long day,
This day for ever to me holy is,
250 Poure out the wine without restraint or stay,
Poure not by cups, but by the belly full,
Poure out to all that wull,°   *want it*
And sprinkle all the postes and wals with wine,
That they may sweat, and drunken be withall.
255 Crowne ye God Bacchus[5] with a coronall,°   *flower garland*
And Hymen also crowne with wreathes of vine,
And let the Graces daunce unto the rest;
For they can doo it best:
The whiles the maydens doe theyr carroll sing,
260 To which the woods shall answer and theyr Eccho ring.

Ring ye the bels, ye young men of the towne,
And leave your wonted° labors for this day: *usual*
This day is holy; doe ye write it downe,
That ye for ever it remember may.
265 This day the sunne is in his chiefest hight,
With Barnaby the bright,[6]
From whence declining daily by degrees,
He somewhat loseth of his heat and light,
When once the Crab[7] behind his back he sees.
270 But for this time it ill ordainèd was,
To chose the longest day in all the yeare,

4. I.e., the glory of gaining her.
5. God of wine.
6. St. Barnabas' Day, at the time of the summer solstice.

7. The constellation Cancer between Gemini and Leo. The sun, passing through the zodiac, leaves the Crab behind toward the end of July.

And shortest night, when longest fitter weare:
Yet never day so long, but late° would passe.   *at last*
Ring ye the bels, to make it weare away,
275 And bonefiers make all day,
And daunce about them, and about them sing:
That all the woods may answer, and your Eccho ring.

Ah when will this long weary day have end,
And lende me leave to come unto my love?
280 How slowly do the houres theyr numbers spend?
How slowly does sad Time his feathers move?
Hast thee O fayrest Planet to thy home
Within the Westerne fome:
Thy tyred steedes long since have need of rest.[8]
285 Long though it be, at last I see it gloome,
And the bright evening star[9] with golden creast
Appeare out of the East.
Fayre childe of beauty, glorious lampe of love
That all the host of heaven in rankes doost lead,
290 And guydest lovers through the nightès dread,
How chearefully thou lookest from above,
And seemst to laugh atweene thy twinkling light
As joying in the sight
Of these glad many which for joy doe sing,
295 That all the woods them answer and theyr Eccho ring.

Now ceasse ye damsels your delights forepast;
Enough is it, that all the day was youres:
Now day is doen, and night is nighing fast:
Now bring the Bryde into the brydall boures.
300 Now night is come, now soone her disaray,
And in her bed her lay;
Lay her in lillies and in violets,
And silken courteins over her display,°   *spread*
And odourd sheetes, and Arras° coverlets.   *tapestry*
305 Behold how goodly my faire love does ly
In proud humility;
Like unto Maia,[1] when as Jove her tooke,
In Tempe, lying on the flowry gras,
Twixt sleepe and wake, after she weary was,
310 With bathing in the Acidalian brooke.
Now it is night, ye damsels may be gon,
And leave my love alone,
And leave likewise your former lay to sing:
The woods no more shall answere, nor your Eccho ring.

---

8. The sun's chariot completes its daily course in   9. Hesperus
the western sea.   1. The eldest and most beautiful of the Pleiades.

315   Now welcome night, thou night so long expected,
        That long daies labour doest at last defray,°   *pay*
        And all my cares, which cruell love collected,
        Hast sumd in one, and cancellèd for aye:
        Spread thy broad wing over my love and me,
320   That no man may us see,
        And in thy sable mantle us enwrap,
        From feare of perrill and foule horror free.
        Let no false treason seeke us to entrap,
        Nor any dread disquiet once annoy
325   The safety of our joy:
        But let the night be calme and quietsome,
        Without tempestuous storms or sad afray:
        Lyke as when Jove with fayre Alcmena[2] lay,
        When he begot the great Tirynthian groome:
330   Or lyke as when he with thy selfe[3] did lie,
        And begot Majesty.
        And let the mayds and yongmen cease to sing:
        Ne let the woods them answer, nor theyr Eccho ring.

        Let no lamenting cryes, nor dolefull teares,
335   Be heard all night within nor yet without.
        Ne let false whispers, breeding hidden feares,
        Breake gentle sleepe with misconceivèd dout.°   *fear*
        Let no deluding dreames, nor dreadful sights
        Make sudden sad affrights;
340   Ne let housefyres, nor lightnings helpelesse harmes,
        Ne let the Pouke,[4] nor other evill sprights,
        Ne let mischivous witches with theyr charmes,
        Ne let hob Goblins, names whose sence we see not,
        Fray° us with things that be not.   *terrify*
345   Let not the shriech Oule, nor the Storke be heard:
        Nor the night Raven that still° deadly yels,[5]   *continuously*
        Nor damnèd ghosts cald up with mighty spels,
        Nor griesly° vultures make us once affeard: *horrid*
        Ne let th' unpleasant Quyre of Frogs still croking
350   Make us to wish theyr choking.
        Let none of these theyr drery accents sing;
        Ne let the woods them answer, nor theyr Eccho ring.

        But let stil Silence trew night watches keepe,
        That sacred peace may in assurance rayne,
355   And tymely sleep, when it is tyme to sleepe,
        May poure his limbs forth on your pleasant playne,

2. The mother of Hercules ("the great Tirynthian groome"). Jove made that one night last as long as three.
3. I.e., night. This is Spenser's own myth.
4. Puck, Robin Goodfellow—here more powerful and evil than Shakespeare made him.
5. The owl and the night raven were birds of ill omen; the stork, in Chaucer's *Parliament of Fowls*, is called an avenger of adultery. "Still": always.

The whiles an hundred little wingèd loves,[6]
Like divers fethered doves,
Shall fly and flutter round about your bed,
360   And in the secret darke, that none reproves,
Their prety stealthes shal worke, and snares shal spread
To filch away sweet snatches of delight,
Conceald through covert night.
Ye sonnes of Venus, play your sports at will,
365   For greedy pleasure, carelesse of your toyes,°   *amorous dallying*
Thinks more upon her paradise of joyes,
Then what ye do, albe it good or ill.
All night therefore attend your merry play,
For it will soone be day:
370   Now none doth hinder you, that say or sing,
Ne will the woods now answer, nor your Eccho ring.

Who is the same, which at my window peepes?
Or whose is that faire face, that shines so bright,
Is it not Cinthia,[7] she that never sleepes,
375   But walkes about high heaven al the night?
O fayrest goddesse, do thou not envy
My love with me to spy:
For thou likewise didst love, though now unthought,°   *unsuspected*
And for a fleece of woll,° which privily,   *wool*
380   The Latmian shephard[8] once unto thee brought,
His pleasures with thee wrought,
Therefore to us be favorable now;
And sith of wemens labours thou hast charge,[9]
And generation goodly dost enlarge,
385   Encline thy will t' effect our wishfull vow,
And the chast wombe informe° with timely seed,   *give life to*
That may our comfort breed:
Till which we cease our hopefull hap[1] to sing,
Ne let the woods us answer, nor our Eccho ring.

390   And thou great Juno, which with awful might
The lawes of wedlock still dost patronize,
And the religion° of the faith first plight   *sanctity*
With sacred rites hast taught to solemnize:
And eeke° for comfort often callèd art   *also*
395   Of women in their smart,°   *labor*
Eternally bind thou this lovely band,
And all thy blessings unto us impart.
And thou glad Genius,[2] in whose gentle hand,
The bridale bowre and geniall bed remaine,

---

6. Cupids (or amoretti).
7. I.e., the moon.
8. Endymion, beloved by the moon. The "fleece of woll," however, comes from another story—that of Pan's enticement of the moon.

9. Diana (the moon, "Cinthia") is, as Lucina, patroness of births; the "labours" are, of course, those of childbirth.
1. The fortune we hope for.
2. Patron of sex, pregnancy, reproduction.

400 Without blemish or staine,
And the sweet pleasures of theyr loves delight
With secret ayde doest succour and supply,
Till they bring forth the fruitfull progeny,
Send us the timely fruit of this same night.
405 And thou fayre Hebe,[3] and thou Hymen free,
Grant that it may so be.
Til which we cease your further prayse to sing,
Ne any woods shall answer, nor your Eccho ring.

And ye high heavens, the temple of the gods,
410 In which a thousand torches flaming bright
Doe burne, that to us wretched earthly clods,
In dreadful darknesse lend desirèd light;
And all ye powers which in the same remayne,
More than we men can fayne,°   *imagine*
415 Poure out your blessing on us plentiously,
And happy influence upon us raine,
That we may raise a large posterity,
Which from the earth, which they may long possesse,
With lasting happinesse,
420 Up to your haughty pallaces may mount,
And for the guerdon° of theyr glorious merit   *reward*
May heavenly tabernacles there inherit,
Of blessed Saints for to increase the count.
So let us rest, sweet love, in hope of this,
425 And cease till then our tymely joyes to sing,
The woods no more us answer, nor our Eccho ring.

Song made in lieu of many ornaments,
With which my love should duly have bene dect,°   *adorned*
Which cutting off through hasty accidents,
430 Ye would not stay your dew time to expect,°   *await*
But promist both to recompens,
Be unto her a goodly ornament,
And for short time an endlesse moniment.[4]

1595

3. Patron of youth and freedom.
4. The envoy is traditionally apologetic in tone: the poem is offered as a substitute for wedding presents ("ornaments") that did not arrive in time for the wedding. But this elaborate poem is itself a "goodly ornament," for it stands as a timeless monument of art to the passing day which it celebrates.

SIR WALTER RALEGH
1552-1618

The brilliant and versatile Ralegh was a soldier, courtier, philosopher, explorer and colonist, student of science, historian, and poet. He is popularly known now as the founder of Virginia and the introducer of tobacco into Europe, but in his own time he was known for his violent temper, his dramatic sense of life, his extravagant dress, and his great favor with Queen Elizabeth, interrupted in 1592 when he seduced, and then married, one of her ladies-in-waiting. His long poem to the queen, *The Ocean to Cynthia*, was not published but remains in fragments of manuscript, one of more than five hundred lines. Ralegh did publish a few shorter poems, mostly commendatory sonnets, including two to Spenser, whom he visited in Ireland and brought to court in England. His reply to Marlowe's *Passionate Shepherd* circulated widely. His own poem *The Lie*, with its attack on social classes and institutions, in turn provoked many answers.

As a soldier and sailor Ralegh fought against Spain and he retained a bitter hatred of that country all his life. When James came to the throne in 1603, with a pacific policy, he threw Ralegh into the Tower of London on trumped-up charges of treason. There he remained for the rest of his life, except for the ill-fated last voyage to Guiana in 1617. In prison he wrote his long, unfinished *History of the World*; it confines itself to the earliest times and does not deal with recent events because, as Ralegh remarked, he who follows truth too closely at the heels might get kicked in the teeth. Ralegh intended to dedicate his great book to Henry, Prince of Wales, his most powerful friend, who said "Only my father would keep such a bird in a cage." But Prince Henry died in 1612.

Ralegh was a passionate man, like Hotspur and Hamlet. In fact, he was, like them, something of an actor, and he saw the world as his stage. His zeal and passion earned him enemies. Yet by 1618 popular sympathy was so much in his favor that, as the historian Trevelyan said, "the ghost of Ralegh pursued the House of Stuart to the scaffold." On his own scaffold Ralegh described himself as "a seafaring man, a soldier and a courtier," but he was described by his friend the poet Spenser as "the sommers nightingale" who

tooke in hond°	*hand*
My pipe, before that aemulèd of° many,	*was imitated by*
And plaid thereon; (for well that skil he cond°)	*knew*
Himself as skilfull in that art as any.	

The Nymph's Reply to the Shepherd

> If all the world and love were young,
> And truth in every shepherd's tongue,
> These pretty pleasures might me move
> To live with thee and be thy love.
>
> Time drives the flocks from field to fold   5
> When rivers rage and rocks grow cold,
> And Philomel[1] becometh dumb;
> The rest complains of cares to come.
>
> The flowers do fade, and wanton fields
> To wayward winter reckoning yields;   10

1. The nightingale.

A honey tongue, a heart of gall,
Is fancy's spring, but sorrow's fall.

Thy gowns, thy shoes, thy beds of roses,
Thy cap, thy kirtle,[2] and thy posies
Soon break, soon wither, soon forgotten—   15
In folly ripe, in reason rotten.

Thy belt of straw and ivy buds,
Thy coral clasps and amber studs,
All these in me no means can move
To come to thee and be thy love.   20

But could youth last and love still breed,
Had joys no date[3] nor age no need,
Then these delights my mind might move
To live with thee and be thy love.

[On the Life of Man]

What is our life? a play of passion;
Our mirth the music of division;[1]
Our mothers' wombs the tiring-houses[2] be
Where we are dressed for this short comedy.
Heaven the judicious sharp spectator is,   5
That sits and marks still who doth act amiss;
Our graves that hide us from the searching sun
Are like drawn curtains when the play is done.
Thus march we, playing, to our latest rest,
Only we die in earnest—that's no jest.   10

1612

[Sir Walter Ralegh to His Son]

Three things there be that prosper up apace
And flourish, whilst they grow asunder far,
But on a day, they meet all in one place,
And when they meet, they one another mar;
And they be these: the wood, the weed, the wag.   5
The wood is that which makes the gallow tree;
The weed is that which strings the hangman's bag;
The wag, my pretty knave, betokeneth thee.
Mark well, dear boy, whilst these assemble not,

---

2. Skirt, outer petticoat.
3. Ending.
1. The more rapid accompaniment to, or varia-

tion on, a musical theme.
2. Dressing rooms in an Elizabethan theater.

Green springs the tree, hemp grows, the wag is wild,   10
But when they meet, it makes the timber rot;
It frets the halter, and it chokes the child.
Then bless thee, and beware, and let us pray
We part not with thee at this meeting day.

ca. 1600

The Lie

Go, soul, the body's guest,
Upon a thankless errand;
Fear not to touch the best;
The truth shall be thy warrant.
Go, since I needs must die,   5
And give the world the lie.

Say to the court, it glows
And shines like rotten wood;
Say to the church, it shows
What's good, and doth no good.   10
If church and court reply,
Then give them both the lie.

Tell potentates, they live
Acting by others' action;
Not loved unless they give,   15
Not strong but by a faction.
If potentates reply,
Give potentates the lie.

Tell men of high condition,
That manage the estate,   20
Their purpose is ambition,
Their practice only hate.
And if they once reply,
Then give them all the lie.

Tell them that brave it[1] most,   25
They beg for more by spending,
Who, in their greatest cost,
Seek nothing but commending.
And if they make reply,
Then give them all the lie.   30

Tell zeal it wants devotion;
Tell love it is but lust;
Tell time it is but motion;

1. I.e., those who spend much on clothes.

Tell flesh it is but dust.
And wish them not reply,   35
For thou must give the lie.

Tell age it daily wasteth;
Tell honor how it alters;
Tell beauty how she blasteth;
Tell favor how it falters.   40
And as they shall reply,
Give every one the lie.

Tell wit how much it wrangles
In tickle[2] points of niceness;
Tell wisdom she entangles   45
Herself in overwiseness.
And when they do reply,
Straight give them both the lie.

Tell physic of her boldness;
Tell skill it is pretension;   50
Tell charity of coldness;
Tell law it is contention.
And as they do reply,
So give them still the lie.

Tell fortune of her blindness;   55
Tell nature of decay;
Tell friendship of unkindness;
Tell justice of delay.
And if they will reply,
Then give them all the lie.   60

Tell arts they have no soundness,
But vary by esteeming;
Tell schools they want profoundness,
And stand too much on seeming.
If arts and schools reply,   65
Give arts and schools the lie.

Tell faith it's fled the city;
Tell how the country erreth;
Tell manhood shakes off pity;
Tell virtue least preferreth.   70
And if they do reply,
Spare not to give the lie.

So when thou hast, as I
Commanded thee, done blabbing—

2. Delicate.

Although to give the lie   75
Deserves no less than stabbing—
Stab at thee he that will,
No stab the soul can kill.

ca. 1592

Farewell, False Love

Farewell, false love, the oracle of lies,
A mortal foe and enemy to rest;
An envious boy, from whom all cares arise,
A bastard vile, a beast with rage possessed;
A way of error, a temple full of treason,   5
In all effects contrary unto reason.

A poisoned serpent covered all with flowers,
Mother of sighs and murtherer of repose,
A sea of sorrows from whence are drawn such showers
As moisture lends to every grief that grows;   10
A school of guile, a net of deep deceit,
A gilded hook that holds a poisoned bait.

A fortress foiled[1] which reason did defend,
A siren song, a fever of the mind,
A maze wherein affection finds no end,   15
A raging cloud that runs before the wind,
A substance like the shadow of the sun,
A goal of grief for which the wisest run.

A quenchless fire, a nurse of trembling fear,
A path that leads to peril and mishap;   20
A true retreat of sorrow and despair,
An idle boy that sleeps in pleasure's lap,
A deep distrust of that which certain seems,
A hope of that which reason doubtful deems.

Sith[2] then thy trains my younger years betrayed,   25
And for my faith ingratitude I find,
And sith repentance hath my wrongs bewrayed[3]
Whose course was ever contrary to kind—
False love, desire, and beauty frail, adieu!
Dead is the root whence all these fancies grew.   30

1588

1. Overthrown.   3. Revealed.
2. Since; "trains": tricks, stratagems.

Nature, That Washed Her Hands in Milk

Nature, that washed her hands in milk,
And had forgot to dry them,
Instead of earth took snow and silk,
At love's request to try them,
If she a mistress could compose   5
To please love's fancy out of those.

Her eyes he would should be of light,
A violet breath, and lips of jelly;
Her hair not black, nor overbright,
And of the softest down her belly;   10
As for her inside he'd have it
Only of wantonness and wit.

At love's entreaty such a one
Nature made, but with her beauty
She hath framed a heart of stone;   15
So as love, by ill destiny,
Must die for her whom nature gave him,
Because her darling would not save him.

But time (which nature doth despise,
And rudely gives her love the lie,   20
Makes hope a fool, and sorrow wise)
His hands do neither wash nor dry;
But being made of steel and rust,
Turns snow and silk and milk to dust.

The light, the belly, lips, and breath,   25
He dims, discolors, and destroys;
With those he feeds but fills not death,
Which sometimes were the food of joys.
Yea, time doth dull each lively wit,
And dries all wantonness with it.   30

Oh, cruel time! which takes in trust
Our youth, our joys, and all we have,
And pays us but with age and dust;
Who in the dark and silent grave
When we have wandered all our ways   35
Shuts up the story of our days.

c. 1592   1902

Methought I Saw the Grave Where Laura Lay[1]

Methought I saw the grave where Laura lay,
Within that temple where the vestal[2] flame
Was wont to burn; and passing by that way
To see that buried dust of living fame,
Whose tomb fair love and fairer virtue kept,   5
All suddenly I saw the Fairy Queen;
At whose approach the soul of Petrarch wept,
And from thenceforth those graces were not seen,
For they this Queen attended; in whose stead
Oblivion laid him down on Laura's hearse.   10
Hereat the hardest stones were seen to bleed,
And groans of buried ghosts the heavens did pierce;
Where Homer's sprite[3] did tremble all for grief,
And cursed th' access of that celestial thief.

1590

The Author's Epitaph, Made By Himself[4]

Even such is time, which takes in trust
Our youth, our joys, and all we have,
And pays us but with age and dust,
Who in the dark and silent grave
When we have wandered all our ways   5
Shuts up the story of our days,
And from which earth, and grave, and dust
The Lord shall raise me up, I trust.

1628

From The History of the World[1]

That Man Is, As It Were, A Little World: With A Digression Touching Our Mortality.

Man, thus compounded and formed by God, was an abstract or model, or brief story of the universal, in whom God concluded the creation and work of the world, and whom he made the last and most excellent of his creatures, being internally endued with[2] a divine understanding, by which

1. A commendatory sonnet to the first 3 books of *The Faerie Queene* by Ralegh's friend Spenser. Laura was the lady celebrated in the sonnets of Petrarch (1304–1374).
2. Celebrating virginity.
3. The spirit of Homer. Ralegh is giving extravagant praise to Spenser's poem as an epic, the type of poem Homer wrote.

4. In the 17th century it was thought that Ralegh composed this poem the night before his execution and wrote it in his Bible. It is actually a version of the last stanza of the love poem, "Nature, That Washed Her Hands in Milk." (above). Only the first three words and the final couplet are changed.
1. Book 1, chapter 2, section 5.
2. Possessed of.

he might contemplate and serve his Creator, after whose image he was formed, and endued with the powers and faculties of reason and other abilities, that thereby also he might govern and rule the world, and all other God's creatures therein. And whereas God created three sorts of living natures, to wit, angelical, rational, and brutal; giving to angels an intellectual, and to beasts a sensual nature, he vouchsafed unto man both the intellectual of angels, the sensitive of beasts, and the proper rational belonging unto man, and therefore, saith Gregory Nazianzen,[3] *Homo est utriusque naturae vinculum:* "Man is the bond and chain which tieth together both natures." And because in the little frame of man's body there is a representation of the universal, and (by allusion)[4] a kind of participation of all the parts thereof, therefore was man called *microcosmos,* or the little world. *Deus igitur hominem factum, velut alterum quendam mundum, in brevi magnum, atque exiguo totum, in terris statuit:* "God therefore placed in the earth the man whom he had made, as it were another world, the great and large world in the small and little world."[5] For out of earth and dust was formed the flesh of man, and therefore heavy and lumpish; the bones of his body we may compare to the hard rocks and stones, and therefore strong and durable, of which Ovid:[6]

> Inde genus durum sumus, experiensque laborum,
> Et documenta damus qua simus origine nati.

> From thence our kind hard-hearted is,
>   Enduring pain and care,
> Approving, that our bodies of
>   A stony nature are.

His blood, which disperseth itself by the branches of veins through all the body, may be resembled to those waters which are carried by brooks and rivers over all the earth; his breath to the air; his natural heat to the enclosed warmth which the earth hath in itself—which, stirred up by the heat of the sun, assisteth nature in the speedier procreation of those varieties which the earth bringeth forth; our radical moisture, oil, or balsamum (whereon the natural heat feedeth and is maintained) is resembled to the fat and fertility of the earth; the hairs of man's body, which adorns, or overshadows it, to the grass, which covereth the upper face and skin of the earth; our generative power, to nature, which produceth all things; our determinations,[7] to the light, wandering, and unstable clouds, carried every where with uncertain winds; our eyes, to the light of the sun and moon; and the beauty of our youth, to the flowers of the spring, which either in a very short time, or with the sun's heat, dry up and wither away, or the fierce puffs of wind blow them from the stalks; the thoughts of our mind, to the motion of angels; and our pure under-

---

3. St. Gregory (328–390), bishop and theologian
4. Symbolical likeness.
5. St. Augustine, *Retractions,* 1.1.

6. *Metamorphoses* 1, 414–15.
7. Efforts to reach a decision.

standing (formerly called *mens*,[8] and that which always looketh upwards) to those intellectual natures which are always present with God; and, lastly, our immortal souls (while they are righteous); are by God himself beautified with the title of his own image and similitude. And although, in respect of God, there is no man just, or good, or righteous (for, *in angelis deprehensa est stultitia*, "Behold, he found folly in his angels," saith Job[9]) yet, with such a kind of difference as there is between the substance and the shadow, there may be found a goodness in man: which God being pleased to accept, hath therefore called man the image and similitude of his own righteousness. In this also is the little world of man compared, and made more like the universal (man being the measure of all things—*Homo est mensura omnium rerum*, saith Aristotle[1] and Pythagoras) that the four complexions resemble the four elements,[2] and the seven ages of man the seven planets; whereof our infancy is compared to the moon, in which we seem only to live and grow, as plants; the second age to Mercury, wherein we are taught and instructed; our third age to Venus, the days of love, desire, and vanity; the fourth to the sun, the strong, flourishing, and beautiful age of man's life; the fifth to Mars, in which we seek honor and victory, and in which our thoughts travel to ambitious ends; the sixth age is ascribed to Jupiter, in which we begin to take account of our times, judge of ourselves, and grow to the perfection of our understanding; the last and seventh to Saturn, wherein our days are sad, and overcast, and in which we find by dear[3] and lamentable experience, and by the loss which can never be repaired, that of all our vain passions and affections past, the sorrow only abideth: our attendants are sicknesses, and variable infirmities; and by how much the more we are accompanied with plenty, by so much the more greedily is our end desired, whom when time hath made unsociable to others, we become a burden to ourselves: being of no other use, than to hold the riches we have from our successors. In this time it is, when (as aforesaid) we, for the most part, and never before, prepare for our eternal habitation, which we pass on unto with many sighs, groans, and sad thoughts, and in the end, by the workmanship of death, finish the sorrowful business of a wretched life; towards which we always travel both sleeping and waking; neither have those beloved companions of honor and riches any power at all to hold us any one day by the glorious promise of entertainments; but by what crooked path soever we walk, the same leadeth on directly to the house of death, whose doors lie open at all hours, and to all persons. For this tide of man's life, after it once turneth and declineth, ever runneth with a perpetual ebb and falling stream, but never floweth again: our leaf once fallen, springeth no more; neither doth the sun or the summer adorn us again, with the garments of new leaves and flowers.

---

8. Intellect.
9. Job 4:18.
1. *Metaphysics* 1, 1053b. Aristotle there refers to Protagoras, a Sophist, not to the more celebrated

Pythagoras, the philosopher and mathematician.
2. Ancient science recognized four elements: earth, air, fire, and water.
3. Grievous.

Redditur arboribus florens revirentibus aetas;
Ergo non homini, quod fuit ante, redit.[4]

To which I give this sense.

The plants and trees made poor and old
By winter envious,
The spring-time bounteous
Covers again from shame and cold:
But never man repaired again
His youth and beauty lost,
Though art, and care, and cost,
Do promise nature's help in vain.

And of which Catullus, Epigram 53.

Soles occidere et redire possunt:
Nobis cum semel occidit brevis lux,
Nox est perpetua una dormienda.

The sun may set and rise:
But we contrarywise
Sleep after our short light
One everlasting night.

For if there were any baiting place, or rest, in the course or race of man's life, then, according to the doctrine of the Academics,[5] the same might also perpetually be maintained. But as there is a continuance of motion in natural living things, and as the sap and juice, wherein the life of plants is preserved, doth evermore ascend or descend; so is it with the life of man, which is always either increasing towards ripeness and perfection, or declining and decreasing towards rottenness and dissolution.

[Conclusion: On Death]

It is therefore Death alone that can suddenly make man to know himself. He tells the proud and insolent that they are but abjects,[6] and humbles them at the instant; makes them cry, complain, and repent, yea, even to hate their forepast happiness. He takes the account of the rich, and proves him a beggar, a naked beggar, which hath interest in nothing but in the gravel that fills his mouth. He holds a glass before the eyes of the most beautiful, and makes them see therein their deformity and rottenness, and they acknowledge it.

O eloquent, just, and mighty Death! Whom none could advise, thou hast persuaded; whom none hath dared, thou hast done;[7] and whom all the world hath flattered, thou hast cast out of the world and despised; thou hast drawn together all the far-fetched greatness, all the pride, cru-

---

4. From an elegy by Albinovinus, a minor poet and friend of Ovid.
5. Followers of Plato, who taught in a grove called Academia.
6. Castoffs.
7. Accomplished.

elty, and ambition of man, and covered it all over with these two narrow
words: *Hic jacet!*[8]

1614

8. Latin for "Here lies . . ." often carved on tombstones.

CHRISTOPHER MARLOWE
1564–1593

ca. 1587:   *Tamburlaine* produced, introducing blank verse,
                "Marlowe's mighty line," to the stage.
ca. 1592–93:   *Dr. Faustus, Hero and Leander.*

Christopher Marlowe was born two months before William Shakespeare.
He was the son of a Canterbury shoemaker; in 1580 he went to Corpus
Christi College, Cambridge, on a scholarship which was ordinarily awarded
to students preparing for the ministry. He held the scholarship for the maximum time, six years, but did not take holy orders. Instead, he began to
write plays. When he came to supplicate for his Master of Arts degree in
1587, the university was about to deny it to him on the grounds that he
intended to go abroad to Reims, the center of Catholic intrigue and propaganda against Elizabeth, and remain there. But the Privy Council intervened and requested that, since Marlowe had done the queen good service,
he be granted his degree at the next commencement "because it is not Her
Majesty's pleasure that anyone employed as he had been in matters touching
the benefit of his country should be defamed by those that are ignorant in
the affairs he went about." Although much sensational information about
Marlowe has been discovered in modern times, we are still "ignorant in the
affairs he went about."

Before he left Cambridge, he had certainly written his tremendously successful play *Tamburlaine* and perhaps also, in collaboration with his younger
Cambridge contemporary, Thomas Nashe, the tragedy of *Dido, Queen of
Carthage. Tamburlaine*, which soon was followed by a sequel (*Tamburlaine*, part 2), dramatizes the exploits of a fourteenth-century Scythian shepherd who conquered much of the known world, as Alexander had before
him. In some sixteenth-century narratives Tamburlaine is represented as the
type of modern (i.e., Renaissance) man, and in others he is portrayed as
God's Scourge. In Marlowe's play he is the vehicle for the expression of
boundless energy and ambition, the impulse to strive constantly upward to
absolute power. When one of his victims accuses him of bloody cruelty,
Tamburlaine answers that ambition to rule is embedded in the laws of nature
and in basic human psychology:

> Nature, that framed us of four elements
> Warring within our breasts for regiment,
> Doth teach us all to have aspiring minds;

Our souls, whose faculties can comprehend
The wondrous architecture of the world
And measure every planet's wandering course,
Still climbing after knowledge infinite,
And always moving as the restless spheres,
Wills us to wear ourselves and never rest
Until we reach the ripest fruit of all,
That perfect bliss and sole felicity,
The sweet fruition of an earthly crown.

The English theater had heard nothing like this before. Here is a resonant, rhetorical blank verse, eminently suited to projection from the stage,
and appropriate also, as it turned out, for the robust talents of the actor
Edward Alleyn who happily appeared in time to portray Marlowe's heroes.

From the time of his first great success, when he was twenty-three, Marlowe had only six years to live. They were not calm years. In 1589 he was
involved in a brawl with one William Bradley, in which the poet Thomas
Watson intervened and killed Bradley. Both poets were jailed, but Watson
got off on a plea of self-defense and Marlowe was released. In 1591 Marlowe
was living in London with the playwright Thomas Kyd, who later gave information to the Privy Council accusing Marlowe of atheism and treason. On
May 30, 1593, at the inn of the Widow Bull in Deptford, Marlowe was
killed by a dagger thrust in an argument over the bill. In these six violent
years, Marlowe composed five more plays: his sequel to *Tamburlaine*; *The
Massacre at Paris*; two major tragedies, *The Jew of Malta* and *Dr. Faustus*;
and a chronicle history play, *Edward II*.

Hero and Leander Marlowe's mythological erotic poem, is a free

and original treatment of a classic tale of two tragic lovers. The story had
been told by the 5th-century Alexandrian poet Musaeus. Marlowe's poem,
however, is in the manner of Ovid, who had told the story in two epistles of
his *Heroides* and who refers to it in one of his *Elegies* that Marlowe translated.

George Chapman, the playwright and translator of Homer, undertook to
complete Marlowe's poem. His continuation, with his division of the poem
into "Sestiads" (named after Sestos, where Hero lived) and verse summaries
preceding each, was published shortly after the first surviving edition of Marlowe's poem. For a long time Chapman's altered version remained the standard form of the poem. Thanks to Louis L. Martz, however, Marlowe's
poem has recently been freed of its accretions and can now be read as he left
it. As Martz points out, the poem has a 3-part structure: the meeting of the
lovers at the Feast of Adonis; the inserted tale of Mercury and the Fates; and
the narrative of the consummation.

The narrative serves mainly as a framework on which to hang the poetry,
and the characters are not intended to be consistent or psychologically credible; they inhabit a world of fancy and delight, of strange contrasts between
innocence and the wild riot of amorous intrigues among the gods which is
Ovid's subject matter. Hero is paradoxically a nun vowed to chastity and a
devotee of Venus, the love goddess; Leander is both a sharp, sophisticated

seducer and an incredibly innocent novice in sex. The gravely spoken asides, sometimes platitudes and sometimes cynical remarks about women, in the manner of Ovid, give a distance or disengagement to the experience of reading about the ill-fated lovers. The poem is rich in many ways: it is comic, erotic, decorative, now swiftly narrative, now deliberate and, in a light way, philosophical.

Hero and Leander[1]

On Hellespont, guilty of true-loves'[2] blood,
In view and opposite, two cities stood,
Sea-borderers, disjoined by Neptune's might;
The one Abydos, the other Sestos hight.[3]
At Sestos Hero dwelt; Hero the fair,　　　　　　　　　　　5
Whom young Apollo courted for her hair,
And offered as a dower his burning throne,
Where she should sit for men to gaze upon.
The outside of her garments were of lawn,[4]
The lining purple silk, with gilt stars drawn;　　　　　　10
Her wide sleeves green, and bordered with a grove
Where Venus in her naked glory strove
To please the careless and disdainful eyes
Of proud Adonis, that before her lies;[5]
Her kirtle blue, whereon was many a stain,　　　　　　　15
Made with the blood of wretched lovers slain.[6]
Upon her head she ware a myrtle wreath,
From whence her veil reached to the ground beneath.
Her veil was artificial flowers and leaves,
Whose workmanship both man and beast deceives;　　　20
Many would praise the sweet smell as she passed,
When 'twas the odor which her breath forth cast;
And there for honey, bees have sought in vain,
And, beat from thence, have lighted there again.
About her neck hung chains of pebble-stone,　　　　　　25
Which, lightened[7] by her neck, like diamonds shone.
She ware no gloves, for neither sun nor wind
Would burn or parch her hands, but to her mind[8]

1. *Hero and Leander* cannot be dated precisely. It was entered in the Stationers' Register on Sept. 28, 1593, just 4 months after the poet's death, but the earliest known edition was not published until 1598. The poem has something in common with Marlowe's translation of Ovid's *Elegies*, generally thought to be early work, possibly done while he was still at Cambridge. The same verse form, the closed couplet, is used in both, though the versification is much more expert in *Hero and Leander*. Not much can be inferred about the interrelationship of Marlowe's poem with Shakespeare's *Venus and Adonis*, probably composed in late 1592. They are different in verse form (Shakespeare used a 6-line stanza) and somewhat different in tone, though they belong to the same genre of erotic narrative, along with about a dozen other Elizabethan poems.
2. Sweethearts'.
3. Called.
4. A kind of fine linen or thin cambric.
5. Venus's love for the young hunter, Adonis, and his death in the boar hunt are told by Ovid and by Shakespeare in *Venus and Adonis*. "Kirtle": skirt.
6. The extravagant claim is made that many "wretched lovers" had committed suicide at her feet because Hero would not have them.
7. Illuminated.
8. As she wished.

Or warm or cool them, for they took delight
To play upon those hands, they were so white.   30
Buskins[9] of shells all silvered, usèd she,
And branched with blushing coral to the knee,
Where sparrows perched, of hollow pearl and gold,
Such as the world would wonder to behold;
Those with sweet water oft her handmaid fills,   35
Which, as she went, would chirrup through the bills.
Some say, for her the fairest Cupid pined,
And looking in her face, was strooken blind.
But this is true: so like was one the other,
As he imagined Hero was his mother;[1]   40
And oftentimes into her bosom flew,
About her naked neck his bare arms threw,
And laid his childish head upon her breast,
And with still[2] panting rocked, there took his rest.
So lovely fair was Hero, Venus' nun,[3]   45
As Nature wept, thinking she was undone,
Because she took more from her than she left
And of such wondrous beauty her bereft;
Therefore, in sign her treasure suffered wrack,
Since Hero's time hath half the world been black.   50
Amorous Leander, beautiful and young,
(Whose tragedy divine Musaeus[4] sung)
Dwelt at Abydos; since him dwelt there none
For whom succeeding times make greater moan.
His dangling tresses that were never shorn,   55
Had they been cut and unto Colchos[5] borne,
Would have allured the vent'rous youth of Greece
To hazard more than for the Golden Fleece.
Fair Cynthia[6] wished his arms might be her sphere;
Grief makes her pale, because she moves not there.   60
His body was as straight as Circe's wand;[7]
Jove might have sipped out nectar from his hand.
Even as delicious meat is to the taste,
So was his neck in touching, and surpassed
The white of Pelops' shoulder.[8] I could tell ye   65
How smooth his breast was, and how white his belly,
And whose immortal fingers did imprint
That heavenly path, with many a curious[9] dint,

9. High shoes or boots.
1. I.e., Venus.
2. Continual.
3. The connotations of these two words are contradictory; Marlowe gets a similar effect elsewhere in the poem. Hero is a maiden in attendance at the temple of Venus, who is, of course, the goddess of love.
4. I.e., the author of the Greek poem upon which *Hero and Leander* is remotely based. He was sometimes confused with a legendary early

Musaeus, supposed son of Orpheus—hence Marlowe calls him "divine."
5. A country in Asia where the Argonauts ("the ven'trous youth of Greece") found the Golden Fleece.
6. The moon; "sphere": orbit.
7. The wand with which Circe, in the *Odyssey*, turned men into beasts.
8. Pelops, according to Ovid, had a shoulder of ivory.
9. Exquisite.

That runs along his back; but my rude pen
Can hardly blazon forth the loves of men,   70
Much less of powerful gods; let it suffice
That my slack[1] muse sings of Leander's eyes,
Those orient cheeks and lips, exceeding his
That leapt into the water for a kiss
Of his own shadow, and despising many,   75
Died ere he could enjoy the love of any.[2]
Had wild Hippolytus[3] Leander seen,
Enamored of his beauty had he been;
His presence made the rudest peasant melt,
That in the vast uplandish country dwelt;   80
The barbarous Thracian soldier, moved with naught,
Was moved with him, and for his favor sought.
Some swore he was a maid in man's attire,
For in his looks were all that men desire:
A pleasant smiling cheek, a speaking[4] eye,   85
A brow for love to banquet royally;
And such as knew he was a man, would say,
"Leander, thou art made for amorous play;
Why art thou not in love, and loved of all?
Though thou be fair, yet be not thine own thrall."   90
    The men of wealthy Sestos every year,
For his sake whom their goddess held so dear,
Rose-cheeked Adonis, kept a solemn feast.
Thither resorted many a wandering guest
To meet their loves; such as had none at all   95
Came lovers home from this great festival;
For every street, like to a firmament,
Glistered with breathing stars, who, where they went,
Frighted the melancholy earth, which deemed
Eternal heaven to burn, for so it seemed   100
As if another Phaëton[5] had got
The guidance of the sun's rich chariot.
But, far above the loveliest, Hero shined,
And stole away th' enchanted gazer's mind;
For like sea nymphs' inveigling harmony,   105
So was her beauty to the standers by.
Nor that night-wandering pale and watery star[6]
(When yawning dragons draw her thirling[7] car
From Latmus' mount up to the gloomy sky,
Where, crowned with blazing light and majesty,   110
She proudly sits) more over-rules[8] the flood
Than she the hearts of those that near her stood.
Even as when gaudy nymphs pursue the chase,

1. Dull. "Orient": shining.
2. An allusion to Narcissus.
3. Like Adonis, he preferred hunting to love.
4. Expressive.
5. A son of the sun god, he drove his father's chariot across the sky and almost burned up the world.
6. The moon.
7. Flying like a spear. Latmus was the mountain
where the moon visited her lover, Endymion.
8. Rules over.

Wretched Ixion's shaggy-footed race,[9]
Incensed with savage heat, gallop amain   115
From steep pine-bearing mountains to the plain,
So ran the people forth to gaze upon her,
And all that viewed her were enamored on her.
And as in fury of a dreadful fight,
Their fellows being slain or put to flight,   120
Poor soldiers stand with fear of death dead-strooken,
So at her presence all, surprised and tooken,
Await the sentence of her scornful eyes;
He whom she favors lives, the other dies.
There might you see one sigh, another rage,   125
And some, their violent passions to assuage,
Compile sharp satires; but alas, too late,
For faithful love will never turn to hate.
And many, seeing great princes were denied,
Pined as they went, and thinking on her, died.   130
On this feast day, oh, cursèd day and hour!
Went Hero thorough[1] Sestos, from her tower
To Venus' temple, where unhappily,
As after chanced, they did each other spy.
So fair a church as this had Venus none;   135
The walls were of discolored[2] jasper stone,
Wherein was Proteus carvèd, and o'erhead
A lively[3] vine of green sea-agate spread,
Where, by one hand, light-headed Bacchus hung,
And with the other, wine from grapes out-wrung.   140
Of crystal shining fair the pavement was;
The town of Sestos called it Venus' glass;
There might you see the gods in sundry shapes,
Committing heady[4] riots, incest, rapes;
For know that underneath this radiant floor   145
Was Danaë's statue in a brazen tower,[5]
Jove slyly stealing from his sister's bed
To dally with Idalian Ganymed,[6]
And for his love Europa bellowing loud,
And tumbling with the rainbow in a cloud;   150
Blood-quaffing Mars heaving the iron net
Which limping Vulcan and his Cyclops set;[7]
Love kindling fire to burn such towns as Troy;
Silvanus weeping for the lovely boy[8]

9. I.e., the centaurs, fathered by Ixion upon a cloud. For his presumption in loving Juno, Ixion was chained to a wheel—hence "wretched."
1. Through.
2. Of various colors.
3. Lifelike.
4. Passionate, violent. In the next lines, specific examples of the "riots, incest, rapes" are given.
5. Danaë, imprisoned in a tower, was visited by Jove in the form of a shower of gold. "His sister's":
i.e., Juno's; she was also Jove's wife.
6. A beautiful youth whom Jove kidnaped from Mt. Ida (hence "Idalian"). In order to seduce Europa, Jove took the form of a "bellowing" bull.
7. Vulcan used a net to trap Venus, his wife, and Mars, "blood-quaffing" god of war, in the act of love.
8. I.e., Cyparissus, beloved of the wood god Sylvanus.

That now is turned into a cypress tree,   155
Under whose shade the wood-gods love to be.
And in the midst a silver altar stood;
There Hero sacrificing turtles'[9] blood,
Veiled to the ground, veiling her eyelids close,
And modestly they opened as she rose;   160
Thence flew love's arrow with the golden head,[1]
And thus Leander was enamorèd.
Stone still he stood, and evermore he gazed,
Till with the fire that from his countenance blazed,
Relenting Hero's gentle heart was strook;   165
Such force and virtue hath an amorous look.
    It lies not in our power to love or hate,
For will in us is overruled by fate.
When two are stripped, long ere the course[2] begin
We wish that one should lose, the other win;   170
And one especially do we affect[3]
Of two gold ingots, like in each respect.
The reason no man knows, let it suffice,
What we behold is censured[4] by our eyes.
Where both deliberate, the love is slight;   175
Who ever loved, that loved not at first sight?[5]
    He kneeled, but unto her devoutly prayed.
Chaste Hero to herself thus softly said,
"Were I the saint he worships, I would hear him,"
And as she spake those words, came somewhat near him.   180
He started up; she blushed as one ashamed,
Wherewith Leander much more was inflamed.
He touched her hand; in touching it she trembled:
Love deeply grounded hardly[6] is dissembled.
These lovers parlèd[7] by the touch of hands;   185
True love is mute, and oft amazèd stands.
Thus, while dumb signs their yielding hearts entangled,
The air with sparks of living fire was spangled,
And Night, deep drenched in misty Acheron,[8]
Heaved up her head, and half the world upon   190
Breathed darkness forth. (Dark night is Cupid's day.)
And now begins Leander to display
Love's holy fire, with words, with sighs and tears,
Which like sweet music entered Hero's ears,
And yet at every word she turned aside   195
And always cut him off as he replied.
At last, like to a bold sharp sophister,[9]

---

9. Turtledoves, symbolic of constancy in love.
1. The "golden head" of some of Cupid's arrows
produced love; he had others, of lead, that produced dislike.
2. Race.
3. Have affection for.
4. Judged.

5. Shakespeare quotes this line in As You Like It
(3.5.82).
6. With difficulty.
7. Parleyed, spoke.
8. One of the rivers of Hades.
9. A second- or third-year Cambridge student,
trained in logic and argument. "Accosted": wooed.

With cheerful hope thus he accosted her:
    "Fair creature, let me speak without offense;
I would my rude words had the influence   200
To lead my thoughts, as thy fair looks do mine,
Then shouldst thou be his prisoner who is thine.
Be not unkind and fair—misshapen stuff[1]
Are of behavior boisterous and rough.
O shun me not, but hear me ere you go;   205
God knows I cannot force[2] love, as you do.
My words shall be as spotless as my youth,
Full of simplicity and naked truth.
This sacrifice, whose sweet perfume descending
From Venus' altar to your footsteps bending,[3]   210
Doth testify that you exceed her far
To whom you offer and whose nun you are.
Why should you worship her? Her you surpass
As much as sparkling diamonds flaring[4] glass.
A diamond set in lead his worth retains;   215
A heavenly nymph, beloved of human swains,
Receives no blemish but ofttimes more grace;
Which makes me hope, although I am but base—
Base in respect of thee, divine and pure,
Dutiful service may thy love procure,   220
And I in duty will excel all other,
As thou in beauty dost exceed Love's mother.
Nor heaven, nor thou, were made to gaze upon;
As heaven preserves all things, so save thou one.
A stately builded ship, well rigged and tall,   225
The ocean maketh more majestical.
Why vowest thou then to live in Sestos here,
Who on Love's seas more glorious wouldst appear?
Like untuned golden strings all women are,
Which long time lie untouched, will harshly jar.[5] 230
Vessels of brass, oft handled, brightly shine.
What difference betwixt the richest mine[6]
And basest mold, but use, for both not used
Are of like worth. Then treasure is abused
When misers keep it; being put to loan,   235
In time it will return us two for one.
Rich robes themselves and others do adorn;
Neither themselves nor others, if not worn.
Who builds a palace and rams up the gate
Shall see it ruinous and desolate.   240
Ah, simple Hero, learn thyself to cherish;
Lone women, like to empty houses, perish.

---

1. Persons.
2. Compel.
3. Turning.
4. Gaudy.

5. I.e., instruments not played upon will be out of tune and harsh.
6. Ore; "mold": earth.

Less sins the poor rich man that starves himself
In heaping up a mass of drossy pelf,
Than such as you: his golden earth remains,   245
Which after his decease some other gains.
But this fair gem, sweet in the loss alone,
When you fleet hence can be bequeathed to none.
Or if it could, down from th' enameled[7] sky
All heaven would come to claim this legacy,   250
And with intestine[8] broils the world destroy
And quite confound Nature's sweet harmony.
Well therefore by the gods decreed it is,
We human creatures should enjoy that bliss.
One is no number;[9] maids are nothing then   255
Without the sweet society of men.
Wilt thou live single still? One shalt thou be,
Though never-singling[1] Hymen couple thee.
Wild savages, that drink of running springs,
Think water far excels all earthly things;   260
But they that daily taste neat[2] wine despise it.
Virginity, albeit some highly prize it,
Compared with marriage, had you tried them both,
Differs as much as wine and water doth.
Base bullion for the stamp's sake[3] we allow: 265
Even so for men's impression do we you;
By which alone, our reverend fathers[4] say,
Women receive perfection every way.
This idol which you term Virginity,
Is neither essence,[5] subject to the eye—   270
No, nor to any one exterior sense,
Nor hath it any place of residence,
Nor is 't of earth or mold[6] celestial,
Or capable of any form at all.
Of that which hath no being do not boast: 275
Things that are not at all are never lost.
Men foolishly do call it virtuous:
What virtue is it that is born with us?[7]
Much less can honor be ascribed thereto:
Honor is purchased by the deeds we do.   280
Believe me, Hero, honor is not won
Until some honorable deed be done.
Seek you for chastity, immortal fame,
And know that some have wronged Diana's name?[8]
Whose name is it, if she be false or not,   285

---

7. Beautiful, many-colored.
8. Internal, civil.
9. A traditional concept, going back to Aristotle.
1. I.e., who never separates, but always joins.
Hymen was the god of marriage.
2. Undiluted.
3. For the impression which makes metal ("bul-

lion") into a coin.
4. Ancient philosophers, like Aristotle.
5. Something that exists, is real.
6. Form.
7. I.e., a virtue is not a virtue unless it is acquired.
8. I.e., no fame for chastity is secure. Even Diana,
goddess of chastity, has been slandered.

So she be fair, but some vile tongues will blot?
But you are fair, aye me! so wondrous fair,
So young, so gentle, and so debonair,[9]
As Greece will think, if thus you live alone,
Some one or other keeps you as his own.   290
Then, Hero, hate me not, nor from me fly
To follow swiftly-blasting infamy.
Perhaps thy sacred priesthood makes thee loath.
Tell me, to whom madest thou that heedless oath?"
    "To Venus," answered she, and as she spake,   295
Forth from those two tralucent cisterns[1] brake
A stream of liquid pearl, which down her face
Made milk-white paths whereon the gods might trace[2]
To Jove's high court. He thus replied: "The rites
In which Love's beauteous empress most delights   300
Are banquets, Doric music,[3] midnight revel,
Plays, masques, and all that stern age counteth evil.
Thee as a holy idiot doth she scorn;
For thou, in vowing chastity, hast sworn
To rob her name and honor, and thereby   305
Commit'st a sin far worse than perjury—
Even sacrilege against her Deity,
Through regular and formal purity.
To expiate which sin, kiss and shake hands;
Such sacrifice as this Venus demands."   310
    Thereat she smiled and did deny him so
As, put[4] thereby, yet might he hope for mo.
Which makes him quickly reinforce his speech
And her in humble manner thus beseech:
    "Though neither gods nor men may thee deserve,   315
Yet for her sake whom you have vowed to serve,
Abandon fruitless, cold Virginity,
The gentle Queen of Love's sole enemy.
Then shall you most resemble Venus' nun,
When Venus' sweet rites are performed and done.   320
Flint-breasted Pallas[5] joys in single life,
But Pallas and your mistress are at strife.
Love, Hero, then, and be not tyrannous,
But heal the heart that thou hast wounded thus,
Nor stain thy youthful years with avarice;   325
Fair fools delight to be accounted nice.[6]
The richest corn dies, if it be not reaped;
Beauty alone is lost, too warily kept."
    These arguments he used, and many more,
Wherewith she yielded, that was won before.   330

9. Affable, agreeable.
1. Translucent eyes; "stream": i.e., of tears.
2. Go.
3. A solemn, military mode. Marlowe presumably meant "Lydian" (as in Milton's L'Allegro, line 136); Lydian music was soft and sensual.
4. Put off; "mo": more.
5. Athena, a rival goddess, usually portrayed in armor.
6. Shy, reluctant.

Hero's looks yielded, but her words made war:
Women are won when they begin to jar.[7]
Thus, having swallowed Cupid's golden hook,
The more she strived, the deeper was she strook.
Yet, evilly feigning anger, strove she still   335
And would be thought to grant against her will.
So having paused a while, at last she said:
"Who taught thee rhetoric to deceive a maid?
Aye me, such words as these should I abhor,
And yet I like them for the orator."   340
    With that, Leander stooped to have embraced her,
But from his spreading arms away she cast her,[8]
And thus bespake him: "Gentle youth, forbear
To touch the sacred garments which I wear.
    "Upon a rock, and underneath a hill,   345
Far from the town, where all is whist[9] and still,
Save that the sea, playing on yellow sand,
Sends forth a rattling murmur to the land,
Whose sound allures the golden Morpheus[1]
In silence of the night to visit us,   350
My turret stands, and there, God knows, I play
With Venus' swans and sparrows[2] all the day.
A dwarfish beldame[3] bears me company,
That hops about the chamber where I lie
And spends the night, that might be better spent,   355
In vain discourse and apish[4] merriment.
Come thither." As she spake this, her tongue tripped,
For unawares "Come thither" from her slipped;
And suddenly her former color changed
And here and there her eyes through anger ranged.   360
And like a planet, moving several ways,[5]
At one self instant, she, poor soul, assays[6]
Loving, not to love at all, and every part
Strove to resist the motions of her heart;
And hands so pure, so innocent, nay, such   365
As might have made heaven stoop to have a touch,
Did she uphold to Venus, and again
Vowed spotless chastity, but all in vain.
Cupid beat down her prayers with his wings;
Her vows above the empty air he flings.   370
All deep enraged, his sinewy[7] bow he bent,
And shot a shaft that burning from him went,
Wherewith she, strooken, looked so dolefully

7. Dispute.
8. Withdrew.
9. Silent.
1. God of sleep; "golden slumbers" was a common expression.
2. Venus was often portrayed in a chariot drawn by swans, and sparrows were associated with her because of their traditional lechery.

3. Old hag.
4. Silly.
5. In Ptolemaic astronomy each planet moved in its own orbit or sphere, but was also carried in other directions by a surrounding sphere.
6. Attempts.
7. Strong.

As made Love sigh to see his tyranny.
And as she wept, her tears to pearl he turned, 375
And wound them on his arm, and for her mourned.
Then towards the palace of the Destinies,[8]
Laden with languishment and grief, he flies,
And to those stern nymphs humbly made request
Both might enjoy each other and be blessed. 380
But with a ghastly dreadful countenance,
Threatening a thousand deaths at every glance,
They answered Love, nor would vouchsafe so much
As one poor word, their hate to him was such.
Harken a while, and I will tell you why: 385
Heaven's wingèd herald, Jove-born Mercury,
The selfsame day that he asleep had laid
Enchanted Argus,[9] spied a country maid
Whose careless hair, instead of pearl t' adorn it,
Glistered with dew, as one that seemed to scorn it,[1] 390
Her breath as fragrant as the morning rose,
Her mind pure, and her tongue untaught to glose.[2]
Yet proud she was, for lofty pride that dwells
In towered courts is oft in shepherds' cells,[3]
And too-too well the fair vermilion knew 395
And silver tincture of her cheeks, that drew
The love of every swain. On her, this god
Enamored was, and with his snaky rod[4]
Did charm her nimble feet and made her stay;
The while upon a hillock down he lay, 400
And sweetly on his pipe began to play,
And with smooth speech, her fancy to assay,
Till in his twining arms he locked her fast,
And then he wooed with kisses, and at last,
As shepherds do, her on the ground he laid, 405
And tumbling in the grass, he often strayed
Beyond the bounds of shame, in being bold
To eye those parts which no eye should behold;
And, like an insolent commanding lover,
Boasting his parentage, would needs discover 410
The way to new Elysium; but she,
Whose only dower was her chastity,
Having striven in vain, was now about to cry
And crave the help of shepherds that were nigh.
Herewith he stayed his fury,[5] and began 415
To give her leave to rise. Away she ran;
After went Mercury, who used such cunning
As she, to hear his tale, left off her running.

8. The Fates.
9. Mercury, or Hermes, the messenger god with winged feet, put to sleep Argus, the 100-eyed monster whom Juno had placed as a guard over Io, with whom her husband Jupiter was in love.

1. I.e., pearl or other jewelry.
2. Speak insincerely.
3. Huts.
4. Caduceus (now the symbol of medicine).
5. Passion.

Maids are not won by brutish force and might
But speeches full of pleasure and delight.   420
And knowing Hermes courted her, was glad
That she such loveliness and beauty had
As could provoke his liking, yet was mute,
And neither would deny nor grant his suit.
Still vowed he love; she, wanting no excuse   425
To feed him with delays, as women use,[6]
Or thirsting after immortality
(All women are ambitious naturally),
Imposed upon her lover such a task
As he ought not perform, nor yet she ask.   430
A draft of flowing nectar she requested
Wherewith the king of gods and men is feasted.
He, ready to accomplish what she willed,
Stole some from Hebe (Hebe Jove's cup filled),
And gave it to his simple rustic love,   435
Which being known (as what is hid from Jove?)
He inly stormed and waxed more furious
Than for the fire filched by Prometheus
And thrusts him down from heaven. He, wandering here,
In mournful terms,[7] with sad and heavy cheer   440
Complained to Cupid. Cupid for his sake,
To be revenged on Jove did undertake;
And those on whom heaven, earth, and hell relies
(I mean the adamantine[8] Destinies)
He wounds with love and forced them equally   445
To dote upon deceitful Mercury.
They offered him the deadly fatal knife
That shears the slender threads of human life;[9]
At his fair feathered feet the engines laid
Which th' earth from ugly Chaos' den upweighed.[1]   450
These he regarded not, but did entreat
That Jove, usurper of his father's seat,
Might presently be banished into hell
And agèd Saturn in Olympus dwell.
They granted what he craved, and once again   455
Saturn and Ops began their golden reign.
Murder, rape, war, lust, and treachery
Were with Jove closed in Stygian empery.
But long this blessèd time continued not;
As soon as he his wishèd purpose got,   460
He, reckless of his promise, did despise
The love of th' everlasting Destinies.
They seeing it, both Love and him abhorred

6. Practice.
7. Condition; "cheer": countenance.
8. Of extreme hardness (so called because the Destinies' decrees were irrevocable).
9. According to classical mythology, the Fates spun

and cut the threads that measure each human life.
1. The Fates also controlled the supports ("beams") that had supported ("upweighed") the earth since it arose out of Chaos, the yawning abyss from which all things came.

And Jupiter unto his place restored.[2]
And but that Learning, in despite of Fate,   465
Will mount aloft and enter heaven gate,
And to the seat of Jove itself advance,
Hermes had slept in hell with Ignorance.
Yet as a punishment they added this,
That he and Poverty should always kiss.[3]   470
And to this day is every scholar poor;
Gross gold from them runs headlong to the boor.
Likewise the angry sisters, thus deluded,
To venge themselves on Hermes, have concluded
That Midas' brood[4] shall sit in Honor's chair,   475
To which the Muses' sons are only heir.
And fruitful wits that inaspiring[5] are
Shall discontent run into regions far;
And few great lords in virtuous deeds shall joy,
But be surprised with every garish toy,   480
And still enrich the lofty servile clown[6]
Who, with encroaching guile, keeps learning down.
Then muse not[7] Cupid's suit no better sped,
Seeing in their loves the Fates were injurèd.
By this, sad Hero, with love unacquainted,   485
Viewing Leander's face, fell down and fainted.
He kissed her and breathed life into her lips,
Wherewith, as one displeased, away she trips.
Yet as she went, full often looked behind,
And many poor excuses did she find   490
To linger by the way, and once she stayed
And would have turned again, but was afraid
In offering parley to be counted light.
So on she goes, and in her idle flight
Her painted fan of curlèd plumes let fall,   495
Thinking to train[8] Leander therewithal.
He, being a novice, knew not what she meant
But stayed, and after her a letter sent,
Which joyful Hero answered in such sort
As he had hope to scale the beauteous fort   500
Wherein the liberal Graces[9] locked their wealth,

2. The story in lines 451–64 may be summarized as follows: Mercury scorns the gifts offered by the Fates but asks instead that Jove be dethroned (Jove had overthrown his father Saturn, who ruled heaven during the Golden Age). Mercury persuades the Fates to reverse this revolution, so Saturn and his wife Ops return to Olympus and Jove is thrust down into "Stygian empery" (line 458) or Hades. During the Golden Age there was no murder, rape, war, lust, or treachery; these came in with Jove, so when he is sent to Hades these crimes go with him. But this second Golden Age did not last long, because once he got what he wanted, Mercury (Hermes) forgot the Destinies and they restored Jove.
3. Marlowe invents the mythology that Mercury,

the god of learning, would have slept in hell with Ignorance, but Learning is so divine that it always mounts up, even to heaven, the "seat of Jove." But it was not beyond the Fates' power to make learning and poverty go together, which they decreed in revenge for Mercury's neglect.
4. The rich, since everything Midas touched turned to gold.
5. Not ambitious for riches or power.
6. Ignorant person.
7. I.e., don't be surprised.
8. Entice.
9. Three goddesses associated with everything beautiful.

And therefore to her tower he got by stealth.
Wide open stood the door; he need not climb,
And she herself before the pointed[1] time
Had spread the board,[2] with roses strewed the room, 505
And oft looked out, and mused he did not come.
At last he came; O who can tell the greeting
These greedy lovers had at their first meeting?
He asked, she gave, and nothing was denied;
Both to each other quickly were affied.[3] 510
Look how their hands, so were their hearts united,
And what he did, she willingly requited.
(Sweet are the kisses, the embracements sweet,
When like desires and affections meet,
For from the earth to heaven is Cupid raised 515
Where fancy is in equal balance peised.)[4]
Yet she this rashness suddenly repented
And turned aside and to herself lamented,
As if her name and honor had been wronged
By being possessed of him for whom she longed. 520
Ay, and she wished, albeit not from her heart,
That he would leave her turret and depart.
The mirthful god of amorous pleasure smiled
To see how he this captive nymph beguiled,
For hitherto he did but fan the fire 525
And kept it down that it might mount the higher.
Now waxed she jealous[5] lest his love abated,
Fearing her own thoughts made her to be hated.
Therefore unto him hastily she goes
And, like light Salmacis,[6] her body throws 530
Upon his bosom where, with yielding eyes,
She offers up herself a sacrifice
To slake his anger; if he were displeased,
O what god would not therewith be appeased?
Like Aesop's cock,[7] this jewel he enjoyed, 535
And as a brother with his sister toyed,
Supposing nothing else was to be done
Now he her favor and good will had won.
But know you not that creatures wanting sense[8]
By nature have a mutual appetence,[9] 540
And wanting organs to advance a step,
Moved by love's force, unto each other leap?
Much more in subjects having intellect,
Some hidden influence breeds like effect.
Albeit Leander, rude in[1] love and raw, 545

1. Appointed.
2. Set the table.
3. Affianced, engaged. "Look how": just as.
4. Weighed.
5. Fearful.
6. An amorous nymph in Ovid's *Metamorphoses*.

7. In the Aesopic fable a cock, scratching in the barnyard, uncovers a jewel, but prefers a barley corn to it.
8. Intelligence.
9. Attraction, as iron to a magnet.
1. Untutored.

Long dallying with Hero, nothing saw
That might delight him more, yet he suspected
Some amorous rites or other were neglected.
Therefore unto his body, hers he clung;
She, fearing on the rushes[2] to be flung,   550
Strived with redoubled strength. The more she strived,
The more a gentle, pleasing heat revived,
Which taught him all that elder lovers know.
And now the same gan so to scorch and glow,
As, in plain terms, yet cunningly,[3] he craved it.   555
(Love always makes those eloquent that have it.)
She, with a kind of granting, put him by it
And, ever as he thought himself most nigh it,
Like to the tree of Tantalus,[4] she fled
And, seeming lavish, saved her maidenhead.   560
Ne'er king more sought to keep his diadem
Than Hero this inestimable gem.
Above our life we love a steadfast friend;
Yet, when a token of great worth we send,
We often kiss it, often look thereon,   565
And stay the messenger that would be gone.
No marvel then, though Hero would not yield
So soon to part from that she dearly held.
Jewels being lost are found again, this never;
'Tis lost but once and once lost, lost forever.   570

  Now had the Morn espied her lover's steeds,[5]
Whereat she starts, puts on her purple weeds,[6]
And, red for anger that he stayed so long,
All headlong throws herself the clouds among.
And now Leander, fearing to be missed,   575
Embraced her suddenly, took leave, and kissed;
Long was he taking leave, and loath to go,
And kissed again, as lovers use to do.
Sad Hero wrung him by the hand and wept,
Saying, "Let your vows and promises be kept."   580
Then, standing at the door, she turned about,
As loath to see Leander going out.
And now the sun that through th' horizon peeps,
As pitying these lovers, downward creeps,
So that in silence of the cloudy night,   585
Though it was morning, did he take his flight.
But what the secret trusty night concealed,
Leander's amorous habit[7] soon revealed.
With Cupid's myrtle[8] was his bonnet crowned;
About his arms the purple riband[9] wound   590

2. Reeds used as carpeting in Elizabethan homes.
3. Skillfully.
4. Tantalus was punished in Hades by constantly
reaching for fruit from a tree that eluded him.
5. The horses that pull the chariot of the sun.

6. Clothes.
7. Dress.
8. A flower sacred to Venus or Cupid, symbolic
of love. "Bonnet": hat.
9. Ribbon.

Wherewith she wreathed her largely spreading hair;
Nor could the youth abstain but he must wear
The sacred ring wherewith she was endowed
When first religious chastity she vowed;
Which made his love through Sestos to be known,   595
And thence unto Abydos sooner blown
Than he could sail, for incorporeal Fame,
Whose weight consists in nothing but her name,
Is swifter than the wind, whose tardy plumes
Are reeking water and dull earthly fumes.[1]   600
Home when he came, he seemed not to be there,
But like exilèd air thrust from his sphere,
Set in a foreign place, and straight from thence,
Alcides-like,[2] by mighty violence
He would have chased away the swelling main   605
That him from her unjustly did detain.
Like as the sun in a diameter[3]
Fires and inflames objects removèd far,
And heateth kindly, shining lat'rally;
So beauty sweetly quickens when 'tis nigh.   610
But being separated and removed,
Burns where it cherished, murders where it loved.[4]
Therefore, even as an index to a book,
So to his mind was young Leander's look.
O none but gods have power their love to hide: 615
Affection by the count'nance is descried.
The light of hidden fire itself discovers,
And love that is concealed betrays[5] poor lovers.
His secret flame apparently[6] was seen;
Leander's father knew where he had been   620
And for the same mildly rebuked his son,
Thinking to quench the sparkles new begun.
But love resisted, once[7] grows passionate
And nothing more than counsel, lovers hate.
For as a hot, proud horse highly disdains   625
To have his head controlled, but breaks the reins,
Spits forth the ringled[8] bit, and with his hooves
Checks[9] the submissive ground; so he that loves,
The more he is restrained, the worse he fares.
What is it now but mad Leander dares?[1]   630
"O Hero, Hero!" thus he cried full oft,
And then he got him to a rock aloft,
Where, having spied her tower, long stared he on 't
And prayed the narrow toiling Hellespont
To part in twain, that he might come and go,   635

---

1. I.e., fame is as incorporeal as mist or smoke.
2. Like Hercules, with brute force.
3. I.e., shining straight down.
4. I.e., inaccessible beauty can burn and murder.
5. Gives away.
6. Openly.
7. At once.
8. With rings at the ends.
9. Stamps.
1. I.e., what is there now Leander dares not do?

But still the rising billows answered "No!"
With that he stripped him to the ivory skin
And crying, "Love, I come!" leapt lively in.
Whereat the sapphire-visaged god[2] grew proud
And made his capering Triton[3] sound aloud;   640
Imagining that Ganimed,[4] displeased,
Had left the heavens, therefore on him seized.
Leander strived; the waves about him wound
And pulled him to the bottom, where the ground
Was strewed with pearl, and in low coral groves.   645
Sweet singing mermaids sported with their loves
On heaps of heavy gold and took great pleasure
To spurn in careless sort[5] the shipwrack treasure;
For here the stately azure palace stood
Where kingly Neptune and his train abode.   650
The lusty god embraced him, called him love,
And swore he never should return to Jove.
But when he knew it was not Ganimed,
For under water he was almost dead,
He heaved him up, and looking on his face,   655
Beat down the bold waves with his triple mace,[6]
Which mounted up, intending to have kissed him,
And fell in drops like tears because they missed him.
Leander being up, began to swim
And, looking back, saw Neptune follow him.   660
Whereat aghast, the poor soul gan to cry,
"O let me visit Hero ere I die!"
The god put Helle's bracelet[7] on his arm
And swore the sea should never do him harm.
He clapped his plump cheeks, with his tresses played   665
And, smiling wantonly, his love bewrayed.[8]
He watched his arms, and as they opened wide,
At every stroke betwixt them he would slide
And steal a kiss, and then run out and dance
And, as he turned, cast many a lustful glance   670
And throw him gaudy toys to please his eye,
And dive into the water and there pry
Upon his breast, his thighs, and every limb,
And up again and close beside him swim
And talk of love. Leander made reply,   675
"You are deceived; I am no woman, I."
Thereat smiled Neptune and then told a tale
How that a shepherd, sitting in a vale,

---

2. Neptune, god of the sea.
3. A subordinate sea god who blew on a conch shell.
4. A beautiful boy, taken by Jove to be his cup-bearer.
5. Manner.
6. The 3-pronged fork carried by Neptune.

7. Helle was the daughter of King Athamas of Thebes. To escape a cruel stepmother, she fled on a winged, golden-fleeced ram but fell off into the Hellespont, which was named for her. Marlowe apparently invents the detail of the bracelet.
8. Revealed.

Played with a boy so fair and so kind
As, for his love, both earth and heaven pined;   680
That of the cooling river durst not drink
Lest water nymphs should pull him from the brink.
And when he sported in the fragrant lawns,
Goat-footed satyrs and up-staring fawns[9]
Would steal him thence. Ere half this tale was done   685
"Ay me!" Leander cried, "th' enamored sun
That now should shine on Thetis' glassy bower[1]
Descends upon my radiant Hero's tower.
O that these tardy arms of mine were wings!"
And as he spake, upon the waves he springs.   690
Neptune was angry that he gave no ear,
And in his heart revenging malice bare.
He flung at him his mace, but as it went
He called it in, for love made him repent.
The mace returning back, his own hand hit,   695
As meaning to be venged for darting it.
When this fresh bleeding wound Leander viewed,
His color went and came, as if he rued
The grief[2] which Neptune felt. In gentle breasts
Relenting thoughts, remorse, and pity rests;   700
And who have hard hearts and obdurate minds
But vicious, harebrained, and illit'rate hinds?[3]
The god, seeing him with pity to be moved,
Thereon concluded that he was beloved.
(Love is too full of faith, too credulous,   705
With folly and false hope deluding us.)
Wherefore Leander's fancy to surprise,[4]
To the rich ocean for gifts he flies.
'Tis wisdom to give much; a gift prevails
When deep persuading oratory fails.   710
By this[5] Leander, being near the land,
Cast down his weary feet and felt the sand.
Breathless albeit he were, he rested not
Till to the solitary tower he got.
And knocked and called; at which celestial noise,   715
The longing heart of Hero much more joys
Than nymphs and shepherds when the timbrel rings,
Or crooked dolphin[6] when the sailor sings.
She stayed not for her robes, but straight arose
And, drunk with gladness, to the door she goes;   720
Where, seeing a naked man, she screeched for fear
(Such sights as this to tender maids are rare),

9. *Fauni*, woodland spirits, who prophesied by looking up to the heavens.
1. I.e., the sea; Thetis was a sea nymph, mother of the hero Achilles.
2. Pain.
3. Rustics, boors.

4. Love to capture.
5. At this time.
6. "Crooked" because of the undulating path of the dolphin in the water. The musician Arion was saved from drowning by a dolphin charmed by his music. "Timbrel": tambourine.

And ran into the dark herself to hide.
Rich jewels in the dark are soonest spied.
Unto her was he led, or rather drawn   725
By those white limbs which sparkled through the lawn.[7]
The nearer that he came, the more she fled
And, seeking refuge, slipped into her bed.
Whereon Leander sitting, thus began,
Through numbing cold, all feeble, faint, and wan: 730
      "If not for love, yet, love, for pity's sake
Me in thy bed and maiden bosom take;
At least vouchsafe these arms some little room
Who, hoping to embrace thee, cheerly[8] swum.
This head was beat with many a churlish billow,   735
And therefore let it rest upon thy pillow."
Herewith affrighted Hero shrunk away
And in her lukewarm place Leander lay;
Whose lively heat, like fire from heaven fet,[9]
Would animate gross clay, and higher set   740
The drooping thoughts of base declining souls
Than dreary Mars[1] carousing nectar bowls.
His hands he cast upon her like a snare;
She, overcome with shame and sallow[2] fear,
Like chaste Diana when Actaeon spied her,[3]   745
Being suddenly betrayed, dived down to hide her,
And as her silver body downward went,
With both her hands she made the bed a tent,
And in her own mind thought herself secure,
O'ercast with dim and darksome coverture.   750
And now she lets him whisper in her ear,
Flatter, entreat, promise, protest, and swear;
Yet ever as he greedily assayed
To touch those dainties, she the Harpy[4] played,
And every limb did, as a soldier stout,   755
Defend the fort and keep the foeman out.
For though the rising ivory mount he scaled,
Which is with azure circling lines empaled,[5]
Much like a globe (a globe may I term this
By which love sails to regions full of bliss),   760
Yet there with Sisyphus[6] he toiled in vain
Till gentle parley did the truce obtain.
Wherein Leander on her quivering breast,
Breathless spoke something and sighed out the rest;
Which so prevailed, as he, with small ado,   765

---

7. Fine linen or cambric.
8. Gladly.
9. Fetched.
1. God of war; "dreary": bloody.
2. Pale, yellowish.
3. Actaeon, a hunter, came upon Diana bathing; she turned him into a stag, and he was killed by his own hounds.
4. A monster, half bird, half woman, who snatches away banquets in Virgil's *Aeneid* and Shakespeare's *Tempest*.
5. Surrounded.
6. Condemned in Hades to endlessly roll a stone uphill.

Enclosed her in his arms and kissed her, too.
And every kiss to her was as a charm
And to Leander as a fresh alarm.[7]
So that the truce was broke, and she, alas,
Poor silly[8] maiden, at his mercy was.   770
Love is not full of pity, as men say,
But deaf and cruel, where he means to prey.
Even as a bird which in our hands we wring[9]
Forth plungeth and oft flutters with her wing.
She trembling strove; this strife of hers, like that   775
Which made the world,[1] another world begat
Of unknown joy. Treason was in her thought,
And cunningly to yield herself she sought.
Seeming not won, yet won she was, at length.
(In such wars women use but half their strength.)   780
Leander now, like Theban Hercules,
Entered the orchard of th' Hesperides,
Whose fruit none rightly can describe but he
That pulls or shakes it from the golden tree.[2]
And now she wished this night were never done,   785
And sighed to think upon th' approaching sun,
For much it grieved her that the bright daylight
Should know the pleasure of this blessèd night,
And them like Mars and Erycine[3] displayed,
Both in each other's arms chained as they laid.   790
Again she knew not how to frame her look
Or speak to him who in a moment took
That which so long so charily she kept;
And fain by stealth away she would have crept
And to some corner secretly have gone,   795
Leaving Leander in the bed alone.
But as her naked feet were whipping out,
He on the sudden clinged her so about
That mermaidlike unto the floor she slid:
One half appeared, the other half was hid.   800
Thus near the bed she blushing stood upright;
And from her countenance behold ye might
A kind of twilight break, which through the hair,
As from an orient[4] cloud, glims here and there,
And round about the chamber this false morn   805
Brought forth the day before the day was born.
So Hero's ruddy cheek Hero betrayed,
And her all naked to his sight displayed,

---

7. Call to battle.
8. Innocent.
9. Hold firmly.
1. The Greek philosopher Empedocles held that creation was the result of love and strife.
2. One of Hercules's labors was to get the golden

apples of the Hesperides, guarded by a dragon. Hercules was born in Thebes.
3. A name for Venus, who was caught in bed with Mars by her husband Vulcan, who cast a fine chain net over them.
4. Bright, shining; "glims": gleams.

Whence his admiring eyes more pleasure took
Than Dis,[5] on heaps of gold fixing his look.   810
By this Apollo's golden harp began
To sound forth music to the Ocean,
Which watchful Hesperus[6] no sooner heard
But he the day's bright-bearing car prepared,
And ran before, as harbinger of light,   815
And with his flaring beams mocked ugly Night,
Till she, o'ercome with anguish, shame and rage,
Danged[7] down to hell her loathsome carriage.

1598

The Passionate Shepherd to His Love[1]

Come live with me and be my love,
And we will all the pleasures prove[2]
That valleys, groves, hills, and fields,
Woods, or steepy mountain yields.

And we will sit upon the rocks,   5
Seeing the shepherds feed their flocks,
By shallow rivers to whose falls
Melodious birds sing madrigals.

And I will make thee beds of roses
And a thousand fragrant posies,   10
A cap of flowers, and a kirtle
Embroidered all with leaves of myrtle;

A gown made of the finest wool
Which from our pretty lambs we pull;
Fair lined slippers for the cold,   15
With buckles of the purest gold;

A belt of straw and ivy buds,
With coral clasps and amber studs:
And if these pleasures may thee move,
Come live with me, and be my love.   20

The shepherds' swains shall dance and sing
For thy delight each May morning:

5. Pluto, god of the underworld and of wealth.
6. The evening star; apparently Marlowe's error for Lucifer, the morning star.
7. Hurled.
1. This pastoral lyric of invitation is one of the most famous of Elizabethan songs, and a few lines from it are sung in Shakespeare's *Merry Wives of Windsor*. Many poets have written replies to it, the finest of which is by that other great Elizabethan romantic, Sir Walter Ralegh, above.
2. Test, experience.

If these delights thy mind may move,
Then live with me and be my love.

1599, 1600

Dr. Faustus   Marlowe's major tragedies, *Tamburlaine*, *The Jew of Malta*, and *Dr. Faustus*, all portray a hero who passionately seeks power—the power of rule, the power of money, and the power of knowledge, respectively. Each of the heroes is an "overreacher," striving beyond the bounds of human capacity, or at least the limits imposed upon human achievement.

Unlike Tamburlaine, whose aim and goal is "the sweet fruition of an earthly crown," and Barabas, the Jew of Malta, who lusts for "infinite riches in a little room," Faustus seeks the power that comes from knowledge, no matter at what cost that knowledge is acquired. To get this power Faustus must make (or chooses to make) a bargain with the devil. Such a situation is an old folklore motif, but it would have been taken seriously in a time when everyone believed in the reality of devils. Faustus on his part is in search of the power that comes from black magic, but the devil on his side exacts a fearful price in exchange—the eternal damnation of Faustus's soul. This, like the reality of devils, would have been taken literally by an Elizabethan audience. Faustus aspires to be more than a man—a demigod, a deity. His fall is caused by the same pride and ambition that caused the fall of the angels in heaven, and of humanity in the Garden of Eden. So to aspire is to incur inevitable defeat, but it is characteristic of Marlowe that he makes those aspirations nonetheless magnificent.

The immediate source of the play is a German narrative called, in its English translation, *The History of the Damnable Life and Deserved Death of Doctor John Faustus*. It contains those scenes of horseplay and low practical joking which, in the drama, contrast so markedly with the passages of grand aspiration. It is quite possible that these low scenes are the work of a collaborator, and the early records from the theater and the early editions of the play (1604 and 1616, both long after Marlowe's death) show that the true text of the play is difficult to establish. What does seem clear is that no other Elizabethan could have written the first scene (which projects the insatiable aspiring mind of the hero), the famous address to Helen of Troy, or the final scene of Faustus's last hour.

The Tragical History
of the Life and Death of Doctor Faustus

Dramatis Personae

CHORUS
DR. JOHN FAUSTUS, *of the University of Wittenberg*
WAGNER, *his servant*
GOOD ANGEL *and* BAD ANGEL
VALDES and CORNELIUS, *magicians and friends of* FAUSTUS
THREE SCHOLARS, *students at the university*
LUCIFER, MEPHISTOPHILIS, *and* BELZEBUB, *devils*

ROBIN *and* DICK, *rustic clowns*
THE SEVEN DEADLY SINS
POPE ADRIAN
RAYMOND, *King of Hungary*
BRUNO, *a rival Pope, appointed by the* EMPEROR
CARDINALS OF FRANCE *and* PADUA
ARCHBISHOP OF RHEIMS
MARTINO, FREDERICK, *and* BENVOLIO, *gentlemen at the* EMPEROR'S *court*
CAROLUS (CHARLES) THE FIFTH, EMPEROR
DUKE OF SAXONY
DUKE *and* DUCHESS OF VANHOLT
HORSE-COURSER
CARTER
HOSTESS *of a tavern*
OLD MAN
SPIRITS *of* DARIUS, ALEXANDER *and his* PARAMOUR, *and* HELEN OF TROY
ATTENDANTS, MONKS *and* FRIARS, SOLDIERS, PIPER, *two* CUPIDS

Act 1

[*Enter* CHORUS.[1]]

CHO. Not marching in the fields of Trasimene[2]
    Where Mars did mate the warlike Carthagens,
    Nor sporting in the dalliance of love
    In courts of kings where state[3] is overturned,
    Nor in the pomp of proud audacious deeds   5
    Intends our Muse to vaunt his heavenly verse:
    Only this, gentles, we must now perform
    The form of Faustus' fortunes good or bad.
    And so to patient judgments we appeal
    And speak for Faustus in his infancy.   10
    Now is he born, his parents base of stock,
    In Germany within a town called Rhode;[4]
    At riper years to Wittenberg he went
    Whereas his kinsmen chiefly brought him up;
    So much he profits in divinity,   15
    The fruitful plot of scholarism graced,[5]
    That shortly he was graced with Doctor's name,
    Excelling all whose sweet delight disputes[6]
    In th' heavenly matters of theology,
    Till, swollen with cunning,[7] of a self-conceit,   20
    His waxen wings did mount above his reach
    And melting, heavens conspired his overthrow.[8]

1. A single actor who recited a prologue to an act or a whole play, and occasionally delivered an epilogue.
2. The battle of Lake Trasimene (217 B.C.) was one of the Carthaginian leader Hannibal's great victories. "Mate": join with.
3. Political power.
4. Roda. Wittenberg, in the next line, was the famous university where Martin Luther studied, as did Shakespeare's Hamlet and Horatio; "whereas": where.
5. Grazed. In line 17 "graced" refers to the Cambridge word for permission to proceed to a degree.
6. The usual academic exercises were disputations, which took the place of examinations.
7. Learning.
8. The reference is to the Greek myth of Icarus, who flew too near the sun on wings of feathers and wax made by his father Daedalus. The wax melted and he fell into the sea and was drowned.

For, falling to a devilish exercise
And glutted more with learning's golden gifts,
He surfeits upon cursèd necromancy;[9]   25
Nothing so sweet as magic is to him,
Which he prefers before his chiefest bliss[1]—
And this the man that in his study sits.

    [*Draws the curtain[2] and exit.*]

SCENE 1

[FAUSTUS *in his study.*]

FAUST. Settle thy studies, Faustus, and begin
    To sound the depth of that thou wilt profess.
    Having commenced,[3] be a divine in show,
    Yet level at the end of every art
    And live and die in Aristotle's works: 5
    Sweet Analytics,[4] 'tis thou hast ravished me!   [*Reads.*]
    Bene disserere est finis logicis—
    Is to dispute well logic's chiefest end?
    Affords this art no greater miracle?
    Then read no more; thou hast attained that end.   10
    A greater subject fitteth Faustus' wit:
    Bid *on kaì mē on*[5] farewell, Galen come,
    Seeing *ubi desinit philosophus, ibi incipit medicus;*[6]
    Be a physician, Faustus, heap up gold
    And be eternized for some wondrous cure.   [*Reads.*] 15
    Summum bonum medicinae sanitas[7]—
    The end of physic is our bodies' health:
    Why, Faustus, hast thou not attained that end?
    Is not thy common talk sound aphorisms?[8]
    Are not thy bills hung up as monuments   20
    Whereby whole cities have escaped the plague
    And thousand desperate maladies been eased?
    Yet art thou still but Faustus, and a man.
    Couldst thou make men to live eternally
    Or, being dead, raise them to life again,   25
    Then this profession were to be esteemed.
    Physic, farewell. Where is Justinian?[9]   [*Reads.*]
    Si una eademque res legatur duobus,
    Alter rem, alter valorem rei, etc.[1]—

---

9. Black magic.
1. The salvation of his soul.
2. A curtain to the enclosed space at the rear of the stage.
3. "Commenced": graduated, i.e., received the doctor's degree; "in show": in external appearance; "level": aim.
4. The title of a treatise on logic by Aristotle. The Latin means, "To carry on a disputation well is the end or purpose of logic."
5. "Being and not being," i.e., philosophy. Galen: the ancient authority on medicine (2nd century A.D.).

6. "Where the philosopher leaves off the physician begins."
7. "Good health is the object of medicine" (or "physic").
8. I.e., reliable medical pronouncements. "Bills": prescriptions.
9. Roman emperor and authority on law (483–565), author of the *Institutes*.
1. "If something is bequeathed to two persons, one shall have the thing itself, the other something of equal value." The next Latin phrase means: "A father cannot disinherit his son unless."

A pretty case of paltry legacies!   30
Exhaereditare filium non potest pater nisi—
Such is the subject of the Institute
And universal body of the law.
This study fits a mercenary drudge
Who aims at nothing but external trash,   35
Too servile and illiberal for me.
When all is done, divinity is best.
Jerome's Bible,[2] Faustus, view it well: [*Reads.*]
Stipendium peccati mors est—Ha! *Stipendium, etc.*
The reward of sin is death? That's hard.   40
Si pecasse negamus, fallimur, et nulla est in nobis veritas[3]—
If we say that we have no sin
We deceive ourselves, and there's no truth in us.
Why then belike
We must sin and so consequently die,   45
Aye, we must die an everlasting death.
What doctrine call you this, *Che sera, sera:*[4]
What will be, shall be? Divinity, adieu!
These metaphysics[5] of magicians
And necromantic books are heavenly: 50
Lines, circles, signs, letters, and characters—
Aye, these are those that Faustus most desires.
O what a world of profit and delight,
Of power, of honor, of omnipotence,
Is promised to the studious artisan![6]   55
All things that move between the quiet[7] poles
Shall be at my command. Emperors and kings
Are but obeyed in their several provinces,
Nor can they raise the wind or rend the clouds;
But his dominion that exceeds in this   60
Stretcheth as far as doth the mind of man.
A sound magician is a demigod:
Here tire my brains to gain a deity!
Wagner!

        [*Enter* WAGNER.]

Commend me to my dearest friends,   65
The German Valdes and Cornelius;
Request them earnestly to visit me.
WAG. I will, sir.   [*Exit.*]
FAUST. Their conference will be a greater help to me
Than all my labors, plod I ne'er so fast.   70

        [*Enter the* GOOD ANGEL *and the* BAD ANGEL.]

G. ANG. O Faustus, lay that damnèd book aside
And gaze not on it, lest it tempt thy soul

---

2. The Latin translation, or "Vulgate," of St. Jerome (ca. 340–420). The Latin (Romans vi.23) is translated in line 40.
3. 1 John i.8, translated in the next 2 lines.
4. Translated in the first half of the next line.

5. Basic principles.
6. I.e., a master of the occult arts, such as necromancy.
7. Unmoving.

And heap God's heavy wrath upon thy head.
Read, read the Scriptures! That is blasphemy.
B. ANG. Go forward, Faustus, in that famous art   75
    Wherein all nature's treasury is contained:
    Be thou on earth, as Jove[8] is in the sky,
    Lord and commander of these elements.

    [*Exeunt* ANGELS.]

FAUST. How am I glutted with conceit[9] of this!
    Shall I make spirits fetch me what I please,   80
    Resolve me of all ambiguities,
    Perform what desperate enterprise I will?
    I'll have them fly to India[1] for gold,
    Ransack the ocean for orient pearl,
    And search all corners of the new-found world[2]   85
    For pleasant fruits and princely delicates;
    I'll have them read me strange philosophy
    And tell the secrets of all foreign kings;
    I'll have them wall all Germany with brass
    And make swift Rhine circle fair Wittenberg;   90
    I'll have them fill the public schools[3] with silk
    Wherewith the students shall be bravely clad;
    I'll levy soldiers with the coin they bring,
    And chase the Prince of Parma[4] from our land
    And reign sole king of all our provinces;   95
    Yea, stranger engines for the brunt of war
    Than was the fiery keel[5] at Antwerp's bridge
    I'll make my servile spirits to invent!

    [*Enter* VALDES *and* CORNELIUS.]

    Come, German Valdes and Cornelius,
    And make me blest with your sage conference.   100
    Valdes, sweet Valdes and Cornelius,
    Know that your words have won me at the last
    To practice magic and concealèd arts;
    Yet not your words only, but mine own fantasy
    That will receive no object,[6] for my head   105
    But ruminates on necromantic skill.
    Philosophy is odious and obscure,
    Both law and physic are for petty wits,
    Divinity is basest of the three,
    Unpleasant, harsh, contemptible, and vile;   110
    'Tis magic, magic, that hath ravished me!
    Then, gentle friends, aid me in this attempt,
    And I, that have with concise syllogisms

---

8. God (a common substitution in Elizabethan drama).
9. Filled with the idea.
1. "India" could mean the West Indies, America, or Ophir (in the east).
2. The western hemisphere.
3. The university lecture rooms.

4. The duke of Parma was the Spanish governor general of the Low Countries from 1579 to 1592.
5. A reference to the burning ship sent by the Netherlanders in 1585 against the barrier on the river Scheldt which Parma had built as a part of the blockade of Antwerp.
6. That will pay no attention to physical reality.

Graveled[7] the pastors of the German church,
And made the flowering pride of Wittenberg
Swarm to my problems[8] as the infernal spirits   115
On sweet Musaeus when he came to hell,
Will be as cunning as Agrippa[9] was
Whose shadows made all Europe honor him.

VALD. Faustus, these books, thy wit, and our experience   120
    Shall make all nations to canonize us.
    As Indian Moors[1] obey their Spanish lords
    So shall the spirits of every element
    Be always serviceable to us three:
    Like lions shall they guard us when we please.   125
    Like Almain rutters[2] with their horsemen's staves,
    Or Lapland giants trotting by our sides;
    Sometimes like women, or unwedded maids,
    Shadowing[3] more beauty in their airy brows
    Than in the white breasts of the queen of love;   130
    From Venice shall they drag huge argosies
    And from America the golden fleece
    That yearly stuffs old Philip's[4] treasury,
    If learned Faustus will be resolute.

FAUST. Valdes, as resolute am I in this   135
    As thou to live; therefore object it not.[5]

CORN. The miracles that magic will perform
    Will make thee vow to study nothing else.
    He that is grounded in astrology,
    Enriched with tongues, well seen[6] in minerals,   140
    Hath all the principles magic doth require.
    Then doubt not, Faustus, but to be renowned
    And more frequented for this mystery[7]
    Than heretofore the Delphian oracle.
    The spirits tell me they can dry the sea   145
    And fetch the treasure of all foreign wrecks—
    Aye, all the wealth that our forefathers hid
    Within the massy[8] entrails of the earth.
    Then tell me, Faustus, what shall we three want?

FAUST. Nothing, Cornelius. O this cheers my soul!   150
    Come, show me some demonstrations magical
    That I may conjure in some lusty[9] grove
    And have these joys in full possession.

VALD. Then haste thee to some solitary grove
    And bear wise Bacon's[1] and Abanus' works,   155

---

7. Confounded.
8. Lectures in logic and mathematics. Musaeus was a mythical singer, son of Orpheus; it was, however, the latter who charmed the denizens of hell with his music.
9. Cornelius Agrippa, German author of *The Vanity and Uncertainty of Arts and Sciences,* popularly supposed to have the power of calling up shades ("shadows") of the dead.
1. I.e., dark-skinned American Indians.
2. German horsemen.

3. Harboring.
4. Philip II, king of Spain.
5. I.e., don't make it a condition.
6. Expert.
7. Craft. The "Delphian oracle" was the oracle of Apollo at Delphi, much frequented in antiquity.
8. Massive.
9. Flourishing, beautiful.
1. Roger Bacon, the medieval friar and scientist, popularly thought a magician. "Abanus" is Pietro d'Abano, 13th-century alchemist.

The Hebrew Psalter and New Testament;
And whatsoever else is requisite
We will inform thee ere our conference cease.
CORN. Valdes, first let him know the words of art,
    And then, all other ceremonies learned,   160
    Faustus may try his cunning by himself.
VALD. First I'll instruct thee in the rudiments,
    And then wilt thou be perfecter than I.
FAUST. Then come and dine with me, and after meat
    We'll canvass every quiddity² thereof;   165
    For ere I sleep I'll try what I can do:
    This night I'll conjure³ though I die therefore.   [*Exeunt.*]

SCENE 2

[Enter two SCHOLARS.]

1 SCH. I wonder what's become of Faustus, that was wont to make
    our schools ring with *sic probo.*⁴
2 SCH. That shall we presently know; here comes his boy.⁵

[Enter WAGNER carrying wine.]

1 SCH. How now, sirrah; where's thy master?
WAG. God in heaven knows.   5
2 SCH. Why, dost not thou know then?
WAG. Yes, I know; but that follows not.
1 SCH. Go to, sirrah; leave your jesting and tell us where he is.
WAG. That follows not by force of argument, which you, being
    licentiate,⁶ should stand upon; therefore acknowledge your error   10
    and be attentive.
2 SCH. Then you will not tell us?
WAG. You are deceived, for I will tell you. Yet if you were not
    dunces you would never ask me such a question, for is he not
    corpus naturale, and is not that *mobile?*⁷ Then wherefore should   15
    you ask me such a question? But that I am by nature phleg-
    matic,⁸ slow to wrath and prone to lechery (to love, I would say),
    it were not for you to come within forty foot of the place of
    execution,⁹ although I do not doubt to see you both hanged the
    next sessions. Thus having triumphed over you, I will set my   20
    countenance like a precisian,¹ and begin to speak thus: Truly,
    my dear brethren, my master is within at dinner with Valdes and
    Cornelius, as this wine, if it could speak, would inform your
    worships; and so the Lord bless you, preserve you, and keep you,
    my dear brethren.   25

[Exit.]

---

2. Essential feature.
3. Call up spirits.
4. "Thus I prove," a phrase in scholastic disputation.
5. Poor student earning his keep.
6. I.e., graduate students.
7. *Corpus naturale et mobile* (natural, movable matter) was a scholastic definition of the subject

matter of physics. Wagner is here parodying the language of learning he hears around the university.
8. Dominated by the phlegm, one of the 4 humors of medieval medicine and psychology.
9. I.e., the dining room.
1. A Puritan. The rest of his speech is in the style of the Puritans.

1 SCH. O Faustus, then I fear that which I have long suspected,
      That thou art fallen into that damnèd art
      For which they two are infamous through the world.
2 SCH. Were he a stranger, not allied to me,
      The danger of his soul would make me mourn.   30
      But come, let us go and inform the Rector,[2]
      It may be his grave counsel may reclaim him.
1 SCH. I fear me nothing will reclaim him now.
2 SCH. Yet let us see what we can do.   [*Exeunt.*]

SCENE 3

[*Enter* FAUSTUS *to conjure.*]

FAUST. Now that the gloomy shadow of the night,
      Longing to view Orion's drizzling look,[3]
      Leaps from the antarctic world unto the sky
      And dims the welkin[4] with her pitchy breath,
      Faustus, begin thine incantations   5
      And try if devils will obey thy hest,
      Seeing thou hast prayed and sacrificed to them.
      Within this circle is Jehovah's name

[*He draws the circle[5] on the ground.*]

      Forward and backward anagrammatized,
      The breviated names of holy saints,   10
      Figures of every adjunct[6] to the heavens
      And characters of signs and erring stars,
      By which the spirits are enforced to rise.
      Then fear not, Faustus, but be resolute
      And try the uttermost magic can perform.   [*Thunder.*]   15
      Sint mihi dei Acherontis propitii! Valeat numen triplex Iehovae!
      Ignei aerii aquatici terreni spiritus, salvete! Orientis princeps Lucifer
      Belzebub, inferni ardentis monarcha, et Demogorgon, propitia-
      mus vos, ut appareat et surgat Mephistophilis![7]

[*FAUSTUS pauses. Thunder still.*]

Quid tu moraris?[8] Per Iehovam, Gehennam et consecratam aquam
quam nunc spargo, signumque crucis quod nunc facio, et per vota
nostra, ipse nunc surgat nobis dicatus Mephistophilis!

[*Enter* MEPHISTOPHILIS *in the shape of a dragon.*]

      I charge thee to return and change thy shape;   25
      Thou art too ugly to attend on me.

2. The head of a German university.
3. Orion appears at the beginning of winter. The phrase is a reminiscence of Virgil.
4. Sky.
5. I.e., the magic circle on the ground within which the spirits rise.
6. Heavenly body, thought to be joined to the solid firmament. "Characters of signs" are signs of the zodiac and the planets; "erring": wandering.
7. This first part of the incantation means: "May the gods of the lower regions favor me! Goodbye to the Trinity! Hail, spirits of fire, air, water, and earth! Prince of the East, Belzebub, monarch of burning hell, and Demogorgon, we pray to you that Mephistophilis may appear and rise."
8. Nothing has happened, so Faustus asks, "What are you waiting for?" and continues to conjure: "By Jehovah, Gehenna, and the holy water which I now sprinkle, and the sign of the cross which I now make, and by our vows, may Mephistophilis himself now rise to serve us."

Go, and return an old Franciscan friar;
That holy shape becomes a devil best.   [*Exit* MEPH.]
I see there's virtue in my heavenly words:
Who would not be proficient in this art?   30
How pliant is this Mephistophilis,
Full of obedience and humility!
Such is the force of magic and my spells.
Now, Faustus, thou art conjurer laureate
That canst command great Mephistophilis: 35
Quin redis, Mephistophilis, fratris imagine![9]

[*Re-enter* MEPHISTOPHILIS *like a Friar.*]

MEPH. Now, Faustus, what wouldst thou have me do?
FAUST. I charge thee wait upon me whilst I live
    To do whatever Faustus shall command,
    Be it be make the moon drop from her sphere   40
    Or the ocean to overwhelm the world.
MEPH. I am a servant to great Lucifer
    And may not follow thee without his leave:
    No more than he commands must we perform.
FAUST. Did not he charge thee to appear to me?   45
MEPH. No, I came now hither of my own accord.
FAUST. Did not my conjuring speeches raise thee?
    Speak!
MEPH. That was the cause, but yet *per accidens*,[1]
    For when we hear one rack[2] the name of God,   50
    Abjure the Scriptures and his Saviour Christ,
    We fly in hope to get his glorious soul;
    Nor will we come unless he use such means
    Whereby he is in danger to be damned;
    Therefore the shortest cut for conjuring   55
    Is stoutly to abjure the Trinity
    And pray devoutly to the prince of hell.
FAUST. So I have done, and hold this principle,
    There is no chief but only Belzebub
    To whom Faustus doth dedicate himself.   60
    This word "damnation" terrifies not me
    For I confound hell in Elysium;
    My ghost be with the old philosophers![3]
    But leaving these vain trifles of men's souls—
    Tell me, what is that Lucifer thy lord?   65
MEPH. Arch-regent and commander of all spirits.
FAUST. Was not that Lucifer an angel once?
MEPH. Yes, Faustus, and most dearly loved of God.
FAUST. How comes it, then, that he is prince of devils?   70
MEPH. O, by aspiring pride and insolence,
    For which God threw him from the face of heaven.

---

9. "Return, Mephistophilis, in the shape of a friar."
1. By the immediate, not ultimate, cause.
2. Torture (by anagrammatizing).

3. I.e., I consider the true hell to be the classical Elysium, where philosophy is discussed, not the Christian place of punishment for sinners.

FAUST. And what are you that live with Lucifer?
MEPH. Unhappy spirits that fell with Lucifer,
　　Conspired against our God with Lucifer,
　　And are forever damned with Lucifer.   75
FAUST. Where are you damned?
MEPH. In hell.
FAUST. How comes it, then, that thou art out of hell?
MEPH. Why, this is hell, nor am I out of it: 80
　　Thinkst thou that I who saw the face of God
　　And tasted the eternal joys of heaven
　　Am not tormented with ten thousand hells
　　In being deprived of everlasting bliss?[4]
　　O Faustus, leave these frivolous demands   85
　　Which strike a terror to my fainting soul!
FAUST. What, is great Mephistophilis so passionate
　　For being deprivèd of the joys of heaven?
　　Learn thou of Faustus manly fortitude
　　And scorn those joys thou never shalt possess.   90
　　Go, bear these tidings to great Lucifer:
　　Seeing Faustus hath incurred eternal death
　　By desperate thoughts against Jove's deity,
　　Say he surrenders up to him his soul
　　So he will spare him four and twenty years,   95
　　Letting him live in all voluptuousness,
　　Having thee ever to attend on me:
　　To give me whatsoever I shall ask,
　　To tell me whatsoever I demand,
　　To slay mine enemies and aid my friends,   100
　　And always be obedient to my will.
　　Go, and return to mighty Lucifer,
　　And meet me in my study at midnight
　　And then resolve me of thy master's mind.[5]
MEPH. I will, Faustus.   [Exit.]   105
FAUST. Had I as many souls as there be stars
　　I'd give them all for Mephistophilis!
　　By him I'll be great emperor of the world,
　　And make a bridge thorough the moving air
　　To pass the ocean with a band of men;   110
　　I'll join the hills that bind the Afric shore
　　And make that country continent to Spain,
　　And both contributory to my crown;
　　The Emperor[6] shall not live but by my leave,
　　Nor any potentate of Germany.   115
　　Now that I have obtained what I desire
　　I'll live in speculation[7] of this art
　　Till Mephistophilis return again.   [Exit.]

---

4. This is the *poena damni*, or punishment of loss, supposed to constitute the greatest spiritual suffering.
5. Give me his decision.
6. The Holy Roman Emperor.
7. Contemplation.

SCENE 4

[*Enter* WAGNER *and the* CLOWN ⟨ROBIN.⟩[8]]

WAG. Come hither, sirrah boy.

CLOWN. Boy! O disgrace to my person! Zounds, boy in your face!
You have seen many boys with such pickadevaunts, I am sure.[9]

WAG. Sirrah, hast thou no comings in?[1]

CLOWN. Yes, and goings out too; you may see, sir.   5

WAG. Alas, poor slave. See how poverty jests in his nakedness:
the villain's out of service, and so hungry that I know he would
give his soul to the devil for a shoulder of mutton, though it were
blood-raw.

CLOWN. Not so, neither; I had need to have it well-roasted, and   10
good sauce to it, if I pay so dear, I can tell you.

WAG. Sirrah, wilt thou be my man and wait on me? And I will
make thee go like *Qui mihi discipulus*.[2]

CLOWN. What, in verse?

WAG. No, slave, in beaten silk and staves-acre.[3]   15

CLOWN. Staves-acre! that's good to kill vermin. Then, belike, if I
serve you I shall be lousy.

WAG. Why, so thou shalt be, whether thou dost it or no; for, sirrah,
if thou dost not presently bind thyself to me for seven years, I'll
turn all the lice about thee into familiars[4] and make them tear   20
thee in pieces.

CLOWN. Nay, sir, you may save yourself a labor, for they are as
familiar with me as if they paid for their meat and drink, I can
tell you.

WAG. Well, sirrah, leave your jesting and take these guilders.[5]   25

CLOWN. Yes, marry, sir, and I thank you, too.

WAG. So, now thou art to be at an hour's warning whenever and
wheresoever the devil shall fetch thee.

CLOWN. Here, take your guilders again, I'll none of 'em.

WAG. Not I, thou art pressed;[6] prepare thyself, for I will presently   30
raise up two devils to carry thee away. Banio! Belcher!

CLOWN. Belcher? And Belcher come here I'll belch him. I am not
afraid of a devil.

[*Enter two* DEVILS, *and the* CLOWN *runs up and down crying.*]

WAG. How now, sir! Will you serve me now?

CLOWN. Aye, good Wagner, take away the devil then.   35

WAG. Spirits, away!   [DEVILS *exeunt.*]
                    Now, sirrah, follow me.

8. Not a court jester (as in some of Shakespeare's
plays), but the older-fashioned stock character, a
rustic buffoon. The name "Robin" has been interpolated by later editors of the text; all such inter-
polations, introduced for clarity of understanding,
are indicated by the special brackets used here.
9. The point of the Clown's retort is that he is a
man and wears a beard ("pickadevant"). "Zounds":
an oath ("God's wounds").
1. Income, but the Clown then puns on the literal

meaning.
2. "You who are my pupil" (the opening phrase
of a poem on how students should behave, from
Lily's *Latin Grammar*). Wagner means, "like a
proper servant of a learned man."
3. A kind of delphinium used for killing vermin.
4. Familiar spirits, demons.
5. Money.
6. Impressed, i.e., hired.

CLOWN. I will, sir. But hark you, master, will you teach me this
  conjuring occupation?

WAG. Aye, sirrah, I'll teach thee to turn thyself to a dog, or a cat,   40
  or a mouse, or a rat, or anything.

CLOWN. A dog, or a cat, or a mouse, or a rat! O brave[7] Wagner!

WAG. Villain, call me Master Wagner; and see that you walk attentively, and let your right eye be always diametrally[8] fixed upon
  my left heel, that thou mayst *quasi vestigiis nostris insistere.*[9]   45

CLOWN. Well, sir, I warrant you.   [*Exeunt.*]

Act 2

SCENE 1

[*Enter* FAUSTUS *in his study.*]

FAUST. Now, Faustus, must thou needs be damned,
  And canst thou not be saved.
  What boots[1] it, then, to think of God or heaven?
  Away with such vain fancies, and despair—
  Despair in God and trust in Belzebub.   5
  Now go not backward, no, be resolute!
  Why waverest thou? O something soundeth in mine ears:
  "Abjure this magic, turn to God again!"
  Aye, and Faustus will turn to God again.
  To God? He loves thee not;   10
  The God thou servest is thine own appetite,
  Wherein is fixed the love of Belzebub.
  To him I'll build an altar and a church
  And offer lukewarm blood of newborn babes.

[*Enter* GOOD ANGEL *and* BAD ANGEL.]

G. ANG. Sweet Faustus, leave that execrable art.   15
B. ANG. Go forward, Faustus, in that famous art.
FAUST. Contrition, prayer, repentance—what of them?
G. ANG. O they are means to bring thee unto heaven!
B. ANG. Rather illusions, fruits of lunacy,
  That makes men foolish that do use them most.   20
G. ANG. Sweet Faustus, think of heaven and heavenly things.
B. ANG. No, Faustus, think of honor and of wealth.

[⟨*Exeunt* ANGELS.⟩]

FAUST. Of wealth!
  Why, the signiory of Emden[2] shall be mine.
  When Mephistophilis shall stand by me   25
  What power can hurt me? Faustus, thou art safe;
  Cast no more doubts. Come, Mephistophilis,
  And bring glad tidings from great Lucifer.

7. Marvelous, wonderful.   1. Avails.
8. Diametrically.   2. A wealthy German trade center.
9. A pedantic way of saying "follow my footsteps."

Is 't not midnight? Come, Mephistophilis!
Veni, veni, Mephistophile![3]   30

    [*Enter* MEPHISTOPHILIS.]

Now tell me what saith Lucifer, thy lord?
MEPH. That I shall wait on Faustus whilst I live,
  So he will buy my service with his soul.
FAUST. Already Faustus hath hazarded that for thee.
MEPH. But, Faustus, thou must bequeath it solemnly   35
  And write a deed of gift with thine own blood,
  For that security craves Lucifer.
  If thou deny it, I must back to hell.
FAUST. Stay, Mephistophilis, and tell me what good
  Will my soul do thy lord?
MEPH.   Enlarge his kingdom.   40
FAUST. Is that the reason why he tempts us thus?
MEPH. *Solamen miseris socios habuisse doloris.*[4]
FAUST. Why, have you any pain that tortures others?
MEPH. As great as have the human souls of men.
  But tell me, Faustus, shall I have thy soul?   45
  And I will be thy slave, and wait on thee,
  And give thee more than thou hast wit to ask.
FAUST. Aye, Mephistophilis, I'll give it him.
MEPH. Then, Faustus, stab thine arm courageously,
  And bind thy soul that at some certain day   50
  Great Lucifer may claim it as his own,
  And then be thou as great as Lucifer.
FAUST. Lo, Mephistophilis, for love of thee

    [*Stabbing his arm.*]

Faustus hath cut his arm, and with his proper[5] blood
Assures his soul to be great Lucifer's.   55
Chief lord and regent of perpetual night,
View here the blood that trickles from mine arm
And let it be propitious for my wish!
MEPH. But, Faustus,
  Write it in manner of a deed of gift.   60
FAUST. Aye, so I do. [*Writes.*] But, Mephistophilis,
  My blood congeals and I can write no more.
MEPH. I'll fetch thee fire to dissolve it straight.   [*Exit.*]
FAUST. What might the staying of my blood portend?
  Is it unwilling I should write this bill?[6]   65
  Why streams it not, that I may write afresh?
  "Faustus gives to thee his soul"—ah, there it stayed.
  Why shouldst thou not? Is not thy soul thine own?
  Then write again: "Faustus gives to thee his soul."

    [*Enter* MEPHISTOPHILIS *with a chafer*[7] *of fire.*]

---

3. "Come, come, Mephistophilis!"   6. Contract.
4. "Misery loves company."   7. A portable grate.
5. Own.

MEPH. See, Faustus, here is fire; set it on.   70
FAUST. So: now the blood begins to clear again;
  Now will I make an end immediately.   [⟨*Writes.*⟩]
MEPH. [*aside*] What will not I do to obtain his soul!
FAUST. *Consummatum est*[8]—this bill is ended;
  And Faustus hath bequeathed his soul to Lucifer.   75
  But what is this inscription on mine arm?
  "*Homo, fuge!*"[9] Whither should I fly?
  If unto God, he'll throw me down to hell.
  My senses are deceived; here's nothing writ.
  O yes, I see it plain: even here is writ   80
  "*Homo, fuge!*" Yet shall not Faustus fly.
MEPH. I'll fetch him somewhat to delight his mind.   [*Exit.*]

    [*Re-enter* MEPHISTOPHILIS *with* DEVILS, *giving crowns and
    rich apparel to* FAUSTUS, *and dance, and then depart.*]

FAUST. What means this show?
  Speak, Mephistophilis.
MEPH. Nothing, Faustus, but to delight thy mind   85
  And let thee see what magic can perform.
FAUST. But may I raise such spirits when I please?
MEPH. Aye, Faustus, and do greater things than these.
FAUST. Then, Mephistophilis, receive this scroll,
  A deed of gift of body and of soul;   90
  But yet conditionally that thou perform
  All covenant-articles between us both.
MEPH. Faustus, I swear by hell and Lucifer
  To effect all promises between us made.
FAUST. Then hear me read it, Mephistophilis.   [⟨*Reads.*⟩] 95
  "On these conditions following:
  First, that Faustus may be a spirit in form and substance.
  Secondly, that Mephistophilis shall be his servant and at his
  command.
  Thirdly, that Mephistophilis shall do for him, and bring him   100
  whatsoever.
  Fourthly, that he shall be in his chamber or house invisible.
  Lastly, that he shall appear to the said John Faustus at all times,
  in what form or shape soever he please.
  I, John Faustus of Wittenberg, Doctor, by these presents do give 105
  both body and soul to Lucifer, Prince of the East, and his minister Mephistophilis, and furthermore grant unto them, that four
  and twenty years being expired, the articles above written inviolate, full power to fetch or carry the said John Faustus, body and
  soul, flesh, blood, or goods, into their habitation wheresoever.   110
                        By me John Faustus."
MEPH. Speak, Faustus, do you deliver this as your deed?
FAUST. Aye, take it, and the devil give thee good of it.

8. "It is finished." A blasphemy, as these are the   9. "O man, fly!"
words of Christ on the Cross (see John 19.30).

MEPH. Now, Faustus, ask what thou wilt.

FAUST. First will I question with thee about hell.   115
    Tell me, where is the place that men call hell?

MEPH. Under the heavens.

FAUST. Aye, so are all things else, but whereabout?

MEPH. Within the bowels of these elements,
    Where we are tortured and remain forever.   120
    Hell hath no limits, nor is circumscribed
    In one self place, for where we are is hell,
    And where hell is there must we ever be;
    And, to be short, when all the world dissolves
    And every creature shall be purified,   125
    All places shall be hell that is not heaven.

FAUST. I think hell's a fable.

MEPH. Aye, think so still, till experience change thy mind.

FAUST. Why, thinkst thou that Faustus shall be damned?

MEPH. Aye, of necessity, for here's the scroll   130
    In which thou hast given thy soul to Lucifer.

FAUST. Aye, and body too; but what of that?
    Thinkst thou that Faustus is so fond[1] to imagine
    That after this life there is any pain?
    Tush, no, these are trifles and mere old wives' tales.   135

MEPH. But I am an instance to prove the contrary,
    For I tell thee I am damned and now in hell.

FAUST. Nay, and this be hell I'll willingly be damned.
    What, sleeping, eating, walking, and disputing?
    But leaving off this, let me have a wife,   140
    The fairest maid in Germany,
    For I am wanton and lascivious
    And cannot live without a wife.

MEPH. I prithee, Faustus, talk not of a wife.[2]

FAUST. Nay, sweet Mephistophilis, fetch me one, for I will have   145
one.

MEPH. Well, thou shalt have a wife. Sit there till I come. [⟨*Exit.*⟩]

    [*Re-enter* MEPHISTOPHILIS *with a* DEVIL *dressed like a woman,
    with fireworks.*]

FAUST. What sight is this?

MEPH. Now, Faustus, how dost thou like thy wife?

FAUST. Here's a hot whore indeed! No, I'll no wife.   150

MEPH. Marriage is but a ceremonial toy,
    And if thou lovest me, think no more of it.
    I'll cull thee out the fairest courtesans
    And bring them every morning to thy bed;
    She whom thine eye shall like thy heart shall have,   155
    Were she as chaste as was Penelope,[3]
    As wise as Saba, or as beautiful

---

1. Foolish.
2. Mephistophilis cannot produce a wife for Faustus because marriage is a sacrament.
3. The wife of Ulysses, famed for chastity and fidelity. "Saba": the Queen of Sheba.

As was bright Lucifer before his fall.
Hold, take this book: peruse it thoroughly.
The iterating[4] of these lines brings gold,   160
The framing[5] of this circle on the ground
Brings whirlwinds, tempests, thunder, and lightning;
Pronounce this thrice devoutly to thyself
And men in harness[6] shall appear to thee,
Ready to execute what thou desirest.   165

FAUST. Thanks, Mephistophilis, yet fain would I have a book wherein
I might behold all spells and incantations, that I might raise up
spirits when I please.

MEPH. Here they are in this book.   [*There turn to them.*]

FAUST. Now would I have a book where I might see all characters   170
and planets of the heavens, that I might know their motions and
dispositions.

MEPH. Here they are too.   [*Turn to them.*]

FAUST. Nay, let me have one book more, and then I have done,
wherein I might see all plants, herbs, and trees that grow upon   175
the earth.

MEPH. Here they be.

FAUST. O thou art deceived!

MEPH. Tut, I warrant thee.   [*Turn to them.*]

　　　　[⟨*Exeunt.*⟩][7]

SCENE 2

[*Enter* FAUSTUS *in his study and* MEPHISTOPHILIS.]

FAUST. When I behold the heavens then I repent
And curse thee, wicked Mephistophilis,
Because thou hast deprived me of those joys.

MEPH. 'Twas thine own seeking, Faustus, thank thyself.
But thinkest thou heaven is such a glorious thing?   5
I tell thee, Faustus, it is not half so fair
As thou or any man that breathes on earth.

FAUST. How provest thou that?

MEPH. 'Twas made for man; then he's more excellent.

FAUST. If heaven was made for man 'twas made for me.   10
I will renounce this magic and repent.

[*Enter* GOOD ANGEL *and* BAD ANGEL.]

G. ANG. Faustus, repent; yet God will pity thee.

B. ANG. Thou art a spirit; God cannot pity thee.

FAUST. Who buzzeth in mine ears I am a spirit?[8]
Be I a devil, yet God may pity me.   15
Yea, God will pity me, if I repent.

B. ANG. Aye, but Faustus never shall repent.

4. Repeating.
5. Drawing.
6. Armor.
7. After this a comic scene has been lost from the text. In it, apparently the Clown, Robin, stole one of Faustus's conjuring books and left Wagner's service. He then became an hostler at an inn.
8. Evil spirit, devil.

[*Exeunt* ANGELS.]

FAUST. My heart is hardened; I cannot repent.
  Scarce can I name salvation, faith, or heaven,
  But fearful echoes thunder in mine ears: 20
  "Faustus, thou are damned!" Then guns and knives,
  Swords, poison, halters, and envenomed steel
  Are laid before me to dispatch myself,
  And long ere this I should have done the deed
  Had not sweet pleasure conquered deep despair.   25
  Have I not made blind Homer sing to me
  Of Alexander's love and Oenon's death,[9]
  And hath not he that built the walls of Thebes
  With ravishing sound of his melodious harp[1]
  Made music with my Mephistophilis?   30
  Why should I die, then, or basely despair?
  I am resolved Faustus shall not repent.
  Come, Mephistophilis, let us dispute again
  And reason of divine astrology.
  Speak, are there many spheres above the moon?   35
  Are all celestial bodies but one globe
  As is the substance of this centric earth?[2]
MEPH. As are the elements, such are the heavens,
  Even from the moon unto the empyreal orb,
  Mutually folded in each other's spheres,   40
  And jointly move upon one axletree
  Whose termine[3] is termed the world's wide pole;
  Nor are the names of Saturn, Mars, or Jupiter
  Feigned, but are erring stars.
FAUST. But tell me, have they all one motion, both *situ et tem-*   45
  pore?[4]
MEPH. All move from east to west in four and twenty hours upon
  the poles of the world, but differ in their motions upon the poles
  of the zodiac.[5]
FAUST. These slender questions Wagner can decide.   50
  Hath Mephistophilis no greater skill?
  Who knows not the double motion of the planets?
  That the first is finished in a natural day;
  The second thus, Saturn in thirty years, Jupiter in twelve, Mars
  in four, the Sun, Venus, and Mercury in a year, the Moon in   55
  twenty-eight days. These are freshmen's suppositions. But tell
  me, hath every sphere a dominion or *intelligentia?*[6]
MEPH. Aye.

9. Alexander is another name for Paris, the lover of Oenone; later he deserted her and abducted Helen, causing the Trojan War. Oenone refused to heal the wounds Paris received in battle, and when he died of them she killed herself in remorse.
1. I.e., the legendary musician Amphion.
2. "Faustus asks whether all the apparently different heavenly bodies form really one globe, like the earth. Mephistophilis answers that like the elements, which are separate but combined, the heavenly bodies are separate, though their spheres

are infolded, and they move on one axletree. Hence we are not in error in giving individual names to Saturn, Mars, or Jupiter; they are separate planets" (F. S. Boas). The "empyreal orb," or outermost sphere, was also called the empyrean.
3. End.
4. In position and time.
5. I.e., the common axletree on which all the spheres revolve.
6. I.e., an angel or intelligence (thought to be the source of motion in each sphere).

FAUST. How many heavens or spheres are there?

MEPH. Nine: the seven planets, the firmament, and the empyreal   60
heaven.

FAUST. But is there not *coelum igneum, et crystallinum?*[7]

MEPH. No, Faustus, they be but fables.

FAUST. Resolve me then in this one question: why are not conjunctions, oppositions, aspects, eclipses, all at one time, but in some   65
years we have more, in some less?

MEPH. *Per inequalem motum respectu totius.*[8]

FAUST. Well, I am answered. Tell me, who made the world?

MEPH. I will not.

FAUST. Sweet Mephistophilis, tell me.   70

MEPH. Move[9] me not, Faustus.

FAUST. Villain, have I not bound thee to tell me anything?

MEPH. Aye, that is not against our kingdom; this is.
Thou art damned; think thou of hell.

FAUST. Think, Faustus, upon God that made the world!   75

MEPH. Remember this!   [*Exit.*]

FAUST. Aye, go, accursèd spirit, to ugly hell;
'Tis thou has damned distressèd Faustus' soul.
Is 't not too late?

[*Enter* GOOD ANGEL *and* BAD ANGEL.]

B. ANG. Too late.   80

G. ANG. Never too late, if Faustus will repent.

B. ANG. If thou repent, devils will tear thee in pieces.

G. ANG. Repent, and they shall never raze[1] thy skin.

[*Exeunt* ANGELS.]

FAUST. O Christ, my Saviour! my Saviour!
Help to save distressèd Faustus' soul.   85

[*Enter* LUCIFER, BELZEBUB, *and* MEPHISTOPHILIS.]

LUC. Christ cannot save thy soul, for he is just;
There's none but I have interest in the same.

FAUST. O what art thou that lookst so terrible?

LUC. I am Lucifer,
And this is my companion prince in hell.

FAUST. O Faustus, they are come to fetch thy soul!   90

BEL. We are come to tell thee thou dost injure us.

LUC. Thou call'st on Christ, contrary to thy promise.

BEL. Thou shouldst not think on God.

LUC. Think on the devil.   95

BEL. And his dam too.[2]

FAUST. Nor will I henceforth. Pardon me in this,
And Faustus vows never to look to heaven,
Never to name God or pray to him,

7. The "heaven of fire" and the "crystalline sphere," introduced by some of the old authorities to explain the precession of the equinoxes.

8. "Because of their unequal velocities within the system."

9. Anger.

1. Scratch.

2. "The devil and his dam" was a common colloquial expression.

   To burn his Scriptures, slay his ministers,   100
   And make my spirits pull his churches down.
LUC. So shalt thou show thyself an obedient servant, and we will
   highly gratify thee for it.
BEL. Faustus, we are come from hell in person to show thee some
   pastime. Sit down, and thou shalt behold the Seven Deadly Sins   105
   appear to thee in their own proper shapes and likeness.
FAUST. That sight will be as pleasant to me as Paradise was to Adam,
   the first day of his creation.
LUC. Talk not of Paradise or Creation, but mark the show. Go,
   Mephistophilis, fetch them in.   110

      [Enter the SEVEN DEADLY SINS,[3] led by a piper.]

   Now, Faustus, question them of their names and dispositions.
FAUST. That shall I soon. What art thou, the first?
PRIDE. I am Pride. I disdain to have any parents. I am like to Ovid's
   flea:[4] I can creep into every corner of a wench; sometimes like a
   periwig I sit upon her brow; next like a necklace I hang about her   115
   neck; then like a fan of feathers I kiss her lips; and then turning
   myself to a wrought smock[5] do what I list. But fie, what a smell
   is here! I'll not speak another word except the ground be perfumed and covered with cloth of arras.[6]
FAUST. Thou art a proud knave indeed. What art thou, the second?   120
COVET. I am Covetousness, begotten of an old churl in a leather
   bag; and, might I now obtain my wish, this house, you and all,
   should turn to gold, that I might lock you safe into my chest. O
   my sweet gold!
FAUST. And what art thou, the third?   125
ENVY. I am Envy, begotten of a chimney-sweeper and an oyster-
   wife. I cannot read, and therefore wish all books were burned. I
   am lean with seeing others eat. O that there would come a famine over all the world, that all might die, and I live alone; then
   thou shouldst see how fat I'd be! But must thou sit and I stand?   130
   Come down, with a vengeance!
FAUST. Out, envious wretch! But what art thou, the fourth?
WRATH. I am Wrath. I had neither father nor mother; I leapt out of
   a lion's mouth when I was scarce an hour old, and ever since
   have run up and down the world with these case of rapiers,   135
   wounding myself when I could get none to fight withal. I was
   born in hell; and look to it, for some of you shall be my father.
FAUST. And what art thou, the fifth?
GLUT. I am Gluttony. My parents are all dead, and the devil a
   penny they have left me but a small pension, and that buys me   140
   thirty meals a day and ten bevers[7]—a small trifle to suffice nature.
   I come of a royal pedigree: my father was a gammon[8] of bacon,
   and my mother was a hogshead of claret wine. My godfathers

3. The Seven Deadly Sins are pride, avarice, gluttony, lust, sloth, envy, and anger. (They are deadly
because other sins grow out of them.) They were
frequently represented in medieval plays, sometimes in the rather grimly comic tone used here;
in the old morality plays all the characters, not
merely the sins, were abstractions.

4. A salacious medieval poem *Carmen de Pulice*
("The Flea") was attributed to Ovid.
5. A decorated or ornamented petticoat.
6. Arras in Flanders exported fine cloth used for
tapestry hangings.
7. Snacks.
8. The lower side of pork, including the leg.

were these: Peter Pickle-herring and Martin Martlemas-beef. But
my godmother, O, she was a jolly gentlewoman, and well beloved   145
in every good town and city: her name was mistress Margery
March-beer. Now, Faustus, thou hast heard all my progeny;[9]
wilt thou bid me to supper?

FAUST. Not I. Thou wilt eat up all my victuals.

GLUT. Then the devil choke thee!   150

FAUST. Choke thyself, glutton. What art thou, the sixth?

SLOTH. Heigh ho! I am Sloth. I was begotten on a sunny bank,
where I have lain ever since, and you have done me great injury
to bring me from thence; let me be carried thither again by Gluttony and Lechery. Heigh ho! I'll not speak word more for a king's   155
ransom.

FAUST. And what are you, mistress minx, the seventh and last?

LECHERY. Who, I, sir? I am one that loves an inch of raw mutton[1]
better than an ell of fried stockfish, and the first letter of my name
begins with Lechery.   160

LUC. Away, to hell, away! On, piper![2]

[*Exeunt the* SINS.]

FAUST. O how this sight doth delight my soul!

LUC. Tut, Faustus, in hell is all manner of delight.

FAUST. O might I see hell and return again safe, how happy were I
then!   165

LUC. Faustus, thou shalt. At midnight I will send for thee. In meantime peruse this book, and view it throughly, and thou shalt turn
thyself into what shape thou wilt.

FAUST. Thanks, mighty Lucifer; this will I keep as chary[3] as my life.

LUC. Now Faustus, farewell.   170

FAUST. Farewell, great Lucifer. Come, Mephistophilis.

[*Exeunt* OMNES.]

SCENE 3

[*Enter the* CLOWN (ROBIN).]

ROBIN. What, Dick, look to the horses there till I come again. I
have gotten one of Dr. Faustus' conjuring books, and now we'll
have such knavery as 't passes.

[*Enter* DICK.]

DICK. What, Robin, you must come away and walk the horses.

ROBIN. I walk the horses! I scorn 't, faith: I have other matters in   5
hand; let the horses walk themselves and they will. "A *per se*[4] a;
t, h, e, the; o *per se* o; deny orgon, gorgon." Keep further from
me, O thou illiterate and unlearned hostler.

---

9. Ancestry, lineage.

1. Frequently a word of indecent meaning in
Elizabethan English; here it means the penis. "Ell":
45 inches; "stockfish": dried cod.

2. The command to the piper who led the procession of the Deadly Sins onto the stage to strike up
a tune for their exit.

3. Carefully.

4. "A by itself," a method of reading the letters of
the alphabet taught to children. Robin's semiliter-
acy is being satirized. "Deny orgon, gorgon" is a
parody of Faustus' invocation of Demogorgon in
1.3.

DICK. 'Snails,[5] what has thou got there? a book? Why, thou canst
    not tell ne'er a word on 't.   10

ROBIN. That thou shalt see presently. Keep out of the circle, I say,
    lest I send you into the ostry[6] with a vengeance.

DICK. That's like, faith! You had best leave your foolery, for an my
    master come, he'll conjure you, faith.

ROBIN. My master conjure me! I'll tell thee what; an my master   15
    come here, I'll clap as fair a pair of horns on 's head as e'er thou
    sawest in thy life.[7]

DICK. Thou needst not do that, for my mistress hath done it.

ROBIN. Aye, there be of us here have waded as deep into matters as
    other men, if they were disposed to talk.   20

DICK. A plague take you! I thought you did not sneak up and down
    after her for nothing. But I prithee tell me in good sadness, Robin,
    is that a conjuring book?

ROBIN. Do but speak what thou 't have me do, and I'll do 't. If thou
    't dance naked, put off thy clothes, and I'll conjure thee about   25
    presently. Or if thou 't but to the tavern with me, I'll give thee
    white wine, red wine, claret wine, sack, muscadine, malmesey,
    and whippincrust,[8] hold-belly-hold, and we'll not pay one penny
    for it.

DICK. O brave! Prithee let's to it presently, for I am as dry as a dog.   30

ROBIN. Come then, let's away.   [*Exeunt.*]

Act 3

[*Enter* CHORUS.]

CHO. Learned Faustus,
    To find the secrets of astronomy
    Graven in the book of Jove's high firmament,
    Did mount himself to scale Olympus' top.
    Where sitting in a chariot burning bright   5
    Drawn by the strength of yokèd dragons' necks,
    He views the clouds, the planets, and the stars,
    The tropics, zones, and quarters of the sky
    From the bright circle of the hornèd moon
    Even to the height of *Primum Mobile;*[9]   10
    And whirling round with this circumference
    Within the concave compass of the pole,
    From east to west his dragons swiftly glide
    And in eight days did bring him home again.
    Not long he stayed within his quiet house   15
    To rest his bones after his weary toil
    But new exploits do hale him out again;
    And mounted then upon a dragon's back
    That with his wings did part the subtle air,

5. I.e., God's nails (on the Cross).
6. Hostelry, inn.
7. A wife's infidelity was supposed in legend, and
in the standard Elizabethan joke, to cause her husband to grow horns.
8. Robin's pronunciation of "hippocras," a spiced
wine; "hold-belly-hold": as much as we can drink.
9. The outermost sphere, the empyrean.

He now is gone to prove cosmography[1]   20
That measures coasts and kingdoms of the earth:
And, as I guess, will first arrive at Rome
To see the Pope and manner of his court
And take some part of holy Peter's feast,
The which this day is highly solemnized.   25

    [*Exit.*]

SCENE 1

[*Enter* FAUSTUS *and* MEPHISTOPHILIS.]

FAUST. Having now, my good Mephistophilis,
  Passed with delight the stately town of Trier[2]
  Environed round with airy mountain tops,
  With walls of flint and deep-entrenchèd lakes,[3]
  Not to be won by any conquering prince;   5
  From Paris next coasting the realm of France,
  We saw the river Main fall into Rhine,
  Whose banks are set with groves of fruitful vines;
  Then up to Naples, rich Campania,
  With buildings fair and gorgeous to the eye,   10
  Whose streets straight forth and paved with finest brick
  Quarter the town in four equivalents.
  There saw we learned Maro's[4] golden tomb,
  The way he cut, an English mile in length,
  Thorough a rock of stone in one night's space.   15
  From thence to Venice, Padua, and the rest,
  In midst of which a sumptuous temple[5] stands
  That threats the stars with her aspiring top,
  Whose frame is paved with sundry colored stones
  And roofed aloft with curious work in gold.   20
  Thus hitherto hath Faustus spent his time.
  But tell me now, what resting place is this?
  Hast thou, as erst I did command,
  Conducted me within the walls of Rome?
MEPH. I have, my Faustus, and for proof thereof   25
  This is the goodly palace of the Pope,
  And 'cause we are no common guests
  I choose his privy chamber for our use.
FAUST. I hope his Holiness will bid us welcome.
MEPH. All's one, for we'll be bold with his venison.   30
  But now, my Faustus, that thou mayst perceive
  What Rome contains for to delight thine eyes,
  Know that this city stands upon seven hills
  That underprop the groundwork of the same;
  Just through the midst runs flowing Tiber's stream,   35

---

1. I.e., to test the accuracy of maps.
2. Treves (in Prussia).
3. Moats.
4. Virgil's. In medieval legend the Roman poet Virgil was considered a magician, and a tunnel
("way") on the promontory of Posilippo at Naples, near his tomb, was accredited to his magical powers.
5. I.e., St. Mark's in Venice.

With winding banks that cut it in two parts
Over the which four stately bridges lean
That make safe passage to each part of Rome.
Upon the bridge called Ponte Angelo
Erected is a castle passing strong,   40
Where thou shalt see such store of ordnance
As that the double cannons forged of brass
Do match the number of the days contained
Within the compass of one complete year;
Besides the gates and high pyramides[6]   45
That Julius Caesar brought from Africa.
FAUST. Now by the kingdoms of infernal rule,
   Of Styx, Acheron, and the fiery lake
   Of ever-burning Phlegethon,[7] I swear
   That I do long to see the monuments   50
   And situation of bright-splendent Rome.
   Come, therefore, let's away.
MEPH. Nay, stay, my Faustus; I know you'd see the Pope
   And take some part of holy Peter's feast,
   The which in state and high solemnity   55
   This day is held through Rome and Italy
   In honor of the Pope's triumphant victory.
FAUST. Sweet Mephistophilis, thou pleasest me;
   Whilst I am here on earth let me be cloyed
   With all things that delight the heart of man.   60
   My four and twenty years of liberty
   I'll spend in pleasure and in dalliance,
   That Faustus' name, whilst this bright frame doth stand,
   May be admirèd through the furthest land.
MEPH. 'Tis well said, Faustus; come then, stand by me   65
   And thou shalt see them come immediately.
FAUST. Nay, stay, my gentle Mephistophilis,
   And grant me my request, and then I go.
   Thou knowst, within the compass of eight days
   We viewed the face of heaven, of earth, of hell;   70
   So high our dragons soared into the air
   That, looking down, the earth appeared to me
   No bigger than my hand in quantity.
   There did we view the kingdoms of the world,
   And what might please mine eye I there beheld.   75
   Then in this show let me an actor be,
   That this proud Pope may Faustus' cunning see.
MEPH. Let it be so, my Faustus, but first stay
   And view their triumphs[8] as they pass this way,
   And then devise what best contents thy mind,   80
   By cunning of thine art to cross the Pope
   Or dash the pride of this solemnity,
   To make his monks and abbots stand like apes

---

6. *Py-rám-i-des*, a singular noun, meaning an
obelisk.
7. Classical names for rivers of the underworld;

symbolic of hell, they are appropriate as oaths for
Faustus.
8. Parades.

And point like antics[9] at his triple crown,
To beat the beads about the friars' pates   85
Or clap huge horns upon the cardinals' heads,
Or any villainy thou canst devise,
And I'll perform it, Faustus. Hark, they come!
This day shall make thee be admired in Rome.

> [*Enter the* CARDINALS *and* BISHOPS, *some bearing crosiers,*
> *some the pillars;* MONKS *and* FRIARS *singing their procession;*
> *then the* POPE *and* RAYMOND, *King of Hungary, with* BRUNO
> *led in chains.*][1]

POPE. Cast down our footstool.
RAY.   Saxon Bruno, stoop,   90
   Whilst on thy back his Holiness ascends
   St. Peter's chair and state pontifical.
BRUNO. Proud Lucifer, that state belongs to me;
   But thus I fall, to Peter, not to thee.
POPE. To me and Peter shalt thou groveling lie   95
   And crouch before the papal dignity.
   Sound trumpets, then, for thus St. Peter's heïr
   From Bruno's back ascends St. Peter's chair.

> [*A flourish while he ascends.*]

Thus as the gods creep on with feet of wool
Long ere with iron hands they punish men,   100
So shall our sleeping vengeance now arise
And smite with death thy hated enterprise.
Lord Cardinals of France and Padua,
Go forthwith to our holy consistory
And read among the statutes decretal   105
What, by the holy council held at Trent,[2]
The sacred synod hath decreed for him
That doth assume the papal government
Without election and a true consent.
Away and bring us word with speed.   110
1 CARD. We go, my lord.   [*Exeunt* CARDINALS.]
POPE. Lord Raymond—
FAUST. Go, haste thee, gentle Mephistophilis,
   Follow the cardinals to the consistory,
   And as they turn their superstitious books,
   Strike them with sloth and drowsy idleness   115
   And make them sleep so sound that in their shapes
   Thyself and I may parley with this Pope,
   This proud confronter of the Emperor,[3]
   And in despite of all his holiness   120
   Restore this Bruno to his liberty

9. Grotesque figures.
1. "Crosiers": crosses borne before prelates; "the pillars" (of silver), however, are known to have been used by only two English cardinals, Wolsey and De la Pole. "Raymond, King of Hungary" is unknown to history. "Bruno" is likewise fictitious; he is the German pretender to the papal throne over whom the Pope has just triumphed (line 57).
2. The famous council of the Catholic Church which lasted from 1545 to 1563.
3. Holy Roman Emperor. Faustus refers to the conflict between the Pope and the Emperor; the former was victorious and captured the Emperor's choice for Pope, "Saxon Bruno."

And bear him to the states of Germany.
MEPH. Faustus, I go.
FAUST.   Dispatch it soon.
The Pope shall curse that Faustus came to Rome.

[*Exeunt* FAUSTUS *and* MEPHISTOPHILIS.]

BRUNO. Pope Adrian, let me have some right of law;   125
    I was elected by the Emperor.
POPE. We will depose the Emperor for that deed
    And curse the people that submit to him;
    Both he and thou shalt stand excommunicate
    And interdict from church's privilege   130
    And all society of holy men.
    He grows too proud in his authority,
    Lifting his lofty head above the clouds,
    And like a steeple overpeers the church,
    But we'll pull down his haughty insolence.   135
    And as Pope Alexander,[4] our progenitor,
    Trod on the neck of German Frederick,
    Adding this golden sentence to our praise,
    That Peter's heirs should tread on emperors
    And walk upon the dreadful adder's back,   140
    Treading the lion and the dragon down,
    And fearless spurn the killing basilisk;[5]
    So will we quell that haughty schismatic,
    And by authority apostolical
    Depose him from his regal government.   145
BRUNO. Pope Julius swore to princely Sigismond,
    For him and the succeeding popes of Rome,
    To hold the emperors their lawful lords.
POPE. Pope Julius did abuse the church's rights,
    And therefore none of his decrees can stand.   150
    Is not all power on earth bestowed on us?
    And therefore though we would we cannot err.
    Behold this silver belt, whereto is fixed
    Seven golden keys fast sealed with seven seals
    In token of our sevenfold power from heaven,   155
    To bind or loose, lock fast, condemn, or judge,
    Resign or seal, or whatso pleaseth us.
    Then he and thou and all the world shall stoop,
    Or be assurèd of our dreadful curse
    To light as heavy as the pains of hell.   160

[*Enter* FAUSTUS *and* MEPHISTOPHILIS *like cardinals.*]

MEPH. Now tell me, Faustus, are we not fitted well?
FAUST. Yes, Mephistophilis, and two such cardinals
    Ne'er served a holy pope as we shall do.
    But whilst they sleep within the consistory
    Let us salute his reverend Fatherhood.   165

4. Pope Alexander III (1159–81) compelled the Emperor Frederick Barbarossa to submit to him.
5. A mythical monster capable of killing by a look.

RAY. Behold, my lord, the cardinals are returned.
POPE. Welcome, grave fathers, answer presently;[6]
    What have our holy council there decreed
    Concerning Bruno and the Emperor
    In quittance of their late conspiracy   170
    Against our state and papal dignity?
FAUST. Most sacred patron of the church of Rome,
    By full consent of all the synod
    Of priests and prelates it is thus decreed:
    That Bruno and the German Emperor   175
    Be held as lollards[7] and bold schismatics
    And proud disturbers of the church's peace.
    And if that Bruno by his own assent,
    Without enforcement of the German peers,
    Did seek to wear the triple diadem   180
    And by your death to climb St. Peter's chair,
    The statutes decretal have thus decreed:
    He shall be straight condemned of heresy
    And on a pile of fagots burned to death.
POPE. It is enough. Here, take him to your charge   185
    And bear him straight to Ponte Angelo,
    And in the strongest tower enclose him fast.
    Tomorrow, sitting in our consistory
    With all our college of grave cardinals,
    We will determine of his life or death.   190
    Here, take his triple crown along with you
    And leave it in the church's treasury.
    Make haste again, my good lord cardinals,
    And take our blessing apostolical.
MEPH. So, so. Was never devil thus blessed before!   195
FAUST. Away, sweet Mephistophilis, be gone;
    The cardinals will be plagued for this anon.

      [*Exeunt* FAUSTUS *and* MEPHISTOPHILIS *with* BRUNO.]

POPE. Go presently and bring a banquet forth,
    That we may solemnize St. Peter's feast
    And with Lord Raymond, King of Hungary,   200
    Drink to our late and happy victory.   [*Exeunt.*]

SCENE 2

    [*The banquet is brought in, and then enter* FAUSTUS *and*
    MEPHISTOPHILIS *in their own shapes.*]

MEPH. Now Faustus, come prepare thyself for mirth;
    The sleepy cardinals are hard at hand
    To censure Bruno, that is posted hence
    And on a proud-paced steed as swift as thought

6. Immediately.
7. Protestants, usually English followers of Wycliffe, the 14th-century religious reformer.

Flies o'er the Alps to fruitful Germany,   5
There to salute the woeful Emperor.
FAUST. The Pope will curse them for their sloth today
That slept both Bruno and his crown away.
But now, that Faustus may delight his mind
And by their folly make some merriment,   10
Sweet Mephistophilis, so charm me here
That I may walk invisible to all
And do whate'er I please unseen of any.
MEPH. Faustus, thou shalt; then kneel down presently,
          Whilst on thy head I lay my hand   15
          And charm thee with this magic wand.
          First wear this girdle, then appear
          Invisible to all are here.
          The planets seven, the gloomy air,
          Hell, and the Furies' forkèd hair,   20
          Pluto's blue fire and Hecate's[8] tree
          With magic spells so compass thee
          That no eye may thy body see.
So, Faustus, now, for all their holiness,
   Do what thou wilt thou shalt not be discerned.   25
FAUST. Thanks, Mephistophilis. Now friars, take heed
Lest Faustus make your shaven crowns to bleed.
MEPH. Faustus, no more; see where the cardinals come.

          [Enter POPE and all the lords, with KING RAYMOND and the
          ARCHBISHOP OF RHEIMS. Enter the two CARDINALS with a
          book.]

POPE. Welcome, lord cardinals; come, sit down.
   Lord Raymond, take your seat. Friars, attend,   30
   And see that all things be in readiness
   As best beseems this solemn festival.
1 CARD. First may it please your sacred holiness
   To view the sentence of the reverend synod
   Concerning Bruno and the Emperor.   35
POPE. What needs this question? Did I not tell you
   Tomorrow we would sit i' th' consistory
   And there determine of his punishment?
   You brought us word, even now, it was decreed
   That Bruno and the cursèd Emperor   40
   Were by the holy council both condemned
   For loathèd lollards and base schismatics;
   Then wherefore would you have me view that book?
1 CARD. Your Grace mistakes; you gave us no such charge.
RAY. Deny it not; we all are witnesses   45
   That Bruno here was late delivered you,
   With his rich triple crown to be reserved
   And put into the church's treasury.
BOTH CARD. By holy Paul we saw them not.

8. The goddess of magic and witchcraft, whose name the Elizabethans pronounced *Héc-at*. She is not known to have any special "tree"; the word may be a mistake for "three," since she was often represented as a triple goddess—of heaven, earth, and hell.

POPE. By Peter, you shall die   50
   Unless you bring them forth immediately.
   Hale them to prison! Lade their limbs with gyves![9]
   False prelates, for this hateful treachery,
   Cursed be your souls to hellish misery.   [*Exeunt* CARDINALS.]
FAUST. So they are safe. Now, Faustus, to the feast;   55
   The Pope had never such a frolic guest.
POPE. Lord Archbishop of Rheims, sit down with us.
ARCH. I thank your Holiness.
FAUST. Fall to! The devil choke you an you spare!
POPE. Who's that spoke? Friars, look about.   60
   Lord Raymond, pray fall to. I am beholden
   To the Bishop of Milan for this so rare a present.
FAUST. I thank you, sir.

     [FAUSTUS *snatches the meat from the* POPE.]

POPE. How now! Who snatched the meat from me? Villains, why
   speak you not?   65
FRIAR. Here's nobody, if it like your Holiness.
POPE. My good Lord Archbishop, here's a most dainty dish
   Was sent me from a cardinal in France.
FAUST. I'll have that, too.

     [FAUSTUS *snatches the dish from the* POPE.]

POPE. What lollards do attend our Holiness   70
   That we receive such great indignity?
   Fetch me some wine.
FAUST. Aye, pray do, for Faustus is adry.
POPE. Lord Raymond, I drink unto your Grace.
FAUST. I pledge your Grace.   75

     [FAUSTUS *snatches the cup from the* POPE.]

POPE. My wine gone, too? Ye lubbers, look about
   And find the man that doth this villainy,
   Or by my sanctitude you all shall die.
   I pray, my lords, have patience at this troublesome banquet.
ARCH. Please your Holiness, I think it be some ghost crept out of   80
   purgatory and now is come unto your Holiness for his pardon.
POPE. It may be so;
   Go then, command our priests to sing a dirge
   To lay the fury of this same troublesome ghost.
   Once again, my lord, fall to.   85

     [*The* POPE *crosses himself.*]

FAUST. How now!
   Must every bit be spicèd with a cross?
   Well, use that trick no more, I would advise you.

     [*The* POPE *crosses himself.*]

---

9. I.e., load their limbs with prisoners' shackles.

Well, there's the second time; aware the third;
I give you fair warning.   90

    [*The* POPE *crosses himself again.*]

Nay then, take that!

    [FAUSTUS *hits the* POPE *a box on the ear.*]

POPE. O, I am slain! Help me, my lords!
  O come and help to bear my body hence!
  Damned be his soul forever for this deed.

    [*Exeunt the* POPE *and his train.*]

MEPH. Now Faustus, what will you do now? For I can tell you   95
  you'll be cursed with bell, book, and candle.[1]
FAUST. Bell, book, and candle; candle, book, and bell
  Forward and backward, to curse Faustus to hell!

    [*Enter all the* FRIARS *with bell, book, and candle to sing the
    dirge.*]

FRIAR. Come, brethren, let's about our business with good devotion.

    [ALL *sing this:*]
Cursèd be he that stole away his Holiness' meat from the table—   100
maledicat dominus![2]
Cursèd be he that struck his Holiness a blow on the face—*maledicat dominus!*
Cursèd be he that took Friar Sandelo a blow on the face—*maledicat dominus!*   105
Cursèd be he that disturbeth our holy dirge—*maledicat dominus!*
Cursèd be he that took away his Holiness' wine—*maledicat dominus! Et omnes sancti!*[3] Amen.

    [FAUSTUS *and* MEPHISTOPHILIS *beat the* FRIARS, *and fling
    fireworks among them, and so exeunt.*]

SCENE 3

    [*Enter* CLOWN (ROBIN) *and* DICK *with a cup.*]

DICK. Sirrah Robin, we were best look that your devil can answer
  the stealing of this same cup, for the vintner's boy follows us at
  the hard heels.
ROBIN. 'Tis no matter, let him come! An he follow us I'll so conjure
  him as he was never conjured in his life, I warrant him. Let me   5
  see the cup.

    [*Enter* VINTNER.]

DICK. Here 'tis. Yonder he comes. Now, Robin, now or never show
  thy cunning.

---

1. The traditional paraphernalia for cursing and
excommunication.
2. "May the Lord curse him!"
3. And all saints (also curse him).

VINT. O, are you here? I am glad I have found you. You are a
couple of fine companions! Pray, where's the cup you stole from   10
the tavern?

ROBIN. How, how? We steal a cup? Take heed what you say! We
look not like cup-stealers, I can tell you.

VINT. Never deny it, for I know you have it, and I'll search you.

ROBIN. Search me? Aye, and spare not. Hold the cup, Dick! Come,   15
come; search me, search me.

VINT. Come on, sirrah, let me search you now.

DICK. Aye, aye, do; do. Hold the cup, Robin, I fear not your searching. We scorn to steal your cups, I can tell you.

VINT. Never outface me for the matter, for sure the cup is between   20
you two.

ROBIN. Nay, there you lie. 'Tis beyond us both.

VINT. A plague take you! I thought 'twas your knavery to take it
away. Come, give it me again.

ROBIN. Aye, much! When, can you tell?[4] Dick, make me a circle,   25
and stand close at my back and stir not for thy life. Vintner, you
shall have your cup anon. Say nothing, Dick. O *per se* O; Demogorgon, Belcher and Mephistophilis!

[*Enter* MEPHISTOPHILIS.]

MEPH. Monarch of hell, under whose black survey
    Great potentates do kneel with awful fear,   30
    Upon whose altars thousand souls do lie,
    How am I vexèd with these villains' charms!
    From Constantinople am I hither brought
    Only for pleasure of these damnèd slaves.   [*Exit* VINTNER.]

ROBIN. By Lady, sir, you have had a shrewd journey of it; will it   35
please you to take a shoulder of mutton to supper and a tester[5] in
your purse, and go back again?

DICK. Aye, I pray you heartily, sir; for we called you but in jest, I
promise you.

MEPH. To purge the rashness of this cursèd deed,   40
    First be thou turnèd to this ugly shape:
    For apish deeds transformèd to an ape.

ROBIN. O brave! an ape! I pray, sir, let me have the carrying of him
about to show some tricks.

MEPH. And so thou shalt. Be thou transformed to a dog and carry   45
him upon thy back. Away! Be gone!

ROBIN. A dog! That's excellent! Let the maids look well to their
porridge pots, for I'll into the kitchen presently. Come, Dick,
come.

[*Exeunt* ROBIN *and* DICK.]

MEPH. Now with the flames of ever-burning fire   50
    I'll wing myself and forthwith fly amain
    Unto my Faustus, to the Great Turk's court.   [*Exit.*]

4. A common Elizabethan scornful retort.   5. Sixpence.

Act 4

[*Enter* CHORUS.]

CHO. When Faustus had with pleasure ta'en the view
   Of rarest things and royal courts of kings,
   He stayed his course and so returnèd home,
   Where such as bear his absence but with grief,
   I mean his friends and nearest companións,   5
   Did gratulate his safety with kind words,
   And in their conference of what befell
   Touching his journey through the world and air,
   They put forth questions of astrology
   Which Faustus answered with such learned skill   10
   As they admired and wondered at his wit.
   Now is his fame spread forth in every land:
   Amongst the rest the Emperor is one,
   Carolus the Fifth,[6] at whose palace now
   Faustus is feasted 'mongst his noblemen.   15
   What there he did in trial of his art
   I leave untold, your eyes shall see performed.   [*Exit.*]

SCENE 1

[*Enter* MARTINO *and* FREDERICK *at several doors.*[7]]

MART. What ho! Officers, gentlemen!
   Hie to the presence to attend the Emperor.
   Good Frederick, see the rooms be voided straight;
   His Majesty is coming to the hall.
   Go back, and see the state in readiness.   5
FRED. But where is Bruno, our elected Pope,
   That on a fury's back came post from Rome?
   Will not his Grace consort[8] the Emperor?
MART. O yes, and with him comes the German conjurer,
   The learned Faustus, fame of Wittenberg,   10
   The wonder of the world for magic art;
   And he intends to show great Carolus
   The race of all his stout progenitors
   And bring in presence of his majesty
   The royal shapes and warlike semblances   15
   Of Alexander and his beauteous paramour.[9]
FRED. Where is Benvolio?
MART. Fast asleep, I warrant you;
   He took his rouse with stoups[1] of Rhenish wine
   So kindly yesternight to Bruno's health   20
   That all this day the sluggard keeps his bed.
FRED. See, see; his window's ope; we'll call to him.
MART. What ho, Benvolio!

---

6. I.e., Emperor Charles V (1519–56).
7. I.e., at different entrances.
8. Accompany.

9. Alexander the Great and his mistress Thaïs.
1. Drank many full glasses.

[*Enter* BENVOLIO *above at a window, in his nightcap, but-toning.*]

BENV. What a devil ail you two?

MART. Speak softly, sir, lest the devil hear you;   25
    For Faustus at the court is late arrived
    And at his heels a thousand furies wait
    To accomplish whatsoever the Doctor please.

BENV. What of this?

MART. Come, leave thy chamber first and thou shalt see   30
    This conjurer perform such rare exploits
    Before the Pope[2] and royal Emperor
    As never yet was seen in Germany.

BENV. Has not the Pope enough of conjuring yet?
    He was upon the devil's back late enough,   35
    And if he be so far in love with him
    I would he would post home to Rome with him again.

FRED. Speak, wilt thou come and see this sport?

BENV. Not I.

MART. Wilt thou stand in thy window and see it, then?   40

BENV. Aye, an, I fall not asleep i' th' meantime.

MART. The Emperor is at hand, who comes to see
    What wonders by black spells may compassed be.

BENV. Well, go you attend the Emperor. I am content for this once
    to thrust my head out a window, for they say if a man be drunk   45
    overnight the devil cannot hurt him in the morning. If that be
    true, I have a charm in my head shall control him as well as the
    conjurer, I warrant you.

[*Exit* MARTINO *and* FREDERICK.]

SCENE 2

[*A* sennet.[3] *Enter* CHARLES THE GERMAN EMPEROR, BRUNO,
the DUKE OF SAXONY, FAUSTUS, MEPHISTOPHILIS, FREDER-
ICK, MARTINO *and* ATTENDANTS. BENVOLIO *remains at his
window.*]

EMP. Wonder of men, renowned magician,
    Thrice-learned Faustus, welcome to our court.
    This deed of thine, in setting Bruno free
    From his and our professèd enemy,
    Shall add more excellence unto thine art   5
    Than if by powerful necromantic spells
    Thou couldst command the world's obedience.
    Forever be beloved of Carolus;
    And if this Bruno thou hast late redeemed
    In peace possess the triple diadem   10
    And sit in Peter's chair despite of chance,
    Thou shalt be famous through all Italy
    And honored of the German Emperor.

FAUST. These gracious words, most royal Carolus,

2. Bruno.   3. A trumpet signal.

    Shall make poor Faustus to his utmost power   15
    Both love and serve the German Emperor
    And lay his life at holy Bruno's feet.
    For proof whereof, if so your Grace be pleased,
    The Doctor stands prepared by power of art
    To cast his magic charms that shall pierce through   20
    The ebon gates of ever-burning hell
    And hale the stubborn furies from their caves
    To compass whatsoe'er your Grace commands.

BENV. [*aside*] Blood! He speaks terribly, but for all that I do not
    greatly believe him. He looks as like a conjurer as the Pope to a   25
    costermonger.[4]

EMP. Then Faustus, as thou late didst promise us,
    We would behold that famous conqueror,
    Great Alexander and his paramour,
    In their true shapes and state majestical,   30
    That we may wonder at their excellence.

FAUST. Your Majesty shall see them presently.
    Mephistophilis, away!
    And with a solemn noise of trumpets' sound
    Present before this royal Emperor   35
    Great Alexander and his beauteous paramour.

MEPH. Faustus, I will.   [*Exit.*]

BENV. [*aside*] Well, master Doctor, an your devils come not away
    quickly, you shall have me asleep presently. Zounds, I could eat
    myself for anger to think I have been such an ass all this while to   40
    stand gaping after the devil's governor, and can see nothing.

FAUST. [*aside*] I'll make you feel something anon if my art fail me
    not.—
    My lord, I must forewarn your Majesty
    That when my spirits present the royal shapes   45
    Of Alexander and his paramour,
    Your Grace demand no questions of the King,
    But in dumb silence let them come and go.

EMP. Be it as Faustus please; we are content.

BENV. [*aside*] Aye, Aye, and I am content, too. And thou bring   50
    Alexander and his paramour before the Emperor, I'll be Actaeon[5]
    and turn myself into a stag.

FAUST. [*aside*] And I'll play Diana and send you the horns presently.

        [*Sennet. Enter at one door the emperor* ALEXANDER, *at the
        other* DARIUS. *They meet;* DARIUS *is thrown down;* ALEXAN-
        DER *kills him, takes off his crown and, offering to go out,
        his* PARAMOUR *meets him; he embraceth her and sets* DARIUS'
        crown upon her head and, coming back, both salute the
        EMPEROR, who, leaving his state,[6] offers to embrace them,
        which* FAUSTUS *seeing, suddenly stays him. Then trumpets
        cease and music sounds.*]

---

4. Fruitseller.
5. The hunter of classical legend who happened
to see the goddess Diana bathing. In punishment

he was changed into a stag and pursued by his own
hounds.
6. Throne.

FAUST. My gracious lord, you do forget yourself;   55
    These are but shadows, not substantial.
EMP. O pardon me; my thoughts are ravished so
    With sight of this renownèd Emperor
    That in mine arms I would have compassed him.
    But Faustus, since I may not speak to them   60
    To satisfy my longing thoughts at full,
    Let me this tell thee: I have heard it said
    That this fair lady, whilst she lived on earth,
    Had on her neck a little wart or mole.
    How may I prove that saying to be true?   65
FAUST. Your Majesty may boldly go and see.
EMP. Faustus, I see it plain;
    And in this sight thou better pleasest me
    Than if I gained another monarchy.
FAUST. Away, be gone!   *[Exit* SHOW.*]*   70
    See, see, my gracious lord, what strange beast is yon, that thrusts
    its head out at the window!
EMP. O wondrous sight! See, Duke of Saxony, two spreading horns
    most strangely fastened upon the head of young Benvolio.
SAX. What, is he asleep, or dead?   75
FAUST. He sleeps, my lord, but dreams not of his horns.
EMP. This sport is excellent. We'll call and wake him. What ho!
    Benvolio!
BENV. A plague upon you! Let me sleep a while
EMP. I blame thee not to sleep, much, having such a head of thine   80
    own.
SAX. Look up, Benvolio. 'Tis the Emperor calls.
BENV. The Emperor! Where? O zounds, my head!
EMP. Nay, and thy horns hold 'tis no matter for thy head, for that's
    armed sufficiently.   85
FAUST. Why, how now, sir knight! What, hanged by the horns?
    This is most horrible. Fie, fie! Pull in your head, for shame! Let
    not all the world wonder at you.
BENV. Zounds, Doctor, is this your villainy?
FAUST. O, say not so, sir. The Doctor has no skill,   90
    No art, no cunning to present these lords
    Or bring before this royal Emperor
    The mighty monarch, warlike Alexander?
    If Faustus do it, you are straight resolved
    In bold Actaeon's shape to turn a stag?   95
    And therefore, my lord, so please your Majesty,
    I'll raise a kennel of hounds shall hunt him so
    As all his footmanship shall scarce prevail
    To keep his carcass from their bloody fangs.
    Ho, Belimote, Argiron, Asterote!   100
BENV. Hold, hold! Zounds, he'll raise up a kennel of devils, I think,
    anon. Good my lord, entreat for me. 'Sblood, I am never able
    to endure these torments.
EMP. Then good master Doctor,
    Let me entreat you to remove his horns;   105

He has done penance now sufficiently.

FAUST. My gracious lord, not so much for injury done to me, as to
delight your Majesty with some mirth, hath Faustus justly requited
this injurious knight; which, being all I desire, I am content to
remove his horns.—Mephistophilis, transform him.—And here-   110
after, sir, look you speak well of scholars.

BENV. [aside] Speak well of ye! 'Sblood, and scholars be such cuck-
oldmakers to clap horns of honest men's heads o' this order, I'll
ne'er trust smooth faces and small ruffs[7] more. But an I be not
revenged for this, would I might be turned to a gaping oyster and   115
drink nothing but salt water!

EMP. Come, Faustus. While the Emperor lives,
    In recompense of this thy high desert,
    Thou shalt command the state of Germany
    And live beloved of mighty Carolus.   [Exeunt OMNES.]   120

SCENE 3

[Enter BENVOLIO, MARTINO, FREDERICK, and SOLDIERS.]

MART. Nay, sweet Benvolio, let us sway thy thoughts
    From this attempt against the conjurer.

BENV. Away! You love me not to urge me thus.
    Shall I let slip so great an injury
    When every servile groom jests at my wrongs   5
    And in their rustic gambols proudly say,
    "Benvolio's head was graced with horns today"?
    O, may these eyelids never close again
    Till with my sword I have that conjurer slain.
    If you will aid me in this enterprise,   10
    Then draw your weapons and be resolute;
    If not, depart. Here will Benvolio die,
    But Faustus' death shall quit[8] my infamy.

FRED. Nay, we will stay with thee, betide what may,
    And kill that Doctor if he come this way.   15

BENV. Then gentle Frederick, hie thee to the grove
    And place our servants and our followers
    Close in an ambush there behind the trees.
    By this I know the conjurer is near;
    I saw him kneel and kiss the Emperor's hand   20
    And take his leave laden with rich rewards.
    Then, soldiers, boldly fight. If Faustus die,
    Take you the wealth, leave us the victory.

FRED. Come, soldiers, follow me unto the grove;
    Who kills him shall have gold and endless love.   25

[Exit FREDERICK with the SOLDIERS.]

BENV. My head is lighter than it was by th' horns,
    But yet my heart's more ponderous than my head

7. I.e., scholars, who were often smooth-shaven
and did not wear the large "ruffs" (collars) of courtiers. But Faustus has a beard; see the next scene.
8. Avenge.

And pants until I see that conjurer dead.

MART. Where shall we place ourselves, Benvolio?

BENV. Here will we stay to bide the first assault.   30
O, were that damnèd hell-hound but in place
Thou soon shouldst see me quit my foul disgrace.

     [*Enter* FREDERICK.]

FRED. Close, close! The hated conjurer is at hand
And all alone comes walking in his gown;
Be ready then and strike the peasant down.   35

BENV. Mine be that honor then. Now, sword, strike home!
For horns he gave I'll have his head anon.

     [*Enter* FAUSTUS *wearing a false head.*]

MART. See, see, he comes.

BENV.   No words; this blow ends all;
Hell take his soul, his body thus must fall.

FAUST. O!   40

FRED. Groan you, master Doctor?

BENV. Break may his heart with groans. Dear Frederick, see
Thus will I end his griefs immediately.

     [*Cuts off the false head.*]

MART. Strike with a willing hand! His head is off.

BENV. The devil's dead; the furies now may laugh.   45

FRED. Was this that stern aspect, that awful frown,
Made the grim monarch of infernal spirits
Tremble and quake at his commanding charms?

MART. Was this that damnèd head whose art conspired
Benvolio's shame before the Emperor?   50

BENV. Aye, that's the head, and here the body lies
Justly rewarded for his villainies.

FRED. Come, let's devise how we may add more shame
To the black scandal of his hated name.

BENV. First, on his head, in quittance of my wrongs,   55
I'll nail huge forkèd horns and let them hang
Within the window where he yoked me first,
That all the world may see my just revenge.

MART. What use shall we put his beard to?

BENV. We'll sell it to a chimney-sweeper; it will wear out ten birchen   60
brooms, I warrant you.

FRED. What shall his eyes do?

BENV. We'll put out his eyes, and they shall serve for buttons to his
lips to keep his tongue from catching cold.

MART. An excellent policy. And now, sirs, having divided him,   65
what shall the body do?

     [FAUSTUS *rises.*]

BENV. Zounds, the devil's alive again!

FRED. Give him his head, for God's sake!

FAUST. Nay, keep it. Faustus will have heads and hands,

Aye, all your hearts, to recompense this deed.   70
Knew you not, traitors, I was limited
For four and twenty years to breathe on earth?
And had you cut my body with your swords
Or hewed this flesh and bones as small as sand,
Yet in a minute had my spirit returned   75
And I had breathed a man made free from harm.
But wherefore do I dally my revenge?
Asteroth, Belimoth, Mephistophilis!

        [*Enter* MEPHISTOPHILIS *and other* DEVILS.]

Go, horse these traitors on your fiery backs
And mount aloft with them as high as heaven,   80
Then pitch them headlong to the lowest hell.
Yet stay, the world shall see their misery,
And hell shall after plague their treachery.
Go, Belimoth, and take this caitiff[9] hence
And hurl him in some lake of mud and dirt;   85
Take thou this other, drag him through the woods
Amongst the pricking thorns and sharpest briars,
Whilst with my gentle Mephistophilis
This traitor flies unto some steepy rock
That rolling down may break the villain's bones   90
As he intended to dismember me.
Fly hence, dispatch my charge immediately.
FRED. Pity us, gentle Faustus; save our lives!
FAUST. Away!
FRED. He must needs go that the devil drives.   95

                    [*Exeunt* SPIRITS *with the* KNIGHTS.]
        [*Enter the ambushed* SOLDIERS.]

1 SOLD. Come, sirs, prepare yourselves in readiness;
    Make haste to help these noble gentlemen;
    I heard them parley with the conjurer.
2 SOLD. See where he comes; dispatch, and kill the slave!
FAUST. What's here? An ambush to betray my life?   100
    Then, Faustus, try thy skill. Base peasants, stand!
    For lo, these trees remove at my command
    And stand as bulwarks 'twixt yourselves and me
    To shield me from your hated treachery;
    Yet to encounter this, your weak attempt,   105
    Behold an army comes incontinent.[1]

        [FAUSTUS *strikes the door, and enter a* DEVIL *playing on a
        drum; after him another bearing an ensign, and divers with
        weapons;* MEPHISTOPHILIS *with fireworks. They set upon the*
        SOLDIERS *and drive them out. Exeunt.*]

9. Wretch.   1. Immediately.

SCENE 4

[*Enter at several doors* BENVOLIO, FREDERICK, *and* MAR-
TINO, *their heads and faces bloody and besmeared with mud
and dirt, all having horns on their heads.*]

MART. What ho, Benvolio!
BENV. Here! What, Frederick, ho!
FRED. O help me, gentle friend. Where is Martino?
MART. Dear Frederick, here—
    Half smothered in a lake of mud and dirt   5
    Through which the furies dragged me by the heels.
FRED. Martino, see! Benvolio's horns again.
MART. O misery! How now, Benvolio!
BENV. Defend me, heaven! Shall I be haunted still?
MART. Nay, fear not, man; we have no power to kill.   10
BENV. My friends transformèd thus! O hellish spite!
    Your heads are all set with horns.
FRED. You hit it right;
    It is your own you mean; feel on your head.
BENV. Zounds, horns again!   15
MART. Nay, chafe not, man; we are all sped.[2]
BENV. What devil attends this damned magician
    That spite of spite our wrongs are doublèd?
FRED. What may we do that we may hide our shames?
BENV. If we should follow him to work revenge,   20
    He'd join long asses' ears to those huge horns
    And make us laughingstocks to all the world.
MART. What shall we then do, dear Benvolio?
BENV. I have a castle joining near these woods,
    And thither we'll repair and live obscure   25
    Till time shall alter this our brutish shapes.
    Sith black disgrace hath thus eclipsed our fame,
    We'll rather die with grief than live with shame.

                        [*Exeunt* OMNES.]

SCENE 5

[*Enter* FAUSTUS *and the* HORSE-COURSER.[3]]

HOR. I beseech your Worship, accept of these forty dollars.[4]
FAUST. Friend, thou canst not buy so good a horse for so small a
    price. I have no great need to sell him, but if thou likest him for
    ten dollars more, take him, because I see thou hast a good mind
    to him.   5
HOR. I beseech you, sir, accept of this; I am a very poor man and
    have lost very much of late by horseflesh, and this bargain will
    set me up again.

---

2. Don't fret, man, we are all done for.
3. Horse trader, traditionally a sharp bargainer or cheat.

4. Common German coins; the word originally comes from the German *Joachimsthaler*.

FAUST. Well, I will not stand with thee; give me the money. Now,
sirrah, I must tell you that you may ride him o'er hedge and ditch   10
and spare him not; but—do you hear?—in any case ride him not
into the water.

HOR. How, sir, not into the water? Why, will he not drink of all
waters?

FAUST. Yes, he will drink of all waters, but ride him not into the   15
water; o'er hedge and ditch or where thou wilt, but not into the
water. Go bid the hostler deliver him unto you, and remember
what I say.

HOR. I warrant you, sir. O joyful day! Now am I a made man forever.   20

    [Exit.]

FAUST. What art thou, Faustus, but a man condemned to die?
   Thy fatal time draws to a final end;
   Despair doth drive distrust into my thoughts.
   Confound these passions with a quiet sleep.
   Tush, Christ did call the thief upon the cross;[5]   25
   Then rest thee, Faustus, quiet in conceit.

              [He sits to sleep in his chair.]
    [Enter the HORSE-COURSER *wet.]*

HOR. O, what a cozening Doctor was this! I riding my horse into
the water, thinking some hidden mystery had been in the horse,
I had nothing under me but a little straw, and had much ado to
escape drowning. Well, I'll go rouse him and make him give me   30
my forty dollars again. Ho! sirrah Doctor, you cozening scab!
Master Doctor, awake and rise, and give me my money again,
for your horse is turned to a bottle[6] of hay. Master Doctor—

    [He pulls off his leg.]

Alas, I am undone! What shall I do? I have pulled off his leg.

FAUST. O help! Help! The villain hath murdered me!   35

HOR. Murder or not murder, now he has but one leg I'll outrun
him and cast this leg into some ditch or other.

    [Exit.]

FAUST. Stop him, stop him, stop him! Ha ha ha! Faustus hath his
leg again, and the horse-courser a bundle of hay for his forty
dollars.   40

    [Enter WAGNER.*]*

FAUST. How now, Wagner! What news with thee?

WAG. If it please you, the Duke of Vanholt doth earnestly entreat
your company and hath sent some of his men to attend you with
provision fit for your journey.

---

5. In Luke 23.39–43 one of the two thieves cru-   ceit": in mind.
cified with Jesus is promised Paradise. "In con-   6. Bundle.

FAUST. The Duke of Vanholt's an honorable gentleman, and one   45
to whom I must be no niggard of my cunning. Come, away!

    [*Exeunt* OMNES.]

SCENE 6

    [*Enter* ROBIN, DICK, HORSE-COURSER, *and a* CARTER.]

CART. Come, my masters, I'll bring you to the best beer in Europe—
What ho, Hostess!—Where be these whores?[7]

    [*Enter* HOSTESS.]

HOST. How now! What lack you? What, my old guests, welcome.
ROBIN. Sirrah Dick, dost thou know why I stand so mute?
DICK. No, Robin, why is 't?   5
ROBIN. I am eighteen pence on the score,[8] but say nothing; see if
she have forgotten me.
HOST. Who's this that stands so solemnly by himself? What, my
old guest!
ROBIN. O, hostess, how do you do? I hope my score stands still.   10
HOST. Aye, there's no doubt of that, for methinks you make no
haste to wipe it out.
DICK. Why, hostess, I say, fetch us some beer.
HOST. You shall presently; look up into th' hall. There, ho!

    [*Exit.*]

DICK. Come, sirs; what shall we do now till mine hostess comes?   15
CART. Marry, sir, I'll tell you the bravest tale how a conjurer served
me. You know Dr. Faustus?
HOR. Aye, a plague take him! Here's some on 's have cause to know
him. Did he conjure thee too?
CART. I'll tell you how he served me. As I was going to Wittenberg   20
t' other day, he met me and asked me what he should give me
for as much hay as he could eat. Now, sir, I, thinking that a little
would serve his turn, bade him take as much as he would for
three farthings. So he presently gave me my money and fell to
eating; and, as I am a cursen[9] man, he never left eating till he   25
had eat up all my load of hay.
ALL. O monstrous; eat a whole load of hay!
ROBIN. Yes, yes; that may be, for I have heard of one that has eat a
load of logs.[1]
HOR. Now, sirs, you shall hear how villainously he served me. I   30
went to him yesterday to buy a horse of him, and he would by
no means sell him under forty dollars. So, sir, because I knew
him to be such a horse as would run over hedge and ditch and
never tire, I gave him his money. So, when I had my horse, Dr.
Faustus bade me ride him night and day and spare him no time;   35

---

7. I.e., the hostess and maids of the inn.
8. Charged, not paid for.
9. Mispronunciation of "Christian."

1. Comic expression for being drunk—to carry a
jag (or load) of logs.

"But," quoth he, "in any case ride him not into the water." Now sir, I thinking the horse had had some quality that he would not have me know of, what did I but ride him into a great river, and when I came just in the midst my horse vanished away and I sat straddling upon a bottle of hay.   40

ALL. O brave Doctor!

HOR. But you shall hear how bravely I served him for it. I went me home to his house, and there I found him asleep; I kept a hallowing and whooping in his ears, but all could not wake him. I seeing that, took him by the leg and never rested pulling till I   45 had pulled me his leg quite off, and now 'tis at home in mine hostry.

DICK. And has the Doctor but one leg then? That's excellent, for one of his devils turned me into the likeness of an ape's face.

CART. Some more drink, hostess!   50

ROBIN. Hark you, we'll into another room and drink awhile, and then we'll go seek out the Doctor.

[*Exeunt* OMNES.]

SCENE 7

[*Enter the* DUKE OF VANHOLT, *his* DUCHESS, FAUSTUS, *and* MEPHISTOPHILIS.]

DUKE. Thanks, master Doctor, for these pleasant sights; nor know I how sufficiently to recompense your great deserts in erecting that enchanted castle in the air, the sight whereof so delighted me as nothing in the world could please me more.

FAUST. I do think myself, my good lord, highly recompensed that   5 it pleaseth your Grace to think but well of that which Faustus hath performed. But gracious lady, it may be that you have taken no pleasure in those sights; therefore I pray you tell me what is the thing you most desire to have; be it in the world it shall be yours. I have heard that great-bellied women do long for things   10 that are rare and dainty.

DUCH. True, master Doctor, and since I find you so kind, I will make known unto you what my heart desires to have; and were it now summer, as it is January, a dead time of winter, I would request no better meat than a dish of ripe grapes.   15

FAUST. This is but a small matter.—Go, Mephistophilis, away!—

[*Exit* MEPHISTOPHILIS.]

Madam, I will do more than this for your content.

[*Enter* MEPHISTOPHILIS *again with the grapes.*]

Here, now taste ye these; they should be good, for they come from a far country, I can tell you.

DUKE. This makes me wonder more than all the rest, that at this   20 time of year, when every tree is barren of his fruit, from whence you had these ripe grapes.

FAUST. Please it your Grace, the year is divided into two circles over

the whole world, so that when it is winter with us, in the contrary
circle it is likewise summer with them, as in India, Saba,[2] and   25
such countries that lie far east, where they have fruit twice a year.
From whence, by means of a swift spirit that I have, I had these
grapes brought as you see.

DUCH. And trust me they are the sweetest grapes that e'er I tasted.

[*The* CLOWNS *bounce*[3] *at the gate within.*]

DUKE. What rude disturbers have we at the gate?   30
    Go pacify their fury, set it ope,
    And then demand of them what they would have.

[*They knock again and call out to talk with* FAUSTUS.]

A SERVANT. Why, how now, masters, what a coil[4] is there!
    What is the reason you disturb the Duke?

DICK. We have no reason for it, therefore a fig[5] for him!   35

SERV. Why, saucy varlets! Dare you be so bold?

HOR. I hope, sir, we have wit enough to be more bold than wel-
    come.

SERV. It appears so; Pray be bold elsewhere
    And trouble not the Duke.

DUKE. What would they have?   40

SERV. They all cry out to speak with Dr. Faustus.

CART. Aye, and we will speak with him.

DUKE. Will you, sir? Commit[6] the rascals!

DICK. Commit with us? He were as good commit with his father as
    commit with us.   45

FAUST. I do beseech your Grace, let them come in;
    They are good subject for a merriment.

DUKE. Do as thou wilt, Faustus; I give thee leave.

FAUST. I thank your Grace.

[*Enter* ROBIN, DICK, CARTER, *and* HORSE-COURSER.]

                    Why, how now, my good friends?   50
'Faith you are too outrageous; but come near,
    I have procured your pardons. Welcome all!

ROBIN. Nay, sir, we will be welcome for our money, and we will
    pay for what we take. What ho! Give 's half a dozen of beer here,
    and be hanged.   55

FAUST. Nay, hark you, can you tell me where you are?[7]

CART. Aye, marry, can I; we are under heaven.

SERV. Aye, but, sir saucebox, know you in what place?

HOR. Aye, aye, the house is good enough to drink in. Zounds, fill
    us some beer, or we'll break all the barrels in the house and dash   60
    out all your brains with your bottles.

FAUST. Be not so furious; come, you shall have beer.

---

2. Sheba.
3. Bang.
4. Disturbance.
5. An obscene gesture, implying contempt.
6. Put in jail. Dick puns on its other meaning
("commit adultery"), from the Ten Commandments.
7. At the end of 4.6, the clowns thought they were
stepping into another room, but Faustus has had
them transported to the court of the Duke of Vanholt.

My lord, beseech you give me leave awhile;
I'll gage my credit 'twill content your Grace.

DUKE. With all my heart, kind Doctor, please thyself;   65
Our servants and our court's at thy command.

FAUST. I humbly thank your Grace. Then fetch some beer.

HOR. Aye, marry, there spake a doctor indeed; and, faith, I'll drink
a health to thy wooden leg for that word.

FAUST. My wooden leg! What dost thou mean by that?   70

CART. Ha ha ha, dost hear him, Dick? He has forgot his leg.

HOR. Aye, he does not stand much upon that.

FAUST. No, faith, not much upon a wooden leg.

CART. Good lord, that flesh and blood should be so frail with your
worship! Do you not remember a horse-courser you sold a horse   75
to?

FAUST. Yes, I remember I sold one a horse.

CART. And do you remember you bid he should not ride him into
the water?

FAUST. Yes, I do very well remember that.   80

CART. And do you remember nothing of your leg?

FAUST. No, in good sooth.

CART. Then I pray remember your courtesy.

FAUST. I thank you, sir.

CART. 'Tis not so much worth. I pray you tell me one thing.   85

FAUST. What's that?

CART. Be both of your legs bedfellows every night together?

FAUST. Wouldst thou make a colossus[8] of me, that thou askest me
such questions?

CART. No, truly, sir, I would make nothing of you, but I would fain   90
know that.

         [*Enter* HOSTESS *with drink.*]

FAUST. Then I assure thee certainly they are.

CART. I thank you; I am fully satisfied.

FAUST. But wherefore dost thou ask?

CART. For nothing, sir; but methinks you should have a wooden   95
bedfellow to one of 'em.

HOR. Why, do you hear, sir, did not I pull off one of your legs
when you were asleep?

FAUST. But I have it again now I am awake; look you here, sir.

ALL. O horrible! Had the doctor three legs?   100

CART. Do you remember, sir, how you cozened me and eat up my
load of——

         [FAUSTUS *charms him dumb.*]

DICK. Do you remember how you made me wear an ape's——

HOR. You whoreson conjuring scab, do you remember how you
cozened me of a ho——   105

8. The huge statue which stood at the entrance to   and Dr. Faustus is suggesting that the clowns are
the harbor at Rhodes; boats sailed between its legs,   making his legs as important.

ROBIN. Ha' you forgotten me? You think to carry it away with your
hey-pass and your re-pass;[9] do you remember the dog's fa——

    [*Exeunt* CLOWNS.]

HOST. Who pays for the ale? Hear you, master Doctor, now you
have sent away my guests, I pray who shall pay me for my a——

    [*Exit* HOSTESS.]

DUCH. My lord,   110
  We are much beholding to this learned man.
DUKE. So are we, madam, which we will recompense
  With all the love and kindness that we may;
  His artful sport drives all sad thoughts away.   [*Exeunt.*]

Act 5

SCENE 1

[*Thunder and lightning. Enter* DEVILS *with covered dishes;*
MEPHISTOPHILIS *leads them into* FAUSTUS' *study. Then enter*
WAGNER.]

WAG. I think my master means to die shortly;
  He has made his will and given me his wealth,
  His house, his goods, and store of golden plate,
  Besides two thousand ducats ready coined.
  And yet I wonder, for if death were nigh   5
  He would not banquet and carouse and swill
  Amongst the students as even now he doth,
  Who are at supper with such belly-cheer
  As Wagner ne'er beheld in all his life.
  See where they come; belike the feast is ended.   [*Exit.*] 10

    [*Enter* FAUSTUS *and* MEPHISTOPHILIS *with two or three*
    SCHOLARS.]

1 SCH. Master Doctor Faustus, since our conference about fair ladies,
which was the beautifullest in all the world, we have determined
with ourselves that Helen of Greece was the admirablest lady that
ever lived. Therefore, master Doctor, if you will do us that favor
as to let us see that peerless dame of Greece whom all the world   15
admires for majesty, we should think ourselves much beholding
unto you.
FAUST. Gentlemen,
  For that I know your friendship is unfeigned,
  And Faustus' custom is not to deny   20
  The just requests of those that wish him well,
  You shall behold that peerless dame of Greece,
  No otherways for pomp and majesty
  Than when Sir Paris crossed the seas with her

---

9. Traditional exclamations of a conjurer.

And brought the spoils to rich Dardania.[1]   25
Be silent, then, for danger is in words.

> [*Music sounds.* MEPHISTOPHILIS *brings in* HELEN; *she pas-
> seth over the stage.*]

2 SCH. Too simple is my wit to tell her praise
      Whom all the world admires for majesty.
3 SCH. No marvel though the angry Greeks pursued
      With ten years' war the rape of such a queen   30
      Whose heavenly beauty passeth all compare.
1 SCH. Since we have seen the pride of Nature's works
      And only paragon of excellence,
      Let us depart, and for this glorious deed
      Happy and blest be Faustus evermore.   35
FAUST. Gentlemen, farewell; the same I wish to you.

> [*Exeunt* SCHOLARS.]

> [*Enter an* OLD MAN.]

OLD MAN. O gentle Faustus, leave this damnèd art,
      This magic, that will charm thy soul to hell
      And quite bereave[2] thee of salvation.
      Though thou hast now offended like a man,   40
      Do not persèver in it like a devil.
      Yet, yet, thou hast an amiable soul
      If sin by custom grow not into nature;
      Then, Faustus, will repentance come too late;
      Then thou art banished from the sight of heaven.   45
      No mortal can express the pains of hell.
      It may be this my exhortation
      Seems harsh and all unpleasant; let it not;
      For, gentle son, I speak it not in wrath
      Or envy of thee, but in tender love   50
      And pity of thy future misery,
      And so have hope that this my kind rebuke,
      Checking thy body, may amend thy soul.
FAUST. Where art thou, Faustus? Wretch, what hast thou done?
      Damned art thou, Faustus, damned! Despair and die.   55

> [MEPHISTOPHILIS *gives him a dagger.*]

      Hell claims his right, and with a roaring voice
      Says, "Faustus, come; thine hour is almost come!"
      And Faustus now will come to do thee right.
OLD MAN. O stay, good Faustus, stay thy desperate steps!
      I see an angel hovers o'er thy head   60
      And with a vial full of precious grace
      Offers to pour the same into thy soul:
      Then call for mercy and avoid despair.
FAUST. Ah my sweet friend, I feel thy words
      To comfort my distressèd soul.   65
      Leave me awhile to ponder on my sins.

---

1. Troy.   2. Deprive.

OLD MAN. Faustus, I leave thee, but with grief of heart,
    Fearing the ruin of thy hapless soul.   [*Exit.*]
FAUST. Accursèd Faustus, where is mercy now?
    I do repent and yet I do despair: 70
    Hell strives with grace for conquest in my breast.
    What shall I do to shun the snares of death?
MEPH. Thou traitor, Faustus, I arrest thy soul
    For disobedience to my sovereign lord.
    Revolt, or I'll in piecemeal tear thy flesh.   75
FAUST. I do repent I e'er offended him.
    Sweet Mephistophilis, entreat thy lord
    To pardon my unjust presumption,
    And with my blood again I will confirm
    The former vow I made to Lucifer.   80
MEPH. Do it then, Faustus, with unfeignèd heart
    Lest greater danger do attend thy drift.
FAUST. Torment, sweet friend, that base and aged man
    That durst dissuade me from thy Lucifer,
    With greatest torments that our hell affords.   85
MEPH. His faith is great; I cannot touch his soul;
    But what I may afflict his body with
    I will attempt, which is but little worth.
FAUST. One thing, good servant, let me crave of thee
    To glut the longing of my heart's desire: 90
    That I might have unto my paramour
    That heavenly Helen which I saw of late,
    Whose sweet embracings may extinguish clear
    These thoughts that do dissuade me from my vow,
    And keep mine oath I made to Lucifer.   95
MEPH. This, or what else my Faustus shall desire
    Shall be performed in twinkling of an eye.

    [*Enter* HELEN *again, passing over between two* CUPIDS.]

FAUST. Was this the face that launched a thousand ships
    And burnt the topless[3] towers of Ilium?
    Sweet Helen, make me immortal with a kiss.   100
    Her lips suck forth my soul—see where it flies!
    Come, Helen, come, give me my soul again.
    Here will I dwell, for heaven is in these lips
    And all is dross that is not Helena.

    [*Enter* OLD MAN *and stands watching* FAUSTUS.]

    I will be Paris, and for love of thee   105
    Instead of Troy shall Wittenberg be sacked,
    And I will combat with weak Menelaus
    And wear thy colors on my plumèd crest;
    Yea, I will wound Achilles in the heel
    And then return to Helen for a kiss.   110

3. So high they seemed to have no tops.

O thou art fairer than the evening air
Clad in the beauty of a thousand stars!
Brighter art thou than flaming Jupiter
When he appeared to hapless Semele,[4]
More lovely than the monarch of the sky   115
In wanton Arethusa's azured arms,[5]
And none but thou shalt be my paramour!

[*Exeunt* ALL *except the* OLD MAN.]

OLD MAN. Accursèd Faustus, miserable man,
    That from thy soul exclud'st the grace of heaven
    And fliest the throne of his tribunal seat.   120

[*Enter the* DEVILS *to torment him.*]

Satan begins to sift me with his pride.[6]
As in this furnace God shall try my faith,
My faith, vile hell, shall triumph over thee!
Ambitious fiends, see how the heavens smiles
At your repulse, and laughs your state to scorn.   125
Hence, hell! for hence I fly unto my God.   [*Exeunt.*]

SCENE 2

[*Thunder. Enter* LUCIFER, BELZEBUB, *and* MEPHISTOPHILIS.]

LUC. Thus from infernal Dis[7] do we ascend
    To view the subjects of our monarchy,
    Those souls which sin seals the black sons of hell.
    'Mong which as chief, Faustus, we come to thee,
    Bringing with us lasting damnation   5
    To wait upon thy soul; the time is come
    Which makes it forfeit.
MEPH.   And this gloomy night
    Here in this room will wretched Faustus be.
BEL. And here we'll stay
    To mark him how he doth demean himself.   10
MEPH. How should he but with desperate lunacy?
    Fond worldling, now his heart-blood dries with grief,
    His conscience kills it, and his laboring brain
    Begets a world of idle fantasies
    To overreach the devil, but all in vain.   15
    His store of pleasure must be sauced with pain.
    He and his servant Wagner are at hand;
    Both come from drawing Faustus' latest will.
    See where they come!

[*Enter* FAUSTUS *and* WAGNER.]

FAUST. Say, Wagner, thou has perused my will;   20

4. A Theban girl, loved by Jupiter and destroyed
by the fire of his lightning when he appeared to
her in his full splendor.
5. Arethusa was the nymph of a fountain, as well
as the fountain itself; no classical myth, however,
records her love affair with Jupiter, the "monarch
of the sky."
6. I.e., to test me with his strength.
7. The underworld.

How dost thou like it?
WAG.   Sir, so wondrous well
As in all humble duty I do yield
My life and lasting service for your love.

[*Enter the* SCHOLARS.]

FAUST. Gramercies, Wagner.—Welcome, gentlemen.
1 SCH. Now, worthy Faustus, methinks your looks are changed.   25
FAUST. Ah, gentlemen!
2 SCH. What ails Faustus?
FAUST. Ah, my sweet chamber-fellow, had I lived with thee, then
   had I lived still, but now must die eternally. Look, sirs! Comes
   he not? Comes he not?   30
1 SCH. O my dear Faustus, what imports this fear?
2 SCH. Is all our pleasure turned to melancholy?
3 SCH. He is not well with being over-solitary.
2 SCH. If it be so, we'll have physicians, and Faustus shall be cured.
3 SCH. 'Tis but a surfeit,[8] sir; fear nothing.   35
FAUST. A surfeit of deadly sin that hath damned both body and soul.
2 SCH. Yet, Faustus, look up to heaven: remember God's mercies
   are infinite.
FAUST. But Faustus' offense can ne'er be pardoned; the Serpent that
   tempted Eve may be saved, but not Faustus. Ah, gentlemen,   40
   hear me with patience, and tremble not at my speeches. Though
   my heart pants and quivers to remember that I have been a student here these thirty years, O would I had never seen Wittenberg, never read book! And what wonders I have done all Germany
   can witness, yea all the world, for which Faustus hath lost both   45
   Germany and the world, yea heaven itself—heaven the seat of
   God, the throne of the blessed, the kingdom of joy, and must
   remain in hell forever, hell, ah hell, forever! Sweet friends, what
   shall become of Faustus, being in hell forever?
3 SCH. Yet, Faustus, call on God.   50
FAUST. On God, whom Faustus hath abjured? on God, whom
   Faustus hath blasphemed? Ah, my God, I would weep, but the
   devil draws in my tears! Gush forth, blood, instead of tears, yea
   life and soul! O he stays my tongue; I would lift up my hands
   but, see, they hold 'em, they hold 'em!   55
ALL. Who, Faustus?
FAUST. Why, Lucifer and Mephistophilis.
   Ah gentlemen, I gave them my soul for my cunning.
ALL. God forbid!
FAUST. God forbade it indeed, but Faustus hath done it: for the vain   60
   pleasure of four and twenty years hath Faustus lost eternal joy
   and felicity. I writ them a bill with mine own blood; the date is
   expired, this is the time, and he will fetch me.
1 SCH. Why did not Faustus tell us of this before, that divines might
   have prayed for thee?   65
FAUST. Oft have I thought to have done so, but the devil threatened
   to tear me in pieces if I named God, to fetch both body and soul

8. Indigestion; the effects of overindulgence.

if I once gave ear to divinity; and now 'tis too late. Gentlemen,
away, lest you perish with me!

2 SCH. O what may we do to save Faustus?   70

FAUST. Talk not of me, but save yourselves and depart.

3 SCH. God will strengthen me: I will stay with Faustus.

1 SCH. Tempt not God, sweet friend, but let us into the next room,
and there pray for him.

FAUST. Aye, pray for me, pray for me! And what noise soever ye   75
hear, come not unto me, for nothing can rescue me.

2 SCH. Pray thou, and we will pray that God may have mercy upon
thee.

FAUST. Gentlemen, farewell. If I live till morning I'll visit you; if
not, Faustus is gone to hell.   80

ALL. Faustus, farewell.   [*Exeunt* SCHOLARS.]

MEPH. Aye, Faustus, now thou hast no hope of heaven;
　　　Therefore despair, think only upon hell,
　　　For that must be thy mansion, there to dwell.

FAUST. O thou bewitching fiend, 'twas thy temptation   85
　　　Hath robbed me of eternal happiness.

MEPH. I do confess it, Faustus, and rejoice.
　　　'Twas I, that when thou wert i' the way to heaven
　　　Damned up thy passage; when thou tookest the book
　　　To view the scriptures, then I turned the leaves   90
　　　And led thine eye.
　　　What, weepst thou? 'tis too late. Despair, farewell!
　　　Fools that will laugh on earth must weep in hell.   [*Exit.*]

[*Enter the* GOOD ANGEL *and the* BAD ANGEL *at several doors.*]

G. ANG. Ah Faustus, if thou hadst given ear to me,
　　　Innumerable joys had followed thee,   95
　　　But thou didst love the world.

B. ANG.　　　　　　　　　　Gave ear to me
　　　And now must taste hell's pains perpetually.

G. ANG. O what will all thy riches, pleasures, pomps
　　　Avail thee now?

B. ANG.　　　　　　Nothing but vex thee more,
　　　To want in hell, that had on earth such store.   100

[*Music while the throne descends.*[9]]

G. ANG. O, thou hast lost celestial happiness,
　　　Pleasures unspeakable, bliss without end.
　　　Hadst thou affected sweet divinity
　　　Hell or the devil had had no power on thee.
　　　Hadst thou kept on that way, Faustus, behold   105
　　　In what resplendent glory thou hadst sit
　　　In yonder throne, like those bright shining saints,
　　　And triumphed over hell; that hast thou lost.
　　　And now, poor soul, must thy good angel leave thee;
　　　The jaws of hell are open to receive thee.   110

9. A throne suspended by ropes descended to the stage near the end of many Elizabethan plays and was an expected theatrical display. Here the throne clearly symbolizes heaven, as the next speech shows.

[*Exit. Hell is discovered.*]

B. ANG. Now Faustus, let thine eyes with horror stare
 Into that vast perpetual torture-house.
 There are the furies, tossing damnèd souls
 On burning forks; their bodies boil in lead.
 There are live quarters[1] broiling on the coals   115
 That ne'er can die; this ever-burning chair
 Is for o'ertortured souls to rest them in;
 These that are fed with sops of flaming fire
 Were gluttons and loved only delicates
 And laughed to see the poor starve at their gates.   120
 But yet all these are nothing; thou shalt see
 Ten thousand tortures that more horrid be.
FAUST. O, I have seen enough to torture me.
B. ANG. Nay, thou must feel them, taste the smart of all;
 He that loves pleasure must for pleasure fall.   125
 And so I leave thee, Faustus, till anon;
 Then wilt thou tumble in confusiòn.[2]

[*Exit. The clock strikes eleven.*]

FAUST. Ah, Faustus,
 Now hast thou but one bare hour to live
 And then thou must be damned perpetually!   130
 Stand still, you ever-moving spheres of heaven,
 That time may cease and midnight never come;
 Fair Nature's eye, rise, rise again, and make
 Perpetual day; or let this hour be but
 A year, a month, a week, a natural day,   135
 That Faustus may repent and save his soul!
 O lente lente currite noctis equi.[3]
 The stars move still, time runs, the clock will strike,
 The devil will come, and Faustus must be damned.
 O, I'll leap up to my God! Who pulls me down?   140
 See, see, where Christ's blood streams in the firmament!—
 One drop would save my soul—half a drop! ah, my Christ!
 Rend not my heart for naming of my Christ;
 Yet will I call on him—O, spare me, Lucifer!
 Where is it now? 'Tis gone; and see where God   145
 Stretcheth out his arm and bends his ireful brows.
 Mountains and hills, come, come and fall on me
 And hide me from the heavy wrath of God,
 No, no?
 Then will I headlong run into the earth: 150
 Earth, gape! O no, it will not harbor me.
 You stars that reigned at my nativity,
 Whose influence hath allotted death and hell,
 Now draw up Faustus like a foggy mist
 Into the entails of yon laboring cloud   155
 That when you vomit forth into the air,

---

1. Bodies.
2. Destruction, perdition.

3. "Slowly, slowly run, O horses of the night," adapted from a line in Ovid's *Amores*.

My limbs may issue from your smoky mouths,
So that my soul may but ascend to heaven.[4]

[*The watch strikes.*]

Ah, half the hour is past; 'twill all be past anon.
O God,   160
If thou wilt not have mercy on my soul,
Yet for Christ's sake whose blood hath ransomed me
Impose some end to my incessant pain:
Let Faustus live in hell a thousand years,
A hundred thousand, and at last be saved!   165
O, no end is limited to damnèd souls!
Why wert thou not a creature wanting soul?
Or why is this immortal that thou hast?
Ah, Pythagoras' *metempsychosis*[5]—were that true,
This soul should fly from me, and I be changed   170
Unto some brutish beast. All beasts are happy,
For when they die
Their souls are soon dissolved in elements,
But mine must live still[6] to be plagued in hell.
Cursèd be the parents that engendered me!   175
No, Faustus, curse thyself, curse Lucifer
That hath deprived thee of the joys of heaven.

[*The clock strikes twelve.*]

It strikes, it strikes! Now, body, turn to air
Or Lucifer will bear thee quick[7] to hell!

[*Thunder and lightning.*]

O soul, be changed to little water drops   180
And fall into the ocean, ne'er be found.
My God, my God, look not so fierce on me!

[*Enter* DEVILS.]

Adders and serpents, let me breathe awhile!
Ugly hell, gape not—come not, Lucifer—
I'll burn my books—ah, Mephistophilis!   185

[*Exeunt* DEVILS *with* FAUSTUS.]

SCENE 3

[*Enter the* SCHOLARS.]

1 SCH. Come, gentlemen, let us go visit Faustus,
For such a dreadful night was never seen
Since first the world's creation did begin,
Such fearful shrieks and cries were never heard.

---

4. Faustus begs his natal stars to draw him up into
the cloud, where his body may be compacted into
a thunderstone and fall to earth, so that his soul,
thus purified, may ascend to heaven.

5. Pythagoras' doctrine of the transmigration of
souls.
6. Always.
7. Alive.

Pray heaven the Doctor have escaped the danger.   5
2 SCH. O, help us heaven! See, here are Faustus' limbs
    All torn asunder by the hand of death.
3 SCH. The devils whom Faustus served have torn him thus;
    For 'twixt the hours of twelve and one, methought
    I heard him shriek and call aloud for help.   10
    At which self[8] time the house seemed all on fire
    With dreadful horror of these damnèd fiends.
2 SCH. Well, gentlemen, though Faustus' end be such
    As every Christian heart laments to think on,
    Yet for he was a scholar once admired   15
    For wondrous knowledge in our German schools,
    We'll give his mangled limbs due burial;
    And all the students, clothed in mourning black,
    Shall wait upon his heavy[9] funeral.   [*Exeunt.*]

        [*Enter* CHORUS.]

CHO. Cut is the branch that might have grown full straight,   20
    And burnèd is Apollo's laurel bough[1]
    That sometime grew within this learnèd man.
    Faustus is gone: regard his hellish fall,
    Whose fiendful fortune may exhort the wise
    Only to wonder at[2] unlawful things   25
    Whose deepness doth entice such forward wits
    To practice more than heavenly power permits.   [*Exit.*]

                                        1604, 1616

8. Same, exact.
9. Tragic, sorrowful.
1. Laurel is a symbol of wisdom and learning; Apollo was the god of divination, one of whose shrines was the oracle at Delphi. The image, though it sounds classical, is really Marlowe's.
2. I.e., to be content with observing with awe. "Fiendful fortune": devilish fate.

WILLIAM SHAKESPEARE
1564–1616

ca. 1588–92:   In London as actor and playwright.
ca. 1592–98:   Devotes himself mainly to chronicle histories and comedies.
ca. 1601–9:   Period of the great tragedies and romantic comedies.
ca. 1610:   Retires to Stratford.

William Shakespeare was born in Stratford-on-Avon in April (probably April 23), 1564. His father was a citizen of some prominence who became an alderman and bailiff, but who later suffered financial reverses. Shakespeare presumably attended the Stratford grammar school, where he could have acquired a respectable knowledge of Latin, but he did not proceed to Oxford or Cambridge. There are legends about Shakespeare's youth but no documented facts. The first record we have of his life after his christening is that of his marriage in 1582 to Anne Hathaway. A daughter was born to the young Shakespeares in 1583 and twins, a boy and a girl, in 1585. We possess no information about his activities for the next seven years, but by 1592 he was in London as an actor and apparently well known as a playwright, for Robert Greene refers to him resentfully in A *Groatsworth of Wit* as "an upstart crow, beautified with our feathers," who, "being an absolute *Johannes Factotum*, is in his own conceit the only Shake-scene in a country."

At this time, there were several companies of actors in London and in the provinces. What connection Shakespeare had with one or more of them before 1592 is conjectural, but we do know of his long and fruitful connection with the most successful troupe, the Lord Chamberlain's Men, who later, when James I came to the throne, became the King's Men. Shakespeare not only acted with this company, but eventually became a leading shareholder and the principal playwright. The company included some of the most famous actors of the day, such as Richard Burbage, who no doubt created the roles of Hamlet, Lear, and Othello, and Will Kempe and Robert Armin, who acted Shakespeare's clowns and fools. In 1599 the Chamberlain's Men built and occupied that best known of Elizabethan theaters, the Globe.

Shakespeare did not, in his early years, confine himself to the theater. In 1593 he published a mythological-erotic poem, *Venus and Adonis*, dedicated to the earl of Southampton; in the next year he dedicated a "graver labor," *The Rape of Lucrece*, to the same noble patron. By 1597 Shakespeare had so prospered that he was able to purchase New Place, a handsome house in Stratford; he could now call himself a gentleman, as his father had been granted a coat of arms in the previous year.

Our first record of the playwright's actual work occurs in Francis Meres' *Palladis Tamia: Wit's Treasury* (1598), in which Meres compared English poets with the ancients; of Shakespeare he says, "As Plautus and Seneca are accounted the best for Comedy and Tragedy among the Latins, so Shakespeare among the English is the most excellent in both kinds for the stage." He goes on to list *Richard II, Richard III, Henry IV, King John, Titus Andronicus*, and *Romeo and Juliet* for tragedy and *Two Gentlemen of Verona, The Comedy of Errors, A Midsummer Night's Dream, The Merchant of Venice, Love's Labor's Lost*, and the unknown (or perhaps retitled) *Love's Labor's Won* as comedy. All of the plays Meres lists as tragedy (except for *Romeo and Juliet* and the very early *Titus Andronicus*) we would call chronicle history plays, a popular kind of drama based upon history books like Raphael Holinshed's *Chronicle* and presenting dramatically the events in the reigns of various English kings. About the turn of the century Shakespeare wrote his great romantic comedies, *As You Like It, Twelfth Night*, and *Much Ado About Nothing*, and his concluding history play in the Prince Hal series, *Henry V*. The next decade was the period of the great tragedies: *Hamlet, Macbeth, Othello, King Lear*, and *Antony and Cleopatra*.

About 1610 Shakespeare apparently retired to Stratford, though he continued to write, both by himself (*The Tempest*) and in collaboration (*Henry VIII*). This is the period of the "romances" or "tragicomedies," which include, besides *The Tempest, Cymbeline* and *The Winter's Tale*. Aside from his two early nondramatic poems, Shakespeare devoted his genius primarily to the stage. Meres mentioned in 1598, however, that he was known for "his sugared sonnets among his private friends"; the sonnets were published in 1609. The publisher, Thomas Thorpe, included a strange dedication "To the only begetter of these ensuing sonnets, Master W. H." that has puzzled Shakespeare scholars ever since.

The sonnets are Shakespeare's contribution to a popular vogue, but his cycle is quite unlike the other sonnet sequences of his day. Shakespeare's cycle suggests a story, though the details are vague, and there is doubt even whether the sonnets as published in 1609 are in the correct order. Certain motifs are clear: a series celebrating the beauty of a young man and urging him to marry; some sonnets to a lady; some sonnets (like 144) about a strange triangle of love involving two men and a woman; sonnets on the destructive power of time and the permanence of poetry; sonnets about a rival poet; and incidental sonnets of moral insight, like 129 and 146. The biographical background of the sonnets has aroused much speculation, but very little of it is convincing. The poems themselves are what is important. Though the vocabulary is often simple, the metaphorical style of the sonnets is rich. "Shall I compare thee to a summer's day" is a question which might lead to a very ordinary conceit; instead it introduces a profound meditation on time, change, and beauty.

The structure of the sonnet frequently reinforces the power of the metaphors; each quatrain in 73 develops an image of lateness, of approaching extinction—of a season, of a day, and of a fire, but they also apply to a life. The three quatrains may be equally and successively at work preparing for the conclusion in the couplet, or the first eight lines may contain a catalogue an the last six turn in quite a different direction, as in sonnet 29. The rhetorical strategy of the sonnets is also worth careful attention. Some begin with a purported reminiscence; some are imperative; others make an almost proverbial statement, then elaborate it. The imagery comes from a wide variety of sources: gardening, navigation, law, farming, business, pictorial art, astrology, domestic affairs. The moods are also not confined to what the Renaissance thought were those of the despairing Petrarchan lover; they include delight, pride, melancholy, shame, disgust, fear. It is evident that the poet of the sonnets is also the author of the great plays.

The plays contain some of the finest songs ever written. They are of various types: the aubade, or morning song, the gay pastoral invitation, love songs of various kinds, the ballad sung by wandering minstrels, and the funeral dirge. They illustrate many sides of Shakespeare's genius—his incomparable lyric gift, his ready humor, and his marvelous sensitivity to the sights and sounds of English life, especially the life of the country.

When Shakespeare died, in Stratford in 1616, no collected edition of his plays had been published. Some of them had been printed in separate editions ("quartos") without his editorial supervision, sometimes from his manuscripts, sometimes from playhouse prompt books, sometimes from pirated texts secured by shorthand reports of a performance or from reconstruction from memory by an actor or spectator.

In 1623, two members of Shakespeare's company, John Heminges and Henry Condell, published the great collection of all the plays they considered authentic; it is called the First Folio. They printed the best texts they had, according to their lights. The Folio contains an epistle "to the great variety of readers" which urges us to read Shakespeare again and again; if we do not like him, say Heminges and Condell, it is evident that we do not understand him. Another preliminary document in the First Folio is a poem

by Shakespeare's great rival, critic, and opposite, Ben Jonson. In it he asserts
the superiority of Shakespeare not only to other English playwrights but to
the Greek and Latin masters. Jonson first states what has come to be a universal opinion:

> Triumph, my Britain, thou hast one to show
> To whom all scenes of Europe homage owe.
> He was not of an age, but for all time!

SONGS FROM THE PLAYS
When Daisies Pied[1]

Spring

When daisies pied, and violets blue,
   And lady-smocks all silver-white
And cuckoo-buds of yellow hue
   Do paint the meadows with delight,
The cuckoo then, on every tree,   5
Mocks married men;[2] for thus sings he,
              "Cuckoo;
Cuckoo, cuckoo": Oh word of fear,
Unpleasing to a married ear!

When shepherds pipe on oaten straws,[3]   10
   And merry larks are plowmen's clocks,
When turtles tread,[4] and rooks, and daws,
   And maidens bleach their summer smocks,
The cuckoo then, on every tree,
Mocks married men; for thus sings he,   15
              "Cuckoo;
Cuckoo, cuckoo": Oh word of fear,
Unpleasing to a married ear!

Winter

When icicles hang by the wall,
   And Dick the shepherd blows his nail,[5]   20
And Tom bears logs into the hall,
   And milk comes frozen home in pail,
When blood is nipped and ways be foul,

1. This song concludes *Love's Labour's Lost* (1594–
95), one of Shakespeare's earliest comedies.
Announced as a "Dialogue . . . in praise of the
Owl and the Cuckoo," it provides a lyric commentary on the bittersweet mood that dominates the
play's last scene. "Pied": variegated.

2. The cuckoo's song—"Cuckoo!"—is taken to
mean "Cuckold!"
3. The reed pipes played by shepherds.
4. Turtledoves mate. The "larks" are "plowmen's
clocks" because they sing at sunrise.
5. Warms his fingers by blowing on them.

Then nightly sings the staring owl,
"Tu-whit, tu-who": a merry note,   25
While greasy Joan doth keel[6] the pot.

When all aloud the wind doth blow,
    And coughing drowns the parson's saw,[7]
And birds sit brooding in the snow,
    And Marian's nose looks red and raw,   30
When roasted crabs[8] hiss in the bowl,
Then nightly sings the staring owl,
"Tu-whit, tu-who": a merry note
While greasy Joan doth keel the pot.

Tell Me Where Is Fancy Bred[1]

    Tell me where is fancy bred,
    Or in the heart or in the head?
    How begot, how nourishèd?
        Reply, reply.
    It is engendered in the eyes,   5
    With gazing fed; and fancy dies
    In the cradle where it lies.
        Let us all ring fancy's knell:
    I'll begin it—Ding, dong, bell.
    Ding, dong, bell.   10

Under the Greenwood Tree[1]

Under the greenwood tree
Who loves to lie with me,
And turn his merry note
Unto the sweet bird's throat,[2]
Come hither, come hither, come hither: 5
    Here shall he see
    No enemy
But winter and rough weather.

Who doth ambition shun
And loves to live i' th' sun,   10

6. Stir, to prevent boiling over.
7. Wise saying.
8. Crabapples.
1. *The Merchant of Venice* (1596–97) 3.2.63 ff.;
sung while Bassanio is trying to choose between
the caskets of gold, silver, and lead—one of which
contains the token that will enable him to gain
Portia as his wife. The song is perhaps intended to
help Bassanio's choice: notice the number of words

that rhyme with "lead." "Fancy" is a superficial
love or liking for something attractive.
1. *As You Like It* (1599–1600) 2.5.1 ff.; this song
provides a comment on the happy existence of the
banished Duke and his followers in the Forest of
Arden, where life is "more sweet / Than that of
painted pomp."
2. I.e., improvise his song in harmony with the
bird's.

Seeking the food he eats,
And pleased with what he gets,
Come hither, come hither, come hither!
    Here shall he see
    No enemy   15
But winter and rough weather.

Blow, Blow, Thou Winter Wind[1]

Blow, blow, thou winter wind,
Thou art not so unkind
    As man's ingratitude;
Thy tooth is not so keen,
Because thou art not seen,   5
    Although thy breath be rude.
Heigh-ho! sing, heigh-ho! unto the green holly:
Most friendship is feigning, most loving mere folly:
    Then, heigh-ho, the holly!
    This life is most jolly.   10

Freeze, freeze, thou bitter sky,
That dost not bite so nigh
    As benefits forgot:
Though thou the waters warp,[2]
Thy sting is not so sharp   15
    As friend remembered not.
Heigh-ho! sing, etc.

It Was a Lover and His Lass[1]

It was a lover and his lass,
    With a hey, and a ho, and a hey nonino,
That o'er the green corn-field[2] did pass,
    In spring time, the only pretty ring
    time,[3]
When birds do sing, hey ding a ding, ding,   5
Sweet lovers love the spring.

Between the acres of the rye,[4]
    With a hey, and a ho, and a hey nonino,

1. From *As You Like It* 2.7. 174 ff. The contrast here between nature and man's willful behavior is one of the continuing themes of the play.
2. I.e., roughen by freezing.
1. Sung by two pages to the clown Touchstone and his "country wench," Audrey, in *As You Like It* 5.3.16 ff. This *carpe diem* ("seize the time") song anticipates the happy marriages that will conclude the play.
2. Wheat field.
3. I.e., marriage season.
4. I.e., on unplowed ground separating the planted fields.

These pretty country folks would lie,
   In spring time, etc.   10

This carol they began that hour,
   With a hey, and a ho, and a hey nonino,
How that a life was but a flower,
   In spring time, etc.

And therefore take[5] the present time,   15
   With a hey, and a ho, and a hey nonino,
For love is crownèd with the prime,[6]
   In spring time, etc.

Oh Mistress Mine[1]

Oh mistress mine! where are you roaming?
O, stay and hear; your true love's coming,
   That can sing both high and low.
Trip no further, pretty sweeting;
Journeys end in lovers meeting,
   Every wise man's son doth know.   5

What is love? 'tis not hereafter;
Present mirth hath present laughter;
   What's to come is still unsure:
In delay there lies no plenty;
Then come kiss me, sweet and twenty,   10
   Youth's a stuff will not endure.

Fear No More the Heat o' the Sun[1]

Fear no more the heat o' the sun,
   Nor the furious winter's rages;
Thou thy worldly task hast done,
   Home art gone, and ta'en thy wages.
Golden lads and girls all must,   5
As[2] chimney-sweepers, come to dust.

Fear no more the frown o' the great;
   Thou art past the tyrant's stroke;
Care no more to clothe and eat;
   To thee the reed is as the oak: 10

5. Seize.
6. Springtime.
1. *Twelfth Night* (1601–2) 2.3. 40 ff.

1. A lament for the supposedly dead Imogen, sung in *Cymbeline* 4.2.258 ff.
2. Like.

The scepter, learning, physic,[3] must
All follow this, and come to dust.

Fear no more the lightning flash,
    Nor the all-dreaded thunder stone;[4]
Fear not slander, censure rash;   15
    Thou hast finished joy and moan:
All lovers young, all lovers must
Consign to thee, and come to dust.

No exorciser harm thee!
Nor no witchcraft charm thee!   20
Ghost unlaid forbear thee!
Nothing ill come near thee!
Quiet consummation have;
And renownèd be thy grave!

Full Fathom Five[1]

Full fathom five thy father lies;
    Of his bones are coral made;
Those are pearls that were his eyes:
    Nothing of him that doth fade,
But doth suffer a sea change   5
Into something rich and strange.
Sea nymphs hourly ring his knell:
    Ding-dong.
Hark! now I hear them—Ding-dong, bell.

Where the Bee Sucks, There Suck I[1]

Where the bee sucks, there suck I:
In a cowslip's bell I lie;
There I couch when owls do cry.
On the bat's back I do fly
After summer merrily.   5
Merrily, merrily shall I live now
Under the blossom that hangs on the bough.

---

3. Medical science.
4. The sound of thunder was commonly thought
to be caused by the falling of stones or meteorites.
1. *The Tempest* (1611–12) 1.2.396 ff. Ariel, the
airy spirit of the enchanted isle, sings this song to
Ferdinand, prince of Naples. Ferdinand wonders

at it: "The ditty does remember my drowned father.
/ This is no mortal business, nor no sound/ That
the earth owes [owns]."
1. Also from *The Tempest* 5.1.88 ff.: Ariel is happily anticipating the freedom of his future life.

SONNETS

3

Look in thy glass and tell the face thou viewest
Now is the time that face should form another,
Whose fresh repair if now thou not renewest,
Thou dost beguile the world, unbless some mother.
For where is she so fair whose uneared[1] womb   5
Disdains the tillage of thy husbandry?
Or who is he so fond[2] will be the tomb
Of his self-love, to stop posterity?
Thou art thy mother's glass,[3] and she in thee
Calls back the lovely April of her prime;   10
So thou through windows of thine age shalt see,
Despite of wrinkles, this thy golden time.
    But if thou live rememb'red not to be,
    Die single, and thine image dies with thee.

                                                      1609

12

When I do count the clock that tells the time
And see the brave[1] day sunk in hideous night,
When I behold the violet past prime
And sable curls all silvered o'er with white,
When lofty trees I see barren of leaves,   5
Which erst[2] from heat did canopy the herd
And summer's green all girded up in sheaves
Borne on the bier with white and bristly beard:
Then of thy beauty do I question make
That thou among the wastes of time must go,   10
Since sweets and beauties do themselves forsake,
And die as fast as they see others grow,
    And nothing 'gainst Time's scythe can make defense
    Save breed,[3] to brave him when he takes thee hence.

                                                      1609

15

When I consider every thing that grows
Holds[1] in perfection but a little moment;

---

1. Unplowed.   2. Formerly.
2. Foolish.   3. Offspring; "to brave": to defy.
3. Mirror.   1. Remains.
1. Splendid.

That this huge stage presenteth naught but shows
Whereon the stars in secret influence comment;[2]
When I perceive that men as plants increase,   5
Cheerèd and checked[3] even by the selfsame sky,
Vaunt[4] in their youthful sap, at height decrease,
And wear their brave state out of memory;[5]
Then the conceit[6] of this inconstant stay
Sets you most rich in youth before my sight,   10
Where wasteful Time debateth[7] with Decay
To change your day of youth to sullied[8] night,
     And all in war with Time for love of you,
     As he takes from you, I ingraft[9] you new.

                                      1609

18

Shall I compare thee to a summer's day?
Thou art more lovely and more temperate:
Rough winds do shake the darling buds of May,
And summer's lease hath all too short a date:
Sometime too hot the eye of heaven shines   5
And often is his gold complexion dimmed;
And every fair from fair sometimes declines,
By chance or nature's changing course untrimmed;[1]
But thy eternal summer shall not fade,
Nor lose possession of that fair thou ow'st;[2]   10
Nor shall death brag thou wander'st in his shade,
When in eternal lines to time thou grow'st:[3]
     So long as men can breathe, or eyes can see,
     So long lives this, and this gives life to thee.[4]

                                      1609

19

Devouring Time, blunt thou the lion's paws,
And make the earth devour her own sweet brood;
Pluck the keen teeth from the fierce tiger's jaws,
And burn the long-lived phoenix in her blood;[1]

---

2. The stars in an occult way affect human actions.
"Shows": (1) appearances (2) performances.
3. Encouraged and reproached or stopped.
4. Exult, display themselves.
5. Wear their showy splendor out and are forgotten.
6. Conception.
7. Discusses.
8. Soiled, blackened.
9. Renew by grafting, implant beauty again (by my verse).

1. Stripped of gay apparel.
2. Ownest.
3. When in [this] immortal poetry you become even with time.
4. The boast of immortality for one's verse was a Renaissance convention and goes back to the classics. It implies, not egotism on the part of the poet, but a faith in the permanence of poetry.
1. In full vigor of life (a hunting term). The phoenix was a mythical bird that lived five hundred years, then died in flames, to rise again from its ashes.

Make glad and sorry seasons as thou fleet'st,   5
And do what e'er thou wilt, swift-footed Time,
To the wide world and all her fading sweets:
But I forbid thee one most heinous crime,
O carve not with thy hours my love's fair brow,
Nor draw no lines there with thine antique[2] pen;   10
Him in thy course untainted[3] do allow,
For beauty's pattern to succeeding men.
    Yet do thy worst, old Time: despite thy wrong,
    My love shall in my verse ever live young.

                                                         1609

20

A woman's face with Nature's own hand painted[1]
Hast thou, the master mistress of my passion;[2]
A woman's gentle heart but not acquainted
With shifting change as is false women's fashion;
An eye more bright than theirs, less false in rolling,[3]   5
Gilding the object whereupon it gazeth;
A man in hue all hues in his controlling,
Which steals men's eyes and women's souls amazeth.
And for a woman wert thou first created,
Till Nature as she wrought thee fell a-doting,[4]   10
And by addition me of thee defeated,
By adding one thing to my purpose nothing.
    But since she pricked thee out for women's pleasure,[5]
    Mine be thy love, and thy love's use their treasure.[6]

                                                         1609

29

When, in disgrace[1] with Fortune and men's eyes,
I all alone beweep my outcast state,
And trouble deaf heaven with my bootless[2] cries,
And look upon myself and curse my fate,
Wishing me like to one more rich in hope,   5
Featured like him, like him with friends possessed,
Desiring this man's art and that man's scope,
With what I most enjoy contented least;
Yet in these thoughts myself almost despising,

---

2. (1) Old, (2) fantastic.
3. (1) Undefiled, (2) untouched by a weapon (a term from tilting).
1. I.e., not made up with cosmetics.
2. (1) Strong feeling, (2) poem.
3. Roving.

4. (1) Crazy, (2) infatuated.
5. Marked, with obvious sexual pun.
6. (1) Sexual enjoyment, (2) interest (as in usury).
1. Out of favor.
2. Futile.

Haply I think on thee, and then my state[3]   10
(Like to the lark at break of day arising
From sullen earth) sings hymns at heaven's gate;
    For thy sweet love remembered such wealth brings
    That then I scorn to change my state with kings.

                                                                       1609

30

When to the sessions[1] of sweet silent thought
I summon up remembrance of things past,
I sigh the lack of many a thing I sought,
And with old woes new wail[2] my dear time's waste:
Then can I drown an eye (unused to flow)   5
For precious friends hid in death's dateless[3] night,
And weep afresh love's long since canceled woe,
And moan th' expense[4] of many a vanished sight:
Then can I grieve at grievances foregone,[5]
And heavily from woe to woe tell o'er   10
The sad account of fore-bemoanèd moan,
Which I new pay as if not paid before.
But if the while I think on thee, dear friend,
All losses are restored and sorrows end.

                                                                       1609

35

No more be grieved at that which thou hast done:
Roses have thorns, and silver fountains mud.
Clouds and eclipses stain[1] both moon and sun,
And loathsome canker[2] lives in sweetest bud.
All men make faults, and even I in this,   5
Authorizing thy trespass with compare,
Myself corrupting, salving thy amiss,
Excusing thy sins more than thy sins are;
For to thy sensual fault I bring in sense[3]—
Thy adverse party is thy advocate—   10
And 'gainst myself a lawful plea commence.

---

3. Condition, state of mind; but in line 14 there
is a pun on "state" meaning chair of state, throne.
1. Sittings of court; "summon up" (line 2) continues the metaphor.
2. Bewail anew.
3. Endless.

4. Loss.
5. Old subjects for grief. "Tell": count.
1. Dim.
2. Rose worm.
3. Reason.

Such civil war is in my love and hate,
   That I an accessary needs must be
   To that sweet thief which sourly robs from me.

1609

55

Not marble, nor the gilded monuments
Of princes, shall outlive this powerful rhyme;
But you shall shine more bright in these contents
Than unswept stone, besmeared with sluttish time.[1]
When wasteful war shall statues overturn,   5
And broils root out the work of masonry,
Nor Mars his[2] sword nor war's quick fire shall burn
The living record of your memory.
'Gainst death and all-oblivious enmity[3]
Shall you pace forth; your praise shall still find room   10
Even in the eyes of all posterity
That wear this world out to the ending doom.[4]
   So, till the judgment that yourself arise,
   You live in this, and dwell in lovers' eyes.

1609

60

Like as the waves make towards the pibbled[1] shore,
So do our minutes hasten to their end;
Each changing place with that which goes before,
In sequent toil all forwards do contend.[2]
Nativity, once in the main[3] of light,   5
Crawls to maturity, wherewith being crowned,
Crooked eclipses 'gainst his glory fight,
And Time that gave doth now his gift confound.
Time doth transfix the flourish[4] set on youth
And delves the parallels in beauty's brow,   10
Feeds on the rarities of nature's truth,
And nothing stands but for his scythe to mow.

1. I.e., than in a stone tomb or effigy which time
wears away and covers with dust.
2. Mars's.
3. The enmity of oblivion, of being forgotten.
4. Judgment Day. The next line is paraphrased,
"Until you rise from the dead on Judgment Day."
1. Pebbled.

2. Toiling and following each other, the waves
struggle to press forward.
3. Broad expanse.
4. Remove the embellishment. "Delves the parallels": digs the parallel furrows (wrinkles). To
"flourish" is also to blossom.

And yet to times in hope[5] my verse shall stand,
Praising thy worth, despite his cruel hand.

1609

65

Since[1] brass, nor stone, nor earth, nor boundless sea,
But sad mortality o'ersways their power,
How with this rage[2] shall beauty hold a plea,
Whose action is no stronger than a flower?
O how shall summer's honey breath hold out   5
Against the wrackful[3] siege of batt'ring days,
When rocks impregnable are not so stout,
Nor gates of steel so strong, but Time decays?
O fearful meditation! where, alack,
Shall Time's best jewel from Time's chest lie hid?[4]   10
Or what strong hand can hold his swift foot back?
Or who his spoil[5] of beauty can forbid?
     O none, unless this miracle have might,
     That in black ink my love may still shine bright.

1609

71

No longer mourn for me when I am dead
Than you shall hear the surly sullen bell[1]
Give warning to the world that I am fled
From this vile world, with vilest worms to dwell:
Nay, if you read this line, remember not   5
The hand that writ it; for I love you so,
That I in your sweet thoughts would be forgot,
If thinking on me then should make you woe.
Oh, if, (I say,) you look upon this verse
When I (perhaps) compounded am with clay,   10
Do not so much as my poor name rehearse,
But let your love even with my life decay;
     Lest the wise world should look into your moan,
     And mock you with me after I am gone.

1609

---

5. Future times.
1. I.e., since there is neither.
2. Destructive power.
3. Destructive.
4. Time, like any wealthy person, keeps his jewels in a chest. Once it is taken out, where can his best

jewel be hidden from destructive forces?
5. Ravaging.
1. The bell was tolled to announce the death of a member of the parish—one stroke for each year of his life.

73

That time of year thou mayst in me behold
When yellow leaves, or none, or few, do hang
Upon those boughs which shake against the cold,
Bare ruined choirs, where late the sweet birds sang.
In me thou seest the twilight of such day   5
As after sunset fadeth in the west;
Which by and by black night doth take away,
Death's second self that seals up all in rest.
In me thou seest the glowing of such fire,
That on the ashes of his youth doth lie,   10
As the deathbed whereon it must expire,
Consumed with that which it was nourished by.[1]
    This thou perceiv'st, which makes thy love more strong,
    To love that well, which thou must leave ere long.

                            1609

74

But be contented; when that fell[1] arrest
Without all bail shall carry me away,
My life hath in this line[2] some interest,
Which for memorial still[3] with thee shall stay.
When thou reviewest this, thou dost review   5
The very part was[4] consecrate to thee.
The earth can have but earth, which is his due;
My spirit is thine, the better part of me.
So then thou hast but lost the dregs of life,
The prey of worms, my body being dead,   10
The coward conquest of a wretch's knife,[5]
Too base of thee to be rememberèd.
    The worth of that is that which it contains.[6]
    And that is this, and this with thee remains.

                            1609

87

Farewell: thou art too dear[1] for my possessing,
And like enough thou know'st thy estimate.[2]

---

1. Choked by the ashes of that which once nourished its flame.
1. Cruel. Hamlet says, "this fell sergeant Death is strict in his arrest" (5.2.337–38).
2. I.e., poetry; "interest": share, participation.
3. Always.

4. I.e., which was.
5. Death's weapon (like Time's scythe).
6. I.e., the only value of the body is that it contains the spirit.
1. Expensive, beloved.
2. Value.

The charter[3] of thy worth gives thee releasing;
My bonds in thee are all determinate.[4]
For how do I hold thee but by thy granting,   5
And for that riches where is my deserving?
The cause of this fair gift in me is wanting,
And so my patent[5] back again is swerving.
Thy self thou gav'st, thy own worth then not knowing,
Or me, to whom thou gav'st it, else mistaking;   10
So thy great gift, upon misprision[6] growing,
Comes home again, on better judgment making.
    Thus have I had thee as a dream doth flatter,
    In sleep a king, but waking no such matter.

                                                    1609

94

They that have power to hurt and will do none,
That do not do the thing they most do show,[1]
Who, moving others, are themselves as stone,
Unmovèd, cold, and to temptation slow;
They rightly do inherit heaven's graces   5
And husband nature's riches from expense;[2]
They are the lords and owners of their faces,
Others but stewards of their excellence.
The summer's flower is to the summer sweet,
Though to itself it only live and die,   10
But if that flower with base infection meet,
The basest weed outbraves[3] his dignity:
    For sweetest things turn sourest by their deeds;
    Lilies that fester smell far worse than weeds.[4]

                                                    1609

97

How like a winter hath my absence been
From thee, the pleasure of the fleeting year!
What freezings have I felt, what dark days seen!
What old December's bareness everywhere!
And yet this time removed was summer's time,   5
The teeming autumn, big with rich increase,
Bearing the wanton burthen of the prime,[1]

---

3. Deed, contract for property.
4. Expired.
5. Title.
6. Mistake, oversight.
1. Seem to do.
2. I.e., they do not squander nature's gifts.
3. Surpasses. Gerard's *Herbal* (1597) says "the lil-

ies of the field outbraved him."
4. This line appears in *Edward III* (2.1.451), an apocryphal Shakespearean play licensed Dec. 1, 1595.
1. Spring, which has engendered the lavish crop ("wanton burthen") that autumn is now left to bear.

Like widowed wombs after their lords' decease;
Yet this abundant issue seemed to me
But hope of orphans and unfathered fruit;   10
For summer and his pleasures wait on thee,
And, thou away, the very birds are mute;
   Or, if they sing, 'tis with so dull a cheer[2]
   That leaves look pale, dreading the winter's near.

1609

98

From you have I been absent in the spring,
When proud-pied[1] April, dressed in all his trim,
Hath put a spirit of youth in everything,
That heavy Saturn[2] laughed and leapt with him.
Yet nor the lays of birds, nor the sweet smell   5
Of different flowers in odor and in hue,
Could make me any summer's story tell,
Or from their proud lap pluck them where they grew;
Nor did I wonder at[3] the lily's white,
Nor praise the deep vermilion in the rose;   10
They were but sweet, but figures of delight,
Drawn after you, you pattern of all those.
   Yet seemed it winter still, and, you away,
   As with your shadow I with these did play.

1609

106

When in the chronicle of wasted[1] time
I see descriptions of the fairest wights,[2]
And beauty making beautiful old rhyme
In praise of ladies dead and lovely knights,
Then, in the blazon[3] of sweet beauty's best,   5
Of hand, of foot, of lip, of eye, of brow,
I see their antique pen would have expressed
Even such a beauty as you master now.
So all their praises are but prophecies
Of this our time, all you prefiguring;   10
And, for they looked but with divining eyes,[4]
They had not still enough your worth to sing:

---

2. Disposition.
1. Magnificent in many colors.
2. God of melancholy.
3. Admire.
1. Past.

2. Persons.
3. Display.
4. Because ("for") they were able *only* ("but") to
foresee prophetically.

For we, which now behold these present days,
Have eyes to wonder, but lack tongues to praise.

1609

107

Not mine own fears, nor the prophetic soul
Of the wide world dreaming on things to come,[1]
Can yet the lease of my true love control,
Supposed as forfeit to a confinèd doom.[2]
The mortal moon hath her eclipse endured,   5
And the sad augurs mock their own presage;[3]
Incertainties now crown themselves assured,
And peace[4] proclaims olives of endless age.
Now with the drops of this most balmy time
My love looks fresh, and death to me subscribes,[5]   10
Since, spite of him, I'll live in this poor rhyme,
While he insults o'er dull and speechless tribes:
    And thou in this shalt find thy monument,
    When tyrants' crests and tombs of brass are spent.[6]

1609

116

Let me not to the marriage of true minds
Admit impediments;[1] love is not love
Which alters when it alteration finds,
Or bends with the remover to remove:
O, no, it is an ever-fixèd mark,[2]   5
That looks on tempests and is never shaken;
It is the star to every wand'ring bark,
Whose worth's unknown, although his highth[3] be taken.
Love's not Time's fool,[4] though rosy lips and cheeks
Within his[5] bending sickle's compass come;   10
Love alters not with his brief hours and weeks,

---

1. This sonnet refers to contemporary events and
the prophecies, common in Elizabethan almanacs, of disaster.
2. I.e., can yet put an end to my love, which I
thought doomed to early forfeiture.
3. The "mortal moon" is Queen Elizabeth; her
"eclipse" is probably her climacteric year, her 63rd
(thought meaningful because the product of two
"significant" numbers, 7 and 9), which ended in
September 1596. The sober astrologers ("sad
augurs") now ridicule their own predictions ("presage") of catastrophe, since they turned out to be
false.

4. Probably an agreement between Henry IV of
France and Elizabeth.
5. Submits.
6. Wasted away.
1. From the Marriage Service: "If any of you know
cause or just impediment why these persons should
not be joined together . . ."
2. Sea-mark (cf. "landmark").
3. The star's value is not known, though the star's
"highth" (altitude) may be known and used for
practical investigation.
4. I.e., slave or victim.
5. I.e., Time's (as also in line 11).

But bears it out even to the edge of doom.[6]
If this be error and upon me proved,
I never writ, nor no man ever loved.

1609

126

O thou, my lovely boy, who in thy power
Dost hold Time's fickle glass,[1] his sickle, hour;
Who hast by waning grown and therein show'st
Thy lovers withering as thy sweet self grow'st;
If Nature (sovereign mistress over wrack)[2]   5
As thou goest onwards still will pluck thee back,
She keeps thee to this purpose, that her skill
May Time disgrace and wretched minutes kill.
Yet fear her, O thou minion[3] of her pleasure,
She may detain, but not still[4] keep, her treasure!   10
Her audit[5] (though delayed) answered must be,
And her quietus is to render[6] thee.

1609

128

How oft when thou, my music, music play'st
Upon that blessèd wood[1] whose motion sounds
With thy sweet fingers when thou gently sway'st[2]
The wiry concord that mine ear confounds,[3]
Do I envy those jacks[4] that nimble leap   5
To kiss the tender inward of thy hand,
Whilst my poor lips, which should that harvest reap,
At the wood's boldness by thee blushing stand.
To be so tickled they would change their state
And situation[5] with those dancing chips,   10
O'er whom thy fingers walk with gentle gait,
Making dead wood more blessed than living lips.
    Since saucy jacks[6] so happy are in this,
    Give them thy fingers, me thy lips to kiss.

1609

6. Brink of the Last Judgment.
1. (1) Mirror, fickle because as the subject ages the mirror reflects a changed image, (2) an hour glass.
2. Destruction, ruin.
3. Darling.
4. Always, forever.
5. Accounting.
6. Surrender; "quietus": settlement.
1. Keys of the spinet or virginal.

2. Governest.
3. The harmony from the strings which overcomes my ear with delight.
4. I.e., keys (actually, "jacks" are the plectra which pluck the strings when activated by the keys).
5. Physical location; "state": place in the order of things.
6. With a quibble on the sense "impertinent fellows."

129

Th' expense of spirit in a waste of shame
Is lust in action;[1] and till action, lust
Is perjured, murd'rous, bloody, full of blame,
Savage, extreme, rude, cruel, not to trust;
Enjoyed no sooner but despisèd straight: 5
Past reason hunted; and no sooner had,
Past reason hated, as a swallowed bait,
On purpose laid to make the taker mad:
Mad in pursuit, and in possession so;
Had, having, and in quest to have, extreme;   10
A bliss in proof[2] and proved, a very woe;
Before, a joy proposed; behind, a dream.
  All this the world well knows; yet none knows well
  To shun the heaven that leads men to this hell.

1609

130

My mistress' eyes are nothing like the sun;[1]
Coral is far more red than her lips' red;
If snow be white, why then her breasts are dun;
If hairs be wires, black wires grow on her head.
I have seen roses damasked,[2] red and white,   5
But no such roses see I in her cheeks;
And in some perfumes is there more delight
Than in the breath that from my mistress reeks.
I love to hear her speak, yet well I know
That music hath a far more pleasing sound;   10
I grant I never saw a goddess go;[3]
My mistress, when she walks, treads on the ground.
  And yet, by heaven, I think my love as rare[4]
  As any she belied[5] with false compare.

1609

135

Whoever hath her wish, thou hast thy *Will*,[1]
And *Will* to boot, and *Will* in overplus;

---

1. The word order here is inverted and slightly obscures the meaning. Lust, when put into action, expends "spirit" (life, vitality) in a "waste" (desert, with a possible pun on "waist," also) of shame.
2. A bliss during the experience.
1. An anti-Petrarchan sonnet. All of the details commonly attributed by other Elizabethan sonneteers to their ladies are here denied to the poet's mistress.

2. Variegated. The damask rose (supposedly from Damascus, originally) is pink.
3. Walk.
4. Admirable, extraordinary.
5. Misrepresented.
1. (1) Wishes, (2) carnal desire, (3) the male and female sexual organs, (4) one or more persons named Will. This is one of 3, possibly 4, sonnets punning on the word.

More than enough am I that vex thee still,
To thy sweet will making addition thus.
Wilt thou, whose will is large and spacious,   5
Not once vouchsafe to hide my will in thine?
Shall will in others seem right gracious,
And in my will no fair acceptance shine?
The sea, all water, yet receives rain still,
And in abundance addeth to his store,[2]   10
So thou being rich in *Will* add to thy *Will*
One will of mine to make thy large Will more.
     Let no unkind, no fair beseechers kill;[3]
     Think all but one, and me in that one *Will*.

                                          1609

138

When my love swears that she is made of truth,
I do believe her, though I know she lies,
That she might think me some untutored youth,
Unlearnèd in the world's false subtleties.
Thus vainly thinking that she thinks me young,   5
Although she knows my days are past the best,[1]
Simply I credit her false-speaking tongue:
On both sides thus is simple truth suppressed.
But wherefore says she not she is unjust?[2]
And wherefore say not I that I am old?   10
Oh, love's best habit[3] is in seeming trust,
And age in love loves not to have years told.
     Therefore I lie with her and she with me,
     And in our faults by lies we flattered be.

                                     1599, 1609

144

Two loves I have of comfort and despair,
Which like two spirits do suggest me still:[1]
The better angel is a man right fair,
The worser spirit a woman, colored ill.[2]
To win me soon to hell, my female evil   5
Tempteth my better angel from my side,
And would corrupt my saint to be a devil,

---

2. Plenty.
3. I.e., do not kill with unkindness any of your
wooers.
1. Shakespeare was 35 or younger when he wrote
this sonnet (it first appeared in *The Passionate Pil-*

grim, 1599). "Simply": like a simpleton.
2. Unfaithful.
3. Appearance, deportment.
1. Tempt me constantly.
2. Dark.

Wooing his purity with her foul pride.
And whether that my angel be turned fiend
Suspect I may, yet not directly tell;   10
But being both from[3] me, both to each friend,
I guess one angel in another's hell.
    Yet this shall I ne'er know, but live in doubt,
    Till my bad angel fire[4] my good one out.

                         1599, 1609

146

Poor soul, the center of my sinful earth,
Lord of[1] these rebel powers that thee array,[2]
Why dost thou pine within and suffer dearth,
Painting thy outward walls so costly gay?
Why so large cost, having so short a lease,   5
Dost thou upon thy fading mansion spend?
Shall worms, inheritors of this excess,
Eat up thy charge? Is this thy body's end?
Then, soul, live thou upon thy servant's loss,
And let that pine to aggravate thy store;[3]   10
Buy terms[4] divine in selling hours of dross;
Within be fed, without be rich no more.
    So shalt thou feed on death, that feeds on men,
    And death once dead, there's no more dying then.

                         1609

147

My love is as a fever, longing still[1]
For that which longer nurseth[2] the disease,
Feeding on that which doth preserve the ill,[3]
Th' uncertain sickly appetite[4] to please.
My reason, the physician to my love,   5
Angry that his prescriptions are not kept,
Hath left me, and I desperate now approve
Desire is death, which physic did except.[5]
Past cure I am, now reason is past care,[6]

---

3. Away from; "each": each other.
4. Drive out by fire.
1. An emendation. The Quarto repeats the last 3 words of line 1. Other suggestions are "Thrall to," "Starved by," "Pressed by," and leaving the repetition but dropping "that thee" in line 2.
2. Dress out, often used in a military sense.
3. Let "that" (i.e., the body) deteriorate to increase ("aggravate") the soul's riches ("thy store").

4. Long periods; "dross": refuse, rubbish.
1. Continually.
2. (1) Nourishes, (2) takes care of.
3. Maintain the illness.
4. (1) Desire for food, (2) lust.
5. I.e., learn by experience, that desire, which medicine forbade, is death.
6. I.e., medical care (of me). The line is a version of the proverb "past cure, past care."

And frantic mad with evermore unrest;   10
My thoughts and my discourse as madmen's are,
At random from the truth vainly expressed;[7]
For I have sworn thee fair, and thought thee bright,
Who art as black as hell, as dark as night.

1609

1 Henry IV

The title page of the first quarto edition of Shakespeare's *1 Henry IV*, published in 1598, reads: "THE HISTORY OF HENRIE THE FOURTH; With the battell at Shrewsburie, *betweene the King and Lord* Henry Percy, surnamed Henrie Hotspur of the North. *With the humorous conceits of Sir* John Falstalffe." It had been performed on the stage and at court before publication, and from that time to this it has remained one of Shakespeare's most popular plays.

Shakespeare had already inaugurated a new dramatic type by writing four plays dealing with fairly recent English history, and had then gone back to a period two centuries earlier to portray, in *Richard II*, the downfall of the weak, effeminate, and poetic young King Richard ("that sweet lovely rose," as he is called in this play) at the hands of the hard, efficient Bullingbrook, who came to the throne as Henry IV. Before this seizure of the crown there had been a prophecy, put by Shakespeare into the mouth of the bishop of Carlisle in *Richard II* (4.1.136–44), of the dire consequences to follow:

> And if you crown him, let me prophesy,
> The blood of English shall manure the ground
> And future ages groan for this foul act;
> Peace shall go sleep with Turks and infidels,
> And in this seat of peace tumultuous wars
> Shall kin with kin and kind with kind confound;
> Disorder, horror, fear, and mutiny
> Shall here inhabit, and this land be called
> The field of Golgotha and dead men's skulls.

Shakespeare drew his historical material from the prose chronicle histories, specifically Raphael Holinshed's *Chronicles of England, Scotland, and Ireland*, Samuel Daniel's historical poem *Civil Wars*, and an earlier play, either the popular farcical piece called *The Famous Victories of Henry V* or a lost play which was its source. His sources gave him the portrait of a madcap and reckless Prince of Wales and his roistering companions. Chief of these was a fat knight, Sir John Oldcastle; Shakespeare at first used this name, but later, because of protests from the descendants of that Protestant martyr, changed the name to Sir John Falstaff. This character, whose "humorous conceits" are advertised on the title page, is one of the greatest comic creations in all literature. Shakespeare continued to exploit his inexhaustible exuberance through a sequel, *The Second Part of Henry IV*, and a comedy of middle-class life, supposed to have been written at Queen Elizabeth's command, *The Merry Wives of Windsor*.

7. Wide of the mark and senselessly uttered.

The ominous wars of Carlisle's prophecy could thus be mixed with hilarious fooling, but *1 Henry IV* succeeds, not only as a comedy, but as a serious play about character and history. The real hero is not King Henry IV, nor the fat Falstaff, but Prince Hal, the handsome playboy who in time of crisis reforms and saves his father's throne. He is the prince who later became Henry V, the English national hero who reconquered France.

Shakespeare's theme in all his history plays is the importance of order and degree, of the disruptive effects of civil strife and rebellion. But as he matured as a dramatist (and *1 Henry IV* stands at the beginning of his great period of maturity), he found character to be more interesting than the philosophy or events of history. How to demonstrate the kind of character that would make the English national hero was his problem, and he solved it by a method of comparison and contrast, utilizing four men of different types. At one extreme is Falstaff, who loves to eat, drink, joke, and dramatize himself, and to whom anything as intangible as honor is a mere word, a breath of air. Opposite in every way is Hotspur, fiery and impatient, completely ambitious for honor and fame, scornful of the soft, civilized arts of poetry and music, a hardheaded fanatic. A third type is the wild Welshman Glendower, a believer in magic and a practitioner of it, an accomplished poet yet a valiant, if superstitious, warrior, and an egotist like his ally Hotspur. Finally there is Prince Hal, whose sense of humor rivals Falstaff's, but who turns out to be the match for Hotspur in valor and his superior in knightly courtesy. It is worth noting that Shakespeare changed history in order to make this dramatic contrast: in Holinshed's *Chronicle* Hotspur is older than Prince Hal's father, but Shakespeare makes Hal and Hotspur contemporaries. It is in the excesses of the other three that we see the merits of the Prince's character illuminated. The four characters represent not only men but ways of life. And these ways of life are all relevant to fundamental questions about social and political responsibility, honor, and loyalty to a cause.

Some background in fifteenth-century English history, as Shakespeare understood it, is needed if we are to respond readily to the play. Henry Hereford, called Bullingbrook, was in exile in France when his father, John of Gaunt, died. He returned to England to claim his inheritance, and profited from the aid of the Percy family, powerful nobles in the north. The two brothers, Henry Percy, earl of Northumberland, and Thomas Percy, earl of Worcester, together with Northumberland's son Henry (called Hotspur) received Bullingbrook's oath at Doncaster (see 5.1.32–58) to seize only his inheritance. But King Richard II was in Ireland fighting, having named Edmund Mortimer, earl of March, his successor if he did not return. In the confused situation in England, Bullingbrook was able to collect enough power so that on Richard's return he could force him to abdicate and then have him killed in prison. Various troubles on the borders made the throne of the new king (Henry IV) insecure. Hotspur managed to defeat the Scots under Douglas at Holmedon (see 1.1.62–75) and took many important prisoners. But Mortimer, in fighting against Glendower in Wales, was taken captive and married Glendower's daughter. Henry IV refused to ransom Mortimer, and the indignation of Mortimer's brother-in-law, Hotspur, led him to refuse to turn over his prisoners to the king. So came the conspiracy into being— and such a formidable opposition as that of the Percies, Douglas, Glendower, and certain disaffected churchmen like the archbishop of York meant a critical danger to Henry's throne. The Battle of Shrewsbury, the climax of this play, decides the conflict.

Much critical comment has been devoted to the character of Falstaff. He has certain resemblances to the traditional *miles gloriosus* (braggart soldier) of Latin comedy, but he far transcends the type; he sometimes resembles the Vice, a comic character in the old morality plays, who is usually an allegorical personification of extreme self-indulgence or of a particular sin; and he often uses, or parodies, the language of the Puritans. Critics differ on whether Falstaff is really a coward or not, and on the question of how much he expects his lies to be believed. But everyone agrees about his inexhaustible vitality and resilience. It is not surprising that he, like other immortal characters in literature, remains something of a mystery.

The First Part of
King Henry the Fourth

Dramatis Personae

KING HENRY THE FOURTH
HENRY, *Prince of Wales*
PRINCE JOHN OF LANCASTER   } *Sons to the* KING
EARL OF WESTMORELAND
SIR WALTER BLUNT
THOMAS PERCY, *Earl of Worcester*
HENRY PERCY, *Earl of Northumberland*
HENRY PERCY, *surnamed* HOTSPUR, *his son*
EDMUND MORTIMER, *Earl of March*
RICHARD SCROOP, *Archbishop of York*
ARCHIBALD, *Earl of Douglas*
OWEN GLENDOWER
SIR RICHARD VERNON
SIR MICHAEL, *a friend to the* ARCHBISHOP OF YORK
SIR JOHN FALSTAFF
POINS
GADSHILL
PETO
BARDOLPH
LADY PERCY, *wife to* HOTSPUR, *and sister to* MORTIMER
LADY MORTIMER, *daughter to* GLENDOWER, *and wife to* MORTIMER
MISTRESS QUICKLY, *hostess of a tavern in Eastcheap*
LORDS, OFFICERS, SHERIFF, VINTNER, CHAMBERLAIN, DRAWERS, *two* CARRIERS, TRAVELERS, *and* ATTENDANTS

Act 1

SCENE 1

[*Enter the* KING, PRINCE JOHN OF LANCASTER, THE EARL OF WESTMORELAND, SIR WALTER BLUNT, *with others.*]

KING. So shaken as we are, so wan with care,
 Find we a time for frighted peace to pant,[1]

---

1. I.e., let us allow peace to catch her breath.

And breathe short-winded accents of new broils[2]
To be commenced in stronds afar remote.
No more the thirsty entrance[3] of this soil   5
Shall daub her lips with her own children's blood;
No more shall trenching war channel her fields,
Nor bruise her flow'rets with the armèd hoofs
Of hostile paces:[4] those opposèd eyes,
Which, like the meteors of a troubled heaven,   10
All of one nature, of one substance bred,
Did lately meet in the intestine shock[5]
And furious close of civil butchery,
Shall now, in mutual well-beseeming ranks,
March all one way and be no more opposed   15
Against acquaintance, kindred, and allies.
The edge of war, like an ill-sheathèd knife,
No more shall cut his master: Therefore, friends,
As far as to the sepulchre of Christ,—
Whose soldier now, under whose blessed cross   20
We are impressèd and engaged to fight,
Forthwith a power[6] of English shall we levy,
Whose arms were molded in their mother's womb
To chase these pagans in those holy fields
Over whose acres walked those blessed feet   25
Which fourteen hundred years ago were nailed
For our advantage on the bitter cross.
But this our purpose now is twelve month old,
And bootless[7] 'tis to tell you we will go.
Therefore we meet not now.[8] Then let me hear   30
Of you, my gentle cousin Westmoreland,
What yesternight our Council did decree
In forwarding this dear expedience.[9]
WEST. My liege, this haste was hot in questiòn,[1]
And many limits of the charge set down   35
But yesternight, when all athwart[2] there came
A post from Wales loaden with heavy news,
Whose worst was that the noble Mortimer,
Leading the men of Herefordshire to fight
Against the irregular[3] and wild Glendower,   40
Was by the rude hands of that Welshman taken,
A thousand of his people butcherèd,
Upon whose dead corpse[4] there was such misuse,
Such beastly shameless transformatiòn,
By those Welshwomen done as may not be   45
Without much shame retold or spoken of.

---

2. I.e., news of new wars; "stronds": strands, regions.
3. Surface.
4. The tread of war horses.
5. Internal violence; "close": encounter.
6. Army. He is planning a crusade, in expiation of his guilt for the death of Richard II.
7. Useless.
8. I.e., that is not the reason for our present meet-

ing. "Cousin": kinsman.
9. Important, urgent matter.
1. Actively discussed. "Limits of the charge": assignment of commands.
2. Interrupting, crossing our purpose. "Post": messenger.
3. Guerilla.
4. Bodies.

KING. It seems then that the tidings of this broil
    Brake off our business for the Holy Land.
WEST. This matched with other did, my gracious lord,
    For more uneven and unwelcome news   50
    Came from the north, and thus it did import:
    On Holyrood Day[5] the gallant Hotspur there,
    Young Harry Percy, and brave Archibald,
    That ever-valiant and approvèd Scot,
    At Holmedon met,   55
    Where they did spend a sad and bloody hour;
    As by discharge of their artillery,
    And shape of likelihood,[6] the news was told;
    For he that brought them[7] in the very heat
    And pride of their contention did take horse,   60
    Uncertain of the issue any way.
KING. Here is a dear, a true industrious friend,
    Sir Walter Blunt, new lighted from his horse,
    Stained with the variation of each soil
    Betwixt that Holmedon and this seat of ours;   65
    And he hath brought us smooth and welcome news.
    The Earl of Douglas is discomfited;
    Ten thousand bold Scots, two and twenty knights
    Balked[8] in their own blood did Sir Walter see
    On Holmedon's plains. Of prisoners Hotspur took   70
    Mordake Earl of Fife, and eldest son
    To beaten Douglas, and the Earl of Athol,
    Of Murray, Angus, and Menteith;
    And is not this an honorable spoil,
    A gallant prize? Ha, cousin, is it not?   75
WEST. In faith,
    It is a conquest for a prince to boast of.
KING. Yea, there thou mak'st me sad and mak'st me sin
    In envy that my Lord Northumberland
    Should be the father to so blest a son,   80
    A son who is the theme of honor's tongue,
    Amongst a grove the very straightest plant,
    Who is sweet Fortune's minion[9] and her pride;
    Whilst I, by looking on the praise of him,
    See riot and dishonor stain the brow   85
    Of my young Harry. O that it could be proved
    That some night-tripping fairy had exchanged
    In cradle-clothes our children where they lay,
    And called mine Percy, his Plantagenet!
    Then would I have his Harry, and he mine.   90
    But let him from my thoughts. What think you, coz,
    Of this young Percy's pride? The prisoners
    Which he in this adventure hath surprised
    To his own use he keeps, and sends me word

[handwritten marginal note: King's dislike for harry]

---

5. Holy Cross Day (September 14).
6. Probable inference. "As": since.
7. I.e., the news (usually a plural in Shakespeare). "Pride": height; literally, the top of a falcon's flight.
8. Heaped.
9. Favorite.

I shall have none but Mordake Earl of Fife.   95
WEST. This is his uncle's teaching, this is Worcester,
    Malevolent to you in all aspects,[1]
    Which makes him prune himself,[2] and bristle up
    The crest of youth against your dignity.
KING. But I have sent for him to answer this;   100
    And for this cause awhile we must neglect
    Our holy purpose to Jerusalem.
    Cousin, on Wednesday next our council we
    Will hold at Windsor, so inform the lords;
    But come yourself with speed to us again,   105
    For more is to be said and to be done
    Than out of anger can be utterèd.
WEST. I will, my liege.   [Exeunt.]

SCENE 2

[Enter HENRY, PRINCE OF WALES, and SIR JOHN FALSTAFF.]

FAL. Now Hal, what time of day is it, lad?
PRINCE. Thou art so fat-witted with drinking of old sack,[3] and
    unbuttoning thee after supper, and sleeping upon benches after
    noon, that thou hast forgotten to demand that truly which thou
    wouldst truly know. What a devil hast thou to do with the time   5
    of the day? Unless hours were cups of sack, and minutes capons,
    and clocks the tongues of bawds, and dials the signs of leaping-
    houses,[4] and the blessed sun himself a fair hot wench in flame-
    colored taffeta, I see no reason why thou shouldst be so superflu-
    ous to demand the time of the day.   10
FAL. Indeed you come near me now, Hal, for we that take purses
    go by the moon and the seven stars, and not by Phoebus,[5] he,
    "that wandering knight so fair." And I prithee, sweet wag, when
    thou art king, as, God save thy grace—majesty I should say, for
    grace[6] thou wilt have none—   15
PRINCE. What, none?
FAL. No, by my troth, not so much as will serve to be prologue to
    an egg and butter.
PRINCE. Well, how then? come, roundly, roundly.[7]
FAL. Marry then, sweet wag, when thou art king, let not us that are   20
    squires of the night's body[8] be called thieves of the day's beauty;
    let us be Diana's foresters, gentlemen of the shade, minions of
    the moon; and let men say we be men of good government,
    being governed as the sea is, by our noble and chaste mistress the
    moon, under whose countenance we steal.   25

1. Hostile in every way. The figure is from astrology.
2. Plume himself. "Bristle up" and "crest" continue the image, which is that of a fighting cock.
3. Sherry.
4. Whorehouses.
5. The sun. Falstaff then quotes from a popular
ballad.
6. A triple pun: (1) "your Grace," the correct
manner of addressing a prince or duke; (2) the divine

influence which produces sanctity; and (3) a short
prayer before a meal—hence Falstaff's allusion to
"egg and butter," a common hasty breakfast.
7. Plainly.
8. Two puns are involved: a "squire of the body"
was an attendant on a knight, and "body" would
be pronounced bawdy. "Beauty" also puns with
"booty" (which thieves take); Diana is, of course,
the moon goddess.

PRINCE. Thou sayest well, and it holds well too, for the fortune of us that are the moon's men doth ebb and flow like the sea, being governed as the sea is by the moon. As for proof now: a purse of gold most resolutely snatched on Monday night and most dissolutely spent on Tuesday morning, got with swearing "Lay by" 30 and spent with crying "Bring in," now in as low an ebb as the foot of the ladder and by and by in as high a flow as the ridge of the gallows.[9]

FAL. By the Lord thou sayest true, lad. And is not my hostess of the tavern a most sweet wench? 35

PRINCE. As the honey of Hybla,[1] my old lad of the castle. And is not a buff jerkin a most sweet robe of durance?[2]

FAL. How now, how now, mad wag! what, in thy quips and thy quiddities?[3] what a plague have I to do with a buff jerkin?

PRINCE. Why, what a pox have I to do with my hostess of the tav- 40 ern?

FAL. Well, thou hast called her to a reckoning many a time and oft.

PRINCE. Did I ever call for thee to pay thy part?

FAL. No, I'll give thee thy due, thou hast paid all there.

PRINCE. Yea, and elsewhere, so far as my coin would stretch, and 45 where it would not I have used my credit.

FAL. Yea, and so used it that were it not here apparent that thou art heir apparent[4]—but I prithee, sweet wag, shall there be gallows standing in England when thou art king? and resolution thus fobbed as it is with the rusty curb of old father antic the law?[5] Do 50 not thou, when thou art king, hang a thief.

PRINCE. No, thou shalt.

FAL. Shall I? O rare! By the Lord, I'll be a brave judge.

PRINCE. Thou judgest false already; I mean thou shalt have the hanging of the thieves and so become a rare hangman. 55

FAL. Well, Hal, well; and in some sort it jumps with my humor[6] as well as waiting in the court, I can tell you.

PRINCE. For obtaining of suits?[7]

FAL. Yea, for obtaining of suits, whereof the hangman hath no lean wardrobe. 'Sblood,[8] I am as melancholy as a gib cat or a lugged 60 bear.

PRINCE. Or an old lion, or a lover's lute.

FAL. Yea, or the drone of a Lincolnshire bagpipe.

PRINCE. What sayest thou to a hare, or the melancholy of Moorditch?[9] 65

FAL. Thou hast the most unsavory similes and art indeed the most

9. "Lay by": i.e., hand over (a robber's command to his victim); "bring in": a customer's command for more drink at a tavern. The "foot of the ladder" is at the bottom of the gallows (robbery was a hanging offense); the "ridge" is the crosspiece at the top.
1. A town in Sicily, famous for honey; "old lad of the castle" is a reference to Falstaff's original name, Oldcastle.
2. A "buff jerkin" was the leather jacket worn by a sheriff's sergeant; "durance" is a pun: (1) lasting quality and (2) imprisonment.
3. Quibbles.
4. "Here" and "heir" would pun in Elizabethan pronunciation.
5. "Resolution": bravery; "fobbed": cheated; "antic": a clown.
6. I.e., agrees with my disposition.
7. Special favors, but "clothing" in the next line. The hangman was given the clothes of his victims.
8. God's blood, a common oath. "Gib cat": tomcat; "lugged": baited (in the bear-baiting pits a bear was attacked by dogs as a public amusement).
9. The "hare" was traditionally associated with melancholy; Moorditch was a foul-smelling ditch on the outskirts of London.

comparative,[1] rascalliest, sweet young prince. But Hal, I prithee,
trouble me no more with vanity. I would to God thou and I knew
where a commodity of good names were to be bought. An old
lord of the council rated[2] me the other day in the street about   70
you, sir, but I marked him not; and yet he talked very wisely, but
I regarded him not; and yet he talked wisely, and in the street
too.

PRINCE. Thou didst well, for wisdom cries out in the streets and no
man regards it.[3]   75

FAL. O, thou hast damnable iteration[4] and art indeed able to corrupt a saint. Thou hast done much harm upon me, Hal, God
forgive thee for it! Before I knew thee, Hal, I knew nothing, and
now am I, if a man should speak truly, little better than one of
the wicked. I must give over this life, and I will give it over; by   80
the Lord, an[5] I do not, I am a villain; I'll be damned for never a
king's son in Christendom.

PRINCE. Where shall we take a purse tomorrow, Jack?

FAL. Zounds, where thou wilt, lad; I'll make one; an I do not, call
me villain and baffle[6] me.   85

PRINCE. I see a good amendment of life in thee—from praying to
purse-taking.

FAL. Why, Hal, 'tis my vocation,[7] Hal; 'tis no sin for a man to labor
in his vocation.

[*Enter* POINS.]

Poins! Now shall we know if Gadshill[8] have set a match. O, if   90
men were to be saved by merit, what hole in hell were hot enough
for him? This is the most omnipotent villain that ever cried "stand"
to a true man.

PRINCE. Good morrow, Ned.

POINS. Good morrow, sweet Hal. What says Monsieur Remorse?   95
what says Sir John Sack and Sugar? Jack! how agrees the devil
and thee about thy soul, that thou soldest him on Good Friday
last for a cup of Madeira and a cold capon's leg?

PRINCE. Sir John stands to his word; the devil shall have his bargain,
for he was never yet a breaker of proverbs; he will give the devil   100
his due.

POINS. Then art thou damned for keeping thy word with the devil.

PRINCE. Else he had been damned for cozening[9] the devil.

POINS. But my lads, my lads, tomorrow morning by four o'clock,
early at Gadshill, there are pilgrims going to Canterbury with   105
rich offerings, and traders riding to London with fat purses. I

---

1. Affecting wit, dealing in comparisons.
2. Scolded, berated.
3. Prince Hal is quoting Proverbs 1.20 and 24.
4. Repetition, especially of sacred texts.
5. If.
6. A knight in the days of chivalry was "baffled" or disgraced by having his shield hung upside down. Falstaff may mean "hang me up by the heels." "Zounds": a common oath, a contraction of "by God's wounds" (i.e., Jesus's wounds on the Cross).

7. Falstaff is here making fun of the Puritan doctrine of "calling" or vocation, based on the parable of the talents (see Matthew 25.25 ff.).
8. Gadshill is both a man and a place: the place is a hill 27 miles from London on the road to Rochester; it was notorious for robberies. The man, so called from the place, is the thieves' "setter," who arranges when and where the robbery will occur.
9. Cheating.

have vizards[1] for you all, you have horses for yourselves; Gadshill
lies tonight in Rochester; I have bespoke supper tomorrow night
in Eastcheap; we may do it as secure as sleep. If you will go, I
will stuff your purses full of crowns; if you will not, tarry at home   110
and be hanged.

FAL. Hear ye, Yedward, if I tarry at home and go not, I'll hang you
for going.

POINS. You will, chops?[2]

FAL. Hal, wilt thou make one?   115

PRINCE. Who, I rob? I a thief? not I, by my faith.

FAL. There's neither honesty, manhood, nor good fellowship in
thee, nor thou camest not of the blood royal,[3] if thou darest not
stand for ten shillings.

PRINCE. Well then, once in my days I'll be a madcap.   120

FAL. Why, that's well said.

PRINCE. Well, come what will, I'll tarry at home.

FAL. By the Lord, I'll be a traitor then, when thou art king.

PRINCE. I care not.

POINS. Sir John, I prithee leave the prince and me alone; I will lay   125
him down such reasons for this adventure that he shall go.

FAL. Well, God give thee the spirit of persuasion and him the ears
of profiting, that what thou speakest may move and what he
hears may be believed, that the true prince may (for recreation
sake) prove a false thief; for the poor abuses of the time want counte-   130
nance.[4] Farewell; you shall find me in Eastcheap.

PRINCE. Farewell, thou latter spring, farewell, Allhallown summer![5]

[⟨*Exit* FALSTAFF.⟩][6]

POINS. Now, my good sweet honey lord, ride with us tomorrow; I
have a jest to execute that I cannot manage alone. Falstaff, Bar-   135
dolph, Peto, and Gadshill shall rob those men that we have already
waylaid;[7] yourself and I will not be there, and when they have
the booty, if you and I do not rob them, cut this head off from
my shoulders.

PRINCE. How shall we part with them in setting forth?   140

POINS. Why, we will set forth before or after them, and appoint
them a place of meeting, wherein it is at our pleasure to fail, and
then will they adventure upon the exploit themselves, which they
shall have no sooner achieved but we'll set upon them.

PRINCE. Yea, but 'tis like that they will know us by our horses,   145
by our habits,[8] and by every other appointment to be ourselves.

---

1. Masks.
2. Fat face.
3. A pun: the coin called a "royal" was worth 10
shillings. "Stand for" also puns: it means both
"represent" and "fight for."
4. A satirical reference to the common complaint
that the nobility did not properly give "countenance" to (i.e., encourage) good causes, and to the
Puritan habit of attacking the "abuses of the time."
This entire speech parodies the language of the
Puritans.

5. I.e., Indian summer. The 2 epithets are intended
to suggest how unseasonable it is for Falstaff, an
old man, to be engaged in youthful, hoodlum
exploits.
6. This stage direction, like some others in the play,
does not appear in the earliest editions; it was added
by a later editor. All such interpolated directions
are indicated in our text by the special brackets
used here.
7. Set an ambush for.
8. Clothes.

POINS. Tut, our horses they shall not see—I'll tie them in the wood;
  our vizards we will change after we leave them: and, sirrah, I
  have cases of buckram for the nonce,[9] to immask our noted outward garments.   150
PRINCE. Yea, but I doubt[1] they will be too hard for us.
POINS. Well, for two of them, I know them to be as true-bred cowards as ever turned back; and for the third, if he fight longer than
  he sees reason, I'll forswear arms. The virtue of this jest will be
  the incomprehensible lies that this same fat rogue will tell us   155
  when we meet at supper: how thirty at least he fought with; what
  wards,[2] what blows, what extremities he endured; and in the
  reproof[3] of this lies the jest.
PRINCE. Well, I'll go with thee. Provide us all things necessary and
  meet me tomorrow night[4] in Eastcheap; there I'll sup. Farewell.   160
POINS. Farewell, my lord.   [*Exit* POINS.]
PRINCE. I know you all, and will awhile uphold
    The unyoked humor[5] of your idleness;
    Yet herein will I imitate the sun,
    Who doth permit the base contagious clouds   165
    To smother up his beauty from the world,
    That, when he please again to be himself,
    Being wanted, he may be more wondered at
    By breaking through the foul and ugly mists
    Of vapors that did seem to strangle him.   170
    If all the year were playing holidays,
    To sport would be as tedious as to work;
    But when they seldom come, they wished for come,
    And nothing pleaseth but rare accidents.
    So, when this loose behavior I throw off   175
    And pay the debt I never promisèd,
    By how much better than my word I am,
    By so much shall I falsify men's hopes,
    And like bright metal on a sullen ground,[6]
    My reformation, glitt'ring o'er my fault,   180
    Shall show more goodly and attract more eyes
    Than that which hath no foil[7] to set it off.
    I'll so offend to make offense a skill,[8]
    Redeeming time when men think least I will.   [*Exit.*]

---

9. I.e., outer clothes (of a coarse, stiff cloth) for
the occasion.
1. Suspect.
2. Guards in fencing.
3. Disproof.
4. Either the text should read "tonight" (before the
robbery) or else Shakespeare intends to show Prince
Hal's mind intent, not on the robbery, but on its
aftermath. The soliloquy of the Prince that follows
has provoked much critical discussion. Read psychologically, it makes Hal seem like a prig and a
self-conscious schemer, but this surely was not

Shakespeare's intention. Rather, the speech belongs
to the old dramatic convention in which the speaker
steps out of character for a moment to deliver a
message from the playwright to the audience.
5. Undisciplined whim.
6. Dull background.
7. I.e., contrast.
8. Piece of good policy. "Redeeming time": making good use of time, following the advice given to
Christians in a non-Christian world. See Ephesians 5.16.

SCENE 3

[*Enter the* KING, NORTHUMBERLAND, WORCESTER, HOTSPUR, SIR WALTER BLUNT, *with others.*]

KING. My blood hath been too cold and temperate,
    Unapt to stir at these indignities,
    And you have found me,[9] for accordingly
    You tread upon my patience; but be sure
    I will from henceforth rather be myself,   5
    Mighty and to be feared, than my condition,[1]
    Which hath been smooth as oil, soft as young down,
    And therefore lost that title of respect
    Which the proud soul ne'er pays but to the proud.
WOR. Our house, my sovereign liege, little deserves   10
    The scourge of greatness to be used on it,
    And that same greatness too which our own hands
    Have holp[2] to make so portly.
NORTH. My lord—
KING. Worcester, get thee gone, for I do see   15
    Danger and disobedience in thine eye;
    O, sir, your presence is too bold and peremptory,
    And majesty might never yet endure
    The moody frontier of a servant brow.[3]
    You have good leave to leave us; when we need   20
    Your use and counsel we shall send for you.   [*Exit* WOR.]
    You were about to speak.   [⟨*to* NORTH.⟩]
NORTH.   Yea, my good lord.
    Those prisoners in your highness' name demanded,
    Which Harry Percy here at Holmedon took,
    Were, as he says, not with such strength denied   25
    As is delivered to your majesty.
    Either envy therefore or misprisiòn[4]
    Is guilty of this fault, and not my son.
HOT. My liege, I did deny no prisoners.
    But I remember, when the fight was done,   30
    When I was dry with rage and extreme toil,
    Breathless and faint, leaning upon my sword,
    Came there a certain lord, neat and trimly dressed,
    Fresh as a bridegroom, and his chin new reaped
    Showed like a stubble-land at harvest-home;   35
    He was perfumèd like a milliner,[5]
    And 'twixt his finger and his thumb he held
    A pouncet box,[6] which ever and anon
    He gave his nose and took 't away again;
    Who therewith angry, when it next came there,   40

9. Discovered this to be true.
1. Disposition.
2. Helped; "portly": stately.
3. I.e., a servant's brow showing defiance, like a fortification ("frontier").

4. "Envy": malice; "misprision": mistake.
5. Not a maker of hats, but a dealer in perfumes, women's gloves, etc.
6. Perfume box.

Took it in snuff;[7] and still he smiled and talked,
And as the soldiers bore dead bodies by,
He called them untaught knaves, unmannerly,
To bring a slovenly[8] unhandsome corse
Betwixt the wind and his nobility.   45
With many holiday and lady terms[9]
He questioned me; amongst the rest, demanded
My prisoners in your majesty's behalf.
I then, all smarting with my wounds being cold,
To be so pestered with a popinjay,[1]   50
Out of my grief and my impatience
Answered neglectingly I know not what,
He should, or he should not—for he made me mad
To see him shine so brisk and smell so sweet
And talk so like a waiting-gentlewoman   55
Of guns and drums and wounds, God save the mark!
And telling me the sovereign'st thing on earth
Was parmaceti[2] for an inward bruise,
And that it was great pity, so it was,
This villanous saltpeter[3] should be digged   60
Out of the bowels of the harmless earth,
Which many a good tall[4] fellow had destroyed
So cowardly, and but for these vile guns
He would himself have been a soldier.
This bald[5] unjointed chat of his, my lord,   65
I answered indirectly as I said,
And I beseech you, let not his report
Come current[6] for an accusation
Betwixt my love and your high majesty.

BLUNT. The circumstance considered, good my lord,   70
    Whate'er Lord Harry Percy then had said
    To such a person and in such a place,
    At such a time, with all the rest retold,
    May reasonably die and never rise
    To do him wrong or any way impeach   75
    What then he said, so he unsay it now.

KING. Why, yet[7] he doth deny his prisoners,
    But with proviso and exceptiòn,
    That we at our own charge shall ransom straight
    His brother-in-law, the foolish Mortimer,   80
    Who, on my soul, hath willfully betrayed
    The lives of those that he did lead to fight
    Against that great magician, damned Glendower,
    Whose daughter, as we hear, the Earl of March
    Hath lately married. Shall our coffers then   85

---

7. I.e., was annoyed at it, with a pun on "snuffing it up."
8. Nasty, disgusting; "corse": corpse, body.
9. Affected and effeminate language (not "every-day" English).
1. Parrot.
2. Spermaceti, whale oil used as an ointment.

3. Used in gunpowder.
4. Brave.
5. Trivial. "Indirectly": negligently.
6. Be considered valid.
7. I.e., even after all this (the strong use of "yet"). "But": except. "Straight": immediately.

Be emptied to redeem a traitor home?
Shall we buy treason? and indent with fears,[8]
When they have lost and forfeited themselves?
No, on the barren mountains let him starve;
For I shall never hold that man my friend   90
Whose tongue shall ask me for one penny cost
To ransom home revolted Mortimer.
HOT. Revolted Mortimer!
He never did fall off, my sovereign liege,
But by the chance of war. To prove that true   95
Needs no more but one tongue for all those wounds,
Those mouthèd wounds[9] which valiantly he took
When on the gentle Severn's sedgy bank
In single opposition, hand to hand,
He did confound the best part of an hour   100
In changing hardiment[1] with great Glendower;
Three times they breathed[2] and three times did they drink
Upon agreement of swift Severn's flood,
Who then, affrighted with their bloody looks,
Ran fearfully among the trembling reeds,   105
And hid his crisp[3] head in the hollow bank
Bloodstainèd with these valiant combatants.
Never did bare and rotten policy[4]
Color her working with such deadly wounds,
Nor never could the noble Mortimer   110
Receive so many, and all willingly;
Then let not him be slandered with revolt.
KING. Thou dost belie him, Percy, thou dost belie him;
He never did encounter with Glendower.
I tell thee,   115
He durst as well have met the devil alone
As Owen Glendower for an enemy.
Art thou not ashamed? But, sirrah,[5] henceforth
Let me not hear you speak of Mortimer;
Send me your prisoners with the speediest means,   120
Or you shall hear in such a kind from me
As will displease you. My Lord Northumberland,
We license your departure with your son.
Send us your prisoners, or you will hear of it.

[*Exeunt* KING, ⟨BLUNT, *and train.*⟩]

HOT. An if the devil come and roar for them   125
I will not send them; I will after straight

---

8. Enter into a contract with cowards.
9. Wounds are often likened to mouths in Shakespeare. The image may derive from their appearance and from the idea that they could speak as
witnesses to what caused them. Cf. *Julius Caesar*
3.2.229–31 and *Richard III* 1.2.55–56.
1. Testing prowess and exchanging blows. "Confound": spend.

2. Paused for breath.
3. I.e., curly (because of the waves).
4. Craftiness or conspiracy; "color": disguise.
5. A form of "sir," but used familiarly, and sometimes, as here, with a tone of contempt. "Speak
of": i.e., even mention (an emphatic sense of
"speak").

And tell him so, for I will ease my heart
Albeit I make a hazard of my head.
NORTH. What, drunk with choler?[6] stay and pause awhile.
    Here comes your uncle.

      [*Enter* WORCESTER.]

HOT.   Speak of Mortimer!   130
    Zounds, I will speak of him, and let my soul
    Want mercy if I do not join with him;
    Yea, on his part[7] I'll empty all these veins,
    And shed my dear blood drop by drop in the dust,
    But I will lift the downtrod Mortimer   135
    As high in the air as this unthankful king,
    As this ingrate and cankered[8] Bullingbrook.
NORTH. Brother, the king hath made your nephew mad.
WOR. Who struck this heat up after I was gone?
HOT. He will, forsooth, have all my prisoners;   140
    And when I urged the ransom once again
    Of my wife's brother, then his cheek looked pale,
    And on my face he turned an eye of death,
    Trembling even at the name of Mortimer.
WOR. I cannot blame him; was not he proclaimed   145
    By Richard, that dead is, the next of blood?
NORTH. He was—I heard the proclamatiòn;
    And then it was when the unhappy king
    (Whose wrongs in us God pardon![9]) did set forth
    Upon his Irish expeditiòn;   150
    From whence he intercepted did return
    To be deposed and shortly murderèd.
WOR. And for whose death we in the world's wide mouth
    Live scandalized and foully spoken of.
HOT. But soft, I pray you; did King Richard then   155
    Proclaim my brother[1] Edmund Mortimer
    Heir to the crown?
NORTH.   He did; myself did hear it.
HOT. Nay, then I cannot blame his cousin king
    That wished him on the barren mountains starve.
    But shall it be that you, that set the crown   160
    Upon the head of this forgetful man
    And for his sake wear the detested blot
    Of murderous subornation[2]—shall it be
    That you a world of curses undergo,
    Being the agents, or base second means,[3]   165
    The cords, the ladder, or the hangman rather?
    O pardon me that I descend so low
    To show the line and the predicament
    Wherein you range[4] under this subtle king!

6. Anger.
7. Behalf.
8. Ungrateful and malignant.
9. I.e., God pardon in us the wrongs we did to him.

1. Brother-in-law.
2. I.e., the stain of aiding and abetting murder.
3. Tools, helpers.
4. I.e., to show the position and the category (or class) in which you are placed.

Shall it for shame be spoken in these days,   170
Or fill up chronicles in time to come,
That men of your nobility and power
Did gage[5] them both in an unjust behalf,
As both of you—God pardon it!—have done,
To put down Richard, that sweet lovely rose,   175
And plant this thorn, this canker,[6] Bullingbrook?
And shall it in more shame be further spoken,
That you are fooled, discarded, and shook off
By him for whom these shames ye underwent?
No; yet time serves wherein you may redeem   180
Your banished honors and restore yourselves
Into the good thoughts of the world again,
Revenge the jeering and disdained[7] contempt
Of this proud king, who studies day and night
To answer all the debt he owes to you   185
Even with the bloody payment of your deaths:
Therefore, I say—

WOR.   Peace, cousin, say no more;
And now I will unclasp a secret book,
And to your quick-conceiving discontents
I'll read you matter deep and dangerous,   190
As full of peril and adventurous spirit
As to o'er-walk a current roaring loud
On the unsteadfast footing of a spear.[8]

HOT. If he fall in, good night, or sink or swim;
Send danger from the east unto the west,   195
So[9] honor cross it from the north to south,
And let them grapple; O, the blood more stirs
To rouse a lion than to start[1] a hare!

NORTH. Imagination of some great exploit
Drives him beyond the bounds of patience.   200

HOT. By heaven, methinks it were an easy leap
To pluck bright honor from the pale-faced moon,
Or dive into the bottom of the deep,
Where fathom line could never touch the ground,
And pluck up drownèd honor by the locks,   205
So he that doth redeem her thence might wear
Without corrival[2] all her dignities;
But out upon this half-faced fellowship![3]

WOR. He apprehends a world of figures[4] here,
But not the form of what he should attend.   210
Good cousin, give me audience for a while.

HOT. I cry you mercy.[5]

WOR.   Those same noble Scots
That are your prisoners—

---

5. Pledge; "behalf": cause.
6. "Canker" meant not only a wild rose but also a
diseased spot in a nose.
7. Disdainful.
8. A spear laid down as a foot-bridge.
9. Provided that.

1. Arouse, in hunting.
2. Rival.
3. Miserable sharing (of honor) with someone else.
4. Rhetorical figures of speech.
5. Beg your pardon.

HOT.   I'll keep them all;
    By God, he shall not have a Scot of them;
    No, if a Scot would save his soul he shall not.   215
    I'll keep them, by his hand.
WOR.   You start away
    And lend no ear unto my purposes.
    Those prisoners you shall keep.
HOT.   Nay, I will; that's flat.
    He said he would not ransom Mortimer,
    Forbade my tongue to speak of Mortimer,   220
    But I will find him when he lies asleep,
    And in his ear I'll holla "Mortimer!"
    Nay,
    I'll have a starling shall be taught to speak[6]
    Nothing but "Mortimer," and give it him   225
    To keep his anger still in motion.
WOR. Hear you, cousin, a word.
HOT. All studies here I solemnly defy,
    Save how to gall[7] and pinch this Bullingbrook,
    And that same sword-and-buckler[8] Prince of Wales,   230
    But that I think his father loves him not
    And would be glad he met with some mischance,
    I would have him poisoned with a pot of ale.[9]
WOR. Farewell, kinsman; I'll talk to you
    When you are better tempered to attend.   235
NORTH. Why, what a wasp-stung and impatient fool
    Art thou to break into this woman's mood,
    Tying thine ear to no tongue but thine own!
HOT. Why, look you, I am whipped and scourged with rods,
    Nettled and stung with pismires,[1] when I hear   240
    Of this vile politician Bullingbrook.
    In Richard's time—what do you call the place?—
    A plague upon it, it is in Gloucestershire—
    'Twas where the madcap duke his uncle kept,[2]
    His uncle York, where I first bow'd my knee   245
    Unto this king of smiles, this Bullingbrook
    'Sblood!—
    When you and he came back from Ravenspurgh.
NORTH. At Berkeley castle.
HOT. You say true.   250
    Why, what a candy deal of courtesy
    This fawning greyhound[3] then did proffer me!
    "Look when his infant fortune came to age,"
    And "gentle Harry Percy," and "kind cousin";
    O, the devil take such cozeners![4] God forgive me!   255

---

6. Starlings used to be taught to speak, as parrots are now.
7. Irritate.
8. Weapons used not by gentlemen but by servants or rustic clowns.
9. The drink of the lower classes.
1. Ants.
2. Lived.

3. A complex image which occurs in Shakespeare several times (cf. *Hamlet* 3.2.1.65–67 and *Antony and Cleopatra* 4.12.20–23). The idea of fawning or flattery called up to Shakespeare's mind the image of a dog begging for sweetmeats ("candy").
4. Cheaters, with of course a pun on the word "cousin."

Good uncle, tell your tale; I have done.

WOR. Nay, if you have not, to it again;
We will stay your leisure.

HOT.   I have done, i' faith.

WOR. Then once more to your Scottish prisoners.
Deliver them up without their ransom straight,   260
And make the Douglas' son your only mean
For powers in Scotland, which, for divers reasons
Which I shall send you written, be assured
Will easily be granted. You, my lord, [⟨*to* NORTHUMBERLAND⟩]
Your son in Scotland being thus employed,   265
Shall secretly into the bosom creep
Of that same noble prelate well beloved,
The archbishop.

HOT. Of York, is it not?

WOR. True; who bears hard   270
His brother's death at Bristol, the Lord Scroop.
I speak not this in estimation,[5]
As what I think might be, but what I know
Is ruminated, plotted, and set down,
And only stays but to behold the face   275
Of that occasion that shall bring it on.

HOT. I smell it; upon my life, it will do well.

NORTH. Before the game is afoot, thou still let'st slip.[6]

HOT. Why, it cannot choose but be a noble plot;
And then the power of Scotland and of York   280
To join with Mortimer, ha?

WOR.   And so they shall.

HOT. In faith, it is exceedingly well aimed.

WOR. And 'tis no little reason bids us speed,
To save our heads by raising of a head;[7]
For, bear ourselves as even as we can,   285
The king will always think him in our debt,
And think we think ourselves unsatisfied,
Till he hath found a time to pay us home;
And see already how he doth begin
To make us strangers to his looks of love.   290

HOT. He does, he does; we'll be revenged on him.

WOR. Cousin, farewell. No further go in this
Than I by letters shall direct your course.
When time is ripe, which will be suddenly,
I'll steal to Glendower and Lord Mortimer,   295
Where you and Douglas and our powers at once,
As I will fashion it, shall happily meet,
To bear our fortunes in our own strong arms,
Which now we hold at much uncertainty.

NORTH. Farewell, good brother; we shall thrive, I trust.   300

HOT. Uncle, adieu; O, let the hours be short
Till fields and blows and groans applaud our sport! [*Exeunt.*]

5. I.e., guessing.
6. An image from hunting. The meaning is: "You
always ('still') release the dogs before we are ready
to pursue the game."
7. Raising an army.

Act 2

SCENE 1

[*Enter a* CARRIER *with a lantern in his hand.*]

FIRST CAR. Heigh-ho! an it be not four by the day, I'll be hanged; Charles' wain[1] is over the new chimney, and yet our horse not packed. What, ostler!

OST. [*within*] Anon, anon.

FIRST CAR. I prithee, Tom, beat Cut's saddle,[2] put a few flocks in   5 the point; poor jade, is wrung in the withers out of all cess.[3]

[*Enter another* CARRIER.]

SEC. CAR. Peas and beans are as dank here as a dog, and that is the next way to give poor jades the bots;[4] this house is turned upside down since Robin Ostler died.

FIRST CAR. Poor fellow, never joyed since the price of oats rose; it   10 was the death of him.

SEC. CAR. I think this be the most villainous house in all London road for fleas; I am stung like a tench.[5]

FIRST CAR. Like a tench! by the mass, there is ne'er a king christen[6] could be better bit than I have been since the first cock.   15

SEC. CAR. Why, they will allow us ne'er a jordan, and then we leak in your chimney, and your chamber-lye breeds fleas like a loach.[7]

FIRST CAR. What, ostler! come away and be hanged, come away!

SEC. CAR. I have a gammon[8] of bacon and two razes of ginger, to be delivered as far as Charing Cross.   20

FIRST CAR. God's body! the turkeys in my pannier[9] are quite starved. What, ostler! A plague on thee, hast thou never an eye in thy head? canst not hear? An 'twere not as good deed as drink to break the pate on thee, I am a very villain. Come and be hanged! hast no faith in thee?   25

[*Enter* GADSHILL.]

GADS. Good morrow, carriers. What's o'clock?

FIRST CAR. I think it be two o'clock.

GADS. I prithee lend me thy lantern to see my gelding in the stable.

FIRST CAR. Nay, by God, soft; I know a trick worth two of that, i' faith.   30

GADS. I pray thee lend me thine.

SEC. CAR. Aye, when? canst tell?[1] Lend me thy lantern, quoth he? marry, I'll see thee hanged first.

GADS. Sirrah carrier, what time do you mean to come to London?

SEC. CAR. Time enough to go to bed with a candle, I warrant thee.   35

1. The constellation of the Great Bear or Big Dipper.
2. The saddle was beaten to make it soft; "Cut" is a name for a horse with a docked tail. "Flocks in the point": pieces of wool under the point of the saddle.
3. I.e., is sore in the shoulders excessively.
4. I.e., that is the easiest way to give poor nags worms in the stomach.
5. A fish covered with red spots, like fleabites.
6. Christian king.
7. "Jordan": chamber pot; "chamber-lye": urine. The "loach" is a fish which breeds prolifically.
8. Haunch; "razes": roots.
9. Basket.
1. A colloquial expression of contemptuous refusal.

Come, neighbor Mugs, we'll call up the gentlemen; they will
along with company, for they have great charge.[2]

[*Exeunt* ⟨CARRIERS.⟩]

GADS. What ho! chamberlain!

[*Enter* CHAMBERLAIN.]

CHAM. At hand, quoth pickpurse.

GADS. That's even as fair as At hand, quoth the chamberlain, for   40
  thou variest no more from picking of purses than giving direction[3]
  doth from laboring; thou layest the plot how.

CHAM. Good morrow, Master Gadshill. It holds current[4] that I told
  you yesternight; there's a franklin[5] in the weald of Kent hath
  brought three hundred marks with him in gold—I heard him tell   45
  it to one of his company last night at supper—a kind of auditor,[6]
  one that hath abundance of charge too, God knows what. They
  are up already and call for eggs and butter; they will away presently.[7]

GADS. Sirrah, if they meet not with Saint Nicholas' clerks,[8] I'll give   50
  thee this neck.

CHAM. No, I'll none of it; I pray thee, keep that for the hangman,
  for I know thou worshipest Saint Nicholas as truly as a man of
  falsehood may.

GADS. What talkest thou to me of the hangman? if I hang, I'll make   55
  a fat pair of gallows; for if I hang, old Sir John hangs with me,
  and thou knowest he is no starveling. Tut! there are other Trojans[9]
  that thou dream'st not of, the which for sport sake are content to
  do the profession some grace, that would, if matters should be
  looked into, for their own credit sake make all whole. I am joined   60
  with no foot land-rakers,[1] no long-staff sixpenny strikers, none of
  these mad mustachio purple-hued maltworms,[2] but with nobility
  and tranquility, burgomasters and great oneyers, such as can hold
  in, such as will strike sooner than speak, and speak sooner than
  drink, and drink sooner than pray; and yet, zounds, I lie, for they   65
  pray continually to their saint, the commonwealth, or rather, not
  pray to her but prey on her, for they ride up and down on her
  and make her their boots.[3]

CHAM. What, the commonwealth their boots? will she hold out
  water in foul way?   70

GADS. She will, she will; justice hath liquored her. We steal as in a
  castle, cocksure; we have the receipt of fern seed,[4] we walk invisible.

2. Valuable cargo.
3. A pun: "giving direction" means supervising,
as contrasted with "laboring," but it was also the
name for informing thieves about the journeys of
prospective victims (laying "the plot how").
4. Remains true.
5. A freeholder, just below a gentleman in rank.
"Weald of Kent": a section of that county, formerly wooded.
6. Revenue officer; "abundance of charge": con-

siderable property.
7. At once.
8. Highwaymen.
9. Roisterers, good fellows.
1. Footpads; "sixpenny strikers": small-time thieves.
2. Flushed, swaggering barflies. "Oneyers": dignitaries; "hold in": keep secret.
3. Booty.
4. I.e., we have the recipe for fern seed (supposed
to make one invisible). "Liquored": greased.

CHAM. Nay, by my faith, I think you are more beholding to the
night than to fern seed for your walking invisible.   75
GADS. Give me thy hand; thou shalt have a share in our purchase,[5]
as I am a true man.
CHAM. Nay, rather let me have it, as you are a false thief.
GADS. Go to; *homo* is a common name to all men. Bid the ostler
bring my gelding out of the stable. Farewell, you muddy[6] knave.   80
                                                       [*Exeunt.*]

SCENE 2

[*Enter* PRINCE *and* POINS.]

POINS. Come shelter, shelter; I have removed Falstaff's horse, and
he frets like a gummed velvet.[7]
PRINCE. Stand close.

[*Enter* FALSTAFF.]

FAL. Poins! Poins, and be hanged! Poins!
PRINCE. Peace, ye fat-kidneyed rascal! what a brawling dost thou   5
keep!
FAL. Where's Poins, Hal?
PRINCE. He is walked up to the top of the hill; I'll go seek him.

[⟨*He pretends to go, but hides onstage with* POINS.⟩]

FAL. I am accursed to rob in that thief's company; the rascal hath
removed my horse, and tied him I know not where. If I travel   10
but four foot by the squier[8] further afoot, I shall break my wind.
Well, I doubt not but to die a fair death for all this, if I 'scape
hanging for killing that rogue. I have forsworn his company hourly
any time this two and twenty years, and yet I am bewitched with
the rogue's company. If the rascal have not given me medicines   15
to make me love him, I'll be hanged; it could not be else; I have
drunk medicines. Poins! Hal! a plague upon you both! Bardolph!
Peto! I'll starve ere I'll rob a foot further. An 'twere not as good a
deed as drink to turn true man and to leave these rogues, I am
the veriest varlet that ever chewed with a tooth. Eight yards of   20
uneven ground is threescore and ten miles afoot with me, and
the stony-hearted villains know it well enough; a plague upon it
when thieves cannot be true one to another! [*They whistle.*] Whew!
A plague upon you all! Give me my horse, you rogues; give me
my horse, and be hanged!   25
PRINCE. Peace, ye fat-guts! lie down; lay thine ear close to the ground
and list if thou canst hear the tread of travelers.
FAL. Have you any levers to lift me up again, being down? 'Sblood,
I'll not bear my own flesh so far afoot again for all the coin in
thy father's exchequer. What a plague mean ye to colt[9] me thus?   30
PRINCE. Thou liest; thou art not colted, thou art uncolted.

---

5. Takings.   "Stand close": hide.
6. Muddle-headed.   8. Ruler, yardstick.
7. Cheap velvet was treated with gum to make the   9. Trick.
pile stiff; as a result it soon fretted or wore away.

FAL. I prithee, good Prince, Hal, help me to my horse, good king's
son.

PRINCE. Out, ye rogue! shall I be your ostler?

FAL. Go hang thyself in thine own heir-apparent garters![1] If I be 35
ta'en, I'll peach for this. An I have not ballads made on you all
and sung to filthy tunes, let a cup of sack be my poison; when a
jest is so forward, and afoot too! I hate it.

[*Enter* GADSHILL.]

GADS. Stand.

FAL. So I do, against my will. 40

POINS. [*Coming forward with* BARDOLPH *and* PETO] O, 'tis our setter;
I know his voice. Bardolph, what news?

BARD. Case[2] ye, case ye, on with your vizards; there's money of the
king's coming down the hill; 'tis going to the king's exchequer.

FAL. You lie, you rogue; 'tis going to the king's tavern. 45

GADS. There's enough to make us all.

FAL. To be hanged.

PRINCE. Sirs, you four shall front them in the narrow lane; Ned
Poins and I will walk lower; if they 'scape from your encounter,
then they light on us. 50

PETO. How many be there of them?

GADS. Some eight or ten.

FAL. Zounds, will they not rob us?

PRINCE. What, a coward, Sir John Paunch?

FAL. Indeed, I am not John of Gaunt, your grandfather, but yet no 55
coward, Hal.

PRINCE. Well, we leave that to the proof.

POINS. Sirrah Jack, thy horse stands behind the hedge; when thou
need'st him, there thou shalt find him. Farewell, and stand fast.

FAL. Now cannot I strike him, if I should be hanged. 60

PRINCE. [⟨*aside to* POINS⟩] Ned, where are our disguises?

POINS. [⟨*aside*⟩] Here, hard by; stand close.

[⟨*Exeunt* PRINCE *and* POINS.⟩]

FAL. Now, my masters, happy man be his dole,[3] say I; every man
to his business.

[*Enter the* TRAVELERS.]

FIRST TRAV. Come, neighbor, the boy shall lead our horses down 65
the hill; we'll walk afoot awhile, and ease our legs.

THIEVES. Stand!

TRAVELERS. Jesus bless us!

FAL. Strike; down with them; cut the villains' throats. Ah, whoreson
caterpillars,[4] bacon-fed knaves, they hate us youth! Down with 70
them, fleece them.

TRAVELERS. O, we are undone, both we and ours forever!

---

1. As heir apparent to the throne, Hal would of
course be a knight of the Order of the Garter.
2. Mask.
3. I.e., good luck!

4. "Caterpillars of the commonwealth" was a
common phrase, referring to rogues. Falstaff here
applies ridiculously inappropriate terms to the
travelers and to himself (e.g., "youth").

FAL. Hang ye, gorbellied[5] knaves, are ye undone? No, ye fat chuffs,
I would your store were here! On, bacons, on! What, ye knaves,
young men must live! You are grand jurors, are ye? we'll jure ye,   75
faith.

[*Here they rob them and bind them. Exeunt.*]
[*Enter the* PRINCE *and* POINS *in buckram.*]

PRINCE. The thieves have bound the true men. Now could thou
and I rob the thieves and go merrily to London; it would be
argument[6] for a week, laughter for a month, and a good jest
forever.   80
POINS. Stand close; I hear them coming.

[*Enter the* THIEVES *again.*]

FAL. Come, my masters, let us share, and then to horse before day.
An the Prince and Poins be not two arrant cowards, there's no
equity stirring;[7] there's no more valor in that Poins than in a wild
duck.   85
PRINCE. Your money!
POINS. Villains!

[*As they are sharing, the* PRINCE *and* POINS *set upon them;
they all run away; and* FALSTAFF, *after a blow or two, runs
away too, leaving the booty behind them.*]

PRINCE. Got with much ease. Now merrily to horse;
The thieves are all scattered and possessed with fear
So strongly that they dare not meet each other;   90
Each takes his fellow for an officer.
Away, good Ned. Falstaff sweats to death,
And lards the lean earth as he walks along;
Were't not for laughing, I should pity him.
POINS. How the fat rogue roared!   [*Exeunt.*]   95

SCENE 3

[*Enter* HOTSPUR, *alone, reading a letter.*]

HOT. "But for mine own part, my lord, I could be well contented
to be there, in respect of the love I bear your house." He could
be contented; why is he not, then? In respect of the love he bears
our house, he shows in this, he loves his own barn better than
he loves our house. Let me see some more. "The purpose you   5
undertake is dangerous." Why, that's certain. 'Tis dangerous to
take a cold, to sleep, to drink; but I tell you, my lord fool, out of
this nettle, danger, we pluck this flower, safety.[8] "The purpose
you undertake is dangerous, the friends you have named uncertain, the time itself unsorted,[9] and your whole plot too light for   10

---

5. Fat; "chuffs": misers.
6. Subject of stories.
7. There's no justice.

8. The nettle if touched tenderly will sting; if
grasped firmly, will not.
9. Unsuitable.

the counterpoise of so great an opposition." Say you so, say you
so? I say unto you again, you are a shallow cowardly hind,[1] and
you lie. What a lackbrain is this! By the Lord, our plot is a good
plot as ever was laid, our friends true and constant; a good plot,
good friends, and full of expectation; an excellent plot, very good   15
friends. What a frosty-spirited rogue is this! Why, my lord of
York[2] commends the plot and the general course of the action.
Zounds, an I were now by this rascal I could brain him with his
lady's fan. Is there not my father, my uncle, and myself? Lord
Edmund Mortimer, my lord of York, and Owen Glendower? is   20
there not besides the Douglas? have I not all their letters to meet
me in arms by the ninth of the next month, and are they not
some of them set forward already? What a pagan rascal is this,
an infidel! Ha! you shall see now in very sincerity of fear and
cold heart, will he to the king and lay open all our proceedings.   25
O, I could divide myself and go to buffets,[3] for moving such a
dish of skim milk with so honorable an action! Hang him! let
him tell the king. We are prepared; I will set forward tonight.

      [*Enter his* LADY.]

How now, Kate! I must leave you within these two hours.
LADY. O, my good lord, why are you thus alone?   30
  For what offense have I this fortnight been
  A banished woman from my Harry's bed?
  Tell me, sweet lord, what is 't that takes from thee
  Thy stomach,[4] pleasure, and thy golden sleep?
  Why dost thou bend thine eyes upon the earth,   35
  And start so often when thou sit'st alone?
  Why hast thou lost the fresh blood in thy cheeks,
  And given my treasures and my rights of thee
  To thick-eyed musing and cursed melancholy?
  In thy faint slumbers I by thee have watched   40
  And heard thee murmur tales of iron wars,
  Speak terms of manage[5] to thy bounding steed,
  Cry "Courage! to the field!" And thou hast talked
  Of sallies and retires, of trenches, tents,
  Of palisadoes, frontiers, parapets,   45
  Of basilisks, of cannon, culverin,[6]
  Of prisoners' ransom and of soldiers slain,
  And all the currents of a heady fight.
  Thy spirit within thee hath been so at war
  And thus hath so bestirred thee in thy sleep   50
  That beads of sweat have stood upon thy brow
  Like bubbles in a late-disturbèd stream,
  And in thy face strange motions have appeared
  Such as we see when men restrain their breath

1. Peasant.
2. The archbishop of York.
3. Split myself in two and let the parts fight each
other; "moving": urging.
4. Appetite.
5. Horsemanship.
6. Three kinds of artillery (named here in decreasing order of weight).

On some great sudden hest.[7] O, what portents are these?   55
Some heavy business hath my lord in hand
And I must know it, else he loves me not.
HOT. What, ho!

      [⟨*Enter* SERVANT.⟩]

         Is Gilliams with the packet gone?
SERV. He is, my lord, an hour ago.   60
HOT. Hath Butler brought those horses from the sheriff?
SERV. One horse, my lord, he brought even now.
HOT. What horse? a roan, a crop-ear, is it not?
SERV. It is, my lord.
HOT.   That roan shall be my throne.
  Well, I will back[8] him straight; O Esperance![9]   65
  Bid Butler lead him forth into the park.   [⟨*Exit* SERVANT.⟩]
LADY. But hear you, my lord.
HOT. What say'st thou, my lady?
LADY. What is it carries you away?
HOT. Why, my horse, my love, my horse.   70
LADY. Out, you mad-headed ape!
  A weasel hath not such a deal of spleen[1]
  As you are tossed with. In faith
  I'll know your business, Harry, that I will.
  I fear my brother Mortimer doth stir   75
  About his title, and hath sent for you
  To line his enterprise; but if you go[2]—
HOT. So far afoot, I shall be weary, love.
LADY. Come, come, you paraquito, answer me
  Directly unto this question that I ask;   80
  In faith, I'll break thy little finger, Harry,
  An if thou wilt not tell me all things true.
HOT. Away,
  Away, you trifler! Love! I love thee not,
  I care not for thee, Kate; this is no world   85
  To play with mammets and to tilt with lips;
  We must have bloody noses and cracked crowns,[3]
  And pass them current too. God's me, my horse!
  What say'st thou, Kate? what wouldst thou have with me?
LADY. Do you not love me? do you not, indeed?   90
  Well, do not then, for since you love me not
  I will not love myself. Do you not love me?
  Nay, tell me if you speak in jest or no.
HOT. Come, wilt thou see me ride?
  And when I am o' horseback, I will swear   95
  I love thee infinitely. But hark you, Kate,

---

7. Command.
8. Mount.
9. The battle cry of the Percies: "Hope!"
1. The spleen was supposed to be the source of sudden and violent emotions; the weasel was considered a very impetuous animal.

2. Besides its ordinary sense, which Lady Percy uses, "go" also meant "walk," the sense in which Hotspur takes it. "Line": support.
3. Broken heads, with a pun on "crowns" as coins. "Mammets": dolls.

I must not have you henceforth question me
Whither I go, nor reason whereabout;
Whither I must, I must; and, to conclude,
This evening must I leave you, gentle Kate.   100
I know you wise, but yet no farther wise
Than Harry Percy's wife; constant you are,
But yet a woman, and for secrecy
No lady closer; for I well believe
Thou wilt not utter what thou dost not know,   105
And so far will I trust thee, gentle Kate.
LADY. How! so far?
HOT. Not an inch further. But hark you, Kate,
Whither I go, thither shall you go too;
Today will I set forth, tomorrow you.   110
Will this content you, Kate?
LADY.   It must of force.[4]   [*Exeunt.*]

SCENE 4

[*Enter the* PRINCE *and* POINS.]

PRINCE. Ned, prithee come out of that fat[5] room, and lend me thy
hand to laugh a little.
POINS. Where hast been, Hal?
PRINCE. With three or four loggerheads[6] amongst three or four-score
hogsheads. I have sounded the very bass string of humility. Sir-   5
rah, I am sworn brother to a leash of drawers,[7] and can call them
all by their christen names, as Tom, Dick, and Francis. They
take it already upon their salvation, that though I be but Prince
of Wales, yet I am the king of courtesy, and tell me flatly I am
no proud Jack, like Falstaff, but a Corinthian,[8] a lad of mettle, a   10
good boy—by the Lord, so they call me—and when I am king of
England I shall command all the good lads in Eastcheap. They
call drinking deep, dyeing scarlet, and when you breathe in your
watering[9] they cry "hem!" and bid you play it off. To conclude,
I am so good a proficient in one quarter of an hour that I can   15
drink with any tinker in his own language during my life. I tell
thee, Ned, thou hast lost much honor, that thou wert not with
me in this action. But, sweet Ned—to sweeten which name of
Ned, I give thee this pennyworth of sugar, clapped even now into
my hand by an underskinker,[1] one that never spake other English   20
in his life than "Eight shillings and sixpence," and "You are
welcome," with this shrill addition, "Anon, anon, sir! Score a
pint of bastard in the Half-Moon,"[2] or so. But, Ned, to drive
away the time till Falstaff come, I prithee do thou stand in some
by-room, while I question my puny drawer to what end he gave   25

4. Of necessity.
5. Vat. This establishes that the scene is a tavern.
6. Blockheads.
7. Group of tapsters, waiters.
8. Good fellow.
9. Drinking.

1. Assistant waiter.
2. I.e., charge a pint of "bastard" (a sweet Spanish wine) to a customer in the room called "Half-Moon." "Anon": immediately (the reply of a servant when called, equivalent to "Coming!").

me the sugar, and do thou never leave calling "Francis," that his
tale to me may be nothing but "Anon." Step aside, and I'll show
thee a precedent.

POINS. Francis!

PRINCE. Thou art perfect.   30

POINS. Francis!   [⟨*Exit* POINS.⟩]

[*Enter* DRAWER.]

FRAN. Anon, anon, sir. Look down into the Pomgarnet,[3] Ralph.

PRINCE. Come hither, Francis.

FRAN. My lord?

PRINCE. How long hast thou to serve,[4] Francis?   35

FRAN. Forsooth, five years, and as much as to—

POINS. [*Within*] Francis!

FRAN. Anon, anon, sir.

PRINCE. Five year! by 'r Lady, a long lease for the clinking of pew-
ter. But, Francis, darest thou be so valiant as to play the coward   40
with thy indenture and show it a fair pair of heels and run from it?

FRAN. O Lord, sir, I'll be sworn upon all the books[5] in England, I
could find in my heart—

POINS. [*within*] Francis!

FRAN. Anon, sir.   45

PRINCE. How old art thou, Francis?

FRAN. Let me see— about Michaelmas[6] next I shall be—

POINS. [*within*] Francis!

FRAN. Anon, sir. Pray stay a little, my lord.

PRINCE. Nay, but hark you, Francis: for the sugar thou gavest me,   50
'twas a pennyworth, was't not?

FRAN. O Lord, I would it had been two!

PRINCE. I will give thee for it a thousand pound; ask me when thou
wilt, and thou shalt have it.

POINS. [*within*] Francis!   55

FRAN. Anon, anon.

PRINCE. Anon, Francis? No, Francis, but tomorrow, Francis; or
Francis, o' Thursday, or indeed, Francis, when thou wilt. But,
Francis!

FRAN. My lord?   60

PRINCE. Wilt thou rob this leathern-jerkin,[7] crystal-button, not-pated,
agate-ring, puke-stocking, caddis-garter, smooth-tongue, Span-
ish-pouch—

FRAN. O Lord, sir, who do you mean?

PRINCE. Why, then, your brown bastard is your only drink, for look 65
you, Francis, your white canvas doublet will sully. In Barbary,
sir, it cannot come to so much.[8]

FRAN. What, sir?

---

3. Pomegranate (another room in the tavern).

4. I.e., to finish out his apprenticeship, usually a
seven-year period under an "indenture" or agreement.

5. I.e., Bibles.

6. September 29.

7. Leather-jacketed; "not-pated": with short hair;
"puke": dark gray; "caddis": worsted tape.

8. Deliberate nonsense to confuse Francis, and one
of the first instances of doubletalk in English literature.

POINS. [*within*] Francis!

PRINCE. Away, you rogue, dost thou not hear them call?   70

> [*Here they both call him; the drawer stands amazed, not knowing which way to go.*]
> [*Enter* VINTNER.]

VINT. What, stand'st thou still, and hear'st such a calling? Look to the guests within. [*Exit* FRANCIS.] My lord, old Sir John with half-a-dozen more are at the door; shall I let them in?

PRINCE. Let them alone awhile, and then open the door. [*Exit* VINTNER.] Poins!   75

> [*Enter* POINS.]

POINS. Anon, anon, sir.

PRINCE. Sirrah, Falstaff and the rest of the thieves are at the door; shall we be merry?

POINS. As merry as crickets, my lad. But hark ye, what cunning match have you made with this jest of the drawer? come, what's the issue?   80

PRINCE. I am now of all humors[9] that have showed themselves humors since the old days of goodman Adam to the pupil[1] age of this present twelve o'clock at midnight.

> [⟨*Enter* FRANCIS.⟩]

What's o'clock, Francis?   85

FRAN. Anon, anon, sir.   [⟨*Exit.*⟩]

PRINCE. That ever this fellow should have fewer words than a parrot, and yet the son of a woman! His industry is upstairs and downstairs, his eloquence the parcel[2] of a reckoning. I am not yet of Percy's mind, the Hotspur of the north, he that kills me some six or seven dozen of Scots at a breakfast, washes his hands, and says to his wife "Fie upon this quiet life! I want work." "O my sweet Harry," says she, "how many hast thou killed today?" "Give my roan horse a drench," says he, and answers "Some fourteen," an hour after, "a trifle, a trifle." I prithee, call in Falstaff; I'll play Percy, and that damned brawn shall play Dame Mortimer his wife. "Rivo!"[3] says the drunkard. Call in ribs, call in tallow.   90   95

> [*Enter* FALSTAFF, ⟨GADSHILL, BARDOLPH, *and* PETO, FRANCIS *following with wine.*⟩]

POINS. Welcome, Jack; where hast thou been?

FAL. A plague of all cowards, I say, and a vengeance too, marry and amen! Give me a cup of sack, boy. Ere I lead this life long, I'll sew nether stocks[4] and mend them and foot them too. A plague of all cowards! Give me a cup of sack, rogue. Is there no virtue extant?   [*He drinks.*]   100

PRINCE. Didst thou ever see Titan[5] kiss a dish of butter, pitiful-   105

---

9. Temperaments, dispositions.
1. Youthful.
2. Item.

3. Drink up!
4. Stockings.
5. The sun.

hearted butter that melted at the sweet tale of the sun's? If thou
didst, then behold that compound.

FAL. You rogue, here's lime in this sack too;[6] there is nothing but
roguery to be found in villainous man, yet a coward is worse than
a cup of sack with lime in it. A villainous coward! Go thy ways,   110
old Jack, die when thou wilt; if manhood, good manhood, be
not forgot upon the face of the earth, then am I a shotten herring.[7] There lives not three good men unhanged in England, and
one of them is fat and grows old. God help the while; a bad
world, I say. I would I were a weaver; I could sing psalms[8] or   115
anything. A plague of all cowards, I say still.

PRINCE. How now, woolsack, what mutter you?

FAL. A king's son! If I do not beat thee out of thy kingdom with a
dagger of lath,[9] and drive all thy subjects afore thee like a flock
of wild geese, I'll never wear hair on my face more. You Prince   120
of Wales!

PRINCE. Why, you whoreson round man, what's the matter?

FAL. Are not you a coward? answer me to that; and Poins there?

POINS. Zounds, ye fat paunch, an ye call me coward, by the Lord
I'll stab thee.   125

FAL. I call thee coward! I'll see thee damned ere I call thee coward;
but I would give a thousand pound I could run as fast as thou
canst. You are straight enough in the shoulders, you care not
who sees your back; call you that backing of your friends? A
plague upon such backing! give me them that will face me.   130
Give me a cup of sack; I am a rogue if I drunk today.

PRINCE. O villain! thy lips are scarce wiped since thou drunk'st last.

FAL. All's one for that. [*He drinks.*] A plague of all cowards, still say
I.

PRINCE. What's the matter?   135

FAL. What's the matter! there be four of us here have ta'en a thousand pound this day morning.

PRINCE. Where is it, Jack? where is it?

FAL. Where is it? taken from us it is—a hundred upon poor four of
us.   140

PRINCE. What, a hundred, man?

FAL. I am a rogue if I were not at half-sword[1] with a dozen of them
two hours together. I have 'scaped by miracle. I am eight times
thrust through the doublet, four through the hose,[2] my buckler
cut through and through, my sword hacked like a handsaw—*ecce*   145
signum![3] I never dealt better since I was a man; all would not do.
A plague of all cowards! Let them speak; if they speak more or
less than truth, they are villains and the sons of darkness.

PRINCE. Speak, sirs; how was it?

GADS. We four set upon some dozen—   150

FAL. Sixteen at least, my lord.

GADS. And bound them.

---

6. Lime was used to make wine sparkle.
7. A herring that has cast its spawn and is lean.
8. Protestant weavers from Flanders were notorious for singing psalms.

9. A stick used by Vice in the old morality plays.
1. At half a sword's length.
2. Breeches.
3. Here's the proof!

PETO. No, no, they were not bound.

FAL. You rogue, they were bound, every man of them, or I am a
Jew else, an Ebrew Jew.   155

GADS. As we were sharing, some six or seven fresh men set upon
us—

FAL. And unbound the rest, and then come in the other.

PRINCE. What, fought you with them all?

FAL. All! I know not what you call all, but if I fought not with fifty   160
of them, I am a bunch of radish; if there were not two or three
and fifty upon poor old Jack, then am I no two-legged creature.

PRINCE. Pray God you have not murdered some of them.

FAL. Nay, that's past praying for; I have peppered two of them. Two
I am sure I have paid, two rogues in buckram suits. I tell thee   165
what, Hal, if I tell thee a lie, spit in my face, call me horse.
Thou knowest my old ward;[4] here I lay, and thus I bore my
point. Four rogues in buckram let drive at me—

PRINCE. What, four? thou saidst but two even now.

FAL. Four, Hal; I told thee four.   170

POINS. Aye, aye, he said four.

FAL. These four came all a-front, and mainly[5] thrust at me. I made
me no more ado but took all their seven points in my target,[6]
thus.

PRINCE. Seven? why, there were but four even now.   175

FAL. In buckram?

POINS. Aye, four, in buckram suits.

FAL. Seven, by these hilts, or I am a villain else.

PRINCE. Prithee, let him alone; we shall have more anon.

FAL. Dost thou hear me, Hal?   180

PRINCE. Aye, and mark thee too, Jack.

FAL. Do so, for it is worth the listening to. These nine in buckram
that I told thee of—

PRINCE. So, two more already.

FAL. Their points being broken—   185

POINS. Down fell their hose.[7]

FAL. Began to give me ground; but I followed me close, came in
foot and hand, and with a thought[8] seven of the eleven I paid.

PRINCE. O monstrous! eleven buckram men grown out of two!

FAL. But, as the devil would have it, three misbegotten knaves in   190
Kendal green came at my back and let drive at me, for it was so
dark, Hal, that thou couldst not see thy hand.

PRINCE. These lies are like their father that begets them—gross as a
mountain, open, palpable. Why, thou clay-brained guts, thou
knotty-pated fool, thou whoreson, obscene, greasy tallow-catch[9]—   195

FAL. What, art thou mad? art thou mad? is not the truth the truth?

PRINCE. Why, how couldst thou know these men in Kendal green,
when it was so dark thou couldst not see thy hand? come, tell us
your reason. What sayest thou to this?

---

4. Defense; "here I lay": this was my stance.
5. Strongly.
6. Shield.
7. Poins puns on the other meaning of "points":

the laces used to tie up trousers ("hose").
8. As quick as thought.
9. Piece of tallow from which chandlers made
candles.

POINS. Come, your reason, Jack, your reason.   200

FAL. What, upon compulsion? Zounds, an I were at the strappado,[1]
or all the racks in the world, I would not tell you on compulsion.
Give you a reason on compulsion! if reasons[2] were as plentiful
as blackberries, I would give no man a reason upon compulsion,
I.   205

PRINCE. I'll be no longer guilty of this sin; this sanguine coward,
this bed-presser, this horseback-breaker, this huge hill of flesh—

FAL. 'Sblood, you starveling, you eelskin, you dried neat's tongue,
you bull's pizzle, you stockfish![3] O for breath to utter what is like
thee! you tailor's yard, you sheath, you bow case, you vile stand-   210
ing-tuck[4]

PRINCE. Well, breathe awhile, and then to it again; and when thou
hast tired thyself in base comparisons, hear me speak but this.

POINS. Mark, Jack.

PRINCE. We two saw you four set on four and bound them, and   215
were masters of their wealth. Mark now, how a plain tale shall
put you down. Then did we two set on you four; and, with a
word, outfaced you from your prize, and have it, yea, and can
show it you here in the house; and, Falstaff, you carried your
guts away as nimbly, with as quick dexterity, and roared for mercy   220
and still run and roared, as ever I heard bullcalf. What a slave
art thou, to hack thy sword as thou hast done, and then say it
was in fight! What trick, what device, what starting-hole,[5] canst
thou now find out to hide thee from this open and apparent
shame?   225

POINS. Come, let's hear, Jack; what trick hast thou now?

FAL. By the Lord, I knew ye as well as he that made ye. Why, hear
you, my masters: was it for me to kill the heir apparent? should I
turn upon the true prince? why, thou knowest I am as valiant as
Hercules; but beware instinct; the lion will not touch the true   230
prince.[6] Instinct is a great matter; I was now a coward on instinct.
I shall think the better of myself and thee during my life; I for a
valiant lion, and thou for a true prince. But, by the Lord, lads, I
am glad you have the money. Hostess, clap to the doors; watch[7]
tonight, pray tomorrow. Gallants, lads, boys, hearts of gold, all   235
the titles of good fellowship come to you! What, shall we be
merry? shall we have a play extempore?

PRINCE. Content; and the argument[8] shall be thy running away.

FAL. Ah, no more of that, Hal, an thou lovest me!

[*Enter* HOSTESS.]

HOST. O Jesu, my lord the prince!   240

PRINCE. How now, my lady the hostess! what sayest thou to me?

HOST. Marry, my lord, there is a nobleman of the court at door
would speak with you; he says he comes from your father.

---

1. A method of torture; "racks": another method.
2. A pun on the word "raisin," which was spelled
and pronounced like "reason" in Elizabethan
England.
3. I.e., you ox tongue, you bull's penis, you dried
cod!
4. Stiff rapier.
5. Evasion.
6. In many medieval romances the lion, as king
of beasts, shows respect for royalty.
7. Stay up.
8. Plot or story.

PRINCE. Give him as much as will make him a royal⁹ man, and
send him back again to my mother.   245

FAL. What manner of man is he?

HOST. An old man.

FAL. What doth gravity out of his bed at midnight? Shall I give him
his answer?

PRINCE. Prithee, do, Jack.   250

FAL. Faith, and I'll send him packing.   [*Exit.*]

PRINCE. Now, sirs. By 'r Lady, you fought fair; so did you, Peto; so
did you, Bardolph; you are lions too, you ran away upon instinct,
you will not touch the true prince; no, fie!

BARD. Faith, I ran when I saw others run.   255

PRINCE. Faith, tell me now in earnest, how came Falstaff's sword
so hacked?

PETO. Why, he hacked it with his dagger, and said he would swear
truth out of England but he would make you believe it was done
in fight, and persuaded us to do the like.   260

BARD. Yea, and to tickle our noses with speargrass to make them
bleed, and then to beslubber our garments with it and swear it
was the blood of true men. I did that I did not this seven year
before, I blushed to hear his monstrous devices.

PRINCE. O villain, thou stolest a cup of sack eighteen years ago, and   265
wert taken with the manner,¹ and ever since thou hast blushed
extempore. Thou hadst fire² and sword on thy side, and yet thou
ran'st away; what instinct hadst thou for it?

BARD. My lord, do you see these meteors? do you behold these
exhalations?   270

PRINCE. I do.

BARD. What think you they portend?

PRINCE. Hot livers and cold purses.³

BARD. Choler, my lord, if rightly taken.

PRINCE. No, if rightly taken, halter.   275

[*Enter* FALSTAFF.]

Here comes lean Jack, here comes bare-bone. How now, my
sweet creature of bombast,⁴ how long is 't ago, Jack, since thou
sawest thine own knee?

FAL. My own knee! when I was about thy years, Hal, I was not an
eagle's talon in the waist; I could have crept into any alderman's   280
thumb ring. A plague of sighing and grief—it blows a man up
like a bladder. There's villainous news abroad; here was Sir John
Bracy from your father; you must to the court in the morning.
That same mad fellow of the north, Percy, and he of Wales, that
gave Amamon⁵ the bastinado and made Lucifer cuckold and swore   285
the devil his true liegeman upon the cross of a Welsh hook⁶—
what a plague call you him?

POINS. O, Glendower.

9. A "royal" was half of a pound sterling, a "noble"
was a third.
1. In the act.
2. "Fire" and the allusions to "meteors" and
"exhalations" (shooting stars) refer to Bardolph's red
nose.
3. I.e., drunkenness and poverty.
4. Padding, stuffing.
5. A devil. "Bastinado": a beating, cudgelling.
6. A long spear with a hook on it.

FAL. Owen, Owen, the same; and his son-in-law Mortimer, and
old Northumberland, and that sprightly Scot of Scots, Douglas, 290
that runs o' horseback up a hill perpendicular—
PRINCE. He that rides at high speed and with his pistol kills a spar-
row flying.
FAL. You have hit it.
PRINCE. So did he never the sparrow. 295
FAL. Well, that rascal hath good mettle in him; he will not run.
PRINCE. Why, what a rascal art thou then, to praise him so for
running!
FAL. O' horseback, ye cuckoo; but afoot he will not budge a foot.
PRINCE. Yes, Jack, upon instinct. 300
FAL. I grant ye, upon instinct. Well, he is there too, and one Mor-
dake, and a thousand blue-caps[7] more. Worcester is stolen away
tonight; thy father's beard is turned white with the news; you may
buy land now as cheap as stinking mackerel.
PRINCE. Why then, it is like, if there come a hot June, and this civil 305
buffeting hold, we shall buy maidenheads as they buy hobnails,
by the hundreds.
FAL. By the mass, lad, thou sayest true; it is like we shall have good
trading that way. But tell me, Hal, art not thou horrible afeard?
thou being heir apparent, could the world pick thee out three 310
such enemies again as that fiend Douglas, that spirit Percy, and
that devil Glendower? Art thou not horribly afraid? doth not thy
blood thrill at it?
PRINCE. Not a whit, i' faith; I lack some of thy instinct.
FAL. Well, thou wilt be horribly chid tomorrow when thou comest 315
to thy father; if thou love me, practice an answer.
PRINCE. Do thou stand for[8] my father and examine me upon the
particulars of my life.
FAL. Shall I? Content. This chair shall be my state,[9] this dagger my
scepter, and this cushion my crown. 320
PRINCE. Thy state is taken for a joint-stool,[1] thy golden scepter for
a leaden dagger, and thy precious rich crown for a pitiful bald
crown!
FAL. Well, an the fire of grace be not quite out of thee, now shalt
thou be moved. Give me a cup of sack to make my eyes look 325
red, that it may be thought I have wept, for I must speak in
passion, and I will do it in King Cambyses'[2] vein.
PRINCE. Well, here is my leg.[3]
FAL. And here is my speech. Stand aside, nobility.
HOST. O Jesu, this is excellent sport, i' faith! 330
FAL. Weep not, sweet queen, for trickling tears are vain.
HOST. O, the father, how he holds his countenance!
FAL. For God's sake, lords, convey my tristful queen,
For tears do stop the floodgates of her eyes.[4]

---

7. Scots.
8. Represent.
9. Throne.
1. An ordinary stool, made by a joiner (cabinet maker).

2. Like the bombastic hero of the old play Cambyses.
3. I.e., he bows, makes an obeisance.
4. Falstaff's blank verse lines parody the old-fashioned tragedies of the 1570s and 80s.

HOST. O Jesu, he doth it as like one of these harlotry players as ever I see!   335

FAL. Peace, good pint pot, peace, good ticklebrain. Harry, I do not only marvel where thou spendest thy time, but also how thou art accompanied, for though the camomile,[5] the more it is trodden on the faster it grows, so youth, the more it is wasted the sooner it wears. That thou art my son, I have partly thy mother's word, partly my own opinion, but chiefly a villainous trick of thine eye and a foolish hanging of thy nether lip that doth warrant[6] me. If then thou be son to me, here lies the point; why, being son to me, art thou so pointed at? Shall the blessed sun of heaven prove a micher[7] and eat blackberries? a question not to be asked. Shall the son of England prove a thief and take purses? a question to be asked. There is a thing, Harry, which thou hast often heard of and it is known to many in our land by the name of pitch. This pitch, as ancient writers do report, doth defile; so doth the company thou keepest: for, Harry, now I do not speak to thee in drink but in tears, not in pleasure but in passion, not in words only, but in woes also: and yet there is a virtuous man whom I have often noted in thy company, but I know not his name.   340, 345, 350

PRINCE. What manner of man, an it like your majesty?   355

FAL. A goodly portly man, i' faith, and a corpulent; of a cheerful look, a pleasing eye and a most noble carriage, and, as I think, his age some fifty, or, by 'r Lady, inclining to threescore; and now I remember me, his name is Falstaff. If that man should be lewdly given, he deceiveth me, for, Harry, I see virtue in his looks. If then the tree may be known by the fruit, as the fruit by the tree, then, peremptorily I speak it, there is virtue in that Falstaff; him keep with, the rest banish. And tell me now, thou naughty varlet, tell me, where hast thou been this month?   360

PRINCE. Dost thou speak like a king? Do thou stand for me, and I'll play my father.   365

FAL. Depose me? if thou dost it half so gravely, so majestically, both in word and matter, hang me up by the heels for a rabbit-sucker[8] or a poulter's hare.

PRINCE. Well, here I am set.[9]   370

FAL. And here I stand; judge, my masters.

PRINCE. Now, Harry, whence come you?

FAL. My noble lord, from Eastcheap.

PRINCE. The complaints I hear of thee are grievous.

FAL. 'Sblood, my lord, they are false: nay, I'll tickle ye for a young prince, i' faith.   375

PRINCE. Swearest thou, ungracious boy? Henceforth ne'er look on me. Thou art violently carried away from grace; there is a devil haunts thee in the likeness of an old fat man; a tun[1] of man is thy companion. Why dost thou converse with that trunk of humors, that bolting-hutch[2] of beastliness, that swollen parcel of   380

---

5. An aromatic herb. The style in this speech is a parody of Euphuism, the ornate, elaborate, balanced style made popular by Lyly's *Euphues*. See pp. 1033–35.
6. Assure.

7. Truant.
8. Suckling rabbit.
9. Seated.
1. Large barrel.
2. Trough; "bombard": leather wine vessel.

dropsies, that huge bombard of sack, that stuffed cloak-bag of
guts, that roasted Manningtree[3] ox with the pudding in his belly,
that reverend vice, that gray iniquity, that father ruffian, that
vanity in years? Wherein is he good, but to taste sack and drink   385
it? wherein neat and cleanly, but to carve a capon and eat it?
wherein cunning, but in craft? wherein crafty, but in villainy?
wherein villainous, but in all things? wherein worthy, but in
nothing?

FAL. I would your grace would take me with you; whom means   390
your grace?

PRINCE. That villainous abominable misleader of youth, Falstaff,
that old white-bearded Satan.

FAL. My lord, the man I know.

PRINCE. I know thou dost.   395

FAL. But to say I know more harm in him than in myself were to
say more than I know. That he is old the more the pity, his white
hairs do witness it; but that he is, saving your reverence, a whoremaster, that I utterly deny. If sack and sugar be a fault, God help
the wicked! if to be old and merry be a sin, then many an   400
old host that I know is damned; if to be fat be to be hated, then
Pharaoh's lean kine[4] are to be loved. No, my good lord, banish
Peto, banish Bardolph, banish Poins, but for sweet Jack Falstaff,
kind Jack Falstaff, true Jack Falstaff, valiant Jack Falstaff, and
therefore more valiant, being as he is old Jack Falstaff, banish   405
not him thy Harry's company, banish not him thy Harry's company; banish plump Jack, and banish all the world.

PRINCE. I do, I will.   [⟨A knocking heard.⟩]

                     [⟨Exeunt HOSTESS and BARDOLPH.⟩]
        [Enter BARDOLPH, running.]

BARD. O, my lord, my lord, the sheriff with a most monstrous watch
is at the door.   410

FAL. Out, ye rogue! Play out the play; I have much to say in the
behalf of that Falstaff.

        [Enter the HOSTESS.]

HOST. O Jesu, my lord, my lord!

FAL. Heigh, heigh! the devil rides upon a fiddlestick;[5] what's the   415
matter?

HOST. The sheriff and all the watch are at the door; they are come
to search the house. Shall I let them in?

FAL. Dost thou hear, Hal? never call a true piece of gold a counterfeit; thou art essentially mad, without seeming so.[6]

PRINCE. And thou a natural coward, without instinct.   420

FAL. I deny your major;[7] if you will deny the sheriff, so; if not, let

---

3. Town in Essex, noted for barbecues; "pudding": sausage. The "vice" was a comic character
in the old morality plays. Falstaff is in some respects
a descendant of this type-character.
4. In the dream Joseph interpreted. See Genesis
41.19–21.
5. I.e., there's a commotion.

6. I.e., don't give a true man (me, Falstaff) away
as a thief. He goes on to accuse the prince, in his
reversal of values in the play scene, of being out of
his mind, though he appears rational.
7. Your major premise (that I, Falstaff, am a coward).

him enter. If I become not a cart as well as another man, a
plague on my bringing up! I hope I shall as soon be strangled
with a halter as another.[8]

PRINCE. Go hide thee behind the arras;[9] the rest walk up above.   425
Now, my masters, for a true face and good conscience.

FAL. Both which I have had; but their date is out,[1] and therefore I'll
hide me.

PRINCE. Call in the sheriff.

[*Exeunt ⟨all except the* PRINCE *and* POINS.⟩]
[*Enter* SHERIFF *and the* CARRIER.]

Now, master sheriff, what is your will with me?   430
SHER. First pardon me, my lord. A hue and cry
Hath followed certain men unto this house.
PRINCE. What men?
SHER. One of them is well known, my gracious lord,
A gross fat man.
CAR.   As fat as butter.   435
PRINCE. The man, I do assure you, is not here,
For I myself at this time have employed him,
And, sheriff, I will engage my word to thee
That I will by tomorrow dinnertime
Send him to answer thee or any man   440
For anything he shall be charged withal;
And so let me entreat you leave the house.
SHER. I will, my lord. There are two gentlemen
Have in this robbery lost three hundred marks.
PRINCE. It may be so; if he have robbed these men   445
He shall be answerable; and so farewell.
SHER. Good night, my noble lord.
PRINCE. I think it is good morrow, is it not?
SHER. Indeed, my lord, I think it be two o'clock.

[*Exeunt ⟨*SHERIFF *and* CARRIER.⟩]

PRINCE. This oily rascal is known as well as Paul's.[2] Go call him   450
forth.
POINS. Falstaff!—Fast asleep behind the arras, and snorting like a
horse.
PRINCE. Hark, how hard he fetches breath. Search his pockets. [*He
searcheth his pockets, and findeth certain papers.*] What hast thou   455
found?
POINS. Nothing but papers, my lord.
PRINCE. Let's see what they be: read them.
POINS. [*reads*] "Item, a capon. . . . . 2s. 2d.
          Item, sauce. . . . . .   4d.
          Item, sack, two gallons. . 5s. 8d.

8. I.e., I hope my fat neck will not make the process of strangling on the gallows longer for me than
for the rest of you. The "cart" is the wagon on
which criminals were taken to be hanged.

9. The hangings or draperies which covered the
walls. "Up above": on the balcony.
1. Lease has expired.
2. St. Paul's Cathedral.

> Item, anchovies and sack
>   after supper. . . . . 2s. 6d.
> Item, bread. . . . . ob."[3]

PRINCE. O monstrous! but one halfpennyworth of bread to this   465
   intolerable deal of sack! What there is else, keep close; we'll read
   it at more advantage; there let him sleep till day. I'll to the court
   in the morning. We must all to the wars, and thy place shall be
   honorable. I'll procure this fat rogue a charge of foot,[4] and I
   know his death will be a march of twelvescore. The money shall   470
   be paid back again with advantage. Be with me betimes[5] in the
   morning, and so good morrow, Poins.
POINS. Good morrow, good my lord.   [*Exeunt.*]

Act 3

SCENE 1

[*Enter* HOTSPUR, WORCESTER, LORD MORTIMER, *and* OWEN
   GLENDOWER.]

MORT. These promises are fair, the parties sure,
   And our induction[1] full of prosperous hope.
HOT. Lord Mortimer, and cousin Glendower,
   Will you sit down?
   And uncle Worcester; a plague upon it,   5
   I have forgot the map.
GLEND.   No, here it is.
   Sit, cousin Percy, sit, good cousin Hotspur,
   For by that name as oft as Lancaster[2]
   Doth speak of you, his cheek looks pale and with
   A rising sigh he wisheth you in heaven.   10
HOT. And you in hell as often as he hears Owen Glendower spoke
   of.
GLEND. I cannot blame him; at my nativity
   The front[3] of heaven was full of fiery shapes,
   Of burning cressets, and at my birth   15
   The frame and huge foundation of the earth
   Shaked like a coward.
HOT. Why, so it would have done at the same season if your moth-
   er's cat had but kittened, though yourself had never been born.
GLEND. I say the earth did shake when I was born.   20
HOT. And I say the earth was not of my mind,
   If you suppose as fearing you it shook.
GLEND. The heavens were all on fire, the earth did tremble.
HOT. O then the earth shook to see the heavens on fire,
   And not in fear of your nativity.   25
   Diseasèd nature oftentimes breaks forth

---

3. Oble, a halfpenny.
4. Company of infantry. "Twelvescore": i.e., 240
yards.
5. Early.

1. Initial step.
2. I.e., King Henry IV. To call him by his lesser
title is insulting.
3. The forehead. "Cressets": lamps.

In strange eruptions; oft the teeming earth
Is with a kind of colic pinched and vexed
By the imprisoning of unruly wind
Within her womb, which for enlargement striving   30
Shakes the old beldam[4] earth and topples down
Steeples and moss-grown towers. At your birth
Our grandam earth, having this distemperature,[5]
In passion shook.

GLEND.   Cousin, of many men
I do not bear these crossings. Give me leave   35
To tell you once again that at my birth
The front of heaven was full of fiery shapes,
The goats ran from the mountains, and the herds
Were strangely clamorous to the frighted fields.
These signs have marked me extraordinary,   40
And all the courses of my life do show
I am not in the roll of common men.
Where is he living, clipped in with[6] the sea
That chides the banks of England, Scotland, Wales,
Which calls me pupil or hath read to me?   45
And bring him out that is but woman's son
Can trace me in the tedious ways of art[7]
And hold me pace in deep experiments.

HOT. I think there's no man speaks better Welsh. I'll to dinner.

MORT. Peace, cousin Percy; you will make him mad.   50

GLEND. I can call spirits from the vasty deep.

HOT. Why, so can I, or so can any man;
But will they come when you do call for them?

GLEND. Why, I can teach you, cousin, to command
The devil.   55

HOT. And I can teach thee, coz, to shame the devil
By telling truth; tell truth and shame the devil.[8]
If thou have power to raise him, bring him hither,
And I'll be sworn I have power to shame him hence.
O, while you live, tell truth and shame the devil!   60

MORT. Come, come, no more of this unprofitable chat.

GLEND. Three times hath Henry Bullingbrook made head
Against my power, thrice from the banks of Wye
And sandy-bottomed Severn have I sent him
Bootless[9] home and weather-beaten back.   65

HOT. Home without boots, and in foul weather too!
How 'scapes he agues,[1] in the devil's name?

GLEND. Come, here is the map; shall we divide our right
According to our threefold order ta'en?[2]

MORT. The archdeacon hath divided it   70

4. Old woman.
5. Ailment.
6. Within the limits of.
7. Follow me in practicing difficult magic.
8. A proverb.

9. Unsuccessful; but Hotspur takes it in the other sense.
1. Fevers and chills.
2. Divide our property according to the arrangement for division into 3 parts.

Into three limits very equally:
England, from Trent and Severn hitherto,
By south and east is to my part assigned;
All westward, Wales beyond the Severn shore,
And all the fertile land within that bound,   75
To Owen Glendower; and, dear coz, to you
The remnant northward lying off from Trent;
And our indentures tripartite are drawn,
Which being sealèd interchangeably,
A business that this night may execute,   80
Tomorrow, cousin Percy, you and I
And my good Lord of Worcester will set forth
To meet your father and the Scottish power,
As is appointed us, at Shrewsbury.
My father[3] Glendower is not ready yet,   85
Nor shall we need his help these fourteen days.
Within that space you may have drawn together
Your tenants, friends, and neighboring gentlemen.
GLEND. A shorter time shall send me to you, lords,
And in my conduct shall your ladies come,   90
From whom you now must steal and take no leave,
For there will be a world of water shed
Upon the parting of your wives and you.
HOT. Methinks my moiety,[4] north from Burton here,
In quantity equals not one of yours;   95
See how this river comes me cranking[5] in,
And cuts me from the best of all my land
A huge half-moon, a monstrous cantle[6] out.
I'll have the current in this place dammed up;
And here the smug[7] and silver Trent shall run   100
In a new channel, fair and evenly;
It shall not wind with such a deep indent
To rob me of so rich a bottom[8] here.
GLEND. Not wind? it shall, it must; you see it doth.
MORT. Yea, but   105
Mark how he bears his course, and runs me up
With like advantage on the other side;
Gelding the opposèd continent[9] as much
As on the other side it takes from you.
WOR. Yea, but a little charge will trench him here   110
And on this north side win this cape of land,
And then he runs straight and even.
HOT. I'll have it so; a little charge will do it.
GLEND. I'll not have it altered.
HOT.   Will not you?
GLEND. No, nor you shall not.

---

3. Father-in-law.
4. Part, share.
5. Curving.
6. Corner.

7. Smooth.
8. Valley.
9. I.e., cutting off from the opposite side.

HOT.   Who shall say me nay?   115
GLEND. Why, that will I.
HOT. Let me not understand you then; speak it in Welsh.
GLEND. I can speak English, lord, as well as you,
 For I was trained up in the English court,
 Where, being but young, I framèd to the harp   120
 Many an English ditty lovely well
 And gave the tongue a helpful ornament,
 A virtue that was never seen in you.
HOT. Marry,
 And I am glad of it with all my heart;   125
 I had rather be a kitten and cry mew
 Than one of these same meter ballad-mongers;
 I had rather hear a brazen canstick turned,[1]
 Or a dry wheel grate on the axletree,
 And that would set my teeth nothing on edge,   130
 Nothing so much as mincing[2] poetry;
 'Tis like the forced gait of a shuffling nag.
GLEND. Come, you shall have Trent turned.
HOT. I do not care; I'll give thrice so much land
 To any well-deserving friend;   135
 But in the way of bargain, mark ye me,
 I'll cavil[3] on the ninth part of a hair.
 Are the indentures drawn? shall we be gone?
GLEND. The moon shines fair; you may be away by night.
 I'll haste the writer, and withal   140
 Break with[4] your wives of your departure hence.
 I am afraid my daughter will run mad,
 So much she doteth on her Mortimer.   [Exit.]
MORT. Fie, cousin Percy, how you cross my father!
HOT. I cannot choose; sometime he angers me   145
 With telling me of the moldwarp[5] and the ant,
 Of the dreamer Merlin and his prophecies,
 And of a dragon and a finless fish,
 A clip-winged griffin and a molten raven,
 A couching lion and a ramping[6] cat,   150
 And such a deal of skimble-skamble stuff
 As puts me from my faith. I tell you what;
 He held me last night at least nine hours
 In reckoning up the several devils' names
 That were his lackeys. I cried "hum" and "well, go to," 155
 But marked him not a word. O, he is as tedious
 As a tired horse, a railing[7] wife,

1. A brass candlestick turned on a lathe.
2. Affected. "Shuffling": hobbled.
3. Quibble.
4. Inform.
5. Mole. According to the chronicler Holinshed there were prophecies in which Henry IV was referred to as "a moldwarp, cursed of God." Mer-

lin was the famous prophet of King Arthur's court; many later prophecies were attributed to him.
6. "Couching" and "ramping" are Hotspur's versions of the heraldic terms "couchant" (lying down) and "rampant" (erect, on hind feet).
7. Nagging.

Worse than a smoky house. I had rather live
With cheese and garlic in a windmill,[8] far,
Than feed on cates and have him talk to me　　　160
In any summer house in Christendom.
MORT. In faith, he is a worthy gentleman,
　　Exceedingly well read, and profited
　　In strange concealments,[9] valiant as a lion
　　And wondrous affable and as bountiful　　　165
　　As mines of India. Shall I tell you, cousin?
　　He holds your temper[1] in a high respect
　　And curbs himself even of his natural scope
　　When you come 'cross his humor; faith, he does.
　　I warrant you that man is not alive　　　170
　　Might so have tempted him as you have done
　　Without the taste of danger and reproof;
　　But do not use it oft, let me entreat you.
WOR. In faith, my lord, you are too willful-blame,
　　And since your coming hither have done enough　　　175
　　To put him quite beside his patience.
　　You must needs learn, lord, to amend this fault.
　　Though sometimes it show greatness, courage, blood[2]—
　　And that's the dearest grace it renders you—
　　Yet oftentimes it doth present harsh rage,　　　180
　　Defect of manners, want of government,[3]
　　Pride, haughtiness, opinion, and disdain;
　　The least of which haunting a nobleman
　　Loseth men's hearts and leaves behind a stain
　　Upon the beauty of all parts besides,　　　185
　　Beguiling them of commendation.
HOT. Well, I am schooled; good manners be your speed!
　　Here come our wives, and let us take our leave.

[*Enter* GLENDOWER *with the ladies.*]

MORT. This is the deadly spite that angers me;
　　My wife can speak no English, I no Welsh.　　　190
GLEND. My daughter weeps; she will not part with you,
　　She'll be a soldier too, she'll to the wars.
MORT. Good father, tell her that she and my aunt Percy
　　Shall follow in your conduct speedily.

[GLENDOWER *speaks to her in Welsh, and she answers him
in the same.*]

GLEND. She is desperate here; a peevish self-willed harlotry,[4] one　　　195
　　that no persuasion can do good upon.

[*The lady speaks in Welsh.*]

8. Cheese and garlic would be smelly, and the living quarters in a mill would be noisy. "Cates":
delicacies.
9. Experienced in secret mysteries.
1. Character.

2. Breeding, blood-lines.
3. Self-control. "Opinion": arrogance.
4. Wench; used affectionately, not seriously (Juliet's
father applies the same phrase to her in *Romeo and
Juliet*).

MORT. I understand thy looks; that pretty Welsh
   Which thou pour'st down from these swelling heavens[5]
   I am too perfect in; and, but for shame,
   In such a parley should I answer thee.   200

       [*The lady speaks again in Welsh.*]

   I understand thy kisses and thou mine,
   And that's a feeling disputation,
   But I will never be a truant, love,
   Till I have learned thy language, for thy tongue
   Makes Welsh as sweet as ditties highly penned,   205
   Sung by a fair queen in a summer's bower,
   With ravishing division,[6] to her lute.
GLEND. Nay, if you melt, then will she run mad.

       [*The lady speaks again in Welsh.*]

MORT. O, I am ignorance itself in this!
GLEND. She bids you on the wanton rushes[7] lay you down   210
   And rest your gentle head upon her lap,
   And she will sing the song that pleaseth you
   And on your eyelids crown the god of sleep,
   Charming your blood with pleasing heaviness,[8]
   Making such difference 'twixt wake and sleep   215
   As is the difference betwixt day and night
   The hour before the heavenly-harnessed team[9]
   Begins his golden progress in the east.
MORT. With all my heart I'll sit and hear her sing;
   By that time will our book,[1] think, be drawn.   220
GLEND. Do so:
   And those musicians that shall play to you
   Hang in the air a thousand leagues from hence,
   And straight they shall be here; sit, and attend.
HOT. Come, Kate, thou art perfect in lying down; come, quick,   225
   quick, that I may lay my head in thy lap.
LADY P. Go, ye giddy goose.

       [*The music plays.*]

HOT. Now I perceive the devil understands Welsh,
   And 'tis no marvel, he is so humorous.[2]
   By 'r Lady, he is a good musician.   230
LADY P. Then should you be nothing but musical, for you are alto-
   gether governed by humors. Lie still, ye thief, and hear the lady
   sing in Welsh.
HOT. I had rather hear Lady, my brach,[3] howl in Irish.
LADY P. Wouldst thou have thy head broken?   235
HOT. No.
LADY P. Then be still.

---

5. I.e., tears from her eyes. "Answer thee": cry
likewise.
6. Musical variation.
7. The dry reeds used as a floor covering in Elizabethan England.

8. Drowsiness.
9. The horses of the sun.
1. The indenture.
2. Capricious, governed by humors.
3. My bitch hound, Lady.

HOT. Neither; 'tis a woman's fault.[4]
LADY P. Now God help thee.
HOT. To the Welsh lady's bed.   240
LADY P. What's that?
HOT. Peace! she sings.

[Here the lady sings a Welsh song.]

HOT. Come, Kate, I'll have your song too.
LADY P. Not mine, in good sooth.[5]
HOT. Not yours, in good sooth! Heart! you swear like a comfitmaker's[6]   245
    wife. "Not you, in good sooth," and "as true as I live," and "as
    God shall mend me," and "as sure as day,"
    And givest such sarcenet[7] surety for thy oaths
    As if thou never walk'st further than Finsbury.
    Swear me, Kate, like a lady as thou art,   250
    A good mouth-filling oath, and leave "in sooth,"
    And such protest of pepper-gingerbread,[8]
    To velvet-guards and Sunday citizens.
    Come, sing.
LADY P. I will not sing.   255
HOT. 'Tis the next way to turn tailor, or be redbreast teacher.[9] An
    the indentures be drawn, I'll away within these two hours; and
    so, come in when ye will.   [Exit.]
GLEND. Come, come, Lord Mortimer, you are as slow
    As hot Lord Percy is on fire to go.   260
    By this our book is drawn; we will but seal,
    And then to horse immediately.
MORT.   With all my heart.   [Exeunt.]

SCENE 2

[Enter the KING, PRINCE OF WALES, and others.]

KING. Lords, give us leave; the Prince of Wales and I
    Must have some private conference; but be near at hand,
    For we shall presently have need of you.   [Exeunt LORDS.]
    I know not whether God will have it so
    For some displeasing service I have done,   5
    That, in his secret doom, out of my blood[1]
    He'll breed revengement and a scourge for me;
    But thou dost in thy passages[2] of life
    Make me believe that thou art only marked
    For the hot vengeance and the rod of heaven   10

---

4. Hotspur sarcastically reverses the usual saying about women and talkativeness.
5. Truth.
6. Confectioner's.
7. Thin silk. Finsbury: a recreation ground outside London, frequented by citizens and their wives on Sundays, but not by ladies of Lady Percy's class.
8. I.e., such tame oaths, as crumbly and unsubstantial as gingerbread. "Velvet-guards": respectable people of the middle class, who wore velvet

stripes on their clothes; "Sunday citizens": city folk out for a stroll on Sunday.
9. I.e., it is the easiest way to become a tailor (supposedly tailors sang at their work) or a person who teaches birds to sing. Hotspur is equally scornful of music and of people who work for a living.
1. Unknown judgment, through my son.
2. Actions.

To punish my mistreadings.[3] Tell me else,
Could such inordinate and low desires,
Such poor, such bare, such lewd,[4] such mean attempts,
Such barren pleasures, rude society
As thou art matched withal and grafted to   15
Accompany the greatness of thy blood
And hold their level with thy princely heart?
PRINCE. So please your majesty, I would I could
    Quit[5] all offenses with as clear excuse
    As well as I am doubtless I can purge   20
    Myself of many I am charged withal;
    Yet such extenuation let me beg,
    As, in reproof of many tales devised
    (Which oft the ear of greatness needs must hear)
    By smiling pickthanks[6] and base newsmongers,   25
    I may, for some things true, wherein my youth
    Hath faulty wandered and irregular,
    Find pardon on my true submissiòn.
KING. God pardon thee; yet let me wonder, Harry,
    At thy affections, which doth hold a wing   30
    Quite from the flight of all thy ancestors.
    Thy place in council thou hast rudely lost,
    Which by thy younger brother is supplied,
    And art almost an alien to the hearts
    Of all the court and princes of my blood.   35
    The hope and expectation of thy time[7]
    Is ruined, and the soul of every man
    Prophetically do forethink thy fall.
    Had I so lavish of my presence been,
    So common-hackneyed[8] in the eyes of men,   40
    So stale and cheap to vulgar company,
    Opinion,[9] that did help me to the crown,
    Had still kept loyal to possessiòn
    And left me in reputeless banishment,
    A fellow of no mark nor likelihood.   45
    By being seldom seen, I could not stir
    But like a comet I was wondered at,
    That men would tell their children "This is he";
    Others would say "Where, which is Bullingbrook?"
    And then I stole all courtesy from heaven,   50
    And dressed myself in such humility.
    That I did pluck allegiance from men's hearts,
    Loud shouts and salutations from their mouths,
    Even in the presence of the crownèd king.
    Thus did I keep my person fresh and new,   55
    My presence like a robe pontifical,
    Ne'er seen but wondered at; and so my state,[1]

3. False steps, misdeeds.
4. Low.
5. Acquit myself of. "Doubtless": sure.
6. Flatterers; "newsmongers": tattletales.
7. Lifetime.
8. Cheapened, vulgarized.
9. Popularity, public opinion.
1. Public ceremonial appearances.

Seldom but sumptuous, showed like a feast
And wan[2] by rareness such solemnity.
The skipping king, he ambled up and down   60
With shallow jesters and rash bavin wits,[3]
Soon kindled and soon burnt, carded his state,
Mingled his royalty with cap'ring fools,
Had his great name profanèd with their scorns
And gave his countenance[4] against his name   65
To laugh at gibing boys and stand the push
Of every beardless vain comparative,[5]
Grew a companion to the common streets,
Enfeoffed himself to popularity,[6]
That, being daily swallowed by men's eyes,   70
They surfeited with honey and began
To loathe the taste of sweetness, whereof a little
More than a little is by much too much.
So when he had occasion to be seen
He was but as the cuckoo is in June,[7]   75
Heard, not regarded, seen, but with such eyes
As, sick and blunted with community,[8]
Afford no extraordinary gaze
Such as is bent on sunlike majesty
When it shines seldom in admiring eyes,   80
But rather drowsed and hung their eyelids down,
Slept in his face[9] and rendered such aspèct
As cloudy men use to their adversaries,
Being with his presence glutted, gorged, and full.
And in that very line, Harry, standest thou,   85
For thou hast lost thy princely privilege
With vile participation.[1] Not an eye
But is a-weary of thy common sight,
Save mine, which hath desired to see thee more,
Which now doth that I would not have it do,   90
Make blind itself with foolish tenderness.
PRINCE. I shall hereafter, my thrice gracious lord,
    Be more myself.
KING.   For all the world
    As thou art to this hour was Richard then
    When I from France set foot at Ravenspurgh,   95
    And even as I was then is Percy now.

---

2. Won. "Such solemnity": i.e., the greatest possible majestic effect (an intensive use of "such").
King Henry's theory of public relations is of course
not based upon the assumption of a democratic
society.
3. "Rash": quick; "bavin": brushwood; the image
is explained in the next line. "Carded his state":
degraded his royal dignity; "card" also means "to
adulterate wine."
4. Authority; "name": reputation.

5. Shallow satirical pretender to wit.
6. Made himself the common property of the
public.
7. The cuckoo is noticed in April, when its song
is first heard; by June it is commonplace.
8. Commonness.
9. I.e., yawned in his face. "Aspect": looks;
"cloudy": sullen.
1. Association with vile companions.

Now, by my scepter and my soul to boot,
He hath more worthy interest to the state
Than thou the shadow of succession;[2]
For of no right, nor color like to right,   100
He doth fill fields with harness in the realm,
Turns head against the lion's armèd jaws,[3]
And, being no more in debt to years than thou,
Leads ancient lords and reverend bishops on
To bloody battles and to bruising arms.   105
What never-dying honor hath he got
Against renownèd Douglas! whose high deeds,
Whose hot incursions and great name in arms
Holds from all soldiers chief majority
And military title capital[4]   110
Through all the kingdoms that acknowledge Christ.
Thrice hath this Hotspur, Mars in swaddling clothes,
This infant warrior, in his enterprises
Discomfited great Douglas, ta'en him once,
Enlargèd[5] him and made a friend of him,   115
To fill the mouth of deep defiance up[6]
And shake the peace and safety of our throne.
And what say you to this? Percy, Northumberland,
The Archbishop's grace of York, Douglas, Mortimer,
Capitulate[7] against us and are up.   120
But wherefore do I tell these news to thee?
Why, Harry, do I tell thee of my foes,
Which art my nearest and dearest enemy?
Thou that art like enough through vassal fear,
Base inclinatiòn and the start of spleen,[8]   125
To fight against me under Percy's pay,
To dog his heels and curtsy at his frowns,
To show how much thou art degenerate.
PRINCE. Do not think so; you shall not find it so;
And God forgive them that so much have swayed   130
Your majesty's good thoughts away from me.
I will redeem all this on Percy's head
And in the closing of some glorious day
Be bold to tell you that I am your son,
When I will wear a garment all of blood   135
And stain my favors[9] in a bloody mask,
Which, washed away, shall scour my shame with it;
And that shall be the day, whene'er it lights,

---

2. I.e., Hotspur's claim to the throne is more solid,
because of his achievements, than is Hal's, which
rests only on shadowy rights of succession by birth.
"Color": false pretense.
3. I.e., takes military action against the king's army.
"Harness": armor.
4. Has the greatest reputation among soldiers.

"Incursions": raids; "majority": superiority.
5. Freed.
6. I.e., to make the voice of defiance full in volume.
7. Raise a head, revolt.
8. Unreasoning impulse.
9. Features.

That this same child of honor and renown,
This gallant Hotspur, this all-praisèd knight,   140
And your unthought-of Harry chance to meet.
For every honor sitting on his helm—
Would they were multitudes, and on my head
My shames redoubled!—for the time will come
That I shall make this northern youth exchange   145
His glorious deeds for my indignities.
Percy is but my factor,[1] good my lord,
To engross up glorious deeds on my behalf,
And I will call him to so strict account,
That he shall render every glory up,   150
Yea, even the slightest worship[2] of his time,
Or I will tear the reckoning from his heart.
This in the name of God I promise here,
The which if He be pleased I shall perform,
I do beseech your majesty, may salve   155
The long-grown wounds of my intemperance;
If not, the end of life cancels all bands,[3]
And I will die a hundred thousand deaths
Ere break the smallest parcel of this vow.

KING. A hundred thousand rebels die in this;   160
  Thou shalt have charge and sovereign trust herein.

    [*Enter* BLUNT.]

How now, good Blunt? thy looks are full of speed.

BLUNT. So hath the business that I come to speak of.
  Lord Mortimer of Scotland hath sent word
  That Douglas and the English rebels met   165
  The eleventh of this month at Shrewsbury;
  A mighty and a fearful head[4] they are,
  If promises be kept on every hand,
  As ever offered foul play in a state.

KING. The Earl of Westmoreland set forth today,   170
  With him my son, Lord John of Lancaster,
  For this advertisement[5] is five days old.
  On Wednesday next, Harry, you shall set forward;
  On Thursday we ourselves will march. Our meeting
  Is Bridgenorth and, Harry, you shall march   175
  Through Gloucestershire, by which account,[6]
  Our business valued, some twelve days hence
  Our general forces at Bridgenorth shall meet.
  Our hands are full of business: let's away;
  Advantage feeds him fat while men delay.[7]   [*Exeunt.*]   180

1. Agent; "engross up": collect, acquire.
2. Honor.
3. Bonds, debts.
4. Power.
5. News.

6. Method. "Our business valued": according to estimates.
7. I.e., the rebels' "advantage" (opportunity) grows as the king's men delay.

scene 3

[*Enter* FALSTAFF *and* BARDOLPH.]

FAL. Bardolph, am I not fall'n away vilely since this last action?[8] do
I not bate? do I not dwindle? Why, my skin hangs about me like
an old lady's loose gown; I am withered like an old applejohn.[9]
Well, I'll repent, and that suddenly, while I am in some liking;
I shall be out of heart shortly, and then I shall have no strength   5
to repent. An I have not forgotten what the inside of a church is
made of, I am a peppercorn, a brewer's horse. The inside of a
church! Company, villainous company, hath been the spoil of
me.

BARD. Sir John, you are so fretful you cannot live long.   10

FAL. Why, there is it; come sing me a bawdy song, make me merry.
I was as virtuously given as a gentleman need to be: virtuous
enough: swore little; diced not above seven times a week; went to
a bawdyhouse not above once in a quarter—of an hour; paid
money that I borrowed three or four times; lived well and in good   15
compass; and now I live out of all order, out of all compass.

BARD. Why, you are so fat, Sir John, that you must needs be out of
all compass, out of all reasonable compass, Sir John.

FAL. Do thou amend thy face, and I'll amend my life; thou art our
admiral,[1] thou bearest the lantern in the poop, but 'tis in the   20
nose of thee; thou art the Knight of the Burning Lamp.

BARD. Why, Sir John, my face does you no harm.

FAL. No, I'll be sworn; I make as good use of it as many a man doth
of a death's-head or a *memento mori*.[2] I never see thy face but I
think upon hell-fire and Dives[3] that lived in purple, for there he   25
is in his robes, burning, burning. If thou wert any way given to
virtue, I would swear by thy face; my oath should be "By this
fire, that's God's angel"; but thou art altogether given over, and
wert indeed, but for the light in thy face, the son of utter darkness. When thou ran'st up Gadshill in the night to catch my   30
horse, if I did not think thou hadst been an *ignis fatuus*[4] or a ball
of wildfire, there's no purchase in money. O, thou art a perpetual triumph,[5] an everlasting bonfire light! Thou hast saved me a
thousand marks in links[6] and torches, walking with thee in the
night betwixt tavern and tavern, but the sack that thou hast drunk   35
me would have bought me lights as good cheap at the dearest
chandler's[7] in Europe. I have maintained that salamander of yours
with fire any time this two and thirty years, God reward me for
it.

BARD. 'Sblood, I would my face were in your belly!   40

FAL. God-a-mercy! so should I be sure to be heartburnt.

---

8. I.e., the Gadshill robbery; "bate": lose weight.
9. A keeping apple with a wrinkled skin. "In some
liking": in good condition, in the mood.
1. Flagship.
2. I.e., a skull or some other reminder of death.
3. The rich man who would not give food to Lazarus and was punished in hell for it. See Luke

16.19–31.
4. Will-o'-the-wisp; "wildfire": a firework used for
military purposes.
5. Illumination at a public festival.
6. Small torches carried at night.
7. Candlemaker's. "Salamanders" were lizards that
supposedly lived in fire and ate it.

[*Enter* HOSTESS.]

How now, Dame Partlet[8] the hen! have you inquired yet who
picked my pocket?

HOST. Why, Sir John, what do you think, Sir John? do you think I
keep thieves in my house? I have searched, I have inquired, so   45
has my husband, man by man, boy by boy, servant by servant;
the tithe[9] of a hair was never lost in my house before.

FAL. Ye lie, hostess; Bardolph was shaved and lost many a hair, and
I'll be sworn my pocket was picked. Go to, you are a woman,
go.   50

HOST. Who, I? no, I defy thee; God's light, I was never called so in
mine own house before.

FAL. Go to, I know you well enough.

HOST. No, Sir John; you do not know me, Sir John. I know you,
Sir John; you owe me money, Sir John, and now you pick a   55
quarrel to beguile me of it; I bought you a dozen of shirts to your
back.

FAL. Dowlas,[1] filthy dowlas; I have given them away to bakers' wives,
and they have made bolters of them.

HOST. Now, as I am a true woman, holland[2] of eight shillings an   60
ell. You owe money here besides, Sir John, for your diet and by-
drinkings,[3] and money lent you, four and twenty pound.

FAL. He had his part of it; let him pay.

HOST. He? alas, he is poor; he hath nothing.

FAL. How! poor? look upon his face; what call you rich? let them   65
coin his nose, let them coin his cheeks; I'll not pay a denier.[4]
What, will you make a younker of me? shall I not take mine ease
in mine inn but I shall have my pocket picked? I have lost a seal
ring of my grandfather's worth forty mark.[5]

HOST. O Jesu, I have heard the prince tell him I know not how oft   70
that ring was copper.

FAL. How! the prince is a Jack,[6] a sneak-up; 'sblood, an he were
here, I would cudgel him like a dog if he would say so.

[*Enter the* PRINCE ⟨*and* POINS⟩, *marching, and* FALSTAFF
meets them playing upon his truncheon like a fife.]

How now, lad, is the wind in that door, i' faith? must we all
march?   75

BARD. Yea, two and two, Newgate fashion.[7]

HOST. My lord, I pray you hear me.

PRINCE. What say'st thou, Mistress Quickly? How doth thy husband? I love him well; he is an honest man.

HOST. Good my lord, hear me.   80

FAL. Prithee let her alone, and list to me.

PRINCE. What say'st thou, Jack?

FAL. The other night I fell asleep here behind the arras and had my

---

8. A nickname from the hen in Chaucer's Nun's
Priest's Tale; in Shakespeare's time a conventional
name for a scolding woman.
9. Tenth part.
1. A coarse cloth. "Bolters": sieves for flour.
2. Fine linen; "ell": 45 inches.

3. Drinks between meals.
4. French penny, worth a tenth of an English
penny. "Younker": youngster, novice.
5. A mark was worth two thirds of a pound.
6. Rascal; "sneak-up": a sneak.
7. Chained together, like prisoners at Newgate.

pocket picked; this house is turned bawdyhouse, they pick pockets.

85

PRINCE. What didst thou lose, Jack?

FAL. Wilt thou believe me, Hal? three or four bonds of forty pound apiece, and a seal ring of my grandfather's.

PRINCE. A trifle, some eightpenny matter.

HOST. So I told him, my lord, and I said I heard your grace say so; and, my lord, he speaks most vilely of you, like a foulmouthed man as he is, and said he would cudgel you.

90

PRINCE. What, he did not?

HOST. There's neither faith, truth, nor womanhood in me else.

FAL. There's no more faith in thee than in a stewed prune,[8] nor no more truth in thee than in a drawn fox, and for womanhood Maid Marian may be the deputy's wife of the ward to thee.[9] Go, you thing, go.

95

HOST. Say, what thing, what thing?

FAL. What thing! why, a thing to thank God on.

100

HOST. I am no thing to thank God on, I would thou shouldst know it; I am an honest man's wife, and, setting thy knighthood aside,[1] thou art a knave to call me so.

FAL. Setting thy womanhood aside, thou art a beast to say otherwise.

105

HOST. Say, what beast, thou knave, thou?

FAL. What beast? why, an otter.

PRINCE. An otter, Sir John, why an otter?

FAL. Why, she's neither fish nor flesh, a man knows not where to have her.[2]

110

HOST. Thou art an unjust man in saying so; thou or any man knows where to have me, thou knave, thou!

PRINCE. Thou sayest true, hostess, and he slanders thee most grossly.

HOST. So he doth you, my lord, and said this other day you ought[3] him a thousand pound.

115

PRINCE. Sirrah, do I owe you a thousand pound?

FAL. A thousand pound, Hal! A million. Thy love is worth a million; thou owest me thy love.

HOST. Nay, my lord, he called you Jack, and said he would cudgel you.

120

FAL. Did I, Bardolph?

BARD. Indeed, Sir John, you said so.

FAL. Yea, if he said my ring was copper.

PRINCE. I say 'tis copper; darest thou be as good as thy word now?

FAL. Why, Hal, thou knowest, as thou art but man, I dare; but as thou art prince, I fear thee as I fear the roaring of the lion's whelp.

125

PRINCE. And why not as the lion?

---

8. Stewed prunes were commonly served in bawdyhouses, as a supposed protection against venereal disease. "Drawn": hunted.

9. "Maid Marian" was a female character of low morals in the popular Robin Hood plays; a "deputy's wife of the ward" would be a respectable woman.

1. I.e., ignoring, or intending no disrespect to, the rank of knighthood. Falstaff intentionally misunderstands the phrase.

2. I.e., how to understand her. But the Hostess' retort is, unconsciously, equivalent to saying that she is completely promiscuous.

3. Owed.

FAL. The king himself is to be feared as the lion; dost thou think I'll
fear thee as I fear thy father? Nay, an I do, I pray God my girdle[4]   130
break.

PRINCE. O, if it should, how would thy guts fall about thy knees!
But, sirrah, there's no room for faith, truth, nor honesty in this
bosom of thine; it is all filled up with guts and midriff. Charge
an honest woman with picking thy pocket! Why, thou whoreson,   135
impudent, embossed rascal[5] if there were anything in thy pocket
but tavern-reckonings, memorandums of bawdyhouses, and one
poor pennyworth of sugar candy to make thee long-winded, if
thy pocket were enriched with any other injuries but these, I am
a villain. And yet you will stand to it, you will not pocket up   140
wrong; art thou not ashamed?

FAL. Dost thou hear, Hal? thou knowest in the state of innocency
Adam fell, and what should poor Jack Falstaff do in the days of
villainy? Thou seest I have more flesh than another man, and
therefore more frailty. You confess then, you picked my pocket?   145

PRINCE. It appears so by the story.

FAL. Hostess, I forgive thee; go make ready breakfast, love thy husband, look to thy servants, cherish thy guests; thou shalt find me
tractable to any honest reason; thou seest I am pacified still. Nay,
prithee begone. [*Exit* HOSTESS.] Now, Hal, to the news at court;   150
for the robbery, lad, how is that answered?

PRINCE. O, my sweet beef, I must still be good angel to thee; the
money is paid back again.

FAL. O, I do not like that paying back; 'tis a double labor.

PRINCE. I am good friends with my father and may do anything.   155

FAL. Rob me the exchequer the first thing thou doest, and do it
with unwashed hands too.

BARD. Do, my lord.

PRINCE. I have procured thee, Jack, a charge of foot.[6]

FAL. I would it had been of horse. Where shall I find one that can   160
steal well? O for a fine thief, of the age of two and twenty or
thereabouts! I am heinously unprovided. Well, God be thanked
for these rebels, they offend none but the virtuous; I laud them,
I praise them.

PRINCE. Bardolph!   165

BARD. My lord?

PRINCE. Go bear this letter to Lord John of Lancaster, to my brother
John; this to my Lord of Westmoreland. [*Exit* BARDOLPH.] Go,
Poins, to horse, to horse; for thou and I have thirty miles to ride
yet ere dinnertime. [*Exit* POINS.] Jack, meet me tomorrow in the   170
Temple Hall at two o'clock in the afternoon.
There shalt thou know thy charge, and there receive
Money and order for their furniture.[7]
The land is burning, Percy stands on high,
And either we or they must lower lie.   [⟨*Exit.*⟩]   175

---

4. Belt.
5. Swollen rascal; "embossed" was also a technical term in hunting, applied to a deer which was
exhausted and foaming at the mouth.

6. Command of a company of foot-soldiers.
"Horse": cavalry.
7. Furnishings, equipment.

FAL. Rare words, brave world! Hostess, my breakfast, come.
  O, I could wish this tavern were my drum![8]   *Exit.*]

Act 4

SCENE 1

[*Enter* HOTSPUR, WORCESTER, *and* DOUGLAS.]

HOT. Well said, my noble Scot. If speaking truth
  In this fine age were not thought flattery,
  Such attribution should the Douglas have
  As not a soldier of this season's stamp
  Should go so general current[1] through the world.   5
  By God, I cannot flatter; I do defy
  The tongues of soothers,[2] but a braver place
  In my heart's love hath no man than yourself;
  Nay, task me to my word,[3] approve me, lord.
DOUG. Thou art the king of honor;   10
  No man so potent breathes upon the ground
  But I will beard him.[4]
HOT.   Do so, and 'tis well.

[*Enter a* MESSENGER *with letters.*]

  What letters hast thou there?—I can but thank you.
MESS. These letters come from your father.
HOT. Letters from him! why comes he not himself?   15
MESS. He cannot come, my lord; he is grievous sick.
HOT. Zounds! how has he the leisure to be sick
  In such a justling[5] time? Who leads his power?
  Under whose government come they along?
MESS. His letters bears his mind, not I, my lord.   20
WOR. I prithee tell me, doth he keep his bed?
MESS. He did, my lord, four days ere I set forth,
  And at the time of my departure thence
  He was much feared by[6] his physiciáns.
WOR. I would the state of time had first been whole   25
  Ere he by sickness had been visited;
  His health was never better worth than now.
HOT. Sick now! droop now! this sickness doth infect
  The very lifeblood of our enterprise;
  'Tis catching hither, even to our camp.   30
  He writes me here that inward sickness—
  And that his friends by deputation could not
  So soon be drawn,[7] nor did he think it meet
  To lay so dangerous and dear a trust

8. Headquarters.
1. I.e., that not a soldier of this year's coinage should achieve such currency. "Attribution": praise.
2. Flatterers; "braver": more distinguished.
3. Compare my actions with my speech. "Approve": prove, test.

4. I.e., I will take on anybody, however powerful.
5. Turbulent.
6. Feared for by. "State of time": public affairs.
7. Could not quickly be organized under a deputy. "Soul removed": other person.

On any soul removed but on his own.   35
Yet doth he give us bold advertisement
That with our small conjunction[8] we should on
To see how fortune is disposed to us;
For, as he writes, there is no quailing now,
Because the king is certainly possessed[9]   40
Of all our purposes. What say you to it?

WOR. Your father's sickness is a maim to us.

HOT. A perilous gash, a very limb lopped off;
    And yet in faith it is not; his present want[1]
    Seems more than we shall find it. Were it good   45
    To set the exact wealth of all our states
    All at one cast, to set so rich a main[2]
    On the nice hazard of one doubtful hour?
    It were not good, for therein should we read
    The very bottom and the soul of hope,[3]   50
    The very list, the very utmost bound
    Of all our fortunes.

DOUG.   Faith, and so we should,
    Where now remains a sweet reversiòn.[4]
    We may boldly spend upon the hope of what
    Is to come in;   55
    A comfort of retirement[5] lives in this.

HOT. A rendezvous, a home to fly unto,
    If that the devil and mischance look big
    Upon the maidenhead of our affairs.[6]

WOR. But yet I would your father had been here.   60
    The quality and hair[7] of our attempt
    Brooks no division; it will be thought
    By some that know not why he is away
    That wisdom, loyalty, and mere dislike
    Of our proceedings kept the earl from hence.   65
    And think how such an apprehensiòn
    May turn the tide of fearful factiòn[8]
    And breed a kind of question in our cause,
    For well you know we of the off'ring[9] side
    Must keep aloof from strict arbitrement,   70
    And stop all sight-holes, every loop[1] from whence
    The eye of reason may pry in upon us.
    This absence of your father's draws a curtain,
    That shows the ignorant a kind of fear
    Before not dreamt of.

HOT.   You strain too far.   75
    I rather of his absence make this use:
    It lends a luster and more great opinion,

---

8. Unified forces.
9. Informed.
1. Our present awareness of his absence.
2. Stake, in betting; "nice hazard": risky chance.
3. Foundation and essence of our expectations.
"List": limit.
4. A fund to be inherited in the future.

5. Sustaining place to fall back on.
6. I.e., threaten the beginning of our affairs.
7. Character; "brooks": allows.
8. Conspiracy.
9. Challenging. "Arbitrement": investigation.
1. Loophole.

A larger dare to our great enterprise,
Than if the earl were here, for men must think,
If we without his help can make a head   80
To push against a kingdom, with his help
We shall o'erturn it topsy-turvy down.
Yet all goes well, yet all our joints are whole.
DOUG. As heart can think; there is not such a word
Spoke of in Scotland as this term of fear.   85

[Enter SIR RICHARD VERNON.]

HOT. My cousin Vernon, welcome, by my soul!
VER. Pray God my news be worth a welcome, lord.
The Earl of Westmoreland, seven thousand strong,
Is marching hitherwards; with him Prince John.
HOT. No harm; what more?
VER.   And further I have learned   90
The king himself in person is set forth,
Or hitherwards intended speedily,
With strong and mighty preparation.
HOT. He shall be welcome too. Where is his son,
The nimble-footed madcap Prince of Wales,   95
And his comrades that daft² the world aside
And bid it pass?
VER.   All furnished, all in arms,
All plumed like estridges that with the wind
Bated, like eagles having lately bathed,³
Glittering in golden coats like images,   100
As full of spirit as the month of May,
And gorgeous as the sun at midsummer,
Wanton as youthful goats, wild as young bulls.
I saw young Harry, with his beaver⁴ on,
His cushes on his thighs, gallantly armed,   105
Rise from the ground like feathered Mercury,
And vaulted with such ease into his seat,
As if an angel dropped down from the clouds,
To turn and wind⁵ a fiery Pegasus
And witch the world with noble horsemanship.   110
HOT. No more, no more. Worse than the sun in March
This praise doth nourish agues.⁶ Let them come;
They come like sacrifices in their trim,
And to the fire-eyed maid of smoky war⁷
All hot and bleeding will we offer them;   115
The mailèd Mars shall on his altar sit
Up to the ears in blood. I am on fire
To hear this rich reprisal⁸ is so nigh
And yet not ours. Come, let me taste my horse,

---

2. Push.
3. Eagles were supposed to renew their youth by bathing in the ocean. "Estridges": ostriches; "bated": fluttering their wings.
4. Helmet. "Cushes": cuisses, armor for the thighs.
5. Direct. "Pegasus": winged horse.

6. Fevers. Malaria was thought to be caused by vapors from the marshes, drawn up by the sun in spring.
7. Bellona, goddess of war.
8. Prize.

Who is to bear me like a thunderbolt   120
Against the bosom of the Prince of Wales;
Harry to Harry shall, hot horse to horse,
Meet and ne'er part till one drop down a corse.
O that Glendower were come!
VER.   There is more news;
I learned in Worcester, as I rode along,   125
He cannot draw his power[9] this fourteen days.
DOUG. That's the worst tidings that I hear of yet.
WOR. Aye, by my faith, that bears a frosty sound.
HOT. What may the king's whole battle[1] reach unto?
VER. To thirty thousand.
HOT.   Forty let it be;   130
My father and Glendower being both away,
The powers of us may serve so great a day.
Come, let us take a muster speedily;
Doomsday is near; die all, die merrily.
DOUG. Talk not of dying; I am out of fear   135
Of death or death's hand for this one-half year.   [Exeunt.]

                              SCENE 2

                    [Enter FALSTAFF and BARDOLPH.]

FAL. Bardolph, get thee before to Coventry; fill me a bottle of sack,
     our soldiers shall march through. We'll to Sutton Co'fil'[2] tonight.
BARD. Will you give me money, captain?
FAL. Lay out, lay out.
BARD. This bottle makes an angel.[3]   5
FAL. An if it do, take it for thy labor; and if it make twenty, take
     them all; I'll answer the coinage. Bid my lieutenant Peto meet
     me at town's end.
BARD. I will, captain; farewell.   [Exit.]
FAL. If I be not ashamed of my soldiers, I am a soused gurnet.[4] I   10
     have misused the king's press damnably. I have got in exchange
     of a hundred and fifty soldiers three hundred and odd pounds. I
     press me none but good householders, yeomen's sons, inquire
     me out contracted bachelors, such as had been asked twice on
     the banns,[5] such a commodity[6] of warm slaves as had as lieve   15
     hear the devil as a drum, such as fear the report of a caliver worse
     than a struck fowl or a hurt wild duck. I pressed me none but
     such toasts-and-butter[7] with hearts in their bellies no bigger than
     pins' heads, and they have bought out their services, and now
     my whole charge consists of ancients,[8] corporals, lieutenants,   20
     gentlemen of companies, slaves as ragged as Lazarus in the painted
     cloth where the glutton's dogs licked his sores, and such as indeed

9. Assemble his forces.
1. Army.
2. Sutton Coldfield, about 25 miles from Coventry.
3. Ten shillings' worth.
4. Pickled anchovy. "Press": the draft or impress-
ment of soldiers into service.

5. Notice of approaching marriage, announced
three times publicly in church before the marriage
could take place.
6. "Commodity": collection; "warm": well-to-do;
"caliver": musket.
7. Sissies.
8. Ensigns.

were never soldiers, but discarded unjust serving-men, younger
sons to younger brothers, revolted tapsters and ostlers trade-fall'n,[9]
the cankers of a calm world and a long peace, ten times more   25
dishonorable ragged than an old-fac'd ancient,[1] and such have I
to fill up the rooms of them that have bought out their services,
that you would think that I had a hundred and fifty tattered prodigals lately come from swine-keeping, from eating draff[2] and husks.
A mad fellow met me on the way and told me I had unloaded   30
all the gibbets and pressed the dead bodies. No eye hath seen
such scarecrows. I'll not march through Coventry with them,
that's flat; nay, and the villains march wide betwixt the legs, as if
they had gyves[3] on, for indeed I had the most of them out of
prison. There's but a shirt and a half in all my company, and the   35
half shirt is two napkins tacked together and thrown over the
shoulders like a herald's coat without sleeves, and the shirt, to
say the truth, stolen from my host at Saint Alban's, or the red-
nose innkeeper of Daventry. But that's all one; they'll find linen
enough on every hedge.[4]   40

[*Enter the* PRINCE *and the* LORD OF WESTMORELAND.]

PRINCE. How now, blown Jack! how now, quilt![5]

FAL. What, Hal, how now, mad wag! what a devil dost thou in
    Warwickshire? My good Lord of Westmoreland, I cry you mercy;
    I thought your honor had already been at Shrewsbury.

WEST. Faith, Sir John, 'tis more than time that I were there, and   45
    you too; but my powers are there already. The king, I can tell
    you, looks for us all; we must away all night.

FAL. Tut, never fear me; I am as vigilant as a cat to steal cream.

PRINCE. I think, to steal cream indeed, for thy theft hath already
    made thee butter. But tell me, Jack, whose fellows are these that   50
    come after?

FAL. Mine, Hal, mine.

PRINCE. I did never see such pitiful rascals.

FAL. Tut, tut, good enough to toss,[6] food for powder, food for pow-
    der; they'll fill a pit as well as better; tush, man, mortal men,   55
    mortal men.

WEST. Aye, but, Sir John, methinks they are exceeding poor and
    bare, too beggarly.

FAL. Faith, for their poverty I know not where they had that, and
    for their bareness I am sure they never learned that of me.   60

PRINCE. No, I'll be sworn, unless you call three fingers[7] on the ribs
    bare. But, sirrah, make haste; Percy is already in the field.

FAL. What, is the king encamped?

WEST. He is, Sir John; I fear we shall stay too long.

FAL. Well,   65
    To the latter end of a fray and the beginning of a feast
    Fits a dull fighter and a keen guest.   [*Exeunt.*]

---

9. Hostlers out of work; "cankers": canker worms.
1. Frayed flag.
2. Garbage. The prodigal son, in the Bible, fed
on husks before returning to the paternal board.
3. Leg-irons.

4. Laundry was customarily hung on hedges to dry.
5. Padded material, a substitute for armor.
6. I.e., on a pike, or long spear.
7. Layers of fat. A finger was ¾ of an inch.

SCENE 3

[Enter HOTSPUR, WORCESTER, DOUGLAS, *and* VERNON.]

HOT. We'll fight with him tonight.
WOR.   It may not be.
DOUG. You give him then advantage.
VER.   Not a whit.
HOT. Why say you so? looks he not for supply?
VER. So do we.
HOT.   His is certain, ours is doubtful.
WOR. Good cousin, be advised; stir not tonight.   5
VER. Do not, my lord.
DOUG.   You do not counsel well;
   You speak it out of fear and cold heart.
VER. Do me no slander, Douglas; by my life,
   And I dare well maintain it with my life,
   If well-respected honor[8] bid me on,   10
   I hold as little counsel with weak fear
   As you, my lord, or any Scot that this day lives.
   Let it be seen tomorrow in the battle
   Which of us fears.
DOUG.   Yea, or tonight.
VER.   Content.
HOT. Tonight, say I.   15
VER. Come, come, it may not be. I wonder much,
   Being men of such great leading as you are,
   That you foresee not what impediments
   Drag back our expedition;[9] certain horse
   Of my cousin Vernon's are not yet come up,   20
   Your uncle Worcester's horse came but today,
   And now their pride and mettle is asleep,
   Their courage with hard labor tame and dull,
   That not a horse is half the half of himself.
HOT. So are the horses of the enemy   25
   In general, journey-bated[1] and brought low;
   The better part of ours are full of rest.
WOR. The number of the king exceedeth ours;
   For God's sake, cousin, stay till all come in.

   [The trumpet sounds a parley. Enter SIR WALTER BLUNT.]

BLUNT. I come with gracious offers from the king,   30
   If you vouchsafe me hearing and respect.
HOT. Welcome, Sir Walter Blunt; and would to God
   You were of our determinatìon!
   Some of us love you well, and even those some
   Envy your great deservings and good name   35
   Because you are not of our quality,[2]
   But stand against us like an enemy.

8. Well-considered (not rash, like Hotspur's).   1. Tired from travel.
9. Retard our speed.   2. Fellowship, party.

BLUNT. And God defend[3] but still I should stand so,
    So long as out of limit and true rule
    You stand against anointed majesty.
    But to my charge. The king hath sent to know   40
    The nature of your griefs, and whereupon
    You conjure from the breast of civil peace
    Such bold hostility, teaching his duteous land
    Audacious cruelty. If that the king   45
    Have any way your good deserts forgot,
    Which he confesseth to be manifold,
    He bids you name your griefs, and with all speed
    You shall have your desires with interest
    And pardon absolute for yourself and these   50
    Herein misled by your suggestiòn.[4]
HOT. The king is kind, and well we know the king
    Knows at what time to promise, when to pay.
    My father and my uncle and myself
    Did give him that same royalty he wears;   55
    And when he was not six and twenty strong,
    Sick in the world's regard, wretched and low,
    A poor unminded outlaw sneaking home,
    My father gave him welcome to the shore;
    And when he heard him swear and vow to God   60
    He came but to be Duke of Lancaster,
    To sue his livery[5] and beg his peace,
    With tears of innocency and terms of zeal,
    My father, in kind heart and pity moved,
    Swore him assistance and performed it too.   65
    Now when the lords and barons of the realm
    Perceived Northumberland did lean to him,
    The more and less came in with cap and knee,[6]
    Met him in boroughs, cities, villages,
    Attended him on bridges, stood in lanes,   70
    Laid gifts before him, proffered him their oaths,
    Gave him their heirs as pages, followed him
    Even at the heels in golden multitudes.
    He presently, as greatness knows itself,
    Steps me a little higher than his vow,   75
    Made to my father while his blood was poor
    Upon the naked shore at Ravenspurgh,
    And now, forsooth, takes on him to reform
    Some certain edicts and some strait[7] decrees
    That lie too heavy on the commonwealth,   80
    Cries out upon abuses, seems to weep
    Over his country's wrongs, and by this face,[8]
    This seeming brow of justice, did he win
    The hearts of all that he did angle for;

3. Forbid; "still": always.
4. Temptation.
5. I.e., claim title to his late father's lands (held by King Richard II).
6. Cap in hand and on bended knee; i.e., offering homage.
7. Strict.
8. Pretense.

Proceeded further, cut me off the heads   85
Of all the favorites that the absent king
In deputation left behind him here,
When he was personal[9] in the Irish war.
BLUNT. Tut, I came not to hear this.
HOT.   Then to the point.
    In short time after he deposed the king,   90
    Soon after that deprived him of his life,
    And in the neck of that tasked[1] the whole state;
    To make that worse, suffered his kinsman March
    (Who is, if every owner were well placed,
    Indeed his king) to be engaged[2] in Wales,   95
    There without ransom to lie forfeited;
    Disgraced[3] me in my happy victories,
    Sought to entrap me by intelligence,[4]
    Rated mine uncle from the council board,
    In rage dismissed my father from the court,   100
    Broke oath on oath, committed wrong on wrong,
    And in conclusion drove us to seek out
    This head of safety,[5] and withal to pry
    Into his title, the which we find
    Too indirect for long continuance.   105
BLUNT. Shall I return this answer to the king?
HOT. Not so, Sir Walter; we'll withdraw awhile.
    Go to the king, and let there be impawned[6]
    Some surety for a safe return again,
    And in the morning early shall mine uncle   110
    Bring him our purposes; and so farewell.
BLUNT. I would you would accept of grace and love.
HOT. And may be so we shall.
BLUNT.   Pray God you do.   [Exeunt.]

SCENE 4

[Enter the ARCHBISHOP OF YORK and SIR MICHAEL.]

ARCH. Hie, good Sir Michael; bear this sealèd brief[7]
    With wingèd haste to the lord marshal,
    This to my cousin Scroop, and all the rest
    To whom they are directed. If you knew
    How much they do import you would make haste.   5
SIR M. My good lord,
    I guess their tenor.
ARCH.   Like enough you do.
    Tomorrow, good Sir Michael, is a day
    Wherein the fortune of ten thousand men
    Must bide the touch;[8] for, sir, at Shrewsbury,   10

---

9. Actively participating in person.   5. Army for our safety.
1. I.e., immediately after that, (he) taxed.   6. Pledged; "surety": guarantee.
2. Pawned as a hostage.   7. Letter.
3. I.e., did not favor.   8. Stand the test.
4. Spying; "rated": angrily dismissed.

As I am truly given to understand,
The king with mighty and quick-raisèd power
Meets with Lord Harry; and I fear, Sir Michael,
What with the sickness of Northumberland,
Whose power was in the first proportiòn,[9]   15
And what with Owen Glendower's absence thence,
Who with them was a rated[1] sinew too
And comes not in, o'er-ruled by prophecies—
I fear the power of Percy is too weak
To wage an instant trial with the king.   20

SIR M. Why, my good lord, you need not fear;
    There is Douglas and Lord Mortimer.

ARCH. No, Mortimer is not there.

SIR M. But there is Mordake, Vernon, Lord Harry Percy,
    And there is my Lord of Worcester and a head   25
    Of gallant warriors, noble gentlemen.

ARCH. And so there is; but yet the king hath drawn
    The special head[2] of all the land together:
    The Prince of Wales, Lord John of Lancaster,
    The noble Westmoreland, and warlike Blunt,
    And many more corrivals[3] and dear men   30
    Of estimation and command in arms.

SIR M. Doubt not, my lord, they shall be well opposed.

ARCH. I hope no less, yet needful 'tis to fear,
    And to prevent[4] the worst, Sir Michael, speed;
    For if Lord Percy thrive not, ere the king   35
    Dismiss his power, he means to visit[5] us,
    For he hath heard of our confederacy,
    And 'tis but wisdom to make strong against him;
    Therefore make haste. I must go write again
    To other friends; and so farewell, Sir Michael.   [Exeunt.]   40

Act 5

SCENE 1

[Enter the KING, PRINCE OF WALES, PRINCE JOHN OF LAN-
CASTER, SIR WALTER BLUNT, and FALSTAFF.]

KING. How bloodily the sun begins to peer
    Above yon busky[1] hill! The day looks pale
    At his distemp'rature.[2]

PRINCE.   The southern wind
    Doth play the trumpet to his purposes,[3]
    And by his hollow whistling in the leaves
    Foretells a tempest and a blustering day.   5

KING. Then with the losers let it sympathize,
    For nothing can seem foul to those that win.

---

9. The largest part.
1. Highly regarded.
2. Principal army.
3. Associates; "dear": noble.
4. Forestall.

5. Attack.
1. Wooded.
2. I.e., the sun's illness or malevolence.
3. I.e., the sun's intentions; the southern wind
supports them.

[*The trumpet sounds. Enter* WORCESTER ⟨*and* VERNON.⟩]

How now, my lord of Worcester! 'Tis not well
That you and I should meet upon such terms   10
As now we meet. You have deceived our trust
And made us doff our easy robes of peace,
To crush[4] our old limbs in ungentle steel;
This is not well, my lord, this is not well.
What say you to it? will you again unknit   15
This churlish knot of all-abhorrèd war
And move in that obedient orb[5] again
Where you did give a fair and natural light,
And be no more an exhaled meteor,[6]
A prodigy of fear and a portent   20
Of broachèd mischief to the unborn times?[7]
WOR. Hear me, my liege:
For mine own part I could be well content
To entertain the lag end of my life
With quiet hours, for I do protest   25
I have not sought the day of this dislike.
KING. You have not sought it! how comes it then?
FAL. Rebellion lay in his way, and he found it.
PRINCE. Peace, chewet,[8] peace!
WOR. It pleased your majesty to turn your looks   30
Of favor from myself and all our house,
And yet I must remember[9] you, my lord,
We were the first and dearest of your friends.
For you my staff of office did I break
In Richard's time, and posted day and night   35
To meet you on the way and kiss your hand
When yet you were in place and in account
Nothing so strong and fortunate as I.
It was myself, my brother, and his son
That brought you home and boldly did outdare   40
The dangers of the time. You swore to us,
And you did swear that oath at Doncaster,
That you did nothing purpose 'gainst the state
Nor claim no further than your new-fall'n[1] right,
The seat of Gaunt, dukedom of Lancaster.   45
To this we swore our aid. But in short space
It rained down fortune showering on your head
And such a flood of greatness fell on you,
What with our help, what with the absent king,
What with the injuries of a wanton time,   50
The seeming sufferances[2] that you had borne,

---

4. Enfold, cramp.
5. Regular orbit, as of a planet.
6. Meteors were thought to be made of gas exhaled by a planet and were commonly associated with civil commotion.
7. I.e., of harm or disaster opened up ("broached") to plague the future. Note that "mischief" conveyed a stronger meaning to Shakespeare than it does to us.
8. Chattering bird.
9. Remind.
1. Recently inherited.
2. Sufferings.

And the contrarious winds that held the king
So long in his unlucky Irish wars
That all in England did repute him dead;
And from this swarm of fair advantages   55
You took occasion to be quickly wooed
To gripe the general sway[3] into your hand,
Forgot your oath to us at Doncaster,
And being fed by us you used us so
As that ungentle gull[4] the cuckoo's bird   60
Useth the sparrow, did oppress our nest,
Grew by our feeding to so great a bulk
That even our love durst not come near your sight
For fear of swallowing;[5] but with nimble wing
We were enforced for safety sake to fly   65
Out of your sight and raise this present head,
Whereby we stand opposèd by such means
As you yourself have forged against yourself
By unkind usage, dangerous countenance,[6]
And violation of all faith and troth   70
Sworn to us in your younger enterprise.
KING. These things indeed you have articulate,[7]
Proclaimed at market crosses, read in churches,
To face[8] the garment of rebelliòn
With some fine color that may please the eye   75
Of fickle changelings and poor discontents,
Which gape and rub the elbow at the news
Of hurlyburly innovatiòn;
And never yet did insurrection want
Such water colors to impaint his cause,   80
Nor moody beggars starving for a time
Of pellmell havoc and confusiòn.
PRINCE. In both our armies there is many a soul
Shall pay full dearly for this encounter,
If once they join in trial. Tell your nephew   85
The Prince of Wales doth join with all the world
In praise of Henry Percy; by my hopes,
This present enterprise set off his head,[9]
I do not think a braver gentleman,
More active-valiant or more valiant-young,   90
More daring or more bold, is now alive
To grace this latter age with noble deeds.
For my part, I may speak it to my shame,
I have a truant been to chivalry—
And so I hear he doth account me too—   95
Yet this before my father's majesty:
I am content that he shall take the odds

3. Seize power over the whole state.
4. Rude nestling; the cuckoo hatches its young in
other birds' nests.
5. Being swallowed.

6. Threatening looks.
7. Drawn up in detail.
8. Decorate.
9. Deducted from his account.

Of his great name and estimatìon,
And will, to save the blood on either side,
Try fortune with him in a single fight.   100
KING. And, Prince of Wales, so dare we venture thee,
Albeit considerations infinite
Do make[1] against it. No, good Worcester, no,
We love our people well; even those we love
That are misled upon your cousin's part;   105
And, will they take the offer of our grace,
Both he and they and you, yea, every man
Shall be my friend again and I'll be his.
So tell your cousin, and bring me word
What he will do; but if he will not yield,   110
Rebuke and dread correction wait on[2] us
And they shall do their office. So, be gone;
We will not now be troubled with reply.
We offer fair; take it advisedly.

        [*Exit* WORCESTER ⟨*and* VERNON.⟩]

PRINCE. It will not be accepted, on my life;   115
The Douglas and the Hotspur both together
Are confident against the world in arms.
KING. Hence, therefore, every leader to his charge,
For on their answer will we set on them,
And God befriend us, as our cause is just!   120

        [*Exeunt all but the* PRINCE *and* FALSTAFF.]

FAL. Hal, if thou see me down in the battle and bestride me, so; 'tis
a point of friendship.
PRINCE. Nothing but a colossus can do thee that friendship. Say thy
prayers, and farewell.
FAL. I would 'twere bedtime, Hal, and all well.   125
PRINCE. Why, thou owest God a death.   [⟨*Exit.*⟩]
FAL. 'Tis not due yet; I would be loath to pay him before his day.
What need I be so forward with him that calls not on me? Well,
'tis no matter; honor pricks me on. Yea, but how if honor prick
me off when I come on? How then? can honor set to a leg? No.   130
Or an arm? No. Or take away the grief[3] of a wound? No. Honor
hath no skill in surgery, then? No. What is honor? A word. What
is in that word honor? what is that honor? Air. A trim reckoning![4]
Who hath it? He that died o' Wednesday. Doth he feel it? No.
Doth he hear it? No. 'Tis insensible,[5] then? Yea, to the dead. 135
But will it not live with the living? No. Why? Detraction will not
suffer it. Therefore I'll none of it; Honor is a mere scutcheon.[6]
And so ends my catechism.   [*Exit.*]

1. Weigh.   4. A fine totaling of the bill.
2. Accompany.   5. Not capable of being felt.
3. Pain.   6. A coat of arms, as often put on a tombstone.

SCENE 2

[*Enter* WORCESTER *and* SIR RICHARD VERNON.]

WOR. O no, my nephew must not know, Sir Richard,
　The liberal and kind offer of the king.
VER. 'Twere best he did.
WOR.　　　　　　　Then are we all undone.
　It is not possible, it cannot be,
　The king should keep his word in loving us; 　　　　5
　He will suspect us still and find a time
　To punish this offense in other faults.
　Suspicion all our lives shall be stuck full of eyes,
　For treason is but trusted like the fox
　Who, ne'er so tame, so cherished and locked up, 　10
　Will have a wild trick of his ancestors;
　Look how we can, or sad or merrily,
　Interpretation will misquote[7] our looks,
　And we shall feed like oxen at a stall,
　The better cherished, still the nearer death. 　　15
　My nephew's trespass may be well forgot;
　It hath the excuse of youth and heat of blood
　And an adopted name of privilege,[8]
　A harebrained Hotspur, governed by a spleen.
　All his offenses live upon my head 　　　　　　20
　And on his father's; we did train him on,
　And, his corruption being ta'en from us,[9]
　We, as the spring of all, shall pay for all.
　Therefore, good cousin, let not Harry know
　In any case the offer of the king. 　　　　　　25
VER. Deliver what you will; I'll say 'tis so.
　Here comes your cousin.

[*Enter* HOTSPUR ⟨*and* DOUGLAS.⟩]

HOT. My uncle is returned;
　Deliver up my Lord of Westmoreland.
　Uncle, what news? 　　　　　　　　　　　30
WOR. The king will bid you battle presently.[1]
DOUG. Defy him by the Lord of Westmoreland.
HOT. Lord Douglas, go you and tell him so.
DOUG. Marry, and shall, and very willingly. 　　[*Exit.*]
WOR. There is no seeming mercy in the king. 　　35
HOT. Did you beg any? God forbid!
WOR. I told him gently of our grievances,
　Of his oath-breaking, which he mended thus,
　By now forswearing[2] that he is forsworn;
　He calls us rebels, traitors, and will scourge 　40
　With haughty arms this hateful name in us.

7. Misinterpret.
8. A nickname which gives him privileges.
"Spleen": impetuous temperament.

9. Being attributed to. "Train": entice.
1. Immediately.
2. Swearing falsely.

[*Enter* DOUGLAS.]

DOUG. Arm, gentlemen, to arms! for I have thrown
     A brave defiance in King Henry's teeth,
     And Westmoreland, that was engaged,[3] did hear it,
     Which cannot choose but bring him quickly on.   45
WOR. The Prince of Wales stepped forth before the king,
     And, nephew, challenged you to single fight.
HOT. O, would the quarrel lay upon our heads,
     And that no man might draw short breath today
     But I and Harry Monmouth! Tell me, tell me,   50
     How showed his tasking?[4] seemed it in contempt?
VER. No, by my soul; I never in my life
     Did hear a challenge urged more modestly,
     Unless a brother should a brother dare
     To gentle exercise and proof of arms.   55
     He gave you all the duties[5] of a man,
     Trimmed up your praises with a princely tongue,
     Spoke your deservings like a chronicle,
     Making you ever better than his praise
     By still dispraising praise valued with[6] you;   60
     And, which became him like a prince indeed,
     He made a blushing cital[7] of himself,
     And chid his truant youth with such a grace
     As if he mastered there a double spirit
     Of teaching and of learning instantly.   65
     There did he pause; but let me tell the world,
     If he outlive the envy[8] of this day,
     England did never owe[9] so sweet a hope,
     So much misconstrued in his wantonness.[1]
HOT. Cousin, I think thou art enamoured   70
     On his follies; never did I hear
     Of any prince so wild a liberty.[2]
     But be he as he will, yet once ere night
     I will embrace him with a soldier's arm,
     That he shall shrink under my courtesy.   75
     Arm, arm with speed; and, fellows, soldiers, friends,
     Better consider what you have to do
     Than I, that have not well the gift of tongue,
     Can lift your blood up with persuasiòn.

          [*Enter a* MESSENGER.]

MESS. My lord, here are letters for you.   80
HOT. I cannot read them now.
     O gentlemen, the time of life is short!
     To spend that shortness basely were too long,
     If life did ride upon a dial's point,[3]

3. Held as a hostage.
4. Challenge.
5. Good qualities.
6. Compared to.
7. Mention, recital.
8. Malice.

9. Own.
1. Frivolity.
2. Reckless dissipation.
3. Hand of a clock; "still": always. Hotspur's
meaning (in lines 83–85) is that a base life would
be too long even if it lasted only an hour.

Still ending at the arrival of an hour;   85
And if we live, we live to tread on kings,
If die, brave death when princes die with us!
Now, for our consciences, the arms are fair,
When the intent of bearing them is just.

    [*Enter another* MESSENGER.]

MESS. My lord, prepare; the king comes on apace.   90
HOT. I thank him that he cuts me from my tale,
  For I profess not talking; only this—
  Let each man do his best; and here draw I
  A sword whose temper I intend to stain
  With the best blood that I can meet withal   95
  In the adventure of this perilous day.
  Now, *Esperance! Percy!*[4] and set on.
  Sound all the lofty instruments of war,
  And by that music let us all embrace;
  For, heaven to earth,[5] some of us never shall   100
  A second time do such a courtesy.

    [*The trumpets sound. They embrace and exeunt.*]

SCENE 3

    [*The* KING *enters with his power. Alarum*[6] *to the battle.*
    Then enter DOUGLAS *and* SIR WALTER BLUNT.]

BLUNT. What is thy name, that in the battle thus
  Thou crossest me? what honor dost thou seek
  Upon my head?
DOUG.   Know then, my name is Douglas,
  And I do haunt thee in the battle thus
  Because some tell me that thou art a king.[7]   5
BLUNT. They tell thee true.
DOUG. The Lord of Stafford dear[8] today hath bought
  Thy likeness, for instead of thee, King Harry,
  This sword hath ended him; so shall it thee,
  Unless thou yield thee as my prisoner.   10
BLUNT. I was not born a yielder, thou proud Scot,
  And thou shalt find a king that will revenge
  Lord Stafford's death.   [*They fight.* DOUGLAS *kills* BLUNT.]

    [*Enter* HOTSPUR.]

HOT. O Douglas, hadst thou fought at Holmedon thus,
  I never had triumphed upon a Scot.   15
DOUG. All's done, all's won; here breathless lies the king.
HOT. Where?
DOUG. Here.
HOT. This, Douglas? No, I know this face full well;
  A gallant knight he was, his name was Blunt;   20

---

4. Hope, Percy! (the family motto).
5. I.e., the odds are heaven to earth that.
6. Trumpet signal.
7. Blunt and others are dressed to look like the king.
8. Expensively.

Semblably furnished like the king himself.

DOUG. Ah fool, go with thy soul whither it goes!
A borrowed title hast thou bought too dear;
Why didst thou tell me that thou wert a king?

HOT. The king hath many marching in his coats. 25

DOUG. Now, by my sword, I will kill all his coats;
I'll murder all his wardrobe, piece by piece,
Until I meet the king.

HOT.   Up and away!
Our soldiers stand full fairly for the day.   [Exeunt.]

              [Alarum. Enter FALSTAFF alone.]

FAL. Though I could 'scape shot-free[9] at London, I fear the shot   30
here; here's no scoring but upon the pate. Soft, who are you? Sir
Walter Blunt; there's honor for you, here's no vanity! I am as hot
as molten lead, and as heavy too; God keep lead out of me! I
need no more weight than mine own bowels. I have led my
ragamuffins where they are peppered; there's not three of my   35
hundred and fifty left alive, and they are for the town's end, to
beg during life. But who comes here?

              [Enter the PRINCE.]

PRINCE. What, stand'st thou idle here? lend me thy sword;
Many a nobleman lies stark and stiff
Under the hoofs of vaunting enemies,   40
Whose deaths are yet unrevenged; I prithee, lend me thy sword.

FAL. O Hal, I prithee give me leave to breathe awhile. Turk Gregory[1]
never did such deeds in arms as I have done this day. I have paid
Percy, I have made him sure.

PRINCE. He is indeed, and living to kill thee. I prithee, lend me thy   45
sword.

FAL. Nay, before God, Hal, if Percy be alive, thou get'st not my
sword; but take my pistol if thou wilt.

PRINCE. Give it me; what, is it in the case?

FAL. Aye, Hal; 'tis hot, 'tis hot; there's that will sack a city.   50

     [The PRINCE draws it out, and finds it to be a bottle of sack.]

PRINCE. What, is it a time to jest and dally now?

              [He throws the bottle at him. Exit.]

FAL. Well, if Percy be alive, I'll pierce him. If he do come in my
way, so; if he do not, if I come in his willingly, let him make a
carbonado[2] of me. I like not such grinning honor as Sir Walter
hath; give me life, which if I can save, so; if not, honor comes   55
unlooked for, and there's an end.   [Exit.]

---

9. Scot-free, without paying the bill at a tavern;
"scoring" continues the pun; it means (1) marking
up a charge, (2) cutting with a sword.
1. Falstaff combines Pope Gregory VII, of whom

fantastic stories were told, with "Turk" (the Turks
were noted for ferocity).
2. A cubed steak.

SCENE 4

[*Alarum. Excursions.*[3] *Enter the* KING, *the* PRINCE, PRINCE
JOHN OF LANCASTER, *and* EARL OF WESTMORELAND.]

KING. I prithee,
  Harry, withdraw thyself; thou bleed'st too much.
  Lord John of Lancaster, go you with him.
LAN. Not I, my lord, unless I did bleed too.
PRINCE. I beseech your majesty, make up,[4]   5
  Lest your retirement do amaze your friends.
KING. I will do so.
  My Lord of Westmoreland, lead him to his tent.
WEST. Come, my lord, I'll lead you to your tent.
PRINCE. Lead me, my lord? I do not need your help,   10
  And God forbid a shallow scratch should drive
  The Prince of Wales from such a field as this,
  Where stained nobility lies trodden on,
  And rebels' arms triumph in massacres!
LAN. We breathe too long; come, cousin Westmoreland,   15
  Our duty this way lies; for God's sake, come.

      [⟨*Exeunt* PRINCE JOHN *and* WESTMORELAND.⟩]

PRINCE. By God, thou hast deceived me, Lancaster;
  I did not think thee lord of such a spirit.
  Before, I loved thee as a brother, John,
  But now I do respect thee as my soul.   20
KING. I saw him hold Lord Percy at the point
  With lustier maintenance than I did look for
  Of such an ungrown warrior.
PRINCE.   O, this boy
  Lends mettle to us all!   [*Exit.*]
      [*Enter* DOUGLAS.]

DOUG. Another king! they grow like Hydra's heads.[5]   25
  I am the Douglas, fatal to all those
  That wear those colors on them; what art thou,
  That counterfeit'st the person of a king?
KING. The king himself, who, Douglas, grieves at heart
  So many of his shadows[6] thou hast met   30
  And not the very king. I have two boys
  Seek Percy and thyself about the field,
  But seeing thou fall'st on me so luckily
  I will assay thee; so defend thyself.
DOUG. I fear thou art another counterfeit,   35
  And yet, in faith, thou bearest thee like a king;
  But mine I am sure thou art, whoe'er thou be.
  And thus I win thee.

3. Brief appearances and exits of soldiers fighting.   faster than they could be cut off.
4. Advance; "amaze": dismay.   6. Likenesses.
5. The heads of this fabulous monster grew back

[*They fight; the* KING *being in danger, enter* PRINCE OF WALES.]

PRINCE. Hold up thy head, vile Scot, or thou art like
Never to hold it up again! the spirits   40
Of valiant Shirley, Stafford, Blunt, are in my arms;
It is the Prince of Wales that threatens thee,
Who never promiseth but he means to pay.

[*They fight;* DOUGLAS *flieth.*]

Cheerly, my lord; how fares your grace?
Sir Nicholas Gawsey hath for succor sent,   45
And so hath Clifton; I'll to Clifton straight.
KING. Stay, and breathe awhile.
Thou hast redeemed thy lost opinìon,
And showed thou makest some tender of[7] my life
In this fair rescue thou hast brought to me.   50
PRINCE. O God, they did me too much injury
That ever said I hearkened for your death.
If it were so, I might have let alone
The insulting hand of Douglas over you,
Which would have been as speedy in your end   55
As all the poisonous potions in the world
And saved the treacherous labor of your son.
KING. Make up to Clifton; I'll to Sir Nicholas Gawsey.   [*Exit.*]

[*Enter* HOTSPUR.]

HOT. If I mistake not, thou art Harry Monmouth.
PRINCE. Thou speak'st as if I would deny my name.   60
HOT. My name is Harry Percy.
PRINCE.   Why then I see
A very valiant rebel of the name.
I am the Prince of Wales, and think not, Percy,
To share with me in glory any more:
Two stars keep not their motion in one sphere,[8]   65
Nor can one England brook a double reign
Of Harry Percy and the Prince of Wales.
HOT. Nor shall it, Harry, for the hour is come
To end the one of us; and would to God
Thy name in arms were now as great as mine!   70
PRINCE. I'll make it greater ere I part from thee,
And all the budding honors on thy crest
I'll crop to make a garland for my head.
HOT. I can no longer brook thy vanities.   [*They fight.*]

[*Enter* FALSTAFF.]

FAL. Well said, Hal, to it, Hal! Nay, you shall find no boy's play   75
here, I can tell you.

[*Enter* DOUGLAS: *he fighteth with* FALSTAFF. *who falls down*

7. I.e., you have some concern for. "Opinion":   8. Orbit. "Brook": endure.
reputation.

as if he were dead. ⟨*Exit* DOUGLAS.⟩ *The* PRINCE *killeth* PERCY.]

HOT. O Harry, thou hast robbed me of my youth!
    I better brook the loss of brittle life
    Than those proud titles thou hast won of me;
    They wound my thoughts worse than thy sword my flesh; 80
    But thought's the slave of life, and life time's fool,
    And time, that takes survey of all the world,
    Must have a stop. O, I could prophesy,
    But that the earthy and cold hand of death
    Lies on my tongue; no, Percy, thou art dust,   85
    And food for—   [⟨*Dies.*⟩]
PRINCE. For worms, brave Percy; fare thee well, great heart!
    Ill-weaved ambition, how much art thou shrunk!
    When that this body did contain a spirit
    A kingdom for it was too small a bound,   90
    But now two paces of the vilest earth
    Is room enough; this earth that bears thee dead
    Bears not alive so stout[9] gentleman.
    If thou wert sensible of courtesy,
    I should not make so dear[1] show of zeal;   95
    But let my favors hide thy mangled face[2]
    And, even in thy behalf, I'll thank myself
    For doing these fair rites of tenderness.
    Adieu, and take thy praise with thee to heaven;
    Thy ignominy sleep with thee in the grave,   100
    But not remembered in thy epitaph!

    [*He spieth* FALSTAFF *on the ground.*]

    What, old acquaintance, could not all this flesh
    Keep in a little life? Poor Jack, farewell;
    I could have better spared a better man.
    O, I should have a heavy miss of thee,   105
    If I were much in love with vanity![3]
    Death hath not struck so fat a deer today,
    Though many dearer,[4] in this bloody fray.
    Emboweled will I see thee by and by;
    Till then in blood by noble Percy lie.   [*Exit.*] 110
FAL. [*rising up*] Emboweled! if thou embowel me today, I'll give
    you leave to powder[5] me and eat me tomorrow. 'Sblood, 'twas
    time to counterfeit, or that hot termagant[6] Scot had paid me scot
    and lot too. Counterfeit? I lie, I am no counterfeit; to die is to be
    a counterfeit, for he is but the counterfeit of a man who hath not 115
    the life of a man; but to counterfeit dying when a man thereby
    liveth is to be no counterfeit, but the true and perfect image of
    life indeed. The better part[7] of valor is discretion, in the which
    better part I have saved my life. Zounds, I am afraid of this gun-

9. Valiant.
1. Open.
2. Prince Hal here covers Hotspur's face with a scarf.
3. Frivolity.

4. Nobler. "Emboweled": embalmed.
5. Pickle.
6. Violent; "scot and lot": completely.
7. Quality, not "portion."

powder Percy, though he be dead; how if he should counterfeit   120
too and rise? By my faith, I am afraid he would prove the better
counterfeit. Therefore I'll make him sure; yea, and I'll swear I
killed him. Why may not he rise as well as I? Nothing confutes
me but eyes, and nobody sees me. Therefore, sirrah [*stabbing
him*], with a new wound in your thigh, come you along with   125
me.

> [*He takes up* HOTSPUR *on his back.*]
> [*Enter the* PRINCE *and* JOHN OF LANCASTER.]

PRINCE. Come, brother John, full bravely hast thou fleshed[8]
  Thy maiden sword.
LAN.   But soft, whom have we here?
  Did you not tell me this fat man was dead?
PRINCE. I did; I saw him dead,   130
  Breathless and bleeding on the ground. Art thou alive?
  Or is it fantasy[9] that plays upon our eyesight?
  I prithee speak; we will not trust our eyes
  Without our ears; thou art not what thou seem'st.
FAL. No, that's certain, I am not a double man; but if I be not Jack   135
  Falstaff, then am I a Jack.[1] There is Percy [*throwing the body
  down*]; if your father will do me any honor, so; if not, let him kill
  the next Percy himself. I look to be either earl or duke, I can
  assure you.
PRINCE. Why, Percy I killed myself and saw thee dead.   140
FAL. Didst thou? Lord, Lord, how this world is given to lying! I
  grant you I was down and out of breath, and so was he; but we
  rose both at an instant and fought a long hour by Shrewsbury
  clock. If I may be believed, so; if not, let them that should reward
  valor bear the sin upon their own heads. I'll take it upon my   145
  death, I gave him this wound in the thigh; if the man were alive
  and would deny it, zounds, I would make him eat a piece of my
  sword.
LAN. This is the strangest tale that ever I heard.
PRINCE. This is the strangest fellow, brother John.   150
  Come, bring your luggage nobly on your back;
  For my part, if a lie may do thee grace,
  I'll gild it with the happiest terms I have.

> [*A retreat is sounded.*]

  The trumpet sounds retreat;[2] the day is ours.
  Come, brother, let us to the highest[3] of the field,   155
  To see what friends are living, who are dead.

> [*Exeunt ⟨*PRINCE OF WALES *and* LANCASTER.⟩]

FAL. I'll follow, as they say, for reward. He that rewards me, God
  reward him! If I do grow great,[4] I'll grow less, for I'll purge and
  leave sack, and live cleanly as a nobleman should do. [*Exit.*]

---

8. Initiated.
9. Illusion.
1. I.e., a worthless fellow.
2. The signal to stop pursuit of the defeated enemy.

3. Highest part.
4. I.e., become "either earl or duke." "Purge": take
cleansing medicines.

SCENE 5

[*The trumpets sound. Enter the* KING, PRINCE OF WALES,
PRINCE JOHN OF LANCASTER, EARL OF WESTMORELAND, *with*
WORCESTER *and* VERNON *prisoners.*]

KING. Thus ever did rebellion find rebuke,
  Ill-spirited Worcester, did not we send grace,
  Pardon, and terms of love to all of you?
  And wouldst thou turn our offers contrary,
  Misuse the tenor of thy kinsman's trust?   5
  Three knights upon our party slain today,
  A noble earl and many a creature else
  Had been alive this hour,
  If like a Christian thou hadst truly borne
  Betwixt our armies true intelligence.   10
WOR. What I have done my safety urged me to,
  And I embrace this fortune patiently,
  Since not to be avoided it falls on me.
KING. Bear Worcester to the death and Vernon too;
  Other offenders we will pause upon.   15

[*Exeunt* WORCESTER *and* VERNON ⟨*guarded.*⟩]

  How goes the field?
PRINCE. The noble Scot, Lord Douglas, when he saw
  The fortune of the day quite turned from him,
  The noble Percy slain, and all his men
  Upon the foot of fear,[5] fled with the rest,   20
  And falling from a hill he was so bruised
  That the pursuers took him. At my tent
  The Douglas is, and I beseech your grace
  I may dispose of him.
KING.   With all my heart.
PRINCE. Then, brother John of Lancaster, to you   25
  This honorable bounty shall belong;
  Go to the Douglas and deliver him
  Up to his pleasure, ransomless and free;
  His valor shown upon our crests today
  Hath taught us how to cherish such high deeds   30
  Even in the bosom of our adversaries.
LAN. I thank your grace for this high courtesy,
  Which I shall give away immediately.
KING. Then this remains, that we divide our power.
  You, son John and my cousin Westmoreland,   35
  Towards York shall bend you with your dearest[6] speed
  To meet Northumberland and the prelate Scroop,
  Who, as we hear, are busily in arms;
  Myself and you, son Harry, will towards Wales
  To fight with Glendower and the Earl of March.   40

---

5. Fleeing in panic.   6. Greatest.

Rebellion in this land shall lose his sway,
Meeting the check[7] of such another day;
And since this business so fair is done,
Let us not leave till all our own be won.   [*Exeunt.*]

1598

7. (1) Hindrance, (2) rebuke.

THOMAS NASHE
1567–1601

Nashe, a Cambridge graduate, was a versatile writer of controversial pamphlets, satire, plays, a novel, and lyric verse. He was one of the university wits who came to London and wrote for the stage and the press. They lived short and precarious lives: Nashe was about thirty-three when he died; his friend Christopher Marlowe died at twenty-nine, George Peele at thirty, and Robert Greene at thirty-two. Nashe's personal enemy was an older man, Gabriel Harvey, Spenser's friend; with him he exchanged a series of vituperative and slanderous pamphlets in which Nashe's talent for invective was exploited to the fullest, until the ecclesiastical authorities ordered, in June 1599, that "all Nashe's books and Doctor Harvey's books be taken wheresoever they may be found and that none of their books be ever printed hereafter."

Nashe's picaresque narrative, *The Unfortunate Traveler, or the Life of Jack Wilton*, is a rambling account of escapades all over Europe, including some fictional exploits attributed to the poet Surrey. He wrote a festive comedy, *Summer's Last Will and Testament*; an attack upon women called *The Anatomy of Absurdity*; an attack on social abuses of every kind entitled *Pierce Penniless His Supplication to the Devil*; and a strident comparison between the sins of the Jews which led to the destruction of Jerusalem and the current morals and manners of London, called *Christ's Tears Over Jerusalem*. Nashe's outlook, like that of many satirists, was conservative: he praised the past in comparison with the present. But his prose style sometimes sounds quite modern. It is headlong, impatient, colloquial, and vivid. One of his own phrases best describes it: "No wind that blows strong but is boisterous."

Spring, the Sweet Spring[1]

Spring, the sweet spring, is the year's pleasant king,
Then blooms each thing, then maids dance in a ring,
Cold doth not sting, the pretty birds do sing:
Cuckoo, jug-jug, pu-we, to-witta-woo![2]

1. This and the following lyric are from *A Pleasant Comedy Called Summer's Last Will and Testament*, acted before the archbishop of Canterbury in his palace at Croydon in 1592, and published in 1600.
2. The calls of the cuckoo, the nightingale, the lapwing, and the owl respectively.

The palm and may make country houses gay,   5
Lambs frisk and play, the shepherds pipe all day,
And we hear aye birds tune this merry lay:
    Cuckoo, jug-jug, pu-we, to-witta-woo!

The fields breathe sweet, the daisies kiss our feet,
Young lovers meet, old wives a-sunning sit,   10
In every street these tunes our ears do greet:
    Cuckoo, jug-jug, pu-we, to-witta-woo!
      Spring, the sweet spring!

1592   1600

A Litany in Time of Plague

Adieu, farewell, earth's bliss;
This world uncertain is;
Fond[1] are life's lustful joys;
Death proves them all but toys;[2]
None from his darts can fly;   5
I am sick, I must die.
    Lord, have mercy on us!

Rich men, trust not in wealth,
Gold cannot buy you health;
Physic himself must fade.   10
All things to end are made,
The plague full swift goes by;
I am sick, I must die.
    Lord, have mercy on us!

Beauty is but a flower
Which wrinkles will devour;   15
Brightness falls from the air;
Queens have died young and fair;
Dust hath closèd Helen's eye.
I am sick, I must die.   20
    Lord, have mercy on us!

Strength stoops unto the grave,
Worms feed on Hector brave;
Swords may not fight with fate,
Earth still holds ope her gate.   25
"Come, come!" the bells do cry.
I am sick, I must die.
    Lord, have mercy on us.

1. Foolish.   2. Trifles.

Wit with his wantonness
Tasteth death's bitterness;　　　　　　　　　　30
Hell's executioner
Hath no ears for to hear
What vain art can reply.
I am sick, I must die.
　　Lord, have mercy on us.　　　　　　　　　35

Haste, therefore, each degree,
To welcome destiny;
Heaven is our heritage,
Earth but a player's stage;
Mount we unto the sky.　　　　　　　　　　40
I am sick, I must die.
　　Lord, have mercy on us.

1592　　　　　　　　　　　　　　　　　　　1600

From Pierce Penniless, His Supplication to the Devil

An Invective Against Enemies of Poetry

With the enemies of poetry I care not if I have a bout, and those are they that term our best writers but babbling ballad-makers, holding them fantastical fools, that have wit but cannot tell how to use it. I myself have been so censured among some dull-headed divines,[1] who deem it no more cunning to write an exquisite poem than to preach pure Calvin or distill the juice of a commentary in a quarter sermon.[2] Prove it when you will, you slow-spirited Saturnists,[3] that have nothing but the pilferies of your pen to polish an exhortation withal; no eloquence but tautologies to tie the ears of your auditory unto you; no invention but "here it is to be noted, I stole this note out of Beza or Marlorat";[4] no wit to move, no passion to urge, but only an ordinary form of preaching, blown up by use of often hearing and speaking; and you shall find there goes more exquisite pains and purity of wit to the writing of one such rare poem as *Rosamond*[5] than to a hundred of your dunstical sermons.

Should we (as you) borrow all out of others, and gather nothing of ourselves our names should be baffuld[6] on every bookseller's stall, and not a chandler's mustard pot but would wipe his mouth with our waste paper. "New herrings, new!"[7] we must cry, every time we make ourselves public, or else we shall be christened with a hundred new titles of

---

1. Specifically, the Reverend Richard Harvey, brother of Gabriel, in an epistle prefixed to some copies of *The Lamb of God* (1590).
2. I.e., plagiarize from Calvin or another commentator on those rare (once a quarter) occasions when you preach at all.
3. Dull, morose persons.
4. Theodore Beza (1519–1605), successor of Cal-

vin at Geneva; most eminent Protestant divine in Europe. Augustine Marlorat (1506–1563), another of the Geneva reformers.
5. Samuel Daniel's *The Complaint of Rosamond* (1592).
6. Treated with scorn.
7. A fishmonger's street cry.

idiotism. Nor is poetry an art whereof there is no use in a man's whole life but to describe discontented thoughts and youthful desires; for there is no study but it doth illustrate and beautify. How admirably shine those divines above the common mediocrity, that have tasted the sweet springs of Parnassus!

Silver-tongued Smith,[8] whose well-tuned style hath made thy death the general tears of the Muses, quaintly couldst thou devise heavenly ditties to Apollo's lute, and teach stately verse to trip it as smoothly as if Ovid and thou had but one soul. Hence alone did it proceed that thou wert such a plausible pulpit man, that before thou enteredst into the rough ways of theology thou refinedst, preparedst, and purifiedst thy mind with sweet poetry. If a simple man's censure[9] may be admitted to speak in such an open theater of opinions, I never saw abundant reading better mixed with delight, or sentences which no man can challenge of profane affectation sounding more melodious to the ear or piercing more deep to the heart.

To them that demand what fruits the poets of our time bring forth, or wherein they are able to prove themselves necessary to the state, thus I answer: first and foremost, they have cleansed our language from barbarism and made the vulgar sort[1] here in London (which is the fountain whose rivers flow round about England) to aspire to a richer purity of speech than is communicated with the commonality of any nation under heaven. The virtuous by their praises they encourage to be more virtuous; to vicious men they are as infernal hags to haunt their ghosts with eternal infamy after death. The soldier, in hope to have his high deeds celebrated by their pens, despiseth a whole army of perils, and acteth wonders exceeding all human conjecture. Those that care neither for God nor the devil, by their quills are kept in awe. *Multi famam*, saith one, *pauci conscientiam verentur.*[2]

Let God see what he will, they would be loath to have the shame of the world. What age will not praise immortal Sir Philip Sidney, whom noble Salustius[3] (that thrice singular French poet) hath famoused; together with Sir Nicholas Bacon, Lord Keeper, and merry Sir Thomas More, for the chief pillars of our English speech. Not so much but Chaucer's host, Bailly in Southwark, and his wife of Bath he keeps such a stir with, in his *Canterbury Tales*, shall be talked of whilst the Bath is used, or there be ever a bad house in Southwark.[4] Gentles, it is not your lay chronographers, that write of nothing but of mayors and sheriffs and the dear year[5] and the great frost, that can endow your names with never-dated glory; for they want the wings of choice words to fly to heaven, which we have; they cannot sweeten a discourse, or wrest admiration

---

8. Henry Smith (1550–1591), a very popular preacher. He published some verse in Latin.
9. Judgment.
1. Common people.
2. "Many respect fame; only a few, conscience," Pliny, *Epistles* 3.20.
3. Guillaume de Saluste du Bartas (1544–1590),

an immensely popular religious poet, both in French and in English translation. It is in his *Second Sepmaine* that he praises Sidney, Bacon, and More.
4. Southwark was notorious for its brothels.
5. Year of high prices.

from men reading, as we can, reporting the meanest accident. Poetry is the honey of all flowers, the quintessence of all sciences, the marrow of wit, and the very phrase of angels. How much better is it, then, to have an elegant lawyer to plead one's cause, than a stutting[6] townsman that loseth himself in his tale and doth nothing but make legs;[7] so much it is better for a nobleman or gentleman to have his honor's story related, and his deeds emblazoned, by a poet, than a citizen.

Alas, poor Latinless authors, they are so simple they know not what they do; they no sooner spy a new ballad, and his name to it that compiled it, but they put him in for one of the learned men of our time. I marvel how the masterless men, that set up their bills in Paul's[8] for services, and such as paste up their papers on every post, for arithmetic and writing schools, 'scape eternity amongst them. I believe both they and the knight marshal's men, that nail up mandates[9] at the court gate for annoying the palace with filth or making water, if they set their names to the writing, will shortly make up the number of the learned men of our time, and be as famous as the rest. For my part, I do challenge[1] no praise of learning to myself, yet have I worn a gown in the University, and so hath *caret tempus non habet moribus;*[2] but this I dare presume, that if any Maecenas[3] bind me to him by his bounty or extend some sound liberality to me worth the speaking of, I will do him as much honor as any poet of my beardless years shall in England. Not that I am so confident what I can do, but that I attribute so much to my thankful mind above others, which I am persuaded would enable me to work miracles.

On the contrary side, if I be evil intreated, or sent away with a flea in mine ear,[4] let him look that I will rail on him soundly; not for an hour or a day, whiles the injury is fresh in my memory; but in some elaborate polished poem, which I will leave to the world when I am dead, to be a living image to all ages of his beggarly parsimony and ignoble illiberality; and let him not (whatsoever he be) measure the weight of my words by this book, where I write *quicquid in buccam venerit,*[5] as fast as my hand can trot; but I have terms (if I be vexed) laid in steep in *aqua fortis*[6] and gunpowder, that shall rattle through the skies and make an earthquake in a peasant's ears. Put case[7] (since I am not yet out of the theme of wrath) that some tired jade belonging to the press, whom I never wronged in my life, hath named me expressly in print[8] (as I will not do him) and accuse me of want of learning, unbraiding me for reviving in an epistle of mine, the reverent memory of Sir Thomas More, Sir John Cheke,

6. Stuttering.
7. Bow and scrape.
8. Advertisements for jobs were commonly posted on the west door of the cathedral.
9. Proclamations.
1. Claim.
2. (Bad Latin) i.e., even unlearned persons have worn a university gown.
3. Roman patron of poets, especially Virgil and Horace.

4. Stinging reproof (proverbial).
5. Whatever occurs to me.
6. Soaking in nitric acid.
7. Suppose.
8. I.e., Richard Harvey in *The Lamb of God*. Nashe has a marginal note at this point which reads. "I would tell you in what book it is, but I am afraid it would make his book sell in his latter days, which hitherto hath lain dead and been a great loss to the printer."

Doctor Watson, Doctor Haddon, Doctor Carr, Master Ascham,[9] as if they were no meat but for his mastership's mouth, or none but some such as the son of a ropemaker were worthy to mention them. To show how I can rail, thus would I begin to rail on him, "Thou that hadst thy hood turned over thy ears when thou wert a bachelor,[1] for abusing of Aristotle and setting him upon the school gates painted with ass's ears on his head, is it any discredit for me, thou great babound,[2] thou pygmy braggart, thou pamphleter of nothing but paeans,[3] to be censured by thee, that hast scorned the prince of philosophers? Thou that in thy dialogues sold'st honey for a halfpenny, and the choicest writers extant for cues[4] apiece, that camest to the logic schools when thou wert a freshman and writ'st phrases, off with thy gown and untruss, for I mean to lash thee mightily. Thou hast a brother,[5] hast thou not, student in almanacs, go to, I'll stand to it, fathered one of thy bastards (a book, I mean) which being of thy begetting was set forth under his name?"

* * *

The Defense of Plays

That state or kingdom that is in league with all the world, and hath no foreign sword to vex it, is not half so strong or confirmed to endure as that which lives every hour in fear of invasion. There is a certain waste of the people for whom there is no use but war; and these men must have some employment still to cut them off; *Nam si foras hostem non habent, domi invenient.*[6] If they have no service abroad, they will make mutinies at home. Or if the affairs of the state be such as cannot exhale all these corrupt excrements, it is very expedient they have some light toys to busy their heads withal, cast before them as bones to gnaw upon, which may keep them from having leisure to intermeddle with higher matters.

To this effect, the policy of plays is very necessary, howsoever some shallow-brained censurers (not the deepest searchers into the secrets of government) mightily oppugn them. For whereas the afternoon being idlest time of the day, wherein men that are their own masters (as gentlemen of the court, the Inns of the Court,[7] and the number of captains and soldiers about London) do wholly bestow themselves upon pleasure, and that pleasure they divide (how virtuously, it skills[8] not) either into gaming, following of harlots, drinking, or seeing a play; is it not then better (since of four extremes all the world cannot keep them but they will choose one) that they should betake them to the least, which is plays? Nay, what if I prove plays to be no extreme, but a rare exercise of virtue? First, for the subject of them, (for the most part) it is borrowed

9. Humanists praised by Nashe in his preface to Greene's *Menaphon* (1589).
1. Bachelor of Arts, recent graduate.
2. Baboon.
3. A reference to Richard Harvey's *Ephemeron, Sive Paean* (1583).
4. Quadrans, ⅛ of a penny.

5. John Harvey, who published almanacs for 1583 and 1589.
6. Adapted from Livy, book 30, 9. Nashe translates.
7. Law schools.
8. Matters.

out of our English chronicles, wherein our forefathers' valiant acts (that have lain long buried in rusty brass and worm-eaten books) are revived, and they themselves raised from the grave of oblivion, and brought to plead their aged honors in open presence; than which, what can be a sharper reproof to these degenerate effeminate days of ours?

How would it have joyed brave Talbot,[9] the terror of the French, to think that after he had lain two hundred years in his tomb, he should triumph again on the stage, and have his bones new embalmed with the tears of ten thousand spectators at least (at several times) who in the tragedian that represents his person imagine they behold him fresh bleeding.

I will defend it against any collian[1] or clubfisted usurer of them all, there is no immortality can be given a man on earth like unto plays. What talk I to them of immortality, that are the only underminers of honor, and do envy any man that is not sprung up by base brokery like themselves. They care not if all the ancient houses were rooted out, so that like the burgomasters of the Low Countries they might share the government amongst them as states, and be quartermasters of our monarchy. All arts to them are vanity; and if you tell them what a glorious thing it is to have Henry the Fifth represented on the stage leading the French king prisoner, and forcing both him and the Dolphin[2] to swear fealty, "Aye, but," will they say, "what do we get by it?" Respecting neither the right of fame that is due to true nobility deceased, nor what hopes of eternity are to be proposed to adventurous minds, to encourage them forward, but only their execrable lucre and filthy unquenchable avarice.

They know when they are dead they shall not be brought upon the stage for any goodness, but in a merriment of the usurer and the devil, or buying arms of the herald, who gives them the lion without tongue, tail, or talons, because his master whom he must serve is a townsman and a man of peace, and must not keep any quarreling beasts to annoy his honest neighbors.

In plays, all cozenages,[3] all cunning drifts over-gilded with outward holiness, all stratagems of war, all the cankerworms that breed on the rust of peace, are most lively anatomized; they show the ill success of treason, the fall of hasty climbers, the wretched end of usurpers, the misery of civil dissension, and how just God is evermore in punishing of murther. And to prove every one of these allegations could I propound the circumstances of this play and that play, if I meant to handle this theme otherwise than *obiter*.[4] What should I say more? They are sour pills of reprehension wrapped up in sweet words. Whereas some petitioners of the counsel against them object,[5] they corrupt the youth

---

9. In the play *Harey the VI* produced by Strange's men for Henslowe on Mar. 3, 1592. What relation this play had to the Shakespearean *1 Henry VI* is uncertain, but Nashe's reference would fit 1.4.39–43, and 2.3.14–24.
1. Rascal (the usual form is "cullion").

2. Dauphin (son of the king of France).
3. Deceptions, cheats.
4. By the way.
5. "The confutation of citizens' objections against players" [Nashe's marginal note].

of the city and withdraw prentices from their work; they heartily wish they might be troubled with none of their youth nor their prentices; for some of them (I mean the ruder handicrafts' servants) never come abroad but they are in danger of undoing; and as for corrupting them when they come, that's false; for no play they have encourageth any man to tumults or rebellion, but lays before such the halter and the gallows; or praiseth or approveth pride, lust, whoredom, prodigality, or drunkenness, but beats them down utterly. As for the hindrance of trades and traders of the city by them, that is an article foisted in by the vintners, alewives, and victualers, who surmise if there were no plays they should have all the company that resort to them lie boozing and beer-bathing in their houses every afternoon. Nor so, nor so, good brother bottle-ale, for there are other places besides where money can bestow itself; the sign of the smock[6] will wipe your mouth clean; and yet I have heard ye have made her a tenant to your taphouses. But what shall he do that hath spent himself? Where shall he haunt? Faith, when dice, lust, and drunkenness, and all, have dealt upon him, if there be never a play for him to go to for his penny, he sits melancholy in his chamber, devising upon felony or treason, and how he may best exalt himself by mischief.

In Augustus' time (who was the patron of all witty sports) there happened a great fray in Rome about a player, insomuch as all the city was in an uproar; whereupon, the emperor (after the broil was somewhat overblown) called the player before him, and asked what was the reason that a man of his quality durst presume to make such a brawl about nothing. He smilingly replied, "It is good for thee, Oh Caesar, that the people's heads are troubled with brawls and quarrels about us and our light matters; for otherwise they would look into thee and thy matters." Read Lipsius[7] or any profane or Christian politician, and you shall find him of this opinion. Our players are not as the players beyond sea, a sort of squirting bawdy comedians, that have whores and common courtesans to play women's parts, and forbear no immodest speech or unchaste action that may procure laughter; but our scene is more stately furnished than ever it was in the time of Roscius, our representations honorable and full of gallant resolution, not consisting like theirs of pantaloon, a whore, and a zany,[8] but of emperors, kings, and princes; whose true tragedies (*Sophocleo cothurno*)[9] they do vaunt.

Not Roscius nor Aesope,[1] those admired tragedians that have lived ever since before Christ was born, could ever perform more in action than famous Ned Allen.[2] I must accuse our poets of sloth and partiality that they will not boast in large impressions what worthy men (above all nations) England affords. Other countries cannot have a fiddler break a string but they will put it in print, and the old Romans in the writings

6. I.e., of a prostitute.
7. Justus Lipsius (1547–1606), Belgian scholar and historian.
8. Type parts in the *commedia dell' arte*.
9. "With Sophoclean dignity."
1. These two Roman actors flourished about 70

B.C.
2. Edward Alleyn (1566–1626), partner and son-in-law of Henslowe, the manager. He retired from the stage about 1603–4. He founded Dulwich College.

they published thought scorn to use any but domestical examples of their own home-bred actors, scholars, and champions, and them they would extol to the third and fourth generation; cobblers, tinkers, fencers, none escaped them, but they mingled them all in one gallimaufry of glory.

Here I have used a like method, not of tying myself to mine own country, but by insisting in the experience of our time; and if I ever write anything in Latin (as I hope one day I shall), not a man of any desert here amongst us, but I will have up. Tarlton, Ned Allen, Knell, Bentley,[3] shall be made known to France, Spain, and Italy; and not a part that they surmounted in, more than other, but I will there note and set down, with the manner of their habits and attire.[4]

1592

3. Actors older than Alleyn, and famous in the period before 1588. Richard Tarlton (d. 1588) was the most popular Elizabethan comedian.
4. Nashe never fulfilled this resolution.

Songs and Poems of the Sixteenth Century

The sixteenth century was one of the great ages for lyric poetry in English. J. J. Jusserand in his *Literary History of the English People* declares that the poets of this period "sing verses worthy of remembrance, on every subject, amorous, religious, epic, satirical, pastoral, didactic, moving from the world of insects to the world of heroes. Songs rise naturally to their lips, no one knows why, they do not know why."

The lyrics written by courtiers, in the first half of the century as well as later, were poems intended to be set to music and sung. In the courts of all the Tudor sovereigns music flourished; skill in composition was an excellent qualification for a servant, and noblemen, even kings and queens themselves, pursued the art. The songs of Wyatt and other courtiers collected in *Tottel's Miscellany* (1557), the first great sixteenth-century anthology, are only a remnant of the large amount of lyrical verse written in the courts of Henry VIII and Edward VI. The courtly "makers," as they have been called, sometimes composed new words to a popular tune. Often they imitated and borrowed foreign stanza forms and popular themes from the poetry of Italy and France. But at their best they wrote lyrics in the native English tradition also, and the fusion of native and foreign strains contributed to the flourishing of lyric poetry in the last decades of the century.

In Shakespeare's *Twelfth Night*, the duke calls upon a court jester to repeat a song he has heard him sing:

> O fellow, come, the song we had last night.
> Mark it, Cesario; it is old and plain.
> The spinsters and the knitters in the sun,
> And the free maids that weave their thread with bones,
> Do use to chant it. It is silly sooth,
> And dallies with the innocence of love,
> Like the old age.

Singing at court is described in these lines, which also illustrate another source of lyric poetry in Elizabethan England: the drama. Acting companies used boys to play female parts, and as these boys had often been trained as singers, the playwrights provided them opportunities to display their talents. In Shakespeare's plays, the gravedigger in *Hamlet* sings while he works; the court in exile in Shakespeare's *As You Like It* brings along its singer whose songs include *Blow, Blow, Thou Winter Wind* (p. 870); and the spirit Ariel in Shakespeare's *The Tempest* sings many lovely songs, among them *Full Fathom Five* (p. 872).

The popular ballad, with its simple four-line stanza form, of anonymous or perhaps composite authorship, can be traced back to the fifteenth century. With the invention of printing, a more commercial form, the broadside ballad, became popular. Copies of broadside ballads were sold by travelling peddlers like Autolycus in Shakespeare's *Winter's Tale*; they were often crude, exploiting the latest murder or scandal like the sensational newspaper of modern times.

At the other extreme were two kinds of art song, the madrigal and the air. A madrigal is a song for two or more voices in counterpoint, usually a setting of a poem expressing the woes of the Petrarchan lover, although any subject is possible. The music imitates in musical terms the meaning of the words, but since the separate voices usually do not sing the same word at the same time, the text is often difficult for the listener to understand. Because the complex musical rendering involved much repetition and extension of the words and lines, the madrigal text was a short poem, most often an epigram or a single stanza. There is evidence that many Elizabethans could sing a part in a madrigal at sight—a feat which now requires a high degree of musical training.

The air, a much less complicated musical form, was a single, recurring melody for the voice with a three-note harmonic accompaniment on the lute. This musical form allowed for the use of longer poems, sometimes in several stanzas, and excellent lyric poems were more often written for the lute-song or air than for madrigals. The finest poet of airs was Thomas Campion, who was also a composer with a remarkably sensitive ear and a thorough understanding of the problems of versification and musical setting. The genius of Campion and of Ben Jonson solved the vexed problem of whether English quantitative verse (verse which relies upon length and duration of syllables rather than accent) could be successful.

The sixteenth century produced more anonymous lyrics than lyrics whose authors can be identified. Many poems circulated in manuscript and were copied into manuscript books without particular care for identifying authorship. Sometimes publishers obtained such collections and printed them, either not knowing or not caring about the authorship of individual poems. *Tottel's Miscellany* attributes a large number of poems to "Uncertain Authors," only a few of whom have been identified; and at the end of the century another popular anthology, *The Phoenix Nest*, gives no author for some poems and attributes others to "Ignoto." Lyrics for songs were most often anonymous: the composer published his musical settings with words for singing, but few publishers gave credit to the authors of such lyrics. Thomas Campion was an exception.

All this reflects a casualness about authorship that seems strange to us, harking back to the medieval idea that individual authorship is unimportant. Moreover, while aristocrats and courtiers wrote poetry they often did not publish their verse—it would be beneath them. On the other hand, the art was less specialized then: lawyers, statesmen, explorers, parsons, soldiers, merchants—it was a rare Elizabethan who would not try his hand at verse.

Another very important feature of the poetic scene throughout the sixteenth century was verse translation—from the classics (Surrey's Virgil, Chapman's Homer, Golding's Ovid), and from the Bible, especially the Book of Psalms. The first complete metrical psalter in English verse appeared in 1549; the enormously popular Sternhold-Hopkins version was adopted for congregational singing in the liturgy; and by 1640 there were well over 300 editions of metrical psalms in several versions. Such experiments (and notably that by Sir Philip Sidney and the countess of Pembroke) contributed significantly to the flowering of English religious lyric in the late sixteenth and seventeenth centuries.

We begin our selections with examples of translation from the classics and from the Psalms. Thereafter, the selections are ordered with primary attention to the period in which the poets wrote their major lyrics, rather than strictly by birthdate.

ARTHUR GOLDING
1536–1605

A prolific translator, especially from Latin and French into English, Golding belonged to a wealthy family in Essex and was educated at Jesus College, Cambridge. His half sister married the sixteenth earl of Oxford and Golding dedicated several of his translations to their son, the seventeenth earl, whom he may have tutored. Sir Philip Sidney chose Golding to complete the translation, begun by Sidney, of Philippe de Mornay's *Trueness of the Christian Religion*. Golding was an ardent Puritan; he translated seven separate works of Calvin into English. His most celebrated translation, however, was of Ovid's *Metamorphoses*. That long poem, in fifteen books, narrates many classical myths about gods and mortal maidens, nymphs and their lovers, all of which involved transformations (metamorphoses). Ovid's pagan erotic poem had been moralized or interpreted allegorically centuries before, so Golding was doing nothing new when he wrote six hundred lines of moralizing interpretation and dedicated it to the earl of Leicester. According to a recent critic, Gordon Braden, "Despite the moralistic packaging Golding's translation is solidly humanistic in its content, and his scholarly and antiquarian interests, at least here, are far more important than his religious alliances." Golding's Ovid was one of Shakespeare's favorite books; although the playwright was able to read the Latin original, his references to the classical myths related by Ovid often reflect Golding's English version. Shakespeare, like most Elizabethans, would have been familiar with Ovid's description of the Four Ages of Man.

From Ovid's *Metamorphoses*[1]
[*The Four Ages*]

Then sprang up first the golden age, which of itself maintained
The truth and right of everything unforced and unconstrained.
There was no fear of punishment, there was no threatening law   105
In brazen tables nailèd up, to keep the folk in awe.
There was no man would crouch or creep to judge with cap in hand,
They livèd safe without a judge, in every realm and land.

---

1. Our selection is drawn from book 1, lines 103–70.

The lofty pinetree was not hewn from mountains where it stood,
In seeking strange and foreign lands, to rove upon the flood.   110
Men knew none other countries yet than where themselves did keep;
There was no town enclosèd yet, with walls and ditches deep.
No horn nor trumpet was in use, no sword nor helmet worn;
The world was such that soldiers' help might easily be forborn.
The fertile earth as yet was free, untouched of spade or plow,   115
And yet it yielded of itself of every things enow.[2]
And men themselves contented well with plain and simple food
That on the earth of nature's gift without their travail stood,
Did live by raspès, hips, and haws, by cornels,[3] plums, and cherries,
By sloes and apples, nuts and pears, and loathsome bramble berries,   120
And by the acorns dropped on ground from Jove's broad tree[4] in field.
The springtime lasted all the year, and Zephyr with his mild
And gentle blast did cherish things that grew of own accord;
The ground untilled all kinds of fruits did plenteously afford.
No muck nor tillage was bestowed on lean and barren land,   125
To make the corn[5] of better head and ranker for to spread.
Then streams ran milk, then streams ran wine, and yellow honey flowed
From each green tree whereon the rays of fiery Phoebus glowed.
But when that into limbo once Saturnus[6] being thrust,
The rule and charge of all the world was under Jove unjust.   130
And that the silver age came in, more somewhat base than gold,
More precious yet than freckled[7] brass, immediately the old
And ancient spring did Jove abridge,[8] and made thereof anon
Four seasons, winter, summer, spring, and autumn off and on.
Then first of all began the air with fervent heat to swelt,[9]   135
Then icicles hung roping[1] down; then for the cold was felt,
Men gan to shroud themselves in house. Their houses were the thicks[2]
And bushy queaches,[3] hollow caves, or hardels made of sticks.
Then first of all were furrows drawn, and corn was cast in ground.
The simple ox, with sorry sighs, to heavy yoke was bound.   140
Next after this succeeded straight[4] the third and brazen age,
More hard of nature, somewhat bent to cruel wars and rage,
But yet not wholly past all grace. Of iron is the last,
In no part good and tractable as former ages past.
For when that of this wicked age once opened was the vein,   145
Therein all mischief rushèd forth; then faith and truth were fain,
And honest shame, to hide their heads, for whom crept stoutly in,
Craft, treason, violence, envy, pride, and wicked lust to win.
The shipman hoist his sails to wind, whose names he did not know,
And ships that erst[5] in tops of hills and mountains had ygrow,   150
Did leap and dance on uncouth[6] waves, and men began to bound

2. Enough.
3. Raspberries, hips of wild roses, hawthorn buds,
fruit of cornelian cherry.
4. Oak (called *Arbor Jovis* in Latin).
5. Grain.
6. Saturn, father of Jove.
7. Light brown, mottled.
8. Shorten.

9. Swelter.
1. Dangling, like the end of a rope.
2. Thickets.
3. Dense growth of bushes; "hardels": woven huts.
4. Immediately.
5. Formerly.
6. Unfamiliar.

With dools[7] and ditches drawn in length the free and fertile ground
Which was as common as the air and light of sun before.
Not only corn and other fruits, for sustenance and for store,
Were now exacted[8] of the earth, but eft they gan to dig   155
And in the bowels of the ground unsatiably to rig
For riches couched and hidden deep, in places near to Hell,
The spurs and stirrers unto vice and foes to doing well.
Then hurtful iron came abroad, then came forth yellow gold,
More hurtful than the iron far; then came forth battle bold,   160
That fights with both, and shakes his sword in cruel bloody hand.
Men live by ravine[9] and by stealth; the wandering guest doth stand
In danger of his host, the host in danger of his guest,
And fathers of their son-in-laws, yet seldom time doth rest
Between born brothers such accord and love as ought to be.   165
The goodman seeks the goodwife's death, and his again seeks she.
The stepdames fell[1] their husband's sons with poison do assail.
To see their fathers live so long the children do bewail.
All godliness lies under foot, And Lady Astre[2] last
Of heavenly virtues, from this earth in slaughter drownèd past.   170

1567

7. Boundary marks between fields.
8. Extracted; "eft": soon.
9. Violence.
1. Evil, wicked.

2. Astrea, goddess of justice. In classical mythology she lived on earth in the Golden Age, but when wickedness increased, she withdrew to heaven.

MARY (SIDNEY) HERBERT, COUNTESS
OF PEMBROKE
1562–1621

Mary, countess of Pembroke, was a major Elizabethan literary patron, as were her brothers Sir Philip Sidney and Sir Robert Sidney (of Penshurst), and her eldest son William, third earl of Pembroke. After her marriage in 1577, she gathered a notable group of poets, clergy, alchemists, naturalists, and musicians at the Pembroke country estate, Wilton. Her literary works include a few original poems, a composite edition of Sidney's *Arcadia* (combining the unfinished *New Arcadia* with the last part of the *Old Arcadia*), a translation in terza rima of Petrarch's *Triumph of Death*, a translation in quantitative verse of Robert Garnier's neoclassical French tragedy *Antonius*, and a prose translation of the religious tract, *A Discourse of Life and Death* by the French Protestant Du Plessis Mornay. She also contributed the largest number (107) of the series of 150 poetic psalm versions begun by Sir Philip Sidney. Her very free renderings recreate the psalms as English poems, using an amazing variety of stanzaic and metrical patterns and some strikingly effective images. This widely circulated and influential volume was an important bridge between the many metrical paraphrases of psalms in this period and the great religious lyric poets of the seventeenth century, especially George Herbert. Donne's poem, *Upon the Translation of the Psalmes by Sir Philip Sidney and the Countess of Pembroke His Sister*, testifies to that importance: "They tell us *why*, and teach us *how* to sing."

Psalm 58 *Si Vere Utique*

And call ye this to utter what is just
    You that of justice hold the sovereign throne?
And call ye this, to yield, O sons of dust,
    To wrongèd brethren every man his own?
O no! It is your long malicious will   5
    Now to the world to make by practice known
With whose oppression you the balance fill:
    Just to yourselves, indifferent[1] else to none.

But what could they, who even in birth declined
    From truth and right to lies and injuries?   10
To show the venom of their cankered mind
    The adder's image scarcely can suffice;
Nay, scarce the aspic[2] may with them contend,
    On whom the charmer all in vain applies
His skilfull'st spells, aye missing of his end,   15
    While she, self-deaf and unaffected, lies.

Lord, crack their teeth! Lord, crush these lions' jaws!
    So let them sink as water in the sand.
When deadly bow their aiming fury draws,
    Shiver the shaft ere past the shooter's hand.   20
So make them melt as the dishousèd snail,
    Or as the embryo whose vital band
Breaks ere it holds, and formless eyes do fail
    To see the sun, though brought to lightful land.

O let their brood, a brood of springing thorns,   25
    Be by untimely rooting overthrown;
Ere bushes waxed,[3] they push with pricking horns,
    As fruits yet green are oft by tempest blown.
The good with gladness this revenge shall see
    And bathe his feet in blood of wicked one   30
While all shall say, "The just rewarded be;
    There is a God that carves to each his own."

1820

---

1. Impartial.
2. The asp, a small poisonous snake.
3. Grew; "pricking horns": thorns.

QUEEN ELIZABETH
1533–1603

Queen Elizabeth was a well-educated woman of letters who found time to study and write throughout her eventful and brilliant public career. She took pride in displaying her considerable knowledge of the Latin and Greek languages, and her wide reading in the classics, begun under the tutelage of Roger Ascham and other humanist scholars. Her literary work includes speeches on several state occasions; poetic translations of selections from the Psalms, Petrarch, Seneca, and Horace; prose translations from Boethius, Plutarch, and the French Protestant Queen Margaret of Navarre; and a few original poems. The original poems known to be hers deal with actual events in her life. They are chiefly in octosyllabics or poulter's couplets (rhyming couplets in which the first line has twelve and the second line fourteen syllables) and are rough-hewn, vigorous, and moralistic.

The Doubt of Future Foes[1]

The doubt of future foes exiles my present joy,
And wit me warns to shun such snares as threaten mine annoy.[2]
For falsehood now doth flow, and subject faith doth ebb,[3]
Which would not be, if reason ruled or wisdom weaved the web.
But clouds of toys untried do cloak aspiring minds,   5
Which turn to rain of late repent, by course of changèd winds.[4]
The top of hope supposed, the root of ruth will be,
And fruitless all their graffèd guiles, as shortly ye shall see.[5]
The dazzled eyes with pride, which great ambition blinds,
Shall be unsealed by worthy wights whose foresight falsehood finds.   10
The daughter of debate,[6] that eke discord doth sow
Shall reap no gain where former rule[7] hath taught still peace to grow.
No foreign banished wight[8] shall anchor in this port,
Our realm it brooks no stranger's force, let them elsewhere resort.
Our rusty sword with rest,[9] shall first his edge employ   15
To poll their tops that seek such change and gape for joy.

ca. 1568

1. The poem concerns Elizabeth's Roman Catholic cousin Mary Stuart, queen of Scotland, who in 1568 sought refuge in England from her rebellious subjects. Mary was the focus of several Roman Catholic conspiracies to place her on the English throne in place of Elizabeth. "Doubt": fear.
2. I.e., threaten to harm ("annoy") me. "Wit": intelligence.
3. I.e., the tide of faith (loyalty) is ebbing, because it is now subject to the rising tide of falsehood.
4. I.e., clouds of tricks ("toys") not yet tested and detected ("untried") hide the "aspiring minds" of ambitious foes, but those clouds will turn at last into rains of repentance.
5. I.e., the deceptions ("guiles") grafted ("graffed") into them will not bear fruit. "Ruth": sorrow.
6. Mary Stuart, also sometimes called "Mother of Debate" because she was constantly the focus of conspiracies and plots; "eke": also.
7. Either the reign of Henry VIII or Edward VI, which established the Reformation in England. "Still": stable.
8. Person.
9. I.e., sword rusty from disuse; in the next line, "poll the tops": strike off their heads.

On Monsieur's Departure[1]

I grieve and dare not show my discontent,
I love and yet am forced to seem to hate,
I do, yet dare not say I ever meant,
I seem stark mute but inwardly do prate.[2]
    I am and not, I freeze and yet am burned,   5
    Since from myself another self I turned.

My care is like my shadow in the sun,
Follows me flying, flies when I pursue it,
Stands and lies by me, doth what I have done.[3]
His too familiar care[4] doth make me rue it.   10
    No means I find to rid him from my breast,
    Till by the end of things it be suppressed.

Some gentler passion slide into my mind,
For I am soft and made of melting snow;
Or be more cruel, love, and so be kind.   15
Let me or float or sink, be high or low.
    Or let me live with some more sweet content,
    Or die and so forget what love ere meant.

ca. 1582

---

1. The heading, present in two manuscripts, identifies the occasion of this poem as the breaking-off of marriage negotiations between Queen Elizabeth and the French duke of Anjou in 1582. A third manuscript implies instead an association with Elizabeth's favorite, the earl of Essex, who led an abortive rebellion and was executed for treason in 1601.
2. Chatter.
3. Does everything I do.
4. I.e., my own care (i.e., sorrow) which he caused; "rue": regret.

GEORGE GASCOIGNE
1539–1578

Gascoigne was a pioneer translator of plays from the Italian, the first composer of a sonnet sequence in English, the first writer of an original poem in blank verse (Surrey's earlier blank verse was a translation), and, according to some, the author of *The Adventures of Master F. J.* (1573)—according to some, the first English novel. He was educated at Cambridge and the Inns of Court. He had a military career in the low countries and he adopted as his motto *Tam Marti Quam Mercurio* (as much to Mars—god of war—as to Mercury—god of eloquence, patron of thieves and travelers, messenger of the gods). There is an engraving of him, armed with sword and pike, kneeling before Queen Elizabeth and presenting her with one of his works. In 1572 a petition was circulated that prevented him from taking his seat in Parliament, where he had already served twice, on the ground that he was a common rhymer, spy, atheist, and Godless person, as well as a notorious ruffian. Whatever the truth of these charges about the real-life Gascoigne, his poetry sometimes shows an affecting zeal for repentance.

The Lullaby of a Lover

Sing lullaby, as women do,
Wherewith they bring their babes to rest,
And lullaby can I sing too,
As womanly as can the best.
With lullaby they still the child,   5
And if I be not much beguiled,[1]
Full many wanton babes have I,
Which must be stilled with lullaby.

First, lullaby, my youthful years,
It is now time to go to bed,   10
For crooked age and hoary hairs
Have won the haven within my head.
With lullaby then, youth, be still,
With lullaby content thy will,
Since courage quails and comes behind,   15
Go sleep, and so beguile thy mind.

Next, lullaby, my gazing eyes,
Which wonted[2] were to glance apace.
For every glass may now suffice
To show the furrows in my face.   20
With lullaby then wink[3] awhile,
With lullaby your looks beguile.
Let no fair face nor beauty bright
Entice you eft[4] with vain delight.

And lullaby, my wanton will,   25
Let reason's rule now rein thy thought,
Since all too late I find by skill
How dear I have thy fancies bought.
With lullaby now take thine ease,
With lullaby thy doubts appease.   30
For trust to this, if thou be still,
My body shall obey thy will.

Eke[5] lullaby, my loving boy,
My little Robin,[6] take thy rest.
Since age is cold and nothing coy,   35

1. Deceived.
2. Accustomed.
3. Close the eyes (not momentarily).
4. Again.

5. Also.
6. A jocular name for the speaker's penis; "coy": lascivious.

Keep close thy coin, for so is best.
With lullaby be thou content,
With lullaby thy lusts relent.
Let others pay which hath mo pence;
Thou art too poor for such expense. 40

Thus, lullaby, my youth, mine eyes,
My will, my ware,[7] and all that was.
I can no mo delays devise,
But welcome pain, let pleasure pass.
With lullaby now take your leave, 45
With lullaby your dreams deceive,
And when you rise with waking eye,
Remember then this lullaby.

1573

7. Sexual organ.

ROBERT SOUTHWELL
1561–1595

Robert Southwell, the younger son of a prominent Roman Catholic family, went to the English seminary for Catholics at Douai, France, in his youth, then to Rome where he entered the Society of Jesus (the Jesuits). In 1586 he returned to England to minister to English Catholics. His mission was a dangerous one because of laws that proscribed Roman Catholic worship and banished priests; in 1592 he was apprehended, imprisoned, tortured, and three years later executed as a traitor in the usual grisly manner—by being hanged, disemboweled, and then beheaded. Southwell wrote a good deal of religious prose and verse; the most famous of his lyrics is *The Burning Babe*. Ben Jonson told William Drummond of Hawthornden that if he had written *The Burning Babe* he would willingly destroy many of his own poems.

The Burning Babe

As I in hoary winter's night stood shivering in the snow,
Surprised I was with sudden heat which made my heart to glow;
And lifting up a fearful eye to view what fire was near,
A pretty babe all burning bright did in the air appear;
Who, scorchèd with excessive heat, such floods of tears did shed 5
As though his floods should quench his flames which with his tears
    were fed.
"Alas," quoth he, "but newly born in fiery heats I fry,[1]
Yet none approach to warm their hearts or feel my fire but I!

1. Burn.

My faultless breast the furnace is, the fuel wounding thorns,
Love is the fire, and sighs the smoke, the ashes shame and scorns;   10
The fuel justice layeth on, and mercy blows the coals,
The metal in this furnace wrought are men's defilèd souls,
For which, as now on fire I am to work them to their good,
So will I melt into a bath to wash them in my blood."
With this he vanished out of sight and swiftly shrunk away,   15
And straight I callèd unto mind that it was Christmas day.

                                                         1602

THOMAS CAMPION
1567–1620

Thomas Campion was a law student, a physician, a composer, a writer of
masques, and a poet. His first poetic attempts were in Latin. His love of
quantitative versification in classical Latin poems carried over into his English
poems and songs. In quantitative verse the syllables are arranged in patterns
according to their length and duration (that is, according to the length of
time it takes to pronounce them) rather than according to accent or stress;
see, for instance, Campion's *Rose-Cheeked Laura*. In his *Observations In
the Art of English Poesy* he defended quantitative verse and disparaged the
accentual, rhymed verse characteristic of poetry in English and the other
vernacular languages. But his finest achievements as a lyric poet—and he is
one of the very best in the language—arise from the fact that he was both
poet and composer. In the preface to one of his books, he wrote, "I have
chiefly aimed to couple my words and notes lovingly together, which will
be much for him to do that hath not power over both."

My Sweetest Lesbia[1]

My sweetest Lesbia, let us live and love,
And though the sager sort our deeds reprove,
Let us not weigh them. Heaven's great lamps do dive
Into their west, and straight again revive,
But soon as once set is our little light,   5
Then must we sleep one ever-during night.

If all would lead their lives in love like me,
Then bloody swords and armor should not be;
No drum nor trumpet peaceful sleeps should move,
Unless alarm came from the camp of love.   10
But fools do live, and waste their little light,
And seek with pain their ever-during night.

1. Imitated and partly translated from a poem by
Catullus (87–ca. 54 B.C.), the Latin lyric poet who
often celebrated the charms of Lesbia in his verses.

This and the two lyrics which follow appeared in
A Book of Airs, which contains Campion's first work
as a composer.

When timely death my life and fortune ends,
Let not my hearse be vexed with mourning friends,
But let all lovers, rich in triumph, come   15
And with sweet pastimes grace my happy tomb;
And Lesbia, close up thou my little light,
And crown with love my ever-during night.

1601

When to Her Lute Corinna Sings

When to her lute Corinna sings,
Her voice revives the leaden strings,
And doth in highest notes appear
As any challenged echo clear;
But when she doth of mourning speak,   5
Ev'n with her sighs the strings do break.

And as her lute doth live or die,
Led by her passion, so must I:
For when of pleasure she doth sing,
My thoughts enjoy a sudden spring,   10
But if she doth of sorrow speak,
Ev'n from my heart the strings do break.

1601

Rose-Cheeked Laura[1]

Rose-cheeked Laura, come,
Sing thou smoothly with thy beauty's
Silent music, either other
          Sweetly gracing.

Lovely forms do flow   5
From concent[2] divinely framed;
Heav'n is music, and thy beauty's
          Birth is heavenly.

These dull notes we sing
Discords need for helps to grace them;   10
Only beauty purely loving
          Knows no discord,

1. Written by Campion to illustrate his theories of versification in *Observations in the Art of English Poesy*, this song is a brilliant example of quantita-tive verse made musically effective in English.
2. Playing or singing together in harmony.

But still moves delight,
Like clear springs renewed by flowing,
Ever perfect, ever in them-   15
  Selves eternal.

          1602

There Is a Garden in Her Face

There is a garden in her face,
Where roses and white lilies grow,
A heavenly paradise is that place,
Wherein all pleasant fruits do flow.
There cherries grow, which none may buy   5
Till "Cherry ripe!"[1] themselves do cry.

Those cherries fairly do enclose
Of orient pearl a double row;
Which when her lovely laughter shows,
They look like rosebuds filled with snow.   10
Yet them nor peer nor prince can buy,
Till "Cherry ripe!" themselves do cry.

Her eyes like angels watch them still;
Her brows like bended bows do stand,
Threatening with piercing frowns to kill   15
All that attempt with eye or hand
Those sacred cherries to come nigh,
Till "Cherry ripe!" themselves do cry.

          1617

Think'st Thou to Seduce Me Then[1]

Think'st thou to seduce me then with words that have no meaning?
Parrots so can learn to prate, our speech by pieces gleaning;
Nurses teach their children so about the time of weaning.

Learn to speak first, then to woo; to wooing much pertaineth;
He that courts us, wanting art, soon falters when he feigneth,   5
Looks asquint on his discourse,[2] and smiles when he complaineth.

---

1. A familiar cry of London street vendors.
1. In this poem and the one following, Campion assumes the voice of a female speaker; the procedure is rare among early poets. Both poems are

written in the old-fashioned metrical form known as "fourteeners"—verses of 14 or 15 syllables, with 7 accented beats.
2. Looks away from the lady to check on his script.

Skillful anglers hide their hooks, fit baits for every season;
But with crooked pins fish thou, as babes do that want reason:
Gudgeons[3] only can be caught with such poor tricks of treason.

Ruth[4] forgive me, if I erred from human heart's compassion,   10
When I laughed sometimes too much to see thy foolish fashion;
But, alas, who less could do that found so good occasion?

1617

Fain Would I Wed

Fain would I wed a fair young man that night and day could please
     me,
When my mind or body grieved that had the power to ease me.
Maids are full of longing thoughts that breed a bloodless sickness,
And that, oft I hear men say, is only cured by quickness.
Oft I have been wooed and praised, but never could be movèd;   5
Many for a day or so I have most dearly lovèd,
But this foolish mind of mine straight loathes the thing resolvèd;
If to love be sin in me, that sin is soon absolvèd.
Sure I think I shall at last fly to some holy order;
When I once am settled there, then can I fly no farther.   10
Yet I would not die a maid, because I had a mother,
As I was by one brought forth, I would bring forth another.

1617

I Care Not for These Ladies

I care not for these ladies that must be wooed and prayed.
Give me kind Amaryllis, the wanton country maid.
Nature art disdaineth; her beauty is her own,
Who when we court and kiss, she cries "Forsooth, let go!"
But when we come where comfort is, she never will say no.   5

If I love Amaryllis, she gives me fruit and flowers;
But if we love these ladies, we must give golden showers.
Give them gold that sell love, give me the nutbrown lass,
Who when we court and kiss, she cries "Forsooth, let go!"
But when we come where comfort is, she never will say no.   10

These ladies must have pillows and beds by strangers wrought.
Give me a bower of willows, of moss and leaves unbought,
And fresh Amaryllis, with milk and honey fed,

3. Small fish.
4. Pity, which misled the girl into seeming too complaisant.

Who when we court and kiss, she cries "Forsooth, let go!"
But when we come where comfort is, she never will say no.   15

1601

SAMUEL DANIEL
1562–1619

Samuel Daniel, poet, historian, and translator, was a member of the circle
of the countess of Pembroke, Sir Philip Sidney's sister. He wrote tragedies
closely imitating Senecan form, court masques, a historical epic on the *Civil
Wars Between the Two Houses of Lancaster and York* (1594–1609), a defense
of learning *(Musophilus)*, and one of the better Elizabethan sonnet sequences,
Delia (1592). His *Defense of Rhyme* (1603), an answer to Thomas Campion's strictures on the use of rhyme, is an important contribution to the
critical debates of the period. Daniel's lyrics are marked by clarity, restraint,
and a quiet eloquence.

From Delia

33

When men shall find thy flower, thy glory pass,
And thou, with careful brow sitting alone,
Receivèd hast this message from thy glass,
That tells thee truth, and says that all is gone,
Fresh shalt thou see in me the wounds thou madest,   5
Though spent thy flame, in me the heat remaining,
I that have loved thee thus before thou fadest,
My faith shall wax, when thou art in thy waning.
The world shall find this miracle in me,
That fire can burn when all the matter's spent;   10
Then what my faith hath been thyself shall see,
And that thou wast unkind thou mayst repent.
Thou mayst repent that thou hast scorned my tears,
When winter snows upon thy golden hairs.

45

Care-charmer Sleep, son of the sable Night,
Brother to Death, in silent darkness born,
Relieve my languish and restore the light;
With dark forgetting of my cares, return.
And let the day be time enough to mourn   5
The shipwreck of my ill-adventured youth;
Let waking eyes suffice to wail their scorn

Without the torment of the night's untruth.
Cease, dreams, th' imagery of our day desires,
To model forth the passions of the morrow;   10
Never let rising sun approve you liars,
To add more grief to aggravate my sorrow.
Still let me sleep, embracing clouds in vain,
And never wake to feel the day's disdain.

                                                        1592

Ulysses and the Siren[1]

Siren: Come, worthy Greek, Ulysses, come,
Possess these shores with me;
The winds and seas are troublesome,
And here we may be free.
Here may we sit and view their toil   5
That travail in the deep,
And joy the day in mirth the while,
And spend the night in sleep.

Ulysses: Fair nymph, if fame or honor were
To be attained with ease,   10
Then would I come and rest me there,
And leave such toils as these.
But here it dwells, and here must I
With danger seek it forth;
To spend the time luxuriously   15
Becomes not men of worth.

Siren: Ulysses, Oh be not deceived
With that unreal name;
This honor is a thing conceived,
And rests on others' fame.   20
Begotten only to molest
Our peace, and to beguile
The best thing of our life, our rest,
And give us up to toil.

Ulysses: Delicious nymph, suppose there were   25
Nor honor nor report,
Yet manliness would scorn to wear
The time in idle sport.
For toil doth give a better touch,
To make us feel our joy;   30

1. Ulysses, the hero of Homer's *Odyssey*, was tempted by several nymphs to lead a life of ease and abandon his arduous struggle to return to his own land, Ithaca.

And ease finds tediousness, as much
As labor yields annoy.

Siren: Then pleasure likewise seems the shore
Whereto tends all your toil,
Which you forgo to make it more,   35
And perish oft the while.
Who may disport them diversly,
Find never tedious day,
And ease may have variety
As well as action may.   40

Ulysses: But natures of the noblest frame
These toils and dangers please,
And they take comfort in the same
As much as you in ease,
And with the thoughts of actions past   45
Are recreated still;
When pleasure leaves a touch at last
To show that it was ill.

Siren: That doth opinion only cause
That's out of custom bred,   50
Which makes us many other laws
Than ever nature did.
No widows wail for our delights,
Our sports are without blood;
The world, we see, by warlike wights   55
Receives more hurt than good.

Ulysses: But yet the state of things require
These motions of unrest,
And these great spirits of high desire
Seem born to turn them best,   60
To purge the mischiefs that increase
And all good order mar;
For oft we see a wicked peace
To be well changed for war.

Siren: Well, well, Ulysses, then I see   65
I shall not have thee here,
And therefore I will come to thee,
And take my fortunes there.
I must be won that cannot win,
Yet lost were I not won;   70
For beauty hath created been
T' undo, or be undone.

MICHAEL DRAYTON
1563–1631

Drayton was born about a year before Shakespeare and in the same county, Warwickshire, and had a long career as poet, extending from the early 1590s until well into the seventeenth century. He collaborated on plays, wrote sonnets, pastorals, odes, poetic epistles, and a historical "epic" called *The Barons' Wars*. His self-styled masterpiece, however, is *Poly-Olbion*, a 30,000-line historical-geographical poem about the English countryside. His life-long devotion to Anne Goodyere, Lady Rainsford (in the manner of a courtly lover) is memorialized in his sonnets addressed to "Idea," e.g., the embodiment of the Platonic Idea of virtue and beauty. He revised and added to his sonnets and poems as they were republished, so one can trace his development from an Elizabethan to a seventeenth-century poet. He wrote of himself:

> My muse is rightly of the English strain
> That cannot long one fashion entertain.

From Idea

To the Reader of These Sonnets

Into these loves who but for passion looks,
At this first sight here let him lay them by,
And seek elsewhere, in turning other books
Which better may his labor satisfy.
No farfetched sigh shall ever wound my breast,   5
Love from mine eye a tear shall never wring,
Nor in *Ah me's* my whining sonnets dressed;
A libertine, fantastically I sing.
My verse is the true image of my mind,
Ever in motion, still desiring change;   10
And as thus to variety inclined,
So in all humors sportively I range;
My muse is rightly of the English strain,
That cannot long one fashion entertain.

1599

6

How many paltry, foolish, painted things,
That now in coaches trouble every street,
Shall be forgotten, whom no poet sings,
Ere they be well wrapped in their winding sheet?

Where[1] I to thee eternity shall give   5
When nothing else remaineth of these days,
And queens hereafter shall be glad to live
Upon the alms of thy superfluous praise.
Virgins and matrons, reading these my rhymes,
Shall be so much delighted with thy story   10
That they shall grieve they lived not in these times
To have seen thee, their sex's only glory;
So shalt thou fly above the vulgar throng,
Still to survive in my immortal song.

1619

61

Since there's no help, come let us kiss and part;
Nay, I have done, you get no more of me,
And I am glad, yea glad with all my heart
That thus so cleanly I myself can free;
Shake hands forever, cancel all our vows,   5
And when we meet at any time again,
Be it not seen in either of our brows
That we one jot of former love retain.
Now at the last gasp of love's latest breath,
When, his pulse failing, passion speechless lies,   10
When faith is kneeling by his bed of death,
And innocence is closing up his eyes;
Now if thou wouldst, when all have given him over,
From death to life thou mightst him yet recover.

1619

Ode. To the Virginian Voyage[1]

You brave heroic minds
Worthy your country's name,
    That honor still pursue,
    Go, and subdue
Whilst loit'ring hinds   5
Lurk here at home, with shame.

Britons, you stay too long;
Quickly aboard bestow you,
    And with a merry gale
    Swell your stretched sail,   10
With vows as strong
As the winds that blow you.

1. Whereas.
1. The expedition was ordered in April 1606. Three   ships set out in December, after Drayton's poem
                                                      was published.

Your course securely steer,
West and by south forth keep,
   Rocks, lee shores, nor shoals,
   When Aeolus[2] scowls,   15
You need not fear,
So absolute the deep.

And cheerfully at sea,
Success you still entice,[3]   20
   To get the pearl and gold,
   And ours to hold,
Virginia,
Earth's only paradise,

Where nature hath in store   25
Fowl, venison, and fish,
   And the fruitful'st soil
   Without your toil
Three harvests more,
All greater than your wish.   30

And the ambitious vine
Crowns with his purple mass,
   The cedar reaching high
   To kiss the sky,
The cypress, pine,   35
And useful sassafras.

To whose the golden age
Still nature's laws doth give,
   No other cares that tend,
   But them to defend
From winter's age,   40
That long there doth not live.

Whenas the luscious smell
Of that delicious land,
   Above the seas that flows,
   The clear wind throws,   45
Your hearts to swell
Approaching the dear strand,

In kenning[4] of the shore,
Thanks to God first given,   50
   Oh you, the happi'st men,
   Be frolic then,

---

2. In Greek mythology, the controller of the winds.   4. Sighting.
3. Pursue.

Let cannons roar,
Frighting the wide heaven.

And in regions far   55
Such heroes bring ye forth
    As those from whom we came,
    And plant our name
Under that star
Not known unto our north.   60

And as there plenty grows
Of laurel everywhere,
    Apollo's sacred tree,
    You it may see
A poet's brows   65
To crown, that may sing there.

Thy voyages attend,
Industrious Hakluyt,[5]
    Whose reading shall enflame
    Men to seek fame,   70
And much commend
To after times thy wit.

1606

5. Richard Hakluyt (1553–1616) geographer and
author of *The Principal Navigations, Traffics,
Voyages and Discoveries of the English Nation*
(1589). Drayton evidently pronounced his name
with three syllables, "Hack-loo-it."

SIR JOHN DAVIES
1569–1626

Sir John Davies was a law student at the Middle Temple when he wrote
*Orchestra, or A Poem of Dancing, Judicially proving the true observation of
time and measure in the authentical and laudable use of dancing.* In the
next year, 1595, Davies was called to the bar. He had a distinguished legal
career, becoming successively solicitor-general for Ireland, attorney general
for Ireland, and finally, just before his death in 1626, lord chief justice of
the King's Bench in England. Five years after writing *Orchestra* he published
a serious philosophical poem called *Nosce Teipsum* ("Know Thyself"). He
is also the author of some amusing parodies on Elizabethan sonnets, his so-
called *Gulling* ("Fooling") *Sonnets.*

Orchestra pretends to be a light, even frivolous poem, but it is really a
serious expression of some important Elizabethan concepts. (The title has
the original Greek meaning, a dance floor.) The courtier was supposed to
learn to dance, not merely as a social accomplishment, but as a part of his

liberal education. Dancing was considered allegorical; as Sir Thomas Elyot said in his treatise on the ideal Elizabethan gentleman, dancing "betokeneth concord." It reconciles and harmonizes such moral and psychological opposites as fierceness and mildness, boldness and fearfulness, arrogance and modesty.

The poem purports to be an account of an episode which for some reason was left out of Homer's *Odyssey*; that classical epic and others were considered by the Elizabethans to be moral and didactic in purpose. In Davies' invented episode, the chaste Penelope, Ulysses' queen, who has been waiting patiently for the return of her husband (although suitors have tried to persuade her that she is really a widow and should therefore remarry), is endowed with special beauty by the goddess Athena. The foremost suitor, Antinous, begs her to dance; she refuses, and an extended debate ensues, in which Antinous claims that the whole universe is organized in a dance— the sun, the moon, the fixed stars, the elements in descending order beneath the moon, the winds, even the rivers and brooks.

The idea that the universe is bound together by a kind of harmony or concord is fundamental in Elizabethan cosmology. The music of the spheres orders the heavens, and music alike orders and tempers human passions and social forces. *Orchestra* also reflects another great Elizabethan idea—that of degree or rank, the orderly arrangement of all things in the universe from the highest to the lowest. If Davies had finished his poem, he would have shown Queen Elizabeth surrounded by a dance at court, and this would have seemed to sixteenth-century readers the culminating and perfect image of political order and harmony.

From Orchestra, or A Poem of Dancing

[*Dancing Justified*]

16

"Sole heir of virtue, and of beauty both,
Whence cometh it," Antinous replies,
"That your imperious virtue is so loath
To grant your beauty her chief exercise?
Or from what spring doth your opinion rise   110
    That dancing is a frenzy and a rage,
      First known and used in this new-fangled age?

17

"Dancing, bright lady, then began to be
When the first seeds whereof the world did spring,
The fire, air, earth and water did agree,   115
By Love's persuasion, nature's mighty king,
To leave their first disordered combating
    And in a dance such measure to observe
      As all the world their motion should preserve.

18

"Since when they still are carried in a round,   120
And changing come one in another's place,

Yet do they neither mingle nor confound,
But every one doth keep his bounded space
Wherein the dance doth bid it turn or trace.
   This wondrous miracle did Love devise,   125
   For dancing is Love's proper exercise.

19

"Like this he framed the gods' eternal bower
And of a shapeless and confusèd mass,
By his through-piercing and digesting power
The turning vault of heaven formèd was,   130
Whose starry wheels he hath so made to pass
   As that their movings do a music frame
   And they themselves still dance unto the same.

20

"Or if this all[1] which round about we see,
As idle Morpheus[2] some sick brains have taught,   135
Of undivided motes[3] compacted be,
How was this goodly architecture wrought?
Or by what means were they together brought?
   They err that say they did concur by chance;
   Love made them meet in a well-ordered dance.   140

21

"As when Amphion[4] with his charming lyre
Begot so sweet a siren of the air
That with her rhetoric made the stones conspire
The ruins of a city to repair,
A work of wit, and reason's wise affair,   145
   So Love's smooth tongue the motes such measures taught
   That they joined hands, and so the world was wrought.

22

"How justly then is dancing termèd new,
Which with the world in point of time begun?
Yea, time itself, whose birth Jove never knew,   150
And which indeed is elder than the sun,
Had not one moment of his age outrun,
   When out leaped dancing from the heap of things
   And lightly rode upon his nimble wings.

23

"Reason hath both their pictures in her treasure,   155
Where time the measure of all moving is,
And dancing is a moving all in measure.
Now if you do resemble that to this
And think both one, I think you think amiss;
   But if you judge them twins, together got,   160
   And time first born, your judgment erreth not.

---

1. The universe.
2. The god of dreams.
3. Atoms.

4. A Greek hero who was given a lyre by the god Hermes; he played on it so beautifully that stones moved to build a wall around Thebes.

24

"Thus doth it equal age with age enjoy,
And yet in lusty youth forever flowers,
Like Love, his sire, whom painters make a boy,
Yet is he eldest of the heavenly powers,   165
Or like his brother time, whose wingèd hours
   Going and coming, will not let him die,
   But still preserve him in his infancy."

1596

FULKE GREVILLE, LORD BROOKE
1554–1628

Greville was a close friend and biographer of Sir Philip Sidney. He came
from a wealthy family, was educated at Shrewsbury and Cambridge, and
was a courtier under three sovereigns, Elizabeth, James I, and Charles I. He
wrote a sonnet cycle, *Caelica*, under the influence of Sidney, and several
closet dramas (plays meant to be read, not acted on a stage). His most famous
poem is a chorus from one of these dramas, *Mustapha*.

Chorus Sacerdotum[1]

O wearisome condition of humanity!
Born under one law, to another bound;
Vainly begot and yet forbidden vanity;
Created sick, commanded to be sound.
What meaneth nature by these diverse laws?   5
Passion and reason, self-division cause.
Is it the mark or majesty of power
To make offenses that it may forgive?
Nature herself doth her own self deflower
To hate those errors she herself doth give.   10
For how should man think that he may not do,
If nature did not fail and punish, too?
Tyrant to others, to herself unjust,
Only commands things difficult and hard,
Forbids us all things which it knows is lust,[2]   15
Makes easy pains, unpossible reward.
If nature did not take delight in blood,
She would have made more easy ways to good.
We that are bound by vows and by promotion,[3]

---

1. Chorus of the priests, from *Mustapha*, one of
Greville's 2 surviving closet tragedies. He may have
composed a version of the play as early as 1600,
but whether the chorus was in that version or written about 1609 is uncertain.
2. Pleasure.
3. Motion or stirring of the mind.

With pomp of holy sacrifice and rites,   20
To teach belief in good and still[4] devotion,
To preach of heaven's wonders and delights;
Yet when each of us in his own heart looks
He finds the God there, far unlike his books.

1609

4. Instill.

LADY MARY WROTH
1587?–1651?

Lady Mary Wroth was the most accomplished and prolific woman poet and
writer of prose fiction in Renaissance England. She was surrounded by poets,
writers, and patrons of literature: her uncle was the famous poet Sir Philip
Sidney, her aunt was the countess of Pembroke, and her father, Sir Robert
Sidney (of Penshurst), also wrote poetry. So too did her first cousin and
lover, William Herbert, earl of Pembroke (to whom she bore two illegitimate
children). She danced in some of Ben Jonson's court masques, and Jonson
celebrated her and her husband, Sir Robert Wroth, in several poems.

Her very long but unfinished prose romance, *The Countess of Montgomery's Urania*, is modeled in some respects upon Sir Philip Sidney's *Arcadia*,
but it also alludes covertly to several scandals and personages of the Jacobean
court. The storm of criticism attending its publication in 1621 caused her to
withdraw it from circulation, and evidently kept her from publishing a continuation of that work (the manuscript has only recently been discovered) as
well as her pastoral play *Love's Victorie*. Appended to *Urania* is a Petrarchan
sonnet sequence, *Pamphilia to Amphilanthus*, consisting of one hundred
and three sonnets and songs; as the speaker is a woman, the conventional
sonnet roles of male lover and female beloved are reversed. In addition,
some seventy-four poems are interspersed throughout the two parts of the
Urania, and a few others exist in manuscript.

Song from *Urania*

Love what art thou? A vain thought
    In our minds by fant'sy wrought,
    Idle smiles did thee beget
    While fond wishes made the net
    Which so many fools have caught;   5

Love what art thou? light, and faire,
    Fresh as morning, clear as th' Air,
    But too soon thy evening change
    Makes thy worth with coldness range
    Still thy joy is mixt with care: 10

Love what art thou? A sweet flower
  Once full blown,[1] dead in an hour,
  Dust in wind as staid remains
  As thy pleasure, or our gains
  If thy humor[2] change, to lour.   15

Love what art thou? childish, vain,
  Firm as bubbles made by rain:
  Wantonness thy greatest pride,
  These foul faults thy virtues hide
  But babes can no staidness gain.   20

Love what art thou? causeless cursed
  Yet alas these not the worst
  Much more of thee may be said
  But thy law I once obeyed
  Therefore say no more at first.   25

1621

From Pamphilia to Amphilanthus[1]

Am I Thus Conquered?

Am I thus conquered? have I lost the powers
  That to withstand, which joys to ruin me?[2]
  Must I be still while it my strength devours
  And captive leads me prisoner, bound, unfree?

Love[3] first shall leave mens fant'sies to them free,   5
  Desire shall quench loves flames, spring hate sweet showers,
  Love shall loose all his darts, have sight, and see
  His shame, and wishings hinder happy hours;

Why should we not loves purblind[4] charms resist?
  Must we be servile, doing what he list?[5]   10
  No, seek some host to harbor thee: I fly

Thy babish tricks, and freedom do profess;
  But O my hurt, makes my lost heart confess
  I love, and must: So farewell liberty.

1621

1. In full bloom.
2. Whim.
1. Pamphilia is the protagonist of the *Urania*. Her
name means "all loving"; her unfaithful beloved's
name means "lover of two."

2. I.e., have I lost the power to withstand love
("that"), whose joys ruin me.
3. I.e., blind Cupid.
4. Totally blind.
5. Wishes.

False Hope Which Feeds But to Destroy

False hope which feeds but to destroy, and spill
    What it first breeds;[1] unnatural to the birth
    Of thine own womb; conceiving but to kill,
    And plenty gives to make the greater dearth,[2]

So tyrants do who falsely ruling earth   5
    Outwardly grace them, and with profits fill,
    Advance those who appointed are to death[3]
    To make their greater fall to please their will.

Thus shadow[4] they their wicked vile intent
    Coloring evil with a show of good   10
    While in fair shows their malice so is spent;
    Hope kills the heart, and tyrants shed the blood.

For hope deluding brings us to the pride
Of our desires the farther down to slide.

1621

From A Crown of Sonnets Dedicated to Love

IN THIS STRANGE LABYRINTH HOW SHALL I TURN?[1]

In this strange labyrinth how shall I turn?
    Ways are on all sides while the way I miss:
    If to the right hand, there, in love I burn;
    Let me go forward, therein danger is;

If to the left, suspicion hinders bliss,   5
    Let me turn back, shame cries I ought return
    Nor faint though crosses with my fortunes kiss;
    Stand still is harder, although sure to mourn;[2]

Then let me take the right, or left hand way;
    Go forward, or stand still, or back retire;   10
    I must these doubts endure without allay[3]
    Or help, but travail find for my best hire;[4]

---

1. "Spill": kill; the image is of miscarriage or infanticide.
2. Famine.
3. I.e., first advance those whom they intend to destroy.
4. Cloud over, cover up.
1. This is the first in a set of fourteen sonnets in the *corona* form, in which the last line of each sonnet serves as the first line of the succeeding one, with the last line of the final sonnet rounding back to repeat the first line of the first sonnet (hence the name "corona," a crown or circlet). This sequence comprises the poems numbered 77–90 in *Pamphilia to Amphilanthus*.
2. I.e., although certain to make me mourn.
3. Relief.
4. I.e., I find suffering ("travail"—with a pun on both labor and travel) to be the best recompense ("hire") I can gain.

Yet that which most my troubled sense doth move
Is to leave all, and take the thread of love.[5]

1621

ANONYMOUS LYRICS

Back and Side Go Bare, Go Bare[1]

Back and side go bare, go bare,
   Both foot and hand go cold;
But, belly, God send thee good ale enough,
   Whether it be new or old.

I cannot eat but little meat,   5
   My stomach is not good;
But sure I think that I can drink
   With him that wears a hood.[2]
Though I go bare, take ye no care,
   I am nothing a-cold;   10
I stuff my skin so full within
   Of jolly good ale and old.
Back and side go bare, go bare, etc.

I love no roast but a nut-brown toast,[3]
   And a crab laid in the fire;   15
A little bread shall do me stead,
   Much bread I not desire.
No frost nor snow, no wind, I trow,[4]
   Can hurt me if I would,
I am so wrapped, and throughly lapped   20
   Of jolly good ale and old.
Back and side go bare, etc.

And Tib my wife, that as her life
   Loveth well good ale to seek,
Full oft drinks she, till ye may see   25
   The tears run down her cheeks.
Then doth she troll[5] to me the bowl,
   Even as a maltworm should,
And saith, "Sweetheart, I took my part
   Of this jolly good ale and old."   30

5. The allusion is to the thread that Ariadne gave Theseus to guide him out of the labyrinth and so save him from the Minotaur.
1. One of the best English drinking songs, this is sung in *Gammer Gurton's Needle*, a pioneer play in the development of native English comedy. The play is often ascribed to a "Mr. S., Master of Art," who probably wrote it for performance at Cambridge University.
2. With a monk, i.e., I can match anyone in drinking.
3. Toast was often dipped in beverages; "crab": crab apple.
4. Think, suppose.
5. Pass.

Back and side go bare, etc.

Now let them drink, till they nod and wink,
    Even as good fellows should do;
They shall not miss to have the bliss
    Good ale doth bring men to;   35
And all poor souls that have scoured bowls
    Or have them lustily trolled,
God save the lives of them and their wives,
    Whether they be young or old.

Back and side go bare, go bare,   40
    Both foot and hand go cold;
But, belly, God send thee good ale enough,
    Whether it be new or old.

1575

In Praise of a Contented Mind[1]

My mind to me a kingdom is;
    Such perfect joy therein I find
That it excels all other bliss
    That world affords or grows by kind.[2]
Though much I want[3] which most men have,   5
Yet still my mind forbids to crave.

No princely pomp, no wealthy store,
    No force to win the victory,
No wily wit to salve a sore,
    No shape to feed each gazing eye;   10
To none of these I yield as thrall.
For why[4] my mind doth serve for all.

I see how plenty suffers oft,
    How hasty climbers soon do fall;
I see that those that are aloft   15
    Mishap doth threaten most of all;
They get with toil, they keep with fear.
Such cares my mind could never bear.

1. This is one of the most popular of Elizabethan lyrics. It was long attributed to the courtier-poet and friend of Sidney, Sir Edward Dyer, but a recent study ascribes it more plausibly to Edward de Vere, seventeenth earl of Oxford, also a courtier, poet, and patron of writers. Several manuscripts of the poem survive. In 1588 the great Elizabethan composer William Byrd set it to music in his *Psalms, Sonnets, and Songs of Sadness and Piety;* there were other musical settings later. The poem was also printed as a broadside ballad and remained popular down through the seventeenth century. It may be regarded as the culmination in the sixteenth century of the ideal of *otium,* or the contented mind. It is embodied in the idyllic simplicity of pastoral and in the glorification of the "mean estate" (moderate living) in such poems as Surrey's *My Friend, the Things That Do Attain.*
2. Nature.
3. Lack.
4. Because.

Content I live, this is my stay;
　　I see no more than may suffice;   20
I press to bear no haughty sway;
　　Look what⁵ I lack my mind supplies;
Lo, thus I triumph like a king,
Content with that my mind doth bring.

Some have too much, yet still do crave;   25
　　I little have, and seek no more.
They are but poor, though much they have,
　　And I am rich with little store.
They poor, I rich; they beg, I give;
They lack, I leave;⁶ they pine, I live.   30

I laugh not at another's loss;
　　I grudge not at another's gain;
No worldly waves my mind can toss;
　　My state at one doth still remain.
I fear no foe, nor fawning friend;   35
I loathe not life, nor dread my end.

Some weigh their pleasure by their lust,⁷
　　Their wisdom by their rage of will,⁸
Their treasure is their only trust;
　　And cloakèd craft their store of skill.   40
But all the pleasure that I find
Is to maintain a quiet mind.

My wealth is health and perfect ease;
　　My conscience clear my chief defense;
I neither seek by bribes to please,   45
　　Nor by deceit to breed offense.
Thus do I live; thus will I die.
Would all did so as well as I!

1581   1588

Though Amaryllis Dance in Green¹

　　Though Amaryllis dance in green
　　　　Like fairy queen;
　　　　And sing full clear
　　Corinna can, with smiling, cheer.

---

5. Whatever.
6. Bequeath, as in a will; "pine": dwindle away.
7. Sensual delight.
8. I.e., wild desires.
1. William Byrd set this anonymous lyric to music

in his song book entitled *Psalms, Sonnets, and Songs of Sadness and Piety*. It is a "ballet"—a dance-song of short stanzas with refrain—an appropriate form for this quaint rustic song about the renunciation of love.

Yet since their eyes make heart so sore,   5
Heigh ho, heigh ho, 'chill[2] love no more.

My sheep are lost for want of food,
        And I so wood,[3]
        That all the day
I sit and watch a herdmaid gay,   10
Who laughs to see me sigh so sore,
Heigh ho, heigh ho, 'chill love no more.

Her loving looks, her beauty bright
        Is such delight,
        That all in vain   15
I love to like and lose my gain,
For her that thanks me not therefor,
Heigh ho, heigh ho, 'chill love no more.

Ah wanton eyes, my friendly foes,
        And cause of woes,   20
        Your sweet desire
Breeds flames of ice and freeze in fire.
Ye scorn to see me weep so sore,
Heigh ho, heigh ho, 'chill love no more.

Love ye who list, I force him not,   25
        Sith, God it wot,
        The more I wail,
The less my sighs and tears prevail.
What shall I do but say therefore,
Heigh ho, heigh ho, 'chill love no more.   30

1588

Come Away, Come, Sweet Love![1]

Come away, come, sweet love! The golden morning breaks;
All the earth, all the air of love and pleasure speaks.
        Teach thine arms then to embrace,
        And sweet rosy lips to kiss,
        And mix our souls in mutual bliss;   5
        Eyes were made for beauty's grace,
        Viewing, rueing love-long pain,
        Procured by beauty's rude disdain.

---

2. The rustic dialect form for "I will": (i)ch (w)ill.
3. Frantic.
1. An aubade (or morning song to one's lady), set to music by John Dowland in his *First Book of Songs or Airs.* Dowland (1563–1626) was a famous composer and lutenist.

Come away, come, sweet love! The golden morning wastes,
While the sun from his sphere his fiery arrows casts   10
    Making all the shadows fly,
    Playing, staying in the grove
    To entertain the stealth of love.
    Thither, sweet love, let us hie,
    Flying, dying in desire,   15
    Winged with sweet hopes and heavenly fire.

Come away, come, sweet love! Do not in vain adorn
Beauty's grace, that should rise like to the naked morn.
    Lilies on the riverside
    And fair Cyprian[2] flowers new-blown   20
    Desire no beauties but their own,
    Ornament is nurse of pride;
    Pleasure measure love's delight.
    Haste then, sweet love, our wishèd flight!

1597

Thule, the Period of Cosmography[1]

Thule, the period of cosmography,
    Doth vaunt of Hecla,[2] whose sulphurious fire
Doth melt the frozen clime and thaw the sky;
    Trinacrian Aetna's[3] flames ascend not higher.
These things seem wondrous, yet more wondrous I,   5
Whose heart with fear doth freeze, with love doth fry.

The Andalusian[4] merchant, that returns
    Laden with cochineal and China dishes,
Reports in Spain how strangely Fogo[5] burns
    Amidst an ocean full of flying fishes.   10
These things seem wondrous, yet more wondrous I,
Whose heart with fear doth freeze, with love doth fry.

1600

2. Pertaining to Venus, the Cyprian goddess; hence, spring flowers.

1. "Thule" or "Ultima Thule" was a general name for the Arctic; "period of cosmography" suggests the end point of navigation, a full stop. This remarkable poem, which draws upon Elizabethan interest in exploration and discovery to illustrate the conventional pangs of a lover, first appeared in a book of madrigals by Thomas Weelkes.

2. A volcano in Iceland.

3. Mt. Etna, a volcano on the island of Sicily. The poet is quoting Virgil, *Aeneid* 3.554: *e fluctu Trinacria cernitur Aetna* ("out of the waves appears Trinacrian [i.e. Sicilian] Aetna").

4. From southern Spain. "Cochineal": a red dye.

5. One of the Cape Verde Islands, 300 miles off the coast of Africa, west of Dakar. Francis Drake visited it in 1578; the account in Hakluyt's *Principal Navigations* includes details used here: "The Isle of Fogo . . . called by the Portingals *Ila del fogo*, that is, the burning Island: in the Northside whereof is a consuming fire, the matter is sayd to bee of Sulphure. . . . Being departed from these Islands, we drew towards the line [the Equator], where wee were becalmed the space of 3. weekes . . . we had the commoditie of great store [plenty] of fish, as Dolphin, Bonitas, and flying fishes, whereof some fell into our shippes, where hence they could not rise againe for want of moisture, for when their wings are drie, they cannot flie."

Madrigal[1]

My love in her attire doth show her wit,
  It doth so well become her;
For every season she hath dressings fit,
  For winter, spring, and summer.
  No beauty she doth miss   5
  When all her robes are on;
  But beauty's self she is
  When all her robes are gone.

1602

The Silver Swan[1]

The silver swan, who living had no note.
When death approached, unlocked her silent throat;
Leaning her breast against the reedy shore,
Thus sung her first and last, and sung no more:
"Farewell, all joys; Oh death, come close mine eyes;   5
More geese than swans now live, more fools than wise."

1612

Constant Penelope Sends to Thee[1]

Constant Penelope sends to thee, careless Ulysses.
Write not again, but come, sweet mate, thyself to revive me.
Troy we do much envy, we desolate lost ladies of Greece,
Not Priamus, nor yet all Troy can us recompense make.
Oh, that he had, when he first took shipping to Lacedaemon,[2]   5
That adulter I mean, had been o'erwhelmed with waters.
Then had I not lain now all alone, thus quivering for cold,
Nor used this complaint, nor have thought the day to be so long.

1588

---

1. This sophisticated courtly lyric was printed in an anthology entitled *A Poetical Rhapsody* (1602).
1. From Orlando Gibbons' *First Set of Madrigals and Motets*. In this short lyric, Gibbons, who was one of the last of the madrigalists, may be mourning the demise of his art.
1. A translation (perhaps by Thomas Watson), from book 1 of Ovid's *Heroides*, into purely quantitative

English verse. It was set to music by William Byrd in his *Psalms, Sonnets, and Songs of Sadness and Piety* (1588). Penelope was the wife of Ulysses, away at the Trojan War. "Priamus" (line 4) was king of Troy.
2. Sparta. Paris, the "adulter" of line 6, stole Helen from her husband Menelaus, king of Sparta; this rape was the cause of the Trojan War.

Prose of the Sixteenth Century

English prose in the fifteenth century was not much used for works of "high" literature. Malory was the sole exception, writing as he did a variety of prose akin to early epic poetry—spare, understated, but highly evocative. A modern prose style was forged only gradually during the sixteenth century. Contributing to its formation were translations of classical and Continental works such as Plutarch's *Lives* (by Sir Thomas North) and Castiglione's *The Courtier* (by Sir Thomas Hoby), and most notably, vernacular translations of the Bible. Important also were experiments in prose fiction ranging from romances such as Sidney's *Arcadia* and Thomas Lodge's *Rosalynde* to picaresque adventure tales such as Thomas Nashe's *Unfortunate Traveller*. The exploration and exposition of issues and problems posed by the Reformation, by the discovery of new continents and new civilizations, and by the beginnings of experimental science also contributed to the evolution of English prose.

In the course of the sixteenth century, the Bible was rendered in several English versions. The Reformation, with its insistence upon the responsibilities of the private conscience informed by a personal reading of Scripture, gave an enormous impetus to translations for the Bible from the Hebrew and Greek originals into the vernacular tongues. In the Middle Ages, the Roman Catholic Church as infallible authority interpreted the Bible and directed public, ceremonial worship for a generally illiterate laity. But in England as elsewhere, the first reformers gave the production of a vernacular Bible the highest priority, and were themselves among the first translators. William Tyndale, boldest and most influential of the English translators, was burned at the stake for his efforts; yet within three years of his death in 1536, an English Bible was on public sale everywhere in the land. There can be no doubt that the impulse to read the Bible, the book which held the key to salvation, was responsible for a tremendous rise in the literacy of the nation.

The Reformation also gave impetus to the writing and publication of many kinds of instructional and devotional writing, intended to provide spiritual direction for a Protestant nation. Such works included sermons, biblical commentaries, books on moral problems (called Cases of Conscience), instruction in and models for prayer and meditation, analyses of the course of the Christian life. A great deal of controversial and polemical writing was addressed to theological and ecclesiastical issues disputed among Roman Catholics, adherents of the Church of England, and the everincreasing group of radical Protestants (or Puritans) who wanted a more thoroughgoing reformation in doctrine and worship than that accomplished by the English Church. Roman Catholic controversial writings were generally suppressed after 1570, in the wake of a papal decree denying that Elizabeth was the rightful sovereign of England and absolving her subjects of allegiance to her; many such "recusant" works by Catholics were, however, published abroad and circulated in England underground. On the Puritan side, the most notable controversial works were the so-called Marprelate Tracts, a series of brilliant, wittily satiric, and often scurrilous underground pamphlets ascribed to one Martin Marprelate (the pseudonym Mar-prelate points to the satiric intention and thrust). The style of these was brash, popular, and colloquial, and from the viewpoint of the government this made them all the more dangerous. Elizabeth's officers sought out the secret press on which the tracts were printed (it was carried about the country on the back of a haywagon); several of those responsible were imprisoned and died awaiting trial. However, the principal author of the Marprelate tracts, Job Throckmorton, managed to escape detection and died in his own bed in 1600.

But far and away the most influential polemics were two massive works supporting the established Church under Elizabeth. John Foxe, one of the many Protestants who had gone into exile during the reign of the Catholic Mary Tudor and returned at the accession of Elizabeth, published in several editions an enormous collection of records and tales of the Marian martyrs—the Protestants executed during Mary's reign. Titled *Acts and Monuments* and familiarly known as "The Book of Martyrs," this prodigiously popular work fomented hatred for the Church of Rome and all its actions. In a very different spirit, characterized by rigorous logic, a moderate tone, and many expressions of Christian charity, was Richard Hooker's monumental *Laws of Ecclesiastical Polity*, intended to defend the established church order and the episcopal government of the Church of England against the scripture-based attacks of the Puritan Presbyterians. Hooker's book has particular importance for its development of a broadly conceived Elizabethan version of the "natural law" philosophy inherited from the medieval scholastics as a basis for the interlocking system of laws governing the cosmos, humankind, civil government, and the church. This work fully deserves its reputation as the first finished monument of modern English prose.

Polemics were of course addressed to topics other than religious controversy. One striking example is the vigorous defense of women against common assumptions about their moral and spiritual inferiority to men, mounted by Aemilia Lanyer in the *Epistle* to her volume of religious poetry. Another is Sir Philip Sidney's urbane, closely argued, and witty *Defence of Poesy* against Puritan attacks on it as false and immoral.

Other kinds of prose developed from the challenge of exploring and exploiting the New World. The English were relative latecomers to this enterprise: the Spanish and Portuguese had been entrenched in South and North America fully a hundred years by the time Sir Walter Ralegh planted the first unsuccessful English Colony in Virginia. But the voyages of discovery sparked the English imagination almost as soon as they were known, and gave rise to a steady stream of travelers' tales, colonists' reports, and entrepreneurs' advertisements that were often a curious mixture of fact and myth.

In addition, plain practical prose, often on technical or scientific topics and cast in the common, vernacular speech, flourished during the latter years of Elizabeth. The lectures on science and related topics, established by Sir Thomas Gresham in the City of London, were free to all and mostly in English, providing a foundation for a vernacular idiom mingling learned theory with practical explanation. In 1628 Sir William Harvey announced the circulation of the blood in Latin, but twelve years before this publication to the learned world the theory had been set forth in English lectures.

Throughout the century writers paid increasing attention to the resources of the language and to issues of style. One focus for this concern during the latter half of the century was the so-called inkhorn controversy, a dispute over whether and how to enrich the language by anglicizing learned words from Greek and Latin; and a related dispute centered upon French and Italian. Some such terms were evidently recognized as artificial and pretentious, and were dropped, but others were permanently adopted into the language, along with many new word coinages. In fact, Richard Mulcaster, Spenser's schoolmaster, saw the expanding vocabulary of English as a parallel to England's emergence as a world power through exploration and colonization. Another issue involved the status of the Roman rhetorician Cicero as the most exalted model for prose, and the use of Seneca and other classical stylists as alternative models. There was also a short-lived fad for "Euphuism"—an experiment in exaggerated, aphoristic, sententious prose begun by John Lyly in 1579, which had become a ripe subject for parody by 1598 (see Shakespeare's *1 Henry IV*, 2.4.347–63). Such experiments and controversies gave rise to a heightened sense of the stylistic possibilities of English prose.

During the sixteenth century, then, English prose was vindicated as a medium for God's word, and was recognized as a suitable vehicle to present the sufferings of Protestant martyrs, to instruct ambitious courtiers, to describe newly explored countries, to defend poetry against its detractors. It also made available the treasures of classical and continental learning and literature to those who knew no Latin, Greek, or modern European languages. Richard Carew's *Epistle on the Excellency of the English Tongue*, written in the last decade of the sixteenth century, praised the large resources of English for literary expression: "neither can any tongue (as I am persuaded) deliver a matter with more variety than ours, both plainly and by proverbs and metaphors."

TRANSLATING THE BIBLE
Isaiah 53:3-6

The Reformation made it imperative to read the Bible for oneself; hence, translating the Bible from its Greek and Hebrew originals into the vernacular was a matter of the first importance. William Tyndale began an English translation in 1523, but he had to do it surreptitiously, outside the country, and he finally suffered martyrdom for his efforts. In 1530 a royal proclamation condemned Tyndale's translation and all other versions in the vernacular. In 1535 Miles Coverdale published, in Zurich, the first complete Bible in English. But by this time Henry VIII had broken with Rome and the official attitude was changing. In 1540 the so-called Great Bible—essentially a composite of the Tyndale and Coverdale versions—was issued with official sanction, the first English Bible to be so recognized.

The Geneva Bible (1560) was the work of Protestant refugees who fled to the Continent in the reign of the Catholic Queen Mary. This was the first Bible to divide the chapters into verses in the modern manner, and the first English Bible to be printed in Roman type rather than the old black letter or Gothic type. It was handy in size, and in many instances more accurate than its predecessors, but the marginal commentary was strongly Protestant. The Bishops' Bible (1568) was an attempt on the part of the Elizabethan church to counter the extreme Protestantism of the Geneva Bible. The bishops who sponsored it directed that their Bible be the official one used in churches, but the people continued to read the Geneva Bible at home, and its influence remained very great throughout the sixteenth and early seventeenth centuries. A Catholic translation into English, based upon the Latin Vulgate, was a belated concession to the demand for the scriptures in the vernacular. It was published by English Catholic refugees abroad, the New Testament at Rheims in 1582 and the Old Testament at Douai in 1609-10.

King James did not like the popular Geneva Bible (some of its commentary was quite critical of kings). As part of the religious settlement which took place early in his reign, he authorized a distinguished group of forty-seven translators to make a new version in English. The resulting work, which owes more to Tyndale than to any other predecessor, has been called "the noblest monument of English prose." We have chosen to reprint a passage from Isaiah in the several versions described above, to indicate some of the stylistic features characteristic of each translation.

Translating the Bible (Isaiah 53.3-6)

From *The Coverdale Bible*

He shall be the most simple and despised of all, which yet hath good experience of sorrows and infirmities. We shall reckon him so simple and so vile that we shall hide our faces from him.

Howbeit (of a truth) he only taketh away our infirmity, and beareth our pain: Yet we shall judge him, as though he were plagued and cast down of God:

whereas he (notwithstanding) shall be wounded for our offenses, and smitten for our wickedness. For the pain of our punishment shall be laid upon him, and with his stripes shall we be healed.

As for us, we go all astray (like sheep), everyone turneth his own way. But through him, the Lord pardoneth all our sins.

1535

From *The Great Bible*

He is despised and abhorred of men. He is such a man as is afull of sorrow and as hath good experience of infirmities. We have reckoned him so vile that we hid our faces from him. Yea, he was despised and therefore we regarded him not.

Howbeit he only hath taken on him our infirmities and borne our pains. Yet we did judge him, as though he were plagued and cast down of God and punished.

Whereas he (notwithstanding) was wounded for our offenses and smitten for our wickedness. For the chastisement of our peace was laid upon him and with his stripes we are healed.

As for us, we have gone all astray, like sheep; every one hath turned his own way. But the Lord hath heaped together upon him the iniquity of us all.

1539–40

From *The Geneva Bible*

He is despised and rejected of men. He is a man full of sorrows and hath experience of infirmities. We hid as it were our faces from him. He was despised and we esteemed him not.

Surely he hath borne our infirmities and carried our sorrows; yet we did judge him as plagued, and smitten of God, and humbled.

But he was wounded for our transgressions; he was broken for our iniquities; the chastisement of our peace was upon him, and with his stripes we are healed.

All we like sheep have gone astray. We have turned every one to his own way, and the Lord hath laid upon him the iniquity of us all.

1560

From *The Rheims-Douai Bible*

Despised, and most abject of men, a man of sorrows, and knowing infirmity. And his look as it were hid and despised, whereupon neither have we esteemed him.

He surely hath borne our infirmities, and our sorrows he hath carried. And we have thought him as it were a leper, and stricken of God and humbled.

But he was wounded for our iniquities; he was broken for our sins. The discipline of our peace upon him, and with the wail of his stripe we are healed.

All we have strayed as sheep; everyone hath declined into his own way, and our Lord hath put upon him the iniquity of all us.

1609

From *The King James Bible*

He is despised and rejected of men; a man of sorrows, and acquainted with grief. And we hid as it were our faces from him. He was despised, and we esteemed him not.

Surely he hath borne our griefs and carried our sorrows; yet we did esteem him stricken, smitten of God, and afflicted.

But he was wounded for our transgressions; he was bruised for our iniquities. The chastisement of our peace was upon him, and with his stripes we are healed.

All we like sheep have gone astray; we have turned every one to his own way; and the Lord hath laid on him the iniquity of us all.

1611

SIR THOMAS HOBY
1530–1566

One of the great and influential books of the Renaissance was *Il Cortegiano* ("The Courtier") published in 1528 in Italian by Count Baldasarre Castiglione (1478–1529) and soon translated into all the other European languages. The English translation, by the humanist and diplomat Sir Thomas Hoby, was not published until 1561, but had been written earlier, probably during the reign of Queen Mary (1553–58) when Hoby lived abroad as a Protestant exile. The style of the translation makes it an important landmark in English prose; Hoby, like his master Sir John Cheke, preferred words from the native Anglo-Saxon element of the language, rather than borrowings from French or Italian.

The book describes, by means of dialogues between actual persons living at the court of the duke of Urbino in the years 1504–8, the qualities and characteristics of the ideal courtier. Spenser's friend Gabriel Harvey, in his copy of Hoby's translation, summarized the contents of this great "courtesy book" as follows: "Above all things it importeth a courtier to be graceful and lovely in countenance and behavior; fine and discreet in discourse and entertainment; skillful and expert in letters and arms; active and gallant in every courtly exercise; nimble and speedy of body and mind; resolute, industrious and valorous in action, as profound and invincible in action as is possible; and withal ever generously bold, wittily pleasant, and full of life in his sayings and doings." Shakespeare's Hamlet was such an ideal courtier, as Ophelia testifies when she finds in him,

The courtier's, soldier's, scholar's eye, tongue, sword;
The expectancy and rose of the fair state,
The glass of fashion and the mold of form. (3.1.151–53)

The Elizabethans thought of Sir Philip Sidney as the example of an ideal courtier in real life.

Probably the most famous passage in *The Courtier* is Peter Bembo's classic statement of the Neoplatonic ideal of love in book 4. Bembo declares that love is not the mere gratification of the senses, but is the yearning of the soul after beauty. Furthermore, the beautiful is finally identical with the good. Love properly understood is therefore a kind of ladder by which the soul progresses from lower to higher things. As he pursues his theme Bembo becomes more and more enraptured, and ends with a prayer to Love as a god. Although the dialogue form permits his auditors to voice criticism of Bembo's doctrine, the eloquence of his speech carries the day.

From The Courtier

From *Book 4*

[THE LADDER OF LOVE]

Then M. Peter[1] after a while's silence, somewhat settling himself as though he should entreat upon a weighty matter, said thus: "My Lords, to show that old men may love not only without slander, but otherwhile[2] more happily than young men, I must be enforced to make a little discourse to declare what love is, and wherein consisteth the happiness that lovers may have. Therefore I beseech you give the hearing with heedfulness, for I hope to make you understand that it were not unfitting for any man here to be a lover, in case he were fifteen or twenty years elder than M. Morello."[3]

And here, after they had laughed awhile, M. Peter proceeded: "I say, therefore, that according as it is defined of the wise men of old time, love is nothing else but a certain coveting to enjoy beauty; and forsomuch as coveting longeth for nothing but for things known, it is requisite that knowledge go evermore before coveting, which of his own nature willeth the good, but of himself is blind and knoweth it not. Therefore hath nature so ordained that to every virtue of knowledge there is annexed a virtue of longing. And because in our soul there be three manner[4] ways to know, namely, by sense, reason, and understanding: of sense ariseth appetite or longing, which is common to us with brute beasts; of reason ariseth election or choice, which is proper to man; of understanding, by the which man may be partner with angels, ariseth will. Even as therefore the sense knoweth not but sensible matters and that which may be felt, so the appetite or coveting only desireth the same; and even as

---

1. Peter Bembo (1470–1547) poet, Platonist, grammarian and historian, later a cardinal.
2. Occasionally.

3. Morello da Ortona, a courtier and musician, later a speaker in the discussion.
4. Kinds of.

the understanding is bent but to behold things that may be understood, so is that will only fed with spiritual goods. Man of nature endowed with reason, placed, as it were, in the middle between these two extremities, may, through his choice inclining to sense or reaching to understanding, come nigh to the coveting, sometime of the one, sometime of the other part. In these sorts therefore may beauty be coveted, the general name whereof may be applied to all things, either natural or artificial, that are framed in good proportion and due temper,[5] as their nature beareth. But speaking of the beauty that we mean, which is only it that appeareth in bodies, and especially in the face of man, and moveth this fervent coveting which we call love, we will term it an influence of the heavenly bountifulness, the which for all it stretcheth over all things that be created (like the light of the sun), yet when it findeth out a face well proportioned, and framed with a certain lively agreement of several colors, and set forth with lights and shadows, and with an orderly distance and limits of lines, thereinto it distilleth itself and appearth most well favored, and decketh out and lighteneth the subject where it shineth with a marvelous grace and glistering, like the sunbeams that strike against beautiful plate of fine gold wrought and set with precious jewels, so that it draweth unto it men's eyes with pleasure, and piercing through them imprinteth himself in the soul, and with an unwonted sweetness all to-stirreth[6] her and delighteth, and setting her on fire maketh her to covet him. When the soul then is taken with coveting to enjoy this beauty as a good thing, in case she suffer herself to be guided with the judgment of sense, she falleth into most deep errors, and judgeth the body in which beauty is discerned to be the principal cause thereof; whereupon to enjoy it she reckoneth it necessary to join as inwardly as she can with that body, which is false; and therefore whoso thinketh in possessing the body to enjoy beauty, he is far deceived, and is moved to it, not with true knowledge by the choice of reason, but with false opinion by the longing of sense. Whereupon the pleasure that followeth it is also false and of necessity full of errors. And therefore into one of the two vices run all those lovers that satisfy their unhonest lusts with the women whom they love; for either as soon as they come to the coveted end, they not only feel a fullness and loathsomeness, but also conceive a hatred against the right beloved, as though longing repented him of his offense and acknowledged the deceit wrought him by the false judgment of sense, that made him believe the ill to be good, or else they continue in the very same coveting and greediness, as though they were not indeed come to the end which they sought for. And albeit through the blind opinion that hath made them drunken (to their seeming) in that instant they feel a contentation,[7] as the diseased otherwhile, that dream they drink of some clear spring, yet they are not satisfied, nor leave off so. And because of possessing coveted goodness there arises always quietness and satisfaction in the possessor's mind, in case this were the true and right end of

---

5. The right mixture or combination of elements.   7. Satisfaction.
6. Moves violently.

their coveting, when they possess it they would be at quietness and throughly satisfied, which they be not: but rather deceived through that likeness, they forthwith return again to unbridled coveting, and with the very same trouble which they felt at the first, they fall again into the raging and most burning thirst of the thing, that they hope in vain to possess perfectly. These kind of lovers therefore love most unluckily for either they never come by their covetings, which is a great unluckiness, or else if they do come by them, they find they come by their hurt and end their misery with other greater miseries, for both in the beginning and middle of this love, there is never other thing felt but afflictions, torments, griefs, pining travail, so that to be wan, vexed with continual tears and sighs, to live with a discontented mind, to be always dumb, or to lament, to covet death, in conclusion to be most unlucky are the properties which, they say, belong to lovers. The cause therefore of this wretchedness in men's minds is principally sense, which in youthful age beareth most sway, because the lustiness of the flesh and of the blood in that season addeth unto him even so much force as it withdraweth from reason. Therefore doth it easily train[8] the soul to follow appetite or long-ing, for when she seeth herself drowned in the earthly prison, because she is set in the office to govern the body, she cannot of herself under-stand plainly at the first the truth of spiritual beholding. Wherefore to compass the understanding of things, she must go beg the beginning at the senses, and therefore she believeth them and giveth ear to them, and is contented to be led by them, especially when they have so much courage, that (in a manner) they enforce her, and because they are deceitful they fill her with errors and false opinions. Whereupon most commonly it happeneth that young men be wrapped in this sensual love, which is a very rebel against reason, and therefore they make them-selves unworthy to enjoy the favors and benefits which love bestows upon his true subjects, neither in love feel they any other pleasures than what beasts without reason do, but much more grievous afflictions. Setting case therefore this to be so, which is most true, I say that the contrary chanceth to them of a more ripe age. For in case they, when the soul is not now so much weighted down with the bodily burden, and when the natural burning assuageth and draweth to a warmth, if they be inflamed with beauty, and to it bend their coveting guided by reasonable choice, they be not deceived, and possess beauty perfectly, and therefore through the possessing of it, always goodness ensueth to them. Because beauty is good and consequently the true love of it is most good and holy, and evermore bringeth forth good fruits in the souls of them that with the bridle of reason restrain the ill disposition of sense, the which old men can much sooner do than young. It is not therefore out of reason to say that old men may also love without slander and more happily than young men, taking notwithstanding this name old, not for the age at the pit's brink, nor when the canals of the body be so feeble, that the soul cannot

8. Entice.

through them work her feats, but when knowledge in us is in his right strength. And I will not also hide this from you: namely, that I suppose where sensual love in every age is naught, yet in young men it deserveth excuse, and perhaps in some case leeful;[9] for although it puts them in afflictions, dangers, travails, and the unfortunateness that is said, yet are there many that to win them the goodwill of their ladies practice virtuous things, which for all they be not bent to a good end, yet are they good of themselves; and so of that much bitterness they pick out a little sweetness, and through the adversities which they sustain, in the end they acknowledge their error. As I judge therefore those young men that bridle their appetites, and love with reason, to be godly; so do I hold excused such as yield to sensual love, whereunto they be so inclined through the weakness and frailty of man—so they show therein meekness, courtesy, and prowess, and the other worthy conditions that these Lords have spoken of; and when those youthful years be gone and past, leave it off clean, keeping aloof from this sensual coveting as from the lowermost step of the stairs, by which a man may ascend to true love. But in case after they draw in years once, they reserve in their cold heart the fire of appetites, and bring stout reason in subjection to feeble sense, it cannot be said how much they are to be blamed: for like men without sense they deserve with an everlasting shame to be put in the number of unreasonable living creatures, because the thoughts and ways of sensual love be far unfitting for ripe age."

Here Bembo paused awhile, and when all things were whist[1] M. Morello of Ortona said: "And in case there were some old man more fresh and lusty and of a better complexion[2] than many young men, why would you not have it lawful for him to love with the love that young men love?"

The Duchess[3] laughed, and said: "If the love of young men be so unlucky, why would you, M. Morello, that old men should also love with this unluckiness? But in case you were old, as these men say you be, you would not thus procure the hurt of old men."

M. Morello answered: "The hurt of old men, meseemeth, M. Peter Bembo procureth, who will have them to love after a sort that I for my part understand not; and, methink, the possessing of this beauty which he praiseth so much, without the body, is a dream."

"Do you believe, M. Morello," quoth then Count Lewis,[4] "that beauty is always so good a thing as M. Peter Bembo speaketh of?"

"Not I, in good sooth," answered M. Morello. "But I remember rather that I have seen many beautiful women of a most ill inclination, cruel and spiteful, and it seemeth that, in a manner, it happeneth always so, for beauty maketh them proud, and pride, cruel."

Count Lewis said, smiling: "To you perhaps they seem cruel, because they content you not with it that you would have. But cause M. Peter

9. Permissible.
1. Quiet.
2. Bodily vigor.

3. Elizabeth Gonzaga, wife of the duke of Urbino.
4. Lodovico Canossa, later bishop of Bayeux.

Bembo to teach you in what sort old men ought to covet beauty, and what to seek at their ladies' hands, and what to content themselves withal; and in not passing out of these bounds ye shall see that they shall be neither proud nor cruel, and will satisfy you with what you shall require."

M. Morello seemed then somewhat out of patience, and said: "I will not know the thing that toucheth me not. But cause you to be taught how the young men ought to covet this beauty that are not so fresh and lusty as old men be."

Here Sir Frederick,[5] to pacify M. Morello and to break their talk, would not suffer Count Lewis to make answer, but interrupting him said: "Perhaps M. Morello is not altogether out of the way in saying that beauty is not always good, for the beauty of women is many times cause of infinite evils in the world—hatred, war, mortality, and destruction, whereof the razing of Troy[6] can be a good witness; and beautiful women for the most part be either proud and cruel, as is said, or unchaste; but M. Morello would find no fault with that. There be also many wicked men that have the comeliness of a beautiful countenance, and it seemeth that nature hath so shaped them because they may be the readier to deceive, and that this amiable look were like a bait that covereth the hook."

Then M. Peter Bembo: "Believe not," quoth he, "but beauty is always good."

Here Count Lewis, because he would return again to his former purpose, interrupted him and said: "Since M. Morello passeth not to understand that which is so necessary for him, teach it me, and show me how old men may come by this happiness of love, for I will not care to be counted old, so it may profit me."

M. Peter Bembo laughed, and said: "First will I take the error out of these gentlemen's mind, and afterward will I satisfy you also." So beginning afresh: "My Lords," quoth he, "I would not that with speaking ill of beauty, which is a holy thing, any of us as profane and wicked should purchase him the wrath of God. Therefore, to give M. Morello and Sir Frederick warning, that they lose not their sight, as Stesichorus[7] did—a pain most meet for whoso dispraiseth beauty—I say that beauty cometh of God and is like a circle, the goodness whereof is the center. And therefore, as there can be no circle without a center, no more can beauty be without goodness. Whereupon doth very seldom an ill soul dwell in a beautiful body. And therefore is the outward beauty a true sign of the inward goodness, and in bodies this comeliness is imprinted, more and less, as it were, for a mark of the soul, whereby she is outwardly known; as in trees, in which the beauty of the buds giveth a testimony of the goodness of the fruit. And the very same happeneth in bodies, as it is seen that palmisters[8] by the visage know many times the conditions and

---

5. Federico Fregoso, later archbishop of Salerno.
6. The destruction of Troy by the Greeks, celebrated in Homer's *Iliad*, was caused by the Trojan Paris's abduction of Helen, the most beautiful woman in the world.

7. "A notable poet which lost his sight for writing against Helena and recanting had his sight restored him again" [Hoby's note].
8. Fortune tellers.

otherwhile the thoughts of men. And, which is more, in beasts also a man may discern by the face the quality of the courage, which in the body declareth itself as much as it can. Judge you how plainly in the face of a lion, a horse, and an eagle, a man shall discern anger, fierceness, and stoutness; in lambs and doves, simpleness and very innocency; the crafty subtlety in foxes and wolves; and the like, in a manner, in all other living creatures. The foul,[9] therefore, for the most part be also evil, and the beautiful good. Therefore it may be said that beauty is a face pleasant, merry, comely, and to be desired for goodness; and foulness a face dark, uglesome,[1] unpleasant, and to be shunned for ill. And in case you will consider all things, you shall find that whatsoever is good and profitable hath also evermore the comeliness of beauty. Behold the state of this great engine of the world, which God created for the health and preservation of everything that was made: the heaven round beset with so many heavenly lights; and in the middle the earth environed with the elements and upheld with the very weight of itself; the sun, that compassing about giveth light to the whole, and in winter season draweth to the lowermost sign, afterward by little and little climbeth again to the other part; the moon, that of him taketh her light, according as she draweth nigh or goeth farther from him; and the other five stars that diversely keep the very same course. These things among themselves have such force by the knitting together of an order so necessarily framed that, with altering them any one jot, they should all be loosed and the world would decay. They have also such beauty and comeliness that all the wits men have cannot imagine a more beautiful matter.

"Think now of the shape of man, which may be called a little world, in whom every parcel of his body is seen to be necessarily framed by art and not by hap, and then the form altogether most beautiful, so that it were a hard matter to judge whether the members (as the eyes, the nose, the mouth, the ears, the arms, the breast, and in like manner the other parts) give either more profit to the countenance and the rest of the body, or comeliness. The like may be said of all other living creatures. Behold the feathers of fowls, the leaves and boughs of trees, which be given them of nature to keep them in their being, and yet have they withal a very great sightliness. Leave nature, and come to art. What thing is so necessary in sailing vessels as the forepart, the sides, the main yards, the mast, the sails, the stern, oars, anchors, and tacklings? All these things notwithstanding are so wellfavored in the eye that unto whoso beholdeth them they seem to have been found out as well for pleasure as for profit. Pillars and great beams uphold high buildings and palaces, and yet are they no less pleasureful unto the eyes of the beholders than profitable to the buildings. When men began first to build, in the middle of temples and houses they reared the ridge of the roof, not to make the works to have a better show, but because the water might the more commodi-

9. Ugly.   1. Horribly ugly (apparently first used by Hoby).

ously avoid[2] on both sides; yet unto profit there was forthwith adjoined a fair sightliness, so that if, under the sky where there falleth neither hail nor rain, a man should build a temple without a reared ridge, it is to be thought that it could have neither a sightly show nor any beauty. Besides other things, therefore, it giveth a great praise to the world in saying that it is beautiful. It is praised in saying the beautiful heaven, beautiful earth, beautiful sea, beautiful rivers, beautiful woods, trees, gardens, beautiful cities, beautiful churches, houses, armies. In conclusion, this comely and holy beauty is a wondrous setting out of everything. And it may be said that good and beautiful be after a sort one self thing, especially in the bodies of men; of the beauty whereof the nighest cause, I suppose, is the beauty of the soul; the which, as a partner of the right and heavenly beauty, maketh sightly and beautiful whatever she toucheth, and most of all, if the body, where she dwelleth, be not of so vile a matter that she cannot imprint in it her property.[3] Therefore beauty is the true monument and spoil of the victory of the soul, when she with heavenly influence beareth rule over material and gross nature, and with her light overcometh the darkness of the body. It is not, then, to be spoken that beauty maketh women proud or cruel, although it seem so to M. Morello. Neither yet ought beautiful women to bear the blame of that hatred, mortality, and destruction which the unbridled appetites of men are the cause of. I will not now deny but it is possible also to find in the world beautiful women unchaste; yet not because beauty inclineth them to unchaste living, for it rather plucketh them from it, and leadeth them into the way of virtuous conditions, through the affinity that beauty hath with goodness; but otherwhile[4] ill bringing up, the continual provocations of lovers' tokens, poverty, hope, deceits, fear, and a thousand other matters, overcome the steadfastness, yea, of beautiful and good women; and for these and like causes may also beautiful men become wicked."

Then said the Lord Cesar:[5] "In case the Lord Gaspar's saying be true of yesternight, there is no doubt but the fair women be more chaste than the foul."

"And what was my saying?" quoth the Lord Gaspar.

The Lord Cesar answered: "If I do well bear in mind, your saying was that the women that are sued to always refuse to satisfy him that sueth to them, but those that are not sued to, sue to others. There is no doubt but the beautiful women have always more suitors, and be more instantly laid at[6] in love, than the foul. Therefore the beautiful always deny, and consequently be more chaste than the foul, which, not being sued to, sue unto others."

M. Peter Bembo laughed, and said: "This argument cannot be answered to."

Afterward he proceeded: "It chanceth also, oftentimes, that as the

---

2. Escape.
3. Attribute, quality.
4. Sometimes.

5. Cesar Gonzaga, cousin of Castiglione.
6. Pursued.

other senses, so the sight is deceived and judgeth a face beautiful which indeed is not beautiful. And because in the eyes and in the whole countenance of some woman a man beholdeth otherwhile a certain lavish wantonness painted, with dishonest flickerings, many, whom that manner delighteth because it promiseth them an easiness to come by the thing that they covet, call it beauty; but indeed it is a cloaked unshamefastness,[7] unworthy of so honorable and holy a name."

M. Peter Bembo held his peace, but those lords still were earnest upon him to speak somewhat more of this love and of the way to enjoy beauty aright, and at the last: "Methink," quoth he, "I have showed plainly enough that old men may love more happily than young, which was my drift; therefore it belongeth not to me to enter any farther."

Count Lewis answered: "You have better declared the unluckiness of young men than the happiness of old men, whom you have not as yet taught what way they must follow in this love of theirs; only you have said that they must suffer themselves to be guided by reason, and the opinion of many is that it is unpossible for love to stand with reason."

Bembo notwithstanding sought to make an end of reasoning, but the Duchess desired him to say on, and he began thus afresh: "Too unlucky were the nature of man, if our soul, in which this so fervent coveting may lightly arise, should be driven to nourish it with that only which is common to her with beasts, and could not turn it to the other noble part, which is proper to her.[8] Therefore, since it is so your pleasure, I will not refuse to reason upon this noble matter. And because I know myself unworthy to talk of the most holy mysteries of Love, I beseech him to lead my thought and my tongue so that I may show this excellent Courtier how to love contrary to the wonted manner of the common ignorant sort. And even as from my childhood I have dedicated all my whole life unto him, so also now that my words may be answerable to the same intent, and to the praise of him: I say, therefore, that since the nature of man in youthful age is so much inclined to sense, it may be granted the Courtier, while he is young, to love sensually; but in case afterward also, in his riper years, he chance to be set on fire with this coveting of love, he ought to be good and circumspect, and heedful that he beguile not himself to be led willfully into the wretchedness that in young men deserveth more to be pitied than blamed and contrariwise in old men, more to be blamed than pitied. Therefore when an amiable countenance of a beautiful woman cometh in his sight, that is accompanied with noble conditions and honest behaviors, so that, as one practiced in love, he wotteth[9] well that his hue hath an agreement with hers, as soon as he is aware that his eyes snatch that image and carry it to the heart, and that the soul beginneth to behold it with pleasure, and feeleth within herself the influence that stirreth her and by little and little setteth her in heat, and that those lively spirits that twinkle out through the eyes put continually fresh nourishment to the fire, he ought in this beginning

---

7. Immodesty.
8. "I.e., Reason" [Hoby's note].

9. Knows.

to seek a speedy remedy and to raise up reason, and with her to fence the fortress of his heart, and to shut in such wise the passages against sense and appetites that they may enter neither with force nor subtle practice. Thus, if the flame be quenched, the jeopardy is also quenched. But in case it continue or increase, then must the Courtier determine, when he perceiveth he is taken, to shun throughly[1] all filthiness of common love, and so enter into the holy way of love with the guide of reason, and first consider that the body where that beauty shineth is not the fountain from whence beauty springeth, but rather because beauty is bodiless and, as we have said, an heavenly shining beam, she loseth much of her honor when she is coupled with that vile subject[2] and full of corruption, because the less she is partner thereof, the more perfect she is, and, clean sundered from it, is most perfect. And as a man heareth not with his mouth, nor smelleth with his ears, no more can he also in any manner wise enjoy beauty, nor satisfy the desire that she stirreth up in our minds, with feeling, but with the sense unto whom beauty is the very butt to level at,[3] namely, the virtue of seeing. Let him lay aside, therefore, the blind judgment of the sense, and enjoy with his eyes the brightness, the comeliness, the loving sparkles, laughters, gestures, and all the other pleasant furnitures of beauty, especially with hearing the sweetness of her voice, the tunableness[4] of her words, the melody of her singing and playing on instruments (in case the woman beloved be a musician), and so shall he with most dainty food feed the soul through the means of these two senses which have little bodily substance in them and be the ministers of reason, without entering farther toward the body with coveting unto any longing otherwise than honest. Afterward let him obey, please, and honor with all reverence his woman, and reckon her more dear to him than his own life, and prefer all her commodities[5] and pleasures before his own, and love no less in her the beauty of the mind than of the body. Therefore let him have a care not to suffer her to run into any error, but with lessons and good exhortations seek always to frame her to modesty, to temperance, to true honesty, and so to work that there may never take place in her other than pure thoughts and far wide from all filthiness of vices. And thus in sowing of virtue in the garden of that mind, he shall also gather the fruits of most beautiful conditions, and savor them with a marvelous good relish. And this shall be the right engendering and imprinting of beauty in beauty, the which some hold opinion to be the end of love. In this manner shall our Courtier be most acceptable to his lady, and she will always show herself toward him tractable, lowly,[6] and sweet in language, and as willing to please him as to be beloved of him; and the wills of them both shall be most honest and agreeable, and they consequently shall be most happy."

Here M. Morello: "The engendering," quoth he, "of beauty in beauty aright were the engendering of a beautiful child in a beautiful woman;

---

1. Completely.
2. I.e., the body.
3. Target to aim at.

4. Musical quality.
5. Conveniences.
6. Modest.

and I would think it a more manifest token a great deal that she loved her lover, if she pleased him with this than with the sweetness of language that you speak of."

M. Peter Bembo laughed, and said: "You must not, M. Morello, pass your bounds. I may tell you it is not a small token that a woman loveth when she giveth unto her lover her beauty, which is so precious a matter; and by the ways that be a passage to the soul (that is to say, the sight and the hearing) sendeth the looks of her eyes, the image of her countenance, and the voice of her words, that pierce into the lover's heart and give a witness of her love."

M. Morello said: "Looks and words may be, and oftentimes are, false witnesses. Therefore whoso hath not a better pledge of love, in my judgment he is in an ill assurance. And surely I looked still that you would have made this woman of yours somewhat more courteous and free toward the Courtier than my Lord Julian[7] hath made his; but meseemeth ye be both of the property of those judges that, to appear wise, give sentence against their own."

Bembo said: "I am well pleased to have this woman much more courteous toward my Courtier not young than the Lord Julian's is to the young; and that with good reason, because mine coveteth but honest matters, and therefore may the woman grant him them all without blame. But my Lord Julian's woman, that is not so assured of the modesty of the young man, ought to grant him the honest matters only, and deny him the dishonest. Therefore more happy is mine, that hath granted him whatsoever he requireth, than the other, that hath part granted and part denied. And because you may moreover the better understand that reasonable love is more happy than sensual, I say unto you that selfsame things in sensual ought to be denied otherwhile, and in reasonable granted; because in the one they be honest, and in the other dishonest. Therefore the woman, to please her good lover, besides the granting him merry countenances, familiar and secret talk, jesting, dallying, hand-in-hand, may also lawfully and without blame come to kissing, which in sensual love, according to the Lord Julian's rules, is not lawful. For since a kiss is a knitting together both of body and soul, it is to be feared lest the sensual lover will be more inclined to the part of the body than of the soul; but the reasonable lover wotteth well that although the mouth be a parcel[8] of the body, yet is it an issue for the words that be the interpreters of the soul, and for the inward breath, which is also called the soul; and therefore hath a delight to join his mouth with the woman's beloved with a kiss—not to stir him to any unhonest desire, but because he feeleth that that bond is the opening of an entry to the souls, which, drawn with a coveting the one of the other, pour themselves by turn the one into the other's body, and be so mingled together that each of them hath two souls, and one alone so framed of them both ruleth, in a manner, two bodies. Whereupon a kiss may be said to be rather a coupling

7. Giuliano de Medici, younger son of Lorenzo the Magnificent.   8. Part.

together of the soul than of the body, because it hath such force in her that it draweth her unto it, and, as it were, separateth her from the body. For this do all chaste lovers covet a kiss as a coupling of souls together. And therefore Plato,[9] the divine lover, saith that in kissing his soul came as far as his lips to depart out of the body. And because the separating of the soul from the matters of the sense, and the thorough coupling of her with matters of understanding, may be betokened by a kiss, Solomon saith[1] in his heavenly book of ballads, 'Oh that he would kiss me with a kiss of his mouth,' to express the desire he had that his soul might be ravished through heavenly love to the beholding of heavenly beauty in such manner that, coupling herself inwardly with it, she might forsake the body."

They stood all hearkening heedfully to Bembo's reasoning, and after he had stayed a while and saw that none spake, he said: "Since you have made me to begin to show our not young Courtier this happy love, I will lead him yet somewhat farther forwards, because to stand still at this stay were somewhat perilous for him, considering, as we have oftentimes said, the soul is most inclined to the senses, and for all reason with discourse chooseth well, and knoweth that beauty not to spring of the body, and therefore setteth a bridle to the unhonest desires, yet to behold it always in that body doth oftentimes corrupt the right judgment. And where no other inconvenience ensueth upon it, one's absence from the wight beloved carrieth a great passion with it; because the influence of that beauty when it is present giveth a wondrous delight to the lover, and, setting his heart on fire, quickeneth and melteth certain virtues in a trance and congealed in the soul, the which, nourished with the heat of love, flow about and go bubbling nigh the heart, and thrust out through the eyes those spirits which be most fine vapors made of the purest and clearest part of the blood, which receive the image of beauty and deck it with a thousand sundry furnitures. Whereupon the soul taketh a delight, and with a certain wonder is aghast, and yet enjoyeth she it, and, as it were, astonied[2] together with the pleasure, feeleth the fear and reverence that men accustomably have toward holy matters, and thinketh herself to be in paradise. The lover, therefore, that considereth only the beauty in the body, loseth this treasure and happiness as soon as the woman beloved with her departure leaveth the eyes without their brightness, and consequently the soul as a widow without her joy. For since beauty is far off, that influence of love setteth not the heart on fire, as it did in presence. Whereupon the pores be dried up and withered, and yet doth the remembrance of beauty somewhat stir those virtues of the soul in such wise that they seek to scatter abroad the spirits, and they, finding the ways closed up, have no issue, and still they seek to get out, and so with those shootings enclosed prick the soul and torment her bitterly, as young children when in their tender gums they begin to breed teeth. And hence come the tears, sighs, vexations, and torments of lovers; because the soul is always in affliction and travail and, in a manner, waxeth wood,[3] until the beloved beauty cometh before her once again, and then she is immediately pacified and taketh breath, and, throughly bent to it, is nourished with most dainty food, and by her will would never depart from so sweet a sight. To avoid, therefore, the torment of this absence, and to enjoy beauty without passion, the Courtier by the help of reason must full and wholly call back again the coveting of the body to beauty alone, and, in what he can, behold it in itself simple and pure, and frame it within his imagination sundered from all matter, and so make it friendly and loving to his soul, and there enjoy it, and have it with him day and night, in every time and place, without mistrust ever to lose it; keeping always fast in mind that the body is a most diverse thing from beauty, and not only not increaseth but diminisheth the perfection of it. In this wise shall our not young Courtier be out of all bitterness and wretchedness that young men feel, in a manner continually, as jealousies, suspicions, disdains, angers, desperations, and certain rages full of madness, whereby many times they be led into so great error that some do not only beat the women whom they love, but rid themselves out of their life. He shall do no wrong to the husband, father, brethren, or kinsfolk of the woman beloved. He shall not bring her in slander. He shall not be in case with much ado otherwhile to refrain his eyes and tongue from discovering his desires to others. He shall not take thought at departure or in absence, because he shall evermore carry his precious treasure about with him shut fast within his heart. And besides, through the virtue of imagination, he shall fashion within himself that beauty much more fair than it is indeed. But among these commodities the lover shall find another yet far greater, in case he will take this love for a stair, as it were, to climb up to another far higher than it. The which he shall bring to pass, if he will go and consider with himself what a strait bond it is to be always in the trouble to behold the beauty of one body alone. And therefore, to come out of this so narrow a room, he shall gather in his thought by little and little so many ornaments that meddling[4] all beauties together he shall make a universal concept, and bring the multitude of them to the unity of one alone, that is generally spread over all the nature of man. And thus shall he behold no more the particular beauty of one woman, but an universal, that decketh out all bodies. Whereupon, being made dim with this greater light, he shall not pass upon[5] the lesser, and, burning in a more excellent flame, he shall little esteem it that he set great store by at the first. This stair of love, though it be very noble and such as few arrive at it, yet is it not in this sort to be called perfect, forsomuch as where the imagination is of force to make conveyance and hath no knowledge but through those beginnings that the senses help her withal, she is not clean purged from gross darkness; and therefore, though she do consider that universal beauty in sunder and in itself alone, yet doth she not well and clearly discern

3. Mad, crazy.
4. Mingling.   5. Make his destination.

it, nor without some doubtfulness, by reason of the agreement that the fancies have with the body. Wherefore such as come to this love are like young birds almost flush,[6] which for all they flutter a little their tender wings, yet dare they not stray far from the nest, nor commit themselves to the wind and open weather. When our Courtier, therefore, shall be come to this point, although he may be called a good and happy lover, in respect of them that be drowned in the misery of sensual love, yet will I not have him to set his heart at rest, but boldy proceed farther, following the highway after his guide, that leadeth him to the point of true happiness. And thus, instead of going out of his wit with thought, as he must do that will consider the bodily beauty, he may come into his wit to behold the beauty that is seen with the eyes of the mind, which then begin to be sharp and through-seeing, when the eyes of the body lose the flower of their sightliness.

"Therefore the soul, rid of vices, purged with the studies of true philosophy, occupied in spiritual, and exercised in matters of understanding, turning her to the beholding of her own substance, as it were raised out of a most deep sleep, openeth the eyes that all men have and few occupy,[7] and seeth in herself a shining beam of that light which is the true image of the angel-like beauty partened with her, whereof she also partneth[8] with the body a feeble shadow; therefore, waxed blind about earthly matters, is made most quick of sight about heavenly. And otherwhile when the stirring virtues of the body are withdrawn alone through earnest beholding, either fast bound through sleep, when she is not hindered by them, she feeleth a certain privy[9] smell of the right angel-like beauty, and, ravished with the shining of that light, beginneth to be inflamed, and so greedily followeth after, that in a manner she waxeth drunken and beside herself, for coveting to couple herself with it, having found, to her weening,[1] the footsteps of God, in the beholding of whom, as in her happy end, she seeketh to settle herself. And therefore, burning in this most happy flame, she ariseth to the noblest part of her, which is the understanding, and there, no more shadowed with the dark night of earthly matters, seeth the heavenly beauty; but yet doth she not for all that enjoy it altogether perfectly, because she beholdeth it only in her particular understanding, which cannot conceive the passing great universal beauty; whereupon, not throughly satisfied with this benefit, love giveth unto the soul a greater happiness. For like as through the particular beauty of one body he guideth her to the universal beauty of all bodies, even so in the last degree of perfection through particular understanding he guideth her to the universal understanding. Thus the soul kindled in the most holy fire of heavenly love fleeth to couple herself with the nature of angels, and not only clean forsaketh sense, but hath no more need of the discourse of reason, for, being changed into an angel, she understandeth all things that may be understood; and without

6. Fledged, fit to fly.   9. Intimate.
7. Use.   1. Opinion, thought.
8. Shares.

any veil or cloud she seeth the main sea of the pure heavenly beauty, and receiveth it into her, and enjoyeth that sovereign happiness that cannot be comprehended of the senses. Since, therefore, the beauties which we daily see with these our dim eyes in bodies subject to corruption, that nevertheless be nothing else but dreams and most thin shadows of beauty, seem unto us so well-favored and comely that oftentimes they kindle in us a most burning fire, and with such delight that we reckon no happiness may be compared to it that we feel otherwhile through the only look which the beloved countenance of a woman casteth at us; what happy wonder, what blessed abashment, may we reckon that to be that taketh the souls which come to have a sight of the heavenly beauty? What sweet flame, what sweet incense, may a man believe that to be which ariseth of the fountain of the sovereign and right beauty? Which is the origin of all other beauty, which never increaseth nor diminisheth, always beautiful, and of itself, as well on the one part as on the other, most simple, only like itself, and partner of none other, but in such wise beautiful that all other beautiful things be beautiful because they be partners of the beauty of it.

"This is the beauty unseparable from the high bounty which with her voice calleth and draweth to her all things; and not only to the endowed with understanding giveth understanding, to the reasonable reason, to the sensual sense and appetite to live, but also partaketh with plants and stones, as a print of herself, stirring, and the natural provocation of their properties. So much, therefore, is this love greater and happier than others as the cause that stirreth it is more excellent. And therefore, as common fire trieth gold and maketh it fine, so this most holy fire in souls destroyeth and consumeth whatsoever is mortal in them, and relieveth and maketh beautiful the heavenly part, which at the first by reason of the sense was dead and buried in them. This is the great fire in the which, the poets write, that Hercules was burned on the top of the mountain Oeta,[2] and, through that consuming with fire, after his death was holy and immortal. This is the fiery bush of Moses;[3] the divided tongues of fire; the inflamed chariot of Elias; which doubleth grace and happiness in their souls that be worthy to see it, when they forsake this earthly baseness and flee up into heaven. Let us, therefore, bend all our force and thoughts of soul to this most holy light, which showeth us the way which leadeth to heaven; and after it, putting off the affections we were clad withal at our coming down, let us climb up the stairs which at the lowermost step have the shadow of sensual beauty, to the high mansion place where the heavenly, amiable, and right beauty dwelleth, which lieth hid in the innermost secrets of God, lest unhallowed eyes should come to the sight of it; and there shall we find a most happy end

2. "A mountain between Thessalia and Macedonia where is the sepulchre of Hercules" [Hoby's note].
3. "And the angel of the Lord appeared unto (Moses) in a flame of fire out of the midst of a bush; and he looked, and, behold, the bush burned with fire, and the bush was not consumed" (Exodus 3.2). "And it came to pass, as they still went on, and talked, that, behold there appeared a chariot of fire, and horses of fire, and parted them both asunder; and Elijah went up by a whirlwind into heaven" (2 Kings 2.11).

for our desires, true rest for our travails, certain remedy for miseries, a most healthful medicine for sickness, a most sure haven in the troublesome storms of the tempestuous sea of this life.

"What tongue mortal is there then, Oh most holy love, that can sufficiently praise thy worthiness? Thou most beautiful, most good, most wise, art derived of the unity of heavenly beauty, goodness, and wisdom, and therein dost thou abide, and unto it through it, as in a circle, turnest about. Thou the most sweet bond of the world, a mean betwixt heavenly and earthly things, with a bountiful temper bendest the high virtues to the government of the lower, and turning back the minds of mortal men to their beginning, couplest them with it. Thou with agreement bringest the elements in one, and stirrest nature to bring forth that which ariseth and is born for the succession of the life. Thou bringest severed matters into one, to the unperfect givest perfection, to the unlike likeness, to enmity amity, to the earth fruits, to the sea calmness, to the heaven lively light. Thou art the father of true pleasures, of grace, peace, lowliness, and goodwill, enemy to rude wildness and sluggishness—to be short, the beginning and end of all goodness. And forsomuch as thou delightest to dwell in the flower of beautiful bodies and beautiful souls, I suppose that thy abiding-place is now here among us, and from above otherwhile showest thyself a little to the eyes and minds of them that be worthy to see thee. Therefore vouchsafe, Lord, to hearken to our prayers, pour thyself into our hearts, and with the brightness of thy most holy fire lighten our darkness, and, like a trusty guide in this blind maze, show us the right way; reform the falsehood of the senses, and after long wandering in vanity give us the right and sound joy. Make us to smell those spiritual savors that relieve the virtues of the understanding, and to hear the heavenly harmony so tunable that no discord of passion take place any more in us. Make us drunken with the bottomless fountain of contentation that always doth delight and never giveth fill, and that giveth a smack of the right bliss unto whoso drinketh of the running and clear water thereof. Purge with the shining beams of thy light our eyes from misty ignorance, that they may no more set by mortal beauty, and well perceive that the things which at the first they thought themselves to see be not indeed, and those that they saw not to be in effect. Accept our souls that be offered unto thee for a sacrifice. Burn them in the lively flame that wasteth all gross filthiness, that after they be clean sundered from the body they may be coupled with an everlasting and most sweet bond to the heavenly beauty. And we, severed from ourselves, may be changed like right lovers into the beloved, and, after we be drawn from the earth, admitted to the feast of the angels, where, fed with immortal ambrosia and nectar,[4] in the end we may die a most happy and lively death, as in times past died the fathers of old time, whose souls with most fervent zeal of beholding thou didst hale from the body and coupledst them with God."

---

4. The food and drink of the gods in classical legend.

When Bembo had hitherto spoken with such vehemency that a man would have thought him, as it were, ravished and beside himself, he stood still without once moving, holding his eyes toward heaven as astonied, when the Lady Emilia, which together with the rest gave most diligent ear to this talk, took him by the plait of his garment and plucking him a little, said: "Take heed, M. Peter, that these thoughts make not your soul also to forsake the body."

"Madam," answered M. Peter, "it should not be the first miracle that love hath wrought in me."

Then the Duchess and all the rest began afresh to be instant upon M. Bembo that he would proceed once more in his talk, and every one thought he felt in his mind, as it were, a certain sparkle of that godly love that pricked him, and they all coveted to hear farther; but M. Bembo: "My Lords," quoth he, "I have spoken what the holy fury of love hath, unsought for, indited[5] to me; now that, it seemeth, he inspireth me no more, I wot not what to say. And I think verily that love will not have his secrets discovered any farther, nor that the Courtier should pass the degree that his pleasure is I should show him, and therefore it is not perhaps lawful to speak any more in this matter."

"Surely," quoth the Duchess, "if the not young Courtier be such a one that he can follow this way which you have showed him, of right he ought to be satisfied with so great a happiness, and not to envy the younger."

Then the Lord Cesar Gonzaga: "The way," quoth he, "that leadeth to this happiness is so steep, in my mind, that I believe it will be much ado to get to it."

The Lord Gaspar said: "I believe it be hard to get up for men, but unpossible for women."

The Lady Emilia laughed, and said: "If you fall so often to offend us, I promise you you shall be no more forgiven."

The Lord Gaspar answered: "It is no offense to you in saying that women's souls be not so purged from passions as men's be, nor accustomed in beholdings, as M. Peter hath said is necessary for them to be that will taste of the heavenly love. Therefore it is not read that ever woman hath had this grace; but many men have had it, as Plato, Socrates, Plotinus,[6] and many other, and a number of our holy fathers, as Saint Francis, in whom a fervent spirit of love imprinted the most holy seal of the five wounds. And nothing but the virtue of love could hale up Saint Paul the Apostle to the sight of those secrets which is not lawful for man to speak of; nor show Saint Stephen the heavens open."[7]

Here answered the Lord Julian: "In this point men shall nothing pass women, for Socrates himself doth confess that all the mysteries of love which he knew were oped unto him by a woman, which was Diotima.

5. Dictated.
6. Famous ancient philosophers, especially on the subject of love. St. Francis of Assisi (1182–1226) is supposed to have received the stigmata resembling the 5 wounds that Christ suffered.

7. The first Christian martyr. Just before he was stoned to death he said, "Behold, I see the heavens opened, and the Son of man standing on the right hand of God" (Acts 7.56). St. Paul's praise of love is in 1 Corinthians 13.

And the angel that with the fire of love imprinted the five wounds in Saint Francis hath also made some women worthy of the same print in our age. You must remember, moreover, that Saint Mary Magdalen[8] had many faults forgiven her, because she loved much; and perhaps with no less grace than Saint Paul was she many times through angelic love haled up to the third heaven. And many other, as I showed you yesterday more at large, that for love of the name of Christ have not passed upon life, nor feared torments, nor any other kind of death how terrible and cruel ever it were. And they were not, as M. Peter will have his Courtier to be, aged, but soft and tender maidens, and in the age when he saith that sensual love ought to be borne withal in men."

The Lord Gaspar began to prepare himself to speak, but the Duchess: "Of this," quoth she, "let M. Peter be judge, and the matter shall stand to his verdict, whether women be not as meet for heavenly love as men. But because the plead between you may happen be too long, it shall not be amiss to defer it until tomorrow."

"Nay, tonight," quoth the Lord Cesar Gonzaga.

And how can it be tonight?" quoth the Duchess.

The Lord Cesar answered: "Because it is day already," and showed her the light that began to enter in at the clefts of the windows. Then every man arose upon his feet with much wonder, because they had not thought that the reasonings had lasted longer than the accustomed wont, saving only that they were begun much later, and with their pleasantness had deceived so the lords' minds that they wist not of the going away of the hours. And not one of them felt any heaviness of sleep in his eyes, the which often happeneth when a man is up after his accustomed hour to go to bed. When the windows then were opened on the side of the palace that hath his prospect toward the high top of Mount Catri, they saw already risen in the east a fair morning like unto the color of roses, and all stars voided, saving only the sweet governess of the heaven, Venus, which keepeth the bounds of the night and the day, from which appeared to blow a sweet blast that, filling the air with a biting cold, began to quicken the tunable notes of the pretty birds among the hushing woods of the hills at hand. Whereupon they all, taking their leave with reverence of the Duchess, departed toward their lodgings without torch, the light of the day sufficing.

And as they were now passing out at the great chamber door, the Lord General turned him to the Duchess and said: "Madam, to take up the variance between the Lord Gaspar and the Lord Julian, we will assemble this night with the judge sooner than we did yesterday."

The Lady Emilia answered: "Upon condition that in case my Lord Gaspar will accuse women, and give them, as his wont is, some false report, he will also put us in surety to stand to trial, for I reckon him a wavering starter."

1561

8. A converted harlot who became one of Jesus' most faithful followers.

ROGER ASCHAM
1515–1568

When she heard of the death of her former tutor and Latin secretary, Queen Elizabeth is said to have exclaimed, "I would rather have cast ten thousand pounds in the sea than parted from my Ascham." He had been one of the second generation of English Humanists, along with Sir Thomas Elyot, Sir John Cheke, and Sir Thomas Wilson. These men strongly believed in the study of the Greek and Latin classics, not merely for erudition and aesthetic pleasure, but for guidance in moral values and in political activity. Ascham published *Toxophilus*, a dialogue in praise of archery with the longbow, a traditional English weapon, and *A Report and Discourse of the State of Germany*, based upon his experience as secretary to the English ambassador there in 1550–53. His most famous work in English was *The Schoolmaster*, with its advocacy of "double translation" as the most effective way of acquiring a sound Latin style.

He wrote these books in English, because he wanted to influence his countrymen, whether they read Latin or not. His correspondence with learned men on the continent was very extensive; it was all in Latin. *The Schoolmaster* was not intended to be merely a treatise on Latin and English composition. It was in many ways a conduct book for youth, and their teachers as well, in which the ideals of the Renaissance and the Reformation were combined to develop a dignified and well-ordered character, based upon "truth in religion, honesty of living, and right order in learning."

The moral emphasis in Ascham's humanistic doctrine is best displayed in his unfavorable view of Italy. This attitude became common among Englishmen; a generation later than Ascham, Thomas Nashe has the hero of his tale *The Unfortunate Traveler* (1594) describe Italy as follows: "Italy, the paradise of the earth and the epicure's heaven, how does it form our young master? It makes him kiss his hand like an ape, cringe his neck like a starveling, and play at hey-pass-repass-come-aloft when he salutes a man. From thence he brings the art of atheism, the art of epicurising, the art of whoring, the art of poisoning, the art of sodomitry. . . . It is now a privy note amongst the better sort of men, when they would set a singular mark or brand on a notorious villain, to say 'He hath been in Italy.' "

From The Schoolmaster

From *The First Book for the Youth*

[TEACHING LATIN]

There is a way, touched in the first book of Cicero *De oratore*,[1] which, wisely brought into schools, truly taught, and constantly used, would not only take wholly away this butcherly fear in making of Latins but would also, with ease and pleasure and in short time, as I know by

1. Cicero wrote three books *On the Orator*.

good experience, work a true choice and placing of words, a right ordering of sentences, an easy understanding of the tongue, a readiness to
speak, a facility to write, a true judgment both of his own and other
men's doings, what tongue soever he doth use.

The way is this. After the three concordances[2] learned, as I touched
before, let the master read unto him the epistles of Cicero gathered together
and chosen out by Sturmius[3] for the capacity of children.

First let him teach the child, cheerfully and plainly, the cause and
matter of the letter; then, let him construe it into English so oft as the
child may easily carry away the understanding of it; lastly, parse[4] it over
perfectly. This done thus, let the child, by and by, both construe and
parse it over again so that it may appear that the child doubteth in nothing that his master taught him before. After this, the child must take a
paper book and, sitting in some place where no man shall prompt him,
by himself, let him translate into English his former lesson. Then, showing
it to his master, let the master take from him his Latin book, and, pausing an hour at the least, then let the child translate his own English into
Latin again in another paper book. When the child bringeth it turned
into Latin, the master must compare it with Tully's[5] book and lay them
both together, and where the child doth well, either in choosing or true
placing of Tully's words, let the master praise him and say, "Here ye do
well." For I assure you, there is no such whetstone to sharpen a good
wit and encourage a will to learning as is praise.

But if the child miss, either in forgetting a word, or in changing a
good with a worse, or misordering the sentence, I would not have the
master either frown or chide with him, if the child have done his diligence and used no truantship therein. For I know by good experience
that a child shall take more profit of two faults gently warned of than of
four things rightly hit. For then the master shall have good occasion to
say unto him:

> N[omen],[6] Tully would have used such a word, not this; Tully would
> have placed this word here, not there; would have used this case,
> this number, this person, this degree, this gender; he would have
> used this mood, this tense, this simple rather than this compound;
> this adverb here, not there; he would have ended the sentence with
> this verb, not with that noun or participle, etc.

In these few lines I have wrapped up the most tedious part of grammar
and also the ground of almost all the rules that are so busily taught by
the master, and so hardly learned by the scholar, in all common schools,
which after this sort, the master shall teach without all error, and the
scholar shall learn without great pain, the master being led by so sure a

---

2. Agreement of noun and adjective, verb and
noun, relative with antecedent.
3. Johannes Sturm (1507–1589) German scholar
and educator.

4. Give a grammatical analysis.
5. Common English name for Marcus Tullius
Cicero.
6. Substituting the child's name.

guide, and the scholar being brought into so plain and easy a way. And therefore we do not contemn rules, but we gladly teach rules, and teach them more plainly, sensibly, and orderly than they be commonly taught in common schools. For when the master shall compare Tully's book with his scholar's translation, let the master at the first lead and teach his scholar to join the rules of his grammar book with the examples of his present lesson, until the scholar by himself be able to fetch out of his grammar every rule for every example, so as the grammar book be ever in the scholar's hand also used of him, as a dictionary, for every present use. This is a lively and perfect way of teaching of rules, where the common way, used in common schools, to read the grammar alone by itself, is tedious for the master, hard for the scholar, cold and uncomfortable to them both.

Let your scholar be never afraid to ask you any doubt, but use discreetly the best allurements ye can to encourage him to the same, lest his overmuch fearing of you drive him to seek some misorderly shift,[7] as to seek to be helped by some other book, or to be prompted by some other scholar, and so go about to beguile you much and himself more.

[A TALK WITH LADY JANE GREY]

Therefore, to love or to hate, to like or contemn, to ply this way or that way to good or to bad, ye shall have as ye use a child in his youth.

And one example, whether love or fear doth work more in a child for virtue and learning, I will gladly report; which may be heard with some pleasure and followed with more profit. Before I went into Germany, I came to Broadgate in Leicestershire to take my leave of that noble Lady Jane Grey,[8] to whom I was exceeding much beholding. Her parents, the duke and the duchess, with all the household, gentlemen and gentlewomen, were hunting in the park. I found her in her chamber reading *Phaedon Platonis*[9] in Greek, and that with as much delight as some gentleman would read a merry tale in Boccaccio.[1] After salutation and duty done, with some other talk, I asked her why she would lose such pastime in the park. Smiling she answered me, "Iwis,[2] all their sport in the park is but a shadow to that pleasure that I find in Plato. Alas, good folk, they never felt what true pleasure meant." "And how came you, madame," quoth I, "to this deep knowledge of pleasure, and what did chiefly allure you unto it, seeing not many women, but very few men, have attained thereunto?" "I will tell you," quoth she, "and tell you a truth which perchance ye will marvel at. One of the greatest benefits that ever God gave me is that he sent me so sharp and severe parents and so gentle a schoolmaster. For when I am in presence either of father

7. Subterfuge.
8. (1537–1554), daughter of the duke of Suffolk. On the death of King Edward VI she was proclaimed queen by the Protestant faction but was overthrown by the Catholic Mary and executed. See the account of her death in the selection from

Foxe's *Acts and Monuments*, pp. 1029–30.
9. Plato's dialogue *Phaedo*.
1. Boccaccio's *Decameron* (1348–53) a collection of 100 "merry," sometimes licentious, tales, not translated into English in Ascham's time.
2. Truly.

or mother, whether I speak, keep silence, sit, stand, or go, eat, drink, be merry or sad, be sewing, playing, dancing, or doing anything else, I must do it, as it were, in such weight, measure, and number, even so perfectly as God made the world, or else I am so sharply taunted, so cruelly threatened, yea, presently sometimes, with pinches, nips, and bobs, and other ways which I will not name for the honor I bear them, so without measure misordered, that I think myself in hell till time come that I must go to Master Aylmer,[3] who teacheth me so gently, so pleasantly, with such fair allurements to learning, that I think all the time nothing whilst I am with him. And when I am called from him, I fall on weeping because whatsoever I do else but learning is full of grief, trouble, fear, and whole misliking unto me. And thus my book hath been so much my pleasure, and bringeth daily to me more pleasure and more, that in respect of it all other pleasures in very deed be but trifles and troubles unto me." I remember this talk gladly, both because it is so worthy of memory and because also it was the last talk that ever I had, and the last time that ever I saw, that noble and worthy lady.

[THE ITALIANATE ENGLISHMAN]

But I am afraid that overmany of our travelers into Italy do not eschew the way to Circe's[4] court but go and ride and run and fly thither; they make great haste to come to her; they make great suit to serve her; yea, I could point out some with my finger that never had gone out of England but only to serve Circe in Italy. Vanity and vice and any license to ill-living in England was counted stale and rude unto them. And so, being mules and horses before they went, returned very swine and asses home again; yet everywhere very foxes with subtle and busy heads and, where they may, very wolves with cruel malicious hearts. A marvelous monster which for filthiness of living, for dullness to learning himself, for wiliness in dealing with others, for malice in hurting without cause, should carry at once in one body the belly of a swine, the head of an ass, the brain of a fox, the womb of a wolf. If you think we judge amiss and write too sore against you, hear what the Italian saith of the Englishman, what the master reporteth of the scholar, who uttereth plainly what is taught by him and what is learned by you, saying, *Inglese italianato è un diavolo incarnato*; that is to say, "You remain men in shape and fashion but become devils in life and condition." This is not the opinion of one for some private spite but the judgment of all in a common proverb which riseth of that learning and those manners which you gather in Italy, a good schoolhouse of wholesome doctrine, and worthy masters of commendable scholars, where the master had rather defame himself for his teaching than not shame his scholar for his learning. A good

3. John Aylmer (1521–1594). As a schoolboy he attracted the notice of Henry Grey, marquis of Dorset, later duke of Suffolk, who provided for his education. After graduating from Cambridge in 1541 he became chaplain to Dorset and tutor to his children. Queen Elizabeth made him bishop of London in 1577.
4. An enchantress in Homer's *Odyssey* who changes men into swine.

nature of the master and fair conditions of the scholars. And now choose you, you Italian Englishmen, whether you will be angry with us for calling you monsters, or with the Italians for calling you devils, or else with your own selves, that take so much pains and go so far to make yourselves both. If some yet do not well understand what is an Englishman Italianated, I will plainly tell him: he that by living and traveling in Italy bringeth home into England out of Italy the religion, the learning, the policy,[5] the experience, the manners of Italy. That is to say, for religion, papistry or worse; for learning, less, commonly, than they carried out with them; for policy, a factious heart, a discoursing head, a mind to meddle in all men's matters; for experience, plenty of new mischiefs never known in England before; for manners, variety of vanities and change of filthy living. These be the enchantments of Circe brought out of Italy to mar men's manners in England: much by example of ill life but more by precepts of fond books, of late translated out of Italian into English, sold in every shop in London, commended by honest titles the sooner to corrupt honest manners, dedicated overboldly to virtuous and honorable personages, the easilier to beguile simple and innocent wits. It is pity that those which have authority and charge to allow and disallow books to be printed be no more circumspect herein than they are. Ten sermons at Paul's Cross[6] do not so much good for moving men to true doctrine as one of those books do harm with enticing men to illliving. Yea, I say farther, those books tend not so much to corrupt honest living as they do to subvert true religion. More papists be made by your merry books of Italy than by your earnest books of Louvain.[7] And because our great physicians do wink at the matter and make no count of this sore, I, though not admitted one of their fellowship, yet having been many years a prentice to God's true religion, and trust to continue a poor journeyman therein all days of my life, for the duty I owe and love I bear both to true doctrine and honest living, though I have no authority to amend the sore myself, yet I will declare my good will to discover the sore to others.

St. Paul saith that sects and ill opinions be the works of the flesh and fruits of sin.[8] This is spoken no more truly for the doctrine than sensibly for the reason. And why? For ill-doings breed ill-thinkings, and of corrupted manners spring perverted judgments. And how? There be in man two special things: man's will, man's mind. Where will inclineth to goodness the mind is bent to truth; where will is carried from goodness to vanity the mind is soon drawn from truth to false opinion. And so the readiest way to entangle the mind with false doctrine is first to entice the will to wanton living. Therefore, when the busy and open papists abroad could not by their contentious books turn men in England fast enough from truth and right judgment in doctrine, then the subtle and secret

5. Trickery, deceit.
6. An outdoor pulpit near St. Paul's Cathedral where important and eloquent ministers preached.
7. Town in Belgium noted in the 16th century for its Catholic university, especially its theological faculty.
8. In Galatians 5:19–21.

papists at home procured bawdy books to be translated out of the Italian tongue, whereby overmany young wills and wits, allured to wantonness, do now boldly contemn all severe books that sound to honesty and godliness. In our forefathers' time, when papistry as a standing pool covered and overflowed all England, few books were read in our tongue, saving certain books of chivalry, as they said, for pastime and pleasure, which, as some say, were made in monasteries by idle monks or wanton canons; as one for example, *Morte Darthur*,[9] the whole pleasure of which book standeth in two special points—in open manslaughter and bold bawdry; in which book those be counted the noblest knights that do kill most men without any quarrel and commit foulest adulteries by subtlest shifts: as Sir Lancelot with the wife of King Arthur his master, Sir Tristram with the wife of King Mark his uncle, Sir Lamorak with the wife of King Lot that was his own aunt. This is good stuff for wise men to laugh at or honest men to take pleasure at. Yet I know when God's Bible was banished the court and *Morte Darthur* received into the prince's chamber. * * *

1570

9. Sir Thomas Malory's Arthurian romance. See above, p. 392.

JOHN FOXE
1516–1587

John Foxe's career at Oxford University, where he had become a fellow of Magdalen College, was interrupted when his Puritan convictions led him to protest energetically against some college rules and practices. He then served as tutor to the children of various great houses, but when Mary became queen in 1553 and the persecutions of Protestants began, he fled to the Continent. His great book was already under way: its first version (Strasbourg, 1554) was in Latin, and dealt with the persecutions suffered by the early Protestants, particularly Wycliffe and John Hus. But the book grew and grew as Foxe received from England accounts of the hideous tortures and persecutions being inflicted on the Protestants there. When Elizabeth came to the throne in 1558, Foxe returned at once to England, and there he translated his Latin volume, adding to it hundreds of stories of the Marian martyrs (many true, some doubtful, some ridiculous). The English edition was published in 1563; its title was *Acts and Monuments of these latter and perilous days, touching matters of the church, wherein are comprehended and described the great persecution and horrible troubles that have been wrought and practices by the Romish prelates from the year of Our Lord a thousand to the time now present.*

It was immediately and enormously popular. Foxe saw life melodramatically, in terms of black and white; his book is a compendium of memoirs, stories, eye-witness accounts, personal letters, and the like, rendering the words, acts, and sufferings of some hundreds of martyrs in graphic—if often fictionalized—detail. The final version of the book is massive—over six thousand folio pages, containing four million words. Apart from fanning the flames of anti-Catholic feeling, Foxe had an immense influence upon English nationalism. His stories, from the medieval crypto-Protestants burned for heresy to the Protestant martyrs who passed through the fiery trials of the Marian persecutions, tended to show that England was the land of a new chosen people, destined to lead the way toward the kingdom of God on earth. Foxe's second edition (1570) was so impressive that a copy of it was placed, with the Bible, in every English church.

From Acts and Monuments

The Words and Behavior of the Lady Jane [Grey][1] upon the Scaffold

These are the words that the Lady Jane spake upon the scaffold, at the hour of her death. First, when she mounted upon the scaffold, she said to the people standing thereabout, "Good people, I am come hither to die, and by a law I am condemned to the same. The fact against the queen's highness was unlawful, and the consenting thereunto by me; but, touching the procurement and desire thereof by me, or on my behalf, I do wash my hands thereof in innocency before God and the face of you, good Christian people, this day." And therewith she wrung her hands, wherein she had her book. Then said she, "I pray you all, good Christian people, to bear me witness that I die a true Christian woman, and that I do look to be saved by no other mean, but only by the mercy of God, in the blood of his only Son Jesus Christ; and I confess that when I did know the word of God I neglected the same, loved myself and the world; and therefore this plague and punishment is happily and worthily happened unto me for my sins; and yet I thank God of his goodness that he hath thus given me a time and respite to repent. And now, good people, while I am alive, I pray you assist me with your prayers." And then, kneeling down, she turned her to Fecknam,[2] saying, "Shall I say this psalm?" And he said, "Yea." Then said she the psalm of *Miserere mei Deus*[3] in English, in the most devout manner, throughout to the end; and then she stood up, and gave her maiden, Mistress Ellen, her gloves and handkerchief, and her book to Master Bruges.[4] And then she untied her gown, and the hangman pressed upon her to help her off with it; but she, desiring him to let her alone, turned towards her two gentlewomen, who helped her off therewith, and also with her frows paste,[5] and neckerchief, giving her a fair handkerchief to knit about her eyes.

1. Daughter of the duke of Suffolk. On the death of King Edward VI she was proclaimed queen by the Protestant faction but was overthrown by the Catholic Mary. For an account of her educational accomplishments see the selection from Ascham's *Schoolmaster* pp. 1025–26.
2. John de Feckenham, last abbot of Westmin-

ster, employed by Queen Mary to convert obdurate heretics. He had tried in vain to convert Lady Jane to Catholicism.
3. Psalm 51.
4. Thomas Bridges, vice-lieutenant of the Tower of London.
5. Elaborate headdress.

Then the hangman kneeled down and asked her forgiveness, whom she forgave most willingly. Then he willed her to stand upon the straw; which doing, she saw the block. Then she said, "I pray you, despatch me quickly." Then she kneeled down, saying, "Will you take it off before I lay me down?" And the hangman said, "No, madam." Then tied she the kerchief about her eyes, and feeling for the block she said, "What shall I do? Where is it? Where is it?" One of the standers-by guiding her thereunto she laid her head down upon the block, and then stretched forth her body and said, "Lord, into thy hands I commend my spirit"; and so finished her life, in the year of our Lord God 1553, the twelfth day of February.

1563

JOHN LYLY
1554–1606

John Lyly was the grandson of William Lily, the author of the standard Latin grammar which every schoolboy studied. After receiving the A. M. degree at Oxford, Lyly went to London and sought the patronage of Lord Burleigh and his son-in-law, the earl of Oxford. With the publication of *Euphues* he became instantly famous. The title of the book is Greek for "well-endowed," but a fuller explanation may be found in Ascham's *Schoolmaster*, where perhaps Lyly got it: "*Euphues* is he that by goodness of wit and appliable by readiness of will, to learning, having all other qualities of the mind and parts of the body that must another day serve learning." The subtitle, "Anatomy of Wit," means something like "analysis of intelligence."

The prose style of Lyly's book is called Euphuism, from its title that names its hero. This style has two features: an especially elaborate sentence structure and a wealth of ornament of various kinds. Sentence structure is based on parallel figures from the ancient rhetorics. Ornament includes incidents from history or poetry, proverbs, and similes drawn from pseudoscience, from Pliny, from textbooks, or from the author's imagination.

Euphuism became a rage for a while, especially at court. The publisher of Lyly's *Six Court Comedies* in 1632 informed his readers that "All our ladies were then his [Euphues' or Lyly's] scholars, and the beauty in court who could not parley Euphuism was as little regarded as she which now there speaks not French." In Shakespeare's *1 Henry IV*, 2.4.346–365, Falstaff, when he is pretending to be the king admonishing his wayward son, Prince Hal, speaks Euphuistic prose.

This highly artificial and elaborate style did not last, of course, but it is an example of a fascination with language and its possible artifices that extended to all classes of Elizabethans. "It is a world to see," wrote Lyly, "how Englishmen desire to hear finer speech than the language will allow, to eat finer bread than is made of wheat, to wear finer cloth than is wrought of wool."

Euphues: The Anatomy of Wit

[*Euphues Introduced*]

There dwelt in Athens a young gentleman of great patrimony, and of so comely a personage, that it was doubted[1] whether he were more bound to Nature for the lineaments of his person, or to Fortune for the increase of his possessions. But Nature impatient of comparisons, and as it were disdaining a companion or copartner in her working, added to this comeliness of his body such a sharp capacity of mind, that not only she proved Fortune counterfeit, but was half of that opinion that she herself was only current. This young gallant, of more wit than wealth, and yet of more wealth than wisdom, seeing himself inferior to none in pleasant conceits, thought himself superior to all in honest conditions, insomuch that he deemed himself so apt to all things, that he gave himself almost to nothing, but practicing of those things commonly which are incident to these sharp wits, fine phrases, smooth quipping, merry taunting, using jesting without mean,[2] and abusing mirth without measure. As therefore the sweetest rose hath his prickle, the finest velvet his brack,[3] the fairest flower his bran,[4] so the sharpest wit hath his wanton will, and the holiest head his wicked way. And true it is that some men write and most men believe, that in all perfect shapes, a blemish bringeth rather a liking every way to the eyes, than a loathing any way to the mind. Venus had her mole in her cheek which made her more amiable: Helen[5] her scar on her chin which Paris called *cos amoris*, the whetsone of love. Aristippus[6] his wart, Lycurgus his wen: So likewise in the disposition of the mind, either virtue is overshadowed with some vice, or vice overcast with some virtue. Alexander valiant in war, yet given to wine. Tully eloquent in his glozes, yet vainglorious: Solomon wise, yet too too wanton: David holy but yet an homicide:[7] none more witty than Euphues, yet at the first none more wicked. The freshest colors soonest fade, the teenest[8] razor soonest turneth his edge, the finest cloth is soonest eaten with moths, and the cambric sooner stained than the coarse canvas: which appeared well in this Euphues, whose wit being like wax apt to receive any impression, and having the bridle in his own hands, either to use the rein or the spur, disdaining counsel, leaving his country, loathing his old acquaintance, thought either by wit to obtain some conquest, or by shame to abide some conflict, and leaving the rule of reason, rashly ran unto destruction. Who preferring fancy before friends, and his pres-

1. Wondered.
2. Moderation.
3. Break, flaw.
4. Husk.
5. Greek queen whom Paris abducted to Troy; supposedly the most beautiful woman in the world.
6. Greek philosopher, known for his pursuit of pleasure. Lycurgus was a Spartan lawmaker.
7. Alexander was a Macedonian king, conqueror of Asia and Egypt; he killed his friend Clitus in a drunken brawl. Tully (Marcus Tullius Cicero) was the great Roman orator, famous for his glozes (flattering speeches). Solomon was the third king of Israel, famous for his wisdom and his many wives. His father, David, got Bath-Sheba pregnant and had her husband, Uriah, killed so he could marry her.
8. Keenest.

ent humor, before honor to come, laid reason in water being too salt
for his taste, and followed unbridled affection,[9] most pleasant for his
tooth. When parents have more care how to leave their children wealthy
than wise, and are more desirous to have them maintain the name, than
the nature of a gentleman: when they put gold into the hands of youth,
where they should put a rod under their girdle,[1] when instead of awe
they make them past grace, and leave them rich executors of goods, and
poor executors of godliness, then is it no marvel, that the son being left
rich by his father's will, become retchless by his own will.[2]

It hath been an old said saw,[3] and not of less truth than antiquity, that
wit is the better if it be the dearer bought: as in the sequel of this history
shall most manifestly appear. It happened this young imp[4] to arrive at
Naples (a place of more pleasure than profit, and yet of more profit than
piety) the very walls and windows whereof shewed it rather to be the
Tabernacle of Venus, than the Temple of Vesta.[5]

There was all things necessary and in readiness that might either allure
the mind to lust, or entice the heart to folly, a court more meet for an
atheist, than for one of Athens, for Ovid than for Aristotle, for a graceless
lover than for a godly liver: more fitter for Paris than Hector, and meeter
for Flora than Diana.[6]

Here my youth (whether for weariness he could not, or for wantonness would not go any further) determined to make his abode: whereby
it is evidently seen that the fleetest fish swalloweth the delicatest bait,
that the highest soaring hawk traineth[7] to the lure, and that the wittiest
sconce[8] is inveigled with the sudden view of alluring vanities.

Here he wanted no companions which courted him continually with
sundry kinds of devices, whereby they might either soak his purse to reap
commodity, or sooth his person to win credit, for he had guests and
companions of all sorts.

There frequented to this lodging and mansion house as well the spider
to suck poison of his fine wit, as the bee to gather honey as well the
drone, as the dove, the fox as the lamb, as well Damocles[9] to betray
him, as Damon[1] to be true to him: Yet he behaved himself so warily,
that he singled his game wisely. He could easily discern Apollo's music,
from Pan his pipe, and Venus's beauty from Juno's bravery,[2] and the
faith of Laelius, from the flattery of Aristippus,[3] he welcomed all, but
trusted none, he was merry but yet so wary, that neither the flatterer

---

9. Passion.
1. Whip them.
2. Appetite, the opposite of reason; "retchless":
reckless.
3. Saying, proverb.
4. Novice.
5. Symbolizing chastity, in contrast to Venus.
6. Ovid was famous for his love poems, Aristotle
for his profound, serious philosophical works. Paris
was the lover of Helen, in contrast to his brother
Hector, a great Trojan soldier. Flora was a fertility
goddess, whose annual celebrations were noted for
lasciviousness; Diana was the goddess of chastity.
7. Is attracted to.

8. Head, brain.
9. Famous as a flatterer of Dionysius, who gave
him a gorgeous banquet, but made him sit with a
sword suspended over his head by a single hair, to
show how dangerous eminence is.
1. Famous in classical legend as the friend of
Phintias, so loyal to him that he offered to be executed in his place.
2. Splendid attire.
3. A disciple of Socrates who was nevertheless given
to luxurious living. Laelius was famous as the
faithful friend of Scipio Africanus the younger;
central figure in Cicero's treatise on friendship.

could take advantage to entrap him in his talk, nor the wisest any assurance of his friendship: who being demanded of one what countryman he was, he answered, "What countryman am I not? if I be in Crete, I can lie, if in Greece I can shift, if in Italy I can court it:[4] if thou ask whose son I am also, I ask thee whose son I am not. I can carouse with Alexander, abstain with Romulus, eat with the Epicure, fast with the Stoic, sleep with Endymion, watch with Chrysippus,"[5] using these speeches and other like. An old gentleman in Naples seeing his pregnant wit, his eloquent tongue somewhat taunting, yet with delight, his mirth without measure, yet not without wit, his sayings vainglorious, yet pithy, began to bewail his nurture: and to muse at his nature, being incensed against the one as most pernicious, and enflamed with the other as most precious: for he well knew that so rare a wit would in time either breed an intolerable trouble, or bring an incomparable treasure to the common weal: at the one he greatly pitied, at the other he rejoiced.

1578

4. Inhabitants of the island of Crete early had a reputation as liars. Lyly is elaborating or inventing when he says that the Greeks "shift" (practice or live by deceit) and that the Italians "court it" (behave in a courtly manner).
5. Romulus was the legendary founder and first king of Rome. Exposed as an infant with his brother Remus, he was rescued and suckled by a she-wolf and became a symbol of abstinence. The followers

of Epicurus (Epicureans) were simplistically thought to care for nothing but pleasure; the more austere Stoics venerated duty. Endymion was a youth in Greek legend renowned for his beauty and his eternal sleep on Mt. Latmus, where the moon goddess fell in love with him. Chrysippus was a celebrated Stoic philosopher, devoted to study so that he would watch (stay up all night) with his books.

RICHARD HOOKER
1554–1600

Out of the long and bitter controversy over the government of the church in sixteenth-century England emerged one literary masterpiece. It is a long work in eight books called *Of the Laws of Ecclesiastical Polity* (that is, the governmental system of the church). The author was Richard Hooker, scholar and minister. In 1585 Hooker was master of the temple (in modern terms, a dean of a law school); one of his subordinates was a Puritan lecturer named Walter Travers. Between them a running debate developed on the burning question of how the church should be governed. The Puritan view was that no organization or authority in the church was valid unless it was based clearly and specifically upon the Bible; the whole hierarchical system of the English church, with its deacons, priests, bishops, and archbishops, was accordingly wrong. The position Hooker undertook to defend was that the Scriptures, or divine revelation, are not the only guide given to Christians for organizing and administering the church. Another guide is the law of nature, also divinely given, which can be discerned by the use of human reason.

In his great book, which grew out of his controversy with Travers, Hooker therefore explained how the law of nature affords principles that justify the existing organization of the English church. Book 1 of *Ecclesiastical Polity* deals with laws in general and their various kinds, picturing a universe operating under natural and divine law and founded upon reason. Book 2 deals with the nature, authority, and adequacy of Scripture. Books 3 to 5 explain and defend the rites, ceremonies, worship and government of the English church; and books 6, 7, and 8 deal with various embodiments of authority—elders, bishops, kings, and popes.

Hooker was a close and effective reasoner; avoiding the fiery invective or impassioned rhetoric that characterized most disputants of his time, his manner was calm, reasonable, tolerant. His defense of existing ecclesiastical practices went back to fundamental principles, to a philosophy of nature and our place in it, our relation to God and to other human beings. It is this world view which makes Hooker's book of enduring interest. And Hooker sets forth this world view in what is perhaps the finest prose of the Elizabethan age. King James 1 is quoted by Izaak Walton, Hooker's seventeenth-century biographer, as saying, "I observe there is in Mr. Hooker no affected language; but a grave, comprehensive, clear manifestation of reason, and that backed with the authority of the Scriptures, the fathers and schoolmen, and with all law both sacred and civil. . . . Doubtless there is in every page of Mr. Hooker's book the picture of a divine soul, such pictures of truth and reason, and drawn in so sacred colors, that they shall never fade but give an immortal memory to the author."

From Of the Laws of Ecclesiastical Polity

From *The Preface*

[ON MODERATION IN CONTROVERSY]

* * * Amongst ourselves, there was in King Edward's days some question moved by reason of a few men's scrupulosity touching certain things.[1] And beyond seas, of them which fled in the days of Queen Mary, some contenting themselves abroad with the use of their own service book at home authorized before their departure out of the realm, others liking better the common prayer book of the Church of Geneva translated, those smaller contentions before begun were by this mean somewhat increased. Under the happy reign of Her Majesty which now is, the greatest matter a while contended for was the wearing of the cap and surplice,[2] till there came *Admonitions Directed unto the High Court of Parliament*, by men who, concealing their names, thought it glory enough to discover their minds and affections, which were now universally bent

1. During the short reign of the boy king, Edward VI (1547–53), the reformation begun under Henry VIII was carried further. Services were held in English, images were banished from the church, and the use of holy water was forbidden. During the following reign of Mary, a Catholic, many Protestant reformers fled abroad and there were influenced by the Calvinist doctrines and practices of the "Church of Geneva."
2. The extreme Protestants or "Puritans" were opposed to the daily wearing of cap and gown by the clergy and the wearing of the surplice in church. This "Vestiarian controversy" was at its height in the 1560s. The "*Admonitions Directed unto the High Court of Parliament*," by John Field and Thomas Wilcox (1572), attacked not only conventional clerical dress but the Prayer Book, episcopacy, and the whole structure of the Church of England.

even against all the orders and laws wherein this Church is found unconformable to the platform of Geneva. Concerning the defender of which admonitions, all that I mean to say is this: "There will come a time when three words uttered with charity and meekness shall receive a far more blessed reward than three thousand volumes written with disdainful sharpness of wit." But the manner of men's writing must not alienate our hearts from the truth if it appear they have the truth, as the followers of the same defender do think he hath, and in that persuasion they follow him no otherwise than himself doth Calvin, Beza,[3] and others, with the like persuasion that they in this cause had the truth. We being as fully persuaded otherwise, it resteth that some kind of trial be used to find out which part is in error.

The first mean whereby Nature teacheth men to judge good from evil, as well in laws as in other things, is the force of their own discretion. Hereunto therefore Saint Paul referreth oftentimes his own speech to be considered by them that heard him, "I speak as to them which have understanding; judge ye what I say."[4] Again, afterward, "Judge in yourselves, is it comely that a woman pray uncovered?" The exercise of this kind of judgment our Saviour requireth in the Jews.[5] In them of Berea the Scripture commendeth it. Finally, whatsoever we do, if our own secret judgment consent not unto it as fit and good to be done, the doing of it, to us, is sin, although the thing itself be allowable. Saint Paul's rule therefore generally is, "Let every man in his own mind be fully persuaded of that thing which he either alloweth or doth."[6] Some things are so familiar and plain that truth from falsehood and good from evil is most easily discerned in them, even by men of no deep capacity. And of that nature, for the most part are things absolutely unto all men's salvation necessary, either to be held or denied, either to be done or avoided. For which cause Saint Augustine acknowledgeth that they are not only set down, but also plainly set down in scripture, so that he which heareth or readeth may, without any great difficulty, understand. Other things also there are belonging, though in a lower degree of importance, unto the offices of Christian men, which, because they are more obscure, more intricate and hard to be judged of, therefore God hath appointed some to spend their whole time principally in the study of things divine, to the end that in these more doubtful cases their understanding might be a light to direct others. "If the understanding power or faculty of the soul be," saith the Grand Physician,[7] "like unto the bodily sight, not of equal sharpness in all, what can be more convenient than that, even as the dark-sighted man is directed by the clear about things visible, so likewise in matters of deeper discourse the wise

3. John Calvin (1509–1564) and Theodore Beza (1519–1605), two leading Protestant reformers on the Continent.
4. 1 Corinthians 10.15. The next quotation is from I Corinthians 11.13.
5. See Luke 12.57. "Them of Berea": the inhabitants of the Macedonian city of Berea who "received

the word with all readiness of mind" when Paul preached to them, according to Acts 14.10–11.
6. See Romans 14.5
7. I.e., Galen, Greek physician of the 2d century A.D., whose works were long accepted as the highest medical authority.

in heart do show the simple where his way lieth?" In the doubtful cases of law, what man is there who seeth not how requisite it is that professors of skill in that faculty be our directors? So is it in all other kinds of knowledge. And even in this kind likewise the Lord hath himself appointed that "the Priest's lips should preserve knowledge, and that other men should seek the truth at his mouth, because he is the messenger of the Lord of Hosts."[8] Gregory Nazianzen, offended at the people's too great presumption in controlling the judgment of them to whom in such cases they should rather have submitted their own, seeketh by earnest entreaty to stay them within their bounds: "Presume not, ye that are sheep, to make yourselves guides of them that should guide you; neither seek ye to overskip the fold which they about you have pitched. It sufficeth for your part, if ye can well frame yourselves to be ordered. Take not upon you to judge your judges, nor to make them subject to your laws who should be a law to you. For God is not a God of sedition and confusion but of order and of peace." But ye will say that if the guides of the people be blind, the common sort of men must not close up their own eyes and be led by the conduct of such; if the priest be partial in the law, the flock must not therefore depart from the ways of sincere truth, and in simplicity yield to be followers of him for his place' sake and office over them. Which thing, though in itself most true, is in your defense notwithstanding weak; because the matter wherein ye think that ye see and imagine that your ways are sincere is of far deeper consideration than any one amongst five hundred of you conceiveth. Let the vulgar sort amongst you know that there is not the least branch of the cause wherein they are so resolute but to the trial of it a great deal more appertaineth than their concept doth reach unto. I write not this in disgrace of the simplest that way given,[9] but I would gladly they knew the nature of that cause wherein they think themselves thoroughly instructed and are not; by means whereof they daily run themselves, without feeling their own hazard, upon the dint of the Apostle's sentence against evil speakers as touching things wherein they are ignorant.[1] If it be granted a thing unlawful for private men, not called into public consultation, to dispute which is the best state of civil polity, with a desire of bringing in some other kind than that under which they already live, for of such disputes I take it his meaning was—if it be a thing confessed that of such questions they cannot determine without rashness, inasmuch as a great part of them consisteth in special circumstances, and for one kind as many reasons may be brought as for another—is there any reason in the world why they should better judge what kind of regiment[2] ecclesiastical is the fittest? For in the civil state more insight and, in those affairs, more experience a great deal needs be granted them, than in this they can

---

8. See Malachi 2.7. "Gregory Nazianzen" is St. Gregory of Nazianzus, a 4th-century bishop.

9. I.e., I am not disparaging ordinary, uneducated people.

1. Ignorant people run the risk of the condemnation of the apostle Peter: "But these, as natural brute beasts, made to be taken and destroyed, speak evil of the things that they understand not; and shall utterly perish in their own corruption" (2 Peter 2.12).

2. Government.

possibly have. When they which write in defense of your discipline and commend it unto the highest[3] not in the least cunning manner, are forced notwithstanding to acknowledge that with whom the truth is they know not, they are not certain—what certainty or knowledge can the multitude have thereof? Weigh what doth move the common sort so much to favor this innovation and it shall soon appear unto you that the force of particular reasons which for your several opinions are alleged is a thing whereof the multitude never did nor could consider as to be therewith wholly carried; but certain general inducements are used to make salable your cause in gross; and when once men have cast a fancy towards it, any slight declaration of specialties will serve to lead forward men's inclinable and prepared minds. The method of winning the people's affection unto a general liking of "the Cause," for so ye term it, hath been this: First, in the hearing of the multitude, the faults, especially of higher callings, are ripped up with marvelous exceeding severity and sharpness of reproof, which being oftentimes done, begetteth a great good opinion of integrity, zeal, and holiness to such constant reprovers of sin as by likelihood would never be so much offended at that which is evil, unless themselves were singularly good. The next thing hereunto is to impute all faults and corruptions wherewith the world aboundeth unto the kind of ecclesiastical government established. Wherein, as by reproving faults, they purchased unto themselves with the multitude a name to be virtuous; so by finding out this kind of cause they obtain to be judged wise above others, whereas in truth unto the form even of Jewish government, which the Lord himself, they all confess, did establish, with like show of reason they might impute those faults which the prophets condemn in the governors of that commonwealth as to the English kind of regiment ecclesiastical (whereof also God himself though in other sort is author), the stains and blemishes found in our state, which springing from the root of human frailty and corruption, not only are, but have always been more or less—yea, and for anything we know to the contrary will be till the world's end—complained of, what form of government soever take place. Having gotten thus much sway in the hearts of men, a third step is to propose their own form of church government as the only sovereign remedy of all evils, and to adorn it with all the glorious titles that may be. And the nature, as of men that have sick bodies, so likewise of the people in the crazedness of their minds possessed with dislike and discontentment at things present, is to imagine that anything the virtue whereof they hear commended would help them, but that most which they least have tried. The fourth degree of inducement is by fashioning the very notions and conceits[4] of men's minds in such sort that when they read the Scriptures they may think that everything soundeth towards the advancement of that discipline and to the utter disgrace of the contrary. Pythagoras, by bringing up his scholars

---

3. I.e., Queen Elizabeth. The *Humble Petition of the Commonalty* (1588) said, "we are very babes and children, not knowing our right hand from our left in matters that concern the Kingdom of Heaven." "Cunning": learned.
4. Concepts.

in the speculative knowledge of numbers, made their conceits therein so strong that when they came to the contemplation of things natural they imagined that in every particular thing they even beheld, as it were with their eyes, how the elements of number gave essence and being to the works of nature. A thing in reason impossible, which notwithstanding through their misfashioned preconceit appeared unto them no less certain than if nature had written it in the very foreheads of all the creatures of God. * * *

From *Book 1, Chapter 3*

[ON THE SEVERAL KINDS OF LAW, AND ON THE NATURAL LAW]

I am not ignorant that by law eternal the learned for the most part do understand the order, not which God hath eternally purposed himself in all his works to observe, but rather that which with himself he hath set down as expedient to be kept by all his creatures, according to the several[5] condition wherewith he hath indued them. They who thus are accustomed to speak apply the name of *Law* unto that only rule of working which superior authority imposeth, whereas we, somewhat more enlarging the sense thereof, term any kind of rule or canon whereby actions are framed a law. Now that law, which as it is laid up in the bosom of God they call *eternal*, receiveth according unto the different kinds of things which are subject unto it different and sundry kinds of names. That part of it which ordereth natural agents, we call usually *nature's* law; that which angels do clearly behold, and without any swerving observe, is a law *celestial* and heavenly; the law of *reason* that which bindeth creatures reasonable in this world, and with which by reason they may most plainly perceive themselves bound; that which bindeth them, and is not known but by special revelation from God, *divine* law; *human* law, that which out of the law either of reason or of God, men probably gathering to be expedient, they make it a law. All things, therefore, which are as they ought to be, are conformed unto *this second law eternal*, and even those things which to this *eternal* law are not conformable are notwithstanding in some sort ordered by *the first eternal law*. For what good or evil is there under the sun, what action correspondent to or repugnant unto the law which God hath imposed upon his creatures, but in or upon it God doth work according to the law which himself hath eternally purposed to keep, that is to say, the *first law eternal?* So that a twofold law eternal being thus made, it is not hard to conceive how they both take place in all things. Wherefore to come to the law of nature, albeit thereby we sometimes mean that manner of working which God hath set for each created thing to keep: yet forasmuch as those things are termed most properly natural agents, which keep the law of their kind unwittingly, as the heavens and elements of the world, which can do no otherwise than they do, and forasmuch as

5. Different.

we give unto intellectual natures the name of voluntary agents, that so we may distinguish them from the other, expedient it will be that we sever the law of nature observed by the one from that which the other is tied unto. Touching the former, their strict keeping of one tenure statute[6] and law is spoken of by all, but hath in it more than men have as yet attained to know, or perhaps ever shall attain, seeing the travail of wading herein is given of God to the sons of men, that perceiving how much the least thing in the world hath in it more than the wisest are able to reach unto, they may by this means learn humility. Moses in describing the work of creation, attributeth speech unto God: "God said, Let there be light, Let there be a firmament; Let the waters under the heaven be gathered together into one place; Let the earth bring forth; Let there be lights in the firmament of heaven."[7] Was this only the intent of Moses, to signify the greatness of God's power by the easiness of his accomplishing such effects without travail, pain, or labor? Surely it seemeth that Moses had herein besides this a further purpose: namely, first to teach that God did not work as a necessary, but a voluntary, agent, intending beforehand and decreeing with himself that which did outwardly proceed from him; secondly, to show that God did then institute a law natural to be observed by creatures, and therefore according to the manner of laws, the institution thereof is described as being established by solemn injunction. His commanding those things to be which are, and to be in such sort as they are, to keep that tenure and course which they do, importeth the establishment of nature's law. This world's first creation, and the preservation since of things created, what is it but only so far forth a manifestation by execution, what the eternal law of God is concerning things natural? And as it cometh to pass in a kingdom rightly ordered, that after a law is once published, it presently takes effect far and wide, all states[8] framing themselves thereunto; even so let us think it fareth in the natural course of the world; since the time that God did first proclaim the edicts of his law upon it, heaven and earth have hearkened unto his voice, and their labor hath been to do his will. He made a law for the rain. He gave his decree unto the sea, that the waters should not pass his commandment.

Now if Nature should intermit her course and leave altogether, though it were but for a while, the observation of her own laws; if those principal and mother elements of the world, whereof all things in this lower world are made, should lose the qualities which now they have; if the frame of that heavenly arch erected over our heads should loosen and dissolve itself; if celestial spheres should forget their wonted motions and by irregular volubility turn themselves any way as it might happen; if the prince of the lights of heaven which now as a giant doth run his unwearied course, should as it were through a languishing faintness begin to

6. Decree establishing the domains of the various creatures, and the conditions of service by which they hold these domains.

7. Genesis 1.3, 6, 9, 11, 14. In this period, Moses was generally assumed to be the author of the Book of Genesis.

8. Conditions.

stand and to rest himself; if the moon should wander from her beaten way, the times and seasons of the year blend themselves by disordered and confused mixture, the winds breathe out their last gasp, the clouds yield no rain, the earth be defeated of heavenly influence, the fruits of the earth pine away as children at the withered breasts of their mother no longer able to yield them relief, what would become of man himself, whom these things now do all serve? See we not plainly that obedience of creatures unto the law of Nature is the stay of the whole world? Notwithstanding with Nature it cometh sometimes to pass as with art. Let Phidias[9] have rude and obstinate stuff to carve, though his art do that it should, his work will lack that beauty which otherwise in fitter matter it might have had. He that striketh an instrument with skill may cause notwithstanding a very unpleasant sound if the string whereon he striketh chance to be uncapable of harmony. In the matter whereof natural things consist, that of Theophrastus[1] taketh place, "much of it is oftentimes such as will by no means yield to receive that impression which were best and most perfect." Which defect in the matter of things natural, they who gave themselves unto the contemplation of Nature among the heathen observed often; but the true original cause thereof divine malediction,[2] laid for the sin of man upon those creatures which God had made for the use of man. This, being an article of that saving truth which God hath revealed unto his church, was above the reach of their merely natural capacity and understanding. But howsoever these swervings are now and then incident into the course of Nature, nevertheless so constantly the laws of Nature are by natural agents observed, that no man denieth but those things which Nature worketh are wrought either always or for the most part after one and the same manner. * * *

From *Book I, Chapter* 8

[ON THE SCOPE OF THE SEVERAL LAWS]

* * * The general and perpetual voice of men is as the sentence[3] of God himself. For that which all men have at all times learned, Nature herself must needs have taught, and God being the author of Nature, her voice is but his instrument. By her from Him we receive whatsoever in such sort we learn. Infinite duties there are, the goodness whereof is by this rule sufficiently manifested, although we had no warrant besides to approve them. The apostle St. Paul having speech concerning the heathen saith of them "They are a law unto themselves."[4] His meaning is, that by force of the light of reason wherewith God illuminateth everyone which cometh into the world, men being enabled to know truth from falsehood, and good from evil, do thereby learn in many things what the will of God is; which will himself not revealing by any extraor-

9. The greatest of ancient Greek sculptors (5th century B.C.).
1. Greek writer of the 3rd century B.C., a follower of Aristotle and inventor of the type of essay called the "character," which in concise form delineated a type of person.
2. God's curse in Eden, which fell not only upon sinful man but upon the earth as well.
3. Decree.
4. Romans 2.14.

dinary means unto them, but they be natural discourse attaining the knowledge thereof, seem the makers of those laws which indeed are his, and they but only the finders of them out. A law therefore generally taken is a directive rule unto goodness of operation. The rule of divine operations outward is the definite appointment of God's own wisdom set down within himself. The rule of natural agents that work by simple necessity is the determination of the wisdom of God, known to God himself, the principal director of them, but not unto them that are directed to execute the same. The rule of natural agents which work after a sort of their own accord, as the beasts do, is the judgment of common sense or fancy concerning the sensible[5] goodness of those objects wherewith they are moved. The rule of ghostly or immaterial natures, as spirits and angels, is their intuitive intellectual judgment concerning the amiable beauty and high goodness of that object, which with unspeakable joy and delight doth set them on work. The rule of voluntary agents on earth is the sentence that reason giveth concerning the goodness of those things which they are to do. And the sentences which reason giveth are some more, some less general, before it come to define in particular actions what is good. The main principles of reason are in themselves apparent. For to make nothing evident of itself unto man's understanding were to take away all possibility of knowing anything. And herein that of Theophrastus is true, "They that seek a reason of all things do utterly overthrow reason." * * *

From *Book I, Chapter 10*

[THE FOUNDATIONS OF SOCIETY]

That which hitherto we have set down is, I hope, sufficient to show their brutishness which imagine that religion and virtue are only as men will accompt of[6] them, that we might make as much accompt, if we would, of the contrary, without any harm unto ourselves, and that in Nature they are as indifferent one as the other. We see then how Nature itself teacheth laws and statutes to live by. The laws which have been hitherto mentioned do bind men absolutely, even as they are men, although they have never any settled fellowship, never any solemn agreement amongst themselves what to do or not to do. But forasmuch as we are not by ourselves sufficient to furnish ourselves with competent store of things needful for such a life as our nature doth desire, a life fit for the dignity of man, therefore to supply those defects and imperfections which are in us living single and solely, by ourselves, we are naturally induced to seek communion and fellowship with others. This was the cause of men's uniting themselves at the first in politic societies, which societies could not be without government, nor government without a distinct kind of law from that which hath been already declared. Two foundations there are which bear up public societies, the one a

5. Perceptible by the senses.   6. Value.

natural inclination whereby all men desire a sociable life and fellowship, the other an order expressly or secretly agreed upon, touching the manner of their union in living together. The latter is that which we call the law of a commonweal,[7] the very soul of a politic body, the parts whereof are by law animated, held together and set on work in such actions as the common good requireth. Laws politic, ordained for external order and regiment amongst men, are never framed as they should be, unless presuming the will of man to be inwardly obstinate, rebellious, and averse from all obedience unto the sacred laws of his nature—in a word, unless presuming man to be in regard of his depraved mind little better than a wild beast—they do accordingly provide notwithstanding so to frame his outward actions that they be no hindrance unto the common good for which societies are instituted; unless they do this, they are not perfect. It resteth therefore that we consider how Nature findeth out such laws of government as serve to direct even nature depraved to a right end. All men desire to lead in this world an happy life. That life is led most happily, wherein all virtue is exercised without impediment or let. The Apostle[8] in exhorting men to contentment, although they have in this world no more than very bare food and raiment, giveth us thereby to understand that those are even the lowest of things necessary; that if we should be stripped of all those things without which we might possibly be, yet these must be left, that destitution in these is such an impediment, as till it be removed, suffereth not the mind of man to admit any other care. For this cause first God assigned Adam maintenance of life and then appointed him a law to observe. For this cause after men began to grow to a number, the first thing we read they gave themselves unto was the tilling of the earth and the feeding of cattle. Having by this mean whereon to live, the principal actions of their life afterward are noted by the exercise of their religion. True it is that the Kingdom of God must be the first thing in our purposes and desires. But inasmuch as righteous life presupposeth life, inasmuch as to live virtuously it is impossible except we live, therefore the first impediment which naturally we endeavor to remove is penury and want of things without which we cannot live. Unto life many implements are necessary; moe,[9] if we seek, as all men naturally do, such a life as hath in it joy, comfort, delight and pleasure. To this end we see how quickly sundry arts mechanical were found out in the very prime of the world. As things of greatest necessity are always first provided for, so things of greatest dignity are most accompted of by all such as judge rightly. Although therefore riches be a thing which every man wisheth, yet no man of judgment can esteem it better to be rich than wise, virtuous, and religious. If we be both or either of these, it is not because we are so born. For into the world we come as empty of the one as of the other, as naked in mind as we are in body. Both which necessities of man had at the first no other helps and supplies than only domestical, such as that which the prophet[1] implieth, saying, "Can a mother forget her child?" such as that which the Apostle[2] mentioneth, saying, "He that careth not for his own is worse than an infidel"; such as that concerning Abraham, "Abraham will command his sons and his household after him that they keep the way of the Lord."[3] But neither that which we learn of ourselves, nor that which others teach us, can prevail where wickedness and malice have taken deep root. If therefore when there was but as yet one only family in the world, no means of instruction human or divine could prevent effusion of blood, how could it be chosen but that when families were multiplied and increased upon earth, after separation each providing for itself, envy, strife, contention, and violence must grow amongst them? For hath not Nature furnished man with wit and valor, as it were with armor, which may be used as well unto extreme evil as good? Yea, were they not used by the rest of the world unto evil, unto the contrary only by Seth, Enoch, and those few the rest in that line?[4] We all make complaint of the iniquity of our times; not unjustly, for the days are evil. But compare them with those times wherein there were no civil societies, with those times wherein there was as yet no manner of public regiment established, with those times wherein there were not above eight persons righteous living upon the face of the earth, and we have surely good cause to think that God hath blessed us exceedingly and hath made us behold most happy days. To take away all such mutual grievances, injuries, and wrongs, there was no way but only by growing into composition and agreement amongst themselves by ordaining some kind of government public and by yielding themselves subject thereunto, that unto whom they granted authority to rule and govern, by them the peace, tranquility, and happy estate of the rest might be procured. * * *

From *Book I, Chapter* 12

[THE NEED FOR REVEALED LAW]

* * * The first principles of the law of nature are easy: hard it were to find men ignorant of them; but concerning the duty which Nature's law doth require at the hands of men in a number of things particular, so far hath the natural understanding even of sundry whole nations been darkened, that they have not discerned—no, not gross iniquity—to be sin. Again, being so prone as we are to fawn upon ourselves, and to be ignorant as much as may be of our own deformities, without the feeling sense whereof we are most wretched, even so much the more because not knowing them we cannot as much as desire to have them taken away, how should our festered sores be cured but that God hath delivered a

1. Isaiah (49.17).
2. Paul, in 1 Timothy 5.8.
3. Genesis 18.19.
4. The virtuous line of Seth is described in Genesis 4.25–26. It was in the time of Seth and his son Enos that "men began to call upon the name of the Lord."

law as sharp as the two-edged sword, piercing the very closest and most unsearchable corners of the heart which the law of nature can hardly, human laws by no means possible, reach unto? Hereby we know even secret concupiscence to be sin, and are made fearful to offend, though it be but in a wandering cogitation.[5] * * *

1593

5. A reference to Hebrews 4.12: "For the word of God is quick, and powerful, and sharper than any two-edged sword, piercing even to the dividing asunder of soul and spirit and of the joints and marrow, and is a discerner of the thoughts and intents of the heart."

RALPH LANE
ca. 1530–1603

Sir Ralph Lane accompanied an expedition to the new world organized by Sir Water Ralegh and led by Sir Richard Grenville in 1585. As the governor of the Virginia colony established on Roanoke Island that year, Lane was the first English governor in America. The next year, however, shortages of provisions and difficulties with the Indians caused the Roanoke colonists to abandon the settlement and return to England. Lane's letter, a hyperbolic description of the wonders and benefits of the new colony, was one of many such accounts intended to promote settlement and financial investment in the colonies. It was published by Richard Hakluyt, geographer, clergyman, and promoter of colonization, in his three-volume collection, *The Principal Narrations, Traffics, Voyages, and Discoveries of the English Nation* (1598–1600). Hakluyt's work was a major repository of accounts by adventurers, explorers, and travellers, exemplifying and promoting interest in the new world, its exotic curiosities and its attractions for colonists. The nineteenth-century historian J. A. Froude termed the work "the prose epic of the English Nation."

From Hakluyt's *Voyages*

An Extract of Master Ralph Lane's Letter to M[aster] Richard Hakluyt, Esquire, and Another Gentleman of the Middle Temple, from Virginia

In the meanwhile, you shall understand that since Sir Richard Grenville's departure from us, as also before, we have discovered the main to be the goodliest soil under the cope[1] of heaven, so abounding with sweet trees that bring such sundry rich and pleasant gums, grapes of such greatness, yet wild, as France, Spain, nor Italy have no greater, so many sorts of apothecary drugs, such several kinds of flax, and one kind like silk, the same gathered of a grass as common there as grass is here. And now within these few days we have found here maize or guinea wheat,

1. Vault.

whose ear yieldeth corn for bread, four hundred upon one ear, and the cane maketh very good and perfect sugar; also *terra samia*, otherwise *terra sigillata*.[2] Besides that, it is the goodliest and most pleasing territory of the world; for the continent is of a huge and unknown greatness, and very well peopled and towned, though savagely, and the climate so wholesome that we had not one sick since we touched the land here. To conclude, if Virginia had but horses and kine[3] in some reasonable proportion, I dare assure myself, being inhabited with English, no realm in Christendom were comparable to it.

For this already we find that what commodities soever Spain, France, Italy, or the East parts do yield unto us, in wines of all sorts, in oils, in flax, in rosins,[4] pitch, frankincense, currants, sugars, and such like, these parts do abound with the growth of them all; but, being savages that possess the land, they know no use of the same. And sundry other rich commodities that no parts of the world, be they West or East Indies, have, here we find great abundance of. The people naturally are most courteous, and very desirous to have clothes, but especially of coarse cloth rather than silk; coarse canvas they also like well of, but copper carrieth the price of all, so it be made red. Thus good Master Hakluyt and M. H., I have joined you both in one letter of remembrance, as two that I love dearly well, and commending me most heartily to you both, I commit you to the tuition of the Almighty. From the new fort in Virginia, this third of September, 1585.

Your most assured friend,
RALPH LANE

1585   1600

2. Two kinds of earth valued for their medicinal properties.
3. Cattle.

4. Resin, a residue of turpentine, used in making varnish.

AEMILIA LANYER
1569–1645

Aemilia Lanyer, one of the very few published women poets of the Renaissance, was the daughter of, and wife of, gentlemen musicians attached to the courts of Elizabeth I and James I. Her single volume of poems, *Salve Deus Rex Judaeorum* (1611) has a decided feminist thrust. A series of dedicatory poems to patronesses praises them as a community of contemporary good women; the title poem on Christ's Passion contrasts the good women associated with the Passion story with the weak and evil men, and incorporates a defense of Eve; the final poem *To Cookham* celebrates the estate of her patroness, Margaret countess of Cumberland, as an Edenic paradise of women, now lost. The Epistle *To the Virtuous Reader* is a spirited and forceful contribution to the so-called *querelle des femmes*, a massive body of writings which argue the issue of women's worthiness or faultiness, beginning in the Middle Ages and extending over several centuries. Such writings—both serious and satiric and in several languages—included sermons, tracts, manuals of domestic advice, poems, and plays. Some notable examples are The Wife of Bath's Prologue and Tale; John Knox's denunciation of Mary Queen of Scots, *The Monstrous Regiment of Women*; and Shakespeare's *Taming of the Shrew*.

From Salve Deus Rex Judaeorum[1]

To the Virtuous Reader

Often have I heard, that it is the property of some women, not only to emulate the virtues and perfections of the rest, but also by all their powers of ill speaking, to eclipse the brightness of their deserved fame: now contrary to their custom, which men I hope unjustly lay to their charge, I have written this small volume, or little book, for the general use of all virtuous ladies and gentlewomen of this kingdom; and in commendation of some particular persons of our own sex, such as for the most part, are so well known to myself, and others, that I dare undertake Fame dares not to call any better. And this have I done, to make known to the world, that all women deserve not to be blamed though some forgetting they are women themselves, and in danger to be condemned by the words of their own mouths, fall into so great an error, as to speak unadvisedly against the rest of their sex; which if it be true, I am persuaded they can show their own imperfection in nothing more: and therefore could wish (for their own ease, modesties, and credit) they would refer such points of folly, to be practised by evil disposed men, who forgetting they were born of women, nourished of women, and that if it were not by the means of women, they would be quite extinguished out of the world, and a final end of them all, do like vipers deface the wombs wherein they were bred, only to give way and utterance to their want of discretion and goodness. Such as these, were they that dishonoured Christ his Apostles and Prophets, putting them to shameful deaths. Therefore we are not to regard any imputations, that they undeservedly lay upon us, no otherwise than to make use of them to our own benefits, as spur to virtue, making us fly all occasions that may colour their unjust speeches to pass current. Especially considering that they have tempted even the patience of God himself, who gave power to wise and virtuous women, to bring down their pride and arrogancy. As was cruel Cesarus by the discreet counsel of noble Deborah, judge and prophetess of Israel: and resolution of Jael wife of Heber the Kenite:[2] wicked Haman, by the

---

1. Hail God, King of the Jews.
2. Sisera (Canaanite "leader," hence "cesarus," i.e., "caesar") was a Canaanite military commander (12th century b.c.) routed in battle by the Israelites under the leadership of the prophetess Deborah. Sisera was subsequently killed by the Kenite woman Jael, who enticed him to her tent and then drove a tent spike through his temples while he slept (Judges 4).

divine prayers and prudent proceedings of beautiful Hester:[3] blasphemous Holofernes, by the invincible courage, rare wisdom, and confident carriage of Judeth: and the unjust Judges, by the innocency of chaste Susanna:[4] with infinite others, which for brevity sake I will omit. As also in respect it pleased our Lord and Saviour Jesus Christ, without the assistance of man, being free from original and all other sins, from the time of his conception, till the hour of his death, to be begotten of a woman, born of a woman, nourished of a woman, obedient to a woman; and that he healed women, pardoned women, comforted women: yea, even when he was in his greatest agony and bloody sweat, going to be crucified, and also in the last hour of his death, took care to dispose of a woman:[5] after his resurrection, appeared first to a woman, sent a woman to declare his most glorious resurrection to the rest of his Disciples.[6] Many other examples I could allege of divers faithful and virtuous women, who have in all ages, not only been confessors, but also indured most cruel martyrdom for their faith in Jesus Christ. All which is sufficient to inforce all good Christians and honourable-minded men to speak reverently of our sex, and especially of all virtuous and good women. To the modest censures of both which, I refer these my imperfect indeavours, knowing that according to their own excellent dispositions, they will rather, cherish, nourish, and increase the least spark of virtue where they find it, by their favourable and best interpretations, than quench it by wrong constructions. To whom I wish all increase of virtue, and desire their best opinions.

1611

3. Esther, the Jewish wife (5th century B.C.) of the Persian King Ahasuerus (Xerxes I), who by her wit and courage subverted the plot of the King's minister, Haman, to annihilate the Jews (Esther 1–7). Judith in the 5th century B.C. delivered her Judean countrymen from the Assyrians by captivating their leader, Holofernes, with her charms and then decapitating him while he was drunk (*Apocrypha*, Book of Judith).
4. Jewish wife and example of chastity (6th century B.C.). She was falsely accused of adultery by two Jewish elders, in revenge for refusing their sexual advances, and condemned to death. The wise judge Daniel saved her by uncovering the elders' perjury (*Apocrypha*, Book of Susanna).
5. I.e., Christ asked his apostle John to care for his mother Mary (John 19.25–27). "Dispose of": provide for.
6. Mary Magdalen (John 20.1–18).

The Early
Seventeenth Century
1603-1660

1603: Death of Elizabeth Tudor, accession of James I, first Stuart king of England.

1605: The Gunpowder Plot, a failed effort by Catholic extremists to blow up Parliament and the King. Responsible for prolonged and bitter anti-Catholic feeling: "Guy Fawkes Day" (November 5) still preserves the memory of one of the conspirators.

1620: Arrival of the Pilgrim Fathers in the New World.

1625: Death of James I, accession of Charles I.

1642: Outbreak of civil war: theaters closed.

1649: Execution of Charles I, beginning of Commonwealth and Protectorate, known inclusively as the Interregnum (1649–1660).

1660: End of the Protectorate, Restoration of Charles II.

In its narrowest definition, the "early seventeenth century" extends from the accession of the first Stuart king (James I) in 1603 to the coronation of the third (Charles II) in 1660. But the events of those years are historically meaningful only if seen in a pattern extending from 1588 to 1688. Between these two outer dates occurred those massive social events which, in their cumulative effect, bridge the gap between the Tudor "tyranny-by-consent" of the sixteenth century and the equally ill-defined but equally functional constitutional monarchy of the eighteenth century. At the center of the period lies the Puritan Revolution of 1640–1660. The quarrels and controversies that culminated in this upheaval began to reach an inflammatory stage shortly after 1588; its tremors and aftershocks largely subsided after 1688. In more senses than one, the Revolution was the central event of the century.

Armada year, 1588, marked a decisive turning point in the reign of Elizabeth. Like most of her subjects, she had expected the nation's supreme triumph over a long-awaited, much-hated invader to release a tide of patriotic good feeling. Nothing of the sort happened: quite the contrary. Social problems that had long lain suppressed in the interests of national unity suddenly surfaced when the nation was secure. They gave rise to bitter and divisive quarrels, fought out for the most part between the aging queen and her successive parliaments, but also in local encounters throughout the land. Wherever a stiff-necked parson encountered a strong-willed bishop, a grumbling consumer confronted an unjust monopoly, or a truculent House-of-Commons man complained that his freedom of speech was being abridged, the frictions of society built up. Individually, perhaps, they were minor grievances, but, being neglected, they festered, tending over the years to reinforce one another. The queen's traditional measures of cajolery and grandiose rhetoric failed to placate the malcontents; and the peaceful accession of James, first English monarch of the Stuart family, did nothing to mollify them. By pleas and remonstrations, and by voting to withhold taxes from the royal administration, Parliament sought redress, but to little avail. Agitation against the authoritarian episcopal church continued, mostly subsurface, but flaring up occasionally in acts of fierce despair, as when the Pilgrim Fathers left their native land forever, rather than submit to episcopal rule. (They went to Amsterdam in 1608 and then in 1620 to the wilderness of Plymouth, Massachusetts.) Under the increasingly strict rule of James's son, Charles, discontents spread more widely if even less openly; they expanded from Puritan preachers and their relatively small congregations to the merchant classes, the lawyers, the Parliament-men, and the gentry—to Scotland, to the mercantile towns, through the cloth-making countryside of East Anglia. By the late 1630s tempers were strained, and in 1637 an episode in Edinburgh led to the first of two half-hearted wars between England and Scotland. But domestic peace was an ingrained habit in most of England, and it was not till 1642, after five years of muted struggle and negotiation, that open conflict broke out.

In the wars that followed, the forces of insurrection (the Parliamentary, Puritan, or Roundhead armies) were successful in one of their aims: they rendered Charles powerless, brought him to trial, and executed him (1649). But they failed to set up a stable government of their own, free from the faults of the one they had destroyed, and they failed to set up a new national church, to replace the episcopacy that they had long criticized. The military dictatorship (1649–1660) established first by Oliver Cromwell under the name of Commonwealth and then maintained as a Protectorate, even after his death in 1658, was no more than a makeshift effort to contain a political instability that had got out of hand. When Charles II was recalled from exile (1660) and put back on his father's throne but without his father's powers, it became clear that England was bound to have, in religion and politics, some sort of organization looser than anyone had anticipated, looser than anyone really wanted. But its exact form was subject to constant pulling and hauling among the parties, and no solid settlement was reached till 1688, when Charles's brother and successor, James II, was ejected from the throne and sent into exile. After 1688, its social problems compromised if not solved, the country settled down to a long constitutional nap under a series of monarchs who made little trouble for their parliaments and therefore had little trouble with their thrones. The crisis was over.

Though infinitely complex in details, the main social problems that exercised the seventeenth century can be broadly stated, with their solutions, in two sentences. In the religious sphere, the basic issue was: How far should the reformation of the Protestant church be carried? and the solution accomplished in 1688 was, "As far as each individual self-defined religious group wants." In the sphere of constitutional politics, the basic issue was: How much authority should the monarch have independent of Parliament? and the solution accomplished in 1688 was, "Almost none."

To visualize the immense changes wrought by the crisis years of the Puritan Revolt, and their relation to the quality of English literature, it may be useful to anatomize very roughly the value structure of English society before and after the event. Oversimplifications are inevitable but necessary, to point up a set of broad changes which actually took place; and definitions are possible because the Revolution was preceded and followed by periods of relative order and tranquility. Under Elizabeth Tudor the court was the undisputed center of national authority, influence, power, reward, and intellectual inspiration. Careers were made and fortunes established through court connections. London was the center of the kingdom, and the court was the unchallenged center of London. Particularly was this true in matters of the intellect, of literature and the arts. The characteristic forms of literature under Elizabeth were courtly. Courtiers patronized the theater by attending plays (of which the middle class generally disapproved) and by lending the prestige of their names to different acting companies. The sonnet sequence, the pastoral romance (Sidney's *Arcadia*), the chivalric allegory (Spenser's *Faerie Queene*), the learned sermon, the erotic idyll *(Hero and Leander* or *Venus and Adonis)*, the masque, the epic—all these were courtly forms, implying courtly readers and writers who were either courtiers themselves or concerned to please courtiers. For patronage flowed, when it flowed at all, from courtly donors; and, apart from the precarious rewards of the theater, patronage was almost the only way for the writer to live by writing. The same pattern continued under the first two Stuarts, James I and Charles I. Whether in his sermons or in his poems, a man like Donne wrote primarily for courtiers. Versatile and various as he was, Ben Jonson channeled almost all his energies into writing for court and courtiers. Carew, Suckling, Lovelace, and a host of lesser writers were themselves courtiers, simply in the sense that they spent much of their time at court. A man like George Herbert was much remarked because he could have been a courtier and chose not to be. There were exceptions, of course: country doctors and rural parsons sometimes exercised themselves in literature. But the court influence was predominant, and so far as a literary society existed, it took its tone from the court. Because court circles were narrow, a poet did not have to wait for publication in order to be widely known among his fellow poets. Manuscript collections of poems by one author, or by several, circulated through the court; a poem could become popular, be set to music several times over, and yet never appear in print. The books that were printed generally appeared in small editions, and, being destined for a particular audience, could take a good deal for granted in the way of special background and training. A court preacher like Lancelot Andrewes assumed in his hearers acquaintance with at least the rudiments of three ancient languages; Sir Philip Sidney in the *Arcadia* assumed familiarity not only with the codes of learned pastoralism, but with the traditions and conventions of courtly behavior. For court society had many characteristic and distinctive values. It implied a belief in hierarchical order within a strict framework of uniformity, involving obedience to the national church, loyalty to the national monarch. Within that framework, it tended to produce intricate, allusive, and highly decorative writing. Courtiers generally valued the heroic passions—love (but not necessarily marriage), warfare (largely free of a political context), and devotional piety (quite apart from practical morality). The controlling principle behind all these distinctions was an emphasis upon honor as the supreme principle in life, not to be estimated in any way by criteria of mere prudence. Literature written within this framework and primarily for readers who accepted it tended generally to reflect its arrangement of values.

After 1660, and even more strikingly after 1688, the pattern of values was quite different. For one thing, the court was no longer an unchallenged center of intellectual and literary influence. It did not have the power, social and financial, to be anything of the sort. For now money and influence no longer flowed exclusively from the court. London City (a network of banks and merchants, jobbers, financiers, brokers, tradesmen, and credit-managers) was one rival source of power and influence; Parliament itself, which in 1688 would assert decisive power over the throne by expelling James II and appointing a Dutchman to be his successor as William III, was another. Instead of standing above interest as the sole fountain of honor, the court thus became in effect one of several competing interests. The relatively conservative "landed interest" tended toward the court, as the more innovative "money interest" found its chief support in the City; and Parliament-men, ranking themselves under the deliberately meaningless nicknames of "Tory" and "Whig," sided with either interest as they chose or with both as they found the occasion proper. One's connection with an interest was not through the inflexible principle of honor, but through the flexible one of . . . interest.

In precisely the same way, the established church, which had once claimed to be sole guardian of men's spiritual welfare and therefore of their worldly behavior—the authoritative voice disciplining every Englishman's private interests—became after 1660 simply one of many possible religious communities. (It was the most powerful, the most socially acceptable, and for the moment the largest one; but it was not, and could not be made, the only one.) The Puritan sects, originally factions within the English church, had been freed to multiply and develop their independence during the Interregnum; after the Restoration, they could not be got back into the episcopal (Anglican) church by force or persuasion. When several sects exist side by side in open competition, they are all voluntary. Each interprets Scripture after its own fashion, each follows its own moral code, each tries to attract proselytes, all agree in not trying to persecute one another. But that creates problems of discipline; if a member does not like the social code of his sect, he transfers to a more understanding sect, or out of them all. When neither monarch nor church could control social and economic behavior, most of it passed out of control altogether. For morality in a social or business sense applies mainly to people, considered as responsible economic agents; and the new forms of economic organization involved either artificial personalities or legal fictions to which moral laws do not apply. Corporations and joint-stock companies, cartels and syndicates, mutual-aid societies and credit unions, banks and bankers' combines (a whole gamut of anonymous voluntary associations) began to develop England piecemeal, amorphously, after the fashion of a modern capitalist nation. New money brought to the fore new men, enterprising and respectable, but with few pretensions to courtly manners or intellectual sophistication. The literature that appealed to them was less dogmatic and moralistic than the old hell-and-damnation puritanism; it was more serious than the frankly bawdy wit of the Restoration stage. Observing these and other divergencies of taste, enterprising publishers began to aim their products at a particular market, in which they specialized. Before long, they were hiring writers to turn out titles on order. The "booksellers," as they were called, thus began to replace the older courtly patrons as makers of public taste. Authors who wrote to order at the bidding of publishers became known collectively, from the cheap lodgings where they congregated, as Grub Street authors. For them, at least, the change from a society organized around honor to one organized around interest was very palpable indeed.

Around the broad social changes sketched above there took place a set of intellectual and spiritual changes, no less striking and significant. The Elizabethan monarchy and church had been hierarchical in organization because that was thought to be the inevitable structure of things, the natural pattern of the world. Every creature had his place in the great order of divine appointments; and the different families of being were bound together by a chain of universal analogy. The king was to his subjects as Michael was to the other archangels, as the bishop was to his pastors, as the lion was to other beasts, as the eagle was to other birds, as the diamond was to other stones, as gold was to other metals. The head ruled the other parts of the body because, as the seat of reason, it was nobler. Reason, which ruled in man, made him natural head of the family because passion was thought to rule in woman. The king was head of the body politic; in him, reason ruled as it ought, over the passionate and tumultuous multitude. And all this ruling was necessary because of Adam's fall, as a result of which not only human psychology but the whole structure of the universe had been disordered. Though they differed over the form of the rule and the name of the ruler, almost all the contestants in the civil wars agreed that the people needed strict discipline of some sort, because in themselves they were radically imperfect. While the various leaders were disputing over details, the people, simply as a result of slow experience (by living under an "illegitimate" authority, without any sort of religious conformity), demonstrated that they were less imperfect, and needed less rigid discipline, than had been supposed.

One universal truth emerged from the revolution and civil wars—that no one universal truth was to be had, whether by sword, by prayer, or by study. Nor was it really needed. Individuals, it seemed, could hold differing views about foreign policy, the nature of Christ's presence in the sacrament, or the lawfulness of infant baptism, without necessarily precipitating social chaos. A single true belief in these matters, and in many, many others, was evidently unnecessary. And thus the whole notion of human beings as radically fallen creatures, who needed a special saving truth and a dose of stiff discipline to redeem their faults, began fading toward obsolescence. A reasonable person (one who behaved sensibly and didn't bother his or her neighbor) seemed to be almost as good as need be. In a long list of controversies, over which people had once been willing to slit throats, it turned out that nobody was right and nobody was wrong. And thus the English community changed from one founded on the concepts of hierarchy, uniformity, and personal relatedness, to one founded on the concepts of multiplicity, disparity, and toleration. In less than a hundred years the nation had passed from a strict authoritarian regime legitimated (in its own eyes) by eternal divine constitutions—to a vigorous, materialistic community of competing pressure groups within an accepted framework of political, religious, and social differences. Slowly the notion that a critic of the government must be a heretic and a traitor gave way to a gentler formula which in the nineteenth century became classic: one could be "a member of His Majesty's loyal opposition."

LITERARY CROSSCURRENTS

With the obvious and immensely important exception of Milton (and perhaps his friend Marvell), hardly any of the high literature of the early seventeenth century was the work of Puritans or men sympathetic to the Puritan cause. The great Puritan art forms of the age were the sermon and the religious tract. This is not just the joke it seems; Puritan sermons, of which there were many thousands, explored in intimate detail the psychology of the Christian trying to be sure of his own salvation, and Puritan tracts developed dramatic new ways of exciting the zeal of their readers. Yet on the whole the Puritans mistrusted *belles-lettres*, on the same principle that they mistrusted graven idols (statues, stained-glass windows, or paintings), music, and religious rituals. These were all allurements and enticements of the sensual world; they threatened to contaminate and diffuse the pure spiritual energy of divinely infused faith. The Puritans, therefore, did not directly compete with the old courtly forms of literature; they subjected those who did follow the old forms to heavy moral and social pressure. A sense of deep disquiet, of ancient traditions under challenge, is felt everywhere in the early seventeenth century; and it can hardly be accounted for except as a response to the growing discontents that ultimately erupted in the Revolt.

One may well think of Metaphysical poets who followed Donne (such as Herbert, Crashaw, Vaughan, Cowley) as trying to deepen the traditional lyric forms of love and devotion by stretching them to comprehend new and extreme intellectual energies. In the other direction, Jonson and his "sons" the Cavalier poets (Herrick, Suckling, Lovelace, Waller, Denham) generally tried to compress and limit their poems, giving them a high finish and a strong sense of easy domination at the expense (occasionally) of their explicit intellectual content. Though these alternate "schools" do not by any means represent watertight compartments (Donne wrote some poems that sound like Jonson, Jonson some in the manner of Donne), the common contrast of "Cavalier" with "Metaphysical" does describe two major poetic alternatives of the early century. Yet both styles were wholly inadequate containers for the sort of gigantic energy that Milton, for example, was trying to express.

For Milton, with his deep sense of moral imperative, his heroic ambitions for poetry, and his proud Englishness, the fashionable verses of his contemporaries must have seemed unbearably constricting. Like any great artist, Milton was capable of profiting from the study of craftsmen whom he had no intention of imitating; and in different ways, he did profit by a study of Donne and Jonson, we may be sure. But for his central inspiration Milton reached back beyond both Metaphysicals and Jonsonians to the figure of Spenser. In youth particularly his mind ran to Spenserian projects—chivalric romances based on Arthurian themes or sometimes on scriptural stories. Milton's style was fully formed by the late 1630s—it is usual to say that he found his voice in *Lycidas* (1637); and he might well have proceeded to complete one or more of these semi-Spenserian projects. But it is not altogether a loss that the civil war intervened, and prevented him for twenty years from putting his mind full-time to poetic work.

Agonizing as they were, the wars did not involve constant bloodshed;

rather, they were intervals of fighting separated by periods of negotiation and argument, and accompanied by a constant, deep-seated turmoil of popular agitation. Especially on the parliamentary side, enthusiasts for a wide array of causes, political, social, and religious, began appealing for public support in the only way available to them, through the printing press. Most of their pamphlets, broadsheets, and newsletters were not literary at all; but many achieved a direct and forceful prose style that can be sampled in the excerpt we reprint from John Lilburne's *Picture of the Council of State* (below, p. 1737); and a few attained not only a high level of eloquence, but some distinction of thought. The pamphlet wars, in which over twenty thousand verbal shots were fired off, wrought a mighty change in English public life. They accustomed thousands of Englishmen, whose mental life had previously been guarded by strict censorship, to free reading and open argumentation; they created something close to what we now call public opinion. And the experience of Puritanism gave to English life a strong steady moral tone, never so widely or deeply established before.

Thus, when Milton returned to his epic ambitions after 1660, neither he nor his potential audience was anything like what they had been before the war. Chivalric romance was out of the question; the issue on Milton's mind, and the nation's, was whether God maintained, behind the chaotic reversals of history, a sustaining plan for his favored people. That theme could not be addressed through the favorite metaphors of Spenser, jousting knights, lovely ladies, dark enchanters, and hospitals for sick souls. It had to be approached through the central and very simple narrative of mainline Christianity. As the work of Milton's fifties, *Paradise Lost* was deeper, larger, more evangelical than anything he might have written in his thirties; it was well suited to appeal to a nation which had just passed through a massive spiritual crisis. Its author could not have risen so confidently above the twin temptations of pride and despair, had he himself not experienced both in full measure.

But *Paradise Lost* was also, and could not help being, the product of Milton's surpassingly thorough classical education. It is thus a major monument—one of the last perhaps, certainly one of the most impressive—of the Renaissance tradition of Christian humanism. This is the assurance, shared by many writers of the period, that the classical virtues, such as justice, magnanimity, and temperance, when joined in the service of the Christian faith, strengthen both it and themselves. Gathering together in a grasp of unparalleled amplitude these major strands of European culture, and forming them into a poised and balanced structure of epic dimensions, Milton forged a poem that would remain for centuries to come a supreme literary achievement.

During the twenty years of Puritan rule at mid-century, most of the theaters were closed and hardly anything was written for the stage; during this period, most of the old actors and playwrights died, and the revival of the English stage after 1660 depended very largely on the work of one man, Sir William Davenant, and on the example of the French stage, then at its height. Shakespeare's emulators and successors under the first two Stuarts had been much influenced by the melancholy then so largely prevalent; the dark, oppressive mood is almost unbroken in the work of tragic writers such as Webster, Ford, Tourneur, and Middleton. But alongside this somber and sometimes morbid tragedy, and serving as relief from it, flourished a great variety of tragicomic spectacles, romantic comedies, and pastoral fantasies.

Very often these plays were influenced by the masques so popular at court—
that is, they included a great deal in the way of spectacle, display, pageant,
music, and sometimes fantasy. Though Shakespeare was long dead, though
Jonson was in his dotage, and though none of the successors to these two
men quite met their measure, the stage continued vigorously active right up
to the civil war. But then the theaters were shut, abruptly and apparently
forever. When they reopened in 1660, they were forced at first to rely on a
backlog of twenty-year-old plays. But gradually they built up a repertoire of
comedies (generally bawdy) and tragedies in the rhetorical, declamatory
manner which gave them, and the couplets in which they were cast, the
name of "heroic." Both these fashions, like so much else in the Restoration,
were extreme and temporary. Dryden, who practiced both modes, lived to
see them both at an end—the heroic tragedies under the weight of their own
pomposity, the bawdy comedies under the attack of an infuriated clergyman,
Jeremy Collier.

Beyond, perhaps outside, literature as such lies a change in the intellectual tone of the century which cannot be ignored, hard as it is to describe.
The great minds of the early century were lawyers and theologians. Coke,
Bacon, Selden, and Spelman among the lawyers, Laud, Andrewes, Cud-
worth, Ussher, and Chillingworth among the theologians were men famous
in their generation. Among the lawyers, some are still consulted as authorities to this day—Coke is a name to conjure with in English law, and Selden's treatise on *Titles of Honor* is obsolete only because the subject itself is.
As for the theologians, their work too has ceased to be "relevant"; but a brief
browsing expedition through the *Library of Anglo-Catholic Theology* cannot
fail to convince the student that they were men who worked—in their chosen trade—to very high standards of precise and authoritative scholarship.
And yet, as the century's intellectual weather changed, these disciplines ceased
to be at the center of things. There were great lawyers after 1660, but they
were not the makers and shakers of society; there were famous clergymen,
but they were not the builders of society's central codes of belief. Starting
about mid-century, the great names belong to other disciplines—they are
scientists like the astronomers Hooke and Halley, the physicist Robert Boyle,
Locke the physician-philosopher, John Wallis and Sir Isaac Newton the
mathematicians, William Harvey the anatomist. Few of them set out consciously to reconstruct an entire view of the cosmos, and Sir Isaac, who did
so most successfully, retained to the end streaks and patches of the old beliefs.
(He wrote a commentary on the Book of Revelation that has rather baffled
those who admire his scientific work.) But the coming of a secular, materialist world view was in the air; even before the Puritans were forced to give
up their dream of a community of saints, the tide had set and was ebbing
rapidly another way.

BIRTH AND DEATH OF LITERARY FORMS

The stress and strain of a revolutionary age can thus be read at large in the
century's literature, from the somber, sluggish melancholy of the early decades,
through the hoarse, incoherent warfare of the middle years, to the slow
firming up of new standards of decorum and correctness after 1660. Still
another mark of violent change is provided by the number of literary forms
which perished or dropped from favor in the course of the century, even as
others were being born.

Sonnets, for example, were all the rage in the last years of Elizabeth, the first years of James. Almost always they dealt with erotic themes, often they were linked together in sequences to suggest, if not tell, a story. Donne turned the sonnet primarily to religious themes; Milton's sonnets are mostly on religion and politics. And thereafter sonnets largely faded from the poetic repertory; like epic poetry in our own day, they practically disappeared. Allegory suffered an even more curious fate. It was of course the essential method of Spenser's *Faerie Queene*, and the figures of Sin and Death in the midst of *Paradise Lost* testify to its survival. But when Dryden used allegory (exceptionally, as in *The Hind and the Panther*), there was a kind of grotesque comedy about it, as if the form were fundamentally a joke. Serious allegory had slid far down the social scale; it was now the natural mode for an inspired primitive like Bunyan.

Blighted by the frosts of Puritan disapproval, the masque and madrigal both perished. The one was a courtly, the other a popular form; but both were suspect as vain, sensual, and worldly. Madrigals, as a blend of folk- and art-songs, were particularly to be regretted. For many years they had been sung in the yeoman's home or merchant's parlor, to the accompaniment of lutes, viols, and recorders. Many developed complex polyphonic harmonies; many had been composed by distinguished musicians. But they faded away, with other folk arts and folk customs—rounds and carols and morris-dancing, Maypoles, and rural pageants, and country games—to make way for psalm singing and sermon listening. For the gentry, indigenous music was replaced by oratorios and operas, many of them imported from Italy, Germany, or France.

As the many intricate stanzaic forms of the early century lost favor, rhymed couplets came to the fore. They are a superb meter for verse argumentation; they can combine the stinging effect of epigrams with the impetus of cumulative rhythms that build into splendid verse paragraphs. Whether coincidentally or as a consequence, the rise of strict and regular couplets accompanied a perceptible decline of the lyric impulse. Elizabethan and Jacobean lyrics make up (in the ancient phrase) a paradise of dainty devices; Restoration lyrics, though occasionally elegant and sometimes magnificently obscene, are far less numerous as well as less expressive.

Formal verse satire, which had been a self-conscious novelty at the start of the century, was a well-established mode of poetry by the end. Under the molding of many hands, satire grew subtler and more various; the satirist recognized his responsibility to divert his reader as well as to insult his antagonist. Indeed, a whole new mode of gentlemanly discourse grew up after the Restoration; it went sometimes by the name of "raillery," sometimes "banter," and amounted to nothing more than light irony. But serious things could be said in it, about which nonetheless a gentleman might not want to show himself too earnest. Below satire, burlesque was another literary mode which the seventeenth century nurtured, with the aid of France. After the unrelieved earnestness of the Puritans, derision and buffoonery became the order of the day; and with the advent of burlesque, we find ourselves on the very threshold of the modern novel, one vein of which reaches as far back as *Don Quixote*.

Alongside perishing forms, new ones sprang up, many involving prose rather than verse, and reaching out toward a popular readership. As the century passed, preachers found that they could no longer entertain audiences with intricate similitudes and microscopic, word-by-word explication of texts; ranting and raving (known more politely as "zeal") were equally out of fashion. Instead, they turned increasingly to plainly phrased, common-sense discussions of practical morality, and found that such discourses pleased their audiences about as well as anything. Prose in general grew simpler and less artful; as it did so, its applications multiplied. In Walton we have the first intimate English biographer, in Clarendon the first large-scale political historian. The diarists Pepys and Evelyn, the scandalmongers Wood and Aubrey, the "character-writers" Overbury and Earle, professed psychologists like Robert Burton, and quizzical self-explorers like Sir Thomas Browne all contribute liberally and originally to the arts of human personality. Less than a hundred years elapsed between the early publications of Francis Bacon, England's first secular philosopher, and those of John Locke, one of her greatest. For better or worse, the first English newspapers sprang up during the civil wars; under the familiar rubric of "A Letter to a Friend in the Country," political commentators made themselves heard. Abraham Cowley, better as a writer of prose than a poet, produced a series of personal essays, more relaxed than those of Bacon, and soon to be followed by many others. The second great age of English translation began in 1660; it introduced Englishmen not only to the classics, and to works written in French or Italian, but to works of their own past—as when Dryden "translated" into modern English some of Chaucer's *Canterbury Tales*.

All these developments were predicated on a reading audience responsive, alert, and eager to be informed; not necessarily instructed in foreign tongues or trained in courtly conventions, but ready to follow a sustained discourse in unrhetorical, commonsense English. Such an audience, so tuned and so motivated, not expecting too much from its reading, but responsive to acute arguments or vivid touches of the imagination, is a first premise of modern literature. We are apt to think it as normal and natural a phenomenon as the air we breathe, but it is not. In fact, it had to be created slowly, hesitantly, without much conscious direction on anyone's part, by a process of gradual accretion and expansion. Its existence is the foundation of the new age, and the culminating achievement of the early seventeenth century.

Being diverse out of harsh necessity and tolerant only reluctantly, the later seventeenth century was often halting and unsteady in its taste. It was forging new standards, not accepting the guidance of old ones; its hallmark is a widening eclecticism. Women, freed by the civil wars to assume previously unfamiliar roles, struggled to find a voice of their own; despite striking many false notes at first, they made their presence felt, and the age to come would speak out more assuredly because of them. Science also advanced gropingly through a series of corrected errors and inspired guesses. The same age saw Sir Kenelm Digby's solemn proposal that one could cure wounds by medicating the sword that caused them, and William Harvey's proclamation of the circulation of the blood. Though much of Inigo Jones's work in architecture was destroyed, some of his actual structures and more of his important translations of Italian books on architecture survived, to provide a lead for neoclassical building in England and North America during the eighteenth century. Though the Puritan commonwealth went to smash as a political organization, many of the ideas expressed during those hectic mid-century years maintained an underground existence, and blossomed at the time of the American Revolution, more than a century later.

Thus the early seventeenth century brought to its culmination much that had been characteristic from the beginning of the English Renaissance, and at the same time advanced boldly across the threshold of the next age, whatever one prefers to call it. Though its elapsed time is relatively brief, the period changed not only the tone of literature, but the very definition of what literature could be. Like all great cultural shifts, this one was too complex to be captured in a single phrase or attributed to a single cause. It had neither a fixed beginning nor a precise end. But in the seamless web of history we can hardly fail to notice new colors and textures which, over the short course of the early seventeenth century, enter into the warp and woof of the nation's literary as of its social life, to make it look and feel like a whole new piece of cloth.

JOHN DONNE
1572–1631

1601: Secret marriage to Ann More.
1615: Becomes an Anglican priest.
1621: Appointed dean of St. Paul's Cathedral.
1633: First publication of *Poems*.

Donne himself originated an observation about his life and character which, though only partly accurate, has become commonplace. In a private letter, he distinguished Jack Donne, an adventurous young spark who wrote bawdy and cynical verses to an assortment of mistresses, from the grave and eloquent divine, Doctor Donne, the dean of St. Paul's. The contrast is striking, but the key to both characters is the same; it is a restless, searching energy that scorns the easy platitude and the smooth, vacant phrase; that is vivid, immediate, troubling. Whether he is flaunting his pleasure at chasing every girl in sight (as in *The Indifferent*), or voicing total repentance and devotion to God (as in the *Holy Sonnets*), Donne's poetry demands imaginative effort of the reader, and absorbs him in a tense, complex experience.

Donne was born into an old Roman Catholic family, at a time when anti-Catholic feeling in England was near its height and Catholics were subject to constant harassment by the Elizabethan secret police. His faith barred him from many of the usual avenues of success, and his point of view was always that of an insecure outsider. Though he attended both Oxford and Cambridge Universities, as well as Lincoln's Inn (where lawyers got their training), he never took any academic degrees and never practiced law. After quietly abandoning Catholicism some time during the 1590s, he had scruples about becoming an Anglican. He had no gift for commerce, and though he inherited money from his father (who died when Donne was only four), it was far from enough to render him independent. Hence he had to make his way in the world indirectly—by wit, charm, learning, valor, and above all, favor. Partly from sheer intellectual curiosity, he read enormously in divinity, medicine, law, and the classics; he wrote to display his learning and wit. He traveled on the Continent, especially, it would seem, to Spain; even in later years, he did a good deal of moving around. With Ralegh and Essex he took part in two hit-and-run expeditions against Cadiz and the Azores. He put himself in the way of court employment, danced attendance on great court ladies, and generally lived the life of a brilliant young man hopeful of preferment.

When in 1598 Donne was appointed private secretary to Sir Thomas Egerton, one of the highest officials in the queen's court, his prospects for worldly advancement seemed good. He sat in Elizabeth's last Parliament; he cultivated those who wielded power and had patronage to dispense. But in 1601 he secretly married Lady Egerton's niece, seventeen-year-old Ann More, and thereby ruined his own worldly hopes. The marriage turned out happily, but Donne's bad faith to his employer was neither forgotten nor forgiven. Sir George More had Donne imprisoned and dismissed from his post; and for the next dozen years the poet had to struggle at a series of makeshift employments to support his growing family. In his middle thirties, Donne was far from the brilliant young gallant of the 1590s; sick, poor, and unhappy, he wrote, but dared not publish, a treatise of the lawfulness of suicide (*Biathanatos*). As he approached forty, he published two anti-Catholic polemics (*Pseudo-Martyr*, 1610; *Ignatius his Conclave*, 1611); they sealed publicly his renunciation of the Catholic faith. In return for patronage from Sir Robert Drury, he wrote in 1611 and 1612 a pair of long poems, the *Anniversaries*, on the death of Sir Robert's daughter Elizabeth. None of these activities represented a full employment of Donne's pent-up intellectual energy. To be sure, his social position should not be painted too blackly. He still had friends among courtiers, politicians, poets, and the great ladies around court, like Lucy Countess of Bedford and Magdalen Herbert with her two poet-sons, George and Edward. Donne was never quite without resources; yet, broadly speaking, the middle years of his life were a period of uncertainty and discontent.

Though Donne had flatly refused in 1607 to take Anglican orders, King James was certain that he would some day make a great Anglican preacher. Hence he declared that Donne could have no preferment or employment from him, except in the church. Finally, in 1615, Donne overcame his scruples, not the least of which was the fear of seeming ambitious, and entered the ministry. He was in due course appointed Reader in Divinity at Lincoln's Inn. In the seventeenth century, among court circles and at the Inns of Court where lawyers congregated, preaching was at once a form of spiritual devotion, an intellectual exercise, and a dramatic entertainment. Donne's metaphorical style, bold erudition, and dramatic wit at once established him as a great preacher in an age of great preachers. Fully one hundred sixty of his sermons survive. In 1621 he was made dean of St. Paul's, where he preached to great congregations of "City" lawyers, courtiers, merchants, and tradesmen. In addition, his private devotions were published in 1624, and he continued to write sacred poetry till within a few years of his death. Obsessed with the idea of death, Donne preached what was called his own funeral sermon just a few weeks before he died. It is a terrifyingly personal meditation on dissolution, as befits a man who arranged for a final portrait of himself to be painted, dressed in his shroud.

The poetry of Donne represents a sharp break with that written by his predecessors and most of his contemporaries. Much Elizabethan verse is decorative and flowery. Its images adorn, its rhythm is mellifluous. Its frequent "conceits" (elaborately sustained metaphors) are often variations on comparisons passed down through generations of poets in a line from Petrarch in the fourteenth century. But Donne, taking his cue from recent Continental poets who had freshened the Petrarchan tradition by developing a more intellectualized form of conceit, created highly concentrated images which involve a major element of dramatic contrast or of intellectual strain. The clichés of earlier love poetry—bleeding hearts, cheeks like roses, lips like cherries, Cupid shooting the arrows of love—appear in Donne's poetry only to be mocked, or in some ingenious transmutation. The tears which flow in *A Valediction: of Weeping* are different from, and more complex than, the ordinary saline fluid of unhappy lovers; they are ciphers, naughts, symbols of the world's emptiness without the beloved; or else, suddenly reflecting her image, they are globes, worlds, they contain the sum of things. By using such conceits, the poet not only displays his own ingenuity; he may express a deep vision of the world and the strands of analogy that seem to hold it together. Donne's conceits leap continually in a restless orbit from the personal to the cosmic and back again.

Donne likes to twist and distort not only images and ideas, but traditional rhythmic and stanzaic patterns. His speech patterns are colloquial and various. Ben Jonson expressed the shock of some contemporaries by saying that "Donne, for not keeping of accent [i.e., metrical uniformity], deserved hanging"—though he also said that Donne was "the first poet in the world in some things." While Donne sometimes uses traditional verse forms, and indeed very simple ones, he is also fond of inventing elaborate and intricate stanzas. His penchant for compressed and elliptical expression often produces difficulty for the reader. In the satires, which Renaissance writers understood to be "harsh" and "crabbed" as a genre, Donne's distortions often threaten to choke off the stream of expression entirely. But in the lyrics (both those which are worldly and those which are religious in theme), as in the elegies and sonnets, the verse repeatedly achieves a complex and memorable melody. Donne had an unusual gift, rather like that of a modern poet, T. S. Eliot, for striking off phrases which ring in the mind like a silver coin. They are two masters of the colloquial style, removed alike from the dignified, weighty manner of Milton and the sugared sweetness of the Elizabethans.

Donne and his followers are known to literary history as the "Metaphysical school" of poets. Strictly speaking, this is a misnomer. There was no organized group of poets who imitated Donne, and if there had been, they would not have called themselves "Metaphysical" poets. That term was invented by John Dryden and Samuel Johnson. But the influence of Donne's poetic style was widely felt, especially by men whose taste was formed before 1660. George Herbert, Richard Crashaw, Henry Vaughan, Andrew Marvell, and Abraham Cowley are only the best known of those in whom this influence is recognizable. The great change of taste which took place in 1660 threw Donne and the "conceited" style out of fashion; during the eighteenth and nineteenth centuries both he and his followers were rarely read and still more rarely appreciated. Finally, in the late nineteenth and early twentieth centuries, three new editions of Donne appeared, of which Sir H. J. C. Grierson's, published in 1912, was quickly accepted as standard. By clarifying and purifying the often-garbled text, Grierson did a great deal to make Donne's poetry more available to the modern reader. Almost at once it started to exert an influence on modern poetic practice, the modern poets being hungry for a "tough" style which would free them from the worn-out rhetoric of late nineteenth-century Romanticism. And Donne's status among the English poets quickly climbed from that of a curiosity to that of an acknowledged master.

No more than a couple of the poems on which Donne's modern reputation is built were published during his lifetime, though most of them were widely circulated through court and literary circles in handwritten copies. There were practical reasons for this halfway state of affairs. Many of the poems would have constituted black marks on Donne's reputation as an earnest and godly divine; and because they were difficult and allusive, only a few people wanted to read them. Thus Donne was known, outside the relatively limited circles which had access to manuscript collections, primarily as a preacher and devotional writer. His collected poems were first published in 1633; in the second edition (1635), the poems were divided into nine generic groups (one of which includes only a single long poem,

The Progress of the Soul). The *Songs and Sonnets*, which open the volume, are generally amorous in theme; the *Divine Poems*, which close it, are described by their title. In between fall groups of epigrams, love elegies, epithalamia (wedding songs), satires, verse letters, and funeral elegies. For convenience, our selections, like those of most other editors, follow the order of the 1635 edition, though this is distinctly *not* the order in which Donne wrote the poems. Indeed, a detailed chronology is impossible to construct. The basic text for most of the poems, though, is that of the first, 1633, edition, sometimes supplemented and corrected by reference to other early editions and to manuscript materials. Recent editions, especially those by Helen Gardner and W. Milgate, have also been consulted.

The Good-Morrow[1]

I wonder, by my troth, what thou and I
Did, till we loved? Were we not weaned till then,
But sucked on country pleasures, childishly?
Or snorted we in the seven sleepers' den?[2]
'Twas so; but this, all pleasures fancies be.   5
If ever any beauty I did see,
Which I desired, and got, 'twas but a dream of thee.

And now good morrow to our waking souls,
Which watch not one another out of fear;
For love all love of other sights controls,   10
And makes one little room an everywhere.
Let sea-discoverers to new worlds have gone,
Let maps to others, worlds on worlds have shown:[3]
Let us possess one world; each hath one, and is one.

My face in thine eye, thine in mine appears,   15
And true plain hearts do in the faces rest;
Where can we find two better hemispheres,
Without sharp North, without declining West?
Whatever dies was not mixed equally;[4]
If our two loves be one, or thou and I   20
Love so alike that none do slacken, none can die.

1633

---

1. This is the first poem of the *Songs and Sonnets* in the 1635 edition. Confusingly, the group doesn't include any sonnets in our sense: in Donne's time, the term often meant simply "love lyric." Though precise dating is impossible, it is safe to suppose that Donne wrote all, or almost all, of the 53 poems in the 1590s and the first decade of the 17th century.

2. Many ancient authors recite the legend of 7 youths of Ephesus who hid in a cave from their pagan persecutors and slept there for 187 years,

awakening to find, amazedly, that the world had become Christian while they slept. "But" (line 5): except for.

3. I.e., let us concede that maps (or charts of the heavens) have shown to other investigators, etc. In line 14 an alternative reading is "Let us possess *our* world."

4. Scholastic philosophy taught that when the elements were imperfectly ("not equally") mixed, matter was mutable and mortal, but when they were perfectly mixed, it was unchanging and undying.

Song

Go and catch a falling star,
   Get with child a mandrake root,[1]
Tell me where all past years are,
   Or who cleft the Devil's foot,
Teach me to hear mermaids[2] singing,   5
Or to keep off envy's stinging,
     And find
     What wind
Serves to advance an honest mind.

If thou beest born to strange sights,   10
   Things invisible to see,
Ride ten thousand days and nights,
   Till age snow white hairs on thee,
Thou, when thou return'st, wilt tell me
All strange wonders that befell thee,   15
     And swear
     No where
Lives a woman true, and fair.

If thou find'st one, let me know,
   Such a pilgrimage were sweet;   20
Yet do not, I would not go,
   Though at next door we might meet;
Though she were true when you met her,
And last till you write your letter,
     Yet she   25
     Will be
False, ere I come, to two, or three.

1633

The Undertaking

I have done one braver thing
   Than all the Worthies[1] did,
And yet a braver thence doth spring,
   Which is, to keep that hid.

1. The mandrake root, or mandragora, is often forked like the lower part of the male body. Legend has it that when pulled from the ground, the root is castrated and shrieks in agony; its shriek is death to hear. Getting such a vegetable with child presents obvious difficulties.
2. Identified with the sirens, whose song only the wily Odysseus survived.
1. According to medieval legend, the Nine Worthies, or supreme heroes of history, included three Jews (Joshua, David, Judas Maccabeus), three pagans (Hector, Alexander, Julius Caesar), and three Christians (Arthur, Charlemagne, Godfrey of Bouillon).

It were but madness now t' impart   5
　　The skill of specular stone,[2]
When he which can have learned the art
　　To cut it, can find none.

So, if I now should utter this,
　　Others (because no more   10
Such stuff to work upon, there is)
　　Would love but as before.

But he who loveliness within
　　Hath found, all outward loathes,
For he who color loves, and skin,   15
　　Loves but their[3] oldest clothes.

If, as I have, you also do
　　Virtue attirèd in woman see,
And dare love that, and say so too,
　　And forget the He and She;   20

And if this love, though placèd so,
　　From profane men you hide,
Which will no faith on this bestow,
　　Or, if they do, deride;

Then you have done a braver thing   25
　　Than all the Worthies did;
And a braver thence will spring,
　　Which is, to keep that hid.

1633

The Sun Rising

Busy old fool, unruly sun,
　　Why dost thou thus,
Through windows and through curtains call on us?
Must to thy motions lovers' seasons run?
　　Saucy pedantic wretch, go chide   5
　　Late schoolboys and sour prentices,
　Go tell court huntsmen that the King will ride,[1]
　Call country ants to harvest offices;
Love, all alike, no season knows nor clime,
Nor hours, days, months, which are the rags of time.   10

2. A transparent or translucent material, reputed
to have been used in antiquity for windows, but no
longer known.
3. I.e., women's.

1. King James was addicted to hunting. "Harvest
offices": autumn chores. The "country ants" may
imply an allusion to the old fable of the ant and
the grasshopper.

Thy beams, so reverend and strong
　　Why shouldst thou think?
I could eclipse and cloud them with a wink,
But that I would not lose her sight so long;
　　　　If her eyes have not blinded thine, 　　　　　　　　15
　　　　Look, and tomorrow late, tell me,
　　Whether both th' Indias of spice and mine[2]
　　Be where thou leftst them, or lie here with me.
Ask for those kings whom thou saw'st yesterday,
And thou shalt hear, All here in one bed lay. 　　　　　　20

　　　She is all states,[3] and all princes I,
　　　　Nothing else is.
Princes do but play us; compared to this,
All honor's mimic, all wealth alchemy.[4]
　　　　Thou, sun, art half as happy as we, 　　　　　　　　25
　　　　In that the world's contracted thus;
　　Thine age asks ease, and since thy duties be
　　To warm the world, that's done in warming us.
Shine here to us, and thou art everywhere;
This bed thy center is,[5] these walls thy sphere. 　　　　30

1633

The Indifferent

I can love both fair and brown,[1]
Her whom abundance melts, and her whom want betrays,[2]
Her who loves loneness best, and her who masks and plays,
Her whom the country formed, and whom the town,
Her who believes, and her who tries, 　　　　　　　　　　5
Her who still weeps with spongy eyes,
And her who is dry cork, and never cries;
I can love her, and her, and you, and you,
I can love any, so she be not true.

Will no other vice content you? 　　　　　　　　　　　　10
Will it not serve your turn to do as did your mothers?
Or have you all old vices spent, and now would find out others?
Or doth a fear that men are true torment you?
O we are not, be not you so;
Let me, and do you, twenty know. 　　　　　　　　　　　15

2. The India of "spice" is East India, that of "mine"
(gold) the West Indies.
3. All the nations of the world.
4. I.e., fraudulent.
5. As the earth was the center of the sun's orbit
(according to the old Ptolemaic astronomy), so the
bed will be the new center of the sun's activities,
and the walls of the bedroom will outline its motion.
1. Both blonde and brunette.
2. The girl with lots of lovers, the girl with none
at all; also, perhaps, the plump girl and the thin
girl.

Rob me, but bind me not, and let me go.
Must I, who came to travail[3] thorough you,
Grow your fixed subject, because you are true?

Venus heard me sigh this song,
And by love's sweetest part, variety, she swore,   20
She heard not this till now; and that it should be so no more.
She went, examined, and returned ere long,
And said, Alas, some two or three
Poor heretics in love there be,
Which think to 'stablish dangerous constancy.   25
But I have told them, Since you will be true,
You shall be true to them who are false to you.

                                                            1633

The Canonization

For God's sake hold your tongue, and let me love,
    Or chide my palsy, or my gout,
My five gray hairs, or ruined fortune, flout,
        With wealth your state, your mind with arts improve,
            Take you a course, get you a place,[1]   5
            Observe His Honor, or His Grace,
Or the King's real, or his stampèd face[2]
        Contemplate; what you will, approve,[3]
    So you will let me love.

Alas, alas, who's injured by my love?   10
    What merchant's ships have my sighs drowned?
Who says my tears have overflowed his ground?
        When did my colds a forward spring remove?[4]
            When did the heats which my veins fill
            Add one man to the plaguy bill?[5]   15
Soldiers find wars, and lawyers find out still
    Litigious men, which quarrels move,
        Though she and I do love.

Call us what you will, we are made such by love;
    Call her one, me another fly,   20
We're tapers too, and at our own cost die,[6]

---

3. "Grief, sorrow," but also "journey, travel."
1. "Take you a course": in the general sense of "settle yourself in life." A "place" is an appointment, at court or elsewhere.
2. On coins.
3. Put to proof, find by experience.
4. Petrarchan lovers traditionally sigh, weep, and are frozen by their mistresses' neglect. The "forward spring" is either a fountain or a season.
5. Deaths from the hot-weather plague were recorded, by parish, in weekly bills.
6. We're both fly (the ephemeral moth) and the self-consuming candle that attracts it. Donne hints here at the old superstition that intercourse shortens life. (To "die" in the punning terminology of the 17th century was to experience orgasm.)

And we in us find the eagle and the dove.[7]
    The phoenix riddle hath more wit
    By us:[8] we two being one, are it.
So, to one neutral thing both sexes fit.   25
    We die and rise the same, and prove
    Mysterious by this love.

We can die by it, if not live by love,
    And if unfit for tombs and hearse
Our legend be, it will be fit for verse;   30
    And if no piece of chronicle we prove,
    We'll build in sonnets pretty rooms;[9]
    As well a well-wrought urn becomes
The greatest ashes, as half-acre tombs,
    And by these hymns,[1] all shall approve   35
    Us canonized for love:

And thus invoke us: You whom reverend love
    Made one another's hermitage;
You, to whom love was peace, that now is rage;
    Who did the whole world's soul contract,[2] and
        drove   40
        Into the glasses of your eyes
        (So made such mirrors, and such spies,
    That they did all to you epitomize)
Countries, towns, courts: Beg from above
    A pattern of your love![3]   45

                      1633

Air and Angels

Twice or thrice had I loved thee,
Before I knew thy face or name;
So in a voice, so in a shapeless flame,
Angels affect us oft, and worshipped be;
    Still when, to where thou wert, I came,   5

---

7. The eagle signifies such qualities as strength and vision; the dove, meekness and mercy. The phoenix was a fabulous Arabian bird, only one of which existed at any one time. After living 500 years, it lit its nest of spices, jumped in, and sang its funeral song as it was consumed—then rose triumphantly from its ashes, a new bird. Thus it was a symbol of immortality, and was sometimes associated with Christ. "Eagle" and "dove" are also alchemical terms for processes leading to the rise of "phoenix," a stage in the transmutation of metals.
8. I.e., the story of the phoenix seems more plausible, now that we've shown how male and female can fuse.
9. The "rooms" (punning on the Italian meaning

of "stanza") will hold the ashes—i.e., record their exploits—as prose history records great deeds in other spheres. "Becomes": befits.
1. The lover's own poems, which become hymns for a new love religion. "All" (posterity) shall "approve" (confirm) us as love's saints.
2. An alternative reading is "extract."
3. The poet and his mistress, turned to saints, are implored by the rest of the population to get from heaven ("above") a pattern of their love for general distribution. "Countries, towns, courts" are objects of the verb "drove"; the notion that eyes both see and reflect the outside world, and so "contain" it doubly, was very delightful to Donne.

Some lovely glorious nothing I did see.
    But since my soul, whose child love is,
Takes limbs of flesh, and else could nothing do,[1]
    More subtle than the parent is
Love must not be, but take a body too;   10
    And therefore what thou wert, and who,
        I bid love ask, and now
That it assume thy body I allow,
And fix itself in thy lip, eye, and brow.

Whilst thus to ballast love I thought,   15
And so more steadily to have gone,
With wares which would sink admiration,
I saw I had love's pinnace overfraught;[2]
    Every thy hair for love to work upon
Is much too much, some fitter must be sought;   20
    For, nor in nothing, nor in things
Extreme and scatt'ring[3] bright, can love inhere.
    Then as an angel, face and wings
Of air, not pure as it, yet pure doth wear,
    So thy love may be my love's sphere;   25
        Just such disparity
As is 'twixt air and angels' purity,
'Twixt women's love and men's will ever be.[4]

                             1633

Break of Day[1]

'Tis true, 'tis day; what though it be?
O wilt thou therefore rise from me?
Why should we rise because 'tis light?
Did we lie down because 'twas night?
Love, which in spite of darkness brought us hither,   5
Should in despite of light keep us together.

Light hath no tongue, but is all eye;
If it could speak as well as spy,
This were the worst that it could say,
That being well, I fain would stay,   10

1. As my soul could not function unless it were in a body, so love, which is the soul's child, must also be corporeal.
2. Her physical beauty (his "wares") would sink admiration—i.e., overwhelm wonder itself. This is too much ballast for love's "pinnace" (a small boat).
3. Diffused, dazzling.
4. Some Scholastic philosophers held that angels, when they appeared to humans, assumed a body of air. Such a body, though pure, was less so than the angel's spiritual being. Similarly, women's love, which Donne assumes to be *less* pure than that of men, may serve as the "sphere" within which the love of men moves as a governing angel. It is not unusual for a Donne poem to reverse itself in this way.
1. Recalling the Provençal aubade or song of the lovers' parting at dawn, this poem is a departure for Donne in that it assumes a feminine point of view.

And that I loved my heart and honor so
That I would not from him, that had them, go.

Must business thee from hence remove?
O, that's the worst disease of love.
The poor, the foul, the false, love can   15
Admit, but not the busied man.
He which hath business, and makes love, doth do
Such wrong, as when a married man doth woo.

1633

A Valediction: Of Weeping

            Let me pour forth
My tears before thy face whilst I stay here,
For thy face coins them,[1] and thy stamp they bear,
And by this mintage they are something worth,
            For thus they be   5
            Pregnant of thee;
Fruits of much grief they are, emblems of more—
When a tear falls, that Thou falls which it bore,
So thou and I are nothing then, when on a diverse shore.[2]

            On a round ball   10
A workman that hath copies by can lay
An Europe, Afric, and an Asia,
And quickly make that, which was nothing, all;[3]
            So doth each tear
            Which thee doth wear,   15
A globe, yea world, by that impression grow,
Till thy tears mixed with mine do overflow
This world; by waters sent from thee, my heaven dissolvèd so.

            O more than moon,
Draw not up seas to drown me in thy sphere;   20
Weep me not dead in thine arms, but forbear
To teach the sea what it may do too soon.
            Let not the wind
            Example find
To do me more harm than it purposeth;   25
Since thou and I sigh one another's breath,
Whoe'er sighs most is cruelest, and hastes the other's death.

1633

---

1. I.e., they reflect her face.
2. The extinction of the lovers in their separation
is prefigured in the fall of a tear that contains the
image of the mistress.

3. I.e., on a blank globe an artist can paste maps
of the continents, and so convert a cipher, the image
of nothingness, to the whole world. "Thee doth
wear": bears your image.

Love's Alchemy

Some that have deeper digged love's mine than I,
Say where his centric happiness doth lie:
   I have loved, and got, and told,
But should I love, get, tell, till I were old,
I should not find that hidden mystery;   5
     O, 'tis imposture all:
And as no chemic yet the elixir got,[1]
    But glorifies his pregnant pot[2]
    If by the way to him befall
Some odoriferous thing, or medicinal;   10
   So lovers dream a rich and long delight,
   But get a winter-seeming summer's night.[3]

Our ease, our thrift, our honor, and our day,
Shall we for this vain bubble's shadow pay?
   Ends love in this, that my man   15
Can be as happy as I can, if he can
Endure the short scorn of a bridegroom's play?
    That loving wretch that swears
'Tis not the bodies marry, but the minds,
    Which he in her angelic finds,
    Would swear as justly that he hears,   20
In that day's rude hoarse minstrelsy, the spheres.[4]
   Hope not for mind in women; at their best
   Sweetness and wit they are but mummy possessed.[5]

1633

The Flea

Mark but this flea, and mark in this,
How little that which thou deniest me is;
Me it sucked first, and now sucks thee,
And in this flea our two bloods mingled be;
Thou know'st that this cannot be said   5
A sin, or shame, or loss of maidenhead,
   Yet this enjoys before it woo,

---

1. "Chemic": alchemist. "The elixir": a magic medicine sought by alchemists and reputed to heal all ills.
2. Praises his fertile (and womb-shaped) retort.
3. A night cold as in winter and short as in summer.
4. The perfect harmony of the planets, moving in concentric crystalline spheres, is contrasted with the charivari, a boisterous serenade for pots, pans, and trumpets, performed on the wedding night.

5. The syntax of the last two lines is very dark; the last line in particular may be read with a comma after "wit," after "are," or after "mummy." The final word may modify "mummy," to signify "mummy with a demon in it," or "they," to signify "women who when you have possessed them." A comma after "best" would change the whole balance of the ending. Some sort of mysogyny is almost certainly expressed.

And pampered swells with one blood made of two,
And this, alas, is more than we would do.[1]

Oh stay, three lives in one flea spare,   10
Where we almost, nay more than married are.
This flea is you and I, and this
Our marriage bed and marriage temple is;
Though parents grudge, and you, we are met,
And cloistered in these living walls of jet.   15
    Though use[2] make you apt to kill me
    Let not to that, self-murder added be,
    And sacrilege, three sins in killing three.

Cruel and sudden, hast thou since
Purpled thy nail in blood of innocence?[3]   20
Wherein could this flea guilty be,
Except in that drop which it sucked from thee?
Yet thou triumph'st, and say'st that thou
Find'st not thy self nor me the weaker now;
    'Tis true; then learn how false fears be: 25
    Just so much honor, when thou yield'st to me,
    Will waste, as this flea's death took life from thee.

                                                        1633

A Nocturnal upon Saint Lucy's Day, Being the Shortest Day[1]

'Tis the year's midnight and it is the day's,
Lucy's, who scarce seven hours herself unmasks;
    The sun is spent, and now his flasks
    Send forth light squibs,[2] no constant rays.
        The world's whole sap is sunk;   5
The general balm th' hydroptic[3] earth hath drunk,
Whither, as to the bed's feet, life is shrunk,
Dead and interred; yet all these seem to laugh,
Compared with me, who am their epitaph.

---

1. I.e., we, alas, don't dare hope for this consummation of our love, which the flea freely accepts. The idea of swelling suggests pregnancy.
2. Habit.
3. Like Herod, Donne's mistress has slaughtered the innocents and is now clothed in imperial purple.
1. A "nocturnal" seems to suggest a dreamy, meditative poem about dark thoughts; but the more common 17th-century usage alluded to a kind of astrolabe for finding one's latitude or telling the time at night. Donne probably wanted both meanings. St. Lucy's Day falls on December 13, which under the old calendar was very close to the winter solstice (December 21 under our modern calendar). At this time of year the sun rises after eight in the latitude of London, and sets well before four.
2. The sun is compared to a gun shooting powder from powder flasks, but in small "squibs" like firecrackers.
3. Dropsical, thus insatiably thirsty. "General balm": the supposed life-preserving essence of all things.

Study me, then, you who shall lovers be   10
At the next world, that is, at the next spring;
  For I am every dead thing
   In whom love wrought new alchemy.
    For his art did express[4]
A quintessence even from nothingness,   15
From dull privations and lean emptiness.
He ruined me, and I am re-begot
Of absence, darkness, death: things which are not.

All others from all things draw all that's good,
Life, soul, form, spirit, whence they being have;   20
  I, by love's limbeck,[5] am the grave
   Of all that's nothing. Oft a flood
    Have we two wept, and so
Drowned the whole world, us two; oft did we grow
To be two chaoses when we did show   25
Care to aught else; and often absences
Withdrew our souls, and made us carcasses.

But I am by her death (which word wrongs her)[6]
Of the first nothing the elixir grown;[7]
  Were I a man, that I were one   30
   I needs must know; I should prefer,
    If I were any beast,
Some ends, some means; yea plants, yea stones detest
And love.[8] All, all some properties invest.
If I an ordinary nothing were,   35
As shadow, a light and body must be here.

But I am none; nor will my sun renew.
You lovers, for whose sake the lesser sun
  At this time to the Goat[9] is run
   To fetch new lust and give it you,
    Enjoy your summer all.   40
Since she enjoys her long night's festival,
Let me prepare towards her, and let me call
This hour her vigil and her eve, since this
Both the year's and the day's deep midnight is.   45

1633

4. Squeeze out.
5. Alembic, retort; a vessel used in distilling.
6. To speak of her death "wrongs" her by implying that she is not now among the immortals, a
saint.
7. He is now "grown" (become) the "elixir of the
first nothing," i.e., the quintessence of that absolute nothingness that existed before the creation.
8. Beasts have intentions, plants instincts, even
stones (like loadstones) attractions and antipathies.
9. The sign of Capricorn, which the sun enters at
the winter solstice; the goat is an emblem of sexual
vigor. The "lesser sun" is the real, everyday sun;
"my sun" is the dead mistress.

The Bait[1]

Come live with me and be my love,
And we will some new pleasures prove,
Of golden sands and crystal brooks,
With silken lines and silver hooks.

There will the river whispering run,   5
Warmed by thine eyes more than the sun.
And there the enamored fish will stay,
Begging themselves they may betray.

When thou wilt swim in that live bath,
Each fish, which every channel hath,   10
Will amorously to thee swim,
Gladder to catch thee, than thou him.

If thou, to be so seen, beest loath,
By sun or moon, thou darkenest both;
And if myself have leave to see,   15
I need not their light, having thee.

Let others freeze with angling reeds,
And cut their legs with shells and weeds,
Or treacherously poor fish beset
With strangling snare or windowy net.   20

Let coarse bold hands from slimy nest
The bedded fish in banks out-wrest,
Or curious traitors, sleave-silk flies,[2]
Bewitch poor fishes' wandering eyes.

For thee, thou needest no such deceit,   25
For thou thyself art thine own bait;
That fish that is not catched thereby,
Alas, is wiser far than I.

1633

The Apparition

When by thy scorn, O murderess, I am dead,
And that thou thinkst thee free
From all solicitation from me,

1. This poem is Donne's response to Marlowe's *Passionate Shepherd to his Love* (above, p. 813). Another of the many replies was Ralegh's *Nymph's Reply to the Shepherd* (above, p. 782).
2. Flies of unravelled silk, floss silk. "Curious": exquisitely made.

Then shall my ghost come to thy bed,
And thee, feigned vestal,[1] in worse arms shall see;   5
Then thy sick taper will begin to wink,
And he whose thou art then, being tired before,
Will, if thou stir, or pinch to wake him, think
    Thou call'st for more,
And in false sleep will from thee shrink,   10
And then, poor aspen wretch,[2] neglected thou
Bathed in a cold quicksilver sweat[3] wilt lie
    A verier ghost than I;
What I will say, I will not tell thee now,
Lest that preserve thee; and since my love is spent,   15
I had rather thou shouldst painfully repent,
Than by my threatenings rest still innocent.

1633

A Valediction: Forbidding Mourning[1]

As virtuous men pass mildly away,
    And whisper to their souls to go,
Whilst some of their sad friends do say
    The breath goes now, and some say, No;

So let us melt, and make no noise,   5
    No tear-floods, nor sigh-tempests move,
'Twere profanation of our joys
    To tell the laity our love.

Moving of th' earth brings harms and fears,
    Men reckon what it did and meant;   10
But trepidation of the spheres,
    Though greater far, is innocent.[2]

Dull sublunary[3] lovers' love
    (Whose soul[4] is sense) cannot admit
Absence, because it doth remove   15
    Those things which elemented[5] it.

1. In Roman history the "vestals" were sacred virgins. "Wink": flicker (from the presence of a ghost).
2. Aspen leaves flutter in the slightest breeze.
3. Sweating in terror; quicksilver (mercury) was a
stock prescription for venereal disease, and sweating was part of the cure.
1. The particularly serious and steady tone of this
poem may be due to the circumstances of its composition. Izaak Walton tells us it was addressed to
Donne's wife on the occasion of his trip to the
Continent in 1611. Donne had many forebodings
of misfortune, which were verified when his wife
gave birth to a stillborn child during his absence.

Still, Walton's linkage of these events with this poem
is only a speculation.
2. Earthquakes cause damage, and were thought
portentous. "Trepidation" (in the Ptolemaic cosmology, an oscillation of the ninth or "crystalline"
sphere, imparted to all the inner spheres), though
a vastly greater motion than an earthquake, is neither destructive nor sinister.
3. Beneath the moon, therefore mundane and
subject to change.
4. Essence.
5. Composed.

But we, by a love so much refined
   That our selves know not what it is,
Inter-assurèd of the mind,
   Care less, eyes, lips, and hands to miss.   20

Our two souls therefore, which are one,
   Though I must go, endure not yet
A breach, but an expansion,
   Like gold to airy thinness beat.

If they be two, they are two so   25
   As stiff twin compasses[6] are two;
Thy soul, the fixed foot, makes no show
   To move, but doth, if th' other do.

And though it in the center sit,
   Yet when the other far doth roam,   30
It leans and hearkens after it,
   And grows erect, as that comes home.

Such wilt thou be to me, who must
   Like th' other foot, obliquely run;
Thy firmness makes my circle just,   35
   And makes me end where I begun.

                                          1633

The Ecstasy[1]

Where, like a pillow on a bed,
   A pregnant bank swelled up to rest
The violet's reclining head,
   Sat we two, one another's best.

Our hands were firmly cemented   5
   With a fast balm[2] which thence did spring,
Our eye-beams twisted, and did thread
   Our eyes upon one double string;[3]

So to intergraft our hands, as yet
   Was all our means to make us one,   10

6. I.e., drawing compasses—an emblem of constancy in change, as the circle they produce signifies perfection. This simile is the most famous example of the "metaphysical conceit" (see "Poetic Forms," below).
1. For Donne's readers the word "ecstasy" implied, not wild delight, as it commonly does nowadays, but a standing apart, a movement of the soul outside of the body.
2. I.e., perspiration. "Fast": strong.
3. Joining hands and eyes is the only intercourse of the lovers: "eyebeams" are invisible shafts of light, thought of as going out of the eyes and so enabling one to see things.

And pictures in our eyes[4] to get
    Was all our propagation.

As 'twixt two equal armies Fate
    Suspends uncertain victory,
Our souls (which to advance their state   15
    Were gone out) hung 'twixt her and me;

And whilst our souls negotiate there,
    We like sepulchral statues lay;
All day the same our postures were,
    And we said nothing all the day.   20

If any, so by love refined
    That he soul's language understood,
And by good love were grown all mind,[5]
    Within convenient distance stood,

He (though he know not which soul spake,   25
    Because both meant, both spake the same)
Might thence a new concoction[6] take,
    And part far purer than he came.

This ecstasy doth unperplex,
    We said, and tell us what we love;
We see by this it was not sex;   30
    We see we saw not what did move;[7]

But as all several souls contain
    Mixture of things, they know not what,
Love these mixed souls doth mix again,   35
    And makes both one, each this and that.

A single violet transplant,
    The strength, the color, and the size
(All which before was poor and scant)
    Redoubles still, and multiplies.   40

When love with one another so
    Interinanimates two souls,
That abler soul, which thence doth flow,
    Defects of loneliness controls.[8]

---

4. I.e., reflections of each other, often called "babies." "Get": beget.
5. On this kind of "good" love, see Castiglione, pp. 1006 ff.
6. Literally, ingredients "cooked together"; the word has alchemical overtones.

7. I.e., we see that we did not understand before what motivated ("did move") us. "Several": separate.
8. The "abler soul" which derives from the union of two lesser ones can eliminate the defects with which each of the component souls is afflicted.

We then, who are this new soul, know   45
    Of what we are composed and made,
For, th' atomies[9] of which we grow
    Are souls, whom no change can invade.

But O alas, so long, so far
    Our bodies why do we forbear?   50
They are ours, though they are not we; we are
    The intelligences, they the sphere.[1]

We owe them thanks because they thus
    Did us to us at first convey,
Yielded their forces, sense, to us,   55
    Nor are dross to us, but allay.[2]

On man heaven's influence works not so
    But that it first imprints the air:[3]
So soul into the soul may flow,
    Though it to body first repair.   60

As our blood labors to beget
    Spirits as like souls as it can,[4]
Because such fingers need to knit
    That subtle knot which makes us man,

So must pure lovers' souls descend   65
    T' affections, and to faculties
Which sense may reach and apprehend;
    Else a great Prince in prison lies.

To our bodies turn we then, that so
    Weak men on love revealed may look;   70
Love's mysteries in souls do grow,
    But yet the body is his book.[5]

And if some lover, such as we,
    Have heard this dialogue of one,[6]
Let him still mark us; he shall see   75
    Small change when we are to bodies gone.

                                                          1633

---

9. Units.
1. In Ptolemaic astronomy, each planet, set in a transparent globe ("sphere") that revolved and so carried it round the earth, was inhabited by a controlling angelic "intelligence." Similarly, Donne says, our bodies are guided and controlled by our souls.
2. "Dross" is an impurity that weakens metal, "allay" (alloy) an impurity that strengthens it. Our bodies contribute sensation ("sense") to the soul, and so reinforce it.

3. Astrological influences were thought to work on mankind through the surrounding air.
4. "Spirits" were subtle substances thought to be begotten by the blood to serve as intermediaries between body and soul. "Need": are needed.
5. I.e., Love puts forth in the body a book where his mysteries may be read (as God's mysteries may be read in the book of Nature and the book of Scripture).
6. "Dialogue of one" because "both meant, both spake the same" (line 26).

The Funeral

Whoever comes to shroud me, do not harm
    Nor question much
That subtle wreath of hair which crowns my arm;
The mystery, the sign you must not touch,
    For 'tis my outward soul,   5
Viceroy to that, which then to heaven being gone,
    Will leave this to control,
And keep these limbs, her[1] provinces, from dissolution.

For if the sinewy thread[2] my brain lets fall
    Through every part   10
Can tie those parts and make me one of all;
These hairs which upward grew, and strength and art
    Have from a better brain,
Can better do it; except she meant that I
    By this should know my pain,   15
As prisoners then are manacled, when they're condemned to die.

Whate'er she meant by it, bury it with me,
    For since I am
Love's martyr, it might breed idolatry,
If into others' hands these relics came: 20
    As 'twas humility[3]
To afford to it all that a soul can do,
    So 'tis some bravery,
That since you would save none of me, I bury some of you.

          1633

The Blossom

    Little think'st thou, poor flower,
      Whom I have watched six or seven days,
And seen thy birth, and seen what every hour
Gave to thy growth, thee to this height to raise,
And now dost laugh and triumph on this bough,   5
      Little think'st thou
That it will freeze anon, and that I shall
Tomorrow find thee fall'n, or not at all.

    Little think'st thou, poor heart,
      That labor'st yet to nestle thee   10

1. The soul's, but also the mistress's; compare "she," below, line 14.
2. The spinal cord and nervous system.
3. It was humility to grant, in the first part of the poem, that her hair could act as a soul; it is also "bravery" (defiance) to bury a part of the mistress in revenge for her cruelty.

And think'st by hovering here to get a part
In a forbidden or forbidding tree,[1]
And hop'st her stiffness by long siege to bow,
    Little think'st thou
That thou tomorrow, ere that sun[2] doth wake,   15
Must with this sun and me a journey take.

    But thou, which lov'st to be
      Subtle to plague thyself, wilt say,
Alas, if you must go, what's that to me?
Here lies my business, and here I will stay: 20
You go to friends whose love and means present
      Various content
To your eyes, ears, and tongue, and every part.
If then your body go, what need you a heart?

    Well, then, stay here; but know,   25
      When thou hast stayed and done thy most,
A naked thinking heart that makes no show
Is to a woman but a kind of ghost.
How shall she know my heart; or, having none,
      Know thee for one?   30
Practice may make her know some other part,
But take my word, she doth not know a heart.

    Meet me at London, then,
      Twenty days hence, and thou shalt see
Me fresher and more fat by being with men[3]   35
Than if I had stayed still with her and thee.
For God's sake, if you can, be you so too:
      I would give you
There to another friend, whom we shall find
As glad to have my body as my mind.   40

                                      1633

The Relic

    When my grave is broke up again
    Some second guest to entertain
    (For graves have learned that woman-head[1]
    To be to more than one a bed),
      And he that digs it, spies   5
A bracelet of bright hair about the bone,
      Will he not let us alone,

---

1. The fruit of this tree is "forbidden" (presumably because the woman is married) or "forbidding" (because she is unwilling).
2. I.e., the woman.

3. I.e., with people (not necessarily just males).
1. I.e., characteristic of women. Graves were often used to inter successive corpses, the bones of previous occupants being deposited in charnel houses.

And think that there a loving couple lies,
Who thought that this device might be some way
To make their souls, at the last busy day,[2]
Meet at this grave, and make a little stay?   10

    If this fall in a time, or land,
    Where mis-devotion[3] doth command,
    Then he that digs us up, will bring
    Us to the Bishop and the King,   15
      To make us relics; then
Thou shalt be a Mary Magdalen, and I
    A something else[4] thereby;
All women shall adore us, and some men;
And since at such times, miracles are sought,   20
I would have that age by this paper taught
What miracles we harmless lovers wrought.

    First, we loved well and faithfully,
    Yet knew not what we loved, nor why,
    Difference of sex no more we knew,   25
    Than our guardian angels do;
      Coming and going, we
Perchance might kiss, but not between those meals;[5]
    Our hands ne'er touched the seals
Which nature, injured by late law, sets free:[6]
These miracles we did: but now, alas,
All measure and all language I should pass,
Should I tell what a miracle she was.

                          1633

A Lecture Upon the Shadow

Stand still, and I will read to thee
A lecture, Love, in love's philosophy.
   These three hours that we have spent
   Walking here, two shadows went
Along with us, which we ourselves produced;   5
But, now the sun is just above our head,
   We do those shadows tread
   And to brave clearness all things are reduced.
So, whilst our infant loves did grow,
Disguises did and shadows flow   10
From us and our care;[1] but now, 'tis not so.

2. Judgment Day.
3. False devotion, superstition. Donne seems to have in mind Roman Catholicism.
4. What the indefinite subterfuge "something else" stands for, Donne leaves deliberately unclear; the reader may—and indeed, must—speculate.
5. The kiss of salutation and parting was, in the 17th century, a peculiarly English custom.
6. "Late": recent (comparatively speaking). Human law forbids the free love permitted by nature.
1. Metaphorically, morning shadows were the disguises with which they anxiously concealed their love from outsiders.

That love hath not attained the high'st degree
Which is still diligent lest others see.

Except[2] our loves at this noon stay,
We shall new shadows make the other way.   15
   As the first were made to blind
   Others, these which come behind
Will work upon ourselves, and blind our eyes.
If our loves faint and westwardly decline,
   To me thou falsely thine   20
   And I to thee mine actions shall disguise.
The morning shadows wear away,
But these grow longer all the day,
But, oh, love's day is short if love decay.

Love is a growing or full constant light,   25
And his first minute after noon is night.

1635

Elegy 16.[1] On His Mistress

By our first strange and fatal interview,
By all desires which thereof did ensue,
By our long starving hopes, by that remorse
Which my words' masculine persuasive force
Begot in thee, and by the memory   5
Of hurts which spies and rivals threatened me,
I calmly beg; but by thy father's wrath,
By all pains which want and divorcement hath,
I conjure thee: and all the oaths which I
And thou have sworn to seal joint constancy   10
Here I unswear and overswear them thus:
Thou shalt not love by ways so dangerous.
Temper, oh fair love, love's impetuous rage;
Be my true mistress still, not my feigned page.[2]
I'll go, and, by thy kind leave, leave behind   15
Thee, only worthy to nurse in my mind

---

2. Unless.

1. In Latin poetry, an elegy is not necessarily a funeral lament, but may be simply a discursive or reflective poem written in "elegiacs" (unrhymed couplets of alternating dactylic hexameters and pentameters). In fact the subject matter primarily associated with this meter was not death but sex, the most famous collection of elegies being Ovid's *Amores*. Donne's elegies—some 15 poems, almost all written in the 1590s—take Ovid as their principal model, and resemble him in ingenious wit and, for the most part, in frank and unapologetic eroticism. Elegy 16 is uncharacteristically tender. (We retain Grierson's numbering, though he included among the elegies some poems that are probably not Donne's.)

2. Evidently Donne's mistress (nothing positively identifies her with Ann More, who became his wife) wanted to accompany him abroad, disguised as a page boy. Such escapades occasionally took place in real life; in 1605, Elizabeth Southwell, disguised as a page, went abroad with the scapegrace Sir Robert Dudley.

Thirst to come back. Oh, if thou die before,
My soul from other lands to thee shall soar.
Thy (else almighty) beauty cannot move
Rage from the seas, nor thy love teach them love,   20
Nor tame wild Boreas' harshness.[3] Thou hast read
How roughly he in pieces shiverèd
Fair Orithea, whom he swore he loved.
Fall ill or good, 'tis madness to have proved[4]
Dangers unurged; feed on this flattery,   25
That absent lovers one in th' other be.
Dissemble nothing, not a boy, nor change
Thy body's habit, nor mind's; be not strange
To thyself only; all will spy in thy face
A blushing womanly discovering grace.   30
Richly clothed apes are called, and as soon
Eclipsed as bright we call the moon the moon.[5]
Men of France, changeable chameleons,
Spitals[6] of diseases, shops of fashions,
Love's fuellers and the rightest company   35
Of players which upon the world's stage be,
Will quickly know thee, and know thee; and alas!
Th' indifferent Italian, as we pass
His warm land, well content to think thee page,
Will hunt[7] thee with such lust and hideous rage   40
As Lot's fair guests were vexed.[8] But none of these
Nor spongy, hydroptic[9] Dutch shall thee displease
If thou stay here. O stay here, for, for thee,
England is only a worthy gallery
To walk in expectation, till from thence   45
Our greatest king call thee to his presence.[1]
When I am gone, dream me some happiness,
Nor let thy looks our long-hid love confess;
Nor praise nor dispraise me, bless nor curse
Openly love's force, nor in bed fright thy nurse   50
With midnight's startings, crying out "Oh, oh!
Nurse, oh my love is slain, I saw him go
O'er the white Alps alone; I saw him, I,
Assailed, fight, taken, stabbed, bleed, fall, and die."
Augur me better chance, except dread Jove   55
Think it enough for me t' have had thy love.

3. Boreas is god of the north wind; Ovid in the 6th
book of the *Metamorphoses* describes his boisterous abduction of Orithea.
4. Sought out.
5. I.e., we recognize the moon as easily when it's
in eclipse as when it's not.
6. Hospitals.
7. An alternative reading is "haunt."

8. The inhabitants of Sodom brought destruction
on themselves when they tried to rape two angels
who visited Lot (Genesis 19.1–11).
9. Dropsical, thus insatiably thirsty ("spongy").
1. Throne rooms commonly had antechambers
(galleries) where visitors waited until the monarch
was ready to see them. The world itself is such a
gallery for the greatest king of all, God.

Elegy 19. Going to Bed

Come, Madam, come, all rest my powers defy,
Until I labor, I in labor lie.[1]
The foe oft-times, having the foe in sight,
Is tired with standing though he never fight.
Off with that girdle, like heaven's zone[2] glistering,   5
But a far fairer world encompassing.
Unpin that spangled breastplate which you wear
That th' eyes of busy fools may be stopped there.
Unlace yourself, for that harmonious chime
Tells me from you that now it is bed-time.   10
Off with that happy busk,[3] which I envy,
That still can be and still can stand so nigh.
Your gown going off, such beauteous state reveals
As when from flowery meads th' hill's shadow steals.
Off with that wiry coronet and show   15
The hairy diadem which on you doth grow;
Now off with those shoes, and then safely tread
In this love's hallowed temple, this soft bed.
In such white robes, heaven's angels used to be
Received by men; thou, angel, bring'st with thee   20
A heaven like Mahomet's paradise;[4] and though
Ill spirits walk in white, we easily know
By this these angels from an evil sprite,
Those set our hairs, but these our flesh upright.
    License my roving hands, and let them go   25
Before, behind, between, above, below.
O my America! my new-found-land,
My kingdom, safeliest when with one man manned,
My mine of precious stones, my empery,
How blest am I in this discovering thee!   30
To enter in these bonds is to be free;
There where my hand is set, my seal shall be.[5]
    Full nakedness! All joys are due to thee,
As souls unbodied, bodies unclothed must be,
To taste whole joys. Gems which you women use   35
Are like Atalanta's balls,[6] cast in men's views,
That when a fool's eye lighteth on a gem,
His earthly soul may covet theirs, not them.
Like pictures, or like books' gay coverings, made
For laymen, are all women thus arrayed;   40
Themselves are mystic books, which only we

---

1. "Labor" is the sense of "get to work" and in the sense of "distress."
2. The zodiac.
3. Bodice.
4. Populated by seductive houris, for the delectation of the faithful.
5. The jokes mingle law with sex; having signed the document with his hand, he will now seal it, and in the bonds of her arms he will find freedom.
6. Atalanta, running a race against her suitor Hippomenes, was beaten when he dropped golden balls (apples) for her to pick up. Donne reverses the story.

(Whom their imputed grace will dignify)
Must see revealed.[7] Then since that I may know,
As liberally as to a midwife show
Thyself: cast all, yea, this white linen hence,   45
There is no penance due to innocence.[8]
　　To teach thee, I am naked first; why then
What need'st thou have more covering than a man?

                                                        1669

Satire 3, Religion

Satire 3, Religion　　Like his elegies, Donne's five satires were written
in his twenties, and follow, though remotely, in classical footsteps. The
essence of satire is an attitude: the author holds his subject up to laughter or
scorn. Elements of such an attitude appear in many works of prose and
poetry that are not, as a whole, satiric—in Chaucer, in Langland, as early
as the figure of Thersites in Homer's *Iliad*. But the great examples of formal
satiric writing in classical times were the Roman poets Horace and Juvenal,
models respectively of the urbanely jocose and the indignant satire. During
the sixteenth century their satires were imitated on the continent by the
Italian poet Ariosto and some of his contemporaries. Even in England, Sir
Thomas Wyatt felt through an Italian intermediary the influence of Juvenal:
see, for example, *Mine Own John Poins*, pp. 471–473. Yet satiric poems as
such remained rare in English till the 1590s; their sudden appearance at that
time evidently grew out of moods of skepticism, discontent, and melancholy
that marked the last years of the sixteenth and the first years of the seventeenth century.
　　Donne's third satire is not conventional, in terms of the genre, because it
does not assume a position of derisive superiority to its victim—indeed, it
does not have a proper victim. It is a strenuous, inconclusive discussion of
an acute theological problem: How may a man recognize the true Christian
church among the many competing sects? Its theme was of paramount
importance to Donne as an ex-Catholic, and to the men of his age, for
whom religious polemic was a passion. The poem offers no easy answer to
the problem it raises; the point it makes most forcefully is the folly of not
thinking about the matter. Its language and meter are harsh and rough, as
was traditional in the genre, its concentration is complete; it is a powerful
piece of wrought-iron work in poetry.

Satire 3, Religion

Kind pity chokes my spleen;[1] brave scorn forbids
Those tears to issue which swell my eyelids;
I must not laugh,[2] nor weep sins, and be wise:

---

7. By granting favors to their lovers, women impute
to them grace which they don't deserve, as God
imputes grace to undeserving sinners. Laymen can
only look at the covers of mystic books (women);
but "we" who have saving grace can read them.

8. An alternative reading is "Here is no penance,
much less innocence."
1. The seat of bile, hence scorn and ridicule.
2. Mock.

Can railing then cure these worn maladies?
Is not our mistress, fair Religion,   5
As worthy of all our souls' devotion
As virtue was to the first blinded age?[3]
Are not heaven's joys as valiant to assuage
Lusts, as earth's honor was to them?[4] Alas,
As we do them in means, shall they surpass   10
Us in the end, and shall thy father's spirit
Meet blind philosophers in heaven, whose merit
Of strict life may be imputed faith,[5] and hear
Thee, whom he taught so easy ways and near
To follow, damned? O, if thou dar'st, fear this;   15
This fear great courage and high valor is.
Dar'st thou aid mutinous Dutch,[6] and dar'st thou lay
Thee in ships, wooden sepulchers, a prey
To leaders' rage, to storms, to shot, to dearth?
Dar'st thou dive seas and dungeons of the earth?   20
Hast thou courageous fire to thaw the ice
Of frozen North discoveries? and thrice
Colder than salamanders,[7] like divine
Children in the oven, fires of Spain, and the line,
Whose countries limbecks to our bodies be,   25
Canst thou for gain bear?[8] And must every he
Which cries not, "Goddess!" to thy mistress, draw,[9]
Or eat thy poisonous words? Courage of straw!
O desperate coward, wilt thou seem bold, and
To thy foes and his[1] (who made thee to stand   30
Sentinel in his world's garrison) thus yield,
And for forbidden wars leave th' appointed field?
Know thy foes: The foul Devil (whom thou
Strivest to please) for hate, not love, would allow
Thee fain his whole realm to be quit;[2] and as   35
The world's all parts wither away and pass,[3]
So the world's self, thy other loved foe, is
In her decrepit wane, and thou, loving this,
Dost love a withered and worn strumpet; last,
Flesh (itself's death) and joys which flesh can taste   40
Thou lovest; and thy fair goodly soul, which doth

---

3. The age of paganism, blind to Christianity but capable of natural morality ("virtue").

4. I.e., hope of heaven should be as strong ("valiant") against our lusts as earthly honor was against theirs, the pagans'.

5. Specially virtuous pagans, it was felt, might achieve heaven by behavior so good that it virtually implied faith.

6. English volunteers took frequent part with the Dutch in their wars against Spain. Donne himself had sailed in two raiding expeditions against the Spanish (see below, *The Storm*, pp. 1088–1090).

7. The salamander was traditionally so cold-blooded that it could live even in a fire. The "divine children in the oven" are Shadrach, Meshach, and Abednego, rescued from the fiery furnace in Daniel 3.

8. The object of "bear" is "fires of Spain, and the line"—Inquisitorial and equatorial heats, which roast men as chemists heat materials in "limbecks" (alembics, or retorts for distilling).

9. I.e., fight a duel.

1. God's.

2. I.e., the Devil would gladly give you a free hand with his whole kingdom.

3. It was a common belief in the 17th century that the world was getting old and decrepit.

Give this flesh power to taste joy, thou dost loathe.
Seek true religion. O, where? Mirreus,[4]
Thinking her unhoused here, and fled from us,
Seeks her at Rome; there, because he doth know   45
That she was there a thousand years ago.
He loves her rags so, as we here obey
The statecloth[5] where the Prince sat yesterday.
Crantz to such brave loves will not be enthralled,
But loves her only, who at Geneva is called   50
Religion—plain, simple, sullen, young,
Contemptuous, yet unhandsome; as among
Lecherous humors,[6] there is one that judges
No wenches wholesome but coarse country drudges.
Graius stays still at home here, and because   55
Some preachers, vile ambitious bawds, and laws
Still new, like fashions, bid him think that she
Which dwells with us is only perfect, he
Embraceth her whom his godfathers will
Tender to him, being tender, as wards still   60
Take such wives as their guardians offer, or
Pay values.[7] Careless Phrygius doth abhor
All, because all cannot be good, as one
Knowing some women whores, dares marry none.
Graccus loves all as one, and thinks that so   65
As women do in divers countries go
In divers habits, yet are still one kind,
So doth, so is religion; and this blind-
ness too much light breeds; but unmoved thou
Of force must one, and forced but one allow;   70
And the right;[8] ask thy father which is she,
Let him ask his; though truth and falsehood be
Near twins, yet truth a little elder is;[9]
Be busy to seek her, believe me this,
He's not of none, nor worst, that seeks the best.[1]   75
To adore, or scorn an image, or protest,
May all be bad; doubt wisely; in strange way
To stand inquiring right, is not to stray;
To sleep, or run wrong, is. On a huge hill,
Cragged and steep, Truth stands, and he that will   80
Reach her, about must, and about must go,

---

4. The imaginary characters in this passage represent different creeds. "Mirreus" is a Roman Catholic, "Crantz" a Geneva Presbyterian, "Graius" an Erastian (i.e., believing in any religion sponsored by the state), "Phrygius" a skeptic, and "Graccus" a Universalist.
5. The royal canopy, a symbol of kingly power.
6. Tempers, temperaments.
7. Young men (of "tender" years) might reject the wives offered ("tendered") them by their guardians; but, if they did so, had to pay "values," i.e., fines.

8. I.e., being blind to the differences between religions, Graccus has too much light to see anything (lines 68–69). But the poet insists that without being swayed by human pressures, we must find just one true religion, "the right" true religion.
9. I.e., the true church is the one most like the primitive church.
1. The man who seeks the best church is neither an unbeliever nor the worst sort of believer.

And what the hill's suddenness resists, win so;
Yet strive so, that before age, death's twilight,
Thy soul rest, for none can work in that night.
To will[2] implies delay, therefore now do.　　　　　　85
Hard deeds, the body's pains; hard knowledge too
The mind's endeavors reach,[3] and mysteries
Are like the sun, dazzling, yet plain to all eyes.
Keep the truth which thou hast found; men do not stand
In so ill case here, that God hath with his hand　　　　90
Signed kings' blank charters to kill whom they hate,
Nor are they vicars, but hangmen to fate.[4]
Fool and wretch, wilt thou let thy soul be tied
To man's laws, by which she shall not be tried
At the last day? O, will it then boot thee　　　　　　95
To say a Philip, or a Gregory,
A Harry, or a Martin taught thee this?[5]
Is not this excuse for mere contraries
Equally strong? Cannot both sides say so?
That thou mayest rightly obey power, her bounds know;　　100
Those passed, her nature and name is changed; to be
Then humble to her is idolatry.
As streams are, power is; those blest flowers that dwell
At the rough stream's calm head, thrive and prove well,
But having left their roots, and themselves given　　　105
To the stream's tyrannous rage, alas, are driven
Through mills, and rocks, and woods, and at last, almost
Consumed in going, in the sea are lost:
So perish souls, which more choose men's unjust
Power from God claimed, than God himself to trust.　　110

1633

The Storm[1]

To Mr. Christopher Brooke

Thou which art I ('tis nothing to be so),
Thou which art still thyself, by these shalt know

2. To intend a future action.
3. I.e., the body's pains achieve ("reach") hard deeds; the mind's endeavors will reach hard knowledge.
4. Human authority does not represent divine justice on earth; men are not God's vicars on earth (the hit here is at both the Pope and the secular monarch), but his hangmen at best—agents through whom his justice is fulfilled without carte blanche ("blank charters") to use their own judgments.
5. "Philip" is Philip II of Spain, and "Gregory" any one of several Pope Gregories (VII, XIII, XIV); "Harry" is England's Henry VIII, and "Martin" is Martin Luther. Laymen and clergy, Protestants and

Catholics, all are covered. "Boot": profit.
1. The Storm is a display of virtuoso wit, but it is also factual reporting of a specific historical event. In 1597, Elizabeth, alarmed by reports of a second Armada being prepared by Philip II of Spain, authorized a preemptive strike under the primary leadership of Essex and Ralegh; Donne went along as a gentleman-volunteer. Having started against Cadiz, the fleet ran into a violent storm, a result of which was this verse letter; later in the summer, after refitting at Plymouth, the fleet sailed again toward the Azores. But there the adventurers ran into exactly the opposite weather problem, a prolonged calm spell, about which Donne wrote a

Part of our passage; and a hand or eye
By Hilliard[2] drawn is worth an history
By a worse painter made; and (without pride)   5
When by thy judgment they are dignified,
My lines are such: 'tis the preeminence
Of friendship only to impute excellence.
    England, to whom we owe what we be and have,
Sad that her sons did seek a foreign grave   10
(For Fate's or Fortune's drifts[3] none can soothsay,
Honor and misery have one face and way),
From out her pregnant entrails sighed a wind
Which at th' air's middle marble[4] room did find
Such strong resistance that itself it threw   15
Downward again; and so when it did view
How in the port our fleet dear time did leese,[5]
Withering like prisoners which lie but for fees,
Mildly it kissed our sails, and fresh and sweet
As to a stomach sterved[6] whose insides meet   20
Meat comes, it came; and swole our sails, when we
So joyed, as Sara her swelling joyed to see.[7]
    But 'twas but so kind as our countrymen
Which bring friends one day's way, and leave them then.
Then like two mighty kings, which dwelling far   25
Asunder, meet against a third to war,
The south and west winds joined, and as they blew,
Waves like a rolling trench before them threw.
    Sooner than you read this line did the gale,
Like shot, not feared till felt, our sails assail;   30
And what at first was called a gust, the same
Hath now a storm's, anon a tempest's name.
Jonas, I pity thee, and curse those men
Who when the storm raged most did wake thee then;[8]
Sleep is pain's easiest salve, and doth fulfill   35
All offices of death except to kill.
But when I waked, I saw that I saw not;
I and the sun which should teach me had forgot
East, west, day, night, and I could only say,
If the world had lasted, now it had been day.   40
Thousands our noises were, yet we 'mongst all
Could none by his right name but thunder call.

second verse letter. It was probably addressed, like
the first one, to Christopher Brooke, a law school
friend. The two poems were in fact the only significant achievements of this ill-fated venture.
2. Nicholas Hilliard, the most famous portrait
painter of the Elizabethan age.
3. Intentions. The parenthesis explains "grave";
they thought they were seeking honor.
4. With an overtone from the Greek root, meaning "glistening."
5. Lose. Prisoners often languished in jail for lack
of money to pay the fees.

6. The old word "sterved" had a wider meaning
than modern "starved;" it means here, and in the
poem's last line, enfeebled, languishing. Donne's
fondness for repeating in immediate proximity the
same sound or word, not always as puns, is apparent here (meet / meat; comes, it came); see also line
30, sails assail.
7. Sarah, wife of Abraham, bore him a son (Isaac)
when she was 90 and he 103.
8. Jonah, asleep in his storm-tossed vessel, was
awakened and accused of bringing bad luck: (Jonah
1.5–6).

Lightning was all our light, and it rained more
Than if the sun had drunk the sea before.
Some coffined in their cabins lie, equally   45
Grieved that they are not dead and yet must die;
And as sin-burdened souls from graves will creep
At the last day, some forth their cabins peep,
And tremblingly ask what news, and do hear so
Like jealous husbands what they would not know.   50
Some sitting on the hatches would seem there
With hideous gazing to fear away fear.
Then note they the ship's sicknesses, the mast
Shaked with this ague, and the hold and waist
With a salt dropsy clogged, and all our tacklings   55
Snapping, like too-high-stretched treble strings.
And from our tattered sails rags drop down so
As from one hanged in chains a year ago.⁹
Even our ordinance, placed for our defense,
Strive to break loose and 'scape away from thence.   60
    Pumping hath tired our men, and what's the gain?
Seas into seas thrown we suck in again.
Hearing hath deafed our sailors, and if they
Knew how to hear, there's none knows what to say.
Compared to these storms, death is but a qualm,   65
Hell somewhat lightsome, and the Bermuda calm.¹
Darkness, light's elder brother, his birth-right
Claims o'er this world, and to heaven hath chased light.
All things are one, and that one none² can be
Since all forms uniform deformity   70
Doth cover, so that we, except God say
Another *Fiat*, shall have no more day.³
So violent yet long these furies be,
That though thine absence sterve me, I wish not thee.

1597   1633

An Anatomy of the World

Donne composed this poem in 1611 to mark the first anniversary of the death of Elizabeth, fourteen-year-old daughter of his patron and friend Sir Robert Drury. The plan was to write a poem every year on the death of Elizabeth; but after two such exercises, the project meeting with considerable criticism, the poet called a halt. Ben Jonson voiced the sentiments of many when he told William Drummond that "Donne's *Anniversary* was profane and full of blasphemies; that he told Mr. Donne, if it had been written of the Virgin Mary it had been something; to

9. After being hanged in chains, criminals were often left indefinitely on the gallows, as a warning to others. Cannon ("ordinance"), mounted on wheeled carriages but torn loose of their moorings, were a fearful peril in a rough sea.
1. The Bermudas lie in a turbulent area of ocean;

compare Shakespeare, "the still-vex'd Bermoothes" in *The Tempest* 1.2, and the modern-day "Bermuda triangle."
2. I.e., no thing.
3. By saying "Let there be light" (*Fiat lux*), God created the first day.

which he answered that he described the Idea of a Woman, and not as she was."

The basic themes of Donne's poem are in fact more philosophic than elegiac. They are the decay and disintegration of the world as a whole (the word "anatomy" implies a postmortem dissection), caused by the breaking of those slender but precious lines of correspondent sympathy which used to hold it together. (See above, the period introduction.) An ancient harmony is gone, of which Elizabeth Drury is but one symbol. Other aspects, developed in the poem, are the story of the Garden of Eden and the Fall of Man, the myth of the Golden Age, and the disintegration of the old geocentric cosmos in which humanity and its moral life were the focus of universal attention. Five separate meditations on these and similar themes are surrounded by an introduction and a conclusion. Each meditation concludes with a eulogy of the dead girl, a two-line refrain beginning "She, she is dead," and a moral. We give the introduction (lines 1–90) and the first two meditations (lines 91–190, 191–246). Since both Donne's *Anniversaries* were several times printed during the poet's lifetime, as well as in the posthumous 1633 volume of *Poems*, they exist in several slightly different versions; our text is based on the first edition of 1611.

From An Anatomy of the World[1]

The First Anniversary

<table>
<tr><td>The entry into
the work.</td><td>When that rich soul which to her heaven is gone,
Whom all they celebrate who know they have one
(For who is sure he hath a soul, unless
It see, and judge, and follow worthiness,
And by deeds praise it? He who doth not this,
May lodge an inmate soul, but 'tis not his);
When that queen ended here her progress time,[2]
And, as to her standing house,[3] to heaven did climb,
Where, loath to make the saints attend[4] her long,
She's now a part both of the choir and song,
This world in that great earthquake languishèd;
For in a common bath of tears it bled,
Which drew the strongest vital spirits[5] out:
But succored then with a perplexèd doubt,
Whether the world did lose or gain in this
(Because since now no other way there is
But goodness to see her, whom all would see,
All must endeavor to be good as she),
This great consumption to a fever turned,
And so the world had fits; it joyed, it mourned.</td><td>

5

10

15

20</td></tr>
</table>

1. The marginal glosses are by Donne, added in 1612.
2. "That queen" is Elizabeth Drury, but the phrase would also recall Queen Elizabeth, who liked to go on "progresses," formal visits from one country house to another.

3. I.e., a house that stands open and waiting for its owner.
4. Await.
5. "Vital spirits" were essential, if mysterious, agents, supposed to link soul with body. "Succored": comforted.

And as men think that agues physic are,[6]
And the ague being spent, give over care,
So thou, sick world, mistak'st thyself to be
Well, when, alas, thou art in a lethargy.
Her death did wound and tame thee then, and then
Thou might'st have better spared the sun, or man;   26
That wound was deep, but 'tis more misery
That thou hast lost thy sense and memory.
'Twas heavy[7] then to hear thy voice of moan,
But this is worse, that thou art speechless grown.   30
Thou hast forgot thy name thou hadst; thou wast
Nothing but she, and her thou hast o'erpast.[8]
For as a child kept from the font,[9] until
A prince, expected long, come to fulfill
The ceremonies, thou unnamed had'st laid,   35
Had not her coming, thee her palace made:[1]
Her name defined thee, gave thee form and frame,
And thou forget'st to celebrate thy name.
     Some months she hath been dead (but being dead,
Measures of times are all determinèd),[2]   40
But long she hath been away, long, long, yet none
Offers to tell us who it is that's gone.
But as in states doubtful of future heirs,
When sickness without remedy impairs
The present prince, they're loath it should be said   45
The prince doth languish, or the prince is dead:
So mankind, feeling now a general thaw,
A strong example gone, equal to law,
The cèment which did faithfully compact
And glue all virtues, now resolved,[3] and slacked,   50
Thought it some blasphemy to say she was dead,
Or that our weakness was discoverèd[4]
In that confession; therefore spoke no more
Than tongues, the soul being gone, the loss deplore.
But though it be too late to succor thee,   55
Sick world, yea, dead, yea, putrefied, since she,
Thy intrinsic balm and thy preservative,[5]
Can never be renewed, thou never live,
I (since no man can make thee live) will try
What we may gain by thy anatomy.[6]   60
Her death hath taught us dearly that thou art
Corrupt and mortal in thy purest part.
     Let no man say, the world itself being dead,

6. Ague is chills and fever, physic medicine. Some people think the fever stage of the disease, as most disagreeable, is itself a cure.
7. Mournful, depressing.
8. Outlived.
9. Baptismal font.
1. The sick world is still being addressed; until it was made her palace, the world was nameless nothing.
2. Terminated.
3. Melted.
4. Disclosed.
5. I.e., a medicine that preserved one in perfect health forever.
6. I.e., by dissecting and analyzing the world's corpse, now its soul is gone.

'Tis labor lost to have discoverèd
The world's infirmities, since there is none   65
Alive to study this dissection;

What life the   For there's a kind of world remaining still,
world hath still.   Though she which did inanimate and fill
The world be gone, yet in this last long night,
Her ghost doth walk; that is, a glimmering light,   70
A faint weak love of virtue and of good
Reflects from her on them which understood
Her worth; and though she have shut in all day,
The twilight of her memory doth stay;
Which, from the carcass of the old world free,   75
Creates a new world; and new creatures be
Produced: the matter and the stuff of this,
Her virtue, and the form our practice is;
And though to be thus elemented,[7] arm
These creatures, from home-born intrinsic harm   80
(For all assumed[8] unto this dignity
So many weedless Paradises be,
Which of themselves produce no venomous sin,
Except some foreign serpent bring it in),
Yet, because outward storms the strongest break,   85
And strength itself by confidence grows weak,
This new world may be safer, being told

The sickness   The dangers and diseases of the old:
of the world.   For with due temper[9] men do then forgo
Or covet things, when they their true worth know.   90

Impossibility of   There is no health; physicians say that we
health.   At best enjoy but a neutrality.
And can there be worse sickness than to know
That we are never well, nor can be so?
We are born ruinous;[1] poor mothers cry   95
That children come not right, nor orderly,
Except they headlong come and fall upon
An ominous precipitation.[2]
How witty's ruin! how importunate
Upon mankind! It labored to frustrate   100
Even God's purpose; and made Woman, sent
For man's relief, cause of his languishment.
They were to good ends, and they are so still,
But accessory, and principal in ill.[3]
For that first marriage was our funeral: 105
One woman at one blow then killed us all,

---

7. Constituted.
8. Raised.
9. Moderation.
1. Falling into ruin.
2. "We do not make account that a child comes right, except it come with the head forward, and thereby prefigure that headlong falling into calam-

ities which it must suffer after" (Donne, *Sermons*, ed. Potter & Simpson, 4.333). "Witty": ingenious.
3. Women are only helpers in good but leaders in evil. This sort of exaggerated antifeminism went hand in hand with an equally exaggerated idolizing of women. "That first marriage": Adam and Eve's.

And singly, one by one, they kill us now.
We do delightfully ourselves allow
To that consumption; and profusely blind,
We kill ourselves to propagate our kind.[4]   110
   And yet we do not that; we are not men:
There is not now that mankind which was then
When as the sun and man did seem to strive

Shortness of life. (Joint tenants of the world) who should survive;
When stag and raven and the long-lived tree,[5]   115
Compared with man, died in minority;
When, if a slow-paced star had stolen away
From the observer's marking, he might stay
Two or three hundred years to see it again,
And then make up[6] his observation plain;   120
When, as the age was long, the size was great;
Man's growth confessed and recompensed the meat;[7]
So spacious and large, that every soul
Did a fair kingdom and large realm control;
And when the very stature, thus erect,   125
Did that soul a good way towards Heaven direct.
Where is this mankind now? who lives to age
Fit to be made Methusalem his page?
Alas, we scarce live long enough to try
Whether a new-made clock run right, or lie.   130
Old grandsires talk of yesterday with sorrow,
And for our children we reserve tomorrow.
So short is life that every peasant strives,
In a torn house, or field, to have three lives.[8]
   And as in lasting, so in length is man   135

Smallness of Contracted to an inch, who was a span;[9]
stature. For had a man at first in forests strayed,
Or shipwrecked in the sea, one would have laid
A wager that an elephant or whale
That met him would not hastily assail   140
A thing so equal to him: now, alas,
The fairies and the pygmies well may pass
As credible; mankind decays so soon,
We're scarce our fathers' shadows cast at noon.
Only death adds to our length:[1] nor are we grown   145
In stature to be men, till we are none.
But this were light,[2] did our less volume hold

---

4. Popular superstition had it that every act of sex shortened one's life by a day.

5. Stags and ravens were thought to live particularly long; but, compared with early men, they, and even oak-trees, died in youth.

6. Complete.

7. Early man was thought to have eaten better than modern man, lived longer, and grown to greater stature. Methuselah (below) is said to have lived 969 years (Genesis 5.27).

8. Leases of farmland were often made for "three lives," i.e., through the longest-lived of three designated persons.

9. I.e., the distance from tip of thumb to tip of little finger, about 9 inches.

1. The corpse of a person is said to measure a little more than his height when alive.

2. I.e., this would be a trifle. The word "volume" puns on the senses of "bulk" and "book."

All the old text, or had we changed to gold
Their silver; or disposed into less glass
Spirits of virtue,[3] which then scattered was.   150
But 'tis not so: we're not retired, but damped;[4]
And as our bodies, so our minds are cramped:
'Tis shrinking, not close weaving, that hath thus
In mind and body both bedwarfèd us.
We seem ambitious, God's whole work to undo;   155
Of nothing He made us, and we strive, too,
To bring ourselves to nothing back; and we
Do what we can to do it so soon as He.
With new diseases on ourselves we war,
And with new physic,[5] a worse engine far.   160
　　Thus man, this world's vice-emperor, in whom
All faculties, all graces are at home—
And if in other creatures they appear,
They're but man's ministers and legates there,
To work on their rebellions, and reduce   165
Them to civility, and to man's use—
This man, whom God did woo, and loath to attend[6]
Till man came up, did down to man descend,
This man, so great, that all that is, is his,
Oh what a trifle, and poor thing he is!   170
If man were anything, he's nothing now:
Help, or at least some time to waste, allow
To his other wants, yet when he did depart[7]
With her whom we lament, he lost his heart.
　　She, of whom th' ancients seemed to prophesy   175
When they called virtues by the name of *she*;[8]
She in whom virtue was so much refined
That for allay unto so pure a mind
She took the weaker sex,[9] she that could drive
The poisonous tincture, and the stain of Eve,   180
Out of her thoughts and deeds, and purify
All, by a true religious alchemy;
She, she is dead; she's dead: when thou knowest this,
Thou knowest how poor a trifling thing man is.
And learn'st thus much by our anatomy,   185
The heart being perished, no part can be free.
And that except thou feed (not banquet) on
The supernatural food, religion,
Thy better growth grows witherèd and scant;
Be more than man, or thou'rt less than an ant.   190

3. I.e., distilled virtue, which would fit in a small bottle. The word "virtue" includes the sense of "power" as well as that of "goodness."
4. I.e., not compressed, but deadened.
5. Medications. Modern medicine is said to be the worst enemy of human health.
6. Wait. God wooed man by descending to earth in order to redeem him.
7. I.e., part with, lose. Though man has other wants, which God might help him to satisfy, or allow him to squander himself on ("waste"), yet when she is lost all is lost.
8. The virtues are all represented in Latin by feminine nouns and portrayed as female figures.
9. Her mind was so pure that she mingled it with the corruption and frailty of "the weaker sex."

Then, as mankind, so is the world's whole frame
Quite out of joint, almost created lame:
For, before God had made up all the rest,
Corruption entered and depraved the best.
It seized the angels,[1] and then first of all   195
The world did in her cradle take a fall,
And turned her brains, and took a general maim,
Wronging each joint of th' universal frame.
The noblest part, man, felt it first; and then

Decay of nature   Both beasts and plants, cursed in the curse of
in other parts.   man.[2]   200
So did the world from the first hour decay,
That evening was beginning of the day,[3]
And now the springs and summers which we see
Like sons of women after fifty be.[4]
And new philosophy calls all in doubt: 205
The element of fire is quite put out;[5]
The sun is lost, and the earth, and no man's wit[6]
Can well direct him where to look for it.
And freely men confess that this world's spent,
When in the planets and the firmament   210
They seek so many new;[7] they see that this
Is crumbled out again to his atomies.
'Tis all in pieces, all coherence gone;
All just supply, and all relation:
Prince, subject; father, son,[8] are things forgot,   215
For every man alone thinks he hath got
To be[9] a phoenix, and that there can be
None of that kind of which he is, but he.[1]

       This is the world's condition now, and now
She that should all parts to reunion bow,   220
She that had all magnetic force alone,
To draw and fasten sundered parts in one;
She whom wise nature had invented then
When she observed that every sort of men
Did in their voyage in this world's sea stray,   225
And needed a new compass for their way;
She that was best, and first original

1. I.e., the rebel angels who fell from heaven with Satan, and became demons.
2. For a similar account of the way man's fall corrupted the physical universe, see *Paradise Lost* 10.706 ff.
3. I.e., the world's day began with the darkness of sin.
4. Women giving birth after the age of 50 were supposed to produce feeble or defective children.
5. The Polish astronomer Copernicus, of the 16th century, and the Italian Galileo of the 17th, led the argument of the "new philosophy" that the sun, not the earth, is the center of the cosmos as they defined it. Among other things, this new theory contradicted the notion that a realm of fire surrounded the earth beyond the air.
6. "Wit": intellect. "Spent": exhausted.
7. Galileo's first accounts of his telescopic observations were published in 1610, intensifying speculation on the perennial question whether there are other inhabited worlds. "Atomies": atoms.
8. I.e., all traditional relationships.
9. Has become.
1. The fabulous phoenix was supposed to be unique, i.e., there was only one phoenix on earth at any one time. The loss of relation leaves each man thinking he is unique of his "kind."

Of all fair copies, and the general
Steward to Fate;[2] she whose rich eyes and breast
Gilt the West Indies, and perfumed the East;[3]   230
Whose having breathed in this world did bestow
Spice on those isles, and bade them still smell so,
And that rich Indie which doth gold inter
Is but as single money,[4] coined from her;
She to whom this world must itself refer   235
As suburbs,[5] or the microcosm of her,
She, she is dead; she's dead: when thou know'st this,
Thou know'st how lame a cripple this world is.
And learn'st thus much by our anatomy,
That this world's general sickness doth not lie   240
In any humor,[6] or one certain part;
But, as thou sawest it rotten at the heart,
Thou seest a hectic[7] fever hath got hold
Of the whole substance, not to be controlled,
And that thou hast but one way not to admit   245
The world's infection, to be none of it.[8]

* * *

1611

From Holy Sonnets[1]

1

Thou hast made me, and shall thy work decay?
Repair me now, for now mine end doth haste;
I run to death, and death meets me as fast,
And all my pleasures are like yesterday.
I dare not move my dim eyes any way,   5
Despair behind, and death before doth cast
Such terror, and my feeble flesh doth waste
By sin in it, which it towards hell doth weigh.
Only thou art above, and when towards thee
By thy leave I can look, I rise again;   10

2. Fate or Providence disposes of the world, but
"she" was chief officer ("steward") under Fate.
3. The West Indies (i.e., the Americas) were a
source of gold, the East Indies a source of spices
and perfumes.
4. Small change.
5. She is the center of everything, the world a mere
appendage or suburb.
6. The four bodily "humors" or dispositions combined to make up a temperament; when they were
badly tempered, a person was sick. So with the
world.
7. Consumptive.

8. I.e., the world.
1. Donne's religious poetry is collectively known
as the *Divine Poems*. Among these, the largest group
is that of the 19 *Holy Sonnets*. Like others of
Donne's poems, these sonnets reflect his interest
in the formal meditative exercises of the Jesuits—
though Donne began writing them around 1609,
at least a decade after leaving the Catholic church.
    Our selections are numbered as in Sir Herbert
Grierson's influential edition (1912), since it is his
numbers that the sonnets usually go by; but there
is no reason to suppose that this is the order Donne
intended.

But our old subtle foe so tempteth me
That not one hour myself I can sustain.
Thy grace may wing me to prevent his art,
And thou like adamant draw mine iron heart.[2]

                                                              1635

5

I am a little world made cunningly
Of elements, and an angelic sprite;[1]
But black sin hath betrayed to endless night
My world's both parts, and O, both parts must die.
You which beyond that heaven which was most high   5
Have found new spheres, and of new lands can write,[2]
Pour new seas in mine eyes, that so I might
Drown my world with my weeping earnestly,
Or wash it if it must be drowned no more.[3]
But O, it must be burnt! Alas, the fire   10
Of lust and envy have burnt it heretofore,
And made it fouler; let their flames retire,
And burn me, O Lord, with a fiery zeal
Of thee and thy house, which doth in eating heal.[4]

                                                              1635

7

At the round earth's imagined corners,[1] blow
Your trumpets, angels; and arise, arise
From death, you numberless infinities
Of souls, and to your scattered bodies go:
All whom the flood did, and fire shall, o'erthrow,   5
All whom war, dearth, age, agues, tyrannies,
Despair, law, chance hath slain, and you whose eyes
Shall behold God, and never taste death's woe.[2]
But let them sleep, Lord, and me mourn a space;
For, if above all these, my sins abound,   10
'Tis late to ask abundance of thy grace
When we are there. Here on this lowly ground,
Teach me how to repent; for that's as good
As if thou hadst sealed my pardon with thy blood.

                                                              1633

2. "Wing": give wings to. "Prevent": forestall.
"Adamant": loadstone.
1. Both body and soul—the former made of elements, the latter an "angelic sprite" (spirit).
2. Astronomers and explorers are to find new oceans for tears to weep or waters to wash away the poet's sins.
3. After Noah's experience, God promised (Genesis 9.11) never to flood the earth again.

4. See Psalm 69.9: "For the zeal of thine house hath eaten me up." The passage involves three sorts of flame—those of the Last Judgment; those of lust and envy; and those of zeal, which alone save.
1. Compare Revelation 7.1: "I saw four angels standing on the four corners of the earth. . . ."
2. I.e., those who will be alive at the Second Coming.

9

If poisonous minerals, and if that tree
Whose fruit threw death on else-immortal us,
If lecherous goats, if serpents envious
Cannot be damned, alas! why should I be?
Why should intent or reason, born in me,   5
Make sins, else equal, in me more heinous?
And, mercy being easy and glorious
To God, in his stern wrath why threatens he?
But who am I that dare dispute with thee
O God? Oh,[1] of thine only worthy blood   10
And my tears, make a heavenly Lethean[2] flood,
And drown in it my sin's black memory.
That thou remember them some claim as debt;
I think it mercy if thou wilt forget.

                                                    1633

10

Death, be not proud, though some have callèd thee
Mighty and dreadful, for thou art not so;
For those whom thou think'st thou dost overthrow
Die not, poor Death, nor yet canst thou kill me.
From rest and sleep, which but thy pictures be,   5
Much pleasure; then from thee much more must flow,
And soonest our best men with thee do go,
Rest of their bones, and soul's delivery.[1]
Thou art slave to fate, chance, kings, and desperate men,
And dost with poison, war, and sickness dwell,   10
And poppy[2] or charms can make us sleep as well
And better than thy stroke; why swell'st thou then?[3]
One short sleep past, we wake eternally
And death shall be no more; Death, thou shalt die.

                                                    1633

13

What if this present were the world's last night?
Mark in my heart, O soul, where thou dost dwell,
The picture of Christ crucified, and tell
Whether that countenance can thee affright.
Tears in his eyes quench the amazing light,   5

---

1. The 1st edition punctuates as follows: "thee? /
O God, oh!"
2. In classical mythology, the waters of the river
Lethe in the underworld caused total forgetfulness.

1. I.e., to find rest for their bones and freedom
("delivery") for their souls.
2. Opium.
3. Why do you puff with pride?

Blood fills his frowns, which from his pierced head fell;
And can that tongue adjudge thee unto hell
Which prayed forgiveness for his foes' fierce spite?
No, no; but as in my idolatry
I said to all my profane[1] mistresses,   10
Beauty of pity, foulness only is
A sign of rigor:[2] so I say to thee,
To wicked spirits are horrid shapes assigned,
This beauteous form assures a piteous mind.

1633

14

Batter my heart, three-personed God; for you
As yet but knock, breathe, shine, and seek to mend;
That I may rise and stand, o'erthrow me, and bend
Your force to break, blow, burn, and make me new.
I, like an usurped town, to another due,   5
Labor to admit you, but O, to no end;
Reason, your viceroy in me, me should defend,
But is captived, and proves weak or untrue.
Yet dearly I love you, and would be loved fain,
But am betrothed unto your enemy.   10
Divorce me, untie or break that knot again;
Take me to you, imprison me, for I,
Except you enthrall me, never shall be free,
Nor ever chaste, except you ravish me.

1633

17

Since she whom I loved hath paid her last debt
To Nature, and to hers, and my good is dead,[1]
And her soul early into heaven ravishèd,
Wholly on heavenly things my mind is set.
Here the admiring her my mind did whet   5
To seek thee, God; so streams do show the head;
But though I have found thee, and thou my thirst hast fed,
A holy thirsty dropsy melts me yet.
But why should I beg more love, whenas thou
Dost woo my soul, for hers offering all thine: 10
And dost not only fear lest I allow
My love to saints and angels, things divine,

---

1. Worldly.
2. Beautiful features are a sign of a gentle disposition, ugliness of the contrary.
1. Donne's wife died in 1617 at the age of 33,

having just borne her 12th child. This rough and
very personal sonnet, and the following one, survive in a single manuscript, which came to light
only in 1892.

But in thy tender jealousy dost doubt
Lest the world, flesh, yea, devil put thee out.[2]

1899

18

Show me, dear Christ, thy spouse so bright and clear.[1]
What! is it she which on the other shore
Goes richly painted? or which, robbed and tore,
Laments and mourns in Germany and here?[2]
Sleeps she a thousand, then peeps up one year?   5
Is she self-truth, and errs? now new, now outwore?
Doth she, and did she, and shall she evermore
On one, on seven, or on no hill appear?[3]
Dwells she with us, or like adventuring knights
First travel we to seek, and then make love?   10
Betray, kind husband, thy spouse to our sights,
And let mine amorous soul court thy mild dove,
Who is most true and pleasing to thee then
When she is embraced and open to most men.[4]

1899

Good Friday, 1613. Riding Westward

Let man's soul be a sphere, and then, in this,
The intelligence that moves, devotion is,[1]
And as the other spheres, by being grown
Subject to foreign motions, lose their own,
And being by others hurried every day,   5
Scarce in a year their natural form[2] obey;
Pleasure or business, so, our souls admit
For their first mover, and are whirled by it.[3]
Hence is 't, that I am carried towards the West

2. Donne seems to imply that God took away Ann More in order to have a monopoly of John Donne's love. The last lines even suggest that the bereaved husband saw his wife as having been a temptation to deadly sin.

1. This sonnet embodies Donne's lifelong distress at the fragmentation of the church ("the bride of Christ"). Whether it also embodies doubts as to the superiority of the Anglican church has been a subject of dispute.

2. I.e., neither the painted woman (the Church of Rome) nor the ravished virgin (the Protestant churches) seems very like a bride. "Robbed and tore" may allude to a military defeat suffered by German Protestants in 1620.

3. The church on seven hills is, inescapably, that of Rome; that "on no hill" could be either the presbyterian church of Geneva or the episcopal church of England, with its head at Canterbury. But what then is the church on one hill that could conceivably be the bride of Christ? It is a crux, not easy of solution.

4. The final lines echo the Song of Solomon (5.2), which was often interpreted as the song of love between Christ and the church: "Open to me, my sister, my love, my dove, my undefiled."

1. As angelic intelligences guide the celestial spheres, so devotion is or should be the guiding principle of man's life.

2. Moving principle.

3. I.e., spheres are deflected from their true orbits by outside influences; so our souls are deflected by business or pleasure.

This day, when my soul's form bends toward the East.   10
There I should see a Sun,[4] by rising, set,
And by that setting endless day beget:
But that Christ on this cross did rise and fall,
Sin had eternally benighted all.
Yet dare I almost be glad I do not see   15
That spectacle, of too much weight for me.
Who sees God's face, that is self-life, must die;[5]
What a death were it then to see God die?
It made his own lieutenant, Nature, shrink;
It made his footstool crack, and the sun wink.[6]   20
Could I behold those hands which span the poles,
And tune[7] all spheres at once, pierced with those holes?
Could I behold that endless height which is
Zenith to us, and t'our antipodes,[8]
Humbled below us? Or that blood which is   25
The seat[9] of all our souls, if not of his,
Make dirt of dust, or that flesh which was worn
By God for his apparel, ragg'd and torn?
If on these things I durst not look, durst I
Upon his miserable mother cast mine eye,   30
Who was God's partner here, and furnished thus
Half of that sacrifice which ransomed us?
Though these things, as I ride, be from mine eye,
They are present yet unto my memory,
For that looks towards them; and thou look'st towards me,   35
O Savior, as thou hang'st upon the tree.
I turn my back to thee but to receive
Corrections, till thy mercies bid thee leave.[1]
O think me worth thine anger; punish me;
Burn off my rusts and my deformity;   40
Restore thine image so much, by thy grace,
That thou may'st know me, and I'll turn my face.

                                                        1633

A Hymn to Christ, at the Author's Last Going into Germany[1]

In what torn ship soever I embark,
That ship shall be my emblem of thy ark;

---

4. The sun-Son pun was an ancient one. Christ, the Son of God, set when he rose on the Cross, and his setting (death) gave rise to the Christian era, with the hope of ultimate immortality.
5. God told Moses, "Thou canst not see my face: for there shall no man see me, and live" (Exodus 33.20).
6. An earthquake and eclipse supposedly accompanied the Crucifixion.
7. Some manuscripts read "turn."

8. "Zenith" is the highest reach of heaven; the "antipodes" are the opposite side of the earth.
9. Center (as of magnetic attraction).
1. Cease.
1. Donne went to Germany in 1619 as chaplain to the Earl of Doncaster. The mission was a diplomatic one, to the king and queen of Bohemia, King James's son-in-law and daughter, who at that time were mainstays of the Protestant cause on the Continent.

What sea soever swallow me, that flood
Shall be to me an emblem of thy blood;
Though thou with clouds of anger do disguise   5
Thy face, yet through that mask I know those eyes,
    Which, though they turn away sometimes, they never
      will despise.[2]

I sacrifice this island unto thee,
And all whom I loved there, and who loved me;
When I have put our seas twixt them and me,   10
Put thou thy sea[3] betwixt my sins and thee.
As the tree's sap doth seek the root below
In winter, in my winter now I go
    Where none but thee, th' eternal root of true love, I
      may know.

Nor thou nor thy religion dost control   15
The amorousness of an harmonious soul,
But thou wouldst have that love thyself; as thou
Art jealous, Lord, so I am jealous now.
Thou lov'st not, till from loving more[4] thou free
My soul; whoever gives, takes liberty;   20
    Oh, if thou car'st not whom I love, alas, thou lov'st not
      me.

Seal then this bill of my divorce to all
On whom those fainter beams of love did fall;
Marry those loves which in youth scattered be
On fame, wit, hopes (false mistresses) to thee.   25
Churches are best for prayer that have least light:
To see God only, I go out of sight,
    And to 'scape stormy days, I choose an everlasting night.

1633

Hymn to God My God, in My Sickness[1]

Since I am coming to that holy room
    Where, with thy choir of saints for evermore,
I shall be made thy music; as I come
    I tune the instrument here at the door,
    And what I must do then, think now before.   5

2. Printed texts break in two parts (an unrhymed
tetrameter and a trimeter) the long last line of each
stanza. Unrhymed lines would be unique in
Donne's poetry, and the manuscripts are unanimous for the "fourteeners" as we print them.
3. An alternate reading is "blood," reemphasizing
the metaphor of lines 3 and 4.

4. From loving elsewhere. The idea is, "To give
me true love, you must take away my freedom to
love anyone else."
1. Though Izaak Walton, Donne's pious biographer, assigns this poem to the last days of his life,
it was probably written in December 1623.

Whilst my physicians by their love are grown
   Cosmographers, and I their map, who lie
Flat on this bed, that by them may be shown
   That this is my southwest discovery[2]
     Per fretum febris,[3] by these straits to die,   10

I joy, that in these straits, I see my West;[4]
   For, though their currents yield return to none,
What shall my West hurt me? As West and East
   In all flat maps (and I am one) are one,
     So death doth touch the resurrection.   15

Is the Pacific Sea my home? Or are
   The Eastern riches? Is Jerusalem?
Anyan,[5] and Magellan, and Gibraltar,
   All straits, and none but straits, are ways to them,
     Whether where Japhet dwelt, or Cham, or Shem.[6]   20

We think that Paradise and Calvary,
   Christ's cross and Adam's tree, stood in one place;
Look, Lord and find both Adams[7] met in me;
   As the first Adam's sweat surrounds my face,
     May the last Adam's blood my soul embrace.   25

So, in his purple wrapped,[8] receive me, Lord;
   By these his thorns give me his other crown;
And, as to others' souls I preached thy word,
   Be this my text, my sermon to mine own:
     Therefore that he may raise the Lord throws down.   30

                                            1635

A Hymn to God the Father[1]

Wilt thou forgive that sin where I begun,
   Which is my sin, though it were done before?[2]
Wilt thou forgive that sin through which I run,
   And do run still, though still I do deplore?
     When thou hast done, thou hast not done,   5
       For I have more.

2. The Strait of Magellan, or something spiritual that is analogous to it.
3. I.e., through the strait of fever.
4. Where the sun sets, hence where life ends.
5. The Bering Strait. Behind these anxious questions lie many ancient speculations about the location of Paradise—which is analogous to Heaven, as the various straits are to death.
6. Japhet, Cham (Ham), and Shem were the three sons of Noah by whom the world was repopulated after the Flood (Genesis 10). The descendants of Japhet were thought to inhabit Europe, those of Ham Africa, and those of Shem Asia.
7. I.e., Adam and Christ.
8. The purple of Christ is his blood.
1. Izaak Walton tells us that this short hymn was written during Donne's illness of 1623. Donne had it set to music and frequently performed by the choir and organist of St. Paul's Cathedral.
2. I.e., through his parents he inherits the original sin of Adam and Eve.

Wilt thou forgive that sin by which I have won
    Others to sin? and made my sin their door?
Wilt thou forgive that sin which I did shun
    A year or two, but wallowed in a score?   10
        When thou hast done, thou hast not done,
            For I have more.

I have a sin of fear, that when I have spun
    My last thread, I shall perish on the shore;
Swear by thy self, that at my death thy Son   15
    Shall shine as he shines now and heretofore;
        And, having done that, thou hast done,
           I fear[3] no more.

1633

From Devotions upon Emergent Occasions[1]

Meditation 4

Medicusque vocatur.
The physician is sent for.[2]

It is too little to call man a little world; except God, man is a diminutive to nothing.[3] Man consists of more pieces, more parts, than the world; than the world doth, nay, than the world is. And if those pieces were extended and stretched out in man as they are in the world, man would be the giant and the world the dwarf; the world but the map, and the man the world. If all the veins in our bodies were extended to rivers, and all the sinews to veins of mines, and all the muscles that lie upon one another to hills, and all the bones to quarries of stones, and all the other pieces to the proportion of those which correspond to them in the world, the air would be too little for this orb of man to move in, the firmament would be but enough for this star. For as the whole world hath nothing to which something in man doth not answer,[4] so hath man many pieces of which the whole world hath no representation. Enlarge this meditation upon this great world, man, so far as to consider the

---

3. An alternative reading is "have."

1. Donne's *Devotions* were written in the aftermath of a serious illness in the winter of 1623—though Donne characteristically writes as if the events of the illness were happening at the moment he describes them. The *Devotions* recount the stages of his disease and recovery; each stage comprises a "meditation upon our human condition," an "expostulation and debatement with God," and a prayer to Him. The book was published almost immediately it was written, and to great effect—the blend of private feeling and public moralizing rendering it particularly accessible to 17th-century readers. And its eloquent, richly metaphorical sentences have provided a title for at least one major modern novel (see Meditation 17).

"Emergent" occasions are those which arise casually or unexpectedly.

2. Donne's Latin epigraphs are followed by his English translations, some of them very free ones indeed.

3. Donne's meditation is built on the Renaissance notion that man is a microcosm, a little world, analogous in every respect to the macrocosm, or big world, outside. But in playing with this notion, Donne paradoxically reverses it, arguing for a moment that man (though without God he is nothing) may be a giant and the world his diminished representation.

4. Correspond.

immensity of the creatures this world produces. Our creatures are our thoughts, creatures that are born giants, that reach from east to west, from earth to heaven, that do not only bestride all the sea and land, but span the sun and firmament at once: my thoughts reach all, comprehend all.

Inexplicable mystery! I their creator am in a close prison, in a sick bed, anywhere, and any one of my creatures, my thoughts, is with the sun, and beyond the sun, overtakes the sun, and overgoes the sun in one pace, one step, everywhere. And then as the other world produces serpents and vipers, malignant and venomous creatures, and worms and caterpillars, that endeavor to devour that world which produces them, and monsters compiled and complicated[5] of divers parents and kinds, so this world, our selves, produces all these in us, in producing diseases and sicknesses of all those sorts; venomous and infectious diseases, feeding and consuming diseases, and manifold and entangled diseases made up of many several ones. And can the other world name so many venomous, so many consuming, so many monstrous creatures, as we can diseases of all these kinds? O miserable abundance, O beggarly riches! How much do we lack of having remedies for every disease when as yet we have not names for them?

But we have a Hercules against these giants, these monsters: that is the physician. He musters up all the forces of the other world to succor this, all nature to relieve man. We have the physician but we are not the physician. Here we shrink in our proportion, sink in our dignity in respect of very mean creatures who are physicians to themselves. The hart that is pursued and wounded, they say, knows an herb which, being eaten, throws off the arrow: a strange kind of vomit.[6] The dog that pursues it, though he be subject to sickness, even proverbially knows his grass that recovers him. And it may be true that the drugger[7] is as near to man as to other creatures; it may be that obvious and present simples, easy to be had, would cure him; but the apothecary is not so near him, nor the physician so near him, as they two are to other creatures. Man hath not that innate instinct to apply these natural medicines to his present danger, as those inferior creatures have. He is not his own apothecary, his own physician, as they are. Call back therefore thy meditation again, and bring it down.[8] What's become of man's great extent and proportion, when himself shrinks himself and consumes himself to a handful of dust? What's become of his soaring thoughts, his compassing thoughts, when himself brings himself to the ignorance, to the thoughtlessness, of the grave? His diseases are his own, but the physician is not; he hath them at home, but he must send for the physician.

---

5. Folded or twisted together.
6. Deer supposedly expelled arrows by eating the herb dittany.

7. Druggist. "Simples": medicinal plants.
8. I.e., apply it to the present situation.

Meditation 17

Nunc lento sonitu dicunt, morieris.
Now this bell tolling softly for another, says to me, Thou must die.

Perchance he for whom this bell[1] tolls may be so ill as that he knows not it tolls for him; and perchance I may think myself so much better than I am, as that they who are about me and see my state may have caused it to toll for me, and I know not that. The church is catholic, universal, so are all her actions; all that she does belongs to all. When she baptizes a child, that action concerns me; for that child is thereby connected to that head which is my head too, and ingrafted into that body[2] whereof I am a member. And when she buries a man, that action concerns me: all mankind is of one author and is one volume; when one man dies, one chapter is not torn out of the book, but translated[3] into a better language; and every chapter must be so translated. God employs several translators; some pieces are translated by age, some by sickness, some by war, some by justice; but God's hand is in every translation, and his hand shall bind up all our scattered leaves again for that library where every book shall lie open to one another. As therefore the bell that rings to a sermon calls not upon the preacher only, but upon the congregation to come, so this bell calls us all; but how much more me, who am brought so near the door by this sickness. There was a contention as far as a suit[4] (in which piety and dignity, religion and estimation, were mingled) which of the religious orders should ring to prayers first in the morning; and it was determined that they should ring first that rose earliest. If we understand aright the dignity of this bell that tolls for our evening prayer, we would be glad to make it ours by rising early, in that application, that it might be ours as well as his whose indeed it is. The bell doth toll for him that thinks it doth; and though it intermit again, yet from that minute that that occasion wrought upon him, he is united to God. Who casts not up his eye to the sun when it rises? but who takes off his eye from a comet when that breaks out? Who bends not his ear to any bell which upon any occasion rings? but who can remove it from that bell which is passing a piece of himself out of this world? No man is an island, entire of itself; every man is a piece of the continent, a part of the main.[5] If a clod be washed away by the sea, Europe is the less, as well as if a promontory were, as well as if a manor of thy friend's or of thine own were. Any man's death diminishes me, because I am involved in mankind; and therefore never send to know for whom the bell tolls; it tolls for thee. Neither can we call this a begging of misery or a borrowing of misery, as though we were not miserable enough of ourselves but must fetch in more from the next house, in

---

1. The "passing bell" for the dying.
2. The church.
3. Punning on the literal sense, "carried across."

4. Controversy which went as far as a lawsuit. "Estimation": self-esteem.
5. Mainland.

taking upon us the misery of our neighbors. Truly it were an excusable covetousness if we did; for affliction is a treasure, and scarce any man hath enough of it. No man hath affliction enough that is not matured and ripened by it, and made fit for God by that affliction. If a man carry treasure in bullion, or in a wedge of gold, and have none coined into current moneys, his treasure will not defray him as he travels. Tribulation is treasure in the nature of it, but it is not current money in the use of it, except we get nearer and nearer our home, heaven, by it. Another man may be sick too, and sick to death, and this affliction may lie in his bowels as gold in a mine and be of no use to him; but this bell that tells me of his affliction digs out and applies that gold to me, if by this consideration of another's danger I take mine own into contemplation and so secure myself by making my recourse to my God, who is our only security.

From *Expostulation* 19

[THE LANGUAGE OF GOD]

My God, my God, thou art a direct God, may I not say a literal God, a God that wouldst be understood literally and according to the plain sense of all that thou sayest. But thou art also (Lord, I intend it to thy glory, and let no profane misinterpreter abuse it to thy diminution), thou art a figurative, a metaphorical God too: a God in whose words there is such a height of figures, such voyages, such peregrinations to fetch remote and precious metaphors, such extensions, such spreadings, such curtains of allegories, such third heavens of hyperboles, so harmonious elocutions, so retired and so reserved expressions, so commanding persuasions, so persuading commandments, such sinews even in thy milk and such things in thy words, as all profane[1] authors seem of the seed of the serpent that creeps; thou art the dove that flies. Oh, what words but thine can express the inexpressible texture and composition of thy word; in which, to one man, that argument that binds his faith to believe that to be the word of God is the reverent simplicity of the word, and to another, the majesty of the word; and in which two men, equally pious, may meet, and one wonder that all should not understand it, and the other as much that any man should. So, Lord, thou givest us the same earth to labor on and to lie in; a house and a grave of the same earth; so, Lord, thou givest us the same word for our satisfaction and for our inquisition,[2] for our instruction and for our admiration too. For there are places that thy servants Jerome and Augustine would scarce believe (when they grew warm by mutual letters) of one another that they understood them, and yet both Jerome and Augustine call upon persons whom they knew to be far weaker than they thought one another

---

1. Secular.
2. Investigation.

(old women and young maids) to read thy Scriptures without confining them to these or those places.[3]

Neither art thou thus a figurative, a metaphorical God, in thy word only but in thy works too. The style of thy works, the phrase of thine actions, is metaphorical. The institution of thy whole worship in the old law was a continual allegory; types[4] and figures overspread all, and figures flowed into figures, and poured themselves out into further figures. Circumcision carried a figure of baptism,[5] and baptism carries a figure of that purity which we shall have in perfection in the New Jerusalem. Neither didst thou speak and work in this language only in the time of the prophets; but since thou spokest in thy son it is so too. How often, how much more often, doth thy son call himself a way and a light and a gate and a vine and bread than the son of God or of man? How much oftener doth he exhibit a metaphorical Christ than a real, a literal? This hath occasioned thine ancient servants, whose delight it was to write after thy copy,[6] to proceed the same way in their expositions of the Scriptures, and in their composing both of public liturgies and of private prayers to thee, to make their accesses to thee in such a kind of language as thou was pleased to speak to them, in a figurative, in a metaphorical language; in which manner I am bold to call the comfort which I receive now in this sickness, in the indication of the concoction[7] and maturity thereof, in certain clouds[8] and residences which the physicians observe, a discovering of land from sea after a long and tempestuous voyage. But wherefore, Oh my God, hast thou presented to us the afflictions and calamities of this life in the name of waters? so often in the name of waters and deep waters and seas of waters? Must we look to be drowned? Are they bottomless, are they boundless? That's not the dialect of thy language; thou hast given a remedy against the deepest water, by water; against the inundation of sin, by baptism; and the first life that thou gavest to any creatures was in waters; therefore thou dost not threaten us with an irremediableness when our affliction is a sea. * * *

1623   1624

---

3. Saints Jerome and Augustine did in fact differ over the proper way of interpreting the Bible, yet encouraged its use by the unlearned.

4. Anticipations, prefigurations. The next sentence exemplifies the common practice of interpreting Scripture by viewing one event or theme as analogically related to another. For a rich and very beautiful poem exemplifying this process, see

Herbert, *The Bunch of Grapes*, p. 1347.

5. Both circumcision and baptism are rites of admission to a religious community.

6. Text.

7. Digestion.

8. "Clouds" are discolorations in fluids. "Residences": an old form of "residues."

From Sermon 76[1]

[*On Falling out of God's Hand*]

* * * when God's hand is bent to strike, "it is a fearful thing to fall into the hands of the living God";[2] but to fall out of the hands of the living God is a horror beyond our expression, beyond our imagination. That God should let my soul fall out of his hand into a bottomless pit and roll an unremovable stone upon it and leave it to that which it finds there (and it shall find that there which it never imagined till it came thither) and never think more of that soul, never have more to do with it; that of that providence of God that studies the life and preservation of every weed and worm and ant and spider and toad and viper there should never, never any beam flow out upon me; that that God who looked upon me when I was nothing and called me when I was not, as though I had been, out of the womb and depth of darkness, will not look upon me now, when though a miserable and a banished and a damned creature, yet I am his creature still and contribute something to his glory even in my damnation; that that God who hath often looked upon me in my foulest uncleanness, and when I had shut out the eye of the day, the sun, and the eye of the night, the taper, and the eyes of all the world with curtains and windows and doors, did yet see me and see me in mercy by making me see that he saw me, and sometimes brought me to a present remorse and (for that time) to a forbearing of that sin, should so turn himself from me to his glorious saints and angels as that no saint nor angel nor Christ Jesus himself should ever pray him to look towards me, never remember[3] him that such a soul there is; that that God who hath so often said to my soul, *Quare morieris?* why wilt thou die? and so often sworn to my soul, *Vivit Dominus*, as the Lord liveth, I would not have thee die but live, will neither let me die nor let me live, but die an everlasting life and live an everlasting death; that that God who, when he could not get into me by standing and knocking, by his ordinary means of entering, by his Word, his mercies, hath applied his judgments and hath shaked the house, this body, with agues and palsies, and set

---

1. The reasons for Donne's popularity as a preacher are clear. His sermons concentrate in often hair-raising (though sometimes hair-splitting) fashion on the fundamental Christian issues of sin, guilt, repentance, death, damnation, and salvation; and (like his poems, which they often illuminatingly parallel) they are personal and particular, rich in learning and curious lore, and dazzling in verbal ingenuity and metaphor. Like the *Devotions*, they are crafted for the most part of sentences that are long, sinuous, and elaborate. And then there was the delivery, which Izaak Walton describes: Donne "preaching the Word so, as showed his own heart was possessed with those very thoughts and joys that he labored to distill into others: a preacher in earnest; weeping sometimes for his auditory,

sometimes with them; always preaching to himself, like an angel from a cloud, but in none; carrying some, as St. Paul was, to heaven in holy raptures, and enticing others by a sacred art and courtship to amend their lives: here picturing a vice so as to make it ugly to those that practiced it; and a virtue so as to make it be beloved, even by those that loved it not; and all this with a most particular grace and an unexpressible addition of comeliness."

The present selection, a purple passage from one of the 160 long sermons that survive, comes from the conclusion of a sermon on the text Mark 16.16: "He that believeth not, shall be damned."

2. Hebrews 10.31.

3. Remind.

this house on fire with fevers and calentures,[4] and frighted the master of
the house, my soul, with horrors and heavy apprehensions and so made
an entrance into me; that that God should lose and frustrate all his own
purposes and practices upon me and leave me and cast me away as
though I had cost him nothing; that this God at last should let this soul
go away as a smoke, as a vapor, as a bubble, and that then this soul
cannot be a smoke, nor a vapor, nor a bubble, but must lie in darkness
as long as the Lord of light is light itself, and never a spark of that light
reach to my soul; what Tophet is not Paradise, what brimstone is not
amber, what gnashing is not a comfort, what gnawing of the worm is
not a tickling, what torment is not a marriage bed to this damnation, to
be secluded eternally, eternally, eternally from the sight of God? * * *

1622?   1640

4. Fever with delirium.

BEN JONSON
1572–1637

1598: *Every Man in his Humor,* Jonson's first published play.
1606: *Volpone.*
1616: Jonson appointed poet laureate; publishes his *Works.*
1629: Decisive failure of *The New Inn.*

Ben Jonson did so many different things in the literary world of the early
seventeenth century, and made use of so many different styles to do them,
that he is difficult to see as a whole person. Actor, playwright, poet and poet
laureate, scholar, critic, translator, man of letters, and head, for the first
time in English, of a literary "school," the so-called "sons of Ben," he was
a giant of a man. Yet we cannot easily take a perspective of him.

Jonson's life was tough and turbulent. The posthumous child of a clergyman, he was stepson to a master bricklayer of Westminster. He was educated at Westminster School by the great classical scholar and antiquarian
William Camden, worked briefly at his stepfather's trade, and then entered
the army. In Flanders, where the Dutch with English help were warring
against the Spaniards, he fought single-handed with one of the enemy before
the massed armies, and killed his man. Returning to England about 1594,
he began to work as an actor and playwright but was drawn from one storm
center to another. He killed a fellow-actor in a duel, and escaped the gallows
only by pleading "benefit of clergy" (i.e., by proving he could read and
write, which entitled him to plead before a more lenient ecclesiastical court).
He was jailed for insulting the Scottish nation at a time when King James
was newly arrived from Scotland. He took furious part in an intricate set of
literary wars with his fellow-playwrights. Having converted to Catholicism,
he was the object of deep suspicion after the Gunpowder Plot of Guy Fawkes

(1605), when the phobia against his religion reached its height. Yet he rode out all these troubles, growing mellower as he grew older (and re-converting to Anglicanism); in his latter years he became the unofficial literary dictator of London, the king's pensioned poet, a favorite around the court, and the good friend of men like Shakespeare, Donne, Francis Beaumont, John Selden, Francis Bacon, dukes, diplomats, and distinguished folk generally. In addition, he engaged the affection of younger men (poets like Robert Herrick, Thomas Carew, and Sir John Suckling, speculative thinkers like Lord Falkland and Sir Kenelm Digby), who delighted to christen themselves "sons of Ben." Sons of Ben provided the nucleus of the entire "Cavalier school" of English poets.

The first of Jonson's great plays was *Every Man in His Humor,* in which Shakespeare acted a leading role. It was also the first of the so-called "comedies of humors," in which the prevailing eccentricities and ruling passions of men (i.e., their "humors") were exposed to satiric deflation. Though Jonson's classical tragedy *Sejanus* (1603) has not been much liked (it is gloomy in mood, static in action, and weighty with antiquarian lore), *Volpone* (1606) and *The Alchemist* (1610) are two supreme satiric comedies of the English stage. Both have been repeatedly "adapted" and "modernized," but even now the original texts are likely to seem more lively and vital than the doctored versions. Meanwhile, starting in 1605, Jonson began writing for the court a series of masques—elaborate semitheatrical displays involving spectacle, allegory, and compliment to the king or queen. Thus he became closely involved with the life of the court, a connection which was formalized in 1616, when he was appointed poet laureate with a substantial pension. In the same year, he published in a splendid volume his collected *Works,* a body of poetry to which he kept adding in the years before his death. Though his later plays were not very successful, he turned out many occasional poems, verse letters, translations, complimentary verses before other poets' volumes—finding in all these different forms a grave, incisive pattern of formal speech through which the reverberations of his immense classical learning make themselves heard.

The bulk of Jonson's poetry falls, without undue strain, into five groups, based mostly on stylistic qualities. He wrote a number of poems of festive ceremony, poems which celebrate those qualities of ordered richness and dignified delight which represent his image of the good life. A poem like *To Penshurst* turns a physical building and its surrounding countryside into an emblem of modest yet noble opulence; the poem *Inviting a Friend to Supper* is an imitation of Horace, yet its tonality is thoroughly English, and the "modest little supper" to which he invites his friend would scandalize a modern weight-watcher. Quite a different side of Jonson's talent is represented by his elegies and epitaphs; they are brief, full, simple poems, such as one could imagine being carved on a marble slab—direct, impersonal, inevitable. Allied to these are his compliments and tributes; often prefixed to his friends' books, but sometimes simple tributes of friendship and admiration, they summarize warmly yet judiciously a man's character and achievement. Jonson the pure poet finds expression in his songs, sometimes occurring in the plays and masques but sometimes standing alone, often intended for musical accompaniment, but generally beautifully melodic, even without it. Finally, Jonson wrote (in imitation of the Roman poet Martial) a great number of epigrams, sometimes lewd, sometimes nasty, occasionally funny. We have largely lost the taste for this sort of thing today, but epigrams were a vital Renaissance genre, and Jonson's profane epigrams can usefully be compared to Crashaw's sacred ones.

Jonson took his calling as a poet with the greatest seriousness, asserting the dignity of the profession with (sometimes) a kind of pedantry and emphasis that contrasts with Shakespeare's extraordinary anonymity. When Jonson published in 1616 his collected works—*The Works of Benjamin Jonson*—it was the first time an English author had been so presumptuous. Yet he succeeded in making the fact of professional authorship somehow respectable; an author like John Dryden, who owed so much to Jonson on stylistic grounds, owed him a social debt as well. His career stood on foundations which Ben, with his pedantry and his pugnacity, was the first to lay down.

Volpone   Though Jonson was reputed a slow composer, *Volpone* was created in little more than a month, and performed by the King's Men in the spring of 1606. It was a great success, and despite occasional lapses has held the stage ever since. (A Broadway adaptation, under the title of *Sly Fox*, transferred the action to San Francisco in the 1890s, but retained most of the original play's outlines; an adaptation for the French cinema, made by Stefan Zweig and featuring Harry Baur and Louis Jouvet, is by now technically old-fashioned but still dramatically superb.) The text was printed separately in a quarto of 1607 and reprinted with a few minor changes amid the rest of Jonson's *Works* in the Folio of 1616 as well as the posthumous Folio of 1640. Our modernized text includes a number of stage directions first introduced by William Gifford in his edition of 1816, and a few more added by the present editors for the better understanding of the action.

Jonson's central topic—sordid greed deluded by ruthless guile—dictated the tonality of his play, which is cruelly funny. Classical satire, in the form of passages in Horace, Juvenal, Petronius, and Lucian, provided him with hints toward the basic action of legacy-chasing, and the reputation of Venice as a worldly, commercial, cosmopolitan center served to darken his comedy. But his own fondness for unscrupulous rascals, combined with deep indignation at the spreading prostitution of life to commercial interest, provided the real dynamic of the play. Because they prey on loathsome forms of life, Jonson's sharks are admired quite as much as they are despised; the murky social waters through which they cruise are not so ambiguous.

The play makes use of many traditional elements. Surely the medieval legend of Reynard the Fox contributed to the pervasive animal imagery; and figures like Mosca the wily parasite, Voltore the shyster lawyer, the avaricious dotard Corbaccio, and voluble Lady Would-Be have recognizable analogues in classical literature. Some characters and scenes (such as that in which Volpone, disguised as a mountebank, woos Celia at her window) reflect Jonson's knowledge of Italian *commedia dell'arte*. *Volpone's* mode of cloaking serious moral points in voluminous comic exaggeration was practiced by many previous Renaissance authors, such as Erasmus *(The Praise of Folly)* and Rabelais *(Gargantua and Pantagruel)*. Yet nowhere does an author triumph more splendidly over his materials than in *Volpone:* the play is instinct with a spirit of mischief and fun, a delight in the con game for its own sake, that renders all talk of sources and traditions very secondary indeed.

"The love of money is the root of all evil"—it had been the steady theme of preachers and teachers for thousands of years. But for Jonson, as for

Shakespeare and Donne and for Thomas More before them all, the commercializing of life that began with the rise of a money economy and the development of an ethic dominated by self-interest was particularly disturbing. Like his fellows, Jonson protested in *Volpone* the inhumanity, not just of greedy men, but of greedy laws—laws made by the greedy to protect the acquisitions of the greedy. In many ways the state of Venice is shown, in *Volpone*, to be a worse criminal than the criminals it prosecutes; and Jonson's vigorous social morality would not have rejected the implication that what Venice is in the play, England is about to become, in the city of London, the year of our lord 1606.

Volpone

or
The Fox

The Persons of the Play[1]

VOLPONE, *a magnifico*
MOSCA, *his parasite*
VOLTORE, *an advocate*
CORBACCIO, *an old gentleman*
CORVINO, *a merchant*
BONARIO, *son to Corbaccio*
SIR POLITIC WOULD-BE, *a knight*
PEREGRINE, *a gentleman traveler*
NANO, *a dwarf*
CASTRONE, *an eunuch*
ANDROGYNO, *an hermaphrodite*

GREGE (*or Mob*)

COMMENDATORI, *officers of justice*
MERCATORI, *three merchants*
AVOCATORI, *four magistrates*
NOTARIO, *the register*

LADY WOULD-BE, SIR POLITIC'S *Wife*
CELIA, CORVINO'S *Wife*
SERVITORI, *Servants, two* WAITING-WOMEN, &c.

---

1. Most of the names are Italian, and in that language many of them signify animals. Volpone: "fox." "Magnifico" is not a formal title; it simply means "gentleman." Mosca: "fly." The figure of the parasite implies scavenging, as well as fawning dependence. The client-patron relationship in ancient Rome fostered parasitical dependents, and Jonson saw something similar, not only around the English court, but around the big money men of London city. Voltore: "vulture." Corbaccio: "raven." Corvino: "crow." Bonario: "good-natured." Sir Politic Would-be: in the 17th century the word "politic" carried overtones of devious and subtle calculation. His name spells out, almost too explicitly, Sir Politic's character; and in its abbreviation ("Pol") suggests further the parrot he is. Peregrine: in English, "a falcon," but the word also associates with "pilgrim," i.e., "traveler." Nano: "dwarf." Castrone: "gelding." Androgyno: from the Greek, "man-woman," i.e., "hermaphrodite." Grege: from the Latin, "mob" or "crowd." Commendatori: a not very distinguished title of honor: Jonson assigns them a function akin to sergeants or marshals of a court. Mercatori: "merchants." Avocatori: properly, in Italian, "prosecutors"; Jonson makes them judges. Notario: "recorder." Celia: literally, "heavenly."

THE SCENE, Venice

The Argument[2]

Volpone, childless, rich, feigns sick, despairs,
Offers his state to hopes of several heirs,
Lies languishing; his parasite receives
Presents of all, assures, deludes; then weaves
Other cross plots, which ope themselves, are told.   5
New tricks for safety are sought; they thrive: when bold,
Each tempts the other again, and all are sold.[3]

Prologue

Now, luck yet send us, and a little wit
    Will serve to make our play hit;
According to the palates of the season,
    Here is rhyme, not empty of reason.
This we were bid to credit from our poet,   5
    Whose true scope, if you would know it,
In all his poems still hath been this measure,
    To mix profit with your pleasure;[4]
And not as some, whose throats their envy failing,
    Cry hoarsely, All he writes is railing;[5]   10
And when his plays come forth, think they can flout them,
    With saying, He was a year about them.
To these there needs no lie[6] but this his creature,
    Which was, two months since, no feature;
And though he dares give them five lives to mend it,   15
    'Tis known, five weeks fully penned it,
From his own hand, without a coadjutor,
    Novice, journey man,[7] or tutor.
Yet thus much I can give you as a token
    Of his play's worth: no eggs are broken,   20
Nor quaking custards with fierce teeth affrighted,[8]
    Wherewith your rout[9] are so delighted;
Nor hales he in a gull,[1] old ends reciting,
    To stop gaps in his loose writing;
With such a deal of monstrous and forced action,   25
    As might make Bedlam[2] a faction;
Nor made he his play for jests stolen from each table,
    But makes jests to fit his fable;

2. A capsule summary of the plot.
3. Deceived.
4. That the task of the poet is to mix profit with pleasure was an idea dating back to Horace's *Art of Poetry*, lines 343–44.
5. Abuse, invective.
6. "To give the lie" was to deny flatly; we would use here the word "disproof."
7. Piece worker, apprentice, or assistant.
8. Comic routines—thrown eggs or custard pies—

which had popular success on the low Elizabethan stage. A giant custard pie was also served at city feasts inaugurating the Lord Mayor; sometimes an attendant fool jumped into it.
9. Mob, common herd.
1. Buffoon. Elizabethans were fond of wise saws and ancient adages, and often put characters into plays who recited them.
2. Bethlehem Hospital, the madhouse.

And so presents quick comedy refined,
　　As best critics have designed;   30
The laws of time, place, persons he observeth,[3]
　　From no needful rule he swerveth.
All gall and copperas from his ink he draineth,
　　Only a little salt remaineth,[4]
Wherewith he'll rub your cheeks till, red with laughter,   35
　　They shall look fresh a week after.

Act 1

SCENE 1. *A room in* VOLPONE's *house.*

[*Enter* VOLPONE *and* MOSCA.]

VOLPONE. Good morning to the day; and next, my gold!
　　Open the shrine,[1] that I may see my saint.

　　　　[MOSCA *withdraws the curtain, and discovers piles of gold, plate,*
　　　　jewels, &c.]

Hail the world's soul, and mine! more glad than is
The teeming earth to see the longed-for sun
Peep through the horns of the celestial ram,[2]   5
Am I, to view thy splendor darkening his;
That lying here, amongst my other hoards,
Show'st like a flame by night, or like the day
Struck out of chaos, when all darkness fled
Unto the center. O thou son of Sol,[3]   10
But brighter than thy father, let me kiss,
With adoration, thee, and every relic
Of sacred treasure in this blessèd room.
Well did wise poets by thy glorious name
Title that age which they would have the best;[4]   15
Thou being the best of things, and far transcending
All style of joy, in children, parents, friends,
Or any other waking dream on earth.
Thy looks when they to Venus did ascribe,

---

3. The so-called Aristotelian unities, actually imposed as prescripts by the Renaissance critics Castelvetro and Scaliger, placed limits of time and place on a dramatic action; the limitation on persons was less strict.
4. Gall and copperas (i.e., green vitriol) are traditional ingredients of ink: both are corrosive and bitter to the taste. Salt, though not an ingredient of ink, is a classical metaphor for wit, that which gives flavor to speech or writing.
1. Though there was no proscenium curtain in the Elizabethan theater, such as rises on a modern play, there was a small curtained inner area, and that is what Mosca unveils. By "the world's soul and mine" Volpone means the soul of the universe and his own immortal essence, both identi-

fied with gold.
2. In the spring. The sun peeps through the horns of the Ram (Aries) late in March, and (as the opening of *The Canterbury Tales* reminds us) is halfway through the zodiacal sign in early April.
3. The circle of a gold coin is compared to the created cosmos, i.e., the world with sun, moon, and stars, created by god in Genesis 1. When the sun illumined the outer universe, darkness "fled to the center," i.e., to hell, underground. Gold is said to be "the son of Sol" (the sun) because in Renaissance lore, the fertilizing rays of the sun, penetrating the ground, were supposed responsible for developing the "seeds of gold" naturally found there.
4. The "Age of Gold."

They should have given her twenty thousand Cupids,[5]　　　20
Such are thy beauties and our loves! Dear saint,
Riches, the dumb god, that givest all men tongues,
That canst do nought, and yet mak'st men do all things;
The price of soul; even hell, with thee to boot,
Is made worth heaven. Thou art virtue, fame,　　　25
Honor and all things else. Who can get thee,
He shall be noble, valiant, honest, wise—

MOSCA. And what he will, sir. Riches are in fortune
A greater good than wisdom is in nature.

VOLPONE. True, my belovèd Mosca. Yet I glory　　　30
More in the cunning purchase[6] of my wealth
Than in the glad possession, since I gain
No common way; I use no trade, no venture;
I wound no earth with plowshares, fat no beasts
To feed the shambles; have no mills for iron,　　　35
Oil, corn, or men, to grind them into powder;[7]
I blow no subtle glass, expose no ships
To threat'nings of the furrow-facèd sea;
I turn no moneys[8] in the public bank,
Nor usure private—

MOSCA.　　　　　　No, sir, nor devour　　　40
Soft prodigals. You shall have some will swallow
A melting heir as glibly as your Dutch
Will pills of butter, and ne'er purge[9] for it;
Tear forth the fathers of poor families
Out of their beds, and coffin them alive　　　45
In some kind clasping prison, where their bones
May be forth-coming when the flesh is rotten.
But your sweet nature doth abhor these courses;
You loathe the widow's or the orphan's tears
Should wash your pavements, or their piteous cries　　　50
Ring in your roofs, and beat the air for vengeance.

VOLPONE. Right, Mosca; I do loathe it.

MOSCA.　　　　　　　　And besides, sir,
You are not like the thresher that doth stand
With a huge flail, watching a heap of corn,
And, hungry, dares not taste the smallest grain,　　　55
But feeds on mallows and such bitter herbs;
Nor like the merchant who hath filled his vaults
With Romagnìa and rich Candian wines,

5. Lines 16–20 are translated from a fragment of Euripides; Seneca tells us that when they were pronounced onstage, the audience was so indignant that it would allow the play to continue only after Euripides provided assurance that the speakers would be badly punished in the course of the play. A traditional epithet of Venus is "golden"; but Volpone is not satisfied with her minting a single golden boy; he wants a lot of them.

6. I.e., acquisition.

7. As Jonson wrote, household industries were just starting to be converted, in a few places, to factory industries run by water power. Glass was a Venetian specialty, in Jonson's day as now, but in England it was just starting to be used for glazing.

8. I.e., take no interest. Banking and money lending were more important in Venice, where long voyages were common mercantile practice, than in England.

9. Suffer indigestion. Many jokes were made in the 17th century on the Dutch appetite for butter. Loan sharks swallowed up heirs by lending them money at exorbitant rates against their future inheritance.

Yet drinks the lees of Lombard's vinegar.[1]
You will not lie in straw, whilst moths and worms   60
Feed on your sumptuous hangings and soft beds.
You know the use of riches, and dare give now
From that bright heap, to me, your poor observer,
Or to your dwarf, or your hermaphrodite,
Your eunuch, or what other household trifle   65
Your pleasure allows maintenance—

VOLPONE.   Hold thee, Mosca, [*Gives him money.*]
Take of my hand; thou strik'st on truth in all,
And they are envious term thee parasite.
Call forth my dwarf, my eunuch, and my fool,
And let them make me sport. [*Exit* MOSCA.] What should I do,   70
But cocker up[2] my genius and live free
To all delights my fortune calls me to?
I have no wife, no parent, child, ally,
To give my substance to, but whom I make
Must be my heir; and this makes men observe me.   75
This draws new clients daily to my house,
Women and men of every sex and age,
That bring me presents, send me plate, coin, jewels,
With hope that when I die (which they expect
Each greedy minute) it shall then return   80
Tenfold upon them; whilst some, covetous
Above the rest, seek to engross me whole,[3]
And counter-work the one unto the other,
Contend in gifts, as they would seem in love.
All which I suffer, playing with their hopes,   85
And am content to coin them into profit,
And look upon their kindness, and take more,
And look on that; still bearing them in hand,
Letting the cherry knock against their lips,
And draw it by their mouths, and back again.[4]—How now!   90

SCENE 2

[*Enter* MOSCA *with* NANO, ANDROGYNO, *and* CASTRONE.]

NANO. *Now, room for fresh gamesters, who do will you to know,*
    They do bring you neither play nor university show;
And therefore do entreat you, that whatsoever they rehearse,
    May not fare a whit the worse, for the false pace of the verse.[5]
If you wonder at this, you will wonder more ere we pass,   5

1. Romagnia was a sweet wine from Greece; Candian is wine from Crete (Candia). During the Renaissance good wine was thought to come from the eastern Mediterranean, or else from Spain (sack and canary). French and Italian wines ("Lombard's vinegar") were not much appreciated, and the "lees" (dregs) were of course the worst part of any bottle.
2. Pamper, indulge.
3. An engrosser bought up an entire crop of grain,

held it for hard times, then sold it at exorbitant prices.
4. "Chop-cherry" is a country game in which a cherry hung from a string is dangled before a player who tries to catch it with his teeth.
5. This little interlude tells us something about the tastes of the man for whom it is performed. The loose, jogtrot meter that the characters recite is reminiscent of the vices in the old morality plays.

> *For know, here[6] is enclosed the soul of Pythagoras,*
> *That juggler divine, as hereafter shall follow;*
> > *Which soul, fast and loose, sir, came first from Apollo,*
> *And was breathed into Aethalides,[7] Mercurius his son,*
> > *Where it had the gift to remember all that ever was done,*   10
> *From thence it fled forth, and made quick transmigration*
> > *To goldy-locked Euphorbus,[8] who was killed in good fashion*
> *At the siege of old Troy by the cuckold of Sparta.*
> > *Hermotimus was next (I find it in my charta)[9]*
> *To whom it did pass, where no sooner it was missing,*   15
> > *But with one Pyrrhus of Delos it learned to go a-fishing;*
> *And thence did it enter the sophist of Greece.*
> > *From Pythagore, she went into a beautiful piece*
> *Hight Aspasia, the meretrix;[1] and the next toss of her*
> > *Was again of a whore she became a philosopher,*   20
> *Crates the cynic,[2] as itself doth relate it;*
> > *Since, kings, knights, and beggars, knaves, lords, and fools gat it,*
> *Besides ox and ass, camel, mule, goat, and brock,[3]*
> > *In all which it hath spoke, as in the cobbler's cock.*
> *But I come not here to discourse of that matter,*   25
> > *Or his one, two, or three, or his great oath, BY QUATER!*
> *His musics, his trigon, his golden thigh,[4]*
> > *Or his telling how elements shift; but I*
> *Would ask how of late thou hast suffered translation,*
> > *And shifted thy coat in these days of reformation?*   30

ANDROGYNO. *Like one of the reformed, a fool, as you see,*
   Counting all old doctrine heresy.

NANO. *But not on thine own forbid meats hast thou ventured?*

ANDROGYNO. *On fish, when first a Carthusian I entered.[5]*

NANO. *Why, then thy dogmatical silence hath left thee?*   35

ANDROGYNO. *Of that an obstreperous lawyer bereft me.[6]*

NANO. *O wonderful change! When sir lawyer forsook thee,*
   For Pythagore's sake, what body then took thee?

ANDROGYNO. *A good dull mule.*

NANO.   *And how! by that means*

---

6. He points at Androgyno. The Greek philosopher Pythagoras put forward the doctrine of transmigration of souls, and fantastic lineages were a frequent comic exercise in the Renaissance. Nano's comic story is copied from the life of Pythagoras by Diogenes Laertius.

7. Herald of the Argonauts.

8. Trojan hero, killed by Menelaus, "the cuckold of Sparta"; Pythagoras specifically claimed to have been Euphorbus, and to recall the event.

9. Hermotimus is indeed mentioned in Nano's "charta," i.e., the text of Diogenes Laertius, but hardly anywhere else. Pyrrhus of Delos is an equally obscure figure, a fisherman mentioned only in Diogenes. The "sophist of Greece" is Pythagoras himself.

1. Whore; but Aspasia was simply the mistress of Pericles.

2. Crates was a philosopher of the Cynic school, a follower of Diogenes who professed a particularly bitter brand of scepticism.

3. Badger. Lucian's comic dialogue, *Gallus, or the Cock*, which reproduces much of this material about Pythagoras, is a dialogue between a cobbler and a chicken.

4. Pythagorean theories about music and numerology, the Pythagorean theorem about right triangles, and the myth that Pythagoras had a golden thigh are glanced at here. A trigon is a triangle; the oath "by Quater" (four) is reported in Plutarch, *On the Sayings of the Philosophers.*

5. As a Carthusian monk (of a particularly strict sect), he learned to eat fish, which as a Pythagorean was forbidden to him.

6. Having taken a vow of silence as a Carthusian, he became a lawyer and learned to blabber.

Thou wert brought to allow of the eating of beans?[7]   40
ANDROGYNO. *Yes.*
NANO.   *But from the mule into whom didst thou pass?*
ANDROGYNO. *Into a very strange beast, by some writers called an ass;*
By others, a precise, pure, illuminate brother,[8]
  Of those devour flesh, and sometimes one another;
And will drop you forth a libel, or a sanctified lie,   45
  Betwixt every spoonful of a nativity-pie.[9]
NANO. *Now quit thee, for heaven, of that profane nation,*
  And gently report thy next transmigration.
ANDROGYNO. *To the same that I am.*
NANO.   *A creature of delight,*
  And, what is more than a fool, an hermaphrodite!   50
Now, prithee, sweet soul, in all thy variation,
  Which body wouldst thou choose, to take up thy station?
ANDROGYNO. *Troth, this I am in, even here would I tarry.*
NANO. *'Cause here the delight of each sex thou canst vary?*
ANDROGYNO. *Alas, those pleasures be stale and forsaken;*   55
  No, 'tis your fool wherewith I am so taken,
The only one creature that I can call blessed;[1]
  For all other forms I have proved most distressed.
NANO. *Spoke true, as thou wert in Pythagoras still.*
  This learned opinion we celebrate will,   60
Fellow eunuch, as behooves us, with all our wit and art,
  To dignify that whereof ourselves are so great and special a part.
VOLPONE. Now, very, very pretty! Mosca, this
  Was thy invention?
MOSCA.   If it please my patron,
  Not else.
VOLPONE. It doth, good Mosca,
MOSCA.   Then it was, sir.   65

  [NANO *and* CASTRONE *sing.*][2]

            Fools, they are the only nation
            Worth men's envy or admiration;
            Free from care or sorrow-taking,
            Selves and others merry making,
            All they speak or do is sterling,   70
            Your fool he is your great man's darling,
            And your ladies' sport and pleasure;
            Tongue and bauble are his treasure.
            E'en his face begetteth laughter,
            And he speaks truth free from slaughter;   75

7. Pythagoras forbade the eating of beans. All these prohibitions and special observances were supposed to have occult or mystical meaning.
8. All these adjectives would be understood as pointing at the Puritans, for whom Jonson had a standing aversion.
9. The Puritans did not like the old word "Christmas" because it included the "idolatrous" word "mass," so they began using the neutral word "Nativity," which Jonson here derides.
1. Jonson is drawing here on one of the wellsprings of Renaissance thought, Erasmus's mock-oration, *The Praise of Folly.*
2. The song is a patchwork of passages from Erasmus.

He's the grace of every feast,
And sometimes the chiefest guest;
Hath his trencher[3] *and his stool.*
When wit waits upon the fool,
 O, who would not be   80
 He, he, he?   *[Knocking without.]*
VOLPONE. Who's that? Away!   *[Exeunt* NANO *and* CASTRONE.*]*
     Look, Mosca.
MOSCA. Fool, begone!   *[Exit* ANDROGYNO.*]*
   'Tis Signor Voltore, the advocate;
 I know him by his knock.
VOLPONE.   Fetch me my gown,
 My furs, and night-caps; say my couch is changing,
 And let him entertain himself awhile   85
 Without i' the gallery. *[Exit* MOSCA.*]* Now, now my clients
 Begin their visitation! Vulture, kite,
 Raven, and gor-crow, all my birds of prey[4]
 That think me turning carcass, now they come;
 I am not for them yet.

  [Re-enter MOSCA, *with the gown, &c.]*

     How now? The news?   90
MOSCA. A piece of plate,[5] sir.
VOLPONE.   Of what bigness?
MOSCA.   Huge,
 Massy, and antique, with your name inscribed,
 And arms engraven.
VOLPONE.   Good! and not a fox
 Stretched on the earth, with fine delusive sleights 95
 Mocking a gaping crow?[6] ha, Mosca!
MOSCA.   Sharp, sir.
VOLPONE. Give me my furs.   *[Puts on his sick dress.]*
    Why dost thou laugh so, man?
MOSCA. I cannot choose, sir, when I apprehend
 What thoughts he has without now, as he walks:
 That this might be the last gift he should give;
 That this would fetch you; if you died today,   100
 And gave him all, what he should be tomorrow;
 What large return would come of all his ventures;
 How he should worshipped be, and reverenced;
 Ride with his furs and foot cloths;[7] waited on
 By herds of fools and clients; have clear way   105
 Made for his mule, as lettered as himself;

---

3. Dish.

4. Volpone foresees his visitors precisely in the order they come: Lady Politic is the kite, Corvino the gorcrow ("gor": filth). They are not, however, birds of prey, but all carrion eaters.

5. A solid silver platter. In those days, when banks were uncertain and display important, families often put much of their wealth in massive silver dinner-ware.

6. Of the several fox-and-crow stories, the less familiar one, which has the fox feigning death in order to catch the carrion crow, seems to work best here.

7. Ornate tapestries, laid upon the beast, not his rider; the furs would be for the lawyer.

Be called the great and learnèd advocate:
And then concludes, there's nought impossible.
VOLPONE. Yes, to be learnèd, Mosca.
MOSCA.   O, no; rich   110
   Implies it. Hood an ass with reverend purple,
   So you can hide his two ambitious ears,
   And he shall pass for a cathedral doctor.[8]
VOLPONE. My caps, my caps, good Mosca. Fetch him in.
MOSCA. Stay, sir; your ointment for your eyes.
VOLPONE.   That's true;   115
   Dispatch, dispatch![9] I long to have possession
   Of my new present.
MOSCA.   That, and thousands more,
   I hope to see you lord of.
VOLPONE.   Thanks, kind Mosca.
MOSCA. And that, when I am lost in blended dust,
   And hundred such as I am, in succession—   120
VOLPONE. Nay, that were too much, Mosca.
MOSCA.   You shall live,
   Still, to delude these harpies.
VOLPONE.   Loving Mosca!
   'Tis well. My pillow now, and let him enter.   [Exit MOSCA.]
   Now, my feigned cough, my phthisic, and my gout,
   My apoplexy, palsy, and catarrhs,   125
   Help, with your forcèd functions, this my posture,
   Wherein, this three year, I have milked their hopes.
   He comes; I hear him—Uh! [coughing] uh! uh! uh! O—

SCENE 3

[Enter MOSCA, introducing VOLTORE with a piece of plate.]

MOSCA. You still are what you were, sir. Only you,
   Of all the rest, are he commands his love,
   And you do wisely to preserve it thus,
   With early visitation, and kind notes
   Of your good meaning to him, which, I know,   5
   Cannot but come most grateful. Patron! Sir!
   Here's Signor Voltore is come—
VOLPONE. [faintly]   What say you?
MOSCA. Sir, Signor Voltore is come this morning
   To visit you.
VOLPONE.   I thank him.
MOSCA.   And hath brought
   A piece of antique plate, bought of St. Mark,[1]   10
   With which he here presents you.
VOLPONE.   He is welcome.
   Pray him to come more often.

---

8. The power of money to make the stupid wise,
the ugly beautiful, and, in general, black white
had been a satiric commonplace since antiquity.
"Cathedral doctor": a doctor of theology (with the

implication that he's not only the most pompous
but the most stupid of the lot).
9. Hurry.
1. I.e., bought in Saint Mark's square.

MOSCA.   Yes.
VOLTORE.   What says he?
MOSCA. He thanks you, and desires you see him often.
VOLPONE. Mosca.
MOSCA.   My patron?
VOLPONE.   Bring him near, where is he?
   I long to feel his hand.
MOSCA.   The plate is here, sir.   15
VOLTORE. How fare you, sir?
VOLPONE.   I thank you, Signor Voltore.
   Where is the plate? mine eyes are bad.
VOLTORE. [*putting it into his hands*]   I'm sorry
   To see you still thus weak.
MOSCA. [*aside*]   That he's not weaker.
VOLPONE. You are too munificent.
VOLTORE.   No, sir; would to heaven
   I could as well give health to you, as that plate!   20
VOLPONE. You give, sir, what you can; I thank you. Your love
   Hath taste in this, and shall not be unanswered;
   I pray you see me often.
VOLTORE.   Yes, I shall, sir.
VOLPONE. Be not far from me.
MOSCA.   Do you observe that, sir?
VOLPONE. Hearken unto me still; it will concern you.   25
MOSCA. You are a happy man, sir; know your good.
VOLPONE. I cannot now last long—
MOSCA.   You are his heir, sir.
VOLTORE. Am I?
VOLPONE.   I feel me going; Uh! uh! uh! uh!
   I'm sailing to my port, Uh! uh! uh! uh!
   And I am glad I am so near my haven.   30
MOSCA. Alas, kind gentleman! Well, we must all go—
VOLTORE. But, Mosca—
MOSCA.   Age will conquer.
VOLTORE.   Pray thee, hear me:
   Am I inscribed his heir for certain?
MOSCA.   Are you!
   I do beseech you, sir, you will vouchsafe
   To write me in your family.[2] All my hopes   35
   Depend upon your worship. I am lost,
   Except the rising sun do shine on me.
VOLTORE. It shall both shine and warm thee, Mosca.
MOSCA.   Sir,
   I am a man that have not done your love
   All the worst offices.[3] Here I wear your keys,   40
   See all your coffers and your caskets locked,
   Keep the poor inventory of your jewels,
   Your plate and moneys; am your steward, sir,
   Husband[4] your goods here.

2. I.e., inscribe me on the list of your servants.   4. Safeguard.
3. Services.

VOLTORE.   But am I sole heir?
MOSCA. Without a partner, sir; confirmed this morning.   45
   The wax is warm yet, and the ink scarce dry
   Upon the parchment.
VOLTORE.   Happy, happy me!
   By what good chance, sweet Mosca?
MOSCA.   Your desert, sir;
   I know no second cause.
VOLTORE.   Thy modesty
   Is loath to know it; well, we shall requite it.   50
MOSCA. He ever liked your course, sir; that first took him.
   I oft have heard him say how he admired
   Men of your large profession, that could speak
   To every cause, and things mere contraries,
   Till they were hoarse again, yet all be law;   55
   That with most quick agility could turn
   And return; make knots, and undo them;
   Give forkèd counsel;[5] take provoking gold
   On either hand, and put it up. These men,
   He knew, would thrive with their humility.   60
   And, for his part, he thought he should be blessed
   To have his heir of such a suffering spirit,
   So wise, so grave, of so perplexed a tongue,
   And loud withal, that would not wag, nor scarce
   Lie still, without a fee; when every word   65
   Your worship but lets fall is a sequin!—[6]

                                      [Knocking without.]

   Who's that? One knocks; I would not have you seen, sir.
   And yet—pretend you came and went in haste;
   I'll fashion an excuse—and, gentle sir,
   When you do come to swim in golden lard,   70
   Up to the arms in honey, that your chin
   Is born up stiff with fatness of the flood,
   Think on your vassal; but remember me:
   I have not been your worst of clients.
VOLTORE.   Mosca—
MOSCA. When will you have your inventory brought, sir?   75
   Or see a copy of the will? *[Knocking again.]* Anon![7]
   I'll bring them to you, sir. Away, be gone;
   Put business in your face.   *[Exit* VOLTORE.*]*
VOLPONE. *[springing up]*   Excellent Mosca!
   Come hither, let me kiss thee.
MOSCA.   Keep you still, sir.
   Here is Corbaccio.
VOLPONE   Set the plate away.   80
   The vulture's gone, and the old raven's come.

---

5. Ambiguous, ambivalent advice. This ironic praise of lawyers is probably from Cornelius Agrippa's influential book *On the Uncertainty and Vanity of the Sciences and Arts* (1531).
6. Zecchino, a gold coin.

7. Said in response to a sharp rap at the door; a modern Mosca would say, "Coming!" See the game played by Prince Hal and Poins with a waiter who says nothing but "Anon!" in *1 Henry IV* 2.4.

SCENE 4

MOSCA. Betake you to your silence and your sleep.
  [*Puts the plate away.*] Stand there and multiply. Now shall we see
  A wretch who is indeed more impotent
  Than this can feign to be; yet hopes to hop
  Over his grave. [*Enter* CORBACCIO.] Signor Corbaccio!   5
  You're very welcome, sir.
CORBACCIO.   How does your patron?
MOSCA. Troth, as he did, sir; no amends.
CORBACCIO.   What! mends he?
MOSCA. No, sir, he's rather worse.
CORBACCIO.   That's well. Where is he?
MOSCA. Upon his couch, sir, newly fallen asleep.
CORBACCIO. Does he sleep well?
MOSCA.   No wink, sir, all this night,   10
  Nor yesterday; but slumbers.[8]
CORBACCIO.   Good! He should take
  Some counsel of physicians. I have brought him
  An opiate here, from mine own doctor.
MOSCA. He will not hear of drugs.
CORBACCIO.   Why? I myself
  Stood by while it was made, saw all the ingredients,   15
  And know it cannot but most gently work.
  My life for his, 'tis but to make him sleep.
VOLPONE. [*aside*] Ay, his last sleep, if he would take it.
MOSCA.   Sir,
  He has no faith in physic.
CORBACCIO.   Say you, say you?
MOSCA. He has no faith in physic. He does think   20
  Most of your doctors are the greater danger,
  And worse disease, t' escape. I often have
  Heard him protest that your physician
  Should never be his heir.
CORBACCIO.   Not I his heir?
MOSCA. Not your physician, sir.
CORBACCIO.   O, no, no, no,   25
  I do not mean it.
MOSCA.   No, sir, nor their fees
  He cannot brook; he says, they flay a man,
  Before they kill him.
CORBACCIO.   Right, I do conceive you.
MOSCA. And then they do it by experiment;
  For which the law not only doth absolve them,   30
  But gives them great reward; and he is loath
  To hire his death so.
CORBACCIO.   It is true, they kill
  With as much license as a judge.
MOSCA.   Nay, more;

8. Dozes.

For he but kills, sir, where the law condemns,
And these can kill him too.

CORBACCIO.   Ay, or me,   35
Or any man. How does his apoplex?
Is that strong on him still?

MOSCA.   Most violent.
His speech is broken, and his eyes are set,
His face drawn longer than 'twas wont—

CORBACCIO.   How? How?
Stronger than he was wont?

MOSCA.   No, sir: his face   40
Drawn longer than 'twas wont.

CORBACCIO.   O, good!

MOSCA.   His mouth
Is ever gaping, and his eyelids hang.

CORBACCIO.   Good.

MOSCA. A freezing numbness stiffens all his joints,
And makes the color of his flesh like lead.

CORBACCIO.   'Tis good.

MOSCA. His pulse beats slow and dull.

CORBACCIO.   Good symptoms still.   45

MOSCA. And from his brain—

CORBACCIO.   Ha? How? Not from his brain?

MOSCA. Yes, sir, and from his brain—

CORBACCIO.   I conceive you; good.

MOSCA. Flows a cold sweat, with a continual rheum,
Forth the resolvèd corners of his eyes.

CORBACCIO. Is 't possible? Yet I am better, ha!   50
How does he with the swimming of his head?

MOSCA. O, sir, 'tis past the scotomy;[9] he now
Hath lost his feeling, and hath left to snort.
You hardly can perceive him, that he breathes.

CORBACCIO. Excellent, excellent! Sure I shall outlast him!   55
This makes me young again, a score of years.

MOSCA. I was a-coming for you, sir.

CORBACCIO.   Has he made his will?
What has he given me?

MOSCA.   No, sir.

CORBACCIO.   Nothing? ha!

MOSCA. He has not made his will, sir.

CORBACCIO.   Oh, oh, oh!
What then did Voltore, the lawyer, here?   60

MOSCA. He smelt a carcass, sir, when he but heard
My master was about his testament,
As I did urge him to it for your good.

CORBACCIO. He came unto him, did he? I thought so.

MOSCA. Yes, and presented him this piece of plate.   65

CORBACCIO. To be his heir?

MOSCA.   I do not know, sir.

9. Dizziness, with dimness of sight.

CORBACCIO.   True,
  I know it too.
MOSCA. [*aside*] By your own scale, sir.[1]
CORBACCIO.   Well,
  I shall prevent him yet. See, Mosca, look:
  Here I have brought a bag of bright sequins,
  Will quite weigh down his plate.
MOSCA. [*taking the bag*]   Yea, marry, sir.   70
  This is true physic, this your sacred medicine;
  No talk of opiates, to this great elixir![2]
CORBACCIO. 'Tis *aurum palpabile*,[3] if not *potabile*.
MOSCA. It shall be ministered to him, in his bowl.
CORBACCIO. Ay, do, do, do.
MOSCA.   Most blessèd cordial!   75
  This will recover him.
CORBACCIO.   Yes, do, do, do.
MOSCA. I think it were not best, sir.
CORBACCIO.   What?
MOSCA.   To recover him.
CORBACCIO. O, no, no, no; by no means.
MOSCA.   Why, sir, this
  Will work some strange effect, if he but feel it.
CORBACCIO. 'Tis true, therefore forbear; I'll take my venture.   80
  Give me it again.
MOSCA.   At no hand; pardon me.
  You shall not do yourself that wrong, sir. I
  Will so advise you, you shall have it all.
CORBACCIO.   How?
MOSCA. All, sir; 'tis your right, your own; no man
  Can claim a part; 'tis yours without a rival,   85
  Decreed by destiny.
CORBACCIO.   How, how, good Mosca?
MOSCA. I'll tell you, sir. This fit he shall recover—
CORBACCIO. I do conceive you.
MOSCA.   And, on first advantage
  Of his gained sense, will I re-importune him
  Unto the making of his testament,   90
  And show him this.   [*Pointing to the money.*]
CORBACCIO.   Good, good.
MOSCA.   'Tis better yet,
  If you will hear, sir.
CORBACCIO.   Yes, with all my heart.
MOSCA. Now, would I counsel you, make home with speed;
  There, frame a will, whereto you shall inscribe
  My master your sole heir.

1. The phrase seems to imply, "You think so because that's the sort of creature you are yourself."
2. No comparison of sedatives ("opiates") to this great medicine is possible. The elixir was supposed to be the supreme, universal medicine, capable of prolonging life indefinitely as well as of transforming baser metals to gold.
3. I.e., palpable, material gold; *aurum potabile*, or drinkable gold, was the elixir.

CORBACCIO.   And disinherit   95
    My son?
MOSCA.   O, sir, the better: for that color
    Shall make it much more taking.[4]
CORBACCIO.   O, but color?
MOSCA. This will, sir, you shall send it unto me.
    Now, when I come to enforce, as I will do,
    Your cares, your watchings, and your many prayers,   100
    Your more than many gifts, your this day's present,
    And last, produce your will; where, without thought
    Or least regard unto your proper issue,
    A son so brave and highly meriting,
    The stream of your diverted love hath thrown you   105
    Upon my master, and made him your heir:
    He cannot be so stupid, or stone dead,
    But out of conscience and mere gratitude—
CORBACCIO. He must pronounce me his?
MOSCA.   'Tis true.
CORBACCIO.   This plot
    Did I think on before.
MOSCA.   I do believe it.   110
CORBACCIO. Do you not believe it?
MOSCA.   Yes, sir.
CORBACCIO.   Mine own project.
MOSCA. Which, when he hath done, sir—
CORBACCIO.   Published me his heir?
MOSCA. And you so certain to survive him—
CORBACCIO.   Ay.
MOSCA. Being so lusty a man—
CORBACCIO.   'Tis true.
MOSCA.   Yes, sir—
CORBACCIO. I thought on that too. See, how he should be   115
    The very organ to express my thoughts!
MOSCA. You have not only done yourself a good—
CORBACCIO. But multiplied it on my son?
MOSCA.   'Tis right, sir.
CORBACCIO. Still my invention.
MOSCA.   'Las, sir! heaven knows
    It hath been all my study, all my care   120
    (I e'en grow gray withal), how to work things—
CORBACCIO. I do conceive, sweet Mosca.
MOSCA.   You are he
    For whom I labor here.
CORBACCIO.   Ay, do, do, do:
    I'll straight about it.   [Going.]
MOSCA.   Rook go with you, raven![5]

4. That circumstance or appearance ("color") will   and thievish; but Mosca is playing on a secondary
make the trick more effective.   meaning—cheat or deception: "May you be
5. The rook is a common crowlike bird, raucous   deceived, you raven!"

CORBACCIO. I know thee honest.
MOSCA. [aside]   You do lie, sir!
CORBACCIO.   And—   125
MOSCA. Your knowledge is no better than your ears, sir.
CORBACCIO. I do not doubt to be a father to thee.
MOSCA. Nor I to gull my brother of his blessing.[6]
CORBACCIO. I may have my youth restored to me, why not?
MOSCA. Your worship is a precious ass!
CORBACCIO.   What sayest thou?   130
MOSCA. I do desire your worship to make haste, sir.
CORBACCIO. 'Tis done, 'tis done; I go.   [Exit.]
VOLPONE. [leaping from his couch] O, I shall burst!
    Let out my sides, let out my sides—
MOSCA.   Contain
    Your flux of laughter, sir; you know this hope
    Is such a bait it covers any hook.   135
VOLPONE. O, but thy working, and thy placing it!
    I cannot hold; good rascal, let me kiss thee:
    I never knew thee in so rare a humor.
MOSCA. Alas, sir, I but do as I am taught;
    Follow your grave instructions; give them words;   140
    Pour oil into their ears, and send them hence.
VOLPONE. 'Tis true, 'tis true. What a rare punishment
    Is avarice to itself![7]
MOSCA.   Ay, with our help, sir.
VOLPONE. So many cares, so many maladies,
    So many fears attending on old age,   145
    Yea, death so often called on, as no wish
    Can be more frequent with them, their limbs faint,
    Their senses dull, their seeing, hearing, going,
    All dead before them; yea, their very teeth,
    Their instruments of eating, failing them: 150
    Yet this is reckoned life! Nay, here was one,
    Is now gone home, that wishes to live longer!
    Feels not his gout, nor palsy; feigns himself
    Younger by scores of years, flatters his age
    With confident belying it, hopes he may,   155
    With charms, like Aeson,[8] have his youth restored;
    And with these thoughts so battens, as if fate
    Would be as easily cheated on, as he,
    And all turns air! [Knocking within.] Who's that there, now? a
        third?
MOSCA. Close, to your couch again; I hear his voice: 160
    It is Corvino, our spruce merchant.
VOLPONE. [lies down as before]   Dead.[9]

6. Jacob robbed Esau of his blessing by impersonating him before blind old Isaac (Genesis 27).
7. Seneca, Epistle 115, par. 16. Volpone is liberated, at least intellectually, from the vices on which he plays.
8. Aeson, Jason's father, was restored to life by the charms of Medea the witch.
9. I.e., "Pretend that I'm dead." The "bout . . . with your eyes" is a dose of gummy medicine.

MOSCA. Another bout, sir, with your eyes. [*anointing them*]—Who's there?

SCENE 5

[*Enter* CORVINO.]

    Signor Corvino! come most wished for! O,
How happy were you, if you knew it, now!
CORVINO. Why? What? Wherein?
MOSCA.   The tardy hour is come, sir.
CORVINO. He is not dead?
MOSCA.   Not dead, sir, but as good;
    He knows no man.
CORVINO.   How shall I do then?
MOSCA.   Why, sir?   5
CORVINO. I have brought him here a pearl.
MOSCA.   Perhaps he has
    So much remembrance left as to know you, sir.
    He still calls on you; nothing but your name
    Is in his mouth. Is your pearl orient,[1] sir?
CORVINO. Venice was never owner of the like.   10
VOLPONE. [*faintly*] Signor Corvino!
MOSCA.   Hark.
VOLPONE.   Signor Corvino!
MOSCA. He calls you; step and give it him.—He's here, sir,
    And he has brought you a rich pearl.
CORVINO.   How do you, sir?
    Tell him it doubles the twelfth carat.[2]
MOSCA.   Sir,
    He cannot understand, his hearing's gone;   15
    And yet it comforts him to see you—
CORVINO.   Say
    I have a diamond for him, too.
MOSCA.   Best show it, sir;
    Put it into his hand; 'tis only there
    He apprehends:[3] he has his feeling, yet.
    See how he grasps it!
CORVINO.   'Las, good gentleman!   20
    How pitiful the sight is!
MOSCA.   Tut! forget, sir.
    The weeping of an heir should still be laughter
    Under a visor.[4]
CORVINO.   Why, am I his heir?
MOSCA. Sir, I am sworn, I may not show the will
    Till he be dead: but here has been Corbaccio,   25
    Here has been Voltore, here were others too,

---

1. Lustrous, therefore precious.
2. I.e., weighs 24 carats, or more than a third of an ounce—a huge pearl. "24-carat" has other overtones, as a measure of perfect purity in gold.
3. In English "apprehends" means "to understand intellectually," but the root Latin sense is "to grasp physically."
4. An heir should look sad by way of concealing his jubilation.

I cannot number 'em, they were so many,
All gaping here for legacies; but I,
Taking the vantage of his naming you,
Signor Corvino, Signor Corvino, took   30
Paper and pen and ink, and there I asked him
Whom he would have his heir? *Corvino*. Who
Should be executor? *Corvino*. And
To any question he was silent to,
I still interpreted the nods he made,   35
Through weakness, for consent, and sent home th' others,
Nothing bequeathed them but to cry and curse.
CORVINO. O, my dear Mosca! [*They embrace.*] Does he not
    perceive us?
MOSCA. No more than a blind harper.[5] He knows no man,
No face of friend, nor name of any servant,   40
Who 'twas that fed him last, or gave him drink;
Not those he hath begotten, or brought up,
Can he remember.
CORVINO.   Has he children?
MOSCA.   Bastards,
Some dozen or more, that he begot on beggars,
Gypsies, and Jews, and black-moors, when he was drunk.   45
Knew you not that, sir? 'Tis the common fable,
The dwarf, the fool, the eunuch, are all his;[6]
He's the true father of his family,
In all save me; but he has given them nothing.
CORVINO. That's well, that's well! Art sure he does not hear us?   50
MOSCA. Sure, sir! Why, look you, credit your own sense.

                                            [*Shouts in* VOLPONE'S *ear.*]

The pox approach and add to your diseases,
If it would send you hence the sooner, sir.
For your incontinence, it hath deserved it
Throughly and throughly, and the plague to boot!—   55
You may come near, sir—Would you would once close
Those filthy eyes of yours, that flow with slime
Like two frog-pits; and those same hanging cheeks,
Covered with hide instead of skin—Nay, help, sir—
That look like frozen dish-clouts set on end!   60
CORVINO. Or like an old smoked wall, on which the rain
    Ran down in streaks!
MOSCA.   Excellent, sir! Speak out.
You may be louder yet; a culverin[7]
Dischargèd in his ear would hardly bore it.
CORVINO. His nose is like a common sewer, still running.   65
MOSCA. 'Tis good! And what his mouth?
CORVINO.   A very draught.[8]

---

5. Playing the harp and singing ballads to it were traditional devices of blind beggars; but blindness in poets is sometimes accompanied by second sight, and Mosca knows that Volpone sees the situation clearly.

6. The suggestion that Volpone's playmates are his own children is never really contradicted.
7. Cannon.
8. Cesspool.

MOSCA. O, stop it up—
CORVINO.   By no means.
MOSCA.   Pray you, let me:
  Faith, I could stifle him rarely with a pillow,
  As well as any woman that should keep him.[9]
CORVINO. Do as you will; but I'll be gone.
MOSCA.   Be so;   70
  It is your presence makes him last so long.
CORVINO. I pray you, use no violence.
MOSCA.   No, sir? Why?
  Why should you be thus scrupulous, pray you, sir?
CORVINO. Nay, at your discretion.
MOSCA.   Well, good sir, begone.
CORVINO. I will not trouble him now, to take my pearl?   75
MOSCA. Puh! nor your diamond. What a needless care
  Is this afflicts you? Is not all here yours?
  Am not I here? whom you have made? your creature?
  That owe my being to you?
CORVINO.   Grateful Mosca!
  Thou art my friend, my fellow, my companion,   80
  My partner, and shalt share in all my fortunes.
MOSCA. Excepting one.
CORVINO.   What's that?
MOSCA.   Your gallant wife, sir.—

                                                    [Exit CORVINO.]

  Now is he gone: we had no other means
  To shoot him hence, but this.
VOLPONE.   My divine Mosca!
  Thou hast today outgone thyself. [Knocking within.]
    Who's there?   85
  I will be troubled with no more. Prepare
  Me music, dances, banquets, all delights;
  The Turk is not more sensual in his pleasures
  Than will Volpone. [Exit MOSCA.] Let me see; a pearl!
  A diamond! plate! sequins! Good morning's purchase.   90
  Why, this is better than rob churches,[1] yet;
  Or fat by eating, once a month, a man—[Enter MOSCA.]
  Who is 't?
MOSCA.   The beauteous Lady Would-be, sir,
  Wife to the English knight, Sir Politic Would-be
  (This is the style, sir, is directed me),[2]   95
  Hath sent to know how you have slept tonight,
  And if you would be visited?
VOLPONE.   Not now:
  Some three hours hence—
MOSCA.   I told the squire so much.
VOLPONE. When I am high with mirth and wine, then, then.

9. I.e., "I could smother him as well as a nurse."   2. I.e., "this is the way I've been told to announce
1. I.e., easy money.   her."

'Fore heaven, I wonder at the desperate valor   100
Of the bold English, that they dare let loose
Their wives to all encounters!
MOSCA.   Sir, this knight
Had not his name for nothing: he is *politic*,[3]
And knows, howe'er his wife affect strange airs,
She hath not yet the face to be dishonest.[4]   105
But had she Signor Corvino's wife's face—
VOLPONE. Has she so rare a face?
MOSCA.   O, sir, the wonder,
The blazing star of Italy! a wench
Of the first year! a beauty ripe as harvest![5]
Whose skin is whiter than a swan all over,   110
Than silver, snow, or lilies! a soft lip,
Would tempt you to eternity of kissing!
And flesh that melteth in the touch to blood!
Bright as your gold, and lovely as your gold!
VOLPONE. Why had not I known this before?
MOSCA.   Alas, sir,   115
Myself but yesterday discovered it.
VOLPONE. How might I see her?
MOSCA.   O, not possible;
She's kept as warily as is your gold;
Never does come abroad, never takes air,
But at a window. All her looks are sweet
As the first grapes or cherries, and are watched   120
As near as they are.
VOLPONE.   I must see her.
MOSCA.   Sir,
There is a guard of ten spies thick upon her,
All his whole household; each of which is set
Upon his fellow, and have all their charge,   125
When he goes out, when he comes in, examined.
VOLPONE. I will go see her, though but at her window.
MOSCA. In some disguise, then.
VOLPONE.   That is true; I must
Maintain mine own shape still the same; we'll think.

                                              [*Exeunt.*]

Act 2

SCENE 1. St. *Mark's Place, before* CORVINO's *house.*

[*Enter* SIR POLITIC WOULD-BE, *and* PEREGRINE.]

SIR POLITIC. Sir, to a wise man, all the world's his soil.
It is not Italy, nor France, nor Europe

---

3. Devious, subtle.
4. I.e., "she's not beautiful enough to be unchaste."
5. A blazing star is literally a comet, hence a heavenly object of special attention. "A wench of the first year" seems to be a metaphor from wine-making, implying that the first crop of grapes makes the best wine.

That must bound me, if my fates call me forth.
Yet, I protest, it is no salt[6] desire
Of seeing countries, shifting a religion,   5
Nor any disaffection to the state
Where I was bred, and unto which I owe
My dearest plots,[7] hath brought me out; much less
That idle, antique, stale, gray-headed project
Of knowing men's minds and manners, with Ulysses![8]   10
But a peculiar humor of my wife's,
Laid for this height[9] of Venice, to observe,
To quote, to learn the language, and so forth.—
I hope you travel, sir, with license?[1]

PEREGRINE.   Yes.
SIR POLITIC. I dare the safelier converse—How long, sir,   15
  Since you left England?
PEREGRINE.   Seven weeks.
SIR POLITIC.   So lately!
  You have not been with my lord ambassador?
PEREGRINE. Not yet, sir.
SIR POLITIC.   Pray you, what news, sir, vents our climate?[2]
  I heard last night a most strange thing reported
  By some of my lord's followers, and I long   20
  To hear how 'twill be seconded.
PEREGRINE.   What was 't, sir?
SIR POLITIC. Marry, sir, of a raven that should build
  In a ship royal of the king's.[3]
PEREGRINE. [aside]   This fellow,
  Does he gull me,[4] trow? or is gulled?—Your name, sir?
SIR POLITIC. My name is Politic Would-be.
PEREGRINE. [aside]   O, that speaks him.—   25
  A knight, sir?
SIR POLITIC.   A poor knight, sir.
PEREGRINE.   Your lady
  Lies here in Venice for intelligence
  Of tires and fashions and behavior
  Among the courtesans?[5] the fine Lady Would-be?
SIR POLITIC. Yes, sir; the spider and the bee ofttimes   30
  Suck from one flower.
PEREGRINE.   Good Sir Politic,
  I cry you mercy; I have heard much of you.
  'Tis true, sir, of your raven.
SIR POLITICS.   On your knowledge?

---

6. Wanton, frivolous.
7. Projects, notions.
8. Ulysses (Homer says) knew the minds of many men and saw many cities. The "humor" of Sir Politic's wife was exactly calculated, he thinks, to bring her to Venice.
9. Latitude.
1. I.e., special permission to travel abroad.

2. I.e., "What news does our climate give off?"
3. A raven is a bird of ill omen.
4. To "gull" is constantly used in the sense of to fool or deceive. "Trow?": do you think?
5. Attires, costumes. Venetian prostitutes were for hundreds of years reputed to be the most desirable in Europe, perhaps because Pietro Aretino advertised them so flatteringly in his pornographic poems.

PEREGRINE. Yes, and your lion's whelping in the Tower.[6]
SIR POLITIC. Another whelp!
PEREGRINE.   Another, sir.
SIR POLITIC.   Now, heaven!   35
  What prodigies be these? The fires at Berwick![7]
  And the new star! these things concurring, strange
  And full of omen! Saw you those meteors?
PEREGRINE. I did, sir.
SIR POLITIC.   Fearful! Pray you, sir, confirm me,
  Were there three porpoises seen above the bridge,   40
  As they give out?[8]
PEREGRINE   Six, and a sturgeon, sir.
SIR POLITIC. I am astonished!
PEREGRINE.   Nay, sir, be not so;
  I'll tell you a greater prodigy than these—
SIR POLITIC. What should these things portend?
PEREGRINE.   The very day
  (Let me be sure) that I put forth from London,   45
  There was a whale discovered in the river,
  As high as Woolwich, that had waited there,
  Few know how many months, for the subversion
  Of the Stade fleet.[9]
SIR POLITIC.   Is't possible? Believe it,
  'Twas either sent from Spain, or the Archduke's: 50
  Spinola's whale, upon my life, my credit![1]
  Will they not leave these projects? Worthy sir,
  Some other news.
PEREGRINE.   Faith, Stone the fool is dead,
  And they do lack a tavern fool extremely.
SIR POLITIC. Is Mas' Stone dead?[2]
PEREGRINE.   He's dead, sir; why, I hope   55
  You thought him not immortal? [Aside.] O, this knight,
  Were he well known, would be a precious thing
  To fit our English stage. He that should write
  But such a fellow, should be thought to feign
  Extremely, if not maliciously.
SIR POLITIC.   Stone dead!   60
PEREGRINE. Dead. Lord! how deeply, sir, you apprehend it!
  He was no kinsman to you?

---

6. Lions were kept caged in the Tower of London, and cubs were whelped from time to time. Most of the events to which Sir Politic alludes had in fact occurred shortly before the time of the play's first production, and would have been familiar to the audience.

7. The end of 1604 was astronomically active. A new star appeared in September, and the aurora borealis over Berwick in December was said to resemble armies of fighting men.

8. It was unusual for deep-sea creatures to venture up the Thames, past London Bridge.

9. The fleet of the English Merchant Adventur-ers, an import/export company based at Stade on the Elbe estuary. How a whale in the Thames could subvert it is not very clear.

1. Sir Politic's suggestions about the origin of the whale all involve Spain. It comes either from Spain itself, or from the Archduke Albert, ruler of the Spanish Netherlands in the name of Philip II, or from Ambrosio Spinola, general of the Spanish armies in Holland.

2. Stone the fool was an actual figure, about whom various anecdotes survive. "Mas' ": short for Master, the common denomination of fools and boys.

SIR POLITIC.   That I know of.
  Well, that same fellow was an unknown fool.
PEREGRINE. And yet you knew him, it seems?
SIR POLITIC.   I did so. Sir,
  I knew him one of the most dangerous heads   65
  Living within the state, and so I held him.
PEREGRINE. Indeed, sir?
SIR POLITIC.   While he lived, in action.
  He has received weekly intelligence,
  Upon my knowledge, out of the Low Countries,
  For all parts of the world, in cabbages;[3]   70
  And those dispensed again to ambassadors,
  In oranges, musk melons, apricots,
  Lemons, pome-citrons, and suchlike; sometimes
  In Colchester oysters, and your Selsey cockles.[4]
PEREGRINE. You make me wonder!
SIR POLITIC.   Sir, upon my knowledge.   75
  Nay, I've observed him, at your public ordinary,[5]
  Take his advertisement from a traveler
  (A concealed statesman) in a trencher of meat;
  And instantly, before the meal was done,
  Convey an answer in a toothpick.
PEREGRINE.   Strange!   80
  How could this be, sir?
SIR POLITIC.   Why, the meat was cut
  So like his character, and so laid, as he
  Must easily read the cipher.
PEREGRINE.   I have heard
  He could not read, sir.
SIR POLITIC.   So 'twas given out,
  In polity,[6] by those that did employ him: 85
  But he could read, and had your languages,
  And to 't,[7] as sound a noddle—
PEREGRINE.   I have heard, sir,
  That your baboons were spies, and that they were
  A kind of subtle nation near to China.
SIR POLITIC. Ay, ay, your Mamaluchi.[8] Faith, they had   90
  Their hand in a French plot or two; but they
  Were so extremely given to women, as
  They made discovery of all; yet I
  Had my advices here, on Wednesday last,
  From one of their own coat, they were returned,   95
  Made their relations, as the fashion is,
  And now stand fair for fresh employment.
PEREGRINE. [aside]   'Heart!

3. Cabbages were a recent importation from Holland.
4. "Pome-citrons" we would call simply "citrons." The oysters and cockles specified were the best shellfish to be had in England and were often served to royalty.
5. Common tavern. "Advertisement": secret message, tip.

6. For political reasons, as part of his cover story.
7. In addition.
8. Mameluchi is the Italian form of *mamelukes*, a group of slaves and warriors originally from Circassia, in Asia Minor, who held or controlled the throne of Egypt for many years. They had nothing to do with baboons, China, or French plots.

This Sir Politic will be ignorant of nothing.
—It seems, sir, you know all.
SIR POLITIC.   Not all, sir; but
  I have some general notions. I do love   100
  To note and to observe; though I live out,
  Free from the active torrent, yet I'd mark
  The currents and the passages of things
  For mine own private use, and know the ebbs
  And flows of state.
PEREGRINE.   Believe it, sir, I hold   105
  Myself in no small tie unto my fortunes
  For casting me thus luckily upon you,
  Whose knowledge, if your bounty equal it,
  May do me great assistance in instruction
  For my behavior and my bearing, which   110
  Is yet so rude and raw.
SIR POLITIC.   Why, came you forth
  Empty of rules for travel?
PEREGRINE.   Faith, I had
  Some common ones from out that vulgar grammar
  Which he that cried Italian to me taught me.[9]
SIR POLITIC. Why this it is that spoils all our brave bloods,   115
  Trusting our hopeful gentry unto pedants,
  Fellows of outside and mere bark.[1] You seem
  To be a gentleman, of ingenuous race:
  I not profess it, but my fate hath been
  To be where I have been consulted with,   120
  In this high kind, touching some great men's sons,
  Persons of blood and honor—
PEREGRINE. [seeing people approach] Who be these, sir?

SCENE 2

  [Enter MOSCA and NANO disguised, followed by persons with
  materials for erecting a stage.]

MOSCA. Under that window, there 't must be. The same.
SIR POLITIC. Fellows to mount a bank. Did your instructor
  In the dear tongues never discourse to you
  Of the Italian mountebanks?[2]
PEREGRINE.   Yes, sir.
SIR POLITIC.   Why,
  Here you shall see one.
PEREGRINE.   They are quacksalvers,   5
  Fellows that live by venting[3] oils and drugs?
SIR POLITIC. Was that the character he gave you of them?
PEREGRINE. As I remember.

---

9. Trained me in the pronunciation of Italian.
1. Superficial and ignorant teachers.
2. The word "mountebank" comes from the Italian *monta in banco*, meaning "to mount the bench." Mountebanks were a mixture of street
entertainer and patent-medicine salesman who gave a very considerable semidramatic, improvised performance before delivering their pitch.
3. Vending.

SIR POLITIC.   Pity his ignorance.
  They are the only knowing men of Europe!
  Great general scholars, excellent physicians,   10
  Most admired statesmen, professed favorites,
  And cabinet counselors to the greatest princes;
  The only languaged men of all the world![4]
PEREGRINE. And I have heard they are most lewd impostors;
  Made all of terms and shreds; no less beliers   15
  Of great men's favors than their own vile medicines;
  Which they will utter upon monstrous oaths,
  Selling that drug for twopence, ere they part,
  Which they have valued at twelve crowns before.
SIR POLITIC. Sir, calumnies are answered best with silence.   20
  Yourself shall judge.—Who is it mounts, my friends?
MOSCA. Scoto of Mantua, sir.[5]
SIR POLITIC.   Is't he? Nay, then
  I'll proudly promise, sir, you shall behold
  Another man than has been phant'sied[6] to you.
  I wonder, yet, that he should mount his bank   25
  Here in this nook, that has been wont t'appear
  In face of the Piazza!—Here he comes.

      [*Enter* VOLPONE *disguised as a mountebank and followed by a
      crowd of people.*]

VOLPONE. [*to* NANO] Mount, zany.
  MOB.   Follow, follow, follow, follow, follow!
SIR POLITIC. See how the people follow him! He's a man
  May write ten thousand crowns in bank here. Note,

                              [VOLPONE *mounts the stage.*]

  Mark but his gesture: I do use to observe   30
  The state he keeps in getting up.
PEREGRINE.   'Tis worth it, sir.
VOLPONE. *Most noble gentlemen, and my worthy patrons! It may seem
  strange, that I, your Scoto Mantuano, who was ever wont to fix my
  bank in face of the public Piazza, near the shelter of the Portico to the
  Procuratia,[8] should now, after eight months' absence from this illus-
  trious city of Venice, humbly retire myself into an obscure nook of the
  Piazza.*
SIR POLITIC. Did not I now object the same?
PEREGRINE.   Peace, sir.
VOLPONE. *Let me tell you: I am not, as your Lombard proverb saith, cold
  on my feet;[9] or content to part with my commodities at a cheaper rate*

---

4. The best talkers.
5. Scoto of Mantua was a real person, a juggler,
magician, and performer at legerdemain; he actually
visited England and performed before Queen Elizabeth, about a quarter of a century before *Volpone*
had its first performance.
6. Described.
7. "Zany": from the Italian name *Giovanni*; a
generic term for a fool, clown, performer. The

speech of the crowd is intended to mimic a confused hubbub.
8. The arcade along the north side of Piazza San
Marco, where the Procurators (senior government
officials) resided. Jonson takes great pains to make
his Venetian details specific and accurate.
9. There is in fact an Italian proverb, "*Haver freddo
a'piedi,*" meaning "to be so hard up that one has
to sell one's goods at a loss."

than I accustomed: look not for it. Nor that the calumnious reports of that impudent detractor and shame to our profession (Alessandro But-tone, I mean), who gave out in public I was condemned a sforzato to the galleys, for poisoning the Cardinal Bembo's—[1] cook, hath at all attached, much less dejected, me. No, no, worthy gentlemen; to tell you true, I cannot endure to see the rabble of these ground ciarlitani,[2] that spread their cloaks on the pavement as if they meant to do feats of activity, and then come in lamely with their moldy tales out of Boc-caccio,[3] like stale Tabarin, the fabulist: some of them discoursing their travels, and of their tedious captivity in the Turks' galley, when, indeed, were the truth known, they were the Christians' galleys, where very temperately they ate bread and drunk water, as a wholesome penance enjoined them by their confessors for base pilferies.[4]

SIR POLITIC. Note but his bearing, and contempt of these.

VOLPONE. These turdy-facy-nasty-paty-lousy-fartical rogues, with one poor groat's-worth of unprepared antimony, finely wrapped up in several scartoccios,[5] are able very well to kill their twenty a week, and play; yet these meager, starved spirits, who have half stopped the organs of their minds with earthy oppilations,[6] want not their favorers among your shrivelled salad-eating artisans, who are overjoyed that they may have their ha'p'orth[7] of physic; though it purge them into another world, it makes no matter.

SIR POLITIC. Excellent! Have you heard better language, sir?

VOLPONE. Well, let them go. And, gentlemen, honorable gentlemen, know that for this time our bank, being thus removed from the clamors of the canaglia,[8] shall be the scene of pleasure and delight; for I have nothing to sell, little or nothing to sell.

SIR POLITIC. I told you, sir, his end.

PEREGRINE.   You did so, sir.

VOLPONE. I protest, I and my six servants are not able to make of this precious liquor so fast as it is fetched away from my lodging by gentle-men of your city; strangers of the Terra-firma;[9] worshipful merchants; ay, and senators too: who, ever since my arrival, have detained me to their uses by their splendidous liberalities. And worthily; for what avails your rich man to have his magazines stuffed with moscadelli,[1] or of the purest grape, when his physicians prescribe him, on pain of death, to drink nothing but water cocted[2] with aniseeds? O, health! health! the blessing of the rich! the riches of the poor! who can buy thee at too dear a rate, since there is no enjoying this world without thee? Be not

---

1. Alessandro Buttone is an imaginary rival who has dreamed up a slander against Scoto—but the tale is most unlikely, since Cardinal Bembo died in 1547, more than 50 years before the play is sup-posed to be taking place. A *sforzato* is a galley-slave; the dash before "cook" is supposed to indi-cate that the title of "cook" is just a euphemism.
2. Ground *ciarlatani* or charlatans put on their acts and sold their nostrums at street level.
3. Boccaccio told in the *Decameron* a great many popular stories; as he lived in the 14th century, the tales were "moldy" by the 17th. Like Scoto, Tabarine was an actual Italian comedian of the time who performed in France (not so far as we know, in England) during the 1570s.
4. Venetian galleys required many oars, often

operated by captive Turks or condemned crimi-nals, chained to the bench, fed miserable food, and whipped mercilessly.
5. Antimony was the basis of most common emet-ics. *Scartoccios* were little paper envelopes in which drugs were placed.
6. Obstructions.
7. Half-pennyworth.
8. The common mob.
9. *Terra firma* is still the Venetian term for land across the lagoon, the mainland.
1. Muscadel or muscatel is wine made from cer-tain grapes, in Italian *moscatini*, which seem to have the perfume of musk.
2. Cooked.

*then so sparing of your purses, honorable gentlemen, as to abridge the
natural course of life—*

PEREGRINE. You see his end?

SIR POLITIC.   Ay, is 't not good?

VOLPONE. *For when a humid flux, or catarrh, by the mutability of air,
falls from your head into an arm or shoulder, or any other part; take
you a ducat, or your sequin of gold, and apply to the place affected:
see what good effect it can work.*[3] *No, no, tis this blessed* unguento,
*this rare extraction, that hath only power to disperse all malignant
humors that proceed either of hot, cold, moist, or windy causes—*

PEREGRINE. I would he had put in dry too.[4]

SIR POLITIC.   Pray you, observe.

VOLPONE. *To fortify the most indigest and crude stomach, ay, were it of
one that, through extreme weakness, vomited blood, applying only a
warm napkin to the place, after the unction and fricace;*[5] *for the ver-
tigine in the head, putting but a drop into your nostrils, likewise behind
the ears; a most sovereign and approved remedy: the* Mal Caduco,
cramps, convulsions, paralyses, epilepsies, Tremor-Cordia, *retired nerves,
ill vapors of the spleen, stoppings of the liver, the stone, the strangury,*
Hernia Ventosa, Iliaca Passio; *stops a* Dysenteria *immediately; easeth
the torsion of the small guts, and cures* Melancholia Hypochondriaca,[6] *being taken and applied, according to my printed receipt.*
[Pointing to his bill and his vial.] *For this is the physician, this the
medicine; this counsels, this cures; this gives the direction, this works
the effect; and, in sum, both together may be termed an abstract of the
theoric and practic*[7] *in the Aesculapian art. 'Twill cost you eight crowns.
And,* Zan Fritada,[8] *prithee sing a verse extempore in honor of it.*

SIR POLITIC. How do you like him, sir?

PEREGRINE.   Most strangely, I!

SIR POLITIC. Is not his language rare?

PEREGRINE.   But alchemy,[9]
I never heard the like; or Broughton's books.

[NANO *sings.*]

> *Had old Hippocrates, or Galen,*[1]
> *That to their books put med'cines all in,*
> *But known this secret, they had never*
> *(Of which they will be guilty ever)*
> *Been murderers of so much paper,*
> *Or wasted many a hurtless taper;*
> *No Indian drug had e'er been famed,*

3. I.e., money won't cure your cold when you catch it (but my "blessed unguent" will).
4. Of the four "humors" or ingredients of a balanced human complexion, "Scoto" has left out one, as Peregrine drily observes.
5. Anointing and massage.
6. "*Melancholia Hypochondriaca*" is black depression. The other ailments are: *Mal Caduco,* falling sickness, epilepsy; *Tremor Cordia,* palpitations of the heart; strangury, painful urination; *Hernia Ventosa,* gassy hernia; *Iliaca Passio* cramps of the small intestine.
7. Theory and practice. "The Aesculapian art": medicine (from Aesculapius, Greek god of medicine).
8. Literally, "Johnny Omelet," obviously one of the mountebank's stooges.
9. Except for alchemy, Jonson had no use for the books of Hugh Broughton, a Puritan divine and rabbinical scholar.
1. Famous doctors of the classical world.

Tobacco, sassafras not named;
Ne yet, of guacum²one small stick, sir,
Nor Raymond Lully's great elixir.
Ne had been known the Danish Gonswart,
*Or Paracelsus, with his long sword.*³

PEREGRINE. All this, yet, will not do; eight crowns is high.

VOLPONE. No more. Gentlemen, *if I had but time to discourse to you the miraculous effects of this my oil, surnamed oglio del Scoto;*⁴ *with the countless catalogue of those I have cured of the aforesaid, and many more diseases; the patents and privileges of all the princes and commonwealths of Christendom; or but the depositions of those that appeared on my part before the signory of the Sanita*⁵ *and most learned College of Physicians; where I was authorized, upon notice taken of the admirable virtues of my medicaments, and mine own excellency in matter of rare and unknown secrets, not only to disperse them publicly in this famous city, but in all the territories that happily joy under the government of the most pious and magnificent states of Italy. But may some other gallant fellow say, "O, there be divers that make profession to have as good and as experimented receipts as yours." Indeed, very many have essayed, like apes, in imitation of that which is really and essentially in me, to make of this oil; bestowed great cost in furnaces, stills, alembics,*⁶ *continual fires, and preparation of the ingredients (as indeed there goes to it six hundred several simples,*⁷ *besides some quantity of human fat, for the conglutination, which we buy of the anatomists); but when these practitioners come to the last decoction, blow, blow, puff, puff, and all flies in fumo:*⁸ *ha, ha, ha! Poor wretches, I rather pity their folly and indiscretion than their loss of time and money; for those may be recovered by industry: but to be a fool born is a disease incurable.*

*For myself, I always from my youth have endeavored to get the rarest secrets, and book them, either in exchange or for money: I spared nor cost nor labor, where anything was worthy to be learned. And, gentlemen, honorable gentlemen, I will undertake, by virtue of chemical art, out of the honorable hat that covers your head to extract the four elements; that is to say, the fire, air, water, and earth, and return you your felt without burn or stain. For, whilst others have been at the balloo,*⁹ *I have been at my book; and am now past the craggy paths of study, and come to the flowery plains of honor and reputation.*

SIR POLITIC. I do assure you, sir, that is his aim.

VOLPONE. *But to our price—*

PEREGRINE.   And that withal, Sir Pol.

---

2. Modern guaiacum, obtained from the bark of a South American tree.

3. Raymond Lully or Lull was a Spanish mystic philosopher of the 13th century who claimed to have discovered the elixir. "The Danish Gonswart": unidentifiable. Paracelsus, the famous German doctor of the 16th century, had a sword in the handle of which he kept, according to legend, familiar spirits, and according to history, medications and herbs.

4. Scoto's oil.

5. The Board of Medical Examiners in Venice.

6. Distilleries, retorts.

7. Medicinal plants.

8. In smoke. "Decoction": boiling down.

9. Balloon, ball; i.e., while others have been diverting themselves with ball games.

VOLPONE. *You all know, honorable gentlemen, I never valued this* ampulla, *or vial, at less than eight crowns; but for this time I am content to be deprived of it for six: six crowns is the price, and less in courtesy I know you cannot offer me; take it or leave it, howsoever, both it and I am at your service. I ask you not as the value of the thing, for then I should demand of you a thousand crowns: so the Cardinals Montalto, Farnese, the great Duke of Tuscany, my gossip,[1] with divers other princes, have given me; but I despise money. Only to show my affection to you, honorable gentlemen, and your illustrious state here, I have neglected the messages of these princes, mine own offices, framed my journey hither, only to present you with the fruits of my travels.* [To NANO *and* MOSCA.]—*Tune your voices once more to the touch of your instruments, and give the honorable assembly some delightful recreation.*

PEREGRINE. What monstrous and most painful circumstance
Is here, to get some three or four *gazettes,*[2]
Some three pence in the whole—for that 'twill come to.

Song

> *You that would last long, list to my song,*
> *Make no more coil,[3] but buy of this oil.*
> *Would you be ever fair and young?*
> *Stout of teeth and strong of tongue?*
> *Tart of palate? quick of ear?*
> *Sharp of sight? of nostril clear?*
> *Moist of hand and light of foot?*
> *Or, I will come nearer to 't,*
> *Would you live free from all diseases?*
> *Do the act your mistress pleases,*
> *Yet fright all aches from your bones?*
> *Here's a med'cine for the nones.[4]*

VOLPONE. *Well, I am in a humor at this time to make a present of the small quantity my coffer contains, to the rich in courtesy, and to the poor for God's sake. Wherefore, now mark: I asked you six crowns; and six crowns, at other times, you have paid me; you shall not give me six crowns, nor five, nor four, nor three, nor two, nor one; nor half a ducat; no, nor a moccenigo.[5] Six pence it will cost you, or six hundred pound— expect no lower price, for, by the banner of my front, I will not bate a bagatine[6]—that I will have, only, a pledge of your loves, to carry something from amongst you to show I am not contemned by you. Therefore, now, toss your handkerchiefs, cheerfully, cheerfully;[7] and be*

---

1. My good friend. Cardinal Montalto became Pope as Sixtus V in 1585; Alessandro Farnese had been Pope as Paul III in 1534; "the great Duke of Tuscany" was Cosimo de Medici, who died in 1587.
2. The smallest Venetian coins, worth less than an English penny.
3. Stir, fuss.
4. For the occasion.

5. A Venetian coin, worth about nine English pennies.
6. A tiny coin.
7. When business was brisk at the mountebank's stand, customers sometimes knotted their money in a handkerchief or glove and tossed it on stage; the money was taken out, replaced with the medicine, and the handkerchief tossed back to the purchaser.

*advertised that the first heroic spirit that deigns to grace me with a
handkerchief, I will give it a little remembrance of something beside,
shall please it better than if I had presented it with a double* pistolet.[8]

PEREGRINE. Will you be that heroic spark, Sir Pol?

[CELIA, *at a window above, throws down her handkerchief.*]

O, see! the window has prevented[9] you.

VOLPONE. *Lady, I kiss your bounty; and for this timely grace you have
done your poor Scoto of Mantua, I will return you, over and above my
oil, a secret of that high and inestimable nature shall make you forever
enamored on that minute wherein your eye first descended on so mean,
yet not altogether to be despised, an object. Here is a powder concealed
in this paper, of which, if I should speak to the worth, nine thousand
volumes were but as one page, that page as a line, that line as a word;
so short is this pilgrimage of man (which some call life) to the expressing
of it. Would I reflect on the price? why, the whole world were but as
an empire, that empire as a province, that province as a bank, that
bank as a private purse to the purchase of it. I will only tell you: it is
the powder that made Venus a goddess (given her by Apollo), that kept
her perpetually young, cleared her wrinkles, firmed her gums, filled her
skin, colored her hair; from her derived to Helen, and at the sack of
Troy unfortunately lost; till now, in this our age, it was as happily
recovered, by a studious antiquary, out of some ruins of Asia, who sent
a moiety[1] of it to the court of France (but much sophisticated), wherewith the ladies there now color their hair. The rest, at this present,
remains with me; extracted to a quintessence, so that wherever it but
touches, in youth it perpetually preserves, in age restores the complexion; seats your teeth, did they dance like virginal jacks,[2] firm as a wall;
makes them white as ivory, that were black as—*

SCENE 3

[*Enter* CORVINO.]

CORVINO. Spite o' the devil, and my shame! [*To* VOLPONE.] Come
    down here;
Come down! No house but mine to make your scene?
Signor Flaminio,[3] will you down, sir? down?
What, is my wife your Franciscina, sir?
No windows on the whole Piazza here   5
To make your properties, but mine? but mine? [*Beats away* VOL-
    PONE, NANO, &c.]
'Heart! ere tomorrow I shall be new christened,
And called the *Pantalone di Bisognosi*[4]
About the town. [*Exit* CORVINO; *and the crowd disperses.*]

---

8. A double pistolet was a Spanish coin of some
value, worth not much less than an English pound.
9. Forestalled, anticipated.
1. Fraction. "Sophisticated": diluted.
2. In virginals (early harpsichords), the strings were
plucked by quills set in bits of wood called "jacks";
their leaping motion provides the term for "Scoto's" comparison.

3. Flaminio was one of the stock characters—a
lover—in the *commedia dell'arte*; Franciscina the
always available servant girl, in the same class of
play.
4. Pantaloon of the Paupers. Pantaloon, in the
tradition of *commedia dell'arte*, is a doddering old
fool in perpetual terror of being cuckolded.

PEREGRINE.   What should this mean, Sir Pol?
SIR POLITIC. Some trick of state, believe it; I will home.   10
PEREGRINE. It may be some design on you.
SIR POLITIC.   I know not.
   I'll stand upon my guard.
PEREGRINE.   It is your best, sir.
SIR POLITIC. This three weeks, all my advices, all my letters,
   They have been intercepted.
PEREGRINE.   Indeed, sir!
   Best have a care.
SIR POLITIC.   Nay, so I will.
PEREGRINE.   This knight,   15
   I may not lose him, for my mirth, till night.   [*Exeunt.*]

                SCENE 4. A *room in* VOLPONE's *house.*

            [*Enter* VOLPONE *and* MOSCA.]

VOLPONE. O, I am wounded!
MOSCA.   Where, sir?
VOLPONE.   Not without;
   Those blows were nothing; I could bear them ever.
   But angry Cupid, bolting from her eyes,
   Hath shot himself into me like a flame,
   Where now he flings about his burning heat,   5
   As in a furnace an ambitious[5] fire
   Whose vent is stopped. The fight is all within me.
   I cannot live, except thou help me, Mosca;
   My liver melts, and I, without the hope
   Of some soft air from her refreshing breath,   10
   Am but a heap of cinders.
MOSCA.   'Las, good sir,
   Would you had never seen her!
VOLPONE.   Nay, would thou
   Hadst never told me of her!
MOSCA.   Sir, 'tis true;
   I do confess I was unfortunate,
   And you unhappy: but I'm bound in conscience,   15
   No less than duty, to effect my best
   To your release of torment, and I will, sir.
VOLPONE. Dear Mosca, shall I hope?
MOSCA.   Sir, more than dear,
   I will not bid you to despair of aught
   Within a human compass.
VOLPONE.   O, there spoke   20
   My better angel. Mosca, take my keys,
   Gold, plate, and jewels, all 's at thy devotion;[6]
   Employ them how thou wilt; nay, coin me too,
   So thou in this but crown my longings. Mosca?

5. Aspiring, growing. Most of Volpone's erotic   by Petrarch.
torments are of the sort popularized 300 years before 6. At your service.

MOSCA. Use but your patience.

VOLPONE. So I have.

MOSCA. I doubt not 25
To bring success to your desires.

VOLPONE. Nay, then,
I not repent me of my late disguise.

MOSCA. If you can horn[7] him, sir, you need not.

VOLPONE. True:
Besides, I never meant him for my heir.—
Is not the color of my beard and eyebrows 30
To make me known?

MOSCA. No jot.

VOLPONE. I did it well.

MOSCA. So well, would I could follow you in mine,
With half the happiness!— and yet I would
Escape your epilogue.[8]

VOLPONE. But were they gulled
With a belief that I was Scoto?

MOSCA. Sir, 35
Scoto himself could hardly have distinguished!
I have not time to flatter you now; we'll part:
And as I prosper, so applaud my art. [*Exeunt.*]

SCENE 5. *A room* in CORVINO's *house.*

[*Enter* CORVINO, *sword in his hand, dragging in* CELIA.]

CORVINO. Death of mine honor, with the city's fool!
A juggling, tooth-drawing, prating mountebank!
And at a public window! where, whilst he,
With his strained action and his dole[9] of faces,
To his drug-lecture draws your itching ears, 5
A crew of old, unmarried, noted lechers
Stood leering up like satyrs: and you smile
Most graciously, and fan your favors forth,
To give your hot spectators satisfaction!
What, was your mountebank their call?[1] their whistle? 10
Or were you enamored on his copper rings,
His saffron jewel with the toad-stone in 't?
Or his embroidered suit with the cope-stitch,
Made of a hearse cloth?[2] or his old tilt-feather?
Or his starched beard? Well! you shall have him, yes! 15
He shall come home and minister unto you
The fricace for the mother.[3] Or, let me see,
I think you'd rather mount;[4] would you not mount?
Why, if you'll mount, you may; yes, truly, you may:

7. Cuckold.
8. Avoid the beating you got.
9. Guile, trickery; the suggestion is of false faces or masks.
1. I.e., did you arrange the appearance of Scoto deliberately to draw a crowd?
2. Copper rings and toad-stone jewelry are Corvino's sneers at the cheap and flashy dress of the mountebank, whose suit (he imagines) is made of coarse brown burlap ("hearse-cloth") prettied up with embroidery.
3. Massage for the womb.
4. I.e., both on the man and on the stage.

And so you may be seen down to the foot.   20
Get you a cittern,[5] Lady Vanity,
And be a dealer with the virtuous man;
Make one: I'll but protest myself a cuckold,
And save your dowry.[6] I'm a Dutchman, I!
For if you thought me an Italian,   25
You would be damned ere you did this, you whore!
Thou'dst tremble to imagine that the murder
Of father, mother, brother, all thy race,
Should follow, as the subject of my justice.

CELIA. Good sir, have patience.

CORVINO.   What couldst thou propose   30
Less to thyself, than in this heat of wrath,
And stung with my dishonor, I should strike
This steel into thee, with as many stabs
As thou wert gazed upon with goatish eyes?

CELIA. Alas, sir, be appeased! I could not think   35
My being at the window should more now
Move your impatience than at other times.

CORVINO. No? not to seek and entertain a parley
With a known knave, before a multitude?
You were an actor with your handkerchief,   40
Which he most sweetly kissed in the receipt,
And might, no doubt, return it with a letter,
And 'point the place where you might meet—your sister's,
Your mother's, or your aunt's might serve the turn.

CELIA. Why, dear sir, when do I make these excuses,   45
Or ever stir abroad, but to the church?
And that so seldom—

CORVINO.   Well, it shall be less;
And thy restraint before was liberty
To what I now decree: and therefore mark me.
First, I will have this bawdy light dammed up;[7]   50
And till 't be done, some two or three yards off,
I'll chalk a line, o'er which if thou but chance
To set thy desperate foot, more hell, more horror,
More wild remorseless rage shall seize on thee
Than on a conjuror that had heedless left   55
His circle's safety ere his devil was laid.[8]
Then, here's a lock[9] which I will hang upon thee,
And, now I think on 't, I will keep thee backwards;
Thy lodging shall be backwards; thy walks backwards;
Thy prospect—all be backwards; and no pleasure   60
That thou shalt know but backwards. Nay, since you force
My honest nature, know, it is your own,

---

5. A kind of guitar, with which she could set up business with the mountebank—she a whore, he a pimp. "Lady Vanity" is a stock figure out of the old morality plays.
6. In the event of her infidelity, Celia's dowry would be forfeited to her husband. "I'm a Dutch-man": the stolidity, not to say complacency, of Dutch men was a common theme of satire—Ital-

ians, on the other hand, were reputed to be fiercely jealous.
7. I.e., brick up the window.
8. When a warlock raised the devil, he was well advised to draw around himself a magic circle, over which the devil could not step.
9. Chastity belt.

Being too open, makes me use you thus.
Since you will not contain your subtle nostrils
In a sweet room, but they must snuff the air   65
Of rank and sweaty passengers—[*Knocking within.*] One
  knocks.
Away, and be not seen, pain of thy life;
Nor look toward the window: if thou dost—
Nay, stay, hear this: let me not prosper, whore,
But I will make thee an anatomy,[1]   70
Dissect thee mine own self, and read a lecture
Upon thee to the city, and in public.
Away!—[*Exit* CELIA.] Who's there? [*Enter* SERVANT.]
SERVANT.   'Tis Signor Mosca, sir.

SCENE 6

CORVINO. Let him come in. [*Exit* SERVANT.] His master's dead:
  there's yet
  Some good to help the bad. [*Enter* MOSCA.] My Mosca, wel-
  come!
  I guess your news.
MOSCA.   I fear you cannot, sir.
CORVINO. Is 't not his death?
MOSCA.   Rather the contrary.
CORVINO. Not his recovery?
MOSCA.   Yes, sir.
CORVINO.   I am cursed,   5
  I am bewitched, my crosses meet to vex me.
  How? how? how? how?
MOSCA.   Why, sir, with Scoto's oil!
  Corbaccio and Voltore brought of it,
  Whilst I was busy in an inner room—
CORVINO. Death! that damned mountebank! But for the law   10
  Now I could kill the rascal: it cannot be
  His oil should have that virtue.[2] Have not I
  Known him a common rogue, come fiddling in
  To the *osteria*,[3] with a tumbling whore,
  And, when he has done all his forced tricks, been glad   15
  Of a poor spoonful of dead wine, with flies in 't?
  It cannot be. All his ingredients
  Are a sheep's gall, a roasted bitch's marrow,
  Some few sod[4] earwigs, pounded caterpillars,
  A little capon's grease, and fasting spittle: 20
  I know them to a dram.
MOSCA.   I know not, sir;
  But some on 't, there, they poured into his ears,
  Some in his nostrils, and recovered him,
  Applying but the fricace.[5]

1. A corpse for anatomical demonstrations.
2. Efficacy.
3. The Italian word for "tavern."

4. Boiled. "Fasting spittle": as it implies, spit taken
from a hungry man.
5. I.e., all they had to do was rub it in.

CORVINO.   Pox o' that fricace!

MOSCA. And since, to seem the more officious   25
   And flattering of his health, there they have had,
   At extreme fees, the college of physicians
   Consulting on him, how they might restore him;
   Where one would have a cataplasm[6] of spices,
   Another a flayed ape clapped to his breast,   30
   A third would have it a dog, a fourth an oil
   With wild cats' skins; at last, they all resolved
   That to preserve him was no other means
   But some young woman must be straight sought out,
   Lusty, and full of juice, to sleep by him;   35
   And to this service, most unhappily
   And most unwillingly, am I now employed,
   Which here I thought to pre-acquaint you with,
   For your advice, since it concerns you most;
   Because I would not do that thing might cross   40
   Your ends, on whom I have my whole dependence, sir.
   Yet, if I do it not, they may delate[7]
   My slackness to my patron, work me out
   Of his opinion; and there all your hopes,
   Ventures, or whatsoever, are all frustrate!   45
   I do but tell you, sir. Besides, they are all
   Now striving who shall first present him; therefore—
   I could entreat you, briefly conclude somewhat;
   Prevent[8] them if you can.

CORVINO.   Death to my hopes,
   This is my villainous fortune! Best to hire   50
   Some common courtesan.

MOSCA.   Ay, I thought on that, sir;
   But they are all so subtle, full of art,
   And age again doting and flexible,
   So as—I cannot tell—we may perchance
   Light on a quean[9] may cheat us all.

CORVINO.   'Tis true.   55

MOSCA. No, no: it must be one that has no tricks, sir,
   Some simple thing, a creature made unto it;
   Some wench you may command. Have you no kinswoman?
   God's so—Think, think, think, think, think, think, think, sir.
   One o' the doctors offered there his daughter.   60

CORVINO. How!

MOSCA.   Yes, Signor Lupo,[1] the physician.

CORVINO. His daughter!

MOSCA.   And a virgin, sir. Why, alas,
   He knows the state of 's body, what it is;
   That nought can warm his blood, sir, but a fever;
   Nor any incantation raise his spirit:[2]   65
   A long forgetfulness hath seized that part.

---

6. Poultice.
7. Denounce, complain of.
8. Forestall.

9. Trollop.
1. Doctor Wolf.
2. With a pun on spirit, meaning "semen."

Besides, sir, who shall know it? Some one or two—
CORVINO. I pray thee give me leave. [*Walks aside.*] If any man
    But I had had this luck—The thing in itself,
    I know, is nothing—Wherefore should not I   70
    As well command my blood and my affections
    As this dull doctor? In the point of honor,
    The cases are all one of wife and daughter.
MOSCA. [*aside*] I hear him coming.
CORVINO.   She shall do 't: 'tis done.
    'Slight! if this doctor, who is not engaged,   75
    Unless 't be for his counsel, which is nothing,
    Offer his daughter, what should I, that am
    So deeply in? I will prevent him. Wretch!
    Covetous wretch![3]—Mosca, I have determined.
MOSCA. How, sir?
CORVINO.   We'll make all sure. The party you wot of[4]   80
    Shall be mine own wife, Mosca.
MOSCA.   Sir, the thing,
    But that I would not seem to counsel you,
    I should have motioned[5] to you at the first:
    And, make your count, you have cut all their throats.
    Why, 'tis directly taking a possession!   85
    And in his next fit, we may let him go.
    'Tis but to pull the pillow from his head,
    And he is throttled: it had been done before,
    But for your scrupulous doubts.
CORVINO.   Ay, a plague on 't,
    My conscience fools my wit! Well, I'll be brief,   90
    And so be thou, lest they should be before us:
    Go home, prepare him, tell him with what zeal
    And willingness I do it; swear it was
    On the first hearing, as thou mayst do truly,
    Mine own free motion.
MOSCA.   Sir, I warrant you,   95
    I'll so possess him with it, that the rest
    Of his starved clients shall be banished all,
    And only you received. But come not, sir,
    Until I send, for I have something else
    To ripen for your good; you must not know it.   100
CORVINO. But do not you forget to send now.
MOSCA.   Fear not.[*Exit* MOSCA.]

SCENE 7

CORVINO. Where are you, wife? my Celia! wife!

    [*Enter* CELIA, *weeping.*]

---

3. Whether Corvino in this passionate outburst is
thinking of Doctor Lupo, or, more dramatically,
of himself, Jonson leaves unclear.

4. Know about.
5. Suggested.

                                              What, blubbering?
Come, dry those tears. I think thou thought'st me in earnest.
Ha! by this light I talked so but to try thee.
Methinks the lightness of the occasion
Should have confirmed thee.[6] Come, I am not jealous.   5
CELIA. No?
CORVINO.   Faith I am not, I, nor never was;
It is a poor unprofitable humor.
Do not I know, if women have a will,
They'll do 'gainst all the watches of the world,
And that the fiercest spies are tamed with gold?[7]   10
Tut, I am confident in thee, thou shalt see 't;
And see, I'll give thee cause too, to believe it.
Come, kiss me. Go, and make thee ready straight,
In all thy best attire, thy choicest jewels,
Put them all on, and, with them, thy best looks: 15
We are invited to a solemn feast
At old Volpone's, where it shall appear
How far I am free from jealousy or fear.   [Exeunt.]

                                  Act 3

                          SCENE 1. A street.

        [Enter MOSCA.]

MOSCA. I fear I shall begin to grow in love
    With my dear self and my most prosperous parts,
    They do so spring and burgeon; I can feel
    A whimsy in my blood: I know not how,
    Success hath made me wanton. I could skip   5
    Out of my skin, now, like a subtle snake,
    I am so limber. O! your parasite[8]
    Is a most precious thing, dropped from above,
    Not bred 'mongst clods and clodpoles here on earth.
    I muse the mystery[9] was not made a science,   10
    It is so liberally professed! Almost
    All the wise world is little else, in nature,
    But parasites or sub-parasites. And yet
    I mean not those that have your bare town-art,
    To know who's fit to feed them; have no house,   15
    No family, no care, and therefore mold
    Tales for men's ears, to bait[1] that sense; or get
    Kitchen-invention, and some stale receipts
    To please the belly, and the groin; nor those,

---

6. You should have seen I was joking because the occasion was so trivial.
7. Immemorial commonplaces on the lust and treachery of women.
8. The comedies of Terence and Plautus, with which Jonson was thoroughly familiar, swarm with parasites; the very idea of the relationship was repugnant to his sturdy, Stoic independence of spirit.
9. Craft. Mosca is playing on the idea of the liberal arts and sciences.
1. The parasite who talks for a living "baits" (teases, gratifies) the sense of hearing; others gratify the bellies and groins of their patrons. "Receipts": recipes.

With their court dog-tricks, that can fawn and fleer,   20
Make their revènue out of legs and faces,[2]
Echo my lord, and lick away a moth:
But your fine elegant rascal, that can rise
And stoop almost together, like an arrow;
Shoot through the air as nimbly as a star;   25
Turn short as doth a swallow; and be here,
And there, and here, and yonder, all at once;
Present to any humor, all occasion;
And change a visor[3] swifter than a thought!
This is the creature had the art born with him;   30
Toils not to learn it, but doth practice it
Out of most excellent nature: and such sparks
Are the true parasites, others but their zanies.

SCENE 2

[*Enter* BONARIO.]

MOSCA. [*aside*] Who's this? Bonario, old Corbaccio's son?
   The person I was bound to seek.—Fair sir,
   You are happily met.
BONARIO.   That cannot be by thee.
MOSCA. Why, sir?
BONARIO.   Nay, pray thee know thy way, and leave me:
   I would be loath to interchange discourse
   With such a mate as thou art.   5
MOSCA.   Courteous sir,
   Scorn not my poverty.
BONARIO.   Not I, by heaven;
   But thou shalt give me leave to hate thy baseness.
MOSCA. Baseness!
BONARIO.   Ay; answer me, is not thy sloth
   Sufficient argument? thy flattery?   10
   Thy means of feeding?
MOSCA.   Heaven be good to me!
   These imputations are too common, sir,
   And easily stuck on virtue when she's poor.
   You are unequal to me, and howe'er
   Your sentence may be righteous, yet you are not,   15
   That, ere you know me, thus proceed in censure:
   St. Mark bear witness 'gainst you, 'tis inhuman. [*Weeps.*]
BONARIO. [*aside*] What! does he weep? The sign is soft and good;
   I do repent me that I was so harsh.
MOSCA. 'Tis true that, swayed by strong necessity,   20
   I am enforced to eat my careful bread
   With too much obsequy;[4] 'tis true, beside,
   That I am fain to spin mine own poor raiment
   Out of my mere observance,[5] being not born

---

2. Scrapings and looks of admiration.
3. I.e., the mask of his expression.

4. Flattery, obsequiousness.
5. Service.

To a free fortune: but that I have done 25
Base offices, in rending friends asunder,
Dividing families, betraying counsels,
Whispering false lies, or mining men with praises,
Trained their credulity with perjuries,
Corrupted chastity, or am in love 30
With mine own tender ease, but would not rather
Prove the most rugged and laborious course
That might redeem my present estimation,
Let me here perish in all hope of goodness.

BONARIO. [*aside*] This cannot be a personated passion.— 35
I was to blame, so to mistake thy nature;
Pray thee forgive me and speak out thy business.

MOSCA. Sir, it concerns you; and though I may seem
At first to make a main offense in manners,
And in my gratitude unto my master, 40
Yet for the pure love which I bear all right,
And hatred of the wrong, I must reveal it.
This very hour your father is in purpose
To disinherit you—

BONARIO.   How!

MOSCA.   And thrust you forth
As a mere stranger to his blood; 'tis true, sir. 45
The work no way engageth me, but as
I claim an interest in the general state
Of goodness and true virtue, which I hear
T' abound in you; and for which mere respect,
Without a second aim, sir, I have done it. 50

BONARIO. This tale hath lost thee much of the late trust
Thou hadst with me; it is impossible.
I know not how to lend it any thought,
My father should be so unnatural.

MOSCA. It is a confidence that well becomes 55
Your piety; and formed, no doubt, it is
From your own simple innocence, which makes
Your wrong more monstrous and abhorred. But, sir,
I now will tell you more. This very minute,
It is or will be doing; and, if you 60
Shall be but pleased to go with me, I'll bring you,
I dare not say where you shall see, but where
Your ear shall be a witness of the deed;
Hear yourself written bastard and professed
The common issue of the earth.[6]

BONARIO.   I'm mazed. 65

MOSCA. Sir, if I do it not, draw your just sword,
And score your vengeance on my front and face;
Mark me your villain: you have too much wrong,
And I do suffer for you, sir. My heart

---

6. A man without recognized father was known to the Romans as a *filius terrae*, "son of earth." "Mazed": dazed, bewildered.

Weeps blood in anguish—
BONARIO.   Lead; I follow thee.   [*Exeunt.*]   70

    SCENE 3. A *room in* VOLPONE'S *house.*

      [*Enter* VOLPONE.]

VOLPONE. Mosca stays long, methinks. Bring forth your sports,
    And help to make the wretched time more sweet.

      [*Enter* NANO, ANDROGYNO, *and* CASTRONE.]

NANO. *Dwarf, fool, and eunuch, well met here we be.*
    A question it were now, whether of us three,
    Being, all, the known delicates[7] of a rich man,
      In pleasing him, claim the precedency can?   5
CASTRONE. *I claim for myself.*
ANDROGYNO.   *And so doth the fool.*
NANO. *'Tis foolish indeed: let me set you both to school.*
    First for your dwarf, he's little and witty,
      And everything, as it is little, is pretty;   10
    Else why do men say to a creature of my shape,
      So soon as they see him, "It's a pretty little ape?"
    And why a pretty ape, but for pleasing imitation
      Of greater men's action, in a ridiculous fashion?
    Beside, this feat[8] body of mine doth not crave   15
      Half the meat, drink, and cloth one of your bulks will have.
    Admit your fool's face be the mother of laughter,
      Yet, for his brain, it must always come after:
    And though that do feed him, it's a pitiful case
      His body is beholding to such a bad face. [*Knocking within.*]   20
VOLPONE. Who's there? my couch; away! Look, Nano, see—

      [*Exeunt* ANDROGYNO *and* CASTRONE.]

    Give me my caps, first—go, enquire. [*Exit* NANO.] Now,
      Cupid
    Send it be Mosca, and with fair return!
NANO. [*within*] It is the beauteous madam—
VOLPONE.   Would-be—is it?
NANO. The same.
VOLPONE.   Now torment on me! Squire her in;   25
    For she will enter, or dwell here forever:
    Nay, quickly. [*Retires to his couch.*]—That my fit were past!
      I fear
    A second hell too, that my loathing this
    Will quite expel my appetite to the other:[9]
    Would she were taking now her tedious leave.   30
    Lord, how it threats me what I am to suffer!

7. Favorites.
8. Trim.
                            9. I.e., his loathing for Lady Politic may destroy
                            his appetite for Celia.

SCENE 4

[*Enter* NANO *with* LADY POLITIC WOULD-BE.]

LADY POLITIC. I thank you, good sir. Pray you signify
  Unto your patron I am here.—This band
  Shows not my neck enough.—I trouble you, sir.
  Let me request you, bid one of my women   5
  Come hither to me. In good faith, I am dressed
  Most favorably today. It is no matter;
  'Tis well enough.[1]

    [*Enter 1st* WAITING-WOMAN.]

                    Look, see, these petulant[2] things,
  How they have done this!
VOLPONE. [*aside*]   I do feel the fever
  Entering in at mine ears; O, for a charm   10
  To fright it hence!
LADY POLITIC.   Come nearer: is this curl
  In his right place? or this? Why is this higher
  Than all the rest? You have not washed your eyes yet?
  Or do they not stand even in your head?
  Where's your fellow? Call her. [*Exit 1st* WOMAN.]
NANO. [*aside*]   Now, St. Mark   15
  Deliver us! Anon she'll beat her women,
  Because her nose is red.

    [*Re-enter 1st with 2nd* WOMAN.]

LADY POLITIC.   I pray you, view
  This tire,[3] forsooth: are all things apt, or no?
2 WOMAN. One hair a little, here, sticks out, forsooth.
LADY POLITIC. Does 't so, forsooth! And where was your dear sight   20
  When it did so, forsooth![4] What now! bird-eyed?
  And you, too? Pray you both approach and mend it.
  Now, by that light, I muse you're not ashamed!
  I, that have preached these things so oft unto you,
  Read you the principles, argued all the grounds,   25
  Disputed every fitness, every grace,
  Called you to counsel of so frequent dressings—
NANO. [*aside*] More carefully than of your fame or honor.
LADY POLITIC. Made you acquainted what an ample dowry
  The knowledge of these things would be unto you,   30
  Able, alone, to get you noble husbands
  At your return; and you thus to neglect it!
  Besides, you seeing what a curious[5] nation
  The Italians are, what will they say of me?
  The English lady cannot dress herself.—   35

---

1. The theme of talkative women was ancient and
traditional; Jonson got a lot of Lady Politic's chatter from a Syrian sophist of the 4th century A.D.,
Libanius, who wrote a talkative book all about
talkative women.

2. Troublesome.
3. Headdress, arrangement of hair.
4. She strikes at them both, and jeers at their
flinching. "Bird-eyed": sharp of sight.
5. Fastidious, particular.

Here's a fine imputation to our country!
Well, go your ways, and stay in the next room.
This fucus[6] was too coarse too; it's no matter.
Good sir, you'll give them entertainment?

[*Exeunt* NANO *and* WAITING-WOMEN.]

VOLPONE. The storm comes toward me.
LADY POLITIC. [*goes to the couch*]   How does my Volpone?   40
VOLPONE. Troubled with noise; I cannot sleep; I dreamt
    That a strange fury entered now my house
    And with the dreadful tempest of her breath
    Did cleave my roof asunder.
LADY POLITIC.   Believe me, and I
    Had the most fearful dream, could I remember 't—   45
VOLPONE. [*aside*] Out on my fate! I have given her the
    occasion
    How to torment me: she will tell me hers.
LADY POLITIC. Methought, the golden mediocrity,[7]
    Polite, and delicate—
VOLPONE   O, if you do love me,
    No more; I sweat and suffer at the mention   50
    Of any dream: feel how I tremble yet.
LADY POLITIC. Alas, good soul! the passion of the heart.[8]
    Seed-pearl were good now, boiled with syrup of apples,
    Tincture of gold, and coral, citron-pills,
    Your elecampane root, myrobalanes[9]—   55
VOLPONE. [*aside*] Ay me, I have ta'en a grasshopper
    by the wing!
LADY POLITIC. Burnt silk, and amber; you have muscadel
    Good in the house—
VOLPONE.   You will not drink and part?
LADY POLITIC. No, fear not that. I doubt we shall not get
    Some English saffron—half a dram would serve;   60
    Your sixteen cloves, a little musk, dried mints,
    Bugloss,[1] and barley-meal—
VOLPONE. [*aside*]   She's in again!
    Before I feigned diseases, now I have one.
LADY POLITIC. And these applied with a right scarlet cloth.
VOLPONE. [*aside*] Another flood of words! a very torrent!   65
LADY POLITIC. Shall I, sir, make you a poultice?
VOLPONE.   No, no, no;
    I'm very well, you need prescribe no more.
LADY POLITIC. I have a little studied physic; but now,
    I'm all for music, save in the forenoons
    An hour or two for painting. I would have   70
    A lady, indeed, to have all letters and arts,
    Be able to discourse, to write, to paint,

---

6. Makeup. The last sentence is spoken to Nano.
7. Lady Would-be's mistake for the golden mean.
8. Heartburn.

9. Plants supposed to supply antidepressant drugs.
"Elecampane": a stimulant.
1. A common herb used as a mild stimulant.

But principal, as Plato holds, your music
(And so does wise Pythagoras, I take it)
Is your true rapture, when there is consent[2]   75
In face, in voice, and clothes: and is, indeed,
Our sex's chiefest ornament.

VOLPONE.   The poet
    As old in time as Plato, and as knowing,
    Says that your highest female grace is silence.[3]

LADY POLITIC. Which of your poets? Petrarch, or Tasso, or Dante?   80
    Guarini? Ariosto? Aretine?
    Cieco di Hadria?[4] I have read them all.

VOLPONE. [aside] Is everything a cause to my destruction?

LADY POLITIC. I think I have two or three of them about me.

VOLPONE. [aside] The sun, the sea, will sooner both stand still   85
    Than her eternal tongue! Nothing can 'scape it.

LADY POLITIC. Here's *Pastor Fido*[5]—

VOLPONE. [aside]   Profess obstinate silence;
    That's now my safest.

LADY POLITIC.   All our English writers,
    I mean such as are happy in th' Italian,
    Will deign to steal out of this author, mainly;   90
    Almost as much as from Montagnié:[6]
    He has so modern and facile a vein,
    Fitting the time, and catching the court-ear!
    Your Petrarch is more passionate, yet he,
    In days of sonneting, trusted them with much: 95
    Dante is hard, and few can understand him.
    But, for a desperate wit, there's Aretine;[7]
    Only, his pictures are a little obscene—
    You mark me not?

VOLPONE.   Alas, my mind's perturbed.

LADY POLITIC. Why, in such cases, we must cure ourselves,   100
    Make use of our philosophy—

VOLPONE.   Oh me!

LADY POLITIC. And as we find our passions do rebel,
    Encounter them with reason, or divert them
    By giving scope unto some other humor
    Of lesser danger; as in politic bodies,   105
    There's nothing more doth overwhelm the judgment,
    And cloud the understanding, than too much
    Settling and fixing and, as 't were, subsiding

---

2. Harmony, concord.
3. The poet as old as Plato is Sophocles (*Ajax*, line 293).
4. All Lady Politic's poets are well known today except Cieco di Hadria ("the blind man of Adria"), Luigi Groto; he was an actor as well as a poet, and made a tremendous impression by playing Oedipus (in Giustiniani's version of Sophocles' play) at the opening of Palladio's Teatro Olimpico at Vicenza (1585).

5. A pastoral by G. B. Guarini (1590), internationally popular.
6. Montaigne's name tended to be given three syllables by English tongues; his *Essays*, first published in 1580, were translated into English by Jonson's friend John Florio (1603).
7. Aretino's dirty poems, written to accompany some obscene drawings by Giulio Romano, were internationally notorious.

Upon one object. For the incorporating
Of these same outward things into that part   110
Which we call mental, leaves some certain feces[8]
That stop the organs and, as Plato says,
Assassinate our knowledge.

VOLPONE. [*aside*]   Now the spirit
Of patience help me!

LADY POLITIC.   Come, in faith, I must
Visit you more a-days, and make you well;   115
Laugh and be lusty.

VOLPONE. [*aside*]   My good angel save me!

LADY POLITIC. There was but one sole man in all the world
With whom I e'er could sympathize; and he
Would lie you often[9] three, four hours together
To hear me speak; and be sometime so rapt,   120
As he would answer me quite from the purpose,
Like you, and you are like him, just. I'll discourse,
An 't be but only, sir, to bring you asleep,
How we did spend our time and loves together,
For some six years.

VOLPONE.   Oh, oh, oh, oh, oh, oh!   125

LADY POLITIC. For we were *coaetanei*,[1] and brought up—

VOLPONE. Some power, some fate, some fortune rescue me!

SCENE 5

[*Enter* MOSCA.]

MOSCA. God save you, madam!

LADY POLITIC.   Good sir.

VOLPONE.   Mosca! welcome,
Welcome to my redemption!

MOSCA.   Why, sir?

VOLPONE. [*aside to* MOSCA]   O,
Rid me of this my torture, quickly, there;
My madam with the everlasting voice:
The bells in time of pestilence ne'er made   5
Like noise, or were in that perpetual motion!
The cockpit comes not near it.[2] All my house
But now steamed like a bath with her thick breath.
A lawyer could not have been heard; nor scarce
Another woman, such a hail of words   10
She has let fall. For hell's sake, rid her hence.

MOSCA. Has she presented?

VOLPONE.   O, I do not care;
I'll take her absence upon any price,
With any loss.

8. Traces. Lady Politic is into orthodox, but very verbose, psychology.
9. Would often lie (if you please).
1. Of an age.

2. When the plague struck, church bells were constantly tolling; at the cockpit spectators constantly shouted bets and encouragement to the birds.

MOSCA.   Madam—
LADY POLITIC.   I have brought your patron
  A toy, a cap here, of mine own work.
MOSCA.   'Tis well.   15
  I had forgot to tell you, I saw your knight,
  Where you would little think it—
LADY POLITIC.   Where?
MOSCA.   Marry,
  Where yet, if you make haste, you may apprehend him,
  Rowing upon the water in a gondola,
  With the most cunning courtesan of Venice.   20
LADY POLITIC. Is 't true?
MOSCA.   Pursue them, and believe your eyes:
  Leave me to make your gift. [*Exit* LADY POLITIC *hastily*.]—I
      knew 'twould take:
  For, lightly,[3] they that use themselves most license
  Are still most jealous.
VOLPONE.   Mosca, hearty thanks
  For thy quick fiction and delivery of me.   25
  Now to my hopes, what sayest thou?

        [*Re-enter* LADY POLITIC.]

LADY POLITIC.   But do you hear, sir?—
VOLPONE. Again! I fear a paroxysm.
LADY POLITIC.   Which way
  Rowed they together?
MOSCA.   Toward the Rialto.
LADY POLITIC. I pray you lend me your dwarf.
MOSCA.   I pray you take him—

                          [*Exit* LADY POLITIC.]

  Your hopes, sir, are like happy blossoms: fair,   30
  And promise timely fruit, if you will stay
  But the maturing; keep you at your couch.
  Corbaccio will arrive straight, with the will;
  When he is gone, I'll tell you more.   [*Exit.*]
VOLPONE.   My blood,
  My spirits are returned; I am alive: 35
  And, like your wanton gamester at primero,[4]
  Whose thought had whispered to him, not go less,
  Methinks I lie, and draw—for an encounter.

        [*The bed-curtains close upon* VOLPONE.]

  SCENE 6. *The Passage Leading to* VOLPONE'*s Chamber*.

        [*Enter* MOSCA *and* BONARIO.]

---

3. Commonly (an old sense of the word).
4. An early form of the Spanish card game later
known as ombre 'he game played in Pope's *Rape*
of the Lock). The phrases "go less," "draw," and
"encounter" are all used in primero.

MOSCA. Sir, here concealed, [*Shows him a closet.*] you may hear
    all. But, pray you,
  Have patience, sir. [*Knocking within.*]—The same's your
    father knocks: 40
  I am compelled to leave you.   [*Exit.*]
BONARIO.   Do so. Yet
  Cannot my thought imagine this a truth.   [*Goes into the closet.*]

SCENE 7. *Another part of the same.*

[*Enter* MOSCA *and* CORVINO, CELIA *following.*]

MOSCA. Death on me! You are come too soon, what meant you?
  Did not I say, I would send?
CORVINO.   Yes, but I feared
  You might forget it, and then they prevent us.
MOSCA. [*aside*] Prevent! Did e'er man haste so for his horns?
  A courtier would not ply it so, for a place.   5
  —Well, now there is no helping it, stay here;
  I'll presently return.

    [*Crosses stage to* BONARIO.]

CORVINO.   Where are you, Celia?
  You know not wherefore I have brought you hither?
CELIA. Not well, except you told me.
CORVINO.   Now, I will:
  Hark hither. [*He leads her apart, and whispers to her.*]
MOSCA. [*to* BONARIO] Sir, your father hath sent word   10
  It will be half an hour ere he come;
  And therefore, if you please to walk the while
  Into that gallery—at the upper end
  There are some books to entertain the time;
  And I'll take care no man shall come unto you, sir.   15
BONARIO. Yes, I will stay there. [*aside.*]—I do doubt this
  fellow.   [*Exit* BONARIO.]
MOSCA. [*looking after him*] There, he is far enough; he can
  hear nothing:
  And, for his father, I can keep him off.

    [*Goes to* VOLPONE'S *couch, opens the curtains, and whispers with
    him.*]

CORVINO. [*to* CELIA] Nay, now, there is no starting back, and
  therefore
  Resolve upon it: I have so decreed.   20
  It must be done. Nor would I move 't afore,
  Because I would avoid all shifts and tricks
  That might deny me.
CELIA.   Sir, let me beseech you,
  Affect not these strange trials;[5] if you doubt

5. Don't tempt me so.

My chastity, why, lock me up forever;   25
Make me the heir of darkness. Let me live
Where I may please your fears, if not your trust.
CORVINO. Believe it, I have no such humor, I.
    All that I speak I mean; yet I'm not mad;
    Not horn-mad, see you? Go to, show yourself   30
    Obedient, and a wife.
CELIA.   O heaven!
CORVINO.   I say it,
    Do so.
CELIA.   Was this the train?[6]
CORVINO.   I've told you reasons:
    What the physicians have set down; how much
    It may concern me; what my engagements are;
    My means; and the necessity of those means,   35
    For my recovery:[7] wherefore, if you be
    Loyal and mine, be won, respect my venture.[8]
CELIA. Before your honor?
CORVINO.   Honor! tut, a breath;[9]
    There's no such thing in nature. A mere term
    Invented to awe fools. What is my gold   40
    The worse for touching, clothes for being looked on?
    Why, this 's no more. An old decrepit wretch,
    That has no sense, no sinew; takes his meat
    With others' fingers; only knows to gape
    When you do scald his gums;[1] a voice; a shadow;   45
    And what can this man hurt you?
CELIA. [aside]   Lord! what spirit
    Is this hath entered him?
CORVINO.   And for your fame,[2]
    That's such a jig; as if I would go tell it,
    Cry it on the Piazza! Who shall know it,
    But he that cannot speak it, and this fellow,[3]   50
    Whose lips are in my pocket? Save yourself
    (If you'll proclaim 't, you may), I know no other
    Should come to know it.
CELIA.   Are heaven and saints then nothing?
    Will they be blind or stupid?
CORVINO.   How!
CELIA.   Good sir,
    Be jealous still, emulate them;[4] and think   55
    What hate they burn with toward every sin.
CORVINO. I grant you; if I thought it were a sin,
    I would not urge you. Should I offer this
    To some young Frenchman, or hot Tuscan blood

6. Is this what you had in mind all the time?
7. Corvino is evidently in financial straits.
8. In the sense of a commercial venture.
9. Like Falstaff (1 Henry IV 5.1), Corvino disposes easily of honor.
1. I.e., the old man has to be fed by others, and

doesn't even know enough to open his own mouth for food.
2. Reputation. "Jig": farce, joke.
3. "He that cannot speak it": Volpone. "This fellow": Mosca.
4. I.e., God and the saints, who hate sin.

That had read Aretine, conned all his prints,[5]   60
Knew every quirk within lust's labyrinth,
And were professed critic in lechery,
And I would look upon him, and applaud him,
This were a sin: but here, 'tis contrary,
A pious work, mere charity, for physic,   65
And honest polity to assure mine own.[6]

CELIA. O heaven! canst thou suffer such a change?

VOLPONE. Thou art mine honor, Mosca, and my pride,
  My joy, my tickling, my delight! Go bring them.

MOSCA. [*advancing*] Please you draw near, sir.

CORVINO.   Come on, what—   70
  You will not be rebellious? By that light—

MOSCA.   Sir,
  Signor Corvino here is come to see you—

VOLPONE.   O!

MOSCA. And hearing of the consultation had,
  So lately, for your health, is come to offer,
  Or rather, sir, to prostitute—

CORVINO.   Thanks, sweet Mosca.   75

MOSCA. Freely, unasked, or unentreated—

CORVINO.   Well.

MOSCA. As the true fervent instance of his love,
  His own most fair and proper wife, the beauty
  Only of price in Venice—

CORVINO.   'Tis well urged.

MOSCA. To be your comfortress, and to preserve you.   80

VOLPONE. Alas, I'm past, already! Pray you, thank him
  For his good care and promptness; but for that,
  'Tis a vain labor e'en to fight 'gainst heaven;
  Applying fire to stone—uh, uh, uh, uh! [*coughing*]—
  Making a dead leaf grow again. I take   85
  His wishes gently, though; and you may tell him
  What I've done for him: marry, my state is hopeless.
  Will him to pray for me; and to use his fortune
  With reverence, when he comes to 't.

MOSCA.   Do you hear, sir?
  Go to him with your wife.

CORVINO. [*to* CELIA]   Heart of my father!   90
  Wilt thou persist thus? Come, I pray thee, come.
  Thou seest 'tis nothing. Celia! By this hand,
  I shall grow violent. Come, do 't, I say.

CELIA. Sir, kill me, rather: I will take down poison,
  Eat burning coals, do anything.

CORVINO.   Be damned!   95
  'Heart! I will drag thee hence, home, by the hair;

---

5. I.e., that had read Aretino's poems and studied the obscene illustrations to them.

6. "Pious work" means it's good for the soul, "mere charity" says it's kindness to the neighbor, "for

physic" says it's good for the health; but "honest policy to assure mine own" gets down to the basic motivation—greed.

Cry thee a strumpet through the streets; rip up
Thy mouth unto thine ears; and slit thy nose,
Like a raw rochet![7]—Do not tempt me; come,
Yield, I am loath—Death! I will buy some slave   100
Whom I will kill, and bind thee to him, alive;
And at my window hang you forth, devising
Some monstrous crime which I, in capital letters,
Will eat into thy flesh with aquafortis
And burning corsives,[8] on this stubborn breast.   105
Now, by the blood thou hast incensed, I'll do it!
CELIA. Sir, what you please you may, I am your martyr.
CORVINO. Be not thus obstinate, I have not deserved it:
   Think who it is entreats you. Pray thee, sweet;
   Good faith, thou shalt have jewels, gowns, attires,   110
   What thou wilt think, and ask. Do but go kiss him.
   Or touch him, but. For my sake. At my suit.
   This once. No? Not? I shall remember this.
   Will you disgrace me thus? Do you thirst my undoing?
MOSCA. Nay, gentle lady, be advised.
CORVINO.   No, no.   115
   She has watched her time. God's precious, this is scurvy,[9]
   'Tis very scurvy; and you are—
MOSCA.   Nay, good sir.
CORVINO. An arrant locust, by heaven, a locust! Whore,
   Crocodile, that hast thy tears prepared,
   Expecting how thou 'lt bid them flow—
MOSCA.   Nay, pray you, sir!   120
   She will consider.
CELIA.   Would my life would serve
   To satisfy—
CORVINO.   'Sdeath! If she would but speak to him,
   And save my reputation, 'twere somewhat;
   But spitefully to affect my utter ruin!
MOSCA. Ay, now you've put your fortune in her hands.   125
   Why, i 'faith, it is her modesty; I must quit[1] her.
   If you were absent, she would be more coming;
   I know it, and dare undertake for her.
   What woman can before her husband? Pray you,
   Let us depart, and leave her here.
CORVINO.   Sweet Celia,   130
   Thou mayst redeem all yet; I'll say no more:
   If not, esteem yourself as lost. Nay, stay there.

                      [Shuts the door, and exit with MOSCA.]

CELIA. O God, and his good angels! whither, whither,
   Is shame fled human breasts? that with such ease

---

7. Like a fish.
8. With acids and corrosives.
9. I.e., by God's precious blood, this is villainous.
For her husband, Celia is a "locust" because a
devouring plague, a "crocodile" because of her
hypocritical tears.
1. Acquit. "Coming": forthcoming.

Men dare put off your honors, and their own?   135
Is that which ever was a cause of life
Now placed beneath the basest circumstance,
And modesty an exile made, for money?
VOLPONE. Ay, in Corvino, and such earth-fed minds, [*leaping from his couch*]
That never tasted the true heaven of love.   140
Assure thee, Celia, he that would sell thee,
Only for hope of gain, and that uncertain,
He would have sold his part of Paradise
For ready money, had he met a cope-man.[2]
Why are thou mazed to see me thus revived?   145
Rather applaud thy beauty's miracle;
'Tis thy great work:[3] that hath, not now alone,
But sundry times raised me, in several shapes,
And, but this morning, like a mountebank,
To see thee at thy window. Ay, before   150
I would have left my practice for thy love,
In varying figures I would have contended
With the blue Proteus, or the hornèd flood.[4]
Now art thou welcome.
CELIA.   Sir!
VOLPONE.   Nay, fly me not.
Nor let thy false imagination   155
That I was bed-rid, make thee think I am so:
Thou shalt not find it. I am now as fresh,
As hot, as high, and in as jovial plight
As when in that so celebrated scene
At recitation of our comedy,   160
For entertainment of the great Valois,[5]
I acted young Antinous; and attracted
The eyes and ears of all the ladies present,
To admire each graceful gesture, note, and footing.

Song[6]   165

        Come, my Celia, let us prove,
        While we can, the sports of love;
        Time will not be ours forever,
        He, at length, our good will sever;
        Spend not then his gifts in vain.   170
        Suns that set may rise again;
        But if once we lose this light,

---

2. Buyer.
3. "The great work" is always the philosopher's stone, which converts base metals to gold.
4. Proteus was a sea god who could take any shape at will; Virgil calls him "blue Proteus." Achelous was a river god who fought with Hercules for possession of Deianira; he fought first as a river, then as a snake, and finally as a bull (hence "the hornèd flood"), but was beaten in all three shapes (Ovid, *Metamorphoses* 9).

5. Henry of Valois, Duke of Anjou, and newly created King Henry III of France, visited Venice in 1574, and was entertained with splendid festivities. Antinous was the favorite (catamite) of Emperor Hadrian, in Roman antiquity.
6. The opening lines are adapted from Catullus, boldest and bawdiest of Latin lyricists, and the whole song emphasises the theme of "*carpe diem*" (clutch the fleeting moment), which is a common erotic incitement.

'Tis with us perpetual night.
Why should we defer our joys?
Fame and rumor are but toys.   175
Cannot we delude the eyes
Of a few poor household spies?
Or his easier ears beguile,
Thus removèd by our wile?
'Tis no sin love's fruits to steal;   180
But the sweet thefts to reveal,
To be taken, to be seen,
These have crimes accounted been.

CELIA. Some sèrene[7] blast me, or dire lightning strike
   This my offending face!
VOLPONE.   Why droops my Celia?   185
   Thou hast, in place of a base husband, found
   A worthy lover: use thy fortune well,
   With secrecy and pleasure. See, behold
   What thou art queen of; not in expectation,
   As I feed others, but possessed and crowned.   190
   See here a rope of pearl, and each more orient
   Than that the brave Egyptian queen caroused:[8]
   Dissolve and drink them. See, a carbuncle[9]
   May put out both the eyes of our St. Mark;
   A diamond, would have bought Lollia Paulina,   195
   When she came in like starlight, hid with jewels
   That were the spoils of provinces;[1] take these,
   And wear, and lose them: yet remains an earring
   To purchase them again, and this whole state.
   A gem but worth a private patrimony   200
   Is nothing: we will eat such at a meal.
   The heads of parrots, tongues of nightingales,
   The brains of peacocks, and of ostriches
   Shall be our food: and, could we get the phoenix,[2]
   Though nature lost her kind, she were our dish.   205
CELIA. Good sir, these things might move a mind affected
   With such delights; but I, whose innocence
   Is all I can think wealthy, or worth th' enjoying,
   And which, once lost, I have nought to lose beyond it,
   Cannot be taken with these sensual baits: 210
   If you have conscience—
VOLPONE.   'Tis the beggar's virtue;
   If thou hast wisdom, hear me, Celia.
   Thy baths shall be the juice of gilly-flowers,[3]

7. Mist from heaven, malignant influence.
8. According to a common story, Cleopatra dissolved a precious pearl in wine and during a banquet with Antony drank it up.
9. Ruby.
1. Lollia Paulina, wife of a Roman governor, is said by Pliny (*Natural History* 9.117) to have worn

in her hair jewels enough to represent the loot of several provinces.
2. Only one phoenix is said to be alive at any one time; eating him would eradicate the species.
3. Clove-scented flowers used to flavor drinks and as a light perfume.

Spirit of roses, and of violets,
The milk of unicorns, and panthers' breath   215
Gathered in bags and mixed with Cretan wines.[4]
Our drink shall be preparèd gold and amber,
Which we will take until my roof whirl round
With the vertigo; and my dwarf shall dance,
My eunuch sing, my fool make up the antic,   220
Whilst we, in changèd shapes, act Ovid's tales,[5]
Thou like Europa now, and I like Jove,
Then I like Mars and thou like Erycine:
So of the rest, till we have quite run through
And wearied all the fables of the gods.   225
Then will I have thee in more modern forms,
Attirèd like some sprightly dame of France,
Brave Tuscan lady, or proud Spanish beauty;
Sometimes, unto the Persian Sophy's wife,[6]
Or the Grand Signor's mistress; and, for change,   230
To one of our most artful courtesans,
Or some quick Negro, or cold Russian;
And I will meet thee in as many shapes:
Where we may so transfuse our wandering souls
Out at our lips, and score up sums of pleasures, [*Sings.*]   235

> That the curious shall not know
>   How to tell them as they flow;
> And the envious, when they find
>   What their number is, be pined.[7]

CELIA. If you have ears that will be pierced; or eyes   240
  That can be opened; a heart may be touched;
  Or any part that yet sounds man about you;
  If you have touch of holy saints, or heaven,
  Do me the grace to let me 'scape. If not,
  Be bountiful and kill me. You do know   245
  I am a creature hither ill betrayed
  By one whose shame I would forget it were.
  If you will deign me neither of these graces,
  Yet feed your wrath, sir, rather than your lust
  (It is a vice comes nearer manliness),   250
  And punish that unhappy crime of nature,
  Which you miscall my beauty; flay my face,
  Or poison it with ointments for seducing
  Your blood to this rebellion. Rub these hands
  With what may cause an eating leprosy,   255
  E'en to my bones and marrow: anything
  That may disfavor[8] me, save in my honor—

4. The most expensive known to Jonson's age.
5. I.e., enact the fables in the *Metamorphoses.*
"Erycine" is one of the epithets of Venus.
6. The "Sophy" is the Shah of Persia, the "Grand
Signor" the Sultan of Turkey.
7. Envious, depressed. The verses, once again, are
adapted from Catullus.
8. Disfigure.

And I will kneel to you, pray for you, pay down
A thousand hourly vows, sir, for your health;
Report, and think you virtuous—   260
VOLPONE.   Think me cold,
Frozen, and impotent, and so report me?
That I had Nestor's hernia,[9] thou wouldst think.
I do degenerate, and abuse my nation,
To play with opportunity thus long;
I should have done the act, and then have parleyed.   265
Yield, or I'll force thee.   [Seizes her.]
CELIA.   O! just God!
VOLPONE.   In vain—
BONARIO. [rushing in] Forbear, foul ravisher! libidinous swine!
Free the forced lady, or thou diest, impostor!
But that I'm loath to snatch thy punishment
Out of the hand of justice, thou shouldst yet   270
Be made the timely sacrifice of vengeance
Before this altar, and this dross, thy idol.
Lady, let's quit the place, it is the den
Of villainy; fear nought, you have a guard:
And he ere long shall meet his just reward. [Exeunt BONARIO and
    CELIA.]   275
VOLPONE. Fall on me, roof, and bury me in ruin!
Become my grave, that wert my shelter! O!
I am unmasked, unspirited, undone,
Betrayed to beggary, to infamy—

SCENE 8

[Enter MOSCA, wounded and bleeding.]

MOSCA. Where shall I run, most wretched shame of men,
To beat out my unlucky brains?
VOLPONE.   Here, here.
What! dost thou bleed?
MOSCA.   O that his well-driven sword
Had been so courteous to have cleft me down
Unto the navel, ere I lived to see   5
My life, my hopes, my spirits, my patron, all
Thus desperately engagèd, by my error!
VOLPONE. Woe on thy fortune!
MOSCA.   And my follies, sir.
VOLPONE. Thou hast made me miserable.
MOSCA.   And myself, sir.
Who would have thought he would have hearkened so?   10
VOLPONE. What shall we do?
MOSCA.   I know not; if my heart
Could expiate the mischance, I'd pluck it out.

---

9. Senile impotence; the phrase is from Juvenal's sixth satire.

Will you be pleased to hang me? or cut my throat?
And I'll requite you, sir. Let's die like Romans,
Since we have lived like Grecians.[1] [*Knocking within.*]
VOLPONE.   Hark! who's there? 15
I hear some footing; officers, the Saffi,[2]
Come to apprehend us! I do feel the brand
Hissing already at my forehead; now
Mine ears are boring.[3]
MOSCA.   To your couch, sir; you
Make that place good, however. [VOLPONE *lies down, as before.*]—
Guilty men   20
Suspect what they deserve still. Signor Corbaccio!

SCENE 9

[*Enter* CORBACCIO *with* VOLTORE *behind, unseen.*]

CORBACCIO. Why, how now, Mosca?
MOSCA.   O, undone, amazed, sir.
Your son, I know not by what accident,
Acquainted with your purpose to my patron
Touching your will, and making him your heir,
Entered our house with violence, his sword drawn,   5
Sought for you, called you wretch, unnatural,
Vowed he would kill you.
CORBACCIO.   Me!
MOSCA.   Yes, and my patron.
CORBACCIO. This act shall disinherit him indeed:
Here is the will.
MOSCA.   'Tis well, sir.
CORBACCIO.   Right and well;
Be you as careful now for me.
MOSCA.   My life, sir,   10
Is not more tendered; I am only yours.
CORBACCIO. How does he? Will he die shortly, think'st thou?
MOSCA.   I fear
He'll outlast May.
CORBACCIO.   Today?
MOSCA.   No, last out May, sir.
CORBACCIO. Couldst thou not give him a dram?
MOSCA.   O, by no means, sir.
CORBACCIO. Nay, I'll not bid you.
VOLTORE. [*coming forward*]   This is a knave, I see.   15
MOSCA. [*seeing* VOLTORE, *aside*] How! Signor Voltore! Did he hear me?
VOLTORE.   Parasite!
MOSCA. Who's that? O, sir, most timely welcome—
VOLTORE.   Scarce

---

1. Greeks, especially Corinthians, were famous for living in luxury; Romans for committing suicide with dignity when life no longer appeared worthy of them.

2. Police officers, investigators.
3. Branding on the face and boring holes in the ears were common criminal punishments.

To the discovery of your tricks, I fear.
You are his, *only?* and mine also, are you not?
MOSCA. Who? I, sir?
VOLTORE.   You, sir. What device is this   20
About a will?
MOSCA.   A plot for you, sir.
VOLTORE.   Come,
Put not your foists[4] upon me; I shall scent them.
MOSCA. Did you not hear it?
VOLTORE.   Yes, I hear Corbaccio
Hath made your patron there his heir.
MOSCA.   'Tis true,
By my device, drawn to it by my plot,   25
With hope—
VOLTORE.   Your patron should reciprocate?
And you have promised?
MOSCA.   For your good, I did, sir.
Nay more, I told his son, brought, hid him here,
Where he might hear his father pass the deed;
Being persuaded to it by this thought, sir,   30
That the unnaturalness, first, of the act,
And then his father's oft disclaiming in him
(Which I did mean t' help on), would sure enrage him
To do some violence upon his parent,
On which the law should take sufficient hold,   35
And you be stated[5] in a double hope:
Truth be my comfort, and my conscience,
My only aim was to dig you a fortune
Out of these two old rotten sepulchres—
VOLTORE. I cry thee mercy, Mosca.
MOSCA.   Worth your patience,   40
And your great merit, sir. And see the change!
VOLTORE. Why, what success?[6]
MOSCA.   Most hapless! you must help, sir.
Whilst we expected the old raven, in comes
Corvino's wife, sent hither by her husband—
VOLTORE. What, with a present?
MOSCA.   No, sir, on visitation   45
(I'll tell you how anon); and, staying long,
The youth he grows impatient, rushes forth,
Seizeth the lady, wounds me, makes her swear
(Or he would murder her, that was his vow)
To affirm my patron to have done her rape: 50
Which how unlike it is, you see! and hence,
With that pretext he's gone to accuse his father,
Defame my patron, defeat you—

4. Tricks, but also bad smells.   6. Result, outcome.
5. Installed.

VOLTORE.   Where's her husband?
  Let him be sent for straight.
MOSCA.   Sir, I'll go fetch him.
VOLTORE. Bring him to the Scrutineo.[7]
MOSCA.   Sir, I will.   55
VOLTORE. This must be stopped.
MOSCA.   O, you do nobly, sir.
  Alas, 'twas labored all, sir, for your good;
  Nor was there want of counsel in the plot:
  But fortune can, at any time, o'erthrow
  The projects of a hundred learnèd clerks,[8] sir.   60
CORBACCIO. [listening] What's that?
VOLTORE.   Will 't please you, sir, to go
    along?   [Exit CORBACCIO followed by VOLTORE.]
MOSCA. Patron, go in, and pray for our success.
VOLPONE. [rising from his couch] Need makes devotion: heaven
    your labor bless!   [Exeunt.]

Act 4

SCENE 1. A street.

[Enter SIR POLITIC WOULD-BE and PEREGRINE.]

SIR POLITIC. I told you, sir, it was a plot; you see
  What observation is! You mentioned[9] me
  For some instructions: I will tell you, sir
  (Since we are met here in this height of Venice),
  Some few particulars I have set down   5
  Only for this meridian, fit to be known
  Of your crude traveler; and they are these.
  I will not touch, sir, at your phrase, or clothes,
  For they are old.
PEREGRINE.   Sir, I have better.
SIR POLITIC.   Pardon,
  I meant, as they are themes.
PEREGRINE.   O, sir, proceed: 10
  I'll slander you no more of wit, good sir.
SIR POLITIC. First, for your garb,[1] it must be grave and serious,
  Very reserved and locked; not tell a secret
  On any terms, not to your father; scarce
  A fable but with caution; make sure choice   15
  Both of your company and discourse; beware
  You never speak a truth—
PEREGRINE.   How!

7. The court of law. Jonson's court, like courts on   8. Scholars.
the Continent generally, has power to look into   9. Asked.
abuses and investigate possible violations of the law,   1. Comportment.
before any particular suit is filed.

SIR POLITIC.   Not to strangers,
  For those be they you must converse with most;
  Others I would not know, sir, but at distance,
  So as I still might be a saver in them:[2]   20
  You shall have tricks, else, passed upon you hourly.
  And then, for your religion, profess none,
  But wonder at the diversity of all;
  And, for your part, protest, were there no other
  But simply the laws o' th' land, you could content you.   25
  Nick Machiavel and Monsieur Bodin both
  Were of this mind.[3] Then must you learn the use
  And handling of your silver fork at meals,[4]
  The metal of your glass (these are main matters
  With your Italian), and to know the hour   30
  When you must eat your melons and your figs.
PEREGRINE. Is that a point of state too?
SIR POLITIC.   Here it is:
  For your Venetian, if he see a man
  Preposterous[5] in the least, he has him straight;
  He has: he strips him. I'll acquaint you, sir.   35
  I now have lived here, 'tis some fourteen months;
  Within the first week of my landing here,
  All took me for a citizen of Venice,
  I knew the forms so well—
PEREGRINE. [aside]   And nothing else.
SIR POLITIC. I had read Contarine,[6] took me a house,   40
  Dealt with my Jews to furnish it with movables—
  Well, if I could but find one man, one man
  To mine own heart, whom I durst trust, I would—
PEREGRINE. What, what, sir?
SIR POLITIC.   Make him rich; make him a fortune;
  He should not think again. I would command it.   45
PEREGRINE. As how?
SIR POLITIC.   With certain projects[7] that I have
  Which I may not discover.
PEREGRINE. [aside]   If I had
  But one to wager with, I would lay odds now,
  He tells me instantly.
SIR POLITIC.   One is (and that
  I care not greatly who knows) to serve the state   50
  Of Venice with red herrings for three years,

---

2. The implication is clear: Don't lend anybody money.

3. The abbreviation "Nick Machiavel" implies casual familiarity; the sentiment attributed to Machiavelli shows complete ignorance of him. Sir Politic Would-be is more nearly right in his estimate of Jean Bodin, the French political philosopher, who did advocate religious toleration.

4. Handling a fork was a new experience for Englishmen who traveled abroad in Jonson's time; back home, fingers were still the preferred instruments. "The metal of your glass": literally, the composition of your glass (perhaps to know what could or couldn't be put in it).

5. In its literal Latin sense, getting things back to front.

6. Contarini wrote a book on Venetian government, which Sir Politic would be quick to know. "My Jews": in the indefinite sense—the usual Jews that everybody goes to for furniture to set up a Venetian apartment.

7. Schemes for social improvement or making money (or preferably both) were favorite targets of 17th-century satire. "Discover": disclose.

And at a certain rate, from Rotterdam,[8]
Where I have correspondence. There's a letter,
Sent me from one o' the States,[9] and to that purpose;
He cannot write his name, but that's his mark.   55
PEREGRINE. He is a chandler?
SIR POLITIC.   No, a cheesemonger.
There are some other too with whom I treat
About the same negotiation;
And I will undertake it: for, 'tis thus,
I'll do't with ease, I've cast it all.[1] Your hoy   60
Carries but three men in her, and a boy;
And she shall make me three returns a year.
So, if there come but one of three, I save;
If two, I can defalk[2]: but this is now
If my main project fail.
PEREGRINE.   Then you have others?   65
SIR POLITIC. I should be loath to draw the subtle air
Of such a place without my thousand aims.
I'll not dissemble, sir; where'er I come,
I love to be considerative; and 'tis true,
I have at my free hours thought upon   70
Some certain goods unto the state of Venice,
Which I do call my *Cautions*; and, sir, which
I mean, in hope of pension, to propound
To the Great Council, then unto the Forty,
So to the Ten.[3] My means are made already—   75
PEREGRINE. By whom?
SIR POLITIC.   Sir, one that, though his place be obscure,
Yet he can sway, and they will hear him. He's
A *commendatore*.
PEREGRINE.   What! a common sergeant?
SIR POLITIC. Sir, such as they are put it in their mouths
What they should say, sometimes, as well as greater.   80
I think I have my notes to show you—[*Searching his pockets.*]
PEREGRINE.   Good, sir.
SIR POLITIC. But you shall swear unto me, on your gentry,[4]
Not to anticipate—
PEREGRINE.   I, sir!
SIR POLITIC.   Nor reveal
A circumstance—My paper is not with me.
PEREGRINE. O, but you can remember, sir.
SIR POLITIC.   My first is   85
Concerning tinder boxes.[5] You must know
No family is here without its box.

---

8. The Venetians have plenty of fresh fish in the Adriatic.

9. I.e., from one of the States-General in Holland.

1. Figured it all out. "Hoy": a small North Sea coastal vessel; such a boat would have great trouble making a trip to Venice, let alone carrying a worthwhile cargo.

2. Reduce the amount, cut back, maybe even go into bankruptcy.

3. Representative legislative bodies, increasingly narrow and increasingly lofty, of the Venetian government. "My means": my approaches to these eminent bodies.

4. As you are a gentleman.

5. As we would say, matchboxes or cigarette lighters.

Now, sir, it being so portable a thing,
Put case that you or I were ill affected
Unto the state; sir, with it in our pockets,   90
Might not I go into the Arsenal,[6]
Or you? come out again? and none the wiser?
PEREGRINE. Except yourself, sir.
SIR POLITIC.   Go to, then. I therefore
Advertise to the state, how fit it were
That none but such as were known patriots,   95
Sound lovers of their country, should be suffered
To enjoy them in their houses; and even those
Sealed at some office, and at such a bigness
As might not lurk in pockets.
PEREGRINE.   Admirable!
SIR POLITIC. My next is, how to inquire, and be resolved   100
By present demonstration, whether a ship
Newly arrived from Syria, or from
Any suspected part of all the Levant,[7]
Be guilty of the plague; and where they use
To lie out forty, fifty days, sometimes,   105
About the Lazaretto,[8] for their trial,
I'll save that charge and loss unto the merchant,
And in an hour clear the doubt.
PEREGRINE.   Indeed, sir!
SIR POLITIC. Or—I will lose my labor.
PEREGRINE.   My faith, that's much.
SIR POLITIC. Nay, sir, conceive me. 'Twill cost me in onions,   110
Some thirty livres—[9]
PEREGRINE.   Which is one pound sterling.
SIR POLITIC. Besides my water works; for this I do, sir:
First, I bring in your ship 'twixt two brick walls;
But those the state shall venture. On the one
I strain[1] me a fair tarpaulin, and in that   115
I stick my onions, cut in halves; the other
Is full of loop holes, out at which I thrust
The noses of my bellows; and those bellows
I keep, with water works,[2] in perpetual motion,
Which is the easiest matter of a hundred.   120
Now, sir, your onion, which doth naturally
Attract the infection, and your bellows blowing
The air upon him, will show instantly,
By his changed color, if there be contagion,

6. Venice being largely a maritime power, the Arsenal where ships were built and repaired was (and still is) an important part of the city.
7. The Middle East.
8. Quarantine hospital. Bubonic plague, carried by fleas living on shipboard rats, was a constant peril in Venice, where trade with the Middle East was particularly busy. Ships had to wait several months in port before debarking crew, passengers, or cargo.

9. A French coin of small value. Onions were reputed to be good against the plague; cut open, they supposedly absorbed the plague germs from the air.
1. Stretch.
2. Sir Politic's waterworks are apparently a water wheel arranged to operate a bellows. Of course there is no spot in the flat country around Venice where streams have enough impetus to turn a wheel.

Or else remain as fair as at the first.   125
—Now 'tis known, 'tis nothing.
PEREGRINE.   You are right, sir.
SIR POLITIC. I would I had my note.
PEREGRINE.   Faith, so would I:
But you have done well for once, sir.
SIR POLITIC.   Were I false,
Or would be made so, I could show you reasons
How I could sell this state now to the Turk,[3]   130
Spite of their galleys, or their—[*Examining his papers.*]
PEREGRINE.   Pray you, Sir Pol.
SIR POLITIC. I have them not about me.
PEREGRINE.   That I feared.
They are there, sir?
SIR POLITIC.   No, this is my diary,
Wherein I note my actions of the day.
PEREGRINE. Pray you let's see, sir. What is here? [*Reads.*] *Notan-*
        dum,[4]   135
A rat had gnawn my spur leathers; notwithstanding,
I put on new and did go forth; but first
I threw three beans over the threshold. Item,
I went, and bought two tooth picks, whereof one
I burst immediately in a discourse   140
With a Dutch merchant 'bout ragion del stato.[5]
From him I went and paid a moccenigo
For piecing my silk stockings; by the way
I cheapened sprats;[6] *and at St. Mark's I urined.*
Faith, these are politic notes!
SIR POLITIC.   Sir, I do slip   145
No action of my life, thus, but I quote it.
PEREGRINE. Believe me, it is wise!
SIR POLITIC.   Nay, sir, read forth.

                              SCENE 2

[*Enter, at a distance,* LADY POLITIC WOULD-BE, NANO, *and two*
WAITING-WOMEN.]

LADY POLITIC. Where should this loose knight be, trow? Sure, he's
        housed.[7]
NANO. Why, then he's fast.
LADY POLITIC.   Ay, he plays both with me.[8]
I pray you stay. This heat will do more harm
To my complexion than his heart is worth.
(I do not care to hinder, but to take him.)   5
How it[9] comes off!   [*Rubbing her cheeks.*]

3. Here Sir Politic is verging on real subversion,
and Peregrine quickly shuts him off.
4. Take special note.
5. Literally, "reason of state," but also the title of
a famous book by Giovanni Botero, presenting a
diluted version of Machiavelli's thought.
6. Bargained over some trifling fish. "Piecing":
mending.
7. Gone into somebody's house. "He's fast" implies
that he's securely fastened and in fast company.
8. Both fast and loose.
9. I.e., her complexion.

1 WOMAN.   My master's yonder.
LADY POLITIC.   Where?
2 WOMAN. With a young gentleman.
LADY POLITIC.   That same's the party,
   In man's apparel! Pray you, sir, jog my knight;
   I will be tender to his reputation,
   However he demerit.
SIR POLITIC. [*seeing her*] My lady!
PEREGRINE.   Where?   10
SIR POLITIC. 'Tis she indeed, sir; you shall know her. She is,
   Were she not mine, a lady of that merit,
   For fashion and behavior; and for beauty
   I durst compare—
PEREGRINE.   It seems you are not jealous,
   That dare commend her.
SIR POLITIC.   Nay, and for discourse—   15
PEREGRINE. Being your wife, she cannot miss that.
SIR POLITIC. [*introducing Peregrine*]   Madam,
   Here is a gentleman; pray you, use him fairly;
   He seems a youth, but he is—
LADY POLITIC.   None.
SIR POLITIC.   Yes, one
   Has put his face as soon into the world—
LADY POLITIC. You mean, as early? but today?
SIR POLITIC.   How's this?   20
LADY POLITIC. Why, in this habit, sir; you apprehend me.
   Well, Master Would-be, this doth not become you;
   I had thought the odor, sir, of your good name
   Had been more precious to you; that you would not
   Have done this dire massacre on your honor;   25
   One of your gravity, and rank besides!
   But knights, I see, care little for the oath
   They make to ladies, chiefly, their own ladies.
SIR POLITIC. Now, by my spurs, the symbol of my knighthood[1]—
PEREGRINE. [*aside*] Lord, how his brain is humbled for an oath!   30
SIR POLITIC. I reach you not.
LADY POLITIC.   Right, sir, your polity
   May bear it through thus. [*To* PEREGRINE.]—Sir, a word with you.
   I would be loath to contest publicly
   With any gentlewoman, or to seem
   Froward, or violent: as *The Courtier* says,[2]   35
   It comes too near rusticity in a lady,
   Which I would shun by all means; and however
   I may deserve from Master Would-be, yet
   T' have one fair gentlewoman thus be made
   The unkind instrument to wrong another,   40
   And one she knows not, ay, and to persèver;
   In my poor judgment, is not warranted

---

1. Because King James created knights indiscrim-   joke in early 17th-century England.
inately at his accession, knighthood was a broad   2. I.e., Castiglione.

From being a solecism in our sex,
If not in manners.

PEREGRINE.   How is this!

SIR POLITIC.   Sweet madam,
Come nearer to your aim.

LADY POLITIC.   Marry, and will, sir.   45
Since you provoke me with your impudence,
And laughter of your light land-siren here,
Your Sporus,[3] your hermaphrodite—

PEREGRINE.   What's here?
Poetic fury and historic[4] storms!

SIR POLITIC. The gentleman, believe it, is of worth,   50
And of our nation.

LADY POLITIC.   Ay, your Whitefriars[5] nation!
Come, I blush for you, Master Would-be, ay;
And am ashamed you should have no more forehead[6]
Than thus to be the patron or St. George
To a lewd harlot, a base fricatrice,[7]   55
A female devil in a male outside.

SIR POLITIC.   Nay,
An[8] you be such a one, I must bid adieu
To your delights. The case appears too liquid. [*Exit.*]

LADY POLITIC. Ay, you may carry 't clear, with your state-face![9]
But for your carnival concupiscence,   60
Who here is fled for liberty of conscience
From furious persecution of the marshal,
Her will I dis'ple.[1]

PEREGRINE.   This is fine, i' faith,
And do you use this often? Is this part
Of your wit's exercise, 'gainst you have occasion?   65
Madam—

LADY POLITIC. Go to, sir.

PEREGRINE.   Do you hear me, lady?
Why, if your knight have set you to beg shirts,
Or to invite me home, you might have done it
A nearer way, by far.[2]

LADY POLITIC.   This cannot work you
Out of my snare.

PEREGRINE.   Why, am I in it, then?   70
Indeed your husband told me you were fair,
And so you are; only your nose inclines,
That side that's next the sun, to the queen-apple.[3]

LADY POLITIC. This cannot be endured by any patience.

---

3. Sporus was a favorite catamite of Nero, who dressed him in drag and married him.
4. With reference to the historical allusion (Sporus), but "hysteric" is not far away.
5. Disreputable quarter of London, inhabited by whores.
6. Sense of shame.
7. Prostitute.

8. If.
9. A solemn expression.
1. Discipline; specifically, whip. In England at least (though not in Venice) the marshal was directly charged with catching and punishing prostitutes.
2. Peregrine implies that the whole situation is a setup, the knight pimping for his wife.
3. Lady Politic has a fiery red nose.

SCENE 3

[*Enter* MOSCA.]

MOSCA. What's the matter, madam?

LADY POLITIC.   If the Senate
Right not my quest in this,[4] I will protest them
To all the world no aristocracy.

MOSCA. What is the injury, lady?

LADY POLITIC.   Why, the callet[5]
You told me of, here I have ta'en disguised.   5

MOSCA. Who? this! What means your ladyship? The creature
I mentioned to you is apprehended now
Before the Senate; you shall see her—

LADY POLITIC.   Where?

MOSCA. I'll bring you to her. This young gentleman,
I saw him land this morning at the port.   10

LADY POLITIC. Is 't possible! How has my judgment wandered?
Sir, I must, blushing, say to you, I have erred,
And plead your pardon.

PEREGRINE.   What, more changes yet!

LADY POLITIC. I hope you've not the malice to remember
A gentlewoman's passion. If you stay   15
In Venice here, please you to use me, sir—

MOSCA. Will you go, madam?

LADY POLITIC.   Pray you, sir, use me; in faith,
The more you see me, the more I shall conceive
You have forgot our quarrel.

[*Exeunt* LADY WOULD-BE, MOSCA, NANO, *and* WAITING-WOMEN.]

PEREGRINE.   This is rare!
Sir Politic Would-be? No, Sir Politic Bawd!   20
To bring me thus acquainted with his wife!
Well, wise Sir Pol, since you have practiced thus
Upon my freshman-ship,[6] I'll try your salt-head,
What proof it is against a counterplot.   [*Exit.*]

SCENE 4. *The Scrutineo.*

[*Enter* VOLTORE, CORBACCIO, CORVINO, *and* MOSCA.]

VOLTORE. Well, now you know the carriage of the business,
Your constancy is all that is required
Unto the safety of it.

MOSCA.   Is the lie[7]
Safely conveyed amongst us? Is that sure?
Knows every man his burden?[8]

CORVINO.   Yes.

4. Don't do me justice.
5. Slut.
6. Innocence, as of a freshman, but in opposition
to Sir Politic's "salt-head": salacity.

7. Untruth, but also the shape of things, as in the
lie or lay of the land.
8. "Part," as in part-singing. Mosca must be sure
everyone has his story straight.

MOSCA.   Then shrink not.   5

CORVINO. [aside to MOSCA] But knows the advocate the truth?

MOSCA.   O, sir,
  By no means; I devised a formal tale
  That salved your reputation. But be valiant, sir.

CORVINO. I fear no one but him, that this his pleading
  Should make him stand for a co-heir—

MOSCA.   Co-halter!   10
  Hang him; we will but use his tongue, his noise,
  As we do Croaker's[9] here.

CORVINO.   Ay, what shall he do?

MOSCA. When we have done, you mean?

CORVINO.   Yes.

MOSCA.   Why, we'll think:
  Sell him for mummia;[1] he's half dust already.
  [To VOLTORE.] Do you not smile to see this buffalo,[2]   15
  How he doth sport it with his head? [Aside.]—I should,
  If all were well and past. [To CORBACCIO.] Sir, only you
  Are he that shall enjoy the crop of all,
  And these know not for whom they toil.

CORBACCIO.   Ay, peace.

MOSCA. [turning to CORVINO] But you shall eat it. [Aside.]
     Much![3] [To VOLTORE.] Worshipful sir,   20
  Mercury sit upon your thundering tongue,
  Or the French Hercules,[4] and make your language
  As conquering as his club, to beat along,
  As with a tempest, flat, our adversaries;
  But much more yours, sir.

VOLTORE.   Here they come, have done.   25

MOSCA. I have another witness, if you need, sir,
  I can produce.

VOLTORE.   Who is it?

MOSCA.   Sir, I have her.

SCENE 5

[Enter AVOCATORI and take their seats; BONARIO, CELIA, NOTARIO,
COMMENDATORI, SAFFI, and other OFFICERS OF JUSTICE.]

1 AVOCATORE. The like of this the Senate never heard of.

2 AVOCATORE. 'Twill come most strange to them when we report it.

4 AVOCATORE. The gentlewoman[5] has been ever held
  Of unreprovèd name,

3 AVOCATORE.   So the young man.[6]

4 AVOCATORE. The more unnatural part that of his father.   5

2 AVOCATORE. More of the husband.[7]

---

9. I.e., Corbaccio's.
1. Allegedly the remains of the Pharaohs, popularly sold as medicine.
2. An allusion to the cuckold's horns worn by Corvino.
3. I.e., "fat chance!"

4. Both Mercury, god of thieves, and the French Hercules were patrons of eloquence; the latter is discussed by the classical burlesque writer Lucian.
5. I.e., Celia.
6. I.e., Bonario.
7. I.e., Corvino.

1 AVOCATORE.   I not know to give
    His act a name, it is so monstrous!
4 AVOCATORE. But the impostor,[8] he's a thing created
    To exceed example!
1 AVOCATORE.   And all after-times!
2 AVOCATORE. I never heard a true voluptuary   10
    Described, but him.
3 AVOCATORE.   Appear yet those were cited?
NOTARIO. All but the old magnifico, Volpone.
1 AVOCATORE. Why is not he here?
MOSCA.   Please your fatherhoods,
    Here is his advocate: himself's so weak,
    So feeble—
4 AVOCATORE. What are you?
BONARIO.   His parasite,   15
    His knave, his pander: I beseech the court
    He may be forced to come, that your grave eyes
    May bear strong witness of his strange impostures.
VOLTORE. Upon my faith and credit with your virtues,
    He is not able to endure the air.   20
2 AVOCATORE. Bring him, however.
3 AVAOCATORE.   We will see him.
4 AVOCATORE.   Fetch him.
VOLTORE. Your fatherhoods' fit pleasures be obeyed;

                                    [*Exeunt* OFFICERS.]

    But sure, the sight will rather move your pities
    Than indignation. May it please the court,
    In the meantime, he may be heard in me.   25
    I know this place most void of prejudice,
    And therefore crave it, since we have no reason
    To fear our truth should hurt our cause.
3 AVOCATORE.   Speak free.
VOLTORE. Then know, most honored fathers, I must now
    Discover to your strangely abusèd ears,   30
    The most prodigious and most frontless[9] piece
    Of solid impudence and treachery,
    That ever vicious nature yet brought forth
    To shame the state of Venice. This lewd woman,
    That wants[1] no artificial looks or tears   35
    To help the visor she has now put on,
    Hath long been known a close adulteress
    To that lascivious youth there; not suspected,
    I say, but known, and taken in the act
    With him; and by this man, the easy husband,   40
    Pardoned; whose timeless[2] bounty makes him now
    Stand here, the most unhappy, innocent person

---

8. I.e., Volpone.
9. Shameless.
1. Lacks. "Visor": artificial features, outward
appearance.
2. Ill-timed.

That ever man's own goodness made accused.
For these, not knowing how to owe a gift
Of that dear grace but with their shame, being placed   45
So above all powers of their gratitude,
Began to hate the benefit; and, in place
Of thanks, devise to extirp[3] the memory
Of such an act. Wherein, I pray your fatherhoods
To observe the malice, yea, the rage of creatures   50
Discovered in their evils; and what heart
Such take, even from their crimes. But that anon
Will more appear. This gentleman, the father,
Hearing of this foul fact, with many others
Which daily struck at his too tender ears,   55
And grieved in nothing more than that he could not
Preserve himself a parent (his son's ills
Growing to that strange flood), at last decreed
To disinherit him.
1 AVOCATORE.   These be strange turns!
2 AVOCATORE. The young man's fame was ever fair and honest.   60
VOLTORE. So much more full of danger is his vice,
That can beguile so under shade of virtue.
But, as I said, my honored sires, his father
Having this settled purpose, by what means
To him betrayed, we know not, and this day   65
Appointed for the deed; that parricide—
I cannot style him better—by confederacy[4]
Preparing this his paramour to be there,
Entered Volpone's house (who was the man,
Your fatherhoods must understand, designed   70
For the inheritance), there sought his father;
But with what purpose sought he him, my lords?
I tremble to pronounce it, that a son
Unto a father, and to such a father,
Should have so foul, felonious intent: 75
It was to murder him! When, being prevented
By his more happy absence, what then did he?
Not check his wicked thoughts; no, now new deeds
(Mischief doth never[5] end where it begins);
An act of horror, fathers! He dragged forth   80
The agèd gentleman that had there lain bed-rid
Three years and more, out of his innocent couch,
Naked upon the floor, there left him; wounded
His servant in the face; and, with this strumpet,
The stale to his forged practice,[6] who was glad   85
To be so active (I shall here desire
Your fatherhoods to note but my collections,[7]

---

3. Wipe out, extirpate.
4. Conspiracy.
5. Jonson's text reads "ever," and the sense is
defensible, but the stronger meaning comes from

"never."
6. The decoy in his contrived scheme.
7. Deductions.

As most remarkable), thought at once to stop
His father's ends, discredit his free choice
In the old gentleman, redeem themselves,   90
By laying infamy upon this man,[8]
To whom, with blushing, they should owe their lives.

1 AVOCATORE. What proofs have you of this?

BONARIO.   Most honored fathers,
I humbly crave there be no credit given
To this man's mercenary tongue.

2 AVOCATORE.   Forbear.   95

BONARIO. His soul moves in his fee.

3 AVOCATORE.   O, sir!

BONARIO.   This fellow,
For six sols more,[9] would plead against his Maker.

1 AVOCATORE. You do forget yourself.

VOLTORE.   Nay, nay, grave fathers,
Let him have scope; can any man imagine
That he will spare his accuser, that would not   100
Have spared his parent?

1 AVOCATORE.   Well, produce your proofs.

CELIA. I would I could forget I were a creature.

VOLTORE. Signor Corbaccio! [CORBACCIO comes forward.]

4 AVOCATORE.   What is he?

VOLTORE.   The father.

2 AVOCATORE. Has he had an oath?

NOTARIO.   Yes.

CORBACCIO.   What must I do now?

NOTARIO. Your testimony's craved.

CORBACCIO.   Speak to the knave?   105
I'll have my mouth first stopped with earth; my heart
Abhors his knowledge:[1] I disclaim in him.

1 AVOCATORE. But for what cause?

CORBACCIO.   The mere portent of nature!
He is an utter stranger to my loins.

BONARIO. Have they made you to this?

CORBACCIO.   I will not hear thee,   110
Monster of men, swine, goat, wolf, parricide!
Speak not, thou viper.

BONARIO.   Sir, I will sit down,
And rather wish my innocence should suffer,
Than I resist the authority of a father.

VOLTORE. Signor Corvino! [CORVINO comes forward.]

2 AVOCATORE.   This is strange.

1 AVOCATORE.   Who's this?   115

NOTARIO. The husband.

4 AVOCATORE. Is he sworn?

NOTARIO.   He is.

---

8. I.e., Corvino.   1. Shudders to recognize him.
9. Three pence.

3 AVOCATORE.   Speak, then.

CORVINO. This woman, please your fatherhoods, is a whore
  Of most hot exercise, more than a partridge,[2]
  Upon record—

1 AVOCATORE.   No more.

CORVINO.   Neighs like a jennet.[3]

NOTARIO. Preserve the honor of the court.

CORVINO.   I shall,   120
  And modesty of your most reverend ears.
  And yet I hope that I may say these eyes
  Have seen her glued unto that piece of cedar,
  That fine well-timbered gallant; and that here[4]
  The letters may be read, through the horn,   125
  That make the story perfect.

MOSCA.   Excellent, sir!

CORVINO. [aside to MOSCA] There is no shame in this now, is there?

MOSCA.   None.

CORVINO. Or if I said, I hoped that she were onward
  To her damnation, if there be a hell
  Greater than whore and woman; a good Catholic   130
  May make the doubt.[5]

3 AVOCATORE.   His grief hath made him frantic.

1 AVOCATORE. Remove him hence.   [CELIA swoons.]

2 AVOCATORE.   Look to the woman.

CORVINO.   Rare!
  Prettily feigned, again!

4 AVOCATORE.   Stand from about her.

1 AVOCATORE. Give her the air.

3 AVOCATORE. [to MOSCA]   What can you say?

MOSCA.   My wound,
  May it please your wisdoms, speaks for me, received   135
  In aid of my good patron, when he missed
  His sought-for father,[6] when that well-taught dame
  Had her cue given her to cry out, A rape!

BONARIO. O most laid impudence! Fathers—

3 AVOCATORE.   Sir, be silent;
  You had your hearing free, so must they theirs.   140

2 AVOCATORE. I do begin to doubt the imposture here.

4 AVOCATORE. This woman has too many moods.

VOLTORE.   Grave fathers,
  She is a creature of a most professed
  And prostituted lewdness.

CORVINO.   Most impetuous,
  Unsatisfied, grave fathers!

---

2. The partridge vied with the sparrow as the most lustful of birds.
3. Mare in heat.
4. Corvino holds two fingers over his head to make the horned sign of the cuckold.
5. If there's any hell worse than being a woman and a whore, Corvino thinks of saying Celia may be headed for it; because he doesn't say flatly that she *is* so headed, he can claim the virtue of charity, and remain a good Catholic. The 1607 quarto reads "Christian" instead of "Catholic."
6. I.e., Corbaccio.

VOLTORE.   May her feignings
  Not take your wisdoms: but this day she baited
  A stranger, a grave knight, with her loose eyes
  And more lascivious kisses. This man [*indicating* MOSCA] saw them
  Together on the water, in a gondola.
MOSCA. Here is the lady herself, that saw them too,   150
  Without; who then had in the open streets
  Pursued them, but for saving her knight's honor.
1 AVOCATORE. Produce that lady.
2 AVOCATORE.   Let her come. [*Exit* MOSCA.]
4 AVOCATORE.   These things,
  They strike with wonder.
3 AVOCATORE.   I am turned a stone.

SCENE 6

[Enter MOSCA with LADY WOULD-BE.]

MOSCA. Be resolute, madam.
LADY POLITIC.   Ay, this same is she.   [*Pointing to* CELIA.]
  Out, thou chameleon[7] harlot! Now thine eyes
  Vie tears with the hyena. Dar'st thou look
  Upon my wrongèd face?—I cry your pardons,
  I fear I have forgettingly transgressed   5
  Against the dignity of the court—
2 AVOCATORE.   No, madam.
LADY POLITIC. And been exorbitant[8]—
2 AVOCATORE.   You have not, lady.
4 AVOCATORE. These proofs are strong.
LADY POLITIC.   Surely, I had no purpose
  To scandalize your honors, or my sex's.
3 AVOCATORE. We do believe it.
LADY POLITIC.   Surely, you may believe it.   10
2 AVOCATORE. Madam, we do.
LADY POLITIC.   Indeed you may; my breeding
  Is not so coarse—
4 AVOCATORE.   We know it.
LADY POLITIC.   To offend
  With pertinacy—
3 AVOCATORE.   Lady—
LADY POLITIC.   Such a presence!
  No, surely.
1 AVOCATORE. We well think it.
LADY POLITIC.   You may think it.
1 AVOCATORE. Let her o'ercome. [*To* BONARIO.] What witnesses
  have you,   15
  To make good your report?
BONARIO.   Our consciences.
CELIA. And heaven, that never fails the innocent.

7. An animal that changes colors. The hyena is   8. Lady Politic doubtless means "excessive."
emblematic of treachery and an eater of carrion.

4 AVOCATORE. These are no testimonies.

BONARIO.   Not in your courts,
  Where multitude, and clamor overcomes.

1 AVOCATORE. Nay, then you do wax insolent.   20

> [*Re-enter* OFFICERS, *bearing* VOLPONE *on a couch.* LADY POLITIC
> *embraces him.*]

VOLTORE.   Here, here,
  The testimony comes that will convince,
  And put to utter dumbness their bold tongues!
  See here, grave fathers, here's the ravisher,
  The rider on men's wives, the great impostor,
  The grand voluptuary! Do you not think   25
  These limbs should affect venery?[9] or these eyes
  Covet a concubine? Pray you mark these hands;
  Are they not fit to stroke a lady's breasts?
  Perhaps he doth dissemble!

BONARIO.   So he does.

VOLTORE. Would you have him tortured?

BONARIO.   I would have him proved.   30

VOLTORE. Best try him then with goads, or burning irons;
  Put him to the strappado.[1] I have heard
  The rack hath cured the gout; 'faith, give it him,
  And help him of a malady; be courteous.
  I'll undertake, before these honored fathers,   35
  He shall have yet as many left diseases
  As she has known adulterers, or thou strumpets.
  O, my most equal hearers, if these deeds,
  Acts of this bold and most exorbitant strain,
  May pass with sufferance, what one citizen   40
  But owes the forfeit of his life, yea, fame,
  To him that dares traduce him? Which of you
  Are safe, my honored fathers? I would ask,
  With leave of your grave fatherhoods, if their plot
  Have any face or color like to truth?   45
  Or if, unto the dullest nostril here,
  It smell not rank and most abhorrèd slander?
  I crave your care of this good gentleman,
  Whose life is much endangered by their fable;
  And as for them, I will conclude with this,   50
  That vicious persons, when they're hot, and fleshed
  In impious acts, their constancy abounds:
  Damned deeds are done with greatest confidence.

1 AVOCATORE. Take them to custody, and sever them. [CELIA *and*
  BONARIO *are taken out.*]

2 AVOCATORE. 'Tis pity two such prodigies should live.   55

1 AVOCATORE. Let the old gentleman be returned with care:

> [*Exeunt* OFFICERS *with* VOLPONE.]

9. Be disposed to lust.
1. A common torture of the time: a man's hands
were tied behind his back, and he was hoisted by
his wrists on a gallows, to the common effect of
dislocating his shoulders.

I'm sorry our credulity hath wronged him.

4 AVOCATORE. These are two creatures!

3 AVOCATORE.   I have an earthquake in me.[2]

2 AVOCATORE. Their shame, even in their cradles, fled their faces.

4 AVOCATORE. [to VOLTORE] You have done a worthy service to the
      state, sir,   60
   In their discovery.

1 AVOCATORE.   You shall hear, ere night,
   What punishment the court decrees upon them.

VOLTORE. We thank your fatherhoods. [Exeunt AVOCATORI, NOTARIO,
   and OFFICERS.] [To MOSCA.]—How like you it?

MOSCA.   Rare.
   I'd have your tongue, sir, tipped with gold for this;
   I'd have you be the heir to the whole city;   65
   The earth I'd have want men, ere you want living:
   They're bound to erect your statue in St. Mark's.
   Signor Corvino, I would have you go
   And show yourself, that you have conquered.

CORVINO.   Yes.

MOSCA. [aside to CORVINO] It was much better that you should
      profess   70
   Yourself a cuckold thus, than that the other
   Should have been proved.

CORVINO.   Nay, I considered that;
   Now it is her fault.

MOSCA.   Then it had been yours.

CORVINO. True; I do doubt this advocate still.

MOSCA.   I' faith,
   You need not; I dare ease you of that care.   75

CORVINO. I trust thee, Mosca.

MOSCA.   As your own soul, sir.

                                             [Exit CORVINO.]

CORBACCIO.   Mosca!

MOSCA. Now for your business, sir.

CORBACCIO.   How! Have you business?

MOSCA. Yes, yours, sir.

CORBACCIO.   O, none else?

MOSCA.   None else, not I.

CORBACCIO. Be careful then.

MOSCA.   Rest you with both your eyes, sir.

CORBACCIO. Dispatch it.[3]

MOSCA.   Instantly.

CORBACCIO.   And look that all,   80
   Whatever, be put in, jewels, plate, moneys,
   Household stuff, bedding, curtains.

MOSCA.   Curtain-rings, sir:
   Only the advocate's fee must be deducted.

CORBACCIO. I'll pay him now; you'll be too prodigal.

2. I'm overwhelmed.
3. I.e., get the will made, with me in it.

MOSCA. Sir, I must tender it.
CORBACCIO.   Two sequins is well?   85
MOSCA. No, six, sir.
CORBACCIO.   'Tis too much.
MOSCA.   He talked a great while;
    You must consider that, sir.
CORBACCIO.   Well, there's three—
MOSCA. I'll give it him.
CORBACCIO.   Do so, and there's for thee.   [Exit.]
MOSCA. Bountiful bones! What horrid strange offense
    Did he commit 'gainst nature, in his youth,   90
    Worthy this age? [To VOLTORE.]—You see, sir, how I work
    Unto your ends; take you no notice.
VOLTORE.   No,
    I'll leave you.
MOSCA.   All is yours [exit VOLTORE]—the devil and all,
    Good advocate!—Madam, I'll bring you home.
LADY POLITIC. No, I'll go see your patron.
MOSCA.   That you shall not.   95
    I'll tell you why. My purpose is to urge
    My patron to reform his will;[4] and for
    The zeal you have shown today, whereas before.
    You were but third or fourth, you shall be now
    Put in the first; which would appear as begged,   100
    If you were present. Therefore—
LADY POLITIC.   You shall sway me.   [Exeunt.]

Act 5

SCENE 1. *A room in* VOLPONE's *house.*

[*Enter* VOLPONE.]

VOLPONE. Well, I am here, and all this brunt[5] is past.
    I ne'er was in dislike with my disguise
    Till this fled moment;[6] here 'twas good, in private,
    But in your public—*cavè*[7] whilst I breathe.
    'Fore God, my left leg 'gan to have the cramp,   5
    And I apprehended[8] straight some power had struck me
    With a dead palsy. Well! I must be merry,
    And shake it off. A many of these fears
    Would put me into some villainous disease,
    Should they come thick upon me: I'll prevent 'em.   10
    Give me a bowl of lusty wine, to fright
    This humor from my heart. [*Drinks.*]—Hum, hum, hum!
    'Tis almost gone already, I shall conquer.
    Any device, now, of rare ingenious knavery,
    That would possess me with a violent laughter,   15

4. Rewrite his testament, though always with the
other connotation of improving his disposition.
5. Trouble.
6. Moment just past.

7. Beware, watch out (Latin).
8. The word is printed in one text and pronounced in all "apprended."

Would make me up again. [*Drinks again.*]—So, so, so, so!
This heat is life; 'tis blood by this time! Mosca!

SCENE 2

[*Enter* MOSCA.]

MOSCA. How now, sir? Does the day look clear again?
   Are we recovered? and wrought out of error
   Into our way, to see our path before us?
   Is our trade free once more?
VOLPONE.   Exquisite Mosca!
MOSCA. Was it not carried learnedly?
VOLPONE.   And stoutly.   5
   Good wits are greatest in extremities.
MOSCA. It were a folly beyond thought, to trust
   Any grand act unto a cowardly spirit.
   You are not taken with it[9] enough, methinks.
VOLPONE. O, more than if I had enjoyed the wench;   10
   The pleasure of all womankind's not like it.
MOSCA. Why now you speak, sir! We must here be fixed;
   Here we must rest. This is our masterpiece;
   We cannot think to go beyond this.
VOLPONE.   True,
   Thou'st played thy prize, my precious Mosca.
MOSCA.   Nay, sir,   15
   To gull the court—
VOLPONE.   And quite divert the torrent
   Upon the innocent.
MOSCA.   Yes, and to make
   So rare a music out of discords—
VOLPONE.   Right.
   That yet to me's the strangest! how thou'st borne it
   That these, being so divided 'mongst themselves,   20
   Should not scent somewhat, or in me or thee,
   Or doubt their own side.
MOSCA.   True, they will not see 't.
   Too much light blinds them, I think.[1] Each of them
   Is so possessed and stuffed with his own hopes
   That anything unto the contrary,   25
   Never so true, or never so apparent,
   Never so palpable, they will resist it—
VOLPONE. Like a temptation of the devil.
MOSCA.   Right, sir.
   Merchants may talk of trade, and your great signors
   Of land that yields well; but if Italy   30
   Have any glebe[2] more fruitful than these fellows,
   I am deceived. Did not your advocate rare?[3]
VOLPONE. O—*My most honored fathers, my grave fathers,*

---

9. Pleased, satisfied with it.   2. Soil.
1. An ancient adage.   3. Did not your advocate (perform) rare(ly)?

Under correction of your fatherhoods,
What face of truth is here? If these strange deeds   35
May pass, most honored fathers—I had much ado
To forbear laughing.

MOSCA.   It seemed to me you sweat, sir.

VOLPONE. In troth, I did a little.

MOSCA.   But confess, sir,
Were you not daunted?

VOLPONE.   In good faith, I was
A little in a mist, but not dejected;   40
Never but still myself.

MOSCA.   I think it, sir.
Now, so truth help me, I must needs say this, sir,
And out of conscience for your advocate—
He has taken pains, in faith, sir, and deserved,
In my poor judgment (I speak it under favor,   45
Not to contrary you, sir) very richly—
Well—to be cozened.

VOLPONE.   Troth, and I think so too,
By that I heard him, in the latter end.

MOSCA. O, but before, sir: had you heard him first
Draw it to certain heads, then aggravate,   50
Then use his vehement figures[4]—I looked still
When he would shift a shirt;[5] and doing this
Out of pure love, no hope of gain—

VOLPONE.   'Tis right.
I cannot answer him, Mosca, as I would,
Not yet; but for thy sake, at thy entreaty,   55
I will begin e'en now to vex them all,
This very instant.

MOSCA.   Good, sir.

VOLPONE.   Call the dwarf
And eunuch forth.

MOSCA.   Castrone, Nano!

[*Enter* CASTRONE *and* NANO.]

NANO.   Here.

VOLPONE. Shall we have a jig now?

MOSCA.   What you please, sir.

VOLPONE.   Go,
Straight give out about the streets, you two,   60
That I am dead; do it with constancy,
Sadly, do you hear? Impute it to the grief
Of this late slander.   [*Exeunt* CASTRONE *and* NANO.]

MOSCA.   What do you mean, sir?

VOLPONE.   O,
I shall have instantly my vulture, crow,
Raven, come flying hither on the news   65

---

4. Terms of legal oratory.   seemed he might have to change his linen.
5. I.e., he sweated so much over his speech, it

To peck for carrion, my she-wolf and all,
Greedy, and full of expectation—
MOSCA. And then to have it ravished from their mouths!
VOLPONE. 'Tis true. I will have thee put on a gown,   70
And take upon thee as thou wert mine heir;
Show them a will. Open that chest and reach
Forth one of those that has the blanks; I'll straight
Put in thy name.
MOSCA.   It will be rare, sir.   [*Gives him a paper.*]
VOLPONE.   Ay,
When they e'en gape, and find themselves deluded—
MOSCA. Yes.
VOLPONE.   And thou use them scurvily! Dispatch,   75
Get on thy gown.
MOSCA.   But what, sir, if they ask
After the body?
VOLPONE.   Say it was corrupted.
MOSCA. I'll say it stunk, sir; and was fain to have it
Coffined up instantly and sent away.
VOLPONE. Anything, what thou wilt. Hold, here's my will.   80
Get thee a cap, a count-book,[6] pen and ink,
Papers afore thee; sit as thou wert taking
An inventory of parcels. I'll get up
Behind the curtain, on a stool, and hearken;
Sometime peep over, see how they do look,   85
With what degrees their blood doth leave their faces.
O, 'twill afford me a rare meal of laughter!
MOSCA. [*putting on a cap, and setting out the table, &c.*] Your
      advocate will turn stark dull upon it.
VOLPONE. It will take off his oratory's edge.
MOSCA. But your clarissimo, old round-back,[7] he   90
Will crump you like a hog-louse with the touch.
VOLPONE. And what Corvino?
MOSCA.   O, sir, look for him
Tomorrow morning with a rope and dagger
To visit all the streets;[8] he must run mad.
My lady too, that came into the court   95
To bear false witness for your worship—
VOLPONE.   Yes,
And kissed me 'fore the fathers, when my face
Flowed all with oils.
MOSCA.   And sweat, sir. Why, your gold
Is such another medicine, it dries up
All those offensive savors; it transforms   100
The most deformèd, and restores them lovely,
As 'twere the strange poetical girdle.[9] Jove
Could not invent t' himself a shroud more subtle

6. Ledger.
7. Corbaccio is a *clarissimo*, a distinguished man
in Venice. "Crump you": curl up on you; there is
a species of wood louse or hog louse (the names
are interchangeable) which curls up in a ball when
touched.
8. I.e., looking for a place to commit suicide.
9. The girdle of Venus (*cestus*) made any wearer
irresistibly beautiful.

To pass Acrisius' guards.[1] It is the thing
Makes all the world her grace, her youth, her beauty.   105
VOLPONE. I think she loves me.
MOSCA.   Who? the lady, sir?
She's jealous of you.
VOLPONE.   Dost thou say so?   [Knocking within.]
MOSCA.   Hark,
There's some already.
VOLPONE.   Look.
MOSCA.   It is the vulture;
He has the quickest scent.
VOLPONE.   I'll to my place,
Thou to thy posture.   [Goes behind the curtain.]
MOSCA.   I am set.
VOLPONE.   But, Mosca,   110
Play the artificer now, torture them rarely.

SCENE 3

[Enter VOLTORE.]

VOLTORE. How now, my Mosca?
MOSCA. [writing]   Turkey carpets, nine[2]—
VOLTORE. Taking an inventory? That is well.
MOSCA. Two suits of bedding, tissue—
VOLTORE.   Where's the will?
Let me read that the while.

[Enter SERVANTS with CORBACCIO in a chair.]

CORBACCIO.   So, set me down,
And get you home.   [Exeunt SERVANTS.]
VOLTORE.   Is he come now to trouble us?   5
MOSCA. Of cloth of gold, two more—
CORBACCIO.   Is it done, Mosca?
MOSCA. Of several velvets, eight—
VOLTORE.   I like his care.
CORBACCIO. Dost thou not hear?

[Enter CORVINO.]

CORVINO.   Ha! is the hour come, Mosca?
VOLPONE. [peeping over the curtain] Ay, now they muster.
CORVINO.   What does
the advocate here,
Or this Corbaccio?
CORBACCIO.   What do these here?

[Enter LADY POLITIC WOULD-BE.]

LADY POLITIC.   Mosca!   10

1. Acrisius was the father of Danaë; he locked her up in a tower till Jove managed to get to her in the form of a shower of gold.
2. Turkey carpets (not necessarily from Turkey) were particularly thick and luxurious; cloth described as tissue often had threads of gold or silver interwoven.

Is his thread spun?
MOSCA.   *Eight chests of linen—*
VOLPONE.   O,
My fine Dame Would-be, too!
CORVINO.   Mosca, the will,
That I may show it these, and rid them hence.
MOSCA. *Six chests of diaper,*[3] *four of damask.*—There. [*Gives them the
    will carelessly, over his shoulder.*]
CORBACCIO. Is that the will?
MOSCA.   *Down-beds, and bolsters—*
VOLPONE.   Rare!   15
Be busy still. Now they began to flutter:
They never think of me. Look, see, see, see!
How their swift eyes run over the long deed,
Unto the name, and to the legacies,
What is bequeathed them there—
MOSCA.   *Ten suits of hangings*[4]—   20
VOLPONE. Ay, in their garters, Mosca. Now their hopes
Are at the gasp.
VOLTORE.   Mosca the heir!
CORBACCIO.   What's that?
VOLPONE. My advocate is dumb; look to my merchant;
He has heard of some strange storm, a ship is lost,
He faints; my lady will swoon. Old glazen-eyes,[5]   25
He hath not reached his despair yet.
CORBACCIO.   All these
Are out of hope; I am, sure, the man. [*Takes the will.*]
CORVINO.   But, Mosca—
MOSCA. *Two cabinets—*
CORVINO.   Is this in earnest?
MOSCA.   *One*
Of ebony—
CORVINO.   Or do you but delude me?
MOSCA. *The other, mother of pearl*—I am very busy.   30
Good faith, it is a fortune thrown upon me—
Item, one salt[6] *of agate*—not my seeking.
LADY POLITIC. Do you hear, sir?
MOSCA.   *A perfumed box*—Pray you forbear,
You see I'm troubled—*made of an onyx—*
LADY POLITIC.   How!
MOSCA. Tomorrow or next day I shall be at leisure   35
To talk with you all.
CORVINO.   Is this my large hope's issue?
LADY POLITIC. Sir, I must have a fairer answer.
MOSCA.   Madam!
Marry, and shall: pray you, fairly[7] quit my house.

3. Fine linen cloth. "Damask" (from Damascus):   5. I.e., Corbaccio.
a rich fabric woven with many figures.   6. Salt cellar.
4. Sets of tapestries on the walls. But Volpone   7. Once and for all.
suggests garters, traditional means of suicide.

Nay, raise no tempest with your looks, but hark you:
Remember what your ladyship offered me   40
To put you in an heir;[8] go to, think on it,
And what you said e'en your best madams did
For maintenance;[9] and why not you? Enough.
Go home, and use the poor Sir Pol, your knight, well,
For fear I tell some riddles; go, be melancholic. [*Exit* LADY
    POLITIC.]   45
VOLPONE. O, my fine devil!
CORVINO.   Mosca, pray you a word.
MOSCA. Lord! will not you take your dispatch hence yet?
Methinks, of all, you should have been the example.
Why should you stay here? With what thought, what promise?
Hear you: do not you know I know you an ass,   50
And that you would most fain have been a wittol,[1]
If fortune would have let you? That you are
A declared cuckold, on good terms? This pearl,
You'll say, was yours? Right. This diamond?
I'll not deny 't, but thank you. Much here else?   55
It may be so. Why, think that these good works
May help to hide your bad. I'll not betray you;
Although you be but extraordinary,[2]
And have it only in title, it sufficeth;
Go home, be melancholic too, or mad. [*Exit* CORVINO.]   60
VOLPONE. Rare Mosca! How his villainy becomes him!
VOLTORE. Certain he doth delude all these for me.
CORBACCIO. Mosca the heir!
VOLPONE.   O, his four eyes have found it![3]
CORBACCIO. I am cozened, cheated, by a parasite slave;
Harlot,[4] thou hast gulled me.
MOSCA.   Yes, sir. Stop your mouth,   65
Or I shall draw the only tooth is left.
Are not you he, that filthy covetous wretch,
With the three legs,[5] that here, in hope of prey,
Have, any time this three year, snuffed about
With your most groveling nose, and would have hired   70
Me to the poisoning of my patron, sir?
Are not you he that have today in court
Professed the disinheriting of your son?
Perjured yourself? Go home, and die, and stink;
If you but croak a syllable, all comes out: 75
Away, and call your porters!   [*Exit* CORBACCIO.]—
                    Go, go stink.
VOLPONE. Excellent varlet!

---

8. This aspect of Lady Politic Jonson has saved for
the present moment.
9. Lady Politic would never say "for money."
1. A pimp for your own wife.
2. I.e., not a full-fledged pimp or cuckold, just
one who did his best to be such.

3. No doubt after much fumbling, Corbaccio has
put on his spectacles.
4. Frequently used of men, in the sense of
"scoundrel."
5. I.e., two plus a cane or crutch.

VOLTORE.   Now, my faithful Mosca,
   I find thy constancy—
MOSCA.   Sir?
VOLTORE.   Sincere.
MOSCA. [writing]   A table
   Of porphyry—I mar'l[6] you'll be thus troublesome.
VOLTORE. Nay, leave off now, they are gone.
MOSCA.   Why, who are you?   80
   What! Who did send for you? O, cry you mercy,
   Reverend sir! Good faith, I am grieved for you
   That any chance of mine should thus defeat
   Your (I must needs say) most deserving travails:
   But I protest, sir, it was cast upon me,   85
   And I could almost wish to be without it,
   But that the will o' the dead must be observed.
   Marry, my joy is that you need it not;
   You have a gift, sir (thank your education),
   Will never let you want while there are men   90
   And malice to breed causes. Would I had
   But half the like, for all my fortune, sir!
   If I have any suits (as I do hope,
   Things being so easy and direct, I shall not),
   I will make bold with your obstreperous aid—   95
   Conceive me—for your fee, sir. In meantime,
   You that have so much law, I know have the conscience
   Not to be covetous of what is mine.
   Good sir, I thank you for my plate; 'twill help
   To set up a young man.[7] Good faith, you look   100
   As you were costive;[8] best go home and purge, sir. [Exit VOLTORE.]
VOLPONE. [comes from behind the curtain] Bid him eat lettuce
      well.[9] My witty mischief,
   Let me embrace thee. O that I could now
   Transform thee to a Venus!—Mosca, go,
   Straight take my habit of clarissimo,[1]   105
   And walk the streets; be seen, torment them more.
   We must pursue, as well as plot. Who would
   Have lost this feast?
MOSCA.   I doubt it will lose them.
VOLPONE. O, my recovery shall recover all.
   That I could now but think on some disguise   110
   To meet them in, and ask them questions;
   How I would vex them still at every turn!
MOSCA. Sir, I can fit you.
VOLPONE.   Canst thou?
MOSCA.   Yes, I know

6. Marvel.
7. I.e., himself.
8. Constipated; "Purge": take a laxative.
9. In classical days, lettuce was thought to have
mild purgative powers.

1. Mosca, in putting on the distinctive dress of a
patrician (clarissimo) is running a big risk—laws
about wearing the costume of one's rank were strict
and severe.

One o' the commendatori, sir, so like you;
  Him will I straight make drunk, and bring you his habit.[2]   115
VOLPONE. A rare disguise, and answering thy brain!
  O, I will be a sharp disease unto them.
MOSCA. Sir, you must look for curses—
VOLPONE.   Till they burst;
  The fox fares ever best when he is cursed.   [Exeunt.]

SCENE 4. A *hall in* SIR POLITIC'S *house.*

[*Enter* PEREGRINE *disguised, and three* MERCHANTS.]

PEREGRINE. Am I enough disguised?
1 MERCHANT.   I warrant you.
PEREGRINE. All my ambition is to fright him only.
2 MERCHANT. If you could ship him away, 'twere excellent.
3 MERCHANT. To Zant, or to Aleppo?[3]
PEREGRINE.   Yes, and have his
  Adventures put i' the Book of Voyages,   5
  And his gulled story[4] registered for truth.
  Well, gentlemen, when I am in a while,
  And that you think us warm in our discourse,
  Know your approaches.
1 MERCHANT.   Trust it to our care.   [*Exeunt* MERCHANTS.]

[*Enter* WAITING-WOMAN.]

PEREGRINE. Save you, fair lady! Is Sir Pol within?   10
WOMAN. I do not know, sir.
PEREGRINE.   Pray you say unto him,
  Here is a merchant upon earnest business
  Desires to speak with him.
WOMAN.   I will see, sir. [*Exit.*]
PEREGRINE.   Pray you.—
  I see the family is all female here.

[*Re-enter* WAITING-WOMAN.]

WOMAN. He says, sir, he has weighty affairs of state   15
  That now require him whole; some other time
  You may possess him.
PEREGRINE.   Pray you say again,
  If those require him whole, these will exact him,
  Whereof I bring him tidings. [*Exit* WOMAN.]—What might be
  His grave affair of state now? How to make   20
  Bolognian sausages[5] here in Venice, sparing
  One o' the ingredients?

[*Re-enter* WAITING-WOMAN.]

2. Volpone will thus assume a common sergeant's uniform, and over it a loose black robe.
3. Zant or (nowadays) Zakynthos is an Ionian island known for its currants; Greek now, it was part of the Venetian empire in the 17th century. Aleppo, in Syria, still carries its old name.
4. The story of his gulling.
5. Sausages of Bologna were so famous that *baloney* is still a word in general use.

WOMAN.   Sir, he says he knows
By your word *tidings* that you are no statesman,[6]
And therefore wills you stay.
PEREGRINE.   Sweet, pray you return him;
I have not read so many proclamations,   25
And studied them for words, as he has done—
But—here he deigns to come. [*Exit* WOMAN.]

      [*Enter* SIR POLITIC.]

SIR POLITIC.   Sir, I must crave
Your courteous pardon. There hath chanced today
Unkind disaster 'twixt my lady and me;
And I was penning my apology,   30
To give her saitsfaction, as you came now.
PEREGRINE. Sir, I am grieved I bring you worse disaster:
The gentleman you met at the port today,
That told you he was newly arrived—
SIR POLITIC.   Ay, was
A fugitive punk?[7]
PEREGRINE.   No, sir, a spy set on you;   35
And he has made relation to the Senate
That you professed to him to have a plot
To sell the state of Venice to the Turk.[8]
SIR POLITIC. O me!
PEREGRINE.   For which, warrants are signed by this time
To apprehend you and to search your study   40
For papers—
SIR POLITIC.   Alas, sir, I have none but notes
Drawn out of play-books[9]—
PEREGRINE.   All the better, sir.
SIR POLITIC. And some essays. What shall I do?
PEREGRINE.   Sir, best
Convey yourself into a sugar-chest;
Or, if you could lie round, a frail[1] were rare,   45
And I could send you aboard.
SIR POLITIC.   Sir, I but talked so,
For discourse' sake merely. [*Knocking within.*]
PEREGRINE.   Hark! they are there.
SIR POLITIC. I am a wretch, a wretch!
PEREGRINE.   What will you do, sir?
Have you ne'er a currant-butt[2] to leap into?
They'll put you to the rack; you must be sudden.   50
SIR POLITIC. Sir, I have an engine[3]—
3 MERCHANT. [*within*]   Sir Politic Would-be!

---

6. "Tidings" were what normal people received; a
secret-service operative would get "intelligence."
7. A whore in flight from the marshal. (For all his
vaunted subtlety, Sir Politic still believes his wife's
deluded charge that Peregrine was a woman in disguise.)
8. See above, 4.1.

9. Sir Pol's exotic information turns out to be very
common stuff. Playbooks in particular had then
about the reputation of comic books now.
1. Flimsy fruit basket.
2. Cask for holding currants.
3. Contrivance.

2 MERCHANT. [*within*] Where is he?

SIR POLITIC.   That I have thought upon before-
    time.

PEREGRINE. What is it?

SIR POLITIC.   I shall ne'er endure the torture.
    Marry, it is, sir, of a tortoise-shell,
    Fitted for these extremities: pray you, sir, help me.   55
    Here I've a place, sir, to put back my legs;
    Please you to lay it on, sir. [*Lies down while* PEREGRINE
        places the shell upon him.]—With this cap
    And my black gloves, I'll lie, sir, like a tortoise,
    Till they are gone.

PEREGRINE.   And call you this an engine?

SIR POLITIC. Mine own device—Good sir, bid my wife's women
    To burn my papers.   [*Exit* PEREGRINE.]

        [*The* MERCHANTS *rush in.*]

1 MERCHANT.   Where is he hid?

MERCHANT.   We must,
    And will, sure, find him.

2 MERCHANT.   Which is his study?

        [*Re-enter* PEREGRINE.]

1 MERCHANT.   What
    Are you, sir?

PEREGRINE.   I am a merchant, that came here
    To look upon this tortoise.

3 MERCHANT.   How!

1 MERCHANT.   St. Mark!
    What beast is this?

PEREGRINE.   It is a fish.

2 MERCHANT.   Come out here!   65

PEREGRINE. Nay, you may strike him, sir, and tread upon him:
    He'll bear a cart.

1 MERCHANT.   What, to run over him?

PEREGRINE.   Yes.

3 MERCHANT. Let's jump upon him.

2 MERCHANT.   Can he not go?

PEREGRINE.   He creeps, sir.

1 MERCHANT. Let's see him creep. [*Pokes him.*]

PEREGRINE.   No, good sir, you will hurt him.

2 MERCHANT. 'Heart, I will see him creep, or prick his guts.   70

3 MERCHANT. Come out here!

PEREGRINE.   Pray you, sir! [*Aside to* SIR POLITIC.]
                    —Creep a little.

1 MERCHANT.   Forth!

2 MERCHANT. Yet farther.

            Good sir! [*Aside to* SIR POLITIC.]
                    —Creep.

2 MERCHANT.   We'll see his legs.

[They pull off the shell and discover him.]

3 MERCHANT. God's so, he has garters!

1 MERCHANT.   Ay, and gloves!

2 MERCHANT.   Is this
  Your fearful tortoise?

PEREGRINE. *[discovering himself]* Now, Sir Pol, we are even;
  For your next project I shall be prepared.   75
  I am sorry for the funeral of your notes, sir.

1 MERCHANT. 'Twere a rare motion[4] to be seen in Fleet Street.

2 MERCHANT. Ay, in the Term.

1 MERCHANT.   Or Smithfield, in the fair.

3 MERCHANT. Methinks 'tis but a melancholic sight.

PEREGRINE. Farewell, most politic tortoise! *[Exeunt PEREGRINE
  and MERCHANTS.]*

    [Re-enter WAITING-WOMAN.]

SIR POLITIC.   Where's my lady?   80
  Knows she of this?

WOMAN.   I know not, sir.

SIR POLITIC.   Inquire.   *[Exit WOMAN.]*
  O, I shall be the fable of all feasts,
  The freight of the gazetti,[5] ship-boys' tale;
  And, which is worst, even talk for ordinaries.   *[Re-enter WOMAN.]*

WOMAN. My lady's come most melancholic home,   85
  And says, sir, she will straight to sea, for physic.[6]

SIR POLITIC. And I, to shun this place and clime forever,
  Creeping with house on back, and think it well
  To shrink my poor head in my politic shell.   *[Exeunt.]*

    SCENE 5. *A room in* VOLPONE's *house.*

    *[Enter MOSCA in the habit of a clarissimo, and VOLPONE in that
  of a commendatore.]*

VOLPONE. Am I then like him?

MOSCA.   O, sir, you are he.
  No man can sever[7] you.

VOLPONE.   Good.

MOSCA.   But what am I?

VOLPONE. 'Fore heaven, a brave *clarissimo*; thou becom'st it!
  Pity thou wert not born one.

MOSCA.   If I hold
  My made one, 'twill be well.

VOLPONE.   I'll go and see   5
  What news first at the court.   *[Exit.]*

MOSCA.   Do so. My fox

4. Puppet show. "Fleet Street": then as now a busy street in central London, particularly busy "in Term," when the law courts were in session. "Smithfield": a district outside the city walls, where many fairs ware held. These Venetian *mercatori* are remarkably familiar with London manners.
5. Subject of the newsletters. "Talk for the ordinaries": tavern gossip.
6. For her health.
7. Distinguish.

Is out of his hole,[8] and ere he shall re-enter
I'll make him languish in his borrowed case,
Except he come to composition with me.—
Androgyno, Castrone, Nano!

[*Enter* ANDROGYNO, CASTRONE, *and* NANO.]

ALL.   Here.   10
MOSCA. Go, recreate yourselves abroad; go, sport.—   [*Exeunt.*]
    So, now I have the keys and am possessed.
    Since he will needs be dead afore his time,
    I'll bury him, or gain by him. I am his heir,
    And so will keep me, till he share at least.   15
    To cozen him of all were but a cheat
    Well placed; no man would cònstrue it a sin:
    Let his sport pay for 't. This is called the fox-trap.   [*Exit.*]

SCENE 6. A *street*.

[*Enter* CORBACCIO *and* CORVINO.]

CORBACCIO. They say the court is set.
CORVINO.   We must maintain
    Our first tale good, for both our reputations.
CORBACCIO. Why, mine's no tale; my son would there have
        killed me.
CORVINO. That's true, I had forgot. [*Aside.*]—Mine is, I'm sure.
    But for your will, sir.
CORBACCIO.   Ay, I'll come upon him   5
    For that hereafter, now his patron's dead.

[*Enter* VOLPONE *in disguise.*]

VOLPONE. Signor Corvino! and Corbaccio! Sir,
    Much joy unto you.
CORVINO.   Of what?
VOLPONE.   The sudden good
    Dropped down upon you—
CORBACCIO.   Where?
VOLPONE.   And none knows how,
    From old Volpone, sir.
CORBACCIO.   Out, arrant knave!   10
VOLPONE. Let not your too much wealth, sir, make you furious.
CORBACCIO. Away, thou varlet.
VOLPONE.   Why, sir?
CORBACCIO.   Dost thou mock me?
VOLPONE. You mock the world, sir; did you not change[9] wills?
CORBACCIO. Out, harlot!
VOLPONE.   O! belike you are the man,
    Signor Corvino? Faith, you carry it well;
    You grow not mad withal; I love your spirit.   15

8. Children play a game called Fox-in-the-Hole. "His borrowed case": his false costume.
9. Exchange.

You are not over-leavened[1] with your fortune.
You should have some would swell now, like a wine-vat,
With such an autumn—Did he give you all, sir?
CORVINO. Avoid, you rascal!
VOLPONE.   Troth, your wife has shown   20
    Herself a very woman;[2] but you are well,
    You need not care, you have a good estate
    To bear it out, sir; better by this chance.
    Except Corbaccio have a share.
CORBACCIO.   Hence, varlet.
VOLPONE. You will not be a'known, sir; why, 'tis wise.   25
    Thus do all gamesters, at all games, dissemble;
    No man will seem to win.   [Exeunt CORVINO and CORBACCIO.]
                         —Here comes my vulture,
    Heaving his beak up in the air, and snuffing.

                          SCENE 7

        [Enter VOLTORE.]

VOLTORE. Outstripped thus, by a parasite! a slave,
    Would run on errands, and make legs[3] for crumbs!
    Well, what I'll do—
VOLPONE.   The court stays for your worship.
    I e'en rejoice, sir, at your worship's happiness,
    And that it fell into so learnèd hands,   5
    That understand the fingering—
VOLTORE.   What do you mean?
VOLPONE. I mean to be a suitor to your worship
    For the small tenement, out of reparations[4]—
    That at the end of your long row of houses,
    By the Pescheria;[5] it was, in Volpone's time,   10
    Your predecessor, ere he grew diseased,
    A handsome, pretty, customed[6] bawdy-house
    As any was in Venice—none dispraised;
    But fell with him. His body and that house
    Decayed together.
VOLTORE.   Come, sir, leave your prating.   15
VOLPONE. Why, if your worship give me but your hand
    That I may have the refusal, I have done.
    'Tis a mere toy to you, sir; candle-rents;[7]
    As your learned worship knows—
VOLTORE.   What do I know?
VOLPONE. Marry, no end of your wealth, sir; God decrease it!   20
VOLTORE. Mistaking knave! what, mock'st thou my misfortune?

---

1. Too puffed up (like a loaf of bread).
2. I.e., promiscuous.
3. Bow and scrape.
4. Repair.
5. The fish market on the Grand Canal.

6. Well patronized. "None dispraised": without
prejudice to any of the other splendid bawdy houses
in Venice.
7. I.e., trivial stuff to a rich man like you.

VOLPONE. His blessing on your heart, sir; would 'twere more!—

[Exit VOLTORE.]

—Now to my first again, at the next corner.   [Exit.]

SCENE 8. Another part of the street.

> [Enter CORBACCIO and CORVINO;—MOSCA passes over the stage, before them.]

CORBACCIO. See, in our habit![8] See the impudent varlet!
CORVINO. That I could shoot mine eyes at him like gun-stones!

> [Enter VOLPONE.]

VOLPONE. But is this true, sir, of the parasite?
CORBACCIO. Again, to afflict us! monster!
VOLPONE.   In good faith, sir,
  I'm heartily grieved a beard of your grave length   5
  Should be so over-reached. I never brooked[9]
  That parasite's hair; methought his nose should cozen.
  There still was somewhat in his look did promise
  The bane of a clarissimo.[1]
CORBACCIO.   Knave—
VOLPONE.   Methinks
  Yet you, that are so traded in the world,   10
  A witty merchant, the fine bird Corvino,
  That have such moral emblems on your name,
  Should not have sung your shame, and dropped your cheese,
  To let the fox laugh at your emptiness.[2]
CORVINO. Sirrah, you think the privilege of the place,   15
  And your red saucy cap, that seems to me
  Nailed to your jolt-head[3] with those two sequins,
  Can warrant your abuses. Come you hither;
  You shall perceive, sir, I dare beat you; approach.
VOLPONE. No haste, sir, I do know your valor well,   20
  Since you durst publish what you are, sir.[4]
CORVINO.   Tarry,
  I'd speak with you.
VOLPONE.   Sir, sir, another time—
CORVINO. Nay, now.
VOLPONE.   O God, sir! I were a wise man,
  Would stand the fury of a distracted cuckold. [As he is running
  off, re-enter MOSCA.]
CORBACCIO. What, come again!
VOLPONE. [aside]   Upon 'em, Mosca; save me.   25
CORBACCIO. The air's infected where he breathes.
CORVINO.   Let's fly him.

8. I.e., in the clothes we patricians are accustomed to wear.
9. Could stand.
1. I.e., trouble for a patrician.

2. The recurrent refrain from Aesop's fable.
3. Blockhead. Volpone's disguise includes a red cap with two brass buttons.
4. A cuckold, liable to run "horn-mad."

                       [*Exeunt* CORVINO *and* CORBACCIO.]

VOLPONE. Excellent basilisk![5] Turn upon the vulture.

SCENE 9

     [*Enter* VOLTORE.]

VOLTORE. Well, flesh-fly, it is summer with you now;
     Your winter will come on.
MOSCA.   Good advocate,
     Pray thee not rail, nor threaten out of place thus;
     Thou 'lt make a solecism, as Madam says.[6]
     Get you a biggen[7] more; your brain breaks loose. [*Exit.*]   5
VOLTORE. Well, sir.
VOLPONE.   Would you have me beat the insolent slave,
     Throw dirt upon his first good clothes?
VOLTORE.   This same
     Is doubtless some familiar.
VOLPONE.   Sir, the court,
     In troth, stays for you. I am mad, a mule
     That never read Justinian[8] should get up   10
     And ride an advocate. Had you no quirk
     To avoid gullage,[9] sir, by such a creature?
     I hope you do but jest; he has not done it;
     This 's but confederacy[1] to blind the rest.
     You are the heir?
VOLTORE.   A strange, officious,   15
     Troublesome knave! Thou dost torment me.
VOLPONE.   I know—
     It cannot be, sir, that you should be cozened;
     'Tis not within the wit of man to do it;
     You are so wise, so prudent; and 'tis fit
     That wealth and wisdom still should go together.   20

                                   [*Exeunt.*]

SCENE 10. *The Scrutineo.*

     [*Enter* AVOCATORI, NOTARIO, BONARIO, CELIA, CORBACCIO, COR-
     VINO, COMMENDATORI, SAFFI, &c.]

1 AVOCATORE. Are all the parties here?
NOTARIO.   All but the advocate.
2 AVOCATORE. And here he comes.

     [*Enter* VOLTORE *and* VOLPONE.]

1 AVOCATORE.   Then bring them forth to sentence.
VOLTORE. O, my most honored fathers, let your mercy

---

5. A mythical creature that kills with its glance.
6. The "solecism" of Lady Politic is above, 4.2.
7. A little skullcap worn by lawyers.
8. I.e., Mosca, wholly ignorant of the legal codes

compiled by the Emperor Justinian.
9. Deceit.
1. Conspiracy, trickery.

Once win upon your justice, to forgive—
I am distracted—

VOLPONE. [*aside*]   What will he do now?

VOLTORE.   O,   5
I know not which to address myself to first;
Whether your fatherhoods, or these innocents—

CORVINO. [*aside*] Will he betray himself?

VOLTORE.   Whom equally
I have abused, out of most covetous ends—

CORVINO. The man is mad!

CORBACCIO.   What's that?

CORVINO.   He is possessed.   10

VOLTORE. For which, now struck in conscience, here I prostrate
Myself at your offended feet, for pardon.

1, 2 AVOCATORI. Arise.

CELIA.   O heaven, how just thou art!

VOLPONE. [*aside*]   I am caught
In mine own noose—

CORVINO. [*to* CORBACCIO] Be constant, sir; naught now
Can help, but impudence.

1 AVOCATORE.   Speak forward.

COMMENDATORE. [*to the courtroom*]   Silence!   15

VOLTORE. It is not passion in me, reverend fathers,
But only conscience, conscience, my good sires,
That makes me now tell truth. That parasite,
That knave, hath been the instrument of all.

1 AVOCATORE. Where is that knave? Fetch him.

VOLPONE.   I go.   [*Exit.*]

CORVINO.   Grave fathers,   20
This man's distracted; he confessed it now;
For, hoping to be old Volpone's heir,
Who now is dead—

3 AVOCATORE.   How!

2 AVOCATORE.   Is Volpone dead?

CORVINO. Dead since, grave fathers.

BONARIO.   O sure vengeance!

1 AVOCATORE.   Stay!
Then he was no deceiver?

VOLTORE.   O no, none;   25
The parasite, grave fathers.

CORVINO.   He does speak
Out of mere envy, 'cause the servant's made
The thing he gaped for. Please your fatherhoods,
This is the truth, though I'll not justify
The other[2] but he may be some-deal faulty.   30

VOLTORE. Ay, to your hopes, as well as mine, Corvino.
But I'll use modesty. Pleaseth your wisdoms
To view these certain notes, and but confer them;
As I hope favor, they shall speak clear truth.

CORVINO. The devil has entered him!

2. I.e., Mosca.

BONARIO.   Or bides in you.   35
4 AVOCATORE. We have done ill, by a public officer
    To send for him, if he be heir.
2 AVOCATORE.   For whom?
4 AVOCATORE. Him that they call the parasite.
3 AVOCATORE.   'Tis true,
    He is a man of great estate now left.[3]
4 AVOCATORE. Go you and learn his name, and say the court   40
    Entreats his presence here, but to the clearing
    Of some few doubts.   [*Exit* NOTARIO.]
2 AVOCATORE.   This same's a labyrinth!
1 AVOCATORE. [*To* CORVINO.] Stand you unto your first report?
CORVINO.   My
    state,
    My life, my fame—
BONARIO.   Where is it?
CORVINO.   Are at the stake.
1 AVOCATORE. [*to* CORBACCIO] Is yours so too?
CORBACCIO.   The advocate's a knave;   45
    And has a forkèd tongue—
                                 Speak to the point.
CORBACCIO. So is the parasite too.
1 AVOCATORE.   This is confusion.
VOLTORE. I do beseech your fatherhoods, read but those—

                                          [*Giving them papers.*]

CORVINO. And credit nothing the false spirit hath writ;
    It cannot be but he's possessed,[4] grave fathers.   50

SCENE 11. *A street.*

[*Enter* VOLPONE.]

VOLPONE. To make a snare for mine own neck! and run
    My head into it, wilfully! with laughter!
    When I had newly 'scaped, was free and clear!
    Out of mere wantonness! O, the dull devil
    Was in this brain of mine, when I devised it,   5
    And Mosca gave it second; he must now
    Help to sear up this vein,[5] or we bleed dead.

[*Enter* NANO, ANDROGYNO, *and* CASTRONE.]

    How now! Who let you loose? Whither go you now?
    What? to buy gingerbread, or to drown kitlings?
NANO. Sir, Master Mosca called us out of doors,   10
    And bid us all go play, and took the keys.
ANDROGYNO.   Yes.
VOLPONE. Did Master Mosca take the keys? Why, so!

---

3. As a patrician (which he automatically is if he
has a lot of money), Mosca is not to be summoned
by a common official.
4. I.e., demonically possessed by a devil inside him

(not wholly incredible in those days, when witchcraft was an accepted fact).
5. Cautery was frequent medical procedure in the
days before antisepsis.

I'm farther in. These are my fine conceits!
I must be merry, with a mischief to me!
What a vile wretch was I, that could not bear   15
My fortune soberly! I must have my crotchets,
And my conundrums! Well, go you and seek him.
His meaning may be truer than my fear.
Bid him, he straight come to me, to the court;
Thither will I, and, if 't be possible,   20
Unscrew my advocate, upon new hopes.
When I provoked him, then I lost myself.   [*Exeunt.*]

SCENE 12. *The Scrutineo.*

[AVOCATORI, BONARIO, CELIA, CORBACCIO, CORVINO, VOLTORE,
COMMENDATORI, SAFFI, &c. *as before.*]

1 AVOCATORE. [*showing the papers*] These things can ne'er be recon-
   ciled. He here
Professeth that the gentleman was wronged,
And that the gentlewoman was brought thither,
Forced by her husband, and there left.
VOLTORE.   Most true.
CELIA. How ready is heaven to those that pray!
1 AVOCATORE.   But that   5
   Volpone would have ravished her, he holds
   Utterly false, knowing his impotence.
CORVINO. Grave fathers, he's possessed; again, I say,
   Possessed; nay, if there be possession and
   Obsession, he has both.[6]
3 AVOCATORE.   Here comes our officer.   10

   [*Enter* VOLPONE, *still in disguise.*]

VOLPONE. The parasite will straight be here, grave fathers.
4 AVOCATORE. You might invent some other name, sir varlet.
3 AVOCATORE. Did not the notary meet him?
VOLPONE.   Not that I know.
4 AVOCATORE. His coming will clear all.
2 AVOCATORE.   Yet, it is misty,
VOLTORE. May 't please your fatherhoods—
VOLPONE. [*whispers to* VOLTORE]   Sir, the parasite   15
   Willed me to tell you that his master lives;
   That you are still the man; your hopes the same;
   And this was only a jest—
VOLTORE.   How?
VOLPONE.   Sir, to try
   If you were firm, and how you stood affected.
VOLTORE. Art sure he lives?
VOLPONE.   Do I live, sir?
VOLTORE.   O me!   20

---

6. Possession is a devil attacking the mind from within, obsession is the same temptation from without.

I was too violent.

VOLPONE. Sir, you may redeem it.
They said you were possessed: fall down, and seem so.
I'll help to make it good. [VOLTORE *falls.*]—God bless the man!
[*Aside.*] Stop your wind hard, and swell.—See, see, see, see!
He vomits crooked pins![7] His eyes are set,   25
Like a dead hare's hung in a poulter's[8] shop!
His mouth's running away! Do you see, signor?
Now it is in his belly.

CORVINO. Ay, the devil!

VOLPONE. Now in his throat.

CORVINO. Ay, I perceive it plain.

VOLPONE. 'Twill out, 'twill out! Stand clear! See where it flies;   30
In shape of a blue toad with a bat's wings!
Do not you see it, sir?

CORBACCIO. What? I think I do.

CORVINO. 'Tis too manifest.

VOLPONE. Look! he comes to himself!

VOLTORE. Where am I?

VOLPONE. Take good heart, the worst is past, sir.
You are dispossessed.

1 AVOCATORE. What accident is this?   35

2 AVOCATORE. Sudden and full of wonder!

3 AVOCATORE. If he were
Possessed, as it appears, all this is nothing. [*He waves the notes.*]

CORVINO. He has been often subject to these fits.

1 AVOCATORE. Show him that writing.—Do you know it, sir?

VOLPONE. [*whispers to* VOLTORE] Deny it, sir, forswear it;
know it not.   40

VOLTORE. Yes, I do know it well, it is my hand;
But all that it contains is false.

BONARIO. O practice![9]

2 AVOCATORE. What maze is this?

1 AVOCATORE. Is he not guilty then,
Whom you there name the parasite?

VOLTORE. Grave fathers,
No more than his good patron, old Volpone.   45

4 AVOCATORE. Why, he is dead.

VOLTORE. O no, my honored fathers,
He lives—

1 AVOCATORE. How! Lives?

VOLTORE. Lives.

2 AVOCATORE. This is subtler yet!

3 AVOCATORE. You said he was dead.

VOLTORE. Never.

AVOCATORE. [*to* CORVINO] You said so!

---

7. The symptoms that Volpone "sees," and persuades others to see, were standard. The "blue toad with bat's wings" below is the demon himself.

8. A dealer in fowl and small game.

9. Deceit.

CORVINO.   I heard so.
4 AVOCATORE. Here comes the gentleman; make him way.[1]

[*Enter* MOSCA *as a clarissimo.*]

3 AVOCATORE.   A stool.
4 AVOCATORE. [*aside*] A proper man; and, were Volpone dead,   50
    A fit match for my daughter.
3 AVOCATORE.   Give him way.
VOLPONE. [*aside to* MOSCA] Mosca, I was almost lost; the advocate
    Had betrayed all; but now it is recovered;
    All's on the hinge again—say I am living.
MOSCA. What busy knave is this! Most reverend fathers,   55
    I sooner had attended your grave pleasures,
    But that my order for the funeral
    Of my dear patron did require me—
VOLPONE. [*aside*]   Mosca!
MOSCA. Whom I intend to bury like a gentleman.
VOLPONE. [*aside*] Ay, quick,[2] and cozen me of all.
2 AVOCATORE.   Still stranger!   60
    More intricate!
1 AVOCATORE.   And come about again!
4 AVOCATORE. [*aside*] It is a match, my daughter is bestowed.
MOSCA. [*aside to* VOLPONE] Will you give me half?
VOLPONE.   First I'll be hanged.
MOSCA. [*aside*]   I know
    Your voice is good, cry not so loud.
1 AVOCATORE.   Demand
    The advocate.—Sir, did you not affirm   65
    Volpone was alive?
VOLPONE.   Yes, and he is;
    This gentleman[3] told me so. [*Aside to* MOSCA.] Thou shalt have
    half.
MOSCA. Whose drunkard is this same? Speak, some that know him:
    I never saw his face. [*Aside to* VOLPONE.] I cannot now
    Afford it you so cheap.
VOLPONE. [*aside*]   No?
1 AVOCATORE. [*To* VOLTORE] What say you?   70
VOLTORE. The officer told me.
VOLPONE.   I did, grave fathers,
    And will maintain he lives, with mine own life,
    And that this creature [*points to* MOSCA] told me. [*Aside.*] I was
    born
    With all good stars my enemies.
MOSCA.   Most grave fathers,
    If such an insolence as this must pass   75
    Upon me, I am silent: 'twas not this
    For which you sent, I hope.

---

1. Jonson's audience would be scandalized at the instant transformation of a parasite into a gentleman, partly because they had seen it happen frequently in their own land.
2. Alive.
3. I.e., Mosca.

2 AVOCATORE.   Take him away.

VOLPONE. [*aside*] Mosca!

3 AVOCATORE.   Let him be whipped—

VOLPONE. [*aside*]   Wilt thou betray me?
     Cozen me?

3 AVOCATORE. And taught to bear himself
     Toward a person of his rank.
                              Away. [*The* OFFICERS *seize* VOLPONE.]   80

MOSCA. I humbly thank your fatherhoods.

VOLPONE. [*aside*]   Soft, soft. Whipped?
     And lose all that I have? If I confess,
     It cannot be much more.

4 AVOCATORE. [*to* MOSCA]   Sir, are you married?[4]

VOLPONE. [*aside*] They'll be allied anon; I must be resolute.
     The fox shall here uncase.[5] [*Throws off his disguise.*]

MOSCA.   Patron!

VOLPONE.   Nay, now   85
     My ruins shall not come alone; your match
     I'll hinder sure: my substance shall not glue you
     Nor screw you into a family.

MOSCA.   Why, patron!

VOLPONE. I am Volpone, and this [*pointing to* MOSCA] is my knave;
     This, [*to* VOLTORE] his own knave; this, [*to* CORBACCIO] avarice's
          fool;   90
     This, [*to* CORVINO] a chimera[6] of wittol, fool, and knave.
     And, reverend fathers, since we all can hope
     Nought but a sentence, let's not now despair it.
     You hear me brief.

CORVINO.   May it please your fatherhoods—

COMMENDATORE. Silence!

1 AVOCATORE.   The knot is now undone by miracle!   95

2 AVOCATORE. Nothing can be more clear.

3 AVOCATORE.   Or can more prove
     These innocent.

1 ADVOCATORE.   Give them their liberty.

BONARIO. Heaven could not long let such gross crimes be hid.

2 AVOCATORE. If this be held the highway to get riches,
     May I be poor!

3 AVOCATORE.   This is not gain, but torment.   100

1 AVOCATORE. These possess wealth as sick men possess fevers,
     Which trulier may be said to possess them.[7]

2 AVOCATORE.   Disrobe that parasite.

CORVINO, MOSCA.   Most honored fathers!

1 AVOCATORE. Can you plead aught to stay the course of justice?
     If you can, speak.

---

4. The question is addressed to Mosca.
5. Remove his mask.
6. The chimera was an unnatural imaginary creature compounded of lion, goat, and serpent.
7. The aphorism is Seneca's (Epistle 119, par. 12).

CORVINO, VOLTORE. We beg favor.

CELIA. And mercy. 105

1 AVOCATORE. You hurt your innocence, suing for the guilty.
Stand forth; and first the parasite. You appear
T' have been the chiefest minister, if not plotter,
In all these lewd impostures; and now, lastly,
Have with your impudence abused the court, 110
And habit of a gentleman of Venice,
Being a fellow of no birth or blood:[8]
For which our sentence is, first, thou be whipped;
Then live perpetual prisoner in our galleys.

VOLPONE. I thank you for him.

MOSCA. Bane[9] to thy wolfish nature! 115

1 AVOCATORE. Deliver him to the Saffi. [MOSCA *is led out.*]
—Thou, Volpone,
By blood and rank a gentleman, canst not fall
Under like censure; but our judgment on thee
Is that thy substance all be straight confiscate
To the hospital of the Incurabili.[1] 120
And, since the most was gotten by imposture,
By feigning lame, gout, palsy, and such diseases,
Thou art to lie in prison, cramped with irons,
Till thou be'st sick and lame indeed. Remove him. [*He is led aside.*]

VOLPONE. This is called mortifying of a fox.[2] 125

1 AVOCATORE. Thou, Voltore, to take away the scandal
Thou hast given all worthy men of thy profession,
Art banished from their fellowship, and our state.
Corbaccio!—bring him near—we here possess
Thy son of all thy state,[3] and confine thee 130
To the monastery of San Spirito;
Where, since thou knew'st not how to live well here,
Thou shalt be learned[4] to die well.

CORBACCIO. Ha! what said he?

COMMENDATORE. You shall know anon, sir.

1 AVOCATORE. Thou, Corvino, shalt
Be straight embarked from thine own house, and rowed 135
Round about Venice, through the Grand Canal,
Wearing a cap with fair long ass's ears
Instead of horns; and so to mount, a paper
Pinned on thy breast, to the Berlina[5]—

8. Justice in Venice makes no pretense to equality; Mosca's sentence is most severe, and for snob reasons.
9. Poison. It was legitimate to poison wolves, not foxes.
1. There was a Hospital of the Incurables in Venice, but the sentence carries an irony: these are the only people in Venice who can be trusted with money.
2. "Mortifying": not just humiliating, but killing. Both the galleys and the dungeons of Venice were widely reputed the most horrible in Europe; neither Mosca nor Volpone is long for this world.
3. I.e., convey to your son your entire estate.
4. Taught.
5. Pillory.

CORVINO.   Yes,
   And have mine eyes beat out with stinking fish,   140
   Bruised fruit, and rotten eggs—'Tis well: I'm glad
   I shall not see my shame yet.
1 AVOCATORE.   And to expiate
   Thy wrongs done to thy wife, thou art to send her
   Home, to her father, with her dowry trebled:
   And these are all your judgments—
ALL.   Honored fathers!   145
1 AVOCATORE. Which may not be revoked. Now you begin,
   When crimes are done, and past, and to be punished,
   To think what your crimes are: away with them!
   Let all that see these vices thus rewarded,
   Take heart, and love to study 'em! Mischiefs feed   150
   Like beasts, till they be fat, and then they bleed.   [*Exeunt.*]

          [VOLPONE *comes forward.*]

   The seasoning of a play is the applause.
   Now, though the fox be punished by the laws,
   He yet doth hope, there is no suffering due
   For any fact which he hath done 'gainst you.   155
   If there be, censure him; here he doubtful stands.
   If not, fare jovially, and clap your hands.
                                                         [Exit.]

                                                         1606

To My Book[1]

It will be looked for, book, when some but see
     Thy title, *Epigrams*, and named of me,
Thou should'st be bold, licentious, full of gall,
     Wormwood and sulphur, sharp and toothed[2] withal,
Become a petulant thing, hurl ink and wit   5
     As madmen stones, not caring whom they hit.
Deceive their malice who could wish it so,
     And by thy wiser temper let men know
Thou art not covetous of least self-fame
     Made from the hazard of another's shame—   10
Much less with lewd, profane, and beastly phrase
     To catch the world's loose laughter or vain gaze.

---

1. Epigrams are commonly thought of as short, incisive poems of personal invective; but when Jonson included in his collected *Works* of 1616 a separate section headed "Epigrams (Book 1)," he was using the word in a more liberal sense. His "epigrams" included (besides some sharp and sarcastic verses) several poems of compliment and courtesy, some memorial epitaphs, and a verse letter, *Inviting a Friend to Supper*. In our anthology, *To My Book* and the next several poems (through *Epitaph on Elizabeth, L. H.*) come from this sec-tion. The "Book 1" of Jonson's title implied at least the promise of a "Book 2," and there are, scattered through his later poetry, a number of verses that might have entered into such a book. But, for whatever reason, Jonson never assembled them under any such title.

2. The distinction between toothed (biting) and toothless (general) satires, originally made by Joseph Hall, who claimed to be the first English satirist, was a commonplace of Jonson's age.

He that departs[3] with his own honesty
  For vulgar praise, doth it too dearly buy.

1616

On Something, That Walks Somewhere

At court I met it, in clothes brave[4] enough
  To be a courtier, and looks grave enough
To seem a statesman: as I near it came,
  It made me a great face. I asked the name.
"A lord," it cried, "buried in flesh and blood,   5
  And such from whom let no man hope least good,
For I will do none; and as little ill,
  For I will dare none." Good lord, walk dead still.

1616

To William Camden[1]

Camden, most reverend head, to whom I owe
  All that I am in arts, all that I know
(How nothing's that!), to whom my country owes
  The great renown and name wherewith she goes;[2]
Than thee the age sees not that thing more grave,   5
  More high, more holy, that she more would crave.
What name, what skill, what faith hast thou in things!
  What sight in searching the most antique springs!
What weight and what authority in thy speech!
  Man scarce can make that doubt, but thou canst teach.[3] 10
Pardon free truth and let thy modesty,
  Which conquers all, be once o'ercome by thee.
Many of thine[4] this better could than I;
  But for their powers, accept my piety.

1616

On My First Daughter

Here lies, to each her parents' ruth,[1]
  Mary, the daughter of their youth;

---

3. I.e., parts.
4. Fine.
1. Though first printed among the *Epigrams*, this affectionate tribute to a distinguished scholar and Jonson's old teacher has few of the qualities of an epigram, except brevity. It is just the size (though not the shape) of a sonnet.
2. Camden's antiquarian studies of his native land

in *Britannia* (1586) and *Remains of a Greater Work Concerning Britain* (1605) ran into several editions and were translated abroad.
3. I.e., man can scarcely ask a question to which you don't know the answer.
4. I.e., your pupils. "But for": but in lieu of.
1. Grief. There is no positive date of composition for this poem.

Yet all heaven's gifts being heaven's due,
It makes the father less to rue.
At six months' end she parted hence   5
With safety of her innocence;
Whose soul heaven's queen, whose name she bears,
In comfort of her mother's tears,
Hath placed amongst her virgin-train:
Where, while that severed doth remain,   10
This grave partakes the fleshly birth;
Which cover lightly, gentle earth!

                                                              1616

On My First Son

Farewell, thou child of my right hand,[1] and joy;
My sin was too much hope of thee, loved boy:
Seven years thou wert lent to me, and I thee pay,
Exacted by thy fate, on the just day.
O could I lose all father[2] now! For why   5
Will man lament the state he should envy,
To have so soon 'scaped world's and flesh's rage,
And, if no other misery, yet age?
Rest in soft peace, and asked, say, "Here doth lie
Ben Jonson his best piece of poetry."   10
For whose sake henceforth all his vows be such
As what he loves may never like too much.[3]

                                                              1616

To John Donne

Donne, the delight of Phoebus and each Muse,
Who, to thy one, all other brains refuse;[1]
Whose every work, of thy most early wit,
Came forth example and remains so yet;
Longer a-knowing than most wits do live,   5
And which no affection praise enough can give.
To it[2] thy language, letters, arts, best life,
Which might with half mankind maintain a strife.

---

1. "Child of the right hand" is a literal translation of the Hebrew name "Benjamin," which implies the meanings "dexterous," or "fortunate." The boy was born in 1596 and died on his birthday in 1603.
2. Relinquish all fatherly thoughts.
3. The obscure grammar of the last lines seems to recapitulate the feeling in line 2, that too much affection is fatal to the loved one. "Whose sake" is the boy's; "like" may carry the sense of "please."
1. I.e., the muses shower their favors exclusively on you.
2. The verb "add" is understood.

All which I meant to praise, and yet I would,
But leave, because I cannot as I should.   10

On Don Surly

Don Surly,[1] to aspire the glorious name
  Of a great man, and to be thought the same,
Makes serious use of all great trade[2] he knows.
  He speaks to men with a Rhinocerotes' nose,[3]
Which he thinks great; and so reads verses too,   5
  And that is done as he saw great men do.
He has timpanies[4] of business in his face,
  And can forget men's names with a great grace.
He will both argue and discourse in oaths,
  Both which are great; and laugh at ill-made clothes—   10
That's greater yet—to cry his own up neat.
  He doth, at meals, alone his pheasant eat,
Which is main greatness; and at his still board[5]
  He drinks to no man; that's, too, like a lord.
He keeps another's wife, which is a spice[6]   15
  Of solemn greatness. And he dares, at dice,
Blaspheme God greatly, or some poor hind[7] beat
  That breathes in his dog's way; and this is great.
Nay more, for greatness' sake, he will be one
  May hear my epigrams, but like of none.   20
Surly, use other arts; these only can
  Style thee a most great fool, but no great man.

On Giles and Joan

Who says that Giles and Joan at discord be?
  Th' observing neighbors no such mood can see.
Indeed, poor Giles repents he married ever,
  But that his Joan doth too. And Giles would never
By his free will be in Joan's company;   5
  No more would Joan he should. Giles riseth early,
And having got him out of doors is glad;
  The like is Joan. But turning home is sad,

---

1. "Don" is a Spanish title, and the Spanish were
thought to have pompous manners. "Aspire": attain.
2. Tricks.
3. I.e., looking down his nose like a rhinoceros.
4. Figuratively, a kettle-drum; fullness, empti-

ness, and hollow noises are implied.
5. I.e., his lonely dinner-table.
6. Species, kind.
7. Yokel.

And so is Joan. Ofttimes, when Giles doth find
    Harsh sights at home, Giles wisheth he were blind: 10
All this doth Joan. Or that his long-yearned[1] life
    Were quite outspun. The like wish hath his wife.
The children that he keeps Giles swears are none
    Of his begetting; and so swears his Joan.
In all affections she concurreth still.   15
    If now, with man and wife, to will and nill[2]
The self-same things a note of concord be,
    I know no couple better can agree.

                                1616

To Lucy, Countess of Bedford, with Mr. Donne's Satires[1]

Lucy, you brightness of our sphere, who are
    Life of the Muses' day, their morning star!
If works, not th' authors, their own grace should look,
    Whose poems would not wish to be your book?
But these, desired by you, the maker's ends   5
    Crown with their own. Rare poems ask rare friends.
Yet satires, since the most of mankind be
    Their unavoided subject, fewest see:
For none e'er took that pleasure in sin's sense,
    But, when they heard it taxed, took more offense.   10
They then that, living where the matter is bred,
    Dare for these poems yet both ask and read
And like them too, must needfully, though few,
    Be of the best: and 'mongst those, best are you;
Lucy, you brightness of our sphere, who are   15
    The Muses' evening, as their morning star.

                                1616

Inviting a Friend to Supper

Tonight, grave sir, both my poor house and I
    Do equally desire your company:
Not that we think us worthy such a guest,
    But that your worth will dignify our feast
With those that come; whose grace may make that seem   5

---

1. Spun from long skeins of yarn, but with the extra implication of long and futile yearning.
2. To desire and reject; cf. modern "willy-nilly."
1. The Countess of Bedford was a famous patroness of the age, to whom both Jonson and Donne addressed poems of compliment. With this poem, Jonson was not offering a printed volume of Donne's Satires, but simply a manuscript collection, such as commonly passed from hand to hand in court circles.

Something, which else could hope for no esteem.
It is the fair acceptance, Sir, creates
   The entertainment perfect: not the cates.[1]
Yet shall you have, to rectify your palate,
   An olive, capers, or some better salad   10
Ushering the mutton; with a short-legged hen,
   If we can get her, full of eggs, and then
Lemons and wine for sauce; to these, a coney[2]
   Is not to be despaired of for our money;
And though fowl now be scarce, yet there are clerks,[3]
   The sky not falling, think we may have larks.
I'll tell you of more, and lie, so you will come:
   Of partridge, pheasant, woodcock, of which some
May yet be there; and godwit if we can,
   Knot, rail, and ruff, too.[4] Howsoe'er, my man   20
Shall read a piece of Virgil, Tacitus,
   Livy, or of some better book to us,
Of which we'll speak our minds amidst our meat;
   And I'll profess[5] no verses to repeat:
To this, if aught appear which I not know of,   25
   That will the pastry, not my paper, show off.[6]
Digestive cheese and fruit there sure will be;
   But that which most doth take my muse and me
Is a pure cup of rich Canary wine,
   Which is the Mermaid's[7] now, but shall be mine;   30
Of which, had Horace or Anacreon tasted,
   Their lives, as do their lines, till now had lasted.
Tobacco, Nectar, or the Thespian spring
   Are all but Luther's beer to this I sing.[8]
Of this we will sup free but moderately,   35
   And we will have no Pooly or Parrot[9] by;
Nor shall our cups make any guilty men,
   But at our parting we will be as when
We innocently met. No simple word
   That shall be uttered at our mirthful board   40
Shall make us sad next morning; or affright
   The liberty that we'll enjoy tonight.

1616

---

1. Dishes.
2. Rabbit.
3. Scholars (pronounced "clarks").
4. The treat of the feast will be these various game birds.
5. Promise.
6. I.e., papers may appear, but they will be under pies (to keep them from sticking to the pan), not for declamation. "To this": add to this.
7. The Mermaid tavern, favorite haunt of the poets; sweet wine from the Canary Islands was popular in England. Horace and Anacreon (one in Latin, the other in Greek) wrote many poems in praise of wine.
8. One of two springs on Mount Helicon near the village of Thespiae, both reputed to be sources of poetic inspiration. Compared to Canary, all these other intoxicants are no better than Luther's beer, i.e., weak stuff.
9. Pooly and Parrot were government spies, though their conjunction also suggests a talkative bird, Poll Parrot. While a Roman Catholic and even after he formally left that communion, Jonson had reason to be wary of undercover agents.

Epitaph on Salomon Pavy, a Child of Queen Elizabeth's Chapel[1]

Weep with me, all you that read
   This little story;
And know for whom a tear you shed,
   Death's self is sorry.
'Twas a child that so did thrive   5
   In grace and feature,
As Heaven and Nature seemed to strive
   Which owned the creature.
Years he numbered scarce thirteen
   When Fates turned cruel,   10
Yet three filled zodiacs[2] had he been
   The stage's jewel;
And did act (what now we moan)
   Old men so duly,
As, sooth, the Parcae[3] thought him one,   15
   He played so truly.
So, by error, to his fate
   They all consented;
But, viewing him since (alas, too late),
   They have repented,   20
And have sought (to give new birth)
   In baths[4] to steep him;
But, being so much too good for earth,
   Heaven vows to keep him.

1616

Epitaph on Elizabeth, L. H.[1]

Wouldst thou hear what man can say
   In a little? Reader, stay.
Underneath this stone doth lie
   As much beauty as could die;
Which in life did harbor give   5
   To more virtue than doth live.
If at all she had a fault,
   Leave it buried in this vault.
One name was Elizabeth;

1. Salomon Pavy, a boy actor in the troupe known as the Children of Queen Elizabeth's Chapel, had appeared in several of Jonson's plays; he died in 1602.
2. I.e., had been on the stage for three seasons.
3. The Fates, one of whose functions was to determine the length of lives.

4. Jonson may have had in mind such magic baths as that of Medea, which restored old Aeson, Jason's father, to his first youth (Ovid, *Metamorphoses* 7).
1. The subject of this epitaph has not been identified; her full name (though we can guess that the L. probably stood for "Lady") has slept with death.

Th' other, let it sleep with death: 10
  Fitter, where it died, to tell,
    Than that it lived at all. Farewell!

                                                              1616

To Penshurst[1]

Thou art not, Penshurst, built to envious show,
  Of touch[2] or marble; nor canst boast a row
Of polished pillars, or a roof of gold;
  Thou hast no lantern[3] whereof tales are told,
Or stair, or courts; but stand'st an ancient pile,   5
  And, these grudged at,[4] art reverenced the while.
Thou joy'st in better marks, of soil, of air,
  Of wood, of water; therein thou art fair.
Thou hast thy walks for health, as well as sport;
  Thy mount, to which the dryads[5] do resort,   10
Where Pan and Bacchus their high feasts have made,
  Beneath the broad beech and the chestnut shade;
That taller tree, which of a nut was set
  At his great birth where all the Muses met.[6]
There in the writhèd bark are cut the names   15
  Of many a sylvan, taken with his flames;[7]
And thence the ruddy satyrs oft provoke
  The lighter fauns to reach thy Lady's Oak.[8]
Thy copse too, named of Gamage,[9] thou hast there,
  That never fails to serve thee seasoned deer   20
When thou wouldst feast or exercise thy friends.
  The lower land, that to the river bends,
Thy sheep, thy bullocks, kine, and calves do feed;
  The middle grounds thy mares and horses breed.
Each bank doth yield thee conies;[1] and the tops,   25
  Fertile of wood, Ashore and Sidney's copse,[2]
To crown thy open table, doth provide
  The purpled pheasant with the speckled side;

---

1. The country seat of the Sidney family (famous for Sir Philip) in Kent. Jonson's is one of the first English poems celebrating a specific place. Later examples are *Cooper's Hill* by Sir John Denham and *Windsor Forest* by Alexander Pope; some modern poets have celebrated their favorite subway stations or particularly atrocious (but fondly remembered) bits of suburbia.

In the 1616 *Works*, Jonson grouped some of his non-epigrammatic poems under the heading *The Forest*. This was a translation of the term *Silvae*, used by the late Latin poet Statius to designate a poetical miscellany. *To Penshurst* and the two following poems are from that grouping.

2. Touchstone, a fine black (and expensive) variety of basalt.

3. Cupola.

4. More pretentious houses attract criticism.

5. Wood nymphs.

6. Sir Philip Sidney was born at Penshurst; an oak tree, planted the day of his birth, is still shown as "Sidney's oak."

7. Woodsman, in love because of reading Sidney's poems. "His flames" are the fires of love.

8. Lady Leicester's oak, named after a lady of the house who once entered into labor under its branches. "Provoke": challenge to a race.

9. Lady Barbara Gamage gave her name to a grove near the park entrance.

1. Rabbits.

2. Little woods and thickets of the estate, still surviving under their ancient names.

The painted partridge lies in every field,
    And for thy mess is willing to be killed.   30
And if the high-swollen Medway[3] fail thy dish,
    Thou hast thy ponds, that pay thee tribute fish:
Fat aged carps that run into thy net,
    And pikes, now weary their own kind to eat,
As loath the second draught or cast to stay,   35
    Officiously at first themselves betray;
Bright eels that emulate them, and leap on land
    Before the fisher, or into his hand.
Then hath thy orchard fruit, thy garden flowers,
    Fresh as the air, and new as are the hours.   40
The early cherry, with the later plum,
    Fig, grape, and quince, each in his time doth come;
The blushing apricot and woolly peach
    Hang on thy walls, that every child may reach.
And though thy walls be of the country stone,   45
    They are reared with no man's ruin, no man's groan;
There's none that dwell about them wish them down;
    But all come in, the farmer and the clown,[4]
And no one empty-handed, to salute
    Thy lord and lady, though they have no suit.   50
Some bring a capon, some a rural cake,
    Some nuts, some apples; some that think they make
The better cheeses bring them, or else send
    By their ripe daughters, whom they would commend
This way to husbands, and whose baskets bear   55
    An emblem of themselves in plum or pear.
But what can this (more than express their love)
    Add to thy free provisions, far above
The need of such? whose liberal board doth flow
    With all that hospitality doth know;   60
Where comes no guest but is allowed to eat,
    Without his fear, and of thy lord's own meat;
Where the same beer and bread, and selfsame wine,
    That is his lordship's shall be also mine,
And I not fain to sit (as some this day   65
    At great men's tables), and yet dine away.[5]
Here no man tells[6] my cups; nor, standing by,
    A waiter doth my gluttony envy,
But gives me what I call, and lets me eat;
    He knows below he shall find plenty of meat.   70
Thy tables hoard not up for the next day;
    Nor, when I take my lodging, need I pray
For fire, or lights, or livery;[7] all is there,

---

3. The local river.
4. Yokel.
5. When tables were large, different courses might be served at the two ends; hence one could sit at a man's table and dine away, eating different food entirely.
6. Counts.
7. In the old sense, provisions, food.

As if thou then wert mine, or I reigned here:
There's nothing I can wish, for which I stay.[8]   75
 That found King James when, hunting late this way
With his brave son, the Prince, they saw thy fires
 Shine bright on every hearth, as the desires
Of thy Penates[9] had been set on flame
 To entertain them; or the country came   80
With all their zeal to warm their welcome here.
 What (great I will not say, but) sudden cheer
Didst thou then make 'em! and what praise was heaped
 On thy good lady then, who therein reaped
The just reward of her high housewifery;   85
 To have her linen, plate, and all things nigh,
When she was far; and not a room but dressed
 As if it had expected such a guest!
These, Penshurst, are thy praise, and yet not all.
 Thy lady's noble, fruitful, chaste withal.   90
His children thy great lord may call his own,
 A fortune in this age but rarely known.
They are, and have been, taught religion; thence
 Their gentler spirits have sucked innocence.
Each morn and even they are taught to pray,   95
 With the whole household, and may, every day,
Read in their virtuous parents' noble parts
 The mysteries of manners, arms, and arts.
Now, Penshurst, they that will proportion[1] thee
 With other edifices, when they see   100
Those proud, ambitious heaps, and nothing else,
 May say, their lords have built, but thy lord dwells.

1616

Song: To Celia[1]

Drink to me only with thine eyes,
 And I will pledge with mine;
Or leave a kiss but in the cup,
 And I'll not look for wine.
The thirst that from the soul doth rise   5
 Doth ask a drink divine:
But might I of Jove's nectar sup,
 I would not change for thine.

---

8. Wait.
9. Roman household gods. A room in the house is still known as "King James's room."
1. Compare.
1. These famous lines are a patchwork of 5 separate prose passages by Philostratus, a Greek sophist (3rd century A.D.). Jonson very carefully reworded the phrases (there are several manuscript versions of the poem) into this classic lyric. The music which has made it a barroom favorite is by an anonymous 18th-century composer.

I sent thee late a rosy wreath,
    Not so much honoring thee,   10
As giving it a hope that there
    It could not withered be.
But thou thereon did'st only breathe,
    And sent'st it back to me;
Since when it grows and smells, I swear,   15
    Not of itself, but thee.

                        1616

To Heaven

Good and great God, can I not think of thee
    But it must straight my melancholy be?
Is it interpreted in me disease
    That, laden with my sins, I seek for ease?
Oh, be thou witness, that the reins[1] dost know   5
    And hearts of all, if I be sad for show,
And judge me after, if I dare pretend
    To aught but grace, or aim at other end.
As thou art all, so be thou all to me,
    First, midst, and last, converted[2] one and three,   10
My faith, my hope, my love; and in this state,
    My judge, my witness, and my advocate.
Where have I been this while exiled from thee,
    And whither rapt, now thou but stoop'st[3] to me?
Dwell, dwell here still: Oh, being everywhere,   15
    How can I doubt to find thee ever here?
I know my state, both full of shame and scorn,
    Conceived in sin and unto labor born,
Standing with fear, and must with horror fall,
    And destined unto judgment after all.   20
I feel my griefs too, and there scarce is ground
    Upon my flesh to inflict another wound.
Yet dare I not complain or wish for death
    With holy Paul,[4] lest it be thought the breath
Of discontent; or that these prayers be   25
    For weariness of life, not love of thee.

                        1616

1. Literally, kidneys, but also the seat of the affections, with a further glance at Psalm 7.9: "the righteous God trieth the hearts and reins."
2. Interchanging.
3. Falcons stoop (i.e., dive from the heavens) to snatch their quarry.
4. In Romans 7.24, Paul cries out despairingly, "Who shall deliver me from the body of this death?"

In the Person of Womankind[1]
(In Defense of their Inconstancy)

Hang up those dull and envious fools
    That talk abroad of woman's change;
We were not bred to sit on stools,
    Our proper virtue is to range:
        Take that away, you take our lives,   5
        We are no women then, but wives.

Such as in valor would excel
    Do change, though man, and often fight,
Which we in love must do as well
    If ever we will love aright.   10
        The frequent varying of the deed
        Is that which doth perfection breed.

Nor is 't inconstancy to change
    For what is better, or to make
(By searching) what before was strange   15
    Familiar for the use's sake.
        The good from bad is not descried
        But as 'tis often vexed[2] and tried.

And this profession of a store[3]
    In love doth not alone help forth
Our pleasure, but preserves us more   20
    From being forsaken than doth worth:
        For were the worthiest woman cursed
        To love one man, he'd leave her first.

              1640–41

My Picture Left in Scotland[1]

I now think Love is rather deaf than blind,
    For else it could not be
        That she
Whom I adore so much should so slight me
    And cast my love behind;   5

---

1. Preparing a second edition of his *Works* (published posthumously in 1640–41), Jonson added a third section of poems, *The Underwood*, "out of the analogy they hold to *The Forest* in my former book." Of its 89 poems we reprint just 3, this and the following two.
2. Examined severely.

3. Abundance.
1. After his walking tour of Scotland in 1618–19, Jonson sent a manuscript version of this poem to William Drummond, with whom he had stayed. No one knows who the woman of the poem was, or if she existed at all.

I'm sure my language to her was as sweet,
        And every close[2] did meet
     In sentence of as subtle feet,
        As hath the youngest he
That sits in shadow of Apollo's tree.   10

O, but my conscious fears
        That fly my thoughts between,
        Tell me that she hath seen
     My hundreds of gray hairs,
        Told seven and forty years,   15
Read so much waste[3] as she cannot embrace
My mountain belly and my rocky face;
And all these through her eyes have stopped her ears.

1619   1640–41

The Ode on Cary and Morison

The ode was originally a classical form, and was therefore always in English a learned and slightly artificial one. It is defined as a serious lyric poem, dignified by its theme, its occasion, or the person to whom it is addressed. The Greek poet Pindar wrote many odes for winners of the Olympic games; because of their exalted style, they are known as "Great Odes." Later, the Latin poet Horace wrote more modest poems that he actually called Carmina (Songs), but which everyone has agreed to call by the equivalent Greek word, Odes—though Horace's are called "Lesser Odes" to distinguish them from those of Pindar.

The Renaissance brought odes into the modern European languages through the agency of Petrarch in Italian and Ronsard in French; but in England the formal ode was slow to appear. Michael Drayton referred to some of his poems as "odes," but they are more like ballads. Jonson's ode to Cary and Morison is the first Great Ode in English; its relation to Pindar is most apparent in the matter of formal structure.

Pindar's odes were designed to be sung by a chorus, and like other Greek choral odes, they often follow a three-part scheme of strophe, antistrophe, and epode: the chorus moved in one direction while chanting the strophe, reversed direction for the antistrophe, and stood still for the epode. This pattern Jonson imitates with his triple division of turn, counterturn, and stand—the terms more or less literally translated from the original Greek. All Jonson's stanzas follow a fixed pattern, the turns and counterturns rhyming in couplets, line lengths varying in all stanzas according to a fixed and uniform schema. The twelve-line stands follow a more complex but equally strict design. Later in the century, under the influence of Abraham Cowley, who thought he was imitating the essential Pindar, odes became more vehement in tone and more irregular in form. But modern opinion views this lawless and extravagant quality as a misunderstanding of the Greek original. So, equally, would be any indulgence in personal details concerning the

---

2. Cadence. "Sentence": judgment or opinion. Jonson claims his words to the lady were as eloquent and profound as any younger poet's.

3. "Waist" is understood behind "waste," and may have been the primary meaning.

two central figures; Jonson's emphasis falls, as Pindar's in like circumstances
would have, on moral generalizations and dignified, impersonal consolato-
ries. His poem thus rises nearer to the lofty vein of the "Great Ode" than
any other in the language. For an example of the Lesser Ode, see Andrew
Marvell's *Horatian Ode Upon Cromwell's Return from Ireland*, below, p.
1397.

To the Immortal Memory and Friendship of That Noble Pair, Sir Lucius Cary and Sir H. Morison[1]

The Turn

Brave infant of Saguntum, clear[2]
Thy coming forth in that great year
When the prodigious Hannibal did crown
His rage, with razing your immortal town.
Thou, looking then about   5
Ere thou wert half got out,
Wise child, didst hastily return
And mad'st thy mother's womb thine urn.
How summed a circle[3] didst thou leave mankind
Of deepest lore, could we the center find!   10

The Counter-Turn

Did wiser nature draw thee back
From out the horror of that sack,
Where shame, faith, honor, and regard of right
Lay trampled on?—the deeds of death and night
Urged, hurried forth, and hurled   15
Upon th' affrighted world?
Sword, fire, and famine, with fell fury met,
And all on utmost ruin set:
As, could they but life's miseries foresee,
No doubt all infants would return like thee.   20

The Stand

For what is life if measured by the space,
Not by the act?
Or maskèd man, if valued by his face,
Above his fact?[4]
Here's one outlived his peers   25

1. Henry Morison died in 1629 at the age of only
20; his good friend Lucius Cary was a year or two
younger. He lived on, as Jonson could not foresee,
to die bravely and perhaps deliberately, fighting for
his king in the first years of the civil war.
2. Explain, describe. Pliny tells the story of the
infant born while Sagunto, in Spain, was being
assaulted by Hannibal; he dived back into his
mother's womb (setting a record for brevity), and
was buried there.
3. How complete a lesson.
4. Deeds.

And told forth fourscore years:
He vexèd time, and busied the whole state,
Troubled both foes and friends,
But ever to no ends:
What did this stirrer but die late?   30
How well at twenty had he fall'n or stood!
For three of his four score, he did no good.

The Turn

He[5] entered well, by virtuous parts,
Got up and thrived with honest arts:
He purchased friends and fame and honors then,   35
And had his noble name advanced with men;
But, weary of that flight,
He stooped in all men's sight
To sordid flatteries, acts of strife,
And sunk in that dead sea of life   40
So deep, as he did then death's waters sup;
But that the cork of title buoyed him up.

The Counter-Turn

Alas, but Morison fell young;—
He never fell, thou fall'st,[6] my tongue.
He stood, a soldier, to the last right end,   45
A perfect patriot and a noble friend,
But most a virtuous son.
All offices[7] were done
By him, so ample, full, and round
In weight, in measure, number, sound,   50
As, though his age imperfect might appear,
His life was of humanity the sphere.

The Stand

Go now, and tell out[8] days summed up with fears,
And make them years;
Produce thy mass of miseries on the stage   55
To swell thine age;
Repeat of things a throng,
To show thou hast been long,
Not lived; for life doth her great actions spell,
By what was done and wrought   60
In season, and so brought

---

5. I.e., another man, a separate example.   7. Duties of life.
6. Slip, with a latent pun on Latin *fallo*, "to make   8. Count, number.
a mistake."

To light: her measures are, how well
Each syllab'e answered, and was formed how fair;
These make the lines of life, and that's her air.[9]

The Turn

It is not growing like a tree   65
In bulk, doth make man better be,
Or standing long an oak, three hundred year,
To fall a log at last, dry, bald, and sere:
A lily of a day
Is fairer far in May   70
Although it fall and die that night;
It was the plant and flower of light.
In small proportions we just beauties see,
And in short measures life may perfect be.

The Counter-Turn

Call, noble Lucius, then for wine,   75
And let thy looks with gladness shine:
Accept this garland, plant it on thy head,
And think, nay, know, thy Morison's not dead.
He leaped the present age,
Possessed with holy rage,   80
To see that bright eternal day,
Of which we priests and poets say
Such truths as we expect for happy men,
And there he lives with memory: and Ben

The Stand

Jonson, who sung this of him ere he went   85
Himself to rest,
Or taste a part of that full joy he meant
To have expressed
In this bright asterism:[1]
Where it were friendship's schism   90
(Were not his Lucius long with us to tarry)
To separate these twi-
Lights, the Dioscuri;[2]
And keep the one half from his Harry.
But fate doth so alternate the design,   95
Whilst that in heaven, this light on earth must shine.

9. Life is a poem set to music, the music of its meaning. Life's "measures" are its metrical patterns, as well as the standards by which it is judged.
1. Constellation.

2. Castor and Pollux, the Dioscuri, are the principal stars of the constellation of Gemini, or the twins.

The Turn

And shine as you exalted are,
Two names of friendship, but one star,
Of hearts the union. And those not by chance
Made, or indentured,[3] or leased out t' advance   100
The profits for a time.
No pleasures vain did chime
Of rhymes or riots at your feasts,
Orgies of drink, or feigned protests;
But simple love of greatness and of good   105
That knits brave minds and manners, more than blood.

The Counter-Turn

This made you first to know the Why
You liked, then after to apply
That liking; and approach so one the tother,
Till either grew a portion of the other;   110
Each stylèd by his end,
The copy of his friend.
You lived to be the great surnames
And titles by which all made claims
Unto the virtue. Nothing perfect done,   115
But as a Cary or a Morison.

The Stand

And such a force the fair example had,
As they that saw
The good and durst not practice it, were glad
That such a law   120
Was left yet to mankind;
Where they might read and find
Friendship in deed was written, not in words.
And with the heart, not pen,
Of two so early[4] men,   125
Whose lives her rolls were, and records,
Who, ere the first down bloomèd on the chin
Had sowed these fruits, and got the harvest in.

1629   1640–41

3. Contracted for.
4. Youthful.

Slow, Slow, Fresh Fount[1]

Slow, slow, fresh fount, keep time with my salt tears;
Yet slower, yet, O faintly, gentle springs!
List to the heavy part the music bears,
Woe weeps out her division,[2] when she sings.
      Droop herbs and flowers;   5
      Fall grief in showers;
      Our beauties are not ours.
        O, I could still,
Like melting snow upon some craggy hill,
      Drop, drop, drop, drop,   10
Since nature's pride is now a withered daffodil.

                                       1600

Queen and Huntress[1]

Queen and huntress, chaste and fair,
Now the sun is laid to sleep,
Seated in thy silver chair,
State in wonted manner keep;
Hesperus entreats thy light,   5
Goddess excellently bright.

Earth, let not thy envious shade
Dare itself to interpose;
Cynthia's shining orb was made
Heaven to clear, when day did close.   10
Bless us then with wishèd sight,
Goddess excellently bright.

Lay thy bow of pearl apart,
And thy crystal-shining quiver;   15
Give unto the flying hart
Space to breathe, how short soever.
Thou that mak'st a day of night,
Goddess excellently bright.

                                       1600

1. From the satiric comedy *Cynthia's Revels*. The play deals with the sin of self-love, and this lyric is a lament sung by Echo for Narcissus, who was entranced by his own reflection and ultimately transformed into a flower.
2. Grief at parting, but also a rapid melodic passage of music.

1. Also from *Cynthia's Revels*, this song is sung by Hesperus, the evening star, to Cynthia or Diana, goddess of chastity and the moon—with whom Queen Elizabeth was, almost automatically, equated.

Still to Be Neat[1]

Still to be neat, still to be dressed
As you were going to a feast,
Still to be powdered, still perfumed;
Lady, it is to be presumed,
Though art's hid causes are not found,   5
All is not sweet, all is not sound.

Give me a look, give me a face
That makes simplicity a grace;
Robes loosely flowing, hair as free—
Such sweet neglect more taketh me   10
Than all the adulteries of art.
They strike mine eyes, but not my heart.

1609

Though I Am Young[1]

Though I am young and cannot tell
    Either what Death or Love is well,
Yet I have heard they both bear darts,
    And both do aim at human hearts.
And then again, I have been told   5
    Love wounds with heat, as Death with cold;
So that I fear they do but bring
    Extremes to touch, and mean one thing.

As in a ruin we it call
    One thing to be blown up or fall;   10
Or to our end like way may have
    By a flash of lightning or a wave;
So Love's inflamèd shaft or brand
    May kill as soon as Death's cold hand;
Except[2] Love's fires the virtue have   15
    To fright the frost out of the grave.

1640–41

---

1. This song is sung in the play *Epicoene* at the
request of Clerimont, supposed to be its composer;
he is irked at the Lady Haughty, who, he says,
overdoes the art of makeup.

1. This song is sung in *The Sad Shepherd* by Karo-
lin; the pastoral simplicity of his character is caught
in the naive monosyllables of the poem.
2. Unless.

To the Memory of My Beloved, The Author, Mr. William Shakespeare, and What He Hath Left Us[1]

To draw no envy, Shakespeare, on thy name
   Am I thus ample to thy book and fame,
While I confess thy writings to be such
   As neither man nor Muse can praise too much.
'Tis true, and all men's suffrage.[2] But these ways   5
   Were not the paths I meant unto thy praise;
For silliest[3] ignorance on these may light,
   Which, when it sounds at best, but echoes right;
Or blind affection,[4] which doth ne'er advance
   The truth, but gropes, and urgeth all by chance;   10
Or crafty malice might pretend this praise,
   And think to ruin where it seemed to raise.
These are as some infamous bawd or whore
   Should praise a matron. What could hurt her more?
But thou art proof against them, and, indeed,   15
   Above th' ill fortune of them, or the need.
I therefore will begin. Soul of the age!
   The applause! delight! the wonder of our stage!
My Shakespeare, rise; I will not lodge thee by
   Chaucer or Spenser, or bid Beaumont lie   20
A little further to make thee a room:[5]
   Thou art a monument without a tomb,
And art alive still while thy book doth live,
   And we have wits to read and praise to give.
That I not mix thee so, my brain excuses,   25
   I mean with great, but disproportioned[6] Muses;
For, if I thought my judgment were of years,
   I should commit thee surely with thy peers,
And tell how far thou didst our Lyly outshine,
   Or sporting Kyd, or Marlowe's mighty line.[7]   30
And though thou hadst small Latin and less Greek,[8]
   From thence to honor thee I would not seek
For names, but call forth thund'ring Aeschylus,
   Euripides, and Sophocles to us,
Pacuvius, Accius, him of Cordova dead,[9]   35

---

1. This poem was prefixed to the first folio of Shakespeare's plays, published in 1623.
2. Consent.
3. Emptiest.
4. Prejudice.
5. Chaucer, Spenser, and Francis Beaumont were buried in Westminster Abbey; Shakespeare, of course, in Stratford. Jonson endorses the separation; Shakespeare should not be crowded.
6. Not comparable.
7. John Lyly, Thomas Kyd, and Christopher Marlowe, Elizabethan dramatists put in the shade by Shakespeare.

8. Shakespeare had, by modern standards, a very adequate command of Latin; Jonson is speaking from the lofty height of his own remarkable scholarship. Shakespeare's French and Italian (he was competent in both tongues) Jonson does not think worthy of mention. "Seek": be short of, lacking in.
9. Marcus Pacuvius and Lucius Accius (2nd century B.C.) and "him of Cordova," Seneca the Younger (1st century A.D.), the greatest of the Latin tragedians. Only fragments survive of the plays of Pacuvius and Accius; Jonson's comparisons are more pedantic, in these instances, than relevant.

To life again, to hear thy buskin[1] tread
And shake a stage; or, when thy socks were on,
   Leave thee alone for the comparison
Of all that insolent Greece or haughty Rome
   Sent forth, or since did from their ashes come.   40
Triumph, my Britain; thou hast one to show
   To whom all scenes[2] of Europe homage owe.
He was not of an age, but for all time!
   And all the Muses still were in their prime
When like Apollo he came forth to warm   45
   Our ears, or like a Mercury to charm.
Nature herself was proud of his designs,
   And joyed to wear the dressing of his lines,
Which were so richly spun, and woven so fit,
   As, since, she will vouchsafe no other wit: 50
The merry Greek, tart Aristophanes,
   Neat Terence, witty Plautus[3] now not please,
But antiquated and deserted lie,
   As they were not of Nature's family.
Yet must I not give Nature all; thy Art,   55
   My gentle Shakespeare, must enjoy a part.
For though the poet's matter Nature be,
   His Art doth give the fashion;[4] and that he
Who casts to write a living line must sweat
   (Such as thine are) and strike the second heat   60
Upon the muses' anvil; turn the same,
   And himself with it, that he thinks to frame,
Or for the laurel he may gain a scorn;
   For a good poet's made as well as born.
And such wert thou! Look how the father's face   65
   Lives in his issue; even so the race
Of Shakespeare's mind and manners brightly shines
   In his well-turned and true-filed lines,
In each of which he seems to shake a lance,[5]
   As brandished at the eyes of ignorance.   70
Sweet swan of Avon, what a sight it were
   To see thee in our waters yet appear,
And make those flights upon the banks of Thames
   That so did take Eliza and our James![6]
But stay; I see thee in the hemisphere   75
   Advanced and made a constellation there![7]
Shine forth, thou star of poets, and with rage
   Or influence[8] chide or cheer the drooping stage,

---

1. The symbol of tragedy, as contrasted with "socks" (in the next line), symbols of comedy.
2. Stages.
3. Aristophanes, the Greek satirist and comic writer; Terence and Plautus (2nd and 3rd centuries B.C.), Roman writers of comedy.
4. Form, style. "Casts": undertakes.
5. Pun on Shake-speare.
6. Queen Elizabeth and King James.
7. Heroes and demigods were typically exalted after death to a place among the stars.
8. "Rage" and "influence" describe the supposed effects of the planets on earthly affairs. "Rage" also implies poetic inspiration.

Which, since thy flight from hence, hath mourned like night,
   And despairs day, but for thy volume's light.   80

1623

Ode to Himself[1]

   Come, leave the loathèd stage,
     And the more loathsome age,
Where pride and impudence, in faction knit,
     Usurp the chair of wit,
Indicting and arraigning every day   5
     Something they call a play.
     Let their fastidious, vain
     Commission of the brain
Run on and rage, sweat, censure, and condemn:
They were not made for thee, less thou for them.   10

     Say that thou pour'st them wheat,
     And they will acorns eat;
'Twere simple fury still thyself to waste
     On such as have no taste!
To offer them a surfeit of pure bread,   15
     Whose appetites are dead!
     No, give them grains their fill,
     Husks, draff to drink and swill:[2]
If they love lees, and leave the lusty wine,
Envy them not; their palate's with the swine.   20

     No doubt some moldy tale
     Like *Pericles*,[3] and stale
As the shrieve's crusts, and nasty as his fish—
     Scraps, out of every dish
Thrown forth and raked into the common tub,   25
     May keep up the Play-club:
     There, sweepings do as well
     As the best-ordered meal;
For who the relish of these guests will fit
Needs set them but the alms basket of wit.   30

     And much good do 't you then:
     Brave plush and velvet men
Can feed on orts;[4] and, safe in your stage clothes,

1. The failure of Jonson's *The New Inn* (1629) inspired this assault on criticism and the public taste. For Thomas Carew's affectionate, mocking rebuke, see p. 1642.
2. Jonson gets into one line three words suggestive of pig-food.
3. Shakespeare's play, at least in part (printed 1609).

"Shrieve": sheriff. The basket left outside the jail to receive food for the poor was called the sheriff's tub.
4. Scraps. Actors often wore on the stage clothes cast off by the gentry; these parasites, Jonson seems to be saying, wear clothes cast off by actors (cf. line 40, "you [share] their stuff").

Dare quit,[5] upon your oaths,
The stagers and the stage-wrights[6] too, your peers,   35
    Of larding your large ears
With their foul comic socks,[7]
    Wrought upon twenty blocks;
Which, if they're torn, and turned, and patched enough,
The gamesters share your guilt, and you their stuff.   40

    Leave things so prostitute
    And take th' Alcaic lute;[8]
Or thine own Horace, or Anacreon's lyre;
    Warm thee by Pindar's fire:
And though thy nerves be shrunk, and blood be cold,   45
    Ere years have made thee old,
    Strike that disdainful heat
    Throughout, to their defeat,
As curious fools, and envious of thy strain,
May, blushing, swear no palsy's in thy brain.   50

    But when they hear thee sing
    The glories of thy king,
His zeal to God and his just awe o'er men,
    They may, blood-shaken then,
Feel such a flesh-quake to possess their powers   55
    As they shall cry, "Like ours,
    In sound of peace or wars,
    No harp e'er hit the stars
In tuning forth the acts of his sweet reign,
And raising Charles his chariot 'bove his Wain."[9]   60

1629   1631, 1640–41

Pleasure Reconciled to Virtue

In the opening pages of his famous study, *The Civilization of the Renaissance in Italy*, Jacob Burckhardt eloquently describes the many pageants, tourneys, triumphs, and festal displays that were a striking feature of courtly and urban life in those days. England too, and as late as the first third of the seventeenth century, fostered these semidramatic ceremonials, under the title of masques. In its whole social and literary structure the masque stood quite apart from the stage play. It was performed by noble amateurs, not professional players, and performed, as a rule, only once, perhaps as the climax of "revels" which were tied

---

5. Acquit.
6. "Stagers": actors (also "gamesters," below). "Stage-wrights": playwrights.
7. Socks were the traditional footwear of comic actors, buskins of tragedians.
8. That of Alcaeus, who lived ca. 600 B.C., and

became famous, along with Horace, Anacreon, and Pindar, among the greatest lyric poets.
9. Jonson's poetry will elevate the chariot of Charles I (symbol of his royal power) above Charles's Wain (Wagon)—the seven bright stars of Ursa Major.

strictly to a calendar date. The aim of the masque was not to make money, but to lose it, in great quantities and with maximum splendor. The masque did not try to create or maintain an intact illusion by separating the audience sharply from the action; rather, it mingled the audience offstage with the actors onstage, either inviting the audience to join the dance (as in *Pleasure Reconciled to Virtue*) or leading the players off the stage in an act of homage or deference to the chief person in the audience (as in Milton's *Comus*). The masque had many elements of an audience-participation game. Especially when produced at court, it made use of elaborate and expensive "machinery"—sets far more intricate than any the playhouses could afford. It involved many musicians, special dancers, and extravagant costumes; it jumbled the heraldic and mythical figures together in strange profusion; it was both comic and serious, and anything but realistic. The three constant elements of the masque were rich spectacle (with both song and dance), moral allegory, and courtly compliment. In weaving these traditional ingredients together, Jonson, with his special gifts of learning, fantasy, and lucid eloquence, showed particular mastery. He wrote nearly thirty masques in all, of which *Pleasure Reconciled to Virtue* may be taken as typical.

The reader should not look for too much narrative logic in Jonson's masque, which shifts scenes and characters, not according to the sequences of a story, but to provide good "production numbers." Comus appears at the beginning of the masque, but only to sing a song and do a wild dance with his "crew." Hercules is present, because he once had to make a hard choice between pleasure and virtue; but as this choice is no longer necessary, he soon fades into the role of a spectator. There is another grotesque dance (an "antimasque" or "antic masque") of pygmies. This comic dance serves to prepare for, and contrast with, the elegant and polished dances performed by the gentry at the end of the masque; its specific form in Jonson's masque was probably determined by the presence of some dwarfs among the court jesters who wanted a part in the action. Finally, the true masquers take possession of the stage; they are a group of court lords, led by Prince Charles, richly dressed and wearing masks, but obviously recognizable in their own persons. They perform a series of intricate figures, descend into the audience to invite forth their ladies, and perform one other formal dance before the festivities become general.

These last dances of the masque are all under the guidance of Daedalus, the master craftsman of ancient Greece, who is shown to be capable of reconciling pleasure with virtue, life with artifice, and the court with its own fantastic mirror-image in the masque. If Hercules in the masque reminds us of Jonson himself (teased by spiteful but impotent pygmies), the figure of Daedalus can scarcely fail to suggest Jonson's partner in masque making, Inigo Jones. Jones was a student of continental art and architecture, a practicing architect under the special influence of Palladio, the Italian master, and an adviser to many aristocratic art collectors; in his own line, he was quite as remarkable and influential a man as Jonson himself. The two men quarrelled violently and permanently in later years; but Jones was far and away the most sophisticated stage designer and deviser of stage effects in his time; we know he was responsible for the production of *Pleasure Reconciled to Virtue*; and Jonson would have enjoyed paying this elegant tribute to him as Daedalus, the fabulous artificer.

Pleasure Reconciled to Virtue

A MASQUE. AS IT WAS PRESENTED AT COURT BEFORE KING
JAMES. 1618.

*The scene was the mountain Atlas, who had his top ending
in the figure of an old man, his head and beard all hoary and frost as if
his shoulders were covered with snow; the rest wood and rock. A grove of
ivy at his feet, out of which, to a wild music of cymbals, flutes, and
tabors, is brought forth Comus,[1] the god of cheer, or the belly, riding in
triumph, his head crowned with roses and other flowers, his hair curled;
they that wait upon him crowned with ivy, their javelins done about
with it; one of them going with Hercules his bowl bare before him, while
the rest presented him with this*

HYMN

Room, room! make room for the bouncing belly,
First father of sauce, and deviser of jelly;
Prime master of arts, and the giver of wit,
That found out the excellent engine, the spit,
The plow and the flail, the mill and the hopper,   5
The hutch and the bolter, the furnace and copper,
The oven, the bavin, the mawkin, the peel,
The hearth and the range, the dog and the wheel.[2]
He, he first invented the hogshead and tun,
The gimlet and vice, too, and taught them to run.   10
And since, with the funnel, an Hippocras bag
He's made of himself, that now he cries swag.[3]
Which shows, though the pleasure be but of four inches,
Yet he is a weasel, the gullet that pinches,
Of any delight, and not spares from the back   15
Whatever to make of the belly a sack.[4]
Hail, hail, plump paunch! O the founder of taste
For fresh meats, or powdered, or pickle, or paste;
Devourer of broiled, baked, roasted, or sod,[5]
And emptier of cups, be they even or odd;   20

1. Comus is the traditional classical and Renaissance figure of sensual indulgence; many of his properties here (ivy, wild music, and the flowing bowl) suggest his kinship with Dionysus. The bowl of Hercules, given him by the Sun-god, was so big that the hero sailed across the ocean in it. At the root of the masque is the ancient story that early in his life Hercules had to choose between a life of easy pleasure and one of strenuous virtue. But now, under King James, the two principles are at last going to be reconciled.
2. "Hutch" (bin), "mill," and "hopper" were used in grinding grain; "bavin," "mawkin," and "peel" are different sorts of apparatus used in a bake shop. A dog harnessed to a wheel served to keep a roasting-spit turning.
3. "Gimlet" and "vice" are tools for tapping a keg. A "Hippocras bag" is a cloth filter for clearing wine; and to "cry swag" is to reveal a drooping, pendulous belly.
4. The gullet, though only four inches long, is a harsh master; it imposes the belly's great weight on the back.
5. Boiled.

All which have now made thee so wide i' the waist
As scarce with no pudding thou art to be laced;
But eating and drinking until thou dost nod,
Thou break'st all thy girdles, and break'st forth a god.

To this, the Bowl-bearer.

Do you hear, my friends? to whom did you sing all this now? Pardon   25
me only that I ask you, for I do not look for an answer; I'll answer
myself. I know it is now such a time as the Saturnals[6] for all the
world, that every man stands under the eaves of his own hat and
sings what pleases him; that's the right and the liberty of it. Now   30
you sing of god Comus here, the Belly-god. I say it is well, and I say
it is not well. It is well as it is a ballad, and the belly worthy of it, I
must needs say, an 'twere forty yards of ballad more—as much ballad as tripe. But when the belly is not edified by it, it is not well; for
where did you ever read or hear that the belly had any ears? Come,   35
never pump for an answer, for you are defeated. Our fellow Hunger
there, that was as ancient a retainer to the belly as any of us, was
turned away for being unseasonable—not unreasonable, but unseasonable—and now is he (poor thin-gut) fain to get his living with
teaching of starlings, magpies, parrots, and jackdaws, those things   40
he would have taught the belly. Beware of dealing with the belly;
the belly will not be talked to, especially when he is full. Then there
is no venturing upon Venter;[7] he will blow you all up; he will thunder indeed, la: some in derision call him the father of farts. But I
say he was the first inventor of great ordnance, and taught us to   45
discharge them on festival days. Would we had a fit feast for him, i'
faith, to show his activity: I would have something now fetched in
to please his five senses, the throat; or the two senses, the eyes.
Pardon me for my two senses; for I that carry Hercules' bowl[8] in the
service may see double by my place, for I have drunk like a frog   50
today. I would have a tun now brought in to dance, and so many
bottles about him. Ha! You look as if you would make a problem of
this. Do you see? Do you see? a problem: why bottles? and why a
tun? and why a tun and why bottles to dance? I say that men that
drink hard and serve the belly in any place of quality (as *The Jovial*   55
Tinkers, or *The Lusty Kindred*)[9] are living measures of drink, and
can transform themselves, and do every day, to bottles or tuns when
they please; and when they have done all they can, they are, as I say
again (for I think I said somewhat like it afore) but moving measures
of drink; and there is a piece in the cellar can hold more than all   60
they. This will I make good if it please our new god but to give a
nod; for the belly does all by signs, and I am all for the belly, the
truest clock in the world to go by.

---

6. The Roman Saturnalia, which came about the
end of the year, were a time of license; Jonson
compares them to the twelfth-night festivities in
the English court, at which this masque was produced.

7. Belly, in Latin.
8. To carry Hercules' bowl would clearly imply
drinking a lot. "Tun": barrel.
9. These seem to be names of taverns.

Here the first antimasque[1] *[danced by men in the shape of bottles, tuns, etc.], after which,*

HERCULES. What rites are these? Breeds earth more monsters yet?　65
　　Antaeus[2] scarce is cold: what can beget
　　This store?—and stay! such contraries upon her?
　　Is earth so fruitful of her own dishonor?
　　Or 'cause his vice was inhumanity,
　　Hopes she by vicious hospitality　　　　　　　70
　　To work an expiation first?[3] and then
　　(Help, Virtue!) these are sponges and not men.
　　Bottles? mere vessels? half a tun of paunch?
　　How? and the other half thrust forth in haunch?
　　Whose feast? the belly's! Comus'! and my cup　75
　　Brought in to fill the drunken orgies up
　　And here abused! that was the crowned reward
　　Of thirsty heroes after labor hard!
　　Burdens and shames of nature, perish, die;
　　For yet you never lived, but in the sty　　　　80
　　Of vice have wallowed, and in that swine's strife
　　Been buried under the offense of life.
　　Go, reel and fall under the load you make,
　　Till your swoll'n bowels burst with what you take.
　　Can this be pleasure, to extinguish man?　　85
　　Or so quite change him in his figure? Can
　　The belly love his pain, and be content
　　With no delight but what's a punishment?
　　These monsters plague themselves, and fitly, too,
　　For they do suffer what and all they do.　　　90
　　But here must be no shelter, nor no shroud
　　For such: sink grove, or vanish into cloud!

At this the whole grove vanished, and the whole music was discovered, sitting at the foot of the mountain, with Pleasure and Virtue seated above them. The choir invited Hercules to rest with this

SONG

　　Great friend and servant of the good,
　　　Let cool awhile thy heated blood,
　　　And from thy mighty labor cease.　　　　　　95
　　　　Lie down, lie down,
　　And give thy troubled spirits peace,

1. The antimasque, or antic masque, was a group of dancers, grotesquely or comically dressed, who served to contrast with the main group of masquers.
2. Antaeus, an earth-born giant, whom Hercules destroyed in the course of his labors. As his favored sport was wrestling, and he grew stronger every time he touched the ground, Hercules had to kill him by holding him in the air till he died. "Store": abundance.
3. I.e., has earth, to compensate for the inhumanity of her monstrous son Antaeus, produced other monsters, but this time of indulgence (Comus and his companions)?

Whilst Virtue, for whose sake
Thou dost this godlike travail take,
May of the choicest herbage[4] make,   100
Here on this mountain bred,
A crown, a crown
For thy immortal head.

Here Hercules being laid down at their feet, the second antimasque,
which was of pygmies, appeared.

1ST PYGMY. Antaeus dead and Hercules yet live!
Where is this Hercules? What would I give   105
To meet him now? Meet him? nay three such other,
If they had hand in murder of our brother![5]
With three? with four, with ten, nay, with as many
As the name yields! Pray anger there be any
Whereon to feed my just revenge, and soon!   110
How shall I kill him? Hurl him 'gainst the moon,
And break him in small portions! Give to Greece
His brain, and every tract of earth a piece!
2ND PYGMY. He is yonder.
1ST PYGMY.   Where?
3RD PYGMY.   At the hill foot, asleep.
1ST PYGMY. Let one go steal his club.
2ND PYGMY.   My charge; I'll creep.   15
4TH PYGMY. He's ours.
1ST PYGMY.   Yes, peace.
3RD PYGMY.   Triumph, we have him, boy.
4TH PYGMY. Sure, sure, he's sure.
1ST PYGMY.   Come, let us dance for joy.

At the end of their dance they thought to surprise him, when suddenly,
being awaked by the music, he roused himself, and they all ran into
holes.

SONG

CHOIR. Wake, Hercules, awake: but heave up thy black eye,
'Tis only asked from thee to look and these will die,
          Or fly.   120
Already they are fled,
Whom scorn had else left dead.

At which Mercury descended from the hill with a garland of poplar to
crown him.

---

4. Plants and branches. "Travail": labor, trouble.
5. Pygmies and giants, minimals and maximals, are disproportioned offspring of mere earth, therefore brothers to one another. The pygmies don't know how many Hercules-figures there are, because so many tales were told about the hero that even Renaissance mythographers were forced to think there must have been several persons of that name.

MERCURY. Rest still, thou active friend of Virtue: these
   Should not disturb the peace of Hercules.
   Earth's worms and honor's dwarfs, at too great odds,   125
   Prove or provoke the issue of the gods.
   See here a crown the agèd hill hath sent thee,
   My grandsire Atlas, he that did present thee
   With the best sheep that in his fold were found,
   Or golden fruit in the Hesperian ground,   130
   For rescuing his fair daughters, then the prey
   Of a rude pirate, as thou cam'st this way;
   And taught thee all the learning of the sphere,
   And how, like him, thou might'st the heavens up-bear,
   As that thy labor's virtuous recompense.[6]   135
   He, though a mountain now, hath yet the sense
   Of thanking thee for more, thou being still
   Constant to goodness, guardian of the hill;
   Antaeus, by thee suffocated here,
   And the voluptuous Comus, god of cheer,   140
   Beat from his grove, and that defaced. But now
   The time's arrived that Atlas told thee of: how
   By unaltered law, and working of the stars,
   There should be a cessation of all jars[7]
   'Twixt Virtue and her noted opposite,   145
   Pleasure; that both should meet here in the sight
   Of Hesperus, the glory of the west,[8]
   The brightest star, that from his burning crest
   Lights all on this side the Atlantic seas
   As far as to thy pillars, Hercules.[9]   150
   See where he shines, Justice and Wisdom placed
   About his throne, and those with Honor graced,
   Beauty and Love! It is not with his brother
   Bearing the world, but ruling such another
   Is his renown.[1] Pleasure, for his delight   155
   Is reconciled to Virtue, and this night
   Virtue brings forth twelve princes have been bred
   In this rough mountain and near Atlas' head,
   The hill of knowledge; one and chief of whom
   Of the bright race of Hesperus is come,   160
   Who shall in time the same that he is be,
   And now is only a less light than he.[2]
   These now she trusts with Pleasure, and to these

6. When Hercules was seeking the golden apples
of the Hesperides, he took for a while Atlas' job of
holding up the heavens, so the giant could wade
out in the ocean and get the apples. Atlas himself
was originally an astronomer, and thus knew "all
the learning of the sphere."
7. Quarrels.
8. Jonson followed the mythographers in making
Hesperus a brother of Atlas; as the evening star and
guardian of the western isles, he identifies easily

with King James.
9. The "pillars of Hercules" are the Straits of
Gibraltar.
1. As Hesperus, King James does not hold up the
sky, like his brother Atlas, but rules over a special
world of his own, England.
2. Tradition has it that Prince Charles was one of
the masquers; he was just 18 at the time, and it
was his first masque.

She gives an entrance to the Hesperides,
Fair Beauty's garden; neither can she fear   165
They should grow soft or wax effeminate here,
Since in her sight and by her charge all's done,
Pleasure the servant, Virtue looking on.[3]

*Here the whole choir of music called the twelve masquers forth from the
lap of the mountain, which then opened with this*

SONG

Ope, agèd Atlas, open then thy lap,
And from thy beamy bosom strike a light,   170
That men may read in thy mysterious map
   All lines
   And signs
Of royal education and the right,
  See how they come and show,   175
  That are but born to know.
    Descend,
    Descend,
Though pleasure lead,
   Fear not to follow: 180
They who are bred
   Within the hill
   Of skill
May safely tread
   What path they will,   185
No ground of good is hollow.

*In their descent from the hill Daedalus[4] came down before them, of
whom Hercules questioned Mercury.*

HERCULES. But Hermes, stay a little, let me pause:
 Who's this that leads?
MERCURY.   A guide that gives them laws
 To all their motions: Daedalus the wise.
HERCULES. And doth in sacred harmony comprise   190
 His precepts?
MERCURY.   Yes.
HERCULES.   They may securely prove,[5]
 Then, any labyrinth, though it be of love.

Here, while they put themselves in form, Daedalus had his first

3. Having grown up inside Atlas itself, so that virtue comes naturally to them, the masquers can now be allowed to mingle freely with the daughters of Hesperus, in pursuit of pleasure.
4. Daedalus, the mythical Greek maker of mazes, acts here as master of the intricate dance steps that interweave pleasure with virtue under the guidance of art. Hercules questions Mercury in order to identify for the audience a personage whom they might not recognize.
5. Experience.

SONG

Come on, come on! and where you go,
    So interweave the curious knot,
As ev'n th' observer scarce may know   195
    Which lines are Pleasure's and which not.

First, figure out the doubtful way
    At which awhile all youth should stay,[6]
Where she and Virtue did contend
    Which should have Hercules to friend.   200

Then, as all actions of mankind
    Are but a labyrinth or maze,
So let your dances be entwined,
    Yet not perplex men unto gaze;

But measured, and so numerous too,   205
    As men may read each act you do,
And when they see the graces meet,
    Admire the wisdom of your feet.

For dancing is an exercise
    Not only shows the mover's wit,   210
But maketh the beholder wise,
    As he hath power to rise to it.

The first dance.

After which Daedalus again.

SONG 2

O more, and more! this was so well
    As praise wants half his voice to tell;
        Again yourselves compose;   215
And now put all the aptness on
    Of figure, that proportion
        Or color can disclose.

That if those silent arts were lost,
    Design and picture, they might boast   220
        From you a newer ground;[7]
Instructed to the height'ning sense
    Of dignity and reverence
        In your true motions found:

---

6. The dancers are to "figure out" the doubtful moment of Hercules' choice in the sense of illustrating it; they are beyond the occasion of making it themselves, having already reconciled pleasure with virtue.

7. Put on the "aptness of figure," i.e., significance of expression, of which art (proportion or color) is capable; thus, if design and picture, the silent arts, were lost, they could be rebuilt out of the dance alone.

Begin, begin; for look, the fair   225
Do longing listen to what air
   You form your second touch;[8]
That they may vent their murmuring hymns
Just to the tune you move your limbs,
   And wish their own were such.   230

Make haste, make haste, for this
  The labyrinth of beauty is.

   The second dance:

   That ended, Daedalus.

SONG 3

It follows now you are to prove
  The subtlest maze of all, that's love,
   And if you stay too long,   235
   The fair will think you do 'em wrong.

Go choose among—but with a mind
  As gentle as the stroking wind
   Runs o'er the gentler flowers.
And so let all your actions smile   240
  As if they meant not to beguile
   The ladies, but the hours.

Grace, laughter, and discourse may meet,
  And yet the beauty not go less:
For what is noble should be sweet,   245
  But not dissolved in wantonness.

Will you that I give the law
  To all your sport, and sum it?
It should be such should envy draw,
  But ever overcome it.   250

*Here they danced with the ladies, and the whole revels[9] followed; which
ended, Mercury called to Daedalus in this following speech, which was
after repeated in song by two trebles, two tenors, a bass, and the whole
chorus.*

SONG 4

An eye of looking back were well,
 Or any murmur that would tell
  Your thoughts, how you were sent

---

8. Perhaps "set of figures." The three dances were
performed to three different tunes; but Daedalus is
addressing the dancers, not the musicians.
9. Group of onlookers and courtiers.

And went,
To walk with Pleasure, not to dwell.   255

These, these are hours by Virtue spared
    Herself, she being her own reward,
        But she will have you know
            That though
    Her sports be soft, her life is hard.   260

    You must return unto the hill,
            And there advance
    With labor, and inhabit still
            That height and crown
    From whence you ever may look down   265
            Upon triùmphed Chance.

She, she it is, in darkness shines.
    'Tis she that still herself refines
        By her own light, to every eye
More seen, more known when Vice stands by.   270
    And though a stranger here on earth,
        In heaven she hath her right of birth.
            There, there is Virtue's seat,
Strive to keep her your own;
        'Tis only she can make you great,   275
Though place here make you known.

*After which, they danced their last dance, and returned into the scene,
which closed and was a mountain again as before.*

The End.

This pleased the king so well, as he would see it again; when it was
presented with these additions.[1]

1618   1640–41

---

1. The "additions" were another short masque, *For
the Honor of Wales*. Masques were not usually
repeated; in this instance, the second showing seems
to have been an effort to get it right.

JOHN WEBSTER
1580?–1625?

Though Shakespeare seems, in our eyes, to tower above all his contemporaries, and was by no means without honor in his own day, it is only by
comparison with him that the Stuart playwrights look small. In any age other

than Shakespeare's a group of writers that included not only Ben Jonson but John Ford, John Webster, Cyril Tourneur, Francis Beaumont, John Marston, John Fletcher, and Thomas Middleton would have been the climactic glory of the English stage. Such a galaxy of talent, working at a level just short of supreme, we shall not see again. Among them John Webster stands out as second only to Jonson—not as a contriver of well-articulated stage actions, but for the dark poetry of his tragic imagination.

By a process brilliantly sketched in a series of essays by Mario Praz (*The Flaming Heart*, 1958), the Jacobean age had built up a view of Roman Catholic Italy as a land of sophisticated, morbid corruption, sumptuous and evil. (Few Italians take or ever took such a view of themselves; they are puzzled and amused by it.) Webster, who never visited Italy, based *The Duchess of Malfi* on a scandal of the early sixteenth century, which he encountered in various sensationalized English, French, and Italian accounts. But over the basic narrative Webster drew the veil of his dark imagination, and enhanced the horrors of his borrowed story in order to set off the figure of his Duchess, one of the freest and most positive women in all English drama. In this respect, he quite reversed the attitude of his sources. Most of them condemn the Duchess as headstrong and libidinous. Webster boldly asserts her right to choose a husband without regard to her family or the codes of her social class. And he clearly invites us to admire both the assured sensitivity of her impulses and the perfect self-command with which she meets her fate. Though he is not skilled at articulating persuasive plots, Webster is capable of tremendous poetic flashes. His scenes of brooding, stagnant terror give new depth and meaning to that favorite Jacobean word, "melancholy." Their darkness is lit by frequent imaginative lightnings, as when Ferdinand, faced with his sister's corpse, at last sees what his insane furies have meant.

As for the man who created these lurid nightmares, he remains very obscure. His father was a member of the merchant tailors, but apparently rented out carts and wagons for a living. Webster may have studied law, but made no name for himself in the profession. He collaborated with other playwrights, and came into his own style only gradually. The evidence is that he was a slow, painful writer, who drew heavily on his reading in the course of composition. Modern scholarship has found a literary source for nearly every phrase and concept in his plays. But what he made of his reading is distinctively his own. His art is one of brilliant highlights and black shadows, of furtive and dangerous intrigue carried out in the flickering light of hell fire; it serves to illumine one clear character who accepts without faltering or cringing the ultimate test.

The Duchess of Malfi

Dramatis Personae

FERDINAND, *Duke of Calabria*
THE CARDINAL, *his brother*
ANTONIO BOLOGNA, *steward of the household to the* DUCHESS
DELIO, *his friend*
DANIEL DE BOSOLA, *gentleman of the horse to the* DUCHESS

CASTRUCCIO, *an old Lord*
MARQUIS OF PESCARA
COUNT MALATESTE
SILVIO, *a Lord, of Milan*
RODERIGO ⎫
GRISOLAN ⎬ *gentlemen attending on the* DUCHESS
DOCTOR ⎭
Several MADMEN, PILGRIMS, EXECUTIONERS, OFFICERS, ATTENDANTS
&c.
THE DUCHESS OF MALFI, *sister of* FERDINAND *and the* CARDINAL
CARIOLA, *her woman*
JULIA, CASTRUCCIO'S *wife, and the* CARDINAL'S *mistress*
OLD LADY, LADIES, *and* CHILDREN

   SCENE. *Amalfi, Rome, Loreto, and Milan*

Act 1

   SCENE 1. *Amalfi; a hall in the* DUCHESS' *palace.*

   [*Enter* ANTONIO *and* DELIO.]

DELIO. You are welcome to your country, dear Antonio;
   You have been long in France, and you return
   A very formal Frenchman in your habit.[1]
   How do you like the French court?
ANTONIO.   I admire it:
   In seeking to reduce both state and people   5
   To a fixed order, their judicious king
   Begins at home; quits[2] first his royal palace
   Of flattering sycophants, of dissolute
   And infamous persons—which he sweetly terms
   His Master's masterpiece, the work of heaven—   10
   Considering duly that a prince's court
   Is like a common fountain, whence should flow
   Pure silver drops in general, but if 't chance
   Some cursed example poison 't near the head,
   Death and diseases through the whole land spread.   15
   And what is 't makes this blessed government
   But a most provident council; who dare freely
   Inform him the corruption of the times.
   Though some o' th' court hold it presumption
   To instruct princes what they ought to do,   20
   It is a noble duty to inform them
   What they ought to foresee.—Here comes Bosola,
   The only court-gall;[3] yet I observe his railing
   Is not for simple love of piety.
   Indeed, he rails at those things which he wants;   25
   Would be as lecherous, covetous, or proud,
   Bloody, or envious, as any man,
   If he had means to be so. Here's the Cardinal.

---

1. An absolute Frenchman in your manners.
2. Liberates, frees.

3. One who frets the court, but with the overtone of a disease, a blight.

[*Enter the* CARDINAL *and* BOSOLA.]

BOSOLA. I do haunt you still.

CARDINAL. So.   30

BOSOLA. I have done you better service than to be slighted thus.
Miserable age, where the only reward of doing well is the doing
of it!

CARDINAL. You enforce your merit too much.

BOSOLA. I fell into the galleys[4] in your service; where, for two years   35
together, I wore two towels instead of a shirt, with a knot on the
shoulder, after the fashion of a Roman mantle. Slighted thus? I
will thrive some way. Blackbirds fatten best in hard weather; why
not I in these dog-days?[5]

CARDINAL. Would you could become honest!   40

BOSOLA. With all your divinity do but direct me the way to it. I
have known many travel far for it, and yet return as arrant knaves
as they went forth, because they carried themselves always along
with them. [*Exit* CARDINAL.] Are you gone? Some fellows, they
say, are possessed with the devil, but this great fellow were able   45
to possess the greatest devil, and make him worse.

ANTONIO. He hath denied thee some suit?

BOSOLA. He and his brother are like plum trees that grow crooked
over standing pools; they are rich and o'erladen with fruit, but
none but crows, pies, and caterpillars feed on them.[6] Could I be   50
one of their flattering panders, I would hang on their ears like a
horseleech till I were full and then drop off. I pray, leave me.
Who would rely upon these miserable dependencies, in expectation to be advanced tomorrow? What creature ever fed worse
than hoping Tantalus?[7] Nor ever died any man more fearfully   55
than he that hoped for a pardon. There are rewards for hawks
and dogs when they have done us service; but for a soldier that
hazards his limbs in a battle, nothing but a kind of geometry is
his last supportation.

DELIO. Geometry?   60

BOSOLA. Aye, to hang in a fair pair of slings, take his latter swing in
the world upon an honorable pair of crutches, from hospital to
hospital. Fare ye well, sir: and yet do not you scorn us; for places
in the court are but like beds in the hospital, where this man's
head lies at that man's foot, and so lower and lower.   [*Exit.*]   65

DELIO. I knew this fellow seven years[8] in the galleys
For a notorious murder; and 'twas thought
The Cardinal suborned it. He was released
By the French general, Gaston de Foix,
When he recovered Naples.[9]   70

---

4. Service at the oar of a Mediterranean galley was
the last penalty this side of torture and execution,
a 50 percent death sentence.
5. The hot, sultry season of midsummer. Being
naturally an ill-omened creature, like a blackbird,
Bosola thinks he may thrive under oppression.
6. "Standing pools": stagnant, therefore poisonous, waters. "Pies": magpies, birds of evil omen
like blackbirds.
7. Tantalus, in classical mythology, was "tanta-

lized" by the constant presence under his nose of
delectable food and drink which, though desperate, he could never reach.
8. In speaking to the Cardinal himself (line 35),
Bosola had mentioned only two years.
9. Gaston de Foix, French commander, was active
in Italy during the early 1500s; hence, the time of
the tragedy is about 100 years before Webster wrote.
Ferdinand and the Cardinal are Spaniards established in Italy, like the house of Borgia (inces-

ANTONIO.   'Tis great pity
   He should be thus neglected; I have heard
   He's very valiant. This foul melancholy
   Will poison all his goodness; for, I'll tell you,
   If too immoderate sleep be truly said   75
   To be an inward rust unto the soul,
   It then doth follow want of action
   Breeds all black malcontents; and their close rearing,
   Like moths in cloth, do hurt for want of wearing.[1]

SCENE 2

[*Enter* CASTRUCCIO, SILVIO, RODERIGO, *and* GRISOLAN.]

DELIO. The presence[2] 'gins to fill: you promised me
   To make me the partaker of the natures
   Of some of your great courtiers.
ANTONIO.   The Lord Cardinal's,
   And other strangers' that are now in court?
   I shall. Here comes the great Calabrian duke.   5

[*Enter* FERDINAND *and* ATTENDANTS.]

FERDINAND. Who took the ring oftenest?[3]
SILVIO. Antonio Bologna, my lord.
FERDINAND. Our sister duchess' great-master of her household?
   Give him the jewel. When shall we leave this sportive action,
   and fall to action indeed?   10
CASTRUCCIO. Methinks, my lord, you should not desire to go to war
   in person.
FERDINAND. Now for some gravity. Why, my lord?
CASTRUCCIO. It is fitting a soldier arise to be a prince, but not nec-
   essary a prince descend to be a captain.   15
FERDINAND. No?
CASTRUCCIO. No, my lord, he were far better do it by a deputy.
FERDINAND. Why should he not as well sleep or eat by a deputy?
   This might take idle, offensive, and base office from him, whereas
   the other deprives him of honor.   20
CASTRUCCIO. Believe my experience, that realm is never long in
   quiet where the ruler is a soldier.
FERDINAND. Thou told'st me thy wife could not endure fighting.
CASTRUCCIO. True, my lord.
FERDINAND. And of a jest she broke of a captain she met full of   25
   wounds. I have forgot it.
CASTRUCCIO. She told him, my lord, he was a pitiful fellow, to lie,
   like the children of Israel, all in tents.[4]
FERDINAND. Why, there's a wit were able to undo all the chirurgeons[5]
   o' the city; for although gallants should quarrel and had drawn   30

---

tuous, simoniacal Pope Alexander VI and his two
illegitimate children Cesare and Lucrezia).
1. I.e., malcontents, being unemployed, suffer
from psychic moths, like clothes not worn for a
long time.
2. Audience hall.

3. A common game around court, used in training for tourneys, involved catching a hanging ring
on the tip of a lance. But some of Webster's audience would have caught a sexual analogy.
4. Lint bandages were called "tents."
5. Surgeons.

their weapons and were ready to go to it, yet her persuasions
would make them put up.

CASTRUCCIO. That she would, my lord.

FERDINAND. How do you like my Spanish gennet?[6]

RODERIGO. He is all fire.   35

FERDINAND. I am of Pliny's opinion, I think he was begot by the
wind; he runs as if he were ballassed[7] with quicksilver.

SILVIO. True, my lord, he reels from the tilt often.[8]

RODERIGO *and* GRISOLAN. Ha, ha, ha!

FERDINAND. Why do you laugh? Methinks, you that are courtiers   40
should be my touchwood, take fire when I give fire; that is, laugh
but when I laugh, were the subject never so witty.

CASTRUCCIO. True, my lord, I myself have heard a very good jest,
and have scorned to seem to have so silly a wit as to understand it.

FERDINAND. But I can laugh at your fool, my lord.   45

CASTRUCCIO. He cannot speak, you know, but he makes faces: my
lady cannot abide him.

FERDINAND. No?

CASTRUCCIO. Nor endure to be in merry company, for she says too
much laughing and too much company fills her too full of the   50
wrinkle.

FERDINAND. I would, then, have a mathematical instrument made
for her face, that she might not laugh out of compass.[9] I shall
shortly visit you at Milan, Lord Silvio.

SILVIO. Your grace shall arrive most welcome.   55

FERDINAND. You are a good horseman, Antonio. You have excellent riders in France. What do you think of good horsemanship?

ANTONIO. Nobly, my lord: as out of the Grecian horse issued many
famous princes, so out of brave horsemanship arise the first sparks
of growing resolution that raise the mind to noble action.   60

FERDINAND. You have bespoke it worthily.

SILVIO. Your brother, the Lord Cardinal, and sister duchess.

[*Re-enter* CARDINAL, *with* DUCHESS, CARIOLA, *and* JULIA.]

CARDINAL. Are the galleys come about?

GRISOLAN.   They are, my lord.

FERDINAND. Here's the Lord Silvio, is come to take his leave.

DELIO. Now, sir, your promise. What's that Cardinal?   65
I mean his temper? They say he's a brave fellow,
Will play[1] his five thousand crowns at tennis, dance,
Court ladies, and one that hath fought single combats.

ANTONIO. Some such flashes superficially hang on him for form;
but observe his inward character: he is a melancholy churchman;   70
the spring in his face is nothing but the engendering of toads;
where he is jealous of any man, he lays worse plots for them than
ever was imposed on Hercules, for he strews in his way flatterers,

---

6. Sometimes "jennet": a small Spanish horse of
Arabian stock.
7. Ballasted. Pliny in his *Natural History* tells about
some Spanish horses generated by a swift wind
(8.67).
8. "Reeling from the tilt" involves a double mean-

ing: recoiling from the shock of a charge, and rolling about like quicksilver on a tilted table.
9. Excessively; with a pun on the draftsman's
compass.
1. Wager.

panders, intelligencers, atheists, and a thousand such political
monsters.[2] He should have been Pope; but instead of coming to   75
it by the primitive decency of the Church, he did bestow bribes
so largely and so impudently as if he would have carried it away
without heaven's knowledge. Some good he hath done—

DELIO. You have given too much of him. What's his brother?

ANTONIO. The duke there? A most perverse and turbulent nature.   80
    What appears in him mirth is merely outside;
    If he laugh heartily, it is to laugh
    All honesty out of fashion.

DELIO.   Twins?

ANTONIO.   In quality.
    He speaks with others' tongues, and hears men's suits
    With others' ears; will seem to sleep o' th' bench   85
    Only to entrap offenders in their answers;
    Dooms men to death by information;[3]
    Rewards by hearsay.

DELIO.   Then the law to him
    Is like a foul black cobweb to a spider:
    He makes of it his dwelling and a prison   90
    To entangle those shall feed him.

ANTONIO.   Most true:
    He ne'er pays debts unless they be shrewd turns,[4]
    And those he will confess that he doth owe.
    Last, for his brother there, the Cardinal,
    They that do flatter him most say oracles   95
    Hang at his lips; and verily I believe them,
    For the devil speaks in them.
    But for their sister, the right noble duchess,
    You never fixed your eye on three fair medals
    Cast in one figure, of so different temper.   100
    For her discourse, it is so full of rapture,
    You only will begin then to be sorry
    When she doth end her speech, and wish, in wonder,
    She held it less vainglory to talk much,
    Than your penance to hear her: whilst she speaks,   105
    She throws upon a man so sweet a look,
    That it were able to raise one to a galliard[5]
    That lay in a dead palsy, and to dote
    On that sweet countenance; but in that look
    There speaketh so divine a continence   110
    As cuts off all lascivious and vain hope.
    Her days are practiced in such noble virtue
    That sure her nights, nay, more, her very sleeps,
    Are more in heaven than other ladies' shrifts.[6]
    Let all sweet ladies break their flattering glasses,   115

---

2. "Intelligencers": spies.
3. On the basis of secret reports.
4. Hurtful acts.

5. A gay and lively dance.
6. Confessions.

And dress themselves in her.

DELIO.   Fie, Antonio,
You play the wire-drawer[7] with her commendations.

ANTONIO. I'll case the picture up only thus much;
All her particular worth grows to this sum,
She stains[8] the time past, lights the time to come.   120

CARDINAL. You must attend my lady in the gallery,
Some half an hour hence.

ANTONIO.   I shall.

[Exeunt ANTONIO *and* DELIO.*]*

FERDINAND. Sister, I have a suit to you.

DUCHESS.   To me, sir?

FERDINAND. A gentleman here, Daniel de Bosola,
One that was in the galleys—

DUCHESS.   Yes, I know him.   125

FERDINAND. A worthy fellow he is. Pray, let me entreat for
The provisorship of your horse.

DUCHESS.   Your knowledge of him
Commends him and prefers him.

FERDINAND.   Call him hither.

[Exit ATTENDANT.*]*

We are now upon parting. Good Lord Silvio,
Do us commend to all our noble friends   130
At the leaguer.[9]

SILVIO.   Sir, I shall.

DUCHESS.   You are for Milan?

SILVIO. I am.

DUCHESS. Bring the caroches. We'll bring you down
To the haven.[1]   *[Exeunt all but* FERDINAND *and the* CARDINAL.*]*

CARDINAL. Be sure you entertain that Bosola
For your intelligence:[2] I would not be seen in 't;   135
And therefore many times I have slighted him
When he did court our furtherance, as this morning.

FERDINAND. Antonio, the great-master of her household,
Had been far fitter.

CARDINAL.   You are deceived in him:
His nature is too honest for such business.   140
He comes: I'll leave you.   *[Exit.]*

[Re-enter BOSOLA.*]*

BOSOLA.   I was lured to you.

FERDINAND. My brother here the Cardinal could never
Abide you.

BOSOLA.   Never since he was in my debt.

FERDINAND. Maybe some oblique character in your face
Made him suspect you.

---

7. Draw out her praises excessively. "Case the picture": frame it.
8. Darkens (by comparison with her brilliance).

9. A gathering of the armies, as at a siege.
1. Harbor. "Caroches": carriages.
2. I.e., be sure to hire Bosola as your spy.

BOSOLA.   Doth he study physiognomy?   145
   There's no more credit to be given to th' face
   Than to a sick man's urine, which some call
   The physician's whore, because she cozens[3] him.
   He did suspect me wrongfully.
FERDINAND.   For that
   You must give great men leave to take their times.   150
   Distrust doth cause us seldom be deceived:
   You see, the oft shaking of the cedar tree
   Fastens it more at root.
BOSOLA.   Yet, take heed;
   For to suspect a friend unworthily
   Instructs him the next way to suspect you,   155
   And prompts him to deceive you.
FERDINAND. [*giving him money*]   There's gold.
BOSOLA.   So:
   What follows? Never rained such showers as these
   Without thunderbolts i' th' tail of them. Whose throat must
     I cut?
FERDINAND. Your inclination to shed blood rides post
   Before my occasion to use you. I give you that   160
   To live i' th' court here, and observe the duchess;
   To note all the particulars of her 'havior,
   What suitors do solicit her for marriage,
   And whom she best affects. She's a young widow:
   I would not have her marry again.
BOSOLA.   No, sir?   165
FERDINAND. Do not you ask the reason, but be satisfied
   I say I would not.
BOSOLA.   It seems you would create me
   One of your familiars.[4]
FERDINAND.   Familiar? What's that?
BOSOLA. Why, a very quaint invisible devil in flesh,
   An intelligencer.
FERDINAND.   Such a kind of thriving thing   170
   I would wish thee, and ere long thou may'st arrive
   At a higher place by 't.
BOSOLA.   Take your devils,
   Which hell calls angels;[5] these cursed gifts would make
   You a corrupter, me an impudent traitor;
   And should I take these, they'd take me to hell.   175
FERDINAND. Sir, I'll take nothing from you that I have given:
   There is a place that I procured for you
   This morning, the provisorship o' th' horse;
   Have you heard on 't?
BOSOLA.   No.
FERDINAND.   'Tis yours. Is 't not worth thanks?
BOSOLA. I would have you curse yourself now, that your bounty,   180
   Which makes men truly noble, e'er should make me

---

3. Tricks.
4. Diabolic spirits, who serve a magician.

5. Gold coins, marked with the image of the archangel Michael.

A villain. Oh, that to avoid ingratitude
For the good deed you have done me, I must do
All the ill man can invent! Thus the devil
Candies all sins o'er; and what heaven terms vile,   185
That names he complimental.

FERDINAND.   Be yourself;
Keep your old garb of melancholy; 'twill express
You envy those that stand above your reach,
Yet strive not to come near 'em: this will gain
Access to private lodgings, where yourself   190
May, like a politic dormouse—

BOSOLA.   As I have seen some
Feed in a lord's dish, half asleep, not seeming
To listen to any talk; and yet these rogues
Have cut his throat in a dream. What's my place?
The provisorship o' th' horse? Say, then, my corruption   195
Grew out of horse-dung. I am your creature.

FERDINAND.   Away!

BOSOLA. Let good men, for good deeds, covet good fame,
Since place and riches oft are bribes of shame:
Sometimes the devil doth preach.   [*Exit.*]

    [*Enter* DUCHESS, CARDINAL, *and* CARIOLA.]

CARDINAL. We are to part from you, and your own discretion   200
Must now be your director.

FERDINAND.   You are a widow:
You know already what man is; and therefore
Let not youth, high promotion, eloquence—

CARDINAL. No, nor any thing without the addition, honor,
Sway your high blood.

FERDINAND.   Marry! They are most luxurious   205
Will wed twice.

CARDINAL.   Oh, fie!

FERDINAND.   Their livers are more spotted
Than Laban's sheep.[6]

DUCHESS.   Diamonds are of most value,
They say, that have passed through most jewelers' hands.

FERDINAND. Whores by that rule are precious.

DUCHESS.   Will you hear me?
I'll never marry.

CARDINAL.   So most widows say;   210
But commonly that motion[7] lasts no longer
Than the turning of an hour-glass; the funeral sermon
And it end both together.

FERDINAND.   Now hear me:
You live in a rank pasture, here, i' th' court;
There is a kind of honey-dew[8] that's deadly;   215

---

6. Dividing his flock with Jacob, Laban took the
speckled sheep (Genesis 30.31–33); the liver as seat
of the passions was thought to be diseased when
discolored.

7. Impulse, notion.
8. A sweet, sticky substance left on plants by aphids.
"Fame": reputation.

'Twill poison your fame; look to 't; be not cunning;
For they whose faces do belie their hearts
Are witches ere they arrive at twenty years,
Aye, and give the devil suck.

DUCHESS.   This is terrible good counsel.

FERDINAND. Hypocrisy is woven of a fine small thread,   220
Subtler than Vulcan's engine:[9] yet, believe 't,
Your darkest actions, nay, your privatest thoughts,
Will come to light.

CARDINAL.   You may flatter yourself,
And take your own choice; privately be married
Under the eaves of night—

FERDINAND.   Think 't the best voyage   225
That e'er you made; like the irregular crab,
Which, though 't goes backward, thinks that it goes right
Because it goes its own way; but observe,
Such weddings may more properly be said
To be executed than celebrated.

CARDINAL.   The marriage night   230
Is the entrance into some prison.

FERDINAND.   And those joys,
Those lustful pleasures, are like heavy sleeps
Which do forerun man's mischief.

CARDINAL.   Fare you well.
Wisdom begins at the end: remember it.   [Exit.]

DUCHESS. I think this speech between you both was studied,   235
It came so roundly off.

FERDINAND.   You are my sister;
This was my father's poniard,[1] do you see?
I'd be loth to see 't look rusty, 'cause 'twas his.
I would have you to give o'er these chargeable[2] revels:
A visor and a mask are whispering-rooms   240
That were ne'er built for goodness—fare ye well—
And women like that part which, like the lamprey,[3]
Hath never a bone in 't.

DUCHESS.   Fie, sir!

FERDINAND.   Nay,
I mean the tongue; variety of courtship.
What cannot a neat knave with a smooth tale   [Exit.]   245
Make a woman believe? Farewell, lusty widow.

DUCHESS. Shall this move me? If all my royal kindred
Lay in my way unto this marriage,
I'd make them my low footsteps; and even now,
Even in this hate, as men in some great battles,   250
By apprehending danger, have achieved
Almost impossible actions (I have heard soldiers say so),
So I through frights and threatenings will assay

9. The net in which Vulcan, Venus's husband,
caught her misbehaving with Mars.
1. Dagger.
2. Expensive. "Visor": a half-mask, worn by ladies
at carnivals, theaters, and other dubious resorts.
3. Like sharks, lamprey eels (which are also ver-
tebrates) have a cartilaginous, not a bony, skeleton.

This dangerous venture. Let old wives report
I winked and chose a husband. Cariola,   255
To thy known secrecy I have given up
More than my life—my fame.
CARIOLA.   Both shall be safe,
  For I'll conceal this secret from the world
  As warily as those that trade in poison
  Keep poison from their children.
DUCHESS.   Thy protestation   260
  Is ingenious and hearty:[4] I believe it.
  Is Antonio come?
CARIOLA.   He attends you.
DUCHESS.   Good dear soul,
  Leave me, but place thyself behind the arras,[5]
  Where thou mayst overhear us. Wish me good speed,
  For I am going into a wilderness   265
  Where I shall find nor path nor friendly clue
  To be my guide.   [CARIOLA *goes behind the arras.*]

          [*Enter* ANTONIO.]

                    I sent for you: sit down;
  Take pen and ink, and write. Are you ready?
ANTONIO.   Yes.
DUCHESS. What did I say?
ANTONIO. That I should write somewhat.
DUCHESS.   Oh, I remember: 270
  After these triumphs and this large expense,
  It's fit, like thrifty husbands,[6] we inquire
  What's laid up for tomorrow.
ANTONIO. So please your beauteous excellence.
DUCHESS.   Beauteous?
  Indeed, I thank you: I look young for your sake;   275
  You have ta'en my cares upon you.
ANTONIO.   I'll fetch your grace
  The particulars of your revenue and expense.
DUCHESS. Oh, you are an upright treasurer: but you mistook;
  For when I said I meant to make inquiry
  What's laid up for tomorrow, I did mean   280
  What's laid up yonder for me.
ANTONIO.   Where?
DUCHESS.   In heaven.
  I am making my will (as 'tis fit princes should,
  In perfect memory), and I pray sir, tell me,
  Were not one better make it smiling thus
  Than in deep groans and terrible ghastly looks,   285
  As if the gifts we parted with procured[7]
  That violent distraction?

4. Sincere.
5. Tapestries were often hung in Renaissance palaces to moderate the chill of the bare walls.
6. Though used here in its original sense of one
who preserves and safeguards property, the word
shows where the Duchess' thoughts are tending.
7. Brought on.

ANTONIO.   O, much better.

DUCHESS. If I had a husband now, this care were quit:
    But I intend to make you overseer.
    What good deed shall we first remember? Say.   290

ANTONIO. Begin with that first good deed begun i' th' world
    After man's creation, the sacrament of marriage:
    I'd have you first provide for a good husband;
    Give him all.

DUCHESS.   All?

ANTONIO.   Yes, your excellent self.

DUCHESS. In a winding-sheet?

ANTONIO.   In a couple.   295

DUCHESS. Saint Winfred, that were a strange will![8]

ANTONIO. 'Twere stranger if there were no will in you
    To marry again.

DUCHESS.   What do you think of marriage?

ANTONIO. I take 't, as those that deny purgatory;
    It locally contains or heaven or hell;   300
    There's no third place in 't.

DUCHESS.   How do you affect it?[9]

ANTONIO. My banishment, feeding my melancholy,
    Would often reason thus—

DUCHESS.   Pray, let's hear it.

ANTONIO. Say a man never marry, nor have children,
    What takes that from him? Only the bare name   305
    Of being a father, or the weak delight
    To see the little wanton ride a cock-horse
    Upon a painted stick, or hear him chatter
    Like a taught starling.

DUCHESS.   Fie, fie, what's all this?
    One of your eyes is bloodshot; use my ring to 't,   310
    They say 'tis very sovereign.[1] 'Twas my wedding-ring,
    And I did vow never to part with it
    But to my second husband.

ANTONIO.   You have parted with it now.

DUCHESS. Yes, to help your eyesight.

ANTONIO.   You have made me stark blind.

DUCHESS.   How?

ANTONIO. There is a saucy and ambitious devil   315
    Is dancing in this circle.[2]

DUCHESS.   Remove him.

ANTONIO.   How?

DUCHESS. There needs small conjuration, when your finger
    May do it: thus; is it fit?

               [*She puts the ring upon his finger; he kneels.*]

---

8. Saint Winifred, Welsh virgin and martyr, is an odd saint for the Duchess of Malfi to swear on.
9. Feel about it.
1. Healing, but with an additional overtone implying royal power.
2. To conjure up a devil, the necromancer first draws a charmed circle on the ground—like the Duchess' ring.

ANTONIO.   What said you?

DUCHESS.   Sir,
This goodly roof of yours[3] is too low built;
I cannot stand upright in 't nor discourse,   320
Without I raise it higher: raise yourself;
Or, if you please, my hand to help you: so.   [*Raises him.*]

ANTONIO. Ambition, madam, is a great man's madness,
That is not kept in chains and close-pent rooms,
But in fair lightsome lodgings, and is girt   325
With the wild noise of prattling visitants,
Which makes it lunatic beyond all cure.
Conceive not I am so stupid but I aim
Whereto your favors tend; but he's a fool
That, being a-cold, would thrust his hands i' th' fire   330
To warm them.

DUCHESS.   So, now the ground's broke,
You may discover what a wealthy mine
I make you lord of.

ANTONIO.   O my unworthiness!

DUCHESS. You were ill to sell yourself:
This darkening of your worth is not like that   335
Which tradesmen use i' th' city; their false lights
Are to rid bad wares off:[4] and I must tell you,
If you will know where breathes a complete man
(I speak it without flattery), turn your eyes,
And progress through yourself.

ANTONIO.   Were there nor heaven   340
Nor hell, I should be honest: I have long served virtue,
And ne'er ta'en wages of her.

DUCHESS.   Now she pays it.
The misery of us that are born great!
We are forced to woo, because none dare woo us;
And as a tyrant doubles with his words   345
And fearfully equivocates, so we
Are forced to express our violent passions
In riddles and in dreams, and leave the path
Of simple virtue, which was never made
To seem the thing it is not. Go, go brag   350
You have left me heartless; mine is in your bosom:
I hope 'twill multiply love there. You do tremble:
Make not your heart so dead a piece of flesh,
To fear more than to love me. Sir, be confident:
What is 't distracts you? This is flesh and blood, sir;   355
'Tis not the figure cut in alabaster
Kneels at my husband's tomb. Awake, awake, man!
I do here put off all vain ceremony,
And only do appear to you a young widow
That claims you for her husband, and, like a widow,   360
I use but half a blush in 't.

---

3. His head as he kneels before her.
4. Tradesmen in the city display their goods in a poor light, so the defects won't be seen.

ANTONIO. Truth speak for me,
  I will remain the constant sanctuary
  Of your good name.
DUCHESS. I thank you, gentle love:
  And 'cause you shall not come to me in debt,
  Being now my steward, here upon your lips   365
  I sign your *Quietus est.*[5] This you should have begged now;
  I have seen children oft eat sweetmeats thus,
  As fearful to devour them too soon.
ANTONIO. But for your brothers?
DUCHESS. Do not think of them.
  All discord without this circumference[6]   370
  Is only to be pitied, and not feared;
  Yet, should they know it, time will easily
  Scatter the tempest.
ANTONIO. These words should be mine,
  And all the parts you have spoke, if some part of it
  Would not have savored flattery.
DUCHESS. Kneel.

  [CARIOLA *comes from behind the arras.*]

ANTONIO. Ha!   375
DUCHESS. Be not amazed; this woman's of my counsel:
  I have heard lawyers say, a contract in a chamber
  Per verba de presenti[7] is absolute marriage.

  [*She and* ANTONIO *kneel.*]

  Bless, heaven, this sacred gordian,[8] which let violence
  Never untwine!   380
ANTONIO. And may our sweet affections, like the spheres,
  Be still in motion!
DUCHESS. Quickening, and make
  The like soft music!
ANTONIO. That we may imitate the loving palms,
  Best emblem of a peaceful marriage, that ne'er   385
  Bore fruit, divided!
DUCHESS. What can the Church force more?
ANTONIO. That fortune may not know an accident,
  Either of joy or sorrow, to divide
  Our fixèd wishes!
DUCHESS. How can the Church bind faster?[9]
  We now are man and wife, and 'tis the Church   390
  That must but echo this. Maid, stand apart:
  I now am blind.[1]

5. The legal formula for marking a bill "Paid" or "Acquitted."
6. Their arms around one another. "Without": outside.
7. "By words concerning the present (fact)"—not, as commonly supposed, and perhaps by Webster himself, "On the words of one present." In canon law, the Duchess is right; the agreement of two parties to consider themselves married is a valid

contract with or without priest, ceremony, or witness.
8. Knot.
9. Tighter, with a pun on "swifter."
1. The phrase, "Maid, stand apart" is addressed to Cariola. In shutting her eyes and rejecting all support, the Duchess dramatizes the quality of her choice. "Conceit": notion.

ANTONIO.   What's your conceit in this?
DUCHESS. I would have you lead your fortune by the hand
     Unto your marriage bed
     (You speak in me this, for we now are one);   395
     We'll only lie, and talk together, and plot
     To appease my humorous[2] kindred; and if you please,
     Like the old tale in *Alexander and Lodowick*,
     Lay a naked sword between us, keep us chaste.
     Oh, let me shroud my blushes in your bosom,   400
     Since 'tis the treasury of all my secrets!

                                   [*Exeunt* DUCHESS *and* ANTONIO.]

CARIOLA. Whether the spirit of greatness or of woman
     Reign most in her, I know not; but it shows
     A fearful madness: I owe her much of pity.   [*Exit.*]

Act 2

SCENE 1

[*Enter* BOSOLA *and* CASTRUCCIO.]

BOSOLA. You say you would fain be taken for an eminent courtier?
CASTRUCCIO. 'Tis the very main of my ambition.
BOSOLA. Let me see: you have a reasonable good face for 't already,
     and your nightcap expresses your ears sufficient largely. I would
     have you learn to twirl the strings of your band[3] with a good   5
     grace, and in a set speech, at th' end of every sentence, to hum
     three or four times, or blow your nose till it smart again, to recover
     your memory. When you come to be a president in criminal
     causes, if you smile upon a prisoner, hang him, but if you frown
     upon him and threaten him, let him be sure to 'scape the gal-   10
     lows.
CASTRUCCIO. I would be a very merry president.
BOSOLA. Do not sup o' nights; 'twill beget you an admirable wit.
CASTRUCCIO. Rather it would make me have a good stomach to
     quarrel; for they say, your roaring boys[4] eat meat seldom, and   15
     that makes them so valiant. But how shall I know whether the
     people take me for an eminent fellow?
BOSOLA. I will teach a trick to know it: give out you lie a-dying, and
     if you hear the common people curse you, be sure you are taken
     for one of the prime nightcaps.[5]   20

          [*Enter an* OLD LADY.]

     You come from painting now.
OLD LADY. From what?
BOSOLA. Why, from your scurvy face-physic. To behold thee not

---

2. I.e., my difficult, troublesome brothers. Alexander and Lodowick were look-alike friends in an
old ballad. For purely virtuous reasons, one slept
with the wife of the other, but with the precaution
indicated.

3. The elaborate ruff of the day had strings attached
to it.
4. London town-bullies. (Webster's Amalfi has
about it an occasional touch of Cheapside.)
5. Roughs who roamed the streets at night.

painted inclines somewhat near a miracle; these in thy face here
were deep ruts and foul sloughs the last progress.[6] There was a   25
lady in France that, having had the smallpox, flayed the skin off
her face to make it more level; and whereas before she looked
like a nutmeg grater, after she resembled an abortive hedgehog.

OLD LADY. Do you call this painting?

BOSOLA. No, no, but you call it careening of an old morphewed   30
lady, to make her disembogue again:[7] there's rough-cast phrase
to your plastic.

OLD LADY. It seems you are well acquainted with my closet.

BOSOLA. One would suspect it for a shop of witchcraft, to find in it
the fat of serpents, spawn of snakes, Jews' spittle, and their young   35
children's ordure; and all these for the face. I would sooner eat a
dead pigeon taken from the soles of the feet of one sick of the
plague than kiss one of you fasting.[8] Here are two of you, whose
sin of your youth is the very patrimony of the physician; makes
him renew his foot-cloth with the spring,[9] and change his high-   40
prized courtesan with the fall of the leaf. I do wonder you do not
loathe yourselves. Observe my meditation now:
What thing is in this outward form of man
To be beloved? We account it ominous,
If nature do produce a colt, or lamb,   45
A fawn, or goat, in any limb resembling
A man, and fly from 't as a prodigy:
Man stands amazed to see his deformity
In any other creature but himself.
But in our own flesh, though we bear diseases   50
Which have their true names only ta'en from beasts—
As the most ulcerous wolf and swinish measle[1]—
Though we are eaten up of lice and worms,
And though continually we bear about us
A rotten and dead body, we delight   55
To hide it in rich tissue: all our fear,
Nay, all our terror, is lest our physician
Should put us in the ground to be made sweet—
Your wife's gone to Rome: you two couple, and get you
To the wells at Lucca to recover your aches.[2]   60

[*Exeunt* CASTRUCCIO *and* OLD LADY.]

I have other work on foot. I observe our duchess
Is sick a-days: she pukes, her stomach seethes,

---

6. A progress was a formal royal journey of state.

7. Scraping ("careening") of an old, scaly ("morphewed") ship ("lady") to fit her for the ocean
("making her disembogue") again. All these metaphors are language cast in rough bronze on the
clay model ("plastic") of the lady's condition.

8. Centuries of traditional invective about wom-
en's cosmetic practices, and some contemporary
practices and superstititions, lie behind this speech.
Freshly killed pigeons were indeed applied to the
feet of plague victims, and fasting was supposed to
cause bad breath.

9. The physician grows rich on those who have
outworn their youth; every spring he buys a new
harness for his horse and every fall a new mistress
for himself.

1. "Wolf" and "measle": an ulcerous skin disease
(lupus) and an infection of swine.

2. The wells at Lucca are the mineral springs at
nearby Montecatini, then as now renowned as a
place to "take the cure."

The fins of her eyelids look most teeming blue,
She wanes i' th' cheek, and waxes fat i' th' flank,
And contrary to our Italian fashion,   70
Wears a loose-bodied gown: there's somewhat in 't.
I have a trick may chance discover it,
A pretty one; I have bought some apricocks,[3]
The first our spring yields.

[*Enter* ANTONIO *and* DELIO, *talking apart.*]

DELIO.   And so long since married?
   You amaze me.
ANTONIO.   Let me seal your lips forever: 70
   For, did I think that anything but th' air
   Could carry these words from you, I should wish
   You had no breath at all.

         [*Turning to* BOSOLA.]

Now, sir, in your contemplation? You are studying to become a
great wise fellow?   75
BOSOLA. Oh, sir, the opinion of wisdom is a foul tetter[4] that runs
   all over a man's body. If simplicity direct us to have no evil, it
   directs us to a happy being, for the subtlest folly proceeds from
   the subtlest wisdom. Let me be simply honest.
ANTONIO. I do understand your inside.
BOSOLA.   Do you so?   80
ANTONIO. Because you would not seem to appear to th' world
   Puffed up with your preferment, you continue
   This out-of-fashion melancholy. Leave it, leave it.
BOSOLA. Give me leave to be honest in any phrase, in any compli-
   ment whatsoever. Shall I confess myself to you? I look no higher   85
   than I can reach: they are the gods that must ride on winged
   horses. A lawyer's mule of a slow pace will both suit my disposi-
   tion and business; for, mark me, when a man's mind rides faster
   than his horse can gallop, they quickly both tire.
ANTONIO. You would look up to heaven, but I think   90
   The devil, that rules i' th' air, stands in your light.
BOSOLA. Oh, sir, you are lord of the ascendant,[5] chief man with the
   duchess; a duke was your cousin-german removed. Say you were
   lineally descended from King Pepin,[6] or he himself, what of this?
   Search the heads of the greatest rivers in the world, you shall find 95
   them but bubbles of water. Some would think the souls of princes
   were brought forth by some more weighty cause than those of
   meaner persons: they are deceived, there's the same hand to them;
   the like passions sway them; the same reason that makes a vicar
   go to law for a tithe-pig,[7] and undo his neighbors, makes them   100

3. The old spelling of "apricots," emphasizing the
derivation of the name from Latin *praecox*, "early
ripener."
4. Scab.
5. In astrology, the predominating influence.

6. Father of Charlemagne, hence source of a great
dynasty.
7. A parson was entitled to a tenth (tithe) of his
parishioners' annual profit, but was thought mean
if he sued for a petty sum.

spoil a whole province, and batter down goodly cities with the cannon.

[*Enter* DUCHESS *and* LADIES.]

DUCHESS. Your arm, Antonio; do I not grow fat?
  I am exceeding short-winded. Bosola,
  I would have you, sir, provide for me a litter,   105
  Such a one as the Duchess of Florence rode in.
BOSOLA. The duchess used one when she was great with child.
DUCHESS. I think she did. Come hither, mend my ruff;
  Here, when? Thou art such a tedious lady, and
  Thy breath smells of lemon peels;[8] would thou hadst done;   110
  Shall I swoon under thy fingers? I am
  So troubled with the mother![9]
BOSOLA. [*aside*] I fear too much.
DUCHESS. I have heard you say
  That the French courtiers wear their hats on 'fore   115
  The king.
ANTONIO.   I have seen it.
DUCHESS.   In the presence?
ANTONIO.   Yes.
DUCHESS. Why should not we bring up that fashion? 'Tis
  Ceremony more than duty that consists
  In the removing of a piece of felt.
  Be you the example to the rest o' th' court;   120
  Put on your hat first.
ANTONIO.   You must pardon me.
  I have seen, in colder countries than in France,
  Nobles stand bare to th' prince, and the distinction
  Methought showed reverently.
BOSOLA. I have a present for your grace.
DUCHESS.   For me, sir?   125
BOSOLA. Apricocks, madam.
DUCHESS.   O, sir, where are they?
  I have heard of none to-year.
BOSOLA. [*aside*]   Good: her color rises.
DUCHESS. Indeed, I thank you: they are wondrous fair ones.
  What an unskillful fellow is our gardener!
  We shall have none this month.
BOSOLA. Will not your grace pare them?   130
DUCHESS. No. They taste of musk, methinks; indeed they do.
BOSOLA. I know not: yet I wish your grace had pared 'em.
DUCHESS. Why?
BOSOLA. I forgot to tell you, the knave gardener,   135
  Only to raise his profit by them the sooner,
  Did ripen them in horse-dung.[1]

---

8. Lemon peels, chewed to sweeten the breath. "Tedious": clumsy.
9. Heartburn, but with a second meaning not lost on Bosola.

1. The heat of decomposing manure was widely supposed to have special virtues; but Bosola is thinking also of his post as provisor of the horse.

DUCHESS.   O, you jest.
  You shall judge: pray taste one.
ANTONIO.   Indeed, madam,
  I do not love the fruit.
DUCHESS.   Sir, you are loath
  To rob us of our dainties: 'tis a delicate fruit;   140
  They say they are restorative.
BOSOLA.   'Tis a pretty art,
  This grafting.
DUCHESS.   'Tis so; a bettering of nature.
BOSOLA. To make a pippin grow upon a crab,
  A damson on a blackthorn. [*Aside.*] How greedily she eats
    them!   145
  A whirlwind strike off these bawd farthingales![2]
  For, but for that and the loose-bodied gown,
  I should have discovered apparently[3]
  The young springal[4] cutting a caper in her belly.
DUCHESS. I thank you, Bosola. They were right good ones,   150
  If they do not make me sick.
ANTONIO.   How now, madam?
DUCHESS. This green fruit and my stomach are not friends;
  How they swell me!
BOSOLA. [*aside*]   Nay, you are too much swelled already.
DUCHESS. Oh, I am in an extreme cold sweat!
BOSOLA.   I am very sorry.
DUCHESS. Lights to my chamber! O good Antonio,   155
  I fear I am undone!
DELIO.   Lights there, lights!

[*Exeunt* DUCHESS *and* LADIES. *Exit, on the other side,* BOSOLA.]

ANTONIO. O my most trusty Delio, we are lost!
  I fear she's fall'n in labor; and there's left
  No time for her remove.
DELIO.   Have you prepared
  Those ladies to attend her? and procured   160
  That politic safe conveyance for the midwife
  Your duchess plotted?
ANTONIO. I have.
DELIO.   Make use, then, of this forced occasion:
  Give out that Bosola hath poisoned her
  With these apricocks; that will give some color   165
  For her keeping close.
ANTONIO.   Fie, fie, the physicians
  Will then flock to her.
DELIO.   For that you may pretend
  She'll use some prepared antidote of her own,
  Lest the physicians should re-poison her.

---

2. Early hoop-skirts, capable of concealing the   3. Easily, certainly.
figure.   4. Fellow.

ANTONIO. I am lost in amazement: I know not what to think
    on 't.   [*Exeunt.*]   170

SCENE 2

    [*Enter* BOSOLA.]

BOSOLA. So, so, there's no question but her tetchiness[5] and most
    vulturous eating of the apricocks are apparent signs of breeding.

    [*Enter an* OLD LADY.]

    Now?

OLD LADY. I am in haste, sir.

BOSOLA. There was a young waiting-woman had a monstrous   5
    desire to see the glass-house[6]—

OLD LADY. Nay, pray let me go.

BOSOLA. And it was only to know what strange instrument it was
    should swell up a glass to the fashion of a woman's belly.

OLD LADY. I will hear no more of the glass-house. You are still   10
    abusing women?

BOSOLA. Who, I? No; only by the way now and then, mention your
    frailties. The orange tree bears ripe and green fruit and blossoms
    all together; and some of you give entertainment for pure love,
    but more for more precious reward. The lusty spring smells well,   15
    but drooping autumn tastes well. If we have the same golden
    showers that rained in the time of Jupiter the thunderer, you
    have the same Danaës still,[7] to hold up their laps to receive them.
    Didst thou never study the mathematics?

OLD LADY. What's that sir?   20

BOSOLA. Why, to know the trick how to make a many lines meet in
    one center. Go, go, give your foster-daughters good counsel: tell
    them that the devil takes delight to hang at a woman's girdle, like
    a false rusty watch, that she cannot discern how the time passes.
                                             [*Exit* OLD LADY.]

    [*Enter* ANTONIO, DELIO, RODERIGO, *and* GRISOLAN.]

ANTONIO. Shut up the court-gates.

RODERIGO.   Why, sir? what's the danger?   25

ANTONIO. Shut up the posterns presently,[8] and call
    All the officers o' th' court.

GRISOLAN.   I shall instantly.   [*Exit.*]

ANTONIO. Who keeps the key o' th' park gate?

RODERIGO.   Forobosco.

ANTONIO. Let him bring 't presently.

    [*Re-enter* GRISOLAN *with* SERVANTS.]

1 SERVANT. O, gentlemen o' the court, the foulest treason!   30

---

5. Irritability.
6. Where bottles were blown, near the theater in
Blackfriars.

7. Jupiter's success in wooing Danaë in a shower
of gold traditionally illustrates female venality.
8. Outer gates at once.

BOSOLA. [*aside*] If that these apricocks should be poisoned now,
  Without my knowledge!
1 SERVANT.   There was taken even now
  A Switzer[9] in the duchess' bedchamber—
2 SERVANT.   A Switzer?
1 SERVANT. With a pistol in his great codpiece.[1]
BOSOLA.   Ha, ha, ha!
1 SERVANT. The codpiece was the case for 't.
2 SERVANT.   There was   35
  A cunning traitor: who would have searched his codpiece?
1 SERVANT. True, if he had kept out of the ladies' chambers.
  And all the molds of his buttons were leaden bullets.
2 SERVANT. O wicked cannibal!
  A fire-lock in 's codpiece!
1 SERVANT.   'Twas a French plot,   40
  Upon my life.
2 SERVANT.   To see what the devil can do!
ANTONIO. Are all the officers here?
SERVANTS.   We are.
ANTONIO.   Gentlemen,
  We have lost much plate[2] you know, and but this evening
  Jewels, to the value of four thousand ducats,
  Are missing in the duchess' cabinet.   45
  Are the gates shut?
SERVANT.   Yes.
ANTONIO.   'Tis the duchess' pleasure
  Each officer be locked into his chamber
  Till the sun-rising; and to send the keys
  Of all their chests and of their outward doors
  Into her bedchamber. She is very sick.   50
RODERIGO. At her pleasure.
ANTONIO.   She entreats you take 't not ill:
  The innocent shall be the more approved by it.
BOSOLA. Gentlemen o' th' wood-yard, where's your Switzer now?
1 SERVANT. By this hand, 'twas credibly reported by one o' th'
  black guard.[3]   [*Exeunt all except* ANTONIO *and* DELIO.] 55
DELIO. How fares it with the duchess?
ANTONIO.   She's exposed
  Unto the worst of torture, pain, and fear.
DELIO. Speak to her all happy comfort.
ANTONIO. How I do play the fool with mine own danger!
  You are this night, dear friend, to post to Rome;   60
  My life lies in your service.
DELIO.   Do not doubt me.
ANTONIO. Oh, 'tis far from me, and yet fear presents me
  Somewhat that looks like danger.
DELIO.   Believe it,

9. Swiss guard.
1. An outsize flap worn on the front of men's trunk
hose.
2. Massive gold and silver dishes, a frequent form

of wealth in the days before banks.
3. Kitchen scullions. The "wood-yard" is a source
of firewood for kitchen and fireplaces.

'Tis but the shadow of your fear, no more;
How superstitiously we mind our evils!   65
The throwing down salt, or crossing of a hare,
Bleeding at nose, the stumbling of a horse,
Or singing of a cricket, are of power
To daunt whole man in us. Sir, fare you well:
I wish you all the joys of a blessed father: 70
And, for my faith, lay this unto your breast,
Old friends, like old swords, still are trusted best.   [*Exit.*]

> [*Enter* CARIOLA.]

CARIOLA. Sir, you are the happy father of a son:
  Your wife commends him to you.
ANTONIO.   Blessed comfort!
  For heaven's sake tend her well: I'll presently   75
  Go set a figure for 's nativity.[4]   [*Exeunt.*]

SCENE 3

> [*Enter* BOSOLA, *with a dark lantern.*]

BOSOLA. Sure I did hear a woman shriek: list, ha!
  And the sound came, if I received it right,
  From the duchess' lodgings. There's some stratagem
  In the confining all our courtiers
  To their several wards: I must have part of it;   5
  My intelligence will freeze else.[5] List, again!
  It may be 'twas the melancholy bird,
  Best friend of silence and of solitariness,
  The owl, that screamed so. Ha! Antonio?

> [*Enter* ANTONIO *with a candle, his sword drawn.*]

ANTONIO. I heard some noise. Who's there? What art thou?
    Speak.   10
BOSOLA. Antonio? Put not your face nor body
  To such a forced expression of fear.
  I am Bosola, your friend.
ANTONIO.   Bosola!
  [*Aside.*] This mole does undermine me.—Heard you not
  A noise even now?
BOSOLA.   From whence?
ANTONIO.   From the duchess' lodging.   15
BOSOLA. Not I. Did you?
ANTONIO.   I did, or else I dreamed.
BOSOLA. Let's walk towards it.
ANTONIO.   No, it may be 'twas
  But the rising of the wind.
BOSOLA.   Very likely.
  Methinks 'tis very cold, and yet you sweat:
  You look wildly.

---

4. Cast his horoscope.
5. All my news will be cold.

ANTONIO.   I have been setting a figure[6]   20
  For the duchess' jewels.
BOSOLA.   Ah, and how falls your question?
  Do you find it radical?[7]
ANTONIO.   What's that to you?
  'Tis rather to be questioned what design,
  When all men were commanded to their lodgings,
  Makes you a night-walker.
BOSOLA.   In sooth, I'll tell you: 25
  Now all the court's asleep, I thought the devil
  Had least to do here; I came to say my prayers;
  And if it do offend you I do so,
  You are a fine courtier.
ANTONIO. [Aside.]   This fellow will undo me.
  You gave the duchess apricocks today: 30
  Pray heaven they were not poisoned!
BOSOLA.   Poisoned? A Spanish fig[8]
  For the imputation!
ANTONIO.   Traitors are ever confident
  Till they are discovered. There were jewels stolen, too;
  In my conceit, none are to be suspected
  More than yourself.
BOSOLA.   You are a false steward.   35
ANTONIO. Saucy slave, I'll pull thee up by the roots.
BOSOLA. Maybe the ruin will crush you to pieces.
ANTONIO. You are an impudent snake indeed, sir:
  Are you scarce warm, and do you show your sting?
  You libel well, sir.
BOSOLA.   No, sir: copy it out,   40
  And I will set my hand to 't.[9]
ANTONIO. [aside]   My nose bleeds.
  One that were superstitious would count
  This ominous, when it merely comes by chance:
  Two letters, that are wrought here for my name,
  Are drowned in blood!   45
  Mere accident. For you, sir, I'll take order
  I' th' morn you shall be safe. [Aside.] 'Tis that must color
  Her lying-in.— Sir, this door you pass not:
  I do not hold it fit that you come near
  The duchess' lodgings, till you have quit yourself.   50
  [Aside.] The great are like the base, nay, they are the same,
  When they seek shameful ways to avoid shame.   [Exit.]
BOSOLA. Antonio hereabout did drop a paper:
  Some of your help, false friend: [Opening his lantern.] Oh,
    here it is.
  What's here? A child's nativity calculated?   [Reads.] 55
  "The duchess was delivered of a son, 'tween the hours twelve

6. Establishing the loss involved. But Bosola takes the expression astrologically, as if Antonio were casting a horoscope.
7. Indicative, significant.
8. An obscene gesture, which Bosola doubtless makes onstage.
9. Bosola denies the charge, not by denying malignancy, but by offering to publish it.

and one in the night, *Anno Dom.* 1504,"— that's this year—
"*decimo nono Decembris.*"[1]—that's this night—"taken according
to the meridian of Malfi,"—that's our duchess: happy discovery!
"The lord of the first house being combust[2] in the ascendant,   60
signifies short life; and Mars being in a human sign, joined to
the tail of the Dragon, in the eighth house, doth threaten a vio-
lent death. *Caetera non scrutantur.*"[3]
Why, now 'tis most apparent: this precise[4] fellow
Is the duchess' bawd: I have it to my wish!   65
This is a parcel of intelligency
Our courtiers were cased up for: it needs must follow
That I must be committed on pretense
Of poisoning her; which I'll endure, and laugh at.
If one could find the father now! But that   70
Time will discover. Old Castruccio
I' th' morning posts to Rome: by him I'll send
A letter that shall make her brothers' galls
O'erflow their livers. This was a thrifty way.
Though lust do mask in ne'er so strange disguise,   75
She's oft found witty, but is never wise.   [*Exit.*]

SCENE 4. *The palace of the* CARDINAL *at Rome.*

[*Enter* CARDINAL *and* JULIA.]

CARDINAL. Sit. Thou art my best of wishes. Prithee, tell me
  What trick didst thou invent to come to Rome
  Without thy husband.
JULIA.   Why, my lord, I told him
  I came to visit an old anchorite[5]
  Here for devotion.
CARDINAL.   Thou are a witty false one—   5
  I mean, to him.
JULIA.   You have prevailed with me
  Beyond my strongest thoughts! I would not now
  Find you inconstant.
CARDINAL.   Do not put thyself
  To such a voluntary torture, which proceeds
  Out of your own guilt.
JULIA.   How, my lord?
CARDINAL.   You fear   10
  My constancy, because you have approved[6]
  Those giddy and wild turnings in yourself.
JULIA. Did you e'er find them?
CARDINAL.   Sooth, generally for women;
  A man might strive to make glass malleable,
  Ere he should make them fixed.

---

1. December 19.
2. Burnt up; i.e., the ruling planet is close to the sun.
3. The rest is not to be seen. Mars and the Dragon

are sinister signs, even separately; fatal together.
4. Meticulous, fussy. "Bawd": procurer.
5. Hermit.
6. Experienced.

JULIA.   So, my lord.   15
CARDINAL. We had need go borrow that fantastic glass
   Invented by Galileo the Florentine[7]
   To view another spacious world i' th' moon,
   And look to find a constant woman there.
JULIA. This is very well, my lord.
CARDINAL.   Why do you weep?   20
   Are tears your justification? The self-same tears
   Will fall into your husband's bosom, lady,
   With a loud protestation that you love him
   Above the world. Come, I'll love you wisely,
   That's jealously, since I am very certain   25
   You cannot make me cuckold.
JULIA.   I'll go home
   To my husband.
CARDINAL.   You may thank me, lady,
   I have taken you off your melancholy perch,
   Bore you upon my fist, and showed you game,
   And let you fly at it.[8] I pray thee, kiss me.   30
   When thou wast with thy husband, thou wast watched
   Like a tame elephant: still you are to thank me:
   Thou hadst only kisses from him and high feeding;
   But what delight was that? 'Twas just like one
   That hath a little fingering on the lute,   35
   Yet cannot tune it: still you are to thank me.
JULIA. You told me of a piteous wound i' th' heart
   And a sick liver, when you wooed me first,
   And spake like one in physic.[9]   [A *knock is heard*.]
CARDINAL.   Who's that?
   Rest firm, for my affection to thee,   40
   Lightning moves slow to 't.[1]

         [*Enter* SERVANT.]

SERVANT.   Madam, a gentleman,
   That's come post from Malfi, desires to see you.
CARDINAL. Let him enter. I'll withdraw.   [*Exit*.]
SERVANT.   He says
   Your husband, old Castruccio, is come to Rome,
   Most pitifully tired with riding post.[2]   45

         [*Enter* DELIO.]   [*Exit*.]

JULIA. Signor Delio! [*Aside*.]—'tis one of my old suitors.
DELIO. I was bold to come and see you.
JULIA.   Sir, you are welcome.
DELIO. Do you lie here?
JULIA.   Sure, your own experience
   Will satisfy you no: our Roman prelates

7. In 1504, Galileo's telescope was more than 100
years in the future, but the reference was topical
for Webster's audience.
8. The Cardinal speaks of himself as a falcon
training a bird (Julia).

9. Like a man under a doctor's care.
1. By comparison.
2. When riding post, one changed horses at regular intervals without stopping to rest oneself.

Do not keep lodging for ladies.

DELIO.   Very well.   50
I have brought you no commendations from your husband,
For I know none by him.

JULIA.   I hear he's come to Rome.

DELIO. I never knew man and beast, of a horse and a knight,
So weary of each other: if he had had a good back,
He would have undertook to have borne his horse,   55
His breech was so pitifully sore.

JULIA.   Your laughter
Is my pity.

DELIO.   Lady, I know not whether
You want money, but I have brought you some.

JULIA. From my husband?

DELIO.   No, from mine own allowance.

JULIA. I must hear the condition, ere I be bound to take it.   60

DELIO. Look on 't, 'tis gold: hath it not a fine color?

JULIA. I have a bird more beautiful.

DELIO. Try the sound on 't.

JULIA.   A lute-string far exceeds it:
It hath no smell, like cassia or civet;
Nor is it physical,³ though some fond doctors   65
Persuade us seethe 't in cullises:⁴ I'll tell you,
This is a creature bred by—

          [*Re-enter* SERVANT.]

SERVANT.   Your husband's come,
Hath delivered a letter to the Duke of Calabria
That, to my thinking, hath put him out of his wits.   [*Exit.*]

JULIA. Sir, you hear: 70
Pray, let me know your business and your suit
As briefly as can be.

DELIO. With good speed: I would wish you,
At such time as you are non-resident
With your husband, my mistress.   75

JULIA. Sir, I'll go ask my husband if I shall,
And straight return your answer.   [*Exit.*]

DELIO.   Very fine!
Is this her wit, or honesty, that speaks thus?
I heard one say the duke was highly moved
With a letter sent from Malfi. I do fear   80
Antonio is betrayed: how fearfully
Shows his ambition now! Unfortunate fortune!
They pass through whirlpools, and deep woes do shun,
Who the event weigh ere the action's done.⁵   [*Exit.*]

---

3. Medicinally valuable.   5. I.e., who judge of actions before seeing their
4. Boil it up in a broth.   final consequences.

SCENE 5

[*Enter* CARDINAL, *and* FERDINAND *with a letter.*]

FERDINAND. I have this night digged up a mandrake.[6]

CARDINAL.   Say you?

FERDINAND. And I am grown mad with 't.

CARDINAL.   What's the prodigy?

FERDINAND. Read there—a sister damned: she's loose i' th' hilts;[7]
   Grown a notorious strumpet.

CARDINAL.   Speak lower.

FERDINAND.   Lower?
   Rogues do not whisper 't now, but seek to publish 't   5
   (As servants do the bounty of their lords)
   Aloud; and with a covetous searching eye,
   To mark who note them. O, confusion seize her!
   She hath had most cunning bawds to serve her turn,
   And more secure conveyances for lust   10
   Than towns of garrison for service.

CARDINAL.   Is 't possible?
   Can this be certain?

FERDINAND.   Rhubarb, oh, for rhubarb[8]
   To purge this choler! Here's the cursèd day
   To prompt my memory, and here 't shall stick
   Till of her bleeding heart I make a sponge   15
   To wipe it out.

CARDINAL.   Why do you make yourself
   So wild a tempest?

FERDINAND.   Would I could be one,
   That I might toss her palace 'bout her ears,
   Root up her goodly forests, blast her meads,[9]
   And lay her general territory as waste   20
   As she hath done her honors.

CARDINAL.   Shall our blood,
   The royal blood of Aragon and Castile,
   Be thus attainted?

FERDINAND.   Apply desperate physic:
   We must not now use balsamum,[1] but fire,
   The smarting cupping-glass, for that 's the mean   25
   To purge infected blood, such blood as hers.
   There is a kind of pity in mine eye,
   I'll give it to my handkercher; and now 'tis here,
   I'll bequeath this to her bastard.

CARDINAL.   What to do?

FERDINAND. Why, to make soft lint for his mother's wounds,   30
   When I have hewed her to pieces.

---

6. A fabulous root, violently aphrodisiac but also deadly poison. Both aspects apply to Ferdinand.
7. I.e., promiscuous.
8. Rhubarb, as a laxative, was thought curative of the high pressures of hot rage.

9. Open fields.
1. Balm, a gentle remedy, gives way to cautery ("fire") and the "cupping-glass," by which people were bled.

CARDINAL.   Cursèd creature!
  Unequal nature, to place women's hearts
  So far upon the left side![2]
FERDINAND.   Foolish men,
  That e'er will trust their honor in a bark
  Made of so slight weak bulrush as is woman,   35
  Apt every minute to sink it!
CARDINAL. Thus ignorance, when it hath purchased honor,
  It cannot wield it.
FERDINAND.   Methinks I see her laughing—
  Excellent hyena! Talk to me somewhat, quickly,
  Or my imagination will carry me   40
  To see her in the shameful act of sin.
CARDINAL. With whom?
FERDINAND. Haply[3] with some strong-thighed bargeman,
  Or one o' th' wood-yard that can quoit the sledge
  Or toss the bar,[4] or else some lovely squire   45
  That carries coal up to her privy lodgings.
CARDINAL. You fly beyond your reason.
FERDINAND.   Go to, mistress!
  'Tis not your whore's milk that shall quench my wild fire,
  But your whore's blood.
CARDINAL. How idly shows this rage, which carries you,   50
  As men conveyed by witches through the air,
  On violent whirlwinds! This intemperate noise
  Fitly resembles deaf men's shrill discourse,
  Who talk aloud, thinking all other men
  To have their imperfection.
FERDINAND.   Have not you   55
  My palsy?
CARDINAL.   Yes, I can be angry, but
  Without this rupture: there is not in nature
  A thing that makes man so deformed, so beastly,
  As doth intemperate anger. Chide yourself.
  You have divers men who never yet expressed   60
  Their strong desire of rest but by unrest,
  By vexing of themselves. Come, put yourself
  In tune.
FERDINAND. So; I will only study to seem
  The thing I am not. I could kill her now,
  In you, or in myself; for I do think   65
  It is some sin in us heaven doth revenge
  By her.
CARDINAL. Are you stark mad?
FERDINAND.   I would have their bodies
  Burnt in a coal-pit with the ventage stopped,
  That their cursed smoke might not ascend to heaven;

---

2. The left is the sinister side, associated with bad
luck and deceit. (Why women should be thought
more subject to these defects than men, the brothers are too furious to ask.)
3. Perhaps.

4. Beefy fellows, employed to carry firewood,
imagined as competing in gross tests of strength
(throwing the sledge, tossing the bar), the winner
to be promoted to the Duchess' bed.

Or dip the sheets they lie in in pitch or sulphur,   70
Wrap them in 't, and then light them like a match;
Or else to-boil their bastard to a cullis,
And give 't his lecherous father to renew
The sin of his back.[5]

CARDINAL.   I'll leave you.

FERDINAND.   Nay, I have done.
I am confident, had I been damned in hell,   75
And should have heard of this, it would have put me
Into a cold sweat. In, in; I'll go sleep.
Till I know who leaps my sister, I'll not stir:
That known, I'll find scorpions to string my whips,[6]
And fix her in a general eclipse.   80

[Exeunt.]

Act 3

SCENE 1. Amalfi.

[Enter ANTONIO and DELIO.]

ANTONIO. Our noble friend, my most belovèd Delio!
Oh, you have been a stranger long at court;
Came you along with the Lord Ferdinand?

DELIO. I did, sir. And how fares your noble duchess?

ANTONIO. Right fortunately well: she's an excellent   5
Feeder of pedigrees; since you last saw her,
She hath had two children more, a son and daughter.

DELIO. Methinks 'twas yesterday: let me but wink,
And not behold your face, which to mine eye
Is somewhat leaner, verily I should dream   10
It were within this half-hour.

ANTONIO. You have not been in law, friend Delio,
Nor in prison, nor a suitor at the court,
Nor begged the reversion of some great man's place,
Nor troubled with an old wife, which doth make   15
Your time so insensibly hasten.[7]

DELIO.   Pray, sir, tell me,
Hath not this news arrived yet to the ear
Of the Lord Cardinal?

ANTONIO.   I fear it hath:
The Lord Ferdinand, that's newly come to court,
Doth bear himself right dangerously.

DELIO.   Pray, why?   20

ANTONIO. He is so quiet that he seems to sleep
The tempest out, as dormice do in winter.
Those houses that are haunted are most still
Till the devil be up.

5. Only boiling down the bastard to a broth ("cullis") and feeding him to his father, as Atreus did to Thyestes in Greek legend, will satisfy Ferdinand. Thus the father will be made to "renew" (repair, atone for) the sin of his back in begetting the child.
6. Tipping the thongs of a whip with "scorpions" (tips of jagged steel or lead that sting and bite the flesh) is an old metaphor for aggravated punishment.
7. I.e., this is what makes one's time pass imperceptibly ("insensibly") by.

DELIO.   What say the common people?
ANTONIO. The common rabble do directly say   25
  She is a strumpet.
DELIO.   And your graver heads
  Which would be politic, what censure they?
ANTONIO. They do observe I grow to infinite purchase,
  The left-hand way,[8] and all suppose the duchess
  Would amend it, if she could; for, say they,   30
  Great princes, though they grudge their officers
  Should have such large and unconfinèd means
  To get wealth under them, will not complain,
  Lest thereby they should make them odious
  Unto the people; for other obligation   35
  Of love or marriage between her and me
  They never dream of.
DELIO.   The Lord Ferdinand
  Is going to bed.

    [*Enter* DUCHESS, FERDINAND, *and* BOSOLA.]

FERDINAND.   I'll instantly to bed,
  For I am weary.—I am to bespeak
  A husband for you.
DUCHESS.   For me, sir? Pray, who is 't?   40
FERDINAND. The great Count Malateste.
DUCHESS.   Fie upon him!
  A count? He's a mere stick of sugar-candy;
  You may look quite through him. When I choose
  A husband, I will marry for your honor.
FERDINAND. You shall do well in 't.—How is 't, worthy Antonio?   45
DUCHESS. But, sir, I am to have private conference with you
  About a scandalous report is spread
  Touching mine honor.
FERDINAND.   Let me be ever deaf to 't:
  One of Pasquil's paper bullets,[9] court-calumny,
  A pestilent air, which princes' palaces   50
  Are seldom purged of. Yet, say that it were true,
  I pour it in your bosom, my fixed love
  Would strongly excuse, extenuate, nay, deny
  Faults, were they apparent in you. Go, be safe
  In your own innocency.
DUCHESS. [*aside*]   O blessèd comfort!   55
  This deadly air is purged.

    [*Exeunt* DUCHESS, ANTONIO, *and* DELIO.]

FERDINAND.   Her guilt treads on
  Hot-burning coulters.[1] Now, Bosola,
  How thrives our intelligence?

---

8. I.e., they think I am getting rich dishonestly.
9. Anonymous satires were traditionally pasted on
the statue of Pasquillo, or Pasquino, near Piazza
Navona in Rome, and attributed to his authorship.

1. Medieval virginity inquests customarily required
the questioned lady to walk barefoot over red-hot
plowshares ("coulters").

BOSOLA.   Sir, uncertainly:
  'Tis rumored she hath had three bastards, but
  By whom, we may go read i' th' stars.
FERDINAND.   Why, some   60
  Hold opinion all things are written there.
BOSOLA. Yes, if we could find spectacles to read them.
  I do suspect there hath been some sorcery
  Used on the duchess.
FERDINAND.   Sorcery? To what purpose?
BOSOLA. To make her dote on some desertless fellow   65
  She shames to acknowledge.
FERDINAND.   Can your faith give way
  To think there's power in potions or in charms,
  To make us love whether we will or no?
BOSOLA. Most certainly.
FERDINAND. Away! These are mere gulleries,[2] horrid things,   70
  Invented by some cheating mountebanks
  To abuse us. Do you think that herbs or charms
  Can force the will? Some trials have been made
  In this foolish practice, but the ingredients
  Were lenitive poisons,[3] such as are of force   75
  To make the patient mad; and straight the witch
  Swears by equivocation they are in love.
  The witchcraft lies in her rank blood. This night
  I will force confession from her. You told me
  You had got, within these two days, a false key   80
  Into her bedchamber.
BOSOLA.   I have.
FERDINAND.   As I would wish.
BOSOLA. What do you intend to do?
FERDINAND.   Can you guess?
BOSOLA.   No.
FERDINAND. Do not ask, then:
  He that can compass me, and know my drifts,
  May say he hath put a girdle 'bout the world,   85
  And sounded all her quicksands.
BOSOLA.   I do not
  Think so.
FERDINAND. What do you think, then, pray?
BOSOLA.   That you
  Are your own chronicle too much, and grossly
  Flatter yourself.
FERDINAND.   Give me thy hand; I thank thee:
  I ne'er gave pension but to flatterers,   90
  Till I entertained thee. Farewell.
  That friend a great man's ruin strongly checks,
  Who rails into his belief all his defects.   [*Exeunt.*]

2. Deceits.
3. Secret, slow-working poisons.

SCENE 2. *The Bedchamber of the* DUCHESS.

[*Enter* DUCHESS, ANTONIO, *and* CARIOLA.]

DUCHESS. Bring me the casket hither, and the glass.
    You get no lodging here tonight, my lord.
ANTONIO. Indeed, I must persuade one.
DUCHESS.   Very good:
    I hope in time 'twill grow into a custom,
    That noblemen shall come with cap and knee   5
    To purchase a night's lodging of their wives.
ANTONIO. I must lie here.
DUCHESS.   Must! You are a lord of misrule.[4]
ANTONIO. Indeed, my rule is only in the night.
DUCHESS. To what use will you put me?
ANTONIO.   We'll sleep together.
DUCHESS. Alas, what pleasure can two lovers find in sleep?   10
CARIOLA. My lord, I lie with her often, and I know
    She'll much disquiet you.
ANTONIO.   See, you are complained of.
CARIOLA. For she's the sprawling'st bedfellow.
ANTONIO.   I shall like her
    The better for that.
CARIOLA.   Sir, shall I ask you a question?
ANTONIO. I pray thee, Cariola.
CARIOLA.   Wherefore still, when you lie
    with my lady,   15
    Do you rise so early?
ANTONIO.   Laboring men
    Count the clock oftenest, Cariola,
    Are glad when their task's ended.
DUCHESS.   I'll stop your mouth.

                                        [*Kisses him.*]

ANTONIO. Nay, that's but one; Venus had two soft doves
    To draw her chariot; I must have another—   20

                                        [*She kisses him again.*]

    When wilt thou marry, Cariola?
CARIOLA.   Never, my lord.
ANTONIO. Oh, fie upon this single life! Forgo it.
    We read how Daphne, for her peevish flight,
    Became a fruitless bay tree; Syrinx turned
    To the pale empty reed; Anaxarete   25
    Was frozen into marble: whereas those
    Which married, or proved kind unto their friends,
    Were by a gracious influence transhaped
    Into the olive, pomegranate, mulberry,

---

4. The mock-monarch of a carnival festival.

Became flowers, precious stones, or eminent stars.[5]   30
CARIOLA. This is a vain poetry, but I pray you tell me,
   If there were proposed me, wisdom, riches, and beauty,
   In three several young men, which should I choose?
ANTONIO. 'Tis a hard question: this was Paris' case,
   And he was blind in 't, and there was great cause;   35
   For how was 't possible he could judge right,
   Having three amorous goddesses in view,
   And they stark naked? 'Twas a motion[6]
   Were able to benight the apprehension
   Of the severest counsellor of Europe.   40
   Now I look on both your faces so well formed,
   It puts me in mind of a question I would ask.
CARIOLA. What is 't?
ANTONIO.   I do wonder why hard-favored ladies,
   For the most part, keep worse-favored waiting-women
   To attend them, and cannot endure fair ones.   45
DUCHESS. Oh, that's soon answered.
   Did you ever in your life know an ill painter
   Desire to have his dwelling next door to the shop
   Of an excellent picture-maker? 'Twould disgrace
   His face-making, and undo him. I prithee,   50
   When were we so merry?—My hair tangles.
ANTONIO. Pray thee, Cariola, let's steal forth the room,
   And let her talk to herself: I have divers times
   Served her the like, when she hath chafed extremely.
   I love to see her angry. Softly, Cariola.   55

                              [*Exeunt* ANTONIO *and* CARIOLA.]

DUCHESS. Doth not the color of my hair 'gin to change?
   When I wax gray, I shall have all the court
   Powder their hair with arras,[7] to be like me.
   You have cause to love me; I entered you into my heart
   Before you would vouchsafe to call for the keys.   60

      [*Enter* FERDINAND *behind.*]

   We shall one day have my brothers take you napping;
   Methinks his presence, being now in court,
   Should make you keep your own bed; but you'll say
   Love mixed with fear is sweetest. I'll assure you,
   You shall get no more children till my brothers   65
   Consent to be your gossips.[8] Have you lost your tongue?

                              [*She turns and sees* FERDINAND.]

---

5. The olive was created by Athene; the mulberry
gained its color from the blood of Pyramus and
Thisbe; the pomegranate seems to have no particular mythological origin. Most of the other stories
of ladies being transformed for complying, or not
complying, with the solicitations of a god are from
Ovid, *Metamorphoses.*

6. Spectacle. Paris had to choose between Hera,
Athena, and Aphrodite, goddesses of marriage,
wisdom, and love; his selecting the third led to the
Trojan war.
7. Orris root, used in powdered form to make hair
artificially gray.
8. Sponsors in baptism.

'Tis welcome:
For know, whether I am doomed to live or die,
I can do both like a prince.
FERDINAND.   Die, then, quickly! [*Giving her a poniard.*]
Virtue, where art thou hid? What hideous thing   70
Is it that doth eclipse thee?
DUCHESS.   Pray, sir, hear me.
FERDINAND. Or is it true thou art but a bare name,
And no essential thing?
DUCHESS.   Sir—
FERDINAND.   Do not speak.
DUCHESS. No, sir: I will plant my soul in mine ears, to hear you.
FERDINAND. O most imperfect light of human reason,   75
That mak'st us so unhappy to foresee
What we can least prevent! Pursue thy wishes,
And glory in them: there's in shame no comfort
But to be past all bounds and sense of shame.
DUCHESS. I pray, sir, hear me. I am married.
FERDINAND.   So!   80
DUCHESS. Haply,[9] not to your liking: but for that,
Alas, your shears do come untimely now
To clip the bird's wings that's already flown!
Will you see my husband?
FERDINAND.   Yes, if I could change
Eyes with a basilisk.[1]
DUCHESS.   Sure, you came hither   85
By his confederacy.
FERDINAND.   The howling of a wolf
Is music to thee, screech-owl: prithee, peace.
Whate'er thou art that hast enjoyed my sister,
For I am sure thou hear'st me, for thine own sake
Let me not know thee. I came hither prepared   90
To work thy discovery; yet am now persuaded
It would beget such violent effects
As would damn us both. I would not for ten millions
I had beheld thee: therefore use all means
I never may have knowledge of thy name;   95
Enjoy thy lust still, and a wretched life,
On that condition. And for thee, vile woman,
If thou do wish thy lecher may grow old
In thy embracements, I would have thee build
Such a room for him as our anchorites   100
To holier use inhabit. Let not the sun
Shine on him till he's dead; let dogs and monkeys
Only converse with him, and such dumb things
To whom nature denies use to sound his name;
Do not keep a paraquito,[2] lest she learn it;   105
If thou do love him, cut out thine own tongue,
Lest it bewray him.

9. Perhaps.   glance.
1. The mythical basilisk was fabled to kill with a   2. Parrot.

DUCHESS.   Why might not I marry?
   I have not gone about in this to create
   Any new world or custom.
FERDINAND.   Thou art undone;
   And thou hast ta'en that massy sheet of lead   110
   That hid thy husband's bones, and folded it
   About my heart.
DUCHESS.   Mine bleeds for 't.
FERDINAND.   Thine? Thy heart?
   What should I name 't unless a hollow bullet
   Filled with unquenchable wild-fire?
DUCHESS.   You are in this
   Too strict, and were you not my princely brother,   115
   I would say, too willful. My reputation
   Is safe.
FERDINAND. Dost thou know what reputation is?
   I'll tell thee—to small purpose, since the instruction
   Comes now too late.   120
   Upon a time, Reputation, Love, and Death
   Would travel o'er the world; and it was concluded
   That they should part, and take three several ways.
   Death told them, they should find him in great battles,
   Or cities plagued with plagues. Love gives them counsel   125
   To inquire for him 'mongst unambitious shepherds,
   Where dowries were not talked of, and sometimes
   'Mongst quiet kindred that had nothing left
   By their dead parents. "Stay," quoth Reputation,
   "Do not forsake me; for it is my nature,   130
   If once I part from any man I meet,
   I am never found again." And so for you:
   You have shook hands with Reputation,
   And made him invisible. So, fare you well.
   I will never see you more.
DUCHESS.   Why should only I,   135
   Of all the other princes of the world,
   Be cased up, like a holy relic? I have youth
   And a little beauty.
FERDINAND.   So you have some virgins
   That are witches. I will never see thee more.   [*Exit.*]

     [*Enter* ANTONIO *with a pistol, and* CARIOLA.]

DUCHESS. You saw this apparition?
ANTONIO.   Yes. We are   140
   Betrayed. How came he hither? I should turn
   This to thee, for that.   [*Pointing the pistol at* CARIOLA.]
CARIOLA.   Pray, sir, do; and when
   That you have cleft my heart, you shall read there
   Mine innocence.
DUCHESS.   That gallery gave him entrance.
ANTONIO. I would this terrible thing would come again,
   That, standing on my guard, I might relate   145

My warrantable³ love.   [*She shows the poniard.*]
                    Ha! What means this?
DUCHESS. He left this with me.
ANTONIO.   And it seems did wish
    You would use it on yourself.
DUCHESS.   His action seemed
    To intend so much.
ANTONIO.   This hath a handle to 't   150
    As well as a point: turn it towards him, and
    So fasten the keen edge in his rank gall.   [*Knocking within.*]
    How now! Who knocks? More earthquakes?
DUCHESS.   I stand
    As if a mine beneath my feet were ready
    To be blown up.
CARIOLA.   'Tis Bosola.
DUCHESS.   Away!   155
    O misery! Methinks unjust actions
    Should wear these masks and curtains, and not we.
    You must instantly part hence: I have fashioned it
    Already.   [*Exit* ANTONIO.]

        [*Enter* BOSOLA.]

BOSOLA. The duke your brother is ta'en up in a whirlwind,   160
    Hath took horse, and 's rid post to Rome.
DUCHESS.   So late?
BOSOLA. He told me, as he mounted into th' saddle,
    You were undone.
DUCHESS.   Indeed, I am very near it.
BOSOLA. What's the matter?
DUCHESS. Antonio, the master of our household,   165
    Hath dealt so falsely with me in 's accounts:
    My brother stood engaged with me for money
    Ta'en up of certain Neapolitan Jews,
    And Antonio lets the bonds be forfeit.⁴
BOSOLA. Strange!—[*Aside.*] This is cunning.
DUCHESS.   And hereupon   170
    My brother's bills at Naples are protested
    Against.⁵—Call up our officers.
BOSOLA.   I shall.   [*Exit.*]

        [*Re-enter* ANTONIO.]

DUCHESS. The place that you must fly to is Ancona:⁶
    Hire a house there; I'll send after you
    My treasure and my jewels. Our weak safety   175
    Runs upon enginous wheels: short syllables

3. Legitimate, defensible.
4. I.e., my brother stood security for some money
I borrowed from Neapolitan money lenders; now
Antonio has let them call on the Duke for payment.

5. I.e., the Duke of Calabria's checks have
bounced.
6. Ancona lies on the Adriatic coast of Italy, across
the peninsula from Amalfi and well to the north.

Must stand for periods.[7] I must now accuse you
Of such a feignèd crime as Tasso calls
Magnanima menzogna, a noble lie,
'Cause it must shield our honors. Hark! They are coming.   180

    [*Re-enter* BOSOLA *and* OFFICERS.]

ANTONIO. Will your grace hear me?
DUCHESS. I have got well by you; you have yielded me
  A million of loss: I am like to inherit
  The people's curses for your stewardship.
  You had the trick in audit-time to be sick,   185
  Till I had signed your *quietus*;[8] and that cured you
  Without help of a doctor.—Gentlemen,
  I would have this man be an example to you all;
  So shall you hold my favor; I pray, let him;[9]
  For he's done that, alas, you would not think of,   190
  And, because I intend to be rid of him,
  I mean not to publish. [*To* ANTONIO.] Use your fortune elsewhere.
ANTONIO. I am strongly armed to brook my overthrow;
  As commonly men bear with a hard year,
  I will not blame the cause on 't; but do think   195
  The necessity of my malevolent star
  Procures this, not her humor. Oh, the inconstant
  And rotten ground of service! You may see,
  'Tis even like him that in a winter night
  Takes a long slumber o'er a dying fire,   200
  As loth to part from 't; yet parts thence as cold
  As when he first sat down.
DUCHESS.   We do confiscate,
  Towards the satisfying of your accounts,
  All that you have.
ANTONIO.   I am yours, and 'tis very fit
  All mine should be so.
DUCHESS.   So, sir, you have your pass.[1]   205
ANTONIO. You may see, gentlemen, what 'tis to serve
  A prince with body and soul.   [*Exit.*]
BOSOLA. Here's an example for extortion: what moisture is drawn
  out of the sea, when foul weather comes, pours down, and runs
  into the sea again.   210
DUCHESS. I would know what are your opinions of this Antonio.
SECOND OFFICER. He could not abide to see a pig's head gaping: I
  thought your grace would find him a Jew.[2]
THIRD OFFICER. I would you had been his officer, for your own
  sake.   215
FOURTH OFFICER. You would have had more money.

7. Full sentences. "Enginous": delicately balanced, as in clockwork. The allusion to Tasso is literally accurate (*Gerusalemme liberata*, 2.22) but anachronistic, since Tasso's poem was not published till 1574.
8. Receipt.

9. Release him.
1. Passport, leave to depart.
2. Jews were identified by their antipathy to pork; but the assumptions here are deliberately ridiculous.

FIRST OFFICER. He stopped his ears with black wool, and to those came to him for money said he was thick of hearing.

SECOND OFFICER. Some said he was an hermaphrodite, for he could not abide a woman.   220

FOURTH OFFICER. How scurvy proud he would look when the treasury was full! Well, let him go!

FIRST OFFICER. Yes, and the chippings of the buttery fly after him, to scour his gold chain![3]

DUCHESS. Leave us. [*Exeunt* OFFICERS.] What do you think of these?   225

BOSOLA. That these are rogues that in 's prosperity, but to have waited on his fortune, could have wished his dirty stirrup riveted through their noses, and followed after 's mule, like a bear in a ring; would have prostituted their daughters to his lust; made their first-born intelligencers; thought none happy but such as   230 were born under his blessed planet, and wore his livery: and do these lice drop off now? Well, never look to have the like again:[4] he hath left a sort of flattering rogues behind him; their doom must follow. Princes pay flatterers in their own money: flatterers dissemble their vices, and they dissemble their lies; that's justice.   235 Alas, poor gentleman!

DUCHESS. Poor? He hath amply filled his coffers.

BOSOLA. Sure, he was too honest. Pluto, the god of riches, when he 's sent by Jupiter to any man, he goes limping, to signify that wealth that comes on God's name comes slowly; but when he's   240 sent on the devil's errand, he rides post and comes in by scuttles.[5] Let me show you what a most unvalued jewel you have in a wanton humor thrown away, to bless the man shall find him. He was an excellent courtier and most faithful; a soldier that thought it as beastly to know his own value too little as devilish   245 to acknowledge it too much. Both his virtue and form deserved a far better fortune: his discourse rather delighted to judge itself than show itself; his breast was filled with all perfection, and yet it seemed a private whispering-room, it made so little noise of 't.

DUCHESS. But he was basely descended.   250

BOSOLA. Will you make yourself a mercenary herald, rather to examine men's pedigrees than virtues? You shall want[6] him: for know, an honest statesman to a prince is like a cedar planted by a spring; the spring bathes the tree's root, the grateful tree rewards it with his shadow: you have not done so. I would sooner swim to   255 the Bermoothes[7] on two politicians' rotten bladders, tied together with an intelligencer's heartstring, than depend on so changeable a prince's favor. Fare thee well, Antonio! Since the malice of the world would needs down with thee, it cannot be said yet that any ill happened unto thee, considering thy fall was accompanied   260 with virtue.

DUCHESS. Oh, you render me excellent music!

BOSOLA.   Say you?

3. A gold chain was the steward's traditional badge
of office. Bread crumbs (the "chippings of the buttery") were used to polish gold and silver plate.
4. I.e., a servant as good as he was.
5. In haste. "Unvalued": invaluable.

6. Miss.
7. The Bermudas, unknown at the time of the
action, but very topical a hundred years later, when
the play was written.

DUCHESS. This good one that you speak of is my husband.
BOSOLA. Do I not dream? Can this ambitious age
   Have so much goodness in 't as to prefer   265
   A man merely for worth, without these shadows
   Of wealth and painted honors? Possible?
DUCHESS. I have had three children by him.
BOSOLA.   Fortunate lady!
   For you have made your private nuptial bed   270
   The humble and fair seminary of peace.
   No question but many an unbeneficed scholar[8]
   Shall pray for you for this deed, and rejoice
   That some preferment in the world can yet
   Arise from merit. The virgins of your land   275
   That have no dowries shall hope your example
   Will raise them to rich husbands. Should you want
   Soldiers, 'twould make the very Turks and Moors
   Turn Christians, and serve you for this act.
   Last, the neglected poets of your time,   280
   In honor of this trophy of a man,
   Raised by that curious engine, your white hand,
   Shall thank you, in your grave, for 't; and make that
   More reverend than all the cabinets[9]
   Of living princes. For Antonio,   285
   His fame shall likewise flow from many a pen,
   When heralds shall want coats to sell to men.
DUCHESS. As I taste comfort in this friendly speech,
   So would I find concealment.
BOSOLA. Oh, the secret of my prince,   290
   Which I will wear on th' inside of my heart!
DUCHESS. You shall take charge of all my coin and jewels,
   And follow him; for he retires himself
   To Ancona.
BOSOLA.   So.
DUCHESS.   Whither, within few days,
   I mean to follow thee.
BOSOLA.   Let me think: 295
   I would wish your grace to feign a pilgrimage
   To our Lady of Loreto,[1] scarce seven leagues
   From fair Ancona; so may you depart
   Your country with more honor, and your flight
   Will seem a princely progress, retaining   300
   Your usual train about you.
DUCHESS.   Sir, your direction
   Shall lead me by the hand.
CARIOLA.   In my opinion,
   She were better progress to the baths at Lucca,

---

8. A scholar without an official appointment.
9. Council-chambers. She will be more honored
in her grave than living princes in their courts.

1. The shrine of the Virgin at Loreto was famous
throughout Europe.

Or go visit the Spa in Germany;
For, if you will believe me, I do not like   305
This jesting with religion, this feigned
Pilgrimage.
DUCHESS.   Thou art a superstitious fool.
Prepare us instantly for our departure.
Past sorrows, let us moderately lament them;
For those to come, seek wisely to prevent them.   310

                          [*Exit* DUCHESS, *with* CARIOLA.]

BOSOLA. A politician is the devil's quilted anvil;
He fashions all sins on him, and the blows
Are never heard: he may work in a lady's chamber,
As here for proof. What rests but I reveal
All to my lord? Oh, this base quality   315
Of intelligencer! Why, every quality i' th' world
Prefers but gain or commendation:
Now for this act I am certain to be raised,
And men that paint weeds to the life are praised.

SCENE 3. *Rome.*

[*Enter* CARDINAL, FERDINAND, MALATESTE, PESCARA, SILVIO,
DELIO.]

CARDINAL. Must we turn soldier, then?
MALATESTE.   The Emperor,[2]
Hearing your worth that way, ere you attained
This reverend garment, joins you in commission
With the right fortunate soldier the Marquis of Pescara,
And the famous Lannoy.
CARDINAL.   He that had the honor   5
Of taking the French king prisoner?[3]
MALATESTE.   The same.
Here's a plot drawn for a new fortification
At Naples.   [*They talk apart.*]
FERDINAND. This great Count Malateste, I perceive,
Hath got employment?
DELIO.   No employment, my lord;   10
A marginal note in the muster-book, that he is
A voluntary lord.
FERDINAND.   He's no soldier?
DELIO. He has worn gunpowder in 's hollow tooth for the tooth-
    ache.[4]
SILVIO. He comes to the leaguer[5] with a full intent

2. The Spanish Emperor, Charles V. The transformation of the Cardinal to a soldier (which has
no consequence for the action of the play) recalls
Cesare Borgia, who was created a cardinal by his
father, Alexander VI, before he resigned the office
and became famous, or infamous, as a soldier.
3. Charles de Lannoy, Belgian by origin, did

indeed capture Francis I at Pavia, but only in 1525,
about two decades after the date of the play's supposed action.
4. Saltpeter was sometimes used against the toothache.
5. Gathering of the armies.

To eat fresh beef and garlic, means to stay   15
Till the scent be gone, and straight return to court.

DELIO. He hath read all the late service[6] as the city chronicle relates it, and keeps two painters going, only to express battles in model.

SILVIO. Then he'll fight by the book.

DELIO. By the almanac, I think, to choose good days and shun the   20
critical. That's his mistress' scarf.

SILVIO. Yes, he protests he would do much for that taffeta.

DELIO. I think he would run away from a battle, to save it from taking prisoner.

SILVIO. He is horribly afraid gunpowder will spoil the perfume on 't.

DELIO. I saw a Dutchman break his pate once for calling him pot-   26
gun;[7] he made his head have a bore in 't like a musket.

SILVIO. I would he had made a touchhole to 't. He is indeed a guarded sumpter-cloth,[8] only for the remove of the court.   30

[*Enter* BOSOLA *and speaks to* FERDINAND *and the* CARDINAL.]

PESCARA. Bosola arrived? What should be the business?
Some falling-out amongst the cardinals.
These factions amongst great men, they are like
Foxes; when their heads are divided,
They carry fire in their tails, and all the country   35
About them goes to wrack for 't.[9]

SILVIO.   What's that Bosola?

DELIO. I knew him in Padua—a fantastical scholar, like such who study to know how many knots were in Hercules' club, of what color Achilles' beard was, or whether Hector were not troubled with the toothache. He hath studied himself half blear-eyed to   40
know the true symmetry of Caesar's nose by a shoeing-horn; and this he did to gain the name of a speculative man.[1]

PESCARA. Mark Prince Ferdinand:
A very salamander lives in 's eye,
To mock the eager violence of fire.[2]   45

SILVIO. That Cardinal hath made more bad faces with his oppression than ever Michael Angelo[3] made good ones: he lifts up 's nose, like a foul porpoise before a storm.

PESCARA. The Lord Ferdinand laughs.

DELIO. Like a deadly cannon that lightens ere it smokes.   50

PESCARA. These are your true pangs of death,
The pangs of life, that struggle with great statesmen.

DELIO. In such a deformed silence witches whisper
Their charms.

CARDINAL. Doth she make religion her riding-hood   55

---

6. Recent military operations.
7. Loudmouth.
8. Decorated saddle-cloth; i.e., a mere formality. "Touchhole": where the match was applied to set off a cannon.
9. Samson once tied some foxes together by the tail and set them afire to burn down the cornfields of the Philistines (Judges 15).

1. Scholarship was a traditional cause of melancholy, especially when exercised on impossible, useless questions like these.
2. The salamander, or water lizard, was supposed to be so cold and wet of constitution that it could live in fire; Ferdinand is cold in his rage.
3. Michelangelo Buonarroti, the great Florentine painter and sculptor, another anachronism.

To keep her from the sun and tempest?

FERDINAND.   That,
That damns her. Methinks her fault and beauty,
Blended together, show like leprosy,
The whiter, the fouler. I make it a question
Whether her beggarly brats were ever christened.   60

CARDINAL. I will instantly solicit the state of Ancona
To have them banished.

FERDINAND.   You are for Loreto?
I shall not be at your ceremony; fare you well.
Write to the Duke of Malfi, my young nephew
She had by her first husband, and acquaint him   65
With 's mother's honesty.

BOSOLA.   I will.

FERDINAND.   Antonio!
A slave that only smelled of ink and counters,
And never in 's life looked like a gentleman,
But in the audit-time. Go, go presently,[4]
Draw me out an hundred and fifty of our horse,   70
And meet me at the fort-bridge.   [*Exeunt.*]

SCENE 4. *The Shrine of Our Lady of Loreto.*

[*Enter* TWO PILGRIMS.]

FIRST PILGRIM. I have not seen a goodlier shrine than this;
Yet I have visited many.

SECOND PILGRIM.   The Cardinal of Aragon
Is this day to resign his cardinal's hat:
His sister duchess likewise is arrived
To pay her vow of pilgrimage. I expect   5
A noble ceremony.

FIRST PILGRIM. No question. They come.

[*Here the ceremony of the* CARDINAL'*s installment in the habit
of a soldier: performed in delivering up his cross, hat, robes,
and ring at the shrine, and investing him with sword, helmet, shield, and spurs; then* ANTONIO, *the* DUCHESS, *and
their children, having presented themselves at the shrine, are,
by a form of banishment in dumb-show expressed towards
them by the* CARDINAL *and the state of Ancona, banished:
during all which ceremony, this ditty is sung, to very solemn
music, by divers churchmen.*]

Arms and honors deck thy story,
To thy fame's eternal glory!
Adverse fortune ever fly thee;   10
No disastrous fate come nigh thee!

I alone will sing thy praises,
Whom to honor virtue raises;

4. At once.

And thy study, that divine is,
Bent to martial discipline is.   15
Lay aside all those robes lie by thee;
Crown thy arts with arms, they'll beautify thee.

O worthy of worthiest name, adorned in this manner,
Lead bravely thy forces on under war's warlike banner!
Oh, mayst thou prove fortunate in all martial courses!   20
Guide thou still by skill in arts and forces!
Victory attend thee nigh, whilst fame sings loud thy powers;
Triumphant conquest crown thy head, and blessings pour
     down showers![5]   [*Exeunt all except the* TWO PILGRIMS.]

FIRST PILGRIM. Here's a strange turn of state! Who would have
     thought
So great a lady would have matched herself   25
Unto so mean a person? Yet the Cardinal
Bears himself much too cruel.
SECOND PILGRIM.   They are banished.
FIRST PILGRIM. But I would ask what power hath this state
     Of Ancona to determine of a free prince?
SECOND PILGRIM. They are a free state, sir, and her brother
     showed   30
How that the Pope, fore-hearing of her looseness,
Hath seized into the protection of the Church
The dukedom which she held as dowager.[6]
FIRST PILGRIM. But by what justice?
SECOND PILGRIM.   Sure, I think by none,
Only her brother's instigation.   35
FIRST PILGRIM. What was it with such violence he took
     Off from her finger?
SECOND PILGRIM.   'Twas her wedding ring,
Which he vowed shortly he would sacrifice
To his revenge.
FIRST PILGRIM.   Alas, Antonio!
If that a man be thrust into a well,   40
No matter who sets hands to 't, his own weight
Will bring him sooner to th' bottom. Come, let's hence.
Fortune makes this conclusion general,
All things do help th' unhappy man to fall.   [*Exeunt.*]

SCENE 5. *Near Loreto.*

[*Enter* DUCHESS, ANTONIO, CHILDREN, CARIOLA, *and* SERVANTS.]

DUCHESS. Banished Ancona!
ANTONIO.   Yes, you see what power
     Lightens in great men's breath.
DUCHESS.   Is all our train
     Shrunk to this poor remainder?

---

5. This song is not very suitable to the scene, and
Webster, in the edition of 1623, denied writing it.

6. The Duchess held Malfi only as guardian for
her son, the still youthful Duke.

ANTONIO.   These poor men,
   Which have got little in your service, vow
   To take your fortune, but your wiser buntings,[7]   5
   Now they are fledged, are gone.
DUCHESS.   They have done wisely.
   This puts me in mind of death: physicians thus,
   With their hands full of money, use to give o'er
   Their patients.
ANTONIO.   Right[8] the fashion of the world:
   From decayed fortunes every flatterer shrinks;   10
   Men cease to build where the foundation sinks.
DUCHESS. I had a very strange dream tonight.
ANTONIO.   What was 't?
DUCHESS. Methought I wore my coronet of state,
   And on a sudden all the diamonds
   Were changed to pearls.
ANTONIO.   My interpretation   15
   Is, you'll weep shortly, for to me the pearls
   Do signify your tears.
DUCHESS.   The birds that live
   I' th' field on the wild benefit of nature
   Live happier than we; for they may choose their mates,
   And carol their sweet pleasures to the spring.   20

    [*Enter* BOSOLA *with a letter.*]

BOSOLA. You are happily o'erta'en.
DUCHESS.   From my brother?
BOSOLA. Yes, from the Lord Ferdinand your brother
   All love and safety.
DUCHESS.   Thou dost blanch[9] mischief,
   Wouldst make it white. See, see, like to calm weather
   At sea before a tempest, false hearts speak fair   25
   To those they intend most mischief.   [*Reads.*]
   "Send Antonio to me; I want his head in a business."
   A politic equivocation!
   He doth not want your counsel, but your head;
   That is, he cannot sleep till you be dead.   30
   And here's another pitfall that's strewed o'er
   With roses: mark it, 'tis a cunning one:
   "I stand engaged for your husband for several debts at Naples:
   let not that trouble him; I had rather have his heart than his
   money."
   And I believe so too.
BOSOLA.   What do you believe?
DUCHESS. That he so much distrusts my husband's love,
   He will by no means believe his heart is with him
   Until he see it: the devil is not cunning

---

7. Migratory birds. "Take": accept.   9. Whitewash, cover up.
8. Exactly.

Enough to circumvent us in riddles.   40

BOSOLA. Will you reject that noble and free league
   Of amity and love which I present you?

DUCHESS. Their league is like that of some politic kings,
   Only to make themselves of strength and power
   To be our after-ruin: tell them so.   45

BOSOLA. And what from you?

ANTONIO.   Thus tell him: I will not come.

BOSOLA. And what of this?   [*Pointing to the letter.*]

ANTONIO.   My brothers have dispersed
   Bloodhounds abroad; which till I hear are muzzled,
   No truce, though hatched with ne'er such politic skill,
   Is safe, that hangs upon our enemies' will.   50
   I'll not come at them.

BOSOLA.   This proclaims your breeding:
   Every small thing draws a base mind to fear,
   As the adamant[1] draws iron. Fare you well, sir;
   You shall shortly hear from 's.   [*Exit.*]

DUCHESS.   I suspect some ambush;
   Therefore, by all my love I do conjure you   55
   To take your eldest son, and fly towards Milan.
   Let us not venture all this poor remainder
   In one unlucky bottom.[2]

ANTONIO.   You counsel safely.
   Best of my life, farewell. Since we must part,
   Heaven hath a hand in 't, but no otherwise   60
   Than as some curious artist[3] takes in sunder
   A clock or watch, when it is out of frame,
   To bring 't in better order.

DUCHESS. I know not which is best,
   To see you dead, or part with you: farewell, boy.   65
   Thou art happy that thou hast not understanding
   To know thy misery; for all our wit
   And reading brings us to a truer sense
   Of sorrow. In the eternal church, sir,
   I do hope we shall not part thus.

ANTONIO.   Oh, be of comfort!   70
   Make patience a noble fortitude,
   And think not how unkindly we are used:
   Man, like to cassia, is proved best being bruised.[4]

DUCHESS. Must I, like to a slave-born Russian,
   Account it praise to suffer tyranny?   75
   And yet, O heaven, thy heavy hand is in 't!
   I have seen my little boy oft scourge his top,[5]
   And compared myself to 't: naught made me e'er

1. Loadstone.
2. The metaphor is mercantile; let's not load all
our cargo in one ship ("bottom").
3. Clever craftsman. "Out of frame": not working.

4. Man, like cinnamon bark, is most aromatic
(virtuous) when pressed (oppressed).
5. Children used to make tops spin by whipping
them.

Go right but heaven's scourge-stick.

ANTONIO.   Do not weep:
Heaven fashioned us of nothing, and we strive   80
To bring ourselves to nothing. Farewell, Cariola,
And thy sweet armful. If I do never see thee more,
Be a good mother to your little ones,
And save them from the tiger. Fare you well.

DUCHESS. Let me look upon you once more, for that speech   85
Came from a dying father. Your kiss is colder
Than that I have seen an holy anchorite
Give to a dead man's skull.

ANTONIO. My heart is turned to a heavy lump of lead,
With which I sound my danger. Fare you well.   90

                        [*Exeunt* ANTONIO *and his son.*]

DUCHESS. My laurel is all withered.

CARIOLA. Look, madam, what a troop of armèd men
Make toward us.

DUCHESS.   Oh, they are very welcome:
When Fortune's wheel[6] is over-charged with princes,
The weight makes it move swift: I would have my ruin   95
Be sudden.

          [*Enter* BOSOLA *vizarded,*[7] *with a guard.*]

                    I am your adventure,[8] am I not?

BOSOLA. You are. You must see your husband no more.

DUCHESS. What devil art thou that counterfeits heaven's thunder?

BOSOLA. Is that terrible? I would have you tell me whether
Is that note worse that frights the silly birds   100
Out of the corn, or that which doth allure them
To the nets? You have hearkened to the last too much.

DUCHESS. Oh, misery! Like to a rusty o'erchargèd cannon,
Shall I never fly in pieces?—Come, to what prison?

BOSOLA. To none.

DUCHESS.   Whither, then?

BOSOLA.   To your palace.

DUCHESS.   I have heard   105
That Charon's boat serves to convey all o'er[9]
The dismal lake, but brings none back again.

BOSOLA. Your brothers mean you safety and pity.

DUCHESS.   Pity!
With such a pity men preserve alive
Pheasants and quails, when they are not fat enough   110
To be eaten.

BOSOLA. These are your children?

DUCHESS.   Yes.

BOSOLA.   Can they prattle?

---

6. The wheel of fortune is an ancient emblem of
mutability; men have their fixed positions on it,
and rise or fall as it turns.

7. I.e., wearing a mask.

8. I.e., I am what you're looking for, am I not?

9. In classical mythology, Charon transports the
souls of the dead across the river Styx to Hades.

DUCHESS.   No.
    But I intend, since they were born accursed,
    Curses shall be their first language.
BOSOLA.   Fie, madam!
    Forget this base, low fellow—
DUCHESS.   Were I a man,   115
    I'd beat that counterfeit face into thy other.[1]
BOSOLA. One of no birth.[2]
DUCHESS.   Say that he was born mean,
    Man is most happy when 's own actions
    Be arguments and examples of his virtue.
BOSOLA. A barren, beggarly virtue!   120
DUCHESS. I prithee, who is greatest? Can you tell?
    Sad tales befit my woe: I'll tell you one.
    A salmon, as she swam unto the sea,
    Met with a dog-fish, who encounters her
    With this rough language: "Why art thou so bold   125
    To mix thyself with our high state of floods,
    Being no eminent courtier, but one
    That for the calmest and fresh time o' th' year
    Dost live in shallow rivers, rank'st thyself
    With silly smelts and shrimps? And darest thou   130
    Pass by our dog-ship without reverence?"
    "Oh!" quoth the salmon, "sister, be at peace:
    Thank Jupiter we both have passed the net!
    Our value never can be truly known,
    Till in the fisher's basket we be shown: 135
    I' th' market then my price may be the higher,
    Even when I am nearest to the cook and fire."
    So to great men the moral may be stretchèd;
    Men oft are valued high, when they're most wretched.
    But come, whither you please. I am armed 'gainst misery;   140
    Bent to all sways of the oppressor's will:
    There's no deep valley but near some great hill.   [*Exeunt.*]

Act 4

SCENE 1. *Amalfi.*

[*Enter* FERDINAND *and* BOSOLA.]

FERDINAND. How doth our sister duchess bear herself
    In her imprisonment?
BOSOLA.   Nobly. I'll describe her.
    She's sad as one long used to 't, and she seems
    Rather to welcome the end of misery
    Than shun it; a behavior so noble   5
    As gives a majesty to adversity:
    You may discern the shape of loveliness
    More perfect in her tears than in her smiles;

---

1. I.e., I'd push your mask down your throat.
2. Of low rank by birth.

She will muse four hours together; and her silence,
Methinks, expresseth more than if she spake.   10
FERDINAND. Her melancholy seems to be fortified
  With a strange disdain.
BOSOLA.   'Tis so; and this restraint,
  Like English mastiffs that grow fierce with tying,
  Makes her too passionately apprehend
  Those pleasures she's kept from.
FERDINAND.   Curse upon her!   15
  I will no longer study in the book
  Of another's heart. Inform her what I told you.   [*Exit.*]

          [*Enter* DUCHESS.]

BOSOLA. All comfort to your grace!
DUCHESS.   I will have none.
  Pray thee, why dost thou wrap thy poisoned pills
  In gold and sugar?   20
BOSOLA. Your elder brother, the Lord Ferdinand,
  Is come to visit you, and sends you word,
  'Cause once he rashly made a solemn vow
  Never to see you more, he comes i' th' night,
  And prays you gently neither torch nor taper   25
  Shine in your chamber. He will kiss your hand
  And reconcile himself, but for his vow
  He dares not see you.
DUCHESS.   At his pleasure.
  Take hence the lights: he's come.

          [*Enter* FERDINAND.]

FERDINAND. Where are you?
DUCHESS.   Here, sir.   30
FERDINAND. This darkness suits you well.
DUCHESS. I would ask your pardon.
FERDINAND.   You have it;
  For I account it the honorabl'st revenge,
  Where I may kill, to pardon. Where are your cubs?
DUCHESS. Whom?
FERDINAND.   Call them your children;   35
  For though our national law distinguish bastards
  From true legitimate issue, compassionate nature
  Makes them all equal.
DUCHESS.   Do you visit me for this?
  You violate a sacrament o' th' Church
  Shall make you howl in hell for 't.
FERDINAND.   It had been well   40
  Could you have lived thus always; for, indeed,
  You were too much i' th' light—but no more—
  I come to seal my peace with you. Here's a hand

                          [*Gives her a dead man's hand.*]

To which you have vowed much love; the ring upon 't
You gave.   45
DUCHESS. I affectionately kiss it.
FERDINAND. Pray, do, and bury the print of it in your heart.
  I will leave this ring with you for a love-token,
  And the hand as sure as the ring; and do not doubt
  But you shall have the heart, too. When you need a friend,   50
  Send it to him that owed[3] it; you shall see
  Whether he can aid you.
DUCHESS.   You are very cold;
  I fear you are not well after your travel.
  Ha! Lights! Oh, horrible!
FERDINAND.   Let her have lights enough.   [Exit.]
DUCHESS. What witchcraft doth he practice, that he hath left   55
  A dead man's hand here?

> [Here is discovered, behind a traverse,[4] the artificial figures of
> Antonio and his children, appearing as if they were dead.]

BOSOLA. Look you, here's the piece from which 'twas ta'en.
  He doth present you this sad spectacle,
  That, now you know directly they are dead,
  Hereafter you may wisely cease to grieve   60
  For that which cannot be recovered.
DUCHESS. There is not between heaven and earth one wish
  I stay for after this: it wastes[5] me more
  Than were 't my picture, fashioned out of wax,
  Stuck with a magical needle, and then buried   65
  In some foul dunghill; and yond's an excellent property[6]
  For a tyrant, which I would account mercy.
BOSOLA.   What's that?
DUCHESS. If they would bind me to that lifeless trunk
  And let me freeze to death.
BOSOLA.   Come, you must live.
DUCHESS. That's the greatest torture souls feel in hell,   70
  In hell: that they must live, and cannot die.
  Portia,[7] I'll new-kindle thy coals again,
  And revive the rare and almost dead example
  Of a loving wife.
BOSOLA.   Oh, fie! Despair? Remember
  You are a Christian.
DUCHESS.   The Church enjoins fasting: 75
  I'll starve myself to death.
BOSOLA.   Leave this vain sorrow.
  Things being at the worst begin to mend: the bee

3. Owned.
4. A screen or curtain, through which the Duchess can see, without being tempted to examine or touch, the bodies of her family.
5. Consumes, as by secret disease; witches were supposed to be able to "waste" their enemies by

making wax images and tormenting them as indicated below.
6. There's an excellent scheme.
7. Portia, the wife of Brutus, committed suicide by swallowing hot coals.

When he hath shot his sting into your hand, may then
Play with your eyelid.
DUCHESS.   Good comfortable fellow,
  Persuade a wretch that's broke upon the wheel   80
  To have all his bones new set; entreat him live
  To be executed again. Who must dispatch me?
  I account this world a tedious theater,
  For I do play a part in 't 'gainst my will.
BOSOLA. Come, be of comfort; I will save your life.
DUCHESS.   Indeed,   85
  I have not leisure to tend so small a business.
BOSOLA. Now, by my life, I pity you.
DUCHESS.   Thou art a fool, then,
  To waste thy pity on a thing so wretched
  As cannot pity itself. I am full of daggers.
  Puff, let me blow these vipers from me.   90

      [*Enter* SERVANT.]

  What are you?
SERVANT.   One that wishes you long life.
DUCHESS. I would thou wert hanged for the horrible curse
  Thou hast given me. I shall shortly grow one
  Of the miracles of pity. I'll go pray—
  No, I'll go curse.
BOSOLA.   Oh, fie!
DUCHESS.   I could curse the stars—   95
BOSOLA. Oh, fearful!
DUCHESS. And those three smiling seasons of the year
  Into a Russian winter, nay, the world
  To its first chaos.[8]
BOSOLA.   Look you, the stars shine still.
DUCHESS. Oh, but you must   100
  Remember, my curse hath a great way to go.
  Plagues, that make lanes through largest families,
  Consume them!
BOSOLA.   Fie, lady!
DUCHESS.   Let them, like tyrants,
  Never be remembered but for the ill they have done;
  Let all the zealous prayers of mortified   105
  Churchmen forget them!
BOSOLA.   Oh, uncharitable!
DUCHESS. Let Heaven a little while cease crowning martyrs
  To punish them!
  Go, howl them this, and say, I long to bleed:
  It is some mercy when men kill with speed.   110

                        [*Exeunt* DUCHESS *and* SERVANT.]

    [*Re-enter* FERDINAND.]

8. A Russian winter would last all year long.

FERDINAND. Excellent, as I would wish; she's plagued in art:
    These presentations are but framed in wax
    By the curious master in that quality,
    Vincentio Lauriola,[9] and she takes them
    For true substantial bodies.
BOSOLA.   Why do you do this?   115
FERDINAND. To bring her to despair.
BOSOLA.   'Faith, end here,
    And go no farther in your cruelty.
    Send her a penitential garment to put on
    Next to her delicate skin, and furnish her
    With beads and prayer-books.
FERDINAND.   Damn her! That body of hers,   120
    While that my blood ran pure in 't, was more worth
    Than that which thou wouldst comfort, called a soul.
    I will send her masks of common courtesans,
    Have her meat served up by bawds and ruffians,
    And, 'cause she'll needs be mad, I am resolved   125
    To remove forth the common hospital
    All the mad-folk, and place them near her lodging;
    There let them practice together, sing and dance,
    And act their gambols to the full o' th' moon:
    If she can sleep the better for it, let her.   130
    Your work is almost ended.
BOSOLA. Must I see her again?
FERDINAND.   Yes.
BOSOLA.   Never.
FERDINAND.   You must.
BOSOLA. Never in mine own shape;
    That's forfeited by my intelligence[1]
    And this last cruel lie. When you send me next,   135
    The business shall be comfort.
FERDINAND.   Very likely.
    Thy pity is nothing of kin to thee.[2] Antonio
    Lurks about Milan: thou shalt shortly thither
    To feed a fire as great as my revenge,
    Which ne'er will slack till it have spent his fuel.   140
    Intemperate agues make physicians cruel.   [*Exeunt.*]

SCENE 2

[*Enter* DUCHESS *and* CARIOLA.]

DUCHESS. What hideous noise was that?
CARIOLA.   'Tis the wild consort
    Of madmen, lady, which your tyrant brother
    Hath placed about your lodging. This tyranny,
    I think, was never practiced till this hour.

9. The art of wax modeling was common enough, but the name of the artist seems to be imaginary.
1. I.e., I can't do that because she knows now I've played the spy on her.
2. I.e., pity doesn't suit you very well.

DUCHESS. Indeed, I thank him. Nothing but noise and folly   5
    Can keep me in my right wits, whereas reason
    And silence make me stark mad. Sit down;
    Discourse to me some dismal tragedy.
CARIOLA. Oh, 'twill increase your melancholy.
DUCHESS.   Thou art deceived:
    To hear of greater grief would lessen mine.   10
    This is a prison?
CARIOLA.   Yes, but you shall live
    To shake this durance off.
DUCHESS.   Thou art a fool:
    The robin-redbreast and the nightingale
    Never live long in cages.
CARIOLA.   Pray, dry your eyes.
    What think you of, madam?
DUCHESS.   Of nothing: 15
    When I muse thus, I sleep.
CARIOLA. Like a madman, with your eyes open?
DUCHESS. Dost thou think we shall know one another in th' other
    world?
CARIOLA. Yes, out of question.
DUCHESS.   Oh that it were possible we might   20
    But hold some two days' conference with the dead!
    From them I should learn somewhat, I am sure,
    I never shall know here. I'll tell thee a miracle;
    I am not mad yet, to my cause of sorrow:
    Th' heaven o'er my head seems made of molten brass,   25
    The earth of flaming sulphur, yet I am not mad.
    I am acquainted with sad misery
    As the tanned galley-slave is with his oar;
    Necessity makes me suffer constantly,
    And custom makes it easy. Who do I look like now?   30
CARIOLA. Like to your picture in the gallery,
    A deal of life in show, but none in practice;
    Or rather like some reverend monument
    Whose ruins are even pitied.
DUCHESS.   Very proper.
    And Fortune seems only to have her eyesight   35
    To behold my tragedy.
    How now! What noise is that?

        [*Enter* SERVANT.]

SERVANT.   I am come to tell you
    Your brother hath intended you some sport.
    A great physician, when the Pope was sick
    Of a deep melancholy, presented him   40
    With several sorts of madmen, which wild object
    Being full of change and sport, forced him to laugh,
    And so the imposthume[3] broke. The self-same cure
    The duke intends on you.

3. Abscess.

DUCHESS.   Let them come in.
SERVANT. There's a mad lawyer; and a secular priest;   45
  A doctor that hath forfeited his wits
  By jealousy; an astrologian
  That in his works said such a day o' the' month
  Should be the day of doom, and, failing of 't,
  Ran mad; an English tailor crazed i' th' brain   50
  With the study of new fashions; a gentleman-usher[4]
  Quite beside himself with care to keep in mind
  The number of his lady's salutations
  Or "How do you's" she employed him in each morning;
  A farmer, too, an excellent knave in grain,   55
  Mad 'cause he was hindered transportation:
  And let one broker that's mad loose to these,
  You'd think the devil were among them.[5]
DUCHESS. Sit, Cariola. Let them loose when you please,
  For I am chained to endure all your tyranny.   60

[*Enter* MADMEN.]
[*Here by a* MADMAN *this Song is sung to a dismal kind of music.*]

    Oh, let us howl some heavy note,
      Some deadly dogged howl,
    Sounding as from the threatening throat
      Of beasts and fatal fowl!
    As ravens, screech-owls, bulls, and bears,   65
      We'll bell and bawl our parts,
    Till irksome noise have cloyed your ears
      And corrosived your hearts.
    At last, whenas our choir wants breath,
      Our bodies being blest,   70
    We'll sing, like swans, to welcome death,
      And die in love and rest.

FIRST MADMAN. Doomsday not come yet? I'll draw it nearer by a
  perspective,[6] or make a glass that shall set all the world on fire
  upon an instant. I cannot sleep; my pillow is stuffed with a litter   75
  of porcupines.
SECOND MADMAN. Hell is a mere glass-house, where the devils are
  continually blowing up women's souls on hollow irons, and the
  fire never goes out.
THIRD MADMAN. I will lie with every woman in my parish the tenth   80
  night; I will tithe them over like haycocks.
FOURTH MADMAN. Shall my pothecary outgo me because I am a
  cuckold? I have found out his roguery; he makes alum of his
  wife's urine, and sells it to puritans that have sore throats with
  overstraining.   85
FIRST MADMAN. I have skill in heraldry.
SECOND MADMAN. Hast?

4. Doorkeeper.
5. All the madmen have lost their wits in the pursuit of their trades; set among them a broker, who
might get them back to work again, and they'll be
madder than ever.
6. Telescope.

FIRST MADMAN. You do give for your crest a woodcock's head with the brains picked out on 't; you are a very ancient gentleman.

THIRD MADMAN. Greek is turned Turk: we are only to be saved by the Helvetian translation.[7]   90

FIRST MADMAN. Come on, sir, I will lay the law to you.

SECOND MADMAN. Oh, rather lay a corrosive: the law will eat to the bone.

THIRD MADMAN. He that drinks but to satisfy nature is damned.   95

FOURTH MADMAN. If I had my glass[8] here, I would show a sight should make all the women here call me mad doctor.

FIRST MADMAN. What's he? A rope-maker?

SECOND MADMAN. No, no, no, a snuffling knave that, while he shows the tombs, will have his hand in a wench's placket.[9]   100

THIRD MADMAN. Woe to the caroche that brought home my wife from the masque at three o'clock in the morning! It had a large featherbed in it.

FOURTH MADMAN. I have pared the devil's nails forty times, roasted them in raven's eggs, and cured agues with them.   105

THIRD MADMAN. Get me three hundred milchbats, to make possets to procure sleep.[1]

FOURTH MADMAN. All the college may throw their caps at me: I have made a soap boiler costive; it was my masterpiece.

> [*Here the dance, consisting of eight* MADMEN, *with music answerable thereunto; after which* BOSOLA, *like an old man, enters.*]

DUCHESS. Is he mad too?

SERVANT.   Pray, question him. I'll leave you.   110

> [*Exeunt* SERVANT *and* MADMEN.]

BOSOLA. I am come to make thy tomb.

DUCHESS.   Ha! My tomb?
Thou speak'st as if I lay upon my deathbed,
Gasping for breath. Dost thou perceive me sick?

BOSOLA. Yes, and the more dangerously, since thy sickness is insen-   115
sible.[2]

DUCHESS. Thou art not mad, sure. Dost know me?

BOSOLA. Yes.

DUCHESS.   Who am I?

BOSOLA. Thou art a box of worm-seed, at best but a salvatory of green mummy.[3] What's this flesh? A little crudded milk, fantastical puff-paste. Our bodies are weaker than those paper-prisons   120
boys use to keep flies in, more contemptible, since ours is to preserve earthworms. Didst thou ever see a lark in a cage? Such is the soul in the body: this world is like her little turf of grass,

---

7. The Geneva Bible; but how it would help with the Greeks and Turks is clear only to the lunatic.
8. Looking glass.
9. Slit in a skirt. "Caroche": carriage.
1. It is a mad idea indeed that toddies ("possets") made of bat's milk would put people to sleep.
2. Imperceptible.

3. "Worm-seed" is a matter whose ultimate end is the generation of worms. "A salvatory of green mummy": the substance of mummified bodies was considered medicinal. The living body is a box ("salvatory") of such medicine, only not yet ready for use. "Crudded": curdled.

and the heaven o'er our heads, like her looking-glass, only gives
us a miserable knowledge of the small compass of our prison.   125
DUCHESS. Am not I thy duchess?
BOSOLA. Thou art some great woman, sure, for riot[4] begins to sit on
thy forehead, clad in gray hairs, twenty years sooner than on a
merry milkmaid's. Thou sleep'st worse than if a mouse should
be forced to take up her lodging in a cat's ear: a little infant that   130
breeds its teeth,[5] should it lie with thee, would cry out, as if thou
wert the more unquiet bedfellow.
DUCHESS. I am Duchess of Malfi still.
BOSOLA. That makes thy sleep so broken:
 Glories, like glow-worms, afar off shine bright,   135
 But, looked to near, have neither heat nor light.
DUCHESS. Thou art very plain.
BOSOLA. My trade is to flatter the dead, not the living; I am a
tomb-maker.
DUCHESS. And thou com'st to make my tomb?   140
BOSOLA. Yes.
DUCHESS. Let me be a little merry. Of what stuff wilt thou make
it?
BOSOLA. Nay, resolve me first, of what fashion?
DUCHESS. Why, do we grow fantastical in our deathbed? Do we   145
affect fashion in the grave?
BOSOLA. Most ambitiously. Princes' images on their tombs do not
lie, as they were wont, seeming to pray up to heaven, but with
their hands under their cheeks, as if they died of the toothache.
They are not carved with their eyes fixed upon the stars, but as   150
their minds were wholly bent upon the world, the self-same way
they seem to turn their faces.
DUCHESS. Let me know fully therefore the effect
 Of this thy dismal preparation,
 This talk fit for a charnel.
BOSOLA.   Now I shall.   155

  [*Enter* EXECUTIONERS, *with a coffin, cords, and a bell.*]

Here is a present from your princely brothers;
And may it arrive welcome, for it brings
Last benefit, last sorrow.
DUCHESS.   Let me see it:
 I have so much obedience in my blood,
 I wish it in their veins to do them good.   160
BOSOLA. This is your last presence-chamber.[6]
CARIOLA. O my sweet lady!
DUCHESS.   Peace, it affrights not me.
BOSOLA. I am the common bellman,
 That usually is sent to condemned persons
 The night before they suffer.
DUCHESS.   Even now thou said'st   165

4. Debauchery.   6. A noble person's reception room.
5. A teething infant.

Thou wast a tomb-maker.
BOSOLA.   'Twas to bring you
  By degrees to mortification.[7] Listen.

                                        [*Rings the bell.*]

              Hark, now every thing is still
              The screech-owl and the whistler[8] shrill
              Call upon our dame aloud,   170
              And bid her quickly don her shroud!
              Much you had of land and rent:
              Your length in clay's now competent.[9]
              A long war disturbed your mind:
              Here your perfect peace is signed.   175
              Of what is 't fools make such vain keeping?
              Sin their conception, their birth weeping,
              Their life a general mist of error,
              Their death a hideous storm of terror.
              Strew your hair with powders sweet,   180
              Don clean linen, bathe your feet,
              And (the foul fiend more to check)
              A crucifix let bless your neck:
              'Tis now full tide 'tween night and day;
              End your groan, and come away.   185

CARIOLA. Hence, villains, tyrants, murderers! Alas!
  What will you do with my lady? Call for help.
DUCHESS. To whom? To our next neighbors? They are mad-folks.
BOSOLA. Remove that noise.
DUCHESS.   Farewell, Cariola.
  In my last will I have not much to give: 190
  A many hungry guests have fed upon me;
  Thine will be a poor reversion.
CARIOLA.   I will die with her.
DUCHESS. I pray thee, look thou giv'st my little boy
  Some syrup for his cold, and let the girl
  Say her prayers ere she sleep.   195

            [CARIOLA *is forced out by the* EXECUTIONERS.]

                          Now what you please.
  What death?
BOSOLA.   Strangling: here are your executioners.
DUCHESS. I forgive them:
  The apoplexy, catarrh, or cough o' th' lungs
  Would do as much as they do.
BOSOLA. Doth not death fright you?
DUCHESS.   Who would be afraid on 't,   200
  Knowing to meet such excellent company
  In th' other world?

7. Repentance, also death and decomposition.   9. Sufficient.
8. A bird premonitory of death.

BOSOLA.   Yet, methinks,
The manner of your death should much afflict you:
This cord should terrify you.
DUCHESS.   Not a whit.
What would it pleasure me to have my throat cut   205
With diamonds? Or to be smothered
With cassia?[1] Or to be shot to death with pearls?
I know death hath ten thousand several doors
For men to take their exits, and 'tis found
They go on such strange geometrical hinges,   210
You may open them both ways.—Any way, for heaven sake,
So I were out of your whispering. Tell my brothers
That I perceive death, now I am well awake,
Best gift is they can give or I can take.
I would fain put off my last woman's fault,   215
I'd not be tedious to you.
EXECUTIONER.   We are ready.
DUCHESS. Dispose my breath how please you, but my body
Bestow upon my women, will you?
EXECUTIONER.   Yes.
DUCHESS. Pull, and pull strongly, for your able strength
Must pull down heaven upon me—   220
Yet stay; heaven-gates are not so high arched
As princes' palaces; they that enter there
Must go upon their knees. [*Kneels.*] Come, violent death.
Serve for mandragora[2] to make me sleep!
Go tell my brothers, when I am laid out,   225
They then may feed in quiet.   [*They strangle her.*]
BOSOLA. Where's the waiting woman?
Fetch her. Some other strangle the children.

[*Exeunt* EXECUTIONERS, *some of whom return with* CARIOLA.]

Look you, there sleeps your mistress.
CARIOLA.   Oh, you are damned
Perpetually for this! My turn is next.   230
Is 't not so ordered?
BOSOLA.   Yes, and I am glad
You are so well prepared for 't.
CARIOLA.   You are deceived, sir,
I am not prepared for 't, I will not die;
I will first come to my answer, and know
How I have offended.
BOSOLA.   Come, dispatch her.   235
You kept her counsel; now you shall keep ours.
CARIOLA. I will not die, I must not; I am contracted
To a young gentleman.
EXECUTIONER.   Here's your wedding ring.
CARIOLA. Let me but speak with the Duke; I'll discover
Treason to his person.

1. Cinnamon.
2. The word is used loosely for a stupefying drug.

BOSOLA.   Delays! Throttle her.   240
EXECUTIONER. She bites and scratches.
CARIOLA.   If you kill me now,
   I am damned; I have not been at confession
   This two years.
BOSOLA. [to EXECUTIONERS] When!
CARIOLA.   I am quick with child.
BOSOLA.   Why, then,
   Your credit's saved.[3]   [They strangle CARIOLA.]
          Bear her into th' next room;
   Let this lie still.

      [Exeunt the EXECUTIONERS with the body of CARIOLA.]
      [Enter FERDINAND.]

FERDINAND.   Is she dead?
BOSOLA.   She is what   245
   You'd have her. But here begin your pity.

                  [Shows the children strangled.]

   Alas, how have these offended?
FERDINAND.   The death
   Of young wolves is never to be pitied.
BOSOLA.   Fix
   Your eye here.
FERDINAND.   Constantly.
BOSOLA.   Do you not weep?
   Other sins only speak; murder shrieks out: 250
   The element of water moistens the earth,
   But blood flies upwards and bedews the heavens.
FERDINAND. Cover her face; mine eyes dazzle: she died young.
BOSOLA. I think not so; her infelicity
   Seemed to have years too many.
FERDINAND.   She and I were twins;   255
   And should I die this instant, I had lived
   Her time to a minute.
BOSOLA.   It seems she was born first:
   You have bloodily approved[4] the ancient truth,
   That kindred commonly do worse agree
   Than remote strangers.
FERDINAND.   Let me see her face again.   260
   Why didst not thou pity her? What an excellent
   Honest man mightst thou have been,
   If thou hadst borne her to some sanctuary!
   Or, bold in a good cause, opposed thyself,
   With thy advancèd sword above thy head,   265
   Between her innocence and my revenge!
   I bade thee, when I was distracted of my wits,
   Go kill my dearest friend, and thou hast done 't.
   For let me but examine well the cause:

3. Your reputation will now be safe.
4. Given proof of.

What was the meanness of her match to me?   270
Only I must confess I had a hope,
Had she continued widow, to have gained
An infinite mass of treasure by her death:
And that was the main cause, her marriage,
That drew a stream of gall quite through my heart.   275
For thee, as we observe in tragedies
That a good actor many times is cursed
For playing a villain's part, I hate thee for 't,
And, for my sake, say thou hast done much ill well.

BOSOLA. Let me quicken your memory, for I perceive   280
  You are falling into ingratitude: I challenge
  The reward due to my service.

FERDINAND.   I'll tell thee
  What I'll give thee.

BOSOLA.   Do.

FERDINAND.   I'll give thee a pardon
  For this murder.

BOSOLA.   Ha!

FERDINAND.   Yes, and 'tis
  The largest bounty I can study to do thee.   285
  By what authority didst thou execute
  This bloody sentence?

BOSOLA.   By yours.

FERDINAND.   Mine! Was I her judge?
  Did any ceremonial form of law
  Doom her to not-being? Did a complete jury
  Deliver her conviction up i' th' court?   290
  Where shalt thou find this judgment registered,
  Unless in hell? See, like a bloody fool,
  Thou'st forfeited thy life, and thou shalt die for 't.

BOSOLA. The office of justice is perverted quite
  When one thief hangs another. Who shall dare   295
  To reveal this?

FERDINAND.   Oh, I'll tell thee;
  The wolf shall find her grave, and scrape it up,
  Not to devour the corpse, but to discover
  The horrid murder.

BOSOLA.   You, not I, shall quake for 't.

FERDINAND. Leave me.

BOSOLA.   I will first receive my pension.   300

FERDINAND. You are a villain.

BOSOLA.   When your ingratitude
  Is judge, I am so.

FERDINAND.   Oh, horror!
  That not the fear of Him which binds the devils
  Can prescribe man obedience!
  Never look upon me more.

BOSOLA.   Why, fare thee well.   305
  Your brother and your self are worthy men:
  You have a pair of hearts are rotten graves,

Rotten, and rotting others; and your vengeance,
Like two chained bullets, still goes arm in arm.
You may be brothers, for treason, like the plague,   310
Doth take much in a blood.[5] I stand like one
That long hath ta'en a sweet and golden dream.
I am angry with myself, now that I wake
FERDINAND. Get thee into some unknown part o' th' world,
That I may never see thee.
BOSOLA.   Let me know   315
Wherefore I should be thus neglected. Sir,
I served your tyranny, and rather strove
To satisfy yourself than all the world,
And though I loathed the evil, yet I loved
You that did counsel it; and rather sought   320
To appear a true servant than an honest man.
FERDINAND. I'll go hunt the badger by owl-light:
'Tis a deed of darkness.   [Exit.]
BOSOLA. He's much distracted. Off, my painted honor!
While with vain hopes our faculties we tire,   325
We seem to sweat in ice and freeze in fire.
What would I do, were this to do again?
I would not change my peace of conscience
For all the wealth of Europe.—She stirs; here's life.
Return, fair soul, from darkness, and lead mine   330
Out of this sensible[6] hell.—She's warm, she breathes.
Upon thy pale lips I will melt my heart,
To store them with fresh color.—Who's there!
Some cordial[7] drink!—Alas! I dare not call:
So pity would destroy pity.—Her eye opes,   335
And heaven in it seems to ope, that late was shut,
To take me up to mercy.
DUCHESS. Antonio!
BOSOLA.   Yes, madam, he is living;
The dead bodies you saw were but feigned statues:
He's reconciled to your brothers: the Pope hath wrought   340
The atonement.
DUCHESS.   Mercy!   [She dies.]
BOSOLA. Oh, she's gone again! There the cords of life broke.
Oh, sacred innocence, that sweetly sleeps
On turtles'[8] feathers, whilst a guilty conscience
Is a black register wherein is writ   345
All our good deeds and bad, a perspective[9]
That shows us hell! That we cannot be suffered
To do good when we have a mind to it!
This is manly sorrow:
These tears, I am very certain, never grew   350
In my mother's milk. My estate is sunk
Below the degree of fear. Where were

---

5. Treason and plague run in certain families.   8. Turtle doves, emblems of a loving couple.
6. Material, tangible.   9. Picture.
7. Restorative.

These penitent fountains while she was living?
Oh, they were frozen up! Here is a sight
As direful to my soul as is the sword   355
Unto a wretch hath slain his father. Come,
I'll bear thee hence,
And execute thy last will; that's deliver
Thy body to the reverend dispose[1]
Of some good women: that the cruel tyrant   360
Shall not deny me. Then I'll post to Milan,
Where somewhat I will speedily enact
Worth my dejection.   [*Exit with the body.*]

Act 5

SCENE 1. A *Public Place in Milan.*

[*Enter* ANTONIO *and* DELIO.]

ANTONIO. What think you of my hope of reconcilement
    To the Aragonian brethren?
DELIO.   I misdoubt it;
    For though they have sent their letters of safe-conduct
    For your repair to Milan, they appear
    But nets to entrap you. The Marquis of Pescara,   5
    Under whom you hold certain land in cheat,[2]
    Much 'gainst his noble nature hath been moved
    To seize those lands, and some of his dependents
    Are at this instant making it their suit
    To be invested in your revenues.[3]   10
    I cannot think they mean well to your life
    That do deprive you of your means of life,
    Your living.
ANTONIO.   You are still an heretic
    To any safety I can shape myself.[4]
DELIO. Here comes the Marquis. I will make myself   15
    Petitioner for some part of your land,
    To know whither it is flying.
ANTONIO.   I pray do.   [*Withdraws.*]

[*Enter* PESCARA.]

DELIO. Sir, I have a suit to you.
PESCARA.   To me?
DELIO. An easy one.
    There is the citadel of Saint Bennet,[5]   20
    With some demesnes, of late in the possession
    Of Antonio Bologna; please you bestow them on me.
PESCARA. You are my friend, but this is such a suit,
    Nor fit for me to give, nor you to take.

1. Disposition.
2. Escheat, i.e., subject to forfeiture under certain conditions.
3. I.e., to be given your rents.

4. I.e., you still don't give me any hope of safety that I can believe in. "Heretic": unbeliever.
5. Saint Benedict. "Demesnes": associated estates.

DELIO. No, sir?

PESCARA.   I will give you ample reason for 't   25
Soon in private.—Here's the Cardinal's mistress.

     [*Enter* JULIA.]

JULIA. My lord, I am grown your poor petitioner,
And should be an ill beggar, had I not
A great man's letter here, the Cardinal's,
To court you in my favor.   [*Gives a letter.*]

PESCARA.   He entreats for you   30
The citadel of Saint Bennet, that belonged
To the banished Bologna.

JULIA.   Yes.

PESCARA.   I could not
Have thought of a friend I could rather pleasure with it;
'Tis yours.

JULIA.   Sir, I thank you; and he shall know
How doubly I am engaged both in your gift,   35
And speediness of giving, which makes your grant
The greater.   [*Exit.*]

ANTONIO. [*aside*] How they fortify themselves
With my ruin!

DELIO.   Sir, I am little bound to you.

PESCARA.   Why?

DELIO. Because you denied this suit to me, and gave 't
To such a creature.

PESCARA.   Do you know what it was?   40
It was Antonio's land, not forfeited
By course of law, but ravished from his throat
By the Cardinal's entreaty. It were not fit
I should bestow so main a piece of wrong
Upon my friend; 'tis a gratification   45
Only due to a strumpet, for it is injustice.
Shall I sprinkle the pure blood of innocents
To make those followers I call my friends
Look ruddier upon me? I am glad
This land, ta'en from the owner by such wrong,   50
Returns again unto so foul an use
As salary for his lust. Learn, good Delio,
To ask noble things of me, and you shall find
I'll be a noble giver.

DELIO.   You instruct me well.

ANTONIO. [*aside*] Why, here's a man now would fright impudence   55
From sauciest beggars.

PESCARA.   Prince Ferdinand's come to Milan,
Sick, as they give out, of an apoplexy,
But some say 'tis a frenzy. I am going
To visit him.   [*Exit.*]

ANTONIO.   'Tis a noble old fellow.

DELIO. What course do you mean to take, Antonio?   60

ANTONIO. This night I mean to venture all my fortune,

Which is no more than a poor lingering life,
To the Cardinal's worst of malice. I have got
Private access to his chamber, and intend
To visit him about the mid of night,   65
As once his brother did our noble duchess.
It may be that the sudden apprehension
Of danger—for I'll go in mine own shape—
When he shall see it fraught with love and duty,
May draw the poison out of him, and work   70
A friendly reconcilement. If it fail,
Yet it shall rid me of this infamous calling,
For better fall once than be ever falling.
DELIO. I'll second you in all danger, and, howe'er,
    My life keeps rank with yours.   75
ANTONIO. You are still my loved and best friend.   [*Exeunt.*]

SCENE 2

[*Enter* PESCARA *and* DOCTOR.]

PESCARA. Now, doctor, may I visit your patient?
DOCTOR. If 't please your lordship: but he's instantly[6]
    To take the air here in the gallery
    By my direction.
PESCARA.   Pray thee, what's his disease?
DOCTOR. A very pestilent disease, my lord,   5
    They call lycanthropia.[7]
PESCARA.   What's that?
    I need a dictionary to 't.
DOCTOR.   I'll tell you.
    In those that are possessed with 't there o'erflows
    Such melancholy humor, they imagine
    Themselves to be transformèd into wolves;   10
    Steal forth to churchyards in the dead of night,
    And dig dead bodies up: as two nights since
    One met the Duke 'bout midnight in a lane
    Behind Saint Mark's Church, with the leg of a man
    Upon his shoulder; and he howled fearfully;   15
    Said he was a wolf, only the difference
    Was, a wolf's skin was hairy on the outside,
    His on the inside; bade them take their swords,
    Rip up his flesh, and try. Straight I was sent for,
    And, having ministered to him, found his grace   20
    Very well recovered.
PESCARA.   I'm glad on 't.
DOCTOR. Yet not without some fear
    Of a relapse. If he grow to his fit again,
    I'll go a nearer way to work with him

6. Very shortly.
7. The mental aberration that produces werewolves—as the Doctor will shortly explain.

Than ever Paracelsus[8] dreamed of: if   25
They'll give me leave, I'll buffet his madness
Out of him. Stand aside; he comes.

[*Enter* FERDINAND, MALATESTE, CARDINAL, *and* BOSOLA *apart.*]

FERDINAND.   Leave me.
MALATESTE. Why doth your lordship love this solitariness?
FERDINAND. Eagles commonly fly alone: they are crows, daws, and
    starlings that flock together. Look, what's that follows me?   30
MALATESTE. Nothing, my lord.
FERDINAND. Yes.
MALATESTE. 'Tis your shadow.
FERDINAND. Stay it; let it not haunt me.
MALATESTE. Impossible, if you move, and the sun shine.   35
FERDINAND. I will throttle it.   [*Throws himself on the ground.*]
MALATESTE. O, my lord, you are angry with nothing.
FERDINAND. You are a fool: how is 't possible I should catch my
    shadow, unless I fall upon 't? When I go to hell, I mean to carry
    a bribe; for, look you, good gifts evermore make way for the worst   40
    persons.
PESCARA. Rise, good my lord.
FERDINAND. I am studying the art of patience.
PESCARA. 'Tis a noble virtue.
FERDINAND. To drive six snails before me from this town to Mos-   45
    cow; neither use goad nor whip to them, but let them take their
    own time—the patient'st man i' th' world match me for an exper-
    iment—and I'll crawl after like a sheep-biter.[9]
CARDINAL. Force him up.   [*They raise him.*]
FERDINAND. Use me well, you were best. What I have done, I have   50
    done: I'll confess nothing.
DOCTOR. Now let me come to him. Are you mad, my lord: Are you
    out of your princely wits?
FERDINAND. What's he?
PESCARA. Your doctor.   55
FERDINAND. Let me have his beard sawed off, and his eyebrows filed
    more civil.
DOCTOR. I must do mad tricks with him, for that's the only way
    on 't. I have brought your grace a salamander's skin to keep you
    from sunburning.[1]   60
FERDINAND. I have cruel sore eyes.
DOCTOR. The white of a cockatrix's[2] egg is present remedy.
FERDINAND. Let it be a new-laid one, you were best. Hide me
    from him: physicians are like kings—they brook no contradic-
    tion.   65
DOCTOR. Now he begins to fear me: now let me alone with him.

---

8. Paracelsus, the great Swiss alchemist, famous
for his cures by sympathetic magic. Though
anachronistic in this play, he would be well known
to Webster's audience.
9. A sheepdog, nipping at the heels of his flock.

1. The ideas are deliberately crazy: the Doctor is
trying to enter into Ferdinand's frenzy in order
gradually to draw him out.
2. A fabulous, and deadly poisonous, serpent,
supposed to be hatched of a cock's egg.

CARDINAL. How now? Put off your gown?

DOCTOR. Let me have some forty urinals filled with rosewater: he
and I'll go pelt one another with them. Now he begins to fear
me. Can you fetch a frisk, sir?[3] Let him go, let him go, upon my   70
peril: I find by his eye he stands in awe of me; I'll make him as
tame as a dormouse.

FERDINAND. Can you fetch your frisks, sir? I will stamp him into a
cullis, flay off his skin, to cover one of the anatomies[4] this
rogue hath set i' th' cold yonder in Barber-Chirurgeons' Hall.   75
Hence, hence! You are all of you like beasts for sacrifice: there's
nothing left of you but tongue and belly, flattery and lechery.

                                                              [*Exit.*]

PESCARA. Doctor, he did not fear you throughly.

DOCTOR.   True;
I was somewhat too forward.

BOSOLA. [*aside*]   Mercy upon me,   80
What a fatal judgment hath fall'n upon this Ferdinand!

PESCARA. Knows your grace what accident hath brought
Unto the prince this strange distraction?

CARDINAL. [*aside*] I must feign somewhat.—Thus they say it grew:
You have heard it rumored, for these many years   85
None of our family dies but there is seen
The shape of an old woman, which is given
By tradition to us to have been murdered
By her nephews for her riches. Such a figure
One night, as the prince sat up late at 's book,   90
Appeared to him; when, crying out for help,
The gentlemen of 's chamber found his grace
All on a cold sweat, altered much in face
And language; since which apparition,
He hath grown worse and worse, and I much fear   95
He cannot live.

BOSOLA.   Sir, I would speak with you.

PESCARA. We'll leave your grace,
Wishing to the sick prince, our noble lord,
All health of mind and body.

CARDINAL.   You are most welcome.

                    [*Exeunt* PESCARA, MALATESTE, *and* DOCTOR.]

Are you come? So. [*Aside.*] This fellow must not know   100
By any means I had intelligence[5]
In our duchess' death; for, though I counseled it,
The full of all th' engagement seemed to grow
From Ferdinand.—Now, sir, how fares our sister?
I do not think but sorrow makes her look   105
Like to an oft-dyed garment: she shall now
Taste comfort from me. Why do you look so wildly?

---

3. Cut a caper, dance a jig.   the Doctor's flayed skin.
4. Anatomical skeletons hung up in the surgeon's   5. Had a hand in.
college, which Ferdinand proposes to cover with

Oh, the fortune of your master here the prince
Dejects you, but be you of happy comfort:
If you'll do one thing for me I'll entreat,   110
Though he had a cold tombstone o'er his bones,
I'll make you what you would be.
BOSOLA.   Anything;
Give it me in a breath, and let me fly to 't:
They that think long, small expedition win,
For musing much o' th' end cannot begin.   115

      [*Enter* JULIA.]

JULIA. Sir, will you come in to supper?
CARDINAL.   I am busy;
Leave me.
JULIA. [*aside*] What an excellent shape hath that fellow! [*Exit.*]
CARDINAL. 'Tis thus. Antonio lurks here in Milan:
Inquire him out, and kill him. While he lives,   120
Our sister cannot marry, and I have thought
Of an excellent match for her. Do this, and style me
Thy advancement.[6]
BOSOLA. But by what means shall I find him out?
CARDINAL. There is a gentleman called Delio   125
Here in the camp, that hath been long approved
His loyal friend. Set eye upon that fellow;
Follow him to mass; maybe Antonio,
Although he do account religion
But a school-name,[7] for fashion of the world   130
May accompany him; or else go inquire out
Delio's confessor, and see if you can bribe
Him to reveal it. There are a thousand ways
A man might find to trace him; as to know
What fellows haunt the Jews for taking up   135
Great sums of money, for sure he's in want;
Or else to go to th' picture-makers, and learn
Who bought her picture lately. Some of these
Haply may take.
BOSOLA.   Well, I'll not freeze i' th' business:
I would see that wretched thing, Antonio,   140
Above all sights i' th' world.
CARDINAL.   Do, and be happy.   [*Exit.*]
BOSOLA. This fellow doth breed basilisks in 's eyes,
He's nothing else but murder; yet he seems
Not to have notice of the duchess' death.
'Tis his cunning: I must follow his example;   145
There cannot be a surer way to trace
Than that of an old fox.

      [*Re-enter* JULIA, *with a pistol.*]

6. Look to me for your promotion.
7. Just an idle phrase.

JULIA.   So, sir, you are well met.

BOSOLA. How now?

JULIA.   Nay, the doors are fast enough.
  Now, sir, I will make you confess your treachery.

BOSOLA. Treachery?

JULIA.   Yes, confess to me   150
  Which of my women 'twas, you hired to put
  Love-powder into my drink?

BOSOLA.   Love-powder?

JULIA. Yes, when I was at Malfi.
  Why should I fall in love with such a face else?
  I have already suffered for thee so much pain,   155
  The only remedy to do me good
  Is to kill my longing.

BOSOLA.   Sure, your pistol holds
  Nothing but perfumes or kissing-comfits.[8]
  Excellent lady! You have a pretty way on 't
  To discover your longing. Come, come, I'll disarm you,   160
  And arm you thus:[9] yet this is wondrous strange.

JULIA. Compare thy form and my eyes together, you'll find
  My love no such great miracle. Now you'll say
  I am wanton: this nice modesty in ladies
  Is but a troublesome familiar[1] that haunts them.   165

BOSOLA. Know you me, I am a blunt soldier.

JULIA.   The better:
  Sure, there wants[2] fire where there are no lively sparks
  Of roughness.

BOSOLA.   And I want compliment.[3]

JULIA.   Why, ignorance
  In courtship cannot make you do amiss,
  If you have a heart to do well.

BOSOLA.   You are very fair.   170

JULIA. Nay, if you lay beauty to my charge,
  I must plead unguilty.

BOSOLA.   Your bright eyes
  Carry a quiver of darts in them, sharper
  Than sunbeams.

JULIA.   You will mar me with commendation,
  Put yourself to the charge of courting me,   175
  Whereas now I woo you.

BOSOLA. [aside] I have it, I will work upon this creature;—
  Let us grow most amorously familiar.
  If the great Cardinal now should see me thus,
  Would he not count me a villain?   180

JULIA. No, he might count me a wanton,
  Not lay a scruple of offence on you;
  For if I see and steal a diamond,

---

8. Candies to sweeten the breath.
9. Disarm (by taking away her pistol and kissing her); arm (by embracing her).

1. An irksome ghost.
2. Lacks, is missing.
3. I don't have the gift of flattery.

The fault is not i' th' stone, but in me the thief
That purloins it. I am sudden with you.   185
We that are great women of pleasure, use to cut off
These uncertain wishes and unquiet longings,
And in an instant join the sweet delight
And the pretty excuse together. Had you been i' th' street,
Under my chamber window, even there   190
I should have courted you.

BOSOLA.   Oh, you are an excellent lady!

JULIA. Bid me do somewhat for you presently[4]
To express I love you.

BOSOLA.   I will, and if you love me,
Fail not to effect it.
The Cardinal is grown wondrous melancholy;   195
Demand the cause, let him not put you off
With feigned excuse; discover the main ground on 't.

JULIA. Why would you know this?

BOSOLA.   I have depended on him,
And I hear he is fallen in some disgrace
With the Emperor: if he be, like the mice   200
That forsake falling houses, I would shift
To other dependence.

JULIA. You shall not need follow the wars;
I'll be your maintenance.

BOSOLA.   And I your loyal servant;
But I cannot leave my calling.

JULIA.   Not leave   205
An ungrateful general for the love of a sweet lady?
You are like some cannot sleep in featherbeds,
But must have blocks for their pillows.

BOSOLA.   Will you do this?

JULIA. Cunningly.

BOSOLA.   Tomorrow I'll expect th' intelligence.

JULIA. Tomorrow? Get you into my cabinet,   210
You shall have it with you. Do not delay me,
No more than I do you. I am like one
That is condemned: I have my pardon promised,
But I would see it sealed. Go, get you in;
You shall see me wind my tongue about his heart   215
Like a skein of silk.   [*Exit* BOSOLA.]

                    [*Re-enter* CARDINAL.]

CARDINAL.   Where are you?

                    [*Enter* SERVANTS.]

SERVANTS.   Here.

CARDINAL. Let none, upon your lives,
Have conference with the Prince Ferdinand,
Unless I know it. [*Aside.*] In this distraction   219
He may reveal the murder.   [*Exeunt* SERVANTS.]

4. Right away.

Yond's my lingering consumption:
I am weary of her, and by any means
Would be quit of.
JULIA.   How now, my lord?
   What ails you?
CARDINAL.   Nothing.
JULIA.   Oh, you are much altered:
   Come, I must be your secretary, and remove   225
   This lead from off your bosom.[5] What's the matter?
CARDINAL. I may not tell you.

JULIA. Are you so far in love with sorrow
   You cannot part with part of it? Or think you
   I cannot love your grace when you are sad   230
   As well as merry? Or do you suspect
   I, that have been a secret to your heart
   These many winters, cannot be the same
   Unto your tongue?
CARDINAL.   Satisfy thy longing—
   The only way to make thee keep my counsel   235
   Is not to tell thee.
JULIA.   Tell your echo this,
   Or flatterers, that like echoes still report
   What they hear though most imperfect, and not me;
   For if that you be true unto yourself,
   I'll know.
CARDINAL. Will you rack[6] me?
JULIA.   No, judgment shall   240
   Draw it from you: it is an equal fault,
   To tell one's secrets unto all or none.
CARDINAL. The first argues folly.
JULIA.   But the last, tyranny.
CARDINAL. Very well. Why, imagine I have committed
   Some secret deed which I desire the world   245
   May never hear of.
JULIA.   Therefore may not I know it?
   You have concealed for me as great a sin
   As adultery. Sir, never was occasion
   For perfect trial of my constancy
   Till now: sir, I beseech you—
CARDINAL.   You'll repent it.   250
JULIA. Never.
CARDINAL. It hurries thee to ruin: I'll not tell thee.
   Be well advised, and think what danger 'tis
   To receive a prince's secrets: they that do,
   Had need have their breasts hooped with adamant   255
   To contain them. I pray thee, yet be satisfied;
   Examine thine own frailty; 'tis more easy

5. Secretaries opened letters addressed to their   6. Will you put me to the torture?
masters by removing the heavy lead seals.

To tie knots than unloose them: 'tis a secret
That, like a lingering poison, may chance lie
Spread in thy veins, and kill thee seven year hence.   260
JULIA. Now you dally with me.
CARDINAL.   No more; thou shalt know it.
By my appointment the great Duchess of Malfi
And two of her young children, four nights since,
Were strangled.
JULIA.   O Heaven! Sir, what have you done?
CARDINAL. How now? How settles this? Think you your bosom   265
Will be a grave dark and obscure enough
For such a secret?
JULIA.   You have undone yourself, sir.
CARDINAL. Why?
JULIA.   It lies not in me to conceal it.
CARDINAL.   No?
Come, I will swear you to 't upon this book.
JULIA. Most religiously.
CARDINAL.   Kiss it.   [*She kisses the book.*]
                        Now you shall   270
Never utter it; thy curiosity
Hath undone thee: thou'rt poisoned with that book.
Because I knew thou couldst not keep my counsel,
I have bound thee to 't by death.

        [*Re-enter* BOSOLA.]

BOSOLA.   For pity sake,
Hold!
CARDINAL. Ha! Bosola?
JULIA.   I forgive you   275
This equal piece of justice you have done;
For I betrayed your counsel to that fellow:
He overheard it; that was the cause I said
It lay not in me to conceal it.
BOSOLA.   O foolish woman,
Couldst not thou have poisoned him?
JULIA.   'Tis weakness,   280
Too much to think what should have been done. I go
I know not whither.   [*Dies.*]
CARDINAL.   Wherefore com'st thou hither?
BOSOLA. That I might find a great man like yourself,
Not out of his wits as the Lord Ferdinand,
To remember my service.
CARDINAL.   I'll have thee hewed in pieces.   285
BOSOLA. Make not yourself such a promise of that life
Which is not yours to dispose of.
CARDINAL.   Who placed thee here?
BOSOLA. Her lust, as she intended.
CARDINAL.   Very well.
Now you know me for your fellow-murderer.

BOSOLA. And wherefore should you lay fair marble colors[7]   290
    Upon your rotten purposes to me?
    Unless you imitate some that do plot great treasons,
    And when they have done, go hide themselves i' th' graves
    Of those were actors in 't?
CARDINAL.   No more; there is
    A fortune attends thee.   295
BOSOLA. Shall I go sue to Fortune any longer?
    'Tis the fool's pilgrimage.
CARDINAL.   I have honors in store for thee.
BOSOLA. There are a many ways that conduct to seeming
    Honor, and some of them very dirty ones.
CARDINAL.   Throw to the devil
    Thy melancholy; the fire burns well,   300
    What need we keep a stirring of 't, and make
    A greater smother? Thou wilt kill Antonio?
BOSOLA. Yes.
CARDINAL.   Take up that body.
BOSOLA.   I think I shall
    Shortly grow the common bier for churchyards!
CARDINAL. I will allow thee some dozen of attendants   305
    To aid thee in the murder.
BOSOLA. Oh, by no means. Physicians that apply horse-leeches to
    any rank swelling use to cut off their tails, that the blood may
    run through them the faster. Let me have no train[8] when I go to
    shed blood, lest it make me have a greater when I ride to the   310
    gallows.
CARDINAL. Come to me after midnight, to help to remove that body
    to her own lodging. I'll give out she died of the plague; 'twill
    breed the less inquiry after her death.
BOSOLA. Where's Castruccio her husband?   315
CARDINAL. He's rode to Naples to take possession of Antonio's cita-
    del.
BOSOLA. Believe me, you have done a very happy turn.
CARDINAL. Fail not to come. There is the master-key of our lodg-
    ings, and by that you may conceive what trust I plant in you.   320
BOSOLA. You shall find me ready.   [*Exit* CARDINAL.]
    Oh poor Antonio, though nothing be so needful
    To thy estate as pity, yet I find
    Nothing so dangerous. I must look to my footing;
    In such slippery ice-pavements men had need   325
    To be frost-nailed well; they may break their necks else;
    The precedent's here afore me. How this man
    Bears up in blood! Seems fearless! Why, 'tis well:
    Security some men call the suburbs of hell,
    Only a dead wall between.[9] Well, good Antonio,   330

---

7. Plaster was often painted to look like marble.
8. Followers. Criminals, carted through the streets
to be hanged at Tyburn, were followed by crowds
of the idle, the sadistic, and their own fellow criminals.
9. False security brings you next door to hell, with
only a bare wall between.

I'll seek thee out, and all my care shall be
To put thee into safety from the reach
Of these most cruel biters that have got
Some of thy blood already. It may be,
I'll join with thee in a most just revenge: 335
The weakest arm is strong enough that strikes
With the sword of justice. Still methinks the duchess
Haunts me. There, there, 'tis nothing but my melancholy.
O Penitence, let me truly taste thy cup.
That throws men down only to raise them up!   [*Exit.*]   340

SCENE 3. *A Fortification at Milan.*

[*Enter* ANTONIO *and* DELIO. *Echo from the* DUCHESS' *grave.*]

DELIO. Yond's the Cardinal's window. This fortification
  Grew from the ruins of an ancient abbey;
  And to yond side o' th' river lies a wall,
  Piece of a cloister, which in my opinion
  Gives the best echo that you ever heard,   5
  So hollow and so dismal, and withal
  So plain in the distinction of our words,
  That many have supposed it is a spirit
  That answers.
ANTONIO.   I do love these ancient ruins.
  We never tread upon them but we set   10
  Our foot upon some reverend history:
  And, questionless, here in this open court,
  Which now lies naked to the injuries
  Of stormy weather, some men lie interred
  Loved the church so well, and gave so largely to 't,   15
  They thought it should have canopied their bones
  Till doomsday; but all things have their end:
  Churches and cities, which have diseases like to men,
  Must have like death that we have.
ECHO.   "Like death that we have."
DELIO. Now the echo hath caught you.
ANTONIO.   It groaned, methought, and gave   20
  A very deadly accent.
ECHO.   "Deadly accent."
DELIO. I told you 'twas a pretty one: you may make it
  A huntsman, or a falconer, a musician,
  Or a thing of sorrow.
ECHO.   "A thing of sorrow."
ANTONIO. Aye, sure, that suits it best.
ECHO.   "That suits it best."   25
ANTONIO. 'Tis very like my wife's voice.
ECHO.   "Aye, wife's voice."
DELIO. Come, let's walk further from 't. I would not have you
  Go to th' Cardinal's tonight: do not.
ECHO.   "Do not."

DELIO. Wisdom doth not more moderate wasting sorrow
    Than time: take time for 't; be mindful of thy safety.   30
ECHO. "Be mindful of thy safety."
ANTONIO.   Necessity compels me:
    Make scrutiny throughout the passes
    Of your own life, you'll find it impossible
    To fly your fate.
ECHO.   "Oh, fly your fate."
DELIO. Hark! The dead stones seem to have pity on you,   35
    And give you good counsel.
ANTONIO. Echo, I will not talk with thee,
    For thou art a dead thing.
ECHO.   "Thou art a dead thing."
ANTONIO. My duchess is asleep now,
    And her little ones, I hope sweetly: O heaven,   40
    Shall I never see her more?
ECHO.   "Never see her more."
ANTONIO. I marked not one repetition of the echo
    But that, and on the sudden a clear light
    Presented me a face folded in sorrow.
DELIO. Your fancy merely.
ANTONIO.   Come, I'll be out of this ague,   45
    For to live thus is not indeed to live;
    It is a mockery and abuse of life.
    I will not henceforth save myself by halves;
    Lose all, or nothing.
DELIO.   Your own virtue save you!
    I'll fetch your eldest son, and second[1] you: 50
    It may be that the sight of his own blood
    Spread in so sweet a figure[2] may beget
    The more compassion.
ANTONIO.   However, fare you well.
    Though in our miseries Fortune have a part,
    Yet in our noble sufferings she hath none: 55
    Contempt of pain, that we may call our own.   [*Exeunt.*]

SCENE 4. A *Room in the* CARDINAL'*s Palace.*

[*Enter* CARDINAL, PESCARA, MALATESTE, RODERIGO, *and* GRISO-
LAN.]

CARDINAL. You shall not watch tonight by the sick prince;
    His grace is very well recovered.
MALATESTE. Good my lord, suffer[3] us.
CARDINAL.   Oh, by no means;
    The noise and change of object in his eye
    Doth more distract him. I pray, all to bed;
    And though you hear him in his violent fit,   5
    Do not rise, I entreat you.

1. Back you up.   3. Allow.
2. Image.

PESCARA.   So, sir; we shall not.
CARDINAL. Nay, I must have you promise upon your honors,
   For I was enjoined to 't by himself; and he seemed
   To urge it sensibly.[4]
PESCARA.   Let our honors bind   10
   This trifle.
CARDINAL.   Nor any of your followers.
MALATESTE.   Neither.
CARDINAL. It may be, to make trial of your promise,
   When he's asleep, myself will rise and feign
   Some of his mad tricks, and cry out for help,
   And feign myself in danger.
MALATESTE.   If your throat were cutting,   15
   I'd not come at you, now I have protested against it.
CARDINAL. Why, I thank you.   [*Withdraws.*]
GRISOLAN.   'Twas a foul storm tonight.
RODERIGO. The Lord Ferdinand's chamber shook like an osier.[5]
MALATESTE. 'Twas nothing but pure kindness in the devil,
   To rock his own child.   [*Exeunt all except the* CARDINAL.] 20
CARDINAL. The reason why I would not suffer these
   About my brother, is, because at midnight
   I may with better privacy convey
   Julia's body to her own lodging. Oh, my conscience!
   I would pray now, but the devil takes away my heart   25
   For having any confidence in prayer.
   About this hour I appointed Bosola
   To fetch the body: when he hath served my turn,
   He dies.   [*Exit.*]

     Enter BOSOLA.]

BOSOLA. Ha! 'Twas the Cardinal's voice; I heard him name   30
   Bosola and my death. Listen! I hear
   One's footing.

     [*Enter* FERDINAND.]

FERDINAND.   Strangling is a very quiet death.
BOSOLA. [*aside*] Nay, then, I see I must stand upon my guard.
FERDINAND. What say to that? Whisper softly; do you agree to 't?
   So; it must be done i' th' dark: the Cardinal would not for a   35
   thousand pounds the doctor should see it.   [*Exit.*]
BOSOLA. My death is plotted; here's the consequence of murder.
   We value not desert nor Christian breath,
   When we know black deeds must be cured with death.

     [*Enter* ANTONIO *and* SERVANT.]

SERVANT. Here stay, sir, and be confident, I pray: 40
   I'll fetch you a dark lantern.   [*Exit.*]
ANTONIO. Could I take him at his prayers,
   There were hope of pardon.

4. With real feeling.
5. A willow wand.

BOSOLA.   Fall right, my sword!   [*Stabs him.*]
  I'll not give thee so much leisure as to pray.
ANTONIO. Oh, I am gone! Thou hast ended a long suit[6]   45
  In a minute.
BOSOLA.   What art thou?
ANTONIO.   A most wretched thing,
  That only have thy benefit in death,
  To appear myself.

[*Re-enter* SERVANT *with a lantern.*]

SERVANT.   Where are you, sir?
ANTONIO. Very near my home. Bosola?
SERVANT.   Oh, misfortune!
BOSOLA. Smother thy pity; thou art dead else. Antonio?   50
  The man I would have saved 'bove mine own life!
  We are merely the stars' tennis balls, struck and bandied
  Which way please them.[7] O good Antonio,
  I'll whisper one thing in thy dying ear
  Shall make thy heart break quickly! Thy fair duchess   55
  And two sweet children—
ANTONIO.   Their very names
  Kindle a little life in me.
BOSOLA.   Are murdered.
ANTONIO. Some men have wished to die
  At the hearing of sad tidings; I am glad
  That I shall do 't in sadness: I would not now   60
  Wish my wounds balmed nor healed, for I have no use
  To put my life to. In all our quest of greatness,
  Like wanton boys, whose pastime is their care,
  We follow after bubbles blown in th' air.
  Pleasure of life, what is't? Only the good hours   65
  Of an ague; merely a preparative to rest,
  To endure vexation. I do not ask
  The process of my death; only commend me
  To Delio.
BOSOLA.   Break, heart!
ANTONIO. And let my son fly the courts of princes.   [*Dies.*] 70
BOSOLA. Thou seem'st to have loved Antonio?
SERVANT.   I brought him hither.
  To have reconciled him to the Cardinal.
BOSOLA. I do not ask thee that.
  Take him up, if thou tender thine own life,
  And bear him where the lady Julia   75
  Was wont to lodge. Oh, my fate moves swift;
  I have this Cardinal in the forge already;
  Now I'll bring him to th' hammer. Oh direful misprision![8]
  I will not imitate things glorious,
  No more than base; I'll be mine own example.   80

6. Antonio thinks it is the Cardinal, to whom he
was addressing his "suit" (plea for reconciliation),
who has murdered him.

7. The power of the stars over men's lives was a
Renaissance commonplace.
8. Error.

On, on, and look thou represent, for silence,
The thing thou bear'st.[9]　　　　　　　　　　　　　　　　*[Exeunt.]*

SCENE 5

[Enter CARDINAL, *with a book.]*

CARDINAL. I am puzzled in a question about hell:
　He says, in hell there's one material fire,
　And yet it shall not burn all men alike.
　Lay him by. How tedious is a guilty conscience!
　When I look into the fish-ponds in my garden,　　　　　　　5
　Methinks I see a thing armed with a rake,
　That seems to strike at me.

[Enter BOSOLA, *and* SERVANT *bearing* ANTONIO's *body.]*

　　　　　　　　　　　Now, art thou come?
　Thou look'st ghastly:
　There sits in thy face some great determination
　Mixed with some fear.

BOSOLA.　　　　　　　Thus it lightens into action:　　　　10
　I am come to kill thee.

CARDINAL.　　　　　　Ha! Help! Our guard!

BOSOLA. Thou art deceived; they are out of thy howling.

CARDINAL. Hold; and I will faithfully divide
　Revenues with thee.

BOSOLA.　　　　　　　Thy prayers and proffers
　Are both unseasonable.

CARDINAL.　　　　　　Raise the watch!　　　　　15
　We are betrayed!

BOSOLA.　　　　　I have confined your flight:[1]
　I'll suffer your retreat to Julia's chamber,
　But no further.

CARDINAL.　　　Help! We are betrayed!

[Enter, above, PESCARA, MALATESTE, RODERIGO, *and* GRISOLAN.]

MALATESTE.　　　　　　　　　　　　Listen.

CARDINAL. My dukedom for rescue!

RODERIGO.　　　　　　　　　Fie upon his counterfeiting!

MALATESTE. Why, 'tis not the Cardinal.

RODERIGO.　　　　　　　　　Yes, yes, 'tis he,　　　20
　But I'll see him hanged ere I'll go down to him.

CARDINAL. Here's a plot upon me. I am assaulted! I am lost,
　Unless some rescue.

GRISOLAN.　　　　　He doth this pretty well,
　But it will not serve to laugh me out of my honor.

CARDINAL. The sword's at my throat!

RODERIGO.　　　　　　　　You would not bawl so loud
　then.　　　　　　　　　　　　　　　　　　　　　　25

---

9. Be still as the corpse you're carrying.
1. I.e., I've cut off your escape.

MALATESTE. Come, come, let's go to bed. He told us thus much
    aforehand.
PESCARA. He wished you should not come at him; but, believe 't,
    The accent of the voice sounds not in jest:
    I'll down to him, howsoever, and with engines.[2]
    Force ope the doors.   *[Exit above.]*
RODERIGO.   Let's follow him aloof,[3]   30
    And note how the Cardinal will laugh at him.

      [Exeunt, above, MALATESTE, RODERIGO, *and* GRISOLAN.]

BOSOLA. There's for you first,   *[He kills the* SERVANT.]
    'Cause you shall not unbarricade the door
    To let in rescue.
CARDINAL. What cause hast thou to pursue my life?
BOSOLA.   Look there.   35
CARDINAL. Antonio?
BOSOLA.   Slain by my hand unwittingly.
    Pray, and be sudden: when thou killed'st thy sister,
    Thou took'st from Justice her most equal balance,
    And left her naught but her sword.
CARDINAL.   Oh, mercy!
BOSOLA. Now it seems thy greatness was only outward;   40
    For thou fall'st faster of thyself than calamity
    Can drive thee. I'll not waste longer time: there!   *[Stabs him.]*
CARDINAL. Thou hast hurt me.
BOSOLA.   Again!   *[Stabs him again.]*
CARDINAL.   Shall I die like a leveret,[4]
    Without any resistance? Help, help, help!
    I am slain!   45

      [Enter FERDINAND.]

FERDINAND. Th' alarum? Give me a fresh horse;
    Rally the vaunt-guard, or the day is lost.
    Yield, yield! I give you the honor of arms,
    Shake my sword over you; will you yield?[5]
CARDINAL. Help me; I am your brother!
FERDINAND.   The devil!   50
    My brother fight upon the adverse party?

      [He wounds the CARDINAL, *and, in the scuffle, gives* BOSOLA *his
      death-wound.]*

    There flies your ransom.
CARDINAL.   O justice!
    I suffer now for what hath former been:
    Sorrow is held the eldest child of sin.
FERDINAND. Now you're brave fellows. Caesar's fortune was harder
    than Pompey's; Caesar died in the arms of prosperity, Pompey at   55

2. Bars and beams.
3. At a distance.
4. A baby hare, a defenseless creature.
5. It won't do to look for too much sense in Fer-

dinand's wild cries; he thinks he's on the field of
battle and offering the "honor of arms" (liberal surrender terms) to his foes.

the feet of disgrace. You both died in the field. The pain's nothing: pain many times is taken away with the apprehension of
greater, as the toothache with the sight of a barber that comes to
pull it out: there's philosophy for you.

BOSOLA. Now my revenge is perfect. Sink, thou main cause   60

[*He kills* FERDINAND.]

Of my undoing! The last part of my life
Hath done me best service.
FERDINAND. Give me some wet hay; I am broken-winded. I do
account this world but a dog-kennel: I will vault credit and affect
high pleasures beyond death.[6]   65
BOSOLA. He seems to come to himself, now he's so near
The bottom.
FERDINAND. My sister, O my sister! There's the cause on 't.
Whether we fall by ambition, blood, or lust,
Like diamonds we are cut with our own dust.   [*Dies.*]   70
CARDINAL. Thou hast thy payment, too.
BOSOLA. Yes, I hold my weary soul in my teeth.
'Tis ready to part from me. I do glory
That thou, which stood'st like a huge pyramid
Begun upon a large and ample base,   75
Shalt end in a little point, a kind of nothing.

[*Enter, below,* PESCARA, MALATESTE, RODERIGO, *and* GRISOLAN.]

PESCARA. How now, my lord?
MALATESTE.   O sad disaster!
RODERIGO.   How
Comes this?
BOSOLA. Revenge for the Duchess of Malfi murdered
By th' Aragonian brethren; for Antonio   80
Slain by this hand; for lustful Julia
Poisoned by this man; and lastly for myself,
That was an actor in the main of all,
Much 'gainst mine own good nature, yet i' th' end
Neglected.
PESCARA.   How now, my lord?
CARDINAL.   Look to my brother: 85
He gave us these large wounds as we were struggling
Here i' the rushes.[7] And now, I pray,
Let me be laid by and never thought of.   [*Dies.*]
PESCARA. How fatally, it seems, he did withstand
His own rescue!
MALATESTE.   Thou wretched thing of blood,   90
How came Antonio by his death?
BOSOLA. In a mist: I know not how;
Such a mistake as I have often seen
In a play. Oh, I am gone!

6. Worn-out horses are said to be broken-winded.
The last sentence implies that he expects no more
of this life and looks forward only to the next one.

7. Leafy plants, strewn over Elizabethan floors in
lieu of carpets.

We are only like dead walls or vaulted graves,   95
That, ruined, yield no echo. Fare you well.
It may be pain, but no harm to me to die
In so good a quarrel. Oh, this gloomy world,
In what a shadow or deep pit of darkness
Doth, womanish and fearful, mankind live!   100
Let worthy minds ne'er stagger in distrust
To suffer death or shame for what is just:
Mine is another voyage.   [*Dies.*]
PESCARA. The noble Delio, as I came to the palace,
Told me of Antonio's being here, and showed me   105
A pretty gentleman, his son and heir.

      [*Enter* DELIO *with* ANTONIO'S SON.]

MALATESTE. O, sir, you come too late.
DELIO.   I heard so, and
Was armed[8] for it ere I came. Let us make noble use
Of this great ruin, and join all our force
To establish this young hopeful[9] gentleman   110
In 's mother's right. These wretched eminent things
Leave no more fame behind 'em, than should one
Fall in a frost, and leave his print in snow;
As soon as the sun shines, it ever melts
Both form and matter. I have ever thought   115
Nature doth nothing so great for great men
As when she's pleased to make them lords of truth:
Integrity of life is fame's best friend,
Which nobly, beyond death, shall crown the end.   [*Exeunt.*]

performed 1613   *published* 1623

8. Inwardly prepared.
9. Promising.

ROBERT HERRICK
1591–1674

1648: *Hesperides* and *Noble Numbers.*

What little personal history Robert Herrick had was always too much for
him; the decisions he had to take were mostly forced on him, and he accepted
them as misfortunes. Yet he is the happiest of English poets. The son of a
prosperous London goldsmith, he was slow in taking his degrees, slower still
in finding himself a career. Clearly he would have liked nothing better than
a life of leisured study in London, talking literature and drinking sack with
his hero Ben Jonson, while polishing his verses. But social pressures were
insistent; he took orders in the church and moved reluctantly to a parish at
Dean Prior, in Devonshire.

As a Londoner, he did not much like the rough West Country or its people, but he gradually adapted to both, settling placidly into his bachelor quarters and accumulating poems, one after another, without making any effort to publish them. For purely poetic purposes, he invented for himself dozens of imaginary mistresses—hectic, bewitching creatures with exotic names; but the maid who kept house for him was prophetically named Prudence. At the top of his poetic bent, in *Corinna's Going A-Maying*, Herrick produced a truly major lyric on the central theme of his life, the happy reconciliation of nature and nature's god. But much of his poetic work seems casual, even trivial, though one can easily be misled by his apparent off-handedness into overlooking a serious strain that lies subsurface. He wrote against Devonshire, and then for it; about his cat, and his spaniel Tracy, and his maid Prudence; a farewell to sack (heart-rending) and a return to it (joyous). A recurrent theme in his work is a deftly balanced personal paganism—private sacrifices to household gods, tiny rituals and allusions to ancient creeds only half-seriously taken. The Puritans would have been scandalized had they realized that this minister of the holy gospel was at least half a pagan, and didn't even have the grace to be ashamed of the fact.

Herrick himself did not advertise his beliefs; but when the storm of civil war broke, and the Puritans came to power, they dispossessed him anyhow, and Herrick came down to London with the fruits of his exile. They were published early in 1648 in a fat little octavo volume with two titles, *Hesperides* for the secular poems, and *Noble Numbers* for those with sacred subjects. Altogether, there were over 1,400 poems in this one volume, the only publication of Herrick's life. But the time was not right for tiny, playful lyrics; few readers noticed *Hesperides*, either to applaud or deplore; and Herrick disappeared in silence and oblivion, not to be restored to English literature till the nineteenth century. He did manage to survive the harsh weather of Puritanism till King Charles was restored in 1660; and that restoration brought him back to Dean Prior, where he lived out his last years quietly, dying at the ripe age of eighty-three.

For all his indebtedness to Jonson and the classical authors whom Jonson also idolized, Herrick's playfulness is his own, and so is his light, quiet poetic touch. Though he took life as a sacrament, he did not take it, or himself, solemnly. His poems, seemingly light as snowflakes, often feel as if they had been chiselled in marble. Since they were all published in 1648, we do not give the date for each one.

The Argument[1] of His Book

> I sing of brooks, of blossoms, birds, and bowers,
> Of April, May, of June, and July flowers.
> I sing of Maypoles, hock carts, wassails, wakes,[2]
> Of bridegrooms, brides, and of their bridal cakes.
> I write of youth, of love, and have access   5
> By these to sing of cleanly wantonness.[3]

1. Subject matter.
2. "Hock carts" carried home the last load of the harvest; therefore adorned and celebrated. "Wakes": festive, not funerary occasions, to commemorate the dedication of a parish church.
3. Good fun, but already tinged with the lascivious overtone the word carries today.

I sing of dews, of rains, and, piece by piece,
Of balm, of oil, of spice, and ambergris.[4]
I sing of times trans-shifting, and I write
How roses first came red and lilies white.   10
I write of groves, of twilights, and I sing
The court of Mab and of the fairy king.[5]
I write of hell; I sing (and ever shall)
Of heaven, and hope to have it after all.

Upon the Loss of His Mistresses[1]

I have lost, and lately, these
Many dainty mistresses:
Stately Julia, prime of all;
Sappho next, a principal;
Smooth Anthea, for a skin   5
White and heaven-like crystalline;
Sweet Electra, and the choice
Myrrha, for the lute and voice;
Next Corinna for her wit
And the graceful use of it,   10
With Perilla; all are gone,
Only Herrick's left alone,
For to number sorrows by
Their departures hence, and die.

The Vine

I dreamed this mortal part of mine
Was metamorphosed to a vine,
Which, crawling one and every way,
Enthralled my dainty Lucia.[1]
Methought, her long small legs and thighs   5
I with my tendrils did surprise;
Her belly, buttocks, and her waist
By my soft nervelets were embraced.
About her head I writhing hung, ⎫
And with rich clusters (hid among ⎬   10
The leaves) her temples I behung, ⎭
So that my Lucia seemed to me
Young Bacchus ravished by his tree.[2]

4. Ambergris is used in making perfumes; hence
it carries the overtone of something rare and
delectable.
5. Mab was by long-standing tradition queen of
the fairies and wife of King Oberon. See Shakespeare, A Midsummer Night's Dream.
1. The ladies are entirely imaginary; their names

chosen to fit within the poet's neat metrical patterns.
1. For the sake of both rhyme and meter, the name
of this imaginary lady must be given three syllables
here in line 4, though below in line 12 it has only
two.
2. Bacchus' tree is the grapevine.

My curls about her neck did crawl,
And arms and hands they did enthrall,   15
So that she could not freely stir
(All parts there made one prisoner).
But when I crept with leaves to hide
Those parts which maids keep unespied,
Such fleeting pleasures there I took   20
That with the fancy I awoke,
And found (ah me!) this flesh of mine
More like a stock than like a vine.

Dreams

Here we are all, by day; by night, we're hurled
By dreams, each one into a several[1] world.

Delight in Disorder

A sweet disorder in the dress
Kindles in clothes a wantonness.[1]
A lawn[2] about the shoulders thrown
Into a fine distractiòn;
An erring[3] lace, which here and there   5
Enthralls the crimson stomacher;[4]
A cuff neglectful, and thereby
Ribbons to flow confusedly;
A winning wave, deserving note,
In the tempestuous petticoat;   10
A careless shoestring, in whose tie
I see a wild civility:
Do more bewitch me than when art
Is too precise[5] in every part.

His Farewell to Sack[1]

Farewell, thou thing, time-past so known, so dear
To me as blood to life and spirit; near,
Nay, thou more near than kindred, friend, man, wife,
Male to the female, soul to body, life

1. Separate.
1. Most of the terms used to describe the ladies' clothing have an ethical or social overtone. Compare Jonson's *Still to Be Neat*, p. 1226.
2. A scarf of fine linen.
3. Wandering, floating.
4. The lower part of the bodice.
5. "Precise" and "precision" were terms used freely of Puritans; Herrick, in praising feminine disarray,

is defining the "sprezzatura," or careless grace, of his own Cavalier art.
1. Sack is sherry wine, imported from Spain or the Canaries; serious drinkers like Falstaff and Herrick made it a staple of their cellars. The depth of Herrick's feeling about sack should be contrasted with the feelings he expresses about his various mistresses.

To quick action, or the warm soft side   5
Of the resigning yet resisting bride.
The kiss of virgins; first-fruits of the bed;
Soft speech, smooth touch, the lips, the maidenhead;
These and a thousand sweets could never be
So near or dear as thou wast once to me.   10
O thou, the drink of gods and angels! Wine
That scatterest spirit and lust;[2] whose purest shine
More radiant than the summer's sunbeams shows,
Each way illustrious, brave; and like to those
Comets we see by night, whose shagg'd portents   15
Foretell the coming of some dire events,
Or some full flame which with a pride aspires,
Throwing about his wild and active fires.
'Tis thou, above nectar, O divinest soul!
(Eternal in thyself) that canst control   20
That which subverts whole nature: grief and care,
Vexation of the mind, and damned despair.
'Tis thou alone who with thy mystic fan[3]
Work'st more than wisdom, art, or nature can
To rouse the sacred madness,[4] and awake   25
The frost-bound blood and spirits, and to make
Them frantic with thy raptures, flashing through
The soul like lightning, and as active too.
'Tis not Apollo can, or those thrice three
Castalian sisters sing,[5] if wanting thee.   30
Horace, Anacreon both had lost their fame
Had'st thou not filled them with thy fire and flame.[6]
Phoebean splendor! and thou Thespian spring![7]
Of which sweet swans must drink before they sing
Their true-paced numbers and their holy lays   35
Which makes them worthy cedar[8] and the bays.
But why? why longer do I gaze upon
Thee with the eye of admiration?
Since I must leave thee, and enforced must say
To all thy witching beauties, Go, Away.   40
But if thy whimpering looks do ask me why,
Then know that nature bids thee go, not I.
'Tis her erroneous self has made a brain
Uncapable of such a sovereign
As is thy powerful self. Prithee not smile,   45
Or smile more inly, lest thy looks beguile

2. Pleasure.
3. Instrument for winnowing grain; associated with
Bacchus, god of wine.
4. Poetic inspiration or frenzy, often likened to
intoxication.
5. I.e., Apollo, god of poetry, and the nine muses
would all fall mute if deprived of wine.
6. Both Horace and Anacreon wrote about the
pleasures of wine bibbing.

7. In addition to being an epithet of Apollo, *phoebus* in Greek is also an adjective, meaning bright,
pure. The inhabitants of Thespiae in Boeotia worshipped the muses, and held an annual festival in
their honor at the spring of Hippocrene, nearby.
8. I.e., worth preserving: in antiquity, cedar oil
was used to preserve papyrus; the poet's crown is
woven of bay (i.e., laurel) leaves.

My vows denounced[9] in zeal, which thus much show thee,
That I have sworn but by thy looks to know thee.
Let others drink thee freely, and desire
Thee and their lips espoused, while I admire   50
And love thee but not taste thee. Let my muse
Fail of thy former helps, and only use
Her inadulterate strength. What's done by me
Hereafter shall smell of the lamp, not thee.[1]

Corinna's Going A-Maying

Get up! get up for shame! the blooming morn
Upon her wings presents the god unshorn.[1]
   See how Aurora throws her fair
   Fresh-quilted colors through the air:[2]
   Get up, sweet slug-a-bed, and see   5
   The dew bespangling herb and tree.
Each flower has wept and bowed toward the east
Above an hour since, yet you not dressed;
   Nay, not so much as out of bed?
   When all the birds have matins said,   10
   And sung their thankful hymns, 'tis sin,
   Nay, profanation to keep in,
Whenas a thousand virgins on this day
Spring, sooner than the lark, to fetch in May.[3]

Rise, and put on your foliage, and be seen   15
To come forth, like the springtime, fresh and green,
   And sweet as Flora.[4] Take no care
   For jewels for your gown or hair;
   Fear not; the leaves will strew
   Gems in abundance upon you;   20
Besides, the childhood of the day has kept,
Against you come, some orient[5] pearls unwept;
   Come and receive them while the light
   Hangs on the dew-locks of the night,
   And Titan[6] on the eastern hill   25
   Retires himself, or else stands still

---

9. Proclaimed.
1. To "smell of the lamp" is a proverbial expression for a laborious and uninspired literary production.
1. Apollo, the sun god, whose hair (the rays of the sun) is never cut.
2. Aurora, goddess of the dawn, is both tossing her blankets aside, like one anxious to be up, and spreading over the earth a freshly composed coverlet of light.

3. On May Day morning, it was the custom to gather whitethorn blossoms and trim the house with them (see below, lines 30–35).
4. Flora, Italian goddess of flowers, had her festival in the spring.
5. Eastern, as pearls come from the Orient, but also rosy and glowing like the rising sun. "Against": until.
6. The sun.

Till you come forth. Wash, dress, be brief in praying:
Few beads[7] are best when once we go a-Maying.

Come, my Corinna, come; and, coming, mark
How each field turns a street,[8] each street a park   30
   Made green and trimmed with trees; see how
   Devotion gives each house a bough
   Or branch: each porch, each door ere this,
   An ark, a tabernacle is,[9]
Made up of whitethorn neatly interwove,   35
As if here were those cooler shades of love.
   Can such delights be in the street
   And open fields, and we not see 't?
   Come, we'll abroad; and let's obey
   The proclamation made for May,   40
And sin no more, as we have done, by staying;
But, my Corinna, come, let's go a-Maying.

There's not a budding boy or girl this day
But is got up and gone to bring in May;
   A deal of youth, ere this, is come   45
   Back, and with whitethorn laden home.
   Some have dispatched their cakes and cream
   Before that we have left to dream;
And some have wept, and wooed, and plighted troth,
And chose their priest, ere we can cast off sloth.   50
   Many a green-gown[1] has been given,
   Many a kiss, both odd and even;[2]
   Many a glance, too, has been sent
   From out the eye, love's firmament;
Many a jest told of the keys betraying   55
This night, and locks picked; yet we're not a-Maying.

Come, let us go while we are in our prime,
And take the harmless folly of the time.
   We shall grow old apace, and die
   Before we know our liberty.   60
   Our life is short, and our days run
   As fast away as does the sun;
And, as a vapor or a drop of rain
Once lost, can ne'er be found again,
   So when or you or I are made   65
   A fable, song, or fleeting shade,

7. A casual term for prayers, but with overtones of
the old (Catholic) religion, which in the next stanza
is playfully converted into, and identified with, the
worship of nature.
8. Turns into a street.
9. The doorways, ornamented with whitethorn, are
like the Hebrew Ark of the Covenant, or the sanctuary that housed it; May sprigs are the central
mystery of the religion of nature.
1. Got by rolling in the grass.
2. Kisses odd and even in kissing games.

All love, all liking, all delight
Lies drowned with us in endless night.
Then while time serves, and we are but decaying,
Come, my Corinna, come, let's go a-Maying.   70

The Lily in a Crystal

You have beheld a smiling rose
   When virgins' hands have drawn
   O'er it a cobweb-lawn;[1]
And here you see, this lily shows,
   Tombed in a crystal stone,   5
More fair in this transparent case
   Than when it grew alone
   And had but single grace.

You see how cream but naked is,
   Nor dances in the eye   10
   Without a strawberry;
Or some fine tincture,[2] like to this,
   Which draws the sight thereto,
More by that wantoning[3] with it
   Than when the paler hue   15
   No mixture did admit.

You see how amber through the streams
   More gently strokes the sight
   With some concealed delight[4]
Than when he darts his radiant beams   20
   Into the boundless air,
Where either too much life his worth
   Doth all at once impair
   Or set it little forth.

Put purple grapes or cherries in-   25
   To glass, and they will send
   More beauty to commend
Them from that clean and subtle skin
   Than if they naked stood,
And had no other pride at all   30
   But their own flesh and blood
   And tinctures natural.

Thus lily, rose, grape, cherry, cream,
   And strawberry do stir

1. A very fine, transparent linen.
2. Slight coloration.
3. Toying, sporting.

4. Some varieties of cloudy amber do in fact look
more attractive under water.

More love when they transfer   35
A weak, a soft, a broken beam,
 Than if they should discover
At full their proper excellence
 Without some scene[5] cast over
 To juggle with the sense.   40

Thus let this crystaled lily be
 A rule how far to teach
 Your nakedness must reach,
And that no further than we see
 Those glaring colors laid   45
By art's wise hand, but to this end
 They should obey a shade
 Lest they too far extend.

So, though you're white as swan or snow
 And have the power to move   50
 A world of men to love,
Yet when your lawns and silks shall flow
 And that white cloud divide
Into a doubtful twilight, then,
 Then will your hidden pride   55
 Raise greater fires in men.

To the Virgins, to Make Much of Time

Gather ye rosebuds while ye may,
 Old time is still a-flying;
And this same flower that smiles today,
 Tomorrow will be dying.

The glorious lamp of heaven, the sun,   5
 The higher he's a-getting,
The sooner will his race be run,
 And nearer he's to setting.

That age is best which is the first,
 When youth and blood are warmer;   10
But being spent, the worse, and worst
 Times still succeed the former.

Then be not coy, but use your time,
 And while ye may, go marry;
For having lost but once your prime,   15
 You may forever tarry.

5. Veil.

The Hock-Cart,[1] or Harvest Home

to the Right Honorable Mildmay, Earl of Westmoreland

Come, sons of summer, by whose toil
We are the lords of wine and oil;[2]
By whose tough labors and rough hands
We rip up first, then reap our lands.
Crowned with the ears of corn, now come   5
And, to the pipe, sing harvest home.
Come forth, my Lord, and see the cart
Dressed up with all the country art.
See here a maukin,[3] there a sheet,
As spotless pure as it is sweet,   10
The horses, mares, and frisking fillies
Clad all in linen, white as lilies,
The harvest swains and wenches bound
For joy to see the hock-cart crowned.
    About the cart, hear how the rout   15
Of rural younglings raise the shout,
Pressing before, some coming after,
Those with a shout and these with laughter.
Some bless the cart, some kiss the sheaves,
Some prank[4] them up with oaken leaves;   20
Some cross the fill-horse,[5] some with great
Devotion stroke the home-borne wheat;
While other rustics, less attent
To prayers than to merriment,
Run after with their breeches rent.   25
    Well, on, brave boys, to your Lord's hearth,
Glittering with fire; where, for your mirth,
Ye shall see first the large and chief
Foundation of your feast, fat beef;
With upper stories, mutton, veal,   30
And bacon, which makes full the meal,
With several dishes standing by,
As here a custard, there a pie,
And here all-tempting frumenty.[6]
And for to make the merry cheer,   35
If smirking wine be wanting here,[7]
There's that which drowns all care, stout beer:

---

1. The last cart carrying home the harvest; hence the occasion of a rural festival, traditional throughout Europe and the classical world. Mildmay was the second member of the Fane family to be earl of Westmoreland (from 1628 to 1666).
2. Wine and oil are the yields of Mediterranean farming; Herrick uses them to suggest the universality of his local English feast.
3. Scarecrow.

4. Dress, adorn.
5. The fill-horse is harnessed between the shafts of the cart. Crossing the horse and kissing the sheaves are old pre-Reformation practices, to which Herrick applies the emphatically placed word "Devotion." Puritans would have used, with equal emphasis, the word "Superstition."
6. Pudding.
7. If bubbling wine is not in good supply.

Which freely drink to your Lord's health,
Then to the plough (the common-wealth),[8]
Next to your flails, your fans, your vats,   40
Then to the maids with wheaten hats,
To the rough sickle and crook'd scythe,
Drink, frolic boys, till all be blithe.
    Feed, and grow fat; and, as ye eat,
Be mindful that the lab'ring neat,[9]   45
As you, may have their fill of meat.
And know, besides, ye must revoke[1]
The patient ox unto his yoke,
And all go back unto the plough
And harrow, though they're hanged up now.   50
And you must know, your Lord's word's true,
Feed him ye must whose food fills you,
And that this pleasure is like rain,
Not sent ye for to drown your pain
But for to make it spring again.[2]   55

Upon the Nipples of Julia's Breast

Have ye beheld (with much delight)
A red rose peeping through a white?
Or else a cherry (double graced)
Within a lily center-placed?
Or ever marked the pretty beam   5
A strawberry shows half drowned in cream?
Or seen rich rubies blushing through
A pure smooth pearl, and orient too?
So like to this, nay all the rest,
Is each neat niplet of her breast.   10

To Blossoms

Fair pledges of a fruitful tree,
    Why do ye fall so fast?
    Your date is not so past
But you may stay yet here a while,
    To blush and gently smile,   5
        And go at last.

---

8. The plough is the common (universal, vulgar) source of everybody's wealth; as the whole poem is tinged with anti-Puritan feeling, the word "commonwealth" in this earthy sense may be used to contrast with Puritan republican theories. "Fans" were used to separate grain from chaff.
9. Cattle; their "meat" is of course grain or hay.

1. Call back.
2. Spring is the rainy season, figured in the present liquid showers; but the sentence intimates a darker meaning as well: pain and labor, for the working man, are continually renewed, i.e., made to "spring again."

What, were ye born to be
    An hour or half's delight,
    And so to bid good night?
'Twas pity Nature brought you forth   10
    Merely to show your worth,
        And lose you quite.

But you are lovely leaves, where we
    May read how soon things have
    Their end, though ne'er so brave;   15
And after they have shown their pride
    Like you a while, they glide
        Into the grave.

To the Water Nymphs Drinking at the Fountain

Reach with your whiter hands to me
    Some crystal of the spring;
And I about the cup shall see
    Fresh lilies flourishing.

Or else, sweet nymphs, do you but this—   5
    To the glass your lips incline;
And I shall see by that one kiss
    The water turned to wine.

Upon Jack and Jill. Epigram[1]

When Jill complains to Jack for want of meat,
Jack kisses Jill, and bids her freely eat.
Jill says, Of what? Says Jack, On that sweet kiss,
Which full of nectar and ambrosia is,
The food of poets. So I thought, says Jill;   5
That makes them look so lank, so ghost-like still.
Let poets feed on air or what they will;
Let me feed full till that I fart, says Jill.

To Marygolds

Give way, an[1] ye be ravished by the sun,
And hang the head whenas the act is done.
Spread as he spreads; wax less as he does wane,
And as he shuts, close up to maids again.

---

1. Compare Jonson, *On Giles and Joan*, p. 1211.
1. If.

His Prayer to Ben Jonson

When I a verse shall make,
Know I have prayed thee,
For old religion's sake,[1]
Saint Ben to aid me.

Make the way smooth for me   5
When I, thy Herrick,
Honoring thee, on my knee,
Offer my lyric.

Candles I'll give to thee
And a new altar;   10
And thou Saint Ben shalt be
Writ in my psalter.

The Bad Season Makes the Poet Sad[1]

Dull to myself and almost dead to these
My many fresh and fragrant mistresses,
Lost to all music now, since every thing
Puts on the semblance here of sorrowing.[2]
Sick is the land to the heart, and doth endure   5
More dangerous faintings by her desperate cure.
But if that golden age would come again,
And Charles here rule as he before did reign,
If smooth and unperplexed the seasons were,
As when the sweet Maria livèd here,   10
I should delight to have my curls half drowned
In Tyrian dews,[3] and head with roses crowned,
And once more yet (ere I am laid out dead)
Knock at a star with my exalted head.[4]

The Night-Piece to Julia

Her eyes the glow-worm lend thee,
The shooting stars attend thee;

1. The Puritans were hostile to the invocation of saints, above all such "saints" as Ben Jonson. Herrick plays on the fact that Jonson was for a while a Catholic (of the "old religion"), as well as a saint in the mock-religion of poetry.
1. The bad season is evidently political, not meteorological. If line 10 refers to Charles's queen Henrietta Maria, the poem must have been written after 1644, when her highness was forced to retire to France.

2. The absence of verbs from the first three lines is surely deliberate; Herrick aims at an effect of languor and passivity.
3. Perfume from Tyre was one of many Middle Eastern luxuries proverbial in Roman times.
4. The last line translates literally the last line of Horace's first ode, to Maecenas. Herrick hopes once more to have enlightened readers and an enlightened patron.

And the elves also,
Whose little eyes glow
Like the sparks of fire, befriend thee.   5

No Will-o'th'-Wisp mislight thee,
Nor snake or slow-worm[1] bite thee;
But on, on thy way,
Not making a stay,
Since ghost there's none to affright thee.   10

Let not the dark thee cumber;
What though the moon does slumber?
The stars of the night
Will lend thee their light
Like tapers clear without number.   15

Then, Julia, let me woo thee
Thus, thus to come unto me:
And when I shall meet
Thy silv'ry feet,
My soul I'll pour into thee.   20

Upon His Verses

What offspring other men have got,
The how, where, when I question not.
These are the children I have left;
Adopted some, none got by theft.
But all are touched (like lawful plate)[1]   5
And no verse illegitimate.

His Return to London

From the dull confines of the drooping West,
To see the day spring from the pregnant East,
Ravished in spirit, I come, nay more, I fly
To thee, blest place of my nativity!
Thus, thus with hallowed foot I touch the ground   5
With thousand blessings by thy fortune crowned.
O fruitful Genius![1] that bestowest here
An everlasting plenty, year by year.
O place! O people! Manners! framed to please

---

1. Will-o'-the-wisp traditionally draws travelers astray by holding a false light before them. "Slow-worm": a limbless lizard.
1. A special variety of quartz, known as basanite, was used to test gold and silver objects; the color of the smear left by the object on the touchstone served as evidence of its purity.
1. The Genius of a place was its guardian deity; the phrase and concept were originally Latin.

All nations, customs, kindreds, languages!   10
I am a free-born Roman;[2] suffer then
That I amongst you live a citizen.
London my home is, though by hard fate sent
Into a long and irksome banishment;
Yet since called back, henceforward let me be,   15
O native country, repossessed by thee!
For, rather than I'll to the West return,
I'll beg of thee first here to have mine urn.
Weak I am grown, and must in short time fall;
Give thou my sacred relics burial.[3]   20

1647?

Upon Julia's Clothes

Whenas in silks my Julia goes,
Then, then, methinks, how sweetly flows
That liquefaction of her clothes.

Next, when I cast mine eyes and see
That brave[1] vibration each way free,   5
Oh, how that glittering taketh me!

Upon Prue, His Maid

In this little urn is laid
Prudence Baldwin, once my maid,
From whose happy spark here let
Spring the purple violet.

To His Book's End[1]

To his book's end this last line he'd have placed:
Jocund his muse was, but his life was chaste.

To His Conscience[1]

Can I not sin, but thou wilt be
My private protonotary?[2]

2. An ancient Roman born in the city was said to
be "free of it," i.e., entitled to its special rights and
privileges, including residence there.
3. As a priest and a poet, Herrick might fairly claim
that his relics were "sacred."
1. Glorious, splendid.

1. The last poem of *Hesperides*.
1. This and the following poem are from *Noble
Numbers*, the collection of Herrick's religious poems
that was bound together with *Hesperides*.
2. Chief recording clerk of a court.

Can I not woo thee to pass by
A short and sweet iniquity?
I'll cast a mist and cloud upon   5
My delicate transgression
So utter dark as that no eye
Shall see the hugged impiety.
Gifts blind the wise, and bribes do please
And wind[3] all other witnesses: 10
And wilt not thou with gold be tied
To lay thy pen and ink aside?
That in the mirk[4] and tongueless night
Wanton I may, and thou not write?
It will not be; and therefore now   15
For times to come I'll make this vow,
From aberrations to live free,
So I'll not fear the Judge, or thee.

A Grace for a Child

Here a little child I stand,
Heaving up my either hand;
Cold as paddocks[1] though they be,
Here I lift them up to thee,
For a benison[2] to fall   5
On our meat and on us all. *Amen.*

---

3. Entangle.   1. Frogs.
4. Black, with an added overtone of filth.   2. Blessing.

GEORGE HERBERT
1593–1633

1633: *The Temple.*

George Herbert was the fifth son of an ancient and eminent Welsh family.
His father died when he was young, and he was brought up by his mother,
Magdalen Herbert, a lady notable for her piety and for her patronage of
literary men like Donne. After taking his degrees with distinction at Cambridge, George Herbert was elected Public Orator of the university. It was a
post carrying dignity and even some authority: its incumbent was called on
to express, in the florid Latin of the day, the sentiments of the university on
public occasions. Other men had used the position as a stepping stone to
high political office; and this idea certainly tantalized Herbert, who also
served twice, during the early 1620s, as a member of Parliament. But the
death of his influential patrons, and the bent of his own temper, drew him

in another direction. In 1626 he took a minor office in the church; in 1629 he married Jane Danvers; and in 1630 he accepted the living of Bemerton near Salisbury, and took holy orders.

Many younger sons of highly connected houses entered the church in those days—picking up a sinecure here and a nonresident ministry there; accepting the pay, and letting the work be done by underpaid curates; filling the offices of the church, perhaps without scandal, but also without the least breath of spiritual fervor. At Bemerton, on the contrary, George Herbert became at once what the age delighted to recognize as "a learned, godly, and painful [painstaking] divine." He preached and prayed; he rebuilt the church out of his own pocket; he visited the poor, consoled the sick, and sat by the bed of the dying—administering true pastoral care to the plowman and the peer alike. "Holy Mr. Herbert" became the talk of the countryside in the three short years of his ministry, before he died of consumption. And during these years, he completed the volume of poems known as *The Temple*, which was published shortly after his death, in 1633, by the friend to whom it had been left. His fame rests on this volume, and all our selections are taken from it.

Technically, Herbert is so deft that a casual reader risks dismissing him as merely ingenious. Like Donne, he enjoys complicated stanzas and titles that imply a distant figurative relation to the poems themselves (e.g., *The Pulley*). Though not all the poems of the volume he titled *The Temple* bear analogy to the specific parts or occasions of a church structure, enough do so to intimate a recurrent parallel. Herbert is a master of the unexpected, climactic quiet simplicity (e.g., *Prayer* [1]). He enjoys applying homely images— from commerce, law, or a game of cards—to spiritual matters; in the same spirit of humorous reverence, he delighted in collecting homely proverbs from the mouths of country folk. Strikingly among English authors, he is a poet of silence and humility (e.g., *The Altar* and *Love* [3]). Yet he is no docile lamb. The awful experience of spiritual barrenness Herbert knows and renders (e.g., in *Denial* and *The Flower*) as no one will render it till Gerard Manley Hopkins in the nineteenth century. Herbert was profoundly, traditionally Anglican—devoted to church music, stained glass windows, and the established rituals; yet a major theme in his work is the recovery of fresh feeling from old and apparently sterile formulas. No English poet makes more frequent or more subtle use of the ancient analogical patterns known as "types." Through these analogies, developed over the centuries by preachers, poets, and philosophers of the church, one can see events of the Old Testament as foreshadowing events of the New, and these in turn as describing actions of the individual Christian heart in its perpetual search for renewal and redemption. Working within this tradition, Herbert delights in using ancient devices and traditional images to achieve a spiritual feeling remarkably pure and personal, fresh and free.

A recurrent theme is contrast between art's complexity and feeling's direct simplicity (e.g., the two *Jordan* poems, which hark back to Sidney's treatment of the same theme, in a different context, in the first of the *Astrophil and Stella* sonnets). But Herbert not only plays *with* form, he plays *against* it, as in *Denial*, where each last line of the first five stanzas fails to rhyme, ending on a deliberate dead note—until, in the final stanza, the rhyme is triumphantly completed. *Church Monuments* is another poem that is enriched by seeing in it a counter-form.

Because Herbert is as much an ecclesiastical as a religious poet, one would not expect him to make much appeal to an age as secular as our own; but it has not proved so. All sorts of readers, not otherwise noticeably devout, have responded to his quiet intensity; and the opinion has even been voiced that if Donne was the supreme metaphysical poet for readers of the 1930s, Herbert occupies that position for the 1980s.

Because all Herbert's poems have the same publication date (1633), we do not bother repeating it for each separate one.

The Altar[1]

A broken ALTAR, Lord, thy servant rears,
  Made of a heart, and cemented with tears:
    Whose parts are as thy hand did frame;
    No workman's tool hath touched the same.[2]
          A HEART alone   5
          Is such a stone,
          As nothing but
          Thy power doth cut.
          Wherefore each part
          Of my hard heart   10
          Meets in this frame,
          To praise thy Name:
  That, if I chance to hold my peace,
    These stones to praise thee may not cease.[3]
Oh let thy blessed SACRIFICE be mine,   15
And sanctify this ALTAR to be thine.

Redemption[1]

Having been tenant long to a rich lord,
  Not thriving, I resolvèd to be bold,
And make a suit unto him, to afford
  A new small-rented lease, and cancel th' old.[2]

In heaven at his manor I him sought: 5
  They told me there that he was lately gone

---

1. This poem and *Easter Wings* (below) are "shaped verses," which represent, by the typographical shape of the poem on the page, some part of the subject. Though sometimes condemned as "false wit," this sort of poem has appealed to an occasional author from Hellenistic times to the present. Among recent examples are *Vision and Prayer* by Dylan Thomas and *Un Coup de Dés* by Stéphane Mallarmé.

2. A reference to Exodus 20.25, in which the Lord enjoins Moses to build an altar without using cut stone or any tools.

3. Herbert wants his poem to praise God whether or not it is being read or spoken. There is also a reference to Luke 19.40: "I tell you that, if these should hold their peace, the stones would immediately cry out." Herbert's poetry, like Milton's, is rich to overflowing in Scriptural echoes.

1. "Redemption" means literally "buying back." In this beautifully concise sonnet, Herbert figures God as a landlord, himself as a discontented tenant.

2. I.e., to ask him for a new lease, involving a smaller rent, and to cancel the old lease. Herbert is often concerned to put spiritual relationships in terms of humble, everyday business transactions, over which he casts a sacramental coloring.

About some land which he had dearly bought
   Long since on earth, to take possession.

I straight returned, and knowing his great birth,
   Sought him accordingly in great resorts—
     In cities, theaters, gardens, parks, and courts: 10
At length I heard a ragged noise and mirth

   Of thieves and murderers; there I him espied,
   Who straight, "Your suit is granted," said, and died.

Easter[1]

Rise, heart, thy lord is risen. Sing his praise
         Without delays,
Who takes thee by the hand, that thou likewise
         With him may'st rise;
That, as his death calcinèd[2] thee to dust,   5
His life may make thee gold, and much more, just.

Awake, my lute, and struggle for thy part
         With all thy art.
The cross taught all wood to resound his name
         Who bore the same.   10
His stretchèd sinews taught all strings what key
Is best to celebrate this most high day.

Consort, both heart and lute, and twist a song
         Pleasant and long;
Or, since all music is but three parts vied[3]   15
         And multiplied,
Oh let thy blessèd spirit bear a part,
And make up our defects with his sweet art.

The Song

   I got me flowers to strew thy way,
   I got me boughs off many a tree;   20
   But thou wast up by break of day
   And brought'st thy sweets along with thee.

   The sun arising in the east,
   Though he give light and th' east perfume,
   If they should offer to contest   25
   With thy arising, they presume.

1. Herbert's Easter poem consists of an invitation to song, and then of the song itself.
2. Burned to powder.
3. Increased by repetition. Harmony is based on the triad.

Can there be any day but this,
Though many suns to shine endeavor?
We count three hundred, but we miss:[4]
There is but one, and that one ever.   30

Easter Wings[1]

Lord, who createdst man in wealth and store,[2]
  Though foolishly he lost the same,
    Decaying more and more
      Till he became
        Most poor: 5
        With thee
      O let me rise
    As larks, harmoniously,
  And sing this day thy victories:
Then shall the fall further the flight in me.   10

My tender age in sorrow did begin:
  And still with sicknesses and shame
    Thou didst so punish sin,
      That I became
        Most thin.   15
        With thee
      Let me combine,
    And feel this day thy victory;
  For, if I imp[3] my wing on thine,
Affliction shall advance the flight in me.   20

Affliction (1)

When first thou didst entice to thee my heart,
    I thought the service brave:[1]
So many joys I writ down for my part,
    Besides what I might have
Out of my stock of natural delights,   5
Augmented with thy gracious benefits.

I lookèd on thy furniture so fine,
    And made it fine to me;
Thy glorious household stuff did me entwine,
    And 'tice me unto thee.   10

---

4. The 300-plus days of the year are all but a single day suffused with the light of the rising Son.
1. Early editions of Herbert print *Easter Wings* with the lines running vertically.

2. Abundance.
3. Graft (a technical term from falconry).
1. Splendid.

Such stars I counted mine: both heaven and earth
Paid me my wages in a world of mirth.

What pleasures could I want, whose king I served,
        Where joys my fellows were?
Thus argued into hopes, my thoughts reserved   15
        No place for grief or fear;
Therefore my sudden soul caught at the place,
And made her youth and fierceness seek thy face.

At first thou gav'st me milk and sweetnesses;
        I had my wish and way:
My days were strawed[2] with flowers and happiness;   20
        There was no month but May.
But with my years sorrow did twist and grow,
And made a party unawares for woe.

My flesh began unto my soul in pain,   25
        Sicknesses cleave my bones;
Consuming agues dwell in every vein,
        And tune my breath to groans.
Sorrow was all my soul; I scarce believed,
Till grief did tell me roundly, that I lived.   30

When I got health, thou took'st away my life,
        And more; for my friends die:
My mirth and edge was lost: a blunted knife
        Was of more use than I.
Thus thin and lean without a fence or friend,   35
I was blown through with every storm and wind.

Whereas my birth and spirit rather took
        The way that takes the town,
Thou didst betray me to a lingering book,
        And wrap me in a gown.   40
I was entangled in the world of strife,
Before I had the power to change my life.

Yet, for I threatened oft the siege to raise,
        Not simpering all mine age,
Thou often didst with academic praise   45
        Melt and dissolve my rage.
I took thy sweetened pill, till I came where
I could not go away, nor persevere.

Yet lest perchance I should too happy be
        In my unhappiness,   50

2. Strewn.

Turning my purge to food, thou throwest me
    Into more sicknesses.
Thus doth thy power cross-bias[3] me, not making
Thine own gift good, yet me from my ways taking.

Now I am here, what thou wilt do with me   55
    None of my books will show:
I read, and sigh, and wish I were a tree,
    For sure then I should grow
To fruit or shade; at least, some bird would trust
Her household to me, and I should be just.   60

Yet, though thou troublest me, I must be meek;
    In weakness must be stout:
Well, I will change the service, and go seek
    Some other master out.
Ah, my dear God! though I am clean forgot,   65
Let me not love thee, if I love thee not.

Prayer (1)[1]

Prayer, the church's banquet; angels' age,
    God's breath in man returning to his birth;
The soul in paraphrase, heart in pilgrimage;
    The Christian plummet, sounding heaven and earth;

Engine against th' Almighty, sinner's tower,   5
    Reversèd thunder, Christ-side-piercing spear,
The six-days' world transposing in an hour;
    A kind of tune which all things hear and fear:

Softness and peace and joy and love and bliss;
    Exalted manna, gladness of the best;   10
    Heaven in ordinary,[2] man well dressed,
The milky way, the bird of paradise,

    Church-bells beyond the stars heard, the soul's blood,
    The land of spices; something understood.

---

3. Frustrate.
1. Herbert often uses the same title for several different poems; editors distinguish them by adding numbers. This extraordinary sonnet without a verb gains many of its effects from the pace at which one reads its metaphorical phrases. The punctuation as printed suggests only one of many possible patterns.
2. I.e., "everyday heaven"; the word was used specifically of the meal set out each day in a public eating house.

Jordan (1)[1]

Who says that fictions only and false hair
Become a verse? Is there in truth no beauty?
Is all good structure in a winding stair?
May no lines pass, except they do their duty
    Not to a true, but painted chair?[2]   5

Is it no verse, except enchanted groves
And sudden arbors shadow coarse-spun lines?[3]
Must purling streams refresh a lover's loves?
Must all be veiled, while he that reads, divines,
    Catching the sense at two removes?   10

Shepherds are honest people; let them sing:
Riddle who list, for me, and pull for prime:[4]
I envy no man's nightingale or spring;
Nor let them punish me with loss of rhyme,
    Who plainly say, *My God, My King.*   15

Church Monuments[1]

While that my soul repairs to her devotion,
Here I entomb my flesh, that it betimes
May take acquaintance of this heap of dust
To which the blast of death's incessant motion,
Fed with the exhalation of our crimes,   5
Drives all at last. Therefore I gladly trust

My body to this school, that it may learn
To spell his elements and find his birth[2]
Written in dusty heraldry and lines
Which dissolution sure doth best discern,   10
Comparing dust with dust and earth with earth.
These[3] laugh at jet and marble, put for signs

1. "Crossing Jordan" is a symbol for entering into the Promised Land, and it seems likely that Herbert means to indicate by his title that for a poet who has crossed the river (i.e., come into God's country), the complexities (and the clichés) of worldly poetry cease to be necessary or desirable.
2. May no poems ("lines") pass as good unless they make a reverence ("do their duty") to a false throne? It has often been the custom for men to bow before a throne, whether it was occupied or not (see Donne, *Satire* 3, lines 47–48); but to require bowing to a throne in a painting would be excessive. Herbert implies that earthly love is a mere painted imitation of divine love.
3. "Sudden": i.e., that appear unexpectedly (an artificial effect much sought after in landscape gar-

dening). "Shadow": shade, but also overshadow, cause to be overlooked. Herbert is suggesting that flashy dramatic effects and inherited images ("enchanted groves," "purling streams," and so on) obscure poor craftsmanship.
4. To draw a lucky card in the game of "primero." Herbert implies that anyone who understands one of the complex poems he is describing (and parodying) has made a wild and lucky guess. "For me": as far as I'm concerned.
1. The earlier, manuscript version of the poem does not divide it into stanzas.
2. I.e., the elements and birth (lineage) of the body, which comes ultimately from dust for noble and plebian alike.
3. Dust and earth.

To sever the good fellowship of dust
And spoil the meeting. What shall point out them[4]
When they shall bow and kneel and fall down flat   15
To kiss those heaps which now they have in trust?
Dear flesh, while I do pray, learn here thy stem
And true descent, that, when thou shalt grow fat

And wanton in thy cravings, thou mayest know
That flesh is but the glass which holds the dust   20
That measures all our time, which also shall
Be crumbled into dust. Mark here below
How tame these ashes are, how free from lust,
That thou mayest fit thyself against thy fall.

The Windows[1]

Lord, how can man preach thy eternal word?
    He is a brittle, crazy[2] glass,
Yet in thy temple thou dost him afford
    This glorious and transcendent place,
    To be a window through thy grace.   5

But when thou dost anneal[3] in glass thy story,
    Making thy life to shine within
The holy preachers, then the light and glory
    More reverend grows, and more doth win,
    Which else shows wat'rish, bleak, and thin.   10

Doctrine and life, colors and light, in one
    When they combine and mingle, bring
A strong regard and awe; but speech alone
    Doth vanish like a flaring thing,
    And in the ear, not conscience, ring.   15

Denial

When my devotions could not pierce
    Thy silent ears,
Then was my heart broken, as was my verse:
    My breast was full of fears
        And disorder: 5

---

4. I.e., the inhabitants of the tombs. On the Day of Judgment they may crave to be covered from the wrath of God.
1. From his little parish at Bemerton, George Herbert used to walk twice a week across Salisbury Plain to the great cathedral, where he delighted not only in the music but in the stained-glass windows. For the Puritans, both music and pictures were forms of idolatry; and Herbert's last stanza seems to challenge directly Puritan belief in the efficacy of the spoken word alone.
2. Flawed, therefore distorting.
3. Heat, in order to fix laid-on colors.

My bent thoughts, like a brittle bow,
   Did fly asunder:
Each took his way; some would to pleasures go,
  Some to the wars and thunder
    Of alarms.   10

As good go anywhere, they say,
   As to benumb
Both knees and heart in crying night and day,
  Come, come, my God, O come!
    But no hearing.   15

O that thou shouldst give dust a tongue
   To cry to thee,
And then not hear it crying! All day long
  My heart was in my knee,[1]
    But no hearing.   20

Therefore my soul lay out of sight,
   Untuned, unstrung:
My feeble spirit, unable to look right,
  Like a nipped blossom, hung
    Discontented.   25

O cheer and tune my heartless breast;
   Defer no time,
That so thy favors granting my request,
  They and my mind may chime,[2]
    And mend my rhyme.   30

Virtue

Sweet day, so cool, so calm, so bright,
The bridal of the earth and sky:
The dew shall weep thy fall tonight;
  For thou must die.

Sweet rose, whose hue, angry and brave,[1] 5
Bids the rash gazer wipe his eye:
Thy root is ever in its grave,
  And thou must die.

Sweet spring, full of sweet days and roses,
A box where sweets[2] compacted lie; 10

---

1. I.e., my heart was bowed and bent, like my knee, in reverence.
2. Agree.

1. "Angry": having the hue of anger, red. "Brave": splendid.
2. Perfumes.

My music shows ye have your closes,[3]
    And all must die.

Only a sweet and virtuous soul,
Like seasoned timber, never gives;
But though the whole world turn to coal,[4]   15
    Then chiefly lives.

Man

My God, I heard this day
That none doth build a stately habitation,
    But he that means to dwell therein.
    What house more stately hath there been,
Or can be, than is man? to[1] whose creation   5
    All things are in decay.

For man is every thing
And more; he is a tree, yet bears more[2] fruit;
    A beast, yet is or should be more;
    Reason and speech we only bring.
Parrots may thank us, if they are not mute:
    They go upon the score.[3]

Man is all symmetry,
Full of proportions, one limb to another,
    And all to all the world besides;   15
    Each part may call the farthest, brother;
For head with foot hath private amity,
    And both with moons and tides.

Nothing hath got so far
But man hath caught and kept it as his prey.   20
    His eyes dismount the highest star:
    He is in little all the sphere.
Herbs gladly cure our flesh; because that they
    Find their acquaintance there.

For us the winds do blow,   25
The earth doth rest, heav'n move, and fountains flow;
    Nothing we see but means our good,
    As our delight, or as our treasure.

3. Concluding cadences. The expression shows that
Herbert intended his poem to be sung—as it has,
in fact, often been.
4. Be reduced to a cinder at the Last Judgment.
See 2 Peter 3.10.
1. Compared to.

2. An alternative reading is "no."
3. Man has a vegetable, an animal, and a spiritual
nature; he's the only creature which speaks and
reasons. Parrots may seem to be an exception to
the first of these rules, but they talk on credit
(because we taught them how).

The whole is either our cupboard of food,
　　　Or cabinet of pleasure.　　　　　　　　　　　30

　　　The stars have us to bed;
Night draws the curtain which the sun withdraws,
　　　Music and light attend our head.
　　　All things unto our flesh are kind
In their descent and being; to our mind　　　　35
　　　In their ascent and cause.

　　　Each thing is full of duty.
Waters united are our navigation,
　　　Distinguished, our habitation;
　　　Below, our drink; above, our meat;
Both are our cleanliness. Hath one such beauty?[4]　40
　　　Then how are all things neat!

　　　More servants wait on man
Than he'll take notice of; in every path,
　　　He treads down that which doth befriend him,
　　　When sickness makes him pale and wan.[5]　45
O mighty love! Man is one world, and hath
　　　Another to attend him.

　　　Since then, my God, thou hast
So brave a palace built, O, dwell in it,　　　　　50
　　　That it may dwell with thee at last!
　　　Till then, afford us so much wit,
That, as the world serves us, we may serve thee,
　　　And both thy servants be.

Jordan (2)[1]

When first my lines of heavenly joys made mention,
Such was their luster, they did so excel,
That I sought out quaint words, and trim invention;
My thoughts began to burnish,[2] sprout, and swell,
Curling with metaphors a plain intention,　　　　5
Decking the sense, as if it were to sell.[3]

Thousands of notions in my brain did run,
Offering their service, if I were not sped:[4]
I often blotted what I had begun;

4. All the elements serve us multiply, for instance water. Oceans are valuable for navigation; the earth was created by dividing waters from waters (Genesis 1.6–7); on earth water is drink, from above (as dew or manna), food. If one element can serve so richly, how beautiful is the sum of things.

5. Man thoughtlessly treads down the herb that will cure him when he's sick.
1. Cf. *Jordan (1)*, p. 1341.
2. Expand, burgeon.
3. For sale.
4. Supplied, satisfied.

This was not quick[5] enough, and that was dead.   10
Nothing could seem too rich to clothe the sun,
Much less those joys which trample on his head.[6]

As flames do work and wind when they ascend,
So did I weave myself into the sense;
But while I bustled, I might hear a friend   15
Whisper, "How wide[7] is all this long pretense!
There is in love a sweetness ready penned:
Copy out only that, and save expense."

Time

Meeting with Time, "Slack thing," said I,
"Thy scythe is dull; whet it for shame."
"No marvel, sir," he did reply,
"If it at length deserve some blame;
    But where one man would have me grind it,   5
    Twenty for one too sharp do find it."

"Perhaps some such of old did pass[1]
Who above all things loved this life;
To whom thy scythe a hatchet was,
Which now is but a pruning knife.[2]   10
    Christ's coming hath made man thy debtor,
    Since by thy cutting he grows better.

"And in his blessing thou art blessed,
For where thou only wert before
An executioner at best,   15
Thou art a gardener now, and more,
    An usher to convey our souls
    Beyond the utmost stars and poles.

"And this is that makes life so long,
While it detains us from our God.   20
Ev'n pleasures here increase the wrong,
And length of days lengthens the rod.[3]
    Who wants the place where God doth dwell
    Partakes already half of hell.

"Of what strange length must that needs be,   25
Which ev'n eternity excludes!"—

---

5. Lively, alive.
6. The "joys which trample on" the sun's head
are those of the Son.
7. Irrelevant, "wide of the mark."
1. Herbert is understood to be the speaker in stanzas 2, 3, 4, and the first two lines of stanza 5.

2. A hatchet kills, a pruning knife improves growing things like souls.
3. I.e., long life on earth is a punishment because
it keeps us from bliss. "Wants": lacks, does not
enjoy.

Thus far Time heard me patiently,
    Then chafing said, "This man deludes:
      What do I here before his door?
      He doth not crave less time, but more."   30

The Bunch of Grapes[1]

Joy, I did lock thee up;[2] but some bad man
    Hath let thee out again,
And now methinks I am where I began
    Sev'n years ago:[3] one vogue and vein,
    One air of thoughts usurps my brain.   5
I did towards Canaan draw, but now I am
Brought back to the Red Sea, the sea of shame.[4]

For as the Jews of old by God's command
    Traveled, and saw no town,
So now each Christian hath his journeys spanned;   10
    Their story pens and sets us down.[5]
    A single deed is small renown.
God's works are wide, and let in future times;
His ancient justice overflows our crimes.

Then have we too our guardian fires and clouds;   15
    Our Scripture-dew[6] drops fast;
We have our sands and serpents, tents and shrouds;[7]
    Alas! our murmurings come not last.
    But where's the cluster? where's the taste[8]
Of mine inheritance? Lord, if I must borrow,   20
Let me as well take up their[9] joy as sorrow.

But can he want[1] the grape who hath the wine?
    I have their fruit and more.
Blessèd be God, who prospered Noah's vine[2]
    And made it bring forth grapes good store.   25
    But much more him I must adore

1. When the children of Israel were desponding in the wilderness, God inspired Moses to send forth scouts, who returned to report that Canaan was a land of milk and honey. In evidence they carried back a single bunch of grapes so big they had to carry it between them on a pole (Numbers 13.23). Herbert, fainting in the desert of this world, asks for a similar token of his reward in the next.
2. I.e., I did take (as I thought) secure possession of thee.
3. The "seven years" may be an allusion to Herbert's personal history; he took holy orders in 1626, but no doubt dated his religious vocation from an earlier time. "Vogue": tendency.
4. The Red Sea, blushing, is the sea of shame; it is also the place to which the Lord remitted the querulous and plaintive Jews, as punishment.
5. The wandering of the Hebrews in the wilderness was thought to be a type (prefiguration) of the Christian's trials on his path to salvation.
6. I.e., manna.
7. Shelters.
8. I.e., token.
9. I.e., the Hebrews'.
1. Lack.
2. Noah's vine (Genesis 9) is taken as a type of the earth being replenished by God's command after the Flood.

Who of the Law's sour juice[3] sweet wine did make,
Even God himself being pressèd for my sake.

The Pilgrimage

I traveled on, seeing the hill where lay
    My expectation.
A long it was and weary way.
    The gloomy cave of desperation
I left on th' one, and on the other side   5
    The rock of pride.[1]

And so I came to fancy's meadow, strowed
    With many a flower;
Fain would I here have made abode,
    But I was quickened by my hour.   10
So to care's copse I came, and there got through
    With much ado.

That led me to the wild of passion, which
    Some call the wold[2]—
A wasted place but sometimes rich.   15
    Here I was robbed of all my gold
Save one good angel,[3] which a friend had tied
    Close to my side.

At length I got unto the gladsome hill
    Where lay my hope,   20
Where lay my heart; and, climbing still,
    When I had gained the brow and top,
A lake of brackish waters on the ground
    Was all I found.

With that abashed, and struck with many a sting   25
    Of swarming fears,
I fell, and cried, "Alas, my king!
    Can both the way and end be tears?"
Yet taking heart I rose, and then perceived
    I was deceived: 30

My hill was further; so I flung away,
    Yet heard a cry,

---

3. The severe and detailed rules of the Old Testament, as contrasted with the sweeter and more tolerant covenant of the New Testament. Christ himself was a Jewish grape crushed to make wholesome doctrine.

1. The spiritual pilgrimage or search through allegorical perils was a frequent literary motif long before Bunyan's *Pilgrim's Progress*; compare Henry Vaughan's *Regeneration*, below.

2. A "wold" is hill country, often treeless; irregular and barren, it emblematizes the wilderness of feeling.

3. A golden coin as well as (punningly) a guardian angel.

Just as I went: *None goes that way*
And lives: "If that be all," said I,
"After so foul a journey, death is fair,   35
And but a chair."[4]

The Collar

I struck the board[1] and cried, "No more;
                    I will abroad!
What? shall I ever sigh and pine?
My lines and life are free, free as the road,
    Loose as the wind, as large as store.
            Shall I be still in suit?[2]   5
Have I no harvest but a thorn
To let me blood, and not restore
What I have lost with cordial[3] fruit?
                    Sure there was wine   10
        Before my sighs did dry it; there was corn
        Before my tears did drown it.
    Is the year only lost to me?
        Have I no bays[4] to crown it,
No flowers, no garlands gay? all blasted?   15
                    All wasted?
    Not so, my heart; but there is fruit,
                    And thou hast hands.
            Recover all thy sigh-blown age
On double pleasures: leave thy cold dispute   20
Of what is fit and not. Forsake thy cage,
                    Thy rope of sands,[5]
Which petty thoughts have made, and made to thee
    Good cable, to enforce and draw,
                    And be thy law,   25
    While thou didst wink[6] and wouldst not see.
                    Away! take heed;
                    I will abroad.
Call in thy death's-head[7] there; tie up thy fears.
                    He that forbears   30
        To suit and serve his need,
                    Deserves his load."
But as I raved and grew more fierce and wild
                    At every word,

4. "Chair" implies rest and immobility, but also,
in the sense of "sedan chair," a conveyance.
1. Table.
2. In attendance, waiting on someone for a favor.
3. Giving heart's ease, restorative.
4. The poet's laurel wreath, here used as a general
symbol of festivity.

5. Christian restrictions on behavior, which the
"petty thoughts" of the docile believer have made
"good cable," i.e., strong.
6. Shut your eyes (to the real weakness of the
church's injunctions).
7. The skull which reminds the penitent of
approaching death.

Methought I heard one calling, *Child!*   35
And I replied, *My Lord*.

The Pulley

When God at first made man,
Having a glass of blessings standing by,
"Let us," said he, "pour on him all we can:
Let the world's riches, which dispersèd lie,
     Contract into a span."   5

So strength first made a way;
Then beauty flowed, then wisdom, honor, pleasure.
When almost all was out, God made a stay,
Perceiving that, alone of all his treasure,
     Rest in the bottom lay.[1]   10

"For if I should," said he,
"Bestow this jewel also on my creature,
He would adore my gifts instead of me,
And rest in Nature, not the God of Nature;
     So both should losers be.   15

"Yet let him keep the rest,
But keep them with repining restlessness:
Let him be rich and weary, that at least,
If goodness lead him not, yet weariness
     May toss him to my breast."   20

The Flower

How fresh, O Lord, how sweet and clean
Are thy returns! even as the flowers in spring;
     To which, besides their own demesne,[1]
The late-past frosts tributes of pleasure bring.
         Grief melts away   5
         Like snow in May,
     As if there were no such cold thing.

Who would have thought my shriveled heart
Could have recovered greenness? It was gone
         Quite underground; as flowers depart   10
     To see their mother-root, when they have blown,[2]

---

1. "Rest" in the poem has two senses ("remainder" and "repose"); Herbert works them against one another. This balance of forces suggests the pulley, which can draw us to God one way or the other.

1. Estate of one's own (here, beauty or pleasure). The word, spelled *demean* in the original text, may also be a short form of "demeanor," i.e., bearing.
2. Bloomed.

Where they together
All the hard weather,
Dead to the world, keep house unknown.

These are thy wonders, Lord of power,   15
Killing and quickening, bringing down to hell
    And up to heaven in an hour,
Making a chiming of a passing-bell.[3]
            We say amiss
            This or that is:
Thy word is all, if we could spell.   20

Oh that I once past changing were,
Fast in thy Paradise, where no flower can wither!
    Many a spring I shoot up fair,
Offering[4] at heaven, growing and groaning thither;   25
            Nor doth my flower
            Want a spring shower,[5]
My sins and I joining together.

But while I grow in a straight line,
Still upwards bent, as if heaven were mine own,   30
    Thy anger comes, and I decline:
What frost to that? what pole is not the zone
            Where all things burn,
            When thou dost turn,
And the least frown of thine is shown?[6]   35

And now in age I bud again,
After so many deaths I live and write;
    I once more smell the dew and rain,
And relish versing. Oh, my only light,
            It cannot be   40
            That I am he
On whom thy tempests fell all night.

These are thy wonders, Lord of love,
To make us see we are but flowers that glide;[7]
    Which when we once can find and prove,[8]   45
Thou hast a garden for us where to bide;
            Who would be more,
            Swelling through store,
Forfeit their Paradise by their pride.

---

3. The "passing-bell," intended to mark the death
of a parishioner, is tolled in a monotone; a chiming offers pleasant variety.
4. Aiming.
5. The tears of contrition produced by the "joining together" of the poet's conscience and his sins.

6. Lines 32–35 may be paraphrased: "What cold
compares to God's anger? Compared to God's
wrath, what polar chill would not seem like the
heat of the equator?"
7. Pass silently away.
8. Experience.

The Forerunners

The harbingers are come: see, see their mark;
White is their color, and behold my head.[1]
But must they have my brain? must they dispark[2]
Those sparkling notions which therein were bred?
   Must dullness turn me to a clod?   5
Yet have they left me "Thou art still my God."

Good men ye be to leave me my best room,
Even all my heart and what is lodgèd there:
I pass not,[3] I, what of the rest become,
So "Thou art still my God" be out of fear.   10
   He will be pleasèd with that ditty;
And if I please Him, I write fine and witty.

Farewell, sweet phrases, lovely metaphors:
But will ye leave me thus? when ye before
Of stews and brothels only knew the doors,   15
Then did I wash you with my tears, and more,
   Brought you to church well-dressed and clad:
My God must have my best, even all I had.

Lovely enchanting language, sugarcane,
Honey of roses, whither wilt thou fly?   20
Hath some fond lover 'ticed thee to thy bane?
And wilt thou leave the church and love a sty?
   Fie! thou wilt soil thy 'broidered coat,
And hurt thyself and him that sings the note.

Let foolish lovers, if they will love dung,   25
With canvas, not with arras,[4] clothe their shame:
Let Folly speak in her own native tongue.
True Beauty dwells on high; ours is a flame
   But borrowed thence to light us thither:
Beauty and beauteous words should go together.   30

Yet, if you go, I pass not; take your way.
For "Thou art still my God" is all that ye
Perhaps with more embellishment can say.
Go, birds of spring; let winter have his fee;

---

1. Great men when they traveled in the 17th century often had "harbingers" (cf. French, *auberge*, lodging), who rode ahead of the main party to commandeer resting places for the night. Customarily they marked the doors of the houses they had selected with chalk. Herbert's conceit is that he has been so marked, by the appearance of his first white hairs—a sign that all his fine language must be dispossessed, to make room for the great Lord to come.
2. Turn out.
3. I.e., I don't care. All the other thoughts in my house (my mind, my soul) can be turned out of doors, as long as you leave "my best room," my heart, and its one inhabitant, the thought "Thou art still my God."
4. I.e., with coarse cloth, not with fine tapestry.

Let a bleak paleness chalk the door,   35
So all within be livelier than before.

Discipline

Throw away thy rod,
Throw away thy wrath:
        O my God,
Take the gentle path.

For my heart's desire   5
Unto thine is bent:
        I aspire
To a full consent.

Not a word or look
I affect to own,   10
        But by book,
And thy book alone.[1]

Though I fail, I weep:
Though I halt in pace,
        Yet I creep   15
To the throne of grace.

Then let wrath remove;
Love will do the deed:
        For with love
Stony hearts will bleed.   20

Love is swift of foot;
Love's a man of war,[2]
        And can shoot,
And can hit from far.

Who can 'scape his bow?   25
That which wrought on thee,
        Brought thee low,
Needs must work on me.

Throw away thy rod;
Though man frailties hath,   30
        Thou art God:
Throw away thy wrath.

1. Disclaiming all independence, Herbert describes himself as an actor, who will speak only "by the book."
2. The jubilant song sung by Moses in Exodus 15 calls the Lord "a man of war"; but Herbert is thinking also, and without any apparent sense of contradiction, about Cupid, another divine bowman.

Death

Death, thou wast once an uncouth, hideous thing,
          Nothing but bones,
     The sad effect of sadder groans:
Thy mouth was open, but thou couldst not sing.

For we considered thee as at some six   5
          Or ten years hence,
     After the loss of life and sense,
Flesh being turned to dust and bones to sticks.

We looked on this side of thee, shooting short,
          Where we did find   10
     The shells of fledge-souls left behind[1]—
Dry dust, which sheds no tears, but may extort.

But since our Savior's death did put some blood
          Into thy face,
     Thou art grown fair and full of grace,   15
Much in request, much sought for as a good.

For we do now behold thee gay and glad
          As at doomsday,
     When souls shall wear their new array,
And all thy bones with beauty shall be clad.   20

Therefore we can go die as sleep, and trust
          Half that we have
     Unto an honest faithful grave,
Making our pillows either down or dust.

Love (3)

Love bade me welcome: yet my soul drew back,
          Guilty of dust and sin.
But quick-eyed Love, observing me grow slack[1]
          From my first entrance in,
Drew nearer to me, sweetly questioning   5
          If I lacked anything.[2]

"A guest," I answered, "worthy to be here":
          Love said, "You shall be he."

1. Souls which have left the body and gone to heaven are like fledgling chicks that have left the shell behind. That shell (the corpse), though it sheds no tears itself, can draw ("extort") them from the survivors.

1. Hesitant, as one feeling misgivings.
2. The first question of shopkeepers and tavern waiters to an entering customer would be "What d'ye lack?" (i.e., want).

"I, the unkind, ungrateful? Ah, my dear,
    I cannot look on thee."
Love took my hand, and smiling did reply,   10
    "Who made the eyes but I?"

"Truth, Lord; but I have marred them; let my shame
    Go where it doth deserve."
"And know you not," says Love, "who bore the blame?"   15
    "My dear, then I will serve."
"You must sit down," says Love, "and taste my meat."
    So I did sit and eat.

RICHARD CRASHAW
ca. 1613–1649

1644:   Fled from the Puritans to the Continent, where he embraced
        Roman Catholicism.

Richard Crashaw is a phenomenon unique in Anglo-Saxon taste; there is
really no other English poet who is much like him. His roots seem to be
sunk less in English literature than in Italian, Spanish, and neo-Latin writings. His personal background was thoroughly English (his father was a noted
Puritan clergyman, and his academic training was at Cambridge), but from
the first he was devoted to ritual, ceremony, and ecclesiastical exercise. This
habit of mind ultimately led him out of the English church altogether, and
into Roman Catholicism—the church, as many Englishmen considered it,
of the scarlet woman and of Antichrist himself. But, for one of Crashaw's
ardent devotional temperament, it was a natural home. In terms of chronological time, Crashaw spent only the last five or six years of his life on the
Continent and in the church of Rome; but in terms of his spiritual development, he never belonged anywhere else.

Poetically, Crashaw was a follower of George Herbert, as the title of his
second volume (Steps to the Temple) suggests. But the feeling one gets from
the two poets is altogether different. There is a little streak of quaint and
homely imagery in Herbert; Crashaw exaggerates it toward the grotesque. In
this practice he was following the writers of emblem-books—volumes in
which a picture with allegorical meanings stood at the head of a poem
explaining those meanings. He was also influenced by a widespread school
of Jesuit writers of sacred Latin epigrams, and by the great Italian writer of
conceits (concetti) Giambattista Marino, the first book of whose poem The
Massacre of the Innocents Crashaw translated. All these influences—plus,
of course, his own ardent temperament—pushed Crashaw toward the
exploitation of far-fetched, almost perverse parallels, in which familiar physical objects not only stood for, but were sometimes distorted by, extravagant
spiritual pressures. The method hardly allowed for any interest in "decorum," in the traditional sense of tonal harmony—and that, of course, is an

assumption about the proper character of poetry that has prevailed very generally, until recent times. Thus Crashaw was bitterly ridiculed during the nineteenth and early twentieth centuries for lines like those in *The Weeper*, his poem on the tears of Saint Mary Magdalen:

> And now where'er he strays
> Among the Galilean mountains
> Or more unwelcome ways,
> He's followed by two faithful fountains;
> Two walking baths; two weeping motions;
> Portable and compendious oceans.

The ludicrous effect produced by these lines isn't open to question, any more than is the macabre effect produced by that little epigram *On Our Crucified Lord, Naked and Bloody* (below). But in seeking these effects, it is evident that Crashaw was a conscious and deliberate craftsman working in an established tradition which on the Continent often goes by the name of "baroque." Whether this term is worth importing into English literary history in order to take care of a largely isolated figure like Crashaw may be argued. Undeniably, it opens the way to make suggestive parallels, with Continental poetry and with developments in the sister arts. In any event, we of the modern world, with the violent and unresolved images of modern literature and the surrealist pyrotechnics behind us, seem better equipped to appreciate the poetry of Crashaw than readers have been for several hundred years past.

Since the image is so violent in Crashaw, the structure of his poems is often less strict than an English reader is used to; they wander from image to image, without seeming to "get anywhere." He wrote many of his poems several times over, in differing versions; the same images and stanzas will recur, but in an entirely different order, without any sign that the poem "as a whole" (if it is a whole) has suffered in any way. For the effect at which he aims is a phantasmagoria, a blurring together of erotic and spiritual, tortured and ecstatic, infantile and sadistic themes. This doesn't preclude wit, even cheerful wit, but it's wit under the impulsion of a more consuming religious passion than English devotional writers before Gerard Manley Hopkins generally display. Like Saint Teresa of Avila, the Spanish mystic whom Crashaw admired so much, he yearned to be eaten up by the zeal of God's house— a spiritual act of faith to whose ecstatic paradoxes his best poetry does spectacular justice.

Crashaw's publications were not many. In 1634 he published a book of *Sacred Epigrams* in Latin (a posthumous second edition added some in Greek); a combined volume, *Steps to the Temple* and *The Delights of the Muses* (secular poems) appeared in 1646; and in 1652, a volume published in Paris under the title of *Carmen Deo Nostro* collected his final writings. Some new material has since been added from manuscript collections; and Crashaw has enjoyed, of late years, a genuine revival of favor after long years of hostility, neglect, and at best, condescension. His cause has been much aided by a new understanding of baroque art, architecture, and music.

A special feature of Crashaw's poetry, in the manuscripts as well as the printed volumes, is the styling of his poems' titles. They are elaborately constructed in different sorts of lettering, the lines piled on top of one another, to create outsize typographical facades, like the weighty fronts of baroque churches. The titles to *The Flaming Heart* and the poem *To the Countess of Denbigh* are reproduced here from the 1652 edition.

To the Infant Martyrs[1]

Go, smiling souls, your new-built cages[2] break,
In heaven you'll learn to sing, ere here to speak,
Nor let the milky fonts that bathe your thirst
        Be your delay;
The place that calls you hence is, at the worst,   5
        Milk all the way.[3]

1646

I Am the Door

And now th' art set wide ope, the spear's sad art,
Lo! hath unlocked thee at the very heart;
   He to himself (I fear the worst)
     And his own hope
Hath shut these doors of heaven, that durst   5
     Thus set them ope.

1646

On the Wounds of Our Crucified Lord

O these wakeful wounds of thine!
   Are they mouths? or are they eyes?
Be they mouths, or be they eyne,[1]
   Each bleeding part some one supplies.[2]

Lo! a mouth, whose full-bloomed lips   5
   At too dear a rate are roses.
Lo! a bloodshot eye! that weeps
   And many a cruel tear discloses.

O thou that on this foot hast laid
   Many a kiss and many a tear,   10
Now thou shalt have all repaid,
   Whatsoe'er thy charges were.

1. This poem, and the two that follow, were originally written in Latin, as sacred epigrams; but also appeared in *Steps to the Temple*, translated into English.
2. I.e., the bodies that confine them to an earthly existence.

3. The Milky Way will replace their mothers' milk, at the worst; at best, they may rise even higher in the heavens.
1. An old plural form of "eyes."
2. I.e., each wound of Christ's supplies either an eye or a mouth.

This foot hath got a mouth and lips
    To pay the sweet sum of thy kisses;
To pay thy tears, an eye that weeps   15
    Instead of tears such gems as this is.

The difference only this appears
    (Nor can the change offend),
The debt is paid in ruby-tears
    Which thou in pearls didst lend.   20

                      1646

On Our Crucified Lord, Naked and Bloody

Th' have left thee naked, Lord, O that they had;
This garment too I would they had denied.
Thee with thyself they have too richly clad,
Opening the purple wardrobe of thy side.
    O never could be found garments too good   5
    For thee to wear, but these, of thine own blood.

                      1646

In the Holy Nativity of Our Lord God: A Hymn Sung as by the Shepherds[1]

CHORUS.   Come we shepherds whose blest sight
        Hath met Love's noon in Nature's night;
            Come lift we up our loftier song,
        And wake the sun that lies too long.

        To all our world of well-stol'n joy   5
            He[2] slept, and dreamt of no such thing,
        While we found out Heaven's fairer Eye,
            And kissed the cradle of our King.
        Tell him he rises now too late
        To show us aught worth looking at.   10

        Tell him we now can show him more
            Than he e'er showed to mortal sight;
        Than he himself e'er saw before,
            Which to be seen needs not his light.

1. Had it appeared during the Restoration, when Italian music and Italian musical terminology were familiar in England, Crashaw's *Hymn* would have been recognized at once as an oratorio. The interweaving of chorus and alternating soloists is structurally comparable to the pattern of Dryden's *Ode for St. Cecilia's Day* (below, p. 1831); another interesting comparison (thematic rather than structural) is with Milton's poem *On The Morning of Christ's Nativity* (below, p. 1403). The version of this poem printed in 1646 differs considerably from that printed in 1652; we follow the latter.
2. The sun.

Tell him, Tityrus,[3] where th' hast been;   15
Tell him, Thyrsis, what th' hast seen.

TITYRUS.   Gloomy night embraced the place
                    Where the noble infant lay.
            The babe looked up and showed his face:
                    In spite of darkness, it was day.   20
            It was thy day, Sweet! and did rise,
            Not from the East, but from thine eyes.
                    CHORUS.   It was thy day, Sweet, *etc.*

THYRSIS.   Winter chid aloud, and sent
                    The angry North to wage his wars;   25
            The North forgot his fierce intent,
                    And left perfumes instead of scars.
            By those sweet eyes' persuasive powers,
            Where he meant frost, he scattered flowers.
                    CHORUS.   By those sweet eyes', *etc.*   30

BOTH.   We saw thee in thy balmy nest,
                    Young dawn of our eternal day!
            We saw thine eyes break from their East
                    And chase the trembling shades away.
            We saw thee; and we blessed the sight;   35
            We saw thee by thine own sweet light.

TITYRUS.   Poor world (said I), what wilt thou do
                    To entertain this starry stranger?
            Is this the best thou canst bestow,
                    A cold, and not too cleanly, manger?   40
            Contend, ye powers of heaven and earth,
            To fit a bed for this huge birth.
                    CHORUS.   Contend, ye powers, *etc.*

THYRSIS.   Proud world (said I), cease your contèst,
                    And let the Mighty Babe alone;   45
            The phoenix[4] builds the phoenix' nest;
                    Love's architecture is his own.
            The Babe whose birth embraves[5] this morn
            Made his own bed ere he was born.
                    CHORUS.   The Babe whose, *etc.*   50

TITYRUS.   I saw the curl'd drops, soft and slow,
                    Come hovering o'er the place's head,
            Offering their whitest sheets of snow
                    To furnish the fair Infant's bed:

---

3. "Tityrus" and "Thyrsis"—shepherds' names in classical poetry—are comically inappropriate for shepherds on the hillsides around Bethlehem, but Crashaw does not care; his Christ came to bring redemption to all the peoples.

4. Like the phoenix, marvelous bird of ancient Egypt, Christ was unique of his kind; as the son of God, he was present at, and took part in, the making of the world long before his incarnation.
5. Makes brave, i.e., splendid.

Forbear (said I), be not too bold;   55
Your fleece is white, but 'tis too cold.
    CHORUS.   Forbear (said I), *etc.*

THYRSIS.   I saw the obsequious Seraphims[6]
        Their rosy fleece of fire bestow,
For well they now can spare their wings   60
        Since Heaven itself lies here below.
Well done (said I), but are you sure
Your down so warm will pass for pure?
    CHORUS.   Well done (said I), *etc.*

TITYRUS.   No, no; your King's not yet to seek   65
        Where to repose his royal head;
See, see; how soon his new-bloomed cheek
        Twixt mother's breasts is gone to bed.
Sweet choice (said we), no way but so
Not to lie cold, yet sleep in snow.   70
      CHORUS.   Sweet choice (said we), *etc.*

BOTH.   We saw thee in thy balmy nest,
        Bright dawn of our eternal day!
We saw thine eyes break from their East
        And chase the trembling shades away.   75
We saw thee; and we blessed the sight.
We saw thee, by thine own sweet light.
      CHORUS.   We saw thee, *etc.*

FULL CHORUS

Welcome, all wonders in one sight!
        Eternity shut in a span.   80
Summer in winter. Day in night.
        Heaven in earth, and God in man.
Great little one! whose all-embracing birth
Lifts earth to Heaven, stoops Heaven to earth.

Welcome! though not to gold nor silk,   85
        To more than Caesar's birthright is;
Two sister-seas of Virgin-milk,
        With many a rarely-tempered kiss
That breathes at once both maid and mother,
Warms in the one, cools in the other.   90

Welcome! though not to those gay flies[7]
        Gilded i' th' beams of earthly kings—
Slippery souls in smiling eyes;
        But to poor shepherds, homespun things,
Whose wealth's their flock, whose wit to be   95
Well read in their simplicity.

6. Fiery angelic ministers of the Lord.   as ephemeral, worldly, and hypocritical.
7. Courtiers, stigmatized in three compressed lines

Yet when young April's husband showers
    Shall bless the fruitful Maia's bed,[8]
We'll bring the first-born of her flowers
    To kiss thy feet and crown thy head.   100
To thee, dread Lamb! whose love must keep
The shepherds more than they the sheep.

To Thee, meek Majesty! soft King
    Of simple graces and sweet loves,
Each of us his lamb will bring,
    Each his pair of silver doves,   105
Till burnt at last in fire of Thy fair eyes,
Ourselves become our own best sacrifice.

1646, 1652

N O N V I.[1]

'Tis not the work of force but skill
To find the way into man's will.
'Tis loue alone can hearts unlock.
Who knowes the WORD, *he needs not knock.*

T O T H E
Noblest & best of Ladyes, the
Countesse of Denbigh.

Perswading her to Resolution in Religion,
& to render her selfe without further
delay into the Communion of
the Catholick Church.[2]

8. The showers of April make fruitful the bed of May (from Maia, identified by the Romans with an ancient Italian goddess of the spring).

1. Not by force. "Emblems" were popular throughout Europe in the late Renaissance. Their elements were generally three: an image, an adage, and a poem explaining the relation of the two. The image was often an enigma, and the poem limited itself to moralizing its various elements, in line with the adage. Crashaw's poem takes its departure from an enigmatic image, but, like the best of the emblem-poems, goes far beyond it. The heart here has a hinge on the right to show that it can be opened, but is sealed on the left with a scroll or phylactery inscribed with letters standing for the Word or the Law. Only knowledge of the Word enables one to open the heart.

2. Lords and ladies with religious doubts and scruples were the object of tremendous attention during the 17th century. Anxious conferences were held, with priests of all faiths eager to put their views before a possible influential convert; accounts of these conferences were published, disputed, analyzed, and presented to the perplexed for their guidance. Susan, Countess of Denbigh, had been widowed in 1643, when her husband was killed fighting for the king; she had gone with the queen to Paris in 1644, and there, in a thoroughly Cath-

What heaven-entreated heart is this,
Stands trembling at the gate of bliss,
Holds fast the door, yet dares not venture
Fairly to open it, and enter?
Whose definition is a doubt   5
'Twixt life and death, 'twixt in and out.
Say, lingering fair! why comes the birth
Of your brave soul so slowly forth?
Plead your pretenses (O you strong
In weakness!) why you choose so long   10
In labor of your self to lie,
Not daring quite to live nor die.
Ah, linger not, loved soul! a slow
And late consent was a long no;
Who grants at last, long time tried   15
And did his best to have denied.
What magic bolts, what mystic bars,
Maintain the will in these strange wars!
What fatal yet fantastic bands
Keep the free heart from its own hands!   20
So when the year takes cold, we see
Poor waters their own prisoners be.
Fettered and locked up fast they lie
In a sad self-captivity.
Th' astonished nymphs their flood's strange fate deplore,   25
To see themselves their own severer shore.
    Thou that alone canst thaw this cold,
And fetch the heart from its stronghold,
Almighty Love! end this long war,
And of a meteor make a star.   30
O fix this fair Indefinite;
And 'mongst thy shafts of sovereign light
Choose out that sure decisive dart
Which has the key of this close heart,
Knows all the corners of 't, and can control   35
The self-shut cabinet of an unsearched soul.
O let it be at last love's hour!
Raise this tall trophy of thy power;
Come once the conquering way, not to confute,
But kill this rebel-word, *irresolute*,   40
That so, in spite of all this peevish strength
Of weakness, she may write, *resolved at length*.
    Unfold at length, unfold, fair flower,
And use the season of love's shower.
Meet his well-meaning wounds, wise heart,   45

---

olic environment, had begun contemplating conversion. The queen was a lifelong Catholic,
Crashaw, though simply another member of the
court in exile, was a new convert; pressure on the
lady was therefore very strong to abjure her Anglicanism. As is his wont, Crashaw uses all the imagery
of erotic persuasion in urging the Countess to "yield
the fort and let life in."

And haste to drink the wholesome dart,
That healing shaft which heaven till now
Hath in love's quiver hid for you.
O dart of love! arrow of light!
O happy you, if it hit right;   50
It must not fall in vain, it must
Not mark the dry, regardless dust.
Fair one, it is your fate, and brings
Eternal worlds upon its wings.
Meet it with wide-spread arms, and see   55
Its seat your soul's just center be.
Disband dull fears; give faith the day.
To save your life, kill your delay.
It is love's siege, and sure to be
Your triumph, though his victory.   60
'Tis cowardice that keeps this field,
And want of courage not to yield.
Yield, then, O yield, that love may win
The fort at last, and let life in.
Yield quickly, lest perhaps you prove   65
Death's prey before the prize of love.
This fort of your fair self, if 't be not won,
He is repulsed indeed; but you are undone.

                                                          1652

The Flaming Heart   Saint Teresa of Avila, a sixteenth-century
Spanish mystic, was one of the great figures of the Catholic Counter-
Reformation. Her autobiography, describing not only her practical problems
in establishing her ascetic order of barefoot Carmelites, but a series of ecstatic
trances and visitations which brought her close to the Heavenly Vision itself,
was immediately popular throughout all Europe. Gian Lorenzo Bernini, the
great Italian sculptor and architect, created the ultimate baroque statue of
Saint Teresa, which stands to this day in the church of Santa Maria della
Vittoria, in Rome. It shows the saint in an attitude of ecstatic, swooning
abandonment, while a somewhat juvenile seraph stands over her, in the act
of plunging a golden arrow into her heart. The statue is based on a famous
passage of the autobiography.

   Bernini's statue was not actually unveiled till after Crashaw's death, and
though the poet was in Rome and could easily have learned about the statue,
or seen it by visiting Bernini's studio, there is no definite proof that he actually
did so. In any case, what he says in the poem about a "picture" applies
perfectly to Bernini's statue: the seraph *is* a weak and childish figure, the
saint an embodiment of sensual and religious passion. The reversal of roles
with which the poet plays in the first part of his poem makes an effective
literary game; but it isn't clear what sort of picture or statue would express
his preferred conception of the saint. What excites him—and Bernini too,
for that matter—is the moment of total absorption in the divine, the ecstatic
union. For Puritans this is too fleshly an experience to be sacred, but for

those who respond to imaginative challenge, holding these two elements in balance is a special and perilous delight.

THE
FLAMING HEART

VPON THE BOOK AND
Picture of the seraphicall saint

TERESA,

(AS SHE IS VSVALLY EX-
pressed with a SERAPHIM
biside her.)[1]

Well-meaning readers! you that come as friends,
And catch the precious name this piece pretends;[2]
Make not too much haste to admire
That fair-cheeked fallacy of fire.
That is a Seraphim, they say,   5
And this the great Teresia.
Readers, be ruled by me, and make
Here a well-placed and wise mistake:
You must transpose the picture quite
And spell it wrong to read it right;   10
Read *him* for *her* and *her* for *him*,
And call the Saint the Seraphim.
    Painter, what didst thou understand,
To put her dart into his hand!
See, even the years and size of him   15
Shows this the Mother Seraphim.
This is the mistress-flame; and duteous he,
Her happy fire-works here comes down to see.
O most poor-spirited of men!
Had thy cold pencil kissed her pen[3]   20
Thou couldst not so unkindly err
To show us this faint shade for her.
Why, man, this speaks pure mortal frame,
And mocks with female frost love's manly flame.
One would suspect thou meant'st to paint   25
Some weak, inferior, woman saint.
But had thy pale-faced purple took
Fire from the burning cheeks of that bright book,
Thou wouldst on her have heaped up all
That could be found seraphical: 30

1. Crashaw does not know (or perhaps care) that "seraphim" is the plural form of the singular "seraph"; "seraphs" are distinguished among angels by dwelling continually in the fire of divine love.

2. Puts forward.
3. I.e., if you'd only been properly inspired by her book.

Whate'er this youth of fire wears fair,
Rosy fingers, radiant hair,
Glowing cheek and glistering wings,
All those fair and flagrant[4] things,
But before all, that fiery dart   35
Had filled the hand of this great heart.
    Do then as equal right requires,
Since his the blushes be, and hers the fires,
Resume and rectify thy rude design,
Undress thy seraphim into mine.   40
Redeem this injury of thy art,
Give him the veil, give her the dart.
    Give him the veil, that he may cover
The red cheeks of a rivaled lover,
Ashamed that our world now can show   45
Nests of new Seraphims here below.[5]
    Give her the dart, for it is she
(Fair youth) shoots both thy shaft and thee.
Say, all ye wise and well-pierced hearts
That live and die amidst her darts,[6]   50
What is 't your tasteful spirits do prove
In that rare life of her and love?
Say and bear witness. Sends she not
A Seraphim at every shot?
What magazines of immortal arms there shine!   55
Heaven's great artillery in each love-spun line.
Give then the dart to her who gives the flame,
Give him the veil who kindly takes the shame.
    But if it be the frequent fate
Of worst faults to be fortunate;   60
If all's prescription,[7] and proud wrong
Hearkens not to an humble song,
For all the gallantry of him,
Give me the suffering Seraphim.[8]
His be the bravery of all those bright things,   65
The glowing cheeks, the glistering wings,
The rosy hand, the radiant dart;
Leave her alone the Flaming Heart.
    Leave her that, and thou shalt leave her
Not one loose shaft, but love's whole quiver.   70
For in love's field was never found
A nobler weapon than a wound.
Love's passives are his activ'st part,
The wounded is the wounding heart.
O heart! the equal poise of love's both parts,   75

4. Burning (from Latin *flagrare*).
5. Teresa burns on earth in the element of fire, as seraphim do in heaven.
6. I.e., her writings. "Prove": experience.
7. I.e., settled beforehand, by the decision of the artist.
8. If Teresa can't be transformed into the angel, as he would like, Crashaw still prefers her as the "suffering Seraphim."

Big alike with wounds and darts,
Live in these conquering leaves,[9] live all the same;
And walk through all tongues one triumphant flame.
Live here, great heart; and love and die and kill,
And bleed and wound; and yield and conquer still.   80
Let this immortal life, where'er it comes,
Walk in a crowd of loves and martyrdoms.
Let mystic deaths wait on 't, and wise souls be
The love-slain witnesses of this life of thee:
O sweet incendiary! show here thy art,   85
Upon this carcass of a hard, cold heart;[1]
Let all thy scattered shafts of light, that play
Among the leaves of thy large books of day,[2]
Combined against this breast, at once break in
And take away from me myself and sin!
This gracious robbery shall thy bounty be,   90
And my best fortunes such fair spoils of me.[3]
O thou undaunted daughter of desires!
By all thy dower of lights and fires;
By all the eagle in thee, all the dove;[4]
By all thy lives and deaths of love;   95
By thy large draughts of intellectual day,
And by thy thirsts of love more large than they;
By all thy brim-filled bowls of fierce desire,
By thy last morning's draught of liquid fire;   100
By the full kingdom of that final kiss
That seized thy parting soul, and sealed thee His;
By all the heavens thou hast in Him,
Fair sister of the seraphim,
By all of Him we have in thee,   105
Leave nothing of myself in me!
Let me so read thy life that I
Unto all life of mine may die!

1652

9. I.e., the leaves of St. Teresa's book.
1. After being Saint Teresa's, the heart (now hard and cold) has become Crashaw's.
2. Books filled with intellectual and spiritual light.
3. I.e., my best fortune will be to be despoiled in this way.
4. The eagle symbolizes wisdom, for its lofty flight and ability to look into the sun's eye; the dove symbolizes mercy. Cf. Donne's *The Canonization*, line 22.

HENRY VAUGHAN
1621–1695

1650, 1655:   *Silex Scintillans.*

The doctrine of mystic correspondence (i.e., of analogical relations between the world of creatures and the world of spirits)—which had been accepted philosophy during the Middle Ages, and into which poets like Donne and Herbert had breathed new life during the early seventeeth century—faded during the second half of the century before a rising tide of materialism and rationalism. One of the last figures to give full-voiced expression to the old doctrine was a Welsh country doctor with special interests in the occult, Henry Vaughan.

Vaughan enjoyed only a brief interlude of poetry in his long life. He spent two years at Oxford, and then went to London to study law. But his studies were interrupted by the civil wars, in which he took a brief part on the king's side. After the royal defeat, he retired to his native Wales and began to practice medicine—without many preliminaries, as men could do in those days. (If the volume of *Hermetical Physic* which he translated from the Latin in 1655 is any index to his practice, the "good success" he said he enjoyed must have been due to the sturdy constitution of his patients.) In 1646 he published a very slender volume of secular verse. This was followed in 1650 by a somewhat larger collection of sacred poems, *Silex Scintillans,* and in 1651 by a volume of occasional poems and translations, *Olor Iscanus.* (*Silex Scintillans,* or The Fiery Flint, refers to the stony hardness of his heart, from which divine steel strikes fire; *Olor Iscanus,* or The Swan of Usk, refers to a little river that flows near Vaughan's native town of Scethrog hard by Llansantffraed.) *Silex Scintillans* was reprinted in 1655 with the addition of a second part; and that closed Vaughan's poetic career.

Two major influences marked Vaughan's early development. George Herbert's poetry made a great impression on him, and the religious poetry, on which his reputation largely depends, is full of echoes from *The Temple.* In addition, Vaughan's twin brother Thomas was an esoteric, hermetic philosopher, an alchemist, and a student of occult correspondences. Vaughan's poems often imply some knowledge of these "secret doctrines"—doctrines in which folklore, sympathetic magic, religious symbolism, and the rudiments of chemical affinity rub elbows under the aegis of the mythical Egyptian teacher Hermes Trismegistus.

But though they are "occult" in their under- and over-tones, Vaughan's best poems are direct and untangled in their expression. They tend to start with a brilliant phrase or set of phrases and trail off into relatively prosaic meditations. Sparkles of poetic brightness attend most of his writings; but they glow irregularly and fade under the unsteady breath of the poet's personal inspiration. When that inspiration is up, he sees, or tries to see, through the veil of things, to the spiritual quick of life lying just under its commonplace, material surface. There is a kind of silver-gray purity in Vaughan's finest work, which, though comparable to Herbert's and tangibly influenced by it, is more nervous and restive, more apt to dissolve the physical book under our hands, turning it into the living mind and immediate soul of a man.

Except for the first poem, all our selections come from the two parts of *Silex Scintillans*.

A Rhapsody

Occasionally written[1] upon a meeting with some of his friends at the Globe Tavern, in a chamber painted overhead with a cloudy sky and some few dispersed stars and on the sides with landscapes, hills, shepherds, and sheep.

Darkness and stars i' the mid-day! they invite
Our active fancies to believe it night;
For taverns need no sun but for a sign,
Where rich tobacco and quick tapers shine,
And royal, witty sack,[2] the poet's soul,   5
With brighter suns than he doth gild the bowl;
As though the pot and poet did agree
Sack should to both illuminator be.
That artificial cloud with its curled brow
Tells us 'tis late; and that blue space below   10
Is fired with many stars; mark, how they break
In silent glances o'er the hills and speak
The evening to the plains; where, shot from far,
They meet in dumb salutes, as one great star.

    The room, methinks, grows darker, and the air   15
Contracts a sadder color and less fair;
Or is 't the drawer's skill,[3] hath he no arts
To blind us so we can't know pints from quarts?
No, no, 'tis night; look where the jolly clown[4]
Musters his bleating herd and quits the down.   20
Hark! how his rude pipe frets the quiet air
Whilst every hill proclaims Lycoris fair.[5]
Rich, happy man! that canst thus watch and sleep,
Free from all cares, but thy wench, pipe, and sheep.

    But see, the moon is up; view where she stands   25
Sentinel o'er the door, drawn by the hands
Of some base painter that for gain hath made
Her face the landmark to the tippling trade.
This cup to her, that to Endymion give,[6]

---

1. I.e., on a casual occasion. A "rhapsody" need imply nothing more than an emotional fantasy. Vaughan is so often a poet of solitary, mystic visions, this poem is welcome in placing him in London, amid a merry company, with a glass in his hand.
2. Sherry, the favored wine of Jonson and Herrick, among others.
3. Drawer: the artist, and the tapster.

4. Rustic.
5. The shepherd painted on the wall is piping the praises of his imagined mistress Lycoris; the imaginary tune echoes from the painted hills.
6. In mythology, Artemis the moon goddess fell in love with the shepherd Endymion, and he with her.

'Twas wit at first, and wine, that made them live.   30
Choke may the painter! and his box disclose
No other colors than his fiery nose;
And may we no more of his pencil see
Than two churchwardens and mortality.[7]

    Should we go now a-wandering, we should meet   35
With catchpoles,[8] whores, and carts in every street,
Now when each narrow lane, each nook and cave,
Sign-posts and shop-doors pimp for every knave,
When riotous sinful plush and telltale spurs
Walk Fleet Street and the Strand,[9] when the soft stirs   40
Of bawdy, ruffled silks turn night to day,
And the loud whip and coach scolds all the way,
When lust of all sorts and each itchy blood
From the Tower-wharf to Cymbeline and Lud[1]
Hunts for a mate, and the tired footman reels   45
'Twixt chairmen, torches, and the hackney-wheels:
    Come, take the other dish; it is to him
That made his horse a senator.[2] Each brim
Look big as mine! The gallant, jolly beast
Of all the herd (you'll say) was not the least.   50

    Now crown the second bowl, rich as his worth,
I'll drink it to; he! that like fire broke forth[3]
Into the Senate's face, crossed Rubicon,
And the state's pillars, with their laws thereon,
And made the dull gray beards and furred gowns fly   55
Into Brundisium, to consult and lie.

    This to brave Sulla![4] Why should it be said
We drink more to the living than the dead?
Flatt'rers and fools do use it. Let us laugh
At our own honest mirth; for they that quaff   60
To honor others do like those that sent
Their gold and plate to strangers to be spent.

    Drink deep; this cup be pregnant; and the wine
Spirit of wit to make us all divine,
That big with sack and mirth we may retire   65
Possessors of more souls and nobler fire,
And by the influx of this painted sky
And labored forms, to higher matters fly;
So, if a nap shall take us, we shall all
After full cups have dreams poetical.   70

---

7. The two churchwardens would record the painter's death (mortality).
8. Petty officers of the law.
9. Busy streets of downtown London.
1. I.e., from the eastern to the western side of London. Statues of Lud and Cymbeline, legendary kings of ancient Britain, stood at Ludgate, near St. Paul's Cathedral.
2. The Roman emperor Caligula made his horse Incitatus a priest, a senator, and a consul.

3. Julius Caesar.
4. Lucius Cornelius Sulla did as much as any man before Caesar to destroy the ancient constitution of Rome. The poem was written and published under the parliamentary regime against which Vaughan had borne arms; the combination of antirepublican, antisenatorial Romans being toasted suggests that a certain amount of covert treason may have been talked in the old Globe Tavern.

> *Let's laugh now, and the pressed grape drink*
> *Till the drowsy day-star wink,*
> *And in our merry, mad mirth run*
> *Faster and farther than the sun;*
> *And let none his cup forsake*   75
> *Till that star again doth wake;*
> *So we men below shall move*
>   *Equally with the gods above.*

1646

Regeneration

A ward, and still in bonds, one day
    I stole abroad;
It was high spring, and all the way
   Primrosed and hung with shade;
   Yet was it frost within,   5
    And surly winds
Blasted my infant buds, and sin
   Like clouds eclipsed my mind.

Stormed thus, I straight perceived my spring
   Mere stage and show,   10
My walk a monstrous, mountained thing,
   Roughcast with rocks and snow;
   And as a pilgrim's eye,
    Far from relief,
Measures the melancholy sky,   15
   Then drops and rains for grief,

So sighed I upwards still; at last
   'Twixt steps and falls
I reached the pinnacle, where placed
   I found a pair of scales;   20
   I took them up and laid
    In th' one, late pains;
The other smoke and pleasures weighed,
   But proved the heavier grains.[1]

With that some cried, "Away!" Straight I   25
   Obeyed, and led
Full east, a fair, fresh field could spy;
   Some called it Jacob's bed,[2]

---

1. Vaughan's spiritual adventure can only be described darkly. After his purgatorial ascent, smoke and pleasures prove heavier than "late pains"— apparently because the vanity of his mind out- weighs its recent turning to repentance.
2. Jacob slept in an open field with stones for pillows (Genesis 28.11–19) and was rewarded with a vision of the Lord, who prophesied his future.

A virgin soil which no
    Rude feet ere trod,   30
Where, since he stepped there, only go
    Prophets and friends of God.

Here I reposed; but scarce well set,
    A grove descried
Of stately height, whose branches met   35
    And mixed on every side;
    I entered, and once in,
      Amazed to see 't,
Found all was changed, and a new spring
    Did all my senses greet.   40

The unthrift sun shot vital gold,
    A thousand pieces,
And heaven its azure did unfold,
    Checkered with snowy fleeces;
    The air was all in spice,   45
      And every bush
A garland wore; thus fed my eyes,
    But all the ear lay hush.[3]

Only a little fountain lent
    Some use for ears,   50
And on the dumb shades language spent,
    The music of her tears;
    I drew her near, and found
      The cistern full
Of divers stones, some bright and round,   55
    Others ill-shaped and dull.[4]

The first, pray mark, as quick as light
    Danced through the flood,
But the last, more heavy than the night,
    Nailed to the center stood;   60
    I wondered much, but tired
      At last with thought,
My restless eye that still desired
    As strange an object brought:

It was a bank of flowers, where I descried,   65
    Though 'twas midday,
Some fast asleep, others broad-eyed
    And taking in the ray;
    Here musing long, I heard
      A rushing wind   70

---

3. Quiet. Some editors emend "ear" to "earth."
4. Proposed explanations for the stones in the fountain (none altogether satisfactory) are ideas, images, and souls.

Which still increased, but whence it stirred
   No where I could not find.

I turned me round, and to each shade
    Dispatched an eye
To see if any leaf had made   75
   Least motion or reply;
   But while I listening sought
     My mind to ease
By knowing where 'twas, or where not,
   It whispered, "Where I please."[5]   80

"Lord," then said I, "on me one breath,
And let me die before my death!"

                            1650

The Retreat

Happy those early days! when I
Shined in my angel infancy.
Before I understood this place
Appointed for my second race,[1]
Or taught my soul to fancy aught   5
But a white, celestial thought;
When yet I had not walked above
A mile or two from my first love,
And looking back, at that short space,
Could see a glimpse of His bright face;   10
When on some gilded cloud or flower
My gazing soul would dwell an hour,
And in those weaker glories spy
Some shadows of eternity;
Before I taught my tongue to wound   15
My conscience with a sinful sound,
Or had the black art to dispense
A several[2] sin to every sense,
But felt through all this fleshly dress
Bright shoots of everlastingness.   20
   O, how I long to travel back,
And tread again that ancient track!
That I might once more reach that plain
Where first I left my glorious train,
From whence th' enlightened spirit sees   25

---

5. John 3.8: "The wind bloweth where it listeth, and thou hearest the sound thereof, but canst not tell whence it cometh, and whither it goeth: so is every one that is born of the Spirit." Cf. also the inspiring breath by which God breathed life into man (Genesis 2.7).

1. The "second race" suggests, dimly, a doctrine of pre-existence. Comparisons are often made with Wordsworth's *Ode: Intimations of Immortality*.

2. Different.

That shady city of palm trees.[3]
But, ah! my soul with too much stay[4]
Is drunk, and staggers in the way.
Some men a forward motion love;
But I by backward steps would move,   30
And when this dust falls to the urn,
In that state I came, return.

1650

Silence and Stealth of Days!

Silence and stealth of days! 'tis now
    Since thou art gone[1]
Twelve hundred hours, and not a brow
    But clouds hang on.
As he that in some cave's thick damp,   5
    Locked from the light,
Fixeth a solitary lamp
    To brave the night,
And walking from his sun, when past
    That glimmering ray,   10
Cuts through the heavy mists in haste
    Back to his day,[2]
So o'er fled minutes I retreat
    Unto that hour
Which showed thee last, but did defeat   15
    Thy light and power;
I search and rack my soul to see
    Those beams again,
But nothing but the snuff[3] to me
    Appeareth plain,   20
That dark and dead sleeps in its known
    And common urn;
But those[4] fled to their maker's throne,
    There shine and burn.
O could I track them! but souls must   25
    Track one the other,
And now the spirit, not the dust,
    Must be thy brother.
Yet I have one Pearl,[5] by whose light
    All things I see,   30

3. The New Jerusalem, the Heavenly City (for its identification with Jericho see Deuteronomy 34.3).
4. Delay.
1. As indicated below, lines 27–28, the poem is on the loss of Vaughan's brother—not his twin brother, Thomas, the hermetic philosopher, who did not die till 1666, but his younger brother, William, who died in July 1648.

2. The miner fixes his lamp halfway down the dark shaft, ventures a little beyond it, but then beats a hasty retreat.
3. The burnt wick of the lamp or candle; also, metaphorically, the bodily form of the brother.
4. The reference is back to "light and power."
5. The Bible.

And in the heart of earth and night,
    Find heaven and thee.

1648   1650

Corruption

Sure it was so. Man in those early days
    Was not all stone and earth;
He shined a little, and by those weak rays
    Had some glimpse of his birth.
He saw heaven o'er his head, and knew from whence   5
    He came, condemnèd, hither;
And, as first love draws strongest, so from hence
    His mind sure progressed thither.
Things here were strange unto him: sweat and till,
    All was a thorn or weed: 10
Nor did those last, but (like himself) died still
    As soon as they did seed.
They seemed to quarrel with him, for that act
    That felled him foiled them all:
He drew the curse upon the world, and cracked   15
    The whole frame with his fall.[1]
This made him long for home, as loath to stay
    With murmurers and foes;
He sighed for Eden, and would often say,
    "Ah! what bright days were those!"   20
Nor was heaven cold unto him; for each day
    The valley or the mountain
Afforded visits, and still Paradise lay
    In some green shade or fountain.
Angels lay lieger[2] here; each bush and cell,   25
    Each oak and highway knew them;
Walk but the fields, or sit down at some well,
    And he was sure to view them.
Almighty Love! where art thou now? Mad man
    Sits down and freezeth on;   30
He raves, and swears to stir nor fire, nor fan,
    But bids the thread be spun.[3]
I see, thy curtains are close-drawn; thy bow
    Looks dim, too, in the cloud;
Sin triumphs still, and man is sunk below   35
    The center, and his shroud.

---

1. Compare Donne, *Anatomy of the World*, lines
199–200.
2. As resident ambassadors (from heaven).

3. Man will do nothing for himself, but trusts to
Fate.

All's in deep sleep and night: thick darkness lies
    And hatcheth o'er thy people—
But hark! what trumpet's that? what angel cries,
    "Arise! thrust in thy sickle"?[4]   40

1650

The World

I saw eternity the other night
Like a great ring of pure and endless light,
    All calm as it was bright;
And round beneath it, Time, in hours, days, years,
    Driven by the spheres,[1]   5
Like a vast shadow moved, in which the world
    And all her train were hurled.
The doting lover in his quaintest[2] strain
    Did there complain;
Near him, his lute, his fancy, and his flights,   10
    Wit's sour delights,
With gloves and knots,[3] the silly snares of pleasure,
    Yet his dear treasure,
All scattered lay, while he his eyes did pour
    Upon a flower.   15

The darksome statesman hung with weights and woe
Like a thick midnight fog moved there so slow
    He did nor stay nor go;
Condemning thoughts, like sad eclipses, scowl
    Upon his soul,   20
And clouds of crying witnesses without
    Pursued him with one shout.
Yet digged the mole, and, lest his ways be found,
    Worked underground,
Where he did clutch his prey. But one did see   25
    That policy:[4]
Churches and altars fed him; perjuries
    Were gnats and flies;
It rained about him blood and tears; but he
    Drank them as free.[5]   30

---

4. Revelation 14.15: "And another angel came out of the temple, crying with a loud voice to him that sat on the cloud, 'Thrust in thy sickle, and reap . . .'" The time to harvest is now.
1. The concentric spheres of Ptolemaic astronomy.
2. Most elaborate.

3. Love knots.
4. Strategy. The "mole" (i.e., the "darksome statesman," line 16) worked underground to avoid detection: but He who marks the fall of a sparrow was not deceived.
5. I.e., as freely as they rained.

The fearful miser on a heap of rust
Sat pining all his life there, did scarce trust
    His own hands with the dust;
Yet would not place[6] one piece above, but lives
    In fear of thieves.   35
Thousands there were as frantic as himself,
    And hugged each one his pelf:
The downright epicure placed heaven in sense,[7]
    And scorned pretense;
While others, slipped into a wide excess,   40
    Said little less;
The weaker sort, slight, trivial wares enslave,
    Who think them brave;[8]
And poor, despisèd Truth sat counting by[9]
    Their victory.   45

Yet some, who all this while did weep and sing,
And sing and weep, soared up into the ring;
    But most would use no wing.
"O fools!" said I, "thus to prefer dark night
    Before true light!   50
To live in grots and caves, and hate the day
    Because it shows the way,
The way which from this dead and dark abode
    Leads up to God,
A way where you might tread the sun and be   55
    More bright than he!"
But, as I did their madness so discuss,
    One whispered thus:
"This ring the bridegroom did for none provide,
    But for his bride."[1]   60

                                1650

They Are All Gone into the World of Light!

They are all gone into the world of light!
    And I alone sit ling'ring here;
Their very memory is fair and bright,
    And my sad thoughts doth clear.

It glows and glitters in my cloudy breast   5
    Like stars upon some gloomy grove,

---

6. Invest.
7. Found his heaven in the senses.
8. Fine, flashy.

9. Recording.
1. See Revelation 19.7–9 and 21 for the marriage of the Lamb and the bride (Christ and His church).

Or those faint beams in which this hill is dressed
　　After the sun's remove.

I see them walking in an air of glory,
　　Whose light doth trample on my days;　　　　　　　　10
My days, which are at best but dull and hoary,
　　Mere glimmering and decays.

O holy hope, and high humility,
　　High as the heavens above!
These are your walks, and you have showed them me　　15
　　To kindle my cold love.

Dear, beauteous death! the jewel of the just,
　　Shining nowhere but in the dark;
What mysteries do lie beyond thy dust,
　　Could man outlook that mark![1]　　　　　　　　　　20

He that hath found some fledged bird's nest may know
　　At first sight if the bird be flown;
But what fair well[2] or grove he sings in now,
　　That is to him unknown.

And yet, as angels in some brighter dreams　　　　　25
　　Call to the soul when man doth sleep,
So some strange thoughts transcend our wonted themes,
　　And into glory peep.

If a star were confined into a tomb,
　　Her captive flames must needs burn there;　　　　30
But when the hand that locked her up gives room,
　　She'll shine through all the sphere.

O Father of eternal life, and all
　　Created glories under thee!
Resume thy spirit from this world of thrall[3]　　　　35
　　Into true liberty!

Either disperse these mists, which blot and fill
　　My pèrspective[4] still as they pass;
Or else remove me hence unto that hill[5]
　　Where I shall need no glass.　　　　　　　　　　　40

　　　　　　　　　　　　　　　　　　　　　　　1655

1. Limit.
2. Spring.
3. I.e., take back from this world of slavery the
spirit which you have made.

4. Literally, "telescope," but more freely, "distant
vision."
5. Sion hill (figuratively, Abraham's bosom).

The Night

John 3.2[1]

Through that pure virgin-shrine,
That sacred veil drawn o'er thy glorious noon,
That men might look and live as glow-worms shine
    And face the moon,
  Wise Nicodemus saw such light   5
  As made him know his God by night.

    Most blest believer he!
Who in that land of darkness and blind eyes
Thy long-expected healing wings could see,
    When thou didst rise,   10
  And what can never more be done,
  Did at midnight speak with the Sun!

    Oh who will tell me where
He found thee at that dead and silent hour?
What hallowed solitary ground did bear   15
    So rare a flower,
  Within whose sacred leaves did lie
  The fullness of the Deity?

    No mercy-seat of gold,
No dead and dusty cherub nor carved stone,[2]   20
But his own living works did my Lord hold
    And lodge alone;
  Where trees and herbs did watch and peep
  And wonder while the Jews did sleep.

    Dear night! this world's defeat,[3]   25
The stop to busy fools; care's check and curb;
The day of spirits; my soul's calm retreat
    Which none disturb!
  Christ's progress and his prayer time;
  The hours to which high heaven doth chime;   30

    God's silent, searching flight,
When my Lord's head is filled with dew, and all
His locks are wet with the clear drops of night;
    His still, soft call;

---

1. John 3.2 describes how a Pharisee named Nicodemus came to Jesus by night and said, "Rabbi, we know that thou art a teacher come from God."
2. God commanded the Israelites to cover the Ark of the Covenant with "a mercy seat of pure gold.

. . . And two cherubims of gold, of beaten work . . . , in the two ends of the mercy seat" (Exodus 25.17–19).
3. This stanza and the next seem to be modeled on George Herbert's *Prayer (1)*.

His knocking time; the soul's dumb watch,   35
When spirits their fair kindred catch.

    Were all my loud, evil days
Calm and unhaunted as is thy dark tent,
Whose peace but by some angel's wing or voice
        Is seldom rent,   40
  Then I in heaven all the long year
  Would keep, and never wander here.

    But living where the sun
Doth all things wake, and where all mix and tire
Themselves and others, I consent and run   45
      To every mire,[4]
  And by this world's ill-guiding light
  Err more than I can do by night.

    There is in God (some say)
A deep but dazzling darkness, as men here   50
Say it is late and dusky because they
      See not all clear.
  Oh for that night, where I in him
  Might live invisible and dim!

                                    1655

The Waterfall

With what deep murmurs through time's silent stealth
Doth thy transparent, cool, and watery wealth
        Here flowing fall,
        And chide, and call,
As if his liquid, loose retinue stayed   5
Ling'ring, and were of this steep place afraid,[1]
        The common pass
        Where, clear as glass,
        All must descend,
        Not to an end,   10
But quickened by this steep and rocky grave,
Rise to a longer course more bright and brave.

Dear stream! dear bank! where often I
Have sat and pleased my pensive eye—
Why, since each drop of thy quick store   15

4. The basic image is that of the will-o'-the-wisp, which leads night wanderers astray and founders them in bogs.

1. The waterfall is for Vaughan an emblem of death, when the soul leaps from one sphere to another—not lower, as appearances suggest, but higher.

Runs thither whence it flowed before,
Should poor souls fear a shade or night,
Who came, sure, from a sea of light?
Or since those drops are all sent back
So sure to thee that none doth lack,   20
Why should frail flesh doubt any more
That what God takes he'll not restore?
O useful element and clear!
My sacred wash and cleanser here,
My first consigner unto those   25
Fountains of life where the Lamb goes!
What sublime truths and wholesome themes
Lodge in thy mystical deep streams!
Such as dull man can never find
Unless that Spirit lead his mind   30
Which first upon thy face did move
And hatched all with his quickening love.[2]
As this loud brook's incessant fall
In streaming rings restagnates all
Which reach by course the bank, and then   35
Are no more seen, just so pass men.[3]
Oh my invisible estate,
My glorious liberty, still late!
Thou art the channel my soul seeks,
Not this with cataracts and creeks.   40

                                                    1655

2. The echo is from Genesis 1.2: "And the Spirit   3. I.e., human beings are as evanescent as ripples
of God moved upon the face of the waters."   on water.

ANDREW MARVELL
1621–1678

1681: *Miscellaneous Poems.*

Andrew Marvell was one of those quiet men whose voices generally go unheard during the storm and turmoil of revolution. He attended Cambridge, graduated B. A. in 1638, and remained for a couple of years more in residence; after traveling abroad for some years, he disappears from the biographer's view, turning up around 1650 as tutor to the daughter of Sir Thomas Fairfax, Lord-General of the parliamentary forces. At the Yorkshire seat of this family, Nun Appleton House, Marvell seems to have written, over a period of about three years, most of his non-satiric English poems. The learning of these poems, like their serious intent, is hidden beneath a graceful, humorous surface, and they suggest that Marvell must have been a delightful tutor to the little girl who was growing up to be the daughter of a great house.

In 1657 Marvell was appointed assistant to the blind Latin Secretary for the Commonwealth, John Milton; and in his quiet way he seems to have been helpful after the Restoration in saving Milton from an extended jail term and possible execution. Starting in 1659, Marvell was elected M.P. for his home town of Hull, and he continued to represent it in a businesslike way till his death. He was a good committee man and devoted to the interests of Hull. His letters to his constituents, regular as clockwork, are useful historical documents; but one would never guess from reading them that their author was an accomplished poet.

And in fact, when Marvell died, he was known to the world simply as the author of a few rough-and-ready satires in prose and verse which had been printed during the Restoration. His "serious" verse was published three years after his death, by a woman who gave herself out as his widow but had probably been his housekeeper. The reputation of these poems has made its way slowly, but steadily; and it has never stood higher than in our own time. For it is now clear that Marvell's is the most major minor verse in English. Playful, casual, and witty in tone, always light on its metrical feet and exact in its diction, it displays depth and intellectual hardness in unexpected places; its texture is extraordinarily rich. For example, the four poems about a mower seem almost to mock the tiny, conventional figures of Damon the susceptible mower and his hardhearted girl Juliana. They are conventional figures, and Damon voices the conventional complaints about her chilly responses to his ardent proposals. Yet the poems move so persistently and allusively around the old metaphor that all flesh is grass that we can hardly avoid sensing the presence of those other sinister scythemen, Old Father Time and the Grim Reaper. The poems have no more unity than is implied in the phrase "variations on a theme"; but their combination of a light touch, a vein of mockery, and the shadow of a dark thought is perfectly Marvellian.

As all Marvell's poems were published in 1681, this date will not be repeated for each individual poem.

The Coronet

When for the thorns with which I long, too long,
     With many a piercing wound,
     My Savior's head have crowned,
I seek with garlands to redress that wrong,
     Through every garden, every mead,   5
I gather flowers (my fruits are only flowers),
     Dismantling all the fragrant towers
That once adorned my shepherdess's head:
And now, when I have summed up all my store,
     Thinking (so I myself deceive)   10
     So rich a chaplet[1] thence to weave
As never yet the King of Glory wore,
     Alas! I find the serpent old,
     That, twining in his speckled breast,

---

1. Wreath Marvell's garlands, without ceasing to be literal wreaths, also imply poems of praise.

About the flowers disguised does fold   15
  With wreaths of fame and interest.[2]
Ah, foolish man, that wouldst debase with them
And mortal glory, heaven's diadem!
But thou who only couldst the serpent tame,
  Either his slippery knots at once untie,   20
And disentangle all his winding snare,
  Or shatter too with him my curious frame,[3]
And let these wither, so that he may die,
  Though set with skill and chosen out with care;
That they, while thou on both their spoils dost tread,   25
  May crown thy feet, that could not crown thy head.[4]

Bermudas

Where the remote Bermudas ride,
In th' ocean's bosom unespied,
From a small boat that rowed along,
The listening winds received this song:

"What should we do but sing his praise   5
That led us through the wat'ry maze
Unto an isle so long unknown,
And yet far kinder than our own?
Where he the huge sea monsters wracks,[1]
That lift the deep upon their backs;   10
He lands us on a grassy stage,
Safe from the storms, and prelate's rage.[2]
He gave us this eternal spring
Which here enamels everything,
And sends the fowls to us in care,   15
On daily visits through the air;
He hangs in shades the orange bright,
Like golden lamps in a green night,
And does in the pomegranates close
Jewels more rich than Ormus[3] shows;   20
He makes the figs our mouths to meet,
And throws the melons at our feet;
But apples[4] plants of such a price,
No tree could ever bear them twice;
With cedars, chosen by his hand,   25
From Lebanon, he stores the land;
And makes the hollow seas that roar

---

2. Self-glorification, self-advancement.
3. I.e., my elaborate ("curious") wreath of flowers; but "my curious frame" could also be my physical body.
4. Compare the curse of Genesis 3.15, that the seed of Eve shall bruise the serpent's head.

1. Shipwrecks, destroys.
2. Storms at sea are quietly equated with bishops as sources of peril.
3. Pearl- and jewel-trading center in the Persian Gulf.
4. Pineapples.

Proclaim the ambergris[5] on shore;
He cast (of which we rather[6] boast)
The Gospel's pearl upon our coast,   30
And in these rocks for us did frame
A temple, where to sound his name.
O let our voice his praise exalt
Till it arrive at heaven's vault,
Which, thence (perhaps) rebounding, may   35
Echo beyond the Mexique Bay."[7]

    Thus sung they in the English boat
An holy and a cheerful note;
And all the way, to guide their chime,
With falling oars they kept the time.   40

A Dialogue Between the Soul and Body

SOUL.   O, who shall from this dungeon raise
A soul enslaved so many ways?[1]
With bolts of bones, that fettered stands
In feet; and manacled in hands.
Here blinded with an eye; and there   5
Deaf with the drumming of an ear;
A soul hung up, as 'twere, in chains
Of nerves, and arteries, and veins;
Tortured, besides each other part,
In a vain head and double heart.   10

BODY.   O, who shall me deliver whole
From bonds of this tyrannic soul?
Which, stretched upright, impales me so
That mine own precipice[2] I go;
And warms and moves this needless frame[3]   15
(A fever could but do the same),
And, wanting where[4] its spite to try,
Has made me live to let me die.
A body that could never rest
Since this ill spirit it possessed.   20

SOUL.   What magic could me thus confine
Within another's grief to pine?

---

5. "Proclaim" suggests the seas roaring to announce their bounty. Ambergris is an expensive, mysterious, soapy substance found in sperm whales and used in the manufacture of perfumes (see *Moby-Dick*, chap. 92).
6. More properly.
7. The Gulf of Mexico.
1. The soul speaks almost in the words of St. Paul's Epistle to the Romans 7.24: "O wretched man that I am! who shall deliver me from the body of this death?"
2. Possession of a soul is the reason why man walks erect, facing the heavens, instead of prowling the earth like a brute; but it is also the reason why he can fall and be damned, as brutes cannot; so the soul is an interior precipice.
3. This frame, which does not need it.
4. Lacking an object.

Where, whatsoever it complain,
I feel, that cannot feel,[5] the pain;
And all my care itself employs,   25
That to preserve which me destroys;
Constrained not only to endure
Diseases, but, what's worse, the cure;
And, ready oft the port to gain,
Am shipwracked into health again.   30

BODY.   But physic[6] yet could never reach
The maladies thou me dost teach;
Whom first the cramp of hope does tear,
And then the palsy shakes of fear;
The pestilence of love does heat,   35
Or hatred's hidden ulcer eat;
Joy's cheerful madness does perplex,
Or sorrow's other madness vex;
Which knowledge forces me to know,
And memory will not forego;   40
What but a soul could have the wit
To build me up for sin so fit?
So architects do square and hew
Green trees that in the forest grew.[7]

The Nymph Complaining for The Death of Her Fawn

The wanton troopers riding by
Have shot my fawn, and it will die.
Ungentle men! They cannot thrive
To kill thee. Thou ne'er didst alive
Them any harm; alas, nor could   5
Thy death yet do them any good.
I'm sure I never wished them ill,
Nor do I for all this; nor will:
But if my simple prayers may yet
Prevail with heaven to forget   10
Thy murder, I will join my tears
Rather than fail. But, O my fears!
It cannot die so. Heaven's king
Keeps register of everything,
And nothing may we use in vain.   15
Even beasts must be with justice slain,
Else men are made their deodands.[1]

---

5. The soul can "feel" (sympathize) even though
it "cannot feel" (has no power of physical sensation).
6. Medicine.
7. The outsize last stanza, the inconclusive ending, and the fact that the body has the last word,
all suggest that the poem as we have it is incomplete.
1. Objects (or, in this case, persons) forfeit to God
because they are the immediate occasion of someone's death.

Though they should wash their guilty hands
In this warm life-blood, which doth part
From thine, and wound me to the heart,   20
Yet could they not be clean; their stain
Is dyed in such a purple grain
There is not such another in
The world to offer for their sin.

   Unconstant Sylvio, when yet   25
I had not found him counterfeit,[2]
One morning (I remember well),
Tied in this silver chain and bell,
Gave it to me; nay, and I know
What he said then, I'm sure I do.   30
Said he, Look how your huntsman here
Hath taught a fawn to hunt his dear.
But Sylvio soon had me beguiled;
This waxèd tame, while he grew wild,
And quite regardless of my smart,   35
Left me his fawn, but took his heart.

   Thenceforth I set myself to play
My solitary time away
With this; and very well content
Could so mine idle life have spent.   40
For it was full of sport, and light
Of foot and heart, and did invite
Me to its game. It seemed to bless
Itself in me; how could I less
Than love it? Oh, I cannot be   45
Unkind t' a beast that loveth me.

   Had it lived long, I do not know
Whether it too might have done so
As Sylvio did; his gifts might be
Perhaps as false or more than he.   50
But I am sure, for aught that I
Could in so short a time espy,
Thy love was far more better than
The love of false and cruel men.

   With sweetest milk and sugar first   55
I it at mine own fingers nursed.
And as it grew, so every day
It waxed more sweet and white than they.
It had so sweet a breath! and oft
I blushed to see its foot more soft   60
And white—shall I say than my hand?—
Nay, any lady's of the land.

   It is a wondrous thing how fleet
'Twas on those little silver feet,

2. False, deceitful.

With what a pretty skipping grace   65
It oft would challenge me the race;
And when it had left me far away,
'Twould stay, and run again, and stay.
For it was nimbler much than hinds,[3]
And trod, as on the four winds.   70
    I have a garden of my own
But so with roses overgrown
And lilies that you would it guess
To be a little wilderness.
And all the springtime of the year   75
It only lovèd to be there.
Among the beds of lilies, I
Have sought it oft where it should lie,
Yet could not, till itself would rise,
Find it, although before mine eyes.   80
For in the flaxen lilies' shade
It like a bank of lilies laid.
Upon the roses it would feed,
Until its lips ev'n seemed to bleed;
And then to me 'twould boldly trip   85
And print those roses on my lip.
But all its chief delight was still
On roses thus itself to fill,
And its pure virgin limbs to fold
In whitest sheets of lilies cold.   90
Had it lived long, it would have been
Lilies without, roses within.
    Oh help! Oh help! I see it faint,
And die as calmly as a saint.
See how it weeps. The tears do come   95
Sad, slowly dropping like a gum.
So weeps the wounded balsam,[4] so
The holy frankincense doth flow.
The brotherless Heliades
Melt in such amber tears as these.[5]   100
    I in a golden vial will
Keep these two crystal tears, and fill
It till it do o'erflow with mine,
Then place it in Diana's shrine.
    Now my sweet fawn is vanished to   105
Whither the swans and turtles[6] go,
In fair Elysium to endure

---

3. I.e., full-grown deer.
4. Both balsam and frankincense are fragrant resins obtained a drop at a time from wounded trees.
5. The three daughters of the sun, Helios, so
bewailed the death of their rash brother Phaethon
that they were transformed into black poplar trees,
shedding tears of amber.

6. "Turtles": turtledoves. "Elysium": the Elysian
fields, a pagan version of heaven. Whether there
is a significant Christian element in the poem, if
so of what sort, and whether (it it exists) it enriches
the poem or muddles it, has been subject to scholarly dispute.

With milk-white lambs and ermines pure.
Oh, do not run too fast, for I
Will but bespeak thy grave, and die.   110
    First my unhappy statue shall
Be cut in marble, and withal,
Let it be weeping too; but there
Th' engraver sure his art may spare,
For I so truly thee bemoan   115
That I shall weep, though I be stone:
Until my tears, still dropping, wear
My breast, themselves engraving there.
There at my feet shalt thou be laid,
Of purest alabaster made;   120
For I would have thine image be
White as I can, though not as thee.

To His Coy Mistress

    Had we but world enough, and time,
This coyness, lady, were no crime.
We would sit down, and think which way
To walk, and pass our long love's day.
Thou by the Indian Ganges' side   5
Shouldst rubies find; I by the tide
Of Humber would complain.[1] I would
Love you ten years before the Flood,
And you should, if you please, refuse
Till the conversion of the Jews.[2]   10
My vegetable love should grow
Vaster than empires, and more slow;
An hundred years should go to praise
Thine eyes, and on thy forehead gaze;
Two hundred to adore each breast,   15
But thirty thousand to the rest;
An age at least to every part,
And the last age should show your heart.
For, lady, you deserve this state,[3]
Nor would I love at lower rate.   20
    But at my back I always hear
Time's wingèd chariot hurrying near;
And yonder all before us lie
Deserts of vast eternity.
Thy beauty shall no more be found,   25

1. Compared to the gorgeous Oriental Ganges, the
Humber (which flows past Marvell's home town of
Hull) is a muddy estuary, where one is more likely
to encounter herring-boats and coal scows than
rubies. "Complain" implies ditties of plaintive,
unavailing love.
2. According to popular chronology, the Jews were
to be converted just before the Last Judgment.
3. Dignity.

Nor, in thy marble vault, shall sound
My echoing song; then worms shall try
That long-preserved virginity,
And your quaint honor turn to dust,
And into ashes all my lust: 30
The grave's a fine and private place,
But none, I think, do there embrace.
   Now therefore, while the youthful hue
Sits on thy skin like morning dew,[4]
And while thy willing soul transpires   35
At every pore with instant fires,[5]
Now let us sport us while we may,
And now, like amorous birds of prey,
Rather at once our time devour
Than languish in his slow-chapped[6] power.   40
Let us roll all our strength and all
Our sweetness up into one ball,
And tear our pleasures with rough strife
Thorough the iron gates of life:
Thus, though we cannot make our sun   45
Stand still, yet we will make him run.[7]

The Definition of Love

My Love is of a birth as rare
As 'tis, for object, strange and high;
It was begotten by Despair
Upon Impossibility.

Magnanimous Despair alone   5
Could show me so divine a thing,
Where feeble Hope could ne'er have flown
But vainly flapped its tinsel wing.

And yet I quickly might arrive
Where my extended soul is fixed;[1]   10
But Fate does iron wedges drive,
And always crowds itself betwixt.

For Fate with jealous eye does see
Two perfect loves, nor lets them close;[2]

---

4. The text reads "glew," a reading as odious in
Marvell's time as in ours. Efforts have been made
to salvage "glew" by declaring it a dialectal form of
"glow"; and "lew," meaning "warmth," has been
suggested. But the simplest and most natural
emendation is probably the best.
5. Immediate, present enthusiasm. "Transpires":
breathes forth.
6. Slow-jawed. Time is envisaged as slowly chewing up the world and its people.
7. In the final lines, lover and mistress triumphantly reverse the field, eating time avidly instead
of being eaten by it, forcing the sun to race them
instead of vainly imploring it to stand still.
1. Marvell thinks of his soul as having gone out of
his body ("extended") and attached ("fixed") itself
to his mistress.
2. Unite.

Their union would her ruin be,   15
And her tyrannic power depose.[3]

And therefore her decrees of steel
Us as the distant poles have placed
(Though Love's whole world on us doth wheel),
Not by themselves to be embraced,   20

Unless the giddy heaven fall,
And earth some new convulsion tear,
And, us to join, the world should all
Be cramped into a planisphere.[4]

As lines, so loves oblique may well   25
Themselves in every angle greet;[5]
But ours, so truly parallel,
Though infinite, can never meet.

Therefore the love which us doth bind,
But Fate so enviously debars,   30
Is the conjunction of the mind,
And opposition of the stars.[6]

The Picture of Little T. C. in a Prospect of Flowers[1]

See with what simplicity
This nymph begins her golden days!
In the green grass she loves to lie,
And there with her fair aspect tames
The wilder flowers and gives them names,   5
But only with the roses plays,
        And them does tell
What color best becomes them and what smell.

Who can foretell for what high cause
This darling of the gods was born?   10
Yet this is she whose chaster laws
The wanton Love shall one day fear,
And under her command severe

3. Fate, and its agents Time and Change, would none of them have any power against a perfect mixture of the elements.
4. A flat sphere, literally absurd, but describing a kind of cartographic projection in which the world was represented in two dimensions and the poles were united.
5. "Oblique" includes the meaning of "deviating from right conduct or thought"; oblique loves, like oblique lines, touch in angles (corners), but Mar-vell's love and the lady's, being parallel and perfect, can never touch.
6. "Conjunction" and "opposition" are technical terms from astrology, here yoked to Marvell's "definition."
1. We do not know who T. C. was, though speculation has not been idle; all we need know is that she was a little girl. "Prospect": landscape, background scene.

See his bow broke and ensigns[2] torn.
    Happy who can   15
Appease this virtuous enemy of man!

O then let me in time compound
And parley with those conquering eyes
Ere they have tried their force to wound,
Ere with their glancing wheels they drive   20
In triumph over hearts that strive
And them that yield but more despise:
    Let me be laid
Where I may see thy glories from some shade.

Meantime, whilst every verdant thing   25
Itself does at thy beauty charm,
Reform the errors of the spring;
Make that the tulips may have share
Of sweetness, seeing they are fair;
And roses of their thorns disarm: 30
    But most procure
That violets may a longer age endure.

But O, young beauty of the woods,
Whom Nature courts with fruit and flowers,
Gather the flowers but spare the buds,   35
Lest Flora,[3] angry at thy crime
To kill her infants in their prime,
Do quickly make th' example yours;
    And ere we see,
Nip in the blossom all our hopes and thee.   40

The Mower Against Gardens

Luxurious man,[1] to bring his vice in use,
    Did after him the world seduce,
And from the fields the flowers and plants allure,
    Where Nature was most plain and pure.
He first enclosed within the garden's square   5
    A dead and standing pool of air,
And a more luscious earth for them did knead,
    Which stupefied them while it fed.
The pink grew then as double as his mind;[2]
    The nutriment did change the kind.   10
With strange perfumes he did the roses taint;

---

2. Flags, pennants.
3. Roman goddess of flowers.
1. Voluptuous man, who wants to popularize
("bring in use") his own vices.

2. The double pink or carnation is a product of
sophisticated, therefore hypocritical ("double"),
minds.

And flowers themselves were taught to paint.
The tulip white did for complexion seek,
   And learned to interline its cheek;
Its onion root they then so high did hold,   15
   That one was for a meadow sold;[3]
Another world was searched through oceans new,
   To find the marvel of Peru;[4]
And yet these rarities might be allowed
   To man, that sovereign thing and proud,   20
Had he not dealt between the bark and tree,[5]
   Forbidden mixtures there to see.
No plant now knew the stock from which it came;
   He grafts upon the wild the tame,
That the uncertain and adult'rate fruit   25
   Might put the palate in dispute.
His green seraglio has its eunuchs too,
   Lest any tyrant him outdo;
And in the cherry he does Nature vex,
   To procreate without a sex.[6]   30
'Tis all enforced, the fountain and the grot,
   While the sweet fields do lie forgot,
Where willing Nature does to all dispense
   A wild and fragrant innocence;
And fauns and fairies do the meadows till   35
   More by their presence than their skill.
Their statues polished by some ancient hand
   May to adorn the gardens stand;
But, howsoe'er the figures do excel,
   The gods themselves with us do dwell.   40

Damon the Mower

Hark how the mower Damon[1] sung,
With love of Juliana stung!
While everything did seem to paint
The scene more fit for his complaint.[2]
Like her fair eyes the day was fair,   5
But scorching like his amorous care;
Sharp, like his scythe, his sorrow was,
And withered, like his hopes, the grass.

---

3. A great boom in tulip bulbs took place in Holland during the 17th century; Marvell's line was therefore, on occasion, strictly accurate.
4. *Mirabilis Jalapa*, the four o'clock, a flower found originally in tropical America.
5. By grafting.
6. Cherries are commonly propagated by budding on the stocks of sturdier but less productive varieties.

1. Damon is a pastoral name familiar since Virgil's time; Juliana gets her name, if anywhere, from July (lines 23–24).
2. Love song. The word "complaint," used casually, carries a fine mockery with it, as does its cognate in "To his Coy Mistress," line 7.

"Oh what unusual heats are here,
Which thus our sunburned meadows sear!   10
The grasshopper its pipe gives o'er,
And hamstringed frogs can dance no more:
But in the brook the green frog wades,
And grasshoppers seek out the shades.
Only the snake, that kept within,   15
Now glitters in its second skin.

"This heat the sun could never raise,
Nor dog star so inflame the days;[3]
It from an higher beauty grow'th,
Which burns the fields and mower both;   20
Which mads the dog, and makes the sun
Hotter than his own Phaëton;[4]
Not July causeth these extremes,
But Juliana's scorching beams.

"Tell me where I may pass the fires   25
Of the hot day or hot desires,
To what cool cave shall I descend,
Or to what gelid[5] fountain bend?
Alas! I look for ease in vain,
When remedies themselves complain:[6]   30
No moisture but my tears do rest,
No cold but in her icy breast.

"How long wilt thou, fair shepherdess,
Esteem me and my presents less?
To thee the harmless snake I bring,   35
Disarmèd of its teeth and sting;
To thee chameleons, changing hue,
And oak leaves tipped with honey dew;
Yet thou, ungrateful, hast not sought
Nor what they are, nor who them brought.   40

"I am the mower Damon, known
Through all the meadows I have mown.
On me the morn her dew distills
Before her darling daffodils,
And if at noon my toil me heat,   45
The sun himself licks off my sweat;
While, going home, the evening sweet
In cowslip-water bathes my feet.

---

3. The dog star (Sirius in the constellation Canis Major) rises with the sun in late summer; coincidentally, this is the season when dogs most often develop rabies.
4. Son of Helios, the sun god of Greek mythology, he tried to drive his father's chariot, but let the horses run away, and scorched the world.
5. Icy.
6. I.e., fountain and cave themselves complain of unusual heat.

"What though the piping shepherd stock
The plains with an unnumbered flock,   50
This scythe of mine discovers wide
More ground than all his sheep do hide.
With this the golden fleece I shear
Of all these closes every year,[7]
And though in wool more poor than they,   55
Yet I am richer far in hay.

"Nor am I so deformed to sight
If in my scythe I lookèd right;
In which I see my picture done
As in a crescent moon the sun.   60
The deathless fairies take me oft
To lead them in their dances soft,
And when I tune myself to sing,
About me they contract their ring.[8]

"How happy might I still have mowed,   65
Had not Love here his thistles sowed!
But now I all the day complain,
Joining my labor to my pain;
And with my scythe cut down the grass,
Yet still my grief is where it was;   70
But when the iron blunter grows,
Sighing, I whet my scythe and woes."

While thus he threw his elbow round,
Depopulating all the ground,
And with his whistling scythe does cut   75
Each stroke between the earth and root,
The edgèd steel, by careless chance,
Did into his own ankle glance,
And there among the grass fell down
By his own scythe the mower mown.   80

"Alas!" said he, "these hurts are slight
To those that die by Love's despite.
With shepherd's purse and clown's all-heal[9]
The blood I stanch and wound I seal.
Only for him no cure is found   85
Whom Juliana's eyes do wound;
'Tis Death alone that this must do;
For, Death, thou art a mower too."

---

7. Hay is the "wool" of the fields ("closes").
8. I.e., the "fairy-ring," a discolored circle of grass, popularly supposed to result from fairies dancing there.

9. Folk-names for popular remedies found in fields and hedges. Like a good Petrarchan lover, the mower falls with an erotic conceit and a sentimental morality on his lips.

The Mower to the Glow-Worms

Ye living lamps, by whose dear light
The nightingale does sit so late,
And studying all the summer night
Her matchless songs does meditate,

Ye country comets, that portend   5
No war nor prince's funeral,
Shining unto no higher end
Than to presage the grass's fall;

Ye glow-worms, whose officious[1] flame
To wand'ring mowers shows the way,   10
That in the night have lost their aim,
And after foolish fires[2] do stray;

Your courteous fires in vain you waste,
Since Juliana here is come,
For she my mind hath so displaced   15
That I shall never find my home.

The Mower's Song

My mind was once the true survey
Of all these meadows fresh and gay,
And in the greenness of the grass
Did see its hopes as in a glass;[1]
When Juliana came, and she,   5
What I do to the grass, does to my thoughts and me.

But these, while I with sorrow pine,
Grew more luxuriant still and fine,
That not one blade of grass you spied
But had a flower on either side;   10
When Juliana came, and she,
What I do to the grass, does to my thoughts and me.

Unthankful meadows, could you so
A fellowship so true forego,
And in your gaudy May-games[2] meet,   15
While I lay trodden under feet?
When Juliana came, and she,
What I do to the grass, does to my thoughts and me.

1. Obliging, zealous.
2. Will-o'-the-wisps, swampfires.
1. Looking glass, mirror.

2. Festivals and merrymaking marked the first of
May—and still do for the heartless grass, though
not for the melancholy mower.

But what you in compassion ought
Shall now by my revenge be wrought,   20
And flowers, and grass, and I, and all,
Will in one common ruin fall;
For Juliana comes, and she,
What I do to the grass, does to my thoughts and me.

And thus ye meadows, which have been   25
Companions of my thoughts more green,
Shall now the heraldry become
With which I shall adorn my tomb.
For Juliana comes, and she,
What I do to the grass, does to my thoughts and me.   30

The Garden

How vainly men themselves amaze
To win the palm, the oak, or bays,[1]
And their uncessant labors see
Crowned from some single herb or tree,
Whose short and narrow-vergèd shade   5
Does prudently their toils upbraid;
While all flowers and all trees do close[2]
To weave the garlands of repose!

Fair Quiet, have I found thee here,
And Innocence, thy sister dear?   10
Mistaken long, I sought you then
In busy companies of men.
Your sacred plants, if here below,
Only among the plants will grow;
Society is all but rude,   15
To this delicious solitude.

No white nor red[3] was ever seen
So amorous as this lovely green.
Fond lovers, cruel as their flame,
Cut in these trees their mistress' name: 20
Little, alas, they know or heed
How far these beauties hers exceed!
Fair trees, wheresoe'er your barks I wound,
No name shall but your own be found.[4]

When we have run our passion's heat,   25
Love hither makes his best retreat.

1. Honors, respectively, for military, civic, and
poetic achievement.
2. Unite, agree.
3. Colors traditionally associated with female
beauty.
4. Marvell proposes to carve in the bark of trees,
not "Sylvia" or "Laura," but "Beech" and "Oak."

The gods, that mortal beauty chase,
Still in a tree did end their race:
Apollo hunted Daphne so,
Only that she might laurel grow;[5]   30
And Pan did after Syrinx speed,
Not as a nymph, but for a reed.

What wondrous life in this I lead!
Ripe apples drop about my head;
The luscious clusters of the vine   35
Upon my mouth do crush their wine;
The nectarine and curious[6] peach
Into my hands themselves do reach;
Stumbling on melons as I pass,
Insnared with flowers, I fall on grass.   40

Meanwhile the mind, from pleasure less,[7]
Withdraws into its happiness;
The mind, that ocean where each kind
Does straight its own resemblance find;[8]
Yet it creates, transcending these,   45
Far other worlds and other seas,
Annihilating all that's made
To a green thought in a green shade.[9]

Here at the fountain's sliding foot,
Or at some fruit tree's mossy root,   50
Casting the body's vest[1] aside,
My soul into the boughs does glide:
There like a bird it sits and sings,
Then whets[2] and combs its silver wings,
And, till prepared for longer flight,   55
Waves in its plumes the various light.[3]

Such was that happy garden-state,
While man there walked without a mate:
After a place so pure and sweet,
What other help could yet be meet![4]   60
But 'twas beyond a mortal's share
To wander solitary there:

5. Apollo chased Daphne until she turned into a laurel, and Pan pursued Syrinx until she became a reed, out of which he made Panpipes. The gods' motives were, of course, sexual, not horticultural.
6. Exquisite. (The nectarine *is* a curious variety of peach.) In line 39, "melons," which have their etymological roots in the Greek word for "apple," may be intended to recall a particularly remote apple over which all mankind once stumbled.
7. "Less" may modify either pleasure or mind. In the latter sense ("drawn in on itself") it chimes on "withdraws" and "annihilating" later in the stanza.

8. As the ocean supposedly contained a counterpart of every creature on land, so also the ocean of the mind.
9. A famous instance of Marvell's endlessly evocative simplicity.
1. Garment.
2. Preens.
3. The many-colored light of this world, contrasted with the white radiance of eternity.
4. Genesis 2.18 records the Lord's decision to make "an help meet" for Adam, i.e., Eve.

Two paradises 'twere in one
To live in paradise alone.

How well the skillful gardener drew   65
Of flowers and herbs this dial new,[5]
Where from above the milder sun
Does through a fragrant zodiac run;
And as it works, th' industrious bee
Computes its time as well as we!   70
How could such sweet and wholesome hours
Be reckoned but with herbs and flowers?

An Horatian Ode

Upon Cromwell's Return from Ireland[1]

The forward youth that would appear,
Must now forsake his Muses dear,
            Nor in the shadows sing
            His numbers languishing:

'Tis time to leave the books in dust,   5
And oil th' unusèd armor's rust;
            Removing from the wall
            The corselet of the hall.[2]

So restless Cromwell could not cease
In the inglorious arts of peace,   10
            But through adventurous war
            Urgèd his active star;

And, like the three-forked lightning, first
Breaking the clouds where it was nursed,
            Did thorough his own side   15
            His fiery way divide:[3]

---

5. The garden itself, enlarged metaphorically to a sundial. While the sun keeps time on it, the bee (below, line 69) is busy with the thyme in it.
1. Cromwell returned from conquering Ireland in May 1650, about 18 months after the execution of Charles I. The two events were vaguely but persistently connected: Cromwell's victory over the Irish was somehow a "vindication" of his career to this point, a sign that God did not disapprove of his laying violent hands on the sacred person of the monarch. The title phrase, "An Horatian Ode," promises a poem of cool and balanced judgment, not "enthusiastic" or heroic like the odes of Pindar. Balanced judgments of Cromwell were not politic in the Restoration: the poem was cancelled from all but two known copies of the 1681 edition.

2. The "forward youth" who removes armor from the wall owes something to a similar figure in the first book of Lucan's *Pharsalia*, which is also a poem about force, justice, and civil war. Andrew Marvell was not by any means dropping books and picking up armor in 1650.
3. Cromwell had begun as a relatively inconspicuous Presbyterian, but soon became the leader of the more radical group variously known as the "Rump" or the "Independents." The "three-forked lightning" he wields identifies him with Zeus; and his giving birth (to himself, presumably) through his own side (party, of course, but a part of the body, too) might remind a reader of Athena's birth through Zeus' ear.

For 'tis all one to courage high,
The emulous, or enemy;
    And with such, to enclose
    Is more than to oppose;   20

Then burning through the air he went,
And palaces and temples rent;
    And Caesar's head at last
    Did through his laurels blast.[4]

'Tis madness to resist or blame   25
The force of angry heaven's flame;
    And if we would speak true,
    Much to the man is due,

Who from his private gardens, where
He lived reservèd and austere,   30
    As if his highest plot
    To plant the bergamot;[5]

Could by industrious valor climb
To ruin the great work of Time,
    And cast the kingdom old   35
    Into another mold;

Though Justice against Fate complain,
And plead the ancient rights in vain:
    But those do hold or break,
    As men are strong or weak.   40

Nature that hateth emptiness,
Allows of penetration[6] less,
    And therefore must make room
    Where greater spirits come.

What field of all the civil wars   45
Where his were not the deepest scars?
    And Hampton shows what part
    He had of wiser art;[7]

Where, twining subtle fears with hope,
He wove a net of such a scope   50

---

4. Laurels were used for royal crowns precisely
because they were supposed to protect from lightning. "Caesar," of course, is Charles I.
5. Bergamot is a variety of pear; but its etymology
(from the Turkish, "prince's pear") may conceal
the insinuation that Cromwell had been plotting
for power even in his early days of "private" life.
The whole poem is full of puns (cf. "enclose," line
19, "mold," line 36) for the reader to seek out.

6. I.e., simultaneous occupation of the same space
by two bodies.
7. Hampton Court, where Charles I was confined
shortly before his execution. It was popularly said
that Cromwell connived at his momentary escape
to Carisbrooke Castle on the Isle of Wight in order
to convince the doubtful Parliament that the king
could not be trusted and must be executed.

That Charles himself might chase
To Caresbrooke's narrow case,

That thence the royal actor borne,
The tragic scaffold might adorn;
    While round the armèd bands   55
    Did clap their bloody hands.

He nothing common did or mean
Upon that memorable scene,
    But with his keener eye
    The ax's edge did try;[8]   60

Nor called the gods with vulgar spite
To vindicate his helpless right;
    But bowed his comely head
    Down, as upon a bed.

This was that memorable hour,   65
Which first assured the forcèd power;
    So when they did design
    The capitol's first line,

A bleeding head where they begun
Did fright the architects to run;   70
    And yet in that the state
    Foresaw its happy fate.[9]

And now the Irish are ashamed
To see themselves in one year tamed;
    So much one man can do,   75
    That does both act and know.

They can affirm his praises best,
And have, though overcome, confessed
    How good he is, how just,
    And fit for highest trust.[1]   80

Nor yet grown stiffer with command,
But still in the republic's hand—
    How fit he is to sway,
    That can so well obey.

8. Latin uses one word, *acies,* for the front of a battle line, the edge of a sword- or ax-blade, and the beam of an eye.
9. When foundations were being dug for the temple of Jupiter at Rome, Pliny tells us, the workmen uncovered a bloody head. They at first thought it an ill omen but then were persuaded to consider it a token that Rome would be the head (*caput*) of an empire; hence the name of the temple, Jupiter Capitolinus, and of the hill on which it stood, the Capitoline. The tale may well imply a generic relation between civilization and violence.
1. Not surprisingly, no such testimonials are known.

He to the Commons' feet presents   85
A kingdom for his first year's rents;
    And, what he may, forbears
    His fame to make it theirs;

And has his sword and spoils ungirt,
To lay them at the public's skirt: 90
    So, when the falcon high
    Falls heavy from the sky,

She, having killed, no more does search,
But on the next green bough to perch;
    Where, when he first does lure,   95
    The falconer has her sure.

What may not then our isle presume,
While victory his crest does plume!
    What may not others fear,
    If thus he crown each year!   100

A Caesar he ere long to Gaul,
To Italy an Hannibal,
    And to all states not free,
    Shall climactèric be.[2]

The Pict no shelter now shall find   105
Within his party-colored mind,
    But from this valor sad,[3]
    Shrink underneath the plaid;[4]

Happy if in the tufted brake
The English hunter him mistake,   110
    Nor lay his hounds in near
    The Caledonian[5] deer.

But thou, the war's and Fortune's son,
March indefatigably on;
    And for the last effect,   115
    Still keep thy sword erect;[6]

Besides the force it has to fright
The spirits of the shady night,[7]

---

2. Neither Caesar nor Hannibal brought, or pretended to bring, freedom to the lands they attacked. "Climacteric": a period of crucial change in human life (for better or worse).
3. Primarily, "severe."
4. Early inhabitants of Scotland were called Picts because their warriors painted themselves many colors (Latin, *pictus*: painted); Marvell is playing with an image of the Scots as divided by factions (parties) into as many colors as Scottish plaids.

5. Scottish.
6. The sword is being carried "erect," i.e., with the bare blade up, not the cross of the handle. Naked power, not religion, is to be the ensign of Cromwell's rule.
7. In classical tradition, underworld spirits fear cold iron. The last two lines may recall the saying of Christ that they who take the sword shall perish by the sword.

> The same arts that did gain
> A power must it maintain.   120

1650

JOHN MILTON
1608–1674

1637:   *Lycidas*.
1640–1660: The pamphlet wars.
1651:   Blindness.
1667:   *Paradise Lost*.

The life of John Milton falls conveniently into three divisions. There is a period of youthful education and apprenticeship, which culminates in the writing of *Lycidas* (1637) and Milton's foreign travels (1638–39). There is a period of prose and controversy (1640–60), when almost all his verse was the by-product of events public or private, and when his major preoccupations were political and social; and finally, there are the last fourteen years of his life, when he returned to literature, a mature and somewhat embittered figure, to publish his three major poems, *Paradise Lost* (1667), *Paradise Regained* (1671), and *Samson Agonistes* (1671).

Milton was born in Bread Street, Cheapside, the elder son of a self-made businessman, who, under the title of scrivener, drew up contracts, lent money at interest, and dealt in real estate. From the beginning, young Milton showed prodigious gifts as a student of languages. At St. Paul's School he mastered Latin and Greek, and before long he was adept in most modern European tongues, as well as Hebrew. Sent to Christ's College, Cambridge, he graduated A. B. in 1629 and A. M. in 1632, meanwhile continuing to read voraciously and writing (too infrequently for his own satisfaction) an occasional poem. In the normal course of events, a career like this would have culminated in ordination to the ministry and a career in the church. But after his A. M., Milton, who disliked the trend of religious and civil affairs in England, did not take orders; leaving the university, first for London, then for his father's country house at Horton in Buckinghamshire, he read, day and night, under his own direction, for six more years. It seems likely that Milton in his time read just about everything of importance written in English, Latin, Greek, and Italian. (Of course, he had the Bible by heart.) In 1634 he wrote, at the invitation of a noble family in Shropshire, the masque known as *Comus*; and in 1637 he contributed to a volume memorializing a college classmate the elegy *Lycidas*. Finally, in 1638, his most indulgent father sent this most avid of students abroad, to put the finishing touches on an already splendid education. For a little over a year Milton traveled on the Continent, visiting famous literary figures and scenes; then, hearing rumors of impending troubles in England, he returned home.

Of Milton's complex and troubled career in controversy, we need not say much. It too is divided into three major phases. He began by publishing antiprelatical tracts, against government of the church by bishops. These are rough, knockabout, name-calling tracts in the style of the times, which take a popular position on a relatively popular issue. In 1644, responding to a book by a German exile in England named Samuel Hartlib, he wrote a short essay *Of Education*; later in the same year, responding to a severe if ineffectual parliamentary ordinance to regulate printing, he published his defense of a free press, *Areopagitica*. But in the meanwhile his personal circumstances had led to a second series of pamphlets that earned Milton a reputation as a radical. In May or June 1642, he had married Mary Powell, daughter of a royalist country squire. The bride was just seventeen years old, half her husband's age. Within a few weeks she left him, to return to her parents' house; and from 1643 to 1645, Milton published a series of pamphlets arguing that divorce should be granted on grounds of incompatibility. Respectable Englishmen, already disturbed by the social troubles of the time, took a dim view of what they called "divorce at pleasure"; it looked like the end of all social order. In fact, Milton's position appears moderate today, and is accepted practice in many modern societies; but it was scandalous in his time, and Milton was much embittered by ridicule of his ideas. After the execution of Charles I in 1649, he published a third set of pamphlets; they were Latin disputations against Continental critics of the Cromwell regime, and they explicitly defended the execution of Charles. In the middle of this work he went blind, as a result of eyestrain continued over many years. With the help of assistants, however, he was able to fulfill his duties as Latin Secretary to Cromwell's Council of State, and to contribute very substantially to the diplomatic dignity of the new government.

Meanwhile, his wife had returned to him in 1645, and having borne him three daughters, died in 1652. In 1656 Milton married Katherine Woodcock, who died in childbirth in 1658. Finally, in 1660, the whole political movement for which Milton had sacrificed so much went to smash. Though Milton boldly published pamphlets in its support to the very last minute, the Good Old Cause was defeated, and Charles II recalled from his travels. For a time under the Restoration, Milton was imprisoned and in danger of his life; but friends intervened (among them, Andrew Marvell), and he escaped with a fine and the loss of most of his property.

In 1663 Milton married his third wife, Elizabeth Minshull; and in blindness, poverty, defeat, and relative isolation, he set about completing a poem "justifying the ways of God to men," which he had first envisaged many years before. It was published in 1667, as *Paradise Lost*; and despite the many difficulties which it presented, despite its unfamiliar meter (blank verse was rare outside drama), despite the unpopularity of its attitudes and Milton's reputation as a dangerous man, it was recognized at once as a supreme epic achievement. In 1671 Milton published *Paradise Regained*, an epic poem in four books describing Christ's temptation in the wilderness, and *Samson Agonistes*, a "closet" tragedy (i.e., not intended for the stage). He died, of complications arising from gout, in 1674.

In the writings of Milton, the work of two tremendous intellectual and social movements comes to a head. The Renaissance is responsible for the rich and complex texture of Milton's style, the multiplicity of its classical references, its wealth of ornament and decoration. *Paradise Lost*, being an epic, not only challenges comparison with Homer and Virgil, it undertakes to encompass the whole life of mankind—war, love, religion, Hell, Heaven, the cosmos. It is a poem vastly capacious of worldly experience. On the other hand, the Reformation speaks with equal, if not greater, authority in Milton's earnest and individually minded Christianity. The great epic, which resounds with the grandeur and multiplicity of the world, is also a poem whose central actions take place inwardly, at the core of man's conscience. Adam's fate culminates in an act of passive suffering, not of active heroism. He does not kill Hector or Turnus, much less Satan, he picks up the burden of worldly existence, and triumphs over his guilt by admitting it and repenting of it.

These two contrasting aspects of Milton's life and thought place him within the long tradition of Renaissance Christian humanism. His literary art places him in the small circle of great epic writers.

On the Morning of Christ's Nativity[1]

1

This is the month, and this the happy morn
Wherein the son of Heaven's eternal King,
Of wedded maid and virgin mother born,
Our great redemption from above did bring;
For so the holy sages once did sing,[2]   5
   That he our deadly forfeit should release,
And with his Father work us a perpetual peace.

2

That glorious form, that light unsufferable,[3]
And that far-beaming blaze of majesty
Wherewith he wont at Heaven's high council-table   10
To sit the midst of Trinal Unity,[4]
He laid aside; and here with us to be,
   Forsook the courts of everlasting day,
And chose with us a darksome house of mortal clay.

3

Say, heavenly Muse, shall not thy sacred vein   15
Afford a present to the infant God?
Hast thou no verse, no hymn, or solemn strain,
To welcome him to this his new abode,
Now while the heaven by the sun's team untrod[5]
   Hath took no print of the approaching light,   20
And all the spangled host keep watch in squadrons bright?

4

See how from far upon the eastern road
The star-led wizards[6] haste with odors sweet:

1. This ode was written at Christmas 1629, a few weeks after Milton's 21st birthday. The poem was not only the largest (physically and thematically) that he had so far attempted, either in English or Latin; it was also the best sustained. Milton gave it pride of place in the 1645 edition of his poems, no doubt because it had confirmed him in his vocation as a poet.
2. For example, the prophet Isaiah (chaps. 9 and 40) and the Book of Job (chap. 19) were thought to have foretold the Messiah. "Our deadly forfeit" is the sentence of death consequent upon the Fall.
3. Bright beyond endurance.
4. The Trinity, of which Christ is the middle member (Father, Son, and Holy Ghost).
5. In classical mythology, the sun drove across heaven in a chariot drawn by horses. Milton's poem begins (and ends) in the darkness of predawn.
6. I.e., the magi or "wise men," who came to adore the Christ child. "Prevent" (line 24): anticipate.

O run, prevent them with thy humble ode,
And lay it lowly at his blessèd feet;   25
Have thou the honor first thy Lord to greet,
    And join thy voice unto the angel choir,
From out his secret altar touched with hallowed fire.[7]

The Hymn

1

It was the winter wild
While the Heaven-born child   30
    All meanly wrapped in the rude manger lies;
Nature in awe to him
Had doffed her gaudy trim[8]
    With her great Master so to sympathize;
It was no season then for her   35
To wanton with the sun, her lusty paramour.

2

Only with speeches fair
She woos the gentle air
    To hide her guilty front with innocent snow,
And on her naked shame,   40
Pollute with sinful blame,
    The saintly veil of maiden white to throw,[9]
Confounded that her Maker's eyes
Should look so near upon her foul deformities.

3

But he her fears to cease   45
Sent down the meek-eyed Peace;
    She, crowned with olive green, came softly sliding
Down through the turning sphere,[1]
His ready harbinger,
    With turtle[2] wing the amorous clouds dividing,   50
And waving wide her myrtle wand,
    She strikes a universal peace through sea and land.

4

No war or battle's sound
Was heard the world around;[3]
    The idle spear and shield were high up-hung;   55
The hookèd chariot[4] stood
Unstained with hostile blood,
    The trumpet spake not to the armèd throng,

---

7. The prophet whose lips are touched by a coal from the altar, and whose works are thus authenticated, is described in Isaiah 6.7.
8. I.e., the leaves had fallen from the trees.
9. The "metaphysical" intentions attributed to Nature are of the sort that would one day be described by John Ruskin as "pathetic fallacies."
1. I.e., through the heavenly spheres, containing the planets, and surrounding the earth.

2. Like a turtledove; dove and myrtle wand are special attributes of Venus, as a crown of olive emblematizes peace.
3. Around the time of Christ's birth, the entire civilized world rejoiced in the "Peace of Augustus," when for many years no major wars disturbed the Roman empire.
4. War chariots were built with scythe-like hooks on the axles, for murderous purposes.

And kings sat still with aweful eye,
As if they surely knew their sovereign Lord was by.   60

5

But peaceful was the night
Wherein the Prince of light
    His reign of peace upon the earth began:
The winds, with wonder whist,[5]
Smoothly the waters kissed,   65
    Whispering new joys to the mild oceàn,
Who now hath quite forgot to rave,
While birds of calm[6] sit brooding on the charmèd wave.

6

The stars with deep amaze
Stand fixed in steadfast gaze,   70
    Bending one way their precious influence,
And will not take their flight
For all the morning light,
    Or Lucifer[7] that often warned them thence;
But in their glimmering orbs did glow   75
Until their Lord himself bespake, and bid them go.

7

And though the shady gloom
Had given day her room,
    The sun himself withheld his wonted speed,
And hid his head for shame   80
As his inferior flame
    The new-enlightened world no more should need;
He saw a greater Sun[8] appear
Than his bright throne or burning axletree could bear.

8

The shepherds on the lawn   85
Or ere the point of dawn
    Sat simply chatting in a rustic row;
Full little thought they than
That the mighty Pan[9]
    Was kindly come to live with them below;   90
Perhaps their loves or else their sheep
Was all that did their silly[1] thoughts so busy keep.

9

When such music sweet
Their hearts and ears did greet
    As never was by mortal finger struck,   95
Divinely warbled voice
Answering the stringèd noise,
    As all their souls in blissful rapture took;

---

5. Hushed.
6. Halcyon birds, reputed to bring calm weather.
7. Not Satan, but the morning star.
8. The familiar pun. The sun's axletree is his chariot.

9. Pan, patron of shepherds, is a merry goatfoot god; but his name, which in Greek means "All," suggests a more august deity. "Than" and "then" were 17th-century equivalents.
1. Not "foolish," just "humble."

The air, such pleasure loath to lose,
With thousand echoes still prolongs each heavenly close.[2]   100

10

Nature that heard such sound
Beneath the hollow round
   Of Cynthia's seat[3] the airy region thrilling,
Now was almost won
To think her part was done,   105
   And that her reign had here its last fulfilling;
She knew such harmony alone
Could hold all heaven and earth in happier uniòn.

11

At last surrounds their sight
A globe of circular light   110
   That with long beams the shamefaced night arrayed;[4]
The helmèd cherubim
And sworded seraphim
   Are seen in glittering ranks with wings displayed,
Harping in loud and solemn choir   115
With unexpressive [5] notes to Heaven's newborn heir.

12

Such music (as 'tis said)
Before was never made,
   But when of old the sons of morning sung,[6]
While the Creator great   120
His constellations set,
   And the well-balanced world on hinges hung,
And cast the dark foundations deep,
And bid the weltering waves their oozy channel keep.

13

Ring out, ye crystal spheres,   125
Once bless our human ears
   (If ye have power to touch our senses so),
And let your silver chime
Move in melodious time,
   And let the bass of Heaven's deep organ blow;   130
And with your ninefold harmony[7]
Make up full consort to th' angelic symphony.

14

For if such holy song
Enwrap our fancy long,
   Time will run back and fetch the age of gold;[8]   135

2. Cadence.
3. "Cynthia" is the moon; nature below the moon's sphere (sublunary nature) was thought to be different from, and inferior to, nature above that sphere.
4. In a rather special sense, "drove back." The "cherubim" and "seraphim" are special classes of angels.
5. Inexpressible.

6. The phrase is from Job 38.6–7.
7. Though there are ten heavenly spheres, the harmony they make is ninefold, because one of them, the *primum mobile* or prime mover, does not itself move.
8. The first age, of human innocence; classical mythology's equivalent to the garden of Eden.

And speckled Vanity
Will sicken soon and die,
    And leprous Sin will melt from earthly mold,
And Hell itself will pass away,
And leave her dolorous mansions to the peering day.   140

15

Yea, Truth and Justice then
Will down return to men,[9]
    Th' enameled arras of the rainbow wearing,
And Mercy set between,[1]
Throned in celestial sheen,   145
    With radiant feet the tissued clouds down steering;
And Heaven, as at some festival,
Will open wide the gates of her high palace hall.

16

But wisest Fate says no,
This must not yet be so   150
    The Babe lies yet in smiling infancy[2]
That on the bitter cross
Must redeem our loss,
    So both himself and us to glorify;
Yet first to those ychained in sleep   155
The wakeful trump of doom must thunder through the deep,

17

With such a horrid clang
As on Mount Sinai rang
    While the red fire and smoldering clouds outbrake;[3]
The agèd earth, aghast   160
With terror of that blast,
    Shall from the surface to the center shake,
When at the world's last sessiòn,
The dreadful Judge in middle air shall spread his throne.

18

And then at last our bliss   165
Full and perfect is,
    But now begins; for from this happy day
Th' old dragon under ground,[4]
In straiter limits bound,
    Not half so far casts his usurpèd sway,   170
And wroth to see his kingdom fail,
Swinges[5] the scaly horror of his folded tail.

9. According to classic myth, Astraea, goddess of justice, lived on earth during the golden age, but when men grew corrupt, she fled to heaven, from where we still hope she may some day return. An "arras" is a hanging or tapestry.
1. In the 1673 edition of his poems, Milton changed lines 143–44 to read: "Orbed in a rainbow; and, like glories wearing, / Mercy will sit between."
2. The Latin word *infans* means literally non-speaker. Till Christ has fulfilled his mission, the greatest Word of God has not been spoken.
3. Moses received the Ten Commandments amid thunders and lightnings atop Sinai (Exodus 19); the Last Judgment (good for some, bad for others) will take place amid similar uproar.
4. I.e., the devil.
5. Lashes.

19

The oracles are dumb;[6]
No voice or hideous hum
   Runs through the archèd roof in words deceiving.   175
Apollo from his shrine
Can no more divine,
   With hollow shriek the steep of Delphos leaving.[7]
No nightly trance or breathèd spell
Inspires the pale-eyed priest from the prophetic cell.   180

20

The lonely mountains o'er
And the resounding shore
   A voice of weeping heard and loud lament;
From haunted spring and dale
Edged with the poplar pale,   185
   The parting Genius[8] is with sighing sent;
With flower-inwoven tresses torn,
The nymphs in twilight shade of tangled thickets mourn.

21

In consecrated earth
And on the holy hearth,   190
   The Lars and Lemures[9] moan with midnight plaint;
In urns and altars round
A drear and dying sound
   Affrights the flamens at their service quaint;
And the chill marble seems to sweat,   195
While each peculiar power forgoes his wonted seat.[1]

22

Peor and Baalim[2]
Forsake their temples dim,
   With that twice-battered god of Palestine,[3]
And moonèd Ashtaroth,[4]   200
Heaven's queen and mother both,
   Now sits not girt with tapers' holy shine;
The Libyc Hammon[5] shrinks his horn;
In vain the Tyrian maids their wounded Thammuz mourn.[6]

---

6. The most famous classical account of the failure of the oracles at the birth of Christ is that of the Greek essayist and biographer Plutarch.
7. Apollo's main shrine was at Delphi on the steep slopes of Mount Parnassus.
8. For classical antiquity the "Genius" of a place or person was a tutelary deity. With the coming of Christ all these picturesque local deities are dismissed, and the poet clearly regrets their departure.
9. Lars are domestic gods, Lemures the spirits of the dead.
1. Flamens are Roman priests. As the inward spirit evaporates from marble statues, they seem to sweat.

2. Peor was a place in the land of Canaan where one of the many Baals or Baalim (fertility gods) was worshipped; Milton uses the name for the god himself.
3. Dagon, the Philistine god whose image at Ashdod was twice knocked down by Jehovah; see 1 Samuel 5.3–4.
4. Ashtaroth, also known as Astarte, was a Phoenician fertility goddess, identified with the moon.
5. Ammon or Hammon, formed like a ram, had his main shrine in Libya.
6. Thammuz, lover of Ashtaroth, was annually lamented by the Phoenician women; he was later adopted into the Greek pantheon as Adonis.

23

And sullen Moloch,[7] fled,   205
Hath left in shadows dread
   His burning idol all of blackest hue;
In vain with cymbals' ring
They call the grisly king
   In dismal dance about the furnace blue;   210
The brutish gods of Nile as fast,[8]
Isis and Orus and the dog Anubis haste.

24

Nor is Osiris seen
In Memphian grove or green,
   Trampling the unshowered grass with lowings loud,[9]   215
Nor can he be at rest
Within his sacred chest;[1]
   Naught but profoundest Hell can be his shroud.
In vain with timbreled anthems dark
The sable-stolèd sorcerers bear his worshipped ark.   220

25

He feels from Judah's land
The dreaded Infant's hand,
   The rays of Bethlehem blind his dusky eyn;[2]
Nor all the gods beside
Longer dare abide,   225
   Not Typhon huge,[3] ending in snaky twine;
Our Babe, to show his godhead true,
Can in his swaddling bands control the damnèd crew.

26

So when the sun in bed,
Curtained with cloudy red,   230
   Pillows his chin upon an orient[4] wave,
The flocking shadows pale
Troop to th' infernal jail;
   Each fettered ghost slips to his several grave;[5]
And the yellow-skirted fays   235
Fly after the night-steeds, leaving their moon-loved maze.

---

7. Moloch was worshipped by the Phoenicians and their colonists the Carthaginians in the form of a brazen idol with a human body and a calf's head; the statue was heated flaming hot, and children thrown into its embrace as sacrifices—or so the story goes.
8. Egyptian gods often had some of the features of animals; for example, Isis was represented with cow's horns, Orus or Horus with a hawk's head.
9. Osiris was sometimes given the shape of a bull, and known in that guise as Apis.
1. The Greek historian Herodotus tells (2.63) how the image of Osiris was carried from temple to temple in a small wooden container (Milton calls it a "chest" and an "ark"). The priests of Osiris accompanied it with tambourines ("timbrels").

2. An obsolete plural form of "eyes," used for the sake of the rhyme.
3. Typhon, who bears the same name in both Greek and Egyptian mythology, is a disagreeable figure in both contexts; in Egypt he is the murderer of Osiris, in Greek legend, he is like an enormous serpent, a trait suggesting "th' old dragon under ground" (above, line 168). The Christian Babe, destroying serpents in his swaddling bands, recalls the infant Hercules, who strangled two giant serpents in his cradle.
4. Only the adjective "orient" (eastern) suggests that it is morning, not evening.
5. Like ghosts at sunrise, the pagan gods, geniuses, and fays (fairies) are all bound to disappear at the rising of the Christian sun.

27

But see ! the Virgin blessed
Hath laid her Babe to rest.
    Time is our tedious song should here have ending.
Heaven's youngest-teemèd star[6]   240
Hath fixed her polished car,
    Her sleeping Lord with handmaid lamp attending:
And all about the courtly stable
Bright-harnessed angels sit in order serviceàble.

1629   1645

On Shakespeare[1]

What needs my Shakespeare for his honored bones
The labor of an age in pilèd stones,
Or that his hallowed relics should be hid
Under a star-ypointing pyramid?[2]
Dear son of memory, great heir of fame,   5
What need'st thou such weak witness of thy name?
Thou in our wonder and astonishment
Hast built thyself a livelong monument.
For whilst to th' shame of slow-endeavoring art
Thy easy numbers flow, and that each heart   10
Hath from the leaves of thy unvalued book[3]
Those Delphic lines with deep impression took,
Then thou, our fancy of itself bereaving,
Dost make us marble with too much conceiving;[4]
And so sepùlchered in such pomp dost lie,   15
That kings for such a tomb would wish to die.

1630   1632

6. The newest star of heaven is that which guided the wise men to Bethlehem. By contrast with Richard Crashaw's poem on the same theme (above, p. 1358), Milton's has devoted very little attention to the physical baby and his physical mother. What this shows about Puritan and Catholic attitudes toward the Incarnation has been the subject of much critical discussion.

1. Milton's tribute to Shakespeare appeared in the Second Folio of the plays.

2. "Star-ypointing" uses one of Spenser's archaic "y-" prefixes to eke out the meter. (Note also the interpolated "that" in line 10, serving the same purpose.) Milton's poem begins by answering the common complaint of the day, that Shakespeare should have been buried in some place more splendid than Stratford. Shakespeare is described as the "son of memory" because that makes him a brother of the muses, daughters of Mnemosyne (four syllables; the word means "memory") by Zeus.

3. Beyond all value, invaluable book.

4. The monuments of Shakespeare's tomb are all the enchanted and motionless readers of his book.

L'Allegro[1]

Hence loathèd Melancholy,
   Of Cerberus[2] and blackest midnight born,
In Stygian[3] cave forlorn
   'Mongst horrid shapes, and shrieks, and sights unholy,
Find out some uncouth cell,   5
   Where brooding Darkness spreads his jealous wings,
And the night-raven sings;
   There under ebon shades and low-browed rocks,
As ragged as thy locks,
   In dark Cimmerian[4] desert ever dwell.   10
But come thou goddess fair and free,
In heaven yclept Euphrosyne,[5]
And by men, heart-easing Mirth,
Whom lovely Venus at a birth
With two sister Graces more   15
To ivy-crownèd Bacchus bore;[6]
Or whether (as some sager sing)[7]
The frolic wind that breathes the spring,
Zephyr with Aurora playing,
As he met her once a-Maying,   20
There on beds of violets blue,
And fresh-blown[8] roses washed in dew,
Filled her with thee a daughter fair,
So buxom,[9] blithe, and debonair.
Haste thee nymph, and bring with thee   25
Jest and youthful Jollity,
Quips and Cranks,[1] and wanton Wiles,
Nods, and Becks, and wreathèd Smiles,
Such as hang on Hebe's[2] cheek,
And love to live in dimple sleek;   30

1. *L'Allegro* and *Il Penseroso* are companion poems, written in those dancing tetrameter couplets which are so hard to keep from sinking into singsong, so delightful when controlled. Milton's handling of this difficult meter may be compared with other virtuoso performances like Marvell's *To His Coy Mistress*, Keats's *Lines on the Mermaid Tavern*, and Housman's *Terence, This Is Stupid Stuff*.
   The titles are almost untranslatable. Within the framework of two contrasted yet parallel days we see the cheerful, social man and the melancholy, contemplative man in their typical postures. Milton's interest in the typical accounts for the striking generality of the pictures; they are in effect "characters" in verse. Melancholy has been much analyzed; in addition to Burton's famous *Anatomy*, it is discussed in Erwin Panofsky's *Albrecht Dürer* (1945), where it arises in connection with Dürer's magnificent engraving *Melencolia*, as well as in the immense study by Saxl, Panofsky, and Klibansky, *Saturn and Melancholy* (1964). There is a history of literary cheerfulness too—*The Happy Man*, by Maren Sofie Røstvig (1954).

2. The three-headed hell hound of classical mythology.
3. I.e., near the river Styx, in the underworld.
4. The Cimmerians, who gave their name to Crimea, were supposed to live on the outer edge of the world, in perpetual twilight.
5. Euphrosyne, Aglaia, and Thalia (four syllables, three, and two) were the Graces, goddesses of beauty and delight; antiquity assigned them a variety of parents, though they were most often regarded as products as Zeus' leisure hours.
6. Bacchus is god of wine.
7. The "sager" poets who describe the Graces as born of Zephyr (the west wind) and Aurora (the dawn) are in fact John Milton himself; the story is his invention.
8. Newly opened.
9. Lively.
1. Jokes.
2. Goddess of youth and cupbearer to the other gods. Pronounced *Hee-bee*.

Sport that wrinkled Care derides,
And Laughter holding both his sides.
Come, and trip it as ye go
On the light fantastic toe,
And in thy right hand lead with thee   35
The mountain nymph, sweet Liberty;
And if I give thee honor due,
Mirth, admit me of thy crew
To live with her and live with thee,
In unreprovèd pleasures free;   40
To hear the lark begin his flight,
And, singing, startle the dull night,
From his watch-tower in the skies,
Till the dappled dawn doth rise;
Then to come[3] in spite of sorrow,   45
And at my window bid good morrow,
Through the sweetbriar or the vine,
Or the twisted eglantine.
While the cock with lively din
Scatters the rear of darkness thin,   50
And to the stack or the barn door,
Stoutly struts his dames before;
Oft listening how the hounds and horn
Cheerly rouse the slumbering morn,
From the side of some hoar hill,   55
Through the high wood echoing shrill.
Sometime walking not unseen
By hedgerow elms, on hillocks green,
Right against the eastern gate,
Where the great sun begins his state,[4]   60
Robed in flames and amber light,
The clouds in thousand liveries dight;[5]
While the plowman near at hand
Whistles o'er the furrowed land,
And the milkmaid singeth blithe,   65
And the mower whets his scythe,
And every shepherd tells his tale
Under the hawthorn in the dale.
Straight mine eye hath caught new pleasures
Whilst the landscape round it measures,   70
Russet lawns and fallows gray,
Where the nibbling flocks do stray,
Mountains on whose barren breast
The laboring clouds do often rest;
Meadows trim with daisies pied,[6]   75
Shallow brooks, and rivers wide.
Towers and battlements it sees

---

3. I.e., then admit me to come.   5. Dressed.
4. Procession.   6. Dappled.

Bosomed high in tufted trees,
Where perhaps some beauty lies,
The cynosure[7] of neighboring eyes.   80
Hard by, a cottage chimney smokes
From betwixt two agèd oaks,
Where Corydon and Thyrsis[8] met
Are at their savory dinner set
Of herbs and other country messes,   85
Which the neat-handed Phyllis dresses;
And then in haste her bower she leaves,
With Thestylis to bind the sheaves;
Or if the earlier season lead
To the tanned haycock in the mead.   90
Sometimes with secure delight
The upland hamlets will invite,
When the merry bells ring round
And the jocund rebecks[9] sound
To many a youth and many a maid,   95
Dancing in the checkered shade;
And young and old come forth to play
On a sunshine holiday,
Till the livelong daylight fail;
Then to the spicy nut-brown ale,   100
With stories told of many a feat,
How fairy Mab[1] the junkets eat;
She was pinched and pulled, she said,
And he, by friar's lantern led,
Tells how the drudging goblin[2] sweat   105
To earn his cream-bowl duly set,
When in one night, ere glimpse of morn,
His shadowy flail hath threshed the corn
That ten day-laborers could not end;
Then lies him down the lubber fiend,[3]   110
And stretched out all the chimney's length,
Basks at the fire his hairy strength;
And crop-full out of doors he flings
Ere the first cock his matin rings.
Thus done the tales, to bed they creep,   115
By whispering winds soon lulled asleep.
Towered cities please us then,
And the busy hum of men,
Where throngs of knights and barons bold
In weeds[4] of peace high triumphs hold,   120

7. Literally, the bright polestar, by which mariners steer; here, a splendid, eminent object, much gazed at.
8. Since the days of Theocritus, "Corydon," "Thyrsis," "Phyllis," and "Thestylis" have been traditional shepherds' names.
9. A rebeck is a small three-stringed fiddle; "jocund" implies a festive occasion.

1. Queen Mab, wife of Oberon, the fairy king. "She" and "he" in the next two lines are country folk, telling of their experiences with the fairies. "Junkets": sweetmeats, especially with cream.
2. Robin Goodfellow, alias Puck, Pook, or Hobgoblin. "Friar's lantern": will-o'-the-wisp.
3. Drudging spirit.
4. Garments. "Triumphs": festive ceremonies.

With store of ladies, whose bright eyes
Rain influence,[5] and judge the prize
Of wit or arms, while both contend
To win her grace, whom all commend.
There let Hymen[6] oft appear   125
In saffron robe, with taper clear,
And pomp and feast and revelry,
With masque and antique pageantry;
Such sights as youthful poets dream
On summer eves by haunted stream.   130
Then to the well-trod stage anon,
If Jonson's learned sock[7] be on,
Or sweetest Shakespeare, fancy's child,
Warble his native wood-notes wild.
And ever against eating cares[8]   135
Lap me in soft Lydian airs,[9]
Married to immortal verse
Such as the meeting soul may pierce
In notes with many a winding bout[1]
Of linkèd sweetness long drawn out,   140
With wanton heed and giddy cunning,
The melting voice through mazes running;
Untwisting all the chains that tie
The hidden soul of harmony;
That Orpheus' self[2] may heave his head   145
From golden slumber on a bed
Of heaped Elysian flowers, and hear
Such strains as would have won the ear
Of Pluto, to have quite set free
His half-regained Eurydice.   150
These delights if thou canst give,
Mirth, with thee I mean to live.

ca. 1631   1645

Il Penseroso

Hence vain deluding Joys,
    The brood of Folly without father bred,

---

5. The ladies' eyes are stars, and so have astrological influence over the men.
6. Roman god of marriage, wearing an orange-
yellow ("saffron") robe.
7. A low-heeled slipper, worn by actors in classical comedy, and often contrasted with the buskin
(high-heeled boot) appropriate to tragedy. The
contrast of Jonson as a "learned" poet with Shakespeare as a "natural" one was conventional.
8. "Eating cares" is but one of many classical
phrases in the poem; it is from Horace, *Odes*
2.11.18 (*curas edaces*).

9. "Lydian" airs in music would be soft, languishing, sensual—unlike those in the chaste Dorian
and brisk Ionian modes.
1. Turn, involution.
2. Orpheus went to the underworld to regain his
wife Eurydice (four syllables, accent on the second) and by his music dissolved the guardians of
Hades in tears. But as they left, he violated the
condition of her release by looking back at her,
and so lost her again. Milton uses the Orpheus
story again in *Il Penseroso*, *Lycidas*, and *Paradise
Lost* 7.32 ff.

How little you bestead,[1]
　　Or fill the fixèd mind with all your toys;[2]
Dwell in some idle brain,　　　　　　　　　　　5
　　And fancies fond[3] with gaudy shapes possess,
As thick and numberless
　　As the gay motes that people the sunbeams,
Or likest hovering dreams,
　　The fickle pensioners[4] of Morpheus' train.　　10
But hail thou Goddess sage and holy,
Hail, divinest Melancholy,
Whose saintly visage is too bright
To hit[5] the sense of human sight,
And therefore to our weaker view,　　　　　　15
O'erlaid with black, staid Wisdom's hue;
Black, but such as in esteem,
Prince Memnon's sister[6] might beseem,
Or that starred Ethiope queen[7] that strove
To set her beauty's praise above　　　　　　　20
The sea nymphs, and their powers offended.
Yet thou art higher far descended;
Thee bright-haired Vesta long of yore
To solitary Saturn bore;[8]
His daughter she (in Saturn's reign　　　　　25
Such mixture was not held a stain).
Oft in glimmering bowers and glades
He met her, and in secret shades
Of woody Ida's inmost grove,
While yet there was no fear of Jove.　　　　　30
Come pensive nun, devout and pure,
Sober, steadfast, and demure,
All in a robe of darkest grain,[9]
Flowing with majestic train,
And sable stole of cypress lawn[1]　　　　　　35
Over thy decent shoulders drawn.
Come, but keep thy wonted state,
With even step and musing gait,
And looks commercing with the skies,
Thy rapt soul sitting in thine eyes:　　　　　40

1. Avail, help.
2. Trifles.
3. Foolish.
4. Followers. Morpheus is the god of sleep; the melancholy man feels the cheerful man lives in a dream.
5. Suit, agree with.
6. Memnon in *Odyssey* 11 was a handsome Ethiopian prince who fought for Troy; his sister, not mentioned by Homer but by later commentators, was Himera.
7. Cassiopeia was turned into a constellation ("starred") for bragging that her daughter Andromeda or she herself (Milton follows this second version) was more beautiful than the sea-nymphs.
8. Vesta was goddess of the household, and virgin, as were her priestesses; Milton invented the story of her connection with Saturn on Mt. Ida in Crete, and of her giving birth to Melancholy. But Saturn helps out the poem because he was a primitive deity (hence melancholy is "natural"), and because a saturnine complexion is said to evidence a dark and melancholy disposition.
9. Color.
1. "Cypress lawn": a delicate cloth (originally Cyprus, from the island; but the cypress is also the tree of death). "Decent": comely, proper.

There held in holy passion still,
Forget thyself to marble, till
With a sad leaden downward cast
Thou fix them on the earth as fast.
And join with thee calm Peace and Quiet,   45
Spare Fast, that oft with gods doth diet,
And hears the Muses in a ring
Aye round about Jove's altar sing.
And add to these retired Leisure,
That in trim gardens takes his pleasure;   50
But first, and chiefest, with thee bring
Him that yon soars on golden wing,
Guiding the fiery-wheelèd throne,
The cherub Contemplatiòn;[2]
And the mute Silence hist[3] along,   55
'Less Philomel[4] will deign a song,
In her sweetest, saddest plight,
Smoothing the rugged brow of night,
While Cynthia[5] checks her dragon yoke
Gently o'er th' accustomed oak;   60
Sweet bird that shunn'st the noise of folly,
Most musical, most melancholy!
Thee chantress oft the woods among
I woo to hear thy evensong;
And missing thee, I walk unseen   65
On the dry smooth-shaven green,
To behold the wandering moon,
Riding near her highest noon,
Like one that had been led astray
Through the heaven's wide pathless way;   70
And oft as if her head she bowed,
Stooping through a fleecy cloud.
Oft on a plat[6] of rising ground,
I hear the far-off curfew sound
Over some wide-watered shore,   75
Swinging slow with sullen roar;
Or if the air will not permit,
Some still removèd place will fit,
Where glowing embers through the room
Teach light to counterfeit a gloom,   80
Far from all resort of mirth,
Save the cricket on the hearth,
Or the bellman's[7] drowsy charm,
To bless the doors from nightly harm;

2. The special function of cherubim is contemplation; the fiery-wheeled throne recalls the Biblical vision of Ezekiel.
3. Summon.
4. The nightingale, whose song is traditionally one of grief.

5. Goddess of the moon and of the underworld as well, she drives a pair of sleepless dragons.
6. Plot, open space.
7. The night watchman in towns rang a bell to mark the hours.

Or let my lamp at midnight hour 85
Be seen in some high lonely tower,
Where I may oft outwatch the Bear,[8]
With thrice-great Hermes,[9] or unsphere
The spirit of Plato to unfold
What words or what vast regions hold 90
The immortal mind that hath forsook
Her mansion in this fleshly nook;
And of those demons[1] that are found
In fire, air, flood, or under ground,
Whose power hath a true consent[2] 95
With planet, or with element.
Sometime let gorgeous Tragedy
In sceptered pall[3] come sweeping by,
Presenting Thebes, or Pelops' line,
Or the tale of Troy divine,[4] 100
Or what (though rare) of later age
Ennobled hath the buskined[5] stage.
But, O sad virgin, that thy power
Might raise Musaeus[6] from his bower,
Or bid the soul of Orpheus[7] sing 105
Such notes as, warbled to the string,
Drew iron tears down Pluto's cheek,
And made Hell grant what Love did seek.
Or call up him[8] that left half told
The story of Cambuscan bold, 110
Of Camball and of Algarsife,
And who had Canacee to wife,
That owned the virtuous[9] ring and glass,
And of the wondrous horse of brass,
On which the Tartar king did ride; 115
And if aught else great bards beside
In sage and solemn tunes have sung,
Of tourneys and of trophies hung,
Of forests and enchantments drear,
Where more is meant than meets the ear.[1] 120
Thus, Night, oft see me in thy pale career,

8. Since the Great Bear never sets, outwatching it is a major enterprise.
9. The Egyptian god Thoth or Hermes, to whom were attributed various esoteric books of the 3rd and 4th centuries; under the name Hermes Trismegistus ("thrice-great"), he later became a patron of magicians and alchemists. To "unsphere" Plato is to bring him magically back to earth from the sphere he now inhabits.
1. Not devils but halfway beings, between gods and men. There were four sorts of demons, corresponding with the four elements.
2. Sympathetic agreement.
3. Royal robe (from Latin *palla*, the robe of tragic actors).

4. Tragedies about Thebes would include Sophocles' Oedipus cycle; those about the line of Pelops, Aeschylus' *Oresteia*; and those about Troy, Euripides' *Trojan Women*.
5. The buskin of tragedy, contrasted with the sock of comedy.
6. A mythical poet-priest of the pre-Homeric age, supposedly son or pupil of the equally mythical Orpheus.
7. For the story of Orpheus, see *L'Allegro*, line 145, and note.
8. I.e., Chaucer, who in the Squire's Tale left the tale of Cambuscan unfinished.
9. Having special power.
1. A capsule description of allegory.

Till civil-suited Morn appear,[2]
Not tricked and frounced as she was wont
With the Attic boy to hunt,
But kerchiefed in a comely cloud,   125
While rocking winds are piping loud,
Or ushered with a shower still,
When the gust hath blown his fill,
Ending on the rustling leaves,
With minute drops from off the eaves.   130
And when the sun begins to fling
His flaring beams, me, Goddess, bring
To archèd walks of twilight groves,
And shadows brown that Sylvan[3] loves
Of pine or monumental oak,   135
Where the rude ax with heavèd stroke
Was never heard the nymphs to daunt,
Or fright them from their hallowed haunt.
There in close covert by some brook,
Where no profaner eye may look,   140
Hide me from day's garish eye,
While the bee with honeyed thigh,
That at her flowery work doth sing,
And the waters murmuring
With such consort[4] as they keep,   145
Entice the dewy-feathered sleep;
And let some strange mysterious dream
Wave at his wings in airy stream
Of lively portraiture displayed
Softly on my eyelids laid.[5]   150
And as I wake, sweet music breathe
Above, about, or underneath,
Sent by some spirit to mortals good,
Or th' unseen genius[6] of the wood.
But let my due feet never fail   155
To walk the studious cloister's pale,[7]
And love the high embowèd roof,
With antic[8] pillars massy proof,
And storied windows[9] richly dight,
Casting a dim religious light.   160
There let the pealing organ blow
To the full-voiced choir below,
In service high and anthems clear,

---

2. The goddess Aurora, who once fell in love with
Cephalus ("the Attic boy," line 124), and used to
go hunting with him. "Tricked and frounced":
adorned and frizzled.
3. Roman god of the woodlands.
4. Accompaniment.
5. Milton's syntax gets loose and dreamy too, here.
He means, "Let some strange dream wave at the
wings of sleep, while a stream of vivid pictures passes

softly over my eyelids."
6. Guardian deity.
7. Enclosure.
8. I.e., covered with quaint, grotesque, or antic
carvings; but "antique," which derives from the
same Latin root, was not excluded from the sense.
"Massy proof": massive and strong.
9. I.e., with stories told by stained-glass images.
"Dight": dressed.

As may with sweetness, through mine ear,
Dissolve me into ecstasies, 165
And bring all heaven before mine eyes.
And may at last my weary age
Find out the peaceful hermitage,
The hairy gown and mossy cell,
Where I may sit and rightly spell[1] 170
Of every star that heaven doth shew,
And every herb that sips the dew,
Till old experience do attain
To something like prophetic strain.
These pleasures, Melancholy, give, 175
And I with thee will choose to live.

ca. 1631 1645

Lycidas This poem is a pastoral elegy; that is, it uses the sometimes artificial imagery supplied by an idyllic shepherd's existence to bewail the loss of a friend. Among its many predecessors in the Renaissance and in classical antiquity are poems by Spenser, Ronsard, Castiglione, Mantuan, Petrarch, Virgil, Theocritus, Moschus, and Bion; its successors include poems like *Adonais* by Shelley and *Thyrsis* by Matthew Arnold. T. P. Harrison and H. J. Leon have collected in *The Pastoral Elegy* (1939) a selection of poems from the tradition.

All pastoral poems enjoy the privilege of saying something about the world as a whole while seeming to talk simply of an artificial play-society; they are irresistibly allegorical. They have certain conventions—the swain (i.e., the shepherd) is ignorant but unspoiled, naturally virtuous, inherently poetic; life is pleasant and easy, yet just for this reason the basic human preoccupations stand out. The pastoral elegy has a further list of conventions—a history of past friendship, a questioning of destiny, a procession of mourners, a laying-on of flowers, a consolation, and usually a refrain. Milton adapted all but the last of these to *Lycidas*.

Edward King, who was the occasion of the poem if not its subject, was a junior contemporary of Milton's at Cambridge. He had written a few short Latin poems, and intended to enter the ministry. On his way to visit family in his native Ireland, he was drowned, in 1637; and Milton joined with his school fellows the following year to produce a little memorial volume. *Justa Edouardo King (For Edward King)* includes thirty-six poems, twenty in Latin, three in Greek, the rest in English; only *Lycidas* is of literary consequence.

It is written in a flowing, extended manner, with many run-on lines and great impetus, predominantly in pentameter but with a number of trimeter lines mixed in, and an irregular rhyme scheme, including ten unrhymed lines and two perfectly formed stanzas of ottava rima. Many of these technical qualities are reminiscent of the Italian *canzone* or song, already domesticated in English by poems like Spenser's *Epithalamion*.

There are usually taken to be three explicit climaxes in *Lycidas*, each

1. Study. The melancholy man wants to think his way into the cosmos until he becomes a prophet.

having to do with an aspect of the shepherd's life and with a problem which Milton wished to pose regarding the meaning of existence. Apollo answers his first question about the reward of poetry; St. Peter answers a second question, about the spiritual shepherd who betrays his flock; and finally Lycidas is translated into the Christian Paradise, to be at one with the Lamb of God, the Good Shepherd, the supreme giver of poetic fame, and the proper subject of all song.

For some of the author's revisions while composing *Lycidas*, see "Poems in Process," below.

Lycidas

IN THIS MONODY[1] THE AUTHOR BEWAILS A LEARNED FRIEND, UNFORTUNATELY DROWNED IN HIS PASSAGE FROM CHESTER ON THE IRISH SEAS, 1637. AND BY OCCASION FORETELLS THE RUIN OF OUR CORRUPTED CLERGY, THEN IN THEIR HEIGHT.

Yet once more, O ye laurels, and once more
Ye myrtles brown, with ivy never sere,[2]
I come to pluck your berries harsh and crude,[3]
And with forced fingers rude,
Shatter your leaves before the mellowing year.   5
Bitter constraint, and sad occasion dear,[4]
Compels me to disturb your season due;
For Lycidas is dead, dead ere his prime,
Young Lycidas, and hath not left his peer.
Who would not sing for Lycidas? He knew   10
Himself to sing, and build the lofty rhyme.
He must not float upon his watery bier
Unwept, and welter to the parching wind,
Without the meed[5] of some melodious tear.
Begin then, sisters of the sacred well[6]   15
That from beneath the seat of Jove doth spring,
Begin, and somewhat loudly sweep the string.
Hence with denial vain, and coy excuse;
So may some gentle Muse
With lucky words favor my destined urn,[7]   20
And as he passes turn,
And bid fair peace be to my sable shroud.
For we were nursed upon the selfsame hill,
Fed the same flock, by fountain, shade, and rill.

1. A dirge sung by a single voice. This Miltonic headnote was added in the edition of 1645.
2. "Laurels" for the crown of poetry given by Apollo; "myrtles" for the undying love granted by Venus; "ivy," the plant of Bacchus, also the reward of learning. All three plants are evergreens associated with poetic inspiration.
3. Unripe.
4. Heartfelt, profoundly moving; but also, in the 17th century, with overtones of "dire."
5. Reward.
6. The nine sister Muses were reported to dwell by various springs or "wells"; most likely Milton had in mind that of Aganippe near Mt. Helicon.
7. The speaker suggests that if he sings for Lycidas, "some gentle Muse" (i.e., poet) may some day sing for him.

Together both, ere the high lawns[8] appeared   25
Under the opening eyelids of the morn,
We drove afield, and both together heard
What time the grayfly winds her sultry horn,[9]
Battening our flocks with the fresh dews of night,
Oft till the star that rose at evening bright   30
Toward heaven's descent had sloped his westering wheel.
Meanwhile the rural ditties were not mute,
Tempered to th' oaten flute,[1]
Rough satyrs danced, and fauns with cloven heel
From the glad sound would not be absent long,   35
And old Damoetas[2] loved to hear our song.

   But O the heavy change, now thou art gone,
Now thou art gone, and never must return!
Thee, shepherd, thee the woods and desert caves,
With wild thyme and the gadding[3] vine o'ergrown,   40
And all their echoes mourn.
The willows and the hazel copses green
Shall now no more be seen,
Fanning their joyous leaves to thy soft lays.
As killing as the canker[4] to the rose,   45
Or taint-worm to the weanling herds that graze,
Or frost to flowers that their gay wardrobe wear
When first the white-thorn blows;[5]
Such, Lycidas, thy loss to shepherd's ear.

   Where were ye, nymphs,[6] when the remorseless deep   50
Closed o'er the head of your loved Lycidas?
For neither were ye playing on the steep
Where your old bards, the famous Druids,[7] lie,
Nor on the shaggy top of Mona high,[8]
Nor yet where Deva spreads her wizard stream: 55
Ay me! I fondly dream—
Had ye been there—for what could that have done?
What could the Muse[9] herself that Orpheus bore,
The Muse herself, for her inchanting[1] son
Whom universal Nature did lament,   60
When by the rout[2] that made the hideous roar

---

8. Upland pastures.
9. I.e., heard the grayfly when she buzzes ("winds her sultry horn"). "Battening": feeding.
1. Traditional Panpipes, played by shepherds.
2. A type name from pastoral poetry, possibly referring to some specific tutor at Cambridge.
3. Straggling.
4. Cankerworm.
5. Blossoms (as in the surviving expression, "full-blown").
6. Nature deities.
7. The Druids, priestly poet-kings of Celtic Britain, worshiped the forces of nature. They lie dead in their burying ground on the mountain ("steep") Kerig-y-Druidion in Wales.
8. "Mona" is the island of Anglesey. "Deva" is

the river Dee in Cheshire. The Dee was magic ("wizard") because the size and position of its shifting stream foretold prosperity or dearth for the land. All the places mentioned in lines 52–55 are in the West Country, near where King drowned.
9. Calliope, Muse of epic poetry, was the mother of Orpheus.
1. "Inchanting" implies both song and magic; the root word survives as "incantation."
2. Orpheus was torn to pieces by a mob ("rout") of screaming Thracian women (Bacchantes), who threw his gory head into the river Hebrus, down which it floated, still singing, and out to Lesbos in the Aegean. The fate of Orpheus and the Druids suggests that nature everywhere is indifferent to the destruction of the priest-poet.

His gory visage down the stream was sent,
Down the swift Hebrus to the Lesbian shore?
　　Alas! What boots[3] it with incessant care
To tend the homely slighted shepherd's trade,   65
And strictly meditate the thankless Muse?[4]
Were it not better done as others use,
To sport with Amaryllis in the shade,
Or with the tangles of Neaera's hair?[5]
Fame is the spur that the clear spirit doth raise   70
(That last infirmity of noble mind)
To scorn delights, and live laborious days;
But the fair guerdon[6] when we hope to find,
And think to burst out into sudden blaze,
Comes the blind Fury[7] with th' abhorrèd shears,   75
And slits the thin-spun life. "But not the praise,"
Phoebus[8] replied, and touched my trembling ears;
"Fame is no plant that grows on mortal soil,
Nor in the glistering foil[9]
Set off to th' world, nor in broad rumor lies,   80
But lives and spreads aloft by those pure eyes,
And perfect witness of all-judging Jove;
As he pronounces lastly on each deed,
Of so much fame in heaven expect thy meed."
　　O fountain Arethuse,[1] and thou honored flood,   85
Smooth-sliding Mincius, crowned with vocal reeds,
That strain I heard was of a higher mood.
But now my oat[2] proceeds,
And listens to the herald of the sea[3]
That came in Neptune's plea.   90
He asked the waves, and asked the felon winds,
"What hard mishap hath doomed this gentle swain?"
And questioned every gust of rugged wings
That blows from off each beakèd promontory;
They knew not of his story,   95
And sage Hippotades[4] their answer brings,
That not a blast was from his dungeon strayed;
The air was calm, and on the level brine,

---

3. Profits.
4. Study to write poetry (the phrase is Virgil's).
5. "Amaryllis" and "Neaera" (*Nee-eye-ra*), conventional names for pretty shepherdesses, a passing hour's diversion for idle shepherds.
6. Reward.
7. Atropos, one of the three Fates, bearing scissors with which she cuts the thread of human life. Milton, to suggest the bitterness of death, makes her an avenging Fury.
8. Phoebus Apollo, god of poetic inspiration. Touching the ears of one's hearers was a traditional Roman way of asking them to remember something that had been said.
9. Flashy metal, used to add glitter to gems.

1. Arethusa was a fountain in Sicily, Mincius a river in Lombardy, the former associated with the pastorals of Theocritus, the latter with those of Virgil. Arethusa was originally a nymph who went bathing in the river Alpheus, in Arcadian Greece. The river god grew enamored, and gave chase; she dove into the ocean and fled undersea to Sicily, where she came up as a fountain. Milton plays here with the idea of his pastoral going underground while the "strain of a higher mood" (line 87) is heard.
2. Pipe, hence song.
3. Neptune's "herald" is Triton, pleading his master's innocence in the death of Lycidas.
4. Aeolus, god of winds, and son of Hippotas.

Sleek Panope[5] with all her sisters played.
It was that fatal and perfidious bark,   100
Built in th' eclipse,[6] and rigged with curses dark,
That sunk so low that sacred head of thine.
    Next Camus,[7] reverend sire, went footing slow,
His mantle hairy, and his bonnet sedge,
Inwrought with figures dim, and on the edge   105
Like to that sanguine flower inscribed with woe.[8]
"Ah! who hath reft," quoth he, "my dearest pledge?"
Last came and last did go
The pilot of the Galilean lake;[9]
Two massy keys he bore of metals twain   110
(The golden opes, the iron shuts amain).[1]
He shook his mitered locks,[2] and stern bespake:
"How well could I have spared for thee, young swain,
Enow[3] of such as for their bellies' sake
Creep and intrude and climb into the fold!   115
Of other care they little reckoning make,
Than how to scramble at the shearers' feast,
And shove away the worthy bidden guest.
Blind mouths![4] that scarce themselves know how to hold
A sheep-hook,[5] or have learned aught else the least   120
That to the faithful herdsman's art belongs!
What recks it them?[6] What need they? They are sped;
And when they list,[7] their lean and flashy songs
Grate on their scrannel[8] pipes of wretched straw.
The hungry sheep look up, and are not fed,   125
But swoln with wind, and the rank mist they draw,
Rot inwardly, and foul contagion spread,
Besides what the grim wolf with privy paw[9]
Daily devours apace, and nothing said.
But that two-handed engine at the door[1]   130
Stands ready to smite once, and smite no more."

---

5. The chief Nereid or sea nymph.
6. I.e., time of the worst possible luck.
7. God of the river Cam (properly, Granta), representing the ancient University of Cambridge, but slow and shaggy like the stream.
8. The bonnet and mantle of Camus have marks of woe on the edge like the AI AI supposedly found on the hyacinth, a "sanguine flower" sprung from the blood of a youth killed accidentally by Apollo.
9. St. Peter, originally a fisherman on Lake Tiberias (the Sea of Galilee), was first founder and bishop of the Christian church; his keys open and shut the gates to heaven.
1. Literally, "in full force," "exceedingly"; in this context, "for good," "once and for all."
2. He wears the bishop's miter.
3. An old plural form of "enough," used here with contemptuous intensification, as if to say, "enough and more than enough."
4. This audacious metaphor, as of tapeworms, takes on new depth when one notes that the word *epis-*

copus (bishop) originally meant "over-seer" and that a "pastor" is properly one who feeds his flock.
5. The bishop's staff, or crozier, is made in the form of a shepherd's crook.
6. What do they care? "They are sped": i.e., they have prospered in a worldly sense; but also, "their doom is sealed."
7. Choose (that is, choose to play on their pipes, as shepherds should); but with the secondary meaning of "listen."
8. Harsh, meager. Milton's is the first recorded literary use of the word in English; it existed previously only in a North Country dialect.
9. I.e., Roman Catholicism, whose agents operated in secret.
1. Many guesses as to the specific meaning of the "two-handed engine" are on record; it may be St. Peter's keys, the two houses of Parliament, or a big sword, but there is no harm in letting it remain an indistinct, apocalyptic instrument of revenge.

Return, Alpheus,[2] the dread voice is past,
That shrunk thy streams; return, Sicilian muse,
And call the vales, and bid them hither cast
Their bells and flowerets of a thousand hues.   135
Ye valleys low where the mild whispers use,[3]
Of shades and wanton winds, and gushing brooks,
On whose fresh lap the swart star[4] sparely looks,
Throw hither all your quaint enameled eyes,
That on the green turf suck the honeyed showers,   140
And purple all the ground with vernal flowers.
Bring the rathe[5] primrose that forsaken dies,
The tufted crow-toe, and pale jessamine,
The white pink, and the pansy freaked[6] with jet,
The glowing violet,   145
The musk-rose, and the well-attired woodbine,
With cowslips wan that hang the pensive head,
And every flower that sad embroidery wears:
Bid amaranthus[7] all his beauty shed,
And daffadillies fill their cups with tears,   150
To strew the laureate hearse[8] where Lycid lies.
For so to interpose a little ease,
Let our frail thoughts dally with false surmise.[9]
Ay me! whilst thee the shores and sounding seas
Wash far away, where'er thy bones are hurled,   155
Whether beyond the stormy Hebrides,[1]
Where thou perhaps under the whelming tide
Visit'st the bottom of the monstrous world;
Or whether thou, to our moist vows denied,
Sleep'st by the fable of Bellerus old,[2]   160
Where the great vision of the guarded mount
Looks toward Namancos and Bayona's hold;[3]
Look homeward angel now, and melt with ruth:[4]
And, O ye dolphins,[5] waft the hapless youth.
    Weep no more, woeful shepherds, weep no more,   165
For Lycidas your sorrow is not dead,

2. With the return of Alpheus, the pastoral mode of the poem revives (see above, lines 85–87), and a catalogue of flowers serves, as in Castiglione's *Alcon*, to "interpose a little ease."

3. I.e., are used or accustomed to be heard.

4. The Dog Star, Sirius, associated with the heats of late summer, looks but "sparely" (gently) on the shady valleys. It may not be irrelevant that Edward King drowned on August 10.

5. Early.

6. Flecked (the early verb survives in our word "freckle").

7. The amaranth is an imaginary flower that never fades; but for Lycidas it will.

8. Bier decked with laurels (see line 1).

9. The "false surmise" is that the body of Lycidas has been recovered and can receive Christian burial.

1. Islands off the coast of Scotland, representing the northern terminus of the Irish Sea.

2. The fabulous giant Bellerus is supposed to lie buried on Land's End in Cornwall.

3. St. Michael's Mount, in Cornwall, from which the archangel is envisioned as looking south, over miles of open Atlantic, across the Bay of Biscay, to Bayona (not far from Vigo) and the district of Nemancos, near Cape Finisterre in northern Spain, where the historical Catholic enemy of Protestant England lay entrenched.

4. Michael is implored to look homeward, relaxing his stern guard for a moment of grief and pity ("ruth").

5. Dolphins, admirable sea beasts, brought the Greek poet Arion safely ashore for love of his verses, and also wafted the dead body of Melicertes to land, where he was promptly transformed to a sea god, Palaemon.

Sunk though he be beneath the wat'ry floor;
So sinks the day-star[6] in the ocean bed,
And yet anon repairs his drooping head,
And tricks[7] his beams, and with new-spangled ore   170
Flames in the forehead of the morning sky:
So Lycidas sunk low, but mounted high,
Through the dear might of him that walked the waves,
Where, other groves and other streams along,
With nectar pure his oozy locks he laves,   175
And hears the unexpressive nuptial song,[8]
In the blest kingdoms meek of joy and love.
There entertain him all the saints above,
In solemn troops and sweet societies
That sing, and singing in their glory move,   180
And wipe the tears forever from his eyes.
Now, Lycidas, the shepherds weep no more;
Henceforth thou art the genius[9] of the shore,
In thy large recompense, and shalt be good
To all that wander in that perilous flood.   185
    Thus sang the uncouth swain[1] to th' oaks and rills,
While the still morn went out with sandals gray;
He touched the tender stops of various quills,[2]
With eager thought warbling his Doric[3] lay:
And now the sun had stretched out all the hills,   190
And now was dropped into the western bay;
At last he rose, and twitched his mantle blue:
Tomorrow to fresh woods, and pastures new.

November 1637   1638

From The Reason of Church Government
Urged Against Prelaty[1]

[*Plans and Projects*]

* * * Concerning therefore this wayward[2] subject against prelaty, the
touching whereof is so distasteful and disquietous[3] to a number of men,

---

6. The sun.
7. Dresses.
8. Inexpressible hymn of joy, sung at "the marriage supper of the Lamb" (Revelation 19).
9. Protective deity.
1. Unknown, unlettered shepherd (a stock convention of this supremely literary form).
2. The oaten stalks of Panpipes.
3. Rustic, simple.
1. When Milton published *The Reason of Church Government* in 1642, he had had some experience of controversial prose, and knew that it was not his natural medium of full expression. Controversial prose in behalf of the Presbyterian cause—so his

conscience told him—was what the circumstances of England in 1642 called for; and that was what, in his tracts against church-government by bishops, he undertook to provide. But his mind was still full of the poetry which for years he had been planning and training to write; and in an extraordinary digression, he took the reader into his confidence, revealing what he really wanted to do in a literary way. There could be no better introduction to *Paradise Lost,* a poem still nearly a quarter of century in the future.
2. Contrary to my real wishes. "Prelaty": government by prelates, i.e., bishops.
3. Distressing.

as by what hath been said I may deserve of charitable readers to be credited that neither envy nor gall hath entered me upon this controversy, but the enforcement of conscience only and a preventive fear lest the omitting of this duty should be against me when I would store up to myself the good provision of peaceful hours; so lest it should be still imputed to me, as I have found it hath been, that some self-pleasing humor of vainglory hath incited me to contest with men of high estimation, now while green years are upon my head; from this needless surmisal I shall hope to dissuade the intelligent and equal[4] auditor, if I can but say successfully that which in this exigent behooves me; although I would be heard only, if it might be, by the elegant and learned reader, to whom principally for a while I shall beg leave I may address myself. To him it will be no new thing though I tell him that if I hunted after praise by the ostentation of wit and learning, I should not write thus out of mine own season when I have neither yet completed to my mind the full circle of my private studies, although I complain not of any insufficiency to the matter in hand; or, were I ready to my wishes, it were a folly to commit anything elaborately composed to the careless and interrupted listening of these tumultuous times. Next, if I were wise only to mine own ends, I would certainly take such a subject as of itself might catch applause, whereas this hath all the disadvantages on the contrary, and such a subject[5] as the publishing whereof might be delayed at pleasure, and time enough to pencil[6] it over with all the curious touches of art, even to the perfection of a faultless picture; whenas in this argument the not deferring is of great moment to the good speeding, that if solidity have leisure to do her office, art cannot have much. Lastly, I should not choose this manner of writing, wherein knowing myself inferior to myself, led by the genial[7] power of nature to another task, I have the use, as I may account it, but of my left hand. And though I shall be foolish in saying more to this purpose, yet, since it will be such a folly as wisest men going about to commit have only confessed and so committed, I may trust with more reason, because with more folly, to have courteous pardon. For although a poet, soaring in the high region of his fancies with his garland and singing robes about him, might without apology speak more of himself than I mean to do, yet for me sitting here below in the cool element of prose, a mortal thing among many readers of no empyreal conceit,[8] to venture and divulge unusual things of myself, I shall petition to the gentler sort, it may not be envy to me.

I must say, therefore, that after I had from my first years by the ceaseless diligence and care of my father (whom God recompense) been exercised to the tongues and some sciences, as my age would suffer,[9] by sundry masters and teachers both at home and at the schools, it was

---

4. Impartial.
5. "Subject" is the object of "take."
6. Paint. The old meaning of "pencil" was "a small brush."
7. A man's "genius" was either his guardian angel or his natural gift or bent of mind. Milton clearly has the second use in mind here.
8. Of no exalted intelligence.
9. Admit.

found that whether aught was imposed me by them that had the over-looking, or betaken to of mine own choice in English or other tongue, prosing or versing (but chiefly this latter), the style, by certain vital signs it had, was likely to live. But much latelier in the private academies of Italy, whither I was favored to resort—perceiving that some trifles which I had in memory, composed at under twenty or thereabout (for the manner is that everyone must give some proof of his wit and reading there) met with acceptance above what was looked for, and other things which I had shifted in scarcity of books and conveniences to patch up amongst them, were received with written encomiums, which the Italian is not forward to bestow on men of this side the Alps—I began thus far to assent both to them and divers of my friends here at home, and not less to an inward prompting which now grew daily upon me, that by labor and intent study (which I take to be my portion in this life) joined with the strong propensity of nature, I might perhaps leave something so written to aftertimes, as they should not willingly let it die. These thoughts at once possessed me, and these other: that if I were certain to write as men buy leases, for three lives and downward,[1] there ought no regard be sooner had than to God's glory by the honor and instruction of my country. For which cause, and not only for that I knew it would be hard to arrive at the second rank among the Latins, I applied myself to that resolution which Ariosto followed against the persuasions of Bembo,[2] to fix all the industry and art I could unite to the adorning of my native tongue; not to make verbal curiosities the end—that were a toilsome vanity—but to be an interpreter and relater of the best and sagest things among mine own citizens throughout this island in the mother dialect. That what the greatest and choicest wits of Athens, Rome, or modern Italy, and those Hebrews of old did for their country, I, in my proportion, with this over and above of being a Christian, might do for mine; not caring to be once named abroad, though perhaps I could attain to that, but content with these British islands as my world; whose fortune hath hitherto been that if the Athenians, as some say, made their small deeds great and renowned by their eloquent writers, England hath had her noble achievements made small by the unskillful handling of monks and mechanics.

Time serves not now, and perhaps I might seem too profuse to give any certain account of what the mind at home in the spacious circuits of her musing hath liberty to propose to herself, though of highest hope and hardest attempting; whether that epic form whereof the two poems of Homer and those other two of Virgil and Tasso are a diffuse, and the book of Job a brief, model:[3] or whether the rules of Aristotle herein are strictly to be kept, or nature to be followed, which in them that know art

---

1. Leases were often drawn for a tenancy to run through the longest-lived of three named persons.
2. Rejecting Cardinal Bembo's advice, Ariosto said he would rather be first among the Italian poets than second among those writing Latin.

3. Much the same reasons that led Milton to see in the book of Job a concise epic evidently entered into the design of *Paradise Regained:* the exterior action is slight, the moral issues are tremendous.

and use judgment is no transgression but an enriching of art: and lastly, what king or knight before the conquest[4] might be chosen in whom to lay the pattern of a Christian hero. And as Tasso gave to a prince of Italy his choice whether he would command him to write of Godfrey's expedition against the infidels, or Belisarius against the Goths, or Charlemagne against the Lombards;[5] if to the instinct of nature and the emboldening of art aught may be trusted, and that there be nothing adverse in our climate or the fate of this age, it haply would be no rashness from an equal diligence and inclination to present the like offer in our own ancient stories; or whether those dramatic constitutions[6] wherein Sophocles and Euripides reign shall be found more doctrinal and exemplary to a nation. The Scripture also affords us a divine pastoral drama in the Song of Solomon, consisting of two persons and a double chorus, as Origen[7] rightly judges. And the Apocalypse of St. John is the majestic image of a high and stately tragedy, shutting up and intermingling her solemn scenes and acts with a sevenfold chorus of hallelujahs and harping symphonies; and this my opinion the grave authority of Paraeus, commenting that book, is sufficient to confirm. [8] Or if occasion shall lead to imitate those magnific odes and hymns wherein Pindarus and Callimachus[9] are in most things worthy, some others in their frame judicious, in their matter most an end[1] faulty. But those frequent songs throughout the law and prophets beyond all these, not in their divine argument alone, but in the very critical art of composition, may be easily made appear over all the kinds of lyric poesy to be incomparable. These abilities, wheresoever they be found, are the inspired gift of God rarely bestowed, but yet to some (though most abuse) in every nation; and are of power beside the office of a pulpit to inbreed and cherish in a great people the seeds of virtue and public civility, to allay the perturbations of the mind and set the affections in right tune, to celebrate in glorious and lofty hymns the throne and equipage of God's almightiness, and what he works and what he suffers to be wrought with high providence in his church, to sing the victorious agonies of martyrs and saints, the deeds and triumphs of just and pious nations doing valiantly through faith against the enemies of Christ, to deplore the general relapses of kingdoms and states from justice and God's true worship. Lastly, whatsoever in religion is holy and sublime, in virtue amiable or grave, what-

---

4. King Arthur, who fought against invading Saxons, and King Alfred, who was a Saxon warring with invading Danes, appealed to Milton's early imagination as potential epic heroes; his limiting the period for such a hero to "before the conquest" is striking. He never considered Norman, Angevin, or Plantagenet heroes, far less the Tudor queen who glitters at the center of Spenser's epic romance.
5. The Italian poet Torquato Tasso offered this generous choice to Alfonso II d'Este, duke of Ferrara.
6. Plays. Sophocles and Euripides, approximate contemporaries in the 5th century B.C., are cited as supreme exponents of Greek tragic drama.
7. Origen, of the 3rd century A.D., was an Alex-

andrian scholar and father of the church, who wrote many books analyzing and commenting on the Old Testament.
8. David Paraeus, a German theologian of the late 16th and early 17th centuries, wrote a number of commentaries on books of the Bible, including one on Revelation.
9. Pindar, a Greek poet of the 5th century B.C., wrote numerous odes, especially on winners of the Olympic games; Callimachus, an Alexandrian Greek of the 3rd century B.C., wrote elegant elegiac verses on the origins of various myths and rituals.
1. Almost entirely.

soever hath passion or admiration in all the changes of that which is called fortune from without or the wily subtleties and refluxes of man's thoughts from within, all these things with a solid and treatable smoothness to paint out and describe. Teaching over the whole book of sanctity and virtue through all the instances of example, with such delight to those especially of soft and delicious temper[2] who will not so much as look upon truth herself unless they see her elegantly dressed, that whereas the paths of honesty and good life appear now rugged and difficult, though they be indeed easy and pleasant, they would then appear to all men both easy and pleasant, though they were rugged and difficult indeed. And what a benefit this would be to our youth and gentry may be soon guessed by what we know of the corruption and bane which they suck in daily from the writings and interludes of libidinous and ignorant poetasters,[3] who, having scarce ever heard of that which is the main consistence of a true poem, the choice of such persons as they ought to introduce, and what is moral and decent to each one, do for the most part lap up vicious principles in sweet pills to be swallowed down, and make the taste of virtuous documents harsh and sour.

But because the spirit of man cannot demean[4] itself lively in this body without some recreating intermission of labor and serious things, it were happy for the commonwealth if our magistrates, as in those famous governments of old, would take into their care, not only the deciding of our contentious law cases and brawls, but the managing of our public sports and festival pastimes, that they might be, not such as were authorized a while since, the provocations of drunkenness and lust,[5] but such as may inure and harden our bodies by martial exercises to all warlike skill and performance, and may civilize, adorn, and make discreet our minds by the learned and affable meeting of frequent academies, and the procurement of wise and artful recitations sweetened with eloquent and graceful enticements to the love and practice of justice, temperance, and fortitude, instructing and bettering the nation at all opportunities, that the call of wisdom and virtue may be heard everywhere, as Solomon saith: "She crieth without, she uttereth her voice in the streets, in the top of high places, in the chief concourse, and in the openings of the gates."[6] Whether this may not be, not only in pulpits, but after another persuasive method, at set and solemn panegyries,[7] in theaters, porches,[8] or what other place or way may win most upon the people to receive at once both recreation and instruction, let them in authority consult.

The thing which I had to say, and those intentions which have lived within me ever since I could conceive myself anything worth to my country, I return to crave excuse that urgent reason hath plucked from me by an abortive and foredated discovery. And the accomplishment of

2. Temperament.
3. Mini-poets or pseudo-poets.
4. Comport.
5. The Stuart regime of James I had published in 1617 a Book of Sports, encouraging archery and dancing on Sundays; Puritans of Milton's kidney

fiercely opposed it.
6. The phrases are from Proverbs 1 and 8.
7. "Panegyric" means literally (in the Greek) "fit for a public assembly."
8. Porticos.

them lies not but in a power above man's to promise; but that none hath by more studious ways endeavored, and with more unwearied spirit that none shall, that I dare almost aver of myself as far as life and free leisure will extend; and that the land had once enfranchised herself from this impertinent yoke of prelaty, under whose inquisitorious and tyrannical duncery no free and splendid wit can flourish. Neither do I think it shame to covenant with any knowing reader that for some few years yet I may go on trust with him toward the payment of what I am now indebted, as being a work not to be raised from the heat of youth or the vapors of wine, like that which flows at waste from the pen of some vulgar amorist or the trencher fury of a rhyming parasite,[9] nor to be obtained by the invocation of Dame Memory and her siren daughters,[1] but by devout prayer to that Eternal Spirit who can enrich with all utterance and knowledge, and sends out his seraphim with the hallowed fire of his altar to touch and purify the lips of whom he pleases.[2] To this must be added industrious and select reading, steady observation, insight into all seemly and generous arts and affairs, till which in some measure be compassed, at mine own peril and cost I refuse not to sustain this expectation.[3] * * * But were it the meanest under-service, if God by his secretary conscience enjoin it, it were sad for me if I should draw back, for me especially, now when all men offer their aid to help ease and lighten the difficult labors of the church, to whose service by the intentions of my parents and friends I was destined of a child, and in mine own resolutions: till coming to some maturity of years and perceiving what tyranny had invaded the church, that he who would take orders must subscribe slave and take an oath withal, which, unless he took with a conscience that would retch, he must either straight perjure or split his faith; I thought it better to prefer a blameless silence before the sacred office of speaking, bought and begun with servitude and forswearing. Howsoever, thus church-outed by the prelates, hence may appear the right I have to meddle in these matters, as before the necessity and constraint appeared.

1642

Areopagitica   This pamphlet appeared on November 24, 1644. The title, which Milton took from a famous oration delivered by Isocrates in 355 B.C., means "things to be said before the Areopagus." The Areopagus was an ancient, powerful, and much-respected tribunal in Athens, and Milton's title thus implies a comparison between the Greek institution and the English Parliament, and between Isocrates' role and his own. These comparisons may be thought to validate the florid, oratorical tone of the tract—which was, in fact, subtitled "A Speech," and is structured in accordance with the precepts of classical rhetoric.

---

9. Courtly poets, limited (as Milton rather crossly sees it) to themes of adulterous love and social flattery.
1. The siren daughters of Dame Memory (Mnemosyne) are no other than the nine muses.
2. The coal from the altar which purifies the prophet's lips is from Isaiah 6.6–7.
3. To set aside these visions, in order to take part in political squabbles with ignorant opponents has been, Milton declares, a painful and disagreeable necessity.

Areopagitica is a plea for the liberty of unlicensed printing; its occasion was a severe ordinance for the control of printing which had been passed by Parliament on June 14, 1643. This ordinance, however disagreeable at the moment, was no striking novelty in English history. On the contrary, control of the press had been actively exercised by all the Tudors and both the early Stuarts. The aim of this government regulation was traditionally defined as the preservation of order and uniformity in church and state; but it also had an economic motive. Unlicensed printers threatened a monopoly enjoyed by the twenty licensed printers of London. Thus the censorship laws familiar to Englishmen had generally been strictly defined and had bristled with penalties. But to enforce them was another matter entirely. Tudor and Stuart police forces being what they were, few printers or authors had to worry about the consequences of going to print without a license. As a matter of fact, *Areopagitica* was itself unlicensed, Milton's third unlicensed pamphlet since the passage of the Ordinance for Printing only seventeen months before.

Thus the practical effects of the Ordinance for Printing were less important (particularly, we may be sure, in Milton's eyes) than the principle involved. Having taken the lead in destroying the licensing system of the Stuarts, Parliament was now setting up a censorship of its own. Milton's first effort was to show, through a condensed history of censorship, that the institution was only fit for, and only used by, degenerate cultures. His next argument is still more general, that censorship is evil and un-Christian in itself. As God left man free to choose among the many physical foods of this world, urging only temperance, so (Milton argues) he left man free to pick and choose for himself among ideas.

From Areopagitica

* * * Good and evil we know in the field of this world grow up together almost inseparably; and the knowledge of good is so involved and interwoven with the knowledge of evil, and in so many cunning resemblances hardly to be discerned, that those confused seeds which were imposed on Psyche as an incessant labor to cull out and sort asunder,[1] were not more intermixed. It was from out the rind of one apple tasted, that the knowledge of good and evil, as two twins cleaving together, leaped forth into the world. And perhaps this is that doom which Adam fell into of knowing good and evil, that is to say of knowing good by evil.

As therefore the state of man now is, what wisdom can there be to choose, what continence to forbear, without the knowledge of evil? He that can apprehend and consider vice with all her baits and seeming pleasures, and yet abstain, and yet distinguish, and yet prefer that which is truly better, he is the true wayfaring[2] Christian. I cannot praise a fugitive and cloistered virtue, unexercised and unbreathed, that never sallies out and sees her adversary, but slinks out of the race where that immortal garland[3] is to be run for, not without dust and heat. Assuredly

1. Angry at her son Cupid's love for Psyche, Venus set Psyche to sorting out a vast mound of mixed seeds; but the ants took pity on her, and did the work. See Apuleius, *The Golden Ass.*
2. There has been debate whether this word should

be "wayfaring" or "warfaring," but in the image of Christian life as a pilgrimage, a crusade, the two ideas are united.
3. The crown of righteousness, the garland of virtue.

we bring not innocence into the world, we bring impurity much rather; that which purifies us is trial, and trial is by what is contrary. That virtue therefore which is but a youngling in the contemplation of evil, and knows not the utmost that vice promises to her followers, and rejects it, is but a blank virtue, not a pure; her whiteness is but an excremental[4] whiteness; which was the reason why our sage and serious poet Spenser (whom I dare be known to think a better teacher than Scotus or Aquinas),[5] describing true temperance under the person of Guyon, brings him in with his palmer through the cave of Mammon and the bower of earthly bliss, that he might see and know, and yet abstain.

Since therefore the knowledge and survey of vice is in this world so necessary to the constituting of human virtue, and the scanning of error to the confirmation of truth, how can we more safely, and with less danger, scout into the regions of sin and falsity than by reading all manner of tractates and hearing all manner of reason? And this is the benefit which may be had of books promiscuously read.

But of the harm that may result hence, three kinds are usually reckoned. First is feared the infection that may spread; but then all human learning and controversy in religious points must remove out of the world, yea, the Bible itself; for that ofttimes relates blasphemy not nicely,[6] it describes the carnal sense of wicked men not unelegantly, it brings in holiest men passionately murmuring against providence through all the arguments of Epicurus;[7] in other great disputes it answers dubiously and darkly to the common reader; and ask a Talmudist what ails the modesty of his marginal Keri, that Moses and all the prophets cannot persuade him to pronounce the textual Chetiv.[8] For these causes we all know the Bible itself put by the papist into the first rank of prohibited books. The ancientest Fathers must be next removed, as Clement of Alexandria, and that Eusebian book of evangelic preparation, transmitting our ears through a hoard of heathenish obscenities to receive the Gospel.[9] Who finds not that Irenaeus, Epiphanius, Jerome, and others discover[1] more heresies than they well confute, and that oft for heresy which is the truer opinion?[2] * * *

*   *   *

Impunity and remissness, for certain, are the bane of a commonwealth; but here the great art lies, to discern in what the law is to bid

---

4. Exterior (like a whited sepulcher, covering corruption within).
5. Duns Scotus and Thomas Aquinas, taken as types of the Scholastic theologian. The Cave of Mammon is described in *The Faerie Queene* 2.7, the Bower of Bliss in 2.12.
6. Daintily.
7. See the Book of Ecclesiastes.
8. "Keri" are the marginal comments of rabbinical scholars on the "Chetiv" of the Bible, the text itself. When the text was too free-spoken for later commentators, Keri was sometimes read in place of Chetiv.

9. Eusebius' *Preparatio Evangelica*, like many early Christian books of polemic, describes heathen wickedness in fascinating detail, as an encouragement to Christian faith. St. Irenaeus, St. Jerome, and even that ancient and edifying convert, Clement of Alexandria, are all subject to this charge.
1. Describe (and so preserve, report).
2. Milton now argues that books cannot pervert men unless they are given force and vitality by a teacher, who, if he is a good teacher, needs no books. A fool, he urges, can find material for his folly in the best books, and a wise man material for his wisdom in the worst. Plato, indeed, rec-

restraint and punishment, and in what things persuasion only is to work. If every action which is good or evil in man at ripe years were to be under pittance[3] and prescription and compulsion, what were virtue but a name, what praise could be then due to well-doing, what gramercy[4] to be sober, just, or continent?

Many there be that complain of divine providence for suffering Adam to transgress; foolish tongues! when God gave him reason, he gave him freedom to choose, for reason is but choosing; he had been else a mere artificial Adam, such an Adam as he is in the motions.[5] We ourselves esteem not of that obedience, or love, or gift, which is of force: God therefore left him free, set before him a provoking object, ever almost in his eyes; herein consisted his merit, herein the right of his reward, the praise of his abstinence. Wherefore did he create passions within us, pleasures round about us, but that these rightly tempered are the very ingredients of virtue? They are not skillful considerers of human things, who imagine to remove sin by removing the matter of sin; for, besides that it is a huge heap increasing under the very act of diminishing, though some part of it may for a time be withdrawn from some persons, it cannot from all, in such a universal thing as books are; and when this is done, yet the sin remains entire. Though ye take from a covetous man all his treasure, he has yet one jewel left: ye cannot bereave him of his covetousness. Banish all objects of lust, shut up all youth into the severest discipline that can be exercised in any hermitage, ye cannot make them chaste that came not thither so: such great care and wisdom is required to the right managing of this point.

Suppose we could expel sin by this means; look how much we thus expel of sin, so much we expel of virtue: for the matter of them both is the same; remove that, and ye remove them both alike. This justifies the high providence of God, who, though he commands us temperance, justice, continence, yet pours out before us, even to a profuseness, all desirable things, and gives us minds that can wander beyond all limit and satiety. Why should we then affect a rigor contrary to the manner of God and of nature, by abridging or scanting those means, which books freely permitted are, both to the trial of virtue and the exercise of truth?[6] * * *

* * *

Well knows he who uses to consider, that our faith and knowledge thrives by exercise, as well as our limbs and complexion.[7] Truth is compared in Scripture to a streaming fountain; if her waters flow not in a

---

ommended censorship in his *Laws*; but in real life one cannot censor books without censoring ballads, fiddlers, clothing, conversation, and social life as a whole.

3. Rationing.

4. Reward, thanks.

5. Puppet shows.

6. Censorship, Milton urges, is a vulgar, mechanical job; no man of intelligence will undertake it, and a dunderhead will make serious blunders. Besides, putting stupid men in authority over intelligent ones will discourage the pursuit of learning on every hand, except so far as censorship, by giving authority to banned books, will encourage men to seek out and cling to perverse opinions.

7. Constitution, regarded as the proper mingling of certain qualities in one's body.

perpetual progression, they sicken into a muddy pool of conformity and tradition. A man may be a heretic in the truth; and if he believe things only because his pastor says so, or the Assembly so determines, without knowing other reason, though his belief be true, yet the very truth he holds becomes his heresy. There is not any burden that some would gladlier post off to another than the charge and care of their religion. There be, who knows not that there be, of Protestants and professors[8] who live and die in as arrant an implicit faith as any lay papist of Loretto.[9] A wealthy man, addicted to his pleasure and to his profits, finds religion to be a traffic so entangled, and of so many piddling accounts, that of all mysteries he cannot skill[1] to keep a stock going upon that trade. What should he do? Fain he would have the name to be religious, fain he would bear up with his neighbors in that. What does he therefore, but resolves to give over toiling, and to find himself out some factor,[2] to whose care and credit he may commit the whole managing of his religious affairs; some divine of note and estimation that must be. To him he adheres, resigns the whole warehouse of his religion, with all the locks and keys, into his custody; and indeed makes the very person of that man his religion; esteems his associating with him a sufficient evidence and commendatory of his own piety. So that a man may say his religion is now no more within himself, but is become a dividual[3] movable, and goes and comes near him, according as that good man frequents the house. He entertains him, gives him gifts, feasts him, lodges him; his religion comes home at night, prays, is liberally supped, and sumptuously laid to sleep, rises, is saluted, and after the malmsey, or some well-spiced brewage, and better breakfasted than He whose morning appetite would have gladly fed on green figs between Bethany and Jerusalem,[4] his religion walks abroad at eight, and leaves his kind entertainer in the shop trading all day without his religion.

Another sort there be who, when they hear that all things shall be ordered, all things regulated and settled, nothing written but what passes through the custom-house of certain publicans that have the tonnaging and poundaging[5] of all free-spoken truth, will straight give themselves up into your hands, make 'em and cut 'em out what religion ye please: there be delights, there be recreations and jolly pastimes that will fetch the day about from sun to sun, and rock the tedious year as in a delightful dream. What need they torture their heads with that which others have taken so strictly and so unalterably into their own purveying? These are the fruits which a dull ease and cessation of our knowledge will bring forth among the people. How goodly and how to be wished were such

---

8. "Professors" in this context are people professing the Protestant faith.
9. A famous Catholic shrine.
1. In no way can he manage.
2. Agent.
3. I.e., separate or separable. Milton is describing the common institution of the household chaplain.

4. Mark 11.12–13. Jesus, hungry, found nothing but leaves on the fig tree, for the time of the figs was not yet.
5. "Publicans": tax collectors. Tonnage and poundage were excise taxes levied illegally by the king before 1641, and therefore specially odious to Milton's readers.

an obedient unanimity as this, what a fine conformity would it starch us all into! Doubtless a staunch and solid piece of framework, as any January could freeze together.[6] * * *

* * *

Truth indeed came once into the world with her Divine Master, and was a perfect shape most glorious to look on: but when he ascended, and his apostles after him were laid asleep, then straight arose a wicked race of deceivers, who, as that story goes of the Egyptian Typhon with his conspirators, how they dealt with the good Osiris,[7] took the virgin Truth, hewed her lovely form into a thousand pieces, and scattered them to the four winds. From that time ever since, the sad friends of Truth, such as durst appear, imitating the careful search that Isis made for the mangled body of Osiris, went up and down gathering up limb by limb, still as they could find them. We have not yet found them all, Lords and Commons, nor ever shall do, till her Master's second coming; he shall bring together every joint and member, and shall mold them into an immortal feature of loveliness and perfection. Suffer not these licensing prohibitions to stand at every place of opportunity, forbidding and disturbing them that continue seeking, that continue to do our obsequies to the torn body of our martyred saint.

We boast our light; but if we look not wisely on the sun itself, it smites us into darkness. Who can discern those planets that are oft combust,[8] and those stars of brightest magnitude that rise and set with the sun, until the opposite motion of their orbs bring them to such a place in the firmament where they may be seen evening or morning? The light which we have gained was given us, not to be ever staring on, but by it to discover onward things more remote from our knowledge. It is not the unfrocking of a priest, the unmitering of a bishop, and the removing him from off the Presbyterian shoulders, that will make us a happy nation. No, if other things as great in the church, and in the rule of life both economical[9] and political, be not looked into and reformed, we have looked so long upon the blaze that Zwinglius[1] and Calvin hath beaconed up to us, that we are stark blind.

There be who perpetually complain of schisms and sects, and make it such a calamity that any man dissents from their maxims. 'Tis their own pride and ignorance which causes the disturbing, who neither will hear with meekness, nor can convince; yet all must be suppressed which is not found in their syntagma.[2] They are the troublers, they are the dividers of unity, who neglect and permit not others to unite those dissevered

---

6. To set barriers in the way of fresh truths implies that a nation has all the truth it needs; but this, Milton argues, is far from the case. England has no grounds for smugness; the nation needs every bit of truth it can discover.

7. Plutarch tells, in his *Isis and Osiris*, of Typhon's scattering the fragments of his brother Osiris, and of Isis' efforts to recover them.

8. Literally, burned up; in astrology, so close to the sun as not to be visible.

9. Domestic.

1. Zwingli and Calvin, both radical Swiss reformers, were mainstays of the Presbyterian cause, which Milton was already feeling to be a little narrow.

2. Compilation of beliefs, creed.

pieces which are yet wanting to the body of Truth. To be still searching what we know not by what we know, still closing up truth to truth as we find it (for all her body is homogeneal and proportional), this is the golden rule in theology as well as in arithmetic, and makes up the best harmony in a church; not the forced and outward union of cold and neutral and inwardly divided minds.

Lords and Commons of England, consider what nation it is whereof ye are, and whereof ye are the governors: a nation not slow and dull, but of a quick, ingenious, and piercing spirit, acute to invent, subtle and sinewy to discourse, not beneath the reach of any point the highest that human capacity can soar to. Therefore the studies of learning in her deepest sciences have been so ancient and so eminent among us, that writers of good antiquity and ablest judgment have been persuaded that even the school of Pythagoras and the Persian wisdom took beginning from the old philosophy of this island.[3] And that wise and civil Roman, Julius Agricola, who governed once here for Caesar, preferred the natural wits of Britain before the labored studies of the French. Nor is it for nothing that the grave and frugal Transylvanian sends out yearly from as far as the mountainous borders of Russia, and beyond the Hercynian wilderness, not their youth, but their staid men, to learn our language and our theologic arts.

Yet that which is above all this, the favor and the love of heaven we have great argument[4] to think in a peculiar manner propitious and propending towards us. Why else was this nation chosen before any other, that out of her, as out of Zion,[5] should be proclaimed and sounded forth the first tidings and trumpet of Reformation to all Europe? And had it not been the obstinate perverseness of our prelates against the divine and admirable spirit of Wycliffe to suppress him as a schismatic and innovator, perhaps neither the Bohemian Huss and Jerome,[6] no, nor the name of Luther or of Calvin, had been ever known: the glory of reforming all our neighbors had been completely ours. But now, as our obdurate clergy have with violence demeaned[7] the matter, we are become hitherto the latest and the backwardest scholars of whom God offered to have made us the teachers.

Now once again by all concurrence of signs, and by the general instinct of holy and devout men, as they daily and solemnly express their thoughts, God is decreeing to begin some new and great period in his church, even to the reforming of Reformation itself; what does he then but reveal himself to his servants, and as his manner is, first to his Englishmen? I say, as his manner is, first to us, though we mark not the method of his

---

3. So far as it concerns Pythagoras and the Persians, this sentence is better patriotism than it is intellectual history. Agricola's opinion of the British intellect (referred to next) is found in Tacitus' *Life of Agricola*; "civil" means "cultured, civilized." The Transylvanians, being Protestants, did sometimes come to England from "beyond the Hercynian wilderness" (the Harz mountains) to

study.
4. Reason. "Propending": inclining, favorable.
5. Mt. Zion, in Jerusalem, the site of the temple, the holy of holies.
6. Jerome of Prague (martyred in 1416) was a follower of Huss and so of Wycliffe.
7. Conducted.

counsels, and are unworthy. Behold now this vast city: a city of refuge, the mansion house of liberty, encompassed and surrounded with his protection; the shop of war hath not there more anvils and hammers waking, to fashion out the plates[8] and instruments of armed justice in defense of beleaguered truth, than there be pens and heads there, sitting by their studious lamps, musing, searching, revolving new notions and ideas wherewith to present, as with their homage and their fealty, the approaching Reformation: others as fast reading, trying all things, assenting to the force of reason and convincement.

What could a man require more from a nation so pliant and so prone to seek after knowledge? What wants there to such a towardly[9] and pregnant soil, but wise and faithful laborers, to make a knowing people, a nation of prophets, of sages, and of worthies? We reckon more than five months yet to harvest; there need not be five weeks; had we but eyes to lift up, the fields are white already.[1] Where there is much desire to learn, there of necessity will be much arguing, much writing, many opinions; for opinion in good men is but knowledge in the making. Under these fantastic terrors of sect and schism we wrong the earnest and zealous thirst after knowledge and understanding which God hath stirred up in this city.

What some lament of, we rather should rejoice at, should rather praise this pious forwardness among men, to reassume the ill-deputed care of their religion into their own hands again. A little generous prudence, a little forbearance of one another, and some grain of charity might win all these diligences to join, and unite into one general and brotherly search after truth; could we but forego this prelatical tradition of crowding free consciences and Christian liberties into canons and precepts of men. I doubt not, if some great and worthy stranger should come among us, wise to discern the mold and temper of a people, and how to govern it, observing the high hopes and aims, the diligent alacrity of our extended thoughts and reasonings in the pursuance of truth and freedom, but that he would cry out as Pyrrhus did, admiring the Roman docility and courage: "If such were my Epirots, I would not despair the greatest design that could be attempted, to make a church or kingdom happy."[2] Yet these are the men cried out against for schismatics and sectaries;[3] as if, while the temple of the Lord was building, some cutting, some squaring the marble, others hewing the cedars, there should be a sort of irrational men, who could not consider there must be many schisms and many dissections[4] made in the quarry and in the timber, ere the house of God can be built. And when every stone is laid artfully together, it cannot be united into a continuity, it can but be contiguous in this world; neither can every piece of the building be of one form; nay rather the perfection consists in this, that out of many moderate varieties and brotherly dissi-

8. Plate mail, armor plate.
9. Favorable.
1. Milton is paraphrasing Christ's words to the disciples (John 4.35).
2. Though King Pyrrhus of Epirus beat the Roman

armies at Heraclea in 280 B.C., he was much impressed by their discipline.
3. Sectarians, dividers of the church.
4. Literally, cuttings-up, figuratively dissensions and divisions.

militudes that are not vastly disproportional, arises the goodly and the graceful symmetry that commends the whole pile and structure. Let us therefore be more considerate builders, more wise in spiritual architecture, when great reformation is expected. For now the time seems come, wherein Moses the great prophet may sit in heaven rejoicing to see that memorable and glorious wish of his fulfilled, when not only our seventy elders, but all the Lord's people, are become prophets.[5]

* * *

Methinks I see in my mind a noble and puissant nation rousing herself like a strong man after sleep, and shaking her invincible locks: methinks I see her as an eagle mewing[6] her mighty youth, and kindling her undazzled eyes at the full midday beam; purging and unscaling her longabused sight at the fountain itself of heavenly radiance; while the whole noise of timorous and flocking birds, with those also that love the twilight, flutter about, amazed at what she means, and in their envious gabble would prognosticate a year of sects and schisms.

What should ye do then, should ye suppress all this flowery crop of knowledge and new light sprung up and yet springing daily in this city? Should ye set an oligarchy of twenty engrossers[7] over it, to bring a famine upon our minds again, when we shall know nothing but what is measured to us by their bushel? Believe it, Lords and Commons, they who counsel ye to such a suppressing do as good as bid ye suppress yourselves; and I will soon show how.[8]

* * *

And now the time in special is by privilege to write and speak what may help to the further discussing of matters in agitation. The temple of Janus with his two controversial faces might now not unsignificantly be set open.[9] And though all the winds of doctrine were let loose to play upon the earth, so Truth be in the field, we do injuriously by licensing and prohibiting to misdoubt her strength. Let her and Falsehood grapple; who ever knew Truth put to the worse in a free and open encounter? Her confuting is the best and surest suppressing. He who hears what praying there is for light and clearer knowledge to be sent down among us would think of other matters to be constituted beyond the discipline of Geneva framed and fabricked already to our hands.[1]

5. In Numbers 11.29 Moses expresses the wish that not only the Sanhedrin, or council of seventy, but the whole people of Israel should be prophets.
6. Molting, shaking off. Or the word may be "newing," i.e., renewing.
7. Engrossers, much hated in the English countryside, bought great quantities of grain and held it for times of famine and consequent high prices.
8. By its liberal and enlightened policies, Milton argues, Parliament has actually created the vigorous and enquiring minds that censorship seeks to suppress. For Parliament to destroy its own creation would be like a father killing his own children.

9. Janus, who gives us our month of January, had two faces looking in opposite directions, because he was god of beginnings and endings. A special door in Rome, dedicated to him, was kept open in times of war, closed in times of peace.
1. Milton's Calvinism, a major ingredient of which was hostility to English bishops, was fading fast in 1644, since bishops had been abolished; within a year or two he would be writing his sonnet (below, p. 1442) On the New Forcers of Conscience, meaning by them the Presbyterians.

Yet when the new light which we beg for shines in upon us, there be who envy and oppose if it come not first in at their casements. What a collusion is this, whenas we are exhorted by the wise man to use diligence, to seek for wisdom as for hidden treasures early and late,[2] that another order shall enjoin us to know nothing but by statute. When a man hath been laboring the hardest labor in the deep mines of knowledge, hath furnished out his findings in all their equipage, drawn forth his reasons as it were a battle[3] ranged, scattered and defeated all objections in his way, calls out his adversary into the plain, offers him the advantage of wind and sun if he please, only that he may try the matter by dint of argument; for his opponents then to skulk, to lay ambushments, to keep a narrow bridge of licensing where the challenger should pass, though it be valor enough in soldiership, is but weakness and cowardice in the wars of Truth.

For who knows not that Truth is strong, next to the Almighty? She needs no policies nor stratagems nor licensings to make her victorious—those are the shifts and the defenses that error uses against her power. Give her but room, and do not bind her when she sleeps, for then she speaks not true, as the old Proteus[4] did, who spake oracles only when he was caught and bound, but then rather she turns herself into all shapes except her own, and perhaps tunes her voice according to the time, as Micaiah did before Ahab,[5] until she be adjured into her own likeness.

Yet it is not impossible that she may have more shapes than one. What else is all that rank of things indifferent, wherein Truth may be on this side or on the other without being unlike herself? What but a vain shadow else is the abolition of those ordinances, that handwriting nailed to the cross?[6] what great purchase is this Christian liberty which Paul so often boasts of? His doctrine is that he who eats or eats not, regards a day or regards it not, may do either to the Lord.[7] How many other things might be tolerated in peace and left to conscience, had we but charity, and were it not the chief stronghold of our hypocrisy to be ever judging one another? I fear yet this iron yoke of outward conformity hath left a slavish print upon our necks; the ghost of a linen decency[8] yet haunts us. We stumble and are impatient at the least dividing of one visible congregation from another, though it be not in fundamentals; and through our forwardness to suppress and our backwardness to recover any enthralled piece of truth out of the gripe of custom, we care not[9] to keep truth separated from truth, which is the fiercest rent and disunion of all. We do not see that while we still affect by all means a rigid and

2. Solomon was the wise man; the allusion is to Proverbs 8.11.

3. Line of battle, array, Wind and sun were significant advantages in a fight with swords.

4. The old man of the sea, who tried to escape capture by changing shapes, in *Odyssey* 4.

5. The story of Micaiah, who tried to disguise an unpleasant prophecy from King Ahab, is in 1 Kings 22.

6. The locution, from Colossians 2.14, implies that the crucifixion canceled out all the rules and penalties of Mosaic law. Paul's doctrine is expressed in Galatians 5.

7. In the Lord's service.

8. Strips of white linen at neck and wrist were worn by many men in the 17th century, especially (under the name of "bands") by clergymen. Milton uses them as emblems of formal purity.

9. Scruple not.

external formality, we may as soon fall again into a gross conforming stupidity, a stark and dead congealment of "wood and hay and stubble,"[1] forced and frozen together, which is more to the sudden degenerating of a church than many sub-dichotomies of petty schisms.

Not that I can think well of every light separation, or that all in a church is to be expected "gold and silver and precious stones." It is not possible for man to sever the wheat from the tares, the good fish from the other fry; that must be the angels' ministry at the end of mortal things.[2] Yet if all cannot be of one mind—as who looks they should be?—this doubtless is more wholesome, more prudent, and more Christian, that many be tolerated rather than all compelled. I mean not tolerated popery and open superstition, which, as it extirpates all religions and civil supremacies, so itself should be extirpate, provided first that all charitable and compassionate means be used to win and regain the weak and the misled; that also which is impious or evil absolutely, either against faith or manners, no law can possibly permit that intends not to unlaw itself; but those neighboring differences or rather indifferences are what I speak of, whether in some point of doctrine or of discipline, which though they may be many yet need not interrupt "the unity of spirit," if we could but find among us the "bond of peace."[3]

In the meanwhile, if anyone would write and bring his helpful hand to the slow-moving reformation which we labor under, if truth have spoken to him before others, or but seemed at least to speak, who hath so bejesuited us that we should trouble that man with asking license to do so worthy a deed? And not consider this, that if it come to prohibiting, there is not aught more likely to be prohibited than truth itself; whose first appearance to our eyes bleared and dimmed with prejudice and custom is more unsightly and unplausible than many errors, even as the person is of many a great man slight and contemptible to see to. And what do they tell us vainly of new opinions, when this very opinion of theirs, that none must be heard but whom they like, is the worst and newest opinion of all others, and is the chief cause why sects and schisms do so much abound, and true knowledge is kept at distance from us; besides yet a greater danger which is in it. For when God shakes a kingdom with strong and healthful commotions to a general reforming, it is not untrue that many sectaries and false teachers are then busiest in seducing; but yet more true it is that God then raises to his own work men of rare abilities and more than common industry, not only to look back and revise what hath been taught heretofore, but to gain further and go on some new enlightened steps in the discovery of truth.[4]

*   *   *

1644

1. The contrast between "wood, hay, stubble" and "gold, silver, precious stones" is from 1 Corinthians 3.12.
2. This is the parable of the wheat and the tares (weeds) in Matthew 13.24–30, 36–43.
3. The phrases are from Paul's letter to the Ephesians.
4. After a few final thoughts, *Areopagitica* ends with an exhortation to Parliament. In practical terms, the argument was unsuccessful; the ordi-

Sonnets   Between 1630 and 1658 Milton wrote twenty-four sonnets.
Five he wrote in Italian, no doubt partly as linguistic exercises, the rest in
English, on a variety of occasions, both public and private. Unlike the sonnets of Sidney, Spenser, and Shakespeare, those of Milton do not form any
sort of sequence, and they lay very little emphasis on erotic themes. Neither
are they devotional like the *Holy Sonnets* of Donne. They are more often
public and political than simply personal. Yet, whatever their theme, they
speak with a massive and authoritative voice like none other in English.

The form of the sonnets is Petrarchan rather than Shakespearean (see the
appendix on poetic forms); and one is a "tailed" sonnet, with two little extra
units, each consisting of a half line and a couplet. A special feature of Milton's later sonnets is the way he runs on the sense from line to line, deliberately avoiding end-stopped lines (see particularly that *On the Late Massacre
in Piedmont*). In this as in other respects, Milton was following the example
of an Italian sonneteer, Giovanni Della Casa, who broke sharply with the
Petrarchan tradition of metrical regularity. Milton's break with his English
predecessors was just as sharp.

Sonnets

How Soon Hath Time

How soon hath Time, the subtle thief of youth,
   Stol'n on his wing my three and twentieth year!
   My hasting days fly on with full career,
   But my late spring no bud or blossom show'th.
Perhaps my semblance might deceive the truth,   5
   That I to manhood am arrived so near,
   And inward ripeness doth much less appear,
   That some more timely-happy spirits endu'th.[1]
Yet be it less or more, or soon or slow,
   It shall be still in strictest measure even[2]   10
   To that same lot, however mean or high,
Toward which Time leads me, and the will of Heaven;
   All is, if I have grace to use it so,
   As ever in my great Taskmaster's eye.[3]

1632?   1645

nance against which Milton protested was not
repealed, though it was never effectively enforced.
In time, Milton himself became for a while a
licenser of news sheets under Cromwell, commissioned to give editorial supervision to a small, pro-
government paper. But this biographical fact need
not be taken as a retraction of the position assumed
in *Areopagitica*, which moves throughout on a lofty
plane of policy far above mundane details of politics.

1. Endoweth.
2. Equal, adequate. Whenever it appears and
however much it amounts to, Milton's inner growth
will be adequate to the destiny that time and heaven
are preparing.
3. I.e., nothing has been lost in God's eyes—if
only I can see ("use") it that way.

On the New Forcers of Conscience Under the Long Parliament[1]

Because you have thrown off your prelate lord,[2]
    And with stiff vows renounced his liturgy,
    To seize the widowed whore Plurality[3]
From them whose sin ye envied, not abhorred,
Dare ye for this adjure the civil sword   5
    To force our consciences that Christ set free,
    And ride us with a classic hierarchy[4]
Taught ye by mere A. S. and Rutherford?[5]
Men whose life, learning, faith, and pure intent
    Would have been held in high esteem with Paul   10
    Must now be named and printed heretics
By shallow Edwards and Scotch what-d'ye-call:[6]
    But we do hope to find out all your tricks,
    Your plots and packing worse than those of Trent,[7]
            That so the Parliament   15
May with their wholesome and preventive shears
Clip your phylacteries,[8] though balk your ears,
            And succor our just fears
When they shall read this clearly in your charge:
New presbyter is but *old priest* writ large.   20

ca. 1646   1673

To the Lord General Cromwell

Cromwell, our chief of men, who through a cloud
    Not of war only, but detractions rude,

1. "The new forcers of conscience" are Presbyterians, whom Milton at first supported against the Episcopalians (Church of England men). Now, under the Puritan-dominated Long Parliament, he finds them as bad as their predecessors ("whose sin ye envied, not abhorred"). The sonnet proper has 14 lines followed by two "tails" of three lines each; in Italy, where it was common, this was called a *sonetto caudato*, or "tailed sonnet."
2. Bishop.
3. I.e., the comfortable, and sometimes necessary, practice of one priest's holding several livings at once.
4. A church discipline made up on the Presbyterian model of synods or classes, ecclesiastical governing boards with strong powers over the laity.
5. Adam Stuart and Samuel Rutherford, Presbyterian pamphleteers, whose full names Milton does not deign to give.
6. Thomas Edwards, alarmed by the spread of heresies, began to describe them in a book picturesquely titled *Gangraena* (1645–46). Before giving

up in despair, he wrote three fat volumes, including a denunciation of Milton, whom he described unjustly as an advocate of "divorce at pleasure." "Scotch what-d'ye-call" is Milton's humanistic sneer at the unpronounceability of Scottish names.
7. I.e., of the Council of Trent, held by the Papacy in consequence of the Reformation; it was widely reported to have been the scene of political jockeying.
8. Little scrolls, containing texts from the Pentateuch, worn by orthodox Jews to remind them of the Law. Milton uses them here as symbols of superstition. Mutilation by having one's ears cut off was a common punishment for sedition, and several Presbyterian leaders had suffered it. Milton's MS. read, "Crop ye as close as marginal P——'s ears," but the jeer was too brutal. William Prynne, whose books had many notes in the margins, and whose ears had twice been cropped, had suffered for a cause in which Milton at the time believed. "Balk": spare.

Guided by faith and matchless fortitude
   To peace and truth thy glorious way hast ploughed,
And on the neck of crownèd Fortune proud   5
   Hast reared God's trophies, and his work pursued,
   While Darwen stream with blood of Scots imbrued[1]
And Dunbar field resounds thy praises loud,
And Worcester's laureate wreath; yet much remains
   To conquer still; peace hath her victories   10
   No less renowned than war; new foes arise,
Threatening to bind our souls with secular chains:[2]
   Help us to save free conscience from the paw
   Of hireling wolves whose gospel is their maw.

1652   1694

When I Consider How My Light Is Spent[1]

When I consider how my light is spent,
   Ere half my days, in this dark world and wide,
   And that one talent which is death to hide,[2]
   Lodged with me useless, though my soul more bent
To serve therewith my Maker, and present   5
   My true account, lest he returning chide;
   "Doth God exact day-labor, light denied?"
I fondly[3] ask; but Patience to prevent
That murmur, soon replies, "God doth not need
   Either man's work or his own gifts; who best   10
   Bear his mild yoke, they serve him best. His state
Is kingly. Thousands at his bidding speed
   And post o'er land and ocean without rest:
   They also serve who only stand and wait."

1652?   1673

1. The river Darwen runs through Preston, where
Cromwell defeated the Scots in 1648; in 1650 he
defeated them again at Dunbar, and in 1651 at
Worcester. "Imbrued": stained.
2. A move was made in 1652 to impose licensing
requirements on hitherto-unsupervised preachers;
Cromwell opposed it, to Milton's satisfaction. This
theme and the outspoken praise of Cromwell prevented the poem from being published till twenty
years after Milton's death.
1. Milton's sonnet on his blindness is close in
theme to *How Soon Hath Time*; but his affliction
(fresh at the time of writing) represents a far more
severe test.

2. The parable of the talents (Matthew 25) loomed
large in Puritan minds, and particularly in Milton's. The servants who put their master's money
(talents of gold and silver) out to earn interest while
he was away were called "good and faithful"; the
one who simply returned what he had been given
was deprived of everything and cast into outer
darkness. Usury, which under Catholic theology
had been a deadly sin, changed its meaning for the
Puritans; it became a metaphor, and sometimes
more than a metaphor, for "working out one's salvation."
3. Foolishly. "Prevent": forestall.

On the Late Massacre in Piedmont[1]

Avenge, O Lord, thy slaughtered saints, whose bones
  Lie scattered on the Alpine mountains cold;
  Even them who kept thy truth so pure of old
  When all our fathers worshipped stocks and stones,
Forget not: in thy book record their groans   5
  Who were thy sheep and in their ancient fold
  Slain by the bloody Piemontese that rolled
  Mother with infant down the rocks. Their moans
The vales redoubled to the hills, and they
  To heaven. Their martyred blood and ashes sow   10
  O'er all th' Italian fields, where still doth sway
The triple tyrant:[2] that from these may grow
  A hundredfold, who having learnt thy way
  Early may fly the Babylonian woe.[3]

1655   1673

Methought I Saw My Late Espousèd Saint

Methought I saw my late espousèd saint
  Brought to me like Alcestis[1] from the grave,
  Whom Jove's great son to her glad husband gave,
  Rescued from death by force though pale and faint.
Mine, as whom washed from spot of childbed taint,   5
  Purification in the old law did save,[2]
  And such, as yet once more I trust to have
  Full sight of her in heaven without restraint,
Came vested all in white, pure as her mind.
  Her face was veiled, yet to my fancied sight   10
  Love, sweetness, goodness, in her person shined
So clear, as in no face with more delight.
  But O, as to embrace me she inclined,
  I waked, she fled, and day brought back my night.

1658   1673

1. The Waldenses were a heretical sect, probably of Eastern origin by way of Venice: they lived in the valleys of northern Italy ("the Piedmont") and southern France, professing a creed which was particularly akin to Protestantism in its avoidance of graven images ("stocks and stones"). The understanding which had allowed them freedom of worship was terminated in 1655, and the massacre which ensued was widely protested by the Protestant powers of Europe. Milton, as Latin secretary to Cromwell, wrote several indignant letters.
2. I.e., the Pope, wearing his tiara with three crowns.

3. Protestants in Milton's day frequently identified the Roman Church with the "whore of Babylon" (Revelation 17, 18).
1. Alcestis, wife of Admetus, was rescued from the underworld by Hercules ("Jove's great son").
2. The Mosaic law prescribing periods for the purification of women after childbirth is found in Leviticus 12. Line 5 is very compressed; expanded, it would read, "My wife, like the woman whom, when washed from spot of childbed taint," etc. Milton's second wife died after childbirth.

Paradise Lost   Milton's epic begins with a rush. Carried along by the
impetus of Satan's tremendous adventures, readers are apt to forget there is
any other part to the poem. Indeed, while we are getting acclimated to the
Miltonic world, there is no reason to hold back our sympathy with Satan,
our admiration for his heroic energy. It is energy in a bad cause, clearly; but
it is energy, it is heroically exercised, and there is as yet no source of virtuous
power to oppose or offset it. With the appearance of Christ the Son, at the
opening of Book 3, we begin to see in heavenly Love the counterpoise of
Satan's hellish Hate; and in Book 4, as we are introduced not only to Adam
and Eve but to Paradise, our sympathies gradually shift. Satan is no longer
a glamorous underdog, fighting his adventurous way through the universe
against enormous odds; he is a menacing vulture, a cormorant, a toad, a
snake. He is not only dangerous, he is dull; whatever richness and variety
he discovers in the universe serve only to produce in him envious hatred
and destructiveness. His sin is incestuous, as the allegory of Sin and Death
points out; it breeds out of itself ever fresh occasions of sin. Adam and Eve,
who are weaker, less active, and less spectacular in every way, finally outweigh Satan in our interest and sympathy simply because they can respond
to life, and to the terrifying experience of guilt, more vigorously than Satan
can.

Seen overall—from above, as it were—*Paradise Lost* is a vast but delicately balanced structure. Its first half rises from Hell through Chaos to
Heaven, and takes place mostly in these cosmic locales; its second half opens
with the word "Descend," and is largely confined to earth, ending with
Adam and Eve's descent from the Mount of Paradise to the "subjected plain"
of our world. The adventure of the fallen Satan in the opening books balances the history of fallen mankind in the closing ones. Book 4, the entry of
Satan (and the reader) into Paradise, balances Book 9, describing the loss of
Paradise. Books 5 and 10 provide contrasting views of life in Eden before
and after the Fall. At the center of the poem, balanced as on a fulcrum, are
the account of the destructive war in Heaven (Book 6), and that of the Creation (Book 7).

Within the poem's larger structure, there are all sorts of secondary balances which readers will recognize for themselves. The consult in Hell (Book
2) is paralleled by a consult in Heaven (Book 3); Eve is generated from Adam
as Sin is generated from Satan; Satan's fall parallels Adam's fall, and the
parallel is prolonged into that extended series of falls and recoveries which
is the history of mankind. Moloch contrasts with Mammon; the Son's mercy
with the Father's justice; Raphael's affability with Michael's severity; and so
on, almost without limit.

The structure of the poem is at once massive and delicate; its language is
also both rich and strong. Milton's range of classical reference and gift for
epithet are undoubtedly staggering at first view, and his long, complexly
subordinated sentences are sometimes hard to follow. Footnotes, alas, provide the only proper solution to this problem. But one need not equal, or
even follow, all Milton's learning in order to appreciate his poem, especially
at a first reading. The poem progresses as through a garden of metaphor and
reference which stretches away on either side of one, as far as the eye can
see; on a first tour, it is enough to get the general prospect clear, without
learning the name of each particular blossom. Ultimately, the reader who is

experienced in the poem comes to appreciate its details—epic similes like Leviathan the seabeast (1.201), no less than the one-eyed Arimaspians and the gryphon (2.943); its epithets and circumlocutions like Mulciber (1.740), who is Vulcan, and Amram's son (1.339) who is Moses—without sense of strain or strangeness. Milton himself moved securely through the literatures of half a dozen languages and as many cultures; it is one of the supreme rewards of literary study to be able to follow him with an equivalent security.

Paradise Lost is at once a deeply traditional and a boldly original poem. Milton takes pains to fulfill the traditional prescriptions of the epic form; he gives us love, war, supernatural characters, a descent into Hell, a catalogue of warriors, all the conventional items of epic machinery. Yet no poem in which the climax of the central action is a woman eating a piece of fruit can be a conventional epic. Similarly, Milton himself defined his moral purpose as being to "justify the ways of God to men." This seems no more than conventionally meek. Yet we cannot even think of equating the message of Milton's poem with Pope's injunction to "submit" because "whatever is is right." The way of life which Adam and Eve take up as the poem ends is that of the Christian pilgrimage through this world. Expelled from Eden, our first "grand parents" pick up the burdens of humanity as we know them, sustained by a faith which we also know, and go forth to seek a blessing that we do not know yet. They are to become wayfaring, warfaring Christians, like John Milton; and in this condition, with its weaknesses and strivings and inevitable defeats, there is a glory that no devil can ever understand. Thus Milton strikes, humanly as well as artistically, a grand resolving chord. It is the careful, triumphant balancing and tempering of this conclusion which completes the noble architecture of Milton's poem; and which makes of the end a richer, if not a more exciting, experience than the beginning.

From PARADISE LOST

Book 1

The Argument[1]

This first book proposes, first in brief, the whole subject, man's disobedience, and the loss thereupon of Paradise, wherein he was placed: then touches the prime cause of his fall, the serpent, or rather Satan in the serpent; who, revolting from God, and drawing to his side many legions of angels, was, by the command of God, driven out of Heaven with all his crew, into the great deep. Which action passed over, the poem hastes into the midst of things;[2] presenting Satan, with his angels, now fallen into Hell—described here not in the center (for heaven and earth may be supposed as yet not made, certainly not yet accursed), but

---

1. *Paradise Lost* appeared originally without any sort of prose aid to the reader; but, since many readers found the poem hard going, the printer asked Milton for some prose "Arguments" or summary explanations of the action in the various books,

and prefixed them to later issues of the poem. We reprint those for the first two books and the ninth.
2. Adapted from Horace's prescription that the epic poet should start *"in medias res."*

in a place of utter darkness, fitliest called Chaos. Here Satan with his angels lying on the burning lake, thunderstruck and astonished, after a certain space recovers, as from confusion; calls up him who, next in order and dignity, lay by him; they confer of their miserable fall. Satan awakens all his legions, who lay till then in the same manner confounded. They rise: their numbers; array of battle; their chief leaders named, according to the idols known afterwards in Canaan and the countries adjoining. To these Satan directs his speech; comforts them with hope yet of regaining Heaven; but tells them, lastly, of a new world and new kind of creature to be created, according to an ancient prophecy or report in Heaven; for that angels were long before this visible creation was the opinion of many ancient fathers.[3] To find out the truth of this prophecy, and what to determine[4] thereon, he refers to a full council. What his associates thence attempt. Pandemonium, the palace of Satan, rises, suddenly built out of the deep: the infernal peers there sit in council.

Of man's first disobedience, and the fruit[5]
Of that forbidden tree whose mortal[6] taste
Brought death into the world, and all our woe,
With loss of Eden, till one greater Man[7]
Restore us, and regain the blissful seat,   5
Sing, Heavenly Muse,[8] that on the secret top
Of Oreb, or of Sinai, didst inspire
That shepherd who first taught the chosen seed
In the beginning how the heavens and earth
Rose out of Chaos: or, if Sion hill[9]   10
Delight thee more, and Siloa's brook that flowed
Fast[1] by the oracle of God, I thence
Invoke thy aid to my adventurous song,
That with no middle flight intends to soar
Above th' Aonian mount,[2] while it pursues   15
Things unattempted yet in prose or rhyme.
And chiefly thou, O Spirit,[3] that dost prefer
Before all temples th' upright heart and pure,
Instruct me, for thou know'st; thou from the first

3. I.e., Church Fathers, the Christian writers of the first few centuries of the church.
4. I.e., what action to take upon their information.
5. Eve's apple, of course; but also all the consequences of eating it.
6. Deadly; but also "to mortals" (i.e., human beings).
7. Christ, the second Adam.
8. In Greek mythology, Urania, Muse of astronomy; but here identified, by references to Oreb and Sinai, with the Holy Spirit of the Bible, which inspired Moses ("that shepherd") to write Genesis and the other four books of the Pentateuch for the instruction of the Jews ("the chosen seed").
9. The hill of Sion and the brook of Siloa are two features of the landscape around Jerusalem likely to appeal to a Muse whose natural haunts are springs and mountains (see *Lycidas*, line 15). Milton's aim is to show that poetry is everywhere recognized as an inspiration close to that of religion.
1. Close.
2. Helicon, home of the classical Muses; Milton is deliberately courting comparison with Homer and Virgil. In the very line ("Things unattempted yet in prose or rhyme") where he vaunts his originality, Milton is translating a line in the invocation of Ariosto's *Orlando Furioso*—thus acknowledging, and challenging, another of his predecessors.
3. The Spirit is an impulse or voice of God, by which the Hebrew prophets were directly inspired.

Wast present, and, with mighty wings outspread,   20
Dovelike sat'st brooding[4] on the vast abyss,
And mad'st it pregnant: what in me is dark
Illumine; what is low, raise and support;
That to the height of this great argument[5]
I may assert Eternal Providence,   25
And justify the ways of God to men.
   Say first (for Heaven hides nothing from thy view,
Nor the deep tract of Hell), say first what cause
Moved our grand[6] parents, in that happy state,
Favored of Heaven so highly, to fall off   30
From their Creator, and transgress his will
For[7] one restraint, lords of the world besides?[8]
Who first seduced them to that foul revolt?
   Th' infernal serpent; he it was, whose guile,
Stirred up with envy and revenge, deceived   35
The mother of mankind, what time[9] his pride
Had cast him out from Heaven, with all his host
Of rebel angels, by whose aid aspiring
To set himself in glory above his peers,[1]
He trusted to have equaled the Most High,   40
If he opposed; and with ambitious aim
Against the throne and monarchy of God
Raised impious war in Heaven and battle proud,
With vain attempt. Him the Almighty Power
Hurled headlong flaming from th' ethereal sky   45
With hideous ruin and combustion down
To bottomless perdition, there to dwell
In adamantine chains and penal fire,
Who durst defy th' Omnipotent to arms.
   Nine times the space that measures day and night   50
To mortal men, he with his horrid crew
Lay vanquished, rolling in the fiery gulf
Confounded though immortal. But his doom
Reserved him to more wrath; for now the thought
Both of lost happiness and lasting pain   55
Torments him; round he throws his baleful[2] eyes,
That witnessed huge affliction and dismay,
Mixed with obdùrate pride and steadfast hate.

---

4. A composite of phrases and ideas from Genesis 1.2 ("And the earth was without form, and void; and darkness was upon the face of the deep. And the Spirit of God moved upon the face of the waters"); Matthew 3.16 ("and he saw the Spirit of God descending like a dove, and lighting upon him"); and Luke 3.22 ("and the Holy Ghost descended in a bodily shape like a dove upon him"). Milton's mind as he wrote was impregnated with expressions from the King James Bible, only a few of which can be indicated in the notes.
5. Theme.
6. First in importance; by implication, in time also.

7. Because of.
8. In every other respect.
9. I.e., at the time when.
1. His equals. The sentence mimics Satan's action, piling clause loosely upon clause, and building ever higher, till "with vain attempt" (line 44) brings the whole structure crashing down. It is a dramatic entry into "the midst of things," where epics begin. Book 6 will recount more largely the war in Heaven, in the full narrative form which Aeneas used to tell Dido of the last days of Troy (Aeneid 2).
2. Malignant, as well as suffering.

At once, as far as angels ken,[3] he views
The dismal situation waste and wild: 60
A dungeon horrible, on all sides round
As one great furnace flamed; yet from those flames
No light,[4] but rather darkness visible
Served only to discover sights of woe,
Regions of sorrow, doleful shades, where peace   65
And rest can never dwell, hope never comes
That comes to all,[5] but torture without end
Still urges,[6] and a fiery deluge, fed
With ever-burning sulphur unconsumed:
Such place Eternal Justice had prepared   70
For those rebellious; here their prison ordained
In utter[7] darkness and their portion set
As far removed from God and light of Heaven
As from the center[8] thrice to th' utmost pole.
O how unlike the place from whence they fell!   75
There the companions of his fall, o'erwhelmed
With floods and whirlwinds of tempestuous fire,
He soon discerns; and, weltering by his side,
One next himself in power, and next in crime,
Long after known in Palestine, and named   80
Beëlzebub.[9] To whom th' arch-enemy,
And thence in Heaven called Satan,[1] with bold words
Breaking the horrid silence thus began:
    "If thou beëst he—but O how fallen! how changed
From him who in the happy realms of light   85
Clothed with transcendent brightness didst outshine
Myriads, though bright! if he whom mutual league,
United thoughts and counsels, equal hope
And hazard in the glorious enterprise,
Joined with me once, now misery hath joined   90
In equal ruin; into what pit thou seest[2]
From what height fallen, so much the stronger proved
He with his thunder:[3] and till then who knew

3. As far as angels can see.
4. Omitting the verb conveys abruptly the paradox: fire-without-light.
5. The phrase echoes an expression in Dante ("All hope abandon, ye who enter here"), but Milton expresses it as a logical absurdity. Hope comes to "all" but not to Helldwellers; they are not included in "all."
6. Afflicts.
7. "Complete" but also "outer."
8. The earth. Milton makes use in *Paradise Lost* of two images of the cosmos: (1) the earth is the center of the *created* (Ptolemaic) cosmos of ten concentric spheres; but (2) the earth and the whole created cosmos are a mere appendage, hanging from Heaven by a golden chain, in the larger, aboriginal, and less shapely cosmos. In the present passage, the fall from Heaven to Hell (through the aboriginal universe) is described as thrice as far as the distance (in the created universe) from the center (earth) to the outermost sphere.
9. A Phoenician deity, or Baal (the name means "Lord of flies"); traditionally, a prince of devils and enemy of Jehovah. The Phoenician Baal, a sun god, had many aspects and so many names; most Baals were nature deities. But in the poem's time scheme all this lies in the future; Beelzebub's angelic name, whatever it was, has been erased from the Book of Life, and as he has not yet got another one, he must be called by the name he will have later on.
1. In Hebrew, the name means "Adversary."
2. Satan's syntax, like that of a man recovering from a stunning blow, is not of the clearest.
3. God with his thunderbolts.

The force of those dire arms? Yet not for those,
Nor what the potent Victor in his rage   95
Can else inflict, do I repent or change,
Though changed in outward luster, that fixed mind
And high disdain, from sense of injured merit,
That with the Mightiest raised me to contend,
And to the fierce contention brought along   100
Innumerable force of spirits armed,
That durst dislike his reign, and me preferring,
His utmost power with adverse power opposed
In dubious battle on the plains of Heaven,
And shook his throne. What though the field be lost?   105
All is not lost: the unconquerable will,
And study[4] of revenge, immortal hate,
And courage never to submit or yield:
And what is else not to be overcome?[5]
That glory never shall his wrath or might   110
Extort from me. To bow and sue for grace
With suppliant knee, and deify his power[6]
Who from the terror of this arm so late
Doubted[7] his empire—that were low indeed;
That were an ignominy and shame beneath   115
This downfall; since, by fate, the strength of gods[8]
And this empyreal substance cannot fail;
Since, through experience of this great event,
In arms not worse, in foresight much advanced,
We may with more successful hope resolve   120
To wage by force or guile eternal war,
Irreconcilable to our grand Foe,
Who now triùmphs, and in th' excess of joy
Sole reigning holds the tyranny[9] of Heaven."
    So spake th' apostate angel, though in pain,   125
Vaunting aloud, but racked with deep despair;
And him thus answered soon his bold compeer:[1]
    "O prince, O chief of many thronèd powers,
That led th' embattled seraphim[2] to war
Under thy conduct, and in dreadful deeds   130
Fearless, endangered Heaven's perpetual King,
And put to proof his high supremacy,

---

4. Pursuit.
5. I.e., what else does it mean not to be beaten?
"That glory" is the glory of hearing Satan confess
himself overcome.
6. I.e., deify the power of him who. Milton sometimes writes English as if it were an inflected language.
7. Feared for. In the next line, "ignominy" is pronounced "ignomy."
8. The essence of Satan's fault is his claim to the
position of a god, subject to fate but to nothing
else. His substance is "empyreal" (heavenly, from
the empyrean), and cannot be destroyed; but, as

he learns in the poem, it can be confounded by
God's greater power and weakened by its own corruption and self-contradictions. "Fail": cease to
exist.
9. The accusation is bold, but one of the aims of
the poem is to show that Satan is a tyrant and God
is not.
1. Comrade and equal
2. According to tradition, there were nine orders
of angels—seraphim, cherubim, thrones, dominions, virtues, powers, principalities, archangels, and
angels; but Milton does not use these systematic
categories systematically.

Whether upheld by strength, or chance, or fate![3]
Too well I see and rue the dire event[4]
That with sad overthrow and foul defeat   135
Hath lost us Heaven, and all this mighty host
In horrible destruction laid thus low,
As far as gods and heavenly essences
Can perish: for the mind and spirit remains
Invincible, and vigor soon returns,   140
Though all our glory extinct, and happy state
Here swallowed up in endless misery.
But what if he our Conqueror (whom I now
Of force[5] believe almighty, since no less
Than such could have o'erpowered such force as ours)   145
Have left us this our spirit and strength entire,
Strongly to suffer and support our pains,
That we may so suffice[6] his vengeful ire,
Or do him mightier service as his thralls
By right of war, whate'er his business be,   150
Here in the heart of Hell to work in fire,
Or do his errands in the gloomy deep?
What can it then avail though yet we feel
Strength undiminished, or eternal being
To undergo eternal punishment?"   155
     Whereto with speedy words th' arch-fiend[7] replied:
"Fallen cherub, to be weak is miserable,
Doing or suffering:[8] but of this be sure,
To do aught good never will be our task,
But ever to do ill our sole delight,   160
As being the contrary to his high will
Whom we resist. If then his providence
Out of our evil seek to bring forth good,
Our labor must be to pervert that end,
And out of good still to find means of evil;   165
Which ofttimes may succeed, so as perhaps
Shall grieve him, if I fail not,[9] and disturb
His inmost counsels from their destined aim.
But see! the angry Victor hath recalled
His ministers of vengeance and pursuit   170
Back to the gates of Heaven; the sulphurous hail,
Shot after us in storm, o'erblown hath laid
The fiery surge that from the precipice
Of Heaven received us falling; and the thunder,
Winged with red lightning and impetuous rage,   175
Perhaps hath spent his shafts, and ceases now
To bellow through the vast and boundless deep.

3. The devils can conceive of any reason for God's
continuing rule, except goodness and justice.
4. Outcome.
5. Perforce, necessarily.
6. Satisfy.

7. A fiend is an enemy, one who hates; the word
is an antonym of "friend."
8. Whether one is active or passive.
9. "Unless I'm mistaken" (direct from the Latin,
nisi fallor).

Let us not slip[1] th' occasion, whether scorn
Or satiate fury yield it from our Foe.
Seest thou yon dreary plain, forlorn and wild,   180
The seat of desolation, void of light,
Save what the glimmering of these livid flames
Casts pale and dreadful? Thither let us tend
From off the tossing of these fiery waves;
There rest, if any rest can harbor there;   185
And reassembling our afflicted powers,[2]
Consult how we may henceforth most offend
Our enemy, our own loss how repair,
How overcome this dire calamity,
What reinforcement we may gain from hope,   190
If not, what resolution from despair."[3]

    Thus Satan talking to his nearest mate
With head uplift above the wave, and eyes
That sparkling blazed; his other parts besides
Prone on the flood, extended long and large   195
Lay floating many a rood,[4] in bulk as huge
As whom[5] the fables name of monstrous size,
Titanian or Earth-born, that warred on Jove,
Briareos or Typhon,[6] whom the den
By ancient Tarsus held, or that sea beast   200
Leviathan,[7] which God of all his works
Created hugest that swim th' ocean-stream.
Him, haply, slumbering on the Norway foam,
The pilot of some small night-foundered[8] skiff,
Deeming some island, oft, as seamen tell,   205
With fixèd anchor in his scaly rind
Moors by his side under the lee, while night
Invests[9] the sea, and wishèd morn delays:
So stretched out huge in length the arch-fiend lay,
Chained on the burning lake; nor ever thence   210
Had risen or heaved his head, but that the will
And high permission of all ruling Heaven
Left him at large to his own dark designs,
That with reiterated crimes he might
Heap on himself damnation, while he sought   215

1. I.e., let slip.
2. Stricken armies.
3. Of the last nine lines of Satan's speech, no fewer than five rhyme. Milton may have felt the need for something like the couplet with which blank-verse dramatists cut off their scenes.
4. An old unit of measure, between six and eight yards.
5. I.e., as those whom.
6. Both the Titans, led by Briareos, and the earth-born Giants, represented by Typhon (who lived in Cilicia near Tarsus), fought with Jove. Briareos was said to have a hundred hands, and Typhon a hundred heads; and both were said, by different

authors, to have been punished for their rebellion (like Satan for his) by being thrown into the underworld. Briareos and Typhon are still heard grumbling from time to time under Mt. Etna.
7. The great sea monster of Isaiah 27.1 or Job 41; for Milton and us, simply a whale, but scaly (line 206).
8. Overtaken by darkness.
9. Wraps, covers. The story of sailors mooring to whales was an old one, but the reference to Norway suggests that Milton was thinking of a 16th-century version by Olaus Magnus, the Swedish historian.

Evil to others, and enraged might see
How all his malice served but to bring forth
Infinite goodness, grace, and mercy shown
On man by him seduced, but on himself
Treble confusion, wrath, and vengeance poured.   220
    Forthwith upright he rears from off the pool
His mighty stature; on each hand the flames
Driven backward slope their pointing spires,[1] and rolled
In billows, leave i' th' midst a horrid[2] vale.
Then with expanded wings he steers his flight   225
Aloft, incumbent on[3] the dusky air,
That felt unusual weight; till on dry land
He lights, if it were land that ever burned
With solid, as the lake with liquid fire,
And such appeared in hue; as when the force   230
Of subterranean wind transports a hill
Torn from Pelorus[4] or the shattered side
Of thundering Etna, whose combustible
And fuelèd entrails thence conceiving fire,
Sublimed[5] with mineral fury, aid the winds,   235
And leave a singèd bottom all involved[6]
With stench and smoke: such resting found the sole
Of unblest feet. Him followed his next mate,
Both glorying to have 'scaped the Stygian[7] flood
As gods, and by their own recovered strength,   240
Not by the sufferance[8] of supernal power.
    "Is this the region, this the soil, the clime,"
Said then the lost archangel, "this the seat
That we must change for Heaven? this mournful gloom
For that celestial light? Be it so, since he   245
Who now is sovereign can dispose and bid
What shall be right: farthest from him is best,
Whom reason hath equaled, force hath made supreme
Above his equals.[9] Farewell, happy fields,
Where joy forever dwells! Hail, horrors! hail,   250
Infernal world! and thou, profoundest Hell,
Receive thy new possessor, one who brings
A mind not to be changed by place or time.
The mind is its own place, and in itself
Can make a Heaven of Hell, a Hell of Heaven.[1]   255
What matter where, if I be still the same,

1. Points of flame.
2. Not simply "ghastly," but in the Latin sense,
"bristling."
3. Resting upon.
4. Pelorus and Etna are volcanic mountains in
Sicily, which Milton pictures as exploding under
pressure of underground winds.
5. Vaporized.
6. Wrapped.
7. Of the river Styx, i.e., demonic, hellish.

8. Permission.
9. Satan likes to think that by "reason" he is God's
equal; this only shows how far he is from "right
reason," that is, reason directed and corrected by
a proper sense of religious values.
1. Satan's heroic resolution here, where he fancies he can convert Hell into a kind of plastic
Heaven, takes another turn when in Book 4 we
find him bringing the Hell of his own mind into
Paradise.

And what I should be, all but less[2] than he
Whom thunder hath made greater? Here at least
We shall be free; th' Almighty hath not built
Here for his envy, will not drive us hence.   260
Here we may reign secure; and in my choice
To reign is worth ambition, though in Hell:
Better to reign in Hell than serve in Heaven.
But wherefore let we then our faithful friends,
Th' associates and copartners of our loss,   265
Lie thus astonished[3] on th' oblivious pool,
And call them not to share with us their part
In this unhappy mansion, or once more
With rallied arms to try what may be yet
Regained in Heaven, or what more lost in Hell?"   270
    So Satan spake: and him Beëlzebub
Thus answered: "Leader of those armies bright,
Which but th' Omnipotent none could have foiled!
If once they hear that voice, their liveliest pledge
Of hope in fears and dangers, heard so oft   275
In worst extremes, and on the perilous edge[4]
Of battle when it raged, in all assaults
Their surest signal, they will soon resume
New courage and revive, though now they lie
Groveling and prostrate on yon lake of fire,   280
As we erewhile, astounded and amazed;
No wonder, fallen such a pernicious height!"
    He scarce had ceased when the superior fiend
Was moving toward the shore; his ponderous shield,
Ethereal temper,[5] massy, large, and round,   285
Behind him cast; the broad circumference
Hung on his shoulders like the moon, whose orb
Through optic glass the Tuscan artist[6] views
At evening, from the top of Fesolè,
Or in Valdarno, to descry new lands,   290
Rivers, or mountains in her spotty globe.
His spear, to equal which the tallest pine
Hewn on Norwegian hills, to be the mast
Of some great admiral,[7] were but a wand,
He walked with, to support uneasy steps   295
Over the burning marl,[8] not like those steps
On Heaven's azure; and the torrid clime
Smote on him sore besides, vaulted with fire.

2. Second only to. The expression "all but less than" telescopes "all but equal to" and "only less than."

3. Stunned. The epithet "oblivious" is transferred from the fallen angels to the pool in which they have fallen.

4. Not the fringe of battle but the front line (Latin *acies*).

5. Tempered in celestial fire.

6. Galileo, who looked through a telescope ("optic glass") from the hill town of Fiesole outside Florence in the Val d'Arno, is the only contemporary mentioned by Milton in *Paradise Lost*.

7. Not the naval commander, but his flagship, usually the biggest of the fleet.

8. Soil.

Nathless[9] he so endured, till on the beach
Of that inflamèd[1] sea he stood, and called   300
His legions, angel forms, who lay entranced,
Thick as autumnal leaves that strow the brooks
In Vallombrosa,[2] where th' Etrurian shades
High over-arched embower;[3] or scattered sedge
Afloat, when with fierce winds Orion armed   305
Hath vexed the Red-Sea coast, whose waves o'erthrew
Busiris and his Memphian chivalry,
While with perfidious hatred they pursued
The sojourners of Goshen, who beheld
From the safe shore their floating carcasses   310
And broken chariot wheels;[4] so thick bestrown,
Abject and lost, lay these, covering the flood,
Under amazement of their hideous change.
He called so loud that all the hollow deep
Of Hell resounded: "Princes, potentates,   315
Warriors, the flower of Heaven, once yours, now lost,
If such astonishment as this can seize
Eternal spirits! or have ye chosen this place
After the toil of battle to repose
Your wearied virtue,[5] for the ease you find   320
To slumber here, as in the vales of Heaven?
Or in this abject posture have ye sworn
To adore the Conqueror, who now beholds
Cherub and seraph rolling in the flood
With scattered arms and ensigns,[6] till anon   325
His swift pursuers from Heaven-gates discern
Th' advantage, and descending tread us down
Thus drooping, or with linkèd thunderbolts
Transfix us to the bottom of this gulf?
Awake, arise, or be forever fallen!"   330
    They heard, and were abashed, and up they sprung
Upon the wing, as when men wont to watch
On duty, sleeping found by whom they dread,
Rouse and bestir themselves ere well awake.
Nor did they not perceive[7] the evil plight   335
In which they were, or the fierce pains not feel;
Yet to their general's voice they soon obeyed
Innumerable. As when the potent rod

9. A compressed, archaic form of "nonetheless."
1. Flaming, of course, but also fevered.
2. "Shady Valley," high in the Apennines about twenty miles from Florence, "Etruria" is Etruscan land, i.e., Tuscany.
3. I.e., form bowers by enclosing space.
4. Orion is a constellation, whose rising near sunset in late summer and autumn was associated with storms; in the Red Sea, where sedge grows thick, these storms result in much floating seaweed. This reminds Milton of how the sea must have looked after the Israelites ("sojourners of Goshen") passed through it while escaping from Egypt, when it was covered with the littered corpses of Pharaoh ("Busiris") and his pursuing horsemen ("Memphian chivalry").
5. Strength, but Satan's sarcasm makes use of the other connotation too.
6. Standards, battle flags.
7. The double negatives make a positive: they did indeed perceive both plight and pains. (Latin, *neque non*, "nor . . . not," "and.")

Of Amram's son[8] in Egypt's evil day
Waved round the coast, up called a pitchy cloud   340
Of locusts, warping[9] on the eastern wind,
That o'er the realm of impious Pharaoh hung
Like night, and darkened all the land of Nile;
So numberless were those bad angels seen
Hovering on wing under the cope[1] of Hell   345
'Twixt upper, nether, and surrounding fires;
Till, as a signal given, th' uplifted spear
Of their great sultan[2] waving to direct
Their course, in even balance down they light
On the firm brimstone, and fill all the plain;   350
A multitude like which the populous North[3]
Poured never from her frozen loins to pass
Rhene or the Danaw, when her barbarous sons
Came like a deluge on the South, and spread
Beneath Gibraltar to the Libyan sands.   355
    Forthwith from every squadron and each band
The heads and leaders thither haste where stood
Their great commander; godlike shapes and forms
Excelling human; princely dignities,
And powers that erst in Heaven sat on thrones,   360
Though of their names in Heavenly records now
Be no memorial, blotted out and rased[4]
By their rebellion from the Books of Life.
Nor had they yet among the sons of Eve
Got them new names, till, wandering o'er the earth,   365
Through God's high sufferance for the trial of man,
By falsities and lies the greatest part
Of mankind they corrupted to forsake
God their Creator, and th' invisible
Glory of him that made them to transform   370
Oft to the image of a brute, adorned
With gay religions[5] full of pomp and gold,
And devils to adore for deities:
Then were they known to men by various names,
And various idols through the heathen world.   375
    Say, Muse, their names then known, who first, who last,[6]
Roused from the slumber on that fiery couch,
At their great emperor's call, as next in worth

8. Moses, who drew down a plague of locusts on
Egypt (Exodus 10.12–15). Milton's learned locution is designed to keep Moses out of Hell, as well
as from appearing too often in the poem (compare
above, 307–11).
9. Floating.
1. Roof.
2. A first use of the image, which will be reinforced later, of Satan as an Oriental despot.
3. The barbarian invasions of falling Rome began

with crossings of the Rhine ("Rhene") and Danube ("Danaw") Rivers, and spread across Spain,
via Gibraltar, to North Africa.
4. Erased. See above, line 81. Though reluctant
to state the view strongly, Milton believed all the
pagan deities had been devils in disguise.
5. Ceremonies.
6. The catalogue of gods here is an epic convention; Homer catalogues ships, Virgil warriors.

Came singly[7] where he stood on the bare strand,
While the promiscuous crowd stood yet aloof.   380
    The chief were those who, from the pit of Hell
Roaming to seek their prey on Earth, durst fix
Their seats, long after, next the seat of God,[8]
Their altars by his altar, gods adored
Among the nations round, and durst abide   385
Jehovah thundering out of Sion, throned
Between the cherubim; yea, often placed
Within his sanctuary itself their shrines,
Abominations; and with cursèd things
His holy rites and solemn feasts profaned,   390
And with their darkness durst affront his light.
First Moloch,[9] horrid king, besmeared with blood
Of human sacrifice, and parents' tears;
Though, for the noise of drums and timbrels loud,
Their children's cries unheard, that passed through fire   395
To his grim idol. Him the Ammonite[1]
Worshiped in Rabba and her watery plain,
In Argob and in Basan, to the stream
Of utmost Arnon. Nor content with such
Audacious neighborhood, the wisest heart   400
Of Solomon he led by fraud to build
His temple right against the temple of God
On that opprobrious hill,[2] and made his grove
The pleasant valley of Hinnom, Tophet thence
And black Gehenna called, the type of Hell.   405
Next Chemos,[3] th' obscene dread of Moab's sons,
From Aroar to Nebo and the wild
Of southmost Abarim; in Hesebon
And Horonaim, Seon's realm, beyond
The flowery dale of Sibma clad with vines,   410
And Elealè to th' asphaltic pool:
Peor[4] his other name, when he enticed
Israel in Sittim, on their march from Nile,
To do him wanton rites, which cost them woe.

---

7. One at a time. The diabolical aristocrats rally round Satan, while the "promiscuous crowd," the vulgar devils, stand apart.
8. The first group of devils come from the Near East, close neighbors and intimate enemies of Jehovah at Jerusalem.
9. A sun god, sometimes represented as a roaring bull or with a calf's head, within whose brazen image living children might be burned as sacrifices (for a lurid fictional account, see Flaubert's *Salammbô*). "Timbrels": tambourines.
1. The Ammonites lived east of the Jordan, and Milton uses uncouth place names ("Rabba," "Argob," "Basan," "utmost Arnon") to suggest wildness.

2. The rites of Moloch on "that opprobrious hill" (the Mount of Olives) right opposite the Jewish temple, and in the valley of Hinnom, so polluted these places that they were turned into the refuse dump of Jerusalem. Thus they became "types" (analogies) of Hell, under the names "Tophet" and "Gehenna."
3. Chemos or Chemosh was another name for Moloch, used in Moab, a nation lying south and east of the Dead Sea ("th' asphaltic pool"). Many of the geographical names clustered here come from Isaiah 15–16.
4. For the story of how Peor seduced "Israel in Sittim," see Numbers 25.

Yet thence his lustful orgies he enlarged   415
Even to that hill of scandal, by the grove
Of Moloch homicide,[5] lust hard by hate,
Till good Josiah drove them thence to Hell.
With these came they who, from the bordering flood
Of old Euphrates to the brook that parts   420
Egypt from Syrian ground,[6] had general names
Of Baalim and Ashtaroth, those male,
These feminine.[7] For spirits when they please
Can either sex assume, or both; so soft
And uncompounded is their essence pure,   425
Not tied or manacled with joint or limb,
Nor founded on the brittle strength of bones,
Like cumbrous flesh; but in what shape they choose,
Dilated or condensed, bright or obscure,
Can execute their airy purposes,   430
And works of love or enmity fulfill.
For those the race of Israel oft forsook
Their Living Strength,[8] and unfrequented left
His righteous altar, bowing lowly down
To bestial gods; for which their heads as low   435
Bowed down in battle, sunk before the spear
Of despicable foes. With these in troop
Came Astoreth, whom the Phoenicians called
Astartè, queen of heaven, with crescent horns;
To whose bright image nightly by the moon   440
Sidonian virgins[9] paid their vows and songs;
In Sion also not unsung, where stood
Her temple on th' offensive mountain,[1] built
By that uxorious king[2] whose heart, though large,
Beguiled by fair idolatresses, fell   445
To idols foul. Thammuz[3] came next behind,
Whose annual wound in Lebanon allured
The Syrian damsels to lament his fate
In amorous ditties all a summer's day,
While smooth Adonis[4] from his native rock   450
Ran purple to the sea, supposed with blood
Of Thammuz yearly wounded: the love-tale

---

5. An epithet was often joined to a god's name as
a surname (e.g., *Jupiter Tonans*, Jove the Thunderer); Milton's epithet involves almost a parody,
Moloch the Mankiller. The story of "good Josiah"
and his campaign against pagan gods is told in 2
Kings 23 and in 2 Chronicles 34.
6. Palestine lies between the Euphrates and "the
brook Besor" (1 Samuel 30.10).
7. I.e., plural forms, masculine and feminine
respectively, for Baal and Astarte. As Baals were
aspects of the sun god, Astartes (Ishtars) were manifestations of the moon goddess.
8. The Jews lost battles, Milton says, when they
neglected Jehovah.

9. Sidon and Tyre were the chief cities of Phoeni-
cia.
1. The Mount of Olives again (see above, lines
403 and 416).
2. Solomon, who "loved many strange women"
(2 Kings 11.1–8).
3. A Syrian god, who was supposed to have been
killed by a boar in Lebanon; annual festivals
mourned his death and celebrated his revival, imitating the cycle of vegetable life. In his Greek form
he was Adonis, god of the solar year.
4. A Lebanese river, named after the deity because
every spring it turned blood-red with sedimentary
mud.

Infected Sion's daughters with like heat,
Whose wanton passions in the sacred porch
Ezekiel[5] saw, when, by the vision led,   455
His eye surveyed the dark idolatries
Of alienated Judah. Next came one
Who mourned in earnest, when the captive ark
Maimed his brute image, head and hands lopped off
In his own temple, on the grunsel-edge,[6]   460
Where he fell flat, and shamed his worshipers:
Dagon his name, sea monster, upward man
And downward fish; yet had his temple high
Reared in Azotus, dreaded through the coast
Of Palestine, in Gath and Ascalon,   465
And Accaron and Gaza's frontier bounds.[7]
Him followed Rimmon, whose delightful seat
Was fair Damascus, on the fertile banks
Of Abbana and Pharphar, lucid streams.
He also 'gainst the house of God was bold: 470
A leper once he lost, and gained a king,
Ahaz,[8] his sottish conqueror, whom he drew
God's altar to disparage and displace
For one of Syrian mode, whereon to burn
His odious offerings, and adore the gods   475
Whom he had vanquished. After these appeared
A crew who, under names of old renown,
Osiris, Isis, Orus,[9] and their train,
With monstrous shapes[1] and sorceries abused
Fanatic Egypt and her priests to seek   480
Their wandering gods disguised in brutish forms
Rather than human. Nor did Israel 'scape
Th' infection, when their borrowed gold composed
The calf in Oreb;[2] and the rebel king
Doubled that sin in Bethel and in Dan,   485
Likening his Maker to the grazèd ox[3]—
Jehovah, who in one night when he passed
From Egypt marching, equaled[4] with one stroke

---

5. Ezekiel complained that the Jewish women of his day were worshiping Thammuz (Ezekiel 8.14).
6. When the Philistines stole the ark of God, they tried to store it in the temple of their sea god, Dagon; but in the morning the mutilated statue of Dagon was found on the threshold ("grunsel-edge"). See 1 Samuel 5.1–5.
7. Milton names the five chief cities of the Philistines as places where Dagon was worshiped.
8. A Syrian general, Naaman, was cured of leprosy and converted from worship of Rimmon by the waters of the Jordan (2 Kings 5). King Ahaz, on the other hand, an Israelite monarch who conquered Damascus, was converted there to worship of Rimmon (2 Kings 16).
9. The second group of devils includes those from

Egypt, driven in terror from heaven by the revolt of the giants (so Ovid tells us in *Metamorphoses* 5), and forced to wander through Egypt in animal disguises.
1. Monstrous, because often represented with animals' heads.
2. Aaron made a golden calf in the wilderness (Exodus 32); Milton thought it an idol of the Egyptian god Apis because the gold of which it was made had been borrowed from the Egyptians.
3. Jeroboam, "the rebel king," doubled Aaron's sin by making *two* golden calves (1 Kings 12.28–30).
4. Leveled. See Exodus 12.12 for Jehovah's vengeance on the first-born of Egypt and their gods.

Both her first-born and all her bleating gods.
Belial[5] came last; than whom a spirit more lewd   490
Fell not from Heaven, or more gross to love
Vice for itself. To him no temple stood
Or altar smoked; yet who more oft than he
In temples and at altars, when the priest
Turns atheist, as did Eli's sons,[6] who filled   495
With lust and violence the house of God?
In courts and palaces he also reigns,
And in luxurious cities, where the noise
Of riot ascends above their loftiest towers,
And injury and outrage; and when night   500
Darkens the streets, then wander forth the sons
Of Belial, flown[7] with insolence and wine.
Witness the streets of Sodom,[8] and that night
In Gibeah, when the hospitable door
Exposed a matron, to avoid worse rape.   505
    These were the prime in order and in might;
The rest were long to tell, though far renowned,
Th' Ionian gods, of Javan's issue held
Gods, yet confessed later than Heaven and Earth,
Their boasted parents;[9] Titan, Heaven's first-born,   510
With his enormous brood, and birthright seized
By younger Saturn; he from mightier Jove,
His own and Rhea's son, like measure found;
So Jove usurping reigned.[1] These, first in Crete
And Ida known, thence on the snowy top   515
Of cold Olympus ruled the middle air,
Their highest heaven; or on the Delphian cliff,
Or in Dodona, and through all the bounds
Of Doric land; or who with Saturn old
Fled over Adria to th' Hesperian fields,   520
And o'er the Celtic roamed the utmost isles.
    All these and more came flocking; but with looks
Downcast and damp,[2] yet such wherein appeared

5. Belial was never worshiped as a god; his name was originally an abstract noun meaning "wickedness"; hence used mainly in set phrases like "sons of Belial." He comes last, because weak and slothful.
6. The misdeeds of Eli's sons, and the epithet "sons of Belial" applied to them, will be found in 1 Samuel 2.12–17.
7. Flushed. Puritans liked to call their enemies sons of Belial; this passage, with its present tense verbs, may reflect Milton's view of Restoration London.
8. In Sodom and Gibeah ancient outrages befell, described in Genesis 19 and Judges 19.
9. The Titans were regarded as gods by the Greeks ("Javan's issue," i.e., offspring of Javan, son of Japhet, son of Noah), but were admittedly created later than Heaven and Earth (Uranus and Ge),

whose children they were said to be. Milton's Christian humanism naturally led him, wherever possible, to use classic myths as analogues (parallels or reflections) of Christian history.
1. Cronos or Saturn, one of the Titans, deposed his elder brother, married his sister Rhea, and ruled until Zeus, who had been reared in secret on Mt. Ida in Crete, overthrew his own father and came to rule on Mt. Olympus. The Olympic gods, headed by Zeus, were also worshiped in Delphi, Dodona, and throughout the "Doric (Grecian) land." Meanwhile Saturn (lines 519–21), after his downfall, fled across the Adriatic Sea ("Adria") to Italy ("th' Hesperian fields"), crossed "the Celtic" (fields) of France, and finally reached Britain ("the utmost isles").
2. Depressed.

Obscure some glimpse of joy, to have found their chief
Not in despair, to have found themselves not lost   525
In loss itself; which on his countenance cast
Like doubtful hue.[3] But he, his wonted pride
Soon recollecting, with high words that bore
Semblance of worth, not substance, gently raised
Their fainting courage, and dispelled their fears: 530
Then straight commands that at the warlike sound
Of trumpets loud and clarions[4] be upreared
His mighty standard. That proud honor claimed
Azazel[5] as his right, a cherub tall:
Who forthwith from the glittering staff unfurled   535
Th' imperial ensign; which, full high advanced,
Shone like a meteor streaming to the wind,
With gems and golden luster rich emblazed,
Seraphic arms and trophies; all the while
Sonorous metal[6] blowing martial sounds: 540
At which the universal host up sent
A shout that tore Hell's concave,[7] and beyond
Frighted the reign of Chaos and old Night.[8]
All in a moment through the gloom were seen
Ten thousand banners rise into the air,   545
With orient[9] colors waving: with them rose
A forest huge of spears; and thronging helms
Appeared, and serried[1] shields in thick array
Of depth immeasurable. Anon they move
In perfect phalanx to the Dorian[2] mood   550
Of flutes and soft recorders; such as raised
To height of noblest temper heroes old
Arming to battle, and instead of rage
Deliberate valor breathed, firm and unmoved
With dread of death to flight or foul retreat;   555
Nor wanting power to mitigate and swage[3]
With solemn touches troubled thoughts, and chase
Anguish and doubt and fear and sorrow and pain
From mortal or immortal minds. Thus they,
Breathing united force with fixèd thought,   560
Moved on in silence to soft pipes that charmed
Their painful steps o'er the burnt soil. And now
Advanced in view they stand, a horrid[4] front

---

3. Their comfort is the chilly one of finding themselves not completely annihilated; and at first it is
reflected in Satan's face.
4. Small, shrill, treble trumpets.
5. Among the historians of angels and devils, a
traditional diabolic leader.
6. Reverberant trumpets.
7. Vault.
8. Disorder and darkness, the first materials of the
cosmos, still maintain a kingdom between Heaven

and Hell.
9. Lustrous, like the colors of a pearl.
1. Locked together.
2. Severe, simple. The shrill trumpet, which first
roused the courage of the devils, now gives way to
firm, martial tones, played on instruments of softer
timbre, in the Spartan manner.
3. Assuage.
4. Bristling.

Of dreadful length and dazzling arms, in guise
Of warriors old with ordered spear and shield,   565
Awaiting what command their mighty chief
Had to impose. He through the armèd files
Darts his experienced eye, and soon traverse[5]
The whole battalion views, their order due,
Their visages and stature as of gods;   570
Their number last he sums. And now his heart
Distends with pride, and hardening in his strength
Glories: for never, since created man,[6]
Met such embodied force as named with these
Could merit more than that small infantry   575
Warred on by cranes:[7] though all the giant brood
Of Phlegra with th' heroic race were joined
That fought at Thebes and Ilium, on each side
Mixed with auxiliar[8] gods; and what resounds
In fable or romance of Uther's son,   580
Begirt with British and Armoric knights;
And all who since, baptized or infidel,
Jousted in Aspramont or Montalban,
Damasco, or Marocco, or Trebisond;
Or whom Biserta sent from Afric shore   585
When Charlemagne with all his peerage fell
By Fontarabbia.[9] Thus far these beyond
Compare of mortal prowess, yet observed[1]
Their dread commander. He above the rest
In shape and gesture proudly eminent   590
Stood like a tower. His form had yet not lost
All her[2] original brightness, nor appeared
Less than archangel ruined, and th' excess
Of glory obscured: as when the sun new-risen
Looks through the horizontal[3] misty air   595
Shorn of his beams, or from behind the moon
In dim eclipse[4] disastrous twilight sheds
On half the nations, and with fear of change
Perplexes monarchs. Darkened so, yet shone
Above them all th' archangel; but his face   600

5. Across. Satan glances, like a reviewing officer, down the files and columns.
6. I.e., since the creation of man.
7. The pygmies had periodic fights with the cranes, which (according to Pliny) they won by riding to battle on pigs and goats. This would make them cavalry; but Milton wanted the pun on "infants." His idea is that, compared with the devils, all other armies that ever were would look puny.
8. Allied.
9. The Giants of Greek mythology were born at Phlegra (line 577); Milton imagines them joined with the Seven who fought against Thebes, and the whole Greek host that besieged Troy ("Ilium"), plus the various gods who helped on both sides.

He even adds the knights "British or Armoric" (from Brittany) who fought with King Arthur ("Uther's son"), and includes a list of proper names taken from the cycles of romance and suggesting vast, remote armies. Fontarabbia, the best known, was reputed to be the scene of Roland's last stand in the *Chanson de Roland*; Milton thus mingles the fall of Charlemagne with that of his best-known knight.
1. Obeyed.
2. *Forma*, in Latin, is feminine; hence "her."
3. The rays of the sun as it first rises are almost horizontal.
4. Time of ill omen. "Disastrous": threatening disaster.

Deep scars of thunder had intrenched, and care
Sat on his faded cheek, but under brows
Of dauntless courage, and considerate[5] pride
Waiting revenge. Cruel his eye, but cast
Signs of remorse and passion[6] to behold   605
The fellows of his crime, the followers rather
(Far other once beheld in bliss), condemned
Forever now to have their lot in pain;
Millions of spirits for his fault amerced[7]
Of Heaven, and from eternal splendors flung   610
For his revolt; yet faithful how they stood,
Their glory withered; as when Heaven's fire
Hath scathed the forest oaks or mountain pines,
With singèd top their stately growth, though bare,
Stands on the blasted heath. He now prepared   615
To speak; whereat their doubled ranks they bend
From wing to wing, and half enclose him round
With all his peers: attention held them mute.
Thrice he essayed, and thrice, in spite of scorn,
Tears such as angels weep burst forth; at last   620
Words interwove with sighs found out their way:
     "O myriads of immortal spirits! O powers
Matchless, but with th' Almighty!—and that strife
Was not inglorious, though th' event[8] was dire,
As this place testifies, and this dire change,   625
Hateful to utter. But what power of mind,
Foreseeing or presaging, from the depth
Of knowledge past or present, could have feared
How such united force of gods, how such
As stood like these, could ever know repulse?   630
For who can yet believe, though after loss,
That all these puissant[9] legions, whose exile
Hath emptied Heaven, shall fail to reascend,
Self-raised, and repossess their native seat?
For me, be witness all the host of Heaven,   635
If counsels different,[1] or danger shunned
By me, have lost our hopes. But he who reigns
Monarch in Heaven, till then as one secure
Sat on his throne, upheld by old repute,
Consent or custom, and his regal state   640
Put forth at full, but still his strength concealed,
Which tempted our attempt,[2] and wrought our fall.
Henceforth his might we know, and know our own,
So as not either to provoke or dread

5. Thoughtful, conscious.
6. Compassion.
7. Deprived.
8. Outcome, result.
9. Potent, powerful.

1. Contradictory or even selfish, but also, in an obsolete sense, delaying.
2. Satan is an inveterate punster and player on words.

New war provoked: our better part remains   645
To work in close design,[3] by fraud or guile,
What force effected not; that he no less
At length from us may find, who overcomes
By force hath overcome but half his foe.
Space may produce new worlds; whereof so rife   650
There went a fame[4] in Heaven that he ere long
Intended to create, and therein plant
A generation whom his choice regard
Should favor equal to the sons of Heaven.
Thither, if but to pry, shall be perhaps   655
Our first eruption—thither, or elsewhere;
For this infernal pit shall never hold
Celestial spirits in bondage, nor th' abyss
Long under darkness cover. But these thoughts
Full counsel must mature. Peace is despaired,   660
For who can think submission? War, then, war
Open or understood,[5] must be resolved."
        He spake; and, to confirm his words, out flew
Millions of flaming swords, drawn from the thighs
Of mighty cherubim; the sudden blaze   665
Far round illumined Hell. Highly they raged
Against the Highest, and fierce with graspèd arms,
Clashed on their sounding shields the din of war,[6]
Hurling defiance toward the vault of Heaven.
        There stood a hill not far, whose grisly[7] top   670
Belched fire and rolling smoke; the rest entire
Shone with a glossy scurf,[8] undoubted sign
That in his womb was hid metallic ore,
The work of sulphur.[9] Thither, winged with speed,
A numerous brìgade hastened: as when bands   675
Of pioneers[1] with spade and pickax armed
Forerun the royal camp, to trench a field
Or cast a rampart. Mammon led them on,
Mammon, the least erected[2] spirit that fell
From Heaven; for even in Heaven his looks and thoughts   680
Were always downward bent, admiring more
The riches of Heaven's pavement, trodden gold,
Than aught divine or holy else enjoyed
In vision beatific. By him first
Men also, and by his suggestion taught,   685
Ransacked the center, and with impious hands
Rifled the bowels of their mother Earth

---

3. I.e., our best choice is to achieve by secret schemes.
4. Rumor. "Rife": common.
5. Agreed-upon, tacit, hence secret.
6. Like Roman legionaries, the fallen angels applaud by beating swords on shields.
7. Horrible.
8. Crust.
9. Suphur and mercury were considered the basic substances of all metals.
1. Sappers, engineers.
2. Elevated. Mammon is not a god but an abstract word meaning "wealth"; cf. Belial.

For treasures better hid. Soon had his crew
Opened into the hill a spacious wound
And digged out ribs[3] of gold. Let none admire   690
That riches grow in Hell; that soil may best
Deserve the precious bane. And here let those
Who boast in mortal things, and wondering tell
Of Babel, and the works of Memphian kings,
Learn how their greatest monuments of fame   695
And strength and art are easily outdone
By spirits reprobate,[4] and in an hour
What in an age they with incessant toil
And hands innumerable scarce perform.
Nigh on the plain, in many cells prepared,   700
That underneath had veins of liquid fire
Sluiced from the lake, a second multitude
With wondrous art founded the massy ore,
Severing each kind, and scummed the bullion-dross.
A third as soon had formed within the ground   705
A various mold, and from the boiling cells
By strange conveyance filled each hollow nook:[5]
As in an organ, from one blast of wind
To many a row of pipes the soundboard breathes.
Anon out of the earth a fabric huge   710
Rose like an exhalation, with the sound
Of dulcet symphonies and voices sweet,
Built like a temple, where pilasters[6] round
Were set, and Doric pillars[7] overlaid
With golden architrave; nor did there want   715
Cornice or frieze, with bossy[8] sculptures graven;
The roof was fretted[9] gold. Not Babylon
Nor great Alcairo such magnificence
Equaled in all their glories,[1] to enshrine
Belus or Serapis their gods, or seat   720
Their kings, when Egypt with Assyria strove
In wealth and luxury. Th' ascending pile
Stood fixed[2] her stately height; and straight the doors
Opening their brazen folds discover, wide
Within, her ample spaces o'er the smooth   725
And level pavement: from the archèd roof,
Pendent by subtle magic, many a row
Of starry lamps and blazing cressets[3] fed

3. Bars, of course, but also suggesting golden-haired Eve, who was a "precious bane" (sweet poison) dug out of Adam's side. "Admire": wonder.
4. The tower of Babel and the Pyramids of Egypt ("works of Memphian kings") are easily outdone by the devils ("spirits reprobate").
5. After melting the gold with fire from the lake and pouring it into molds, the devils cause their building to rise by a sort of spiritual-musical magic.
6. Columns set in a wall.
7. Doric pillars are severe and plain.
8. Embossed.
9. Patterned.
1. At Babylon in Assyria there were temples to "Belus" or Baal; at Alcairo (modern Cairo, ancient Memphis) in Egypt, they were to Osiris, one of whose names was Serapis (here, but not ordinarily, accented on the first syllable).
2. Complete. "Straight": straightway.
3. Basketlike lamps, hung from the ceiling.

With naphtha and asphaltus yielded light
As from a sky. The hasty multitude   730
Admiring entered; and the work some praise,
And some the architect. His hand was known
In Heaven by many a towered structure high,
Where sceptered angels held their residence,
And sat as princes, whom the sùpreme King   735
Exalted to such power, and gave to rule,
Each in his hierarchy, the orders bright.
Nor was his name unheard or unadored
In ancient Greece; and in Ausonian land
Men called him Mulciber;[4] and how he fell   740
From Heaven they fabled, thrown by angry Jove
Sheer o'er the crystal battlements: from morn
To noon he fell, from noon to dewy eve,
A summer's day, and with the setting sun
Dropped from the zenith like a falling star,   745
On Lemnos th' Aegean isle. Thus they relate,
Erring;[5] for he with this rebellious rout
Fell long before; nor aught availed him now
To have built in Heaven high towers; nor did he 'scape
By all his engines, but was headlong sent   750
With his industrious crew to build in Hell.
    Meanwhile the wingèd heralds, by command
Of sovereign power, with awful ceremony
And trumpet's sound, throughout the host proclaim
A solemn council forthwith to be held   755
At Pandemonium,[6] the high capital
Of Satan and his peers.[7] Their summons called
From every band and squarèd regiment
By place or choice the worthiest; they anon
With hundreds and with thousands trooping came   760
Attended.[8] All access was thronged, the gates
And porches wide, but chief the spacious hall
(Though like a covered field, where champions bold
Wont ride in armed, and at the soldan's[9] chair
Defied the best of paynim chivalry   765
To mortal combat, or career with lance)
Thick swarmed, both on the ground and in the air,
Brushed with the hiss of rustling wings. As bees
In springtime, when the sun with Taurus[1] rides,
Pour forth their populous youth about the hive   770

---

4. Hephaestus, or Vulcan, was sometimes known
in "Ausonian land" (Italy) by the secondary epithet
of "Mulciber." The story of Jove's tossing him out
of Heaven is told, to the accompaniment of much
Homeric laughter, in *Iliad* 1.
5. Milton tells the story, and gives it six lines of
splendid poetry (740–46), but in the end condemns it as a corrupt version of the Biblical truth.

6. "Pandemonium" (a Miltonic coinage) means
literally "All-Demons"; an inversion of Pantheon,
"All-Gods."
7. Nobility.
8. I.e., each with his bodyguards.
9. Sultan's. "Paynim": pagan.
1. The sun is in the Zodiacal sign of Taurus from
about April 19 to May 20.

In clusters; they among fresh dews and flowers
Fly to and fro, or on the smoothèd plank,
The suburb of their straw-built citadel,
New rubbed with balm, expatiate, and confer[2]
Their state-affairs: so thick the airy crowd   775
Swarmed and were straitened; till, the signal given,
Behold a wonder! They but now who seemed
In bigness to surpass Earth's giant sons,
Now less than smallest dwarfs, in narrow room
Throng numberless—like that pygmean race   780
Beyond the Indian mount;[3] or fairy elves,
Whose midnight revels by a forest side
Or fountain some belated peasant sees,
Or dreams he sees, while overhead the Moon
Sits arbitress,[4] and nearer to the Earth   785
Wheels her pale course; they, on their mirth and dance
Intent, with jocund[5] music charm his ear;
At once with joy and fear his heart rebounds.
Thus incorporeal spirits to smallest forms
Reduced their shapes immense, and were at large,   790
Though without number still, amidst the hall
Of that infernal court. But far within,
And in their own dimensions like themselves,
The great seraphic lords and cherubim
In close recess and secret conclave sat,   795
A thousand demigods on golden seats,
Frequent and full.[6] After short silence then,
And summons read, the great consult began.

Book 2

The Argument

The consultation begun, Satan debates whether another battle be to
be hazarded for the recovery of Heaven: some advise it, others dissuade.
A third proposal is preferred, mentioned before by Satan—to search the
truth of that prophecy or tradition in Heaven concerning another world,
and another kind of creature, equal or not much inferior to themselves,
about this time to be created. Their doubt who shall be sent on this
difficult search; Satan, their chief, undertakes alone the voyage; is honored and applauded. The council thus ended, the rest betake them several ways and to several employments, as their inclinations lead them,
to entertain[1] the time till Satan return. He passes on his journey to Hell-

---

2. Spread out and discuss, bring together. The
simile of bees prepares for the sudden contraction
of the devils' size; they can shrink or dilate at will.
3. The pygmies were supposed to live beyond the
Himalayas, "the Indian mount."

4. Witness.
5. Merry.
6. Crowded ("frequent") and in full complement
("full"); all present and accounted for.
1. Pass.

gates; finds them shut, and who sat there to guard them; by whom at
length they are opened, and discover[2] to him the great gulf between Hell
and Heaven; with what difficulty he passes through, directed by Chaos,
the power of that place, to the sight of this new world which he sought.

High on a throne of royal state, which far
Outshone the wealth of Ormus[3] and of Ind,
Or where the gorgeous East with richest hand
Showers on her kings barbaric pearl and gold,
Satan exalted sat, by merit raised   5
To that bad eminence; and from despair
Thus high uplifted beyond hope, aspires
Beyond thus high, insatiate to pursue
Vain war with Heaven; and by success[4] untaught,
His proud imaginations thus displayed: 10
   "Powers and dominions, deities of Heaven!
For since no deep within her gulf can hold
Immortal vigor, though oppressed and fallen,
I give not Heaven for lost: from this descent
Celestial virtues rising will appear   15
More glorious and more dread than from no fall,
And trust themselves to fear no second fate.
Me though just right and the fixed laws of Heaven
Did first create your leader, next, free choice,
With what besides, in council or in fight,   20
Hath been achieved of merit, yet this loss
Thus far at least recovered, hath much more
Established in a safe unenvied throne
Yielded with full consent.[5] The happier state
In Heaven, which follows dignity, might draw   25
Envy from each inferior; but who here
Will envy whom the highest place exposes
Foremost to stand against the Thunderer's aim,
Your bulwark, and condemns to greatest share
Of endless pain? Where there is then no good   30
For which to strive, no strife can grow up there
From faction; for none sure will claim in Hell
Precèdence, none, whose portion is so small
Of present pain, that with ambitious mind
Will covet more. With this advantage then   35
To union and firm faith and firm accord,
More than can be in Heaven, we now return
To claim our just inheritance of old,
Surer to prosper than prosperity

---

2. Disclose.
3. An island in the Persian Gulf, modern Hor-
muz, famous for pearls. "Ind": India.
4. Outcome, result; experience of either sort, good

or bad.
5. He lays claim to the throne by just right, fixed
laws, free choice—and the fact that no one else
will want such a dangerous job.

Could have assured us;[6] and by what best way,   40
Whether of open war or covert guile,
We now debate; who can advise, may speak."
    He ceased, and next him Moloch, sceptered king,
Stood up, the strongest and the fiercest spirit
That fought in Heaven, now fiercer by despair.   45
His trust was with th' Eternal to be deemed
Equal in strength, and rather than be less
Cared not to be at all; with that care lost
Went all his fear: of God, or Hell, or worse
He recked[7] not, and these words thereafter spake: 50
    "My sentence[8] is for open war: of wiles,
More unexpert,[9] I boast not: them let those
Contrive who need, or when they need, not now.
For while they sit contriving, shall the rest,
Millions that stand in arms and longing wait   55
The signal to ascend, sit lingering here
Heaven's fugitives, and for their dwelling place
Accept this dark opprobrious den of shame,
The prison of his tyranny who reigns
By our delay? No! let us rather choose,   60
Armed with Hell-flames and fury, all at once
O'er Heaven's high towers to force resistless way,
Turning our tortures into horrid arms
Against the Torturer; when to meet the noise
Of his almighty engine[1] he shall hear   65
Infernal thunder, and for lightning see
Black fire and horror shot with equal rage
Among his angels, and his throne itself
Mixed with Tartarean[2] sulphur and strange fire,
His own invented torments. But perhaps   70
The way seems difficult and steep to scale
With upright wing against a higher foe.
Let such bethink them, if the sleepy drench[3]
Of that forgetful lake benumb not still,
That in our proper motion[4] we ascend   75
Up to our native seat; descent and fall
To us is adverse. Who but felt of late,
When the fierce foe hung on our broken rear
Insulting,[5] and pursued us through the deep,
With what compulsion and laborious flight   80

6. Note the play on "sure—prosper—prosperity—
assured." An Elizabethan critic famous for his picturesque terminology, George Puttenham, calls this
figure "*epanalepsis*, or the echo sound, otherwise
the slow return." It is a favorite device of Milton's.
7. Cared.
8. Judgment.
9. Inexperienced. Moloch never had to be clever,

and is proud of it.
1. The thunderbolt.
2. Tartarus is a classical name for Hell.
3. A draught of physic, as for animals; hence, used
contemptuously here.
4. Natural impulse.
5. With the Latin sense of stamping or dancing
on.

We sunk thus low? Th' ascent is easy then;
Th' event[6] is feared: should we again provoke
Our stronger,[7] some worse way his wrath may find
To our destruction; if there be in Hell
Fear to be worse destroyed! What can be worse   85
Than to dwell here, driven out from bliss, condemned
In this abhorrèd deep to utter woe;
Where pain of unextinguishable fire
Must exercise us without hope of end,
The vassals[8] of his anger, when the scourge   90
Inexorably, and the torturing hour,
Calls us to penance? More destroyed than thus,
We should be quite abolished, and expire.
What fear we then? What[9] doubt we to incense
His utmost ire? Which, to the height enraged,   95
Will either quite consume us, and reduce
To nothing this essential,[1] happier far
Than miserable to have eternal being!
Or if our substance be indeed divine,
And cannot cease to be, we are at worst   100
On this side nothing;[2] and by proof we feel
Our power sufficient to disturb his Heaven,
And with perpetual inroads to alarm,
Though inaccessible, his fatal throne:
Which, if not victory, is yet revenge."   105
     He ended frowning, and his look denounced
Desperate revenge, and battle dangerous
To less than gods.[3] On th' other side up rose
Belial, in act more graceful and humane;
A fairer person lost not Heaven; he seemed   110
For dignity composed, and high exploit.
But all was false and hollow; though his tongue
Dropped manna,[4] and could make the worse appear
The better reason, to perplex and dash
Maturest counsels: for his thoughts were low,   115
To vice industrious, but to nobler deeds
Timorous and slothful: yet he pleased the ear,
And with persuasive accent thus began:
     "I should be much for open war, O peers,
As not behind in hate, if what was urged   120
Main reason to persuade immediate war
Did not dissuade me most, and seem to cast
Ominous conjecture on the whole success;[5]

6. Outcome.
7. The word "enemy" is understood.
8. Servants, underlings; but perhaps also—or
alternatively—"vessels."
9. Why.
1. Essence.
2. I.e., we are now as badly off as we can be without being nothing, and so need have no fear.
3. Only gods could have withstood Moloch.
4. His tongue was honeyed. To "make the worse
appear / The better reason" was characteristic of
Sophists—mercenary logic-choppers of ancient
Greece. "Dash": confuse.
5. As above, line 9, outcome. "Fact": feat.

When he who most excels in fact of arms,
In what he counsels and in what excels   125
Mistrustful, grounds his courage on despair
And utter dissolution, as the scope
Of all his aim, after some dire revenge.
First, what revenge? The towers of Heaven are filled
With armèd watch, that render all access   130
Impregnable; oft on the bordering deep
Encamp their legions, or with òbscure wing
Scout far and wide into the realm of Night,
Scorning surprise. Or could we break our way
By force, and at our heels all Hell should rise   135
With blackest insurrection, to confound
Heaven's purest light, yet our great enemy
All incorruptible would on his throne
Sit unpolluted, and th' ethereal mold[6]
Incapable of stain would soon expel   140
Her mischief, and purge off the baser fire,
Victorious. Thus repulsed, our final hope
Is flat despair: we must exasperate
Th' almighty Victor to spend all his rage,
And that must end us, that must be our cure,   145
To be no more. Sad cure! for who would lose,
Though full of pain, this intellectual being,
Those thoughts that wander through eternity,
To perish rather, swallowed up and lost
In the wide womb of uncreated Night,   150
Devoid of sense and motion? And who knows,
Let this be good,[7] whether our angry Foe
Can give it, or will ever? How he can
Is doubtful; that he never will is sure.
Will he, so wise, let loose at once his ire,   155
Belike[8] through impotence, or unaware,
To give his enemies their wish, and end
Them in his anger, whom his anger saves
To punish endless? 'Wherefore cease we then?'
Say they who counsel war, 'we are decreed,   160
Reserved and destined to eternal woe;
Whatever doing, what can we suffer more,
What can we suffer worse?' Is this then worst,
Thus sitting, thus consulting, thus in arms?
What when we fled amain,[9] pursued and strook   165
With Heaven's afflicting thunder, and besought
The deep to shelter us? this Hell then seemed
A refuge from those wounds. Or when we lay
Chained on the burning lake? that sure was worse.

---

6. Substance. "Ethereal" substance, derived from "ether," the fifth and purest element, is thought to be incorruptible.

7. I.e., suppose it is good to be destroyed.
8. Ironically, in the sense of "I dare say."
9. Headlong. "Strook": struck.

What if the breath that kindled those grim fires,   170
Awaked, should blow them into sevenfold rage
And plunge us in the flames? or from above
Should intermitted[1] vengeance arm again
His red right hand to plague us? What if all
Her[2] stores were opened, and this firmament   175
Of Hell should spout her cataracts of fire,
Impendent[3] horrors, threatening hideous fall
One day upon our heads; while we perhaps
Designing or exhorting glorious war,
Caught in a fiery tempest shall be hurled,   180
Each on his rock transfixed, the sport and prey
Of racking whirlwinds, or forever sunk
Under yon boiling ocean, wrapped in chains;
There to converse with everlasting groans,
Unrespited, unpitied, unreprieved,   185
Ages of hopeless end! This would be worse.
War therefore, open or concealed, alike
My voice dissuades; for what can force or guile[4]
With him, or who deceive his mind, whose eye
Views all things at one view? He from Heaven's height   190
All these our motions[5] vain sees and derides,
Not more almighty to resist our might
Than wise to frustrate all our plots and wiles.
Shall we then live thus vile, the race of Heaven
Thus trampled, thus expelled to suffer here   195
Chains and these torments? Better these than worse,
By my advice; since fate inevitable
Subdues us, and omnipotent decree,
The Victor's will. To suffer, as to do,
Our strength is equal,[6] nor the law unjust   200
That so ordains: this was at first resolved,
If we were wise, against so great a foe
Contending, and so doubtful what might fall.
I laugh when those who at the spear are bold
And venturous, if that fail them, shrink and fear   205
What yet they know must follow, to endure
Exile, or ignominy, or bonds, or pain,
The sentence of their Conqueror. This is now
Our doom; which if we can sustain and bear,
Our sùpreme Foe in time may much remit   210
His anger, and perhaps, thus far removed,

1. Momentarily suspended.
2. Those of Hell.
3. In the Latin sense, hanging down, threatening.
4. The verb "accomplish" or "achieve" is understood.
5. Proposals, plots.

6. I.e., passive endurance and active energy are both in the devils' power. Belial points out, with dangerous good sense, that they must have known from the beginning that they might have to exercise both (lines 201–3).

Not mind us not offending, satisfied
With what is punished;[7] whence these raging fires
Will slacken, if his breath stir not their flames.
Our purer essence then will overcome   215
Their noxious vapor, or inured[8] not feel,
Or changed at length, and to the place conformed
In temper and in nature, will receive
Familiar the fierce heat, and void of pain;
This horror will grow mild, this darkness light;   220
Besides what hope the never-ending flight
Of future days may bring, what chance, what change
Worth waiting, since our present lot appears
For happy though but ill, for ill not worst,[9]
If we procure not to ourselves more woe."   225
    Thus Belial, with words clothed in reason's garb,
Counseled ignoble ease and peaceful sloth,
Not peace; and after him thus Mammon spake:
    "Either to disenthrone the King of Heaven
We war, if war be best, or to regain   230
Our own right lost: him to unthrone we then
May hope, when everlasting Fate shall yield
To fickle Chance, and Chaos judge the strife.
The former, vain to hope, argues[1] as vain
The latter; for what place can be for us   235
Within Heaven's bound, unless Heaven's Lord supreme
We overpower? Suppose he should relent
And publish grace to all, on promise made
Of new subjection; with what eyes could we
Stand in his presence humble, and receive   240
Strict laws imposed, to celebrate his throne
With warbled hymns, and to his Godhead sing
Forced Halleluiahs; while he lordly sits
Our envied Sovereign, and his altar breathes
Ambrosial odors and ambrosial flowers,   245
Our servile offerings? This must be our task
In Heaven, this our delight; how wearisome
Eternity so spent in worship paid
To whom we hate! Let us not then pursue,
By force impossible, by leave obtained   250
Unàcceptable, though in Heaven, our state
Of spendid vassalage;[2] but rather seek
Our own good from ourselves, and from our own
Live to ourselves, though in this vast recess,
Free, and to none accountable, preferring   255

---

7. A Latinism, *quod punitum est*; God will be satisfied with the punishment that has been inflicted.
8. Accustomed.
9. I.e., from the point of view of happiness, the
devils are but ill off; from the point of view of evil,
they could be worse. This is diabolic relativism.
1. Proves.
2. Servitude.

Hard liberty before the easy yoke
Of servile pomp. Our greatness will appear
Then most conspicuous, when great things of small,
Useful of hurtful, prosperous of adverse,
We can create, and in what place soe'er   260
Thrive under evil, and work ease out of pain
Through labor and endurance. This deep world
Of darkness do we dread? How oft amidst
Thick clouds and dark doth Heaven's all-ruling Sire
Choose to reside, his glory unobscured,   265
And with the majesty of darkness round
Covers his throne; from whence deep thunders roar,
Mustering their rage, and Heaven resembles Hell!
As he our darkness, cannot we his light
Imitate when we please? This desert soil   270
Wants³ not her hidden luster, gems and gold;
Nor want we skill or art, from whence to raise
Magnificence; and what can Heaven show more?
Our torments also may in length of time
Become our elements, these piercing fires   275
As soft as now severe, our temper changed
Into their temper; which must needs remove
The sensible of pain.⁴ All things invite
To peaceful counsels, and the settled state
Of order, how in safety best we may   280
Compose our present evils, with regard
Of what we are and where, dismissing quite
All thoughts of war. Ye have what I advise."
    He scarce had finished, when such murmur filled
Th' assembly, as when hollow rocks retain   285
The sound of blustering winds, which all night long
Had roused the sea, now with hoarse cadence lull
Seafaring men o'erwatched,⁵ whose bark by chance,
Or pinnace, anchors in a craggy bay
After the tempest: such applause was heard   290
As Mammon ended, and his sentence pleased,
Advising peace; for such another field
They dreaded worse than Hell; so much the fear
Of thunder and the sword of Michaël⁶
Wrought still within them; and no less desire   295
To found this nether empire, which might rise
By policy, and long process of time,
In emulation opposite to Heaven.
Which when Beëlzebub perceived, than whom,
Satan except, none higher sat, with grave   300

---

3. Lacks. Mammon proposes a tawdry imitation-
Heaven in Hell; this is the ultimate in diabolic
degradation.
4. The aspect of pain that is apprehended by the

senses; physical pain.
5. Tired out with watching.
6. The warrior angel, chief stay of the angelic
armies.

Aspect he rose, and in his rising seemed
A pillar of state; deep on his front[7] engraven
Deliberation sat and public care;
And princely counsel in his face yet shone,
Majestic though in ruin. Sage he stood   305
With Atlantean[8] shoulders fit to bear
The weight of mightiest monarchies; his look
Drew audience and attention still as night
Or summer's noontide air, while thus he spake:
    "Thrones and imperial powers, offspring of Heaven,   310
Ethereal virtues; or these titles now
Must we renounce, and, changing style, be called
Princes of Hell? For so the popular vote
Inclines, here to continue, and build up here
A growing empire—Doubtless! while we dream,   315
And know not that the King of Heaven hath doomed
This place our dungeon, not our safe retreat
Beyond his potent arm, to live exempt
From Heaven's high jurisdiction, in new league
Banded against his throne, but to remain   320
In strictest bondage, though thus far removed,
Under th' inevitable curb, reserved
His captive multitude. For he, be sure,
In height or depth, still first and last will reign
Sole King, and of his kingdom lose no part   325
By our revolt, but over Hell extend
His empire, and with iron scepter rule
Us here, as with his golden those in Heaven.
What[9] sit we then projecting peace and war?
War hath determined us,[1] and foiled with loss   330
Irreparable; terms of peace yet none
Vouchsafed or sought; for what peace will be given
To us enslaved, but custody severe,
And stripes, and arbitrary punishment
Inflicted? and what peace can we return,   335
But, to our power,[2] hostility and hate,
Untamed reluctance,[3] and revenge, though slow,
Yet ever plotting how the Conqueror least
May reap his conquest, and may least rejoice
In doing what we most in suffering feel?[4]   340
Nor will occasion want, nor shall we need
With dangerous expedition to invade
Heaven, whose high walls fear no assault or siege,
Or ambush from the deep. What if we find

---

7. Forehead, brow.
8. Worthy of Atlas, one of the Titans, who as a
punishment for rebellion was condemned to stand
in North Africa and hold up the heavens.
9. Why.
1. I.e., war has decided the question for (but also,

limited) us.
2. I.e., to the best of our power.
3. Resistance (in the Latin sense, struggling back).
4. How God may get least pleasure from our pain—
a devil's view of the deity.

Some easier enterprise? There is a place   345
(If ancient and prophetic fame[5] in Heaven
Err not), another world, the happy seat
Of some new race called *Man*, about this time
To be created like to us,[6] though less
In power and excellence, but favored more   350
Of him who rules above; so was his will
Pronounced among the gods, and by an oath,
That shook Heaven's whole circumference, confirmed.
Thither let us bend all our thoughts, to learn
What creatures there inhabit, of what mold   355
Or substance, how endued,[7] and what their power,
And where their weakness, how attempted[8] best,
By force or subtlety. Though Heaven be shut,
And Heaven's high Arbitrator sit secure
In his own strength, this place may lie exposed,   360
The utmost border of his kingdom, left
To their defense who hold it;[9] here perhaps
Some advantageous act may be achieved
By sudden onset: either with Hell-fire
To waste[1] his whole creation, or possess   365
All as our own, and drive, as we were driven,
The puny habitants; or if not drive,
Seduce them to our party, that their God
May prove their foe, and with repenting hand
Abolish his own works. This would surpass   370
Common revenge, and interrupt his joy
In our confusion, and our joy upraise
In his disturbance; when his darling sons,
Hurled headlong to partake with us, shall curse
Their frail original,[2] and faded bliss,   375
Faded so soon! Advise if this be worth
Attempting, or to sit in darkness here
Hatching vain empires." Thus Beëlzebub
Pleaded his devilish counsel, first devised
By Satan, and in part proposed; for whence   380
But from the author of all ill could spring
So deep a malice, to confound[3] the race
Of mankind in one root, and Earth with Hell
To mingle and involve, done all to spite
The great Creator? But their spite still serves   385
His glory to augment. The bold design
Pleased highly those infernal states,[4] and joy

---

5. Report, rumor.
6. The created (Ptolemaic) cosmos came into existence only after the fall of Satan, and the fallen angels, being otherwise occupied, could not know of it.
7. Endowed.
8. Attacked, but also "tempted."

9. To be defended by the occupants.
1. Lay waste.
2. Originator, parent; or, perhaps, "their original condition."
3. Destroy, ruin. Adam, the first man, is the "root" of mankind.
4. Estates, territorial dignitaries of Hell.

Sparkled in all their eyes; with full assent
They vote: whereat his speech he thus renews:
     "Well have ye judged, well ended long debate,   390
Synod of gods, and, like to what ye are,
Great things resolved; which from the lowest deep
Will once more lift us up, in spite of Fate,
Nearer our ancient seat; perhaps in view
Of those bright confines, whence with neighboring arms   395
And opportune excursion we may chance
Re-enter Heaven; or else in some mild zone
Dwell not unvisited of Heaven's fair light,
Secure, and at the brightening orient beam
Purge off this gloom; the soft delicious air,   400
To heal the scar of these corrosive fires,
Shall breathe her balm. But first, whom shall we send
In search of this new world? whom shall we find
Sufficient? who shall tempt[5] with wandering feet
The dark unbottomed infinite abyss,   405
And through the palpable obscure find out
His uncouth[6] way, or spread his airy flight
Upborne with indefatigable wings
Over the vast abrupt,[7] ere he arrive
The happy isle?[8] What strength, what art, can then   410
Suffice, or what evasion bear him safe
Through the strict senteries[9] and stations thick
Of angels watching round? Here he had need
All circumspection, and we now no less
Choice in our suffrage;[1] for on whom we send   415
The weight of all, and our last hope, relies."
     This said, he sat; and expectation held
His look suspense,[2] awaiting who appeared
To second, or oppose, or undertake
The perilous attempt; but all sat mute,   420
Pondering the danger with deep thoughts; and each
In others' countenance read his own dismay,
Astonished. None among the choice and prime
Of those Heaven-warring champions could be found
So hardy as to proffer or accept   425
Alone the dreadful voyage; till at last
Satan, whom now transcendent glory raised
Above his fellows, with monarchal pride
Conscious of highest worth, unmoved thus spake:
     "O progeny of Heaven, empyreal thrones!   430

---

5. Attempt, venture upon (from Latin *temptare*). The "palpable obscure" is darkness so thick it can be felt.
6. Unknown.
7. Chaos; a striking example of sound imitating sense.

8. Wherever man is (for the fallen angels do not yet know of Earth).
9. Old spelling of *sentries*, necessary here for the meter.
1. Care in our voting.
2. I.e., everyone sat waiting in suspense.

With reason hath deep silence and demur[3]
Seized us, though undismayed. Long is the way
And hard, that out of Hell leads up to light;
Our prison strong, this huge convex[4] of fire,
Outrageous to devour, immures us round   435
Ninefold,[5] and gates of burning adamant
Barred over us prohibit all egress.
These passed, if any pass, the void profound
Of unessential[6] Night receives him next,
Wide gaping, and with utter loss of being   440
Threatens him, plunged in that abortive gulf.
If thence he 'scape into whatever world,
Or unknown region, what remains him less[7]
Than unknown dangers and as hard escape?
But I should ill become this throne, O peers,   445
And this imperial sovereignty, adorned
With splendor, armed with power, if aught proposed
And judged of public moment,[8] in the shape
Of difficulty or danger, could deter
Me from attempting. Wherefore do I assume   450
These royalties,[9] and not refuse to reign,
Refusing to accept as great a share
Of hazard as of honor, due alike
To him who reigns, and so much to him due
Of hazard more, as he above the rest   455
High honored sits?[1] Go therefore, mighty powers,
Terror of Heaven, though fallen; intend[2] at home,
While here shall be our home, what best may ease
The present misery, and render Hell
More tolerable; if there be cure or charm   460
To respite or deceive or slack the pain
Of this ill mansion; intermit no watch
Against a wakeful foe, while I abroad
Through all the coasts of dark destruction seek
Deliverance for us all: this enterprise   465
None shall partake with me." Thus saying rose
The monarch, and prevented[3] all reply;
Prudent, lest, from his resolution raised,[4]
Others among the chief might offer now
(Certain to be refused) what erst they feared,   470
And so refused might in opinion stand
His rivals, winning cheap the high repute

---

3. Delay.
4. Vault.
5. Walls us in with nine thicknesses. See below, lines 645 ff.
6. Without real being, darkness being merely the absence of light. The "abortive gulf" expresses again this completely negative quality of Chaos and Night.
7. I.e., what awaits him except.
8. Importance.

9. Insignia of royalty. "Refusing": i.e., if I refuse.
1. Satan's argument, simple though entangled in rhetoric, is that rulers must share in the dangers as well as the rewards of an enterprise.
2. Consider.
3. Forestalled, anticipated.
4. After their courage had been raised by his resolution.

Which he through hazard huge must earn. But they
Dreaded not more th' adventure than his voice
Forbidding; and at once with him they rose;   475
Their rising all at once was as the sound
Of thunder heard remote. Towards him they bend
With awful[5] reverence prone; and as a god
Extol him equal to the highest in Heaven.
Nor failed they to express how much they praised,   480
That for the general safety he despised
His own; for neither do the spirits damned
Lose all their virtue; lest bad men should boast
Their specious deeds on Earth, which glory excites,
Or close ambition varnished o'er with zeal.[6]   485
　　Thus they their doubtful consultations dark
Ended, rejoicing in their matchless chief:
As when from mountain tops the dusky clouds
Ascending, while the north wind sleeps, o'erspread
Heaven's cheerful face, the lowering element   490
Scowls o'er the darkened landscape snow or shower;
If chance the radiant sun with farewell sweet
Extend his evening beam, the fields revive,
The birds their notes renew, and bleating herds
Attest their joy, that hill and valley rings.   495
O shame to men! Devil with devil damned
Firm concord holds, men only disagree
Of creatures rational, though under hope
Of heavenly grace; and, God proclaiming peace,[7]
Yet live in hatred, enmity, and strife   500
Among themselves, and levy cruel wars,
Wasting the earth, each other to destroy:
As if (which might induce us to accord)
Man had not hellish foes enow[8] besides,
That day and night for his destruction wait!   505
　　The Stygian council thus dissolved; and forth
In order came the grand infernal peers.
Midst came their mighty paramount,[9] and seemed
Alone th' antagonist of Heaven, nor less
Than Hell's dread emperor, with pomp supreme   510
And godlike imitated state; him round
A globe[1] of fiery seraphim enclosed
With bright emblazonry[2] and horrent arms.
Then of their session ended they bid cry
With trumpets' regal sound the great result: 515
Toward the four winds four speedy cherubim

---

5. Full of respect and awe.
6. The sense is that damned spirits still retain some virtues; lest bad men boast of good deeds they have done out of glory and ambition, Milton has shown us that devils do just as much. "Specious": pretending virtue. "Close": secret.
7. I.e., though God proclaims peace.
8. I.e., enough; the old plural emphatic form.
9. Champion, chief.
1. Band or crowd.
2. Decorated shields. "Horrent": bristling.

Put to their mouths the sounding alchemy[3]
By herald's voice explained; the hollow abyss
Heard far and wide, and all the host of Hell
With deafening shout returned them loud acclaim.   520
Thence more at ease their minds and somewhat raised
By false presumptuous hope, the rangèd[4] powers
Disband; and wandering, each his several way
Pursues, as inclination or sad choice
Leads him perplexed where he may likeliest find   525
Truce to his restless thoughts, and entertain
The irksome hours, till his great chief return.
Part on the plain, or in the air sublime[5]
Upon the wing, or in swift race contend,
As at th' Olympian games or Pythian fields;[6]   530
Part curb their fiery steeds, or shun the goal
With rapid wheels, or fronted brìgades form.
As when to warn proud cities war appears
Waged in the troubled sky, and armies rush
To battle in the clouds;[7] before each van   535
Prick forth the airy knights, and couch their spears
Till thickest legions close; with feats of arms
From either end of Heaven the welkin[8] burns.
Others with vast Typhoean[9] rage more fell
Rend up both rocks and hills, and ride the air   540
In whirlwind; Hell scarce holds the wild uproar;
As when Alcides, from Oechalia crowned
With conquest, felt th' envenomed robe, and tore
Through pain up by the roots Thessalian pines,
And Lichas from the top of Oeta threw   545
Into th' Euboic sea.[1] Others more mild,
Retreated in a silent valley, sing
With notes angelical to many a harp
Their own heroic deeds and hapless fall
By doom of battle; and complain that Fate   550
Free Virtue should enthrall to Force or Chance.
Their song was partial,[2] but the harmony
(What could it less when spirits immortal sing?)
Suspended[3] Hell, and took with ravishment
The thronging audience. In discourse more sweet   555
(For eloquence the soul, song charms the sense)

---

3. I.e., resonant trumpets (made of the alloy brass
by a marriage of metals which Milton associates
with alchemy).
4. Arrayed in ranks.
5. Aloft, uplifted (the adjective modifies the flyer,
not the air).
6. The Olympic games were held at Olympia, the
Pythian games at Delphi. To "shun the goal" is to
drive a chariot as close as possible around a column without hitting it.
7. Warfare in the skies, portending trouble on

earth. "Van": vanguard. "Prick": spur.
8. Sky.
9. Like that of Typhon, the hundred-headed Titan.
See above 1.199.
1. Poisoned by the malicious centaur Nessus,
Hercules in his dying agonies threw his beloved
companion Lichas, along with a good part of Mount
Oeta, into the sea of Euboea, near Thermopylae.
2. Prejudiced.
3. Held in suspense.

Others apart sat on a hill retired,
In thoughts more elevate, and reasoned high
Of providence, foreknowledge, will, and fate,
Fixed fate, free will, foreknowledge absolute,   560
And found no end, in wandering mazes lost.
Of good and evil much they argued then,
Of happiness and final misery,
Passion and apathy,[4] and glory and shame,
Vain wisdom all, and false philosophy![5]   565
Yet with a pleasing sorcery could charm
Pain for a while or anguish, and excite
Fallacious hope, or arm th' obdurèd[6] breast
With stubborn patience as with triple steel.
Another part, in squadrons and gross[7] bands,   570
On bold adventure to discover wide
That dismal world, if any clime perhaps
Might yield them easier habitation, bend
Four ways their flying march, along the banks
Of four infernal rivers that disgorge   575
Into the burning lake their baleful streams:[8]
Abhorrèd Styx, the flood of deadly hate;
Sad Acheron of sorrow, black and deep;
Cocytus, named of lamentation loud
Heard on the rueful stream; fierce Phlegethon   580
Whose waves of torrent fire inflame with rage.
Far off from these a slow and silent stream,
Lethe, the river of oblivion, rolls
Her watery labyrinth, whereof who drinks
Forthwith his former state and being forgets,   585
Forgets both joy and grief, pleasure and pain.
Beyond this flood a frozen continent
Lies dark and wild, beat with perpetual storms
Of whirlwind and dire hail, which on firm land
Thaws not, but gathers heap,[9] and ruin seems   590
Of ancient pile; all else deep snow and ice,
A gulf profound as that Serbonian bog[1]
Betwixt Damiata and Mount Casius old,
Where armies whole have sunk: the parching air
Burns frore,[2] and cold performs th' effect of fire.   595
Thither by harpy-footed[3] Furies haled,

4. Feeling and lack of feeling; the angels are dabbling in Stoicism.
5. Milton means, not that the subjects themselves are vain (he himself, in the present poem, has a good deal to say on these topics), but that the very premises with which devils start are bound to land them in error.
6. Hardened.
7. Solid, dense.
8. The four rivers are traditional in hellish geography; Milton takes pains to distinguish them by the original meanings of their Greek names (Styx means "hateful," Acheron "woeful," etc.). Lethe is "far off" and very different from the others, oblivion being relatively a blessed state in hell.
9. In a heap, so that it looks like the ruin of an old building ("ancient pile").
1. Lake Serbonis, once famous for its quicksands but today dried up, used to lie on the coast of Egypt, just east of the Nile, between Damiata and Mt. Cassius.
2. Frosty.
3. With hooked claws.

At certain revolutions[4] all the damned
Are brought; and feel by turns the bitter change
Of fierce extremes, extremes by change more fierce,
From beds of raging fire to starve[5] in ice   600
Their soft ethereal warmth, and there to pine
Immovable, infixed, and frozen round
Periods of time; thence hurried back to fire.
They ferry over this Lethean sound
Both to and fro, their sorrow to augment,   605
And wish and struggle, as they pass, to reach
The tempting stream, with one small drop to lose
In sweet forgetfulness all pain and woe,
All in one moment, and so near the brink;
But Fate withstands, and to oppose th' attempt   610
Medusa[6] with Gorgonian terror guards
The ford, and of itself the water flies
All taste of living wight, as once it fled
The lips of Tantalus.[7] Thus roving on
In cònfused march forlorn, th' adventurous bands   615
With shuddering horror pale, and eyes aghast
Viewed first their lamentable lot, and found
No rest. Through many a dark and dreary vale
They passed, and many a region dolorous,
O'er many a frozen, many a fiery alp,[8]   620
Rocks, caves, lakes, fens, bogs, dens, and shades of death,
A universe of death, which God by curse
Created evil, for evil only good,
Where all life dies, death lives, and Nature breeds,
Perverse, all monstrous, all prodigious things,   625
Abominable, unutterable, and worse
Than fables yet have feigned, or fear conceived,
Gorgons, and Hydras, and Chimeras[9] dire.
    Meanwhile the adversary of God and man,
Satan with thoughts inflamed of highest design,   630
Puts on swift wings,[1] and toward the gates of Hell
Explores his solitary flight; sometimes
He scours the right-hand coast, sometimes the left;
Now shaves with level wing the deep, then soars
Up to the fiery concave[2] towering high.   635
As when far off at sea a fleet descried
Hangs in the clouds, by equinoctial winds

---

4. I.e., of time.
5. Benumb.
6. One of the three Gorgons, women with snaky hair, scaly bodies, and boar's tusks, the very sight of whose faces changed men to stone.
7. Tantalus, afflicted with a raging thirst, stood in the middle of a lake, the water of which always receded when he tried to drink it (hence, "tantalize").

8. A "fiery alp" is a volcano.
9. The Hydra was a serpent with nine heads, slain by Hercules; the Chimera was a fire-breathing creature, part lion, part dragon, part goat. They exemplify abominations of nature.
1. Satan does not fasten on his wings; he takes swiftly to wing.
2. Vault.

Close sailing from Bengala,[3] or the isles
Of Ternate and Tidore,[4] whence merchants bring
Their spicy drugs; they on the trading flood   640
Through the wide Ethiopian[5] to the Cape
Ply stemming nightly toward the pole: so seemed
Far off the flying fiend. At last appear
Hell bounds, high reaching to the horrid roof,
And thrice threefold the gates; three folds were brass,   645
Three iron, three of adamantine rock,
Impenetrable, impaled with circling fire,
Yet unconsumed. Before the gates there sat
On either side a formidable shape;[6]
The one seemed woman to the waist, and fair,   650
But ended foul in many a scaly fold
Voluminous and vast, a serpent armed
With mortal sting. About her middle round
A cry[7] of Hellhounds never ceasing barked
With wide Cerberean[8] mouths full loud, and rung   655
A hideous peal; yet, when they list, would creep,
If aught disturbed their noise, into her womb,
And kennel there, yet there still barked and howled
Within unseen. Far less abhorred than these
Vexed Scylla,[9] bathing in the sea that parts   660
Calabria from the hoarse Trinacrian shore;
Nor uglier follow the night-hag,[1] when, called
In secret, riding through the air she comes,
Lured with the smell of infant blood, to dance
With Lapland witches, while the laboring moon   665
Eclipses at their charms.[2] The other shape,
If shape it might be called that shape had none
Distinguishable in member, joint, or limb,
Or substance might be called that shadow seemed,
For each seemed either; black it stood as night,   670
Fierce as ten Furies, terrible as Hell,
And shook a dreadful dart; what seemed his head
The likeness of a kingly crown had on.
Satan was now at hand, and from his seat

---

3. An old form of "Bengal."
4. Two of the Molucca or "Spice" Islands, modern Indonesia.
5. The Indian Ocean, east of Africa. "The Cape" is of course the Cape of Good Hope; "the pole," the South Pole.
6. The allegorical figures of Sin and Death are founded on James 1.15: "Then when lust hath conceived, it bringeth forth sin: and sin, when it is finished, bringeth forth death." But the incestuous relations of Sin and Death are Milton's own invention. Physically, Sin is modeled on Virgil's or Ovid's Scylla, with some touches adopted from Spenser's Error; Death is a traditional figure, vague

and vast.
7. Pack.
8. Like Cerberus, the traditional hound of Hell.
9. Circe out of jealousy threw poison into the water where Scylla bathed, in the straits between Calabria and Sicily ("Trinacria"); as a result of the poison, Scylla developed a ring of barking, snapping dogs around her waist.
1. Hecate (three syllables), goddess of sorcery. She attends the orgies of witches in the home of all witchcraft, Lapland, whither she is drawn by the blood of babies sacrificed for the occasion.
2. Magic formulas, not allurements.

The monster moving onward came as fast,   675
With horrid strides; Hell trembled as he strode.
Th' undaunted fiend what this might be admired,[3]
Admired, not feared; God and his Son except,
Created thing naught valued he nor shunned;
And with disdainful look thus first began: 680
   "Whence and what art thou, execrable shape,
That dar'st, though grim and terrible, advance
Thy miscreated front[4] athwart my way
To yonder gates? Through them I mean to pass,
That be assured, without leave asked of thee.   685
Retire, or taste thy folly, and learn by proof,
Hell-born, not to contend with spirits of Heaven."
   To whom the goblin full of wrath replied:
"Art thou that traitor angel, art thou he,
Who first broke peace in Heaven, and faith, till then   690
Unbroken, and in proud rebellious arms
Drew after him the third part of Heaven's sons
Conjured[5] against the Highest, for which both thou
And they, outcast from God, are here condemned
To waste eternal days in woe and pain?   695
And reckon'st thou thyself with spirits of Heaven,
Hell-doomed, and breath'st defiance here and scorn,
Where I reign king, and, to enrage thee more,
Thy king and lord? Back to thy punishment,
False fugitive, and to thy speed add wings,   700
Lest with a whip of scorpions I pursue
Thy ling'ring, or with one stroke of this dart
Strange horror seize thee, and pangs unfelt before."
   So spake the grisly terror, and in shape,
So speaking and so threatening, grew tenfold   705
More dreadful and deform. On th' other side,
Incensed with indignation Satan stood
Unterrified, and like a comet burned
That fires the length of Ophiucus[6] huge
In th' arctic sky, and from his horrid hair   710
Shakes pestilence and war. Each at the head
Leveled his deadly aim; their fatal hands
No second stroke intend,[7] and such a frown
Each cast at th' other, as when two black clouds,
With Heaven's artillery fraught,[8] come rattling on   715
Over the Caspian,[9] then stand front to front
Hovering a space, till winds the signal blow
To join their dark encounter in mid-air:

---

3. Wondered.
4. Misshapen forehead, or face.
5. Sworn together by an oath.
6. A vast Northern constellation, "The Serpent-Holder" (also called "Serpentarius"). Satan will soon

appear as a snake; and, like a comet, he portends "pestilence and war."
7. I.e., the first stroke will do the business.
8. Loaded with thunderbolts.
9. The Caspian is a particularly stormy area.

So frowned the mighty combatants, that Hell
Grew darker at their frown; so matched they stood;   720
For never but once more was either like
To meet so great a foe.[1] And now great deeds
Had been achieved, whereof all Hell had rung,
Had not the snaky sorceress that sat
Fast by Hell-gate, and kept the fatal key,   725
Ris'n, and with hideous outcry rushed between.
    "O father, what intends thy hand," she cried,
"Against thy only son?[2] What fury, O son,
Possesses thee to bend that mortal dart
Against thy father's head? and know'st for whom?   730
For Him who sits above and laughs the while
At thee ordained his drudge, to execute
Whate'er his wrath, which he calls Justice, bids;
His wrath which one day will destroy ye both!"
    She spake, and at her words the hellish pest   735
Forbore; then these to her Satan returned:
    "So strange thy outcry, and thy words so strange
Thou interposest, that my sudden hand
Prevented[3] spares to tell thee yet by deeds
What it intends, till first I know of thee,   740
What thing thou art, thus double-formed, and why,
In this infernal vale first met, thou call'st
Me father, and that phantasm call'st my son?
I know thee not, nor ever saw till now
Sight more detestable than him and thee."   745
    T' whom thus the portress of Hell-gate replied:
"Hast thou forgot me then, and do I seem
Now in thine eye so foul? once deemed so fair
In Heaven, when at th' assembly, and in sight
Of all the seraphim with thee combined   750
In bold conspiracy against Heaven's King,
All on a sudden miserable pain
Surprised thee; dim thine eyes, and dizzy swum
In darkness, while thy head flames thick and fast
Threw forth, till on the left side opening wide,   755
Likest to thee in shape and countenance bright,
Then shining heavenly fair, a goddess armed
Out of thy head I sprung.[4] Amazement seized
All th' host of Heaven; back they recoiled afraid
At first, and called me *Sin*, and for a sign   760
Portentous held me; but, familiar grown,
I pleased, and with attractive graces won
The most averse, thee chiefly, who full oft

1. I.e., the Son of God.
2. Sin, Death, and Satan, in their various inter-
relations, parody obscenely the relations between
God and the Son, Adam and Eve.

3. Forestalled.
4. As Athena sprang full-grown from the head of
Zeus.

Thyself in me thy perfect image viewing
Becam'st enamored;[5] and such joy thou took'st   765
With me in secret, that my womb conceived
A growing burden. Meanwhile war arose,
And fields were fought in Heaven; wherein remained
(For what could else?) to our almighty foe
Clear victory, to our part loss and rout   770
Through all the empyrean. Down they fell,
Driven headlong from the pitch[6] of Heaven, down
Into this deep, and in the general fall
I also; at which time this powerful key
Into my hand was given, with charge to keep   775
These gates forever shut, which none can pass
Without my opening. Pensive here I sat
Alone, but long I sat not, till my womb
Pregnant by thee, and now excessive grown,
Prodigious motion felt and rueful throes.   780
At last this odious offspring whom thou seest,
Thine own begotten, breaking violent way
Tore through my entrails, that with fear and pain
Distorted, all my nether shape thus grew
Transformed; but he, my inbred enemy,   785
Forth issued, brandishing his fatal dart,
Made to destroy. I fled, and cried out *Death!*
Hell trembled at the hideous name, and sighed
From all her caves, and back resounded *Death!*
I fled; but he pursued (though more, it seems,   790
Inflamed with lust than rage) and swifter far,
Me overtook, his mother, all dismayed,
And in embraces forcible and foul
Engendering with me, of that rape begot
These yelling monsters that with ceaseless cry   795
Surround me, as thou sawest, hourly conceived
And hourly born, with sorrow infinite
To me; for when they list, into the womb
That bred them they return, and howl and gnaw
My bowels, their repast; then bursting forth   800
Afresh, with conscious terrors vex me round,
That rest or intermission none I find.
Before mine eyes in opposition sits
Grim Death, my son and foe, who sets them on,
And me his parent would full soon devour   805
For want of other prey, but that he knows
His end with mine involved; and knows that I
Should prove a bitter morsel, and his bane,
Whenever that shall be; so Fate pronounced.
But thou, O father, I forewarn thee, shun   810

---

5. Sin looks attractive at first, being a lovely woman at the top of her body; but she is a serpent below, and ends in a "mortal sting," i.e., death.
6. Height.

His deadly arrow; neither vainly hope
To be invulnerable in those bright arms,
Though tempered heavenly; for that mortal dint,
Save he who reigns above, none can resist."[7]
    She finished, and the subtle fiend his lore   815
Soon learned, now milder, and thus answered smooth:
"Dear daughter, since thou claimest me for thy sire,
And my fair son here show'st me, the dear pledge
Of dalliance had with thee in Heaven, and joys
Then sweet, now sad to mention, through dire change   820
Befallen us unforeseen, unthought of; know
I come no enemy, but to set free
From out this dark and dismal house of pain,
Both him and thee, and all the heavenly host
Of spirits that, in our just pretenses[8] armed,   825
Fell with us from on high. From them I go
This uncouth errand sole,[9] and one for all
Myself expose, with lonely steps to tread
Th' unfounded[1] deep, and through the void immense
To search with wandering quest a place foretold   830
Should be, and, by concurring signs, ere now
Created vast and round, a place of bliss
In the purlieus[2] of Heaven, and therein placed
A race of upstart creatures, to supply
Perhaps our vacant room, though more removed,   835
Lest Heaven surcharged[3] with potent multitude
Might hap to move new broils. Be this or aught
Than this more secret now designed, I haste
To know; and this once known, shall soon return,
And bring ye to the place where thou and Death   840
Shall dwell at ease, and up and down unseen
Wing silently the buxom[4] air, embalmed
With odors: there ye shall be fed and filled
Immeasurably; all things shall be your prey."
He ceased, for both seemed highly pleased, and Death   845
Grinned horrible a ghastly smile, to hear
His famine[5] should be filled, and blessed his maw
Destined to that good hour. No less rejoiced
His mother bad, and thus bespake her sire:
    "The key of this infernal pit by due   850
And by command of Heaven's all-powerful King
I keep, by him forbidden to unlock
These adamantine gates; against all force
Death ready stands to interpose his dart,
Fearless to be o'ermatched by living might.   855

---

7. I.e., only God is immune to death.
8. Pretensions, claims.
9. Alone on a desolate journey.
1. Bottomless.
2. Outskirts, suburbs.

3. Too full. "Broils": controversies.
4. Yielding. "Embalmed": made fragrant, but also with a thought of the process associated with death.
5. Hunger, belly.

But what owe I to his commands above
Who hates me, and hath hither thrust me down
Into this gloom of Tartarus profound,
To sit in hateful office here confined,
Inhabitant of Heaven and heavenly-born,   860
Here in perpetual agony and pain,
With terrors and with clamors compassed round
Of mine own brood that on my bowels feed?
Thou art my father, thou my author, thou
My being gav'st me; whom should I obey   865
But thee? whom follow? Thou wilt bring me soon
To that new world of light and bliss, among
The gods who live at ease, where I shall reign
At thy right hand voluptuous,[6] as beseems
Thy daughter and thy darling, without end."   870
    Thus saying, from her side the fatal key,
Sad instrument of all our woe, she took;
And towards the gate rolling her bestial train,[7]
Forthwith the huge portcullis high up-drew,
Which but herself not all the Stygian powers[8]   875
Could once have moved; then in the keyhole turns
Th' intricate wards, and every bolt and bar
Of massy iron or solid rock with ease
Unfastens: on a sudden open fly
With impetuous recoil and jarring sound   880
Th' infernal doors, and on their hinges grate
Harsh thunder, that the lowest bottom shook
Of Erebus.[9] She opened, but to shut
Excelled[1] her power; the gates wide open stood,
That with extended wings a bannered host,   885
Under spread ensigns[2] marching, might pass through
With horse and chariots ranked in loose array;
So wide they stood, and like a furnace-mouth
Cast forth redounding[3] smoke and ruddy flame.
Before their eyes in sudden view appear   890
The secrets of the hoary deep, a dark
Illimitable ocean without bound,
Without dimension; where length, breadth, and height,
And time and place are lost; where eldest Night
And Chaos, ancestors of Nature, hold   895
Eternal anarchy, amidst the noise
Of endless wars, and by confusion stand.
For Hot, Cold, Moist, and Dry, four champions fierce,
Strive here for mastery, and to battle bring

---

6. As the Son sits at God's right hand, Sin will at
Satan's; a blasphemous parody of the Creed.
7. I.e., accompanied by her yelping offspring.
8. The powers of Hell.

9. Another classical name for Hell.
1. Exceeded.
2. Standards, flags.
3. Billowing.

Their embryon atoms;[4] they around the flag   900
Of each his faction, in their several clans,
Light-armed or heavy, sharp, smooth, swift, or slow,
Swarm populous, unnumbered as the sands
Of Barca or Cyrene's torrid soil,[5]
Levied to side with warring winds, and poise[6]   905
Their lighter wings. To whom these most adhere,
He rules a moment; Chaos[7] umpire sits,
And by decision more embroils the fray
By which he reigns: next him, high arbiter,
Chance governs all. Into this wild abyss—   910
The womb of Nature and perhaps her grave,
Of neither sea, nor shore, nor air, nor fire,
But all these in their pregnant causes[8] mixed
Confusedly, and which thus must ever fight,
Unless th' Almighty Maker them ordain   915
His dark materials to create more worlds[9]—
Into this wild abyss the wary fiend
Stood on the brink of Hell and looked awhile,
Pondering his voyage; for no narrow frith[1]
He had to cross. Nor was his ear less pealed[2]   920
With noises loud and ruinous (to compare
Great things with small) than when Bellona[3] storms,
With all her battering engines bent to raze
Some capital city; or less than if this frame
Of Heaven were falling, and these elements   925
In mutiny had from her axle torn
The steadfast earth. At last his sail-broad vans[4]
He spreads for flight, and in the surging smoke
Uplifted spurns the ground; thence many a league,
As in a cloudy chair ascending, rides   930
Audacious; but that seat soon failing, meets
A vast vacuity: all unawares,
Fluttering his pennons[5] vain, plumb down he drops
Ten thousand fathom deep, and to this hour
Down had been falling, had not by ill chance   935
The strong rebuff[6] of some tumultuous cloud
Instinct[7] with fire and niter hurried him
As many miles aloft; that fury stayed,

---

4. The four elements, fire, earth, water, and air,
struggle endlessly in Chaos. "Embryon": embryo,
unformed.
5. Barca and Cyrene were cities built on the shifting sands of North Africa.
6. Give weight to.
7. Chaos is both the place where confusion reigns
and personified confusion itself.
8. Chaos is not organized to the point of being
matter; it is the seeds of all forms of matter.

9. God must impose order on Chaos to create
worlds from it.
1. Channel, firth.
2. Rung.
3. Goddess of war.
4. Wings.
5. Pinions, from Latin *pennae*, "wings."
6. Puff or blast.
7. Filled. "Niter": saltpeter.

Quenched in a boggy Syrtis,[8] neither sea,
Nor good dry land, nigh foundered on he fares,   940
Treading the crude consistence, half on foot,
Half flying; behoves[9] him now both oar and sail.
As when a gryphon through the wilderness
With wingèd course o'er hill or moory dale
Pursues the Arimaspian, who by stealth   945
Had from his wakeful custody purloined
The guarded gold:[1] so eagerly the fiend
O'er bog or steep, through strait, rough, dense, or rare,
With head, hands, wings, or feet pursues his way,
And swims, or sinks, or wades, or creeps, or flies.   950
At length a universal hubbub wild
Of stunning sounds and voices all confused
Borne through the hollow dark assaults his ear
With loudest vehemence. Thither he plies
Undaunted, to meet there whatever power   955
Or spirit of the nethermost abyss
Might in that noise reside, of whom to ask
Which way the nearest coast of darkness lies
Bordering on light; when straight behold the throne
Of Chaos, and his dark pavilion spread   960
Wide on the wasteful deep! With him enthroned
Sat sable-vested Night, eldest of things,
The consort of his reign; and by them stood
Orcus and Ades,[2] and the dreaded name
Of Demogorgon;[3] Rumor next and Chance,   965
And Tumult and Confusion all embroiled,
And Discord with a thousand various mouths.
     T' whom Satan turning boldly, thus: "Ye powers
And spirits of this nethermost abyss,
Chaos and ancient Night, I come no spy,   970
With purpose to explore or to disturb
The secrets of your realm; but by constraint
Wandering this darksome desert, as my way
Lies through your spacious empire up to light,
Alone and without guide, half lost, I seek   975
What readiest path leads where your gloomy bounds
Confine with[4] Heaven; or if some other place
From your dominion won, th' Ethereal King
Possesses lately, thither to arrive
I travel this profound.[5] Direct my course: 980

---

8. Quicksand, form the North African gulfs, famous for their shifting sandbars.
9. Befits.
1. Gryphons, fabulous creatures, half eagle, half lion, lived in northern Europe, and were said to hoard gold. When it was stolen from them by the one-eyed Arimaspians, they pursued these curious malefactors, hopping, flapping, and squawking. The

story is a piece of moralized natural history, directed against the love of money.
2. Latin and Greek names of Pluto, god of Hell.
3. A mysterious subdeity, stronger than Fate itself, publicized by Boccaccio.
4. Border on.
5. Deep pit.

Directed, no mean recompense it brings
To your behoof,[6] if I that region lost,
All usurpation thence expelled, reduce
To her original darkness and your sway
(Which is my present journey),[7] and once more   985
Erect the standard there of ancient Night.
Yours be th' advantage all, mine the revenge!"
    Thus Satan; and him thus the anarch[8] old,
With faltering speech and visage incomposed,[9]
Answered: "I know thee, stranger, who thou art,   990
That mighty leading angel, who of late
Made head against Heaven's King, though overthrown.
I saw and heard; for such a numerous host
Fled not in silence through the frighted deep
With ruin upon ruin, rout on rout,   995
Confusion worse confounded; and Heaven-gates
Poured out by millions her victorious bands
Pursuing. I upon my frontiers here
Keep residence; if all I can will serve
That little which is left so to defend,   1000
Encroached on still through our intestine broils[1]
Weakening the scepter of old Night: first Hell,
Your dungeon, stretching far and wide beneath;
Now lately Heaven and Earth,[2] another world
Hung o'er my realm, linked in a golden chain   1005
To that side Heaven from whence your legions fell.
If that way be your walk, you have not far;
So much the nearer danger. Go, and speed!
Havoc and spoil and ruin are my gain."
    He ceased; and Satan stayed not to reply,   1010
But glad that now his sea should find a shore,
With fresh alacrity and force renewed
Springs upward like a pyramid of fire
Into the wild expanse, and through the shock
Of fighting elements, on all sides round   1015
Environed, wins his way; harder beset
And more endangered than when Argo[3] passed
Through Bosporus betwixt the jostling rocks;
Or when Ulysses on the larboard shunned

6. On your behalf.
7. I.e., the purpose of my present journey.
8. Chaos is not "monarch" of his realm, but "anarch," i.e., nonruler.
9. Disturbed.
1. I.e., the territory of Chaos is continually shrinking because of our civil wars ("intestine broils"). Without textual authority, but with a certain logical force, some students have proposed to amend "our" to "your."
2. Our human cosmos, recently carved out of Chaos, and having a little heaven of its own, as

distinguished from "Heaven," as used in line 1006 to mean the eternal empyrean, the abode of the deity and his angels.
3. Jason and his fifty Argonauts, sailing through the Bosporus to the Black Sea in pursuit of the Golden Fleece, had to pass through the Symplegades, or clashing rocks. Ulysses also had a tight squeeze to pass between Scylla and Charybdis, where Italy almost touches Sicily. Charybdis was a whirlpool, but Scylla, the dog-monster who ate alive six of Ulysses' best men, is called by Milton "th' other whirlpool."

Charybdis, and by th' other whirlpool steered: 1020
So he with difficulty and labor hard
Moved on, with difficulty and labor he;
But, he once past, soon after when man fell,
Strange alteration! Sin and Death amain,[4]
Following his track (such was the will of Heaven),   1025
Paved after him a broad and beaten way
Over the dark abyss, whose boiling gulf
Tamely endured a bridge of wondrous length
From Hell continued reaching th' utmost orb[5]
Of this frail world; by which the spirits perverse   1030
With easy intercourse pass to and fro
To tempt or punish mortals, except whom
God and good angels guard by special grace.
But now at last the sacred influence
Of light appears, and from the walls of Heaven   1035
Shoots far into the bosom of dim Night
A glimmering dawn. Here Nature first begins
Her farthest verge,[6] and Chaos to retire,
As from her outmost works a broken foe
With tumult less and with less hostile din;   1040
That[7] Satan with less toil and now with ease
Wafts on the calmer wave by dubious light,
And like a weather-beaten vessel holds[8]
Gladly the port, though shrouds and tackle torn;
Or in the emptier waste, resembling air,   1045
Weighs his spread wings, at leisure to behold
Far off th' empyreal Heaven, extended wide
In circuit, undetermined[9] square or round,
With opal towers and battlements adorned
Of living sapphire, once his native seat;   1050
And fast by, hanging in a golden chain,
This pendant world,[1] in bigness as a star
Of smallest magnitude close by the moon.
Thither, full fraught with mischievous revenge,
Accursed, and in a cursèd hour, he hies.   1055

---

4. At full speed, vigorously.
5. The world is surrounded by ten spheres, the whole concentric construction making up the created universe. The bridge built by Sin and Death ends on the outermost of these spheres.
6. Threshold. The end of Chaos is the beginning of (created) Nature.
7. So that.
8. Makes for.

9. Heaven is so vast that simply by looking at it one cannot tell its shape.
1. Homer first imagined the world as hanging from Heaven by a golden chain (*Iliad* 8). As Milton uses the image, it has a symbolic meaning as well: earth is dependent on Heaven. The world which hangs from Heaven is not just our earth, but earth and all its ten spheres.

From Book 3

[*The Invocation, the Council in Heaven, and the
Conclusion of Satan's Journey*]

Hail, holy Light, offspring of Heaven first-born!
Or of th' Eternal coeternal beam,
May I express thee unblamed?[1] since God is light,
And never but in unapproachèd light
Dwelt from eternity, dwelt then in thee,   5
Bright effluence of bright essence increate![2]
Or hear'st thou rather[3] pure ethereal stream,
Whose fountain who shall tell? Before the sun,
Before the heavens, thou wert, and at the voice
Of God, as with a mantle didst invest[4]   10
The rising world of waters dark and deep,
Won from the void and formless infinite.
Thee I revisit now with bolder wing,
Escaped the Stygian pool, though long detained
In that obscure sojourn, while in my flight,   15
Through utter and through middle darkness[5] borne,
With other notes than to th' Orphean lyre[6]
I sung of Chaos and eternal Night;
Taught by the Heavenly Muse[7] to venture down
The dark descent, and up to reascend,   20
Though hard and rare. Thee I revisit safe,
And feel thy sovereign vital lamp; but thou
Revisit'st not these eyes, that roll in vain
To find thy piercing ray, and find no dawn;
So thick a drop serene[8] hath quenched their orbs,   25
Or dim suffusion veiled. Yet not the more
Cease I to wander where the Muses haunt
Clear spring, or shady grove, or sunny hill,
Smit with the love of sacred song;[9] but chief
Thee, Sion,[1] and the flowery brooks beneath,   30
That wash thy hallowed feet, and warbling flow,
Nightly I visit: nor sometimes forget[2]
Those other two equaled with me in fate,[3]

1. Milton feels some hesitation at calling Light
coeternal with God himself; his reasons for doing
so follow.
2. Uncreated, i.e., eternal.
3. I.e., would you rather be called. The construction is a Latinism.
4. Cover, wrap.
5. Hell and Chaos.
6. One of the so-called Orphic Hymns is *To Night*,
and Orpheus himself visited the underworld. But
Milton's song, being Christian, is of a different kind.
7. Urania. The following lines echo Aeneid 6.
126–29, where the Sybil tells Aeneas that the

descent to hell is easy: getting back is the hard part.
8. *Gutta serena* was the medical term for the kind
of blindness from which Milton suffered. "Dim
suffusion" was cataract—*suffusio nigra*.
9. Again the phrase is Virgilian, "[*Musarum*]
ingenti percussus amore (*Georgics* 2. 476); but the
adjective "sacred" is Milton's own reservation.
1. The mountain of Scriptural inspiration, with
its brooks Siloa and Kidron.
2. I.e., and never forget: therefore always remember.
3. Blind like me.

So were I equaled with them in renown,
Blind Thamyris and blind Maeonides,   35
And Tiresias and Phineus, prophets old:[4]
Then feed on thoughts that voluntary move
Harmonious numbers; as the wakeful bird[5]
Sings darkling, and in shadiest covert hid
Tunes her nocturnal note. Thus with the year   40
Seasons return; but not to me returns
Day, or the sweet approach of even or morn,
Or sight of vernal bloom, or summer's rose,
Or flocks, or herds, or human face divine;
But cloud instead and ever-during dark   45
Surrounds me, from the cheerful ways of men
Cut off, and for the book of knowledge fair
Presented with a universal blank
Of Nature's works to me expunged and rased,[6]
And wisdom at one entrance quite shut out.   50
So much the rather thou, Celestial Light,
Shine inward, and the mind through all her powers
Irradiate; there plant eyes; all mist from thence
Purge and disperse, that I may see and tell
Of things invisible to mortal sight.   55
      Now had th' Almighty Father from above,
From the pure empyrean where he sits
High throned above all height, bent down his eye,
His own works and their works at once to view:
About him all the sanctities of Heaven   60
Stood thick as stars, and from his sight[7] received
Beatitude past utterance; on his right
The radiant image of his glory sat,
His only Son. On Earth he first beheld
Our two first parents, yet the only two   65
Of mankind, in the happy garden placed,
Reaping immortal fruits of joy and love,
Uninterrupted joy, unrivaled love,
In blissful solitude. He then surveyed
Hell and the gulf between, and Satan there   70
Coasting the wall of Heaven on this side Night,
In the dun air sublime,[8] and ready now
To stoop, with wearied wings and willing feet,
On the bare outside of this world, that seemed
Firm land embosomed without firmament,   75

---

4. Thamyris was a blind Thracian poet, who lived
before Homer. "Maeonides" is an epithet of Homer,
either as a son of Maeon or as a native of Maeonia.
Tiresias was the blind prophet of Thebes; Phineus
was a blind king and seer (*Aeneid* 3). For Milton
poetry and prophecy were intimately joined; blindness of the outer eye rendered more acute the sight
of the inner eye.
5. The nightingale. "Darkling": in the dark.

6. Shaved off (like a Roman tablet), erased.
7. From sight of him.
8. From the aspect of God's radiance the air is
"dun," i.e., dusky; Satan is literally "sublime" in
it, i.e., lifted up, aloft. But from where Satan hangs,
outside the world's outer shell, he cannot be sure
the world and its ten concentric spheres are not a
single solid (line 75). The points of view are precisely distinguished.

Uncertain which, in ocean or in air.
Him God beholding from his prospect high,
Wherein past, present, future he beholds,
Thus to his only Son foreseeing spake:
    "Only begotten Son, seest thou what rage   80
Transports our adversary? whom no bounds
Prescribed, no bars of Hell, nor all the chains
Heaped on him there, nor yet the main abyss
Wide interrupt,[9] can hold; so bent he seems
On desperate revenge, that shall redound   85
Upon his own rebellious head. And now
Through all restraint broke loose he wings his way
Not far off Heaven, in the precincts of light,
Directly towards the new-created world,
And man there placed, with purpose to essay   90
If him by force he can destroy, or worse,
By some false guile pervert: and shall pervert;
For man will hearken to his glozing[1] lies,
And easily transgress the sole command,
Sole pledge of his obedience; so will fall   95
He and his faithless progeny. Whose fault?
Whose but his own? Ingrate, he had of me
All he could have; I made him just and right,
Sufficient to have stood, though free to fall.
Such I created all th' ethereal powers   100
And spirits, both them who stood and them who failed:
Freely they stood who stood, and fell who fell.
Not free, what proof could they have given sincere[2]
Of true allegiance, constant faith, or love,
Where only what they needs must do appeared,   105
Not what they would? What praise could they receive,
What pleasure I, from such obedience paid,
When Will and Reason (Reason also is Choice),
Useless and vain, of freedom both despoiled,
Made passive both, had served Necessity,   110
Not me? They therefore as to right belonged,
So were created, nor can justly accuse
Their Maker or their making or their fate,
As if predestination overruled
Their will, disposed by absolute decree   115
Or high foreknowledge. They themselves decreed
Their own revolt, not I. If I foreknew,
Foreknowledge had no influence on their fault,
Which had no less proved certain unforeknown.[3]
So without least impulse or shadow of fate,   120
Or aught by me immutably foreseen,

---

9. Dividing, in between.
1. Flattering.
2. The delayed modifier is a favorite stylistic device
of Milton's. "Sincere" goes with "proof."
3. I.e., if I had not foreknown it.

They trespass, authors to themselves in all,
Both what they judge and what they choose; for so
I formed them free, and free they must remain
Till they enthrall themselves: I else must change   125
Their nature, and revoke the high decree
Unchangeable, eternal, which ordained
Their freedom; they themselves ordained their fall.
The first sort[4] by their own suggestion fell,
Self-tempted, self-depraved; man falls, deceived   130
By the other first: man therefore shall find grace;
The other, none. In mercy and justice both,[5]
Through Heaven and Earth, so shall my glory excel;
But mercy, first and last, shall brightest shine."
    Thus while God spake ambrosial fragrance filled   135
All Heaven, and in the blessèd spirits elect
Sense of new joy ineffable diffused.
Beyond compare the Son of God was seen
Most glorious; in him all his Father shone
Substantially expressed; and in his face   140
Divine compassion visibly appeared,
Love without end, and without measure grace;
Which uttering, thus he to his Father spake:
    "O Father, gracious was that word which closed
Thy sovereign sentence, that man should find grace;   145
For which both Heaven and Earth shall high extol
Thy praises, with th' innumerable sound
Of hymns and sacred songs, wherewith thy throne
Encompassed shall resound thee ever blest.
For should man finally be lost, should man   150
Thy creature late so loved, thy youngest son,
Fall circumvented thus by fraud, though joined
With his own folly? That be from thee far,
That far be from thee, Father, who art judge
Of all things made, and judgest only right!   155
Or shall the adversary[6] thus obtain
His end, and frustrate thine? Shall he fulfill
His malice, and thy goodness bring to naught,
Or proud return, though to his heavier doom,
Yet with revenge accomplished, and to Hell   160
Draw after him the whole race of mankind,
By him corrupted? Or wilt thou thyself
Abolish thy creation, and unmake
For him, what for thy glory thou hast made?
So should thy goodness and thy greatness both   165
Be questioned and blasphemed without defense."[7]

4. The bad angels, Satan and his crew.
5. Mercy and justice are key terms in the poem. Their personifications here are separate: God is justice (he claims to be merciful, but his speech does not have this tone at all); the Son is mercy;

but by Book 12 Milton intends to show their identity.
6. "Satan" in Hebrew means "adversary."
7. The Son correctly intuits the motives overtly expressed by Beëlzebub in the great consult.

    To whom the great Creator thus replied:
"O Son, in whom my soul hath chief delight,
Son of my bosom, Son who art alone
My word, my wisdom, and effectual might,   170
All hast thou spoken as my thoughts are, all
As my eternal purpose hath decreed.[8]
Man shall not quite be lost, but saved who will;
Yet not of will in him, but grace in me
Freely vouchsafed. Once more I will renew   175
His lapsèd powers, though forfeit, and enthralled
By sin to foul exorbitant desires:
Upheld by me, yet once more he shall stand
On even ground against his mortal foe,
By me upheld,[9] that he may know how frail   180
His fallen condition is, and to me owe
All his deliverance, and to none but me.
Some I have chosen of peculiar grace,
Elect above the rest; so is my will:
The rest shall hear me call, and oft be warned   185
Their sinful state,[1] and to appease betimes
Th' incensèd Deity, while offered grace
Invites; for I will clear their senses dark
What may suffice,[2] and soften stony hearts
To pray, repent, and bring obedience due.   190
To prayer, repentance, and obedience due,
Though but endeavored with sincere intent,
Mine ear shall not be slow, mine eye not shut.
And I will place within them as a guide
My umpire Conscience; whom if they will hear,   195
Light after light well used they shall attain,[3]
And to the end persisting, safe arrive.
This my long sufferance and my day of grace
They who neglect and scorn shall never taste;
But hard be hardened, blind be blinded more,   200
That they may stumble on, and deeper fall;
And none but such from mercy I exclude.
    But yet all is not done. Man, disobeying,
Disloyal breaks his fealty, and sins
Against the high supremacy of Heaven,   205
Affecting[4] godhead, and so losing all,
To expiate his treason hath naught left,
But to destruction sacred and devote,
He with his whole posterity must die;
Die he or Justice must; unless for him   210

8. The Lord's speech is notably rhythmic, even rhymed.

9. Note the ambiguity: the second "by me upheld" (line 180) may modify either "he" (line 178) or "his mortal foe" (line 179). Both divine and hellish energy are ultimately divine.

1. I.e., warned about their sinful state.

2. I.e., as much as need be.

3. By using light well, they will reach even more light, and, in the end, salvation.

4. Pretending to. "Devote": dedicated, given up to.

Some other, able and as willing,[5] pay
The rigid satisfaction, death for death.
Say, heavenly powers, where shall we find such love?
Which of ye will be mortal to redeem
Man's mortal crime,[6] and just th' unjust to save?   215
Dwells in all Heaven charity so dear?"
    He asked, but all the heavenly choir stood mute,[7]
And silence was in Heaven: on man's behalf
Patron or intercessor none appeared,
Much less that durst upon his own head draw   220
The deadly forfeiture and ransom set.
And now without redemption all mankind
Must have been lost, adjudged to Death and Hell
By doom severe, had not the Son of God,
In whom the fullness dwells of love divine,   225
His dearest mediation[8] thus renewed:
    "Father, thy word is passed, man shall find grace;
And shall Grace not find means, that finds her way,
The speediest of thy wingèd messengers,
To visit all thy creatures, and to all   230
Comes unprevented,[9] unimplored, unsought?
Happy for man, so coming! He her aid
Can never seek, once dead in sins and lost;
Atonement for himself, or offering meet,
Indebted and undone, hath none to bring.   235
Behold me, then: me for him, life for life,
I offer; on me let thine anger fall;
Account me man: I for his sake will leave
Thy bosom, and this glory next to thee
Freely put off, and for him lastly die   240
Well pleased; on me let Death wreak all his rage;
Under his gloomy power I shall not long
Lie vanquished. Thou hast given me to possess
Life in myself forever; by thee I live;
Though now to Death I yield, and am his due,   245
All that of me can die, yet that debt paid,
Thou wilt not leave me in the loathsome grave
His prey, nor suffer my unspotted soul
Forever with corruption there to dwell;
But I shall rise victorious, and subdue   250
My vanquisher, spoiled of his vaunted spoil.
Death his death's wound shall then receive, and stoop[1]
Inglorious, of his mortal sting disarmed;
I through the ample air in triumph high

---

5. I.e., able to pay, and as willing as he is able.
6. Note that "mortal" means "human" (line 214) but "deadly" (line 215).
7. The silence of the good angels in face of a difficult task parallels that of the devils in the great consult (2.420–26).
8. Intercession.
9. Unanticipated.
1. Be humbled, fall.

Shall lead Hell captive maugre[2] Hell, and show   255
The powers of darkness bound. Thou at the sight
Pleased, out of Heaven shalt look down and smile,
While, by thee raised, I ruin[3] all my foes,
Death last, and with his carcass glut the grave;
Then with the multitude of my redeemed   260
Shall enter Heaven, long absent, and return,
Father, to see thy face, wherein no cloud
Of anger shall remain, but peace assured
And reconcilement: wrath shall be no more
Thenceforth, but in thy presence joy entire."   265
    His words here ended, but his meek aspèct
Silent yet spake, and breathed immortal love
To mortal men, above which only shone
Filial obedience: as a sacrifice
Glad to be offered, he attends the will   270
Of his great Father. Admiration[4] seized
All Heaven, what this might mean, and whither tend,
Wondering; but soon th' Almighty thus replied:
    "O thou in Heaven and Earth the only peace
Found out for mankind under wrath,[5] O thou   275
My sole complacence![6] well thou know'st how dear
To me are all my works; nor man the least,
Though last created, that for him I spare
Thee from my bosom and right hand, to save,
By losing thee a while, the whole race lost!   280
Thou, therefore, whom thou only canst redeem,
Their nature also to thy nature join,[7]
And be thyself man among men on Earth,
Made flesh, when time shall be, of virgin seed
By wondrous birth; be thou in Adam's room[8]   285
The head of all mankind, though Adam's son.[9]
As in him perish all men, so in thee,
As from a second root, shall be restored
As many as are restored; without thee, none.
His crime makes guilty all his sons; thy merit   290
Imputed shall absolve them who renounce
Their own both righteous and unrighteous deeds,[1]

---

2. In spite of (French, *malgré*). The Son's triumph
is represented in a series of fantastic paradoxes—a
vanquisher vanquished, a spoiler spoiled, death
dead, Hell captured in all Hell's despite.
3. In the Latin sense, throw down.
4. Wonder, curiosity.
5. The Lord is looking to the future, when mankind will be under his wrath.
6. Contentment.
7. I.e., join the nature of those people (mankind)
whom you alone can save to your own nature; in
other words, "Become a man and suffer the pains
of mortality." The antecedent of "whom" is, loosely
construed, the "their" which follows it.

8. Place.
9. Adam is, properly, the "Old Adam"; Christ is
the Second Adam (there was an old tradition that
the Forbidden Tree and the Cross of Christ stood
on the same spot). The Son of God, who long
antedates the creation of Adam, and who is actually
the first created being (3.383), is historical Jesus
Christ in one sense, an eternal spiritual principle
in another.
1. I.e., the merit of Christ, imputed to men, frees
from original sin those who renounce their own
deeds both good and bad and hope to be saved by
faith.

And live in thee transplanted, and from thee
Receive new life. So man, as is most just,
Shall satisfy for man, be judged and die, 295
And dying rise, and rising with him raise
His brethren, ransomed with his own dear life.
So heavenly love shall outdo hellish hate,
Giving to death, and dying to redeem,
So dearly to redeem, what hellish hate 300
So easily destroyed, and still destroys
In those who, when they may, accept not grace.
Nor shalt thou, by descending to assume
Man's nature, lessen or degrade thine own.
Because thou hast, though throned in highest bliss 305
Equal to God, and equally enjoying
Godlike fruition,[2] quitted all to save
A world from utter loss, and hast been found
By merit more than birthright Son of God,[3]
Found worthiest to be so by being good, 310
Far more than great or high; because in thee
Love hath abounded more than glory abounds;
Therefore thy humiliation shall exalt
With thee thy manhood also to this throne:
Here shalt thou sit incarnate, here shalt reign 315
Both God and man, Son both of God and man,
Anointed[4] universal King. All power
I give thee; reign forever, and assume
Thy merits; under thee, as Head Supreme,
Thrones, princedoms, powers, dominions, I reduce: 320
All knees to thee shall bow of them that bide
In Heaven, or Earth, or under Earth in Hell.
When thou, attended gloriously from Heaven,
Shalt in the sky appear, and from thee send
The summoning archangels to proclaim 325
Thy dread tribunal, forthwith from all winds[5]
The living, and forthwith the cited dead
Of all past ages, to the general doom
Shall hasten; such a peal shall rouse their sleep.
Then, all thy saints assembled, thou shalt judge 330
Bad men and angels; they arraigned shall sink
Beneath thy sentence; Hell, her numbers full,
Thenceforth shall be forever shut. Meanwhile
The world shall burn, and from her ashes spring
New Heaven and Earth, wherein the just shall dwell,[6] 335
And after all their tribulations long
See golden days, fruitful of golden deeds,

---

2. Godlike pleasures, rewards.
3. An audacious doctrine, that Christ was Son of God by merit. Satan, one notes, was sultan of Hell on the same principle. (See above, 2.5).
4. "The Anointed," in Hebrew, is the Messiah.
5. From all directions. "Cited": summoned.
6. The burning of the earth is based on 2 Peter 3.12, 13.

With Joy and Love triùmphing, and fair Truth.
Then thou thy regal scepter shalt lay by;
For regal scepter then no more shall need;[7]   340
God shall be all in all. But all ye gods,[8]
Adore him who, to compass all this, dies;
Adore the Son, and honor him as me."
    No sooner had th' Almighty ceased, but all
The multitude of angels with a shout   345
Loud as from numbers without number, sweet
As from blest voices, uttering joy, Heaven rung[9]
With jubilee, and loud hosannas filled
Th' eternal regions. Lowly reverent
Towards either throne[1] they bow, and to the ground   350
With solemn adoration down they cast
Their crowns inwove with amarant[2] and gold;
Immortal amarant, a flower which once
In Paradise, fast by the Tree of Life,
Began to bloom, but soon for man's offense   355
To Heaven removed, where first it grew, there grows
And flowers aloft, shading the Fount of Life,
And where the River of Bliss through midst of Heaven
Rolls o'er Elysian[3] flowers her amber stream.
With these, that never fade, the spirits elect   360
Bind their resplendent locks enwreathed with beams;
Now in loose garlands thick thrown off, the bright
Pavement, that like a sea of jasper shone,
Empurpled with celestial roses smiled.
Then, crowned again, their golden harps they took,   365
Harps ever tuned, that glittering by their side
Like quivers hung; and with preamble sweet
Of charming symphony they introduce
Their sacred song, and waken raptures high:
No voice exempt,[4] no voice but well could join   370
Melodious part; such concord is in Heaven.
    Thee, Father, first they sung, Omnipotent,
Immutable, Immortal, Infinite,[5]
Eternal King; thee, Author of all being,
Fountain of light, thyself invisible   375
Amidst the glorious brightness where thou sitt'st
Throned inaccessible, but when thou shad'st

---

7. Be needed.
8. In addressing the angels as gods, the Lord is merely indicating their share in his divinity; the word is not literal.
9. "Multitude" (line 345) is subject of the sentence, "rung" the verb, and "Heaven" the object.
1. Those of God and the Son.
2. Or "amaranth"; in Greek, "unwithering"—an unfading flower and hence a type of immortality, which could not continue on earth after man became subject to death.

3. Milton draws freely, and with no sense of incongruity, on pagan properties for his Christian Heaven. "Amber": not "yellow," but "clear." Milton's epithets are not always visually strong.
4. Abstaining.
5. Joshua Sylvester, in translating the long, pedestrian poem of Du Bartas on the creation, makes use of this line. It is the only example, and not a very striking one, of Milton's paralleling an English predecessor for ten consecutive syllables.

The full blaze of thy beams, and through a cloud
Drawn round about thee like a radiant shrine
Dark with excessive bright thy skirts appear,[6]   380
Yet dazzle Heaven, that brightest seraphim
Approach not, but with both wings veil their eyes.
Thee next they sang, of all creation first,
Begotten Son, divine similitude,
In whose conspicuous countenance, without cloud   385
Made visible, th' Almighty Father shines,
Whom else[7] no creature can behold: on thee
Impressed th' effulgence of his glory abides;
Transfused on thee his ample spirit rests.
He Heaven of Heavens, and all the powers therein,   390
By thee created; and by thee threw down
Th' aspiring dominations.[8] Thou that day
Thy Father's dreadful thunder didst not spare,
Nor stop thy flaming chariot wheels that shook
Heaven's everlasting frame, while o'er the necks   395
Thou drov'st of warring angels disarrayed.
Back from pursuit, thy powers with loud acclaim
Thee only extolled, Son of thy Father's might,
To execute fierce vengeance on his foes.
Not so on man: him through their malice fallen,   400
Father of mercy and grace, thou didst not doom
So strictly, but much more to pity incline.
No sooner did thy dear and only Son
Perceive thee purposed not to doom frail man
So strictly, but much more to pity inclined,[9]   405
He, to appease thy wrath, and end the strife
Of mercy and justice in thy face discerned,
Regardless of the bliss wherein he sat
Second to thee, offered himself to die
For man's offense. O unexampled love!   410
Love nowhere to be found less than divine!
Hail, Son of God, Savior of men! Thy name
Shall be the copious matter of my[1] song
Henceforth, and never shall my harp thy praise
Forget, nor from thy Father's praise disjoin!   415
　　　Thus they in Heaven, above the starry sphere,
Their happy hours in joy and hymning spent.
Meanwhile, upon the firm opacous globe
Of this round world, whose first convex divides

6. In this hymn, for the first time, we get a sense
of the majesty and mystery of the Godhead; hitherto, he has seemed rather querulous and legalistic.
7. Except for whom (if it were not for the Son, no
creature could see God).
8. I.e., the rebel angels.
9. A "than" or "but" is understood at the end of
line 405. The repetition (lines 402, 405) suggests
the choral nature of the psalm. Note in 407 the re-
emphasis on a conflict of mercy and justice.
1. Either the angels are singing as a single chorus,
or Milton wishes to associate himself with them;
possibly both. The change of pronoun is deliberate
and striking.

The luminous inferior orbs, enclosed   420
From chaos and th' inroad of darkness old,
Satan alighted walks.[2] A globe far off
It seemed; now seems a boundless continent,
Dark, waste, and wild, under the frown of night
Starless exposed, and ever-threatening storms   425
Of chaos blustering round, inclement sky,
Save on that side which from the wall of Heaven,
Though distant far, some small reflection gains
Of glimmering air less vexed with tempest loud.
Here walked the fiend at large in spacious field.   430
As when a vulture on Imaus bred,
Whose snowy ridge the roving Tartar bounds,[3]
Dislodging from a region scarce of prey
To gorge the flesh of lambs or yeanling[4] kids
On hills where flocks are fed, flies toward the springs   435
Of Ganges or Hydaspes, Indian streams,
But in his way lights on the barren plains
Of Sericana, where Chineses drive
With sails and wind their cany wagons light;[5]
So, on this windy sea of land, the fiend   440
Walked up and down alone, bent on his prey:
Alone, for other creature in this place,
Living or lifeless, to be found was none;—
None yet; but store hereafter from the earth
Up hither like aërial vapors flew   445
Of all things transitory and vain, when sin
With vanity had filled the works of men:
Both all things vain, and all who in vain things
Built their fond hopes of glory or lasting fame,
Or happiness in this or th' other life.[6]   450
All who have their reward on earth, the fruits
Of painful superstition and blind zeal,
Naught seeking but the praise of men, here find
Fit retribution, empty as their deeds;
All th' unaccomplished works of nature's hand,   455
Abortive, monstrous, or unkindly[7] mixed,
Dissolved on earth, fleet hither, and in vain,
Till final dissolution, wander here—

---

2. Satan is not on the earth's surface but on the
outermost of the ten concentric spheres that make
up the created cosmos. This sphere is "opacous"
(opaque) by contrast with the inner nine (containing the planets and the fixed stars), which are crystalline and transparent.
3. Imaus, a ridge of mountains beyond the modern Himalayas, is described by Pliny (*Natural History* 6.17), and shown in Mercator's *Atlas*, as
running north through Asia from modern Afghan-
istan to the Arctic Circle.
4. Newborn.
5. Both the Ganges and Hydaspes (a tributary of

the river Indus) rise from the mountains of northern India; Sericana is an area in what is now Sin-
kiang province, in China.
6. Milton's Paradise of Fools (named in line 496)
was probably inspired by Ariosto's equivalent valley on the moon (*Orlando Furioso*, canto 34; see
below, line 459); it serves much the same function
as Dante's Limbo, to dispose of those who deserve
neither salvation nor damnation. But, instead of
indifferents, Milton's region is reserved for deluded
victims of misplaced devotion, chiefly Roman
Catholics.
7. Against "kind," against their own natures.

Not in the neighboring moon, as some have dreamed:
Those argent fields more likely habitants,[8]   460
Translated saints, or middle spirits hold,
Betwixt th' angelical and human kind.
Hither, of ill-joined sons and daughters born,
First from the ancient world those giants came,
With many a vain exploit, though then renowned:[9]   465
The builders next of Babel on the plain
Of Sennaar,[1] and still with vain design
New Babels, had they wherewithal, would build;
Others came single; he who, to be deemed
A god, leaped fondly into Etna flames,   470
Empedocles, and he who, to enjoy
Plato's Elysium, leaped into the sea,
Cleombrotus;[2] and many more, too long,
Embryos and idiots, eremites and friars,
White, black, and gray, with all their trumpery.[3]   475
Here pilgrims roam, that strayed so far to seek
In Golgotha him dead who lives in Heaven;
And they who to be sure of paradise,
Dying put on the weeds of Dominic,
Or in Franciscan think to pass disguised.[4]   480
They pass the planets seven, and pass the fixed,
And that crystàlline sphere whose balance weighs
The trepidation talked, and that first moved;[5]
And now Saint Peter at Heaven's wicket seems
To wait them with his keys, and now at foot   485
Of Heaven's ascent they lift their feet, when, lo!
A violent cross wind from either coast
Blows them transverse ten thousand leagues awry
Into the devious air. Then might ye see
Cowls, hoods, and habits, with their wearers, tossed   490
And fluttered into rags; then relics, beads,
Indulgences, dispenses, pardons, bulls,[6]

---

8. Argent: silver. The moon Milton imagines, though only briefly, as a kind of middle Paradise.
9. The "giants in the earth," born of unnatural marriages between the "sons of God" and the daughters of men, are creatures "unkindly mixed," therefore sent to the Paradise of Fools, "though then renowned," as Genesis 6.4 tells us.
1. Shinär, the plain of Babel, as in Genesis 11.2–9. Babel for Milton is an emblem of human pride and folly.
2. Both Empedocles and Cleombrotus carried piety to the point of folly and suicide. Hell is reserved for the wilfully malicious, the Paradise of Fools for the merely misguided.
3. Unnatural mixtures produce embryos and idiots; Milton adds to them hermits and friars (the white are Carmelites, the black Dominicans, and the gray Franciscans); he thinks they exemplify unnatural piety, frustrated by its very nature.
4. Pilgrims also are unnatural in their piety, since

they worship the relic and forget the spirit. So are those who try to trick God into granting them salvation by wearing religious garb on their death-beds. The traveler Thomas Coryat reported (1619), with severe Protestant disapproval, that Venetians often buried sinners in the cowls of Franciscan friars, hoping thus to slip them into heaven.
5. Milton follows their souls through the spheres of the moon and sun and the five then-known planets, that of the fixed stars, and the sphere responsible for what astronomers call "the trepidation," a periodic corrective shudder of the cosmos. This brings them to the outermost sphere, the prime mover, or *primum mobile*—the next step seems to be the empyrean itself.
6. All that Milton considered the "trumpery," that is, the exterior and legal manifestations of ecclesiasticism, is here cast aside as vanity. Milton certainly means "backside" (line 494) to have its vulgar connotation.

The sport of winds: all these upwhirled aloft
Fly o'er the backside of the world far off
Into a limbo large and broad, since called   495
The Paradise of Fools; to few unknown
Long after, now unpeopled and untrod.
    All this dark globe the fiend found as he passed;
And long he wandered, till at last a gleam
Of dawning light turned thitherward in haste   500
His traveled steps. Far distant he descries,
Ascending by degrees magnificent
Up to the wall of Heaven, a structure high;
At top whereof, but far more rich, appeared
The work as of a kingly palace-gate,   505
With frontispiece[7] of diamond and gold
Embellished; thick with sparkling orient gems
The portal shone, inimitable on earth
By model, or by shading pencil drawn.
The stairs were such as whereon Jacob saw   510
Angels ascending and descending, bands
Of guardians bright, when he from Esau fled
To Padan-Aram, in the field of Luz
Dreaming by night under the open sky,
And waking cried, *This is the gate of Heaven.*   515
Each stair mysteriously was meant, nor stood
There always, but drawn up to Heaven sometimes
Viewless;[8] and underneath a bright sea flowed
Of jasper, or of liquid pearl, whereon
Who after came from earth sailing arrived   520
Wafted by angels, or flew o'er the lake
Rapt in a chariot drawn by fiery steeds.
The stairs were then let down, whether to dare
The fiend by easy ascent, or aggravate
His sad exclusion from the doors of bliss.[9]   525
Direct against which opened from beneath,
Just o'er the blissful seat of Paradise,
A passage down to th' earth—a passage wide,
Wider by far than that of after-times
Over Mount Sion, and, though that were large,   530
Over the Promised Land to God so dear,
By which, to visit oft those happy tribes,
On high behests his angels to and fro
Passed frequent,[1] and his eye with choice regard
From Paneas, the fount of Jordan's flood,   535

7. Portico.
8. Invisible. The story of Jacob's vision is summarized from Genesis 28.1–19. The stairs of the
ladder were meant "mysteriously"—each represented a stage of spiritual growth.
9. In either case, Milton implies, heavenly
authorities were aware of Satan's approach.

1. The crystalline spheres would be impenetrable
if there weren't passages, or holes, in them, through
which heavenly—and, alas, diabolic—spirits could
make their way. The visiting angels (act as) his eye
(in maintaining) a choice regard over the chosen
people.

To Beërsaba, where the Holy Land
Borders on Egypt and the Arabian shore.[2]
So wide the opening seemed, where bounds were set
To darkness, such as bound the ocean wave.
Satan from hence, now on the lower stair   540
That scaled by steps of gold to Heaven-gate,
Looks down with wonder at the sudden view
Of all this world at once. As when a scout,
Through dark and desert ways with peril gone
All night, at last by break of cheerful dawn   545
Obtains the brow of some high-climbing hill,
Which to his eye discovers unaware
The goodly prospect of some foreign land
First seen, or some renowned metropolis
With glistering spires and pinnacles adorned,   550
Which now the rising sun gilds with his beams;
Such wonder seized, though after Heaven seen,
The spirit malign, but much more envy seized,
At sight of all this world beheld so fair.
Round he surveys (and well might, where he stood   555
So high above the circling canopy
Of night's extended shade) from eastern point
Of Libra to the fleecy star that bears
Andromeda far off Atlantic seas[3]
Beyond th' horizon; then from pole to pole   560
He views in breadth—and, without longer pause,
Down right into the world's first region throws
His flight precipitant, and winds with ease
Through the pure marble air his oblique way[4]
Amongst innumerable stars, that shone   565
Stars distant, but nigh-hand seemed other worlds.
Or other worlds they seemed, or happy isles,
Like those Hesperian gardens famed of old,
Fortunate fields, and groves, and flowery vales;[5]
Thrice happy isles! But who dwelt happy there   570
He stayed not to inquire: above them all
The golden sun, in splendor likest Heaven,
Allured his eye. Thither his course he bends,
Through the calm firmament (but up or down,
By center or eccentric, hard to tell,   575
Or longitude),[6] where the great luminary,
Aloof the vulgar constellations thick,

---

2. From Paneas (or Dan) in northern Palestine to
Beersaba, or Beersheba, near the Egyptian border—the whole land.
3. In the Zodiac, Libra or the Scales are diametrically opposite the Ram ("the fleecy star"), which
seems to carry the constellation Andromeda on its
back.
4. "Marble" derives from the Greek word for

"shining," but there's also a sense of solidity in the
adjective to contrast with Satan's "oblique"
approach.
5. The gardens of the Hesperides and the "fortunate isles" of Greek mythology lay far out in the
Atlantic, almost like separate miniature worlds.
6. Milton is cautious about saying whether the sun
or the earth is at the center of the created cosmos.

That from his lordly eye keep distance due,
Dispenses light from far; they, as they move
Their starry dance in numbers that compute   580
Days, months, and years, towards his all-cheering lamp
Turn swift their various motions, or are turned
By his magnetic beam, that gently warms
The universe, and to each inward part
With gentle penetration, though unseen,   585
Shoots invisible virtue even to the deep;[7]
So wondrously was set his station bright.

Summary   Landing on the bright orb of the sun, Satan disguises himself as a youthful cherub, and approaches the solar guardian, the archangel
Uriel. Pretending interest in the new great works of God, he gets directions
toward earth and Adam's bower, then spirals down and lands on Mount
Niphates (in modern Iran) overlooking the site of Paradise.

From Book 4

[*Satan's Entry into Paradise; Adam and Eve
in their Bower of Bliss*]

O for that warning voice which he who saw
Th' Apocalypse heard cry in Heaven aloud,
Then when the dragon, put to second rout,
Came furious down to be revenged on men,
Woe to the inhabitants on Earth![1] that now,   5
While time was, our first parents had been warned
The coming of their secret foe, and scaped,
Haply so scaped, his mortal snare![2] For now
Satan, now first inflamed with rage, came down,
The tempter ere th' accuser of mankind,   10
To wreak on innocent frail man his loss
Of that first battle, and his flight to Hell.
Yet not rejoicing in his speed though bold
Far off and fearless, nor with cause to boast,
Begins his dire attempt; which nigh the birth   15
Now rolling, boils in his tumultuous breast,
And like a devilish engine back recoils
Upon himself. Horror and doubt distract
His troubled thoughts, and from the bottom stir

7. "Virtue" in the sense of "influence," "strength."
For example, gold was thought to grow in the depths
of the earth as a result of solar influence.
1. John of Patmos, in Revelation 12, describes a
war in heaven between dragon and angels, in the
course of which a voice cries from heaven, "Woe

to the inhabitants of the earth and of the sea!"
2. "Haply": by good luck, happily. "Mortal":
deadly. The reiterated "first" 's in lines 6, 9, and 12
refer back to "second" in line 3; Milton wants us
to remember that his story was the first of all the
Bible stories, and is, as it were, their root.

The Hell within him; for within him Hell   20
He brings, and round about him, nor from Hell
One step no more than from himself can fly
By change of place.[3] Now conscience wakes despair
That slumbered, wakes the bitter memory
Of what he was, what is, and what must be   25
Worse; of worse deeds worse sufferings must ensue.
Sometimes towards Eden, which now in his view
Lay pleasant, his grieved look he fixes sad;
Sometimes towards heaven and the full-blazing sun,
Which now sat high in his meridian tower;[4]   30
Then, much revolving, thus in sighs began:
    "O thou that with surpassing glory crowned
Look'st from thy sole dominion like the god
Of this new world—at whose sight all the stars
Hide their diminished heads—to thee I call,   35
But with no friendly voice, and add thy name,
O sun, to tell thee how I hate thy beams,
That bring to my remembrance from what state
I fell, how glorious once above thy sphere,
Till pride and worse ambition threw me down,   40
Warring in Heaven against Heaven's matchless King!
Ah, wherefore? He deserved no such return
From me, whom he created what I was
In that bright eminence, and with his good
Upbraided none;[5] nor was his service hard.   45
What could be less than to afford him praise,
The easiest recompense, and pay him thanks,
How due! Yet all his good proved ill in me,
And wrought but malice. Lifted up so high,
I 'sdained[6] subjection, and thought one step higher   50
Would set me highest, and in a moment quit
The debt immense of endless gratitude,
So burdensome, still paying, still to owe,
Forgetful what from him I still received;
And understood not that a grateful mind   55
By owing owes not, but still pays, at once
Indebted and discharged—what burden then?
Oh, had his powerful destiny ordained
Me some inferior angel, I had stood
Then happy; no unbounded hope had raised   60
Ambition. Yet why not? Some other power
As great might have aspired, and me, though mean,
Drawn to his part. But other powers as great

---

3. Satan's proud statement that "the mind is its own place" (1.254) finds here its bitter ironic echo.
4. Midday, the height of noon. Milton's nephew Edward Phillips tells us that the speech which follows was the first part of the poem that existed,

when Milton still thought of making it into the drama of "Adam Unparadised."
5. Demanded no return for his benefits; the phrase echoes James 1.5.
6. Disdained. "Quit": acquit, pay off.

Fell not, but stand unshaken, from within
Or from without to all temptations armed!   65
Hadst thou[7] the same free will and power to stand?
Thou hadst. Whom hast thou then, or what, to accuse,
But Heaven's free love dealt equally to all?
Be then his love accursed, since, love or hate,
To me alike it deals eternal woe.   70
Nay, cursed be thou; since against his thy will
Chose freely what it now so justly rues.
Me miserable![8] which way shall I fly
Infinite wrath and infinite despair?
Which way I fly is Hell; myself am Hell;   75
And in the lowest deep a lower deep
Still threatening to devour me opens wide,
To which the Hell I suffer seems a Heaven.
O then at last relent! Is there no place
Left for repentance, none for pardon left?   80
None left but by submission; and that word
Disdain forbids me, and my dread of shame
Among the spirits beneath, whom I seduced
With other promises and other vaunts
Than to submit, boasting I could subdue   85
Th' omnipotent. Ay me! they little know
How dearly I abide that boast so vain,
Under what torments inwardly I groan.
While they adore me on the throne of Hell,
With diadem and scepter high advanced,   90
The lower still I fall, only supreme
In misery: such joy ambition finds!
But say I could repent and could obtain
By act of grace[9] my former state, how soon
Would height recall high thoughts, how soon unsay   95
What feigned submission swore! Ease would recant
Vows made in pain, as violent and void.
For never can true reconcilement grow
Where wounds of deadly hate have pierced so deep;
Which would but lead me to a worse relapse   100
And heavier fall: so should I purchase dear
Short intermission, bought with double smart.
This knows my punisher; therefore as far
From granting he, as I from begging, peace.
All hope excluded thus, behold, instead   105
Of us outcast, exiled, his new delight,
Mankind created, and for him this world!
So farewell hope, and with hope farewell fear,

---

7. Satan addresses himself directly, as Adam will
do under parallel circumstances in Book 10, line
758 ff.

8. "Me miserable!": an exact Latinism, "me mi-

serum!"

9. The correct technical term for a formal pardon
is an "act of grace."

Farewell remorse! All good to me is lost;
Evil, be thou my good: by thee at least   110
Divided empire with Heaven's king I hold,
By thee, and more than half perhaps will reign;
As man ere long, and this new world, shall know."
   Thus while he spake, each passion dimmed his face,
Thrice changed with pale—ire, envy, and despair;   115
Which marred his borrowed visage, and betrayed
Him counterfeit, if any eye beheld:
For heavenly minds from such distempers foul
Are ever clear. Whereof he soon aware
Each perturbation smoothed with outward calm,   120
Artificer of fraud; and was the first
That practiced falsehood under saintly show,
Deep malice to conceal, couched with revenge:
Yet not enough had practiced to deceive
Uriel, once warned; whose eye pursued him down   125
The way he went, and on th' Assyrian mount
Saw him disfigured, more than could befall
Spirit of happy sort: his gestures fierce
He marked and mad demeanor, then alone,
As he supposed, all unobserved, unseen.   130
   So on he fares, and to the border comes
Of Eden, where delicious Paradise,
Now nearer, crowns with her enclosure green
As with a rural mound the champaign[1] head
Of a steep wilderness, whose hairy sides   135
With thicket overgrown, grotesque[2] and wild,
Access denied; and overhead up grew
Insuperable height of loftiest shade,
Cedar, and pine, and fir, and branching palm,
A sylvan scene, and as the ranks ascend   140
Shade above shade, a woody theater[3]
Of stateliest view. Yet higher than their tops
The verdurous wall of Paradise up sprung;
Which to our general sire[4] gave prospect large
Into his nether empire neighboring round.   145
And higher than that wall a circling row
Of goodliest trees loaden with fairest fruit,
Blossoms and fruits at once of golden hue,
Appeared, with gay enameled colors mixed;
On which the sun more glad impressed his beams   150
Than in fair evening cloud, or humid bow,[5]

1. From French *champs*, open countryside. Paradise is an open garden on top of a hill straddling
a river in the east of Eden.
2. One of the earliest uses of the word in English
to mean "romantic" or "picturesque."
3. As if in a Greek amphitheater, the trees are set

row on row.
4. Adam.
5. The rainbow. There is a thick wall of trees
around Paradise, which "access denied"; then above
them, the shaggy sides of Paradise itself ("the verdurous wall"), and above it the garden of fruit trees.

When God hath showered the earth: so lovely seemed
That landscape. And of pure now purer air[6]
Meets his approach, and to the heart inspires
Vernal delight and joy, able to drive[7]   155
All sadness but despair. Now gentle gales,
Fanning their odoriferous wings, dispense
Native perfumes, and whisper whence they stole
Those balmy spoils. As when to them who sail
Beyond the Cape of Hope, and now are past   160
Mozambic, off at sea northeast winds blow
Sabean odors from the spicy shore
Of Araby the Blest,[8] with such delay
Well pleased they slack their course, and many a league
Cheered with the grateful smell old Ocean smiles;   165
So entertained those odorous sweets the fiend
Who came their bane, though with them better pleased
Than Asmodëus with the fishy fume
That drove him, though enamored, from the spouse
Of Tobit's son,[9] and with a vengeance sent   170
From Media post to Egypt, there fast bound.
    Now to th' ascent of that steep savage[1] hill
Satan had journeyed on, pensive and slow;
But further way found none; so thick entwined,
As one continued brake, the undergrowth   175
Of shrubs and tangling bushes had perplexed
All path of man or beast that passed that way.
One gate there only was, and that looked east
On th' other side; which when th' arch-felon saw,
Due entrance he disdained, and in contempt   180
At one slight bound high overleaped all bound[2]
Of hill or highest wall, and sheer within
Lights on his feet. As when a prowling wolf,
Whom hunger drives to seek new haunt for prey,
Watching where shepherds pen their flocks at eve   185
In hurdled cotes[3] amid the field secure,
Leaps o'er the fence with ease into the fold;
Or as a thief, bent to unhoard the cash
Of some rich burgher, whose substantial doors,
Cross-barred and bolted fast, fear no assault,   190

6. After breathing pure air, Satan now breathes
even purer.
7. Scatter.
8. Coasting up East Africa after doubling the Cape
of Good Hope, Milton supposes off "Mozambic"
(Mozambique) one might meet "Sabean" (i.e., as
from Sheba) odors coming from "Araby the Blest"
(Arabia Felix). This is the fantasy of a man who
learned his geography from medieval atlases and
Diodorus Siculus, for the distance between Mozambique and Arabia is close to 2,000 miles.

9. Milton retells briefly here the story of Tobias,
Tobit's son, who married Sara and was saved from
the fate of her seven previous husbands by the advice
of Raphael, who showed him how to make a fishy
smell that would drive away the devil Asmodeus.
See the Book of Tobit among the Apocrypha.
1. Wooded, entangled (from Latin, *silvaticus*,
through Italian *selvaggio*, and French *sauvage*).
2. Satan enters Paradise, not only illegally, but with
a contemptuous pun.
3. Pens made of woven reeds.

In at the window climbs, or o'er the tiles;
So clomb[4] this first grand thief into God's fold:
So since into his church lewd hirelings[5] climb.
Thence up he flew, and on the Tree of Life,
The middle tree and highest there that grew,   195
Sat like a cormorant; yet not true life
Thereby regained, but sat devising death
To them who lived; nor on the virtue thought
Of that life-giving plant, but only used
For prospect,[6] what, well used, had been the pledge   200
Of immortality. So little knows
Any, but God alone, to value right
The good before him, but perverts best things
To worst abuse, or to their meanest use.
    Beneath him with new wonder now he views   205
To all delight of human sense exposed
In narrow room Nature's whole wealth; yea more,
A Heaven on Earth; for blissful Paradise
Of God the garden was, by him in the east
Of Eden planted. Eden stretched her line   210
From Auran eastward to the royal towers
Of great Seleucia, built by Grecian kings,
Or where the sons of Eden long before
Dwelt in Telassar.[7] In this pleasant soil
His far more pleasant garden God ordained.   215
Out of the fertile ground he caused to grow
All trees of noblest kind for sight, smell, taste;
And all amid them stood the Tree of Life,
High eminent, blooming ambrosial fruit
Of vegetable gold; and next to life,   220
Our death, the Tree of Knowledge, grew fast by—
Knowledge of good bought dear by knowing ill.
Southward through Eden went a river large,
Nor changed his course, but through the shaggy hill
Passed underneath engulfed; for God had thrown   225
That mountain, as his garden-mold,[8] high raised
Upon the rapid current, which, through veins
Of porous earth with kindly[9] thirst up drawn,
Rose a fresh fountain, and with many a rill

---

4. Old past tense of "climb," but used with a special feeling of ungainly energy. The whole metaphor, of God as a rich citizen hoarding Adam and
Eve from Satan the second-story-man, is instinct
with comic feeling. On the devil as a thief, see
John 10.1.
5. Base men interested only in money; Milton felt
strongly that churchmen should be unsalaried to
insure the purity of their motives.
6. Perspective, lookout.
7. By suggesting alternate boundaries of Eden,
Milton invokes a hazy sense of the richness, vast-

ness, and antiquity of the Middle East. "Auran" is
an area in Syria, to the south of Damascus;
"Seleucia," a powerful city founded by one of
Alexander's generals (hence, "built by Grecian
kings"), lies near modern Bagdad; and "Telassar"
is another Near Eastern kingdom, this one probably on the east bank of the Euphrates.
8. The mountain is God's topsoil, out of which
grows Paradise. The river (identified as the Tigris
in Book 9, line 71) flowed under the hill.
9. Natural.

Watered the garden; thence united fell   230
Down the steep glade, and met the nether flood,
Which from his darksome passage now appears,
And now, divided into four main streams,
Runs diverse, wandering many a famous realm
And country, whereof here needs no account;[1]   235
But rather to tell how, if art could tell,
How from that sapphire fount the crispèd[2] brooks,
Rolling on orient pearl and sands of gold,
With mazy error[3] under pendant shades
Ran nectar, visiting each plant, and fed   240
Flowers worthy of Paradise; which not nice[4] art
In beds and curious knots, but Nature boon[5]
Poured forth profuse on hill and dale and plain,
Both where the morning sun first warmly smote
The open field, and where the unpierced shade   245
Embrowned[6] the noontide bowers. Thus was this place,
A happy rural seat of various view:[7]
Groves whose rich trees wept odorous gums and balm;
Others whose fruit, burnished with golden rind,
Hung amiable[8]—Hesperian fables true,   250
If true, here only—and of delicious taste.
Betwixt them lawns, or level downs, and flocks
Grazing the tender herb, were interposed,
Or palmy hillock; or the flowery lap
Of some irriguous[9] valley spread her store,   255
Flowers of all hue, and without thorn the rose.[1]
Another side, umbrageous[2] grots and caves
Of cool recess, o'er which the mantling vine
Lays forth her purple grape, and gently creeps
Luxuriant; meanwhile murmuring waters fall   260
Down the slope hills dispersed, or in a lake,
That to the fringèd bank with myrtle crowned
Her crystal mirror holds, unite their streams.
The birds their choir apply;[3] airs, vernal airs,
Breathing the smell of field and grove, attune   265
The trembling leaves, while universal Pan,[4]
Knit with the Graces and the Hours in dance,
Led on th' eternal spring.[5] Not that fair field

1. Milton has in mind Genesis 2.10; but the expression "whereof here needs no account" dodges many questions about the correct translation of this passage.
2. Wavy, ruffled.
3. From Latin *errare*, "wandering."
4. Particular, careful.
5. Liberal, bounteous.
6. Darkened.
7. Aspect.
8. Lovely. These were real golden apples like those said to have existed in the Hesperides, fabulous islands of the Western Ocean; Paradise was the only place where the fable of the Hesperides was literally true.
9. Well-watered.
1. Figuratively and literally, there was no need for thorns in Paradise.
2. Shady.
3. Practice their song. "Airs" may be either "breezes" or "melodies," and probably are both.
4. The god of all nature. "Pan" in Greek means "all," but it is also the name of the goat-legged nature god.
5. The god of nature dances with the Graces and Hours, an image of perfect harmony.

Of Enna, where Proserpin gathering flowers,
Herself a fairer flower, by gloomy Dis   270
Was gathered, which cost Ceres all that pain
To seek her through the world; nor that sweet grove
Of Daphne,[6] by Orontes and th' inspired
Castalian spring, might with this Paradise
Of Eden strive; nor that Nyseian isle,   275
Girt with the river Triton, where old Cham,
Whom Gentiles Ammon call and Libyan Jove,
Hid Amalthea and her florid son
Young Bacchus from his stepdame Rhea's eye;[7]
Nor where Abassin kings their issue guard   280
Mount Amara[8] (though this by some supposed
True Paradise) under the Ethiop line
By Nilus' head, enclosed with shining rock,
A whole day's journey high, but wide remote
From this Assyrian garden, where the fiend   285
Saw undelighted all delight, all kind
Of living creatures, new to sight and strange.
Two of far nobler shape, erect and tall,
Godlike erect,[9] with native honor clad
In naked majesty, seemed lords of all,   290
And worthy seemed; for in their looks divine,
The image of their glorious Maker, shone
Truth, wisdom, sanctitude severe and pure—
Severe, but in true filial freedom[1] placed,
Whence true authority in men; though both   295
Not equal, as their sex not equal seemed;
For contemplation he and valor formed,
For softness she and sweet attractive grace;
He for God only, she for God in him.[2]
His fair large front[3] and eye sublime declared   300
Absolute rule; and hyacinthine[4] locks

6. Milton is comparing Paradise with the famous beauty spots of antiquity. Enna in Sicily was a lovely meadow from which "Proserpin" was kidnapped by "gloomy Dis" (i.e., Pluto); her mother Ceres sought her throughout the world. The grove of Daphne, near Antioch and the Orontes river in the Near East, had a spring called "Castalia" in imitation of the Muses' fountain near Delphi.

7. The isle of Nysa in the river Triton in Tunisia was where Ammon hid Bacchus, his bastard child by Amalthea, from the eye of his wife Rhea. "Florid" (wine-flushed) Bacchus, when he grew up, received the name of Dionysus in honor of his birthplace. The identification of the Egyptian god Ammon or Hammon with Cham or Ham, the son of Noah, is a piece of comparative anthropology like that in 10.580 ff.

8. Finally, Paradise ("this Assyrian garden," line 285) is finer than the royal residences atop Mt. Amara, where the "Abassin" (Abyssinian) kings had a splendid palace. Milton's authority for this exotic

scene was Peter Heylyn (*Cosmographie* 4.64), from whom he took several phrases direct. His passage then had a continuing influence on the names and phrasings of Coleridge's *Kubla Khan*.

9. By emphasizing the word "erect," Milton means to distinguish man from the beasts of the field, who went "prone."

1. Though almost a paradox, the phrase suggests Milton's idea that true freedom always involves respect for authority and hierarchy. Cf. Eve's foolish question, "For, inferior, who is free?" (9.825)

2. Milton's ideas on the relations between the sexes were the strict ones of his time, and of Christian tradition: "The head of every man is Christ; and the head of the woman is the man" (1 Corinthians 11.3).

3. Forehead.

4. A classical metaphor, often applied to hair, and implying "dark" or perhaps "flowing," but actually not very definite in its import.

Round from his parted forelock manly hung
Clustering, but not beneath his shoulders broad:
She, as a veil down to the slender waist,
Her unadornèd golden tresses wore   305
Disheveled, but in wanton ringlets waved
As the vine curls her tendrils,[5] which implied
Subjection, but required with gentle sway,
And by her yielded, by him best received,
Yielded with coy[6] submission, modest pride,   310
And sweet, reluctant, amorous delay.
Nor those mysterious parts were then concealed;
Then was not guilty shame. Dishonest shame
Of Nature's works, honor dishonorable,
Sin-bred, how have ye troubled all mankind   315
With shows instead, mere shows of seeming pure,
And banished from man's life his happiest life,
Simplicity and spotless innocence!
So passed they naked on, nor shunned the sight
Of God or angel; for they thought no ill;   320
So hand in hand they passed, the loveliest pair
That ever since in love's embraces met:
Adam the goodliest man of men since born
His sons; the fairest of her daughters Eve.[7]
Under a tuft of shade that on a green   325
Stood whispering soft, by a fresh fountain-side,
They sat them down; and after no more toil
Of their sweet gardening labor than sufficed
To recommend cool Zephyr,[8] and made ease
More easy, wholesome thirst and appetite   330
More grateful, to their supper fruits they fell,
Nectarine fruits which the compliant boughs
Yielded them, sidelong as they sat recline
On the soft downy bank damasked with flowers.
The savory pulp they chew, and in the rind   335
Still as they thirsted scoop the brimming stream;
Nor gentle purpose,[9] nor endearing smiles
Wanted, nor youthful dalliance, as beseems
Fair couple linked in happy nuptial league,
Alone as they. About them frisking played   340
All beasts of th' earth, since wild, and of all chase[1]
In wood or wilderness, forest or den.
Sporting the lion ramped,[2] and in his paw
Dandled the kid; bears, tigers, ounces, pards,[3]

---

5. Eve's hair is curly, abundant, uncontrolled; like
the vegetation in Paradise, it clings seductively about
a severe and masculine virtue.
6. Shy.
7. Logically these constructions are absurd; Adam
was not born since his day, Eve was not one of her
own daughters. Milton combines comparative with

superlative forms for emphatic effect.
8. I.e., to make a cool breeze welcome.
9. Conversation. "Wanted": lacked.
1. Who lurk in every sort of cover.
2. Reared up.
3. Lynxes and leopards.

Gamboled before them; th' unwieldy elephant   345
To make them mirth used all his might, and wreathed
His lithe proboscis; close the serpent sly,
Insinuating,[4] wove with Gordian twine
His braided train,[5] and of his fatal guile
Gave proof unheeded. Others on the grass   350
Couched and now filled with pasture, gazing sat,
Or bedward ruminating;[6] for the sun,
Declined, was hasting now with prone career
To th' ocean isles,[7] and in th' ascending scale
Of heaven the stars that usher evening rose: 355
When Satan, still in gaze as first he stood,
Scarce thus at length failed speech recovered sad:[8]
    "O Hell! what do mine eyes with grief behold?
Into our room of bliss thus high advanced
Creatures of other mold, Earth-born perhaps,   360
Not spirits, yet to heavenly spirits bright
Little inferior; whom my thoughts pursue
With wonder, and could love; so lively shines
In them divine resemblance, and such grace
The hand that formed them on their shape hath poured.[9]   365
Ah! gentle pair, ye little think how nigh
Your change approaches, when all these delights
Will vanish, and deliver ye to woe,
More woe, the more your taste is now of joy:
Happy, but for so happy[1] ill secured   370
Long to continue, and this high seat, your Heaven,
Ill fenced for Heaven to keep out such a foe
As now is entered; yet no purposed foe
To you, whom I could pity thus forlorn,
Though I unpitied. League with you I seek,   375
And mutual amity so strait, so close,
That I with you must dwell, or you with me,
Henceforth.[2] My dwelling, haply, may not please,
Like this fair Paradise, your sense; yet such
Accept your Maker's work; he gave it me,   380
Which I as freely give. Hell shall unfold,
To entertain you two, her widest gates,
And send forth all her kings; there will be room,
Not like these narrow limits, to receive
Your numerous offspring; if no better place,   385

4. Writhing and twisting, but with a glance at the Tempter's rhetorical techniques.
5. Checkered body. "Gordian twine": knots, like the Gordian knot, cut by Alexander the Great.
6. The animals are chewing their cuds before bedtime; in Paradise, where the animal kingdom is not yet subject to death, they are perforce vegetarians.
7. The Azores.
8. The choked, laborious line mirrors Satan's heavy, congested mind.
9. Though Satan's moral values are topsy-turvy ("Evil, be thou my good," he has said in the first part of Book 4), his aesthetic values are strictly orthodox.
1. Such happiness.
2. Though it starts in simple admiration, Satan's friendship for mankind is, at the end, grisly and sardonic. The turning point seems to be "though I unpitied" (line 375).

Thank him who puts me, loath, to this revenge
On you, who wrong me not, for him who wronged.[3]
And should I at your harmless innocence
Melt, as I do, yet public reason just—
Honor and empire with revenge enlarged   390
By conquering this new world—compels me now
To do what else, though damned, I should abhor."[4]
　　So spake the fiend, and with necessity,
The tyrant's plea, excused his devilish deeds.
Then from his lofty stand on that high tree   395
Down he alights among the sportful herd
Of those four-footed kinds, himself now one,
Now other, as their shape served best his end
Nearer to view his prey, and unespied,
To mark what of their state he more might learn   400
By word or action marked. About them round
A lion now he stalks with fiery glare;
Then as a tiger, who by chance hath spied
In some purlieu[5] two gentle fawns at play,
Straight couches close; then, rising, changes oft   405
His couchant watch, as one who chose his ground,
Whence rushing he might surest seize them both
Gripped in each paw; when Adam first of men
To first of women Eve thus moving speech,
Turned him all ear to hear new utterance flow.   410
　　"Sole partner and sole part of all these joys,[6]
Dearer thyself than all; needs must the power
That made us, and for us this ample world,
Be infinitely good, and of his good
As liberal and free as infinite,   415
That raised us from the dust and placed us here
In all this happiness, who at his hand
Have nothing merited, nor can perform
Aught of which he hath need; he who requires
From us no other service than to keep   420
This one, this easy charge, of all the trees
In Paradise that bear delicious fruit
So various, not to taste that only Tree
Of Knowledge, planted by the Tree of Life,
So near grows death to life, whate'er death is,   425
Some dreadful thing, no doubt; for well thou know'st
God hath pronounced it death to taste that tree,
The only sign of our obedience left
Among so many signs of power and rule
Conferred upon us, and dominion given   430

3. I.e., it is not my fault; Satan's favorite evasion.
4. Satan's final reason for destroying Adam and
Eve is thoroughly Satanic; it is *ragione di stato*,
reason of state, the public interest.
5. The outskirt of a forest. Note that Satan can
and does enter any animal he wants; it is only for
the special purposes of the temptation that he finds
the serpent specially convenient.
6. Eve shares Adam's joys, and is herself the principal part of them.

Over all other creatures that possess
Earth, air, and sea. Then let us not think hard
One easy prohibition, who enjoy
Free leave so large to all things else, and choice
Unlimited of manifold delights;   435
But let us ever praise him, and extol
His bounty, following our delightful task
To prune these growing plants and tend these flowers,
Which were it toilsome, yet with thee were sweet."
    To whom thus Eve replied: "O thou for whom   440
And from whom I was formed flesh of thy flesh,
And without whom am to no end, my guide
And head, what thou hast said is just and right.
For we to him indeed all praises owe
And daily thanks, I chiefly who enjoy   445
So far the happier lot, enjoying thee
Preeminent by so much odds, while thou
Like consort to thyself canst nowhere find.
That day I oft remember, when from sleep
I first awaked, and found myself reposed   450
Under a shade on flowers, much wondering where
And what I was, whence thither brought, and how.
Not distant far from thence a murmuring sound
Of waters issued from a cave and spread
Into a liquid plain, then stood unmoved,   455
Pure as th' expanse of heaven; I thither went
With unexperienced thought, and laid me down
On the green bank, to look into the clear
Smooth lake that to me seemed another sky.
As I bent down to look, just opposite,   460
A shape within the wat'ry gleam appeared,
Bending to look on me. I started back,
It started back; but pleased I soon returned,
Pleased it returned as soon with answering looks
Of sympathy and love. There I had fixed   465
Mine eyes till now, and pined with vain desire,[7]
Had not a voice thus warned me: 'What thou seest,
What there thou seest, fair creature, is thyself;
With thee it came and goes. But follow me,
And I will bring thee where no shadow stays   470
Thy coming, and thy soft embraces, he
Whose image thou art, him thou shalt enjoy
Inseparably thine, to him shalt bear
Multitudes like thyself, and thence be called
Mother of human race.' What could I do   475
But follow straight, invisibly thus led?

---

7. The fate of Narcissus, who fell in love with his own reflection, is hinted at. Like most men of his day, Milton followed the apostle Peter in thinking woman "the weaker vessel," and the attitude pervades his treatment of Eve.

Till I espied thee, fair indeed and tall
Under a platan,[8] yet methought less fair,
Less winning soft, less amiably mild
Than that smooth wat'ry image. Back I turned;   480
Thou following cried'st aloud, 'Return, fair Eve,
Whom fli'st thou? whom thou fli'st, of him thou art,
His flesh, his bone; to give thee being I lent
Out of my side to thee, nearest my heart,
Substantial life, to have thee by my side   485
Henceforth an individual solace dear.
Part of my soul I seek thee, and thee claim
My other half.' With that, thy gentle hand
Seized mine, I yielded, and from that time see
How beauty is excelled by manly grace   490
And wisdom, which alone is truly fair."
    So spake our general mother, and with eyes
Of conjugal attraction unreproved
And meek surrender, half embracing leaned
On our first father; half her swelling breast   495
Naked met his under the flowing gold
Of her loose tresses hid. He in delight
Both of her beauty and submissive charms
Smiled with superior love, as Jupiter
On Juno smiles, when he impregns the clouds   500
That shed May flowers, and pressed her matron lip
With kisses pure. Aside the Devil turned
For envy, yet with jealous leer malign
Eyed them askance, and to himself thus plained:[9]
    "Sight hateful, sight tormenting! thus these two   505
Imparadised in one another's arms,
The happier Eden, shall enjoy their fill
Of bliss on bliss, while I to Hell am thrust,
Where neither joy nor love, but fierce desire,
Among our other torments not the least,   510
Still unfulfilled with pain of longing pines.
Yet let me not forget what I have gained
From their own mouths: all is not theirs, it seems.
One fatal tree there stands, of knowledge called,
Forbidden them to taste. Knowledge forbidden?   515
Suspicious, reasonless. Why should their lord
Envy them that? Can it be sin to know,
Can it be death? and do they only stand
By ignorance, is that their happy state,
The proof of their obedience and their faith?   520
O fair foundation laid whereon to build
Their ruin! Hence I will excite their minds
With more desire to know, and to reject

8. Plane tree, with broad leaves and spreading branches.
9. Complained.

Envious commands, invented with design
To keep them low whom knowledge might exalt   525
Equal with gods. Aspiring to be such,
They taste and die; what likelier can ensue?
But first with narrow search I must walk round
This garden, and no corner leave unspied;
A chance but chance[1] may lead where I may meet   530
Some wandering spirit of heaven, by fountain side
Or in thick shade retired, from him to draw
What further would be learnt. Live while ye may,
Yet happy pair; enjoy, till I return,
Short pleasures, for long woes are to succeed."   535
    So saying, his proud step he scornful turned,
But with sly circumspection, and began
Through wood, through waste, o'er hill, o'er dale his roam.
Meanwhile, in utmost longitude, where heaven
With earth and ocean meets, the setting sun   540
Slowly descended, and with right aspèct
Against the eastern gate of Paradise
Levelled his evening rays.[2] It was a rock
Of alabaster piled up to the clouds,
Conspicuous far, winding with one ascent   545
Accessible from earth, one entrance high;
The rest was craggy cliff that overhung
Still as it rose, impossible to climb.
Betwixt these rocky pillars Gabriel sat,
Chief of th' angelic guards, awaiting night;   550
About him exercised heroic games
Th' unarmèd youth of Heaven, but nigh at hand
Celestial armory, shields, helms, and spears,
Hung high with diamond flaming and with gold.
Thither came Uriel, gliding through the even   555
On a sunbeam, swift as a shooting star
In autumn thwarts[3] the night when vapors fired
Impress the air, and shows the mariner
From what point of his compass to beware
Impetuous winds.[4] He thus began in haste: 560
    "Gabriel, to thee thy course by lot hath given
Charge and strict watch that to this happy place
No evil thing approach or enter in.
This day at height of noon came to my sphere
A spirit, zealous (as he seemed) to know   565
More of th' Almighty's works and chiefly man,
God's latest image. I described his way
Bent all on speed, and marked his airy gait;[5]

---

1. An opportunity, even if only an accident.
2. Setting in the west, the sun can strike the eastern gate only from the inside. "Right aspèct": direct view.
3. Flies across. "Vapors fired": heat lightning.
4. Meteors were thought to indicate by the direction of their fall the source of oncoming storms.
5. Course. "Described": descried.

But in the mount that lies from Eden north,
Where he first lighted, soon discerned his looks   570
Alien from Heaven, with passions foul obscured.
Mine eye pursued him still, but under shade
Lost sight of him. One of the banished crew
I fear hath ventured from the deep to raise
New troubles; him thy care must be to find."   575
　　To whom the wingèd warrior thus returned:
"Uriel, no wonder if thy perfect sight
Amid the sun's bright circle where thou sitst
See far and wide. In at this gate none pass
The vigilance here placed, but such as come   580
Well known from Heaven; and since meridian hour[6]
No creature thence. If spirit of other sort
So minded have o'erleaped these earthy bounds
On purpose, hard thou know'st it to exclude
Spiritual substance with corporeal bar.   585
But if within the circuit of these walks
In whatsoever shape he lurk of whom
Thou tell'st, by morrow dawning I shall know."
　　So promised he, and Uriel to his charge
Returned on that bright beam, whose point now raised   590
Bore him slope downward to the sun now fallen
Beneath th' Azores, whether the prime orb,
Incredible how swift had thither rolled
Diurnal, or this less volùble earth
By shorter flight to th' east,[7] had left him there   595
Arraying with reflected purple and gold
The clouds that on his western throne attend.
Now came still evening on, and twilight gray
Had in her sober livery all things clad.
Silence accompanied, for beast and bird,   600
They to their grassy couch, these to their nests,
Were slunk, all but the wakeful nightingale;
She all night long her amorous descant[8] sung.
Silence was pleased; now glowed the firmament
With living sapphires; Hesperus that led   605
The starry host rode brightest, till the moon,
Rising in clouded majesty, at length
Apparent queen unveiled her peerless light
And o'er the dark her silver mantle threw.
　　When Adam thus to Eve: "Fair consort, th' hour   610
Of night and all things now retired to rest
Mind us of like repose, since God hath set

---

6. Noon.
7. Again Milton avoids the question whether sun moves around earth or vice versa; he clearly enjoys Uriel's trick of sliding down a sunbeam to reach the earth, and then (relative positions having changed) down the same beam back to his sunny post. "Volùble": swift-turning.
8. Melody. ("Descant" has more technical meanings as well, but not here.)

Labor and rest as day and night to men
Successive, and the timely dew of sleep
Now falling with soft slumbrous weight inclines   615
Our eyelids. Other creatures all day long
Rove idle unemployed, and less need rest;
Man hath his daily work of body or mind
Appointed, which declares his dignity
And the regard of Heaven on all his ways,   620
While other animals unactive range,
And of their doings God takes no account.
Tomorrow ere fresh morning streak the east
With first approach of light, we must be risen
And at our pleasant labor, to reform   625
Yon flow'ry arbors, yonder alleys green,
Our walk at noon, with branches overgrown
That mock our scant manuring,[9] and require
More hands than ours to lop their wanton growth.
Those blossoms also and those dropping gums   630
That lie bestrown unsightly and unsmooth
Ask riddance, if we mean to tread with ease;
Meanwhile, as nature wills, night bids us rest."
    To whom thus Eve with perfect beauty adorned:
"My author and disposer, what thou bidd'st   635
Unargued I obey; so God ordains.
God is thy law, thou mine; to know no more
Is woman's happiest knowledge and her praise.
With thee conversing I forget all time,
All seasons and their change, all please alike.[1]   640
Sweet is the breath of morn, her rising sweet,
With charm of earliest birds; pleasant the sun
When first on this delightful land he spreads
His orient beams on herb, tree, fruit, and flower
Glistering with dew; fragrant the fertile earth   645
After soft showers; and sweet the coming on
Of grateful evening mild, then silent night
With this her solemn bird and this fair moon
And these the gems of heaven, her starry train:
But neither breath of morn when she ascends   650
With charm of earliest birds, nor rising sun
On this delightful land, nor herb, fruit, flower
Glistering with dew, nor fragrance after showers,
Nor grateful evening mild, nor silent night
With this her solemn bird, nor walk by moon   655
Or glittering starlight without thee is sweet.
But wherefore all night long shine these, for whom
This glorious sight, when sleep hath shut all eyes?"

9. Cultivating.
1. As there are no seasons in Paradise, Eve must   mean the times of day. Her incantatory repetitions
                                                      echo similar effects in the Song of Solomon.

    To whom our general ancestor replied:
"Daughter of God and Man, accomplished Eve,   660
Those have their course to finish round the earth
By morrow evening, and from land to land
In order, though to nations yet unborn,
Minist'ring light prepared, they set and rise,
Lest total darkness should by night regain   665
Her old possession, and extinguish life
In nature and all things, which these soft fires
Not only enlighten, but with kindly heat
Of various influence foment[2] and warm,
Temper or nourish, or in part shed down   670
Their stellar virtue on all kinds that grow
On earth, made hereby apter to receive
Perfection from the sun's more potent ray.[3]
These, then, though unbeheld in deep of night,
Shine not in vain; nor think, though men were none,   675
That heaven would want spectators, God want praise.
Millions of spiritual creatures walk the earth
Unseen, both when we wake and when we sleep;
All these with ceaseless praise his works behold
Both day and night. How often from the steep   680
Of echoing hill or thicket have we heard
Celestial voices to the midnight air
Sole or responsive each to other's note,
Singing their great Creator: oft in bands
While they keep watch or nightly rounding walk,   685
With heavenly touch of instrumental sounds
In full harmonic number joined, their songs
Divide the night and lift our thoughts to Heaven."
    Thus talking, hand in hand alone they passed
On to their blissful bower. It was a place   690
Chos'n by the sovereign planter when he framed
All things to man's delightful use; the roof
Of thickest covert was inwoven shade,
Laurel and myrtle, and what higher grew
Of firm and fragrant leaf; on either side,   695
Acanthus and each odorous bushy shrub
Fenced up the verdant wall. Each beauteous flower,
Iris all hues, roses, and jessamine
Reared high their flourished heads between, and wrought
Mosaic; underfoot the violet,   700
Crocus, and hyacinth with rich inlay
Broidered the ground, more colored than with stone
Of costliest emblem.[4] Other creature here,
Beast, bird, insect, or worm durst enter none,

2. Cherish, nurture.
3. The stars were thought to have their own occult
influence and also to modulate that of the sun.

Before the Fall, all these influences were "kindly"
(benign).
4. Inlaid work.

Such was their awe of man. In shadier bower,   705
More sacred and sequestered, though but feigned,
Pan or Silvanus never slept, nor Nymph
Nor Faunus haunted.[5] Here in close recess
With flowers, garlands, and sweet-smelling herbs
Espousèd Eve decked first her nuptial bed,   710
And heavenly choirs the hymenaean[6] sung,
What day the genial angel to our sire
Brought her in naked beauty more adorned,
More lovely than Pandora, whom the gods
Endowed with all their gifts, and O too like   715
In sad event, when to th' unwiser son
Of Japhet brought by Hermes, she ensnared
Mankind with her fair looks, to be avenged
On him who had stole Jove's authentic fire.[7]
    Thus at their shady lodge arrived, both stood,   720
Both turned, and under open sky adored
The god that made both sky, air, earth, and heaven
Which they beheld, the moon's resplendent globe
And starry pole: "Thou also mad'st the night,
Maker omnipotent, and thou the day,   725
Which we in our appointed work employed
Have finished happy in our mutual help
And mutual love, the crown of all our bliss
Ordained by thee, and this delicious place
For us too large, where thy abundance wants   730
Partakers, and uncropped falls to the ground.
But thou hast promised from us two a race
To fill the earth, who shall with us extol
Thy goodness infinite, both when we wake
And when we seek, as now, thy gift of sleep."   735
    This said unanimous, and other rites
Observing none but adoration pure
Which God likes best,[8] into their inmost bower
Handed they went; and, eased the putting off
Those troublesome disguises which we wear,   740
Straight side by side were laid. Nor turned, I ween,
Adam from his fair spouse, nor Eve the rites
Mysterious of connubial love refused—
Whatever hypocrites austerely talk
Of purity and place and innocence,   745

---

5. Forest-and-field divinities of classical mythology.
6. Marriage hymn.
7. Pandora was a lovely girl, bestowed by the gods on Epimetheus, brother of Prometheus. ("Epimetheus" means "hind-sighted," "Prometheus" means "fore-sighted," "Pandora" means "All-Gifts.") The brothers were sons of Iapetos, whom Milton identifies with Japhet, Noah's third son. Pandora's dowry consisted of a closed box, which foolish Epimetheus opened; all the ills of the human race flew out, leaving only hope behind. The Eve-Pandora parallel was often used by learned misogynists.
8. Like many Puritans, Milton hated set forms of prayer. Adam and Eve pray spontaneously, hence (we are to think) sincerely. "Handed": hand in hand; "eased": spared. (As they wore no clothes, they did not have to undress.)

Defaming as impure what God declares
Pure and commands to some, leaves free to all.
Our Maker bids increase,[9] who bids abstain
But our destroyer, foe to God and man?
Hail wedded love, mysterious law, true source   750
Of human offspring, sole propriety[1]
In Paradise of all things common else.
By thee adulterous lust was driven from men
Among the bestial herds to range, by thee
Founded in reason, loyal, just, and pure,   755
Relations dear and all the charities[2]
Of father, son, and brother first were known.
Far be 't that I should write thee sin or blame,
Or think thee unbefitting holiest place,
Perpetual fountain of domestic sweets,   760
Whose bed is undefiled and chaste pronounced,
Present or past, as saints and patriarchs used.[3]
Here Love his golden shafts employs, here lights
His constant lamp and waves his purple wings,
Reigns here and revels; not in the bought smile   765
Of harlots, loveless, joyless, unindeared,
Casual fruition, nor in court amours,
Mixed dance or wanton masque or midnight ball
Or serenade, which the starved lover sings
To his proud fair, best quitted with disdain.   770
These, lulled by nightingales, embracing slept,
And on their naked limbs the flowery roof
Showered roses, which the morn repaired.[4] Sleep on,
Blest pair; and O yet happiest if ye seek
No happier state, and know to know no more.[5]   775

Summary   Fulfilling his promise to Uriel, Gabriel divides his night watch into search parties, assigning Ithuriel and Zephon to guard closely the bower of Adam and Eve. They find Satan in the bower, whispering in the ear of the sleeping Eve, and bring him before Gabriel. A battle impends, but is averted by a heavenly signal, and Satan flees out of Paradise.

From Book 5

[*Eve's Dream: Trouble in Paradise*]

Now Morn her rosy steps in th' eastern clime
Advancing, sowed the earth with orient pearl,

9. Genesis 1.28.
1. Property, specifically private property.
2. Affections.
3. Throughout history ("present or past"), Milton says, matrimony has been an honorable estate. The

"golden shafts" (arrows) of Cupid produce true love.
4. Replaced.
5. I.e., know enough to be content with what you know.

When Adam waked, so customed, for his sleep
Was airy light, from pure digestion bred
And temperate vapors bland, which the only sound   5
Of leaves and fuming rills, Aurora's fan,[1]
Lightly dispersed, and the shrill matin song
Of birds on every bough; so much the more
His wonder was to find unwakened Eve
With tresses discomposed and glowing cheek   10
As through unquiet rest; he on his side
Leaning half-raised with looks of cordial love
Hung over her enamored, and beheld
Beauty which whether waking or asleep
Shot forth peculiar[2] graces; then with voice   15
Mild as when Zephyrus on Flora breathes,
Her soft hand touching, whispered thus. "Awake,
My fairest, my espoused, my latest found,
Heaven's last best gift, my ever new delight,
Awake, the morning shines, and the fresh field   20
Calls us: we lose the prime, to mark how spring
Our tended plants, how blows the citron grove,
What drops the myrrh and what the balmy reed,
How nature paints her colors, how the bee
Sits on the bloom extracting liquid sweet."[3]   25
    Such whispering waked her, but with startled eye
On Adam, whom embracing, thus she spake:
    "Oh sole in whom my thoughts find all repose,
My glory, my perfection, glad I see
Thy face, and morn returned, for I this night—   30
Such night till this I never passed—have dreamed,
If dreamed, not as I oft am wont, of thee,
Works of day past or morrow's next design,
But of offense and trouble, which my mind
Knew never till this irksome night. Methought   35
Close at mine ear one called me forth to walk
With gentle voice; I thought it thine; it said,
'Why sleepest thou, Eve? Now is the pleasant time,
The cool, the silent, save where silence yields
To the night-warbling bird, that now awake   40
Tunes sweetest his love-labored song; now reigns
Full-orbed the moon, and with more pleasing light
Shadowy sets off the face of things—in vain
If none regard. Heaven wakes with all his eyes,[4]
Whom to behold but thee, nature's desire,   45
In whose sight all things joy with ravishment

---

1. The fan of Aurora (goddess of dawn) is the rustling leaves, as the "orient pearl" of line 2 is dewdrops. "Matin": morning.
2. Distinctive. Zephyrus is god of the gentle west

wind, Flora goddess of flowers.
3. Adam's good morning to Eve is phrased after
the Song of Solomon.
4. The stars.

Attracted by thy beauty still to gaze.'
I rose as at thy call, but found thee not;
To find thee I directed then my walk;
And on, methought, alone I passed through ways   50
That brought me on a sudden to the tree
Of interdicted knowledge: fair it seemed,
Much fairer to my fancy than by day;
And as I wondering looked, beside it stood
One shaped and winged like one of those from Heaven   55
By us oft seen. His dewy locks distilled
Ambrosia;[5] on that tree he also gazed:
And 'Oh, fair plant,' said he, 'with fruit surcharged,
Deigns none to ease thy load and taste thy sweet,
Nor god nor man? is knowledge so despised?   60
Or envy or what reserve forbids to taste?[6]
Forbid who will, none shall from me withhold
Longer thy offered good, why else set here?'
This said, he paused not, but with venturous arm
He plucked, he tasted; me damp horror chilled   65
At such bold words vouched with a deed so bold.
But he thus overjoyed: 'Oh fruit divine,
Sweet of thyself, but much more sweet thus cropped,
Forbidden here, it seems, as only fit
For gods, yet able to make gods of men: 70
And why not gods of men, since good, the more
Communicated, more abundant grows,
The author not impaired, but honored more?
Here, happy creature, fair angelic Eve,
Partake thou also; happy though thou art,   75
Happier thou may'st be, worthier canst not be.
Taste this, and be henceforth among the gods
Thyself a goddess, not to earth confined,
But sometimes in the air, as we, sometimes
Ascend to heaven, by merit thine, and see   80
What life the gods live there, and such live thou.'
So saying, he drew nigh, and to me held,
Even to my mouth of that same fruit held part
Which he had plucked; the pleasant savory smell
So quickened appetite that I, methought,   85
Could not but taste. Forthwith up to the clouds
With him I flew, and underneath beheld
The earth outstretched immense, a prospect wide
And various: wondering at my flight and change
To this high exaltation, suddenly   90
My guide was gone, and I, methought, sunk down
And fell asleep. But Oh how glad I waked

5. Technically, the food of the gods; used here of   6. I.e., does either envy or some other barrier
perfume.   ("reserve") forbid to taste?

To find this but a dream!" Thus Eve her night
Related, and thus Adam answered sad:[7]
   "Best image of myself and dearer half,   95
The trouble of thy thoughts this night in sleep
Affects me equally; nor can I like
This uncouth dream, of evil sprung, I fear;
Yet evil whence? In thee can harbor none,
Created pure. But know that in the soul   100
Are many lesser faculties that serve
Reason as chief; among these fancy next
Her office holds. Of all external things
Which the five watchful senses represent
She forms imaginations, airy shapes   105
Which reason, joining or disjoining, frames
All what we affirm or what deny, and call
Our knowledge or opinion; then retires
Into her private cell when nature rests.
Oft in her absence mimic fancy wakes   110
To imitate her; but, misjoining shapes,
Wild work produces oft, and most in dreams,
Ill matching words and deeds long past or late.
Some such resemblances methinks I find
Of our last evening's talk in this thy dream,[8]   115
But with addition strange. Yet be not sad,
Evil into the mind of god[9] or man
May come and go, so unapproved, and leave
No spot or blame behind; which gives me hope
That what in sleep thou didst abhor to dream,   120
Waking thou never wilt consent to do.
Be not disheartened then, nor cloud those looks
That wont to be more cheerful and serene
Than when fair morning first smiles on the world;
And let us to our fresh employments rise   125
Among the groves, the fountains, and the flowers
That open now their choicest bosomed smells
Reserved from night, and kept for thee in store."
   So cheered he his fair spouse, and she was cheered,
But silently a gentle tear let fall   130
From either eye, and wiped them with her hair;
Two other precious drops that ready stood,
Each in their crystal sluice, he ere they fell
Kissed as the gracious signs of sweet remorse
And pious awe that feared to have offended.   135

---

7. Grave, serious.
8. Adam recalls his own words in 4.411–39.
9. Probably "angel," as elsewhere; but perhaps also

"God," whose omniscience must encompass evil
as well as good.

Summary   Before going to work at their rural tasks, Adam and Eve
recite their spontaneous morning prayers. God, seeing and pitying their
unprotected innocence, dispatches Raphael to warn them of approaching
dangers. The affable archangel enters the bower just about noontime and is
promptly invited to join the midday meal, an invitation which he gladly
accepts.

[A Visit with the Angel: The Scale of Nature]

       * * * So to the sylvan lodge
They came, that like Pomona's arbor[1] smiled
With flowerets decked and fragrant smells; but Eve,
Undecked save with herself, more lovely fair   380
Than wood nymph or the fairest goddess feigned
Of three that on Mount Ida naked strove,[2]
Stood t' entertain her guest from Heaven; no veil
She needed, virtue-proof, no thought infirm
Altered her cheek. On whom the Angel "Hail"   385
Bestowed, the holy salutation used
Long after to blessed Mary, second Eve.
   "Hail mother of mankind, whose fruitful womb
Shall fill the world more numerous with thy sons
Than with these various fruits the trees of God   390
Have heaped this table." Raised of grassy turf
Their table was, and mossy seats had round,
And on her ample square from side to side
All autumn piled, though spring and autumn here
Danced hand in hand. A while discourse they hold—   395
No fear lest dinner cool—when thus began
Our author.[3] "Heavenly stranger, please to taste
These bounties which our nourisher, from whom
All perfect good, unmeasured-out, descends,
To us for food and for delight hath caused   400
The earth to yield;[4] unsavory food perhaps
To spiritual natures; only this I know,
That one celestial Father gives to all."
   To whom the Angel: "Therefore what he gives
(Whose praise be ever sung) to man in part   405
Spiritual, may of purest spirits be found
No ungrateful food;[5] and food alike those pure
Intelligential substances require
As doth your rational; and both contain

---

1. Pomona, Roman goddess of fruit trees and gardens, dwelt in an orchard.
2. Aphrodite, Hera, and Athena were judged for their beauty on Mount Ida by Paris, son of Priam. Milton reminds us that the goddesses were only "feigned," i.e., not true in the sense that the Christian god is true.
3. Our creator (i.e., Adam).

4. I.e., please to taste these bounties which God ("our nourisher") has caused the earth to yield to us for food and for delight.
5. I.e., food that is proper for man, who is partly spiritual, will be proper also for the very purest spirits. The idea that within the hierarchical universe higher powers include and comprehend lower powers is the key to the entire passage that follows.

Within them every lower faculty　　　　　　　　　410
Of sense, whereby they hear, see, smell, touch, taste,
Tasting concoct,[6] digest, assimilate,
And corporeal to incorporeal turn.
For know, whatever was created needs
To be sustained and fed; of elements　　　　　　415
The grosser feeds the purer, earth the sea,
Earth and the sea feed air, the air those fires
Ethereal, and as lowest first the moon—
Whence in her visage round those spots, unpurged
Vapors not yet into her substance turned.[7]　　420
Nor doth the moon no nourishment exhale
From her moist continent to higher orbs.
The sun, that light imparts to all, receives
From all his alimental recompense
In humid exhalations, and at even　　　　　　　425
Sups with the ocean.[8] Though in Heaven the trees
Of life ambrosial[9] fruitage bear, and vines
Yield nectar, though from off the boughs each morn
We brush mellifluous dews, and find the ground
Covered with pearly grain, yet God hath here　　430
Varied his bounty so with new delights
As may compare with Heaven; and to taste
Think not I shall be nice."[1] So down they sat,
And to their viands fell, nor seemingly
The Angel, nor in mist (the common gloss　　　435
Of theologians),[2] but with keen dispatch
Of real hunger and concoctive heat
To transubstantiate;[3] what redounds, transpires
Through spirits with ease: nor wonder: if by fire
Of sooty coal the empiric alchemist　　　　　　440
Can turn, or holds it possible to turn,
Metals of drossiest ore to perfect gold
As from the mine. Meanwhile at table Eve
Ministered naked, and their flowing cups
With pleasant liquors crowned. O innocence　　445
Deserving Paradise! if ever, then,

---

6. Make ready by heat, warm up.

7. Raphael voices an archaic theory of lunar spots as still-undigested vapors, drawn up as food from the inferior planet, earth. This theory fits with Raphael's exposition of the universal hierarchy, but Milton knew better: he had referred to Galileo's correct explanation of the spots—as landscape features—in 1.287–91.

8. The phenomenon of evaporation Milton interprets as the sun dining off the moisture exhaled from oceans.

9. Ambrosia and nectar are the traditional diet of angelic creatures.

1. Scrupulous, finicky.

2. Theologians intent on maintaining the pure spirituality of angels say they experience only the likeness of eating or loving—seemingly, or in a mist; Milton will have none of this evasion: the angel ate with real hunger.

3. In common theological use, transubstantiation is the Roman Catholic doctrine that the bread and wine of the eucharist really become the body and blood of Christ; Milton would vigorously have denied that doctrine as it applied to the sacrament, but says that here, by transforming material food to spiritual substance, the angel performed an act of true transubstantiation. The excess ("what redounds") is exhaled through spiritual pores.

Then had the sons of God excuse t' have been
Enamored at that sight; but in those hearts
Love unlibidinous reigned, nor jealousy
Was understood, the injured lover's hell.   450
   Thus when with meats and drinks they had sufficed,
Not burdened nature, sudden mind arose
In Adam, not to let th' occasion pass
Giv'n him by this great conference to know
Of things above his world, and of their being   455
Who dwell in Heaven, whose excellence he saw
Transcend his own so far, whose radiant forms
Divine effulgence,[4] whose high power so far
Exceeded human, and his wary speech
Thus to th' empyreal[5] minister he framed: 460
   "Inhabitant with God, now know I well
Thy favor in this honor done to man,
Under whose lowly roof thou hast vouchsafed
To enter and these earthly fruits to taste,
Food not of angels, yet accepted so   465
As that more willingly thou couldst not seem
At Heav'n's high feasts t' have fed: yet what compare?"
   To whom the wingèd hierarch replied:
"O Adam, one Almighty is, from whom
All things proceed and up to him return,   470
If not depraved from good, created all
Such to perfection, one first matter all,
Endued with various forms, various degrees
Of substance, and in things that live, of life;[6]
But more refined, more spiritous, and pure,   475
As nearer to him placed or nearer tending,
Each in their several active spheres assigned,
Till body up to spirit work, in bounds
Proportioned to each kind. So from the root
Springs lighter the green stalk, from thence the leaves   480
More airy, last the bright consummate flower
Spirits odorous breathes:[7] flowers and their fruit,
Man's nourishment, by gradual scale sublimed,[8]
To vital spirits aspire, to animal,
To intellectual[9]—give both life and sense,   485
Fancy[1] and understanding, whence the soul

---

4. A verb to the general effect of "diffused" or "radiated" is omitted.

5. A minister from the empyrean, the highest or fiery level of heaven; with a perhaps accidental touch on "imperial," as well.

6. Behind Raphael's speech lies the traditional division of natural things into inanimate objects, vegetable, animal, human, and angelic natures; they all derive from one matter, created by God, but are differentiated by Him into distinct levels of

purity.

7. As the flower is the consummation of a plant's existence, its odors are efflorescences analogous to man's spiritual life, the consummation of *his* existence.

8. Purified.

9. Man was thought to have three "souls"—vegetative, sensitive, and rational—each of which worked through subtle fluids called spirits.

1. Imagination.

Reason receives, and reason is her being,
Discursive or intuitive;[2] discourse
Is oftest yours, the latter most is ours,
Differing but in degree, of kind the same.   490
Wonder not then, what God for you saw good
If I refuse not,[3] but convert, as you,
To proper substance; time may come when men
With angels may participate, and find
No inconvenient diet, nor too light fare;   495
And from these corporal nutriments perhaps
Your bodies may at last turn all to spirit,
Improved by tract of time, and winged ascend
Ethereal as we,[4] or may at choice
Here or in heavenly paradises dwell;   500
If ye be found obedient, and retain
Unalterably firm his love entire
Whose progeny you are. Meanwhile, enjoy
Your fill what happiness this happy state
Can comprehend, incapable of more."   505
    To whom the patriarch of mankind replied:
"O favorable spirit, propitious guest,
Well hast thou taught the way that might direct
Our knowledge, and the scale of nature set
From center to circumference, whereon   510
In contemplation of created things
By steps we may ascend to God. * * *"

Summary   After this mingled explanation and warning, Raphael, by way of emphasizing the danger that threatens Adam and Eve, enters upon the story of Satan's revolt and fall. Satan, pretending that God's exaltation of the Son was an offense to angelic dignity, persuaded a host of his fellow angels to withdraw their allegiance to God and set up a camp in the north of Heaven. When open war on God was declared, however, one of these angels was able to repent. The seraph Abdiel, though scorned by his fellow rebels, denounced the rebellion, and returned, heroically alone, to the ranks of God's followers.

Book 6 Summary   Continuing the story of the war in Heaven, Raphael describes the assembling of the armies and a first skirmish in which Satan is both insulted and wounded by Abdiel. After the first day's battle, the evil

2. For Milton, discursive reason, which must be learned by rules and study, is quite different from the intuitive reason that especially characterizes angels.
3. I.e., don't be surprised if I accept ("refuse not")

what God thought would be good for you.
4. Raphael is talking to unfallen man, who might in time very well turn all spirit; Milton's view of fallen man, strongly idealistic in an early poem like *Comus*, darkened with time and experience.

angels retire discomfited; but overnight Satan invents cannon with which, on the second day, the good angels are put to some disorder. In the fury of the fight, however, they pull up mountains by the roots and bury the cannon beneath them; thus the issue remains inconclusive. On the third day, God withdraws all his armies and sends the Son alone into battle; the Son drives his enemies irresistibly over the wall of Heaven, and after falling nine days through Chaos they are swallowed up in Hell.

From Book 7

[*The Invocation*]

Descend from Heaven, Urania,[1] by that name
If rightly thou art called,[2] whose voice divine
Following, above th' Olympian hill I soar,
Above the flight of Pegasean wing![3]
The meaning, not the name I call: for thou   5
Nor of the Muses nine, nor on the top
Of old Olympus dwell'st, but heavenly born,
Before the hills appeared, or fountain flowed,
Thou with eternal Wisdom didst converse,
Wisdom thy sister, and with her didst play   10
In presence of th' Almighty Father,[4] pleased
With thy celestial song. Up led by thee
Into the Heaven of Heavens I have presumed,
An earthly guest, and drawn empyreal air,
Thy tempering;[5] with like safety guided down,   15
Return me to my native element:
Lest from this flying steed unreined (as once
Bellerophon,[6] though from a lower clime),
Dismounted, on th' Aleian field I fall,
Erroneous[7] there to wander and forlorn.   20
Half yet remains unsung, but narrower bound
Within the visible diurnal sphere;
Standing on earth, not rapt above the pole,
More safe I sing with mortal voice, unchanged
To hoarse or mute, though fall'n on evil days,   25

---

1. To start the second half of his poem, Milton must counterbalance the destruction of the war in Heaven with the creation by God of a new universe, centering on the Earth. Book 7 is devoted to this topic; and to approach so vast a subject, Milton once more invokes his Muse.
2. Milton has only the names of classical Muses with which to invoke the spiritual principles of Christian theology. Properly the Muse of astronomy, Urania is also the symbol of heavenly love and of divine wisdom.
3. Pegasus, the flying horse of poetry, suggests (in connection with Bellerophon, line 18) Milton's sense of his own perilous audacity in writing so

vast a poem.
4. In Proverbs 8.30, Wisdom is made to speak of "playing always before God," previous even to the Creation. Milton makes his Muse coeval with divine wisdom.
5. Tempered (i.e., mixed and softened) by thee.
6. Bellerophon tried to explore the stars astride Pegasus the flying horse; but Zeus sent a gadfly to sting Pegasus, and his rider, after falling onto the Aleian plain in Lycia, wandered about there till he died.
7. From Latin *errare*, "to wander," as well as "to be mistaken."

On evil days though fall'n, and evil tongues,
In darkness, and with dangers compassed round,
And solitude; yet not alone, while thou
Visit'st my slumbers nightly, or when morn
Purples the east:[8] still govern thou my song,   30
Urania, and fit audience find, though few.
But drive far off the barbarous dissonance
Of Bacchus and his revelers, the race
Of that wild rout that tore the Thracian bard[9]
In Rhodope, where woods and rocks had ears   35
To rapture, till the savage clamor drowned
Both harp and voice; nor could the Muse defend
Her son. So fail not thou, who thee implores:
For thou art heavenly, she an empty dream.

Summary   At Adam's request, Raphael continues his narration and
describes how God, to replace the fallen angels, created the world, its creatures, and finally man, in the course of six days; the story of the creation
concludes, on the seventh day, with a chorus of thanksgiving by the angels.

From Book 8

Summary   Adam, to prolong his visit with Raphael, asks why so many
and such splendid stars seem to be at the service of the earth, which appears
smaller and less noble than they. At this point Eve discreetly takes her leave.
In answer to Adam's question, Raphael proposes various astronomical possibilities, but gives no conclusive answer, advising Adam to concern himself
with matters closer to home. The angel, on the other hand, is much interested to hear the story, which Adam proposes to tell, of his own creation.

[*Adam Describes His Own Creation and that of Eve;
Having Repeated His Warning, the Angel Departs*]

So spake the godlike power, and thus our sire:
"For man to tell how human life began   250
Is hard; for who himself beginning knew?
Desire with thee still longer to converse
Induced me. As new waked from soundest sleep,
Soft on the flowery herb I found me laid
In balmy sweat, which with his beams the sun   255
Soon dried, and on the reeking moisture fed.
Straight toward heaven my wondering eyes I turned,

---

8. Milton composed mostly at night or very early
in the morning.
9. The Thracian Bacchantes, female worshipers
of Bacchus, tore Orpheus to pieces in Rhodope,
though even the rocks and trees were so impressed
with his music that they refused to be used against
the poet. See *Lycidas*, lines 58–63. Orpheus was
son of Calliope, the epic Muse.

And gazed a while the ample sky, till raised
By quick instinctive motion up I sprung
As thitherward endeavoring, and upright   260
Stood on my feet; about me round I saw
Hill, dale, and shady woods, and sunny plains
And liquid lapse of murmuring streams; by these,
Creatures that lived and moved, and walked or flew,
Birds on the branches warbling. All things smiled,   265
With fragrance and with joy my heart o'erflowed.
Myself I then perused,[1] and limb by limb
Surveyed, and sometimes went and sometimes ran
With supple joints as lively vigor led:
But who I was, or where, or from what cause,   270
Knew not. To speak I tried, and forthwith spake,
My tongue obeyed, and readily could name
Whate'er I saw. 'Thou sun,' said I, 'fair light,
And thou enlightened earth, so fresh and gay,
Ye hills and dales, ye rivers, woods, and plains,   275
And ye that live and move, fair creatures, tell,
Tell, if ye saw, how came I thus, how here?
Not of myself; by some great maker, then,
In goodness and in power preëminent.
Tell me how may I know him, how adore,   280
From whom I have that thus I move and live,
And feel that I am happier than I know.'
     "While thus I called, and strayed I knew not whither
From where I first drew air and first beheld
This happy light, when answer none returned,   285
On a green shady bank profuse of flowers
Pensive I sat me down; there gentle sleep
First found me and with soft oppression seized
My drowsèd sense—untroubled, though I thought
I then was passing to my former state   290
Insensible, and forthwith to dissolve;
When suddenly stood at my head a dream,
Whose inward apparition gently moved
My fancy to believe I yet had being
And lived. One came, methought, of shape divine,   295
And said, 'Thy mansion[2] wants thee, Adam, rise,
First man, of men innumerable ordained
First father; called by thee I come thy guide
To the garden of bliss, thy seat prepared.'
So saying, by the hand he took me raised,   300
And over fields and waters, as in air
Smooth sliding without step, last led me up
A woody mountain whose high top was plain,
A circuit wide, enclosed, with goodliest trees

1. Inspected.   2. Habitation.

Planted, with walks and bowers, that what I saw   305
Of earth before scarce pleasant seemed. Each tree
Loaden with fairest fruit that hung to the eye
Tempting, stirred in me sudden appetite
To pluck and eat; whereat I waked, and found
Before mine eyes all real, as the dream   310
Had lively shadowed. Here had new begun
My wandering, had not he who was my guide
Up hither, from among the trees appeared,
Presence divine. Rejoicing, but with awe,
In adoration at his feet I fell   315
Submiss: he reared me, and, 'Whom thou soughtest I am,'
Said mildly, 'author of all this thou seest
Above or round about thee or beneath.
This Paradise I give thee, count it thine
To till and keep, and of the fruit to eat.   320
Of every tree that in the garden grows
Eat freely with glad heart; fear here no dearth.
But of the tree whose operation brings
Knowledge of good and ill, which I have set
The pledge of thy obedience and thy faith   325
Amid the garden by the Tree of Life,
Remember what I warn thee, shun to taste
And shun the bitter consequence: for know
The day thou eat'st thereof, my sole command
Transgressed, inevitably thou shalt die,   330
From that day mortal, and this happy state
Shalt lose, expelled from hence into a world
Of woe and sorrow.' Sternly he pronounced
The rigid interdiction, which resounds
Yet dreadful in mine ear, though in my choice   335
Not to incur; but soon his clear aspèct
Returned, and gracious purpose[3] thus renewed:
'Not only these fair bounds, but all the Earth
To thee and to thy race I give; as lords
Possess it, and all things that therein live,   340
Or live in sea or air, beast, fish, and fowl.
In sign whereof each bird and beast behold
After their kinds; I bring them to receive
From thee their names, and pay thee fealty
With low subjection; understand the same   345
Of fish within their watery residence,
Not hither summoned, since they cannot change
Their element to draw the thinner air.'
As thus he spake, each bird and beast behold
Approaching two and two, these[4] cowering low   350
With blandishment, each bird stooped on his wing.

---

3. Speech.   4. I.e., the beasts.

I named them as they passed, and understood
Their nature, with such knowledge God endued
My sudden apprehension. But in these
I found not what methought I wanted still,   355
And to the heavenly vision thus presumed:
    " 'Oh by what name, for thou above all these,
Above mankind, or aught than mankind higher,
Surpassest far my naming, how may I
Adore thee, author of this universe   360
And all this good to man, for whose well-being
So amply and with hands so liberal
Thou hast provided all things? But with me
I see not who partakes. In solitude
What happiness? Who can enjoy alone,   365
Or all enjoying, what contentment find?'
Thus I presumptuous; and the vision bright,
As with a smile more brightened, thus replied:
    " 'What callest thou solitude? Is not the earth
With various living creatures, and the air,   370
Replenished, and all these at thy command
To come and play before thee? Knowest thou not
Their language and their ways?[5] They also know
And reason not contemptibly; with these
Find pastime and bear rule; thy realm is large.'   375
So spake the universal lord, and seemed
So ordering. I with leave of speech implored
And humble deprecation, thus replied:
    " 'Let not my words offend thee, heavenly power,
My maker; be propitious while I speak.   380
Hast thou not made me here thy substitute,
And these inferior far beneath me set?
Among unequals what society
Can sort,[6] what harmony or true delight?
Which must be mutual, in proportion due   385
Given and received. But in disparity,
The one intense, the other still remiss,[7]
Cannot well suit with either, but soon prove
Tedious alike. Of fellowship I speak
Such as I seek, fit to participate   390
All rational delight, wherein the brute
Cannot be human consort. They rejoice
Each with their kind, lion with lioness,
So fitly them in pairs thou hast combined;
Much less can bird with beast, or fish with fowl   395
So well converse, nor with the ox the ape;

---

5. Adam in the state of innocence knows instinctively, not only the earliest language (for Milton
and his age, that was Hebrew), but also the languages of all the creatures.

6. Agree.
7. "Intense . . . remiss": taut . . . slack, continuing the musical metaphor begun with "harmony"
(line 384).

Worse then can man with beast, and least of all.'
    "Whereto the Almighty answered, not displeased:
'A nice[8] and subtle happiness I see
Thou to thyself proposest, in the choice   400
Of thy associates, Adam, and wilt taste
No pleasure, though in pleasure, solitary.
What thinkest thou then of me and this my state?
Seem I to thee sufficiently possessed
Of happiness or not? who am alone   405
From all eternity, for none I know
Second to me or like, equal much less.
How have I then with whom to hold converse
Save with the creatures which I made, and those
To me inferior, infinite descents   410
Beneath what other creatures are to thee?'
    "He ceased, I lowly answered: 'To attain
The height and depth of thy eternal ways
All human thoughts come short, supreme of things.
Thou in thyself art perfect, and in thee   415
Is no deficience found; not so is man,
But in degree, the cause of his desire[9]
By conversation with his like to help
Or solace his defects. No need that thou
Shouldst propagate, already infinite,   420
And through all numbers absolute, though one.[1]
But man by number is to manifest
His single imperfection,[2] and beget
Like of his like, his image multiplied,
In unity defective, which requires   425
Collateral love and dearest amity.
Thou in thy secrecy although alone,
Best with thyself accompanied, seekest not
Social communication; yet, so pleased,
Canst raise thy creature to what height thou wilt   430
Of union or communion, deified;
I by conversing cannot these erect
From prone, nor in their ways complacence find.'
Thus I emboldened spake, and freedom used
Permissive, and acceptance found, which gained   435
This answer from the gracious voice divine:
    " 'Thus far to try thee, Adam, I was pleased,
And find thee knowing, not of beasts alone
Which thou hast rightly named, but of thyself,
Expressing well the spirit within thee free,   440
My image, not imparted to the brute,

---

8. Delicate, discriminating—with perhaps an
overtone of the sense "finicky."
9. Though perfect "in degree" (i.e., for his sort of
creature), man is far from God's perfection, (which

is) the cause of his desire, etc.
1. God, as infinity, contains all numbers, though
he is also and especially one.
2. Imperfection in being single.

Whose fellowship, therefore unmeet for thee,
Good reason was thou freely shouldst dislike;
And be so minded still. I, ere thou spak'st,
Knew it not good for man to be alone,   445
And no such company as then thou sawest
Intended thee, for trial only brought,
To see how thou couldst judge of fit and meet.
What next I bring shall please thee, be assured:
Thy likeness, thy fit help, thy other self,   450
Thy wish exactly to thy heart's desire.'
    "He ended, or I heard no more, for now,
My earthly by his heavenly overpowered
Which it had long stood under, strained to the height
In that celestial colloquy sublime,   455
As with an object that excels³ the sense
Dazzled and spent, sunk down and sought repair
Of sleep, which instantly fell on me, called
By nature as in aid, and closed mine eyes.
Mine eyes he closed, but open left the cell   460
Of fancy, my internal sight, by which
Abstract as in a trance methought I saw,
Though sleeping, where I lay, and saw the shape
Still glorious before whom awake I stood;
Who stooping opened my left side, and took   465
From thence a rib, with cordial⁴ spirits warm
And life-blood streaming fresh. Wide was the wound,
But suddenly with flesh filled up and healed.
The rib he formed and fashioned with his hands;
Under his forming hands a creature grew,   470
Manlike, but different sex, so lovely fair
That what seemed fair in all the world seemed now
Mean, or in her summed up, in her contained,
And in her looks, which from that time infused
Sweetness into my heart, unfelt before,   475
And into all things from her air inspired
The spirit of love and amorous delight.
She disappeared, and left me dark; I waked
To find her or forever to deplore
Her loss, and other pleasures all abjure;   480
When out of hope, behold her, not far off,
Such as I saw her in my dream, adorned
With what all earth or heaven could bestow
To make her amiable. On she came,
Led by her heavenly maker, though unseen,   485
And guided by his voice, nor uninformed
Of nuptial sanctity and marriage rites.
Grace was in all her steps, heaven in her eye,
In every gesture dignity and love.

3. Exceeds.   4. "Cordial": from the heart.

I overjoyed could not forbear aloud: 490
    " 'This turn hath made amends; thou hast fulfilled
Thy words, Creator bounteous and benign,
Giver of all things fair, but fairest this
Of all thy gifts; nor enviest.[5] I now see
Bone of my bone, flesh of my flesh, my self   495
Before me; woman is her name, of man
Extracted; for this cause he shall forego
Father and mother, and to his wife adhere,
And they shall be one flesh, one heart, one soul.'[6]
    "She heard me thus, and though divinely brought,   500
Yet innocence and virgin modesty,
Her virtue and the conscience[7] of her worth
That would be wooed and not unsought be won,
Not obvious, not obtrusive, but retired,
The more desirable—or, to say all,   505
Nature herself, though pure of sinful thought,
Wrought in her so that, seeing me, she turned.
I followed her; she what was honor knew,
And with obsequious[8] majesty approved
My pleaded reason. To the nuptial bower   510
I led her blushing like the morn. All heaven
And happy constellations on that hour
Shed their selectest influence; the earth
Gave sign of gratulation, and each hill;
Joyous the birds; fresh gales and gentle airs   515
Whispered it to the woods, and from their wings
Flung rose, flung odors from the spicy shrub,
Disporting, till the amorous bird of night[9]
Sung spousal, and bid haste the evening star
On his hill-top, to light the bridal lamp.   520
    "Thus have I told thee all my state, and brought
My story to the sum of earthly bliss
Which I enjoy, and must confess to find
In all things else delight indeed, but such
As, used or not, works in the mind no change,   525
Nor vehement desire—these delicacies
I mean of taste, sight, smell, herbs, fruits, and flowers,
Walks and the melody of birds. But here,
Far otherwise, transported I behold,
Transported touch; here passion first I felt,   530
Commotion strange, in all enjoyments else
Superior and unmoved, here only weak

---

5. Unlike some other gods (Jove, for example), Milton's deity does not lust after the females he bestows on men.
6. Adam's speech to Eve is largely an expansion of Genesis 2.23–24.
7. Consciousness. Note that Adam cannot find a verb for what Eve does in consequence of her innocence and virgin modesty. The poet's touch at this juncture is delicate in the extreme.
8. Compliant.
9. The nightingale, present on this auspicious occasion, as he was in the more doubtful scene of Eve's tempting dream (5.40).

Against the charm of beauty's powerful glance.
Or[1] nature failed in me and left some part
Not proof enough such object to sustain,   535
Or from my side subducting[2] took perhaps
More than enough; at least on her bestowed
Too much of ornament, in outward show
Elaborate, of inward less exact.
For well I understand in the prime end   540
Of nature her th' inferior, in the mind
And inward faculties which most excel,
In outward also her resembling less
His image who made both, and less expressing
The character of that dominion given   545
O'er other creatures. Yet when I approach
Her loveliness, so absolute she seems
And in herself complete, so well to know
Her own, that what she wills to do or say
Seems wisest, virtuousest, discreetest, best.   550
All higher knowledge in her presence falls
Degraded; wisdom in discourse with her
Loses discountenanced, and like folly shows;
Authority and reason on her wait
As one intended first, not after made   555
Occasionally;[3] and to consùmmate all,
Greatness of mind and nobleness their seat
Build in her loveliest, and create an awe
About her as a guard angelic placed."
    To whom the Angel with contracted brow: 560
"Accuse not nature, she hath done her part;
Do thou but thine, and be not diffident[4]
Of wisdom; she deserts thee not if thou
Dismiss not her when most thou need'st her nigh
By àttributing overmuch to things   565
Less excellent, as thou thyself perceiv'st.
For what admir'st thou, what transports thee so?
An outside? Fair no doubt, and worthy well
Thy cherishing, thy honoring, and thy love;
Not thy subjection. Weigh her with thyself,   570
Then value. Ofttimes nothing profits more
Then self-esteem, grounded on just and right
Well managed. Of that skill the more thou know'st,
The more she will acknowledge thee her head,
And to realities yield all her shows—   575
Made so adorn for thy delight the more,
So aweful[5] that with honor thou may'st love
Thy mate, who sees when thou art seen least wise.

1. Either.
2. Subtracting.
3. Incidentally.

4. Mistrustful, without faith.
5. Awe-inspiring.

But if the sense of touch whereby mankind
Is propagated seem such dear delight   580
Beyond all other, think the same vouchsafed
To cattle and each beast; which would not be
To them made common and divulged if aught
Therein enjoyed were worthy to subdue
The soul of man, or passion in him move.   585
What higher in her society thou find'st
Attractive, human, rational—love still;
In loving thou dost well, in passion not,
Wherein true love consists not. Love refines
The thoughts, and heart enlarges, hath his seat   590
In reason, and is judicious, is the scale[6]
By which to heavenly love thou may'st ascend,
Not sunk in carnal pleasure, for which cause
Among the beasts no mate for thee was found."
    To whom thus half abashed Adam replied: 595
"Neither her outside formed so fair, nor aught
In procreation common to all kinds
(Though higher of the genial[7] bed by far
And with mysterious reverence I deem)
So much delights me as those graceful acts,   600
Those thousand decencies that daily flow
From all her words and actions, mixed with love
And sweet compliance, which declare unfeigned
Union of mind or in us both one soul,
Harmony to behold in wedded pair   605
More grateful than harmonious sound to the ear.
Yet these subject not; I to thee disclose
What inward thence I feel, not therefore foiled,
Who meet with various objects from the sense
Variously representing; yet still free   610
Approve the best, and follow what I approve.[8]
    "To love thou blam'st me not, for love thou say'st
Leads up to heaven, is both the way and guide;
Bear with me then, if lawful what I ask:
Love not the heavenly spirits, and how their love   615
Express they, by looks only, or do they mix
Irradiance, virtual or immediate touch?"
    To whom the Angel with a smile that glowed
Celestial rosy red, love's proper hue,
Answered: "Let it suffice thee that thou know'st   620
Us happy, and without love no happiness.
Whatever pure thou in the body enjoy'st

6. The scale of nature, as in 5.509 above, but with
an important overtone from Latin or Italian *scala*,
meaning "ladder." The ladder of love was a Neoplatonic metaphor, ardently described by Cardinal
Bembo in Castiglione's *Courtier* (above, p. 1006).

7. Procreative, progenitive.
8. The sense of these last few lines is not quite
clear; Milton seems to be miming Adam's embar-
rassment, from which he escapes with an acute
question for the angel.

(And pure thou wert created), we enjoy
In eminence, and obstacle find none
Of membrane, joint, or limb, exclusive bars.   625
Easier than air with air, if spirits embrace,
Total they mix, union of pure with pure
Desiring; nor restrained conveyance need
As flesh to mix with flesh or soul with soul.
But I can now no more; the parting sun   630
Beyond the earth's green cape and verdant isles[9]
Hesperian sets, my signal to depart.
Be strong, live happy, and love, but first of all
Him whom to love is to obey, and keep
His great command; take heed lest passion sway   635
Thy judgment to do aught which else free will
Would not admit; thine and of all thy sons
The weal or woe in thee is placed: beware.
I in thy persevering shall rejoice,
And all the blest. Stand fast; to stand or fall   640
Free in thine own arbitrement it lies.
Perfect within, no outward aid require;
And all temptation to transgress repel."[1]
  So saying, he arose; whom Adam thus
Followed with benediction: "Since to part,   645
Go, heavenly guest, ethereal messenger,
Sent from whose[2] sovereign goodness I adore.
Gentle to me and affable hath been
Thy condescension, and shall be honored ever
With grateful memory. Thou to mankind   650
Be good and friendly still, and oft return."
  So parted they, the Angel up to Heaven
From the thick shade, and Adam to his bower.

Book 9

The Argument

Satan, having compassed the Earth, with meditated guile returns as a mist by night into Paradise; enters into the serpent sleeping. Adam and Eve in the morning go forth to their labors, which Eve proposes to divide in several places, each laboring apart: Adam consents not, alleging the danger lest that enemy of whom they were forewarned should attempt her found alone. Eve, loath to be thought not circumspect or firm enough,

9. Cape Verde near Dakar and the Islas Verdes off that coast are the westernmost ("Hesperian") points of Africa, and so of the Old World as a whole.
1. "Require" (i.e., look for, depend on) and "repel" are the two strong imperative verbs with which the angel concludes his mission. *Don't* look for help

from outsiders; *do* repel temptation on your own. It is a curious touch that Eve, though she overhears, at least in part, this most forceful of divine warnings (9.276), is not present to be addressed directly by the admonitory angel.
2. I.e., from Him whose goodness I adore.

urges her going apart, the rather desirous to make trial of her strength;
Adam at last yields. The serpent finds her alone: his subtle approach,
first gazing, then speaking, with much flattery extolling Eve above all
other creatures. Eve, wondering to hear the serpent speak, asks how he
attained to human speech and such understanding not till now; the serpent answers that by tasting of a certain tree in the garden he attained
both to speech and reason, till then void of both. Eve requires him to
bring her to that tree, and finds it to be the Tree of Knowledge forbidden:
the serpent, now grown bolder, with many wiles and arguments induces
her at length to eat. She, pleased with the taste, deliberates a while
whether to impart thereof to Adam or not; at last brings him of the fruit;
relates what persuaded her to eat thereof. Adam, at first amazed, but
perceiving her lost, resolves, through vehemence of love, to perish with
her, and, extenuating[1] the trespass, eats also of the fruit. The effects
thereof in them both; they seek to cover their nakedness; then fall to
variance and accusation of one another.

   No more of talk where God[2] or angel guest
With man, as with his friend, familiar used
To sit indulgent, and with him partake
Rural repast, permitting him the while
Venial[3] discourse unblamed. I now must change   5
Those notes to tragic; foul distrust and breach
Disloyal on the part of man, revolt
And disobedience; on the part of Heaven
Now alienated, distance and distaste,
Anger and just rebuke, and judgment given,   10
That brought into this world a world of woe,
Sin and her shadow Death, and Misery,
Death's harbinger. Sad task! yet argument
Not less but more heroic than the wrath
Of stern Achilles on his foe pursued   15
Thrice fugitive about Troy wall; or rage
Of Turnus for Lavinia disespoused;
Or Neptune's ire, or Juno's, that so long
Perplexed the Greek and Cytherea's son:[4]
If answerable style I can obtain   20
Of my celestial Patroness,[5] who deigns
Her nightly visitation unimplored,
And dictates to me slumbering, or inspires
Easy my unpremeditated verse,[6]

1. Not "diminishing" or "excusing" as in customary English usage, but carrying further, drawing
out.
2. God, of course, has not been lunching with
Adam; but since man is about to fall, the age is
now over when such an occasion could be contemplated.
3. Permissible.
4. In the *Iliad* (22), Achilles pursues Hector three
times around Troy wall before catching him. In

the *Aeneid*, Aeneas must fight with Turnus for the
hand of Lavinia. Neptune (or Poseidon) was
unfriendly to Odysseus (the Greek); Juno (or Hera)
to Aeneas, who was Cytherea's, i.e., Aphrodite's,
son by Anchises.
5. The Muse, Urania.
6. Milton, we are told by his nephew Edward
Phillips, used to wake up in the morning with lines
of poetry full-formed in his head; he would then
dictate them to an amanuensis.

Since first this subject for heroic song   25
Pleased me, long choosing and beginning late,[7]
Not sedulous by nature to indite
Wars, hitherto the only argument
Heroic deemed, chief mastery to dissect[8]
With long and tedious havoc fabled knights   30
In battles feigned (the better fortitude
Of patience and heroic martyrdom
Unsung), or to describe races and games,
Or tilting furniture,[9] emblazoned shields,
Impresses quaint, caparisons and steeds,   35
Bases and tinsel trappings, gorgeous knights
At joust and tournament; then marshaled feast
Served up in hall with sewers and seneschals:[1]
The skill of artifice or office mean;
Not that which justly gives heroic name   40
To person or to poem. Me of these
Nor skilled nor studious, higher argument
Remains,[2] sufficient of itself to raise
That name,[3] unless an age too late, or cold
Climate, or years, damp my intended wing   45
Depressed; and much they may if all be mine,
Not hers who brings it nightly to my ear.
    The sun was sunk, and after him the star
Of Hesperus, whose office is to bring
Twilight upon the Earth, short arbiter   50
'Twixt day and night, and now from end to end
Night's hemisphere had veiled the horizon round,
When Satan, who late fled before the threats
Of Gabriel out of Eden,[4] now improved
In meditated fraud and malice, bent   55
On man's destruction, maugre what might hap
Of heavier on himself,[5] fearless returned.
By night he fled, and at midnight returned
From compassing the Earth—cautious of day
Since Uriel, regent of the sun, descried   60
His entrance, and forewarned the cherubim
That kept their watch.[6] Thence, full of anguish, driven,
The space of seven continued nights he rode

7. Milton's early plans for epics, preserved in manuscript, did center on national heroes; his choice of a sacred subject, though not wholly without precedent, was a relative novelty. "Sedulous": eager.
8. I.e., in describing wars one's chief task is to dissect; dissect, in its strict Latin sense of "cut apart," but perhaps also with a comic overtone from the anatomy table.
9. The equipment of tournaments; "impresses quaint": elaborate devices on shields; "bases": trappings for horses.
1. Waiters and stewards, who also dissect.

2. I.e., for me, when these things are set aside which I neither can nor want to do, there remains a higher argument.
3. I.e., the name of heroic poet. "Age too late": not Milton's age, but the age of the world. Milton felt a "cold climate" was inimical to epic poetry. "Damp": stupefy, benumb.
4. At the end of Book 4.
5. Despite the peril of heavier (punishments).
6. In Book 4. These connections with Book 4 not only bridge the intervening narration, but emphasize a balancing of the whole epic; see the headnote.

With darkness; thrice the equinoctial line[7]
He circled, four times crossed the car of Night   65
From pole to pole, traversing each colure;
On the eighth returned, and on the coast averse
From entrance or cherubic watch by stealth
Found unsuspected way. There was a place
(Now not, though sin, not time, first wrought the change)   70
Where Tigris at the foot of Paradise
Into a gulf shot under ground, till part
Rose up a fountain by the Tree of Life.
In with the river sunk and with it rose
Satan, involved in rising mist; then sought   75
Where to lie hid. Sea he had searched and land
From Eden over Pontus, and the pool
Maeotis, up beyond the river Ob;[8]
Downward as far antarctic; and, in length,
West from Orontes to the ocean barred   80
At Darien, thence to the land where flows
Ganges and Indus.[9] Thus the orb he roamed
With narrow search, and with inspection deep
Considered every creature, which of all
Most opportune might serve his wiles, and found   85
The serpent subtlest beast of all the field.[1]
Him, after long debate, irresolute
Of thoughts revolved,[2] his final sentence chose
Fit vessel, fittest imp[3] of fraud, in whom
To enter, and his dark suggestions hide   90
From sharpest sight; for in the wily snake
Whatever sleights none would suspicious mark,
As from his wit and native subtlety
Proceeding, which, in other beasts observed,
Doubt[4] might beget of diabolic power   95
Active within beyond the sense of brute.
Thus he resolved, but first from inward grief
His bursting passion into plaints thus poured:
     "O Earth, how like to Heaven, if not preferred
More justly, seat worthier of gods, as built   100
With second thoughts, reforming what was old!
For what god, after better, worse would build?
Terrestrial heaven, danced round by other heavens
That shine, yet bear their bright officious lamps,
Light above light, for thee alone, as seems,   105

---

7. The equator. The colures are the two great circles of the celestial sphere which intersect at the poles. By circling the globe, either from east to west or over the north and south poles, Satan can remain continually hidden in darkness.

8. Pontus is the Black Sea, the pool Maeotis the swamps of the Sea of Azov; the river Ob flows north through Siberia into the Arctic Ocean.

9. Flying west from Orontes in Syria, Satan crossed the Atlantic to the Isthmus of Panama (Darien), then the Pacific and southeast Asia to India.
1. Genesis 3.1 so describes the serpent.
2. I.e., unable to decide among his revolving thoughts. "Sentence": decision.
3. Craft, offshoot.
4. Suspicion.

In thee concent'ring all their precious beams
Of sacred influence![5] As God in Heaven
Is center, yet extends to all, so thou
Cent'ring receiv'st from all those orbs; in thee,
Not in themselves, all their known virtue appears,   110
Productive in herb, plant, and nobler birth
Of creatures animate with gradual life
Of growth, sense, reason,[6] all summed up in man.
With what delight could I have walked thee round,
If I could joy in aught; sweet interchange   115
Of hill and valley, rivers, woods, and plains,
Now land, now sea, and shores with forest crowned,
Rocks, dens, and caves! But I in none of these
Find place or refuge; and the more I see
Pleasures about me, so much more I feel   120
Torment within me, as from the hateful siege[7]
Of contraries; all good to me becomes
Bane,[8] and in Heaven much worse would be my state.
But neither here seek I, no, nor in Heaven,
To dwell, unless by mastering Heaven's Supreme;   125
Nor hope to be myself less miserable
By what I seek, but others to make such
As I, though thereby worse to me redound.
For only in destroying I find ease
To my relentless thoughts, and him[9] destroyed,   130
Or won to what may work his utter loss,
For whom all this was made, all this[1] will soon
Follow, as to him linked in weal or woe:
In woe then, that destruction wide may range!
To me shall be the glory sole among   135
The infernal powers, in one day to have marred
What he, Almighty styled, six nights and days
Continued making, and who knows how long
Before had been contriving? though perhaps
Not longer than since I in one night freed   140
From servitude inglorious well-nigh half
Th' angelic name, and thinner left the throng
Of his adorers. He to be avenged,
And to repair his numbers thus impaired,
Whether such virtue,[2] spent of old, now failed   145
More angels to create (if they at least
Are his created),[3] or to spite us more,

5. Satan, like Adam in Book 8, is impressed that so many heavenly bodies center on (and "serve") the earth—as the old Ptolemaic astronomy taught that they did. "Officious": dutiful.
6. Life on earth is gradual, or graduated, from the herb which merely grows, to the animal which grows and feels, to man, who grows, feels, and thinks.
7. Conflict.
8. Poison. This is exactly what he willed in 4.110, just reversed.
9. I.e., man.
1. I.e., the created cosmos.
2. Strength, energy.
3. Satan never likes to admit that the angels were created by God: he faces the fact squarely only once, in his soliloquy at the beginning of Book 4 (line 43).

Determined to advance into our room
A creature formed of earth, and him endow,
Exalted from so base original,   150
With heavenly spoils, our spoils. What he decreed
He effected; man he made, and for him built
Magnificent this world, and Earth his seat,
Him lord pronounced, and, O indignity!
Subjected to his service angel-wings   155
And flaming ministers, to watch and tend
Their earthy charge. Of these the vigilance
I dread, and to elude, thus wrapped in mist
Of midnight vapor glide obscure, and pry
In every bush and brake, where hap may find   160
The serpent sleeping in whose mazy folds
To hide me, and the dark intent I bring.
O foul descent! that I, who erst contended
With gods to sit the highest, am now constrained
Into a beast, and mixed with bestial slime,   165
This essence to incarnate and imbrute,[4]
That to the height of deity aspired!
But what will not ambition and revenge
Descend to? Who aspires must down as low
As high he soared, obnoxious[5] first or last   170
To basest things. Revenge, at first though sweet,
Bitter ere long back on itself recoils.
Let it; I reck not, so it light well aimed,
Since higher I fall short, on him who next
Provokes my envy, this new favorite   175
Of Heaven, this man of clay, son of despite,
Whom, us the more to spite,[6] his Maker raised
From dust: spite then with spite is best repaid."
    So saying, through each thicket dank or dry,
Like a black mist low-creeping, he held on   180
His midnight search, where soonest he might find
The serpent. Him fast sleeping soon he found
In labyrinth of many a round self-rolled,
His head the midst, well stored with subtle wiles:
Not yet in horrid shade or dismal den,   185
Nor nocent[7] yet, but on the grassy herb,
Fearless, unfeared, he slept. In at his mouth
The devil entered, and his brutal sense,
In heart or head possessing, soon inspired
With act intelligential; but his sleep   190
Disturbed not, waiting close[8] th' approach of morn.
    Now whenas sacred light began to dawn

---

4. Satan's incarnation in a snake is a grotesque   creature.
parody of the Son of God's incarnation in Christ. 7. Harmful.
5. Subject to.   8. In secret.
6. Satan sees God in his own image, as a spiteful

In Eden on the humid flowers, that breathed
Their morning incense, when all things that breathe
From th' Earth's great altar send up silent praise   195
To the Creator, and his nostrils fill
With grateful smell, forth came the human pair
And joined their vocal worship to the choir
Of creatures wanting voice; that done, partake
The season,[9] prime for sweetest scents and airs;   200
Then còmmune how that day they best may ply
Their growing work; for much their work outgrew
The hands' dispatch of two gardening so wide:
And Eve first to her husband thus began:
    "Adam, well may we labor still[1] to dress   205
This garden, still to tend plant, herb, and flower,
Our pleasant task enjoined; but till more hands
Aid us, the work under our labor grows,
Luxurious by restraint: what we by day
Lop overgrown, or prune, or prop, or bind,   210
One night or two with wanton growth derides,
Tending to wild. Thou, therefore, now advise,
Or hear what to my mind first thoughts present.
Let us divide our labors; thou where choice
Leads thee, or where most needs, whether to wind   215
The woodbine round this arbor, or direct
The clasping ivy where to climb; while I
In yonder spring[2] of roses intermixed
With myrtle find what to redress till noon.
For while so near each other thus all day   220
Our task we choose, what wonder if so near
Looks intervene and smiles, or object new
Casual discourse draw on, which intermits
Our day's work, brought to little, though begun
Early, and th' hour of supper comes unearned!"   225
    To whom mild answer Adam thus returned:
"Sole Eve, associate sole, to me beyond
Compare above all living creatures dear!
Well hast thou motioned,[3] well thy thoughts employed
How we might best fulfil the work which here   230
God hath assigned us, nor of me shalt pass
Unpraised; for nothing lovelier can be found
In woman than to study household good,
And good works in her husband to promote.[4]
Yet not so strictly hath our Lord imposed   235
Labor as to debar us when we need
Refreshment, whether food or talk between,

9. I.e., go forth into the morning air. "Prime":   3. Suggested.
the best.   4. Proverbs 31 is devoted to the praise of a good
1. Continually.   wife, and Milton doubtless had it in mind here.
2. Growth.

Food of the mind, or this sweet intercourse
Of looks and smiles; for smiles from reason flow,
To brute denied, and are of love the food,   240
Love, not the lowest end of human life.
For not to irksome toil, but to delight
He made us, and delight to reason joined.
These paths and bowers doubt not but our joint hands
Will keep from wilderness with ease, as wide   245
As we need walk, till younger hands ere long
Assist us. But if much convèrse perhaps
Thee satiate, to short absence I could yield;
For solitude sometimes is best society,
And short retirement urges sweet return.   250
But other doubt possesses me, lest harm
Befall thee, severed from me; for thou know'st
What hath been warned us, what malicious foe,
Envying our happiness, and of his own
Despairing, seeks to work us woe and shame   255
By sly assault; and somewhere nigh at hand
Watches, no doubt, with greedy hope to find
His wish and best advantage, us asunder,[5]
Hopeless to circumvent us joined, where each
To other speedy aid might lend at need.   260
Whether his first design be to withdraw
Our fealty from God, or to disturb
Conjugal love, than which perhaps no bliss
Enjoyed by us excites his envy more;
Or this, or worse,[6] leave not the faithful side   265
That gave thee being, still shades thee and protects.
The wife, where danger or dishonor lurks,
Safest and seemliest by her husband stays,
Who guards her, or with her the worst endures."
  To whom the virgin[7] majesty of Eve,   270
As one who loves, and some unkindness meets,
With sweet austere composure thus replied:
  "Offspring of Heaven and Earth, and all Earth's lord!
That such an enemy we have, who seeks
Our ruin, both by thee informed I learn,   275
And from the parting angel overheard
As in a shady nook I stood behind,
Just then returned at shut of evening flowers.
But that thou shouldst my firmness therefore doubt
To God or thee, because we have a foe   280
May tempt it, I expected not to hear.
His violence thou fear'st not, being such
As we, not capable of death or pain,

5. I.e., to find us apart, which will answer his wishes and serve his advantage.
6. I.e., whether this or something worse be his intent.
7. Unspotted.

Can either not receive, or can repel.
His fraud is, then, thy fear; which plain infers   285
Thy equal fear that my firm faith and love
Can by his fraud be shaken or seduced:
Thoughts, which how found they harbor in thy breast,
Adam, misthought of her to thee so dear?"[8]
   To whom with healing words Adam replied: 290
"Daughter of God and man, immortal Eve,
For such thou art, from sin and blame entire;[9]
Not diffident of thee do I dissuade
Thy absence from my sight, but to avoid
Th' attempt itself, intended by our foe.   295
For he who tempts, though in vain, at least asperses[1]
The tempted with dishonor foul, supposed
Not incorruptible of faith, not proof
Against temptation. Thou thyself with scorn
And anger wouldst resent the offered wrong   300
Though ineffectual found; misdeem not, then,
If such affront I labor to avert
From thee alone, which on us both at once
The enemy, though bold, will hardly dare;
Or, daring, first on me th' assault shall light.   305
Nor thou his malice and false guile contemn—
Subtle he needs must be who could seduce
Angels—nor think superfluous others' aid.
I from the influence of thy looks receive
Access[2] in every virtue; in thy sight   310
More wise, more watchful, stronger, if need were
Of outward strength; while shame, thou looking on,
Shame to be overcome or overreached,[3]
Would utmost vigor raise, and raised unite.
Why shouldst not thou like sense within thee feel   315
When I am present, and thy trial choose
With me, best witness of thy virtue tried?"
   So spake domestic Adam in his care
And matrimonial love; but Eve, who thought
Less[4] àttributed to her faith sincere,   320
Thus her reply with accent sweet renewed:
   "If this be our condition, thus to dwell
In narrow circuit straitened by a foe,
Subtle or violent, we not endued
Single with like defense wherever met,   325
How are we happy, still in fear of harm?
But harm precedes not sin: only our foe

---

8. I.e., these thoughts were misthought of (misapplied to) her to thee so dear (me).
9. "Entire" is from Latin *integer*, untouched.
"Diffident": the usual English meaning is "shy,"
"timid"; Milton emphasizes the Latin roots, *dis* +
fides = mistrustful.

1. The word is from Latin *spargere*, to sprinkle,
with overtones from English "aspersion," an ugly
insinuation.
2. Extra strength.
3. Overpowered or outwitted.
4. Too little.

Tempting affronts us with his foul esteem
Of our integrity: his foul esteem
Sticks no dishonor on our front,[5] but turns   330
Foul on himself; then wherefore shunned or feared
By us, who rather double honor gain
From his surmise proved false, find peace within,
Favor from Heaven, our witness, from th' event?
And what is faith, love, virtue, unassayed   335
Alone, without exterior help sustained?
Let us not then suspect our happy state
Left so imperfect by the Maker wise
As not secure to single or combined.
Frail is our happiness, if this be so;   340
And Eden were no Eden, thus exposed."
    To whom thus Adam fervently replied:
"O woman, best are all things as the will
Of God ordained them; his creating hand
Nothing imperfect or deficient left   345
Of all that he created, much less man,
Or aught that might his happy state secure,
Secure from outward force. Within himself
The danger lies, yet lies within his power;
Against his will he can receive no harm.   350
But God left free the will; for what obeys
Reason is free; and reason he made right,
But bid her well beware, and still erect,[6]
Lest by some fair appearing good surprised,
She dictate false, and misinform the will   355
To do what God expressly hath forbid.
Not then mistrust, but tender love, enjoins
That I should mind[7] thee oft; and mind thou me.
Firm we subsist, yet possible to swerve,
Since reason not impossibly may meet   360
Some specious object by the foe suborned,
And fall into deception unaware,
Not keeping strictest watch, as she was warned.
Seek not temptation, then, which to avoid
Were better, and most likely if from me   365
Thou sever not: trial will come unsought.
Wouldst thou approve thy constancy, approve[8]
First thy obedience; th' other who can know,
Not seeing thee attempted, who attest?
But if thou think trial unsought may find   370
Us both securer[9] than thus warned thou seem'st,
Go; for thy stay, not free, absents thee more.

---

5. Forehead.
6. Remain alert.
7. Remind; in the next phrase, "mind" means "pay heed to."

8. Prove, give evidence of.
9. The Latin word *securus* can mean either "free from care" or "careless." Adam's warning is at once reassuring and ominous.

Go in thy native innocence; rely
On what thou hast of virtue; summon all;
For God towards thee hath done his part: do thine."   375
    So spake the patriarch of mankind; but Eve
Persisted; yet submiss, though last, replied:
    "With thy permission,[1] then, and thus forewarned,
Chiefly by what thy own last reasoning words
Touched only, that our trial, when least sought,   380
May find us both perhaps far less prepared,
The willinger I go, nor much expect
A foe so proud will first the weaker seek;
So bent, the more shall shame him his repulse."
Thus saying, from her husband's hand her hand   385
Soft she withdrew, and like a wood nymph light,
Oread or dryad, or of Delia's train,[2]
Betook her to the groves, but Delia's self
In gait surpassed and goddesslike deport,
Though not as she with bow and quiver armed,   390
But with such gardening tools as art yet rude,
Guiltless of fire[3] had formed, or angels brought.
To Pales, or Pomona, thus adorned,
Likest she seemed, Pomona when she fled
Vertumnus, or to Ceres in her prime,   395
Yet virgin of Proserpina from Jove.[4]
Her long with ardent look his eye pursued
Delighted, but desiring more her stay.
Oft he to her his charge of quick return
Repeated; she to him as oft engaged   400
To be returned by noon amid the bower,
And all things in best order to invite
Noontide repast, or afternoon's repose.
O much deceived, much failing, hapless Eve,
Of thy presumed return![5] Event perverse!   405
Thou never from that hour in Paradise
Found'st either sweet repast, or sound repose;
Such ambush hid among sweet flowers and shades
Waited with hellish rancor imminent[6]
To intercept thy way, or send thee back   410
Despoiled of innocence, of faith, of bliss.
For now, and since first break of dawn, the fiend,
Mere serpent in appearance, forth was come,

1. Eve takes a reluctant and extorted permission as free leave to do what she wants. Though apparently submissive, she gets the last word.
2. An "oread" is a nymph of the mountain, a "dryad" one of the wood. "Delia" is Diana or Artemis, goddess of the chase, who when she hunted was accompanied by a train of nymphs.
3. There was no need of fire in Paradise; but that fire is a possession which renders one "guilty" suggests an overtone of the Prometheus myth.

4. Pales is a Roman goddess of flocks, Pomona a Roman divinity of fruits and orchards. Pomona was wooed by Vertumnus, god of the turning year, who assumed all sorts of shapes to win her. Ceres, the Mother Nature of the ancients (hence, the word "cereal"), bore Proserpina to Jupiter. All three goddesses are patronesses of agriculture, like Eve.
5. "Much deceived" carries over; Eve was "much deceived of" (about) her "presumed return."
6. Threatening.

And on his quest, where likeliest he might find
The only two of mankind, but in them   415
The whole included race, his purposed prey.
In bower and field he sought, where any tuft
Of grove or garden-plot more pleasant lay,
Their tendance[7] or plantation for delight;
By fountain or by shady rivulet   420
He sought them both, but wished his hap might find
Eve separate; he wished, but not with hope
Of what so seldom chanced; when to his wish,
Beyond his hope, Eve separate he spies,
Veiled in a cloud of fragrance, where she stood,   425
Half spied, so thick the roses bushing round
About her glowed, oft stooping to support
Each flower of slender stalk, whose head though gay
Carnation, purple, azure, or specked with gold,
Hung drooping unsustained; them she upstays   430
Gently with myrtle band, mindless[8] the while
Herself, though fairest unsupported flower,
From her best prop so far, and storm so nigh.
Nearer he drew, and many a walk traversed
Of stateliest covert, cedar, pine, or palm;   435
Then voluble[9] and bold, now hid, now seen
Among thick-woven arborets[1] and flowers
Embordered on each bank, the hand of Eve:
Spot more delicious than those gardens feigned
Or of revived Adonis,[2] or renowned   440
Alcinous, host of old Laertes' son,
Or that, not mystic, where the sapient king[3]
Held dalliance with his fair Egyptian spouse.
Much he the place admired, the person more.
As one who long in populous city pent,   445
Where houses thick and sewers annoy[4] the air,
Forth issuing on a summer's morn to breathe
Among the pleasant villages and farms
Adjoined, from each thing met conceives delight,
The smell of grain, or tedded[5] grass, or kine,   450
Or dairy, each rural sight, each rural sound:
If chance with nymphlike step fair virgin pass,[6]

---

7. Object of their tending.
8. Heedless. The conceit of the flower gatherer
who is herself gathered is repeated here from 4.270,
where it was applied to Proserpina.
9. Rolling; with a hint from the second sense of
"glib, fluent."
1. Bushes. "Hand": handiwork.
2. The garden of Adonis was a heavenly bower
where Venus' lover was supposed still to lie in secret,
recovering from his wound received on earth (Venus
would not allow him to die). Alcinous was king of
the Phaeacians. His garden, visited by Odysseus

("old Laertes' son"), is described in *Odyssey* 7.
3. Solomon; his "fair Egyptian spouse" is Pharaoh's daughter: Milton is referring to the Song of
Solomon 6.2. The fact that it is "not mystic" (i.e.,
not mythical) distinguishes the Scriptural garden
from the "feigned" (line 439) ones of classical legend.
4. Make noisome, befoul.
5. Tossed and drying in the sun. "Kine": cows.
6. I.e., if by chance with nymphlike step a fair
virgin should pass.

What pleasing seemed, for her now pleases more,
She most, and in her look sums all delight.[7]
Such pleasure took the serpent to behold   455
This flowery plat,[8] the sweet recess of Eve
Thus early, thus alone; her heavenly form
Angelic, but more soft and feminine,
Her graceful innocence, her every air
Of gesture or least action overawed   460
His malice, and with rapine[9] sweet bereaved
His fierceness of the fierce intent it brought:
That space the evil one abstracted stood
From his own evil, and for the time remained
Stupidly good,[1] of enmity disarmed,   465
Of guile, of hate, of envy, of revenge.
But the hot Hell that always in him burns,
Though in mid Heaven, soon ended his delight,
And tortures him now more, the more he sees
Of pleasure not for him ordained: then soon   470
Fierce hate he recollects, and all his thoughts
Of mischief, gratulating,[2] thus excites:
    "Thoughts, whither have ye led me? with what sweet
Compulsion thus transported to forget
What hither brought us? hate, not love, nor hope   475
Of Paradise for Hell, hope here to taste[3]
Of pleasure, but all pleasure to destroy,
Save what is in destroying; other joy
To me is lost. Then let me not let pass
Occasion which now smiles: behold alone   480
The woman, opportune to all attempts,
Her husband, for I view far round, not nigh,
Whose higher intellectual more I shun,
And strength, of courage haughty, and of limb
Heroic built, though of terrestrial mold;[4]   485
Foe not informidable, exempt from wound,[5]
I not; so much hath Hell debased and pain
Enfeebled me to what I was in Heaven.
She fair, divinely fair, fit love for gods,
Not terrible, though terror be in love   490
And beauty, not approached by stronger hate,
Hate stronger, under show of love well feigned,
The way which to her ruin now I tend."[6]
    So spake the enemy of mankind, enclosed

---

7. I.e., in her look epitomizes all delight.
8. Meadow.
9. It is a deliberate paradox that her sweetness can ravish his malice; the word "rapine" is deliberately overviolent.
1. I.e., he is momentarily stunned into a kind of vacant goodness.
2. Exulting.

3. A "nor" is understood before "hope," carried over from the negatives of the previous line.
4. Made of earth.
5. Adam in the state of innocence is invulnerable.
6. I.e., love and beauty are terrible unless counteracted by hate—as they are being counteracted in Satan, to the ruin of Eve.

In serpent, inmate bad, and toward Eve   495
Addressed his way, not with indented wave,
Prone on the ground, as since, but on his rear,
Circular base of rising folds, that towered
Fold above fold a surging maze; his head
Crested aloft, and carbuncle[7] his eyes;   500
With burnished neck of verdant gold, erect
Amidst his circling spires,[8] that on the grass
Floated redundant. Pleasing was his shape,
And lovely; never since of serpent kind
Lovelier, not those that in Illyria changed   505
Hermione and Cadmus,[9] or the god
In Epidaurus;[1] nor to which transformed
Ammonian Jove, or Capitoline was seen,
He with Olympias, this with her who bore
Scipio, the height of Rome.[2] With tract oblique   510
At first, as one who sought accèss, but feared
To interrupt, sidelong he works his way.
As when a ship by skillful steersman wrought
Nigh river's mouth or foreland, where the wind
Veers oft, as oft so steers and shifts her sail: 515
So varied he, and of his tortuous train
Curled many a wanton wreath in sight of Eve,
To lure her eye: she busied heard the sound
Of rustling leaves, but minded not, as used
To such disport before her through the field,   520
From every beast, more duteous at her call
Than at Circean call the herd disguised.[3]
He bolder now, uncalled before her stood:
But as in gaze admiring; oft he bowed
His turret crest, and sleek enameled neck,   525
Fawning, and licked the ground whereon she trod.
His gentle dumb expression turned at length
The eye of Eve to mark his play: he, glad
Of her attention gained, with serpent tongue
Organic, or impulse of vocal air,[4]   530
His fraudulent temptation thus began:
    "Wonder not, sovereign mistress, if perhaps
Thou canst, who art sole wonder; much less arm
Thy looks, the heaven of mildness, with disdain,

---

7. Deep red, inflamed.
8. Coils. "Redundant": abundantly, to excess.
9. Ovid tells how Cadmus and Harmonia (Milton's "Hermione") were changed to serpents after they retired (in despair at the misfortunes of their children) to Illyria.
1. Aesculapius, god of medicine, had a temple at Epidaurus, from which he sometimes emerged in the form of a serpent.
2. Jupiter Ammon ("Ammonian Jove"), in the form of a snake, was said to have consorted with Olym-

pias to beget Alexander the Great; and in the same way, the Jupiter of the Roman capitol (Jove "Capitoline") was thought to have begotten Scipio Africanus, the savior and greatest leader ("height") of Rome.
3. Circe, who enchanted men into the shape of beasts, was attended by an obedient herd in the *Odyssey*.
4. I.e., Satan either used the actual tongue of the serpent or himself impressed the air with speech.

Displeased that I approach thee thus, and gaze   535
Insatiate, I thus single, nor have feared
Thy awful brow, more awful thus retired.
Fairest resemblance of thy Maker fair,
Thee all things living gaze on, all things thine
By gift, and thy celestial beauty adore   540
With ravishment beheld, there best beheld
Where universally admired: but here
In this enclosure wild, these beasts among,
Beholders rude and shallow to discern
Half what in thee is fair, one man except,   545
Who sees thee?[5] (and what is one?) who shouldst be seen
A goddess among gods, adored and served
By angels numberless, thy daily train."
    So glozed[6] the tempter, and his proem tuned;
Into the heart of Eve his words made way,   550
Though at the voice much marveling: at length,
Not unamazed, she thus in answer spake:
"What may this mean? Language of man pronounced
By tongue of brute, and human sense expressed?
The first at least of these I thought denied   555
To beasts, whom God on their creation-day
Created mute to all articulate sound;
The latter I demur,[7] for in their looks
Much reason, and in their actions oft appears.
Thee, serpent, subtlest beast of all the field   560
I knew, but not with human voice endued:[8]
Redouble then this miracle, and say,
How cam'st thou speakable of mute,[9] and how
To me so friendly grown above the rest
Of brutal kind, that daily are in sight?   565
Say, for such wonder claims attention due."
    To whom the guileful tempter thus replied:
"Empress of this fair world, resplendent Eve!
Easy to me it is to tell thee all
What thou command'st and right thou shouldst be obeyed: 570
I was at first as other beasts that graze
The trodden herb, of abject thoughts and low,
As was my food, nor aught but food discerned
Or sex, and apprehended nothing high:
Till on a day, roving the field, I chanced   575
A goodly tree far distant to behold
Loaden with fruit of fairest colors mixed,
Ruddy and gold; I nearer drew to gaze;
When from the boughs a savory odor blown,

---

5. The beasts cannot see the beauty of Eve's soul, only Adam can, Satan's entire speech is couched in the extravagant phrases of the Petrarchan love convention.
6. Flattered. "Proem": introduction.
7. I.e., as to whether rational sense was denied to brutes, I am doubtful.
8. Endowed.
9. To have speech after being dumb.

Grateful to appetite, more pleased my sense　　　　　　580
Than smell of sweetest fennel,[1] or the teats
Of ewe or goat dropping with milk at even,
Unsucked of lamb or kid, that tend their play.
To satisfy the sharp desire I had
Of tasting those fair apples, I resolved　　　　　　585
Not to defer: hunger and thirst at once,
Powerful persuaders, quickened at the scent
Of that alluring fruit, urged me so keen.
About the mossy trunk I wound me soon,
For, high from ground, the branches would require　　　　　　590
Thy utmost reach, or Adam's: round the tree
All other beasts that saw, with like desire
Longing and envying stood, but could not reach.
Amid the tree now got, where plenty hung
Tempting so nigh, to pluck and eat my fill　　　　　　595
I spared not;[2] for such pleasure till that hour
At feed or fountain never had I found.
Sated at length, ere long I might perceive
Strange alteration in me, to degree
Of reason in my inward powers, and speech　　　　　　600
Wanted not long, though to this shape retained.[3]
Thenceforth to speculations high or deep
I turned my thoughts, and with capacious mind
Considered all things visible in Heaven,
Or Earth, or middle, all things fair and good:　　　　　　605
But all that fair and good in thy divine
Semblance, and in thy beauty's heavenly ray
United I beheld: no fair[4] to thine
Equivalent or second, which compelled
Me thus, though importune perhaps, to come　　　　　　610
And gaze, and worship thee of right declared
Sovereign of creatures, universal dame."
　　So talked the spirited[5] sly snake: and Eve
Yet more amazed, unwary thus replied:
　　"Serpent, thy overpraising leaves in doubt　　　　　　615
The virtue of that fruit, in thee first proved.
But say, where grows the tree, from hence how far?
For many are the trees of God that grow
In Paradise, and various, yet unknown
To us; in such abundance lies our choice,　　　　　　620
As leaves a greater store of fruit untouched,
Still hanging incorruptible, till men

---

1. Milton learned, probably from Pliny, the natural historian, that serpents were fond of fennel; popular superstition had it that they drank the milk of sheep and goats.
2. Refrained not.

3. His inward powers, his mental constitution and gift of speech, were changed; but he retained his exterior shape as before.
4. Beauty.
5. Possessed by a spirit, inspired.

Grow up to their provision, and more hands
Help to disburden Nature of her bearth."[6]
   To whom the wily adder, blithe and glad: 625
"Empress, the way is ready, and not long,
Beyond a row of myrtles, on a flat,
Fast by a fountain, one small thicket past
Of blowing[7] myrrh and balm: if thou accept
My conduct, I can bring thee thither soon."   630
   "Lead then," said Eve. He leading swiftly rolled
In tangles, and made intricate seem straight,
To mischief swift.[8] Hope elevates, and joy
Brightens his crest; as when a wandering fire
Compact of unctuous vapor,[9] which the night   635
Condenses, and the cold environs round,
Kindled through agitation to a flame
(Which oft, they say, some evil spirit attends),
Hovering and blazing with delusive light,
Misleads th' amazed night-wanderer from his way   640
To bogs and mires, and oft through pond or pool,
There swallowed up and lost, from succor far:
So glistered the dire snake, and into fraud
Led Eve our credulous mother, to the tree
Of prohibition,[1] root of all our woe: 645
Which when she saw, thus to her guide she spake:
   "Serpent, we might have spared our coming hither,
Fruitless to me, though fruit be here to excess,
The credit of whose virtue rest with thee;[2]
Wondrous indeed, if cause of such effects!   650
But of this tree we may not taste nor touch:
God so commanded, and left that command
Sole daughter of his voice;[3] the rest, we live
Law to ourselves; our reason is our law."
   To whom the tempter guilefully replied: 655
"Indeed? Hath God then said that of the fruit
Of all these garden trees ye shall not eat,
Yet lords declared of all in earth or air?"
   To whom thus Eve, yet sinless: "Of the fruit
Of each tree in the garden we may eat,   660
But of the fruit of this fair tree amidst
The garden, God hath said, 'Ye shall not eat
Thereof, nor shall ye touch it, lest ye die.' "
   She scarce had said, though brief, when now more bold

---

6. So spelled to pun on the idea of trees bearing
fruit and thus in a way giving birth to young.
7. Blooming.
8. Milton's physical descriptions of the serpent often
have distinct moral overtones, as here.
9. Composed of oily vapor; Milton's theory of the
ignis fatuus, or will-o'-the-wisp, is strikingly mate-

rial and "scientific."
1. Prohibited tree (a Hebraism).
2. I.e., you must remain the only evidence of the
fruit's power.
3. His one injunction (a Hebraism). "The rest":
in everything else.

The tempter, but with show of zeal and love 665
To man, and indignation at his wrong,
New part puts on, and as to passion moved,
Fluctuates disturbed, yet comely, and in act
Raised,[4] as of some great matter to begin.
As when of old some orator renowned 670
In Athens or free Rome, where eloquence
Flourished, since mute, to some great cause addressed,
Stood in himself collected, while each part,
Motion, each act, won audience ere the tongue,
Sometimes in height began, as no delay 675
Of preface brooking,[5] through his zeal of right.
So standing, moving, or to height upgrown
The tempter all impassioned thus began:
    "O sacred, wise, and wisdom-giving plant,
Mother of science![6] now I feel thy power 680
Within me clear, not only to discern
Things in their causes, but to trace the ways
Of highest agents, deemed however wise.
Queen of this universe! do not believe
Those rigid threats of death. Ye shall not die; 685
How should ye? by the fruit? it gives you life
To knowledge;[7] by the Threatener? look on me,
Me who have touched and tasted, yet both live,
And life more perfect have attained than Fate
Meant me, by venturing higher than my lot. 690
Shall that be shut to man, which to the beast
Is open? Or will God incense his ire
For such a petty trespass, and not praise
Rather your dauntless virtue, whom the pain
Of death denounced, whatever thing death be, 695
Deterred not from achieving what might lead
To happier life, knowledge of good and evil?
Of good, how just![8] Of evil, if what is evil
Be real, why not known, since easier shunned?
God therefore cannot hurt ye, and be just; 700
Not just, not God; not feared then, nor obeyed:
Your fear itself of death removes the fear.[9]
Why then was this forbid? Why but to awe,
Why but to keep ye low and ignorant,
His worshipers? He knows that in the day 705
Ye eat thereof, your eyes that seem so clear,
Yet are but dim, shall perfectly be then

---

4. Poised in posture.
5. The orator, as if too much moved to be bothered with a preface, bursts into the middle of his speech.
6. Knowledge.
7. Life in addition to knowledge; or, life with which

to enlarge your knowledge.
8. I.e., how just to have knowledge of good!
9. I.e., your fear of death removes your fear of God; since if God inflicts death, he will not be just and hence not God. The serpent's sophism is visible.

Opened and cleared, and ye shall be as gods,
Knowing both good and evil, as they know.
That ye should be as gods, since I as man,   710
Internal man,[1] is but proportion meet,
I, of brute, human; ye, of human, gods.
So ye shall die perhaps, by putting off
Human, to put on gods:[2] death to be wished,
Though threatened, which no worse than this can bring.   715
And what are gods that man may not become
As they, participating godlike food?
The gods are first, and that advantage use
On our belief, that all from them proceeds.
I question it; for this fair Earth I see,   720
Warmed by the sun, producing every kind,
Them nothing: if they all things,[3] who enclosed
Knowledge of good and evil in this tree,
That whoso eats thereof forthwith attains
Wisdom without their leave? And wherein lies   725
Th' offense, that man should thus attain to know?
What can your knowledge hurt him, or this tree
Impart against his will, if all be his?
Or is it envy, and can envy dwell
In heavenly breasts?[4] These, these, and many more   730
Causes import your need of this fair fruit.
Goddess humane,[5] reach then, and freely taste!"
    He ended, and his words, replete with guile,
Into her heart too easy entrance won:
Fixed on the fruit she gazed, which to behold   735
Might tempt alone, and in her ears the sound
Yet rung of his persuasive words, impregned[6]
With reason, to her seeming, and with truth;
Meanwhile the hour of noon drew on, and waked
An eager appetite, raised by the smell   740
So savory of that fruit, which with desire,
Inclinable now grown to touch or taste,
Solicited her longing eye;[7] yet first
Pausing a while, thus to herself she mused:
    "Great are thy virtues, doubtless, best of fruits,   745
Though kept from man, and worthy to be admired,
Whose taste, too long forborne, at first essay
Gave elocution to the mute, and taught
The tongue not made for speech to speak thy praise:
Thy praise he also who forbids thy use   750

1. Man in intellectual powers.
2. The devil can quote Scripture to his purpose, and here he is perverting Saint Paul, who told the Colossians (3.9–10) to put off the old man and put on the new. "Participating" (line 717): sharing.
3. The verb "produced" is understood. Satan is talking now, not about "God," but "the gods."
4. Adapted from Virgil, *Aeneid* 1.15. "Import": imply, suggest.
5. Not so much "human goddess" (a Satanic paradox) as "kindly," "gracious" goddess.
6. Impregnated.
7. The five senses of Eve—sight, hearing, smell, taste, and touch—are all solicited by the fruit.

Conceals not from us,[8] naming thee the Tree
Of Knowledge, knowledge both of good and evil;
Forbids us then to taste; but his forbidding
Commends thee more, while it infers the good
By thee communicated, and our want: 755
For good unknown, sure is not had, or had
And yet unknown, is as not had at all.[9]
In plain then, what forbids he but to know?
Forbids us good, forbids us to be wise!
Such prohibitions bind not. But if death   760
Bind us with after-bands, what profits then
Our inward freedom? In the day we eat
Of this fair fruit, our doom is, we shall die.
How dies the serpent? He hath eaten and lives,
And knows, and speaks, and reasons, and discerns,   765
Irrational till then. For us alone
Was death invented? Or to us denied
This intellectual food, for beasts reserved?
For beasts it seems: yet that one beast which first
Hath tasted, envies not, but brings with joy   770
The good befallen him, author unsuspect,[1]
Friendly to man, far from deceit or guile.
What fear I then, rather what know to fear[2]
Under this ignorance of good and evil,
Of God or death, of law or penalty?   775
Here grows the cure of all, this fruit divine,
Fair to the eye, inviting to the taste,
Of virtue[3] to make wise: what hinders then
To reach and feed at once both body and mind?"
    So saying, her rash hand in evil hour   780
Forth reaching to the fruit, she plucked, she eat.[4]
Earth felt the wound, and nature from her seat[5]
Sighing through all her works gave signs of woe,
That all was lost. Back to the thicket slunk
The guilty serpent, and well might, for Eve,   785
Intent now wholly on her taste, naught else
Regarded; such delight till then, as seemed,
In fruit she never tasted, whether true
Or fancied so, through expectation high
Of knowledge; nor was godhead from her thought.[6]   790
Greedily she engorged without restraint,
And knew not eating death:[7] satiate at length,

---

8. God himself, by naming it, has called attention
to the tree's magic powers.
9. An unknown good is like no good at all. "In
plain": i.e., in plain language.
1. A witness beyond suspicion.
2. In her ignorance, Eve does not really know what
to fear and what not to fear—at least, so she says.
3. Power.

4. In the 17th century, an accepted past tense of
"eat."
5. Wherever Nature is hidden, in the heart of
things, she sighs.
6. She expected to achieve godhead immediately.
7. A grim pun. She is eating death and does not
know it; but death is eating her too. Compare "eating cares" (*L'Allegro*, line 135).

And heightened as with wine, jocund and boon,[8]
Thus to herself she pleasingly began:
   "O sovereign, virtuous, precious of all trees   795
In Paradise! of operation blest
To sapience,[9] hitherto obscured, infamed,
And thy fair fruit let hang, as to no end
Created; but henceforth my early care,
Not without song each morning, and due praise   800
Shall tend thee, and the fertile burden ease
Of thy full branches offered free to all;
Till dieted by thee I grow mature
In knowledge, as the gods who all things know;
Though others[1] envy what they cannot give: 805
For had the gift been theirs, it had not here
Thus grown. Experience, next to thee I owe,
Best guide; not following thee I had remained
In ignorance; thou open'st Wisdom's way,
And giv'st accèss, though secret she retire.   810
And I perhaps am secret; Heaven is high,
High and remote to see from thence distinct
Each thing on Earth; and other care perhaps
May have diverted from continual watch
Our great Forbidder,[2] safe with all his spies   815
About him. But to Adam in what sort[3]
Shall I appear? Shall I to him make known
As yet my change, and give him to partake
Full happiness with me, or rather not,
But keep the odds[4] of knowledge in my power   820
Without copartner? so to add what wants
In female sex, the more to draw his love,
And render me more equal, and perhaps,
A thing not undesirable, sometime
Superior: for, inferior, who is free?[5]   825
This may be well: but what if God have seen
And death ensue? Then I shall be no more,
And Adam, wedded to another Eve,
Shall live with her enjoying, I extinct;
A death to think. Confirmed then I resolve,   830
Adam shall share with me in bliss or woe:
So dear I love him, that with him all deaths
I could endure, without him live no life."[6]
   So saying, from the tree her step she turned,

---

8. Joyous and liberal.
9. To wisdom, for the wise and those of good taste.
(Latin *sapere*, to be wise, has its root in the verb
"to taste.") "Infamed": defamed, i.e., maligned.
1. The gods, i.e., other gods. In saying that God
did not give the tree, Eve is merely echoing a lesson learned from the serpent.
2. Now that Eve has fallen, God is a "great Forbidder," and all his gifts in Paradise are forgotten.

3. Guise.
4. Balance.
5. Eve's fatal foolishness implies that the only person in the world who can ever be free is an absolute tyrant.
6. Her affection is not unlike Satan's (4.374–85)
in its destructiveness. In reality, there is no chance
of her living "without him," since she is already
under sentence of death.

But first low reverence done,[7] as to the power   835
That dwelt within, whose presence had infused
Into the plant sciential[8] sap, derived
From nectar, drink of gods. Adam the while
Waiting desirous her return, had wove
Of choicest flowers a garland to adorn   840
Her tresses, and her rural labors crown,
As reapers oft are wont their harvest queen.
Great joy he promised to his thoughts, and new
Solace in her return, so long delayed:
Yet oft his heart, divine[9] of something ill,   845
Misgave him; he the faltering measure[1] felt;
And forth to meet her went, the way she took
That morn when first they parted. By the Tree
Of Knowledge he must pass; there he her met,
Scarce from the tree returning; in her hand   850
A bough of fairest fruit that downy smiled,
New gathered, and ambrosial smell diffused.
To him she hasted, in her face excuse
Came prologue, and apology to prompt,[2]
Which with bland words at will she thus addressed: 855
    "Hast thou not wondered, Adam, at my stay?
Thee I have missed, and thought it long, deprived
Thy presence, agony of love till now
Not felt, nor shall be twice; for never more
Mean I to try what rash untried I sought,   860
The pain of absence from thy sight. But strange
Hath been the cause, and wonderful to hear:
This tree is not as we are told, a tree
Of danger tasted,[3] nor to evil unknown
Opening the way, but of divine effect   865
To open eyes, and make them gods who taste;
And hath been tasted such. The serpent wise,
Or not restrained as we, or not obeying,
Hath eaten of the fruit, and is become,
Not dead, as we are threatened, but thenceforth   870
Endued with human voice and human sense,
Reasoning to admiration,[4] and with me
Persuasively hath so prevailed, that I
Have also tasted, and have also found
Th' effects to correspond, opener mine eyes   875
Dim erst, dilated spirits, ampler heart,
And growing up to godhead;[5] which for thee
Chiefly I sought, without thee can despise.

---

7. Eve's first physical act after falling is idolatry.
8. Knowledge-giving.
9. Foreboding, suspicious.
1. I.e., of his pulse.
2. Her face had an excuse in it, as prologue to an

apology which followed after.
3. If tasted.
4. Admirably. "Persuasively": by persuasion.
5. Everything that Eve says she feels is what Satan has told her she will feel.

For bliss, as thou hast part, to me is bliss;
Tedious, unshared with thee, and odious soon.   880
Thou therefore also taste, that equal lot
May join us, equal joy, as equal love;
Lest, thou not tasting, different degree[6]
Disjoin us, and I then too late renounce
Deity for thee, when Fate will not permit.[7]   885
    Thus Eve with countenance blithe her story told;
But in her cheek distemper[8] flushing glowed.
On th' other side, Adam, soon as he heard
The fatal trespass done by Eve, amazed,
Astonied[9] stood and blank, while horror chill   890
Ran through his veins, and all his joints relaxed;
From his slack hand the garland wreathed for Eve
Down dropped, and all the faded roses shed.
Speechless he stood and pale, till thus at length
First to himself he inward silence broke: 895
    "O fairest of creation, last and best
Of all God's works, creature in whom excelled
Whatever can to sight or thought be formed,
Holy, divine, good, amiable, or sweet!
How art thou lost, how on a sudden lost,   900
Defaced, deflowered, and now to death devote?[1]
Rather how hast thou yielded to transgress
The strict forbiddance, how to violate
The sacred fruit forbidden! Some cursèd fraud
Of enemy hath beguiled thee, yet unknown,[2]   905
And me with thee hath ruined, for with thee
Certain my resolution is to die.
How can I live without thee, how forego
Thy sweet converse and love so dearly joined,
To live again in these wild woods forlorn?[3]   910
Should God create another Eve, and I
Another rib afford, yet loss of thee
Would never from my heart; no, no! I feel
The link of nature draw me: flesh of flesh,
Bone of my bone thou art, and from thy state   915
Mine never shall be parted, bliss or woe."
    So having said, as one from sad dismay
Recomforted, and after thoughts disturbed
Submitting to what seemed remediless,
Thus in calm mood his words to Eve he turned: 920
    "Bold deed thou hast presumed, adventurous Eve,
And peril great provoked, who thus hath dared

6. Differing rank in the hierarchy of creatures.
7. Contrast Eve's logic when she is alone (lines 817–25).
8. The proportion of Eve's humors—which, in the state of innocence, gave her perfect health—has been disturbed, and she is running a fever.
9. Astonished, "petrified." "Blank": empty of mind.
1. Doomed.
2. "Yet unknown" modifies "enemy."
3. Without Eve, Paradise itself would be a wilderness.

Had it been only coveting to eye
That sacred fruit, sacred[4] to abstinence,
Much more to taste it, under ban to touch.   925
But past who can recall, or done undo?
Not God omnipotent, nor Fate! Yet so
Perhaps thou shalt not die, perhaps the fact[5]
Is not so heinous now, foretasted fruit,
Profaned first by the serpent, by him first   930
Made common and unhallowed ere our taste,
Nor yet on him found deadly; he yet lives,
Lives, as thou saidst, and gains to live as man
Higher degree of life: inducement strong
To us, as likely tasting to attain   935
Proportional ascent, which cannot be
But to be gods, or angels, demigods.[6]
Nor can I think that God, Creator wise,
Though threatening, will in earnest so destroy
Us his prime creatures, dignified so high,   940
Set over all his works, which in our fall,
For us created, needs with us must fail,
Dependent made; so God shall uncreate,
Be frustrate, do, undo, and labor lose;
Not well conceived of God,[7] who, though his power   945
Creation could repeat, yet would be loath
Us to abolish, lest the adversary
Triùmph and say: 'Fickle their state whom God
Most favors; who can please him long? Me first
He ruined, now mankind; whom will he next?'   950
Matter of scorn, not to be given the foe.
However, I with thee have fixed my lot,
Certain to undergo like doom: if death
Consort with thee, death is to me as life;
So forcible within my heart I feel   955
The bond of nature draw me to my own,
My own in thee, for what thou art is mine;
Our state cannot be severed; we are one,
One flesh; to lose thee were to lose myself."
    So Adam, and thus Eve to him replied: 960
"O glorious trial of exceeding love,
Illustrious evidence, example high!
Engaging me to emulate; but short
Of thy perfection, how shall I attain,
Adam? from whose dear side I boast me sprung,   965
And gladly of our union hear thee speak,
One heart, one soul in both; whereof good proof

4. Devoted.
5. Act.
6. Note how Adam agrees first in Eve's harmless
errors about the serpent, then in her sinful ambi-

tion to achieve a higher form of life.
7. I.e., not a proper conception of God (as making his actions dependent on those of an inferior).

This day affords, declaring thee resolved,
Rather than death or aught than death more dread
Shall separate us, linked in love so dear,   970
To undergo with me one guilt, one crime,
If any be, of tasting this fair fruit;
Whose virtue (for of good still good proceeds,
Direct, or by occasion)[8] hath presented
This happy trial of thy love, which else   975
So eminently never had been known.
Were it I thought death menaced would ensue[9]
This my attempt, I would sustain alone
The worst, and not persuade thee, rather die
Deserted, than oblige[1] thee with a fact   980
Pernicious to thy peace, chiefly assured
Remarkably so late of thy so true,
So faithful love unequaled;[2] but I feel
Far otherwise th' event;[3] not death, but life
Augmented, opened eyes, new hopes, new joys,   985
Taste so divine, that what of sweet before
Hath touched my sense, flat seems to this, and harsh.
On my experience, Adam, freely taste,
And fear of death deliver to the winds."
    So saying, she embraced him, and for joy   990
Tenderly wept, much won that he his love
Had so ennobled, as of choice to incur
Divine displeasure for her sake, or death.
In recompense (for such compliance bad
Such recompense best merits), from the bough   995
She gave him of that fair enticing fruit
With liberal hand; he scrupled not to eat,
Against his better knowledge, not deceived,
But fondly overcome with female charm.[4]
Earth trembled from her entrails, as again   1000
In pangs, and Nature gave a second groan,
Sky lowered, and muttering thunder, some sad drops
Wept at completing of the mortal sin
Original; while Adam took no thought,
Eating his fill, nor Eve to iterate   1005
Her former trespass feared, the more to soothe
Him with her loved society; that now
As with new wine intoxicated both,
They swim in mirth, and fancy that they feel
Divinity within them breeding wings   1010
Wherewith to scorn the earth. But that false fruit

8. Indirectly.
9. Result from.
1. Render liable, involve.
2. Touched by Adam's devotion, Eve feels a little belated remorse at the damage she may have inflicted on him.
3. Result (of eating the apple).
4. See 1 Timothy 2.14: "And Adam was not deceived, but the woman being deceived was in the transgression."

Far other operation first displayed,
Carnal desire inflaming; he on Eve
Began to cast lascivious eyes, she him
As wantonly repaid; in lust they burn,   1015
Till Adam thus 'gan Eve to dalliance move:
    "Eve, now I see thou art exact[5] of taste,
And elegant, of sapience no small part,
Since to each meaning savor we apply,
And palate call judicious. I the praise   1020
Yield thee, so well this day thou hast purveyed.[6]
Much pleasure we have lost while we abstained
From this delightful fruit, nor known till now
True relish, tasting; if such pleasure be
In things to us forbidden, it might be wished   1025
For this one tree had been forbidden ten.
But come; so well refreshed, now let us play,
As meet is, after such delicious fare;
For never did thy beauty since the day
I saw thee first and wedded thee, adorned   1030
With all perfections, so enflame my sense
With ardor to enjoy thee, fairer now
Than ever, bounty of this virtuous tree."
    So said he, and forbore not glance or toy[7]
Of amorous intent, well understood   1035
Of[8] Eve, whose eye darted contagious fire.
Her hand he seized, and to a shady bank,
Thick overhead with verdant roof embowered
He led her, nothing loath; flowers were the couch,
Pansies, and violets, and asphodel,   1040
And hyacinth, Earth's freshest, softest lap.
There they their fill of love and love's disport
Took largely, of their mutual guilt the seal,
The solace of their sin, till dewy sleep
Oppressed them, wearied with their amorous play.   1045
    Soon as the force of that fallacious fruit,
That with exhilarating vapor bland
About their spirits had played, and inmost powers
Made err, was now exhaled, and grosser sleep
Bred of unkindly fumes,[9] with conscious dreams   1050
Encumbered, now had left them, up they rose
As from unrest, and each the other viewing,
Soon found their eyes how opened, and their minds
How darkened. Innocence, that as a veil
Had shadowed them from knowing ill, was gone;   1055

---

5. Exacting, demanding. "Sapience" means wisdom, but the word comes from Latin *sapere*, "to
taste," which gives rise, via another etymology, to
the word "savor." Adam's sentence plays rather
heavily on these two meanings of *sapere*.

6. Provided for us, provisioned us.
7. Caress.
8. By.
9. Unnatural vapors.

Just confidence, and native righteousness,
And honor from about them, naked left
To guilty Shame; he covered, but his robe
Uncovered more.[1] So rose the Danite strong,
Herculean Samson, from the harlot-lap   1060
Of Philistean Dalilah, and waked
Shorn of his strength;[2] they destitute and bare
Of all their virtue. Silent, and in face
Confounded, long they sat, as strucken mute;
Till Adam, though not less than Eve abashed,   1065
At length gave utterance to these words constrained:
    "O Eve, in evil hour[3] thou didst give ear
To that false worm,[4] of whomsoever taught
To counterfeit man's voice, true in our fall,
False in our promised rising; since our eyes   1070
Opened we find indeed, and find we know
Both good and evil, good lost and evil got:
Bad fruit of knowledge, if this be to know,
Which leaves us naked thus, of honor void,
Of innocence, of faith, of purity,   1075
Our wonted ornaments now soiled and stained,
And in our faces evident the signs
Of foul concupiscence; whence evil store,[5]
Even shame, the last of evils; of the first
Be sure then.[6] How shall I behold the face   1080
Henceforth of God or angel, erst with joy
And rapture so oft beheld? Those heavenly shapes
Will dazzle now this earthly[7] with their blaze
Insufferably bright. O might I here
In solitude live savage, in some glade   1085
Obscured, where highest woods, impenetrable
To star or sunlight, spread their umbrage broad,
And brown[8] as evening! Cover me, ye pines,
Ye cedars, with innumerable boughs
Hide me, where I may never see them more![9]   1090
But let us now, as in bad plight, devise
What best may for the present serve to hide
The parts of each from other that seem most
To shame obnoxious,[1] and unseemliest seen;
Some tree whose broad smooth leaves together sewed,   1095
And girded on our loins, may cover round

1. They were covered with shame, which made
them conscious of their nakedness as they had never
been before.
2. See the story of Samson and Delilah, Judges
16.4–20.
3. Even in his misery, Adam cannot resist the word
play on Eve-evil.
4. Serpent, with a connotation of disgust. "Of":
by.
5. A store of evil.

6. I.e., since we now feel shame, the last of evils,
we shall soon experience the first ones.
7. A noun such as "vision" is understood.
8. Dark.
9. Cf. Revelation 6.16: "And said to the mountains and rocks, Fall on us, and hide us from the
face of him that sitteth on the throne, and from
the wrath of the Lamb."
1. Vulnerable, liable.

Those middle parts, that this newcomer, Shame,
There sit not, and reproach us as unclean."
　　So counseled he, and both together went
Into the thickest wood; there soon they chose   1100
The figtree,[2] not that kind for fruit renowned,
But such as at this day, to Indians known,
In Malabar or Deccan[3] spreads her arms
Branching so broad and long, that in the ground
The bended twigs take root, and daughters grow   1105
About the mother tree, a pillared shade
High overarched, and echoing walks between;
There oft the Indian herdsman, shunning heat,
Shelters in cool, and tends his pasturing herds
At loopholes cut through thickest shade. Those leaves   1110
They gathered, broad as Amazonian targe,[4]
And with what skill they had, together sewed,
To gird their waist; vain covering, if to hide
Their guilt and dreaded shame! O how unlike
To that first naked glory! Such of late   1115
Columbus found th' American so girt
With feathered cincture,[5] naked else and wild
Among the trees on isles and woody shores.
Thus fenced, and, as they thought, their shame in part
Covered, but not at rest or ease of mind,   1120
They sat them down to weep; nor only tears
Rained at their eyes, but high winds worse within
Began to rise, high passions, anger, hate,
Mistrust, suspicion, discord, and shook sore
Their inward state of mind, calm region once   1125
And full of peace, now tossed and turbulent:
For Understanding ruled not, and the Will
Heard not her lore, both in subjection now
To sensual Appetite, who from beneath
Usurping over sovereign Reason claimed   1130
Superior sway.[6] From thus distempered breast,
Adam, estranged in look and altered style,
Speech intermitted thus to Eve renewed:
　　"Would thou hadst hearkened to my words, and stayed
With me, as I besought thee, when that strange   1135
Desire of wandering, this unhappy morn,
I know not whence possessed thee! we had then
Remained still happy, not as now, despoiled
Of all our good, shamed, naked, miserable.

---

2. The banyan, or Indian fig. It has, in fact, small
leaves, but Milton's knowledge of it came from
Gerard's *Herball*, where all the details of lines 1104–
11 may be found.
3. Sections of southern India.
4. Shield. The Amazons, mythical female war-

riors, carried large crescent-shaped shields.
5. Belt.
6. The psychology of the Fall is made explicit here.
The higher faculties of reason are in subjection to
the lower faculties of appetite. Moreover, Adam
has lost his superiority over Eve.

Let none henceforth seek needless cause to approve[7]   1140
The faith they owe; when earnestly they seek
Such proof, conclude they then begin to fail."
    To whom, soon moved with touch of blame, thus Eve:
"What words have passed thy lips, Adam severe?
Imput'st thou that to my default or will   1145
Of wandering, as thou call'st it, which who knows
But might as ill have happened, thou being by,
Or to thyself perhaps? Hadst thou been there,
Or here th' attempt, thou couldst not have discerned
Fraud in the serpent, speaking as he spake;   1150
No ground of enmity between us known,
Why he should mean me ill, or seek to harm?
Was I to have never parted from thy side?
As good have grown there still, a lifeless rib.
Being as I am, why didst not thou, the head,[8]   1155
Command me absolutely not to go,
Going into such danger, as thou saidst?
Too facile[9] then, thou didst not much gainsay,
Nay, didst permit, approve, and fair dismiss.
Hadst thou been firm and fixed in thy dissent,   1160
Neither had I transgressed, nor thou with me."
    To whom, then first incensed, Adam replied:
"Is this the love, is this the recompense
Of mine to thee, ingrateful Eve, expressed
Immutable[1] when thou were lost, not I,   1165
Who might have lived and joyed immortal bliss,
Yet willingly chose rather death with thee?
And am I now upbraided as the cause
Of thy transgressing? not enough severe,
It seems, in thy restraint? What could I more?   1170
I warned thee, I admonished thee, foretold
The danger, and the lurking enemy
That lay in wait; beyond this had been force,
And force upon free will hath here no place.
But confidence then bore thee on, secure   1175
Either to meet no danger, or to find
Matter of glorious trial; and perhaps
I also erred in overmuch admiring
What seemed in thee so perfect, that I thought
No evil durst attempt thee! but I rue   1180
That error now, which is become my crime,
And thou th' accuser. Thus it shall befall
Him who, to worth in women overtrusting,
Lets her will rule; restraint she will not brook,[2]

---

7. Test, prove. "Owe": own.
8. Head of the family, but also the rational director, as the head is to the rest of the body. Cf. 1 Corinthians 11.3, "the head of the woman is the man."
9. Easy, permissive.
1. Shown to be unchangeable.
2. Accept.

And, left to herself, if evil thence ensue,   1185
She first his weak indulgence will accuse."
    Thus they in mutual accusation spent
The fruitless hours, but neither self-condemning;[3]
And of their vain contèst appeared no end.

From Book 10

Summary   When it is known in Heaven that man has fallen, God sends
his Son to pass judgment on the sinners. Having found them in the garden,
he hears their confession and passes instant sentence, cursing the serpent,
condemning Eve to the pains of childbirth and Adam to those of daily toil;
but in mercy he clothes the human couple both outwardly with the skins of
beasts and inwardly with his righteousness. Meanwhile Sin and Death, sitting by Hell-gate, feel new strength, and pass across Chaos, leaving a great
bridge behind them. On their way they meet with their parent, Satan, learn
of his success on earth, and press eagerly forward in hopes of destroying man
altogether. Satan, on the other hand, continues his flight back toward Hell,
where he is to report to his constituents.

[*Consequences of the Fall*]

    * * * Th' other way Satan went down
The causey[1] to Hell-gate; on either side   415
Disparted Chaos overbuilt exclaimed,
And with rebounding surge the bars assailed,
That scorned his indignation.[2] Through the gate,
Wide open and unguarded, Satan passed,
And all about found desolate; for those   420
Appointed to sit there[3] had left their charge,
Flown to the upper world; the rest were all
Far to the inland retired, about the walls
Of Pandemonium, city and proud seat
Of Lucifer, so by allusion called   425
Of that bright star to Satan paragoned.[4]
There kept their watch the legions, while the Grand
In council sat, solicitous what chance
Might intercept their emperor sent; so he
Departing gave command, and they observed.   430
As when the Tartar from his Russian foe,
By Astracan, over the snowy plains
Retires, or Bactrian Sophi, from the horns

---

3. Sterile recrimination is an early fruit of the forbidden tree; only self-condemnation can turn the
Fall from a mind-closing to a mind-opening event.
1. Causeway.
2. Chaos, as the instinctive enemy of order, is
hostile to the bridge built across its gulf by Sin and
Death, even though it means an increase in the

kingdom of Chaos itself.
3. I.e., Sin and Death.
4. Satan is called Lucifer, the light-bringer, because
bright as the morning star (before he fell). The
Grand (line 427) are the superior devils, Hell's
aristocracy.

Of Turkish crescent, leaves all waste beyond
The realm of Aladule, in his retreat   435
To Tauris or Casbeen;[5] so these, the late
Heaven-banished host, left desert utmost Hell
Many a dark league, reduced in careful watch
Round their metropolis, and now expecting
Each hour their great adventurer from the search   440
Of foreign worlds. He through the midst unmarked,
In show plebeian angel militant[6]
Of lowest order, passed, and from the door
Of that Plutonian hall, invisible
Ascended his high throne, which, under state[7]   445
Of richest texture spread, at th' upper end
Was placed in regal luster. Down a while
He sat, and round about him saw, unseen.
At last, as from a cloud, his fulgent[8] head
And shape star-bright appeared, or brighter, clad   450
With what permissive glory since his fall
Was left him, or false glitter. All amazed
At that so sudden blaze, the Stygian throng
Bent their aspèct, and whom they wished beheld,
Their mighty chief returned: loud was th' acclaim.   455
Forth rushed in haste the great consulting peers,
Raised from their dark divan,[9] and with like joy
Congratulant approached him, who with hand
Silence, and with these words attention, won:
    "Thrones, Dominations, Princedoms, Virtues, Powers!   460
For in possession such, not only of right,[1]
I call ye and declare ye now, returned
Successful beyond hope, to lead ye forth
Triumphant out of this infernal pit
Abominable, accursed, the house of woe,   465
And dungeon of our tyrant! Now possess,
As lords, a spacious world, to our native Heaven
Little inferior, by my adventure hard
With peril great achieved. Long were to tell
What I have done, what suffered, with what pain   470
Voyaged th' unreal, vast, unbounded deep
Of horrible confusion, over which
By Sin and Death a broad way now is paved
To expedite your glorious march; but I

5. The comparison is with Tartars retreating before
attacking Russians, and Persians before predatory
Turks. "Bactrian": Persian; "Tauris": Tabriz;
"Casbeen": Kazvin. Milton wants his simile to
convey a mingled sense of barbaric oriental splendor, cruelty, and desolation in hell.
6. Literally, an angelic footsoldier or private, but
with an ironic overtone from the phrase "church
militant."
7. Canopy.

8. Glittering, refulgent.
9. The Turkish council of state; the oriental theme
continues.
1. Satan makes a distinction much in men's minds
since the days of Cromwell and Charles I; a kingdom could be claimed either by right (in law, *de
jure*) or in act (by possession, *de facto*). The devils
now have both claims to their titles. "Returned"
(line 462) modifies "I" at the beginning of the line:
"now that I have returned."

Toiled out my uncouth passage, forced to ride   475
Th' untractable abyss, plunged in the womb
Of unoriginal² Night and Chaos wild,
That, jealous of their secrets, fiercely opposed
My journey strange, with clamorous uproar
Protesting Fate supreme; thence how I found   480
The new-created world, which fame in Heaven
Long had foretold, a fabric wonderful
Of absolute perfection; therein man
Placed in a paradise, by our exile
Made happy. Him by fraud I have seduced   485
From his creator, and, the more to increase
Your wonder, with an apple! He³ thereat
Offended—worth your laughter!—hath given up
Both his belovèd man and all his world
To Sin and Death a prey, and so to us,   490
Without our hazard, labor, or alarm,
To range in, and to dwell, and over man
To rule, as over all he should have ruled.
True is, me also he hath judged; or rather
Me not, but the brute serpent in whose shape   495
Man I deceived. That which to me belongs
Is enmity, which he will put between
Me and mankind: I am to bruise his heel;
His seed (when, is not set) shall bruise my head.⁴
A world who would not purchase with a bruise,   500
Or much more grievous pain? Ye have th' account
Of my performance; what remains, ye gods,
But up and enter now into full bliss?"
  So having said, a while he stood, expecting
Their universal shout and high applause   505
To fill his ear; when, contrary, he hears,
On all sides from innumerable tongues
A dismal universal hiss, the sound
Of public scorn. He wondered, but not long
Had leisure, wondering at himself now more.   510
His visage drawn he felt to sharp and spare,
His arms clung to his ribs, his legs entwining
Each other, till, supplanted,⁵ down he fell
A monstrous serpent on his belly prone,
Reluctant,⁶ but in vain; a greater power   515
Now ruled him, punished in the shape he sinned,

---

2. Without source or origin, primeval.
3. God.
4. Satan seems to have overheard or understood
the curse pronounced by God on the serpent, even
though he was not present at the time.
5. The word is used with its Latin force of "tripped
up by the heels." Ovid (*Metamorphoses* 4.576 ff.),
Lucan (*Pharsalia* 9.700 ff.), and Dante (*Inferno* 25)
had made set pieces about people being transformed into serpents. Whether Milton's editorial
hand does not intervene against Satan too directly
in this scene has been the subject of considerable
critical debate.
6. The Latin sense is felt again, "struggling against
the change."

According to his doom. He would have spoke,
But hiss for hiss returned with forkèd tongue
To forkèd tongue; for now were all transformed
Alike, to serpents all, as accessories   520
To his bold riot.[7] Dreadful was the din
Of hissing through the hall, thick-swarming now
With complicated monsters, head and tail—
Scorpion, and asp, and amphisbaena dire,[8]
Cerastes horned, hydrus, and ellops drear,   525
And dipsas (not so thick swarmed once the soil
Bedropped with blood of Gorgon, or the isle
Ophiusa); but still greatest he the midst,
Now dragon grown, larger than whom the sun
Engendered in the Pythian vale on slime,   530
Huge Python;[9] and his power no less he seemed
Above the rest still to retain. They all
Him followed, issuing forth to th' open field,
Where all yet left of that revolted rout,
Heaven-fallen, in station or just array,   535
Sublime[1] with expectation when to see
In triumph issuing forth their glorious chief.
They saw, but other sight instead, a crowd
Of ugly serpents. Horror on them fell,
And horrid sympathy; for what they saw   540
They felt themselves now changing. Down their arms,
Down fell both spear and shield; down they as fast,
And the dire hiss renewed, and the dire form
Catched by contagion, like in punishment
As in their crime. Thus was th' applause they meant   545
Turned to exploding hiss, triumph to shame
Cast on themselves from their own mouths. There stood
A grove hard by, sprung up with this their change,
His will who reigns above,[2] to aggravate
Their penance, laden with fair fruit, like that   550
Which grew in Paradise, the bait of Eve
Used by the tempter. On that prospect strange
Their earnest eyes they fixed, imagining
For one forbidden tree a multitude
Now risen, to work them further woe or shame;[3]   555
Yet, parched with scalding thirst and hunger fierce,

7. Revolt.
8. "Complicated": again a Latinism, meaning "twined together." The "amphisbaena" was alleged to have a head at each end of its body; "cerastes" was a horned snake, "hydrus" a water-snake, "ellops" perhaps the swordfish, and "dipsas" a snake whose bite was supposed to create outrageous thirst. When Perseus flew over Libya with the head of the snaky-haired Gorgon, the drops of her blood fell to the ground and became serpents. The "isle Ophiusa" is Snake Island, in the Balearics.

9. Python was a gigantic mythological serpent engendered by Apollo, the sun god, from the slime left by Deucalion's flood, and slain by Apollo in a great contest.
1. On tiptoes. The ordinary devils are standing in ranks outside Pandemonium, trying to catch a glimpse of Satan.
2. "By the will of him who reigns above."
3. The punishment of the devils not only fits the crime, it *is* the crime (the eating of forbidden fruit) repeated again and again, in disgust and loathing.

Though to delude them sent, could not abstain,
But on they rolled in heaps, and up the trees
Climbing, sat thicker than the snaky locks
That curled Megaera.[4] Greedily they plucked   560
The fruitage fair to sight, like that which grew
Near that bituminous lake where Sodom flamed;[5]
This more delusive, not the touch, but taste
Deceived; they fondly[6] thinking to allay
Their appetite with gust, instead of fruit   565
Chewed bitter ashes, which th' offended taste
With spattering noise rejected. Oft they assayed,
Hunger and thirst constraining: drugged as oft,
With hatefulest disrelish writhed their jaws
With soot and cinders filled: so oft they fell   570
Into the same illusion, not as man
Whom they triùmphed once lapsed.[7] Thus were they plagued,
And worn with famine long and ceaseless hiss,
Till their lost shape, permitted, they resumed—
Yearly enjoined, some say, to undergo   575
This annual humbling certain numbered days,
To dash their pride, and joy for man seduced.[8]
However, some tradition they dispersed
Among the heathen of their purchase got,
And fabled how the serpent, whom they called   580
Ophion, with Eurynome (the wide-
Encroaching Eve perhaps),[9] had first the rule
Of high Olympus, thence by Saturn driven
And Ops, ere yet Dictaean[1] Jove was born.

Summary   Sin and Death proceed without further interruption to the
earth, and enter into possession of it. God sees their arrival and declines to
interfere, but prophesies that their triumph will be only temporary; in due
course they will be forced back to hell again, and forever. Meanwhile, the
angels are ordered to twist the earth on its axis, disorder the planets so their
influence will in future be bad as well as good, and rearrange the cosmos
generally. In consequence, the temperate climate of Paradise at once gives
way to extremes of heat and cold, and furious winds begin to blow across the
ruined planet.

4. Megaera, like her sister Furies, had snakes
instead of hair on her head.
5. Sodom apples grew (legend had it) on the spot
where that accursed city once stood; though good
to look at, they dissolved into ashes when plucked.
6. Foolishly. "Gust": taste.
7. They fell again and again into delusion, though
they had felt superior to man, who fell just once.
8. There are many folktales about fairies, devils,
incubi, and the like, who are forced periodically
to take on the shape of some loathsome creature.

9. There is a mythological story about the Titan
Ophion (the name means "snake") and his wife
Eurynome ("the wide-reacher"), who ruled Olympus till Saturn and his wife Rhea (or Ops) drove
them away. Milton feels this story may be a vague,
pagan reminiscence of the real truth, the fall of
Satan. But there is an unresolved suggestion here
that Eve fell with Satan, becoming a kind of Proserpina to his role as Pluto, King of Hell.
1. Zeus was raised in a cave on Mount Dicte, in
Crete; hence, "Dictaean Jove."

[Adam, Eve, and the First Steps to Redemption]

* * * Thus began
Outrage from lifeless things; but Discord first,
Daughter of Sin, among th' irrational
Death introduced through fierce antipathy:[1]
Beast now with beast 'gan war, and fowl with fowl,   710
And fish with fish: to graze the herb[2] all leaving,
Devoured each other; nor stood much in awe
Of man, but fled him, or with countenance grim
Glared on him passing. These were from without
The growing miseries, which Adam saw   715
Already in part, though hid in gloomiest shade,
To sorrow abandoned, but worse felt within,
And in a troubled sea of passion tossed,
Thus to disburden sought with sad complaint:
    "O miserable of happy![3] Is this the end   720
Of this new glorious world, and me so late
The glory of that glory? who now, become
Accursed of blessèd, hide me from the face
Of God, whom to behold was then my height
Of happiness! Yet well, if here would end   725
The misery; I deserved it, and would bear
My own deservings; but this will not serve.
All that I eat or drink, or shall beget,
Is propagated curse.[4] O voice, once heard
Delightfully, 'Increase and multiply,'   730
Now death to hear! for what can I increase
Or multiply, but curses on my head?
Who of all ages to succeed, but, feeling
The evil on him brought by me, will curse
My head: 'Ill fare our ancestor impure!   735
For this we may thank Adam!' but his thanks
Shall be the execration;[5] so besides
Mine own that bide upon me, all from me
Shall with a fierce reflux on me redound,
On me, as on their natural center, light   740
Heavy, though in their place.[6] O fleeting joys
Of Paradise, dear bought with lasting woes!
Did I request thee, Maker, from my clay
To mold me man? Did I solicit thee
From darkness to promote me, or here place   745
In this delicious garden? As my will

---

1. "Discord" is the subject of the sentence, "Death" the object. "Th' irrational" are the beasts.
2. Grass.
3. I.e., change, to misery from happiness.
4. Whatever prolongs life extends the curse.
5. The only thanks for Adam will be mankind's curses.
6. Adam plays with the notion that natural objects have weight only as long as they are above their "natural" positions; so all curses will flow naturally to him, but they will still be heavy when they have lighted.

Concurred not to my being, it were but right
And equal[7] to reduce me to my dust,
Desirous to resign and render back
All I received, unable to perform   750
Thy terms too hard, by which I was to hold
The good I sought not. To the loss of that,
Sufficient penalty, why hast thou added
The sense of endless woes? Inexplicable
Thy justice seems; yet to say truth, too late   755
I thus contèst; then should have been refused
Those terms whatever, when they were proposed.
Thou[8] didst accept them; wilt thou enjoy the good,
Then cavil the conditions? And though God
Made thee without thy leave, what if thy son   760
Prove disobedient, and reproved, retort,
'Wherefore didst thou beget me? I sought it not.'
Wouldst thou admit for his contempt of thee
That proud excuse? Yet him not thy election,[9]
But natural necessity begot.   765
God made thee of choice his own, and of his own
To serve him; thy reward was of his grace;
Thy punishment then justly is at his will.
Be it so, for I submit; his doom is fair,
That dust I am and shall to dust return.   770
O welcome hour whenever! Why delays
His hand to execute what his decree
Fixed on this day? Why do I overlive?
Why am I mocked with death, and lengthened out
To deathless pain? How gladly would I meet   775
Mortality, my sentence, and be earth
Insensible! how glad would lay me down
As in my mother's lap![1] There I should rest
And sleep secure; his dreadful voice no more
Would thunder in my ears; no fear of worse   780
To me and to my offspring would torment me
With cruel expectation. Yet one doubt
Pursues me still, lest all I cannot die;[2]
Lest that pure breath of life, the spirit of man
Which God inspired, cannot together perish   785
With this corporeal clod; then in the grave,
Or in some other dismal place, who knows
But I shall die a living death? O thought
Horrid, if true! Yet why? It was but breath
Of life that sinned; what dies but what had life   790

---

7. Just.
8. "Thou," which referred to God in lines 753
and 755 ("Thy"), here shifts as Adam suddenly
addresses himself.
9. Choice.

1. Adam's lamentations owe a good deal to the
Book of Job 3.
2. Direct from Horace, *Odes* 3.30.6: *non omnis
moriar.*

And sin? the body properly hath neither.
All of me then shall die: let this appease
The doubt, since human reach no further knows.[3]
For though the Lord of all be infinite,
Is his wrath also? Be it, man is not so,   795
But mortal doomed. How can he exercise
Wrath without end on man whom death must end?
Can he make deathless death? That were to make
Strange contradiction, which to God himself
Impossible is held, as argument   800
Of weakness, not of power.[4] Will he draw out,
For anger's sake, finite to infinite
In punished man, to satisfy his rigor
Satisfied never? That were to extend
His sentence beyond dust and nature's law,   805
By which all causes else according still
To the reception of their matter act,
Not to th' extent of their own sphere.[5] But say
That death be not one stroke, as I supposed,
Bereaving[6] sense, but endless misery   810
From this day onward, which I feel begun
Both in me and without me, and so last
To perpetuity—Ay me! that fear
Comes thundering back with dreadful revolution
On my defenseless head! Both death and I   815
Am found eternal, and incorporate[7] both:
Nor I on my part single; in me all
Posterity stands cursed. Fair patrimony
That I must leave ye, sons! O, were I able
To waste it all myself, and leave ye none!   820
So disinherited, how would ye bless
Me, now your curse! Ah, why should all mankind
For one man's fault thus guiltless be condemned,
If guiltless? But from me what can proceed,
But all corrupt, both mind and will depraved,   825
Not to do only, but to will the same
With me?[8] How can they then acquitted stand
In sight of God? Him, after all disputes,
Forced[9] I absolve. All my evasions vain
And reasonings, though through mazes, lead me still   830
But to my own conviction: first and last

---

3. Adam convinces himself, as Milton was convinced, that both soul and body die at death; the
corollary is that they are resurrected together.
4. For a man in a state of nature, Adam displays
a fine command of theological argument. He holds
that if God contradicts himself, it is a sign of weakness.
5. An axiom of traditional philosophy: all agents
act according to the capacity of the object, not to

the extent of their inherent powers.
6. Taking away.
7. In the same body. Adam is appalled to find that
he has become death incarnate; the grammar ("both
death and I/Am") displays his shock.
8. Not only will men repeat Adam's sin; their will
is corrupted and they will *want* to be fallen like
Adam.
9. Perforce.

On me, me only, as the source and spring
Of all corruption, all the blame lights due;[1]
So might the wrath! Fond[2] wish! Couldst thou support
That burden, heavier than the earth to bear;   835
Than all the world much heavier, though divided
With that bad woman? Thus, what thou desir'st,
And what thou fear'st, alike destroys all hope
Of refuge, and concludes thee miserable[3]
Beyond all past example and futùre;   840
To Satan only like, both crime and doom.
O Conscience! into what abyss of fears
And horrors hast thou driven me; out of which
I find no way, from deep to deeper plunged!"
    Thus Adam to himself lamented loud   845
Through the still night, not now, as ere man fell,
Wholesome and cool and mild, but with black air
Accompanied, with damps and dreadful gloom;
Which to his evil conscience represented
All things with double terror. On the ground   850
Outstretched he lay, on the cold ground, and oft
Cursed his creation; Death as oft accused
Of tardy execution, since denounced
The day of his offense. "Why comes not Death,"
Said he, "with one thrice-acceptable stroke   855
To end me? Shall Truth fail to keep her word,
Justice divine not hasten to be just?
But Death comes not at call; Justice divine
Mends not her slowest pace for prayers or cries.
O woods, O fountains, hillocks, dales, and bowers!   860
With other echo late I taught your shades
To answer, and resound far other song."
Whom thus afflicted when sad Eve beheld,
Desolate where she sat, approaching nigh,
Soft words to his fierce passion she essayed;   865
But her with stern regard he thus repelled:
    "Out of my sight, thou serpent! that name best
Befits thee, with him leagued, thyself as false
And hateful: nothing wants, but that thy shape,
Like his, and color serpentine, may show   870
Thy inward fraud, to warn all creatures from thee
Henceforth; lest that too heavenly form, pretended[4]
To hellish falsehood, snare them. But for thee
I had persisted happy, had not thy pride
And wandering vanity, when least was safe,   875
Rejected my forewarning, and disdained

---

1. In this discovery that he alone must accept the
guilt of mankind, Adam has chosen crucially to be
like Christ and unlike Satan—at the very moment
when he feels exactly the opposite.

2. Foolish.
3. Shows thee to be miserable.
4. Serving as a mask; literally, "held out before."

Not to be trusted, longing to be seen
Though by the devil himself, him overweening[5]
To overreach, but, with the serpent meeting,
Fooled and beguiled; by him thou, I by thee,   880
To trust thee from my side, imagined wise,
Constant, mature, proof against all assaults;
And understood not all was but a show
Rather than solid virtue, all but a rib
Crooked by nature—bent, as now appears,   885
More to the part sinìster[6]—from me drawn;
Well if thrown out, as supernumerary
To my just number found![7] Oh, why did God,
Creator wise, that peopled highest Heaven
With spirits masculine, create at last   890
This novelty on earth, this fair defect
Of nature, and not fill the world at once
With men, as angels, without feminine;
Or find some other way to generate
Mankind?[8] This mischief had not then befallen,   895
And more that shall befall—innumerable
Disturbances on earth through female snares,
And strait conjunction[9] with this sex. For either
He never shall find out fit mate, but such
As some misfortune brings him, or mistake;   900
Or whom he wishes most shall seldom gain,
Through her perverseness, but shall see her gained
By a far worse, or, if she love, withheld
By parents, or his happiest choice too late
Shall meet, already linked and wedlock-bound   905
To a fell[1] adversary, his hate or shame:
Which infinite calamity shall cause
To human life, and household peace confound."
    He added not, and from her turned; but Eve,
Not so repulsed, with tears that ceased not flowing,   910
And tresses all disordered, at his feet
Fell humble, and embracing them besought
His peace, and thus proceeded in her plaint:
    "Forsake me not thus, Adam! witness Heaven
What love sincere and reverence in my heart   915
I bear thee, and unweeting[2] have offended,
Unhappily deceived! Thy suppliant[3]
I beg, and clasp thy knees; bereave me not,
Whereon I live, thy gentle looks, thy aid,
Thy counsel in this uttermost distress,   920

---

5. Overconfident.
6. "On the left hand," as in Latin; also "unlucky."
7. Since men visibly have twelve ribs on both sides,
it was supposed that Adam originally had thirteen
ribs on his left side, so that he could give up one
and still have twelve, the proper ("just") number.

8. Ancient traditions of antifeminist thought lie
behind these ungenerous questions.
9. Close connections, i.e., matrimony.
1. Bitter.
2. Unintentionally.
3. As a suppliant to thee.

My only strength and stay: forlorn of thee,
Whither shall I betake me, where subsist?
While yet we live, scarce one short hour perhaps,
Between us two let there be peace; both joining,
As joined in injuries, one enmity   925
Against a foe by doom express assigned us,
That cruel serpent. On me exercise not
Thy hatred for this misery befallen;
On me already lost, me than thyself
More miserable. Both have sinned, but thou   930
Against God only; I against God and thee,
And to the place of judgment will return,
There with my cries importune Heaven, that all
The sentence, from thy head removed, may light
On me, sole cause to thee of all this woe,   935
Me, me only, just object of his ire."[4]
     She ended weeping; and her lowly plight,
Immovable till peace obtained from fault
Acknowledged and deplored,[5] in Adam wrought
Commiseration. Soon his heart relented   940
Towards her, his life so late and sole delight,
Now at his feet submissive in distress,
Creature so fair his reconcilement seeking,
His counsel, whom she had displeased, his aid;
As one disarmed, his anger all he lost,   945
And thus with peaceful words upraised her soon:
     "Unwary, and too desirous, as before,
So now, of what thou know'st not,[6] who desir'st
The punishment all on thyself! Alas!
Bear thine own first, ill able to sustain   950
His full wrath, whose thou feel'st as yet least part,[7]
And my displeasure bear'st so ill. If prayers
Could alter high decrees, I to that place
Would speed before thee, and be louder heard,
That on my head all might be visited,   955
Thy frailty and infirmer sex forgiven,
To me committed, and by me exposed.
But rise; let us no more contend, nor blame
Each other, blamed enough elsewhere, but strive
In offices of love, how we may lighten   960
Each other's burden in our share of woe;
Since this day's death denounced, if aught I see,
Will prove no sudden, but a slow-paced evil,

---

4. Eve too now offers to accept the blame for the
Fall; and the moral regeneration of man is henceforth possible.
5. Her suppliant posture ("lowly plight") would not
be changed till she obtained forgiveness ("peace")
from her admission of her fault and repentance for
it.

6. Adam's remark is rueful but affectionate; Eve is
still looking for more trouble than she knows how
to handle.
7. I.e., ill able to sustain the full wrath of God—
of whose wrath, so far, you have felt only the least
part.

A long day's dying to augment our pain,
And to our seed (O hapless seed!) derived."[8]   965
   To whom thus Eve, recovering heart, replied:
"Adam, by sad experiment I know
How little weight my words with thee can find,
Found so erroneous, thence by just event
Found so unfortunate; nevertheless,   970
Restored by thee, vile as I am, to place
Of new acceptance, hopeful to regain
Thy love, the sole contentment of my heart
Living or dying, from thee I will not hide
What thoughts in my unquiet breast are risen,   975
Tending to some relief of our extremes,
Or end, though sharp and sad, yet tolerable,
As in our evils,[9] and of easier choice.
If care of our descent perplex us most,
Which must be born to certain woe, devoured   980
By Death at last—and miserable it is
To be to others cause of misery,
Our own begotten, and of our loins to bring
Into this cursèd world a woeful race
That after wretched life must be at last   985
Food for so foul a monster—in thy power
It lies yet ere conception to prevent[1]
The race unblessed, to being yet unbegot.
Childless thou art, childless remain: so Death
Shall be deceived his glut, and with us two   990
Be forced to satisfy his ravenous maw.
But if thou judge it hard and difficult,
Conversing, looking, loving, to abstain
From love's due rites, nuptial embraces sweet,
And with desire to languish without hope   995
Before the present object[2] languishing
With like desire, which would be misery
And torment less than none of what we dread,
Then both our selves and seed at once to free
From what we fear for both, let us make short;   1000
Let us seek Death, or he not found, supply
With our own hands his office on ourselves.
Why stand we longer shivering under fears
That show no end but Death, and[3] have the power,
Of many ways to die the shortest choosing,   1005
Destruction with destruction to destroy?"
   She ended here, or vehement despair

8. Handed down.
9. A Latinism. The English meaning is something like "given the evil plight in which we find ourselves."
1. Literally, in the Latin root, come before, forestall.

2. The present object is of course Eve herself, referring to herself obliquely because she is ashamed to admit that she would pine for Adam, as he for her.
3. I.e., when we.

Broke off the rest; so much of death her thoughts
Had entertained as dyed her cheeks with pale.
But Adam, with such counsel nothing swayed,   1010
To better hopes his more attentive mind
Laboring had raised, and thus to Eve replied:
    "Eve, thy contempt of life and pleasure seems
To argue in thee something more sublime
And excellent than what thy mind contemns;[4]   1015
But self-destruction therefore[5] sought refutes
That excellence thought in thee, and implies,
Not thy contempt, but anguish and regret
For loss of life and pleasure overloved.
Or if thou covet death as utmost end   1020
Of misery, so thinking to evade
The penalty pronounced, doubt not but God
Hath wiselier armed his vengeful ire than so
To be forestalled; much more I fear lest death
So snatched will not exempt us from the pain   1025
We are by doom to pay; rather such acts
Of contumacy[6] will provoke the Highest
To make death in us live. Then let us seek
Some safer resolution, which methinks
I have in view, calling to mind with heed   1030
Part of our sentence, that thy seed shall bruise
The serpent's head; piteous amends, unless
Be meant, whom I conjecture, our grand foe
Satan, who in the serpent hath contrived
Against us this deceit. To crush his head   1035
Would be revenge indeed, which will be lost
By death brought on ourselves or childless days
Resolved, as thou proposest; so our foe
Shall 'scape his punishment ordained, and we
Instead shall double ours upon our heads.   1040
No more be mentioned then of violence
Against ourselves and willful barrenness
That cuts us off from hope, and savors only
Rancor and pride, impatience and despite,
Reluctance[7] against God and his just yoke   1045
Laid on our necks. Remember with what mild
And gracious temper he both heard and judged,
Without wrath or reviling; we expected
Immediate dissolution, which we thought
Was meant by death that day, when lo, to thee   1050
Pains only in childbearing were foretold,
And bringing forth, soon recompensed with joy,
Fruit of thy womb. On me the curse aslope

4. Despises.   7. From Latin *luctare*, to struggle; here, to oppose
5. For this motive.   (the will of God).
6. Contempt.

Glanced on the ground:[8] with labor I must earn
My bread. What harm? Idleness had been worse.   1055
My labor will sustain me; and lest cold
Or heat should injure us, his timely care
Hath unbesought provided, and his hands
Clothed us unworthy, pitying while he judged.
How much more, if we pray him, will his ear   1060
Be open and his heart to pity incline,
And teach us further by what means to shun
Th' inclement seasons, rain, ice, hail, and snow,
Which now the sky with various face begins
To show us in this mountain, while the winds   1065
Blow moist and keen, shattering the graceful locks
Of these fair spreading trees—which bids us seek
Some better shroud, some better warmth to cherish
Our limbs benumbed, ere this diurnal star[9]
Leave cold the night, how we his gathered beams,   1070
Reflected, may with matter sere foment,
Or by collision of two bodies grind
The air attrite to fire,[1] as late the clouds,
Justling or pushed with winds rude in their shock,
Tine[2] the slant lightning, whose thwart flame driven down   1075
Kindles the gummy bark of fir or pine,
And sends a comfortable heat from far,
Which might supply[3] the sun. Such fire to use,
And what may else be remedy or cure
To evils which our own misdeeds have wrought,   1080
He will instruct us praying, and of grace
Beseeching him, so as we need not fear
To pass commodiously this life, sustained
By him with many comforts, till we end
In dust, our final rest and native home.   1085
    "What better can we do than to the place
Repairing where he judged us, prostrate fall
Before him reverent, and there confess
Humbly our faults, and pardon beg, with tears
Watering the ground, and with our sighs the air   1090
Frequenting,[4] sent from hearts contrite, in sign
Of sorrow unfeigned, and humiliation meek?
Undoubtedly he will relent and turn
From his displeasure; in whose look serene,
When angry most he seemed and most severe,   1095
What else but favor, grace, and mercy shone?"
    So spake our father penitent, nor Eve

---

8. The curse, like a spear that almost missed its
target, glanced aside and stuck in the ground.
9. The sun.
1. Adam is inventing the burning glass ("matter
sere" is dry leaves, twigs, etc.) and the use of flint
and steel to start fires. "Attrite": rubbed or worn
down; in this sense, the word is more Latin than
English.
2. Kindle, light.
3. Take the place of.
4. Filling.

Felt less remorse: they forthwith to the place
Repairing where he judged them, prostrate fell
Before him reverent, and both confessed   1100
Humbly their faults, and pardon begged, with tears
Watering the ground, and with their sighs the air
Frequenting, sent from hearts contrite, in sign
Of sorrow unfeigned, and humiliation meek.[5]

Book 11. Summary The prayers of Adam and Eve prove acceptable
to God. But while man may now hope for ultimate redemption, he may no
longer dwell in Paradise; and Michael, the warrior archangel, is dispatched
to explain the sentence, offer some hope for the future, and dismiss mankind
from the happy garden. Adam is at first overcome with grief; but the angel
encourages him, and while Eve is put in a trance, Adam is raised to the
peak of a high hill and shown in a vision the future of the human race as far
as the flood of Noah.

From Book 12

Summary Continuing his instruction of Adam, Michael relates the
history of the world from the time of Noah through the coming of Christ,
whose ascent into Heaven and triumph over Death after the Crucifixion he
describes.

[The Departure from Eden]

So spake th' archangel Michaël; then paused,
As at the world's great period;[1] and our sire,
Replete with joy and wonder, thus replied:
    "O goodness infinite, goodness immense!
That all this good of evil shall produce,   470
And evil turn to good; more wonderful
Than that which by creation first brought forth
Light out of darkness! Full of doubt I stand,
Whether I should repent me now of sin
By me done and occasioned, or rejoice   475
Much more that much more good thereof shall spring;
To God more glory, more good will to men
From God, and over wrath grace shall abound.
But say, if our Deliverer up to Heaven
Must reascend, what will betide the few,   480
His faithful, left among th' unfaithful herd,
The enemies of truth? Who then shall guide

---

5. The deliberate repetition of six consecutive lines,
almost word for word, with only six lines in
between, is a very strong mark of closure. Adam
and Eve have reached most of the major decisions

which will separate their fate from that of Satan.
1. Conclusion. Michael has just given a brief prophetic glimpse of the Second Coming and the Last
Judgment.

His people, who defend? Will they not deal
Worse with his followers than with him they dealt?"
     "Be sure they will," said th' angel; "but from Heaven   485
He to his own a Comforter will send,
The promise of the Father, who shall dwell,
His Spirit, within them, and the law of faith,
Working through love, upon their hearts shall write,
To guide them in all truth, and also arm   490
With spiritual armor, able to resist
Satan's assaults, and quench his fiery darts,
What[2] man can do against them, not afraid,
Though to the death; against such cruelties
With inward consolations recompensed,   495
And oft supported so as shall amaze
Their proudest persecutors.[3] For the Spirit,
Poured first on his apostles, whom he sends
To evangelize the nations, then on all
Baptized, shall them with wondrous gifts endue[4]   500
To speak all tongues, and do all miracles,
As did their Lord before them. Thus they win
Great numbers of each nation to receive
With joy the tidings brought from Heaven: at length,
Their ministry performed, and race well run,   505
Their doctrine and their story written left,
They die; but in their room, as they forewarn,
Wolves shall succeed for teachers, grievous wolves,[5]
Who all the sacred mysteries of Heaven
To their own vile advantages shall turn   510
Of lucre and ambition, and the truth
With superstitions and traditions taint,
Left only in those written records pure,
Though not but by the Spirit understood.
Then shall they seek to avail themselves of names,   515
Places, and titles,[6] and with these to join
Secular power, though feigning still to act
By spiritual; to themselves appropriating
The Spirit of God, promised alike and given
To all believers; and, from that pretense,   520
Spiritual laws by carnal[7] power shall force
On every conscience, laws which none shall find
Left them enrolled, or what the Spirit within
Shall on the heart engrave.[8] What will they then,
But force the Spirit of Grace itself, and bind   525

2. As much as.
3. Milton briefly summarizes here the story of the Christian martyrs.
4. Endow.
5. To profit by religion was for Milton the lowest of crimes. In addition, he regularly uses the wolf as an emblem of the Papacy; see *Lycidas*, line 128.

6. The name "Catholic," the place of court preacher, and the title of "bishop," for example.
7. Fleshly, i.e., secular, of this world.
8. I.e., the wolves will enforce laws which have no ancient authority or appeal to the conscience.

His consort, Liberty? what but unbuild
His living temples,[9] built by faith to stand,
Their own faith, not another's? for, on Earth,
Who against faith and conscience can be heard
Infallible? Yet many will presume: 530
Whence heavy persecution shall arise
On all who in the worship persevere
Of Spirit and Truth; the rest, far greater part,
Will deem in outward rites and specious[1] forms
Religion satisfied; Truth shall retire   535
Bestuck with slanderous darts, and works of faith
Rarely be found. So shall the world go on,
To good malignant, to bad men benign,
Under her own weight groaning,[2] till the day
Appear of respiration[3] to the just   540
And vengeance to the wicked, at return
Of Him so lately promised to thy aid,
The Woman's Seed,[4] obscurely then foretold,
Now amplier known thy Savior and thy Lord;
Last in the clouds from Heaven to be revealed   545
In glory of the Father, to dissolve
Satan with his perverted world; then raise
From the conflagrant mass,[5] purged and refined,
New Heavens, new Earth, ages of endless date
Founded in righteousness and peace and love,   550
To bring forth fruits, joy and eternal bliss."
    He ended, and thus Adam last replied:
"How soon hath thy prediction, seer blest,
Measured this transient world, the race of Time,
Till Time stand fixed! Beyond is all abyss,   555
Eternity, whose end no eye can reach.
Greatly instructed I shall hence depart,
Greatly in peace of thought, and have my fill
Of knowledge, what[6] this vessel can contain,
Beyond which was my folly to aspire.   560
Henceforth I learn that to obey is best,
And love with fear the only God, to walk
As in his presence, ever to observe
His providence, and on him sole depend,
Merciful over all his works, with good   565
Still overcoming evil, and by small
Accomplishing great things, by things deemed weak

---

9. Individual believers. Milton's strict Protestant individualism speaks throughout this passage of protest against persecution.
1. Fair-seeming.
2. This passage, which in isolation appears to offer some justification for viewing the end of the poem as essentially pessimistic, should be set against Adam's earlier statement (lines 470–78) that the Fall was really a fortunate event, and gave rise to more good than evil.
3. Relief, refreshment.
4. Christ, whose Second Coming is here foreseen.
5. The burning world.
6. As much as.

Subverting worldly-strong, and worldly-wise
By simply meek; that suffering for truth's sake
Is fortitude to highest victory,   570
And to the faithful, death the gate of life;
Taught this by his example whom I now
Acknowledge my Redeemer ever blest."
    To whom thus also th' angel last replied:
"This having learned, thou hast attained the sum[7]   575
Of wisdom; hope no higher, though all the stars
Thou knew'st by name,[8] and all th' ethereal powers,
All secrets of the deep, all Nature's works,
Or works of God in heaven, air, earth, or sea,
And all the riches of this world enjoy'dst,   580
And all the rule, one empire. Only add
Deeds to thy knowledge answerable;[9] add faith,
Add virtue, patience, temperance; add love,
By name to come called charity, the soul
Of all the rest: then wilt thou not be loath   585
To leave this Paradise, but shalt possess
A Paradise within thee, happier far.
Let us descend now, therefore, from this top
Of speculation;[1] for the hour precise
Exacts[2] our parting hence; and, see! the guards,   590
By me encamped on yonder hill, expect
Their motion,[3] at whose front a flaming sword,
In signal of remove, waves fiercely round.
We may no longer stay. Go, waken Eve;
Her also I with gentle dreams have calmed,   595
Portending good, and all her spirits composed
To meek submission: thou, at season fit,
Let her with thee partake what thou hast heard;
Chiefly what may concern her faith to know,
The great deliverance by her seed to come   600
(For by the Woman's Seed)[4] on all mankind;
That ye may live, which will be many days,[5]
Both in one faith unanimous; though sad
With cause for evils past, yet much more cheered
With meditation on the happy end."   605
    He ended, and they both descend the hill;
Descended, Adam to the bower where Eve
Lay sleeping ran before, but found her waked;
And thus with words not sad she him received:
    "Whence thou return'st and whither went'st, I know; 610

---

7. Total.
8. Michael glances back at Raphael's cool warning (in Book 8) that Adam should concern himself with matters closer to home than the stars.
9. Corresponding.
1. Hill of vision.
2. Requires.

3. Await their order to move. "At whose front": before whom.
4. The parenthesis seems incomplete; perhaps something like "deliverance was foretold" is understood.
5. Adam lived to be 930 (Genesis 5.5).

For God is also in sleep, and dreams advise,
Which he hath sent propitious, some great good
Presaging, since with sorrow and heart's distress
Wearied I fell asleep. But now lead on;
In me is no delay; with thee to go   615
Is to stay here; without thee here to stay
Is to go hence unwilling; thou to me
Art all things under Heaven, all places thou,[6]
Who for my willful crime art banished hence.
This further consolation yet secure   620
I carry hence: though all by me is lost,
Such favor I unworthy am vouchsafed,
By me the Promised Seed shall all restore."
    So spake our mother Eve; and Adam heard
Well pleased, but answered not; for now too nigh   625
Th' archangel stood, and from the other hill
To their fixed station, all in bright array
The cherubim descended; on the ground
Gliding meteorous, as evening mist
Risen from a river o'er the marish[7] glides,   630
And gathers ground fast at the laborer's heel
Homeward returning. High in front advanced,
The brandished sword of God before them blazed,
Fierce as a comet; which with torrid heat,
And vapor as the Libyan air adust,[8]   635
Began to parch that temperate clime; whereat
In either hand the hastening angel caught
Our lingering parents, and to th' eastern gate
Led them direct, and down the cliff as fast
To the subjected[9] plain; then disappeared.   640
They, looking back, all th' eastern side beheld
Of Paradise, so late their happy seat,[1]
Waved over by that flaming brand;[2] the gate
With dreadful faces thronged and fiery arms.
Some natural tears they dropped, but wiped them soon;   645
The world was all before them, where to choose
Their place of rest, and Providence their guide.
They, hand in hand, with wandering steps and slow,
Through Eden took their solitary way.

1667, 1674

Samson Agonistes   The figure of Samson, as one finds him in the
Book of Judges, does not seem at first glance particularly adaptable to the

---

6. Once more, "The mind is its own place . . ."
(1.254). Eve's resolution may also owe something
to the book of Ruth 1.16.
7. Marsh (an old form).
8. The scorched climate of Libya, in North Africa,

was proverbial.
9. Low-lying.
1. Home.
2. "Sword," with the extra overtone of "burning."

elevated mode of tragedy. He is a promiscuous, violent fellow, given to riddles and practical jokes—the last of which puts a gruesome end to himself and his enemies. His long shaggy hair, his name (Samson, in Hebrew *Shimshun*), which includes the Hebrew word for "sun," and a persistent association with fire, all suggest a connection with some primitive solar cult, such as can be seen behind the equivalent figure of Hercules. A burly, truculent, and not-very-clever giant, in short; one would not easily see in him the dignified and purifying figure of the tragic sufferer.

But though Samson's rude vigor and vengeful nature appealed to Milton on one level; the story of his fall through the treachery of a woman on another; and the fact of his blindness on still another; there was a last level on which he could in fact be represented as the type and precursor of the Christian hero. He suffered for his people; in the very pit of despair he was rendered suddenly capable of God's revivifying grace; long exercised in physical warfare, he gave evidence in his last heroic action of having learned the principles of spiritual warfare.

Milton approached the idea of tragedy with hesitations and misgivings; for a Puritan of his day, the very idea of a stage play was instinct with moral danger. But the example of the Greeks and of his much-admired Tasso prevailed; he wrote a "closet drama," a drama intended not for the actual stage but for reading. *When* he wrote it is not clear: it was published, with *Paradise Regained*, in 1671, but may have been begun years earlier. The work is closely modeled on Greek tragedy. Unmoved by this noble ancestry, Samuel Johnson proclaimed it deficient as a play: it had, he said, a beginning and an end but no proper middle. Modern criticism, dissenting as usual from Johnson and stimulated as usual by his judgment, has exercised itself to find in Samson's spiritual progression during the successive visits of Manoa, Dalila, and Harapha ample psychological movement to sustain both action and interest. This is beyond doubt a useful exercise; but it is useful also to reflect that Samson acts in the end by direction of an inward spirit, a private, intimate inspiration; and that for the coming of this spirit there is no sufficient preparation. "The wind bloweth where it listeth, and thou hearest the sound thereof, but canst not tell whence it cometh, and whither it goeth: so is every one that is born of the Spirit" (John 3.8).

The story of Samson is told in Judges 13–16. "Agonistes" means "in struggle" or "under trial"; it is a term derived from the Greek word for a wrestler and suggests not only that Samson is an athlete of the Lord but that he will wrestle with the pillars.

Samson Agonistes

A DRAMATIC POEM

Of That Sort of Dramatic Poem Which Is Called Tragedy

Tragedy, as it was anciently composed, hath been ever held the gravest, moralest, and most profitable of all other poems: therefore said by Aristotle to be of power, by raising pity and fear, or terror, to purge the mind of those and such like passions, that is, to temper and reduce them to just measure with a kind of delight, stirred up by reading or seeing those passions well imitated.[1] Nor is Nature wanting in her own effects to make good his assertion; for so, in physic, things of melancholic hue and quality are used against melancholy, sour against sour, salt to remove salt humors.[2] Hence philosophers and other gravest writers, as Cicero, Plutarch, and others, frequently cite out of tragic poets, both to adorn and illustrate their discourse. The Apostle Paul himself thought it not unworthy to insert a verse of Euripides into the text of Holy Scripture, 1 Cor. 15.33; and Paraeus, commenting on the Revelation, divides the whole book, as a tragedy, into acts, distinguished each by a chorus of heavenly harpings and song between.[3] Heretofore men in highest dignity have labored not a little to be thought able to compose a tragedy. Of that honor Dionysius the elder was no less ambitious, than before of his attaining to the tyranny.[4] Augustus Caesar also had begun his *Ajax*, but unable to please his own judgment with what he had begun, left it unfinished. Seneca the philosopher is by some thought the author of those tragedies (at least the best of them) that go under that name. Gregory Nazianzen, a Father of the Church, thought it not unbeseeming the sanctity of his person to write a tragedy, which he entitled *Christ Suffering*.[5] This is mentioned to vindicate tragedy from the small esteem, or rather infamy, which in the account of many it undergoes at this day, with other common interludes[6]—happening through the poet's error of intermixing comic stuff with tragic sadness and gravity, or introducing trivial and vulgar persons, which by all judicious hath been counted absurd, and brought in without discretion, corruptly to gratify the people. And, though ancient tragedy use no prologue,[7] yet using sometimes, in case of self-defense or explanation, that which Martial calls an epistle,[8] in behalf of this tragedy, coming forth after the ancient manner, much different from what among us passes for best, thus much beforehand may be epistled: that chorus is here introduced after the Greek manner, not ancient only, but modern, and still in use among the Italians.[9] In the modeling therefore of this poem, with good reason, the ancients and Italians are rather followed, as of much more authority and fame. The measure of verse used in the chorus is of all sorts, called by the Greeks *monostrophic*,[1] or rather *apolelymenon*,[2] without regard had to strophe, antistrophe, or epode, which were a kind of stanzas framed only for the music, then used with the chorus that sung; not essential to the poem, and therefore not material; or, being divided into stanzas or

1. Milton is paraphrasing Aristotle's *Poetics* 6.
2. Italian critics like Minturno had applied notions of homeopathic medicine (like cures like) to tragedy; the idea is not Aristotelean. "Physic": medicine.
3. David Paraeus was a German Calvinist who wrote Biblical commentaries.
4. Dionysius (4th century B.C.) won a prize at Athens for tragedy, after becoming tyrant of Syracuse.
5. Seneca the philosopher was indeed the author of tragedies; but Gregory Nazianzen, a Greek ecclesiastic of the 4th century, did not write the tragedy *Christ Suffering*, which scholarly opinion

of Milton's day attributed to him.
6. Stage plays.
7. Prologues and epilogues were frequent on the Restoration stage; Milton sets himself apart from contemporary styles.
8. Martial, the Roman epigrammatist of the 1st century A.D., prefixed an epistle to his book of epigrams.
9. For example, Torquato Tasso's tragedy *Re Torrismondo* was modeled closely on classical examples.
1. Not divided into strophe, antistrophe, and epode.
2. Free from stanzaic patterns altogether.

pauses, they may be called *allaeostropha*.[3] Division into act and scene, referring chiefly to the stage (to which this work never was intended), is here omitted.[4] It suffices if the whole drama be found not produced[5] beyond the fifth act.

Of the style and uniformity, and that commonly called the plot, whether intricate or explicit[6]—which is nothing indeed but such economy, or disposition of the fable, as may stand best with verisimilitude and decorum—they only will best judge who are not unacquainted with Aeschylus, Sophocles, and Euripides, the three tragic poets unequaled yet by any, and the best rule to all who endeavor to write tragedy. The circumscription of time wherein the whole drama begins and ends is, according to ancient rule and best example, within the space of twenty-four hours.[7]

The Argument

Samson, made captive, blind, and now in the prison at Gaza,[8] there to labor as in a common workhouse, on a festival day, in the general cessation from labor, comes forth into the open air, to a place nigh, somewhat retired, there to sit a while and bemoan his condition. Where he happens at length to be visited by certain friends and equals[9] of his tribe, which make the chorus, who seek to comfort him what they can; then by his old father, Manoa, who endeavors the like, and withal tells him his purpose to procure his liberty by ransom; lastly, that this feast was proclaimed by the Philistines as a day of thanksgiving for their deliverance from the hands of Samson—which yet more troubles him. Manoa then departs to prosecute his endeavor with the Philistian lords for Samson's redemption; who in the meanwhile is visited by other persons, and, lastly, by a public officer to require his coming to the feast before the lords and people, to play or show his strength in their presence. He at first refuses, dismissing the public officer with absolute denial to come; at length persuaded inwardly that this was from God, he yields to go along with him, who came now the second time with great threatenings to fetch him. The chorus yet remaining on the place, Manoa returns full of joyful hope to procure ere long his son's deliverance: in the midst of which discourse an Hebrew comes in haste, confusedly at first, and afterwards more distinctly, relating the catastrophe—what Samson had done to the Philistines, and by accident to himself; wherewith the tragedy ends.

---

3. With various forms of strophe, irregular.

4. The reader who cares will not find Milton's drama hard to divide into the customary five acts, each ending with a chorus: Act 1 (Samson and chorus) lines 1–325; 2 (Samson and Manoa) 326–709; 3 (Samson and Dalila) 710–1060; 4 (Samson and Harapha) 1061–1296; 5 (Catastrophe) 1297–the end.

5. Drawn out.

6. Complex or simple. "Decorum," for a Renaissance writer, is not simply solemn or sedate behavior but the use of appropriate and suitable style, depending on speaker, subject, setting, genre, and so on.

7. The so-called unity of time, limiting dramatic action to 24 hours, was derived from Aristotle's *Poetics* by the Renaissance critic Castelvetro.

8. The Philistines, warlike and commercial, lived in southwest Palestine (the southern coast of modern Israel between, approximately, Tel Aviv and Gaza) in five great cities splendidly named Ashdod, Eshkol, Gaza, Gath, and Ashkalon. They were a wholly urban people as against the largely rural Israelites.

9. People of about the same age.

The Persons

SAMSON
MANOA, *the father of
Samson*
DALILA, *his wife*

HARAPHA *of Gath*
Public Officer
Messenger
Chorus of Danites[1]

The Scene, before the Prison in Gaza.

SAMSON. A little onward lend thy guiding hand
    To these dark steps, a little further on;
    For yonder bank hath choice of sun or shade.
    There I am wont to sit, when any chance
    Relieves me from my task of servile toil,   5
    Daily in the common prison else enjoined me,[2]
    Where I, a prisoner chained, scarce freely draw
    The air, imprisoned also, close and damp,
    Unwholesome draught. But here I feel amends—
    The breath of heaven fresh blowing, pure and sweet,   10
    With day-spring[3] born; here leave me to respire.
    This day a solemn feast the people hold
    To Dagon[4] their sea-idol, and forbid
    Laborious works. Unwillingly this rest
    Their superstition yields me; hence, with leave   15
    Retiring from the popular noise, I seek
    This unfrequented place, to find some ease—
    Ease to the body some, none to the mind
    From restless thoughts, that like a deadly swarm
    Of hornets armed, no sooner found alone   20
    But rush upon me thronging, and present
    Times past, what once I was, and what am now.
    Oh, wherefore was my birth from Heaven foretold
    Twice by an angel,[5] who at last, in sight
    Of both my parents, all in flames ascended   25
    From off the altar where an offering burned,
    As in a fiery column charioting
    His godlike presence, and from some great act
    Or benefit revealed to Abraham's race?
    Why was my breeding ordered and prescribed   30
    As of a person separate to God,
    Designed for great exploits,[6] if I must die
    Betrayed, captived, and both my eyes put out,

1. Hebrews of the tribe of Dan, Samson's tribe.
When the land of Canaan was divided among the
twelve tribes, they received the southern portion,
adjacent to the Philistines.
2. The metrical pattern of this line, with its many
unaccented syllables and careful placement of the
strong word "else," merits careful study. Similar
bold effects are found throughout.
3. Break of day.
4. Dagon's name comes from *dag*, fish, and he

seems to have had a fishy shape. His would thus
be a marine cult to correspond with that of the
many Baals, or land gods, of the Philistines. See
Paradise Lost 1.457–66.
5. Before Samson was born an angel foretold that
he would begin the delivery of Israel from the
Philistines (Judges 13.5).
6. Samson was a Nazarite, member of an ascetic
group specially dedicated to the service of God.
See Numbers 6.

Made of my enemies the scorn and gaze,
To grind in brazen fetters under task   35
With this heaven-gifted strength? O glorious strength,
Put to the labor of a beast, debased
Lower than bondslave! Promise was that I
Should Israel from Philistian yoke deliver;
Ask for this great deliverer now, and find him   40
Eyeless in Gaza at the mill with slaves,
Himself in bonds under Philistian yoke.
Yet stay; let me not rashly call in doubt
Divine prediction. What if all foretold
Had been fulfilled but through mine own default?   45
Whom have I to complain of but myself,
Who this high gift of strength committed to me,
In what part lodged, how easily bereft me,
Under the seal of silence could not keep,[7]
But weakly to a woman must reveal it,   50
O'ercome with importunity and tears?
O impotence of mind in body strong!
But what is strength without a double share
Of wisdom? Vast, unwieldy, burdensome,
Proudly secure,[8] yet liable to fall   55
By weakest subtleties; not made to rule,
But to subserve where wisdom bears command.
God, when he gave me strength, to show withal
How slight the gift was, hung it in my hair.
But peace! I must not quarrel with the will   60
Of highest dispensation,[9] which herein
Haply had ends above my reach to know.
Suffices that to me strength is my bane,
And proves the source of all my miseries,
So many, and so huge, that each apart   65
Would ask a life to wail. But, chief of all,
O loss of sight, of thee I most complain!
Blind among enemies! O worse than chains,
Dungeon, or beggary, or decrepit age!
Light, the prime work of God,[1] to me is extinct,   70
And all her various objects of delight
Annulled, which might in part my grief have eased.
Inferior to the vilest now become
Of man or worm, the vilest here excel me:
They creep, yet see; I, dark in light, exposed   75
To daily fraud, contempt, abuse, and wrong,
Within doors or without, still as a fool,
In power of others, never in my own—

7. I.e., who could not keep silent about the high gift of strength committed to me, or about where it was located, or about how easily it could be taken from me.
8. Confident, free from care (Latin, *cura*).

9. Providence.
1. God's first ("prime") act in creating the world was to say "Let there be light" (Genesis 1.3), a phrase Milton paraphrases below.

Scarce half I seem to live, dead more than half.
O dark, dark, dark, amid the blaze of noon,   80
Irrecoverably dark, total eclipse
Without all hope of day!
O first-created beam, and thou great Word,
"Let there be light, and light was over all,"
Why am I thus bereaved thy prime decree?[2]   85
The sun to me is dark
And silent[3] as the moon,
When she deserts the night,
Hid in her vacant interlunar cave.[4]
Since light so necessary is to life,   90
And almost life itself, if it be true
That light is in the soul,
She all in every part,[5] why was the sight
To such a tender ball as th' eye confined,
So obvious[6] and so easy to be quenched,   95
And not, as feeling, through all parts diffused,
That she might look at will through every pore?
Then had I not been thus exiled from light,
As in the land of darkness, yet in light,
To live a life half dead, a living death,   100
And buried; but, O yet more miserable!
Myself my sepulcher, a moving grave;
Buried, yet not exempt
By privilege of death and burial
From worst of other evils, pains, and wrongs;   105
But made hereby obnoxious[7] more
To all the miseries of life,
Life in captivity
Among inhuman foes.
But who are these? for with joint pace I hear   110
The tread of many feet steering this way;
Perhaps my enemies, who come to stare
At my affliction, and perhaps to insult,
Their daily practice to afflict me more.
CHORUS. This, this is he; softly a while;   115
    Let us not break in upon him.
    O change beyond report, thought, or belief!
    See how he lies at random, carelessly diffused,[8]
    With languished head unpropped,
    As one past hope, abandoned,   120
    And by himself given over,

---

2. I.e., why am I thus deprived of the first-created (and most important) thing?
3. I.e., unperceived.
4. Ancient astronomers supposed that during its dark ("interlunar") phase, the moon hid in a cave. "Vacant": i.e., where the moon is at ease (Latin *vacare*, whence modern "vacation").

5. A famous formula of Plotinus (*Ennead* 4.2.1) describes the soul as "all in all and all in every part."
6. Exposed.
7. Vulnerable, subject.
8. Literally, "poured forth," sprawled.

In slavish habit, ill-fitted weeds[9]
O'er-worn and soiled.
Or do my eyes misrepresent? Can this be he,
That heroic, that renowned,
Irresistible Samson? whom, unarmed,   125
No strength of man, or fiercest wild beast, could withstand:[1]
Who tore the lion as the lion tears the kid;
Ran on embattled armies clad in iron,
And, weaponless himself,
Made arms ridiculous, useless the forgery[2]   130
Of brazen shield and spear, the hammered cuirass,
Chalýbean-tempered[3] steel, and frock of mail
Adamantean proof;
But safest he who stood aloof,
When insupportably[4] his foot advanced,   135
In scorn of their proud arms and warlike tools,
Spurned them to death by troops. The bold Ascalonite[5]
Fled from his lion ramp; old warriors turned
Their plated backs under his heel,
Or groveling soiled their crested helmets in the dust.   140
Then with what trivial weapon came to hand,
The jaw of a dead ass, his sword of bone,
A thousand foreskins fell, the flower of Palestine,
In Ramath-lechi, famous to this day;[6]
Then by main force pulled up, and on his shoulders bore,   145
The gates of Azza, post and massy bar,
Up to the hill by Hebron, seat of giants old,
No journey of a Sabbath day, and loaded so,
Like whom the Gentiles feign to bear up heaven.[7]   150
Which shall I first bewail,
Thy bondage or lost sight,
Prison within prison
Inseparably dark?
Thou art become (O worst imprisonment!)   155
The dungeon of thyself; thy soul
(Which men enjoying sight oft without cause complain),
Imprisoned now indeed,
In real darkness of the body dwells,
Shut up from outward light   160
To incorporate with gloomy night;

---

9. Rags.
1. Judges 14.5–6 tells the story of Samson ripping apart a lion with his bare hands.
2. Weapons of forged steel, but also fraudulent, exterior protections.
3. The Chalybes lived on the Black Sea and were famous ironworkers. "Adamantean proof": hard as adamant, i.e., diamond.
4. Irresistibly.
5. A man from Ascalon, or Ashkalon, one of the five great Philistine cities. "Lion ramp": a lion in the act of attacking its prey, rampant.
6. On one occasion Samson killed a thousand Philistines (i.e., "foreskins," uncircumcised warriors), using the jawbone of an ass (Judges 15.15–17). Judges 16.3 tells how Samson, to escape his enemies, picked up and carried off the gates of Gaza (Azza).
7. In Greek (or, as Milton calls it, Gentile) mythology, Atlas supports the heavens. From Gaza to Hebron would be about 40 miles—no journey for the day of rest.

For inward light, alas!
Puts forth no visual beam.[8]
O mirror of our fickle state,
Since man on earth unparalleled![9]   165
The rarer thy example stands,
By how much from the top of wondrous glory,
Strongest of mortal men,
To lowest pitch of abject fortune thou art fallen!
For him I reckon not in high estate   170
Whom long descent of birth,
Or the sphere[1] of fortune, raises;
But thee, whose strength, while virtue was her mate,
Might have subdued the Earth,
Universally crowned with highest praises.   175

SAMSON. I hear the sound of words; their sense the air
    Dissolves unjointed ere it reach my ear.

CHORUS. He speaks: let us draw nigh. Matchless in might,
    The glory late of Israel, now the grief!
    We come, thy friends and neighbors not unknown,   180
    From Eshtaol and Zora's fruitful vale,
    To visit or bewail thee; or, if better,
    Counsel or consolation we may bring,
    Salve to thy sores: apt words have power to swage[2]
    The tumors of a troubled mind,   185
    And are as balm to festered wounds.

SAMSON. Your coming, friends, revives me; for I learn
    Now of my own experience, not by talk,
    How counterfeit a coin they are who "friends"
    Bear in their superscription (of the most   190
    I would be understood). In prosperous days
    They swarm, but in adverse withdraw their head,
    Not to be found, though sought. Ye see, O friends,
    How many evils have enclosed me round;
    Yet that which was the worst now least afflicts me,   195
    Blindness; for, had I sight, confused with shame,
    How could I once look up, or heave[3] the head,
    Who like a foolish pilot have shipwrecked
    My vessel trusted to me from above,
    Gloriously rigged, and for a word, a tear,   200
    Fool! have divulged the secret gift of God
    To a deceitful woman? Tell me, friends,
    Am I not sung and proverbed for a fool
    In every street? Do they not say, "How well

---

8. Renaissance physiologists supposed the eye saw by sending forth a "visual beam" which it directed at various objects.
9. I.e., no such example (has been seen) since man (was) on earth. "Fickle": changeable.
1. "Sphere": wheel. Fortune was described as possessing a wheel which merely by rotating automat-

ically interchanged the highest and lowest social positions. Milton's definition of "high estate" is interior and spiritual; he has no interest in the old "Fall of Princes" theme. In fact, the play exactly reverses that theme.
2. Assuage.
3. Lift.

Are come upon his deserts"? Yet why?   205
Immeasurable strength they might behold
In me; of wisdom nothing more than mean. [4]
This with the other should at least have paired; [5]
These two, proportioned ill, drove me transverse. [6]

CHORUS. Tax not divine disposal. Wisest men   210
  Have erred, and by bad women been deceived;
  And shall again, pretend they ne'er so wise. [7]
  Deject not then so overmuch thyself,
  Who hast of sorrow thy full load besides.
  Yet, truth to say, I oft have heard men wonder   215
  Why thou should'st wed Philistian women rather
  Than of thine own tribe fairer, or as fair,
  At least of thy own nation, and as noble.

SAMSON. The first I saw at Timna, and she pleased
  Me, not my parents, that I sought to wed   220
  The daughter of an infidel. [8] They knew not
  That what I motioned [9] was of God; I knew
  From intimate impulse, and therefore urged
  The marriage on, that, by occasion hence, [1]
  I might begin Israel's deliverance,   225
  The work to which I was divinely called.
  She proving false, the next I took to wife
  (O that I never had! fond wish too late!)
  Was in the vale of Sorec, Dàlila, [2]
  That specious monster, my accomplished snare.   230
  I thought it lawful from my former act
  And the same end, still watching to oppress
  Israel's oppressors. Of what now I suffer
  She was not the prime cause, but I myself,
  Who, vanquished with a peal of words (O weakness!),   235
  Gave up my fort of silence to a woman.

CHORUS. In seeking just occasion to provoke
  The Philistine, thy country's enemy,
  Thou never wast remiss, I bear thee witness;
  Yet Israel still serves with all his sons. [3]   240

SAMSON. That fault I take not on me, but transfer
  On Israel's governors and heads of tribes,
  Who, seeing those great acts which God had done
  Singly by me against their conquerors,
  Acknowledged not, or not at all considered   245
  Deliverance offered. I, on th' other side,
  Used no ambition to commend my deeds; [4]

4. Average.
5. Been equal.
6. Off the true course.
7. I.e., however they profess to be wise.
8. Judges 14.1–4 tells the story of Samson's first decision to marry outside his own tribe and nation.
9. Intended.

1. I.e., so that it might provide an occasion for me to begin Israel's deliverance.
2. Judges 16.4.
3. I.e., Israel and the children of Israel are still in servitude.
4. I.e., sought for no testimonials to my actions.

The deeds themselves, though mute, spoke loud the doer.
But they persisted deaf, and would not seem
To count them things worth notice, till at length   250
Their lords, the Philistines, with gathered powers,
Entered Judea seeking me, who then
Safe to the rock of Etham was retired,
Not flying, but forecasting in what place
To set upon them, what advantaged best.   255
Meanwhile the men of Judah, to prevent
The harass of their land, beset me round;
I willingly on some conditions came
Into their hands, and they as gladly yield me
To the uncircumcised[5] a welcome prey,   260
Bound with two cords. But cords to me were threads
Touched with the flame: on their whole host I flew
Unarmed, and with a trivial weapon felled
Their choicest youth; they only lived who fled.[6]
Had Judah that day joined, or one whole tribe,   265
They had by this[7] possessed the towers of Gath,
And lorded over them whom now they serve.
But what more oft, in nations grown corrupt,
And by their vices brought to servitude,
Than to love bondage more than liberty,   270
Bondage with ease than strenuous liberty,[8]
And to despise, or envy, or suspect,
Whom God hath of his special favor raised
As their deliverer? If he aught begin,
How frequent to desert him, and at last   275
To heap ingratitude on worthiest deeds!
CHORUS. Thy words to my remembrance bring
How Succoth and the fort of Penuel
Their great deliverer contemned,
The matchless Gideon, in pursuit   280
Of Madian and her vanquished kings;[9]
And how ingrateful Ephraim
Had dealt with Jephtha, who by argument,
Not worse than by his shield and spear,
Defended Israel from the Ammonite,   285
Had not his prowess quelled their pride
In that sore battle when so many died
Without reprieve, adjudged to death
For want of well pronouncing *Shibboleth*.[1]
SAMSON. Of such examples add me to the roll.   290

---

5. Foreigners, the people outside the covenant of Abraham.
6. Judges 15.8–17 tells the tale of Samson's single-handed victory, using a "trivial weapon," the jawbone of an ass.
7. By this time.

8. Milton appears to have in mind, not only early Israel, but also contemporary England.
9. Judges 8: Succoth and Penuel refused aid to Gideon when he was pursuing the common foe, and he punished them.
1. Judges 11 and 12.

Me easily indeed mine[2] may neglect,
But God's proposed deliverance not so.
CHORUS. Just are the ways of God,
    And justifiable to men,
    Unless there be who think not God at all.   295
    If any be, they walk obscure;
    For of such doctrine never was there school,
    But the heart of the fool,
    And no man therein doctor but himself.[3]
        Yet more there be who doubt his ways not just,   300
    As to his own edìcts found contradicting;
    Then give the reins to wandering thought,
    Regardless of his glory's diminution,
    Till, by their own perplexities involved,
    They ravel[4] more, still less resolved,   305
    But never find self-satisfying solution.
    As if they would confine th' Interminable,[5]
    And tie him to his own prescript,
    Who made our laws to bind us, not himself,
    And hath full right to exempt   310
    Whomso it pleases him by choice
    From national obstriction,[6] without taint
    Of sin, or legal debt;
    For with his own laws he can best dispense.
        He would not else, who never wanted means,   315
    Nor in respect of the enemy just cause
    To set his people free,
    Have prompted this heroic Nazarite,
    Against his vow of strictest purity,
    To seek in marriage that fallacious bride,   320
    Unclean, unchaste.
        Down, Reason, then; at least, vain reasonings down;
    Though Reason here aver
    That moral verdict quits her of unclean:
    Unchaste was subsequent; her stain, not his.[7]   325
        But see! here comes thy reverend sire,
    With careful step, locks white as down,[8]
    Old Manoa: advise[9]
    Forthwith how thou ought'st to receive him.
SAMSON. Ay me! another inward grief, awaked   330
    With mention of that name, renews th' assault.

2. My people.
3. Psalm 14 deals with the fool who says in his heart there is no God. "Doctor": teacher.
4. Become entangled.
5. Infinite.
6. Obligation, i.e., the law against marrying Gentiles (Deuteronomy 7.3). The chorus here accepts Samson's argument that God had prompted him inexplicably to marry the woman of Timna.

7. The chorus, having accused the woman of Timna of being unclean (i.e., Gentile and taboo) and unchaste, now admits that since Samson married her at God's instigation she was not unclean to him; and that she was unchaste only after Samson left her. Reason is therefore puzzled.
8. "Careful": full of care. "Down": swan's down.
9. Reflect, consider inwardly.

MANOA. Brethren and men of Dan (for such ye seem,
    Though in this uncouth[1] place), if old respect,
    As I suppose, towards your once gloried friend,
    My son, now captive, hither hath informed[2]   335
    Your younger feet, while mine, cast back with age,
    Came lagging after, say if he be here.
CHORUS. As signal[3] now in low dejected state
    As erst in highest, behold him where he lies.
MANOA. O miserable change! Is this the man,   340
    That invincible Samson, far renowned,
    The dread of Israel's foes, who with a strength
    Equivalent to angels' walked their streets,
    None offering fight; who, single combatant,
    Dueled their armies ranked in proud array,   345
    Himself an army—now unequal match
    To save himself against a coward armed
    At one spear's length? O ever-failing trust
    In mortal strength! and, oh, what not in man
    Deceivable and vain?[4] Nay, what thing good   350
    Prayed for, but often proves our woe, our bane?
    I prayed for children, and thought barrenness
    In wedlock a reproach; I gained a son,
    And such a son as all men hailed me happy:
    Who would be now a father in my stead?   355
    O wherefore did God grant me my request,
    And as a blessing with such pomp adorned?
    Why are his gifts desirable, to tempt
    Our earnest prayers, then, given with solemn hand
    As graces, draw a scorpion's tail behind?   360
    For this did the angel twice descend?[5] for this
    Ordained thy nurture holy, as of a plant
    Select and sacred? glorious for a while,
    The miracle of men; then in an hour
    Ensnared, assaulted, overcome, led bound,   365
    Thy foes' derision, captive, poor and blind,
    Into a dungeon thrust, to work with slaves!
    Alas! methinks whom God hath chosen once
    To worthiest deeds, if he through frailty err,
    He should not so o'erwhelm, and as a thrall   370
    Subject him to so foul indignities,
    Be it but for honor's sake of former deeds.
SAMSON. Appoint not heavenly disposition,[6] father.
    Nothing of all these evils hath befallen me
    But justly; I myself have brought them on;   375

---

1. Unknown, unfamiliar.
2. Directed.
3. Notable, eminent.
4. I.e., what is there in man that is not deceivable and vain?
5. The angel who announced Samson's birth was

sent a second time, in answer to Manoa's request, to give instructions concerning his education and training.
6. I.e., do not presume to control heaven's decisions.

Sole author I, sole cause.[7] If aught seem vile,
As vile hath been my folly, who have profaned
The mystery of God, given me under pledge
Of vow, and have betrayed it to a woman,
A Canaanite, my faithless enemy.   380
This well I knew, nor was at all surprised,
But warned by oft experience. Did not she
Of Timna first betray me, and reveal
The secret wrested from me in her height
Of nuptial love professed, carrying it straight   385
To them who had corrupted her, my spies
And rivals?[8] In this other was there found
More faith, who, also in her prime of love,
Spousal embraces, vitiated with gold,
Though offered only, by the scent conceived   390
Her spurious first-born, treason against me?[9]
Thrice she essayed, with flattering prayers and sighs,
And amorous reproaches, to win from me
My capital secret,[1] in what part my strength
Lay stored, in what part summed, that she might know;   395
Thrice I deluded her, and turned to sport
Her importunity, each time perceiving
How openly and with what impudence
She purposed to betray me, and (which was worse
Than undissembled hate) with what contempt   400
She sought to make me traitor to myself.[2]
Yet the fourth time, when, mustering all her wiles,
With blandished parleys, feminine assaults,
Tongue-batteries, she surceased[3] not day nor night
To storm me, over-watched and wearied out   405
At times when men seek most repose and rest,
I yielded, and unlocked her all my heart,
Who, with a grain of manhood well resolved,
Might easily have shook off all her snares;
But foul effeminacy[4] held me yoked   410
Her bondslave. O indignity, O blot
To honor and religion! servile mind
Rewarded well with servile punishment!
The base degree to which I now am fallen,
These rags, this grinding, is not yet so base   415
As was my former servitude, ignoble,
Unmanly, ignominious, infamous,
True slavery; and that blindness worse than this,

7. Like Adam, in *Paradise Lost 10*, Samson proves his own resurgent virtue by accepting responsibility for his own faults.

8. Samson's first wife, the woman of Timna, revealed Samson's riddle to his enemies (Judges 14.8–19).

9. At the mere scent of gold, Dalila conceived a bastard ("spurious") offspring for Samson—trea-

son.

1. The secret Dalila learned was of capital importance; also, it involved the hair on Samson's head (*caput*).

2. Judges 16.5–20.

3. Forbore.

4. "Effeminacy": uxoriousness, overfondness, the fault of Adam.

That saw not how degenerately I served.
MANOA. I cannot praise thy marriage-choices, son,   420
    Rather approved them not; but thou didst plead
    Divine impulsion[5] prompting how thou might'st
    Find some occasion to infest our foes.
    I state not that; this I am sure, our foes
    Found soon occasion thereby to make thee   425
    Their captive, and their triumph; thou the sooner
    Temptation found'st, or over-potent charms,
    To violate the sacred trust of silence
    Deposited within thee; which to have kept
    Tacit was in thy power. True; and thou bear'st   430
    Enough, and more, the burden of that fault;
    Bitterly hast thou paid, and still art paying,
    That rigid score.[6] A worse thing yet remains:
    This day the Philistines a popular feast
    Here celebrate in Gaza, and proclaim   435
    Great pomp and sacrifice and praises loud,
    To Dagon, as their god who hath delivered
    Thee, Samson, bound and blind, into their hands,
    Them out of thine, who slew'st them many a slain.[7]
    So Dagon shall be magnified,[8] and God,   440
    Besides whom is no god, compared with idols,
    Disglorified, blasphemed, and had in scorn
    By th' idolatrous rout amidst their wine;
    Which to have come to pass by means of thee,
    Samson, of all thy sufferings think the heaviest,   445
    Of all reproach the most with shame that ever
    Could have befallen thee and thy father's house.
SAMSON. Father, I do acknowledge and confess
    That I this honor, I this pomp, have brought
    To Dagon, and advanced his praises high   450
    Among the heathen round; to God have brought
    Dishonor, obloquy, and oped the mouths
    Of idolists and atheists; have brought scandal
    To Israel, diffidence[9] of God, and doubt
    In feeble hearts, propense[1] enough before   455
    To waver, or fall off and join with idols:
    Which is my chief affliction, shame and sorrow,
    The anguish of my soul, that suffers not
    Mine eye to harbor sleep, or thoughts to rest.
    This only hope relieves me, that the strife   460
    With me hath end. All the contèst is now
    'Twixt God and Dagon. Dagon hath presumed,

---

5. Samson's repeated reliance on extraordinary divine inspiration aligns him, for Milton, with the godly party of the 17th century—as against worldlings who doubted or disliked the idea of recurring divine intervention. "Infest": attack.

6. Debt.
7. I.e., who slew many a one of them.
8. Glorified.
9. Mistrust.
1. Inclined.

Me overthrown, to enter lists[2] with God,
His deity comparing and preferring
Before the God of Abraham. He, be sure,   465
Will not connive[3] or linger, thus provoked,
But will arise, and his great name assert.
Dagan must stoop, and shall ere long receive
Such a discomfit as shall quite despoil him
Of all these boasted trophies won on me,   470
And with confusion blank[4] his worshipers.
MANOA. With cause this hope relieves thee; and these words
   I as a prophecy receive; for God
   (Nothing more certain) will not long defer
   To vindicate the glory of his name   475
   Against all competition, nor will long
   Endure it doubtful whether God be Lord,
   Or Dagon. But for thee what shall be done?
   Thou must not in the meanwhile, here forgot,
   Lie in this miserable loathsome plight   480
   Neglected. I already have made way
   To some Philistian lords, with whom to treat
   About thy ransom. Well they may by this[5]
   Have satisfied their utmost of revenge
   By pains and slaveries, worse than death, inflicted   485
   On thee, who now no more canst do them harm.
SAMSON. Spare that proposal, father; spare the trouble
   Of that solicitation. Let me here,
   As I deserve, pay on my punishment,
   And expiate, if possible, my crime,   490
   Shameful garrulity. To have revealed
   Secrets of men, the secrets of a friend,
   How heinous had the fact been, how deserving
   Contempt and scorn of all; to be excluded
   All friendship, and avoided as a blab,   495
   The mark of fool set on his front![6] But I
   God's counsel have not kept, his holy secret
   Presumptuously have published, impiously,
   Weakly at least and shamefully: a sin
   That Gentiles in their parables condemn   500
   To their abyss and horrid pains confined.[7]
MANOA. Be penitent, and for thy fault contrite;
   But act not in thy own affliction, son.
   Repent the sin; but if the punishment
   Thou canst avoid, self-preservation bids;   505
   Or th' execution leave to high disposal,

2. Jousting courts as in medieval tourneys.
3. Hesitate, palter.
4. Confound, turn pale.
5. By this time.
6. Forehead.

7. In classical legend, Tantalus was confined to hell and torment because he betrayed the secrets of the gods, and Prometheus was savagely punished for giving to mankind the secret of fire.

And let another hand, not thine, exact
Thy penal forfeit from thyself. Perhaps
God will relent, and quit[8] thee of all his debt;
Who ever more approves and more accepts   510
(Best pleased with humble and filial submission)
Him who, imploring mercy, sues for life,
Than who, self-rigorous, chooses death as due;[9]
Which argues over-just, and self-displeased
For self-offense more than for God offended.   515
Reject not, then, what offered means who knows
But God hath set before us to return thee
Home to thy country and his sacred house,
Where thou may'st bring thy offerings, to avert
His further ire, with prayers and vows renewed.   520
SAMSON. His pardon I implore; but, as for life,
To what end should I seek it? When in strength
All mortals I excelled, and great in hopes,
With youthful courage, and magnanimous thoughts
Of birth from Heaven foretold and high exploits,   525
Full of divine instinct, after some proof
Of acts indeed heroic, far beyond
The sons of Anak,[1] famous now and blazed,
Fearless of danger, like a petty god
I walked about, admired of all, and dreaded   530
On hostile ground, none daring my affront.
Then, swoll'n with pride, into the snare I fell
Of fair fallacious looks, venereal trains,[2]
Softened with pleasure and voluptuous life;
At length to lay my head and hallowed pledge   535
Of all my strength in the lascivious lap
Of a deceitful concubine, who shore me,
Like a tame wether,[3] all my precious fleece,
Then turned me out ridiculous, despoiled,
Shaven, and disarmed among my enemies.   540
CHORUS. Desire of wine and all delicious drinks,
Which many a famous warrior overturns,
Thou could'st repress; nor did the dancing ruby,
Sparkling out-poured, the flavor or the smell,
Or taste, that cheers the heart of gods and men,   545
Allure thee from the cool crystàlline stream.
SAMSON. Wherever fountain or fresh current flowed
Against the eastern ray, translucent pure
With touch ethereal of Heaven's fiery rod,[4]
I drank, from the clear milky juice allaying   550

8. Cancel.
9. This is similar to Adam's argument against suicide in *Paradise Lost* 10.1013–19.
1. Giants, described in Numbers 13.
2. Sensual, sexual lures.
3. A castrated male sheep.

4. The rays of the sun. Samson is saying that
wherever water was purest and cleanest, he drank
of it—never of wine; "rod" intimates a parallel with
Moses, who like Samson brought forth a spring in
the middle of the desert.

Thirst, and refreshed; nor envied them the grape
Whose heads that turbulent liquor fills with fumes.
CHORUS. O madness! to think use of strongest wines
  And strongest drinks our chief support of health,
  When God with these forbidden made choice to rear   555
  His mighty champion, strong above compare,
  Whose drink was only from the liquid brook![5]
SAMSON. But what availed this temperance, not complete
  Against another object more enticing?
  What boots it at one gate to make defense,   560
  And at another to let in the foe,
  Effeminately vanquished? by which means,
  Now blind, disheartened, shamed, dishonored, quelled,
  To what can I be useful? wherein serve
  My nation, and the work from Heaven imposed?   565
  But to sit idle on the household hearth,
  A burdenous drone; to visitants a gaze,[6]
  Or pitied object; these redundant[7] locks,
  Robustious to no purpose, clustering down,
  Vain monument of strength; till length of years   570
  And sedentary numbness craze [8] my limbs
  To a contemptible old age obscure.
  Here rather let me drudge, and earn my bread,
  Till vermin, or the draff of servile food,[9]
  Consume me, and oft-invocated death   575
  Hasten the welcome end of all my pains.
MANOA. Wilt thou then serve the Philistines with that gift
  Which was expressly given thee to annoy them?
  Better at home lie bed-rid, not only idle,
  Inglorious, unemployed, with age outworn.   580
  But God, who caused a fountain at thy prayer
  From the dry ground to spring, thy thirst to allay
  After the brunt of battle,[1] can as easy
  Cause light again within thy eyes to spring,
  Wherewith to serve him better than thou hast.   585
  And I persuade me so. Why else this strength
  Miraculous yet remaining in those locks?
  His might continues in thee not for naught,
  Nor shall his wondrous gifts be frustrate thus.
SAMSON. All otherwise to me my thoughts portend,   590
  That these dark orbs no more shall treat with light,
  Nor th' other light of life continue long,
  But yield to double darkness nigh at hand;
  So much I feel my genial spirits[2] droop,

---

5. Samson's calling as a Nazarite forbade him the use of wine.
6. Spectacle.
7. In its Latin sense, "redundant" means "flowing," in the English sense "unnecessary," "unemployed." "Robustious": strong.
8. Weaken, twist.
9. Garbage given to slaves as food.
1. The story of how Samson, with divine aid, created a spring in the desert after the battle with the ass's jawbone, is told in Judges 15.18–19.
2. Life forces, vital energy.

My hopes all flat. Nature within me seems   595
In all her functions weary of herself;
My race of glory run, and race of shame,
And I shall shortly be with them that rest.
MANOA. Believe not these suggestions, which proceed
From anguish of the mind, and humors black   600
That mingle with thy fancy.[3] I, however,
Must not omit a father's timely care
To prosecute the means of thy deliverance
By ransom or how else: meanwhile be calm,
And healing words from these thy friends admit.   605
SAMSON. Oh, that torment should not be confined
To the body's wounds and sores,
With maladies innumerable
In heart, head, breast, and reins,
But must secret passage find   610
To th' inmost mind,
There exercise all his fierce accidents,[4]
And on her purest spirits prey,
As on entrails, joints, and limbs,
With answerable pains, but more intense,   615
Though void of corporal sense!
    My griefs not only pain me
As a lingering disease,
But, finding no redress, ferment and rage;
Nor less than wounds immedicable   620
Rankle, and fester, and gangrene,
To black mortification.[5]
Thoughts, my tormentors, armed with daily stings,
Mangle my apprehensive tenderest parts,
Exasperate, exulcerate, and raise   625
Dire inflammation which no cooling herb
Or med'cinal liquor can assuage,
Nor breath of vernal air from snowy alp.
Sleep hath forsook and given me o'er
To death's benumbing opium as my only cure;   630
Thence faintings, swoonings of despair,
And sense of Heaven's desertion.[6]
    I was his nursling once and choice delight,
His destined from the womb,
Promised by heavenly message[7] twice descending.   635
Under his special eye
Abstemious I grew up and thrived amain;
He led me on to mightiest deeds,

---

3. Black bile, the melancholy humor, was supposed to have specially ill effects on the imagination.
4. I.e., there put into effect all the fierce qualities
(of torment).

5. A medical term for decay.
6. Samson comes close here to suggesting that
religious despair is the symptom of a physical condition; compare Burton's *Anatomy of Melancholy.*
7. Messenger.

Above the nerve[8] of mortal arm,
Against the uncircumcised, our enemies: 640
But now hath cast me off as never known,
And to those cruel enemies,
Whom I by his appointment had provoked,
Left me all helpless with th' irreparable loss
Of sight, reserved alive to be repeated[9]   645
The subject of their cruelty or scorn.
Nor am I in the list of them that hope;
Hopeless are all my evils, all remèdiless.
This one prayer yet remains, might I be heard,
No long petition—speedy death,   650
The close of all my miseries and the balm.
CHORUS. Many are the sayings of the wise,
    In ancient and in modern books enrolled,
    Extolling patience as the truest fortitude,
    And to the bearing well of all calamities,   655
    All chances incident to man's frail life;
    Consolatories writ
    With studied argument, and much persuasion sought,
    Lenient[1] of grief and anxious thought.
    But with th' afflicted in his pangs their sound   660
    Little prevails, or rather seems a tune
    Harsh, and of dissonant mood[2] from his complaint,
    Unless he feel within
    Some source of consolation from above,
    Secret refreshings that repair his strength   665
    And fainting spirits uphold.[3]
        God of our fathers! what is man,
    That thou towards him with hand so various—
    Or might I say contrarious?—
    Temper'st thy providence through his short course: 670
    Not evenly, as thou rul'st
    The angelic orders, and inferior creatures mute,
    Irrational and brute?[4]
    Nor do I name of men the common rout,
    That, wandering loose about,   675
    Grow up and perish as the summer fly,
    Heads without name, no more remembered;
    But such as thou hast solemnly elected,
    With gifts and graces eminently adorned,
    To some great work, thy glory,   680
    And people's safety, which in part they effect.

---

8. Sinew, hence, strength.
9. Repeatedly, continually.
1. Soothing (from Latin, *leniens*).
2. The musical mode, or psychological mood, of the comforter jars on that of the sufferer.
3. Compare Job's answers to his comforters, espe-

cially in chapter 14.
4. The chorus feels that the beings above and below man on the Great Chain of Being (the nine orders of angels above, the many mute beasts below) are ruled by a less capricious code than man.

Yet toward these, thus dignified, thou oft,
Amidst their height of noon,
Changest thy countenance and thy hand, with no regard
Of highest favors past   685
From thee on them, or them to thee of service.[5]
    Nor only dost degrade them, or remit
To life obscured, which were a fair dismission,
But throw'st them lower than thou didst exalt them high,
Unseemly falls in human eye,   690
Too grievous for the trespass or omission;
Oft leav'st them to the hostile sword
Of heathen and profane, their carcasses
To dogs and fowls a prey, or else captived,
Or to the unjust tribunals, under change of times,   695
And condemnation of the ingrateful multitude.[6]
If these they 'scape, perhaps in poverty
With sickness and disease thou bow'st them down,
Painful diseases and deformed,
In crude[7] old age;   700
Though not disordinate,[8] yet causeless suffering
The punishment of dissolute days. In fine,
Just or unjust alike seem miserable,
For oft alike both come to evil end.
    So deal not with this once thy glorious champion,   705
The image of thy strength, and mighty minister.[9]
What do I beg? how hast thou dealt already!
Behold him in this state calamitous, and turn
His labors, for thou canst, to peaceful end.
    But who is this? what thing of sea or land—   710
Female of sex it seems—
That, so bedecked, ornate, and gay,
Comes this way sailing
Like a stately ship
Of Tarsus, bound for th' isles   715
Of Javan or Gadire,[1]
With all her bravery on, and tackle trim,
Sails filled, and streamers waving,
Courted by all the winds that hold them play;
An amber[2] scent of odorous perfume   720
Her harbinger, a damsel train behind?
Some rich Philistian matron she may seem;

5. Manoa has already voiced this plaint, lines 368–72.
6. After the Restoration, many Puritan leaders were executed, jailed, or exiled, while even the corpses of some were exhumed, beheaded, and publicly exhibited.
7. Literally, "raw," but, figuratively, "premature."
8. I.e., though they have not been dissipated (disordinate). Milton resented having the gout, supposed to be a disease of the luxurious.

9. Agent, but with a religious connotation as well.
1. Tarsus (the birthplace of St. Paul) is a trading city in modern Turkey; the isles of Javan are the isles of Greece, supposed to be populated by descendants of Javan, son of Noah's son Japhet. Gadire is modern Cadiz in Spain. "Ships of Tarshish" is a common Old Testament emblem of pride and worldliness (e.g., Isaiah 23, Psalm 48).
2. Ambergris.

And now, at nearer view, no other certain
Than Dàlila thy wife.[3]

SAMSON. My wife! my traitress! let her not come near me.   725

CHORUS. Yet on she moves; now stands and eyes thee fixed,
About t' have spoke; but now, with head declined
Like a fair flower surcharged with dew, she weeps,
And words addressed seem into tears dissolved,
Wetting the borders of her silken veil.   730
But now again she makes address to speak.

DALILA. With doubtful feet and wavering resolution
I came, still dreading thy displeasure, Samson;
Which to have merited, without excuse,
I cannot but acknowledge. Yet if tears   735
May expiate (though the fact more evil drew
In the perverse event than I foresaw),[4]
My penance hath not slackened, though my pardon
No way assured. But conjugal affection,
Prevailing over fear and timorous doubt,   740
Hath led me on, desirous to behold
Once more thy face, and know of thy estate,[5]
If aught in my ability may serve
To lighten what thou suffer'st, and appease
Thy mind with what amends is in my power—   745
Though late, yet in some part to recompense
My rash but more unfortunate misdeed.

SAMSON. Out, out, hyena![6] These are thy wonted arts,
And arts of every woman false like thee,
To break all faith, all vows, deceive, betray;   750
Then, as repentant, to submit, beseech,
And reconcilement move with feigned remorse,
Confess, and promise wonders in her change,
Not truly penitent, but chief to try
Her husband, how far urged his patience bears,   755
His virtue or weakness which way to assail:
Then, with more cautious and instructed skill,
Again transgresses, and again submits;
That wisest and best men, full oft beguiled,
With goodness principled not to reject   760
The penitent, but ever to forgive,
Are drawn to wear out miserable days,
Entangled with a poisonous bosom-snake,
If not by quick destruction soon cut off,
As I by thee, to ages an example.   765

DALILA. Yet hear me, Samson; not that I endeavor
To lessen or extenuate my offense,

3. The circling, mocking, derisive description of the chorus carefully holds Samson in suspense till the last minute.
4. I.e., my action turned out worse than intended.
5. Condition.

6. Apart from being an animal of odious habits and appearance, the hyena was a traditional beast of hypocrisy, supposed to entice men to destruction by its power of imitating the human voice.

But that, on th' other side, if it be weighed
By itself, with aggravations not surcharged,
Or else with just allowance counterpoised,   770
I may, if possible, thy pardon find
The easier towards me, or thy hatred less.
First granting, as I do, it was a weakness
In me, but incident to all our sex,
Curiosity, inquisitive, importùne   775
Of secrets, then with like infirmity
To publish them, both common female faults;
Was it not weakness also to make known,
For importunity, that is for naught,
Wherein consisted all thy strength and safety?   780
To what I did thou show'dst me first the way.
But I to enemies revealed, and should not!
Nor should'st thou have trusted that to woman's frailty:[7]
Ere I to thee, thou to thyself wast cruel.
Let weakness then with weakness come to parle,[8]   785
So near related, or the same of kind;
Thine forgive mine, that men may censure thine
The gentler, if severely thou exact not
More strength from me than in thyself was found.
And what if love, which thou interpret'st hate,   790
The jealousy of love, powerful of sway
In human hearts, nor less in mine towards thee,
Caused what I did? I saw thee mutable
Of fancy; feared lest one day thou would'st leave me,
As her at Timna; sought by all means therefore,   795
How to endear, and hold thee to me firmest:
No better way I saw than by importuning
To learn thy secrets, get into my power
Thy key of strength and safety. Thou wilt say,
"Why, then, revealed?" I was assured by those   800
Who tempted me that nothing was designed
Against thee but safe custody and hold.
That made for me; I knew that liberty
Would draw thee forth to perilous enterprises,
While I at home sat full of cares and fears,   805
Wailing thy absence in my widowed bed;
Here I should still enjoy thee, day and night,
Mine and love's prisoner, not the Philistines',
Whole to myself, unhazarded abroad,
Fearless at home of partners in my love.   810
These reasons in love's law have passed for good,
Though fond[9] and reasonless to some perhaps;
And love hath oft, well meaning, wrought much woe,

---

7. Like Eve, who wore down Adam with importunity, then blamed him for giving in (*Paradise
Lost* 9.1155–61), Dalila blames Samson for doing
what she herself had demanded.
8. Parley, agreement.
9. Foolish.

Yet always pity or pardon hath obtained.
Be not unlike all others, not austere   815
As thou art strong, inflexible as steel.
If thou in strength all mortals dost exceed,
In uncompassionate anger do not so.
SAMSON. How cunningly the sorceress displays
    Her own transgressions, to upbraid me mine!   820
    That malice, not repentance, brought thee hither,
    By this appears. I gave, thou say'st, th' example,
    I led the way—bitter reproach, but true;
    I to myself was false ere thou to me.
    Such pardon, therefore, as I give my folly   825
    Take to thy wicked deed; which when thou seest
    Impartial, self-severe, inexorable,
    Thou wilt renounce thy seeking, and much rather
    Confess it feigned. Weakness is thy excuse,
    And I believe it, weakness to resist   830
    Philistian gold. If weakness may excuse,
    What murderer, what traitor, parricide,
    Incestuous, sacrilegious, but may plead it?
    All wickedness is weakness; that plea, therefore,
    With God or man will gain thee no remission.   835
    But love constrained thee? Call it furious rage
    To satisfy thy lust. Love seeks to have love;
    My love how could'st thou hope, who took'st the way
    To raise in me inexpiable[1] hate,
    Knowing, as needs I must, by thee betrayed?   840
    In vain thou striv'st to cover shame with shame,
    Or by evasions thy crime uncover'st more.
DALILA. Since thou determin'st weakness for no plea
    In man or woman, though to thy own condemning,
    Hear what assaults I had, what snares besides,   845
    What sieges girt me round, ere I consented;
    Which might have awed the best-resolved of men,
    The constantest, to have yielded without blame.
    It was not gold, as to my charge thou lay'st,
    That wrought with me.[2] Thou know'st the magistrates   850
    And princes of my country came in person,
    Solicited, commanded, threatened, urged,
    Adjured by all the bonds of civil duty
    And of religion—pressed how just it was,
    How honorable, how glorious, to entrap   855
    A common enemy, who had destroyed
    Such numbers of our nation: and the priest
    Was not behind, but ever at my ear,
    Preaching how meritorious with the gods
    It would be to ensnare an irreligious   860

---

1. Inextinguishable.
2. Judges 16 is very explicit that Dalila betrayed Samson for money—eleven hundred pieces of silver offered her by each one of the Philistine lords.

Dishonorer of Dagon. What had I
To oppose against such powerful arguments?
Only my love of thee held long debate,
And combated in silence all these reasons
With hard contest. At length, that grounded maxim,   865
So rife and celebrated in the mouths
Of wisest men, that to the public good
Private respects must yield,[3] with grave authority
Took full possession of me, and prevailed;
Virtue, as I thought, truth, duty, so enjoining.   870
SAMSON. I thought where all thy circling wiles would end,
    In feigned religion, smooth hypocrisy!
    But had thy love, still odiously pretended,
    Been, as it ought, sincere, it would have taught thee
    Far other reasonings, brought forth other deeds.   875
    I before all the daughters of my tribe
    And of my nation chose thee from among
    My enemies, loved thee, as too well thou knew'st;
    Too well; unbosomed all my secrets to thee,
    Not out of levity, but overpowered   880
    By thy request, who could deny thee nothing;
    Yet now am judged an enemy. Why then
    Didst thou at first receive me for thy husband,
    Then, as since then, thy country's foe professed?
    Being once a wife, for me thou wast to leave   885
    Parents and country; nor was I their subject,
    Nor under their protection, but my own;
    Thou mine, not theirs.[4] If aught against my life
    Thy country sought of thee, it sought unjustly,
    Against the law of nature, law of nations;   890
    No more thy country, but an impious crew
    Of men conspiring to uphold their state
    By worse than hostile deeds, violating the ends
    For which our country is a name so dear;
    Not therefore to be obeyed. But zeal moved thee;   895
    To please thy gods thou didst it! Gods unable
    To acquit themselves and prosecute their foes
    But by ungodly deeds, the contradiction
    Of their own deity, gods cannot be;
    Less therefore to be pleased, obeyed, or feared.   900
    These false pretexts and varnished colors failing,
    Bare in thy guilt, how foul must thou appear!
DALILA. In argument with men a woman ever
    Goes by the worse,[5] whatever be her cause.
SAMSON. For want of words, no doubt, or lack of breath!   905
    Witness when I was worried with thy peals.

---

3. Reason of state, political "necessity," was in
Milton's eyes the worst of all possible motives for
an action. Compare *Paradise Lost* 4.393–94.

4. I.e., you were under my protection, not theirs.
5. Comes off second best.

DALILA. I was a fool, too rash, and quite mistaken
   In what I thought would have succeeded best.
   Let me obtain forgiveness of thee, Samson;
   Afford me place to show what recompense   910
   Towards thee I intend for what I have misdone,
   Misguided. Only what remains past cure
   Bear not too sensibly,[6] nor still insist
   To afflict thyself in vain. Though sight be lost,
   Life yet hath many solaces, enjoyed   915
   Where other senses want not their delights
   At home, in leisure and domestic ease,
   Exempt from many a care and chance to which
   Eyesight exposes, daily, men abroad.
   I to the lords will intercede, not doubting   920
   Their favorable ear, that I may fetch thee
   From forth this loathsome prison-house, to abide
   With me, where my redoubled love and care,
   With nursing diligence, to me glad office,
   May ever tend about thee to old age,   925
   With all things grateful cheered, and so supplied
   That what by me thou hast lost thou least shalt miss.
SAMSON. No, no; of my condition take no care;
   It fits not; thou and I long since are twain;
   Nor think me so unwary or accursed[7]   930
   To bring my feet again into the snare
   Where once I have been caught. I know thy trains,
   Though dearly to my cost, thy gins, and toils.[8]
   Thy fair enchanted cup, and warbling charms,
   No more on me have power; their force is nulled;   935
   So much of adder's wisdom I have learnt,
   To fence my ear against thy sorceries.[9]
   If in my flower of youth and strength, when all men
   Loved, honored, feared me, thou alone could hate me,
   Thy husband, slight me, sell me, and forgo me,   940
   How would'st thou use me now, blind, and thereby
   Deceivable, in most things as a child,
   Helpless, thence easily contemned and scorned,
   And last neglected! How would'st thou insult,
   When I must live uxorious to thy will   945
   In perfect thraldom! how again betray me,
   Bearing my words and doings to the lords
   To gloss upon, and, censuring, frown or smile![1]
   This jail I count the house of liberty
   To thine,[2] whose doors my feet shall never enter.   950

6. "Too sensibly": with too great sensitivity.
7. I.e., so neglectful or bewitched.
8. "Trains": tricks; "gins": snares; "toils": nets. The traditional images for female wiles are heightened by reference to an enchanting cup and warbled charms reminiscent of Homer's Circe (*Odyssey* 10).

9. Psalm 58 verses 4 and 5 describes the "deaf adder that stoppeth her ear; which will not hearken to the voice of charmers, charming never so wisely."
1. Milton's libertarian hatred of censorship and managed liberty is apparent. "Gloss": comment.
2. Compared to thine.

DALILA. Let me approach at least, and touch thy hand.
SAMSON. Not for thy life, lest fierce remembrance wake
    My sudden rage to tear thee joint by joint.[3]
    At distance I forgive thee, go with that;
    Bewail thy falsehood, and the pious works   955
    It hath brought forth to make thee memorable
    Among illustrious women, faithful wives;
    Cherish thy hastened widowhood with the gold
    Of matrimonial treason: so farewell.
DALILA. I see thou art implacable, more deaf   960
    To prayers than winds and seas. Yet winds to seas
    Are reconciled at length, and sea to shore:
    Thy anger, unappeasable, still rages,
    Eternal tempest never to be calmed.
    Why do I humble thus myself, and, suing   965
    For peace, reap nothing but repulse and hate,
    Bid go with evil omen,[4] and the brand
    Of infamy upon my name denounced?
    To mix with thy concernments I desist
    Henceforth, nor too much disapprove my own.   970
    Fame, if not double-faced, is double-mouthed,
    And with contràry blast proclaims most deeds;[5]
    On both his wings, one black, th' other white,
    Bears greatest names in his wild airy flight.
    My name, perhaps, among the circumcised   975
    In Dan, in Judah, and the bordering tribes,
    To all posterity may stand defamed,
    With malediction mentioned, and the blot
    Of falsehood most unconjugal traduced.
    But in my country, where I most desire,   980
    In Ekron, Gaza, Asdod, and in Gath,
    I shall be named among the famousest
    Of women, sung at solemn festivals,
    Living and dead recorded, who to save
    Her country from a fierce destroyer chose   985
    Above the faith of wedlock bands; my tomb
    With odors[6] visited and annual flowers;
    Not less renowned than in Mount Ephraim
    Jael, who, with inhospitable guile,
    Smote Sisera sleeping,[7] through the temples nailed.   990
    Nor shall I count it heinous to enjoy
    The public marks of honor and reward
    Conferred upon me for the piety

3. What Samson might remember, at the touch of Dalila, which would lead him to tear her to pieces, is a problem in domestic psychology.
4. I.e., dismissed with predictions of ill fame.
5. The figure of Fame, in Milton's youthful poem *On the Fifth of November*, does indeed have a double tongue, one for truth and one for lies. Fame or Rumor was a favorite grotesque allegorical figure in classical poets like Ovid (*Metamorphoses* 12.43 ff.) and Virgil (*Aeneid* 4.173 ff.).
6. Perfumes.
7. Jael lured Sisera, who saw in her the wife of his ally and friend, into a tent, and there drove a large nail into his head (Judges 4.17–21).

Which to my country I was judged to have shown.
At this whoever envies or repines,   995
I leave him to his lot, and like my own.
CHORUS. She's gone, a manifest serpent by her sting
    Discovered in the end, till now concealed.
SAMSON. So let her go. God sent her to debase me,
    And aggravate my folly, who committed   1000
    To such a viper his most sacred trust
    Of secrecy, my safety, and my life.
CHORUS. Yet beauty, though injurious, hath strange power,
    After offense returning, to regain
    Love once possessed, nor can be easily   1005
    Repulsed, without much inward passion[8] felt,
    And secret sting of amorous remorse.
SAMSON. Love-quarrels oft in pleasing concord end;
    Not wedlock-treachery, endangering life.
CHORUS. It is not virtue, wisdom, valor, wit,   1010
    Strength, comeliness of shape, or amplest merit
    That woman's love can win, or long inherit;[9]
    But what it is hard is to say,
    Harder to hit,
    Which way soever men refer it   1015
    (Much like thy riddle, Samson),[1] in one day
    Or seven though one should musing sit.
        If any of these, or all, the Timnian bride
    Had not so soon preferred
    Thy paranymph, worthless to thee compared,   1020
    Successor in thy bed,[2]
    Nor both so loosely disallied
    Their nuptials,[3] nor this last so treacherously
    Had shorn the fatal harvest of thy head.
    Is it for that[4] such outward ornament   1025
    Was lavished on their sex, that inward gifts
    Were left for haste unfinished, judgment scant,
    Capacity not raised to apprehend
    Or value what is best
    In choice, but oftest to affect[5] the wrong?   1030
    Or was too much of self-love mixed,
    Of constancy no root infixed,
    That either they love nothing, or not long?
        Whate'er it be, to wisest men and best,
    Seeming at first all heavenly under virgin veil,   1035
    Soft, modest, meek, demure,
    Once joined, the contrary she proves, a thorn

8. Suffering.
9. Possess.
1. Samson's riddle is propounded and answered in Judges 14, verses 14 and 18.
2. I.e., if any of these (virtue, etc., lines 1010–11) sufficed, Samson's first wife (the Timnian bride)

would not have preferred to marry his "para-nymph" (best man). See Judges 14.
3. I.e., nor would both your wives have been so careless about their marriage vows.
4. Because.
5. Desire.

Intestine,[6] far within defensive arms
A cleaving[7] mischief, in his way to virtue
Adverse and turbulent; or by her charms   1040
Draws him awry, enslaved
With dotage, and his sense depraved
To folly and shameful deeds, which ruin ends.
What pilot so expert but needs must wreck,
Embarked with such a steers-mate at the helm?   1045
    Favored of Heaven who finds
One virtuous, rarely found,
That in domestic good combines:
Happy that house! his way to peace is smooth:
But virtue which breaks through all opposition,   1050
And all temptation can remove,
Most shines and most is acceptable above.
    Therefore God's universal law
Gave to the man despotic power
Over his female in due awe,   1055
Nor from that right to part an hour,
Smile she or lour:
So shall he least confusion draw
On his whole life, not swayed
By female usurpation, nor dismayed.   1060
    But had we best retire? I see a storm.
SAMSON. Fair days have oft contracted[8] wind and rain.
CHORUS. But this another kind of tempest brings.
SAMSON. Be less abstruse; my riddling days are past.
CHORUS. Look now for no enchanting voice, nor fear   1065
    The bait of honeyed words; a rougher tongue
    Draws hitherward, I know him by his stride,
    The giant Harapha[9] of Gath, his look
    Haughty, as is his pile[1] high-built and proud.
    Comes he in peace? What wind hath blown him hither   1070
    I less conjecture than when first I saw
    The sumptuous Dalila floating this way:[2]
    His habit carries peace, his brow defiance.
SAMSON. Or peace or not, alike to me he comes.
CHORUS. His fraught[3] we soon shall know: he now arrives.   1075
HARAPHA. I come not, Samson, to condole thy chance,
    As these[4] perhaps, yet wish it had not been,
    Though for no friendly intent. I am of Gath;

6. An inward thorn, a viper in the bosom.
7. Clinging; a traditional emblem of marriage was
the elm and the vine.
8. Drawn after them.
9. Harapha does not appear at all within the story
told in the Book of Judges; Milton invented him
with the help of some hints from the image of
Goliath in 1 Samuel 17 and some other giants in
2 Samuel 21. *Rapha* means giant in Hebrew.
1. Body; with the suggestion that he is tall as a

tower.
2. That the various visitors of Samson are blown
hither and yon by the winds of occasion serves to
emphasize the deep steadiness of Samson's final
resolution. "Habit": garb. (He's not dressed for
fighting.)
3. Freight, i.e., business.
4. The chorus of Danites, naturally sympathetic
to Samson.

Men call me Harapha, of stock renowned
As Og, or Anak, and the Emims old   1080
That Kiriathaim held.[5] Thou know'st me now,
If thou at all art known.[6] Much I have heard
Of thy prodigious might and feats performed,
Incredible to me, in this displeased,
That I was never present on the place   1085
Of those encounters, where we might have tried
Each other's force in camp or listed field;[7]
And now am come to see of whom such noise
Hath walked about, and each limb to survey,
If thy appearance answer loud report.   1090
SAMSON. The way to know were not to see, but taste.[8]
HARAPHA. Dost thou already single[9] me? I thought
   Gyves and the mill had tamed thee. O that fortune
   Had brought me to the field where thou art famed
   To have wrought such wonders with an ass's jaw!   1095
   I should have forced thee soon wish[1] other arms,
   Or left thy carcass where the ass lay thrown;
   So had the glory of prowess been recovered
   To Palestine, won by a Philistine
   From the unforeskinned race, of whom thou bear'st   1100
   The highest name for valiant acts. That honor,
   Certain to have won by mortal duel from thee,
   I lose, prevented by thy eyes put out.
SAMSON. Boast not of what thou would'st have done, but do
   What then thou would'st; thou seest it in thy hand.   1105
HARAPHA. To combat with a blind man I disdain,
   And thou hast need much washing to be touched.
SAMSON. Such usage as your honorable lords
   Afford me, assassinated[2] and betrayed;
   Who durst not with their whole united powers   1110
   In fight withstand me single and unarmed,
   Nor in the house with chamber ambushes[3]
   Close-banded durst attack me, no, not sleeping,
   Till they had hired a woman with their gold,
   Breaking her marriage-faith, to circumvent me.   1115
   Therefore, without feigned shifts, let be assigned
   Some narrow place enclosed, where sight may give thee,
   Or rather flight, no great advantage on me;
   Then put on all thy gorgeous arms, thy helmet

---

5. Og was a giant King of Bashan in Deuteronomy 3.11; Anak and his sons were giants in Numbers 13.33; the Emims were giants in Deuteronomy 2.10–11 and Genesis 14.5.
6. I.e., you know me now if you know anything; but also "if you are anyone worth knowing." Compare Satan's brag to Zephon and Ithuriel, "Not to know me argues yourselves unknown." *Paradise Lost* 4.830.
7. "Camp": field of battle (from Latin, *campus*).

"Listed field": lists, tourney ground.
8. Make a trial of.
9. Challenge. "Gyves": chains.
1. Eighteenth-century editors changed "wish" to "with," easing the grammar at the expense of the sense.
2. Treacherously assailed.
3. Samson refers to the four occasions on which Philistines hid in his bedroom while Dalila tried unsuccessfully to betray him to them.

And brigandine of brass, thy broad habergeon,   1120
Vant-brace and greaves and gauntlet;[4] add thy spear,
A weaver's beam, and seven-times-folded shield:
I only with an oaken staff will meet thee,
And raise such outcries on thy clattered iron,
Which long shall not withhold me from thy head,   1125
That in a little time, while breath remains thee,
Thou oft shalt wish thyself at Gath, to boast
Again in safety what thou would'st have done
To Samson, but shalt never see Gath more.

HARAPHA. Thou durst not thus disparage glorious arms,   1130
Which greatest heroes have in battle worn,
Their ornament and safety, had not spells
And black enchantments, some magician's art,
Armed thee or charmed thee strong, which thou from Heaven
Feign'dst at thy birth was given thee in thy hair,   1135
Where strength can least abide, though all thy hairs
Were bristles ranged like those that ridge the back
Of chafed wild boars or ruffled porcupines.

SAMSON. I know no spells, use no forbidden arts;
My trust is in the Living God, who gave me   1140
At my nativity this strength, diffused
No less through all my sinews, joints, and bones,
Than thine, while I preserved these locks unshorn,
The pledge of my unviolated vow.
For proof hereof, if Dagon be thy god,   1145
Go to his temple, invocate his aid
With solemnest devotion, spread before him
How highly it concerns his glory now
To frustrate and dissolve these magic spells,
Which I to be the power of Israel's God   1150
Avow, and challenge Dagon to the test,
Offering to combat thee, his champion bold,
With th' utmost of his godhead seconded:
Then thou shalt see, or rather to thy sorrow
Soon feel, whose God is strongest, thine or mine.   1155

HARAPHA. Presume not on thy God. Whate'er he be,
Thee he regards not, owns not, hath cut off
Quite from his people, and delivered up
Into thy enemies' hand; permitted them
To put out both thine eyes, and fettered send thee   1160
Into the common prison, there to grind
Among the slaves and asses, thy comràdes,
As good for nothing else, no better service
With those thy boisterous locks; no worthy match

---

4. "Brigandine": a padded chest-protector, covered with iron scales or rings; "habergeon": a coat
of mail, a hauberk; "vant-brace": a steel cuff for
the forearm; greaves protect the shins and thighs,
and gauntlets the hands. A weaver's beam, emblem
of weightiness, is used to keep threads hanging tautly
in a loom. All these military details are from the
description of Goliath, 1 Samuel 17.4–7.

For valor to assail, nor by the sword   1165
  Of noble warrior, so to stain his honor,
  But by the barber's razor best subdued.
SAMSON. All these indignities, for such they are
  From thine,[5] these evils I deserve and more,
  Acknowledge them from God inflicted on me   1170
  Justly, yet despair not of his final pardon,
  Whose ear is ever open, and his eye
  Gracious to re-admit the suppliant;
  In confidence whereof I once again
  Defy thee to the trial of mortal fight,   1175
  By combat to decide whose god is God,
  Thine, or whom I with Israel's sons adore.
HARAPHA. Fair honor that thou dost thy God, in trusting
  He will accept thee to defend his cause,
  A murderer, a revolter, and a robber!   1180
SAMSON. Tongue-doughty giant, how dost thou prove me these?
HARAPHA. Is not thy nation subject to our lords?
  Their magistrates confessed it when they took thee
  As a league-breaker, and delivered bound
  Into our hands;[6] for hadst thou not committed   1185
  Notorious murder on those thirty men
  At Ascalon, who never did thee harm,
  Then, like a robber, stripp'dst them of their robes?
  The Philistines, when thou hadst broke the league,
  Went up with armèd powers thee only seeking,   1190
  To others did no violence nor spoil.
SAMSON. Among the daughters of the Philistines
  I chose a wife, which argued me no foe,
  And in your city held my nuptial feast;
  But your ill-meaning politician lords,   1195
  Under pretense of bridal friends and guests,
  Appointed to await me thirty spies,
  Who, threatening cruel death, constrained the bride
  To wring from me, and tell to them, my secret,
  That solved the riddle which I had proposed.   1200
  When I perceived all set on enmity,
  As on my enemies, wherever chanced,
  I used hostility, and took their spoil,
  To pay my underminers in their coin.
  My nation was subjected to your lords![7]   1205
  It was the force of conquest; force with force
  Is well ejected when the conquered can.
  But I, a private person, whom my country

---

5. Thy people.
6. Judges 14.8–20 and 15.9–15 describe the episode. Samson when he came to Timna to be married proposed a riddle and a bet to the marriage guests; they got his intended bride to reveal the riddle, and in revenge he killed thirty of their peo-

ple and left the lady to the "paranymph," or best man. Old Testament Samson is indeed a rude and savage figure; Milton, with characteristic confidence, undertakes his legal defense in everything.
7. I.e., you argue that my nation was subjected to your lords.

As a league-breaker gave up bound, presumed
Single rebellion, and did hostile acts!   1210
I was no private,[8] but a person raised,
With strength sufficient, and command from Heaven,
To free my country. If their servile minds
Me, their deliverer sent, would not receive,
But to their masters gave me up for naught,   1215
Th' unworthier they; whence to this day they serve.
I was to do my part from Heaven assigned,
And had performed it if my known offense
Had not disabled me, not all your force.
These shifts refuted, answer thy appellant,[9]   1220
Though by his blindness maimed for high attempts,
Who now defies thee thrice to single fight,
As a petty enterprise of small enforce.[1]

HARAPHA. With thee, a man condemned, a slave enrolled,
Due by the law to capital punishment?   1225
To fight with thee no man of arms will deign.

SAMSON. Cam'st thou for this, vain boaster, to survey me,
To descant on my strength, and give thy verdict?
Come nearer; part not hence so slight informed;
But take good heed my hand survey not thee.   1230

HARAPHA. O Baal-zebub![2] can my ears unused
Hear these dishonors, and not render death?

SAMSON. No man withholds thee; nothing from thy hand
Fear I incurable; bring up thy van;[3]
My heels are fettered, but my fist is free.   1235

HARAPHA. This insolence other kind of answer fits.

SAMSON. Go, baffled coward, lest I run upon thee,
Though in these chains, bulk without spirit vast,
And with one buffet lay thy structure low,
Or swing thee in the air, then dash thee down,   1240
To the hazard of thy brains and shattered sides.

HARAPHA. By Astaroth,[4] ere long thou shalt lament
These braveries,[5] in irons loaden on thee.

CHORUS. His giantship is gone somewhat crestfallen,
Stalking with less unconscionable[6] strides,   1245
And lower looks, but in a sultry chafe.

SAMSON. I dread him not, nor all his giant brood,
Though fame divulge him father of five sons,
All of gigantic size, Goliath chief.[7]

8. I.e., lawless individual.
9. I.e., now that we've disposed of these dodges,
answer your challenger. "Apellant": literally, caller,
one who calls you out.
1. Difficulty.
2. Baal-zebub is Beëlzebub, god of the flies.
3. The vanguard of an army was, naturally, the
first group engaged. Samson invites Harapha to start
the fight.

4. Moon-goddess of the Philistines, consort of
Dagon. See *Paradise Lost* 1.437–46.
5. Boasts.
6. Excessive.
7. 2 Samuel 21 describes four giants "born to the
giant in Gath" and brothers of Goliath, slain by
David's men; Milton makes the identification with
Harapha on his own.

CHORUS. He will directly to the lords, I fear,   1250
   And with malicious counsel stir them up
   Some way or other yet further to afflict thee.
SAMSON. He must allege some cause, and offered fight
   Will not dare mention, lest a question rise
   Whether he durst accept the offer or not;   1255
   And that he durst not plain enough appeared.
   Much more affliction than already felt
   They cannot well impose, nor I sustain,
   If they intend advantage of my labors,
   The work of many hands, which earns my keeping,   1260
   With no small profit daily to my owners.
   But come what will; my deadliest foe will prove
   My speediest friend, by death to rid me hence;
   The worst that he can give, to me the best.
   Yet so it may fall out, because their end   1265
   Is hate, not help to me, it may with mine
   Draw their own ruin who attempt the deed.
CHORUS. Oh, how comely it is, and how reviving
   To the spirits of just men long oppressed,
   When God into the hands of their deliverer   1270
   Puts invincible might
   To quell the mighty of the earth, th' oppressor,
   The brute and boisterous force of violent men,
   Hardy and industrious to support
   Tyrannic power, but raging to pursue   1275
   The righteous, and all such as honor truth!
   He all their ammunition
   And feats of war defeats,[8]
   With plain heroic magnitude of mind
   And celestial vigor armed;   1280
   Their armories and magazines[9] contemns,
   Renders them useless, while
   With wingèd expedition[1]
   Swift as the lightning glance he executes
   His errand on the wicked, who, surprised,   1285
   Lose their defense, distracted and amazed.
     But patience is more oft the exercise
   Of saints, the trial of their fortitude,
   Making them each his own deliverer,
   And victor over all   1290
   That tyranny or fortune can inflict.
   Either of these is in thy lot,[2]
   Samson, with might endued
   Above the sons of men; but sight bereaved
   May chance to number thee with those   1295

8. A touch of the pervasive Miltonic punning.   1. Haste.
9. Storerooms, hence the contents, military stores.   2. Fate.

Whom patience finally must crown.[3]
   This idol's day hath been to thee no day of rest,
Laboring thy mind
More than the working day thy hands.
And yet, perhaps, more trouble is behind;   1300
For I descry this way
Some other tending; in his hand
A scepter or quaint[4] staff he bears,
Comes on amain, speed in his look.
By his habit I discern him now   1305
A public officer, and now at hand.
His message will be short and voluble.[5]

OFFICER. Hebrews, the prisoner Samson here I seek.

CHORUS. His manacles remark[6] him; there he sits.

OFFICER. Samson, to thee our lords thus bid me say: 1310
   This day to Dagon is a solemn feast,
   With sacrifices, triumph, pomp, and games;
   Thy strength they know surpassing human rate,
   And now some public proof thereof require
   To honor this great feast, and great assembly.   1315
   Rise, therefore, with all speed, and come along,
   Where I will see thee heartened and fresh clad,
   To appear as fits before th' illustrious lords.

SAMSON. Thou know'st I am an Hebrew; therefore tell them
   Our Law forbids at their religious rites   1320
   My presence; for that cause I cannot come.

OFFICER. This answer, be assured, will not content them.

SAMSON. Have they not sword-players, and every sort
   Of gymnic artists, wrestlers, riders, runners,
   Jugglers and dancers, antics, mummers, mimics,[7]   1325
   But they must pick me out, with shackles tired,
   And over-labored at their public mill,
   To make them sport with blind activity?
   Do they not seek occasion of new quarrels,
   On my refusal, to distress me more,   1330
   Or make a game of my calamities?
   Return the way thou cam'st; I will not come.

OFFICER. Regard thyself; this will offend them highly.

SAMSON. Myself? my conscience, and internal peace.
   Can they think me so broken, so debased   1335
   With corporal servitude, that my mind ever
   Will condescend to such absurd commands?
   Although their drudge, to be their fool or jester,
   And in my midst of sorrow and heart-grief
   To show them feats, and play before their god,   1340

---

3. The Christian tragedy, like the Christian epic, must center ultimately on an act of passive, not active, fortitude. It is the special achievement of Samson to combine in a single dramatic action both qualities.

4. Ornamented.
5. To the point.
6. Distinguish.
7. "Gymnic artists": gymnasts; "antics": clowns; "mummers": actors.

The worst of all indignities, yet on me
Joined[8] with supreme contempt! I will not come.
OFFICER. My message was imposed on me with speed,
  Brooks no delay: is this thy resolution?
SAMSON. So take it with what speed thy message needs.   1345
OFFICER. I am sorry what this stoutness[9] will produce.
SAMSON. Perhaps thou shalt have cause to sorrow indeed.
CHORUS. Consider, Samson; matters now are strained
  Up to the height, whether to hold or break.
  He's gone, and who knows how he may report   1350
  Thy words by adding fuel to the flame?
  Expect another message, more imperious,
  More lordly thundering than thou well wilt bear.
SAMSON. Shall I abuse this consecrated gift
  Of strength, again returning with my hair   1355
  After my great transgression, so requite
  Favor renewed, and add a greater sin
  By prostituting holy things to idols,
  A Nazarite in place abominable
  Vaunting my strength in honor to their Dagon?   1360
  Besides how vile, contemptible, ridiculous,
  What act more execrably unclean,[1] profane?
CHORUS. Yet with this strength thou serv'st the Philistines,
  Idolatrous, uncircumcised, unclean.
SAMSON. Not in their idol-worship, but by labor   1365
  Honest and lawful to deserve my food
  Of those who have me in their civil power.
CHORUS. Where the heart joins not, outward acts defile not.
SAMSON. Where outward force constrains, the sentence holds:[2]
  But who constrains me to the temple of Dagon,   1370
  Not dragging? The Philistian lords command:
  Commands are no constraints. If I obey them,
  I do it freely, venturing to displease
  God for the fear of man, and man prefer,
  Set God behind; which, in his jealousy,   1375
  Shall never, unrepented, find forgiveness.
  Yet that he may dispense with me, or thee,
  Present in temples at idolatrous rites
  For some important cause,[3] thou need'st not doubt.
CHORUS. How thou wilt here come off surmounts my reach.   1380
SAMSON. Be of good courage; I begin to feel
  Some rousing motions in me which dispose
  To something extraordinary my thoughts.
  I with this messenger will go along—
  Nothing to do, be sure, that may dishonor   1385

8. Enjoined, ordered.
9. Defiance.
1. Taboo.
2. I.e., where outward force constrains, your maxim may be right.

3. God will make a special dispensation for Samson to attend idolatrous ceremonies "for some important cause," which Samson cannot yet define but which he intuits.

Our Law or stain my vow of Nazarite.
If there be aught of presage in the mind,
This day will be remarkable in my life
By some great act, or of my days the last.[4]

CHORUS. In time thou hast resolved: the man returns.   1390

OFFICER. Samson, this second message from our lords
  To thee I am bid say: Art thou our slave,
  Our captive, at the public mill our drudge,
  And dar'st thou, at our sending and command,
  Dispute thy coming? Come without delay;   1395
  Or we shall find such engines to assail
  And hamper thee, as thou shalt come of force,
  Though thou wert firmlier fastened than a rock.

SAMSON. I could be well content to try their art,
  Which to no few of them would prove pernicious;   1400
  Yet, knowing their advantages too many,
  Because[5] they shall not trail me through their streets
  Like a wild beast, I am content to go.
  Masters' commands come with a power resistless
  To such as owe them absolute subjection;   1405
  And for a life who will not change his purpose?
  (So mutable are all the ways of men!)
  Yet this be sure, in nothing to comply
  Scandalous or forbidden in our Law.

OFFICER. I praise thy resolution.[6] Doff these links: 1410
  By this compliance thou wilt win the lords
  To favor, and perhaps to set thee free.

SAMSON. Brethren, farewell. Your company along
  I will not wish, lest it perhaps offend them
  To see me girt with friends; and how the sight   1415
  Of me, as of a common enemy,
  So dreaded once, may now exasperate them
  I know not. Lords are lordliest in their wine;
  And the well-feasted priest then soonest fired
  With zeal, if aught religion seem concerned;[7]   1420
  No less the people, on their holy-days,
  Impetuous, insolent, unquenchable.
  Happen what may, of me expect to hear
  Nothing dishonorable, impure, unworthy
  Our God, our Law, my nation, or myself;   1425
  The last of me or no I cannot warrant.

CHORUS. Go, and the Holy One
  Of Israel be thy guide
  To what may serve his glory best, and spread his name

---

4. By a classic device of dramatic irony, Samson proposes as alternatives two events which will both simultaneously come true. "Presage": premonition, presight.
5. So that.
6. Decision. "Doff these links": take off these chains.
7. Milton's animus against paid priests, whom he considers particularly likely to contaminate the Word of God with their own private interests and worldly desires, comes out plainly here.

Great among the heathen round;   1430
Send thee the angel of thy birth, to stand
Fast by thy side, who from thy father's field
Rode up in flames after his message told
Of thy conception, and be now a shield
Of fire; that Spirit that first rushed on thee   1435
In the camp of Dan,
Be efficacious in thee now at need![8]
For never was from Heaven imparted
Measure of strength so great to mortal seed
As in thy wondrous actions hath been seen.   1440
But wherefore comes old Manoa in such haste
With youthful steps? Much livelier than erewhile
He seems: supposing here to find his son,
Or of him bringing to us some glad news?
MANOA. Peace with you, brethren! My inducement hither   1445
Was not at present here to find my son,
By order of the lords new parted hence
To come and play before them at their feast.
I heard all as I came; the city rings,
And numbers thither flock: I had no will,   1450
Lest I should see him forced to things unseemly.
But that which moved my coming now was chiefly
To give ye part with me[9] what hope I have
With good success to work his liberty.
CHORUS. That hope would much rejoice us to partake   1455
With thee. Say, reverend sire; we thirst to hear.
MANOA. I have attempted, one by one, the lords,
Either at home, or through the high street passing,
With supplication prone and father's tears,
To accept of ransom for my son, their prisoner.   1460
Some much averse I found, and wondrous harsh,
Contemptuous, proud, set on revenge and spite;
That part most reverenced Dagon and his priests:
Others more moderate seeming, but their aim
Private reward, for which both God and State   1465
They easily would set to sale: a third
More generous far and civil, who confessed
They had enough revenged, having reduced
Their foe to misery beneath their fears;
The rest was magnanimity to remit,   1470
If some convenient ransom were proposed.[1]
What noise or shout was that? It tore the sky.
CHORUS. Doubtless the people shouting to behold
Their once great dread, captive and blind before them,

---

8. As a Nazarite (specially consecrated person), Samson had been frequently inspired by the "Spirit of the Lord."
9. I.e., to impart to you.

1. The three parties are in effect bigots, swindlers, and gentlemen—three types common enough in Restoration England, with whom Milton and the defeated Puritans must have had frequently to deal.

Or at some proof of strength before them shown.   1475
MANOA. His ransom, if my whole inheritance
    May compass it, shall willingly be paid
    And numbered down. Much rather I shall choose
    To live the poorest in my tribe, than richest
    And he in that calamitous prison left.   1480
    No, I am fixed not to part hence without him.
    For his redemption all my patrimony,
    If need be, I am ready to forgo
    And quit. Not wanting him, I shall want nothing.
CHORUS. Fathers are wont to lay up for their sons;   1485
    Thou for thy son art bent to lay out all:
    Sons wont to nurse their parents in old age;
    Thou in old age car'st how to nurse thy son,
    Made older than thy age through eyesight lost.
MANOA. It shall be my delight to tend his eyes,   1490
    And view him sitting in the house, ennobled
    With all those high exploits by him achieved,
    And on his shoulders waving down those locks
    That of a nation armed the strength contained.
    And I persuade me God hath not permitted   1495
    His strength again to grow up with his hair
    Garrisoned round about him like a camp
    Of faithful soldiery, were not his purpose
    To use him further yet in some great service—
    Not to sit idle with so great a gift   1500
    Useless, and thence ridiculous, about him.[2]
    And since his strength with eyesight was not lost,
    God will restore him eyesight to[3] his strength.
CHORUS. Thy hopes are not ill-founded, nor seem vain,
    Of his delivery, and thy joy thereon   1505
    Conceived, agreeable to a father's love;
    In both which we, as next,[4] participate.
MANOA. I know your friendly minds, and—O, what noise!
    Mercy of Heaven! what hideous noise was that?
    Horribly loud, unlike the former shout.   1510
CHORUS. Noise call you it, or universal groan,
    As if the whole inhabitation perished?
    Blood, death, and deathful deeds are in that noise,
    Ruin,[5] destruction at the utmost point.
MANOA. Of ruin indeed methought I heard the noise.   1515
    Oh! it continues; they have slain my son.
CHORUS. Thy son is rather slaying them; that outcry
    From slaughter of one foe could not ascend.
MANOA. Some dismal accident it needs must be.

---

2. Much of the play deals with the concept of relevance and irrelevance; outward weapons and outward strength are often beside the point
("ridiculous") in the face of inward and spiritual

powers.
3. To accompany.
4. "As next": as kinsmen.
5. From Latin *ruina*, downfall.

What shall we do, stay here, or run and see?   1520
CHORUS. Best keep together here, lest running thither
   We unawares run into danger's mouth.
   This evil on the Philistines is fallen:
   From whom could else a general cry be heard?
   The sufferers then will scarce molest us here;   1525
   From other hands we need not much to fear.
   What if, his eyesight (for to Israel's God
   Nothing is hard) by miracle restored,
   He now be dealing dole[6] among his foes,
   And over heaps of slaughtered walk his way?   1530
MANOA. That were a joy presumptuous to be thought.
CHORUS. Yet God hath wrought things as incredible
   For his people of old; what hinders now?
MANOA. He can, I know, but doubt to think he will;
   Yet hope would fain subscribe, and tempts belief.   1535
   A little stay will bring some notice hither.
CHORUS. Of good or bad so great, of bad the sooner;
   For evil news rides post, while good news baits.[7]
   And to our wish I see one hither speeding—
   An Hebrew, as I guess, and of our tribe.   1540
MESSENGER.[8] O, whither shall I run, or which way fly
   The sight of this so horrid spectacle,
   Which erst[9] my eyes beheld, and yet behold?
   For dire imagination still pursues me.
   But providence or instinct of nature seems,   1545
   Or reason, though disturbed, and scarce consulted,
   To have guided me aright, I know not how,
   To thee first, reverend Manoa, and to these
   My countrymen, whom here I knew remaining,
   As[1] at some distance from the place of horror,   1550
   So in the sad event too much concerned.
MANOA. The accident was loud, and here before thee
   With rueful cry; yet what it was we hear not.
   No preface needs; thou seest we long to know.
MESSENGER. It would burst forth; but I recover breath,   1555
   And sense distract, to know well what I utter.
MANOA. Tell us the sum; the circumstance defer.
MESSENGER. Gaza yet stands; but all her sons are fallen,
   All in a moment overwhelmed and fallen.
MANOA. Sad, but thou know'st to Israelites not saddest,   1560
   The desolation of a hostile city.
MESSENGER. Feed on that first; there may in grief be surfeit.[2]
MANOA. Relate by whom.

---

6. Grief, pain, with perhaps a pun on "dole," that which is handed out.

7. Pauses to renew (bait) the horses.

8. Greek tragedy forbade the representation on stage of actual bloodshed; a messenger is therefore a frequent figure at the end of these plays, arriving posthaste from the scene of the final catastrophe, to deliver in a long set speech a descriptive report.

9. A moment ago.

1. The construction "as . . . so . . ." is equivalent to a "though . . . yet. . . ."

2. I.e., there may be all too much grief to follow.

MESSENGER.　　　　　By Samson.

MANOA.　　　　　　　　　　　That still lessens
The sorrow, and converts it nigh to joy.

MESSENGER. Ah! Manoa, I refrain too suddenly　　　　　　1565
To utter what will come at last too soon,
Lest evil tidings, with too rude irruption
Hitting thy agèd ear, should pierce too deep.

MANOA. Suspense in news is torture; speak them out.

MESSENGER. Then take the worst in brief: Samson is dead.　　1570

MANOA. The worst indeed! O, all my hope's defeated
To free him hence! but Death who sets all free
Hath paid his ransom now and full discharge.
What windy[3] joy this day had I conceived,
Hopeful of his delivery, which now proves　　　　　　1575
Abortive as the first-born bloom of spring
Nipped with the lagging rear of winter's frost!
Yet ere I give the reins to grief, say first
How died he; death to life is crown or shame.
All by him fell, thou say'st; by whom fell he?　　　　1580
What glorious hand gave Samson his death's wound?

MESSENGER. Unwounded of his enemies he fell.

MANOA. Wearied with slaughter, then, or how? Explain.

MESSENGER. By his own hands.

MANOA.　　　　　　　　Self-violence! What cause
Brought him so soon at variance with himself　　　　　1585
Among his foes?

MESSENGER.　　　Inevitable cause
At once both to destroy and be destroyed.
The edifice, where all were met to see him,
Upon their heads and on his own he pulled.

MANOA. O lastly over-strong against thyself!　　　　　1590
A dreadful way thou took'st to thy revenge.
More than enough we know; but while things yet
Are in confusion, give us, if thou canst,
Eyewitness of what first or last was done,
Relation more particular and distinct.　　　　　　1595

MESSENGER. Occasions drew me early to this city;
And as the gates I entered with sunrise,
The morning trumpets festival proclaimed
Through each high street. Little I had dispatched,
When all abroad was rumored that this day　　　　　1600
Samson should be brought forth, to show the people
Proof of his mighty strength in feats and games.
I sorrowed at his captive state, but minded
Not to be absent at that spectacle.
The building was a spacious theater,　　　　　　1605
Half round on two main pillars vaulted high,

---

3. Empty and talky.

With seats where all the lords, and each degree
Of sort,[4] might sit in order to behold;
The other side was open, where the throng
On banks and scaffolds under sky might stand:[5]   1610
I among these aloof obscurely stood.
The feast and noon grew high, and sacrifice
Had filled their hearts with mirth, high cheer, and wine,
When to their sports they turned. Immediately
Was Samson as a public servant brought,   1615
In their state livery clad: before him pipes
And timbrels;[6] on each side went armèd guards;
Both horse and foot before him and behind,
Archers and slingers, cataphracts[7] and spears.
At sight of him the people with a shout   1620
Rifted the air, clamoring their god with praise,
Who had made their dreadful enemy their thrall.
He, patient but undaunted, where they led him,
Came to the place; and what was set before him,
Which without help of eye might be essayed,   1625
To heave, pull, draw, or break, he still performed
All with incredible, stupendous force,
None daring to appear antagonist.
At length for intermission sake they led him
Between the pillars; he his guide requested   1630
(For so from such as nearer stood we heard),
As over-tired, to let him lean a while
With both his arms on those two massy pillars,
That to the archèd roof gave main support.
He unsuspicious led him; which when Samson   1635
Felt in his arms, with head a while inclined,
And eyes fast fixed he stood, as one who prayed,
Or some great matter in his mind revolved:
At last, with head erect, thus cried aloud:
"Hitherto, Lords, what your commands imposed   1640
I have performed, as reason was, obeying,
Not without wonder or delight beheld;
Now of my own accord such other trial
I mean to show you of my strength yet greater
As with amaze shall strike all who behold."   1645
This uttered, straining all his nerves,[8] he bowed;
As with the force of winds and waters pent
When mountains tremble,[9] those two massy pillars
With horrible convulsion to and fro

---

4. Of rank.
5. The temple at Gaza comprised a covered pavilion or shell for the gentry, semicircular in shape
and supported at the center of the semicircle by
two pillars; on the open side, under the hot sun,
and behind the stage, as it were, sat the common
people.

6. Tambourines.
7. Armored horsemen on armored horses.
8. Muscles.
9. Earthquakes in Milton's day were supposed to
be the effect of escaping winds and waters imprisoned (pent) beneath the earth.

He tugged, he shook, till down they came, and drew 1650
The whole roof after them with burst of thunder
Upon the heads of all who sat beneath,
Lords, ladies, captains, counselors, or priests,
Their choice nobility and flower, not only
Of this, but each Philistian city round, 1655
Met from all parts to solemnize this feast.
Samson, with these immixed, inevitably
Pulled down the same destruction on himself;
The vulgar[1] only 'scaped, who stood without.
CHORUS. O dearly bought revenge, yet glorious! 1660
  Living or dying thou hast fulfilled
  The work for which thou wast foretold
  To Israel, and now li'st victorious
  Among thy slain self-killed;
  Not willingly, but tangled in the fold 1665
  Of dire Necessity,[2] whose law in death conjoined
  Thee with thy slaughtered foes, in number more
  Than all thy life had slain before.
SEMICHORUS.[3] While their hearts were jocund and sublime,
  Drunk with idolatry, drunk with wine 1670
  And fat regorged[4] of bulls and goats,
  Chaunting their idol, and preferring
  Before our living Dread, who dwells
  In Silo, his bright sanctuary,[5]
  Among them he a spirit of frenzy sent, 1675
  Who hurt their minds,
  And urged them on with mad desire
  To call in haste for their destroyer.
  They, only set on sport and play,
  Unweetingly[6] importuned 1680
  Their own destruction to come speedy upon them.
  So fond are mortal men,
  Fallen into wrath divine,
  As their own ruin on themselves to invite,
  Insensate left, or to sense reprobate, 1685
  And with blindness internal[7] struck.
SEMICHORUS. But he, though blind of sight,
  Despised, and thought extinguished quite,
  With inward eyes illuminated,
  His fiery virtue roused 1690
  From under ashes into sudden flame,
  And as an evening dragon[8] came,

---

1. The common people.
2. Samson must not be supposed guilty of suicide. See above, lines 1586–87.
3. In classical theater a chorus was commonly split in two parts, their speeches to be recited alternately. "Jocund and sublime": joyous and exalted.
4. Greedily devoured.
5. Shiloh, where the Israelites established their tabernacle (Joshua 18.1).
6. Unwittingly.
7. The play accomplishes itself by showing the internal blindness of the Philistines at the very moment of Samson's spiritual illumination.
8. Serpent (from Latin, *draco*).

Assailant on the perchèd roosts
And nests in order ranged
Of tame villatic[9] fowl, but as an eagle   1695
His cloudless thunder bolted on their heads.
So Virtue, given for lost,[1]
Depressed and overthrown, as seemed,
Like that self-begotten bird,[2]
In the Arabian woods embossed,[3]   1700
That no second knows nor third,
And lay erewhile a holocaust,[4]
From out her ashy womb now teemed,
Revives, reflourishes, then vigorous most
When most unactive deemed;   1705
And, though her body die, her fame survives,
A secular[5] bird, ages of lives.

MANOA. Come, come; no time for lamentation now,
    Nor much more cause. Samson hath quit[6] himself
Like Samson, and heroicly hath finished   1710
A life heroic, on his enemies
Fully revenged; hath left them years of mourning
And lamentation to the sons of Caphtor[7]
Through all Philistian bounds; to Israel
Honor hath left and freedom, let but them   1715
Find courage to lay hold on this occasion;
To himself and father's house eternal fame;
And, which is best and happiest yet, all this
With God not parted from him, as was feared,
But favoring and assisting to the end.   1720
Nothing is here for tears, nothing to wail
Or knock the breast; no weakness, no contempt,
Dispraise, or blame; nothing but well and fair,
And what may quiet us in a death so noble.
Let us go find the body where it lies   1725
Soaked in his enemies' blood, and from the stream
With lavers[8] pure, and cleansing herbs, wash off
The clotted gore. I, with what speed the while[9]
(Gaza is not in plight to say us nay),
Will send for all my kindred, all my friends,   1730
To fetch him hence and solemnly attend,
With silent obsequy and funeral train,
Home to his father's house. There will I build him
A monument, and plant it round with shade

---

9. Farmyard (from Latin, *villaticus*). "Bolted": cast as a thunderbolt.
1. "Given up for lost."
2. The mythical phoenix begets itself out of its own ashes; it is unique, in that there is only one phoenix alive at any one time, and it lives in the scrubland of Arabia.
3. Enclosed, hidden.

4. A sacrifice burned whole on the altar.
5. Living through the centuries (Latin, *saecula*).
6. Acquitted.
7. In Amos 9.7 the Philistines are described as immigrants from Caphtor (perhaps Crete).
8. Basins.
9. I.e., with what speed (I may) in the meanwhile.

Of laurel ever green and branching palm,[1]   1735
With all his trophies hung, and acts enrolled
In copious legend, or sweet lyric song.
Thither shall all the valiant youth resort,
And from his memory inflame their breasts
To matchless valor and adventures high;   1740
The virgins also shall, on feastful days,
Visit his tomb with flowers, only bewailing
His lot unfortunate in nuptial choice,
From whence captivity and loss of eyes.

CHORUS.[2] All is best, though we oft doubt   1745
What th' unsearchable dispose[3]
Of Highest Wisdom brings about,
And ever best found in the close.
Oft he seems to hide his face,
But unexpectedly returns,   1750
And to his faithful champion hath in place[4]
Bore witness gloriously; whence Gaza mourns,
And all that band them to resist
His uncontrollable intent.
His servants he, with new acquist[5]   1755
Of true experience from this great event,
With peace and consolation hath dismissed,
And calm of mind, all passion spent.

1671

1. Leaves of laurel were worn by civic conquerors on triumphal occasions; wreaths of palm were given to victors in the Olympic games. Samson, as both an athletic victor in his *agon* and the savior of his people, gets both.

2. The final chorus of the play is cast in the rhyme pattern of a sonnet.

3. Appointment, disposition.

4. On this very spot, at this very instant.

5. Increase, acquisition.

Poetic Modes of the Early Seventeenth Century

More than most literary periods, the first half of the seventeenth century was rich in first-rate poets of the second order. The phrase means simply that they were writers of evident talent but limited scope; either they wrote few poems of any sort, or they struck the resounding chord only once. In the early seventeenth century they numbered as many as fifty or sixty, including some who in a less prolific age might have passed for major figures. Falling as they do in a period dominated by giants like Donne, Jonson, and Milton, these lesser voices are still of interest as they hit upon distinctive themes, develop further established forms, and point the way to styles which will establish themselves more fully in later periods.

Nobody is fully satisfied with the conventional division of early seventeenth-century poets between the "Metaphysicals" and the "Cavaliers," the followers of Donne and the "sons of Ben." On the surface of things, it contrasts a stylistic group with a political group; it corresponds to very little that the seventeenth-century poets thought about themselves; and in poets like Carew and Marvell—who neatly combine metaphysical wit with Jonsonian polish—the contrast comes a cropper altogether. Still, the distinction, though only a first approximation to truth, is not without value as a memory device, which is the chief function of most poetic "schools" and groupings.

If one regards them for the moment as alternatives, Jonson was an easier model to follow than Donne. A few powerful talents like Herbert, Crashaw, and Vaughan found the metaphysical vein really congenial; lesser talents like Cowley made heavy weather out of writing the "conceited" witty style without having the special temperament for it. On the other hand, Jonson's manner of poised, polished, yet "easy" statement developed naturally toward the airy songs of Herrick, Carew, and Suckling; then in Waller and Denham the Jonsonian manner moved toward a correct and formal style marked by two relatively new elements. One was the use of antithetical, balanced couplets, heavily end-stopped and often marked with strong caesural pauses. (After the Restoration stage adapted them for use in "heroic" plays—grandiloquent tragedies—they became, under the name of "heroic couplets," the predominant verse form of the late seventeenth and early eighteenth centuries. The other new element was a specialized, elevated, and often artificial diction, peculiar to verse: poetic diction, so called.

Not everyone picked up these mannerisms all at once; a solitary writer like Traherne was largely immune to changes in poetic fashion. But major poetic changes that nobody planned or even consciously recognized at the time did take place within ten years, either way, of the middle of the century. And in working out these changes the "minor" poets of England played a major role; through their work, small variations developed in a quiet way and cumulatively worked up toward a major alteration of the poetic climate.

HENRY KING
1592–1669

The son of a bishop, Henry King was an intimate of Donne, Jonson, and Izaak Walton. After attending Westminster School and Oxford University, he entered the church and rose without strain or difficulty from prebend to deacon to dean of Rochester, and in 1642 to the bishopric of Chichester. He survived the deprivations of the civil wars, and returned to enjoy his episcopal see for nine years after the Restoration. In 1617 he married Anne Berkeley, who died in 1624, and for whom he wrote *The Exequy*. It was printed anonymously, and without King's consent, with other poems of his, in 1657. Except for Milton's sonnet on his "late espoused saint," the seventeenth century produced no poem so direct and poignant in expressing the sentiments of a married lover for his wife.

The Exequy

Accept, thou shrine of my dead saint,
Instead of dirges, this complaint;
And for sweet flowers to crown thy hearse,
Receive a strew[1] of weeping verse
From thy grieved friend, whom thou might'st see   5
Quite melted into tears for thee.

Dear loss! since thy untimely fate
My task hath been to meditate
On thee, on thee; thou art the book,
The library whereon I look,   10
Though almost blind. For thee, loved clay,
I languish out, not live, the day,
Using no other exercise
But what I practice with mine eyes;
By which wet glasses I find out   15
How lazily time creeps about
To one that mourns: this, only this,
My exercise and business is.
So I compute the weary hours
With sighs dissolvèd into showers.   20

---

1. Scattering.

Nor wonder if my time go thus
Backward and most preposterous;[2]
Thou hast benighted me, thy set
This eve of blackness did beget,
Who wast my day, though overcast   25
Before thou hadst thy noontide passed;
And I remember must in tears,
Thou scarce hadst seen so many years
As day tells hours. By thy clear sun
My love and fortune first did run,   30
But thou wilt never more appear
Folded within my hemisphere,
Since both thy light and motion
Like a fled star is fallen and gone;
And 'twixt me and my soul's dear wish   35
An earth now interposèd is,
Which such a strange eclipse doth make
As ne'er was read in almanac.[3]

I could allow thee for a time
To darken me and my sad clime;   40
Were it a month, a year, or ten,
I would thy exile live till then,
And all that space my mirth adjourn,
So thou wouldst promise to return;
And putting off thy ashy shroud,   45
At length disperse this sorrow's cloud.

But woe is me! the longest date
Too narrow is to calculate
These empty hopes; never shall I
Be so much blest as to descry   50
A glimpse of thee, till that day come
Which shall the earth to cinders doom,
And a fierce fever must calcine[4]
The body of this world—like thine,
My little world! That fit of fire   55
Once off, our bodies shall aspire
To our souls' bliss; then we shall rise
And view ourselves with clearer eyes
In that calm region where no night
Can hide us from each other's sight.   60

Meantime, thou hast her, earth: much good
May my harm[5] do thee. Since it stood

---

2. "Preposterous": from the Latin, literally "hind
side first." "Set": setting, death.
3. The earth, which covers her body and so inter-
venes between her and her husband, is like an
eclipse.
4. Burn down to dust.
5. I.e., this event which harms me so much.
"Stood": agreed.

With heaven's will I might not call
Her longer mine, I give thee all
My short-lived right and interest   65
In her whom living I loved best;
With a most free and bounteous grief
I give thee what I could not keep.
Be kind to her, and prithee look
Thou write into thy doomsday book   70
Each parcel of this rarity
Which in thy casket shrined doth lie.
See that thou make thy reckoning straight,
And yield her back again by weight;
For thou must audit on thy trust   75
Each grain and atom of this dust,
As thou wilt answer Him that lent,
Not gave thee, my dear monument.

So close the ground, and 'bout her shade
Black curtains draw; my bride is laid.   80

Sleep on, my love, in thy cold bed,
Never to be disquieted!
My last good-night! Thou wilt not wake
Till I thy fate shall overtake;
Till age, or grief, or sickness must   85
Marry my body to that dust
It so much loves; and fill the room
My heart keeps empty in thy tomb.
Stay for me there; I will not fail
To meet thee in that hollow vale.   90
And think not much of my delay;
I am already on the way,
And follow thee with all the speed
Desire can make, or sorrows breed.
Each minute is a short degree,   95
And every hour a step towards thee.
At night when I betake to rest,
Next morn I rise nearer my west
Of life, almost by eight hours' sail,
Than when sleep breathed his drowsy gale.   100

Thus from the sun my bottom[6] steers,
And my day's compass downward bears;
Nor labor I to stem the tide
Through which to thee I swiftly glide.

6. Vessel.

'Tis true, with shame and grief I yield,   105
Thou like the van first took'st the field,
And gotten hast the victory
In thus adventuring to die
Before me, whose more years might crave
A just precedence in the grave.   110
But hark! my pulse like a soft drum
Beats my approach, tells thee I come;
And slow howe'er my marches be,
I shall at last sit down by thee.

The thought of this bids me go on,   115
And wait my dissolution
With hope and comfort. Dear (forgive
The crime), I am content to live
Divided, with but half a heart,
Till we shall meet and never part.   120

ca. 1624   1657

THOMAS CAREW
1595–1640

Thomas Carew (pronounced *Carey*) made a point of seeming idle, flippant, and careless; his "profession" as a decorative hanger-on of the Stuart courts made this an easy disguise to adopt. In fact he was one of the most painstaking poetic craftsmen of his age; though he did not produce a great mass of poetry, the care and thought he lavished on each piece were proverbial. For example, his one masque, *Coelum Britannicum* (1634), though full of contemporary jokes and witty allusions, draws for much of its substance on an important work by the subtle sixteenth-century Italian philosopher Giordano Bruno.

Again, much of Carew's poetry was sexually explicit far beyond the norms of his age, and his reputation was that of a libertine; yet he also took time to translate nine of the Psalms, and created what the serious-minded of his age particularly admired, a devout and edifying death-bed scene.

Most interesting of Carew's achievements, from a modern point of view, is his gift for phrasing in verse acute and forceful criticisms of his contemporaries. Formal criticism was in its infancy during the early seventeenth century; commendatory, complimentary, and elegiac poems—of which the greatest is Carew's on the death of Doctor Donne—provide some of our best evidence concerning the literary values of the age.

An Elegy upon the Death of the Dean of Paul's, Dr. John Donne[1]

Can we not force from widowed poetry,
Now thou art dead, great Donne, one elegy
To crown thy hearse? Why yet dare we not trust,
Though with unkneaded dough-baked prose, thy dust,
Such as the unscissored[2] churchman from the flower   5
Of fading rhetoric, short-lived as his hour,
Dry as the sand that measures it,[3] should lay
Upon thy ashes on the funeral day?
Have we no voice, no tune? Didst thou dispense
Through all our language both the words and sense?   10
'Tis a sad truth. The pulpit may her plain
And sober Christian precepts still retain;
Doctrines it may, and wholesome uses, frame,
Grave homilies and lectures; but the flame
Of thy brave soul, that shot such heat and light   15
As burnt our earth and made our darkness bright,
Committed holy rapes upon our will,
Did through the eye the melting heart distill,
And the deep knowledge of dark truths so teach
As sense might judge what fancy could not reach,[4]   20
Must be desired forever. So the fire
That fills with spirit and heat the Delphic choir,[5]
Which, kindled first by thy Promethean[6] breath,
Glowed here a while, lies quenched now in thy death.
The Muses' garden, with pedantic weeds   25
O'erspread, was purged by thee; the lazy seeds
Of servile imitation thrown away,
And fresh invention planted; thou didst pay
The debts of our penurious bankrupt age—
Licentious thefts, that make poetic rage   30
A mimic fury, when our souls must be
Possessed or with Anacreon's ecstasy,
Or Pindar's,[7] not their own. The subtle cheat
Of sly exchanges, and the juggling feat
Of two-edged words,[8] or whatsoever wrong   35

1. First appearing with a number of other elegies in the 1633 edition of Donne's poems, then reprinted in 1640 with some softening changes, Carew's tribute is notable among 17th-century poems on poetry for its effort at technical precision. Our text is from 1633.
2. I.e., with uncut hair. Whether from grief, poverty, or in imitation of Apollo is not clear.
3. The hourglass was used by preachers to keep track of time.
4. I.e., so that things too abstract and elevated even to be imagined might be made plain to sense. "Desired": missed.

5. The choir of poets, inspired by Apollo, whose oracle used to be at Delphi.
6. Donne stole fire from heaven, like Prometheus, and used it to fill with spirit and heat the choir of poets.
7. Anacreon (6th and 5th centuries B.C.) and Pindar (first half of the 5th century B.C.) were famous Greek lyric poets.
8. "Sly exchanges": Carew seems to refer to the habit, frequent in Jonsonian and Miltonic style, of using English words in their Latin senses, e.g., "horrid (bristling) spears." "Two-edged words" might be puns; but as these were a favorite device of

By ours was done the Greek or Latin tongue,
Thou hast redeemed, and opened us a mine
Of rich and pregnant fancy, drawn a line
Of masculine expression, which had good
Old Orpheus[9] seen, or all the ancient brood   40
Our superstitious fools admire, and hold
Their lead more precious than thy burnished gold,
Thou hadst been their exchequer, and no more
They in each other's dust had raked for ore.
Thou shalt yield no precedence but of time   45
And the blind fate of language, whose tuned chime
More charms the outward sense; yet thou mayest claim
From so great disadvantage greater fame,
Since to the awe of thy imperious wit
Our stubborn language bends, made only fit   50
With her tough thick-ribbed hoops to gird about
Thy giant fancy, which had proved too stout
For their soft melting phrases. As in time
They had the start, so did they cull the prime
Buds of invention many a hundred year,   55
And left the rifled fields, besides the fear
To touch their harvest; yet from those bare lands
Of what is purely thine, thy only hands
(And that thy smallest work) have gleanèd more
Than all those times and tongues could reap before.   60
    But thou art gone, and thy strict laws will be
Too hard for libertines in poetry.
They will repeal[1] the goodly exiled train
Of gods and goddesses, which in thy just reign
Were banished nobler poems; now with these   65
The silenced tales o' th' *Metamorphoses*[2]
Shall stuff their lines and swell the windy page,
Till verse, refined by thee in this last age,
Turn ballad-rhyme, or those old idols be
Adored again with new apostasy.   70
    O pardon me, that break with untuned verse
The reverend silence that attends thy hearse,
Whose awful[3] solemn murmurs were to thee,
More than these faint lines, a loud elegy,
That did proclaim in a dumb eloquence   75
The death of all of the arts, whose influence,
Grown feeble, in these panting numbers lies
Gasping short-winded accents, and so dies:
So doth the swiftly turning wheel not stand

Donne's, this cannot be the sense. Perhaps "two-edged words" are not far from "sly exchanges" in meaning.
9. Ancient Greek poet and prophet, so mythical that he is often used as the type of all poets.
1. Recall, as from banishment.

2. Ovid's tales in the *Metamorphoses* had been a favorite stockpile of poetical properties for Renaissance poets; Donne forwent them, but soon they will return.
3. I.e., awesome.

In th' instant we withdraw the moving hand,   80
But some small time maintain a faint weak course
By virtue of the first impulsive force;
And so whilst I cast on thy funeral pile
Thy crown of bays,[4] oh, let it crack awhile
And spit disdain, till the devouring flashes   85
Suck all the moisture up; then turn to ashes.
   I will not draw the envy to engross
All thy perfections, or weep all our loss;
Those are too numerous for an elegy,
And this too great to be expressed by me.   90
Though every pen should take a distinct part,
Yet art thou theme enough to tire[5] all art.
Let others carve the rest; it shall suffice
I on thy tomb this epitaph incise:

   Here lies a king, that ruled as he thought fit   95
   The universal monarchy of wit;
   Here lie two flamens,[6] and both those the best:
   Apollo's[7] first, at last the true God's priest.

1633, 1640

To Ben Jonson

Upon occasion of his Ode of Defiance annexed to his play of The New Inn[1]

'Tis true, dear Ben, thy just chastising hand
Hath fixed upon the sotted age a brand
To their swoll'n pride and empty scribbling due.
It can nor judge nor write; and yet 'tis true
Thy comic Muse from the exalted line   5
Touched by thy *Alchemist*[2] doth since decline
From that her zenith, and foretells a red
And blushing evening when she goes to bed—
Yet such as shall outshine the glimmering light
With which all stars shall gild the following night.   10
Nor think it much (since all thy eaglets may
Endure the sunny trial)[3] if we say,

---

4. The poet's crown.
5. Exhaust. This line and the preceding one were omitted in the 1640 edition.
6. Priests of the Roman religion.
7. I.e., of the god of poetry.
1. Jonson's late play *The New Inn* was hissed from the stage in 1629 and published in 1631 with an angry *Ode to Himself* prefixed (above, p. 1229).

Carew's remonstration must have been written close upon that event.
2. Jonson's play (1610) about three confidence tricksters.
3. To make sure the young birds in his nest are genuine eaglets, the eagle is reputed to fly with them up toward the sun; any bird that isn't an authentic eagle is blinded by the rays.

This hath the stronger wing, or that doth shine
Tricked up in fairer plumes, since all are thine.
Who hath his flock of cackling geese compared   15
With thy tuned choir of swans? or who hath dared
To call thy births deformed? But if thou bind
By city-custom, or by gavel-kind,[4]
In equal shares thy love to all thy race,
We may distinguish of their sex and place: 20
Though one hand shape them and though one brain strike
Souls into all, they are not all alike.
Why should the follies then of this dull age
Draw from thy pen such an immodest rage
As seems to blast thy else-immortal bays,[5]   25
When thine own tongue proclaims thy itch of praise?
Such thirst will argue drought. No, let be hurled
Upon thy works by the detracting world
What malice can suggest; let the rout say
The running sands that, ere thou make a play,   30
Count the slow minutes might a Goodwin frame[6]
To swallow when th' hast done thy shipwrecked name.
Let them the dear[7] expense of oil upbraid,
Sucked by thy watchful lamp that hath betrayed
To theft the blood of martyred authors, spilt   35
Into thy ink, while thou growest pale with guilt.[8]
Repine not at the taper's thrifty waste,
That sleeks thy terser poems; nor is haste
Praise, but excuse; and if thou overcome
A knotty writer, bring the booty home;   40
Nor think it theft if the rich spoils so torn
From conquered authors be as trophies worn.
Let others glut on the extorted praise
Of vulgar breath: trust thou to after days.
Thy labored works shall live when Time devours   45
Th' abortive offspring of their hasty hours.
Thou art not of their rank, the quarrel lies
Within thine own verge[9]—then let this suffice,
The wiser world doth greater thee confess
Than all men else, than thy self only less.   50

ca. 1631   1640

---

4. "City-custom" (i.e., London city custom) and
"gavel-kind" (a system of land tenure once common in Kent) were two legal ways of dividing an
estate equally among all the heirs—as opposed to
the normal English rule of primogeniture (everything to the eldest son).
5. Bays or laurel make up the poet's crown.
6. Goodwin Sands were a sandbar, shifty and
treacherous, on which many ships were lost. Jon-

son's slowness in composition was proverbial.
7. Extravagant.
8. The other great charge against Jonson was that
he copied or translated too liberally from other
authors.
9. I.e., within your own territory, against yourself. Duels cannot properly take place between two
men of different rank, and as Jonson is out of
everyone else's class, he can only fight himself.

Song (Persuasions to Enjoy)

If the quick spirits in your eye
Now languish, and anon must die;
If every sweet and every grace
Must fly from that forsaken face,
    Then, Celia, let us reap our joys   5
    E'er time such goodly fruit destroys.

Or if that golden fleece must grow
For ever, free from agèd snow,
If those bright suns must know no shade,
Nor your fresh beauties ever fade,   10
Then fear not, Celia, to bestow
What still being gathered, still must grow.
    Thus, either Time his sickle brings
    In vain, or else in vain his wings.

1640

A Song[1]

Ask me no more where Jove bestows,
When June is past, the fading rose;
For in your beauties orient deep,
These flowers, as in their causes, sleep.[2]

Ask me no more whither do stray   5
The golden atoms of the day;
For in pure love heaven did prepare
Those powders to enrich your hair.

Ask me no more whither doth haste
The nightingale when May is past;   10
For in your sweet dividing[3] throat
She winters, and keeps warm her note.

Ask me no more where those stars light,
That downwards fall in dead of night;
For in your eyes they sit, and there   15
Fixèd become, as in their sphere.

---

1. Widely popular, and several times set to music, this poem exists in a variety of different forms.
2. Aristotelian philosophy suggested that objects often lay latent in their causes—e.g., that in the seed creating man there was a little man (*homun-culus*). In Carew's compliment, the lady is a summation of last summer and cause of the next one.
3. Harmonious (from the "division," or rapid melodic passage).

Ask me no more if east or west
The phoenix builds her spicy nest;[4]
For unto you at last she flies,
And in your fragrant bosom dies.   20

1640

A Rapture

I will enjoy thee now, my Celia, come
And fly with me to love's Elysium.[1]
The giant, Honor, that keeps cowards out,
Is but a masquer,[2] and the servile rout
Of baser subjects only bend in vain   5
To the vast idol, whilst the nobler train
Of valiant lovers daily sail between
The huge Colossus' legs,[3] and pass unseen
Unto the blissful shore. Be bold and wise,
And we shall enter; the grim Swiss[4] denies   10
Only tame fools a passage, that not know
He is but form and only frights in show
The duller eyes that look from far; draw near,
And thou shalt scorn what we were wont to fear.
We shall see how the stalking pageant[5] goes   15
With borrowed legs, a heavy load to those
That made and bear him—not as we once thought
The seed of gods, but a weak model wrought
By greedy men, that seek to enclose the common,
And within private arms empale free woman.[6]   20
    Come then, and mounted on the wings of love,
We'll cut the flitting air and soar above
The monster's head, and in the noblest seats
Of those blessed shades, quench and renew our heats.
There shall the Queens of Love and Innocence,   25
Beauty, and Nature banish all offense
From our close ivy twines, there I'll behold
Thy barèd snow and thy unbraided gold.
There my enfranchised hand on every side
Shall o'er thy naked polished ivory slide.   30
No curtain there, though of transparent lawn,[7]

---

4. The phoenix, an Arabian bird, builds her nest
from spicy shrubs. She dies every 500 years and a
new bird springs from her ashes.
1. In classical mythology, the abode of the blessed
spirits.
2. I.e., a play actor. "Rout": crowd.
3. The ancient Colossus of Rhodes bestrode the
entrance to that harbor, so that ships entering or
leaving passed between its legs. Or so legend has

it.
4. The Pope's Swiss Guard were so picturesque
that the adjective came in time to stand for the
noun.
5. Figure in a pageant, make-believe giant.
6. To "empale" is to surround with a fence, but
the word has phallic overtones as well.
7. Fine linen.

Shall be before thy virgin treasure drawn,
But the rich mine to the enquiring eye
Exposed, shall ready still for mintage lie,
And we will coin young Cupids.[8] There a bed   35
Of roses and fresh myrtles shall be spread
Under the cooler shade of cypress groves;
Our pillows, of the down of Venus' doves,[9]
Whereon our panting limbs we'll gently lay
In the faint respites of our active play,   40
That so our slumbers may in dreams have leisure
To tell the nimble fancy our past pleasure,
And so our souls that cannot be embraced
Shall the embraces of our bodies taste.
Meanwhile the bubbling stream shall court the shore,   45
Th' enamored chirping wood-choir shall adore
In varied tunes the Deity of Love;
The gentle blasts of western winds shall move
The trembling leaves, and through their close boughs breathe
Still music, while we rest ourselves beneath   50
Their dancing shade; till a soft murmur, sent
From souls entranced in amorous languishment
Rouse us, and shoot into our veins fresh fire
Till we in their sweet ecstasy expire.
    Then, as the empty bee, that lately bore   55
Into the common treasure all her store,
Flies 'bout the painted field with nimble wing,
Deflowering the fresh virgins of the spring,
So will I rifle all the sweets that dwell
In my delicious paradise, and swell   60
My bag with honey, drawn forth by the power
Of fervent kisses from each spicy flower.
I'll seize the rosebuds in their perfumed bed,
The violet knots, like curious mazes spread
O'er all the garden, taste the ripened cherry,   65
The warm, firm apple, tipped with coral berry.
Then will I visit with a wandering kiss
The vale of lilies and the bower of bliss,
And where the beauteous region both divide
Into two milky ways, my lips shall slide   70
Down those smooth alleys, wearing as I go
A track for lovers on the printed snow.
Thence climbing o'er the swelling Apennine,
Retire into thy grove of eglantine,
Where I will all those ravished sweets distill   75
Through love's alembic,[1] and with chemic skill

---

8. Behind this metaphor of mine-mint-and-coin lies the ancient belief that in the creation of children woman contributes matter, man form (*materia* and *forma*).

9. Venus, when she travels, rides in a chariot drawn by a yoke of doves.

1. I.e., retort—a vessel used for distilling.

From the mixed mass one sovereign balm[2] derive,
Then bring that great elixir to thy hive.
    Now in more subtle wreaths I will entwine
My sinewy thighs, my legs and arms with thine;   80
Thou like a sea of milk shalt lie displayed,
Whilst I the smooth, calm Ocèan invade
With such a tempest as when Jove of old
Fell down on Danaë in a storm of gold.[3]
Yet my tall pine shall in the Cyprian strait   85
Ride safe at anchor and unlade her freight;
My rudder with thy bold hand like a tried
And skillful pilot thou shalt steer, and guide
My bark[4] into love's channel, where it shall
Dance as the bounding waves do rise or fall.   90
Then shall thy circling arms embrace and clip
My naked body, and thy balmy lip
Bathe me in juice of kisses, whose perfume
Like a religious incense shall consume
And send up holy vapors to those powers   95
That bless our loves and crown our sportful hours,
That with such halcyon calmness fix our souls
In steadfast peace, as no affright controls.
There no rude sounds shake us with sudden starts,
No jealous ears, when we unrip our hearts,   100
Suck our discourse in, no observing spies
This blush, that glance traduce; no envious eyes
Watch our close meetings, nor are we betrayed
To rivals by the bribèd chambermaid.
No wedlock bonds unwreathe our twisted loves,   105
We seek no midnight arbor, no dark groves
To hide our kisses; there the hated name
Of husband, wife, lust, modest, chaste, or shame
Are vain and empty words, whose very sound
Was never heard in the Elysian ground.   110
All things are lawful there that may delight
Nature or unrestrainèd appetite.
Like and enjoy, to will and act is one;
We only sin when love's rites are not done.
    The Roman Lucrece there reads the divine   115
Lectures of love's great master, Aretine,
And knows as well as Laïs how to move
Her pliant body in the act of love.[5]

---

2. According to alchemical doctrine, skilled distillation could extract from common metals not only the philosopher's stone but a supreme ointment ("sovereign balm"), good to prevent as well as to cure all diseases whatever.
3. In ancient mythology Zeus (or Jove) wooed Danaë in a shower of gold, thereby begetting Perseus. "Pine": mast, and by metonymy, ship; "Cyprian": Cyprus was reputed the birthplace of the goddess of love, sometimes called simply "the Cyprian."
4. Vessel.
5. In Elysium, Lucrece (chastest of Roman matrons, who committed suicide to atone for the disgrace of her rape by Tarquin), reads Aretino (bawdiest of Italian pornographers) to provoke her attacker to new efforts. Laïs was a famous prostitute of Corinth.

To quench the burning ravisher, she hurls
Her limbs into a thousand winding curls,   120
And studies artful postures, such as be
Carved on the bark of every neighboring tree
By learnèd hands, that so adorned the rind
Of those fair plants, which, as they lay entwined
Have fanned their glowing fires. The Grecian dame   125
That in her endless web toiled for a name
As fruitless as her work doth there display
Herself before the youth of Ithaca,
And th' amorous sport of gamesome nights prefer
Before dull dreams of the lost traveler.[6]   130
Daphne hath broke her bark, and that swift foot
Which th' angry gods had fastened with a root
To the fixed earth, doth now unfettered run
To meet th' embraces of the youthful sun.[7]
She hangs upon him like his Delphic lyre,[8]   135
Her kisses blow the old and breathe new fire;
Full of her god, she sings inspired lays,
Sweet odes of love, such as deserve the bays
Which she herself was.[9] Next her, Laura lies
In Petrarch's learnèd arms, drying those eyes   140
That did in such sweet smooth-paced numbers flow,
As made the world enamored of his woe.[1]
These and ten thousand beauties more, that died
Slave to the tyrant,[2] now enlarged, deride
His canceled laws, and for their time misspent   145
Pay into love's exchequer double rent.
    Come then, my Celia, we'll no more forbear
To taste our joys, struck with a panic fear,
But will depose from his imperious sway
This proud usurper and walk free as they,   150
With necks unyoked; nor is it just that he
Should fetter your soft sex with chastity,
Which Nature made unapt for abstinence;
When yet this false impostor can dispense
With human justice and with sacred right,   155
And maugre[3] both their laws, command me fight
With rivals or with emulous loves, that dare
Equal with thine their mistress' eyes or hair.

6. Penelope was the faithful wife of Odysseus ("the lost traveler"); during the 20 years he was away (at Troy, and on the way back), she fended off her importunate suitors by weaving an endless web—she unwove by night what she wove by day—which she said she had to finish before she could marry again. But in Elysium, she welcomes "the youth of Ithaca" (the suitors) and enjoys "gamesome nights" with them.
7. Closely pursued by Apollo, god of poetry and the sun, Daphne with the help of Zeus turned into a laurel bush or bay tree to get away from him.

8. The shrine of Apollo was at Delphi; he carries a lyre as an emblem of poetic harmony.
9. The songs she sings deserve the crown of poetry, woven of laurel or bays; but she herself was a laurel or bay tree.
1. Whether Laura was a real lady or a laurel bush (hence an emblem of poetry) is still in dispute; but Petrarch (1304–74) wrote melancholy poems to and about her, and she was a martyr to honor.
2. The tyrant is Honor; the inhabitants of Elysium are "enlarged" (i.e., liberated) from him.
3. In spite of.

If thou complain of wrong, and call my sword
To carve out thy revenge, upon that word   160
He[4] bids me fight and kill, or else he brands
With marks of infamy my coward hands.
And yet religion bids from bloodshed fly,
And damns me for that act. Then tell me why
This goblin Honor which the world adores   165
Should make men atheists and not women whores.[5]

                                                                    1640

4. I.e., Honor.
5. These last two and a half lines of the poem cast some curious reflections on the first 164.

SIR JOHN SUCKLING
1609–1642

"Natural, easy Suckling," says Millamant rapturously, in Congreve's comedy, *The Way of the World*; he is her ideal of a poet, one who does not take the whole business very seriously. "Brisk" was the adjective that his contemporaries generally applied to Sir John. He was a small man physically, a wit, a gamester, and a courtier, who when he turned to poetry imitated and exaggerated the informal, colloquial qualities of Donne. Many years before, Baldassare Castiglione in his dialogue *The Courtier* (1528) had emphasized a certain fine carelessness (*sprezzatura*) as the natural quality of a great gentleman. It meant that no matter how hard one had worked on some accomplishment—a poem, a costume, swordsmanship—one should treat it always as if it were a natural, easy, spontaneous action. Sir John Suckling, above all the other "Cavalier" poets who gallantly supported the lost cause of Charles Stuart, cultivated this special quality of instinctive, careless poise. Sometimes, indeed, like a Restoration fop, he seems so careful about being careless that the substance of his discourse goes by the board. But his gay trifles have remained current in the language as some others have not; he is the prototype of the Cavalier playboy.

Song[1]

Why so pale and wan, fond lover?
    Prithee, why so pale?
Will, when looking well can't move her,
    Looking ill prevail? ·
    Prithee, why so pale?   5

Why so dull and mute, young sinner?
    Prithee, why so mute?

1. This song was first printed in Suckling's play *Aglaura* (1638).

Will, when speaking well can't win her,
    Saying nothing do 't?
    Prithee, why so mute?   10

Quit, quit, for shame; this will not move,
    This cannot take her.
If of herself she will not love,
    Nothing can make her:
    The devil take her!   15

                                      1638

Loving and Beloved

There never yet was honest man
    That ever drove the trade of love.
It is impossible, nor can
    Integrity our ends promove;[1]
For kings and lovers are alike in this,   5
That their chief art in reign dissembling is.

Here we are loved and there we love:
    Good nature now and passion strive
Which of the two should be above
    And laws unto the other give.   10
So we false fire with art sometimes discover,
And the true fire with the same art do cover.

What rack[2] can fancy find so high?
    Here we must court and here engage,
    Though in the other place we die.   15
    O! 'tis torture all and cozenage:
And which the harder is I cannot tell,
To hide true love, or make false love look well.

Since it is thus, god of desire,
    Give me my honesty again,   20
And take thy brands back and thy fire;
    I'm weary of the state I'm in:
Since (if the very best should now befall)
Love's triumph must be Honor's funeral.

                                      1646

---

1. Promote, move forward.
2. Torture. The question is, what torture can be   worse than being obliged to one woman while lov-
    ing another?

Out upon It!

Out upon it! I have loved
    Three whole days together;
And am like to love three more,
    If it prove fair weather.

Time shall molt away his wings,   5
    Ere he shall discover
In the whole wide world again
    Such a constant lover.

But the spite on 't is, no praise
    Is due at all to me: 10
Love with me had made no stays
    Had it any been but she.

Had it any been but she,
    And that very face,[1]
There had been at least ere this   15
    A dozen dozen in her place.

1656, 1659

1. Other versions of the poem give the line as "that very very face."

RICHARD LOVELACE
1618–1657

Richard Lovelace and Sir John Suckling are commonly bracketed together as the leaders of the "Cavalier" poets; and though they were quite different, both as men and as writers, there is no injustice in the conjunction. Both men fought and suffered for the king; both wrote gallant verses. Perhaps one feels a little more substance in the work of Lovelace; but perhaps that is simply because he was lucky enough to live a little longer. He is best known for his poems of clarion resolution:

> Stone walls do not a prison make,
>   Nor iron bars a cage,

but he is also an affectionate observer of, and gentle moralizer upon, the little creatures—snails, ants, grasshoppers.

    Lovelace was born of an old and wealthy Kentish family, and educated at Oxford; he was an attractive, handsome, and witty young man, the very model of a courtier. King Charles and Queen Henrietta Maria admired his demeanor so much when they visited Oxford in 1636, that they had him created M.A. on the spot. But the civil wars were hard on him; he fought bravely, was imprisoned, exiled, wounded while serving as a soldier of fortune abroad, imprisoned again in England, and finally released, penniless and unemployed. His death followed after a decade of penury and squalor. Lovelace published *Lucasta* in 1649, and a posthumous volume appeared in 1659, with his remaining writings. A special point of interest about Lovelace is that he was one of the few English writers of the seventeenth century to be seriously concerned with the art of painting and the appreciation of good pictures, to which he thought his countrymen disgracefully blind.

To Lucasta, Going to the Wars

Tell me not, sweet, I am unkind
    That from the nunnery
Of thy chaste breast and quiet mind,
    To war and arms I fly.

True, a new mistress now I chase,   5
    The first foe in the field;
And with a stronger faith embrace
    A sword, a horse, a shield.

Yet this inconstancy is such
    As you too shall adore;   10
I could not love thee, dear, so much,
    Loved I not honor more.

                    1649

To Althea, from Prison

When Love with unconfinèd wings
    Hovers within my gates,
And my divine Althea brings
    To whisper at the grates;
When I lie tangled in her hair   5
    And fettered to her eye,
The gods[1] that wanton in the air
    Know no such liberty.

When flowing cups run swiftly round,
    With no allaying Thames,[2]   10
Our careless heads with roses bound,
    Our hearts with loyal flames;
When thirsty grief in wine we steep,

---

1. Some versions read "birds" instead of "gods."   2. No mixture of water in the wine.

When healths and draughts go free,
Fishes that tipple in the deep   15
  Know no such liberty.

When, like committed linnets,[3] I
  With shriller throat shall sing
The sweetness, mercy, majesty,
  And glories of my King;   20
When I shall voice aloud how good
  He is, how great should be,
Enlargèd winds, that curl the flood,
  Know no such liberty.

Stone walls do not a prison make,   25
  Nor iron bars a cage;
Minds innocent and quiet take
  That for an hermitage.
If I have freedom in my love,
  And in my soul am free,   30
Angels alone, that soar above,
  Enjoy such liberty.

1649

The Grasshopper

To My Noble Friend, Mr. Charles Cotton[1]

Oh, thou that swing'st upon the waving hair
  Of some well-fillèd oaten beard,
Drunk every night with a delicious tear
  Dropped thee from heav'n, where now th' art reared,

The joys of earth and air are thine entire,   5
  That with thy feet and wings dost hop and fly;
And when thy poppy[2] works thou dost retire
  To thy carved acorn bed to lie.

Up with the day, the sun thou welcom'st then,
  Sport'st in the gilt-plats[3] of his beams,   10
And all these merry days mak'st merry men,
  Thyself, and melancholy streams.[4]

3. Caged finches.
1. Lovelace's friend Charles Cotton, scholar, man
of letters, and father of Montaigne's translator, may
have appeared to the poet an industrious and prudent ant, compared with himself, the melodious
and improvident grasshopper. The circumstances
of the poem are evidently those of the interreg-

num, when a winter of Puritanism seemed to be
settling over all civilized feeling in England.
2. Opiate, sleeping potion.
3. Golden meadows.
4. The three objects of "mak'st merry" are "men,"
"thyself," and "melancholy streams."

But ah, the sickle! golden ears are cropped,
    Ceres and Bacchus[5] bid goodnight;
Sharp frosty fingers all your flow'rs have topped,   15
    And what scythes spared, winds shave off quite.

Poor verdant fool! and now green ice! thy joys
    Large and as lasting as thy perch of grass,
Bid us lay in 'gainst winter rain, and poise[6]
    Their floods with an o'erflowing glass.   20

Thou best of men and friends! we will create
    A genuine summer in each other's breast;
And spite of this cold time and frozen fate
    Thaw us a warm seat to our rest.

Our sacred hearths shall burn eternally   25
    As vestal flames;[7] the North Wind, he
Shall strike his frost-stretched wings, dissolve, and fly
    This Etna in epitome.[8]

Dropping December shall come weeping in,
    Bewail th' usurping of his reign;   30
But when in showers of old Greek[9] we begin,
    Shall cry, he hath his crown again!

Night as clear Hesper[1] shall our tapers whip
    From the light casements where we play,
And the dark hag from her black mantle strip,   35
    And stick there everlasting day.

Thus richer than untempted kings are we,
    That asking nothing, nothing need:
Though lord of all that seas embrace, yet he
    That wants himself is poor indeed.   40

                                              1649

Love Made in the First Age. To Chloris

        In the nativity of time,
        Chloris, it was not thought a crime
        In direct Hebrew for to woo.[1]

---

5. The grain and the grape.
6. Counter.
7. The vestal virgins, in Rome, were responsible
for tending an eternal flame.
8. Boreas, the north wind, "striking" (i.e., folding
up) his wings, flees from the underground warmth
of Etna, an emblem of the flame of friendship.
9. Greek wine was especially favored in the classical world; drinkers, in classical times, often wore

festive crowns at their carousals; and December
"crowns," i.e., terminates, the year.
1. The tapers are compared to Hesperus, the
morning star, which whips night from the sky.
Hecate, the dark hag, was sometimes described as
the daughter of Night.
1. Hebrew, supposed to be the original language
of mankind, reads "backwards" in our terms, i.e.,
from right to left.

Now we make love as all on fire,
Ring retrograde[2] our loud desire,
   And court in English backward too.

Thrice happy was that golden age,
When compliment was construed rage,[3]
   And fine words in the center hid;
When cursèd *No* stained no maid's bliss,
And all discourse was summed in *Yes*,
   And nought forbade, but to forbid.

Love then unstinted, love did sip,
And cherries plucked fresh from the lip,
   On cheeks and roses free he fed;
Lasses like autumn plums did drop,
And lads indifferently[4] did crop
   A flower and a maidenhead.

Then unconfinèd each did tipple
Wine from the bunch, milk from the nipple;
   Paps tractable as udders were;
Then equally the wholesome jellies
Were squeezed from olive trees and bellies,
   Nor suits of trespass did they fear.

A fragrant bank of strawberries,
Diapered[5] with violet's eyes
   Was table, tablecloth, and fare;
No palace to the clouds did swell,
Each humble princess then did dwell
   In the piazza[6] of her hair.

Both broken faith and th' cause of it,
All-damning gold, was damned to th' pit;
   Their troth, sealed with a clasp and kiss,
Lasted until that extreme day
In which they smiled their souls away,
   And, in each other, breathed new bliss.

Because no fault, there was no tear;
No groan did grate the granting ear;
   No false foul breath their del'cate smell:
No serpent kiss poisoned the taste,
Each touch was naturally chaste,
   And their mere sense a miracle.

2. "Retrograde" is a word with special musical connotations; Lovelace may have in mind a pattern of bell-ringing.
3. Passion. Every compliment in the golden age was understood as an ardent proposition; there was no hypocrisy.
4. Without preference; but also, languidly.
5. Dappled, decorated (in the pattern of diaper cloth).
6. Shadowy porch.

Naked as their own innocence,
And unembroidered[7] from offense
   They went, above poor riches, gay;   45
On softer than the cygnet's down,
In beds they tumbled of their own;
   For each within the other lay.

Thus did they live; thus did they love,
Repeating only joys above;   50
   And angels were, but with clothes on,
Which they would put off cheerfully,
To bathe them in the galaxy,
   Then gird them with the heavenly zone.[8]

Now, Chloris, miserably crave[9]   55
The offered bliss you would not have,
   Which evermore I must deny,
Whilst ravished with these noble dreams
And crownèd with mine own soft beams,[1]
   Enjoying of my self I lie.   60

1659

7. I.e., without the stiff gold braid of rank or authority.
8. Bathing in the Milky Way, belted with the zodiac.
9. Do without.
1. Perhaps moonbeams, in ridicule of this over-idealized image of primitive life.

EDMUND WALLER
1606–1687

Edmund Waller was born to money, and through his long life got steadily richer; he went to Parliament very early, was expelled during the civil wars, but came back after, and stayed there till he was a very old man. In politics he was a moderate Royalist, but without the strength of character or intellect to play a leading role in public affairs.

In poetry too, Waller was a moderating and softening influence. His verses, first published in 1645 while he was in exile, then republished and expanded several times, enjoyed an enormous popularity which nowadays we find hard to explain. At first glance they seem mostly remarkable for their negative qualities. A poem like *The Story of Phoebus and Daphne Applied* is not ingenious or strained in its thinking, but it is not "natural" either—on the contrary, it is highly artificial. Its diction is formal, almost mannered. Its couplets are metrically smooth, frequently end-stopped, and full of balanced antitheses; the caesura is used artfully from time to time to break up the roll of the pentameters, and balance one half-line against another. The poem has "point" in the sense that one word or locution constantly works against another; occasionally it rises to a kind of verbal "counter-point." Waller was one of the first Englishmen to write this way. Though his style drew a little from Donne and a lot from Jonson, though in his lighter lyric moments he sounds a good deal like Carew, he really was a pioneer. And thus the Restoration poets were quite right when they honored old Mr. Waller as one of the chief "improvers of our numbers"—by which they meant that he had brought a new correctness to English metrics and diction. Perhaps Waller had less intellectual energy to be mastered than did earlier poets; but the degree and manner of his mastery were in themselves widely influential.

The Story of Phoebus and Daphne Applied[1]

Thyrsis, a youth of the inspirèd train,
Fair Sacharissa loved, but loved in vain;[2]
Like Phoebus sung the no less amorous boy;
Like Daphne she, as lovely and as coy.
With numbers[3] he the flying nymph pursues,   5
With numbers such as Phoebus' self might use.
Such is the chase when love and fancy leads
O'er craggy mountains and through flowery meads,[4]
Invoked to testify the lover's care
Or form some image of his cruel fair.   10
Urged with his fury, like a wounded deer,
O'er these he fled; and now approaching near,
Had reached the nymph with his harmonious lay,
Whom all his charms could not incline to stay.
Yet what he sung in his immortal strain,   15
Though unsuccessful, was not sung in vain.
All but the nymph that should redress his wrong
Attend his passion and approve his song.
Like Phoebus thus, acquiring unsought praise,
He catched at love, and filled his arms with bays.   20

1645

Song

Go, lovely rose!
Tell her that wastes her time and me
That now she knows,

1. Phoebus (Apollo, god of poetry) fell in love with Daphne, and pursued her till in answer to her prayers she was turned into a laurel tree; the laurel, or bay tree, is, accordingly, an emblem of poetic fame, and successful poets are crowned with laurel leaves ("bays").
2. Since Sacharissa is the constant name of Waller's beloved, it is a fair presumption that Thyrsis is

himself. "A youth of the inspirèd train" is poetic diction for a poet, as "cruel fair," below, is for a mistress. The boy is "no less amorous" than Phoebus, the girl just as "coy" (unwilling) as Daphne.
3. Poetic diction for verses.
4. Meadows. The craggy mountains represent the lover's griefs, the flowery meadows (by neat antithesis) his mistress' beauty.

When I resemble[1] her to thee,
How sweet and fair she seems to be.   5

   Tell her that's young,
And shuns to have her graces spied,
   That hadst thou sprung
In deserts, where no men abide,
Thou must have uncommended died.   10

   Small is the worth
Of beauty from the light retired;
   Bid her come forth,
Suffer herself to be desired,
And not blush so to be admired.   15

   Then die! that she
The common fate of all things rare
   May read in thee;
How small a part of time they share
That are so wondrous sweet and fair!   20

1645

On a Girdle[1]

   That which her slender waist confined,
Shall now my joyful temples bind;
No monarch but would give his crown,
His arms might do what this has done.

   It was my heaven's extremest sphere,[2]   5
The pale[3] which held that lovely deer;
My joy, my grief, my hope, my love
Did all within this circle move!

   A narrow compass! and yet there
Dwelt all that's good, and all that's fair;   10
Give me but what this ribbon bound,
Take all the rest the sun goes round!

1645, 1664

---

1. Compare.
1. Belt or sash.
2. The last of the concentric crystalline spheres which, according to Ptolemaic astronomy, made

up the universe. Hence, the lady's outermost garment.
3. Fence encircling a park. There is, of course, a pun on "dear" in this line.

Of English Verse[1]

Poets may boast, as safely vain,
Their work shall with the world remain;
Both bound together live or die,
The verses and the prophecy.

But who can hope his lines should long   5
Last in a daily changing tongue?
While they are new, envy prevails,
And as that dies, our language fails.

When architects have done their part,
The matter may betray their art;   10
Time, if we use ill-chosen stone,
Soon brings a well-built palace down.

Poets that lasting marble seek
Must carve in Latin or in Greek;
We write in sand, our language grows,   15
And like the tide our work o'erflows.

Chaucer his sense can only boast,
The glory of his numbers[2] lost!
Years have defaced his matchless strain;
And yet he did not sing in vain.   20

The beauties which adorned that age,
The shining subjects of his rage,[3]
Hoping they should immortal prove,
Rewarded with success his love.

This was the generous poet's scope,   25
And all an English pen can hope,
To make the fair approve his flame
That can so far extend their name.

Verse thus designed has no ill fate
If it arrive but at the date   30

---

1. To understand Waller's deprecatory attitude toward English poetry, we must recall that in his day modern English was very new, and was still acquiring new words, forms, and usages at a rapid pace. We write in sand, he says, the tide of language rises, and overflows our work. In those days it was true.
2. Metrics, versification. The belief that Chau-

cer's versification was hopelessly obsolete led to such ventures as Dryden's "translation" of some of his *Canterbury Tales* into modern (i.e., 17th-century) English.
3. Poetic fury, inspiration. As it calls attention to its own artifice, the word "rage" is a piece of poetic diction.

> Of fading beauty, if it prove
> But as long-lived as present love.

1668

SIR JOHN DENHAM
1615–1669

Along with Edmund Waller, Sir John Denham was widely credited with developing during the interregnum the poetic mode that would be popular under the Restoration and in the early eighteenth century. One striking feature of the new mode is the use of balanced and antithetical closed couplets, such as those in which Denham compares the majestic Thames with the sort of verse he would like to write:

> Oh could I flow like thee, and make thy stream
> My great example, as it is my theme!
> Though deep, yet clear, though gentle, yet not dull,
> Strong without rage, without o'erflowing full.

Dryden first singled out these lines of *Cooper's Hill* for praise; generations of poets for the best part of a century to come tried to emulate their polished, pendulum-like versification. (Some were all too successful; the very best metronome does not produce real music.) Apart from its contribution to the developing "heroic couplet," Denham's masterpiece also set the example for an important new genre, the descriptive poetic meditation. From his father, Denham had inherited an estate near the Thames, not far from Windsor Castle; his poem is an account of what one can see from a hill near his house of Egham, and of the reflections inspired in the poet by the details of that view. These reflections constitute the major novelty of the poem; they are sententious and discursive, quite unlike anything found in earlier descriptive poems like Jonson's *To Penshurst*. On the other hand, they are basically historical and political—not inward and personal, like those in various descendants of *Cooper's Hill* written during the Romantic period. Thus Denham's poem occupies a crucial central position in the history of the genre.

Though he developed his one great poem slowly and methodically over a period of nearly thirty years, Denham was not really a quiet, meditative man. From early youth he was a compulsive gambler and all-round rake. During the civil wars he fought (though ineffectually) for the king; and after the Restoration he suffered attacks of periodic insanity—scandal said, because his young and beautiful second wife had been taken as a mistress by the duke of York. None of this personal history can be found in his poem, which celebrates, in stately, leisured verses, the ample charms of the Thames valley and the equally measured tread of the poet's reflective mind.

From Cooper's Hill

[*Chertsey Abbey and the Thames*]

Here should my wonder dwell, and here my praise;[1]
But my fixed thoughts my wandering eye betrays,
Viewing a neighboring hill, whose top of late
A chapel crowned, till in the common fate
The adjoining abbey fell (may no such storm   115
Fall on our times, where ruin must reform).[2]
Tell me, my muse, what monstrous dire offense,
What crime, could any Christian king incense
To such a rage? Was 't luxury or lust?
Was he so temperate, so chaste, so just?   120
Were these their crimes? They were his own much more;
But wealth is crime enough to him that's poor—
Who, having spent the treasures of his crown,
Condemns their luxury to feed his own.
And yet this act, to varnish o'er the shame   125
Of sacrilege, must bear devotion's name.
No crime so bold but would be understood[3]
A real, or at least a seeming good.
Who fears not to do ill, yet fears the name,
And, free from conscience, is a slave to fame.   130
Thus he the church at once protects and spoils;[4]
But princes' swords are sharper than their styles.
And thus to the ages past he makes amends,
Their charity destroys, their faith defends.
Then did religion in a lazy cell   135
In empty, airy contemplations dwell,
And like the block, unmovèd, lay; but ours,
As much too active, like the stork devours.[5]
Is there no temperate region can be known
Between their frigid and our torrid zone?   140
Could we not wake from that lethargic dream
But to be restless in a worse extreme?
And for that lethargy was there no cure
But to be cast into a calenture?[6]

1. Denham's poem has begun by contemplating Windsor Castle, where Edward III founded the knightly order of the Garter, but his attention is distracted (line 112) by the ruins of Chertsey Abbey, dismantled by order of Henry VIII.
  Early versions of the poem, starting in 1642, are notably different from that which was printed in Denham's final volume, *Poems and Translations* (1668). The variants are too many and too extensive to present here; we follow 1668.
2. Parallels between the reformers (Puritans) of Denham's day and those of the early 16th century are prominent in the poet's mind; almost he seems to regret the Reformation, when, to be reformed, the English church had nearly to be ruined.
3. Presented as.
4. Henry still bore the papal title of Defender of the Faith when in later years he became the despoiler of the church.
5. In Aesop's fable, the frogs were dissatisfied with King Log, who did nothing, till they replaced him with King Stork, who gobbled them all up.
6. Tropical fever.

Can knowledge have no bound, but must advance   145
So far, to make us wish for ignorance?
And rather in the dark to grope our way
Than, led by a false guide, to err by day?
   Who sees these dismal heaps but would demand
What barbarous invader sacked the land?   150
But when he hears no Goth, no Turk did bring
This desolation, but a Christian king;
When nothing but the name of zeal appears
'Twixt our best actions and the worst of theirs;
What does he think our sacrilege would spare,   155
When such the effects of our devotions are?
   Parting from thence 'twixt anger, shame, and fear,
Those for what's past and this for what's too near,[7]
My eye, descending from the hill, surveys
Where Thames amongst the wanton valleys strays.   160
Thames, the most loved of all the ocean's sons
By his old sire, to his embraces runs,
Hasting to pay his tribute to the sea
Like mortal life to meet eternity.
Though with those streams he no resemblance hold   165
Whose foam is amber and their gravel gold,[8]
His genuine and less guilty wealth t' explore,
Search not his bottom, but survey his shore,
O'er which he kindly spreads his spacious wing,
And hatches plenty for th' ensuing spring.   170
Nor then destroys it with too fond a stay,
Like mothers which their infants overlay;
Nor with a sudden and impetuous wave,
Like profuse kings, resumes the wealth he gave.
No unexpected inundations spoil   175
The mower's hopes, nor mock the plowman's toil;
But God-like his unwearied bounty flows;
First loves to do, then loves the good he does.
Nor are his blessings to his banks confined,
But free and common as the sea or wind;   180
When he to boast or to disperse his stores,
Full of the tributes of his grateful shores,
Visits the world, and in his flying towers[9]
Brings home to us, and makes the Indies ours;
Finds wealth where 'tis, bestows it where it wants,   185
Cities in deserts, woods in cities plants;
So that to us no thing, no place is strange,
While his fair bosom is the world's exchange.
Oh could I flow like thee, and make thy stream
My great example, as it is my theme!   190

7. Anger and shame for Henry's depredations, fear
for those of Cromwell and his partisans.
8. Several rivers in the Baltic region, and one in
Sicily, were rich in amber; the Tagus was supposed to flow through Portugal on golden sands.
9. Tall ships.

Though deep, yet clear, though gentle, yet not dull,
Strong without rage, without o'erflowing full.

1642, 1668

ABRAHAM COWLEY
1618–1667

Abraham Cowley (pronounced *Cooley*) was ten years younger than Milton, and for a time outshone the greater man by publishing his first volume of verses in 1633, aged just fifteen. Aided by his "correct" (Royalist) political views and a style modeled on Donne's but not so challenging, Cowley maintained a popular literary reputation throughout his life. But the publication of his *Works*, the year after his death, was like the planting of a tombstone; his reputation declined precipitously, and before long Pope could ask, "Who now reads Cowley?" in full assurance that his readers would automatically answer, "Nobody." Yet Cowley was an interesting man, if not a great writer; his *Ode: Of Wit*, though a curiosity, is an interesting poem both for its form and for what it tries to say.

Ben Jonson, in his splendid *Ode to Cary and Morison* (above, p. 1220), gave to England for the first time an equivalent to the Great Ode of Greece's supreme lyric artist, Pindar. Cowley admired Pindar just as ardently as Jonson did, but understood him very differently; the *Pindaric Odes*, of which Cowley published a first installment in 1656, aimed to be irregular, abrupt, and exalted—many readers found them incomprehensible. The *Ode: Of Wit*, however, is more subdued than the average of Cowley's odes; though its subject is the very mainspring of literary energy (as the seventeenth century understood it), the poem is regular in form and judicious in content. In these respects, it is much closer to the Lesser or Horatian Ode than to the Pindaric.

Cowley's poem deals with an elusive yet vital quality of mind, which the seventeenth century referred to repeatedly and in a great variety of contexts—but which only Cowley (who liked to call himself "the Muses' Hannibal") was bold enough to approach directly and analytically. Over the years, "wit," as a word of general appreciation, had acquired dozens of different, and not always congruent, applications. It was used to mean all of the following: genius, wisdom, learning, skill at discovering unexpected comparisons and metaphors, quickness of repartee, imagination, a style of point and antithesis, the power of invention, and any form of verbal cleverness, including puns and smart sexual innuendos. In actual usage, "wit" was a good many of the things that Cowley's ode says it is *not*. So his attempt at a definition must be set down as an ambitious and interesting failure. As a matter of fact, Samuel Johnson, discussing the poem in 1779, showed himself still somewhat bemused by the definition, when he said that in Cowley's day, "*Wit*, which had been till then used for *Intellection*, in contradistinction to *Will*, took the meaning, whatever it be, which it now bears."

Ode: Of Wit

Tell me, O tell, what kind of thing is Wit,
    Thou who master art of it.[1]
For the First Matter loves variety less;
Less women love 't,[2] either in love or dress.
    A thousand different shapes it bears,   5
    Comely in thousand shapes appears.
Yonder we saw it plain; and here 'tis now,
Like spirits in a place, we know not how.

London, that vents of false ware so much store,
    In no ware deceives us more.   10
For men, led by the color and the shape,
Like Zeuxis' birds, fly to the painted grape;[3]
    Some things do through our judgment pass
    As through a multiplying glass,
And sometimes, if the object be too far,   15
We take a falling meteor for a star.

Hence 'tis, a Wit, that greatest word of fame,
    Grows such a common name;
And wits by our creation they become
Just so as tit'lar bishops made at Rome.[4]   20
    'Tis not a tale, 'tis not a jest
    Admired with laughter at a feast,
Nor florid talk which can that title gain;
The proofs of Wit forever must remain.

'Tis not to force some lifeless verses meet   25
    With their five gouty feet.
All everywhere, like man's, must be the soul,[5]
And reason the inferior powers control.
    Such were the numbers which could call
    The stones into the Theban wall.[6]   30
Such miracles are ceased, and now we see
No towns or houses raised by poetry.

Yet 'tis not to adorn and gild each part;
    That shows more cost than art.
Jewels at nose and lips but ill appear;   35

1. The person to whom the poem was addressed is unknown. By "the First Matter" Cowley means the basic material of the universe, given a multiplicity of shapes by the Deity.
2. I.e., women love variety less than wit does.
3. Zeuxis, a Greek painter of the 5th century B.C., reportedly painted grapes so realistic that birds came to peck at them.
4. Certain churches in Rome have as their titular incumbents cardinals whose real duties are elsewhere; so men are often called "wits" by courtesy.
5. An old formula from Plotinus, of which Cowley seems to voice an echo here, has it that the soul is all in all, and all in every part.
6. When Amphion and Zethus were fortifying Thebes, Amphion's performance on the lyre was so moving that the stones rose into place of their own accord.

Rather than all things Wit, let none be there.
  Several lights will not be seen,
  If there be nothing else between.
Men doubt because they stand so thick i' th' sky
If those be stars which paint the galaxy.   40

'Tis not when two like words make up one noise,
  Jests for Dutch men and English boys,[7]
In which who finds out Wit, the same may see
In an'grams and acrostics, poetry.[8]
  Much less can that have any place   45
  At which a virgin hides her face.
Such dross the fire must purge away; 'tis just
The author blush there where the reader must.

'Tis not such lines as almost crack the stage
  When Bajazet begins to rage;[9]   50
Nor a tall met'phor in the bombast way,
Nor the dry chips of short-lunged Seneca.[1]
  Nor upon all things to obtrude
  And force some odd similitude.
What is it then, which like the power divine   55
We only can by negatives define?

In a true piece of Wit all things must be,
  Yet all things there agree,
As in the ark, joined without force or strife,
All creatures dwelt: all creatures that had life;   60
  Or as the primitive forms of all
  (If we compare great things with small)
Which without discord or confusion lie
In that strange mirror of the Deity.[2]

But love, that molds one man up out of two,   65
  Makes me forget and injure you.
I took you for myself, sure, when I thought
That you in anything were to be taught.
  Correct my error with thy pen,
  And if any ask me then   70
What thing right Wit and height of genius is,
I'll only show your lines, and say, *'Tis this.*

                        1656, 1668

---

7. Scorn for a pun mingles with contempt for the Dutch.
8. Anagrams and acrostics never stood very high in critical theory; Cowley here anticipates their rejection as "false wit," in a famous essay by Joseph Addison 50 years later.
9. Bajazet was a grandiloquent character in Mar-lowe's *Tamburlaine.*
1. The "Senecan" style tended toward short, epigrammatic statements.
2. As in line 3 above, Cowley posits a kind of first matter ("that strange mirror of the Deity") which contains potentially all the objects of the world, until they are made actual by the word of God.

THOMAS TRAHERNE
1637–1674

Though the short, obscure life of Thomas Traherne fell squarely in the
middle of the seventeenth century, this retiring clergyman did not become
known as an English author till the first years of the twentieth century, when
a manuscript volume of his poems and prose meditations fell into the hands
of a perceptive bookseller, who published it. Another volume followed within
a few years, other works came to light since, and are still doing so; and
Traherne took his place among the English poets. Though it is sometimes
uneven, there is a freshness and visionary innocence in Traherne's work at
its best that might not have proved uncongenial to the mind of William
Blake, had Traherne's writing been discovered a hundred years earlier.

Wonder

How like an angel came I down!
   How bright are all things here!
When first among his works I did appear,
   O how their glory me did crown!
The world resembled his eternity,   5
     In which my soul did walk,
   And everything that I did see
     Did with me talk.

The skies in their magnificence,
     The lively, lovely air;   10
O how divine, how soft, how sweet, how fair!
   The stars did entertain my sense,
And all the works of God so bright and pure,
     So rich and great did seem,
   As if they ever must endure,   15
     In my esteem.

A native health and innocence
     Within my bones did grow,
And while my God did all his glories show,
   I felt a vigor in my sense   20
That was all Spirit. I within did flow
     With seas of life like wine;
   I nothing in the world did know
     But 'twas divine.

Harsh ragged objects were concealed,   25
   Oppression's tears and cries,

Sins, griefs, complaints, dissensions, weeping eyes,
　　Were hid; and only things revealed
Which heavenly spirits and the angels prize.
　　　The state of innocence   30
　　And bliss, not trades and poverties,
　　　　Did fill my sense.

　　The streets were paved with golden stones,
　　　The boys and girls were mine,
O how did all their lovely faces shine!   35
　　The sons of men were holy ones.
Joy, beauty, welfare did appear to me
　　　And everything which here I found
　　While like an angel I did see,
　　　　Adorned the ground.   40

　　Rich diamond and pearl and gold
　　　In every place was seen;
Rare splendors, yellow, blue, red, white, and green,
　　Mine eyes did everywhere behold.
Great wonders clothed with glory did appear,   45
　　　Amazement was my bliss.
　　That and my wealth was everywhere:
　　　　No joy to this!¹

　　Cursed and devised proprieties,²
　　　With envy, avarice,   50
And fraud, those fiends that spoil even paradise,
　　Fled from the splendor of mine eyes.
And so did hedges, ditches, limits, bounds,
　　　I dreamed not aught of those,
　　But wandered over all men's grounds,   55
　　　　And found repose.

　　Proprieties themselves were mine,
　　　And hedges ornaments;
Walls, boxes, coffers, and their rich contents
　　Did not divide my joys, but shine.   60
Clothes, ribbons, jewels, laces, I esteemed
　　　My joys by others worn;
　　For me they all to wear them seemed
　　　　When I was born.

1903

---

1. Compared to this.
2. Properties. It is not simply private property, but

more importantly the individual self from which
Traherne in his vision has escaped.

On Leaping over the Moon

I saw new worlds beneath the water lie,
  New people, and another sky
    And sun, which seen by day
    Might things more clear display.
      Just such another   5
      Of late my brother[1]
Did in his travel see, and saw by night,
  A much more strange and wondrous sight;
Nor could the world exhibit such another
  So great a sight, but in a brother.   10

Adventure strange! no such in story we
  New or old, true or feignèd see.
    On earth he seemed to move,
    Yet heaven went above;
      Up in the skies   15
      His body flies,
In open, visible, yet magic sort:
  As he along the way did sport,
Like Icarus over the flood he soars
  Without the help of wings or oars.   20

As he went tripping o'er the king's highway,
  A little pearly river lay
    O'er which, without a wing
    Or oar, he dared to swim,
      Swim through the air   25
      On body fair;
He would not use nor trust Icarian wings[2]
  Lest they should prove deceitful things;
For had he fallen, it had been wondrous high,
  Not from, but from above, the sky.   30

He might have dropped through that thin element
  Into a fathomless descent
    Unto the nether sky
    That did beneath him lie
      And there might tell   35
      What wonders dwell
On earth above. Yet bold he briskly runs,
  And soon the danger overcomes,
Who, as he leapt, with joy related soon
  How happy he o'erleaped the moon.   40

1. Traherne's brother Philip.
2. The waxen wings of Icarus melted in the sun and dropped him fatally into the sea.

What wondrous things upon the earth are done
   Beneath and yet above the sun!
     Deeds all appear again
     In higher spheres; remain
      In clouds as yet: 45
      But there they get
Another light, and in another way
   Themselves to us above display.
The skies themselves this earthly globe surround;
   We're even here within them found.   50

On heavenly ground within the skies we walk,
   And in this middle center talk:
     Did we but wisely move
     On earth in heaven above,
      We then should be   55
      Exalted high
Above the sky: from whence whoever falls,
   Through a long dismal precipice,
Sinks to the deep abyss where Satan crawls,
   Where horrid Death and Dèspair lies.   60

As much as others thought themselves to lie
   Beneath the moon, so much more high
     Himself he thought to fly
     Above the starry sky,
      As that he spied   65
      Below the tide.
Thus did he yield me in the shady night
   A wondrous and instructive light,
Which taught me that under our feet there is,
   As o'er our heads, a place of bliss.   70

1910

Prose of the Early Seventeenth Century

The history of English prose up to the end of the sixteenth century is by no means simple, but it can be written and has been written. One can trace across the decades a fairly clear-cut contrast between courtly or learned, and homely or vulgar styles. Sidney's *Arcadia* is a disciplined example of the ornate courtly style, which in lesser hands tended to verbal extravagance or display; the Puritan polemicist who called himself Martin Marprelate wrote in the vulgar style at its raciest and most vigorous, but this was also the idiom for popular entertainers like Nashe, Deloney, and Dekker. A style which looks forward to modern English at its best—dignified, unmannered, fluent, and consecutive—first makes its presence felt in Richard Hooker's massive polemic *Of the Laws of Ecclesiastical Polity* (above, pp. 1034–1044). Hooker is so much respected because he is both majestic and colloquial, learned and direct, strong and gentle. He is specially adept at balancing concessions and subordinate qualifications against the massive tree-trunk of his assertion; the impression he gives of seeing completely around his subject is the reason why he was known from the beginning as "judicious Mr. Hooker."

But in the wake of Hooker's great achievement, English started to take more different intermediate forms than can be practically arranged in an historical narrative. Especially prominent were an assortment of plain and direct styles modeled on the writing of the Roman philosopher Seneca. This sort of prose uses short, irregular phrases, connected logically but not grammatically; it makes little effort at subordination, balance, or smoothness. Rather, a central idea is stated, often in the form of an adage or apothegm; separate aspects of it are then explored in separate clauses; and the sentence as a whole is sometimes known, picturesquely, as an "exploded period," because secondary thoughts are, as it were, exploded out of the primary one. Modern scholars distinguish two varieties of Senecan style, the curt and the loose, while confessing that most writers used a mixture of both. Francis Bacon, for example, employs the curt style primarily in his *Essays*; Robert Burton generally uses the loose style, though he is fond of sprinkling his page with proverbial sayings and nuggets of wisdom from the philosophers. Burton brings us very close to the plain prose of common folk, who had no conscious ideas of prose style at all, and would have been astonished (like Monsieur Jourdain in Molière's play *The Bourgeois Gentleman*) to learn they had been speaking prose all their lives without knowing it. Homely or even vulgar English could of course be deliberately adopted or imitated; since the Middle Ages, there had been a tradition of popular preaching which used the idiom of the tribe to bring spiritual light into the lives of earnest, unsophisticated folk. Puritans were particularly given to such direct, strong discourse; generations of preachers, famous in their day and forgotten in ours, labored in this way to instill godly zeal in their hearers.

On the other hand, when it was directed to a dignified or erudite audience, a good deal of prose both ecclesiastical and secular took on the devices of rhetorical ornament. As a rule, such prose was not formally balanced, but nervous, irregular, and energetic, as if the writer's next words sprang directly out of his last ones. Bold imagery and complex verbal artifice were hallmarks of the manner. In public rhetoric the master of this style was Donne; he had many followers, of whom Jeremy Taylor distinguished himself by adapting the epic simile to pulpit rhetoric. (For epic similes, see the section on Poetic Forms, below). Taylor's "so have I seen" comparisons, though admired at the time, are of interest nowadays chiefly as showing the taste of his day for highly adorned prose. "Witty" writing was much admired, in prose as in verse. "Characters," a popular genre in the early century, amounted to prose portraits, often sarcastic, of a particular human type; and for such writing the curt, epigrammatic Senecan style was appropriate. Thomas Fuller even carried the witty style into such sad and serious subjects as the church history of Britain. On the other hand, the wit of Sir Thomas Browne is subdued to his meditative and inward manner of thought; he uses, accordingly, a conglomerate style that resembles only remotely that of any of his predecessors. One can identify its various ingredients, but the mixture is distinctive, individual.

And this is one trend traceable through the prose styles of the early seventeenth century: they are increasingly individual. Writers have started, as we say, to have "styles of their own." Yet, paradoxically, the outcome of extreme stylistic diversity was a general increase in stylistic simplicity. In the battles of propaganda that accompanied the civil war, extravagant opinions on a thousand different topics got expressed in an amazing variety of ways; but in the struggle to appeal to a mass audience, one variety or other of plain style generally proved most persuasive. Repeatedly common sense was called on to adjudicate controversies in which private inspiration was helpless. Gradually, the clarity, simplicity, and "naturalness" of an idea became accepted as good evidence of its truth, rather than the contrary. And English prose style, though still as various as that of Dryden compared with that of Bunyan, began to move (in the pulpit, as well as among gentlemen of taste) toward that ideal of smooth, taut simplicity that marks the best work of Swift.

FRANCIS BACON
1561–1626

1597: First edition of the *Essays* (augmented and revised editions in 1612 and 1625).
1605: *The Advancement of Learning.*
1620: *Novum Organum.*
1621: Bacon's disgrace and retirement.

Francis Bacon, the younger son of a highly placed Elizabethan civil servant, studied law at Cambridge and Gray's Inn, entered the legal bureaucracy of

Elizabeth, and rose steadily through it until, under James, he stood at the head of his profession, as lord chancellor of England. But after barely three years in this office, he fell from power and reputation, accused of taking bribes in office and confessing himself guilty of corruption and neglect. The last five years of his life were spent in retirement.

Bacon's only predecessor in the field of the essay was Michel de Montaigne (1533–1592), the French country squire who wrote so volubly, intimately, charmingly—and at such immense length—about himself. Concentration on self was not for Montaigne simply a matter of egotistic display; he thought himself a fair specimen of the whole human race, and proposed that we can learn a good deal about mankind in general by stripping a single example morally as well as physically naked. But Bacon when he set out to write essays had no intention of imitating his unbuttoned predecessor. As a man with a judicial position to maintain, he was not out to discover himself or explore unknown thoughts. His training in law and his reading in the Roman moralists had given him the habit of thinking in axioms; and axioms of prudent, practical conduct were what he wrote. Not only a lawyer but a judge, he laid down the law like a magistrate or a Dutch uncle, and largely concealed his "self"—at least in the way Montaigne defined "self"—under the official robes of worldly wisdom.

Bacon's reticence—not to say inhibition—when writing personal essays contrasts strikingly with the sweep and boldness of his directly philosophical work. Here the importance of his rhetorical persuasiveness is almost impossible to overstate. He was not himself much of a practical scientist, and anyone who tries can comb from his works an amazing collection of superstitious and unfounded beliefs. But his vision of intellectual method was wide if not very deep, and its emphasis on verifiable experiment held immense promise for the future. In fact, simple emphasis on "experience" and "experiment" (the former word was sometimes used where we would employ the latter) was not a novel principle when Bacon put it forth. A man like Paracelsus, the Swiss alchemist of the sixteenth century, had insisted on following his own experience against the authority of the great Galen and other doctors of classical antiquity. That was why Paracelsus and his alchemical followers were called "empirics." But their observations were uncontrolled. They noted the effects of what they called occult sympathies (for example, the peculiar affinity of the sunflower for the sun), and generalized from that single observation by analogy. Bacon recommended controlled and repeated experiments, in which theory worked to direct and focus experience, and in which all experiments were coordinated with one another. And this vision, as most memorably outlined in *The New Atlantis*, represented the ideal of the future. If anything, the great chancellor did not give enough weight to the concept of a controlling hypothesis. A modern scientist, and even a few of Bacon's predecessors, would give more, restricting the role of experiment to that of proof or disproof. But in most other respects, Bacon was well ahead of most thinkers of his day.

Yet, before anything could be built out of scientific hypothesis and verification, a major work of demolition had to be accomplished. The obstacle was the mass of things men already knew, under the name of "science," that weren't so. Bacon first attacked these errors and their causes in *The Advancement of Learning* (1605), and later in the *Novum Organum* or "New Instrument of Knowledge" (1620), under the heading of "idols," or false notions that possess the mind.

From ESSAYS[1]

Of Truth

"What is truth?" said jesting Pilate; and would not stay for an answer.[2] Certainly there be that delight in giddiness,[3] and count it a bondage to fix a belief; affecting free will in thinking, as well as in acting. And though the sects of philosophers of that kind[4] be gone, yet there remain certain discoursing wits, which are of the same veins, though there be not so much blood in them as was in those of the ancients. But it is not only the difficulty and labor which men take in finding out of truth; nor again, that when it is found, it imposeth upon[5] men's thoughts, that doth bring lies in favor; but a natural though corrupt love of the lie itself. One of the later school of the Grecians examineth the matter, and is at a stand to think what should be in it, that men should love lies, where neither they make for pleasure, as with poets, nor for advantage, as with the merchant, but for the lie's sake. But I cannot tell:[6] this same truth is a naked and open daylight, that doth not show the masks and mummeries and triumphs of the world half so stately and daintily as candle lights. Truth may perhaps come to the price of a pearl, that showeth best by day, but it will not rise to the price of a diamond or carbuncle,[7] that showeth best in varied lights. A mixture of a lie doth ever add pleasure. Doth any man doubt that if there were taken out of men's minds vain opinions, flattering hopes, false valuations, imaginations as one would, and the like, but it would leave the minds of a number of men poor shrunken things, full of melancholy and indisposition, and unpleasing to themselves? One of the fathers, in great severity, called poesy *vinum daemonum*,[8] because it filleth the imagination, and yet it is but with the shadow of a lie. But it is not the lie that passeth through the mind, but the lie that sinketh in, and settleth in it, that doth the hurt, such as we spake of before. But howsoever these things are thus in men's depraved judgments and affections, yet truth, which only doth judge itself, teacheth that the inquiry of truth, which is the love-making or wooing of it, the knowledge of truth, which is the presence of it, and the belief of truth, which is the enjoying of it, is the sovereign good of human nature. The first creature[9] of God, in the works of the days, was the light of the sense; the last was the light of reason; and his sabbath work ever since is the illumination of his Spirit. First he breathed light upon the face of the matter, or chaos; then he breathed light into the face of man; and still he breatheth and inspireth light into the face of his chosen. The

---

1. With one exception (below, p. 1680), texts are from the 1625 edition.

2. See John 18.38 for Pilate's idle query to Jesus.

3. Changeability, insecurity of ideas. "That": those who.

4. The Greek Skeptics, who taught the uncertainty of all knowledge. "Discoursing wits": discursive minds.

5. Restricts, limits.

6. "I cannot tell," says Bacon, and tells.

7. Ruby.

8. The wine of devils; St. Augustine is probably being cited.

9. Creation.

poet that beautified the sect that was otherwise inferior to the rest[1] saith yet excellently well: "It is a pleasure to stand upon the shore, and to see ships tossed upon the sea: a pleasure to stand in the window of a castle, and to see a battle, and the adventures thereof below: but no pleasure is comparable to the standing upon the vantage ground of truth" (a hill not to be commanded,[2] and where the air is always clear and serene), "and to see the errors, and wanderings, and mists, and tempests, in the vale below": so always that this prospect[3] be with pity, and not with swelling or pride. Certainly, it is heaven upon earth to have a man's mind move in charity, rest in providence, and turn upon the poles of truth.

To pass from theological and philosophical truth to the truth of civil business; it will be acknowledged even by those that practice it not, that clear and round dealing[4] is the honor of man's nature, and that mixture of falsehood is like alloy in coin of gold and silver, which may make the metal work the better, but it embaseth[5] it. For these winding and crooked courses are the goings of the serpent; which goeth basely upon the belly, and not upon the feet. There is no vice that doth so cover a man with shame as to be found false and perfidious. And therefore Montaigne saith prettily, when he inquired the reason why the word of the lie should be such a disgrace, and such an odious charge, saith he, "If it be well weighed, to say that a man lieth is as much to say as that he is brave towards God and a coward towards men."[6] For a lie faces God, and shrinks from man. Surely the wickedness of falsehood and breach of faith cannot possibly be so highly expressed, as in that it shall be the last peal to call the judgments of God upon the generations of men, it being foretold that when Christ cometh, he shall not "find faith upon the earth."[7]

1625

Of Marriage and Single Life

He that hath wife and children hath given hostages to fortune; for they are impediments to great enterprises, either of virtue or mischief. Certainly the best works, and of greatest merit for the public, have proceeded from the unmarried or childless men, which both in affection and means have married and endowed the public. Yet it were great reason that those that have children should have greatest care of future times, unto which they know they must transmit their dearest pledges. Some there are who, though they lead a single life, yet their thoughts

1. Lucretius' *On the Nature of Things* expressed the Epicurean creed, which Bacon thought inferior because it emphasized pleasure. The passage cited opens Book 2.
2. Dominated.
3. I.e., provided always that this contemplation.

4. The dealing that Bacon calls "round" we should describe as "square."
5. Debases.
6. *Essays* 2.18.
7. Luke 18.8.

do end with themselves, and account future times impertinences.[1] Nay, there are some other that account wife and children but as bills of charges. Nay more, there are some foolish rich covetous men that take a pride in having no children, because they may be thought so much the richer. For perhaps they have heard some talk, "Such an one is a great rich man," and another except to it, "Yea, but he hath a great charge of children"; as if it were an abatement to his riches. But the most ordinary cause of a single life is liberty, especially in certain self-pleasing and humorous[2] minds, which are so sensible of every restraint, as they will go near to think their girdles and garters to be bonds and shackles. Unmarried men are best friends, best masters, best servants, but not always best subjects, for they are light to run away, and almost all fugitives are of that condition. A single life doth well with churchmen, for charity will hardly water the ground where it must first fill a pool. It is indifferent for judges and magistrates, for if they be facile[3] and corrupt, you shall have a servant five times worse than a wife. For soldiers, I find the generals commonly in their hortatives[4] put men in mind of their wives and children; and I think the despising of marriage amongst the Turks maketh the vulgar soldier more base. Certainly wife and children are a kind of discipline of humanity; and single men, though they be many times more charitable, because their means are less exhaust,[5] yet, on the other side, they are more cruel and hard-hearted (good to make severe inquisitors), because their tenderness is not so oft called upon. Grave natures, led by custom, and therefore constant, are commonly loving husbands, as was said of Ulysses, *Vetulam suam praetulit immortalitati.*[6] Chaste women are often proud and froward, as presuming upon the merit of their chastity. It is one of the best bonds, both of chastity and obedience, in the wife if she think her husband wise, which she will never do if she find him jealous. Wives are young men's mistresses, companions for middle age, and old men's nurses, so as a man may have a quarrel[7] to marry when he will. But yet he was reputed one of the wise men that made answer to the question when a man should marry: "A young man not yet, an elder man not at all."[8] It is often seen that bad husbands have very good wives; whether it be that it raiseth the price of their husbands' kindness when it comes, or that the wives take a pride in their patience. But this never fails, if the bad husbands were of their own choosing, against their friends' consent; for then they will be sure to make good their own folly.

1612, 1625

---

1. Irrelevant concerns.
2. Unbalanced, whimsical.
3. Pliable.
4. Exhortations.
5. Exhausted, drained.
6. "He preferred his old wife to immortality." Ulysses might have had immortality in the company of the nymph Calypso, but preferred to go back to Penelope.
7. Pretext.
8. Thales (6th century B.C.) was the confirmed bachelor who made this remark. He was one of the Seven Sages of Greece.

Of Great Place

Men in great place are thrice servants: servants of the sovereign or state, servants of fame, and servants of business. So as they have no freedom, neither in their persons, nor in their actions, nor in their times. It is a strange desire, to seek power and to lose liberty, or to seek power over others and to lose power over a man's self. The rising unto place is laborious, and by pains men come to greater pains; and it is sometimes base, and by indignities men come to dignities. The standing is slippery, and the regress is either a downfall or at least an eclipse, which is a melancholy thing: *Cum non sis qui fueris, non esse cur velis vivere.*[1] Nay, retire men cannot when they would, neither will they when it were reason; but are impatient of privateness,[2] even in age and sickness, which require the shadow; like old townsmen, that will be still sitting at their street door, though thereby they offer age to scorn. Certainly great persons had need to borrow other men's opinions to think themselves happy; for if they judge by their own feeling, they cannot find it; but if they think with themselves what other men think of them, and that other men would fain be as they are, then they are happy, as it were by report; when perhaps they find the contrary within. For they are the first that find their own griefs, though they be the last that find their own faults. Certainly men in great fortunes are strangers to themselves, and while they are in the puzzle of business they have no time to tend their health, either of body or mind. *Illi mors gravis incubat, qui notus nimis omnibus, ignotus moritur sibi.*[3] In place there is license to do good and evil, whereof the latter is a curse; for in evil the best condition is not to will, the second not to can.[4] But power to do good is the true and lawful end of aspiring; for good thoughts (though God accept them) yet towards men are little better than good dreams, except they be put in act; and that cannot be without power and place, as the vantage and commanding ground. Merit and good works is the end of man's motion, and conscience[5] of the same is the accomplishment of man's rest; for if a man can be partaker of God's theater,[6] he shall likewise be partaker of God's rest. *Et conversus Deus, ut aspiceret opera quae fecerunt manus suae, vidit quod omnia essent bona nimis;*[7] and then the sabbath.

In the discharge of thy place set before thee the best examples, for imitation is a globe[8] of precepts. And after a time set before thee thine own example; and examine thyself strictly, whether thou didst not best at first. Neglect not also the examples of those that have carried themselves ill in the same place; not to set off thyself by taxing[9] their memory,

---

1. "When you aren't what you were, there's no reason to live" (Cicero, *Familiar Letters* 7.3).
2. I.e., they object to retirement. "The shadow" is that of retirement, out of the glare of public life.
3. "Death lies heavily on him who, while too well known to everyone else, dies unknown to himself" (Seneca, *Thyestes*).

4. Be able.
5. Consciousness.
6. The world.
7. "And God saw every thing that he had made, and, behold, it was very good" (Genesis 1.31).
8. World.
9. Blaming.

but to direct thyself what to avoid. Reform, therefore, without bravery, or scandal[1] of former times and persons; but yet set it down to thyself, as well to create good precedents as to follow them. Reduce things to the first institution,[2] and observe wherein and how they have degenerate; but yet ask counsel of both times; of the ancient time what is best, and of the latter time what is fittest. Seek to make thy course regular, that men may know beforehand what they may expect; but be not too positive and peremptory, and express thyself well when thou digressest from thy rule. Preserve the right of thy place, but stir not questions of jurisdiction; and rather assume thy right in silence and *de facto*,[3] than voice it with claims and challenges. Preserve likewise the rights of inferior places, and think it more honor to direct in chief than to be busy in all. Embrace and invite helps and advices touching the execution of thy place, and do not drive away such as bring thee information as meddlers, but accept of them in good part. The vices of authority are chiefly four: delays, corruption, roughness, and facility.[4] For delays, give easy access, keep times appointed, go through with that which is in hand, and interlace not business[5] but of necessity. For corruption, do not only bind thine own hands or thy servants' hands from taking, but bind the hands of suitors also from offering. For integrity used doth the one; but integrity professed and with a manifest detestation of bribery, doth the other. And avoid not only the fault, but the suspicion. Whosoever is found variable and changeth manifestly, without manifest cause, giveth suspicion of corruption. Therefore, always when thou changest thine opinion or course, profess it plainly and declare it, together with the reasons that move thee to change; and do not think to steal it.[6] A servant or a favorite, if he be inward,[7] and no other apparent cause of esteem, is commonly thought but a by-way to close[8] corruption. For roughness, it is a needless cause of discontent; severity breedeth fear, but roughness breedeth hate. Even reproofs from authority ought to be grave, and not taunting. As for facility, it is worse than bribery; for bribes come but now and then; but if importunity or idle respects[9] lead a man, he shall never be without. As Solomon saith, "To respect persons is not good, for such a man will transgress for a piece of bread."[1]

It is most true that was anciently spoken, "A place showeth the man"; and it showeth some to the better and some to the worse. *Omnium consensu capax imperii, nisi imperasset*,[2] saith Tacitus of Galba; but of Vespasian he saith, *Solus imperantium Vespasianus mutatus in melius*:[3] though the one was meant of sufficiency, the other of manners and affection. It is an assured sign of a worthy and generous spirit, whom

---

1. Defaming, imputing evil to. "Bravery": ostentation.
2. I.e., go back to first principles.
3. Without debate as to right and wrong, as a matter of course.
4. Docility, too great obligingness.
5. I.e., do not carry on different businesses at the same time.
6. Change your mind without its being noticed.

7. In his master's confidence.
8. Secret.
9. Irrelevant considerations.
1. Cf. Proverbs 28.21.
2. "Everyone would have thought him a good ruler, if he had not ruled."
3. "Of all the emperors, only Vespasian changed for the better." "Sufficiency": abilities. "Affection": disposition.

honor amends.[4] For honor is, or should be, the place of virtue; and as in nature things move violently to their place and calmly in their place, so virtue in ambition is violent, in authority settled and calm. All rising to great place is by a winding stair; and if there be factions, it is good to side a man's self[5] whilst he is in the rising, and to balance himself when he is placed. Use the memory of thy predecessor fairly and tenderly; for if thou dost not, it is a debt will sure be paid when thou art gone. If thou have colleagues, respect them, and rather call them when they look not for it, than exclude them when they have reason to look to be called. Be not too sensible[6] or too remembering of thy place in conversation and private answers to suitors; but let it rather be said, "When he sits in place he is another man."

1612, 1625

Of Superstition[1]

It were better to have no opinion of God at all than such an opinion as is unworthy of him. For the one is unbelief, the other is contumely:[2] and certainly superstition is the reproach of the deity. Plutarch saith well to that purpose: "Surely" (saith he) "I had rather a great deal men should say there was no such man at all as Plutarch, than that they should say that there was one Plutarch that would eat his children as soon as they were born"—as the poets speak of Saturn.[3] And as the contumely is greater towards God, so the danger is greater towards men. Atheism leaves a man to sense, to philosophy, to natural piety, to laws, to reputation, all which may be guides to an outward moral virtue, though religion were not. But superstition dismounts all these, and erecteth an absolute monarchy in the minds of men. Therefore atheism did never perturb states, for it makes men wary of themselves as looking no further,[4] and we see the times inclined to atheism (as the time of Augustus Caesar) were civil times. But superstition hath been the confusion of many states, and bringeth in a new *primum mobile*, that ravisheth all the spheres of government.[5] The master of superstition is the people, and in all superstition wise men follow fools, and arguments are fitted to practice in a reversed order. It was gravely said by some of the prelates in the council of Trent, where the doctrine of the schoolmen bare great sway, *that the schoolmen were like astronomers, which did feign eccentrics*

4. I.e., whom promotion improves.
5. For a man to take sides.
6. Sensitive.
1. By "superstition" Bacon means irrational religious practices founded on fear or ignorance.
2. Contempt.
3. Saturn, identified by the Romans with the Greek Cronos, god of time (among other things), was reputed to eat all his children, as time does. Not only this sentence, but many of the sentiments in Bacon's essay, come from Plutarch's essay *On*

Superstition.
4. I.e., not looking beyond their own personal lifetimes. The rule of Augustus Caesar in the first years of the Christian era was marked by general peace and civil quiet. They were "civil" (i.e., civilized) times; but why Bacon thinks they "inclined to atheism" is less clear.
5. The prime mover *(primum mobile)* was supposed to control the motions of the other heavenly spheres; superstition as a second (and contrary) mover throws all into confusion.

*and epicycles and such engines of orbs to save the phenomena, though
they knew there were no such things;*[6] and in like manner that the schoolmen had framed a number of subtle and intricate axioms and theorems
to save the practice of the church.

The causes of superstition are: pleasing and sensual rites and ceremonies; excess of outward and pharisaical holiness;[7] over-great reverence
of traditions, which cannot but load the church; the stratagems of prelates for their own ambition and lucre; the favoring too much of good
intentions, which openeth the gate to conceits[8] and novelties; the taking
an aim at divine matters by human, which cannot but breed mixture of
imaginations; and lastly barbarous times, especially joined with calamities and disasters. Superstition without a veil is a deformed thing, for as
it addeth deformity to an ape to be so like a man, so the similitude of
superstition to religion makes it the more deformed. And as wholesome
meat corrupteth to little worms, so good forms and orders corrupt into a
number of petty observances. There is a superstition in avoiding superstition, when men think to do best if they go furthest from the superstition formerly received; therefore care would be had that (as it fareth in
ill purgings) the good be not taken away with the bad, which commonly
is done when the people is the reformer.[9]

1612, 1625

Of Negotiating

It is generally better to deal by speech than by letter, and by the
mediation of a third than by a man's self. Letters are good when a man
would draw an answer by letter back again, or when it may serve for a
man's justification afterwards to produce his own letter, or where it may
be danger to be interrupted or heard by pieces. To deal in person is good
when a man's face breedeth regard, as commonly with inferiors, or in
tender[1] cases, where a man's eye upon the countenance of him with
whom he speaketh may give him a direction how far to go; and generally, where a man will reserve to himself liberty either to disavow or to
expound. In choice of instruments, it is better to choose men of a plainer
sort, that are like to do that that is committed to them, and to report
back again faithfully the success,[2] than those that are cunning to contrive out of other men's business somewhat to grace themselves, and will
help the matter in report for satisfaction sake. Use also such persons as
affect[3] the business wherein they are employed, for that quickeneth much;

6. "Saving the phenomena" means explaining
appearances. The elaborate theories of pre-Coper-
nican astronomers (epicycles, trepidation, and such
concepts) aimed at just that. So with the scholastic
philosophers (schoolmen).
7. The Pharisees were the strict party among the
Jews of Christ's time; they emphasized precise
observance of the letter of Mosaic law.

8. Fancies.
9. The final sentence is directed against Puritan
reformers, who particularly loathed ceremonies,
traditions, images, and observances, which they
uniformly called "superstitions."
1. Delicate.
2. Result.
3. Like.

and such as are fit for the matter, as bold men for expostulation, fair-spoken men for persuasion, crafty men for inquiry and observation, froward and absurd men for business that doth not well bear out itself.[4] Use also such as have been lucky, and prevailed before in things wherein you have employed them; for that breeds confidence, and they will strive to maintain their prescription.[5] It is better to sound a person with whom one deals afar off, than to fall upon the point at first, except you mean to surprise him by some short question. It is better dealing with men in appetite,[6] than with those that are where they would be. If a man deal with another upon conditions, the start or first performance is all,[7] which a man cannot reasonably demand, except either the nature of the thing be such which must go before, or else a man can persuade the other party that he shall still need him in some other thing, or else that he be counted the honester man. All practice is to discover or to work.[8] Men discover themselves in trust, in passion, at unawares, and of necessity, when they would have somewhat done and cannot find an apt pretext. If you would work any man, you must either know his nature and fashions, and so lead him; or his ends, and so persuade him; or his weakness and disadvantages, and so awe him; or those that have interest in him, and so govern him. In dealing with cunning persons, we must ever consider their ends, to interpret their speeches; and it is good to say little to them, and that which they least look for. In all negotiations of difficulty, a man may not look to sow and reap at once; but must prepare business, and so ripen it by degrees.

1597, 1625

Of Studies

[1597 version][1]

Studies serve for pastimes, for ornaments, and for abilities. Their chief use for pastime is in privateness[2] and retiring; for ornament, is in discourse; and for ability, is in judgment. For expert men[3] can execute, but learned men are fittest to judge or censure. To spend too much time in them is sloth; to use them too much for ornament is affectation; to make judgment wholly by their rules is the humor[4] of a scholar. They perfect nature, and are perfected by experience. Crafty men contemn them,

4. Bacon suggests that when you have an unjust demand to make, you select a fool to make it.
5. Keep up their reputation.
6. Hungry, i.e., ambitious men.
7. If you're arguing over details, they will have to be settled by reference to the basic agreement, or to some other power relationship.
8. All sharp bargaining aims to find out what men are up to or to make use of them. "Discover" (next sentence): reveal.
1. When Bacon first published a little pamphlet

of essays, in 1597, there were only 10 of them, and the author's effort at epigrammatic concision resulted in brief and occasionally cryptic utterances. Later editions added many more essays, for a final total of 58; Bacon also filled out the abrupt and mannered prose of his early versions.
2. Private life.
3. Men of experience, the English adjective being used in its Latin sense, *experti*.
4. Mannerism, implying absurd error.

simple men admire them, wise men use them, for they teach not their own use; but that is a wisdom without them, and above them, won by observation. Read not to contradict nor to believe, but to weigh and consider. Some books are to be tasted, others to be swallowed, and some few to be chewed and digested; that is, some books are to be read only in parts; others to be read but cursorily; and some few to be read wholly and with diligence and attention. Reading maketh a full man, conference[5] a ready man, and writing an exact man. And therefore, if a man write little, he had need have a great memory; if he confer little, he had need have a present wit;[6] and if he read little, he had need have much cunning, to seem to know that[7] he doth not. Histories make men wise; poets, witty;[8] the mathematics, subtle; natural philosophy,[9] deep; moral, grave; logic and rhetoric, able to contend.

Of Studies

[1625 version]

Studies serve for delight, for ornament, and for ability. Their chief use for delight is in privateness[1] and retiring; for ornament, is in discourse; and for ability, is in the judgment and disposition of business. For expert men[2] can execute, and perhaps judge of particulars, one by one; but the general counsels, and the plots and marshaling of affairs, come best from those that are learned. To spend too much time in studies is sloth; to use them too much for ornament is affectation; to make judgment wholly by their rules is the humor[3] of a scholar. They perfect nature, and are perfected by experience; for natural abilities are like natural plants, that need pruning by study; and studies themselves do give forth directions too much at large, except they be bounded in by experience. Crafty men contemn studies, simple men admire them, and wise men use them, for they teach not their own use; but that is a wisdom without them, and above them, won by observation. Read not to contradict and confute, nor to believe and take for granted, nor to find talk and discourse, but to weigh and consider. Some books are to be tasted, others to be swallowed, and some few to be chewed and digested; that is, some books are to be read only in parts; others to be read, but not curiously;[4] and some few to be read wholly, and with diligence and attention. Some books also may be read by deputy and extracts made of them by others, but that would be only in the less important arguments and the meaner sort of books; else distilled books are like common distilled waters,[5] flashy things. Reading maketh a full man, conference[6] a

---

5. Conversations, meetings.
6. Lively intelligence.
7. That which.
8. Clever.
9. Science; "moral": i.e., moral philosophy.
1. Private life.

2. Men of experience.
3. Mannerism.
4. Attentively.
5. Infusions of herbs, etc., used as home remedies—without real value.
6. Conversations, meetings.

ready man, and writing an exact man. And therefore, if a man write little, he had need have a great memory; if he confer little, he had need have a present wit;[7] and if he read little, he had need have much cunning, to seem to know that[8] he doth not. Histories make men wise; poets, witty;[9] the mathematics, subtle; natural philosophy,[1] deep; moral, grave; logic and rhetoric, able to contend. *Abeunt studia in mores.*[2] Nay, there is no stond or impediment in the wit but may be wrought out by fit studies, like as diseases of the body may have appropriate exercises. Bowling is good for the stone and reins,[3] shooting for the lungs and breast, gentle walking for the stomach, riding for the head, and the like. So if a man's wit be wandering, let him study the mathematics; for in demonstrations, if his wit be called away never so little, he must begin again. If his wit be not apt to distinguish or find differences, let him study the schoolmen,[4] for they are *cumini sectores.* If he be not apt to beat over matters[5] and to call up one thing to prove and illustrate another, let him study the lawyer's cases. So every defect of the mind may have a special receipt.[6]

From The Advancement of Learning

[*The Abuses of Language*][1]

Martin Luther, conducted (no doubt) by an higher providence, but in discourse of reason finding what a province[2] he had undertaken against the bishop of Rome and the degenerate traditions of the church, and finding his own solitude being no ways aided by the opinions of his own time, was enforced to awake all antiquity and to call former times to his succor to make a party against the present time, so that the ancient authors both in divinity and in humanity which had long time slept in libraries began generally to be read and revolved.[3] This by consequence did draw on a necessity of a more exquisite travail in the languages original wherein those authors did write,[4] for the better understanding of those authors and the better advantage of pressing and applying their words. And thereof grew again a delight in their manner of style and phrase, and an admiration of that kind of writing, which was much furthered and precipitated by the enmity and opposition that the pro-

7. Lively intelligence.
8. That which.
9. Clever.
1. Science; "moral": i.e., moral philosophy.
2. "Studies culminate in manners" (Ovid, *Heroides*). "Stond": difficulty.
3. Gall bladder and kidneys.
4. Scholastic philosophers. The Latin means "dividers of cuminseed," i.e., hairsplitters.
5. Discuss a subject thoroughly.
6. Cure, prescription.
1. Among the "three distempers of learning" that Bacon proposes to cure in *The Advancement of Learning*, the most important is that which he

describes as "vain imaginations, vain altercations, and vain affectations"; and to explain precisely the form it has taken of late, he gives a concise history of changes in the language of learned discourse since the Reformation.
2. Task.
3. Circulated. Bacon is ludicrously wrong in attributing to Luther (1483–1546) the humanist revival of the classics—which had begun in the 14th century. But the error does not invalidate his analysis of the vanity of much 16th-century humanist learning.
4. I.e., classical Greek and Latin, as well as Biblical Hebrew. "Travail": labor.

pounders of those (primitive but seeming new) opinions had against the schoolmen, who were generally of the contrary part, and whose writings were altogether in a differing style and form, taking liberty to coin and frame new terms of art to express their own sense and to avoid circuit of speech, without regard to the pureness, pleasantness, and (as I may call it) lawfulness of the phrase or word.[5] And again, because the greatest labor then was with the people (of whom the Pharisees were wont to say, *Execrabilis ista turba, quae non novit legem*),[6] for the winning and persuading of them there grew of necessity in chief price and request eloquence and variety of discourse, as the fittest and forciblest access into the capacity of the vulgar sort. So that these four causes concurring (the admiration of ancient authors, the hate of the schoolmen, the exact study of languages, and the efficacy of preaching) did bring in an affectionate study of eloquence and copy[7] of speech, which then began to flourish. This grew speedily to an excess, for men began to hunt more after words than matter, and more after the choiceness of the phrase, and the round and clean composition of the sentence, and the sweet falling of the clauses, and the varying and illustration of their works with tropes and figures[8] than after the weight of matter, worth of subject, soundness of argument, life of invention, or depth of judgment. Then grew the flowing and watery vein of Osorius, the Portugal bishop, to be in price.[9] Then did Sturmius spend such infinite and curious pains upon Cicero the orator and Hermogenes the rhetorician, besides his own books of periods and imitation and the like. Then did Carr of Cambridge and Ascham[1] with their lectures and writings almost deify Cicero and Demosthenes, and allure all young men that were studious unto that delicate and polished kind of learning. Then did Erasmus take occasion to make the scoffing echo, *Decem annos consumpsi in legendo Cicerone*, and the echo answered in Greek, *one, Asine*.[2] Then grew the learning of the schoolmen to be utterly despised as barbarous. In sum, the whole inclination and bent of those times was rather towards copy than weight.

Here therefore is the first distemper of learning, when men study words and not matter, whereof though I have represented an example of late times, yet it hath been and will be *secundum maius et minus*[3] in all time. And how is it possible but this should have an operation to discredit learning, even with vulgar capacities, when they see learned men's

5. The scholastic philosophers and theologians ("schoolmen") used the living Latin of the Middle Ages; applying it to philosophical matters of great subtlety, they wrenched it even further from classical Latin. The humanists, who were devoted to reviving classical Latin (more elegant, but unfortunately a dead tongue), liked to call the scholastics and their language barbaric.

6. "Execrable is that crowd which knows not the law." The source of the phrase is unknown.

7. Copiousness. "Affectionate": affected.

8. Figurative language.

9. Jerome Osorio was a Spanish bishop who wrote a history of the Portuguese conquests and discoveries. His "flowing and watery vein" caused him

to be known as "the Portuguese Cicero," as his contemporary Sturmius (Johann Sturm) was known as "the German Cicero." Sturmius edited texts of Cicero himself, and of Hermogenes the Greek rhetorician; his own "book of periods" was a rhetorical textbook.

1. Nicholas Carr succeeded Sir John Cheke as professor of Greek at Cambridge; Roger Ascham was tutor to Queen Elizabeth and author of *The Schoolmaster*. Both admired the balanced and polished sentences of Ciceronian style.

2. "I spent ten years in reading Cicero." Echo answers, "Ass!" The joke is in the *Colloquies* of Erasmus, "Echo."

3. More or less.

works like the first letter of a patent or limned[4] book, which though it
hath large flourishes, yet it is but a letter? It seems to me that Pygmalion's frenzy[5] is a good emblem or portraiture of this vanity, for words are
but the images of matter, and except they have life of reason and invention, to fall in love with them is all one as to fall in love with a picture.

But yet notwithstanding, it is a thing not hastily to be condemned to
clothe and adorn the obscurity even of philosophy itself with sensible
and plausible elocution. For hereof we have great examples in Xenophon, Cicero, Seneca, Plutarch, and of Plato also in some degree; and
hereof likewise there is great use, for surely to the severe inquisition of
truth and the deep progress into philosophy it is some hindrance, because
it is too early satisfactory to the mind of man, and quencheth the desire
of further search before we come to a just period; but then if a man be
to have any use of such knowledge in civil occasions of conference,
counsel, persuasion, discourse, or the like, then shall he find it prepared
to his hands in those authors which write in that manner. But the excess
of this is so justly contemptible that as Hercules, when he saw the image
of Adonis, Venus' minion, in a temple, said in disdain, *Nil sacri es;*[6] so
there is none of Hercules' followers in learning, that is, the more severe
and laborious sort of inquirers into truth,[7] but will despise those delicacies and affectations as indeed capable of no divineness.

1605

From Novum Organum[1]

[*The Idols*]

50

But by far the greatest hindrance and aberration of the human understanding proceeds from the dullness, incompetency, and deceptions of
the senses; in that things which strike the sense outweigh things which
do not immediately strike it, though they[2] be more important. Hence it

4. Illuminated, i.e., illustrated, as with elaborate
initial capitals. Royal grants ("patents") were also
engrossed with fancy initial letters.
5. Pygmalion's "frenzy" (delirium) was to fall in
love with a statue he had carved of a beautiful
woman.
6. "You're nothing holy." Adonis was the lover
("minion") of Venus, deified after his death while
boar-hunting.
7. Hercules early in life was offered a choice
between an existence of ignoble ease and one of
strenuous virtue. He chose the latter, and so do his
followers in learning, i.e., authentic scholars.
1. *Novum Organum*, or "The New Instrument of
Learning," is not properly a work of English literature, since it was written in Latin, for an international scholarly audience. (Bacon rather
mistrusted the modern languages, thinking they
would "wear away" in time; but Latin was safe.)
Still, no history of English ideas can afford to ignore

this book; for it was the keystone of Bacon's vast
project to renovate the structure of human learning from the ground up. The translation is that of
Spedding, Ellis, and Heath, from their edition of
the *Works* (1857–74).
    Observation was the essential process of Bacon's
new method; he felt that only observation, long
continued and carefully directed, was capable of
producing certainty about the operations of nature.
As against the true intellectual temper produced by
careful observation and controlled experiment, he
set the frivolity of the skeptics and the unwarranted
confidence of the dogmatists. This argument rises
to its height about halfway through the first
(destructive) part of the book, in an extended
account of the various Idols, or delusive ideas,
which mislead and bewilder the human understanding.
2. The latter.

is that speculation commonly ceases where sight ceases; insomuch that of things invisible there is little or no observation. Hence all the working of the spirits enclosed in tangible bodies lies hid and unobserved of men.[3] So also all the more subtle changes of form in the parts of coarser substances (which they commonly call alteration, though it is in truth local motion through exceedingly small spaces) is in like manner unobserved. And yet unless these two things just mentioned be searched out and brought to light, nothing great can be achieved in nature, as far as the production of works is concerned. So again the essential nature of our common air, and of all bodies less dense than air (which are very many), is almost unknown. For the sense by itself is a thing infirm and erring; neither can instruments for enlarging or sharpening the senses do much; but all the truer kind of interpretation of nature is effected by instances and experiments fit and apposite; wherein the sense decides touching the experiment only, and the experiment touching the point in nature and the thing itself.

51

The human understanding is of its own nature prone to abstractions and gives a substance and reality to things which are fleeting. But to resolve nature into abstractions is less to our purpose than to dissect her into parts; as did the school of Democritus,[4] which went further into nature than the rest. Matter rather than forms should be the object of our attention, its configurations and changes of configuration, and simple action, and law of action or motion; for forms are figments of the human mind, unless you will call those laws of action forms.

52

Such then are the idols which I call *Idols of the Tribe*;[5] and which take their rise either from the homogeneity of the substance of the human spirit, or from its preoccupation, or from its narrowness, or from its restless motion, or from an infusion of the affections, or from the incompetency of the senses, or from the mode of impression.

53

The *Idols of the Cave* take their rise in the peculiar constitution, mental or bodily, of each individual; and also in education, habit, and accident. Of this kind there is a great number and variety; but I will instance those the pointing out of which contains the most important caution, and which have most effect in disturbing the clearness of the understanding.

3. Though his views on scientific method were modern, Bacon's ideas about physical phenomena were those of his age; he believed in subtle spiritual principles which might lie concealed in physical objects, unobserved by men.

4. The school of Democritus, the "laughing philosopher" of ancient Greece (5th century B.C.), held that the world was composed of atoms. Democritus developed the atomic theory, of which Leucip-

pus was the originator; Lucretius (four centuries later) became the great literary exponent of this school.

5. By "Idols" Bacon means delusive images of truth, leading men away from the exact knowledge of science. By "Idols of the Tribe" he denotes particularly readiness to generalize on the basis of inadequate facts—a fault to which all men are prone.

54

Men become attached to certain particular sciences[6] and speculations, either because they fancy themselves the authors and inventors thereof, or because they have bestowed the greatest pains upon them and become most habituated to them. But men of this kind, if they betake themselves to philosophy and contemplations of a general character, distort and color them in obedience to their former fancies; a thing especially to be noticed in Aristotle, who made his natural philosophy a mere bondservant to his logic, thereby rendering it contentious and well nigh useless. The race of chemists[7] again out of a few experiments of the furnace have built up a fantastic philosophy, framed with reference to a few things; and Gilbert also, after he had employed himself most laboriously in the study and observation of the loadstone, proceeded at once to construct an entire system in accordance with his favorite subject.[8]

55

There is one principal and, as it were, radical distinction between different minds in respect of philosophy and the sciences, which is this: that some minds are stronger and apter to mark the differences of things, others to mark their resemblances. The steady and acute mind can fix its contemplations and dwell and fasten on the subtlest distinctions; the lofty and discursive mind recognizes and puts together the finest and most general resemblances. Both kinds however easily err in excess, by catching the one at gradations, the other at shadows.

56

There are found some minds given to an extreme admiration of antiquity, others to an extreme love and appetite for novelty; but few so duly tempered that they can hold the mean, neither carping at what has been well laid down by the ancients, nor despising what is well introduced by the moderns. This however turns to the great injury of the sciences and philosophy; since these affectations of antiquity and novelty are the humors of partisans rather than judgments; and truth is to be sought for not in the felicity of any age, which is an unstable thing, but in the light of nature and experience, which is eternal. These factions therefore must be abjured, and care must be taken that the intellect be not hurried by them into assent.

57

Contemplations of nature and of bodies in their simple form break up and distract the understanding, while contemplations of nature and bodies in their composition and configuration overpower and dissolve the

6. Branches of knowledge.
7. Alchemists.
8. William Gilbert, author of a famous treatise on the magnet (1600), serves Bacon (rather unfairly) as an example of dogmatism founded on a few limited experiments.

understanding:[9] a distinction well seen in the school of Leucippus and Democritus as compared with the other philosophies. For that school is so busied with the particles that it hardly attends to the structure; while the others are so lost in admiration of the structure that they do not penetrate to the simplicity of nature. These kinds of contemplation should therefore be alternated and taken by turns; that so the understanding may be rendered at once penetrating and comprehensive, and the inconveniences above mentioned, with the idols which proceed from them, may be avoided.

58

Let such then be our provision and contemplative prudence for keeping off and dislodging the *Idols of the Cave,* which grow for the most part either out of the predominance of a favorite subject, or out of an excessive tendency to compare or to distinguish, or out of partiality for particular ages, or out of the largeness or minuteness of the objects contemplated. And generally let every student of nature take this as a rule— that whatever his mind seizes and dwells upon with peculiar satisfaction is to be held in suspicion, and that so much the more care is to be taken in dealing with such questions to keep the understanding even and clear.

59

But the *Idols of the Marketplace* are the most troublesome of all: idols which have crept into the understanding through the alliances of words and names. For men believe that their reason governs words; but it is also true that words react on the understanding; and this it is that has rendered philosophy and the sciences sophistical and inactive. Now words, being commonly framed and applied according to the capacity of the vulgar, follow those lines of division which are most obvious to the vulgar understanding. And whenever an understanding of greater acuteness or a more diligent observation would alter those lines to suit the true divisions of nature, words stand in the way and resist the change. Whence it comes to pass that the high and formal discussions of learned men end oftentimes in disputes about words and names; with which (according to the use[1] and wisdom of the mathematicians) it would be more prudent to begin, and so by means of definitions reduce them to order. Yet even definitions cannot cure this evil in dealing with natural and material things; since the definitions themselves consist of words, and those words beget others; so that it is necessary to recur to individual instances, and those in due series and order; as I shall say presently when I come to the method and scheme for the formation of notions and axioms.[2]

9. I.e., reducing nature to general principles is, intellectually, as dangerous as trying to observe all its particulars.
1. Custom.

2. Bacon's mistrust of words, evident here, led the Royal Society to cultivate a plain, stripped prose style for purposes of scientific communication.

60

The idols imposed by words on the understanding are of two kinds. They are either names of things which do not exist (for as there are things left unnamed through lack of observation, so likewise are there names which result from fantastic suppositions and to which nothing in reality corresponds), or they are names of things which exist, but yet confused and ill-defined, and hastily and irregularly derived from realities. Of the former kind are Fortune, the Prime Mover, Planetary Orbits, Element of Fire, and like fictions which owe their origin to false and idle theories.[3] And this class of idols is more easily expelled, because to get rid of them it is only necessary that all theories should be steadily rejected and dismissed as obsolete.[4]

But the other class, which springs out of a faulty and unskillful abstraction, is intricate and deeply rooted. Let us take for example such a word as *humid*; and see how far the several things which the word is used to signify agree with each other; and we shall find the word *humid* to be nothing else than a mark loosely and confusedly applied to denote a variety of actions which will not bear to be reduced to any constant meaning. For it both signifies that which easily spreads itself round any other body; and that which in itself is indeterminate and cannot solidize; and that which readily yields in every direction; and that which easily divides and scatters itself; and that which easily unites and collects itself; and that which readily flows and is put in motion; and that which readily clings to another body and wets it; and that which is easily reduced to a liquid, or being solid easily melts. Accordingly when you come to apply the word—if you take it in one sense, flame is humid; if in another, air is not humid; if in another, fine dust is humid; if in another, glass is humid. So that it is easy to see that the notion is taken by abstraction only from water and common and ordinary liquids, without any due verification.

There are however in words certain degrees of distortion and error. One of the least faulty kinds is that of names of substances, especially of lowest species and well-deduced (for the notion of *chalk* and of *mud* is good, of *earth* bad); a more faulty kind is that of actions, as *to generate, to corrupt, to alter*; the most faulty is of qualities (except such as are the immediate objects of the sense), as *heavy, light, rare, dense*, and the like. Yet in all these cases some notions are of necessity a little better than others, in proportion to the greater variety of subjects that fall within the range of the human sense.

3. The "Prime Mover" was a transparent sphere on the outside of the universe, supposed to move all the other spheres; the "Element of Fire" was an area of pure, invisible fire, supposed to exist above the atmosphere. In the nature of things, these concepts could be based on no observation. "Planetary Orbits," on the other hand, are very real; Bacon may be referring to the old notion of crystalline spheres in which the planets were supposed to be set.

4. Bacon does not really mean "theories" in the inclusive modern sense, but "abstractions loosely invoked to explain particular facts." He is actually restating William of Occam's famous 14th-century principle, known as "Occam's razor," to the effect that "essences must not be multiplied beyond necessity."

61

But the *Idols of the Theater*[5] are not innate, nor do they steal into the understanding secretly, but are plainly impressed and received into the mind from the play-books of philosophical systems and the perverted rules of demonstration. To attempt refutations in this case would be merely inconsistent with what I have already said: for since we agree neither upon principles nor upon demonstrations, there is no place for argument. And this is so far well, inasmuch as it leaves the honor of the ancients untouched. For they are no wise disparaged—the question between them and me being only as to the way. For as the saying is, the lame man who keeps the right road outstrips the runner who takes a wrong one. Nay, it is obvious that when a man runs the wrong way, the more active and swift he is the further he will go astray.

But the course I propose for the discovery of sciences is such as leaves but little to the acuteness and strength of wits, but places all wits and understandings nearly on a level. For as in the drawing of a straight line or a perfect circle, much depends on the steadiness and practice of the hand, if it be done by aim of hand only, but if with the aid of rule or compass, little or nothing; so is it exactly with my plan. But though particular confutations would be of no avail, yet touching the sects and general divisions of such systems I must say something; something also touching the external signs which show that they are unsound; and finally something touching the causes of such great infelicity and of such lasting and general agreement in error; that so the access to truth may be made less difficult, and the human understanding may the more willingly submit to its purgation and dismiss its idols.

62

Idols of the Theater, or of systems, are many, and there can be and perhaps will be yet many more. For were it not that now for many ages men's minds have been busied with religion and theology; and were it not that civil governments, especially monarchies, have been averse to such novelties, even in matters speculative; so that men labor therein to the peril and harming of their fortunes—not only unrewarded, but exposed also to contempt and envy; doubtless there would have arisen many other philosophical sects like to those which in great variety flourished once among the Greeks. For as on the phenomena of the heavens many hypotheses may be constructed, so likewise (and more also) many various dogmas may be set up and established on the phenomena of philosophy. And in the plays of this philosophical theater you may observe the same thing which is found in the theater of the poets, that stories invented for the stage are more compact and elegant, and more as one would wish them to be, than true stories out of history.

In general, however, there is taken for the material of philosophy either a great deal out of a few things, or a very little out of many things;

5. I.e., those derived from previous philosophical systems, which misrepresent life by overdramatiz-ing it and mislead men by pretending to show them reality itself.

so that on both sides philosophy is based on too narrow a foundation of experiment and natural history, and decides on the authority of too few cases. For the rational school of philosophers snatches from experience a variety of common instances, neither duly ascertained nor diligently examined and weighed, and leaves all the rest to meditation and agitation of wit.[6]

There is also another class of philosophers, who having bestowed much diligent and careful labor on a few experiments, have thence made bold to educe and construct systems; wresting all other facts in a strange fashion to conformity therewith.

And there is yet a third class, consisting of those who out of faith and veneration mix their philosophy with theology and traditions; among whom the vanity of some has gone so far aside as to seek the origin of sciences among spirits and genii. So that this parent stock of errors—this false philosophy—is of three kinds: the sophistical, the empirical, and the superstitious.

*   *   *

68

So much concerning the several classes of idols, and their equipage: all of which must be renounced and put away with a fixed and solemn determination, and the understanding thoroughly freed and cleansed; the entrance into the kingdom of man, founded on the sciences, being not much other than the entrance into the kingdom of heaven, whereinto none may enter except as a little child.

1620

From The New Atlantis[1]

[Solomon's House]

We came at our day and hour, and I was chosen by my fellows for the private access.[2] We found him in a fair chamber, richly hanged, and

---

6. Bacon's thought contained a concealed element of anti-intellectualism: his enthusiasm for experiment led him to denigrate the value of reason, as very few modern scientists would feel it necessary to do. What he is opposing here is an excessive concern with the forms of logic, as exemplified, he would say, in "the schoolmen."

1. Sir Thomas More's *Utopia* (1516) set a fashion for accounts of imaginary communities with ideal forms of government, a fashion that was suddenly taken up in the early 17th century. The German Johann Andreae published in 1619 his *Christianopolis*; Thomas Campanella, languishing in a Neapolitan jail, wrote his *City of the Sun* in 1623. Bacon's contribution to the discussion, perhaps because he never completed it, is mainly tangential to the concept of an ideal commonwealth. His

New Atlantis centers in an account of a research establishment which could exist in any society that would tolerate it. Perhaps for that reason, it had an immediate influence beyond that of most full-fledged utopias; and was largely realized, within 30 years of its publication, in the shape of the Philosophical Society which in 1662 became the Royal Society. Bacon begins by describing an imaginary voyage to the island of Bensalem, supposed to lie in the vicinity of the Bering Strait. Here, after learning about the miraculous diffusion of Christianity to the island, and various laws and customs of the Bensalemites, the nameless narrator is invited to visit their most interesting institution, Solomon's House.

2. Audience—with the chief scientist of Solomon's House.

carpeted under foot, without any degrees to the state.[3] He was set upon a low throne richly adorned, and a rich cloth of state over his head, of blue satin embroidered. He was alone, save that he had two pages of honor, on either hand one, finely attired in white. His undergarments were the like that we saw him wear in the chariot; but instead of his gown, he had on him a mantle with a cape of the same fine black, fastened about him. When we came in, as we were taught, we bowed low at our first entrance, and when we were come near his chair, he stood up, holding forth his hand ungloved and in posture of blessing; and we every one of us stooped down, and kissed the hem of his tippet.[4] That done, the rest departed, and I remained. Then he warned the pages forth of the room, and caused me to sit down beside him, and spake to me thus in the Spanish tongue:

"God bless thee, my son; I will give thee the greatest jewel I have. For I will impart unto thee, for the love of God and men, a relation of the true state of Solomon's House. Son, to make you know the true state of Solomon's House, I will keep this order. First, I will set forth unto you the end of our foundation. Secondly, the preparations and instruments we have for our works. Thirdly, the several employments and functions whereto our fellows are assigned. And fourthly, the ordinances and rites which we observe.

"The end of our foundation is the knowledge of causes, and secret motions of things; and the enlarging of the bounds of human empire, to the effecting of all things possible.

"The preparations and instruments are these. We have large and deep caves of several depths: the deepest are sunk six hundred fathom; and some of them are digged and made under great hills and mountains; so that if you reckon together the depth of the hill and the depth of the cave, they are, some of them, above three miles deep. For we find that the depth of a hill, and the depth of a cave from the flat, is the same thing; both remote alike from the sun and heaven's beams, and from the open air. These caves we call the Lower Region, and we use them for all coagulations, indurations,[5] refrigerations, and conservations of bodies. We use them likewise for the imitation of natural mines, and the producing also of new artificial metals, by compositions and materials which we use, and lay there for many years. We use them also sometimes (which may seem strange) for curing of some diseases, and for prolongation of life in some hermits that choose to live there, well accommodated of[6] all things necessary, and indeed live very long; by whom also we learn many things.

"We have burials in several earths, where we put divers cements,[7] as the Chinese do their porcelain. But we have them in greater variety, and some of them more fine. We have also great variety of composts[8] and soils, for the making of the earth fruitful.

---

3. I.e., without stairs leading up to the dais.
4. Scarf.
5. Hardenings.

6. Provided with.
7. Clays and pottery mixtures.
8. Manures.

"We have high towers, the highest about half a mile in height, and some of them likewise set upon high mountains, so that the vantage of the hill, with the tower, is in the highest of them three miles at least. And these places we call the Upper Region, accounting the air between the high places and the low as a Middle Region. We use these towers, according to their several heights and situations, for insolation,[9] refrigeration, conservation, and for the view of divers meteors—as winds, rain, snow, hail;[1] and some of the fiery meteors also. And upon them, in some places, are dwellings of hermits, whom we visit sometimes, and instruct what to observe.

"We have great lakes, both salt and fresh, whereof we have use for the fish and fowl. We use them also for burials of some natural bodies, for we find a difference in things buried in earth, or in air below the earth, and things buried in water. We have also pools, of which some do strain fresh water out of salt, and others by art do turn fresh water into salt. We have also some rocks in the midst of the sea, and some bays upon the shore, for some works wherein is required the air and vapor of the sea. We have likewise violent streams and cataracts, which serve us for many motions; and likewise engines for multiplying and enforcing[2] of winds to set also on going divers motions.

"We have also a number of artificial wells and fountains, made in imitation of the natural sources and baths, as tincted upon[3] vitriol, sulphur, steel, brass, lead, niter, and other minerals; and again, we have little wells for infusions of many things, where the waters take the virtue[4] quicker and better than in vessels or basins. And amongst them we have a water which we call Water of Paradise, being by that we do to it, made very sovereign[5] for health and prolongation of life.

"We have also great and spacious houses, where we imitate and demonstrate meteors—as snow, hail, rain, some artificial rains of bodies and not of water, thunders, lightnings; also generations of bodies in air—as frogs, flies, and divers others.

"We have also certain chambers, which we call Chambers of Health, where we qualify[6] the air as we think good and proper for the cure of divers diseases, and preservation of health.

"We have also fair and large baths, of several mixtures, for the cure of diseases, and the restoring of man's body from arefaction;[7] and others for the confirming of it in strength of sinews, vital parts, and the very juice and substance of the body.

"We have also large and various orchards and gardens, wherein we do not so much respect beauty as variety of ground and soil, proper for divers trees and herbs, and some very spacious, where trees and berries are set, whereof we make divers kinds of drinks, besides the vineyards. In these we practice likewise all conclusions[8] of grafting and inoculating,

9. Exposure to the sun.
1. Anything that fell from the sky was, in Renaissance terminology, a meteor.
2. Re-enforcing, strengthening.
3. Tinctured with.
4. Property (of the substances put into water).
5. Efficacious.
6. Modify.
7. Drying up.
8. Theories.

as well of wild trees as fruit trees, which produceth many effects. And we make (by art) in the same orchards and gardens trees and flowers to come earlier or later than their seasons, and to come up and bear more speedily than by their natural course they do. We make them also by art greater much than their nature; and their fruit greater and sweeter, and of differing taste, smell, color, and figure, from their nature. And many of them we so order as they become of medicinal use.

"We have also means to make divers plants rise by mixtures of earths without seeds, and likewise to make divers new plants, differing from the vulgar,[9] and to make one tree or plant turn into another.

"We have also parks and enclosures of all sorts of beasts and birds; which we use not only for view or rareness, but likewise for dissections and trials,[1] that thereby we may take light what may be wrought upon the body of man. Wherein we find many strange effects: as continuing life in them, though divers parts, which you account vital, be perished and taken forth; resuscitating of some that seem dead in appearance, and the like. We try also all poisons and other medicines upon them, as well of chirurgery[2] as physic. By art likewise, we make them greater or taller than their kind is, and contrariwise dwarf them and stay their growth; we make them more fruitful and bearing than their kind is, and contrariwise barren and not generative. Also, we make them differ in color, shape, activity, many ways. We find means to make commixtures and copulations of different kinds, which have produced many new kinds,[3] and them not barren, as the general opinion is. We make a number of kinds of serpents, worms, fishes, flies, of putrefaction, whereof some are advanced (in effect) to be perfect creatures, like beasts or birds, and have sexes, and do propagate. Neither do we this by chance, but we know beforehand of what matter and commixture what kind of those creatures will arise.

"We have also particular pools where we make trials upon fishes, as we have said before of beasts and birds.

"We have also places for breed and generation of those kinds of worms and flies which are of special use; such as are with you your silkworms and bees."[4]

*   *   *

"For the several employments and offices of our fellows, we have twelve that sail into foreign countries under the names of other nations (for our own we conceal), who bring us the books and abstracts and patterns of experiments of all other parts. These we call Merchants of Light.

"We have three that collect the experiments which are in all books. These we call Depredators.

9. Ordinary.
1. Experiments.
2. Surgery.
3. Species. Mules, the offspring of horses and donkeys, are sterile; it was therefore commonly supposed that all hybrids must be so.
4. The narrator continues to describe the various

bakeries, vineyards, breweries, and kitchens operated by Solomon's House. He enumerates the medicines discovered there, as well as various experiments with heat. The researchers study light, sound, perfumes, mechanics, mathematics, and all ways of deceiving the senses.

"We have three that collect the experiments of all mechanical arts, and also of liberal sciences, and also of practices which are not brought into arts. These we call Mystery-men.

"We have three that try new experiments, such as themselves think good. These we call Pioneers or Miners.

"We have three that draw the experiments of the former four into titles and tables, to give the better light for the drawing of observations and axioms out of them. These we call Compilers.

"We have three that bend themselves, looking into the experiments of their fellows, and cast about how to draw out of them things of use and practice for man's life and knowledge, as well for works as for plain demonstration of causes, means of natural divinations, and the easy and clear discovery of the virtues and parts of bodies. These we call Dowry-men or Benefactors.

"Then after divers meetings and consults of our whole number, to consider of the former labors and collections, we have three that take care out of them to direct new experiments, of a higher light, more penetrating into nature than the former. These we call Lamps.

"We have three others that do execute the experiments so directed, and report them. These we call Inoculators.

"Lastly, we have three that raise the former discoveries by experiments into greater observations, axioms, and aphorisms. These we call Interpreters of Nature.[5]

"We have also, as you must think, novices and apprentices, that the succession of the former employed men do not fail; besides a great number of servants and attendants, men and women. And this we do also: we have consultations, which of the inventions and experiences which we have discovered shall be published, and which not; and take all an oath of secrecy for the concealing of those which we think fit to keep secret; though some of those we do reveal sometimes to the State, and some not.[6]

"For our ordinances and rites, we have two very long and fair galleries: in one of these we place patterns and samples of all manner of the more rare and excellent inventions; in the other we place the statues of all principal inventors. There we have the statue of your Columbus, that discovered the West Indies; also the inventor of ships; your monk that was the inventor of ordnance and of gunpowder;[7] the inventor of music; the inventor of letters; the inventor of printing; the inventor of observations of astronomy; the inventor of works in metal; the inventor of glass; the inventor of silk of the worm; the inventor of wine; the inventor of corn and bread; the inventor of sugars; and all these by more certain tradition than you have. Then we have divers inventors of our own, of

---

5. Though Bacon is clearly stretching his imagination to the limit, his enumeration of the personnel of Solomon's House will seem scanty indeed to anyone aware of research institutes on the modern scale.

6. Observe Bacon's suspicion of the body politic,

and the freedom which he allows to Solomon's House from political pressure.

7. Tradition credits Roger Bacon, a 13th-century monk, with the discovery of gunpowder. Bacon tactfully avoids his name.

excellent works, which since you have not seen, it were too long to make descriptions of them; and besides, in the right understanding of those descriptions you might easily err. For upon every invention of value we erect a statue to the inventor, and give him a liberal and honorable reward. These statutes are some of brass, some of marble and touchstone,[8] some of cedar and other special woods gilt and adorned; some of iron, some of silver, some of gold.

"We have certain hymns and services, which we say daily, of laud and thanks to God for his marvelous works; and forms of prayer, imploring his aid and blessing for the illumination of our labors, and the turning of them into good and holy uses.

"Lastly, we have circuits or visits of divers principal cities of the kingdom; where, as it cometh to pass, we do publish such new profitable inventions as we think good. And we do also declare natural divinations of diseases, plagues, swarms of hurtful creatures, scarcity, tempests, earthquakes, great inundations, comets, temperature of the year, and divers other things; and we give counsel thereupon, what the people shall do for the prevention and remedy of them."

And when he had said this he stood up; and I, as I had been taught, kneeled down; and he laid his right hand upon my head, and said, "God bless thee, my son, and God bless this relation which I have made. I give thee leave to publish it, for the good of other nations; for we here are in God's bosom, a land unknown." And so he left me; having assigned a value of about two thousand ducats for a bounty to me and my fellows. For they give great largesses, where they come, upon all occasions.

The rest was not perfected.

1627

8. A hard basaltic-type rock.

ROBERT BURTON
1577–1640

Robert Burton matriculated at Oxford in 1593, became a scholar of Christ Church College in 1599, and stayed there till he died. He never traveled, never married, never sought "success" or attained it; he existed exclusively among books—old, crabbed books by preference. All this absorption in books was supposed (according to the lore of traditional medicine and the theory of "humors" dating back to the Greeks) to throw his constitution out of balance and produce a "melancholy" temperament in which black bile predominated. And in Burton's case, sure enough, that was what happened. His cure for the desperate condition afflicting him was to write a book about his disease; this project occupied the rest of his life.

It wasn't altogether an eccentric project. There had been many books on melancholy before: because of their sedentary life, it was the favorite disease of scholars, and so got a lot of attention. And the age was interested in taking human nature apart, in finding out what makes it tick. Sir John Davies wrote a long poem on normal psychology, in 1599; it was called *Nosce Teipsum*, or "Know Thyself." Somewhat later, Phineas Fletcher expanded on some Spenserian hints, particularly the "House of Alma" passage in *The Faerie Queene* (book 2, canto 9), to create an allegorical anatomy of man, called *The Purple Island*. (Man's body is an island, rather like England, floating in the purple sea of his own blood; James Joyce was fascinated with the poem, and used it in the composition of *Ulysses*.) Thus Burton was in good company when he began his *Anatomy*. But nobody ever put so much energy into the subject, or handled it in such an epic way. The first edition came out in 1621; later editions, each augmented over the previous one, appeared throughout the next two decades. When he died, in 1640, Burton left behind materials for still another and bigger edition: the book continued to grow, even after the author's death, as if it had acquired a queer vitality of its own.

These cumulative additions do not generally deepen the thought of the book or advance its argument into new territory; they are verbal tags from Burton's immense reading, stuck into the text of the book, after Montaigne's fashion, wherever they seemed more or less appropriate. For though he was perfectly serious in trying to understand the disease of melancholy, Burton wrote like a man intoxicated with his own prolixity. He poured forth words, his own and other people's, as if he were using them to relieve an inner pressure, rather than to express something. He never used one word where dozens would do, never refrained from an erudite citation just because he had said the same thing three times already. He was a humorist and a bit of a buffoon; the role he deliberately assumes in the *Anatomy* is that of a mad scholar choked on his own erudition and in danger of exploding from its inner pressures. Yet he is but mad north-northwest (as Hamlet says); he withholds the discussion of love melancholy, the juiciest part of his treatise, till the last section, then tantalizes the reader with a long justification of his treating the topic at all; next he enters into an account of the affinities of plants and vegetables, considers the mutual attractions of metals, moves on to the love of God, and slowly ventures upon the blissful placidity of happy marriages, before turning to what he has clearly been saving for last, the more extreme and violent manifestations of erotic passion.

From The Anatomy of Melancholy

From *Love Melancholy*

PART 3, SECTION 2, MEMBER 1, SUBSECTION 2: HOW LOVE TYRANNIZETH OVER MEN. LOVE, OR HEROICAL MELANCHOLY, HIS DEFINITION, PART AFFECTED.

'Tis a happy state this[1] indeed, when the fountain is blessed (saith Solomon, Proverbs v.18), "and he rejoiceth with the wife of his youth, and she is to him as the loving hind and pleasant roe,[2] and he delights

---

1. I.e., the state of matrimony.
2. The hind is a female, the roebuck (roe) a male deer.

in her continually." But this love of ours is immoderate, inordinate, and not to be comprehended in any bounds. It will not contain itself within the union of marriage or apply to one object, but is a wandering, extravagant, a domineering, a boundless, an irrefragable, a destructive passion; sometimes this burning lust rageth after marriage, and then it is properly called jealousy; sometimes before, and then it is called heroical melancholy; it extends sometimes to corrivals, etc., begets rapes, incests, murders: *Marcus Antoninus compressit Faustinam sororem, Caracalla Juliam novercam, Nero matrem, Caligula sorores, Cinyras Myrrham filiam*, etc.[3] But it is confined within no terms of blood, years, sex, or whatsoever else. Some furiously rage before they come to discretion or age. Quartilla in Petronius[4] never remembered she was a maid; and the Wife of Bath in Chaucer cracks,

> Since I was twelve years old, believe,
> Husbands at kirk-door had I five.[5]

Aretine's Lucretia sold her maidenhead a thousand times before she was twenty-four years old, *plus millies vendideram virginitatem, etc., neque te celabo, non deerant qui ut integram ambirent*.[6] Rahab, that harlot, began to be a professed quean at ten years of age, and was but fifteen when she hid the spies, as Hugh Broughton proves, to whom Serrarius the Jesuit, *quaest. 6 in cap.* 2 Josue, subscribes. Generally women begin *pubescere* as they call it, or *catulire* as Julius Pollux cites, *lib.* 2, *cap.* 3 *Onomast*,[7] out of Aristophanes, at fourteen years old, then they do offer themselves, and some plainly rage. Leo Afer saith that in Africa a man shall scarce find a maid at fourteen years of age, they are so forward, and many amongst us after they come into the teens do not live without husbands, but linger. What pranks in this kind the middle age have played is not to be recorded, *si mihi sint centum linguae, sint oraque centum*,[8] no tongue can sufficiently delcare, every story is full of men and women's insatiable lust, Neros, Heliogabali, Bonosi, etc.[9] *Coelius Aufilenum, et Quintius Aufilenam depereunt*,[1] etc. They neigh after other men's wives (as Jeremy, *cap.* v.8 complaineth) like fed horses, or range like town bulls, *raptores virginum et viduarum*,[2] as many of our

3. "Marc Antony slept with his sister Faustina, Caracalla with his stepmother Julia, Nero with his mother, Caligula with his sisters, Cinyras with his daughter Myrrha." Burton uses Latin, sometimes euphemistically, as here, but more often just because a Latin tag occurs to him; and he often translates his own Latin phrases, either before or after citing them. When he does so, we don't bother translating again. The notes that follow do not pretend to identify all Burton's quotations and allusions, only to provide minimal materials for comprehension.

4. Quartilla is a character in the *Satyricon* of Petronius Arbiter.

5. Burton cites from memory, and inaccurately; see above, note 3.

6. "Moreover, there were those who could restore it." The tale of Lucretia comes from a set of dialogues published by Pietro Aretino in 1534; they parody the dialogues of Plato, and are set in a brothel. The whore Rahab appears in Joshua 2; Hugh Broughton was a Biblical scholar of Burton's day.

7. *Pubescere*: mature sexually; *catulire*: desire a male. Julius Pollux compiled a dictionary (*Onomasticon*) which Burton cites frequently. Leo Afer or Africanus was a 16th-century Spanish Moor who wrote one of the first accounts of Africa.

8. "If I had a hundred tongues, a hundred mouths."

9. Nero and Heliogabalus were corrupt Roman emperors, their vices described in lurid detail by Roman historians and moralists.

1. "Coelius had an itch for Aufilenus, Quintius for Aufilena." From Catullus, the Roman erotic poet.

2. "Ravishers of maids and widows." Jeremy is Saint Jerome.

great ones do. Solomon's wisdom was extinguished in this fire of lust,
Samson's strength enervated, piety in Lot's daughters quite forgot, gravity of priesthood in Eli's sons, reverend old age in the elders that would
violate Susanna, filial duty in Absalom to his stepmother, brotherly love
in Amnon towards his sister. Human, divine laws, precepts, exhortations, fear of God and men, fair, foul means, fame, fortunes, shame,
disgrace, honor cannot oppose, stave off, or withstand the fury of it,
omnia vincit amor, etc.[3] No cord nor cable can so forcibly draw, or hold
so fast, as love can do with a twined thread. The scorching beams under
the equinoctial or extremity of cold within the circle Arctic, where the
very seas are frozen, cold or torrid zone cannot avoid or expel this heat,
fury, and rage of mortal men.

> *Quo fugis? ah, demens ! nulla est fuga, tu licet usque*
> *Ad Tanaim fugias, usque sequetur amor.*[4]

Of women's unnatural, unsatiable lust, what country, what village
doth not complain? Mother and daughter sometimes dote on the same
man; father and son, master and servant on one woman.

> *Sed amor, sed ineffrenata libido,*
> *Quid castum in terris intentatumque reliquit?*[5]

What breach of vows and oaths, fury, dotage, madness might I reckon
up! Yet this is more tolerable in youth, and such as are still in their hot
blood; but for an old fool to dote, to see an old lecher, what more odious,
what can be more absurd? and yet what so common? who so furious?
Amare ea aetate si occeperint, multo insaniunt acrius.[6] Some dote then
more than ever they did in their youth. How many decrepit, hoary,
harsh, writhen, bursten-bellied, crooked, toothless, bald, blear-eyed,
impotent, rotten old men shall you see flickering still in every place?
One gets him a young wife, another a courtesan, and when he can
scarce lift his leg over a sill and hath one foot already in Charon's boat,[7]
when he hath the trembling in his joints, the gout in his feet, a perpetual
rheum in his head, a continuate cough, "his sight fails him, thick of
hearing, his breath stinks,"[8] all his moisture is dried up and gone, may
not spit from him, a very child again, that cannot dress himself or cut
his own meat, yet he will be dreaming of and honing after wenches;
what can be more unseemly? Worse it is in women than in men; when
she is *aetate declivis, diu vidua, mater olim, parum decore matrimonium
sequi videtur,* an old widow, a mother so long since (in Pliny's opinion),[9]
she doth very unseemly seek to marry; yet whilst she is so old, a crone,

3. "Love conquers all."
4. "Whither away? ah, madman! there is no escape.
Flee to the remotest districts of the river Don, love
will still follow." From Propertius, the Latin ele-
giast.
5. "But love, unbridled passion, leaves nothing on
earth untempted, nothing chaste." From Euripides, the Greek tragedian.
6. "When they start loving at that age, the mad-

ness takes them worse." From Plautus, the Roman
comic dramatist.
7. Charon ferries across the river Styx the souls of
the dead.
8. Cyprian, 3rd-century bishop of Carthage,
became a saint despite this vivid passage.
9. Pliny, *Natural History,* book 8. The Latin is
translated by Burton.

a beldam, she can neither see nor hear, go nor stand, a mere carcass, a witch, and scarce feel, she caterwauls and must have a stallion, a champion, she must and will marry again, and betroth herself to some young man that hates to look on her but for her goods, abhors the sight of her, to the prejudice of her good name, her own undoing, grief of friends, and ruin of her children.

But to enlarge or illustrate this power and effects of love is to set a candle in the sun. It rageth with all sorts and conditions of men, yet is most evident among such as are young and lusty, in the flower of their years, nobly descended, high fed, such as live idly and at ease; and for that cause (which our divines call burning lust) this *ferinus insanus amor*, this mad and beastly passion, as I have said, is named by our physicians heroical love, and a more honorable title put upon it, *amor nobilis* as Savonarola[1] styles it, because noble men and women make a common practice of it and are so ordinarily affected with it. Avicenna,[2] *lib.* 3, *fen.* 1, *tract.* 4, *cap.* 23, calleth this passion *Ilishi* and defines it to be "a disease or melancholy vexation or anguish of mind, in which a man continually meditates of the beauty, gesture, manners of his mistress, and troubles himself about it"; "desiring" (as Savonarola adds) "with all intentions and eagerness of mind to compass or enjoy her; as commonly hunters trouble themselves about their sports, the covetous about their gold and goods, so is he tormented still about his mistress." Arnoldus Villanovanus[3] in his book of heroical love defines it "a continual cogitation of that which he desires, with a confidence or hope of compassing it"; which definition his commentator cavils at. For continual cogitation is not the *genus* but a symptom of love; we continually think of that which we hate and abhor, as well as that which we love; and many things we covet and desire without all hope of attaining. Carolus à Lorme in his *Questions* makes a doubt *an amor sit morbus*, whether this heroical love be a disease: Julius Pollux, *Onomast.* lib. 6, *cap.* 44, determines it. They that are in love are likewise sick; *lascivus, salax, lasciviens, et qui in venerem furit, vere est aegrotus.*[4] Arnoldus will have it improperly so called, and a malady rather of the body than mind. Tully, in his *Tusculans*, defines it a furious disease of the mind; Plato, madness itself; Ficinus, his commentator, *cap.* 12, a species of madness, "for many have run mad for women" (I Esdras iv. 26); but Rhasis,[5] "a melancholy passion"; and most physicians make it a species or kind of melancholy (as will appear by the symptoms), and treat of it apart; whom I mean to imitate, and to discuss it in all his kinds, to examine his several causes, to show his symptoms, indications, prognostics, effects, that so it may be with more facility cured.

The part affected in the meantime, as Arnoldus supposeth, "is the former part of the head for want of moisture," which his commentator

---

1. Not the Florentine reformer, but his grandfather Michele, a Paduan physician.
2. An encyclopedic Arabian physician of the 11th century.
3. Arnold of Villanova was a 14th-century Spanish doctor, astrologer, and alchemist.
4. "One who is lustful, lecherous, lascivious, and mad with desire, is really sick."
5. Rhasis or Rhazes was an Arab physician of the 10th century.

rejects. Langius, *Med. epist. lib.* 1, *cap.* 24, will have this passion sited in the liver, and to keep residence in the heart, "to proceed first from the eyes so carried by our spirits, and kindled with imagination in the liver and heart"; *cogit amare iecur*, as the saying is.[6] *Medium ferit per hepar*, as Cupid in Anacreon. For some such cause belike, Homer feigns Titius' liver (who was enamored of Latona) to be still gnawed by two vultures day and night in hell, "for that young men's bowels thus enamored are so continually tormented by love."[7] Gordonius, *cap.* 2, *part.* 2, "will have the testicles an immediate subject or cause, the liver an antecedent." Fracastorius agrees in this with Gordonius,[8] *inde primitus imaginatio venerea, erectio, etc.; titillatissimam partem vocat, ita ut nisi extruso semine gestiens voluptas non cessat, nec assidua veneris recordatio, addit Guastavinius, Comment.*, 4 *sect.*, *prob.* 27 *Arist.*[9] But properly it is a passion of the brain, as all other melancholy, by reason of corrupt imagination, and so doth Jason Pratensis, cap. 19, *De morb. cerebri* (who writes copiously of this erotical love), place and reckon it amongst the affections of the brain. Melanchthon, *De anima*, confutes those that make the liver a part affected, and Guianerius, *tract.* 15, *cap.* 13 *et* 17, though many put all the affections in the heart, refers it to the brain. Ficinus, *cap.* 7 *In Convivium Platonis*, "will have the blood to be the part affected." Jo. Freitagius, *cap.* 14, *Noct. med.*, supposeth all four affected, heart, liver, brain, blood; but the major part concur upon the brain, 'tis *imaginatio laesa*,[1] and both imagination and reason are misaffected; because of his corrupt judgment and continual meditation of that which he desires, he may truly be said to be melancholy. If it be violent, or his disease inveterate, as I have determined in the precedent partitions, both imagination and reason are misaffected, first one, then the other.

1621, 1651

6. "The liver compels one to love"; and, in the next phrase, "Love strikes through the liver." Anacreon was a Greek lyric poet.

7. *Odyssey* 11.

8. Gordonius, Guastavinius, Jason Pratensis, Guianerius, Freitagius *et al.* are Renaissance physicians from the ragbag of Burton's encyclopedic reading. Two who stand out are Girolamo Fracastoro and Marsilio Ficino—the former a physician still remembered for his work on communicable diseases, the latter known mostly for his learned commentaries on the dialogues of Plato.

9. "Whence at first come erotic imaginings, erection, etc.; it so rouses the most excitable part, adds Guastavinius, that until emission takes place, the longing pleasure does not cease, nor the constant recollection of love-making."

1. A wounded imagination.

THOMAS HOBBES
1588–1679

Thomas Hobbes, the second great philosopher of the seventeenth century, was the acknowledged pupil of the first, Francis Bacon, and the unacknowledged instructor of the third, John Locke. Born in 1588 (Armada year), he had attended Oxford and then served as tutor and secretary to various

noblemen, including several members of the Cavendish family, and Bacon.
When the civil wars broke out he took the Royalist side, though not very
actively, going off to Paris to live in exile from 1640 to 1651. His plan as a
philosopher was to publish one book on physical bodies, one on human
nature, and one on the state; and in fact he wrote books under these three
titles, both in English and Latin. But in reality his career is less symmetrical
and orderly than that fact implies, because the English texts are often quite
different from the Latin, and the book for which he is best known, *Leviathan*, does not fit into the scheme at all. *Leviathan* appeared in Paris in
1651, scandalizing Puritans by its frankly secular tone, and disturbing Royalists because it seemed to make no real distinction between a legal king and
an established usurper. When Hobbes left Paris shortly after the book's publication, returned to England, and made his peace with Cromwell, the worst
fears of the Royalists were realized. But their fury hit a peak after the Restoration, when Hobbes not only went unpunished for his "treason," but was
pensioned by his old friend and former pupil, Charles II. Throughout the
Restoration, his outspoken materialism made him a cause of scandal around
the court; but his caustic tongue made him feared, and the indolent, cynical
king was fond of him. Toward the end of his life he began gathering disciples, some of whom he would just as gladly have done without; for lewd,
swearing, sceptical fellows sometimes took delight in being known as
"Hobbists," not because they had studied or understood his philosophy, but
because it was a name of scandal. He had a deeper influence on his enemies.
A whole generation of theologians and moralists trained themselves by thundering against Hobbes. And in the meanwhile, the quiet, capacious mind
of Locke absorbed what it wanted from the thought of Hobbes and, without
getting involved in the Hobbist controversies, built a structure of incomparable solidity using many of the older philosopher's materials.

From Leviathan

From *The Introduction*

[THE ARTIFICIAL MAN]

Nature (the art whereby God hath made and governs the world) is by
the art of man, as in many other things, so in this also imitated, that it
can make an artificial animal. For seeing life is but a motion of limbs,[1]
the beginning whereof is in some principal part within, why may we not
say that all automata (engines that move themselves by springs and wheels
as doth a watch) have an artificial life? For what is the heart but a spring;
and the nerves but so many strings; and the joints but so many wheels,
giving motion to the whole body such as was intended by the artificer?
Art goes yet further, imitating that rational and most excellent work of
nature, man. For by art is created that great Leviathan called a Common-Wealth or State (in Latin, *Civitas*), which is but an artificial man,

---

1. If motion of limbs is a sufficient definition of
life, the question arises (more timely in the 20th
century than ever before) what is the difference
between the "life" of automata and that of animals, including people?

though of greater stature and strength than the natural, for whose protection and defense it was intended; and in which the sovereignty is an artificial soul,[2] as giving life and motion to the whole body; the magistrates and other officers of judicature and execution, artificial joints; reward and punishment (by which, fastened to the seat of the sovereignty, every joint and member is moved to perform his duty) are the nerves, that do the same in the body natural; the wealth and riches of all the particular members are the strength; *salus populi* (the people's safety) its business; counselors, by whom all things needful for it to know are suggested unto it, are the memory; equity and laws an artificial reason and will; concord, health; sedition, sickness; and civil war, death. Lastly, the pacts and covenants by which the parts of this body politic were at first made, set together, and united, resemble that *Fiat* or the "let us make man," pronounced by God in the creation.

From *Part* 1

CHAPTER 1. OF SENSE

Concerning the thoughts of man, I will consider them first singly and afterwards in train or dependence upon one another. Singly, they are every one a representation or appearance of some quality or other accident of a body without us, which is commonly called an object. Which object worketh on the eyes, ears, and other parts of man's body, and by diversity of working produceth diversity of appearances.

The original of them all is that which we call sense. (For there is no conception in a man's mind which hath not at first, totally or by parts, been begotten upon the organs of sense.)[3] The rest are derived from that original.

To know the natural cause of sense is not very necessary to the business now in hand, and I have elsewhere written of the same at large. Nevertheless, to fill each part of my present method, I will briefly deliver the same in this place.

The cause of sense is the external body or object which presseth the organ proper to each sense, either immediately as in the taste and touch, or mediately, as in seeing, hearing, and smelling; which pressure, by the mediation of nerves and other strings and membranes of the body continued inwards to the brain and heart, causeth there a resistance or counterpressure or endeavor of the heart to deliver itself;[4] which endeavor, because outward, seemeth to be some matter without. And this seeming or fancy is that which men call sense; and consisteth, as to the eye, in a light or color figured; to the ear, in a sound; to the nostril in an odor; to the tongue and palate in a savor; and to the rest of the body in heat, cold,

---

2. In assuming (on the basis of a metaphor) the supreme importance of sovereignty, Hobbes solves at a stroke a great many political problems.
3. The contemporary reader will note that this view of the mind as a blank sheet written on by physical experience leaves no room for the influence of genetic inheritance.
4. Hobbes's physiology of sense, though rudimentary, is, in keeping with his premises, strictly mechanical.

hardness, softness, and such other qualities as we discern by feeling. All which qualities called "sensible"[5] are, in the object that causeth them, but so many several motions of the matter by which it presseth our organs diversely. Neither, in us that are pressed, are they anything else but diverse motions; for motion produceth nothing but motion. But their appearance to us is fancy, the same waking, that dreaming. And as pressing, rubbing, or striking the eye makes us fancy a light; and pressing the ear produceth a din; so do the bodies also we see or hear produce the same by their strong though unobserved actions. For if those colors and sounds were in the bodies or objects that cause them, they could not be severed from them, as by glasses[6] and in echoes by reflection we see they are; where we know the thing we see is in one place, the appearance in another. And though at some certain distance the real and very object seem invested with the fancy it begets in us, yet still the object is one thing, the image or fancy is another. So that sense in all cases is nothing else but original fancy, caused (as I have said) by the pressure, that is by the motion, of external things upon our eyes, ears, and other organs thereunto ordained.

But the philosophy-schools[7] through all the universities of Christendom, grounded upon certain texts of Aristotle, teach another doctrine, and say for the cause of vision, that the thing seen sendeth forth on every side a visible species—in English, a visible show, apparition, or aspect, or a being seen—the receiving whereof into the eye is seeing. And for the cause of hearing, that the thing heard sendeth forth an audible species, that is an audible aspect or audible being seen, which entering at the ear maketh hearing. Nay for the cause of understanding also they say the thing understood sendeth forth intelligible species, that is an intelligible being seen, which coming into the understanding makes us understand. I say not this as disapproving the use of universities, but because I am to speak hereafter of their office in a commonwealth, I must let you see on all occasions by the way what things would be amended in them; amongst which the frequency of insignificant speech is one.

CHAPTER 13. OF THE NATURAL CONDITION OF MANKIND AS CONCERNING THEIR FELICITY AND MISERY

Nature hath made men so equal in the faculties of body and mind as that, though there be found one man sometimes manifestly stronger in body or of quicker mind than another, yet when all is reckoned together, the difference between man and man is not so considerable as that one man can thereupon claim to himself any benefit, to which another may not pretend as well as he. For as to the strength of body, the weakest has strength enough to kill the strongest, either by secret machination, or by confederacy with others that are in the same danger with himself.

And as to the faculties of the mind—setting aside the arts grounded

---

5. I.e., accessible through the senses.
6. Mirrors.

7. The scholastic philosophers (schoolmen), always a ready butt for Bacon and his followers.

upon words, and especially that skill of proceeding upon general and infallible rules, called science; which very few have, and but in few things; as being not a native faculty, born with us; nor attained, as prudence, while we look after somewhat else—I find yet a greater equality amongst men than that of strength. For prudence is but experience, which equal time equally bestows on all men, in those things they equally apply themselves unto. That which may perhaps make such equality incredible is but a vain conceit of one's own wisdom, which almost all men think they have in a greater degree than the vulgar—that is, than all men but themselves and a few others, whom by fame, or for concurring with themselves, they approve. For such is the nature of men, that howsoever they may acknowledge many others to be more witty, or more eloquent, or more learned, yet they will hardly believe there be many so wise as themselves; for they see their own wit at hand, and other men's at a distance. But this proveth rather that men are in that point equal, than unequal. For there is not ordinarily a greater sign of the equal distribution of anything than that every man is contented with his share.

From this equality of ability ariseth equality of hope in the attaining of our ends. And therefore if any two men desire the same thing, which nevertheless they cannot both enjoy, they become enemies; and in the way to their end (which is principally their own conservation, and sometimes their delectation only) endeavor to destroy or subdue one another. And from hence it comes to pass, that where an invader hath no more to fear than another man's single power, if one plant, sow, build, or possess a convenient seat, others may probably be expected to come prepared with forces united, to dispossess and deprive him, not only of the fruit of his labor, but also of his life or liberty. And the invader again is in the like danger of another.

And from this diffidence[8] of one another, there is no way for any man to secure himself so reasonable as anticipation; that is, by force or wiles to master the persons of all men he can, so long, till he see no other power great enough to endanger him; and this is no more than his own conservation requireth, and is generally allowed. Also because there be some, that taking pleasure in contemplating their own power in the acts of conquest, which they pursue farther than their security requires; if others that otherwise would be glad to be at ease within modest bounds, should not by invasion increase their power, they would not be able long time, by standing only on their defense, to subsist. And by consequence, such augmentation of dominion over men being necessary to a man's conservation, it ought to be allowed him.

Again, men have no pleasure, but on the contrary a great deal of grief, in keeping company, where there is no power able to overawe them all. For every man looketh that his companion should value him at the same rate he sets upon himself; and upon all signs of contempt, or undervaluing, naturally endeavors, as far as he dares (which amongst them that

8. Lack of faith, mistrust.

have no common power to keep them in quiet, is far enough to make them destroy each other), to extort a greater value from his contemners by damage, and from others by the example.

So that in the nature of man, we find three principal causes of quarrel. First, competition; secondly, diffidence; thirdly, glory.

The first maketh men invade for gain; the second, for safety; and the third, for reputation. The first use violence to make themselves masters of other men's persons, wives, children, and cattle; the second, to defend them; the third, for trifles, as a word, a smile, a different opinion, and any other sign of undervalue, either direct in their persons, or by reflection in their kindred, their friends, their nation, their profession, or their name.

Hereby it is manifest that during the time men live without a common power to keep them all in awe, they are in that condition which is called war; and such a war as is of every man against every man. For war consisteth not in battle only, or the act of fighting, but in a tract of time wherein the will to contend by battle is sufficiently known; and therefore the notion of time is to be considered in the nature of war, as it is in the nature of weather. For as the nature of foul weather lieth not in a shower or two of rain, but in an inclination thereto of many days together; so the nature of war consisteth not in actual fighting, but in the known disposition thereto, during all the time there is no assurance to the contrary. All other time is peace.

Whatsoever therefore is consequent to a time of war, where every man is enemy to every man, the same is consequent to the time wherein men live without other security than what their own strength and their own invention shall furnish them withal. In such condition there is no place for industry, because the fruit thereof is uncertain, and consequently no culture of the earth; no navigation, nor use of the commodities that may be imported by sea; no commodious building; no instruments of moving, and removing, such things as require much force; no knowledge of the face of the earth; no account of time; no arts; no letters; no society; and, which is worst of all, continual fear, and danger of violent death; and the life of man, solitary, poor, nasty, brutish, and short.

It may seem strange to some man that has not well weighed these things, that nature should thus dissociate and render men apt to invade and destroy one another; and he may therefore, not trusting to this inference, made from the passions, desire perhaps to have the same confirmed by experience. Let him therefore consider with himself, when taking a journey, he arms himself and seeks to go well accompanied; when going to sleep, he locks his doors; when even in his house he locks his chests; and this when he knows there be laws, and public officers, armed, to revenge all injuries shall be done him; what opinion he has of his fellow subjects, when he rides armed; of his fellow citizens, when he locks his doors; and of his children and servants, when he locks his chests. Does he not there as much accuse mankind by his actions, as I do by my words? But neither of us accuse man's nature in it. The desires and other passions of man are in themselves no sin. No more are the actions that proceed from those passions, till they know a law that forbids them, which, till laws be made, they cannot know; nor can any law be made, till they have agreed upon the person that shall make it.

It may peradventure be thought there was never such a time nor condition of war as this; and I believe it was never generally so, over all the world; but there are many places where they live so now. For the savage people in many places of America, except the government of small families, the concord whereof dependeth on natural lust, have no government at all and live at this day in that brutish manner as I said before. Howsoever, it may be perceived what manner of life there would be, where there were no common power to fear, by the manner of life which men that have formerly lived under a peaceful government use to degenerate into in a civil war.[9]

But though there had never been any time wherein particular men were in a condition of war one against another, yet in all times, kings and persons of sovereign authority, because of their independency, are in continual jealousies, and in the state and posture of gladiators; having their weapons pointing, and their eyes fixed on one another; that is, their forts, garrisons, and guns upon the frontiers of their kingdoms, and continual spies upon their neighbors, which is a posture of war. But because they uphold thereby the industry of their subjects, there does not follow from it that misery which accompanies the liberty of particular men.

To this war of every man against every man, this also is consequent: that nothing can be unjust. The notions of right and wrong, justice and injustice, have there no place. Where there is no common power, there is no law; where no law, no injustice. Force and fraud are in war the two cardinal virtues. Justice and injustice are none of the faculties neither of the body nor mind. If they were, they might be in a man that were alone in the world, as well as his senses and passions. They are qualities that relate to men in society, not in solitude. It is consequent also to the same condition that there be no propriety,[1] no dominion, no *mine* and *thine* distinct; but only that to be every man's, that he can get; and for so long as he can keep it. And thus much for the ill condition which man by mere nature is actually placed in; though with a possibility to come out of it, consisting partly in the passions, partly in his reason.

The passions that incline men to peace are fear of death, desire of such things as are necessary to commodious living, and a hope by their industry to obtain them. And reason suggesteth convenient articles of peace, upon which men may be drawn to agreement. These articles are they which otherwise are called the Laws of Nature, whereof I shall speak more particularly in the two following chapters.

---

9. Hobbes may be thinking both of recent events in England and of such famous accounts of savage civil wars as that of Thucydides (whom he translated).
1. Property.

CHAPTER 14. OF THE FIRST AND SECOND NATURAL LAWS

The Right of Nature, which writers commonly call *ius naturale*, is the liberty each man hath to use his own power as he will himself for the preservation of his own nature, that is to say, of his own life; and consequently of doing anything which in his own judgment and reason he shall conceive to be the aptest means thereunto.

By Liberty is understood, according to the proper signification of the word, the absence of external impediments, which impediments may oft take away part of a man's power to do what he would, but cannot hinder him from using the power left him according as his judgment and reason shall dictate to him.

A Law of Nature *(lex naturalis)* is a precept or general rule found out by reason, by which a man is forbidden to do that which is destructive of his life or taketh away the means of preserving the same; and to omit that by which he thinketh it may be best preserved. For though they that speak of this subject use to confound[2] *Ius* and *Lex*, *Right* and *Law*, yet they ought to be distinguished, because Right consisteth in liberty to do or to forbear, whereas Law determineth and bindeth to one of them: so that Law and Right differ as much as obligation and liberty, which in one and the same matter are inconsistent.

And because the condition of man (as hath been declared in the precedent chapter) is a condition of war of every one against every one, in which case every one is governed by his own reason, and there is nothing he can make use of that may not be a help unto him in preserving his life against his enemies: it followeth that in such a condition every man has a right to every thing, even to one another's body. And therefore as long as this natural right of every man to every thing endureth, there can be no security to any man (how strong or wise soever he be) of living out the time which nature ordinarily alloweth men to live. And consequently it is a precept or general rule of reason, *That every man ought to endeavor peace, as far as he has hope of obtaining it; and when he cannot obtain it, that he may seek and use all helps and advantages of war.* The first branch of which rule containeth the first and fundamental law of nature, which is *to seek peace and follow it.* The second, the sum of the right of nature, which is, *by all means we can to defend ourselves.*

From this fundamental law of nature, by which men are commanded to endeavor peace, is derived this second law: *That a man be willing, when others are so too, as far-forth as*[3] *for peace and defense of himself he shall think it necessary, to lay down this right to all things, and be contented with so much liberty against other men as he would allow other men against himself.* For as long as any man holdeth this right of doing anything he liketh, so long are all men in the condition of war. But if other men will not lay down their right, as well as he, then there is no

---

2. Customarily confuse.   3. Insofar as.

reason for anyone to divest himself of his. For that were to expose himself to prey (which no man is bound to) rather than to dispose himself to peace. This is that law of the Gospel: *Whatsoever you require that others should do to you, that do ye to them.*[4]

* * *

From CHAPTER 15. OF OTHER LAWS OF NATURE

From that law of nature by which we are obliged to transfer to another such rights as, being retained, hinder the peace of mankind, there followeth a third, which is this: *That men perform their covenants made:* without which, covenants are in vain, and but empty words; and, the right of all men to all things remaining, we are still in the condition of war.

And in this law of nature consisteth the fountain and original of Justice. For where no covenant hath preceded, there hath no right been transferred, and every man has right to every thing; and consequently no action can be unjust. But when a covenant is made, then to break it is unjust; and the definition of injustice is no other than *the not performance of covenant.* And whatsoever is not unjust is just.

But because covenants of mutual trust, where there is a fear of not performance on either part * * * are invalid; though the original of justice be the making of covenants, yet injustice actually there can be none, till the cause of such fear be taken away; which while men are in the natural condition of war, cannot be done. Therefore, before the names of just and unjust can have place, there must be some coercive power, to compel men equally to the performance of their covenants by the terror of some punishment greater than the benefit they expect by the breach of their covenant, and to make good that propriety[5] which by mutual contract men acquire in recompense of the universal right they abandon: and such power there is none before the erection of a commonwealth. And this is also to be gathered out of the ordinary definition of justice in the schools;[6] for they say that *Justice is the constant will of giving to every man his own.* And therefore where there is no *own,* that is, no propriety, there is no injustice; and where there is no coercive power erected, that is, where there is no commonwealth, there is no propriety, all men having right to all things. Therefore where there is no commonwealth, there nothing is unjust. So that the nature of justice consisteth in keeping of valid covenants; but the validity of covenants begins not but with the constitution of a civil power, sufficient to compel men to keep them. And then it is also that propriety begins.

The fool hath said in his heart, there is no such thing as justice, and

4. The golden rule: Matthew 7.12, Luke 6.31.   6. I.e., among the schoolmen, medieval Aristo-
5. Property, in the sense of right or privilege.   telians like St. Thomas Aquinas.

sometimes also with his tongue;[7] seriously alleging that every man's conservation and contentment being committed to his own care, there could
be no reason why every man might not do what he thought conduced
thereunto: and therefore also, to make or not make, keep or not keep
covenants was not against reason, when it conduced to one's benefit. He
does not therein deny that there be covenants, and that they are sometimes broken, sometimes kept, and that such breach of them may be
called injustice, and the observance of them, justice: but he questioneth
whether injustice, taking away the fear of God (for the same fool hath
said in his heart there is no God), may not sometimes stand with that
reason which dictateth to every man his own good; and particularly then
when it conduceth to such a benefit as shall put a man in a condition to
neglect, not only the dispraise and revilings, but also the power of other
men. The kingdom of God is gotten by violence; but what if it could be
gotten by unjust violence? were it against reason so to get it, when it is
impossible to receive hurt by it? and if it be not against reason, it is not
against justice, or else justice is not to be approved for good. From such
reasoning as this, successful wickedness hath obtained the name of virtue; and some that in all other things have disallowed the violation of
faith, yet have allowed it when it is for the getting of a kingdom. And
the heathen that believed that *Saturn* was deposed by his son *Jupiter*
believed nevertheless the same *Jupiter* to be the avenger of injustice:[8]
somewhat like to a piece of law in Coke's commentaries on Littleton,
where he says, if the right heir of the crown be attainted of treason, yet
the crown shall descend to him and *eo instante*[9] the attainder be void.
From which instances a man will be very prone to infer that when the
heir apparent of a kingdom shall kill him that is in possession, though
his father; you may call it injustice or by what other name you will; yet
it can never be against reason, seeing all the voluntary actions of men
tend to the benefit of themselves, and those actions are most reasonable
that conduce most to their ends. This specious reasoning is nevertheless
false.

For the question is not of promises mutual where there is no security
of performance on either side, as when there is no civil power erected
over the parties promising; for such promises are no covenants. But either
where one of the parties has performed already, or where there is a power
to make him perform: there is the question whether it be against reason,
that is against the benefit of the other, to perform or not. And I say it is

7. It is by no means a common fool who speaks
up at this point; what he is saying is that a man
who breaks his covenant (as Cromwell broke his
oath of allegiance to Charles I) does not act unrea-
sonably, as long as he serves his own interest.
Though Hobbes tries to answer this fool, it is not
clear that he succeeds.
8. In Greek mythology, Saturn was deposed by
Zeus (Jupiter), his son; yet Zeus, though himself
a usurper, became father of the gods and the
spokesman of justice. In all this discussion, the

parallel with Cromwell (a usurper, yet perhaps the
creator of a new justice) is strongly felt. Cf. Marvell's *Horatian Ode*.
9. In that very instant. The heir to a throne is a
traitor when he conspires against his father; but the
instant he is successful, the king is dead, he is the
new king, he cannot commit treason against himself, so the attainder of treason is void. "Coke upon
Littleton" (the commentaries of Sir Edward Coke
on Sir Thomas Littleton's 15th-century law treatise) is a famous legal authority.

not against reason.[1] For the manifestation whereof, we are to consider: first, that when a man doth a thing which (notwithstanding anything can be foreseen and reckoned on) tendeth to his own destruction, howsoever[2] some accident, which he could not expect, arriving may turn it to his benefit; yet such events do not make it reasonably or wisely done. Secondly, that in a condition of war, wherein every man to every man, for want of a common power to keep them all in awe, is an enemy, there is no man can hope by his own strength or wit to defend himself from destruction without the help of confederates; where everyone expects the same defense by the confederation that anyone else does. And therefore he which declares he thinks it reason to deceive those that help him can in reason expect no other means of safety than what can be had from his own single power. He therefore that breaketh his covenant, and consequently declareth that he thinks he may with reason do so, cannot be received into any society that unite themselves for peace and defense, but by the error of them that receive him; nor when he is received be retained in it without seeing the danger of their error; which errors a man cannot reasonably reckon upon as the means of his security. And therefore if he be left or cast out of society, he perisheth; and if he live in society, it is by the errors of other men, which he could not foresee nor reckon upon; and consequently against the reason of his preservation; and so as all men that contribute not to his destruction forbear him only out of ignorance of what is good for themselves.

As for the instance of gaining the secure and perpetual felicity of heaven by any way, it is frivolous: there being but one way imaginable, and that is not breaking, but keeping of covenant.

And for the other instance of attaining sovereignty by rebellion, it is manifest that though the event follow, yet because it cannot reasonably be expected, but rather the contrary; and because by gaining it so others are taught to gain the same in like manner, the attempt thereof is against reason. Justice therefore, that is to say, keeping of covenant, is a rule of reason, by which we are forbidden to do anything destructive to our life, and consequently a law of nature.

* * *

1651

1. I.e., to perform the promise.   2. Even though.

IZAAK WALTON
1593–1683

Izaak Walton, who was "in trade," as people once used to say, is remembered these days as the author of *The Complete Angler*. This is an early

treatise on the art of angling, woven artfully into a quaintly humorous dialogue; it is consulted nowadays not so much by people who want to catch
fish as by people who want to think about fishing from the placid perspective
of a library. But to his own generation, Walton was essentially a pious biographer. A devout Anglican, he first turned to biography in 1640, just as the
civil wars were looming; and all his biographical work was done at a time
when the English church was under attack from the Puritans, or struggling
to re-establish itself after the Restoration. The five men whose lives he wrote—
including Hooker, Donne, and Herbert—were ideally suited to be saints and
martyrs in a roster of Anglican worthies; or, if they were not ideally suited
for the role, Izaak's happy imagination and faculty of forgetting inconvenient
details did much to make them so. But if they are not models of scholarly
objectivity—how could they be, in that age?—the biographies by Walton
are warm and moving compositions of literary art. Certainly he has not been
the last man to feel that a good cause justified a little liberty with exact truth.

The *Life of Donne* is the most celebrated of Walton's biographies. We
print its famous conclusion, in which Donne dies as dramatically as he had
lived. Our text is from the fourth edition (1675), which differs considerably
from the first: "Feb. 15, 1640," the date at the end of the *Life,* is misleading.

From The Life of Dr. John Donne

[*Donne on His Deathbed*]

It is observed that a desire of glory or commendation is rooted in the
very nature of man; and that those of the severest and most mortified[1]
lives, though they may become so humble as to banish self-flattery, and
such weeds as naturally grow there; yet they have not been able to kill
this desire of glory, but that like our radical heat,[2] it will both live and
die with us; and many think it should do so; and we want not sacred
examples to justify the desire of having our memory to outlive our lives;
which I mention, because Dr. Donne, by the persuasion of Dr. Fox,
easily yielded at this very time[3] to have a monument made for him; but
Dr. Fox undertook not to persuade him how, or what monument it
should be; that was left to Dr. Donne himself.

A monument being resolved upon, Dr. Donne sent for a carver to
make for him in wood the figure of an urn, giving him directions for the
compass and height of it; and to bring with it a board, of the just[4] height
of his body. These being got, then without delay a choice painter was
got to be in readiness to draw his picture, which was taken as followeth.
Several charcoal fires being first made in his large study, he brought
with him into that place his winding-sheet in his hand, and having put
off all his clothes, had this sheet put on him, and so tied with knots at
his head and feet and his hands so placed as dead bodies are usually
fitted to be shrouded and put into their coffin or grave. Upon this urn

---

1. Self-denying.
2. Bodily warmth.
3. Toward the end of his life, in 1631. Dr. Simeon

Fox was Donne's physician.
4. Exact.

he thus stood with his eyes shut and with so much of the sheet turned aside as might show his lean, pale, and deathlike face, which was purposely turned toward the east, from whence he expected the second coming of his and our Savior Jesus. In this posture he was drawn at his just height; and when the picture was fully finished, he caused it to be set by his bedside, where it continued and became his hourly object till his death, and was then given to his dearest friend and executor Dr. Henry King,[5] then chief residentiary of St. Paul's, who caused him to be thus carved in one entire piece of white marble, as it now stands in that church;[6] and by Dr. Donne's own appointment, these words were to be affixed to it as his epitaph:

JOHANNES DONNE
Sac. Theol. Profess.

Post varia studia quibus ab annis tenerrimis
fideliter, nec infeliciter incubuit,
instinctu et impulsu Sp. Sancti, monitu
et hortatu

REGIS JACOBI, ordines sacros
amplexus, anno sui Jesu, 1614, et suae aetatis 42,
decanatu huius ecclesiae indutus 27
Novembris, 1621,

exutus morte ultimo die Martii, 1631,
hic licet in occiduo cinere aspicit eum
cuius nomen est Oriens.[7]

And now, having brought him through the many labyrinths and perplexities of a various life, even to the gates of death and the grave, my desire is he may rest till I have told my reader that I have seen many pictures of him in several habits and at several ages and in several postures; and I now mention this because I have seen one picture of him, drawn by a curious[8] hand, at his age of eighteen, with his sword and what other adornments might then suit with the present fashions of youth and the giddy gaieties of that age;[9] and his motto then was—

How much shall I be changed,
Before I am changed![1]

5. This is the poet, son of the bishop of London who had advised Donne to enter holy orders, and himself later bishop of Chichester. A reproduction of the portrait may be found in Grierson's edition of the poems, vol. 1, opp. p. 369.
6. Donne's tomb was destroyed in the great fire of 1666; only the statue survived, and is still seen in St. Paul's.
7. "John Donne, Professor of Sacred Theology. After various studies, which he plied from his tenderest youth faithfully and not unsuccessfully, moved by the instinct and impulse of the Holy Spirit and the admonition and encouragement of King James, he took holy orders in the year of his Jesus 1614 and the year of his age 42. On the 27th of November 1621, he was invested as dean of this church; and divested by death, the last day of March 1631. Here in the decline of ashes he looks to One whose name is a Rising Sun."
8. Skillful.
9. See the portrait reproduced in Grierson, vol. 1, opp. p. 7.
1. Transformed (i.e., by death).

And if that young and his now dying picture were at this time set together, every beholder might say, "Lord! how much is Dr. Donne already changed, before he is changed!" And the view of them might give my reader occasion to ask himself with some amazement, "Lord! how much may I also, that am now in health, be changed before I am changed; before this vile, this changeable body shall put off mortality!" and therefore to prepare for it. But this is not writ so much for my reader's memento as to tell him that Dr. Donne would often in his private discourses, and often publicly in his sermons, mention the many changes both of his body and mind; especially of his mind from a vertiginous giddiness; and would as often say, "his great and most blessed change was from a temporal to a spiritual employment"; in which he was so happy, that he accounted the former part of his life to be lost; and the beginning of it to be from his first entering into sacred orders and serving his most merciful God at his altar.

Upon Monday after the drawing this picture, he took his last leave of his beloved study; and being sensible of his hourly decay, retired himself to his bedchamber; and that week sent at several[2] times for many of his most considerable friends, with whom he took a solemn and deliberate farewell, commending to their considerations some sentences useful for the regulation of their lives; and then dismissed them, as good Jacob did his sons, with a spiritual benediction. The Sunday following, he appointed his servants, that if there were any business yet undone that concerned him or themselves, it should be prepared against Saturday next; for after that day he would not mix his thoughts with anything that concerned this world; nor ever did; but, as Job, so he "waited for the appointed day of his dissolution."[3]

And now he was so happy as to have nothing to do but to die, to do which he stood in need of no longer time; for he had studied it long and to so happy a perfection that in a former sickness he called God to witness, "he was that minute ready to deliver his soul into his hands, if that minute God would determine his dissolution."[4] In that sickness he begged of God the constancy to be preserved in that estate forever; and his patient expectation to have his immortal soul disrobed from her garment of mortality makes me confident he now had a modest assurance that his prayers were then heard and his petition granted. He lay fifteen days earnestly expecting his hourly change; and in the last hour of his last day, as his body melted away and vapored into spirit, his soul having, I verily believe, some revelation of the beatifical vision, he said, "I were miserable if I might not die"; and after those words, closed many periods of his faint breath by saying often, "Thy kingdom come, thy will be done." His speech, which had long been his ready and faithful servant, left him not till the last minute of his life, and then forsook him, not to serve another master (for who speaks like him) but died before him; for

2. Separate.
3. Cf. Job 14.14.

4. Walton quotes from Donne's *Devotions upon Emergent Occasions*.

that it was then become useless to him that now conversed with God on earth as angels are said to do in heaven, only by thoughts and looks. Being speechless, and seeing heaven by that illumination by which he saw it, he did, as St. Stephen, "look steadfastly into it, till he saw the Son of Man standing at the right hand of God his Father";[5] and being satisfied with this blessed sight, as his soul ascended and his last breath departed from him, he closed his own eyes; and then disposed his hands and body into such a posture as required not the least alteration by those that came to shroud him.

Thus variable, thus virtuous was the life: thus excellent, thus exemplary was the death of this memorable man.

He was buried in that place of St. Paul's Church which he had appointed for that use some years before his death; and by which he passed daily to pay his public devotions to Almighty God (who was then served twice a day by a public form of prayer and praises in that place):[6] but he was not buried privately, though he desired it; for, beside an unnumbered number of others, many persons of nobility, and of eminency for learning, who did love and honor him in his life, did show it at his death by a voluntary and sad attendance of his body to the grave, where nothing was so remarkable as a public sorrow.

To which place of his burial some mournful friends repaired, and, as Alexander the Great did to the grave of the famous Achilles, so they strewed his with an abundance of curious and costly flowers; which course they (who were never yet known) continued morning and evening for many days, not ceasing till the stones that were taken up in that church to give his body admission into the cold earth (now his bed of rest) were again by the mason's art so leveled and firmed as they had been formerly, and his place of burial undistinguishable to common view.

The next day after his burial, some unknown friend, some one of the many lovers and admirers of his virtue and learning, wrote this epitaph with a coal on the wall over his grave:

> Reader! I am to let thee know,
> Donne's body only lies below;
> For, could the grave his soul comprise,
> Earth would be richer than the skies!

Nor was this all the honor done to his reverend ashes; for, as there be some persons that will not receive a reward for that for which God accounts himself a debtor, persons that dare trust God with their charity and without a witness; so there was by some grateful unknown friend that thought Dr. Donne's memory ought to be perpetuated, an hundred marks sent to his two faithful friends and executors,[7] towards the making of his monument. It was not for many years known by whom; but after the death of Dr. Fox, it was known that it was he that sent it; and he lived

5. Cf. Acts 7.55.
6. This phrase clearly shows up as one of Walton's later additions to the *Life*; Walton originally wrote when the forms of liturgy had not been changed.
7. "Dr. King and Dr. Monfort" [marginal note].

to see as lively a representation of his dead friend as marble can express: a statue indeed so like Dr. Donne, that (as his friend Sir Henry Wotton hath expressed himself) "it seems to breathe faintly, and posterity shall look upon it as a kind of artificial miracle."

He was of stature moderately tall; of a straight and equally proportioned body, to which all his words and actions gave an unexpressible addition of comeliness.

The melancholy and pleasant humor were in him so contempered that each gave advantage to the other, and made his company one of the delights of mankind.

His fancy was unimitably high, equaled only by his great wit; both being made useful by a commanding judgment.[8]

His aspect was cheerful, and such as gave a silent testimony of a clear knowing soul, and of a conscience at peace with itself.

His melting eye showed that he had a soft heart, full of noble compassion; of too brave a soul to offer injuries and too much a Christian not to pardon them in others.

He did much contemplate (especially after he entered into his sacred calling) the mercies of Almighty God, the immortality of the soul, and the joys of heaven: and would often say in a kind of sacred ecstasy— "Blessed be God that he is God, only and divinely like himself."

He was by nature highly passionate, but more apt to reluct at[9] the excesses of it. A great lover of the offices of humanity, and of so merciful a spirit that he never beheld the miseries of mankind without pity and relief.

He was earnest and unwearied in the search of knowledge, with which his vigorous soul is now satisfied, and employed in a continual praise of that God that first breathed it into his active body: that body, which once was a temple of the Holy Ghost and is now become a small quantity of Christian dust:

But I shall see it reanimated.

Feb. 15, 1640

I.W.
1640, 1675

---

8. Note that "wit" (mental acuity) and "fancy" (imagination) are both regarded as faculties under the command of "judgment."
9. Oppose.

SIR THOMAS BROWNE
1605–1682

Though his life was long, Browne's biography contains few events. Born in London, he attended Oxford and then medical schools on the Continent— at Montpellier in France, Padua in Italy, and Leyden in Holland. Rubbing elbows with people of different religions encouraged Browne to reflect on his own religious stance, and shortly after his return to England (about 1635) he wrote a little essay called *Religio Medici* ("A Doctor's Faith"). Not being intended for publication, it wasn't published for several years, till a printer (prophetically named Andrew Crook) brought out a pirated edition in 1642. Browne had by then married and settled down to practice medicine in the bustling commercial city of Norwich in the marshy countryside of Norfolk. (Norwich was bigger then, in absolute terms, than it is now, and proportionately much bigger; though numbering less than a twentieth of London's population, it ranked among the largest provincial towns in the realm.) Browne's book was thought witty and ingenious, perhaps because it managed to talk at length about religion without ever discussing or even facing any of the great religious issues which were tearing the country apart. What fascinated Browne was a private game he was playing between faith and doubt; he would think of all the most intricate and perplexing questions that his "philosophy" could invent, and then solve them by means of his faith. Absorbed in this curious inner drama of his, Browne never entered the literary "world" (such as it was) of London, and, though he was an outspoken Royalist, never took an active part in the civil wars. Like Thoreau, one of his later admirers, he did not need to move around, because he was traveling widely in Norwich.

Some of his investigations were published in 1646 under the forbidding title of *Pseudodoxia Epidemica*, or "Vulgar Errors." They consisted of immense researches into all the foolish ideas entertained by mankind over the ages—superstitions and oddities of opinion, mythical animals, pious legends, hexes, hoaxes, assorted nonsense of every description. It was characteristic of Browne's mind that he was always more interested in what wasn't knowable than in what was. His thought instinctively moved toward the mysterious, the remote, the legendary; and though, for his day, he was an enlightened man, he accepted almost as many vulgar errors as he exposed. He enjoyed the mysteries of ancient wisdom; he enjoyed even more thinking about the unthinkable. Thus when some workmen near Norwich accidentally dug up some funeral urns dating back hundreds or, for all he cared to know, thousands of years, Doctor Browne took occasion to visit the site, inspect the find, and write (in 1658) a private meditation on death and burial practices. The subject might have produced a morbid (or, worse, a dull) document; but Browne's agile metaphysical wit and sumptuous rhetoric gave an immense, resonant poetry to his treatise *Hydriotaphia, Urn-Burial*.

Whatever the ostensible topic of which he was treating, Browne always turned it toward that curious inward balance of faith and skepticism which fascinated him. "We carry with us," he wrote, "the wonders we seek without us: there is all Africa and her prodigies within us. We are that bold and adventurous piece of nature which he that studies wisely learns in a compendium what others labor at in a divided piece and endless volume." His focus was on himself, rarely on those areas of material, factual information where his age was learning, at a furious pace and with ruthless precision, to discriminate truth from falsehood. During his lifetime, the modern scientific outlook, the modern scientific method, established themselves beyond serious challenge at the center of intellectual life. Browne as a philosopher of the old school hardly gave the new developments a thought. What song the sirens sang, and what name Achilles assumed when he hid himself among women, were subjects more congenial for his speculative, inward mind. No doubt he knew that they were funny subjects to think about; the prose in which he discussed these matters, always polysyllabic and Latinate, sometimes gets so elaborate that one can't help suspecting self-mockery. But these were all essential ingredients in the alchemy of a personality, and it is the fascination of that personality—darker and more mysterious than Burton's, but just as much the deliberate creation of an artist—that has kept Browne's name and books alive over the centuries.

From Religio Medici[1]

From *Part* 1

1. For my religion, though there be several circumstances that might persuade the world I have none at all—as the general scandal of my profession,[2] the natural course of my studies, the indifference of my behavior and discourse in matters of religion, neither violently defending one, nor with that common ardor and contention opposing another—yet in despite hereof I dare without usurpation assume the honorable style of a Christian. Not that I merely owe this title to the font,[3] my education, or clime wherein I was born, as being bred up either to confirm those principles my parents instilled into my unwary understanding, or by a general consent proceed in the religion of my country; but having in my riper years and confirmed judgment seen and examined all, I find myself obliged by the principles of grace and the law of mine own reason to embrace no other name but this. Neither doth herein my zeal so far make me forget the general charity I owe unto humanity, as rather to hate than pity Turks, infidels, and (what is worse) Jews;[4] rather contenting myself to enjoy that happy style than maligning those who refuse so glorious a title.

2. But because the name of a Christian is become too general to express our faith—there being a geography of religions as well as lands, and every clime distinguished not only by their laws and limits, but circumscribed by their doctrines and rules of faith—to be particular, I am of that reformed new-cast religion wherein I mislike nothing but the name;[5] of the same belief our Savior taught, the Apostles disseminated, the Fathers authorized, and the Martyrs confirmed; but by the sinister ends of princes, the ambition and avarice of prelates, and the fatal corruption of times,

1. The title *Religio Medici* means "A Doctor's Faith," and one might well wonder why a doctor should have a special faith of his own, different from a lawyer's or a merchant's. But Browne gives a rather private meaning to the word "faith." Not that he is a doubter; he accepts all the articles and constitutions of the Church of England, both because they are enjoined and because they appeal to his reason. But he is also interested in something more mysterious and personal; this is the believer's relation to the Christian mystery of resurrection and redemption, which he embraces, not because he can explain or defend it, but because he cannot. Browne's position, shared mainly by Catholic skeptics like Montaigne and Charron, is known as "fideism"; by separating philosophy (reason) from faith, it exempts faith from criticism by reason, while at the same time depriving it of reason's support. Many people, including the fideists themselves, recognized the position as a perilous one. But for Browne, who was not engaged in public controversies, it was agreeable in answering a deep temperamental need for equivocation.

2. Doctors, because supposed to know intimately the body's mechanisms, were popularly reputed to be sceptical of a divine maker—i.e., to be atheists.

3. The baptismal font.

4. Browne thought Jews worse than Turks or infidels because, with a better chance to know and accept Christianity, they rejected it.

5. Protestantism, which Browne misliked as a name implying constant protest.

so decayed, impaired, and fallen from its native beauty that it required the careful and charitable hands of these times to restore it to its primitive integrity. Now the accidental occasion whereon, the slender means whereby, the low and abject condition of the person by whom so good a work was set on foot,[6] which in our adversaries beget contempt and scorn, fills me with wonder, and is the very same objection the insolent pagans first cast at Christ and his disciples.

3. Yet have I not so shaken hands[7] with those desperate resolutions—who had rather venture at large their decayed bottom than bring her in to be new trimmed in the dock, who had rather promiscuously retain all than abridge any, and obstinately be what they are than what they have been—as to stand in diameter and sword's point with them. We have reformed from them, not against them; for, omitting those improperations[8] and terms of scurrility betwixt us, which only difference our affections and not our cause, there is between us one common name and appellation, one faith and necessary body of principles common to us both; and therefore I am not scrupulous to converse and live with them, to enter their churches in defect of ours, and either pray with them or for them.[9] I could never perceive any rational consequence from those many texts which prohibit the children of Israel to pollute themselves with the temples of the heathens; we being all Christians, and not divided by such detested impieties as might profane our prayers or the place wherein we make them; or that a resolved conscience may not adore her Maker anywhere, especially in places devoted to his service; where, if their devotions offend him, mine may please him, if theirs profane it, mine may hallow it. Holy water and crucifix, dangerous to the common people, deceive not my judgment nor abuse my devotion at all. I am, I confess, naturally inclined to that which misguided zeal terms superstition.[1] My common conversation I do acknowledge austere, my behavior full of rigor, sometimes not without morosity; yet at my devotion I love to use the civility of my knee, my hat, and hand, with all those outward and sensible motions which may express or promote my invisible devotion. I should violate my own arm rather than a church, nor willingly deface the memory of saint or martyr. At the sight of a cross or crucifix I can dispense with my hat, but scarce with the thought and memory of my Savior. I cannot laugh at, but rather pity, the fruitless journeys of pilgrims, or contemn the miserable condition of friars; for though misplaced in circumstance, there is somewhat in it of devotion. I could never hear the Ave-Maria bell without an elevation,[2] or think it a suffi-

6. Martin Luther, who despite the handicaps noted by Browne, set in motion the Protestant Reformation.

7. Rejected, dismissed. "Desperate resolutions" are Roman Catholics, embarked on a "decayed bottom," i.e., the leaky ship of their church.

8. Reproaches. "Difference" (a verb): differentiate.

9. As a medical student in France and Italy, Browne had faced repeatedly the question of where to worship, in Roman Catholic churches or not at all.

1. Puritans, for whom all "superstition" was anathema, would have been, and were, horrified at this declaration.

2. Exaltation of mind; in addition, Browne does not mind our recalling that the host is elevated just before communion.

cient warrant, because they erred in one circumstance, for me to err in all—that is, in silence and dumb contempt. Whilst, therefore, they directed their devotions to her, I offered mine to God, and rectified the errors of their prayers by rightly ordering mine own. At a solemn procession I have wept abundantly while my consorts,[3] blind with opposition and prejudice, have fallen into an excess of scorn and laughter. There are questionless, both in Greek, Roman, and African churches, solemnities and ceremonies whereof the wiser zeals do make a Christian use; and stand condemned by us, not as evil in themselves, but as allurements and baits of superstition to those vulgar heads that look asquint on the face of truth, and those unstable judgments that cannot consist[4] in the narrow point and center of virtue without a reel or stagger to the circumference.

4. As there were many reformers, so likewise many reformations; every country proceeding in a particular way and method, according as their national interest together with their constitution and clime inclined them: some angrily and with extremity, others calmly and with mediocrity,[5] not rending but easily dividing the community, and leaving an honest possibility of a reconciliation; which, though peaceable spirits do desire, and may conceive that revolution of time and the mercies of God may effect, yet that judgment that shall consider the present antipathies between the two extremes, their contrarieties in condition, affection, and opinion, may with the same hopes expect an union in the poles of heaven.

5. But—to difference myself nearer, and draw into a lesser circle—there is no church whose every part so squares unto my conscience, whose articles, constitutions, and customs seem so consonant unto reason, and as it were framed to my particular devotion, as this whereof I hold my belief: the Church of England, to whose faith I am a sworn subject, and therefore in a double obligation subscribe unto her articles and endeavor to observe her constitutions. Whatsoever is beyond, as points indifferent, I observe according to the rules of my private reason or the humor and fashion of my devotion; neither believing this because Luther affirmed it nor disapproving that because Calvin hath disavouched it. I condemn not all things in the council of Trent nor approve all in the synod of Dort.[6] In brief, where the Scripture is silent, the church is my text; where that speaks, 'tis but my comment; where there is a joint silence of both, I borrow not the rules of my religion from Rome or Geneva, but the dictates of my own reason. It is an unjust scandal of our adversaries and a gross error in ourselves to compute the nativity of our religion from Henry the Eighth, who, though he rejected the Pope, refused not the faith of Rome, and effected no more than what

3. Companions.
4. Stand firm.
5. Moderation. "Extremity": violence.
6. The council of Trent in Italy defined Catholic dogma after the Reformation; it sat from 1545 to 1563. The synod of Dort in Holland (1618–1619) defined Calvinist doctrine.

his own predecessors desired and essayed in ages past, and was conceived the state of Venice would have attempted in our days.[7] It is as uncharitable a point in us to fall upon those popular scurrilities and opprobrious scoffs of the bishop of Rome, to whom as a temporal prince we owe the duty of good language. I confess there is cause of passion between us. By his sentence I stand excommunicated: "heretic" is the best language he affords me, yet can no ear witness I ever returned to him the name of "Antichrist," "Man of Sin," or "Whore of Babylon."[8] It is the method of charity to suffer without reaction. Those usual satires and invectives of the pulpit may perchance produce a good effect on the vulgar, whose ears are opener to rhetoric than logic; yet do they in no wise confirm the faith of wiser believers, who know that a good cause needs not to be patroned by a passion, but can sustain itself upon a temperate dispute.

6. I could never divide myself from any man upon the difference of an opinion, or be angry with his judgment for not agreeing with me in that from which perhaps within a few days I should dissent myself. I have no genius to disputes in religion, and have often thought it wisdom to decline them, especially upon a disadvantage, or when the cause of truth might suffer in the weakness of my patronage. Where we desire to be informed, 'tis good to contest with men above ourselves; but to confirm and establish our opinions, 'tis best to argue with judgments below our own, that the frequent spoils and victories over their reasons may settle in ourselves an esteem and confirmed opinion of our own. Every man is not a proper champion for truth, nor fit to take up the gauntlet in the cause of verity. Many, from the ignorance of these maxims and an inconsiderate zeal unto truth, have too rashly charged the troops of error, and remain as trophies unto the enemies of truth. A man may be in as just possession of truth as of a city, and yet be forced to surrender. 'Tis therefore far better to enjoy her with peace than to hazard her on a battle. If therefore there rise any doubts in my way, I do forget them or at least defer them till my better settled judgment and more manly reason be able to resolve them; for I perceive every man's own reason is his best Oedipus,[9] and will upon a reasonable truce find a way to loose those bonds wherewith the subtleties of error have enchained our more flexible and tender judgments. In philosophy, where truth seems double-faced, there is no man more paradoxical than myself, but in divinity I love to keep the road; and, though not in an implicit, yet an humble faith, follow the great wheel of the church, by which I move, not reserving any proper poles or motion from the epicycle of my own brain.[1] By this means I leave no gap for heresies, schisms, or errors, of which at

7. Henry VIII was for long an ambiguous and uncertain Protestant, though also a rebellious Catholic; similarly the state of Venice retained uncongenial though not belligerent relations with the Holy See.
8. Stock terms of anti-Catholic abuse, used mostly by Puritan preachers.
9. I.e., solver of riddles, as Oedipus solved that of the Sphinx.
1. I.e., I don't have any idiosyncratic quirks or notions. In Ptolemaic astronomy, an "epicycle" was a small circle centered on the larger circle of a planet's orbit, hypothesized to account for minor variations from perfect circularity in the planet's movement.

present I hope I shall not injure truth to say I have no taint or tincture. I must confess my greener studies have been polluted with two or three— not any begotten in the latter centuries, but old and obsolete, such as could never have been revived but by such extravagant and irregular heads as mine. For indeed heresies perish not with their authors, but like the river Arethusa, though they lose their currents in one place, they rise up again in another.[2] One general council is not able to extirpate one singular heresy. It may be canceled for the present, but revolution of time and the like aspects from heaven will restore it, when it will flourish till it be condemned again; for as though there were a metempsychosis, and the soul of one man passed into another, opinions do find after certain revolutions men and minds like those that first begat them. To see ourselves again we need not look for Plato's year.[3] Every man is not only himself; there have been many Diogenes and as many Timons,[4] though but few of that name. Men are lived over again; the world is now as it was in ages past. There was none then but there hath been someone since that parallels him, and is as it were his revived self.

* * *

9. As for those wingy mysteries in divinity and airy subtleties in religion, which have unhinged the brains of better heads, they never stretched the *pia mater*[5] of mine. Methinks there be not impossibilities enough in religion for an active faith. The deepest mysteries ours contains have not only been illustrated but maintained by syllogism and the rule of reason. I love to lose myself in a mystery, to pursue my reason to an *O altitudo!*[6] 'Tis my solitary recreation to pose my apprehension with those involved enigmas and riddles of the Trinity, with Incarnation and Resurrection. I can answer all the objections of Satan and my rebellious reason with that odd resolution I learned of Tertullian, *Certum est quia impossibile est.*[7] I desire to exercise my faith in the difficultest points, for to credit ordinary and visible objects is not faith but persuasion. Some believe the better for seeing Christ his sepulcher, and when they have seen the Red Sea doubt not of the miracle. Now, contrarily, I bless myself and am thankful that I lived not in the days of miracles, that I never saw Christ nor his disciples. I would not have been one of those Israelites that passed the Red Sea, nor one of Christ's patients on whom he wrought his wonders: then had my faith been thrust upon me, nor should I enjoy that greater blessing pronounced to all that believe and saw not. 'Tis an easy and necessary belief to credit what our eye and sense hath examined. I

2. The fountain Arethusa (so mythology declares) was pursued in Greece by the river god Alpheus, dived into the sea to escape him, and came up again in Sicily; see Milton's *Lycidas*, lines 85 and 132.
3. "A revolution of certain thousand years, when all things should return unto their former estate, and he be teaching again in his school as when he delivered this opinion" [Browne's note].
4. "Diogenes" a Cynic philosopher, "Timon" a noted misanthrope; both personages of ancient Greece.
5. A membrane enclosing the brain, often used for the brain itself.
6. From Romans 11.33: "Oh the depths!" But the Latin word is ambiguous; it can also mean "heights."
7. Tertullian, the 3rd-century church father, does not quite say that matters of faith are certain because impossible; he says they should be believed because they are wonderful.

believe he was dead, buried, and rose again; and desire to see him in his glory rather than to contemplate him in his cenotaph or sepulcher. Nor is this much to believe. As we have reason, we owe this faith unto history; they only had the advantage of a bold and noble faith who lived before his coming, who upon obscure prophecies and mystical types[8] could raise a belief and expect apparent impossibilities.

*   *   *

15. * * * I could never content my contemplation with those general pieces of wonder, the flux and reflux of the sea, the increase of Nile, the conversion of the needle to the north; and have studied to match and parallel those in the more obvious and neglected pieces of nature, which without further travel I can do in the cosmography of myself. We carry with us the wonders we seek without us: there is all Africa and her prodigies[9] in us. We are that bold and adventurous piece of nature which he that studies wisely learns in a compendium what others labor at in a divided piece and endless volume.

16. Thus are there two books from whence I collect my divinity: besides that written one of God, another of his servant nature, that universal and public manuscript that lies expansed unto the eyes of all. Those that never saw him in the one have discovered him in the other. This was the scripture and theology of the heathens: the natural motion of the sun made them more admire him than its supernatural station[1] did the children of Israel; the ordinary effects of nature wrought more admiration in them than in the other all his miracles. Surely the heathens knew better how to join and read these mystical letters than we Christians, who cast a more careless eye on these common hieroglyphics, and disdain to suck divinity from the flowers of nature. Nor do I so forget God as to adore the name of nature; which I define not, with the schools, the principle of motion and rest, but that straight and regular line, that settled and constant course the wisdom of God hath ordained the actions of his creatures according to their several kinds. To make a revolution every day is the nature of the sun, because that necessary course which God hath ordained it, from which it cannot swerve but by a faculty from that voice which first did give it motion. Now this course of nature God seldom alters or perverts, but like an excellent artist hath so contrived his work that with the selfsame instrument, without a new creation, he may effect his obscurest designs. Thus he sweetened the water with a wood;[2] preserved the creatures in the Ark, which the blast of his mouth might have as easily created: for God is like a skillful geometrician, who when more easily and with one stroke of his compass he might describe or divide a right line, had yet rather do this in a circle or longer way

---

8. Prophetic insights. Job and Isaiah were among the Old Testament figures supposed to have foreseen, long before the event, Christ's coming.
9. Marvels.

1. Standing still, as at the battle of Gibeon; see Joshua 10.13.
2. Exodus 15.25 tells how the Lord sweetened the bitter waters of Marah with a special tree.

according to the constituted and forelaid principles of his art. Yet this rule of his he doth sometimes pervert, to acquaint the world with his prerogative, lest the arrogancy of our reason should question his power and conclude he could not. And thus I call the effects of nature the works of God, whose hand and instrument she only is; and therefore to ascribe his actions unto her is to devolve the honor of the principal agent upon the instrument: which if with reason we may do, then let our hammers rise up and boast they have built our houses, and our pens receive the honor of our writings. I hold there is a general beauty in the works of God, and therefore no deformity in any kind or species of creature whatsoever. I cannot tell by what logic we call a toad, a bear, or an elephant ugly; they being created in those outward shapes and figures which best express the actions of their inward forms, and having passed that general visitation of God, who saw that all that he had made was good—that is, conformable to his will, which abhors deformity and is the rule of order and beauty. There is therefore no deformity but in monstrosity; wherein notwithstanding there is a kind of beauty, nature so ingeniously contriving the irregular parts as they become sometimes more remarkable than the principal fabric. To speak yet more narrowly, there was never anything ugly or misshapen but the chaos; wherein notwithstanding (to speak strictly) there was no deformity because no form, nor was it yet impregnate by the voice of God. Now, nature is not at variance with art nor art with nature, they both being the servants of his providence: art is the perfection of nature. Were the world now as it was the sixth day, there were yet a chaos: nature hath made one world and art another. In brief, all things are artificial, for nature is the art of God.

*   *   *

34. These[3] are certainly the magisterial and master pieces of the creator; the flower or (as we may say) the best part of nothing; actually existing what we are but in hopes and probability. We are only that amphibious piece between a corporal and spiritual essence; that middle form that links those two together, and makes good the method of God and nature, that jumps not from extremes but unites the incompatible distances by some middle and participating natures. That we are the breath and similitude of God it is indisputable and upon record of holy Scripture; but to call ourselves a microcosm or little world I thought it only a pleasant trope of rhetoric[4] till my nearer judgment and second thoughts told me there was a real truth therein. For first we are a rude mass and in the rank of creatures which only are and have a dull kind of being not yet privileged with life or preferred to sense or reason. Next we live the life of plants, the life of animals, the life of men, and at last the life of spirits; running on, in one mysterious nature, those five kinds of existences which comprehend the creatures not only of the world but of the universe. Thus is man that great and true amphibium whose nature is dis-

---

3. The angels.   4. Figure of speech.

posed to live not only like other creatures in divers elements but in divided
and distinguished worlds. For though there be but one world to sense,
there are two to reason; the one visible, the other invisible, whereof
Moses seems to have left no description,[5] and of the other so obscurely
that some parts thereof are yet in controversy: and truly for the first chapters of Genesis I must confess a great deal of obscurity. Though divines
have, to the power of human reason, endeavored to make all go in a
literal meaning, yet those allegorical interpretations are also probable,
and perhaps the mystical method of Moses bred up in the hieroglyphical
schools of the Egyptians.[6]

* * *

59. Again, I am confident and fully persuaded, yet dare not take my
oath of my salvation. I am as it were sure, and do believe without all
doubt, that there is such a city as Constantinople; yet for me to take my
oath thereon were a kind of perjury, because I hold no infallible warrant
from my own sense to confirm me in the certainty thereof. And truly,
though many pretend an absolute certainty of their salvation, yet when
an humble soul shall contemplate her own unworthiness she shall meet
with many doubts and suddenly find how little we stand in need of the
precept of St. Paul, *Work out your salvation with fear and trembling.*[7]
That which is the cause of my election I hold to be the cause of my
salvation, which was the mercy and beneplacit[8] of God before I was or
the foundation of the world. *Before Abraham was, I am,* is the saying of
Christ;[9] yet is it true in some sense if I say it of myself, for I was not only
before myself but Adam, that is, in the idea of God and the decree of
that synod held from all eternity. And in this sense, I say, the world was
before the creation and at an end before it had a beginning; and thus
was I dead before I was alive. Though my grave be England, my dying
place was Paradise, and Eve miscarried of me before she conceived of
Cain.

* * *

From *Part 2*

11. Now for my life, it is a miracle of thirty years, which to relate
were not an history but a piece of poetry, and would sound to common
ears like a fable. For the world, I count it not an inn but an hospital,
and a place not to live but to die in. The world that I regard is myself; it
is the microcosm of mine own frame that I cast mine eye on; for the
other, I use it but like my globe, and turn it round sometimes for my

---

5. In describing the creation of the world, Genesis (supposedly written by Moses) says nothing of angels. "The other": the visible world.
6. Browne sides with the allegorical interpreters, surmising that Moses learned anagogical (mystical)

methods of writing from the subtle Egyptian priests among whom he was reared.
7. Philippians 2.12.
8. Good pleasure.
9. John 8.58.

recreation. Men that look upon my outside, perusing only my condition and fortunes, do err in my altitude, for I am above Atlas his shoulders.[1] The earth is a point, not only in respect of the heavens above us, but of that heavenly and celestial part within us. That mass of flesh that circumscribes me limits not my mind; that surface that tells the heavens it hath an end cannot persuade me I have any. I take my circle to be above three hundred and sixty. Though the number of the arc do measure my body, it comprehendeth not my mind. Whilst I study to find how I am a microcosm or little world, I find myself something more than the great. There is surely a piece of divinity in us; something that was before the elements, and owes no homage unto the sun. Nature tells me I am the image of God as well as Scripture. He that understands not thus much hath not his introduction or first lesson, and is yet to begin the alphabet of man. Let me not injure the felicity of others if I say I am as happy as any. *Ruat coelum, fiat voluntas tua*, salveth all;[2] so that whatsoever happens, it is but what our daily prayers desire. In brief, I am content, and what should providence add more? Surely this is it we call happiness, and this do I enjoy. With this I am happy in a dream, and as content to enjoy a happiness in a fancy as others in a more apparent truth and reality. There is surely a nearer apprehension of anything that delights us in our dreams than in our awaked senses. Without this I were unhappy, for my awaked judgment discontents me, ever whispering unto me that I am from my friend; but my friendly dreams in the night requite me, and make me think I am within his arms. I thank God for my happy dreams as I do for my good rest, for there is a satisfaction in them unto reasonable desires and such as can be content with a fit of happiness; and surely it is not a melancholy conceit to think we are all asleep in this world, and that the conceits of this life are as mere dreams to those of the next, as the phantasms of the night to the conceits of the day. There is an equal delusion in both, and the one doth but seem to be the emblem or picture of the other. We are somewhat more than ourselves in our sleeps, and the slumber of the body seems to be but the waking of the soul. It is the ligation[3] of sense but the liberty of reason; and our waking conceptions do not match the fancies of our sleeps. At my nativity my ascendant was the watery sign of Scorpius; I was born in the planetary hour of Saturn, and I think I have a piece of that leaden planet in me.[4] I am no way facetious, nor disposed for the mirth and galliardize[5] of company, yet in one dream I can compose a whole comedy, behold the action, apprehend the jests, and laugh myself awake at the conceits thereof. Were my memory as faithful as my reason is then fruitful, I would never study but in my dreams, and this time also would I choose for my devotions; but our grosser memories have then so little hold of our abstracted understandings that they forget the story, and can only

---

1. Atlas, in classical mythology, was a giant who held up the sky on his shoulders.
2. "Let the heavens fall, thy will be done." "Salveth": assuages.
3. Binding, bondage.

4. Browne was born on the 19th of October, when Saturn was in the ascendant.
5. "Galliardize": gaiety (from *galliard*, a French dance).

relate to our awaked souls a confused and broken tale of what hath passed. Aristotle, who hath written a singular tract of sleep, hath not methinks thoroughly defined it, nor yet Galen,[6] though he seem to have corrected it; for those noctambuloes and night-walkers, though in their sleep, do yet enjoy the action of their senses. We must therefore say that there is something in us that is not in the jurisdiction of Morpheus,[7] and that those abstracted and ecstatic souls do walk about in their own corpse, as spirits with the bodies they assume, wherein they seem to hear, see, and feel, though indeed the organs are destitute of sense, and their natures of those faculties that should inform them. Thus it is observed that men sometimes, upon the hour of their departure, do speak and reason above themselves; for then the soul begins to be freed from the ligaments of the body, begins to reason like herself and to discourse in a strain above mortality.

* * *

1635   1642 (pirated)
                                                       1643 (authorized)

From Hydriotaphia, Urn-Burial

Chapter 5

Now since these dead bones have already outlasted the living ones of Methuselah,[1] and in a yard under ground, and thin walls of clay, outworn all the strong and specious buildings above it, and quietly rested under the drums and tramplings of three conquests;[2] what prince can promise such diuturnity unto his relics, or might not gladly say,

Sic ego componi versus in ossa velim?[3]

Time, which antiquates antiquities, and hath an art to make dust of all things, hath yet spared these minor monuments.

In vain we hope to be known by open and visible conservatories, when to be unknown was the means of their continuation, and obscurity their protection. If they died by violent hands, and were thrust into their urns, these bones become considerable, and some old philosophers would honor them, whose souls they conceived most pure, which were thus snatched from their bodies, and to retain a stronger propension[4] unto them; whereas they weariedly left a languishing corpse, and with faint desires of reun-

6. Galen was a Greek physician of the 2nd century A.D. Over his long life, he wrote nearly 500 different treatises.
7. God of sleep.
1. Methuselah lived 969 years (Genesis 5.27).
2. If the bones were Roman (as Browne thought),
the conquests would be Saxon, Danish, and Norman. "Diuturnity": long life.
3. "Thus I, when dead, should wish to go to rest" (Tibullus).
4. Attraction. "They" are the philosophers, who traditionally die in bed.

ion. If they fell by long and aged decay, yet wrapped up in the bundle of time, they fall into indistinction, and make but one blot with infants. If we begin to die when we live, and long life be but a prolongation of death, our life is a sad composition; we live with death, and die not in a moment. How many pulses made up the life of Methuselah, were work for Archimedes: common counters sum up the life of Moses his man.[5] Our days become considerable, like petty sums, by minute accumulations; where numerous fractions make up but small round numbers; and our days of a span long make not one little finger.[6]

If the nearness of our last necessity[7] brought a nearer conformity unto it, there were a happiness in hoary hairs, and no calamity in half-senses. But the long habit of living indisposeth us for dying; when avarice makes us the sport of death, when even David grew politicly cruel, and Solomon could hardly be said to be the wisest of men.[8] But many are too early old, and before the date of age. Adversity stretcheth our days, misery makes Alcmena's nights,[9] and time hath no wings unto it. But the most tedious being is that which can unwish itself, content to be nothing, or never to have been, which was beyond the malcontent of Job, who cursed not the day of his life, but his nativity:[1] content to have so far been as to have a title to future being; although he had lived here but in an hidden state of life, and as it were an abortion.

What song the Sirens sang, or what name Achilles assumed when he hid himself among women, though puzzling questions, are not beyond all conjecture.[2] What time the persons of these ossuaries entered the famous nations of the dead, and slept with princes and counselors, might admit a wide[3] solution. But who were the proprietaries of these bones, or what bodies these ashes made up, were a question above antiquarism; not to be resolved by man, nor easily perhaps by spirits, except we consult the provincial guardians, or tutelary observators.[4] Had they made as good provision for their names as they have done for their relics, they had not so grossly erred in the art of perpetuation. But to subsist in bones, and be but pyramidally extant,[5] is a fallacy in duration. Vain ashes, which in the oblivion of names, persons, times, and sexes, have found unto themselves a fruitless continuation, and only arise unto late posterity, as emblems of mortal vanities, antidotes against pride, vainglory, and madding vices. Pagan vainglories, which thought the world might last forever, had encouragement for ambition; and, finding no

---

5. I.e., the ordinary man, alluded to in Psalm 90, supposed to be by Moses; it says (verse 10), "The days of our years are threescore years and ten."
6. In certain ancient arithmetics, Browne's note tells us, "the little finger of the right hand, contracted, signified an hundred."
7. I.e., death.
8. David suffered in his last years from the rebellion and death of his son Absalom; Solomon was seduced by fair idolatresses to the service of alien gods.
9. Sleeping with Alcmena to beget Hercules, Jove enjoyed himself so much that he forbade the sun to rise for one day; thus there were three nights in

a row.
1. Job 3.
2. Suetonius (*Lives of the Twelve Caesars*) says that Tiberius went to the "silly and laughable extreme" of testing grammarians (whom he admired) with these questions.
3. Approximate.
4. Browne, who believed in witches, also believed in angelic protectors, both personal ("tutelary observators") and of more extended jurisdiction ("provincial guardians").
5. Like a pyramid, famous though the person buried within it is long forgotten.

Atropos[6] unto the immortality of their names, were never damped with the necessity of oblivion. Even old ambitions had the advantage of ours, in the attempts of their vainglories, who, acting early and before the probable meridian[7] of time, have by this time found great accomplishment of their designs, whereby the ancient heroes have already outlasted their monuments and mechanical preservations. But in this latter scene of time, we cannot expect such mummies unto our memories, when ambition may fear the prophecy of Elias,[8] and Charles the Fifth can never hope to live within two Methuselahs of Hector.[9]

And therefore restless inquietude for the diuturnity of our memories unto present considerations seems a vanity almost out of date, and superannuated piece of folly. We cannot hope to live so long in our names as some have done in their persons; one face of Janus[1] holds no proportion unto the other. 'Tis too late to be ambitious. The great mutations of the world are acted, or time may be too short for our designs. To extend our memories by monuments, whose death we daily pray for,[2] and whose duration we cannot hope, without injury to our expectations in the advent of the last day, were a contradiction to our beliefs. We whose generations are ordained in this setting part of time[3] are providentially taken off from such imaginations; and, being necessitated to eye the remaining particle of futurity, are naturally constituted unto thoughts of the next world, and cannot excusably decline the consideration of that duration, which maketh pyramids pillars of snow, and all that's past a moment.

Circles and right lines limit and close all bodies, and the mortal rightlined circle must conclude and shut up all.[4] There is no antidote against the opium of time, which temporally considereth all things: our fathers find their graves in our short memories, and sadly tell us how we may be buried in our survivors. Gravestones tell truth scarce forty years.[5] Generations pass while some trees stand, and old families last not three oaks. To be read by bare inscriptions like many in Gruter,[6] to hope for eternity by enigmatical epithets or first letters of our names, to be studied by antiquaries, who we were, and have new names given us like many of the mummies, are cold consolations unto the students of perpetuity, even by everlasting languages.

To be content that times to come should only know there was such a man, not caring whether they knew more of him, was a frigid ambition

---

6. Of the three Fates, Clotho, Lachesis, and Atropos, the last-named held the scissors. They cut the threads of mortal life.

7. Noon, midday.

8. "That the earth may last but 6,000 years" [Browne's note]. There is no warrant for this in the Bible.

9. Methuselah having lived 969 years, the Trojan Hector had already enjoyed well over "two Methuselahs" of fame before the Emperor Charles V (1500–1558) was born. Since in the 6,000-year chronology the final 2,000 began at the time of Christ, Charles could not hope to be famous for more than 500 years.

1. Janus, Roman god of doorways and beginnings (hence "January"), had two faces looking in opposite directions, the past and the future.

2. We pray for the "death" and destruction of our graves at the Last Judgment.

3. The image is from the sunset.

4. Θ (theta), the first letter of thanatos ("death"), symbolizes it.

5. Because old corpses are dug up and replaced with new; see Hamlet 5.1; and Donne, The Relic, lines 3–4.

6. Jan Gruter (1560–1627) was a Dutch scholar who published a collection of Latin inscriptions.

in Cardan;[7] disparaging his horoscopal inclination and judgment of himself. Who cares to subsist like Hippocrates' patients, or Achilles' horses in Homer, under naked nominations, without deserts and noble acts, which are the balsam of our memories, the *entelechia*[8] and soul of our subsistences? To be nameless in worthy deeds exceeds[9] an infamous history. The Canaanitish woman lives more happily without a name than Herodias with one. And who had not rather have been the good thief than Pilate?[1]

But the iniquity of oblivion blindly scattereth her poppy, and deals with the memory of men without distinction to merit of perpetuity. Who can but pity the founder of the pyramids? Herostratus lives that burnt the temple of Diana;[2] he is almost lost that built it. Time hath spared the epitaph of Adrian's horse,[3] confounded that of himself. In vain we compute our felicities by the advantage of our good names, since bad have equal durations, and Thersites is like to live as long as Agamemnon.[4] Who knows whether the best of men be known, or whether there be not more remarkable persons forgot than any that stand remembered in the known account of time? Without the favor of the everlasting register, the first man had been as unknown as the last, and Methuselah's long life had been his only chronicle.

Oblivion is not to be hired: the greater part must be content to be as though they had not been, to be found in the register of God, not in the record of man. Twenty-seven names make up the first story, and the recorded names ever since contain not one living century.[5] The number of the dead long exceedeth all that shall live. The night of time far surpasseth the day, and who knows when was the equinox? Every hour adds unto that current arithmetic,[6] which scarce stands one moment. And since death must be the Lucina[7] of life, and even pagans could doubt whether thus to live were to die; since our longest sun sets at right descensions, and makes but winter arches, and therefore it cannot be long before we lie down in darkness, and have our light in ashes;[8] since the brother of death daily haunts us with dying mementos, and time that grows old itself bids us hope no long duration; diuturnity is a dream and folly of expectation.

Darkness and light divide the course of time, and oblivion shares with memory a great part even of our living beings; we slightly remember our

7. Girolamo Cardano, a famous Italian mathematician and occultist of the 16th century. Taking his own horoscope, he found himself destined to great things.
8. Essence, perfection.
9. Is better than.
1. The woman of Canaan had faith in Jesus; Herodias asked for the head of John the Baptist (Matthew 15.27–28; Mark 6.22–25). The good thief, crucified beside Christ, had his blessing; Pontius Pilate, the procurator of Judea, typifies the sanctimonious villain.
2. Herostratus of Ephesus set fire to the great temple in that city simply in order to gain a stupid immortality.

3. Adrian (Hadrian) was emperor of Rome in the 2nd century A.D.
4. Thersites, the scurrilous scoffer of the *Iliad*, is contrasted with Agamemnon, the royal leader.
5. Genesis 1–5 tells the story of the human race from the creation to the flood in 27 names; since then, there has never been a time when as many as 100 people whose names are recorded were alive simultaneously.
6. That continual addition.
7. Roman goddess of childbirth, hence, "the deliverance."
8. At funerals, Browne's note says, the Jews place a wax candle in a pot of ashes beside the corpse. The "brother of death" is sleep.

felicities, and the smartest strokes of affliction leave but short smart upon us. Sense endureth no extremities, and sorrows destroy us or themselves. To weep into stones are fables.[9] Afflictions induce callosities;[1] miseries are slippery, or fall like snow upon us, which notwithstanding is no unhappy stupidity. To be ignorant of evils to come, and forgetful of evils past, is a merciful provision in nature, whereby we digest the mixture of our few and evil days, and, our delivered senses not relapsing into cutting remembrances, our sorrows are not kept raw by the edge of repetitions. A great part of antiquity contented their hopes of subsistency with a transmigration of their souls: a good way to continue their memories, while, having the advantage of plural successions, they could not but act something remarkable in such variety of beings, and enjoying the fame of their passed selves, make accumulation of glory unto their last durations. Others, rather than be lost in the uncomfortable night of nothing, were content to recede into the common being, and make one particle of the public soul of all things, which was no more than to return into their unknown and divine original again. Egyptian ingenuity[2] was more unsatisfied, contriving their bodies in sweet consistencies, to attend the return of their souls. But all was vanity, feeding the wind, and folly. The Egyptian mummies, which Cambyses or time hath spared, avarice now consumeth.[3] Mummy is become merchandise, Mizraim cures wounds, and Pharaoh is sold for balsams.

In vain do individuals hope for immortality, or any patent[4] from oblivion, in preservations below the moon; men have been deceived even in their flatteries above the sun, and studied conceits to perpetuate their names in heaven. The various cosmography of that part hath already varied the names of contrived constellations: Nimrod is lost in Orion, and Osiris in the Dog Star.[5] While we look for incorruption in the heavens, we find they are but like the earth, durable in their main bodies, alterable in their parts: whereof beside comets and new stars, perspectives[6] begin to tell tales, and the spots that wander about the sun, with Phaëthon's favor,[7] would make clear conviction.

There is nothing strictly immortal but immortality. Whatever hath no beginning may be confident of no end; all others have a dependent being and within the reach of destruction; which is the peculiar[8] of that necessary essence that cannot destroy itself; and the highest strain of omnipotency, to be so powerfully constituted as not to suffer even from the power of itself. But the sufficiency of Christian immortality frustrates all

9. Like Niobe, whose grief turned her to stone.
1. Calluses, hardness, indifference.
2. The reference is to embalming practices.
3. The story of Cambyses ravaging Egypt is told in Herodotus, Book 3. Powdered mummy was sold in the 17th century as medicine (see Donne, *Love's Alchemy*, line 24). "Mizraim": i.e., Egypt; Mizraim was a son of Ham (Genesis 10.6–14.
4. Protection.
5. I.e., the names of the stars and constellations

change—Osiris to Sirius, Nimrod the mighty hunter (Genesis 10.9) to Orion.
6. Telescopes.
7. Phaethon was an unfortunate son of the Sun, who tried to drive his father's chariot and nearly set the universe on fire. His erratic course reminds Browne of spots which wander across the sun's face, and which had only recently been charted by astronomers, starting with Galileo.
8. Characteristic.

earthly glory, and the quality of either state after death makes a folly of posthumous memory. God, who can only[9] destroy our souls, and hath assured our resurrection, either of our bodies or names hath directly promised no duration. Wherein there is so much of chance that the boldest expectants have found unhappy frustration; and to hold long subsistence seems but a scape in oblivion.[1] But man is a noble animal, splendid in ashes and pompous in the grave, solemnizing nativities and deaths with equal luster, nor omitting ceremonies of bravery[2] in the infamy of his nature.

Life is a pure flame, and we live by an invisible sun within us. A small fire sufficeth for life, great flames seemed too little after death, while men vainly affected precious pyres, and to burn like Sardanapalus;[3] but the wisdom of funeral laws found the folly of prodigal blazes, and reduced undoing fires unto the rule of sober obsequies, wherein few could be so mean as not to provide wood, pitch, a mourner, and an urn.

Five languages secured not the epitaph of Gordianus.[4] The man of God[5] lives longer without a tomb than any by one, invisibly interred by angels, and adjudged to obscurity, though not without some marks directing human discovery. Enoch and Elias,[6] without either tomb or burial, in an anomalous state of being, are the great examples of perpetuity, in their long and living memory, in strict account being still on this side death, and having a late part yet to act upon this stage of earth. If in the decretory term of the world[7] we shall not all die but be changed, according to received translation, the last day will make but few graves; at least quick resurrections will anticipate lasting sepultures; some graves will be opened before they be quite closed, and Lazarus be no wonder.[8] When many that feared to die shall groan that they can die but once, the dismal state is the second and living death, when life puts despair on the damned; when men shall wish the coverings of mountains, not of monuments, and annihilations shall be courted.[9]

While some have studied monuments, others have studiously declined them; and some have been so vainly boisterous that they durst not acknowledge their graves, wherein Alaricus[1] seems most subtle, who had a river turned to hide his bones at the bottom. Even Sulla,[2] that thought himself safe in his urn, could not prevent revenging tongues, and stones thrown at his monument. Happy are they whom privacy makes inno-

---

9. Who alone can.

1. Weak trick against forgetfulness.

2. Proud ceremonies.

3. Sardanapalus burned up a palace full of eunuchs, concubines, and treasures as his funeral pyre; later civilizations often forbade such lavish displays.

4. The epitaph of Gordianus, emperor of Rome (238–244), was written in five languages; but it was obliterated in all of them by his successor, Licinius.

5. Moses (see Deuteronomy 34).

6. Enoch and "Elias" (Elijah) were translated straight to heaven (Genesis 5.24; 2 Kings 2.11).

7. The Last Judgment.

8. Lazarus, the dead man raised by Christ (John 11).

9. The damned soul shrieking for mountains to shield him from the wrath of God was a figure beloved of preachers. See Luke 23.30 and Revelation 6.16.

1. Alaric, the Gothic invader, was buried in the bed of the river Busento (A.D. 410).

2. Roman politician and general, who died 78 B.C.

cent, who deal so with men in this world that they are not afraid to meet them in the next; who, when they die, make no commotion among the dead, and are not touched with that poetical taunt of Isaiah.[3]

Pyramids, arches, obelisks were but the irregularities of vainglory, and wild enormities of ancient magnanimity. But the most magnanimous resolution rests in the Christian religion, which trampleth upon pride, and sits on the neck of ambition, humbly pursuing that infallible perpetuity unto which all others must diminish their diameters, and be poorly seen in angles of contingency.[4]

Pious spirits who passed their days in raptures of futurity made little more of this world than the world that was before it, while they lay obscure in the chaos of pre-ordination, and night of their fore-beings. And if any have been so happy as truly to understand Christian annihilation, ecstasy, exolution,[5] liquefaction, transformation, the kiss of the spouse, gustation of God, and ingression into the divine shadow, they have already had an handsome anticipation of heaven; the glory of the world is surely over, and the earth in ashes unto them.

To subsist in lasting monuments, to live in their productions, to exist in their names and predicament of chimeras,[6] was large satisfaction unto old expectations, and made one part of their Elysiums.[7] But all this is nothing in the metaphysics of true belief. To live indeed is to be again ourselves, which being not only an hope but an evidence in noble believers, 'tis all one to lie in St. Innocent's churchyard,[8] as in the sands of Egypt: ready to be anything, in the ecstasy of being ever, and as content with six foot as the *moles* of Adrianus.[9]

> —*Tabesne cadavera solvat,*
> *An rogus, haud refert.*
> —LUCAN

1658

3. In Isaiah 14 the mighty ones of the earth are taunted with their approaching downfall into hell.
4. The angle of contingency is the smallest possible angle; Browne puns on the idea that all these lesser perpetuities are subject to accident ("contingency").
5. The loosening or freeing of the spirit from the bonds of the body.
6. In the condition of phantasms.
7. The pagan afterworld.
8. In Paris, where bodies soon consume; contrasted with the desert, where they last a long time.
9. Adrian's (Hadrian's) tomb, now Castel San Angelo in Rome, the type of a magnificent mausoleum. The Latin tag is translated, "By the swift funeral pyre or slow decay / (No matter which) the bodies pass away" (Lucan, *Pharsalia* 7.809–10).

EDWARD HYDE, EARL OF CLARENDON
1609–1674

Edward Hyde was educated at Oxford and during the 1630s practiced law. From about 1641 onward, he was among the chief supporters and advisers of Charles I; he went into exile with the boy who was to become Charles II, and remained the center of the Stuart cause during the interregnum. After the Restoration, he became lord chancellor and prime minister to Charles II, but was impeached in 1667 (owing partly to England's ill success in the Dutch War), and spent the last seven years of his life in France.

Clarendon's great *History of the Rebellion* was written in part amid the very events which it describes. For the Muse of history, a short view like this is not an unmixed blessing. But Clarendon's learning—legal, classical, and historical—and the formality of his method save him from many of the failings of partisanship. He wrote as a lord chancellor should, with imperial dignity, and he wrote for posterity, which he envisaged as a senatorial assemblage of lord chancellors. His *History*, which first appeared in print thirty years after his death, was remarkable not only for the largeness of its canvas, but for the force and coherence of the social philosophy informing it— which, under the name of Toryism, retains an influence even to the present day. As an historical rhetorician and portrait painter, there can be no doubt that Clarendon ranks among the very greatest.

From The History of the Rebellion

[*The Character of Oliver Cromwell*][1]

About the middle of August he was seized on by a common tertian ague, from which he believed a little ease and divertissement[2] at Hampton Court would have freed him; but the fits grew stronger and his spirits much abated, so that he returned again to Whitehall,[3] when his physicians began to think him in danger, though the preachers who prayed always about him and told God Almighty what great things he had done for Him, and how much more need He had still of his service, declared as from God that he should recover, and he himself did not think he should die, till even the time that his spirits failed him, and then declared to them that he did appoint his son to succeed him, his eldest son Richard. And so expired upon the third day of September (a day he thought always very propitious to him, and on which he had triumphed for several victories),[4] 1658, a day very memorable for the greatest storm of wind that had been ever known for some hours before and after his death, which overthrew trees, houses, and made great wrecks at sea, and was so universal that there were terrible effects of it both in France and Flanders, where all people trembled at it, besides the wrecks all along the coast, many boats having been cast away in the very rivers; and within few days after, that circumstance of his death that accompanied that storm was known.

He was one of those men *quos vituperare ne inimici quidem possunt,*

1. After the manner of ancient historians, Clarendon describes the last days, sickness, and death of Cromwell, then summarizes his character. The Protector, who had been depressed for some time by the death of a favorite daughter, first grew ill in the summer of 1658.

2. Diversion. Hampton Court, built by Cardinal Wolsey and ceded by him to Henry VIII, was (and is) a splendid old palace up the Thames from London.

3. Whitehall, in London, was the traditional residence of the head of state.

4. Dunbar and Worcester were important battles that Cromwell had won on September 3rd.

nisi ut simul laudent,[5] for he could never have done half that mischief without great parts of courage and industry and judgment, and he must have had a wonderful understanding in the natures and humors of men, and as great a dexterity in the applying them, who from a private and obscure birth (though of a good family) without interest of estate, alliance, or friendships, could raise himself to such a height, and compound and knead such opposite and contradictory tempers, humors, and interests into a consistence that contributed to his designs and to their own destruction, whilst himself grew insensibly powerful enough to cut off those by whom he had climbed in the instant that they projected to demolish their own building.[6] What Velleius Paterculus said of Cinna may very justly be said of him, *Ausum eum quae nemo auderet bonus, perfecisse quae a nullo nisi fortissimo perfici possunt.*[7] Without doubt no man with more wickedness ever attempted anything, or brought to pass what he desired more wickedly, more in the face and contempt of religion and moral honesty; yet wickedness as great as his could never have accomplished those trophies without the assistance of a great spirit, an admirable circumspection and sagacity, and a most magnanimous resolution. When he appeared first in the Parliament he seemed to have a person in no degree gracious, no ornament of discourse, none of those talents which use to reconcile the affections of the standers-by; yet as he grew into place and authority, his parts[8] seemed to be renewed, as if he had concealed faculties till he had occasion to use them, and when he was to act the part of a great man, he did it without any indecency[9] through the want of custom.

After he was confirmed and invested Protector by the Humble Petition and Advice,[1] he consulted with very few upon any action of importance, nor communicated any enterprise he resolved upon with more than those who were to have principal parts in the execution of it, nor to them sooner than was absolutely necessary. What he once resolved, in which he was not rash, he would not be dissuaded from, nor endure any contradiction of his power and authority, but extorted obedience from them who were not willing to yield it.

When he had laid some very extraordinary tax upon the city,[2] one Cony, an eminent fanatic, and one who had heretofore served him very notably, positively refused to pay his part and loudly dissuaded others from submitting to it, as an imposition notoriously against the law and the property of the subject, which all honest men were bound to defend. Cromwell sent for him and cajoled him with the memory of the old kindness and friendship that had been between them, and that of all

5. "Whom not even his enemies could curse without praising him." The source of the phrase is unknown.

6. Clarendon's judgment can be compared with that of Andrew Marvell in the *Horatian Ode*, (above, p. 1397).

7. "He dared undertake what no good man would have tried, and triumphed where only the strongest of men could have succeeded." Velleius Pater-

culus (died 30 A.D.) wrote a concise *History of Rome*; the quotation is from 2.24.

8. Personal qualities.

9. Indecorum.

1. I.e., in the last months of 1653. The *Humble Petition* was one of several documents of that period leading to the naming of Cromwell as Protector.

2. London city.

men he did not expect this opposition from him in a matter that was so necessary for the good of the commonwealth. But it was always his fortune to meet with the most rude and obstinate behavior from those who had formerly been absolutely governed by him, and they commonly put him in mind of some expressions and sayings of his own in cases of the like nature. So this man remembered[3] him how great an enemy he had expressed himself to such grievances, and declared that all who submitted to them and paid illegal taxes were more to blame, and greater enemies to their country, than they who imposed them; and that the tyranny of princes could never be grievous but by the tameness and stupidity of the people.

When Cromwell saw that he could not convert him, he told him that he had a will as stubborn as his, and he would try which of them two should be master, and thereupon with some terms of reproach and contempt he committed the man to prison—whose courage was nothing abated by it, but as soon as the term came, he brought his *habeas corpus*[4] in the King's Bench, which they then called the Upper Bench. Maynard, who was of counsel with the prisoner, demanded his liberty with great confidence, both upon the illegality of the commitment and the illegality of the imposition,[5] as being laid without any lawful authority. The judges could not maintain or defend either, but enough declared what their sentence would be, and therefore the Protector's attorney required a further day to answer what had been urged. Before that day, Maynard was committed to the Tower for presuming to question or make doubt of his authority, and the judges were sent for and severely reprehended for suffering that license; and when they with all humility mentioned the law, and Magna Charta, Cromwell told them their Magna Farta should not control his actions, which he knew were for the safety of the commonwealth. He asked them who made them judges; whether they had any authority to sit there but what he gave them, and that if his authority were at an end, they knew well enough what would become of themselves. And therefore advised them to be more tender of that which could only preserve them, and so dismissed them with caution that they should not suffer the lawyers to prate what it would not become them to hear.

Thus he subdued a spirit that had been often troublesome to the most sovereign power, and made Westminster Hall[6] as obedient and subservient to his commands as any of the rest of his quarters. In all other matters which did not concern the life of his jurisdiction, he seemed to have great reverence for the law, and rarely interposed between party and party; and as he proceeded with this kind of indignation and haughtiness with those who were refractory and dared to contend with his greatness, so towards those who complied with his good pleasure and

3. Reminded.
4. Writ to release a prisoner.
5. I.e., the original tax.
6. The center of the law courts and legal profes-

sion. Clarendon never tells us what happened to poor George Cony; the lawyer and judges made their submission and got off, but the fate of the plaintiff remains (as frequently) obscure.

courted his protection he used a wonderful civility, generosity, and bounty.

To reduce three nations which perfectly hated him to an entire obedience to all his dictates, to awe and govern those nations by an army that was indevoted[7] to him and wished his ruin, was an instance of a very prodigious address; but his greatness at home was but a shadow of the glory he had abroad. It was hard to discover which feared him most, France, Spain, or the Low Countries, where his friendship was current at the value he put upon it; and as they did all sacrifice their honor and their interest to his pleasure, so there is nothing he could have demanded that either of them would have denied him.

* * *

He was not a man of blood, and totally declined Machiavel's method, which prescribes upon any alteration of a government, as a thing absolutely necessary, to cut off all the heads of those, and extirpate their families, who are friends to the old;[8] and it was confidently reported in the Council of Officers, it was more than once proposed that there might be a general massacre of all the royal party as the only expedient to secure the government, but Cromwell would never consent to it, it may be out of too much contempt of his enemies. In a word, as he had all the wickednesses against which damnation is denounced and for which hell-fire is prepared, so he had some virtues which have caused the memory of some men in all ages to be celebrated, and he will be looked upon by posterity as a brave, bad man.

1702–4

7. Clarendon's word, carefully coined to express the far from unanimous feelings of the army. "Address": skill.

8. See *The Prince*; chap. 3 for the precept, chap. 7 for the example.

JOHN LILBURNE
1615?–1657

The iron determination of the revolutionary often comes out most vividly in conflict with his fellow revolutionaries. John Lilburne was a natural-born agitator who had suffered for propagandizing against the bishops and had fought in the parliamentary army against the king, but who achieved perhaps his finest moment in a direct confrontation with Oliver Cromwell during the early months of 1649.

Charles I had just been executed (January 30, 1649), and Cromwell, with a picked council of army officers and trusted allies from the House of Commons, was trying to set up a new form of governmental authority. But his plan was simply to keep power in his own hands. Lilburne and the Levelers (a name given them originally in derision because of their democratic principles) wanted a radically new political deal. They wanted, for instance, free elections; by one device or another, they estimated, nineteen of every twenty potential voters were being disenfranchised. They wanted freedom of speech; they wanted the political, legal, and social rights for which, as they thought, the whole war had been fought. When they saw Cromwell moving the other way, toward a tight personal dictatorship, they protested violently. A pamphlet titled *England's New Chains Discovered* denounced the betrayal of the revolution in unmeasured terms, and determined Cromwell to suppress a movement which seemed to be making dangerous headway against him. Toward the end of March he ordered troops to arrest the four leading Levelers (Lilburne, Prince, Overton, and Walwyn), and bring them before his Council of State for examination.

The whole proceeding stood on very dubious legal ground. Cromwell was general of the parliamentary armies, but that fact gave him no right to arrest ordinary citizens. The Council of State existed on Cromwell's say-so; it had never been created legally by an official body. With the king dead, the House of Lords abolished, and the House of Commons reduced by purges to a fraction of its original size, the Levelers were quite justified in arguing that nothing could set up a stable legal authority in England except new elections.

Being arrested was therefore a great opportunity for Lilburne—a headstrong, fearless, melodramatic man with a strong sense of national pride. He saw at once that the tribunal before which he was forced to appear must itself be put on trial; and he lectured his judges unmercifully. He said he would not plead his great services to the parliamentary cause, and then referred to them constantly, for the rest of his speech. Thrown into jail by the Council, as he actually asked them to do, he and his fellow Levelers published a long and passionate pamphlet titled *The Picture of the Council of State*, in which they represented at length their own eloquence and logic, while contrasting it with the harsh and narrow behavior of their persecutors. And in fact the blunt, hammer-like phrases of Lilburne's prose, unencumbered with niceties of grammar or learned decoration, strike with the force of a man driving spikes. Like John Bunyan (see below, p. 1857), Lilburne is a prose artist in the grip of a moral idea that makes all the tricks of art appear small. Our excerpt begins at the moment when Lilburne has just been asked by Mr. John Bradshaw, President of the Council, what he has to say for himself.

From The Picture of the Council of State

[*Lilburne Defies the Authorities*]

* * * "Well, then, Mr. Bradshaw," said I, "if it please you and these gentlemen to afford me the same liberty and privilege that the Cavaliers did at Oxford, when I was arraigned before them for my life, for levying war in the quarrel of the commonwealth against the late king and his party (which was liberty of speech, to speak my mind freely without interruption), I shall speak and go on; but without the grant of liberty of speech, I shall not say a word more to you."

To which he replied, "That is already granted you, and therefore you may go on to speak what you can or will say for yourself, if you please; or if you will not, you may hold your peace and withdraw."

"Well, then," said I, "Mr. Bradshaw, with your favor, thus. I am an Englishman born, bred, and brought up, and England is a nation governed, bounded, and limited by laws and liberties: and for the liberties of England I have both fought and suffered much. But truly, sir, I judge it now infinitely below me, and the glory and excellency of my late actions, now to plead merit or desert unto you, as though I were forced to fly to the merit of my former actions, to lay in a counter-scale, to weigh down your indignation against me for my pretended late offenses. No, sir, I scorn it, I abhor it. And therefore, sir, I now stand before you upon the bare, naked, and single account of an Englishman, as though I had never said, done, or acted anything that tended to the preservation of the liberties thereof; but yet, have never done any act that did put me out of a legal capacity to claim the utmost punctilio, benefit, and privilege that the laws and liberties of England will afford to any of you here present, or any other man in the whole nation. And the laws and liberties of England are my inheritance and birthright.

"And in your late declaration, published about four or five days ago, wherein you lay down the grounds and reasons (as I remember) of your doing justice upon the late king, and why you have abolished kingly government and the House of Lords, you declare in effect the same, and promise to maintain the laws of England in reference to the people's liberties and freedoms. And amongst other things therein contained, you highly commend and extol the Petition of Right,[1] made in the third year of the late king, as one of the most excellent and glorious laws in reference to the people's liberties that ever was made in this nation; and you there very much blame and cry out upon the king for robbing and denying the people of England the benefit of that law. And sure I am (for I have read and studied it), there is one clause in it that saith expressly, That no freeman of England ought to be adjudged for life, limb, liberty, or estate but by the laws already in being established and declared. And truly, sir, if this be good and sound legal doctrine (as undoubtedly it is, or else your own declarations are false and lies), I wonder what you gentlemen are. For the declared and known laws of England know you not, neither by names nor qualifications, as persons endowed with any power either to imprison or try me, or the meanest freeman of England. And truly, were it not that I know the faces of divers of you, and honor the persons of some of you, as members of the House of Commons that have stood pretty firm in shaking times to the interest of the nation, I should wonder what you are, or before whom I am, and should not in the least honor or reverence you so much as with civil respect, especially considering the manner of my being brought before you, with armed men, and the manner of your close[2] sitting, contrary to all courts of justice. * * *

"Sir, by the law of England, let me tell you, what the House votes,

---

1. In the so-called Petition of Right (1628), Parliament drew up and presented to Charles I a formal statement of the rights and privileges to which they laid claim in the name of the people of England.
2. Closed, secret.

orders, and enacts within their walls is nothing to me, I am not at all bound by them, nor in law can take any cognizance of them as laws, although twenty members come out of the House and tell me such things are done, till they be published and declared by sound of trumpet, proclamation, or the like, by a public officer or magistrate, in the public and open places of the nation. But truly, sir, I never saw any law in print or writing that declares your power so proclaimed or published. And therefore, sir, I know not what more to make of you than a company of private men, being neither able to own you as a court of justice, because the law speaks nothing of you; nor as a council of state, till I see and read or hear your commission, which I desire (if you please) to be acquainted with."[3]

* * *

Mr. Bradshaw * * * said unto me to this effect: "Lieut. Colonel Lilburne, this Council hath considered what you have said, and what they have been informed of concerning you, and also of that duty that lies upon them by the command of the House, which enjoins them to improve their utmost ability to find out the author of this book; and therefore to effect that end, they judge themselves bound to demand of you this question: Whether you made not this book, or were privy to the making of it, or no?"

And after some pause, and wondering at the strangeness of the question, I answered, and said: "Mr. Bradshaw, I cannot but stand amazed that you should ask me such a question as this, at this time of the day, considering what you said unto me at my first being before you; and considering it is now about eight years ago since this very Parliament annihilated the court of Star Chamber, Council Board, and High Commission,[4] and that for such proceedings as these. And truly, sir, I have been a contestor and sufferer for the liberties of England these twelve years together, and I should now look upon myself as the basest fellow in the world if now in one moment I should undo all that I have been doing all this while, which I must of necessity do if I should answer to you questions against myself. For in the first place, by answering this question against myself, I should betray the liberties of England in acknowledging you to have a legal jurisdiction over me to try and adjudge me; which I have already proved to your faces you have not in the least. And if you have forgot what you said to me thereupon, yet I have not forgot what I said to you. And secondly, sir, if I should answer to questions against myself and to betray myself, I should do that which not only law but nature abhors. And therefore I cannot but wonder that you yourselves are not ashamed to demand so illegal and unworthy a thing

3. After a great deal of haggling over whether the Council really exists in a legal sense, Mr. Bradshaw finally gets around to asking the question which is at the root of the whole affair.
4. These were all courts which had become infamous under the 11-year period of unparliamentary government (1629–1640). Star Chamber and High Commission were particularly hateful as ecclesiastical courts which reminded their victims of the Inquisition. Lilburne himself had suffered imprisonment and whipping at their hands.

of me as this is. And therefore in short were it that I owned your power (which I do not in the least) I would be hanged before I would do so base and un-Englishman-like an action, to betray my liberty, which I must of necessity do in answering questions to accuse myself. But, sir, this I will say to you, my late actions have not been done in a hole or a corner, but on the housetop in the face of the sun, before hundreds and some thousands of people. And therefore why ask you me any questions? Go to those that have heard me and seen me, and it is possible you may find some hundreds of witnesses to tell you what I have said and done. For I hate holes and corners. My late actions need no covers nor hidings, they have been more honest than so, and I am not sorry for what I have done, for I did look well about me before I did what I did, and I am ready to lay down my life to justify what I have done. And so much in answer to your question.

"But now, sir, with your favor one word more, to mind you again of what I said before, in reference to my martial imprisonment. And truly, sir, I must tell you, circumstantials of my liberty at this time I shall not much dispute, but for the essentials of them I shall die. I am now in the soldiers' custody, where to continue in silence and patience is absolutely to betray my liberty. For they have nothing to do with me, nor the meanest freeman in England in this case. And besides, sir, they have no rules to walk by but their wills and their swords, which are two dangerous things. It may be I may be of an hasty, choleric temper, and not able nor willing to bear their affronts; and peradventure[5] they may be as willing to put them upon me as I am unwilling to bear them. And for you in this case to put fire and tinder together, to burn up one another, will not be much commendable, nor tend much to the accomplishment of your ends. But if for all this you shall send me back to the military sword again, either to Whitehall or any other suchlike garrisoned place in England, I do solemnly protest before the Eternal God of Heaven and Earth, I will fire it and burn it down to the ground, if possibly I can, although I be burnt to ashes with the flames thereof. For, sir, I say again, the soldiers have nothing to do to be my jailers; and besides, it is a maxim among the soldiers, that they must obey without dispute all the commands of their officers, be they right or wrong; and it is also the maxim amongst the officers, that if they do not do it, they must hang for it. Therefore if the officers command them to cut my throat, they must either do it or hang for it. And truly, sir (looking wishfully[6] upon Cromwell, that sat just against me), I must be plain with you, I have not found so much honor, honesty, justice, or conscience in any of the principal officers of the army as to trust my life under their protection or to think it can be safe under their immediate fingers. And therefore, not knowing nor very much caring what you will do with me, I earnestly

5. Perhaps.   6. Intently. "Against": opposite.

entreat you, if you will again imprison me, send me to a civil jail that the law knows, as Newgate, the Fleet, or the Gatehouse."[7]

*   *   *

So after we were all come out, and all four in a room close by them, all alone, I laid my ear to their door and heard Lieutenant General Cromwell (I am sure of it) very loud, thumping his fist upon the Council table till it rang again, and heard him speak in these very words or to this effect: "I tell you, sir, you have no other way to deal with these men but to break them in pieces." And thumping upon the Council table again, he said: "Sir, let me tell you that which is true, if you do not break them, they will break you; yea, and bring all the guilt of the blood and treasure shed and spent in this kingdom upon your head and shoulders; and frustrate and make void all that work that with so many years' industry, toil, and pains you have done, and so render you to all rational men in the world as the most contemptiblest generation of silly, low-spirited men in the earth, to be broken and routed by such a despicable contemptible generation of men as they are; and therefore, sir, I tell you again, you are necessitated to break them." * * * Upon which discourse of Cromwell's, the blood run up and down my veins, and I heartily wished myself in again amongst them (being scarce able to contain myself), that so I might have gone five or six stories higher than I did before.[8]

*   *   *

I know they have an army at command, but if every hair on the head of that officer or soldier they have at their command were a legion of men, I would fear them no more than so many straws, for the Lord Jehovah is my rock and defense, under the assured shelter of whose wings I am safe and secure, and therefore will sing and be merry; and do hereby sound an eternal trumpet of defiance to all the men and devils in earth and hell, but[9] only those men that have the image of God in them, and demonstrate it among men by their just, honest, merciful, and righteous actions. And as for all those vile actions their saint-like agents have fixed upon me[1] of late, I know before God that none is righteous, no, not one, but only he that is clothed with the glorious righteousness of Jesus Christ, which I assuredly know my soul hath been, and now is clothed with, in the strength of which I have walked for above twelve years together, and through the strength of which I have been able at any time in all that time to lay down my life on a quarter of an hour's warning. But as to man, I bid defiance to all my adversaries upon earth, to search my ways and goings with a candle and to lay any

---

7. After being questioned by the Council, and uniformly refusing to answer, Lilburne and his three associates are shut up in a room alongside the Council chamber.

8. Lilburne concludes his narration with a direct personal appeal to his reader and to his own religious conscience.

9. Except.

1. Attributed to me.

one base action to my charge in any kind whatsoever, since the first day that I visibly made profession of the fear of God, which is now above twelve years. Yea, I bid defiance to him or them to proclaim it upon the housetops, provided he will set his hand to it, and proclaim a public place where before indifferent men in the face of the sun his accusation may be scanned. Yea, I here declare that if any man or woman in England, either in reference to my public actions, to the state's money, or in reference to my private dealings in the world, shall come in and prove against me that ever I defrauded him or her of twelvepence, and for every twelvepence that I have so done, I will make him or her twenty shillings worth of amends, so far as all the estate I have in the world will extend.

Courteous reader and dear countryman, excuse I beseech thee my boasting and glorying, for I am necessitated to it, my adversaries' base and lying calumniations putting me upon it, and Paul and Samuel did it before me: and so I am thine, if thou art for the just freedoms and liberties of the land of thy nativity.

> JOHN LILBURNE, that never yet changed his principles from better to worse, nor could never be threatened out of them, nor courted from them, that never feared the rich nor mighty, nor never despised the poor nor needy, but always hath, and hopes by God's goodness to continue, *semper idem.*[2]

From the Tower of London, April 3, 1649

1649

2. Ever the same. John Lilburne was an authentically brave man, and a splendid popular agitator; but his story appears in a somewhat different light when seen from the perspective of his wife Elizabeth. See Antonia Fraser, *The Weaker Vessel,* chap. 12.

LADY ANNE HALKETT
1622–1699

Lady Anne Halkett, née Anne Murray, was born into a family of the royal household; her father was a tutor to Prince Charles, later Charles I. Thus was determined her allegiance to the royalist cause, an attachment by comparison with which her several sentimental complications were mere incidents. She was a tough and active partisan, and more directly than most women of her day engaged in the intrigues of the civil war. With one of her particular admirers, Colonel Bamfield, she assisted the young duke of York (future King James II of England) in making his escape from parliamentary custody. Her account of this adventure appeared in her memoirs, published many years later. We pick up the story in April 1648, with the question of Colonel Bamfield's intentions.

From The Memoirs

[*Springing the Duke*]

This gentleman came to see me sometimes in the company of ladies who had been my mother's neighbors in St. Martin's Lane, and sometimes alone, but whenever he came his discourse was serious, handsome, and tending to impress the advantages of piety, loyalty, and virtue; and these subjects were so agreeable to my own inclination that I could not but give them a good reception, especially from one that seemed to be so much an owner of them himself. After I had been used to freedom of discourse with him, I told him I approved much of his advice to others, but I thought his own practice contradicted much of his profession, for one of his acquaintance had told me he had not seen his wife in a twelvemonth, and it was impossible in my opinion for a good man to be an ill husband; and therefore he must defend himself from one before I could believe the other of him. He said it was not necessary to give everyone that might condemn him the reason of his being so long from her, yet to satisfy me he would tell me the truth, which was that, he being engaged in the King's service, he was obliged to be at London where it was not convenient for her to be with him, his stay in any place being uncertain; besides, she lived amongst her friends who, though they were kind to her, yet were not so to him, for most of that country had declared for the Parliament and were enemies to all that had or did serve the King, and therefore his wife, he was sure, would not condemn him for what he did by her own consent. This seeming reasonable, I did insist no more upon that subject.

At this time he had frequent letters from the King,[1] who employed him in several affairs, but that of the greatest concern which he was employed in was to contrive the Duke of York's escape out of St. James[2] (where his Highness and the Duke of Gloucester and the Princess Elizabeth lived under the care of the Earl of Northumberland and his lady). The difficulties of it was represented by Colonel Bamfield; but his Majesty still pressed it, and I remember this expression was in one of the letters: "I believe it will be difficult, and if he miscarry in the attempt, it will be the greatest affliction that can arrive to me; but I look upon James's escape as Charles's preservation,[3] and nothing can content me more; therefore be careful what you do."

This letter, amongst others, he showed me, and where the King approved of his choice of me to entrust with it, for to get the Duke's clothes made and to dress him in his disguise. So now all Colonel Bam-

---

1. Charles I, currently close prisoner of the parliamentary army under Cromwell. In less than a year he would be executed.
2. St. James's Palace, the present royal residence.
3. As James was a boy of 14 when this letter was written, his father must have had in mind the possibility of the parliamentarians assassinating the older son, Charles. Such an act would not have threatened the royal succession if the younger son, James, were alive and at liberty.

field's business and care was how to manage this business of so important concern, which could not be performed without several persons' concurrence in it, for he being generally known as one whose stay at London was in order to serve the King, few of those who were entrusted by the Parliament in public concerns durst own converse or hardly civility to him, lest they should have been suspect by their party, which made it difficult for him to get access to the Duke. But, to be short, having communicated the design to a gentleman attending his Highness who was full of honor and fidelity, by his means he had private access to the Duke, to whom he presented the King's letter and order to his Highness for consenting to act what Colonel Bamfield should contrive for his escape, which was so cheerfully entertained and so readily obeyed, that being once designed there was nothing more to do than to prepare all things for the execution. I had desired him to take a ribbon with him and bring me the bigness of the Duke's waist and his length, to have clothes made fit for him. In the meantime, Colonel Bamfield was to provide money for all necessary expense, which was furnished by an honest citizen. When I gave the measure to my tailor to inquire how much mohair would serve to make a petticoat and waistcoat to a young gentlewoman of that bigness and stature, he considered it a long time, and said he had made many gowns and suits, but he had never made any to such a person in his life. I thought he was in the right; but his meaning was he had never seen any woman of so low a stature have so big a waist. However, he made it as exactly fit as if he had taken the measure himself. It was a mixed mohair of a light hair color and black, and the underpetticoat was scarlet.

All things being now ready, upon the 20th of April 1648 in the evening was the time resolved for the Duke's escape. And in order to that, it was designed for a week before every night as soon as the Duke had supped he and those servants that attended his Highness (till the Earl of Northumberland and the rest of the house had supped) went to a play called *hide and seek*,[4] and sometimes he would hide himself so well that in half an hour's time they could not find him. His Highness had so used them to this that when he went really away they thought he was but at the usual sport. A little before the Duke went to supper that night, he called for the gardener, who only had a treble key besides that which the Duke had, and bid him give him that key till his own was mended, which he did. And after his Highness had supped, he immediately called to go to the play, and went down the privy stairs into the garden, and opened the gate that goes into the park, treble locking all the doors behind him. And at the garden gate Colonel Bamfield waited for his Highness, and putting on a cloak and periwig, hurried him away to the park gate, where a coach waited that carried them to the waterside, and, taking the boat that was appointed for that service, they rowed to the stairs next the

4. As a boy, James could have played such a game without exciting suspicion; he could also have passed more readily in female dress.

bridge, where I and Miriam[5] waited in a private house hard by that Colonel Bamfield had prepared for dressing his Highness, where all things were in a readiness. But I had many fears, for Colonel Bamfield had desired me, if they came not there precisely by ten o'clock to shift for myself, for then I might conclude they were discovered, and so my stay there could do no good but prejudice myself. Yet this did not make me leave the house though ten o'clock did strike, and he that was entrusted often went to the landing place and saw no boat coming was much discouraged, and asked me what I would do. I told him I came there with a resolution to serve his Highness, and I was fully determined not to leave that place till I was out of hopes of doing what I came there for, and would take my hazard. He left me to go again to the waterside, and while I was fortifying myself against what might arrive to me, I heard a great noise of many as I thought coming upstairs, which I expected to be soldiers to take me, but it was a pleasing disappointment, for the first that came in was the Duke, who with much joy I took in my arms and gave God thanks for his safe arrival. His Highness called "Quickly, quickly, dress me!"; and, putting off his clothes, I dressed him in the women's habit that was prepared, which fitted his Highness very well, and was very pretty in it.

After he had eaten something I made ready while I was idle, lest his Highness should be hungry, and having sent for a Wood-street cake (which I knew he loved) to take in the barge, with as much haste as could be his Highness went cross the bridge to the stairs where the barge lay, Colonel Bamfield leading him; and immediately the boatmen plied the oar so well that they were soon out of sight, having both wind and tide with them. But I afterwards heard the wind changed, and was so contrary that Colonel Bamfield told me he was terribly afraid they should have been blown back again. And the Duke said, "Do anything with me rather than let me go back again," which put Colonel Bamfield to seek help where it was only to be had, and, after he had most fervently supplicated assistance from God, presently the wind blew fair, and they came safely to their intended landing place. But I heard there was some difficulty before they got to the ship at Gravesend, which had like to have discovered them had not Colonel Washington's lady assisted them.

After the Duke's barge was out of sight of the bridge, I and Miriam went where I appointed the coach to stay for me, and made drive as fast as the coachman could to my brother's house, where I stayed. I met none in the way that gave me any apprehension that the design was discovered, nor was it noised abroad till the next day, for (as I related before) the Duke having used to play at hide and seek, and to conceal himself a long time, when they missed him at the same play, thought he would have discovered himself as formerly when they had given over seeking him. But a much longer time being passed than usually was

5. Mistress Murray's personal maid servant.

spent in that divertissement, some began to apprehend that his Highness was gone in earnest past their finding, which made the Earl of Northumberland (to whose care he was committed), after strict search made in the house of St. James and all thereabouts to no purpose, to send and acquaint the Speaker of the House of Commons that the Duke was gone, but how or by what means he knew not, but desired that there might be orders sent to the Cinque Ports[6] for stopping all ships going out till the passengers were examined and search made in all suspected places where his Highness might be concealed.

Though this was gone about with all the vigilancy imaginable, yet it pleased God to disappoint them of their intention by so infatuating those several persons who were employed for writing orders that none of them were able to write one right, but ten or twelve of them were cast by before one was according to their mind. This account I had from Mr. N. who was mace-bearer to the Speaker all that time and a witness of it. This disorder of the clerks contributed much to the Duke's safety, for he was at sea before any of the orders came to the ports, and so was free from what was designed if they had taken his Highness. Though several were suspected for being accessory to the escape, yet they could not charge any with it but the person who went away, and he being out of their reach, they took no notice as either to examine or imprison others.[7]

1778

6. A group of channel ports, originally five in number (hence the name); most English shipping to or from the Continent used to pass through them.
7. Despite this romantic beginning to their friendship, Colonel Bamfield and Mistress Murray never did get together. His wife was the problem; he never could discover for sure whether she was alive or dead. So in 1656 Anne Murray married Sir James Halkett.

DOROTHY OSBORNE
1627–1695

Dorothy Osborne met William Temple early in 1648, when she was twenty-one and he a year younger. Both came from "gentle" families that had suffered financially during the civil wars—hers on the royalist side, his on the Puritan. Since both William and Dorothy were attractive young people, conventional wisdom supposed they would renew the family fortunes by marrying, somewhere, anyhow, large sums of fresh money. Accordingly, when they fell in love with each other, the families were scandalized, and made every effort to separate them. Not until the very end of 1654 were they able to marry. In the meanwhile, they had been forced to communicate by clandestine letters; and while Temple's side of the correspondence is lost, Dorothy Osborne's in large part survives. Among many other points of interest, it shows how during those uncertain years of the interregnum, different political, religious, and social opinions accommodated to one another within the spacious bosom of the extended English family.

As for Dorothy Osborne herself, her style, wit, and poise in the presence of difficulties speak for themselves. Like most women in those days, she was the prisoner of her family; all she had to fight with was her wit and subtlety of spirit. But she was a fierce and in the end successful fighter. Two points to be especially noted are the lightness of her ironic touch, for example in describing negotiations with the "Emperor Justinian"; a little later in the century, this style, under the name of "raillery," would become generally popular. And in describing the great fight with her brother, how ready and natural is her access to the emotions! Neither Henry Osborne nor any other man of his day could have written such an account of a family quarrel.

To complete the story, we should recall that during the second half of the century, Sir William Temple became the ablest and most respected diplomat of his day; his married life was long and (except for the deaths of his seven children) happier than either of the busybody families would have predicted. The Osborne letters were not published till the late nineteenth century.

From The Letters of Dorothy Osborne

["Servants"]

Saturday 11 June 1653[1]

Sir,

If to know I wish you with me pleases you, 'tis a satisfaction you may always have, for I do it perpetually; but were it really in my power to make you happy, I could not miss being so myself, for I know nothing else I want towards it. You are admitted to all my entertainments, and 'twould be a pleasing surprise to me to see you among my shepherd-esses.[2] I meet some there sometimes that look very like gentlemen (for 'tis a road), and when they are in good humor they give us a compliment as they go by; but you would be so courteous as to stay, I hope, if we entreated you. 'Tis in your way to this place, and just before the house. 'Tis our Hyde Park, and every fine evening anybody that wanted a mistress[3] might be sure to find one there. I have wondered often to meet my fair lady Ruthin there alone, methinks it should be dangerous for an heir.[4] I could find in my heart to steal her away myself, but it should be rather for her person than her fortune. My brother says not a word of you nor your service, nor do I expect he should; if I could forget you, he would not help my memory. You would laugh sure if I could tell you how many servants[5] he has offered me since he came down, but one above all the rest I think he is in love with himself, and may marry him too if he pleases—I shall not hinder him. 'Tis one Talbot, the finest gentle-man he has seen this seven year, but the mischief on 't is he has not

---

1. Written from her parents' home at Chicksands in county Bedford, about 40 miles outside London. The first sentence picks up a phrase in a previous letter of Temple's.
2. Girls of the household, also mentioned in a previous letter. They used to sit in the open fields of an evening, chattering and singing songs.

3. Obviously, in the 20th-century sense of "girl friend."
4. I.e., an heiress, hence a likely victim of abduction if outdoors and unprotected.
5. Possible husbands. Her brother John had been in the house only a week, but was already busy rounding up alternatives to Temple.

above fifteen or sixteen hundred pound a year, though he swears he begins to think one might bate £500 a year for such a husband. I tell him I am glad to hear it, and that if I were as much taken as he with Mr. Ta: I should not be less gallant, but I doubted the first extremely.

I have spleen[6] enough to carry me to Epsom this summer, but yet I think I shall not go. If I make one journey, I must make more, for then I have no excuse, and rather than be obliged to that, I'll make none. You have so often reproached me with the loss of your liberty that to make you some amends I am contented to be your prisoner this summer; but you shall do one favor for me into the bargain. When your father goes into Ireland, lay your commands upon some of his servants to get you an Irish greyhound. I have one that was the General's,[7] but 'tis a bitch and those are always much less than the dogs. I got it in the time of my favor there, and it was all they had. H. C.[8] undertook to write to his brother Fleetwood for another for me, but I have lost my hopes there. Whomsoever it is that you employ, he will need no other instructions but to get the biggest he can meet with. 'Tis all the beauty of those dogs or of any, indeed I think; a Masty[9] is handsomer to me than the most exact little dog that ever lady played withal. You will not offer to take it ill that I employ you in such a commission since I have told you that the General's son did not refuse it; but I shall take it ill if you do not take the same freedom whensoever I am capable of serving you.

The town must needs be unpleasant now, and methinks you might contrive some way of having your letters sent to you without giving your-self the trouble of coming to town for them when you have no other business; you must pardon me if I think they cannot be worth it.

I am told that R: Spencer is a servant to a lady of my acquaintance, a daughter of my lady Lexington.[1] Is it true? and if it be, what is become of the £2500 lady?

Would you think it, that I have an ambassador from the Emperor Justinian,[2] that comes to renew the treaty? In earnest, 'tis true, and I want your counsel extremely what to do in it. You told me once that of all my servants you liked him the best; if I could do so too, there were no dispute in 't. Well, I'll think on 't, and if it succeed I will be as good as my word, you shall take your choice of my four daughters. Am I not beholding to him, think you? He says that he has made addresses ('tis true) in several places since we parted, but could not fix anywhere, and in his opinion he sees nobody that would make so fit a wife for him as I. He has often inquired after me to hear if I were not marrying, and somebody told him I had an ague,[3] and he presently fell sick of one too,

6. Fits of ill temper supposed to be caused by an ailing spleen. The waters of Epsom Wells in Surrey were alleged to ease the condition.
7. I.e., Oliver Cromwell's.
8. Henry, Cromwell's youngest son, once mentioned as a husband for Dorothy, is now discarded—hence her "lost hopes" there.
9. Mastiff. "Exact": dainty.

1. These matters were also discussed in a previous letter. Note how Dorothy, in a phrase like "the £2500 lady," mocks the commercial standards of her social class.
2. Sir Justinian Isham, an elderly widower with four grown daughters, had previously been offered to Dorothy as a husband, and now reappears.
3. Chills and fever.

so natural a sympathy there is between us. And yet for all this, on my conscience, we shall never marry. He desires to know whether I am at liberty or not: what shall I tell him? or shall I send him to you to know? I think that will be best. I'll say that you are much my friend, and that I have resolved not to dispose of myself but with your consent and approbation, and therefore he must make all his court to you; and when he can bring me a certificate under your hand that you think him a fit husband for me, 'tis very likely I may have him—till then I am his humble servant, and your faithful friend.

[Fighting with Brother John]

Saturday 4 February 1654

'Tis well you have given over your reproaches. I can allow you to tell me of my faults kindly and like a friend. Possibly it is a weakness in me to aim at the world's esteem, as if I could not be happy without it; but there are certain things that custom has made almost of absolute necessity, and reputation I take to be one of those. If one could be invisible, I should choose that, but since all people are seen and known, and shall be talked of in spite of their teeth, who is it that does not desire at least that nothing of ill may be said of them, whether justly or otherwise? I never knew any so satisfied with their own innocence as to be content the world should think them guilty. Some out of pride have seemed to contemn ill reports when they found they could not avoid them, but none out of strength of reason, though many have pretended to it—no, not my lady Newcastle with all her philosophy.[1] Therefore you must not expect it from me. I shall never be ashamed to own that I have a particular value for you above any other, but 'tis not the greatest merit of person will excuse a want of fortune. In some degree I think it will, at least with the most rational part of the world, and as far as that will reach, I desire it should.

I would not have the world believe I married out of interest and to please my friends; I had much rather they should know I chose the person and took his fortune because 'twas necessary, and that I prefer a competency[2] with one I esteem, infinitely before a vast estate in other hands. 'Tis much easier sure to get a good fortune than a good husband, but whosoever marries without any consideration of fortune shall never be allowed to do it out of so reasonable an apprehension. The whole world (without any reserve) shall pronounce they did it merely to satisfy their giddy humor. Besides, though you imagine 'twere a great argument of my kindness[3] to consider nothing but you, in earnest I believe 'twould

---

1. Margaret Duchess of Newcastle had published in 1653 her *Philosophical Fancies*. Dorothy had no great opinion of her ladyship, and once said that many inhabitants of Bedlam (the madhouse) had better sense.

2. Sufficiency.

3. Note that Dorothy, though clearly devoted to Temple, avoids the sticky word "love" as applied to herself; others may use it, but what she has for Temple is a "kindness."

be an injury to you. I do not see that it puts any value upon men when women marry them for love (as they term it); 'tis not their merit but our folly that is always presumed to cause it, and would it be any advantage to you to have your wife thought an indiscreet person?

All this I can say to you, but when my brother disputes it with me, I have other arguments for him, and I drove him up so close t' other night that for want of a better gap to get out at, he was fain to say that he feared as much your having a fortune as your having none, for he saw you held my lord Lisle's principles,[4] that religion or honor were things you did not consider at all, and that he was confident you would take any engagement, serve in any employment, or do anything to advance yourself. I had no patience with this. To say you were a beggar, your father not worth £4,000 in the whole world, was nothing in comparison of having no religion nor no honor. I forgot all my disguise, and we talked ourselves weary; he renounced me again and I defied him, but both in as civil language as it would permit, and parted in great anger with the usual ceremony of a leg and a curtsey,[5] that you would have died with laughing to have seen us. The next day I, not being at dinner, saw him not till night; then he came into my chamber, where I supped, but he did not. Afterwards, Mr. Gibson and he and I talked of indifferent things till all but we two went to bed. There he sat half an hour and said not one word, nor I to him; at last in a pitiful tone, "Sister," says he, "I have heard you say that when anything troubles you, of all things you apprehend going to bed, because there it increases upon you and you lie at the mercy of all your sad thoughts which the silence and darkness of the night adds a horror to. I am at that pass now, I vow to God I would not endure another night like the last to gain a crown." I, who resolved to take no notice what ailed him, said 'twas a knowledge[6] I had raised from my spleen only; and so fell into a discourse of melancholy and the causes, and from that (I know not how) into religion, and we talked so long of it and so devoutly that it allayed all our anger. We grew to a calm and peace with all the world; two hermits conversing in a cell they equally inhabit never expressed more humble, charitable kindness toward one another than we. He asked my pardon and I his, and he has promised me never to speak of it to me whilst he lives, but leave the event to God Almighty, and till he sees it done he will be always the same to me that he is. Then he shall leave me, he says, not out of want of kindness to me, but because he cannot see the ruin of a person that he loves so passionately and in whose happiness he had laid up all his. These are the terms we are at, and I am confident he will keep his word with me; so that you have no reason to fear him in any respect, for though he should break his promise he should never make me break mine. No, let

---

4. John Lisle earned himself the name of a renegade by an excess of servility to Cromwell. His "lordship" was synthetic as well; he had been a judge at the trial of Charles I, and earned by that service a seat in Cromwell's House of Lords.
5. Masculine and feminine gestures of polite obeisance.
6. Belief, or even opinion.

me assure you, this rival nor any other shall ever alter me. Therefore, spare your jealousy, or turn it all into kindness.

1888

TERMINI: JOHN LOCKE AND ISAAC NEWTON

The Romans, who had a happy gift for devising special-purpose gods, created a number of them, called Termini, whose function was to preside over boundaries and frontiers. As the early seventeenth century, with its hoarse conflicts and extravagant aspirations, gives way to the calmer atmosphere of the Restoration and the eighteenth century, two such giant figures stand forth, to help memory mark a moment of major transition: John Locke and Isaac Newton. Their major works were not published till later in the century (Locke's big *Essay* in 1690, Newton's *Principia Mathematica* in 1687— though not in English till 1729), but their minds were formed during the vital intellectual period of the interregnum. Their thinking developed out of the intellectual conflicts and questionings of the early century; their ideas underlay and authenticated the intellectual activity of centuries to come.

Even his worst enemies conceded that under Oliver Cromwell the universities and learned societies of England flourished as never before. Intellectually, the tide was setting toward a new philosophy of scientific materialism—not just in fields like mathematics, chemistry, and mechanics, but in psychology and cosmology, where ancient intricate structures of mysterious correspondence and astral influence were brushed away like cobwebs by work done to a new standard of exact observation and rational analysis. Locke's emphasis on verifiable evidence interpreted by common sense, and on mutual toleration growing from mistrust of rash generalizations, laid the cornerstone of a new social ethos. Larger and more far-reaching, but basically congruent, was Newton's vision of the cosmos as an intricately designed yet essentially simple and self-contained machine controlled by a set of majestic, impersonal, universal laws.

Thus Locke and Newton are no less notable for what they built anew than for what they destroyed. After demolishing the old theories of humors and temperaments, Locke replaced them with a radically uncluttered view of the mind's workings. His conception of knowledge—and, hardly less important, the tone of his voice when discussing knowledge—reached far beyond the narrow sphere of professional philosophers to become the ideal of an entire culture. Much that the eighteenth century summarized as "candor" in dealing with experience and interpreting evidence implies Lockean assumptions. Similarly Newton, after clearing out a tangle of superstitions and half-truths that had been accumulating for centuries, restructured not only the heavens but men's primary intuitions of how things are put together and what makes them work. Both men dug their foundations deep, and built solidly upon them. They are indeed massive termini who can be seen as marking the end of the Renaissance and the onset of what we call (not without gathering reservations) the modern world.

JOHN LOCKE
1632–1704

1667:   Physician to the first earl of Shaftesbury.
1684:   Expelled from Oxford post as part of intrigues against Shaftesbury.
1690:   Publication of the *Essay, Letter Concerning Toleration,* and *Two Treatises of Government.*

Locke's *Essay Concerning Human Understanding,* which is a pretty formidable book of technical philosophy, drew some protests over its title, and others of a contrary tendency over its method. It seemed too heavy, hard, and long to be a mere essay. On the other hand, its basic material was described as too trifling to merit so much analysis. For all Mr. Locke proposed to do in several hundred knotty pages was to analyze a few ideas that he found lying about in his own mind.

As usual, the philosopher, who was nothing if not a long-headed man, had considered these criticisms already and had devised a single answer for both. His book was an essay because, like that of Montaigne, it aimed to explore the mind of mankind in general through a discriminating analysis of one mind in particular. When Locke analyzed the ideas of his mind, the ways they were acquired and put together, he found they were clear when they were based on direct experience, and adequate when they were clear. Usually, it appeared, problems occurred when the basic ideas with which he was trying to calculate were blurred or confused or did not refer to anything determinate. Thus a critical analysis of the ideas in an individual mind could lead straight to a rule about adequate ideas in general and the sort of subject where adequate ideas were possible. On the basis of such a limitation, individuals might reach rational agreement with one another, and so set up an area of natural law, within which a common rule of understanding was available.

The clergy were naturally upset over Locke's new "way of ideas," which invited people to discard from their minds any ideas that they could not reduce to clear, distinct, i.e., determinate, form. "Mysteries of faith" were essential to the mental economy of churchmen. How could the Trinity or the doctrine of predestination be reduced to clear, distinct ideas? If they couldn't, must one then discard them? On this last point, Locke was polite but very firm. Yes, if one wanted to discourse reasonably and understandably, one really must discard any idea which could not be given a determinate shape and meaning. The philosopher had evidently performed this operation on any unclear and indistinct ideas he found in his own mind. What was left of Christianity when one got rid of all its "unreasonable" elements was a cool, general, undemanding creed, which did not commit one to much more than a belief in the existence of God, and was therefore known as "Deism." Locke did not like labels, but he was a kind of Deist. Though a scandalous idea in the late seventeenth century, Deism was a quite respectable creed by the time of Pope.

Like most philosophers, Locke had a minimum of personal history. His background and connections were all with the Puritan movement, but he was early disillusioned with the enthusiastic moods and dogmatic persecutions to which he found the Puritans prone. Having a small but steady private income, he became a student, chiefly at Oxford, learning enough medicine to act as a physician, holding an occasional appointive office, but never allowing any of these activities to limit his controlling passion, which was simply for thought. After 1667, he was personal physician and tutor in the household of a violent, crafty politician, the first earl of Shaftesbury (Dryden's "Achitophel"). But Locke himself was always a grave, dispassionate man, almost frighteningly judicious. On one occasion, Shaftesbury's political enemies at Oxford had Locke watched for several years on end, during which he was not heard to say one word either critical of the government or favorable to it. When times are turbulent, so much discretion is suspicious in itself; and Locke found it convenient to go abroad for several years during the 1680s. He lived quietly in Holland, and pursued his thoughts. The Glorious Revolution of 1688–89 and the accession of William III brought him back to England, and made possible the publication of the *Essay*, on which he had been working for many years. Its publication foreshadowed the coming age of reason, not only in the positive ideas that the book advanced, but in the quiet way it set aside as insoluble a range of problems about absolute authority and absolute assurance to which the seventeenth century had prodigally sacrificed its best resources of mind and heart.

From An Essay Concerning Human Understanding

From *The Epistle to the Reader*

Reader,

I here put into thy hands what has been the diversion of some of my idle and heavy hours; if it has the good luck to prove so of any of thine, and thou hast but half so much pleasure in reading as I had in writing it, thou wilt as little think thy money, as I do my pains, ill bestowed. Mistake not this for a commendation of my work; nor conclude, because I was pleased with the doing of it, that therefore I am fondly taken with it now it is done. He that hawks at larks and sparrows, has no less sport, though a much less considerable quarry, than he that flies at nobler game: and he is little acquainted with the subject of this treatise, the Understanding, who does not know, that as it is the most elevated faculty of the soul, so it is employed with a greater and more constant delight than any of the other. Its searches after truth are a sort of hawking and hunting, wherein the very pursuit makes a great part of the pleasure. Every step the mind takes in its progress towards knowledge makes some discovery, which is not only new, but the best, too, for the time at least.

For the understanding, like the eye, judging of objects only by its own sight, cannot but be pleased with what it discovers, having less regret for what has escaped it, because it is unknown. Thus he who has raised himself above the alms-basket, and not content to live lazily on scraps of begged opinions, sets his own thoughts on work to find and follow truth, will (whatever he lights on) not miss the hunter's satisfaction; every moment of his pursuit will reward his pains with some delight, and he will have reason to think his time not ill spent, even when he cannot much boast of any great acquisition.

This, reader, is the entertainment of those who let loose their own thoughts, and follow them in writing; which thou oughtest not to envy them, since they afford thee an opportunity of the like diversion, if thou wilt make use of thy own thoughts in reading. It is to them, if they are thy own, that I refer myself; but if they are taken upon trust from others, it is no great matter what they are, they not following truth, but some meaner consideration; and it is not worth while to be concerned what he says or thinks, who says or thinks only as he is directed by another. If thou judgest for thyself, I know thou wilt judge candidly; and then I shall not be harmed or offended, whatever be thy censure. For, though it be certain that there is nothing in this treatise of the truth whereof I am not fully persuaded, yet I consider myself as liable to mistakes as I can think thee; and know that this book must stand or fall with thee, not by any opinion I have of it, but thy own. If thou findest little in it new or instructive to thee, thou art not to blame me for it. It was not meant for those that had already mastered this subject, and made a thorough acquaintance with their own understandings, but for my own information, and the satisfaction of a few friends, who acknowledged themselves not to have sufficiently considered it. Were it fit to trouble thee with the history of this Essay, I should tell thee, that five or six friends, meeting at my chamber, and discoursing on a subject very remote from this, found themselves quickly at a stand by the difficulties that rose on every side. After we had awhile puzzled ourselves, without coming any nearer a resolution of those doubts which perplexed us, it came into my thoughts, that we took a wrong course; and that, before we set ourselves upon inquiries of that nature, it was necessary to examine our own abilities, and see what objects our understandings were or were not fitted to deal with. This I proposed to the company, who all readily assented; and thereupon it was agreed, that this should be our first inquiry. Some hasty and undigested thoughts, on a subject I had never before considered, which I set down against our next meeting, gave the first entrance into this discourse, which, having been thus begun by chance, was continued by entreaty; written by incoherent parcels; and, after long intervals of neglect, resumed again, as my humor or occasions permitted; and at last, in a retirement, where an attendance on my health gave me leisure, it was brought into that order thou now seest it.

This discontinued way of writing may have occasioned, besides others, two contrary faults; viz., that too little and too much may be said in it. If thou findest anything wanting, I shall be glad, that what I have writ gives thee any desire that I should have gone farther: if it seems too much to thee, thou must blame the subject; for when I first put pen to paper, I thought all I should have to say on this matter would have been contained in one sheet of paper; but the farther I went, the larger prospect I had: new discoveries led me still on, and so it grew insensibly to the bulk it now appears in. I will not deny but possibly it might be reduced to a narrower compass than it is; and that some parts of it might be contracted; the way it has been writ in, by catches, and many long intervals of interruption, being apt to cause some repetitions. But, to confess the truth, I am now too lazy or too busy to make it shorter.

* * * I pretend not to publish this Essay for the information of men of large thoughts and quick apprehensions; to such masters of knowledge, I profess myself a scholar, and therefore warn them beforehand not to expect anything here but what, being spun out of my own coarse thoughts,[1] is fitted to men of my own size, to whom, perhaps, it will not be unacceptable that I have taken some pains to make plain and familiar to their thoughts some truths, which established prejudice or the abstractness of the ideas themselves, might render difficult. * * *

* * * The commonwealth of learning is not at this time without master-builders, whose mighty designs in advancing the sciences will leave lasting monuments to the admiration of posterity: but every one must not hope to be a Boyle or a Sydenham; and in an age that produces such masters as the great Huygenius, and the incomparable Mr. Newton, with some other of that strain,[2] it is ambition enough to be employed as an under-laborer in clearing the ground a little, and removing some of the rubbish that lies in the way to knowledge; which certainly had been very much more advanced in the world, if the endeavors of ingenious and industrious men had not been much cumbered with the learned but frivolous use of uncouth, affected, or unintelligible terms introduced into the sciences, and there made an art of to that degree, that philosophy, which is nothing but the true knowledge of things, was thought unfit or uncapable to be brought into well-bred company and polite conversation.[3] Vague and insignificant forms of speech, and abuse of language, have so long passed for mysteries of science; and hard or misapplied words, with little or no meaning, have, by prescription, such a right to be mistaken for deep learning and height of speculation; that it will not be easy to persuade either those who speak or those who hear them, that they are but the covers of ignorance, and hindrance of true knowledge. * * *

The booksellers, preparing for the fourth edition of my Essay, gave me notice of it, that I might, if I had leisure, make any additions or

---

1. Locke's mock-modest confession that his philosophy had been "spun out of his own coarse thoughts" gave rise to a good deal of critical ridicule, echoes of which are heard in the debate between the spider and the bee in Swift's *Battle of the Books*.

2. Robert Boyle is the great Anglo-Irish chemist and physicist; Thomas Sydenham, a physician and authority on the cure of fevers; Christiaan Huygens was a Dutch mathematician and astronomer; and Newton is of course Sir Isaac. Locke's choice of scientists to illustrate the great minds of his time is certainly tendentious. A generation or two ear-

lier a list of "great men" would have consisted largely of theologians and perhaps lawyers.

3. Locke was tutor to Anthony Ashley Cooper, third earl of Shaftesbury, whose philosophical writings make of genteel social conversation and civilized good humor something like guides to ultimate truth. Whatever can't be spoken in a drawing room without exposing a gentleman to ridicule—so Shaftesbury comes close to saying—is not likely to be true. Locke's basic hostility to cant and jargon has been extended by Shaftesbury, but its original source is apparent.

alterations I should think fit. Whereupon I thought it convenient to advertise the reader, that besides several corrections I had made here and there, there was one alteration which it was necessary to mention, because it ran through the whole book, and is of consequence to be rightly understood. What I thereupon said, was this:—

"Clear and distinct ideas" are terms which, though familiar and frequent in men's mouths, I have reason to think every one who uses does not perfectly understand. And possibly it is but here and there one who gives himself the trouble to consider them so far as to know what he himself or others precisely mean by them. I have therefore, in most places, chose to put "determinate" or "determined," instead of "clear" and "distinct," as more likely to direct men's thoughts to my meaning in this matter. By those denominations, I mean some object in the mind, and consequently determined, i.e., such as it is there seen and perceived to be. This, I think, may fitly be called a "determinate" or "determined" idea, when such as it is at any time objectively in the mind, and so determined there, it is annexed, and without variation determined, to a name or articulate sound which is to be steadily the sign of that very same object of the mind, or determinate idea.

To explain this a little more particularly: By "determinate," when applied to a simple idea, I mean that simple appearance which the mind has in its view, or perceives in itself, when that idea is said to be in it. By "determined," when applied to a complex idea, I mean such an one as consists of a determinate number of certain simple or less complex ideas, joined in such a proportion and situation as the mind has before its view, and sees in itself, when that idea is present in it, or should be present in it when a man gives a name to it. I say "should be"; because it is not every one, nor perhaps any one, who is so careful of his language as to use no word till he views in his mind the precise determined idea which he resolves to make it the sign of. The want of this is the cause of no small obscurity and confusion in men's thoughts and discourses.

I know there are not words enough in any language to answer all the variety of ideas that enter into men's discourses and reasonings. But this hinders not but that when anyone uses any term, he may have in his mind a determined idea which he makes it the sign of, and to which he should keep it steadily annexed during that present discourse. Where he does not or cannot do this, he in vain pretends to clear or distinct ideas: it is plain his are not so; and therefore there can be expected nothing but obscurity and confusion, where such terms are made use of which have not such a precise determination.

Upon this ground I have thought "determined ideas" a way of speaking less liable to mistake than "clear and distinct"; and where men have got such determined ideas of all that they reason, inquire, or argue about, they will find a great part of their doubts and disputes at an end. The greatest part of the questions and controversies that perplex mankind, depending on the doubtful and uncertain use of words, or (which is the same) indetermined ideas, which they are made to stand for: I have made choice of these terms to signify, 1. Some immediate object of the mind, which it perceives and has before it, distinct from the sound it uses as a sign of it. 2. That this idea, thus determined, i.e., which the mind has in itself, and knows and sees there, be determined without any change to that name, and that name determined to that precise idea. If men had such determined ideas in their inquiries and discourses, they would both discern how far their own inquiries and discourses went, and avoid the greatest part of the disputes and wranglings they have with others.

* * *

1690, 1700

SIR ISAAC NEWTON
1642–1727

Isaac Newton was the posthumous son of a small farmer in Lincolnshire; as a boy, he invented machines, as an undergraduate he was making discoveries in optics and the higher mathematics, and in 1667, aged barely twenty-five, he was elected a fellow of Trinity College, Cambridge. It would be generous to describe intellectual life in Restoration universities as "torpid," and Newton got little in the way of stimulus from his colleagues. Even the Royal Society, after an initial burst of activity in the 1660s, sank during the latter part of the century into lethargy and triviality. But Newton was a man whose mind worked incessantly and at the very highest level of insight; apart from specific discoveries in the fields of mathematics, physics, and astronomy, he generated an entire world view that was outdated only in the twentieth century by the work of Einstein. The importance of Newton's thought cannot be described or even indicated here: interested readers should refer to a suitable history of philosophy or of scientific thought, or to a full-scale biography.

Much of Sir Isaac's scientific work was reported in Latin, still the language of international scholarship; but when he chose, the great thinker could express himself in notably lucid and trenchant English. The first of his important experiments, having to do with light and color, took form as a letter to the Royal Society, which appeared in the Society's *Journal*, dated February 19, 1672. The experiments and reasoning are described in language of perfect clarity; and when, as the last word of his summary, he drops a very heavy word indeed, he clinches the point like a carpenter nailing shut a box.

In point of fact, not all Newton's conclusions in the *Letter* have held absolutely solid. But for a young man just five years out of college, his command of a rigorous experimental method is extraordinary. We are, evidently, in a world diametrically different from that of Sir Thomas Browne, who also thought himself a man of science.

From A Letter of Mr. Isaac Newton, Professor of the Mathematics in the University of Cambridge, Containing His New Theory about Light and Colors

Sent by the Author to the Publisher from Cambridge, Febr. 6, 1672, in order to Be Communicated to the Royal Society

Sir,

To perform my late promise to you, I shall without further ceremony acquaint you that in the beginning of the year 1666 (at which time I applied myself to the grinding of optic glasses of other figures than spherical) I procured me a triangular glass prism to try therewith the celebrated phenomena of colors. And in order thereto having darkened my chamber and made a small hole in my window-shuts to let in a convenient quantity of the sun's light, I placed my prism at his entrance that it might be thereby refracted to the opposite wall. It was at first a very pleasing divertissement to view the vivid and intense colors produced thereby; but after a while, applying myself to consider them more circumspectly, I became surprised to see them in an *oblong* form, which according to the received laws of refraction I expected should have been *circular*.

They were terminated at the sides with straight lines, but at the ends the decay of light was so gradual that it was difficult to determine justly what was their figure; yet they seemed *semicircular*.

Comparing the length of this colored spectrum with its breadth, I found it about five times greater, a disproportion so extravagant that it excited me to a more than ordinary curiosity of examining from whence it might proceed. I could scarce think that the various thickness of the glass or the termination with shadow or darkness could have any influence on light to produce such an effect; yet I thought it not amiss first to examine those circumstances, and so tried what would happen by transmitting light through parts of the glass of divers thicknesses, or through holes in the window of divers bignesses, or by setting the prism without, so that the light might pass through it and be refracted before it was terminated by the hole. But I found none of those circumstances material. The fashion of the colors was in all these cases the same.

Then I suspected whether by any unevenness in the glass or other contingent irregularity these colors might be thus dilated. And to try this, I took another prism like the former and so placed it that the light, passing through them both, might be refracted contrary ways, and so by the latter returned into that course from which the former had diverted it. For by this means I thought the regular effects of the first prism would be destroyed by the second prism but the irregular ones more augmented by the multiplicity of refractions. The event was that the light which by the first prism was diffused into an oblong form was by the second reduced into an orbicular one with as much regularity as when it did not at all pass through them. So that, whatever was the cause of that length, 'twas not any contingent irregularity.[1]

* * *

The gradual removal of these suspicions at length led me to the *experimentum crucis*,[2] which was this: I took two boards, and placed one of them close behind the prism at the window, so that the light might pass through a small hole made in it for the purpose and fall on the other board, which I placed at about 12 feet distance, having first made a small hole in it also, for some of that incident[3] light to pass through. Then I placed another prism behind this second board so that the light, trajected through both the boards, might pass through that also, and be again refracted before it arrived at the wall. This done, I took the first prism in my hand, and turned it to and fro slowly about its axis, so much as to make the several parts of the image cast on the second board successively pass through the hole in it, that I might observe to what places on the wall the second prism would refract them. And I saw by the variation of those places that the light tending to that end of the image towards which the refraction of the first prism was made did in the second prism suffer a refraction considerably greater than the light tending to the other end. And so the true cause of the length of that image was detected to be no other than that light consists of rays *differently refrangible*, which, without any respect to a difference in their incidence, were, according to their degrees of refrangibility, transmitted towards divers parts of the wall.[4]

* * *

I shall now proceed to acquaint you with another more notable difformity in its rays, wherein the *origin of colors* is unfolded: concerning which I shall lay down the doctrine first and then for its examination give you an instance or two of the experiments, as a specimen of the rest.

The doctrine you will find comprehended and illustrated in the following propositions.

1. As the rays of light differ in degrees of refrangibility, so they also differ in their disposition to exhibit this or that particular color. Colors are not qualifications of light, derived from refractions or reflections of natural bodies (as 'tis generally believed), but original and connate properties which in divers rays are divers. Some rays are disposed to exhibit a red color and no other; some a yellow and no other, some a green and

1. Newton goes on to describe several experiments and calculations by which he disposed of alternative theories—that rays coming from different parts of the sun caused the diffusion of light into an oblong, or that the rays of light traveled in curved paths after leaving the prism.
2. Crucial experiment, turning point.
3. From Latin *incidere*, to fall into or onto. Newton uses it of light striking an obstacle.
4. At this point Newton digresses to a discussion of the optical consequences of his view of light (especially for the improvement of telescopes), adding in passing that his experiments were interrupted for two years by the plague; but at last he returns to some further and even more important characteristics of light.

no other, and so of the rest. Nor are there only rays proper and particular to the more eminent colors, but even to all their intermediate gradations.

2. To the same degree of refrangibility ever belongs the same color, and to the same color ever belongs the same degree of refrangibility. The least refrangible rays are all disposed to exhibit a red color, and contrarily those rays which are disposed to exhibit a red color are all the least refrangible. So the most refrangible rays are all disposed to exhibit a deep violet color, and contrarily those which are apt to exhibit such a violet color are all the most refrangible. And so to all the intermediate colors in a continued series belong intermediate degrees of refrangibility. And this analogy 'twixt colors and refrangibility is very precise and strict; the rays always either exactly agreeing in both or proportionally disagreeing in both.

3. The species of color and degree of refrangibility proper to any particular sort of rays is not mutable by refraction nor by reflection from natural bodies nor by any other cause that I could yet observe. When any one sort of rays hath been well parted from those of other kinds, it hath afterwards obstinately retained its color, notwithstanding my utmost endeavors to change it. I have refracted it with prisms and reflected it with bodies which in daylight were of other colors; I have intercepted it with the colored film of air interceding two compressed plates of glass; transmitted it through colored mediums and through mediums irradiated with other sorts of rays, and diversely terminated it; and yet could never produce any new color out of it. It would by contracting or dilating become more brisk or faint and by the loss of many rays in some cases very obscure and dark; but I could never see it changed *in specie*.[5]

4. Yet seeming transmutations of colors may be made, where there is any mixture of divers sorts of rays. For in such mixtures, the component colors appear not, but by their mutual allaying each other constitute a middling color. And therefore if by refraction or any other of the aforesaid causes the difform rays latent in such a mixture be separated, there shall emerge colors different from the color of the composition. Which colors are not new generated, but only made apparent by being parted; for if they be again entirely mixed and blended together, they will again compose that color which they did before separation. And for the same reason, transmutations made by the convening of divers colors are not real; for when the difform rays are again severed, they will exhibit the very same colors which they did before they entered the composition— as you see blue and yellow powders when finely mixed appear to the naked eye green, and yet the colors of the component corpuscles are not thereby transmuted, but only blended. For, when viewed with a good microscope, they still appear blue and yellow interspersedly.

5. There are therefore two sorts of colors: the one original and simple, the other compounded of these. The original or primary colors are red,

---

5. In kind.

yellow, green, blue, and a violet-purple, together with orange, indigo, and an indefinite variety of intermediate graduations.

6. The same colors *in specie* with these primary ones may be also produced by composition. For a mixture of yellow and blue makes green; or red and yellow makes orange; of orange and yellowish green makes yellow. And in general if any two colors be mixed which, in the series of those generated by the prism, are not too far distant one from another, they by their mutual alloy compound that color which in the said series appeareth in the mid-way between them. But those which are situated at too great a distance, do not so. Orange and indigo produce not the intermediate green, nor scarlet and green the intermediate yellow.

7. But the most surprising and wonderful composition was that of whiteness. There is no one sort of rays which alone can exhibit this. 'Tis ever compounded, and to its composition are requisite all the aforesaid primary colors, mixed in a due proportion. I have often with admiration beheld that, all the colors of the prism being made to converge and thereby to be again mixed as they were in the light before it was incident upon the prism, reproduced light, entirely and perfectly white, and not at all sensibly differing from a direct light of the sun, unless when the glasses I used were not sufficiently clear; for then they would a little incline it to *their* color.

8. Hence therefore it comes to pass that whiteness is the usual color of light, for light is a confused aggregate of rays endued with all sorts of colors, as they are promiscuously darted from the various parts of luminous bodies. And of such a confused aggregate, as I said, is generated whiteness, if there be a due proportion of the ingredients; but if any one predominate, the light must incline to that color, as it happens in the blue flame of brimstone, the yellow flame of a candle, and the various colors of the fixed stars.

9. These things considered, the manner how colors are produced by the prism is evident. For of the rays constituting the incident light, since those which differ in color proportionally differ in refrangibility, they by their unequal refractions must be severed and dispersed into an oblong form in an orderly succession from the least refracted scarlet to the most refracted violet. And for the same reason it is that objects, when looked upon through a prism, appear colored. For the difform rays, by their unequal refractions, are made to diverge towards several parts of the retina, and there express the images of things colored, as in the former case they did the sun's image upon a wall. And by this inequality of refractions they become not only colored, but also very confused and indistinct.

10. Why the colors of the rainbow appear in falling drops of rain is also from hence evident. For those drops which refract the rays disposed to appear purple in greatest quantity to the spectator's eye, refract the rays of other sorts so much less as to make them pass beside it;[6] and such

6. I.e., disappear alongside it.

are the drops on the inside of the primary bow and on the outside of the secondary or exterior one. So those drops which refract in greatest plenty the rays apt to appear red toward the spectator's eye, refract those of other sorts so much more as to make them pass beside it; and such are the drops on the exterior part of the primary and interior part of the secondary bow.

*   *   *

13. I might add more instances of this nature, but I shall conclude with this general one, that the colors of all natural bodies have no other origin than this, that they are variously qualified to reflect one sort of light in greater plenty than another. And this I have experimented in a dark room by illuminating those bodies with uncompounded light of divers colors. For by that means any body may be made to appear of any color. They have there no appropriate color, but ever appear of the color of the light cast upon them, but yet with this difference, that they are most brisk and vivid in the light of their own daylight color. *Minium*[7] appeareth there of any color indifferently with which 'tis illustrated, but yet most luminous in red, and so *Bise*[8] appeareth indifferently of any color with which 'tis illustrated, but yet most luminous in blue. And therefore *minium* reflecteth rays of any color, but most copiously those endued with red; and consequently when illustrated with daylight, that is, with all sorts of rays promiscuously blended, those qualified with red shall abound most in the reflected light, and by their prevalence cause it to appear of that color. And for the same reason *bise*, reflecting blue most copiously, shall appear blue by the excess of those rays in its reflected light; and the like of other bodies. And that this is the entire and adequate cause of their colors is manifest, because they have no power to change or alter the colors of any sort of rays incident apart, but put on all colors indifferently with which they are enlightened.

These things being so, it can no longer be disputed whether there be colors in the dark, nor whether they be the qualities of the objects we see, no, nor perhaps whether light be a body. For since colors are the qualities of light, having its rays for their entire and immediate subject, how can we think those rays qualities also, unless one quality may be the subject of and sustain another—which in effect is to call it substance. We should not know bodies for substances were it not for their sensible qualities, and the principal of those being now found due to something else, we have as good reason to believe that to be a substance also.[9]

Besides, who ever thought any quality to be a heterogeneous aggregate, such as light is discovered to be? But to determine more absolutely

7. Red lead.
8. Azurite blue.
9. I.e., the only way we know bodies are substances is that our senses perceive their qualities. The chief of these qualities, color, is now known to be a quality of light, not body; our conclusion can perfectly well be that light is a form of substance, as well as body, and that we know it to be so through its quality, color.

what light is, after what manner refracted, and by what modes or actions it produceth in our minds the phantasms of colors, is not so easy. And I shall not mingle conjectures with certainties.

*   *   *

1672

The Restoration and the Eighteenth Century
1660-1798

1660:	Charles II restored to the English throne.
1688–89:	The Glorious Revolution: deposition of James II and accession of William of Orange.
1700:	Death of John Dryden.
1707:	Act of Union unites Scotland and England, which thus become "Great Britain."
1714:	Rule by house of Hanover begins with accession of George I.
1744–45:	Deaths of Pope and Swift.
1784:	Death of Samuel Johnson.
1789:	The French Revolution begins.

The England to which Charles Stuart returned in 1660 was a nation divided against itself, exhausted by twenty years of civil war and revolution. Early in Charles's reign, the people were visited by two frightful calamities that seemed to the superstitious to be the work of a divine Providence outraged by rebellion and regicide: the plague of 1665, ravaging the country, carried off over 70,000 souls in London alone; and in September 1666, a fire which raged for four days destroyed a large part of the City (more than 13,000 houses), leaving about two thirds of the population homeless. Yet the nation rose from its ashes, in the century that followed, to become an empire. Within two decades of the king's return, the Royal Navy had defeated the navy of Holland, England's greatest maritime and commercial rival; and, in a series of wars fought between 1689 and 1763 against France, the British acquired dominions that stretched around the world, from Canada in the west to India in the east. Internally, moreover, the nation became whole again. The Glorious Revolution of 1689 established a rule of law, and the Act of Union of 1707 a political alliance, under which England was transformed into Great Britain in fact as well as name—a larger country to which people of widely differing backgrounds and origins felt they owed allegiance. Many of the great British writers of the eighteenth century, like Swift, Burke, Sheridan, and Goldsmith, came from Ireland; many, like Thomson, Boswell, and Hume, came from Scotland. Strengthened from without and from within, Great Britain was able to endure the loss of her thirteen American colonies and to enter the final struggle with Revolutionary and Napoleonic France as a world power.

Charles came home to the almost universal satisfaction of his subjects, for after the abdication of Richard Cromwell in 1659 the country had seemed at the brink of chaos, and Britons were eager to believe that the king would bring order, peace, freedom under law, and a spirit of mildness back into the national life. But no political settlement could be stable until the religious issues of the age had been resolved. The restoration of the monarchy meant, inevitably, the restoration of the Established Church; and though Charles had promised mildness toward all but a few of his late father's enemies, the bishops and Anglican clergy felt anything but Christian charity toward their Dissenting brothers. In 1662 Parliament reimposed the Book of Common Prayer on all ministers and congregations, and in 1664 religious meetings in which the forms of the Established Church were not followed were declared illegal. Thousands of clergymen resigned their livings, and the jails were filled with Nonconformist preachers who, like John Bunyan, refused to be silenced. In 1673 the triumph of the Establishment was completed by the Test Act, which required all holders of civil and military offices to receive the sacrament according to the Anglican rite and to declare their disbelief in transubstantiation. Thus the two adversaries of the Anglican Church, Protestant Dissenters and Roman Catholics, were alike excluded from public life, though the practice of occasional conformity (i.e., receiving the sacrament in an Anglican church at rare intervals) enabled many Dissenters to comply with the law. Throughout the closing decades of the 17th century, Anglicans associated Nonconformity with revolution, regicide, republicanism, and the rule of the Puritan Saints—hence, with subversion; and with excessive zeal, "enthusiasm" (i.e., belief in private revelation), and irrationality—hence, with absurdity. The scorn and detestation in which Dissenters were held may be measured by the delight that readers took in Samuel Butler's caricature of Presbyterians and Independents in *Hudibras* (1663), an attitude that persisted unchanged for the rest of the century, as Jonathan Swift's *Tale of a Tub*, written about 1697, makes clear. As for the English Catholics, they appeared always as potential traitors of whom anything evil could be believed. Few doubted, for example, that the Great Fire of 1666 had been set by Catholics.

Although ecclesiastical problems seemed to have been quickly and effectively solved, the constitutional issues which had divided Charles I and Parliament were not so readily settled. Charles II had promised to govern through Parliament, but like other members of his family he held strong views on the power and prerogatives of the Crown. Nevertheless, he was content to avoid crises whenever he could, and since he was an astute politician he frequently could. He concealed from his subjects his Catholic sympathies (on his deathbed he received the last rites of the Roman Church), for he had no wish "to go on his travels" again. The one great religious and constitutional crisis of his reign was the Popish Plot and its political consequences (1678–81)—the unsuccessful attempt of a faction in Parliament to force Charles to accept a bill excluding his Catholic brother, James, Duke of York, from the succession. Except in this instance, where he was successful because of his courage, duplicity, and political skill, Charles allowed no opportunity for a test of strength between Crown and Parliament.

One important result of the political and religious turmoils of the decade following the Popish Plot was the emergence of two clearly defined political parties, Whig and Tory. The party of the court, which supported the king in 1681, came to be called Tories; the king's opponents, Whigs. By the end of the century the two parties had developed opposed attitudes on other important issues. The Tories drew their strength largely from the landed gentry and the country clergy. They were the conservatives of the period: strong supporters of the Crown and of the Established Church as the two great sources of political and social stability, they bitterly (though futilely) opposed toleration of Dissenters and successfully supported the Test Act. They were hostile to the new moneyed interests, whether among the newer nobility or the increasingly well-to-do middle class, for they held that landed wealth is the only responsible wealth. The Whigs were a less homogeneous group: many powerful nobles, jealous of the powers of the Crown, the merchants and financiers of London, a number of bishops and Low Church clergymen, and the Dissenters; these varied groups were united by their policies of toleration and support of commerce.

After James II came to the throne in 1685, determined to advance the cause of the Roman Church in England, an atmosphere of crisis rapidly developed. Claiming the right to set aside laws and to overrule Parliament, he issued in 1687 a Declaration of Indulgence, suspending the Tests and penal laws against both Catholics and Dissenters, and he began to fill the army and government—not to mention the universities—with his coreligionists. Matters came to a crisis in the summer of 1688, when a son was born to the queen and the prospect of a succession of Catholic monarchs confronted the nation. Secret negotiations paved the way for the arrival in England of the Dutchman William of Orange at the head of a small armed force. He was the leading champion of Protestantism on the Continent and the husband of James's Protestant daughter Mary. Finding resistance to his hostile subjects impossible, James, after sending his wife and the infant prince out of the country, fled to France on December 11. There he was cordially received by Louis XIV, granted a subsidy, and established with his court at St. Germain. For over half a century the possibility of invasion and the forcible restoration first of James, later of his son "the Old Pretender," and finally of his grandson Prince Charles Edward, was a source of anxiety to the English government. Many of the English and a great many more Scots remained loyal to the house of Stuart until there was nothing left of their cause (called Jacobite from the Latin *Jacobus*, James) but a pleasant sentiment. Two serious Jacobite rebellions actually occurred: in 1715, when the Old Pretender arrived in Scotland to support an uprising against the newly crowned Hanoverian, George I, and more threateningly in 1745, when Prince Charles Edward (the "Bonnie Prince Charlie" of romantic story) came dangerously close to success in his invasion of England, an event which affects the fortunes of the hero in Henry Fielding's novel *Tom Jones.*

It was only with the flight of James that England could begin to bury the past and to turn toward her destiny in the next age. The coming in of William and Mary and the settlement achieved in 1689 were known as the Glorious or Bloodless Revolution, all the more glorious for being bloodless. A more tolerant era was opening, as was made apparent in important acts passed by Parliament in the first year of the new reign. In 1689 the Bill of Rights limited the powers of the Crown, reaffirmed the supremacy of Parliament, and guaranteed important legal rights to individuals. Moreover, the

Toleration Act, although it did not repeal the Test, did grant freedom of worship to Dissenters. A number of the conflicting elements in the national life were thus reconciled through what proved to be a workable compromise; and with the passage of the Act of Settlement in 1701, settling the succession to the throne upon Sophia, Electress of Hanover, and her descendants (as the granddaughter of James I, she was the closest Protestant relative of the Princess Anne, James II's younger daughter, whose sole surviving child died in that year), the difficult problems that had so long divided England seemed resolved. The principles established in 1689 endured unaltered in essentials until the Reform Bill of 1832.

During the reign of Anne, the last Stuart monarch (1702–14), a renewal of tension embittered the political atmosphere. On the Continent England led her allies, Holland, Austria, and Bavaria, to victory in the War of the Spanish Succession against France and Spain (1702–13). The hero of the war was the brilliant Captain-General John Churchill, duke of Marlborough, who, with his duchess, dominated the queen until 1710. The war was a Whig war, supported by powerful Whig lords and the Whig merchants of London, who grew increasingly rich on war profits and who stood to gain by any weakening of the power of France and Spain. The Whigs were anxious to reward the Dissenters for their loyalty by removing the Test. Unfortunately for them, Anne was especially devoted to the church, and when, in 1710, they were made to appear to threaten the health of the Establishment, she dismissed her Whig ministers and called in Robert Harley as Lord Treasurer and the brilliant young Henry St. John as Secretary of State (in charge of foreign relations) to form the Tory ministry which governed England during the last four years of her reign. The Marlboroughs were dismissed, the duke even losing his command in 1711, but not before the royal favor and a grateful nation had made him immensely rich and had given him the land on which he built his famous palace, Blenheim (pronounced *Blen'm*) in memory of the most brilliant victory (pronounced *Blén-hime*) of the war.

It was these Tory ministers whom Defoe and Swift served in their different ways; it was for them that Matthew Prior negotiated the Peace of Utrecht, ratified in 1713. To Swift's despair, a bitter rivalry developed between Harley (then earl of Oxford) and St. John (then Viscount Bolingbroke) during 1713–14, and as the queen's life faded in the summer of 1714, Bolingbroke succeeded in ousting Oxford, only to have his own ambitions thwarted by the death of Anne and the return to power of the vindictive Whigs with the accession of George I, son of the late Sophia, Electress of Hanover. For a moment it seemed as if this event might not occur without bloodshed, but the crisis quickly passed, the Protestant succession was not immediately opposed by Jacobites, and the Whigs turned happily to investigating the conduct of the former ministers. Harley was imprisoned in the Tower of London (where he remained until 1717), and Bolingbroke, charged with treasonable correspondence with the Pretender, fled to France, where he actually became, for a while, secretary of state to the Jacobite court. Pardoned in 1723, but denied his seat in the House of Lords, he returned to England and directed the opposition to Robert Walpole, while seeing much of Pope and playing the gentleman-farmer-philosopher at Dawley Farm.

The three Georges who occupied the throne during the rest of the century presided over a nation that grew increasingly prosperous through war trade, and the beginnings of industrialism. George I (reigned 1714–27) and George II (reigned 1727–60) spoke broken English and had little interest in the affairs of the country. In their hearts they remained petty German prince-lings even when they were kings of Great Britain, spending as much time as possible in Hanover. Under such circumstances it was inevitable that min-isters should become more important and more independent of the Crown than they had been under stronger and more intelligent monarchs. Through the indifference of two kings and the ambition and great abilities of the Whig prime minister Sir Robert Walpole, the modern system of ministerial gov-ernment began to develop. This was the last important contribution of the age to British political institutions. Walpole's long ascendency (1721–42) brought a period of peace and prosperity and of capable government based, paradoxically, on flagrant political corruption. Although Walpole strength-ened the importance of the House of Commons in British politics, he none-theless continued, if he did not increase, the corruption of its members through bribery. He was a practical man and cared little for literature, pre-ferring to spend money on useful journalists and voting Members of Parlia-ment rather than on poets. Thus with two kings who knew nothing of literature and a prime minister who was indifferent to it, English writers could not expect the shower of offices and government sinecures that had made the age of Anne the great age of patronage: Congreve, Steele, Addison, Prior, Swift had expected and obtained such rewards both for their literary emin-ence and for their service to party. But after 1715, as patronage declined, authors found that they must turn to the publishers, who could pay them well because of the growing reading public. Indeed, Johnson was accus-tomed to declare that the booksellers of the midcentury had become the patrons of literature.

The long reign of George III (1760–1820) was dominated by two great concerns: the emergence of Britain as a colonial power and the cry for a new social order based on liberty and radical reform. In 1763 the Peace of Paris consolidated British rule over Canada and India, and not even the loss of the American colonies could stem the rise of the Empire. Great Britain was no longer an isolated island but a nation with interests and responsibilities around the world. At home, however, there was discontent. The wealth brought to England by industrialism and foreign trade did not spread to the working classes. In 1780 the Gordon Riots temporarily put London under mob rule. The king, the first Hanoverian monarch born in England, was popular with his subjects, and tried to take government into his own hands. Meanwhile reformers such as John Wilkes and Richard Price called for a new political democracy. Fear of their radicalism contributed to the British reaction against the French Revolution after 1789. In the last decades of the century British authors were torn between two opposing attitudes: loyalty to the old traditions of subordination and local self-sufficiency, and yearning for a new dispensation on principles of liberty, the rule of reason, and human rights. These conflicts within the nation were not easy to resolve, but they were submerged by the long war with France that broke out in 1793.

INTELLECTUAL BACKGROUND

The political turbulence of the seventeenth century subsided only gradually during the last decades of the century, and during the Restoration period (1660–1700) literature also reflected a conflict of values. Milton's major poems, a culmination of Renaissance art, appeared at the same time that John Dryden was establishing himself as the laureate of a new age of ele-gance. Bunyan's *Pilgrim's Progress* expressed the Nonconformist conscience at the same time that such court wits as Rochester and Sedley expressed a libertine creed. The town and the country followed different ideas about art and the conduct of life. The Restoration is best known as a period dominated by a fun-loving, dissolute court, whose style of life was reflected in rakish comedies. But the ordinary life of the nation did not radically change. Rural manners remained conservative and old-fashioned. The London citizens, middle class and respectable, cherishing much of the independence and piety of Dissent, were scandalized by the behavior of upper-class rakes who regarded them with contempt and considered their wives and daughters fair game. Even good royalists like John Evelyn and Samuel Pepys often speak anxiously in their diaries of the moral laxity of the court and the danger to the country of the king's example.

Charles himself was easy going, pleasure loving, and amorous, more fond of the society of boon companions—and mistresses—than he was of state business. But he also had serious intellectual interests and was a patron of the arts. He dabbled in chemistry and was interested in the progress of science. A characteristic act was his chartering in 1662 the Royal Society of London for the Improving of Natural Knowledge, thus giving official approval to the scientific movement that Francis Bacon had initiated early in the century and that was just then coming to maturity. The king's love of music and painting led him to import from the Continent composers, musicians, new musical instruments, the French and Italian opera, and painting and painters largely from the Low Countries. His interest in the theater was demonstrated by the chartering of two companies of actors in 1660, both under royal patronage, the King's Players, and the Duke's—the duke being James, duke of York.

It is natural, therefore, that the most characteristic art of the period reflected the interests and tastes of those who supported it. Artists addressed themselves to court and "town," the western suburbs which were the center of fashion. The middle-class tradespeople, who lodged over their shops in the City (i.e., that part of greater London which was once within the city walls and which was then thickly populated), were scorned as tasteless barbarians. Except in the theater, literature was not in itself a gainful profession (as it was to become in the eighteenth century), and writers looked for patronage from the court and the great nobles. Milton, for example, received only £10 for the first edition of *Paradise Lost*. By the end of the century, however, thanks to the enterprise of the bookseller Jacob Tonson and the new device of publishing books through subscription (i.e., soliciting payment in advance for deluxe copies of a work, in addition to publishing a regular trade edition), Dryden was able to earn between £1000 and £1200 by his translation of the works of Virgil (1697). And Pope's Homer, similarly published between 1715 and 1726, was to prove even more profitable.

Perhaps the most important aspect of the Restoration period is the increasing challenge of various forms of secular thought to the old religious orthodoxies which had been matters of life and death since the Reformation. As the contentious voices of Roman, Anglican, and Dissenter grew more and more subdued, other interests attracted adventurous minds. Thomas Hobbes, in *Leviathan* (1651), had taught a philosophic materialism and advocated an absolute government as the most efficacious check to human nature, which he described as wholly driven by egoistic and predatory passions. Detested by the church and attacked on all sides, these ideas nonetheless played their role in the lives and writings of some of the more advanced young people, and they provoked by way of reaction in the next century an optimistic insistence on the natural goodness of humanity. A soberer and more ancient tradition was philosophic skepticism. Originating in ancient Greece, skepticism had found its most persuasive recent statement in the essays of the Frenchman Michel de Montaigne (1533–1592), whose influence was widespread throughout seventeenth-century Europe. The skeptic argued that all our knowledge is derived from our senses, but that our senses do not report the world around us accurately, and that therefore reliable knowledge is an impossibility. The safest course is to affirm nothing as absolutely true, to remember that most beliefs are mere opinions, and, where possible, to be guided by the traditional in matters intellectual, political, and ethical. Butler, Dryden, and Rochester, among others, more or less adhered to this doctrine. But though skeptics remained in doubt about the results of human reasoning, they were not precluded from religious beliefs, for they could assert (as did Dryden after his conversion to Catholicism) that faith alone is necessary for accepting the mysteries of the Christian religion.

The new science, advanced by members of the Royal Society, was rapidly altering views of nature. Science in the seventeenth century was principally concerned with the physical sciences—with astronomy, physics, and, to a lesser degree, chemistry; and the discoveries in these sciences were reassuring in their evidence of universal and immutable law and order, clear proof of the wisdom and goodness of God in His creation. Such laws of nature as Boyle's law of the behavior of gases under pressure or Newton's law of gravitation seemed obviously to support the idea that a beneficent, divine intelligence created and directs the universe. The truest truths proved to be the clearest, the simplest, the most general. Such truths seemed to promise a time, not remote, when mystery would be banished entirely from religion as well as from nature. Indeed, Deism or Natural Religion, which had an increasingly wide appeal to "enlightened" minds, deduced its simple rationalistic creed from the Book of Nature, God's first and, to many in the eighteenth century, only valid revelation. The Deists deduced the existence of a Supreme Being or First Cause from the existence of the universe: a creature presupposes a Creator. The laws of nature sufficiently proved the reasonableness, goodness, and wisdom of this Creator. Him we can and must revere; but, good though He is, it is demonstrable that He does not punish vice and reward virtue in this life; and therefore, being good and just, He must do so in some future life: hence, we must believe in immortality. Meanwhile, here on earth, it is our duty to cooperate with Nature and the Deity, cultivating as best we can wisdom, virtue, and benevolence. This creed is as simple and as rational as one of Newton's laws; but its omission of the "second revelation" of the Scriptures, the scheme of salvation in which Christ died to redeem our sins, made it unacceptable to many Christians, although many others found it possible to accept both Natural Religion and revealed Christianity.

As the seventeenth century drew to a close, its temper became more secular, tolerant, and moderate. The new age was willing to settle for the possible within the limits of human intelligence and of the material world. Its temper was expressed by its most influential philosopher, John Locke (1632–1704), in his *Essay Concerning Human Understanding* (1690):

> If by this inquiry into the nature of the understanding, I can discover the powers thereof; how far they reach; to what things they are in any

degree proportionate; and where they fail us, I suppose it may be of use to prevail with the busy mind of man to be more cautious in meddling with things exceeding its comprehension; to stop when it is at the utmost extent of its tether; and to sit down in a quiet ignorance of those things which, upon examination, are found to be beyond the reach of our capacities. . . . Our business here is not to know all things, but those which concern our conduct.

These words might be taken as the creed of eighteenth-century England. Such a position is Swift's, when he inveighs against metaphysics, abstract logical deductions, and theoretical science; it is similar to Pope's in the *Essay on Man*; it prompts Samuel Johnson to talk of "the business of living"; it helps to account for the emphasis that the Anglican clergy put on good works, rather than faith, as the way to salvation, and for their dislike of emotion and "enthusiasm" in religion.

But if the eighteenth century brought a recognition of human limitations, it also took an optimistic view of human nature. Rejecting Hobbes, some eighteenth-century philosophers asserted that human beings are naturally good and find their highest happiness in the exercise of virtue and benevolence. Such a view of human nature we describe as "sentimental." It found the source of virtue in instinctive and social impulses rather than in a code of conduct sanctioned by divine law. And people began to feel—or to fancy that they felt—exquisite pleasure in the exercise of benevolent impulses. Sentimentalism fostered a benevolence that led to social reforms seldom envisioned in earlier times—to the improvement of jails, to the relief of imprisoned debtors, to the establishment of foundling hospitals and of homes for penitent prostitutes, and ultimately to the abolition of the slave trade; but it also encouraged a ready flow of feeling and tears and a capacity to respond to the joys and sorrows of others. The doctrine of natural goodness seemed to many to suggest that it is civilization which corrupts us and that "noble savages," those who live in a state of nature, might be models of innocence and virtue. Such notions encouraged an interest in primitive societies and even helped to prepare, late in the century, for the warm reception given the peasant poet Robert Burns, an "original genius," as well as for William Wordsworth's interest in children and in simple, rural people.

As the wave of sentimentalism mounted, a parallel rise of religious feeling occurred after about 1740. The great religious revival known as Methodism was led by John Wesley (1703–1791), his brother Charles (1707–1788), and George Whitefield (1714–1770), all Oxford graduates. The Methodists took their gospel to the common people, preaching the necessity of a conviction of sin, and of conversion, and the joy of the "blessed assurance" of being saved. Often denied the privilege of preaching in village churches, they preached to thousands in the open fields and in barns. The somnolent Anglican Church and the self-assured upper classes were repelled by the emotionalism aroused by Methodist preachers among the lower orders. It seemed as if the irrationality, zeal, and enthusiasm of the Puritan sects were being revived. But the religious awakening persisted, and affected many clergymen and laymen within the Establishment, who, as "Evangelicals," reanimated the church and promoted unworldliness and piety. And yet the insistence of Methodists on faith over works as the way to salvation did not prevent them or their Anglican counterparts from playing important roles in many of the social reforms of the time, especially in helping to abolish slavery and the slave trade.

The literature of the period between 1660 and 1785 can conveniently, though perhaps too schematically, be considered as falling into three lesser periods of about forty years each: the first, extending to the death of Dryden in 1700, may be thought of as the period in which English "neoclassical" literature came into being and its critical principles were formulated; the second, ending with the death of Pope in 1744 and of Swift in 1745, brought to its culmination the literary movement initiated by Dryden and his generation; the third, concluding with the death of Johnson in 1784 and the publication of William Cowper's *The Task* in 1785, was a period in which the old principles were confronted by new ideas which contained within themselves the origins of the Romantic movement of the late eighteenth and early nineteenth centuries.

Apparently a sudden change of taste took place about 1660; but the change was not so sudden as it appears. Like the English Renaissance, it was part of a general movement in European culture, seen perhaps at its most impressive in seventeenth-century France. Described most simply, it was a reaction against the intricacy and occasional obscurity, boldness, and extravagance of European literature of the late Renaissance, in favor of greater simplicity, clarity, restraint, regularity, and good sense. This tendency is most readily to be observed in the preference of Dryden and his contemporaries for "easy, natural" wit, which aims to surprise rather than to shock. It accompanied, though it was not necessarily caused by, the development of certain rationalistic philosophies and the rise of experimental science, as well as a desire for peace and order after an era of violent extremism.

This movement produced in France the impressive body of classical literature that distinguished the age of Louis XIV. In England it produced a literature often termed "neoclassical," or "Augustan," because it was strongly influenced by the writers of the reign of the first Roman emperor, Augustus Caesar, just before the beginning of the Christian era. Rome's Augustan Age was a period of stability and peace after the civil war that followed the death of Julius Caesar. Its chief poets, Virgil, Horace, and Ovid, addressed their polished works to a sophisticated aristocracy, among whom they found generous patrons. Dryden's generation was aware of an analogy between the situations of post–Civil War England and Augustan Rome. Later generations would be suspicious of that analogy; after 1700 most writers stressed that Augustus had been a tyrant who thought himself greater than the law. But in 1660 there was hope that Charles would be a better Augustus, bringing to England the civilized virtues of an Augustan age without its vices.

Charles and his followers inevitably brought back from France an admiration of contemporary French literature as well as of French fashions and elegance. The theories of such writers as Pierre Corneille, René Rapin, and Nicolas Boileau also came into vogue. But English literature remained stubbornly English: English writers took what they required from France, but used it for their own ends. It was not Dryden's aim merely to imitate the French poets or for that matter the Latin, but to produce in England works that would be worthy to stand beside theirs. He knew that this could be done only if English literature remained true to its living tradition: Chaucer, Spenser,

Shakespeare, Jonson, Donne entered into his literary consciousness as well as Virgil, Horace, Longinus, or Corneille.

It is likely that, had Charles never lived abroad, English literature would still have turned toward an ideal of simplicity and elegance. Ben Jonson's poems and criticism had brought the classicizing tendencies of the English Renaissance to a focus. His closed heroic couplets are the model for those of Edmund Waller and Sir John Denham, whom Dryden considered the principal "refiners" of English metrics. One of the lesser "Sons of Ben," Sir John Beaumont, at least as early as 1625—and incidentally in couplets that might have been the very pattern of those of Dryden and Pope—proposed critical standards that became dominant after 1660:

> Pure phrase, fit epithets, a sober care
> Of metaphors, descriptions clear, yet rare,
> Similitudes contracted, smooth and round,
> Not vexed by learning, but with Nature crowned:
> Strong figures drawn from deep inventions, springs,
> Consisting less in words, and more in things:
> A language not affecting ancient times,
> Nor Latin shreds, by which the pedant climbs.
> [*To His Late Majesty, Concerning the True Form
> of English Poetry*]

Such standards, alien to the poetry of Donne, Crashaw, or Milton, prefigure the poetry of the Augustans, and suggest that a native "classicism" existed side by side with metaphysical poetry. The emphasis on the correct ("pure"), the appropriate ("fit"), restraint and discipline ("sober care"), clarity, the fresh and surprising ("rare"), Nature, strength, freedom from pedantry—these indicate exactly the direction English literature was to take after the Restoration.

Above all, the new simplicity of style aimed to give pleasure to the common reader—to write about passions that everyone could recognize in language that everyone could understand. From Dryden to Johnson, English critics value poetry according to its power to affect an audience. Readers, in turn, were supposed to cooperate with authors through the exercise of their own imaginations, creating pictures in the mind. Much poetry of the period comes alive only when it is visualized. A phrase from Horace's *Art of Poetry*, *ut pictura poesis* (as in painting, so in poetry), was interpreted to mean that poetry ought to be a visual as well as a verbal art. Eighteenth-century readers tended to be extremely skilled at translating words into pictures; and a modern reader who wants to appreciate eighteenth-century poems as more than dead words on a page must learn to *see* their images in the mind's eye.

What poets tried to see and represent was "Nature"—a word of many meanings. The Augustans were especially conscious of one meaning: Nature as the universal, permanent, and representative elements in human experience. External nature—the landscape—both as a source of aesthetic pleasure and as an object of scientific inquiry or religious contemplation attracted attention throughout the eighteenth century. But Pope's injunction to the critic, "First follow Nature," has primarily *human* nature and *human* experience in view. Nature is truth in the sense that it includes the enduring, general truths that have been, are, and will be true for everyone in all times, everywhere. Johnson, in chapter 10 of *Rasselas*, says that the poet is to examine "not the individual, but the species; to remark general properties and large appearances . . . to exhibit in his portraits of nature such prominent and striking features as recall the original to every mind." Historians during this period studied the particulars of history in order to observe the universal human nature which those particulars reveal; and scientists formulated, after experiment and observation of particulars, universal and permanent laws of nature. Indeed, Sir Isaac Newton's *Principia* (1687) did much to reinforce scientifically the idea of Nature as order, which underlies such a typical eighteenth-century work as Pope's *Essay on Man*.

But it would be wrong to assume that this emphasis on the general and the representative excluded the particular from the arts. If human nature was held to be uniform, human beings were known to be infinitely varied; and the task of the artist was so to treat the particular as to render it representative. Thus Pope, after praising the characters of Shakespeare because they are "Nature herself," continued: "But every single character in Shakespeare is as much an individual as those in life itself; it is . . . impossible to find any two alike." And Johnson praised the poet James Thomson because he looked on external nature "with a mind that at once comprehends the vast, and attends to the minute."

To study Nature was also to study the ancients—the great artists and thinkers of Greece and imperial Rome. They had expressed the enduring forms of life. Homer and Nature, according to Pope, were the same; and both Pope and his readers found Horace's satires on Roman society thoroughly applicable to their own world, for Horace had followed Nature, "one clear, unchanged, and universal light." Moreover, modern poets could also learn from the ancients how to practice their craft. If a poem is an object to be made, the *poet* (a word derived from a Greek word meaning "maker") must follow sound principles or botch the job. The ancients—for instance, Aristotle in his *Poetics* and Horace in his *Art of Poetry*—had deduced such principles from the practice of early masters like Homer and Sophocles, and during the sixteenth and seventeenth centuries Italian and French critics codified those "rules" and invented new rules of their own. The rules directed poets to plan their works in one of the literary "kinds" or genres: epic, tragedy, comedy, pastoral, satire, ode; to choose a language appropriate to that genre; to select the right style and tone and rhetorical figures. Such rules could serve as a short cut to Nature, for as Pope said, they "are Nature methodized."

In England, however, the rules were followed in rather a casual way. Almost everyone acknowledged that Shakespeare had written the greatest body of drama in modern literature without obeying the formulas of ancients or moderns. He had followed Nature directly, impelled by his wit. "Wit," like "Nature," is a complicated word of many meanings. Here it implies quickness and liveliness of mind, inventiveness, a readiness to perceive resemblances between things apparently unlike and so to enliven literary discourse with appropriate images, similes, and metaphors. This faculty was often identified with "fancy" or "imagination," and was thought to be irregular, wayward, extravagant, unless curbed and disciplined by another and soberer faculty, "judgment." Many poets sought to tame what seemed the wildness of metaphysical wit into a sense of "decorum" or the appropriate. Hence Dryden defined wit as "a propriety of thoughts and words; or, in other terms, thoughts and words elegantly adapted to the subject." Similarly, Pope insists in the *Essay on Criticism*, lines 80–83, on the necessity of a harmonious union of judgment and fancy (which he calls "wit") in a work of literature. Though judgment was to tame, it was not to suppress passion, energy, or originality, but to make them more effective through discipline: "The winged courser, like a generous horse, / Shows most true mettle when you check his course."

The test of mettle in a poet is language. When Wordsworth, in the Preface to *Lyrical Ballads* (1800), declared that the poems were written "in a selection of the language really used by men," he went on to attack eighteenth-century poets for their use of an artificial and stock "diction." Many poets did employ a special language. It is characterized by personification, representing a thing or abstraction in a human form, as when an "Ace of Hearts steps forth" or "Melancholy frowns"; by periphrasis (a roundabout and elegant way of avoiding homely words: "finny tribe" for "fish," or "household feathery people" for "chickens"); frequently used stock phrases, such as "shining sword," "verdant mead," "bounding main," "checkered shade"; words used in their original Latin sense, such as "genial," "gelid," "horrid"; and a fondness for adjectives ending in *y*. This language originated in the attempt of Renaissance poets all over Europe to rival the elegant and golden diction of Virgil and other Roman writers. Milton depended on it to help him obtain "answerable style" for the lofty theme of *Paradise Lost*. Used with discretion it could be both subtle and expressive; but when it became a mannerism, or a dead and conventional language used mechanically, as it did with scores of mere versifiers, it properly became an object of contempt. "Hay and straw were burned in the fields of Thessaly," for instance, was translated into poetic diction:

> There at his words devouring Vulcan feasts
> On all the tribute which Thessalian meads
> Yield to the scythe, and riots on the heaps
> Of Ceres, emptied of the ripened grain.
>
> [Glover's *Leonidas*, 1737]

But such extremes of mannerism are seldom to be found in the works of the good poets of the century.

Versification also tests the poet's skill. The prevailing form was the "closed" heroic couplet—i.e., a pentameter couplet which more often than not contains within itself a complete statement and so is closed by a semicolon, period, question mark, or exclamation point. Within these two lines it was possible to attain certain rhetorical or witty effects by the use of parallelism, balance, or antithesis within the couplet as a whole or the individual line. The second line of the couplet might be made closely parallel in structure and meaning to the first, or the two could be played off against each other in antithesis; taking advantage of the fact that normally a pentameter line of English verse contains at some point a slight pause called a "caesura," one part of a line so divided can be made parallel with or antithetical to the other or even to one of the two parts of the following line. This can be illustrated by a passage from Sir John Denham's *Cooper Hill* (1642), which was quoted and parodied for many years. The poem addresses the Thames and builds up a witty comparison between the flow of a river and the flow of verse (italics are ours, to illustrate the rhetorical effects):

O could I flow like thee, ‖ and make thy stream
Parallelism: *My great example,* ‖ as it is *my theme!*
Double balance: Though *deep,* yet *clear,* ‖ though *gentle,* yet not *dull,*
Double balance: *Strong* without *rage,* ‖ without *o'erflowing, full.*

It only remained for Dryden and Pope to bind such passages more tightly together with alliteration and assonance, and the typical metrical-rhetorical wit of the new age had been perfected.

Shortly after the beginning of the eighteenth century began the vogue of blank verse—the other metrical form most favored by the age. Philosophical poems, descriptive poems, meditative poems, and original or translated epics employed blank verse of one sort or another from Thomson's *Seasons* (1726–30) to Cowper's *The Task* (1785); and the tradition determined Wordsworth's use of the form in *Tintern Abbey* and *The Prelude.* The two chief patterns of blank verse available to the age were the blank verse of Milton in *Paradise Lost* and the dramatic blank verse of Dryden and other Restoration tragic poets. The influence of Milton is easily detected, not by the success with which his manner was imitated, but by the amateur performance of most of those who try to play on his instrument. The dramatic blank verse of the Restoration too often led in eighteenth-century poetry to mannerism or bombast. But gradually a more lyrical blank verse developed, of which William Cowper is the master; and this more plastic metrical line had a formative influence on the blank verse of William Wordsworth.

RESTORATION LITERATURE, 1660–1700

The period between 1660 and 1700 was remarkably varied and vigorous. Dryden was the dominant figure, writing in all the important contemporary forms—occasional verse, comedy, tragedy, heroic play, ode, satire, translation, and critical essay—and both his example and his precepts had great influence. He gave to the England of his day a *modern* literature, cosmopolitan but possessing the richness and variety that he admired in the Elizabethans, the "God's plenty" that he praised in Chaucer's *Canterbury Tales.*

The prose of the Restoration is a clear indication of the direction in which literature was moving. The styles of Donne's sermons, of Milton's pamphlets, or of Sir Thomas Browne's writings had come to seem too elaborate, too involved, too insistently musical, or too wittily rhetorical and pointed for mere exposition or social intercourse. The Royal Society decreed that its members must employ only a plain, concise, and utilitarian prose style suitable to the clear communication of scientific truths. Metaphors, similes, and rhetorical flourishes were disapproved because they engaged the emotions, not the reason, and though they were tolerable in poetry, they had no place in rational discourse. In polite literature, thanks to the example of such writers as Abraham Cowley, Dryden, and Sir William Temple, the ideal of good prose came to be a clear, simple, and natural style which has the ease and poise of well-bred urbane conversation. This is a social prose, designed for a social age. Later, it was available to the writers of periodical essays, such as Addison or Steele, to the novelists of the eighteenth century, and to the many practitioners of the delightful art of letter-writing, one of the minor literary achievements of the eighteenth century; the brilliant but intimate letters of Lady Mary Wortley Montagu, Horace Walpole, Thomas Gray, and William Cowper have never been surpassed. This movement toward clarity and simplicity in prose accompanied a similar movement away from the intricacies of metaphysical wit in verse, which found an early statement in Dryden's *Essay of Dramatic Poesy*.

But if prose was simplified and wit was tamed, the Restoration did not break wholly with the immediate past. It retained the Renaissance admiration for the typically aristocratic heroic ideal. Most Restoration readers associated the "heroic poem" or epic with "fierce wars and faithful loves" and expected it to offer patterns of ideal virtue for the emulation of princes and generals. But the romantic idealism of the heroic mode was most characteristically expressed during the Restoration not in the heroic poem but in the heroic play, which Dryden, its foremost practitioner, defined as "a heroic poem in little." The theme of these plays (their vogue lasted from about 1664 to about 1675) was the conflict between love and honor in the hearts of impossibly valorous heroes and impossibly high-minded and attractive ladies.

Dryden's one undoubted masterpiece in serious drama is his blank verse tragedy *All for Love* (produced 1677), based on the story of Antony and Cleopatra. Instead of Shakespeare's world-wide panorama, his rapid shifts of scene and complex characters, we have the last hours of the tragic lovers presented according to the unities of action, place, and time, in a neatly symmetrical plot. The two other eminent tragic poets of the period were Nathaniel Lee (ca. 1649–1692), known for violent plots, the wild emotions of his characters, and the extravagance of his rhetoric; and Thomas Otway (1652–1685), who excelled in pathos. Not one enduring tragedy was written during the eighteenth century. Addison's *Cato* (produced in 1713) is a museum piece, illustrating the frigidity of "correct" and rule-bound tragedy. George Lillo's *London Merchant* (produced in 1731), dealing with commonplace characters in mercantile life, took a feeble step in the direction of the sort of realistic, middle-class drama with which we are familiar today.

The real distinction of Restoration drama was comedy. The best plays of Sir George Etherege (ca. 1635–1691), William Wycherley (ca. 1640–1716), William Congreve, and the less accomplished but witty Sir John Vanbrugh (pronounced Vánbroo or Vanbróok, 1664–1726) and George Farquhar (ca. 1677–1707) still hold the stage today. These writers excelled in representing—and critically evaluating—the social behavior of the fashionable upper classes of the town. This sort of comedy—brilliantly witty, cynical in its view of human nature, which it shows to be sensual, egoistic, and predatory—is known as "the comedy of manners," since its concern is to bring the moral and social behavior of its characters to the test of comic laughter. The male hero lives not for military glory but for pleasure and the conquests that he can achieve in his amorous campaigns. The object of his very practical game of sexual intrigue is a beautiful, witty, pleasure-loving, and emancipated lady, every bit his equal in the strategies of love. The two are distinguished not for virtue, but for the true wit and well-bred grace with which they conduct the often complicated intrigue that makes up the plot. The best examples of the comedy of manners before William Congreve's *The Way of the World* (produced in 1700) are Etherege's *The Man of Mode* (produced in 1676), William Wycherley's *The Country Wife* (produced ca. 1672–74), and Congreve's earlier *Love for Love* (produced in 1695).

During the 1690s a considerable demand arose for moral reform in both literature and daily life, partly because of the nature of Restoration comedy. "Societies for the Reformation of Manners" were founded with the support of the soberer Anglicans and the resurgent Nonconformists. Their members served not only as propagandists of moral respectability, but also as spies and informers who brought offenders to trial for blasphemy, obscenity, and sexual immorality. The most effective attack on the indecencies of language and situation in comedy was made by the Anglican clergyman Jeremy Collier, whose *Short View of the Immorality and Profaneness of the English Stage* (1698) bore hard on Dryden and Congreve, among others. Collier spoke for the outraged moral sense of the godly middle classes as well as for the church, and his attack helped to discredit "wit" and the wits as subversive of religion and morals. One of the tasks that Steele and Addison undertook in the *Tatler* and *Spectator* and Pope in his *Essay on Criticism*, early in the next century, was to rehabilitate "wit" by making it the servant of social and moral decorum. When Dryden died, a more respectable (if not actually more virtuous) society was coming into being.

Decorum was also enforced by the clubs where literary people tended to gather. From 1652 and increasingly during the first half of the eighteenth century, the coffee houses of London served as informal meeting places. There men could smoke, drink chocolate or coffee, read the newspapers, write and receive letters, exchange news, gossip, and opinions, and observe the oddities of character that the English have always been happy to cultivate. Eventually clubs not unlike Addison's imaginary Spectator Club came to preside over literary life. The groups who frequented them helped to determine the tone of literature, the critical reputation of writers, the success or failure of plays, and the character of such periodicals as the *Tatler* and the *Spectator*. At first women were excluded. Around 1750, however, some intellectual women known as bluestockings because of their informal dress (not black silk hose but blue worsted) established clubs of their own under the leadership of the wealthy Mrs. Elizabeth Montague, and gradually men began to join them for literary conversation.

EIGHTEENTH-CENTURY LITERATURE, 1700–45

During the forty-five years between the deaths of Dryden and Swift, the literature that Dryden and his contemporaries had created attained full maturity. A new and brilliant group of writers took the stage: Swift, with *A Tale of a Tub* (1704–10); Addison, with his popular poetic celebration of Marlborough's victory at Blenheim, *The Campaign* (1705); Prior, with *Poems on Several Occasions* (1707); Steele, with the *Tatler* (1709); and the youthful Pope, in the same year, with his *Pastorals*. On the whole, the literature of this period is chiefly a literature of wit, concerned with civilization and social relationships; and consequently it is critical and in some degree moral or satiric. It preserves the earlier period's interest in the heroic, but apart from Pope's translations of Homer, no writer succeeded in heroic poetry. On the other hand some of the finest works of the period are mock-heroic (individual passages in Swift's *Battle of the Books* and *A Description of a City Shower* and Pope's *Rape of the Lock* and *The Dunciad*) or humorous burlesques of serious classic or modern modes (John Gay's delightful town mock-Georgic, *Trivia, or the Art of Walking the Streets of London*, 1716, or his burlesque of the heroics of Italian opera, *The Beggar's Opera*, produced in 1728). Such literature is addressed to highly sophisticated and cultivated readers, and it reminds us that earlier eighteenth-century literature retained the aristocratic bias that had marked the literature of the seventeenth century.

Nevertheless a body of writing that reached a wider audience was coming into being. The reading public expanded steadily throughout the eighteenth century, and its new recruits were upper-class women and the increasingly numerous rich and leisured people of both sexes in the trading middle class. The popular press flourished, producing a succession of newspapers, literary periodicals in the manner of the *Tatler*, miscellanies of various sorts, and finally, in 1731, the first magazine in the modern sense, the *Gentleman's Magazine*, which was to be followed not only by imitations but also by the appearance of such successful literary reviews as the *Monthly Review* (1749) and the *Critical Review* (1756). The new journalism satisfied a hunger for all sorts of information about politics, science, philosophy, literature, as well as for scandal and gossip. It also created a demand for writers—not necessarily for geniuses—who began to subsist, often on harsh terms, as hacks and compilers in a milieu that came to be called Grub Street, from the name of an actual street. To such authors as Pope and Swift, Grub Street with all its denizens (it was to gain the services of both Johnson and Oliver Goldsmith) represented a serious threat to humanistic learning, urbane enlightenment, and good taste. But literature became in this period of expanding publication and increasingly numerous readers a gainful profession. The novel as we know it—a long prose narrative concerned with the actual world and the men and women who inhabit it—very probably could not have come into existence had not these new readers existed. The eighteenth-century novel supplied the place in the life of the common reader that the heroic poem had occupied in the life of the courtly reader of the past.

During this period new literary kinds took the place of the old. The lyric, one of the glories of the Elizabethan age and the first half of the seventeenth century, had become in the Restoration a minor and graceful mode, appropriate to a song or a "paper of verses" addressed to a mistress. The wits of Charles II's court could turn out accomplished, conventional poems of this sort which do not lack distinction; and Matthew Prior was their counterpart in the time of William of Orange and Queen Anne. But between 1700 and 1740 lyric poetry declined, and comedy too lost its edge. The moral reform of the 1690s, together with the increasingly optimistic and flattering view of human nature, made the rakes of Restoration comedy seem distasteful libels on humanity. The old comedy of manners was replaced by a new kind, called "sentimental" not only because of its faith in the triumph of a good heart over vice, but also because its dialogue deals in high moral sentiments rather than wit, and because its virtuous heroines and virtuous (or penitent) heroes suffer misfortunes which move the audience not to laughter but to tears. One of the pleasures invented in eighteenth-century Europe was the delicious pleasure of weeping, and sentimental comedy (or, as the French phrased it, *la comédie larmoyante*, "weeping comedy") brought that pleasure to playgoers through many decades. As tragedy froze into rhetoric, comedy dissolved in tears. And the successes enjoyed by John Gay's comic ballad opera *The Beggar's Opera* (1728), or the laughing comedies of Goldsmith and Sheridan later in the century, could not eradicate the taste for sentimentality. Although during the eighteenth century the *theater* prospered and the stage was adorned by a succession of great actors and actresses (such as David Garrick and Sarah Siddons) the authors of *drama* lapsed into obscurity.

On the other hand satire flourished, its most distinguished practitioners being Pope and Swift, though they are only two among many effective writers. Satirists are usually conservative, using their weapons against those deviations from norms of conduct which threaten to undermine traditional and socially approved behavior. Both Pope and Swift wrote their major satires as Tories, at a time when Britain was dominated by the Whig party. The Tories resisted, but resisted futilely, the social and economic changes which were taking place as England grew from an island kingdom into a world power, and transformed its agrarian into a mercantile economy. They looked with gloomy forebodings on the rising tide of popular taste, on what they considered the invasion and debasement of the polite world by the barbarians from the middle classes, and the idle rich, and on the increase of corruption in public life. The satire of both Swift and Pope is great because it was animated by moral urgency and heightened by a tragic sense of doom. Pope saw the issue as a struggle between Darkness and Light, Chaos and Order, Barbarism and Civilization: a vision which he expressed in his greatest work, *The Dunciad*. For Swift the issue was one between "right reason" and "madness"—not clinical insanity, of course, but a blindness to anything but one's own private illusions, which is an abandonment of practical reality.

But the great age of satire also produced a wholly different sort of poetry from that which Pope was writing in the 1730s. After 1726, when James Thomson published the first of his nature poems, *Winter*, the poetry of natural description flourished and the characteristic eighteenth-century English taste for natural and picturesque beauty found expression—not only in poetry, but also in that typical Georgian art, landscape gardening, and finally in the beginning of the art of landscape in water color or oils, which has been England's principal achievement in painting. A love of external nature inspired many eighteenth-century poets, and Wordsworth was their heir. *Tintern Abbey* (1798) not only was written *within* the century, but in most respects is very much a poem *of* the century.

In the course of the century, Britons not only admired tamed and ordered nature, in large landscape gardens or cultivated fields, but also early learned to enjoy the more thrilling, emotional pleasure which they began to feel in the presence of what they called "the sublime" in nature: vast spaces, mountainous country, wild and untamed landscape. Whether enthusiasts of nature went to landscape for evidence of the presence of the Deity or merely to enjoy natural beauty, they inevitably learned to feel emotions in the presence of external nature and to examine the quality of their feelings. Before the death of Pope and Swift, in the poetry of Thomson and others, a literature of feeling had come into existence alongside the dominant literature of wit. The development of such a literature of sentiment is perhaps the crucial fact in the literary history of the century after the deaths of Pope and Swift.

THE EMERGENCE OF NEW LITERARY THEMES AND MODES, 1740–85

When Matthew Arnold, speaking for Victorian taste, called the eighteenth century an "Age of Prose," he meant to cast doubt upon its poetry; but the later part of the century might indeed be honored as an age of prose. Never before nor since have so many great writers of prose flourished at once, nor so many kinds of intellectual prose been perfected: literary criticism, with Samuel Johnson; biography, James Boswell; philosophy, David Hume; politics, Edmund Burke; history, Edward Gibbon; aesthetics, Sir Joshua Reynolds; economics, Adam Smith; natural history, Gilbert White. Each of these authors is a master stylist, whose effort to express himself clearly and fully creates an art as difficult to achieve, and as precise, as poetry. Indeed, the prose style of the period often seems to build upon the principles of neoclassical verse: its elaborately balanced use of parallels and antitheses, its elegant allusions to a classical literature, its public, rhetorical manner, its craving for generality. At its best, however, such prose depends less on formal virtues than on its weight of thought. Unlike the earlier masters of simplicity in prose—Addison, Swift, Defoe—the authors of the Age of Johnson have little confidence in plain speaking. Readers will not be convinced of the truth, they suspect, merely by having the facts laid before them; they must be offered scientific demonstration or passionate eloquence. Some comments by Johnson on the prose of Swift make the point by example as well as precept:

> His style was well suited to his thoughts, which are never subtilized by nice disquisitions, decorated by sparkling conceit, elevated by ambitious sentences, or variegated by far-sought learning. He pays no court to the passions, he excites neither surprise nor admiration; he always understands himself, and his readers always understand him. . . . This easy and safe conveyance of meaning it was Swift's desire to attain, and for having attained he deserves praise, though perhaps not the highest praise. For purposes merely didactic, when something is to be told that was not known before, it is the best mode; but against that inattention by which known truths are suffered to lie neglected, it makes no provision; it instructs, but does not persuade.

Johnson's prose bristles with long words, qualifications of thought, and "ambitious sentences" that are the very opposite of the style he describes; he attempts not merely to be understood, not merely to instruct, but to persuade. And similar ambitions motivate many of the authors of his time. An unprecedented effort to formulate the first principles of philosophy, history, psychology, and art required a whole new language of persuasion, more subtle, logical, and accurate than English had ever been before.

An age of great prose, however, can put a burden on its poets. Many of the generation of talented young poets who emerged about the time of Pope's death, a group that includes William Collins, Thomas Gray, Mark Akenside, and the brothers Joseph and Thomas Warton, are haunted by the fear that the spirit of poetry may have passed away—driven out by the spirit of prose, by an ideal of mere "correctness," by the end of superstitions that had once peopled the landscape with fairies and demons, the stuff of poetry. In an age barren of magic, they ask, where is poetry to be found? That question becomes obsessive in many poems of the period, suffusing them with melancholy. Indeed, more and more poetry itself was associated with melancholy, a sweet sadness, a yearning for another time and place. The prototype of the mid-eighteenth-century melancholy poet was Milton's *Il Penseroso*, a night-loving solitary, who sucks pensive sadness from the "far-off curfew" or the swelling organ in the twilight of a Gothic church. Such a figure is most unlike the Augustan poet, a social being, living in a crowded world and little given to the impropriety of the public confession of private feelings. The idea of the poet was changing from that of a maker to that of an introspective, brooding confessor; the materials of poetry were becoming rather the inner life and private vision of the poet than public, social affairs.

Poets who brood in silence are never far from thoughts of death; and an often morbid fascination with death, suicide, and the grave preoccupies the poets of midcentury. The clergyman Edward Young (1683–1765) wrote an immensely long and popular poem in blank verse, *The Complaint: or Night Thoughts on Life, Death, and Immortality* (1742–46), to supplement the Christian optimism of Pope's *Essay on Man* with a darker view of Christianity based on fear of the life to come. But the "graveyard school" is less concerned with religion than with horror and decay. Within an elaborate stage setting of medieval ruins and fleshless bodies, the soul of the graveyard poet self-consciously acts out its secret fears. The revival of Gothic architectural styles, most famously Horace Walpole's tiny and precious pseudo-Gothic castle, Strawberry Hill, helped influence literary styles as well. The Gothic vogue, like a similar vogue for Chinese decor, seemed to suggest that old-fashioned canons of taste—proportion, balance, simplicity, and harmony—might count for less in art than the pleasures of fancy and extravagance—intricacy, asymmetry, a willful excess. Poets began to cultivate archaic language and antique literary forms; especially, after Thomas Percy's edition of *Reliques of Ancient English Poetry* (1765), the ballad. Thus Thomas Chatterton (1752–1770), whom the Romantics later idolized for his precocious genius and his tragic early death, composed sham medieval ballads he pretended to have found in an old manuscript. The most remarkable literary consequence of such medievalizing, however, was the invention of the Gothic romance. Horace Walpole's *Castle of Otranto* (1765), a dreamlike tale of terror inspired by the physical appearance of Strawberry Hill, created a mode of fiction that retains its popularity to the present day. In the typical Gothic romance, set amidst the glooms and intricacies of a medieval castle, the laws of nightmare replace the laws of probability. Forbidden themes—incest, murder, necrophilia, atheism, the torments of sexual desire—are allowed free play; repressed feelings, morbid fears rise to the surface of the narrative. Although most such romances, like William Beckford's *Vathek* (1786) and Matthew Lewis's *The Monk* (1796), depend on sensationalism and the grotesque, Gothicism also resulted in works, like Anne Radcliffe's, that temper romance with reality, as well as in serious novels of social purpose, like William Godwin's *Caleb Williams* (1794); and Godwin's daughter, Mary Shelley, eventually composed a romantic nightmare, *Frankenstein* (1816), that continues to haunt our dreams.

Ultimately, it was not to a medieval revival that poets looked for a renewal of poetry, but to their own imaginations and feelings. In his *Ode to Fancy* (1746), Joseph Warton associated "fancy" with the natural, the wild and spontaneous, with solitude, and with enthusiasm and the passions. Such a concept of the fancy or imagination emphasizes not rules and crafts of the maker, but original genius, the poet as the seer or nature's priest. True poets, Warton suggests, should not be conversationalists or orators but singers. "The public has seen all that art can do," William Shenstone wrote in 1761, welcoming James Macpherson's bardic *Ossian*, "and they want the more striking efforts of wild, original, enthusiastic genius." But genius is easier to call for than to recognize; when it does come, people are apt to call it madness. Many of the best poets of the period—Collins, Christopher Smart, later William Cowper—suffered from mental illness, and others, like Chatterton, were scorned by society. Nor did many readers so much as notice the extraordinary work of Smart, or later of William Blake. The apocalyptic strain of poetry, bursting the bonds of logical transition, of grammar, and even of the natural world, proved difficult to approach. Cowper, the most popular poet of the latter part of the century, won his readers with a more modest, intimate kind of verse, never departing far from the accents of friendly conversation. Nevertheless, it was to visionary poetry, and to genius, that the future belonged. "The road of excess," Blake notes in a Proverb of Hell, "leads to the palace of wisdom." As the eighteenth century drew to an end amid revolutions in society and thought, poets began to travel that road.

THE BEGINNING OF THE NOVEL

To say that the modern novel came into existence in the eighteenth century is not to say that there was no prose fiction before 1700. There were the ancient Greek romances and their modern European imitators; the courtly *Arcadia* of Sidney and the humbler fiction of Deloney and Nashe and other Elizabethans; the interminable French romances of the seventeenth century and their English translations and imitations, loosely constructed, blending aristocratic refinement, chivalric adventure, and courtly love; the tales of the adventures of rogues and the careers of famous criminals; and, in a world apart, Bunyan's vivid allegories of the spiritual adventures of wayfaring and militant Christians and their adversaries. But it remains true that, if we except Daniel Defoe, the creator of the modern novel was Samuel Richardson (1689–1761). Both Defoe and Richardson belonged to the middle class and expressed in their works middle-class interests and attitudes. They also wrote about and for women. To a large extent, the development of the novel is identical with the attempt to interest the growing number of female readers by shaping their lives into literature. Defoe simply ignored the sentimental and aristocratic refinements of the earlier romances and was content to show his readers not a world as it might be, a heroic world, but their world as it was, populated with believable people who were motivated by the practical concerns that dominate our daily lives. He did not seek—and except through *Robinson Crusoe* (1719) did not often find—readers among the upper classes. He was content to interest shopkeepers, apprentices, and servants, who were already avid readers of tales of crime and adventure, usually heavily laced with pious moral observations.

Richardson, however, caught the attention of all literate Europe, and once for all established the novel as we know it, a solid and enduring object in the literary landscape. His three novels were strikingly new in their minute and subtle analysis of emotions and states of mind. It was while he was compiling a little book of model letters that he conceived the idea of *Pamela*, or *Virtue Rewarded* (1740), a story told in a series of letters, in which a virtuous servant girl who resists her master's base designs on her virtue eventually wins him as her husband. Richardson's masterpiece, *Clarissa* (1747–48), carries the same epistolary method, moral instruction, and sexual titillation to new heights. In the conflict between the libertine Lovelace, an attractive and diabolical aristocrat, and the angelic Clarissa, the perfection of middle-class values, Richardson created a fiction that embodied the ideals and the tensions of his society. No earlier author had involved his readers so fully in the thoughts and emotions of his characters; nor had any author paid such close attention to the pressures on women. Such later novelists as Fanny Burney (1752–1840) and Jane Austen would profit from his example. Richardson's final novel, *Sir Charles Grandison* (1753–54), turns to a model of male perfection with less success.

Henry Fielding (1707–1754), who loved virtue as much as Richardson did, but to whom goodness was a matter of spontaneity and fellow feeling, not of conformity to a code, considered *Pamela* a misleading image of virtue;

therefore, in 1742, he published *Joseph Andrews*, which begins as a hilarious burlesque of *Pamela* by describing the staunch resistance offered to the lewd advances of Lady Booby by her servant, the virtuous Joseph, brother of Pamela. Expelled for his chastity from Lady Booby's household, he takes to the road, joining the guileless Parson Adams, who is walking to London to try to sell a bundle of his sermons to a publisher. Their adventures make up what Fielding called "a comic epic in prose." His great novel is *The History of Tom Jones, A Foundling* (1749). The protagonist became the pattern of the good-natured hero of the age: a young man of manly virtues, generous, high-spirited, loyal, and courageous, but impulsive, wanting prudence, full of animal spirits and sensuality. The novel is crowded with incident and with varied types of men and women; and critics have agreed with Coleridge's praise of its brilliantly constructed plot. Fielding's other important novel, *Amelia* (1751), having as its heroine a long-suffering woman, almost wholly passive, is an example of pathos rather than of Fielding's comic vigor and gusto.

The picaresque tradition was continued by Tobias Smollett (1721–1771) in *Roderick Random* (1748), *Peregrine Pickle* (1751), and *Ferdinand, Count Fathom* (1753). Smollett delighted to depict the grotesque side of eighteenth-century life, its brutality, coarse practical jokes, and strong odors. His masterpiece is *Humphrey Clinker* (1771), which recounts, through letters written by several members of a traveling party, the comic incidents of a journey through England and Scotland. But the most original novelist of the period was Laurence Sterne (1713–1768), an unclerical clergyman, a humorist, a sentimentalist, and an author who reminds us that one of the roots of the novel is the word "novelty." *The Life and Opinions of Tristram Shandy*, produced between 1760 and 1767, deliberately frustrated all the stock expectations of its readers. The plot has not the logical order of a beginning, a middle, and an end; instead it abandons clock time for psychological time, interrupts scenes in order to digress or to recount past or future events, follows whimsically any apparently chance association, digresses for several chapters—in fact, it is designed as an elaborate joke at the reader's expense. And yet the method gets us inside the consciousness of the narrator and the other characters, and into a world peopled by the most engaging of comic characters.

Fielding, Smollett, and Sterne gave to English literature not only vivid scenes from the life of their times, but a gallery of eccentric and original characters that illustrate the interest of the age not only in the ideal and the general, but also in the individual and the unique. The novels of Dickens and of Thackeray in the nineteenth century owe much to their forerunners in the eighteenth.

THE CONTINUITY OF THE AUGUSTAN TRADITION

Despite the emergence of new literary forms, materials, and methods after the death of Pope and Swift, the Augustan line continued vigorously throughout the last half of the eighteenth and even into the nineteenth century. If the years between 1745 and 1784 were years of change and experiment, they were also the period of Samuel Johnson's greatest achievement and influence. A conservative in literature as in politics and religion, Johnson defended in conversation and in his critical writings the principles that he had inherited from the older generation. His two major poems, *London* (1738) and *The Vanity of Human Wishes* (1749), are satirical and ethical and show little influence of the new sensibility of the midcentury. He was loyal to the heroic couplet and to the use of generalized diction. His *Dictionary* (1755) was designed not to fix our language permanently but certainly to retard the process of change and to censure words which he considered superfluous. His critical writings sufficiently reveal his devotion to the standards of Dryden and Pope. But his conservatism was saved from pedantry by the empirical bent of his mind and his broad and humanistic learning.

If Johnson speaks for his age, the reason is partly that he shares a faith, with many of his contemporaries, in common sense and the common reader. "By the common sense of readers uncorrupted with literary prejudices," he wrote in the last of his great *Lives of the Poets* (1780), "must be finally decided all claim to poetical honors." A similar respect for common sense, and for standards of taste and behavior based upon responses that all of us share, marks many of the grandest achievements of the century; for instance, the political writings of Edmund Burke, the great Whig statesman and orator, or the *Discourses on Art* (1769–90) of Sir Joshua Reynolds, who drew the best aesthetic theory of his day into an elegant whole. Moreover, the poets whom everyone read relied less upon apocalyptic visions than upon a verse that could do justice to the ordinary feelings of ordinary people. Gray's *Elegy*, Goldsmith's *The Deserted Village*, Crabbe's *The Village*, and the lyrics of Robert Burns are only a few of the poems that strive to make poetry from and for the lives of the common man. Nor did Goldsmith, Crabbe, and Burns, for all their attachment to the growing wave of sentimentalism, desert the verse forms—the careful craftsmanship, the rhyming couplets—developed by the earlier Augustan masters. Even Cowper's *The Task* (1785), which brings us to the threshold of the Romantic movement, belongs most definitely in the eighteenth century. Indeed, the Augustan age did not die on that day in 1798 when a small and unsuccessful volume of poems, *Lyrical Ballads*, was published by Wordsworth and Coleridge. We hear the accents of that age from time to time in the poems of both Wordsworth and Coleridge, in many of the poems of Byron, and in Byron's ardent defense of Pope and Dryden, when the new age finally brought those masters to judgment. And we hear its old verities expressed in its own vocabulary in the criticism of that arch-enemy of the Romantic movement, Francis Jeffrey, editor of the *Edinburgh Review*, as when, for example, in a review (1808) of a volume of poems by George Crabbe, he paused to rebuke the (as he believed) affectedly eccentric poet Wordsworth for having written *The Thorn* and one of the Lucy poems:

> Now we leave it to any reader of common candor and discernment to say whether these representations of character and sentiment are drawn from the eternal and universal standard of truth and nature, which every one is knowing enough to recognize, and no one great enough to depart from with impunity; or whether they are not formed . . . upon certain fantastic and affected peculiarities in the mind or fancy of the author, into which it is most improbable that many of his readers will enter, and which cannot, in some cases, be comprehended without much effort and explanation.

JOHN DRYDEN
1631–1700

1668:	Made poet laureate.
1681:	*Absalom and Achitophel*.
ca. 1686:	Conversion to Catholicism.
1689:	Loss of court offices upon accession of William and Mary.
1697:	Translation of Virgil.

Although John Dryden's parents seem to have sided with Parliament against the king, there is no evidence that the poet grew up in a strict Puritan family. His father, a country gentleman of moderate fortune, gave his son a gentleman's education at Westminster School, under the renowned Dr. Richard Busby, who used the rod as a pedagogical aid in imparting a sound knowledge of the learned languages and literatures to his charges (among others John Locke and Matthew Prior). From Westminster, Dryden went to Trinity College, Cambridge, where he took his A.B. in 1654. His first important and impressive poem, *Heroic Stanzas* (1659), was written to commemorate the death of Cromwell. The next year, however, in *Astraea Redux*, Dryden joined his countrymen in celebrating the return of Charles II to his throne. During the rest of his life Dryden was to remain entirely loyal to Charles and to his successor James II.

Dryden is the commanding literary figure of the last four decades of the seventeenth century. He is that rare phenomenon, the man of letters in whose work the image of an age can be discerned. Every important aspect of the life of his times—political, religious, philosophical, artistic—finds expression somewhere in his writings. Dryden is the least personal of our poets. He is not at all the solitary, subjective poet listening to the murmur of his own voice and preoccupied with his own personal view of experience, but rather a citizen of the world commenting publicly on matters of public concern.

From the beginning to the end of his literary career, Dryden's original nondramatic poems are most typically occasional poems, which celebrate particular events of a public character—a coronation, a military victory, a death, a political crisis. Such poems are social and ceremonial, written not for the self but the nation. Dryden's principal achievements in this form are the two poems on the king's return and his coronation; *Annus Mirabilis* (1667), which celebrates the English naval victory over the Dutch and the fortitude of the people of London and the king during the Great Fire, both events of that "wonderful year," 1666; the political poems; the lines on the death of Oldham (1684); the odes; and the masque printed below.

Between 1664 and 1681, however, Dryden was mainly a playwright. The newly chartered theaters needed a modern repertory, and he set out to supply the need. Dryden wrote his plays, as he frankly confessed, to please his audiences, which were not heterogeneous, like Shakespeare's, but were largely drawn from the court and from people of fashion. In the style of the time, he produced rhymed heroic plays, in which incredibly noble heroes and heroines face incredibly difficult choices between love and honor; comedies, in which male and female rakes engage in intrigue and bright repartee; and, later, libretti for the newly introduced dramatic form, the opera. His one great tragedy, *All for Love* (1677), in blank verse, adapts Shakespeare's *Antony and Cleopatra* to the unities of time, place, and action. As his *Essay of Dramatic Poesy* (1668) shows, Dryden had studied the works of the great playwrights of Greece and Rome, of the English Renaissance, and of contemporary France, seeking sound theoretical principles on which to construct the new drama that the age demanded. Indeed his fine critical intelligence always supported his creative powers, and because he took literature seriously and enjoyed discussing it, he became, it appears almost casually, what Samuel Johnson called him: "the father of English criticism." His abilities as both poet and dramatist brought him to the attention of the king, who in 1668 made him poet laureate. Two years later the post of Historiographer Royal was added to the laureateship at a combined stipend of £200, enough money to live on.

Between 1678 and 1681, when he was nearing fifty, Dryden discovered his great gift for writing formal verse satire. A quarrel with Thomas Shadwell, a playwright of some talent, prompted the mock-heroic episode *Mac Flecknoe*, which was probably written about 1678 but which was not published until 1682. Out of the stresses occasioned by the Popish Plot (1678) and its political aftermath came his major political satires, *Absalom and Achitophel* (1681), and *The Medal* (1682), his final attack on the villain of *Absalom and Achitophel*, the earl of Shaftesbury. Twenty years' experience as poet and playwright had prepared him technically for the triumph of *Absalom and Achitophel*. He had completely mastered the heroic couplet, having fashioned it into an instrument suitable in his hands for every sort of discourse from the thrust and parry of quick logical argument, to lyric feeling, rapid narrative, or forensic declamation. Thanks to this long discipline, he was able in one stride to assume his proper place beside the masters of verse satire: Horace, Juvenal, Persius, in ancient Rome, and Boileau, his French contemporary.

The consideration of religious and political questions that the events of 1678–81 forced on Dryden brought a new seriousness to his mind and works. In 1682 he published *Religio Laici*, a poem in which he examined the grounds of his religious faith and defended the middle way of the Anglican Church against the rationalism of Deism on the one hand and the authoritarianism of Rome on the other. But he had moved closer to Rome than he perhaps realized when he wrote the poem. Charles II died in 1685 and was succeeded by his Catholic brother, James II. Within less than a year Dryden and his two sons were converted to Catholicism. Though his enemies accused him of opportunism, he proved his sincerity by his steadfast loyalty to the Roman Church after James abdicated and the Protestant William and Mary came in; as a result he was to lose his offices and their much-needed stipends. From his new position as a Roman Catholic, Dryden wrote in 1687 *The Hind and the Panther*, in which a milk-white Hind (the Roman Church) and a spotted Panther (the Anglican Church) eloquently debate theology. The Hind has the better of the argument; but Dryden already knew that James's policies were failing, and with them the Catholic cause in England.

Dryden was now nearing sixty, with a family to support on a much-diminished income. To earn a living, he resumed writing plays and turned to translations. In 1693 appeared his versions of Juvenal and Persius, with the long dedicatory epistle on satire; and in 1697, his greatest achievement in this mode, the works of Virgil. At the very end, two months before his death, came the *Fables Ancient and Modern*, prefaced by one of the finest of his critical essays and made up of translations from Ovid, Boccaccio, and Chaucer.

What was the nature of Dryden's achievement? His drama, by and large, belongs entirely to his age, though its influence persisted into the next century. His critical writings established canons of taste and theoretical principles that determined the character of neoclassic literature in the next century. He helped establish a new sort of prose—easy, lucid, plain, and shaped to the cadences of natural speech. This is the prose that we like to think of as "modern." Johnson praised it for its informality and apparent artlessness: "every word seems to drop by chance, though it falls into its proper place. Nothing is cold or languid; the whole is airy, animated, and vigorous . . . though all is easy, nothing is feeble; though all seems careless, there is nothing harsh." His satire, as vital today as it was three hundred years ago, exerted a fruitful influence on the most brilliant verse satirist of the next century, Alexander Pope. The vigor and variety of his metrics made inevitable the long-enduring vogue of the heroic couplet among his successors. At the same time, he created a poetic language that remained the basic language of poetry until the early nineteenth century and that even the Romantic movement did not wholly destroy. His poems represent the superbly civilized language of the Augustan style at its best: dignified, unaffected, precise and always musical—a noble instrument of public speech. Johnson's final estimate remains valid: "By him we were taught *sapere et fari*, to think naturally and express forcibly. . . . What was said of Rome, adorned by Augustus, may be applied by an easy metaphor to English poetry embellished by Dryden, *lateritiam invenit, marmoream reliquit*, he found it brick, and he left it marble."

From Annus Mirabilis[1]

[*London Reborn*]

Yet London, empress of the northern clime,   845
    By an high fate thou greatly didst expire;
Great as the world's, which at the death of time
    Must fall, and rise a nobler frame by fire.[2]

---

1. 1666 was a "year of wonders" (*annus mirabilis*): war, plague, the great fire of London. According to the enemies of Charles II, God was visiting His wrath upon the English people to signify that the reign of an unholy king would soon come to an end. Dryden's long "historical poem" *Annus Mirabilis*, written the same year, interprets the wonders differently: as trials sent by God to punish rebellious spirits and to bind the king and his people together. "Never had prince or people more mutual reason to love each other," Dryden wrote, "if suffering for each other can endear affection."

Charles had endured rejection and exile, England had been torn by civil war. Dryden views these sufferings as a covenant, pledge of better times to come. Out of Charles' troubles, he predicts in heroic stanzas modeled on Virgil, the king shall arise like a new Augustus, the ruler of a great empire; and out of fire London shall arise like the phoenix, ready to take her place as trade center for the world, in the glory of a new Augustan age.
2. Ovid, whom Dryden quotes, foretells, in book 1 of *The Metamorphoses*, that the world will be purged by fire.

As when some dire usurper Heaven provides,
    To scourge his country with a lawless sway:[3]   850
His birth, perhaps, some petty village hides,
    And sets his cradle out of fortune's way:

Till fully ripe his swelling fate breaks out,
    And hurries him to mighty mischiefs on:
His Prince, surprised at first, no ill could doubt,[4]   855
    And wants the power to meet it when 'tis known:

Such was the rise of this prodigious fire,
    Which in mean buildings first obscurely bred,
From thence did soon to open streets aspire,
    And straight to palaces and temples spread.   860

*   *   *

Me-thinks already, from this chymic[5] flame,
    I see a city of more precious mold: 1170
Rich as the town which gives the Indies name,[6]
    With silver paved, and all divine with gold.

Already, laboring with a mighty fate,
    She shakes the rubbish from her mounting brow,
And seems to have renewed her charter's date,   1175
    Which Heaven will to the death of time allow.

More great than human, now, and more August,[7]
    New deified she from her fires does rise:
Her widening streets on new foundations trust,
    And, opening, into larger parts she flies.   1180

Before, she like some shepherdess did show,
    Who sat to bathe her by a river's side:
Not answering to her fame, but rude and low,
    Nor taught the beauteous arts of modern pride.

Now, like a Maiden Queen, she will behold,   1185
    From her high turrets, hourly suitors come:
The East with incense, and the West with gold,
    Will stand, like suppliants, to receive her doom.[8]

The silver Thames, her own domestic flood,
    Shall bear her vessels like a sweeping train;   1190

3. Probably a reference to Oliver Cromwell.
4. Fear.
5. Alchemic or transmuting. The fire of London, which utterly consumed the central city, burned for 4 days, September 2–6. By September 10 Christopher Wren had already submitted a plan, much of it later adopted, for rebuilding the city on a grander scale.
6. Mexico.
7. Augusta, the old name of London [Dryden's note].
8. Judgment, decree.

And often wind (as of his mistress proud)
    With longing eyes to meet her face again.

The wealthy Tagus, and the wealthier Rhine,
    The glory of their towns no more shall boast;
And Seine, that would with Belgian rivers join,[9]   1195
    Shall find her luster stained, and traffic lost.

The venturous merchant, who designed[1] more far,
    And touches on our hospitable shore,
Charmed with the splendor of this northern star,
    Shall here unlade him, and depart no more.   1200

Our powerful navy shall no longer meet,
    The wealth of France or Holland to invade;
The beauty of this Town, without a fleet,
    From all the world shall vindicate[2] her trade.

And while this famed emporium we prepare,   1205
    The British ocean shall such triumphs boast,
That those who now disdain our trade to share,
    Shall rob like pirates on our wealthy coast.

Already we have conquered half the war,
    And the less dangerous part is left behind: 1210
Our trouble now is but to make them dare,
    And not so great to vanquish as to find.

Thus to the eastern wealth through storms we go,
    But now, the Cape once doubled,[3] fear no more;
A constant trade-wind will securely blow,   1215
    And gently lay us on the spicy shore.

1666   1667

Song from *Marriage à la Mode*

1

Why should a foolish marriage vow,
    Which long ago was made,
Oblige us to each other now,
    When passion is decayed?
We loved, and we loved, as long as we could,   5
    Till our love was loved out in us both;

---

9. France and Holland (which then included Belgium) had made an alliance for trade, as well as war, against England. The river Tagus flows into the Atlantic at Lisbon.

1. Intended to go.
2. Defend, protect.
3. Sailed around.

But our marriage is dead when the pleasure is fled:
  'Twas pleasure first made it an oath.

2

If I have pleasures for a friend,
  And farther love in store,   10
What wrong has he whose joys did end,
  And who could give no more?
'Tis a madness that he should be jealous of me,
  Or that I should bar him of another:
For all we can gain is to give ourselves pain,   15
  When neither can hinder the other.

ca. 1672   1673

Absalom and Achitophel   In 1678 a dangerous crisis, both religious and political, threatened to undo the Restoration settlement and to
precipitate England once again into civil war. The Popish Plot and its aftermath not only whipped up extreme anti-Catholic passions, but led between
1679 and 1681 to a bitter political struggle between Charles II (whose adherents came to be called Tories) and the earl of Shaftesbury (whose followers
were termed Whigs). The issues were nothing less than the prerogatives of
the Crown and the possible exclusion of the king's Catholic brother, James,
duke of York, from his rightful position as heir-presumptive to the throne.
Charles's cool courage and brilliant, if unscrupulous, political genius saved
the throne for his brother and gave at least temporary peace to his people.

Charles was a Catholic at heart—he received the last rites of that church
on his deathbed—and was eager to do what he could do discreetly for the
relief of his Catholic subjects, who suffered severe civil and religious disa-
bilities imposed by their numerically superior Protestant countrymen. James
openly professed the Catholic religion, an awkward fact politically, for he
was next in line of succession since Charles had no legitimate children. The
household of the duke, as well as that of Charles's neglected queen, Catherine of Braganza, inevitably became the center of Catholic life and intrigue
at court and consequently of Protestant prejudice and suspicion.

No one understood, however, that the situation was explosive until 1678,
when Titus Oates (a renegade Catholic convert and a man of the most infamous character) offered sworn testimony of the existence of a Jesuit plot to
assassinate the king, burn London, massacre Protestants, and reestablish the
Roman Church.

The country might have kept its head and come to realize (what no historian has doubted) that Oates and his confederates were perjured rascals, as
Charles himself quickly perceived. But panic was created by the discovery
of the murdered body of a prominent London justice of the peace, Sir Edmund
Berry Godfrey, who a few days before had received for safekeeping a copy of
Oates's testimony. The crime, immediately ascribed to the Catholics, has
never been solved. Fear and indignation reached a hysterical pitch when the
seizure of the papers of the duke of York's secretary revealed that he had
been in correspondence with the confessor of Louis XIV regarding the re-
establishment of the Roman Church in England. Before the terror subsided

many innocent men were executed on the increasingly bold and always false evidence of Oates and his fellows.

The earl of Shaftesbury, the duke of Buckingham, and others quickly took advantage of the situation. With the support of the Commons and the City of London, they moved to exclude the duke of York from the succession. Between 1679 and 1681 Charles and Shaftesbury were engaged in a mighty struggle. The Whigs found a candidate of their own in the king's favorite illegitimate son, the handsome and engaging duke of Monmouth, whom they advanced as a proper successor to his father. They urged Charles to legitimize him, and when he refused they whispered that there was proof that the king had secretly married Monmouth's mother. The young man allowed himself to be used against his father. He was sent on a triumphant progress through western England, where he was enthusiastically received. Twice an Exclusion Bill nearly passed both houses. But by early 1681 Charles had secured his own position by secretly accepting from Louis XIV a three-year subsidy that made him independent of Parliament, which had tried to force his hand by refusing to vote him funds. He summoned Parliament to meet at Oxford in the spring of 1681, and, a few moments after the Commons had passed the Exclusion Bill, in a bold stroke he abruptly dissolved Parliament, which never met again during his reign. Already, as Charles was aware, a reaction had set in against the violence of the Whigs. In mid-summer, when he felt it safe to move against his enemies, Shaftesbury was sent to the Tower, charged with high treason. In November the grand jury, packed with Whigs, threw out the indictment, and the earl was free; but his power was broken, and he lived only two more years.

Shortly before the grand jury acted, Dryden published anonymously the first part of *Absalom and Achitophel,* apparently hoping to influence their verdict. It is worthy of the occasion which produced it. The issues in question were grave; the chief actors, the most important men in the realm. Dryden, therefore, could not use burlesque and caricature as had Butler, or the mock-heroic as he himself had done in *Mac Flecknoe.* Only a heroic style and manner were appropriate to his weighty material, and the poem is most original in its blending of the heroic and the satiric. Dryden's task called for all his tact and literary skill; he had to mention, but to gloss over, the king's faults: his indolence and love of pleasure; his neglect of his wife and his devotion to his mistresses—conduct which had left him with many children, but no heir except his Catholic brother. He had to deal gently with Monmouth, whom Charles still loved. And he had to present, or appear to present, the king's case objectively.

The remarkable parallels between the rebellion of Absalom against his father King David (2 Samuel 13–18) had already been remarked in sermons, satires, and pamphlets. Dryden took the hint and gave contemporary events a due distance and additional dignity by approaching them indirectly through their biblical analogues. The poem is famous for its brilliant portraits of the king's enemies and friends; but equally admirable are the temptation scene (which, like other passages, is indebted to *Paradise Lost*) and the remarkably astute analysis of the Popish Plot itself.

A second part of *Absalom and Achitophel* appeared in 1682. Most of it is the work of Nahum Tate, but lines 310–509, which include the devastating portraits of Doeg and Og (two Whig poets, Elkanah Settle and Thomas Shadwell) are certainly by Dryden.

Absalom and Achitophel: A Poem

In pious times, ere priestcraft did begin,
Before polygamy was made a sin;
When man on many multiplied his kind,
Ere one to one was cursedly confined;
When nature prompted and no law denied   5
Promiscuous use of concubine and bride;
Then Israel's monarch after Heaven's own heart,[1]
His vigorous warmth did variously impart
To wives and slaves; and, wide as his command,
Scattered his Maker's image through the land.   10
Michal,[2] of royal blood, the crown did wear,
A soil ungrateful to the tiller's care:
Not so the rest; for several mothers bore
To godlike David several sons before.
But since like slaves his bed they did ascend,   15
No true succession could their seed attend.
Of all this numerous progeny was none
So beautiful, so brave, as Absalom:[3]
Whether, inspired by some diviner lust,
His father got him with a greater gust,[4]   20
Or that his conscious destiny made way,
By manly beauty, to imperial sway.
Early in foreign fields he won renown,
With kings and states allied to Israel's crown:[5]
In peace the thoughts of war he could remove,   25
And seemed as he were only born for love.
Whate'er he did, was done with so much ease,
In him alone 'twas natural to please;
His motions all accompanied with grace;
And paradise was opened in his face.   30
With secret joy indulgent David viewed
His youthful image in his son renewed:
To all his wishes nothing he denied;
And made the charming Annabel[6] his bride.
What faults he had (for who from faults is free?) 35
His father could not, or he would not see.
Some warm excesses which the law forbore,
Were cònstrued youth that purged by boiling o'er:
And Amnon's murther,[7] by a specious name,

1. David ("a man after [God's] own heart," according to 1 Samuel 13.14) represents Charles II.
2. "Michal," one of David's wives, represents the childless queen, Catherine of Braganza.
3. James Scott, duke of Monmouth (1649–1685).
4. Relish, pleasure.
5. Monmouth had won repute as a soldier fighting for France against Holland and for Holland against France.
6. Anne Scott, duchess of Buccleuch (pronounced Bue-cloo), a beauty and a great heiress.
7. Absalom killed his half-brother Amnon, who had raped Absalom's sister Tamar (2 Samuel 13.28–29). The parallel with Monmouth is vague. He is known to have committed acts of violence in his youth, but certainly not fratricide.

Was called a just revenge for injured fame. 40
Thus praised and loved the noble youth remained,
While David, undisturbed, in Sion[8] reigned.
But life can never be sincerely[9] blest;
Heaven punishes the bad, and proves[1] the best.
The Jews,[2] a headstrong, moody, murmuring race, 45
As ever tried the extent and stretch of grace;
God's pampered people, whom, debauched with ease,
No king could govern, nor no God could please
(Gods they had tried of every shape and size
That god-smiths could produce, or priests devise);[3] 50
These Adam-wits,[4] too fortunately free,
Began to dream they wanted liberty;
And when no rule, no precedent was found,
Of men by laws less circumscribed and bound,
They led their wild desires to woods and caves, 55
And thought that all but savages were slaves.
They who, when Saul[5] was dead, without a blow,
Made foolish Ishbosheth the crown forgo;
Who banished David did from Hebron[6] bring,
And with a general shout proclaimed him king: 60
Those very Jews, who, at their very best,
Their humor[7] more than loyalty expressed,
Now wondered why so long they had obeyed
An idol monarch, which their hands had made;
Thought they might ruin him they could create, 65
Or melt him to that golden calf,[8] a state.
But these were random bolts;[9] no formed design
Nor interest made the factious crowd to join:
The sober part of Israel, free from stain,
Well knew the value of a peaceful reign; 70
And, looking backward with a wise affright,
Saw seams of wounds, dishonest[1] to the sight:
In contemplation of whose ugly scars
They cursed the memory of civil wars.
The moderate sort of men, thus qualified,[2] 75
Inclined the balance to the better side;
And David's mildness managed it so well,
The bad found no occasion to rebel.

8. London.
9. Wholly.
1. Tests.
2. The English.
3. Dryden recalls the political and religious controversies which, since the Reformation, had divided England and finally caused civil war.
4. Adam rebelled because he felt that he lacked ("wanted") liberty, since he was forbidden to eat the fruit of one tree.
5. Oliver Cromwell. "Ishbosheth": Saul's son; he stands for Richard Cromwell, who succeeded his

father as Lord Protector.
6. Where David reigned over Judah after the death of Saul and before he became king of Israel (2 Samuel 1–5). Charles had been crowned in Scotland in 1651.
7. Caprice.
8. The image worshiped by the Children of Israel during the period that Moses spent on Mt. Sinai, receiving the law from God. "A state": a republic.
9. Shots.
1. Disgraceful.
2. Assuaged.

But when to sin our biased[3] nature leans,
The careful Devil is still at hand with means;   80
And providently pimps for ill desires:
The Good Old Cause[4] revived, a plot requires.
Plots, true or false, are necessary things,
To raise up commonwealths and ruin kings.

    The inhabitants of old Jerusalem   85
Were Jebusites;[5] the town so called from them;
And theirs the native right.
But when the chosen people[6] grew more strong,
The rightful cause at length became the wrong;
And every loss the men of Jebus bore,   90
They still were thought God's enemies the more.
Thus worn and weakened, well or ill content,
Submit they must to David's government:
Impoverished and deprived of all command,
Their taxes doubled as they lost their land;   95
And, what was harder yet to flesh and blood,
Their gods disgraced, and burnt like common wood.[7]
This set the heathen priesthood[8] in a flame;
For priests of all religions are the same:
Of whatsoe'er descent their godhead be,   100
Stock, stone, or other homely pedigree,
In his defense his servants are as bold,
As if he had been born of beaten gold.
The Jewish rabbins,[9] though their enemies,
In this conclude them honest men and wise: 105
For 'twas their duty, all the learned think,
To espouse his cause, by whom they eat and drink.
From hence began that Plot, the nation's curse,
Bad in itself, but represented worse;
Raised in extremes, and in extremes decried;   110
With oaths affirmed, with dying vows denied;
Not weighed or winnowed by the multitude;
But swallowed in the mass, unchewed and crude.
Some truth there was, but dashed[1] and brewed with lies,
To please the fools, and puzzle all the wise.   115
Succeeding times did equal folly call,
Believing nothing, or believing all.
The Egyptian[2] rites the Jebusites embraced,
Where gods were recommended by their taste.
Such savory deities must needs be good,   120
As served at once for worship and for food.

---

3. Inclined. Cf. *Mac Flecknoe*, line 189 and note.
4. The Commonwealth. Dryden stigmatizes the Whigs by associating them with subversion.
5. Roman Catholics. The original name of Jerusalem (here, London) was Jebus.
6. Protestants.
7. Such oppressive laws against Roman Catholics date from the time of Elizabeth I.
8. Roman Catholic clergy.
9. Anglican clergy.
1. Adulterated.
2. French, therefore Catholic. In the next line Dryden sneers at the doctrine of transubstantiation.

By force they could not introduce these gods,
For ten to one in former days was odds;
So fraud was used (the sacrificer's trade):
Fools are more hard to conquer than persuade.   125
Their busy teachers mingled with the Jews,
And raked for converts even the court and stews:[3]
Which Hebrew priests the more unkindly took,
Because the fleece accompanies the flock.[4]
Some thought they God's anointed[5] meant to slay   130
By guns, invented since full many a day:
Our author swears it not; but who can know
How far the Devil and Jebusites may go?
This Plot, which failed for want of common sense,
Had yet a deep and dangerous consequence: 135
For, as when raging fevers boil the blood,
The standing lake soon floats into a flood,
And every hostile humor, which before
Slept quiet in its channels, bubbles o'er;
So several factions from this first ferment   140
Work up to foam, and threat the government.
Some by their friends, more by themselves thought wise,
Opposed the power to which they could not rise.
Some had in courts been great, and thrown from thence,
Like fiends were hardened in impenitence;   145
Some, by their monarch's fatal mercy, grown
From pardoned rebels kinsmen to the throne,
Were raised in power and public office high;
Strong bands, if bands ungrateful men could tie.
      Of these the false Achitophel[6] was first;   150
A name to all succeeding ages cursed:
For close designs, and crooked counsels fit;
Sagacious, bold, and turbulent of wit;[7]
Restless, unfixed in principles and place;
In power unpleased, impatient of disgrace: 155
A fiery soul, which, working out its way, ⎤
Fretted the pygmy body to decay,   ⎬
And o'er-informed the tenement of clay.[8] ⎦
A daring pilot in extremity;
Pleased with the danger, when the waves went high,   160
He sought the storms; but, for a calm unfit,

---

3. Brothels.
4. Dryden charges that the Anglican clergy ("Hebrew priests") resented proselytizing by Catholics chiefly because they stood to lose their tithes ("fleece").
5. The King.
6. Anthony Ashley Cooper, 1st earl of Shaftesbury (1621–1683). He had served in the parliamentary army and been a member of Cromwell's Council of State. He later helped bring back Charles, and in 1670 was made a member of the notorious Cabal Ministry, which formed an alliance with Louis XIV in which England betrayed her ally, Holland, and joined France in war against that country. In 1672 he became lord chancellor, but with the dissolution of the Cabal in 1673 he was removed from office. Lines 146–49 apply perfectly to him.
7. Unruly imagination.
8. The soul is thought of as the animating principle, the force that puts the body in motion. Shaftesbury's body seemed too small to house his fiery, energetic soul.

Would steer too nigh the sands, to boast his wit.
Great wits[9] are sure to madness near allied,
And thin partitions do their bounds divide;
Else why should he, with wealth and honor blest,   165
Refuse his age the needful hours of rest?
Punish a body which he could not please;
Bankrupt of life, yet prodigal of ease?
And all to leave what with his toil he won,
To that unfeathered two-legged thing,[1] a son;   170
Got, while his soul did huddled[2] notions try;
And born a shapeless lump, like anarchy.
In friendship false, implacable in hate,
Resolved to ruin or to rule the state.
To compass this the triple bond[3] he broke,   175
The pillars of the public safety shook,
And fitted Israel for a foreign yoke;
Then seized with fear, yet still affecting fame,
Usurped a patriot's all-atoning name.
So easy still it proves in factious times,   180
With public zeal to cancel private crimes.
How safe is treason, and how sacred ill,
Where none can sin against the people's will!
Where crowds can wink, and no offense be known,
Since in another's guilt they find their own!   185
Yet fame deserved, no enemy can grudge;
The statesman we abhor, but praise the judge.
In Israel's courts ne'er sat an Abbethdin[4]
With more discerning eyes, or hands more clean;
Unbribed, unsought, the wretched to redress;   190
Swift of dispatch, and easy of access.
Oh, had he been content to serve the crown,
With virtues only proper to the gown;
Or had the rankness of the soil been freed
From cockle, that oppressed the noble seed;   195
David for him his tuneful harp had strung,
And Heaven had wanted one immortal song.[5]
But wild Ambition loves to slide, not stand,
And Fortune's ice prefers to Virtue's land.
Achitophel, grown weary to possess   200
A lawful fame, and lazy happiness,

---

9. Men of genius. That genius and madness are akin is a very old idea.
1. Cf. Plato's definition of man: "a featherless biped."
2. Confused, hurried.
3. The Triple Alliance of England, Sweden, and Holland against France, 1668. Shaftesbury helped to bring about the war against Holland in 1672.
4. The chief of the seventy elders who composed the Jewish supreme court. The allusion is to Shaftesbury's serving as Lord Chancellor in 1672–73. Dryden's praise of Shaftesbury's integrity in this office, by suggesting a balanced judgment, makes his condemnation of the statesman more effective than it might otherwise have been.
5. I.e., David would have had occasion to write one less song of praise to Heaven. The reference may be to 2 Samuel 22 or to Psalm 4.

Disdained the golden fruit to gather free,
And lent the crowd his arm to shake the tree.
Now, manifest of[6] crimes contrived long since,
He stood at bold defiance with his prince;   205
Held up the buckler of the people's cause
Against the crown, and skulked behind the laws.
The wished occasion of the Plot he takes;
Some circumstances finds, but more he makes.
By buzzing emissaries fills the ears   210
Of listening crowds with jealousies[7] and fears
Of arbitrary counsels brought to light,
And proves the king himself a Jebusite.
Weak arguments! which yet he knew full well
Were strong with people easy to rebel.   215
For, governed by the moon, the giddy Jews
Tread the same track when she the prime renews;[8]
And once in twenty years, their scribes record,
By natural instinct they change their lord.
Achitophel still wants a chief, and none   220
Was found so fit as warlike Absalom:
Not that he wished his greatness to create
(For politicians neither love nor hate),
But, for he knew his title not allowed,
Would keep him still depending on the crowd,   225
That kingly power, thus ebbing out, might be
Drawn to the dregs of a democracy.[9]
Him he attempts with studied arts to please,
And sheds his venom in such words as these:
    "Auspicious prince, at whose nativity   230
Some royal planet[1] ruled the southern sky;
Thy longing country's darling and desire;
Their cloudy pillar and their guardian fire:[2]
Their second Moses, whose extended wand
Divides the seas, and shows the promised land;   235
Whose dawning day in every distant age
Has exercised the sacred prophet's rage:
The people's prayer, the glad diviners' theme,
The young men's vision, and the old men's dream![3]
Thee, savior, thee, the nation's vows[4] confess,   240

---

6. Detected in.

7. Suspicions.

8. The moon "renews her prime" when her several phases recur on the same day of the solar calendar—i.e., complete a cycle—as happens approximately every 20 years. The crisis between Charles I and Parliament began to grow acute about 1640; Charles II returned in 1660; it is now 1680 and a full cycle has been completed.

9. To Dryden, "democracy" meant popular government. The "dregs of a democracy" would be mob rule.

1. A planet whose influence destines him to kingship.

2. After their exodus from Egypt under the leadership of Moses, whose "extended wand" separated the waters of the Red Sea so that they crossed over on dry land, the Israelites were led in their 40-year wandering in the wilderness by a pillar of cloud by day and a pillar of fire by night. See Exodus 13–14.

3. Cf. Joel 2.28.

4. Solemn promises of fidelity.

And, never satisfied with seeing, bless:
Swift unbespoken pomps thy steps proclaim,
And stammering babes are taught to lisp thy name.
How long wilt thou the general joy detain,
Starve and defraud the people of thy reign?   245
Content ingloriously to pass thy days
Like one of Virtue's fools that feeds on praise;
Till thy fresh glories, which now shine so bright,
Grow stale and tarnish with our daily sight.
Believe me, royal youth, thy fruit must be   250
Or gathered ripe, or rot upon the tree.
Heaven has to all allotted, soon or late,
Some lucky revolution of their fate;
Whose motions if we watch and guide with skill
(For human good depends on human will),   255
Our Fortune rolls as from a smooth descent,
And from the first impression takes the bent;
But, if unseized, she glides away like wind,
And leaves repenting Folly far behind.
Now, now she meets you with a glorious prize,   260
And spreads her locks before her as she flies.⁵
Had thus old David, from whose loins you spring,
Not dared, when Fortune called him, to be king,
At Gath⁶ an exile he might still remain,
And heaven's anointing⁷ oil had been in vain.   265
Let his successful youth your hopes engage;
But shun the example of declining age;
Behold him setting in his western skies,
The shadows lengthening as the vapors rise.
He is not now, as when on Jordan's sand⁸   270
The joyful people thronged to see him land,
Covering the beach, and blackening all the strand;
But, like the Prince of Angels, from his height
Comes tumbling downward with diminished light;⁹
Betrayed by one poor plot to public scorn   275
(Our only blessing since his cursed return),
Those heaps of people which one sheaf did bind,
Blown off and scattered by a puff of wind.
What strength can he to your designs oppose,
Naked of friends, and round beset with foes?   280
If Pharaoh's¹ doubtful succor he should use,

---

5. Achitophel gives to Fortune the traditional attributes of the allegorical personification of Opportunity: bald except for a forelock, she can be seized only as she approaches.
6. Brussels, where Charles spent his last years in exile. David took refuge from Saul in Gath (1 Samuel 27.4).
7. After God rejected Saul, He sent Samuel to anoint the boy David, as a token that he should finally come to the throne (1 Samuel 16.1–13).
8. The seashore at Dover, where Charles landed (May 25, 1660).
9. Cf. the fall of Satan in *Paradise Lost*, which dims the brightness of the archangel. The choice of the undignified word "tumbling" is deliberate.
1. Louis XIV of France.

A foreign aid would more incense the Jews:
Proud Egypt would dissembled friendship bring;
Foment the war, but not support the king:
Nor would the royal party e'er unite   285
With Pharaoh's arms to assist the Jebusite;
Or if they should, their interest soon would break,
And with such odious aid make David weak.
All sorts of men by my successful arts,
Abhorring kings, estrange their altered hearts   290
From David's rule: and 'tis the general cry,
'Religion, commonwealth, and liberty.'[2]
If you, as champion of the public good,
Add to their arms a chief of royal blood,
What may not Israel hope, and what applause   295
Might such a general gain by such a cause?
Not barren praise alone, that gaudy flower
Fair only to the sight, but solid power;
And nobler is a limited command,
Given by the love of all your native land,   300
Than a successive title,[3] long and dark,
Drawn from the moldy rolls of Noah's ark."
      What cannot praise effect in mighty minds,
When flattery soothes, and when ambition blinds!
Desire of power, on earth a vicious weed,   305
Yet, sprung from high, is of celestial seed:
In God 'tis glory; and when men aspire,
'Tis but a spark too much of heavenly fire.
The ambitious youth, too covetous of fame,
Too full of angels' metal[4] in his frame,   310
Unwarily was led from virtue's ways,
Made drunk with honor, and debauched with praise.
Half loath, and half consenting to the ill
(For loyal blood within him struggled still),
He thus replied: "And what pretense have I   315
To take up arms for public liberty?
My father governs with unquestioned right;
The faith's defender, and mankind's delight,
Good, gracious, just, observant of the laws:
And heaven by wonders has espoused his cause.   320
Whom has he wronged in all his peaceful reign?
Who sues for justice to his throne in vain?
What millions has he pardoned of his foes.
Whom just revenge did to his wrath expose?
Mild, easy, humble, studious of our good,   325
Inclined to mercy, and averse from blood;

2. Cf. line 82 and note.
3. A title to the crown based on succession.
4. An alternative spelling of *mettle*, (i.e., spirit). But a pun on "metal" is intended, as is obvious from the pun "angel" (a purely intellectual being and a coin). Ambition caused the revolt of the angels in heaven.

If mildness ill with stubborn Israel suit,
His crime is God's beloved attribute.
What could he gain, his people to betray,
Or change his right for arbitrary sway?   330
Let haughty Pharaoh curse with such a reign
His fruitful Nile, and yoke a servile train.
If David's rule Jerusalem displease,
The Dog Star[5] heats their brains to this disease.
Why then should I, encouraging the bad,   335
Turn rebel and run popularly mad?
Were he a tyrant, who, by lawless might
Oppressed the Jews, and raised the Jebusite,
Well might I mourn; but nature's holy bands
Would curb my spirits and restrain my hands: 340
The people might assert[6] their liberty,
But what was right in them were crime in me.
His favor leaves me nothing to require,
Prevents my wishes, and outruns desire.
What more can I expect while David lives?   345
All but his kingly diadem he gives:
And that"—But there he paused; then sighing, said—
"Is justly destined for a worthier head.
For when my father from his toils shall rest
And late augment the number of the blest,   350
His lawful issue shall the throne ascend,
Or the collateral line,[7] where that shall end.
His brother, though oppressed with vulgar spite,
Yet dauntless, and secure of native right,
Of every royal virtue stands possessed;   355
Still dear to all the bravest and the best.
His courage foes, his friends his truth proclaim;
His loyalty the king, the world his fame.
His mercy even the offending crowd will find,
For sure he comes of a forgiving kind.[8]   360
Why should I then repine at heaven's decree,
Which gives me no pretense to royalty?
Yet O that fate, propitiously inclined,
Had raised my birth, or had debased my mind;
To my large soul not all her treasure lent,   365
And then betrayed it to a mean descent!
I find, I find my mounting spirits bold,
And David's part disdains my mother's mold.
Why am I scanted by a niggard birth?[9]
My soul disclaims the kindred of her earth;   370
And, made for empire, whispers me within,

5. Sirius, which in midsummer rises and sets with the sun and is thus associated with the maddening heat of the "dog days."
6. Claim.
7. In the event of Charles's dying without legiti- mate issue, the throne would constitutionally pass to his brother James, or his descendants, the "collateral line."
8. Race, in the sense of family.
9. I.e., why am I limited by a sordid birth?

'Desire of greatness is a godlike sin.' "
    Him staggering so when hell's dire agent found,[1]
While fainting Virtue scarce maintained her ground,
He pours fresh forces in, and thus replies: 375
    "The eternal god, supremely good and wise,
Imparts not these prodigious gifts in vain:
What wonders are reserved to bless your reign!
Against your will, your arguments have shown,
Such virtue's only given to guide a throne.   380
Not that your father's mildness I contemn,
But manly force becomes the diadem.
'Tis true he grants the people all they crave;
And more, perhaps, than subjects ought to have:
For lavish grants suppose a monarch tame,   385
And more his goodness than his wit[2] proclaim.
But when should people strive their bonds to break,
If not when kings are negligent or weak?
Let him give on till he can give no more,
The thrifty Sanhedrin[3] shall keep him poor;   390
And every shekel which he can receive,
Shall cost a limb of his prerogative.[4]
To ply him with new plots shall be my care;
Or plunge him deep in some expensive war;
Which when his treasure can no more supply,   395
He must, with the remains of kingship, buy.
His faithful friends our jealousies and fears
Call Jebusites, and Pharaoh's pensioners;
Whom when our fury from his aid has torn,
He shall be naked left to public scorn.   400
The next successor, whom I fear and hate,
My arts have made obnoxious to the state;
Turned all his virtues to his overthrow,
And gained our elders[5] to pronounce a foe.
His right, for sums of necessary gold,   405
Shall first be pawned, and afterward be sold;
Till time shall ever-wanting David draw,
To pass your doubtful title into law:
If not, the people have a right supreme
To make their kings; for kings are made for them.   410
All empire is no more than power in trust,
Which, when resumed, can be no longer just.
Succession, for the general good designed,
In its own wrong a nation cannot bind;

---

1. Observe the Miltonic inversion, which helps to maintain the epic tone.
2. Intelligence.
3. The highest judicial counsel of the Jews; here, Parliament.
4. The Whigs hoped to limit the special privileges of the Crown (the royal "prerogative") by refusing to vote money to Charles. He circumvented them by living on French subsidies and refusing to summon Parliament.
5. The chief magistrates and rulers of the Jews. Shaftesbury had won over ("gained") country gentlemen and nobles to his hostile view of James.

If altering that the people can relieve,   415
Better one suffer than a nation grieve.
The Jews well know their power: ere Saul they chose,[6]
God was their king, and God they durst depose.
Urge now your piety,[7] your filial name,
A father's right and fear of future fame;   420
The public good, that universal call,
To which even heaven submitted, answers all.
Nor let his love enchant your generous mind;
'Tis Nature's trick to propagate her kind.
Our fond begetters, who would never die,   425
Love but themselves in their posterity.
Or let his kindness by the effects be tried,
Or let him lay his vain pretense aside.
God said he loved your father; could he bring
A better proof than to anoint him king?   430
It surely showed he loved the shepherd well,
Who gave so fair a flock as Israel.
Would David have you thought his darling son?
What means he then, to alienate[8] the crown?
The name of godly he may blush to bear: 435
'Tis after God's own heart[9] to cheat his heir.
He to his brother gives supreme command;
To you a legacy of barren land,[1]
Perhaps the old harp, on which he thrums his lays,
Or some dull Hebrew ballad in your praise.   440
Then the next heir, a prince severe and wise,
Already looks on you with jealous eyes;
Sees through the thin disguises of your arts,
And marks your progress in the people's hearts.
Though now his mighty soul its grief contains,   445
He meditates revenge who least complains;
And, like a lion, slumbering in the way,
Or sleep dissembling, while he waits his prey,
His fearless foes within his distance draws,
Constrains his roaring, and contracts his paws;   450
Till at the last, his time for fury found,
He shoots with sudden vengeance from the ground;
The prostrate vulgar[2] passes o'er and spares,
But with a lordly rage his hunters tears.
Your case no tame expedients will afford: 455
Resolve on death, or conquest by the sword,
Which for no less a stake than life you draw;

---

6. Before Saul, the first king of Israel, came to the
throne, the Jews were governed by judges. Similarly Oliver Cromwell ("Saul") as Lord Protector
took over the reins of government, after he had
dissolved the Rump Parliament in 1653.
7. Dutifulness to a parent.
8. In law, to convey the title to property to another

person.
9. An irony: cf. line 7, note.
1. James was given the title of generalissimo in
1678. In 1679 Monmouth was banished and withdrew to Holland.
2. Common people.

And self-defense is nature's eldest law.
Leave the warm people no considering time;
For then rebellion may be thought a crime.   460
Prevail yourself of what occasion gives,
But try your title while your father lives;
And that your arms may have a fair pretense,[3]
Proclaim you take them in the king's defense;
Whose sacred life each minute would expose   465
To plots, from seeming friends, and secret foes.
And who can sound the depth of David's soul?
Perhaps his fear his kindness may control.
He fears his brother, though he loves his son,
For plighted vows too late to be undone.   470
If so, by force he wishes to be gained,
Like women's lechery, to seem constrained.[4]
Doubt not; but when he most affects the frown,
Commit a pleasing rape upon the crown.
Secure his person to secure your cause: 475
They who possess the prince, possess the laws."
       He said, and this advice above the rest
With Absalom's mild nature suited best:
Unblamed of life (ambition set aside),
Not stained with cruelty, nor puffed with pride,   480
How happy had he been, if destiny
Had higher placed his birth, or not so high!
His kingly virtues might have claimed a throne,
And blest all other countries but his own.
But charming greatness since so few refuse,   485
'Tis juster to lament him than accuse.
Strong were his hopes a rival to remove,
With blandishments to gain the public love;
To head the faction while their zeal was hot,
And popularly prosecute the Plot.   490
To further this, Achitophel unites
The malcontents of all the Israelites;
Whose differing parties he could wisely join,
For several ends, to serve the same design:
The best (and of the princes some were such),   495
Who thought the power of monarchy too much;
Mistaken men, and patriots in their hearts;
Not wicked, but seduced by impious arts.
By these the springs of property were bent,
And wound so high, they cracked the government.   500
The next for interest sought to embroil the state,
To sell their duty at a dearer rate;
And make their Jewish markets of the throne,
Pretending public good, to serve their own.

---

3. Pretext.   4. Forced.

Others thought kings an useless heavy load,   505
Who cost too much, and did too little good.
These were for laying honest David by,
On principles of pure good husbandry.[5]
With them joined all the haranguers of the throng,
That thought to get preferment by the tongue.   510
Who follow next, a double danger bring,
Not only hating David, but the king:
The Solymaean rout,[6] well-versed of old
In godly faction, and in treason bold;
Cowering and quaking at a conqueror's sword,   515
But lofty to a lawful prince restored;
Saw with disdain an ethnic[7] plot begun,
And scorned by Jebusites to be outdone.
Hot Levites[8] headed these; who, pulled before
From the ark, which in the Judges' days they bore,   520
Resumed their cant, and with a zealous cry
Pursued their old beloved theocracy:
Where Sanhedrin and priest enslaved the nation,
And justified their spoils by inspiration:[9]
For who so fit for reign as Aaron's race,[1]   525
If once dominion they could found in grace?
These led the pack; though not of surest scent,
Yet deepest-mouthed[2] against the government.
A numerous host of dreaming saints[3] succeed,
Of the true old enthusiastic breed: 530
'Gainst form and order they their power employ,
Nothing to build, and all things to destroy.
But far more numerous was the herd of such,
Who think too little, and who talk too much.
These out of mere instinct, they knew not why,   535
Adored their fathers' God and property;
And, by the same blind benefit of fate,
The Devil and the Jebusite did hate:
Born to be saved, even in their own despite,
Because they could not help believing right.   540
Such were the tools; but a whole Hydra more

---

5. Economy.
6. I.e., London rabble. Solyma was a name for Jerusalem.
7. Gentile; here, Roman Catholic.
8. I.e., Presbyterian clergymen. The tribe of Levi, assigned to duties in the tabernacle, carried the ark of the covenant during the 40-year sojourn in the wilderness (Numbers 4). Under the Commonwealth ("in the Judges' days") Presbyterianism became the state religion, and its clergy therefore "bore the ark." The Act of Uniformity (1662) forced the Presbyterian clergy out of their livings: in short, before the Popish Plot, they had been "pulled from the ark." They are represented here as joining the Whigs in the hope of restoring the Common-

wealth, "their old beloved theocracy."
9. Observe in these lines the cluster of disparaging words: "cant," "zealous," "inspiration." Dryden shared Samuel Butler's contempt for the irrationality of Dissenters.
1. Priests had to be descendants of Aaron (Exodus 28.1; Numbers 18.7).
2. Loudest. The phrase is applied to hunting dogs. "Pack" and "scent" sustain the image.
3. A term used by certain Dissenters for those elected to salvation. The extreme fanaticism of the "saints" and their claims to inspiration are characterized as a form of religious madness ("enthusiastic").

Remains, of sprouting heads too long to score.
Some of their chiefs were princes of the land:
In the first rank of these did Zimri[4] stand;
A man so various, that he seemed to be   545
Not one, but all mankind's epitome:
Stiff in opinions, always in the wrong;
Was everything by starts, and nothing long;
But, in the course of one revolving moon,
Was chymist,[5] fiddler, statesman, and buffoon: 550
Then all for women, painting, rhyming, drinking,
Besides ten thousand freaks that died in thinking.
Blest madman, who could every hour employ,
With something new to wish, or to enjoy!
Railing[6] and praising were his usual themes;   555
And both (to show his judgment) in extremes:
So over-violent, or over-civil,
That every man, with him, was God or Devil.
In squandering wealth was his peculiar art:
Nothing went unrewarded but desert.   560
Beggared by fools, whom still he found[7] too late,
He had his jest, and they had his estate.
He laughed himself from court; then sought relief
By forming parties, but could ne'er be chief;
For, spite of him, the weight of business fell   565
On Absalom and wise Achitophel:
Thus, wicked but in will, of means bereft,
He left not faction, but of that was left.

    Titles and names 'twere tedious to rehearse
Of lords, below the dignity of verse.   570
Wits, warriors, Commonwealth's men, were the best;
Kind husbands, and mere nobles, all the rest.
And therefore, in the name of dullness, be
The well-hung Balaam and cold Caleb, free;
And canting Nadab[8] let oblivion damn,   575
Who made new porridge for the paschal lamb,
Let friendship's holy band some names assure;
Some their own worth, and some let scorn secure.

---

4. George Villiers, 2nd duke of Buckingham (1628–1687), wealthy, brilliant, dissolute, unstable. He had been an influential member of the Cabal, but after 1673 had joined Shaftesbury in opposition to the Court party. This is the least political of the satirical portraits in the poem. Buckingham had been the chief author of *The Rehearsal* (1671), the play which satirized the heroic play and ridiculed Dryden in the character of Mr. Bayes. Politics gave Dryden an opportunity to retaliate. He comments on this portrait in his *Discourse Concerning the Original and Progress of Satire*. Dryden had two biblical Zimris in mind: the Zimri destroyed for his lustfulness and blasphemy (Numbers 25) and the conspirator and regicide of 1 Kings 16.8–20 and 2 Kings 9.31.

5. Chemist.
6. Reviling, abusing.
7. Found out; "still": constantly.
8. The identities of Balaam, Caleb, and Nadab have not been certainly established, although various Whig nobles have been suggested. For Balaam see Numbers 22–24; for Caleb, Numbers 13–14; for Nadab, Leviticus 10.1–2. "Well-hung" may mean "fluent of speech" or "sexually potent" or both; "cold" would contrast with the second meaning of "well-hung." "Canting" points to a Nonconformist, as does the obscure line 576, for Dissenters referred to the Book of Common Prayer contemptuously as "porridge," a hodge-podge, unsubstantial stuff. The "paschal lamb," the lamb slain at the Passover, is Christ.

Nor shall the rascal rabble here have place,
Whom kings no titles gave, and God no grace: 580
Not bull-faced Jonas,[9] who could statutes draw
To mean rebellion, and make treason law.
But he, though bad, is followed by a worse,
The wretch who heaven's anointed dared to curse:
Shimei,[1] whose youth did early promise bring 585
Of zeal to God and hatred to his king,
Did wisely from expensive sins refrain,
And never broke the Sabbath, but for gain;
Nor ever was he known an oath to vent,
Or curse, unless against the government. 590
Thus heaping wealth, by the most ready way
Among the Jews, which was to cheat and pray,
The city, to reward his pious hate
Against his master, chose him magistrate.
His hand a vare[2] of justice did uphold; 595
His neck was loaded with a chain of gold.
During his office, treason was no crime;
The sons of Belial[3] had a glorious time;
For Shimei, though not prodigal of pelf,
Yet loved his wicked neighbor as himself. 600
When two or three were gathered to declaim ⎤
Against the monarch of Jerusalem, ⎬
Shimei was always in the midst of them; ⎦
And if they cursed the king when he was by,
Would rather curse than break good company. 605
If any durst his factious friends accuse,
He packed a jury of dissenting Jews;
Whose fellow-feeling in the godly cause
Would free the suffering saint from human laws.
For laws are only made to punish those 610
Who serve the king, and to protect his foes.
If any leisure time he had from power
(Because 'tis sin to misemploy an hour),
His business was, by writing, to persuade
That kings were useless, and a clog to trade; 615
And, that his noble style he might refine,
No Rechabite[4] more shunned the fumes of wine.
Chaste were his cellars, and his shrieval board[5]

---

9. Sir Williams Jones, attorney general, had been largely responsible for the passage of the first Exclusion Bill by the House of Commons. He prosecuted the accused in the Popish Plot.
1. Shimei cursed and stoned David when he fled into the wilderness during Absalom's revolt (2 Samuel 16.5–14); his name is used here for one of the two sheriffs of London, Slingsby Bethel, a Whig, former republican, and virulent enemy of Charles. He packed juries with Whigs and so secured the acquittal of enemies of the court, among them

Shaftesbury himself.
2. Staff.
3. Sons of wickedness. Cf. Milton, *Paradise Lost* 1.490–505. Dryden probably intended a pun on Balliol, the Oxford college in which leading Whigs stayed during the brief and fateful meeting of Parliament at Oxford in 1681.
4. An austere Jewish sect that drank no wine (Jeremiah 35.2–19).
5. Sheriff's dinner table.

The grossness of a city feast abhorred:
His cooks, with long disuse, their trade forgot;   620
Cool was his kitchen, though his brains were hot,
Such frugal virtue malice may accuse,
But sure 'twas necessary to the Jews:
For towns once burnt[6] such magistrates require
As dare not tempt God's providence by fire.   625
With spiritual food he fed his servants well,
But free from flesh that made the Jews rebel;
And Moses' laws he held in more account,
For forty days of fasting in the mount.[7]
To speak the rest, who better are forgot,   630
Would tire a well-breathed witness of the Plot.
Yet, Corah,[8] thou shalt from oblivion pass:
Erect thyself, thou monumental brass,
High as the serpent of thy metal made,[9]
While nations stand secure beneath thy shade.   635
What though his birth were base, yet comets rise
From earthy vapors, ere they shine in skies.
Prodigious actions may as well be done
By weaver's issue,[1] as by prince's son.
This arch-attestor for the public good   640
By that one deed ennobles all his blood.
Who ever asked the witnesses' high race
Whose oath with martyrdom did Stephen grace?[2]
Ours was a Levite, and as times went then,
His tribe were God Almighty's gentlemen.   645
Sunk were his eyes, his voice was harsh and loud,
Sure signs he neither choleric[3] was nor proud:
His long chin proved his wit; his saintlike grace
A church vermilion, and a Moses' face.[4]
His memory, miraculously great,   650
Could plots, exceeding man's belief, repeat;
Which therefore cannot be accounted lies,
For human wit could never such devise.
Some future truths are mingled in his book;
But where the witness failed, the prophet spoke: 655
Some things like visionary flights appear;
The spirit caught him up, the Lord knows where,
And gave him his rabbinical degree,
Unknown to foreign university.[5]

6. London burned in 1666.
7. Mt. Sinai, where, during a fast of 40 days, Moses received the law (Exodus 34.28).
8. Or Korah, a rebellious Levite, swallowed up by the earth because of his crimes (Numbers 16). Corah is Titus Oates, the self-appointed, perjured, and "well-breathed" (long-winded) witness of the Plot.
9. Moses erected a brazen serpent to heal the Jews bitten by fiery serpents (Numbers 21.4–9). "Brass" also means "impudence" or "shamelessness."

1. Oates's father, a clergyman, belonged to an obscure family of ribbon weavers.
2. The first Christian martyr, accused by false witnesses (Acts 6–7).
3. Prone to anger.
4. Moses's face shone when he came down from Mt. Sinai with the tables of the law (Exodus 34.29–30). Oates's face suggests high living, not spiritual illumination.
5. Oates falsely claimed to be a Doctor of Divinity in the University of Salamanca.

His judgment yet his memory did excel; 660
Which pieced his wondrous evidence so well,
And suited to the temper of the times,
Then groaning under Jebusitic crimes.
Let Israel's foes suspect his heavenly call,
And rashly judge his writ apocryphal;[6] 665
Our laws for such affronts have forfeits made:
He takes his life, who takes away his trade.
Were I myself in witness Corah's place,
The wretch who did me such a dire disgrace
Should whet my memory, though once forgot, 670
To make him an appendix of my plot.
His zeal to heaven made him his prince despise,
And load his person with indignities;
But zeal peculiar privilege affords,
Indulging latitude to deeds and words; 675
And Corah might for Agag's murder[7] call,
In terms as coarse as Samuel used to Saul.
What others in his evidence did join
(The best that could be had for love or coin),
In Corah's own predicament will fall; 680
For *witness* is a common name to all.
　　Surrounded thus with friends of every sort,
Deluded Absalom forsakes the court:
Impatient of high hopes, urged with renown,
And fired with near possession of a crown. 685
The admiring crowd are dazzled with surprise,
And on his goodly person feed their eyes:
His joy concealed, he sets himself to show,
On each side bowing popularly[8] low;
His looks, his gestures, and his words he frames, 690
And with familiar ease repeats their names.
Thus formed by nature, furnished out with arts,
He glides unfelt into their secret hearts.
Then, with a kind compassionating look,
And sighs, bespeaking pity ere he spoke, 695
Few words he said; but easy those and fit,
More slow than Hybla-drops,[9] and far more sweet.
　　"I mourn, my countrymen, your lost estate;
Though far unable to prevent your fate:
Behold a banished man, for your dear cause 700
Exposed a prey to arbitrary laws!
Yet oh! that I alone could be undone,
Cut off from empire, and no more a son!

6. Not inspired, and hence excluded from Holy Writ.
7. Agag is probably one of the 5 Catholic peers executed for the Popish Plot in 1680, most likely Lord Stafford, against whom Oates fabricated testimony; almost certainly not, as is usually sug-

gested, Sir Edmund Berry Godfrey (cf. title note). For "Agag's murder" and Samuel's coarse terms to Saul, see 1 Samuel 15.
8. "So as to please the crowd" (Johnson's *Dictionary*).
9. The famous honey of Hybla in Sicily.

Now all your liberties a spoil are made; ⎤
Egypt and Tyrus[1] intercept your trade, ⎬ 705
And Jebusites your sacred rites invade. ⎦
My father, whom with reverence yet I name,
Charmed into ease, is careless of his fame;
And, bribed with petty sums of foreign gold,
Is grown in Bathsheba's[2] embraces old; 710
Exalts his enemies, his friends destroys;
And all his power against himself employs.
He gives, and let him give, my right away;
But why should he his own, and yours betray?
He only, he can make the nation bleed, 715
And he alone from my revenge is freed.
Take then my tears (with that he wiped his eyes),
'Tis all the aid my present power supplies:
No court-informer can these arms accuse;
These arms may sons against their fathers use: 720
And 'tis my wish, the next successor's reign
May make no other Israelite complain."
    Youth, beauty, graceful action seldom fail;
But common interest always will prevail;
And pity never ceases to be shown 725
To him who makes the people's wrongs his own.
The crowd (that still believe their kings oppress),
With lifted hands their young Messiah bless:
Who now begins his progress to ordain
With chariots, horsemen, and a numerous train; 730
From east to west his glories he displays,[3]
And, like the sun, the promised land surveys.
Fame runs before him as the morning star,
And shouts of joy salute him from afar:
Each house receives him as a guardian god, 735
And consecrates the place of his abode:
But hospitable treats did most commend
Wise Issachar,[4] his wealthy western friend.
This moving court, that caught the people's eyes,
And seemed but pomp, did other ends disguise: 740
Achitophel had formed it, with intent
To sound the depths, and fathom where it went,
The people's hearts; distinguish friends from foes,
And try their strength, before they came to blows.
Yet all was colored with a smooth pretense 745
Of specious love, and duty to their prince.
Religion, and redress of grievances,
Two names that always cheat and always please,

1. France and Holland.
2. With whom David committed adultery (2 Samuel 11); here, Charles II's French mistress, Louise de Keroualle, duchess of Portsmouth.
3. In 1680 Monmouth made a progress through the west of England, seeking popular support for his cause.
4. Thomas Thynne of Longleat. He entertained Monmouth on his journey in the west. "Wise" is, of course, ironic.

Are often urged; and good King David's life
Endangered by a brother and a wife.[5]   750
Thus, in a pageant show, a plot is made,
And peace itself is war in masquerade.
O foolish Israel! never warned by ill,
Still the same bait, and circumvented still!
Did ever men forsake their present ease,   755
In midst of health imagine a disease;
Take pains contingent mischiefs to foresee,
Make heirs for monarchs, and for God decree?
What shall we think![6] Can people give away
Both for themselves and sons, their native sway?   760
Then they are left defenseless to the sword
Of each unbounded, arbitrary lord:
And laws are vain, by which we right enjoy,
If kings unquestioned can those laws destroy.
Yet if the crowd be judge of fit and just,   765
And kings are only officers in trust,
Then this resuming covenant was declared
When kings were made, or is forever barred.
If those who gave the scepter could not tie
By their own deed their own posterity,   770
How then could Adam bind his future race?
How could his forfeit on mankind take place?
Or how could heavenly justice damn us all,
Who ne'er consented to our father's fall?
Then kings are slaves to those whom they command,   775
And tenants to their people's pleasure stand.
Add, that the power for property allowed
Is mischievously seated in the crowd;
For who can be secure of private right,
If sovereign sway may be dissolved by might?   780
Nor is the people's judgment always true:
The most may err as grossly as the few;
And faultless kings run down, by common cry,
For vice, oppression, and for tyranny.
What standard is there in a fickle rout,   785
Which, flowing to the mark,[7] runs faster out?
Nor only crowds, but Sanhedrins may be
Infected with this public lunacy,
And share the madness of rebellious times,
To murder monarchs for imagined crimes.[8]   790
If they may give and take whene'er they please,

---

5. Titus Oates had sworn that both James, duke
of York, and the queen were involved in a plot to
poison Charles II.
6. In the passage that follows, Dryden states his
political philosophy. He bases the royal authority
on a covenant entered into by the governor and
the governed.

7. Highwater mark. The fickle crowd flows and
ebbs like the tide, which is pulled back and forth
by the moon (hence *lunacy* after Latin "luna" or
moon).
8. An allusion to the execution of Charles I.

Not kings alone (the Godhead's images),
But government itself at length must fall
To nature's state, where all have right to all.
Yet, grant our lords the people kings can make,   795
What prudent men a settled throne would shake?
For whatsoe'er their sufferings were before,
That change they covet makes them suffer more.
All other errors but disturb a state,
But innovation is the blow of fate.   800
If ancient fabrics nod, and threat to fall,
To patch the flaws, and buttress up the wall,
Thus far 'tis duty; but here fix the mark;
For all beyond it is to touch our ark.[9]
To change foundations, cast the frame anew,   805
Is work for rebels, who base ends pursue,
At once divine and human laws control,
And mend the parts by ruin of the whole.
The tampering world is subject to this curse,
To physic their disease into a worse.   810
    Now what relief can righteous David bring?
How fatal 'tis to be too good a king!
Friends he has few, so high the madness grows:
Who dare be such, must be the people's foes:
Yet some there were, even in the worst of days;   815
Some let me name, and naming is to praise.
    In this short file Barzillai[1] first appears;
Barzillai, crowned with honor and with years:
Long since, the rising rebels he withstood
In regions waste, beyond the Jordan's flood: 820
Unfortunately brave to buoy the State;
But sinking underneath his master's fate:
In exile with his godlike prince he mourned;
For him he suffered, and with him returned.
The court he practiced, not the courtier's art: 825
Large was his wealth, but larger was his heart:
Which well the noblest objects knew to choose,
The fighting warrior, and recording Muse.
His bed could once a fruitful issue boast;
Now more than half a father's name is lost.   830
His eldest hope,[2] with every grace adorned,
By me (so Heaven will have it) always mourned,
And always honored, snatched in manhood's prime
By unequal fates, and Providence's crime:

9. Uzzah was struck dead because he sacrile-
giously touched the Ark of the Covenant. 2 Samuel 6. 6–7.
1. James Butler, duke of Ormond (1610–1688).
He was famous for his loyalty to the Stuart cause.
He fought for Charles I in Ireland, and when that
cause was hopeless, he joined Charles II in his exile

abroad. He spent a large fortune in behalf of the
king and continued to serve him loyally after the
Restoration.
2. Ormond's son, Thomas, earl of Ossory (1634–
1680), a famous soldier, and like his father devoted
to Charles II.

Yet not before the goal of honor won,   835
All parts fulfilled of subject and of son;
Swift was the race, but short the time to run.
O narrow circle, but of power divine,
Scanted in space, but perfect in thy line!
By sea, by land, thy matchless worth was known,   840
Arms thy delight, and war was all thy own:
Thy force, infused, the fainting Tyrians[3] propped;
And haughty Pharaoh found his fortune stopped.
Oh ancient honor! Oh unconquered hand,
Whom foes unpunished never could withstand!   845
But Israel was unworthy of thy name:
Short is the date of all immoderate fame.
It looks as Heaven our ruin had designed,
And durst not trust thy fortune and thy mind.
Now, free from earth, thy disencumbered soul   850
Mounts up, and leaves behind the clouds and starry pole:
From thence thy kindred legions mayst thou bring,
To aid the guardian angel of thy king.
Here stop my Muse, here cease thy painful flight;
No pinions can pursue immortal height: 855
Tell good Barzillai thou canst sing no more,
And tell thy soul she should have fled before:
Or fled she with his life, and left this verse
To hang on her departed patron's hearse?
Now take thy steepy flight from heaven, and see   860
If thou canst find on earth another *he*:
Another *he* would be too hard to find;
See then whom thou canst see not far behind.
Zadoc the priest,[4] whom, shunning power and place,
His lowly mind advanced to David's grace: 865
With him the Sagan of Jerusalem,
Of hospitable soul, and noble stem;
Him of the western dome, whose weighty sense
Flows in fit words and heavenly eloquence.
The prophets' sons, by such example led,   870
To learning and to loyalty were bred:
For colleges on bounteous kinds depend,
And never rebel was to arts a friend.
To these succeed the pillars of the laws,
Who best could plead, and best can judge a cause.   875
Next them a train of loyal peers ascend;
Sharp-judging Adriel, the Muses' friend,
Himself a Muse—in Sanhedrin's debate
True to his prince, but not a slave of state:

---

3. The Dutch.
4. William Sancroft, archbishop of Canterbury; the Sagan is Henry Compton, bishop of London; "Him of the western dome" is John Dolben, dean of Westminster; "The prophets' sons" are the boys of Westminster School, which Dryden had attended; Adriel is John Sheffield, earl of Mulgrave; Jotham, George Savile, marquis of Halifax; Hushai, Laurence Hyde, earl of Rochester; and Amiel is Edward Seymour, speaker of the House of Commons.

Whom David's love with honors did adorn,   880
That from his disobedient son were torn.
Jotham of piercing wit, and pregnant thought,
Indued by nature, and by learning taught
To move assemblies, who but only tried,
The worse a while, then chose the better side;   885
Nor chose alone, but turned the balance too;
So much the weight of one brave man can do.
Hushai, the friend of David in distress,
In public storms, of manly steadfastness:
By foreign treaties he informed his youth,   890
And joined experience to his native truth.
His frugal care supplied the wanting throne,
Frugal for that, but bounteous of his own:
'Tis easy conduct when exchequers flow,
But hard the task to manage well the low;   895
For sovereign power is too depressed or high,
When kings are forced to sell, or crowds to buy.
Indulge one labor more, my weary Muse,
For Amiel: who can Amiel's praise refuse?
Of ancient race by birth, but nobler yet   900
In his own worth, and without title great:
The Sanhedrin long time as chief he ruled,
Their reason guided, and their passion cooled:
So dexterous was he in the crown's defence,
So formed to speak a loyal nation's sense,   905
That, as their band was Israel's tribes in small,
So fit was he to represent them all.
Now rasher charioteers the seat ascend,
Whose loose careers his steady skill commend:
They like the unequal ruler of the day,   910
Misguide the seasons, and mistake the way;
While he withdrawn at their mad labor smiles,
And safe enjoys the sabbath of his toils.
　　These were the chief, a small but faithful band ⎫
Of worthies, in the breach who dared to stand,   ⎬   915
And tempt the united fury of the land.   ⎭
With grief they viewed such powerful engines bent,
To batter down the lawful government:
A numerous faction, with pretended frights,
In Sanhedrins to plume the regal rights;   920
The true successor from the court removed:[5]
The Plot, by hireling witnesses, improved.
These ills they saw, and, as their duty bound,
They showed the king the danger of the wound:
That no concessions from the throne would please,   925
But lenitives[6] fomented the disease;

---

5. The duke of York had been banished from Eng-   6. Any medicine that relieves pain.
land.

That Absalom, ambitious of the crown,
Was made the lure to draw the people down;
That false Achitophel's pernicious hate
Had turned the Plot to ruin Church and State: 930
The council violent, the rabble worse;
That Shimei taught Jerusalem to curse.
    With all these loads of injuries oppressed,
And long revolving in his careful breast,
The event of things, at last, his patience tired,   935
Thus from his royal throne, by Heaven inspired,
The godlike David spoke: with awful fear
His train their Maker in their master hear.
    "Thus long have I, by native mercy swayed,
My wrongs dissembled, my revenge delayed: 940
So willing to forgive the offending age,
So much the father did the king assuage.
But now so far my clemency they slight,
The offenders question my forgiving right.
That one was made for many, they contend;   945
But 'tis to rule; for that's a monarch's end.
They call my tenderness of blood, my fear;
Though manly tempers can the longest bear.
Yet, since they will divert my native course,
'Tis time to show I am not good by force.   950
Those heaped affronts that haughty subjects bring,
Are burdens for a camel, not a king:
Kings are the public pillars of the State,
Born to sustain and prop the nation's weight:
If my young Samson will pretend a call   955
To shake the column, let him share the fall:[7]
But, oh, that yet he would repent and live!
How easy 'tis for parents to forgive!
With how few tears a pardon might be won
From nature, pleading for a darling son!   960
Poor pitied youth, by my paternal care
Raised up to all the height his frame could bear:
Had God ordained his fate for empire born,
He would have given his soul another turn:
Gulled[8] with a patriot's name, whose modern sense
Is one that would by law supplant his prince: 965
The people's brave, the politician's tool;
Never was patriot yet, but was a fool.
Whence comes it that religion and the laws
Should more be Absalom's than David's cause?   970
His old instructor, ere he lost his place,
Was never thought indued with so much grace.[9]
Good heavens, how faction can a patriot paint!

---

7. Judges 16.
8. Deceived.

9. The earl of Shaftesbury.

My rebel ever proves my people's saint:
Would *they* impose an heir upon the throne?   975
Let Sanhedrins be taught to give their own.
A king's at least a part of government,
And mine as requisite as their consent;
Without my leave a future king to choose,
Infers a right the present to depose: 980
True, they petition me to approve their choice;
But Esau's hands suit ill with Jacob's voice.[1]
My pious subjects for my safety pray,
Which to secure, they take my power away.
From plots and treasons Heaven preserve my years,   985
But save me most from my petitioners.
Unsatiate as the barren womb or grave;
God cannot grant so much as they can crave.
What then is left but with a jealous eye
To guard the small remains of royalty?   990
The law shall still direct my peaceful sway,
And the same law teach rebels to obey:
Votes shall no more established power control—
Such votes as make a part exceed the whole:
No groundless clamors shall my friends remove,   995
Nor crowds have power to punish ere they prove:
For gods and godlike kings, their care express,
Still to defend their servants in distress.
O that my power to saving were confined: ⎤
Why am I forced, like Heaven, against my mind, ⎬   1000
To make examples of another kind? ⎦
Must I at length the sword of justice draw?
O curst effects of necessary law!
How ill my fear they by my mercy scan!
Beware the fury of a patient man.   1005
Law they require, let Law then show her face;
They could not be content to look on Grace,
Her hinder parts, but with a daring eye
To tempt the terror of her front and die.[2]
By their own arts, 'tis righteously decreed,   1010
Those dire artificers of death shall bleed.
Against themselves their witnesses will swear,
Till viper-like their mother Plot they tear:
And suck for nutriment that bloody gore,
Which was their principle of life before.   1015
Their Belial with their Belzebub[3] will fight;
Thus on my foes, my foes shall do me right:
Nor doubt the event; for factious crowds engage,
In their first onset, all their brutal rage.

---

1. Genesis 27.22.
2. Moses was not allowed to see the countenance of Jehovah. Exodus 33. 20–23.

3. Belial, the incarnation of all evil; Beelzebub, a god of the Philistines.

Then let 'em take an unresisted course,   1020
Retire and traverse, and delude their force:
But when they stand all breathless, urge the fight,
And rise upon 'em with redoubled might:
For lawful power is still superior found,
When long driven back, at length it stands the ground."   1025
    He said. The Almighty, nodding, gave consent;
And peals of thunder shook the firmament.
Henceforth a series of new time began,
The mighty years in long procession ran:
Once more the godlike David was restored,   1030
And willing nations knew their lawful lord.

[handwritten annotation: About a father picking one of his sons to succeed him in king of Dullness — Picks Flacknoe, says he is the best of all sons — Bards will write songs about him]

1681

Mac Flecknoe[1]
OR A SATIRE UPON THE TRUE-BLUE-PROTESTANT POET, T. S.

All human things are subject to decay,
And when fate summons, monarchs must obey.
This Flecknoe found, who, like Augustus,[2] young
Was called to empire, and had governed long;
In prose and verse, was owned, without dispute,   5

1. The victim of this superb satire, which is cast in the form of a mock-heroic episode, is Thomas Shadwell (1640–1692), the playwright, with whom Dryden had been on good terms for a number of years, certainly as late as March 1678. Shadwell considered himself the successor of Ben Jonson and the champion of the type of comedy that Jonson had written, the "comedy of humors," in which each character is presented under the domination of a single psychological trait or eccentricity, his humor. His plays are not without merit, but they are often clumsy and prolix, and certainly much inferior to Jonson's. For many years he had conducted a public argument with Dryden on the merits of Jonson's comedies, which he thought Dryden undervalued. Exactly what moved Dryden to attack him is a matter of conjecture: he may simply have grown progressively bored and irritated by Shadwell and his tedious argument. The poem seems to have been written in late 1678 or 1679 and to have circulated only in manuscript, until it was printed in 1682 in a pirated edition by an obscure publisher. By that time, the two playwrights were alienated by politics as well as by literary quarrels. Shadwell was a violent Whig and the reputed author of a sharp attack on Dryden as the Tory author of *Absalom and Achitophel* and *The Medal*. It was probably for this reason that the printer added the subtitle referring to Shadwell's Whiggism in the phrase "true-blue-Protestant poet." Political passions were running high and sales would be helped if the poem seemed to refer to the events of the day.

Whereas Butler had debased and degraded his victims by using burlesque, caricature, and the grotesque, Dryden exposed Shadwell to ridicule by using the devices of mock-epic, which treats the low, mean, or absurd in the grand language, lofty style, and solemn tone of epic poetry. The obvious disparity between subject and style makes the satiric point. In 1678 an execrable Irish poet and playwright, Richard Flecknoe, died. Dryden conceived the idea of presenting Shadwell (the self-proclaimed heir of Ben Jonson, the laureate) as the son and successor of Flecknoe—hence *Mac* (i.e., son of) *Flecknoe*—from whom he inherits the throne of dullness. Flecknoe in the triple role of king, priest, and poet hails his successor, pronounces a panegyric on his perfect fitness for the throne, anoints and crowns him, foretells his glorious reign, and, as he sinks (leaden dullness cannot soar), leaves his mantle to fall symbolically upon Shadwell's shoulders. The poem abounds in literary allusions—to Roman legend and history and to the *Aeneid*; to Cowley's fragmentary epic, *The Davideis*, and to *Paradise Lost*; and to Shadwell's own plays. Biblical allusions add an unexpected dimension of incongruous dignity to the low scene. The coronation takes place in the City, to the plaudits of the citizens, who are fit to admire only what is dull. In 217 lines Dryden created an image of Shadwell which has fixed his reputation to this day.

2. In 31 B.C. Octavian became the first Roman emperor at the age of 32. He assumed the title Augustus in 27 B.C.

Through all the realms of Nonsense, absolute.
This aged prince, now flourishing in peace,
And blest with issue of a large increase,
Worn out with business, did at length debate
To settle the succession of the state;   10
And, pondering which of all his sons was fit
To reign, and wage immortal war with wit,
Cried: " 'Tis resolved; for nature pleads that he
Should only rule, who most resembles me.
Sh——[3] alone my perfect image bears,   15
Mature in dullness from his tender years:
Sh—— alone, of all my sons, is he
Who stands confirmed in full stupidity.
The rest to some faint meaning make pretense,
But Sh—— never deviates into sense.   20
Some beams of wit on other souls may fall,
Strike through, and make a lucid interval;
But Sh——'s genuine night admits no ray,
His rising fogs prevail upon the day.
Besides, his goodly fabric[4] fills the eye,   25
And seems designed for thoughtless majesty:
Thoughtless as monarch oaks that shade the plain,
And, spread in solemn state, supinely reign.
Heywood and Shirley[5] were but types of thee,
Thou last great prophet of tautology.[6]   30
Even I, a dunce of more renown than they,
Was sent before but to prepare thy way;
And, coarsely clad in Norwich drugget,[7] came
To teach the nations in thy greater name.[8]
My warbling lute, the lute I whilom[9] strung,   35
When to King John of Portugal I sung,
Was but the prelude to that glorious day,
When thou on silver Thames didst cut thy way,
With well-timed oars before the royal barge,
Swelled with the pride of thy celestial charge;   40
And big with hymn, commander of a host,
The like was ne'er in Epsom blankets tossed.[1]
Methinks I see the new Arion[2] sail,

3. Thomas Shadwell. The initial and second letter of the name followed by a dash give the appearance, but only the appearance, of protecting Dryden's victim by concealing his name. A common device in the satire of the period.
4. His body. Shadwell was a corpulent man.
5. Thomas Heywood (ca. 1570–1641) and James Shirley (1596–1666), playwrights popular before the closing of the theaters in 1642 but now out of fashion. They are introduced here as "types" (i.e., prefigurings) of Shadwell, in the sense that Solomon was regarded as an Old Testament prefiguring of Christ, the "last [final] great prophet."
6. Unnecessary repetition of meaning in different words.

7. A coarse woolen cloth.
8. The parallel between Flecknoe, as forerunner of Shadwell, and John the Baptist, as forerunner of Jesus, is made plain in lines 32–34 by the use of details and even words taken from Matthew 3.3–4 and John 1.23.
9. Formerly. Flecknoe boasted of the patronage of the Portuguese king.
1. A reference to Shadwell's comedy Epsom Wells and to the farcical scene in his Virtuoso, in which Sir Samuel Hearty is tossed in a blanket.
2. A legendary Greek poet. Returning home by sea, he was robbed and thrown overboard by the sailors, but was saved by a dolphin which had been charmed by his music.

The lute still trembling underneath thy nail.
At thy well-sharpened thumb from shore to shore   45
The treble squeaks for fear, the basses roar;
Echoes from Pissing Alley Sh—— call,
And Sh—— they resound from Aston Hall.
About thy boat the little fishes throng,
As at the morning toast[3] that floats along.   50
Sometimes, as prince of thy harmonious band,
Thou wield'st thy papers in thy threshing hand,
St. André's[4] feet ne'er kept more equal time,
Not ev'n the feet of thy own *Psyche's* rhyme;
Though they in number as in sense excel: 55
So just, so like tautology, they fell,
That, pale with envy, Singleton[5] forswore
The lute and sword, which he in triumph bore,
And vowed he ne'er would act Villerius[6] more."
Here stopped the good old sire, and wept for joy   60
In silent raptures of the hopeful boy.
All arguments, but most his plays, persuade,
That for anointed[7] dullness he was made.
   Close to the walls which fair Augusta[8] bind
(The fair Augusta much to fears inclined),   65
An ancient fabric[9] raised to inform the sight,
There stood of yore, and Barbican it hight:
A watchtower once; but now, so fate ordains,
Of all the pile an empty name remains.
From its old ruins brothel houses rise,   70
Scenes of lewd loves, and of polluted joys,
Where their vast courts the mother-strumpets keep,
And, undisturbed by watch, in silence sleep.
Near these a Nursery[1] erects its head,
Where queens are formed, and future heroes bred;   75
Where unfledged actors learn to laugh and cry,
Where infant punks[2] their tender voices try,
And little Maximins[3] the gods defy.
Great Fletcher[4] never treads in buskins here,
Nor greater Jonson dares in socks appear;   80
But gentle Simkin[5] just reception finds
Amidst this monument of vanished minds:

---

3. Sewage.
4. A French dancer who designed the choreography of Shadwell's opera *Psyche* (1675). Dryden's sneer in the next line at the mechanical metrics of the songs in *Psyche* is justified.
5. John Singleton (d. 1686), a musician at the Theatre Royal.
6. A character in Sir William Davenant's *Siege of Rhodes* (1656), the first English opera.
7. The anticipated phrase is "anointed *majesty*." English kings are anointed with oil at their coronations.
8. London. The next line alludes to the fears excited by the Popish Plot (cf. *Absalom and Achitophel*).
9. Building.
1. The name of a training school for young actors.
2. Prostitutes.
3. Maximin is the cruel emperor in Dryden's *Tyrannic Love* (1669), notorious for his bombast.
4. John Fletcher (1579–1625), the playwright and collaborator with Francis Beaumont (ca. 1584–1616). "Buskins" and "socks" were the symbols of tragedy and comedy.
5. A popular character in low farces.

Pure clinches[6] the suburbian Muse affords,
And Panton[7] waging harmless war with words.
Here Flecknoe, as a place to fame well known,   85
Ambitiously design'd his Sh——'s throne;
For ancient Dekker[8] prophesied long since, ⎤
That in this pile would reign a mighty prince, ⎬
Born for a scourge of wit, and flail of sense; ⎦
To whom true dullness should some *Psyches* owe,   90
But worlds of *Misers* from his pen should flow;
Humorists and *Hypocrites*[9] it should produce,
Whole Raymond families, and tribes of Bruce.
    Now Empress Fame had published the renown
Of Sh——'s coronation through the town.   95
Roused by report of Fame, the nations meet,
From near Bunhill, and distant Watling Street.[1]
No Persian carpets spread the imperial way,
But scattered limbs of mangled poets lay;
From dusty shops neglected authors come,   100
Martyrs of pies, and relics of the bum.[2]
Much Heywood, Shirley, Ogilby[3] there lay,
But loads of Sh—— almost choked the way.
Bilked stationers[4] for yeomen stood prepared,
And Herringman was captain of the guard.   105
The hoary prince in majesty appeared,
High on a throne of his own labors reared.
At his right hand our young Ascanius[5] sate,
Rome's other hope, and pillar of the state.
His brows thick fogs, instead of glories, grace,   110
And lambent dullness played around his face.
As Hannibal did to the altars come,
Sworn by his sire a mortal foe to Rome,[6]
So Sh——swore, nor should his vow be vain,
That he till death true dullness would maintain;   115
And, in his father's right, and realm's defense,
Ne'er to have peace with wit, nor truce with sense.
The king himself the sacred unction[7] made,

---

6. Puns.
7. Said to have been a celebrated punster.
8. Thomas Dekker (ca. 1572–1632), the playwright, whom Jonson had satirized in *The Poetaster*.
9. Three of Shadwell's plays; *The Hypocrite*, a failure, was not published. "Raymond" and "Bruce" (line 94) are characters in *The Humorists* and *The Virtuoso* respectively.
1. Since Bunhill is about a quarter of a mile and Watling Street little more than half a mile from the site of the Nursery, where the coronation is held, Shadwell's fame is narrowly circumscribed. Moreover, his subjects live in the heart of the City, regarded by men of wit and fashion as the abode of bad taste and middle-class vulgarity.
2. Unsold books eventually went to bakers' shops

and privies.
3. John Ogilby, a translator of Homer and Virgil, ridiculed by both Dryden and Pope as a bad poet.
4. Cheated publishers, who acted as "yeomen" of the guard, led by Henry Herringman, who until 1679 was the publisher of both Shadwell and Dryden.
5. Or Ïulus, son of Aeneas; Virgil referred to him as "*spes altera Romae*" ("Rome's other hope"; *Aeneid* 12.168). As Troy fell, he was marked as favored by the gods when a flickering ("lambent") flame played round his head (*Aeneid* 2.680–84).
6. Hannibal, who almost conquered Rome in 216 B.C., during the 2nd Punic War, took this oath at the age of 9 (Livy 21.1).
7. The sacramental oil, used in the coronation.

As king by office, and as priest by trade.
In his sinister[8] hand, instead of ball,   120
He placed a mighty mug of potent ale;
Love's Kingdom to his right he did convey,
At once his scepter, and his rule of sway;
Whose righteous lore the prince had practiced young,
And from whose loins recorded *Psyche* sprung.   125
His temples, last, with poppies were o'erspread,
That nodding seemed to consecrate his head.
Just at that point of time, if fame not lie,
On his left hand twelve reverend owls did fly.[9]
So Romulus, 'tis sung, by Tiber's brook,   130
Presage of sway from twice six vultures took.
The admiring throng loud acclamations make,
And omens of his future empire take.
The sire then shook the honors[1] of his head,
And from his brows damps of oblivion shed   135
Full on the filial dullness: long he stood,
Repelling from his breast the raging god;
At length burst out in this prophetic mood:
     "Heavens bless my son, from Ireland let him reign
To far Barbadoes on the western main;[2]   140
Of his dominion may no end be known,
And greater than his father's be his throne;
Beyond *Love's Kingdom* let him stretch his pen!"
He paused, and all the people cried, "Amen."
Then thus continued he: "My son, advance   145
Still in new impudence, new ignorance.
Success let others teach, learn thou from me
Pangs without birth, and fruitless industry.
Let V*irtuosos* in five years be writ;
Yet not one thought accuse thy toil of wit.   150
Let gentle George[3] in triumph tread the stage,
Make Dorimant betray, and Loveit rage;
Let Cully, Cockwood, Fopling, charm the pit,
And in their folly show the writer's wit.
Yet still thy fools shall stand in thy defense,   155
And justify their author's want of sense.
Let 'em be all by thy own model made
Of dullness, and desire no foreign aid;
That they to future ages may be known,
Not copies drawn, but issue of thy own.   160

8. Left. During his coronation a British monarch holds two symbols of kingship: a globe ("ball") representing the world in his left hand, a scepter in his right. In lines 121–27, Shadwell's symbols of monarchy—a mug of ale; Flecknoe's dreary play, *Love's Kingdom*; a crown of poppies—suggest heaviness, dullness, drowsiness. The poppies also refer obliquely to Shadwell's addiction to opium.
9. Birds of night, appropriate substitutes for the 12 vultures whose flight confirmed to Romulus the destined site of Rome, of which he was founder and king.
1. Ornaments, hence locks.
2. Shadwell's empire is vast but empty.
3. Sir George Etherege (ca. 1635–1691), a writer of brilliant comedies. In the next couplet Dryden names characters from his plays.

Nay, let thy men of wit too be the same,
All full of thee, and differing but in name.
But let no alien S—dl—y[4] interpose,
To lard with wit[5] thy hungry *Epsom* prose.
And when false flowers of rhetoric thou wouldst cull,   165
Trust nature, do not labor to be dull;
But write thy best, and top; and, in each line,
Sir Formal's[6] oratory will be thine:
Sir Formal, though unsought, attends thy quill,
And does thy northern dedications[7] fill.   170
Nor let false friends seduce thy mind to fame,
By arrogating Jonson's hostile name.
Let father Flecknoe fire thy mind with praise,
And uncle Ogilby thy envy raise.
Thou art my blood, where Jonson has no part: 175
What share have we in nature, or in art?
Where did his wit on learning fix a brand,
And rail at arts he did not understand?
Where made he love in Prince Nicander's vein,[8]
Or swept the dust in *Psyche's* humble strain?   180
Where sold he bargains,[9] 'whip-stitch, kiss my arse,'
Promised a play and dwindled to a farce?[1]
When did his Muse from Fletcher scenes purloin,
As thou whole Eth'rege dost transfuse to thine?
But so transfused, as oil on water's flow,   185
His always floats above, thine sinks below.
This is thy province, this thy wondrous way,
New humors to invent for each new play:
This is that boasted bias[2] of thy mind,
By which one way, to dullness, 'tis inclined;   190
Which makes thy writings lean on one side still,
And, in all changes, that way bends thy will.
Nor let thy mountain-belly make pretense
Of likeness; thine's a tympany[3] of sense.
A tun[4] of man in thy large bulk is writ,   195
But sure thou'rt but a kilderkin of wit.
Like mine, thy gentle numbers feebly creep;
Thy tragic Muse gives smiles, thy comic sleep.
With whate'er gall thou sett'st thyself to write,
Thy inoffensive satires never bite.   200

4. Sir Charles Sedley (1638–1701), wit, rake, poet, playwright. Dryden hints that he contributed more than the prologue to Shadwell's *Epsom Wells*.
5. The phrase "lard with wit" recalls a sentence in Burton's *Anatomy of Melancholy*: "They lard their lean books with the fat of others' works."
6. Sir Formal Trifle, the ridiculous and vapid orator in *The Virtuoso*.
7. Shadwell frequently dedicated his works to the duke of Newcastle and members of his family.
8. In *Psyche*.
9. To "sell bargains" is to answer an innocent question with a coarse or indecent phrase as in this line. "Whipstitch" is a nonsense word frequently used by Sir Samuel Hearty in *The Virtuoso*.
1. Low comedy which depends largely on situation rather than wit, consistently condemned by Dryden and other serious playwrights.
2. In bowling, the spin given to the bowl that causes it to swerve. Dryden closely parodies a passage in Shadwell's epilogue to *The Humorists*.
3. A swelling in some part of the body caused by wind.
4. A large wine cask. "Kilderkin": a very small cask.

In thy felonious heart though venom lies,
It does but touch thy Irish pen,[5] and dies.
Thy genius calls thee not to purchase fame
In keen iambics,[6] but mild anagram.
Leave writing plays, and choose for thy command   205
Some peaceful province in acrostic land.
There thou may'st wings display and altars raise,
And torture one poor word ten thousand ways.[7]
Or, if thou wouldst thy different talent suit,
Set thy own songs, and sing them to thy lute."   210
  He said: but his last words were scarcely heard⎫
For Bruce and Longville had a trap prepared,   ⎬
And down they sent the yet declaiming bard.[8]   ⎭
Sinking he left his drugget robe behind,
Borne upwards by a subterranean wind.   215
The mantle fell to the young prophet's part,[9]
With double portion of his father's art.

ca. 1679   1682

To the Memory of Mr. Oldham[1]

Farewell, too little, and too lately known,
Whom I began to think and call my own:
For sure our souls were near allied, and thine
Cast in the same poetic mold with mine.
One common note on either lyre did strike,
And knaves and fools[2] we both abhorred alike.   5
To the same goal did both our studies drive;
The last set out the soonest did arrive.
Thus Nisus[3] fell upon the slippery place,
While his young friend performed and won the race.   10
O early ripe! to thy abundant store
What could advancing age have added more?
It might (what nature never gives the young)
Have taught the numbers[4] of thy native tongue.
But satire needs not those, and wit will shine   15

5. Flecknoe was Irish, and so his son must be Irish. Ireland suggested only poverty, superstition, and barbarity to 17th-century Londoners.
6. Sharp satire.
7. "Anagram": the transposition of letters in a word so as to make a new one; "acrostic": a poem in which the first letter of each line, read downward, makes up the name of the person or thing that is the subject of the poem; "wings" and "altars" refer to poems in the shape of these objects as in George Herbert's *Easter Wings* and *The Altar.* Dryden is citing instances of triviality and overingenuity in literature.
8. In *The Virtuoso,* Bruce and Longville play this trick on Sir Formal Trifle while he makes a speech.

9. When the prophet Elijah was carried to heaven in a chariot of fire borne on a whirlwind, his mantle fell on his successor, the younger prophet Elisha (2 Kings 2.8–14). Flecknoe, prophet of dullness, naturally cannot ascend, but must sink.
1. John Oldham (1653–1683), the young poet whose *Satires upon the Jesuits* (1681) won Dryden's admiration. This elegy was published in Oldham's *Remains in Verse and Prose* (1684).
2. The objects of satire.
3. Nisus, on the point of winning a foot race, slipped in a pool of blood; his "young friend" was Euryalus (Virgil, *Aeneid* 5.315–39).
4. Metrics, verse.

Through the harsh cadence of a rugged line.[5]
A noble error, and but seldom made,
When poets are by too much force betrayed.
Thy generous fruits, though gathered ere their prime, ⎫
Still showed a quickness;[6] and maturing time   ⎬ 20
But mellows what we write to the dull sweets of rhyme. ⎭
Once more, hail and farewell;[7] farewell, thou young,
But ah too short, Marcellus[8] of our tongue;
Thy brows with ivy, and with laurels bound;[9]
But fate and gloomy night encompass thee around.   25

1684

Ode to Mrs. Anne Killigrew   Like Milton's *Lycidas*, Dryden's
ode to Anne Killigrew is not so much the expression of private grief as it is a
decorous ceremonial gesture dignifying a public occasion. In both poems
the death of an individual becomes the point of departure for the treatment
of larger topics. Killigrew's modest talent for poetry and painting prompted
Dryden to consider the arts themselves, their present state in a corrupt age,
their central role in civilization, their service to virtue and religion. In the
course of the poem, the dead woman is transformed into a symbol of the
sister arts themselves, what they are, and what, on earth, they might become.
Although *Lycidas* is cast in the traditional mode of the pastoral lament, and
Anne Killigrew in the form of a eulogistic memorial, both poems develop
classical and Christian themes which had become conventions of the funeral
poem: the death of the young and promising, the praise of their genius and
virtues, a lament for the times which suffer such loss, and a consolation,
offered by describing the reception of the soul of the dead into heaven.

Dryden's poem, in form, is an irregular ode, a lyric poem which develops
a serious theme in a dignified or exalted manner. The "greater ode," of
which this is the finest example in seventeenth-century poetry, was associated with the odes of Pindar, the lyric poet of fifth-century Greece, whose
intricate metrics, bold imagery, and intense and energetic power were aspired
to (seldom with success) by English poets throughout our period. (See headnote above to Ben Jonson's *To the Immortal Memory . . . of . . . Sir Lucius
Cary and Sir Henry Morison*.)

In 1656 Abraham Cowley published loose paraphrases of two of Pindar's
odes in which he abandoned the formal structure of the originals in favor of
irregular meters and irregularly constructed stanzas, while trying to preserve
Pindar's rapture, boldness, and sublimity. Thanks to Cowley's popularity,
his irregular Pindarics became the standard of what the age considered the
loftiest sort of lyric poetry. But Dryden declared that Cowley's odes lacked

---

5. Dryden repeats the Renaissance idea that the
satirist should avoid smoothness and affect rough
meters ("harsh cadence").
6. Sharpness of flavor.
7. Dryden echoes the famous words that conclude
Catullus's elegy to his brother: "*Atque in perpe-
tuum, frater, ave atque vale*" ("And forever, brother,
hail and farewell!").

8. The nephew of Augustus, adopted by him as
his successor. After winning military fame as a
youth, he died at the age of 20. Virgil celebrated
him in the *Aeneid* 6.854–86; the last line of Dryden's poem is a reminiscence of *Aeneid* 6.866.
9. The poet's wreath. Cf. Milton's *Lycidas*, lines
1–2.

"somewhat of a finer turn and more lyrical verse," which should consist in "the warmth and vigor of fancy, the masterly figures, and the copiousness of imagination" (Ker, *Essays* 1.267–268). In this poem he tries to raise the greater ode to its proper heights.

"Mrs." is an abbreviation of "Mistress," used at this time for our "Miss."

To the Pious Memory of the Accomplished Young Lady Mrs. Anne Killigrew

EXCELLENT IN THE TWO SISTER ARTS OF POESY AND PAINTING.

AN ODE

1

Thou youngest virgin-daughter of the skies,
Made in the last promotion of the blest,
Whose palms,[1] new plucked from paradise,
In spreading branches more sublimely rise,
Rich with immortal green above the rest;   5
Whether, adopted to some neighboring star,
Thou roll'st above us in thy wandering race,
     Or in procession fixed and regular,
     Moved with the heavens' majestic pace,
     Or called to more superior bliss,   10
Thou tread'st with seraphims the vast abyss:[2]
Whatever happy region is thy place,
Cease thy celestial song a little space;
Thou wilt have time enough for hymns divine,
     Since heaven's eternal year is thine.   15
Hear then a mortal Muse thy praise rehearse,
     In no ignoble verse;
But such as thy own voice did practice here,
When thy first fruits of poesy were given,
To make thyself a welcome inmate there,   20
        While yet a young probationer,
        And candidate of heaven.

2

If by traduction came thy mind,
     Our wonder is the less to find
A soul so charming from a stock so good;   25
Thy father was transfused into thy blood:[3]

---

1. The symbol of victory (cf. Revelation 7.9).
2. Dryden is speculating on where the soul of the dead poetess has come to rest: is she the tutelary deity of a planet ("neighboring star")? or of one of the remote "fixed" stars? or does she enjoy the higher ("superior") bliss of having joined the "seraphim," the guardians of the throne of God? (cf. Isaiah 6). Like Milton, Dryden makes use of the Ptolemaic universe of concentric spheres moving around the earth "in procession fixed and regular."
3. The idea that the soul is transmitted by the father at the moment of conception. Since Henry Killigrew had written a tragedy, his daughter is said to have inherited a poet's soul from him. In lines 29–32, Dryden proposes the theory that the soul exists before birth, and less seriously that through the ages it transmigrates from body to body.

So wert thou born into the tuneful strain
(An early, rich, and inexhausted vein).
   But if thy pre-existing soul
   Was formed at first with myriads more,   30
It did through all the mighty poets roll
   Who Greek or Latin laurels wore,
And was that Sappho last, which once it was before.[4]
   If so, then cease thy flight, O heaven-born mind!
   Thou hast no dross to purge from thy rich ore;   35
   Nor can thy soul a fairer mansion find
   Than was the beauteous frame she left behind:
Return, to fill or mend the choir of thy celestial kind.

3

   May we presume to say that at thy birth
New joy was sprung in heaven, as well as here on earth?   40
    For sure the milder planets did combine ⎫
    On thy auspicious horoscope to shine,[5] ⎬
    And even the most malicious were in trine. ⎭
   Thy brother-angels at thy birth
    Strung each his lyre, and tuned it high,   45
    That all the people of the sky
   Might know a poetess was born on earth.
    And then, if ever, mortal ears
    Had heard the music of the spheres!
   And if no clustering swarm of bees   50
   On thy sweet mouth distilled their golden dew,[6]
    'Twas that such vulgar miracles
    Heaven had not leisure to renew:
   For all the blest fraternity of love
Solemnized there thy birth, and kept thy holiday above.   55

4

   O gracious God! how far have we
Profaned thy heavenly gift of poesy!
Made prostitute and profligate the Muse,
Debased to each obscene and impious use,
Whose harmony was first ordained above   60
For tongues of angels, and for hymns of love!
O wretched we! why were we hurried down
   This lubric and adulterate[7] age
(Nay, added fat pollutions of our own)
   To increase the steaming ordures of the stage?   65
What can we say to excuse our second fall?

<hr/>

4. Mrs. Killigrew is said to have been Sappho (the Greek lyric poetess of the 7th century B.C.) twice: "once before," when her soul transmigrated into Sappho's body, and most recently ("last"), when it inhabited the body of the modern Sappho, Anne Killigrew.
5. The familiar idea that character and destiny are determined by the position of the planets at the moment of birth ("horoscope"). Mrs. Killigrew's horoscope was fortunate ("auspicious"): even those planets that are usually baleful ("malicious") were "in trine"—120 degrees apart and hence favorable in their influence.
6. It was said that bees clustered on the lips of the infant Pindar, thus foretelling his greatness as a lyric poet.
7. Lewd and corrupted.

Let this thy vestal,[8] Heaven, atone for all:
Her Arethusan stream remains unsoiled,
Unmixed with foreign filth, and undefiled;
Her wit was more than man, her innocence a child!　　　70

5

Art she had none, yet wanted none,
For nature did that want supply;
So rich in treasures of her own,
She might our boasted stores defy:
Such noble vigor did her verse adorn　　　75
That it seemed borrowed where 'twas only born.
Her morals too were in her bosom bred,
　By great examples daily fed,
What in the best of books, her father's life, she read. ⎬
And to be read herself she need not fear;　　　80
Each test and every light her Muse will bear, ⎬
Though Epictetus with his lamp were there.[9]
Even love (for love sometimes her Muse expressed)
Was but a lambent flame[1] which played about her breast,
Light as the vapors of a morning dream;　　　85
So cold herself, whilst she such warmth expressed,
'Twas Cupid bathing in Diana's stream.

6

Born to the spacious empire of the Nine,[2]
One would have thought she should have been content
To manage well that mighty government;　　　90
But what can young ambitious souls confine?
　To the next realm she stretched her sway, ⎬
　For Painture[3] near adjoining lay,
A plenteous province, and alluring prey. ⎬
A chamber of dependences[4] was framed　　　95
(As conquerors will never want pretense,
　When armed, to justify the offense)
And the whole fief in right of Poetry she claimed.
The country open lay without defense;
For poets frequent inroads there had made,　　　100
　And perfectly could represent
　The shape, the face, with every lineament;

---

8. I.e., thy virgin. The Roman "vestal" virgins guarded the fire in the Temple of Vesta, goddess of the hearth. For "Arethusan stream," cf. Milton's *Lycidas*, line 85.
9. A collector is said to have paid a large sum for the lamp of the philosopher Epictetus in the faith that owning it would make him wise. Dryden merely means that Anne Killigrew's poems would appear pure even if judged in the light of the most severe Stoic ethical standards.
1. I.e., "a flickering flame." Cf. Dryden's *Mac Flecknoe*, line 111 and note on line 108.
2. The nine Muses, who preside over the arts of

literature, the dance, music, and astronomy.
3. The art of painting (a Gallicism).
4. In the elaborate figure that dominates lines 95–98, Dryden alludes to recent peaceful annexations by Louis XIV of France, who in 1679 added most of Alsace, Lorraine, and Luxembourg to his realm through his policy of "*réunions*," by setting up "*Chambres de Réunions*." These chambers by quasi-legal means awarded to Louis, as overlord, towns, cities, and estates with all their "dependences" or fiefs, i.e., estates held under the feudal system from overlords, to whom the holders owed services and rents.

And all the large demains[5] which the dumb Sister swayed,
   All bowed beneath her government,
    Received in triumph wheresoe'er she went.   105
Her pencil[6] drew whate'er her soul designed,
And oft the happy draft surpassed the image in her mind.
   The sylvan scenes[7] of herds and flocks
   And fruitful plains and barren rocks;
   Of shallow brooks that flowed so clear   110
   The bottom did the top appear;
   Of deeper too and ampler floods,
   Which, as in mirrors, showed the woods;
   Of lofty trees, with sacred shades
   And pèrspectives[8] of pleasant glades,   115
   Where nymphs of brightest form appear, ⎫
   And shaggy satyrs standing near,   ⎬
   Which them at once admire and fear; ⎭
   The ruins, too, of some majestic piece,
   Boasting the power of ancient Rome or Greece,   120
   Whose statues, friezes, columns broken lie,
   And, though defaced, the wonder of the eye:[9]
   What nature, art, bold fiction e'er durst frame,
   Her forming hand gave feature to the name.
   So strange a concourse ne'er was seen before   125
But when the peopled ark the whole creation bore.[1]

7

   The scene then changed: with bold erected look
Our martial king[2] the sight with reverence strook;
For, not content to express his outward part,
   Her hand called out the image of his heart: 130
   His warlike mind, his soul devoid of fear, ⎫
   His high-designing thoughts were figured there, ⎬
   As when by magic, ghosts are made appear. ⎭
   Our phoenix queen[3] was portrayed, too, so bright,
   Beauty alone could beauty take[4] so right: 135
   Her dress, her shape, her matchless grace
   Were all observed, as well as heavenly face.
   With such a peerless majesty she stands
   As in that day she took the crown from sacred hands;[5]

5. I.e., an estate held in one's own right, as opposed to "fief" (line 98). The "dumb Sister" is the Muse of painting.
6. Painter's brush.
7. Cf. Milton, *Paradise Lost* 4.140.
8. Vistas.
9. Mrs. Killigrew's landscapes are typical of the ideal classical landscape of 17th-century Italian painters: contrasts of fruitful plains and barren rocks, water that reflects trees, vistas, classical ruins, and mythological figures.
1. Noah's ark, which contained all that survived of created beings.

2. James II, who, as duke of York, had won a reputation for courage and skill while fighting as a soldier with the French armies in the 1650s and serving as an admiral during the English-Dutch wars of the 1660s.
3. Mary of Modena, wife of James II, whose unique beauty is expressed by the reference to the "phoenix," the fabulous bird, only one of which exists during each thousand years.
4. I.e., take the likeness of.
5. The queen was crowned by the "sacred hands" of the archbishop of Canterbury.

Before a train of heroines was seen, 140
In beauty foremost, as in rank the queen.
Thus nothing to her genius was denied,
    But like a ball of fire, the further thrown,
    Still with a greater blaze she shone,
And her bright soul broke out on every side. 145
What next she had designed, heaven only knows;[6] ⎫
To such immoderate growth her conquest rose ⎬
That fate alone its progress could oppose. ⎭

8

    Now all those charms, that blooming grace,
The well-proportioned shape, and beauteous face, 150
Shall never more be seen by mortal eyes:
In earth the much-lamented virgin lies!
    Not wit nor piety could fate prevent;
    Nor was the cruel destiny content
    To finish all the murder at a blow, 155
    To sweep at once her life and beauty too;
But, like a hardened felon, took a pride
    To work more mischievously slow,
And plundered first, and then destroyed.
O double sacrilege on things divine, 160
To rob the relic, and deface the shrine!
    But thus Orinda died:[7]
Heaven, by the same disease, did both translate;
As equal were their souls, so equal was their fate.

9

    Meantime her warlike brother[8] on the seas 165
    His waving streamers to the winds displays,
And vows for his return with vain devotion pays.
    Ah, generous youth, that wish forbear;
    The winds too soon will waft thee here!
    Slack all thy sails, and fear to come, 170
Alas, thou know'st not thou art wrecked at home!
No more shalt thou behold thy sister's face;
Thou hast already had her last embrace.
But look aloft, and if thou kenn'st[9] from far,
Among the Pleiads,[1] a new-kindled star, 175
If any sparkles than the rest more bright,
'Tis she that shines in that propitious light.

10

    When in mid-air the golden trump shall sound,
    To raise the nations under ground;

---

6. God alone knows.
7. The poetess Katharine Philips (1631–1664), fancifully referred to by her admirers as "the matchless Orinda," who, like Anne Killigrew, died of the disfiguring disease, smallpox.

8. Henry Killigrew, an officer in the Royal Navy. Pennons ("streamers") fly from the mast of his ship.
9. Perceivest.
1. The Pleiades, a cluster of stars (6 are visible to the unaided eye) in the constellation Taurus.

When in the Valley of Jehosaphat[2]   180
The judging God shall close the book of fate,
    And there the last assizes[3] keep
    For those who wake and those who sleep;
    When rattling bones together fly
    From the four corners of the sky;   185
When sinews o'er the skeletons are spread,
Those clothed with flesh, and life inspires the dead;
The sacred poets first shall hear the sound,
And foremost from the tomb shall bound,
For they are covered with the lightest ground,   190
And straight, with inborn vigor, on the wing,
Like mounting larks, to the new morning sing.
There thou, sweet saint, before the choir shalt go,
As harbinger[4] of heaven, the way to show,
The way which thou so well hast learned below.   195

                                            1686

A Song for St. Cecilia's Day[1]

1

From harmony, from heavenly harmony
        This universal frame began:
        When Nature[2] underneath a heap
            Of jarring atoms lay,
            And could not heave her head,   5
    The tuneful voice was heard from high:
        "Arise, ye more than dead."
    Then cold, and hot, and moist, and dry,
    In order to their stations leap,
            And Music's power obey.   10
    From harmony, from heavenly harmony

2. Joel 3.12; Ezekiel 37.
3. Periodical sessions of superior courts held in each county in England; here, of course, the Last Judgment—at which some will be alive on earth ("wake") and many will have already died ("sleep").
4. One who goes ahead to provide a lodging.
1. St. Cecilia, a Roman lady, was an early Christian martyr. She has long been regarded as the patroness of music and the supposed inventor of the organ. Celebrations of her festival day (November 22) in England were usually devoted to music and the praise of music, and from about 1683 to 1703 a "Musical Society" in London annually commemorated it with a religious service and a public concert. This concert always included an ode written and set to music for the occasion, of which the two by Dryden (A Song for St. Cecil-

ia's Day, 1687, and Alexander's Feast, 1697) are the most distinguished. G. B. Draghi, an Italian brought to England by Charles II, set this ode to music, but Handel's fine score, composed in 1739, has completely obscured the original setting. Like the ode to Mrs. Killigrew, this is an irregular ode in the manner of Cowley. In stanzas 3–6 Dryden boldly attempted to suggest in the sounds of his words the characteristic tones of the instruments mentioned.
2. Created nature, ordered by the Divine Wisdom out of chaos, which Dryden, adopting the physics of the Greek philosopher Epicurus, describes as composed of the warring and discordant ("jarring") atoms of the four elements: earth, fire, water, air ("cold," "hot," "moist," "dry").

This universal frame began:
From harmony to harmony
Through all the compass of the notes it ran,
The diapason[3] closing full in man.   15

2

What passion cannot Music raise and quell![4]
    When Jubal[5] struck the corded shell,
    His listening brethren stood around,
    And, wondering, on their faces fell
    To worship that celestial sound.   20
Less than a god they thought there could not dwell
    Within the hollow of that shell
    That spoke so sweetly and so well.
What passion cannot Music raise and quell!

3

    The trumpet's loud clangor   25
        Excites us to arms,
    With shrill notes of anger,
        And mortal alarms.
    The double double double beat
        Of the thundering drum   30
Cries: "Hark! the foes come;
Charge, charge, 'tis too late to retreat."

4

    The soft complaining flute
    In dying notes discovers
    The woes of hopeless lovers,   35
Whose dirge is whispered by the warbling lute.

5

    Sharp violins[6] proclaim
Their jealous pangs, and desperation,
Fury, frantic indignation,
Depth of pains, and height of passion,   40
    For the fair, disdainful dame.

6

    But O! what art can teach,
    What human voice can reach,
    The sacred organ's praise?
    Notes inspiring holy love,   45

3. The entire compass of tones in the scale. Dryden is thinking of the Chain of Being, the ordered creation from inanimate nature up to man, God's latest and final work. The just gradations of notes in a scale are analogous to the equally just gradations in the ascending scale of created beings. Both are the result of harmony.

4. The power of music to describe, evoke, or subdue emotion ("passion") is a frequent theme in 17th-century literature. In stanzas 2–6 the poet considers music as awakening religious awe, warlike courage, sorrow for unrequited love, jealousy and fury, and the impulse to worship God.

5. According to Genesis 4.21, the inventor of the lyre and the pipe. Dryden imagines Jubal's lyre to have been made of a tortoise shell ("corded shell").

6. A reference to the bright tone of the modern violin, introduced into England at the Restoration. The tone of the old-fashioned viol is much duller (Bronson).

Notes that wing their heavenly ways
　　To mend the choirs above.

7

Orpheus[7] could lead the savage race;
And trees unrooted left their place,
　　Sequacious of the lyre;
But bright Cecilia raised the wonder higher: 50
When to her organ vocal breath was given,
An angel heard, and straight appeared,[8]
　　Mistaking earth for heaven.

GRAND CHORUS

As from the power of sacred lays 55
　　The spheres began to move,[9]
And sung the great Creator's praise
　　To all the blest above;
So, when the last and dreadful hour
This crumbling pageant[1] *shall devour,* 60
The trumpet shall be heard on high,[2] ⎫
The dead shall live, the living die, ⎬
And Music shall untune the sky. ⎭

1687

Epigram on Milton[1]

Three poets, in three distant ages born,
Greece, Italy, and England did adorn.
The first in loftiness of thought surpassed,
The next in majesty, in both the last:
The force of Nature could no farther go; 5
To make a third, she joined the former two.

1688

---

7. A legendary poet, son of one of the Muses, who played so wonderfully on the lyre that wild beasts ("the savage race") grew tame and followed him, as did even rocks and trees. "Sequacious of": following.

8. According to the legend, it was Cecilia's piety, not her music, that brought an angel to visit her.

9. As it was harmony which ordered the universe, so it was angelic song ("sacred lays") which put the celestial bodies ("spheres") in motion. The harmonious chord which results from the traditional "music of the spheres" is a hymn of "praise" sung by created nature to its "Creator."

1. The universe: the stage on which the drama of man's salvation has been acted out.

2. The "last trump" of 1 Corinthians 15.52, which will announce the Resurrection and the Last Judgment. Dryden develops his theme of harmony as order in such a way as to give full emphasis of the splendid paradox ("Music shall *untune*") in the final line of the ode.

1. Engraved beneath the portrait of Milton in Jacob Tonson's edition of *Paradise Lost* (1688). The "three poets" are Homer, Virgil, Milton.

Alexander's Feast[1]

Or the Power of Music; An Ode in Honor of St. Cecilia's Day

1

'Twas at the royal feast, for Persia won
      By Philip's[2] warlike son:
    Aloft in awful state
    The godlike hero sate
      On his imperial throne;   5
His valiant peers were placed around;
Their brows with roses and with myrtles[3] bound:
   (So should desert in arms be crowned).
The lovely Thaïs, by his side,
Sate like a blooming Eastern bride   10
In flower of youth and beauty's pride.
    Happy, happy, happy pair!
    None but the brave,
    None but the brave,
    None but the brave deserves the fair.   15

CHORUS

Happy, happy, happy pair!
None but the brave,
None but the brave,
None but the brave deserves the fair.

2

Timotheus, placed on high   20
   Amid the tuneful choir,
    With flying fingers touched the lyre:
The trembling notes ascend the sky,
     And heavenly joys inspire.
The song began from Jove,   25
Who left his blissful seats above
(Such is the power of mighty love).[4]
A dragon's fiery form belied the god:

---

1. In Dryden's earlier poem for St. Cecilia's Day, music was celebrated primarily as harmony and order, though its power over the passions was also praised. *Alexander's Feast* is devoted entirely to the second theme. It is based upon a well-known episode in the life of Alexander the Great. After the defeat of the Persian Emperor Darius III and the fall of the Persian capital, Persepolis (331 B.C.), Alexander held a great feast for his officers. Thaïs, his Athenian mistress, persuaded him to set fire to the palace in revenge for the burning of Athens by the Persians under Xerxes in 480 B.C. According to Plutarch, Alexander was moved by love and wine, not by music; but Dryden, perhaps altering an old tradition that Alexander's musician Timotheus once caused the hero by his flute-playing to start up and arm himself, attributes the burning of Persepolis to the power of music. The original music was by Jeremiah Clarke, but Handel's score of 1736 is better known.

2. King Philip II of Macedonia, father of Alexander the Great.

3. The Greeks and Romans wore wreaths of flowers at banquets. Roses and myrtles are emblems of love.

4. An oracle had declared that Alexander was the son of Zeus ("Jove") by Philip's wife Olympias (not, as Dryden calls her in line 30, "Olympia"), thus conferring on him that semi-divinity often claimed by heroes. Zeus habitually conducted his amours with mortals in the guise of an animal: in this case a dragon.

Sublime on radiant spires[5] he rode,
   When he to fair Olympia pressed;   30
   And while he sought her snowy breast:
Then, round her slender waist he curled,
And stamped an image of himself, a sovereign of the world.
The listening crowd admire[6] the lofty sound:
"A present deity," they shout around;   35
"A present deity," the vaulted roofs rebound.
      With ravished ears
      The monarch hears,
      Assumes the god,
      Affects to nod,
                      40
And seems to shake the spheres.[7]

CHORUS

With ravished ears
The monarch hears,
Assumes the god,
Affects to nod,   45
And seems to shake the spheres.

3

The praise of Bacchus[8] then the sweet musician sung,
   Of Bacchus ever fair and ever young:
      The jolly god in triumph comes;
      Sound the trumpets; beat the drums;   50
        Flushed with a purple grace
        He shows his honest face:
Now give the hautboys[9] breath; he comes, he comes!
      Bacchus, ever fair and young
        Drinking joys did first ordain;   55
      Bacchus' blessings are a treasure,
      Drinking is a soldier's pleasure;
        Rich the treasure,
        Sweet the pleasure,
      Sweet is pleasure after pain.   60

CHORUS

Bacchus' blessings are a treasure,
Drinking is the soldier's pleasure;
      Rich the treasure,
      Sweet the pleasure,
Sweet is pleasure after pain.   65

4

   Soothed with the sound, the king grew vain;
      Fought all his battles o'er again,

5. High on shining coils ("radiant spires"). "Spires"
for the coils of a serpent is derived from the Latin
word *spira*, which Virgil uses in this sense, *Aeneid*
2.217. Cf. *Paradise Lost* 9.502.
6. Wonder at.

7. According to Virgil (*Aeneid* 10.115) the nod of
Jove causes earthquakes.
8. The god of wine.
9. Oboes.

And thrice he routed all his foes, and thrice he slew the slain.
The master saw the madness rise,
His glowing cheeks, his ardent eyes;   70
And, while he[1] heaven and earth defied,
Changed his hand, and checked his pride.
     He chose a mournful Muse,
       Soft pity to infuse:
He sung Darius great and good,   75
     By too severe a fate
Fallen, fallen, fallen, fallen,
     Fallen from his high estate,
       And weltering in his blood;
Deserted at his utmost need   80
By those his former bounty fed;
On the bare earth exposed he lies,
With not a friend to close his eyes.[2]
With downcast looks the joyless victor sate,
    Revolving[3] in his altered soul   85
     The various turns of chance below;
    And, now and then, a sigh he stole,
     And tears began to flow.

CHORUS

Revolving in his altered soul
  The various turns of chance below;   90
    And, now and then, a sigh he stole,
    And tears began to flow.

5

The mighty master smiled to see
That love was in the next degree;
'Twas but[4] a kindred sound to move,   95
For pity melts the mind to love.
    Softly sweet, in Lydian[5] measures,
    Soon he soothed his soul to pleasures.
    "War," he sung, "is toil and trouble;
    Honor, but an empty bubble.   100
     Never ending, still beginning,
    Fighting still, and still destroying:
     If the world be worth thy winning,
    Think, O think it worth enjoying.
     Lovely Thaïs sits beside thee,   105
      Take the good the gods provide thee."
The many[6] rend the skies with loud applause;

---

1. Alexander; in line 72, "his hand" is the hand of Timotheus, "his pride," the pride of Alexander.
2. After his final defeat by Alexander, Darius was assassinated by his own followers.
3. Pondering.
4. I.e., it was necessary only.

5. In Greek music the Lydian mode expressed the plaintive and the sad.
6. As G. R. Noyes points out, "many" means *meiny*, "a retinue," a spelling that Dryden used elsewhere in his work.

So Love was crowned, but Music won the cause.
   The prince, unable to conceal his pain,
       Gazed on the fair   110
       Who caused his care,
    And sighed and looked, sighed and looked,
   Sighed and looked, and sighed again:
At length, with love and wine at once oppressed,
The vanquished victor sunk upon her breast.   115

CHORUS

The prince, unable to conceal his pain,
   Gazed on the fair
   Who caused his care,
   And sighed and looked, sighed and looked,
  Sighed and looked, and sighed again: 120
At length, with love and wine at once oppressed,
The vanquished victor sunk upon her breast.

6

Now strike the golden lyre again:
A louder yet, and yet a louder strain.
Break his bands of sleep asunder,   125
And rouse him, like a rattling peal of thunder.
    Hark, hark, the horrid[7] sound
     Has raised up his head:
     As waked from the dead,
    And amazed, he stares around,   130
"Revenge, revenge!" Timotheus cries,
   "See the Furies[8] arise!
   See the snakes that they rear,
   How they hiss in their hair,
  And the sparkles that flash from their eyes!   135
   Behold a ghastly band,
   Each a torch in his hand!
Those are Grecian ghosts, that in battle were slain,
    And unburied remain[9]
    Inglorious on the plain: 140
    Give the vengeance due
    To the valiant crew.
Behold how they toss their torches on high,
   How they point to the Persian abodes,
And glittering temples of their hostile gods!"   145
The princes applaud, with a furious joy;
And the king seized a flambeau[1] with zeal to destroy;
    Thaïs led the way,

---

7. Rough, from Latin *horridus.*
8. The Erinyes of the Greeks, avengers of crimes against the natural and the social orders. They are described as women with snakes in their hair and around their waists and arms.
9. According to Greek beliefs, the shades of the dead could not rest until their bodies were buried.
1. Torch.

To light him to his prey,
And, like another Helen, fired another Troy.[2]

150

CHORUS

And the king seized a flambeau with zeal to destroy;
Thaïs led the way,
To light him to his prey,
And, like another Helen, fired another Troy.

7

Thus long ago,   155
Ere heaving bellows learned to blow,
While organs yet were mute;
Timotheus, to his breathing flute,
And sounding lyre,
Could swell the soul to rage, or kindle soft desire.   160
At last, divine Cecilia came,
Inventress of the vocal frame;[3]
The sweet enthusiast,[4] from her sacred store,
Enlarged the former narrow bounds,
And added length to solemn sounds,   165
With nature's mother wit, and arts unknown before.
Let old Timotheus yield the prize,
Or both divide the crown:
He raised a mortal to the skies;
She drew an angel down.   170

GRAND CHORUS

At last, divine Cecilia came,
Inventress of the vocal frame;
The sweet enthusiast, from her sacred store,
Enlarged the former narrow bounds,
And added length to solemn sounds,   175
With nature's mother wit, and arts unknown before.
Let old Timotheus yield the prize,
Or both divide the crown:
He raised a mortal to the skies;
She drew an angel down.   180

1697

---

2. Helen's elopement to Troy with Paris brought on the Trojan War and the ultimate destruction of the city by the Greeks.
3. Organ.
4. Usually at this time a disparaging word, frequently, though not always, applied to a religious zealot or fanatic. Here it is used approvingly and in its literal sense, "possessed by a god," an allusion to Cecilia's angelic companion referred to in line 170. But see note on *Song for St. Cecilia's Day*, line 53.

The Secular Masque[1]

[*Enter* JANUS.[2]]

JANUS. Chronos,[3] Chronos, mend thy pace;
  An hundred times the rolling sun
  Around the radiant belt[4] has run
In his revolving race.
Behold, behold, the goal in sight;   5
Spread thy fans,[5] and wing thy flight.
[*Enter* CHRONOS, *with a scythe in his hand, and a great globe on his back, which he sets down at his entrance.*]

CHRONOS. Weary, weary of my weight,
Let me, let me drop my freight,
  And leave the world behind.
I could not bear   10
Another year
  The load of humankind.

[*Enter* MOMUS,[6] *laughing.*]

MOMUS. Ha! ha! ha! ha! ha! ha! well hast thou done
  To lay down thy pack,
  And lighten thy back;   15
The world was a fool, e'er since it begun,
And since neither Janus, nor Chronos, nor I
  Can hinder the crimes,
  Or mend the bad times,
'Tis better to laugh than to cry.   20

CHORUS OF ALL THREE.
  'Tis better to laugh than to cry.

JANUS. Since Momus comes to laugh below,
  Old Time, begin the show,
That he may see, in every scene,
What changes in this age have been.

    25
CHRONOS. Then, goddess of the silver bow,[7] begin.

[*Horns, or hunting music within.*]
[*Enter* DIANA.]

---

1. A masque is a dramatic performance, usually mythological in character, that combines poetry, music, dance, and spectacle. Unlike the court masques of Ben Jonson (see headnote above to *Pleasure Reconciled to Virtue*), this masque was written for public performance as an afterpiece to the revival of Fletcher's *The Pilgrim*, revised by Sir John Vanbrugh, and produced for the financial benefit of Dryden himself. It is a "secular masque" because it celebrates the end of the century, "secular" being derived from the Latin *saeculares*, applied to the games, plays, and shows celebrated in Rome once an "age," a period of 120 years. It is not certain that Dryden lived to see his masque performed.
2. The god of beginnings, who here presides over the opening of the new century.
3. God of time.
4. The sun, in the course of a year, passes through all twelve signs of the zodiac ("the radiant belt").
5. Wings.
6. God of mockery and faultfinding.
7. Diana, the virgin goddess of the moon, a huntress. She symbolizes England before the Civil War, an allusion to James I's passion for the chase.

DIANA.   With horns and with hounds I waken the day,
     And hie to my woodland walks away;
     I tuck up my robe, and am buskined[8] soon,
     And tie to my forehead a wexing[9] moon.   30
     I course the fleet stag, unkennel the fox,
     And chase the wild goats o'er summits of rocks;
     With shouting and hooting we pierce through the sky,
     And Echo turns hunter, and doubles the cry.

CHORUS OF ALL.
     With shouting and hooting we pierce through the sky,   35
     And Echo turns hunter, and doubles the cry.

JANUS.   Then our age was in its prime:
CHRONOS.   Free from rage:
DIANA.   And free from crime:
MOMUS.   A very merry, dancing, drinking,
     Laughing, quaffing, and unthinking time.   40

CHORUS OF ALL.
     Then our age was in its prime,
     Free from rage, and free from crime;
     A very merry, dancing, drinking,
     Laughing, quaffing, and unthinking time.

         [*Dance of* DIANA's *attendants.*]
            [*Enter* MARS.[1]]

MARS.   Inspire[2] the vocal brass, inspire;   45
     The world is past its infant age:
         Arms and honor,
         Arms and honor,
     Set the martial mind on fire,
     And kindle manly rage.   50
     Mars has looked the sky to red;
     And Peace, the lazy good, is fled.
     Plenty, Peace, and Pleasure fly;
         The sprightly green
     In woodland walks no more is seen;   55
     The sprightly green has drunk the Tyrian dye.[3]

CHORUS OF ALL.
     Plenty, Peace, etc.
MARS.   Sound the trumpet, beat the drum;
         Through all the world around,
         Sound a reveille, sound, sound,   60
     The warrior god is come.

CHORUS OF ALL.
     Sound the trumpet, etc.
MOMUS.   Thy sword within the scabbard keep,
         And let mankind agree;

---

8. Wearing hunting boots.
9. Waxing (i.e., increasing, because in the first quarter).
1. God of war, who represents the period of the civil war and the Commonwealth.

2. Breathe into.
3. I.e., the costume has changed from the green of the hunter to the crimson of the soldier (at once the color of blood and of "Tyrian dye," known to the ancients as "purple").

Better the world were fast asleep,   65
    Than kept awake by thee.
The fools are only thinner,
    With all our cost and care;
But neither side a winner,
    For things are as they were.   70

CHORUS OF ALL.
    The fools are only, etc.

[*Enter* VENUS.[4]]

VENUS.   Calms appear when storms are past,
Love will have his hour at last:
Nature is my kindly care;
Mars destroys, and I repair;   75
Take me, take me, while you may;
Venus comes not every day.

CHORUS OF ALL.
    Take her, take her, etc.

CHRONOS.   The world was then so light,
I scarcely felt the weight;
Joy ruled the day, and Love the night.   80
But since the Queen of Pleasure left the ground,[5]
    I faint, I lag,
    And feebly drag
The ponderous orb around.   85

MOMUS.   All, all of a piece throughout:

[*Pointing to* DIANA.]

Thy chase had a beast in view;

[*To* MARS.]

Thy wars brought nothing about;

[*To* VENUS.]

Thy lovers were all untrue.

JANUS.   'Tis well an old age is out: 90
CHRONOS.   And time to begin a new.

CHORUS OF ALL.
    All, all of a piece throughout: 95
    Thy chase had a beast in view;
    Thy wars brought nothing about;
    Thy lovers were all untrue.
    'Tis well an old age is out,
    And time to begin a new.

[*Dance of huntsmen, nymphs, warriors, and lovers.*]

1700

4. Goddess of love and beauty, representing the licentious reigns of Charles II and James II.
5. Sir Walter Scott suggested that this line refers to the exiled Queen Mary of Modena, wife of James II.

Criticism   Because Dryden liked to talk about literature, he became a critic, indeed the first comprehensive critic in England. The Elizabethans, largely impelled by the example of Italian humanists, had produced an interesting and unsystematic body of critical writings. Dryden could look back to such pioneer works as George Puttenham's *Art of English Poesy* (1589), Sir Philip Sidney's *Defence of Poesy* (1595), Samuel Daniel's *Defense of Rhyme* (ca. 1603), and Ben Jonson's *Timber, or Discoveries* (1641). These and later writings Dryden knew, as he knew the ancients and the important contemporary French critics, notably Corneille, Rapin, and Boileau. Taken as a whole, his critical prefaces and dedications, which appeared between 1664 and 1700, are the work of a man of independent mind who has made his own synthesis of critical canons from wide reading, a great deal of thinking, and the constant practice of the art of writing. As a critic he is no one's disciple, and he has the saving grace of being always willing to change his mind.

All but a very few of Dryden's critical works (most notably the *Essay of Dramatic Poesy*) grew out of the works to which they served as prefaces: comedies, heroic plays, tragedies, translations, poems of various sorts. Each work posed problems which Dryden was eager to discuss with his readers, and the topics that he treated proved to be important in the development of the new literature of which he was the principal apologist. He dealt with the processes of literary creation, the poet's relation to tradition, the forms of modern drama, the craft of poetry, and above all the genius of earlier poets: Shakespeare, Jonson, Chaucer, Juvenal, Horace, Homer, Virgil. For nearly forty years this voice was heard in the land, and when it was finally silenced, a set of critical standards had come into existence and a new age had been given its direction.

From An Essay of Dramatic Poesy[1]

[*Two Sorts of Bad Poetry*]

* * * "I have a mortal apprehension of two poets,[2] whom this victory, with the help of both her wings, will never be able to escape." " 'Tis

1. With the reopening of the theaters in 1660, older plays were revived, but, despite their power and charm, they seemed old-fashioned. Although new playwrights, ambitious to create a modern English drama, soon appeared, they were uncertain of their direction. What, if anything, useful could they learn from the dramatic practice of the ancients? Should they ignore the English dramatists of the late 16th and early 17th centuries? Should they make their example the vigorous contemporary drama of France? Dryden addresses himself to these and other problems in this essay, his first extended piece of criticism. Its purpose, he tells us, was "chiefly to vindicate the honor of our English writers from the censure of those who unjustly prefer the French before them." Its method is skeptical: Dryden presents several points of view, but imposes none. The form is a dialogue among friends, like the *Tusculan Disputations* or the *Brutus* of Cicero. Crites praises the drama of the ancients; Eugenius protests against their authority and argues for the idea of progress in the arts; Lisideius urges the excel-

lence of French plays; Neander, speaking in the climactic position, defends the native tradition and the greatness of Shakespeare, Fletcher, and Jonson. The dialogue takes place on June 3, 1665, in a boat on the Thames. The four friends are rowed downstream to listen to the cannonading of the English and Dutch fleets, engaged in battle off the Suffolk coast. As the gunfire recedes they are assured of victory and order their boatman to return to London, and naturally enough they fall to discussing the number of bad poems that the victory will evoke.

2. Probably Robert Wilde and possibly Richard Flecknoe, whom Dryden later ridiculed in *Mac Flecknoe*. Their actual identity is unimportant, for they merely represent two extremes in poetry, both deplorable: the fantastic and extravagant manner of decadent metaphysical wit and its opposite, the flat and the dull. The new poetry was to seek a mean between these extremes. Cf. Pope, *Essay on Criticism* 2.239–42 and 289–300.

easy to guess whom you intend," said Lisideius; "and without naming them, I ask you if one of them does not perpetually pay us with clenches[3] upon words, and a certain clownish kind of raillery?[4] if now and then he does not offer at a catachresis[5] or Clevelandism, wresting and torturing a word into another meaning: in fine, if he be not one of those whom the French would call *un mauvais buffon*;[6] one who is so much a well-willer to the satire, that he spares no man; and though he cannot strike a blow to hurt any, yet ought to be punished for the malice of the action, as our witches are justly hanged, because they think themselves so, and suffer deservedly for believing they did mischief, because they meant it."

"You have described him," said Crites, "so exactly that I am afraid to come after you with my other extremity of poetry. He is one of those who, having had some advantage of education and converse, knows better than the other what a poet should be, but puts it into practice more unluckily than any man; his style and matter are everywhere alike: he is the most calm, peaceable writer you ever read: he never disquiets your passions[7] with the least concernment, but still[8] leaves you in as even a temper as he found you; he is a very Leveler[9] in poetry: he creeps along with ten little words in every line, and helps out his numbers with *for to*, and *unto*, and all the pretty expletives[1] he can find, till he drags them to the end of another line; while the sense is left tired halfway behind it: he doubly starves all his verses, first for want of thought, and then of expression; his poetry neither has wit in it, nor seems to have it; like him in Martial:

Pauper videri Cinna vult, et est pauper.[2]

"He affects plainness, to cover his want of imagination: when he writes the serious way, the highest flight of his fancy is some miserable antithesis, or seeming contradiction; and in the comic he is still reaching at some thin conceit, the ghost of a jest, and that too flies before him, never to be caught; these swallows which we see before us on the Thames are the just resemblance of his wit: you may observe how near the water they stoop, how many proffers they make to dip, and yet how seldom they touch it; and when they do, it is but the surface: they skim over it but to catch a gnat, and then mount into the air and leave it."

[The Wit of the Ancients: The Universal]

* * * "A thing well said will be wit in all languages; and though it may lose something in the translation, yet to him who reads it in the

3. Puns.
4. Boorish banter.
5. The use of a word in a sense remote from its normal meaning: a legitimate figure of speech used by all poets, it had been abused by John Cleveland (1613–1658), who was at first admired for his ingenuity, but whose reputation declined rapidly after the Restoration. A Clevelandism: "The marigold, whose courtier's face / Echoes the sun. . . ."
6. A malicious jester.
7. Emotions.
8. Always.
9. The Levelers were radical egalitarians and republicans, a powerful political force in the Puritan Army about 1648. They were suppressed by Cromwell.
1. Words used merely to fill out a line of verse. Cf. Pope, *Essay on Criticism* 2.346–47.
2. "Cinna wishes to seem poor, and he is poor" (*Epigrams* 8.19).

original, 'tis still the same: he has an idea of its excellency, though it cannot pass from his mind into any other expression or words than those in which he finds it. When Phaedria, in the *Eunuch*,[3] had a command from his mistress to be absent two days, and, encouraging himself to go through with it, said, '*Tandem ego non illa caream, si sit opus, vel totum triduum?*'[4]—Parmeno, to mock the softness of his master, lifting up his hands and eyes, cries out, as it were in admiration,[5] '*Hui! universum triduum!*' the elegancy of which *universum*, though it cannot be rendered in our language, yet leaves an impression on our souls: but this happens seldom in him; in Plautus[6] oftener, who is infinitely too bold in his metaphors and coining words, out of which many times his wit is nothing; which questionless was one reason why Horace falls upon him so severely in those verses:

> *Sed proavi nostri Plautinos et numeros et*
> *Laudavere sales, nimium patienter utrumque,*
> *Ne dicam stolide.*[7]

For Horace himself was cautious to obtrude a new word on his readers, and makes custom and common use the best measure of receiving it into our writings:

> *Multa renascentur quae nunc cecidere, cadentque*
> *Quae nunc sunt in honore vocabula, si volet usus,*
> *Quem penes arbitrium est, et jus, et norma loquendi.*[8]

"The not observing this rule is that which the world has blamed in our satirist, Cleveland: to express a thing hard and unnaturally is his new way of elocution. 'Tis true no poet but may sometimes use a catachresis: Virgil does it—

> *Mistaque ridenti colocasia fundet acantho*[9]—

in his eclogue of Pollio; and in his seventh *Aeneid*:

> *mirantur et undae,*
> *Miratur nemus insuetum fulgentia longe*
> *Scuta virum fluvio pictasque innare carinas.*[1]

And Ovid once so modestly that he asks leave to do it:

3. A comedy by the Roman poet Terence (ca. 185–159 B.C.).
4. "Shall I not then do without her, if need be, for three whole days?"
5. Wonder. The wit of Parmeno's exclamation, "Oh, three entire days," depends on *universum*, which suggests that a lover may regard three days as an eternity.
6. Titus Maccus Plautus, Roman comic poet (ca. 254–184 B.C.).
7. "But our ancestors too tolerantly (I do not say foolishly) praised both the verse and the wit of Plautus" (*Art of Poetry*, lines 270–72). Dryden misquotes slightly.

8. "Many words that have perished will be born again, and those shall perish that are now esteemed, if usage wills it, in whose power are the judgment, the law, and the pattern of speech" (*Art of Poetry*, lines 70–72).
9. "[The earth] shall give forth the Egyptian bean, mingled with the smiling acanthus" (*Eclogues* 4.20). "Smiling acanthus" is a catachresis.
1. Actually *Aeneid* 8.91–93. Dryden's paraphrase makes the point clearly: "The woods and waters wonder at the gleam / Of shields and painted ships that stem the stream" (*Aeneis* 8.125–26). "Wonder" is a catachresis.

quem, si verbo audacia detur,
Haud metuam summi dixisse Palatia caeli. [2]

calling the court of Jupiter by the name of Augustus his palace; though in another place he is more bold, where he says, '*et longas visent Capitolia pompas.*'[3] But to do this always, and never be able to write a line without it, though it may be admired by some few pedants, will not pass upon those who know that wit is best conveyed to us in the most easy language; and is most to be admired when a great thought comes dressed in words so commonly received that it is understood by the meanest apprehensions, as the best meat is the most easily digested: but we cannot read a verse of Cleveland's without making a face at it, as if every word were a pill to swallow: he gives us many times a hard nut to break our teeth, without a kernel for our pains. So that there is this difference betwixt his satires and Doctor Donne's; that the one gives us deep thoughts in common language, though rough cadence; the other gives us common thoughts in abstruse words: 'tis true in some places his wit is independent of his words, as in that of the *Rebel Scot*:

> Had Cain been Scot, God would have changed his doom;
> Not forced him wander, but confined him home. [4]

"*Si sic omnia dixisset!*[5] This is wit in all languages: it is like mercury, never to be lost or killed:[6] and so that other—

> For beauty, like white powder, makes no noise,
> And yet the silent hypocrite destroys.

You see that the last line is highly metaphorical, but it is so soft and gentle that it does not shock us as we read it."

[Shakespeare and Ben Jonson Compared]

"To begin, then, with Shakespeare. He was the man who of all modern, and perhaps ancient poets, had the largest and most comprehensive soul. All the images of Nature were still present to him, and he drew them, not laboriously, but luckily; when he describes anything, you more than see it, you feel it too. Those who accuse him to have wanted learning, give him the greater commendation: he was naturally learned; he needed not the spectacles of books to read Nature; he looked inwards, and found her there. I cannot say he is everywhere alike; were he so, I should do him injury to compare him with the greatest of mankind. He is many times flat, insipid; his comic wit degenerating into clenches, his serious swelling into bombast. But he is always great when some great

---

2. "[This is the place] which, if boldness of expression be permitted, I shall not hesitate to call the Palace of high heaven" (*Metamorphoses* 1.175–76).
3. "And the Capitol shall see the long processions" (*Metamorphoses* 1.561).

4. Lines 63–64.
5. "Had he said everything thus!" (Juvenal, *Satires* 10.123–24).
6. Mercury is said to be "killed" if its fluidity is destroyed. The couplet quoted below is from *Rupertismus*, lines 39–40.

occasion is presented to him; no man can say he ever had a fit subject for his wit and did not then raise himself as high above the rest of poets,

Quantum lenta solent inter viburna cupressi[7]

The consideration of this made Mr. Hales of Eton[8] say that there was no subject of which any poet ever writ, but he would produce it much better treated of in Shakespeare; and however others are now generally preferred before him, yet the age wherein he lived, which had contemporaries with him Fletcher and Jonson, never equaled them to him in their esteem: and in the last king's[9] court, when Ben's reputation was at highest, Sir John Suckling,[1] and with him the greater part of the courtiers, set our Shakespeare far above him. . . .

"As for Jonson, to whose character I am now arrived, if we look upon him while he was himself (for his last plays were but his dotages), I think him the most learned and judicious writer which any theater ever had. He was a most severe judge of himself, as well as others. One cannot say he wanted wit, but rather that he was frugal of it. In his works you find little to retrench[2] or alter. Wit, and language, and humor also in some measure, we had before him; but something of art[3] was wanting to the drama till he came. He managed his strength to more advantage than any who preceded him. You seldom find him making love in any of his scenes or endeavoring to move the passions; his genius was too sullen and saturnine[4] to do it gracefully, especially when he knew he came after those who had performed both to such an height. Humor was his proper sphere:[5] and in that he delighted most to represent mechanic people.[6] He was deeply conversant in the ancients, both Greek and Latin, and he borrowed boldly from them: there is scarce a poet or historian among the Roman authors of those times whom he has not translated in *Sejanus* and *Catiline*.[7] But he has done his robberies so openly, that one may see he fears not to be taxed by any law. He invades authors like a monarch; and what would be theft in other poets is only victory in him. With the spoils of these writers he so represents old Rome to us, in its rites, ceremonies, and customs, that if one of their poets had written either of his tragedies, we had seen less of it than in him. If there was any fault in his language, 'twas that he weaved it too closely and laboriously, in his serious plays:[8] perhaps, too, he did a little too much Romanize our tongue, leaving the words which he translated almost as much Latin as he found them: wherein, though he learnedly followed the idiom of

---

7. "As do cypresses among the bending shrubs" (Virgil, *Eclogues* 1.25).
8. The learned John Hales (1584–1656), provost of Eton. He is reputed to have said this to Jonson himself.
9. Charles I.
1. Courtier, poet, playwright, much admired in Dryden's time for his wit and the easy naturalness of his style.
2. Delete.
3. Craftsmanship.
4. Heavy.

5. In Jonson's comedies the characters are seen under the domination of some psychological trait, ruling passion, or affectation—i.e., some "humor"—which makes them unique and ridiculous.
6. I.e., artisans.
7. Jonson's two Roman plays, dated 1605 and 1611 respectively.
8. This is the reading of the first edition. Curiously enough, in the second edition Dryden altered the phrase to "in his comedies especially."

their language, he did not enough comply with the idiom of ours. If I would compare him with Shakespeare, I must acknowledge him the more correct poet, but Shakespeare the greater wit.[9] Shakespeare was the Homer, or father of our dramatic poets; Jonson was the Virgil, the pattern of elaborate writing; I admire him, but I love Shakespeare. To conclude of him; as he has given us the most correct plays, so in the precepts which he has laid down in his *Discoveries*, we have as many and profitable rules for perfecting the stage, as any wherewith the French can furnish us."

1668

From The Author's Apology for Heroic Poetry and Heroic License[1]

["*Boldness*" *of Figures and Tropes Defended: The Appeal to "Nature"*]

* * * They, who would combat general authority with particular opinion, must first establish themselves a reputation of understanding better than other men. Are all the flights of heroic poetry to be concluded bombast, unnatural, and mere madness, because they are not affected with their excellencies? It is just as reasonable as to conclude there is no day, because a blind man cannot distinguish of light and colors. Ought they not rather, in modesty, to doubt of their own judgments, when they think this or that expression in Homer, Virgil, Tasso, or Milton's *Paradise* to be too far strained, than positively to conclude that 'tis all fustian and mere nonsense? 'Tis true there are limits to be set betwixt the boldness and rashness of a poet; but he must understand those limits who pretends to judge as well as he who undertakes to write: and he who has no liking to the whole ought, in reason, to be excluded from censuring of the parts. He must be a lawyer before he mounts the tribunal; and the judicature of one court, too, does not qualify a man to preside in another. He may be an excellent pleader in the Chancery, who is not fit to rule the Common Pleas. But I will presume for once to tell them that the boldest strokes of poetry, when they are managed artfully, are those which most delight the reader.

Virgil and Horace, the severest writers of the severest age, have made frequent use of the hardest metaphors and of the strongest hyperboles; and in this case the best authority is the best argument, for generally to have pleased, and through all ages, must bear the force of universal

---

9. Genius.
1. This essay was prefixed to Dryden's *State of Innocence*, the libretto for an opera (never produced), based on *Paradise Lost*. Dryden had been ridiculed for the extravagant and bold imagery and rhetorical figures that are typical of the style of his rhymed heroic plays. This preface is a defense not only of his own predilection for what Samuel Johnson described as "wild and daring sallies of sentiment, in the irregular and eccentric violence of wit," but also of the theory that heroic and idealized materials should be treated in lofty and boldly metaphorical style; hence his definition of "wit" as propriety.

tradition. And if you would appeal from thence to right reason, you will gain no more by it in effect than, first, to set up your reason against those authors, and, secondly, against all those who have admired them. You must prove why that ought not to have pleased which has pleased the most learned and the most judicious; and, to be thought knowing, you must first put the fool upon all mankind. If you can enter more deeply than they have done into the causes and resorts[2] of that which moves pleasure in a reader, the field is open, you may be heard: but those springs of human nature are not so easily discovered by every superficial judge: it requires philosophy, as well as poetry, to sound the depth of all the passions, what they are in themselves, and how they are to be provoked; and in this science the best poets have excelled. * * * From hence have sprung the tropes[3] and figures, for which they wanted a name who first practiced them and succeeded in them. Thus I grant you that the knowledge of Nature was the original rule, and that all poets ought to study her, as well as Aristotle and Horace, her interpreters.[4] But then this also undeniably follows, that those things which delight all ages must have been an imitation of Nature—which is all I contend. Therefore is rhetoric made an art; therefore the names of so many tropes and figures were invented, because it was observed they had such and such effect upon the audience. Therefore catachreses and hyperboles[5] have found their place amongst them; not that they were to be avoided, but to be used judiciously and placed in poetry as heightenings and shadows are in painting, to make the figure bolder, and cause it to stand off to sight. * * *

[Wit as "Propriety"]

* * * [Wit] is a propriety of thoughts and words; or, in other terms, thought and words elegantly adapted to the subject. If our critics will join issue on this definition, that we may *convenire in aliquo tertio*;[6] if they will take it as a granted principle, it will be easy to put an end to this dispute. No man will disagree from another's judgment concerning the dignity of style in heroic poetry; but all reasonable men will conclude it necessary that sublime subjects ought to be adorned with the sublimest, and, consequently, often with the most figurative expressions. * * *

1677

2. Mechanical springs that set something in motion.
3. The use of a word in a figurative sense; "figures," in this phrase, means such figures of speech as metaphors and similes.
4. In the words of the French critic René Rapin, the rules (largely derived from Aristotle's *Poetics* and Horace's *Art of Poetry*) were made in order to

"reduce Nature to method." Cf. Pope, *Essay on Criticism* 1.88–89.
5. "Catachresis" is the use of a word in a sense remote from its normal meaning; "hyperbole," deliberate overstatement or exaggeration.
6. "To find some means of agreement, in a third term, between the two opposites" [W. P. Ker's note].

From A Discourse Concerning the Original and Progress of Satire[1]

[*The Art of Satire*]

* * * How easy is it to call rogue and villain, and that wittily! But how hard to make a man appear a fool, a blockhead, or a knave without using any of those opprobrious terms! To spare the grossness of the names, and to do the thing yet more severely, is to draw a full face, and to make the nose and cheeks stand out, and yet not to employ any depth of shadowing.[2] This is the mystery of that noble trade, which yet no master can teach to his apprentice; he may give the rules, but the scholar is never the nearer in his practice. Neither is it true that this fineness of raillery[3] is offensive. A witty man is tickled while he is hurt in this manner, and a fool feels it not. The occasion of an offense may possibly be given, but he cannot take it. If it be granted that in effect this way does more mischief; that a man is secretly wounded, and though he be not sensible himself, yet the malicious world will find it out for him; yet there is still a vast difference betwixt the slovenly butchering of a man, and the fineness of a stroke that separates the head from the body, and leaves it standing in its place. A man may be capable, as Jack Ketch's[4] wife said of his servant, of a plain piece of work, a bare hanging; but to make a malefactor die sweetly was only belonging to her husband. I wish I could apply it to myself, if the reader would be kind enough to think it belongs to me. The character of Zimri in my *Absalom*[5] is, in my opinion, worth the whole poem: it is not bloody, but it is ridiculous enough; and he, for whom it was intended, was too witty to resent it as an injury. If I had railed,[6] I might have suffered for it justly; but I managed my own work more happily, perhaps more dexterously. I avoided the mention of great crimes, and applied myself to the representing of blindsides, and little extravagancies; to which, the wittier a man is, he is generally the more obnoxious.[7] It succeeded as I wished; the jest went round, and he was laughed at in his turn who began the frolic. * * *

1693

1. This passage is an excerpt from the long and rambling preface which served as the dedication of a translation of the satires of the Roman satirists Juvenal and Persius to Charles Sackville, 6th earl of Dorset. The translations were made by Dryden and other writers, among them William Congreve. Dryden traces the origin and development of verse satire in Rome, and in a very fine passage contrasts Horace and Juvenal as satiric poets. It is plain that he prefers the "tragic" satire of Juvenal to the urbane and laughing satire of Horace. But in the passage printed here he praises his own satiric character of Zimri (the duke of Buckingham) in *Absalom and Achitophel* for the very reason that it

is modeled on Horatian "raillery," not Juvenalian invective.
2. Early English miniaturists prided themselves on the art of giving roundness to the full face without painting in shadows.
3. Satirical mirth, good-natured satire.
4. A notorious public executioner of Dryden's time (d. 1686). His name later became a generic term for all members of his profession.
5. See *Absalom and Achitophel* 1.544–68.
6. Reviled, abused. Observe that the verb differed in meaning from its noun, defined above.
7. Liable.

From The Preface to *Fables Ancient and Modern*[1]

[*In Praise of Chaucer*]

In the first place, as he is the father of English poetry, I hold him in the same degree of veneration as the Grecians held Homer, or the Romans Virgil. He is a perpetual fountain of good sense; learned in all sciences;[2] and, therefore, speaks properly on all subjects. As he knew what to say, so he knows also when to leave off; a continence which is practiced by few writers, and scarcely by any of the ancients, excepting Virgil and Horace. * * *

Chaucer followed Nature everywhere, but was never so bold to go beyond her; and there is a great difference of being *poeta* and *nimis poeta*,[3] if we may believe Catullus, as much as betwixt a modest behavior and affectation. The verse of Chaucer, I confess, is not harmonious to us; but 'tis like the eloquence of one whom Tacitus commends, it was *auribus istius temporis accommodata:*[4] they who lived with him, and some time after him, thought it musical; and it continues so, even in our judgment, if compared with the numbers[5] of Lydgate and Gower, his contemporaries; there is the rude sweetness of a Scotch tune in it, which is natural and pleasing, though not perfect. 'Tis true I cannot go so far as he who published the last edition of him;[6] for he would make us believe the fault is in our ears, and that there were really ten syllables in a verse where we find but nine; but this opinion is not worth confuting; 'tis so gross and obvious an error that common sense (which is a rule in everything but matters of faith and revelation) must convince the reader that equality of numbers in every verse which we call heroic[7] was either not known, or not always practiced in Chaucer's age. It were an easy matter to produce some thousands of his verses which are lame for want of half a foot, and sometimes a whole one, and which no pronunciation can make otherwise. We can only say that he lived in the infancy of our poetry, and that nothing is brought to perfection at the first. * * *

He must have been a man of a most wonderful comprehensive nature, because, as it has been truly observed of him, he has taken into the

1. Dryden's final work, published in the year of his death, was a collection of translations from Homer, Ovid, Boccaccio, and Chaucer, and one or two other pieces. The Preface, in many ways, is Dryden's ripest and finest critical essay. In it, he is not concerned with critical theory or with a formalistic approach to literature; he is simply a man, grown old in the reading and writing of poetry, who is eager to talk informally with his readers about some of his favorite authors. His praise of Chaucer (unusually sympathetic and perceptive for 1700) is animated by that love of great literature which is manifest in everything that Dryden wrote.
2. Branches of learning.
3. A poet ("*poeta*") and too much of a poet ("*nimis poeta*"). The phrase is not from Catullus but from Martial (*Epigrams* 3.44).
4. "Suitable to the ears of that time." Tacitus was a Roman historian and writer on oratory (A.D. ca. 55–ca. 117).
5. Versification. John Lydgate (ca. 1370–ca. 1449) wrote poetry which shows the influence of Chaucer. John Gower (d. 1408), poet and friend of Chaucer.
6. Thomas Speght's Chaucer, which Dryden used, was first published in 1598; the second edition, published in 1602, was reprinted in 1687.
7. The pentameter line. In Dryden's time few readers knew how to pronounce Middle English, especially the syllabic *e*. Moreover, Chaucer's works were known only in corrupt printed texts. As a consequence Chaucer's verse seemed rough and irregular.

compass of his *Canterbury Tales* the various manners and humors (as we now call them) of the whole English nation in his age. Not a single character has escaped him. All his pilgrims are severally distinguished from each other; and not only in their inclinations but in their very physiognomies and persons. Baptista Porta[8] could not have described their natures better than by the marks which the poet gives them. The matter and manner of their tales, and of their telling, are so suited to their different educations, humors, and callings that each of them would be improper in any other mouth. Even the grave and serious characters are distinguished by their several sorts of gravity: their discourses are such as belong to their age, their calling, and their breeding; such as are becoming of them, and of them only. Some of his persons are vicious, and some virtuous; some are unlearned, or (as Chaucer calls them) lewd, and some are learned. Even the ribaldry of the low characters is different: the Reeve, the Miller, and the Cook are several[9] men, and distinguished from each other as much as the mincing Lady Prioress and the broad-speaking, gap-toothed Wife of Bath. But enough of this; there is such a variety of game springing up before me that I am distracted in my choice, and know not which to follow. 'Tis sufficient to say, according to the proverb, that here is God's plenty. * * *

1700

8. Giambattista della Porta (ca. 1535–1615), author of a Latin treatise on physiognomy.
9. Different.

SAMUEL PEPYS
1633–1703

Samuel Pepys (pronounced "Peeps") was the son of a London tailor. With the help of a scholarship he took a degree at Cambridge; with the help of a cousin he found a place in the Navy Office. Eventually, through hard work and an eye for detail, he rose to secretary of the Admiralty. His defense of the Navy Office and himself before Parliament in 1668 won him a reputation as a good administrator, and his career continued to prosper until it was broken, first by false accusations of treason in 1679 and finally by the deposition of James II in 1688. But Pepys was more than a bureaucrat. A Londoner to his core, he was interested in all the activities of the city: the theater, music, the social whirl, business, religion, literary life, and the scientific experiments of the Royal Society (which he served as president from 1684 to 1686). He also found plenty of chances to indulge his two obsessions: chasing after women and making money.

Pepys kept his diary from 1660 to 1669 (when his eyesight began to fail). Writing in shorthand and sometimes in code, he was utterly frank in recording the events of his day, both public and private, the major affairs of state or his quarrels with his wife. Altogether he wrote about 1.3 million words. When the diary was first deciphered and published in the nineteenth century, it made him newly famous. As a document of social history it is unsurpassed for its rich detail, honesty, and immediacy. But more than that, it gives us a sense of somebody else's world: what it was like to live in the Restoration, and what it was like to see through the eyes of Pepys.

From The Diary

[The Great Fire]

September 2, 1666

Lords day. Some of our maids sitting up late last night to get things ready against our feast today, Jane called us up, about 3 in the morning, to tell us of a great fire they saw in the City.[1] So I rose, and slipped on my nightgown and went to her window, and thought it to be on the back side of Mark Lane[2] at the furthest; but being unused to such fires as followed, I thought it far enough off, and so went to bed again and to sleep. About 7 rose again to dress myself, and there looked out at the window and saw the fire not so much as it was, and further off. So to my closet[3] to set things to rights after yesterday's cleaning. By and by Jane comes and tells me that she hears that above 300 houses have been burned down tonight by the fire we saw, and that it was now burning down all Fish Street by London Bridge. So I made myself ready presently,[4] and walked to the Tower and there got up upon one of the high places, Sir J. Robinson's little son going up with me; and there I did see the houses at that end of the bridge all on fire, and an infinite great fire on this and the other side the end of the bridge—which, among other people, did trouble me for poor little Michell[5] and our Sarah on the Bridge. So down, with my heart full of trouble, to the Lieutenant of the Tower, who tells me that it begun this morning in the King's baker's house in Pudding Lane, and that it hath burned down St. Magnus' Church and most part of Fish Street already. So I down to the waterside and there got a boat and through bridge, and there saw a lamentable fire. Poor Michell's house, as far as the Old Swan,[6] already burned that way and the fire running further, that in a very little time it got as far as the Steelyard while I was there. Everybody endeavoring to remove their goods, and flinging into the river or bringing them into lighters[7] that lay off. Poor people staying in their houses as long as till the very fire touched them, and then running into boats or clambering from one pair of stair by the waterside to another. And among other things, the poor pigeons I perceive were loath to leave their houses, but hovered about the win-

---

1. The Fire of London, which was to destroy four fifths of the central city, had begun an hour earlier. For another description see Dryden's *Annus Mirabilis* above.
2. Mark Lane was near Pepys's own house in Seething Lane.
3. A small private room or study.

4. Immediately.
5. William Michell and his wife, Betty, one of Pepys's old flames, lived near London Bridge. Sarah had been a maid of the Pepys's.
6. A tavern in Thames Street, near the source of the fire.
7. Barges.

dows and balconies till they were some of them burned, their wings, and fell down.

Having stayed, and in an hour's time seen the fire rage every way, and nobody to my sight endeavoring to quench it, but to remove their goods and leave all to the fire; and having seen it get as far as the Steelyard, and the wind mighty high and driving it into the city, and everything, after so long a drought, proving combustible, even the very stones of churches, and among other things, the poor steeple by which pretty Mrs. [8] lives, and whereof my old school-fellow Elborough is parson, taken fire in the very top and there burned till it fell down—I to Whitehall[9] with a gentleman with me who desired to go off from the Tower to see the fire in my boat—to Whitehall, and there up to the King's closet in the chapel, where people came about me and I did give them an account dismayed them all; and word was carried in to the King, so I was called for and did tell the King and Duke of York what I saw, and that unless his Majesty did command houses to be pulled down, nothing could stop the fire. They seemed much troubled, and the King commanded me to go to my Lord Mayor from him and command him to spare no houses but to pull down before the fire every way. The Duke of York bid me tell him that if he would have any more soldiers, he shall; and so did my Lord Arlington afterward, as a great secret. Here meeting with Captain Cocke, I in his coach, which he lent me, and Creed with me, to Paul's;[1] and there walked along Watling Street as well as I could, every creature coming away loaden with goods to save—and here and there sick people carried away in beds. Extraordinary good goods carried in carts and on backs. At last met my Lord Mayor in Canning Street, like a man spent, with a hankercher[2] about his neck. To the King's message, he cried like a fainting woman, "Lord, what can I do? I am spent. People will not obey me. I have been pulling down houses. But the fire overtakes us faster than we can do it." That he needed no more soldiers; and that for himself, he must go and refresh himself, having been up all night. So he left me, and I him, and walked home—seeing people all almost distracted and no manner of means used to quench the fire. The houses too, so very thick thereabouts, and full of matter for burning, as pitch and tar, in Thames Street—and warehouses of oil and wines and brandy and other things. Here I saw Mr. Isaak Houblon, that handsome man—prettily dressed and dirty at his door at Dowgate, receiving some of his brothers' things whose houses were on fire; and as he says, have been removed twice already, and he doubts[3] (as it soon proved) that they must be in a little time removed from his house also—which was a sad consideration. And to see the churches all filling with goods, by people who themselves should have been quietly there at this time.

By this time it was about 12 o'clock, and so home and there find my

---

8. Mrs. Horsely, a beauty admired and pursued by Pepys.
9. Palace in central London.

1. St. Paul's Cathedral, later ravaged by the fire.
2. Handkerchief.
3. Fears.

guests, which was Mr. Wood and his wife, Barbary Shelden, and also Mr. Moone—she mighty fine, and her husband, for aught I see, a likely[4] man. But Mr. Moone's design and mine, which was to look over my closet and please him with the sight thereof, which he hath long desired, was wholly disappointed, for we were in great trouble and disturbance at this fire, not knowing what to think of it. However, we had an extraordinary good dinner, and as merry as at this time we could be.

While at dinner, Mrs. Batelier came to enquire after Mr. Woolfe and Stanes (who it seems are related to them), whose houses in Fish Street are all burned, and they in a sad condition. She would not stay in the fright.

As soon as dined, I and Moone away and walked through the City, the streets full of nothing but people and horses and carts loaden with goods, ready to run over one another, and removing goods from one burned house to another—they now removing out of Canning Street (which received goods in the morning) into Lumbard Street and further; and among others, I now saw my little goldsmith Stokes receiving some friend's goods, whose house itself was burned the day after. We parted at Paul's, he home and I to Paul's Wharf, where I had appointed a boat to attend me; and took in Mr. Carcasse and his brother, whom I met in the street, and carried them below and above bridge, to and again, to see the fire, which was now got further, both below and above, and no likelihood of stopping it. Met with the King and Duke of York in their barge, and with them to Queenhithe[5] and there called Sir Rd. Browne to them. Their order was only to pull down houses apace, and so below bridge at the waterside; but little was or could be done, the fire coming upon them so fast. Good hopes there was of stopping it at the Three Cranes above, and at Buttolph's Wharf below bridge, if care be used; but the wind carries it into the City, so as we know not by the waterside what it doth there. River full of lighters and boats taking in goods, and good goods swimming in the water; and only, I observed that hardly one lighter or boat in three that had the goods of a house in, but there was a pair of virginals[6] in it. Having seen as much as I could now, I away to Whitehall by appointment, and there walked to St. James's Park, and there met my wife and Creed and Wood and his wife and walked to my boat, and there upon the water again, and to the fire up and down, it still increasing and the wind great. So near the fire as we could for smoke; and all over the Thames, with one's face in the wind you were almost burned with a shower of firedrops—this is very true—so as houses were burned by these drops and flakes of fire, three or four, nay five or six houses, one from another. When we could endure no more upon the water, we to a little alehouse on the Bankside over against the Three Cranes, and there stayed till it was dark almost and saw the fire grow; and as it grew darker, appeared more and more, and in corners and upon

4. Promising.
5. Harbor in Thames Street. Sir Richard Browne

was a former lord mayor.
6. Table-size harpsichord, popular at the time.

steeples and between churches and houses, as far as we could see up the
hill of the City, in a most horrid malicious bloody flame, not like the
fine flame of an ordinary fire. Barbary[7] and her husband away before us.
We stayed till, it being darkish, we saw the fire as only one entire arch
of fire from this to the other side the bridge, and in a bow up the hill,
for an arch of above a mile long. It made me weep to see it. The churches,
houses, and all on fire and flaming at once, and a horrid noise the
flames made, and the cracking of houses at their ruin. So home with a
sad heart, and there find everybody discoursing and lamenting the fire;
and poor Tom Hater came with some few of his goods saved out of his
house, which is burned upon Fish Street hill. I invited him to lie at my
house, and did receive his goods: but was deceived in his lying there,[8]
the noise coming every moment of the growth of the fire, so as we were
forced to begin to pack up our own goods and prepare for their removal.
And did by moonshine (it being brave,[9] dry, and moonshine and warm
weather) carry much of my goods into the garden, and Mr. Hater and I
did remove my money and iron chests into my cellar—as thinking that
the safest place. And got my bags of gold into my office ready to carry
away, and my chief papers of accounts also there, and my tallies[1] into a
box by themselves. So great was our fear, as Sir W. Batten had carts
come out of the country to fetch away his goods this night. We did put
Mr. Hater, poor man, to bed a little; but he got but very little rest, so
much noise being in my house, taking down of goods.

September 5, 1666

I lay down in the office again upon W. Hewer's[2] quilt, being mighty
weary and sore in my feet with going till I was hardly able to stand.
About 2 in the morning my wife calls me up and tells of new cries of
"Fire!"—it being come to Barking Church, which is the bottom of our
lane. I up; and finding it so, resolved presently to take her away; and
did, and took my gold (which was about £2350), W. Hewer, and Jane
down by Poundy's boat to Woolwich.[3] But Lord, what a sad sight it was
by moonlight to see the whole City almost on fire—that you might see
it plain at Woolwich, as if you were by it. There when I came, I find
the gates[4] shut, but no guard kept at all; which troubled me, because of
discourses now begun that there is plot in it and that the French had
done it.[5] I got the gates open, and to Mr. Shelden's,[6] where I locked up
my gold and charged my wife and W. Hewer never to leave the room
without one of them in it night nor day. So back again, by the way
seeing my goods well in the lighters at Deptford and watched well by

7. The actress Elizabeth Knepp, another of Pepys's
mistresses. He calls her "Barbary" because she had
enchanted him by singing *Barbary Allen*.
8. I.e., mistaken in asking him to stay.
9. Fine.
1. Receipts notched on sticks.
2. William Hewer, Pepys's chief clerk. Pepys had
packed or sent away all his own goods.

3. Suburb on the east side of London.
4. Dockyard gates.
5. There were rumors that the French had set the
fire and were invading the city.
6. William Shelden, a Woolwich official at whose
home Mrs. Pepys had stayed the year before, during the plague.

people. Home, and whereas I expected to have seen our house on fire, it being now about 7 o'clock, it was not. But to the fire, and there find greater hopes than I expected; for my confidence of finding our office on fire was such, that I durst not ask anybody how it was with us, till I came and saw it not burned. But going to the fire, I find, by the blowing up of houses and the great help given by the workmen out of the King's yards,[7] sent up by Sir W. Penn, there is a good stop given to it, as well at Mark Lane end as ours—it having only burned the dial[8] of Barking Church, and part of the porch, and was there quenched. I up to the top of Barking steeple, and there saw the saddest sight of desolation that I ever saw. Everywhere great fires. Oil cellars and brimstone and other things burning. I became afeared to stay there long; and therefore down again as fast as I could, the fire being spread as far as I could see it, and to Sir W. Penn's and there eat a piece of cold meat, having eaten nothing since Sunday but the remains of Sunday's dinner.

Here I met with Mr. Young and Whistler; and having removed all my things, and received good hopes that the fire at our end is stopped, they and I walked into the town and find Fanchurch Street, Gracious Street, and Lumbard Street all in dust. The Exchange a sad sight, nothing standing there of all the statues or pillars but Sir Tho. Gresham's picture in the corner.[9] Walked into Moorefields (our feet ready to burn, walking through the town among the hot coals) and find that full of people, and poor wretches carrying their goods there, and everybody keeping his goods together by themselves (and a great blessing it is to them that it is fair weather for them to keep abroad[1] night and day); drank there, and paid twopence for a plain penny loaf.

Thence homeward, having passed through Cheapside and Newgate Market, all burned—and seen Anthony Joyce's house in fire. And took up (which I keep by me) a piece of glass of Mercer's Chapel in the street, where much more was, so melted and buckled with the heat of the fire, like parchment. I also did see a poor cat taken out of a hole in the chimney joining to the wall of the Exchange, with the hair all burned off the body and yet alive. So home at night, and find there good hopes of saving our office—but great endeavors of watching all night and having men ready; and so we lodged them in the office and had drink and bread and cheese for them. And I lay down and slept a good night about midnight—though when I rose, I hear that there had been a great alarm of French and Dutch being risen—which proved nothing. But it is a strange thing to see how long this time did look since Sunday, having been always full of variety of actions, and little sleep, that it looked like a week or more. And I had forgot almost the day of the week.[2]

7. Dockyards.
8. Clock.
9. Sir Thomas Gresham had founded the Royal Exchange, a center for shopping and trading, in

1568. It was rebuilt in 1669.
1. Out of doors.
2. A day later the fire was under control. Pepys's own house was spared.

JOHN BUNYAN
1628–1688

1653:   Conversion.
1660–72:   Imprisoned in Bedford jail.
1675:   Second imprisonment in Bedford jail; *The Pilgrim's Progress* composed.

Bunyan is one of the most remarkable figures in seventeenth-century literature. The son of a poor Bedfordshire tinker (a maker and mender of metal pots), he received only meager schooling and then learned his father's craft. Nothing in the circumstances of his early life could have suggested that he would become a writer known the world over.

His inner life is fully chronicled in his spiritual autobiography, *Grace Abounding to the Chief of Sinners* (1666). Here we learn of his humble parentage, his marriage to a woman (he does not tell us her name) whose dowry consisted only of two pious tracts, and of his military service—in the Parliamentary army (though he neglects to say so). But such details scarcely interest him except as he can use them to reveal the purposes of Divine Providence. *Grace Abounding* was written to show the way by which a man, convinced of his sins, is led by God's grace through the agonies of spiritual crises to a new birth and the assurance of salvation; and to record how the obscure and sinful tinker was transformed into the eloquent and fearless Baptist preacher.

Preachers, both male and female, often even less educated than Bunyan, were common phenomena among the sects during the Commonwealth. They wished no ordination but the "call," and they could dispense with learning since they abounded in inspiration, inner light, and the gifts conferred by the Holy Spirit. In November 1660, the Anglican church began to persecute and silence the Dissenting sects. Jails filled with unlicensed Nonconformist preachers, and Bunyan was one of the prisoners. Refusing to keep silent, he chose imprisonment and so for twelve years remained in Bedford jail, preaching to his fellow prisoners and writing religious books. Upon his release, he was called to the pastorate of a Nonconformist group in Bedford. It was during a second imprisonment, in 1675, when the Test Act was once again rigorously enforced against Nonconformists, that he wrote his greatest work, *The Pilgrim's Progress from This World to That Which Is to Come* (1678), revised and augmented in the third edition (1679). Bunyan was a prolific writer: part 2 of *The Pilgrim's Progress*, dealing with the journey of Christian's wife and children, appeared in 1684; *The Life and Death of Mr. Badman*, in 1680; *The Holy War*, in 1682. But these major works form only a small part of all his writings.

The Pilgrim's Progress is the most popular allegory in our literature. Its basic metaphor—life is a journey—is simple and familiar; the objects that the pilgrim Christian meets are homely and commonplace: a quagmire, the highway, the bypaths and short cuts through pleasant meadows; the inn, the steep hill, the town fair on market day; the river that must be forded. Such objects have the immediacy of daily experience, a quality that recalls the equally homely parables of Jesus, but Bunyan's allegorizing of these details charges them with spiritual significance. Moreover, this is a tale of adventure. If the road that Christian travels is the King's Highway, it is also a perilous path along which we encounter giants, wild beasts, hobgoblins, and the terrible Apollyon, "the angel of the bottomless pit," with whom Christian must fight. Bunyan keeps the tale firmly based on human experience—whether in the vivid characterization of other travelers along the way (who represent states of the soul and intellectual or moral attitudes) or in the inevitably right arrangement of Christian's own experiences, from the first sight that we catch of him as his reading in the book convinces him of his sins and evokes his cry of terror, to the moving account of his death with Hopeful in the river. Finally, Bunyan's style, modeled on the prose of the English Bible, together with his concrete language and carefully observed details, enables even the simplest reader to share the experiences of the characters. What could be better than the following sentence? "Some cry out against sin even as the mother cries out against her child in her lap, when she calleth it slut and naughty girl, and then falls to hugging and kissing it." In a secular age like the present, *The Pilgrim's Progress* is no longer a household book; but it survives in the phrases it gave to our language: "the slough of despond," "the house beautiful," "Mr. Worldly-Wiseman," "Vanity Fair." And it lives again for anyone who reads beyond the first page.

From Grace Abounding to the Chief of Sinners

It would be too long for me here to stay, to tell you in particular how God did set me down in all the things of Christ, and how he did, that he might so do, lead me into his words, yea and also how he did open them unto me, make them shine before me, and cause them to dwell with me and comfort me over and over, both of his own being, and the being of his Son, and Spirit, and Word, and Gospel.

Only this, as I said before I will say unto you again, that in general he was pleased to take this course with me, first, to suffer me to be afflicted with temptation concerning them, and then reveal them to me; as sometimes I should lie under great guilt for sin, even crushed to the ground therewith, and then the Lord would shew me the death of Christ, yea and so sprinkle my Conscience with his Blood, that I should find, and that before I was aware, that in that Conscience where but just now did reign and rage the Law, even there would rest and abide the Peace and Love of *God* through Christ.

Now had I an evidence, as I thought, of my salvation from Heaven, with many golden Seals thereon, all hanging in my sight; now could I remember this manifestation, and the other discovery of grace with comfort; and should often long and desire that the last day were come, that I might forever be inflamed with the sight, and joy, and communion of him, whose Head was crowned with Thorns, whose Face was spit on, and Body broken, and Soul made an offering for my sins: for whereas before I lay continually trembling at the mouth of Hell; now me thought

I was got so far therefrom, that I could not, when I looked back, scarce discern it; and O thought I, that I were fourscore years old now, that I might die quickly, that my soul might be gone to rest.

But before I had got thus far out of these my temptations, I did greatly long to see some ancient Godly man's Experience, who had writ some hundred of years before I was born; for, for those who had writ in our days, I thought (but I desire them now to pardon me) that they had Writ only that which others felt, or else had, through the strength of their Wits and Parts, studied to answer such Objections as they perceived others were perplexed with, without going down themselves into the deep. Well, after many such longings in my mind, the God in whose hands are all our days and ways, did cast into my hand, one day, a book of *Martin Luther*, his comment on the *Galathians*, so old that it was ready to fall piece from piece, if I did but turn it over. Now I was pleased much that such an old book had fallen into my hand; the which, when I had but a little way perused, I found my condition in his experience, so largely and profoundly handled, as if his Book had been written out of my heart; this made me marvel: for thus thought I, this man could not know anything of the state of Christians now, but must needs write and speak of the Experience of former days.

Besides, he doth most gravely also, in that book debate of the rise of these temptations, namely, Blasphemy, Desperation, and the like, shewing that the law of *Moses*, as well as the Devil, Death, and Hell, hath a very great hand therein; the which at first was very strange to me, but considering and watching, I found it so indeed. But of Particulars here I intend nothing, only this methinks I must let fall before all men, I do prefer this book of Mr. *Luther* upon the *Galathians*, (excepting the Holy Bible) before all the books that ever I have seen, as most fit for a wounded Conscience.

*   *   *

And now I found, as I thought, that I loved Christ dearly. O me thought my soul cleaved unto him, my affections cleaved unto him. I felt love to him as hot as fire, and now, as Job said, I thought I should die in my nest; but I did quickly find that my great love was but little, and that I, who had as I thought such burning love to Jesus Christ, could let him go again for a trifle. God can tell how to abase us, and can hide pride from man. Quickly after this my love was tried to purpose.

For after the Lord had in this manner thus graciously delivered me from this great and sore temptation, and had set me down so sweetly in the faith of his holy gospel, and had given me such strong consolation and blessed evidence from heaven touching my interest in his love through Christ; the Tempter came upon me again, and that with a more grievous and dreadful temptation than before.

And that was to sell and part with this most blessed Christ, to exchange him for the things of this life, for any thing: the temptation lay upon me for the space of a year, and did follow me so continually that I was not rid of it one day in a month, no not sometimes one hour in many days together, unless I was asleep.

And though in my judgment I was persuaded that those who were once effectually in Christ (as I hoped, through his grace, I had seen myself) could never lose him forever . . . yet it was a continual vexation to me to think I should have so much as one such thought within me against a Christ, a Jesus, that had done for me as he had done; and yet then I had almost none others, but such blasphemous ones.

But it was neither my dislike of the thought, nor yet any desire and endeavor to resist it, that in the least did shake or abate the continuation or force and strength thereof; for it did always in almost whatever I thought intermix itself therewith, in such sort that I could neither eat my food, stoop for a pin, chop a stick, or cast mine eye to look on this or that, but still the temptation would come, *Sell Christ for this, or sell Christ for that; sell him, sell him.*

Sometimes it would run in my thoughts not so little as a hundred times together, Sell him, sell him, sell him; against which, I may say, for whole hours together, I have been forced to stand as continually leaning and forcing my spirit against it, lest haply before I were aware, some wicked thought might arise in my heart that might consent thereto; and sometimes also the Tempter would make me believe I had consented to it, then should I be as tortured on a rack for whole days together.

This temptation did put me to such scares lest I should sometimes, I say, consent thereto and be overcome therewith, that by the very force of my mind in laboring to gainsay and resist this wickedness, my very body also would be put into action or motion, by way of pushing or thrusting with my hands or elbows; still answering, as fast as the destroyer said *Sell him:* I will not, I will not, I will not, I will not, no, not for thousands, thousands, thousands of worlds, thus reckoning lest I should in the midst of these assaults set too low a value of him, even until I scarce well knew where I was, or how to be composed again.

At these seasons he would not let me eat my food at quiet, but forsooth when I was set at the table at my meat, I must go hence to pray, I must leave my food now, just now, so counterfeit holy would this Devil be. When I was thus tempted, I should say in myself, *Now I am at my meat, let me make an end.* No, said he, *you must do it now, or you will displease God and despise Christ.* Wherefore I was much afflicted with these things; and because of the sinfulness of my nature (imagining that these things were impulses from God), I should deny to do it as if I denied God; and then should I be as guilty because I did not obey a temptation of the Devil, as if I had broken the law of God indeed.

But to be brief, one morning, as I did lie in my bed, I was, as at other times, most fiercely assaulted with this temptation, to *sell and part with Christ;* the wicked suggestion still running in my mind, *Sell him, sell him, sell him,* as fast as a man could speak; against which also in my mind, as at other times, I answered, No, no, not for thousands, thousands, thousands, at least twenty times together; but at last, after much striving, even until I was almost out of breath, I felt this thought pass through my heart, *Let him go if he will!* and I thought also that I felt my heart freely consent thereto. Oh, the diligence of Satan! Oh, the desperateness of man's heart!

Now was the battle won, and down I fell, as a bird that is shot from the top of a tree, into great guilt and fearful despair; thus getting out of my bed, I went moping into the field; but God knows with as heavy a heart as mortal man, I think, could bear; where for the space of two hours, I was like a man bereft of life, and as now past all recovery, and bound over to eternal punishment.

* * *

Now was I as one bound, I felt myself shut up unto the judgment to come; nothing now for two years together would abide with me but damnation and an expectation of damnation: I say nothing now would abide with me but this, save some few moments for relief, as in the sequel you will see.

These words were to my soul like fetters of brass to my legs, in the continual sound of which I went for several months together. But about ten or eleven a clock one day, as I was walking under a hedge, full of sorrow and guilt, God knows, and bemoaning myself for this hard hap, that such a thought should arise within me, suddenly this sentence bolted in upon me, *The blood of Christ remits all guilt*; at this I made a stand in my spirit: with that, this word took hold upon me, *The blood of Jesus Christ his son cleanseth us from all sin.*

Now I began to conceive peace in my soul, and methought I saw as if the tempter did leer and steal away from me, as being ashamed of what he had done. At the same time also I had my sin and the blood of Christ thus represented to me, That my sin when compared to the blood of Christ was no more to it than this little clot or stone before me is to this vast and wide field that here I see. This gave me good encouragement for the space of two or three hours, in which time also methought I saw by faith the son of God as suffering for my sins. But because it tarried not, I therefore sunk in my spirit under exceeding guilt again.

* * *

And now I was both a burden and a terror to myself, nor did I ever so know, as now, what it was to be weary of my life and yet afraid to die. Oh, how gladly now would I have been anybody but myself! Anything but a man! and in any condition but mine own! for there was nothing did pass more frequently over my mind, than that it was impossible for me to be forgiven my transgression, and to be saved from the wrath to come.

* * *

Once as I was walking to and fro in a good man's shop, bemoaning to myself in my sad and doleful state, afflicting myself with self-abhorrence for this wicked and ungodly thought, lamenting also for this hard hap of mine, for that I should commit so great a sin, greatly fearing I should not be pardoned; praying also in my heart, That if this sin of mine did differ from that against the Holy Ghost, the Lord would show it to me: and being now ready to sink with fear, suddenly there was as if there had rushed in at the window the noise of wind upon me, but very pleasant, and as if I had heard a voice speaking, *Didst ever refuse to be justified by the blood of Christ?* and withal my whole life of profession[1] past was in a moment opened to me, wherein I was made to see that designedly I had not; so my heart answered groaningly, *No.* Then fell with power that word of God upon me, *See that ye refuse not him that speaketh* (Hebrews 12.25). This made a strange seizure upon my spirit; it brought light with it, and commanded a silence in my heart of all those tumultuous thoughts that before did use, like masterless hellhounds to roar and bellow and make a hideous noise within me. It showed me also that Jesus Christ had yet a work of grace and mercy for me, that he had not, as I had feared, quite forsaken and cast off my soul; yea, this was a kind of chide for my proneness to desperation; a kind of threatening me if I did not, notwithstanding my sins and the heinousness of them, venture my salvation upon the son of God. . . . This lasted in the savor of it, for about three or four days, and then I began to mistrust and to despair again.

* * *

At another time I remember I was again much under the question, Whether the blood of Christ was sufficient to save my soul? In which doubt I continued from morning till about seven or eight at night; and at last when I was, as it were, quite worn out with fear lest it should not lay hold on me, these words did sound suddenly within me, *He is able*: but me thought this word *able* was spoke so loud unto me, it showed such a *great* word, it seemed to be writ in *great* letters, and gave such a justle to my fear and doubt (I mean for the time it tarried with me, which was about a day) as I never had from that, all my life either before or after that.

But one morning when I was again at prayer and trembling under the fear of this, that no word of God could help me, that piece of a sentence darted in upon me, *My grace is sufficient.* At this me thought I felt some stay, as if there might be hopes. But O how good a thing is it for God to send his word! for about a fortnight before, I was looking on this very place, and then I thought it could not come near my soul with comfort, and threw down my book in a pet. Then I thought it was not large enough for me; no, not large enough; but now it was as if it had arms of grace so wide that it could not only enclose me, but many more besides.

By these words I was sustained, yet not without exceeding conflicts, for the space of seven or eight weeks: for my peace would be in and out

---

1. My life as a believing (professing) Christian.

sometimes twenty times a day. Comfort now and trouble presently; peace now, and before I could go a furlong, as full of fear and guilt as ever heart could hold. And this was not only now and then, but my whole seven weeks' experience; for this about the sufficiency of grace and that of Esau's parting with his birthright[2] would be like a pair of scales within my mind, sometimes one end would be uppermost and sometimes again the other, according to which would be my peace or trouble.

1666

From The Pilgrim's Progress

From this World to That Which Is to Come: Delivered Under the Similitude of a Dream

[*Christian Sets out for the Celestial City*]

As I walked through the wilderness of this world, I lighted on a certain place where was a Den, and I laid me down in that place to sleep; and, as I slept, I dreamed a dream. I dreamed, and behold I saw a man clothed with rags, standing in a certain place, with his face from his own house, a book in his hand, and a great burden upon his back (Isaiah lxiv.6; Luke xiv.33; Psalms xxxviii.4; Habakkuk ii.2; Acts xvi.31). I looked and saw him open the book and read therein; and, as he read, he wept, and trembled; and not being able longer to contain, he brake out with a lamentable cry, saying, "What shall I do?" (Acts ii.37).

In this plight, therefore, he went home and refrained himself as long as he could, that his wife and children should not perceive his distress; but he could not be silent long, because that his trouble increased. Wherefore at length he brake his mind to his wife and children; and thus he began to talk to them. O my dear wife, said he, and you the children of my bowels, I your dear friend am in myself undone by reason of a burden that lieth hard upon me; moreover, I am for certain informed that this our city will be burned with fire from heaven, in which fearful overthrow both myself, with thee, my wife, and you, my sweet babes, shall miserably come to ruin, except (the which yet I see not) some way of escape can be found, whereby we may be delivered. At this his relations were sore amazed; not for that they believed that what he had said to them was true, but because they thought that some frenzy distemper[1] had got into his head; therefore, it drawing towards night, and they hoping that sleep might settle his brains, with all haste they got him to bed; but the night was as troublesome to him as the day; wherefore, instead of sleeping, he spent it in sighs and tears. So when the morning was

---

2. Bunyan believed that when the fatal phrase about "letting Christ go if he would" flashed through his mind, all power to share in the Christian blessing was eternally lost to him, as Esau sold his birth-right irrevocably, irretrievably, forever.

1. A malady causing madness; the use of "frenzy" as an adjective was not uncommon in the 17th century.

come, they would know how he did. He told them, Worse and worse; he also set to talking to them again, but they began to be hardened. They also thought to drive away his distemper by harsh and surly carriages[2] to him: sometimes they would deride, sometimes they would chide, and sometimes they would quite neglect him. Wherefore he began to retire himself to his chamber, to pray for and pity them, and also to condole his own misery; he would also walk solitarily in the fields, sometimes reading, and sometimes praying; and thus for some days he spent his time.

Now I saw, upon a time, when he was walking in the fields, that he was (as he was wont) reading in this book, and greatly distressed in his mind; and as he read, he burst out, as he had done before, crying, "What shall I do to be saved?"

I saw also that he looked this way and that way, as if he would run; yet he stood still, because (as I perceived) he could not tell which way to go. I looked then, and saw a man named Evangelist[3] coming to him, who asked, Wherefore dost thou cry? (Job xxxiii.23). He answered, Sir, I perceive by the book in my hand that I am condemned to die, and after that to come to judgment (Hebrews ix.27), and I find that I am not willing to do the first (Job xvi.21), nor able to do the second (Ezekiel xxii.14). . . . .

Then said Evangelist, Why not willing to die, since this life is attended with so many evils? The man answered, Because I fear that this burden that is upon my back will sink me lower than the grave, and I shall fall into Tophet[4] (Isaiah xxx.33). And, sir, if I be not fit to go to prison, I am not fit to go to judgment, and from thence to execution; and the thoughts of these things make me cry.[5]

Then said Evangelist, If this be thy condition, why standest thou still? He answered, Because I know not whither to go. Then he gave him a parchment roll, and there was written within, "Fly from the wrath to come" (Matthew iii.7).

The man therefore read it, and looking upon Evangelist very carefully,[6] said, Whither must I fly? Then said Evangelist, pointing with his finger over a very wide field, Do you see yonder wicketgate?[7] (Matthew vii.13, 14.) The man said, No. Then said the other, Do you see yonder shining light? (Psalms cxix.105; II Peter i.19.) He said, I think I do. Then said Evangelist, Keep that light in your eye, and go up directly thereto; so shalt thou see the gate; at which when thou knockest it shall be told thee what thou shalt do.

So I saw in my dream that the man began to run. Now, he had not run far from his own door, but his wife and children perceiving it, began to cry after him to return; but the man put his fingers in his ears, and ran on, crying, Life! life! eternal life! (Luke xiv.26.) So he looked not

---

2. Behavior.
3. A preacher of the Gospel; literally, a bearer of good news.
4. The place near Jerusalem where bodies and filth were burned; hence, by association, a name for hell.
5. Cry out.
6. Sorrowfully.
7. A small gate in or beside a larger gate.

behind him, but fled towards the middle of the plain (Genesis xix. 17).

The neighbors also came out to see him run (Jeremiah xx. 10); and as he ran some mocked, others threatened, and some cried after him to return; and, among those that did so, there were two that resolved to fetch him back by force. The name of the one was Obstinate, and the name of the other Pliable. Now by this time the man was got a good distance from them; but, however, they were resolved to pursue him, which they did, and in a little time they overtook him. Then said the man, Neighbors, wherefore are ye come? They said, To persuade you to go back with us. But he said, That can by no means be; you dwell, said he, in the City of Destruction (the place also where I was born) I see it to be so; and, dying there, sooner or later, you will sink lower than the grave, into a place that burns with fire and brimstone; be content, good neighbors, and go along with me.

OBST. What! said Obstinate, and leave our friends and our comforts behind us?

CHR. Yes, said Christian (for that was his name), because that ALL which you shall forsake is not worthy to be compared with a little of that which I am seeking to enjoy (II Corinthians v. 17); and, if you will go along with me, and hold it, you shall fare as I myself; for there, where I go, is enough and to spare (Luke xv. 17). Come away, and prove my words.

OBST. What are the things you seek, since you leave all the world to find them?

CHR. I seek an inheritance incorruptible, undefiled, and that fadeth not away (I Peter i. 4), and it is laid up in heaven, and safe there (Hebrews xi. 16), to be bestowed, at the time appointed, on them that diligently seek it. Read it so, if you will, in my book.

OBST. Tush! said Obstinate, away with your book; will you go back with us or no?

CHR. No, not I, said the other, because I have laid my hand to the plow (Luke ix. 62).

OBST. Come, then, neighbor Pliable, let us turn again, and go home without him; there is a company of these crazed-headed coxcombs,[8] that, when they take a fancy by the end, are wiser in their own eyes than seven men that can render a reason (Proverbs xxvi. 16).

PLI. Then said Pliable, Don't revile; if what the good Christian says is true, the things he looks after are better than ours; my heart inclines to go with my neighbor.

OBST. What! more fools still? Be ruled by me, go back; who knows whither such a brain-sick fellow will lead you? Go back, go back, and be wise.

CHR. Nay, but do thou come with thy neighbor, Pliable; there are such things to be had which I spoke of, and many more glories besides. If you believe not me, read here in this book; and for the truth of what

8. Fools; "fancy": delusion.

is expressed therein, behold, all is confirmed by the blood of Him that made it (Hebrews ix.17–22; xiii.20.).

PLI. Well, neighbour Obstinate, said Pliable, I begin to come to a point,[9] I intend to go along with this good man, and to cast in my lot with him: but, my good companion, do you know the way to this desired place?

CHR. I am directed by a man, whose name is Evangelist, to speed me to a little gate that is before us, where we shall receive instructions about the way.

PLI. Come, then, good neighbor, let us be going. Then they went both together. * * *

[The Slough of Despond]

Now I saw in my dream, that just as they had ended this talk they drew near to a very miry slough,[1] that was in the midst of the plain; and they, being heedless, did both fall suddenly into the bog. The name of the slough was Despond. Here, therefore, they wallowed for a time, being grievously bedaubed with dirt; and Christian, because of the burden that was on his back, began to sink in the mire.

PLI. Then said Pliable, Ah, neighbor Christian, where are you now?

CHR. Truly, said Christian, I do not know.

PLI. At that Pliable began to be offended, and angrily said to his fellow, Is this the happiness you have told me all this while of? If we have such ill speed at our first setting out, what may we expect 'twixt this and our journey's end? May I get out again with my life, you shall possess the brave country alone for me. And, with that, he gave a desperate struggle or two, and got out of the mire on that side of the slough which was next[2] to his own house: so away he went, and Christian saw him no more.

Wherefore Christian was left to tumble in the Slough of Despond alone: but still he endeavored to struggle to that side of the slough that was further from his own house, and next to the wicket-gate; the which he did, but could not get out, because of the burden that was upon his back: but I beheld in my dream, that a man came to him, whose name was Help, and asked him what he did there?

CHR. Sir, said Christian, I was bid go this way by a man called Evangelist, who directed me also to yonder gate, that I might escape the wrath to come; and as I was going thither I fell in here.

HELP. But why did not you look for the steps?

CHR. Fear followed me so hard that I fled the next way, and fell in.

HELP. Then said he, Give me thy hand; so he gave him his hand, and he drew him out, and set him upon sound ground, and bid him go on his way.

Then I stepped to him that plucked him out, and said, Sir, wherefore,

9. Decision.
1. Pronounce to rhyme with *now*.   2. Nearest.

since over this place is the way from the City of Destruction to yonder gate, is it that this plat[3] is not mended, that poor travelers might go thither with more security? And he said unto me, This miry slough is such a place as cannot be mended; it is the descent whither the scum and filth that attends conviction for sin doth continually run, and therefore it was called the Slough of Despond; for still, as the sinner is awakened about his lost condition, there ariseth in his soul many fears, and doubts, and discouraging apprehensions, which all of them get together, and settle in his place. And this is the reason of the badness of this ground. * * *

[Vanity Fair][4]

Then I saw in my dream, that when they were got out of the wilderness, they presently saw a town before them, and the name of that town is Vanity; and at the town there is a fair kept, called Vanity Fair; it is kept all the year long; it beareth the name of Vanity Fair because the town where it is kept is lighter than vanity; and also because all that is there sold, or that cometh thither, is vanity. As is the saying of the wise, "All that cometh is vanity" (Ecclesiastes i.2, 14; ii.11, 17; xi.8; Isaiah xl.17).

This fair is no new-erected business, but a thing of ancient standing; I will show you the original of it.

Almost five thousand years agone, there were pilgrims walking to the Celestial City, as these two honest persons are; and Beelzebub, Apollyon, and Legion,[5] with their companions, perceiving by the path that the pilgrims made, that their way to the city lay through this town of Vanity, they contrived here to set up a fair; a fair wherein should be sold all sorts of vanity, and that it should last all the year long. Therefore at this fair are all such merchandise sold, as houses, lands, trades, places, honors, preferments,[6] titles, countries, kingdoms, lusts, pleasures, and delights of all sorts, as whores, bawds, wives, husbands, children, masters, servants, lives, blood, bodies, souls, silver, gold, pearls, precious stones, and what not.

And, moreover, at this fair there is at all times to be seen jugglings, cheats, games, plays, fools, apes, knaves, and rogues, and that of every kind.

3. A plot of ground.

4. In this, perhaps the best-known episode in the book, Bunyan characteristically turns one of the most familiar institutions in contemporary England—annual fairs—into a allegory of universal spiritual significance. Christian and his companion Faithful pass through the town of Vanity at the season of the local fair. "Vanity" means "emptiness" or "worthlessness," and hence the fair is an allegory of worldliness and the corruption of the religious life through the attractions of the world. From earliest times numerous fairs were held for stated periods throughout Britain; to them the most

important merchants from all over Europe brought their wares. The serious business of buying and selling was accompanied by all sorts of diversions—eating, drinking, and other fleshly pleasures, as well as spectacles of strange animals, acrobats, and other wonders.

5. Beelzebub, prince of the devils (Matthew 12.24); Apollyon, the Destroyer, "the Angel of the bottomless pit" (Revelation 9.11); Legion, the "unclean spirit" sent by Jesus into the Gadarene swine (Mark 5.9).

6. Appointments and promotions to political or ecclesiastical positions.

Here are to be seen, too, and that for nothing, thefts, murders, adulteries, false swearers, and that of a blood-red color.

And as in other fairs of less moment, there are the several rows and streets, under their proper names, where such and such wares are vended; so here likewise you have the proper places, rows, streets (viz., countries and kingdoms), where the wares of this fair are soonest to be found. Here is the Britain Row, the French Row, the Italian Row, the Spanish Row, the German Row, where several sorts of vanities are to be sold. But, as in other fairs, some one commodity is as the chief of all the fair, so the ware of Rome and her merchandise[7] is greatly promoted in this fair; only our English nation, with some others, have taken a dislike thereat.

Now, as I said, the way to the Celestial City lies just through this town where this lusty[8] fair is kept; and he that will go to the City, and yet not go through this town, must needs "go out of the world" (I Corinthians v. 10). The Prince of princes himself, when here, went through this town to his own country, and that upon a fair-day too,[9] yea, and as I think, it was Beelzebub, the chief lord of this fair, that invited him to buy of his vanities; yea, would have made him lord of the fair, would he but have done him reverence as he went through the town. (Matthew iv. 8; Luke iv. 5–7.) Yea, because he was such a person of honor, Beelzebub had him from street to street, and showed him all the kingdoms of the world in a little time, that he might, if possible, allure the Blessed One to cheapen[1] and buy some of his vanities; but he had no mind to the merchandise, and therefore left the town, without laying out so much as one farthing upon these vanities. This fair, therefore, is an ancient thing, of long standing, and a very great fair.

Now these pilgrims, as I said, must needs go through this fair. Well, so they did; but, behold, even as they entered into the fair, all the people in the fair were moved, and the town itself as it were in a hubbub about them; and that for several reasons: for

First, The pilgrims were clothed with such kind of raiment as was diverse from the raiment of any that traded in that fair. The people, therefore, of the fair, made a great gazing upon them: some said they were fools, some they were bedlams,[2] and some they are outlandish men. (I Corinthians ii. 7, 8.)

Secondly, And as they wondered at their apparel, so they did likewise at their speech; for few could understand what they said; they naturally spoke the language of Canaan,[3] but they that kept the fair were the men of this world; so that, from one end of the fair to the other, they seemed barbarians[4] each to the other.

Thirdly, But that which did not a little amuse the merchandisers was

7. The usages and the temporal power of the Roman Catholic Church.

8. Merry.

9. The temptation of Jesus in the wilderness (Matthew 4.1–11).

1. Ask the price of.

2. Lunatics from Bethlehem Hospital, the insane asylum in London. "Outlandish": foreign.

3. The Promised Land, ultimately conquered by the Children of Israel (Joshua 4) and settled by them: hence the pilgrims speak the language of the Bible and of the true religion. Dissenters were notorious for their habitual use of biblical language.

4. The Greeks and Romans so designated all those who spoke a foreign tongue.

that these pilgrims set very light by all their wares; they cared not so much as to look upon them; and if they called upon them to buy, they would put their fingers in their ears, and cry, "Turn away mine eyes from beholding vanity," and look upwards, signifying that their trade and traffic was in heaven. (Psalms cxix.37; Philippians iii.19, 20.)

One chanced mockingly, beholding the carriages of the men, to say unto them, What will ye buy? But they, looking gravely upon him, said, "We buy the truth" (Proverbs xxiii.23). At that there was an occasion taken to despise the men the more; some mocking, some taunting, some speaking reproachfully, and some calling upon others to smite them. At last things came to an hubbub and great stir in the fair, insomuch that all order was confounded. Now was word presently brought to the great one of the fair, who quickly came down, and deputed some of his most trusty friends to take these men into examination, about whom the fair was almost overturned. So the men were brought to examination; and they that sat upon them[5] asked them whence they came, whither they went, and what they did there, in such an unusual garb? The men told them that they were pilgrims and strangers in the world, and that they were going to their own country, which was the Heavenly Jerusalem (Hebrews xi.13–16); and that they had given no occasion to the men of the town, nor yet to the merchandisers, thus to abuse them, and to let[6] them in their journey, except it was for that, when one asked them what they would buy, they said they would buy the truth. But they that were appointed to examine them did not believe them to be any other than bedlams and mad, or else such as came to put all things into a confusion in the fair. Therefore they took them and beat them, and besmeared them with dirt, and then put them into the cage, that they might be made a spectacle to all the men of the fair. * * *

[The River of Death and the Celestial City]

So I saw that when they[7] awoke, they addressed themselves to go up to the City; but, as I said, the reflection of the sun upon the City (for the City was pure gold, Revelation xxi.18) was so extremely glorious, that they could not, as yet, with open face behold it, but through an instrument made for that purpose. (II Corinthians iii.18.) So I saw that as I went on, there met them two men, in raiment that shone like gold; also their faces shone as the light.

These men asked the pilgrims whence they came; and they told them. They also asked them where they had lodged, what difficulties and dangers, what comforts and pleasures they had met in the way; and they told them. Then said the men that met them, You have but two difficulties more to meet with, and then you are in the City.

Christian then and his companion asked the men to go along with

5. Interrogated and tried them.
6. Hinder.
7. Christian and his companion, Hopeful. Igno-rance, who appears tragically in the final para-graph, had tried to accompany the two pilgrims, but had dropped behind because of his hobbling gait.

them; so they told them they would. But, said they, you must obtain it by your own faith. So I saw in my dream that they went on together till they came in sight of the gate.

Now I further saw that betwixt them and the gate was a river, but there was no bridge to go over; the river was very deep. At the sight, therefore, of this river, the pilgrims were much stunned;[8] but the men that went with them said, You must go through, or you cannot come at the gate.

The pilgrims then began to inquire if there was no other way to the gate; to which they answered, Yes; but there hath not any, save two, to wit, Enoch and Elijah,[9] been permitted to tread that path, since the foundation of the world, nor shall, until the last trumpet shall sound. (I Corinthians xv.51, 52.) The pilgrims then, especially Christian, began to despond in his mind, and looked this way and that, but no way could be found by them by which they might escape the river. Then they asked the men if the waters were all of a depth. They said no; yet they could not help them in that case; for, said they, you shall find it deeper or shallower, as you believe in the King of the place.

They then addressed themselves to the water; and entering, Christian began to sink, and crying out to his good friend Hopeful, he said, I sink in deep waters; the billows go over my head, all his waves go over me! Selah.[1]

Then said the other, Be of good cheer, my brother, I feel the bottom, and it is good. Then said Christian, Ah, my friend, the sorrows of death have compassed me about; I shall not see the land that flows with milk and honey. And with that a great darkness and horror fell upon Christian, so that he could not see before him. Also here he in great measure lost his senses, so that he could neither remember nor orderly talk of any of those sweet refreshments that he had met with in the way of his pilgrimage. But all the words that he spake still tended to discover that he had horror of mind, and heart-fears that he should die in that river, and never obtain entrance in at the gate. Here also, as they that stood by perceived, he was much in the troublesome thoughts of the sins that he had committed, both since and before he began to be a pilgrim. 'Twas also observed that he was troubled with apparitions of hobgoblins and evil spirits; for ever and anon he would intimate so much by words. Hopeful, therefore, here had much ado to keep his brother's head above water; yea, sometimes he would be quite gone down, and then, ere a while, he would rise up again half dead. Hopeful also would endeavor to comfort him, saying, Brother, I see the gate and men standing by to receive us; but Christian would answer, 'Tis you, 'tis you they wait for; you have been Hopeful ever since I knew you. And so have you, said he to Christian. Ah, brother, said he, surely if I was right he would now arise to help me; but for my sins he hath brought me into the snare, and

---

8. Amazed.
9. Both were "translated" alive to heaven. (Genesis 5.24, Hebrews 11.5, 2 Kings 2.11–12).

1. A word of uncertain meaning that occurs frequently at the end of a verse in the Psalms. Bunyan may have supposed it to signify the end.

hath left me. Then said Hopeful, My brother, you have quite forgot the text, where it is said of the wicked, "There are no bands in their death, but their strength is firm. They are not in trouble as other men, neither are they plagued like other men" (Psalms lxxiii. 4, 5). These troubles and distresses that you go through in these waters are no sign that God hath forsaken you, but are sent to try you, whether you will call to mind that which heretofore you have received of his goodness, and live upon him in your distresses.

Then I saw in my dream that Christian was as in a muse[2] a while, to whom also Hopeful added this word, Be of good cheer. Jesus Christ maketh thee whole. And with that Christian brake out with a loud voice, Oh, I see him again! and he tells me, "When thou passest through the waters, I will be with thee; and through the rivers, they shall not overflow thee" (Isaiah xliii. 2). Then they both took courage, and the Enemy was after that as still as a stone, until they were gone over. Christian therefore presently found ground to stand upon, and so it followed that the rest of the river was but shallow. Thus they got over. Now, upon the bank of the river on the other side, they saw the two Shining Men again, who there waited for them. Wherefore, being come out of the river, they saluted them saying, We are ministering spirits, sent forth to minister for those that shall be heirs of salvation. Thus they went along towards the gate. * * *

Now when they were come up to the gate, there was written over it in letters of gold, "Blessed are they that do his commandments, that they may have right to the tree of life, and may enter in through the gates into the city" (Revelation xxii. 14).

Then I saw in my dream, that the Shining Men bid them call at the gate; the which, when they did, some from above looked over the gate, to wit, Enoch, Moses, and Elijah, etc., to whom it was said, These pilgrims are come from the City of Destruction, for the love that they bear to the King of this place; and then the pilgrims gave in unto them each man his certificate, which they had received in the beginning; those, therefore, were carried in to the King, who, when he had read them, said, Where are the men? To whom it was answered, They are standing without the gate. The King then commanded to open the gate, "That the righteous nation," said he, "which keepeth the truth, may enter in" (Isaiah xxvi. 2).

Now I saw in my dream that these two men went in at the gate; and lo, as they entered, they were transfigured, and they had raiment put on that shone like gold. There was also that met them with harps and crowns, and gave them to them: the harps to praise withal, and the crowns in token of honor. Then I heard in my dream that all the bells in the city rang again for joy, and that it was said unto them, "ENTER YE INTO THE JOY OF OUR LORD" (Matthew xxv. 21). I also heard the men themselves, that they sang with a loud voice, saying, "BLESSING AND HONOR, GLORY

---

2. A deep meditation.

AND POWER, BE TO HIM THAT SITTETH UPON THE THRONE, AND TO THE LAMB FOREVER AND EVER" (Revelation v. 13).

Now just as the gates were opened to let in the men, I looked in after them, and, behold, the City shone like the sun; the streets also were paved with gold, and in them walked many men, with crowns on their heads, palms in their hands, and golden harps to sing praises withal.

There were also of them that had wings, and they answered one another without intermission, saying, "Holy, holy, holy is the Lord" (Revelation iv. 8). And after that they shut up the gates, which when I had seen I wished myself among them.

Now while I was gazing upon all these things, I turned my head to look back, and saw Ignorance come up to the riverside; but he soon got over, and that without half that difficulty which the other two men met with. For it happened that there was then in that place one Vain-hope, a ferryman, that with his boat helped him over; so he, as the other, I saw, did ascend the hill to come up to the gate, only he came alone; neither did any man meet him with the least encouragement. When he was come up to the gate, he looked up to the writing that was above, and then began to knock, supposing that entrance should have been quickly administered to him; but he was asked by the men that looked over the top of the gate, Whence came you? and what would you have? He answered, I have eat and drank in the presence of the King, and he has taught in our streets. Then they asked him for his certificate, that they might go in and show it to the King; so he fumbled in his bosom for one, and found none. Then said they, Have you none? But the man answered never a word. So they told the King, but he would not come down to see him, but commanded the two Shining Ones that conducted Christian and Hopeful to the City, to go out and take Ignorance, and bind him hand and foot, and have him away. Then they took him up, and carried him through the air, to the door that I saw in the side of the hill, and put him in there. Then I saw that there was a way to hell, even from the gates of heaven, as well as from the City of Destruction. So I awoke, and behold it was a dream.

1678

WILLIAM CONGREVE

1670–1729

1693:   First play, *The Old Bachelor*, produced.
1695:   *Love for Love*, a successful comedy.
1700:   Failure of *The Way of the World*; Congreve retires from the stage.

On both sides of his family Congreve was descended from well-to-do and prominent county families. His father, a younger son, obtained a commission as lieutenant in the army and moved to Ireland in 1674. There the future playwright was educated at Kilkenny School and Trinity College, Dublin; at both places he was a younger contemporary of Swift. In 1691 he took rooms in the Middle Temple and began to study law, but soon found he preferred the wit of the coffee houses and the theater. Within a year he had so distinguished himself at Will's Coffeehouse that he had become intimate with the great Dryden himself; and his brief career as a dramatist began shortly thereafter.

The success of *The Old Bachelor* (produced in 1693) immediately established him as the most promising young dramatist in London. It had the then phenomenally long run of fourteen days, and Dryden declared it the best first play he had ever read. *The Double Dealer* (produced in 1693) was a near failure, though it evoked one of Dryden's most graceful and gracious poems, in which he praised Congreve as the superior of Jonson and Fletcher and the equal of Shakespeare. *Love for Love* (produced in 1695) was an unqualified success and remains Congreve's most frequently revived play. In 1697 he brought out a tragedy, *The Mourning Bride*, which enjoyed great popular esteem. Congreve's most elegant comedy of manners, *The Way of the World*, received a brilliant production in 1700. But it did not succeed with audiences, and subsequently he gave up the stage. He held a minor government post, which, though a Whig, he was allowed to keep during the Tory ministry of Oxford and Bolingbroke; after the accession of George I he was given a more lucrative government sinecure. Despite the political animosities of the first two decades of the century, he managed to remain on friendly terms with Swift and Pope, and Pope dedicated to him his translation of the *Iliad*. His final years were perplexed by poor health, but were made bearable by the love of Henrietta, duchess of Marlborough, whose last child, a daughter, was in all probability the playwright's.

The Way of the World is one of the wittiest plays ever written, a play to read slowly and savor. Like an expert jeweler, Congreve polished the Restoration comedy of manners to its ultimate sparkle and gloss. The dialogue is epigrammatic and brilliant, the plot is an intricate puzzle, and the characters shine with surprisingly complex facets. Yet the play is not all dazzling surface; it also has depths. Most Restoration comedies begin with the struggle for power, sex, and money, and end with a marriage. In an age that viewed property, not romance, as the basis of marriage, the hero shows his prowess by catching an heiress. *The Way of the World* reflects that standard plot; it is a battle more over a legacy than over a woman, a battle in which sexual attraction is used as a weapon. Yet Congreve, writing late in the period, reveals the weakness of those who treat love as a war or a game: "each deceiver to his cost may find / That marriage frauds too oft are paid in kind." If "the way of the world" is cynical self-interest, it is also the worldly prudence that sees through the ruses of power and turns them to better ends. In this world generosity and affection win the day and true love conquers— with the help of some clever plotting.

At the center of the action are four fully realized characters—Mirabell and Millamant, the hero and heroine, and Fainall and Mrs. Marwood, the two villains—whose stratagems and relations move the play. Around them are characters who serve in one way or another as foils: Witwoud, the would-be wit, with whom we contrast the true wit of Mirabell and Millamant; Petulant, a "humor" character, who affects bluff candor and cynical realism, but succeeds only in being offensive; and Sir Wilfull Witwoud, the booby squire from the country, who serves with Petulant to throw into relief the high good breeding and fineness of nature of the hero and heroine. Finally there is one of Congreve's finest creations, Lady Wishfort ("wish for it"), who though aging and ugly still longs for love, gallantry, and courtship and who is led by her appetites into the trap that Mirabell lays for her.

Because of the complexity of the plot, a summary of the situation at the rise of the curtain may prove helpful. Mirabell (a reformed rake) is sincerely in love with and wishes to marry Millamant, who, though a coquette and a highly sophisticated wit, is a virtuous woman. Mirabell some time before has married off his former mistress, the daughter of Lady Wishfort, to his friend Fainall. Fainall has grown tired of his wife and has been squandering her money on his mistress, Mrs. Marwood. In order to gain access to Millamant, Mirabell has pretended to pay court to the elderly and amorous Lady Wishfort, who is the guardian of Millamant and as such controls half her fortune. But his game has been spoiled by Mrs. Marwood, who nourishes a secret love for Mirabell, and in order to separate him from Millamant has made Lady Wishfort aware of Mirabell's duplicity. Lady Wishfort now loathes Mirabell for making a fool of her—an awkward situation, since if Millamant should marry without her guardian's consent she would lose half her fortune, and Mirabell cannot afford to marry any but a rich wife. It is at this point that the action begins. Mirabell perfects a plot to get such power over Lady Wishfort as to force her to agree to the marriage, while Millamant continues to doubt whether she wishes to marry at all.

The Way of the World

Dramatis Personae[1]

Men

FAINALL, *in love with* MRS. MARWOOD

MIRABELL, *in love with* MRS. MILLAMANT

WITWOUD
PETULANT } *followers of* MRS. MILLAMANT

SIR WILFULL WITWOUD, *half brother to* WITWOUD, *and nephew to* LADY WISHFORT

WAITWELL, *servant to* MIRABELL

Women

LADY WISHFORT, *enemy to* MIRABELL, *for having falsely pretended love to her*

MRS. MILLAMANT, *a fine lady, niece to* LADY WISHFORT, *and loves* MIRABELL

MRS. MARWOOD, *friend to* MR. FAINALL, *and likes* MIRABELL

1. The names of the principal characters reveal their dominant traits: for example, Fainall would *fain* have *all*, with perhaps also the suggestion that he is the complete hypocrite, who *feigns*; Witwoud is the *would-be wit*; Wishfort suggests, *wish for it*; Millamant is the lady with a thousand lovers (*mille amants*); Marwood *would* willingly *Mar* (injure) the lovers; Mincing has an air of affected gentility (i.e., she *minces*), which sorts ill with her vulgar English. "Mrs." is "Mistress," a title then used by young unmarried ladies as well as by the married Mrs. Fainall.

MRS. FAINALL, *daughter to* LADY WISHFORT, *and wife to* FAINALL, *formerly friend to* MIRABELL
FOIBLE, *woman to* LADY WISHFORT
MINCING, *woman to* MRS. MILLAMANT
BETTY, *waitress at the chocolate house*
PEG, *under-servant to* LADY WISHFORT
DANCERS, FOOTMEN, *and* ATTENDANTS

SCENE—*London.*

Prologue

SPOKEN BY MR. BETTERTON[2]

Of those few fools, who with ill stars are cursed,
Sure scribbling fools, called poets, fare the worst:
For they're a sort of fools which Fortune makes,
And after she has made 'em fools, forsakes.
With nature's oafs 'tis quite a different case,   5
For Fortune favors all her idiot race.
In her own nest the cuckoo eggs we find,
O'er which she broods to hatch the changeling kind.[3]
No portion for her own she has to spare,
So much she dotes on her adopted care.   10
    Poets are bubbles,[4] by the town drawn in,
Suffered at first some trifling stakes to win:
But what unequal hazards do they run! ⎤
Each time they write they venture all they've won: ⎬
The squire that's buttered still,[5] is sure to be undone. ⎦   15
This author, heretofore, has found your favor,
But pleads no merit from his past behavior;
To build on that might prove a vain presumption,
Should grants to poets made, admit resumption:[6]
And in Parnassus he must lose his seat,   20
If that be found a forfeited estate.[7]
    He owns, with toil, he wrought the following scenes,
But if they're naught ne'er spare him for his pains:
Damn him the more; have no commiseration
For dullness on mature deliberation.   25
He swears he'll not resent one hissed-off scene ⎤
Nor, like those peevish wits, his play maintain, ⎬
Who, to assert their sense, your taste arraign. ⎦
Some plot we think he has, and some new thought;

---

2. Thomas Betterton (ca. 1635–1710), the greatest actor of the period, played Fainall in the original production of this play.
3. Simpletons; children supposed to have been secretly exchanged in infancy for others. The "cuckoo" lays its eggs in the nests of other birds.
4. Dupes.

5. Constantly flattered.
6. The crown could both grant and take back ("resume") estates.
7. *Seat* rhymed with *estate*; in the next couplet, *scenes* and *pains* rhymed. A few lines later *scene* is similarly pronounced to rhyme with *maintain*, and *fault* (the *l* being silent) is rhymed with *thought*.

Some humor too, no farce; but that's a fault.   30
Satire, he thinks, you ought not to expect,
For so reformed a town,[8] who dares correct?
To please, this time, has been his sole pretense,
He'll not instruct, lest it should give offense.
Should he by chance a knave or fool expose,   35
That hurts none here; sure here are none of those.
In short, our play shall (with your leave to show it)
Give you one instance of a passive poet
Who to your judgments yields all resignation;
So save or damn after your own discretion.   40

Act 1—A *chocolate house.*

SCENE 1

Mirabell and Fainall rising from cards, Betty waiting.

MIRA. You are a fortunate man, Mr. Fainall.

FAIN. Have we done?

MIRA. What you please. I'll play on to entertain you.

FAIN. No, I'll give you your revenge another time, when you are not so
indifferent; you are thinking of something else now, and play too negligently. The coldness of a losing gamester lessens the pleasure of the
winner. I'd no more play with a man that slighted his ill fortune than
I'd make love to a woman who undervalued the loss of her reputation.

MIRA. You have a taste extremely delicate, and are for refining on your
pleasures.

FAIN. Prithee, why so reserved? Something has put you out of humor.

MIRA. Not at all. I happen to be grave today, and you are gay; that's all.

FAIN. Confess, Millamant and you quarreled last night after I left you;
my fair cousin has some humors that would tempt the patience of a
stoic. What, some coxcomb came in, and was well received by her,
while you were by?

MIRA. Witwoud and Petulant; and what was worse, her aunt, your wife's
mother, my evil genius; or to sum up all in her own name, my old
Lady Wishfort came in.

FAIN. O, there it is then—she has a lasting passion for you, and with
reason. What, then my wife was there?

MIRA. Yes, and Mrs. Marwood and three or four more, whom I never
saw before. Seeing me, they all put on their grave faces, whispered
one another; then complained aloud of the vapors,[9] and after fell into
a profound silence.

FAIN. They had a mind to be rid of you.

MIRA. For which good reason I resolved not to stir. At last the good old
lady broke through her painful taciturnity, with an invective against
long visits. I would not have understood her, but Millamant joining
in the argument, I rose and with a constrained smile told her I thought

8. A sarcasm, directed against the general movement to reform manners and morals and, more
particularly, against Jeremy Collier's attack on actors
and playwrights in his *Short View of the Profaneness and Immorality of the English Stage* (1698).
9. Melancholy, the blues.

nothing was so easy as to know when a visit began to be troublesome. She reddened and I withdrew, without expecting[1] her reply.

FAIN. You were to blame to resent what she spoke only in compliance with her aunt.

MIRA. She is more mistress of herself than to be under the necessity of such a resignation.

FAIN. What? though half her fortune depends upon her marrying with my lady's approbation?

MIRA. I was then in such a humor that I should have been better pleased if she had been less discreet.

FAIN. Now I remember, I wonder not they were weary of you: last night was one of their cabal[2] nights; they have 'em three times a week, and meet by turns, at one another's apartments, where they come together like the coroner's inquest, to sit upon the murdered reputations of the week. You and I are excluded; and it was once proposed that all the male sex should be excepted; but somebody moved that to avoid scandal there might be one man of the community; upon which Witwoud and Petulant were enrolled members.

MIRA. And who may have been the foundress of this sect? My Lady Wishfort, I warrant, who publishes her detestation of mankind, and full of the vigor of fifty-five, declares for a friend and ratafia;[3] and let posterity shift for itself, she'll breed no more.

FAIN. The discovery of your sham addresses to her, to conceal your love to her niece, has provoked this separation. Had you dissembled better, things might have continued in the state of nature.

MIRA. I did as much as man could, with any reasonable conscience: I proceeded to the very last act of flattery with her, and was guilty of a song in her commendation. Nay, I got a friend to put her into a lampoon and compliment her with the imputation of an affair with a young fellow, which I carried so far that I told her the malicious town took notice that she was grown fat of a sudden; and when she lay in of a dropsy, persuaded her she was reported to be in labor. The devil's in't, if an old woman is to be flattered further, unless a man should endeavor downright personally to debauch her; and that my virtue forbade me. But for the discovery of this amour, I am indebted to your friend, or your wife's friend, Mrs. Marwood.

FAIN. What should provoke her to be your enemy, unless she has made you advances, which you have slighted? Women do not easily forgive omissions of that nature.

MIRA. She was always civil to me, till of late. I confess I am not one of those coxcombs who are apt to interpret a woman's good manners to her prejudice, and think that she who does not refuse 'em everything, can refuse 'em nothing.

FAIN. You are a gallant man, Mirabell; and though you may have cruelty enough not to satisfy a lady's longing, you have too much generosity not to be tender of her honor. Yet you speak with an indifference which seems to be affected, and confesses you are conscious of a negligence.

MIRA. You pursue the argument with a distrust that seems to be unaf-

1. Awaiting.
2. Secret organization designed for intrigue.

3. A liqueur flavored with fruit kernels (pronounced *rat-a-fé-a*).

fected, and confesses you are conscious of a concern for which the lady is more indebted to you than is your wife.

FAIN. Fie, fie, friend, if you grow censorious I must leave you.—I'll look upon the gamesters in the next room.

MIRA. Who are they?

FAIN. Petulant and Witwoud.—Bring me some chocolate.

MIRA. Betty, what says your clock?

BET. Turned of the last canonical hour,[4] sir.

MIRA. How pertinently the jade answers me! Ha? almost one a clock! [*looking on his watch*]—O, y'are come—

SCENE 2

Mirabell and Footman.

MIRA. Well, is the grand affair over? You have been something tedious.

FOOT. Sir, there's such coupling at Pancras[5] that they stand behind one another, as 'twere in a country dance. Ours was the last couple to lead up; and no hopes appearing of dispatch, besides, the parson growing hoarse, we were afraid his lungs would have failed before it came to our turn; so we drove around to Duke's Place, and there they were riveted in a trice.

MIRA. So, so, you are sure they are married?

FOOT. Married and bedded, sir. I am witness.

MIRA. Have you the certificate?

FOOT. Here it is, sir.

MIRA. Has the tailor brought Waitwell's clothes home, and the new liveries?

FOOT. Yes, sir.

MIRA. That's well. Do you go home again, d'ye hear, and adjourn the consummation till farther order. Bid Waitwell shake his ears, and Dame Partlet[6] rustle up her feathers, and meet me at one a clock by Rosamond's Pond, that I may see her before she returns to her lady: and as you tender your ears, be secret.

SCENE 2

Mirabell, Fainall, Betty.

FAIN. Joy of your success, Mirabell; you look pleased.

MIRA. Aye, I have been engaged in a matter of some sort of mirth, which is not yet ripe for discovery. I am glad this is not a cabal night. I wonder, Fainall, that you who are married, and of consequence should be discreet, will suffer your wife to be of such a party.

FAIN. Faith, I am not jealous. Besides, most who are engaged are women

4. The hours in which marriage can legally be performed in the Anglican Church, then 8–12 noon.

5. The Church of St. Pancras, like that of St. James in Duke's Place (referred to later in the same speech), was notorious for a thriving trade in unlicensed marriages.

6. Pertelote, the hen-wife of the cock Chauntecleer in Chaucer's Nun's Priest's Tale. Rosamond's Pond was in St. James's Park.

and relations; and for the men, they are of a kind too contemptible to give scandal.

MIRA. I am of another opinion. The greater the coxcomb, always the more the scandal: for a woman who is not a fool can have but one reason for associating with a man who is one.

FAIN. Are you jealous as often as you see Witwoud entertained by Millamant?

MIRA. Of her understanding I am, if not of her person.

FAIN. You do her wrong; for to give her her due, she has wit.

MIRA. She has beauty enough to make any man think so; and complaisance enough not to contradict him who shall tell her so.

FAIN. For a passionate lover, methinks you are a man somewhat too discerning in the failings of your mistress.

MIRA. And for a discerning man, somewhat too passionate a lover; for I like her with all her faults, nay, like her for her faults. Her follies are so natural, are so artful, that they become her, and those affectations which in another woman would be odious, serve but to make her more agreeable. I'll tell thee, Fainall, she once used me with that insolence that in revenge I took her to pieces; sifted her, and separated her failings; I studied 'em, and got 'em by rote. The catalogue was so large that I was not without hopes, one day or other, to hate her heartily: to which end I so used myself to think of 'em that at length, contrary to my design and expectation, they gave me every hour less and less disturbance, till in a few days it became habitual to me to remember 'em without being displeased. They are now grown as familiar to me as my own frailties, and in all probability in a little time longer I shall like 'em as well.

FAIN. Marry her, marry her; be half as well acquainted with her charms as you are with her defects, and my life on't, you are your own man again.

MIRA. Say you so?

FAIN. Aye, aye, I have experience; I have a wife, and so forth.

SCENE 4

[To them] Messenger.

MESS. Is one Squire Witwoud here?

BET. Yes. What's your business?

MESS. I have a letter for him, from his brother Sir Wilfull, which I am charged to deliver into his own hands.

BET. He's in the next room, friend—that way.

SCENE 5

Mirabell, Fainall, Betty.

MIRA. What, is the chief of that noble family in town, Sir Wilfull Witwoud?

FAIN. He is expected today. Do you know him?

MIRA. I have seen him. He promises to be an extraordinary person; I think you have the honor to be related to him.

FAIN. Yes; he is half brother to this Witwoud by a former wife, who was sister to my Lady Wishfort, my wife's mother. If you marry Millamant, you must call cousins too.

MIRA. I had rather be his relation than his acquaintance.

FAIN. He comes to town in order to equip himself for travel.

MIRA. For travel! Why the man that I mean is above forty.[7]

FAIN. No matter for that; 'tis for the honor of England that all Europe should know that we have blockheads of all ages.

MIRA. I wonder there is not an Act of Parliament to save the credit of the nation, and prohibit the exportation of fools.

FAIN. By no means, 'tis better as 'tis; 'tis better to trade with a little loss than to be quite eaten up with being overstocked.

MIRA. Pray, are the follies of this knight-errant, and those of the squire his brother, anything related?

FAIN. Not at all. Witwoud grows by the knight, like a medlar[8] grafted on a crab. One will melt in your mouth, and t'other set your teeth on edge; one is all pulp, and the other all core.

MIRA. So one will be rotten before he be ripe, and the other will be rotten without ever being ripe at all.

FAIN. Sir Wilfull is an odd mixture of bashfulness and obstinacy. But when he's drunk, he's as loving as the monster in the *Tempest*;[9] and much after the same manner. To give t'other his due, he has something of good nature, and does not always want wit.

MIRA. Not always; but as often as his memory fails him, and his commonplace of comparisons.[1] He is a fool with a good memory, and some few scraps of other folks' wit. He is one whose conversation can never be approved, yet it is now and then to be endured. He has indeed one good quality, he is not exceptious,[2] for he so passionately affects the reputation of understanding raillery that he will construe an affront into a jest; and call downright rudeness and ill language, satire and fire.

FAIN. If you have a mind to finish his picture, you have an opportunity to do it at full length. Behold the original.

SCENE 6

[*To them*] Witwoud.

WIT. Afford me your compassion, my dears; pity me, Fainall, Mirabell, pity me.

MIRA. I do from my soul.

FAIN. Why, what's the matter?

---

7. The grand tour of the Continent was rapidly becoming a part of the education of gentlemen, but it was usually made in company with a tutor after a young man had graduated from a university, not after a man had passed the age of 40.

8. A fruit eaten when it is overripe. "Crab": crab apple.

9. Trinculo, in the adaptation of Shakespeare's *Tempest* by Sir William Davenant and Dryden

(1667), having made Caliban drunk, says: "The poor monster is loving in his drink" (2.2).

1. One recognized sign of wit was the ability to discover quickly resemblances between objects apparently unlike. Witwoud specializes in this kind of wit, but Mirabell suggests that they are all obvious and collected from others, like observations copied in a notebook, or "commonplace" book.

2. Quarrelsome.

WIT. No letters for me, Betty?

BET. Did not a messenger bring you one but now, sir?

WIT. Aye, but no other?

BET. No, sir.

WIT. That's hard, that's very hard. A messenger, a mule, a beast of burden, he has brought me a letter from the fool my brother, as heavy as a panegyric in a funeral sermon, or a copy of commendatory verses from one poet to another. And what's worse, 'tis as sure a forerunner of the author as an epistle dedicatory.

MIRA. A fool, and your brother, Witwoud!

WIT. Aye, aye, my half brother. My half brother he is, no nearer upon honor.

MIRA. Then 'tis possible he may be but half a fool.

WIT. Good, good, Mirabell, *le drôle!*[3] Good, good. Hang him, don't let's talk of him. Fainall, how does your lady? Gad. I say anything in the world to get this fellow out of my head. I beg pardon that I should ask a man of pleasure and the town a question at once so foreign and domestic. But I talk like an old maid at a marriage, I don't know what I say: but she's the best woman in the world.

FAIN. 'Tis well you don't know what you say, or else your commendation would go near to make me either vain or jealous.

WIT. No man in town lives well with a wife but Fainall. Your judgment, Mirabell?

MIRA. You had better step and ask his wife, if you would be credibly informed.

WIT. Mirabell.

MIRA. Aye.

WIT. My dear, I ask ten thousand pardons—gad, I have forgot what I was going to say to you.

MIRA. I thank you heartily, heartily.

WIT. No, but prithee excuse me—my memory is such a memory.

MIRA. Have a care of such apologies, Witwoud—for I never knew a fool but he affected to complain, either of the spleen or his memory.

FAIN. What have you done with Petulant?

WIT. He's reckoning his money—my money it was.—I have no luck today.

FAIN. You may allow him to win of you at play—for you are sure to be too hard for him at repartee. Since you monopolize the wit that is between you, the fortune must be his of course.

MIRA. I don't find that Petulant confesses the superiority of wit to be your talent, Witwoud.

WIT. Come, come, you are malicious now, and would breed debates.— Petulant's my friend, and a very honest fellow, and a very pretty fellow, and has a smattering—faith and troth a pretty deal of an odd sort of a small wit: nay, I'll do him justice. I'm his friend, I won't wrong him.—And if he had any judgment in the world—he would not be altogether contemptible. Come, come, don't detract from the merits of my friend.

FAIN. You don't take your friend to be over-nicely bred.

WIT. No, no, hang him, the rogue has no manners at all, that I must

3. The witty fellow.

own—no more breeding than a bum-bailey,[4] that I grant you.—'Tis pity; the fellow has fire and life.

MIRA. What, courage?

WIT. Hum, faith I don't know as to that—I can't say as to that.—Yes, faith, in a controversy he'll contradict anybody.

MIRA. Though 'twere a man whom he feared, or a woman whom he loved.

WIT. Well, well, he does not always think before he speaks—we have all our failings; you are too hard upon him, you are, faith. Let me excuse him—I can defend most of his faults, except one or two. One he has, that's the truth on't, if he were my brother, I could not acquit him.—That indeed I could wish were otherwise.

MIRA. Aye marry, what's that, Witwoud?

WIT. O, pardon me—expose the infirmities of my friend?—No, my dear, excuse me there.

FAIN. What, I warrant he's unsincere, or 'tis some such trifle.

WIT. No. no, what if he be? 'Tis no matter for that, his wit will excuse that. A wit should no more be sincere than a woman constant; one argues a decay of parts, as t'other of beauty.

MIRA. Maybe you think him too positive?

WIT. No, no, his being positive is an incentive to argument, and keeps up conversation.

FAIN. Too illiterate.

WIT. That! that's his happiness.—His want of learning gives him the more opportunities to show his natural parts.

MIRA. He wants words.

WIT. Aye; but I like him for that now; for his want of words gives me the pleasure very often to explain his meaning.

FAIN. He's impudent.

WIT. No, that's not it.

MIRA. Vain.

WIT. No.

MIRA. What, he speaks unseasonable truths sometimes, because he has not wit enough to invent an evasion.

WIT. Truths! Ha, ha, ha! No, no, since you will have it—I mean, he never speaks truth at all—that's all. He will lie like a chambermaid, or a woman of quality's porter. Now that is a fault.

SCENE 7

[To them] Coachman.

COACH. Is Master Petulant here, mistress?

BET. Yes.

COACH. Three gentlewomen in a coach would speak with him.

FAIN. O brave Petulant, three!

BET. I'll tell him.

COACH. You must bring two dishes of chocolate and a glass of cinnamon water.

4. Bumbailiff, the lowest kind of arresting officer.

SCENE 8

Mirabell, Fainall, Witwoud.

WIT. That should be for two fasting strumpets, and a bawd troubled with wind. Now you may know what the three are.

MIRA. You are free with your friend's acquaintance.

WIT. Aye, aye, friendship without freedom is as dull as love without enjoyment, or wine without toasting; but to tell you a secret, these are trulls whom he allows coach-hire, and something more by the week, to call on him once a day at public places.

MIRA. How!

WIT. You shall see he won't go to 'em because there's no more company here to take notice of him.—Why this is nothing to what he used to do, before he found out this way. I have known him call for himself.—

FAIN. Call for himself? What dost thou mean?

WIT. Mean? Why he would slip you out of this chocolate house, just when you had been talking to him.—As soon as your back was turned—whip he was gone—then trip to his lodging, clap on a hood and scarf, and a mask, slap into a hackney coach, and drive hither to the door again in a trice; where he would send in for himself, that I mean, call for himself, wait for himself, nay and what's more, not finding himself, sometimes leave a letter for himself.

MIRA. I confess this is something extraordinary.—I believe he waits for himself now, he is so long a-coming. O, I ask his pardon.

SCENE 9

Petulant, Mirabell, Fainall, Witwoud, Betty.

BET. Sir, the coach stays.

PET. Well, well; I come.—'Sbud,[5] a man had as good be a professed midwife, as a professed whoremaster, at this rate; to be knocked up and raised at all hours, and in all places. Pox on 'em, I won't come.—D'ye hear, tell 'em I won't come.—Let 'em snivel and cry their hearts out.

FAIN. You are very cruel, Petulant.

PET. All's one, let it pass—I have a humor to be cruel.

MIRA. I hope they are not persons of condition[6] that you use at this rate.

PET. Condition, condition's a dried fig, if I am not in humor.— By this hand, if they were your—a—a—your what-dee-call-'ems themselves, they must wait or rub off,[7] if I want appetite.

MIRA. What-de-call-ems! What are they, Witwoud?

WIT. Empresses,[8] my dear.—By your what-dee-call-'ems he means sultana queens.

5. God's body.
6. Rank.
7. Make off.
8. "Empresses," like "sultana queens" and "Rox-

olanas," were terms for prostitutes. Roxolana is the wife of the Sultan in Davenant's *Siege of Rhodes* (1656).

PET. Aye, Roxolanas.

MIRA. Cry you mercy,

FAIN. Witwoud says they are—

PET. What does he say th' are?

WIT. I? Fine ladies I say.

PET. Pass on, Witwoud.—Harkee, by this light his relations—two co-heiresses his cousins, and an old aunt, who loves caterwauling better than a conventicle.[9]

WIT. Ha, ha, ha; I had a mind to see how the rogue would come off.—Ha, ha, ha; gad, I can't be angry with him, if he had said they were my mother and my sisters.

MIRA. No!

WIT. No; the rogue's wit and readiness of invention charm me, dear Petulant.

BET. They are gone, sir, in great anger.

PET. Enough, let 'em trundle. Anger helps complexion, saves paint.

FAIN. This continence is all dissembled; this is in order to have something to brag of the next time he makes court to Millamant, and swear he had abandoned the whole sex for her sake.

MIRA. Have you not left off your impudent pretensions there yet? I shall cut your throat, sometime or other, Petulant, about that business.

PET. Aye, aye, let that pass.—There are other throats to be cut.—

MIRA. Meaning mine, sir?

PET. Not I—I mean nobody.—I know nothing. But there are uncles and nephews in the world—and they may be rivals—What then? All's one for that—

MIRA. How! Harkee, Petulant, come hither—explain, or I shall call your interpreter.

PET. Explain? I know nothing.—Why, you have an uncle, have you not, lately come to town, and lodges by my Lady Wishfort's?

MIRA. True.

PET. Why, that's enough.—You and he are not friends; and if he should marry and have a child, you may be disinherited, ha?

MIRA. Where hast thou stumbled upon all this truth?

PET. All's one for that; why, then, say I know something.

MIRA. Come, thou art an honest fellow, Petulant, and shalt make love to my mistress, thou sha't, faith. What hast thou heard of my uncle?

PET. I, nothing, I. If throats are to be cut, let swords clash; snug's the word, I shrug and am silent.

MIRA. O raillery, raillery. Come, I know thou art in the women's secrets.—What, you're a cabalist. I know you stayed at Millamant's last night, after I went. Was there any mention made of my uncle or me? Tell me; if thou hadst but good nature equal to thy wit, Petulant, Tony Witwoud, who is now thy competitor in fame, would show as dim by thee as a dead whiting's eye by a pearl of Orient. He would no more be seen by thee than Mercury is by the sun: come, I'm sure thou wo't tell me.

9. Nonconformist religious meeting.

PET. If I do, will you grant me common sense then, for the future?

MIRA. Faith, I'll do what I can for thee, and I'll pray that Heaven may grant it thee in the meantime.

PET. Well, harkee.

FAIN. Petulant and you both will find Mirabell as warm a rival as a lover.

WIT. Pshaw, pshaw, that she laughs at Petulant is plain. And for my part—but that it is almost a fashion to admire her, I should—harkee—to tell you a secret, but let it go no further—between friends, I shall never break my heart for her.

FAIN. How!

WIT. She's handsome; but she's a sort of an uncertain woman.

FAIN. I thought you had died for her.

WIT. Umh—no—

FAIN. She has wit.

WIT. 'Tis what she will hardly allow anybody else.—Now, demme, I should hate that, if she were as handsome as Cleopatra. Mirabell is not so sure of her as he thinks for.

FAIN. Why do you think so?

WIT. We stayed pretty late there last night, and heard something of an uncle to Mirabell, who is lately come to town—and is between him and the best part of his estate. Mirabell and he are at some distance, as my Lady Wishfort has been told; and you know she hates Mirabell, worse than a Quaker hates a parrot, or than a fishmonger hates a hard frost. Whether this uncle has seen Mrs. Millamant or not, I cannot say; but there were items of such a treaty being in embryo; and if it should come to life, poor Mirabell would be in some sort unfortunately fobbed[1] i' faith.

FAIN. 'Tis impossible Millamant should harken to it.

WIT. Faith, my dear, I can't tell; she's a woman and a kind of a humorist.[2]

MIRA. And this is the sum of what you could collect last night.

PET. The quintessence. Maybe Witwoud knows more, he stayed longer.— Besides they never mind him; they say anything before him.

MIRA. I thought you had been the greatest favorite.

PET. Aye, *tête à tête*;[3] but not in public, because I make remarks.

MIRA. You do?

PET. Aye, aye, pox, I'm malicious, man. Now he's soft, you know, they are not in awe of him.—The fellow's well bred, he's what you call a—what-d'ye-call-'em. A fine gentleman, but he's silly withal.

MIRA. I thank you, I know as much as my curiosity requires. Fainall, are you for the Mall?[4]

FAIN. Aye, I'll take a turn before dinner.

WIT. Aye, we'll all walk in the park, the ladies talked of being there.

MIRA. I thought you were obliged to watch for your brother Sir Wilfull's arrival.

1. Tricked.
2. A capricious person.
3. Face to face, i.e., in private.

4. A walk in St. James's Park, one of the fashionable resorts of the day.

WIT. No, no, he's come to his aunt's, my Lady Wishfort. Pox on him, I shall be troubled with him too. What shall I do with the fool?

PET. Beg him for his estate, that I may beg you afterwards, and so have but one trouble with you both.

WIT. O rare Petulant; thou art as quick as fire in a frosty morning; thou shalt to the Mall with us; and we'll be very severe.

PET. Enough, I'm in a humor to be severe.

MIRA. Are you? Pray then walk by yourselves.—Let not us be accessory to your putting the ladies out of countenance with your senseless ribaldry, which you roar out aloud as often as they pass by you; and when you have made a handsome woman blush, then you think you have been severe.

PET. What, what? Then let 'em either show their innocence by not understanding what they hear, or else show their discretion by not hearing what they would not be thought to understand.

MIRA. But hast not thou then sense enough to know that thou ought'st to be most ashamed thyself, when thou hast put another out of countenance?

PET. Not I, by this hand.—I always take blushing either for a sign of guilt, or ill breeding.

MIRA. I confess you ought to think so. You are in the right, that you may plead the error of your judgment in defense of your practice.

> Where modesty's ill manners, 'tis but fit
> That impudence and malice pass for wit.

Act 2—St. James's Park.

SCENE 1

Mrs. Fainall and Mrs. Marwood.

MRS. FAIN. Aye, aye, dear Marwood, if we will be happy, we must find the means in ourselves, and among ourselves. Men are ever in extremes; either doting or averse. While they are lovers, if they have fire and sense, their jealousies are insupportable: and when they cease to love (we ought to think at least) they loathe. They look upon us with horror and distaste; they meet us like the ghosts of what we were, and as from such, fly from us.

MRS. MAR. True, 'tis an unhappy circumstance of life that love should ever die before us; and that the man so often should outlive the lover. But say what you will, 'tis better to be left than never to have been loved. To pass over youth in dull indifference, to refuse the sweets of life because they once must leave us, is as preposterous as to wish to have been born old, because we one day must be old. For my part, my youth may wear and waste, but it shall never rust in my possession.

MRS. FAIN. Then it seems you dissemble an aversion to mankind only in compliance to my mother's humor.

MRS. MAR. Certainly. To be free, I have no taste of those insipid dry discourses with which our sex of force must entertain themselves apart

from men. We may affect endearments to each other, profess eternal
friendships, and seem to dote like lovers; but 'tis not in our natures
long to persevere. Love will resume his empire in our breasts, and
every heart, or soon or late, receive and readmit him as its lawful
tyrant.

MRS. FAIN. Bless me, how have I been deceived! Why, you profess a
libertine.

MRS. MAR. You see my friendship by my freedom. Come, be as sincere,
acknowledge that your sentiments agree with mine.

MRS. FAIN. Never.

MRS. MAR. You hate mankind?

MRS. FAIN. Heartily, inveterately.

MRS. MAR. Your husband?

MRS. FAIN. Most transcendently; aye, though I say it, meritoriously.

MRS. MAR. Give me your hand upon it.

MRS. FAIN. There.

MRS. MAR. I join with you. What I have said has been to try you.

MRS. FAIN. Is it possible? Dost thou hate those vipers men?

MRS. MAR. I have done hating 'em, and am now come to despise 'em;
the next thing I have to do is eternally to forget 'em.

MRS. FAIN. There spoke the spirit of an Amazon, a Penthesilea.[5]

MRS. MAR. And yet I am thinking sometimes to carry my aversion further.

MRS. FAIN. How?

MRS. MAR. Faith, by marrying. If I could but find one that loved me very
well, and would be thoroughly sensible of ill usage, I think I should
do myself the violence of undergoing the ceremony.

MRS. FAIN. You would not make him a cuckold?

MRS. MAR. No; but I'd make him believe I did, and that's as bad.

MRS. FAIN. Why had not you as good do it?

MRS. MAR. O, if he should ever discover it, he would then know the
worst, and be out of his pain; but I would have him ever to continue
upon the rack of fear and jealousy.

MRS. FAIN. Ingenious mischief! Would thou wert married to Mirabell.

MRS. MAR. Would I were.

MRS. FAIN. You change color.

MRS. MAR. Because I hate him.

MRS. FAIN. So do I; but I can hear him named. But what reason have
you to hate him in particular?

MRS. MAR. I never loved him; he is and always was insufferably proud.

MRS. FAIN. By the reason you give for your aversion, one would think it
dissembled; for you have laid a fault to his charge of which his enemies must acquit him.

MRS. MAR. O then it seems you are one of his favorable enemies. Methinks you look a little pale, and now you flush again.

MRS. FAIN. Do I? I think I am a little sick o' the sudden.

MRS. MAR. What ails you?

MRS. FAIN. My husband. Don't you see him? He turned short upon me
unawares, and has almost overcome me.

5. Queen of the Amazons (a legendary nation of women warriors).

SCENE 2

[*To them*] *Fainall and Mirabell.*

MRS. MAR. Ha, ha, ha; he comes opportunely for you.

MRS. FAIN. For you, for he has brought Mirabell with him.

FAIN. My dear.

MRS. FAIN. My soul.

FAIN. You don't look well today, child.

MRS. FAIN. D'ye think so?

MIRA. He is the only man that does, madam.

MRS. FAIN. The only man that would tell me so at least; and the only man from whom I could hear it without mortification.

FAIN. O my dear, I am satisfied of your tenderness; I know you cannot resent anything from me, especially what is an effect of my concern.

MRS. FAIN. Mr. Mirabell, my mother interrupted you in a pleasant relation last night. I would fain hear it out.

MIRA. The persons concerned in that affair have yet a tolerable reputation.—I am afraid Mr. Fainall will be censorious.

MRS. FAIN. He has a humor more prevailing than his curiosity, and will willingly dispense with the hearing of one scandalous story to avoid giving an occasion to make another by being seen to walk with his wife. This way, Mr. Mirabell, and I dare promise you will oblige us both.

SCENE 3

Fainall, Mrs. Marwood.

FAIN. Excellent creature! Well, sure if I should live to be rid of my wife, I should be a miserable man.

MRS. MAR. Aye!

FAIN. For having only that one hope, the accomplishment of it of consequence must put an end to all my hopes; and what a wretch is he who must survive his hopes! Nothing remains when that day comes but to sit down and weep like Alexander, when he wanted other worlds to conquer.

MRS. MAR. Will you not follow 'em?

FAIN. Faith, I think not.

MRS. MAR. Pray let us; I have a reason.

FAIN. You are not jealous?

MRS. MAR. Of whom?

FAIN. Of Mirabell.

MRS. MAR. If I am, is it inconsistent with my love to you that I am tender of your honor?

FAIN. You would intimate then, as if there were a fellow-feeling between my wife and him.

MRS. MAR. I think she does not hate him to that degree she would be thought.

FAIN. But he, I fear, is too insensible.

MRS. MAR. It may be you are deceived.

FAIN. It may be so. I do now begin to apprehend it.

MRS. MAR. What?

FAIN. That I have been deceived, Madam, and you are false.

MRS. MAR. That I am false! What mean you?

FAIN. To let you know I see through all your little arts.—Come, you both love him; and both have equally dissembled your aversion. Your mutual jealousies of one another have made you clash till you have both struck fire. I have seen the warm confession reddening on your cheeks, and sparkling from your eyes.

MRS. MAR. You do me wrong.

FAIN. I do not.—'Twas for my ease to oversee[6] and willfully neglect the gross advances made him by my wife; that by permitting her to be engaged I might continue unsuspected in my pleasures; and take you oftener to my arms in full security. But could you think, because the nodding husband would not wake, that e'er the watchful lover slept?

MRS. MAR. And wherewithal can you reproach me?

FAIN. With infidelity, with loving another, with love of Mirabell.

MRS. MAR. 'Tis false. I challenge you to show an instance that can confirm your groundless accusation. I hate him.

FAIN. And wherefore do you hate him? He is insensible, and your resentment follows his neglect. An instance! The injuries you have done him are a proof: your interposing in his love. What cause had you to make discoveries of his pretended passion? To undeceive the credulous aunt, and be the officious obstacle of his match with Millamant?

MRS. MAR. My obligations to my lady urged me. I had professed a friendship to her, and could not see her easy nature so abused by that dissembler.

FAIN. What, was it conscience then? Professed a friendship! O the pious friendships of the female sex!

MRS. MAR. More tender, more sincere, and more enduring than all the vain and empty vows of men, whether professing love to us, or mutual faith to one another.

FAIN. Ha, ha, ha; you are my wife's friend too.

MRS. MAR. Shame and ingratitude! Do you reproach me? You, you upbraid me! Have I been false to her, through strict fidelity to you, and sacrificed my friendship to keep my love inviolate? And have you the baseness to charge me with the guilt, unmindful of the merit! To you it should be meritorious that I have been vicious: and do you reflect that guilt upon me, which should lie buried in your bosom?

FAIN. You misinterpret my reproof. I meant but to remind you of the slight account you once could make of strictest ties, when set in competition with your love to me.

MRS. MAR. 'Tis false, you urged it with deliberate malice.—'Twas spoke in scorn, and I never will forgive it.

FAIN. Your guilt, not your resentment, begets your rage. If yet you loved, you could forgive a jealousy, but you are stung to find you are discovered.

MRS. MAR. It shall be all discovered. You too shall be discovered; be sure

6. Overlook.

you shall. I can but be exposed.—If I do it myself, I shall prevent[7] your baseness.

FAIN. Why, what will you do?

MRS. MAR. Disclose it to your wife; own what has passed between us.

FAIN. Frenzy!

MRS. MAR. By all my wrongs I'll do't—I'll publish to the world the injuries you have done me, both in my fame and fortune: with both I trusted you, you bankrupt in honor, as indigent of wealth.

FAIN. Your fame[8] I have preserved. Your fortune has been bestowed as the prodigality of your love would have it, in pleasures which we both have shared. Yet, had not you been false, I had e'er this repaid it.— 'Tis true—had you permitted Mirabell with Millamant to have stolen their marriage, my lady had been incensed beyond all means of reconcilement: Millamant had forfeited the moiety[9] of her fortune, which then would have descended to my wife—and wherefore did I marry, but to make lawful prize of a rich widow's wealth, and squander it on love and you?

MRS. MAR. Deceit and frivolous pretense.

FAIN. Death, am I not married? What's pretense? Am I not imprisoned, fettered? Have I not a wife? Nay, a wife that was a widow, a young widow, a handsome widow; and would be again a widow, but that I have a heart of proof,[1] and something of a constitution to bustle through the ways of wedlock and this world. Will you yet be reconciled to truth and me?

MRS. MAR. Impossible. Truth and you are inconsistent—I hate you, and shall forever.

FAIN. For loving you?

MRS. MAR. I loathe the name of love after such usage; and next to the guilt with which you would asperse me, I scorn you most. Farewell.

FAIN. Nay, we must not part thus.

MRS. MAR. Let me go.

FAIN. Come, I'm sorry.

MRS. MAR. I care not.—Let me go.—Break my hands, do—I'd leave 'em to get loose.

FAIN. I would not hurt you for the world. Have I no other hold to keep you here?

MRS. MAR. Well, I have deserved it all.

FAIN. You know I love you.

MRS. MAR. Poor dissembling!—O that—Well, it is not yet—

FAIN. What? What is it not? What is it not yet? It is not yet too late—

MRS. MAR. No, it is not yet too late—I have that comfort.

FAIN. It is, to love another.

MRS. MAR. But not to loathe, detest, abhor mankind, myself, and the whole treacherous world.

FAIN. Nay, this is extravagance.—Come, I ask your pardon.—No tears.— I was to blame. I could not love you and be easy in my doubts.—Pray forbear.—I believe you; I'm convinced I've done you wrong; and any

7. Anticipate.
8. Good name.
9. Half.
1. I.e., a proved or tempered heart.

way, every way will make amends.—I'll hate my wife yet more, damn her, I'll part with her, rob her of all she's worth, and we'll retire somewhere, anywhere, to another world. I'll marry thee.—Be pacified.— 'Sdeath, they come, hide your face, your tears.—You have a mask,[2] wear it a moment. This way, this way, be persuaded.

SCENE 4

Mirabell and Mrs. Fainall.

MRS. FAIN. They are here yet.

MIRA. They are turning into the other walk.

MRS. FAIN. While I only hated my husband, I could bear to see him, but since I have despised him, he's too offensive.

MIRA. O, you should hate with prudence.

MRS. FAIN. Yes, for I have loved with indiscretion.

MIRA. You should have just so much disgust for your husband as may be sufficient to make you relish your lover.

MRS. FAIN. You have been the cause that I have loved without bounds, and would you set limits to that aversion, of which you have been the occasion? Why did you make me marry this man?

MIRA. Why do we daily commit disagreeable and dangerous actions? To save that idol, reputation. If the familiarities of our loves had produced that consequence, of which you were apprehensive, where could you have fixed a father's name with credit, but on a husband? I knew Fainall to be a man lavish of his morals, an interested and professing friend, a false and a designing lover; yet one whose wit and outward fair behavior have gained a reputation with the town, enough to make that woman stand excused who has suffered herself to be won by his addresses. A better man ought not to have been sacrificed to the occasion; a worse had not answered to the purpose. When you are weary of him, you know your remedy.

MRS. FAIN. I ought to stand in some degree of credit with you, Mirabell.

MIRA. In justice to you, I have made you privy to my whole design, and put it in your power to ruin or advance my fortune.

MRS. FAIN. Whom have you instructed to represent your pretended uncle?

MIRA. Waitwell, my servant.

MRS. FAIN. He is an humble servant to Foible,[3] my mother's woman, and may win her to your interest.

MIRA. Care is taken for that.—She is won and worn by this time. They were married this morning.

MRS. FAIN. Who?

MIRA. Waitwell and Foible. I would not tempt my servant to betray me by trusting him too far. If your mother, in hopes to ruin me, should consent to marry my pretended uncle, he might, like Mosca in *The Fox*,[4] stand upon terms; so I made him sure beforehand.

MRS. FAIN. So, if my poor mother is caught in a contract, you will dis-

2. Often worn in public places by fashionable women of the time in order to preserve their complexions; they were also useful to disguise a woman and so to protect her reputation when she was carrying on an illicit affair.

3. I.e., he is Foible's lover.
4. The scheming parasite in Ben Jonson's *Volpone*, who in the end tries to blackmail Volpone. "To stand upon terms" means to insist upon conditions—hence, here, to blackmail.

cover the imposture betimes; and release her by producing a certificate of her gallant's former marriage.

MIRA. Yes, upon condition that she consent to my marriage with her niece, and surrender the moiety of her fortune in her possession.

MRS. FAIN. She talked last night of endeavoring at a match between Millamant and your uncle.

MIRA. That was by Foible's direction, and my instruction, that she might seem to carry it more privately.

MRS. FAIN. Well, I have an opinion of your success, for I believe my lady will do anything to get an husband; and when she has this, which you have provided for her, I suppose she will submit to anything to get rid of him.

MIRA. Yes, I think the good lady would marry anything that resembled a man, though 'twere no more than what a butler could pinch out of a napkin.

MRS. FAIN. Female frailty! We must all come to it, if we live to be old, and feel the craving of a false appetite when the true is decayed.

MIRA. An old woman's appetite is depraved like that of a girl—'tis the greensickness[5] of a second childhood; and like the faint offer of a latter spring, serves but to usher in the fall and withers in an affected bloom.

MRS. FAIN. Here's your mistress.

SCENE 5

[To them] Mrs. Millamant, Witwoud, Mincing.

MIRA. Here she comes, i'faith, full sail, with her fan spread and streamers out, and a shoal of fools for tenders.—Ha, no, I cry her mercy.

MRS. FAIN. I see but one poor empty sculler, and he tows her woman after him.

MIRA. You seem to be unattended, madam.—You used to have the *beau monde*[6] throng after you; and a flock of gay fine perukes hovering round you.

WIT. Like moths about a candle—I had like to have lost my comparison for want of breath.

MILLA. O, I have denied myself airs today. I have walked as fast through the crowd—

WIT. As a favorite just disgraced; and with as few followers.

MILLA. Dear Mr. Witwoud, truce with your similitudes: For I am as sick of 'em—

WIT. As a physician of a good air—I cannot help it, madam, though 'tis against myself.

MILLA. Yet again! Mincing, stand between me and his wit.

WIT. Do, Mrs. Mincing, like a screen before a great fire. I confess I do blaze today, I am too bright.

MRS. FAIN. But dear Millamant, why were you so long?

MILLA. Long! Lord, have I not made violent haste? I have asked every living thing I met for you; I have inquired after you, as after a new fashion.

5. The anemia that sometimes affects girls at puberty.
6. Fashionable world. "Perukes": periwigs, worn by fashionable men. Cf. Pope's *Rape of the Lock* 1.101.

WIT. Madam, truce with your similitudes.—No, you met her husband, and did not ask him for her.

MIRA. By your leave, Witwoud, that were like inquiring after an old fashion, to ask a husband for his wife.

WIT. Hum, a hit, a hit, a palpable hit,[7] I confess it.

MRS. FAIN. You were dressed before I came abroad.

MILLA. Aye, that's true.—O, but then I had—Mincing, what had I? Why was I so long?

MINC. O mem, your la'ship stayed to peruse a packet of letters.

MILLA. O, aye, letters—I had letters—I am persecuted with letters—I hate letters.—Nobody knows how to write letters; and yet one has 'em, one does not know why.—They serve one to pin up one's hair.

WIT. Is that the way? Pray, madam, do you pin up your hair with all your letters? I find I must keep copies.

MILLA. Only with those in verse, Mr. Witwoud. I never pin up my hair with prose. I think I tried once, Mincing.

MINC. O mem, I shall never forget it.

MILLA. Aye, poor Mincing tiffed[8] and tiffed all the morning.

MINC. Till I had the cramp in my fingers, I'll vow, mem. And all to no purpose. But when your la'ship pins it up with poetry, it sits so pleasant the next day as anything, and is so pure and so crips.[9]

WIT. Indeed, so crips?

MINC. You're such a critic, Mr. Witwoud.

MILLA. Mirabell, did you take exceptions last night? O, aye, and went away.—Now I think on't I'm angry.—No, now I think on't I'm pleased—for I believe I gave you some pain.

MIRA. Does that please you?

MILLA. Infinitely; I love to give pain.

MIRA. You would affect a cruelty which is not in your nature; your true vanity is in the power of pleasing.

MILLA. O, I ask your pardon for that—one's cruelty is one's power, and when one parts with one's cruelty, one parts with one's power; and when one has parted with that, I fancy one's old and ugly.

MIRA. Aye, aye, suffer your cruelty to ruin the object of your power, to destroy your lover.—And then how vain, how lost a thing you'll be! Nay, 'tis true: you are no longer handsome when you've lost your lover; your beauty dies upon the instant: for beauty is the lover's gift; 'tis he bestows your charms—your glass is all a cheat. The ugly and the old, whom the looking glass mortifies, yet after commendation can be flattered by it, and discover beauties in it: for that reflects our praises, rather than your face.

MILLA. O, the vanity of these men! Fainall, d'ye hear him? If they did not commend us, we were not handsome! Now you must know they could not commend one, if one was not handsome. Beauty the lover's gift?—Lord, what is a lover, that it can give? Why, one makes lovers as fat as one pleases, and they live as long as one pleases, and they die as soon as one pleases: and then if one pleases one makes more.

WIT. Very pretty. Why, you make no more of making of lovers, madam, than of making so many card-matches.[1]

---

7. An allusion to the dueling scene in *Hamlet* 5.2.
8. Dressed the hair.
9. A dialectal form of "crisp," curly.

1. Matches made by dipping pieces of card in melted sulphur.

MILLA. One no more owes one's beauty to a lover than one's wit to an
echo.—They can but reflect what we look and say; vain empty things
if we are silent or unseen, and want a being.

MIRA. Yet, to those two vain empty things, you owe two of the greatest
pleasures of your life.

MILLA. How so?

MIRA. To your lover you owe the pleasure of hearing yourselves praised;
and to an echo the pleasure of hearing yourselves talk.

WIT. But I know a lady that loves talking so incessantly she won't give
an echo fair play; she has that everlasting rotation of tongue, that an
echo must wait till she dies before it can catch her last words.

MILLA. O, fiction; Fainall, let us leave these men.

MIRA. [aside to MRS. FAINALL] Draw off Witwoud.

MRS. FAIN. Immediately; I have a word or two for Mr. Witwoud.

SCENE 5

Millamant, Mirabell, Mincing.

MIRA. I would beg a little private audience too.—You had the tyranny
to deny me last night, though you knew I came to impart a secret to
you that concerned my love.

MILLA. You saw I was engaged.

MIRA. Unkind. You had the leisure to entertain a herd of fools, things
who visit you from their excessive idleness, bestowing on your easiness
that time, which is the encumbrance of their lives. How can you find
delight in such society? It is impossible they should admire you, they
are not capable: or if they were, it should be to you as a mortification;
for sure to please a fool is some degree of folly.

MILLA. I please myself—besides, sometimes to converse with fools is for
my health.

MIRA. Your health! Is there a worse disease than the conversation of
fools?

MILLA. Yes, the vapors; fools are physic for it, next to asafetida.[2]

MIRA. You are not in a course of fools?

MILLA. Mirabell, if you persist in this offensive freedom, you'll displease
me. I think I must resolve after all not to have you.—We shan't agree.

MIRA. Not in our physic, it may be.

MILLA. And yet our distemper in all likelihood will be the same, for we
shall be sick of one another. I shan't endure to be reprimanded nor
instructed; 'tis so dull to act always by advice, and so tedious to be told
of one's faults.—I can't bear it. Well, I won't have you, Mirabell—
I'm resolved—I think—you may go—ha, ha, ha. What would you
give that you could help loving me?

MIRA. I would give something that you did not know I could not help it.

MILLA. Come, don't look grave then. Well, what do you say to me?

MIRA. I say that a man may as soon make a friend by his wit, or a fortune
by his honesty, as win a woman with plain-dealing and sincerity.

MILLA. Sententious Mirabell! prithee don't look with that violent and

2. An evil-smelling drug; "course," regimen.

inflexible wise face, like Solomon at the dividing of the child in an old tapestry hanging.[3]

MIRA. You are merry, madam, but I would persuade you for a moment to be serious.

MILLA. What, with that face? No, if you keep your countenance, 'tis impossible I should hold mine. Well, after all, there is something very moving in a lovesick face. Ha, ha, ha.—Well I won't laugh, don't be peevish—heigho! Now I'll be melancholy, as melancholy as a watch-light.[4] Well, Mirabell, if ever you will win me, woo me now. Nay, if you are so tedious, fare you well; I see they are walking away.

MIRA. Can you not find in the variety of your disposition one moment—

MILLA. To hear you tell me Foible's married and your plot like to speed.— No.

MIRA. But how you came to know it—

MILLA. Without the help of the devil, you can't imagine; unless she should tell me herself. Which of the two it may have been, I will leave you to consider; and when you have done thinking of that, think of me.

SCENE 7

Mirabell alone.

MIRA. I have something more.—Gone!—Think of you! To think of a whirlwind, though 'twere in a whirlwind, were a case of more steady contemplation, a very tranquility of mind and mansion. A fellow that lives in a windmill has not a more whimsical dwelling than the heart of a man that is lodged in a woman. There is no point of the compass to which they cannot turn, and by which they are not turned; and by one as well as another, for motion, not method, is their occupation. To know this, and yet continue to be in love, is to be made wise from the dictates of reason, and yet persevere to play the fool by the force of instinct. O, here come my pair of turtles[5]—what, billing so sweetly! Is not Valentine's Day over with you yet?

SCENE 8

[To him] Waitwell, Foible.

MIRA. Sirrah Waitwell, why sure you think you were married for your own recreation and not for my conveniency.

WAIT. Your pardon, sir. With submission, we have indeed been solacing in lawful delights, but still with an eye to business, sir. I have instructed her as well as I could. If she can take your directions as readily as my instructions, sir, your affairs are in a prosperous way.

MIRA. Give you joy, Mrs. Foible.

---

3. The Judgment of Solomon (1 Kings 3.16–27) was a favorite subject in painting and tapestry.
4. Nightlight.

5. Turtledoves, remarkable for their affectionate billing and cooing. Birds were popularly supposed to choose their mates on St. Valentine's Day.

FOIB. O-las, sir, I'm so ashamed—I'm afraid my lady has been in a thousand inquietudes for me. But I protest, sir, I made as much haste as I could.

WAIT. That she did indeed, sir. It was my fault that she did not make more.

MIRA. That I believe.

FOIB. But I told my lady as you instructed me, sir. That I had a prospect of seeing Sir Rowland your uncle, and that I would put her ladyship's picture in my pocket to show him; which I'll be sure to say has made him so enamored of her beauty that he burns with impatience to lie at her ladyship's feet and worship the original.

MIRA. Excellent, Foible! Matrimony has made you eloquent in love.

WAIT. I think she has profited, sir. I think so.

FOIB. You have seen Madam Millamant, sir?

MIRA. Yes.

FOIB. I told her, sir, because I did not know that you might find an opportunity; she had so much company last night.

MIRA. Your diligence will merit more—in the meantime—

[*Gives money.*]

FOIB. O dear sir, your humble servant.

WAIT. Spouse.

MIRA. Stand off, sir, not a penny. Go on and prosper, Foible. The lease shall be made good and the farm stocked if we succeed.

FOIB. I don't question your generosity, sir. And you need not doubt of success. If you have no more commands, sir, I'll be gone; I'm sure my lady is at her toilet, and can't dress till I come. O dear, I'm sure that [*looking out*] was Mrs. Marwood that went by in a mask; if she has seen me with you I'm sure she'll tell my lady. I'll make haste home and prevent her.[6] Your servant, sir. B'w'y, Waitwell.

SCENE 9

Mirabell, Waitwell.

WAIT. Sir Rowland, if you please. The jade's so pert upon her preferment she forgets herself.

MIRA. Come, sir, will you endeavor to forget yourself—and transform into Sir Rowland.

WAIT. Why, sir, it will be impossible I should remember myself—married, knighted, and attended all in one day! 'Tis enough to make any man forget himself. The difficulty will be how to recover my acquaintance and familiarity with my former self; and fall from my transformation to a reformation into Waitwell. Nay, I shan't be quite the same Waitwell neither—for now I remember me, I'm married and can't be my own man again.

> Aye, there's my grief; that's the sad change of life;
> To lose my title, and yet keep my wife.

6. Arrive before she does. "B'w'y" is a shortened form of "God be with you" (our word "goodbye").

Act 3—*A room in Lady Wishfort's house.*

SCENE 1

Lady Wishfort at her toilet, Peg waiting.

LADY. Merciful, no news of Foible yet?

PEG. No, madam.

LADY. I have no more patience. If I have not fretted myself till I am pale again, there's no veracity in me. Fetch me the red—the red, do you hear, sweetheart? An errant ash color, as I'm a person. Look you how this wench stirs! Why dost thou not fetch me a little red? Didst thou not hear me, mopus?[7]

PEG. The red ratafia does your ladyship mean, or the cherry brandy?

LADY. Ratafia, fool. No, fool. Not the ratafia, fool. Grant me patience! I mean the Spanish paper,[8] idiot—complexion, darling. Paint, paint, paint, dost thou understand that, changeling, dangling thy hands like bobbins before thee? Why dost thou not stir, puppet? Thou wooden thing upon wires.

PEG. Lord, madam, your ladyship is so impatient.—I cannot come at the paint, madam. Mrs. Foible has locked it up and carried the key with her.

LADY. A pox take you both!—Fetch me the cherry brandy then.

SCENE 2

Lady Wishfort.

I'm as pale and as faint, I look like Mrs. Qualmsick, the curate's wife, that's always breeding. Wench, come, come, wench, what art thou doing? Sipping? Tasting? Save thee, dost thou not know the bottle?

SCENE 3

Lady Wishfort, Peg with a bottle and china cup.

PEG. Madam, I was looking for a cup.

LADY. A cup, save thee, and what a cup hast thou brought! Dost thou take me for a fairy, to drink out of an acorn? Why didst thou not bring thy thimble? Hast thou ne'er a brass thimble clinking in thy pocket with a bit of nutmeg? I warrant thee. Come, fill, fill.—So—again. See who that is.—[*One knocks.*]—Set down the bottle first. Here, here, under the table.—What, wouldst thou go with the bottle in thy hand like a tapster? As I'm a person, this wench has lived in an inn upon the road before she came to me, like Maritornes the Asturian[9] in *Don Quixote.* No Foible yet?

PEG. No, madam, Mrs. Marwood.

LADY. O Marwood, let her come in. Come in, good Marwood.

7. Dull, stupid person.
8. Rouge.

9. The servant at the inn where the Don and Sancho Panza are succored.

SCENE 4

[To them] Mrs. Marwood.

MRS. MAR. I'm surprised to find your ladyship in *deshabillé*[1] at this time
of day.

LADY. Foible's a lost thing; has been abroad since morning, and never
heard of since.

MRS. MAR. I saw her but now, as I came masked through the park, in
conference with Mirabell.

LADY. With Mirabell! you call my blood into my face, with mentioning
that traitor. She durst not have the confidence. I sent her to negotiate
an affair, in which if I'm detected I'm undone. If that wheedling villain has wrought upon Foible to detect me, I'm ruined. O my dear
friend, I'm a wretch of wretches if I'm detected.

MRS. MAR. O madam, you cannot suspect Mrs. Foible's integrity.

LADY. O, he carries poison in his tongue that would corrupt integrity
itself. If she has given him an opportunity, she has as good as put her
integrity into his hands. Ah dear Marwood, what's integrity to an
opportunity? Hark! I hear her—dear friend, retire into my closet,[2] that
I may examine her with more freedom. You'll pardon me, dear friend,
I can make bold with you. There are books over the chimney—Quarles
and Prynne, and the *Short View of the Stage*, with Bunyan's works to
entertain you.[3] *[to PEG]* Go, you thing, and send her in.

SCENE 5

Lady Wishfort, Foible.

LADY. O Foible, where hast thou been? What hast thou been doing?

FOIB. Madam, I have seen the party.

LADY. But what hast thou done?

FOIB. Nay, 'tis your ladyship has done, and are to do; I have only promised. But a man so enamored—so transported! Well, if worshiping of
pictures be a sin—poor Sir Rowland, I say.

LADY. The miniature has been counted like[4]—but hast thou not betrayed
me, Foible? Hast thou not detected me to that faithless Mirabell?—
What hadst thou to do with him in the park? Answer me, has he got
nothing out of thee?

FOIB. *[aside]* So, the devil has been beforehand with me. What shall I
say?—Alas, madam, could I help it if I met that confident thing? Was
I in fault? If you had heard how he used me, and all upon your
ladyship's account, I'm sure you would not suspect my fidelity. Nay,
if that had been the worst I could have borne; but he had a fling at
your ladyship too; and then I could not hold; but i' faith I gave him
his own.

1. In negligee.
2. Private retiring room.
3. Francis Quarles (1592–1644), a religious poet,
by 1700 regarded with contempt, but formerly
greatly admired, especially among the Puritans;
William Prynne (1600–1669), Puritan pamphleteer, author of *Histriomastix* (1632), a violent attack

on the stage. For Jeremy Collier's *Short View*, see
the Prologue of this play: Congreve, who had been
the object of much of Collier's vituperation, slyly
identifies his enemy with Puritans and Nonconformists, whom Collier, an ardent high churchman,
despised.
4. Considered a likeness.

LADY. Me? What did the filthy fellow say?

FOIB. O madam; 'tis a shame to say what he said—with his taunts and his fleers, tossing up his nose. Humh (says he) what, you are a-hatching some plot (says he) you are so early abroad, or catering[5] (says he), ferreting for some disbanded officer, I warrant—half pay is but thin subsistence (says he).—Well, what pension does your lady propose? Let me see (says he) what, she must come down pretty deep now, she's superannuated (says he) and—

LADY. Ods my life, I'll have him—I'll have him murdered. I'll have him poisoned. Where does he eat? I'll marry a drawer[6] to have him poisoned in his wine. I'll send for Robin from Locket's—immediately.

FOIB. Poison him? Poisoning's too good for him. Starve him, madam, starve him; marry Sir Rowland, and get him disinherited. O, you would bless yourself, to hear what he said.

LADY. A villain!—superannuated!

FOIB. Humh (says he) I hear you are laying designs against me too (says he) and Mrs. Millamant is to marry my uncle; (he does not suspect a word of your ladyship) but (says he) I'll fit you for that, I warrant you (says he) I'll hamper you for that (says he) you and your old frippery[7] too (says he). I'll handle you—

LADY. Audacious villain! handle me, would he durst—frippery? old frippery! Was there ever such a foul-mouthed fellow? I'll be married tomorrow, I'll be contracted tonight.

FOIB. The sooner the better, madam.

LADY. Will Sir Rowland be here, say'st thou? When, Foible?

FOIB. Incontinently, madam. No new sheriff's wife expects the return of her husband after knighthood, with that impatience in which Sir Rowland burns for the dear hour of kissing your ladyship's hand after dinner.

LADY. Frippery! Superannuated frippery! I'll frippery the villain, I'll reduce him to frippery and rags. A tatterdemalion—I hope to see him hung with tatters, like a Long Lane penthouse,[8] or a gibbet-thief. A slandermouthed railer—I warrant the spendthrift prodigal's in debt as much as the million lottery, or the whole court upon a birthday. I'll spoil his credit with his tailor. Yes, he shall have my niece with her fortune, he shall.

FOIB. He! I hope to see him lodge in Ludgate first, and angle into Blackfriars for brass farthings with an old mitten.[9]

LADY. Aye, dear Foible; thank thee for that, dear Foible. He has put me out of all patience. I shall never recompose my features to receive Sir Rowland with any economy of face. This wretch has fretted me that I am absolutely decayed. Look, Foible.

FOIB. Your ladyship has frowned a little too rashly, indeed, madam. There are some cracks discernible in the white varnish.

LADY. Let me see the glass.—Cracks, say'st thou? Why I am arrantly

---

5. Procuring (i.e., pimping for Lady Wishfort). When a regiment was "disbanded," its officers went on half pay, often for life.

6. One who draws wine from casks and serves it. Locket's was a fashionable tavern near Charing Cross.

7. Old, cast-off clothes; an insulting metaphor to apply to Lady Wishfort.

8. "Tatterdemalion": ragamuffin. Long Lane was a street where old clothes were sold; "penthouse": a shed, supported by the wall toward which it is inclined.

9. Ludgate was a debtor's prison, adjoining the district of Blackfriars in London. Prisoners begged by letting down a mitten on a string; passers-by dropped coins into it.

flayed—I look like an old peeled wall. Thou must repair me, Foible, before Sir Rowland comes, or I shall never keep up to my picture.

FOIB. I warrant you, madam; a little art once made your picture like you and now a little of the same art must make you like your picture. Your picture must sit for you, madam.

LADY. But art thou sure Sir Rowland will not fail to come? Or will a' not fail[1] when he does come? Will he be importunate, Foible, and push? For if he should not be importunate—I shall never break decorums.—I shall die with confusion, if I am forced to advance.—Oh, no, I can never advance.—I shall swoon if he should expect advances. No, I hope Sir Rowland is better bred than to put a lady to the necessity of breaking her forms. I won't be too coy neither—I won't give him despair—but a little disdain is not amiss; a little scorn is alluring.

FOIB. A little scorn becomes your ladyship.

LADY. Yes, but tenderness becomes me best.—A sort of dyingness—You see that picture has a sort of a—Ha, Foible? A swimmingness in the eyes—Yes, I'll look so—my niece affects it; but she wants features. Is Sir Rowland handsome? Let my toilet be removed—I'll dress above. I'll receive Sir Rowland here. Is he handsome? Don't answer me. I won't know: I'll be surprised. I'll be taken by surprise.

FOIB. By storm, madam. Sir Rowland's a brisk man.

LADY. Is he! O, then he'll importune, if he's a brisk man, I shall save decorums if Sir Rowland importunes. I have a mortal terror at the apprehension of offending against decorums. O, I'm glad he's a brisk man. Let my things be removed, good Foible.

SCENE 6

Mrs. Fainall, Foible.

MRS. FAIN. O Foible, I have been in a fright, lest I should come too late. That devil Marwood saw you in the park with Mirabell, and I'm afraid will discover it to my lady.

FOIB. Discover what, madam?

MRS. FAIN. Nay, nay, put not on that strange face. I am privy to the whole design and know Waitwell, to whom thou wert this morning married, is to personate Mirabell's uncle, and as such, winning my lady, to involve her in those difficulties from which Mirabell only must release her, by his making his conditions to have my cousin and her fortune left to her own disposal.

FOIB. O dear madam, I beg your pardon. It was not my confidence in your ladyship that was deficient, but I thought the former good correspondence between your ladyship and Mr. Mirabell might have hindered his communicating this secret.

MRS. FAIN. Dear Foible, forget that.

FOIB. O dear madam, Mr. Mirabell is such a sweet winning gentleman—but your ladyship is the pattern of generosity. Sweet lady, to be so good! Mr. Mirabell cannot choose but to be grateful. I find your ladyship has his heart still. Now, madam, I can safely tell your lady-

---

1. I.e., will *he* not fail?

ship our success. Mrs. Marwood had told my lady; but I warrant I managed myself. I turned it all for the better. I told my lady that Mr. Mirabell railed at her. I laid horrid things to his charge, I'll vow; and my lady is so incensed that she'll be contracted to Sir Rowland tonight, she says—I warrant I worked her up, that he may have her for asking for, as they say of a Welsh maidenhead.

MRS. FAIN. O rare Foible!

FOIB. Madam, I beg your ladyship to acquaint Mr. Mirabell of his success. I would be seen as little as possible to speak to him—besides, I believe Madam Marwood watches me. She has a month's mind;[2] but I know Mr. Mirabell can't abide her.—[Calls.]—John—remove my lady's toilet. Madam, your servant. My lady is so impatient, I fear she'll come for me if I stay.

MRS. FAIN. I'll go with you up the back stairs, lest I should meet her.

SCENE 7

Mrs. Marwood alone.

MRS. MAR. Indeed, Mrs. Engine,[3] is it thus with you? Are you become a go-between of this importance? Yes, I shall watch you. Why, this wench is the *passe-partout*, a very master key to everybody's strong-box. My friend Fainall,[4] have you carried it so swimmingly? I thought there was something in it; but it seems it's over with you. Your loathing is not from a want of appetite, then, but from a surfeit. Else you could never be so cool to fall from a principal to be an assistant; to procure for him! A pattern of generosity, that I confess. Well, Mr. Fainall, you have met with your match. O, man, man! Woman, woman! The devil's an ass: If I were a painter, I would draw him like an idiot, a driveler with a bib and bells. Man should have his head and horns, and woman the rest of him. Poor simple fiend! Madam Marwood has a month's mind, but he can't abide her.—'Twere better for him you had not been his confessor in that affair without you could have kept his counsel closer. I shall not prove another pattern of generosity.— He has not obliged me to that with those excesses of himself; and now I'll have none of him. Here comes the good lady, panting ripe, with a heart full of hope and a head full of care, like any chemist upon the day of projection.[5]

SCENE 8

[*To her*] *Lady Wishfort.*

LADY. O dear Marwood, what shall I say for this rude forgetfulness—but my dear friend is all goodness.

MRS. MAR. No apologies, dear madam. I have been very well entertained.

LADY. As I'm a person I am in a very chaos to think I should so forget

---

2. An inclination (toward Mirabell).
3. A person who serves as an instrument or tool of others in an intrigue.
4. I.e., Mrs. Fainall.
5. An alchemical term denoting the final step in the transmutation of baser metals into gold.

myself—but I have such an olio[6] of affairs really I know not what to do—[*Calls.*]Foible—I expect my nephew Sir Wilfull every moment too.—Why, Foible!—He means to travel for improvement.

MRS. MAR. Methinks Sir Wilfull should rather think of marrying than traveling at his years. I hear he is turned of forty.

LADY. O, he's in less danger of being spoiled by his travels.—I am against my nephew's marrying too young. It will be time enough when he comes back and has acquired discretion to choose for himself.

MRS. MAR. Methinks Mrs. Millamant and he would make a very fit match. He may travel afterwards. 'Tis a thing very usual with young gentlemen.

LADY. I promise you I have thought on't—and since 'tis your judgment, I'll think on't again. I assure you I will; I value your judgment extremely. On my word I'll propose it.

SCENE 9

[*To them*] *Foible.*

LADY. Come, come Foible—I had forgot my nephew will be here before dinner.—I must make haste.

FOIB. Mr. Witwoud and Mr. Petulant are come to dine with your ladyship.

LADY. O dear, I can't appear till I am dressed. Dear Marwood, shall I be free with you again and beg you to entertain 'em? I'll make all imaginable haste. Dear friend, excuse me.

SCENE 10

Mrs. Marwood, Mrs. Millamant, Mincing.

MILLA. Sure never anything was so unbred as that odious man.—Marwood, your servant.

MRS. MAR. You have a color. What's the matter?

MILLA. That horrid fellow Petulant has provoked me into a flame—I have broke my fan.—Mincing, lend me yours; is not all the powder out of my hair?

MRS. MAR. No. What has he done?

MILLA. Nay, he has done nothing; he has only talked.—Nay, he has said nothing neither; but he has contradicted everything that has been said. For my part, I thought Witwoud and he would have quarreled.

MINC. I vow, mem, I thought once they would have fit.

MILLA. Well, 'tis a lamentable thing, I swear, that one has not the liberty of choosing one's acquaintance as one does one's clothes.

MRS. MAR. If we had that liberty, we should be as weary of one set of acquaintance, though never so good, as we are of one suit, though never so fine. A fool and a doily stuff[7] would now and then find days of grace, and be worn for variety.

MILLA. I could consent to wear 'em, if they would wear alike; but fools

6. Hodgepodge.　　　　　　　　　7. A woolen cloth.

never wear out—they are such drap-de-Berry[8] things! Without one could give 'em to one's chambermaid after a day or two.

MRS. MAR. 'Twere better so indeed. Or what think you of the play house? A fine gay glossy fool should be given there, like a new masking habit after the masquerade is over,[9] and we have done with the disguise. For a fool's visit is always a disguise, and never admitted by a woman of wit, but to blind her affair with a lover of sense. If you would but appear barefaced now and own Mirabell, you might as easily put off Petulant and Witwoud as your hood and scarf. And indeed 'tis time, for the town has found it: the secret is grown too big for the pretense: 'tis like Mrs. Primly's great belly; she may lace it down before, but it burnishes[1] on her hips. Indeed, Millamant, you can no more conceal it than my Lady Strammel can her face, that goodly face, which in defiance of her Rhenish-wine tea will not be comprehended in a mask.[2]

MILLA. I'll take my death, Marwood, you are more censorious than a decayed beauty, or a discarded toast.[3] Mincing, tell the men they may come up. My aunt is not dressing here; their folly is less provoking than your malice.

SCENE 11

Millamant, Marwood.

MILLA. "The town has found it." What has it found? That Mirabell loves me is no more a secret than it is a secret that you discovered it to my aunt, or than the reason why you discovered it is a secret.

MRS. MAR. You are nettled.

MILLA. You're mistaken. Ridiculous!

MRS. MAR. Indeed, my dear, you'll tear another fan if you don't mitigate those violent airs.

MILLA. O silly! Ha, ha, ha. I could laugh immoderately. Poor Mirabell! His constancy to me has quite destroyed his complaisance for all the world beside. I swear, I never enjoined it him, to be so coy.—If I had the vanity to think he would obey me, I would command him to show more gallantry.—'Tis hardly well bred to be so particular on one hand and so insensible on the other. But I despair to prevail, and so let him follow his own way. Ha, ha, ha. Pardon me, dear creature, I must laugh, ha, ha, ha; though I grant you 'tis a little barbarous, ha, ha, ha.

MRS. MAR. What pity 'tis, so much fine raillery, and delivered with so significant gesture, should be so unhappily directed to miscarry.

MILLA. Hae? Dear creature, I ask your pardon—I swear I did not mind you.

MRS. MAR. Mr. Mirabell and you both may think it a thing impossible, when I shall tell him by telling you—

MILLA. O dear, what? For it is the same thing, if I hear it—Ha, ha, ha.

---

8. Coarse woolen cloth, made in the Berry district of France.
9. Fine gentlemen and ladies sometimes donated their old clothes to the playhouses.
1. Spreads out.

2. Lady Strammel (the name means "a lean, ill-favored person") reduces by drinking Rhenish wine, but still her face is too large to be contained ("comprehended") in a mask.
3. A lady to whom toasts are no longer drunk.

MRS. MAR. That I detest him, hate him, madam.

MILLA. O madam, why so do I— and yet the creature loves me, ha, ha, ha. How can one forbear laughing to think of it?—I am a sibyl[4] if I am not amazed to think what he can see in me. I'll take my death, I think you are handsomer—and within a year or two as young. If you could but stay for me, I should overtake you.—But that cannot be.— Well, that thought makes me melancholy.—Now I'll be sad.

MRS. MAR. Your merry note may be changed sooner than you think.

MILLA. D'ye say so? Then I'm resolved I'll have a song to keep up my spirits.

SCENE 12.

[To them] Mincing.

MINC. The gentlemen stay but to comb,[5] madam, and will wait on you.

MILLA. Desire Mrs. ———[6] that is in the next room to sing the song I would have learnt yesterday. You shall hear it, madam—not that there's any great matter in it—But 'tis agreeable to my humor.

[Song. Set by Mr. John Eccles]

1

Love's but the frailty of the mind,
    When 'tis not with ambition joined;
A sickly flame, which if not fed expires;
And feeding, wastes in self-consuming fires.

2

'Tis not to wound a wanton boy
    Or amorous youth, that gives the joy;
But 'tis the glory to have pierced a swain,
For whom inferior beauties sighed in vain.

3

Then I alone the conquest prize,
    When I insult a rival's eyes:
If there's delight in love, 'tis when I see
That heart which others bleed for, bleed for me.

SCENE 13

[To them] Petulant, Witwoud.

MILLA. Is your animosity composed, gentlemen?

WIT. Raillery, raillery, madam, we have no animosity. We hit off a little wit now and then, but no animosity. The falling out of wits is like the falling out of lovers—we agree in the main, like treble and bass. Ha, Petulant!

---

4. A prophetess.
5. I.e., to comb their periwigs.
6. The name of the singer was to be inserted. The

music was by John Eccles (d. 1735), a popular composer for the theater.

PET. Aye, in the main. But when I have a humor to contradict—

WIT. Aye, when he has a humor to contradict, then I contradict too. What, I know my cue. Then we contradict one another like two battledores;[7] for contradictions beget one another like Jews.

PET. If he says black's black—if I have a humor to say 'tis blue—let that pass.—All's one for that. If I have a humor to prove it, it must be granted.

WIT. Not positively must—but it may—it may.

PET. Yes, it positively must, upon proof positive.

WIT. Aye, upon proof positive it must; but upon proof presumptive it only may. That's a logical distinction now, madam.

MRS. MAR. I perceive your debates are of importance and very learnedly handled.

PET. Importance is one thing, and learning's another; but a debate's a debate, that I assert.

WIT. Petulant's an enemy to learning; he relies altogether on his parts.[8]

PET. No, I'm no enemy to learning; it hurts not me.

MRS. MAR. That's a sign indeed it's no enemy to you.

PET. No, no, it's no enemy to anybody but them that have it.

MILLA. Well, an illiterate man's my aversion. I wonder at the impudence of any illiterate man, to offer to make love.

WIT. That I confess I wonder at too.

MILLA. Ah! to marry an ignorant! that can hardly read or write.

PET. Why should a man be any further from being married though he can't read than he is from being hanged. The ordinary's[9] paid for setting the Psalm, and the parish priest for reading the ceremony. And for the rest which is to follow in both cases, a man may do it without book.—So all's one for that.

MILLA. D'ye hear the creature? Lord, here's company, I'll be gone.

SCENE 14

Sir Wilfull Witwoud in a riding dress, Mrs. Marwood, Petulant, Witwoud, Footman.

WIT. In the name of Bartlemew and his Fair,[1] what have we here?

MRS. MAR. 'Tis your brother, I fancy. Don't you know him?

WIT. Not I.—Yes, I think it is he—I've almost forgot him; I have not seen him since the Revolution.[2]

FOOT. Sir, my lady's dressing. Here's company; if you please to walk in, in the meantime.

SIR WIL. Dressing! What, it's but morning here, I warrant, with you in London; we should count it towards afternoon in our parts, down in Shropshire. Why, then belike my aunt han't dined yet—ha, friend?

FOOT. Your aunt, Sir?

SIR WIL. My aunt, sir, yes, my aunt, sir, and your lady, sir; your lady is

---

7. Rackets used to strike the shuttlecock, or bird, in the old game from which badminton is descended.
8. Native abilities.
9. The clergyman appointed to prepare condemned prisoners for death.

1. A feature of St. Bartholomew's Fair, held during August in Smithfield, London, was the exhibition of monsters and freaks of nature.
2. The "Glorious" Revolution of 1688 that forced the abdication of James II.

my aunt, sir.—Why, what do'st thou not know me, friend? Why, then send somebody hither that does. How long hast thou lived with thy lady, fellow, ha?

FOOT. A week, sir; longer than anybody in the house, except my lady's woman.

SIR WIL. Why, then belike thou dost not know thy lady, if thou see'st her, ha, friend?

FOOT. Why truly, sir, I cannot safely swear to her face in a morning, before she is dressed. 'Tis like I may give a shrewd guess at her by this time.

SIR WIL. Well, prithee try what thou canst do; if thou canst not guess, inquire her out, do'st hear, fellow? And tell her her nephew, Sir Wilfull Witwoud, is in the house.

FOOT. I shall, sir.

SIR WIL. Hold ye, hear me, friend; a word with you in your ear. Prithee who are these gallants?

FOOT. Really, sir, I can't tell; there come so many here, 'tis hard to know 'em all.

SCENE 15

Sir Wilfull Witwoud, Petulant, Witwoud, Mrs. Marwood.

SIR WIL. Oons,[3] this fellow knows less than a starling; I don't think a'knows his own name.

MRS. MAR. Mr. Witwoud, your brother is not behind hand in forgetfulness—I fancy he has forgot you too.

WIT. I hope so.—The devil take him that remembers first, I say.

SIR WIL. Save you, gentlemen and lady.

MRS. MAR. For shame, Mr. Witwoud; why don't you speak to him?—And you, sir.

WIT. Petulant, speak.

PET. And you, sir.

SIR WIL. [*Salutes*[4] MARWOOD.] No offense, I hope.

MRS. MAR. No sure, sir.

WIT. This is a vile dog, I see that already. No offense! Ha, ha, ha, to him; to him, Petulant, smoke him.[5]

PET. [*surveying him round*] It seems as if you had come a journey, sir. Hem, hem.

SIR WIL. Very likely, sir, that it may seem so.

PET. No offense, I hope, sir.

WIT. Smoke the boots, the boots, Petulant, the boots. Ha, ha, ha.

SIR WIL. Maybe not, sir; thereafter as 'tis meant, sir.

PET. Sir, I presume upon the information of your boots.

SIR WIL. Why, 'tis like you may, sir: If you are not satisfied with the information of my boots, sir, if you will step to the stable, you may inquire further of my horse, sir.

PET. Your horse, sir! Your horse is an ass, sir!

---

3. An uncouth oath: "God's wounds."
4. Kisses.

5. Make fun of him.

SIR WIL. Do you speak by way of offense, sir?

MRS. MAR. The gentleman's merry, that's all, sir.—[*aside*] 'Slife,[6] we shall have a quarrel betwixt an horse and an ass, before they find one another out. [*aloud*] You must not take anything amiss from your friends, sir. You are among your friends, here, though it may be you don't know it.—If I am not mistaken, you are Sir Wilfull Witwoud.

SIR WIL. Right, lady; I am Sir Wilfull Witwoud, so I write myself; no offense to anybody, I hope; and nephew to the Lady Wishfort of this mansion.

MRS. MAR. Don't you know this gentleman, sir?

SIR WIL. Hum! What, sure, 'tis not—yea by'r Lady, but 'tis—'sheart,[7] I know not whether 'tis or no.—Yea but 'tis, by the Wrekin.[8] Brother Antony! What, Tony, i'faith! What, do'st thou not know me? By'r Lady, not I thee, thou art so becravated and so beperriwigged—'sheart, why do'st not speak? Art thou o'erjoyed?

WIT. Odso, brother, is it you? Your servant, brother.

SIR WIL. Your servant! Why, yours, sir. Your servant again—'sheart, and your friend and servant to that—and a—[*Puff*]—and a flapdragon[9] for your service, sir: and a hare's foot, and a hare's scut[1] for your service, sir; an you be so cold and so courtly!

WIT. No offense, I hope, brother.

SIR WIL. 'Sheart, sir, but there is, and much offense. A pox, is this your Inns o'Court[2] breeding, not to know your friends and your relations, your elders and your betters?

WIT. Why, Brother Wilfull of Salop,[3] you may be as short as a Shrewsbury cake, if you please. But I tell you 'tis not modish to know relations in town. You think you're in the country, where great lubberly brothers slabber and kiss one another when they meet, like a call of sergeants.[4]—'Tis not the fashion here; 'tis not indeed, dear brother.

SIR WIL. The fashion's a fool; and you're a fop, dear brother. 'Sheart, I've suspected this—by'r Lady, I conjectured you were a fop, since you began to change the style of your letters and write in a scrap of paper gilt round the edges, no bigger than a subpoena. I might expect this when you left off "Honored Brother" and "hoping you are in good health," and so forth—to begin with a "Rat me, knight, I'm so sick of a last night's debauch"—'od's heart, and then tell a familiar tale of a cock and bull, and a whore and a bottle, and so conclude—You could write news before you were out of your time,[5] when you lived with honest Pumple-Nose, the attorney of Furnival's Inn—You could entreat to be remembered then to your friends round the Wrekin. We could

---

6. "God's life."
7. "God's heart."
8. A solitary mountain peak in Shropshire, near the Welsh border.
9. Something worthless.
1. Rabbit's tail.
2. The buildings—Gray's Inn, Lincoln's Inn, the Inner Temple, the Middle Temple—housing the four legal societies that have the sole right to admit persons to the practice of law.
3. An ancient name of Shropshire. A "Shrews-

bury cake" was a "short" cake, in the modern meaning of the term. Witwoud puns, using "short" also in the sense of "abrupt."
4. Witwoud refers to the mutual greetings and felicitations of a group of barristers ("sergeants") newly admitted to the bar.
5. Before he had served out his apprenticeship. Furnival's Inn was one of the Inns of Chancery, attached to Lincoln's Inn. Attorneys were looked down on socially; hence Petulant's ill-natured mirth in his next speech.

have gazettes[6] then, and Dawks's *Letter*, and the Weekly Bill, till of late days.

PET. 'Slife, Witwoud, were you ever an attorney's clerk? Of the family of the Furnivals. Ha, ha, ha!

WIT. Aye, aye, but that was but for a while. Not long, not long; pshaw, I was not in my own power then. An orphan, and this fellow was my guardian; aye, aye, I was glad to consent to that man to come to London. He had the disposal of me then. If I had not agreed to that, I might have been bound 'prentice to a felt-maker in Shrewsbury; this fellow would have bound me to a maker of felts.

SIR WIL. 'Sheart, and better than to be bound to a maker of fops; where, I suppose, you have served your time; and now you may set up for yourself.

MRS. MAR. You intend to travel, sir, as I'm informed.

SIR WIL. Belike I may, madam. I may chance to sail upon the salt seas, if my mind hold.

PET. And the wind serve.

SIR WIL. Serve or not serve, I shan't ask license of you, sir; nor the weather-cock your companion. I direct my discourse to the lady, sir. 'Tis like my aunt may have told you, madam—Yes, I have settled my concerns, I may say now, and am minded to see foreign parts. If an' how that the peace[7] holds, whereby, that is, taxes abate.

MRS. MAR. I thought you had designed for France at all adventures.

SIR WIL. I can't tell that; 'tis like I may and 'tis like I may not. I am somewhat dainty[8] in making a resolution, because when I make it I keep it, I don't stand shill I, shall I,[9] then; if I say't, I'll do't. But I have thoughts to tarry a small matter in town, to learn somewhat of your lingo first, before I cross the seas. I'd gladly have a spice of your French as they say, whereby to hold discourse in foreign countries.

MRS. MAR. Here's an academy in town for that use.

SIR WIL. There is? 'Tis like there may.

MRS. MAR. No doubt you will return very much improved.

WIT. Yes, refined like a Dutch skipper from a whale-fishing.

SCENE 16

[To them] Lady Wishfort and Fainall.

LADY. Nephew, you are welcome.

SIR WIL. Aunt, your servant.

FAIN. Sir Wilfull, your most faithful servant.

SIR WIL. Cousin Fainall, give me your hand.

LADY. Cousin Witwoud, your servant; Mr. Petulant, your servant.—Nephew, you are welcome again. Will you drink anything after your journey, nephew, before you eat? Dinner's almost ready.

---

6. Newspapers. Dawks's *News-Letter* was a popular source of news in the country. The Weekly Bill was the official list of the deaths occurring in London.

7. The peace established by the Treaty of Ryswick in 1697, which concluded the war against France waged under the leadership of William III by England, the Empire, Spain, and Holland. It endured until the spring of 1702, when the War of the Spanish Succession began.

8. Scrupulous, cautious.

9. Shilly-shally.

SIR WIL. I'm very well, I thank you, aunt. However, I thank you for your courteous offer. 'Sheart, I was afraid you would have been in the fashion too, and have remembered to have forgot your relations. Here's your cousin Tony, belike, I mayn't call him brother for fear of offense.

LADY. O, he's a rallier, nephew—my cousin's a wit; and your great wits always rally their best friends to choose.[1] When you have been abroad, nephew, you'll understand raillery better.

[FAIN. *and* MRS. MARWOOD *talk apart.*]

SIR WIL. Why then let him hold his tongue in the meantime, and rail when that day comes.

SCENE 17

[*To them*] *Mincing.*

MINC. Mem, I come to acquaint your la'ship that dinner is impatient.

SIR WIL. Impatient? Why then belike it won't stay till I pull off my boots. Sweetheart, can you help me to a pair of slippers?—My man's with his horses, I warrant.

LADY. Fie, fie, nephew, you would not pull off your boots here. Go down into the hall.—Dinner shall stay for you. My nephew's a little unbred; you'll pardon him, madam.—Gentlemen, will you walk? Marwood?

MRS. MAR. I'll follow you, madam—before Sir Wilfull is ready.

SCENE 18

Marwood, Fainall.

FAIN. Why then Foible's a bawd, an errant, rank, match-making bawd. And I it seems am a husband, a rank husband; and my wife a very errant, rank wife—all in the way of the world. 'Sdeath, to be a cuckold by anticipation, a cuckold in embryo? Sure I was born with budding antlers like a young satyr, or a citizen's child.[2] 'Sdeath, to be outwitted, to be outjilted—outmatrimonied. If I had kept my speed like a stag, 'twere somewhat, but to crawl after, with my horns like a snail, and be outstripped by my wife 'tis scurvy wedlock.

MRS. MAR. Then shake it off. You have often wished for an opportunity to part, and now you have it. But first prevent their plot.—The half of Millamant's fortune is too considerable to be parted with to a foe, to Mirabell.

FAIN. Damn him, that had been mine—had you not made that fond[3] discovery.—That had been forfeited, had they been married. My wife had added luster to my horns. By that increase of fortune, I could have worn 'em tipped with gold, though my forehead had been furnished like a Deputy-Lieutenant's hall.[4]

1. By choice.
2. "Satyr": a sylvan deity, usually represented with a goat's legs and horns. A cuckold is said to wear horns. Since the wives of "citizens" (merchants living in the old city of London, not the fashionable suburbs) were regarded by the rakes as their natural and easy prey, a "citizen's child" was born to be cuckolded.
3. Foolish.
4. I.e., the great hall in the house of the Deputy Lieutenant of a shire. Fainall imagines it ornamented with numerous antlers taken from deer slain in the hunt.

MRS. MAR. They may prove a cap of maintenance[5] to you still, if you can away with your wife. And she's no worse than when you had her—I dare swear she had given up her game, before she was married.

FAIN. Hum! That may be—She might throw up her cards; but I'll be hanged if she did not put Pam[6] in her pocket.

MRS. MAR. You married her to keep you, and if you can contrive to have her keep you better than you expected, why should you not keep her longer than you intended?

FAIN. The means, the means.

MRS. MAR. Discover to my lady your wife's conduct; threaten to part with her.—My lady loves her and will come to any composition to save her reputation. Take the opportunity of breaking it, just upon the discovery of this imposture. My lady will be enraged beyond bounds and sacrifice niece and fortune and all at that conjuncture. And let me alone to keep her warm; if she should flag in her part, I will not fail to prompt her.

FAIN. Faith, this has an appearance.

MRS. MAR. I'm sorry I hinted to my lady to endeavor a match between Millamant and Sir Wilfull. That may be an obstacle.

FAIN. O, for that matter leave me to manage him; I'll disable him for that; he will drink like a Dane; after dinner, I'll set his hand in.

MRS. MAR. Well, how do you stand affected towards your lady?

FAIN. Why, faith, I'm thinking of it. Let me see—I am married already; so that's over. My wife has placed the jade with me—well, that's over too. I never loved her, or if I had, why that would have been over too by this time. Jealous of her I cannot be, for I am certain; so there's an end of jealousy. Weary of her I am and shall be—no, there's no end of that; no, no, that were too much to hope. Thus far concerning my repose. Now for my reputation. As to my own, I married not for it; so that's out of the question. And as to my part in my wife's—why, she had parted with hers before; so bringing none to me, she can take none from me; 'tis against all rule of play that I should lose to one who has not wherewithal to stake.

MRS. MAR. Besides you forget, marriage is honorable.

FAIN. Hum! Faith, and that's well thought on; marriage is honorable, as you say; and if so, wherefore should cuckoldom be a discredit, being derived from so honorable a root?

MRS. MAR. Nay, I know not; if the root be honorable, why not the branches?[7]

FAIN. So, so, why this point's clear. Well, how do we proceed?

MRS. MAR. I will contrive a letter which shall be delivered to my lady at the time when that rascal who is to act Sir Rowland is with her. It shall come as from an unknown hand—for the less I appear to know of the truth, the better I can play the incendiary. Besides, I would not have Foible provoked if I could help it, because you know she knows some passages—nay, I expect all will come out. But let the mine be sprung first, and then I care not if I am discovered.

FAIN. If the worst come to the worst, I'll turn my wife to grass[8]—I have

---

5. In heraldry, a cap with two points like horns.
6. Jack of clubs, high card in the game of loo.
7. I.e., of the cuckold's horns.

8. Turn out to pasture. A "grass widow" is divorced or separated from her husband.

already a deed of settlement of the best part of her estate; which I wheedled out of her; and that you shall partake at least.

MRS. MAR. I hope you are convinced that I hate Mirabell now: you'll be no more jealous?

FAIN. Jealous, no—by this kiss.—Let husbands be jealous, but let the lover still believe. Or if he doubt, let it be only to endear his pleasure and prepare the joy that follows, when he proves his mistress true. But let husbands' doubts convert to endless jealousy; or if they have belief, let it corrupt to superstition and blind credulity. I am single, and will herd no more with 'em. True, I wear the badge, but I'll disown the order. And since I take my leave of 'em, I care not if I leave 'em a common motto to their common crest.

> All husbands must, or pain, or shame, endure;
> The wise too jealous are, fools too secure.

Act 4—Scene continues.

SCENE 1

Lady Wishfort and Foible.

LADY. Is Sir Rowland coming, say'st thou, Foible? and are things in order?

FOIB. Yes, madam. I have put wax lights in the sconces, and placed the footmen in a row in the hall, in their best liveries, with the coachman and postilion to fill up the equipage.

LADY. Have you pulvilled[9] the coachman and postilion, that they may not stink of the stable, when Sir Rowland comes by?

FOIB. Yes, madam.

LADY. And are the dancers and the music ready, that he may be entertained in all points with correspondence to his passion?

FOIB. All is ready, madam.

LADY. And—well—and how do I look, Foible?

FOIB. Most killing well, madam.

LADY. Well, and how shall I receive him? In what figure shall I give his heart the first impression? There is a great deal in the first impression. Shall I sit?—No, I won't sit—I'll walk.—Aye, I'll walk from the door upon his entrance; and then turn full upon him.—No, that will be too sudden. I'll lie—aye, I'll lie down—I'll receive him in my little dressing-room, there's a couch.—Yes, yes, I'll give the first impression on a couch.—I won't lie neither, but loll and lean upon one elbow; with one foot a little dangling off, jogging in a thoughtful way—yes—and then as soon as he appears, start, aye, start and be surprised, and rise to meet him in a pretty disorder—yes. O, nothing is more alluring than a levee[1] from a couch in some confusion. It shows the foot to advantage and furnishes with blushes and recomposing airs beyond comparison. Hark! There's a coach.

FOIB. 'Tis he, madam.

LADY. O dear, has my nephew made his addresses to Millamant? I ordered him.

9. Sprinkled with perfumed powder.   1. A rising.

FOIB. Sir Wilfull is set in to drinking, madam, in the parlor.

LADY. 'Ods my life, I'll send him to her. Call her down, Foible; bring her hither. I'll send him as I go.—When they are together, then come to me, Foible, that I may not be too long alone with Sir Rowland.

SCENE 2

Mrs. Millamant, Mrs. Fainall, Foible.

FOIB. Madam, I stayed here to tell your ladyship that Mr. Mirabell has waited this half hour for an opportunity to talk with you. Though my lady's orders were to leave you and Sir Wilfull together. Shall I tell Mr. Mirabell that you are at leisure?

MILLA. No—What would the dear man have? I am thoughtful and would amuse myself.—Bid him come another time.

> There never yet was woman made,
> Nor shall, but to be cursed.[2]

[*Repeating and walking about.*]

That's hard!

MRS. FAIN. You are very fond of Sir John Suckling today, Millamant, and the poets.

MILLA. He? Aye and filthy verses—so I am.

FOIB. Sir Wilfull is coming, madam. Shall I send Mr. Mirabell away?

MILLA. Aye, if you please, Foible, send him away—or send him hither, just as you will, dear Foible. I think I'll see him—Shall I? Aye, let the wretch come.

> Thyrsis, a youth of the inspirèd train.[3]

[*Repeating.*]

Dear Fainall, entertain Sir Wilfull.—Thou hast philosophy to undergo a fool, thou art married and hast patience.—I would confer with my own thoughts.

MRS. FAIN. I am obliged to you that you would make me your proxy in this affair, but I have business of my own.

SCENE 3

[To them] Sir Wilfull.

MRS. FAIN. O Sir Wilfull; you are come at the critical instant. There's your mistress up to the ears in love and contemplation. Pursue your point, now or never.

SIR WIL. Yes; my aunt will have it so.—I would gladly have been encouraged with a bottle or two, because I'm somewhat wary at first, before

---

2. The opening lines of a poem by Sir John Suckling. Impelled by her love to accept Mirabell, but reluctant to give herself, Millamant broods over poems that speak of the brief happiness of lovers and the falseness of men.

3. The first line of Edmund Waller's *Story of Phoebus and Daphne Applied*. In the flight of the virgin nymph from the embraces of the amorous god, Millamant finds an emblem of her relations with Mirabell.

I am acquainted; [*This while* MILLA. *walks about repeating to her-self.*]—but I hope, after a time, I shall break my mind—that is upon further acquaintance.—So for the present, cousin, I'll take my leave.—If so be you'll be so kind to make my excuse, I'll return to my company.—

MRS. FAIN. O fie, Sir Wilfull! What, you must not be daunted.

SIR WIL. Daunted, no, that's not it; it is not so much for that—for if so be that I set on't, I'll do't. But only for the present, 'tis sufficient till further acquaintance, that's all.—Your servant.

MRS. FAIN. Nay, I'll swear you shall never lose so favorable an opportunity if I can help it. I'll leave you together and lock the door.

SCENE 4

Sir Wilfull, Millamant.

SIR WIL. Nay, nay, cousin—I have forgot my gloves.—What d'ye do? 'Sheart, a'has locked the door indeed, I think.—Nay, cousin Fainall, open the door.—Pshaw, what a vixen trick is this? Nay, now a'has seen me too.—Cousin, I made bold to pass through, as it were.—I think this door's enchanted.—

MILLA. [*repeating*]

> I prithee spare me, gentle boy,
> Press me no more for that slight toy.[4]

SIR WIL. Anan?[5] Cousin, your servant.

MILLA.—"That foolish trifle of a heart"—Sir Wilfull!

SIR WIL. Yes—your servant. No offense I hope, cousin.

MILLA. [*repeating*]

> I swear it will not do its part,
> Though thou dost thine, employ'st thy power and art.

Natural, easy Suckling!

SIR WIL. Anan? Suckling? No such suckling neither, cousin, nor stripling: I thank heaven I'm no minor.

MILLA. Ah rustic, ruder than Gothic.[6]

SIR WIL. Well, well, I shall understand your lingo one of these days, cousin. In the meanwhile I must answer in plain English.

MILLA. Have you any business with me, Sir Wilfull?

SIR WIL. Not at present, cousin.—Yes, I made bold to see, to come and know if that how you were disposed to fetch a walk this evening, if so be that I might not be troublesome, I would have sought a walk with you.

MILLA. A walk? What then?

SIR WIL. Nay nothing—only for the walk's sake, that's all—

MILLA. I nauseate walking; 'tis a country diversion. I loathe the country and everything that relates to it.

SIR WIL. Indeed! Hah! Look ye, look ye, you do? Nay, 'tis like you may.—

4. The first lines of a song by Suckling.   6. To the new age with its classical taste, medieval
5. "How's that?"   art, especially architecture, seemed crude ("rude").

Here are choice of pastimes here in town, as plays and the like; that must be confessed indeed.—

MILLA. Ah, *l'étourdi.*[7] I hate the town too.

SIR WIL. Dear heart, that's much—Hah! that you should hate 'em both! Hah! 'tis like you may; there are some can't relish the town, and others can't away with the country—'tis like you may be one of those, cousin.

MILLA. Ha, ha, ha. Yes, 'tis like I may. You have nothing further to say to me?

SIR WIL. Not at present, cousin. 'Tis like when I have an opportunity to be more private, I may break my mind in some measure.—I conjecture you partly guess—however, that's as time shall try; but spare to speak and spare to speed, as they say.

MILLA. If it is of no great importance, Sir Wilfull, you will oblige me to leave me. I have just now a little business.

SIR WIL. Enough, enough, cousin. Yes, yes, all a case—when you're disposed, when you're disposed. Now's as well as another time; and another time as well as now. All's one for that.—Yes, yes, if your concerns call you, there's no haste; it will keep cold as they say.— Cousin, your servant. I think this door's locked.

MILLA. You may go this way, sir.

SIR WIL. Your servant—then with your leave I'll return to my company.

MILLA. Aye, aye. Ha, ha, ha.

Like Phoebus sung the no less amorous Boy.[8]

SCENE 5

Millamant, Mirabell.

MIRA.

Like Daphne she, as lovely and as coy.

Do you lock yourself up from me, to make my search more curious?[9] Or is this pretty artifice contrived to signify that here the chase must end, and my pursuit be crowned, for you can fly no further?

MILLA. Vanity! No—I'll fly and be followed to the last moment. Though I am upon the very verge of matrimony, I expect you should solicit me as much as if I were wavering at the grate of a monastery,[1] with one foot over the threshold. I'll be solicited to the very last, nay and afterwards.

MIRA. What, after the last?

MILLA. O, I should think I was poor and had nothing to bestow, if I were reduced to an inglorious ease; and freed from the agreeable fatigues of solicitation.

MIRA. But do not you know that when favors are conferred upon instant and tedious solicitation, that they diminish in their value and that

7. I.e., "Oh, the silly fellow!" The French phrase
forms the title of a comedy by Molière.
8. This, and the line that Mirabell caps it with,
are from Waller's poem mentioned in note 3
(above).
9. Intricate, laborious.
1. The grated door of a convent.

both the giver loses the grace, and the receiver lessens his pleasure?

MILLA. It may be in things of common application, but never sure in love. O, I hate a lover that can dare to think he draws a moment's air, independent on the bounty of his mistress. There is not so impudent a thing in nature as the saucy look of an assured man, confident of success. The pedantic arrogance of a very husband has not so pragmatical[2] an air. Ah! I'll never marry, unless I am first made sure of my will and pleasure.

MIRA. Would you have 'em both before marriage? Or will you be contented with the first now, and stay for the other till after grace?

MILLA. Ah, don't be impertinent.—My dear liberty, shall I leave thee? My faithful solitude, my darling contemplation, must I bid you then adieu? Ay-h adieu—My morning thoughts, agreeable wakings, indolent slumbers, all ye *douceurs*, ye *sommeils du matin*,[3] adieu.—I can't do't, 'tis more than impossible.—Positively, Mirabell, I'll lie abed in a morning as long as I please.

MIRA. Then I'll get up in a morning as early as I please.

MILLA. Ah, idle creature, get up when you will.—and d'ye hear? I won't be called names after I'm married; positively I won't be called names.

MIRA. Names!

MILLA. Aye, as wife, spouse, my dear, joy, jewel, love, sweetheart, and the rest of that nauseous cant, in which men and their wives are so fulsomely familiar—I shall never bear that.—Good Mirabell, don't let us be familiar or fond, nor kiss before folks, like my Lady Fadler[4] and Sir Francis; nor go to Hyde Park together the first Sunday in a new chariot, to provoke eyes and whispers; and then never be seen there together again, as if we were proud of one another the first week, and ashamed of one another ever after. Let us never visit together, nor go to a play together, but let us be very strange[5] and well bred; let us be as strange as if we had been married a great while; and as well bred as if we were not married at all.

MIRA. Have you any more conditions to offer? Hitherto your demands are pretty reasonable.

MILLA. Trifles—as liberty to pay and receive visits to and from whom I please; to write and receive letters, without interrogatories or wry faces on your part; to wear what I please; and choose conversation with regard only to my own taste; to have no obligation upon me to converse with wits that I don't like, because they are your acquaintance; or to be intimate with fools, because they may be your relations. Come to dinner when I please, dine in my dressing room when I'm out of humor, without giving a reason. To have my closet inviolate; to be sole empress of my tea table, which you must never presume to approach without first asking leave. And lastly, wherever I am, you shall always knock at the door before you come in. These articles subscribed, if I continue to endure you a little longer, I may by degrees dwindle into a wife.

MIRA. Your bill of fare is something advanced in this latter account.

---

2. Self-assured, conceited.
3. I.e., soft (pleasures) and morning naps.
4. "Fondler."
5. Reserved.

Well, have I liberty to offer conditions—that when you are dwindled into a wife, I may not be beyond measure enlarged into a husband?

MILLA. You have free leave, propose your utmost, speak and spare not.

MIRA. I thank you. *Imprimis*[6] then, I covenant that your acquaintance be general; that you admit no sworn confidante or intimate of your own sex; no she-friend to screen her affairs under your countenance and tempt you to make trial of a mutual secrecy. No decoy duck to wheedle you a fop—scrambling to the play in a mask—then bring you home in a pretended fright, when you think you shall be found out—and rail at me for missing the play, and disappointing the frolic which you had to pick me up and prove my constancy.

MILLA. Detestable *imprimis!* I go to the play in a mask!

MIRA. *Item,*[7] I article, that you continue to like your own face as long as I shall; and while it passes current with me, that you endeavor not to new coin it. To which end, together with all vizards[8] for the day, I prohibit all masks for the night, made of oiled-skins and I know not what—hog's bones, hare's gall, pig water, and the marrow of a roasted cat. In short, I forbid all commerce with the gentlewoman in what-d'ye-call-it court. *Item*, I shut my doors against all bawds with baskets, and pennyworths of muslin, china, fans, atlases,[9] etc. *Item*, when you shall be breeding—

MILLA. Ah! Name it not.

MIRA. Which may be presumed, with a blessing on our endeavors—

MILLA. Odious endeavors!

MIRA. I denounce against all strait lacing, squeezing for a shape, till you mold my boy's head like a sugar loaf; and instead of a man-child, make me father to a crooked billet.[1] Lastly, to the dominion of the tea table I submit.—But with proviso that you exceed not in your province; but restrain yourself to native and simple tea-table drinks, as tea, chocolate, and coffee. As likewise to genuine and authorized tea-table talk—such as mending of fashions, spoiling reputations, railing at absent friends, and so forth—but that on no account you encroach upon the men's prerogative, and presume to drink healths, or toast fellows; for prevention of which, I banish all foreign forces, all auxiliaries to the tea table, as orange brandy, all aniseed, cinnamon, citron and Barbados waters,[2] together with ratafia and the most noble spirit of clary.—But for cowslip-wine, poppy water, and all dormitives,[3] those I allow. These provisos admitted, in other things I may prove a tractable and complying husband.

MILLA. O, horrid provisos! filthy strong waters! I toast fellows, odious men! I hate your odious provisos.

MIRA. Then we're agreed. Shall I kiss your hand upon the contract? And here comes one to be a witness to the sealing of the deed.

---

6. In the first place, as in legal documents.
7. Used to introduce each item in a list. "I article": I stipulate.
8. Masks. Cosmetics were made of materials as repulsive as those that Mirabell names.
9. Rich silk fabrics.

1. I.e., a crooked piece of firewood.
2. All of these "waters" are alcoholic drinks. "Clary": a sweet liqueur made of wine, honey, and spices.
3. Sleeping draughts.

SCENE 6

[To them] Mrs. Fainall.

MILLA. Fainall, what shall I do? Shall I have him? I think I must have him.

MRS. FAIN. Aye, aye, take him, take him. What should you do?

MILLA. Well then—I'll take my death I'm in a horrid fright—Fainall, I shall never say it—well—I think—I'll endure you.

MRS. FAIN. Fy, fy, have him, have him, and tell him so in plain terms: for I am sure you have a mind to him.

MILLA. Are you? I think I have—and the horrid man looks as if he thought so too.—Well, you ridiculous thing you, I'll have you.—I won't be kissed, nor I won't be thanked.—Here kiss my hand though.—So, hold your tongue now, don't say a word.

MRS. FAIN. Mirabell, there's a necessity for your obedience—you have neither time to talk nor stay. My mother is coming; and in my conscience if she should see you, would fall into fits, and maybe not recover, time enough to return to Sir Rowland; who, as Foible tells me, is in a fair way to succeed. Therefore spare your ecstasies for another occasion, and slip down the back stairs, where Foible waits to consult you.

MILLA. Aye, go, go. In the meantime I suppose you have said something to please me.

MIRA. I am all obedience.

SCENE 7

Millamant, Mrs. Fainall.

MRS. FAIN. Yonder Sir Wilfull's drunk, and so noisy that my mother has been forced to leave Sir Rowland to appease him; but he answers her only with singing and drinking.—What they may have done by this time I know not, but Petulant and he were upon quarreling as I came by.

MILLA. Well, if Mirabell should not make a good husband, I am a lost thing; for I find I love him violently.

MRS. FAIN. So it seems, for you mind not what's said to you.—If you doubt him, you had best take up with Sir Wilfull.

MILLA. How can you name that superannuated lubber? foh!

SCENE 8

[To them] Witwoud from drinking.

MRS. FAIN. So, is the fray made up, that you have left 'em?

WIT. Left 'em? I could stay no longer—I have laughed like ten christenings—I am tipsy with laughing.—If I had stayed any longer, I should have burst—I must have been let out and pieced in the sides like an unsized camlet.[4]—Yes, yes, the fray is composed; my lady came in like a *nolle prosequi*[5] and stopped the proceedings.

MILLA. What was the dispute?

WIT. That's the jest; there was no dispute. They could neither of 'em speak for rage; and so fell a-sputtering at one another like two roasting apples.

SCENE 9

[To them] Petulant drunk.

WIT. Now, Petulant? All's over, all's well? Gad, my head begins to whim it about.—Why dost thou not speak? Thou art both as drunk and as mute as a fish.

PET. Look you, Mrs. Millamant—if you can love me, dear nymph—say it—and that's the conclusion—pass on, or pass off—that's all.

WIT. Thou hast uttered volumes, folios, in less than decimo sexto,[6] my dear Lacedemonian. Sirrah Petulant, thou art an epitomizer of words.

PET. Witwoud—You are an annihilator of sense.

WIT. Thou art a retailer of phrases, and dost deal in remnants of remnants, like a maker of pincushions. Thou art in truth (metaphorically speaking) a speaker of shorthand.

PET. Thou art (without a figure) just one-half of an ass, and Baldwin[7] yonder, thy half brother, is the rest.—A Gemini of asses split, would make just four of you.

WIT. Thou dost bite, my dear mustard-seed; kiss me for that.

PET. Stand off—I'll kiss no more males.—I have kissed your twin yonder in a humor of reconciliation, till he—*[hiccup]*—rises upon my stomach like a radish.

MILLA. Eh! filthy creature.—What was the quarrel?

PET. There was no quarrel—there might have been a quarrel.

WIT. If there had been words enow between 'em to have expressed provocation, they had gone together by the ears like a pair of castanets.

PET. You were the quarrel.

MILLA. Me!

PET. If I have a humor to quarrel, I can make less matters conclude premises.—If you are not handsome, what then, if I have a humor to prove it?—If I shall have my reward, say so; if not, fight for your face the next time yourself.—I'll go sleep.

WIT. Do, wrap thyself up like a woodlouse, and dream revenge—and hear me, if thou canst learn to write by tomorrow morning, pen me a challenge.—I'll carry it for thee.

PET. Carry your mistress's monkey a spider[8]—go flea dogs, and read romances—I'll go to bed to my maid.

4. A fabric made by mixing wool and silk; "unsized" because not stiffened with some glutinous substance.
5. A phrase indicating the withdrawal of a lawsuit.
6. "Folios" are books of the largest size, as "decimo sexto" means a book of the smallest size. The Spartans ("Lacedemonians") were men of few words.
7. The name of the ass in the beast epic, *Reynard the Fox.* "Gemini," the two Roman deities, Castor and Pollux, for whom one of the signs of the zodiac is named.
8. Monkeys were supposed to eat spiders. Petulant scornfully contrasts what he imagines to be Witwoud's technique with his lady and his own more vigorous and direct program for the rest of the evening.

MRS. FAIN. He's horridly drunk—how came you all in this pickle?

WIT. A plot, a plot, to get rid of the knight—your husband's advice; but he sneaked off.

SCENE 10

Sir Wilfull drunk, Lady Wishfort, Witwoud, Millamant, Mrs. Fainall.

LADY. Out upon't, out upon't! At years of discretion, and comport yourself at this rantipole[9] rate!

SIR WIL. No offense, aunt.

LADY. Offense? As I'm a person, I'm ashamed of you.—Fogh! how you stink of wine! D'ye think my niece will ever endure such a borachio![1] you're an absolute borachio.

SIR WIL. Borachio!

LADY. At a time when you should commence an amour, and put your best foot foremost—

SIR WIL. 'Sheart, an you grutch[2] me your liquor, make a bill.—Give me more drink, and take my purse.

[*Sings*]   Prithee fill me the glass
                      'Till it laugh in my face,
          With ale that is potent and mellow;
                      He that whines for a lass
                      Is an ignorant ass,
          For a bumper[3] has not its fellow.

But if you would have me marry my cousin—say the word and I'll do't—Wilfull will do't, that's the word—Wilfull will do't, that's my crest—my motto I have forgot.[4]

LADY. My nephew's a little overtaken, cousin—but 'tis with drinking your health—O' my word you are obliged to him—

SIR WIL. *In vino veritas,*[5] aunt.—If I drunk your health today, cousin—I am a borachio. But if you have a mind to be married, say the word, and send for the piper; Wilfull will do't. If not, dust it away, and let's have t'other round.—Tony, 'ods heart, where's Tony?—Tony's an honest fellow, but he spits after a bumper, and that's a fault—

[*Sings*]   We'll drink and we'll never ha' done, boys,
                      Put the glass then around with the sun, boys,
          Let Apollo's example invite us;
                      For he's drunk every night,
                      And that makes him so bright,
          That he's able next morning to light us.

The sun's a good pimple,[6] an honest soaker, he has a cellar at your Antipodes. If I travel, aunt, I touch at your Antipodes.—Your Anti-

9. Rakish.
1. Drunkard. The word is Spanish.
2. Grudge.
3. A wineglass filled to the brim; the word comes from the custom of touching (bumping) glasses when drinking toasts.

4. A coat of arms had a crest—a helmet surmounting the shield—and a motto. In his drunkenness, Sir Wilfull confuses the two.
5. "In wine [there is] truth."
6. Boon companion.

podes are a good rascally sort of topsy-turvy fellows.—If I had a bumper, I'd stand upon my head and drink a health to 'em.—A match or no match, cousin, with the hard name?—aunt, Wilfull will do't. If she has her maidenhead, let her look to't; if she has not, let her keep her own counsel in the meantime, and cry out at the nine months' end.

MILLA. Your pardon, madam, I can stay no longer—Sir Wilfull grows very powerful. Egh! how he smells! I shall be overcome if I stay. Come, cousin.

SCENE 11

Lady Wishfort, Sir Wilfull Witwoud, Mr. Witwoud, Foible.

LADY. Smells! he would poison a tallow-chandler and his family. Beastly creature, I know not what to do with him. Travel, quoth a'; aye, travel, travel, get thee gone, get thee but far enough, to the Saracens, or the Tartars, or the Turks—for thou art not fit to live in a Christian commonwealth, thou beastly pagan.

SIR WIL. Turks, no; no Turks, aunt. Your Turks are infidels, and believe not in the grape. Your Mahometan, your Mussulman is a dry stinkard.—No offense, aunt. My map says that your Turk is not so honest a man as your Christian.—I cannot find by the map that your Mufti[7] is orthodox—whereby it is a plain case, that orthodox is a hard word, aunt, and—[*hiccup*]—Greek for claret.

[*Sings*]　　To drink is a Christian diversion.
　　　　　　　Unknown to the Turk or the Persian:
　　　　　　　　　Let Mahometan fools
　　　　　　　　　Live by heathenish rules,
　　　　　　　And be damned over tea cups and coffee.
　　　　　　　　　But let British lads sing,
　　　　　　　　　Crown a health to the king,
　　　　　　　And a fig for your sultan and sophy.[8]

Ah, Tony!

[FOIBLE *whispers* LADY W.]

LADY. Sir Rowland impatient? Good lack! what shall I do with this beastly tumbrel?[9]—Go lie down and sleep, you sot—or as I'm a person, I'll have you bastinadoed with broomsticks. Call up the wenches with broomsticks.

SIR WIL. Ahay? Wenches, where are the wenches?

LADY. Dear cousin Witwoud, get him away, and you will bind me to you inviolably. I have an affair of moment that invades me with some precipitation—you will oblige me to all futurity.

WIT. Come, knight.—Pox on him, I don't know what to say to him.—Will you go to a cockmatch?

SIR WIL. With a wench, Tony? Is she a shakebag,[1] sirrah? Let me bite your cheek for that.

---

7. The Grand Mufti, head of the state religion of Turkey. Moslems do not use alcohol.
8. The Shah of Persia.

9. Dung cart. "To bastinado" is to punish by beating the soles of the feet.
1. Gamecock.

WIT. Horrible! He has a breath like a bagpipe.—Aye, aye, come, will you march, my Salopian?[2]

SIR WIL. Lead on, little Tony—I'll follow thee, my Anthony, my Tantony. Sirrah, thou shalt be my Tantony, and I'll be thy pig.[3]

—And a fig for your sultan and sophy.

LADY. This will never do. It will never make a match—at least before he has been abroad.

SCENE 12

Lady Wishfort, Waitwell disguised as for Sir Rowland.

LADY. Dear Sir Rowland, I am confounded with confusion at the retrospection of my own rudeness—I have more pardons to ask than the Pope distributes in the Year of Jubilee. But I hope where there is likely to be so near an alliance—we may unbend the severity of decorum—and dispense with a little ceremony.

WAIT. My impatience, madam, is the effect of my transport—and till I have the possession of your adorable person, I am tantalized on the rack; and do but hang, madam, on the tenter[4] of expectation.

LADY. You have excess of gallantry, Sir Rowland; and press things to a conclusion, with a most prevailing vehemence.—But a day or two for decency of marriage.—

WAIT. For decency of funeral, madam. The delay will break my heart—or if that should fail, I shall be poisoned. My nephew will get an inkling of my designs, and poison me—and I would willingly starve him before I die—I would gladly go out of the world with that satisfaction.—That would be some comfort to me, if I could but live so long as to be revenged on that unnatural viper.

LADY. Is he so unnatural, say you? Truly I would contribute much both to the saving of your life and the accomplishment of your revenge—Not that I respect[5] myself; though he has been a perfidious wretch to me.

WAIT. Perfidious to you!

LADY. O Sir Rowland, the hours that he has died away at my feet, the tears that he has shed, the oaths that he has sworn, the palpitations that he has felt, the trances and the tremblings, the ardors and the ecstasies, the kneelings, and the risings, the heart-heavings and the hand-gripings, the pangs and the pathetic regards of his protesting eyes! Oh, no memory can register.

WAIT. What, my rival! Is the rebel my rival? a'dies.

LADY. No, don't kill him at once, Sir Rowland, starve him gradually inch by inch.

WAIT. I'll do't. In three weeks he shall be barefoot; in a month out at knees with begging an alms—he shall starve upward and upward, till

---

2. Inhabitant of Shropshire.
3. St. Anthony (hence "Tantony"), the patron of swineherds, was represented accompanied by a pig.
4. A frame for stretching cloth on hooks so that it

may dry without losing its original shape (cf. the phrase "to be on tenterhooks").
5. Consider.

he has nothing living but his head, and then go out in a stink like a candle's end upon a saveall.[6]

LADY. Well, Sir Rowland, you have the way.—You are no novice in the labyrinth of love—you have the clue—but as I am a person, Sir Rowland, you must not attribute my yielding to any sinister appetite, or indigestion of widowhood; nor impute my complacency to any lethargy of continuence.—I hope you do not think me prone to any iteration of nuptials.—

WAIT. Far be it from me—

LADY. If you do, I protest I must recede—or think that I have made a prostitution of decorums, but in the vehemence of compassion, and to save the life of a person of so much importance—

WAIT. I esteem it so—

LADY. Or else you wrong my condescension—

WAIT. I do no, I do not—

LADY. Indeed you do.

WAIT. I do not, fair shrine of virtue.

LADY. If you think the least scruple of carnality was an ingredient—

WAIT. Dear madam, no. You are all camphire[7] and frankincense, all chastity and odor.

LADY. Or that—

SCENE 13

[To them] Foible.

FOIB. Madam, the dancers are ready, and there's one with a letter, who must deliver it into your own hands.

LADY. Sir Rowland, will you give me leave? Think favorably, judge candidly, and conclude you have found a person who would suffer racks in honor's cause, dear Sir Rowland, and will wait on you incessantly.[8]

SCENE 14

Waitwell, Foible.

WAIT. Fie, fie!—What a slavery have I undergone; spouse, hast thou any cordial? I want spirits.

FOIB. What a washy rogue art thou, to pant thus for a quarter of an hour's lying and swearing to a fine lady?

WAIT. O, she is the antidote to desire. Spouse, thou wilt fare the worse for't—I shall have no appetite for iteration of nuptials—this eight and forty hours—by this hand I'd rather be a chairman in the dog days[9]—than act Sir Rowland till this time tomorrow.

---

6. A small pan inserted into a candlestick to catch the drippings of the candle.

7. Camphor was considered an effective antidote to sexual desire.

8. Immediately.

9. I.e., one who carries a sedan chair during the hottest part of the summer. July and August were called the "dog days" because during these months the Dog Star, Sirius, rises and sets with the sun.

SCENE 15

[To them] Lady with a letter.

LADY. Call in the dancers.—Sir Rowland, we'll sit, if you please, and see the entertainment.
[Dance.]
Now with your permission, Sir Rowland, I will peruse my letter.—I would open it in your presence, because I would not make you uneasy. If it should make you uneasy, I would burn it—speak if it does—but you may see, the superscription is like a woman's hand.

FOIB. *[to him]* By heaven! Mrs. Marwood's, I know it—my heart aches—get it from her.—

WAIT. A woman's hand? No, madam, that's no woman's hand, I see that already. That's somebody whose throat must be cut.

LADY. Nay, Sir Rowland, since you give me a proof of your passion by your jealousy, I promise you I'll make a return, by a frank communication—you shall see it—we'll open it together—look you here.—*[Reads.]*—*Madam, though unknown to you* (Look you there, 'tis from nobody that I know.)—*I have that honor for your character, that I think myself obliged to let you know you are abused. He who pretends to be Sir Rowland is a cheat and a rascal*—O Heavens! what's this?

FOIB. Unfortunate, all's ruined.

WAIT. How, how, let me see, let me see—*[Reads]*—*A rascal and disguised, and suborned for that imposture*—O villainy! O villainy!—*by the contrivance of*—

LADY. I shall faint, I shall die, oh!

FOIB. *[to him]* Say, 'tis your nephew's hand.—Quickly, his plot, swear, swear it.—

WAIT. Here's a villain! Madam, don't you perceive it, don't you see it?

LADY. Too well, too well. I have seen too much.

WAIT. I told you at first I knew the hand—A woman's hand? The rascal writes a sort of a large hand, your Roman hand—I saw there was a throat to be cut presently. If he were my son, as he is my nephew, I'd pistol him—

FOIB. O treachery! But are you sure, Sir Rowland, it is his writing?

WAIT. Sure? Am I here? Do I live? Do I love this pearl of India? I have twenty letters in my pocket from him in the same character.

LADY. How!

FOIB. O, what luck it is, Sir Rowland, that you were present at this juncture! This was the business that brought Mr. Mirabell disguised to Madam Millamant this afternoon. I thought something was contriving, when he stole by me and would have hid his face.

LADY. How, how!—I heard the villain was in the house indeed; and now I remember, my niece went away abruptly, when Sir Wilfull was to have made his addresses.

FOIB. Then, then, madam, Mr. Mirabell waited for her in her chamber; but I would not tell your ladyship to discompose you when you were to receive Sir Rowland.

WAIT. Enough, his date is short.

FOIB. No, good Sir Rowland, don't incur the law.

WAIT. Law! I care not for law. I can but die, and 'tis in a good cause—my lady shall be satisfied of my truth and innocence, though it cost me my life.

LADY. No, dear Sir Rowland, don't fight. If you should be killed I must never show my face—or be hanged—O, consider my reputation, Sir Rowland—no, you shan't fight—I'll go and examine my niece; I'll make her confess. I conjure you, Sir Rowland, by all your love not to fight.

WAIT. I am charmed, madam, I obey. But some proof you must let me give you—I'll go for a black box, which contains the writings of my whole estate, and deliver that into your hands.

LADY. Aye, dear Sir Rowland, that will be some comfort. Bring the black box.

WAIT. And may I presume to bring a contract to be signed this night? May I hope so far?

LADY. Bring what you will; but come alive, pray come alive. O, this is a happy discovery.

WAIT. Dead or alive I'll come—and married we will be in spite of treachery; aye, and get an heir that shall defeat the last remaining glimpse of hope in my abandoned nephew. Come, my buxom widow:

> E'er long you shall substantial proof receive
> That I'm an arrant[1] knight———

FOIB.   Or arrant knave.

Act 5—Scene continues.

SCENE 1

Lady Wishfort and Foible.

LADY. Out of my house, out of my house, thou viper, thou serpent, that I have fostered; thou bosom traitress, that I raised from nothing.—Begone, begone, begone, go, go—that I took from washing of old gauze and weaving of dead hair,[2] with a bleak blue nose over a chafing dish of starved embers, and dining behind a traverse rag,[3] in a shop no bigger than a bird cage—go, go, starve again, do, do.

FOIB. Dear madam, I'll beg pardon on my knees.

LADY. Away, out, out, go set up for yourself again.—Do, drive a trade, do, with your three-pennyworth of small ware, flaunting upon a packthread, under a brandy-seller's bulk or against a dead wall by a balladmonger. Go, hang out an old frisoneer-gorget,[4] with a yard of yellow colberteen again; do; an old gnawed mask, two rows of pins and a child's fiddle; a glass necklace with the beads broken, and a quilted nightcap with one ear. Go, go, drive a trade—these were your com-

---

1. The two words *errant* ("wandering," as in "knight-errant") and *arrant* ("thorough-going," "notorious") were originally the same and were still pronounced alike. This makes possible Foible's pun.
2. Foible had been a wigmaker.
3. A worn cloth, used to curtain off part of a room.
4. A woolen garment that covers the neck and breast. "Colberteen": a French imitation of Italian lace.

modities, you treacherous trull, this was the merchandise you dealt in when I took you into my house, placed you next myself, and made you governante[5] of my whole family. You have forgot this, have you, now you have feathered your nest?

FOIB. No, no, dear madam. Do but hear me, have but a moment's patience—I'll confess all. Mr. Mirabell seduced me; I am not the first that he has wheedled with his dissembling tongue. Your ladyship's own wisdom has been deluded by him, then how should I, a poor ignorant, defend myself? O madam, if you knew but what he promised me, and how he assured me your ladyship should come to no damage—or else the wealth of the Indies should not have bribed me to conspire against so good, so sweet, so kind a lady as you have been to me.

LADY. No damage? What, to betray me, to marry me to a cast[6] serving-man; to make me a receptacle, an hospital for a decayed pimp? No damage? O, thou frontless[7] impudence, more than a big-bellied actress.

FOIB. Pray do but hear me, madam. He could not marry your ladyship, madam.—No, indeed, his marriage was to have been void in law; for he was married to me first, to secure your ladyship. He could not have bedded your ladyship; for if he had consummated with your ladyship, he must have run the risk of the law, and been put upon his clergy.[8]—Yes, indeed, I inquired of the law in that case before I would meddle or make.[9]

LADY. What, then I have been your property, have I? I have been convenient to you, it seems.—While you were catering for Mirabell, I have been broker for you? What, have you made a passive bawd of me?—This exceeds all precedent; I am brought to fine uses, to become a botcher[1] of second-hand marriages between Abigails and Andrews! I'll couple you. Yes, I'll baste you together, you and your philander.[2] I'll Duke's-Place you, as I'm a person. Your turtle is in custody already: you shall coo in the same cage, if there be constable or warrant in the parish.

FOIB. O, that ever I was born, O, that I was ever married.—A bride, aye, I shall be a Bridewell-bride.[3] Oh!

SCENE 2

Mrs. Fainall, Foible.

MRS. FAIN. Poor Foible, what's the matter?

FOIB. O madam, my lady's gone for a constable. I shall be had to a justice, and put to Bridewell to beat hemp; poor Waitwell's gone to prison already.

5. Housekeeper.
6. Cast off, discharged.
7. Shameless.
8. I.e., pleaded "benefit of clergy," originally the privilege of the clergy to be tried for felony before ecclesiastical, not secular, courts; by Congreve's time it had become the privilege to plead exemption from a penal sentence granted a person who could read and was a first offender.
9. A dialectal phrase; the two words mean approx-imately the same thing.
1. A mender of old clothes; Lady Wishfort means something like "a patcher-up of marriages." "Abigail" and "Andrew" were generic names for maid-servants and servingmen.
2. Lover. For "Duke's Place," see act 1, scene 2, note 5.
3. Bridewell was the house of correction for women in London.

MRS. FAIN. Have a good heart, Foible. Mirabell's gone to give security for him. This is all Marwood's and my husband's doing.

FOIB. Yes, yes, I know it, madam; she was in my lady's closet, and overheard all that you said to me before dinner. She sent the letter to my lady; and that missing effect, Mr. Fainall laid this plot to arrest Waitwell, when he pretended to go for the papers; and in the meantime Mrs. Marwood declared all to my lady.

MRS. FAIN. Was there no mention made of me in the letter?—My mother does not suspect my being in the confederacy? I fancy Marwood has not told her, though she has told my husband.

FOIB. Yes, madam; but my lady did not see that part. We stifled the letter before she read so far. Has that mischievous devil told Mr. Fainall of your ladyship then?

MRS. FAIN. Aye, all's out, my affair with Mirabell, everything discovered. This is the last day of our living together, that's my comfort.

FOIB. Indeed, madam, and so 'tis a comfort if you knew all.—He has been even with your ladyship; which I could have told you long enough since, but I love to keep peace and quietness by my good will. I had rather bring friends together than set 'em at distance. But Mrs. Marwood and he are nearer related than ever their parents thought for!

MRS. FAIN. Say'st thou so, Foible? Canst thou prove this?

FOIB. I can take my oath of it, madam. So can Mrs. Mincing; we have had many a fair word from Madam Marwood, to conceal something that passed in our chamber one evening when you were at Hyde Park—and we were thought to have gone a-walking; but we went up unawares—though we were sworn to secrecy too; Madam Marwood took a book and swore us upon it, but it was but a book of poems.—So long as it was not a Bible-oath, we may break it with a safe conscience.

MRS. FAIN. This discovery is the most opportune thing I could wish. Now, Mincing?

SCENE 3

[To them] Mincing.

MINC. My lady would speak with Mrs. Foible, mem. Mr. Mirabell is with her; he has set your spouse at liberty, Mrs. Foible, and would have you hide yourself in my lady's closet, till my old lady's anger is abated. O, my old lady is in a perilous passion, at something Mr. Fainall has said; he swears, and my old lady cries. There's a fearful hurricane, I vow. He says, mem, how that he'll have my lady's fortune made over to him, or he'll be divorced.

MRS. FAIN. Does your lady or Mirabell know that?

MINC. Yes, mem, they have sent me to see if Sir Wilfull be sober, and to bring him to them. My lady is resolved to have him, I think, rather than lose such a vast sum as six thousand pound. O, come, Mrs. Foible, I hear my old lady.

MRS. FAIN. Foible, you must tell Mincing that she must prepare to vouch when I call her.

FOIB. Yes, yes, madam.

MINC. O yes, mem, I'll vouch anything for your ladyship's service, be what it will.

SCENE 4

Mrs. Fainall, Lady Wishfort, Marwood.

LADY. O my dear friend, how can I enumerate the benefit that I have received from your goodness? To you I owe the timely discovery of the false vows of Mirabell; to you I owe the detection of the imposter Sir Rowland. And now you are become an intercessor with my son-in-law, to save the honor of my house, and compound for the frailties of my daughter. Well, friend, you are enough to reconcile me to the bad world, or else I would retire to deserts and solitudes, and feed harmless sheep by groves and purling streams. Dear Marwood, let us leave the world and retire by ourselves and be shepherdesses.

MRS. MAR. Let us first dispatch the affair in hand, madam. We shall have leisure to think of retirement afterwards. Here is one who is concerned in the treaty.

LADY. O daughter, daughter, is it possible thou should'st be my child, bone of my bone, and flesh of my flesh, and as I may say, another me, and yet transgress the most minute particle of severe virtue? Is it possible you should lean aside to iniquity, who have been cast in the direct mold of virtue? I have not only been a mold but a pattern for you, and a model for you, after you were brought into the world.

MRS. FAIN. I don't understand your ladyship.

LADY. Not understand? Why, have you not been naught?[4] Have you not been sophisticated? Not understand? Here I am ruined to compound[5] for your caprices and your cuckoldoms. I must pawn my plate and my jewels, and ruin my niece, and all little enough—

MRS. FAIN. I am wronged and abused, and so are you. 'Tis a false accusation, as false as hell, as false as your friend there, aye, or your friend's friend, my false husband.

MRS. MAR. My friend, Mrs. Fainall? Your husband my friend, what do you mean?

MRS. FAIN. I know what I mean, madam, and so do you; and so shall the world at a time convenient.

MRS. MAR. I am sorry to see you so passionate, madam. More temper[6] would look more like innocence. But I have done. I am sorry my zeal to serve your ladyship and family should admit of misconstruction, or make me liable to affront. You will pardon me, madam, if I meddle no more with an affair in which I am not personally concerned.

LADY. O dear friend, I am so ashamed that you should meet with such returns.—You ought to ask pardon on your knees, ungrateful creature; she deserves more from you than all your life can accomplish— O, don't leave me destitute in this perplexity—no, stick to me, my good genius.

MRS. FAIN. I tell you, madam, you're abused—Stick to you? aye, like a leech, to suck your best blood—She'll drop off when she's full. Madam,

4. Wicked. "Sophisticated": corrupted.
5. I.e., come to terms by making a monetary settlement.
6. Moderation.

you shan't pawn a bodkin,[7] nor part with a brass counter, in composition for me. I defy 'em all. Let 'em prove their aspersions; I know my own innocence, and dare stand a trial.

SCENE 5

Lady Wishfort, Marwood.

LADY. Why, if she should be innocent, if she should be wronged after all, ha? I don't know what to think—and I promise you, her education has been unexceptionable—I may say it; for I chiefly made it my own care to initiate her very infancy in the rudiments of virtue, and to impress upon her tender years a young odium and aversion to the very sight of men.—Aye, friend, she would have shrieked if she had but seen a man, till she was in her teens. As I'm a person, 'tis true—she was never suffered to play with a male child, though but in coats. Nay, her very babies[8] were of the feminine gender—O, she never looked a man in the face but her own father, or the chaplain, and him we made a shift to put upon her for a woman, by the help of his long garments, and his sleek face; till she was going in her fifteen.

MRS. MAR. 'Twas much she should be deceived so long.

LADY. I warrant you, or she would never have borne to have been catechized by him; and have heard his long lectures against singing and dancing, and such debaucheries; and going to filthy plays; and profane music-meetings, where the lewd trebles squeek nothing but bawdry, and the basses roar blasphemy. O, she would have swooned at the sight or name of an obscene play-book—and can I think after all this, that my daughter can be naught? What, a whore? And thought it excommunication to set her foot within the door of a playhouse? O dear friend, I can't believe it, no, no; as she says, let him prove it, let him prove it.

MRS. MAR. Prove it, madam? What, and have your name prostituted in a public court; yours and your daughter's reputation worried at the bar by a pack of bawling lawyers? To be ushered in with an O Yes[9] of scandal; and have your case opened by an old fumbler lecher in a quoif[1] like a man midwife, to bring your daughter's infamy to light; to be a theme for legal punsters, and quibblers by the statute; and become a jest, against a rule of court, where there is no precedent for a jest in any record, not even in Doomsday Book;[2] to discompose the gravity of the bench, and provoke naughty interrogatories in more naughty law-Latin; while the good judge, tickled with the proceeding, simpers under a gray beard, and fidges off and on his cushion as if he had swallowed cantharides, or sate upon cowhage.[3]

LADY. O, 'tis very hard!

MRS. MAR. And then to have my young revelers of the Temple[4] take

7. An ornamental hairpin. "Counter," an imitation coin, used in games of chance.
8. Dolls.
9. The formula for opening court, a variant of Old French *Oyez*, "Hear ye."
1. The cap of a sergeant-at-law.
2. Or Domesday Book, the survey of England made

in 1085–86 by William the Conqueror.
3. "Fidges": fidgets; "cantharides" (or Spanish fly) is an irritant; "cowhage": a plant that causes intolerable itching.
4. The law students at the Temple, one of the Inns of Court.

notes, like 'prentices at a conventicle; and after talk it over again in commons, or before drawers in an eating house.

LADY. Worse and worse.

MRS. MAR. Nay, this is nothing; if it would end here 'twere well. But it must after this be consigned by the shorthand writers to the public press; and from thence be transferred to the hands, nay into the throats and lungs of hawkers, with voices more licentious than the loud flounderman's or the woman that cries gray peas;[5] and this you must hear till you are stunned; nay, you must hear nothing else for some days.

LADY. O, 'tis insupportable. No, no, dear friend, make it up, make it up; aye, aye, I'll compound. I'll give up all, myself and my all, my niece and her all—anything, everything for composition.

MRS. MAR. Nay, madam, I advise nothing; I only lay before you, as a friend, the inconveniencies which perhaps you have overseen.[6] Here comes Mr. Fainall. If he will be satisfied to huddle up all in silence, I shall be glad. You must think I would rather congratulate than condole with you.

SCENE 6

Fainall, Lady Wishfort, Mrs. Marwood.

LADY. Aye, aye, I do not doubt it, dear Marwood. No, no, I do not doubt it.

FAIN. Well, madam; I have suffered myself to be overcome by the importunity of this lady, your friend, and am content you shall enjoy your own proper estate during life; on condition you oblige yourself never to marry, under such penalty as I think convenient.

LADY. Never to marry?

FAIN. No more Sir Rowlands—the next imposture may not be so timely detected.

MRS. MAR. That condition, I dare answer, my lady will consent to, without difficulty; she has already but too much experienced the perfidiousness of men. Besides, madam, when we retire to our pastoral solitude we shall bid adieu to all other thoughts.

LADY. Aye, that's true; but in case of necessity; as of health, or some such emergency—

FAIN. O, if you are prescribed marriage, you shall be considered; I will only reserve to myself the power to choose for you. If your physic be wholesome, it matters not who is your apothecary. Next, my wife shall settle on me the remainder of her fortune, not made over already; and for her maintenance depend entirely on my discretion.

LADY. This is most inhumanly savage; exceeding the barbarity of a Muscovite husband.

FAIN. I learned it from His Czarish Majesty's retinue,[7] in a winter evening's conference over brandy and pepper, amongst other secrets of matrimony and policy, as they are at present practiced in the northern

---

5. Street vendors celebrated for their stridency.
6. Overlooked.

7. Peter the Great of Russia visited London in 1698.

hemisphere. But this must be agreed unto, and that positively. Lastly, I will be endowed, in right of my wife, with that six thousand pound, which is the moiety of Mrs. Millamant's fortune in your possession; and which she has forfeited (as will appear by the last will and testament of your deceased husband, Sir Jonathan Wishfort) by her disobedience in contracting herself against your consent or knowledge; and by refusing the offered match with Sir Wilfull Witwoud, which you, like a careful aunt, had provided for her.

LADY. My nephew was *non compos*,[8] and could not make his addresses.

FAIN. I come to make demands—I'll hear no objections.

LADY. You will grant me time to consider?

FAIN. Yes, while the instrument is drawing, to which you must set your hand till more sufficient deeds can be perfected: which I will take care shall be done with all possible speed. In the meanwhile I will go for the said instrument, and till my return you may balance this matter in your own discretion.

SCENE 7

Lady Wishfort, Mrs. Marwood.

LADY. This insolence is beyond all precedent, all parallel; must I be subject to this merciless villain?

MRS. MAR. 'Tis severe indeed, madam, that you should smart for your daughter's wantonness.

LADY. 'Twas against my consent that she married this barbarian, but she would have him, though her year was not out.[9]—Ah! her first husband, my son Languish, would not have carried it thus. Well, that was my choice, this is hers; she is matched now with a witness[1]—I shall be mad, dear friend. Is there no comfort for me? Must I live to be confiscated at this rebel-rate?—Here comes two more of my Egyptian plagues,[2] too.

SCENE 8

[*To them*] *Millamant, Sir Wilfull.*

SIR WIL. Aunt, your servant.

LADY. Out, caterpillar, call not me aunt; I know thee not.

SIR WIL. I confess I have been a little in disguise,[3] as they say—'Sheart! and I'm sorry for't. What would you have? I hope I committed no offense, aunt—and if I did, I am willing to make satisfaction; and what can a man say fairer? If I have broke anything, I'll pay for't, an' it cost a pound. And so let that content for what's past, and make no more words. For what's to come, to pleasure you I'm willing to marry my cousin. So, pray, let's all be friends. She and I are agreed upon the matter before a witness.

8. I.e., *non compos mentis*, "of unsound mind."
9. The conventional period of mourning for a widow was one year.
1. With a vengeance.

2. The plagues visited by Moses on Pharaoh until he agreed to release the Israelites from bondage. (Exodus 7–12).
3. Drunk.

LADY. How's this, dear niece? Have I any comfort? Can this be true?

MILLA. I am content to be a sacrifice to your repose, madam; and to convince you that I had no hand in the plot, as you were misinformed, I have laid my commands on Mirabell to come in person, and be a witness that I give my hand to this flower of knighthood; and for the contract that passed between Mirabell and me, I have obliged him to make a resignation of it in your ladyship's presence.—He is without, and waits your leave for admittance.

LADY. Well, I'll swear I am something revived at this testimony of your obedience; but I cannot admit that traitor—I fear I cannot fortify myself to support his appearance. He is as terrible to me as a Gorgon;[4] if I see him, I fear I shall turn to stone, petrify incessantly.

MILLA. If you disoblige him, he may resent your refusal, and insist upon the contract still. Then 'tis the last time he will be offensive to you.

LADY. Are you sure it will be the last time?—If I were sure of that—Shall I never see him again?

MILLA. Sir Wilfull, you and he are to travel together, are you not?

SIR WIL. 'Sheart, the gentleman's a civil gentleman, aunt, let him come in; why, we are sworn brothers and fellow travelers. We are to be Pylades[5] and Orestes, he and I. He is to be my interpreter in foreign parts. He has been overseas once already; and with proviso that I marry my cousin, will cross 'em once again, only to bear my company.— 'Sheart, I'll call him in—an I set on't once, he shall come in; and see who'll hinder him.

[*Goes to the door and hems.*]

MRS. MAR. This is precious fooling, if it would pass; but I'll know the bottom of it.

LADY. O dear Marwood, you are not going?

MAR. Not far, madam; I'll return immediately.

SCENE 9

Lady Wishfort, Millamant, Sir Wilfull, Mirabell.

SIR WIL. [*aside*] Look up, man, I'll stand by you. 'Sbud an she do frown, she can't kill you—besides—harkee, she dare not frown desperately, because her face is none of her own. 'Sheart, an she should her forehead would wrinkle like the coat of a cream cheese; but mum for that, fellow traveler.

MIRA. If a deep sense of the many injuries I have offered to so good a lady, with a sincere remorse, and a hearty contrition, can but obtain the least glance of compassion, I am too happy—Ah madam, there was a time—but let it be forgotten—I confess I have deservedly forfeited the high place I once held of sighing at your feet. Nay kill me not by turning from me in disdain—I come not to plead for favor— nay not for pardon. I am a suppliant only for pity—I am going where I never shall behold you more—

4. In Greek mythology, a hideous monster with snakes in her hair. Her glance turned men to stone.
5. The constant friend who journeyed with Orestes,

the son and avenger of the murdered king Agamemnon.

SIR WIL. *[aside]* How, fellow traveler!—You shall go by yourself then.

MIRA. Let me be pitied first, and afterwards forgotten—I ask no more.

SIR WIL. By'r Lady a very reasonable request, and will cost you nothing, aunt.—Come, come, forgive and forget, aunt. Why you must, an you are a Christian.

MIRA. Consider, madam, in reality you could not receive much prejudice; it was an innocent device, though I confess it had a face of guiltiness.—It was at most an artifice which love contrived—and errors which love produces have ever been accounted venial. At least think it is punishment enough that I have lost what in my heart I hold most dear, that to your cruel indignation, I have offered up this beauty, and with her my peace and quiet; nay, all my hopes of future comfort.

SIR WIL. An he does not move me, would I may never be o' the quorum[6]— An it were not as good a deed as to drink, to give her to him again—I would I might never take shipping.—Aunt, if you don't forgive quickly I shall melt, I can tell you that. My contract went no farther than a little mouth glue,[7] and that's hardly dry.—One doleful sigh more from my fellow traveler and 'tis dissolved.

LADY. Well, nephew, upon your account—Ah, he has a false insinuating tongue.—Well, sir, I will stifle my just resentment at my nephew's request. I will endeavor what I can to forget—but on proviso that you resign the contract with my niece immediately.

MIRA. It is in writing and with papers of concern, but I have sent my servant for it and will deliver it to you, with all acknowledgements for your transcendent goodness.

LADY. *[aside]* O, he has witchcraft in his eyes and tongue; when I did not see him I could have bribed a villain to his assassination; but his appearance rakes the embers which have so long lain smothered in my breast.—

SCENE 10

[To them] Fainall, Mrs. Marwood.

FAIN. Your date of deliberation, madam, is expired. Here is the instrument; are you prepared to sign?

LADY. If I were prepared, I am not empowered. My niece exerts a lawful claim, having matched herself by my direction to Sir Wilfull.

FAIN. That sham is too gross to pass on me—though 'tis imposed on you, madam.

MILLA. Sir, I have given my consent.

MIRA. And, sir, I have resigned my pretensions.

SIR WIL. And, sir, I assert my right; and will maintain it in defiance of you, sir, and of your instrument. 'Sheart, an you talk of an instrument, sir, I have an old fox[8] by my thigh shall hack your instrument of ram vellum to shreds, sir. It shall not be sufficient for a *mittimus*[9] or a tailor's measure; therefore withdraw your instrument, sir, or by'r Lady I shall draw mine.

6. Justices of the peace, who were required to be present at the sessions of a court.
7. Literally, glue to be used by moistening with the tongue, but here the meaning is "glue made of mere words" and therefore not binding.
8. A kind of sword. "Ram vellum": the legal instrument to be signed is written on vellum.
9. A warrant, committing a felon to jail.

LADY. Hold, nephew, hold.

MILLA. Good Sir Wilfull, respite your valor.

FAIN. Indeed? Are you provided of your guard, with your single beefeater[1] there? But I'm prepared for you; and insist upon my first proposal. You shall submit your own estate to my management and absolutely make over my wife's to my sole use, as pursuant to the purport and tenor of this other covenant. I suppose, madam, your consent is not requisite in this case; nor, Mr. Mirabell, your resignation; nor, Sir Wilfull, your right—You may draw your fox if you please, sir, and make a bear garden[2] flourish somewhere else: for here it will not avail. This, my Lady Wishfort, must be subscribed, or your darling daughter's turned adrift, like a leaky hulk to sink or swim, as she and the current of this lewd town can agree.

LADY. Is there no means, no remedy, to stop my ruin? Ungrateful wretch! Dost thou not owe thy being, thy subsistence to my daughter's fortune?

FAIN. I'll answer you when I have the rest of it in my possession.

MIRA. But that you would not accept of a remedy from my hands—I own I have not deserved you should owe any obligation to me; or else perhaps I could advise—

LADY. O, what? what? to save me and my child from ruin, from want, I'll forgive all that's past; nay, I'll consent to anything to come, to be delivered from this tyranny.

MIRA. Aye, madam, but that is too late; my reward is intercepted. You have disposed of her who only could have made me a compensation for all my services; but be it as it may, I am resolved I'll serve you. You shall not be wronged in this savage manner.

LADY. How! Dear Mr. Mirabell, can you be so generous at last! But it is not possible. Harkee, I'll break my nephew's match, you shall have my niece yet, and all her fortune, if you can but save me from this imminent danger.

MIRA. Will you? I take you at your word. I ask no more. I must have leave for two criminals to appear.

LADY. Aye, aye, anybody, anybody.

MIRA. Foible is one, and a penitent.

SCENE 11

[To them] Mrs. Fainall, Foible, Mincing.

MRS. MAR. O, my shame! These corrupt things are brought hither to expose me.

[MIRA. *and* LADY *go to* MRS. FAIN. *and* FOIB.]

FAIN. If it must all come out, why let 'em know it, 'tis but *the way of the world*. That shall not urge me to relinquish or abate one tittle of my terms; no, I will insist the more.

FOIB. Yes, indeed, madam, I'll take my Bible-oath of it.

MINC. And so will I, mem.

LADY. O Marwood, Marwood, art thou false? My friend deceive me? Hast thou been a wicked accomplice with that profligate man?

1. Yeoman of the guard.
2. The place for bearbaiting, frequented by a vulgar and unruly crowd.

MRS. MAR. Have you so much ingratitude and injustice, to give credit against your friend to the aspersions of two such mercenary trulls?

MINC. Mercenary, mem? I scorn your words. 'Tis true we found you and Mr. Fainall in the blue garret; by the same token, you swore us to secrecy upon Messalina's[3] poems. Mercenary? No, if we would have been mercenary, we should have held our tongues; you would have bribed us sufficiently.

FAIN. Go, you are an insignificant thing. Well, what are you the better for this! Is this Mr. Mirabell's expedient? I'll be put off no longer. You, thing that was a wife, shall smart for this. I will not leave thee wherewithal to hide thy shame: your body shall be naked as your reputation.

MRS. FAIN. I despise you and defy your malice.—You have aspersed me wrongfully.—I have proved your falsehood.—Go, you and your treacherous—I will not name it, but starve together—perish.

FAIN. Not while you are worth a groat, indeed, my dear. Madam, I'll be fooled no longer.

LADY. Ah, Mr. Mirabell, this is small comfort, the detection of this affair.

MIRA. O, in good time—Your leave for the other offender and penitent to appear, madam.

SCENE 12

[To them] Waitwell with a box of writings.

LADY. O Sir Rowland—Well, rascal.

WAIT. What your ladyship pleases—I have brought the black box at last, madam.

MIRA. Give it me. Madam, you remember your promise.

LADY. Aye, dear sir.

MIRA. Where are the gentlemen?

WAIT. At hand, sir, rubbing their eyes, just risen from sleep.

FAIN. 'Sdeath, what's this to me? I'll not wait your private concerns.

SCENE 13

[To them] Petulant, Witwoud.

PET. How now? What's the matter? Who's hand's out?

WIT. Heyday! What, are you all got together, like players at the end of the last act?

MIRA. You may remember, gentlemen, I once requested your hands as witnesses to a certain parchment.

WIT. Aye, I do, my hand I remember—Petulant set his mark.

MIRA. You wrong him, his name is fairly written, as shall appear. You do not remember, gentlemen, anything of what that parchment contained—   *[Undoing the box.]*

WIT. No.

3. Mincing means "Miscellany," a collection of poems by various writers, such as Dryden's popular *Miscellanies*. Messalina was the viciously debauched wife of the Roman Emperor Claudius.

PET. Not I. I writ, I read nothing.

MIRA. Very well, now you shall know. Madam, your promise.

LADY. Aye, aye, sir, upon my honor.

MIRA. Mr. Fainall, it is now time that you should know that your lady, while she was at her own disposal, and before you had by your insinuations wheedled her out of a pretended settlement of the greatest part of her fortune—

FAIN. Sir! Pretended!

MIRA. Yes, sir. I say that this lady while a widow, having, it seems, received some cautions respecting your inconstancy and tyranny of temper, which from her own partial opinion and fondness of you she could never have suspected—she did, I say, by the wholesome advice of f.iends and of sages learned in the laws of this land, deliver this same as her act and deed to me in trust, and to the uses within mentioned. You may read if you please—[*Holding out the parchment*]— though perhaps what is written on the back may serve your occasions.

FAIN. Very likely, sir. What's here? Damnation!—[*Reads.*] A *deed of conveyance of the whole estate real of Arabella Languish, widow, in trust to Edward Mirabell.* Confusion!

MIRA. Even so, sir, 'tis the way of the world, sir; of the widows of the world. I suppose this deed may bear an elder date than what you have obtained from your lady.

FAIN. Perfidious fiend! Then thus I'll be revenged.

[*Offers to run at* MRS. FAIN.]

SIR WIL. Hold, sir, now you may make your bear garden flourish somewhere else, sir.

FAIN. Mirabell, you shall hear of this, sir, be sure you shall. Let me pass, oaf.

MRS. FAIN. Madam, you seem to stifle your resentment: you had better give it vent.

MRS. MAR. Yes, it shall have vent—and to your confusion, or I'll perish in the attempt.

SCENE THE LAST

Lady Wishfort, Millamant, Mirabell, Mrs. Fainall, Sir Wilfull, Petulant, Witwoud, Foible, Mincing, Waitwell.

LADY. O daughter, daugher, 'tis plain thou hast inherited thy mother's prudence.

MRS. FAIN. Thank Mr. Mirabell, a cautious friend, to whose advice all is owing.

LADY. Well, Mr. Mirabell, you have kept your promise and I must perform mine. First I pardon for your sake Sir Rowland there and Foible.—The next thing is to break the matter to my nephew—and how to do that—

MIRA. For that, madam, give yourself no trouble—let me have your consent.—Sir Wilfull is my friend; he has had compassion upon lovers, and generously engaged a volunteer in this action, for our service; and now designs to prosecute his travels.

SIR WIL. 'Sheart, aunt, I have no mind to marry. My cousin's a fine
lady, and the gentleman loves her, and she loves him, and they deserve
one another. My resolution is to see foreign parts—I have set on't—
and when I'm set on't, I must do't. And if these two gentlemen would
travel too, I think they may be spared.

PET. For my part, I say little—I think things are best off or on.

WIT. Igad, I understand nothing of the matter—I'm in a maze yet; like
a dog in a dancing school.

LADY. Well, sir, take her, and with her all the joy I can give you.

MILLA. Why does not the man take me? Would you have me give myself
to you over again?

MIRA. Aye, and over and over again—[*Kisses her hand.*]—I would have
you as often as possibly I can. Well, Heaven grant I love you not too
well, that's all my fear.

SIR WIL. 'Sheart, you'll have time enough to toy after you're married; or
if you will toy now, let us have a dance in the meantime; that we who
are not lovers may have some other employment, besides looking on.

MIRA. With all my heart, dear Sir Wilfull. What shall we do for music?

FOIB. O, sir, some that were provided for Sir Rowland's entertainment
are yet within call.

[*A dance.*]

LADY. As I am a person I can hold out no longer.—I have wasted my
spirits so today already, that I am ready to sink under the fatigue; and
I cannot but have some fears upon me yet, that my son Fainall will
pursue some desperate course.

MIRA. Madam, disquiet not yourself on that account; to my knowledge
his circumstances are such, he must of force comply. For my part, I
will contribute all that in me lies to a reunion: in the meantime,
madam—[*to* MRS. FAIN.]—let me before these witnesses restore to you
this deed of trust; it may be a means, well managed, to make you live
easily together.

> From hence let those be warned, who mean to wed;
> Lest mutual falsehood stain the bridal bed:
> For each deceiver to his cost may find,
> That marriage frauds too oft are paid in kind.

[*Exeunt omnes.*]

Epilogue

SPOKEN BY MRS. BRACEGIRDLE[4]

After our Epilogue this crowd dismisses,
I'm thinking how this play'll be pulled to pieces.
But pray consider, e'er you doom its fall,
How hard a thing 'twould be to please you all.
There are some critics so with spleen diseased,
They scarcely come inclining to be pleased;

---

4. Anne Bracegirdle (ca. 1663–1748), the most
brilliant actress of her generation. She created the
role of Millamant. Congreve loved her, and it was
rumored that they were secretly married.

And sure he must have more than mortal skill,
Who pleases anyone against his will.
Then, all bad poets we are sure are foes,
And how their number's swelled the town well knows:
In shoals, I've marked 'em judging in the pit;
Though they're on no pretence for judgment fit,
But that they have been damned for want of wit.
Since when, they by their own offenses taught
Set up for spies on plays, and finding fault.
Others there are whose malice we'd prevent;
Such, who watch plays, with scurrilous intent
To mark out who by characters are meant.
And though no perfect likeness they can trace,
Yet each pretends to know the copied face.
These, with false glosses feed their own ill-nature,
And turn to libel, what was meant a *satire*.[5]
May such malicious fops this fortune find,
To think themselves alone the fools designed:
If any are so arrogantly vain,
To think they singly can support a scene,
And furnish fool enough to entertain.
For well the learn'd and the judicious know,
That satire scorns to stoop so meanly low,
As any one abstracted fop to show.
For, as when painters form a matchless face,
They from each fair one catch some different grace,
And shining features in one portrait blend,
To which no single beauty must pretend:
So poets oft do in one piece expose
Whole *belles assemblées* of coquettes and beaux.

1700

5. Pronounce *nā-ter* and *sā-ter*.

MARY ASTELL
1666–1731

Daughter of a Newcastle merchant, Mary Astell was encouraged and educated by her uncle, a clergyman. She never forgot what he taught her: a confidence in her own reason, and a religious faith entirely compatible with reason. In her twenties she moved to Chelsea, on the outskirts of London, where she spent the rest of her life. There she championed the causes of women and the Church of England, and her vigorous way of arguing (not only in print but in person) won her many admirers, both male and female, as well as a few enemies. Her best-known work, *A Serious Proposal to the Ladies* (1694), was, like the rest of her writings, published anonymously ("by a Lover of her Sex"). It advocates the founding of a monastic school or retreat for women, where a rigorous, wide-ranging education could be combined with moral and religious discipline. Though the idea was never carried out, it had a broad influence on later plans for educating women, as well as on literature. At the end of Johnson's *Rasselas*, both Pekuah's dream of leading a religious order and Nekayah's desire to found a college of learned women owe something to Astell.

To question the customs and laws of marriage is to question society itself, its distribution of money and power and love. During the eighteenth century many of the terms of marriage were renegotiated. The older view of the wife as a chattel, bound by contract to a husband whom others had chosen for her and whom she was sworn to obey, was hotly debated and challenged. The witty arguments of Congreve's *The Way of the World* (1700) reflect this growing debate between the sexes. Another work published in the same year, *Some Reflections upon Marriage*, takes a more independent position. Marriage, according to Astell, is all too often a trap. She insists that a woman should be guided by reason, not only in choosing a mate but in choosing whether or not to marry at all (Astell herself never married). So long as the institution of marriage perpetuates inequality rather than a true partnership of minds, women had better beware of flattery and look to themselves or to God, not to men, for the hope of a better life. The debate on marriage continued throughout the century in works such as Defoe's *Roxana*, the novels of Samuel Richardson, *Rasselas*, and eventually the writings of Mary Wollstonecraft and William Godwin. It still continues today. In her sharp, lively style and the pertinent questions she raised, Astell has come to be seen as ahead of her time.

From Some Reflections upon Marriage[1]

If marriage be such a blessed state, how comes it, may you say, that there are so few happy marriages? Now in answer to this, it is not to be wondered that so few succeed; we should rather be surprised to find so many do, considering how imprudently men engage, the motives they act by, and the very strange conduct they observe throughout.

For pray, what do men propose to themselves in marriage? What qualifications do they look after in a spouse? What will she bring? is the first enquiry: How many acres? Or how much ready coin? Not that this is altogether an unnecessary question, for marriage without a competency,[2] that is, not only a bare subsistence, but even a handsome and plentiful provision, according to the quality[3] and circumstances of the parties, is no very comfortable condition. They who marry for love, as they call it, find time enough to repent their rash folly, and are not long in being convinced, that whatever fine speeches might be made in the heat of passion, there could be no *real kindness* between those who can agree to make each other miserable. But though an estate is to be con-

---

1. The text is excerpted from the first edition.   3. Social position.
2. Sufficient income.

sidered, it should not be the *main*, much less the only consideration; for happiness does not depend on wealth. * * *

* * *

But suppose a man does not marry for money, though for one that does not, perhaps there are thousands that do; suppose he marries for love, an heroic action, which makes a mighty noise in the world, partly because of its rarity, and partly in regard of its extravagancy, what does his marrying for love amount to? There's no great odds between his marrying for the love of money, or for the love of beauty; the man does not act according to reason in either case, but is governed by irregular appetites. But he loves her wit perhaps, and this, you'll say, is more spiritual, more refined: not at all, if you examine it to the bottom. For what is that which nowadays passes under the name of wit? A bitter and ill-natured raillery, a pert repartee, or a confident talking at all; and in such a multitude of words, it's odds if something or other does not pass that is surprising, though every thing that surprises does not please; some things being wondered at for their ugliness, as well as others for their beauty. True wit, durst one venture to describe it, is quite another thing; it consists in such a sprightliness of imagination, such a reach and turn of thought, so properly expressed, as strikes and pleases a judicious taste.[4] * * *

* * *

Thus, whether it be wit or beauty that a man's in love with, there are no great hopes of a lasting happiness; beauty, with all the helps of art, is of no long date; the more it is helped, the sooner it decays; and he, who only or chiefly chose for beauty, will in a little time find the same reason for another choice. Nor is that sort of wit which he prefers, of a more sure tenure; or allowing it to last, it will not always please. For that which has not a real excellency and value in itself, entertains no longer than that giddy humor which recommended it to us holds; and when we can like on no just, or on very little ground, 'tis certain a dislike will arise, as lightly and as unaccountably. And it is not improbable that such a husband may in a little time, by ill usage, provoke such a wife to exercise her wit, that is, her spleen on him, and then it is not hard to guess how very agreeable it will be to him.

* * *

But do the women never choose amiss? Are the men only in fault? That is not pretended; for he who will be just, must be forced to acknowledge, that neither sex are always in the right. A woman, indeed, can't properly be said to choose; all that is allowed her, is to refuse or accept what is offered. And when we have made such reasonable allow-

4. Cf. Pope's *Essay on Criticism* 2. 297–304.

ances as are due to the sex, perhaps they may not appear so much in fault as one would at first imagine, and a generous spirit will find more occasion to pity than to reprove. But sure I must transgress—it must not be supposed that the ladies can do amiss! He is but an ill-bred fellow who pretends that they need amendment! They are, no doubt on't, always in the right, and most of all when they take pity on distressed lovers! Whatever they *say* carries an authority that no reason can resist, and all that they *do* must needs be exemplary! This is the modish language, nor is there a man of honor amongst the whole tribe, that would not venture his life, nay, and his salvation too, in their defense, if any but himself attempts to injure them. But I must ask pardon if I can't come up to these heights, nor flatter them with the having no faults, which is only a malicious way of continuing and increasing their mistakes.

*　　*　　*

But, alas! what poor woman is ever taught that she should have a higher design than to get her a husband? Heaven will fall in of course; and if she makes but an obedient and dutiful wife, she cannot miss of it. A husband indeed is thought by both sexes so very valuable, that scarce a man who can keep himself clean and make a bow, but thinks he is good enough to pretend[5] to any woman; no matter for the difference of birth or fortune, a husband is such a wonder-working name as to make an equality, or something more, whenever it is obtained.

*　　*　　*

To wind up this matter: If a woman were duly principled, and taught to know the world, especially the true sentiments that men have of her, and the traps they lay for her under so many gilded compliments, and such a seemingly great respect, that disgrace would be prevented which is brought upon too many families; women would marry more discreetly, and demean[6] themselves better in a married state, than some people say they do. * * *

*　　*　　*

But some sage persons may perhaps object, that were women allowed to improve themselves, and not, amongst other discouragements, driven back by the wise jests and scoffs that are put upon a woman of sense or learning, a philosophical lady, as she is called by way of ridicule, they would be too wise, and too good for the men. I grant it, for vicious and foolish men. Nor is it to be wondered that he is afraid he should not be able to govern them were their understandings improved, who is resolved not to take too much pains with his own. But these, 'tis to be hoped, are no very considerable number, the foolish at least; and therefore this is so far from being an argument against women's improvement, that it is

---

5. Aspire or lay claim.　　　　　　　6. Behave.

a strong one for it, if we do but suppose the men to be as capable of improvement as the women; but much more, if, according to tradition, we believe they have greater capacities. This, if anything, would stir them up to be what they ought, and not permit them to waste their time and abuse their faculties in the service of their irregular appetites and unreasonable desires, and so let poor contemptible women, who have been their slaves, excel them in all that is truly excellent. This would make them blush at employing an immortal mind no better than in making provision for the flesh to fulfill the lusts thereof, since women, by a wiser conduct, have brought themselves to such a reach of thought, to such exactness of judgment, such clearness and strength of reasoning, such purity and elevation of mind, such command of their passions, such regularity of will and affection, and, in a word, to such a pitch of perfection, as the human soul is capable of attaining in this life by the grace of God; such true wisdom, such real greatness, as though it does not qualify them to make a noise in this world, to found or overturn empires, yet it qualifies them for what is infinitely better, a Kingdom that cannot be moved, an incorruptible crown of glory.

*   *   *

Again, it may be said, if a wife's case be as it is here represented, it is not good for a woman to marry, and so there's an end of human race. But this is no fair consequence, for all that can justly be inferred from hence is that a woman has no mighty obligations to the man who makes love to her; she has no reason to be fond of being a wife, or to reckon it a piece of preferment[7] when she is taken to be a man's upper-servant; it is no advantage to her in this world; if rightly managed it may prove one as to the next. For she who marries purely to do good, to educate souls for heaven, who can be so truly mortified as to lay aside her own will and desires, to pay such an entire submission for life, to one whom she cannot be sure will always deserve it, does certainly perform a more heroic action, than all the famous masculine heroes can boast of, she suffers a continual martyrdom to bring glory to God, and benefit to mankind; which consideration, indeed, may carry her through all difficulties, I know not what else can, and engage her to love him who proves perhaps so much worse than a brute, as to make this condition yet more grievous than it needed to be. She has need of a strong reason, of a truly christian and well-tempered spirit, of all the assistance the best education can give her, and ought to have some good assurance of her own firmness and virtue, who ventures on such a trial; and for this reason 'tis less to be wondered at that women marry off in haste, for perhaps if they took time to consider and reflect upon it, they seldom would marry.

1700

7. Advancement in rank; "upper," high ranking.

DANIEL DEFOE

ca. 1660–1731

1703:   Pilloried and jailed for political pamphleteering.
1704–13:   Editor of the *Review*.
1719:   *Robinson Crusoe*, first of his adventure tales.

By birth, education, and occupations Daniel Defoe was a stranger to the sphere of refined tastes and classical learning that determined the course of English literature during his lifetime. Middle class in his birth, Presbyterian in his religion, he belonged among the hardy Nonconformist tradesfolk who, after the Restoration, slowly increased their wealth and toward the end of the seventeenth century began to achieve political importance.

He began life as a small merchant and for a while prospered; but he was not overscrupulous in his dealings, and in 1692 he found himself bankrupt, with debts amounting to £17,000. This was the first of his many financial crises, crises which drove him to make his way, like his own heroes and heroines, by whatever means presented themselves. And however double his dealings, he seems always to have found the way to reconcile them with his genuine Nonconformist piety. His restless mind was fertile in "projects," both for himself and for the country; and his itch for politics made the role of passive observer impossible for him.

An ardent Whig, he first gained notoriety by political verses and pamphlets, and for one of them, in which he ironically defended the Anglican's hostility to the Dissenter, *The Shortest Way with the Dissenters*, he stood in the pillory three times and was sentenced to jail. He was released through the influence of that astute politician, Robert Harley (later earl of Oxford), who recognized in Defoe, as he was to do in Swift, a useful ally. For the next eleven years Defoe served his benefactor secretly as a political spy and confidential agent, traveling throughout England and Scotland, reporting and perhaps influencing opinion. As founder and editor of the *Review*, his job was to gain support for Harley's policies, and his Whiggism did not seem to make it difficult for him to follow Harley's lead, even when, in 1710, his master became head of a Tory ministry. It is characteristic of Defoe that, after the fall of the Tories in 1714, he went over to the triumphant Whigs and served them as loyally as he had their enemy.

When he was nearly sixty, Defoe's energy and inventiveness enabled him to break new ground, indeed to begin a new career. *Robinson Crusoe*, which appeared in 1719, is the first of a series of tales of adventure for which Defoe is now admired, but which brought him little esteem from the polite world, however much they gratified the less cultivated readers in the City or the servants' hall. In this and other tales which followed, Defoe was able to use all his greatest gifts: the ability to re-create a milieu vividly, through the cumulative effect of carefully observed, often petty details; a special skill in writing relaxed and careless prose, the language of actual speech, which seems to reveal the consciousness of the first-person narrator; his wide knowledge of the society in which he lived, both the trading bourgeoisie and the rogues who preyed on them; and his absorption in the spectacle of lonely human beings, whether Crusoe on his island or Moll Flanders in England and Virginia, somehow bending a stubborn and indifferent environment to their own ends of survival or profits. He was interested in the mere processes of living, and there is something of himself in all his protagonists: enormous vitality, humanity, a scheming and sometimes sneaky ingenuity. In these fictitious autobiographies of adventurers or rogues—*Captain Singleton* (1720), *Moll Flanders* (1722), *Colonel Jack* (1722), and *Roxana* (1724)—Defoe spoke for and to the members of his own class. Like them, he was engrossed by property and success; and his way of writing made all he touched seem true.

From Roxana[1]

[*The Cons of Marriage*]

One morning, in the middle of our unlawful freedoms—that is to say, when we were in bed together—he sighed, and told me he desired my leave to ask me one question, and that I would give him an answer to it with the same ingenuous freedom and honesty that I had used to[2] treat him with. I told him I would. Why, then, his question was, why I would not marry him, seeing I allowed him all the freedom of a husband. "Or," says he, "my dear, since you have been so kind as to take me to your bed, why will you not make me your own, and take me for good and all, that we may enjoy ourselves without any reproach to one another?"

I told him, that as I confessed it was the only thing I could not comply with him in, so it was the only thing in all my actions that I could not give him a reason for; that it was true I had let him come to bed to me, which was supposed to be the greatest favor a woman could grant; but it was evident, and he might see it, that as I was sensible of the obligation I was under to him for saving me from the worst circumstance it was possible for me to be brought to, I could deny him nothing; and if I had had any greater favor to yield him, I should have done it, *that of matrimony only excepted*, and he could not but see that I loved him to an extraordinary degree, in every part of my behavior to him; but that as to marrying, which was giving up my liberty, it was what once he knew I had done, and he had seen how it had hurried me up and down in the world, and what it had exposed me to;[3] that I had an aversion to it, and desired he would not insist upon it. He might easily see I had no aversion to him; and that, if I was with child by him, he should see a testi-

1. *Roxana, or The Fortunate Mistress*, is the story, told by herself, of a beautiful and ambitious courtesan. A bad marriage and early poverty drive her to a career of prostitution, at which she succeeds brilliantly until eventually her past catches up with her. The story is set in the Restoration, and even the title reflects the decadence associated with the period: admirers give "Roxana" her name after she has displayed herself provocatively in Turkish costume at a ball ("Roxalana," a sultana in Davenant's *Siege of Rhodes* [1656], had come to mean "whore"). In this excerpt the narrator, who has been saved from ruin and allowed herself to be seduced by an honest Dutch merchant, expresses her liberated views of marriage.

2. Been accustomed to.

3. The Dutch merchant thinks that Roxana is the widow of a jeweler, whose death had left her alone and friendless; actually she was the jeweler's mistress, and has since been the lover of a French prince.

mony of my kindness to the father, for that I would settle all I had in the world upon the child.

He was mute a good while. At last says he, "Come, my dear, you are the first woman in the world that ever lay with a man and then refused to marry him, and therefore there must be some other reason for your refusal; and I have therefore one other request, and that is, if I guess at the true reason, and remove the objection, will you then yield to me?" I told him, if he removed the objection I must needs comply, for I should certainly do everything that I had no objection against.

"Why then, my dear, it must be that either you are already engaged or married to some other man, or you are not willing to dispose of your money to me, and expect to advance yourself higher with your fortune. Now, if it be the first of these, my mouth will be stopped, and I have no more to say; but if it be the last, I am prepared effectually to remove the objection, and answer all you can say on that subject."

I took him up short at the first of these, telling him he must have base thoughts of me indeed, to think that I could yield to him in such a manner as I had done, and continue it with so much freedom as he found I did, if I had a husband, or were engaged to any other man; and that he might depend upon it that was not my case, nor any part of my case.

"Why then," said he, "as to the other, I have an offer to make to you that shall take off all the objections, viz., that I will not touch one pistole[4] of your estate more than shall be with your own voluntary consent, neither now or at any other time, but you shall settle it as you please for your life, and upon who you please after your death." That I should see he was able to maintain me without it; and that it was not for that that he followed me from Paris.

I was indeed surprised at that part of his offer, and he might easily perceive it; it was not only what I did not expect, but it was what I knew not what answer to make to. He had, indeed, removed my principal objection, nay, all my objections, and it was not possible for me to give any answer; for, if upon so generous an offer I should agree with him, I then did as good as confess that it was upon the account of my money that I refused him; and that though I could give up my virtue, and expose myself, yet I would not give up my money, which, though it was true, yet was really too gross for me to acknowledge, and I could not pretend to marry him upon that principle neither. Then as to having him, and make over all my estate out of his hands, so as not to give him the management of what I had, I thought it would be not only a little Gothic[5] and inhumane, but would be always a foundation of unkindness between us, and render us suspected one to another; so that, upon the whole, I was obliged to give a new turn to it, and talk upon a kind of an elevated strain, which really was not in my thoughts, at first, at all; for I own, as above, the divesting myself of my estate and putting my money

---

4. A Spanish coin.   5. Barbaric.

out of my hand was the sum of the matter that made me refuse to marry; but, I say, I gave it a new turn upon this occasion, as follows.

I told him I had, perhaps, different notions of matrimony from what the received custom had given us of it; that I thought a woman was a free agent as well as a man, and was born free, and could she manage herself suitably, might enjoy that liberty to as much purpose as the men do; that the laws of matrimony were indeed otherwise, and mankind at this time acted quite upon other principles, and those such that a woman gave herself entirely away from herself, in marriage, and capitulated only to be, at best, but an upper[6] servant, and from the time she took the man she was no better or worse than the servant among the Israelites, who had his ears bored—that is, nailed to the doorpost—who by that act gave himself up to be a servant during life. That the very nature of the marriage contract was, in short, nothing but giving up liberty, estate, authority, and everything to the man, and the woman was indeed a mere woman ever after—that is to say, a slave.

He replied, that though in some respects it was as I had said, yet I ought to consider that, as an equivalent to this, the man had all the care of things devolved upon him; that the weight of business lay upon his shoulders, and as he had the trust, so he had the toil of life upon him; his was the labor, his the anxiety of living; that the woman had nothing to do but to eat the fat and drink the sweet; to sit still and look around her, be waited on and made much of, be served and loved and made easy, especially if the husband acted as became him; and that, in general, the labor of the man was appointed to make the woman live quiet and unconcerned in the world; that they had the name of subjection without the thing; and if in inferior families they had the drudgery of the house and care of the provisions upon them, yet they had indeed much the easier part; for in general, the women had only the care of managing—that is, spending what their husbands get—and that a woman had the name of subjection, indeed, but that they very generally commanded not the men only, but all they had; managed all for themselves; and where the man did his duty, the woman's life was all ease and tranquility, and that she had nothing to do but to be easy, and to make all that were about her both easy and merry.

I returned, that while a woman was single, she was a masculine in her politic capacity;[7] that she had then the full command of what she had, and the full direction of what she did; that she was a man in her separated capacity, to all intents and purposes that a man could be so to himself; that she was controlled by none, because accountable to none, and was in subjection to none. So I sung these two lines of Mr ——'s:[8]

> Oh! 'tis pleasant to be free,
> The sweetest Miss is Liberty.

6. High-ranking.
7. A male in her function of making prudent decisions.

8. Unidentified; Defoe himself may have written the lines.

I added, that whoever the woman was that had an estate, and would give it up to be the slave of *a great man*, that woman was a fool, and must be fit for nothing but a beggar; that it was my opinion a woman was as fit to govern and enjoy her own estate without a man as a man was without a woman; and that, if she had a mind to gratify herself as to sexes, she might entertain a man as a man does a mistress; that while she was thus single she was her own, and if she gave away that power she merited to be as miserable as it was possible that any creature could be.

All he could say could not answer the force of this, as to argument; only this, that the other way was the ordinary method that the world was guided by; that he had reason to expect I should be content with that which all the world was contented with; that he was of the opinion that a sincere affection between a man and his wife answered all the objections that I had made about the being a slave, a servant, and the like; and where there was a mutual love, there could be no bondage, but that there was but one interest, one aim, one design, and all conspired to make both very happy.

"Aye," said I, "that is the thing I complain of. The pretense of affection takes from a woman everything that can be called *herself*; she is to have no interest, no aim, no view, but all is the interest, aim, and view of the husband; she is to be the passive creature you spoke of," said I. "She is to lead a life of perfect indolence, and living by faith (not in God, but) in her husband, she sinks or swims, as he is either fool or wise man, unhappy or prosperous; and in the middle of what she thinks is her happiness and prosperity, she is engulfed in misery and beggary, which she had not the least notice, knowledge, or suspicion of. How often have I seen a woman living in all the splendor that a plentiful fortune ought to allow her, with her coaches and equipages, her family and rich furniture, her attendants and friends, her visitors and good company, all about her today; tomorrow surprised with a disaster, turned out of all by a commission of bankrupt,[9] stripped to the clothes on her back; her jointure, suppose she had it, is sacrificed to the creditors so long as her husband lived, and she turned into the street, and left to live on the charity of her friends, *if she has any*, or follow the monarch, her husband, into the Mint,[1] and live there on the wreck of his fortunes, till he is forced to run away from her even there; and then she sees her children starve, herself miserable, breaks her heart, and cries herself to death! This," says I, "is the state of many a lady that has had ten thousand pound to her portion."

He did not know how feelingly I spoke this, and what extremities I had gone through of this kind; how near I was to the very last article above, viz., crying myself to death; and how I really starved for almost two years together.[2]

---

9. A writ of bankruptcy. "Jointure": property settled on a wife.
1. Debtors took refuge in the area near the Mint,
where they could not be arrested.
2. Roxana's first husband, a profligate brewer, had run off, leaving her destitute.

But he shook his head, and said, where had I lived? and what dreadful families had I lived among, that had frighted me into such terrible apprehensions of things? that these things indeed might happen where men run into hazardous things in trade, and without prudence or due consideration, launched their fortunes in a degree beyond their strength, grasping at adventures beyond their stocks, and the like; but that, as he was stated[3] in the world, if I would embark with him, he had a fortune equal with mine; that together we should have no occasion of engaging in business any more; but that in any part of the world where I had a mind to live, whether England, France, Holland, or where I would, we might settle, and live as happily as the world could make any one live; that if I desired the management of our estate, when put together, if I would not trust him with mine, he would trust me with his; that we would be upon one bottom,[4] and I should steer. "Ay," says I, "you'll allow me to steer—that is, hold the helm—but you'll con[5] the ship, as they call it; that is, as at sea, a boy serves to stand at the helm, but he that gives him the orders is pilot."

He laughed at my simile. "No," says he; "you shall be pilot then; you shall con the ship." "Ay," says I, "as long as you please, but you can take the helm out of my hand when you please, and bid me go spin. It is not you," says I, "that I suspect, but the laws of matrimony puts the power into your hands, bids you do it, commands you to command, and binds me, forsooth, to obey. You, that are now upon even terms with me, and I with you," says I, "are the next hour set up upon the throne, and the humble wife placed at your footstool; all the rest, all that you call oneness of interest, mutual affection, and the like, is courtesy and kindness then, and a woman is indeed infinitely obliged where she meets with it; but can't help herself where it fails."

Well, he did not give it over yet, but came to the serious part, and there he thought he should be too many for me. He first hinted, that marriage was decreed by Heaven; that it was the fixed state of life, which God had appointed for man's felicity, and for establishing a legal posterity; that there could be no legal claim of estates by inheritance but by children born in wedlock; that all the rest was sunk under scandal and illegitimacy; and very well he talked upon that subject indeed.

But it would not do; I took him short there. "Look you, sir," said I, "you have an advantage of me there indeed, in my particular case; but it would not be generous to make use of it. I readily grant that it were better for me to have married you than to admit you to the liberty I have given you; but as I could not reconcile my judgment to marriage, for the reasons above, and had kindness enough for you, and obligation too much on me to resist you, I suffered your rudeness and gave up my virtue. But I have two things before me to heal up that breach of honor without that desperate one of marriage, and those are, repentance for what is past, and putting an end to it for time to come."

3. Established, a person of standing.   5. Direct the steering of.
4. One ship (literally, lowest part of a hull).

He seemed to be concerned to think that I should take him in that manner. He assured me that I misunderstood him; that he had more manners as well as more kindness for me, and more justice, than to reproach me with what he had been the aggressor in, and had surprised me into; that what he spoke referred to my words above, that the woman, if she thought fit, might entertain a man, as a man did a mistress; and that I seemed to mention that way of living as justifiable, and setting it as a lawful thing, and in the place of matrimony.

Well, we strained some compliments upon those points, not worth repeating; and I added, I supposed when he got to bed to me he thought himself sure of me; and indeed, in the ordinary course of things, after he had lain with me he ought to think so; but that, upon the same foot of argument which I had discoursed with him upon, it was just the contrary; and when a woman had been weak enough to yield up the last point before wedlock, it would be adding one weakness to another to take the man afterwards, to pin down the shame of it upon herself all the days of her life, and bind herself to live all her time with the only man that could upbraid her with it; that in yielding at first, she must be a fool, but to take the man is to be sure to be called fool; that to resist a man is to act with courage and vigor, and to cast off the reproach, which, in the course of things, drops out of knowledge and dies. The man goes one way and the woman another, as fate and the circumstances of living direct; and if they keep one another's counsel, the folly is heard no more of. "But to take the man," says I, "is the most preposterous thing in nature, and (saving your presence) is to befoul one's self, and live always in the smell of it. No, no," added I; "after a man has lain with me as a mistress, he ought never to lie with me as a wife; that's not only preserving the crime in memory, but it is recording it in the family. If the woman marries the man afterwards, she bears the reproach of it to the last hour; if her husband is not a man of a hundred thousand, he some time or other upbraids her with it. If he has children, they fail not one way or other to hear of it. If the children are virtuous, they do their mother the justice to hate her for it; if they are wicked, they give her the mortification of doing the like, and giving her for the example. On the other hand, if the man and the woman part, there is an end of the crime and an end of the clamor. Time wears out the memory of it; or a woman may remove but a few streets, and she soon outlives it, and hears no more of it."

He was confounded at this discourse, and told me he could not say but I was right in the main. That as to that part relating to managing estates, it was arguing *à la cavalier*;[6] it was in some sense right, if the woman were able to carry it on so, but that in general the sex were not capable of it; their heads were not turned for it, and they had better choose a person capable and honest, that knew how to do them justice

6. Cavalierly, rashly.

as women, as well as to love them; and that then the trouble was all taken off of their hands.

I told him it was a dear way of purchasing their ease; for very often when the trouble was taken off of their hands, so was their money too; and that I thought it was far safer for the sex not to be afraid of the trouble, but to be really afraid of their money; that if nobody was trusted, nobody would be deceived; and the staff in their own hands was the best security in the world.

He replied, that I had started a new thing in the world; that however I might support it by subtle reasoning, yet it was a way of arguing that was contrary to the general practice, and that he confessed he was much disappointed in it; that had he known I would have made such a use of it, he would never have attempted what he did, which he had no wicked design in, resolving to make me reparation, and that he was very sorry he had been so unhappy[7]; that he was very sure he should never upbraid me with it hereafter, and had so good an opinion of me as to believe I did not suspect him; but seeing I was positive in refusing him, notwithstanding what had passed, he had nothing to do but secure me from reproach by going back again to Paris, that so, according to my own way of arguing, it might die out of memory, and I might never meet with it again to my disadvantage.

* * *

Thus blinded by my own vanity, I threw away the only opportunity I then had to have effectually settled my fortunes, and secured them for this world; and I am a memorial to all that shall read my story, a standing monument of the madness and distraction which pride and infatuations from hell run us into; how ill our passions guide us; and how dangerously we act, when we follow the dictates of an ambitious mind.

1724

7. Troublesome.

Poetry: Augustan Modes

SAMUEL BUTLER
1612–1680

Butler passed his middle years during the fury of the civil war and under the Commonwealth, sardonically observing the behavior and lovingly memorizing the faults of the Puritan rulers. He despised them and found relief for his feelings by satirizing them, though, naturally enough, he could not publish while they were in power. He served as clerk to several Puritan justices of the peace in the west of England, one of whom, according to tradition, was the original of Sir Hudibras (the *s* is pronounced). *Hudibras*, part 1, was published late in 1662 (the edition bears the date 1663) and pleased the triumphant Royalists. King Charles II admired and often quoted the poem and rewarded its author with a gift of £300; it was, after all, a relief to laugh at what he had earlier hated and feared. The first part, attacking Presbyterians and Independents, proved more vigorous and effective than parts 2 and 3, which followed in 1664 and 1678 respectively. After his initial success, Butler was neglected by the people he had pleased. He died in poverty, and not until 1721 was a monument to his memory erected in Westminster Abbey.

Hudibras is a travesty, or burlesque: it takes a serious subject and debases it by using a low style or distorts it by grotesque exaggeration. Butler carried this mode even into his verse, for he reduced the iambic tetrameter line (used subtly and seriously by such seventeenth-century poets as John Donne, John Milton, and Andrew Marvell) to something approaching doggerel, and his boldly comic rhymes add to the effect of broad comedy which he sought to create. Burlesque was a popular form of satire during the seventeenth century, especially after the French poet Paul Scarron published his *Virgile Travesti* (1648), which retells the *Aeneid* in slang. Butler's use of burlesque expresses his contempt for the Puritans and their Commonwealth; the history of England from 1642 to 1660 is made to appear mere sound and fury.

Butler took his hero's name from Spenser's *Faerie Queene* 2.2, where Sir Huddibras appears briefly as a rash adventurer and lover. The questing knight of chivalric romance is degraded into the meddling, hypocritical busybody Hudibras, who goes out, like an officer in Cromwell's army, "a-coloneling" against the popular sport of bearbaiting. The knight and his squire, Ralph, suggest Don Quixote and Sancho Panza, but the temper of Butler's mind is as remote from Cervantes's warm humanity as it is from Spenser's ardent idealism. Butler had no illusions; he was skeptical in philosophy and conservative in politics, distrusting theoretical reasoning and the new science, disdainful of claims of inspiration and illumination, contemptuous of Catholicism and dubious of bishops, Anglican no less than Roman. It is difficult to think of anything which he approved unless it was peace, com-

mon sense, and the wisdom that emerges from the experience of mankind
through the ages.

From Hudibras

From *Part 1, Canto 1*

THE ARGUMENT

Sir Hudibras, his passing worth,
The manner how he sallied forth,
His arms and equipage are shown,
His horse's virtues and his own:
The adventure of the Bear and Fiddle
Is sung, but breaks off in the middle.

When civil fury[1] first grew high,
And men fell out, they knew not why;
When hard words, jealousies, and fears
Set folks together by the ears
And made them fight, like mad or drunk,   5
For Dame Religion as for punk,[2]
Whose honesty they all durst swear for,
Though not a man of them knew wherefore;
When gospel-trumpeter,[3] surrounded
With long-eared rout, to battle sounded,   10
And pulpit, drum ecclesiastic,[4]
Was beat with fist instead of a stick;
Then did Sir Knight abandon dwelling,
And out he rode a-coloneling.[5]

    A wight he was whose very sight would   15
Entitle him Mirror of Knighthood;
That never bent his stubborn knee
To anything but chivalry,
Nor put up blow but that which laid
Right worshipful on shoulder blade;[6]   20
Chief of domestic knights and errant,
Either for chartel or for warrant;[7]
Great on the bench, great in the saddle,

---

1. The civil war between Royalists and Parliamentarians (1642–49).
2. I.e., a prostitute.
3. A Presbyterian minister, vehemently preaching rebellion. The "long-eared rout" is a mob of Puritans or Roundheads, so called because they wore their hair short instead of in flowing curls and thus exposed their ears, which to many satirists suggested the long ears of the ass.
4. The Presbyterian clergy were said to have preached the country into civil war. Hence, in pounding their pulpits with their fists, they are said

to beat their ecclesiastical drums.
5. Here pronounced *có-lo-nel-ing*. "Wight:" a creature.
6. When a man is knighted he kneels and is tapped on the shoulder by his overlord's sword.
7. "Chartel," a written challenge to combat, such as a knight-errant sends. But Hudibras, as Justice of the Peace ("domestic knight"), could also issue a "warrant" (a writ authorizing an arrest, a seizure, or a search). Hence he is satirically called "great on the [Justice's] bench" as well as in the saddle. "Errant" was spelled and pronounced *arrant*.

That could as well bind o'er as swaddle.[8]
Mighty he was at both of these,   25
And styled of war as well as peace.
(So some rats of amphibious nature
Are either for the land or water.)
But here our authors make a doubt
Whether he were more wise or stout.   30
Some hold the one and some the other;
But howsoe'er they make a pother,
The difference was so small his brain
Outweighed his rage but half a grain;
Which made some take him for a tool   35
That knaves do work with, called a fool,
And offer to lay wagers that,
As Montaigne, playing with his cat,
Complains she thought him but an ass,[9]
Much more she would Sir Hudibras   40
(For that's the name our valiant knight
To all his challenges did write).
But they're mistaken very much,
'Tis plain enough he was no such.
We grant, although he had much wit,   45
He was very shy of using it;
As being loath to wear it out,
And therefore bore it not about,
Unless on holidays, or so,
As men their best apparel do.   50
Beside, 'tis known he could speak Greek
As naturally as pigs squeak;
That Latin was no more difficile
Than to a blackbird 'tis to whistle.
Being rich in both, he never scanted   55
His bounty unto such as wanted,
But much of either would afford
To many that had not one word.
For Hebrew roots, although they're found
To flourish most in barren ground,[1]   60
He had such plenty as sufficed
To make some think him circumcised;
And truly so perhaps he was,
'Tis many a pious Christian's case.
      He was in logic a great critic,   65
Profoundly skilled in analytic.
He could distinguish and divide

---

8. Both Justice of the Peace and soldier, he is
equally able to "bind over" a malefactor to be tried
at the next sessions or in his role of colonel, to beat
("swaddle") him.
9. In his *Apology for Raymond Sebond*, Michel de
Montaigne (1533–1592), French skeptic and

essayist, wondered whether he played with his cat
or his cat played with him.
1. Hebrew, the language of Adam, was thought of
as the primitive language, the one which men in
a state of nature would naturally speak.

A hair 'twixt south and southwest side;
On either which he would dispute,
Confute, change hands, and still confute.   70
He'd undertake to prove, by force
Of argument, a man's no horse;
He'd prove a buzzard is no fowl,
And that a lord may be an owl,
A calf an alderman, a goose a justice,   75
And rooks committee-men and trustees.[2]
He'd run in debt by disputation,
And pay with ratiocination.
All this by syllogism true,
In mood and figure,[3] he would do.   80
    For rhetoric, he could not ope
His mouth but out there flew a trope;[4]
And when he happened to break off
In the middle of his speech, or cough,[5]
He had hard words ready to show why,   85
And tell what rules he did it by.
Else, when with greatest art he spoke,
You'd think he talked like other folk;
For all a rhetorician's rules
Teach nothing but to name his tools.   90
His ordinary rate of speech
In loftiness of sound was rich,
A Babylonish dialect,[6]
Which learned pedants much affect.
It was a parti-colored dress   95
Of patched and piebald languages;
'Twas English cut on Greek and Latin,
Like fustian heretofore on satin.[7]
It had an odd promiscuous tone,
As if he had talked three parts in one;   100
Which made some think, when he did gabble,
They had heard three laborers of Babel,
Or Cerberus himself pronounce
A leash of languages at once.[8]
This he as volubly would vent   105
As if his stock would ne'er be spent;
And truly, to support that charge,
He had supplies as vast and large.

---

2. Committees were set up in the counties by Parliament and given authority to imprison Royalists and to sequestrate their estates. "Rooks": a kind of blackbird; slang for "cheats."
3. "Mood" is the form of an argument. The "figure" of a syllogism is "the proper disposition of the middle term with the parts of the question."
4. Figure of speech.
5. Some pulpit orators regarded hemming and coughing as ornaments of speech.

6. Pedants affected the use of foreign words. The allusion is to the Tower of Babel (Genesis 11.4–9).
7. Clothes made of coarse cloth ("fustian") were slashed so as to display the richer satin lining.
8. The sporting term "leash" denotes a group of three dogs, hawks, deer, etc.; hence, *three* in general. Cerberus was the three-headed dog that guarded the entrance to Hades.

For he could coin or counterfeit
New words with little or no wit;[9]   110
Words so debased and hard no stone
Was hard enough to touch them on.
And when with hasty noise he spoke 'em,
The ignorant for current took 'em;
That had the orator, who once   115
Did fill his mouth with pebble-stones
When he harangued,[1] but known his phrase,
He would have used no other ways.

    In mathematics he was greater
Than Tycho Brahe,[2] or Erra Pater: 120
For he, by geometric scale,
Could take the size of pots of ale;
Resolve by sines and tangents straight,
If bread or butter wanted weight;
And wisely tell what hour o' the day   125
The clock does strike, by algebra.

    Beside, he was a shrewd philosopher,
And had read every text and gloss over;
Whate'er the crabbed'st author hath,
He understood by implicit faith;   130
Whatever skeptic could inquire for,
For every *why* he had a *wherefore*;
Knew more than forty of them do,
As far as words and terms could go.
All which he understood by rote   135
And, as occasion served, would quote,
No matter whether right or wrong;
They might be either said or sung.
His notions fitted things so well
That which was which he could not tell,   140
But oftentimes mistook the one
For the other, as great clerks have done.[3]
He could reduce all things to acts,
And knew their natures by abstracts;
Where entity and quiddity,[4]   145
The ghosts of defunct bodies, fly;
Where truth in person does appear,
Like words congealed in northern air.[5]

---

9. The Presbyterians and other sects invented a special religious vocabulary, much ridiculed by Anglicans: "out-goings," "workings-out," "gospel-walking-times," etc.
1. Demosthenes cured a stutter by speaking with pebbles in his mouth.
2. A Danish astronomer (1546–1601). "Erra Pater": Butler's contemptuous name for the popular astrologer William Lilly (1602–1681).
3. Elsewhere Butler wrote: "Notions are but pictures of things in the imagination of man, and if

they agree with their originals in nature, they are true, and if not, false." "Clerks": scholars.
4. In the hair-splitting logic of medieval Scholastic philosophy, a distinction was drawn between the "entity" or *being* and the "quiddity" or *essence* of bodies. Butler calls entity and quiddity "ghosts" because they were held to be independent realities and so to survive the bodies in which they lodge.
5. The notion, as old as the Greek wit Lucian, that in arctic regions words freeze as they are uttered and become audible only when they thaw.

He knew what's what, and that's as high
As metaphysic wit can fly.   150
    In school-divinity[6] as able
As he that hight Irrefragable;[7]
Profound in all the nominal
And real ways beyond them all;
And with as delicate a hand   155
Could twist as tough a rope of sand;
And weave fine cobwebs, fit for skull
That's empty when the moon is full;[8]
Such as take lodgings in a head
That's to be let unfurnishèd   160
He could raise scruples dark and nice,[9]
And after solve 'em in a trice;
As if divinity had catched
The itch on purpose to be scratched,
Or, like a mountebank,[1] did wound   165
And stab herself with doubts profound,
Only to show with how small pain
The sores of faith are cured again;
Although by woeful proof we find
They always leave a scar behind.   170
He knew the seat of paradise,[2]
Could tell in what degree it lies;
And, as he was disposed, could prove it
Below the moon, or else above it;
What Adam dreamt of when his bride   175
Came from her closet in his side;
Whether the devil tempted her
By a High Dutch interpreter;
If either of them had a navel;
Who first made music malleable;[3]   180
Whether the serpent at the fall
Had cloven feet or none at all:
All this without a gloss or comment
He could unriddle in a moment,
In proper terms, such as men smatter   185
When they throw out and miss the matter.
    For his religion, it was fit
To match his learning and his wit:

---

6. Scholastic theology.
7. Alexander of Hales (d. 1245) was called "Irrefragable," i.e., unanswerable, because his system seemed incontrovertible. The next couplet refers to the debate, continuous throughout the Middle Ages, as to whether the objects of our concepts exist in nature or are mere intellectual abstractions. The "nominalists" denied their objective reality, the "realists" affirmed it.
8. The frenzies of madmen were supposed to wax and wane with the moon (hence "lunatic").

9. Obscure ("dark") and subtle ("nice") intellectual perplexities ("scruples").
1. A seller of quack medicines.
2. The problem of the precise location of the Garden of Eden and the similar problems listed in the ensuing dozen lines had all been the subject of controversy among theologians.
3. Capable of being fashioned into form. Pythagoras is said to have organized sounds into the musical scale.

'Twas Presbyterian true blue,[4]
For he was of that stubborn crew   190
Of errant[5] saints whom all men grant
To be the true church militant,
Such as do build their faith upon
The holy text of pike and gun;
Decide all controversies by   195
Infallible artillery,
And prove their doctrine orthodox
By apostolic blows and knocks;
Call fire, and sword, and desolation
A godly, thorough reformation,   200
Which always must be carried on
And still be doing, never done;
As if religion were intended
For nothing else but to be mended.
A sect whose chief devotion lies   205
In odd, perverse antipathies;[6]
In falling out with that or this,
And finding somewhat still amiss;
More peevish, cross, and splènetic
Than dog distract or monkey sick;   210
That with more care keep holiday
The wrong, than others the right way;
Compound for sins they are inclined to
By damning those they have no mind to;
Still so perverse and opposite   215
As if they worshiped God for spite.
The selfsame thing they will abhor
One way and long another for.
Free-will they one way disavow,[7]
Another, nothing else allow: 220
All piety consists therein
In them, in other men all sin.
Rather than fail, they will defy
That which they love most tenderly;
Quarrel with minced pies and disparage   225
Their best and dearest friend, plum-porridge;
Fat pig and goose itself oppose,
And blaspheme custard through the nose.[8]

                    *   *   *   1663

4. The Scotch Covenanters adopted blue as their color, in contrast to the Royalist red. Blue is the color of constancy; hence, "true blue," staunch, unwavering. This and the next five couplets bitterly recall the violence and fanaticism of the Parliamentary armies in attempting to reform the Anglican Church.

5. A pun: "arrant," meaning "unmitigated," and "errant," meaning "wandering," were both spelled and pronounced *arrant*. The Puritans frequently called themselves "saints."

6. The hostility of the sects to everything Anglican or Roman Catholic laid them open to the charge of opposing innocent practices out of mere perverse antipathy. Some extreme Presbyterians fasted at Christmas, instead of following the old custom of feasting and rejoicing. Cf. lines 211–12.

7. By the doctrine of predestination.

8. A reference to the nasal whine of the pious sectarians.

JOHN WILMOT,
SECOND EARL OF ROCHESTER
1647–1680

John Wilmot, second earl of Rochester, was the precocious son of one of Charles II's most loyal followers in exile. He won the king's favor at the Restoration and, in 1664, after education at Oxford and on the continent, took a place at court, at the age of seventeen. There he soon distinguished himself as "the man who has the most wit and the least honor in England." For one escapade, the abduction of Elizabeth Malet, an heiress, he was imprisoned in the Tower. But he regained his position by courageous service in the naval war against the Dutch; and in 1667 he married Miss Malet. The rest of his career was no less stormy. His satiric wit, directed not only at ordinary mortals but at Dryden and Charles II himself, embroiled him in constant quarrels and exiles; his practical jokes, his affairs, his dissipation were legendary. He told his biographer, Gilbert Burnet, that "for five years together he was continually drunk." Just before his death, however, he was converted to Christian repentance; and for posterity Rochester became a favorite moral topic: the libertine who had seen the error of his ways.

"Wit," in the Restoration, meant not only a clever turn of phrase but mental capacity, intellectual power. Rochester was famous for both kinds of wit. His fierce intelligence, impatient of sham and convention, helped design a way of life based on style, cleverness, self-interest—a way of life observable in Restoration plays (Dorimant, in Etherege's *The Man of Mode*, strongly resembles Rochester). Philosophically, such behavior may be seen as an experiment in living the life of a "natural man," in accord with Hobbes's doctrine that all laws, even our notions of good and evil, are artificial social checks upon natural human desires. *The Disabled Debauchee*, composed in "heroic stanzas" like those of Dryden's *Annus Mirabilis*, subverts the very notion of heroism by turning conventions upside-down. Yet everything is kept plausible by Rochester's special gift for impersonation, the same talent, according to one enemy, that made him a dangerous seducer—"He enters into all your tastes and your feelings, and makes you believe everything he says, though not a single word is sincere."

The Disabled Debauchee

As some brave admiral, in former war
   Deprived of force, but pressed with courage still,
Two rival fleets appearing from afar,
   Crawls to the top of an adjacent hill;

From whence, with thoughts full of concern, he views   5
   The wise and daring conduct of the fight,
Whilst each bold action to his mind renews
   His present glory and his past delight;

From his fierce eyes flashes of fire he throws,
    As from black clouds when lightning breaks away;   10
Transported, thinks himself amidst the foes,
    And absent, yet enjoys the bloody day;

So, when my days of impotence approach,
    And I'm by pox[1] and wine's unlucky chance
Forced from the pleasing billows of debauch   15
    On the dull shore of lazy temperance,

My pains at least some respite shall afford
    While I behold the battle you maintain
When fleets of glasses sail about the board,[2]
    From whose broadsides[3] volleys of wit shall rain.   20

Nor let the sight of honorable scars,
    Which my too forward valor did procure,
Frighten new-listed[4] soldiers from the wars:
    Past joys have more than paid what I endure.

Should any youth (worth being drunk) prove nice,[5]   25
    And from his fair inviter meanly shrink,
'Twill please the ghost of my departed vice
    If, at my counsel, he repent and drink.

Or should some cold-complexioned sot forbid,
    With his dull morals, our bold night-alarms,   30
I'll fire his blood by telling what I did
    When I was strong and able to bear arms.

I'll tell of whores attacked, their lords at home;
    Bawds' quarters beaten up, and fortress won;
Windows demolished, watches[6] overcome;   35
    And handsome ills by my contrivance done.

Nor shall our love-fits, Chloris, be forgot,
    When each the well-looked linkboy[7] strove t' enjoy,
And the best kiss was the deciding lot
    Whether the boy used you, or I the boy.   40

With tales like these I will such thoughts inspire
    As to important mischief shall incline:
I'll make him long some ancient church to fire,
    And fear no lewdness he's called to by wine.

---

1. Venereal disease.
2. Table.
3. The sides of the table; artillery on a ship; sheets on which satirical verses were printed.
4. Newly enlisted.
5. Coy, fastidious.
6. Watchmen.
7. Good-looking boy employed to light the way with a link or torch.

Thus, statesmanlike, I'll saucily impose,   45
   And safe from action, valiantly advise;
Sheltered in impotence, urge you to blows,
   And being good for nothing else, be wise.

1680

ANNE FINCH,
COUNTESS OF WINCHILSEA
1661–1720

Born into an ancient country family, Anne Kingsmill became a maid of honor at the court of Charles II. There she met Colonel Heneage Finch; in 1684 they married. During the short reign of James II they prospered at court, but at the king's fall in 1688 they were forced to retire, eventually settling on a beautiful family estate at Eastwell, in Kent, near the south coast of England. Here Colonel Finch became, in 1712, earl of Winchilsea; and here Lady Winchilsea wrote most of her poems, influenced, she said, by "the solitude and security of the country," and by "objects naturally inspiring soft and poetical imaginations." Her *Miscellany Poems on Several Occasions, Written by a Lady* were published in 1713; one poem, *The Spleen*, a description of the mysterious melancholic illness from which she and many other fashionable people suffered, achieved some fame. But her larger reputation only began a century later, when Wordsworth praised her for keeping her eye upon external nature, and for a style "often admirable, chaste, tender, and vigorous."

Three things conspired to keep Lady Winchilsea's poems in the shade: she was an aristocrat; her nature was retiring; and she was a woman. Any one of these might have made her shrink from exposing herself to the jeers that still, at the turn of the century, greeted any effort by a "scribbling lady." Many of her best poems, for instance *The Petition for an Absolute Retreat*, celebrate the joys of solitude. Nevertheless, remarkably, she chose to publish. The reason may be found in her contempt for the notion that women are fit for nothing but trivial pursuits. In *The Introduction* to her poems she insists that women are "education's, more than nature's fools," and she often comments on the damaging exclusion of half the human race from public life. But Winchilsea is her own best example of what a woman can be: keen-eyed and self-sufficient and a poet.

The Introduction[1]

Did I my lines intend for public view,
  How many censures would their faults pursue!

---

1. This preface to Winchilsea's work was never published during her lifetime, for reasons explained   in the poem itself.

Some would, because such words they do affect,
Cry they're insipid, empty, uncorrect.
And many have attained, dull and untaught,   5
The name of wit, only by finding fault.[2]
True judges might condemn their want of wit;
And all might say, they're by a woman writ.
Alas! a woman that attempts the pen,
Such an intruder on the rights of men,   10
Such a presumptuous creature is esteemed,
The fault can by no virtue be redeemed.
They tell us we mistake our sex and way;
Good breeding, fashion, dancing, dressing, play
Are the accomplishments we should desire;   15
To write, or read, or think, or to enquire,
Would cloud our beauty, and exhaust our time,
And interrupt the conquests of our prime;
Whilst the dull manage of a servile house
Is held by some our utmost art and use.   20
    Sure 'twas not ever thus, nor are we told
Fables,[3] of women that excelled of old;
To whom, by the diffusive hand of heaven,
Some share of wit and poetry was given.
On that glad day on which the Ark[4] returned,   25
The holy pledge for which the land had mourned,
The joyful tribes attend it on the way,
The Levites do the sacred charge convey,
Whilst various instruments before it play;
Here holy virgins in the concert join,[5]   30
The louder notes to soften and refine,
And with alternate verse[6] complete the hymn divine.
    Lo! the young poet,[7] after God's own heart,
By Him inspired and taught the Muses' art,
Returned from conquest a bright chorus meets.   35
That sing his slain ten thousand in the streets.[8]
In such loud numbers they his acts declare,
Proclaim the wonders of his early war,
That Saul upon the vast applause does frown,
And feels its mighty thunder shake the crown.   40
What can the threatened judgment now prolong?[9]
Half of the kingdom is already gone;
The fairest half, whose judgment guides the rest,
Have David's empire o'er their hearts confessed.

2. Pronounced *fawt*.
3. Idle stories or lies.
4. The Ark of the Covenant, restored to Jerusalem
by David (1 Chronicles 15).
5. Pronounced *jine*.
6. A series of couplets. The choir of virgins, not
mentioned in Chronicles, is imagined by Winchilsea as chanting every other line, responsively,
as in some of the Psalms.
7. David.
8. 1 Samuel 18:6–7. "Numbers," measures of
music and verse.
9. What can now stave off the threatened judgment? Saul's doom ("judgment") had been prophesied: God would replace him with a better king.

A woman here leads fainting Israel on,   45
She fights, she wins, she triumphs with a song, [1]
Devout, majestic, for the subject fit,
And far above her arms, exalts her wit,
Then to the peaceful, shady palm withdraws,
And rules the rescued nation with her laws.   50
     How are we fallen! fallen by mistaken rules,
And education's, more than nature's fools;
Debarred from all improvements of the mind,
And to be dull, expected and designed; [2]
And if some one would soar above the rest,   55
With warmer fancy and ambition pressed,
So strong the opposing faction still appears,
The hopes to thrive can ne'er outweigh the fears.
Be cautioned, then, my Muse, and still retired;
Nor be despised, aiming to be admired;   60
Conscious of wants, still with contracted wing,
To some few friends and to thy sorrows sing.
For groves of laurel thou wert never meant;
Be dark enough thy shades, and be thou there content.

1689?   1903

A Nocturnal Reverie

In such a night, [1] when every louder wind
Is to its distant cavern safe confined;
And only gentle Zephyr fans his wings,
And lonely Philomel, [2] still waking, sings;
Or from some tree, famed for the owl's delight,   5
She, hollowing clear, directs the wanderer right:
In such a night, when passing clouds give place,
Or thinly veil the heavens' mysterious face;
When in some river, overhung with green,
The waving moon and trembling leaves are seen;   10
When freshened grass now bears itself upright,
And makes cool banks to pleasing rest invite,
Whence springs the woodbind, and the bramble-rose,
And where the sleepy cowslip sheltered grows;
Whilst now a paler hue the foxglove takes,   15
Yet checkers still with red the dusky brakes:
When scattered glow-worms, but in twilight fine,
Show trivial beauties watch their hour to shine;
Whilst Salisbury [3] stands the test of every light,

1. The prophetess and judge Deborah sang to praise the Lord for the victory she herself had brought about (Judges 4–5).
2. Marked out, intended.
1. This phrase, repeated twice below, echoes the same repeated phrase in the night-piece that opens act 5 of *The Merchant of Venice*.
2. The nightingale.
3. Probably Lady Salisbury, the daughter of a friend. The sense is that this lady differs from others more trivial, who like glow-worms look fine only one hour a day.

In perfect charms, and perfect virtue bright: 20
When odors, which declined repelling day,
Through temperate air uninterrupted stray;
When darkened groves their softest shadows wear,
And falling waters we distinctly hear;
When through the gloom more venerable shows   25
Some ancient fabric,[4] awful in repose,
While sunburnt hills their swarthy looks conceal,
And swelling haycocks thicken up the vale:
When the loosed horse now, as his pasture leads,
Comes slowly grazing through the adjoining meads,   30
Whose stealing pace, and lengthened shade we fear,
Till torn-up forage in his teeth we hear:
When nibbling sheep at large pursue their food,
And unmolested kine rechew the cud;
When curlews cry beneath the village walls,   35
And to her straggling brood the partridge calls;
Their shortlived jubilee the creatures keep,
Which but endures, whilst tyrant man does sleep;
When a sedate content the spirit feels,
And no fierce light disturbs, whilst it reveals;   40
But silent musings urge the mind to seek
Something, too high for syllables to speak;
Till the free soul to a composedness charmed,
Finding the elements of rage disarmed,
O'er all below a solemn quiet grown,   45
Joys in the inferior world,[5] and thinks it like her own:
In such a night let me abroad remain,
Till morning breaks, and all's confused again;
Our cares, our toils, our clamors are renewed,
Or pleasures, seldom reached, again pursued.   50

                                                                    1713

4. Edifice.
5. The world of nature (compared to the world of the soul).

MATTHEW PRIOR
1664–1721

Prior was a public man. He became a diplomat through the patronage of Dryden's friend the earl of Dorset, wit, courtier, and poet, when he was appointed secretary to the embassy at The Hague. His public career culminated in his negotiating for Oxford's Tory ministry the Treaty of Utrecht (1713), which ended the War of the Spanish Succession; but after the fall of the Tories in 1714, Prior was recalled from Paris, placed under house arrest for over a year, and frequently interrogated in the hope that his evidence could be used to bring Oxford to trial as a traitor. Upon his release he found himself out of place and broken in fortune. But the extraordinary success of such friends as Swift and Pope in supporting the publication by subscription of his *Poems on Several Occasions* (1718) secured him a profit of 4,000 guineas, a very large sum at that time, which enabled him to end his life in comfort.

Prior's poetry was the by-product of a busy life—"the fruits of [his] vacant hours," as he once wrote. As a lyric poet he stands at the end of the long tradition of *vers de société*, such as was written by the "mob of gentlemen who wrote with ease" at the courts of Charles and James. But Prior was no careless writer: his grace and colloquial simplicity of language are the effects of studied art. His finest pieces are his lyrics, not his official odes and panegyrics. Of his two philosophical poems it is not the serious *Solomon* in weighty language and heroic couplets that attracts readers today, but rather the skeptical and delightfully witty *Alma* (written during his arrest in 1715) in deft octosyllabic couplets and homely conversational language that suggest Swift at his best. William Cowper admired Prior's ability to "make verse speak the language of prose, without being prosaic—to marshal the words of it in such an order as they might naturally take in falling from the lips of an extemporary speaker, yet without meanness, harmoniously, elegantly, and without seeming to displace a syllable for the sake of the rhyme . . ."

No poems were more popular, in the seventeenth and eighteenth centuries, than those which praised the virtues of a modest, retired life, sequestered from the ambitions of city and court. According to Johnson, "Perhaps no composition in our language has been oftener perused than Pomfret's *Choice*" (1700), which chooses the Golden Mean: a small estate, old books and wines, a few friends, a prudent female companion, a peaceful death. Yet Prior, who knew well enough the disappointments of public life, also knew that simple country living did not guarantee virtue. *An Epitaph* satirizes not the quiet but the unexamined life. For an epigraph, Prior took a chorus from Seneca's *Thyestes*—"All I seek is to lie still"—to which we might add Tolstoy's judgment of Ivan Ilych, whose "life was most ordinary and most simple and therefore most terrible."

An Epitaph

Interred beneath this marble stone
Lie sauntering Jack and idle Joan.
While rolling threescore years and one
Did round this globe their courses run;
If human things went ill or well;   5
If changing empires rose or fell;
The morning passed, the evening came,
And found this couple still the same.
They walked and ate, good folks: what then?
Why then they walked and ate again.   10
They soundly slept the night away;
They did just nothing all the day;
And having buried children four,
Would not take pains to try for more.

Nor sister either had, nor brother: 15
They seemed just tallied for each other.
    Their moral and economy[1]
Most perfectly they made agree:
Each virtue kept its proper bound,
Nor trespassed on the other's ground.   20
Nor fame, nor censure they regarded:
They neither punished, nor rewarded.
He cared not what the footmen did;
Her maids she neither praised, nor chid:
So every servant took his course;   25
And bad at first, they all grew worse.
Slothful disorder filled his stable,
And sluttish plenty decked her table.
Their beer was strong; their wine was port;
Their meal was large; their grace was short.   30
They gave the poor the remnant-meat
Just when it grew not fit to eat.
    They paid the church and parish rate,[2]
And took, but read not the receipt;
For which they claimed their Sunday's due   35
Of slumbering in an upper pew.
    No man's defects sought they to know,
So never made themselves a foe.
No man's good deeds did they commend,
So never raised themselves a friend.   40
Nor cherished they relations poor:
That might decrease their present store;
Nor barn nor house did they repair:
That might oblige their future heir.
    They neither added, nor confounded;[3]   45
They neither wanted, nor abounded.
Each Christmas they accompts[4] did clear;
And wound their bottom[5] round the year.
Nor tear nor smile did they employ
At news of public grief or joy.   50
When bells were rung and bonfires made,
If asked, they ne'er denied their aid;
Their jug was to the ringers carried,
Whoever either died, or married.
Their billet[6] at the fire was found,   55
Whoever was deposed, or crowned.
    Nor good, nor bad, nor fools, nor wise;
They would not learn, nor could advise;
Without love, hatred, joy, or fear,

1. Morality and household management.
2. Tax.
3. Wasted.
4. Accounts.

5. Wound up their skein of thread; that is, they
set the year nicely to rights.
6. Firewood.

They led—a kind of—as it were;   60
Nor wished, nor cared, nor laughed, nor cried;
And so they lived; and so they died.

                                                        1718

A True Maid

"No, no; for my virginity,
    When I lose that," says Rose, "I'll die."
"Behind the elms, last night," cried Dick,
    "Rose, were you not extremely sick?"

                                                        1718

A Better Answer

To Cloe Jealous

Dear Cloe, how blubbered is that pretty face!
    Thy cheek all on fire, and thy hair all uncurled!
Prithee quit this caprice; and (as old Falstaff says)
    Let us e'en talk a little like folks of this world.[1]

How canst thou presume thou hast leave to destroy   5
    The beauties which Venus but lent to thy keeping?
Those looks were designed to inspire love and joy;
    More ord'nary eyes may serve people for weeping.

To be vexed at a trifle or two that I writ,
    Your judgment at once and my passion you wrong: 10
You take that for fact which will scarce be found wit:
    Od's life! must one swear to the truth of a song?

What I speak, my fair Cloe, and what I write, shows
    The difference there is betwixt nature and art;
I court others in verse, but I love thee in prose;   15
    And they have my whimsies, but thou hast my heart.

The god of us verse-men (you know, child) the Sun,
    How after his journeys he sets up his rest;
If at morning o'er earth 'tis his fancy to run,
    At night he reclines on his Thetis's breast.[2]   20

---

1. Cf. 2 Henry IV 5.3.101–2.
2. Apollo, god of poetry and of the sun, is said to recline at night on the breast of Thetis, one of the Nereids or sea spirits, because the sun seems to sink into the western ocean.

So when I am wearied with wandering all day,
    To thee, my delight, in the evening I come;
No matter what beauties I saw in my way—
    They were but my visits, but thou art my home.

Then finish, dear Cloe, this pastoral war;   25
    And let us like Horace and Lydia agree:[3]
For thou art a girl as much brighter than her,
    As he was a poet sublimer than me.

1718

3. In Horace, *Odes* 3.9, the poet, who has been dallying with a girl named Cloe, makes up with Lydia, his former love.

JOHN GAY
1685–1732

The career of John Gay encompasses most of the ways that a talented but indigent author of the early eighteenth century could try to make a living: publication, patronage, odd jobs at court, the theater. Having been well educated at school in Devon, he came to London at seventeen to try his luck as apprentice to a silk mercer. Five years later he became secretary to his friend Aaron Hill, who introduced him to the publishing world and literary circles. Eventually most of the leading authors in London adopted him as a favorite; with Pope, Swift, and Arbuthnot he helped found the Scriblerus Club, famous for its literary satires and practical jokes. Through the offices of friends like these he obtained the patrons and political appointments that supported him. The same Scriblerian influence may be discerned in his first successful poem, *The Shepherd's Week* (1714), a burlesque pastoral. Two years later a mock-georgic, *Trivia, or the Art of Walking the Streets of London*, showed that the town could be as rough as, and more corrupting than, the country. Gay's popularity and financial security, however, were confirmed only by later works: two sets of verse *Fables*, published in 1727 and 1738; and above all *The Beggar's Opera* (1728). This ballad-opera, suggested by Swift—"what think you of a Newgate pastoral, among the thieves and whores there?"—satirized political corruption and Italian opera; the vitality of its raffish characters, and of its theme that vice is the same in high places as in low, maintains its popularity.

Gay seldom seems to take his verse seriously, yet few poets have looked with deeper irony upon the social fabric; life, not as poets would gild it, but as it is. The playfulness of his mock forms and literary parodies, as in *The Birth of the Squire*, exposes the disparity between high poetic expectations and coarse human reality. The squire, expected to bring about a new Golden Age, will waste his life in hunting and drink. For all his lightness of touch, Gay views society with a clarity and a complexity that many greater poets might envy.

Pope's epitaph on Gay, inscribed in Westminster Abbey, begins this way:

Of manners gentle, of affections mild;
In wit, a man; simplicity, a child;
With native humor tempering virtuous rage,
Formed to delight at once and lash the age.

But Gay wrote an epitaph of his own.

Life is a jest, and all things show it;
I thought so once, but now I know it.

The Birth of the Squire. An Eclogue

In Imitation of the Pollio of Virgil[1]

Ye sylvan Muses, loftier strains recite,
Not all in shades and humble cots[2] delight.
Hark! the bells ring; along the distant grounds
The driving gales convey the swelling sounds;
Th' attentive swain, forgetful of his work,   5
With gaping wonder leans upon his fork.
What sudden news alarms the waking morn?
To the glad squire a hopeful heir is born.
Mourn, mourn, ye stags, and all ye beasts of chase,
This hour destruction brings on all your race.   10
See the pleased tenants duteous offerings bear,
Turkeys, and geese, and grocer's sweetest ware;
With the new health[3] the ponderous tankard flows,
And old October[4] reddens every nose.
Beagles and spaniels round his cradle stand,   15
Kiss his moist lip and gently lick his hand.
He joys to hear the shrill horn's echoing sounds,
And learns to lisp the names of all the hounds.
With frothy ale to make his cup o'erflow,
Barley shall in paternal acres grow;   20
The bee shall sip the fragrant dew from flowers,
To give metheglin[5] for his morning hours;
For him the clustering hop shall climb the poles,
And his own orchard sparkle in his bowls.

His sire's exploits he now with wonder hears,   25
The monstrous tales indulge his greedy ears:
How when youth strung his nerves and warmed his veins,
He rode, the mighty Nimrod[6] of the plains.

---

1. Virgil's famous Fourth Eclogue (dedicated to
Consul Pollio) foretells the birth of a marvelous
child, the hope of Rome. In the Middle Ages it
was assumed that the poet had foreseen the birth
of Christ, and he became known as a great magician.

2. Cottages.
3. Toast.
4. Ale.
5. Mead (made from honey).
6. A great hunter (*Genesis* 10.9).

He leads the staring infant through the hall,
Points out the horny spoils that grace the wall;   30
Tells how this stag through three whole counties fled,
What rivers swam, where bayed, and where he bled.
Now he the wonders of the fox repeats,
Describes the desperate chase, and all his cheats;
How in one day, beneath his furious speed,   35
He tired seven coursers of the fleetest breed;
How high the pale he leapt, how wide the ditch,
When the hound tore the haunches of the witch![7]
These stories, which descend from son to son,
The forward boy shall one day make his own.   40

    Ah, too fond mother, think the time draws nigh
That calls the darling from thy tender eye;
How shall his spirit brook the rigid rules,
And the long tyranny of grammar schools?
Let younger brother o'er dull authors plod,   45
Lashed into Latin by the tingling rod;
No, let him never feel that smart disgrace:
Why should he wiser prove than all his race?

    When ripening youth with down o'ershades his chin,
And every female eye incites to sin,   50
The milkmaid (thoughtless of her future shame)
With smacking lip shall raise his guilty flame;
The dairy, barn, the hayloft, and the grove
Shall oft be conscious of their stolen love.
But think, Priscilla, on that dreadful time   55
When pangs and watery qualms shall own[8] thy crime;
How wilt thou tremble when thy nipple's pressed
To see the white drops bathe thy swelling breast!
Nine moons shall publicly divulge her shame,
And the young squire forestall a father's name.   60

    When twice twelve times the reaper's sweeping hand
With leveled harvests has bestrewn the land,
On famed St. Hubert's feast[9] his winding horn
Shall cheer the joyful hound and wake the morn.
This memorable day his eager speed   65
Shall urge with bloody heel the rising steed.
O check the foamy bit, nor tempt thy fate;
Think on the murders of a five-bar gate!
Yet prodigal of life, the leap he tries,
Low in the dust his groveling honor lies,   70

---

7. "The most common accident to sportsmen; to
hunt a witch in the shape of a hare" [Gay's note].

8. Confess.
9. November 3, which opens the hunting season.

Headlong he falls, and on the rugged stone
Distorts[1] his neck, and cracks the collarbone.
O venturous youth, thy thirst of game allay;
May'st thou survive the perils of this day!
He shall survive; and in late years be sent   75
To snore away debates in Parliament.

The time shall come, when his more solid sense
With nod important shall the laws dispense;
A justice, with grave justices shall sit,
He praise their wisdom, they admire his wit.   80
No greyhound shall attend the tenant's pace,
No rusty gun the farmer's chimney grace;
Salmons shall leave their covers void of fear,
Nor dread the thievish net or triple spear;
Poachers shall tremble at his awful name,   85
Whom vengeance now o'ertakes for murdered game.

Assist me, Bacchus, and ye drunken powers,
To sing his friendships and his midnight hours!

Why dost thou glory in thy strength of beer,
Firm-corked and mellowed till the twentieth year;   90
Brewed or when Phoebus warms the fleecy sign
Or when his languid rays in Scorpio shine?[2]
Think on the mischiefs which from hence have sprung!
It arms with curses dire the wrathful tongue;
Foul scandal to the lying lip affords,   95
And prompts the memory with injurious words.
O where is wisdom, when by this o'erpowered?
The state is censured, and the maid deflowered!
And wilt thou still, O squire, brew ale so strong?
Hear then the dictates of prophetic song.   100

Methinks I see him in his hall appear,
Where the long table floats in clammy beer,
'Midst mugs and glasses shattered o'er the floor,
Dead-drunk, his servile crew supinely snore;
Triumphant, o'er the prostrate brutes he stands,   105
The mighty bumper trembles in his hands;
Boldly he drinks, and like his glorious sires,
In copious gulps of potent ale expires.

1720

1. Wrenches.   2. Either in spring (Aries) or fall (Scorpio).

Songs from *The Beggar's Opera*[1]

Were I Laid on Greenland's Coast

(AIR: OVER THE HILLS AND FAR AWAY)

MACHEATH.	Were I laid on Greenland's coast,
	And in my arms embraced my lass;
	Warm amidst eternal frost,
	Too soon the half year's night would pass.
POLLY.	Were I sold on Indian soil, 5
	Soon as the burning day was closed
	I could mock the sultry toil,
	When on my charmer's breast reposed.
MACHEATH.	And I would love you all the day,
POLLY.	Every night would kiss and play, 10
MACHEATH.	If with me you'd fondly stray
POLLY.	Over the hills and far away.

If the Heart of a Man Is Depressed with Cares

(AIR: WOULD YOU HAVE A YOUNG VIRGIN, &C.)

MACHEATH.	If the heart of a man is depressed with cares,
	The mist is dispelled when a woman appears;
	Like the notes of a fiddle, she sweetly, sweetly
	Raises the spirits, and charms our ears,
	Roses and lilies her cheeks disclose, 5
	But her ripe lips are more sweet than those.
	Press her,
	Caress her
	With blisses,
	Her kisses 10
	Dissolve us in pleasure, and soft repose.

Since Laws Were Made for Every Degree

(AIR: GREEN SLEEVES)

MACHEATH.	Since laws were made for every degree,[2]
	To curb vice in others, as well as me,
	I wonder we han't better company
	Upon Tyburn tree![3]

---

1. In the first act of *The Beggar's Opera*, the highwayman Macheath ("son of the heath") exchanges vows with Polly, his new wife. He sings the next song in a tavern while waiting for whores. Eventually he is caught and sentenced to hang, but is reprieved at the last minute. The lyrics were set to the tunes of folk songs, whose titles are given here in parentheses.
2. Rank in society.
3. Gibbet, where criminals were executed in London.

But gold from law can take out the sting;   5
   And if rich men like us were to swing,
     'Twould thin the land, such numbers to string
      Upon Tyburn tree!

1728

Recitativo and Air from *Acis and Galatea*[1]

POLYPHEMUS. I rage, I melt, I burn,
     The feeble god[2] has stabbed me to the heart.
     Thou trusty pine, prop of my godlike steps,
     I lay thee by.
     Bring me a hundred reeds of decent growth,   5
     To make a pipe[3] for my capacious mouth;
     In soft enchanting accents let me breathe
     Sweet Galatea's beauty, and my love.

Air.

     O ruddier than the cherry!
     O sweeter than the berry!   10
      O nymph, more bright
      Than moonshine night!
     Like kidlings blithe and merry.

     Ripe as the melting cluster,[4]
     No lily has such luster;   15
      Yet hard to tame
      As raging flame,
     And fierce as storms that bluster.

     O ruddier, &c.

1732

1. In this scene from Gay's pastoral opera, with music by Handel, the monstrous giant Polyphemus expresses his yearning for the shepherdess Galatea. A recitative, in a style midway between speaking and singing, serves as prologue to the air or tune.
2. Cupid.
3. Panpipe or set of flutes.
4. Grapes ready to "melt in the mouth."

LADY MARY WORTLEY MONTAGU
1689–1762

In her early teens Lady Mary Pierrepont did something that well-bred young women were not supposed to do: she secretly taught herself Latin. The act reveals many of the traits that would also characterize her as a mature woman: curiosity, love of learning, intelligence, ambition, independence of mind. The eldest daughter of a wealthy Whig peer (he later became marquess of Dorchester), she grew up amid a glittering London circle that included Addison, Steele, Congreve, and later Pope and Gay. But she was not content to live the life of a dutiful aristocratic daughter. Unlike most women in her time, she married for love; and when her husband, Edward Wortley Montagu, was appointed ambassador to Constantinople in 1716, she took advantage of the opportunity by traveling through Europe, studying the language and customs of Turkey, and even visiting Turkish harems. She also pioneered in introducing smallpox inoculation to England (her own son and daughter were among the first to be inoculated). Returning home in 1718, she spent unhappy years that included bitter political quarrels with Pope and the gradual failure of her marriage. Then, in middle age, she fell in love with a young Italian author, Francesco Algarotti. In 1739 she followed him to Italy; but the passion that had kindled in their letters was soon quenched at their meeting. The rest of her life was passed abroad, in Avignon, Brescia, and Venice. She died soon after her return to London in 1762.

As an author Lady Mary is remembered chiefly for her letters. In a century that included most of the great letter writers in English—Gray, Horace Walpole, Cowper, and others—she is one of the greatest. "What fire, what ease, what knowledge of Europe and Asia!" Edward Gibbon commented when her Turkish correspondence was published. But from an early age she had also tried her hand at other literary forms: essays, poems, even a translated play. In her own time she was especially admired as a poet. When Pope, after their quarrel, give her the name of "Sappho" (see *Epistle II. To a Lady*, lines 24–26), he was doubtless betraying the nervousness that most men felt in the presence of intelligent women (the Greek poet Sappho, after all, preferred women to men); yet he was also associating her with the classic author of lyric verse. Lady Mary's verse, though often casual, reveals the mind of a woman who is not willing to accept the stereotypes imposed on her by men. Like her friend Mary Astell, Lady Mary puts her trust in education and reason, not in the opinions of others, and she always insists on preserving her freedom of choice. A woman, her poems suggest, need not defer to a man who is less than her equal; she must look to her own satisfaction before she looks to his; and she always has the right to say no. The verse demands respect by virtue of its sexual candor and punishing wit. Like Lady Mary herself, it is never dull; and at its best it places her in that ideal community defined by E. M. Forster: "Not an aristocracy of power, based upon rank and influence, but an aristocracy of the sensitive, the considerate, and the plucky."

The Lover: A Ballad

At length, by so much importunity pressed,
Take, (Molly),[1] at once, the inside of my breast;
This stupid indifference so often you blame

---

1. Molly Skerrett, a friend of Lady Mary, was the mistress of Sir Robert Walpole. The ideal "lover" of the title, however, is not to be identified with any particular person.

Is not owing to nature, to fear, or to shame;
I am not as cold as a Virgin in lead,[2]   5
Nor is Sunday's sermon so strong in my head;
I know but too well how time flies along,
That we live but few years and yet fewer are young.

But I hate to be cheated, and never will buy
Long years of repentance for moments of joy.   10
Oh was there a man (but where shall I find
Good sense and good nature so equally joined?)
Would value his pleasure, contribute to mine,
Not meanly would boast, nor lewdly design,[3]
Not over severe, yet not stupidly vain,   15
For I would have the power though not give the pain;

No pedant yet learnèd, not rakehelly gay
Or laughing because he has nothing to say,
To all my whole sex obliging and free,
Yet never be fond of any but me;   20
In public preserve the decorums are just,
And show in his eyes he is true to his trust,
Then rarely approach, and respectfully bow,
Yet not fulsomely pert, nor yet foppishly low.

But when the long hours of public are past   25
And we meet with champagne and a chicken at last,
May every fond pleasure that hour endear,
Be banished afar both discretion and fear,
Forgetting or scorning the airs of the crowd
He may cease to be formal, and I to be proud,   30
Till lost in the joy we confess that we live,
And he may be rude, and yet I may forgive.

And that my delight may be solidly fixed,
Let the friend and the lover be handsomely mixed,
In whose tender bosom my soul might confide,   35
Whose kindness can sooth me, whose counsel could guide.
From such a dear lover as here I describe
No danger should fright me, no millions should bribe;
But till this astonishing creature I know,
As I long have lived chaste, I will keep myself so.   40

I never will share with the wanton coquette,
Or be caught by a vain affectation of wit.
The toasters and songsters may try all their art
But never shall enter the pass of my heart.

2. I.e., an image of the Virgin Mary, either as a   in lead.
leaden statue or as a stained glass window framed   3. Plot.

I loathe the lewd rake, the dressed fopling despise;   45
Before such pursuers the nice[4] virgin flies;
And as Ovid has sweetly in parables told
We harden like trees, and like rivers are cold.[5]

1747

Epistle from Mrs. Yonge to Her Husband[1]

Think not this paper comes with vain pretense
To move your pity, or to mourn th' offense.
Too well I know that hard obdurate heart;
No softening mercy there will take my part,
Nor can a woman's arguments prevail,   5
When even your patron's wise example fails.[2]
But this last privilege I still retain;
Th' oppressed and injured always may complain.
   Too, too severely laws of honor bind
The weak submissive sex of womankind.   10
If sighs have gained or force compelled our hand,
Deceived by art, or urged by stern command,
Whatever motive binds the fatal tie,
The judging world expects our constancy.
   Just heaven! (for sure in heaven does justice reign,   15
Though tricks below that sacred name profane)
To you appealing I submit my cause,
Nor fear a judgment from impartial laws.
All bargains but conditional[3] are made;
The purchase void, the creditor unpaid;   20
Defrauded servants are from service free;
A wounded slave regains his liberty.
For wives ill used no remedy remains,
To daily racks condemned, and to eternal chains.
   From whence is this unjust distinction grown?   25
Are we not formed with passions like your own?

---

4. Fastidious.
5. In Ovid's *Metamorphoses* Daphne, to escape
Apollo, was turned into a laurel; and Arethusa,
escaping Alpheus, became a fountain.
1. In 1724 the notorious libertine William Yonge,
separated from his wife Mary, discovered that she
(like him) had committed adultery. He sued her
lover, Colonel Norton, for damages and collected
£1,500. Later that year, according to the law of the
time, he petitioned the Houses of Parliament for a
divorce. The case was tried in public, Mrs. Yonge's
love letters were read aloud, and two men testified
that they had found her and Norton "together in
naked bed." Yonge was granted the divorce, his
wife's dowry, and the greater part of her fortune.
   Though the *Epistle* is obviously based on this
sensational affair, it is also a work of imagination.
Like Pope's *Eloisa to Abelard*—to which the author

himself called Lady Mary's attention—it takes the
form of a heroic epistle, the passionate outcry of
an abandoned woman. The poet, entering into the
feelings of Mrs. Yonge, justifies her conduct with
reasons both of the heart and head. The objects of
her attack include the institution of marriage, which
binds wives in "eternal chains"; the double standard of morality, which requires chastity from
women but not men; the hypocrisy of society, which
condemns the very behavior it secretly lusts after;
and the craven greed and cruelty of the husband
himself. But eighteenth-century women seldom
dared to speak like this in public, and the *Epistle*
was not published until the 1970s.
2. Sir Robert Walpole, Yonge's friend at court,
was rumored to tolerate his own wife's infidelities.
3. Only conditionally.

Nature with equal fire our souls endued,
Our minds as haughty, and as warm our blood;
O'er the wide world your pleasures you pursue,
The change is justified by something new;   30
But we must sigh in silence—and be true.
Our sex's weakness you expose and blame
(Of every prattling fop the common theme),
Yet from this weakness you suppose is due
Sublimer virtue than your Cato[4] knew.   35
Had heaven designed us trials so severe,
It would have formed our tempers then to bear.
    And I have borne (oh what have I not borne!)
The pang of jealousy, the insults of scorn.
Wearied at length, I from your sight remove,   40
And place my future hopes in secret love.
In the gay bloom of glowing youth retired,
I quit the woman's joy to be admired,
With that small pension your hard heart allows,
Renounce your fortune, and release your vows.   45
To custom (though unjust) so much is due;
I hide my frailty from the public view.
My conscience clear, yet sensible of shame,
My life I hazard, to preserve my fame.
And I prefer this low inglorious state   50
To vile dependence on the thing I hate—
But you pursue me to this last retreat.
Dragged into light, my tender crime is shown
And every circumstance of fondness known.
Beneath the shelter of the law you stand,   55
And urge my ruin with a cruel hand,
While to my fault thus rigidly severe,
Tamely submissive to the man you fear.[5]
    This wretched outcast, this abandoned wife,
Has yet this joy to sweeten shameful life: 60
By your mean conduct, infamously loose,
You are at once my accuser and excuse.
Let me be damned by the censorious prude
(Stupidly dull, or spiritually lewd),
My hapless case will surely pity find   65
From every just and reasonable mind.
When to the final sentence I submit,
The lips condemn me, but their souls acquit.
    No more my husband, to your pleasures go,
The sweets of your recovered freedom know.   70
Go: court the brittle friendship of the great,
Smile at his board,[6] or at his levee wait;

4. The asceticism and self-discipline of the Roman
statesman Cato had been emphasized in Addison's
famous tragedy *Cato* (1713).
5. I.e., Walpole. Lady Mary suggests that the whole

political establishment of England takes sides against
Mrs. Yonge.
6. Dining table; "levee": morning reception of
visitors.

And when dismissed, to madam's toilet fly,[7]
More than her chambermaids, or glasses, lie,
Tell her how young she looks, how heavenly fair,   75
Admire the lilies and the roses there.
Your high ambition may be gratified,
Some cousin of her own be made your bride,
And you the father of a glorious race
Endowed with Ch——l's strength and Low——r's face.[8]   80

1724   1972

7. It was fashionable for women like Lady Walpole to receive visitors during the last stages of dressing (their "toilet"). "Glasses": mirrors.
8. General Churchill was rumored to have had an affair with Lady Walpole; Antony Lowther was a notorious gallant. The author implies that Yonge's next wife may be as untrue as his first. Mrs. Yonge remarried immediately after her divorce; five years later Yonge himself (whose divorce had made him rich) married the daughter of a baron.

JONATHAN SWIFT
1667–1745

1704:   A *Tale of a Tub* and *The Battle of the Books*.
1710–14:   Alignment with Tories; political writings in defense of
             the Tory ministry.
1713:   Made Dean of St. Patrick's Cathedral, Dublin.
1726:   Publication of *Gulliver's Travels*.

Swift—a posthumous child—was born of English parents in Dublin. Through the generosity of an uncle he was educated at Kilkenny School and Trinity College, Dublin; but before he could fix on a career, the troubles that followed upon James II's abdication and his subsequent invasion of Ireland drove him along with other Anglo-Irish to England. Between 1689 and 1699 he was more or less continuously a member of the household of his kinsman Sir William Temple, an urbane, civilized man, a retired diplomat, and a friend of King William. During these years Swift read widely; rather reluctantly decided on the church as a career and so took orders; and discovered his astonishing gifts as a satirist. About 1696–97 he wrote his powerful satires on corruptions in religion and learning, *A Tale of a Tub* and *The Battle of the Books*, which were published in 1704 and reached their final form only in the fifth edition of 1710. These were the years in which he slowly came to maturity. When at the age of thirty-two, he returned to Ireland as chaplain to the Lord Justice, the earl of Berkeley, he had a clear sense of his genius.

For the rest of his life Swift devoted his talents to politics and religion—not clearly separated at the time—and most of his works in prose were written to further a specific cause. As a clergyman, a spirited controversialist, and a devoted supporter of the Anglican Church as an institution no less important than the Crown itself, he was hostile to all who seemed to threaten his Church—Deists, freethinkers, Roman Catholics, Nonconformists, or merely Whig politicians. In 1710 he abandoned his old party, the Whig, because he disapproved of its indifference to the welfare of the Anglican Church in Ireland and of its desire to repeal the Test Act, which required all holders of offices of state to take the Sacrament according to the Anglican rites, thus excluding Roman Catholics and Dissenters. Welcomed by the Tories, he became the most brilliant political journalist of the day, serving the government of Oxford and Bolingbroke as editor of the party organ, the *Examiner,* and as author of its most powerful articles, as well as writing longer pamphlets in support of important policies, such as that favoring the Peace of Utrecht (1713). He was greatly valued by the two ministers, who admitted him to social intimacy, though never to their counsels. The reward of his services was not the English bishopric which he had a right to expect, but the deanship of St. Patrick's Cathedral in Dublin, which came to him in 1713, a year before the death of Queen Anne and the fall of the Tories put an end to all his hopes of preferment in England.

In Ireland, where he lived unwillingly, he became not only an efficient ecclesiastical administrator, but also, in 1724, the leader of Irish resistance to English oppression. Under the pseudonym of "M. B. Drapier," he published the famous series of public letters that aroused the country to refuse to accept £100,000 in new copper coins (minted in England by William Wood, who had obtained his patent through court corruption) which, it was feared, would further debase the coinage of the already poverty-stricken kingdom. Although his authorship of the letters was known to all Dublin, no one could be found to earn the £300 offered by the government for information as to the identity of the Drapier. Swift is still venerated in Ireland as a national hero. He earned the right to refer to himself in the epitaph that he wrote for his tomb as a vigorous defender of liberty.

His last years were less happy. Swift had suffered most of his adult life from what we now recognize as Ménière's syndrome, which affects the inner ear, causing dizziness, nausea, and deafness. After 1739, when he was seventy-two years old, his infirmities cut him off from his duties as dean, and from then on his social life dwindled. In 1742 guardians were appointed to administer his affairs, and his last three years were spent in gloom and lethargy. But this dark ending should not put his earlier life, so full of energy and humor, into a shadow. The writer of the satires was a man in full control of great intellectual powers.

He also had a gift for friendship. Swift was admired and loved by many of the distinguished men of his time. His friendships with Addison, Pope, Arbuthnot, Gay, Prior, Oxford, Bolingbroke, not to mention those with his less brilliant but amiable Irish circle, bear witness to his moral integrity and social charm. Nor was he, despite some of his writings, indifferent to women. Esther Johnson (Swift's "Stella") was the daughter of Temple's steward, and when Swift first knew her she was little more than a child. He educated her, formed her character, and came to love her as he was to love no other person. After Temple's death she moved to Dublin, where she and Swift met constantly, but never alone. To her he wrote the famous journal-letters, later published (1766) as *The Journal to Stella,* during his four-year residence in London when he was working with the Tories; and to her he wrote charming poems. Whether they were secretly married or whether they never married—and in either case why—has been often debated. A marriage of any sort seems most unlikely; and however perplexing their relationship was to others, it was obviously satisfying to each of them. Not even the violent passion that Swift awakened, no doubt unwittingly, in a much younger woman, Hester Vanhomrigh (pronounced Van-úm-mer-y), her pleadings and reproaches and early death, could unsettle his devotion to Stella. An enigmatic account of his relations with "Vanessa," as he called Vanhomrigh, is given in his poem *Cadenus and Vanessa*.

For all his involvement in public affairs, Swift seems to stand apart from his contemporaries—a striking figure even among the statesmen of the time, a man who towered above other writers by reason of his imagination, mordant wit, and emotional intensity. He has been called a misanthrope, a hater of mankind; and *Gulliver's Travels* has been considered an expression of savage misanthropy. It is true that Swift proclaimed himself a misanthrope in a letter to Pope, declaring that though he loved individuals, he hated "that animal called man" in general, and offering a new definition of the species as not *animal rationale* ("a rational animal"), but as merely *animal rationis capax* ("an animal *capable* of reason"). This, he declared, is the "great foundation" upon which his "misanthropy" was erected. Swift was stating not his hatred of his fellow creatures, but his antagonism to the current optimistic view that human nature is essentially good. To the "philanthropic" flattery that sentimentalism and Deistic rationalism were paying to human nature, Swift opposed a more ancient and plausible view: that human nature is deeply and permanently flawed, and that we can do nothing with or for the human race until we recognize its moral and intellectual limitations. In his epitaph he spoke of the "fierce indignation" which had torn his heart, an indignation that found superb expression in his greatest satires. It was provoked by the constant spectacle of creatures capable of reason, and therefore of reasonable conduct, steadfastly refusing to live up to their capabilities.

Swift is one of our greatest writers of prose. He defined a good style as "proper words in proper places," a more complex and difficult saying than at first appears. Clear, simple, concrete diction, uncomplicated syntax, economy and conciseness of language mark all of his writings. His is a style that shuns ornaments and singularity of all kinds, a style that grows more tense and controlled the more fierce the indignation that it is called upon to express. The virtues of his prose are those of his poetry, which shocks us with its hard look at the facts of life and the body. It is unpoetic poetry, devoid of, indeed as often as not mocking at, inspiration, romantic love, cosmetic beauty, easily assumed literary attitudes, and conventional poetic language. Like the prose it is predominantly satiric in purpose, but not without its moments of comedy and light-heartedness, though written most often not so much to divert as to reform the reader.

A Description of a City Shower

Careful observers may foretell the hour
(By sure prognostics) when to dread a shower:
While rain depends,[1] the pensive cat gives o'er
Her frolics, and pursues her tail no more.

---

1. Impends, is imminent. An example of elevated diction used frequently throughout the poem in order to gain a mock dignity, comically inappropriate to the homely and realistic subject.

Returning home at night, you'll find the sink[2]   5
Strike your offended sense with double stink.
If you be wise, then go not far to dine;
You'll spend in coach hire more than save in wine.
A coming shower your shooting corns presage,
Old achés throb, your hollow tooth will rage.   10
Sauntering in coffeehouse is Dulman[3] seen;
He damns the climate and complains of spleen.
    Meanwhile the South, rising with dabbled wings,
A sable cloud athwart the welkin flings,
That swilled more liquor than it could contain,   15
And, like a drunkard, gives it up again.
Brisk Susan whips her linen from the rope,
While the first drizzling shower is borne aslope:
Such is that sprinkling which some careless quean[4]
Flirts on you from her mop, but not so clean: 20
You fly, invoke the gods; then turning, stop
To rail; she singing, still whirls on her mop.
Not yet the dust had shunned the unequal strife,
But, aided by the wind, fought still for life,
And wafted with its foe by violent gust,   25
'Twas doubtful which was rain and which was dust.
Ah! where must needy poet seek for aid,
When dust and rain at once his coat invade?
Sole coat, where dust cemented by the rain
Erects the nap, and leaves a mingled stain.   30
    Now in contiguous drops the flood comes down,
Threatening with deluge this devoted town.
To shops in crowds the daggled[5] females fly,
Pretend to cheapen goods, but nothing buy.
The Templar[6] spruce, while every spout's abroach,   35
Stays till 'tis fair, yet seems to call a coach.
The tucked-up sempstress walks with hasty strides,
While streams run down her oiled umbrella's sides.
Here various kinds, by various fortunes led,
Commence acquaintance underneath a shed.   40
Triumphant Tories and desponding Whigs
Forget their feuds,[7] and join to save their wigs.
Boxed in a chair[8] the beau impatient sits,
While spouts run clattering o'er the roof by fits,
And ever and anon with frightful din   45

2. Sewer.
3. A type name (from "dull man"), like Congreve's "Petulant" or "Witwoud." It was commonly believed at this time that the Englishman's tendency to melancholy ("the spleen") was attributable to the rainy climate.
4. Wench, slut.
5. Spattered with mud. "To cheapen": to bargain for.
6. A young man engaged in studying law. In the literature of the period the Templar is usually depicted as neglecting his professional studies for the sake of dissipation and the pursuit of literature. Cf. the Member of the Inner Temple in *Spectator* 2. "Abroach": pouring out water.
7. The Whig ministry had just fallen and the Tories, led by Harley and St. John, were forming the government with which Swift was to be closely associated until the death of the queen in 1714.
8. Sedan chair.

The leather sounds;[9] he trembles from within.
So when Troy chairmen bore the wooden steed,
Pregnant with Greeks impatient to be freed
(Those bully Greeks, who, as the moderns do,
Instead of paying chairmen, run them through),[1]   50
Laocoön struck the outside with his spear,
And each imprisoned hero quaked for fear.[2]
      Now from all parts the swelling kennels[3] flow,
And bear their trophies with them as they go:
Filth of all hues and odors seem to tell   55
What street they sailed from, by their sight and smell.
They, as each torrent drives with rapid force,
From Smithfield or St. Pulchre's shape their course,
And in huge confluence joined at Snow Hill ridge,
Fall from the conduit prone to Holborn Bridge.[4]   60
Sweepings from butchers' stalls, dung, guts, and blood, ⎫
Drowned puppies, stinking sprats,[5] all drenched in mud, ⎬
Dead cats, and turnip tops, come tumbling down the flood.[6] ⎭

1710

Stella's Birthday, 1721[1]

All travelers at first incline
Where'er they see the fairest sign,
And if they find the chambers neat,
And like the liquor and the meat,[2]
Will call again and recommend   5
The Angel Inn to every friend:
And though the painting grows decayed
The house will never lose its trade;
Nay, though the treacherous rascal Thomas
Hangs a new Angel two doors from us[3]   10
As fine as daubers' hands can make it
In hopes that strangers may mistake it,
They think it both a shame and sin

9. The roof of the sedan chair was made of leather.
1. Run them through with their swords. The bully, always prone to violence, was a familiar figure in London streets and places of amusement.
2. *Aeneid* 2.40–53.
3. The open gutters in the middle of the street.
4. An accurate description of the drainage system of this part of London—the eastern edge of Holborn and West Smithfield, which lie outside the old walls west and east of Newgate. The great cattle and sheep markets were in Smithfield. The church of St. Sepulchre ("St. Pulchre's") stood opposite Newgate Prison. Holborn Conduit was at the foot of Snow Hill. It drained into Fleet Ditch, an evil-smelling open sewer, at Holborn Bridge.
5. Small herrings.

6. In Falkner's edition of Swift's *Works* (Dublin, 1735) a note almost certainly suggested by Swift points to the concluding triplet, with its resonant final alexandrine, as a burlesque of a mannerism of Dryden and other Restoration poets, and claims that Swift's ridicule banished the triplet from contemporary poetry.
1. This is the second of Swift's seven birthday poems to "Stella," his dear friend Esther Johnson (see the introduction).
2. The beverages and the food.
3. Thomas Sheridan and his wife Elizabeth (the "new Angel") had recently befriended Swift and often entertained him at their home. Sheridan (1687–1738) was a schoolmaster and grandfather of the playwright Richard Brinsley Sheridan.

To quit the true old Angel Inn.
   Now, this is Stella's case in fact;   15
An angel's face, a little cracked
(Could poets or could painters fix
How angels look at thirty-six);[4]
This drew us in at first to find
In such a form an angel's mind,   20
And every virtue now supplies[5]
The fainting rays of Stella's eyes.
See, at her levee[6] crowding swains
Whom Stella freely entertains
With breeding, humor, wit, and sense,   25
And puts them to so small expense,
Their minds so plentifully fills,
And makes such reasonable bills,
So little gets for what she gives,
We really wonder how she lives;   30
And, had her stock been less, no doubt
She must have long ago run out.
   Then, who can think we'll quit the place
When Doll hangs out a newer face,
Or stop and light at Cloe's head[7]   35
With scraps and leavings to be fed.
   Then, Cloe, still go on to prate
Of thirty-six, and thirty-eight;
Pursue thy trade of scandal picking,
Thy hints that Stella is no chicken,   40
Your innuendos when you tell us
That Stella loves to talk with fellows;
But let me warn thee to believe
A truth for which thy soul should grieve:
That, should you live to see the day   45
When Stella's locks must all be gray,
When age must print a furrowed trace
On every feature of her face;
Though you and all your senseless tribe
Could art or time or nature bribe   50
To make you look like beauty's queen
And hold forever at fifteen,
No bloom of youth can ever blind
The cracks and wrinkles of your mind;
All men of sense will pass your door   55
And crowd to Stella's at fourscore.[8]

1721   1727

4. Though Stella admitted to 36, Swift knew that her real age was 40.
5. Compensates for.
6. Reception of visitors.
7. The picture of a head was often the sign of an inn.

8. I.e., 80. Later that year Stella replied with a poem on Swift's birthday, acknowledging his good influence: "You taught how I might youth prolong / By knowing what was right and wrong; . . . / Your lectures could my fancy fix, / And I can please at thirty-six."

Verses on the Death of Dr. Swift

Occasioned by Reading a Maxim in Rochefoucauld[1]

Dans l'adversité de nos meilleurs amis nous trouvons toujours quelque chose, qui ne nous déplaît pas.[2]

As Rochefoucauld his maxims drew
From nature, I believe 'em true:
They argue no corrupted mind
In him; the fault is in mankind.
    This maxim more than all the rest   5
Is thought too base for human breast:
"In all distresses of our friends
We first consult our private ends,
While Nature, kindly bent to ease us,
Points out some circumstance to please us."   10
    If this perhaps your patience move,[3]
Let reason and experience prove.
    We all behold with envious eyes
Our equal raised above our size.
Who would not at a crowded show   15
Stand high himself, keep others low?
I love my friend as well as you,
But why should he obstruct my view?
Then let me have the higher post;
Suppose it but an inch at most.   20
    If in a battle you should find
One, whom you love of all mankind,
Had some heroic action done,
A champion killed, or trophy won;
Rather than thus be overtopped,   25
Would you not wish his laurels cropped?
    Dear honest Ned is in the gout,
Lies racked with pain, and you without:
How patiently you hear him groan!
How glad the case is not your own!   30
    What poet would not grieve to see
His brethren write as well as he?
But rather than they should excel,
He'd wish his rivals all in hell.
    Her end when Emulation misses,   35
She turns to envy, stings, and hisses:
The strongest friendship yields to pride,

---

1. François de la Rochefoucauld (1613–1680), writer of witty, cynical maxims. Writing to Pope (Nov. 26, 1725), Swift, opposing the optimistic philosophy that Pope and Bolingbroke were at that time developing, professed to have founded his whole character on these maxims.
2. "In the misfortune of our best friends we always find something that does not displease us."
3. Should agitate.

Unless the odds be on our side.
    Vain humankind! fantastic race!
Thy various follies who can trace?   40
Self-love, ambition, envy, pride,
Their empire in our hearts divide,
Give others riches, power, and station;
'Tis all on me an usurpation;
I have no title to aspire,   45
Yet, when you sink, I seem the higher.
In Pope I cannot read a line,
But with a sigh I wish it mine:
When he can in one couplet fix
More sense than I can do in six,   50
It gives me such a jealous fit,
I cry, "Pox take him and his wit!"
    I grieve to be outdone by Gay[4]
In my own humorous biting way.
Arbuthnot is no more my friend,   55
Who dares to irony pretend,
Which I was born to introduce,
Refined it first, and showed its use.
St. John,[5] as well as Pulteney, knows
That I had some repute for prose;   60
And, till they drove me out of date,
Could maul a minister of state.
If they have mortified my pride,
And made me throw my pen aside;
If with such talents Heaven hath blessed 'em,   65
Have I not reason to detest 'em?
    To all my foes, dear Fortune, send
Thy gifts, but never to my friend:
I tamely can endure the first,
But this with envy makes me burst.   70
    Thus much may serve by way of proem;
Proceed we therefore to our poem.
    The time is not remote, when I
Must by the course of nature die;
When, I foresee, my special friends   75
Will try to find their private ends:
Though it is hardly understood
Which way my death can do them good;
Yet thus, methinks, I hear 'em speak:

---

4. John Gay (1685–1732), author of the famous
Beggar's Opera (1728), intimate friend of Swift and
Pope. His *Trivia, or the Art of Walking the Streets
of London* (1716) owes something to Swift's *City
Shower*. Dr. John Arbuthnot, physician and wit,
friend of Swift and Pope. See Pope's *Epistle to Dr.
Arbuthnot*.
5. Henry St. John, Lord Bolingbroke (see note,
Pope's *Essay on Man*. 1.1), though debarred from

the House of Lords and from public office, had
become the center of a group of Tories and discontented young Whigs (of whom William Pulteney
was one) who united in opposing Sir Robert Walpole, the chief minister. They published a political
periodical, the *Craftsman*, thus rivaling Swift in
his role of political pamphleteer and enemy of Sir
Robert.

"See how the Dean begins to break!   80
Poor gentleman! he droops apace!
You plainly find it in his face.
That old vertigo[6] in his head
Will never leave him till he's dead.
Besides, his memory decays;   85
He recollects not what he says;
He cannot call his friends to mind;
Forgets the place where last he dined;
Plies you with stories o'er and o'er,
He told them fifty times before.   90
How does he fancy we can sit
To hear his out-of-fashion wit?
But he takes up with younger folks,
Who for his wine will bear his jokes.
Faith, he must make his stories shorter,   95
Or change his comrades once a quarter;
In half the time he talks them round,
There must another set be found.
       "For poetry, he's past his prime;
He takes an hour to find a rhyme;   100
His fire is out, his wit decayed,
His fancy sunk, his Muse a jade.[7]
I'd have him throw away his pen—
But there's no talking to some men."
       And then their tenderness appears   105
By adding largely to my years:
"He's older than he would be reckoned,
And well remembers Charles the Second.
He hardly drinks a pint of wine;
And that, I doubt, is no good sign.   110
His stomach, too, begins to fail;
Last year we thought him strong and hale;
But now he's quite another thing;
I wish he may hold out till spring."
They hug themselves, and reason thus: 115
"It is not yet so bad with us."
       In such a case they talk in tropes,[8]
And by their fears express their hopes.
Some great misfortune to portend
No enemy can match a friend.   120
With all the kindness they profess,
The merit of a lucky guess
(When daily how-d'ye's come of course,
And servants answer, "Worse and worse!")
Would please 'em better, than to tell   125

6. Johnson in his *Dictionary* authorizes Swift's   winged horse of Greek mythology, emblem of poetic
pronounciation: *ver-ti-go*.   inspiration.
7. A worn-out horse, in contrast to Pegasus, the   8. Figures of speech.

That God be praised! the Dean is well.
Then he who prophesied the best,
Approves his foresight to the rest:
"You know I always feared the worst,
And often told you so at first."   130
He'd rather choose that I should die,
Than his prediction prove a lie.
Not one foretells I shall recover,
But all agree to give me over.

    Yet, should some neighbor feel a pain   135
Just in the parts where I complain,
How many a message would he send!
What hearty prayers that I should mend!
Inquire what regimen I kept;
What gave me ease, and how I slept,   140
And more lament, when I was dead,
Then all the snivelers round my bed.

   My good companions, never fear;
For though you may mistake a year,
Though your prognostics run too fast,   145
They must be verified at last.

   Behold the fatal day arrive!
"How is the Dean?"—"He's just alive."
Now the departing prayer is read.
"He hardly breathes"—"The Dean is dead."   150
Before the passing bell begun,
The news through half the town has run.
"Oh! may we all for death prepare!
What has he left? and who's his heir?"
"I know no more than what the news is;   155
'Tis all bequeathed to public uses."
"To public use! a perfect whim!
What had the public done for him?
Mere envy, avarice, and pride:
He gave it all—but first he died.   160
And had the Dean in all the nation
No worthy friend, no poor relation?
So ready to do strangers good,
Forgetting his own flesh and blood?"
Now Grub Street[9] wits are all employed;   165
With elegies the town is cloyed;
Some paragraph in every paper
To curse the Dean, or bless the Drapier.[1]

   The doctors, tender of their fame,
Wisely on me lay all the blame.   170

---

9. Originally a street in London largely inhabited by hack writers; later, a generic term applied to all such writers.
1. It was in the character of "M. B.," a Dublin drapier, that Swift aroused the Irish people to resistance against the importation of Wood's halfpence. See biographical introduction.

"We must confess his case was nice;[2]
But he would never take advice.
Had he been ruled, for aught appears,
He might have lived these twenty years:
For, when we opened him, we found,   175
That all his vital parts were sound."

From Dublin soon to London spread,
'Tis told at court, "The Dean is dead."
Kind Lady Suffolk,[3] in the spleen,
Runs laughing up to tell the Queen.   180
The Queen, so gracious, mild and good,
Cries, "Is he gone? 'tis time he should.
He's dead, you say; why, let him rot:
I'm glad the medals were forgot.[4]
I promised him, I own; but when?   185
I only was the Princess then;
But now, as consort of the King,
You know, 'tis quite a different thing."

Now Chartres,[5] at Sir Robert's levee,
Tells with a sneer the tidings heavy: 190
"Why, is he dead without his shoes?"
Cries Bob, "I'm sorry for the news:
Oh, were the wretch but living still,
And in his place my good friend Will![6]
Or had a miter on his head,   195
Provided Bolingbroke were dead!"

Now Curll his shop from rubbish drains:[7]
Three genuine tomes of Swift's remains!
And then, to make them pass the glibber,
Revised by Tibbalds, Moore, and Cibber.[8]   200
He'll treat me as he does my betters,
Publish my will, my life, my letters;
Revive the libels born to die,
Which Pope must bear, as well as I.

Here shift the scene, to represent   205
How those I love my death lament.
Poor Pope will grieve a month, and Gay
A week, and Arbuthnot a day.
St. John himself will scarce forbear

2. Delicate; hence demanding careful diagnosis and treatment.
3. George II's mistress, with whom Swift became friendly during his visit to Pope in 1726. "In the spleen": in low spirits. The phrase is ironic, as "laughing" in the next line makes clear.
4. Queen Caroline had promised Swift some medals when she was princess of Wales during the same year.
5. Col. Francis Chartres, a debauchee often satirized by Pope; Sir Robert Walpole.
6. William Pulteney (see line 59 and its note.)
7. Edmund Curll, shrewd and disreputable book-

seller, published pirated works, scandalous biographies, and works falsely ascribed to notable writers of the time.
8. Lewis Theobald (1688–1744), Shakespeare scholar and editor, already enthroned as King of the Dunces in Pope's Dunciad (1728). Like Pope, Swift spells the name phonetically. James Moore-Smyth, poetaster and playwright, an enemy of Pope. Colley Cibber (1671–1757), comic actor, playwright, and supremely untalented poet laureate. He succeeded Theobald as King of the Dunces in the Dunciad of 1743.

To bite his pen, and drop a tear.   210
The rest will give a shrug, and cry,
"I'm sorry—but we all must die!"
    Indifference clad in wisdom's guise
All fortitude of mind supplies:
For how can stony bowels melt   215
In those who never pity felt?
When *we* are lashed, *they* kiss the rod,
Resigning to the will of God.
    The fools, my juniors by a year,
Are tortured with suspense and fear;   220
Who wisely thought my age a screen,
When death approached, to stand between:
The screen removed, their hearts are trembling;
They mourn for me without dissembling.
    My female friends, whose tender hearts   225
Have better learned to act their parts,
Receive the news in doleful dumps:
"The Dean is dead (and what is trumps?)
Then, Lord have mercy on his soul!
(Ladies, I'll venture for the vole.)[9]   230
Six deans, they say, must bear the pall.
(I wish I knew what king to call.)
Madam, your husband will attend
The funeral of so good a friend?"
"No, madam, 'tis a shocking sight;   235
And he's engaged tomorrow night:
My Lady Club would take it ill,
If he should fail her at quadrille.
He loved the Dean—(I lead a heart)
But dearest friends, they say, must part.   240
His time was come; he ran his race;
We hope he's in a better place."
    Why do we grieve that friends should die?
No loss more easy to supply.
One year is past; a different scene!   245
No further mention of the Dean,
Who now, alas! no more is missed,
Than if he never did exist.
Where's now this favorite of Apollo?
Departed—and his works must follow,   250
Must undergo the common fate;
His kind of wit is out of date.
    Some country squire to Lintot[1] goes,
Inquires for Swift in verse and prose.
Says Lintot, "I have heard the name;   255

---

9. The equivalent in the card game quadrille of bidding a grand slam in bridge.

1. Bernard Lintot, the publisher of Pope's Homer and some of his early poems.

He died a year ago."—"The same."
He searches all the shop in vain.
"Sir, you may find them in Duck Lane:[2]
I sent them, with a load of books,
Last Monday to the pastry-cook's.[3]   260
To fancy they could live a year!
I find you're but a stranger here.
The Dean was famous in his time,
And had a kind of knack at rhyme.
His way of writing now is past: 265
The town has got a better taste.
I keep no antiquated stuff;
But spick and span I have enough.
Pray do but give me leave to show 'em:
Here's Colley Cibber's birthday poem.   270
This ode you never yet have seen
By Stephen Duck[4] upon the Queen.
Then here's a letter finely penned.
Against the *Craftsman*[5] and his friend;
It clearly shows that all reflection   275
On ministers is disaffection.
Next, here's Sir Robert's vindication,[6]
And Mr. Henley's last oration.[7]
The hawkers have not got them yet:
Your honor please to buy a set?   280
    "Here's Woolston's tracts,[8] the twelfth edition;
'Tis read by every politician:
The country members, when in town,
To all their boroughs send them down;
You never met a thing so smart;   285
The courtiers have them all by heart;
Those maids of honor (who can read)
Are taught to use them for their creed.
The reverend author's good intention
Has been rewarded with a pension.   290
He does an honor to his gown,
By bravely running priestcraft down;
He shows, as sure as God's in Gloucester,[9]
That Jesus was a grand impostor;
That all his miracles were cheats,   295
Performed as jugglers do their feats:
The Church had never such a writer;

2. London street where second-hand books and publishers' "remainders" were sold.
3. To be used as waste paper for lining baking dishes and wrapping parcels.
4. Stephen Duck, "the thresher poet," an agricultural laborer, whose mild poetic gifts brought him to the notice and patronage of Queen Caroline.
5. See line 59 and its note.
6. "Walpole hires a string of party scribblers who do nothing else but write in his defense" [Swift's note].
7. "Orator" John Henley, an Independent preacher, who dazzled unlearned audiences with his oratory and who wrote treatises on elocution.
8. Thomas Woolston (1670–1733), a freethinker, whose *Discourses on the Miracles of Our Saviour* had recently earned him notoriety.
9. Proverbially, Gloucestershire was full of monks.

A shame he has not got a miter!"
    Suppose me dead; and then suppose
A club assembled at the Rose;[1]   300
Where, from discourse of this and that,
I grow the subject of their chat.
And while they toss my name about,
With favor some, and some without,
One, quite indifferent in the cause,   305
My character impartial draws:
    "The Dean, if we believe report,
Was never ill received at court.
As for his works in verse and prose,
I own myself no judge of those;   310
Nor can I tell what critics thought 'em:
But this I know, all people bought 'em,
As with a moral view designed
To cure the vices of mankind.
    "His vein, ironically grave,   315
Exposed the fool and lashed the knave,
To steal a hint was never known,
But what he writ was all his own.
    "He never thought an honor done him,
Because a duke was proud to own him,   320
Would rather slip aside and choose
To talk with wits in dirty shoes;
Despised the fools with stars and garters,
So often seen caressing Chartres.
He never courted men in station,   325
Nor persons held in admiration;
Of no man's greatness was afraid,
Because he sought for no man's aid.
Though trusted long in great affairs,
He gave himself no haughty airs;   330
Without regarding private ends,
Spent all his credit for his friends;
And only chose the wise and good;
No flatterers, no allies in blood;
But succored virtue in distress,   335
And seldom failed of good success;
As numbers in their hearts must own,
Who, but for him, had been unknown.
    "With princes kept a due decorum,
But never stood in awe before 'em.   340
He followed David's lesson just;
In princes never put thy trust:[2]
And would you make him truly sour,
Provoke him with a slave in power.
The Irish senate if you named,   345

1. A fashionable tavern in Covent Garden.   2. Psalm 146.3.

With what impatience he declaimed!
Fair Liberty was all his cry,
For her he stood prepared to die;
For her he boldly stood alone;
For her he oft exposed his own.   350
Two kingdoms, just as faction led,
Had set a price upon his head,
But not a traitor could be found,
To sell him for six hundred pound.[3]
    "Had he but spared his tongue and pen,   355
He might have rose like other men;
But power was never in his thought,
And wealth he valued not a groat:
Ingratitude he often found,
And pitied those who meant the wound;   360
But kept the tenor of his mind,
To merit well of human kind:
Nor made a sacrifice of those
Who still were true, to please his foes.
He labored many a fruitless hour,   365
To reconcile his friends in power;
Saw mischief by a faction brewing,
While they pursued each other's ruin.
But finding vain was all his care,
He left the court in mere despair.[4]   370
    "And, oh! how short are human schemes!
Here ended all our golden dreams.
What St. John's skill in state affairs,
What Ormonde's[5] valor, Oxford's cares,
To save their sinking country lent,   375
Was all destroyed by one event.[6]
Too soon that precious life was ended,
On which alone our weal depended.
When up a dangerous faction starts,[7]
With wrath and vengeance in their hearts;   380
By solemn League and Covenant bound,
To ruin, slaughter, and confound;
To turn religion to a fable,

---

3. In 1714 the government offered £300 for the discovery of the author of Swift's *Public Spirit of the Whigs*, and in 1724 the Irish government offered a similar amount for the discovery of the author of the fourth of Swift's *Drapier's Letters*.

4. The antagonism between the two chief ministers (his dear friends), Robert Harley, earl of Oxford, and Bolingbroke paralyzed the Tory ministry in the crucial last months of Queen Anne's life and drove Swift to retirement in Ireland, whence he returned in 1714 to make a final effort to heal the breach and save the government. He failed and retired to the country in despair. There he received the news of Anne's death on August 1. The Hanoverian succession brought the Whigs back in triumph,

ruined Swift's friends, and brought Swift's public life to a close.

5. James Butler, duke of Ormonde, who succeeded to the command of the English armies on the Continent, when, in 1711, the duke of Marlborough was stripped of his offices by Anne. He went into exile in 1714 and was active in Jacobite intrigue.

6. The death of Queen Anne.

7. Swift's view of the policies of the "dangerous faction" (the Whig party) is hardly impartial. He feared it especially because of its toleration of Dissenters, and so as an enemy of the Church of England.

And make the government a Babel;
Pervert the laws, disgrace the gown,   385
Corrupt the senate, rob the crown;
To sacrifice old England's glory,
And make her infamous in story:
When such a tempest shook the land,
How could unguarded Virtue stand?   390
With horror, grief, despair, the Dean
Beheld the dire destructive scene:
His friends in exile, or the Tower,[8]
Himself within the frown of power,
Pursued by base envenomed pens,   395
Far to the land of slaves and fens;[9]
A servile race in folly nursed,
Who truckle most, when treated worst.
    "By innocence and resolution,
He bore continual persecution;   400
While numbers to preferment rose,
Whose merits were to be his foes;
When even his own familiar friends,
Intent upon their private ends,
Like renegadoes now he feels,   405
Against him lifting up their heels.
    "The Dean did, by his pen, defeat
An infamous destructive cheat;[1]
Taught fools their interest how to know,
And gave them arms to ward the blow.   410
Envy has owned it was his doing,
To save that hapless land from ruin;
While they who at the steerage[2] stood,
And reaped the profit, sought his blood.
    "To save them from their evil fate,   415
In him was held a crime of state.
A wicked monster on the bench,[3]
Whose fury blood could never quench;
As vile and profligate a villain,
As modern Scroggs, or old Tresilian;[4]   420
Who long all justice had discarded,
Nor feared he God, nor man regarded;
Vowed on the Dean his rage to vent,

8. Bolingbroke was in exile; Oxford was sent to the Tower by the Whigs.
9. Ireland.
1. The scheme to introduce Wood's copper half-pence into Ireland in 1723–24.
2. Literally the steering of a ship. Here the direction and management of public affairs in Ireland.
3. William Whitshed, lord chief justice of the King's Bench of Ireland. In 1720, when the jury refused to find Swift's anonymous pamphlet *Proposal for the Universal Use of Irish Manufacture* wicked and seditious, Whitshed sent them back nine times, hoping to force them to another verdict. In 1724 he presided over the trial of Harding, the printer of Swift's fourth *Drapier's Letter*, but again was unable, despite bullying, to force a verdict of guilty.
4. Sir William Scroggs, lord chief justice of England at the time of the Popish Plot, 1678 (see Dryden's *Absalom and Achitophel*), was impeached for his misdemeanors in office in 1680. Sir Robert Tresilian punished with great severity in 1381 men who had participated in the Peasants' Revolt; he was impeached and in 1387 was hanged.

And make him of his zeal repent:
But Heaven his innocence defends,   425
The grateful people stand his friends;
Not strains of law, nor judge's frown,
Nor topics brought to please the crown,
Nor witness hired, nor jury picked,
Prevail to bring him in convict.   430
　　"In exile, with a steady heart,
He spent his life's declining part;
Where folly, pride, and faction sway,
Remote from St. John, Pope, and Gay.
　　"His friendships there, to few confined,   435
Were always of the middling kind;
No fools of rank, a mongrel breed,
Who fain would pass for lords indeed:
Where titles give no right or power,
And peerage is a withered flower;   440
He would have held it a disgrace,
If such a wretch had known his face.
On rural squires, that kingdom's bane,
He vented oft his wrath in vain;
Biennial squires[5] to market brought: 445
Who sell their souls, and votes for naught;
The nation stripped, go joyful back,
To rob the church, their tenants rack,
Go snacks with rogues and rapparees;[6]
And keep the peace to pick up fees;   450
In every job to have a share,
A jail or barrack to repair;
And turn the tax for public roads,
Commodious to their own abodes.
　　"Perhaps I may allow the Dean   455
Had too much satire in his vein;
And seemed determined not to starve it,
Because no age could more deserve it.
Yet malice never was his aim;
He lashed the vice, but spared the name;   460
No individual could resent,
Where thousands equally were meant;
His satire points at no defect,
But what all mortals may correct;
For he abhorred that senseless tribe   465
Who call it humor when they gibe:
He spared a hump, or crooked nose,
Whose owners set not up for beaux.
True genuine dullness moved his pity,
Unless it offered to be witty.   470
Those who their ignorance confessed,

5. Members of the Irish Parliament.　　　　　6. Highwaymen.

He ne'er offended with a jest;
But laughed to hear an idiot quote
A verse from Horace learned by rote.
　"He knew an hundred pleasant stories, 475
With all the turns of Whigs and Tories:
Was cheerful to his dying day;
And friends would let him have his way.
　"He gave the little wealth he had
To build a house for fools and mad;[7] 480
And showed by one satiric touch,
No nation wanted it so much.
That kingdom he hath left his debtor,
I wish it soon may have a better."

1731   1739

From A Tale of a Tub

A Digression Concerning the Original, the Use, and Improvement of Madness in a Commonwealth[1]

Nor shall it any ways detract from the just reputation of his famous sect,[2] that its rise and institution are owing to such an author as I have described Jack to be, a person whose intellectuals were overturned, and his brain shaken out of its natural position; which we commonly suppose to be a distemper, and call by the name of madness or frenzy. For, if we take a survey of the greatest actions that have been performed in the world, under the influence of single men, which are the establishment of new empires by conquest, the advance and progress of new schemes in philosophy, and the contriving, as well as the propagating, of new religions, we shall find the authors of them all to have been persons whose natural reason had admitted great revolutions from their diet, their education, the prevalency of some certain temper, together with the particular influence of air and climate. Besides, there is something individual in human minds, that easily kindles at the accidental approach and collision of certain circumstances, which, though of paltry and mean appearance, do often flame out into the greatest emergencies of life. For great turns are not always given by strong hands, but by lucky adaption,

7. Swift left funds to endow a hospital for the insane.

1. A Tale of a Tub, Swift's first major work, recounts the adventures of three brothers: Peter (Roman Catholicism), Martin (Luther, here regarded as inspiring the Church of England), and Jack (Calvin, the spirit of Protestant dissent). But the most memorable character of the book is its narrator, who interrupts the story with numerous digressions (including even "A Digression in Praise of Digressions"), and whose pride in learning and lack of common sense represent the zealous modern insanity that Swift takes as his target for satire.

"A Digression Concerning Madness," this narrator's masterpiece, is based on Swift's ironical doctrine of "the mechanical operation of the spirit": the notion that all spiritual and mental states derive from physical causes—in this case, the ascent of "vapors" to the brain. Beneath his whimsy, however, the author raises a fearful question: what right has any human being to trust that he is sane?
2. The Aeolists, who "maintain the original cause of all things to be wind," are equated by Swift with religious dissenters who believe themselves to be inspired.

and at proper seasons; and it is of no import where the fire was kindled, if the vapor has once got up into the brain. For the upper region of man is furnished like the middle region of the air; the materials are formed from causes of the widest difference, yet produce at last the same substance and effect. Mists arise from the earth, steams from dunghills, exhalations from the sea, and smoke from fire; yet all clouds are the same in composition as well as consequences, and the fumes issuing from a jakes[3] will furnish as comely and useful a vapor as incense from an altar. Thus far, I suppose, will easily be granted me; and then it will follow, that as the face of nature never produces rain but when it is overcast and disturbed, so human understanding, seated in the brain, must be troubled and overspread by vapors, ascending from the lower faculties to water the invention and render it fruitful. Now, although these vapors, (as it hath been already said) are of as various original as those of the skies, yet the crop they produce differs both in kind and degree, merely according to the soil. I will produce two instances to prove and explain what I am now advancing.

A certain great prince[4] raised a mighty army, filled his coffers with infinite treasures, provided an invincible fleet, and all this without giving the least part of his design to his greatest ministers or his nearest favorites. Immediately the whole world was alarmed; the neighboring crowns in trembling expectation towards what point the storm would burst; the small politicians everywhere forming profound conjectures. Some believed he had laid a scheme for universal monarchy; others, after much insight, determined the matter to be a project for pulling down the Pope, and setting up the reformed religion, which had once been his own. Some again, of a deeper sagacity, sent him into Asia to subdue the Turk, and recover Palestine. In the midst of all these projects and preparations, a certain state-surgeon,[5] gathering the nature of the disease by these symptoms, attempted the cure, at one blow performed the operation, broke the bag, and out flew the vapor; nor did anything want to render it a complete remedy, only that the prince unfortunately happened to die in the performance. Now, is the reader exceeding curious to learn whence this vapor took its rise, which had so long set the nations at a gaze? What secret wheel, what hidden spring, could put into motion so wonderful an engine? It was afterwards discovered that the movement of this whole machine had been directed by an absent female, whose eyes had raised a protuberancy, and before emission, she was removed into an enemy's country. What should an unhappy prince do in such ticklish circumstances as these? He tried in vain the poet's never-failing receipt of *corpora quaeque*;[6] for,

---

3. Latrine.
4. "This was Harry the Great of France" [Swift's note]. Henry IV (1553–1610), infatuated with the Princesse de Condé, whose husband had removed her to the Spanish Netherlands, prepared an expe-

dition to bring her back.
5. "Ravillac, who stabbed Henry the Great in his coach" [Swift's note].
6. "Any available bodies."

Idque petit corpus mens unde est saucia amore:
Unde feritur, eo tendit, gestitque coire.—LUCRETIUS[7]

Having to no purpose used all peaceable endeavors, the collected part of the semen, raised and inflamed, became adust, converted to choler, turned head upon the spinal duct, and ascended to the brain. The very same principle that influences a bully to break the windows of a whore who has jilted him, naturally stirs up a great prince to raise mighty armies, and dream of nothing but sieges, battles, and victories.

——*Teterrima belli*
Causa——[8]

The other instance is what I·have read somewhere in a very ancient author, of a mighty king,[9] who, for the space of above thirty years, amused himself to take and lose towns, beat armies, and be beaten, drive princes out of their dominions; fright children from their bread and butter; burn, lay waste, plunder, dragoon, massacre subject and stranger, friend and foe, male and female. 'Tis recorded, that the philosophers of each country were in grave dispute upon causes natural, moral, and political, to find out where they should assign an original solution of this phenomenon. At last the vapor or spirit, which animated the hero's brain, being in perpetual circulation, seized upon that region of the human body, so renowned for furnishing the *zibeta occidentalis*,[1] and gathering there into a tumor, left the rest of the world for that time in peace. Of such mighty consequence it is where those exhalations fix, and of so little from whence they proceed. The same spirits which, in their superior progress, would conquer a kingdom, descending upon the anus, conclude in a fistula.[2]

Let us next examine the great introducers of new schemes in philosophy, and search till we can find from what faculty of the soul the disposition arises in mortal man, of taking it into his head to advance new systems with such an eager zeal, in things agreed on all hands impossible to be known; from what seeds this disposition springs, and to what quality of human nature these grand innovators have been indebted for their number of disciples. Because it is plain, that several of the chief among them, both ancient and modern, were usually mistaken by their adversaries, and indeed by all except their own followers, to have been persons crazed, or out of their wits; having generally proceeded, in the common course of their words and actions, by a method very different from the vulgar dictates of unrefined reason; agreeing for the most part in their

---

7. "The body strives for that which sickens the mind with love. . . . Stretches out toward that which smites it, and yearns to couple" (*De Rerum Natura* 4.1048 ff.). "Adust": burned up.
8. "The most abominable cause of war" in olden days, according to Horace, *Satires* 1.3.107–8, was a whore.
9. "This is meant of the present French king"

[Louis XIV] [Swift's note].
1. "Paracelsus, who was so famous for chemistry, tried an experiment upon human excrement, to make a perfume of it, which when he had brought to perfection, he called *zibeta occidentalis*, or western-civet, the back parts of man . . . being the west" [Swift's note].
2. Ulcer shaped like a pipe.

several models, with their present undoubted successors in the academy of modern Bedlam[3] (whose merits and principles I shall farther examine in due place). Of this kind were *Epicurus, Diogenes, Apollonius, Lucretius, Paracelsus, Descartes,*[4] and others, who, if they were now in the world, tied fast, and separate from their followers, would, in this our undistinguishing age, incur manifest danger of phlebotomy,[5] and whips, and chains, and dark chambers, and straw. For what man, in the natural state or course of thinking, did ever conceive it in his power to reduce the notions of all mankind exactly to the same length, and breadth, and height of his own? Yet this is the first humble and civil design of all innovators in the empire of reason. Epicurus modestly hoped, that one time or other a certain fortuitous concourse of all men's opinions, after perpetual justlings, the sharp with the smooth, the light and the heavy, the round and the square, would by certain *clinamina*[6] unite in the notions of atoms and void, as these did in the originals of all things. Cartesius reckoned to see, before he died, the sentiments of all philosophers, like so many lesser stars in his romantic system, wrapped and drawn within his own vortex.[7] Now, I would gladly be informed, how it is possible to account for such imaginations as these in particular men without recourse to my phenomenon of vapors, ascending from the lower faculties to overshadow the brain, and there distilling into conceptions for which the narrowness of our mother-tongue has not yet assigned any other name beside that of madness or frenzy. Let us therefore now conjecture how it comes to pass, that none of these great prescribers do ever fail providing themselves and their notions with a number of implicit disciples. And, I think, the reason is easy to be assigned: for there is a peculiar string in the harmony of human understanding, which in several individuals is exactly of the same tuning. This, if you can dexterously screw up to its right key, and then strike gently upon it, whenever you have the good fortune to light among those of the same pitch, they will, by a secret necessary sympathy, strike exactly at the same time. And in this one circumstance lies all the skill or luck of the matter; for if you chance to jar the string among those who are either above or below your own height, instead of subscribing to your doctrine, they will tie you fast, call you mad, and feed you with bread and water. It is therefore a point of the nicest conduct to distinguish and adapt this noble talent, with respect to the differences of persons and of times. Cicero understood this very well, when writing to a friend in England, with a caution, among other matters, to beware of being cheated by our hackney-coachmen (who, it seems, in those days were as arrant rascals as they are now), has these remarkable words: *Est quod gaudeas te in ista*

3. Bethlehem hospital, London's lunatic asylum.

4. Each of these famous speculative thinkers was known as a materialist, hence suspected by Swift of encouraging atheism.

5. Medical blood-letting.

6. Swerves. The Greek philosopher Epicurus held that the universe was formed by atoms swerving together; Swift implies that a similar miracle would be required for men to join in agreement with Epicurus.

7. The physics of René Descartes (1596–1650) is based on a theory of vortices; Swift considered the theory pure romance.

loca venisse, ubi aliquid sapere viderere.[8] For, to speak a bold truth, it is a fatal miscarriage so ill to order affairs, as to pass for a fool in one company, when in another you might be treated as a philosopher. Which I desire some certain gentlemen of my acquaintance to lay up in their hearts, as a very seasonable *innuendo.*

This, indeed, was the fatal mistake of that worthy gentleman, my most ingenious friend, Mr. W—tt—n,[9] a person, in appearance, ordained for great designs, as well as performances; whether you will consider his notions or his looks. Surely no man ever advanced into the public with fitter qualifications of body and mind, for the propagation of a new religion. Oh, had those happy talents, misapplied to vain philosophy, been turned into their proper channels of dreams and visions, where distortion of mind and countenance are of such sovereign use, the base detracting world would not then have dared to report that something is amiss, that his brain has undergone an unlucky shake; which even his brother modernists themselves, like ungrates, do whisper so loud, that it reaches up to the very garret I am now writing in.

Lastly, whosoever pleases to look into the fountains of enthusiasm,[1] from whence, in all ages, have eternally proceeded such fattening streams, will find the springhead to have been as troubled and muddy as the current. Of such great emolument is a tincture of this vapor, which the world calls madness, that without its help, the world would not only be deprived of those two great blessings, conquests and systems, but even all mankind would unhappily be reduced to the same belief in things invisible. Now, the former *postulatum* being held, that it is of no import from what originals this vapor proceeds, but either in what angles it strikes and spreads over the understanding, or upon what species of brain it ascends; it will be a very delicate point to cut the feather, and divide the several reasons to a nice and curious reader, how this numerical difference in the brain can produce effects of so vast a difference from the same vapor, as to be the sole point of individuation between Alexander the Great, Jack of Leyden[2] and Monsieur Descartes. The present argument is the most abstracted that ever I engaged in; it strains my faculties to their highest stretch; and I desire the reader to attend with utmost perpensity; for I now proceed to unravel this knotty point.

There is in mankind a certain[3] ·   ·   ·   ·   ·

·   ·   ·   ·   ·   ·   ·   ·

Hic multa   ·   ·   ·   ·   ·   ·

---

8. "It is ground for rejoicing that you have come to such places, where anyone can seem wise" (Cicero, *Familiar Epistles* 7.10).

9. William Wotton (who had championed modern authors against Swift's patron, Sir William Temple, a spokesman for the ancients) is ridiculed in Swift's *Battle of the Books*, published in the same volume as *A Tale of a Tub* (1704).

1. For much of the 18th century the word "enthusiasm" (literally, "possessed by a god") signified a deluded belief in personal revelation.

2. John of Leyden, a tailor and prophet, briefly

established a revolutionary Anabaptist community, the "New Jerusalem," in the city of Münster early in the 16th century.

3. "Here is another defect in the manuscript, but I think the author did wisely, and that the matter which thus strained his faculties was not worth a solution; and it were well if all metaphysical cobweb problems were no otherwise answered" [Swift's note]. The Latin phrase ("Much is missing here") indicates a gap in the text Swift pretends to be "editing."

desiderantur.   •   •   •   •   •   •   •
•   •   •   •   •   And this I take to be a clear solution of the matter.

Having therefore so narrowly passed through this intricate difficulty, the reader will, I am sure, agree with me in the conclusion, that if the moderns mean by madness, only a disturbance or transposition of the brain, by force of certain vapors issuing up from the lower faculties, then has this madness been the parent of all those mighty revolutions that have happened in empire, in philosophy, and in religion. For the brain, in its natural position and state of serenity, disposeth its owner to pass his life in the common forms, without any thought of subduing multitudes to his own power, his reasons, or his visions; and the more he shapes his understanding by the pattern of human learning, the less he is inclined to form parties after his particular notions, because that instructs him in his private infirmities, as well as in the stubborn ignorance of the people. But when a man's fancy gets astride on his reason, when imagination is at cuffs with the senses, and common understanding, as well as common sense, is kicked out of doors, the first proselyte he makes is himself; and when that is once compassed, the difficulty is not so great in bringing over others; a strong delusion always operating from without as vigorously as from within. For cant[4] and vision are to the ear and the eye, the same that tickling is to the touch. Those entertainments and pleasures we most value in life, are such as dupe and play the wag with the senses. For, if we take an examination of what is generally understood by happiness, as it has respect either to the understanding or the senses, we shall find all its properties and adjuncts will herd under this short definition, that it is a perpetual possession of being well deceived. And first, with relation to the mind or understanding, 'tis manifest what mighty advantages fiction has over truth; and the reason is just at our elbow, because imagination can build nobler scenes, and produce more wonderful revolutions, than fortune or nature will be at expense to furnish. Nor is mankind so much to blame in his choice thus determining him, if we consider that the debate merely lies between things past and things conceived; and so the question is only this: whether things that have place in the imagination, may not as properly be said to exist, as those that are seated in the memory; which may be justly held in the affirmative, and very much to the advantage of the former, since this is acknowledged to be the womb of things, and the other allowed to be no more than the grave. Again, if we take this definition of happiness, and examine it with reference to the senses, it will be acknowledged wonderfully adapt. How fading and insipid do all objects accost us, that are not conveyed in the vehicle of delusion! How shrunk is everything, as it appears in the glass of nature! So that if it were not for the assistance of artificial mediums, false lights, refracted angles, varnish, and tinsel, there would be a mighty level in the felicity and enjoyments of mortal men.

4. "Sudden exclamations, whining, unusual tones, and in fine all praying and preaching like the unlearned of the Presbyterians" (*Spectator* 147).

If this were seriously considered by the world, as I have a certain reason to suspect it hardly will, men would no longer reckon among their high points of wisdom, the art of exposing weak sides, and publishing infirmities; an employment, in my opinion, neither better nor worse than that of unmasking, which, I think, has never been allowed[5] fair usage, either in the world, or the playhouse.

In the proportion that credulity is a more peaceful possession of the mind than curiosity, so far preferable is that wisdom, which converses about the surface, to that pretended philosophy which enters into the depth of things, and then comes gravely back with informations and discoveries, that in the inside they are good for nothing. The two senses, to which all objects first address themselves, are the sight and the touch; these never examine farther than the color, the shape, the size, and whatever other qualities dwell, or are drawn by art upon the outward of bodies; and then comes reason officiously with tools for cutting, and opening, and mangling, and piercing, offering to demonstrate, that they are not of the same consistence quite through. Now I take all this to be the last degree of perverting nature; one of whose eternal laws it is, to put her best furniture forward. And therefore, in order to save the charges of all such expensive anatomy for the time to come, I do here think fit to inform the reader, that in such conclusions as these, reason is certainly in the right, and that in most corporeal beings, which have fallen under my cognizance, the outside has been infinitely preferable to the in; whereof I have been farther convinced from some late experiments. Last week I saw a woman flayed, and you will hardly believe how much it altered her person for the worse. Yesterday I ordered the carcass of a beau to be stripped in my presence; when we were all amazed to find so many unsuspected faults under one suit of clothes. Then I laid open his brain, his heart, and his spleen; but I plainly perceived at every operation, that the farther we proceeded, we found the defects increase upon us in number and bulk; from all which, I justly formed this conclusion to myself: that whatever philosopher or projector[6] can find out an art to solder and patch up the flaws and imperfections of nature, will deserve much better of mankind, and teach us a more useful science, than that so much in present esteem, of widening and exposing them (like him who held anatomy to be the ultimate end of physic).[7] And he, whose fortunes and dispositions have placed him in a convenient station to enjoy the fruits of this noble art; he that can with Epicurus content his ideas with the films and images that fly off upon his senses from the superficies[8] of things; such a man, truly wise, creams off nature, leaving the sour and the dregs for philosophy and reason to lap up. This is the sublime and refined point of felicity, called the possession of being well deceived; the serene peaceful state of being a fool among knaves.

But to return to madness. It is certain, that according to the system I

---

5. Admitted to be.
6. Someone given to speculative experiments.
7. Medical practice.

8. Surfaces. Epicurus considered the senses, directly affected by objects, more trustworthy than reason.

have above deduced, every species thereof proceeds from a redundancy of vapors; therefore, as some kinds of frenzy give double strength to the sinews, so there are of other species, which add vigor, and life, and spirit to the brain. Now, it usually happens, that these active spirits, getting possession of the brain, resemble those that haunt other waste and empty dwellings, which for want of business, either vanish, and carry away a piece of the house, or else stay at home and fling it all out of the windows. By which are mystically displayed the two principal branches of madness, and which some philosophers, not considering so well as I, have mistaken to be different in their causes, over-hastily assigning the first to deficiency, and the other to redundance.

I think it therefore manifest, from what I have here advanced, that the main point of skill and address is to furnish employment for this redundancy of vapor, and prudently to adjust the season of it; by which means it may certainly become of cardinal and catholic emolument, in a commonwealth. Thus one man, choosing a proper juncture, leaps into a gulf, from thence proceeds a hero, and is called the saver of his country; another achieves the same enterprise, but unluckily timing it, has left the brand of madness fixed as a reproach upon his memory; upon so nice a distinction, are we taught to repeat the name of Curtius[9] with reverence and love, that of Empedocles with hatred and contempt. Thus also it is usually conceived, that the elder Brutus only personated the fool and madman for the good of the public; but this was nothing else than a redundancy of the same vapor long misapplied, called by the Latins, *ingenium par negotiis;*[1] or (to translate it as nearly as I can) a sort of frenzy, never in its right element, till you take it up in business of the state.

Upon all which, and many other reasons of equal weight, though not equally curious, I do here gladly embrace an opportunity I have long sought for, of recommending it as a very noble undertaking to Sir Edward Seymour, Sir Christopher Musgrave, Sir John Bowls, John How, Esq.,[2] and other patriots concerned, that they would move for leave to bring in a bill for appointing commissioners to inspect into Bedlam, and the parts adjacent; who shall be empowered to send for persons, papers, and records, to examine into the merits and qualifications of every student and professor, to observe with utmost exactness their several dispositions and behavior, by which means, duly distinguishing and adapting their talents, they might produce admirable instruments for the several offices in a state, . . .,[3] civil, and military, proceeding in such methods as I shall here humbly propose. And I hope the gentle reader will give some allowance to my great solicitudes in this important affair, upon account of the high esteem I have borne that honorable society, whereof I had some time the happiness to be an unworthy member.

---

9. The Roman hero Marcus Curtius appeased the gods by hurling himself into an ominous crack in the earth of the Forum; Empedocles committed suicide by leaping into the crater of Mount Etna.
1. "A talent for business." Lucius Junius Brutus, like Hamlet, pretended madness to deceive his murderous uncle, Tarquin the Proud.
2. Members of Parliament.
3. Swift omits the third office, Ecclesiastical. "Instruments": useful persons.

Is any student tearing his straw in piece-meal, swearing and blaspheming, biting his grate, foaming at the mouth, and emptying his piss-pot in the spectators' faces? Let the right worshipful the commissioners of inspection give him a regiment of dragoons, and send him into Flanders among the rest. Is another eternally talking, sputtering, gaping, bawling in a sound without period or article? What wonderful talents are here mislaid! Let him be furnished immediately with a green bag and papers, and threepence in his pocket,[4] and away with him to Westminster Hall. You will find a third gravely taking the dimensions of his kennel, a person of foresight and insight, though kept quite in the dark; for why, like Moses, *ecce cornuta erat ejus facies.*[5] He walks duly in one pace, entreats your penny with due gravity and ceremony, talks much of hard times, and taxes, and the whore of Babylon, bars up the wooden window of his cell constantly at eight o'clock, dreams of fire, and shop-lifters, and court-customers, and privileged places. Now, what a figure would all these acquirements amount to, if the owner were sent into the city[6] among his brethren! Behold a fourth, in much and deep conversation with himself, biting his thumbs at proper junctures, his countenance checkered with business and design, sometimes walking very fast, with his eyes nailed to a paper that he holds in his hands; a great saver of time, somewhat thick of hearing, very short of sight, but more of memory; a man ever in haste, a great hatcher and breeder of business, and excellent at the famous art of whispering nothing; a huge idolator of monosyllables and procrastination, so ready to give his word to everybody, that he never keeps it; one that has forgot the common meaning of words, but an admirable retainer of the sound; extremely subject to the looseness,[7] for his occasions are perpetually calling him away. If you approach his grate in his familiar intervals, "Sir," says he, "give me a penny, and I'll sing you a song; but give me the penny first." (Hence comes the common saying, and commoner practice, of parting with money for a song.) What a complete system of court skill is here described in every branch of it, and all utterly lost with wrong application! Accost the hole of another kennel, first stopping your nose, you will behold a surly, gloomy, nasty, slovenly mortal, raking in his own dung, and dabbling in his urine. The best part of his diet is the reversion of his own ordure, which expiring into steams, whirls perpetually about, and at last re-infunds. His complexion is of a dirty yellow, with a thin scattered beard, exactly agreeable to that of his diet upon its first declination, like other insects, who having their birth and education in an excrement, from thence borrow their color and their smell. The student of this apartment is very sparing of his words, but somewhat over-liberal of his breath; he holds his hand out ready to receive your penny, and imme-

---

4. "A lawyer's coach-hire" [Swift's note] from the Inns of Court to Westminster. Most lawyers carried green bags.
5. "Cornutus is either horned or shining, and by this term, Moses is described in the vulgar Latin of the Bible" [Swift's note]. Swift puns on the Latin phrase ("Behold his face was shining") by suggesting someone kept in the dark through being "horned," i.e., a cuckold.
6. The commercial center of London.
7. Diarrhea.

diately upon receipt withdraws to his former occupations. Now, is it not amazing to think, the society of Warwick-lane[8] should have no more concern for the recovery of so useful a member, who, if one may judge from these appearances, would become the greatest ornament to that illustrious body? Another student struts up fiercely to your teeth, puffing with his lips, half squeezing out his eyes, and very graciously holds you out his hand to kiss. The keeper desires you not to be afraid of this professor, for he will do you no hurt; to him alone is allowed the liberty of the antechamber, and the orator of the place gives you to understand, that this solemn person is a tailor run mad with pride. This considerable student is adorned with many other qualities, upon which at present I shall not farther enlarge.------*Hark in your ear*[9]------I am strangely mistaken, if all his address, his motions, and his airs, would not then be very natural, and in their proper element.

I shall not descend so minutely, as to insist upon the vast number of beaux, fiddlers, poets, and politicians, that the world might recover by such a reformation; but what is more material, besides the clear gain redounding to the commonwealth, by so large an acquisition of persons to employ, whose talents and acquirements, if I may be so bold as to affirm it, are now buried, or at least misapplied; it would be a mighty advantage accruing to the public from this inquiry, that all these would very much excel, and arrive at great perfection in their several kinds; which, I think, is manifest from what I have already shown, and shall enforce by this one plain instance: that even I myself, the author of these momentous truths, am a person, whose imaginations are hard-mouthed,[1] and exceedingly disposed to run away with his reason, which I have observed from long experience to be a very light rider, and easily shook off; upon which account, my friends will never trust me alone, without a solemn promise to vent my speculations in this, or the like manner, for the universal benefit of human kind; which perhaps the gentle, courteous, and candid reader, brimful of that modern charity and tenderness usually annexed to his office, will be very hardly persuaded to believe.

1704

AN ARGUMENT TO PROVE THAT THE

Abolishing of Christianity in England

MAY, AS THINGS NOW STAND, BE ATTENDED WITH SOME
INCONVENIENCES, AND PERHAPS NOT PRODUCE THOSE MANY
GOOD EFFECTS PROPOSED THEREBY.[1]

I am very sensible what a weakness and presumption it is, to reason against the general humor and disposition of the world. I remember it

8. Royal College of Physicians.
9. "I cannot conjecture what the author means here, or how this chasm could be filled, though it is capable of more than one interpretation" [Swift's note].

1. (Of a horse) apt to reject control by the bit.
1. The Test Act of 1673 required all holders of public office to take the sacrament of the Lord's Supper according to the usage of the Church of England; it was directed against Dissenters and

was with great justice, and a due regard to the freedom both of the public and the press, forbidden upon several penalties to write, or discourse, or lay wagers against the Union,[2] even before it was confirmed by Parliament, because that was looked upon as a design to oppose the current of the people, which, besides the folly of it, is a manifest breach of the fundamental law that makes this majority of opinion the voice of God. In like manner, and for the very same reasons, it may perhaps be neither safe nor prudent to argue against the abolishing of Christianity at a juncture when all parties appear so unanimously determined upon the point, as we cannot but allow from their actions, their discourses, and their writings. However, I know not how, whether from the affectation of singularity, or the perverseness of human nature, but so it unhappily falls out that I cannot be entirely of this opinion. Nay, though I were sure an order were issued for my immediate prosecution by the attorney-general, I should still confess that in the present posture of our affairs at home or abroad, I do not yet see the absolute necessity of extirpating the Christian religion from among us.

This perhaps may appear too great a paradox even for our wise and paradoxical age to endure: therefore I shall handle it with all tenderness, and with the utmost deference to that great and profound majority which is of another sentiment.

And yet the curious may please to observe how much the genius of a nation is liable to alter in half an age: I have heard it affirmed for certain by some very old people that the contrary opinion was even in their memories as much in vogue as the other is now; and that a project for the abolishing of Christianity would then have appeared as singular, and been thought as absurd, as it would be at this time to write or discourse in its defense.

Therefore I freely own that all appearances are against me. The system of the Gospel, after the fate of other systems, is generally antiquated and exploded; and the mass or body of the common people, among whom it seems to have had its latest credit, are now grown as much ashamed of it as their betters; opinions, like fashions, always descending from those of quality to the middle sort, and thence to the vulgar, where at length they are dropped and vanish.

But here I would not be mistaken, and must therefore be so bold as to borrow a distinction from the writers on the other side, when they make a difference between nominal and real Trinitarians. I hope no reader imagines me so weak to stand up in the defense of real Christianity, such as used in primitive times (if we may believe the authors of those ages) to have an influence upon men's belief and actions: to offer

Roman Catholics. In 1708 the Whigs (with whom Swift was then allied) were seeking to repeal the Test in Ireland and eventually in England, in an effort to consolidate the support of the Dissenters. Swift believed that repeal would do great harm to the Established Church, and as a good Anglican priest he opposed it with this essay.

Swift's technique is to assume blandly that to argue against the Test Act is to argue against Christianity and the Church, and he constructs his essay accordingly. The basic satiric principle is therefore that of the *reductio ad absurdum*, but this device is surrounded by a host of other ironies.

2. The union of Scotland and England under one crown in 1707.

at the restoring of that would indeed be a wild project; it would be to dig up foundations; to destroy at one blow all the wit, and half the learning of the kingdom; to break the entire frame and constitution of things; to ruin trade, extinguish arts and sciences with the professors of them; in short, to turn our courts, exchanges, and shops into deserts; and would be full as absurd as the proposal of Horace,[3] where he advises the Romans all in a body to leave their city and seek a new seat in some remote part of the world, by way of cure for the corruption of their manners.

Therefore I think this caution was in itself altogether unnecessary (which I have inserted only to prevent all possibility of caviling), since every candid reader will easily understand my discourse to be intended only in defense of nominal Christianity, the other having been for some time wholly laid aside by general consent as utterly inconsistent with all other present schemes of wealth and power.

But why we should therefore cast off the name and title of Christians, although the general opinion and resolution be so violent for it, I confess I cannot (with submission) apprehend the consequence necessary. However, since the undertakers propose such wonderful advantages to the nation by this project, and advance many plausible objections against the system of Christianity, I shall briefly consider the strength of both, fairly allow them their greatest weight, and offer such answers as I think most reasonable. After which I will beg leave to show what inconveniences may possibly happen by such an innovation, in the present posture of our affairs.

First, one great advantage proposed by the abolishing of Christianity is that it would very much enlarge and establish liberty of conscience, that great bulwark of our nation, and of the protestant religion, which is still too much limited by priestcraft, notwithstanding all the good intentions of the legislature, as we have lately found by a severe instance. For it is confidently reported that two young gentlemen of real hopes, bright wit, and profound judgment, who upon a thorough examination of causes and effects, and by the mere force of natural abilities, without the least tincture of learning, having made a discovery that there was no God, and generously communicating their thoughts for the good of the public, were some time ago, by an unparalleled severity, and upon I know not what obsolete law, broke only for blasphemy. And as it hath been wisely observed, if persecution once begins, no man alive knows how far it may reach, or where it will end.

In answer to all which, with deference to wiser judgments, I think this rather shows the necessity of a nominal religion among us. Great wits love to be free with the highest objects; and if they cannot be allowed a God to revile or renounce, they will speak evil of dignities, abuse the government, and reflect upon the ministry; which I am sure few will deny to be of much more pernicious consequence, according to the saying of Tiberius, *Deorum offensa diis curae.*[4] As to the particular fact

3. *Epode* 16.
4. "Offenses against the gods are the concern of   the gods" (Tacitus, *Annals* 1.73).

related, I think it is not fair to argue from one instance; perhaps another cannot be produced; yet (to the comfort of all those who may be apprehensive of persecution) blasphemy we know is freely spoken a million of times in every coffeehouse and tavern, or wherever else good company meet. It must be allowed indeed, that to break an English freeborn officer only for blasphemy, was, to speak the gentlest of such an action, a very high strain of absolute power. Little can be said in excuse for the general; perhaps he was afraid it might give offense to the allies[5] among whom, for aught we know, it may be the custom of the country to believe a God. But if he argued, as some have done, upon a mistaken principle, that an officer who is guilty of speaking blasphemy may some time or other proceed so far as to raise a mutiny, the consequence is by no means to be admitted: for, surely the commander of an English army is likely to be but ill obeyed whose soldiers fear and reverence him as little as they do a deity.

It is further objected against the gospel system that it obliges men to the belief of things too difficult for freethinkers, and such who have shaken off the prejudices that usually cling to a confined education. To which I answer that men should be cautious how they raise objections which reflect upon the wisdom of the nation. Is not everybody freely allowed to believe whatever he pleases, and to publish his belief to the world whenever he thinks fit, especially if it serves to strengthen the party which is in the right? Would any indifferent foreigner who should read the trumpery lately written by Asgil, Tindal, Toland, Coward,[6] and forty more, imagine the Gospel to be our rule of faith, and confirmed by parliaments? Does any man either believe, or say he believes, or desire to have it thought that he says he believes one syllable of the matter? And is any man worse received upon that score, or does he find his want of nominal faith a disadvantage to him in the pursuit of any civil or military employment? What if there be an old dormant statute or two against him? Are they not now obsolete to a degree that Empson and Dudley[7] themselves, if they were now alive, would find it impossible to put them in execution?

It is likewise urged that there are by computation in this kingdom above ten thousand parsons whose revenues, added to those of my lords the bishops, would suffice to maintain at least two hundred young gentlemen of wit and pleasure, and freethinking enemies to priestcraft, narrow principles, pedantry, and prejudices; who might be an ornament to the court and town. And then again, so great a number of able (bodied) divines might be a recruit to our fleet and armies. This indeed appears to be a consideration of some weight; but then, on the other side, several things deserve to be considered likewise: as, first, whether it may not be thought necessary that in certain tracts of country, like what

5. England's principal allies against France in the War of the Spanish Succession were Holland, Austria, Prussia, Portugal, and Savoy.
6. Deistic writers.

7. Two corrupt ministers of Henry VII, notorious for reviving obsolete statutes in subservience to that king's greed.

we call parishes, there shall be one man at least of abilities to read and write. Then it seems a wrong computation that the revenues of the Church throughout this island would be large enough to maintain two hundred young gentlemen, or even half that number, after the present refined way of living; that is, to allow each of them such a rent[8] as, in the modern form of speech, would make them easy. But still there is in this project a greater mischief behind; and we ought to beware of the woman's folly who killed the hen that every morning laid her a golden egg. For, pray, what would become of the race of men in the next age if we had nothing to trust to beside the scrofulous, consumptive productions, furnished by our men of wit and pleasure, when, having squandered away their vigor, health, and estates, they are forced by some disagreeable marriage to piece up their broken fortunes, and entail rottenness and politeness on their posterity? Now here are ten thousand persons reduced by the wise regulations of Henry the Eighth to the necessity of a low diet and moderate exercise,[9] who are the only great restorers of our breed, without which the nation would in an age or two become one great hospital.

Another advantage proposed by the abolishing of Christianity is the clear gain of one day in seven, which is now entirely lost, and consequently the kingdom one-seventh less considerable in trade, business, and pleasure; besides the loss to the public of so many stately structures now in the hands of the clergy, which might be converted into playhouses, exchanges, markethouses, common dormitories, and other public edifices.

I hope I shall be forgiven a hard word, if I call this a perfect cavil. I readily own there hath been an old custom, time out of mind, for people to assemble in the churches every Sunday, and that shops are still frequently shut, in order, as it is conceived, to preserve the memory of that ancient practice; but how this can prove a hindrance to business or pleasure is hard to imagine. What if the men of pleasure are forced, one day in the week, to game at home instead of the chocolatehouse? Are not the taverns and coffeehouses open? Can there be a more convenient season for taking a dose of physic? Are fewer claps got upon Sundays than other days? Is not that the chief day for traders to sum up the accounts of the week and for lawyers to prepare their briefs? But I would fain know how it can be pretended that the churches are misapplied? Where are more appointments and rendezvouses of gallantry? Where more care to appear in the foremost box with greater advantage of dress? Where more meetings for business? Where more bargains driven of all sorts? And where so many conveniences or incitements to sleep?

There is one advantage greater than any of the foregoing proposed by the abolishing of Christianity: that it will utterly extinguish parties among

8. Income.
9. Swift refers ironically to Henry VIII's expropriation of church lands at the time of the Reformation. Instead of giving them to the church for the support of the clergy, as Swift thought he should

have done, he bestowed them on laymen, thus impoverishing the lower clergy, who were deprived of the tithes that would otherwise have been their due.

us by removing those factious distinctions of High and Low Church, of Whig and Tory, Presbyterian and Church of England, which are now so many mutual clogs upon public proceedings, and dispose men to prefer the gratifying themselves, or depressing their adversaries, before the most important interest of the state.

I confess, if it were certain that so great an advantage would redound to the nation by this expedient, I would submit and be silent: but will any man say that if the words *whoring, drinking, cheating, lying, stealing*, were by act of Parliament ejected out of the English tongue and dictionaries, we should all awake next morning chaste and temperate, honest and just, and lovers of truth? Is this a fair consequence? Or, if the physicians would forbid us to pronounce the words *pox, gout, rheumatism*, and *stone*, would that expedient serve like so many talismans to destroy the diseases themselves? Are party and faction rooted in men's hearts no deeper than phrases borrowed from religion, or founded upon no firmer principles? And is our language so poor that we cannot find other terms to express them? Are *envy, pride, avarice*, and *ambition* such ill nomenclators that they cannot furnish appellations for their owners? Will not *heydukes* and *mamalukes, mandarins* and *patshaws*, or any other words formed at pleasure, serve to distinguish those who are in the ministry from others who would be in it if they could? What, for instance, is easier than to vary the form of speech, and instead of the *church*, make it a question in politics whether the Monument[1] be in danger? Because religion was nearest at hand to furnish a few convenient phrases, is our invention so barren we can find no others? Suppose, for argument sake, that the Tories favored Margarita, the Whigs Mrs. Tofts, and the Trimmers Valentini,[2] would not *Margaritians, Toftians*, and *Valentinians* be very tolerable marks of distinction? The *Prasini* and *Veniti*,[3] two most virulent factions in Italy, began (if I remember right) by a distinction of colors in ribbons, which we might do with as good a grace about the dignity of the blue and the green, and would serve as properly to divide the court, the Parliament, and the kingdom between them, as any terms of art whatsoever borrowed from religion. Therefore I think there is little force in this objection against Christianity, or prospect of so great an advantage as is proposed in the abolishing of it.

'Tis again objected as a very absurd, ridiculous custom that a set of men should be suffered, much less employed and hired, to bawl one day in seven against the lawfulness of those methods most in use toward the pursuit of greatness, riches, and pleasure, which are the constant practice of all men alive on the other six. But this objection is, I think, a little unworthy so refined an age as ours. Let us argue this matter calmly; I appeal to the breast of any polite freethinker whether in the pursuit of gratifying a predominant passion he hath not always felt a wonderful incitement, by reflecting it was a thing forbidden; and there-

---

1. The column that commemorates the great fire of London, 1666.
2. Singers in the popular Italian opera.

3. Rival factions in the Roman chariot races, violently supported by the populace.

fore we see, in order to cultivate this taste, the wisdom of the nation hath taken special care that the ladies should be furnished with prohibited silks and the men with prohibited wine. And indeed, it were to be wished that some other prohibitions were promoted in order to improve the pleasures of the town; which, for want of such expedients begin already, as I am told, to flag and grow languid, giving way daily to cruel inroads from the spleen.[4]

'Tis likewise proposed as a great advantage to the public that if we once discard the system of the Gospel, all religion will of course be banished for ever; and consequently, along with it, those grievous prejudices of education, which under the names of *virtue, conscience, honor, justice,* and the like, are so apt to disturb the peace of human minds, and the notions whereof are so hard to be eradicated by right reason or freethinking, sometimes during the whole course of our lives.

Here first I observe how difficult it is to get rid of a phrase which the world is once grown fond of, though the occasion that first produced it be entirely taken away. For several years past, if a man had but an ill-favored nose, the deep thinkers of the age would some way or other contrive to impute the cause to the prejudice of his education. From this fountain were said to be derived all our foolish notions of justice, piety, love of our country, all our opinions of God, or a future state, heaven, hell, and the like: and there might formerly perhaps have been some pretense for this charge. But so effectual care hath been since taken to remove those prejudices by an entire change in the methods of education that (with honor I mention it to our polite innovators) the young gentlemen who are now on the scene, seem to have not the least tincture of those infusions, or string of those weeds; and, by consequence, the reason for abolishing nominal Christianity upon that pretext is wholly ceased.

For the rest, it may perhaps admit a controversy whether the banishing of all notions of religion whatsoever would be convenient for the vulgar. Not that I am in the least of opinion with those who hold religion to have been the invention of politicians to keep the lower part of the world in awe by the fear of invisible powers; unless mankind were then very different from what it is now: for I look upon the mass or body of our people here in England to be as freethinkers, that is to say, as staunch unbelievers, as any of the highest rank. But I conceive some scattered notions about a superior power to be of singular use for the common people, as furnishing excellent materials to keep children quiet when they grow peevish, and providing topics of amusement in a tedious winter night.

Lastly, it is proposed as a singular advantage that the abolishing of Christianity will very much contribute to the uniting of Protestants, by enlarging the terms of communion so as to take in all sorts of Dissenters, who are now shut out of the pale upon account of a few ceremonies

---

4. Melancholy; often a real affliction, but as often affected as a fashionable ailment.

which all sides confess to be things indifferent; that this alone will effectually answer the great ends of a scheme for comprehension, by opening
a large noble gate, at which all bodies may enter: whereas the chaffering
with Dissenters, and dodging about this or t' other ceremony, is but like
opening a few wickets[5] and leaving them at jar, by which no more than
one can get in at a time, and that, not without stooping, and sideling,
and squeezing his body.

To all this I answer that there is one darling inclination of mankind,
which usually affects to be a retainer to religion, though she be neither
its parent, its godmother, or its friend; I mean the spirit of opposition,
that lived long before Christinaity, and can easily subsist without it. Let
us, for instance, examine wherein the opposition of sectaries[6] among us
consists; we shall find Christianity to have no share in it at all. Does the
Gospel any where prescribe a starched, squeezed countenance, a stiff,
formal gait, a singularity of manners and habit, or any affected modes
of speech different from the reasonable part of mankind? Yet, if Christianity did not lend its name to stand in the gap, and to employ or divert
these humors, they must of necessity be spent in contraventions to the
laws of the land, and disturbance of the public peace. There is a portion
of enthusiasm assigned to every nation, which, if it hath not proper
objects to work on, will burst out, and set all in a flame. If the quiet of
state can be bought by only flinging men a few ceremonies to devour, it
is a purchase no wise man would refuse. Let the mastiffs amuse themselves about a sheepskin stuffed with hay, provided it will keep them
from worrying the flock. The institution of convents abroad seems in
one point a strain of great wisdom, there being few irregularities in human
passions that may not have recourse to vent themselves in some of those
orders, which are so many retreats for the speculative, the melancholy,
the proud, the silent, the politic and the morose, to spend themselves,
and evaporate the noxious particles; for each of whom we in this island
are forced to provide a several sect of religion, to keep them quiet. And
whenever Christianity shall be abolished, the legislature must find some
other expedient to employ and entertain them. For what imports it how
large a gate you open if there will be always left a number who place a
pride and merit in refusing to enter?

Having thus considered the most important objections against Christianity and the chief advantages proposed by the abolishing thereof, I
shall now with equal deference and submission to wiser judgments as
before, proceed to mention a few inconveniences that may happen if the
Gospel should be repealed; which perhaps the projectors may not have
sufficiently considered.

And first, I am very sensible how much the gentlemen of wit and
pleasure are apt to murmur, and be choked at the sight of so many
daggled-tail parsons who happen to fall in their way, and offend their
eyes. But at the same time, these wise reformers do not consider what

---

5. Small gates.   6. Adherents of one of the dissenting sects.

an advantage and felicity it is for great wits to be always provided with objects of scorn and contempt, in order to exercise and improve their talents, and divert their spleen from falling on each other or on themselves; especially when all this may be done without the least imaginable danger to their persons.

And to urge another argument of a parallel nature: if Christianity were once abolished, how could the freethinkers, the strong reasoners, and the men of profound learning, be able to find another subject so calculated in all points whereon to display their abilities? What wonderful productions of wit should we be deprived of from those whose genius by continual practice hath been wholly turned upon raillery and invectives against religion, and would therefore never be able to shine or distinguish themselves upon any other subject! We are daily complaining of the great decline of wit among us, and would we take away the greatest, perhaps the only, topic we have left? Who would ever have suspected Asgil for a wit, or Toland for a philosopher, if the inexhaustible stock of Christianity had not been at hand to provide them with materials? What other subject, through all art or nature, could have produced Tindal for a profound author, or furnished him with readers? It is the wise choice of the subject that alone adorns and distinguishes the writer. For had a hundred such pens as these been employed on the side of religion, they would have immediately sunk into silence and oblivion.

Nor do I think it wholly groundless, or my fears altogether imaginary, that the abolishing of Christianity may perhaps bring the Church in danger, or at least put the senate to the trouble of another securing vote. I desire I may not be mistaken; I am far from presuming to affirm or think that the Church is in danger at present, or as things now stand; but we know not how soon it may be so when the Christian religion is repealed. As plausible as this project seems, there may a dangerous design lurk under it. Nothing can be more notorious than that the atheists, deists, Socinians,[7] Antitrinitarians, and other subdivisions of freethinkers are persons of little zeal for the present ecclesiastical establishment: their declared opinion is for repealing the Sacramental Test; they are very indifferent with regard to ceremonies; nor do they hold the *jus divinum* of Episcopacy.[8] Therefore this may be intended as one politic step toward altering the constitution of the Church established, and setting up Presbytery[9] in the stead, which I leave to be further considered by those at the helm.

In the last place, I think nothing can be more plain than that by this expedient, we shall run into the evil we chiefly pretend to avoid; and that the abolishment of the Christian religion will be the readiest course we can take to introduce popery. And I am the more inclined to this opinion because we know it has been the constant practice of the Jesuits to send over emissaries with instructions to personate themselves mem-

---

7. The Socinians denied the divinity of Jesus.
8. The divine authority of Anglican bishops, derived from apostolic succession.

9. The Presbyterians opposed episcopacy and set up a democratic form of church government.

bers of the several prevailing sects among us. So it is recorded that they have at sundry times appeared in the guise of Presbyterians, Anabaptists, Independents, and Quakers, according as any of these were most in credit; so, since the fashion hath been taken up of exploding religion, the popish missionaries have not been wanting to mix with the freethinkers; among whom, Toland, the great oracle of the Antichristians, is an Irish priest, the son of an Irish priest; and the most learned and ingenious author of a book called *The Rights of the Christian Church*, was in a proper juncture reconciled to the Romish faith, whose true son, as appears by an hundred passages in his treatise, he still continues. Perhaps I could add some others to the number; but the fact is beyond dispute, and the reasoning they proceed by is right: for, supposing Christianity to be extinguished, the people will never be at ease till they find out some other method of worship; which will as infallibly produce superstition as this will end in popery.

And therefore, if notwithstanding all I have said, it still be thought necessary to have a bill brought in for repealing Christianity, I would humbly offer an amendment; that instead of the word *Christianity* may be put *religion* in general; which I conceive will much better answer all the good ends proposed by the projectors of it. For, as long as we leave in being a God and his providence, with all the necessary consequences which curious and inquisitive men will be apt to draw from such premises, we do not strike at the root of the evil, though we should ever so effectually annihilate the present scheme of the Gospel. For of what use is freedom of thought, if it will not produce freedom of action, which is the sole end, how remote soever in appearance, of all objections against Christianity? And, therefore, the freethinkers consider it as a sort of edifice wherein all the parts have such a mutual dependence on each other that if you happen to pull out one single nail, the whole fabric must fall to the ground. This was happily expressed by him who had heard of a text brought for proof of the Trinity, which in an ancient manuscript was differently read; he thereupon immediately took the hint, and by a sudden deduction of a long *sorites*,[1] most logically concluded, "Why, if it be as you say, I may safely whore and drink on, and defy the parson." From which, and many the like instances easy to be produced, I think nothing can be more manifest than that the quarrel is not against any particular points of hard digestion in the Christian system, but against religion in general; which, by laying restraints on human nature, is supposed the great enemy to the freedom of thought and action.

Upon the whole, if it shall still be thought for the benefit of Church and State that Christianity be abolished, I conceive, however, it may be more convenient to defer the execution to a time of peace, and not venture in this conjuncture to disoblige our allies, who, as it falls out, are all Christians; and many of them, by the prejudices of their education, so bigoted as to place a sort of pride in the appellation. If upon

---

1. "An argument when one proposition is accumulated on another" (Johnson's *Dictionary*).

being rejected by them, we are to trust to an alliance with the Turk, we shall find ourselves much deceived: for, as he is too remote, and generally engaged in war with the Persian emperor, so his people would be more scandalized at our infidelity than our Christian neighbors. Because the Turks are not only strict observers of religious worship, but what is worse, believe a God; which is more than is required of us even while we preserve the name of Christians.

To conclude: whatever some may think of the great advantages to trade by this favorite scheme, I do very much apprehend that in six months time after the act is passed for the extirpation of the Gospel, the Bank and East-India Stock may fall at least one per cent. And since that is fifty times more than ever the wisdom of our age thought fit to venture for the preservation of Christianity, there is no reason we should be at so great a loss merely for the sake of destroying it.

1708   1711

Gulliver's Travels *Gulliver's Travels* is Swift's most universal satire. Although it is full of allusions to recent and contemporary historical events, it is as valid today as it was in 1726, for its objects are man's moral nature and the defective political, economic, and social institutions which human imperfections call into being. Swift adopts an ancient satirical device: the imaginary voyage. Lemuel Gulliver, the narrator, is a ship's surgeon, a reasonably well-educated man, kindly, resourceful, cheerful, inquiring, patriotic, truthful, and rather unimaginative. He is, in short, a reasonably decent example of humanity, with whom we identify ourselves readily enough. He undertakes four voyages, all of which end disastrously among "several remote nations of the world." In the first, Gulliver is shipwrecked in the empire of Lilliput, where he finds himself a giant among a diminutive people, charmed by their miniature city and amused by their toylike prettiness. But in the end they prove to be treacherous, malicious, ambitious, vengeful, and cruel. As we read we grow disenchanted with the inhabitants of this fanciful kingdom, and then gradually we begin to recognize our likeness to them, especially in the disproportion between our natural pettiness and our boundless and destructive passions. In the second voyage, Gulliver is abandoned by his shipmates in Brobdingnag, a land of giants, creatures ten times as large as Europeans. Naturally enough, he assumes that such monsters must be brutes, but the reverse proves to be the case. Brobdingnag is something of a utopia, governed by a humane and enlightened prince who is the embodiment of moral and political wisdom. In the long interview in which Gulliver pridefully enlarges on the glories of England and her political institutions, the King reduces him to resentful silence by asking questions which reveal the difference between what is and what ought to be in human, especially British, institutions. In Brobdingnag, Gulliver finds himself a Lilliputian, his pride humbled by his helpless state and his human vanity diminished by the realization that his body must have seemed as disgusting to the Lilliputians as do the bodies of the Brobdingnagians to him.

In the third voyage, to Laputa, Swift is chiefly concerned with attacking extremes of theoretical and speculative reasoning, whether in science, politics, or economics. Much of this voyage is an allegory of political life under the administration of the Whig minister, Sir Robert Walpole. The final voyage sets Gulliver between a race of horses, Houyhnhnms (prounced *Hwínims*), who live entirely by reason except for a few well-controlled and muted social affections, and their slaves, the Yahoos, whose bodies are obscene caricatures of the human body, and who have no glimmer of reason, but are mere creatures of appetite and passion.

When *Gulliver's Travels* first appeared, everyone read it—children for the story, politicians for the satire of current affairs—and ever since it has retained a hold on readers of every kind. Almost unique in world literature, it is simple enough for a child, complex enough to carry an adult beyond his depth. Swift's art works on many levels. First of all, there is the sheer playfulness of the narrative. Through Gulliver's eyes, we gaze on marvel after marvel: a tiny girl who threads an invisible needle with invisible silk, or a white mare who threads a needle between pastern and hoof. The travels, like a fairy story, transport us to imaginary worlds that function with a perfect, fantastic logic different from our own; Swift exercises our sense of vision. But beyond that, he exercises our perceptions of meaning. In *Gulliver's Travels*, things are seldom what they seem; irony, probing or corrosive, underlies almost every word. During the last chapter, Gulliver insists that the example of the Houyhnhnms has made him incapable of telling a lie— but the oath he swears is quoted from Sinon, whose lies to the Trojans persuaded them to accept the Trojan *horse*. Swift trains us to read alertly, to look beneath the surface. Yet on its deepest level, the book does not offer final meanings, but a question: what sort of thing is man? Voyaging through imaginary worlds, we try to find ourselves. Are we prideful insects, or lords of creation? brutes, or reasonable beings? In the last voyage, Swift pushes such questions, and Gulliver himself, almost beyond endurance; hating his own humanity, Gulliver forgets who he is. For the reader, however, the outcome cannot be so clear. Swift does not set out to satisfy our minds, but to vex and unsettle them. And he leaves us at the moment when the mixed face of humanity—the pettiness of the Lilliputians, the savagery of the Yahoos, the innocence of Gulliver himself—begins to look strangely familiar, like our own faces in a mirror.

From Gulliver's Travels[1]

A *Letter from Captain Gulliver to His Cousin Sympson*

I hope you will be ready to own publicly, whenever you shall be called to it, that by your great and frequent urgency you prevailed on me to

1. Swift's full title for this work was *Travels into Several Remote Nations of the World. In Four Parts. By Lemuel Gulliver, First a Surgeon, and then a Captain of several Ships.* In the first edition (1726), either the bookseller or Swift's friends Charles Ford, Pope, and others, who were concerned in getting the book anonymously into print, altered and omitted so much of the original manuscript (because of its dangerous political implications) that Swift was seriously annoyed. When, in 1735, the Dub- lin bookseller George Faulkner brought out an edition of Swift's works, the dean seems to have taken pains, surreptitiously, to see that a more authentic version of the work was published. This text is the basis of modern editions.

In this letter, first published in 1735, Swift complains, among other matters, of the alterations in his original text made by the publisher, Benjamin Motte, in the interest of what he considered political discretion.

publish a very loose and uncorrect account of my travels; with direction to hire some young gentlemen of either University to put them in order, and correct the style, as my Cousin Dampier[2] did by my advice, in his book called A *Voyage round the World*. But I do not remember I gave you power to consent that anything should be omitted, and much less that anything should be inserted: therefore, as to the latter, I do here renounce everything of that kind; particularly a paragraph about her Majesty the late Queen Anne, of most pious and glorious memory; although I did reverence and esteem her more than any of human species. But you, or your interpolator, ought to have considered that as it was not my inclination, so was it not decent to praise any animal of our composition before my master Houyhnhnm; and besides, the fact was altogether false; for to my knowledge, being in England during some part of her Majesty's reign, she did govern by a chief Minister; nay, even by two successively; the first whereof was the Lord of Godolphin, and the second the Lord of Oxford; so that you have made me *say the thing that was not*. Likewise, in the account of the Academy of Projectors, and several passages of my discourse to my master Houyhnhnm, you have either omitted some material circumstances, or minced or changed them in such a manner, that I do hardly know mine own work. When I formerly hinted to you something of this in a letter, you were pleased to answer that you were afraid of giving offense; that people in power were very watchful over the press; and apt not only to interpret, but to punish everything which looked like an *innuendo* (as I think you called it). But pray, how could that which I spoke so many years ago, and at above five thousand leagues distance, in another reign, be applied to any of the Yahoos, who now are said to govern the herd; especially, at a time when I little thought on or feared the unhappiness of living under them. Have not I the most reason to complain, when I see these very Yahoos carried by Houyhnhnms in a vehicle, as if these were brutes, and those the rational creatures? And, indeed, to avoid so monstrous and detestable a sight was one principal motive of my retirement hither.[3]

Thus much I thought proper to tell you in relation to yourself, and to the trust I reposed in you.

I do in the next place complain of my own great want of judgment, in being prevailed upon by the intreaties and false reasonings of you and some others, very much against mine own opinion, to suffer my travels to be published. Pray bring to your mind how often I desired you to consider, when you insisted on the motive of public good, that the Yahoos were a species of animals utterly incapable of amendment by precepts or examples; and so it hath proved; for instead of seeing a full stop put to all abuses and corruptions, at least in this little island, as I had reason to expect, behold, after above six months warning, I cannot learn that my book hath produced one single effect according to mine intentions; I desired you would let me know by a letter, when party and faction were

2. William Dampier (1652–1715), the explorer, whose account of his circumnavigation of the globe　　Swift had read.
3. To Nottinghamshire.

extinguished; judges learned and upright; pleaders honest and modest, with some tincture of common sense; and Smithfield[4] blazing with pyramids of law books; the young nobility's education entirely changed; the physicians banished; the female Yahoos abounding in virtue, honor, truth, and good sense; courts and levees of great ministers thoroughly weeded and swept; wit, merit, and learning rewarded; all disgracers of the press in prose and verse, condemned to eat nothing but their own cotton,[5] and quench their thirst with their own ink. These, and a thousand other reformations, I firmly counted upon by your encouragement; as indeed they were plainly deducible from the precepts delivered in my book. And, it must be owned that seven months were a sufficient time to correct every vice and folly to which Yahoos are subject; if their natures had been capable of the least disposition to virtue or wisdom; yet so far have you been from answering mine expectation in any of your letters, that on the contrary, you are loading our carrier every week with libels, and keys, and reflections, and memoirs, and second parts; wherein I see myself accused of reflecting upon great statesfolk; of degrading human nature (for so they have still the confidence to style it) and of abusing the female sex. I find likewise, that the writers of those bundles are not agreed among themselves; for some of them will not allow me to be author of mine own travels; and others make me author of books to which I am wholly a stranger.

I find likewise that your printer hath been so careless as to confound the times, and mistake the dates of my several voyages and returns; neither assigning the true year, or the true month, or day of the month; and I hear the original manuscript is all destroyed, since the publication of my book. Neither have I any copy left; however, I have sent you some corrections, which you may insert, if ever there should be a second edition; and yet I cannot stand to them, but shall leave that matter to my judicious and candid readers, to adjust it as they please.

I hear some of our sea Yahoos find fault with my sea language, as not proper in many parts, nor now in use. I cannot help it. In my first voyages, while I was young, I was instructed by the oldest mariners, and learned to speak as they did. But I have since found that the sea Yahoos are apt, like the land ones, to become new fangled in their words; which the latter change every year; insomuch, as I remember upon each return to mine own country, their old dialect was so altered, that I could hardly understand the new. And I observe, when any Yahoo comes from London out of curiosity to visit me at mine own house, we neither of us are able to deliver our conceptions in a manner intelligible to the other.[6]

If the censure of Yahoos could any way affect me, I should have great reason to complain that some of them are so bold as to think my book of travels a mere fiction out of mine own brain; and have gone so far as to drop hints that the Houyhnhnms, and Yahoos have no more existence than the inhabitants of Utopia.

4. A part of London containing many bookshops. 6. Swift was the inveterate enemy of slang.
5. Presumably their paper.

Indeed I must confess that as to the people of Lilliput, Brobdingrag (for so the word should have been spelled, and not erroneously Brobdingnag) and Laputa, I have never yet heard of any Yahoo so presumptuous as to dispute their being, or the facts I have related concerning them; because the truth immediately strikes every reader with conviction. And, is there less probability in my account of the Houyhnhnms or Yahoos, when it is manifest as to the latter, there are so many thousands even in this city, who only differ from their brother brutes in Houyhnhnmland, because they use a sort of a jabber, and do not go naked. I wrote for their amendment, and not their approbation. The united praise of the whole race would be of less consequence to me, than the neighing of those two degenerate Houyhnhnms I keep in my stable; because, from these, degenerate as they are, I still improve in some virtues, without any mixture of vice.

Do these miserable animals presume to think that I am so far degenerated as to defend my veracity; Yahoo as I am, it is well known through all Houyhnhnmland, that by the instructions and example of my illustrious master, I was able in the compass of two years (although I confess with the utmost difficulty) to remove that infernal habit of lying, shuffling, deceiving, and equivocating, so deeply rooted in the very souls of all my species; especially the Europeans.

I have other complaints to make upon this vexatious occasion; but I forbear troubling myself or you any further. I must freely confess that since my last return, some corruptions of my Yahoo nature have revived in me by conversing with a few of your species, and particularly those of mine own family, by an unavoidable necessity; else I should never have attempted so absurd a project as that of reforming the Yahoo race in this kingdom; but I have now done with all such visionary schemes for ever.

1727?   1735

The Publisher to the Reader

The author of these travels, Mr. Lemuel Gulliver, is my ancient and intimate friend; there is likewise some relation between us by the mother's side. About three years ago Mr. Gulliver, growing weary of the concourse of curious people coming to him at his house in Redriff,[1] made a small purchase of land, with a convenient house, near Newark, in Nottinghamshire, his native country; where he now lives retired, yet in good esteem among his neighbors.

Although Mr. Gulliver were born in Nottinghamshire, where his father dwelt, yet I have heard him say his family came from Oxfordshire; to confirm which, I have observed in the churchyard at Banbury, in that county, several tombs and monuments of the Gullivers.

Before he quitted Redriff, he left the custody of the following papers in my hands, with the liberty to dispose of them as I should think fit. I

---

1. Rotherhithe, a district in southern London, below Tower Bridge, then frequented by sailors.

have carefully perused them three times; the style is very plain and simple; and the only fault I find is that the author, after the manner of travelers, is a little too circumstantial. There is an air of truth apparent through the whole; and indeed the author was so distinguished for his veracity, that it became a sort of proverb among his neighbors at Redriff, when anyone affirmed a thing, to say, it was as true as if Mr. Gulliver had spoke it.

By the advice of several worthy persons, to whom, with the author's permission, I communicated these papers, I now venture to send them into the world; hoping they may be, at least for some time, a better entertainment to our young noblemen, than the common scribbles of politics and party.

This volume would have been at least twice as large, if I had not made bold to strike out innumerable passages relating to the winds and tides, as well as to the variations and bearings in the several voyages; together with the minute descriptions of the management of the ship in storms, in the style of sailors; likewise the account of the longitudes and latitudes, wherein I have reason to apprehend that Mr. Gulliver may be a little dissatisfied; but I was resolved to fit the work as much as possible to the general capacity of readers. However, if my own ignorance in sea affairs shall have led me to commit some mistakes, I alone am answerable for them; and if any traveler hath a curiosity to see the whole work at large, as it came from the hand of the author, I will be ready to gratify him.

As for any further particulars relating to the author, the reader will receive satisfaction from the first pages of the book.

RICHARD SYMPSON

Part 1. A Voyage to Lilliput

CHAPTER 1. *The author gives some account of himself and family; his first inducements to travel. He is shipwrecked, and swims for his life; gets safe on shore in the country of Lilliput; is made a prisoner, and carried up the country.*

My father had a small estate in Nottinghamshire; I was the third of five sons. He sent me to Emanuel College in Cambridge, at fourteen years old, where I resided three years, and applied myself close to my studies: but the charge of maintaining me (although I had a very scanty allowance) being too great for a narrow fortune, I was bound apprentice to Mr. James Bates, an eminent surgeon in London, with whom I continued four years; and my father now and then sending me small sums of money, I laid them out in learning navigation, and other parts of the mathematics, useful to those who intend to travel, as I always believed it would be some time or other my fortune to do. When I left Mr. Bates, I went down to my father; where, by the assistance of him and my uncle John, and some other relations, I got forty pounds, and a promise of thirty pounds a year to maintain me at Leyden:[1] there I studied physic two years and seven months, knowing it would be useful in long voyages.

Soon after my return from Leyden, I was recommended by my good master Mr. Bates, to be surgeon to the *Swallow*, Captain Abraham Pannell commander; with whom I continued three years and a half, making a voyage or two into the Levant[2] and some other parts. When I came back, I resolved to settle in London, to which Mr. Bates, my master, encouraged me; and by him I was recommended to several patients. I took part of a small house in the Old Jury; and being advised to alter my condition, I married Mrs.[3] Mary Burton, second daughter to Mr. Edmond Burton, hosier, in Newgate Street, with whom I received four hundred pounds for a portion.

But, my good master Bates dying in two years after, and I having few friends, my business began to fail; for my conscience would not suffer me to imitate the bad practice of too many among my brethren. Having therefore consulted with my wife, and some of my acquaintance, I determined to go again to sea. I was surgeon successively in two ships, and made several voyages, for six years, to the East and West Indies; by which I got some addition to my fortune. My hours of leisure I spent in reading the best authors, ancient and modern, being always provided with a good number of books; and when I was ashore, in observing the manners and dispositions of the people, as well as learning their language; wherein I had a great facility by the strength of my memory.

The last of these voyages not proving very fortunate, I grew weary of the sea, and intended to stay at home with my wife and family. I removed from the Old Jury to Fetter Lane, and from thence to Wapping, hoping to get business among the sailors; but it would not turn to account. After three years' expectation that things would mend, I accepted an advantageous offer from Captain William Prichard, master of the *Antelope*, who was making a voyage to the South Sea. We set sail from Bristol, May 4th, 1699, and our voyage at first was very prosperous.

It would not be proper, for some reasons, to trouble the reader with the particulars of our adventures in those seas: let it suffice to inform him, that in our passage from thence to the East Indies we were driven by a violent storm to the northwest of Van Diemen's Land.[4] By an observation, we found ourselves in the latitude of 30 degrees 2 minutes south. Twelve of our crew were dead by immoderate labor, and ill food, the rest were in a very weak condition. On the fifth of November, which was the beginning of summer in those parts, the weather being very hazy, the seamen spied a rock, within half a cable's length of the ship; but the wind was so strong, that we were driven directly upon it, and immediately split. Six of the crew, of whom I was one, having let down

---

1. The University of Leyden, in Holland, a center for the study of "physic" (medicine).
2. The eastern Mediterranean.
3. "Mrs." (pronounced "Mistress") designated any

woman, married or unmarried. "Old Jury": a street (once "Old Jewry") in the City of London.
4. Tasmania.

the boat into the sea, made a shift to get clear of the ship, and the rock. We rowed by my computation about three leagues, till we were able to work no longer, being already spent with labor while we were in the ship. We therefore trusted ourselves to the mercy of the waves; and in about half an hour the boat was overset by a sudden flurry from the north. What became of my companions in the boat, as well as of those who escaped on the rock, or were left in the vessel, I cannot tell; but conclude they were all lost. For my own part, I swam as fortune directed me, and was pushed forward by wind and tide. I often let my legs drop, and could feel no bottom; but when I was almost gone, and able to struggle no longer, I found myself within my depth; and by this time the storm was much abated. The declivity was so small, that I walked near a mile before I got to the shore, which I conjectured was about eight o'clock in the evening. I then advanced forward near half a mile, but could not discover any sign of houses or inhabitants; at least I was in so weak a condition, that I did not observe them. I was extremely tired, and with that, and the heat of the weather, and about half a pint of brandy that I drank as I left the ship, I found myself much inclined to sleep. I lay down on the grass, which was very short and soft, where I slept sounder than ever I remember to have done in my life, and as I reckoned, above nine hours; for when I awaked, it was just daylight. I attempted to rise, but was not able to stir: for as I happened to lie on my back, I found my arms and legs were strongly fastened on each side to the ground; and my hair, which was long and thick, tied down in the same manner. I likewise felt several slender ligatures across my body, from my armpits to my thighs. I could only look upwards; the sun began to grow hot, and the light offended my eyes. I heard a confused noise about me, but in the posture I lay, could see nothing except the sky. In a little time I felt something alive moving on my left leg, which advancing gently forward over my breast, came almost up to my chin; when bending my eyes downwards as much as I could, I perceived it to be a human creature not six inches high,[5] with a bow and arrow in his hands, and a quiver at his back. In the meantime, I felt at least forty more of the same kind (as I conjectured) following the first. I was in the utmost astonishment, and roared so loud, that they all ran back in a fright; and some of them, as I was afterwards told, were hurt with the falls they got by leaping from my sides upon the ground. However, they soon returned; and one of them, who ventured so far as to get a full sight of my face, lifting up his hands and eyes by way of admiration,[6] cried out in a shrill, but distinct voice, *Hekinah Degul*: the others repeated the same words several times, but I then knew not what they meant. I lay all this while, as the reader may believe, in great uneasiness; at length, struggling to get loose, I had the fortune to break the strings, and wrench out the pegs that fastened my left arm to the ground; for, by lifting it up to my face, I discovered the methods they had taken to bind me; and, at the same

---

5. Lilliput is scaled, fairly consistently, at one-twelfth of Gulliver's world.
6. Wonderment.

time, with a violent pull, which gave me excessive pain, I a little loosened the strings that tied down my hair on the left side; so that I was just
able to turn my head about two inches. But the creatures ran off a second time, before I could seize them; whereupon there was a great shout
in a very shrill accent; and after it ceased, I heard one of them cry aloud,
Tolgo phonac; when in an instant I felt above an hundred arrows discharged on my left hand, which pricked me like so many needles; and
besides they shot another flight into the air, as we do bombs in Europe,
whereof many, I suppose, fell on my body (though I felt them not) and
some on my face, which I immediately covered with my left hand. When
this shower of arrows was over, I fell a groaning with grief and pain; and
then striving again to get loose, they discharged another volley larger
than the first, and some of them attempted with spears to stick me in the
sides; but, by good luck, I had on me a buff jerkin,[7] which they could
not pierce. I thought it the most prudent method to lie still; and my
design was to continue so till night, when, my left hand being already
loose, I could easily free myself: and as for the inhabitants, I had reason
to believe I might be a match for the greatest armies they could bring
against me, if they were all of the same size with him that I saw. But
fortune disposed otherwise of me. When the people observed I was quiet,
they discharged no more arrows: but by the noise increasing, I knew
their numbers were greater; and about four yards from me, over-against
my right ear, I heard a knocking for above an hour, like people at work;
when turning my head that way, as well as the pegs and strings would
permit me, I saw a stage erected about a foot and a half from the ground,
capable of holding four of the inhabitatnts, with two or three ladders to
mount it: from whence one of them, who seemed to be a person of
quality, made me a long speech, whereof I understood not one syllable.
But I should have mentioned, that before the principal person began his
oration, he cried out three times, *Langro Dehul san:* (these words and
the former were afterwards repeated and explained to me). Whereupon
immediately about fifty of the inhabitants came, and cut the strings that
fastened the left side of my head, which gave me the liberty of turning
it to the right, and of observing the person and gesture of him who was
to speak. He appeared to be of a middle age, and taller than any of the
other three who attended him; whereof one was a page who held up his
train, and seemed to be somewhat longer than my middle finger; the
other two stood one on each side to support him. He acted every part of
an orator, and I could observe many periods[8] of threatenings, and others
of promises, pity and kindness. I answered in a few words, but in the
most submissive manner, lifting up my left hand and both my eyes to
the sun, as calling him for a witness; and being almost famished with
hunger, having not eaten a morsel for some hours before I left the ship,
I found the demands of nature so strong upon me, that I could not
forbear showing my impatience (perhaps against the strict rules of decency)

7. Leather jacket.
8. In rhetoric, complete, well-constructed sentences.

by putting my finger frequently on my mouth, to signify that I wanted food. The Hurgo (for so they call a great lord, as I afterwards learned) understood me very well. He descended from the stage, and commanded that several ladders should be applied to my sides, on which above an hundred of the inhabitants mounted, and walked towards my mouth, laden with baskets full of meat, which had been provided and sent thither by the King's orders upon the first intelligence he received of me. I observed there was the flesh of several animals, but could not distinguish them by the taste. There were shoulders, legs, and loins shaped like those of mutton, and very well dressed, but smaller than the wings of a lark. I eat them by two or three at a mouthful, and took three loaves at a time, about the bigness of musket bullets. They supplied me as fast as they could, showing a thousand marks of wonder and astonishment at my bulk and appetite. I then made another sign that I wanted drink. They found by my eating that a small quantity would not suffice me; and being a most ingenious people, they slung up with great dexterity one of their largest hogsheads; then rolled it towards my hand, and beat out the top; I drank it off at a draught, which I might well do, for it hardly held half a pint, and tasted like a small wine of Burgundy, but much more delicious. They brought me a second hogshead, which I drank in the same manner, and made signs for more, but they had none to give me. When I had performed these wonders, they shouted for joy, and danced upon my breast, repeating several times as they did at first, *Hekinah Degul*. They made me a sign that I should throw down the two hogsheads, but first warned the people below to stand out of the way, crying aloud, *Borach Mivola*, and when they saw the vessels in the air, there was an universal shout of *Hekinah Degul*. I confess I was often tempted, while they were passing backwards and forwards on my body, to seize forty or fifty of the first that came in my reach, and dash them against the ground. But the remembrance of what I had felt, which probably might not be the worst they could do; and the promise of honor I made them, for so I interpreted my submissive behavior, soon drove out those imaginations. Besides, I now considered myself as bound by the laws of hospitality to a people who had treated me with so much expense and magnificence. However, in my thoughts I could not sufficiently wonder at the intrepidity of these diminutive mortals, who durst venture to mount and walk on my body, while one of my hands was at liberty, without trembling at the very sight of so prodigious a creature as I must appear to them. After some time, when they observed that I made no more demands for meat, there appeared before me a person of high rank from his Imperial Majesty. His Excellency, having mounted on the small of my right leg, advanced forwards up to my face, with about a dozen of his retinue. And producing his credentials under the Signet Royal, which he applied[9] close to my eyes, spoke about ten minutes, without any signs of anger, but with a kind of determinate resolution;

9. Brought.

often pointing forwards, which, as I afterwards found, was towards the capital city, about half a mile distant, whither it was agreed by his Majesty in council that I must be conveyed. I answered in a few words, but to no purpose, and made a sign with my hand that was loose, putting it to the other (but over his Excellency's head, for fear of hurting him or his train) and then to my own head and body, to signify that I desired my liberty. It appeared that he understood me well enough; for he shook his head by way of disapprobation, and held his hand in a posture to show that I must be carried as a prisoner. However, he made other signs to let me understand that I should have meat and drink enough, and very good treatment. Whereupon I once more thought of attempting to break my bonds; but again, when I felt the smart of their arrows upon my face and hands, which were all in blisters, and many of the darts still sticking in them; and observing likewise that the number of my enemies increased; I gave tokens to let them know that they might do with me what they pleased. Upon this the *Hurgo* and his train withdrew, with much civility and cheerful countenances. Soon after I heard a general shout, with frequent repetitions of the words, *Peplom Selan*, and I felt great numbers of the people on my left side relaxing the cords to such a degree, that I was able to turn upon my right, and to ease myself with making water; which I very plentifully did, to the great astonishment of the people, who conjecturing by my motions what I was going to do, immediately opened to the right and left on that side, to avoid the torrent which fell with such noise and violence from me. But before this, they had daubed my face and both my hands with a sort of ointment very pleasant to the smell, which in a few minutes removed all the smart of their arrows. These circumstances, added to the refreshment I had received by their victuals and drink, which were very nourishing, disposed me to sleep. I slept about eight hours, as I was afterwards assured; and it was no wonder; for the physicians, by the Emperor's order, had mingled a sleeping potion in the hogsheads of wine.

It seems that upon the first moment I was discovered sleeping on the ground after my landing, the Emperor had early notice of it by an express; and determined in council that I should be tied in the manner I have related (which was done in the night while I slept), that plenty of meat and drink should be sent me, and a machine prepared to carry me to the capital city.

This resolution perhaps may appear very bold and dangerous, and I am confident would not be imitated by any prince in Europe on the like occasion; however, in my opinion it was extremely prudent as well as generous. For supposing these people had endeavored to kill me with their spears and arrows while I was asleep; I should certainly have awaked with the first sense of smart, which might so far have roused my rage and strength, as to enable me to break the strings wherewith I was tied; after which, as they were not able to make resistance, so they could expect no mercy.

These people are most excellent mathematicians, and arrived to a great perfection in mechanics by the countenance and encouragement of the Emperor, who is a renowned patron of learning. This prince hath several machines fixed on wheels, for the carriage of trees and other great weights. He often builds his largest men of war, whereof some are nine foot long, in the woods where the timber grows, and has them carried on these engines[1] three or four hundred yards to the sea. Five hundred carpenters and engineers were immediately set at work to prepare the greatest engine they had. It was a frame of wood raised three inches from the ground, about seven foot long and four wide, moving upon twenty-two wheels. The shout I heard was upon the arrival of this engine, which it seems set out in four hours after my landing. It was brought parallel to me as I lay. But the principal difficulty was to raise and place me in this vehicle. Eighty poles, each of one foot high, were erected for this purpose, and very strong cords of the bigness of packthread were fastened by hooks to many bandages, which the workmen had girt round my neck, my hands, my body, and my legs. Nine hundred of the strongest men were employed to draw up these cords by many pulleys fastened on the poles; and thus, in less than three hours, I was raised and slung into the engine, and there tied fast. All this I was told, for while the whole operation was performing, I lay in a profound sleep, by the force of that soporiferous[2] medicine infused into my liquor. Fifteen hundred of the Emperor's largest horses, each about four inches and a half high, were employed to draw me towards the metropolis, which, as I said, was half a mile distant.

About four hours after we began our journey, I awaked by a very ridiculous accident; for, the carriage being stopped a while to adjust something that was out of order, two or three of the young natives had the curiosity to see how I looked when I was asleep; they climbed up into the engine, and advancing very softly to my face, one of them, an officer in the guards, put the sharp end of his half-pike a good way up into my left nostril, which tickled my nose like a straw, and made me sneeze violently: whereupon they stole off unperceived, and it was three weeks before I knew the cause of my awaking so suddenly. We made a long march the remaining part of the day, and rested at night with five hundred guards on each side of me half with torches, and half with bows and arrows, ready to shoot me if I should offer to stir. The next morning at sunrise we continued our march, and arrived within two hundred yards of the city gates about noon. The Emperor and all his court came out to meet us, but his great officers would by no means suffer his Majesty to endanger his person by mounting on my body.

At the place where the carriage stopped, there stood an ancient temple, esteemed to be the largest in the whole kingdom, which having been polluted some years before by an unnatural murder,[3] was, according to the zeal of those people, looked on as profane, and therefore had been applied to common use, and all the ornaments and furniture car-

---

1. Contrivances.
2. Inducing unnatural sleep.

3. Presumably a reference to the execution of Charles I, who was sentenced in Westminster Hall.

ried away. In this edifice it was determined I should lodge. The great gate fronting to the north was about four foot high, and almost two foot wide, through which I could easily creep. On each side of the gate was a small window not above six inches from the ground: into that on the left side, the King's smiths conveyed fourscore and eleven chains, like those that hang to a lady's watch in Europe, and almost as large, which were locked to my left leg with six and thirty padlocks. Over against this temple, on the other side of the great highway, at twenty foot distance, there was a turret at least five foot high. Here the Emperor ascended with many principal lords of his court, to have an opportunity of viewing me, as I was told, for I could not see them. It was reckoned that above an hundred thousand inhabitants came out of the town upon the same errand; and in spite of my guards, I believe there could not be fewer than ten thousand, at several times, who mounted upon my body by the help of ladders. But a proclamation was soon issued to forbid it upon pain of death. When the workmen found it was impossible for me to break loose, they cut all the strings that bound me; whereupon I rose up with as melancholy a disposition as ever I had in my life. But the noise and astonishment of the people at seeing me rise and walk are not to be expressed. The chains that held my left leg were about two yards long, and gave me not only the liberty of walking backwards and forwards in a semicircle; but, being fixed within four inches of the gate, allowed me to creep in, and lie at my full length in the temple.

CHAPTER 2. *The Emperor of Lilliput, attended by several of the nobility, comes to see the author in his confinement. The Emperor's person and habit described. Learned men appointed to teach the author their language. He gains favor by his mild disposition. His pockets are searched, and his sword and pistols taken from him.*

When I found myself on my feet, I looked about me, and must confess I never beheld a more entertaining prospect. The country round appeared like a continued garden, and the inclosed fields, which were generally forty foot square, resembled so many beds of flowers. These fields were intermingled with woods of half a stang,[4] and the tallest trees, as I could judge, appeared to be seven foot high. I viewed the town on my left hand, which looked like the painted scene of a city in a theater.

I had been for some hours extremely pressed by the necessities of nature; which was no wonder, it being almost two days since I had last disburthened myself. I was under great difficulties between urgency and shame. The best expedient I could think on, was to creep into my house, which I accordingly did; and shutting the gate after me, I went as far as the length of my chain would suffer; and discharged my body of that uneasy load. But this was the only time I was ever guilty of so uncleanly an action; for which I cannot but hope the candid reader will give some

---

4. A quarter of an acre.

allowance, after he hath maturely and impartially considered my case, and the distress I was in. From this time my constant practice was, as soon as I rose, to perform that business in open air, at the full extent of my chain, and due care was taken every morning before company came, that the offensive matter should be carried off in wheelbarrows by two servants appointed for that purpose. I would not have dwelt so long upon a circumstance, that perhaps at first sight may appear not very momentous, if I had not thought it necessary to justify my character in point of cleanliness to the world; which I am told some of my maligners have been pleased, upon this and other occasions, to call in question.

When this adventure was at an end, I came back out of my house, having occasion for fresh air. The Emperor was already descended from the tower, and advancing on horseback towards me, which had like to have cost him dear; for the beast, although very well trained, yet wholly unused to such a sight, which appeared as if a mountain moved before him, reared up on his hinder feet: but that prince, who is an excellent horseman, kept his seat, until his attendants ran in, and held the bridle, while his Majesty had time to dismount. When he alighted, he surveyed me round with great admiration, but kept beyond the length of my chains. He ordered his cooks and butlers, who were already prepared, to give me victuals and drink, which they pushed forward in a sort of vehicles upon wheels until I could reach them. I took these vehicles, and soon emptied them all; twenty of them were filled with meat, and ten with liquor; each of the former afforded me two or three good mouthfuls, and I emptied the liquor of ten vessels, which was contained in earthen vials, into one vehicle, drinking it off at a draught; and so I did with the rest. The Empress, and young princes of the blood, of both sexes, attended by many ladies, sat at some distance in their chairs; but upon the accident that happened to the Emperor's horse, they alighted, and came near his person; which I am now going to describe. He is taller, by almost the breadth of my nail, than any of his court, which alone is enough to strike an awe into the beholders. His features are strong and masculine, with an Austrian lip, and arched nose, his complexion olive, his countenance[5] erect, his body and limbs well proportioned, all his motions graceful, and his deportment majestic. He was then past his prime, being twenty-eight years and three quarters old, of which he had reigned about seven, in great felicity, and generally victorious. For the better convenience of beholding him, I lay on my side, so that my face was parallel to his, and he stood but three yards off: however, I have had him since many times in my hand, and therefore cannot be deceived in the description. His dress was very plain and simple, the fashion of it between the Asiatic and the European; but he had on his head a light helmet of gold, adorned with jewels, and a plume on the crest. He held his sword drawn in his hand, to defend himself, if I should happen to break loose; it was almost three inches long, the hilt and scabbard were

---

5. Bearing, appearance. Swift is satirically idealizing George I, whom most of the British thought gross.

gold enriched with diamonds. His voice was shrill, but very clear and articulate, and I could distinctly hear it when I stood up. The ladies and courtiers were all most magnificently clad, so that the spot they stood upon seemed to resemble a petticoat spread on the ground, embroidered with figures of gold and silver. His Imperial Majesty spoke often to me, and I returned answers, but neither of us could understand a syllable. There were several of his priests and lawyers present (as I conjectured by their habits) who were commanded to address themselves to me, and I spoke to them in as many languages as I had the least smattering of, which were High and Low Dutch,[6] Latin, French, Spanish, Italian, and Lingua Franca; but all to no purpose. After about two hours the court retired, and I was left with a strong guard, to prevent the impertinence, and probably the malice of the rabble, who were very impatient to crowd about me as near as they durst; and some of them had the impudence to shoot their arrows at me as I sat on the ground by the door of my house, whereof one very narrowly missed my left eye. But the colonel ordered six of the ringleaders to be seized, and thought no punishment so proper as to deliver them bound into my hands, which some of his soldiers accordingly did, pushing them forwards with the butt-ends of their pikes into my reach; I took them all in my right hand, put five of them into my coat-pocket; and as to the sixth, I made a countenance as if I would eat him alive. The poor man squalled terribly, and the colonel and his officer were in much pain, especially when they saw me take out my penknife: but I soon put them out of fear; for, looking mildly, and immediately cutting the strings he was bound with, I set him gently on the ground, and away he ran. I treated the rest in the same manner, taking them one by one out of my pocket, and I observed both the soldiers and people were highly obliged at this mark of my clemency, which was represented very much to my advantage at court.

Towards night I got with some difficulty into my house, where I lay on the ground, and continued to do so about a fortnight; during which time the Emperor gave orders to have a bed prepared for me. Six hundred beds of the common measure were brought in carriages, and worked up in my house; an hundred and fifty of their beds sewn together made up the breadth and length, and these were four double, which however kept me but very indifferently from the hardness of the floor, that was of smooth stone. By the same computation they provided me with sheets, blankets, and coverlets, tolerable enough for one who had been so long enured to hardships as I.

As the news of my arrival spread through the kingdom, it brought prodigious numbers of rich, idle, and curious people to see me; so that the villages were almost emptied, and great neglect of tillage and household affairs must have ensued, if his Imperial Majesty had not provided by several proclamations and orders of state against this inconveniency. He directed that those who had already beheld me should return home,

---

6. German and Dutch; "lingua franca": a jargon, based on Italian, used by traders in the Mediterranean.

and not presume to come within fifty yards of my house without license from court; whereby the secretaries of state got considerable fees.

In the mean time, the Emperor held frequent councils to debate what course should be taken with me; and I was afterwards assured by a particular friend, a person of great quality, who was as much in the secret as any, that the court was under many difficulties concerning me. They apprehended[7] my breaking loose, that my diet would be very expensive, and might cause a famine. Sometimes they determined to starve me, or at least to shoot me in the face and hands with poisoned arrows, which would soon dispatch me: but again they considered, that the stench of so large a carcass might produce a plague in the metropolis, and probably spread through the whole kingdom. In the midst of these consultations, several officers of the army went to the door of the great council chamber; and two of them being admitted, gave an account of my behavior to the six criminals above-mentioned; which made so favorable an impression in the breast of his Majesty, and the whole board, in my behalf, that an imperial commission was issued out, obliging all the villages nine hundred yards round the city to deliver in every morning six beeves, forty sheep, and other victuals for my sustenance; together with a proportionable quantity of bread and wine, and other liquors: for the due payment of which his Majesty gave assignments[8] upon his treasury. For this prince lives chiefly upon his own demesnes; seldom except upon great occasions raising any subsidies upon his subjects, who are bound to attend him in his wars at their own expense. An establishment was also made of six hundred persons to be my domestics, who had board-wages allowed for their maintenance, and tents built for them very conveniently on each side of my door. It was likewise ordered, that three hundred tailors should make me a suit of clothes after the fashion of the country: that six of his Majesty's greatest scholars should be employed to instruct me in their language: and, lastly, that the Emperor's horses, and those of the nobility, and troops of guards, should be exercised in my sight, to accustom themselves to me. All these orders were duly put in execution; and in about three weeks I made a great progress in learning their language; during which time the Emperor frequently honored me with his visits, and was pleased to assist my masters in teaching me. We began already to converse together in some sort; and the first words I learned, were to express my desire that he would please to give me my liberty; which I every day repeated on my knees.[9] His answer, as I could apprehend, was, that this must be a work of time, not to be thought on without the advice of his council; and that first I must *Lumos kelmin pesso desmar lon emposo*; that is, swear a peace with him and his kingdom. However, that I should be used with all kindness; and he advised me to acquire by my patience and discreet behavior, the good opinion of himself and his subjects. He desired I would not take it ill, if he gave

---

7. Anticipated with fear.
8. Formal mandates of revenue.
9. Gulliver's plea for liberty, and the threat of star-

vation or rebellion he represents to his captors, suggest the situation of Ireland with respect to England.

orders to certain proper officers to search me; for probably I might carry about me several weapons, which must needs be dangerous things, if they answered the bulk of so prodigious a person.[1] I said, his Majesty should be satisfied, for I was ready to strip myself, and turn up my pockets before him. This I delivered part in words, and part in signs. He replied, that by the laws of the kingdom, I must be searched by two of his officers; that he knew this could not be done without my consent and assistance; that he had so good an opinion of my generosity and justice, as to trust their persons in my hands; that whatever they took from me should be returned when I left the country, or paid for at the rate which I would set upon them. I took up the two officers in my hands, put them first into my coat-pockets, and then into every other pocket about me, except my two fobs, and another secret pocket which I had no mind should be searched, wherein I had some little necessaries of no consequence to any but myself. In one of my fobs there was a silver watch, and in the other a small quantity of gold in a purse. These gentlemen, having pen, ink, and paper about them, made an exact inventory of everything they saw; and when they had done, desired I would set them down, that they might deliver it to the Emperor. This inventory I afterwards translated into English, and is word for word as follows.

Imprimis, In the right coat-pocket of the Great Man-Mountain (for so I interpret the words *Quinbus Flestrin*) after the strictest search, we found only one great piece of coarse cloth, large enough to be a foot-cloth for your Majesty's chief room of state. In the left pocket, we saw a huge silver chest, with a cover of the same metal, which we the searchers were not able to lift. We desired it should be opened; and one of us, stepping into it, found himself up to the mid leg in a sort of dust, some part whereof flying up to our faces, set us both a sneezing for several times together. In his right waistcoat-pocket, we found a prodigious bundle of white thin substances, folded one over another, about the bigness of three men, tied with a strong cable, and marked with black figures; which we humbly conceive to be writings; every letter almost half as large as the palm of our hands. In the left there was a sort of engine, from the back of which were extended twenty long poles, resembling the palisados[2] before your Majesty's court; wherewith we conjecture the Man-Mountain combs his head; for we did not always trouble him with questions, because we found it a great difficulty to make him understand us. In the large pocket on the right side of his middle cover (so I translate the word *ranfu-lo*, by which they meant my breeches) we saw a hollow pillar of iron, about the length of a man, fastened to a strong piece of timber, larger than the pillar; and upon one side of the pillar were huge pieces of iron sticking out, cut into strange

---

1. When the Whigs came into power in 1715, the leading Tories, who included Swift's friends Oxford and Bolingbroke (Robert Harley and Henry St. John) as well as Swift himself, were investigated by a Committee of Secrecy.
2. Fences of stakes.

figures; which we know not what to make of. In the left pocket, another engine of the same kind. In the smaller pocket on the right side, were several round flat pieces of white and red metal, of different bulk; some of the white, which seemed to be silver, were so large and heavy, that my comrade and I could hardly lift them. In the left pocket were two black pillars irregularly shaped: we could not, without difficulty, reach the top of them as we stood at the bottom of his pocket. One of them was covered, and seemed all of a piece; but at the upper end of the other, there appeared a white round substance, about twice the bigness of our heads. Within each of these was inclosed a prodigious plate of steel; which, by our orders, we obliged him to show us, because we apprehended they might be dangerous engines. He took them out of their cases, and told us, that in his own country his practice was to shave his beard with one of these, and to cut his meat with the other. There were two pockets which we could not enter: these he called his fobs; they were two large slits cut into the top of his middle cover, but squeezed close by the pressure of his belly. Out of the right fob hung a great silver chain, with a wonderful kind of engine at the bottom. We directed him to draw out whatever was at the end of the chain, which appeared to be a globe, half silver, and half of some transparent metal: for on the transparent side we saw certain strange figures circularly drawn, and thought we could touch them, until we found our fingers stopped with that lucid substance. He put this engine to our ears, which made an incessant noise like that of a watermill. And we conjecture it is either some unknown animal, or the god that he worships: but we are more inclined to the latter opinion, because he assured us (if we understood him right, for he expressed himself very imperfectly), that he seldom did any thing without consulting it. He called it his oracle, and said it pointed out the time for every action of his life. From the left fob he took out a net almost large enough for a fisherman, but contrived to open and shut like a purse, and served him for the same use: we found therein several massy pieces of yellow metal, which if they be of real gold, must be of immense value.

Having thus, in obedience to your Majesty's commands, diligently searched all his pockets, we observed a girdle[3] about his waist made of the hide of some prodigious animal; from which, on the left side, hung a sword of the length of five men; and on the right, a bag or pouch divided into cells; each cell capable of holding three of your Majesty's subjects. In one of these cells were several globes or balls of a most ponderous metal, about the bigness of our heads, and required a strong hand to lift them: the other cell contained a heap of certain black grains, but of no great bulk or weight, for we could hold above fifty of them in the palms of our hands.

3. Belt.

This is an exact inventory of what we found about the body of the Man-Mountain; who used us with great civility, and due respect to your Majesty's commission. Signed and sealed on the fourth day of the eighty-ninth moon of your Majesty's auspicious reign.

CLEFREN FRELOCK, MARSI FRELOCK.

When this inventory was read over to the Emperor, he directed me to deliver up the several particulars. He first called for my scimitar, which I took out, scabbard and all. In the meantime he ordered three thousand of his choicest troops (who then attended him) to surround me at a distance, with their bows and arrows just ready to discharge: but I did not observe it; for my eyes were wholly fixed upon his Majesty. He then desired me to draw my scimitar, which, although it had got some rust by the sea water, was in most parts exceeding bright. I did so, and immediately all the troops gave a shout between terror and surprise; for the sun shone clear, and the reflection dazzled their eyes, as I waved the scimitar to and fro in my hand. His Majesty, who is a most magnanimous[4] prince, was less daunted than I could expect; he ordered me to return it into the scabbard, and cast it on the ground as gently as I could, about six foot from the end of my chain. The next thing he demanded was one of the hollow iron pillars, by which he meant my pocket-pistols. I drew it out, and at his desire, as well as I could, expressed to him the use of it, and charging it only with powder, which by the closeness of my pouch happened to escape wetting in the sea (an inconvenience that all prudent mariners take special care to provide against), I first cautioned the Emperor not to be afraid; and then I let it off in the air. The astonishment here was much greater than at the sight of my scimitar. Hundreds fell down as if they had been struck dead; and even the Emperor, although he stood his ground, could not recover himself in some time. I delivered up both my pistols in the same manner as I had done my scimitar, and then my pouch of powder and bullets; begging him that the former might be kept from fire; for it would kindle with the smallest spark, and blow up his imperial palace into the air. I likewise delivered up my watch, which the Emperor was very curious to see; and commanded two of his tallest yeomen of the guards to bear it on a pole upon their shoulders, as draymen in England do a barrel of ale. He was amazed at the continual noise it made, and the motion of the minute-hand, which he could easily discern; for their sight is much more acute than ours: he asked the opinions of his learned men about him, which were various and remote, as the reader may well imagine without my repeating; although indeed I could not very perfectly understand them. I then gave up my silver and copper money, my purse with nine large pieces of gold, and some smaller ones; my knife and razor, my comb and silver snuffbox, my handkerchief and journal book. My scimitar, pistols, and pouch, were conveyed

---

4. Courageous, great-spirited. Magnanimity, the relation (direct or inverse) between the size of the body and the soul, is a central concern of the first two parts of the *Travels*.

in carriages to his Majesty's stores; but the rest of my goods were returned me.

I had, as I before observed, one private pocket which escaped their search, wherein there was a pair of spectacles (which I sometimes use for the weakness of my eyes), a pocket perspective,[5] and several other little conveniences; which, being of no consequence to the Emperor, I did not think myself bound in honor to discover, and I apprehended they might be lost or spoiled if I ventured them out of my possession.

CHAPTER 3. *The author diverts the Emperor and his nobility of both sexes in a very uncommon manner. The diversions of the court of Lilliput described. The author hath his liberty granted him upon certain conditions.*

My gentleness and good behavior had gained so far on the Emperor and his court, and indeed upon the army and people in general, that I began to conceive hopes of getting my liberty in a short time. I took all possible methods to cultivate this favorable disposition. The natives came by degrees to be less apprehensive of any danger from me. I would sometimes lie down, and let five or six of them dance on my hand. And at last the boys and girls would venture to come and play at hide-and-seek in my hair. I had now made a good progress in understanding and speaking their language. The Emperor had a mind one day to entertain me with several of the country shows; wherein they exceed all nations I have known, both for dexterity and magnificence. I was diverted with none so much as that of the rope-dancers, performed upon a slender white thread, extended about two foot, and twelve inches from the ground. Upon which I shall desire liberty, with the reader's patience, to enlarge a little.

This diversion is only practiced by those persons who are candidates for great employments, and high favor, at court. They are trained in this art from their youth, and are not always of noble birth, or liberal education. When a great office is vacant either by death or disgrace (which often happens) five or six of those candidates petition the Emperor to entertain his Majesty and the court with a dance on the rope; and whoever jumps the highest without falling, succeeds in the office. Very often the chief ministers themselves are commanded to show their skill, and to convince the Emperor that they have not lost their faculty. Flimnap,[6] the Treasurer, is allowed to cut a caper on the strait rope, at least an inch higher than any other lord in the whole empire. I have seen him do the summerset several times together upon a trencher[7] fixed on the rope, which is no thicker than a common packthread in England. My friend Reldresal, Principal Secretary for Private Affairs, is, in my opin-

5. Telescope.
6. Sir Robert Walpole, the Whig head of the government, notorious in Swift's circle for his politi-

cal acrobatics.
7. Plate; "summerset": somersault.

ion, if I am not partial, the second after the Treasurer; the rest of the great officers are much upon a par.

These diversions are often attended with fatal accidents, whereof great numbers are on record. I myself have seen two or three candidates break a limb. But the danger is much greater when the ministers themselves are commanded to show their dexterity; for, by contending to excel themselves and their fellows, they strain so far, that there is hardly one of them who hath not received a fall; and some of them two or three. I was assured, that a year or two before my arrival, Flimnap would have infallibly broke his neck, if one of the King's cushions,[8] that accidentally lay on the ground, had not weakened the force of his fall.

There is likewise another diversion, which is only shown before the Emperor and Empress, and first minister, upon particular occasions. The Emperor lays on a table three fine silken threads of six inches long. One is blue, the other red, and the third green.[9] These threads are proposed as prizes for those persons whom the Emperor hath a mind to distinguish by a peculiar mark of his favor. The ceremony is performed in his Majesty's great chamber of state; where the candidates are to undergo a trial of dexterity very different from the former, and such as I have not observed the least resemblance of in any other country of the old or the new world. The Emperor holds a stick in his hands, both ends parallel to the horizon, while the candidates, advancing one by one, sometimes leap over the stick, sometimes creep under it backwards and forwards several times, according as the stick is advanced or depressed. Sometimes the Emperor holds one end of the stick, and his first minister the other; sometimes the minister has it entirely to himself. Whoever performs his part with most agility, and holds out the longest in *leaping* and *creeping*, is rewarded with the blue-colored silk; the red is given to the next, and the green to the third, which they all wear girt twice round about the middle; and you see few great persons about this court who are not adorned with one of these girdles.

The horses of the army, and those of the royal stables, having been daily led before me, were no longer shy, but would come up to my very feet, without starting. The riders would leap them over my hand as I held it on the ground; and one of the Emperor's huntsmen, upon a large courser, took[1] my foot, shoe and all; which was indeed a prodigious leap. I had the good fortune to divert the Emperor one day after a very extraordinary manner. I desired he would order several sticks of two foot high, and the thickness of an ordinary cane, to be brought me; whereupon his Majesty commanded the master of his woods to give directions accordingly; and the next morning six woodmen arrived with as many carriages, drawn by eight horses to each. I took nine of these sticks, and fixing them firmly in the ground in a quadrangular figure, two foot and a half square, I took four other sticks, and tied them parallel at each

8. A mistress of George I was supposed to have helped restore Walpole to office in 1721.
9. The Orders of the Garter, the Bath, and the

Thistle, conferred for services to the King.
1. Jumped over.

corner, about two foot from the ground; then I fastened my handkerchief to the nine sticks that stood erect, and extended it on all sides till it was as tight as the top of a drum; and the four parallel sticks, rising about five inches higher than the handkerchief, served as ledges on each side. When I had finished my work, I desired the Emperor to let a troop of his best horse, twenty-four in number, come and exercise upon this plain. His Majesty approved of the proposal, and I took them up one by one in my hands, ready mounted and armed, with the proper officers to exercise them. As soon as they got into order, they divided into two parties, performed mock skirmishes, discharged blunt arrows, drew their swords, fled and pursued, attacked and retired; and in short discovered the best military discipline I ever beheld. The parallel sticks secured them and their horses from falling over the stage; and the Emperor was so much delighted, that he ordered this entertainment to be repeated several days; and once was pleased to be lifted up, and give the word of command; and, with great difficulty, persuaded even the Empress herself to let me hold her in her close chair[2] within two yards of the stage, from whence she was able to take a full view of the whole performance. It was my good fortune that no ill accident happened in these entertainments, only once a fiery horse that belonged to one of the captains pawing with his hoof struck a hole in my handkerchief, and his foot slipping, he overthrew his rider and himself; but I immediately relieved them both; for covering the hole with one hand, I set down the troop with the other, in the same manner as I took them up. The horse that fell was strained in the left shoulder, but the rider got no hurt, and I repaired my handkerchief as well as I could; however, I would not trust to the strength of it any more in such dangerous enterprises.

About two or three days before I was set at liberty, as I was entertaining the court with these kinds of feats, there arrived an express to inform his Majesty that some of his subjects, riding near the place where I was first taken up, had seen a great black substance lying on the ground, very oddly shaped, extending its edges round as wide as his Majesty's bedchamber, and rising up in the middle as high as a man; that it was no living creature, as they at first apprehended, for it lay on the grass without motion, and some of them had walked round it several times; that by mounting upon each other's shoulders, they had got to the top, which was flat and even; and stamping upon it they found it was hollow within; that they humbly conceived it might be something belonging to the Man-Mountain, and if his Majesty pleased, they would undertake to bring it with only five horses. I presently[3] knew what they meant; and was glad at heart to receive this intelligence. It seems upon my first reaching the shore after our shipwreck, I was in such confusion, that before I came to the place where I went to sleep, my hat, which I had fastened with a string to my head while I was rowing, and had stuck on all the time I was swimming, fell off after I came to land; the string, as I

2. An enclosed or sedan chair.   3. Immediately.

conjecture, breaking by some accident which I never observed, but thought my hat had been lost at sea. I intreated his Imperial Majesty to give orders it might be brought to me as soon as possible, describing to him the use and the nature of it: and the next day the wagoners arrived with it, but not in a very good condition; they had bored two holes in the brim, within an inch and half of the edge, and fastened two hooks in the holes; these hooks were tied by a long cord to the harness, and thus my hat was dragged along for above half an English mile: but the ground in that country being extremely smooth and level, it received less damage than I expected.

Two days after this adventure, the Emperor, having ordered that part of his army which quarters in and about his metropolis to be in a readiness, took a fancy of diverting himself in a very singular manner. He desired I would stand like a colossus, with my legs as far asunder as I conveniently could. He then commanded his general (who was an old experienced leader, and a great patron of mine) to draw up the troops in close order, and march them under me; the foot[4] by twenty-four in a breast, and the horse by sixteen, with drums beating, colors flying, and pikes advanced. This body consisted of three thousand foot, and a thousand horse. His Majesty gave orders, upon pain of death, that every soldier in his march should observe the strictest decency with regard to my person; which, however, could not prevent some of the younger officers from turning up their eyes as they passed under me. And, to confess the truth, my breeches were at that time in so ill a condition, that they afforded some opportunities for laughter and admiration.

I had sent so many memorials and petitions for my liberty, that his Majesty at length mentioned the matter first in the cabinet, and then in a full council; where it was opposed by none, except Skyresh Bolgolam,[5] who was pleased, without any provocation, to be my mortal enemy. But it was carried against him by the whole board, and confirmed by the Emperor. That minister was *Galbet*, or Admiral of the Realm; very much in his master's confidence, and a person well versed in affairs, but of a morose and sour complexion.[6] However, he was at length persuaded to comply; but prevailed that the articles and conditions upon which I should be set free, and to which I must swear, should be drawn up by himself. These articles were brought to me by Skyresh Bolgolam in person, attended by two under-secretaries, and several persons of distinction. After they were read, I was demanded to swear to the performance of them; first in the manner of my own country, and afterwards in the method prescribed by their laws; which was to hold my right foot in my left hand, to place the middle finger of my right hand on the crown of my head, and my thumb on the tip of my right ear. But because the reader may perhaps be curious to have some idea of the style and manner of expression peculiar to that people, as well as to know the articles upon which I recovered my liberty, I have made a translation of the whole instru-

---

4. Foot-soldiers or infantry.
5. The earl of Nottingham, an enemy of Swift.
6. Disposition.

ment,[7] word for word, as near as I was able; which I here offer to the public.

GOLBASTO MOMAREN EVLAME GURDILO SHEFIN MULLY ULLY GUE, most mighty Emperor of Lilliput, delight and terror of the universe, whose dominions extend five thousand blustrugs (about twelve miles in circumference) to the extremities of the globe; Monarch of all Monarchs; taller than the sons of men; whose feet press down to the center, and whose head strikes against the sun; at whose nod the princes of the earth shake their knees; pleasant as the spring, comfortable as the summer, fruitful as autumn, dreadful as winter. His most sublime Majesty proposeth to the Man-Mountain, lately arrived at our celestial dominions, the following articles, which by a solemn oath he shall be obliged to perform.

First, The Man-Mountain shall not depart from our dominions, without our license under our great seal.

Secondly, He shall not presume to come into our metropolis, without our express order; at which time the inhabitants shall have two hours warning, to keep within their doors.

Thirdly, The said Man-Mountain shall confine his walks to our principal high roads; and not offer to walk or lie down in a meadow, or field of corn.

Fourthly, As he walks the said roads, he shall take the utmost care not to trample upon the bodies of any of our loving subjects, their horses, or carriages, nor take any of our said subjects into his hands, without their own consent.

Fifthly, If an express require extraordinary dispatch, the Man-Mountain shall be obliged to carry in his pocket the messenger and horse, a six days' journey once in every moon, and return the said messenger back (if so required) safe to our Imperial Presence.

Sixthly, He shall be our ally against our enemies in the island of Blefuscu, and do his utmost to destroy their fleet, which is now preparing to invade us.

Seventhly, That the said Man-Mountain shall, at his times of leisure, be aiding and assisting to our workmen, in helping to raise certain great stones, towards covering the wall of the principal park, and other our royal buildings.

Eighthly, That the said Man-Mountain shall, in two moons' time, deliver in an exact survey of the circumference of our dominions by a computation of his own paces round the coast.

Lastly, That upon his solemn oath to observe all the above articles, the said Man-Mountain shall have a daily allowance of meat and drink sufficient for the support of 1,728 of our subjects; with free access to our Royal Person, and other marks of our favor. Given at our palace at Belfaborac the twelfth day of the ninety-first moon of our reign.

7. A formal legal document.

I swore and subscribed to these articles with great cheerfulness and content, although some of them were not so honorable as I could have wished; which proceeded wholly from the malice of Skyresh Bolgolam the High Admiral: whereupon my chains were immediately unlocked, and I was at full liberty: the Emperor himself in person did me the honor to be by at the whole ceremony. I made my acknowledgements by prostrating myself at his Majesty's feet: but he commanded me to rise; and after many gracious expressions, which, to avoid the censure of vanity, I shall not repeat, he added, that he hoped I should prove a useful servant, and well deserve all the favors he had already conferred upon me, or might do for the future.

The reader may please to observe, that in the last article for the recovery of my liberty, the Emperor stipulates to allow me a quantity of meat and drink, sufficient for the support of 1,728 Lilliputians. Some time after, asking a friend at court how they came to fix on that determinate number, he told me, that his Majesty's mathematicians, having taken the height of my body by the help of a quadrant, and finding it to exceed theirs in the proportion of twelve to one, they concluded from the similarity of their bodies, that mine must contain at least 1,728 of theirs, and consequently would require as much food as was necessary to support that number of Lilliputians. By which, the reader may conceive an idea of the ingenuity of that people, as well as the prudent and exact economy of so great a prince.

CHAPTER 4. *Mildendo, the metropolis of Lilliput, described, together with the Emperor's palace. A conversation between the author and a principal secretary, concerning the affairs of that empire; the author's offers to serve the Emperor in his wars.*

The first request I made after I had obtained my liberty, was, that I might have license to see Mildendo, the metropolis; which the Emperor easily granted me, but with a special charge to do no hurt, either to the inhabitants, or their houses. The people had notice by proclamation of my design to visit the town. The wall which encompassed it is two foot and an half high, and at least eleven inches broad, so that a coach and horses may be driven very safely round it; and it is flanked with strong towers at ten foot distance. I stepped over the great western gate, and passed very gently, and sideling[8] through the two principal streets, only in my short waistcoat, for fear of damaging the roofs and eaves of the houses with the skirts of my coat. I walked with the utmost circumspection, to avoid treading on any stragglers, who might remain in the streets, although the orders were very strict, that all people should keep in their houses, at their own peril. The garret windows and tops of houses were so crowded with spectators, that I thought in all my travels I had not seen a more populous place. The city is an exact square, each side of

8. Sideways.

the wall being five hundred foot long. The two great streets, which run cross and divide it into four quarters, are five foot wide. The lanes and alleys, which I could not enter, but only viewed them as I passed, are from twelve to eighteen inches. The town is capable of holding five hundred thousand souls. The houses are from three to five stories. The shops and markets well provided.

The Emperor's palace is in the center of the city, where the two great streets meet. It is enclosed by a wall of two foot high, and twenty foot distant from the buildings. I had his Majesty's permission to step over this wall; and the space being so wide between that and the palace, I could easily view it on every side. The outward court is a square of forty foot, and includes two other courts: in the inmost are the royal apartments, which I was very desirous to see, but found it extremely difficult; for the great gates, from one square into another, were but eighteen inches high, and seven inches wide. Now the buildings of the outer court were at least five foot high; and it was impossible for me to stride over them, without infinite damage to the pile, although the walls were strongly built of hewn stone, and four inches thick. At the same time the Emperor had a great desire that I should see the magnificence of his palace; but this I was not able to do till three days after, which I spent in cutting down with my knife some of the largest trees in the royal park, about an hundred yards distance from the city. Of these trees I made two stools, each about three foot high, and strong enough to bear my weight. The people having received notice a second time, I went again through the city to the palace, with my two stools in my hands. When I came to the side of the outer court, I stood upon one stool, and took the other in my hand: this I lifted over the roof, and gently set it down on the space between the first and second court, which was eight foot wide. I then stepped over the buildings very conveniently from one stool to the other, and drew up the first after me with a hooked stick. By this contrivance I got into the inmost court; and lying down upon my side, I applied my face to the windows of the middle stories, which were left open on purpose, and discovered the most splendid apartments that can be imagined. There I saw the Empress, and the young princes in their several lodgings, with their chief attendants about them. Her Imperial Majesty was pleased to smile very graciously upon me and gave me out of the window her hand to kiss.

But I shall not anticipate the reader with farther descriptions of this kind, because I reserve them for a greater work, which is now almost ready for the press; containing a general description of this empire, from its first erection, through a long series of princes, with a particular account of their wars and politics, laws, learning, and religion; their plants and animals, their peculiar manners and customs, with other matters very curious and useful; my chief design at present being only to relate such events and transactions as happened to the public, or to myself, during a residence of about nine months in that empire.

One morning, about a fortnight after I had obtained my liberty, Reldresal, Principal Secretary (as they style him) of Private Affairs, came to my house, attended only by one servant. He ordered his coach to wait at a distance, and desired I would give him an hour's audience; which I readily consented to, on account of his quality, and personal merits, as well as of the many good offices he had done me during my solicitations at court. I offered to lie down, that he might the more conveniently reach my ear; but he chose rather to let me hold him in my hand during our conversation. He began with compliments on my liberty, said he might pretend to some merit in it; but, however, added, that if it had not been for the present situation of things at court, perhaps I might not have obtained it so soon. For, said he, as flourishing a condition as we appear to be in to foreigners, we labor under two mighty evils; a violent faction at home, and the danger of an invasion by a most potent enemy from abroad. As to the first, you are to understand, that for above seventy moons past, there have been two struggling parties in the empire, under the names of *Tramecksan*, and *Slamecksan*,[9] from the high and low heels on their shoes, by which they distinguish themselves.

It is alleged indeed, that the high heels are most agreeable to our ancient constitution: but however this be, his Majesty hath determined to make use of only low heels in the administration of the government and all offices in the gift of the crown; as you cannot but observe; and particularly, that his Majesty's imperial heels are lower at least by a *drurr* than any of his court; (*drurr* is a measure about the fourteenth part of an inch). The animosities between these two parties run so high, that they will neither eat nor drink, nor talk with each other. We compute the *Tramecksan*, or High-Heels, to exceed us in number; but the power is wholly on our side. We apprehend his Imperial Highness, the heir to the crown, to have some tendency towards the High-Heels; at least we can plainly discover one of his heels higher than the other, which gives him a hobble in his gait.[1] Now, in the midst of these intestine disquiets, we are threatened with an invasion from the island of Blefuscu,[2] which is the other great empire of the universe, almost as large and powerful as this of his Majesty. For as to what we have heard you affirm, that there are other kingdoms and states in the world, inhabited by human creatures as large as yourself, our philosophers are in much doubt; and would rather conjecture that you dropped from the moon, or one of the stars; because it is certain, that an hundred mortals of your bulk would, in a short time, destroy all the fruits and cattle of his Majesty's dominions. Besides, our histories of six thousand moons make no mention of any other regions, than the two great empires of Lilliput and Blefuscu. Which two mighty powers have, as I was going to tell you, been engaged in a most obstinate war for six and thirty moons past. It began upon the following occasion. It is allowed on all hands, that the primitive way of breaking eggs before we eat them, was upon the larger end: but his pre-

9. Tory (High Church) and Whig (Low Church).   in both parties.
1. The Prince of Wales (later George II) had friends   2. France.

sent Majesty's grandfather, while he was a boy, going to eat an egg, and breaking it according to the ancient practice, happened to cut one of his fingers. Whereupon the Emperor his father published an edict, commanding all his subjects, upon great penalties, to break the smaller end of their eggs. The people so highly resented this law, that our histories tell us there have been six rebellions raised on that account; wherein one emperor lost his life, and another his crown.[3] These civil commotions were constantly fomented by the monarchs of Blefuscu; and when they were quelled, the exiles always fled for refuge to that empire. It is computed, that eleven thousand persons have, at several times, suffered death, rather than submit to break their eggs at the smaller end. Many hundred large volumes have been published upon this controversy: but the books of the Big-Endians have been long forbidden, and the whole party rendered incapable by law of holding employments.[4] During the course of these troubles, the emperors of Blefuscu did frequently expostulate by their ambassadors, accusing us of making a schism in religion, by offending against a fundamental doctrine of our great prophet Lustrog, in the fifty-fourth chapter of the *Brundecral* (which is their Alcoran). This, however, is thought to be a mere strain upon the text: for the words are these; *That all true believers shall break their eggs at the convenient end:* and which is the convenient end, seems, in my humble opinion, to be left to every man's conscience, or at least in the power of the chief magistrate[5] to determine. Now the Big-Endian exiles have found so much credit in the Emperor of Blefuscu's court, and so much private assistance and encouragement from their party here at home, that a bloody war hath been carried on between the two empires for six and thirty moons with various success;[6] during which time we have lost forty capital ships, and a much greater number of smaller vessels, together with thirty thousand of our best seamen and soldiers; and the damage received by the enemy is reckoned to be somewhat greater than ours. However, they have now equipped a numerous fleet, and are just preparing to make a descent upon us; and his Imperial Majesty, placing great confidence in your valor and strength, hath commanded me to lay this account of his affairs before you.

I desired the Secretary to present my humble duty to the Emperor, and to let him know, that I thought it would not become me, who was a foreigner, to interfere with parties; but I was ready, with the hazard of my life, to defend his person and state against all invaders.

CHAPTER 5. *The author by an extraordinary stratagem prevents an invasion. A high title of honor is conferred upon him. Ambassadors arrive*

---

3. Swift's satirical allegory of the strife between Catholics (Big-Endians) and Protestants (Little-Endians) touches on Henry VIII (who "broke" with the Pope), Charles I (who lost his life), and James II (who lost his crown).
4. The Test Act (1673) prevented Catholics and Nonconformists from holding office unless they accepted the Anglican sacrament.
5. Ruler, sovereign. Swift himself accepted the right of the king to determine religious observances.
6. Reminiscent of the War of the Spanish Succession (1701–13).

from the Emperor of Blefuscu, and sue for peace. The Empress's apart-
ment on fire by an accident; the author instrumental in saving the rest
of the palace.

The empire of Blefuscu is an island situated to the north north-east
side of Lilliput, from whence it is parted only by a channel of eight
hundred yards wide. I had not yet seen it, and upon this notice of an
intended invasion, I avoided appearing on that side of the coast, for fear
of being discovered by some of the enemy's ships, who had received no
intelligence of me; all intercourse between the two empires having been
strictly forbidden during the war, upon pain of death; and an embargo
laid by our Emperor upon all vessels whatsoever. I communicated to his
Majesty a project I had formed of seizing the enemy's whole fleet; which,
as our scouts assured us, lay at anchor in the harbor ready to sail with
the first fair wind. I consulted the most experienced seamen upon the
depth of the channel, which they had often plumbed; who told me, that
in the middle at high water it was seventy *glumgluffs* deep, which is
about six foot of European measure; and the rest of it fifty *glumgluffs* at
most. I walked to the northeast coast over against Blefuscu; where, lying
down behind a hillock, I took out my small pocket perspective glass, and
viewed the enemy's fleet at anchor, consisting of about fifty men of war,
and a great number of transports: I then came back to my house, and
gave order (for which I had a warrant) for a great quantity of the strongest
cable and bars of iron. The cable was about as thick as packthread, and
the bars of the length and size of a knitting-needle. I trebled the cable to
make it stronger, and for the same reason I twisted three of the iron bars
together, bending the extremities into a hook. Having thus fixed fifty
hooks to as many cables, I went back to the northeast coast, and putting
off my coat, shoes, and stockings, walked into the sea in my leathern
jerkin, about half an hour before high water. I waded with what haste I
could, and swam in the middle about thirty yards until I felt the ground;
I arrived at the fleet in less than half an hour. The enemy was so frighted
when they saw me, that they leaped out of their ships, and swam to
shore, where there could not be fewer than thirty thousand souls. I then
took my tackling, and fastening a hook to the hole at the prow of each,
I tied all the cords together at the end. While I was thus employed, the
enemy discharged several thousand arrows, many of which stuck in my
hands and face; and besides the excessive smart, gave me much disturbance in my work. My greatest apprehension was for my eyes, which I
should have infallibly lost, if I had not suddenly thought of an expedient. I kept, among other little necessaries, a pair of spectacles in a private
pocket, which, as I observed before, had escaped the Emperor's searchers. These I took out, and fastened as strongly as I could upon my nose;
and thus armed went on boldly with my work in spite of the enemy's
arrows; many of which struck against the glasses of my spectacles, but
without any other effect, further than a little to discompose them. I had
now fastened all the hooks, and taking the knot in my hand, began to

pull; but not a ship would stir, for they were all too fast by their anchors, so that the boldest part of my enterprise remained. I therefore let go the cord, and leaving the hooks fixed to the ships, I resolutely cut with my knife the cables that fastened the anchors, receiving about two hundred shots in my face and hands; then I took up the knotted end of the cables to which my hooks were tied; and with great ease drew fifty of the enemy's largest men-of-war after me.

The Blefuscudians, who had not the least imagination of what I intended, were at first confounded with astonishment. They had seen me cut the cables, and thought my design was only to let the ships run adrift, or fall foul on each other: but when they perceived the whole fleet moving in order, and saw me pulling at the end, they set up such a scream of grief and despair, that it is almost impossible to describe or conceive. When I had got out of danger, I stopped a while to pick out the arrows that stuck in my hands and face, and rubbed on some of the same ointment that was given me at my first arrival, as I have formerly mentioned. I then took off my spectacles, and waiting about an hour until the tide was a little fallen, I waded through the middle with my cargo, and arrived safe at the royal port of Lilliput.

The Emperor and his whole court stood on the shore, expecting the issue of this great adventure. They saw the ships move forward in a large half-moon, but could not discern me, who was up to my breast in water. When I advanced to the middle of the channel, they were yet more in pain, because I was under water to my neck. The Emperor concluded me to be drowned, and that the enemy's fleet was approaching in a hostile manner: but he was soon eased of his fears, for the channel growing shallower every step I made, I came in a short time within hearing; and holding up the end of the cable by which the fleet was fastened, I cried in a loud voice, Long live the most puissant Emperor of Lilliput! This great prince received me at my landing with all possible encomiums, and created me a *Nardac* upon the spot, which is the highest title of honor among them.

His Majesty desired I would take some other opportunity of bringing all the rest of his enemy's ships into his ports. And so unmeasurable is the ambition of princes, that he seemed to think of nothing less than reducing the whole empire of Blefuscu into a province, and governing it by a viceroy; of destroying the Big-Endian exiles, and compelling that people to break the smaller end of their eggs, by which he would remain sole monarch of the whole world. But I endeavored to divert him from this design, by many arguments drawn from the topics of policy as well as justice: and I plainly protested, that I would never be an instrument of bringing a free and brave people into slavery. And when the matter was debated in council, the wisest part of the ministry were of my opinion.

This open bold declaration of mine was so opposite to the schemes and politics of his Imperial Majesty, that he could never forgive me; he mentioned it in a very artful manner at council, where I was told that some of the wisest appeared, at least by their silence, to be of my opinion; but others, who were my secret enemies, could not forbear some expressions, which by a side-wind[7] reflected on me. And from this time began an intrigue between his Majesty and a junta of ministers maliciously bent against me, which broke out in less than two months, and had like to have ended in my utter destruction. Of so little weight are the greatest services to princes, when put into the balance with a refusal to gratify their passions.[8]

About three weeks after this exploit, there arrived a solemn embassy from Blefuscu, with humble offers of a peace; which was soon concluded upon conditions very advantageous to our Emperor; wherewith I shall not trouble the reader. There were six ambassadors, with a train of about five hundred persons; and their entry was very magnificent, suitable to the grandeur of their master, and the importance of their business. When their treaty was finished, wherein I did them several good offices by the credit I now had, or at least appeared to have at court, their Excellencies, who were privately told how much I had been their friend, made me a visit in form. They began with many compliments upon my valor and generosity; invited me to that kingdom in the Emperor their master's name; and desired me to show them some proofs of my prodigious strength, of which they had heard so many wonders; wherein I readily obliged them, but shall not interrupt the reader with the particulars.

When I had for some time entertained their Excellencies to their infinite satisfaction and surprise, I desired they would do me the honor to present my most humble respects to the Emperor their master, the renown of whose virtues had so justly filled the whole world with admiration, and whose royal person I resolved to attend before I returned to my own country. Accordingly, the next time I had the honor to see our Emperor, I desired his general license to wait on the Blefuscudian monarch, which he was pleased to grant me, as I could plainly perceive, in a very cold manner; but could not guess the reason, till I had a whisper from a certain person, that Flimnap and Bolgolam had represented my intercourse with those ambassadors as a mark of disaffection, from which I am sure my heart was wholly free. And this was the first time I began to conceive some imperfect idea of courts and ministers.

It is to be observed, that these ambassadors spoke to me by an interpreter; the languages of both empires differing as much from each other as any two in Europe, and each nation priding itself upon the antiquity, beauty, and energy of their own tongues, with an avowed contempt for that of their neighbor; yet our Emperor, standing upon the advantage he had got by the seizure of their fleet, obliged them to deliver their credentials, and make their speech, in the Lilliputian tongue. And it must be

7. Indirectly.
8. After a series of British naval victories, the Treaty of Utrecht (1713) had ended the war with France, but the Tory ministers who engineered the peace were subsequently accused of having sold out to the enemy.

confessed, that from the great intercourse of trade and commerce between both realms, from the continual reception of exiles, which is mutual among them, and from the custom in each empire to send their young nobility and richer gentry to the other, in order to polish themselves, by seeing the world, and understanding men and manners, there are few persons of distinction, or merchants, or seamen, who dwell in the maritime parts, but what can hold conversation in both tongues; as I found some weeks after, when I went to pay my respects to the Emperor of Blefuscu, which in the midst of great misfortunes, through the malice of my enemies, proved a very happy adventure to me, as I shall relate in its proper place.

The reader may remember, that when I signed those articles upon which I recovered my liberty, there were some which I disliked upon account of their being too servile, neither could any thing but an extreme necessity have forced me to submit. But being now a *Nardac*, of the highest rank in that empire, such offices[9] were looked upon as below my dignity, and the Emperor (to do him justice) never once mentioned them to me. However, it was not long before I had an opportunity of doing his Majesty, at least as I then thought, a most signal service. I was alarmed at midnight with the cries of many hundred people at my door; by which being suddenly awaked, I was in some kind of terror. I heard the word *burglum* repeated incessantly; several of the Emperor's court, making their way through the crowd, intreated me to come immediately to the palace, where her Imperial Majesty's apartment was on fire, by the carelessness of a maid of honor, who fell asleep while she was reading a romance. I got up in an instant; and orders being given to clear the way before me, and it being likewise a moonshine night, I made a shift to get to the palace without trampling on any of the people. I found they had already applied ladders to the walls of the apartment, and were well provided with buckets, but the water was at some distance. These buckets were about the size of a large thimble, and the poor people supplied me with them as fast as they could; but the flame was so violent, that they did little good. I might easily have stifled it with my coat, which I unfortunately left behind me for haste, and came away only in my leathern jerkin. The case seemed wholly desperate and deplorable; and this magnificent palace would have infallibly been burnt down to the ground, if, by a presence of mind, unusual to me, I had not suddenly thought of an expedient. I had the evening before drank plentifully of a most delicious wine, called *glimigrim* (the Blefuscudians call it *flunec*, but ours is esteemed the better sort), which is very diuretic. By the luckiest chance in the world, I had not discharged myself of any part of it. The heat I had contracted by coming very near the flames, and by my laboring to quench them, made the wine begin to operate by urine; which I voided in such a quantity, and applied so well to the proper

9. Duties.

places, that in three minutes the fire was wholly extinguished; and the rest of that noble pile, which had cost so many ages in erecting, preserved from destruction.

It was now daylight, and I returned to my house, without waiting to congratulate with the Emperor; because, although I had done a very eminent piece of service, yet I could not tell how his Majesty might resent the manner by which I had performed it: for, by the fundamental laws of the realm, it is capital[1] in any person, of what quality soever, to make water within the precincts of the palace. But I was a little comforted by a message from his Majesty, that he would give orders to the Grand Justiciary for passing my pardon in form; which, however, I could not obtain. And I was privately assured, that the Empress, conceiving the greatest abhorrence of what I had done,[2] removed to the most distant side of the court, firmly resolved that those buildings should never be repaired for her use; and, in the presence of her chief confidents, could not forbear vowing revenge.

CHAPTER 6. *Of the inhabitants of Lilliput; their learning, laws, and customs, the manner of educating their children. The author's way of living in that country. His vindication of a great lady.*

Although I intend to leave the description of this empire to a particular treatise, yet in the mean time I am content to gratify the curious reader with some general ideas. As the common size of the natives is somewhat under six inches, so there is an exact proportion in all other animals, as well as plants and trees: for instance, the tallest horses and oxen are between four and five inches in height, the sheep an inch and a half, more or less; their geese about the bigness of a sparrow; and so the several gradations downwards, till you come to the smallest, which, to my sight, were almost invisible; but nature hath adapted the eyes of the Lilliputians to all objects proper for their view: they see with great exactness, but at no great distance. And to show the sharpness of their sight towards objects that are near, I have been much pleased with observing a cook pulling[3] a lark, which was not so large as a common fly; and a young girl threading an invisible needle with invisible silk. Their tallest trees are about seven foot high; I mean some of those in the great royal park, the tops whereof I could but just reach with my fist clinched. The other vegetables[4] are in the same proportion; but this I leave to the reader's imagination.

I shall say but little at present of their learning, which for many ages hath flourished in all its branches among them: but their manner of writing is very peculiar; being neither from the left to the right, like the Europeans; nor from the right to the left, like the Arabians; nor from up

---

1. Punishable by death.
2. Queen Anne, whom Swift called "a royal prude," strongly objected to the coarseness of A

Tale of a Tub.
3. Plucking.
4. Plants.

to down, like the Chinese; nor from down to up, like the Cascagians;[5] but aslant from one corner of the paper to the other, like ladies in England.

They bury their dead with their heads directly downwards; because they hold an opinion that in eleven thousand moons they are all to rise again; in which period, the earth (which they conceive to be flat) will turn upside down, and by this means they shall, at their resurrection, be found ready standing on their feet. The learned among them confess the absurdity of this doctrine; but the practice still continues, in compliance to the vulgar.

There are some laws and customs in this empire very peculiar; and if they were not so directly contrary to those of my own dear country, I should be tempted to say a little in their justification. It is only to be wished, that they were as well executed. The first I shall mention relateth to informers. All crimes against the state are punished here with the utmost severity; but if the person accused make his innocence plainly to appear upon his trial, the accuser is immediately put to an ignominious death; and out of his goods or lands, the innocent person is quadruply recompensed for the loss of his time, for the danger he underwent, for the hardship of his imprisonment, and for all the charges he hath been at in making his defense. Or, if that fund be deficient, it is largely[6] supplied by the crown. The Emperor doth also confer on him some public mark of his favor; and proclamation is made of his innocence through the whole city.

They look upon fraud as a greater crime than theft, and therefore seldom fail to punish it with death; for they allege, that care and vigilance, with a very common understanding, may preserve a man's goods from thieves; but honesty hath no fence against superior cunning: and since it is necessary that there should be a perpetual intercourse of buying and selling, and dealing upon credit, where fraud is permitted or connived at, or hath no law to punish it, the honest dealer is always undone, and the knave gets the advantage. I remember when I was once interceding with the King for a criminal who had wronged his master of a great sum of money, which he had received by order, and ran away with; and happening to tell his Majesty, by way of extenuation, that it was only a breach of trust, the Emperor thought it monstrous in me to offer, as a defense, the greatest aggravation of the crime: and truly, I had little to say in return, farther than the common answer, that different nations had different customs; for, I confess, I was heartily ashamed.

Although we usually call reward and punishment the two hinges upon which all government turns, yet I could never observe this maxim to be put in practice by any nation, except that of Lilliput. Whoever can there bring sufficient proof that he hath strictly observed the laws of his country for seventy-three moons, hath a claim to certain privileges, according to his quality[7] and condition of life, with a proportionable sum of money

5. Swift's invention.
6. Fully.

7. Social position.

out of a fund appropriated for that use: he likewise acquires the title of *Snilpall*, or *Legal*, which is added to his name, but doth not descend to his posterity. And these people thought it a prodigious defect of policy among us, when I told them that our laws were enforced only by penalties, without any mention of reward. It is upon this account that the image of Justice, in their courts of judicature, is formed with six eyes, two before, as many behind, and on each side one, to signify circumspection; with a bag of gold open in her right hand, and a sword sheathed in her left, to show she is more disposed to reward than to punish.

In choosing persons for all employments, they have more regard to good morals than to great abilities; for, since government is necessary to mankind, they believe that the common size of human understandings is fitted to some station or other; and that Providence never intended to make the management of public affairs a mystery, to be comprehended only by a few persons of sublime genius, of which there seldom are three born in an age: but they suppose truth, justice, temperance, and the like, to be in every man's power; the practice of which virtues, assisted by experience and a good intention, would qualify any man for the service of his country, except where a course of study is required. But they thought the want of moral virtues was so far from being supplied by superior endowments of the mind, that employments could never be put into such dangerous hands as those of persons so qualified; and at least, that the mistakes committed by ignorance in a virtuous disposition would never be of such fatal consequence to the public weal, as the practices of a man whose inclinations led him to be corrupt, and had great abilities to manage, to multiply, and defend his corruptions.

In like manner, the disbelief of a divine Providence renders a man uncapable of holding any public station; for since kings avow themselves to be the deputies of Providence, the Lilliputians think nothing can be more absurd than for a prince to employ such men as disown the authority under which he acteth.

In relating these and the following laws, I would only be understood to mean the original institutions, and not the most scandalous corruptions into which these people are fallen by the degenerate nature of man. For as to that infamous practice of acquiring great employments by dancing on the ropes, or badges of favor and distinction by leaping over sticks, and creeping under them, the reader is to observe, that they were first introduced by the grandfather of the Emperor now reigning; and grew to the present height by the gradual increase of party and faction.

Ingratitude is among them a capital crime, as we read it to have been in some other countries; for they reason thus, that whoever makes ill returns to his benefactor, must needs be a common enemy to the rest of mankind, from whom he hath received no obligation; and therefore such a man is not fit to live.

Their notions relating to the duties of parents and children differ extremely from ours. For, since the conjunction of male and female is founded upon the great law of nature, in order to propagate and continue the species, the Lilliputians will needs have it, that men and women are joined together like other animals, by the motives of concupiscence; and that their tenderness towards their young proceedeth from the like natural principle: for which reason they will never allow, that a child is under any obligation to his father for begetting him, or to his mother for bringing him into the world; which, considering the miseries of human life, was neither a benefit in itself, nor intended so by his parents, whose thoughts in their love-encounters were otherwise employed. Upon these, and the like reasonings, their opinion is, that parents are the last of all others to be trusted with the education of their own children: and therefore they have in every town public nurseries, where all parents, except cottagers[8] and laborers, are obliged to send their infants of both sexes to be reared and educated when they come to the age of twenty moons; at which time they are supposed to have some rudiments of docility. These schools are of several kinds, suited to different qualities, and to both sexes. They have certain professors[9] well skilled in preparing children for such a condition of life as befits the rank of their parents, and their own capacities as well as inclinations. I shall first say something of the male nurseries, and then of the female.

The nurseries for males of noble or eminent birth are provided with grave and learned professors, and their several deputies. The clothes and food of the children are plain and simple. They are bred up in the principles of honor, justice, courage, modesty, clemency, religion, and love of their country; they are always employed in some business, except in the times of eating and sleeping, which are very short, and two hours for diversions, consisting of bodily exercises.[1] They are dressed by men until four years of age, and then are obliged to dress themselves, although their quality be ever so great; and the women attendants, who are aged proportionably to ours at fifty, perform only the most menial offices. They are never suffered to converse with servants, but go together in small or greater numbers to take their diversions, and always in the presence of a professor, or one of his deputies; whereby they avoid those early bad impressions of folly and vice to which our children are subject. Their parents are suffered to see them only twice a year; the visit is not to last above an hour; they are allowed to kiss the child at meeting and parting; but a professor, who always standeth by on those occasions, will not suffer them to whisper, or use any fondling expressions, or bring any presents of toys, sweetmeats, and the like.

The pension from each family for the education and entertainment[2] of a child, upon failure of due payment, is levied by the Emperor's officers.

The nurseries for children of ordinary gentlemen, merchants, traders, and handicrafts, are managed proportionably after the same manner; only those designed for trades are put out apprentices at seven years old; whereas those of persons of quality continue in their exercises until fif-

8. Agricultural workers, peasants.   1. Activities.
9. Professional teachers.   2. Sustenance.

teen, which answers to one and twenty with us: but the confinement is gradually lessened for the last three years.

In the female nurseries, the young girls of quality are educated much like the males, only they are dressed by orderly servants of their own sex, but always in the presence of a professor or deputy, until they come to dress themselves, which is at five years old. And if it be found that these nurses ever presume to entertain the girls with frightful or foolish stories, or the common follies practiced by chambermaids among us, they are publicly whipped thrice about the city, imprisoned for a year, and banished for life to the most desolate parts of the country. Thus the young ladies there are as much ashamed of being cowards and fools as the men; and despise all personal ornaments beyond decency and cleanliness: neither did I perceive any difference in their education, made by their difference of sex, only that the exercises of the females were not altogether so robust; and that some rules were given them relating to domestic life, and a smaller compass of learning was enjoined them: for their maxim is, that among people of quality, a wife should be always a reasonable and agreeable companion, because she cannot always be young. When the girls are twelve years old, which among them is the marriageable age, their parents or guardians take them home, with great expressions of gratitude to the professors, and seldom without tears of the young lady and her companions.

In the nurseries of females of the meaner sort, the children are instructed in all kinds of works proper for their sex, and their several degrees:[3] those intended for apprentices are dismissed at seven years old, the rest are kept to eleven.

The meaner families who have children at these nurseries are obliged, besides their annual pension, which is as low as possible, to return to the steward of the nursery a small monthly share of their gettings, to be a portion for the child; and therefore all parents are limited in their expenses by the law. For the Lilliputians think nothing can be more unjust, than that people, in subservience to their own appetites, should bring children into the world, and leave the burthen of supporting them on the public. As to persons of quality, they give security to appropriate a certain sum for each child, suitable to their condition; and these funds are always managed with good husbandry, and the most exact justice.

The cottagers and laborers keep their children at home, their business being only to till and cultivate the earth; and therefore their education is of little consequence to the public; but the old and diseased among them are supported by hospitals: for begging is a trade unknown in this empire.

And here it may perhaps divert the curious reader, to give some account of my domestic,[4] and my manner of living in this country, during a residence of nine months and thirteen days. Having a head mechanically turned, and being likewise forced by necessity, I had made for

3. Various social ranks.   4. Household.

myself a table and chair convenient enough, out of the largest trees in the royal park. Two hundred sempstresses were employed to make me shirts, and linen for my bed and table, all of the strongest and coarsest kind they could get; which, however, they were forced to quilt together in several folds; for the thickest was some degrees finer than lawn. Their linen is usually three inches wide, and three foot make a piece. The sempstresses took my measure as I lay on the ground, one standing at my neck, and another at my mid-leg, with a strong cord extended, that each held by the end, while the third measured the length of the cord with a rule of an inch long. Then they measured my right thumb, and desired no more; for by a mathematical computation, that twice round the thumb is one round the wrist, and so on to the neck and the waist; and by the help of my old shirt, which I displayed on the ground before them for a pattern, they fitted me exactly. Three hundred tailors were employed in the same manner to make me clothes; but they had another contrivance for taking my measure. I kneeled down, and they raised a ladder from the ground to my neck; upon this ladder one of them mounted, and let fall a plumb-line from my collar to the floor, which just answered the length of my coat; but my waist and arms I measured myself. When my clothes were finished, which was done in my house (for the largest of theirs would not have been able to hold them), they looked like the patchwork made by the ladies in England, only that mine were all of a color.

I had three hundred cooks to dress my victuals, in little convenient huts built about my house, where they and their families lived, and prepared me two dishes apiece. I took up twenty waiters in my hand, and placed them on the table; an hundred more attended below on the ground, some with dishes of meat, and some with barrels of wine, and other liquors, slung on their shoulders; all which the waiters above drew up as I wanted, in a very ingenious manner, by certain cords, as we draw the bucket up a well in Europe. A dish of their meat was a good mouthful, and a barrel of their liquor a reasonable draught. Their mutton yields to ours, but their beef is excellent. I have had a sirloin so large, that I have been forced to make three bites of it; but this is rare. My servants were astonished to see me eat it bones and all, as in our country we do the leg of a lark. Their geese and turkeys I usually eat at a mouthful, and I must confess they far exceed ours. Of their smaller fowl I could take up twenty or thirty at the end of my knife.

One day his Imperial Majesty, being informed of my way of living, desired that himself and his royal consort, with the young princes of the blood of both sexes, might have the happiness (as he was pleased to call it) of dining with me. They came accordingly, and I placed them upon chairs of state on my table, just over against me, with their guards about them. Flimnap the Lord High Treasurer attended there likewise, with his white staff; and I observed he often looked on me with a sour countenance, which I would not seem to regard, but eat more than usual, in honor to my dear country, as well as to fill the court with admiration. I have some private reasons to believe, that this visit from his Majesty gave Flimnap an opportunity of doing me ill offices to his master. That minister had always been my secret enemy, although he outwardly caressed me more than was usual to the moroseness of his nature. He represented to the Emperor the low condition of his treasury; that he was forced to take up money at great discount; that exchequer bills[5] would not circulate under nine per cent below par; that I had cost his Majesty above a million and a half of *sprugs* (their greatest gold coin, about the bigness of a spangle); and upon the whole, that it would be advisable in the Emperor to take the first fair occasion of dismissing me.

I am here obliged to vindicate the reputation of an excellent lady, who was an innocent sufferer upon my account. The Treasurer took a fancy to be jealous of his wife, from the malice of some evil tongues, who informed him that her Grace had taken a violent affection for my person; and the court-scandal ran for some time that she once came privately to my lodging. This I solemnly declare to be a most infamous falsehood, without any grounds, farther than that her Grace was pleased to treat me with all innocent marks of freedom and friendship. I own she came often to my house, but always publicly, nor ever without three more in the coach, who were usually her sister and young daughter, and some particular acquaintance; but this was common to many other ladies of the court. And I still appeal to my servants round, whether they at any time saw a coach at my door without knowing what persons were in it. On those occasions, when a servant had given me notice, my custom was to go immediately to the door; and, after paying my respects, to take up the coach and two horses very carefully in my hands (for if there were six horses, the postillion always unharnessed four) and placed them on a table, where I had fixed a moveable rim quite round, of five inches high, to prevent accidents. And I have often had four coaches and horses at once on my table full of company, while I sat in my chair leaning my face towards them; and when I was engaged with one set, the coachmen would gently drive the others round my table. I have passed many an afternoon very agreeably in these conversations. But I defy the Treasurer, or his two informers (I will name them, and let them make their best of it) Clustril and Drunlo, to prove that any person ever came to me *incognito*, except the Secretary Reldresal, who was sent by express command of his Imperial Majesty, as I have before related. I should not have dwelt so long upon this particular, if it had not been a point wherein the reputation of a great lady is so nearly concerned, to say nothing of my own; although I had the honor to be a *Nardac*, which the Treasurer himself is not; for all the world knows he is only a *Clumglum*, a title inferior by one degree, as that of a marquis is to a duke in England; yet I allow he preceded me in right of his post. These false informations, which I afterwards came to the knowledge of, by an accident not proper to mention, made the Treasurer show his lady for some time an ill

5. Government bills of credit. Walpole was noted as a canny financier.

countenance, and me a worse; for although he was at last undeceived and reconciled to her, yet I lost all credit with him; and found my interest decline very fast with the Emperor himself, who was indeed too much governed by that favorite.

CHAPTER 7. *The author, being informed of a design to accuse him of high treason, makes his escape to Blefuscu. His reception there.*

Before I proceed to give an account of my leaving this kingdom, it may be proper to inform the reader of a private intrigue which had been for two months forming against me.

I had been hitherto all my life a stranger to courts, for which I was unqualified by the meanness of my condition. I had indeed heard and read enough of the dispositions of great princes and ministers; but never expected to have found such terrible effects of them in so remote a country, governed, as I thought, by very different maxims from those in Europe.

When I was just preparing to pay my attendance on the Emperor of Blefuscu, a considerable person at court (to whom I had been very serviceable at a time when he lay under the highest displeasure of his Imperial Majesty) came to my house very privately at night in a close chair, and without sending his name, desired admittance. The chairmen were dismissed; I put the chair, with his Lordship in it, into my coat-pocket; and giving orders to a trusty servant to say I was indisposed and gone to sleep, I fastened the door of my house, placed the chair on the table, according to my usual custom, and sat down by it. After the common salutations were over, observing his Lordship's countenance full of concern, and enquiring into the reason, he desired I would hear him with patience, in a matter that highly concerned my honor and my life. His speech was to the following effect, for I took notes of it as soon as he left me.

You are to know, said he, that several committees of council have been lately called in the most private manner on your account: and it is but two days since his Majesty came to a full resolution.

You are very sensible that Skyresh Bolgolam (*Galbet*, or High Admiral) hath been your mortal enemy almost ever since your arrival. His original reasons I know not; but his hatred is much increased since your great success against Blefuscu, by which his glory, as Admiral, is obscured. This lord, in conjunction with Flimnap the High Treasurer, whose enmity against you is notorious on account of his lady, Limtoc the General, Lalcon the Chamberlain, and Balmuff the Grand Justiciary, have prepared articles of impeachment against you, for treason, and other capital crimes.[6]

This preface made me so impatient, being conscious of my own merits and innocence, that I was going to interrupt; when he entreated me to be silent, and thus proceeded.

6. After the Whigs had investigated Oxford and Bolingbroke, both were impeached for high treason, on charges of being sympathetic to the Jacobites and the French.

Out of gratitude for the favors you have done me, I procured information of the whole proceedings, and a copy of the articles, wherein I venture my head for your service.

Articles of Impeachment against Quinbus Flestrin
(the Man-Mountain).

ARTICLE 1

Whereas, by a statute made in the reign of his Imperial Majesty Calin Deffar Plune, it is enacted, that whoever shall make water within the precincts of the royal palace shall be liable to the pains and penalties of high treason: notwithstanding, the said Quinbus Flestrin, in open breach of the said law, under color of extinguishing the fire kindled in the apartment of his Majesty's most dear imperial consort, did maliciously, traitorously, and devilishly, by discharge of his urine, put out the said fire kindled in the said apartment, lying and being within the precincts of the said royal palace; against the statute in that case provided, etc., against the duty, etc.

ARTICLE 2

That the said Quinbus Flestrin, having brought the imperial fleet of Blefuscu into the royal port, and being afterwards commanded by his Imperial Majesty to seize all the other ships of the said empire of Blefuscu, and reduce that empire to a province, to be governed by a viceroy from hence; and to destroy and put to death not only all the Big-Endian exiles, but likewise all the people of that empire who would not immediately forsake the Big-Endian heresy: he, the said Flestrin, like a false traitor against his most auspicious, serene, Imperial Majesty, did petition to be excused from the said service, upon pretense of unwillingness to force the consciences, or destroy the liberties and lives of an innocent people.

ARTICLE 3

That, whereas certain ambassadors arrived from the court of Blefuscu to sue for peace in his Majesty's court: he the said Flestrin did, like a false traitor, aid, abet, comfort, and divert the said ambassadors; although he knew them to be servants to a prince who was lately an open enemy to his Imperial Majesty, and in open war against his said Majesty.

ARTICLE 4

That the said Quinbus Flestrin, contrary to the duty of a faithful subject, is now preparing to make a voyage to the court and empire of Blefuscu, for which he hath received only verbal license from his Imperial Majesty; and under color of the said license, doth falsely and traitorously intend to take the said voyage, and thereby to aid, comfort, and abet the Emperor of Blefuscu, so late an enemy, and in open war with his Imperial Majesty aforesaid.

There are some other articles, but these are the most important, of which I have read you an abstract.

In the several debates upon this impeachment, it must be confessed that his Majesty gave many marks of his great *lenity*; often urging the services you had done him, and endeavoring to extenuate your crimes. The Treasurer and Admiral insisted that you should be put to the most painful and ignominious death, by setting fire on your house at night; and the General was to attend with twenty thousand men armed with poisoned arrows, to shoot you on the face and hands. Some of your servants were to have private orders to strew a poisonous juice on your shirts and sheets, which would soon make you tear your own flesh, and die in the utmost torture. The General came into the same opinion; so that for a long time there was a majority against you. But his Majesty resolving, if possible, to spare your life, at last brought off[7] the Chamberlain.

Upon this incident, Reldresal, Principal Secretary for Private Affairs, who always approved[8] himself your true friend, was commanded by the Emperor to deliver his opinion, which he accordingly did; and therein justified the good thoughts you have of him. He allowed your crimes to be great; but that still there was room for mercy, the most commendable virtue in a prince, and for which his Majesty was so justly celebrated. He said, the friendship between you and him was so well known to the world, that perhaps the most honorable board might think him partial: however, in obedience to the command he had received, he would freely offer his sentiments. That if his Majesty, in consideration of your services, and pursuant to his own merciful disposition, would please to spare your life, and only give order to put out both your eyes, he humbly conceived, that by this expedient justice might in some measure be satisfied, and all the world would applaud the *lenity* of the Emperor, as well as the fair and generous proceedings of those who have the honor to be his counselors. That the loss of your eyes would be no impediment to your bodily strength, by which you might still be useful to his Majesty. That blindness is an addition to courage, by concealing dangers from us; that the fear you had for your eyes was the greatest difficulty in bringing over the enemy's fleet; and it would be sufficient for you to see by the eyes of the ministers, since the greatest princes do no more.

This proposal was received with the utmost disapprobation by the whole board. Bolgolam, the Admiral, could not preserve his temper; but rising up in fury, said, he wondered how the Secretary durst presume to give his opinion for preserving the life of a traitor: that the services you had

---

7. Won over.   8. Proved.

performed were, by all true reasons of state, the great aggravation of your crimes; that you, who were able to extinguish the fire by discharge of urine in her Majesty's apartment (which he mentioned with horror), might, at another time, raise an inundation by the same means, to drown the whole palace; and the same strength which enabled you to bring over the enemy's fleet might serve, upon the first discontent, to carry it back: that he had good reasons to think you were a Big-Endian in your heart; and as treason begins in the heart before it appears in overt acts, so he accused you as a traitor on that account, and therefore insisted you should be put to death.

The Treasurer was of the same opinion; he showed to what straits his Majesty's revenue was reduced by the charge of maintaining you, which would soon grow insupportable: that the Secretary's expedient of putting out your eyes was so far from being a remedy against this evil, that it would probably increase it; as it is manifest from the common practice of blinding some kind of fowl, after which they fed the faster, and grew sooner fat: that his sacred Majesty, and the council, who are your judges, were in their own consciences fully convinced of your guilt; which was a sufficient argument to condemn you to death, without the formal proofs required by the strict letter of the law.

But his Imperial Majesty, fully determined against capital punishment, was graciously pleased to say, that since the council thought the loss of your eyes too easy a censure, some other may be inflicted hereafter. And your friend the Secretary humbly desiring to be heard again, in answer to what the Treasurer had objected concerning the great charge his Majesty was at in maintaining you, said, that his Excellency, who had the sole disposal of the Emperor's revenue, might easily provide against this evil, by gradually lessening your establishment; by which, for want of sufficient food, you would grow weak and faint, and lose your appetite, and consequently decay and consume in a few months; neither would the stench of your carcass be then so dangerous, when it should become more than half diminished; and immediately upon your death, five or six thousand of his Majesty's subjects might, in two or three days, cut your flesh from your bones, take it away by cart-loads, and bury it in distant parts to prevent infection; leaving the skeleton as a monument of admiration to posterity.

Thus by the great friendship of the Secretary, the whole affair was compromised. It was strictly enjoined, that the project of starving you by degrees should be kept a secret; but the sentence of putting out your eyes was entered on the books; none dissenting except Bolgolam the Admiral, who being a creature of the Empress, was perpetually instigated by her Majesty to insist upon your death; she having borne perpetual malice against you, on account of that infamous and illegal method you took to extinguish the fire in her apartment.

In three days your friend the Secretary will be directed to come to your house, and read before you the articles of impeachment; and then to signify the great lenity and favor of his Majesty and council; whereby you are only condemned to the loss of your eyes, which his Majesty doth not question you will gratefully and humbly submit to; and twenty of his Majesty's surgeons will attend, in order to see the operation well performed, by discharging very sharp-pointed arrows into the balls of your eyes, as you lie on the ground.

I leave to your prudence what measures you will take; and to avoid suspicion, I must immediately return in as private a manner as I came.

His Lordship did so, and I remained alone, under many doubts and perplexities of mind.

It was a custom introduced by this prince and his ministry (very different, as I have been assured, from the practices of former times), that after the court had decreed any cruel execution, either to gratify the monarch's resentment, or the malice of a favorite, the Emperor always made a speech to his whole council, expressing his great lenity and tenderness, as qualities known and confessed by all the world. This speech was immediately published through the kingdom; nor did any thing terrify the people so much as those encomiums on his Majesty's mercy; because it was observed, that the more these praises were enlarged and insisted on, the more inhuman was the punishment, and the sufferer more innocent. Yet as to myself, I must confess, having never been designed for a courtier, either by my birth or education, I was so ill a judge of things, that I could not discover the lenity and favor of this sentence, but conceived it (perhaps erroneously) rather to be rigorous than gentle. I sometimes thought of standing my trial; for although I could not deny the facts alleged in the several articles, yet I hoped they would admit of some extenuations. But having in my life perused many state trials, which I ever observed to terminate as the judges thought fit to direct, I durst not rely on so dangerous a decision, in so critical a juncture, and against such powerful enemies. Once I was strongly bent upon resistance: for while I had liberty, the whole strength of that empire could hardly subdue me, and I might easily with stones pelt the metropolis to pieces; but I soon rejected that project with horror, by remembering the oath I had made to the Emperor, the favors I received from him, and the high title of *Nardac* he conferred upon me. Neither had I so soon learned the gratitude of courtiers, to persuade myself that his Majesty's present severities acquitted me of all past obligations.

At last I fixed upon a resolution, for which it is probable I may incur some censure, and not unjustly; for I confess I owe the preserving my eyes, and consequently my liberty, to my own great rashness and want of experience: because if I had then known the nature of princes and ministers, which I have since observed in many other courts, and their methods of treating criminals less obnoxious than myself, I should with great alacrity and readiness have submitted to so *easy* a punishment. But hurried on by the precipitancy of youth, and having his Imperial Majesty's license to pay my attendance upon the Emperor of Blefuscu, I took this opportunity, before the three days were elapsed, to send a letter to my friend the Secretary, signifying my resolution of setting out that morning for Blefuscu,[9] pursuant to the leave I had got; and without waiting for an answer, I went to that side of the island where our fleet lay. I seized a large man of war, tied a cable to the prow, and lifting up the anchors, I stripped myself, put my clothes (together with my coverlet, which I carried under my arm) into the vessel; and drawing it after me, between wading and swimming, arrived at the royal port of Blefuscu, where the people had long expected me. They lent me two guides to direct me to the capital city, which is of the same name; I held them in my hands until I came within two hundred yards of the gate; and desired them to signify my arrival to one of the secretaries, and let him know, I there waited his Majesty's commands. I had an answer in about an hour, that his Majesty, attended by the royal family, and great officers of the court, was coming out to receive me. I advanced a hundred yards; the Emperor, and his train, alighted from their horses, the Empress and ladies from their coaches; and I did not perceive they were in any fright or concern. I lay on the ground to kiss his Majesty's and the Empress's hand. I told his Majesty that I was come according to my promise, and with the license of the Emperor my master, to have the honor of seeing so mighty a monarch, and to offer him any service in my power, consistent with my duty to my own prince; not mentioning a word of my disgrace, because I had hitherto no regular information of it, and might suppose myself wholly ignorant of any such design; neither could I reasonably conceive that the Emperor would discover the secret while I was out of his power: wherein, however, it soon appeared I was deceived.

I shall not trouble the reader with the particular account of my reception at this court, which was suitable to the generosity of so great a prince; nor of the difficulties I was in for want of a house and bed, being forced to lie on the ground, wrapped up in my coverlet.

CHAPTER 8. *The author, by a lucky accident, finds means to leave Blefuscu; and, after some difficulties, returns safe to his native country.*

Three days after my arrival, walking out of curiosity to the northeast coast of the island, I observed, about half a league off, in the sea, somewhat that looked like a boat overturned. I pulled off my shoes and stockings, and wading two or three hundred yards, I found the object to approach nearer by force of the tide; and then plainly saw it to be a real boat, which I supposed might, by some tempest, have been driven from a ship. Whereupon I returned immediately towards the city, and desired his Imperial Majesty to lend me twenty of the tallest vessels he had left after the loss of his fleet, and three thousand seamen under the command of his Vice Admiral. This fleet sailed round, while I went back the shortest way to the coast where I first discovered the boat; I found the tide had driven it still nearer; the seamen were all provided with cordage, which I had beforehand twisted to a sufficient strength. When

---

9. Before his trial for treason could be held, Bolingbroke had escaped to France.

the ships came up, I stripped myself, and waded till I came within an hundred yards of the boat; after which I was forced to swim till I got up to it. The seamen threw me the end of the cord, which I fastened to a hole in the fore-part of the boat, and the other end to a man of war: but I found all my labor to little purpose; for being out of my depth, I was not able to work. In this necessity, I was forced to swim behind, and push the boat forwards as often as I could, with one of my hands; and the tide favoring me, I advanced so far, that I could just hold up my chin and feel the ground. I rested two or three minutes, and then gave the boat another shove, and so on till the sea was no higher than my armpits. And now the most laborious part being over, I took out my other cables which were stowed in one of the ships, and fastening them first to the boat, and then to nine of the vessels which attended me, the wind being favorable, the seamen towed, and I shoved till we arrived within forty yards of the shore; and waiting till the tide was out, I got dry to the boat, and by the assistance of two thousand men, with ropes and engines,[1] I made a shift to turn it on its bottom, and found it was but little damaged.

I shall not trouble the reader with the difficulties I was under by the help of certain paddles, which cost me ten days making, to get my boat to the royal port of Blefuscu; where a mighty concourse of people appeared upon my arrival, full of wonder at the sight of so prodigious a vessel. I told the Emperor that my good fortune had thrown this boat in my way, to carry me to some place from whence I might return into my native country; and begged his Majesty's orders for getting materials to fit it up, together with license to depart; which, after some kind expostulations, he was pleased to grant.

I did very much wonder, in all this time, not to have heard of any express relating to me from our Emperor to the court of Blefuscu. But I was afterwards given privately to understand, that his Imperial Majesty, never imagining I had the least notice of his designs, believed I was only gone to Blefuscu in performance of my promise, according to the license he had given me, which was well known at our court; and would return in a few days when that ceremony was ended. But he was at last in pain at my long absence; and, after consulting with the Treasurer, and the rest of that cabal, a person of quality was dispatched with the copy of the articles against me. This envoy had instructions to represent to the monarch of Blefuscu the great lenity of his master, who was content to punish me no further than with the loss of my eyes; that I had fled from justice, and if I did not return in two hours, I should be deprived of my title of *Nardac*, and declared a traitor. The envoy further added, that in order to maintain the peace and amity between both empires, his master expected, that his brother of Blefuscu would give orders to have me sent back to Lilliput, bound hand and foot, to be punished as a traitor.

The Emperor of Blefuscu, having taken three days to consult, returned

1. Mechanical contrivances.

an answer consisting of many civilities and excuses. He said, that as for sending me bound, his brother knew it was impossible; that although I had deprived him of his fleet, yet he owed great obligations to me for many good offices I had done him in making the peace. That however, both their Majesties would soon be made easy; for I had found a prodigious vessel on the shore, able to carry me on the sea, which he had given order to fit up with my own assistance and direction; and he hoped in a few weeks both empires would be freed from so insupportable an incumbrance.

With this answer the envoy returned to Lilliput, and the monarch of Blefuscu related to me all that had passed, offering me at the same time (but under the strictest confidence) his gracious protection, if I would continue in his service; wherein although I believed him sincere, yet I resolved never more to put any confidence in princes or ministers, where I could possibly avoid it; and therefore, with all due acknowledgements for his favorable intentions, I humbly begged to be excused. I told him, that since fortune, whether good or evil, had thrown a vessel in my way, I was resolved to venture myself in the ocean, rather than be an occasion of difference between two such mighty monarchs. Neither did I find the Emperor at all displeased; and I discovered by a certain accident, that he was very glad of my resolution, and so were most of his ministers.

These considerations moved me to hasten my departure somewhat sooner than I intended; to which the court, impatient to have me gone, very readily contributed. Five hundred workmen were employed to make two sails to my boat, according to my directions, by quilting thirteen fold of their strongest linen together. I was at the pains of making ropes and cables, by twisting ten, twenty or thirty of the thickest and strongest of theirs. A great stone that I happened to find, after a long search by the seashore, served me for an anchor. I had the tallow of three hundred cows for greasing my boat, and other uses. I was at incredible pains in cutting down some of the largest timber trees for oars and masts, wherein I was, however, much assisted by his Majesty's ship-carpenters, who helped me in smoothing them, after I had done the rough work.

In about a month, when all was prepared, I sent to receive his Majesty's commands, and to take my leave. The Emperor and royal family came out of the palace; I lay down on my face to kiss his hand, which he very graciously gave me: so did the Empress, and young princes of the blood. His Majesty presented me with fifty purses of two hundred *sprugs* apiece, together with his picture at full length, which I put immediately into one of my gloves, to keep it from being hurt. The ceremonies at my departure were too many to trouble the reader with at this time.

I stored the boat with the carcasses of an hundred oxen, and three hundred sheep, with bread and drink proportionable, and as much meat ready dressed as four hundred cooks could provide. I took with me six cows and two bulls alive, with as many ewes and rams, intending to carry them into my own country, and propagate the breed. And to feed them on board, I had a good bundle of hay, and a bag of corn.[2] I would gladly have taken a dozen of the natives; but this was a thing the Emperor would by no means permit; and besides a diligent search into my pockets, his Majesty engaged my honor not to carry away any of his subjects, although with their own consent and desire.

Having thus prepared all things as well as I was able, I set sail on the twenty-fourth day of September, 1701, at six in the morning; and when I had gone about four leagues to the northward, the wind being at southeast, at six in the evening, I descried a small island about half a league to the northwest. I advanced forward, and cast anchor on the lee-side of the island, which seemed to be uninhabited. I then took some refreshment, and went to my rest. I slept well, and as I conjecture at least six hours; for I found the day broke in two hours after I awaked. It was a clear night; I eat my breakfast before the sun was up; and heaving anchor, the wind being favorable, I steered the same course that I had done the day before, wherein I was directed by my pocket compass. My intention was to reach, if possible, one of those islands which I had reason to believe lay to the northeast of Van Diemen's Land. I discovered nothing all that day; but upon the next, about three in the afternoon, when I had by my computation made twenty-four leagues from Blefuscu, I descried a sail steering to the southeast; my course was due east. I hailed her, but could get no answer; yet I found I gained upon her, for the wind slackened. I made all the sail I could, and in half an hour she spied me, then hung out her ancient,[3] and discharged a gun. It is not easy to express the joy I was in upon the unexpected hope of once more seeing my beloved country, and the dear pledges[4] I had left in it. The ship slackened her sails, and I came up with her between five and six in the evening, September 26; but my heart leapt within me to see her English colors. I put my cows and sheep into my coat-pockets and got on board with all my little cargo of provisions. The vessel was an English merchantman, returning from Japan by the North and South Seas;[5] the captain, Mr. John Biddel of Deptford, a very civil man, and an excellent sailor. We were now in the latitude of 30 degrees south; there were about fifty men in the ship; and here I met an old comrade of mine, one Peter Williams, who gave me a good character to the captain. This gentleman treated me with kindness, and desired I would let him know what place I came from last, and whither I was bound; which I did in few words; but he thought I was raving, and that the dangers I underwent had disturbed my head; whereupon I took my black cattle and sheep out of my pocket, which, after great astonishment, clearly convinced him of my veracity. I then showed him the gold given me by the Emperor of Blefuscu, together with his Majesty's picture at full length, and some other rarities of that country. I gave him two purses of two hundred *sprugs* each, and promised, when we arrived in England, to make him a present of a cow and a sheep big with young.

2. Wheat.
3. Flag.

4. Hostages (i.e., his family).
5. North and South Pacific.

I shall not trouble the reader with a particular account of this voyage; which was very prosperous for the most part. We arrived in the Downs[6] on the 13th of April, 1702. I had only one misfortune, that the rats on board carried away one of my sheep; I found her bones in a hole, picked clean from the flesh. The rest of my cattle I got safe on shore, and set them a grazing in a bowling-green at Greenwich, where the fineness of the grass made them feed very heartily, though I had always feared the contrary; neither could I possibly have preserved them in so long a voyage, if the captain had not allowed me some of his best biscuit, which rubbed to powder, and mingled with water, was their constant food. The short time I continued in England, I made a considerable profit by showing my cattle to many persons of quality, and others: and before I began my second voyage, I sold them for six hundred pounds. Since my last return, I find the breed is considerably increased, especially the sheep; which I hope will prove much to the advantage of the woolen manufacture, by the fineness of the fleeces.

I stayed but two months with my wife and family; for my insatiable desire of seeing foreign countries would suffer me to continue no longer. I left fifteen hundred pounds with my wife, and fixed her in a good house at Redriff. My remaining stock I carried with me, part in money, and part in goods, in hopes to improve my fortunes. My eldest uncle, John, had left me an estate in land, near Epping, of about thirty pounds a year; and I had a long lease of the Black Bull in Fetter Lane, which yielded me as much more: so that I was not in any danger of leaving my family upon the parish.[7] My son Johnny, named so after his uncle, was at the grammar school, and a towardly[8] child. My daughter Betty (who is now well married, and has children) was then at her needlework. I took leave of my wife, and boy and girl, with tears on both sides; and went on board the *Adventure*, a merchant-ship of three hundred tons, bound for Surat, Captain John Nicholas of Liverpool, Commander. But my account of this voyage must be referred to the second part of my *Travels*.

Part 2. A Voyage to Brobdingnag

Chapter 1. *A great storm described. The longboat[1] sent to fetch water; the Author goes with it to discover the country. He is left on shore, is seized by one of the natives, and carried to a farmer's house. His reception there, with several accidents that happened there. A description of the inhabitants.*

Having been condemned by nature and fortune to an active and restless life, in ten months after my return I again left my native country,

---

6. A rendezvous for ships off the southeast coast of England.
7. On welfare (living on charity given by the parish).
8. Promising.
1. The largest boat carried by a merchant sailing vessel.

and took shipping in the Downs on the 20th day of June, 1702, in the *Adventure*, Captain John Nicholas, a Cornish man, Commander, bound for Surat.[2] We had a very prosperous gale till we arrived at the Cape of Good Hope, where we landed for fresh water, but discovering a leak we unshipped our goods and wintered there; for the Captain falling sick of an ague, we could not leave the Cape till the end of March. We then set sail, and had a good voyage till we passed the Straits of Madagascar; but having got northward of that island, and to about five degrees south latitude, the winds, which in those seas are observed to blow a constant equal gale between the north and west from the beginning of December to the beginning of May, on the 19th of April began to blow with much greater violence and more westerly than usual, continuing so far twenty days together, during which time we were driven a little to the east of the Molucca Islands and about three degrees northward of the Line, as our Captain found by an observation he took the 2nd of May, at which time the wind ceased, and it was a perfect calm, whereat I was not a little rejoiced. But he, being a man well experienced in the navigation of those seas, bid us all prepare against a storm, which accordingly happened the day following: for a southern wind, called the southern monsoon, began to set in.

Finding it was likely to overblow,[3] we took in our spritsail, and stood by to hand the foresail; but making foul weather, we looked the guns were all fast, and handed the mizzen. The ship lay very broad off, so we thought it better spooning before the sea, than trying or hulling. We reefed the foresail and set him, we hauled aft the foresheet; the helm was hard aweather. The ship wore bravely. We belayed the fore-down-haul; but the sail was split, and we hauled down the yard and got the sail into the ship, and unbound all the things clear of it. It was a very fierce storm; the sea broke strange and dangerous. We hauled off upon the lanyard of the whipstaff, and helped the man at helm. We would not get down our topmast, but let all stand, because she scudded before the sea very well, and we knew that the topmast being aloft, the ship was the wholesomer, and made better way through the sea, seeing we had searoom. When the storm was over, we set foresail and mainsail, and brought the ship to. Then we set the mizzen, main topsail and the fore topsail. Our course was east-northeast, the wind was at southwest. We got the starboard tacks aboard, we cast off our weather braces and lifts; we set in the lee braces, and hauled forward by the weather bowlings, and hauled them tight, and belayed them, and hauled over the mizzen tack to windward, and kept her full and by as near as she would lie.

During this storm, which was followed by a strong wind west-south-

2. In India. The geography of the voyage is simple: The *Adventure*, after sailing up the east coast of Africa to about 5° south of the equator (the "Line"), is blown past India into the Malay Archipelago, north of the islands of Buru and Ceram. The storm then drives the ship northward and eastward, away from the coast of Siberia ("Great Tartary") into the northeast Pacific, at that time unexplored. Brobdingnag lies somewhere in the vicinity of Alaska.

3. This paragraph is taken almost literally from Samuel Sturmy's *Mariner's Magazine* (1669). Swift is ridiculing the use of technical terms by writers of popular voyages.

west, we were carried by my computation about five hundred leagues to the east, so that the oldest sailor on board could not tell in what part of the world we were. Our provisions held out well, our ship was stanch, and our crew all in good health; but we lay in the utmost distress for water. We thought it best to hold on the same course rather than turn more northerly, which might have brought us to the northwest parts of Great Tartary, and into the frozen sea.

On the 16th day of June, 1703, a boy on the topmast discovered land. On the 17th we came in full view of a great island or continent (for we knew not whether) on the south side whereof was a small neck of land jutting out into the sea, and a creek[4] too shallow to hold a ship of above one hundred tons. We cast anchor within a league of this creek, and our Captain sent a dozen of his men well armed in the longboat, with vessels for water if any could be found. I desired his leave to go with them that I might see the country and make what discoveries I could. When we came to land we saw no river or spring, nor any sign of inhabitants. Our men therefore wandered on the shore to find out some fresh water near the sea, and I walked alone about a mile on the other side, where I observed the country all barren and rocky. I now began to be weary, and seeing nothing to entertain my curiosity, I returned gently down towards the creek; and the sea being full in my view, I saw our men already got into the boat, and rowing for life to the ship. I was going to hollow after them, although it had been to little purpose, when I observed a huge creature walking after them in the sea as fast as he could; he waded not much deeper than his knees and took prodigious strides, but our men had the start of him half a league, and the sea thereabouts being full of sharp-pointed rocks, the monster was not able to overtake the boat. This I was afterwards told, for I durst not stay to see the issue of that adventure, but ran as fast as I could the way I first went, and then climbed up a steep hill, which gave me some prospect of the country. I found it fully cultivated; but that which first surprised me was the length of the grass, which, in those grounds that seemed to be kept for hay, was about twenty foot high.[5]

I fell into a highroad, for so I took it to be, although it served to the inhabitants only as a footpath through a field of barley. Here I walked on for some time, but could see little on either side, it being now near harvest, and the corn[6] rising at least forty foot. I was an hour walking to the end of this field, which was fenced in with a hedge of at least one hundred and twenty foot high, and the trees so lofty that I could make no computation of their altitude. There was a stile to pass from this field into the next: it had four steps, and a stone to cross over when you came to the utmost. It was impossible for me to climb this stile, because every step was six foot high, and the upper stone above twenty. I was endeavoring to find some gap in the hedge when I discovered one of the inhabi-

4. A small bay or cove, affording anchorage.
5. Swift's intention, not always carried out accurately, is that everything in Brobdingnag should

be, in relation to our familiar world, on a scale of ten to one.
6. Wheat, not maize.

tants in the next field advancing towards the stile, of the same size with
him whom I saw in the sea pursuing our boat. He appeared as tall as an
ordinary spire-steeple, and took about ten yards at every stride, as near
as I could guess. I was struck with the utmost fear and astonishment,
and ran to hide myself in the corn, from whence I saw him at the top of
the stile, looking back into the next field on the right hand; and heard
him call in a voice many degrees louder than a speaking trumpet; but
the noise was so high in the air that at first I certainly thought it was
thunder. Whereupon seven monsters like himself came towards him
with reaping hooks in their hands, each hook about the largeness of six
scythes. These people were not so well clad as the first, whose servants
or laborers they seemed to be. For, upon some words he spoke, they
went to reap the corn in the field where I lay. I kept from them at as
great a distance as I could, but was forced to move with extreme difficulty, for the stalks of the corn were sometimes not above a foot distant,
so that I could hardly squeeze my body betwixt them. However, I made
a shift to go forward till I came to a part of the field where the corn had
been laid by the rain and wind; here it was impossible for me to advance
a step, for the stalks were so interwoven that I could not creep through,
and the beards of the fallen ears so strong and pointed that they pierced
through my clothes into my flesh. At the same time I heard the reapers
not above an hundred yards behind me. Being quite dispirited with toil,
and wholly overcome by grief and despair, I lay down between two ridges
and heartily wished I might there end my days. I bemoaned my desolate
widow and fatherless children; I lamented my own folly and willfulness
in attempting a second voyage against the advice of all my friends and
relations. In this terrible agitation of mind, I could not forbear thinking
of Lilliput, whose inhabitants looked upon me as the greatest prodigy
that ever appeared in the world; where I was able to draw an imperial
fleet in my hand, and perform those other actions which will be recorded
forever in the chronicles of that empire, while posterity shall hardly believe
them, although attested by millions. I reflected what a mortification it
must prove to me to appear as inconsiderable in this nation as one single
Lilliputian would be among us. But this I conceived was to be the least
of my misfortunes; for as human creatures are observed to be more savage and cruel in proportion to their bulk, what could I expect but to be
a morsel in the mouth of the first among these enormous barbarians
who should happen to seize me? Undoubtedly philosophers are in the
right when they tell us that nothing is great or little otherwise than by
comparison. It might have pleased fortune to let the Lilliputians find
some nation where the people were as diminutive with respect to them
as they were to me. And who knows but that even this prodigious race
of mortals might be equally overmatched in some distant part of the
world, whereof we have yet no discovery?

Scared and confounded as I was, I could not forbear going on with
these reflections; when one of the reapers approaching within ten yeards
of the ridge where I lay, made me apprehend that with the next step I

should be squashed to death under his foot, or cut in two with his reaping hook. And therefore when he was again about to move, I screamed as loud as fear could make me. Whereupon the huge creature trod short, and looking round about under him for some time, at last espied me as I lay on the ground. He considered a while with the caution of one who endeavors to lay hold on a small dangerous animal in such a manner that it shall not be able either to scratch or to bite him, as I myself have sometimes done with a weasel in England. At length he ventured to take me up behind by the middle between his forefinger and thumb, and brought me within three yards of his eyes, that he might behold my shape more perfectly. I guessed his meaning, and my good fortune gave me so much presence of mind that I resolved not to struggle in the least as he held me in the air about sixty foot from the ground, although he grievously pinched my sides, for fear I should slip through his fingers. All I ventured was to raise mine eyes towards the sun, and place my hands together in a supplicating posture, and to speak some words in an humble melancholy tone, suitable to the condition I then was in. For I apprehended every moment that he would dash me against the ground, as we usually do any little hateful animal which we have a mind to destroy. But my good star would have it that he appeared pleased with my voice and gestures, and began to look upon me as a curiosity, much wondering to hear me pronounce articulate words, although he could not understand them. In the meantime I was not able to forbear groaning and shedding tears and turning my head towards my sides, letting him know, as well as I could, how cruelly I was hurt by the pressure of his thumb and finger. He seemed to apprehend my meaning; for, lifting up the lappet[7] of his coat, he put me gently into it, and immediately ran along with me to his master, who was a substantial farmer, and the same person I had first seen in the field.

The farmer having (as I supposed by their talk) received such an account of me as his servant could give him, took a piece of a small straw about the size of a walking staff, and therewith lifted up the lappets of my coat, which it seems he thought to be some kind of covering that nature had given me. He blew my hairs aside to take a better view of my face. He called his hinds[8] about him, and asked them (as I afterwards learned) whether they had ever seen in the fields any little creature that resembled me. He then placed me softly on the ground upon all four; but I got immediately up, and walked slowly backwards and forwards, to let those people see I had no intent to run away. They all sat down in a circle about me, the better to observe my motions. I pulled off my hat, and made a low bow towards the farmer; I fell on my knees, and lifted up my hands and eyes, and spoke several words as loud as I could; I took a purse of gold out of my pocket, and humbly presented it to him. He received it on the palm of his hand, then applied it close to his eye to see what it was, and afterwards turned it several times with the point of

---

7. Flap or fold.　　　　8. Farm servants.

a pin (which he took out of his sleeve), but could make nothing of it. Whereupon I made a sign that he should place his hand on the ground; I then took the purse, and opening it, poured all the gold into his palm. There were six Spanish pieces of four pistoles each, beside twenty or thirty smaller coins. I saw him wet the tip of his little finger upon his tongue, and take up one of my largest pieces, and then another; but he seemed to be wholly ignorant what they were. He made me a sign to put them again into my purse, and the purse again into my pocket, which after offering to him several times, I thought it best to do.

The farmer by this time was convinced I must be a rational creature. He spoke often to me, but the sound of his voice pierced my ears like that of a water mill, yet his words were articulate enough. I answered as loud as I could in several languages, and he often laid his ear within two yards of me, but all in vain, for we were wholly unintelligible to each other. He then sent his servants to their work, and taking his handkerchief out of his pocket, he doubled and spread it on his hand, which he placed flat on the ground with the palm upwards, making me a sign to step into it, as I could easily do, for it was not above a foot in thickness. I thought it my part to obey, and for fear of falling, laid myself at full length upon the handkerchief, with the remainder of which he lapped me up to the head for further security, and in this manner carried me home to his house. There he called his wife, and showed me to her; but she screamed and ran back as women in England do at the sight of a toad or a spider. However, when she had a while seen my behavior, and how well I observed the signs her husband made, she was soon reconciled, and by degrees grew extremely tender of me.

It was about twelve at noon, and a servant brought in dinner. It was only one substantial dish of meat (fit for the plain condition of an husbandman) in a dish of about four-and-twenty foot diameter. The company were the farmer and his wife, three children, and an old grandmother. When they were sat down, the farmer placed me at some distance from him on the table, which was thirty foot high from the floor. I was in a terrible fright, and kept as far as I could from the edge, for fear of falling. The wife minced a bit of meat, then crumbled some bread on a trencher,[9] and placed it before me. I made her a low bow, took out my knife and fork, and fell to eat; which gave them exceeding delight. The mistress sent her maid for a small dram cup, which held about two gallons, and filled it with drink; I took up the vessel with much difficulty in both hands, and in a most respectful manner drank to her ladyship's health, expressing the words as loud as I could in English; which made the company laugh so heartily that I was almost deafened with the noise. This liquor tasted like a small cider,[1] and was not unpleasant. Then the master made me a sign to come to his trencher side; but as I walked on the table, being in great surprise all the time, as the indulgent reader will easily conceive and excuse, I happened to stumble

9. A platter.   1. I.e., weak cider.

against a crust, and fell flat on my face, but received no hurt. I got up immediately, and observing the good people to be in much concern, I took my hat (which I held under my arm out of good manners) and waving it over my head, made three huzzas to show I had got no mischief by my fall. But advancing forwards toward my master (as I shall henceforth call him), his youngest son who sat next him, an arch[2] boy of about ten years old, took me up by the legs, and held me so high in the air that I trembled every limb; but his father snatched me from him, and at the same time gave him such a box on the left ear as would have felled an European troop of horse to the earth, ordering him to be taken from the table. But being afraid the boy might owe me a spite, and well remembering how mischievous all children among us naturally are to sparrows, rabbits, young kittens, and puppy dogs, I fell on my knees, and pointing to the boy, made my master to understand, as well as I could, that I desired his son might be pardoned. The father complied, and the lad took his seat again; whereupon I went to him and kissed his hand, which my master took, and made him stroke me gently with it.

In the midst of dinner, my mistress's favorite cat leaped into her lap. I heard a noise behind me like that of a dozen stocking weavers at work; and turning my head, I found it proceeded from the purring of this animal, who seemed to be three times larger than an ox, as I computed by the view of her head and one of her paws, while her mistress was feeding and stroking her. The fierceness of this creature's countenance altogether discomposed me, although I stood at the farther end of the table, about fifty foot off, and although my mistress held her fast for fear she might give a spring and seize me in her talons. But it happened there was no danger, for the cat took not the least notice of me when my master placed me within three yards of her. And as I have been always told, and found true by experience in my travels, that flying or discovering[3] fear before a fierce animal is a certain way to make it pursue or attack you, so I resolved in this dangerous juncture to show no manner of concern. I walked with intrepidity five or six times before the very head of the cat, and came within half a yard of her; whereupon she drew herself back, as if she were more afraid of me; I had less apprehension concerning the dogs, whereof three or four came into the room, as it is usual in farmers' houses; one of which was a mastiff, equal in bulk to four elephants, and a greyhound, somewhat taller than the mastiff, but not so large.

When dinner was almost done, the nurse came in with a child of a year old in her arms, who immediately spied me, and began a squall that you might have heard from London Bridge to Chelsea, after the usual oratory of infants, to get me for a plaything. The mother out of pure indulgence took me up, and put me towards the child, who presently seized me by the middle, and got my head in his mouth, where I roared so loud that the urchin was frighted and let me drop; and I should

2. Mischievous.   3. Revealing.

infallibly have broke my neck if the mother had not held her apron under me. The nurse to quiet her babe made use of a rattle, which was a kind of hollow vessel filled with great stones, and fastened by a cable to the child's waist: but all in vain, so that she was forced to apply the last remedy by giving it suck. I must confess no object ever disgusted me so much as the sight of her monstrous breast, which I cannot tell what to compare with so as to give the curious reader an idea of its bulk, shape, and color. It stood prominent six foot, and could not be less than sixteen in circumference. The nipple was about half the bigness of my head, and the hue both of that and the dug so varified with spots, pimples, and freckles that nothing could appear more nauseous: for I had a near sight of her, she sitting down the more conveniently to give suck, and I standing on the table. This made me reflect upon the fair skins of our English ladies, who appear so beautiful to us, only because they are of our own size, and their defects not to be seen but through a magnifying glass, where we find by experiment that the smoothest and whitest skins look rough and coarse and ill colored.

I remember when I was at Lilliput, the complexion of those diminutive people appeared to me the fairest in the world; and talking upon this subject with a person of learning there, who was an intimate friend of mine, he said that my face appeared much fairer and smoother when he looked on me from the ground than it did upon a nearer view when I took him up in my hand and brought him close, which he confessed was at first a very shocking sight. He said he could discover great holes in my skin; that the stumps of my beard were ten times stronger than the bristles of a boar, and my complexion made up of several colors altogether disagreeable: although I must beg leave to say for myself that I am as fair as most of my sex and country and very little sunburnt by all my travels. On the other side, discoursing of the ladies in that Emperor's court, he used to tell me one had freckles, another too wide a mouth, a third too large a nose; nothing of which I was able to distinguish. I confess this reflection was obvious enough; which however I could not forbear, lest the reader might think those vast creatures were actually deformed: for I must do them justice to say they are a comely race of people; and particularly the features of my master's countenance, although he were but a farmer, when I beheld him from the height of sixty foot, appeared very well proportioned.

When dinner was done, my master went out to his laborers; and as I could discover by his voice and gesture, gave his wife a strict charge to take care of me. I was very much tired and disposed to sleep, which my mistress perceiving, she put me on her own bed, and covered me with a clean white handkerchief, but larger and coarser than the mainsail of a man-of-war.

I slept about two hours, and dreamed I was at home with my wife and children, which aggravated my sorrows when I awaked and found myself alone in a vast room, between two and three hundred foot wide, and above two hundred high, lying in a bed twenty yards wide. My mistress was gone about her household affairs, and had locked me in. The bed was eight yards from the floor. Some natural necessities required me to get down; I durst not presume to call, and if I had, it would have been in vain with such a voice as mine at so great a distance from the room where I lay to the kitchen where the family kept. While I was under these circumstances, two rats crept up the curtains, and ran smelling backwards and forwards on the bed. One of them came up almost to my face; whereupon I rose in a fright, and drew out my hanger[4] to defend myself. These horrible animals had the boldness to attack me on both sides, and one of them held his forefeet at my collar; but I had the good fortune to rip up his belly before he could do me any mischief. He fell down at my feet; and the other seeing the fate of his comrade, made his escape, but not without one good wound on the back, which I gave him as he fled, and made the blood run trickling from him. After this exploit I walked gently to and fro on the bed, to recover my breath and loss of spirits. These creatures were of the size of a large mastiff, but infinitely more nimble and fierce; so that if I had taken off my belt before I went to sleep, I must have infallibly been torn to pieces and devoured. I measured the tail of the dead rat, and found it to be two yards long, wanting an inch; but it went against my stomach to drag the carcass off the bed, where it lay still bleeding; I observed it had yet some life, but with a strong slash cross the neck, I thoroughly dispatched it.

Soon after, my mistress came into the room, who seeing me all bloody, ran and took me up in her hand. I pointed to the dead rat, smiling and making other signs to show I was not hurt, whereat she was extremely rejoiced, calling the maid to take up the dead rat with a pair of tongs, and throw it out of the window. Then she set me on a table, where I showed her my hanger all bloody, and wiping it on the lappet of my coat, returned it to the scabbard. I was pressed to do more than one thing, which another could not do for me, and therefore endeavored to make my mistress understand that I desired to be set down on the floor; which after she had done, my bashfulness would not suffer me to express myself farther than by pointing to the door, and bowing several times. The good woman with much difficulty at last perceived what I would be at, and taking me up again in her hand, walked into the garden, where she set me down. I went on one side about two hundred yards; and beckoning to her not to look or to follow me, I hid myself between two leaves of sorrel, and there discharged the necessities of nature.

I hope the gentle reader will excuse me for dwelling on these and the like particulars, which however insignificant they may appear to groveling vulgar[5] minds, yet will certainly help a philosopher to enlarge his thoughts and imagination, and apply them to the benefit of public as well as private life, which was my sole design in presenting this and other accounts of my travels to the world; wherein I have been chiefly studious of truth, without affecting any ornaments of learning or of style. But the

4. A short, broad sword.
5. Commonplace, uncultivated, in contrast to the scientist ("philosopher"); an irony.

whole scene of this voyage made so strong an impression on my mind, and is so deeply fixed in my memory, that in committing it to paper I did not omit one material circumstance; however, upon a strict review, I blotted out several passages of less moment which were in my first copy, for fear of being censured as tedious and trifling, whereof travelers are often, perhaps not without justice, accused.

CHAPTER 2. *A description of the farmer's daughter. The Author carried to a market town, and then to the metropolis. The particulars of his journey.*

My mistress had a daughter of nine years old, a child of towardly parts for her age, very dexterous at her needle, and skillful in dressing her baby.[6] Her mother and she contrived to fit up the baby's cradle for me against night: the cradle was put into a small drawer of a cabinet, and the drawer placed upon a hanging shelf for fear of the rats. This was my bed all the time I stayed with those people, although made more convenient by degrees as I began to learn their language, and make my wants known. This young girl was so handy, that after I had once or twice pulled off my clothes before her, she was able to dress and undress me, although I never gave her that trouble when she would let me do either myself. She made me seven shirts, and some other linen of as fine cloth as could be got, which indeed was coarser than sackcloth, and these she constantly washed for me with her own hands. She was likewise my schoolmistress to teach me the language: when I pointed to anything, she told me the name of it in her own tongue, so that in a few days I was able to call for whatever I had a mind to. She was very good-natured, and not above forty foot high, being little for her age. She gave me the name of *Grildrig*, which the family took up, and afterwards the whole kingdom. The word imports what the Latins call *nanunculus*, the Italian *homunceletino*,[7] and the English *mannikin*. To her I chiefly owe my preservation in that country: we never parted while I was there; I called her my *Glumdalclitch*, or little nurse: and I should be guilty of great ingratitude if I omitted this honorable mention of her care and affection towards me, which I heartily wish it lay in my power to requite as she deserves, instead of being the innocent but unhappy instrument of her disgrace, as I have too much reason to fear.

It now began to be known and talked of in the neighborhood that my master had found a strange animal in the field, about the bigness of a *splacknuck*, but exactly shaped in every part like a human creature, which it likewise imitated in all its actions: seemed to speak in a little language of its own, had already learned several words of theirs, went erect upon two legs, was tame and gentle, would come when it was called, do whatever it was bid, had the finest limbs in the world, and a complexion fairer than a nobleman's daughter of three years old. Another farmer

6. Doll.
7. The Latin and Italian words are Swift's own coinages, as, of course, are the various words from the Brobdingnagian language.

who lived hard by, and was a particular friend of my master, came on a
visit on purpose to inquire into the truth of this story. I was immediately
produced, and placed upon a table, where I walked as I was commanded, drew my hanger, put it up again, made my reverence to my
master's guest, asked him in his own language how he did, and told him
he was welcome, just as my little nurse had instructed me. This man,
who was old and dimsighted, put on his spectacles to behold me better,
at which I could not forbear laughing very heartily, for his eyes appeared
like the full moon shining into a chamber at two windows. Our people,
who discovered the cause of my mirth, bore me company in laughing,
at which the old fellow was fool enough to be angry and out of countenance. He had the character of a great miser, and to my misfortune he
well deserved it by the cursed advice he gave my master to show me as
a sight upon a market day in the next town, which was half an hour's
riding, about two and twenty miles from our house. I guessed there was
some mischief contriving when I observed my master and his friend
whispering long together, sometimes pointing at me; and my fears made
me fancy that I overheard and understood some of their words. But the
next morning Glumdalclitch, my little nurse, told me the whole matter,
which she had cunningly picked out from her mother. The poor girl
laid me on her bosom, and fell a weeping with shame and grief. She
apprehended some mischief would happen to me from rude vulgar folks,
who might squeeze me to death, or break one of my limbs by taking me
in their hands. She had also observed how modest I was in my nature,
how nicely I regarded my honor, and what an indignity I should conceive it to be exposed for money as a public spectacle to the meanest of
the people. She said her papa and mamma had promised that Grildrig
should be hers; but now she found they meant to serve her as they did
last year, when they pretended to give her a lamb, and yet, as soon as it
was fat, sold it to a butcher. For my own part, I may truly affirm that I
was less concerned than my nurse. I had a strong hope, which never left
me, that I should one day recover my liberty; and as to the ignominy of
being carried about for a monster, I considered myself to be a perfect
stranger in the country, and that such a misfortune could never be charged
upon me as a reproach, if ever I should return to England; since the
King of Great Britain himself, in my condition, must have undergone
the same distress.

My master, pursuant to the advice of his friend, carried me in a box
the next market day to the neighboring town, and took along with him
his little daughter, my nurse, upon a pillion[8] behind him. The box was
close on every side, with a little door for me to go in and out, and a few
gimlet holes to let in air. The girl had been so careful to put the quilt of
her baby's bed into it, for me to lie down on. However, I was terribly
shaken and discomposed in this journey, although it were but of half an
hour. For the horse went about forty foot at every step, and trotted so

---

8. A pad attached to the hinder part of a saddle, on which a second person, usually a woman, could ride.

high that the agitation was equal to the rising and falling of a ship in a great storm, but much more frequent. Our journey was somewhat further than from London to St. Albans. My master alighted at an inn which he used to frequent; and after consulting a while with the innkeeper, and making some necessary preparations, he hired the *Grultrud*, or crier, to give notice through the town of a strange creature to be seen at the Sign of the Green Eagle, not so big as a *splacknuck* (an animal in that country very finely shaped, about six foot long), and in every part of the body resembling an human creature, could speak several words and perform an hundred diverting tricks.

I was placed upon a table in the largest room of the inn, which might be near three hundred foot square. My little nurse stood on a low stool close to the table, to take care of me, and direct what I should do. My master, to avoid a crowd, would suffer only thirty people at a time to see me. I walked about on the table as the girl commanded; she asked me questions as far as she knew my understanding of the language reached, and I answered them as loud as I could. I turned about several times to the company, paid my humble respects, said they were welcome, and used some other speeches I had been taught. I took up a thimble filled with liquor, which Glumdalclitch had given me for a cup, and drank their health. I drew out my hanger, and flourished with it after the manner of fencers in England. My nurse gave me part of a straw, which I exercised as pike, having learned the art in my youth. I was that day shown to twelve sets of company, and as often forced to go over again with the same fopperies, till I was half dead with weariness and vexation. For those who had seen me made such wonderful reports that the people were ready to break down the doors to come in. My master for his own interest would not suffer anyone to touch me except my nurse; and, to prevent danger, benches were set round the table at such a distance as put me out of everybody's reach. However, an unlucky schoolboy aimed a hazelnut directly at my head, which very narrowly missed me; otherwise, it came with so much violence that it would have infallibly knocked out my brains, for it was almost as large as a small pumpion:[9] but I had the satisfaction to see the young rogue well beaten, and turned out of the room.

My master gave public notice that he would show me again the next market day, and in the meantime he prepared a more convenient vehicle for me, which he had reason enough to do; for I was so tired with my first journey, and with entertaining company for eight hours together, that I could hardly stand upon my legs or speak a word. It was at least three days before I recovered my strength; and that I might have no rest at home, all the neighboring gentlemen from an hundred miles round, hearing of my fame, came to see me at my master's own house. There could not be fewer than thirty persons with their wives and children (for the country is very populous); and my master demanded the rate of a full

9. Pumpkin.

room whenever he showed me at home, although it were only to a single family. So that for some time I had but little ease every day of the week (except Wednesday, which is their Sabbath) although I were not carried to the town.

My master finding how profitable I was like to be, resolved to carry me to the most considerable cities of the kingdom. Having therefore provided himself with all things necessary for a long journey, and settled his affairs at home, he took leave of his wife; and upon the 17th of August, 1703, about two months after my arrival, we set out for the metropolis, situated near the middle of that empire, and about three thousand miles distance from our house. My master made his daughter Glumdalclitch ride behind him. She carried me on her lap in a box tied about her waist. The girl had lined it on all sides with the softest cloth she could get, well quilted underneath, furnished it with her baby's bed, provided me with linen and other necessaries, and made everything as convenient as she could. We had no other company but a boy of the house, who rode after us with the luggage.

My master's design was to show me in all the towns by the way, and to step out of the road for fifty or an hundred miles to any village or person of quality's house where he might expect custom. We made easy journeys of not above seven or eight score miles a day: for Glumdalclitch, on purpose to spare me, complained she was tired with the trotting of the horse. She often took me out of my box at my own desire, to give me air and show me the country, but always held me fast by leading strings. We passed over five or six rivers many degrees broader and deeper than the Nile or the Ganges; and there was hardly a rivulet so small as the Thames at London Bridge. We were ten weeks in our journey, and I was shown in eighteen large towns, besides many large villages and private families.

On the 26th day of October, we arrived at the metropolis, called in their language *Lorbrulgrud*, or Pride of the Universe. My master took a lodging in the principal street of the city, not far from the royal palace, and put out bills in the usual form, containing an exact description of my person and parts. He hired a large room between three and four hundred foot wide. He provided a table sixty foot in diameter, upon which I was to act my part, and palisadoed it round three foot from the edge, and as many high, to prevent my falling over. I was shown ten times a day to the wonder and satisfaction of all people. I could now speak the language tolerably well, and perfectly understood every word that was spoken to me. Besides, I had learned their alphabet, and could make a shift to explain a sentence here and there; for Glumdalclitch had been my instructor while we were at home, and at leisure hours during our journey. She carried a little book in her pocket, not much larger than a Sanson's *Atlas*;[1] it was a common treatise for the use of young

_____
1. I.e., over 2 feet long and about 2 feet wide.

girls, giving a short account of their religion: out of this she taught me my letters, and interpreted the words.

CHAPTER 3. *The Author sent for to Court. The Queen buys him of his master, the farmer, and presents him to the King. He disputes with his Majesty's great scholars. An apartment at Court provided for the Author. He is in high favor with the Queen. He stands up for the honor of his own country. His quarrels with the Queen's dwarf.*

The frequent labors I underwent every day made in a few weeks a very considerable change in my health: the more my master got by me, the more unsatiable he grew. I had quite lost my stomach, and was almost reduced to a skeleton. The farmer observed it, and concluding I soon must die, resolved to make as good a hand of me as he could. While he was thus reasoning and resolving with himself, a *Slardral*, or Gentleman Usher, came from Court, commanding my master to carry me immediately thither for the diversion of the Queen and her ladies. Some of the latter had already been to see me and reported strange things of my beauty, behavior, and good sense. Her Majesty and those who attended her were beyond measure delighted with my demeanor. I fell on my knees and begged the honor of kissing her Imperial foot; but this gracious princess held out her little finger towards me (after I was set on a table), which I embraced in both my arms, and put the tip of it, with the utmost respect, to my lip. She made me some general questions about my country and my travels, which I answered as distinctly and in as few words as I could. She asked whether I would be content to live at Court. I bowed down to the board of the table, and humbly answered that I was my master's slave, but if I were at my own disposal, I should be proud to devote my life to her Majesty's service. She then asked my master whether he were willing to sell me at a good price. He, who apprehended I could not live a month, was ready enough to part with me, and demanded a thousand pieces of gold, which were ordered him on the spot, each piece being about the bigness of eight hundred moidores;[2] but, allowing for the proportion of all things between that country and Europe, and the high price of gold among them, was hardly so great a sum as a thousand guineas would be in England. I then said to the Queen, since I was now her Majesty's most humble creature and vassal, I must beg the favor that Glumdalclitch, who had always tended me with so much care and kindness, and understood to do it so well, might be admitted into her service, and continue to be my nurse and instructor. Her Majesty agreed to my petition, and easily got the farmer's consent, who was glad enough to have his daughter preferred at Court; and the poor girl herself was not able to hide her joy. My late master withdrew, bidding me farewell, and

2. Portuguese coins.

saying he had left me in a good service; to which I replied not a word, only making him a slight bow.

The Queen observed my coldness, and when the farmer was gone out of the apartment, asked me the reason. I made bold to tell her Majesty that I owed no other obligation to my late master than his not dashing out the brains of a poor harmless creature found by chance in his field; which obligation was amply recompensed by the gain he had made in showing me through half the kingdom, and the price he had now sold me for. That the life I had since led was laborious enough to kill an animal of ten times my strength. That my health was much impaired by the continual drudgery of entertaining the rabble every hour of the day; and that if my master had not thought my life in danger, her Majestry would not have got so cheap a bargain. But as I was out of all fear of being ill treated under the protection of so great and good an Empress, the Ornament of Nature, the Darling of the World, the Delight of her Subjects, the Phoenix of the Creation; so I hoped my late master's apprehensions would appear to be groundless, for I already found my spirits to revive by the influence of her most august presence.

This was the sum of my speech, delivered with great improprieties and hesitation; the latter part was altogether framed in the style peculiar to that people, whereof I learned some phrases from Glumdalclitch, while she was carrying me to Court.

The Queen, giving great allowance for my defectiveness in speaking, was however surprised at so much wit and good sense in so diminutive an animal. She took me in her own hand, and carried me to the King, who was then retired to his cabinet.[3] His Majesty, a prince of much gravity, and austere countenance, not well observing my shape at first view, asked the Queen after a cold manner how long it was since she grew fond of a *splacknuck*; for such it seems he took me to be, as I lay upon my breast in her Majesty's right hand. But this princess, who hath an infinite deal of wit and humor, set me gently on my feet upon the scrutore,[4] and commanded me to give his Majesty an account of myself, which I did in a very few words; and Glumdalclitch, who attended at the cabinet door, and could not endure I should be out of her sight, being admitted, confirmed all that had passed from my arrival at her father's house.

The King, although he be as learned a person as any in his dominions, had been educated in the study of philosophy and particularly mathematics; yet when he observed my shape exactly, and saw me walk erect, before I began to speak, conceived I might be a piece of clockwork (which is in that country arrived to a very great perfection) contrived by some ingenious artist. But when he heard my voice, and found what I delivered to be regular and rational, he could not conceal his astonishment. He was by no means satisfied with the relation I gave him of the manner I came into his kingdom, but thought it a story concerted between

3. A private apartment.   4. Writing desk.

Glumdalclitch and her father, who had taught me a set of words to make me sell at a higher price. Upon this imagination he put several other questions to me, and still received rational answers, no otherwise defective than by a foreign accent, and an imperfect knowledge in the language, with some rustic phrases which I had learned at the farmer's house, and did not suit the polite style of a court.

His Majesty sent for three great scholars who were then in their weekly waiting (according to the custom in that country). These gentlemen, after they had a while examined my shape with much nicety, were of different opinions concerning me. They all agreed that I could not be produced according to the regular laws of nature, because I was not framed with a capacity of preserving my life, either by swiftness, or climbing of trees, or digging holes in the earth. They observed by my teeth, which they viewed with great exactness, that I was a carnivorous animal; yet most quadrupeds being an overmatch for me, and field mice, with some others, too nimble, they could not imagine how I should be able to support myself, unless I fed upon snails and other insects; which they offered, by many learned arguments, to evince that I could not possibly do. One of them seemed to think that I might be an embryo, or abortive birth. But this opinion was rejected by the other two, who observed my limbs to be perfect and finished, and that I had lived several years, as it was manifest from my beard, the stumps whereof they plainly discovered through a magnifying glass. They would not allow me to be a dwarf, because my littleness was beyond all degrees of comparison; for the Queen's favorite dwarf, the smallest ever known in that kingdom, was nearly thirty foot high. After much debate, they concluded unanimously that I was only *relplum scalcath*, which is interpreted literally, *lusus naturae*;[5] a determination exactly agreeable to the modern philosophy of Europe, whose professors, disdaining the old evasion of *occult causes*, whereby the followers of Aristotle endeavor in vain to disguise their ignorance, have invented this wonderful solution of all difficulties, to the unspeakable advancement of human knowledge.

After this decisive conclusion, I entreated to be heard a word or two. I applied myself to the King, and assured his Majesty that I came from a country which abounded with several millions of both sexes, and of my own stature, where the animals, trees, and houses were all in proportion, and where by consequence I might be as able to defend myself, and to find sustenance, as any of his Majesty's subjects could do here; which I took for a full answer to those gentlemen's arguments. To this they only replied with a smile of contempt, saying that the farmer had instructed me very well in my lesson. The King, who had a much better understanding, dismissing his learned men, sent for the farmer, who by good fortune was not yet gone out of town; having therefore first examined him privately, and then confronted him with me and the young

---

5. One of nature's sports, or, roughly, freaks. Swift had contempt for both the medieval schoolmen, who discussed "occult causes," the unknown causes of observable effects, and modern scientists, who he believed, often concealed their ignorance by using equally meaningless terms.

girl, his Majesty began to think that what we told him might possibly be true. He desired the Queen to order that a particular care should be taken of me, and was of opinion that Glumdalclitch should still continue in her office of tending me, because he observed we had a great affection for each other. A convenient apartment was provided for her at Court; she had a sort of governess appointed to take care of her education, a maid to dress her, and two other servants for menial offices; but the care of me was wholly appropriated to herself. The Queen commanded her own cabinetmaker to contrive a box that might serve me for a bedchamber, after the model that Glumdalclitch and I should agree upon. This man was a most ingenious artist, and according to my directions, in three weeks finished for me a wooden chamber of sixteen foot square and twelve high, with sash windows, a door, and two closets, like a London bedchamber. The board that made the ceiling was to be lifted up and down by two hinges, to put in a bed ready furnished by her Majesty's upholsterer, which Glumdalclitch took out every day to air, made it with her own hands, and letting it down at night, locked up the roof over me. A nice[6] workman, who was famous for little curiosities, undertook to make me two chairs, with backs and frames, of a substance not unlike ivory, and two tables, with a cabinet to put my things in. The room was quilted on all sides, as well as the floor and the ceiling, to prevent any accident from the carelessness of those who carried me, and to break the force of a jolt when I went in a coach. I desired a lock for my door to prevent rats and mice from coming in: the smith, after several attempts, made the smallest that ever was seen among them, for I have known a larger at the gate of a gentleman's house in England. I made a shift[7] to keep the key in a pocket of my own, fearing Glumdalclitch might lose it. The Queen likewise ordered the thinnest silks that could be gotten, to make me clothes, not much thicker than an English blanket, very cumbersome till I was accustomed to them. They were after the fashion of the kingdom, partly resembling the Persian, and partly the Chinese, and are a very grave, decent habit.

The Queen became so fond of my company that she could not dine without me. I had a table placed upon the same at which her Majesty ate, just at her left elbow, and a chair to sit on. Glumdalclitch stood upon a stool on the floor, near my table, to assist and take care of me. I had an entire set of silver dishes and plates, and other necessaries, which, in proportion to those of the Queen, were not much bigger than what I have seen of the same kind in a London toyshop,[8] for the furniture of a baby-house: these my little nurse kept in her pocket in a silver box and gave me at meals as I wanted them, always cleaning them herself. No person dined with the Queen but the two Princesses Royal, the elder sixteen years old, and the younger at that time thirteen and a month. Her Majesty used to put a bit of meat upon one of my dishes, out of which I carved for myself; and her diversion was to see me eat in min-

6. Exact.
7. Contrived.

8. A shop for selling knickknacks.

iature. For the Queen (who had indeed but a weak stomach) took up at one mouthful as much as a dozen English farmers could eat at a meal, which to me was for some time a very nauseous sight. She would craunch the wing of a lark, bones and all, between her teeth, although it were nine times as large as that of a full-grown turkey; and put a bit of bread into her mouth as big as two twelve-penny loaves. She drank out of a golden cup, above a hogshead at a draught. Her knives were twice as long as a scythe set straight upon the handle. The spoons, forks, and other instruments were all in the same proportion. I remember when Glumdalclitch carried me out of curiosity to see some of the tables at Court, where ten or a dozen of these enormous knives and forks were lifted up together, I thought I had never till then beheld so terrible a sight.

It is the custom that every Wednesday (which, as I have before observed, was their Sabbath) the King and Queen, with the royal issue of both sexes, dine together in the apartment of his Majesty, to whom I was now become a favorite; and at these times my little chair and table were placed at his left hand, before one of the salt-cellars. This prince took a pleasure in conversing with me, inquiring into the manners, religion, laws, government, and learning of Europe; wherein I gave him the best account I was able. His apprehension was so clear, and his judgment so exact, that he made very wise reflections and observations upon all I said. But I confess that after I had been a little too copious in talking of my own beloved country, of our trade and wars by sea and land, of our schisms in religion and parties in the state, the prejudices of his education prevailed so far that he could not forbear taking me up in his right hand, and stroking me gently with the other, after an hearty fit of laughing, asked me whether I were a Whig or a Tory. Then turning to his first minister, who waited behind him with a white staff, near as tall as the mainmast of the *Royal Sovereign*,[9] he observed how contemptible a thing was human grandeur, which could be mimicked by such diminutive insects as I: "and yet," said he, "I dare engage, these creatures have their titles and distinctions of honor; they contrive little nests and burrows, that they call houses and cities; they make a figure in dress and equipage;[1] they love, they fight, they dispute, they cheat, they betray." And thus he continued on, while my color came and went several times with indignation to hear our noble country, the mistress of arts and arms, the scourge of France, the arbitress of Europe, the seat of virtue, piety, honor, and truth, the pride and envy of the world, so contemptuously treated.

But as I was not in a condition to resent injuries, so, upon mature thoughts, I began to doubt whether I were injured or no. For, after having been accustomed several months to the sight and converse of this people, and observed every object upon which I cast my eyes to be of

9. At the English court the Lord Treasurer bore a white staff as the symbol of his office. The *Royal Sovereign* was one of the largest ships in the Royal Navy.
1. A carriage and horses, with attendant footmen.

proportionable magnitude, the horror I had first conceived from their bulk and aspect was so far worn off that if I had then beheld a company of English lords and ladies in their finery and birthday clothes,[2] acting their several parts in the most courtly manner of strutting and bowing and prating, to say the truth, I should have been strongly tempted to laugh as much at them as this King and his grandees did at me. Neither indeed could I forbear smiling at myself when the Queen used to place me upon her hand towards a looking glass, by which both our persons appeared before me in full view together; and there could be nothing more ridiculous than the comparison; so that I really began to imagine myself dwindled many degrees below my usual size.

Nothing angered and mortified me so much as the Queen's dwarf, who being of the lowest stature that was ever in that country (for I verily think he was not full thirty foot high) became so insolent at seeing a creature so much beneath him that he would always affect to swagger and look big as he passed by me in the Queen's antechamber, while I was standing on some table talking with the lords or ladies of the court; and he seldom failed of a smart word or two upon my littleness, against which I could only revenge myself by calling him brother, challenging him to wrestle, and such repartees as are usual in the mouths of Court pages. One day at dinner this malicious little cub was so nettled with something I had said to him that, raising himself upon the frame of Her Majesty's chair, he took me up by the middle, as I was sitting down, not thinking any harm, and let me drop into a large silver bowl of cream, and then ran away as fast as he could. I fell over head and ears, and if I had not been a good swimmer, it might have gone very hard with me; for Glumdalclitch in that instant happened to be at the other end of the room, and the Queen was in such a fright that she wanted presence of mind to assist me. But my little nurse ran to my relief, and took me out, after I had swallowed above a quart of cream. I was put to bed; however, I received no other damage than the loss of a suit of clothes, which was utterly spoiled. The dwarf was soundly whipped, and as further punishment, forced to drink up the bowl of cream into which he had thrown me; neither was he ever restored to favor: for soon after the Queen bestowed him to a lady of high quality, so that I saw him no more, to my very great satisfaction; for I could not tell to what extremity such a malicious urchin might have carried his resentment.

He had before served me a scurvy trick, which set the Queen a laughing, although at the same time she were heartily vexed, and would have immediately cashiered him,[3] if I had not been so generous as to intercede. Her Majesty had taken a marrow bone upon her plate, and after knocking out the marrow, placed the bone again in the dish, erect as it stood before; the dwarf watching his opportunity, while Glumdalclitch was gone to the sideboard, mounted upon the stool she stood on to take care

2. Courtiers dressed with especial splendor on the monarch's birthday.
3. Dismissed him.

of me at meals, took me up in both hands, and squeezing my legs together, wedged them into the marrow bone above my waist, where I stuck for some time, and made a very ridiculous figure. I believe it was near a minute before anyone knew what was become of me, for I thought it below me to cry out. But, as princes seldom get their meat hot, my legs were not scalded, only my stockings and breeches in a sad condition. The dwarf at my entreaty had no other punishment than a sound whipping.

I was frequently rallied by the Queen upon account of my fearfulness, and she used to ask me whether the people of my country were as great cowards as myself. The occasion was this. The kingdom is much pestered with flies in summer, and these odious insects, each of them as big as a Dunstable lark, hardly gave me any rest while I sat at dinner, with their continual humming and buzzing about my ears. They would sometimes alight upon my vituals, and leave their loathsome excrement or spawn behind, which to me was very visible, although not to the natives of that country, whose large optics were not so acute as mine in viewing smaller objects. Sometimes they would fix upon my nose or forehead, where they stung me to the quick, smelling very offensively; and I could easily trace that viscous matter, which our naturalists tell us enables those creatures to walk with their feet upwards upon a ceiling. I had much ado to defend myself against these detestable animals, and could not forbear starting when they came on my face. It was the common practice of the dwarf to catch a number of these insects in his hand, as schoolboys do among us, and let them out suddenly under my nose, on purpose to frighten me, and divert the Queen. My remedy was to cut them in pieces with my knife as they flew in the air, wherein my dexterity was much admired.

I remember one morning when Glumdalclitch had set me in my box upon a window, as she usually did in fair days to give me air (for I durst not venture to let the box be hung on a nail out of the window, as we do with cages in England), after I had lifted up one of my sashes, and sat down at my table to eat a piece of sweet cake for my breakfast, above twenty wasps, allured by the smell, came flying into the room, humming louder than the drones of as many bagpipes. Some of them seized my cake, and carried it piecemeal away; others flew about my head and face, confounding me with the noise, and putting me in the utmost terror of their stings. However, I had the courage to rise and draw my hanger, and attack them in the air. I dispatched four of them, but the rest got away, and I presently shut my window. These insects were as large as partridges; I took out their stings, found them an inch and a half long, and as sharp as needles. I carefully preserved them all, and having since shown them with some other curiosities in several parts of Europe, upon my return to England I gave three of them to Gresham College,[4] and kept the fourth for myself.

4. The Royal Society, in its earliest years, met in Gresham College.

CHAPTER 4. *The country described. A proposal for correcting modern maps.*
The King's palace, and some account of the metropolis. The Author's way
of traveling. The chief temple described.

I now intend to give the reader a short description of this country, as
far as I had traveled in it, which was not above two thousand miles round
Lorbrulgrud the metropolis. For the Queen, whom I always attended,
never went further when she accompanied the King in his progresses,
and there stayed till his Majesty returned from viewing his frontiers. The
whole extent of this prince's dominions reacheth about six thousand
miles in length, and from three to five in breadth. From whence I cannot but conclude that our geographers of Europe are in a great error by
supposing nothing but sea between Japan and California: for it was ever
my opinion that there must be a balance of earth to counterpoise the
great continent of Tartary; and therefore they ought to correct their maps
and charts by joining this vast tract of land to the northwest parts of
America, wherein I shall be ready to lend them my assistance.

The kingdom is a peninsula, terminated to the northeast by a ridge of
mountains thirty miles high, which are altogether impassable by reason
of the volcanoes upon the tops. Neither do the most learned know what
sort of mortals inhabit beyond those mountains, or whether they be
inhabited at all. On the three other sides it is bounded by the ocean.
There is not one seaport in the whole kingdom; and those parts of the
coasts into which the rivers issue are so full of pointed rocks, and the sea
generally so rough, that there is no venturing with the smallest of their
boats; so that these people are wholly excluded from any commerce with
the rest of the world. But the large rivers are full of vessels, and abound
with excellent fish, for they seldom get any from the sea, because the
sea fish are of the same size with those in Europe, and consequently not
worth catching; whereby it is manifest that nature, in the production of
plants and animals of so extraordinary a bulk, is wholly confined to this
continent, of which I leave the reasons to be determined by philosophers. However, now and then they take a whale that happens to be
dashed against the rocks, which the common people feed on heartily.
These whales I have known so large that a man could hardly carry one
upon his shoulders; and sometimes for curiosity they are brought in
hampers to Lorbrulgrud: I saw one of them in a dish at the King's table,
which passed for a rarity, but I did not observe he was fond of it; for I
think indeed the bigness disgusted him, although I have seen one somewhat larger in Greenland.

The country is well inhabited, for it contains fifty-one cities, near an
hundred walled towns, and a great number of villages. To satisfy my
curious reader, it may be sufficient to describe Lorbrulgrud. This city
stands upon almost two equal parts on each side the river that passes
through. It contains above eight thousand houses, and about six hundred
thousand inhabitants. It is in length three *glongluns* (which make about
fifty-four English miles) and two and a half in breadth, as I measured it

myself in the royal map made by the King's order, which was laid on the ground on purpose for me, and extended an hundred feet; I paced the diameter and circumference several times barefoot, and computing by the scale, measured it pretty exactly.

The King's palace is no regular edifice, but an heap of buildings about seven miles round: the chief rooms are generally two hundred and forty foot high, and broad and long in proportion. A coach was allowed to Glumdalclitch and me, wherein her governess frequently took her out to see the town, or go among the shops; and I was always of the party, carried in my box, although the girl at my own desire would often take me out, and hold me in her hand, that I might more conveniently view the houses and the people as we passed along the streets. I reckoned our coach to be about a square of Westminster Hall,[5] but not altogether so high; however, I cannot be very exact. One day the governess ordered our coachman to stop at several shops, where the beggars, watching their opportunity, crowded to the sides of the coach, and gave me the most horrible spectacles that ever an English eye beheld. There was a woman with a cancer in her breast, swelled to a monstrous size, full of holes, in two or three of which I could have easily crept, and covered my whole body. There was a fellow with a wen in his neck, larger than five wool-packs, and another with a couple of wooden legs, each about twenty foot high. But the most hateful sight of all was the lice crawling on their clothes. I could see distinctly the limbs of these vermin with my naked eye, much better than those of an European louse through a micro-scope, and their snouts with which they rooted like swine. They were the first I had ever beheld; and I should have been curious enough to dissect one of them if I had proper instruments (which I unluckily left behind me in the ship), although indeed the sight was so nauseous that it perfectly turned my stomach.

Besides the large box in which I was usually carried, the Queen ordered a smaller one to be made for me, of about twelve foot square and ten high, for the convenience of traveling, because the other was somewhat too large for Glumdalclitch's lap, and cumbersome in the coach; it was made by the same artist, whom I directed in the whole contrivance. This traveling closet was an exact square with a window in the middle of three of the squares, and each window was latticed with iron wire on the outside, to prevent accidents in long journeys. On the fourth side, which had no windows, two strong staples were fixed, through which the per-son that carried me, when I had a mind to be on horseback, put in a leathern belt, and buckled it about his waist. This was always the office of some grave trusty servant in whom I could confide, whether I attended the King and Queen in their progresses, or were disposed to see the gardens, or pay a visit to some great lady or minister of state in the court, when Glumdalclitch happened to be out of order: for I soon began to be known and esteemed among the greatest officers, I suppose more upon

5. The ancient hall, now incorporated into the Houses of Parliament, where the Law Courts then sat. Swift presumably means the square of its breadth (just under 68 feet).

account of their Majesties' favor than any merit of my own. In journeys, when I was weary of the coach, a servant on horseback would buckle my box, and place it on a cushion before him; and there I had a full prospect of the country on three sides from my three windows. I had in this closet a field bed and a hammock hung from the ceiling, two chairs and a table, neatly screwed to the floor to prevent being tossed about by the agitation of the horse or the coach. And having been long used to sea voyages, those motions, although sometimes very violent, did not much discompose me.

When I had a mind to see the town, it was always in my traveling closet, which Glumdalclitch held in her lap in a kind of open sedan, after the fashion of the country, borne by four men, and attended by two others in the Queen's livery. The people, who had often heard of me, were very curious to crowd about the sedan; and the girl was complaisant enough to make the bearers stop, and to take me in her hand that I might be more conveniently seen.

I was very desirous to see the chief temple, and particularly the tower belonging to it, which is reckoned the highest in the kingdom. Accordingly one day my nurse carried me thither, but I may truly say I came back disappointed; for the height is not above three thousand foot, reckoning from the ground to the highest pinnacle top; which, allowing for the difference between the size of those people and us in Europe, is no great matter for admiration, nor at all equal in proportion (if I rightly remember) to Salisbury steeple.[6] But, not to detract from a nation to which during my life I shall acknowledge myself extremely obliged, it must be allowed that whatever this famous tower wants in height is amply made up in beauty and strength. For the walls are near an hundred foot thick, built of hewn stone, whereof each is about forty foot square, and adorned on all sides with statues of gods and emperors cut in marble larger than the life, placed in their several niches. I measured a little finger which had fallen down from one of these statues, and lay unperceived among some rubbish, and found it exactly four foot and an inch in length. Glumdalclitch wrapped it up in a handkerchief, and carried it home in her pocket to keep among other trinkets, of which the girl was very fond, as children at her age usually are.

The King's kitchen is indeed a noble building, vaulted at top, and about six hundred foot high. The great oven is not so wide by ten paces as the cupola at St. Paul's:[7] for I measured the latter on purpose after my return. But if I should describe the kitchen grate, the prodigious pots and kettles, the joints of meat turning on the spits, with many other particulars, perhaps I should be hardly believed; at least a severe critic would be apt to think I enlarged a little, as travelers are often suspected to do. To avoid which censure, I fear I have run too much into the other extreme, and that if this treatise should happen to be translated into the

6. One of the most beautiful Gothic steeples in England is that of Salisbury Cathedral, 404 feet high.

7. The cupola of St. Paul's Cathedral in London is 108 feet in diameter.

language of Brobdingnag (which is the general name of that kingdom) and transmitted thither, the King and his people would have reason to complain that I had done them an injury by a false and diminutive representation.

His Majesty seldom keeps above six hundred horses in his stables: they are generally from fifty-four to sixty foot high. But when he goes abroad on solemn days, he is attended for state by a militia guard of five hundred horse, which indeed I thought was the most splendid sight that could be ever beheld, till I saw part of his army in battalia,[8] whereof I shall find another occasion to speak.

CHAPTER 5. *Several adventures that happened to the Author. The execution of a criminal. The Author shows his skill in navigation.*

I should have lived happy enough in that country if my littleness had not exposed me to several ridiculous and troublesome accidents, some of which I shall venture to relate. Glumdalclitch often carried me into the gardens of the court in my smaller box, and would sometimes take me out of it and hold me in her hand, or set me down to walk. I remember, before the dwarf left the Queen, he followed us one day into those gardens; and my nurse having set me down, he and I being close together near some dwarf apple trees, I must needs show my wit by a silly allusion between him and the trees, which happens to hold in their language as it doth in ours. Whereupon, the malicious rogue watching his opportunity, when I was walking under one of them, shook it directly over my head, by which a dozen apples, each of them near as large as a Bristol barrel, came tumbling about my ears; one of them hit me on the back as I chanced to stoop, and knocked me down flat on my face, but I received no other hurt; and the dwarf was pardoned at my desire, because I had given the provocation.

Another day Glumdalclitch left me on a smooth grassplot to divert myself while she walked at some distance with her governess. In the meantime there suddenly fell such a violent shower of hail that I was immediately by the force of it struck to the ground: and when I was down, the hailstones gave me such cruel bangs all over the body as if I had been pelted with tennis balls;[9] however I made a shift to creep on all four, and shelter myself by lying on my face on the lee side of a border of lemon thyme, but so bruised from head to foot that I could not go abroad in ten days. Neither is this at all to be wondered at, because nature in that country observing the same proportion through all her operations, a hailstone is near eighteen hundred times as large as one in Europe; which I can assert upon experience, having been so curious to weigh and measure them.

But a more dangerous accident happened to me in the same garden when my little nurse, believing she had put me in a secure place, which

8. Battle array.
9. 18th-century tennis balls, unlike the modern, were very hard.

I often entreated her to do that I might enjoy my own thoughts, and having left my box at home to avoid the trouble of carrying it, went to another part of the garden with her governess and some ladies of her acquaintance. While she was absent and out of hearing, a small white spaniel belonging to one of the chief gardeners, having got by accident into the garden, happened to range near the place where I lay. The dog following the scent, came directly up, and taking me in his mouth, ran straight to his master, wagging his tail, and set me gently on the ground. By good fortune he had been so well taught that I was carried between his teeth without the least hurt, or even tearing my clothes. But the poor gardener, who knew me well, and had a great kindness for me, was in a terrible fright. He gently took me up in both his hands, and asked me how I did; but I was so amazed and out of breath that I could not speak a word. In a few minutes I came to myself, and he carried me safe to my little nurse, who by this time had returned to the place where she left me, and was in cruel agonies when I did not appear nor answer when she called; she severely reprimanded the gardener on account of his dog. But the thing was hushed up and never known at court; for the girl was afraid of the Queen's anger; and truly, as to myself, I thought it would not be for my reputation that such a story should go about.

This accident absolutely determined Glumdalclitch never to trust me abroad for the future out of her sight. I had been long afraid of this resolution, and therefore concealed from her some little unlucky adventures that happened in those times when I was left by myself. Once a kite[1] hovering over the garden made a swoop at me, and if I had not resolutely drawn my hanger, and run under a thick espalier,[2] he would have certainly carried me away in his talons. Another time walking to the top of a fresh molehill, I fell to my neck in the hole through which that animal had cast up the earth, and coined some lie, not worth remembering, to excuse myself for spoiling my clothes. I likewise broke my right shin against the shell of a snail, which I happened to stumble over, as I was walking alone, and thinking on poor England.

I cannot tell whether I were more pleased or mortified to observe in those solitary walks that the smaller birds did not appear to be at all afraid of me; but would hop about within a yard distance, looking for worms and other food with as much indifference and security as if no creature at all were near them. I remember a thrush had the confidence to snatch out of my hand with his bill a piece of cake that Glumdalclitch had just given me for my breakfast. When I attempted to catch any of these birds, they would boldly turn against me, endeavoring to pick my fingers, which I durst not venture within their reach; and then they would hop back unconcerned to hunt for worms or snails, as they did before. But one day I took a thick cudgel, and threw it with all my strength so luckily at a linnet that I knocked him down, and seizing him by the neck with

---

1. A bird of prey.   2. A trellis on which fruit trees are trained.

both my hands, ran with him in triumph to my nurse. However, the bird, who had only been stunned, recovering himself, gave me so many boxes with his wings on both sides of my head and body, though I held him at arm's length, and was out of the reach of his claws, that I was twenty times thinking to let him go. But I was soon relieved by one of our servants, who wrung off the bird's neck, and I had him next day for dinner, by the Queen's command. This linnet, as near as I can remember, seemed to be somewhat larger than an English swan.

The Maids of Honor often invited Glumdalclitch to their apartments, and desired she would bring me along with her, on purpose to have the pleasure of seeing and touching me. They would often strip me naked from top to toe and lay me at full length in their bosoms; wherewith I was much disgusted, because, to say the truth, a very offensive smell came from their skins, which I do not mention or intend to the disadvantage of those excellent ladies, for whom I have all manner of respect; but I conceive that my sense was more acute in proportion to my littleness, and that those illustrious persons were no more disagreeable to their lovers, or to each other, than people of the same quality are with us in England. And, after all, I found their natural smell was much more supportable than when they used perfumes, under which I immediately swooned away. I cannot forget that an intimate friend of mine in Lilliput took the freedom in a warm day, when I had used a good deal of exercise, to complain of a strong smell about me, although I am as little faulty that way as most of my sex: but I suppose his faculty of smelling was as nice with regard to me as mine was to that of this people. Upon this point, I cannot forbear doing justice to the Queen, my mistress, and Glumdalclitch, my nurse, whose persons were as sweet as those of any lady in England.

That which gave me most uneasiness among these Maids of Honor, when my nurse carried me to visit them, was to see them use me without any manner of ceremony, like a creature who had no sort of consequence. For they would strip themselves to the skin and put on their smocks in my presence, while I was placed on their toilet[3] directly before their naked bodies; which, I am sure, to me was very far from being a tempting sight, or from giving me any other emotions than those of horror and disgust. Their skins appeared so coarse and uneven, so variously colored, when I saw them near, with a mole here and there as broad as a trencher, and hairs hanging from it thicker than pack-threads, to say nothing further concerning the rest of their persons. Neither did they at all scruple, while I was by, to discharge what they had drunk, to the quantity of at least two hogsheads, in a vessel that held above three tuns. The handsomest among these Maids of Honor, a pleasant frolicsome girl of sixteen, would sometimes set me astride upon one of her nipples, with many other tricks, wherein the reader will excuse me for

3. Toilet table.

not being over particular. But I was so much displeased that I entreated Glumdalclitch to contrive some excuse for not seeing that young lady any more.

One day a young gentleman, who was nephew to my nurse's governess, came and pressed them both to see an execution. It was of a man who had murdered one of that gentleman's intimate acquaintance. Glumdalclitch was prevailed on to be of the company, very much against her inclination, for she was naturally tender-hearted: and as for myself, although I abhorred such kind of spectacles, yet my curiosity tempted me to see something that I thought must be extraordinary. The malefactor was fixed in a chair upon a scaffold erected for the purpose, and his head cut off at a blow with a sword of about forty foot long. The veins and arteries spouted up such a prodigious quantity of blood, and so high in the air, that the great *jet d'eau*[4] at Versailles was not equal for the time it lasted; and the head, when it fell on the scaffold floor, gave such a bounce,[5] as made me start, although I were at least half an English mile distant.

The Queen, who often used to hear me talk of my sea voyages, and took all occasions to divert me when I was melancholy, asked me whether I understood how to handle a sail or an oar, and whether a little exercise of rowing might not be convenient for my health. I answered that I understood both very well. For although my proper employment had been to be surgeon or doctor to the ship, yet often, upon a pinch, I was forced to work like a common mariner. But I could not see how this could be done in their country, where the smallest wherry was equal to a first-rate man-of-war among us, and such a boat as I could manage would never live in any of their rivers. Her Majesty said, if I would contrive a boat, her own joiner[6] should make it, and she would provide a place for me to sail in. The fellow was an ingenious workman and, by my instructions, in ten days finished a pleasure boat with all its tackling, able conveniently to hold eight Europeans. When it was finished, the Queen was so delighted that she ran with it in her lap to the King, who ordered it to be put in a cistern full of water, with me in it, by way of trial; where I could not manage my two sculls, or little oars, for want of room. But the Queen had before contrived another project. She ordered the joiner to make a wooden trough of three hundred foot long, fifty broad, and eight deep; which being well pitched to prevent leaking, was placed on the floor along the wall in an outer room of the palace. It had a cock near the bottom to let out the water when it began to grow stale, and two servants could easily fill it in half an hour. Here I often used to row for my own diversion, as well as that of the Queen and her ladies, who thought themselves well entertained with my skill and agility. Sometimes I would put up my sail, and then my business was only to steer, while the ladies gave me a gale with their fans; and when they were weary, some of the pages would blow my sail forward with their

4. This fountain rose over 40 feet in the air.
5. A sudden noise.
6. A skilled woodworker.

breath, while I showed my art by steering starboard or larboard as I pleased. When I had done, Glumdalclitch always carried my boat into her closet, and hung it on a nail to dry.

In this exercise I once met an accident which had like to have cost me my life. For one of the pages having put my boat into the trough, the governess who attended Glumdalclitch very officiously[7] lifted me up to place me in the boat; but I happened to slip through her fingers, and should have infallibly fallen down forty feet upon the floor, if by the luckiest chance in the world I had not been stopped by a corking-pin[8] that stuck in the good gentlewoman's stomacher; the head of the pin passed between my shirt and the waistband of my breeches, and thus I was held by the middle in the air until Glumdalclitch ran to my relief.

Another time, one of the servants, whose office it was to fill my trough every third day with fresh water, was so careless to let a huge frog (not perceiving it) slip out of his pail. The frog lay concealed till I was put into my boat, but then seeing a resting place, climbed up, and made it lean so much on one side that I was forced to balance it with all my weight on the other, to prevent overturning. When the frog was got in, it hopped at once half the length of the boat, and then over my head, backwards and forwards, daubing my face and clothes with its odious slime. The largeness of its features made it appear the most deformed animal that can be conceived. However, I desired Glumdalclitch to let me deal with it alone. I banged it a good while with one of my sculls, and at last forced it to leap out of the boat.

But the greatest danger I ever underwent in that kingdom was from a monkey, who belonged to one of the clerks of the kitchen. Glumdalclitch had locked me up in her closet, while she went somewhere upon business or a visit. The weather being very warm, the closet window was left open, as well as the windows in the door of my bigger box, in which I usually lived, because of its largeness and conveniency. As I sat quietly meditating at my table, I heard something bounce in at the closet window, and skip about from one side to the other, whereat, although I was much alarmed, yet I ventured to look out, but stirred not from my seat; and then I saw this frolicsome animal, frisking and leaping up and down, till at last he came to my box, which he seemed to view with great pleasure and curiosity, peeping in at the door and every window. I retreated to the farther corner of my room, or box, but the monkey looking in at every side, put me into such a fright that I wanted presence of mind to conceal myself under the bed, as I might easily have done. After some time spent in peeping, grinning, and chattering, he at last espied me, and reaching one of his paws in at the door, as a cat does when she plays with a mouse, although I often shifted place to avoid him, he at length seized the lappet of my coat (which, being made of that country cloth, was very thick and strong) and dragged me out. He took me up in his right forefoot, and held me as a nurse does a child she is going to suckle,

7. Kindly, dutifully.
8. A pin of the largest size. "Stomacher": an ornamental covering for the front and upper part of the body.

just as I have seen the same sort of creature do with a kitten in Europe: and when I offered to struggle, he squeezed me so hard that I thought it more prudent to submit. I have good reason to believe that he took me for a young one of his own species, by his often stroking my face very gently with his other paw. In these diversions he was interrupted by a noise at the closet door, as if somebody were opening it, whereupon he suddenly leaped up to the window at which he had come in, and thence upon the leads and gutters, walking upon three legs, and holding me in the fourth, till he clambered up to a roof that was next to ours. I heard Glumdalclitch give a shriek at the moment he was carrying me out. The poor girl was almost distracted: that quarter of the palace was all in an uproar; the servants ran for ladders; the monkey was seen by hundreds in the court, sitting upon the ridge of a building, holding me like a baby in one of his forepaws and feeding me with the other, by cramming into my mouth some victuals he had squeezed out of the bag on one side of his chaps, and patting me when I would not eat; whereat many of the rabble below could not forebear laughing; neither do I think they justly ought to be blamed, for without question the sight was ridiculous enough to everybody but myself. Some of the people threw up stones, hoping to drive the monkey down; but this was strictly forbidden, or else very probably my brains had been dashed out.

The ladders were now applied, and mounted by several men; which the monkey observing, and finding himself almost encompassed, not being able to make speed enough with his three legs, let me drop on a ridge tile, and made his escape. Here I sat for some time three hundred yards from the ground, expecting every moment to be blown down by the wind, or to fall by my own giddiness, and come tumbling over and over from the ridge to the eaves. But an honest lad, one of my nurse's footmen, climbed up, and putting me into his breeches pocket, brought me down safe.

I was almost choked with the filthy stuff the monkey had crammed down my throat; but my dear little nurse picked it out of my mouth with a small needle, and then I fell a vomiting, which gave me great relief. Yet I was so weak and bruised in the sides with the squeezes given me by this odious animal that I was forced to keep my bed a fortnight. The King, Queen, and all the Court sent every day to inquire after my health, and her Majesty made me several visits during my sickness. The monkey was killed, and an order made that no such animal should be kept about the palace.

When I attended the King after my recovery, to return him thanks for his favors, he was pleased to rally me a good deal upon this adventure. He asked me what my thoughts and speculations were while I lay in the monkey's paw, how I liked the victuals he gave me, his manner of feeding, and whether the fresh air on the roof had sharpened my stomach. He desired to know what I would have done upon such an occasion in my own country. I told his Majesty that in Europe we had no monkeys, except such as were brought for curiosities from other places, and so small that I could deal with a dozen of them together, if they presumed to attack me. And as for that monstrous animal with whom I was so lately engaged (it was indeed as large as an elephant), if my fears had suffered me to think so far as to make use of my hanger (looking fiercely and clapping my hand upon the hilt as I spoke) when he poked his paw into my chamber, perhaps I should have given him such a wound as would have made him glad to withdraw it with more haste than he put it in. This I delivered in a firm tone, like a person who was jealous lest his courage should be called in question. However, my speech produced nothing else besides a loud laughter, which all the respect due to his Majesty from those about him could not make them contain. This made me reflect how vain an attempt it is for a man to endeavor doing himself honor among those who are out of all degree of equality or comparison with him. And yet I have seen the moral of my own behavior very frequent in England since my return, where a little contemptible varlet, without the least title to birth, person, wit, or common sense, shall presume to look with importance, and put himself upon a foot with the greatest persons of the kingdom.

I was every day furnishing the court with some ridiculous story; and Glumdalclitch, although she loved me to excess, yet was arch enough to inform the Queen whenever I committed any folly that she thought would be diverting to her Majesty. The girl, who had been out of order, was carried by her governess to take the air about an hour's distance, or thirty miles from town. They alighted out of the coach near a small footpath in a field, and Glumdalclitch setting down my traveling box, I went out of it to walk. There was a cow dung in the patch, and I must needs try my activity by attempting to leap over it. I took a run, but unfortunately jumped short, and found myself just in the middle up to my knees. I waded through with some difficulty, and one of the footmen wiped me as clean as he could with his handkerchief; for I was filthily bemired, and my nurse confined me to my box till we returned home, where the Queen was soon informed of what had passed and the footmen spread it about the Court, so that all the mirth, for some days, was at my expense.

CHAPTER 6. *Several contrivances of the Author to please the King and Queen. He shows his skill in music. The King inquires into the state of Europe, which the Author relates to him. The King's observations thereon.*

I used to attend the King's levee[9] once or twice a week, and had often seen him under the barber's hand, which indeed was at first very terrible to behold. For the razor was almost twice as long as an ordinary scythe. His Majesty, according to the custom of the country, was only shaved twice a week. I once prevailed on the barber to give me some of the suds or lather, out of which I picked forty or fifty of the strongest stumps of

9. A morning reception held by a prince or nobleman, sometimes while dressing for the day.

hair. I then took a piece of fine wood, and cut it like the back of a comb, making several holes in it at equal distance with as small a needle as I could get from Glumdalclitch. I fixed in the stumps so artificially,[1] scraping and sloping them with my knife towards the points, that I made a very tolerable comb; which was a seasonable supply, my own being so much broken in the teeth that it was almost useless; neither did I know any artist in that country so nice and exact as would undertake to make me another.

And this puts me in mind of an amusement wherein I spent many of my leisure hours. I desired the Queen's woman to save for me the combings of her Majesty's hair, whereof in time I got a good quantity; and consulting with my friend the cabinetmaker, who had received general orders to do little jobs for me, I directed him to make two chair frames, no larger than those I had in my box, and then to bore little holes with a fine awl round those parts where I designed the backs and seats; through these holes I wove the strongest hairs I could pick out, just after the manner of cane chairs in England. When they were finished, I made a present of them to her Majesty, who kept them in her cabinet, and used to show them for curiosities, as indeed they were the wonder of every one that beheld them. The Queen would have made me sit upon one of these chairs, but I absolutely refused to obey her, protesting I would rather die a thousand deaths than place a dishonorable part of my body on those precious hairs that once adorned her Majesty's head. Of these hairs (as I had always a mechanical genius) I likewise made a neat little purse above five foot long, with her Majesty's name deciphered in gold letters, which I gave to Glumdalclitch by the Queen's consent. To say the truth, it was more for show than use, being not of strength to bear the weight of the larger coins; and therefore she kept nothing in it but some little toys[2] that girls are fond of.

The King, who delighted in music, had frequent consorts[3] at court, to which I was sometimes carried, and set in my box on a table to hear them; but the noise was so great that I could hardly distinguish the tunes. I am confident that all the drums and trumpets of a royal army, beating and sounding together just at your ears, could not equal it. My practice was to have my box removed from the places where the performers sat, as far as I could, then to shut the doors and windows of it, and draw the window curtains, after which I found their music not disagreeable.

I had learned in my youth to play a little upon the spinet. Glumdalclitch kept one in her chamber, and a master attended twice a week to teach her: I call it a spinet, because it somewhat resembled that instrument, and was played upon in the same manner. A fancy came into my head that I would entertain the King and Queen with an English tune upon this instrument. But this appeared extremely difficult: for the spinet was near sixty foot long, each key being almost a foot wide; so that, with my arms extended, I could not reach to above five keys, and to

1. Skillfully.
2. Trifles.
3. Concerts.

press them down required a good smart stroke with my fist, which would be too great a labor and to no purpose. The method I contrived was this: I prepared two round sticks about the bigness of common cudgels; they were thicker at one end than the other, and I covered the thicker ends with a piece of a mouse's skin, that by rapping on them I might neither damage the tops of the keys, nor interrupt the sound. Before the spinet a bench was placed, about four foot below the keys, and I was put upon the bench. I ran sideling upon it that way and this, as fast as I could, banging the proper keys with my two sticks; and made a shift to play a jig, to the great satisfaction of both their Majesties: but it was the most violent exercise I ever underwent, and yet I could not strike above sixteen keys, nor, consequently, play the bass and treble together, as other artists do; which was a great disadvantage to my performance.

The King, who, as I before observed, was a prince of excellent understanding, would frequently order that I should be brought in my box and set upon the table in his closet. He would then command me to bring one of my chairs out of the box, and sit down within three yards distance upon the top of the cabinet, which brought me almost to a level with his face. In this manner I had several conversations with him. I one day took the freedom to tell his Majesty that the contempt he discovered towards Europe, and the rest of the world, did not seem answerable to those excellent qualities of mind that he was master of. That reason did not extend itself with the bulk of the body: on the contrary, we observed in our country that the tallest persons were usually least provided with it. That among other animals, bees and ants had the reputation of more industry, art, and sagacity than many of the larger kinds; and that, as inconsiderable as he took me to be, I hoped I might live to do his Majesty some signal service. The King heard me with attention, and began to conceive a much better opinion of me than he had before. He desired I would give him as exact an account of the government of England as I possibly could; because, as fond as princes commonly are of their own customs (for so he conjectured of other monarchs, by my former discourses), he should be glad to hear of anything that might deserve imitation.

Imagine with thyself, courteous reader, how often I then wished for the tongue of Demosthenes or Cicero, that might have enabled me to celebrate the praise of my own dear native country in a style equal to its merits and felicity.

I began my discourse by informing his Majesty that our dominions consisted of two islands, which composed three mighty kingdoms under one sovereign, beside our plantations in America. I dwelt long upon the fertility of our soil, and the temperature[4] of our climate. I then spoke at large upon the constitution of an English Parliament, partly made up of an illustrious body called the House of Peers, persons of the noblest blood, and of the most ancient and ample patrimonies. I described that

4. Temperateness.

extraordinary care always taken of their education in arts and arms, to qualify them for being counselors born to the king and kingdom; to have a share in the legislature, to be members of the highest Court of Judicature, from whence there could be no appeal; and to be champions always ready for the defense of their prince and country, by their valor, conduct, and fidelity. That these were the ornament and bulwark of the kingdom, worthy followers of their most renowned ancestors, whose honor had been the reward of their virtue, from which their posterity were never once known to degenerate. To these were joined several holy persons, as part of that assembly, under the title of Bishops, whose peculiar business it is to take care of religion, and of those who instruct the people therein. These were searched and sought out through the whole nation, by the prince and his wisest counselors, among such of the priesthood as were most deservedly distinguished by the sanctity of their lives and the depth of their erudition, who were indeed the spiritual fathers of the clergy and the people.

That the other part of the Parliament consisted of an assembly called the House of Commons, who were all principal gentlemen, freely picked and culled out by the people themselves, for their great abilities and love of their country, to represent the wisdom of the whole nation. And these two bodies make up the most august assembly in Europe, to whom, in conjunction with the prince, the whole legislature is committed.

I then descended to the Courts of Justice, over which the Judges, those venerable sages and interpreters of the law, presided, for determining the disputed rights and properties of men, as well as for the punishment of vice, and protection of innocence. I mentioned the prudent management of our treasury, the valor and achievements of our forces by sea and land. I computed the number of our people, by reckoning how many millions there might be of each religious sect, or political party among us. I did not omit even our sports and pastimes, or any other particular which I thought might redound to the honor of my country. And I finished all with a brief historical account of affairs and events in England for about an hundred years past.

This conversation was not ended under five audiences, each of several hours, and the King heard the whole with great attention, frequently taking notes of what I spoke, as well as memorandums of several questions he intended to ask me.

When I had put an end to these long discourses, his Majesty in a sixth audience consulting his notes, proposed many doubts, queries, and objections, upon every article. He asked what methods were used to cultivate the minds and bodies of our young nobility, and in what kind of business they commonly spent the first and teachable part of their lives. What course was taken to supply that assembly when any noble family became extinct. What qualifications were necessary in those who were to be created new lords. Whether the humor[5] of the prince, a sum

5. Whim.

of money to a Court lady or a prime minister, or a design of strengthening a party opposite to the public interest, ever happened to be motives
in those advancements. What share of knowledge these lords had in the
laws of their country, and how they came by it, so as to enable them to
decide the properties of their fellow subjects in the last resort. Whether
they were always so free from avarice, partialities, or want that a bribe
or some other sinister view could have no place among them. Whether
those holy lords I spoke of were constantly promoted to that rank upon
account of their knowledge in religious matters, and the sanctity of their
lives, had never been compliers with the times while they were common
priests, or slavish prostitute chaplains to some nobleman, whose opinions they continued servilely to follow after they were admitted into that
assembly.

He then desired to know what arts were practiced in electing those
whom I called Commoners. Whether a stranger with a strong purse
might not influence the vulgar voters to choose him before their own
landlord or the most considerable gentleman in the neighborhood. How
it came to pass that people were so violently bent upon getting into this
assembly, which I allowed to be a great trouble and expense, often to
the ruin of their families, without any salary or pension: because this
appeared such an exalted strain of virtue and public spirit that his Majesty seemed to doubt it might possibly not be always sincere; and he
desired to know whether such zealous gentlemen could have any views
of refunding themselves for the charges and trouble they were at, by
sacrificing the public good to the designs of a weak and vicious prince in
conjunction with a corrupted ministry. He multiplied his questions, and
sifted me thoroughly upon every part of this head, proposing numberless
inquiries and objections, which I think it not prudent or convenient to
repeat.

Upon what I said in relation to our Courts of Justice, his Majesty
desired to be satisfied in several points: and this I was the better able to
do, having been formerly almost ruined by a long suit in chancery,
which was decreed for me with costs. He asked what time was usually
spent in determining between right and wrong, and what degree of
expense. Whether advocates and orators had liberty to plead in causes
manifestly known to be unjust, vexatious, or oppressive. Whether party
in religion or politics were observed to be of any weight in the scale of
justice. Whether those pleading orators were persons educated in the
general knowledge of equity, or only in provincial, national, and other
local customs. Whether they or their judges had any part in penning
those laws which they assumed the liberty of interpreting and glossing
upon at their pleasure. Whether they had ever at different times pleaded
for and against the same cause, and cited precedents to prove contrary
opinions. Whether they were a rich or a poor corporation. Whether they
received any pecuniary reward for pleading or delivering their opinions.
And particularly whether they were ever admitted as members in the
lower senate.

He fell next upon the management of our treasury, and said he thought my memory had failed me, because I computed our taxes at about five or six millions a year, and when I came to mention the issues,[6] he found they sometimes amounted to more than double, for the notes he had taken were very particular in this point; because he hoped, as he told me, that the knowledge of our conduct might be useful to him, and he could not be deceived in his calculations. But if what I told him were true, he was still at a loss how a kingdom could run out of its estate like a private person. He asked me, who were our creditors? and where we should find money to pay them? He wondered to hear me talk of such chargeable and extensive wars; that certainly we must be a quarrelsome people, or live among very bad neighbors, and that our generals must needs be richer than our kings.[7] He asked what business we had out of our own islands, unless upon the score of[8] trade or treaty or to defend the coasts with our fleet. Above all, he was amazed to hear me talk of a mercenary standing army[9] in the midst of peace, and among a free people. He said if we were governed by our own consent in the persons of our representatives, he could not imagine of whom we were afraid, or against whom we were to fight; and would hear my opinion whether a private man's house might not better be defended by himself, his children, and family, than by half a dozen rascals picked up at a venture[1] in the streets for small wages, who might get an hundred times more by cutting their throats.

He laughed at my odd kind of arithmetic (as he was pleased to call it) in reckoning the numbers of our people by a computation drawn from the several sects among us in religion and politics. He said he knew no reason why those who entertain opinions prejudicial to the public should be obliged to change, or should not be obliged to conceal them. And as it was tyranny in any government to require the first, so it was weakness not to enforce the second: for a man may be allowed to keep poisons in his closet, but not to vend them about for cordials.[2]

He observed that among the diversions of our nobility and gentry I had mentioned gaming.[3] He desired to know at what age this entertainment was usually taken up, and when it was laid down; how much of their time it employed; whether it ever went so high as to affect their fortunes; whether mean, vicious people, by their dexterity in that art, might not arrive at great riches, and sometimes keep our very nobles in dependence, as well as habituate them to vile companions, wholly take them from the improvement of their minds, and force them, by the losses they have received, to learn and practice that infamous dexterity upon others.

---

6. Expenditures.
7. An allusion to the enormous fortune gained by the duke of Marlborough, formerly captain-general of the army, whom Swift detested.
8. For the sake of.
9. Since the declaration of the Bill of Rights (1689), a standing army without authorization by Parliament had been illegal. Swift and the Tories in general were vigilant in their opposition to such an army.
1. By chance.
2. Medicines to stimulate the heart, or, equally commonly, liqueurs.
3. Gambling.

He was perfectly astonished with the historical account I gave him of our affairs during the last century, protesting it was only an heap of conspiracies, rebellions, murders, massacres, revolutions, banishments, the very worst effects that avarice, faction, hypocrisy, perfidiousness, cruelty, rage, madness, hatred, envy, lust, malice, or ambition could produce.

His Majesty in another audience was at the pains to recapitulate the sum of all I had spoken; compared the questions he made with the answers I had given; then taking me into his hands, and stroking me gently, delivered himself in these words, which I shall never forget nor the manner he spoke them in. "My little friend Grildrig, you have made a most admirable panegyric[4] upon your country. You have clearly proved that ignorance, idleness, and vice are the proper ingredients for qualifying a legislator. That laws are best explained, interpreted, and applied by those whose interests and abilities lie in perverting, confounding, and eluding them. I observe among you some lines of an institution which in its original might have been tolerable; but these half erased, and the rest wholly blurred and blotted by corruptions. It doth not appear from all you have said how any one virtue is required towards the procurement of any one station among you; much less that men are ennobled on account of their virtue, that priests are advanced for their piety or learning, soldiers for their conduct or valor, judges for their integrity, senators for the love of their country, or counselors for their wisdom. As for yourself," continued the King, "who have spent the greatest part of your life in traveling, I am well disposed to hope you may hitherto have escaped many vices of your country. But by what I have gathered from your own relation, and the answers I have with much pains wringed and extorted from you, I cannot but conclude the bulk of your natives to be the most pernicious race of little odious vermin that nature ever suffered to crawl upon the surface of the earth."

CHAPTER 7. *The Author's love of his country. He makes a proposal of much advantage to the King; which is rejected. The King's great ignorance in politics. The learning of that country very imperfect and confined. Their laws, and military affairs, and parties in the State.*

Nothing but an extreme love of truth could have hindered me from concealing this part of my story. It was in vain to discover my resentments, which were always turned into ridicule: and I was forced to rest with patience while my noble and most beloved country was so injuriously treated. I am heartily sorry as any of my readers can possibly be that such an occasion was given, but this prince happened to be so curious and inquisitive upon every particular that it could not consist either with gratitude or good manners to refuse giving him what satisfaction I was able. Yet thus much I may be allowed to say in my own vindication:

---

4. A formal oration in praise of someone or something.

that I artfully eluded many of his questions, and gave to every point a more favorable turn by many degrees than the strictness of truth would allow. For I have always borne that laudable partiality to my own country, which Dionysius Halicarnassensis[5] with so much justice recommends to an historian. I would hide the frailties and deformities of my political mother, and place her virtues and beauties in the most advantageous light. This was my sincere endeavor in those many discourses I had with that mighty monarch, although it unfortunately failed of success.

But great allowances should be given to a King who lives wholly secluded from the rest of the world, and must therefore be altogether unacquainted with the manners and customs that most prevail in other nations: the want of which knowledge will ever produce many *prejudices*, and a certain *narrowness of thinking*, from which we and the politer countries of Europe are wholly exempted. And it would be hard indeed if so remote a prince's notions of virtue and vice were to be offered as a standard for all mankind.

To confirm what I have now said, and further, to show the miserable effects of a *confined education*, I shall here insert a passage which will hardly obtain belief. In hopes to ingratiate myself farther into his Majesty's favor, I told him of an invention discovered between three and four hundred years ago, to make a certain powder, into an heap of which the smallest spark of fire falling would kindle the whole in a moment, although it were as big as a mountain, and make it all fly up in the air together, with a noise and agitation greater than thunder. That a proper quantity of this powder rammed into an hollow tube of brass or iron, according to its bigness, would drive a ball of iron or lead with such violence and speed as nothing was able to sustain its force. That the largest balls thus discharged would not only destroy whole ranks of an army at once, but batter the strongest walls to the ground; sink down ships with a thousand men in each, to the bottom of the sea; and, when linked together by a chain, would cut through masts and rigging; divide hundreds of bodies in the middle, and lay all waste before them. That we often put this powder into large hollow balls of iron, and discharged them by an engine into some city we were besieging; which would rip up the pavements, tear the houses to pieces, burst and throw splinters on every side, dashing out the brains of all who came near. That I knew the ingredients very well, which were cheap and common; I understood the manner of compounding them, and could direct his workmen how to make those tubes of a size proportionable to all other things in his Majesty's kingdom, and the largest need not be above two hundred foot long; twenty or thirty of which tubes, charged with the proper quantity of powder and balls, would batter down the walls of the strongest town in his dominions in a few hours; or destroy the whole metropolis, if ever it should pretend to dispute his absolute commands. This I humbly offered

---

5. A Greek rhetorician and historian, who flourished ca. 25 B.C. His history of Rome was written to reconcile the Greeks to their Roman masters.

to his Majesty as a small tribute of acknowledgement in return of so many marks that I had received of his royal favor and protection.

The King was struck with horror at the description I had given of those terrible engines and the proposal I had made. He was amazed how so impotent and groveling an insect as I (these were his expressions) could entertain such inhuman ideas, and in so familiar a manner as to appear wholly unmoved at all the scenes of blood and desolation which I had painted as the common effects of those destructive machines; whereof he said some evil genius, enemy to mankind, must have been the first contriver. As for himself, he protested that although few things delighted him so much as new discoveries in art or in nature, yet he would rather lose half his kingdom than be privy[6] to such a secret, which he commanded me, as I valued my life, never to mention any more.

A strange effect of *narrow principles* and *short views!* that a prince possessed of every quality which procures veneration, love, and esteem; of strong parts, great wisdom, and profound learning; endued with admirable talents for government, and almost adored by his subjects; should from a *nice, unnecessary scruple,* whereof in Europe we can have no conception, let slip an opportunity put into his hands that would have made him absolute master of the lives, the liberties, and the fortunes of his people. Neither do I say this with the least intention to detract from the many virtues of that excellent King, whose character I am sensible will on this account be very much lessened in the opinion of an English reader: but I take this defect among them to have risen from their ignorance; they not having hitherto reduced politics into a science, as the more acute wits of Europe have done. For I remember very well, in a discourse one day with the King, when I happened to say there were several thousand books among us written upon the art of government, it gave him (directly contrary to my intention) a very mean opinion of our understandings. He professed both to abominate and despise all *mystery, refinement,* and *intrigue,* either in a prince or a minister. He could not tell what I meant by *secrets of state,* where an enemy or some rival nation were not in the case. He confined the knowledge of governing within very *narrow bounds:* to common sense and reason, to justice and lenity,[7] to the speedy determination of civil and criminal causes, with some other obvious topics which are not worth considering. And he gave it for his opinion that whoever could make two ears of corn or two blades of grass to grow upon a spot of ground where only one grew before would deserve better of mankind and do more essential service to his country than the whole race of politicians[8] put together.

The learning of this people is very defective, consisting only in morality, history, poetry, and mathematics; wherein they must be allowed to excel. But the last of these is wholly applied to what may be useful in life, to the improvement of agriculture and all mechanical arts; so that among us it would be little esteemed. And as to ideas, entities, abstrac-

6. To share secret knowledge.
7. Mildness.

8. By "politicians" Swift means something like our modern "political scientists"—theorists.

tions, and transcendentals,[9] I could never drive the least conception into their heads.

No law of that country must exceed in words the number of letters in their alphabet, which consists only in two and twenty. But indeed few of them extend even to that length. They are expressed in the most plain and simple terms, wherein those people are not mercurial[1] enough to discover above one interpretation. And to write a comment upon any law is a capital crime. As to the decision of civil causes, or proceedings against criminals, their precedents[2] are so few that they have little reason to boast of any extraordinary skill in either.

They have had the art of printing as well as the Chinese, time out of mind. But their libraries are not very large; for that of the King's, which is reckoned the biggest, doth not amount to above a thousand volumes, placed in a gallery of twelve hundred foot long, from whence I had liberty to borrow what books I pleased. The Queen's joiner had contrived in one of the Glumdalclitch's rooms a kind of wooden machine five and twenty foot high, formed like a standing ladder; the steps were each fifty foot long. It was indeed a movable pair of stairs, the lowest end placed at ten foot distance from the wall of the chamber. The book I had a mind to read was put up leaning against the wall. I first mounted to the upper step of the ladder, and turning my face towards the book began at the top of the page, and so walking to the right and left about eight or ten paces according to the length of the lines, till I had gotten a little below the level of mine eyes, and then descending gradually till I came to the bottom: after which I mounted again, and began the other page in the same manner, and so turned over the leaf, which I could easily do with both my hands, for it was as thick and stiff as a pasteboard, and in the largest folios[3] not above eighteen or twenty foot long.

Their style is clear, masculine, and smooth, but not florid; for they avoid nothing more than multiplying unnecessary words or using various expressions. I have perused many of their books, especially those in history and morality. Among the rest, I was much diverted with a little old treatise, which always lay in Glumdalclitch's bedchamber, and belonged to her governess, a grave elderly gentlewoman, who dealt in writings of morality and devotion. The book treats of the weakness of human kind, and is in little esteem, except among the women and the vulgar. However, I was curious to see what an author of that country could say upon such a subject. This writer went through all the usual topics of European moralists: showing how diminutive, contemptible, and helpless an animal was man in his own nature; how unable to defend himself from the inclemencies of the air, or the fury of wild beasts; how much he was excelled by one creature in strength, by another in speed, by a third in foresight, by a fourth in industry. He added that nature was

---

9. In Swift's time, "transcendental" was practically synonymous with "metaphysical."
1. Changeable.
2. A legal decision or a course of action which comes to serve as a rule in determining similar cases in the future. In the Fourth Voyage of *Gulliver's Travels*, Gulliver is made to say: "It is a maxim among these lawyers that whatever hath been done before may legally be done again."
3. A book of the largest size.

degenerated in these latter declining ages of the world, and could now produce only small abortive births in comparison of those in ancient times. He said it was very reasonable to think, not only that the species of men were originally much larger, but also that there must have been giants in former ages; which, as it is asserted by history and tradition, so it hath been confirmed by huge bones and skulls casually dug up in several parts of the kingdom, far exceeding the common dwindled race of man in our days. He argued that the very laws of nature absolutely required we should have been made in the beginning of a size more large and robust, not so liable to destruction from every little accident of a tile falling from a house, or a stone cast from the hand of a boy, or of being drowned in a little brook. From this way of reasoning, the author drew several moral applications useful in the conduct of life, but needless here to repeat. For my own part, I could not avoid reflecting how universally this talent was spread, of drawing lectures in morality, or indeed rather matter of discontent and repining, from the quarrels we raise with nature. And I believe, upon a strict inquiry, those quarrels might be shown as ill grounded among us as they are among that people.

As to their military affairs, they boast that the King's army consists of an hundred and seventy-six thousand foot and thirty-two thousand horse: if that may be called an army which is made up of tradesmen in the several cities, and farmers in the country, whose commanders are only the nobility and gentry, without pay or reward. They are indeed perfect enough in their exercises, and under very good discipline, wherein I saw no great merit; for how should it be otherwise, where every farmer is under the command of his own landlord, and every citizen under that of the principal men in his own city, chosen after the manner of Venice by ballot?

I have often seen the militia of Lorbrulgrud drawn out to exercise in a great field near the city, of twenty miles square. They were in all not above twenty-five thousand foot, and six thousand horse; but it was impossible for me to compute their number, considering the space of ground they took up. A cavalier mounted on a large steed might be about an hundred foot high. I have seen this whole body of horse, upon a word of command, draw their swords at once, and brandish them in the air. Imagination can figure nothing so grand, so surprising, and so astonishing. It looked as if ten thousand flashes of lightning were darting at the same time from every quarter of the sky.

I was curious to know how this prince, to whose dominions there is no access from any other country, came to think of armies, or to teach his people the practice of military discipline. But I was soon informed, both by conversation and reading their histories. For in the course of many ages they have been troubled with the same disease to which the whole race of mankind is subject: the nobility often contending for power, the people for liberty, and the King for absolute dominion. All which, however happily tempered by the laws of the kingdom, have been sometimes violated by each of the three parties, and have more than once occasioned civil wars, the last whereof was happily put an end to by this prince's grandfather in a general composition;[4] and the militia, then settled with common consent, hath been ever since kept in the strictest duty.

CHAPTER 8. *The King and Queen make a progress to the frontiers. The Author attends them. The manner in which he leaves the country very particularly related. He returns to England.*

I had always a strong impulse that I should some time recover my liberty, though it were impossible to conjecture by what means, or to form any project with the least hope of succeeding. The ship in which I sailed was the first ever known to be driven within sight of that coast; and the King had given strict orders that if at any time another appeared, it should be taken ashore, and with all its crew and passengers brought in a tumbrel[5] to Lorbrulgrud. He was strongly bent to get me a woman of my own size, by whom I might propagate the breed: but I think I should rather have died than undergone the disgrace of leaving a posterity to be kept in cages like tame canary birds, and perhaps in time sold about the kingdom to persons of quality for curiosities. I was indeed treated with much kindness: I was the favorite of a great King and Queen, and the delight of the whole Court, but it was upon such a foot as ill became the dignity of human kind. I could never forget those domestic pledges[6] I had left behind me. I wanted to be among people with whom I could converse upon even terms, and walk about the streets and fields without fear of being trod to death like a frog or a young puppy. But my deliverance came sooner than I expected, and in a manner not very common; the whole story and circumstances of which I shall faithfully relate.

I had now been two years in this country; and about the beginning of the third, Glumdalclitch and I attended the King and Queen in progress to the south coast of the kingdom. I was carried as usual in my traveling box, which, as I have already described, was a very convenient closet of twelve foot wide. I had ordered a hammock to be fixed by silken ropes from the four corners at the top, to break the jolts when a servant carried me before him on horseback, as I sometimes desired; and would often sleep in my hammock while we were upon the road. On the roof of my closet, set not directly over the middle of the hammock, I ordered the joiner to cut out a hole of a foot square to give me air in hot weather as I slept, which hole I shut at pleasure with a board that drew backwards and forwards through a groove.

When we came to our journey's end, the King thought proper to pass a few days at a palace he hath near Flanflasnic, a city within eighteen English miles of the seaside. Glumdalclitch and I were much fatigued; I had gotten a small cold, but the poor girl was so ill as to be confined

4. A political settlement based upon general agreement of all parties.
5. A farm wagon.
6. His wife and children.

to her chamber. I longed to see the ocean, which must be the only scene of my escape, if ever it should happen. I pretended to be worse than I really was, and desired leave to take the fresh air of the sea with a page whom I was very fond of, and who had sometimes been trusted with me. I shall never forget with what unwillingness Glumdalclitch consented, nor the strict charge she gave the page to be careful of me, bursting at the same time into a flood of tears, as if she had some foreboding of what was to happen. The boy took me out in my box about half an hour's walk from the palace, towards the rocks on the seashore. I ordered him to set me down, and lifting up one of my sashes, cast many a wistful melancholy look towards the sea. I found myself not very well, and told the page that I had a mind to take a nap in my hammock, which I hoped would do me good. I got in, and the boy shut the window close down, to keep out the cold. I soon fell asleep: and all I can conjecture is that while I slept, the page, thinking no danger could happen, went among the rocks to look for birds' eggs; having before observed him from my window searching about, and picking up one or two in the clefts. Be that as it will, I found myself suddenly awaked with a violent pull upon the ring which was fastened at the top of my box for the conveniency of carriage. I felt my box raised very high in the air, and then borne forward with prodigious speed. The first jolt had like to have shaken me out of my hammock, but afterwards the motion was easy enough. I called out several times as loud as I could raise my voice, but all to no purpose. I looked towards my windows, and could see nothing but the clouds and sky. I heard a noise just over my head like the clapping of wings, and then began to perceive the woeful condition I was in; that some eagle had got the ring of my box in his beak, with an intent to let it fall on a rock, like a tortoise in a shell, and then pick out my body and devour it. For the sagacity and smell of this bird enable him to discover his quarry at a great distance, although better concealed than I could be within a two-inch board.

In a little time I observed the noise and flutter of wings to increase very fast, and my box was tossed up and down like a signpost in a windy day. I heard several bangs or buffets, as I thought, given to the eagle (for such I am certain it must have been that held the ring of my box in his beak), and then all on a sudden felt myself falling perpendicularly down for above a minute, but with such incredible swiftness that I almost lost my breath. My fall was topped by a terrible squash, that sounded louder to mine ears than the cataract of Niagara; after which I was quite in the dark for another minute, and then my box began to rise so high that I could see light from the tops of my windows. I now perceived that I was fallen into the sea. My box, by the weight of my body, the goods that were in, and the broad plates of iron fixed for strength at the four corners of the top and bottom, floated above five foot deep in water. I did then and do now suppose that the eagle which flew away with my box was pursued by two or three others, and forced to let me drop while he was defending himself against the rest, who hoped to share in the prey. The plates of iron fastened at the bottom of the box (for those were the strongest) preserved the balance while it fell, and hindered it from being broken on the surface of the water. Every joint of it was well grooved, and the door did not move on hinges, but up and down like a sash; which kept my closet so tight that very little water came in. I got with much difficulty out of my hammock, having first ventured to draw back the slip-board on the roof already mentioned, contrived on purpose to let in air, for want of which I found myself almost stifled.

How often did I then wish myself with my dear Glumdalclitch, from whom one single hour had so far divided me! And I may say with truth that in the midst of my own misfortune, I could not forbear lamenting my poor nurse, the grief she would suffer for my loss, the displeasure of the Queen, and the ruin of her fortune. Perhaps many travelers have not been under greater difficulties and distress than I was at this juncture, expecting every moment to see my box dashed in pieces, or at least overset by the first violent blast or a rising wave. A breach in one single pane of glass would have been immediate death, nor could anything have preserved the windows but the strong lattice wires placed on the outside against accidents in traveling. I saw the water ooze in at several crannies, although the leaks were not considerable, and I endeavored to stop them as well as I could. I was not able to lift up the roof of my closet, which otherwise I certainly should have done, and sat on the top of it, where I might at least preserve myself from being shut up, as I may call it, in the hold. Or, if I escaped these dangers for a day or two, what could I expect but a miserable death of cold and hunger! I was four hours under these circumstances, expecting and indeed wishing every moment to be my last.

I have already told the reader that there were two strong staples fixed upon that side of my box which had no window and into which the servant, who used to carry me on horseback, would put a leathern belt, and buckle it about his waist. Being in this disconsolate state, I heard, or at least thought I heard, some kind of grating noise on that side of my box where the staples were fixed; and soon after I began to fancy that the box was pulled or towed along in the sea; for I now and then felt a sort of tugging, which made the waves rise near the tops of my windows, leaving me almost in the dark. This gave me some faint hopes of relief, although I was not able to imagine how it could be brought about. I ventured to unscrew one of my chairs, which were always fastened to the floor; and having made a hard shift to screw it down again directly under the slipping-board that I had lately opened, I mounted on the chair, and putting my mouth as near as I could to the hole, I called for help in a loud voice, and in all the languages I understood. I then fastened my handkerchief to a stick I usually carried, and thrusting it up the hole, waved it several times in the air, that if any boat or ship were near, the seamen might conjecture some unhappy mortal to be shut up in the box.

I found no effect from all I could do, but plainly perceived my closet to be moved along; and in the space of an hour or better, that side of the box where the staples were, and had no window, struck against something that was hard. I apprehended it to be a rock, and found myself tossed more than ever. I plainly heard a noise upon the cover of my closet, like that of a cable, and the grating of it as it passed through the ring. I then found myself hoisted up by degrees at least three foot higher than I was before. Whereupon I again thrust up my stick and handkerchief, calling for help till I was almost hoarse. In return to which, I heard a great shout repeated three times, giving me such transports of joy as are not to be conceived but by those who feel them. I now heard a trampling over my head, and somebody calling through the hole with a loud voice in the English tongue: "If there be anybody below, let them speak." I answered, I was an Englishman, drawn by ill fortune into the greatest calamity that ever any creature underwent, and begged, by all that was moving, to be delivered out of the dungeon I was in. The voice replied, I was safe, for my box was fastened to their ship; and the carpenter should immediately come and saw an hole in the cover, large enough to pull me out. I answered, that was needless and would take up too much time, for there was no more to be done but let one of the crew put his finger into the ring, and take the box out of the sea into the ship, and so into the captain's cabin. Some of them, upon hearing me talk so wildly, thought I was mad; others laughed; for indeed it never came into my head that I was now got among people of my own stature and strength. The carpenter came, and in a few minutes sawed a passage about four foot square; then let down a small ladder, upon which I mounted, and from thence was taken into the ship in a very weak condition.

The sailors were all in amazement, and asked me a thousand questions, which I had no inclination to answer. I was equally confounded at the sight of so many pygmies, for such I took them to be, after having so long accustomed my eyes to the monstrous objects I had left. But the Captain, Mr. Thomas Wilcocks, an honest, worthy Shropshire man, observing I was ready to faint, took me into his cabin, gave me a cordial to comfort me, and made me turn in upon his own bed, advising me to take a little rest, of which I had great need. Before I went to sleep I gave him to understand that I had some valuable furniture in my box, too good to be lost, a fine hammock, an handsome field bed, two chairs, a table, and a cabinet; that my closet was hung on all sides, or rather quilted with silk and cotton; that if he would let one of the crew bring my closet into his cabin, I would open it before him and show him my goods. The Captain, hearing me utter these absurdities, concluded I was raving; however (I suppose to pacify me), he promised to give order as I desired, and going upon deck, sent some of his men down into my closet, from whence (as I afterwards found) they drew up all my goods and stripped off the quilting; but the chairs, cabinet, and bedstead, being screwed to the floor, were much damaged by the ignorance of the sea-

men, who tore them up by force. Then they knocked off some of the
boards for the use of the ship; and when they had got all they had a mind
for, let the hulk drop into the sea, which, by reason of many breaches
made in the bottom and sides, sunk to rights.[7] And indeed I was glad
not to have been a spectator of the havoc they made, because I am
confident it would have sensibly touched me, by bringing former passages into my mind, which I had rather forget.

I slept some hours, but perpetually disturbed with dreams of the place
I had left, and the dangers I had escaped. However, upon waking, I
found myself much recovered. It was now about eight o'clock at night,
and the Captain ordered supper immediately, thinking I had already
fasted too long. He entertained me with great kindness, observing me
not to look wildly, or talk inconsistently; and when we were left alone,
desired I would give him a relation of my travels, and by what accident
I came to be set adrift in that monstrous wooden chest. He said that
about twelve o'clock at noon, as he was looking through his glass, he
spied it at a distance, and thought it was a sail, which he had a mind to
make,[8] being not much out of his course, in hopes of buying some
biscuit, his own beginning to fall short. That, upon coming nearer, and
finding his error, he sent out his longboat to discover what I was; that
his men came back in a fright, swearing they had seen a swimming
house. That he laughed at their folly, and went himself in the boat,
ordering his men to take a strong cable along with them. That the weather
being calm, he rowed round me several times, observed my windows,
and the wire lattices that defended them. That he discovered two staples
upon one side, which was all of boards, without any passage for light.
He then commanded his men to row up to that side, and fastening a
cable to one of the staples, ordered his men to tow my chest (as he called
it) towards the ship. When it was there, he gave directions to fasten
another cable to the ring fixed in the cover, and to raise up my chest
with pulleys, which all the sailors were not able to do above two or three
foot. He said they saw my stick and handkerchief thrust out of the hole,
and concluded that some unhappy man must be shut up in the cavity. I
asked whether he or the crew had seen any prodigious birds in the air
about the time he first discovered me. To which he answered that, discoursing this matter with the sailors while I was asleep, one of them said
he had observed three eagles flying towards the north, but remarked
nothing of their being larger than the usual size (which I suppose must
be imputed to the great height they were at), and he could not guess the
reason of my question. I then asked the Captain how far he reckoned we
might be from land; he said, by the best computation he could make,
we were at least an hundred leagues. I assured him that he must be
mistaken by almost half; for I had not left the country from whence I
came above two hours before I dropped into the sea. Whereupon he

7. At once; altogether.   8. Overtake.

began again to think that my brain was disturbed, of which he gave me a hint, and advised me to go to bed in a cabin he had provided. I assured him I was well refreshed with his good entertainment and company, and as much in my senses as ever I was in my life. He then grew serious and desired to ask me freely whether I were not troubled in mind by the consciousness of some enormous crime, for which I was punished at the command of some prince, by exposing me in that chest, as great criminals in other countries have been forced to sea in a leaky vessel without provisions; for although he should be sorry to have taken so ill[9] a man into his ship, yet he would engage his word to set me safe on shore in the first port where we arrived. He added that his suspicions were much increased by some very absurd speeches I had delivered at first to the sailors, and afterwards to himself, in relation to my closet or chest, as well as by my odd looks and behavior while I was at supper.

I begged his patience to hear me tell my story, which I faithfully did from the last time I left England to the moment he first discovered me. And as truth always forceth its way into rational minds, so this honest, worthy gentleman, who had some tincture of learning, and very good sense, was immediately convinced of my candor and veracity. But further to confirm all I had said, I entreated him to give order that my cabinet should be brought, of which I kept the key in my pocket (for he had already informed me how the seamen disposed of my closet). I opened it in his presence and showed him the small collection of rarities I made in the country from whence I had been so strangely delivered. There was the comb I had contrived out of the stumps of the King's beard, and another of the same materials, but fixed into a paring of her Majesty's thumbnail, which served for the back. There was a collection of needles and pins from a foot to half a yard long; four wasp-stings, like joiners' tacks; some combings of the Queen's hair; a gold ring which one day she made me a present of in a most obliging manner, taking it from her little finger, and throwing it over my head like a collar. I desired the Captain would please to accept this ring in return for his civilities, which he absolutely refused. I showed him a corn that I had cut off with my own hand from a Maid of Honor's toe; it was about the bigness of a Kentish pippin,[1] and grown so hard that, when I returned to England, I got it hollowed into a cup and set in silver. Lastly, I desired him to see the breeches I had then on, which were made of a mouse's skin.

I could force nothing on him but a footman's tooth, which I observed him to examine with great curiosity, and found he had a fancy for it. He received it with abundance of thanks, more than such a trifle could deserve. It was drawn by an unskillful surgeon in a mistake from one of Glumdalclitch's men, who was afflicted with the toothache; but it was as sound as any in his head. I got it cleaned, and put it into my cabinet. It was about a foot long, and four inches in diameter.

9. Evil.   1. Apple.

The Captain was very well satisfied with this plain relation I had given him, and said he hoped when we returned to England I would oblige the world by putting it in paper and making it public. My answer was that I thought we were already overstocked with books of travels; that nothing could now pass which was not extraordinary; wherein I doubted some authors less consulted truth than their own vanity or interest, or the diversion of ignorant readers. That my story could contain little besides common events, without those ornamental descriptions of strange plants, trees, birds, and other animals, or the barbarous customs and idolatry of savage people, with which most writers abound. However, I thanked him for his good opinion, and promised to take the matter into my thoughts.

He said he wondered at one thing very much, which was to hear me speak so loud, asking me whether the King or Queen of that country were thick of hearing. I told him it was what I had been used to for above two years past, and that I admired[2] as much at the voices of him and his men, who seemed to me only to whisper, and yet I could hear them well enough. But, when I spoke in that country, it was like a man talking in the street to another looking out from the top of a steeple, unless when I was placed on a table, or held in any person's hand. I told him I had likewise observed another thing: that when I first got into the ship, and the sailors stood all about me, I thought they were the most little contemptible creatures I had ever beheld. For indeed while I was in that prince's country, I could never endure to look in a glass after mine eyes had been accustomed to such prodigious objects, because the comparison gave me so despicable a conceit[3] of myself. The Captain said that while we were at supper he observed me to look at everything with a sort of wonder, and that I often seemed hardly able to contain my laughter; which he knew not well how to take, but imputed it to some disorder in my brain. I answered, it was very true; and I wondered how I could forbear, when I saw his dishes of the size of a silver threepence, a leg of pork hardly a mouthful, a cup not so big as a nutshell; and so I went on, describing the rest of his household stuff and provisions after the same manner. For, although the Queen had ordered a little equipage[4] of all things necessary for me while I was in her service, yet my ideas were wholly taken up with what I saw on every side of me, and I winked at my own littleness, as people do at their own faults. The Captain understood my raillery very well, and merrily replied with the old English proverb, that he doubted[5] mine eyes were bigger than my belly, for he did not observe my stomach so good, although I had fasted all day; and continuing in his mirth, protested he would have gladly given an hundred pounds to have seen my closet in the eagle's bill, and afterwards in its fall from so great an height into the sea; which would certainly have been a most astonishing object, worthy to have the description of it

2. Wondered at.   4. Furnishings.
3. Notion.   5. Feared.

transmitted to future ages: and the comparison of Phaeton[6] was so obvious, that he could not forbear applying it, although I did not much admire the conceit.

The Captain having been at Tonquin,[7] was in his return to England driven northeastward to the latitude of 44 degrees, and of longitude 143. But meeting a trade wind two days after I came on board him, we sailed southward a long time, and coasting New Holland[8] kept our course west-southwest, and then south-southwest till we doubled the Cape of Good Hope. Our voyage was very prosperous, but I shall not trouble the reader with a journal of it. The Captain called in at one or two ports, and sent in his longboat for provisions and fresh water; but I never went out of the ship till we came into the Downs,[9] which was on the third day of June, 1706, about nine months after my escape. I offered to leave my goods in security for payment of my freight; but the Captain protested he would not receive one farthing. We took kind leave of each other, and I made him promise he would come to see me at my house in Redriff.[1] I hired a horse and guide for five shillings, which I borrowed of the Captain.

As I was on the road, observing the littleness of the houses, the trees, the cattle, and the people, I began to think myself in Lilliput. I was afraid of trampling on every traveler I met, and often called aloud to have them stand out of the way, so that I had like to have gotten one or two broken heads for my impertinence.

When I came to my own house, for which I was forced to inquire, one of the servants opening the door, I bent down to go in (like a goose under a gate) for fear of striking my head. My wife ran out to embrace me, but I stooped lower than her knees, thinking she could otherwise never be able to reach my mouth. My daughter kneeled to ask my blessing, but I could not see her till she arose, having been so long used to stand with my head and eyes erect to above sixty foot; and then I went to take her up with one hand by the waist. I looked down upon the servants and one or two friends who were in the house, as if they had been pygmies and I a giant. I told my wife she had been too thrifty; for I found she had starved herself and her daughter to nothing. In short, I behaved myself so unaccountably that they were all of the Captain's opinion when he first saw me, and concluded I had lost my wits. This I mention as an instance of the great power of habit and prejudice.

In a little time I and my family and friends came to a right understanding; but my wife protested I should never go to sea any more, although my evil destiny so ordered that she had not power to hinder me; as the reader may know hereafter. In the meantime I here conclude the second part of my unfortunate voyages.

6. The son of Apollo, whose unsuccessful attempt to drive the chariot of the sun god resulted in his death, when he was hurled by Zeus from the sky and fell into the river Eridanus, where he drowned.
7. Tonkin, in Indochina.

8. Australia.
9. The sheltered anchorage between Goodwin Sands and the coast of Kent, near Deal.
1. Rotherhithe, on the south bank of the Thames, slightly below the City.

From *Part 3. A Voyage to Laputa, Balnibarbi, Glubbdubdrib,*
Luggnagg, and Japan

[*The Flying Island of Laputa*][1]

CHAPTER 2. *The humors and dispositions of the Laputans described. An*
account of their learning. Of the King and his court. The author's recep-
tion there. The inhabitants subject to fears and disquietudes. An account
of the women.

At my alighting I was surrounded by a crowd of people, but those who
stood nearest seemed to be of better quality. They beheld me with all
the marks and circumstances of wonder; neither indeed was I much in
their debt, having never till then seen a race of mortals so singular in
their shapes, habits, and countenances. Their heads were all reclined to
the right, or the left; one of their eyes turned inward, and the other
directly up to the zenith. Their outward garments were adorned with the
figures of suns, moons, and stars, interwoven with those of fiddles, flutes,
harps, trumpets, guitars, harpsichords, and many more instruments of
music, unknown to us in Europe.[2] I observed here and there many in
the habits of servants, with a blown bladder fastened like a flail to the
end of a short stick, which they carried in their hands. In each bladder
was a small quantity of dried pease or little pebbles (as I was afterwards
informed). With these bladders they now and then flapped the mouths
and ears of those who stood near them, of which practice I could not
then conceive the meaning. It seems, the minds of these people are so
taken up with intense speculations, that they neither can speak, or attend
to the discourses of others, without being roused by some external taction[3]
upon the organs of speech and hearing; for which reason those persons
who are able to afford it always keep a flapper (the original is *climenole*)
in their family, as one of their domestics; nor ever walk abroad or make
visits without him. And the business of this officer is, when two or more
persons are in company, gently to strike with his bladder the mouth of
him who is to speak, and the right ear of him or them to whom the
speaker addresseth himself. This flapper is likewise employed diligently
to attend his master in his walks, and upon occasion to give him a soft
flap on his eyes, because he is always so wrapped up in cogitation, that
he is in manifest danger of falling down every precipice, and bouncing
his head against every post; and in the streets, of jostling others, or being
jostled himself into the kennel.[4]

It was necessary to give the reader this information, without which he

---

1. In the first chapter of part 3 Gulliver starts on
his third voyage, but is captured by pirates and set
adrift. Just as he is about to despair, a vast flying
island appears in the sky, and the inhabitants draw
him up with pulleys.
2. The Laputans represent contemporary specu-

lation, deplored by Swift, about abstract theories
of science, mathematics, and music. Both the Royal
Society and Sir Isaac Newton took an interest in
the mathematical basis of music.
3. Touch.
4. Gutter.

would be at the same loss with me, to understand the proceedings of these people, as they conducted me up the stairs to the top of the island, and from thence to the royal palace. While we were ascending, they forgot several times what they were about, and left me to myself, till their memories were again roused by their flappers; for they appeared altogether unmoved by the sight of my foreign habit and countenance, and by the shouts of the vulgar, whose thoughts and minds were more disengaged.

At last we entered the palace, and proceeded into the chamber of presence; where I saw the King seated on his throne, attended on each side by persons of prime quality. Before the throne was a large table filled with globes and spheres, and mathematical instruments of all kinds. His Majesty took not the least notice of us, although our entrance was not without sufficient noise, by the concourse of all persons belonging to the court. But he was then deep in a problem, and we attended at least an hour before he could solve it. There stood by him on each side a young page, with flaps in their hands, and when they saw he was at leisure, one of them gently struck his mouth, and the other his right ear; at which he started like one awaked on the sudden, and looking towards me, and the company I was in, recollected the occasion of our coming, whereof he had been informed before. He spoke some words, where-upon immediately a young man with a flap came up to my side, and flapped me gently on the right ear; but I made signs as well as I could, that I had no occasion for such an instrument; which as I afterwards found gave his Majesty and the whole court a very mean opinion of my understanding. The King, as far as I could conjecture, asked me several questions, and I addressed myself to him in all the languages I had. When it was found that I could neither understand nor be understood, I was conducted by his order to an apartment in his palace (this prince being distinguished above all his predecessors for his hospitality to strangers),[5] where two servants were appointed to attend me. My dinner was brought, and four persons of quality, whom I remembered to have seen very near the King's person, did me the honor to dine with me. We had two courses, of three dishes each. In the first course there was a shoulder of mutton, cut into an equilateral triangle; a piece of beef into a rhomboid; and a pudding into a cycloid. The second course was two ducks, trussed up into the form of fiddles; sausages and pudding resembling flutes and hautboys,[6] and a breast of veal in the shape of a harp. The servants cut our bread into cones, cylinders, parallelograms, and several other mathematical figures.

While we were at dinner, I made bold to ask the names of several things in their language, and those noble persons, by the assistance of their flappers, delighted to give me answers, hoping to raise my admiration of their great abilities, if I could be brought to converse with

5. George I, a patron of music and science, had filled his court with Hanoverians when he came to England in 1714.
6. Oboes.

them. I was soon able to call for bread and drink, or whatever else I wanted.

After dinner my company withdrew, and a person was sent to me by the King's order, attended by a flapper. He brought with him pen, ink, and paper, and three or four books; giving me to understand by signs, that he was sent to teach me the language. We sat together four hours, in which time I wrote down a great number of words in columns, with the translations over against them. I likewise made a shift to learn several short sentences. For my tutor would order one of my servants to fetch something, to turn about, to make a bow, to sit, or stand, or walk, and the like. Then I took down the sentence in writing. He showed me also in one of his books the figures of the sun, moon, and stars, the zodiac, the tropics and polar circles, together with the denominations of many figures of planes and solids. He gave me the names and descriptions of all the musical instruments, and the general terms of art in playing on each of them. After he had left me, I placed all my words with their interpretations in alphabetical order. And thus in a few days, by the help of a very faithful memory, I got some insight into their language.

The word, which I interpret the *Flying* or *Floating Island*, is in the original *Laputa*; whereof I could never learn the true etymology. *Lap* in the old obsolete language signifieth *high*, and *untuh* a *governor*; from which they say by corruption was derived *Laputa*, from *Lapuntuh*. But I do not approve of this derivation, which seems to be a little strained. I ventured to offer to the learned among them a conjecture of my own, that *Laputa* was *quasi Lap outed*; *Lap* signifying properly the dancing of the sunbeams in the sea, and *outed* a wing, which however I shall not obtrude, but submit to the judicious reader.[7]

Those to whom the King had entrusted me, observing how ill I was clad, ordered a tailor to come next morning, and take my measure for a suit of clothes. This operator did his office after a different manner from those of his trade in Europe. He first took my altitude by a quadrant, and then, with rule and compasses, described the dimensions and out-lines of my whole body; all which he entered upon paper, and in six days brought my clothes very ill made, and quite out of shape, by hap-pening to mistake a figure in the calculation. But my comfort was, that I observed such accidents very frequent, and little regarded.

During my confinement for want of clothes, and by an indisposition that held me some days longer, I much enlarged my dictionary; and when I went next to court, was able to understand many things the King spoke, and to return him some kind of answers. His Majesty had given orders that the island should move northeast and by east, to the vertical point over Lagado, the metropolis of the whole kingdom, below upon the firm earth. It was about ninety leagues distant, and our voyage lasted four days and a half. I was not in the least sensible of the progressive motion made in the air by the island. On the second morning, about

---

7. Gulliver overlooks a likelier etymology: Spanish *la puta*, "the whore."

eleven o'clock, the King himself in person, attended by his nobility, courtiers, and officers, having prepared all their musical instruments, played on them for three hours without intermission, so that I was quite stunned with the noise; neither could I possibly guess the meaning, till my tutor informed me. He said, that the people of their island had their ears adapted to hear the music of the spheres, which always played at certain periods; and the court was now prepared to bear their part in whatever instrument they most excelled.

In our journey towards Lagado, the capital city, his Majesty ordered that the island should stop over certain towns and villages, from whence he might receive the petitions of his subjects. And to this purpose, several packthreads were let down with small weights at the bottom. On these packthreads the people strung their petitions, which mounted up directly like the scraps of paper fastened by schoolboys at the end of the string that holds their kite.[8] Sometimes we received wine and victuals from below, which were drawn up by pulleys.

The knowledge I had in mathematics gave me great assistance in acquiring their phraseology, which depended much upon that science and music; and in the latter I was not unskilled. Their ideas are perpetually conversant in lines and figures. If they would, for example, praise the beauty of a woman, or any other animal, they describe it by rhombs, circles, parallelograms, ellipses, and other geometrical terms; or else by words of art drawn from music, needless here to repeat. I observed in the King's kitchen all sorts of mathematical and musical instruments, after the figures of which they cut up the joints that were served to his Majesty's table.

Their houses are very ill built, the walls bevil, without one right angle in any apartment; and this defect ariseth from the contempt they bear for practical geometry; which they despise as vulgar and mechanic, those instructions they give being too refined for the intellectuals of their workmen; which occasions perpetual mistakes. And although they are dextrous enough upon a piece of paper, in the management of the rule, the pencil, and the divider, yet in the common actions and behavior of life I have not seen a more clumsy, awkward, and unhandy people, nor so slow and perplexed in their conceptions upon all other subjects, except those of mathematics and music. They are very bad reasoners, and vehemently given to opposition, unless when they happen to be of the right opinion, which is seldom their case. Imagination, fancy, and invention, they are wholly strangers to, nor have any words in their language by which those ideas can be expressed; the whole compass of their thoughts and mind being shut up within the two forementioned sciences.

Most of them, and especially those who deal in the astronomical part, have great faith in judicial astrology, although they are ashamed to own it publicly. But what I chiefly admired,[9] and thought altogether unac-

---

8. Petitioners, that is, might as well go fly a kite. Throughout this section Swift satirizes the "distance" of George I (who spent much of his time in Hanover) from his English subjects.
9. Wondered at.

countable, was the strong disposition I observed in them towards news and politics; perpetually enquiring into public affairs, giving their judgments in matters of state; and passionately disputing every inch of a party opinion. I have indeed observed the same disposition among most of the mathematicians I have known in Europe; although I could never discover the least analogy between the two sciences; unless those people suppose, that because the smallest circle hath as many degrees as the largest, therefore the regulation and management of the world require no more abilities than the handling and turning of a globe. But I rather take this quality to spring from a very common infirmity of human nature, inclining us to be more curious and conceited in matters where we have least concern, and for which we are least adapted either by study or nature.

These people are under continual disquietudes, never enjoying a minute's peace of mind; and their disturbances proceed from causes which very little affect the rest of mortals. Their apprehensions arise from several changes they dread in the celestial bodies. For instance; that the earth, by the continual approaches of the sun towards it, must in course of time be absorbed or swallowed up. That the face of the sun will by degrees be encrusted with its own effluvia,[1] and give no more light to the world. That the earth very narrowly escaped a brush from the tail of the last comet, which would have infallibly reduced it to ashes; and that the next, which they have calculated for one and thirty years hence, will probably destroy us.[2] For, if in its perihelion it should approach within a certain degree of the sun (as by their calculations they have reason to dread), it will conceive a degree of heat ten thousand times more intense than that of red-hot glowing iron; and in its absence from the sun, carry a blazing tail ten hundred thousand and fourteen miles long; through which if the earth should pass at the distance of one hundred thousand miles from the nucleus, or main body of the comet, it must in its passage be set on fire, and reduced to ashes. That the sun daily spending its rays without any nutriment to supply them, will at last be wholly consumed and annihilated; which must be attended with the destruction of this earth, and of all the planets that receive their light from it.

They are so perpetually alarmed with the apprehensions of these and the like impending dangers, that they can neither sleep quietly in their beds, nor have any relish for the common pleasures or amusements of life. When they meet an acquaintance in the morning, the first question is about the sun's health, how he looked at his setting and rising, and what hopes they have to avoid the stroke of the approaching comet. This conversation they are apt to run into with the same temper that boys discover in delighting to hear terrible stories of sprites and hobgoblins, which they greedily listen to, and dare not go to bed for fear.

1. Sunspots.
2. Halley's comet, some astronomers had feared, might strike the earth on its next appearance (1758).

All the disasters that disquiet the Laputans had occurred to English scientists as possible implications of Newtonian theory.

The women of the island have abundance of vivacity; they contemn their husbands, and are exceedingly fond of strangers, whereof there is always a considerable number from the continent below, attending at court, either upon affairs of the several towns and corporations, or their own particular occasions; but are much despised, because they want the same endowments. Among these the ladies choose their gallants: but the vexation is, that they act with too much ease and security; for the husband is always so rapt in speculation, that the mistress and lover may proceed to the greatest familiarities before his face, if he be but provided with paper and implements, and without his flapper at his side.

The wives and daughters lament their confinement to the island, although I think it the most delicious spot of ground in the world; and although they live here in the greatest plenty and magnificence, and are allowed to do whatever they please, they long to see the world, and take the diversions of the metropolis, which they are not allowed to do without a particular license from the King; and this is not easy to be obtained, because the people of quality have found by frequent experience, how hard it is to persuade their women to return from below. I was told that a great court lady, who had several children, is married to the prime minister, the richest subject in the kingdom, a very graceful person, extremely fond of her, and lives in the finest palace of the island, went down to Lagado, on the pretense of health, there hid herself for several months, till the King sent a warrant to search for her, and she was found in an obscure eating-house all in rags, having pawned her clothes to maintain an old deformed footman, who beat her every day, and in whose company she was taken much against her will. And although her husband received her with all possible kindness, and without the least reproach, she soon after contrived to steal down again with all her jewels, to the same gallant, and hath not been heard of since.

This may perhaps pass with the reader rather for an European or English story, than for one of a country so remote. But he may please to consider, that the caprices of womankind are not limited by any climate or nation; and that they are much more uniform than can be easily imagined.

In about a month's time I had made a tolerable proficiency in their language, and was able to answer most of the King's questions, when I had the honor to attend him. His Majesty discovered not the least curiosity to enquire into the laws, government, history, religion, or manners of the countries where I had been; but confined his questions to the state of mathematics, and received the account I gave him with great contempt and indifference, though often roused by his flapper on each side.[3]

3. In the omitted chapters Gulliver visits countries that show the consequences of modern learning. After an account of the Flying Island, whose power of motion (derived from a giant magnet or loadstone) allows it to dominate the regions below, he descends to Balnibarbi, a once fertile land now ruined by the fanciful projects of impractical scientists. In the Grand Academy of Lagado he meets many professors who are contriving such perverse "improvements" as making clothes from cobwebs or breeding naked sheep. Then he visits the part of the academy devoted to speculative learning.

[*The Academy of Lagado*][4]

The first professor I saw was in a very large room, with forty pupils about him. After salutation, observing me to look earnestly upon a frame, which took up the greatest part of both the length and breadth of the room, he said, perhaps I might wonder to see him employed in a project for improving speculative knowledge by practical and mechanical operations. But the world would soon be sensible[5] of its usefulness, and he flattered himself that a more noble, exalted thought never sprang in any other man's head. Everyone knew how laborious the usual method is of attaining to arts and sciences; whereas by his contrivance the most ignorant person at a reasonable charge, and with a little bodily labor, may write books in philosophy, poetry, politics, law, mathematics, and theology, without the least assistance from genius or study. He then led me to the frame, about the sides whereof all his pupils stood in ranks. It was twenty foot square, placed in the middle of the room. The superficies[6] was composed of several bits of wood, about the bigness of a die, but some larger than others. They were all linked together by slender wires. These bits of wood were covered on every square with papers pasted on them; and on these papers were written all the words of their language in their several moods, tenses, and declensions, but without any order. The professor then desired me to observe, for he was going to set his engine[7] at work. The pupils at his command took each of them hold of an iron handle, whereof there were forty fixed round the edges of the frame; and giving them a sudden turn, the whole disposition[8] of the words was entirely changed. He then commanded six and thirty of the lads to read the several lines softly as they appeared upon the frame; and where they found three or four words together that might make part of a sentence, they dictated to the four remaining boys who were scribes. This work was repeated three or four times, and at every turn the engine was so contrived that the words shifted into new places, as the square bits of wood moved upside down.

Six hours a day the young students were employed in this labor; and the professor showed me several volumes in large folio already collected, of broken sentences, which he intended to piece together, and out of those rich materials to give the world a complete body of all arts and sciences; which however might be still improved, and much expedited, if the public would raise a fund for making and employing five hundred such frames in Lagado, and oblige the managers to contribute in common their several[9] collections.

He assured me, that this invention had employed all his thoughts from his youth, that he had emptied the whole vocabulary into his frame,

4. From Chapter 5. The Grand Academy of Lagado satirizes the Royal Society of London, an organization founded in 1662 to encourage the pursuit of scientific knowledge. Some of the projects described by Swift resemble the experiments or speculations of British scientists at the time, and at least one seems current today.
5. Aware.
6. Surface.
7. Contrivance.
8. Arrangement.
9. Separate.

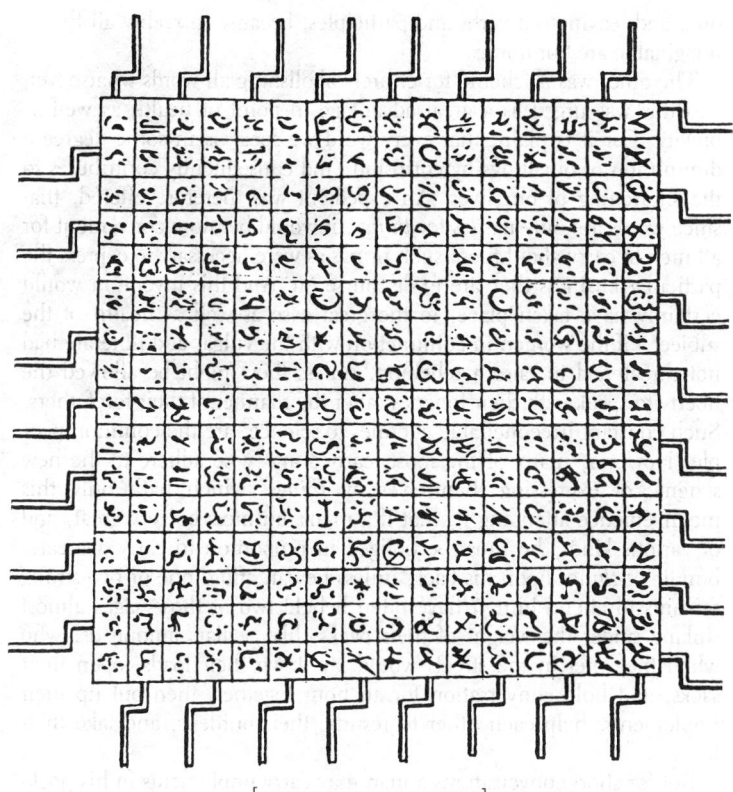

[A PRIMITIVE COMPUTER]

and made the strictest computation of the general proportion there is in books between the numbers of particles, nouns, and verbs, and other parts of speech.

I made my humblest acknowledgments to this illustrious person for his great communicativeness, and promised if ever I had the good fortune to return to my native country, that I would do him justice, as the sole inventor of this wonderful machine; the form and contrivance of which I desired leave to delineate upon paper as in the figure here annexed. I told him, although it were the custom of our learned in Europe to steal inventions from each other, who had thereby at least this advantage, that it became a controversy which was the right owner, yet I would take such caution, that he should have the honor entire without a rival.

We next went to the school of languages, where three professors sat in consultation upon improving that of their own country.[1]

The first project was to shorten discourse by cutting polysyllables into

---

1. Many contemporary scientists had proposed a philosophical language that would eliminate the treacherous disparity between words and things and thus allow accurate scientific discourse.

one, and leaving out verbs and participles, because in reality all things imaginable are but nouns.

The other was a scheme for entirely abolishing all words whatsoever; and this was urged as a great advantage in point of health as well as brevity. For it is plain, that every word we speak is in some degree a diminution of our lungs by corrosion, and consequently contributes to the shortening of our lives. An expedient was therefore offered, that since words are only names for *things*, it would be more convenient for all men to carry about them such *things* as were necessary to express the particular business they are to discourse on. And this invention would certainly have taken place, to the great ease as well as health of the subject,[2] if the women in conjunction with the vulgar and illiterate had not threatened to raise a rebellion, unless they might be allowed the liberty to speak with their tongues, after the manner of their forefathers. Such constant irreconcilable enemies to science[3] are the common people. However, many of the most learned and wise adhere to the new scheme of expressing themselves by *things*, which hath only this inconvenience attending it, that if a man's business be very great, and of various kinds, he must be obliged in proportion to carry a greater bundle of *things* upon his back, unless he can afford one or two strong servants to attend him. I have often beheld two of those sages almost sinking under the weight of their packs, like pedlars among us, who when they met in the streets would lay down their loads, open their sacks, and hold conversation for an hour together, then put up their implements, help each other to resume their burdens, and take their leave.

But for short conversations a man may carry implements in his pockets and under his arms, enough to supply him, and in his house he cannot be at a loss; therefore the room where company meet who practice this art is full of all *things* ready at hand, requisite to furnish matter for this kind of artificial converse.[4]

Another great advantage proposed by this invention was that it would serve as an universal language to be understood in all civilized nations, whose goods and utensils are generally of the same kind, or nearly resembling, so that their uses might easily be comprehended. And thus, ambassadors would be qualified to treat with foreign princes or ministers of state to whose tongues they were utter strangers.

I was at the mathematical school, where the master taught his pupils after a method scarce imaginable to us in Europe. The proposition and demonstration were fairly written on a thin wafer, with ink composed of a cephalic tincture.[5] This the student was to swallow upon a fasting stomach, and for three days following eat nothing but bread and water. As the wafer digested, the tincture mounted to his brain, bearing the

2. a. Person experimented on; b. topic of conversation. "Vulgar": common people.
3. Knowledge.
4. The Royal Society had sponsored a collection intended to contain one specimen of every thing in the world.
5. A solution or dye directed toward the head.

proposition along with it. But the success hath not hitherto been answerable, partly by some error in the *quantum*[6] or composition, and partly by the perverseness of lads, to whom this bolus is so nauseous that they generally steal aside, and discharge it upwards before it can operate; neither have they been yet persuaded to use so long an abstinence as the prescription requires.[7]

[The Struldbruggs]

CHAPTER 10. *The Luggnaggians commended. A particular description of the struldbruggs, with many conversations between the author and some eminent persons upon that subject.*

The Luggnaggians are a polite[8] and generous people, and although they are not without some share of that pride which is peculiar to all eastern countries, yet they show themselves courteous to strangers, especially such who are countenanced by the court. I had many acquaintance among persons of the best fashion, and being always attended by my interpreter, the conversation we had was not disagreeable.

One day in much good company, I was asked by a person of quality, whether I had seen any of their *struldbruggs* or *immortals*. I said I had not; and desired he would explain to me what he meant by such an appellation, applied to a mortal creature. He told me, that sometimes, although very rarely, a child happened to be born in a family with a red circular spot in the forehead, directly over the left eyebrow, which was an infallible mark that it should never die. The spot, as he described it, was about the compass of a silver threepence, but in the course of time grew larger, and changed its color; for at twelve years old it became green, so continued till five and twenty, then turned to a deep blue; at five and forty it grew coal black, and as large as an English shilling; but never admitted any farther alteration. He said these births were so rare, that he did not believe there could be above eleven hundred *struldbruggs* of both sexes in the whole kingdom, of which he computed about fifty in the metropolis, and among the rest a young girl born about three years ago. That these productions were not peculiar to any family, but a mere effect of chance; and the children of the *struldbruggs* themselves were equally mortal with the rest of the people.

I freely own myself to have been struck with inexpressible delight upon hearing this account: and the person who gave it me happening to understand the Balnibarbian language, which I spoke very well, I could not forbear breaking out into expressions perhaps a little too extravagant. I cried out as in a rapture: Happy nation, where every child hath at least a chance for being immortal! Happy people who enjoy so many living

6. Amount. "Bolus": a large pill.
7. In the omitted chapters Gulliver hears projects for improving politics and offers some of his own. He sails to Glubbdubdrib, the Island of Sorcerers, where he talks with the spirits of the dead; he learns that history is a pack of lies and that humanity has degenerated since ancient times. He is then received by the King of Luggnagg.
8. Refined, cultivated.

examples of ancient virtue, and have masters ready to instruct them in the wisdom of all former ages! But happiest beyond all comparison are those excellent *struldbruggs*, who being born exempt from that universal calamity of human nature, have their minds free and disengaged, without the weight and depression of spirits caused by the continual apprehension of death. I discovered my admiration[9] that I had not observed any of these illustrious persons at court; the black spot on the forehead being so remarkable a distinction, that I could not have easily overlooked it; and it was impossible that his Majesty, a most judicious prince, should not provide himself with a good number of such wise and able counselors. Yet perhaps the virtue of those reverend sages was too strict for the corrupt and libertine manners of a court. And we often find by experience that young men are too opinionative[1] and volatile to be guided by the sober dictates of their seniors. However, since the King was pleased to allow me access to his royal person, I was resolved upon the very first occasion to deliver my opinion to him on this matter freely, and at large by the help of my interpreter; and whether he would please to take my advice or no, yet in one thing I was determined, that his Majesty having frequently offered me an establishment in this country, I would with great thankfulness accept the favor, and pass my life here in the conversation of those superior beings the *struldbruggs*, if they would please to admit me.

The gentleman to whom I addressed my discourse, because (as I have already observed) he spoke the language of Balnibarbi, said to me with a sort of a smile, which usually ariseth from pity to the ignorant, that he was glad of any occasion to keep me among them, and desired my permission to explain to the company what I had spoke. He did so; and they talked together for some time in their own language, whereof I understood not a syllable, neither could I observe by their countenances what impression my discourse had made on them. After a short silence the same person told me, that his friends and mine (so he thought fit to express himself) were very much pleased with the judicious remarks I had made on the great happiness and advantages of immortal life; and they were desirous to know in a particular manner, what scheme of living I should have formed to myself, if it had fallen to my lot to have been born a *struldbrugg*.

I answered, it was easy to be eloquent on so copious and delightful a subject, especially to me who have been often apt to amuse myself with visions of what I should do if I were a king, a general, or a great lord; and upon this very case I had frequently run over the whole system how I should employ myself, and pass the time if I were sure to live forever.

That, if it had been my good fortune to come into the world a *struldbrugg*, as soon as I could discover my own happiness by understanding the difference between life and death, I would first resolve by all arts and methods whatsoever to procure myself riches: in the pursuit of which,

9. Wonder.
1. Speculative, impractical. Note, in the next

sentence, Gulliver's own resolve to deliver his opinion.

by thrift and management, I might reasonably expect in about two hundred years to be the wealthiest man in the kingdom. In the second place, I would from my earliest youth apply myself to the study of arts and sciences, by which I should arrive in time to excel all others in learning. Lastly, I would carefully record every action and event of consequence that happened in the public, impartially draw the characters of the several successions of princes, and great ministers of state; with my own observations on every point. I would exactly set down the several changes in customs, languages, fashions of dress, diet and diversions. By all which acquirements, I should be a living treasury of knowledge and wisdom, and certainly become the oracle of the nation.

I would never marry after threescore, but live in an hospitable manner, yet still on the saving side. I would entertain myself in forming and directing the minds of hopeful young men, by convincing them from my own remembrance, experience and observation, fortified by numerous examples, of the usefulness of virtue in public and private life. But my choice and constant companions should be a set of my own immortal brotherhood, among whom I would elect a dozen from the most ancient down to my own contemporaries. Where any of these wanted fortunes, I would provide them with convenient lodges round my own estate, and have some of them always at my table, only mingling a few of the most valuable among you mortals, whom length of time would harden me to lose with little or no reluctance, and treat your posterity after the same manner; just as a man diverts himself with the annual succession of pinks and tulips in his garden, without regretting the loss of those which withered the preceding year.

These *struldbruggs* and I would mutually communicate our observations and memorials[2] through the course of time; remark the several gradations by which corruption steals into the world, and oppose it in every step, by giving perpetual warning and instruction to mankind; which, added to the strong influence of our own example, would probably prevent that continual degeneracy of human nature, so justly complained of in all ages.

Add to all this, the pleasure of seeing the various revolutions of states and empires; the changes in the lower and upper world;[3] ancient cities in ruins; and obscure villages become the seats of kings. Famous rivers lessening into shallow brooks; the ocean leaving one coast dry, and overwhelming another; the discovery of many countries yet unknown. Barbarity overrunning the politest nations, and the most barbarous becoming civilized. I should then see the discovery of the longitude, the perpetual motion, the universal medicine,[4] and many other great inventions brought to the utmost perfection.

What wonderful discoveries should we make in astronomy, by outliv-

2. Memories.
3. Earth and heaven; figuratively, common people and the ruling class. "Revolutions": cycles.
4. The *elixir vitae*, an alchemical formula to preserve life forever, was considered by Swift an impossible dream, like a method for calculating longitude at sea, or a perpetual motion machine.

ing and confirming our own predictions, by observing the progress and returns of comets, with the changes of motion in the sun, moon and stars.

I enlarged upon many other topics, which the natural desire of endless life and sublunary happiness could easily furnish me with. When I had ended, and the sum of my discourse had been interpreted as before to the rest of the company, there was a good deal of talk among them in the language of the country, not without some laughter at my expense. At last the same gentleman who had been my interpreter said, he was desired by the rest to set me right in a few mistakes, which I had fallen into through the common imbecility[5] of human nature, and upon that allowance was less answerable for them. That this breed of *struldbruggs* was peculiar to their country, for there were no such people either in Balnibarbi or Japan, where he had the honor to be ambassador from his Majesty, and found the natives in both those kingdoms very hard to believe that the fact was possible; and it appeared from my astonishment when he first mentioned the matter to me, that I received it as a thing wholly new, and scarcely to be credited. That in the two kingdoms above mentioned, where during his residence he had conversed very much, he observed long life to be the universal desire and wish of mankind. That whoever had one foot in the grave was sure to hold back the other as strongly as he could. That the oldest had still hopes of living one day longer, and looked on death as the greatest evil, from which nature always prompted him to retreat; only in this island of Luggnagg the appetite for living was not so eager, from the continual example of the *struldbruggs* before their eyes.

That the system of living contrived by me was unreasonable and unjust, because it supposed a perpetuity of youth, health, and vigor, which no man could be so foolish to hope, however extravagant he might be in his wishes. That the question therefore was not whether a man would choose to be always in the prime of youth, attended with prosperity and health; but how he would pass a perpetual life under all the usual disadvantages which old age brings along with it. For although few men will avow their desires of being immortal upon such hard conditions, yet in the two kingdoms before mentioned of Balnibarbi and Japan, he observed that every man desired to put off death for some time longer, let it approach ever so late; and he rarely heard of any man who died willingly, except he were incited by the extremity of grief or torture. And he appealed to me whether in those countries I had traveled, as well as my own, I had not observed the same general disposition.

After this preface he gave me a particular account of the *struldbruggs* among them. He said they commonly acted like mortals, till about thirty years old, after which by degrees they grew melancholy and dejected, increasing in both till they came to fourscore. This he learned from their own confession; for otherwise there not being above two or three of that

5. Weakness.

species born in an age, they were too few to form a general observation by. When they came to fourscore years, which is reckoned the extremity of living in this country, they had not only all the follies and infirmities of other old men, but many more which arose from the dreadful prospect of never dying. They were not only opinionative, peevish, covetous, morose, vain, talkative; but uncapable of friendship, and dead to all natural affection, which never descended below their grandchildren. Envy and impotent desires are their prevailing passions. But those objects against which their envy seems principally directed, are the vices of the younger sort, and the deaths of the old. By reflecting on the former, they find themselves cut off from all possibility of pleasure; and whenever they see a funeral, they lament and repine that others are gone to an harbor of rest, to which they themselves never can hope to arrive. They have no remembrance of anything but what they learned and observed in their youth and middle age, and even that is very imperfect. And for the truth or particulars of any fact, it is safer to depend on common traditions than upon their best recollections. The least miserable among them appear to be those who turn to dotage, and entirely lose their memories; these meet with more pity and assistance, because they want[6] many bad qualities which abound in others.

If a *struldbrugg* happen to marry one of his own kind, the marriage is dissolved of course by the courtesy of the kingdom, as soon as the younger of the two comes to be fourscore. For the law thinks it a reasonable indulgence, that those who are condemned without any fault of their own to a perpetual continuance in the world, should not have their misery doubled by the load of a wife.

As soon as they have completed the term of eighty years, they are looked on as dead in law; their heirs immediately succeed to their estates, only a small pittance is reserved for their support; and the poor ones are maintained at the public charge. After that period they are held incapable of any employment of trust or profit; they cannot purchase land, or take leases, neither are they allowed to be witnesses in any cause, either civil or criminal, not even for the decision of meers[7] and bounds.

At ninety they lose their teeth and hair; they have at that age no distinction of taste, but eat and drink whatever they can get, without relish or appetite. The diseases they were subject to still continue without increasing or diminishing. In talking they forget the common appellation of things, and the names of persons, even of those who are their nearest friends and relations. For the same reason they never can amuse themselves with reading, because their memory will not serve to carry them from the beginning of a sentence to the end, and by this defect they are deprived of the only entertainment whereof they might otherwise be capable.

The language of this country being always upon the flux, the *struldbruggs* of one age do not understand those of another; neither are they

---

6. Lack.   7. Boundaries.

able after two hundred years to hold any conversation (farther than by a few general words) with their neighbors the mortals; and thus they lie under the disadvantage of living like foreigners in their own country.

This was the account given me of the *struldbruggs*, as near as I can remember. I afterwards saw five or six of different ages, the youngest not above two hundred years old, who were brought to me at several times by some of my friends; but although they were told that I was a great traveler, and had seen all the world, they had not the least curiosity to ask me a question; only desired I would give them *slumskudask*, or a token of remembrance; which is a modest way of begging, to avoid the law that strictly forbids it, because they are provided for by the public, although indeed with a very scanty allowance.

They are despised and hated by all sorts of people; when one of them is born, it is reckoned ominous, and their birth is recorded very particularly; so that you may know their age by consulting the registry, which however hath not been kept above a thousand years past, or at least hath been destroyed by time or public disturbances. But the usual way of computing how old they are, is by asking them what kings or great persons they can remember, and then consulting history; for infallibly the last prince in their mind did not begin his reign after they were fourscore years old.

They were the most mortifying sight I ever beheld; and the women more horrible than the men. Besides the usual deformities in extreme old age, they acquired an additional ghastliness in proportion to their number of years, which is not to be described; and among half a dozen I soon distinguished which was the oldest, although there were not above a century or two between them.

The reader will easily believe, that from what I had heard and seen, my keen appetite for perpetuity of life was much abated. I grew heartily ashamed of the pleasing visions I had formed; and thought no tyrant could invent a death into which I would not run with pleasure from such a life. The King heard of all that had passed between me and my friends upon this occasion, and rallied[8] me very pleasantly; wishing I would send a couple of *struldbruggs* to my own country, to arm our people against the fear of death; but this it seems is forbidden by the fundamental laws of the kingdom; or else I should have been well content with the trouble and expense of transporting them.

I could not but agree, that the laws of this kingdom relating to the *struldbruggs*, were founded upon the strongest reasons, and such as any other country would be under the necessity of enacting in the like circumstances. Otherwise, as avarice is the necessary consequent of old age, those immortals would in time become proprietors of the whole nation, and engross[9] the civil power; which, for want of abilities to manage, must end in the ruin of the public.[1]

8. Ridiculed.
9. Absorb, monopolize.
1. In the omitted chapter Gulliver sails to Japan, where a Dutch ship provides him passage back to Europe.

Part 4. A Voyage to the Country of the Houyhnhnms[1]

CHAPTER 1. *The Author sets out as Captain of a ship. His men conspire against him, confine him a long time to his cabin, set him on shore in an unknown land. He travels up into the country. The Yahoos, a strange sort of animal, described. The Author meets two Houyhnhnms.*

I continued at home with my wife and children about five months in a very happy condition, if I could have learned the lesson of knowing when I was well. I left my poor wife big with child, and accepted an advantageous offer made me to be Captain of the *Adventure*, a stout merchantman of 350 tons; for I understood navigation well, and being grown weary of a surgeon's employment at sea, which however I could exercise upon occasion, I took a skillful young man of that calling, one Robert Purefoy, into my ship. We set sail from Portsmouth upon the 7th day of September, 1710; on the 14th we met with Captain Pocock of Bristol, at Tenariff,[2] who was going to the Bay of Campeachy[3] to cut logwood. On the 16th he was parted from us by a storm; I heard since my return that his ship foundered and none escaped, but one cabin boy. He was an honest man and a good sailor, but a little too positive in his own opinions, which was the cause of his destruction, as it hath been of several others. For if he had followed my advice, he might at this time have been safe at home with his family as well as myself.

I had several men died in my ship of calentures,[4] so that I was forced to get recruits out of Barbadoes and the Leeward Islands, where I touched by the direction of the merchants who employed me; which I had soon too much cause to repent, for I found afterwards that most of them had been buccaneers. I had fifty hands on board; and my orders were that I should trade with the Indians in the South Sea, and make what discoveries I could. These rogues whom I had picked up debauched my other men, and they all formed a conspiracy to seize the ship and secure me; which they did one morning, rushing into my cabin, and binding me hand and foot, threatening to throw me overboard, if I offered to stir. I told them I was their prisoner, and would submit. This they made me swear to do, and then unbound me, only fastening one of my legs with a chain near my bed, and placed a sentry at my door with his piece charged, who was commanded to shoot me dead if I attempted my liberty. They sent me down victuals and drink, and took the government of the ship to themselves. Their design was to turn pirates and plunder the Spaniards, which they could not do, till they got more men. But first they resolved to sell the goods in the ship, and then go to Madagascar for recruits, several among them having died since my confinement. They sailed many weeks, and traded with the Indians; but I knew not

1. Pronounced *Hwin-ims*. The word suggests the neigh characteristic of a horse.
2. Teneriffe, one of the Canary Islands.
3. In the Gulf of Mexico.

4. "A distemper peculiar to sailors, in hot climates; wherein they imagine the sea to be green fields, and will throw themselves into it, if not restrained" (Johnson's *Dictionary*).

what course they took, being kept close prisoner in my cabin, and expecting nothing less than to be murdered, as they often threatened me.

Upon the 9th day of May, 1711, one James Welch came down to my cabin; and said he had orders from the Captain to set me ashore. I expostulated with him, but in vain; neither would he so much as tell me who their new Captain was. They forced me into the longboat, letting me put on my best suit of clothes, which were as good as new, and a small bundle of linen, but no arms except my hanger; and they were so civil as not to search my pockets, into which I conveyed what money I had, with some other little necessaries. They rowed about a league, and then set me down on a strand. I desired them to tell me what country it was; they all swore, they knew no more than myself, but said that the Captain (as they called him) was resolved, after they had sold the lading, to get rid of me in the first place where they discovered land. They pushed off immediately, advising me to make haste, for fear of being overtaken by the tide, and bade me farewell.

In this desolate condition I advanced forward, and soon got upon firm ground, where I sat down on a bank to rest myself, and consider what I had best to do. When I was a little refreshed, I went up into the country, resolving to deliver myself to the first savages I should meet, and purchase my life from them by some bracelets, glass rings, and other toys, which sailors usually provide themselves with in those voyages, and whereof I had some about me. The land was divided by long rows of trees, not regularly planted, but naturally growing; there was great plenty of grass, and several fields of oats. I walked very circumspectly for fear of being surprised, or suddenly shot with an arrow from behind, or on either side. I fell into a beaten road, where I saw many tracks of human feet, and some of cows, but most of horses. At last I beheld several animals in a field, and one or two of the same kind sitting in trees. Their shape was very singular, and deformed, which a little discomposed me, so that I lay down behind a thicket to observe them better. Some of them coming forward near the place where I lay, gave me an opportunity of distinctly marking their form. Their heads and breasts were covered with a thick hair, some frizzled and others lank; they had beards like goats, and a long ridge of hair down their backs, and the fore parts of their legs and feet; but the rest of their bodies were bare, so that I might see their skins, which were of a brown buff color. They had no tails, nor any hair at all on their buttocks, except about the anus; which, I presume Nature had placed there to defend them as they sat on the ground; for this posture they used, as well as lying down, and often stood on their hind feet. They climbed high trees, as nimbly as a squirrel, for they had strong extended claws before and behind, terminating in sharp points, and hooked. They would often spring, and bound, and leap with prodigious agility. The females were not so large as the males; they had long lank hair on their heads, and only a sort of down on the rest of their bodies, except about the anus, and pudenda. Their dugs hung between their forefeet, and often reached almost to the ground as they walked.

The hair of both sexes was of several colors, brown, red, black, and yellow. Upon the whole, I never beheld in all my travels so disagreeable an animal, or one against which I naturally conceived so strong an antipathy. So that thinking I had seen enough, full of contempt and aversion, I got up and pursued the beaten road, hoping it might direct me to the cabin of some Indian: I had not gone far when I met one of these creatures full in my way, and coming up directly to me. The ugly monster, when he saw me, distorted several ways every feature of his visage, and stared as at an object he had never seen before; then approaching nearer, lifted up his forepaw, whether out of curiosity or mischief, I could not tell; but I drew my hanger, and gave him a good blow with the flat side of it; for I durst not strike him with the edge, fearing the inhabitants might be provoked against me, if they should come to know that I had killed or maimed any of their cattle. When the beast felt the smart, he drew back, and roared so loud, that a herd of at least forty came flocking about me from the near field, howling and making odious faces; but I ran to the body of a tree, and leaning my back against it, kept them off, by waving my hanger. Several of this cursed brood getting hold of the branches behind, leaped up into the tree, from whence they began to discharge their excrements on my head; however, I escaped pretty well, by sticking close to the stem of the tree, but was almost stifled with the filth, which fell about me on every side.

In the midst of this distress, I observed them all to run away on a sudden as fast as they could; at which I ventured to leave the tree, and pursue the road, wondering what it was that could put them into this fright. But looking on my left hand, I saw a horse walking softly in the field; which my persecutors having sooner discovered, was the cause of their flight. The horse started a little when he came near me, but soon recovering himself, looked full in my face with manifest tokens of wonder; he viewed my hands and feet, walking round me several times. I would have pursued my journey, but he placed himself directly in the way, yet looking with a very mild aspect, never offering the least violence. We stood gazing at each other for some time; at last I took the boldness, to reach my hand towards his neck, with a design to stroke it; using the common style and whistle of jockies when they are going to handle a strange horse. But, this animal seeming to receive my civilities with disdain, shook his head, and bent his brows, softly raising up his left forefoot to remove my hand. Then he neighed three or four times, but in so different a cadence, that I almost began to think he was speaking to himself in some language of his own.

While he and I were thus employed, another horse came up; who applying himself to the first in a very formal manner, they gently struck each other's right hoof before, neighing several times by turns, and varying the sound, which seemed to be almost articulate. They went some paces off, as if it were to confer together, walking side by side, backward and forward, like persons deliberating upon some affair of weight; but often turning their eyes towards me, as it were to watch that I might not escape. I was amazed to see such actions and behavior in brute beasts; and concluded with myself that if the inhabitants of this country were endued with a proportionable degree of reason, they must needs be the wisest people upon earth. This thought gave me so much comfort, that I resolved to go forward until I could discover some house or village, or meet with any of the natives, leaving the two horses to discourse together as they pleased. But the first, who was a dapple grey, observing me to steal off, neighed after me in so expressive a tone that I fancied myself to understand what he meant; whereupon I turned back, and came near him, to expect his farther commands; but concealing my fear as much as I could; for I began to be in some pain, how this adventure might terminate; and the reader will easily believe I did not much like my present situation.

The two horses came up close to me, looking with great earnestness upon my face and hands. The grey steed rubbed my hat all round with his right fore hoof, and discomposed it so much that I was forced to adjust it better, by taking it off, and settling it again; whereat both he and his companion (who was a brown bay) appeared to be much surprised; the latter felt the lappet of my coat, and finding it to hang loose about me, they both looked with new signs of wonder. He stroked my right hand, seeming to admire the softness, and color; but he squeezed it so hard between his hoof and his pastern, that I was forced to roar; after which they both touched me with all possible tenderness. They were under great perplexity about my shoes and stockings, which they felt very often, neighing to each other, and using various gestures, not unlike those of a philosopher, when he would attempt to solve some new and difficult phenomenon.

Upon the whole, the behavior of these animals was so orderly and rational, so acute and judicious, that I at last concluded, they must needs be magicians, who had thus metamorphosed themselves upon some design; and seeing a stranger in the way, were resolved to divert themselves with him; or perhaps were really amazed at the sight of a man so very different in habit, feature, and complexion from those who might probably live in so remote a climate. Upon the strength of this reasoning, I ventured to address them in the following manner: "Gentlemen, if you be conjurers, as I have good cause to believe, you can understand any language; therefore I make bold to let your worships know that I am a poor distressed Englishman, driven by his misfortunes upon your coast; and I entreat one of you, to let me ride upon his back, as if he were a real horse, to some house or village, where I can be relieved. In return of which favor, I will make you a present of this knife and bracelet" (taking them out of my pocket). The two creatures stood silent while I spoke, seeming to listen with great attention; and when I had ended, they neighed frequently towards each other, as if they were engaged in serious conversation. I plainly observed, that their language expressed the passions very well, and the words might with little pains be resolved into an alphabet more easily than the Chinese.

I could frequently distinguish the word *Yahoo*,[5] which was repeated by each of them several times; and although it were impossible for me to conjecture what it meant, yet while the two horses were busy in conversation, I endeavored to practice this word upon my tongue; and as soon as they were silent, I boldly pronounced "Yahoo" in a loud voice, imitating, at the same time, as near as I could, the neighing of a horse; at which they were both visibly surprised, and the grey repeated the same word twice, as if he meant to teach me the right accent, wherein I spoke after him as well as I could, and found myself perceivably to improve every time, although very far from any degree of perfection. Then the bay tried me with a second word, much harder to be pronounced; but reducing it to the English orthography, may be spelt thus, *Houyhnhnm*. I did not succeed in this so well as the former, but after two or three farther trials, I had better fortune; and they both appeared amazed at my capacity.

After some farther discourse, which I then conjectured might relate to me, the two friends took their leaves, with the same compliment of striking each other's hoof; and the grey made me signs that I should walk before him; wherein I thought it prudent to comply, till I could find a better director. When I offered to slacken my pace, he would cry, "Hhuun, Hhuun"; I guessed his meaning, and gave him to understand, as well as I could that I was weary, and not able to walk faster; upon which, he would stand a while to let me rest.

CHAPTER 2. *The Author conducted by a Houyhnhnm to his house. The house described. The Author's reception. The food of the Houyhnhnms. The Author in distress for want of meat is at last relieved. His manner of feeding in that country.*

Having traveled about three miles, we came to a long kind of building, made of timber, stuck in the ground, and wattled across; the roof was low, and covered with straw. I now began to be a little comforted, and took out some toys, which travelers usually carry for presents to the savage Indians of America and other parts, in hopes the people of the house would be thereby encouraged to receive me kindly. The horse made me a sign to go in first; it was a large room with a smooth clay floor, and a rack and manger extending the whole length on one side. There were three nags, and two mares, not eating, but some of them sitting down upon their hams, which I very much wondered at; but wondered more to see the rest employed in domestic business; the last seemed but ordinary cattle; however this confirmed my first opinion, that a people who could so far civilize brute animals must needs excel in wisdom all the nations of the world. The grey came in just after, and thereby prevented any ill treatment, which the others might have given

5. Morley suggested that *Yahoo* was compounded from two expressions of disgust, *yah* and *ugh* (or *hoo*) common in the 18th century [Case's note].

me. He neighed to them several times in a style of authority, and received answers.

Beyond this room there were three others, reaching the length of the house, to which you passed through three doors, opposite to each other, in the manner of a vista; we went through the second room towards the third; here the grey walked in first, beckoning me to attend;[6] I waited in the second room, and got ready my presents, for the master and mistress of the house; they were two knives, three bracelets of false pearl, a small looking glass and a bead necklace. The horse neighed three or four times, and I waited to hear some answers in a human voice, but I heard no other returns than in the same dialect, only one or two a little shriller than his. I began to think that this house must belong to some person of great note among them, because there appeared so much ceremony before I could gain admittance. But, that a man of quality should be served all by horses, was beyond my comprehension. I feared my brain was disturbed by my sufferings and misfortunes; I roused myself, and looked about me in the room where I was left alone; this was furnished as the first, only after a more elegant manner. I rubbed my eyes often, but the same objects still occurred. I pinched my arms and sides, to awaken myself, hoping I might be in a dream. I then absolutely concluded that all these appearances could be nothing else but necromancy and magic. But I had no time to pursue these reflections; for the grey horse came to the door, and made me a sign to follow him into the third room; where I saw a very comely mare, together with a colt and foal, sitting on their haunches, upon mats of straw, not unartfully made, and perfectly neat and clean.

The mare soon after my entrance, rose from her mat, and coming up close, after having nicely observed my hands and face, gave me a most contemptuous look; then turning to the horse, I heard the word Yahoo often repeated betwixt them; the meaning of which word I could not then comprehend, although it were the first I had learned to pronounce; but I was soon better informed, to my everlasting mortification: for the horse beckoning to me with his head, and repeating the word, "Hhuun, Hhuun," as he did upon the road, which I understood was to attend him, led me out into a kind of court, where was another building at some distance from the house. Here we entered, and I saw three of those detestable creatures, which I first met after my landing, feeding upon roots, and the flesh of some animals, which I afterwards found to be that of asses and dogs, and now and then a cow dead by accident or disease. They were all tied by the neck with strong withes, fastened to a beam; they held their food between the claws of their forefeet, and tore it with their teeth.

The master horse ordered a sorrel nag, one of his servants, to untie the largest of these animals, and take him into a yard. The beast and I were brought close together; and our countenances diligently compared,

6. To wait.

both by master and servant, who thereupon repeated several times the word "Yahoo." My horror and astonishment are not to be described, when I observed, in this abominable animal, a perfect human figure; the face of it indeed was flat and broad, the nose depressed, the lips large, and the mouth wide; but these differences are common to all savage nations, where the lineaments of the countenance are distorted by the natives suffering their infants to lie groveling on the earth, or by carrying them on their backs, nuzzling with their face against the mother's shoulders. The forefeet of the Yahoo differed from my hands in nothing else but the length of the nails, the coarseness and brownness of the palms, and the hairiness on the backs. There was the same resemblance between our feet, with the same differences, which I knew very well, although the horses did not, because of my shoes and stockings; the same in every part of our bodies, except as to hairiness and color, which I have already described.

The great difficulty that seemed to stick with the two horses was to see the rest of my body so very different from that of a Yahoo, for which I was obliged to my clothes, whereof they had no conception; the sorrel nag offered me a root, which he held (after their manner, as we shall describe in its proper place) between his hoof and pastern; I took it in my hand, and having smelled it, returned it to him again as civilly as I could. He brought out of the Yahoo's kennel a piece of ass's flesh, but it smelled so offensively that I turned from it with loathing; he then threw it to the Yahoo, by whom it was greedily devoured. He afterwards showed me a wisp of hay, and a fetlock full of oats; but I shook my head, to signify that neither of these were food for me. And indeed, I now apprehended that I must absolutely starve, if I did not get to some of my own species; for as to those filthy Yahoos, although there were few greater lovers of mankind, at that time, than myself, yet I confess I never saw any sensitive being so detestable on all accounts; and the more I came near them, the more hateful they grew, while I stayed in that country. This the master horse observed by my behavior, and therefore sent the Yahoo back to his kennel. He then put his forehoof to his mouth, at which I was much surprised, although he did it with ease, and with a motion that appeared perfectly natural; and made other signs to know what I would eat; but I could not return him such an answer as he was able to apprehend; and if he had understood me, I did not see how it was possible to contrive any way for finding myself nourishment. While we were thus engaged, I observed a cow passing by; whereupon I pointed to her, and expressed a desire to let me go and milk her. This had its effect; for he led me back into the house, and ordered a mare-servant to open a room, where a good store of milk lay in earthen and wooden vessels, after a very orderly and cleanly manner. She gave me a large bowl full, of which I drank very heartily, and found myself well refreshed.

About noon I saw coming towards the house a kind of vehicle, drawn like a sledge by four Yahoos. There was in it an old steed, who seemed to be of quality; he alighted with his hind feet forward, having by accident got a hurt in his left forefoot. He came to dine with our horse, who received him with great civility. They dined in the best room, and had oats boiled in milk for the second course, which the old horse eat warm, but the rest cold. Their mangers were placed circular in the middle of the room, and divided into several partitions, round which they sat on their haunches upon bosses of straw. In the middle was a large rack with angles answering to every partition of the manger. So that each horse and mare eat their own hay, and their own mash of oats and milk, with much decency and regularity. The behavior of the young colt and foal appeared very modest; and that of the master and mistress extremely cheerful and complaisant to their guest. The grey ordered me to stand by him; and much discourse passed between him and his friend concerning me, as I found by the stranger's often looking on me, and the frequent repetition of the word Yahoo.

I happened to wear my gloves; which the master grey observing, seemed perplexed; discovering signs of wonder what I had done to my forefeet; he put his hoof three or four times to them, as if he would signify, that I should reduce them to their former shape, which I presently did, pulling off both my gloves, and putting them into my pocket. This occasioned farther talk, and I saw the company was pleased with my behavior, whereof I soon found the good effects. I was ordered to speak the few words I understood; and while they were at dinner, the master taught me the names for oats, milk, fire, water, and some others which I could readily pronounce after him, having from my youth a great facility in learning languages.

When dinner was done, the master horse took me aside, and by signs and words made me understand the concern he was in that I had nothing to eat. Oats in their tongue are called *hlunnh*. This word I pronounced two or three times; for although I had refused them at first, yet upon second thoughts, I considered that I could contrive to make a kind of bread, which might be sufficient with milk to keep me alive, till I could make my escape to some other country, and to creatures of my own species. The horse immediately ordered a white mare-servant of his family to bring me a good quantity of oats in a sort of wooden tray. These I heated before the fire as well as I could, and rubbed them till the husks came off, which I made a shift to winnow from the grain; I ground and beat them between two stones, then took water, and made them into a paste or cake, which I toasted at the fire, and eat warm with milk. It was at first a very insipid diet, although common enough in many parts of Europe, but grew tolerable by time; and having been often reduced to hard fare in my life, this was not the first experiment I had made how easily nature is satisfied. And I cannot but observe that I never had one hour's sickness, while I staid in this island. It is true, I sometimes made a shift to catch a rabbit, or bird, by springes[7] made of Yahoos' hairs; and I often gathered wholesome herbs, which I boiled, or eat as salads with

7. Snares.

my bread; and now and then, for a rarity, I made a little butter, and drank the whey. I was at first at a great loss for salt; but custom soon reconciled the want of it; and I am confident that the frequent use of salt among us is an effect of luxury, and was first introduced only as a provocative to drink; except where it is necessary for preserving of flesh in long voyages, or in places remote from great markets. For we observe no animal to be fond of it but man;[8] and as to myself, when I left this country, it was a great while before I could endure the taste of it in anything that I eat.

This is enough to say upon the subject of my diet, wherewith other travelers fill their books, as if the readers were personally concerned whether we fare well or ill. However, it was necessary to mention this matter, lest the world should think it impossible that I could find sustenance for three years in such a country, and among such inhabitants.

When it grew towards evening, the master horse ordered a place for me to lodge in; it was but six yards from the house, and separated from the stable of the Yahoos. Here I got some straw, and covering myself with my own clothes, slept very sound. But I was in a short time better accommodated, as the reader shall know hereafter, when I come to treat more particularly about my way of living.

CHAPTER 3. *The Author studious to learn the language, the Houyhnhnm his master assists in teaching him. The language described. Several Houyhnhnms of quality come out of curiosity to see the Author. He gives his master a short account of his voyage.*

My principal endeavor was to learn the language, which my master (for so I shall henceforth call him) and his children, and every servant of his house were desirous to teach me. For they looked upon it as a prodigy, that a brute animal should discover such marks of a rational creature. I pointed to everything, and enquired the name of it, which I wrote down in my journal book when I was alone, and corrected my bad accent, by desiring those of the family to pronounce it often. In this employment, a sorrel nag, one of the under servants, was very ready to assist me.

In speaking, they pronounce through the nose and throat, and their language approaches nearest to the High Dutch or German, of any I know in Europe; but is much more graceful and significant. The Emperor Charles V made almost the same observation, when he said, that if he were to speak to his horse, it should be in High Dutch.[9]

The curiosity and impatience of my master were so great, that he spent many hours of his leisure to instruct me. He was convinced (as he afterwards told me) that I must be a Yahoo, but my teachableness, civility, and cleanliness astonished him; which were qualities altogether so

---

8. Gulliver is, of course, in error. Many animals require salt.

9. The emperor is supposed to have said that he would speak to his God in Spanish, to his mistress in Italian, and to his horse in German.

opposite to those animals. He was most perplexed about my clothes, reasoning sometimes with himself whether they were a part of my body; for I never pulled them off till the family were asleep, and got them on before they waked in the morning. My master was eager to learn from whence I came; how I acquired those appearances of reason, which I discovered in all my actions; and to know my story from my own mouth, which he hoped he should soon do by the great proficiency I made in learning and pronouncing their words and sentences. To help my memory, I formed all I learned into the English alphabet, and writ the words down with the translations. This last, after some time, I ventured to do in my master's presence. It cost me much trouble to explain to him what I was doing; for the inhabitants have not the least idea of books or literature.

In about ten weeks time I was able to understand most of his questions; and in three months could give him some tolerable answers. He was extremely curious to know from what part of the country I came, and how I was taught to imitate a rational creature; because the Yahoos (whom he saw I exactly resembled in my head, hands, and face, that were only visible) with some appearance of cunning, and the strongest disposition to mischief, were observed to be the most unteachable of all brutes. I answered that I came over the sea, from a far place, with many others of my own kind, in a great hollow vessel made of the bodies of trees; that my companions forced me to land on this coast, and then left me to shift for myself. It was with some difficulty, and by the help of many signs, that I brought him to understand me. He replied that I must needs be mistaken, or that I *said the thing which was not*. (For they have no word in their language to express lying or falsehood.) He knew it was impossible that there could be a country beyond the sea, or that a parcel of brutes could move a wooden vessel whither they pleased upon water. He was sure no Houyhnhnm alive could make such a vessel, or would trust Yahoos to manage it.

The word Houyhnhnm, in their tongue, signifies a Horse; and in its etymology, the Perfection of Nature. I told my master that I was at a loss for expression, but would improve as fast as I could; and hoped in a short time I should be able to tell him wonders; he was pleased to direct his own mare, his colt, and foal, and the servants of the family to take all opportunities of instructing me; and every day for two or three hours, he was at the same pains himself; several horses and mares of quality in the neighborhood came often to our house, upon the report spread of a wonderful Yahoo, that could speak like a Houyhnhnm, and seemed in his words and actions to discover some glimmerings of reason. These delighted to converse with me; they put many questions, and received such answers as I was able to return. By all which advantages, I made so great a progress, that in five months from my arrival, I understood whatever was spoke, and could express myself tolerably well.

The Houyhnhnms who came to visit my master, out of a design of seeing and talking with me, could hardly believe me to be a right Yahoo, because my body had a different covering from others of my kind. They were astonished to observe me without the usual hair or skin, except on my head, face, and hands; but I discovered that secret to my master, upon an accident, which happened about a fortnight before.

I have already told the reader, that every night when the family were gone to bed, it was my custom to strip and cover myself with my clothes; it happened one morning early, that my master sent for me, by the sorrel nag, who was his valet; when he came, I was fast asleep, my clothes fallen off on one side, and my shirt above my waist. I awaked at the noise he made, and observed him to deliver his message in some disorder; after which he went to my master, and in a great fright gave him a very confused account of what he had seen; this I presently discovered; for going as soon as I was dressed, to pay my attendance upon his honor, he asked me the meaning of what his servant had reported; that I was not the same thing when I slept as I appeared to be at other times; that his valet assured him, some part of me was white, some yellow, at least not so white, and some brown.

I had hitherto concealed the secret of my dress, in order to distinguish myself as much as possible, from that cursed race of Yahoos; but now I found it in vain to do so any longer. Besides, I considered that my clothes and shoes would soon wear out, which already were in a declining condition, and must be supplied by some contrivance from the hides of Yahoos, or other brutes; whereby the whole secret would be known. I therefore told my master, that in the country from whence I came, those of my kind always covered their bodies with the hairs of certain animals prepared by art, as well for decency, as to avoid inclemencies of air both hot and cold; of which, as to my own person I would give him immediate conviction, if he pleased to command me; only desiring his excuse, if I did not expose those parts that Nature taught us to conceal. He said, my discourse was all very strange, but especially the last part; for he could not understand why Nature should teach us to conceal what Nature had given. That neither himself nor family were ashamed of any parts of their bodies; but however I might do as I pleased. Whereupon, I first unbuttoned my coat, and pulled it off. I did the same with my waistcoat; I drew off my shoes, stockings, and breeches. I let my shirt down to my waist, and drew up the bottom, fastening it like a girdle about my middle to hide my nakedness.

My master observed the whole performance with great signs of curiosity and admiration. He took up all my clothes in his pastern, one piece after another, and examined them diligently; he then stroked my body very gently, and looked round me several times; after which he said, it was plain I must be a perfect Yahoo; but that I differed very much from the rest of my species, in the whiteness and smoothness of my skin, my want of hair in several parts of my body, the shape and shortness of my claws behind and before, and my affectation of walking continually on my two hinder feet. He desired to see no more; and gave me leave to put on my clothes again, for I was shuddering with cold.

I expressed my uneasiness at his giving me so often the appellation of Yahoo, an odious animal, for which I had so utter an hatred and contempt. I begged he would forbear applying that word to me, and take the same order in his family, and among his friends whom he suffered to see me. I requested likewise, that the secret of my having a false covering to my body might be known to none but himself, at least as long as my present clothing should last; for as to what the sorrel nag his valet had observed, his honor might command him to conceal it.

All this my master very graciously consented to; and thus the secret was kept till my clothes began to wear out, which I was forced to supply by several contrivances, that shall hereafter be mentioned. In the meantime, he desired I would go on with my utmost diligence to learn their language, because he was more astonished at my capacity for speech and reason, than at the figure of my body, whether it were covered or no; adding that he waited with some impatience to hear the wonders which I promised to tell him.

From thenceforward he doubled the pains he had been at to instruct me; he brought me into all company, and made them treat me with civility, because, as he told them privately, this would put me into good humor, and make me more diverting.

Every day when I waited on him, beside the trouble he was at in teaching, he would ask me several questions concerning myself, which I answered as well as I could; and by those means he had already received some general ideas, although very imperfect. It would be tedious to relate the several steps, by which I advanced to a more regular conversation, but the first account I gave of myself in any order and length was to this purpose:

That, I came from a very far country, as I already had attempted to tell him, with about fifty more of my own species; that we traveled upon the seas, in a great hollow vessel made of wood, and larger than his honor's house. I described the ship to him in the best terms I could; and explained by the help of my handkerchief displayed, how it was driven forward by the wind. That, upon a quarrel among us, I was set on shore on this coast, where I walked forward without knowing whither, till he delivered me from the persecution of those execrable Yahoos. He asked me who made the ship, and how it was possible that the Houyhnhnms of my country would leave it to the management of brutes? My answer was that I durst proceed no farther in my relation, unless he would give me his word and honor that he would not be offended; and then I would tell him the wonders I had so often promised. He agreed; and I went on by assuring him, that the ship was made by creatures like myself, who in all the countries I had traveled, as well as in my own, were the only governing, rational animals; and that upon my arrival hither, I was as much astonished to see the Houyhnhnms act like rational beings, as he or his friends could be in finding some marks of reason in a creature he was pleased to call a Yahoo; to which I owned my resemblance in every part, but could not account for their degenerate and brutal nature. I said farther, that if good fortune ever restored me to my native country, to relate my travels hither, as I resolved to do, everybody would believe that I *said the thing which was not*; that I invented the story out of my own head; and with all possible respect to himself, his family, and friends, and under his promise of not being offended, our countrymen would hardly think it probable, that a Houyhnhnm should be the presiding creature of a nation, and a Yahoo the brute.

CHAPTER 4. *The Houyhnhnms' notion of truth and falsehood. The author's discourse disapproved by his master. The author gives a more particular account of himself, and the accidents of his voyage.*

My master heard me with great appearances of uneasiness in his countenance; because *doubting* or *not believing* are so little known in this country, that the inhabitants cannot tell how to behave themselves under such circumstances. And I remember in frequent discourses with my master concerning the nature of manhood, in other parts of the world, having occasion to talk of *lying* and *false representation*, it was with much difficulty that he comprehended what I meant; although he had otherwise a most acute judgment. For he argued thus: that the use of speech was to make us understand one another, and to receive information of facts; now if anyone *said the thing which was not*, these ends were defeated; because I cannot properly be said to understand him; and I am so far from receiving information, that he leaves me worse than in ignorance; for I am led to believe a thing *black* when it is *white*, and *short* when it is *long*. And these were all the notions he had concerning the faculty of *lying*, so perfectly well understood, and so universally practiced among human creatures.

To return from this digression; when I asserted that the Yahoos were the only governing animals in my country, which my master said was altogether past his conception, he desired to know, whether we had Houyhnhnms among us, and what was their employment; I told him we had great numbers; that in summer they grazed in the fields, and in winter were kept in houses, with hay and oats, where Yahoo servants were employed to rub their skins smooth, comb their manes, pick their feet, serve them with food, and make their beds. "I understand you well," said my master; "it is now very plain from all you have spoken, that whatever share of reason the Yahoos pretend to, the Houyhnhnms are your masters; I heartily wish our Yahoos would be so tractable." I begged his honor would please to excuse me from proceeding any farther, because I was very certain that the account he expected from me would be highly displeasing. But he insisted in commanding me to let him know the best and the worst; I told him he should be obeyed. I owned that the Houyhnhnms among us, whom we called Horses, were the most generous[1] and comely animal we had; that they excelled in

_____

1. Noble.

strength and swiftness; and when they belonged to persons of quality, employed in traveling, racing, and drawing chariots, they were treated with much kindness and care, till they fell into diseases, or became foundered in the feet; but then they were sold, and used to all kind of drudgery till they died; after which their skins were stripped and sold for what they were worth, and their bodies left to be devoured by dogs and birds of prey. But the common race of horses had not so good fortune, being kept by farmers and carriers, and other mean people, who put them to greater labor, and feed them worse. I described as well as I could, our way of riding; the shape and use of a bridle, a saddle, a spur, and a whip; of harness and wheels. I added, that we fastened plates of a certain hard substance called iron at the bottom of their feet, to preserve their hoofs from being broken by the stony ways on which we often traveled.

My master, after some expressions of great indignation, wondered how we dared to venture upon a Houyhnhnm's back; for he was sure, that the weakest servant in his house would be able to shake off the strongest Yahoo; or by lying down, and rolling upon his back, squeeze the brute to death. I answered that our horses were trained up from three or four years old to the several uses we intended them for; that if any of them proved intolerably vicious, they were employed for carriages; that they were severely beaten while they were young for any mischievous tricks; that the males, designed for the common use of riding or draught, were generally castrated about two years after their birth, to take down their spirits, and make them more tame and gentle; that they were indeed sensible of rewards and punishments; but his honor would please to consider that they had not the least tincture of reason any more than the Yahoos in this country.

It put me to the pains of many circumlocutions to give my master a right idea of what I spoke; for their language doth not abound in variety of words, because their wants and passions are fewer than among us. But it is impossible to express his noble resentment at our savage treatment of the Houyhnhnm race; particularly after I had explained the manner and use of castrating horses among us, to hinder them from propagating their kind, and to render them more servile. He said, if it were possible there could be any country where Yahoos alone were endued with reason, they certainly must be the governing animal, because reason will in time always prevail against brutal strength. But, considering the frame of our bodies, and especially mine, he thought no creature of equal bulk was so ill-contrived for employing that reason in the common offices of life; whereupon he desired to know whether those among whom I lived resembled me or the Yahoos of his country. I assured him that I was as well shaped as most of my age; but the younger and the females were much more soft and tender, and the skins of the latter generally as white as milk. He said I differed indeed from other Yahoos, being much more cleanly, and not altogether so deformed; but in point of real advantage, he thought I differed for the worse. That my nails were of no use either to my fore or hinder feet; as to my forefeet, he could not properly call them by that name, for he never observed me to walk upon them; that they were too soft to bear the ground; that I generally went with them uncovered, neither was the covering I sometimes wore on them of the same shape, or so strong as that on my feet behind. That I could not walk with any security; for if either of my hinder feet slipped, I must inevitably fall. He then began to find fault with other parts of my body; the flatness of my face, the prominence of my nose, my eyes placed directly in front, so that I could not look on either side without turning my head; that I was not able to feed myself without lifting one of my forefeet to my mouth; and therefore nature had placed those joints to answer that necessity. He knew not what could be the use of those several clefts and divisions in my feet behind; that these were too soft to bear the hardness and sharpness of stones without a covering made from the skin of some other brute; that my whole body wanted a fence against heat and cold, which I was forced to put on and off every day with tediousness and trouble. And lastly, that he observed every animal in his country naturally to abhor the Yahoos, whom the weaker avoided, and the stronger drove from them. So that supposing us to have the gift of reason, he could not see how it were possible to cure that natural antipathy which every creature discovered against us; nor consequently, how we could tame and render them serviceable. However, he would (as he said) debate the matter no farther, because he was more desirous to know my own story, the country where I was born, and the several actions and events of my life before I came hither.

I assured him how extremely desirous I was that he should be satisfied in every point; but I doubted much whether it would be possible for me to explain myself on several subjects whereof his honor could have no conception, because I saw nothing in his country to which I could resemble them. That however, I would do my best, and strive to express myself by similitudes, humbly desiring his assistance when I wanted proper words; which he was pleased to promise me.

I said, my birth was of honest parents, in an island called England, which was remote from this country, as many days journey as the strongest of his honor's servants could travel in the annual course of the sun. That I was bred a surgeon, whose trade it is to cure wounds and hurts in the body, got by accident or violence. That my country was governed by a female man, whom we called a queen. That I left it to get riches, whereby I might maintain myself and family when I should return. That in my last voyage, I was Commander of the ship and had about fifty Yahoos under me, many of which died at sea, and I was forced to supply them by others picked out from several nations. That our ship was twice in danger of being sunk; the first time by a great storm, and the second, by striking against a rock. Here my master interposed, by asking me, how I could persuade strangers out of different countries to venture with me, after the losses I had sustained, and the hazards I had run. I said, they were fellows of desperate fortunes, forced to fly from the places of their birth, on account of their poverty or their crimes. Some were undone by lawsuits; others spent all they had in drinking, whoring, and gaming; others fled for treason; many for murder, theft, poisoning, robbery, perjury, forgery, coining false money; for committing rapes or sodomy; for flying from their colors, or deserting to the enemy; and most of them had broken prison. None of these durst return to their native countries for fear of being hanged, or of starving in a jail; and therefore were under a necessity of seeking a livelihood in other places.

During this discourse, my master was pleased often to interrupt me. I had made use of many circumlocutions in describing to him the nature of the several crimes, for which most of our crew had been forced to fly their country. This labor took up several days conversation before he was able to comprehend me. He was wholly at a loss to know what could be the use or necessity of practicing those vices. To clear up which I endeavored to give him some ideas of the desire of power and riches; of the terrible effects of lust, intemperance, malice, and envy. All this I was forced to define and describe by putting of cases, and making suppositions. After which, like one whose imagination was struck with something never seen or heard of before, he would lift up his eyes with amazement and indignation. Power, government, war, law, punishment, and a thousand other things had no terms, wherein that language could express them; which made the difficulty almost insuperable to give my master any conception of what I meant; but being of an excellent understanding, much improved by contemplation and converse, he at last arrived at a competent knowledge of what human nature in our parts of the world is capable to perform; and desired I would give him some particular account of that land, which we call Europe, especially, of my own country.

CHAPTER 5. *The Author, at his master's commands, informs him of the state of England. The causes of war among the princes of Europe. The Author begins to explain the English Constitution.*

The reader may please to observe that the following extract of many conversations I had with my master contains a summary of the most material points, which were discoursed at several times for above two years; his honor often desiring fuller satisfaction as I farther improved in the Houyhnhnm tongue. I laid before him, as well as I could, the whole state of Europe; I discoursed of trade and manufactures, of arts and sciences; and the answers I gave to all the questions he made, as they arose upon several subjects, were a fund of conversation not to be exhausted. But I shall here only set down the substance of what passed between us concerning my own country, reducing it into order as well as I can, without any regard to time or other circumstances, while I strictly adhere to truth. My only concern is that I shall hardly be able to do justice to my master's arguments and expressions; which must needs suffer by my want of capacity, as well as by a translation into our barbarous English.

In obedience therefore to his honor's commands, I related to him the Revolution under the Prince of Orange; the long war with France entered into by the said Prince, and renewed by his successor the present queen; wherein the greatest powers of Christendom were engaged, and which still continued. I computed at his request, that about a million of Yahoos might have been killed in the whole progress of it; and perhaps a hundred or more cities taken, and five times as many ships burned or sunk.[2]

He asked me what were the usual causes or motives that made one country to go to war with another. I answered, they were innumerable; but I should only mention a few of the chief. Sometimes the ambition of princes, who never think they have land or people enough to govern; sometimes the corruption of ministers, who engage their master in a war in order to stifle or divert the clamor of the subjects against their evil administration. Difference in opinions hath cost many millions of lives; for instance, whether flesh be bread, or bread be flesh; whether the juice of a certain berry be blood or wine; whether whistling be a vice or a virtue; whether it be better to kiss a post, or throw it into the fire; what is the best color for a coat, whether black, white, red, or grey; and whether it should be long or short, narrow or wide, dirty or clean;[3] with many more. Neither are any wars so furious and bloody, or of so long continuance, as those occasioned by difference in opinion, especially if it be in things indifferent.[4]

Sometimes the quarrel between two princes is to decide which of them shall dispossess a third of his dominions, where neither of them pretend to any right. Sometimes one prince quarreleth with another, for fear the other should quarrel with him. Sometimes a war is entered upon, because the enemy is too strong, and sometimes because he is too weak. Sometimes our neighbors want the things which we have, or have the things which we want; and we both fight, till they take ours or give us theirs. It is a very justifiable cause of war to invade a country after the people have been wasted by famine, destroyed by pestilence, or embroiled by factions amongst themselves. It is justifiable to enter into a war against our nearest ally, when one of his towns lies convenient for us, or a territory of land, that would render our dominions round and compact. If a prince send forces into a nation, where the people are poor and ignorant, he may lawfully put half of them to death, and make slaves of the rest, in order to civilize and reduce them from their barbarous way of living. It is a very kingly, honorable, and frequent practice, when one prince desires the assistance of another to secure him against an invasion, that the assistant, when he hath driven out the invader, should seize on the dominions himself, and kill, imprison, or banish the prince he came to relieve. Alliance by blood or marriage is a sufficient cause of war between princes; and the nearer the kindred is, the greater is their disposition to

2. Gulliver relates recent English history: the Glorious Revolution of 1688 and the War of Spanish Succession (1703–13). He greatly exaggerates the casualties in the war.
3. Gulliver refers to the religious controversies of the Reformation and Counter Reformation: the doctrine of transubstantiation, the use of music in church services, the veneration of the crucifix, and the wearing of priestly vestments.
4. Of little consequence.

quarrel; poor nations are hungry, and rich nations are proud; and pride and hunger will ever be at variance. For these reasons, the trade of a soldier is held the most honorable of all others: because a soldier is a Yahoo hired to kill in cold blood as many of his own species, who have never offended him, as possibly he can.

There is likewise a kind of beggarly princes in Europe, not able to make war by themselves, who hire out their troops to richer nations for so much a day to each man; of which they keep three fourths to themselves, and it is the best part of their maintenance; such are those in many northern parts of Europe.[5]

"What you have told me," said my master, "upon the subject of war, doth indeed discover most admirably the effects of that reason you pretend to; however, it is happy that the shame is greater than the danger; and that Nature hath left you utterly uncapable of doing much mischief; for your mouths lying flat with your faces, you can hardly bite each other to any purpose, unless by consent. Then, as to the claws upon your feet before and behind, they are so short and tender, that one of our Yahoos would drive a dozen of yours before him. And therefore in recounting the numbers of those who have been killed in battle, I cannot but think that you have *said the thing which is not.*"

I could not forbear shaking my head and smiling a little at his ignorance. And, being no stranger to the art of war, I gave him a description of cannons, culverins, muskets, carabines, pistols, bullets, powder, swords, bayonets, battles, sieges, retreats, attacks, undermines, countermines, bombardments, sea fights; ships sunk with a thousand men; twenty thousand killed on each side; dying groans, limbs flying in the air; smoke, noise, confusion, trampling to death under horses' feet; flight, pursuit, victory; fields strewed with carcasses left for food to dogs, and wolves, and birds of prey; plundering, stripping, ravishing, burning, and destroying. And, to set forth the valor of my own dear countrymen, I assured him that I had seen them blow up a hundred enemies at once in a siege, and as many in a ship; and beheld the dead bodies drop down in pieces from the clouds, to the great diversion of all the spectators.

I was going on to more particulars, when my master commanded me silence. He said, whoever understood the nature of Yahoos might easily believe it possible for so vile an animal, to be capable of every action I had named, if their strength and cunning equaled their malice. But, as my discourse had increased his abhorrence of the whole species, so he found it gave him a disturbance in his mind, to which he was wholly a stranger before. He thought his ears being used to such abominable words, might by degrees admit them with less detestation. That, although he hated the Yahoos of this country, yet he no more blamed them for their odious qualities, than he did a *gnnayh* (a bird of prey) for its cruelty, or a sharp stone for cutting his hoof. But, when a creature pretending to reason could be capable of such enormities, he dreaded lest the corrup-

5. A satiric glance at George I, who, as Elector of Hanover, had dealt in this trade.

tion of that faculty might be worse than brutality itself. He seemed therefore confident, that instead of reason, we were only possessed of some quality fitted to increase our natural vices; as the reflection from a troubled stream returns the image of an ill-shapen body, not only larger, but more distorted.

He added that he had heard too much upon the subject of war, both in this and some former discourses. There was another point which a little perplexed him at present. I had said that some of our crew left their country on account of being ruined by law: that I had already explained the meaning of the word; but he was at a loss how it should come to pass, that the law which was intended for every man's preservation, should be any man's ruin. Therefore he desired to be farther satisfied what I meant by law, and the dispensers thereof, according to the present practice in my own country; because he thought Nature and Reason were sufficient guides for a reasonable animal, as we pretended to be, in showing us what we ought to do, and what to avoid.

I assured his honor that law was a science wherein I had not much conversed, further than by employing advocates, in vain, upon some injustices that had been done me. However, I would give him all the satisfaction I was able.

I said there was a society of men among us, bred up from their youth in the art of proving by words multiplied for the purpose, that white is black, and black is white, according as they are paid. To this society all the rest of the people are slaves.

"For example. If my neighbor hath a mind to my cow, he hires a lawyer to prove that he ought to have my cow from me. I must then hire another to defend my right; it being against all rules of law that any man should be allowed to speak for himself. Now in this case, I who am the true owner lie under two great disadvantages. First, my lawyer being practiced almost from his cradle in defending falsehood is quite out of his element when he would be an advocate for justice, which as an office unnatural, he always attempts with great awkwardness, if not with ill-will. The second disadvantage is that my lawyer must proceed with great caution, or else he will be reprimanded by the judges, and abhorred by his brethren, as one who would lessen the practice of the law. And therefore I have but two methods to preserve my cow. The first is to gain over my adversary's lawyer with a double fee; who will then betray his client, by insinuating that he hath justice on his side. The second way is for my lawyer to make my cause appear as unjust as he can; by allowing the cow to belong to my adversary; and this if it be skillfully done, will certainly bespeak the favor of the bench.

"Now, your honor is to know that these judges are persons appointed to decide all controversies of property, as well as for the trial of criminals; and picked out from the most dextrous lawyers who are grown old or lazy; and having been biased all their lives against truth and equity, lie under such a fatal necessity of favoring fraud, perjury, and oppression, that I have known some of them to have refused a large bribe from the side where justice lay, rather than injure the faculty,[6] by doing anything unbecoming their nature or their office.

"It is a maxim among these lawyers, that whatever hath been done before may legally be done again; and therefore they take special care to record all the decisions formerly made against common justice and the general reason of mankind. These, under the name of *precedents*, they produce as authorities to justify the most iniquitous opinions; and the judges never fail of directing accordingly.

"In pleading, they studiously avoid entering into the merits of the cause; but are loud, violent, and tedious in dwelling upon all circumstances which are not to the purpose. For instance, in the case already mentioned, they never desire to know what claim or title my adversary hath to my cow; but whether the said cow were red or black; her horns long or short; whether the field I graze her in be round or square; whether she were milked at home or abroad; what diseases she is subject to, and the like. After which they consult precedents, adjourn the cause, from time to time, and in ten, twenty, or thirty years come to an issue.

"It is likewise to be observed, that this society hath a peculiar cant and jargon of their own, that no other mortal can understand, and wherein all their laws are written, which they take special care to multiply; whereby they have wholly confounded the very essence of truth and falsehood, of right and wrong; so that it will take thirty years to decide whether the field, left me by my ancestors for six generations, belong to me, or to a stranger three hundred miles off.

"In the trial of persons accused for crimes against the state, the method is much more short and commendable: the judge first sends to sound the disposition of those in power; after which he can easily hang or save the criminal, strictly preserving all the forms of law."

Here my master interposing said it was a pity that creatures endowed with such prodigious abilities of mind as these lawyers, by the description I gave of them must certainly be, were not rather encouraged to be instructors of others in wisdom and knowledge. In answer to which, I assured his honor that in all points out of their own trade, they were usually the most ignorant and stupid generation among us, the most despicable in common conversation, avowed enemies to all knowledge and learning; and equally disposed to pervert the general reason of mankind, in every other subject of discourse as in that of their own profession.

CHAPTER 6. *A continuation of the state of England, under Queen Anne. The character of a first minister in the courts of Europe.*

My master was yet wholly at a loss to understand what motives could incite this race of lawyers to perplex, disquiet, and weary themselves by engaging in a confederacy of injustice, merely for the sake of injuring

6. Profession.

their fellow animals; neither could he comprehend what I meant in saying they did it for hire. Whereupon I was at much pains to describe to him the use of money, the materials it was made of, and the value of the metals; that when a Yahoo had got a great store of his precious substance, he was able to purchase whatever he had a mind to; the finest clothing, the noblest houses, great tracts of land, the most costly meats and drinks; and have his choice of the most beautiful females. Therefore since money alone was able to perform all these feats, our Yahoos thought they could never have enough of it to spend or to save, as they found themselves inclined from their natural bent either to profusion or avarice. That the rich man enjoyed the fruit of the poor man's labor, and the latter were a thousand to one in proportion to the former. That the bulk of our people was forced to live miserably, by laboring every day for small wages to make a few live plentifully. I enlarged myself much on these and many other particulars to the same purpose, but his honor was still to seek,[7] for he went upon a supposition that all animals had a title to their share in the productions of the earth; and especially those who presided over the rest. Therefore he desired I would let him know what these costly meats were, and how any of us happened to want[8] them. Whereupon I enumerated as many sorts as came into my head, with the various methods of dressing them, which could not be done without sending vessels by sea to every part of the world, as well for liquors to drink, as for sauces, and innumerable other conveniencies. I assured him, that this whole globe of earth must be at least three times gone round, before one of our better female Yahoos could get her breakfast, or a cup to put it in. He said, "That must needs be a miserable country which cannot furnish food for its own inhabitants." But what he chiefly wondered at, was how such vast tracts of ground as I described, should be wholly without fresh water, and the people put to the necessity of sending over the sea for drink. I replied that England (the dear place of my nativity) was computed to produce three times the quantity of food, more than its inhabitants are able to consume, as well as liquors extracted from grain, or pressed out of the fruit of certain trees, which made excellent drink; and the same proportion in every other convenience of life. But, in order to feed the luxury and intemperance of the males, and the vanity of the females, we sent away the greatest part of our necessary things to other countries, from whence in return we brought the materials of diseases, folly, and vice, to spend among ourselves. Hence it follows of necessity, that vast numbers of our people are compelled to seek their livelihood by begging, robbing, stealing, cheating, pimping, forswearing, flattering, suborning, forging, gaming, lying, fawning, hectoring, voting, scribbling, star gazing, poisoning, whoring, canting, libeling, freethinking, and the like occupations; every one of which terms, I was at much pains to make him understand.

That, wine was not imported among us from foreign countries, to

---

7. Still did not understand.   8. Lack.

supply the want of water or other drinks, but because it was a sort of liquid which made us merry, by putting us out of our senses; diverted all melancholy thoughts, begat wild extravagant imaginations in the brain, raised our hopes, and banished our fears; suspended every office of reason for a time, and deprived us of the use of our limbs, until we fell into a profound sleep; although it must be confessed, that we always awaked sick and dispirited; and that the use of this liquor filled us with diseases, which made our lives uncomfortable and short.

But beside all this, the bulk of our people supported themselves by furnishing the necessities or conveniencies of life to the rich, and to each other. For instance, when I am at home and dressed as I ought to be, I carry on my body the workmanship of an hundred tradesmen; the building and furniture of my house employ as many more; and five times the number to adorn my wife.

I was going on to tell him of another sort of people, who get their livelihood by attending the sick; having upon some occasions informed his honor that many of my crew had died of diseases. But here it was with the utmost difficulty that I brought him to apprehend what I meant. He could easily conceive that a Houyhnhnm grew weak and heavy a few days before his death; or by some accident might hurt a limb. But that nature, who worketh all things to perfection, should suffer any pains to breed in our bodies, he thought impossible; and desired to know the reason of so unaccountable an evil. I told him, we fed on a thousand things which operated contrary to each other; that we eat when we were not hungry, and drank without the provocation of thirst; that we sat whole nights drinking strong liquors without eating a bit, which disposed us to sloth, inflamed our bodies, and precipitated or prevented digestion. That, prostitute female Yahoos acquired a certain malady, which bred rottenness in the bones of those who fell into their embraces; that this and many other diseases were propagated from father to son; so that great numbers come into the world with complicated maladies upon them; that it would be endless to give him a catalogue of all diseases incident to human bodies; for they could not be fewer than five or six hundred, spread over every limb, and joint; in short, every part, external and intestine, having diseases appropriated to each. To remedy which, there was a sort of people bred up among us, in the profession or pretense of curing the sick. And because I had some skill in the faculty, I would in gratitude to his honor let him know the whole mystery and method by which they proceed.

Their fundamental is that all diseases arise from repletion; from whence they conclude, that a great evacuation of the body is necessary, either through the natural passage, or upwards at the mouth. Their next business is, from herbs, minerals, gums, oils, shells, salts, juices, seaweed, excrements, barks of trees, serpents, toads, frogs, spiders, dead men's flesh and bones, birds, beasts and fishes, to form a composition for smell and taste the most abominable, nauseous, and detestable, that they can possibly contrive, which the stomach immediately rejects with loathing, and this they call a vomit. Or else from the same storehouse, with some other poisonous additions, they command us to take in at the orifice above or below (just as the physician then happens to be disposed) a medicine equally annoying and disgustful to the bowels; which relaxing the belly, drives down all before it; and this they call a purge, or a clyster. For nature (as the physicians allege) having intended the superior anterior orifice only for the intromission of solids and liquids, and the inferior posterior for ejection, these artists ingeniously considering that in all diseases nature is forced out of her seat; therefore to replace her in it, the body must be treated in a manner directly contrary, by interchanging the use of each orifice; forcing solids and liquids in at the anus, and making evacuations at the mouth.

But, besides real diseases, we are subject to many that are only imaginary, for which the physicians have invented imaginary cures; these have their several names, and so have the drugs that are proper for them; and with these our female Yahoos are always infested.

One great excellency in this tribe is their skill at prognostics, wherein they seldom fail; their predictions in real diseases, when they rise to any degree of malignity, generally portending death, which is always in their power, when recovery is not, and therefore, upon any unexpected signs of amendment, after they have pronounced their sentence, rather than be accused as false prophets, they know how to approve[9] their sagacity to the world by a seasonable dose.

They are likewise of special use to husbands and wives, who are grown weary of their mates; to eldest sons, to great ministers of state, and often to princes.

I had formerly upon occasion discoursed with my master upon the nature of government in general, and particularly of our own excellent constitution, deservedly the wonder and envy of the whole world. But having here accidently mentioned a minister of state, he commanded me some time after to inform him what species of Yahoo I particularly meant by that appellation.

I told him that a first or chief minister of state, whom I intended to describe, was a creature wholly exempt from joy and grief, love and hatred, pity and anger; at least makes use of no other passions but a violent desire of wealth, power, and titles; that he applies his words to all uses, except to the indication of his mind; that he never tells a truth, but with an intent that you should take it for a lie; nor a lie, but with a design that you should take it for a truth; that those he speaks worst of behind their backs are in the surest way to preferment; and whenever he begins to praise you to others or to yourself, you are from that day forlorn. The worst mark you can receive is a promise, especially when it is confirmed with an oath; after which every wise man retires, and gives over all hopes.

There are three methods by which a man may rise to be chief minis-

9. Prove.

ter: the first is by knowing how with prudence to dispose of a wife, a daughter, or a sister; the second, by betraying or undermining his predecessor; and the third is by a furious zeal in public assemblies against the corruptions of the court. But a wise prince would rather choose to employ those who practice the last of these methods; because such zealots prove always the most obsequious and subservient to the will and passions of their master. That, these ministers having all employments at their disposal, preserve themselves in power by bribing the majority of a senate or great council; and at last by an expedient called an Act of Indemnity[1] (whereof I described the nature to him) they secure themselves from after reckonings, and retire from the public, laden with the spoils of the nation.

The palace of a chief minister is a seminary to breed up others in his own trade; the pages, lackies, and porters, by imitating their master, become ministers of state in their several districts, and learn to excel in the three principal ingredients, of insolence, lying, and bribery. Accordingly, they have a subaltern court paid to them by persons of the best rank; and sometimes by the force of dexterity and impudence, arrive through several gradations to be successors to their lord.

He is usually governed by a decayed wench, or favorite footman, who are the tunnels through which all graces are conveyed, and may properly be called, in the last resort, the governors of the kingdom.

One day, my master, having heard me mention the nobility of my country, was pleased to make me a compliment which I could not pretend to deserve: that, he was sure, I must have been born of some noble family, because I far exceeded in shape, color, and cleanliness, all the Yahoos of his nation, although I seemed to fail in strength, and agility, which must be imputed to my different way of living from those other brutes; and besides, I was not only endowed with the faculty of speech, but likewise with some rudiments of reason, to a degree, that with all his acquaintance I passed for a prodigy.

He made me observe, that among the Houyhnhnms, the white, the sorrel, and the iron grey were not so exactly shaped as the bay, the dapple grey, and the black; nor born with equal talents of mind, or a capacity to improve them; and therefore continued always in the condition of servants, without ever aspiring to match out of their own race, which in that country would be reckoned monstrous and unnatural.

I made his honor my most humble acknowledgments for the good opinion he was pleased to conceive of me; but assured him at the same time, that my birth was of the lower sort, having been born of plain, honest parents, who were just able to give me a tolerable education; that, nobility among us was altogether a different thing from the idea he had of it; that, our young noblemen are bred from their childhood in idleness and luxury; that, as soon as years will permit, they consume their vigor, and contract odious diseases among lewd females; and when their for-

1. An act passed at each session of Parliament to protect ministers of state who in good faith might have acted illegally.

tunes are almost ruined, they marry some woman of mean birth, disagreeable person, and unsound constitution, merely for the sake of money, whom they hate and despise. That, the productions of such marriages are generally scrofulous, rickety or deformed children; by which means the family seldom continues above three generations, unless the wife take care to provide a healthy father among her neighbors, or domestics, in order to improve and continue the breed. That a weak diseased body, a meager countenance, and sallow complexion are the true marks of noble blood; and a healthy robust appearance is so disgraceful in a man of quality, that the world concludes his real father to have been a groom or a coachman. The imperfections of his mind run parallel with those of his body; being a composition of spleen, dullness, ignorance, caprice, sensuality, and pride.

Without the consent of this illustrious body, no law can be enacted, repealed, or altered, and these nobles have likewise the decision of all our possessions without appeal.

CHAPTER 7. *The Author's great love of his native country. His master's observations upon the constitution and administration of England, as described by the Author, with parallel cases and comparisons. His master's observations upon human nature.*

The reader may be disposed to wonder how I could prevail on myself to give so free a representation of my own species, among a race of mortals who were already too apt to conceive the vilest opinion of humankind, from that entire congruity betwixt me and their Yahoos. But I must freely confess that the many virtues of those excellent quadrupeds placed in opposite view to human corruptions had so far opened my eyes, and enlarged my understanding, that I began to view the actions and passions of man in a very different light; and to think the honor of my own kind not worth managing;[2] which, besides, it was impossible for me to do before a person of so acute a judgment as my master, who daily convinced me of a thousand faults in myself, whereof I had not the least perception before, and which with us would never be numbered even among human infirmities. I had likewise learned from his example an utter detestation of all falsehood or disguise; and truth appeared so amiable to me, that I determined upon sacrificing everything to it.

Let me deal so candidly with the reader as to confess that there was yet a much stronger motive for the freedom I took in my representation of things. I had not been a year in this country, before I contracted such a love and veneration for the inhabitants, that I entered on a firm resolution never to return to humankind, but to pass the rest of my life among these admirable Houyhnhnms in the contemplation and practice of every virtue; where I could have no example or incitement to vice. But it was decreed by fortune, my perpetual enemy, that so great a felic-

2. Taking care of.

ity should not fall to my share. However, it is now some comfort to reflect that in what I said of my countrymen, I extenuated their faults as much as I durst before so strict an examiner; and upon every article, gave as favorable a turn as the matter would bear. For, indeed, who is there alive that will not be swayed by his bias and partiality to the place of his birth?

I have related the substance of several conversations I had with my master, during the greatest part of the time I had the honor to be in his service; but have indeed for brevity sake omitted much more than is here set down.

When I had answered all his questions, and his curiosity seemed to be fully satisfied; he sent for me one morning early, and commanding me to sit down at some distance (an honor which he had never before conferred upon me), he said he had been very seriously considering my whole story, as far as it related both to myself and my country; that, he looked upon us as a sort of animals to whose share, by what accident he could not conjecture, some small pittance of reason had fallen, whereof we made no other use than by its assistance to aggravate our natural corruptions, and to acquire new ones which nature had not given us. That we disarmed ourselves of the few abilities she had bestowed; had been very successful in multiplying our original wants, and seemed to spend our whole lives in vain endeavors to supply them by our own inventions. That, as to myself, it was manifest I had neither the strength or agility of a common Yahoo; that I walked infirmly on my hinder feet; had found out a contrivance to make my claws of no use or defense, and to remove the hair from my chin, which was intended as a shelter from the sun and the weather. Lastly, that I could neither run with speed, nor climb trees like my brethren (as he called them) the Yahoos in this country.

That our institutions of government and law were plainly owing to our gross defects in reason, and by consequence, in virtue; because reason alone is sufficient to govern a rational creature; which was therefore a character we had no pretense to challenge, even from the account I had given of my own people; although he manifestly perceived, that in order to favor them, I had concealed many particulars, and often *said the thing which was not*.

He was the more confirmed in this opinion, because he observed that I agreed in every feature of my body with other Yahoos, except where it was to my real disadvantage in point of strength, speed, and activity, the shortness of my claws, and some other particulars where Nature had no part; so, from the representation I had given him of our lives, our manners, and our actions, he found as near a resemblance in the disposition of our minds. He said the Yahoos were known to hate one another more than they did any different species of animals; and the reason usually assigned was the odiousness of their own shapes, which all could see in the rest, but not in themselves. He had therefore begun to think it not unwise in us to cover our bodies, and by that invention, conceal many of our deformities from each other, which would else be hardly support-able. But he now found he had been mistaken; and that the dissentions of those brutes in his country were owing to the same cause with ours, as I had described them. For, if (said he) you throw among five Yahoos as much food as would be sufficient for fifty, they will instead of eating peaceably, fall together by the ears, each single one impatient to have all to itself; and therefore a servant was usually employed to stand by while they were feeding abroad, and those kept at home were tied at a distance from each other. That, if a cow died of age or accident, before a Houyhnhnm could secure it for his own Yahoos, those in the neigh-borhood would come in herds to seize it, and then would ensue such a battle as I had described, with terrible wounds made by their claws on both sides, although they seldom were able to kill one another, for want of such convenient instruments of death as we had invented. At other times the like battles have been fought between the Yahoos of several neighborhoods without any visible cause; those of one district watching all opportunities to surprise the next before they are prepared. But if they find their project hath miscarried, they return home, and for want of enemies, engage in what I call a civil war among themselves.

That, in some fields of his country, there are certain shining stones of several colors, whereof the Yahoos are violently fond; and when part of these stones are fixed in the earth, as it sometimes happeneth, they will dig with their claws for whole days to get them out, and carry them away, and hide them by heaps in their kennels; but still looking round with great caution, for fear their comrades should find out their treasure. My master said he could never discover the reason of this unnatural appetite, or how these stones could be of any use to a Yahoo; but now he believed it might proceed from the same principle of avarice, which I had ascribed to mankind. That he had once, by way of experiment, privately removed a heap of these stones from the place where one of his Yahoos had buried it, whereupon, the sordid animal missing his treas-ure, by his loud lamenting brought the whole herd to the place, there miserably howled, then fell to biting and tearing the rest; began to pine away, would neither eat nor sleep, nor work, till he ordered a servant privately to convey the stones into the same hole, and hide them as before; which when his Yahoo had found, he presently recovered his spirits and good humor; but took care to remove them to a better hiding place; and hath ever since been a very serviceable brute.

My master farther assured me, which I also observed myself, that in the fields where these shining stones abound, the fiercest and most fre-quent battles are fought, occasioned by perpetual inroads of the neigh-boring Yahoos.

He said it was common when two Yahoos discovered such a stone in a field, and were contending which of them should be the proprietor, a third would take the advantage, and carry it away from them both; which my master would needs contend to have some resemblance with our suits at law; wherein I thought it for our credit not to undeceive him;

since the decision he mentioned was much more equitable than many decrees among us; because the plaintiff and defendant there lost nothing beside the stone they contended for; whereas our courts of equity would never have dismissed the cause while either of them had anything left.

My master continuing his discourse said there was nothing that rendered the Yahoos more odious, than their undistinguished appetite to devour everything that came in their way, whether herbs, roots, berries, corrupted flesh of animals, or all mingled together; and it was peculiar in their temper, that they were fonder of what they could get by rapine or stealth at a greater distance, than much better food provided for them at home. If their prey held out, they would eat till they were ready to burst, after which nature had pointed out to them a certain root that gave them a general evacuation.

There was also another kind of root very juicy, but something rare and difficult to be found, which the Yahoos sought for with much eagerness, and would suck it with great delight; it produced the same effects that wine hath upon us. It would make them sometimes hug, and sometimes tear one another; they would howl and grin, and chatter, and reel, and tumble, and then fall asleep in the mud.

I did indeed observe that the Yahoos were the only animals in this country subject to any diseases; which however, were much fewer than horses have among us, and contracted not by any ill treatment they meet with, but by the nastiness and greediness of that sordid brute. Neither has their language any more than a general appellation for those maladies; which is borrowed from the name of the beast, and called *Hnea Yahoo*, or the Yahoo's Evil; and the cure prescribed is a mixture of their own dung and urine, forcibly put down the Yahoo's throat. This I have since often known to have been taken with success, and do here freely recommend it to my countrymen, for the public good, as an admirable specific against all diseases produced by repletion.

As to learning, government, arts, manufactures, and the like, my master confessed he could find little or no resemblance between the Yahoos of that country and those in ours. For he only meant to observe what parity there was in our natures. He had heard indeed some curious Houyhnhnms observe that in most herds there was a sort of ruling Yahoo (as among us there is generally some leading or principal stag in a park) who was always more deformed in body, and mischievous in disposition, than any of the rest. That this leader had usually a favorite as like himself as he could get, whose employment was to lick his master's feet and posteriors, and drive the female Yahoos to his kennel; for which he was now and then rewarded with a piece of ass's flesh. This favorite is hated by the whole herd; and therefore to protect himself, keeps always near the person of his leader. He usually continues in office till a worse can be found; but the very moment he is discarded, his successor, at the head of all the Yahoos in that district, young and old, male and female, come in a body, and discharge their excrements upon him from head to foot.

But how far this might be applicable to our courts and favorites, and ministers of state, my master said I could best determine.

I durst make no return to this malicious insinuation, which debased human understanding below the sagacity of a common hound, who hath judgment enough to distinguish and follow the cry of the ablest dog in the pack, without being ever mistaken.

My master told me there were some qualities remarkable in the Yahoos, which he had not observed me to mention, or at least very slightly, in the accounts I had given him of humankind. He said, those animals, like other brutes, had their females in common; but in this they differed, that the she-Yahoo would admit the male while she was pregnant; and that the hes would quarrel and fight with the females as fiercely as with each other. Both which practices were such degrees of infamous brutality, that no other sensitive creature ever arrived at.

Another thing he wondered at in the Yahoos was their strange disposition to nastiness and dirt; whereas there appears to be a natural love of cleanliness in all other animals. As to the two former accusations, I was glad to let them pass without any reply, because I had not a word to offer upon them in defense of my species, which otherwise I certainly had done from my own inclinations. But I could have easily vindicated humankind from the imputation of singularity upon the last article, if there had been any swine in that country (as unluckily for me there were not) which although it may be a sweeter quadruped than a Yahoo, cannot I humbly conceive in justice pretend to more cleanliness; and so his honor himself must have owned, if he had seen their filthy way of feeding, and their custom of wallowing and sleeping in the mud.

My master likewise mentioned another quality, which his servants had discovered in several Yahoos, and to him was wholly unaccountable. He said, a fancy would sometimes take a Yahoo, to retire into a corner, to lie down and howl, and groan, and spurn away all that came near him, although he were young and fat, and wanted neither food nor water; nor did the servants imagine what could possibly ail him. And the only remedy they found was to set him to hard work, after which he would infallibly come to himself. To this I was silent out of partiality to my own kind; yet here I could plainly discover the true seeds of spleen,[3] which only seizeth on the lazy, the luxurious, and the rich; who, if they were forced to undergo the same regimen, I would undertake for the cure.

His Honor had farther observed, that a female Yahoo would often stand behind a bank or a bush, to gaze on the young males passing by, and then appear, and hide, using many antic gestures and grimaces; at which time it was observed, that she had a most offensive smell; and when any of the males advanced, would slowly retire, looking back, and with a counterfeit show of fear, run off into some convenient place where she knew the male would follow her.

3. Hypochondria.

At other times, if a female stranger came among them, three or four of her own sex would get about her, and stare and chatter, and grin, and smell her all over; and then turn off with gestures that seemed to express contempt and disdain.

Perhaps my master might refine a little in these speculations, which he had drawn from what he observed himself, or had been told by others; however, I could not reflect without some amazement, and much sorrow, that the rudiments of lewdness, coquetry, censure, and scandal, should have place by instinct in womankind.

I expected every moment that my master would accuse the Yahoos of those unnatural appetites in both sexes, so common among us. But Nature it seems hath not been so expert a schoolmistress; and these politer pleasures are entirely the productions of art and reason, on our side of the globe.

CHAPTER 8. *The Author relateth several particulars of the Yahoos. The great virtues of the Houyhnhnms. The education and exercises of their youth. Their general assembly.*

As I ought to have understood human nature much better than I supposed it possible for my master to do, so it was easy to apply the character he gave of the Yahoos to myself and my countrymen; and I believed I could yet make farther discoveries from my own observation. I therefore often begged his honor to let me go among the herds of Yahoos in the neighborhood; to which he always very graciously consented, being perfectly convinced that the hatred I bore those brutes would never suffer me to be corrupted by them; and his honor ordered one of his servants, a strong sorrel nag, very honest and good-natured, to be my guard; without whose protection I durst not undertake such adventures. For I have already told the reader how much I was pestered by those odious animals upon my first arrival. I afterwards failed very narrowly three or four times of falling into their clutches, when I happened to stray at any distance without my hanger. And I have reason to believe, they had some imagination that I was of their own species, which I often assisted myself, by stripping up my sleeves, and shewing my naked arms and breast in their sight, when my protector was with me; at which times they would approach as near as they durst, and imitate my actions after the manner of monkeys, but ever with great signs of hatred; as a tame jackdaw with cap and stockings is always persecuted by the wild ones, when he happens to be got among them.

They are prodigiously nimble from their infancy; however, I once caught a young male of three years old, and endeavored by all marks of tenderness to make it quiet; but the little imp fell a squalling, scratching, and biting with such violence, that I was forced to let it go; and it was high time, for a whole troop of old ones came about us at the noise; but finding the cub was safe (for away it ran) and my sorrel nag being by, they durst not venture near us. I observed the young animal's flesh to smell very rank, and the stink was somewhat between a weasel and a fox, but much more disagreeable. I forgot another circumstance (and perhaps I might have the reader's pardon, if it were wholly omitted) that while I held the odious vermin in my hands, it voided its filthy excrements of a yellow liquid substance, all over my clothes; but by good fortune there was a small brook hard by, where I washed myself as clean as I could; although I durst not come into my master's presence until I were sufficiently aired.

By what I could discover, the Yahoos appear to be the most unteachable of all animals, their capacities never reaching higher than to draw or carry burdens. Yet I am of opinion, this defect ariseth chiefly from a perverse, restive disposition. For they are cunning, malicious, treacherous and revengeful. They are strong and hardy, but of a cowardly spirit, and by consequence insolent, abject, and cruel. It is observed that the red-haired of both sexes are more libidinous and mischievous than the rest, whom yet they much exceed in strength and activity.

The Houyhnhnms keep the Yahoos for present use in huts not far from the house; but the rest are sent abroad to certain fields, where they dig up roots, eat several kinds of herbs, and search about for carrion, or sometimes catch weasels and *luhimuhs* (a sort of wild rat) which they greedily devour. Nature hath taught them to dig deep holes with their nails on the side of a rising ground, wherein they lie by themselves; only the kennels of the females are larger, sufficient to hold two or three cubs.

They swim from their infancy like frogs, and are able to continue long under water, where they often take fish, which the females carry home to their young. And upon this occasion, I hope the reader will pardon my relating an odd adventure.

Being one day abroad with my protector the sorrel nag, and the weather exceeding hot, I entreated him to let me bathe in a river that was near. He consented, and I immediately stripped myself stark naked, and went down softly into the stream. It happened that a young female Yahoo standing behind a bank, saw the whole proceeding; and inflamed by desire, as the nag and I conjectured, came running with all speed, and leaped into the water within five yards of the place where I bathed. I was never in my life so terribly frighted; the nag was grazing at some distance, not suspecting any harm; she embraced me after a most fulsome manner; I roared as loud as I could, and the nag came galloping towards me, whereupon she quitted her grasp, with the utmost reluctancy, and leaped upon the opposite bank, where she stood gazing and howling all the time I was putting on my clothes.

This was matter of diversion to my master and his family, as well as of mortification to myself. For now I could no longer deny that I was a real Yahoo, in every limb and feature, since the females had a natural propensity to me as one of their own species; neither was the hair of this brute of a red color (which might have been some excuse for an appetite a little irregular) but black as a sloe, and her countenance did not make an appearance altogether so hideous as the rest of the kind; for I think, she could not be above eleven years old.

Having already lived three years in this country, the reader I suppose will expect that I should, like other travelers, give him some account of the manners and customs of its inhabitants, which it was indeed my principal study to learn.

As these noble Houyhnhnms are endowed by Nature with a general disposition to all virtues, and have no conceptions or ideas of what is evil in a rational creature; so their grand maxim is to cultivate reason, and to be wholly governed by it. Neither is reason among them a point problematical as with us, where men can argue with plausibility on both sides of a question; but strikes you with immediate conviction; as it must needs do where it is not mingled, obscured, or discolored by passion and interest. I remember it was with extreme difficulty that I could bring my master to understand the meaning of the word "opinion," or how a point could be disputable; because reason taught us to affirm or deny only where we are certain; and beyond our knowledge we cannot do either. So that controversies, wranglings, disputes, and positiveness in false or dubious propositions are evils unknown among the Houyhnhnms. In the like manner when I used to explain to him our several systems of natural philosophy, he would laugh that a creature pretending to reason should value itself upon the knowledge of other people's conjectures, and in things, where that knowledge, if it were certain, could be of no use. Wherein he agreed entirely with the sentiments of Socrates, as Plato delivers them, which I mention as the highest honor I can do that prince of philosophers. I have often since reflected what destruction such a doctrine would make in the libraries of Europe; and how many paths to fame would be then shut up in the learned world.

Friendship and benevolence are the two principal virtues among the Houyhnhnms; and these not confined to particular objects, but universal to the whole race. For a stranger from the remotest part is equally treated with the nearest neighbor, and wherever he goes, looks upon himself as at home. They preserve decency and civility in the highest degrees, but are altogether ignorant of ceremony. They have no fondness for their colts or foals; but the care they take in educating them proceedeth entirely from the dictates of reason. And I observed my master to show the same affection to his neighbor's issue that he had for his own. They will have it that Nature teaches them to love the whole species, and it is reason only that maketh a distinction of persons, where there is a superior degree of virtue.

When the matron Houyhnhnms have produced one of each sex, they no longer accompany with their consorts, except they lose one of their issue by some casualty, which very seldom happens; but in such a case they meet again; or when the like accident befalls a person whose wife is past bearing, some other couple bestows on him one of their own colts, and then go together a second time, until the mother be pregnant.

This caution is necessary to prevent the country from being overburdened with numbers. But the race of inferior Houyhnhnms bred up to be servants is not so strictly limited upon this article; these are allowed to produce three of each sex, to be domestics in the noble families.

In their marriages they are exactly careful to choose such colors as will not make any disagreeable mixture in the breed. Strength is chiefly valued in the male, and comeliness in the female; not upon the account of love, but to preserve the race from degenerating; for, where a female happens to excel in strength, a consort is chosen with regard to comeliness. Courtship, love, presents, jointures, settlements, have no place in their thoughts, or terms whereby to express them in their language. The young couple meet and are joined, merely because it is the determination of their parents and friends; it is what they see done every day; and they look upon it as one of the necessary actions in a reasonable being. But the violation of marriage, or any other unchastity, was never heard of; and the married pair pass their lives with the same friendship and mutual benevolence that they bear to all others of the same species who come in their way, without jealousy, fondness, quarreling, or discontent.

In educating the youth of both sexes, their method is admirable, and highly deserveth our imitation. These are not suffered to taste a grain of oats, except upon certain days, till eighteen years old; nor milk, but very rarely; and in summer they graze two hours in the morning, and as many in the evening, which their parents likewise observe; but the servants are not allowed above half that time; and a great part of the grass is brought home, which they eat at the most convenient hours when they can be best spared from work.

Temperance, industry, exercise, and cleanliness are the lessons equally enjoined to the young ones of both sexes; and my master thought it monstrous in us to give the females a different kind of education from the males, except in some articles of domestic management; whereby, as he truly observed, one half of our natives were good for nothing but bringing children into the world; and to trust the care of their children to such useless animals, he said was yet a greater instance of brutality.

But the Houyhnhnms train up their youth to strength, speed, and hardiness, by exercising them in running races up and down steep hills, or over hard stony grounds; and when they are all in a sweat, they are ordered to leap over head and ears into a pond or a river. Four times a year the youth of certain districts meet to show their proficiency in running, and leaping, and other feats of strength or agility; where the victor is rewarded with a song made in his or her praise. On this festival the servants drive a herd of Yahoos into the field, laden with hay, and oats, and milk for a repast to the Houyhnhnms; after which these brutes are immediately driven back again, for fear of being noisome to the assembly.

Every fourth year, at the vernal equinox, there is a representative council of the whole nation, which meets in a plain about twenty miles from our house, and continueth about five or six days. Here they inquire into the state and condition of the several districts; whether they abound or be deficient in hay or oats, or cows or Yahoos? And wherever there is any want (which is but seldom) it is immediately supplied by unanimous consent and contribution. Here likewise the regulation of children is settled: as for instance, if a Houyhnhnm hath two males, he changeth one of them with another who hath two females, and when a child hath been lost by any casualty, where the mother is past breeding, it is determined what family in the district shall breed another to supply the loss.

CHAPTER 9. *A grand debate at the general assembly of the Houyhnhnms, and how it was determined. The learning of the Houyhnhnms. Their buildings. Their manner of burials. The defectiveness of their language.*

One of these grand assemblies was held in my time, about three months before my departure, whither my master went as the representative of our district. In this council was resumed their old debate, and indeed, the only debate that ever happened in their country; whereof my master after his return gave me a very particular account.

The question to be debated was whether the Yahoos should be exterminated from the face of the earth. One of the members for the affirmative offered several arguments of great strength and weight, alleging that, as the Yahoos were the most filthy, noisome, and deformed animal which nature ever produced, so they were the most restive and indocible, mischievous, and malicious; they would privately suck the teats of the Houyhnhnms' cows; kill and devour their cats, trample down their oats and grass, if they were not continually watched; and commit a thousand other extravagancies. He took notice of a general tradition, that Yahoos had not been always in their country, but that many ages ago, two of these brutes appeared together upon a mountain; whether produced by the heat of the sun upon corrupted mud and slime, or from the ooze and froth of the sea, was never known. That these Yahoos engendered, and their brood in a short time grew so numerous as to overrun and infest the whole nation. That the Houyhnhnms to get rid of this evil, made a general hunting, and at last enclosed the whole herd; and destroying the older, every Houyhnhnm kept two young ones in a kennel, and brought them to such a degree of tameness as an animal so savage by nature can be capable of acquiring, using them for draft and carriage. That there seemed to be much truth in this tradition, and that those creatures could not be *ylnhniamshy* (or aborigines of the land) because of the violent hatred the Houyhnhnms as well as all other animals bore them; which although their evil disposition sufficiently deserved, could never have arrived at so high a degree, if they had been aborigines, or else they would have long since been rooted out. That the inhabitants taking a fancy to use the service of the Yahoos, had very imprudently neglected to cultivate the breed of asses, which were a comely animal, easily kept, more tame and orderly, without any offensive smell, strong enough for labor, although they yield to the other in agility of body; and if their braying be no agreeable sound, it is far preferable to the horrible howlings of the Yahoos.

Several others declared their sentiments to the same purpose, when my master proposed an expedient to the assembly, whereof he had indeed borrowed the hint from me. He approved of the tradition, mentioned by the honorable member, who spoke before; and affirmed, that the two Yahoos said to be first seen among them, had been driven thither over the sea; that coming to land, and being forsaken by their companions, they retired to the mountains, and degenerating by degrees, became in process of time much more savage than those of their own species in the country from whence these two originals came. The reason of his assertion was that he had now in his possession a certain wonderful Yahoo (meaning myself) which most of them had heard of, and many of them had seen. He then related to them how he first found me; that my body was all covered with an artificial composure of the skins and hairs of other animals; that I spoke in a language of my own, and had thoroughly learned theirs; that I had related to him the accidents which brought me thither; that when he saw me without my covering, I was an exact Yahoo in every part, only of a whiter color, less hairy and with shorter claws. He added how I had endeavored to persuade him that in my own and other countries the Yahoos acted as the governing, rational animal, and held the Houyhnhnms in servitude; that he observed in me all the qualities of a Yahoo, only a little more civilized by some tincture of reason, which however was in a degree as far inferior to the Houyhnhnm race as the Yahoos of their country were to me; that among other things, I mentioned a custom we had of castrating Houyhnhnms when they were young, in order to render them tame; that the operation was easy and safe; that it was no shame to learn wisdom from brutes, as industry is taught by the ant, and building by the swallow (for so I translate the world *lyhannh*, although it be a much larger fowl). That this invention might be practiced upon the younger Yahoos here, which, besides rendering them tractable and fitter for use, would in an age put an end to the whole species without destroying life. That in the meantime the Houyhnhnms should be exhorted to cultivate the breed of asses, which, as they are in all respects more valuable brutes, so they have this advantage, to be fit for service at five years old, which the other are not till twelve.

This was all my master thought fit to tell me at that time, of what passed in the grand council. But he was pleased to conceal one particular, which related personally to myself, whereof I soon felt the unhappy effect, as the reader will know in its proper place, and from whence I date all the succeeding misfortunes of my life.

The Houyhnhnms have no letters, and consequently, their knowledge is all traditional. But there happening few events of any moment among a people so well united, naturally disposed to every virtue, wholly governed by reason, and cut off from all commerce with other nations, the historical part is easily preserved without burdening their memories. I have already observed that they are subject to no diseases, and therefore can have no need of physicians. However, they have excellent medicines composed of herbs, to cure accidental bruises and cuts in the pastern or frog of the foot by sharp stones, as well as other maims and hurts in the several parts of the body.

They calculate the year by the revolution of the sun and the moon, but use no subdivisions into weeks. They are well enough acquainted with the motions of those two luminaries, and understand the nature of eclipses; and this is the utmost progress of their astronomy.

In poetry they must be allowed to excel all other mortals; wherein the justness of their similes, and the minuteness, as well as exactness of their descriptions, are indeed inimitable. Their verses abound very much in both of these, and usually contain either some exalted notions of friendship and benevolence, or the praises of those who were victors in races and other bodily exercises. Their buildings, although very rude and simple, are not inconvenient, but well contrived to defend them from all injuries of cold and heat. They have a kind of tree, which at forty years old loosens in the root, and falls with the first storm; it grows very straight, and being pointed like stakes with a sharp stone (for the Houyhnhnms know not the use of iron), they stick them erect in the ground about ten inches asunder, and then weave in oat straw, or sometimes wattles, betwixt them. The roof is made after the same manner, and so are the doors.

The Houyhnhnms use the hollow part between the pastern and the hoof of their forefeet as we do our hands, and this with greater dexterity than I could at first imagine. I have seen a white mare of our family thread a needle (which I lent her on purpose) with that joint. They milk their cows, reap their oats, and do all the work which requires hands in the same manner. They have a kind of hard flints, which by grinding against other stones they form into instruments that serve instead of wedges, axes, and hammers. With tools made of these flints, they likewise cut their hay, and reap their oats, which there groweth naturally in several fields; the Yahoos draw home the sheaves in carriages, and the servants tread them in certain covered huts, to get out the grain, which is kept in stores. They make a rude kind of earthen and wooden vessels, and bake the former in the sun.

If they can avoid casualties, they die only of old age, and are buried in the obscurest places that can be found, their friends and relations expressing neither joy nor grief at their departure; nor does the dying person discover the least regret that he is leaving the world, any more than if he were upon returning home from a visit to one of his neighbors; I remember my master having once made an appointment with a friend and his family to come to his house upon some affair of importance; on the day fixed, the mistress and her two children came very late; she made two excuses, first for her husband, who, as she said, happened that very morning to *lhnuwnh*. The word is strongly expressive in their language, but not easily rendered into English; it signifies, *to retire to his first*

Mother. Her excuse for not coming sooner was that her husband dying late in the morning, she was a good while consulting her servants about a convenient place where his body should be laid; and I observed she behaved herself at our house, as cheerfully as the rest; she died about three months after.

They live generally to seventy or seventy-five years, very seldom to fourscore; some weeks before their death they feel a gradual decay, but without pain. During this time they are much visited by their friends, because they cannot go abroad with their usual ease and satisfaction. However, about ten days before their death, which they seldom fail in computing, they return the visits that have been made by those who are nearest in the neighborhood, being carried in a convenient sledge drawn by Yahoos; which vehicle they use, not only upon this occasion, but when they grow old, upon long journeys, or when they are lamed by any accident. And therefore when the dying Houyhnhnms return those visits, they take a solemn leave of their friends, as if they were going to some remote part of the country, where they designed to pass the rest of their lives.

I know not whether it may be worth observing, that the Houyhnhnms have no word in their language to express anything that is evil, except what they borrow from the deformities or ill qualities of the Yahoos. Thus they denote the folly of a servant, an omission of a child, a stone that cuts their feet, a continuance of foul or unseasonable weather, and the like, by adding to each the epithet of Yahoo. For instance, *hhnm Yahoo, whnaholm Yahoo, ynlhmndwihlma Yahoo,* and an ill-contrived house, *ynholmhnmrohlnw Yahoo.*

I could with great pleasure enlarge farther upon the manners and virtues of this excellent people; but intending in a short time to publish a volume by itself expressly upon that subject, I refer the reader thither. And in the meantime, proceed to relate my own sad catastrophe.

CHAPTER 10. *The Author's economy, and happy life among the Houyhnhnms. His great improvement in virtue, by conversing with them. Their conversations. The Author hath notice given him by his master that he must depart from the country. He falls into a swoon for grief, but submits. He contrives and finishes a canoe, by the help of a fellow servant, and puts to sea at a venture.*

I had settled my little economy to my own heart's content. My master had ordered a room to be made for me after their manner, about six yards from the house; the sides and floors of which I plastered with clay, and covered with rush mats of my own contriving; I had beaten hemp, which there grows wild, and made of it a sort of ticking; this I filled with the feathers of several birds I had taken with springes made of Yahoos' hairs, and were excellent food. I had worked two chairs with my knife, the sorrel nag helping me in the grosser and more laborious part. When my clothes were worn to rags, I made myself others with the skins of rabbits, and of a certain beautiful animal about the same size, called *nnuhnoh*, the skin of which is covered with a fine down. Of these I likewise made very tolerable stockings. I soled my shoes with wood which I cut from a tree, and fitted to the upper leather, and when this was worn out, I supplied it with the skins of Yahoos, dried in the sun. I often got honey out of hollow trees, which I mingled with water, or eat it with my bread. No man could more verify the truth of these two maxims, that *Nature is very easily satisfied*; and, that *Necessity is the mother of invention*. I enjoyed perfect health of body, and tranquility of mind; I did not feel the treachery or inconstancy of a friend, nor the inquiries of a secret or open enemy. I had no occasion of bribing, flattering, or pimping to procure the favor of any great man, or of his minion. I wanted no fence against fraud or oppression; here was neither physician to destroy my body, nor lawyer to ruin my fortune; no informer to watch my words and actions, or forge accusations against me for hire; here were no gibers, censurers, backbiters, pickpockets, highwaymen, housebreakers, attorneys, bawds, buffoons, gamesters, politicians, wits, splenetics, tedious talkers, controvertists, ravishers, murderers, robbers, virtuosos; no leaders or followers of party and faction; no encouragers to vice, by seducement or examples; no dungeons, axes, gibbets, whipping posts, or pillories; no cheating shopkeepers or mechanics; no pride, vanity or affectation; no fops, bullies, drunkards, strolling whores, or poxes; no ranting, lewd, expensive wives; no stupid, proud pedants; no importunate, overbearing, quarrelsome, noisy, roaring, empty, conceited, swearing companions; no scoundrels raised from the dust upon the merit of their vices; or nobility thrown into it on account of their virtues; no lords, fiddlers, judges, or dancing masters.

I had the favor of being admitted to several Houyhnhnms, who came to visit or dine with my master; where his honor graciously suffered me to wait in the room, and listen to their discourse. Both he and his company would often descend to ask me questions, and receive my answers. I had also sometimes the honor of attending my master in his visits to others. I never presumed to speak, except in answer to a question; and then I did it with inward regret, because it was a loss of so much time for improving myself; but I was infinitely delighted with the station of an humble auditor in such conversations, where nothing passed but what was useful, expressed in the fewest and most significant words; where (as I have already said) the greatest decency was observed, without the least degree of ceremony; where no person spoke without being pleased himself, and pleasing his companions; where there was no interruption, tediousness, heat, or difference of sentiments. They have a notion, that when people are met together, a short silence doth much improve conversation; this I found to be true; for during those little intermissions of talk, new ideas would arise in their minds, which very much enlivened the discourse. Their subjects are generally on friendship and benevolence; on order and economy; sometimes upon the visible operations of nature, or ancient traditions; upon the bounds and limits of virtue; upon the unerring rules of reason; or upon some determinations, to be taken at the next great assembly; and often upon the various excellencies of poetry. I may add, without vanity, that my presence often gave them sufficient matter for discourse, because it afforded my master an occasion of letting his friends into the history of me and my country, upon which they were all pleased to descant in a manner not very advantageous to human kind; and for that reason I shall not repeat what they said; only I may be allowed to observe that his honor, to my great admiration, appeared to understand the nature of Yahoos much better than myself. He went through all our vices and follies, and discovered many which I had never mentioned to him; by only supposing what qualities a Yahoo of their country, with a small proportion of reason, might be capable of exerting; and concluded, with too much probability, how vile as well as miserable such a creature must be.

I freely confess, that all the little knowledge I have of any value was acquired by the lectures I received from my master, and from hearing the discourses of him and his friends; to which I should be prouder to listen, than to dictate to the greatest and wisest assembly in Europe. I admired the strength, comeliness, and speed of the inhabitants; and such a constellation of virtues in such amiable persons produced in me the highest veneration. At first, indeed, I did not feel that natural awe which the Yahoos and all other animals bear towards them; but it grew upon me by degrees, much sooner than I imagined, and was mingled with a respectful love and gratitude, that they would condescend to distinguish me from the rest of my species.

When I thought of my family, my friends, my countrymen, or human race in general, I considered them as they really were, Yahoos in shape and disposition, perhaps a little more civilized, and qualified with the gift of speech; but making no other use of reason than to improve and multiply those vices, whereof their brethren in this country had only the share that nature allotted them. When I happened to behold the reflection of my own form in a lake or fountain, I turned away my face in horror and detestation of myself, and could better endure the sight of a common Yahoo than of my own person. By conversing with the Houyhnhnms, and looking upon them with delight, I fell to imitate their gait and gesture, which is now grown into a habit; and my friends often tell me in a blunt way, that I trot like a horse; which, however, I take for a great compliment; neither shall I disown, that in speaking I am apt to fall into the voice and manner of the Houyhnhnms, and hear myself ridiculed on that account without the least mortification.

In the midst of this happiness, when I looked upon myself to be fully settled for life, my master sent for me one morning a little earlier than his usual hour. I observed by his countenance that he was in some perplexity, and at a loss how to begin what he had to speak. After a short silence, he told me, he did not know how I would take what he was going to say; that, in the last general assembly, when the affair of the Yahoos was entered upon, the representatives had taken offense at his keeping a Yahoo (meaning myself) in his family more like a Houyhnhnm than a brute animal. That he was known frequently to converse with me, as if he could receive some advantage of pleasure in my company; that such a practice was not agreeable to reason or nature, or a thing ever heard of before among them. The assembly did therefore exhort him, either to employ me like the rest of my species, or command me to swim back to the place from whence I came. That the first of these expedients was utterly rejected by all the Houyhnhnms who had ever seen me at his house or their own; for, they alleged, that because I had some rudiments of reason, added to the natural pravity of those animals, it was to be feared, I might be able to seduce them into the woody and mountainous parts of the country, and bring them in troops by night to destroy the Houyhnhnms' cattle, as being naturally of the ravenous kind, and averse from labor.

My master added that he was daily pressed by the Houyhnhnms of the neighborhood to have the assembly's exhortation executed, which he could not put off much longer. He doubted it would be impossible for me to swim to another country; and therefore wished I would contrive some sort of vehicle resembling those I had described to him, that might carry me on the sea; in which work I should have the assistance of his own servants, as well as those of his neighbors. He concluded that for his own part he could have been content to keep me in his service as long as I lived; because he found I had cured myself of some bad habits and dispositions, by endeavoring, as far as my inferior nature was capable, to imitate the Houyhnhnms.

I should here observe to the reader, that a decree of the general assembly in this country is expressed by the word *hnhloayn*, which signifies an exhortation, as near as I can render it; for they have no conception how a rational creature can be compelled, but only advised, or exhorted; because no person can disobey reason without giving up his claim to be a rational creature.

I was struck with the utmost grief and despair at my master's discourse; and being unable to support the agonies I was under, I fell into a swoon at his feet; when I came to myself, he told me that he concluded I had been dead (for these people are subject to no such imbecilities of nature). I answered, in a faint voice, that death would have been too great an happiness; that although I could not blame the assembly's exhortation, or the urgency of his friends; yet in my weak and corrupt judgment, I thought it might consist with reason to have been less rigorous. That I could not swim a league, and probably the nearest land to theirs might be distant above an hundred; that many materials, necessary for making a small vessel to carry me off, were wholly wanting in this country, which, however, I would attempt in obedience and gratitude to his honor, although I concluded the thing to be impossible, and therefore looked on myself as already devoted[4] to destruction. That the certain prospect

4. Doomed.

of an unnatural death was the least of my evils; for, supposing I should escape with life by some strange adventure, how could I think with temper[5] of passing my days among Yahoos, and relapsing into my old corruptions, for want of examples to lead and keep me within the paths of virtue. That I knew too well upon what solid reasons all the determinations of the wise Houyhnhnms were founded, not to be shaken by arguments of mine, a miserable Yahoo; and therefore after presenting him with my humble thanks for the offer of his servants' assistance in making a vessel, and desiring a reasonable time for so difficult a work, I told him I would endeavor to preserve a wretched being; and, if ever I returned to England, was not without hopes of being useful to my own species by celebrating the praises of the renowned Houyhnhnms, and proposing their virtues to the imitation of mankind.

My master in a few words made me a very gracious reply, allowed me the space of two months to finish my boat, and ordered the sorrel nag, my fellow servant (for so at this distance I may presume to call him), to follow my instructions, because I told my master that his help would be sufficient, and I knew he had a tenderness for me.

In his company my first business was to go to that part of the coast where my rebellious crew had ordered me to be set on shore. I got upon a height, and looking on every side into the sea, fancied I saw a small island towards the northeast; I took out my pocket glass, and could then clearly distinguish it about five leagues off, as I computed; but it appeared to the sorrel nag to be only a blue cloud; for, as he had no conception of any country besides his own, so he could not be as expert in distinguishing remote objects at sea, as we who so much converse in that element.

After I had discovered this island, I considered no farther; but resolved, it should, if possible, be the first place of my banishment, leaving the consequence to fortune.

I returned home, and consulting with the sorrel nag, we went into a copse at some distance, where I with my knive, and he with a sharp flint fastened very artificially,[6] after their manner, to a wooden handle, cut down several oak wattles about the thickness of a walking staff, and some larger pieces. But I shall not trouble the reader with a particular description of my own mechanics; let it suffice to say, that in six weeks time, with the help of the sorrel nag, who performed the parts that required most labor, I finished a sort of Indian canoe; but much larger, covering it with the skins of Yahoos, well stitched together, with hempen threads of my own making. My sail was likewise composed of the skins of the same animal; but I made use of the youngest I could get, the older being too tough and thick; and I likewise provided myself with four paddles. I laid in a stock of boiled flesh, of rabbits and fowls; and took with me two vessels, one filled with milk, and the other with water.

I tried my canoe in a large pond near my master's house, and then

5. Equanimity.   6. Artfully.

corrected in it what was amiss, stopping all the chinks with Yahoo's tallow, till I found it staunch, and able to bear me and my freight. And when it was as complete as I could possibly make it, I had it drawn on a carriage very gently by Yahoos, to the seaside, under the conduct of the sorrel nag and another servant.

When all was ready, and the day came for my departure, I took leave of my master and lady, and the whole family, my eyes flowing with tears and my heart quite sunk with grief. But his honor, out of curiosity, and perhaps (if I may speak it without vanity) partly out of kindness, was determined to see me in my canoe; and got several of his neighboring friends to accompany him. I was forced to wait above an hour for the tide, and then observing the wind very fortunately bearing towards the island to which I intended to steer my course, I took a second leave of my master; but as I was going to prostrate myself to kiss his hoof, he did me the honor to raise it gently to my mouth. I am not ignorant how much I have been censured for mentioning this last particular. Detractors are pleased to think it improbable that so illustrious a person should descend to give so great a mark of distinction to a creature so inferior as I. Neither have I forgot how apt some travelers are to boast of extraordinary favors they have received. But, if these censurers were better acquainted with the noble and courteous disposition of the Houyhnhnms, they would soon change their opinion. I paid my respects to the rest of the Houyhnhnms in his honor's company; then getting into my canoe, I pushed off from shore.

CHAPTER 11. *The Author's dangerous voyage. He arrives at New Holland, hoping to settle there. Is wounded with an arrow by one of the natives. Is seized and carried by force into a Portuguese ship. The great civilities of the Captain. The Author arrives at England.*

I began this desperate voyage on February 15, 1714 / 5,[7] at 9 o'clock in the morning. The wind was very favorable; however, I made use at first only of my paddles; but considering I should soon be weary, and that the wind might probably chop about, I ventured to set up my little sail, and thus, with the help of the tide, I went at the rate of a league and a half an hour, as near as I could guess. My master and his friends continued on the shore, till I was almost out of sight; and I often heard the sorrel nag (who always loved me) crying out, "*Hnuy illa nyha maiah Yahoo*" ("Take care of thyself, gentle Yahoo").

My design was, if possible, to discover some small island uninhabited, yet sufficient by my labor to furnish me with necessaries of life, which I would have thought a greater happiness than to be first minister in the politest court of Europe, so horrible was the idea I conceived of returning to live in the society and under the government of Yahoos. For in such a solitude as I desired, I could at least enjoy my own thoughts, and

7. I.e., 1714. The year began on March 25.

reflect with delight on the virtues of those inimitable Houyhnhnms, without any opportunity of degenerating into the vices and corruptions of my own species.

The reader may remember what I related when my crew conspired against me, and confined me to my cabin, how I continued there several weeks, without knowing what course we took; and when I was put ashore in the longboat, how the sailors told me with oaths, whether true or false, that they knew not in what part of the world we were. However, I did then believe us to be about 10 degrees southward of the Cape of Good Hope, or about 45 degrees southern latitude, as I gathered from some general words I overheard among them, being I supposed to the southeast in their intended voyage to Madagascar. And although this were but little better than conjecture, yet I resolved to steer my course eastward, hoping to reach the southwest coast of New Holland, and perhaps some such island as I desired, lying westward of it. The wind was full west, and by six in the evening I computed I had gone eastward at least eighteen leagues; when I spied a very small island about half a league off, which I soon reached. It was nothing but a rock with one creek,[8] naturally arched by the force of tempests. Here I put in my canoe, and climbing a part of the rock, I could plainly discover land to the east, extending from south to north. I lay all night in my canoe; and repeating my voyage early in the morning, I arrived in seven hours to the southeast point of New Holland. This confirmed me in the opinion I have long entertained, that the maps and charts place this country at least three degrees more to the east than it really is; which thought I communicated many years ago to my worthy friend Mr. Herman Moll,[9] and gave him my reasons for it, although he hath rather chosen to follow other authors.

I saw no inhabitants in the place where I landed; and being unarmed, I was afraid of venturing far into the country. I found some shellfish on the shore, and eat them raw, not daring to kindle a fire, for fear of being discovered by the natives. I continued three days feeding on oysters and limpets, to save my own provisions; and I fortunately found a brook of excellent water, which gave me great relief.

On the fourth day, venturing out early a little too far, I saw twenty or thirty natives upon a height, not above five hundred yards from me. They were stark naked, men, women, and children round a fire, as I could discover by the smoke. One of them spied me, and gave notice to the rest; five of them advanced towards me, leaving the women and children at the fire. I made what haste I could to the shore, and getting into my canoe, shoved off; the savages observing me retreat, ran after me; and before I could get far enough into the sea, discharged an arrow, which wounded me deeply on the inside of my left knee. (I shall carry the mark to my grave.) I apprehended the arrow might be poisoned; and paddling out of the reach of their darts (being a calm day) I made a shift to suck the wound, and dress it as well as I could.

8. A bay.   9. A famous contemporary map maker.

I was at a loss what to do, for I durst not return to the same landing place, but stood to the north, and was forced to paddle; for the wind, although very gentle, was against me, blowing northwest. As I was looking about for a secure landing place, I saw a sail to the north northeast, which appearing every minute more visible, I was in some doubt whether I should wait for them or no; but at last my detestation of the Yahoo race prevailed; and turning my canoe, I sailed and paddled together to the south, and got into the same creek from whence I set out in the morning, choosing rather to trust myself among these barbarians than live with European Yahoos. I drew up my canoe as close as I could to the shore, and hid myself behind a stone by the little brook, which, as I have already said, was excellent water.

The ship came within half a league of this creek, and sent out her longboat with vessels to take in fresh water (for the place it seems was very well known), but I did not observe it until the boat was almost on shore; and it was too late to seek another hiding place. The seamen at their landing observed my canoe, and rummaging it all over, easily conjectured that the owner could not be far off. Four of them well armed searched every cranny and lurking hole, till at last they found me flat on my face behind the stone. They gazed a while in admiration[1] at my strange uncouth dress; my coat made of skins, my wooden-soled shoes, and my furred stockings; from whence, however, they concluded I was not a native of the place, who all go naked. One of the seamen in Portuguese bid me rise, and asked who I was. I understood that language very well, and getting upon my feet, said I was a poor Yahoo, banished from the Houyhnhnms, and desired they would please to let me depart. They admired to hear me answer them in their own tongue, and saw by my complexion I must be an European; but were at a loss to know what I meant by Yahoos and Houyhnhnms, and at the same time fell a laughing at my strange tone in speaking, which resembled the neighing of a horse. I trembled all the while betwixt fear and hatred; I again desired leave to depart, and was gently moving to my canoe; but they laid hold on me, desiring to know what country I was of? whence I came? with many other questions. I told them I was born in England, from whence I came about five years ago, and then their country and ours was at peace. I therefore hoped they would not treat me as an enemy, since I meant them no harm, but was a poor Yahoo, seeking some desolate place where to pass the remainder of his unfortunate life.

When they began to talk, I thought I never heard or saw any thing so unnatural; for it appeared to me as monstrous as if a dog or a cow should speak in England, or a Yahoo in Houyhnhnmland. The honest Portuguese were equally amazed at my strange dress, and the odd manner of delivering my words, which however they understood very well. They spoke to me with great humanity, and said they were sure their Captain would carry me *gratis* to Lisbon, from whence I might return to my own

---

1. Wonder.

country; that two of the seamen would go back to the ship, to inform the Captain of what they had seen, and receive his orders; in the meantime, unless I would give my solemn oath not to fly, they would secure me by force. I thought it best to comply with their proposal. They were very curious to know my story, but I gave them very little satisfaction; and they all conjectured, that my misfortunes had impaired my reason. In two hours the boat, which went laden with vessels of water, returned with the Captain's commands to fetch me on board. I fell on my knees to preserve my liberty; but all was in vain, and the men having tied me with cords, heaved me into the boat, from whence I was taken into the ship, and from thence into the Captain's cabin.

His name was Pedro de Mendez; he was a very courteous and generous person; he entreated me to give some account of myself, and desired to know what I would eat or drink; said I should be used as well as himself, and spoke so many obliging things, that I wondered to find such civilities from a Yahoo. However, I remained silent and sullen; I was ready to faint at the very smell of him and his men. At last I desired something to eat out of my own canoe; but he ordered me a chicken and some excellent wine, and then directed that I should be put to bed in a very clean cabin. I would not undress myself, but lay on the bedclothes; and in half an hour stole out, when I thought the crew was at dinner; and getting to the side of the ship, was going to leap into the sea, and swim for my life, rather than continue among Yahoos. But one of the seamen prevented me, and having informed the Captain, I was chained to my cabin.

After dinner Don Pedro came to me, and desired to know my reason for so desperate an attempt; assured me he only meant to do me all the service he was able; and spoke so very movingly, that at last I descended to treat him like an animal which had some little portion of reason. I gave him a very short relation of my voyage; of the conspiracy against me by my own men; of the country where they set me on shore, and of my five years residence there. All which he looked upon as if it were a dream or a vision; whereat I took great offense; for I had quite forgot the faculty of lying, so peculiar to Yahoos in all countries where they preside, and consequently the disposition of suspecting truth in others of their own species. I asked him whether it were the custom of his country to *say the thing that was not?* I assured him I had almost forgot what he meant by falsehood; and if I had lived a thousand years in Houyhnhnm-land, I should never have heard a lie from the meanest servant. That I was altogether indifferent whether he believed me or no; but however, in return for his favors, I would give so much allowance to the corruption of his nature, as to answer any objection he would please to make; and he might easily discover the truth.

The Captain, a wise man, after many endeavors to catch me tripping in some part of my story, at last began to have a better opinion of my veracity. But he added that since I professed so inviolable an attachment to truth, I must give him my word of honor to bear him company in this voyage without attempting anything against my life; or else he would continue me a prisoner till we arrived at Lisbon. I gave him the promise he required; but at the same time protested that I would suffer the greatest hardships rather than return to live among Yahoos.

Our voyage passed without any considerable accident. In gratitude to the Captain I sometimes sat with him at his earnest request, and strove to conceal my antipathy against humankind, although it often broke out; which he suffered to pass without observation. But the greatest part of the day, I confined myself to my cabin, to avoid seeing any of the crew. The Captain had often entreated me to strip myself of my savage dress, and offered to lend me the best suit of clothes he had. This I would not be prevailed on to accept, abhorring to cover myself with anything that had been on the back of a Yahoo. I only desired he would lend me two clean shirts, which having been washed since he wore them, I believed would not so much defile me. These I changed every second day, and washed them myself.

We arrived at Lisbon, Nov. 5, 1715. At our landing, the Captain forced me to cover myself with his cloak, to prevent the rabble from crowding about me. I was conveyed to his own house; and at my earnest request, he led me up to the highest room backwards.[2] I conjured him to conceal from all persons what I had told him of the Houyhnhnms; because the least hint of such a story would not only draw numbers of people to see me, but probably put me in danger of being imprisoned, or burned by the Inquisition. The Captain persuaded me to accept a suit of clothes newly made; but I would not suffer the tailor to take my measure; however, Don Pedro being almost of my size, they fitted me well enough. He accounted me with other necessaries, all new, which I aired for twenty-four hours before I would use them.

The Captain had no wife, nor above three servants, none of which were suffered to attend at meals; and his whole deportment was so obliging, added to very good human understanding, that I really began to tolerate his company. He gained so far upon me, that I ventured to look out of the back window. By degrees I was brought into another room, from whence I peeped into the street, but drew my head back in a fright. In a week's time he seduced me down to the door. I found my terror gradually lessened, but my hatred and contempt seemed to increase. I was at last bold enough to walk the street in his company, but kept my nose well stopped with rue, or sometimes with tobacco.

In ten days, Don Pedro, to whom I had given some account of my domestic affairs, put it upon me as a point of honor and conscience that I ought to return to my native country, and live at home with my wife and children. He told me there was an English ship in the port just ready to sail, and he would furnish me with all things necessary. It would be tedious to repeat his arguments, and my contradictions. He said it was altogether impossible to find such a solitary island as I had desired to live

---

2. At the rear.

in; but I might command in my own house, and pass my time in a manner as recluse as I pleased.

I complied at last, finding I could not do better. I left Lisbon the 24th day of November, in an English merchantman, but who was the Master I never inquired. Don Pedro accompanied me to the ship, and lent me twenty pounds. He took kind leave of me, and embraced me at parting; which I bore as well as I could. During this last voyage I had no commerce with the Master, or any of his men; but pretending I was sick kept close in my cabin. On the fifth of December, 1715, we cast anchor in the Downs about nine in the morning, and at three in the afternoon I got safe to my house at Redriff.

My wife and family received me with great surprise and joy, because they concluded me certainly dead; but I must freely confess, the sight of them filled me only with hatred, disgust, and contempt; and the more, by reflecting on the near alliance I had to them. For although since my unfortunate exile from the Houyhnhnm country, I had compelled myself to tolerate the sight of Yahoos, and to converse with Don Pedro de Mendez; yet my memory and imaginations were perpetually filled with the virtues and ideas of those exalted Houyhnhnms. And when I began to consider that by copulating with one of the Yahoo species, I had become a parent of more, it struck me with the utmost shame, confusion, and horror.

As soon as I entered the house, my wife took me in her arms, and kissed me; at which, having not been used to the touch of that odious animal for so many years, I fell in a swoon for almost an hour. At the time I am writing, it is five years since my last return to England; during the first year I could not endure my wife or children in my presence, the very smell of them was intolerable; much less could I suffer them to eat in the same room. To this hour they dare not presume to touch my bread, or drink out of the same cup; neither was I ever able to let one of them take me by the hand. The first money I laid out was to buy two young stone-horses,[3] which I keep in a good stable, and next to them the groom is my greatest favorite; for I feel my spirits revived by the smell he contracts in the stable. My horses understand me tolerably well; I converse with them at least four hours every day. They are strangers to bridle or saddle; they live in great amity with me, and friendship to each other.

CHAPTER 12. *The Author's veracity. His design in publishing this work. His censure of those travelers who swerve from the truth. The Author clears himself from any sinister ends in writing. His native country commended. The right of the crown to those countries described by the Author is justified. The difficulty of conquering them. The Author takes his last leave of the reader; proposeth his manner of living for the future; gives good advice, and concludeth.*

3. Stallions.

Thus gentle reader, I have given thee a faithful history of my travels for sixteen years, and above seven months; wherein I have not been so studious of ornament as of truth. I could perhaps like others have astonished thee with strange improbable tales; but I rather chose to relate plain matter of fact in the simplest manner and style; because my principal design was to inform, and not to amuse thee.

It is easy for us who travel into remote countries, which are seldom visited by Englishmen or other Europeans, to form descriptions of wonderful animals both at sea and land. Whereas a traveler's chief aim should be to make men wiser and better, and to improve their minds by the bad as well as good example of what they deliver concerning foreign places.

I could heartily wish a law were enacted, that every traveler, before he were permitted to publish his voyages, should be obliged to make oath before the Lord High Chancellor that all he intended to print was absolutely true to the best of his knowledge; for then the world would no longer be deceived as it usually is, while some writers, to make their works pass the better upon the public, impose the grossest falsities on the unwary reader. I have perused several books of travels with great delight in my younger days; but, having since gone over most parts of the globe, and been able to contradict many fabulous accounts from my own observation, it hath given me a great disgust against this part of reading, and some indignation to see the credulity of mankind so impudently abused. Therefore, since my acquaintance were pleased to think my poor endeavors might not be unacceptable to my country; I imposed on myself as a maxim, never to be swerved from, that I would *strictly adhere to truth*; neither indeed can I be ever under the least temptation to vary from it, while I retain in my mind the lectures and example of my noble master, and the other illustrious Houyhnhnms, of whom I had so long the honor to be an humble hearer.

> ———*Nec si miserum Fortuna Sinonem*
> *Finxit, vanum etiam, mendacemque improba finget.*[4]

I know very well how little reputation is to be got by writings which require neither genius nor learning, nor indeed any other talent, except a good memory, or an exact *Journal*. I know likewise, that writers of travels, like dictionary-makers, are sunk into oblivion by the weight and bulk of those who come last, and therefore lie uppermost. And it is highly probable that such travelers who shall hereafter visit the countries described in this work of mine, may be detecting my errors (if there be any) and adding many new discoveries of their own, jostle me out of vogue, and stand in my place, making the world forget that ever I was an author. This indeed would be too great a mortification if I wrote for fame; but, as my sole intention was the PUBLIC GOOD, I cannot be altogether disappointed. For, who can read the virtues I have mentioned in the glorious Houyhnhnms, without being ashamed of his own vices,

---

4. Virgil, *Aeneid* 2. 79–80. ". . . nor if Fortune had moulded Sinon for misery, will she also in spite mould him as false and lying."

when he considers himself as the reasoning, governing animal of his country? I shall say nothing of those remote nations where Yahoos preside; amongst which the least corrupted are the Brobdingnagians, whose wise maxims in morality and government it would be our happiness to observe. But I forbear descanting further, and rather leave the judicious reader to his own remarks and applications.

I am not a little pleased that this work of mine can possibly meet with no censurers; for what objections can be made against a writer who relates only plain facts that happened in such distant countries, where we have not the least interest with respect either to trade or negotiations? I have carefully avoided every fault with which common writers of travels are often too justly charged. Besides, I meddle not the least with any party, but write without passion, prejudice, or ill-will against any man or number of men whatsoever. I write for the noblest end, to inform and instruct mankind, over whom I may, without breach of modesty, pretend to some superiority, from the advantages I received by conversing so long among the most accomplished Houyhnhnms. I write without any view towards profit or praise. I never suffer a word to pass that may look like a reflection, or possibly give the least offense even to those who are most ready to take it. So that, I hope, I may with justice pronounce myself an Author perfectly blameless; against whom the tribes of answerers, considerers, observers, reflectors, detecters, remarkers will never be able to find matter for exercising their talents.

I confess it was whispered to me that I was bound in duty as a subject of England, to have given in a memorial to a secretary of state, at my first coming over; because, whatever lands are discovered by a subject, belong to the Crown. But I doubt whether our conquests in the countries I treat of would be as easy as those of Ferdinando Cortez over the naked Americans. The Lilliputians, I think, are hardly worth the charge of a fleet and army to reduce them; and I question whether it might be prudent or safe to attempt the Brobdingnagians; or, whether an English army would be much at their ease with the Flying Island over their heads. The Houyhnhnms, indeed, appear not to be so well prepared for war, a science to which they are perfect strangers, and especially against missive weapons. However, supposing myself to be a minister of state, I could never give my advice for invading them. Their prudence, unanimity, unacquaintedness with fear, and their love of their country would amply supply all defects in the military art. Imagine twenty thousand of them breaking into the midst of an European army, confounding the ranks, overturning the carriages, battering the warriors' faces into mummy,[5] by terrible yerks[6] from their hinder hoofs: for they would well deserve the character given to Augustus, *Recalcitrat undique tutus.*[7] But instead of proposals for conquering that magnanimous nation, I rather wish they were in a capacity or disposition to send a sufficient number of their inhabitants for civilizing Europe; by teaching us the first princi-

5. Pulp.
6. Kicks.

7. Horace, *Satires* 2.1.20. ". . . he kicks backward, at every point on his guard."

ples of Honor, Justice, Truth, Temperance, public Spirit, Fortitude, Chastity, Friendship, Benevolence, and Fidelity. The names of all which Virtues are still retained among us in most languages, and are to be met with in modern as well as ancient authors, which I am able to assert from my own small reading.

But I had another reason which made me less forward to enlarge his majesty's dominions by my discoveries: to say the truth, I had conceived a few scruples with relation to the distributive justice of princes upon those occasions. For instance, a crew of pirates are driven by a storm they know not whither; at length a boy discovers land from the topmast; they go on shore to rob and plunder; they see an harmless people, are entertained with kindness, they give the country a new name, they take formal possession of it for the king, they set up a rotten plank or a stone for a memorial, they murder two or three dozen of the natives, bring away a couple more by force for a sample, return home, and get their pardon. Here commences a new dominion acquired with a title by Divine Right. Ships are sent with the first opportunity; the natives driven out or destroyed, their princes tortured to discover their gold; a free license given to all acts of inhumanity and lust; the earth reeking with the blood of its inhabitants: and this execrable crew of butchers employed in so pious an expedition is a *modern colony* sent to convert and civilize an idolatrous and barbarous people.

But this description, I confess, doth by no means affect the British nation, who may be an example to the whole world for their wisdom, care, and justice in planting colonies; their liberal endowments for the advancement of religion and learning; their choice of devout and able pastors to propagate Christianity; their caution in stocking their provinces with people of sober lives and conversations from this the Mother Kingdom; their strict regard to the distribution of justice, in supplying the civil administration through all their colonies with officers of the greatest abilities, utter strangers to corruption: and to crown all, by sending the most vigilant and virtuous governors, who have no other views than the happiness of the people over whom they preside, and the honor of the king their master.

But, as those countries which I have described do not appear to have any desire of being conquered, and enslaved, murdered, or driven out by colonies, nor abound either in gold, silver, sugar, or tobacco, I did humbly conceive they were by no means proper objects of our zeal, our valor, or our interest. However, if those whom it may concern, think fit to be of another opinion, I am ready to depose, when I shall be lawfully called, that no European did ever visit these countries before me. I mean, if the inhabitants ought to be believed.

But, as to the formality of taking possession in my sovereign's name, it never came once into my thoughts; and if it had, yet as my affairs then stood, I should perhaps in point of prudence and self-preservation have put it off to a better opportunity.

Having thus answered the only objection that can be raised against me as a traveler, I here take a final leave of my courteous readers, and return to enjoy my own speculations in my little garden at Redriff; to apply those excellent lessons of virtue which I learned among the Houyhnhnms; to instruct the Yahoos of my own family as far as I shall find them docible animals; to behold my figure often in a glass, and thus if possible habituate myself by time to tolerate the sight of a human creature; to lament the brutality of Houyhnhnms in my own country, but always treat their persons with respect, for the sake of my noble master, his family, his friends, and the whole Houyhnhnm race, whom these of ours have the honor to resemble in all their lineaments, however their intellectuals came to degenerate.

I began last week to permit my wife to sit at dinner with me, at the farthest end of a long table; and to answer (but with the utmost brevity) the few questions I ask her. Yet the smell of a Yahoo continuing very offensive, I always keep my nose well stopped with rue, lavender, or tobacco leaves. And although it be hard for a man late in life to remove old habits, I am not altogether out of hopes in some time to suffer a neighbor Yahoo in my company, without the apprehensions I am yet under of his teeth or his claws.

My reconcilement to the Yahoo kind in general might not be so difficult, if they would be content with those vices and follies only which nature hath entitled them to. I am not in the least provoked at the sight of a lawyer, a pickpocket, a colonel, a fool, a lord, a gamester, a politician, a whoremonger, a physician, an evidence, a suborner, an attorney, a traitor, or the like: this is all according to the due course of things. But when I behold a lump of deformity, and diseases both in body and mind, smitten with pride, it immediately breaks all the measures of my patience; neither shall I be ever able to comprehend how such an animal and such a vice could tally together. The wise and virtuous Houyhnhnms, who abound in all excellencies that can adorn a rational creature, have no name for this vice in their language, which hath no terms to express anything that is evil, except those whereby they describe the detestable qualities of their Yahoos, among which they were not able to distinguish this of pride, for want of thoroughly understanding human nature, as it showeth itself in other countries, where that animal presides. But I, who had more experience, could plainly observe some rudiments of it among the wild Yahoos.

But the Houyhnhnms, who live under the government of reason, are no more proud of the good qualities they possess, than I should be for not wanting a leg or an arm, which no man in his wits would boast of, although he must be miserable without them. I dwell the longer upon this subject from the desire I have to make the society of an English Yahoo by any means not insupportable; and therefore I here entreat those who have any tincture of this absurd vice, that they will not presume to appear in my sight.

1726, 1735

A Modest Proposal[1]

FOR PREVENTING THE CHILDREN OF POOR PEOPLE IN IRELAND FROM BEING A BURDEN TO THEIR PARENTS OR COUNTRY, AND FOR MAKING THEM BENEFICIAL TO THE PUBLIC

It is a melancholy object to those who walk through this great town[2] or travel in the country, when they see the streets, the roads, and cabin doors, crowded with beggars of the female sex, followed by three, four, or six children, all in rags and importuning every passenger for an alms. These mothers, instead of being able to work for their honest livelihood, are forced to employ all their time in strolling to beg sustenance for their helpless infants, who, as they grow up, either turn thieves for want of work, or leave their dear native country to fight for the Pretender in Spain, or sell themselves to the Barbadoes.[3]

I think it is agreed by all parties that this prodigious number of children in the arms, or on the backs, or at the heels of their mothers, and frequently of their fathers, is in the present deplorable state of the kingdom a very great additional grievance; and therefore whoever could find out a fair, cheap, and easy method of making these children sound, useful members of the commonwealth would deserve so well of the public as to have his statue set up for a preserver of the nation.

But my intention is very far from being confined to provide only for the children of professed beggars; it is of a much greater extent, and shall take in the whole number of infants at a certain age who are born of parents in effect as little able to support them as those who demand our charity in the streets.

As to my own part, having turned my thoughts for many years upon this important subject, and maturely weighed the several schemes of other projectors,[4] I have always found them grossly mistaken in their computation. It is true, a child just dropped from its dam may be supported by her milk for a solar year, with little other nourishment; at most not above the value of two shillings, which the mother may certainly

---

1. A *Modest Proposal* is an example of Swift's favorite satiric devices used with superb effect. Irony (from the deceptive adjective "modest" in the title to the very last sentence) pervades the piece. A rigorous logic deduces ghastly arguments from a shocking premise so quietly assumed that the reader assents before he is aware of what his assent implies. Parody, at which Swift is adept, allows him to glance sardonically at the by then familiar figure of the benevolent humanitarian (forerunner of the modern sociologist, social worker, economic planner) concerned to correct a social evil by means of a theoretically conceived plan. The proposer, as naïve as he is apparently logical and kindly, ignores and therefore emphasizes for the reader the enormity of his plan. The whole is an elaboration of a rather trite metaphor: "The English are devouring the Irish." But there is nothing trite about the pamphlet, which expresses in Swift's most controlled style his pity for the oppressed, ignorant, populous, and hungry Catholic peasants of Ireland, and his anger at the rapacious English absentee landlords, who were bleeding the country white with the silent approbation of Parliament, ministers, and the Crown.

2. Dublin.

3. James Francis Edward Stuart (1688–1766), the son of James II, was claimant ("Pretender") to the throne of England from which the Glorious Revolution had barred his succession. Catholic Ireland was loyal to him, and Irishmen joined him in his exile on the Continent. Because of the poverty in Ireland, many Irishmen emigrated to the West Indies and other British colonies in America; they paid their passage by binding themselves to work for a stated period for one of the planters.

4. Devisers of schemes.

get, or the value in scraps, by her lawful occupation of begging; and it is exactly at one year old that I propose to provide for them in such a manner as instead of being a charge upon their parents or the parish, or wanting food and raiment for the rest of their lives, they shall on the contrary contribute to the feeding, and partly to the clothing, of many thousands.

There is likewise another great advantage in my scheme, that it will prevent those voluntary abortions, and that horrid practice of women murdering their bastard children, alas, too frequent among us, sacrificing the poor innocent babes, I doubt, more to avoid the expense than the shame, which would move tears and pity in the most savage and inhuman breast.

The number of souls in this kingdom[5] being usually reckoned one million and a half, of these I calculate there may be about two hundred thousand couple whose wives are breeders; from which number I subtract thirty thousand couples who are able to maintain their own children, although I apprehend there cannot be so many under the present distresses of the kingdom; but this being granted, there will remain an hundred and seventy thousand breeders. I again subtract fifty thousand for those women who miscarry, or whose children die by accident or disease within the year. There only remain an hundred and twenty thousand children of poor parents annually born. The question therefore is, how this number shall be reared and provided for, which, as I have already said, under the present situation of affairs, is utterly impossible by all the methods hitherto proposed. For we can neither employ them in handicraft or agriculture; we neither build houses (I mean in the country) nor cultivate land. They can very seldom pick up a livelihood by stealing till they arrive at six years old, except where they are of towardly[6] parts; although I confess they learn the rudiments much earlier, during which time they can however be looked upon only as probationers, as I have been informed by a principal gentleman in the county of Cavan, who protested to me that he never knew above one or two instances under the ages of six, even in a part of the kingdom so renowned for the quickest proficiency in that art.

I am assured by our merchants that a boy or a girl before twelve years old is no salable commodity; and even when they come to this age they will not yield above three pounds, or three pounds and half a crown at most on the Exchange; which cannot turn to account either to the parents or the kingdom, the charge of nutriment and rags having been at least four times that value.

I shall now therefore humbly propose my own thoughts, which I hope will not be liable to the least objection.

I have been assured by a very knowing American of my acquaintance in London, that a young healthy child well nursed is at a year old a most delicious, nourishing, and wholesome food, whether stewed, roasted,

5. Ireland.   6. Dutiful, tractable.

baked, or boiled; and I make no doubt that it will equally serve in a fricassee or a ragout.[7]

I do therefore humbly offer it to public consideration that of the hundred and twenty thousand children, already computed, twenty thousand may be reserved for breed, whereof only one fourth part to be males, which is more than we allow to sheep, black cattle, or swine; and my reason is that these children are seldom the fruits of marriage, a circumstance not much regarded by our savages, therefore one male will be sufficient to serve four females. That the remaining hundred thousand may at a year old be offered in sale to the persons of quality and fortune through the kingdom, always advising the mother to let them suck plentifully in the last month, so as to render them plump and fat for a good table. A child will make two dishes at an entertainment for friends; and when the family dines alone, the fore or hind quarter will make a reasonable dish, and seasoned with a little pepper or salt will be very good boiled on the fourth day, especially in winter.

I have reckoned upon a medium that a child just born will weigh twelve pounds, and in a solar year if tolerably nursed increaseth to twenty-eight pounds.

I grant this food will be somewhat dear, and therefore very proper for landlords, who, as they have already devoured most of the parents, seem to have the best title to the children.

Infant's flesh will be in season throughout the year, but more plentiful in March, and a little before and after. For we are told by a grave author, an eminent French physician,[8] that fish being a prolific diet, there are more children born in Roman Catholic countries about nine months after Lent than at any other season; therefore, reckoning a year after Lent, the markets will be more glutted than usual, because the number of popish infants is at least three to one in this kingdom; and therefore it will have one other collateral advantage, by lessening the number of Papists among us.

I have already computed the charge of nursing a beggar's child (in which list I reckon all cottagers, laborers, and four fifths of the farmers) to be about two shillings per annum, rags included; and I believe no gentleman would repine to give ten shillings for the carcass of a good fat child, which, as I have said, will make four dishes of excellent nutritive meat, when he hath only some particular friend or his own family to dine with him. Thus the squire will learn to be a good landlord, and grow popular among the tenants; the mother will have eight shillings net profit, and be fit for the work till she produces another child.

Those who are more thrifty (as I must confess the times require) may flay the carcass; the skin of which artificially[9] dressed will make admirable gloves for ladies, and summer boots for fine gentlemen.

7. A highly seasoned meat stew.
8. François Rabelais (ca. 1494–1553), a humorist   and a satirist, by no means grave.
9. Skillfully.

As to our city of Dublin, shambles[1] may be appointed for this purpose in the most convenient parts of it, and butchers we may be assured will not be wanting; although I rather recommend buying the children alive, and dressing them hot from the knife as we do roasting pigs.

A very worthy person, a true lover of his country, and whose virtues I highly esteem, was lately pleased in discoursing on this matter to offer a refinement upon my scheme. He said that many gentlemen of this kingdom, having of late destroyed their deer, he conceived that the want of venison might be well supplied by the bodies of young lads and maidens, not exceeding fourteen years of age nor under twelve, so great a number of both sexes in every county being now ready to starve for want of work and service; and these to be disposed of by their parents, if alive, or otherwise by their nearest relations. But with due deference to so excellent a friend and so deserving a patriot, I cannot be altogether in his sentiments; for as to the males, my American acquaintance assured me from frequent experience that their flesh was generally tough and lean, like that of our schoolboys, by continual exercise, and their taste disagreeable; and to fatten them would not answer the charge. Then as to the females, it would, I think with humble submission, be a loss to the public, because they soon would become breeders themselves; and besides, it is not improbable that some scrupulous people might be apt to censure such a practice (although indeed very unjustly) as a little bordering upon cruelty; which I confess, hath always been with me the strongest objection against any project, how well soever intended.

But in order to justify my friend, he confessed that this expedient was put into his head by the famous Psalmanazar,[2] a native of the island Formosa, who came from thence to London above twenty years ago, and in conversation told my friend that in his country when any young person happened to be put to death, the executioner sold the carcass to persons of quality as a prime dainty; and that in his time the body of a plump girl of fifteen, who was crucified for an attempt to poison the emperor, was sold to his Imperial Majesty's prime minister of state, and other great mandarins of the court, in joints from the gibbet, at four hundred crowns. Neither indeed can I deny that if the same use were made of several plump young girls in this town, who without one single groat to their fortunes cannot stir abroad without a chair, and appear at the playhouse and assemblies in foreign fineries which they never will pay for, the kingdom would not be the worse.

Some persons of a desponding spirit are in great concern about that vast number of poor people who are aged, diseased, or maimed, and I have been desired to employ my thoughts what course may be taken to ease the nation of so grievous an encumbrance. But I am not in the least

1. Slaughterhouses.
2. George Psalmanazar (ca. 1679–1763), a famous imposter. A Frenchman, he imposed himself on English bishops, noblemen, and scientists as a Formosan. He wrote an entirely fictitious account of Formosa, in which he described human sacrifices and cannibalism.

pain upon that matter, because it is very well known that they are every day dying and rotting by cold and famine, and filth and vermin, as fast as can be reasonably expected. And as to the younger laborers, they are now in almost as hopeful a condition. They cannot get work, and consequently pine away for want of nourishment to a degree that if at any time they are accidentally hired to common labor, they have not strength to perform it; and thus the country and themselves are happily delivered from the evils to come.

I have too long digressed, and therefore shall return to my subject. I think the advantages by the proposal which I have made are obvious and many, as well as of the highest importance.

For first, as I have already observed, it would greatly lessen the number of Papists, with whom we are yearly overrun, being the principal breeders of the nation as well as our most dangerous enemies; and who stay at home on purpose to deliver the kingdom to the Pretender, hoping to take their advantage by the absence of so many good Protestants, who have chosen rather to leave their country than stay at home and pay tithes against their conscience to an Episcopal curate.

Secondly, the poorer tenants will have something valuable of their own, which by law may be made liable to distress,[3] and help to pay their landlord's rent, their corn and cattle being already seized and money a thing unknown.

Thirdly, whereas the maintenance of an hundred thousand children, from two years old and upwards, cannot be computed at less than ten shillings a piece per annum, the nation's stock will be thereby increased fifty thousand pounds per annum, besides the profit of a new dish introduced to the tables of all gentlemen of fortune in the kingdom who have any refinement in taste. And the money will circulate among ourselves, the goods being entirely of our own growth and manufacture.

Fourthly, the constant breeders, besides the gain of eight shillings sterling per annum by the sale of their children, will be rid of the charge of maintaining them after the first year.

Fifthly, this food would likewise bring great custom to taverns, where the vintners will certainly be so prudent as to procure the best receipts for dressing it to perfection, and consequently have their houses frequented by all the fine gentlemen, who justly value themselves upon their knowledge in good eating; and a skillful cook, who understands how to oblige his guests, will contrive to make it as expensive as they please.

Sixthly, this would be a great inducement to marriage, which all wise nations have either encouraged by rewards or enforced by laws and penalties. It would increase the care and tenderness of mothers toward their children, when they were sure of a settlement for life to the poor babes, provided in some sort by the public, to their annual profit instead of

3. Distraint, i.e., the seizing, through legal action, of property for the payment of debts and other obligations.

expense. We should see an honest emulation among the married women, which of them could bring the fattest child to the market. Men would become as fond of their wives during the time of their pregnancy as they are now of their mares in foal, their cows in calf, or sows when they are ready to farrow; nor offer to beat or kick them (as is too frequent a practice) for fear of a miscarriage.

Many other advantages might be enumerated. For instance, the addition of some thousand carcasses in our exportation of barreled beef, the propagation of swine's flesh, and improvement in the art of making good bacon, so much wanted among us by the great destruction of pigs, too frequent at our tables, which are no way comparable in taste or magnificence to a well-grown, fat, yearling child, which roasted whole will make a considerable figure at a lord mayor's feast or any other public entertainment. But this and many others I omit, being studious of brevity.

Supposing that one thousand families in this city would be constant customers for infants' flesh, besides others who might have it at merry meetings, particularly weddings and christenings, I compute that Dublin would take off annually about twenty thousand carcasses, and the rest of the kingdom (where probably they will be sold somewhat cheaper) the remaining eighty thousand.

I can think of no one objection that will probably be raised against this proposal, unless it should be urged that the number of people will be thereby much lessened in the kingdom. This I freely own, and it was indeed one principal design in offering it to the world. I desire the reader will observe, that I calculate my remedy for this one individual kingdom of Ireland and for no other that ever was, is, or I think ever can be upon earth. Therefore let no man talk to me of other expedients: of taxing our absentees at five shillings a pound: of using neither clothes nor household furniture except what is of our own growth and manufacture: of utterly rejecting the materials and instruments that promote foreign luxury: of curing the expensiveness of pride, vanity, idleness, and gaming in our women: of introducing a vein of parsimony, prudence, and temperance: of learning to love our country, in the want of which we differ even from Laplanders and the inhabitants of Topinamboo:[4] of quitting our animosities and factions, nor acting any longer like the Jews, who were murdering one another at the very moment their city was taken:[5] of being a little cautious not to sell our country and conscience for nothing: of teaching landlords to have at least one degree of mercy toward their tenants: lastly, of putting a spirit of honesty, industry, and skill into our shopkeepers; who, if a resolution could now be taken to buy only our native goods, would immediately unite to cheat and exact upon us

4. I.e., even Laplanders love their frozen, infertile country and the savage tribes of Brazil their jungle more than the Anglo-Irish love Ireland.
5. During the siege of Jerusalem by the Roman Emperor Titus, who captured and destroyed the city in A.D. 70, the city was torn by bloody fights between factions of fanatics.

in the price, the measure, and the goodness, nor could ever yet be brought to make one fair proposal of just dealing, though often and earnestly invited to it.[6]

Therefore I repeat, let no man talk to me of these and the like expedients, till he hath at least some glimpse of hope that there will ever be some hearty and sincere attempt to put them in practice.

But as to myself, having been wearied out for many years with offering vain, idle, visionary thoughts, and at length utterly despairing of success, I fortunately fell upon this proposal, which, as it is wholly new, so it hath something solid and real, of no expense and little trouble, full in our own power, and whereby we can incur no danger in disobliging England. For this kind of commodity will not bear exportation, the flesh being of too tender a consistence to admit a long continuance in salt, although perhaps I could name a country which would be glad to eat up our whole nation without it.[7]

After all, I am not so violently bent upon my own opinion as to reject any offer proposed by wise men, which shall be found equally innocent, cheap, easy, and effectual. But before something of that kind shall be advanced in contradiction to my scheme, and offering a better, I desire the author or authors will be pleased maturely to consider two points. First, as things now stand, how they will be able to find food and raiment for an hundred thousand useless mouths and backs. And secondly, there being a round million of creatures in human figure throughout this kingdom, whose sole subsistence put into a common stock would leave them in debt two millions of pounds sterling, adding those who are beggars by profession to the bulk of farmers, cottagers, and laborers, with their wives and children who are beggars in effect; I desire those politicians who dislike my overture, and may perhaps be so bold to attempt an answer, that they will first ask the parents of these mortals whether they would not at this day think it a great happiness to have been sold for food at a year old in the manner I prescribe, and thereby have avoided such a perpetual sense of misfortunes as they have since gone through by the oppression of landlords, the impossibility of paying rent without money or trade, the want of common sustenance, with neither house nor clothes to cover them from the inclemencies of the weather, and the most inevitable prospect of entailing the like or greater miseries upon their breed forever.

I profess, in the sincerity of my heart, that I have not the least personal interest in endeavoring to promote this necessary work, having no other motive than the public good of my country, by advancing our trade, providing for infants, relieving the poor, and giving some pleasure to the rich. I have no children by which I can propose to get a single penny; the youngest being nine years old, and my wife past childbearing.

1729

6. Swift himself had made all these proposals in various pamphlets. In editions printed during his lifetime the various proposals were italicized to indicate that Swift is no longer being ironic.
7. I.e., England.

JOSEPH ADDISON *and* SIR RICHARD STEELE
1672–1719   1672–1729

1709–11:   *Tatler* published.
1711–12:   *Spectator* published.
1714:   *Spectator* resumed (for 80 numbers).

The friendship of Joseph Addison and Richard Steele began when they were schoolboys together in London. Their careers ran parallel courses and brought them for a while into fruitful collaboration. Addison, though charming when among friends, was by nature reserved, calculating, and prudent. Steele was impulsive and rakish when young (but ardently devoted to his beautiful wife), imprudent to a degree, and consequently in frequent financial distress. Addison never stumbled in his progress to financial security, a late marriage to a widowed countess, and a successful political career; walking less surely, Steele experienced many vicissitudes and faced serious financial problems during his last years.

Both men attended Oxford, where Addison took his degree, won a fellowship, and earned a reputation for Latin verse; the less scholarly Steele, however, did not stay for a degree, but left the university to take a commission in the army. For a while he cut a dashing figure in London, even, to his horror, seriously wounding a man in a duel. Both men enjoyed the patronage of the great Whig magnates, and except during the last four years of Queen Anne's reign, when the Tories were in the ascendency, they were generously treated. Steele became editor of the *London Gazette*, an official newspaper that appeared twice a week during the greater part of his editorship, listing government appointments and reporting domestic and foreign news—in short, the first newspaper in the modern sense. Much later, Steele became manager of the Theatre Royal, Drury Lane. Meanwhile he had served in Parliament and been knighted by George I. Addison held more important positions: he was secretary to the Lord Lieutenant of Ireland, and later an under-secretary of state; finally, toward the end of his life, he became secretary of state. Both men wrote plays: Addison's *Cato*, a frigid and very "correct" tragedy, had great success in 1713; and Steele's later plays at Drury Lane (*The Conscious Lovers*, 1722, for instance) were instrumental in establishing the popularity of sentimental comedy throughout the eighteenth century.

Steele's debts and Addison's loss of office in 1710 were the efficient causes of their journalistic enterprises, through which they developed one of the most characteristic types of eighteenth-century literature, the periodical essay. Steele's experience as gazetteer had involved him in journalism, and in 1709, when in need of money, he launched the *Tatler* under the pseudonym Isaac Bickerstaff. He sought to attract the largest possible audience: the title was a bid for female readers, and the mixture of news with personal reflectior soon became popular in coffeehouses and at breakfast tables. The appeared thrice weekly from April 1709 to January 1711. Steele wrot the greater number of *Tatlers*, but Addison contributed helpfully other friends. The *Spectator*, which appeared daily except Sunday fro

1711 to December 1712 (and was briefly resumed by Addison in 1714), was the joint undertaking of the two friends, though it was dominated by Addison. The papers had many imitators in their own day and throughout the rest of the century; Johnson's *Rambler* and *Idler* and Goldsmith's brief *Bee* are distinguished instances.

Both Steele and Addison were conscious moralists and did not disguise their intention of improving the minds, morals, and manners of their readers. The periodical essay they developed is less formal and didactic than the essays of Bacon, less personal than those of Charles Lamb and William Hazlitt in the next century. But it succeeded not only in amusing its audience but in changing it. Moral reform had been in the air since the 1690s, and the new society that was coming into existence (in some degree the creation of Addison and Steele) was attaining a balance between the morality and respectability of the old, rather Puritan middle class (which was too often narrowly Philistine in taste and outlook) and the wit, grace, and enlightenment of the older aristocratic and fashionable class (which, in the previous century, had too often been libertine in morals and thought). The new social ideal, which the two essayists themselves fostered, stressed moderation, reasonableness, self-control, urbanity, and good taste. Steele's *Tatler* essays applied this ideal to any topic that suggested itself as pleasing or useful: the theater, true breeding as against vulgar manners, education, simplicity in dress, the proper use of Sunday, and so on; and he lightly ridiculed common social types such as the prude, the coquette, the "pretty fellow," and the rake. Addison's best *Tatler* essays initiated his study of eccentric or affected characters (to be continued in the *Spectator*), cleverly observed and described with agreeable humor. The *Tatler* papers quickly won an appreciative audience, and when published in book form, they continued (like those of the *Spectator*) to sell throughout the century.

The readers whom Steele had reached and influenced were at hand when the *Spectator* began to appear two months after the last *Tatler*. Steele played a more important role in the paper than Addison had in the *Tatler*, but the *Spectator* is throughout Addisonian. In the second number Steele introduces us to the members of Mr. Spectator's Club: a man about town, a student of law and literature, a churchman, a soldier, a Tory country squire, and, interestingly enough, a London merchant. As a Whig, Steele was ardently sympathetic with the new moneyed class in the City, and it was evidently his intention to pit the merchant, Sir Andrew Freeport, the representative of the new order, against the Tory Sir Roger de Coverley, who is presented as belonging to a vanishing order. Addison, however, preferred to present Sir Roger in episodes set in town and in the country as an endearing, eccentric character, often absurd but always amiable and innocent. He is a prominent ancestor of a long line of similar characters in fiction during the next two centuries. Addison's scholarly interests broadened the material to include not only social criticism but the popularization of current philosophical and scientific notions; and he wrote important critical papers distinguishing true and false wit, an extended series of Saturday essays evaluating *Paradise Lost*, and an influential series on "the pleasures of the imagination" which treated the aesthetics of visual beauty in nature and art. Altogether, the *Spectator* fulfilled his ambition (see *Spectator* 10, below) to be considered an agreeable modern Socrates.

The best description of Addison's prose is Samuel Johnson's in his *Life of Addison*: "His prose is the model of the middle style; on grave subjects not formal, on light occasions not groveling; pure without scrupulosity, and exact without apparent elaboration; always equable, and always easy, without glowing words or pointed sentences." And he concludes: "Whoever wishes to attain an English style, familiar but not coarse, and elegant but not ostentatious, must give his days and nights to the volumes of Addison," a course of study which a good many aspiring writers during the century seem to have undertaken with some success.

THE PERIODICAL ESSAY: MANNERS

STEELE: [The Gentleman; The Pretty Fellow]

From *The Tatler*, No. *21*, *Saturday*, *May 28*, *1709*

> *Quidquid agunt homines——*
> *——nostri est farrago libelli.*[1]
> —JUVENAL, *Satire* 1.85–86

White's Chocolate House,[2] May 26

A gentleman has writ to me out of the country a very civil letter, and said things which I suppress with great violence to my vanity. There are many terms in my narratives which he complains want explaining, and has therefore desired that, for the benefit of my country readers, I would let him know what I mean by a Gentleman, a Pretty Fellow, a Toast, a Coquette, a Critic, a Wit, and all other appellations of those now in the gayer world, who are in possession of these several characters; together with an account of those who unfortunately pretend to them. I shall begin with him we usually call a Gentleman, or man of conversation.

It is generally thought that warmth of imagination, quick relish of pleasure, and a manner of becoming it, are the most essential qualities for forming this sort of man. But anyone that is much in company will observe that the height of good breeding is shown rather in never giving offense, than in doing obliging things. Thus, he that never shocks you, though he is seldom entertaining, is more likely to keep your favor than he who often entertains, and sometimes displeases you. The most necessary talent therefore in a man of conversation, which is what we ordinarily intend by a fine gentleman, is a good judgment. He that has this in perfection is master of his companion, without letting him see it; and has the same advantage over men of any other qualifications whatsoever, as one that can see would have over a blind man of ten times his strength.

This is what makes Sophronius the darling of all who converse with him, and the most powerful with his acquaintance of any man in town. By the light of this faculty, he acts with great ease and dispatch among

1. "Whatever men do . . . shall form the motley subject of my book." Steele used this epigraph for all but a very few of the first 62 *Tatlers*.
2. One of the fashionable chocolate houses, from which Steele, in the earlier numbers of the *Tatler*, dated "accounts of gallantry, pleasure, and entertainment."

the men of business. All which he performs with so much success that, with as much discretion in life as any man ever had, he neither is, nor appears, cunning. But as he does a good office, if he ever does it, with readiness and alacrity, so he denies what he does not care to engage in, in a manner that convinces you that you ought not to have asked it. His judgment is so good and unerring, and accompanied with so cheerful a spirit, that his conversation is a continual feast, at which he helps some, and is helped by others, in such a manner that the equality of society is perfectly kept up, and every man obliges as much as he is obliged: for it is the greatest and justest skill in a man of superior understanding, to know how to be on a level with his companions. This sweet disposition runs through all the actions of Sophronius, and makes his company desired by women, without being envied by men. Sophronius would be as just as he is, if there were no law; and would be as discreet as he is, if there were no such thing as calumny.

In imitation of this agreeable being, is made that animal we call a Pretty Fellow; who being just able to find out that what makes Sophronius acceptable is a natural behavior, in order to the same reputation, makes his own an artificial one. Jack Dimple is his perfect mimic, whereby he is of course the most unlike him of all men living. Sophronius just now passed into the inner room directly forward: Jack comes as fast after as he can for the right and left looking glass, in which he had but just approved himself by a nod at each, and marched on. He will meditate within for half an hour, till he thinks he is not careless enough in his air, and come back to the mirror to recollect his forgetfulness. * * *

STEELE: [Dueling]

From *The Tatler*, No. 25, Tuesday, June 7, 1709

Quidquid agunt homines——
——nostri est farrago libelli.
—Juvenal, *Satire* 1.85–86

White's Chocolate House, June 6

A letter from a young lady, written in the most passionate terms, wherein she laments the misfortune of a gentleman, her lover, who was lately wounded in a duel, has turned my thoughts to that subject, and inclined me to examine into the causes which precipitate men into so fatal a folly. And as it has been proposed to treat of subjects of gallantry in the article from hence, and no one point in nature is more proper to be considered by the company who frequent this place than that of duels, it is worth our consideration to examine into this chimerical groundless humor, and to lay every other thought aside, until we have stripped it of all its false pretenses to credit and reputation amongst men.

But I must confess, when I consider what I am going about, and run over in my imagination all the endless crowd of men of honor who will

be offended at such a discourse, I am undertaking, methinks, a work
worthy an invulnerable hero in romance, rather than a private gentleman with a single rapier; but as I am pretty well acquainted by great
opportunities with the nature of man, and know of a truth that all men
fight against their will, the danger vanishes, and resolution rises upon
this subject. For this reason, I shall talk very freely on a custom which
all men wish exploded, though no man has courage enough to resist it.

But there is one unintelligible word, which I fear will extremely perplex my dissertation, and I confess to you I find very hard to explain,
which is the term "satisfaction." An honest country gentleman had the
misfortune to fall into company with two or three modern men of honor,
where he happened to be very ill treated; and one of the company, being
conscious of his offense, sends a note to him in the morning, and tells
him he was ready to give him satisfaction. "This is fine doing," says the
plain fellow; "last night he sent me away cursedly out of humor, and
this morning he fancies it would be a satisfaction to be run through the
body."

As the matter at present stands, it is not to do handsome actions
denominates a man of honor; it is enough if he dares to defend ill ones.
Thus you often see a common sharper in competition with a gentleman
of the first rank; though all mankind is convinced that a fighting gamester is only a pickpocket with the courage of an highwayman. One cannot
with any patience reflect on the unaccountable jumble of persons and
things in this town and nation, which occasions very frequently that a
brave man falls by a hand below that of a common hangman, and yet
his executioner escapes the clutches of the hangman for doing it. I shall
therefore hereafter consider how the bravest men in other ages and nations
have behaved themselves upon such incidents as we decide by combat;
and show, from their practice, that this resentment neither has its foundation from true reason or solid fame; but is an imposture, made of
cowardice, falsehood, and want of understanding. For this work, a good
history of quarrels would be very edifying to the public, and I apply
myself to the town for particulars and circumstances within their knowledge, which may serve to embellish the dissertation with proper cuts.[1]
Most of the quarrels I have ever known have proceeded from some valiant coxcomb's persisting in the wrong, to defend some prevailing folly,
and preserve himself from the ingenuity[2] of owning a mistake.

By this means it is called "giving a man satisfaction" to urge your
offense against him with your sword; which puts me in mind of Peter's
order to the keeper, in *The Tale of a Tub*:[3] "If you neglect to do all this,
damn you and your generation forever: and so we bid you heartily farewell." If the contradiction in the very terms of one of our challenges
were as well explained and turned into downright English, would it not
run after this manner?

1. Either woodcuts or engravings on copper plates.
2. Honorable candor.
3. In Swift's satire, the Roman Church is attacked
in the character of Peter. The passage (slightly
misquoted) satirizes the Pope's practice of issuing
indulgences.

"SIR,

"Your extraordinary behavior last night, and the liberty you were pleased to take with me, makes me this morning give you this, to tell you, because you are an ill-bred puppy, I will meet you in Hyde Park an hour hence; and because you want both breeding and humanity, I desire you would come with a pistol in your hand, on horseback, and endeavor to shoot me through the head to teach you more manners. If you fail of doing me this pleasure, I shall say you are a rascal, on every post in town: and so, sir, if you will not injure me more, I shall never forgive what you have done already. Pray, sir, do not fail of getting everything ready; and you will infinitely oblige, sir, your most obedient humble servant, etc." * * *

STEELE: [The Spectator's Club]

The Spectator, No. 2, Friday, March 2, 1771

——*Haec alii sex*
Vel plures uno conclamant ore.[1]
—JUVENAL, *Satire* 7.166–67

The first of our society is a gentleman of Worcestershire, of ancient descent, a baronet, his name Sir Roger de Coverley. His great-grand-father was inventor of that famous country-dance which is called after him. All who know the shire are very well acquainted with the parts and merits of Sir Roger. He is a gentleman that is very singular in his behavior, but his singularities proceed from his good sense, and are contradictions to the manners of the world only as he thinks the world is in the wrong. However, this humor creates him no enemies, for he does nothing with sourness or obstinacy; and his being unconfined to modes and forms makes him but the readier and more capable to please and oblige all who know him. When he is in town, he lives in Soho Square. It is said he keeps himself a bachelor by reason he was crossed in love by a perverse, beautiful widow of the next county to him. Before this disappointment, Sir Roger was what you call a fine gentleman, had often supped with my Lord Rochester and Sir George Etherege, fought a duel upon his first coming to town, and kicked Bully Dawson in a public coffeehouse for calling him "youngster."[2] But being ill used by the above-mentioned widow, he was very serious for a year and a half; and though, his temper being naturally jovial, he at last got over it, he grew careless of himself, and never dressed afterward. He continues to wear a coat and doublet of the same cut that were in fashion at the time of his repulse, which, in his merry humors, he tells us, has been in and out twelve

1. "Six more at least join their consenting voice."
2. John Wilmot, earl of Rochester (1647–1680), the poet and rake, an intimate of Charles II; Sir

George Etherege (ca. 1634–1691), playwright, rake, and boon companion of the king and Rochester. Bully Dawson was a notorious sharper of the period.

times since he first wore it. 'Tis said Sir Roger grew humble in his desires after he had forgot this cruel beauty, insomuch that it is reported he has frequently offended in point of chastity with beggars and gypsies; but this is looked upon by his friends rather as matter of raillery than truth. He is now in his fifty-sixth year, cheerful, gay, and hearty; keeps a good house both in town and country; a great lover of mankind; but there is such a mirthful cast in his behavior that he is rather beloved than esteemed. His tenants grow rich, his servants look satisfied, all the young women profess love to him, and the young men are glad of his company; when he comes into a house he calls the servants by their names, and talks all the way upstairs to a visit. I must not omit that Sir Roger is a justice of the quorum,[3] that he fills the chair at a quarter-session with great abilities; and, three months ago, gained universal applause by explaining a passage in the Game Act.

The gentleman next in esteem and authority among us is another bachelor, who is a member of the Inner Temple;[4] a man of great probity, wit, and understanding; but he has chosen his place of residence rather to obey the direction of an old humorsome[5] father, than in pursuit of his own inclinations. He was placed there to study the laws of the land, and is the most learned of any of the house in those of the stage. Aristotle and Longinus are much better understood by him than Littleton or Coke.[6] The father sends up, every post, questions relating to marriage articles, leases, and tenures, in the neighborhood; all which questions he agrees with an attorney to answer and take care of in the lump. He is studying the passions themselves, when he should be inquiring into the debates among men which arise from them. He knows the argument of each of the orations of Demosthenes and Tully,[7] but not one case in the reports of our own courts. No one ever took him for a fool, but none, except his intimate friends, know he has a great deal of wit. This turn makes him at once both disinterested and agreeable; as few of his thoughts are drawn from business, they are most of them fit for conversation. His taste of books is a little too just[8] for the age he lives in; he has read all, but approves of very few. His familiarity with the customs, manners, actions, and writings of the ancients makes him a very delicate observer of what occurs to him in the present world. He is an excellent critic, and the time of the play is his hour of business; exactly at five he passes through New Inn, crosses through Russell Court, and takes a turn at Will's[9] till the play begins; he has his shoes rubbed and his periwig pow-

---

3. A county justice of the peace, presiding over quarterly sessions of the court.
4. One of the Inns of Court, where lawyers resided or had their offices and where students studied law.
5. Full of crotchets.
6. In other words, he is more familiar with the laws of literature than those of England. The *Poetics* of Aristotle and the Greek treatise *On the Sublime* (reputedly by Longinus) were in high favor among the critics of the time. Sir Thomas Littleton, 15th-century jurist, was author of a renowned

treatise on *Tenures*; Sir Edward Coke (1552–1634) was the judge and writer whose *Reports* and *Institutes of the Laws of England* (known as *Coke upon Littleton*) have exerted a great influence on the interpretation of English law.
7. Marcus Tullius Cicero.
8. Exact.
9. The coffeehouse in Covent Garden associated with literature and criticism since Dryden had begun to frequent it in the 1660's.

dered at the barber's as you go into the Rose.[1] It is for the good of the audience when he is at a play, for the actors have an ambition to please him.

The person of next consideration is Sir Andrew Freeport, a merchant of great eminence in the city of London, a person of indefatigable industry, strong reason, and great experience. His notions of trade are noble and generous, and (as every rich man has usually some sly way of jesting which would make no great figure were he not a rich man) he calls the sea the British Common. He is acquainted with commerce in all its parts, and will tell you that it is a stupid and barbarous way to extend dominion by arms; for true power is to be got by arts and industry. He will often argue that if this part of our trade were well cultivated, we should gain from one nation; and if another, from another. I have heard him prove that diligence makes more lasting acquisitions than valor, and that sloth has ruined more nations than the sword. He abounds in several frugal maxims, among which the greatest favorite is, "A penny saved is a penny got." A general trader of good sense is pleasanter company than a general scholar; and Sir Andrew having a natural unaffected eloquence, the perspicuity of his discourse gives the same pleasure that wit would in another man. He has made his fortunes himself, and says that England may be richer than other kingdoms by as plain methods as he himself is richer than other men; though at the same time I can say this of him, that there is not a point in the compass but blows home a ship in which he is an owner.

Next to Sir Andrew in the clubroom sits Captain Sentry, a gentleman of great courage, good understanding, but invincible modesty. He is one of those that deserve very well, but are very awkward at putting their talents within the observation of such as should take notice of them. He was some years a captain, and behaved himself with great gallantry in several engagements and at several sieges; but having a small estate of his own, and being next heir to Sir Roger, he has quitted a way of life in which no man can rise suitably to his merit who is not something of a courtier as well as a soldier. I have heard him often lament that in a profession where merit is placed in so conspicuous a view, impudence should get the better of modesty. When he has talked to this purpose I never heard him make a sour expression, but frankly confess that he left the world because he was not fit for it. A strict honesty and an even, regular behavior are in themselves obstacles to him that must press through crowds who endeavor at the same end with himself—the favor of a commander. He will, however, in his way of talk, excuse generals for not disposing according to men's desert, or inquiring into it, "for," says he, "that great man who has a mind to help me, has as many to break through to come at me as I have to come at him"; therefore he will conclude that the man who would make a figure, especially in a military way, must get over all false modesty, and assist his patron against the

1. A tavern near Drury Lane.

importunity of other pretenders by a proper assurance in his own vindication. He says it is a civil cowardice to be backward in asserting[2] what
you ought to expect, as it is a military fear to be slow in attacking when
it is your duty. With this candor does the gentleman speak of himself
and others. The same frankness runs through all his conversation. The
military part of his life has furnished him with many adventures, in the
relation of which he is very agreeable to the company; for he is never
overbearing, though accustomed to command men in the utmost degree
below him; nor ever too obsequious from an habit of obeying men highly
above him.

But that our society may not appear a set of humorists[3] unacquainted
with the gallantries and pleasures of the age, we have among us the
gallant Will Honeycomb, a gentleman who, according to his years, should
be in the decline of his life, but having ever been very careful of his
person, and always had a very easy fortune, time has made but very little
impression either by wrinkles on his forehead or traces in his brain. His
person is well turned and of a good height. He is very ready at that sort
of discourse with which men usually entertain women. He has all his
life dressed very well, and remembers habits[4] as others do men. He can
smile when one speaks to him, and laughs easily. He knows the history
of every mode, and can inform you from which of the French king's
wenches our wives and daughters had this manner of curling their hair,
that way of placing their hoods; whose frailty was covered by such a sort
of petticoat, and whose vanity to show her foot made that part of the
dress so short in such a year. In a word, all his conversation and knowledge has been in the female world. As other men of his age will take
notice to you what such a minister said upon such and such an occasion,
he will tell you when the Duke of Monmouth[5] danced at court such a
woman was then smitten, another was taken with him at the head of his
troop in the Park. In all these important relations, he has ever about the
same time received a kind glance or a blow of a fan from some celebrated
beauty, mother of the present Lord Such-a-one. If you speak of a young
commoner that said a lively thing in the House, he starts up: "He has
good blood in his veins; Tom Mirabell begot him. The rogue cheated
me in that affair; that young fellow's mother used me more like a dog
than any woman I ever made advances to." This way of talking of his
very much enlivens the conversation among us of a more sedate turn;
and I find there is not one of the company but myself, who rarely speak
at all, but speaks of him as of that sort of man who is usually called a
well-bred, fine gentleman. To conclude his character, where women
are not concerned he is an honest, worthy man.

I cannot tell whether I am to account him whom I am next to speak
of as one of our company, for he visits us but seldom; but when he does,
it adds to every man else a new enjoyment of himself. He is a clergyman,

2. Claiming.
3. Eccentrics.
4. Clothes.

5. The illegitimate son of Charles II, the ill-fated
Absalom of Dryden's *Absalom and Achitophel*.

a very philosophic man, of general learning, great sanctity of life, and the most exact good breeding. He has the misfortune to be of a very weak constitution, and consequently cannot accept of such cares and business as preferments in his function would oblige him to; he is therefore among divines what a chamber-counselor is among lawyers. The probity of his mind and the integrity of his life create him followers, as being eloquent or loud advances others. He seldom introduces the subject he speaks upon; but we are so far gone in years that he observes, when he is among us, an earnestness to have him fall on some divine topic, which he always treats with much authority, as one who has no interest in this world, as one who is hastening to the object of all his wishes and conceives hope from his decays and infirmities. These are my ordinary companions.

ADDISON: [Sir Roger at Church]

The Spectator, No. 112, Monday, July 9, 1711

'Athanátous mèn prōta theoùs, nómo os diákeitai, Tíma.[1]
—PYTHAGORAS

I am always very well pleased with a country Sunday, and think, if keeping holy the seventh day were only a human institution, it would be the best method that could have been thought of for the polishing and civilizing of mankind. It is certain the country people would soon degenerate into a kind of savages and barbarians were there not such frequent returns of a stated time, in which the whole village meet together with their best faces, and in their cleanliest habits, to converse with one another upon indifferent subjects, hear their duties explained to them, and join together in adoration of the Supreme Being. Sunday clears away the rust of the whole week, not only as it refreshes in their minds the notions of religion, but as it puts both the sexes upon appearing in their most agreeable forms, and exerting all such qualities are apt to give them a figure in the eye of the village. A country fellow distinguishes himself as much in the churchyard as a citizen[2] does upon the 'Change, the whole parish politics being generally discussed in that place either after sermon or before the bell rings.

My friend Sir Roger, being a good churchman, has beautified the inside of his church with several texts of his own choosing; he has likewise given a handsome pulpit cloth, and railed in the communion table at his own expense. He has often told me that, at his coming to his estate, he found his parishioners very irregular; and that, in order to make them kneel and join in the responses, he gave every one of them

---

1. "First worship the immortal gods as customarily a merchant. The " 'Change" is the Exchange decrees." The first of the so-called Golden Verses in London, where merchants met to transact business of Pythagoras. ness.
2. A citizen of the City of London, hence com-

a hassock and a Common Prayer book, and at the same time employed an itinerant singing master, who goes about the country for that purpose, to instruct them rightly in the tunes of the Psalms; upon which they now very much value themselves, and indeed outdo most of the country churches that I have ever met.

As Sir Roger is landlord to the whole congregation, he keeps them in very good order, and will suffer nobody to sleep in it besides himself; for if by chance he has been surprised into a short nap at sermon, upon recovering out of it he stands up and looks about him, and if he sees anybody else nodding, either wakes them himself, or sends his servant to them. Several other of the old knight's particularities break out upon these occasions; sometimes he will be lengthening out a verse in the Singing-Psalms half a minute after the rest of the congregation have done with it; sometimes, when he is pleased with the matter of his devotion, he pronounces "Amen" three or four times to the same prayer; and sometimes stands up when everybody else is upon their knees, to count the congregation, or see if any of his tenants are missing.

I was yesterday very much surprised to hear my old friend, in the midst of the service, calling out to one John Matthews to mind what he was about, and not disturb the congregation. This John Matthews, it seems, is remarkable for being an idle fellow, and at that time was kicking his heels for his diversion. This authority of the knight, though exerted in that odd manner which accompanies him in all circumstances of life, has a very good effect upon the parish, who are not polite[3] enough to see anything ridiculous in his behavior; besides that the general good sense and worthiness of his character makes his friends observe these little singularities as foils that rather set off than blemish his good qualities.

As soon as the sermon is finished, nobody presumes to stir till Sir Roger is gone out of the church. The knight walks down from his seat in the chancel between a double row of his tenants, that stand bowing to him on each side, and every now and then inquires how such an one's wife, or mother, or son, or father do, whom he does not see at church—which is understood as a secret reprimand to the person that is absent.

The chaplain has often told me that upon a catechizing day, when Sir Roger has been pleased with a boy that answers well, he has ordered a Bible to be given him next day for his encouragement, and sometimes accompanies it with a flitch of bacon to his mother. Sir Roger has likewise added five pounds a year to the clerk's place; and, that he may encourage the young fellows to make themselves perfect in the church service, has promised, upon the death of the present incumbent, who is very old, to bestow it according to merit.

The fair understanding between Sir Roger and his chaplain, and their mutual concurrence in doing good, is the more remarkable because the

3. Refined.

very next village is famous for the differences and contentions that rise between the parson and the squire, who live in a perpetual state of war. The parson is always preaching at the squire, and the squire, to be revenged on the parson, never comes to church. The squire has made all his tenants atheists and tithe-stealers;[4] while the parson instructs them every Sunday in the dignity of his order, and insinuates to them almost in every sermon that he is a better man than his patron. In short, matters are come to such an extremity that the squire has not said his prayers either in public or private this half year; and that the parson threatens him, if he does not mend his manners, to pray for him in the face of the whole congregation.

Feuds of this nature, though too frequent in the country, are very fatal to the ordinary people, who are so used to be dazzled with riches that they pay as much deference to the understanding of a man of an estate as of a man of learning; and are very hardly brought to regard any truth, how important soever it may be, that is preached to them, when they know there are several men of five hundred a year who do not believe it.

ADDISON: [Sir Roger at the Assizes[1]]

The Spectator, No. 122, Friday, July 20, 1711

Comes jucundus in via pro vehiculo est.[2]
—PUBLILIUS SYRUS, *Fragments*

A man's first care should be to avoid the reproaches of his own heart; his next, to escape the censures of the world. If the last interferes with the former, it ought to be entirely neglected; but otherwise there cannot be a greater satisfaction to an honest mind than to see those approbations which it gives itself seconded by the applauses of the public. A man is more sure of his conduct when the verdict which he passes upon his own behavior is thus warranted and confirmed by the opinion of all that know him.

My worthy friend Sir Roger is one of those who is not only at peace within himself but beloved and esteemed by all about him. He receives a suitable tribute for his universal benevolence to mankind in the returns of affection and good will which are paid him by everyone that lives within his neighborhood. I lately met with two or three odd instances of that general respect which is shown to the good old knight. He would needs carry Will Wimble[3] and myself with him to the county assizes. As we were upon the road, Will Wimble joined a couple of plain men

---

4. Farmers who cheat the parson to whom they are bound to pay annual tithes (i.e., a tenth of the produce of their farms).
1. Periodic sessions of superior courts held by visiting judges throughout England.
2. "An agreeable companion upon the road is as good as a coach." Addison substituted *jucundus* for the original's *facundus* ("eloquent").
3. A character used by Addison to illustrate the injury done to younger sons of gentlemen by not educating them for a profession or to trade.

who rid before us, and conversed with them for some time,, during which my friend Sir Roger acquainted me with their characters.

"The first of them," says he, "that has a spaniel by his side, is a yeoman[4] of about an hundred pounds a year, an honest man. He is just within the Game Act,[5] and qualified to kill an hare or a pheasant. He knocks down a dinner with his gun twice or thrice a week; and by that means lives much cheaper than those who have not so good an estate as himself. He would be a good neighbor if he did not destroy so many partridges; in short he is a very sensible man, shoots flying,[6] and has been several times foreman of the petty jury.[7]

"The other that rides along with him is Tom Touchy, a fellow famous for taking the law of everybody. There is not one in the town where he lives that he has not sued at a quarter sessions. The rogue had once the impudence to go to law with the widow.[8] His head is full of costs, damages, and ejectments; he plagued a couple of honest gentlemen so long for a trespass in breaking one of his hedges, till he was forced to sell the ground it enclosed to defray the charges of the prosecution. His father left him fourscore pounds a year, but he has cast[9] and been cast so often that he is not now worth thirty. I suppose he is going upon the old business of the willow tree."

As Sir Roger was giving me this account of Tom Touchy, Will Wimble and his two companions stopped short till we came up to them. After having paid their respects to Sir Roger, Will told him that Mr. Touchy and he must appeal to him upon a dispute that arose between them. Will, it seems, had been giving his fellow travelers an account of his angling one day in such a hole; when Tom Touchy, instead of hearing out his story, told him that Mr. Such-an-one, if he pleased, might take the law of him for fishing in that part of the river. My friend Sir Roger heard them both, upon a round trot,[1] and after having paused some time, told them, with an air of a man who would not give his judgment rashly, "that much might be said on both sides." They were neither of them dissatisfied with the knight's determination, because neither of them found himself in the wrong by it. Upon which we made the best of our way to the assizes.

The court was sat before Sir Roger came; but notwithstanding all the justices had taken their places upon the bench, they made room for the old knight at the head of them; who, for his reputation in the country, took occasion to whisper in the judge's ear that he was glad his lordship had met with so much good weather in his circuit. I was listening to the proceedings of the court with much attention, and infinitely pleased with that great appearance and solemnity which so properly accompan-

4. A man who owns and cultivates a small estate. His rank is just below that of gentleman.
5. This law restricted the right to kill game to owners of land whose annual income was £100 or more.
6. A true sportsman, he shoots birds only when they are on the wing.
7. The trial jury of twelve in an ordinary civil or criminal case.
8. The woman whom Sir Roger had loved in his youth. She is frequently mentioned in essays that deal with the old knight.
9. Defeated in a lawsuit.
1. While trotting briskly.

ies such a public administration of our laws, when, after about an hour's sitting, I observed to my great surprise, in the midst of a trial, that my friend Sir Roger was getting up to speak. I was in some pain for him, till I found he had acquitted himself of two or three sentences, with a look of much business and great intrepidity.

Upon his first rising the court was hushed, and a general whisper ran among the country people that Sir Roger was up. The speech he made was so little to the purpose that I shall not trouble my readers with an account of it; and I believe was not so much designed by the knight himself to inform the court, as to give him a figure in my eye, and keep up his credit in the country.

I was highly delighted, when the court rose, to see the gentlemen of the country gathering about my old friend, and striving who should compliment him most; at the same time that the ordinary people gazed upon him at a distance, not a little admiring his courage that was not afraid to speak to the judge.

In our return home we met with a very odd accident which I cannot forbear relating, because it shows how desirous all who know Sir Roger are of giving him marks of their esteem. When we were arrived upon the verge of his estate, we stopped at a little inn to rest ourselves and our horses. The man of the house had, it seems, been formerly a servant in the knight's family; and to do honor to his old master, had some time since, unknown to Sir Roger, put him up in a signpost before the door; so that the knight's head had hung out upon the road about a week before he himself knew anything of the matter. As soon as Sir Roger was acquainted with it, finding that his servant's indiscretion proceeded wholly from affection and good will, he only told him that he had made him too high a compliment; and when the fellow seemed to think that could hardly be, added, with a more decisive look, that it was too great an honor for any man under a duke; but told him at the same time that it might be altered with a very few touches, and that he himself would be at the charge of it. Accordingly they got a painter, by the knight's directions, to add a pair of whiskers to the face, and by a little aggravation of the features to change it into the Saracen's Head. I should not have known this story had not the innkeeper, upon Sir Roger's alighting, told him in my hearing that his honor's head was brought back last night with the alterations that he had ordered to be made in it. Upon this my friend, with his usual cheerfulness, related the particulars above-mentioned, and ordered the head to be brought into the room. I could not forbear discovering greater expressions of mirth than ordinary upon the appearance of this monstrous face, under which, notwithstanding it was made to frown and stare in a most extraordinary manner, I could still discover a distant resemblance of my old friend. Sir Roger, upon seeing me laugh, desired me to tell him truly if I thought it possible for people to know him in that disguise. I at first kept my usual silence; but upon the knight's conjuring me to tell him whether it was not still more like himself than a Saracen, I composed my countenance in the best manner I could, and replied that much might be said on both sides.

These several adventures, with the knight's behavior in them, gave me as pleasant a day as ever I met with in any of my travels.

THE PERIODICAL ESSAY: IDEAS

ADDISON: [The Aims of the Spectator]

The Spectator, No. 10, *Monday*, *March* 12, 1711

> *Non aliter quam qui adverso vix flumine lembum*
> *Remigiis subigit, si bracchia forte remisit,*
> *Atque illum in præceps prono rapit alveus amni.*[1]
> —VIRGIL, *Georgics* 1.201–3

It is with much satisfaction that I hear this great city inquiring day by day after these my papers, and receiving my morning lectures with a becoming seriousness and attention. My publisher tells me that there are already three thousand of them distributed every day. So that if I allow twenty readers to every paper, which I look upon as a modest computation, I may reckon about three-score thousand disciples in London and Westminster, who I hope will take care to distinguish themselves from the thoughtless herd of their ignorant and unattentive brethren. Since I have raised to myself so great an audience, I shall spare no pains to make their instruction agreeable, and their diversion useful. For which reasons I shall endeavor to enliven morality with wit, and to temper wit with morality, that my readers may, if possible, both ways find their account in the speculation of the day. And to the end that their virtue and discretion may not be short, transient, intermitting starts of thought, I have resolved to refresh their memories from day to day, till I have recovered them out of that desperate state of vice and folly into which the age is fallen. The mind that lies fallow but a single day sprouts up in follies that are only to be killed by a constant and assiduous culture. It was said of Socrates that he brought philosophy down from heaven, to inhabit among men; and I shall be ambitious to have it said of me that I have brought philosophy out of closets and libraries, schools and colleges, to dwell in clubs and assemblies, at tea tables and in coffeehouses.

I would therefore in a very particular manner recommend these my speculations to all well-regulated families that set apart an hour in every morning for tea and bread and butter; and would earnestly advise them for their good to order this paper to be punctually served up, and to be looked upon as a part of the tea equipage.

---

1. "Like him whose oars can hardly force his boat against the current, if by chance he relaxes his arms, the boat sweeps him headlong down the stream."

Sir Francis Bacon observes that a well-written book, compared with its rivals and antagonists, is like Moses' serpent, that immediately swallowed up and devoured those of the Egyptians.[2] I shall not be so vain as to think that where *The Spectator* appears the other public prints will vanish; but shall leave it to my reader's consideration whether is it not much better to be let into the knowledge of one's self, than to hear what passes in Muscovy or Poland; and to amuse ourselves with such writings as tend to the wearing out of ignorance, passion, and prejudice, than such as naturally conduce to inflame hatreds, and make enmities irreconcilable?

In the next place, I would recommend this paper to the daily perusal of those gentlemen whom I cannot but consider as my good brothers and allies, I mean the fraternity of spectators, who live in the world without having anything to do in it; and either by the affluence of their fortunes or laziness of their dispositions have no other business with the rest of mankind but to look upon them. Under this class of men are comprehended all contemplative tradesmen, titular physicians, fellows of the Royal Society, Templars[3] that are not given to be contentious, and statesmen that are out of business; in short, everyone that considers the world as a theater, and desires to form a right judgment of those who are the actors on it.

There is another set of men that I must likewise lay a claim to, whom I have lately called the blanks of society, as being altogether unfurnished with ideas, till the business and conversation of the day has supplied them. I have often considered these poor souls with an eye of great commiseration, when I have heard them asking the first man they have met with, whether there was any news stirring? and by that means gathering together materials for thinking. These needy persons do not know what to talk of till about twelve o'clock in the morning; for by that time they are pretty good judges of the weather, know which way the wind sits, and whether the Dutch mail be come in.[4] As they lie at the mercy of the first man they meet, and are grave or impertinent all the day long, according to the notions which they have inbibed in the morning. I would earnestly entreat them not to stir out of their chambers till they have read this paper, and do promise them that I will daily instil into them such sound and wholesome sentiments as shall have a good effect on their conversation for the ensuing twelve hours.

But there are none to whom this paper will be more useful than to the female world. I have often thought there has not been sufficient pains taken in finding out proper employments and diversions for the fair ones. Their amusements seem contrived for them, rather as they are women, than as they are reasonable creatures; and are more adapted to the sex than to the species. The toilet is their great scene of business,

---

2. In *The Advancement of Learning*, 2, "To the King." But it was the rod of Aaron, not of Moses, that turned into a devouring serpent (Exodus 7.10–12).

3. Lawyers or students of the law who live or have their offices ("chambers") in the Middle or Inner Temple, one of the Inns of Court.

4. Bringing the latest war news.

and the right adjusting of their hair the principal employment of their lives. The sorting of a suit of ribbons[5] is reckoned a very good morning's work; and if they make an excursion to a mercer's[6] or a toyshop, so great a fatigue makes them unfit for anything else all the day after. Their more serious occupations are sewing and embroidery, and their greatest drudgery the preparation of jellies and sweetmeats. This, I say, is the state of ordinary women; though I know there are multitudes of those of a more elevated life and conversation, that move in an exalted sphere of knowledge and virtue, that join all the beauties of the mind to the ornaments of dress, and inspire a kind of awe and respect, as well as love, into their male beholders. I hope to incease the number of these by publishing this daily paper, which I shall always endeavor to make an innocent if not improving entertainment, and by that means at least divert the minds of my female readers from greater trifles. At the same time, as I would fain give some finishing touches to those which are already the most beautiful pieces in human nature, I shall endeavor to point all those imperfections that are the blemishes, as well as those virtues which are the embellishments, of the sex. In the meanwhile I hope these my gentle readers, who have so much time on their hands, will not grudge throwing away a quarter of an hour in a day on this paper, since they may do it without any hindrance to business.

I know several of my friends and well-wishers are in great pain for me, lest I should not be able to keep up the spirit of a paper which I oblige myself to furnish every day: but to make them easy in this particular, I will promise them faithfully to give it over as soon as I grow dull. This I know will be matter of great raillery to the small wits; who will frequently put me in mind of my promise, desire me to keep my word, assure me that it is high time to give over, with many other little pleasantries of the like nature, which men of a little smart genius cannot forebear throwing out against their best friends, when they have such a handle given them of being witty. But let them remember that I do hereby enter my caveat against this piece of raillery.

ADDISON: [Wit: True, False, Mixed]

The Spectator, No. 62, Friday, March 11, 1711

Scribendi recte sapere est et principium et fons.[1]
—HORACE, *Ars Poetica* 309

Mr. Locke has an admirable reflection upon the difference of wit and judgment, whereby he endeavors to show the reason why they are not always the talents of the same person. His words are as follow: "And hence, perhaps, may be given some reason of that common observation,

---

5. A set of ribbons to be worn together.
6. A seller of such small-wares as tape, ribbon, fringe. A "toyshop" is a shop where baubles and

trifles are sold.
1. "Discernment is the source and fount of writing well."

that men who have a great deal of wit and prompt memories, have not always the clearest judgment, or deepest reason. For wit lying most in the assemblage of ideas, and putting those together with quickness and variety, wherein can be found any resemblance or congruity, thereby to make up pleasant pictures and agreeable visions in the fancy; judgment, on the contrary, lies quite on the other side, in separating carefully one from another, ideas wherein can be found the least difference, thereby to avoid being misled by similitude, and by affinity to take one thing for another. This is a way of proceeding quite contrary to metaphor and allusion; wherein, for the most part, lies that entertainment and pleasantry of wit which strikes so lively on the fancy, and is therefore so acceptable to all people."[2]

This is, I think, the best and most philosophical account that I have ever met with of wit, which generally, though not always, consists in such a resemblance and congruity of ideas as this author mentions. I shall only add to it, by way of explanation, that every resemblance of ideas is not that which we call wit, unless it be such an one that gives delight and surprise to the reader. These two properties seem essential to wit, more particularly the last of them. In order therefore that the resemblance in the ideas be wit, it is necessary that the ideas should not lie too near one another in the nature of things; for where the likeness is obvious, it gives no surprise. To compare one man's singing to that of another, or to represent the whiteness of any object by that of milk and snow, or the variety of its colors by those of the rainbow, cannot be called wit, unless, besides this obvious resemblance, there be some further congruity discovered in the two ideas that is capable of giving the reader some surprise. Thus when a poet tells us, the bosom of his mistress is as white as snow, there is no wit in the comparison; but when he adds, with a sigh, that it is as cold too, it then grows into wit. Every reader's memory may supply him with innumerable instances of the same nature. For this reason, the similitudes in heroic poets, who endeavor rather to fill the mind with great conceptions, than to divert it with such as are new and surprising, have seldom anything in them that can be called wit. Mr. Locke's account of wit, with this short explanation, comprehends most of the species of wit, as metaphors, similitudes, allegories, enigmas, mottoes, parables, fables, dreams, visions, dramatic writings, burlesque, and all the methods of allusion:[3] as there are many other pieces of wit (how remote soever they may appear at first sight from the foregoing description) which upon examination will be found to agree with it.

As true wit generally consists in this resemblance and congruity of ideas, false wit chiefly consists in the resemblance and congruity sometimes of single letters, as in anagrams, chronograms,[4] lipograms, and

---

2. John Locke, *Essay Concerning Human Understanding* (1690) 2.2.
3. Word play; more broadly, any covert or symbolic use of language.
4. Phrase in which certain letters express a date;

e.g., "LorD HaVe MerCIe Vpon Vs": the capital letters, in Roman numerals, add up to 1666, the *annus mirabilis* of fire, plague, and war. "Lipogram": a composition omitting all words that contain a certain letter or letters.

acrostics; sometimes of syllables, as in echoes and doggerel rhymes; sometimes of words, as in puns and quibbles; and sometimes of whole sentences or poems, cast into the figures of eggs, axes, or altars:[5] nay, some carry the notion of wit so far, as to ascribe it even to external mimicry; and to look upon a man as an ingenious person, that can resemble the tone, posture, or face of another.

As true wit consists in the resemblance of ideas, and false wit in the resemblance of words, according to the foregoing instances; there is another kind of wit which consists partly in the resemblance of ideas, and partly in the resemblance of words; which for distinction's sake I shall call mixed wit. This kind of wit is that which abounds in Cowley, more than in any author that ever wrote. Mr. Waller has likewise a great deal of it. Mr. Dryden is very sparing in it. Milton had a genius much above it. Spenser is in the same class with Milton. The Italians, even in their epic poetry, are full of it. Monsieur Boileau, who formed himself upon the ancient poets, has everywhere rejected it with scorn. If we look after mixed wit among the Greek writers, we shall find it nowhere but in the epigrammatists. There are indeed some strokes of it in the little poem ascribed to Musaeus,[6] which by that, as well as many other marks, betrays itself to be a modern composition. If we look into the Latin writers, we find none of this mixed wit in Virgil, Lucretius, or Catullus; very little in Horace, but a great deal of it in Ovid, and scarce anything else in Martial.

Out of the innumerable branches of mixed wit, I shall choose one instance which may be met with in all the writers of this class. The passion of love in its nature has been thought to resemble fire; for which reason the words fire and flame are made use of to signify love. The witty poets therefore have taken an advantage from the doubtful meaning of the word fire, to make an infinite number of witticisms. Cowley, observing the cold regard of his mistress's eyes,[7] and at the same time their power of producing love in him, considers them as burning-glasses made of ice; and finding himself able to live in the greatest extremities of love, concludes the torrid zone to be habitable. When his mistress has read his letter written in juice of lemon by holding it to the fire, he desires her to read it over a second time by love's flames. When she weeps, he wishes it were inward heat that distilled those drops from the limbec.[8] When she is absent he is beyond eighty, that is, thirty degrees nearer the pole than when she is with him. His ambitious love is a fire that naturally mounts upwards; his happy love is the beams of heaven, and his unhappy love flames of hell. When it does not let him sleep, it is a flame that sends up no smoke; when it is opposed by counsel and advice, it is a fire that rages the more by the wind's blowing upon it. Upon the dying of a tree in which he had cut his loves, he observes that

---

5. See *The Altar* and *Easter Wings* by George Herbert.
6. A poem called *Hero and Leander*, attributed to Musaeus, an ancient Greek poet, was first pub-

lished in 1635.
7. In *The Mistress, or Several Copies of Love-Verses* (1647).
8. Alembic, an apparatus used in distilling.

his written flames had burned up and withered the tree. When he resolves to give over his passion, he tells us that one burnt like him for ever dreads the fire. His heart is an Aetna, that instead of Vulcan's shop[9] encloses Cupid's forge in it. His endeavoring to drown his love in wine, is throwing oil upon the fire. He would insinuate to his mistress, that the fire of love, like that of the sun (which produces so many living creatures) should not only warm but beget. Love in another place cooks pleasure at his fire. Sometimes the poet's heart is frozen in every breast, and sometimes scorched in every eye. Sometimes he is drowned in tears, and burnt in love, like a ship set on fire in the middle of the sea.

The reader may observe in every one of these instances, that the poet mixes the qualities of fire with those of love; and in the same sentence speaking of it both as a passion, and as real fire, surprises the reader with those seeming resemblances or contradictions that make up all the wit in this kind of writing. Mixed wit therefore is a composition of pun and true wit, and is more or less perfect as the resemblance lies in the ideas or in the words: its foundations are laid partly in falsehood and partly in truth: reason puts in her claim for one half of it, and extravagance for the other. The only province therefore for this kind of wit, is epigram, or those little occasional poems that in their own nature are nothing else but a tissue of epigrams. I cannot conclude this head of mixed wit, without owning that the admirable poet out of whom I have taken the examples of it, had as much true wit as any author that ever writ; and indeed all other talents of an extraordinary genius.

It may be expected, since I am upon this subject, that I should take notice of Mr. Dryden's definition of wit; which, with all the deference that is due to the judgment of so great a man, is not so properly a definition of wit, as of good writing in general. Wit, as he defines it, is "a propriety of words and thoughts adapted to the subject."[1] If this be a true definition of wit, I am apt to think that Euclid[2] was the greatest wit that ever set pen to paper: it is certain there never was a greater propriety of words and thoughts adapted to the subject, than what that author has made use of in his elements. I shall only appeal to my reader, if this definition agrees with any notion he has of wit: if it be a true one, I am sure Mr. Dryden was not only a better poet, but a greater wit than Mr. Cowley; and Virgil a much more facetious man than either Ovid or Martial.

Bouhours,[3] whom I look upon to be the most penetrating of all the French critics, has taken pains to show that it is impossible for any thought to be beautiful which is not just, and has not its foundation in the nature of things; that the basis of all wit is truth; and that no thought can be

---

9. Mount Etna was supposed to be the workshop of Vulcan, the Roman god of fire and metal-working.

1. Adapted from Dryden's *Apology for Heroic Poetry*

(1677).

2. Hellenic mathematician (ca. 300 B.C.)

3. Dominique Bouhours (1628–1702), who wrote an *Art of Criticism*.

valuable, of which good sense is not the groundwork. Boileau[4] has endeavored to inculcate the same notion in several parts of his writings, both in prose and verse. This is that natural way of writing, that beautiful simplicity, which we so much admire in the compositions of the ancients; and which nobody deviates from, but those who want strength of genius to make a thought shine in its own natural beauties. Poets who want this strength of genius to give that majestic simplicity to nature, which we so much admire in the works of the ancients, are forced to hunt after foreign ornaments, and not to let any piece of wit of what kind soever escape them. I look upon these writers as Goths in poetry, who, like those in architecture, not being able to come up to the beautiful simplicity of the old Greeks and Romans, have endeavored to supply its place with all the extravagances of an irregular fancy. Mr. Dryden makes a very handsome observation on Ovid's writing a letter from Dido to Aeneas, in the following words:[5] "Ovid" (says he, speaking of Virgil's fiction of Dido and Aeneas) "takes it up after him, even in the same age, and makes an ancient heroine of Virgil's new-created Dido; dictates a letter for her just before her death to the ungrateful fugitive; and, very unluckily for himself, is for measuring a sword with a man so much superior in force to him, on the same subject. I think I may be judge of this, because I have translated both. The famous author of the Art of Love[6] has nothing of his own; he borrows all from a greater master in his own profession, and, which is worse, improves nothing which he finds: nature fails him, and being forced to his old shift, he has recourse to witticism. This passes indeed with his soft admirers, and gives him the preference to Virgil in their esteem."

Were not I supported by so great an authority as that of Mr. Dryden, I should not venture to observe, that the taste of most of our English poets, as well as readers, is extremely Gothic. He quotes Monsieur Segrais[7] for a threefold distinction of the readers of poetry: in the first of which he comprehends the rabble of readers, whom he does not treat as such with regard to their quality,[8] but to their numbers and the coarseness of their taste. His words are as follow: "Segrais has distinguished the readers of poetry, according to their capacity of judging, into three classes. [He might have said the same of writers too, if he had pleased.] In the lowest form he places those whom he calls *les petits esprits*,[9] such things as are our upper-gallery audience in a play-house; who like nothing but the husk and rind of wit, prefer a quibble, a conceit, an epigram, before solid sense and elegant expression: these are mob-readers. If Virgil and Martial stood for parliament-men, we know already who would carry it.[1]

4. Nicholas Boileau (1636–1711), a famous French neoclassicist, wrote a verse *Art of Poetry* (1674) translated by Dryden.
5. From Dryden's Dedication to his translation of the *Aeneid* (1697).
6. Ovid.
7. Jean Regnauld de Segrais (1624–1701), who had

translated Virgil into French, is quoted extensively by Dryden.
8. Social standing.
9. The small-minded.
1. That is, the witty Martial would easily defeat the weighty Virgil in an election.

But though they make the greatest appearance in the field, and cry the loudest, the best on 't is they are but a sort of French Huguenots, or Dutch boors,[2] brought over in herds, but not naturalized; who have not lands of two pounds per annum in Parnassus, and therefore are not privileged to poll.[3] Their authors are of the same level, fit to represent them on a mountebank's stage, or to be masters of the ceremonies in a bear-garden: yet these are they who have the most admirers. But it often happens, to their moritification, that as their readers improve their stock of sense (as they may by reading better books, and by conversation with men of judgment), they soon forsake them."

I must not dismiss this subject without observing, that as Mr. Locke in the passage above-mentioned has discovered the most fruitful source of wit, so there is another of a quite contrary nature to it, which does likewise branch itself out into several kinds. For not only the resemblance but the opposition of ideas does very often produce wit; as I could show in several little points, turns, and antitheses, that I may possibly enlarge upon in some future speculation.[4]

ADDISON: [*Paradise Lost:* General Critical Remarks]

The Spectator, No. 267, Saturday, January 5, 1712

Cedite Romani scriptores, cedite Graii.[1]
——PROPERTIUS, *Elegies* 2.34.65

There is nothing in nature so irksome as general discourses, especially when they turn chiefly upon words. For this reason I shall waive the discussion of that point which was started some years since, Whether Milton's *Paradise Lost* may be called an heroic poem? Those who will not give it that title may call it (if they please) a *divine poem*. It will be sufficient to its perfection, if it has in it all the beauties of the highest kind of poetry; and as for those who allege it is not an heroic poem, they advance no more to the diminution of it, than if they should say Adam is not Aeneas, nor Eve Helen.

I shall therefore examine it by the rules of epic poetry,[2] and see whether it falls short of the *Iliad* or *Aeneid*, in the beauties which are essential to that kind of writing. The first thing to be considered in an epic poem is the fable,[3] which is perfect or imperfect, according as the action which

2. Peasants. Huguenots and the Dutch were the largest class of immigrants in England. "On 't": that one can say.
3. Vote. Only freeholders worth 2 pounds a year could go to the polls; and these readers of little taste hold no land in Parnassus (where the Muses live).
4. For such an "enlargement," see Samuel Johnson's remarks on wit in the *Life of Cowley*.
1. "Yield place, ye Roman and ye Grecian writers, yield."

2. The rules for the conduct of an epic poem,, derived out of the poems of Homer and Virgil, the *Poetics* of Aristotle, and the *Art of Poetry* of Horace, had been given their most systematic and complete statement in Père René Le Bossu's *Traité du poème épique* (1675), which was immediately absorbed into English critical thought. Addison writes of *Paradise Lost* with Le Bossu well in sight, but he is no slavish disciple.
3. The plot of a drama or poem.

it relates is more or less so. This action should have three qualifications in it. First, it should be but one action. Secondly, it should be an entire action; and thirdly, it should be a great action. To consider the action of the *Iliad*, *Aeneid*, and *Paradise Lost*, in these three several lights. Homer to preserve the unity of his action hastens into the midst of things, as Horace has observed:[4] had he gone up to Leda's egg, or begun much later, even at the rape of Helen, or the investing of Troy, it is manifest that the story of the poem would have been a series of several actions. He therefore opens his poem with the discord of his princes, and with great art interweaves in the several succeeding parts of it, an account of everything material which relates to them and had passed before that fatal dissension. After the same manner Aeneas makes his first appearance in the Tyrrhene seas,[5] and within sight of Italy, because the action proposed to be celebrated was that of his settling himself in Latium.[6] But because it was necessary for the reader to know what had happened to him in the taking of Troy, and in the preceding parts of his voyage, Virgil makes his hero relate it by way of episode[7] in the second and third books of the *Aeneid*. The contents of both which books come before those of the first book in the thread of the story, though for preserving of this unity of action, they follow them in the disposition of the poem. Milton, in imitation of these two great poets, opens his *Paradise Lost* with an infernal council plotting the fall of man, which is the action he proposed to celebrate; and as for those great actions which preceded, in point of time, the battle of the angels, and the creation of the world (which would have entirely destroyed the unity of his principal action, had he related them in the same order that they happened), he cast them into the fifth, sixth, and seventh books, by way of episode to this noble poem.

Aristotle himself allows that Homer has nothing to boast of as to the unity of his fable, though at the same time that great critic and philosopher endeavors to palliate this imperfection in the Greek poet, by imputing it in some measure to the very nature of an epic poem. Some have been of opinion that the *Aeneid* labors also in this particular, and has episodes which may be looked upon as excrescences rather than as parts of the action. On the contrary, the poem which we have now under our consideration hath no other episodes than such as naturally arise from the subject, and yet is filled with such a multitude of astonishing incidents that it gives us at the same time a pleasure of the greatest variety, and of the greatest simplicity.

I must observe also that as Virgil, in the poem which was designed to

---

4. *Art of Poetry*, 147–49. Helen, whose abduction from her husband Menelaus by the Trojan prince Paris brought on the Trojan War, was the daughter of Leda, who was visited by Zeus in the guise of a swan.

5. That part of the Mediterranean Sea west of Italy, bounded by the islands of Sicily, Sardinia, and Corsica.

6. The kingdom of the Latini, where Aeneas was hospitably received when he landed at the mouth of the Tiber. He married Lavinia, the daughter of King Latinus, and later ruled the kingdom.

7. An incidental narration or digression in an epic which arises naturally from the subject but is separable from the main action.

celebrate the original of the Roman Empire, has described the birth of its great rival, the Carthaginian commonwealth, Milton with the like art in his poem on the Fall of Man, has related the fall of those angels who are his professed enemies. Besides the many other beauties in such an episode, its running parallel with the great action of the poem hinders it from breaking the unity so much as another episode would have done that had not so great an affinity with the principal subject. In short, this is the same kind of beauty which the critics admire in the *Spanish Friar, or The Double Discovery*,[8] where the two different plots look like counterparts and copies of one another.

The second qualification required in the action of an epic poem is, that it should be an *entire* action. An action is entire when it is complete in all its parts; or as Aristotle describes it, when it consists of a beginning, a middle, and an end. Nothing should go before it, be intermixed with it, or follow after it, that is not related to it. As on the contrary, no single step should be omitted in that just and regular process which it must be supposed to take from its original to its consummation. Thus, we see the anger of Achilles in its birth, its continuance, and effects; and Aeneas's settlement in Italy, carried on through all the oppositions in his way to it both by sea and land. The action in Milton excels (I think) both the former in this particular: we see it contrived in hell, executed upon earth, and punished by heaven. The parts of it are told in the most distinct manner, and grow out of one another in the most natural method.

The third qualification of an epic poem is its *greatness*. The anger of Achilles was of such consequence that it embroiled the kings of Greece, destroyed the heroes of Troy, and engaged all the gods in factions. Aeneas's settlement in Italy produced the Caesars, and gave birth to the Roman Empire. Milton's subject was still greater than either of the former; it does not determine the fate of single persons or nations, but of a whole species. The united powers of hell are joined together for the destruction of mankind, which they effected in part, and would have completed, had not Omnipotence itself interposed. The principal actors are man in his greatest perfection, and woman in her highest beauty. Their enemies are the fallen angels: the Messiah their friend, and the Almighty their protector. In short, everything that is great in the whole circle of being, whether within the verge of nature, or out of it, has a proper part assigned it in this noble poem.

In poetry, as in architecture, not only the whole, but the principal members, and every part of them, should be great. I will not presume to say, that the book of games in the *Aeneid,* or that in the *Iliad*, are not of this nature, nor to reprehend Virgil's simile of the top, and many other of the same nature in the *Iliad*, as liable to any censure in this particular; but I think we may say, without derogating from those wonderful performances, that there is an unquestionable magnificence in

8. A comedy by Dryden.

every part of *Paradise Lost*, and indeed a much greater than could have been formed upon any pagan system.

But Aristotle, by the greatness of the action, does not only mean that it should be great in its nature, but also in its duration, or in other words, that it should have a due length in it, as well as what we properly call greatness. The just measure of the kind of magnitude, he explains by the following similitude. An animal, no bigger than a mite, cannot appear perfect to the eye, because the sight takes it in at once, and has only a confused idea of the whole, and not a distinct idea of all its parts: if on the contrary you should suppose an animal of ten thousand furlongs in length, the eye would be so filled with a single part of it, that it would not give the mind an idea of the whole. What these animals are to the eye, a very short or a very long action would be to the memory. The first would be, as it were, lost and swallowed up by it, and the other difficult to be contained in it. Homer and Virgil have shown their principal art in this particular; the action of the *Iliad*, and that of the *Aeneid*, were in themselves exceeding short, but are so beautifully extended and diversified by the invention of episodes, and the machinery[9] of gods, with the like poetical ornaments, that they make up an agreeable story sufficient to employ the memory without overcharging it. Milton's action is enriched with such a variety of circumstances that I have taken as much pleasure in reading the contents of his books as in the best invented story I ever met with. It is possible that the traditions on which the *Iliad* and *Aeneid* were built had more circumstances in them than the history of the Fall of Man, as it is related in Scripture. Besides it was easier for Homer and Virgil to dash the truth with fiction, as they were in no danger of offending the religion of their country by it. But as for Milton, he had not only a very few circumstances upon which to raise his poem, but was also obliged to proceed with the greatest caution in everything that he added out of his own invention. And, indeed, notwithstanding all the restraints he was under, he has filled his story with so many surprising incidents, which bear so close an analogy with what is delivered in Holy Writ, that it is capable of pleasing the most delicate reader, without giving offense to the most scrupulous.

The modern critics have collected from several hints in the *Iliad* and *Aeneid* the space of time which is taken up by the action of each of these poems; but as a great part of Milton's story was transacted in regions that lie out of the reach of the sun and the sphere of day, it is impossible to gratify the reader with such a calculation, which indeed would be more curious than instructive; none of the critics, either ancient or modern, having laid down rules to circumscribe the action of an epic poem with any determined number of years, days, or hours.

This Piece of Criticism on Milton's Paradise Lost *shall be carried on in the following Saturdays' papers.*[1]

---

9. The technical term (from *deus ex machina*) in critical theory for the supernatural beings who oversee and intervene in the affairs of the charac-

ters in epic poems.

1. The series on *Paradise Lost* contains 18 essays.

ADDISON: [On the Scale of Being]

The Spectator, No. 519, October 25, 1712

inde hominum pecudumque genus, vitaeque volantum,
et quae marmoreo fert monstra sub aequore pontus.[1]
—VIRGIL, *Aeneid* 6.728–29

Though there is a great deal of pleasure in contemplating the material world, by which I mean that system of bodies into which nature has so curiously wrought the mass of dead matter, with the several relations which those bodies bear to one another, there is still, methinks, something more wonderful and surprising in contemplations on the world of life, by which I mean all those animals with which every part of the universe is furnished. The material world is only the shell of the universe: the world of life are its inhabitants.

If we consider those parts of the material world which lie the nearest to us and are, therefore, subject to our observations and inquiries, it is amazing to consider the infinity of animals with which it is stocked. Every part of matter is peopled. Every green leaf swarms with inhabitants. There is scarce a single humor in the body of a man, or of any other animal, in which our glasses do not discover myriads of living creatures. The surface of animals is also covered with other animals which are, in the same manner, the basis of other animals that live upon it; nay, we find in the most solid bodies, as in marble itself, innumerable cells and cavities that are crowded with such imperceptible inhabitants as are too little for the naked eye to discover. On the other hand if we look into the more bulky parts of nature, we see the seas, lakes, and rivers teeming with numberless kinds of living creatures. We find every mountain and marsh, wilderness and wood, plentifully stocked with birds and beasts, and every part of matter affording proper necessaries and conveniences for the livelihood of multitudes which inhabit it.

The author of *The Plurality of Worlds*[2] draws a very good argument upon this consideration for the peopling of every planet, as indeed it seems very probable from the analogy of reason that, if no part of matter which we are acquainted with lies waste and useless, those great bodies, which are at such a distance from us, should not be desert and unpeopled, but rather that they should be furnished with beings adapted to their respective situations.

Existence is a blessing to those beings only which are endowed with perception and is, in a manner, thrown away upon dead matter any further than as it is subservient to beings which are conscious of their existence. Accordingly, we find from the bodies which lie under obser-

1. "Thence the race of men and beasts, the life of flying creatures, and the monsters that ocean bears beneath her smooth surface."
2. Bernard de Fontenelle (1657–1757). This delightful book, a series of dialogues between a sci-
entist and a countess concerning the possibility of other inhabited planets and the new astrophysics in general, was published in 1686 in France and beautifully translated by Joseph Glanvill in 1688.

vation that matter is only made as the basis and support of animals and that there is no more of the one than what is necessary for the existence of the other.

Infinite Goodness is of so communicative a nature that it seems to delight in the conferring of existence upon every degree of perceptive being. As this is a speculation which I have often pursued with great pleasure to myself, I shall enlarge farther upon it, by considering that part of the scale of beings which comes within our knowledge.

There are some living creatures which are raised but just above dead matter. To mention only that species of shellfish, which are formed in the fashion of a cone, that grow to the surface of several rocks and immediately die upon their being severed from the place where they grow. There are many other creatures but one remove from these, which have no other sense besides that of feeling and taste. Others have still an additional one of hearing; others of smell, and others of sight. It is wonderful to observe by what a gradual progress the world of life advances through a prodigious variety of species before a creature is formed that is complete in all its senses; and, even among these, there is such a different degree of perfection in the sense which one animal enjoys, beyond what appears in another, that, though the sense in different animals be distinguished by the same common denomination, it seems almost of a different nature. If after this we look into the several inward perfections of cunning and sagacity, or what we generally call instinct, we find them rising after the same manner, imperceptibly, one above another, and receiving additional improvements, according to the species in which they are implanted. This progress in nature is so very gradual that the most perfect of an inferior species comes very near to the most imperfect of that which is immediately above it.

The exuberant and overflowing goodness of the Supreme Being, whose mercy extends to all his works, is plainly seen, as I have before hinted, from his having made so very little matter, at least what falls within our knowledge, that does not swarm with life. Nor is his goodness less seen in the diversity than in the multitude of living creatures. Had he only made one species of animals, none of the rest would have enjoyed the happiness of existence; he has, therefore, *specified* in his creation every degree of life, every capacity of being. The whole chasm in nature, from a plant to a man, is filled up with diverse kinds of creatures, rising one over another by such a gentle and easy ascent that the little transitions and deviations from one species to another are almost insensible. This intermediate space is so well husbanded and managed that there is scarce a degree of perception which does not appear in some one part of the world of life. Is the goodness or wisdom of the Divine Being more manifested in this his proceeding?

There is a consequence, besides those I have already mentioned, which seems very naturally deducible from the foregoing considerations. If the scale of being rises by such a regular progress so high as man, we may by a parity of reason suppose that it still proceeds gradually through those beings which are of a superior nature to him, since there is an infinitely greater space and room for different degrees of perfection between the Supreme Being and man than between man and the most despicable insect. This consequence of so great a variety of beings which are superior to us, from that variety which is inferior to us, is made by Mr. Locke[3] in a passage which I shall here set down after having premised that, notwithstanding there is such infinite room between man and his Maker for the creative power to exert itself in, it is impossible that it should ever be filled up, since there will be still an infinite gap or distance between the highest created being and the Power which produced him:

> That there should be more species of intelligent creatures above us than there are of sensible and material below, is probable to me from hence: That in all the visible corporeal world we see no chasms or no gaps. All quite down from us, the descent is by easy steps and a continued series of things that, in each remove, differ very little from the other. There are fishes that have wings and are not strangers to the airy region; and there are some birds that are inhabitants of the water, whose blood is cold as fishes and their flesh so like in taste that the scrupulous are allowed them on fish days. There are animals so near of kin both to birds and beasts that they are in the middle between both: amphibious animals link the terrestrial and aquatic together; seals live at land and at sea, and porpoises have the warm blood and entrails of a hog, not to mention what is confidently reported of mermaids or seamen. There are some brutes that seem to have as much knowledge and reason as some that are called men; and the animal and vegetable kingdoms are so nearly joined that, if you will take the lowest of one and the highest of the other, there will scarce be perceived any great difference between them; and so on, till we come to the lowest and the most inorganical parts of matter, we shall find everywhere that the several species are linked together and differ but in almost insensible degrees. And when we consider the infinite power and wisdom of the Maker, we have reason to think that it is suitable to the magnificent harmony of the universe and the great design and infinite goodness of the Architect, that the species of creatures should also, by gentle degrees, ascend upward from us toward his infinite perfection, as we see they gradually descend from us downward; which, if it be probable, we have reason to be persuaded that there are far more species of creatures above us than there are beneath, we being in degrees of perfection much more remote from the infinite being of God than we are from the lowest state of being and that which approaches nearest to nothing. And yet of all those distinct species we have no clear distinct ideas.

3. John Locke, in his *Essay Concerning Human Understanding* (1690) 3.6.12.

In this system of being, there is no creature so wonderful in its nature, and which so much deserves our particular attention, as man, who fills up the middle space between the animal and intellectual nature, the visible and invisible world, and is that link in the chain of beings which has been often termed the *nexus utriusque mundi*.[4] So that he who, in one respect, is associated with angels and archangels, may look upon a Being of infinite perfection as his father, and the highest order of spirits as his brethren, and may, in another respect, say to corruption, "Thou art my father," and to the worm, "Thou art my mother and my sister."[5]

4. "The binding together of both worlds."   5. Job 17.14.

ALEXANDER POPE
1688–1744

1711:   *Essay on Criticism.*
1712:   First version of *The Rape of the Lock.*
1713–26: Translating Homer, editing Shakespeare.
1728:   The *Dunciad* begins Pope's career as major verse satirist.
1733–34: The *Essay on Man* begins his career as ethical and philosophical poet.

Pope is the only important writer of his generation who was solely a man of letters. Since he could not, as a Roman Catholic, attend a university, vote, or hold public office, he was excluded from the sort of patronage that was freely bestowed by statesmen on most writers during the reign of Anne. This disadvantage he turned into a positive good, for the translation of Homer's *Iliad* and *Odyssey*, which he undertook for profit as well as for fame, gave him ample means to live the life of an independent suburban gentleman. After 1718 he lived hospitably in his villa by the Thames at Twickenham (then pronounced *Twit'nam*), entertaining his friends and converting his five acres of land into a diminutive landscape garden. Almost exactly a century earlier, Shakespeare had earned enough to retire to a country estate at Stratford—but he had been an actor-manager as well as a playwright; Pope was the first English writer to demonstrate that literature alone could be a gainful profession.

Ill health plagued Pope almost from birth. Delicate as a child, he was early stunted and deformed by tuberculosis of the spine. His father, a well-to-do London merchant, retired from business in the year of the poet's birth, and about 1700 acquired a small property at Binfield in Windsor Forest. In rural surroundings, as the boy's health improved, he early acquired his life-long taste for natural beauty and for gardening. There he completed by wide reading the desultory schooling that both his ill health and his religion had made inevitable, and, encouraged by his father, he began also to develop his precocious talent for poetry. But Pope was never to enjoy good health: in later life he was troubled by violent headaches, and he suffered from easily exacerbated nerves, perhaps a price he had to pay for the sensitive and ardent temperament that helped make him one of our greatest poets.

Pope's first striking success as a poet was the *Essay on Criticism* (1711), which earned him the fame of Addison's approval and the notoriety of an intemperate personal attack from the critic John Dennis, who was angered by a casual reference to himself in the poem. *The Rape of the Lock*, both in its original shorter version of 1712 and in its more elaborate version of 1714, established the author as a master not only of metrics and of language, but also of witty, urbane satire. In the *Essay on Criticism*, Pope had excelled all his predecessors in writing a didactic poem after the example of Horace; in the *Rape*, he had written the most brilliant mock epic in the language. But there was another vein in Pope's youthful poetry, much of which, concerned as it is with natural beauty and love, reveals a temperament that in a later poet might have been called "Romantic." The *Pastorals* (1709), Pope's first publication, and *Windsor Forest* (1713; much of it was written earlier) abound in visual imagery and descriptive passages of ideally ordered nature; they remind us that Pope was an amateur painter. The *Elegy to the Memory of an Unfortunate Lady*, published in the collected poems of 1717, presents the high heroics of romantic love. And even the long task of translating Homer, the "dull duty" of editing Shakespeare, and, in middle age, his preoccupation with ethical and satirical poetry did not extinguish this side of Pope's nature and art. He learned to subordinate, but he did not cease to use, this sensitive awareness of visual beauty in his later poetry.

Pope's early poetry brought him to the attention of literary men, with whom he began to associate in the masculine world of coffeehouse and tavern. His fragile health never permitted him to live the rakish life that he would have liked, but it did not prevent his enjoying the company of some of the most distinguished authors of the time. Between 1706 and 1711 he came to know, among many others, William Congreve, William Walsh, the critic and poet, and Richard Steele and Joseph Addison. As it happened, all were Whigs. Pope could readily ignore politics in the excitement of taking his place among the leading wits of the town. But after the fall of the Whigs in 1710, and the formation of the Tory government under Robert Harley (later earl of Oxford) and Henry St. John (later Viscount Bolingbroke) party loyalties bred bitterness among the wits as among the politicians.

By 1712, Pope had made the acquaintance of another group of writers, all Tories, who soon became his intimate friends: Jonathan Swift, by then the close associate of Harley and St. John and the principal propagandist for their policies; Dr. John Arbuthnot, physician to the queen, a learned scientist, a wit, and a man of humanity and integrity; John Gay, the poet, who in 1728 was to produce the *Beggar's Opera*, the greatest theatrical success of the century; and the poet Thomas Parnell. It was among these men that Pope was to find his lifelong friends; and it was through them that he became the friend and admirer of Oxford, and later the intimate of Bolingbroke. In 1714 this group, at the instigation of Pope, formed a club which was to cooperate in a scheme for satirizing all sorts of false learning and pedantry. The friends proposed to write jointly the biography of a learned fool whom they named Martinus Scriblerus (Martin the Scribbler), whose life and opinions would be a running commentary on whatever they considered the abuses of learning and the follies of the learned. Some amusing episodes were later rewritten and published as the *Memoirs of Martinus Scriblerus* (1741). The real importance of the club, however, is that it fostered a satiric temper which was to find unexpected expression in such mature works of the friends as *Gulliver's Travels*, the *Dunciad*, and even, perhaps, the *Beggar's Opera*.

"The life of a wit is a warfare on earth," said Pope, generalizing from his own experience. His very success as a poet (and his astonishing precocity brought him success very early) made enemies among less talented writers, who were to plague him in pamphlets, verse satires, and squibs in the journals throughout his entire literary career. He was attacked for his writings, his religion, and his physical deformity. Though he smarted under the jibes of his detractors, he was a fighter who struck back, always giving better than he got. Pope's literary warfare began in 1713, when he announced his intention of translating the *Iliad* and sought subscribers to a deluxe edition of the work. Subscribers came in droves, but the Whig writers who surrounded Addison at Button's Coffee House did all they could through anonymous attacks to hinder the success of the venture. The eventual success of the first published installment of his *Iliad* in 1715 did not obliterate Pope's just resentment against Addison and his "little senate"; and this resentment found expression in the damaging portrait of Addison (under the name of Atticus), which, years after it was written, was included in Pope's *Epistle to Dr. Arbuthnot* (1735), lines 193–214. The not unjustified attacks on Pope's edition of Shakespeare (1725), especially those by the learned Shakespeare scholar Lewis Theobald (Pope always spelled and pronounced the name "Tibbald" in his satires), led to Theobald's appearance as king of the dunces in the *Dunciad* (1728). In this impressive poem Pope stigmatized his literary enemies as agents of all that he disliked and feared in the literary tendencies of his time—the vulgarization of taste and the arts consequent on the rapid growth of the reading public, the development of journalism, magazines, and other popular and cheap publications, which spread scandal, sensationalism, and political partisanship—in short the new commercial spirit of the nation, which was corrupting not only the arts, but, as Pope saw it, the national life itself.

In the 1730s Pope moved on to philosophical, ethical, and political subjects in the *Essay on Man*, the *Epistles to Several Persons*, and the *Imitations of Horace*. The reigns of George I and George II appeared to him, as to Swift and other Tories, a period of rapid moral, political, and cultural deterioration. The agents of decay seemed in one way or another related to the spread of moneyed (as opposed to landed) wealth, which accounted for the political corruption encouraged by Sir Robert Walpole and the court party, and the increasing influence in all aspects of the national life of a vulgar class of *nouveaux riches*. Pope assumed the role of the champion of traditional civilization: of right reason, humanistic learning, sound art, good taste, and public virtue. It was fortunate that most of his enemies seem to have been designed by nature to illustrate various degrees of unreason, pedantry, bad art, vulgar taste, and, at best, indifferent morals.

The satirist traditionally deals in generally prevalent evils and generally observable human types, not with particular individuals. So too with Pope; the bulk of his satire can be read and enjoyed without much biographical information. Usually in the late satires, as in the earlier *Rape*, he used fictional or type names, although he most often had an individual in mind— Sappho, Atossa, Atticus, Sporus; and when he named individuals (as he consistently did in the *Dunciad* and occasionally elsewhere), his purpose was to raise his victims to the bad eminence of typifying some sort of obliquity. To judge and censure the age, Pope also created the "I" of the satires (not identical with Alexander Pope of Twickenham). This fictional or semifictional figure is the detached observer, somewhat removed from City, town, and court, the centers of corruption; he is the friend of the virtuous, whose friendship for him testifies to his integrity; he is fond of peace, country life, the arts, morality, and truth, and he detests their opposites which flourish in the great world. In such an age, Pope implies, it is impossible for such a man—honest, truthful, blunt—not to write satire.

Pope was a master of style. From first to last, his verse is notable for its rhythmic variety, despite the apparently rigid metrical unit—the heroic couplet—in which he wrote; the precision of meaning and the harmony (or the expressive disharmony, when necessary) of his language; and the union of maximum conciseness with maximum complexity. Something of Pope's metrical variety and verbal harmony can be observed in even so short a passage as lines 71–76 of the pastoral *Summer* (1709), lines so lyrical that, in *Semele*, Handel set them to music. In the passage quoted below (as also in the following quotation), only those rhetorical stresses which distort the normal iambic flow of the verse have been marked; internal pauses within the line are indicated by single and double bars, alliteration and assonance by italics.

> Óh déign to visit our *fors*aken *se*ats,
> The mossy *fountains* ‖ and the *gr*een re*tre*ats!
>
> Where'er yóu wálk ‖ cóol *gá*les shall *f*an the *g*lade,
>
> Trées whére yóu sít ‖ shall c*r*owd into a sh*a*de:
>
> Where'er yóu tréad ‖ the b*l*ushing *fl*owers shall rise,
>
> And all thíngs *fl*óurish where yóu túrn your eyes.

Pope has attained metrical variety by the free substitution of trochees and spondees for the normal iambs; he has achieved rhythmic variety by arranging phrases and clauses (units of syntax and logic) of different lengths within single lines and couplets, so that the passage moves with the sinuous fluency of thought and feeling; and he has not only chosen musical combinations of words, but has also subtly modulated the harmony of the passage by unobtrusive patterns of alliteration and assonance.

Contrast with this pastoral passage lines 16–25 of the *Epilogue to the Satires, Dialogue* 2 (1738), in which Pope is not making music, but is imitating actual conversation so realistically that the metrical pattern and the integrity of the couplet and individual line seem to be destroyed (though in fact they are very much present). In a dialogue with a friend who warns him that his satire is too personal, indeed mere libel, the poet-satirist replies:

> Yé státesmen, | priests of one religion all!
>
> Yé trádesmen vile ‖ in army, court, or hall!
>
> Yé réverend atheists. ‖ F. Scandal! | name them, | Who?
> P. Why that's the thing you bid me not to do.

Whó stárved a sister, ‖ who foreswore a debt,

Í néver named; ‖ the town's inquiring yet.

The poisoning dame— | F. Yóu méan— | P. I don't— | F. Yóu dó.

   P. Sée, nów Í kéep the secret, ‖ and nót yóu!

The bribing statesman— | F. Hóld, ‖ tóo hígh you go.

   P. The bribed elector— ‖ F. There you stoop tóo lów.

In such a passage the language and rhythms of poetry merge with the language and rhythms of impassioned living speech.

A fine example of Pope's ability to derive the maximum of meaning from the most economic use of language and image is the description of the manor house in which lives old Cotta, the miser (*Epistle to Lord Bathurst*, lines 187–196):

> Like some lone Chartreuse stands the good old Hall,
> Silence without, and fasts within the wall;
> No raftered roofs with dance and tabor sound,
> No noontide bell invites the country round;
> Tenants with sighs the smokeless towers survey,
> And turn the unwilling steeds another way;
> Benighted wanderers, the forest o'er,
> Curse the saved candle and unopening door;
> While the gaunt mastiff growling at the gate,
> Affrights the beggar whom he longs to eat.

The first couplet of this passage, which associates the "Hall," symbol of English rural hospitality, with the Grande Chartreuse, the monastery in the French Alps, which, though a place of "silence" and "fasts" for the monks, afforded food and shelter to all travelers, clashes forcefully with the dismal details of Cotta's miserly dwelling; and the meaning of the scene is concentrated in the grotesque image of the last couplet: the half-starved watchdog and the frightened beggar confronting each other in mutual hunger.

But there is another sort of variety within Pope's work as a whole which derives from the poet's respect for the idea that the different kinds of literature have their different and appropriate styles. Thus the *Essay on Criticism*, an informal discussion of literary theory, is written, like Horace's *Art of Poetry*, a similarly didactic poem, in a plain style, the easy language of well-bred talk. *The Rape of the Lock*, being "a heroi-comical poem" (that is, a comic poem that treats trivial material in an epic style), employs the lofty heroic language that Dryden had perfected in his translation of Virgil, and introduces amusing parodies of passages in *Paradise Lost*; parodies later raised to truly Miltonic sublimity and complexity by the conclusion of the *Dunciad*. *Eloisa to Abelard* renders the brooding, passionate voice of its heroine in a declamatory language, given to sudden outbursts and shifts of tone, that recalls the stage. The grave epistles that make up the *Essay on Man*, a philosophical discussion of such majestic themes as the Creator and his creation, the universe, human nature, society, and happiness, are written in a stately forensic language and tone and constantly employ the traditional rhetorical figures. The *Imitations of Horace*, and, above all, the *Epistle to*

Dr. Arbuthnot, his finest poem "in the Horatian way," reveal Pope's final mastery of the plain style of Horace's epistles and satires and justify his image of himself as the heir of the Roman poet. In short no other poet of the century can equal Pope in the range of his materials, the diversity of his poetic styles, and his mastery of the poet's craft.

An Essay on Criticism   There is no pleasanter introduction to the canons of taste in the English Augustan age than Pope's *Essay on Criticism*. As Addison said in his review in *Spectator* 253, it assembles the "most known and most received observations on the subject of literature and criticism." Pope was attempting to do for his time what Horace, in his *Art of Poetry*, and what Nicolas Boileau (French poet of the age of Louis XIV), in his *L'Art Poétique*, had done for theirs. Horace is not only one of Pope's instructors in the principles of criticism; he is also Pope's model in this poem, especially in the simple, conversational language, the tone of well-bred ease, and the deliberately plain style.

In framing his critical creed, Pope did not try for novelty: he wished merely to give to generally accepted doctrines pleasing and memorable expression and make them useful to modern poets. Here one meets the key words of neoclassical criticism: *wit*, *Nature*, *ancients*, *rules*, *genius*. *Wit* in the poem is a word of many meanings—a clever remark, or the man who makes it; a conceit; liveliness of mind; inventiveness; fancy; genius; a genius; poetry itself, among others. *Nature* is an equally ambiguous word, meaning not "things out there," or "the outdoors," but most importantly that which is representative, universal, permanent in human experience as opposed to the idiosyncratic, the individual, the temporary. In line 21, "Nature" comes close to meaning "intuitive knowledge." In line 52, it means that half-personified power manifested in the cosmic order, which in its modes of working is a model for art. The reverence felt by most Augustans for the works of the great writers of ancient Greece and Rome raised the question how far the authority of these *ancients* extended. Were their works to be received as models to be conscientiously imitated? Were the *rules* received from them or deducible from their works to be accepted as prescriptive laws or merely convenient guides? Was individual *genius* to be bound by what has been conventionally held to be *Nature*, by the authority of the *ancients*, and by the legalistic pedantry of *rules*? Or could it go its own way?

In part 1 of the *Essay* Pope constructs a harmonious system in which he effects a compromise among all these conflicting forces—a compromise which is typically 18th century in spirit. Part 2 analyzes the causes of faulty criticism. Part 3 characterizes the good critic and praises the great critics of the past.

An Essay on Criticism

Part 1

'Tis hard to say, if greater want of skill
Appear in writing or in judging ill;

But of the two less dangerous is the offense
To tire our patience than mislead our sense.
Some few in that, but numbers err in this,   5
Ten censure[1] wrong for one who writes amiss;
A fool might once himself alone expose,
Now one in verse makes many more in prose.
'Tis with our judgments as our watches, none
Go just alike, yet each believes his own.   10
In poets as true genius is but rare,
True taste as seldom is the critic's share;
Both must alike from Heaven derive their light,
These born to judge, as well as those to write.
Let such teach others who themselves excel,   15
And censure freely who have written well.
Authors are partial to their wit, 'tis true,
But are not critics to their judgment too?
    Yet if we look more closely, we shall find
Most have the seeds of judgment in their mind: 20
Nature affords at least a glimmering light;
The lines, though touched but faintly, are drawn right.
But as the slightest sketch, if justly traced, ⎫
Is by ill coloring but the more disgraced,   ⎬
So by false learning is good sense defaced: ⎭   25
Some are bewildered in the maze of schools,
And some made coxcombs[2] Nature meant but fools.
In search of wit these lose their common sense,
And then turn critics in their own defense:
Each burns alike, who can, or cannot write,   30
Or with a rival's or an eunuch's spite.
All fools have still an itching to deride,
And fain would be upon the laughing side.
If Maevius[3] scribble in Apollo's spite,
There are who judge still worse than he can write.   35
    Some have at first for wits, then poets passed,
Turned critics next, and proved plain fools at last.
Some neither can for wits nor critics pass,
As heavy mules are neither horse nor ass.
Those half-learn'd witlings, numerous in our isle,   40
As half-formed insects on the banks of Nile;[4]
Unfinished things, one knows not what to call,
Their generation's so equivocal:
To tell[5] them would a hundred tongues require,
Or one vain wit's, that might a hundred tire.   45
    But you who seek to give and merit fame,
And justly bear a critic's noble name,

1. Judge
2. Superficial pretenders to learning.
3. A silly poet alluded to contemptuously by Virgil in *Eclogue* 3 and by Horace in *Epode* 10.
4. The ancients believed that many forms of life
were spontaneously generated in the fertile mud of
the Nile.
5. Reckon, count.

Be sure yourself and your own reach to know,
How far your genius, taste, and learning go;
Launch not beyond your depth, but be discreet,   50
And mark that point where sense and dullness meet.
    Nature to all things fixed the limits fit,
And wisely curbed proud man's pretending wit.
As on the land while here the ocean gains,
In other parts it leaves wide sandy plains;   55
Thus in the soul while memory prevails,
The solid power of understanding fails;
Where beams of warm imagination play,
The memory's soft figures melt away.
One science[6] only will one genius fit,   60
So vast is art, so narrow human wit.
Not only bounded to peculiar arts,
But oft in those confined to single parts.
Like kings we lose the conquests gained before,
By vain ambition still to make them more;   65
Each might his several province well command,
Would all but stoop to what they understand.
    First follow Nature, and your judgment frame
By her just standard, which is still the same;
Unerring Nature, still divinely bright,   70
One clear, unchanged, and universal light,
Life, force, and beauty must to all impart,
At once the source, and end, and test of art.
Art from that fund each just supply provides,
Works without show, and without pomp presides.   75
In some fair body thus the informing soul
With spirits feeds, with vigor fills the whole,
Each motion guides, and every nerve sustains;
Itself unseen, but in the effects remains.
Some, to whom Heaven in wit has been profuse,   80
Want as much more to turn it to its use;
For wit and judgment often are at strife,
Though meant each other's aid, like man and wife.
'Tis more to guide than spur the Muse's steed,
Restrain his fury than provoke his speed;   85
The wingèd courser,[7] like a generous horse,
Shows most true mettle when you check his course.
    Those rules of old discovered, not devised,
Are Nature still, but Nature methodized;
Nature, like liberty, is but restrained   90
By the same laws which first herself ordained.
    Hear how learn'd Greece her useful rules indites,
When to repress and when indulge our flights:

6. Branch of learning.
7. Pegasus, associated with the Muses and poetic inspiration; "generous": spirited, highly bred.

High on Parnassus' top her sons she showed,
And pointed out those arduous paths they trod;   95
Held from afar, aloft, the immortal prize,
And urged the rest by equal steps to rise.
Just precepts thus from great examples given,
She drew from them what they derived from Heaven.
The generous critic fanned the poet's fire,   100
And taught the world with reason to admire.
Then criticism the Muse's handmaid proved,
To dress her charms, and make her more beloved:
But following wits from that intention strayed,
Who could not win the mistress, wooed the maid;   105
Against the poets their own arms they turned,
Sure to hate most the men from whom they learned.
So modern 'pothecaries, taught the art
By doctors's bills[8] to play the doctor's part,
Bold in the practice of mistaken rules,   110
Prescribe, apply, and call their masters fools.
Some on the leaves of ancient authors prey,
Nor time nor moths e'er spoiled so much as they.
Some dryly plain, without invention's aid,
Write dull receipts[9] how poems may be made.   115
These leave the sense their learning to display,
And those explain the meaning quite away.
    You then whose judgment the right course would steer,
Know well each ancient's proper character;
His fable,[1] subject, scope in every page;   120
Religion, country, genius of his age:
Without all these at once before your eyes,
Cavil you may, but never criticize.
Be Homer's works your study and delight,
Read them by day, and meditate by night;   125
Thence form your judgment, thence your maxims bring,
And trace the Muses upward to their spring.
Still with itself compared, his text peruse;
And let your comment be the Mantuan Muse.[2]
    When first young Maro in his boundless mind   130
A work to outlast immortal Rome designed,
Perhaps he seemed above the critic's law,
And but from Nature's fountains scorned to draw;
But when to examine every part he came,
Nature and Homer were, he found, the same.   135

---

8. Prescriptions.
9. Formulas for preparing a dish; recipes. Pope himself wrote an amusing burlesque *Receipt to Make an Epic Poem*, first published in the *Guardian* 78 (1713).
1. Plot or story of a play or poem; "Scope": aim or purpose.

2. Virgil, the "young Maro" of the following line, was born in a village adjacent to Mantua in Italy; hence "Mantuan Muse." His epic, the *Aeneid*, was modeled on Homer's *Iliad* and *Odyssey* and was considered to be a refinement on the Greek poems. Thus it could be thought of as a commentary ("comment") on Homer's poems.

Convinced, amazed, he checks the bold design,
And rules as strict his labored work confine
As if the Stagirite[3] o'erlooked each line.
Learn hence for ancient rules a just esteem;
To copy Nature is to copy them. 140

    Some beauties yet no precepts can declare,
For there's a happiness as well as care.[4]
Music resembles poetry, in each
Are nameless graces which no methods teach,
And which a master hand alone can reach. 145
If, where the rules not far enough extend
(Since rules were made but to promote their end)
Some lucky license answers to the full
The intent proposed, that license is a rule.
Thus Pegasus, a nearer way to take, 150
May boldly deviate from the common track.
Great wits sometimes may gloriously offend,
And rise to faults true critics dare not mend;
From vulgar bounds with brave disorder part,
And snatch a grace beyond the reach of art, 155
Which without passing through the judgment, gains
The heart, and all its end at once attains.
In prospects thus, some objects please our eyes,
Which out of Nature's common order rise,
The shapeless rock, or hanging precipice. 160
But though the ancients thus their rules invade
(As kings dispense with laws themselves have made)
Moderns, beware! or if you must offend
Against the precept, ne'er transgress its end;
Let it be seldom, and compelled by need; 165
And have at least their precedent to plead.
The critic else proceeds without remorse,
Seizes your fame, and puts his laws in force.
    I know there are, to whose presumptuous thoughts
Those freer beauties, even in them, seem faults.[5] 170
Some figures monstrous and misshaped appear,
Considered singly, or beheld too near,
Which, but proportioned to their light or place,
Due distance reconciles to form and grace.
A prudent chief not always must display 175
His powers in equal ranks and fair array,
But with the occasion and the place comply,
Conceal his force, nay seem sometimes to fly.
Those oft are stratagems which errors seem,
Nor is it Homer nods, but we that dream. 180

---

3. Aristotle, native of Stagira, from whose *Poetics* later critics formulated strict rules for writing tragedy and the epic.
4. I.e., no rules ("precepts") can explain ("declare")
some beautiful effects in a work of art which can be the result only of inspiration or good luck ("happiness"), not of painstaking labor ("care").
5. Pronounced *fawts*.

Still green with bays each ancient altar stands
Above the reach of sacrilegious hands,
Secure from flames, from envy's fiercer rage,
Destructive war, and all-involving age.
See, from each clime the learn'd their incense bring!   185
Here in all tongues consenting[6] paeans ring!
In praise so just let every voice be joined,[7]
And fill the general chorus of mankind.
Hail, bards triumphant! born in happier days,
Immortal heirs of universal praise!   190
Whose honors with increase of ages grow,
As streams roll down, enlarging as they flow;
Nations unborn your mighty names shall sound,
And worlds applaud that must not yet be found!
Oh, may some spark of your celestial fire,   195
The last, the meanest of your sons inspire
(That on weak wings, from far, pursues your flights,
Glows while he reads, but trembles as he writes)
To teach vain wits a science little known,
To admire superior sense, and doubt their own!   200

Part 2

Of all the causes which conspire to blind
Man's erring judgment, and misguide the mind,
What the weak head with strongest bias rules,
Is pride, the never-failing vice of fools.
Whatever Nature has in worth denied,   205
She gives in large recruits[8] of needful pride;
For as in bodies, thus in souls, we find
What wants in blood and spirits swelled with wind:
Pride, where wit fails, steps in to our defense,
And fills up all the mighty void of sense.   210
If once right reason drives that cloud away,
Truth breaks upon us with resistless day.
Trust not yourself: but your defects to know,
Make use of every friend—and every foe.
A little learning is a dangerous thing;   215
Drink deep, or taste not the Pierian spring.[9]
There shallow draughts intoxicate the brain,
And drinking largely sobers us again.
Fired at first sight with what the Muse imparts,
In fearless youth we tempt[1] the heights of arts,   220
While from the bounded level of our mind
Short views we take, nor see the lengths behind;
But more advanced, behold with strange surprise

---

6. Agreeing, concurring.
7. Pronounced *jined*.
8. Supplies.

9. The spring in Pieria on Mt. Olympus, sacred
to the Muses.
1. Attempt.

New distant scenes of endless science rise!
So pleased at first the towering Alps we try,   225
Mount o'er the vales, and seem to tread the sky,
The eternal snows appear already past,
And the first clouds and mountains seem the last;
But, those attained, we tremble to survey
The growing labors of the lengthened way,   230
The increasing prospect tires our wandering eyes,
Hills peep o'er hills, and Alps on Alps arise!
   A perfect judge will read each work of wit
With the same spirit that its author writ:
Survey the whole, nor seek slight faults to find   235
Where Nature moves, and rapture warms the mind;
Nor lose, for that malignant dull delight,
The generous pleasure to be charmed with wit.
But in such lays as neither ebb nor flow,
Correctly cold, and regularly low,   240
That, shunning faults, one quiet tenor keep,
We cannot blame indeed—but we may sleep.
In wit, as nature, what affects our hearts
Is not the exactness of peculiar parts;
'Tis not a lip, or eye, we beauty call,   245
But the joint force and full result of all.
Thus when we view some well-proportioned dome
(The world's just wonder, and even thine, O Rome!),[2]
No single parts unequally surprise,
All comes united to the admiring eyes: 250
No monstrous height, or breadth, or length appear;
The whole at once is bold and regular.
   Whoever thinks a faultless piece to see,
Thinks what ne'er was, nor is, nor e'er shall be.
In every work regard the writer's end,   255
Since none can compass more than they intend;
And if the means be just, the conduct true,
Applause, in spite of trivial faults, is due.
As men of breeding, sometimes men of wit,
To avoid great errors must the less commit,   260
Neglect the rules each verbal critic lays,
For not to know some trifles is a praise.
Most critics, fond of some subservient art,
Still make the whole depend upon a part:
They talk of principles, but notions prize,   265
And all to one loved folly sacrifice.
   Once on a time La Mancha's knight,[3] they say,
A certain bard encountering on the way,
Discoursed in terms as just, with looks as sage,

2. The dome of St. Peter's, designed by Michelangelo.
3. Don Quixote. The story comes not from Cervantes' novel, but from a spurious sequel to it by
Don Alonzo Fernandez de Avellaneda.

As e'er could Dennis,[4] of the Grecian stage;   270
Concluding all were desperate sots and fools
Who durst depart from Aristotle's rules.
Our author, happy in a judge so nice,
Produced his play, and begged the knight's advice;
Made him observe the subject and the plot,   275
The manners, passions, unities; what not?
All which exact to rule were brought about,
Were but a combat in the lists left out.
"What! leave the combat out?" exclaims the knight.
"Yes, or we must renounce the Stagirite."   280
"Not so, by Heaven!" he answers in a rage,
"Knights, squires, and steeds must enter on the stage."
"So vast a throng the stage can ne'er contain."
"Then build a new, or act it in a plain."

    Thus critics of less judgment than caprice,   285
Curious,[5] not knowing, not exact, but nice,
Form short ideas, and offend in arts
(As most in manners), by a love to parts.

    Some to conceit[6] alone their taste confine,
And glittering thoughts struck out at every line;   290
Pleased with a work where nothing's just or fit,
One glaring chaos and wild heap of wit.
Poets, like painters, thus unskilled to trace
The naked nature and the living grace,
With gold and jewels cover every part,   295
And hide with ornaments their want of art.

    True wit is Nature to advantage dressed,
What oft was thought, but ne'er so well expressed;
Something whose truth convinced at sight we find,
That gives us back the image of our mind.   300
As shades more sweetly recommend the light,
So modest plainness sets off sprightly wit;
For works may have more wit than does them good,
As bodies perish through excess of blood.

    Others for language all their care express,   305
And value books, as women men, for dress.
Their praise is still—the style is excellent;
The sense they humbly take upon contènt.[7]
Words are like leaves; and where they most abound,
Much fruit of sense beneath is rarely found.   310
False eloquence, like the prismatic glass,
Its gaudy colors spreads on every place;[8]

---

4. John Dennis (1657–1734), though one of the leading critics of the time, was frequently ridiculed by the wits for his irascibility and his rather solemn pomposity. Pope apparently did not know Dennis personally, but his jibe at him in part 3 of this poem incurred the critic's lasting animosity.
5. Laboriously careful. "Nice": minutely accurate, over refined.

6. Pointed wit, ingenuity and extravagance, or affectation in the use of figures, especially similes and metaphors.
7. Mere acquiescence.
8. A very up-to-date scientific reference. Newton's Optics, which treated of the prism and the spectrum, had been published in 1704, though his theories had been known earlier.

The face of Nature we no more survey,
All glares alike, without distinction gay.
But true expression, like the unchanging sun,   315
Clears and improves whate'er it shines upon;
It gilds all objects, but it alters none.
Expression is the dress of thought, and still
Appears more decent as more suitable.
A vile conceit in pompous words expressed   320
Is like a clown[9] in regal purple dressed:
For different styles with different subjects sort,
As several garbs with country, town, and court.
Some by old words to fame have made pretense,
Ancients in phrase, mere moderns in their sense.   325
Such labored nothings, in so strange a style,
Amaze the unlearn'd, and make the learned smile;
Unlucky as Fungoso[1] in the play,
These sparks with awkward vanity display
What the fine gentleman wore yesterday;   330
And but so mimic ancient wits at best,
As apes our grandsires in their doublets dressed.
In words as fashions the same rule will hold,
Alike fantastic if too new or old:
Be not the first by whom the new are tried,   335
Nor yet the last to lay the old aside.
      But most by numbers[2] judge a poet's song,
And smooth or rough with them is right or wrong.
In the bright Muse though thousand charms conspire,
Her voice is all these tuneful fools admire,   340
Who haunt Parnassus but to please their ear,
Not mend their minds; as some to church repair,
Not for the doctrine, but the music there.
These equal syllables alone require,
Though oft the ear the open vowels tire,[3]   345
While expletives[4] their feeble aid do join,
And ten low words oft creep in one dull line:
While they ring round the same unvaried chimes,
With sure returns of still expected rhymes;
Where'er you find "the cooling western breeze,"   350
In the next line, it "whispers through the trees";
If crystal streams "with pleasing murmurs creep,"
The reader's threatened (not in vain) with "sleep";
Then, at the last and only couplet fraught
With some unmeaning thing they call a thought,   355
A needless Alexandrine[5] ends the song

---

9. Rustic, boor.
1. A character in Ben Jonson's comedy *Every Man out of His Humor* (1599).
2. Versification.
3. In lines 345–57 Pope cleverly contrives to make his own metrics or diction illustrate the faults that

he is exposing.
4. Words used merely to achieve the necessary number of feet in a line of verse.
5. A line of verse containing six iambic feet; it is illustrated in the next line.

That, like a wounded snake, drags its slow length along.
Leave such to tune their own dull rhymes, and know
What's roundly smooth or languishingly slow;
And praise the easy vigor of a line   360
Where Denham's strength and Waller's sweetness join.[6]
True ease in writing comes from art, not chance,
As those move easiest who have learned to dance.
'Tis not enough no harshness gives offense,
The sound must seem an echo to the sense.   365
Soft is the strain when Zephyr gently blows,
And the smooth stream in smoother numbers flows;
But when loud surges lash the sounding shore,
The hoarse, rough verse should like the torrent roar.
When Ajax strives some rock's vast weight to throw,   370
The line too labors, and the words move slow;
Not so when swift Camilla scours the plain,
Flies o'er the unbending corn, and skims along the main.
Hear how Timotheus'[7] varied lays surprise,
And bid alternate passions fall and rise!   375
While at each change the son of Libyan Jove[8]
Now burns with glory, and then melts with love;
Now his fierce eyes with sparkling fury glow,
Now sighs steal out, and tears begin to flow:
Persians and Greeks like turns of nature[9] found   380
And the world's victor stood subdued by sound!
The power of music all our hearts allow,
And what Timotheus was is Dryden now.
    Avoid extremes; and shun the fault of such
Who still are pleased too little or too much.   385
At every trifle scorn to take offense:
That always shows great pride, or little sense.
Those heads, as stomachs, are not sure the best,
Which nauseate all, and nothing can digest.
Yet let not each gay turn thy rapture move;   390
For fools admire,[1] but men of sense approve:
As things seem large which we through mists descry,
Dullness is ever apt to magnify.
    Some foreign writers, some our own despise;
The ancients only, or the moderns prize.   395
Thus wit, like faith, by each man is applied
To one small sect, and all are damned beside.
Meanly they seek the blessing to confine,
And force that sun but on a part to shine,

6. Dryden, whom Pope echoes here, considered
Sir John Denham (1615–1669) and Edmund
Waller (1606–1687) to have been the principal
shapers of the closed pentameter couplet. He had
distinguished the "strength" of the one and the
"sweetness" of the other.
7. The musician in Dryden's *Alexander's Feast*.

Pope retells the story of that poem in the following
lines.
8. Alexander the Great.
9. Alternations of feelings.
1. Wonder. "Approve": judge favorably only after
due deliberation.

Which not alone the southern wit sublimes,   400
But ripens spirits in cold northern climes;
Which from the first has shone on ages past,
Enlights the present, and shall warm the last;
Though each may feel increases and decays,
And see now clearer and now darker days.   405
Regard not then if wit be old or new,
But blame the false and value still the true.
  Some ne'er advance a judgment of their own,
But catch the spreading notion of the town;
They reason and conclude by precedent,   410
And own stale nonsense which they ne'er invent.
Some judge of authors' names, not works, and then
Nor praise nor blame the writings, but the men.
Of all this servile herd the worst is he
That in proud dullness joins with quality,   415
A constant critic at the great man's board,
To fetch and carry nonsense for my lord.
What woeful stuff this madrigal would be
In some starved hackney sonneteer or me!
But let a lord once own the happy lines,   420
How the wit brightens! how the style refines!
Before his sacred name flies every fault,
And each exalted stanza teems with thought!
  The vulgar thus through imitation err;
As oft the learn'd by being singular;   425
So much they scorn the crowd, that if the throng
By chance go right, they purposely go wrong.
So schismatics[2] the plain believers quit,
And are but damned for having too much wit.
Some praise at morning what they blame at night,   430
But always think the last opinion right.
A Muse by these is like a mistress used,
This hour she's idolized, the next abused;
While their weak heads like towns unfortified,
'Twixt sense and nonsense daily change their side.   435
Ask them the cause; they're wiser still, they say;
And still tomorrow's wiser than today.
We think our fathers fools, so wise we grow;
Our wiser sons, no doubt, will think us so.
Once school divines[3] this zealous isle o'erspread;   440
Who knew most sentences was deepest read.
Faith, Gospel, all seemed made to be disputed,
And none had sense enough to be confuted.
Scotists and Thomists now in peace remain

2. Those who have divided the church on points of theology. Pope stressed the first syllable, the pronunciation approved by Johnson in his *Dictionary*.
3. The medieval theologians, such as the follow-ers of Duns Scotus and St. Thomas Aquinas mentioned in line 444; "sentences" alludes to Peter Lombard's *Book of Sentences*, a book esteemed by Scholastic philosophers.

Amidst their kindred cobwebs in Duck Lane.[4]   445
If faith itself has different dresses worn,
What wonder modes in wit should take their turn?
Oft, leaving what is natural and fit,
The current folly proves the ready wit;
And authors think their reputation safe,   450
Which lives as long as fools are pleased to laugh.
    Some valuing those of their own side or mind,
Still make themselves the measure of mankind:
Fondly[5] we think we honor merit then,
When we but praise ourselves in other men.   455
Parties in wit attend on those of state,
And public faction doubles private hate.
Pride, Malice, Folly against Dryden rose,
In various shapes of parsons, critics, beaux;
But sense survived, when merry jests were past;   460
For rising merit will buoy up at last.
Might he return and bless once more our eyes,
New Blackmores and new Milbourns must arise.[6]
Nay, should great Homer lift his awful head,
Zoilus[7] again would start up from the dead.   465
Envy will merit, as its shade, pursue,
But like a shadow, proves the substance true;
For envied wit, like Sol eclipsed, makes known
The opposing body's grossness, not its own.
When first that sun too powerful beams displays,   470
It draws up vapors which obscure its rays;
But even those clouds at last adorn its way,
Reflect new glories, and augment the day.
    Be thou the first true merit to befriend;
His praise is lost who stays till all commend.   475
Short is the date, alas! of modern rhymes,
And 'tis but just to let them live betimes.
No longer now that golden age appears,
When patriarch wits survived a thousand years:
Now length of fame (our second life) is lost,   480
And bare threescore is all even that can boast;
Our sons their fathers' failing language see,
And such as Chaucer is shall Dryden be.[8]
So when the faithful pencil has designed
Some bright idea of the master's mind,   485
Where a new world leaps out at his command,
And ready Nature waits upon his hand;

---

4. Street where publishers' remainders and second-hand books were sold.
5. Foolishly.
6. Sir Richard Blackmore, physician and poet, had
attacked Dryden for the immorality of his plays;
the Rev. Luke Milbourn had attacked his translation of Virgil.
7. A Greek critic of the 4th century B.C., who wrote

a book of carping criticism of Homer.
8. The radical changes that took place in the
English language between the death of Chaucer in
1400 and the death of Dryden in 1700 suggested
that in another 300 years Dryden would be unintelligible. Latin seemed the only means of attaining enduring fame.

When the ripe colors soften and unite,
And sweetly melt into just shade and light;
When mellowing years their full perfection give,   490
And each bold figure just begins to live,
The treacherous colors the fair art betray,
And all the bright creation fades away!
    Unhappy wit, like most mistaken things,
Atones not for that envy which it brings.   495
In youth alone its empty praise we boast,
But soon the short-lived vanity is lost;
Like some fair flower the early spring supplies,
That gaily blooms, but even in blooming dies,
What is this wit, which must our cares employ?   500
The owner's wife, that other men enjoy;
Then most our trouble still when most admired,
And still the more we give, the more required;
Whose fame with pains we guard, but lose with ease,
Sure some to vex, but never all to please;   505
'Tis what the vicious fear, the virtuous shun,
By fools 'tis hated, and by knaves undone!
    If wit so much from ignorance undergo,
Ah, let not learning too commence its foe!
Of old those met rewards who could excel,   510
And such were praised who but endeavored well;
Though triumphs were to generals only due,
Crowns were reserved to grace the soldiers too.
Now they who reach Parnassus' lofty crown
Employ their pains to spurn some others down;   515
And while self-love each jealous writer rules,
Contending wits become the sport of fools;
But still the worst with most regret commend,
For each ill author is as bad a friend.
To what base ends, and by what abject ways,   520
Are mortals urged through sacred[9] lust of praise!
Ah, ne'er so dire a thirst of glory boast,
Nor in the critic let the man be lost!
Good nature and good sense must ever join;
To err is human, to forgive divine.   525
    But if in noble minds some dregs remain
Nor yet purged off, of spleen and sour disdain,
Discharge that rage on more provoking crimes,
Nor fear a dearth in these flagitious[1] times.
No pardon vile obscenity should find,   530
Though wit and art conspire to move your mind;
But dullness with obscenity must prove
As shameful sure as impotence in love.
In the fat age of pleasure, wealth, and ease

9. Accursed. The phrase imitates Virgil's "*auri*
sacra famis," "accursed hunger for gold" (*Aeneid*
3.57).
1. Scandalously wicked.

Sprung the rank weed, and thrived with large increase: 535
When love was all an easy monarch's[2] care,
Seldom at council, never in a war;
Jilts ruled the state, and statesmen farces writ;
Nay, wits had pensions, and young lords had wit;
The fair sat panting at a courtier's play,   540
And not a mask[3] went unimproved away;
The modest fan was lifted up no more,
And virgins smiled at what they blushed before.
The following license of a foreign reign
Did all the dregs of bold Socinus drain;[4]   545
Then unbelieving priests reformed the nation,
And taught more pleasant methods of salvation;
Where Heaven's free subjects might their rights dispute,
Lest God himself should seem too absolute;
Pulpits their sacred satire learned to spare,   550
And Vice admired to find a flatterer there!
Encouraged thus, wit's Titans braved the skies,
And the press groaned with licensed blasphemies.
These monsters, critics! with your darts engage,
Here point your thunder, and exhaust your rage!
Yet shun their fault, who, scandalously nice,
Will needs mistake an author into vice;
All seems infected that the infected spy,
As all looks yellow to the jaundiced eye.

Part 3

Learn then what morals critics ought to show,   560
For 'tis but half a judge's task, to know.
'Tis not enough, taste, judgment, learning, join;
In all you speak, let truth and candor[5] shine:
That not alone what to your sense is due
All may allow; but seek your friendship too.   565
    Be silent always when you doubt your sense;
And speak, though sure, with seeming diffidence:
Some positive, persisting fops we know,
Who, if once wrong, will needs be always so;
But you, with pleasure own your errors past,   570
And make each day a critic[6] on the last.
    'Tis not enough, your counsel still be true;
Blunt truths more mischief than nice falsehoods do;
Men must be taught as if you taught them not,
And things unknown proposed as things forgot.   575
Without good breeding, truth is disapproved;

2. Charles II. The concluding lines of part 2 discuss the corruption of wit and poetry under this monarch.
3. A woman wearing a mask.
4. The "foreign reign" refers to William III, a Dutchman. Socinus was the name of two Italian theologians of the 16th century who denied the divinity of Jesus.
5. Kindness, impartiality.
6. Critique.

That only makes superior sense beloved.
   Be niggards of advice on no pretense;
For the worst avarice is that of sense.
With mean complacence[7] ne'er betray your trust,   580
Nor be so civil as to prove unjust.
Fear not the anger of the wise to raise;
Those best can bear reproof, who merit praise.
   'Twere well might critics still this freedom take;
But Appius reddens at each word you speak,   585
And stares, tremendous! with a threatening eye,
Like some fierce tyrant in old tapestry.[8]
Fear most to tax an honorable fool,
Whose right it is, uncensured to be dull;
Such, without wit, are poets when they please,   590
As without learning they can take degrees.[9]
Leave dangerous truths to unsuccessful satyrs,
And flattery to fulsome dedicators,
Whom, when they praise, the world believes no more,
Than when they promise to give scribbling o'er.   595
'Tis best sometimes your censure to restrain,
And charitably let the dull be vain:
Your silence there is better than your spite,
For who can rail so long as they can write?
Still humming on, their drowsy course they keep,   600
And lashed so long, like tops, are lashed asleep.[1]
False steps but help them to renew the race,
As, after stumbling, jades[2] will mend their pace.
What crowds of these, impenitently bold,
In sounds and jingling syllables grown old,   605
Still run on poets, in a raging vein,
Even to the dregs and squeezings of the brain,
Strain out the last dull droppings of their sense,
And rhyme with all the rage of impotence.
   Such shameless bards we have, and yet 'tis true,   610
There are as mad, abandoned critics too.
The bookful blockhead, ignorantly read,
With loads of learned lumber[3] in his head,
With his own tongue still edifies his ears,
And always listening to himself appears.   615
All books he reads, and all he reads assails,
From Dryden's *Fables* down to Durfey's *Tales*.[4]

---

7. Softness of manners; desire of pleasing.
8. "This picture was taken to himself by John Dennis, a furious old critic by profession, who, upon no other provocation, wrote against this *Essay* and its author, in a manner perfectly lunatic. . . ." [Pope's note, 1744]. Pope *did* intend to ridicule Dennis, whose *Appius and Virginia* had failed on the stage in 1709, and who was known for his stare and his use of the word "tremendous." See line 270 above.

9. Honorary degrees were granted to unqualified men of rank. "Satyrs": satires.
1. Tops "sleep" when they spin so rapidly that they seem not to move.
2. Worthless, worn-out horses.
3. Rubbish.
4. Dryden's *Fables* (1700), a set of translations, were among his most admired works; Thomas D'Urfey's *Tales* (1704) were notorious potboilers.

With him, most authors steal their works, or buy;
Garth did not write his own *Dispensary*.[5]
Name a new play, and he's the poet's friend,   620
Nay showed his faults—but when would poets mend?
No place so sacred from such fops is barred,
Nor is Paul's church more safe than Paul's churchyard:[6]
Nay, fly to altars; *there* they'll talk you dead:
For fools rush in where angels fear to tread.   625
Distrustful sense with modest caution speaks, ⎫
It still looks home, and short excursions makes; ⎬
But rattling nonsense in full volleys breaks, ⎭
And never shocked, and never turned aside,
Bursts out, resistless, with a thundering tide.   630
    But where's the man, who counsel can bestow,
Still pleased to teach, and yet not proud to know?
Unbiased, or[7] by favor, or by spite:
Not dully prepossessed, nor blindly right;
Though learned, well-bred; and though well-bred, sincere; 635
Modestly bold, and humanly severe:
Who to a friend his faults can freely show,
And gladly praise the merit of a foe?
Blessed with a taste exact, yet unconfined;
A knowledge both of books and humankind;   640
Gen'rous converse;[8] a soul exempt from pride;
And love to praise, with reason on his side?
    Such once were critics; such the happy few,
Athens and Rome in better ages knew.
The mighty Stagirite[9] first left the shore,   645
Spread all his sails, and durst the deeps explore;
He steered securely, and discovered far,
Led by the light of the Maeonian star.[1]
Poets, a race long unconfined, and free,
Still fond and proud of savage liberty,   650
Received his laws; and stood convinced 'twas fit,
Who conquered nature, should preside o'er wit.
    Horace still charms with graceful negligence,
And without method talks us into sense;
Will, like a friend, familiarly convey   655
The truest notions in the easiest[2] way.
He, who supreme in judgment, as in wit,
Might boldly censure, as he boldly writ,
Yet judged with coolness, though he sung with fire;
His precepts teach but what his works inspire.   660

5. Samuel Garth (1661–1719), who had been accused of plagiarizing his mock-epic poem, *The Dispensary* (1699), was admired and defended by Pope.
6. Booksellers' district near St. Paul's Cathedral, whose aisles were used as a place to meet and do business.

7. Either.
8. Well-bred conversation.
9. Aristotle, whose *Poetics* founded the art of literary criticism, was born at Stagira.
1. Homer, who was supposed to have been born in Maeonia.
2. Least formal.

Our critics take a contrary extreme,
They judge with fury, but they write with fle'me.[3]
Nor suffers Horace more in wrong translations
By wits, than critics[4] in as wrong quotations.
   See Dionysius[5] Homer's thoughts refine,   665
And call new beauties forth from every line!
   Fancy and art in gay Petronius[6] please,
The scholar's learning, with the courtier's ease.
   In grave Quintilian's[7] copious work, we find
The justest rules, and clearest method joined: 670
Thus useful arms in magazines[8] we place,
All ranged in order, and disposed with grace,
But less to please the eye, than arm the hand,
Still fit for use, and ready at command.
   Thee, bold Longinus![9] all the nine inspire,   675
And bless their critic with a poet's fire.
An ardent judge, who, zealous in his trust,
With warmth gives sentence, yet is always just;
Whose own example strengthens all his laws,
And is himself that great sublime he draws.   680
   Thus long succeeding critics justly reigned,
License repressed, and useful laws ordained.
Learning and Rome alike in empire grew;
And arts still followed where her eagles[1] flew;
From the same foes, at last, both felt their doom,   685
And the same age saw learning fall, and Rome.
With tyranny, then superstition joined,
As that the body, this enslaved the mind;
Much was believed, but little understood,
And to be dull was construed to be good;   690
A second deluge learning thus o'errun,
And the monks finished what the Goths begun.[2]
   At length Erasmus, that great, injured name
(The glory of the priesthood, and the shame!),[3]
Stemmed the wild torrent of a barb'rous age,   695
And drove those holy Vandals off the stage.
   But see! each Muse, in Leo's[4] golden days,
Starts from her trance, and trims her withered bays!

---

3. Phlegmatically.
4. I.e., than by critics. Phrases from Horace's *Art of Poetry* were quoted incessantly by critics.
5. Dionysius of Halicarnassus (1st century B.C.) wrote an important treatise on the artistic arrangement of words.
6. Author of the *Satyricon* (1st century A.D.).
7. Author of the *Institutio Oratoria* (ca. 95 A.D.), a famous treatise on rhetoric. Here as elsewhere, Pope's terms of praise are drawn from the author he is praising.
8. Storehouses or arsenals.
9. Supposed author of the influential treatise *On the Sublime* (1st century A.D.), greatly in vogue at

the time of Pope. "Nine": the muses.
1. Emblems on the standards of the Roman army.
2. Pope thought that the scholastic theologians of the Middle Ages were "holy Vandals" who had "sacked" learning as the Goths and Vandals had sacked Rome.
3. Erasmus (1466–1536), the great humanist scholar, was the "glory" of the priesthood because of his goodness and learning, and its "shame" because he was persecuted.
4. Leo X, pope from 1513 to 1521, was notable for his encouragement of artists. "Bays": the wreath of poetry.

Rome's ancient Genius, o'er its ruins spread,
Shakes off the dust, and rears his reverend head.   700
Then sculpture and her sister-arts revive;
Stones leaped to form, and rocks began to live;
With sweeter notes each rising temple rung;
A Raphael painted, and a Vida[5] sung.
Immortal Vida: on whose honored brow   705
The poet's bays and critic's ivy grow:
Cremona now shall ever boast thy name,
As next in place to Mantua, next in fame![6]
    But soon by impious arms[7] from Latium chased,
Their ancient bounds the banished Muses passed;   710
Thence arts o'er all the northern world advance,
But critic-learning flourished most in France:
The rules a nation, born to serve, obeys;
And Boileau still in right of Horace sways.[8]
But we, brave Britons, foreign laws despised,   715
And kept unconquered—and uncivilized;
Fierce for the liberties of wit, and bold,
We still defied the Romans, as of old.
Yet some there were, among the sounder few
Of those who less presumed, and better knew,   720
Who durst assert the juster ancient cause,
And here restored wit's fundamental laws.
Such was the Muse, whose rules and practice tell,
"Nature's chief masterpiece is writing well."[9]
Such was Roscommon, not more learned than good,   725
With manners gen'rous as his noble blood;
To him the wit of Greece and Rome was known,
And every author's merit, but his own.
Such late was Walsh[1]—the Muse's judge and friend,
Who justly knew to blame or to commend;   730
To failings mild, but zealous for desert;
The clearest head, and the sincerest heart.
This humble praise, lamented shade! receive,
This praise at least a grateful Muse may give:
The Muse, whose early voice you taught to sing,   735
Prescribed her heights, and pruned her tender wing,
(Her guide now lost) no more attempts to rise,
But in low numbers[2] short excursions tries:
Content, if hence the unlearned their wants may view,

5. "M. Hieronymus Vida, an excellent Latin poet, who writ an Art of Poetry in verse. He flourished in the time of Leo the Tenth" [Pope's note]. Raphael (1483–1520) painted many of his greatest works under the patronage of Leo X.
6. Vida came from Cremona, near Mantua, the birthplace of Virgil, his favorite poet.
7. German and Spanish troops sacked Rome in 1527. "Latium": Italy.
8. Boileau's *L'Art Poétique* (1674) regularized and modernized the lessons of Horace's *Art of Poetry*.

9. Quoted from an *Essay on Poetry* by John Sheffield, duke of Buckingham (1648–1721), who had befriended the young Pope. Wentworth Dillon, earl of Roscommon, wrote an important *Essay on Translated Verse* (1684).
1. William Walsh (1663–1708), whom Dryden once called "the best critic of our nation," and who had advised Pope to work at becoming the first great "correct" poet in English. The "Muse" here is Pope himself.
2. Humble verses.

The learned reflect on what before they knew: 740
Careless of censure, nor too fond of fame;
Still pleased to praise, yet not afraid to blame;
Averse alike to flatter, or offend;
Not free from faults, nor yet too vain to mend.

1709   1711

The Rape of the Lock

The Rape of the Lock is based upon an actual episode that provoked a quarrel between two prominent Catholic families. Pope's friend John Caryll, to whom the poem is addressed (line 3), suggested that Pope write it, in the hope that a little laughter might serve to soothe ruffled tempers. Lord Petre had cut off a lock of hair from the head of the lovely Arabella Fermor (often spelled "Farmer" and doubtless so pronounced), much to the indignation of the lady and her relatives. In its original version of two cantos and 334 lines, published in 1712, *The Rape of the Lock* was a great success. In 1713 a new version was undertaken against the advice of Addison, who considered the poem perfect as it was first written. Pope greatly expanded the earlier version, adding the delightful "machinery" (i.e., the supernatural agents in epic action) of the Sylphs, Belinda's toilet, the card game, and the visit to the Cave of Spleen in canto 4. In 1717, with the addition of Clarissa's speech on good humor, the poem assumed its final form.

With supreme tact, delicate fancy, playful wit, and the gentlest satire, Pope elaborated the trivial episode which occasioned the poem into the semblance of an epic in miniature, the most nearly perfect "heroi-comical poem" in English. The poem abounds in parodies and echoes of the *Iliad*, the *Aeneid*, and *Paradise Lost*, thus constantly forcing the reader to compare small things with great. The familiar devices of epic are observed, but the incidents or characters are beautifully proportioned to the scale of mock epic. The *Rape* tells of war, but it is the drawing-room war between the sexes; it has its heroes and heroines, but they are beaux and belles; it has its supernatural characters ("machinery") but they are Sylphs (borrowed, as Pope tells us in his engaging dedicatory letter, from Rosicrucian lore)—creatures of the air, the souls of dead coquettes, with tasks appropriate to their nature—or the Gnome Umbriel, once a prude on earth; it has its epic game, played on the "velvet plain" of the card table, its feasting heroes, who sip coffee and gossip, its battle, fought with the clichés of compliment and conceits, with frowns and angry glances, with snuff and bodkin; it has the traditional epic journey to the underworld—here the Cave of Spleen, emblematic of the peevish ill nature of spoiled and hypochondriacal women. And Pope creates a world in which these actions take place, a world that is dense with beautiful objects: brocades, ivory and tortoise shell, cosmetics and diamonds, lacquered furniture, silver teapot, delicate chinaware. It is a world that is constantly in motion and that sparkles and glitters with light, whether the light of the sun, or of Belinda's eyes, or that light into which the "fluid" bodies of the Sylphs seem to dissolve as they flutter in shrouds and around the mast of Belinda's ship. Though Pope laughs at this world and its creatures—and remembers that a grimmer, darker world surrounds it (3.19–24 and 5.145–48)—he makes us very much aware of its beauty and its charm.

The epigraph may be translated, "I was unwilling, Belinda, to ravish your locks; but I rejoice to have conceded this to your prayers" (Martial, *Epigrams* 12.84.1–2). Pope substituted his heroine for Martial's Polytimus. The epigraph is intended to suggest that the poem was published at Miss Fermor's request.

For some of the author's revisions while composing *The Rape of the Lock*, see "Poems in Process," below.

The Rape of the Lock

An Heroi-Comical Poem

Nolueram, Belinda, tuos violare capillos;
sed juvat hoc precibus me tribuisse tuis.
                                          —MARTIAL

TO MRS. ARABELLA FERMOR

MADAM,

It will be in vain to deny that I have some regard for this piece, since I dedicate it to you. Yet you may bear me witness, it was intended only to divert a few young ladies, who have good sense and good humor enough to laugh not only at their sex's little unguarded follies, but at their own. But as it was communicated with the air of a secret, it soon found its way into the world. An imperfect copy having been offered to a book-seller, you had the good nature for my sake to consent to the publication of one more correct; this I was forced to, before I had executed half my design, for the machinery was entirely wanting to complete it.

The machinery, Madam, is a term invented by the critics, to signify that part which the deities, angels, or demons are made to act in a poem; for the ancient poets are in one respect like many modern ladies: let an action be never so trivial in itself, they always make it appear of the utmost importance. These machines I determined to raise on a very new and odd foundation, the Rosicrucian[1] doctrine of spirits.

I know how disagreeable it is to make use of hard words before a lady; but 'tis so much the concern of a poet to have his works understood, and particularly by your sex, that you must give me leave to explain two or three difficult terms.

The Rosicrucians are a people I must bring you acquainted with. The best account I know of them is in a French book called *Le Comte de Gabalis*,[2] which both in its title and size is so like a novel, that many of the fair sex have read it for one by mistake. According to these gentlemen, the four elements are inhabited by spirits, which they call Sylphs, Gnomes, Nymphs, and Salamanders. The Gnomes or Demons of earth delight in mischief; but the Sylphs, whose habitation is in the air, are the best-conditioned creatures imaginable. For they say, any mortals may enjoy the most intimate familiarities with these gentle spirits, upon a condition very easy to all true adepts, an inviolate preservation of chastity.

---

1. A system of arcane philosophy introduced into England from Germany in the 17th century.

2. By the Abbé de Montfaucon de Villars, published in 1670.

As to the following cantos, all the passages of them are as fabulous as the vision at the beginning, or the transformation at the end; (except the loss of your hair, which I always mention with reverence). The human persons are as fictitious as the airy ones; and the character of Belinda, as it is now managed, resembles you in nothing but in beauty.

If this poem had as many graces as there are in your person, or in your mind, yet I could never hope it should pass through the world half so uncensured as you have done. But let its fortune be what it will, mine is happy enough, to have given me this occasion of assuring you that I am, with the truest esteem,

MADAM,

Your most obedient, humble servant,

A. POPE

Canto 1

What dire offense from amorous causes springs,
What mighty contests rise from trivial things,
I sing—This verse to Caryll, Muse! is due:
This, even Belinda may vouchsafe to view:
Slight is the subject, but not so the praise,   5
If she inspire, and he approve my lays.
     Say what strange motive, Goddess! could compel
A well-bred lord to assault a gentle belle?
Oh, say what stranger cause, yet unexplored,
Could make a gentle belle reject a lord?   10
In tasks so bold can little men engage,
And in soft bosoms dwells such mighty rage?
     Sol through white curtains shot a timorous ray,
And oped those eyes that must eclipse the day.
Now lapdogs give themselves the rousing shake,   15
And sleepless lovers just at twelve awake:
Thrice rung the bell, the slipper knocked the ground,[3]
And the pressed watch returned a silver sound.
Belinda still her downy pillow pressed,
Her guardian Sylph prolonged the balmy rest: 20
'Twas he had summoned to her silent bed
The morning dream that hovered o'er her head.
A youth more glittering than a birthnight beau[4]
(That even in slumber caused her cheek to glow)
Seemed to her ear his winning lips to lay,   25
And thus in whispers said, or seemed to say:
     "Fairest of mortals, thou distinguished care
Of thousand bright inhabitants of air!
If e'er one vision touched thy infant thought,
Of all the nurse and all the priest have taught,   30

---

3. Summons to a maid. A "pressed watch" chimes the hour and the quarter-hour when the stem is pressed down.

4. Courtiers wore especially fine clothes on the sovereign's birthday.

Of airy elves by moonlight shadows seen,
The silver token, and the circled green,[5]
Or virgins visited by angel powers,
With golden crowns and wreaths of heavenly flowers,
Hear and believe! thy own importance know,   35
Nor bound thy narrow views to things below.
Some secret truths, from learned pride concealed,
To maids alone and children are revealed:
What though no credit doubting wits may give?
The fair and innocent shall still believe.   40
Know, then, unnumbered spirits round thee fly,
The light militia of the lower sky:
These, though unseen, are ever on the wing,
Hang o'er the box, and hover round the Ring.[6]
Think what an equipage thou hast in air,   45
And view with scorn two pages and a chair.[7]
As now your own, our beings were of old,
And once enclosed in woman's beauteous mold;
Thence, by a soft transition, we repair
From earthly vehicles to these of air.   50
Think not, when woman's transient breath is fled,
That all her vanities at once are dead:
Succeeding vanities she still regards,
And though she plays no more, o'erlooks the cards.
Her joy in gilded chariots, when alive,   55
And love of ombre,[8] after death survive.
For when the Fair in all their pride expire,
To their first elements[9] their souls retire:
The sprites of fiery termagants in flame
Mount up, and take a Salamander's name.[1]   60
Soft yielding minds to water glide away,
And sip, with Nymphs, their elemental tea.[2]
The graver prude sinks downward to a Gnome,
In search of mischief still on earth to roam.
The light coquettes in Sylphs aloft repair,   65
And sport and flutter in the fields of air.
    "Know further yet; whoever fair and chaste
Rejects mankind, is by some Sylph embraced:
For spirits, freed from mortal laws, with ease
Assume what sexes and what shapes they please.[3]   70

5. According to popular belief fairies skim off the cream from jugs of milk left standing overnight and leave a coin ("silver token") in payment. Rings of bright green grass, which are common in England even in winter, were held to be due to the round dances of fairies.
6. The "box" in the theater and the fashionable circular drive ("Ring") in Hyde Park.
7. Sedan chair.
8. The popular card game. See 3.27 ff. and note.
9. The four elements out of which all things were believed to have been made were fire, water, earth,

and air. One or another of these elements was supposed to be predominant in both the physical and psychological make-up of each human being. In this context they are spoken of as "humors."
1. Pope borrowed his supernatural beings from Rosicrucian mythology. Each element was inhabited by a spirit, as the following lines explain. The salamander is a lizardlike animal, in antiquity believed to live in fire.
2. Pronounce *tay*.
3. Cf. *Paradise Lost* 1.427–31; this is one of many allusions to that poem in the *Rape*.

What guards the purity of melting maids,
In courtly balls, and midnight masquerades,
Safe from the treacherous friend, the daring spark,
The glance by day, the whisper in the dark,
When kind occasion prompts their warm desires,   75
When music softens, and when dancing fires?
'Tis but their Sylph, the wise Celestials know,
Though Honor is the word with men below.
    "Some nymphs there are, too conscious of their face,
For life predestined to the Gnomes' embrace.   80
These swell their prospects and exalt their pride,
When offers are disdained, and love denied:
Then gay ideas[4] crowd the vacant brain,
While peers, and dukes, and all their sweeping train,
And garters, stars, and coronets[5] appear,   85
And in soft sounds, 'your Grace' salutes their ear.
'Tis these that early taint the female soul,
Instruct the eyes of young coquettes to roll,
Teach infant cheeks a bidden blush to know,
And little hearts to flutter at a beau.   90
    "Oft, when the world imagine women stray,
The Sylphs through mystic mazes guide their way,
Through all the giddy circle they pursue,
And old impertinence[6] expel by new.
What tender maid but must a victim fall   95
To one man's treat, but for another's ball?
When Florio speaks what virgin could withstand,
If gentle Damon did not squeeze her hand?
With varying vanities, from every part,
They shift the moving toyshop[7] of their heart;   100
Where wigs with wigs, with sword-knots sword-knots strive,
Beaux banish beaux, and coaches coaches drive.
This erring mortals levity may call;
Oh, blind to truth! the Sylphs contrive it all.
    "Of these am I, who thy protection claim,   105
A watchful sprite, and Ariel is my name.
Late, as I ranged the crystal wilds of air,
In the clear mirror of thy ruling star
I saw, alas! some dread event impend,
Ere to the main this morning sun descend,   110
But Heaven reveals not what, or how, or where:
Warned by the Sylph, O pious maid, beware!
This to disclose is all thy guardian can:
Beware of all, but most beware of Man!"
    He said; when Shock,[8] who thought she slept too long,   115

---

4. Showy images.
5. Emblems of nobility. "Your Grace" would be a duchess.
6. Trifle.

7. A shop stocked with baubles and trifles.
8. Belinda's lapdog; a "shock" was a long-haired poodle.

Leaped up, and waked his mistress with his tongue.
'Twas then, Belinda, if report say true,
Thy eyes first opened on a billet-doux;
Wounds, charms, and ardors were no sooner read,
But all the vision vanished from thy head.   120
    And now, unveiled, the toilet stands displayed,
Each silver vase in mystic order laid.
First, robed in white, the nymph intent adores,
With head uncovered, the cosmetic powers.
A heavenly image in the glass appears;   125
To that she bends, to that her eyes she rears.
The inferior priestess, at her altar's side,
Trembling begins the sacred rites of Pride.
Unnumbered treasures ope at once, and here
The various offerings of the world appear;   130
From each she nicely culls with curious toil,
And decks the goddess with the glittering spoil.
This casket India's glowing gems unlocks,
And all Arabia breathes from yonder box.
The tortoise here and elephant unite,   135
Transformed to combs, the speckled and the white.
Here files of pins extend their shining rows,
Puffs, powders, patches, Bibles,[9] billet-doux.
Now awful Beauty puts on all its arms;
The fair each moment rises in her charms,   140
Repairs her smiles, awakens every grace,
And calls forth all the wonders of her face;
Sees by degrees a purer blush arise,
And keener lightnings quicken in her eyes.
The busy Sylphs surround their darling care,   145
These set the head, and those divide the hair,
Some fold the sleeve, whilst others plait the gown;
And Betty's[1] praised for labors not her own.

Canto 2

    Not with more glories, in the ethereal plain,
The sun first rises o'er the purpled main,
Than, issuing forth, the rival of his beams
Launched on the bosom of the silver Thames.
Fair nymphs and well-dressed youths around her shone,   5
But every eye was fixed on her alone.
On her white breast a sparkling cross she wore,
Which Jews might kiss, and infidels adore.
Her lively looks a sprightly mind disclose,
Quick as her eyes, and as unfixed as those: 10

9. It has been suggested that Pope intended here   1. Belinda's maid, the "inferior priestess" men-
not "Bibles," but "bibelots," (trinkets), but this   tioned in line 127.
interpretation has not gained wide acceptance.

Favors to none, to all she smiles extends;
Oft she rejects, but never once offends.
Bright as the sun, her eyes the gazers strike,
And, like the sun, they shine on all alike.
Yet graceful ease, and sweetness void of pride,   15
Might hide her faults, if belles had faults to hide:
If to her share some female errors fall,
Look on her face, and you'll forget 'em all.
   This nymph, to the destruction of mankind,
Nourished two locks which graceful hung behind   20
In equal curls, and well conspired to deck
With shining ringlets the smooth ivory neck.
Love in these labyrinths his slaves detains,
And mighty hearts are held in slender chains.
With hairy springes[2] we the birds betray,   25
Slight lines of hair surprise the finny prey,
Fair tresses man's imperial race ensnare,
And beauty draws us with a single hair.
   The adventurous Baron the bright locks admired,
He saw, he wished, and to the prize aspired.   30
Resolved to win, he meditates the way,
By force to ravish, or by fraud betray;
For when success a lover's toil attends,
Few ask if fraud or force attained his ends.
   For this, ere Phoebus rose, he had implored   35
Propitious Heaven, and every power adored,
But chiefly Love—to Love an altar built,
Of twelve vast French romances, neatly gilt.
There lay three garters, half a pair of gloves,
And all the trophies of his former loves.   40
With tender billet-doux he lights the pyre,
And breathes three amorous sighs to raise the fire.
Then prostrate falls, and begs with ardent eyes
Soon to obtain, and long possess the prize:
The powers gave ear, and granted half his prayer,   45
The rest the winds dispersed in empty air.
   But now secure the painted vessel glides,
The sunbeams trembling on the floating tides,
While melting music steals upon the sky,
And softened sounds along the waters die.   50
Smooth flow the waves, the zephyrs gently play,
Belinda smiled, and all the world was gay.
All but the Sylph—with careful thoughts oppressed,
The impending woe sat heavy on his breast.
He summons straight his denizens of air;   55
The lucid squadrons round the sails repair:
Soft o'er the shrouds aërial whispers breathe
That seemed but zephyrs to the train beneath.

2. Snares; pronounced *sprin-jez*.

Some to the sun their insect-wings unfold,
Waft on the breeze, or sink in clouds of gold. 60
Transparent forms too fine for mortal sight,
Their fluid bodies half dissolved in light,
Loose to the wind their airy garments flew,
Thin glittering textures of the filmy dew,
Dipped in the richest tincture of the skies, 65
Where light disports in ever-mingling dyes,
While every beam new transient colors flings,
Colors that change whene'er they wave their wings.
Amid the circle, on the gilded mast,
Superior by the head was Ariel placed; 70
His purple[3] pinions opening to the sun,
He raised his azure wand, and thus begun:
  "Ye Sylphs and Sylphids, to your chief give ear!
Fays, Fairies, Genïi, Elves, and Daemons, hear!
Ye know the spheres and various tasks assigned 75
By laws eternal to the aërial kind.
Some in the fields of purest ether play,
And bask and whiten in the blaze of day.
Some guide the course of wandering orbs on high,
Or roll the planets through the boundless sky. 80
Some less refined, beneath the moon's pale light
Pursue the stars that shoot athwart the night,
Or suck the mists in grosser air below,
Or dip their pinions in the painted bow,
Or brew fierce tempests on the wintry main, 85
Or o'er the glebe[4] distill the kindly rain.
Others on earth o'er human race preside,
Watch all their ways, and all their actions guide:
Of these the chief the care of nations own,
And guard with arms divine the British Throne. 90
  "Our humbler province is to tend the Fair,
Not a less pleasing, though less glorious care:
To save the powder from too rude a gale,
Nor let the imprisoned essences exhale;
To draw fresh colors from the vernal flowers; 95
To steal from rainbows e'er they drop in showers
A brighter wash;[5] to curl their waving hairs,
Assist their blushes, and inspire their airs,
Nay oft, in dreams invention we bestow,
To change a flounce, or add a furbelow. 100
  "This day black omens threat the brightest fair,
That e'er deserved a watchful spirit's care;
Some dire disaster, or by force or slight,

3. In 18th-century poetic diction the word might
mean "blood-red," "purple," or simply (as is likely
here) "brightly colored." The word derives from
Virgil, *Eclogue* 9, 40, *purpureum*. An example of

the Latinate nature of some poetic diction of the
period.
4. Cultivated field.
5. Cosmetic lotion.

But what, or where, the Fates have wrapped in night:
Whether the nymph shall break Diana's law,[6]   105
Or some frail china jar receive a flaw,
Or stain her honor or her new brocade,
Forget her prayers, or miss a masquerade,
Or lose her heart, or necklace, at a ball;
Or whether Heaven has doomed that Shock must fall.   110
Haste, then, ye spirits! to your charge repair:
The fluttering fan be Zephyretta's care;
The drops[7] to thee, Brillante, we consign;
And, Momentilla, let the watch be thine;
Do thou, Crispissa,[8] tend her favorite Lock;   115
Ariel himself shall be the guard of Shock.
     "To fifty chosen Sylphs, of special note,
We trust the important charge, the petticoat;
Oft have we known that sevenfold fence to fail,
Though stiff with hoops, and armed with ribs of whale.   120
Form a strong line about the silver bound,
And guard the wide circumference around.
     "Whatever spirit, careless of his charge,
His post neglects, or leaves the fair at large,
Shall feel sharp vengeance soon o'ertake his sins,   125
Be stopped in vials, or transfixed with pins,
Or plunged in lakes of bitter washes lie,
Or wedged whole ages in a bodkin's eye;[9]
Gums and pomatums shall his flight restrain,
While clogged he beats his silken wings in vain,   130
Or alum styptics with contracting power
Shrink his thin essence like a riveled[1] flower:
Or, as Ixion[2] fixed, the wretch shall feel
The giddy motion of the whirling mill,
In fumes of burning chocolate shall glow,   135
And tremble at the sea that froths below!"
     He spoke; the spirits from the sails descend;
Some, orb in orb, around the nymph extend;
Some thread the mazy ringlets of her hair;
Some hang upon the pendants of her ear: 140
With beating hearts the dire event they wait,
Anxious, and trembling for the birth of Fate.

Canto 3

Close by those meads, forever crowned with flowers,
Where Thames with pride surveys his rising towers,

6. Diana was the goddess of chastity.
7. Diamond earrings. Observe the appropriateness of the names of the Sylphs to their assigned functions.
8. From Latin *crispere*, to curl.
9. A "bodkin" is a blunt needle with a large eye, used for drawing ribbon through eyelets in the edging of women's garments.
1. To "rivel" is to "contract into wrinkles and corrugations" (Johnson's *Dictionary*).
2. In the Greek myth Ixion was punished in the underworld by being bound on an everturning wheel.

There stands a structure of majestic frame,
Which from the neighboring Hampton takes its name.[3]
Here Britain's statesmen oft the fall foredoom   5
Of foreign tyrants and of nymphs at home;
Here thou, great Anna! whom three realms obey,
Dost sometimes counsel take—and sometimes tea.
   Hither the heroes and the nymphs resort,
To taste awhile the pleasures of a court;   10
In various talk the instructive hours they passed,
Who gave the ball, or paid the visit last;
One speaks the glory of the British Queen,
And one describes a charming Indian screen;
A third interprets motions, looks, and eyes;   15
At every word a reputation dies.
Snuff, or the fan, supply each pause of chat,
With singing, laughing, ogling, and all that.
   Meanwhile, declining from the noon of day,
The sun obliquely shoots his burning ray;   20
The hungry judges soon the sentence sign,
And wretches hang that jurymen may dine;
The merchant from the Exchange returns in peace,
And the long labors of the toilet cease.
Belinda now, whom thirst of fame invites,   25
Burns to encounter two adventurous knights,
At ombre[4] singly to decide their doom,
And swells her breast with conquests yet to come.
Straight the three bands prepare in arms to join,
Each band the number of the sacred nine.   30
Soon as she spreads her hand, the aërial guard
Descend, and sit on each important card:
First Ariel perched upon a Matadore,
Then each according to the rank they bore;
For Sylphs, yet mindful of their ancient race,   35
Are, as when women, wondrous fond of place.
   Behold, four Kings in majesty revered,
With hoary whiskers and a forky beard;
And four fair Queens whose hands sustain a flower,
The expressive emblem of their softer power;   40
Four Knaves in garbs succinct,[5] a trusty band,
Caps on their heads, and halberts in their hand;
And parti-colored troops, a shining train,

---

3. Hampton Court, the royal palace, about 15 miles up the Thames from London.
4. The game of ombre which Belinda plays against the baron and another young man is too complicated for complete explication here. Pope has carefully arranged the cards so that Belinda wins. The baron's hand is strong enough to be a threat, but the third player's is of little account. The hand is played exactly according to the rules of ombre, and Pope's description of the cards is equally accurate. Each player holds nine cards (line 30). The "Matadores" (line 33), when spades are trumps, are "Spadillio" (line 49), the ace of spades; "Manillio" (line 51), the two of spades; "Basto" (line 53), the ace of clubs; Belinda holds all three of these. (For a more complete description of ombre, see Appendix C, *The Rape of the Lock and Other Poems*, ed. Geoffrey Tillotson, in the Twickenham Edition of Pope's poems, vol. 2.)
5. Girded up.

Draw forth to combat on the velvet plain.
   The skillful nymph reviews her force with care;   45
"Let Spades be trumps!" she said, and trumps they were.
   Now move to war her sable Matadores,
In show like leaders of the swarthy Moors.
Spadillio first, unconquerable lord!
Led off two captive trumps, and swept the board.   50
As many more Manillio forced to yield,
And marched a victor from the verdant field.
Him Basto followed, but his fate more hard
Gained but one trump and one plebeian card.
With his broad saber next, a chief in years,   55
The hoary Majesty of Spades appears,
Puts forth one manly leg, to sight revealed,
The rest his many-colored robe concealed.
The rebel Knave, who dares his prince engage,
Proves the just victim of his royal rage.   60
Even mighty Pam,[6] that kings and queens o'erthrew
And mowed down armies in the fights of loo,
Sad chance of war! now destitute of aid,
Falls undistinguished by the victor Spade.
   Thus far both armies to Belinda yield;   65
Now to the Baron fate inclines the field.
His warlike amazon her host invades,
The imperial consort of the crown of Spades.
The Club's black tyrant first her victim died,
Spite of his haughty mien and barbarous pride.   70
What boots the regal circle on his head,
His giant limbs, in state unwieldy spread?
That long behind he trails his pompous robe,
And of all monarchs only grasps the globe?
   The Baron now his Diamonds pours apace;   75
The embroidered King who shows but half his face,
And his refulgent Queen, with powers combined
Of broken troops an easy conquest find.
Clubs, Diamonds, Hearts, in wild disorder seen,
With throngs promiscuous strew the level green.   80
Thus when dispersed a routed army runs,
Of Asia's troops, and Afric's sable sons,
With like confusion different nations fly,
Of various habit, and of various dye,
The pierced battalions disunited fall   85
In heaps on heaps; one fate o'erwhelms them all.
   The Knave of Diamonds tries his wily arts,
And wins (oh, shameful chance!) the Queen of Hearts.
At this, the blood the virgin's cheek forsook,
A livid paleness spreads o'er all her look;   90

---

6. The knave of clubs, the highest trump in the game of loo.

She sees, and trembles at the approaching ill,
Just in the jaws of ruin, and Codille,[7]
And now (as oft in some distempered state)
On one nice trick depends the general fate.
An Ace of Hearts steps forth: the King unseen   95
Lurked in her hand, and mourned his captive Queen.
He springs to vengeance with an eager pace,
And falls like thunder on the prostrate Ace.
The nymph exulting fills with shouts the sky,
The walls, the woods, and long canals reply.   100
    O thoughtless mortals! ever blind to fate,
Too soon dejected, and too soon elate:
Sudden these honors shall be snatched away,
And cursed forever this victorious day.
    For lo! the board with cups and spoons is crowned,   105
The berries crackle, and the mill turns round;[8]
On shining altars of Japan[9] they raise
The silver lamp; the fiery spirits blaze:
From silver spouts the grateful liquors glide,
While China's earth receives the smoking tide.   110
At once they gratify their scent and taste,
And frequent cups prolong the rich repast.
Straight hover round the fair her airy band;
Some, as she sipped, the fuming liquor fanned,
Some o'er her lap their careful plumes displayed,   115
Trembling, and conscious of the rich brocade.
Coffee (which makes the politician wise,
And see through all things with his half-shut eyes)
Sent up in vapors to the Baron's brain
New stratagems, the radiant Lock to gain.   120
Ah, cease, rash youth! desist ere 'tis too late,
Fear the just Gods, and think of Scylla's fate![1]
Changed to a bird, and sent to flit in air,
She dearly pays for Nisus' injured hair!
    But when to mischief mortals bend their will,   125
How soon they find fit instruments of ill!
Just then, Clarissa drew with tempting grace
A two-edged weapon from her shining case:
So ladies in romance assist their knight,
Present the spear, and arm him for the fight.   130
He takes the gift with reverence, and extends
The little engine on his fingers' ends;
This just behind Belinda's neck he spread,
As o'er the fragrant steams she bends her head.

---

7. The term applied to losing a hand at cards.
8. I.e., coffee is roasted and ground.
9. I.e., small, lacquered tables. The word "altars" suggests the ritualistic character of coffee drinking in Belinda's world.
1. Scylla, daughter of Nisus, was turned into a sea bird because, for the sake of her love for Minos of Crete, who was besieging her father's city of Megara, she cut from her father's head the purple lock on which his safety depended. She is not the Scylla of "Scylla and Charybdis."

Swift to the Lock a thousand sprites repair,   135
A thousand wings, by turns, blow back the hair,
And thrice they twitched the diamond in her ear,
Thrice she looked back, and thrice the foe drew near.
Just in that instant, anxious Ariel sought
The close recesses of the virgin's thought;   140
As on the nosegay in her breast reclined,
He watched the ideas rising in her mind,
Sudden he viewed, in spite of all her art,
An earthly lover lurking at her heart.
Amazed, confused, he found his power expired,   145
Resigned to fate, and with a sigh retired.
     The Peer now spreads the glittering forfex² wide,
To enclose the Lock; now joins it, to divide.
Even then, before the fatal engine closed,
A wretched Sylph too fondly interposed;   150
Fate urged the shears, and cut the Sylph in twain
(But airy substance soon unites again):
The meeting points the sacred hair dissever
From the fair head, forever, and forever!
     Then flashed the living lightning from her eyes,   155
And screams of horror rend the affrighted skies.
Not louder shrieks to pitying heaven are cast,
When husbands, or when lapdogs breathe their last;
Or when rich china vessels fallen from high,
In glittering dust and painted fragments lie!   160
"Let wreaths of triumph now my temples twine,"
The victor cried, "the glorious prize is mine!
While fish in streams, or birds delight in air,
Or in a coach and six the British Fair,
As long as Atalantis³ shall be read,   165
Or the small pillow grace a lady's bed,
While visits shall be paid on solemn days,
When numerous wax-lights in bright order blaze,
While nymphs take treats, or assignations give,
So long my honor, name, and praise shall live!   170
What Time would spare, from Steel receives its date,
And monuments, like men, submit to fate!
Steel could the labor of the Gods destroy,
And strike to dust the imperial towers of Troy;
Steel could the works of mortal pride confound,   175
And hew triumphal arches to the ground.
What wonder then, fair nymph! thy hairs should feel,
The conquering force of unresisted Steel?"

2. Scissors.   rious for its thinly concealed allusions to contem-
3. Mrs. Manley's New Atalantis (1709) was noto-   porary scandals.

Canto 4

But anxious cares the pensive nymph oppressed,
And secret passions labored in her breast.
Not youthful kings in battle seized alive,
Not scornful virgins who their charms survive,
Not ardent lovers robbed of all their bliss,   5
Not ancient ladies when refused a kiss,
Not tyrants fierce that unrepenting die,
Not Cynthia when her manteau's[4] pinned awry,
E'er felt such rage, resentment, and despair,
As thou, sad virgin! for thy ravished hair.   10
    For, that sad moment, when the Sylphs withdrew
And Ariel weeping from Belinda flew,
Umbriel,[5] a dusky, melancholy sprite
As ever sullied the fair face of light,
Down to the central earth, his proper scene,   15
Repaired to search the gloomy Cave of Spleen.[6]
    Swift on his sooty pinions flits the Gnome,
And in a vapor reached the dismal dome.
No cheerful breeze this sullen region knows,
The dreaded east is all the wind that blows.   20
Here in a grotto, sheltered close from air,
And screened in shades from day's detested glare,
She sighs forever on her pensive bed,
Pain at her side, and Megrim[7] at her head.
    Two handmaids wait the throne: alike in place   25
But differing far in figure and in face.
Here stood Ill-Nature like an ancient maid,
Her wrinkled form in black and white arrayed;
With store of prayers for mornings, nights, and noons,
Her hand is filled; her bosom with lampoons.   30
    There Affectation, with a sickly mien,
Shows in her cheek the roses of eighteen,
Practiced to lisp, and hang the head aside,
Faints into airs, and languishes with pride,
On the rich quilt sinks with becoming woe,   35
Wrapped in a gown, for sickness and for show.
The fair ones feel such maladies as these,
When each new nightdress gives a new disease.
    A constant vapor[8] o'er the palace flies,
Strange phantoms rising as the mists arise;   40
Dreadful as hermit's dreams in haunted shades,
Or bright as visions of expiring maids.
Now glaring fiends, and snakes on rolling spires,[9]

4. Negligee or loose robe.
5. The name suggests shade and darkness.
6. Ill humor.
7. Headache.

8. Emblematic of "the vapors," i.e., hypochondria, melancholy, peevishness, often affected by
fashionable women.
9. Coils.

Pale specters, gaping tombs, and purple fires;
Now lakes of liquid gold, Elysian scenes,   45
And crystal domes, and angels in machines.[1]
　Unnumbered throngs on every side are seen
Of bodies changed to various forms by Spleen.
Here living teapots stand, one arm held out,
One bent; the handle this, and that the spout: 50
A pipkin[2] there, like Homer's tripod, walks;
Here sighs a jar, and there a goose pie talks;
Men prove with child, as powerful fancy works,
And maids, turned bottles, call aloud for corks.
　Safe passed the Gnome through this fantastic band,   55
A branch of healing spleenwort[3] in his hand.
Then thus addressed the Power: "Hail, wayward Queen!
Who rule the sex to fifty from fifteen:
Parent of vapors and of female wit,
Who give the hysteric or poetic fit,   60
On various tempers act by various ways,
Make some take physic, others scribble plays;
Who cause the proud their visits to delay,
And send the godly in a pet to pray.
A nymph there is that all your power disdains,   65
And thousands more in equal mirth maintains.
But oh! if e'er thy Gnome could spoil a grace,
Or raise a pimple on a beauteous face,
Like citron-waters[4] matrons' cheeks inflame,
Or change complexions at a losing game;   70
If e'er with airy horns[5] I planted heads,
Or rumpled petticoats, or tumbled beds,
Or caused suspicion when no soul was rude,
Or discomposed the headdress of a prude,
Or e'er to costive lapdog gave disease,   75
Which not the tears of brightest eyes could ease,
Hear me, and touch Belinda with chagrin:[6]
That single act gives half the world the spleen."
　The Goddess with a discontented air
Seems to reject him though she grants his prayer.   80
A wondrous bag with both her hands she binds,
Like that where once Ulysses held the winds;[7]

---

1. Mechanical devices used in the theaters for spectacular effects. The fantasies of neurotic women here merge with the sensational stage effects popular with contemporary audiences.

2. An earthen pot. In *Iliad* 18.373–77, Vulcan furnishes the gods with self-propelling "tripods" (three-legged stools).

3. An herb, efficacious against the spleen. Pope alludes to the golden bough that Aeneas and the Cumaean sybil carry with them for protection into the underworld in *Aeneid* 6.

4. Brandy flavored with orange or lemon peel.

5. Horns, the symbol of the cuckold, the man whose wife has been unfaithful to him; here "airy," because they exist only in the jealous suspicions of the husband, the victim of the mischievous Umbriel.

6. Ill humor.

7. Aeolus (later conceived of as god of the winds) gave Ulysses a bag containing all the winds adverse to his voyage home. When his ship was in sight of Ithaca, his companions opened the bag and the storms that ensued drove Ulysses far away (*Odyssey* 10.19 ff.).

There she collects the force of female lungs,
Sighs, sobs, and passions, and the war of tongues.
A vial next she fills with fainting fears,   85
Soft sorrows, melting griefs, and flowing tears.
The Gnome rejoicing bears her gifts away,
Spreads his black wings, and slowly mounts to day.
   Sunk in Thalestris'[8] arms the nymph he found,
Her eyes dejected and her hair unbound.   90
Full o'er their heads the swelling bag he rent,
And all the Furies issued at the vent.
Belinda burns with more than mortal ire,
And fierce Thalestris fans the rising fire.
"O wretched maid!" she spread her hands, and cried   95
(While Hampton's echoes, "Wretched maid!" replied),
"Was it for this you took such constant care
The bodkin, comb, and essence to prepare?
For this your locks in paper durance bound,
For this with torturing irons wreathed around?   100
For this with fillets strained your tender head,
And bravely bore the double loads of lead?[9]
Gods! shall the ravisher display your hair,
While the fops envy, and the ladies stare!
Honor forbid! at whose unrivaled shrine   105
Ease, pleasure, virtue, all, our sex resign.
Methinks already I your tears survey,
Already hear the horrid things they say,
Already see you a degraded toast,
And all your honor in a whisper lost!   110
How shall I, then, your helpless fame defend?
'Twill then be infamy to seem your friend!
And shall this prize, the inestimable prize,
Exposed through crystal to the gazing eyes,
And heightened by the diamond's circling rays,   115
On that rapacious hand forever blaze?
Sooner shall grass in Hyde Park Circus grow,
And wits take lodgings in the sound of Bow;[1]
Sooner let earth, air, sea, to chaos fall,
Men, monkeys, lapdogs, parrots, perish all!"   120
   She said; then raging to Sir Plume repairs,
And bids her beau demand the precious hairs
(Sir Plume of amber snuffbox justly vain,
And the nice conduct of a clouded cane).
With earnest eyes, and round unthinking face,   125
He first the snuffbox opened, then the case,
And thus broke out—"My Lord, why, what the devil!

---

8. The name is borrowed from a queen of the Amazons, hence a fierce and warlike woman. Thalestris, according to legend, traveled 30 days in order to have a child by Alexander the Great. Plutarch denies the story.

9. The frame on which the elaborate coiffures of the day were arranged.

1. A person born within sound of the bells of St. Mary-le-Bow in Cheapside is said to be a cockney. No fashionable wit would have so vulgar an address.

Z——ds! damn the lock! 'fore Gad, you must be civil!
Plague on 't! 'tis past a jest—nay prithee, pox!
Give her the hair"—he spoke, and rapped his box.   130
    "It grieves me much," replied the Peer again,
"Who speaks so well should ever speak in vain.
But by this Lock, this sacred Lock I swear
(Which never more shall join its parted hair;
Which never more its honors shall renew,   135
Clipped from the lovely head where late it grew),
That while my nostrils draw the vital air,
This hand, which won it, shall forever wear."
He spoke, and speaking, in proud triumph spread
The long-contended honors[2] of her head.   140
    But Umbriel, hateful Gnome, forebears not so;
He breaks the vial whence the sorrows flow.
Then see! the nymph in beauteous grief appears,
Her eyes half languishing, half drowned in tears;
On her heaved bosom hung her drooping head,   145
Which with a sigh she raised, and thus she said:
    "Forever cursed be this detested day,
Which snatched my best, my favorite curl away!
Happy! ah, ten times happy had I been,
If Hampton Court these eyes had never seen!   150
Yet am not I the first mistaken maid,
By love of courts to numerous ills betrayed.
Oh, had I rather unadmired remained
In some lone isle, or distant northern land;
Where the gilt chariot never marks the way,   155
Where none learn ombre, none e'er taste bohea![3]
There kept my charms concealed from mortal eye,
Like roses that in deserts bloom and die.
What moved my mind with youthful lords to roam?
Oh, had I stayed, and said my prayers at home!   160
'Twas this the morning omens seemed to tell,
Thrice from my trembling hand the patch box[4] fell;
The tottering china shook without a wind,
Nay, Poll sat mute, and Shock was most unkind!
A Sylph too warned me of the threats of fate,   165
In mystic visions, now believed too late!
See the poor remnants of these slighted hairs!
My hands shall rend what e'en thy rapine spares.
These in two sable ringlets taught to break,
Once gave new beauties to the snowy neck;   170
The sister lock now sits uncouth, alone,
And in its fellow's fate foresees its own;
Uncurled it hangs, the fatal shears demands,

2. Ornaments, hence locks; a Latinism.   4. A box to hold the ornamental patches of court
3. A costly sort of tea.   plaster worn on the face by both sexes.

And tempts once more thy sacrilegious hands.
Oh, hadst thou, cruel! been content to seize   175
Hairs less in sight, or any hairs but these!"

Canto 5

She said: the pitying audience melt in tears.
But Fate and Jove had stopped the Baron's ears.
In vain Thalestris with reproach assails,
For who can move when fair Belinda fails?
Not half so fixed the Trojan[5] could remain,   5
While Anna begged and Dido raged in vain.
Then grave Clarissa graceful waved her fan;
Silence ensued, and thus the nymph began:
    "Say why are beauties praised and honored most,
The wise man's passion, and the vain man's toast?   10
Why decked with all that land and sea afford,
Why angels called, and angel-like adored?
Why round our coaches crowd the white-gloved beaux,
Why bows the side box from its inmost rows?
How vain are all these glories, all our pains,   15
Unless good sense preserve what beauty gains;
That men may say when we the front box grace,
'Behold the first in virtue as in face!'
Oh! if to dance all night, and dress all day,
Charmed the smallpox, or chased old age away,   20
Who would not scorn what housewife's cares produce,
Or who would learn one earthly thing of use?
To patch, nay ogle, might become a saint,
Nor could it sure be such a sin to paint.
But since, alas! frail beauty must decay,   25
Curled or uncurled, since locks will turn to gray;
Since painted, or not painted, all shall fade,
And she who scorns a man must die a maid;
What then remains but well our power to use,
And keep good humor still whate'er we lose?   30
And trust me, dear, good humor can prevail
When airs, and flights, and screams, and scolding fail.
Beauties in vain their pretty eyes may roll;
Charms strike the sight, but merit wins the soul."[6]
    So spoke the dame, but no applause ensued;   35
Belinda frowned, Thalestris called her prude.
"To arms, to arms!" the fierce virago cries,
And swift as lightning to the combat flies.
All side in parties, and begin the attack;

5. Aeneas, who forsook Dido at the bidding of the gods, despite her reproaches and the supplications of her sister Anna. Virgil compares him to a steadfast oak that withstands a storm (*Aeneid* 4.437–43).

6. The speech is a close parody of Pope's own translation of the speech of Sarpedon to Glaucus, first published in 1709 and slightly revised in his version of the *Iliad* (12.371–96).

Fans clap, silks rustle, and tough whalebones crack;   40
Heroes' and heroines' shouts confusedly rise,
And bass and treble voices strike the skies.
No common weapons in their hands are found,
Like Gods they fight, nor dread a mortal wound.
    So when bold Homer makes the Gods engage,   45
And heavenly breasts with human passions rage;
'Gainst Pallas, Mars; Latona, Hermes arms;
And all Olympus rings with loud alarms:
Jove's thunder roars, heaven trembles all around,
Blue Neptune storms, the bellowing deeps resound: 50
Earth shakes her nodding towers, the ground gives way,
And the pale ghosts start at the flash of day!
    Triumphant Umbriel on a sconce's[7] height
Clapped his glad wings, and sat to view the fight:
Propped on the bodkin spears, the sprites survey   55
The growing combat, or assist the fray.
    While through the press enraged Thalestris flies,
And scatters death around from both her eyes,
A beau and witling perished in the throng,
One died in metaphor, and one in song.   60
"O cruel nymph! a living death I bear,"
Cried Dapperwit, and sunk beside his chair.
A mournful glance Sir Fopling upwards cast,
"Those eyes are made so killing"—was his last.
Thus on Maeander's flowery margin lies   65
The expiring swan, and as he sings he dies.
    When bold Sir Plume had drawn Clarissa down,
Chloe stepped in, and killed him with a frown;
She smiled to see the doughty hero slain,
But, at her smile, the beau revived again.   70
    Now Jove suspends his golden scales in air,
Weighs the men's wits against the lady's hair;
The doubtful beam long nods from side to side;
At length the wits mount up, the hairs subside.
    See, fierce Belinda on the Baron flies,   75
With more than usual lightning in her eyes;
Nor feared the chief the unequal fight to try,
Who sought no more than on his foe to die.
    But this bold lord with manly strength endued,
She with one finger and a thumb subdued: 80
Just where the breath of life his nostrils drew,
A charge of snuff the wily virgin threw;
The Gnomes direct, to every atom just,
The pungent grains of titillating dust.
Sudden, with starting tears each eye o'erflows,   85
And the high dome re-echoes to his nose.

7. Candlestick fastened on the wall.

"Now meet thy fate," incensed Belinda cried,
And drew a deadly bodkin[8] from her side.
(The same, his ancient personage to deck,
Her great-great-grandsire wore about his neck,   90
In three seal rings; which after, melted down,
Formed a vast buckle for his widow's gown:
Her infant grandame's whistle next it grew,
The bells she jingled, and the whistle blew;
Then in a bodkin graced her mother' hairs,   95
Which long she wore, and now Belinda wears.)
    "Boast not my fall," he cried, "insulting foe!
Thou by some other shalt be laid as low.
Nor think to die dejects my lofty mind:
All that I dread is leaving you behind!   100
Rather than so, ah, let me still survive,
And burn in Cupid's flames—but burn alive."
    "Restore the Lock!" she cries; and all around
"Restore the Lock!" the vaulted roofs rebound.
Not fierce Othello in so loud a strain   105
Roared for the handkerchief that caused his pain.[9]
But see how oft ambitious aims are crossed,
And chiefs contend till all the prize is lost!
The lock, obtained with guilt, and kept with pain,
In every place is sought, but sought in vain: 110
With such a prize no mortal must be blessed,
So Heaven decrees! with Heaven who can contest?
    Some thought it mounted to the lunar sphere,
Since all things lost on earth are treasured there.
There heroes' wits are kept in ponderous vases,   115
And beaux' in snuffboxes and tweezer cases.
There broken vows and deathbed alms are found,
And lovers' hearts with ends of riband bound,
The courtier's promises, and sick man's prayers,
The smiles of harlots, and the tears of heirs,   120
Cages for gnats, and chains to yoke a flea,
Dried butterflies, and tomes of casuistry.
    But trust the Muse—she saw it upward rise,
Though marked by none but quick, poetic eyes
(So Rome's great founder to the heavens withdrew,[1]   125
To Proculus alone confessed in view);
A sudden star, it shot through liquid air,
And drew behind a radiant trail of hair.
Not Berenice's locks first rose so bright,[2]
The heavens bespangling with disheveled light.   130

8. An ornamental pin shaped like a dagger, to be
worn in the hair.
9. *Othello* 3.4.
1. Romulus, the "founder" and first king of Rome,
was snatched to heaven in a storm cloud while
reviewing his army in the Campus Martius (Livy

1.16).
2. Berenice, the wife of Ptolemy III, dedicated a
lock of her hair to the gods to ensure her husband's
safe return from war. It was turned into a constellation.

The Sylphs behold it kindling as it flies,
And pleased pursue its progress through the skies.
   This the beau monde shall from the Mall[3] survey,
And hail with music its propitious ray.
This the blest lover shall for Venus take,   135
And send up vows from Rosamonda's Lake.[4]
This Partridge[5] soon shall view in cloudless skies,
When next he looks through Galileo's eyes;
And hence the egregious wizard shall foredoom
The fate of Louis, and the fall of Rome.   140
   Then cease, bright nymph! to mourn thy ravished hair,
Which adds new glory to the shining sphere!
Not all the tresses that fair head can boast,
Shall draw such envy as the Lock you lost.
For, after all the murders of your eye,   145
When, after millions slain, yourself shall die:
When those fair suns shall set, as set they must,
And all those tresses shall be laid in dust,
This Lock the Muse shall consecrate to fame,
And 'midst the stars inscribe Belinda's name.   150

1712   1714

Ode on Solitude[1]

Happy the man whose wish and care
   A few paternal acres bound,
Content to breathe his native air,
      In his own ground.

Whose herds with milk, whose fields with bread,   5
   Whose flocks supply him with attire,
Whose trees in summer yield him shade,
      In winter fire.

Blest, who can unconcernedly find
   Hours, days, and years slide soft away,   10
In health of body, peace of mind,
      Quiet by day,

Sound sleep by night; study and ease,
   Together mixed; sweet recreation;

---

3. A walk laid out by Charles II in St. James's Park, a resort for strollers of all sorts.
4. In St. James's Park; associated with unhappy lovers.
5. John Partridge, the astrologer whose annually published predictions had been amusingly sati-rized by Swift and other wits in 1708. "Galileo's eyes": i.e., a telescope.
1. The hint for this poem was taken from Horace's well-known *Epode* 2, which praises the simplicity and innocence of country life, a favorite literary theme in Pope's time.

And innocence, which most does please   15
            With meditation.

Thus let me live, unseen, unknown;
    Thus unlamented let me die;
Steal from the world, and not a stone
            Tell where I lie.   20

ca. 1700–1709   1717, 1736

Epistle to Miss Blount[1]

On Her Leaving the Town, After the Coronation

As some fond virgin, whom her mother's care
Drags from the town to wholesome country air,
Just when she learns to roll a melting eye,
And hear a spark,[2] yet think no danger nigh;
From the dear man unwilling she must sever,   5
Yet takes one kiss before she parts forever:
Thus from the world fair Zephalinda[3] flew,
Saw others happy, and with sighs withdrew;
Not that their pleasures caused her discontent;
She sighed not that they stayed, but that she went.   10
    She went to plain-work,[4] and to purling brooks,
Old-fashioned halls, dull aunts, and croaking rooks:
She went from opera, park, assembly, play,
To morning walks, and prayers three hours a day;
To part her time 'twixt reading and bohea,[5]   15
To muse, and spill her solitary tea,
Or o'er cold coffee trifle with the spoon,
Count the slow clock, and dine exact at noon;[6]
Divert her eyes with pictures in the fire,
Hum half a tune, tell stories to the squire;   20
Up to her godly garret after seven,
There starve and pray, for that's the way to heaven.
    Some squire, perhaps, you take delight to rack,
Whose game is whist, whose treat a toast in sack;
Who visits with a gun, presents you birds,   25
Then gives a smacking buss, and cries—"No words!"
Or with his hounds comes hollowing from the stable,
Makes love with nods and knees beneath a table;

1. Teresa Blount, sister of Pope's lifelong friend
Martha Blount. The "coronation" was that of
George I (1714).
2. A fop, a beau.
3. A fanciful name adopted by Miss Blount.
4. "Needlework, as distinguished from embroi-

dery" (Johnson's Dictionary).
5. A costly sort of tea.
6. The fashionable hour for dining in London was
three or four o'clock. A noon dinner is a sign of
old-fashioned rusticity.

Whose laughs are hearty, though his jests are coarse,
And loves you best of all things—but his horse.   30
　　In some fair evening, on your elbow laid,
You dream of triumphs in the rural shade;
In pensive thought recall the fancied scene,
See coronations rise on every green:
Before you pass the imaginary sights   35
Of lords and earls and dukes and gartered knights,
While the spread fan o'ershades your closing eyes;
Then give one flirt,[7] and all the vision flies.
Thus vanish scepters, coronets, and balls,
And leave you in lone woods, or empty walls!   40
　　So when your slave,[8] at some dear idle time
(Not plagued with headaches or the want of rhyme)
Stands in the streets, abstracted from the crew,
And while he seems to study, thinks of you;
Just when his fancy points[9] your sprightly eyes,   45
Or sees the blush of soft Parthenia[1] rise,
Gay[2] pats my shoulder, and you vanish quite;
Streets, chairs, and coxcombs rush upon my sight;
Vexed to be still in town, I knit my brow,
Look sour, and hum a tune—as you may now.   50

1717

Eloisa to Abelard[1]

The Argument

Abelard and Eloisa flourished in the twelfth century; they were two of
the most distinguished persons of their age in learning and beauty, but

7. I.e., opens and closes her fan with a jerk.
8. I.e., Pope.
9. Notices.
1. Martha Blount.
2. John Gay, the poet.
1. Like Ovid's *Sappho to Phaon*, which Pope had
translated in his teens, *Eloisa to Abelard* is an heroic
epistle: strictly defined, a versified love letter,
involving historical persons, which dramatizes the
feelings of a woman who has been forsaken. Pope
took his subject from one of the most famous affairs
of history. Peter Abelard (1079–1142), a brilliant
scholastic theologian, seduced a young girl, his
pupil Heloise; eventually she bore him a child, and
they were secretly married. Enraged at the betrayal
of trust, and what he regarded as the casting off of
Heloise, her uncle Fulbert revenged himself by
having Abelard castrated. The lovers separated; each
of them entered a monastery, and went on to a
distinguished career in the Church. Yet their
greatest fame derives from the letters they are supposed to have exchanged late in their lives (modern scholars have cast doubt on the authenticity of
Heloise's letters). It is this correspondence, made

newly popular by French and English translations
of the original Latin, that inspired Pope's poem.
　　The heroic epistle challenges an author in two
ways: he must exert his historical imagination,
projecting himself into another time and place; and
he must enter the mind and passions of a woman,
acting her part, and showing everything through
her point of view. Historically, Pope draws on his
knowledge of Roman Catholic ritual to envelop
Eloisa in a rich medieval atmosphere. The dark
Gothic convent, situated in an imaginary landscape of grottos, mountains, and pine forests,
embodies the 18th-century sense of the "romantic": fantastic, legendary, extravagant. Here Eloisa
is cloistered, not only physically but mentally, by
religious mysticism that surrounds her with a melancholy as palpable as the image of her lover. The
greatest triumph of the poem, however, is psychological. In *Eloisa*, for the only time in his career,
Pope tells a story wholly through another's voice.
Confused and tormented, the heroine tosses
between two kinds of love: an erotic passion for the
earthly lover whose memory she cannot quell; and
the divine, chaste love that must content a nun.

for nothing more famous than for their unfortunate passion. After a long course of calamities, they retired each to a several[2] convent, and consecrated the remainder of their days to religion. It was many years after this separation, that a letter of Abelard's to a friend which contained the history of his misfortune, fell into the hands of Eloisa. This awakening all her tenderness, occasioned those celebrated letters (out of which the following is partly extracted)[3] which give so lively a picture of the struggles of grace and nature, virtue and passion.

In these deep solitudes and awful cells,
Where heavenly-pensive contemplation dwells,
And ever-musing melancholy reigns;
What means this tumult in a vestal's[4] veins?
Why rove my thoughts beyond this last retreat?   5
Why feels my heart its long-forgotten heat?
Yet, yet I love!—From Abelard it[5] came,
And Eloisa yet must kiss the name.
    Dear fatal name! rest ever unrevealed,
Nor pass these lips in holy silence sealed.   10
Hide it, my heart, within that close disguise,
Where mixed with God's, his loved idea[6] lies.
O write it not, my hand—the name appears
Already written—wash it out, my tears!
In vain lost Eloisa weeps and prays,   15
Her heart still dictates, and her hand obeys.
    Relentless walls! whose darksome round contains
Repentant sighs, and voluntary pains:
Ye rugged rocks! which holy knees have worn;
Ye grots and caverns shagged with horrid[7] thorn!   20
Shrines! where their vigils pale-eyed virgins keep,
And pitying saints, whose statues learn to weep![8]
Tho' cold like you, unmoved, and silent grown,
I have not yet forgot myself to stone.
All is not Heaven's while Abelard has part,   25
Still rebel nature holds out half my heart;
Nor prayers nor fasts its stubborn pulse restrain,
Nor tears, for ages taught to flow in vain.

Abelard and God, within her fantasy, compete for her soul. Pope brings these internal struggles to the surface by externalizing them in bold dramatic rhetoric, formal and intense as an aria in an opera (the poem was long a favorite for reading aloud). Eloisa views herself theatrically, if only because, in the letter, she is trying to make Abelard visualize the pathos of her situation. There is literally no way out for her; and at the end of the poem, she can break the static circle of desire and loneliness only by picturing herself in the peace of death. Yet the high reputation of the work, well into the Romantic era, owes less to its theatrics than to its convincing image of a mind in pain. "If you search for passion," Byron wrote more than a century later,

"where is it to be found stronger than in the Epistle from Eloisa to Abelard?"
2. Separate.
3. Pope's source was a highly romanticized English version of the letters by John Hughes, published in 1713.
4. Nun's. Here, as elsewhere, Eloisa substitutes a pagan form for a Christian; nor is she in fact a virgin (vestal).
5. The letter to which Eloisa is replying.
6. Mental image or shape.
7. Bristling.
8. In damp places, stone "weeps" through condensation.

Soon as thy letters trembling I unclose,
That well-known name awakens all my woes.   30
Oh name for ever sad! for ever dear!
Still breathed in sighs, still ushered with a tear.
I tremble too, where'er my own I find,
Some dire misfortune follows close behind.
Line after line my gushing eyes o'erflow,   35
Led through a sad variety of woe:
Now warm in love, now withering in my bloom,
Lost in a convent's solitary gloom!
There stern religion quenched the unwilling flame,
There died the best of passions, love and fame.   40
    Yet write, oh write me all, that I may join
Griefs to thy griefs, and echo sighs to thine.
Nor foes nor fortune take this power away.
And is my Abelard less kind than they?
Tears still are mine, and those I need not spare,   45
Love but demands what else were shed in prayer;
No happier task these faded eyes pursue,
To read and weep is all they now can do.
    Then share thy pain, allow that sad relief;
Ah, more than share it! give me all thy grief.   50
Heaven first taught letters for some wretch's aid,
Some banished lover, or some captive maid;
They live, they speak, they breathe what love inspires,
Warm from the soul, and faithful to its fires,
The virgin's wish without her fears impart,   55
Excuse the blush, and pour out all the heart,
Speed the soft intercourse from soul to soul,
And waft a sigh from Indus[9] to the Pole.
    Thou knowest how guiltless first I met thy flame,
When love approached me under friendship's name;   60
My fancy formed thee of angelic kind,
Some emanation of the all-beauteous Mind.[1]
Those smiling eyes, attempering[2] every ray,
Shone sweetly lambent with celestial day:
Guiltless I gazed; heaven listened while you sung;   65
And truths divine came mended from that tongue.[3]
From lips like those what precept failed to move?
Too soon they taught me 'twas no sin to love.
Back through the paths of pleasing sense I ran,
Nor wished an angel whom I loved a man.   70
Dim and remote the joys of saints I see,
Nor envy them, that heaven I lose for thee.
    How oft, when pressed to marriage, have I said,
Curse on all laws but those which love has made!

---

9. A southern constellation.
1. God, conceived (as is proper to a student of
philosophy) in Platonic terms.

2. Moderating, assuaging.
3. "He was her preceptor in philosophy and divinity" [Pope's note].

Love, free as air, at sight of human ties,   75
Spreads his light wings, and in a moment flies.
Let wealth, let honor, wait the wedded dame,
August her deed, and sacred be her fame;
Before true passion all those views remove,[4]
Fame, wealth, and honor! what are you to love?   80
The jealous god, when we profane his fires,
Those restless passions in revenge inspires,
And bids them make mistaken mortals groan,
Who seek in love for aught but love alone.
Should at my feet the world's great master fall,   85
Himself, his throne, his world, I'd scorn 'em all:
Nor Caesar's empress would I deign to prove;[5]
No, make me mistress to the man I love;
If there be yet another name more free,
More fond than mistress, make me that to thee!   90
Oh happy state! when souls each other draw,
When love is liberty, and nature, law:
All then is full, possessing, and possessed,
No craving void left aching in the breast:
Even thought meets thought ere from the lips it part,   95
And each warm wish springs mutual from the heart.
This sure is bliss (if bliss on earth there be)
And once the lot of Abelard and me.
    Alas how changed! what sudden horrors rise!
A naked lover bound and bleeding lies!   100
Where, where was Eloise? her voice, her hand,
Her poniard, had opposed the dire command.
Barbarian, stay! that bloody stroke restrain;
The crime was common,[6] common be the pain.
I can no more; by shame, by rage suppressed,   105
Let tears, and burning blushes speak the rest.
    Canst thou forget that sad, that solemn day,
When victims at yon altar's foot we lay?
Canst thou forget what tears that moment fell,
When, warm in youth, I bade the world farewell?   110
As with cold lips I kissed the sacred veil,
The shrines all trembled, and the lamps grew pale:
Heaven scarce believed the conquest it surveyed,
And saints with wonder heard the vows I made.
Yet then, to those dread altars as I drew,   115
Not on the Cross my eyes were fixed, but you;
Not grace, or zeal, love only was my call,
And if I lose thy love, I lose my all.
Come! with thy looks, thy words, relieve my woe;
Those still at least are left thee to bestow.   120
Still on that breast enamored let me lie,

4. Depart.   6. Shared; "pain": punishment.
5. Try.

Still drink delicious poison from thy eye,
Pant on thy lip, and to thy heart be pressed;
Give all thou canst—and let me dream the rest.
Ah no! instruct me other joys to prize,   125
With other beauties charm my partial[7] eyes,
Full in my view set all the bright abode,
And make my soul quit Abelard for God.
    Ah think at least thy flock deserves thy care,
Plants of thy hand, and children of thy prayer.   130
From the false world in early youth they fled,
By thee to mountains, wilds, and deserts led.
You raised these hallowed walls;[8] the desert smiled,
And paradise was opened in the wild.
No weeping orphan saw his father's stores   135
Our shrines irradiate,[9] or emblaze the floors;
No silver saints, by dying misers given,
Here bribed the rage of ill-requited heaven:
But such plain roofs as piety could raise,
And only vocal with the Maker's[1] praise.   140
In these lone walls (their day's eternal bound)
These moss-grown domes with spiry turrets crowned,
Where awful arches make a noon-day night,
And the dim windows shed a solemn light,
Thy eyes diffused a reconciling ray,   145
And gleams of glory brightened all the day.
But now no face divine contentment wears,
'Tis all blank sadness, or continual tears.
See how the force of others' prayers I try,
(O pious fraud of amorous charity!)   150
But why should I on others' prayers depend?
Come thou, my father, brother, husband, friend!
Ah let thy handmaid, sister, daughter move,
And all those tender names in one, thy love!
The darksome pines that o'er yon rocks reclined   155
Wave high, and murmur to the hollow wind,
The wandering streams that shine between the hills,
The grots that echo to the tinkling rills,
The dying gales that pant upon the trees,
The lakes that quiver to the curling breeze;   160
No more these scenes my meditation aid,
Or lull to rest the visionary[2] maid.
But o'er the twilight groves and dusky caves,
Long-sounding isles,[3] and intermingled graves,
Black Melancholy sits, and round her throws   165

7. Fond; seeing only a part.
8. "He founded the monastery" [Pope's note].
Abelard erected the "Paraclete," a modest oratory
near Troyes, in 1122; seven years later, when the
nunnery of which Heloise was prioress was evicted
from its property, he ceded the lands of the Para-

clete to her.
9. Adorn with splendor.
1. God's or Abelard's.
2. Given to visions.
3. Sounds reverberate over water as in the *aisles*
of a church.

A death-like silence, and a dread repose:
Her gloomy presence saddens all the scene,
Shades every flower, and darkens every green,
Deepens the murmur of the falling floods,
And breathes a browner horror on the woods.[4]   170
    Yet here for ever, ever must I stay;
Sad proof how well a lover can obey!
Death, only death, can break the lasting chain;
And here, even then, shall my cold dust remain,
Here all its frailties, all its flames resign,   175
And wait, till 'tis no sin to mix with thine.
    Ah wretch! believed the spouse of God in vain,
Confessed within the slave of love and man.
Assist me, heaven! but whence arose that prayer?
Sprung it from piety, or from despair?   180
Even here, where frozen chastity retires,
Love finds an altar for forbidden fires.
I ought to grieve, but cannot what I ought;
I mourn the lover, not lament the fault;
I view my crime, but kindle at the view,   185
Repent old pleasures, and solicit new;
Now turned to heaven, I weep my past offense,
Now think of thee, and curse my innocence.
Of all affliction taught a lover yet,
'Tis sure the hardest science[5] to forget!   190
How shall I lose the sin, yet keep the sense,[6]
And love the offender, yet detest the offense?
How the dear object from the crime remove,
Or how distinguish penitence from love?
Unequal task! a passion to resign,   195
For hearts so touched, so pierced, so lost as mine.
Ere such a soul regains its peaceful state,
How often must it love, how often hate!
How often hope, despair, resent, regret,
Conceal, disdain—do all things but forget.   200
But let heaven seize it, all at once 'tis fired,
Not touched, but rapt; not wakened, but inspired![7]
Oh come! oh teach me nature to subdue,
Renounce my love, my life, my self—and you.
Fill my fond heart with God alone, for he   205
Alone can rival, can succeed to thee.
    How happy is the blameless vestal's lot!
The world forgetting, by the world forgot.
Eternal sun-shine of the spotless mind!
Each prayer accepted, and each wish resigned;   210

4. "The image of the Goddess Melancholy sitting
over the convent, and, as it were, expanding her
dreadful wings over its whole circuit, and diffusing
her gloom all around it, is truly sublime, and
strongly conceived" [Joseph Warton].

5. Knowledge.
6. Both perception and sensation.
7. I.e., when touched, at once rapt; when wakened, at once inspired.

Labor and rest, that equal periods keep;
"Obedient slumbers that can wake and weep;"[8]
Desires composed, affections ever even;
Tears that delight, and sighs that waft to heaven.
Grace shines around her with serenest beams,   215
And whispering angels prompt her golden dreams.
For her the unfading rose of Eden blooms,
And wings of seraphs shed divine perfumes,
For her the Spouse prepares the bridal ring,
For her white virgins hymenaeals[9] sing,   220
To sounds of heavenly harps she dies away,
And melts in visions of eternal day.
    Far other dreams my erring soul employ,
Far other raptures, of unholy joy:
When at the close of each sad, sorrowing day,   225
Fancy restores what vengeance snatched away,
Then conscience sleeps, and leaving nature free,
All my loose soul unbounded springs to thee.
O curst, dear horrors of all-conscious night![1]
How glowing guilt exalts the keen delight!   230
Provoking daemons all restraint remove,
And stir within me every source of love.
I hear thee, view thee, gaze o'er all thy charms,
And round thy phantom glue my clasping arms.
I wake—no more I hear, no more I view,   235
The phantom flies me, as unkind as you.
I call aloud; it hears not what I say;
I stretch my empty arms; it glides away:
To dream once more I close my willing eyes;
Ye soft illusions, dear deceits, arise!   240
Alas, no more!—methinks we wandering go
Through dreary wastes, and weep each other's woe;
Where round some moldering tower pale ivy creeps,
And low-browed rocks hang nodding o'er the deeps.
Sudden you mount! you beckon from the skies;   245
Clouds interpose, waves roar, and winds arise.
I shriek, start up, the same sad prospect find,
And wake to all the griefs I left behind.[2]
    For thee the fates, severely kind, ordain
A cool suspense[3] from pleasure and from pain;   250
Thy life a long dead calm of fixed repose;
No pulse that riots, and no blood that glows.
Still as the sea, ere winds were taught to blow,
Or moving spirit bade the waters flow;
Soft as the slumbers of a saint forgiven,   255

---

8. A quotation from *Description of a Religious House*, by Richard Crashaw.
9. Wedding hymns. Every nun is the bride of Christ, her spouse.
1. The night knows everything; and Eloisa is conscious (guiltily aware) all through the night.
2. Cf. the conclusion to the *Epistle to Miss Blount*, a comic companion-piece to this poem.
3. Suspension.

And mild as opening gleams of promised heaven.
    Come, Abelard! for what hast thou to dread?
The torch of Venus burns not for the dead.
Nature stands checked; religion disapproves;
Even thou art cold—yet Eloisa loves.   260
Ah hopeless, lasting flames! like those that burn
To light the dead, and warm the unfruitful urn.[4]
    What scenes appear where'er I turn my view?
The dear ideas, where I fly, pursue,
Rise in the grove, before the altar rise,   265
Stain all my soul, and wanton in my eyes!
I waste the matin lamp in sighs for thee,
Thy image steals between my God and me,
Thy voice I seem in every hymn to hear,
With every bead I drop too soft a tear.   270
When from the censer clouds of fragrance roll,
And swelling organs lift the rising soul,
One thought of thee puts all the pomp to flight,
Priests, tapers, temples, swim before my sight:
In seas of flame[5] my plunging soul is drowned,   275
While altars blaze, and angels tremble round.
    While prostrate here in humble grief I lie,
Kind, virtuous drops just gathering in my eye,
While praying, trembling, in the dust I roll,
And dawning grace is opening on my soul: 280
Come, if thou dar'st, all charming as thou art!
Oppose thyself to heaven; dispute[6] my heart;
Come, with one glance of those deluding eyes
Blot out each bright idea of the skies.
Take back that grace, those sorrows, and those tears,   285
Take back my fruitless penitence and prayers,
Snatch me, just mounting, from the blest abode,
Assist the fiends and tear me from my God!
    No, fly me, fly me! far as pole from pole;
Rise Alps between us! and whole oceans roll!   290
Ah come not, write not, think not once of me,
Nor share one pang of all I felt for thee.
Thy oaths I quit,[7] thy memory resign,
Forget, renounce me, hate whate'er was mine.
Fair eyes, and tempting looks (which yet I view!)   295
Long loved, adored ideas! all adieu!
O grace serene! oh virtue heavenly fair!
Divine oblivion of low-thoughted care!
Fresh blooming hope, gay daughter of the sky!
And faith, our early immortality!   300
Enter, each mild, each amicable guest;
Receive, and wrap me in eternal rest!

---

4. Perpetual fires were placed in Roman tombs.   6. Contend for.
5. Love, or Hell.   7. Absolve.

See in her cell sad Eloisa spread,
Propped on some tomb, a neighbor of the dead!
In each low wind methinks a spirit calls,   305
And more than echoes talk along the walls.
Here, as I watched the dying lamps around,
From yonder shrine I heard a hollow sound.
"Come, sister, come! (it said, or seemed to say)
Thy place is here, sad sister, come away!   310
Once like thyself, I trembled, wept, and prayed,
Love's victim then, tho' now a sainted maid:
But all is calm in this eternal sleep;
Here grief forgets to groan, and love to weep,
Even superstition loses every fear: 315
For God, not man, absolves our frailties here."
    I come, I come! prepare your roseate bowers,
Celestial palms, and ever-blooming flowers.
Thither, where sinners may have rest, I go,
Where flames refined in breasts seraphic glow.   320
Thou, Abelard! the last sad office pay,
And smooth my passage to the realms of day;
See my lips tremble, and my eyeballs roll,
Suck my last breath, and catch my flying soul!
Ah no—in sacred vestments may'st thou stand,   325
The hallowed taper trembling in thy hand,
Present the Cross before my lifted eye,
Teach me at once, and learn of[8] me to die.
Ah then, thy once-loved Eloisa see!
It will be then no crime to gaze on me.   330
See from my cheek the transient roses fly!
See the last sparkle languish in my eye!
Till every motion, pulse, and breath be o'er;
And even my Abelard be loved no more.
O death all-eloquent! you only prove   335
What dust we doat on, when 'tis man we love.
    Then too, when fate shall thy fair frame destroy,
(That cause of all my guilt, and all my joy)
In trance ecstatic may thy pangs be drowned,
Bright clouds descend, and angels watch thee round,   340
From opening skies may streaming glories shine,
And saints embrace thee with a love like mine.
    May one kind grave unite each hapless name,[9]
And graft my love immortal on thy fame!
Then, ages hence, when all my woes are o'er,   345
When this rebellious heart shall beat no more;
If ever chance two wandering lovers brings
To Paraclete's white walls, and silver springs,
O'er the pale marble shall they join their heads,

8. Learn from.
9. "Abelard and Eloisa were interred in the same
grave, or in monuments adjoining, in the monastery of Paraclete" [Pope's note].

And drink the falling tears each other sheds,   350
Then sadly say, with mutual pity moved,
"Oh may we never love as these have loved!"
From the full choir when loud Hosannas rise,
And swell the pomp of dreadful sacrifice,[1]
Amid that scene if some relenting eye   355
Glance on the stone where our cold relics lie,
Devotion's self shall steal a thought from heaven,
One human tear shall drop, and be forgiven.
And sure if fate some future bard shall join
In sad similitude of griefs to mine,   360
Condemned whole years in absence to deplore,[2]
And image charms he must behold no more,
Such if there be, who loves so long, so well,
Let him our sad, our tender story tell;
The well-sung woes will sooth my pensive ghost;   365
He best can paint 'em, who shall feel 'em most.

1717

An Essay on Man

Pope's philosophical poem, *An Essay on Man*, is a fragment of an ambitious but never completed scheme for what the poet referred to as his "ethic work," which was to have been a large survey of human nature, society, and morals. The work is dedicated to Henry St. John (pronounced *Sín-jun*), Viscount Bolingbroke (1678–1751), the brilliant, though erratic, secretary of state in the Tory ministry of 1710–14, whom Pope had come to know through Swift. After the accession of George I he fled to France, attainted of treason, but was pardoned and allowed to return in 1723. He settled near Pope at Dawley farm and a close friendship developed between the two men. In their conversations Bolingbroke, who fancied himself a philosopher, helped Pope to formulate the optimistic system that is expounded in this poem. Yet it is clear that the poem would have been pretty much what it is had the two men never met, for it expresses doctrines widely circulated and generally accepted at the time by enlightened minds throughout Europe. The *Essay* gives memorable expression to ideas about the nature of the universe and man's place in it, ideas upon which eighteenth-century optimism rested.

Pope's purpose is to "vindicate the ways of God to man," a phrase that consciously echoes *Paradise Lost* 1.26. Like Milton, Pope faces the problem of the existence of evil in a world presumed to be the creation of a good God. *Paradise Lost* is Biblical in content, Christian in doctrine; the *Essay on Man* avoids all specifically Christian doctrines, not because Pope disbelieved them, but because "man," the subject of the poem, includes millions who never heard of Christianity, and Pope is concerned with the universal. Milton tells a mythological story. Pope writes in abstract terms.

---

1. The celebration of the Eucharist (Mass).
2. Lament. Pope, imagining himself imagined by Eloisa, hints that he too is separated from a loved one; perhaps Lady Mary Wortley Montagu, who was in Turkey. Pope and Lady Mary later quarreled, and she appears as Sappho in Epistle 2, *To a Lady*.

The *Essay* is divided into four epistles. In the first Pope asserts the essential order and goodness of the universe and the rightness of our place in it. The other Epistles deal with how man may emulate in his nature and in society the cosmic harmony revealed in the first Epistle. The second seeks to show how he may attain a psychological harmony which can become the basis of a virtuous life through the co-operation of self-love and the passions (both necessary to our complete humanity) with reason, the controller and director. The third is concerned with man in society, which, it teaches, was created through the co-operation of self-love (the egoistic drives that motivate us) and social love (our dependence on others, our inborn benevolence). The fourth is concerned with happiness, which lies within the reach of all, for it is dependent upon virtue, which becomes possible when—though only when—self-love is transmuted into love of others and love of God. Such, in brief summary, are Pope's main ideas, expressed in many phrases so memorable that they have detached themselves from the poem and become a part of our daily speech.

From An Essay on Man

TO HENRY ST. JOHN, LORD BOLINGBROKE

Epistle 1. Of the Nature and State of Man, With Respect to the Universe

> Awake, my St. John! leave all meaner things
> To low ambition, and the pride of kings.
> Let us (since life can little more supply
> Than just to look about us and to die)
> Expatiate free[1] o'er all this scene of man;   5
> A mighty maze! but not without a plan;
> A wild, where weeds and flowers promiscuous shoot,
> Or garden, tempting with forbidden fruit.
> Together let us beat this ample field,
> Try what the open, what the covert yield;   10
> The latent tracts, the giddy heights, explore
> Of all who blindly creep, or sightless soar;
> Eye Nature's walks, shoot folly as it flies,
> And catch the manners living as they rise;
> Laugh where we must, be candid[2] where we can;   15
> But vindicate the ways of God to man.[3]
>
> 1. Say first, of God above, or man below,
> What can we reason, but from what we know?
> Of man, what see we but his station here,
> From which to reason, or to which refer?   20
> Through worlds unnumbered though the God be known,
> 'Tis ours to trace him only in our own.
> He, who through vast immensity can pierce,

---

1. Range freely.   3. Pope deliberately echoes *Paradise Lost* 1.26.
2. Kindly.

See worlds on worlds compose one universe,
Observe how system into system runs,   25
What other planets circle other suns,
What varied being peoples every star,
May tell why Heaven has made us as we are.
But of this frame the bearings, and the ties,
The strong connections, nice dependencies,   30
Gradations just, has thy pervading soul
Looked through? or can a part contain the whole?
    Is the great chain, that draws all to agree,
And drawn supports, upheld by God, or thee?

    2. Presumptuous man! the reason wouldst thou find,   35
Why formed so weak, so little, and so blind?
First, if thou canst, the harder reason guess,
Why formed no weaker, blinder, and no less!
Ask of thy mother earth, why oaks are made
Taller or stronger than the weeds they shade?   40
Or ask of yonder argent fields above,
Why Jove's satellites[4] are less than Jove?
    Of systems possible, if 'tis confessed
That Wisdom Infinite must form the best,
Where all must full or not coherent be,   45
And all that rises, rise in due degree;
Then, in the scale of reasoning life, 'tis plain,
There must be, somewhere, such a rank as man:
And all the question (wrangle e'er so long)
Is only this, if God has placed him wrong?   50
    Respecting man, whatever wrong we call,
May, must be right, as relative to all.
In human works, though labored on with pain,
A thousand movements scarce one purpose gain;
In God's, one single can its end produce;   55
Yet serves to second too some other use.
So man, who here seems principal alone,
Perhaps acts second to some sphere unknown,
Touches some wheel, or verges to some goal;
'Tis but a part we see, and not a whole.   60
    When the proud steed shall know why man restrains
His fiery course, or drives him o'er the plains;
When the dull ox, why now he breaks the clod,
Is now a victim, and now Egypt's god:
Then shall man's pride and dullness comprehend   65
His actions', passions', being's use and end;
Why doing, suffering, checked, impelled; and why
This hour a slave, the next a deity.
    Then say not man's imperfect, Heaven in fault;

---

4. In his *Dictionary* Johnson notes and condemns Pope's giving his word four syllables, as in Latin.

Say rather, man's as perfect as he ought;   70
His knowledge measured to his state and place,
His time a moment, and a point his space.
If to be perfect in a certain sphere,[5]
What matter, soon or late, or here or there?
The blest today is as completely so,   75
As who began a thousand years ago.

   3. Heaven from all creatures hides the book of Fate,
All but the page prescribed, their present state:
From brutes what men, from men what spirits know:
Or who could suffer being here below?   80
The lamb thy riot dooms to bleed today,
Had he thy reason, would he skip and play?
Pleased to the last, he crops the flowery food,
And licks the hand just raised to shed his blood.
O blindness to the future! kindly given,   85
That each may fill the circle marked by Heaven:
Who sees with equal eye, as God of all,
A hero perish, or a sparrow fall,
Atoms or systems[6] into ruin hurled,
And now a bubble burst, and now a world.   90
   Hope humbly then; with trembling pinions soar;
Wait the great teacher Death, and God adore!
What future bliss, he gives not thee to know,
But gives that hope to be thy blessing now.
Hope springs eternal in the human breast: 95
Man never is, but always to be blest:
The soul, uneasy and confined from home,
Rests and expatiates in a life to come.
   Lo! the poor Indian, whose untutored mind
Sees God in clouds, or hears him in the wind;   100
His soul proud Science never taught to stray
Far as the solar walk, or milky way;
Yet simple Nature to his hope has given,
Behind the cloud-topped hill, an humbler heaven;
Some safer world in depth of woods embraced,   105
Some happier island in the watery waste,
Where slaves once more their native land behold,
No fiends torment, no Christians thirst for gold!
To be, contents his natural desire,
He asks no angel's wing, no seraph's fire;   110
But thinks, admitted to that equal sky,
His faithful dog shall bear him company.

   4. Go, wiser thou! and, in thy scale of sense,
Weigh thy opinion against Providence;

---

5. I.e., in one's "state and place."   6. Solar systems.

Call imperfection what thou fancy'st such,   115
Say, here he gives too little, there too much;
Destroy all creatures for thy sport or gust,[7]
Yet cry, if man's unhappy, God's unjust;
If man alone engross not Heaven's high care,
Alone made perfect here, immortal there: 120
Snatch from his hand the balance and the rod,
Rejudge his justice, be the God of God!
In pride, in reasoning pride, our error lies;
All quit their sphere, and rush into the skies.
Pride still is aiming at the blest abodes,   125
Men would be angels, angels would be gods.
Aspiring to be gods, if angels fell,
Aspiring to be angels, men rebel:
And who but wishes to invert the laws
Of order, sins against the Eternal Cause.   130

    5. Ask for what end the heavenly bodies shine,
Earth for whose use? Pride answers, " 'Tis for mine:
For me kind Nature wakes her genial power,
Suckles each herb, and spreads out every flower;
Annual for me, the grape, the rose renew   135
The juice nectareous, and the balmy dew;
For me, the mine a thousand treasures brings;
For me, health gushes from a thousand springs;
Seas roll to waft me, suns to light me rise;
My footstool earth, my canopy the skies."   140
    But errs not Nature from this gracious end,
From burning suns when livid deaths descend,
When earthquakes swallow, or when tempests sweep
Towns to one grave, whole nations to the deep?
"No," 'tis replied, "the first Almighty Cause   145
Acts not by partial, but by general laws;
The exceptions few; some change since all began,
And what created perfect?"—Why then man?
If the great end be human happiness,
Then Nature deviates; and can man do less?   150
As much that end a constant course requires
Of showers and sunshine, as of man's desires;
As much eternal springs and cloudless skies,
As men forever temperate, calm, and wise.
If plagues or earthquakes break not Heaven's design,   155
Why then a Borgia, or a Catiline?[8]
Who knows but he whose hand the lightning forms,
Who heaves old ocean, and who wings the storms,

---

7. "Sense of tasting" (Johnson's *Dictionary*).
8. The Renaissance Italian family of the Borgias were notorious for their crimes: ruthless lust for power, cruelty, rapaciousness, treachery, and murder (especially by poisoning); Cesare Borgia

(1476–1507), son of Pope Alexander VI, is here referred to. Lucius Sergius Catiline (ca. 108–62 B.C.), an ambitious, greedy, and cruel conspirator against the Roman state, was denounced in Cicero's famous orations before the senate and in the Forum.

Pours fierce ambition in a Caesar's mind,
Or turns young Ammon[9] loose to scourge mankind?　160
From pride, from pride, our very reasoning springs;
Account for moral, as for natural things:
Why charge we Heaven in those, in these acquit?
In both, to reason right is to submit.
　Better for us, perhaps, it might appear,　165
Were there all harmony, all virtue here;
That never air or ocean felt the wind;
That never passion discomposed the mind:
But ALL subsists by elemental strife;
And passions are the elements of life.　170
The general ORDER, since the whole began,
Is kept in Nature, and is kept in man.

　6. What would this man? Now upward will he soar,
And little less than angel, would be more;
Now looking downwards, just as grieved appears　175
To want the strength of bulls, the fur of bears.
Made for his use all creatures if he call,
Say what their use, had he the powers of all?
Nature to these, without profusion, kind,
The proper organs, proper powers assigned;　180
Each seeming want compènsated of course,
Here with degrees of swiftness, there of force;
All in exact proportion to the state;
Nothing to add, and nothing to abate.
Each beast, each insect, happy in its own;　185
Is Heaven unkind to man, and man alone?
Shall he alone, whom rational we call,
Be pleased with nothing, if not blessed with all?
　The bliss of man (could pride that blessing find)
Is not to act or think beyond mankind;　190
No powers of body or of soul to share,
But what his nature and his state can bear.
Why has not man a microscopic eye?
For this plain reason, man is not a fly.
Say what the use, were finer optics given,　195
To inspect a mite, not comprehend the heaven?
Or touch, if tremblingly alive all o'er,
To smart and agonize at every pore?
Or quick effluvia[1] darting through the brain,
Die of a rose in aromatic pain?　200
If nature thundered in his opening ears,
And stunned him with the music of the spheres,

9. Alexander the Great.
1. According to the philosophy of Epicurus (adopted by Robert Boyle, the chemist, and other 17th-century scientists), the senses are stirred to perception by being bombarded through the pores by steady streams of "effluvia," incredibly thin and tiny—but material—images of the objects which surround us.

How would he wish that Heaven had left him still
The whispering zephyr, and the purling rill?
Who finds not Providence all good and wise,   205
Alike in what it gives, and what denies?

7. Far as creation's ample range extends,
The scale of sensual,[2] mental powers ascends:
Mark how it mounts, to man's imperial race,
From the green myriads in the peopled grass: 210
What modes of sight betwixt each wide extreme,
The mole's dim curtain, and the lynx's beam:[3]
Of smell, the headlong lioness between,
And hound sagacious[4] on the tainted green:
Of hearing, from the life that fills the flood,   215
To that which warbles through the vernal wood:
The spider's touch, how exquisitely fine!
Feels at each thread, and lives along the line:
In the nice[5] bee, what sense so subtly true
From poisonous herbs extracts the healing dew: 220
How instinct varies in the groveling swine,
Compared, half-reasoning elephant, with thine!
'Twixt that, and reason, what a nice barrier,[6]
Forever separate, yet forever near!
Remembrance and reflection how allied;   225
What thin partitions sense from thought divide:
And middle natures, how they long to join,
Yet never pass the insuperable line!
Without this just gradation, could they be
Subjected, these to those, or all to thee?   230
The powers of all subdued by thee alone,
Is not thy reason all these powers in one?

8. See, through this air, this ocean, and this earth,
All matter quick, and bursting into birth.
Above, how high progressive life may go!   235
Around, how wide! how deep extend below!
Vast Chain of Being! which from God began,
Natures ethereal, human, angel, man,
Beast, bird, fish, insect, what no eye can see,
No glass can reach! from Infinite to thee,   240
From thee to nothing.—On superior powers
Were we to press, inferior might on ours:
Or in the full creation leave a void,
Where, one step broken, the great scale's destroyed:
From Nature's chain whatever link you strike,   245

---

2. Sensory.
3. One of several early theories of vision held that the eye casts a beam of light which makes objects visible.

4. Quick of scent.
5. Exact, accurate.
6. Pronounced *ba-réer*.

Tenth or ten thousandth, breaks the chain alike.
   And, if each system in gradation roll
Alike essential to the amazing Whole,
The least confusion but in one, not all
That system only, but the Whole must fall.   250
Let earth unbalanced from her orbit fly,
Planets and suns run lawless through the sky,
Let ruling angels from their spheres be hurled,
Being on being wrecked, and world on world,
Heaven's whole foundations to their center nod,   255
And Nature tremble to the throne of God:
All this dread ORDER break—for whom? for thee?
Vile worm!—oh, madness, pride, impiety!

   9. What if the foot, ordained the dust to tread,
Or hand, to toil, aspired to be the head?   260
What if the head, the eye, or ear repined
To serve mere engines to the ruling Mind?[7]
Just as absurd, to mourn the tasks or pains,   265
The great directing MIND of ALL ordains.
   All are but parts of one stupendous whole,
Whose body Nature is, and God the soul;
That, changed through all, and yet in all the same,
Great in the earth, as in the ethereal frame,   270
Warms in the sun, refreshes in the breeze,
Glows in the stars, and blossoms in the trees,
Lives through all life, extends through all extent,
Spreads undivided, operates unspent,
Breathes in our soul, informs our mortal part,   275
As full, as perfect, in a hair as heart;
As full, as perfect, in vile man that mourns,
As the rapt seraph that adores and burns;
To him no high, no low, no great, no small;
He fills, he bounds, connects, and equals all.   280

   10. Cease then, nor ORDER imperfection name:
Our proper bliss depends on what we blame.
Know thy own point: this kind, this due degree
Of blindness, weakness, Heaven bestows on thee.
Submit—In this, or any other sphere,   285
Secure to be as blest as thou canst bear:
Safe in the hand of one disposing Power,
Or in the natal, or the mortal hour.
All Nature is but art, unknown to thee;
All chance, direction, which thou canst not see;   290
All discord, harmony not understood;
All partial evil, universal good:

7. Cf. 1 Corinthians 12.14–26.

And, spite of pride, in erring reason's spite,
One truth is clear: Whatever IS, is RIGHT.

From *Epistle 2. Of the Nature and State of Man With Respect to Himself, as an Individual*

1. Know then thyself, presume not God to scan;[8]
The proper study of mankind is Man.
Placed on this isthmus of a middle state,
A being darkly wise, and rudely great:
With too much knowledge for the skeptic side,   5
With too much weakness for the Stoic's pride,
He hangs between; in doubt to act, or rest,
In doubt to deem himself a god, or beast;
In doubt his mind or body to prefer,
Born but to die, and reasoning but to err;   10
Alike in ignorance, his reason such,
Whether he thinks too little, or too much:
Chaos of thought and passion, all confused;
Still by himself abused, or disabused;
Created half to rise, and half to fall;   15
Great lord of all things, yet a prey to all;
Sole judge of truth, in endless error hurled:
The glory, jest, and riddle of the world!

                           *   *   *

                                                              1733

Epistle 2. To a Lady[1]

OF THE CHARACTERS OF WOMEN

Nothing so true as what you once let fall,
"Most women have no characters at all."

8. For the author's revisions while composing this part of *An Essay on Man*, see "Poems in Process," below.

1. This is one of four poems that Pope grouped together under the title *Epistles to Several Persons*, but that have usually been known by the less appropriate title *Moral Essays*. They were conceived as parts of Pope's ambitious "ethic work," of which only the first part, the *Essay on Man*, was completed. *Epistle* 1 treats the characters of men, *Epistle* 2 the characters of women. The other two epistles are concerned with the use of riches, a subject that engaged Pope's attention during the 1730s, since he distrusted the influence on private morals and public life of the rapidly growing wealth of England under the first Hanoverians.

Epistle 2 contains a series of brilliantly executed portraits (the metaphor of portrait painting dominates the poem) which among them illustrate the thesis that women are consistent only in being inconsistent. As we move from portrait to portrait, we not only observe ladies who are changeable and fickle in their own nature, but we also meet a variety of female characters—the affected, the slatternly, the soft-natured, the silly, the lewd, for instance—who remind us that ladies are as variegated as tulips (line 41).

Are the portraits imaginary or do they represent women whom Pope knew and whom his readers could recognize? This question exercised the gossips of Pope's own time and after; and it has occupied the attention of Pope's editors and commentators ever since his death. Many of the portraits indubitably allude to actual women (Sappho); some doubtless are composite (Atossa); others are mere types. Questions of identity, however, pertain rather to Pope's biography and character than to his art. It should matter little if at all to the reader first approaching Pope's satire whether in fact Atossa is Sarah, duchess of Marlborough, or, as is much more likely, Katherine, duchess of Buckinghamshire, or, most likely of all, Katherine combined with a few traits of Sarah. Occasionally, perhaps, a lady's name might have hinted to some of Pope's contemporaries that a real person was

Matter too soft a lasting mark to bear,
And best distinguished by black, brown, or fair.
   How many pictures[2] of one nymph we view,   5
All how unlike each other, all how true!
Arcadia's countess, here, in ermined pride,
Is, there, Pastora by a fountain side.
Here Fannia, leering on her own good man,
And there, a naked Leda with a swan.[3]   10
Let then the fair one beautifully cry,
In Magdalen's loose hair and lifted eye,
Or dressed in smiles of sweet Cecilia shine,[4]
With simpering angels, palms, and harps divine;
Whether the charmer sinner it, or saint it,   15
If folly grow romantic,[5] I must paint it.
   Come then, the colors and the ground[6] prepare!
Dip in the rainbow, trick her off in air;
Choose a firm cloud, before it fall, and in it
Catch, ere she change, the Cynthia[7] of this minute.   20
   Rufa, whose eye quick-glancing o'er the park,
Attracts each light gay meteor of a spark,
Agrees as ill with Rufa studying Locke,[8]
As Sappho's diamonds with her dirty smock,
Or Sappho at her toilet's greasy task,[9]   25
With Sappho fragrant at an evening masque:
So morning insects that in muck begun,
Shine, buzz, and flyblow in the setting sun.
   How soft is Silia! fearful to offend,
The frail one's advocate, the weak one's friend: 30
To her, Calista proved her conduct nice,
And good Simplicius asks of her advice.
Sudden, she storms! she raves! You tip the wink,
But spare your censure; Silia does not drink.
All eyes may see from what the change arose,   35
All eyes may see—a pimple on her nose.
   Papillia,[1] wedded to her amorous spark,
Sighs for the shades—"How charming is a park!"

intended. Today the reader who is not a specialist will do well to neglect particular applications of Pope's satire and to concern himself with the generally, the permanently human, which is always the center of Pope's works.

The "lady" of the title is Martha Blount (1690–1763), Pope's best-loved female friend, to whom he left the bulk of his property.

2. Ladies of the 17th and 18th centuries liked to have themselves painted in the costumes and attitudes of fanciful, mythological, or historical characters.

3. Leda was seduced by Zeus, who approached her in the form of a swan.

4. St. Mary Magdalen was often painted during the 17th century in the attitude described in line

12. St. Cecilia, the reputed inventor of the organ, was traditionally painted in the manner which Pope satirically glances at here.

5. Extravagant.

6. The first coatings of paint on the canvas before the figures in the picture are sketched in.

7. One of the names of Diana, goddess of the moon, a notoriously changeable heavenly body.

8. John Locke, author of *An Essay Concerning Human Understanding* (1690).

9. Lady Mary Wortley Montagu, though beautiful as a young woman, became notorious for her slatternly appearance and personal uncleanliness. Both Sappho and Lady Mary were female poets. "Flyblow": deposit their eggs.

1. The name comes from Latin for "butterfly."

A park is purchased, but the fair he sees
All bathed in tears—"Oh, odious, odious trees!" 40
    Ladies, like variegated tulips, show;
'Tis to their changes half their charms we owe;
Fine by defect, and delicately weak,
Their happy spots the nice admirer take,
'Twas thus Calypso[2] once each heart alarmed, 45
Awed without virtue, without beauty charmed;
Her tongue bewitched as oddly as her eyes,
Less wit than mimic, more a wit than wise;
Strange graces still, and stranger flights she had,
Was just not ugly, and was just not mad; 50
Yet ne'er so sure your passion to create,
As when she touched the brink of all we hate.
    Narcissa's[3] nature, tolerably mild,
To make a wash,[4] would hardly stew a child;
Has even been proved to grant a lover's prayer, 55
And paid a tradesman once to make him stare,
Gave alms at Easter, in a Christian trim,
And made a widow happy, for a whim.
Why then declare good nature is her scorn,
When 'tis by that alone she can be borne? 60
Why pique all mortals, yet affect a name?
A fool to pleasure, yet a slave to fame:
Now deep in Taylor and the *Book of Martyrs*,[5]
Now drinking citron[6] with his Grace and Chartres.
Now conscience chills her, and now passion burns; 65
And atheism and religion take their turns;
A very heathen in the carnal part,
Yet still a sad, good Christian at her heart.
    See Sin in state, majestically drunk;
Proud as a peeress, prouder as a punk; 70
Chaste to her husband, frank[7] to all beside,
A teeming mistress, but a barren bride.
What then? let blood and body bear the fault,
Her head's untouched, that noble seat of thought:
Such this day's doctrine—in another fit 75
She sins with poets through pure love of wit.
What has not fired her bosom or her brain?

---

2. The name is borrowed from the fascinating goddess who detained Odysseus on her island for seven years after the fall of Troy, thus preventing his return to his kingdom, Ithaca.

3. Type of extreme self-love. Narcissus, a beautiful youth, fell in love with his own image when he saw it reflected in a fountain.

4. Cosmetic lotion.

5. Jeremy Taylor, 17th-century Anglican divine, whose *Holy Living and Holy Dying* was often reprinted in the 18th century. John Foxe's *Acts and Monuments* (usually referred to as Foxe's *Book of Martyrs*), 1563, was a household book in most Protestant families in the 17th and 18th centuries; a record of the Protestants who perished for their faith under the persecution of Mary Tudor (1553–58), it was instrumental in keeping anti-Catholic sentiments alive.

6. I.e., citron-water, brandy flavored with lemon or orange peel. "His Grace" is usually said to be the duke of Wharton, an old enemy of Swift's and a notorious libertine; Francis Chartres: a debauchee often mentioned by Pope.

7. "Liberal; generous" (Johnson's *Dictionary*).

Caesar and Tallboy,[8] Charles and Charlemagne.
As Helluo,[9] late dictator of the feast,
The nose of hautgout,[1] and the tip of taste,   80
Criticked your wine, and analyzed your meat,
Yet on plain pudding deigned at home to eat;
So Philomedé,[2] lecturing all mankind
On the soft passion, and the taste refined,
The address, the delicacy—stoops at once,   85
And makes her hearty meal upon a dunce.

    Flavia's a wit, has too much sense to pray;
To toast our wants and wishes, is her way;
Nor asks of God, but of her stars, to give
The mighty blessing, "while we live, to live."   90
Then all for death, that opiate of the soul!
Lucretia's dagger,[3] Rosamonda's bowl.
Say, what can cause such impotence of mind?
A spark too fickle, or a spouse too kind.
Wise wretch! with pleasures too refined to please,   95
With too much spirit to be e'er at ease,
With too much quickness ever to be taught,
With too much thinking to have common thought:
You purchase pain with all that joy can give,
And die of nothing but a rage to live.   100

    Turn then from wits; and look on Simo's mate,
No ass so meek, no ass so obstinate.
Or her, that owns her faults, but never mends,
Because she's honest, and the best of friends:
Or her, whose life the Church and scandal share,   105
Forever in a passion, or a prayer:
Or her, who laughs at hell, but (like her Grace)
Cries, "Ah! how charming, if there's no such place!"
Or who in sweet vicissitude appears
Of mirth and opium, ratafie[4] and tears,   110
The daily anodyne, and nightly draught,
To kill those foes to fair ones, time and thought.
Woman and fool are two hard things to hit,
For true no-meaning puzzles more than wit.

    But what are these to great Atossa's mind?[5]   115
Scarce once herself, by turns all womankind!
Who, with herself, or others, from her birth

---

8. A crude young man in Richard Brome's comedy *The Jovial Crew* (1641) or the opera adapted from the play (1731); "Charles," as F. W. Bateson points out, was a generic name for a footman in the period.
9. Latin for "glutton."
1. "Anything with a strong relish or strong scent, as overkept venison" (Johnson's *Dictionary*).
2. The name is Pope's adaptation of a Greek epithet meaning "laughter-loving," frequently applied to Aphrodite, the goddess of love.

3. Lucretia, violated by Tarquin, committed suicide; according to tradition, the "fair Rosamonda," mistress of Henry II, was forced by Queen Eleanor to drink poison.
4. "A fine liquor, prepared from the kernels of apricots and spirits" (Johnson's *Dictionary*).
5. Atossa, daughter of Cyrus, Emperor of Persia (d. 529 B.C.). If the duchess of Buckinghamshire is alluded to, the name is appropriate, for she was the natural daughter of James II.

Finds all her life one warfare upon earth:
Shines in exposing knaves, and painting fools,
Yet is whate'er she hates and ridicules.   120
No thought advances, but her eddy brain
Whisks it about, and down it goes again.
Full sixty years the world has been her trade,
The wisest fool much time has ever made.
From loveless youth to unrespected age,   125
No passion gratified except her rage.
So much the fury still outran the wit,
The pleasure missed her, and the scandal hit.
Who breaks with her, provokes revenge from hell,
But he's a bolder man who dares be well:[6]   130
Her every turn with violence pursued,
Nor more a storm her hate than gratitude:
To that each passion turns, or soon or late;
Love, if it makes her yield, must make her hate:
Superiors? death! and equals? what a curse!   135
But an inferior not dependent? worse.
Offend her, and she knows not to forgive;
Oblige her, and she'll hate you while you live:
But die, and she'll adore you—Then the bust
And temple rise—then fall again to dust.   140
Last night, her lord was all that's good and great;
A knave this morning, and his will a cheat.
Strange! by the means defeated of the ends,
By spirit robbed of power, by warmth of friends,
By wealth of followers! without one distress   145
Sick of herself through very selfishness!
Atossa, cursed with every granted prayer,
Childless with all her children, wants an heir.
To heirs unknown descends the unguarded store,
Or wanders, Heaven-directed, to the poor.   150
    Pictures like these, dear Madam, to design,
Asks no firm hand, and no unerring line;
Some wandering touches, some reflected light,
Some flying stroke alone can hit 'em right:
For how should equal colors do the knack?[7]   155
Chameleons who can paint in white and black?
    "Yet Chloe sure was formed without a spot—"
Nature in her then erred not, but forgot.
"With every pleasing, every prudent part,
Say, what can Chloe want?"—She wants a heart.   160
She speaks, behaves, and acts just as she ought;
But never, never, reached one generous thought.
Virtue she finds too painful an endeavor,
Content to dwell in decencies forever.

6. Be in her favor.   7. Do the trick.

So very reasonable, so unmoved,   165
As never yet to love, or to be loved.
She, while her lover pants upon her breast,
Can mark[8] the figures on an Indian chest;
And when she sees her friend in deep despair,
Observes how much a chintz exceeds mohair.   170
Forbid it Heaven, a favor or a debt
She e'er should cancel—but she may forget.
Safe is your secret still in Chloe's ear;
But none of Chloe's shall you ever hear.
Of all her dears she never slandered one,   175
But cares not if a thousand are undone.
Would Chloe know if you're alive or dead?
She bids her footman put it in her head.
Chloe is prudent—Would you too be wise?
Then never break your heart when Chloe dies.   180
    One certain portrait may (I grant) be seen,
Which Heaven has varnished out, and made a *Queen*:[9]
The same forever! and described by all
With Truth and Goodness, as with crown and ball.
Poets heap virtues, painters gems at will,   185
And show their zeal, and hide their want of skill.
'Tis well—but, artists! who can paint or write,
To draw the naked is your true delight.
That robe of quality so struts and swells,
None see what parts of Nature it conceals: 190
The exactest traits of body or of mind,
We owe to models of an humble kind.
If Queensberry[1] to strip there's no compelling,
'Tis from a handmaid we must take a Helen.
From peer or bishop 'tis no easy thing   195
To draw the man who loves his God, or king:
Alas! I copy (or my draft would fail)
From honest Mah'met[2] or plain Parson Hale.
    But grant, in public men sometimes are shown,
A woman's seen in private life alone: 200
Our bolder talents in full light displayed;
Your virtues open fairest in the shade.
Bred to disguise, in public 'tis you hide;
There, none distinguish 'twixt your shame or pride,
Weakness or delicacy; all so nice,   205
That each may seem a virtue, or a vice.
    In men, we various ruling passions find;
In women, two almost divide the kind;
Those, only fixed, they first or last obey,

---

8. Pay attention to.
9. Pope refers as usual to Queen Caroline with disapprobation.
1. The duchess of Queensberry, whom Pope valued because of her kindness to his friend John Gay,

had been a famous beauty.
2. Mahomet, a Turkish servant of George I; Dr. Stephen Hales was an Anglican clergyman and friend of Pope.

The love of pleasure, and the love of sway. 210
    That, Nature gives; and where the lesson taught
Is but to please, can pleasure seem a fault?
Experience, this; by man's oppression cursed,
They seek the second not to lose the first.
    Men, some to business, some to pleasure take; 215
But every woman is at heart a rake;
Men, some to quiet, some to public strife;
But every lady would be queen for life.
    Yet mark the fate of a whole sex of queens!
Power all their end, but beauty all the means: 220
In youth they conquer, with so wild a rage,
As leaves them scarce a subject in their age:
For foreign glory, foreign joy, they roam;
No thought of peace or happiness at home.
But wisdom's triumph is well-timed retreat, 225
As hard a science to the fair as great!
Beauties, like tyrants, old and friendless grown,
Yet hate repose, and dread to be alone,
Worn out in public, weary every eye,
Nor leave one sigh behind them when they die. 230
    Pleasures the sex, as children birds, pursue,
Still out of reach, yet never out of view,
Sure, if they catch, to spoil the toy at most,
To covet flying, and regret when lost:
At last, to follies youth could scarce defend, 235
It grows their age's prudence to pretend;
Ashamed to own they gave delight before,
Reduced to feign it, when they give no more:
As hags hold sabbaths,[3] less for joy than spite,
So these their merry, miserable night; 240
Still round and round the ghosts of beauty glide,
And haunt the places where their honor died.
    See how the world its veterans rewards!
A youth of frolics, an old age of cards;
Fair to no purpose, artful to no end, 245
Young without lovers, old without a friend;
A fop their passion, but their prize a sot;
Alive, ridiculous, and dead, forgot!
    Ah friend! to dazzle let the vain design;
To raise the thought, and touch the heart be thine! 250
That charm shall grow, while what fatigues the Ring[4]
Flaunts and goes down, an unregarded thing:
So when the sun's broad beam has tired the sight,
All mild ascends the moon's more sober light,
Serene in virgin modesty she shines, 255
And unobserved the glaring orb declines.

3. Obscene rites popularly supposed to be held by witches ("hags"); "night," in the next line, refers to evenings on which ladies entertained guests.
4. The fashionable drive in Hyde Park.

Oh! blest with temper, whose unclouded ray
Can make tomorrow cheerful as today;
She, who can love a sister's charms, or hear
Sighs for a daughter with unwounded ear;   260
She, who ne'er answers till a husband cools,
Or, if she rules him, never shows she rules;
Charms by accepting, by submitting sways,
Yet has her humor most, when she obeys;
Lets fops or fortune fly which way they will;   265
Disdains all loss of tickets[5] or Codille;
Spleen, vapors, or smallpox, above them all,
And mistress of herself, though China[6] fall.

And yet, believe me, good as well as ill,
Woman's at best a contradiction still.   270
Heaven, when it strives to polish all it can
Its last best work, but forms a softer man;
Picks from each sex, to make the favorite blest,
Your love of pleasure, our desire of rest:
Blends, in exception to all general rules,   275
Your taste of follies, with our scorn of fools:
Reserve with frankness, art with truth allied,
Courage with softness, modesty with pride;
Fixed principles, with fancy ever new;
Shakes all together, and produces—you.   280

Be this a woman's fame: with this unblest,
Toasts live a scorn, and queens may die a jest.
This Phoebus promised (I forget the year)
When those blue eyes first opened on the sphere;
Ascendant Phoebus watched that hour with care,   285
Averted half your parents' simple prayer;
And gave you beauty, but denied the pelf
That buys your sex a tyrant o'er itself.
The generous god, who wit and gold refines,
And ripens spirits as he ripens mines,[7]   290
Kept dross for duchesses, the world shall know it,
To you gave sense, good humor, and a poet.

1735, 1744

Epistle to Dr. Arbuthnot[1]

Advertisement
TO THE FIRST PUBLICATION OF THIS *Epistle*

This paper is a sort of bill of complaint, begun many years since, and
drawn up by snatches, as the several occasions offered. I had no thoughts

5. I.e., lottery tickets; "Codille": the loss of a hand
at the card games of ombre or quadrille.
6. Pope refers punningly to the chinaware which
fashionable women collected enthusiastically.
7. Phoebus Apollo, as god of poetry "ripens wit";

as god of the sun, he "ripens mines," for respectable scientific theory held that the sun's rays mature
precious metals in the earth.
1. Dr. John Arbuthnot (1667–1735), to whom
Pope addressed his best-known verse epistle, was

of publishing it, till it pleased some persons of rank and fortune (the authors of *Verses to the Imitator of Horace*, and of an *Epistle to a Doctor of Divinity from a Nobleman at Hampton Court*) to attack, in a very extraordinary manner, not only my writings (of which, being public, the public is judge) but my person, morals, and family, whereof, to those who know me not, a truer information may be requisite. Being divided between the necessity to say something of myself, and my own laziness to undertake so awkward a task, I thought it the shortest way to put the last hand to this epistle. If it have anything pleasing, it will be that by which I am most desirous to please, the truth and the sentiment; and if anything offensive, it will be only to those I am least sorry to offend, the vicious or the ungenerous.

Many will know their own pictures in it, there being not a circumstance but what is true; but I have, for the most part, spared their names, and they may escape being laughed at, if they please.

I would have some of them know, it was owing to the request of the learned and candid friend to whom it is inscribed, that I make not as free use of theirs as they have done of mine. However, I shall have this advantage, and honor, on my side, that whereas, by their proceeding, any abuse may be directed at any man, no injury can possibly be done by mine, since a nameless character can never be found out, but by its truth and likeness. P.

P. Shut, shut the door, good John![2] (fatigued, I said),
Tie up the knocker, say I'm sick, I'm dead.

distinguished both as a physician and as a man of wit. He had been one of the liveliest members of the Martinus Scriblerus Club, helping his friends to create the character and shape the career of the learned pedant whose *Memoirs* the Club had undertaken to write.

Pope had long been meditating such a poem, which was to be both an attack on his detractors and a defense of his own character and career. In his usual way he had jotted down hints, lines, couplets, fragments over a period of two decades, but the poem might never have been completed had it not been for two events: Arbuthnot, from his deathbed, wrote to urge Pope to continue his abhorrence of vice and to express it in his writings; and during 1733, Pope was the victim of two bitter attacks by "persons of rank and fortune," as the "Advertisement" has it. The *Verses Addressed to the Imitator of Horace* was the work of Lady Mary Wortley Montagu, helped by her friend Lord Hervey (pronounced "Harvey"), a close friend and confidant of Queen Caroline; *An Epistle to a Doctor of Divinity from a Nobleman at Hampton Court* was the work of Lord Hervey alone. Lady Mary, it must be admitted, had provocation enough, especially in Pope's recent reference to her in *The First Satire of the Second Book of Horace*, lines 83–84; but Hervey had little to complain of beyond occasional covert references to him as "Lord Fanny." At any rate, the two scurrilous attacks goaded Pope into action, and the poem was completed by the end of the summer of 1734.

The *Epistle* is a masterpiece of poetic rhetoric. The very fact that it is addressed to Dr. Arbuthnot, a man who had the general approbation of the world because of his kindliness and probity, in some degree seems to guarantee the integrity of the "I" of the poem and to diminish the moral stature of his enemies. This acquisition of virtue through association, an effective stroke, is supported by every device of persuasive rhetoric: reasonable argument and emotional appeals, subtly suggestive imagery, and superbly controlled shifts in tone and style which help to sway the reader's judgment to the side of the speaker. The poem opens in the flat language of commonplace prose discourse, tinged with a wry humor and a tone of exasperation: "Shut, shut the door, good John! (fatigued, I said)" and as it progresses it rises or falls in language and style according to the emotions which the speaker expresses—anger, contempt, amusement, sarcasm, mock self-pity, indignation, hatred, affection, gratitude, tenderness—to return at the end to the homely tone of the opening.

It is not clear that Pope intended the poem to be thought of as a dialogue, as it has usually been printed since Warburton's edition of 1751. The original edition, while suggesting interruptions in the flow of the monologue, kept entirely to the form of a letter. The introduction of the friend, who speaks from time to time, of course converts the original letter into a dramatic dialogue.

2. John Serle, Pope's gardener.

The Dog Star[3] rages! nay 'tis past a doubt
All Bedlam,[4] or Parnassus, is let out:
Fire in each eye, and papers in each hand,   5
They rave, recite, and madden round the land.
    What walls can guard me, or what shades can hide?
They pierce my thickets, through my grot[5] they glide,
By land, by water, they renew the charge,
They stop the chariot, and they board the barge.   10
No place is sacred, not the church is free;
Even Sunday shines no Sabbath day to me:
Then from the Mint[6] walks forth the man of rhyme,
Happy to catch me just at dinner time.
    Is there a parson, much bemused in beer,   15
A maudlin poetess, a rhyming peer,
A clerk foredoomed his father's soul to cross,
Who pens a stanza when he should engross?[7]
Is there who,[8] locked from ink and paper, scrawls
With desperate charcoal round his darkened walls?   20
All fly to Twit'nam,[9] and in humble strain
Apply to me to keep them mad or vain.
Arthur,[1] whose giddy son neglects the laws,
Imputes to me and my damned works the cause:
Poor Cornus[2] sees his frantic wife elope,   25
And curses wit, and poetry, and Pope.
    Friend to my life (which did not you prolong,
The world had wanted many an idle song)
What drop or nostrum[3] can this plague remove?
Or which must end me, a fool's wrath or love?   30
A dire dilemma! either way I'm sped,[4]
If foes, they write, if friends, they read me dead.
Seized and tied down to judge, how wretched I!
Who can't be silent, and who will not lie.
To laugh were want of goodness and of grace,   35
And to be grave exceeds all power of face.
I sit with sad civility, I read
With honest anguish and an aching head,
And drop at last, but in unwilling ears,
This saving counsel, "Keep your piece nine years."[5]   40

---

3. Sirius, associated with the period of greatest heat (and hence of madness) because it sets with the sun in late summer. August, in ancient Rome, was the season for reciting poetry.
4. Bethlehem Hospital for the insane in London.
5. The subterranean passage under the road that separated his house at Twickenham from his garden became, in Pope's hands, a romantic grotto ornamented with shells and mirrors.
6. A place in Southwark where debtors were free from arrest (they could not be arrested anywhere on Sundays).
7. Write out legal documents.
8. Is there some madman who, locked up without ink or paper. . . ?
9. I.e., Twickenham, Pope's villa on the bank of the Thames, a few miles above Hampton Court.
1. Arthur Moore, whose son, James Moore Smythe, dabbled in literature. Moore Smythe had earned Pope's enmity by using in one of his plays some unpublished lines from Pope's *Epistle to a Lady* in spite of Pope's objections.
2. Latin for "horn," the traditional emblem of the cuckold.
3. Medicine.
4. Destroyed; killed (Johnson's *Dictionary*).
5. The advice of Horace in *Art of Poetry* (line 388).

"Nine years!" cries he, who high in Drury Lane,[6]
Lulled by soft zephyrs through the broken pane,
Rhymes ere he wakes, and prints before term[7] ends,
Obliged by hunger and request of friends:
"The piece, you think, is incorrect? why, take it, 45
I'm all submission, what you'd have it, make it."
    Three things another's modest wishes bound,
My friendship, and a prologue, and ten pound.
    Pitholeon[8] sends to me: "You know his Grace,
I want a patron; ask him for a place." 50
Pitholeon libeled me—"but here's a letter
Informs you, sir, 'twas when he knew no better.
Dare you refuse him? Curll[9] invites to dine,
He'll write a Journal, or he'll turn divine."[1]
Bless me! a packet.—" 'Tis a stranger sues, 55
A virgin tragedy, an orphan Muse."
If I dislike it, "Furies, death, and rage!"
If I approve, "Commend it to the stage."
There (thank my stars) my whole commission ends,
The players and I are, luckily, no friends. 60
Fired that the house reject him, " 'Sdeath, I'll print it,
And shame the fools—Your interest, sir, with Lintot!"[2]
Lintot, dull rogue, will think your price too much.
"Not, sir, if you revise it, and retouch."
All my demurs but double his attacks; 65
At last he whispers, "Do; and we go snacks."[3]
Glad of a quarrel, straight I clap the door,
"Sir, let me see your works and you no more."
    'Tis sung, when Midas' ears began to spring
(Midas, a sacred person and a king), 70
His very minister who spied them first,
(Some say his queen) was forced to speak, or burst.[4]
And is not mine, my friend, a sorer case,
When every coxcomb perks them in my face?
    A. Good friend, forbear! you deal in dangerous things. 75
I'd never name queens, ministers, or kings;
Keep close to ears, and those let asses prick;
'Tis nothing——P. Nothing? if they bite and kick?
Out with it, Dunciad! let the secret pass,

6. I.e., living in a garret in Drury Lane, site of one of the theaters and the haunt of the profligate.
7. One of the four annual periods in which the law courts are in session and with which the publishing season coincided.
8. "A foolish poet of Rhodes, who pretended much to Greek" [Pope's note]; he is Leonard Welsted, who translated Longinus and had attacked and slandered Pope. See line 375.
9. Edmund Curll, shrewd and disreputable bookseller, published pirated works, works falsely ascribed to reputable writers, scandalous biographies, and other ephemera. Pope had often attacked him and had assigned to him a low role in the Dunciad.

1. I.e., he will attack Pope in the London Journal or write a treatise on theology, as Welsted in fact did.
2. Bernard Lintot, publisher of Pope's Homer and other early works.
3. Go shares.
4. Midas, king of ancient Lydia, had the bad taste to prefer the flute-playing of Pan to that of Apollo, whereupon the god endowed him with ass's ears. It was his barber (not his wife or his minister) who discovered the secret and whispered it into a hole in the earth. The reference to "queen" and "minister" makes it plain that Pope is alluding to George II, Queen Caroline, and Walpole.

That secret to each fool, that he's an ass: 80
The truth once told (and wherefore should we lie?)
The queen of Midas slept, and so may I.
     You think this cruel? take it for a rule,
No creature smarts so little as a fool.
Let peals of laughter, Codrus! round thee break,   85
Thou unconcerned canst hear the mighty crack.
Pit, box, and gallery in convulsions hurled,
Thou stand'st unshook amidst a bursting world.
Who shames a scribbler? break one cobweb through,
He spins the slight, self-pleasing thread anew: 90
Destroy his fib or sophistry, in vain;
The creature's at his dirty work again,
Throned in the center of his thin designs,
Proud of a vast extent of flimsy lines.
Whom have I hurt? has poet yet or peer   95
Lost the arched eyebrow or Parnassian sneer?
And has not Colley[5] still his lord and whore?
His butchers Henley? his freemasons Moore?
Does not one table Bavius[6] still admit?
Still to one bishop Philips seem a wit?   100
Still Sappho[7]——A. Hold! for god's sake—you'll offend.
No names—be calm—learn prudence of a friend.
I too could write, and I am twice as tall;
But foes like these!——P. One flatterer's worse than all.
Of all mad creatures, if the learn'd are right,   105
It is the slaver kills, and not the bite.
A fool quite angry is quite innocent:
Alas! 'tis ten times worse when they repent.
     One dedicates in high heroic prose,
And ridicules beyond a hundred foes;   110
One from all Grub Street[8] will my fame defend,
And, more abusive, calls himself my friend.
This prints my letters,[9] that expects a bribe,
And others roar aloud, "Subscribe, subscribe!"[1]
     There are, who to my person pay their court: 115
I cough like Horace, and, though lean, am short;
Ammon's great son[2] one shoulder had too high,
Such Ovid's nose, and "Sir! you have an eye—"

---

5. Colley Cibber. The laureate John Henley, known as "Orator" Henley, an independent preacher of marked eccentricity, was popular among the lower orders, especially for his elocution.
6. The bad poet alluded to in Virgil's *Eclogue* 3. The "Bishop" is Hugh Boulter, bishop of Armagh; he had employed as his secretary Ambrose Philips (1674–1749), whose insipid and babbling simplicity of manner in poetry earned him the nickname of "Namby-Pamby."
7. Lady Mary Wortley Montagu.
8. A term denoting the whole society of literary,

political, and journalistic hack writers.
9. In 1726 Curll had surreptitiously acquired and published without permission some of Pope's letters to Henry Cromwell.
1. To ensure the financial success of a work, the public was often asked to "subscribe" to it by taking a certain number of copies before printing was undertaken. Pope's Homer was published thus.
2. Alexander the Great. "Ovid's nose": Ovid's family name Naso suggests the Latin word *nasus* ("nose"), hence the pun.

Go on, obliging creatures, make me see
All that disgraced my betters met in me.   120
Say for my comfort, languishing in bed,
"Just so immortal Maro[3] held his head":
And when I die, be sure you let me know
Great Homer died three thousand years ago.
    Why did I write? what sin to me unknown   125
Dipped me in ink, my parents', or my own?
As yet a child, nor yet a fool to fame,
I lisped in numbers, for the numbers came.
I left no calling for this idle trade,
No duty broke, no father disobeyed.   130
The Muse but served to ease some friend, not wife,
To help me through this long disease, my life,
To second, Arbuthnot! thy art and care,
And teach the being you preserved, to bear.[4]
    A. But why then publish? P. Granville the polite,   135
And knowing Walsh, would tell me I could write;
Well-natured Garth inflamed with early praise,
And Congreve loved, and Swift endured my lays;
The courtly Talbot, Somers, Sheffield, read;
Even mitered Rochester would nod the head,   140
And St. John's self (great Dryden's friends before)
With open arms received one poet more.[5]
Happy my studies, when by these approved!
Happier their author, when by these beloved!
From these the world will judge of men and books,   145
Not from the Burnets, Oldmixons, and Cookes.[6]
    Soft were my numbers; who could take offense
While pure description held the place of sense?
Like gentle Fanny's[7] was my flowery theme,
A painted mistress, or a purling stream.   150
Yet then did Gildon[8] draw his venal quill;
I wished the man a dinner, and sat still.
Yet then did Dennis[9] rave in furious fret;
I never answered, I was not in debt.
If want provoked, or madness made them print,   155
I waged no war with Bedlam or the Mint.
    Did some more sober critic come abroad?

3. Virgil.
4. Endure.
5. The purpose of this list is to establish Pope as the successor of Dryden and thus to place him far above his Grub-Street persecutors. George Granville, Lord Lansdowne, poet and statesman; William Walsh, poet and critic; Sir Samuel Garth, physician and mock-epic poet; William Congreve, the playwright; the statesmen Charles Talbot, duke of Shrewsbury; Lord Sommers; John Sheffield, duke of Buckinghamshire; and Francis Atterbury, bishop of Rochester, had all been associated with Dryden in his later years and had all encouraged the young Pope.
6. Thomas Burnet, John Oldmixon, and Thomas Cooke; Pope identifies them in a note as "authors of secret and scandalous history."
7. John, Lord Hervey, whom Pope satirizes in the character of Sporus, lines 305–33 below.
8. Charles Gildon, minor critic and scribbler, who, Pope believed, early attacked him at the instigation of Addison; hence "venal quill."
9. John Dennis (see Essay on Criticism, line 270 and its note).

If wrong, I smiled; if right, I kissed the rod.
Pains, reading, study are their just pretense,
And all they want is spirit, taste, and sense. 160
Commas and points they set exactly right,
And 'twere a sin to rob them of their mite.
Yet ne'er one sprig of laurel graced these ribalds,
From slashing Bentley down to piddling Tibbalds.[1]
Each wight who reads not, and but scans and spells, 165
Each word-catcher that lives on syllables,
Even such small critics some regard may claim,
Preserved in Milton's or in Shakespeare's name.
Pretty! in amber to observe the forms
Of hairs, or straws, or dirt, or grubs, or worms! 170
The things, we know, are neither rich nor rare,
But wonder how the devil they got there.
    Were others angry? I excused them too;
Well might they rage; I gave them but their due.
A man's true merit 'tis not hard to find; 175
But each man's secret standard in his mind,
That casting weight[2] pride adds to emptiness,
This, who can gratify? for who can guess?
The bard[3] whom pilfered pastorals renown,
Who turns a Persian tale for half a crown, 180
Just writes to make his barrenness appear,
And strains from hard-bound brains eight lines a year:
He, who still wanting, though he lives on theft,
Steals much, spends little, yet has nothing left;
And he who now to sense, now nonsense leaning, 185
Means not, but blunders round about a meaning:
And he whose fustian's so sublimely bad,
It is not poetry, but prose run mad:
All these, my modest satire bade translate,
And owned that nine such poets made a Tate.[4] 190
How did they fume, and stamp, and roar, and chafe!
And swear, not Addison himself was safe.
    Peace to all such! but were there one whose fires
True Genius kindles, and fair Fame inspires;
Blessed with each talent and each art to please, 195
And born to write, converse, and live with ease:
Should such a man, too fond to rule alone,
Bear, like the Turk, no brother near the throne;

1. Richard Bentley (1662–1742), the eminent classical scholar, seemed to both Pope and Swift the perfect type of the pedant: he is called "slashing" because, in his edition of *Paradise Lost* (1732), he had set in square brackets all passages which he disliked on the grounds they had been slipped into the poem without the blind poet's knowledge. Lewis Theobald (1688–1744), whose minute learning in Elizabethan literature had enabled him to expose Pope's defects as an editor of Shakespeare in 1726.

Pope made him King of the Dunces in the *Dunciad* (1728).
2. The weight that turns the scale; here, the "deciding factor."
3. Ambrose Philips, Pope's rival in pastoral poetry in 1709, when their pastorals were published in Tonson's sixth *Miscellany*. Philips had also translated some Persian tales. Cf. line 100.
4. Nahum Tate (1652–1715), poet laureate (1692–1715). His popular rewriting of Shakespeare's's *King*

View him with scornful, yet with jealous eyes,
And hate for arts that caused himself to rise;   200
Damn with faint praise, assent with civil leer,
And without sneering, teach the rest to sneer;
Willing to wound, and yet afraid to strike,
Just hint a fault, and hesitate dislike;
Alike reserved to blame or to commend,   205
A timorous foe, and a suspicious friend;
Dreading even fools; by flatterers besieged,
And so obliging that he ne'er obliged;
Like Cato, give his little senate[5] laws,
And sit attentive to his own applause;   210
While wits and Templars[6] every sentence raise,
And wonder with a foolish face of praise—
Who but must laugh, if such a man there be?
Who would not weep, if Atticus[7] were he?
    What though my name stood rubric[8] on the walls   215
Or plastered posts, with claps, in capitals?
Or smoking forth, a hundred hawkers' load,
On wings of winds came flying all abroad?
I sought no homage from the race that write;
I kept, like Asian monarchs, from their sight: 220
Poems I heeded (now berhymed so long)
No more than thou, great George! a birthday song.
I ne'er with wits or witlings passed my days
To spread about the itch of verse and praise;
Nor like a puppy daggled through the town   225
To fetch and carry sing-song up and down;
Nor at rehearsals sweat, and mouthed, and cried,
With handkerchief and orange at my side;
But sick of fops, and poetry, and prate,
To Bufo[9] left the whole Castalian state.   230
    Proud as Apollo on his forkèd hill,[1]
Sat full-blown Bufo, puffed by every quill;
Fed with soft dedication all day long,
Horace and he went hand in hand in song.
His library (where busts of poets dead   235
And a true Pindar stood without a head)
Received of wits an undistinguished race,

Lear provided a happy ending; he wrote most of part 2 of *Absalom and Achitophel*. The line refers to the old adage that it takes nine tailors to make one man.
5. Addison's tragedy *Cato* had been a sensational success in 1713. Pope had written the prologue, in which occurs the line, "While Cato gives his little senate laws." The satirical reference here is to Addison in the role of arbiter of taste among his friends and admirers, mostly Whigs, at Button's Coffee House. It was these people who had worked against the success of Pope's Homer.

6. Law students.
7. Pope's satiric pseudonym for Addison; Atticus (109–32 B.C.) was a wealthy man of letters and a friend of Cicero, known as a wise and disinterested man.
8. In red letters. "Claps": posters.
9. A type of tasteless patron of the arts. (*Bufo* means "toad" in Latin). The Castalian spring on Mt. Parnassus was sacred to Apollo and the Muses.
1. Mt. Parnassus had two peaks, one sacred to Apollo, one to Bacchus.

Who first his judgment asked, and then a place:
Much they extolled his pictures, much his seat,[2]
And flattered every day, and some days eat: 240
Till grown more frugal in his riper days,
He paid some bards with port, and some with praise;
To some a dry rehearsal was assigned,
And others (harder still) he paid in kind.
Dryden alone (what wonder?) came not nigh;   245
Dryden alone escaped this judging eye:
But still the great have kindness in reserve;
He helped to bury whom he helped to starve.
     May some choice patron bless each gray goose quill!
May every Bavius have his Bufo still!   250
So when a statesman wants a day's defense,
Or Envy holds a whole week's war with Sense,
Or simple Pride for flattery makes demands,
May dunce by dunce be whistled off my hands!
Blessed be the great! for those they take away,   255
And those they left me—for they left me Gay;[3]
Left me to see neglected genius bloom,
Neglected die, and tell it on his tomb;
Of all thy blameless life the sole return
My verse, and Queensberry weeping o'er thy urn!   260
Oh, let me live my own, and die so too!
("To live and die is all I have to do")[4]
Maintain a poet's dignity and ease,
And see what friends, and read what books I please;
Above a patron, though I condescend   265
Sometimes to call a minister my friend.
I was not born for courts or great affairs;
I pay my debts, believe, and say my prayers,
Can sleep without a poem in my head,
Nor know if Dennis be alive or dead,   270
     Why am I asked what next shall see the light?
Heavens! was I born for nothing but to write?
Has life no joys for me? or (to be grave)
Have I no friend to serve, no soul to save?
"I found him close with Swift"—"Indeed? no doubt"   275
Cries prating Balbus, "something will come out."
'Tis all in vain, deny it as I will.
"No, such a genius never can lie still,"
And then for mine obligingly mistakes
The first lampoon Sir Will or Bubo makes.[5]   280

2. Pronounced *sate*, and rhymed in next line with
"eat" *(ate.) Seat* means "estate."
3. John Gay (1685–1732), author of the *Beggar's
Opera* (1728) and other delightful works, dear friend
of Swift and Pope. His failure to obtain patronage
from the court intensified Pope's hostility to the
Whig administration and the queen. Gay spent the
last years of his life under the protection of the
duke and duchess of Queensberry.
4. A quotation from John Denham's poem, *Of
Prudence.*
5. Sir William Yonge, Whig politician and poetaster; George Bubb ("Bubo") Dodington was a
Whig patron of letters.

Poor guiltless I! and can I choose but smile,
When every coxcomb knows me by my style?
    Cursed be the verse, how well soe'er it flow,
That tends to make one worthy man my foe,
Give Virtue scandal, Innocence a fear,   285
Or from the soft-eyed virgin steal a tear!
But he who hurts a harmless neighbor's peace,
Insults fallen worth, or Beauty in distress,
Who loves a lie, lame Slander helps about,
Who writes a libel, or who copies out: 290
That fop whose pride affects a patron's name,
Yet absent, wounds an author's honest fame;
Who can your merit selfishly approve,
And show the sense of it without the love;
Who has the vanity to call you friend,   295
Yet wants the honor, injured, to defend;
Who tells whate'er you think, whate'er you say,
And, if he lie not, must at least betray:
Who to the dean and silver bell can swear,
And sees at Cannons what was never there:[6]   300
Who reads but with a lust to misapply,
Make satire a lampoon, and fiction, lie:
A lash like mine no honest man shall dread,
But all such babbling blockheads in his stead.
    Let Sporus[7] tremble—— A. What? that thing of silk,   305
Sporus, that mere white curd of ass's milk?[8]
Satire or sense, alas! can Sporus feel?
Who breaks a butterfly upon a wheel?
    P. Yet let me flap this bug with gilded wings,
This painted child of dirt, that stinks and stings;   310
Whose buzz the witty and the fair annoys,
Yet wit ne'er tastes, and beauty ne'er enjoys;
So well-bred spaniels civilly delight
In mumbling of the game they dare not bite.
Eternal smiles his emptiness betray,   315
As shallow streams run dimpling all the way.
Whether in florid impotence he speaks,
And, as the prompter breathes, the puppet squeaks;
Or at the ear of Eve,[9] familiar toad,
Half froth, half venom, spits himself abroad,   320
In puns, or politics, or tales, or lies,
Or spite, or smut, or rhymes, or blasphemies.

6. Pope's enemies had accused him of satirizing Cannons, the ostentatious estate of the duke of Chandos, in his description of Timon's villa in the *Epistle to Burlington*. This Pope quite justly denied. The bell of Timon's chapel was of silver, and there preached a dean who "never mentions Hell to ears polite."
7. John, Lord Hervey, effeminate courtier and confidant of Queen Caroline; see title footnote. The original Sporus was a boy, whom the Emperor Nero publicly married (see Suetonius' life of Nero in *The Twelve Caesars*).
8. Ass's milk was drunk by invalids.
9. "Eve" is the queen. The allusion is to *Paradise Lost* 4.799–809.

His wit all seesaw between *that* and *this*, ⎫
Now high, now low, now master up, now miss, ⎬
And he himself one vile antithesis. ⎭　　　　325
Amphibious thing! that acting either part,
The trifling head or the corrupted heart,
Fop at the toilet, flatterer at the board,
Now trips a lady, and now struts a lord.
Eve's tempter thus the rabbins[1] have expressed,　　　330
A cherub's face, a reptile all the rest;
Beauty that shocks you, parts that none will trust,
Wit that can creep, and pride that licks the dust.
　　Not Fortune's worshiper, nor Fashion's fool,
Not Lucre's madman, nor Ambition's tool,　　　　335
Not proud, nor servile, be one poet's praise,
That if he pleased, he pleased by manly ways:
That flattery, even to kings, he held a shame,
And thought a lie in verse or prose the same:
That not in fancy's maze he wandered long,　　　340
But stooped[2] to truth, and moralized his song:
That not for fame, but Virtue's better end,
He stood the furious foe, the timid friend,
The damning critic, half approving wit,
The coxcomb hit, or fearing to be hit;　　　　345
Laughed at the loss of friends he never had,
The dull, the proud, the wicked, and the mad;
The distant threats of vengeance on his head,
The blow unfelt, the tear he never shed;
The tale revived, the lie so oft o'erthrown,　　　350
The imputed trash, and dullness not his own;
The morals blackened when the writings 'scape,
The libeled person, and the pictured shape;[3]
Abuse on all he loved, or loved him, spread,
A friend in exile, or a father dead;　　　　355
The whisper, that to greatness still too near,
Perhaps yet vibrates on his Sovereign's ear—
Welcome for thee, fair Virtue! all the past!
For thee, fair Virtue! welcome even the last!
　　A. But why insult the poor, affront the great?　　　360
P. A knave's a knave to me in every state:
Alike my scorn, if he succeed or fail,
Sporus at court, or Japhet[4] in a jail,
A hireling scribbler, or a hireling peer,
Knight of the post[5] corrupt, or of the shire,　　　365
If on a pillory, or near a throne,
He gain his prince's ear, or lose his own.
　　Yet soft by nature, more a dupe than wit,

---

1. Scholars of and authorities on Jewish law and
doctrine.
2. The falcon is said to "stoop" to its prey when it
swoops down and seizes it in flight.

3. Pope's deformity was frequently ridiculed and
occasionally caricatured.
4. Japhet Crook, a notorious forger.
5. One who lives by selling false evidence.

Sappho[6] can tell you how this man was bit:
This dreaded satirist Dennis will confess   370
Foe to his pride, but friend to his distress:[7]
So humble, he has knocked at Tibbald's door,
Has drunk with Cibber, nay, has rhymed for Moore.
Full ten years slandered, did he once reply?
Three thousand suns went down on Welsted's lie.   375
To please a mistress one aspersed his life;
He lashed him not, but let her be his wife.
Let Budgell charge low Grub Street on his quill,
And write whate'er he pleased, except his will;[8]
Let the two Curlls of town and court,[9] abuse   380
His father, mother, body, soul, and muse.
Yet why? that father held it for a rule,
It was a sin to call our neighbor fool;
That harmless mother thought no wife a whore:
Hear this, and spare his family, James Moore!   385
Unspotted names, and memorable long,
If there be force in virtue, or in song.
     Of gentle blood (part shed in honor's cause,
While yet in Britain honor had applause)
Each parent sprung—— A. What fortune, pray?—— P. Their own,
And better got than Bestia's[1] from the throne.   391
Born to no pride, inheriting no strife,
Nor marrying discord in a noble wife,
Stranger to civil and religious rage,
The good man walked innoxious through his age.   395
No courts he saw, no suits would ever try,
Nor dared an oath,[2] nor hazarded a lie.
Unlearn'd, he knew no schoolman's subtle art,
No language but the language of the heart.
By nature honest, by experience wise,   400
Healthy by temperance, and by exercise;
His life, though long, to sickness passed unknown,
His death was instant, and without a groan.
Oh, grant me thus to live, and thus to die!
Who sprung from kings shall know less joy than I.   405
     O friend! may each domestic bliss be thine!
Be no unpleasing melancholy mine:
Me, let the tender office long engage,
To rock the cradle of reposing Age,
With lenient arts extend a mother's breath,   410

---

6. Lady Mary Wortley Montagu. "Bit": taken in; deceived.
7. Pope wrote the prologue to Cibber's *Provoked Husband* when that play was performed for Dennis's benefit, shortly before the old critic died.
8. Eustace Budgell attacked the *Grub Street Journal* for publishing what he took to be a squib by Pope charging him with having forged the will of Dr. Matthew Tindal.

9. I.e., the publisher and Lord Hervey.
1. Probably the duke of Marlborough, whose vast fortune was made through the favor of Queen Anne. The actual Bestia was a corrupt Roman consul.
2. As a Catholic, Pope's father refused to take the Oaths of Allegiance and Supremacy, and the oath against the Pope. He thus rendered himself vulnerable to the many repressive anti-Catholic laws then in force.

Make Languor smile, and smooth the bed of Death,
Explore the thought, explain the asking eye,
And keep a while one parent from the sky![3]
On cares like these if length of days attend,
May Heaven, to bless those days, preserve my friend,   415
Preserve him social, cheerful, and serene,
And just as rich as when he served a Queen![4]
A. Whether that blessing be denied or given,
Thus far was right—the rest belong to Heaven.

1735

The Dunciad: Book the Fourth

The fourth book of *The Dunciad*, Pope's last major work, was originally intended as a continuation of *An Essay on Man*. To Swift, the spiritual ancestor of the poem, Pope confided in 1736 that he was at work on a series of epistles on the uses of human reason and learning, to conclude with "a satire against the misapplication of all these, exemplified by pictures, characters, and examples." But the epistles never appeared; instead, the satire grew until it took their place. As Pope surveyed England in his last years, the complex literary and social order that had sustained him seemed to be crumbling. It was a time for desperate measures, for satire. And the means of retribution was at hand, in the structure of Pope's own *Dunciad*, the long work that had already impaled so many enemies.

The first *Dunciad*, published in three books in 1728, is a mock-epic reply to Pope's critics and other petty authors. Its hero and victim, Lewis Theobald, had attacked Pope's edition of Shakespeare (1725); other victims had offended Pope either by personal abuse or simply by ineptitude. Inspired by Dryden's *Mac Flecknoe*, the *Dunciad* celebrates the triumph of the hordes of Grub Street. Indeed, so many obscure hacks were mentioned that a *Dunciad Variorum* (1729) was soon required, in which mock-scholarly notes identify the victims, "since it is only in this monument that they must expect to survive." But a modern reader need not catch every reference to enjoy the dazzling wit of the poem, or the sheer sense of fun with which Pope remakes the London literary world into a tiny insane fairground of his own.

The New Dunciad (1742), however, plays a far more serious game: here Pope takes aim at the rot of the whole social fabric. The satire goes deep, and works at many levels. For convenience, these may be divided into four. 1) Politics: From 1721 to 1742 England had been ruled by the Whig supremacy of Robert Walpole, First Minister. To Pope and his circle, the immensely powerful Walpole (no friend of poets) seemed a crass and greedy vulgarian, like his monarch George II. It is no accident, in the kingdom of the *Dunciad*, that Dulness personified sits on a throne. 2) Society: Just as the action of the *Aeneid* had been the removal of the empire of Troy to Latium, the action of the *Dunciad*, according to Pope, is "the removal of the empire of Dulness from the City of London to the polite world, Westminster"; that is,

---

3. Pope was a tender and devoted son. His mother had died in 1733, and the earliest version of these lines dates from 1731, when the poet was nursing her through a serious illness.

4. Pope alludes to the fact that Arbuthnot, a man of strict probity, left the queen's service no wealthier than when he entered it.

the abdication of civility in favor of commerce and financial interests. In modern England authors write for money, and ministers govern for profit; conspicuous consumption (especially the consumption of paper by scribblers) has replaced the old values of the yeoman and the aristocrat. In 1743 Pope revised the original *Dunciad*, substituting the actor and poet laureate Colley Cibber for Theobald as the hero, and incorporating *The New Dunciad* as book four (the version printed here). Dulness, he implies, has achieved her final triumph; Cibber is laureate in England. 3) Education: The word "dunce" is derived from the scholastic philosopher John Duns Scotus (ca. 1265–1308), whose name had come to stand for silly and useless subtlety, logical hair-splitting. Pope, as an heir of the renaissance, believes that the central subject of education must always be its relevance for human behavior: "The proper study of mankind is Man," and moral philosophy, the relation of men to each other and to the world, should be the teacher's first and last concern. By contrast, Dunces waste their time on grammar (words alone) or the "science" of the collector (things alone); they never comprehend that word and thing, like spirit and matter, are essentially dead unless they join. 4) Religion: At its deepest level, the subject of the *Dunciad* is the undoing of God's creation. Many passages from Book Four echo *Paradise Lost*, and one of Pope's starting places seems to be Satan's threat (*Paradise Lost* 2.968–87) to return the world to its original darkness, chaos, and ancient night. The *Dunciad* ends in a great apocalypse, with a yawn that signals the death of *Logos*; as words have become meaningless, so has the whole creation, which the Lord called forth with words. Here Pope invokes, with terrifying intensity, the old idea that God was the first poet, whose poem was the world, and suggests that the sickness of the word has infected all nature. But there is one consolation: out of non-art itself, out of matter without spirit and substance without essence, the poet creates his own final artistic triumph, and makes a poem.

From The Dunciad

From *Book the Fourth*

Yet, yet a moment, one dim ray of light
Indulge, dread Chaos, and eternal Night!
Of darkness visible[1] so much be lent,
As half to show, half veil the deep intent.
Yet Powers![2] whose mysteries restored I sing,   5
To whom Time bears me on his rapid wing,
Suspend a while your force inertly strong,
Then take at once the poet and the song.
   Now flamed the Dog-star's[3] unpropitious ray,
Smote every brain, and withered every bay,[4]   10
Sick was the sun, the owl forsook his bower,

---

1. Cf. *Paradise Lost* 1.63.
2. Chaos and Night, invoked in place of the Muse, since "the restoration of their empire is the action of the poem" [Pope].
3. Sirius, associated with the heat of summer and the madness of poets (see *Epistle to Dr. Arbuthnot*, line 3).
4. The laurel, whose garlands are bestowed on poets.

The moon-struck prophet felt the madding hour:
Then rose the seed[5] of Chaos, and of Night,
To blot out Order, and extinguish Light,
Of dull and venal a new world to mold,   15
And bring Saturnian[6] days of lead and gold.
　　She mounts the throne: her head a cloud concealed,
In broad effulgence all below revealed,
('Tis thus aspiring Dulness ever shines)
Soft on her lap her Laureate son[7] reclines.   20
　　Beneath her foot-stool, Science groans in chains,
And Wit dreads exile, penalties and pains.
There foamed rebellious Logic, gagged and bound,
There, stripped, fair Rhetoric languished on the ground;
His blunted arms by Sophistry are born,   25
And shameless Billingsgate[8] her robes adorn.
Morality, by her false guardians drawn,
Chicane in furs, and Casuistry in lawn,[9]
Gasps, as they straighten at each end the cord,
And dies, when Dulness gives her Page[1] the word.   30

[THE EDUCATOR]

　　Now crowds on crowds around the Goddess press,   135
Each eager to present the first Address.[2]
Dunce scorning dunce beholds the next advance,
But fop shows fop superior complaisance.
When lo! a Specter[3] rose, whose index-hand
Held forth the virtue of the dreadful wand;   140
His beavered brow a birchen garland wears,[4]
Dropping with infant's blood, and mother's tears.
O'er every vein a shuddering horror runs;
Eton and Winton shake through all their sons.
All flesh is humbled, Westminster's bold race[5]   145
Shrink, and confess the Genius[6] of the place:
The pale boy-Senator yet tingling stands,
And holds his breeches close with both his hands.
　　Then thus. "Since Man from beast by words is known,
Words are Man's province, words we teach alone.   150

5. The Goddess Dulness.
6. Saturn ruled during the golden age; the new age of "gold" will be re-established by the dull and venal.
7. Colley Cibber, the poet laureate.
8. Fishmarket slang, which now covers the noble science of rhetoric.
9. Chicanery (legal trickery) wears the ermine robe of a judge; casuistry wears the linen sleeves of a bishop.
1. Sir Francis Page, a notorious "hanging judge"; court page, used to strangle criminals in Turkey; page of writing on which a dull author "kills" moral

sentiments.
2. The Goddess, newly enthroned, is receiving petitions and congratulations.
3. The ghost of Dr. Busby, stern headmaster of Westminster School.
4. He wears a hat (beaver) and a garland of birch twigs, used for flogging. "Wand": cane used for beating.
5. Alumni of Westminster School, with a play on the justices and members of Parliament who meet at Westminster Hall.
6. I.e., admit that Dr. Busby is the presiding deity (Genius).

When reason doubtful, like the Samian letter,[7]
Points him two ways, the narrower is the better.
Placed at the door of learning, youth to guide,
We never suffer it to stand too wide.
To ask, to guess, to know, as they commence,   155
As fancy opens the quick springs of sense,
We ply the memory, we load the brain,
Bind rebel wit, and double chain on chain,
Confine the thought, to exercise the breath;[8]
And keep them in the pale of words till death.   160
Whate'er the talents, or howe'er designed,
We hang one jingling padlock on the mind:
A poet the first day, he dips his quill;
And what the last? a very poet still.
Pity! the charm works only in our wall,   165
Lost, lost too soon in yonder House or Hall."[9]

[THE CARNATION AND THE BUTTERFLY]

Then thick as locusts blackening all the ground,
A tribe,[1] with weeds and shells fantastic crowned,
Each with some wondrous gift approached the Power,
A nest, a toad, a fungus, or a flower.   400
But far the foremost, two, with earnest zeal,
And aspect ardent to the throne appeal.
The first thus opened: "Hear thy suppliant's call,
Great Queen, and common Mother of us all!
Fair from its humble bed I reared this flower,   405
Suckled, and cheer'd, with air, and sun, and shower,
Soft on the paper ruff its leaves I spread,
Bright with the gilded button tipped its head,
Then throned in glass, and named it CAROLINE:[2]
Each maid cried, charming! and each youth, divine!   410
Did Nature's pencil ever blend such rays,
Such varied light in one promiscuous blaze?
Now prostrate! dead! behold that Caroline:
No maid cries, charming! and no youth, divine!
And lo the wretch! whose vile, whose insect lust   415
Laid this gay daughter of the Spring in dust.
Oh punish him, or to th' Elysian shades
Dismiss my soul, where no carnation fades."
He ceased, and wept. With innocence of mien,
The accused stood forth, and thus addressed the Queen.   420

7. The letter Y, which Pythagoras (a native of Samos) used as an emblem of the different roads of virtue and vice.
8. Students are taught only to recite the classic poets by heart.
9. The House of Commons and Westminster Hall, where law cases were heard. The eloquence learned by rote disappears on occasions for public speaking.
1. The Virtuosi, or amateur scientists and collectors.
2. Queen Caroline, an enthusiastic gardener, is an appropriate choice to lend her name to the perfect carnation.

"Of all th' enameled race,[3] whose silvery wing
Waves to the tepid zephyrs of the spring,
Or swims along the fluid atmosphere,
Once brightest shined this child of heat and air.
I saw, and started from its vernal bower   425
The rising game, and chased from flower to flower.
It fled, I followed; now in hope, now pain;
It stopped, I stopped; it moved, I moved again.
At last it fixed, 'twas on what plant it pleased,
And where it fixed, the beauteous bird[4] I seized: 430
Rose or carnation was below my care;
I meddle, Goddess! only in my sphere.
I tell the naked fact without disguise,
And, to excuse it, need but show the prize;
Whose spoils this paper offers to your eye,   435
Fair even in death! this peerless Butterfly."
    "My sons!" she answered, "both have done your parts;
Live happy both, and long promote our arts.
But hear a mother, when she recommends
To your fraternal care, our sleeping friends.   440
The common soul, of heaven's more frugal make,
Serves but to keep fools pert, and knaves awake:
A drowsy watchman, that just gives a knock,
And breaks our rest, to tell us what's a clock.[5]
Yet by some object every brain is stirred;   445
The dull may waken to a hummingbird;
The most recluse, discreetly opened, find
Congenial matter in the cockle-kind;[6]
The mind, in metaphysics at a loss,
May wander in a wilderness of moss;   450
The head that turns at super-lunar things,
Poised with a tail, may steer on Wilkins' wings.[7]
    "O! would the Sons of Men once think their eyes
And reason given them but to study *flies*![8]
See Nature in some partial narrow shape,   455
And let the Author of the whole escape:
Learn but to trifle; or, who most observe,
To wonder at their Maker, not to serve."

[THE TRIUMPH OF DULNESS]

Then blessing all,[9] "Go children of my care!
To practice now from theory repair.   580

---

3. Colored insects.
4. Insect.
5. Eighteenth-century watchmen kept guard in the streets and announced the hours.
6. Cockle-shells, popular with collectors, as were hummingbirds and varieties of moss.
7. John Wilkins (1614–1672), one of the founders of the Royal Society, had speculated "that a man may be able to fly, by the application of wings to his own body."
8. Cf. *An Essay on Man*. 1.189–96: "Say what the use, were finer optics given / T' inspect a mite, not comprehend the heaven?"
9. Having conferred her titles, Dulness bids each of the rulers of England to indulge in the triviality closest to his heart.

All my commands are easy, short, and full:
My sons! be proud, be selfish, and be dull.
Guard my prerogative, assert my throne:
This nod confirms each privilege your own.
The cap and switch be sacred to his Grace;[1]   585
With staff and pumps[2] the Marquis lead the race;
From stage to stage the licensed[3] Earl may run,
Paired with his fellow-charioteer the Sun;
The learned baron butterflies design,
Or draw to silk Arachne's subtle line;[4]   590
The Judge to dance his brother Sergeant[5] call;
The Senator at cricket urge the ball;
The Bishop stow (pontific luxury!)
An hundred souls of turkeys in a pie;[6]
The sturdy squire to Gallic masters[7] stoop,   595
And drown his lands and manors in a Soup.
Others import yet nobler arts from France,
Teach kings to fiddle, and make senates dance.
Perhaps more high some daring son may soar,[8]
Proud to my list to add one monarch more;   600
And nobly conscious, Princes are but things
Born for First Ministers, as slaves for kings,
Tyrant supreme! shall three estates command,
And MAKE ONE MIGHTY DUNCIAD OF THE LAND!"
    More she had spoke, but yawned—All Nature nods: 605
What mortal can resist the Yawn of Gods?
Churches and chapels instantly it reached;
(St. James's first, for leaden Gilbert[9] preached)
Then catched the schools; the Hall scarce kept awake;
The Convocation gaped,[1] but could not speak: 610
Lost was the Nation's Sense,[2] nor could be found,
While the long solemn unison went round:
Wide, and more wide, it spread o'er all the realm;
Even Palinurus[3] nodded at the helm:
The vapor mild o'er each committee crept;   615
Unfinished treaties in each office slept;
And chiefless armies dozed out the campaign;
And navies yawned for orders on the main.
    O Muse! relate (for you can tell alone,
Wits have short memories, and dunces none)   620
Relate, who first, who last resigned to rest;

1. His Grace, a duke who loves horse-racing, is to use the cap and switch of a jockey.
2. Footmen, who wore pumps (low-cut shoes for running), were matched in races.
3. The license required by the owner of a stage-coach; also, privileged or licentious.
4. A spiderweb.
5. A lawyer or legislative officer; formal ceremonies at the Inns of Court are said to have resembled a country dance, "a call of sergeants."
6. According to Pope, a hundred turkeys had been "not unfrequently deposited in one Pye in the Bishopric of Durham."
7. French chefs.
8. A bold, direct attack on Walpole.
9. Dr. John Gilbert, dean of Exeter.
1. The Convocation, an assembly of clergy consulting on ecclesiastical affairs, had been adjourned since 1717.
2. A term for Parliament.
3. The pilot of Aeneas' ship; here Walpole.

Whose heads she partly, whose completely blessed;
What charms could faction, what ambition lull,
The venal quiet, and entrance the dull;
'Till drowned was sense, and shame, and right, and wrong—   625
O sing, and hush the nations with thy song!

    In vain, in vain,—the all-composing Hour
Resistless falls: The Muse obeys the Power.
She comes! she comes![4] the sable throne behold
Of Night primeval, and of Chaos old!   630
Before her, Fancy's gilded clouds decay,
And all its varying rainbows die away.
Wit shoots in vain its momentary fires,
The meteor drops, and in a flash expires.
As one by one, at dread Medea's strain,   635
The sickening stars fade off the ethereal plain;[5]
As Argus' eyes by Hermes' wand oppressed,
Closed one by one to everlasting rest;[6]
Thus at her felt approach, and secret might,
Art after Art goes out, and all is Night.   640
See skulking Truth to her old cavern fled,[7]
Mountains of casuistry heaped o'er her head!
Philosophy, that leaned on Heaven before,
Shrinks to her second cause,[8] and is no more.
Physic[9] of Metaphysic begs defense,   645
And Metaphysic calls for aid on Sense!
See Mystery[1] to Mathematics fly!
In vain! they gaze, turn giddy, rave, and die.
Religion blushing veils her sacred fires,
And unawares Morality expires.   650
Nor public flame, nor private, dares to shine;
Nor human spark is left, nor glimpse divine!
Lo! thy dread Empire, CHAOS is restored;
Light dies before thy uncreating word:[2]
Thy hand, great Anarch! lets the curtain fall;   655
And Universal Darkness buries All.

1743

---

4. Having triumphed in the contemporary world of affairs, Dulness (like her antitype Christ) has a Second Coming, a prophetic vision in which she extinguishes the light of the arts and sciences.
5. In Seneca's *Medea*, the stars obey the curse of Medea, a magician and avenger.
6. Argus, Hera's 100-eyed watchman, was charmed to sleep and slain by Hermes.
7. "Alluding to the saying of Democritus, that Truth lay at the bottom of a deep well" [Pope's note].

8. Science (philosophy) no longer accepts God as the first cause, or final explanation of how all things came to be; instead, it accepts only the second or material cause, and tries to account for all things by physical principles alone.
9. Natural science in general.
1. A religious truth known only through divine revelation.
2. Cf. God's first creating words in Genesis, "Let there be light."

SAMUEL JOHNSON
1709–1784

1737:	Settles in London.
1747–55:	At work on the *Dictionary*.
1762:	Pensioned by the Crown.
1765:	Edition of Shakespeare.
1779, 1781:	*Lives of the Poets*.

Johnson was famous as a talker in his own time, and his conversation (preserved by James Boswell and others) has been famous ever since. But his wisdom survives above all in his writings: a few superb poems; the grave *Rambler* essays, which established his reputation as a stylist and a moralist; the lessons about life in *Rasselas* and the *Lives of the Poets*; and literary criticism that ranks among the best in English. The virtues of the talk and the writings are the same. They come hot from a mind well stored with knowledge, searingly honest, humane, and quick to seize the unexpected but appropriate image of truth. Johnson's wit is timeless, for it deals with the great facts of human experience, with hope and happiness and loss and duty and the fear of death. Whatever topic he addresses, whatever the form in which he writes, he holds to one commanding purpose: to see life as it is.

Two examples must suffice here. When Mrs. Anna Williams wondered why a man should make a beast of himself through drunkenness, Johnson answered that "he who makes a beast of himself gets rid of the pain of being a man." In this reply Mrs. Williams' tired metaphor is so charged with an awareness of the dark aspects of human life that it comes almost unbearably alive. Such moments characterize Johnson's writings as well. For instance, in reviewing the book of a fatuous would-be philosopher who blandly explained away the pains of poverty by declaring that a kindly providence compensates the poor by making them more hopeful, more healthy, more capable of relishing small pleasures and less sensitive to small annoyances than the rich, Johnson retorted: "The poor indeed are insensible of many little vexations which sometimes embitter the possessions and pollute the enjoyment of the rich. They are not pained by casual incivility, or mortified by the mutilation of a compliment; but this happiness is like that of the malefactor who ceases to feel the cords that bind him when the pincers are tearing his flesh."

Johnson had himself known the pains of poverty. During his boyhood and youth, his father's financial circumstances steadily worsened, so that he was forced to leave Oxford before he had taken a degree. An early marriage to a well-to-do widow, Elizabeth ("Tetty") Porter, more than twenty years older than he, enabled him to open a school. But the school failed, and he moved to London to make his way as a writer. The years between 1737, when he first arrived there with his pupil David Garrick (later to become the leading actor of his generation), and 1755, when the publication of the *Dictionary* established his reputation, were very difficult. He supported himself at first as best he could by doing hack work for the *Gentleman's Magazine*, but gradually his own original writings began to attract attention.

In 1747 Johnson published the *Plan* of his *Dictionary*, and the next seven years were occupied in compiling it—although he had been sanguine enough to count on finishing it in three years. When in 1748 Dr. Adams, a friend from Oxford days, questioned his ability to carry out such a work alone in so short a time, and reminded him that the *Dictionary* of the French Academy had been compiled by forty academicians working for forty years, Johnson replied with humorous jingoism: "Sir, thus it is. This is the proportion. Let me see; forty times forty is sixteen hundred. As three to sixteen hundred, so is the proportion of an Englishman to a Frenchman."

Johnson's achievement in compiling the *Dictionary* becomes even greater when it is realized that he was writing some of his best essays and poems during the same period, for although the booksellers who published the *Dictionary* paid him what was then the large sum of £1575, it was not enough to enable him to support his household, buy materials, and pay the wages of the six assistants whom he employed year by year until the task was accomplished. He therefore had to exert himself to earn more money by writing. Thus, in 1749, his early tragedy *Irene* (pronounced *I-re-nĕ*) was produced at long last by his old friend Garrick, by then the manager of Drury Lane. The play was not a success, though Johnson made some profit from it. In the same year appeared his finest poem, *The Vanity of Human Wishes*. With the *Rambler* (1750–52) and the *Idler* (1758–60), two series of periodical essays, Johnson found a devoted audience; but his pleasure in success was tempered by the death of his wife in 1752. He never remarried.

Boswell said of the *Rambler* essays that "in no writings whatever can be found more bark and steel [i.e., quinine and iron] for the mind." Moral strength and health; the importance of applying reason to experience; the test of virtue by what we do, not what we say or "feel"; faith in God: these are the centers to which Johnson's moral writings always return. What Johnson uniquely offers us is the quality of his understanding of the human condition, based on wide reading but always ultimately referred to his own passionate and often anguished experience. Such understanding had to be fought for again and again.

Johnson is thought of as the great generalizer, but what gives his generalizations strength is that they are rooted in the particulars of his self-knowledge. He had constantly to fight against what he called "filling the mind" with illusions, in order to avoid the call of duty, his own black melancholy, and the realities of life. The portrait (largely a self-portrait) of Sober in *Idler* 31 is revealing: he occupies his idle hours with crafts and hobbies, and has now taken up chemistry—he "sits and counts the drops as they come from his retort, and forgets that, whilst a drop is falling, a moment flies away." So clear a vision is some distance away from the secure ease of the Addisonian essay.

His theme of themes is expressed in the title of his poem, *The Vanity of Human Wishes*, by which Johnson means the dangerous but all-pervasive illusion of what we now call wishful thinking, the feverish intrusion of desires and hopes that distort reality and lead to false expectations. Almost all of Johnson's major writings—verse satire, moral essay, or the prose fable *Rasselas* (1759)—express this theme. In *Rasselas* it is called "the hunger of imagination, which preys upon life," the seeing of things as one would like them to be, rather than as they are. The travelers who are the fable's protagonists pursue supposed guarantees of happiness; they reflect our naïve hopefulness, against the accumulation of contrary experience, that one choice of life will make us happy forever.

During this time of great activity, Johnson developed his characteristic style: the rotund periods, proceeding through balanced or parallel words; phrases or clauses moving to carefully controlled rhythms, in language that is characteristically general, often Latinate, and frequently polysyllabic. It is a style at the opposite extreme from Swift's simplicity or Addison's neatness. In Johnson's writings this style never becomes obscure or turgid, for even a very complex sentence reveals—as it should—the structure of the thought, and the learned words are always precisely used. While reading early scientists to collect words for the *Dictionary*, he developed a new vocabulary: for example, *obtund, exuberate, fugacity, frigorific*. But he used many of these strange words in conversation as well as in his writings, often with a peculiarly Johnsonian felicity, describing the operations of the mind with a scientific precision.

After Johnson received his pension in 1762, he no longer had to write for a living, and since he held that "no man but a blockhead" ever wrote for any other reason, he produced as little as he decently could during the last twenty years of his life. His edition of Shakespeare, long delayed, was published in 1765, with its fine preface and its fascinating notes. His last important work is the *Lives of the Poets*, which came out in two parts in 1779 and 1781. These biographical and critical prefaces were commissioned by a group of booksellers who had joined together to publish a large collection of the English poets and who wished to give their venture the prestige that it would acquire if Johnson took part in it. The poets to be included (except for four insisted on by Johnson) were selected by the booksellers according to current fashions. We have, therefore, a collection that begins with Cowley and Milton and ends with Gray and that omits poets whom we regard as "standard," such as Chaucer, Spenser, Sidney, Donne, and Marvell.

In the *Lives of the Poets* and in the earlier *Life of Richard Savage* (1744), Johnson did much to advance the art of biography in England. The public had long been familiar with biography as panegyric or as scandalous memoir, and therefore Johnson's insistence on truth, even about the subject's defects, and on concrete, often minute, details was a new departure, disliked by many readers. "The biographical part of literature is what I love most," Johnson said, for he found every biography useful in revealing human nature and the way we all live. His insistence on truth in biography (and knowing that Boswell intended to write his life, he insisted that he should write it truthfully) was due to his conviction that the more truthful such a work is the more useful it will be to all of us who are concerned with the business of living.

The ideal poet, according to Johnson, has a genius for making the familiar things we see every day seem new. The same might be said of Johnson himself as a critic. He is our great champion, in criticism, of common sense and the common reader. Without denying the right of the poet to flights of imagination, he also insists that poems must make sense, please readers, and help us not only to understand the world but to cope with it. Johnson holds poems to the truth, as he sees it: the principles of nature, logic, religion, and morality. Not even Shakespeare can be excused when "he sacrifices virtue to convenience" and "seems to write without any moral purpose." Yet Johnson is no worshiper of authority or mere "correctness." As a critic he is always the empiricist, testing theory, as he tested all notions, by experience. His determination to judge literature by its truth to life, not by abstract rules, is perfectly illustrated by his treatment of the doctrine of the three unities in the Preface to Shakespeare. Johnson is never afraid to state the obvious, whether the lack of human interest in *Paradise Lost* or Shakespeare's temptation by puns. But at its best, as in the praise of Milton or Shakespeare, his criticism engages some of the deepest questions about literature: why it endures, and how it helps us to endure.

For some of the author's revisions while composing *The Vanity of Human Wishes*, see "Poems in Process," below.

The Vanity of Human Wishes[1]

In Imitation of the Tenth Satire of Juvenal

> Let Observation, with extensive view,
> Survey mankind, from China to Peru;
> Remark each anxious toil, each eager strife,
> And watch the busy scenes of crowded life;
> Then say how hope and fear, desire and hate   5
> O'erspread with snares the clouded maze of fate,
> Where wavering man, betrayed by venturous pride
> To tread the dreary paths without a guide,
> As treacherous phantoms in the mist delude,
> Shuns fancied ills, or chases airy good;   10
> How rarely Reason guides the stubborn choice,
> Rules the bold hand, or prompts the suppliant voice;
> How nations sink, by darling schemes oppressed,
> When Vengeance listens to the fool's request.
> Fate wings with every wish the afflictive dart,   15
> Each gift of nature, and each grace of art;
> With fatal heat impetuous courage glows,
> With fatal sweetness elocution flows,
> Impeachment stops the speaker's powerful breath,
> And restless fire precipitates on death.   20
>   But scarce observed, the knowing and the bold
> Fall in the general massacre of gold;
> Wide-wasting pest! that rages unconfined,
> And crowds with crimes the records of mankind;
> For gold his sword the hireling ruffian draws,   25

1. *The Vanity of Human Wishes* is an imitation of Juvenal's *Satire 10*. Although it closely follows the order and the ideas of the Latin poem, it remains a very personal work, for Johnson has used the Roman Stoic's satire as a means of expressing his own sense of the tragic and comic in human life. He has tried to reproduce in English verse the qualities he thought especially Juvenalian: stateliness, pointed sentences, declamatory grandeur. The poem is difficult because of the extreme compactness of the style: every line is forced to convey the greatest possible amount of meaning. Johnson's poetic theory demanded that the poet should deal in the general rather than the particular (cf. his phrase "the grandeur of generality"), but he certainly did not intend that the general should become the merely abstract: observe, for example, how he makes abstract nouns concrete, active, and dramatic by using them as subjects of active and dramatic verbs: "Hate *dogs* their flight, and Insult *mocks* their end" (line 78). But the difficulty of the poem is also related to its theme, the difficulty of seeing anything clearly on this earth. In a world of blindness and illusion, human beings must struggle to find a point of view that will not deceive them, and a happiness that can last.

For gold the hireling judge distorts the laws;
Wealth heaped on wealth, nor truth nor safety buys,
The dangers gather as the treasures rise.
    Let History tell where rival kings command,
And dubious title shakes the madded land,   30
When statutes glean the refuse of the sword,
How much more safe the vassal than the lord;
Low skulks the hind beneath the rage of power,
And leaves the wealthy traitor[2] in the Tower,
Untouched his cottage, and his slumbers sound,   35
Though Confiscation's vultures hover round.
    The needy traveler, serene and gay,
Walks the wild heath, and sings his toil away.
Does envy seize thee? crush the upbraiding joy,
Increase his riches and his peace destroy;   40
New fears in dire vicissitude invade,
The rustling brake[3] alarms, and quivering shade,
Nor light nor darkness bring his pain relief,
One shows the plunder, and one hides the thief.
    Yet still one general cry the skies assails,   45
And gain and grandeur load the tainted gales;
Few know the toiling statesman's fear or care,
The insidious rival and the gaping heir.
    Once more, Democritus,[4] arise on earth,
With cheerful wisdom and instructive mirth,   50
See motley life in modern trappings dressed,
And feed with varied fools the eternal jest:
Thou who couldst laugh where Want enchained Caprice,
Toil crushed Conceit, and man was of a piece;
Where Wealth unloved without a mourner died;   55
And scarce a sycophant was fed by Pride;
Where ne'er was known the form of mock debate,
Or seen a new-made mayor's unwieldy state;
Where change of favorites made no change of laws,
And senates heard before they judged a cause;   60
How wouldst thou shake at Britain's modish tribe,
Dart the quick taunt, and edge the piercing gibe?
Attentive truth and nature to descry,
And pierce each scene with philosophic eye,
To thee were solemn toys or empty show   65
The robes of pleasures and the veils of woe:
All aid the farce, and all thy mirth maintain,
Whose joys are causeless, or whose griefs are vain.
    Such was the scorn that filled the sage's mind,
Renewed at every glance on human kind;   70
How just that scorn ere yet thy voice declare,

2. Johnson first wrote "bonny traitor," recalling the Jacobite uprising of 1745 and the execution of four of its Scot leaders. "Hind": peasant.
3. Thicket.

4. A Greek philosopher of the late 5th century B.C., remembered as the "laughing philosopher" because men's follies only moved him to mirth.

Search every state, and canvass every prayer.
    Unnumbered suppliants crowd Preferment's gate,
Athirst for wealth, and burning to be great;
Delusive Fortune hears the incessant call,   75
They mount, they shine, evaporate, and fall.
On every stage the foes of peace attend,
Hate dogs their flight, and Insult mocks their end.
Love ends with hope, the sinking statesman's door
Pours in the morning worshiper no more;[5]   80
For growing names the weekly scribbler lies,
To growing wealth the dedicator flies;
From every room descends the painted face,
That hung the bright palladium[6] of the place;
And smoked in kitchens, or in auctions sold,   85
To better features yields the frame of gold;
For now no more we trace in every line
Heroic worth, benevolence divine:
The form distorted justifies the fall,
And Detestation rids the indignant wall.   90
    But will not Britain hear the last appeal,
Sign her foes' doom, or guard her favorites' zeal?
Through Freedom's sons no more remonstrance rings,
Degrading nobles and controlling kings;
Our supple tribes repress their patriot throats,   95
And ask no questions but the price of votes,
With weekly libels and septennial ale.[7]
Their wish is full to riot and to rail.
    In full-blown dignity, see Wolsey[8] stand,
Law in his voice, and fortune in his hand: 100
To him the church, the realm, their powers consign,
Through him the rays of regal bounty shine;
Turned by his nod the stream of honor flows,
His smile alone security bestows:
Still to new heights his restless wishes tower,   105
Claim leads to claim, and power advances power;
Till conquest unresisted ceased to please,
And rights submitted, left him none to seize.
At length his sovereign frowns—the train of state
Mark the keen glance, and watch the sign to hate.   110
Where'er he turns, he meets a stranger's eye,
His suppliants scorn him, and his followers fly;
At once is lost the pride of awful state,
The golden canopy, the glittering plate,

---

5. Statesmen gave interviews and received friends and petitioners at levees, or morning receptions.
6. An image of Pallas Athena, which fell from heaven and was preserved at Troy. Not until it was stolen by Diomedes could the city fall to the Greeks.
7. Ministers and even the king freely bought support by bribing members of Parliament, who in turn won elections by buying votes. "Weekly libels":

politically motivated lampoons published in the weekly newspapers; "septennial ale": the ale given away by candidates at parliamentary elections, held at least every seven years.
8. Thomas Cardinal Wolsey (ca. 1475–1530), lord chancellor and favorite of Henry VIII. Shakespeare dramatized his fall in *Henry VIII*.

The regal palace, the luxurious board,   115
The liveried army, and the menial lord.
With age, with cares, with maladies oppressed,
He seeks the refuge of monastic rest.
Grief aids disease, remembered folly stings,
And his last sighs reproach the faith of kings.   120
      Speak thou, whose thoughts at humble peace repine,
Shall Wolsey's wealth, with Wolsey's end be thine?
Or liv'st thou now, with safer pride content,
The wisest justice on the banks of Trent?
For why did Wolsey, near the steeps of fate,   125
On weak foundations raise the enormous weight?
Why but to sink beneath misfortune's blow,
With louder ruin to the gulfs below?
      What gave great Villiers[9] to the assassin's knife,
And fixed disease on Harley's closing life?   130
What murdered Wentworth, and what exiled Hyde,
By kings protected and to kings allied?
What but their wish indulged in courts to shine,
And power too great to keep or to resign?
      When first the college rolls receive his name,   135
The young enthusiast quits his ease for fame;
Resistless burns the fever of renown
Caught from the strong contagion of the gown:
O'er Bodley's dome his future labors spread,
And Bacon's mansion trembles o'er his head.[1]   140
Are these thy views? proceed, illustrious youth,
And Virtue guard thee to the throne of Truth!
Yet should thy soul indulge the generous heat,
Till captive Science yields her last retreat;
Should Reason guide thee with her brightest ray,   145
And pour on misty Doubt resistless day;
Should no false kindness lure to loose delight,
Nor praise relax, nor difficulty fright;
Should tempting Novelty thy cell refrain,
And Sloth effuse her opiate fumes in vain;   150
Should Beauty blunt on fops her fatal dart,
Nor claim the triumph of a lettered heart;
Should no disease thy torpid veins invade,
Nor Melancholy's phantoms haunt thy shade;
Yet hope not life from grief or danger free,   155
Nor think the doom of man reversed for thee:

9. George Villiers, 1st duke of Buckingham, favorite of James I and Charles I, was assassinated in 1628. Mentioned in the following lines are: Robert Harley, earl of Oxford, chancellor of the exchequer and later lord treasurer under Queen Anne (1710–14), impeached and imprisoned by the Whigs in 1715; Thomas Wentworth, earl of Strafford, intimate and adviser of Charles I, impeached by the Long Parliament and executed 1641; Edward Hyde, earl of Clarendon ("to kings allied" because his daughter married James, duke of York), lord chancellor under Charles II; impeached in 1667, he fled to the Continent.
1. "Bodley's dome" is the Bodleian Library, Oxford. Roger Bacon (ca. 1214–1294), scientist and philosopher, taught at Oxford, where his study, according to tradition, would collapse when a man greater than he should appear at Oxford.

Deign on the passing world to turn thine eyes,
And pause a while from letters, to be wise;
There mark what ills the scholar's life assail,
Toil, envy, want, the patron,[2] and the jail.   160
See nations slowly wise, and meanly just,
To buried merit raise the tardy bust.
If dreams yet flatter, once again attend,
Hear Lydiat's life, and Galileo's end.[3]

Nor deem, when Learning her last prize bestows,   165
The glittering eminence exempt from foes;
See when the vulgar 'scapes, despised or awed,
Rebellion's vengeful talons seize on Laud.[4]
From meaner minds though smaller fines content,
The plundered palace, or sequestered rent;[5]   170
Marked out by dangerous parts he meets the shock,
And fatal Learning leads him to the block:
Around his tomb let Art and Genius weep,
But hear his death, ye blockheads, hear and sleep.

The festal blazes, the triumphal show,   175
The ravished standard, and the captive foe,
The senate's thanks, the gazette's pompous tale,
With force resistless o'er the brave prevail.
Such bribes the rapid Greek[6] o'er Asia whirled,
For such the steady Romans shook the world;   180
For such in distant lands the Britons shine,
And stain with blood the Danube or the Rhine;
This power has praise that virtue scarce can warm,
Till fame supplies the universal charm.
Yet Reason frowns on War's unequal game,   185
Where wasted nations raise a single name,
And mortgaged states their grandsires' wreaths regret
From age to age in everlasting debt;
Wreaths which at last the dear-bought right convey
To rust on medals, or on stones decay.   190

On what foundation stands the warrior's pride,
How just his hopes, let Swedish Charles[7] decide;
A frame of adamant, a soul of fire,
No dangers fright him, and no labors tire;
O'er love, o'er fear, extends his wide domain,   195
Unconquered lord of pleasure and of pain;
No joys to him pacific scepters yield,

---

2. In the first edition, "garret." For the reason of
the change see Boswell's *Life of Johnson*.
3. Thomas Lydiat (1572–1646), Oxford scholar,
died impoverished because of his Royalist sympathies. Galileo (1564–1642), the famous astronomer, was imprisoned as a heretic by the Inquisition
in 1633; he died blind.
4. Appointed archbishop of Canterbury by Charles
I, William Laud followed rigorously high-church
policies and was executed by order of the Long
Parliament in 1645.

5. During the Commonwealth, the estates of many
Royalists were pillaged and their incomes confiscated ("sequestered") by the state.
6. Alexander the Great.
7. Charles XII of Sweden (1682–1718). Defeated
by the Russians at Pultowa (1709), he escaped to
Turkey and tried to form an alliance against Russia
with the sultan. Returning to Sweden, he attacked
Norway and was killed in the attack on Fredriks-
hald.

War sounds the trump, he rushes to the field;
Behold surrounding kings their powers combine,
And one capitulate, and one resign;[8]   200
Peace courts his hand, but spreads her charms in vain;
"Think nothing gained," he cries, "till naught remain,
On Moscow's walls till Gothic standards fly,
And all be mine beneath the polar sky."
The march begins in military state,   205
And nations on his eye suspended wait;
Stern Famine guards the solitary coast,
And Winter barricades the realms of Frost;
He comes, nor want nor cold his course delay—
Hide, blushing Glory, hide Pultowa's day: 210
The vanquished hero leaves his broken bands,
And shows his miseries in distant lands;
Condemned a needy supplicant to wait,
While ladies interpose, and slaves debate.
But did not Chance at length her error mend?   215
Did no subverted empire mark his end?
Did rival monarchs give the fatal wound?
Or hostile millions press him to the ground?
His fall was destined to a barren strand,
A petty fortress, and a dubious hand;   220
He left the name at which the world grew pale,
To point a moral, or adorn a tale.
    All times their scenes of pompous woes afford,
From Persia's tyrant to Bavaria's lord.[9]
In gay hostility, and barbarous pride,   225
With half mankind embattled at his side,
Great Xerxes comes to seize the certain prey,
And starves exhausted regions in his way;
Attendant Flattery counts his myriads o'er,
Till counted myriads soothe his pride no more;   230
Fresh praise is tried till madness fires his mind,
The waves he lashes, and enchains the wind;
New powers are claimed, new powers are still bestowed,
Till rude resistance lops the spreading god;
The daring Greeks deride the martial show,   235
And heap their valleys with the gaudy foe;
The insulted sea with humbler thought he gains,
A single skiff to speed his flight remains;
The encumbered oar scarce leaves the dreaded coast
Through purple billows and a floating host.   240
    The bold Bavarian, in a luckless hour,
Tries the dread summits of Caesarean power,

---

8. Frederick IV of Denmark capitulated to Charles in 1700; Augustus II of Poland resigned his throne to Charles in 1704.
9. Xerxes ("Persia's tyrant") invaded Greece and was totally defeated in the sea battle off Salamis,
480 B.C.; the Elector Charles Albert ("Bavaria's Lord") caused the War of the Austrian Succession (1740–48) when he contested the crown of the Empire with Maria Theresa ("Fair Austria" in line 245).

With unexpected legions bursts away,
And sees defenseless realms receive his sway;
Short sway! fair Austria spreads her mournful charms,   245
The queen, the beauty, sets the world in arms;
From hill to hill the beacon's rousing blaze
Spreads wide the hope of plunder and of praise;
The fierce Croatian, and the wild Hussar,[1]
With all the sons of ravage crowd the war;   250
The baffled prince, in honor's flattering bloom
Of hasty greatness finds the fatal doom;
His foes' derision, and his subjects' blame,
And steals to death from anguish and from shame.

    Enlarge my life with multitude of days!   255
In health, in sickness, thus the suppliant prays;
Hides from himself his state, and shuns to know,
That life protracted is protracted woe.
Time hovers o'er, impatient to destroy,
And shuts up all the passages of joy;   260
In vain their gifts the bounteous seasons pour,
The fruit autumnal, and the vernal flower;
With listless eyes the dotard views the store,
He views, and wonders that they please no more;
Now pall the tasteless meats, and joyless wines,   265
And Luxury with sighs her slave resigns.
Approach, ye minstrels, try the soothing strain,
Diffuse the tuneful lenitives[2] of pain:
No sounds, alas! would touch the impervious ear,
Though dancing mountains witnessed Orpheus[3] near;   270
Nor lute nor lyre his feeble powers attend,
Nor sweeter music of a virtuous friend,
But everlasting dictates crowd his tongue,
Perversely grave, or positively wrong.
The still returning tale, and lingering jest,   275
Perplex the fawning niece and pampered guest,
While growing hopes scarce awe the gathering sneer,
And scarce a legacy can bribe to hear;
The watchful guests still hint the last offense;
The daughter's petulance, the son's expense,   280
Improve his heady rage with treacherous skill,
And mold his passions till they make his will.

    Unnumbered maladies his joints invade,
Lay siege to life and press the dire blockade;
But unextinguished avarice still remains,   285
And dreaded losses aggravate his pains;
He turns, with anxious heart and crippled hands,
His bonds of debt, and mortgages of lands;
Or views his coffers with suspicious eyes,

---

1. Hungarian light cavalry.
2. Medicines that relieve pain.

3. A legendary poet who played on the lyre so
beautifully that wild beasts were spellbound.

Unlocks his gold, and counts it till he dies.   290
But grant, the virtues of a temperate prime
Bless with an age exempt from scorn or crime;
An age that melts with unperceived decay,
And glides in modest innocence away;
Whose peaceful day Benevolence endears,   295
Whose night congratulating Conscience cheers;
The general favorite as the general friend:
Such age there is, and who shall wish its end?
      Yet even on this her load Misfortune flings,
To press the weary minutes' flagging wings;   300
New sorrow rises as the day returns,
A sister sickens, or a daughter mourns.
Now kindred Merit fills the sable bier,
Now lacerated Friendship claims a tear;
Year chases year, decay pursues decay,   305
Still drops some joy from withering life away;
New forms arise, and different views engage,
Superfluous lags the veteran[4] on the stage,
Till pitying Nature signs the last release,
And bids afflicted Worth retire to peace.   310
      But few there are whom hours like these await,
Who set unclouded in the gulfs of Fate.
From Lydia's monarch[5] should the search descend,
By Solon cautioned to regard his end,
In life's last scene what prodigies surprise,   315
Fears of the brave, and follies of the wise!
From Marlborough's eyes the streams of dotage flow,
And Swift expires a driveler and a show.[6]
      The teeming mother, anxious for her race,
Begs for each birth the fortune of a face: 320
Yet Vane could tell what ills from beauty spring;[7]
And Sedley cursed the form that pleased a king.
Ye nymphs of rosy lips and radiant eyes,
Whom Pleasure keeps too busy to be wise,
Whom Joys with soft varieties invite,   325
By day the frolic, and the dance by night;
Who frown with vanity, who smile with art,
And ask the latest fashion of the heart;
What care, what rules your heedless charms shall save,
Each nymph your rival, and each youth your slave?   330
Against your fame with Fondness Hate combines,
The rival batters, and the lover mines.

4. A veteran of life, not of war.
5. Croesus, the wealthy and fortunate king, was warned by Solon not to count himself happy till he ceased to live. He lost his crown to Cyrus the Great of Persia.
6. John Churchill, duke of Marlborough, England's brilliant general during most of the War of the Spanish Succession (1702–13); Jonathan Swift, who passed the last four years of his life in utter senility.
7. Anne Vane, mistress of Frederick, Prince of Wales (son of George II). Catherine Sedley, mistress of James II.

With distant voice neglected Virtue calls,
Less heard and less, the faint remonstrance falls;
Tired with contempt, she quits the slippery reign,   335
And Pride and Prudence take her seat in vain.
In crowd at once, where none the pass defend,
The harmless freedom, and the private friend.
The guardians yield, by force superior plied:
To Interest, Prudence; and to Flattery, Pride.   340
Now Beauty falls betrayed, despised, distressed,
And hissing Infamy proclaims the rest.
　　Where then shall Hope and Fear their objects find?
Must dull Suspense corrupt the stagnant mind?
Must helpless man, in ignorance sedate,   345
Roll darkling down the torrent of his fate?
Must no dislike alarm, no wishes rise,
No cries invoke the mercies of the skies?
Inquirer, cease; petitions yet remain,
Which Heaven may hear, nor deem religion vain.   350
Still raise for good the supplicating voice,
But leave to Heaven the measure and the choice.
Safe in His power, whose eyes discern afar
The secret ambush of a specious prayer.
Implore His aid, in His decisions rest,   355
Secure, whate'er He gives, He gives the best.
Yet when the sense of sacred presence fires,
And strong devotion to the skies aspires,
Pour forth thy fervors for a healthful mind,
Obedient passions, and a will resigned;   360
For love, which scarce collective man can fill;[8]
For patience sovereign o'er transmuted ill;
For faith, that panting for a happier seat,
Counts death kind Nature's signal of retreat:
These goods for man the laws of Heaven ordain,   365
These goods He grants, who grants the power to gain;
With these celestial Wisdom calms the mind,
And makes the happiness she does not find.

1749

Prologue Spoken by Mr. Garrick[1]

At the Opening of the Theatre Royal, Drury Lane, 1747

When Learning's triumph o'er her barbarous foes
First reared the stage, immortal Shakespeare rose;

8. Which mankind as a whole can hardly over-
task.
1. David Garrick, the famous actor, had become
joint patentee and manager of Drury Lane Theatre. Boswell says that this Prologue is unrivaled "for
just and manly dramatic criticism."

Each change of many-colored life he drew,
Exhausted worlds, and then imagined new:
Existence saw him spurn her bounded reign,   5
And panting Time toiled after him in vain.
His powerful strokes presiding Truth impressed,
And unresisted Passion stormed the breast.
    Then Jonson came, instructed from the school
To please in method and invent by rule;   10
His studious patience and laborious art
By regular approach essayed the heart;
Cold Approbation gave the lingering bays,
For those who durst not censure, scarce could praise.[2]
A mortal born, he met the general doom,   15
But left, like Egypt's kings, a lasting tomb.
    The wits of Charles[3] found easier ways to fame,
Nor wished for Jonson's art, or Shakespeare's flame;
Themselves they studied; as they felt, they writ;
Intrigue was plot, obscenity was wit.   20
Vice always found a sympathetic friend;
They pleased their age, and did not aim to mend.
Yet bards like these aspired to lasting praise,
And proudly hoped to pimp in future days.
Their cause was general, their supports were strong,   25
Their slaves were willing, and their reign was long:
Till Shame regained the post that Sense betrayed,
And Virtue called Oblivion to her aid.
    Then, crushed by rules,[4] and weakened as refined,
For years the power of Tragedy declined;   30
From bard to bard the frigid caution crept,
Till Declamation roared while Passion slept;
Yet still did Virtue deign the stage to tread;
Philosophy remained though Nature fled;
But forced at length her ancient reign to quit,   35
She saw great Faustus[5] lay the ghost of Wit;
Exulting Folly hailed the joyous day,
And Pantomime and Song confirmed her sway.
    But who the coming changes can presage,
And mark the future periods of the stage?   40
Perhaps if skill could distant times explore,
New Behns,[6] new Durfeys, yet remain in store;
Perhaps where Lear has raved, and Hamlet died,
On flying cars new sorcerers may ride;[7]
Perhaps (for who can guess the effects of chance?)   45

---

2. Cf. Dryden's contrast of Shakespeare and Ben Jonson in his *Essay of Dramatic Poesy*.
3. The comic poets of the Restoration period.
4. Cf. Johnson's remarks on the dramatic unities in his preface to Shakespeare.
5. Dr. Faustus at that time was a popular subject for both farce and pantomime.

6. Aphra Behn (1640–1689), first Englishwoman to earn her living by writing. Thomas Durfey (1653–1723), satirist and writer of songs and plays.
7. It was a common complaint that the use of increasingly elaborate stage machinery was subordinating drama to mere spectacle.

Here Hunt may box, or Mahomet may dance.[8]
   Hard is his lot that, here by fortune placed,
Must watch the wild vicissitudes of taste;
With every meteor of caprice must play,
And chase the new-blown bubbles of the day.   50
Ah! let not censure term our fate our choice,
The stage but echoes back the public voice;
The drama's laws, the drama's patrons give.
For we that live to please, must please to live.
   Then prompt no more the follies you decry,   55
As tyrants doom their tools of guilt to die;
'Tis yours this night to bid the reign commence
Of rescued Nature and reviving Sense;
To chase the charms of Sound, the pomp of Show,
For useful Mirth and salutary Woe;   60
Bid scenic Virtue form the rising age,
And Truth diffuse her radiance from the stage.

                                   1747

On the Death of Dr. Robert Levet[1]

Condemned to Hope's delusive mine,
   As on we toil from day to day,
By sudden blasts, or slow decline,
   Our social comforts drop away.

Well tried through many a varying year,   5
   See Levet to the grave descend;
Officious,[2] innocent, sincere,
   Of every friendless name the friend.

Yet still he fills Affection's eye,
   Obscurely wise, and coarsely kind;   10
Nor, lettered Arrogance, deny
   Thy praise to merit unrefined.

When fainting Nature called for aid,
   And hovering Death prepared the blow,
His vigorous remedy displayed   15
   The power of art without the show.

In Misery's darkest cavern known,
   His useful care was ever nigh,

8. Edward Hunt, a popular pugilist; Mahomet, a
tightrope dancer.
1. An unlicensed physician, who lived in Johnson's house for many years and who died in 1782.
His practice was among the very poor. Boswell
wrote: "He was of a strange grotesque appearance,
stiff and formal in his manner, and seldom said a
word while any company was present."
2. "Kind, doing good offices" (Johnson's *Dictionary*).

Where hopeless Anguish poured his groan,
   And lonely Want retired to die.   20

No summons mocked by chill delay,
   No petty gain disdained by pride,
The modest wants of every day
   The toil of every day supplied.

His virtues walked their narrow round,   25
   Nor made a pause, nor left a void;
And sure the Eternal Master found
   The single talent well employed.[3]

The busy day, the peaceful night,
   Unfelt, uncounted, glided by;   30
His frame was firm, his powers were bright,
   Though now his eightieth year was nigh.

Then with no throbbing fiery pain,
   No cold gradations of decay,
Death broke at once the vital chain,   35
   And freed his soul the nearest way.

1783

A Short Song of Congratulation

Long expected one and twenty
   Lingering year at last is flown,
Pomp and Pleasure, Pride and Plenty,
   Great Sir John,[1] are all your own.

Loosened from the minor's tether,   5
   Free to mortgage or to sell,
Wild as wind, and light as feather
   Bid the slaves of thrift farewell.

Call the Bettys, Kates, and Jennys
   Every name that laughs at Care,
Lavish of your grandsire's guineas,   10
   Show the spirit of an heir.

All that prey on vice and folly
   Joy to see their quarry fly,

---

3. In the parable of the talents (Matthew 25.14–30), Jesus suggests that salvation will be granted to those who make good use of their abilities, however small.

1. Sir John Lade, nephew of Johnson's friend Henry Thrale. He came into his property in 1780, and, as Johnson foretold, he had squandered it all by his death.

Here the gamester light and jolly   15
    There the lender grave and sly.

Wealth, Sir John, was made to wander,
    Let it wander as it will;
See the jockey, see the pander,
    Bid them come, and take their fill.   20

When the bonny blade carouses,
    Pockets full, and spirits high,
What are acres? What are houses?
    Only dirt, or wet or dry.

If the guardian or the mother   25
    Tell the woes of willful waste,
Scorn their counsel and their pother,
    You can hang or drown at last.

1780   1794

Translation of Horace, *Odes*, Book 4.7[1]

The snow dissolved no more is seen,
The fields, and woods, behold, are green,
The changing year renews the plain,
The rivers know their banks again,
The spritely nymph and naked grace[2]   5
The mazy dance together trace.
The changing year's successive plan
Proclaims mortality to man.
Rough winter's blasts to spring give way,
Spring yields to summer's sovereign ray,   10
Then summer sinks in autumn's reign,
And winter chills the world again.
Her losses soon the moon supplies,
But wretched man, when once he lies
Where Priam[3] and his sons are laid,   15
Is naught but ashes and a shade.
Who knows if Jove who counts our score
Will toss us in a morning more?
What with your friend you nobly share
At least you rescue from your heir.   20
Not you, Torquatus, boast of Rome,
When Minos once has fixed your doom,[4]
Or eloquence, or splendid birth,

---

1. Johnson composed this translation the month before his death.
2. One of the Three Graces, emblematic of beauty.
3. Last king of Troy, slain with his sons at the end of the Trojan War.
4. Sentence. L. Manlius Torquatus, a friend of Horace and an advocate, is represented as pleading his case before Minos, judge of the dead.

Or virtue shall replace on earth.
Hippolytus[5] unjustly slain   25
Diana calls to life in vain,
Nor can the might of Theseus rend
The chains of hell that hold his friend.[6]

1784

Rambler No. 5[1]

[On Spring]

TUESDAY, April 3, 1750

Et nunc omnis ager, nunc omnis parturit arbos,
Nunc frondent silvae, nunc formosissimus annus.
VIRGIL, *Eclogues* 3.5.56

Now ev'ry field, now ev'ry tree is green;
Now genial nature's fairest face is seen.
ELPHINSTON

Every man is sufficiently discontented with some circumstances of his present state, to suffer his imagination to range more or less in quest of future happiness, and to fix upon some point of time, in which, by the removal of the inconvenience which now perplexes him, or acquisition of the advantage which he at present wants, he shall find the condition of his life very much improved.

When this time, which is too often expected with great impatience, at last arrives, it generally comes without the blessing for which it was desired; but we solace ourselves with some new prospect, and press forward again with equal eagerness.

It is lucky for a man, in whom this temper prevails, when he turns his hopes upon things wholly out of his own power; since he forbears then to precipitate[2] his affairs, for the sake of the great event that is to complete his felicity, and waits for the blissful hour, with less neglect of the measures necessary to be taken in the mean time.

I have long known a person of this temper, who indulged his dream of happiness with less hurt to himself than such chimerical wishes commonly produce, and adjusted his scheme with such address, that his hopes were in full bloom three parts of the year, and in the other part never wholly blasted. Many, perhaps, would be desirous of learning by what means he procured to himself such a cheap and lasting satisfaction.

---

5. Phaedra, wife of Theseus, falsely accused his chaste son Hippolytus of rape; Theseus brought about the death of his son, and even Diana, goddess of chastity, could not restore him.
6. Pirithous, held prisoner with Theseus in Hell.
1. The *Rambler*, almost wholly written by Johnson himself, appeared every Tuesday and Saturday from Mar. 20, 1750, to Mar. 14, 1752—years in which Johnson was writing the *Dictionary*. It is a

successor of the *Tatler* and the *Spectator*, but it is much more serious in tone than the earlier periodicals. Johnson's reputation as a moralist and a stylist was established by these essays; because of them Boswell first conceived the ambition to seek Johnson's acquaintance.
2. "To hurry blindly or rashly" (Johnson's *Dictionary*).

It was gained by a constant practice of referring the removal of all his uneasiness to the coming of the next spring; if his health was impaired, the spring would restore it; if what he wanted was at a high price, it would fall in value in the spring.

The spring, indeed, did often come without any of these effects, but he was always certain that the next would be more propitious; nor was ever convinced that the present spring would fail him before the middle of summer; for he always talked of the spring as coming till it was past, and when it was once past, everyone agreed with him that it was coming.

By long converse with this man, I am, perhaps, brought to feel immoderate pleasure in the contemplation of this delightful season; but I have the satisfaction of finding many, whom it can be no shame to resemble, infected with the same enthusiasm; for there is, I believe, scarce any poet of eminence, who has not left some testimony of his fondness for the flowers, the zephyrs, and the warblers of the spring. Nor has the most luxuriant imagination been able to describe the serenity and happiness of the golden age, otherwise than by giving a perpetual spring, as the highest reward of uncorrupted innocence.

There is, indeed, something inexpressibly pleasing, in the annual renovation of the world, and the new display of the treasures of nature. The cold and darkness of winter, with the naked deformity of every object on which we turn our eyes, make us rejoice at the succeeding season, as well for what we have escaped, as for what we may enjoy; and every budding flower, which a warm situation brings early to our view, is considered by us as a messenger to notify the approach of more joyous days.

The spring affords to a mind, so free from the disturbance of cares or passions as to be vacant[3] to calm amusements, almost every thing that our present state makes us capable of enjoying. The variegated verdure of the fields and woods, the succession of grateful odors, the voice of pleasure pouring out its notes on every side, with the gladness apparently conceived by every animal, from the growth of his food, and the clemency of the weather, throw over the whole earth an air of gaiety, significantly expressed by the smile of nature.

Yet there are men to whom these scenes are able to give no delight, and who hurry away from all the varieties of rural beauty, to lose their hours, and divert their thoughts by cards, or assemblies, a tavern dinner, or the prattle of the day.

It may be laid down as a position which will seldom deceive, that when a man cannot bear his own company there is something wrong. He must fly from himself, either because he feels a tediousness in life from the equipoise of an empty mind, which, having no tendency to one motion more than another but as it is impelled by some external power, must always have recourse to foreign objects; or he must be afraid of the intrusion of some unpleasing ideas, and, perhaps, is struggling to

---

3. "At leisure" (Johnson's *Dictionary*).

escape from the remembrance of a loss, the fear of a calamity, or some other thought of greater horror.

Those whom sorrow incapacitates to enjoy the pleasures of contemplation, may properly apply to such diversions, provided they are innocent, as lay strong hold on the attention; and those, whom fear of any future affliction chains down to misery, must endeavor to obviate the danger.

My considerations shall, on this occasion, be turned on such as are burthensome to themselves merely because they want subjects for reflection, and to whom the volume of nature is thrown open, without affording them pleasure or instruction, because they never learned to read the characters.

A French author has advanced this seeming paradox, that *very few men know how to take a walk*; and, indeed, it is true, that few know how to take a walk with a prospect of any other pleasure, than the same company would have afforded them at home.

There are animals that borrow their color from the neighboring body, and, consequently, vary their hue as they happen to change their place. In like manner it ought to be the endeavor of every man to derive his reflections from the objects about him; for it is to no purpose that he alters his position, if his attention continues fixed to the same point. The mind should be kept open to the access of every new idea, and so far disengaged from the predominance of particular thoughts, as easily to accommodate itself to occasional entertainment.

A man that has formed his habit of turning every new object to his entertainment, finds in the productions of nature an inexhaustible stock of materials upon which he can employ himself, without any temptations to envy or malevolence; faults, perhaps, seldom totally avoided by those, whose judgment is much exercised upon the works of art. He has always a certain prospect of discovering new reasons for adoring the sovereign author of the universe, and probable hopes of making some discovery of benefit to others, or of profit to himself. There is no doubt but many vegetables and animals have qualities that might be of great use, to the knowledge of which there is not required much force of penetration, or fatigue of study, but only frequent experiments, and close attention. What is said by the chemists of their darling mercury, is, perhaps, true of everybody through the whole creation, that if a thousand lives should be spent upon it, all its properties would not be found out.

Mankind must necessarily be diversified by various tastes, since life affords and requires such multiplicity of employments, and a nation of naturalists is neither to be hoped, or desired; but it is surely not improper to point out a fresh amusement to those who languish in health, and repine in plenty, for want of some source of diversion that may be less easily exhausted, and to inform the multitudes of both sexes, who are burthened with every new day, that there are many shows which they have not seen.

He that enlarges his curiosity after the works of nature, demonstrably multiplies the inlets to happiness; and, therefore, the younger part of my readers, to whom I dedicate this vernal speculation, must excuse me for calling upon them, to make use at once of the spring of the year, and the spring of life; to acquire, while their minds may be yet impressed with new images, a love of innocent pleasures, and an ardor for useful knowledge; and to remember, that a blighted spring makes a barren year, and that the vernal flowers, however beautiful and gay, are only intended by nature as preparatives to autumnal fruits.

Idler No. 31[1]

[*On Idleness*]

SATURDAY, *November* 18, 1758

Many moralists have remarked, that Pride has of all human vices the widest dominion, appears in the greatest multiplicity of forms, and lies hid under the greatest variety of disguises; of disguises, which, like the moon's *veil of brightness*, are both *its luster and its shade*, and betray it to others, though they hide it from ourselves.

It is not my intention to degrade Pride from this pre-eminence of mischief, yet I know not whether Idleness may not maintain a very doubtful and obstinate competition.

There are some that profess Idleness in its full dignity, who call themselves the Idle, as Busiris in the play "calls himself the Proud";[2] who boast that they do nothing, and thank their stars that they have nothing to do; who sleep every night till they can sleep no longer, and rise only that exercise may enable them to sleep again; who prolong the reign of darkness by double curtains, and never see the sun but to "tell him how they hate his beams";[3] whose whole labor is to vary the postures of indulgence, and whose day differs from their night but as a couch or chair differs from a bed.

These are the true and open votaries of Idleness, for whom she weaves the garlands of poppies, and into whose cup she pours the waters of oblivion; who exist in a state of unruffled stupidity, forgetting and forgotten; who have long ceased to live, and at whose death the survivors can only say, that they have ceased to breathe.

But Idleness predominates in many lives where it is not suspected; for being a vice which terminates in itself, it may be enjoyed without injury to others; and is therefore not watched like Fraud, which endangers property, or like Pride, which naturally seeks its gratifications in another's inferiority. Idleness is a silent and peaceful quality, that neither raises envy by ostentation, nor hatred by opposition; and therefore nobody is busy to censure or detect it.

1. Johnson wrote and published the *Idler*, a periodical similar to the *Rambler*, from 1758 until 1760.

2. Edward Young, *Busiris* (1719), 1.13.

3. *Paradise Lost* 4.37.

As Pride sometimes is hid under humility, Idleness is often covered by turbulence and hurry. He that neglects his known duty and real employment, naturally endeavors to crowd his mind with something that may bar out the remembrance of his own folly, and does any thing but what he ought to do with eager diligence, that he may keep himself in his own favor.

Some are always in a state of preparation, occupied in previous measures, forming plans, accumulating materials, and providing for the main affair. These are certainly under the secret power of Idleness. Nothing is to be expected from the workman whose tools are forever to be sought. I was once told by a great master, that no man ever excelled in painting, who was eminently curious about pencils and colors.

There are others to whom Idleness dictates another expedient, by which life may be passed unprofitably away without the tediousness of many vacant hours. The art is, to fill the day with petty business, to have always something in hand which may raise curiosity, but not solicitude, and keep the mind in a state of action, but not of labor.

This art has for many years been practiced by my old friend Sober, with wonderful success. Sober is a man of strong desires and quick imagination, so exactly balanced by the love of ease, that they can seldom stimulate him to any difficult undertaking; they have, however, so much power, that they will not suffer him to lie quite at rest, and though they do not make him sufficiently useful to others, they make him at least weary of himself.

Mr. Sober's chief pleasure is conversation; there is no end of his talk or his attention; to speak or to hear is equally pleasing; for he still fancies that he is teaching or learning something, and is free for the time from his own reproaches.

But there is one time at night when he must go home, that his friends may sleep; and another time in the morning, when all the world agrees to shut out interruption. These are the moments of which poor Sober trembles at the thought. But the misery of these tiresome intervals, he has many means of alleviating. He has persuaded himself that the manual arts are undeservedly overlooked; he has observed in many trades the effects of close thought, and just ratiocination. From speculation he proceeded to practice, and supplied himself with the tools of a carpenter, with which he mended his coalbox very successfully, and which he still continues to employ, as he finds occasion.

He has attempted at other times the crafts of the shoemaker, tinman, plumber, and potter; in all these arts he has failed, and resolves to qualify himself for them by better information. But his daily amusement is chemistry. He has a small furnace, which he employs in distillation, and which has long been the solace of his life. He draws oils and waters, and essences and spirits, which he knows to be of no use; sits and counts the drops as they come from his retort, and forgets that, whilst a drop is falling, a moment flies away.

Poor Sober![4] I have often teased him with reproof, and he has often promised reformation; for no man is so much open to conviction as the Idler, but there is none on whom it operates so little. What will be the effect of this paper I know not; perhaps he will read it and laugh, and light the fire in his furnace; but my hope is that he will quit his trifles, and betake himself to rational and useful diligence.

Rasselas   Johnson wrote *Rasselas* in January 1759, during the evenings of one week, a remarkable instance of his ability to write rapidly and brilliantly under the pressure of necessity. His mother lay dying in Lichfield. Her son, famous for his *Dictionary*, was nonetheless oppressed by poverty and in great need of ready money with which to make her last days comfortable, pay her funeral expenses, and settle her small debts. He was paid £100 for the first edition of *Rasselas*, but not in time to attend her deathbed or her funeral.

Rasselas is a philosophical fable cast in the popular form of an Oriental tale, a type of fiction that owed its popularity to the vogue of the *Arabian Nights*, first translated into English in the early 18th century. Since the work is a fable, we should not approach it as a novel: psychologically credible characters and a series of intricately involved actions that lead to a necessary resolution and conclusion are not to be found in *Rasselas*. Instead we are meant to reflect on the ideas and to savor the melancholy resonance and intelligence of the stately prose that expresses them. Johnson arranges the incidents of the fable to test a variety of possible solutions to a problem: What choice of life will bring us happiness? (*The Choice of Life* was his working title for the book.) Many ways of life are examined in turn, and each is found wanting. Johnson does not pretend to have solved the problem. Rather, he locates the sources of discontent in a basic principle of human nature: the "hunger of imagination which preys incessantly upon life" (chapter 32) and which lures us to "listen with credulity to the whispers of fancy and pursue with eagerness the phantoms of hope" (chapter 1). The tale is a gentle satire on one of the perennial topics of satirists, the folly of all of us who stubbornly cling to our illusions despite the evidence of experience. *Rasselas* is not all darkness and gloom, for Johnson's theme invites comic as well as tragic treatment, and some of the episodes evoke that laughter of the mind which is the effect of high comedy. In its main theme, however—the folly of cherishing the dream of ever attaining unalloyed happiness in a world which can never wholly satisfy our desires—and in many of the sayings of its characters, especially of the sage Imlac, *Rasselas* expresses some of Johnson's own deepest convictions.

The History of Rasselas, Prince of Abyssinia

Chapter 1. Description of a Palace in a Valley

Ye who listen with credulity to the whispers of fancy, and pursue with eagerness the phantoms of hope; who expect that age will perform the

---

4. Sober represents aspects of Johnson's own character. He was much given to indolence, and he performed chemical experiments in a small laboratory in his garret.

promises of youth, and that the deficiencies of the present day will be supplied by the morrow—attend to the history of Rasselas, prince of Abyssinia.

Rasselas was the fourth son of the mighty emperor in whose dominions the Father of Waters[1] begins his course; whose bounty pours down the streams of plenty, and scatters over half the world the harvests of Egypt.

According to the custom which has descended from age to age among the monarchs of the torrid zone, Rasselas was confined in a private palace, with the other sons and daughters of Abyssinian royalty, till the order of succession should call him to the throne.

The place which the wisdom or policy of antiquity had destined for the residence of the Abyssinian princes was a spacious valley[2] in the kingdom of Amhara, surrounded on every side by mountains, of which the summits overhang the middle part. The only passage by which it could be entered was a cavern that passed under a rock, of which it has long been disputed whether it was the work of nature or of human industry. The outlet of the cavern was concealed by a thick wood, and the mouth which opened into the valley was closed with gates of iron, forged by the artificers of ancient days, so massy that no man could, without the help of engines, open or shut them.

From the mountains on every side rivulets descended that filled all the valley with verdure and fertility, and formed a lake in the middle, inhabited by fish of every species, and frequented by every fowl whom nature has taught to dip the wing in water. This lake discharged its superfluities by a stream, which entered a dark cleft of the mountain on the northern side, and fell with dreadful noise from precipice to precipice till it was heard no more.

The sides of the mountains were covered with trees, the banks of the brooks were diversified with flowers; every blast shook spices from the rocks, and every month dropped fruits upon the ground. All animals that bite the grass, or browse the shrub, whether wild or tame, wandered in this extensive circuit, secured from beasts of prey by the mountains which confined them. On one part were flocks and herds feeding in the pastures, on another all the beasts of chase frisking in the lawns; the sprightly kid was bounding on the rocks, the subtle monkey frolicking in the trees, and the solemn elephant reposing in the shade. All the diversities of the world were brought together, the blessings of nature were collected, and its evils extracted and excluded.

The valley, wide and fruitful, supplied its inhabitants with the necessaries of life, and all delights and superfluities were added at the annual visit which the emperor paid his children, when the iron gate was opened to the sound of music, and during eight days everyone that resided in

1. The Nile.
2. Johnson had read of the Happy Valley in the Portuguese Jesuit Father Lobo's book on Abyssinia, which he translated in 1735. The description in this and the immediately following paragraphs illustrates well enough Johnson's preference for the "general" over the "particular" (see chap. 10, below). It owes something to the description of the Garden in *Paradise Lost* 4, and Coleridge's *Kubla Khan* owes something to it.

the valley was required to propose whatever might contribute to make seclusion pleasant, to fill up the vacancies of attention, and lessen the tediousness of time. Every desire was immediately granted. All the artificers of pleasure were called to gladden the festivity; the musicians exerted the power of harmony, and the dancers showed their activity before the princes, in hope that they should pass their lives in this blissful captivity, to which those only were admitted whose performance was thought able to add novelty to luxury. Such was the appearance of security and delight which this retirement afforded, that they to whom it was new always desired that it might be perpetual; and as those on whom the iron gate had once closed were never suffered to return, the effect of longer experience could not be known. Thus every year produced new schemes of delight and new competitors for imprisonment.

The palace stood on an eminence, raised about thirty paces above the surface of the lake. It was divided into many squares or courts, built with greater or less magnificence according to the rank of those for whom they were designed. The roofs were turned into arches of massy stone, joined with a cement that grew harder by time, and the building stood from century to century, deriding the solstitial rains and equinoctial hurricanes, without need of reparation.

This house, which was so large as to be fully known to none but some ancient officers, who successively inherited the secrets of the place, was built as if suspicion herself had dictated the plan. To every room there was an open and secret passage; every square had a communication with the rest, either from the upper stories by private galleries, or by subterranean passages from the lower apartments. Many of the columns had unsuspected cavities, in which a long race of monarchs had reposited their treasures. They then closed up the opening with marble, which was never to be removed but in the utmost exigencies of the kingdom, and recorded their accumulations in a book, which was itself concealed in a tower, not entered but by the emperor, attended by the prince who stood next in succession.

Chapter 2. The Discontent of Rasselas in the Happy Valley

Here the sons and daughters of Abyssinia lived only to know the soft vicissitudes of pleasure and repose, attended by all that were skillful to delight, and gratified with whatever the senses can enjoy. They wandered in gardens of fragrance, and slept in the fortresses of security. Every art was practiced to make them pleased with their own condition. The sages who instructed them told them of nothing but the miseries of public life, and described all beyond the mountains as regions of calamity, where discord was always raging, and where man preyed upon man.

To heighten their opinion of their own felicity, they were daily entertained with songs, the subject of which was the *happy valley*. Their appetites were excited by frequent enumerations of different enjoyments, and revelry and merriment was the business of every hour, from the dawn of morning to the close of even.

These methods were generally successful; few of the princes had ever wished to enlarge their bounds, but passed their lives in full conviction that they had all within their reach that art or nature could bestow, and pitied those whom fate had excluded from this seat of tranquility, as the sport of chance and the slaves of misery.

Thus they rose in the morning and lay down at night, pleased with each other and with themselves; all but Rasselas, who, in the twenty-sixth year of his age, began to withdraw himself from their pastimes and assemblies, and to delight in solitary walks and silent meditation. He often sat before tables covered with luxury, and forgot to taste the dainties that were placed before him; he rose abruptly in the midst of the song, and hastily retired beyond the sound of music. His attendants observed the change, and endeavored to renew his love of pleasure. He neglected their officiousness, repulsed their invitations, and spent day after day on the banks of rivulets sheltered with trees, where he sometimes listened to the birds in the branches, sometimes observed the fish playing in the stream, and anon cast his eyes upon the pastures and mountains filled with animals, of which some were biting the herbage, and some sleeping among the bushes.

This singularity of his humor made him much observed. One of the sages, in whose conversation he had formerly delighted, followed him secretly, in hope of discovering the cause of his disquiet. Rasselas, who knew not that anyone was near him, having for some time fixed his eyes upon the goats that were browsing among the rocks, began to compare their condition with his own.

"What," said he, "makes the difference between man and all the rest of the animal creation? Every beast that strays beside me has the same corporal necessities with myself; he is hungry, and crops the grass, he is thirsty, and drinks the stream, his thirst and hunger are appeased, he is satisfied, and sleeps; he rises again, and he is hungry, he is again fed, and is at rest. I am hungry and thirsty like him, but when thirst and hunger cease, I am not at rest; I am, like him, pained with want, but am not, like him, satisfied with fullness. The intermediate hours are tedious and gloomy; I long again to be hungry that I may again quicken my attention. The birds peck the berries or the corn, and fly away to the groves, where they sit in seeming happiness on the branches, and waste their lives in tuning one unvaried series of sounds. I likewise can call the lutanist and the singer, but the sounds that pleased me yesterday weary me today, and will grow yet more wearisome tomorrow. I can discover within me no power of perception which is not glutted with its proper pleasure, yet I do not feel myself delighted. Man has surely some latent sense for which this place affords no gratification, or he has some desires distinct from sense, which must be satisfied before he can be happy."

After this he lifted up his head, and seeing the moon rising, walked towards the palace. As he passed through the fields, and saw the animals around him, "Ye," said he, "are happy, and need not envy me that walk thus among you, burthened with myself; nor do I, ye gentle beings, envy your felicity, for it is not the felicity of man. I have many distresses from which ye are free; I fear pain when I do not feel it; I sometimes shrink at evils recollected, and sometimes start at evils anticipated. Surely the equity of Providence has balanced peculiar sufferings with peculiar enjoyments."

With observations like these the prince amused himself as he returned, uttering them with a plaintive voice, yet with a look that discovered him to feel some complacence in his own perspicacity, and to receive some solace of the miseries of life from consciousness of the delicacy with which he felt, and the eloquence with which he bewailed them. He mingled cheerfully in the diversions of the evening, and all rejoiced to find that his heart was lightened.

Chapter 3. The Wants of Him That Wants Nothing

On the next day his old instructor, imagining that he had now made himself acquainted with his disease of mind, was in the hope of curing it by counsel, and officiously sought an opportunity of conference, which the prince, having long considered him as one whose intellects were exhausted, was not very willing to afford. "Why," said he, "does this man thus intrude upon me; shall I be never suffered to forget those lectures which pleased only while they were new, and to become new again must be forgotten?" He then walked into the wood, and composed himself to his usual meditations; when, before his thoughts had taken any settled form, he perceived his pursuer at his side, and was at first prompted by his impatience to go hastily away; but, being unwilling to offend a man whom he had once reverenced and still loved, he invited him to sit down with him on the bank.

The old man, thus encouraged, began to lament the change which had been lately observed in the prince, and to inquire why he so often retired from the pleasures of the palace, to loneliness and silence. "I fly from pleasure," said the prince, "because pleasure has ceased to please; I am lonely because I am miserable, and am unwilling to cloud with my presence the happiness of others." "You, sir," said the sage, "are the first who has complained of misery in the *happy valley*. I hope to convince you that your complaints have no real cause. You are here in full possession of all that the emperor of Abyssinia can bestow; here is neither labor to be endured nor danger to be dreaded, yet here is all that labor or danger can procure or purchase. Look round and tell me which of your wants is without supply; if you want nothing, how are you unhappy?"

"That I want nothing," said the prince, "or that I know not what I want, is the cause of my complaint; if I had any known want, I should have a certain wish; that wish would excite endeavor, and I should not then repine to see the sun move so slowly towards the western mountain, or lament when the day breaks, and sleep will no longer hide me from myself. When I see the kids and the lambs chasing one another, I fancy that I should be happy if I had something to pursue. But, possessing all that I can want, I find one day and one hour exactly like another, except that the latter is still more tedious than the former. Let your experience inform me how the day may now seem as short as in my childhood, while nature was yet fresh and every moment showed me what I never had observed before. I have already enjoyed too much; give me something to desire."

The old man was surprised at this new species of affliction and knew not what to reply, yet was unwilling to be silent. "Sir," said he, "if you had seen the miseries of the world you would know how to value your present state." "Now," said the prince, "you have given me something to desire. I shall long to see the miseries of the world, since the sight of them is necessary to happiness."

Chapter 4. The Prince Continues to Grieve and Muse

At this time the sound of music proclaimed the hour of repast, and the conversation was concluded. The old man went away sufficiently discontented to find that his reasonings had produced the only conclusion which they were intended to prevent. But in the decline of life shame and grief are of short duration; whether it be that we bear easily what we have born long, or that, finding ourselves in age less regarded, we less regard others; or, that we look with slight regard upon afflictions, to which we know that the hand of death is about to put an end.

The prince, whose views were extended to a wider space, could not speedily quiet his emotions. He had been before terrified at the length of life which nature promised him, because he considered that in a long time much must be endured; he now rejoiced in his youth, because in many years much might be done.

This first beam of hope, that had been ever darted into his mind, rekindled youth in his cheeks, and doubled the luster of his eyes. He was fired with the desire of doing something, though he knew not yet with distinctness, either end or means.

He was now no longer gloomy and unsocial; but, considering himself as master of a secret stock of happiness, which he could enjoy only by concealing it, he affected to be busy in all schemes of diversion, and endeavored to make others pleased with the state of which he himself was weary. But pleasures never can be so multiplied or continued, as not to leave much of life unemployed; there were many hours, both of the night and day, which he could spend without suspicion in solitary thought. The load of life was much lightened: he went eagerly into the assemblies, because he supposed the frequency of his presence necessary to the success of his purposes; he retired gladly to privacy, because he had now a subject of thought.

His chief amusement was to picture to himself that world which he had never seen; to place himself in various conditions; to be entangled in imaginary difficulties, and to be engaged in wild adventures: but his benevolence always terminated his projects in the relief of distress, the detection of fraud, the defeat of oppression, and the diffusion of happiness.

Thus passed twenty months of the life of Rasselas. He busied himself so intensely in visionary bustle, that he forgot his real solitude; and, amidst hourly preparations for the various incidents of human affairs, neglected to consider by what means he should mingle with mankind.

One day, as he was sitting on a bank, he feigned to himself an orphan virgin robbed of her little portion[3] by a treacherous lover, and crying after him for restitution and redress. So strongly was the image impressed upon his mind, that he started up in the maid's defense, and ran forward to seize the plunderer with all the eagerness of real pursuit. Fear naturally quickens the flight of guilt. Rasselas could not catch the fugitive with his utmost efforts; but, resolving to weary, by perseverance, him whom he could not surpass in speed, he pressed on till the foot of the mountain stopped his course.

Here he recollected himself, and smiled at his own useless impetuosity. Then raising his eyes to the mountain, "This," said he, "is the fatal obstacle that hinders at once the enjoyment of pleasure, and the exercise of virtue. How long is it that my hopes and wishes have flown beyond this boundary of my life, which yet I never have attempted to surmount!"

Struck with this reflection, he sat down to muse, and remembered, that since he first resolved to escape from his confinement, the sun had passed twice over him in his annual course. He now felt a degree of regret with which he had never been before acquainted. He considered how much might have been done in the time which had passed, and left nothing real behind it. He compared twenty months with the life of man. "In life," said he, "is not to be counted the ignorance of infancy, or imbecility of age. We are long before we are able to think, and we soon cease from the power of acting. The true period of human existence may be reasonably estimated as forty years, of which I have mused away the four and twentieth part. What I have lost was certain, for I have certainly possessed it; but of twenty months to come who can assure me?"

The consciousness of his own folly pierced him deeply, and he was long before he could be reconciled to himself. "The rest of my time," said he, "has been lost by the crime or folly of my ancestors, and the absurd institutions of my country; I remember it with disgust, yet without remorse: but the months that have passed since new light darted into my soul, since I formed a scheme of reasonable felicity, have been squandered by my own fault. I have lost that which can never be restored:

3. Money or goods.

I have seen the sun rise and set for twenty months, an idle gazer on the light of heaven. In this time the birds have left the nest of their mother, and committed themselves to the woods and to the skies: the kid has forsaken the teat, and learned by degrees to climb the rocks in quest of independent sustenance. I only have made no advances, but am still helpless and ignorant. The moon, by more than twenty changes, admonished me of the flux of life; the stream that rolled before my feet upbraided my inactivity. I sat feasting on intellectual luxury, regardless alike of the examples of the earth, and the instructions of the planets. Twenty months are past, who shall restore them!"

These sorrowful meditations fastened upon his mind; he passed four months in resolving to lose no more time in idle resolves, and was awakened to more vigorous exertion by hearing a maid, who had broken a porcelain cup, remark that what cannot be repaired is not to be regretted.

This was obvious; and Rasselas reproached himself that he had not discovered it, having not known, or not considered, how many useful hints are obtained by chance, and how often the mind, hurried by her own ardor to distant views, neglects the truths that lie open before her. He, for a few hours, regretted his regret, and from that time bent his whole mind upon the means of escaping from the valley of happiness.

Chapter 5. The Prince Meditates His Escape

He now found that it would be very difficult to effect that which it was very easy to suppose effected. When he looked round about him, he saw himself confined by the bars of nature which had never yet been broken, and by the gate, through which none that once had passed it were ever able to return. He was now impatient as an eagle in a grate.[4] He passed week after week in clambering the mountains, to see if there was any aperture which the bushes might conceal, but found all the summits inaccessible by their prominence. The iron gate he despaired to open; for it was not only secured with all the power of art, but was always watched by successive sentinels, and was by its position exposed to the perpetual observation of all the inhabitants.

He then examined the cavern through which the waters of the lake were discharged; and, looking down at a time when the sun shone strongly upon its mouth, he discovered it to be full of broken rocks, which, though they permitted the stream to flow through many narrow passages, would stop any body of solid bulk. He returned discouraged and dejected; but, having now known the blessing of hope, resolved never to despair.

In these fruitless searches he spent ten months. The time, however, passed cheerfully away: in the morning he rose with new hope, in the evening applauded his own diligence, and in the night slept sound after his fatigue. He met a thousand amusements which beguiled his labor,

4. Barred cage.

and diversified his thoughts. He discerned the various instincts of animals, and properties of plants, and found the place replete with wonders, of which he purposed to solace himself with the contemplation, if he should never be able to accomplish his flight; rejoicing that his endeavors, though yet unsuccessful, had supplied him with a source of inexhaustible enquiry.

But his original curiosity was not yet abated; he resolved to obtain some knowledge of the ways of men. His wish still continued, but his hope grew less. He ceased to survey any longer the walls of his prison, and spared to search by new toils for interstices which he knew could not be found, yet determined to keep his design always in view, and lay hold on any expedient that time should offer.

Chapter 6. A Dissertation on the Art of Flying

Among the artists that had been allured into the happy valley, to labor for the accommodation and pleasure of its inhabitants, was a man eminent for his knowledge of the mechanic powers, who had contrived many engines[5] both of use and recreation. By a wheel, which the stream turned, he forced the water into a tower, whence it was distributed to all the apartments of the palace. He erected a pavillion in the garden, around which he kept the air always cool by artificial showers. One of the groves, appropriated to the ladies, was ventilated by fans, to which the rivulet that run through it gave a constant motion; and instruments of soft music were placed at proper distances, of which some played by the impulse of the wind, and some by the power of the stream.

This artist was sometimes visited by Rasselas, who was pleased with every kind of knowledge, imagining that the time would come when all his acquisitions should be of use to him in the open world. He came one day to amuse himself in his usual manner, and found the master busy in building a sailing chariot: he saw that the design was practicable upon a level surface, and with expressions of great esteem solicited its completion. The workman was pleased to find himself so much regarded by the prince, and resolved to gain yet higher honors. "Sir," said he, "you have seen but a small part of what the mechanic sciences can perform. I have been long of opinion, that, instead of the tardy conveyance of ships and chariots, man might use the swifter migration of wings; that the fields of air are open to knowledge, and that only ignorance and idleness need crawl upon the ground."

This hint rekindled the prince's desire of passing the mountains; having seen what the mechanist had already performed, he was willing to fancy that he could do more; yet resolved to inquire further before he suffered hope to afflict him by disappointment. "I am afraid," said he to the artist, "that your imagination prevails over your skill, and that you now tell me rather what you wish than what you know. Every animal

5. Machines; "mechanic powers": the forces that cause things to move.

has his element assigned him; the birds have the air, and man and beasts the earth." "So," replied the mechanist, "fishes have the water, in which yet beasts can swim by nature, and men by art. He that can swim needs not despair to fly: to swim is to fly in a grosser fluid, and to fly is to swim in a subtler. We are only to proportion our power of resistance to the different density of the matter through which we are to pass. You will be necessarily upborn by the air, if you can renew any impulse upon it, faster than the air can recede from the pressure."

"But the exercise of swimming," said the prince, "is very laborious; the strongest limbs are soon wearied; I am afraid the act of flying will be yet more violent, and wings will be of no great use, unless we can fly further than we can swim."

"The labor of rising from the ground," said the artist "will be great, as we see it in the heavier domestic fowls; but, as we mount higher, the earth's attraction, and the body's gravity, will be gradually diminished, till we shall arrive at a region where the man will float in the air without any tendency to fall: no care will then be necessary, but to move forwards, which the gentlest impulse will effect. You, Sir, whose curiosity is so extensive, will easily conceive with what pleasure a philosopher, furnished with wings, and hovering in the sky, would see the earth, and all its inhabitants, rolling beneath him, and presenting to him successively, by its diurnal motion, all the countries within the same parallel. How must it amuse the pendent spectator to see the moving scene of land and ocean, cities and deserts! To survey with equal security the marts of trade, and the fields of battle; mountains infested by barbarians, and fruitful regions gladdened by plenty, and lulled by peace! How easily shall we then trace the Nile through all his passage; pass over to distant regions, and examine the face of nature from one extremity of the earth to the other!"

"All this," said the prince, "is much to be desired, but I am afraid that no man will be able to breathe in these regions of speculation and tranquility. I have been told, that respiration is difficult upon lofty mountains, yet from these precipices, though so high as to produce great tenuity of the air, it is very easy to fall: therefore I suspect, that from any height, where life can be supported, there may be danger of too quick descent."

"Nothing," replied the artist, "will ever be attempted, if all possible objections must be first overcome. If you will favor my project I will try the first flight at my own hazard. I have considered the structure of all volant[6] animals, and find the folding continuity of the bat's wings most easily accommodated to the human form. Upon this model I shall begin my task tomorrow, and in a year expect to tower into the air beyond the malice or pursuit of man. But I will work only on this condition, that the art shall not be divulged, and that you shall not require me to make wings for any but ourselves."

"Why," said Rasselas, "should you envy others so great an advantage?

6. Able to fly.

All skill ought to be exerted for universal good; every man has owed much to others, and ought to repay the kindness that he has received."

"If men were all virtuous," returned the artist, "I should with great alacrity teach them all to fly. But what would be the security of the good, if the bad could at pleasure invade them from the sky? Against an army sailing through the clouds neither walls, nor mountains, nor seas, could afford any security. A flight of northern savages might hover in the wind, and light at once with irresistible violence upon the capital of a fruitful region that was rolling under them. Even this valley, the retreat of princes, the abode of happiness, might be violated by the sudden descent of some of the naked nations that swarm on the coast of the southern sea."

The prince promised secrecy, and waited for the performance, not wholly hopeless of success. He visited the work from time to time, observed its progress, and remarked many ingenious contrivances to facilitate motion, and unite levity with strength. The artist was every day more certain that he should leave vultures and eagles behind him, and the contagion of his confidence seized upon the prince.

In a year the wings were finished, and, on a morning appointed, the maker appeared furnished for flight on a little promontory: he waved his pinions a while to gather air, then leaped from his stand, and in an instant dropped into the lake. His wings, which were of no use in the air, sustained him in the water, and the prince drew him to land, half dead with terror and vexation.

Chapter 7. *The Prince Finds a Man of Learning*

The prince was not much afflicted by this disaster, having suffered himself to hope for a happier event, only because he had no other means of escape in view. He still persisted in his design to leave the happy valley by the first opportunity.

His imagination was now at a stand; he had no prospect of entering into the world; and, notwithstanding all his endeavors to support himself, discontent by degrees preyed upon him, and he began again to lose his thoughts in sadness, when the rainy season, which in these countries is periodical, made it inconvenient to wander in the woods.

The rain continued longer and with more violence than had been ever known; the clouds broke on the surrounding mountains, and the torrents streamed into the plain on every side, till the cavern was too narrow to discharge the water. The lake overflowed its banks, and all the level of the valley was covered with the inundation. The eminence, on which the palace was built, and some other spots of rising ground, were all that the eye could now discover. The herds and flocks left the pastures, and both the wild beasts and the tame retreated to the mountains.

This inundation confined all the princes to domestic amusements, and the attention of Rasselas was particularly seized by a poem, which Imlac rehearsed,[7] upon the various conditions of humanity. He com-

7. Recited.

manded the poet to attend him in his apartment, and recite his verses a second time; then entering into familiar talk, he thought himself happy in having found a man who knew the world so well, and could so skilfully paint the scenes of life. He asked a thousand questions about things, to which, though common to all other mortals, his confinement from childhood had kept him a stranger. The poet pitied his ignorance, and loved his curiosity, and entertained him from day to day with novelty and instruction, so that the prince regretted the necessity of sleep, and longed till the morning should renew his pleasure.

As they were sitting together, the prince commanded Imlac to relate his history, and to tell by what accident he was forced, or by what motive induced, to close his life in the happy valley. As he was going to begin his narrative, Rasselas was called to a concert, and obliged to restrain his curiosity till the evening.

Chapter 8. The History of Imlac

The close of the day is, in the regions of the torrid zone, the only season of diversion and entertainment, and it was therefore midnight before the music ceased, and the princesses retired. Rasselas then called for his companion and required him to begin the story of his life.

"Sir," said Imlac, "my history will not be long: the life that is devoted to knowledge passes silently away, and is very little diversified by events. To talk in public, to think in solitude, to read and to hear, to inquire, and answer inquiries, is the business of a scholar. He wanders about the world without pomp or terror, and is neither known nor valued but by men like himself.

"I was born in the kingdom of Goiama, at no great distance from the fountain of the Nile. My father was a wealthy merchant, who traded between the inland countries of Africk and the ports of the red sea. He was honest, frugal and diligent, but of mean sentiments, and narrow comprehension: he desired only to be rich, and to conceal his riches, lest he should be spoiled[8] by the governors of the province."

"Surely," said the prince, "my father must be negligent of his charge, if any man in his dominions dares take that which belongs to another. Does he not know that kings are accountable for injustice permitted as well as done? If I were emperor, not the meanest of my subjects should be oppressed with impunity. My blood boils when I am told that a merchant durst not enjoy his honest gains for fear of losing them by the rapacity of power. Name the governor who robbed the people, that I may declare his crimes to the emperor."

"Sir," said Imlac, "your ardor is the natural effect of virtue animated by youth: the time will come when you will acquit your father, and perhaps hear with less impatience of the governor. Oppression is, in the Abyssinian dominions, neither frequent nor tolerated; but no form of government has been yet discovered, by which cruelty can be wholly

8. Robbed.

prevented. Subordination supposes power on one part and subjection on the other; and if power be in the hands of men, it will sometimes be abused. The vigilance of the supreme magistrate may do much, but much will still remain undone. He can never know all the crimes that are committed, and can seldom punish all that he knows."

"This," said the prince, "I do not understand, but I had rather hear thee than dispute. Continue thy narration."

"My father," proceeded Imlac "originally intended that I should have no other education, than such as might qualify me for commerce; and discovering in me great strength of memory, and quickness of apprehension, often declared his hope that I should be some time the richest man in Abyssinia."

"Why," said the prince, "did thy father desire the increase of his wealth, when it was already greater than he durst discover or enjoy? I am unwilling to doubt thy veracity, yet inconsistencies cannot both be true."

"Inconsistencies," answered Imlac, "cannot both be right, but, imputed to man, they may both be true. Yet diversity is not inconsistency. My father might expect a time of greater security. However, some desire is necessary to keep life in motion, and he, whose real wants are supplied, must admit those of fancy."

"This," said the prince, "I can in some measure conceive. I repent that I interrupted thee."

"With this hope," proceeded Imlac, "he sent me to school; but when I had once found the delight of knowledge, and felt the pleasure of intelligence[9] and the pride of invention, I began silently to despise riches, and determined to disappoint the purpose of my father, whose grossness of conception raised my pity. I was twenty years old before his tenderness would expose me to the fatigue of travel, in which time I had been instructed, by successive masters, in all the literature of my native country. As every hour taught me something new, I lived in a continual course of gratifications; but, as I advanced towards manhood, I lost much of the reverence with which I had been used to look on my instructors; because, when the lesson was ended, I did not find them wiser or better than common men.

"At length my father resolved to initiate me in commerce, and, opening one of his subterranean treasuries, counted out ten thousand pieces of gold. 'This, young man,' said he, 'is the stock with which you must negotiate. I began with less than the fifth part, and you see how diligence and parsimony have increased it. This is your own to waste or to improve. If you squander it by negligence or caprice, you must wait for my death before you will be rich: if, in four years, you double your stock, we will thenceforward let subordination cease, and live together as friends and partners; for he shall always be equal with me, who is equally skilled in the art of growing rich.'

"We laid our money upon camels, concealed in bales of cheap goods,

9. Information or knowledge.

and travelled to the shore of the red sea. When I cast my eye on the expanse of waters my heart bounded like that of a prisoner escaped. I felt an unextinguishable curiosity kindle in my mind, and resolved to snatch this opportunity of seeing the manners of other nations, and of learning sciences unknown in Abyssinia.

"I remembered that my father had obliged me to the improvement of my stock, not by a promise which I ought not to violate, but by a penalty which I was at liberty to incur; and therefore determined to gratify my predominant desire, and by drinking at the fountains of knowledge, to quench the thirst of curiosity.

"As I was supposed to trade without connection with my father, it was easy for me to become acquainted with the master of a ship, and procure a passage to some other country. I had no motives of choice to regulate my voyage; it was sufficient for me that, wherever I wandered, I should see a country which I had not seen before. I therefore entered a ship bound for Surat,[1] having left a letter for my father declaring my intention.

Chapter 9. The History of Imlac Continued

"When I first entered upon the world of waters, and lost sight of land, I looked round about me with pleasing terror, and thinking my soul enlarged by the boundless prospect, imagined that I could gaze round for ever without satiety; but, in a short time, I grew weary of looking on barren uniformity, where I could only see again what I had already seen. I then descended into the ship, and doubted for a while whether all my future pleasures would not end like this in disgust and disappointment. Yet, surely, said I, the ocean and the land are very different; the only variety of water is rest and motion, but the earth has mountains and valleys, deserts and cities: it is inhabited by men of different customs and contrary opinions; and I may hope to find variety in life, though I should miss it in nature.

"With this thought I quieted my mind; and amused myself during the voyage, sometimes by learning from the sailors the art of navigation, which I have never practiced, and sometimes by forming schemes for my conduct in different situations, in not one of which I have been ever placed.

"I was almost weary of my naval amusements when we landed safely at Surat. I secured my money, and purchasing some commodities for show, joined myself to a caravan that was passing into the inland country. My companions, for some reason or other, conjecturing that I was rich, and, by my inquiries and admiration, finding that I was ignorant, considered me as a novice whom they had a right to cheat, and who was to learn at the usual expense the art of fraud. They exposed me to the theft of servants, and the exaction of officers,[2] and saw me plundered

1. A port in India.   2. Officials or agents.

upon false pretences, without any advantage to themselves, but that of rejoicing in the superiority of their own knowledge."

"Stop a moment," said the prince. "Is there such depravity in man, as that he should injure another without benefit to himself? I can easily conceive that all are pleased with superiority; but your ignorance was merely accidental, which, being neither your crime nor your folly, could afford them no reason to applaud themselves; and the knowledge which they had, and which you wanted, they might as effectually have shown by warning, as betraying you."

"Pride," said Imlac, "is seldom delicate, it will please itself with very mean advantages; and envy feels not its own happiness, but when it may be compared with the misery of others. They were my enemies because they grieved to think me rich, and my oppressors because they delighted to find me weak."

"Proceed," said the prince: "I doubt not of the facts which you relate, but imagine that you impute them to mistaken motives."

"In this company," said Imlac, "I arrived at Agra, the capital of Indostan, the city in which the great Mogul commonly resides. I applied myself to the language of the country, and in a few months was able to converse with the learned men; some of whom I found morose and reserved, and others easy and communicative; some were unwilling to teach another what they had with difficulty learned themselves; and some showed that the end of their studies was to gain the dignity of instructing.

"To the tutor of the young princes I recommended myself so much, that I was presented to the emperor as a man of uncommon knowledge. The emperor asked me many questions concerning my country and my travels; and though I cannot now recollect any thing that he uttered above the power of a common man, he dismissed me astonished at his wisdom, and enamored of his goodness.

"My credit was now so high, that the merchants, with whom I had traveled, applied to me for recommendations to the ladies of the court. I was surprised at their confidence of solicitation, and gently reproached them with their practices on the road. They heard me with cold indifference, and showed no tokens of shame or sorrow.

"They then urged their request with the offer of a bribe; but what I would not do for kindness I would not do for money; and refused them, not because they had injured me, but because I would not enable them to injure others; for I knew they would have made use of my credit to cheat those who should buy their wares.

"Having resided at Agra till there was no more to be learned, I traveled into Persia, where I saw many remains of ancient magnificence, and observed many new accommodations[3] of life. The Persians are a nation eminently social, and their assemblies afforded me daily opportunities of remarking characters and manners, and of tracing human nature through all its variations.

---

3. "Conveniences, things requisite to ease or refreshment" (Johnson's *Dictionary*).

"From Persia I passed into Arabia, where I saw a nation at once pastoral and warlike; who live without any settled habitation; whose only wealth is their flocks and herds; and who have yet carried on, through all ages, an hereditary war with all mankind, though they neither covet nor envy their possessions.

Chapter 10. Imlac's History Continued.
A Dissertation upon Poetry

"Wherever I went, I found that poetry was considered as the highest learning, and regarded with a veneration somewhat approaching to that which man would pay to the angelic nature. And yet it fills me with wonder that, in almost all countries, the most ancient poets are considered as the best: whether it be that every other kind of knowledge is an acquisition gradually attained, and poetry is a gift conferred at once; or that the first poetry of every nation surprised them as a novelty, and retained the credit by consent which it received by accident at first; or whether, as the province of poetry is to describe nature and passion, which are always the same, the first writers took possession of the most striking objects for description and the most probable occurrences for fiction, and left nothing to those that followed them, but transcription of the same events, and new combinations of the same images—whatever be the reason, it is commonly observed that the early writers are in possession of nature, and their followers of art; that the first excel in strength and invention, and the latter in elegance and refinement.

"I was desirous to add my name to this illustrious fraternity. I read all the poets of Persia and Arabia, and was able to repeat by memory the volumes that are suspended in the mosque of Mecca. But I soon found that no man was ever great by imitation. My desire of excellence impelled me to transfer my attention to nature and to life. Nature was to be my subject, and men to be my auditors: I could never describe what I had not seen; I could not hope to move those with delight or terror, whose interests and opinions I did not understand.

"Being now resolved to be a poet, I saw everything with a new purpose; my sphere of attention was suddenly magnified; no kind of knowledge was to be overlooked. I ranged mountains and deserts for images and resemblances, and pictured upon my mind every tree of the forest and flower of the valley. I observed with equal care the crags of the rock and the pinnacles of the palace. Sometimes I wandered along the mazes of the rivulet, and sometimes watched the changes of the summer clouds. To a poet nothing can be useless. Whatever is beautiful, and whatever is dreadful, must be familiar to his imagination; he must be conversant with all that is awfully vast or elegantly little. The plants of the garden, the animals of the wood, the minerals of the earth, and meteors of the sky, must all concur to store his mind with inexhaustible variety: for every idea[4] is useful for the enforcement or decoration of moral or reli-

4. Mental image.

gious truth; and he who knows most will have most power of diversifying his scenes, and of gratifying his reader with remote allusions and unexpected instruction.

"All the appearances of nature I was therefore careful to study, and every country which I have surveyed has contributed something to my poetical powers."

"In so wide a survey," said the prince, "you must surely have left much unobserved. I have lived till now within the circuit of these mountains, and yet cannot walk abroad without the sight of something which I have never beheld before, or never heeded."

"The business of a poet," said Imlac, "is to examine, not the individual, but the species; to remark general properties and large appearances; he does not number the streaks of the tulip, or describe the different shades in the verdure of the forest. He is to exhibit in his portraits of nature such prominent and striking features as recall the original to every mind, and must neglect the minuter discriminations, which one may have remarked and another have neglected, for those characteristics which are alike obvious to vigilance and carelessness.

"But the knowledge of nature is only half the task of a poet; he must be acquainted likewise with all the modes of life. His character requires that he estimate the happiness and misery of every condition; observe the power of all the passions in all their combinations, and trace the changes of the human mind, as they are modified by various institutions and accidental influences of climate or custom, from the sprightliness of infancy to the despondence of decrepitude. He must divest himself of the prejudices of his age or country; he must consider right and wrong in their abstracted and invariable state; he must disregard present laws and opinions, and rise to general and transcendental[5] truths, which will always be the same. He must, therefore, content himself with the slow progress of his name, contemn the applause of his own time, and commit his claims to the justice of posterity. He must write as the interpreter of nature and the legislator of mankind, and consider himself as presiding over the thoughts and manner of future generations, as a being superior to time and place.

"His labor is not yet at an end; he must know many languages and many sciences; and, that his style may be worthy of his thoughts, must by incessant practice familiarize to himself every delicacy of speech and grace of harmony."

Chapter 11. Imlac's Narrative Continued. A Hint on Pilgrimage

Imlac now felt the enthusiastic fit, and was proceeding to aggrandize his own profession, when the prince cried out: "Enough! thou hast convinced me that no human being can ever be a poet. Proceed with thy narration."

---

5. "General; pervading many particulars" (Johnson's *Dictionary*).

"To be a poet," said Imlac, "is indeed very difficult." "So difficult," returned the prince, "that I will at present hear no more of his labors. Tell me whither you went when you had seen Persia."

"From Persia," said the poet, "I traveled through Syria, and for three years resided in Palestine, where I conversed with great numbers of the northern and western nations of Europe, the nations which are now in possession of all power and all knowledge, whose armies are irresistible, and whose fleets command the remotest parts of the globe. When I compared these men with the natives of our own kingdom, and those that surround us, they appeared almost another order of beings. In their countries it is difficult to wish for anything that may not be obtained; a thousand arts, of which we never heard, are continually laboring for their convenience and pleasure; and whatever their own climate has denied them is supplied by their commerce."

"By what means," said the prince, "are the Europeans thus powerful, or why, since they can so easily visit Asia and Africa for trade or conquest, cannot the Asiatics and Africans invade their coasts, plant colonies in their ports, and give laws to their natural princes? The same wind that carries them back would bring us thither."

"They are more powerful, sir, than we," answered Imlac, "because they are wiser; knowledge will always predominate over ignorance, as man governs the other animals. But why their knowledge is more than ours, I know not what reason can be given, but the unsearchable will of the Supreme Being."

"When," said the prince with a sigh, "shall I be able to visit Palestine, and mingle with this mighty confluence of nations? Till that happy moment shall arrive, let me fill up the time with such representations as thou canst give me. I am not ignorant of the motive that assembles such numbers in that place, and cannot but consider it as the center of wisdom and piety, to which the best and wisest men of every land must be continually resorting."

"There are some nations," said Imlac, "that send few visitants to Palestine; for many numerous and learned sects in Europe concur to censure pilgrimage as superstitious, or deride it as ridiculous."

"You know," said the prince, "how little my life has made me acquainted with diversity of opinions. It will be too long to hear the arguments on both sides; you, that have considered them, tell me the result."

"Pilgrimage," said Imlac, "like many other acts of piety, may be reasonable or superstitious, according to the principles upon which it is performed. Long journeys in search of truth are not commanded. Truth, such as is necessary to the regulation of life, is always found where it is honestly sought. Change of place is no natural cause of the increase of piety, for it inevitably produces dissipation of mind. Yet, since men go every day to view the fields where great actions have been performed, and return with stronger impressions of the event, curiosity of the same kind may naturally dispose us to view that country whence our religion had its beginning; and I believe no man surveys those awful scenes without some confirmation of holy resolutions. That the Supreme Being may be more easily propitiated in one place than in another is the dream of idle superstition, but that some places may operate upon our own minds in an uncommon manner is an opinion which hourly experience will justify. He who supposes that his vices may be more successfully combated in Palestine, will, perhaps, find himself mistaken, yet he may go thither without folly; he who thinks they will be more freely pardoned, dishonors at once his reason and religion."

"These," said the prince, "are European distinctions. I will consider them another time. What have you found to be the effect of knowledge? Are those nations happier than we?"

"There is so much infelicity," said the poet, "in the world that scarce any man has leisure from his own distresses to estimate the comparative happiness of others. Knowledge is certainly one of the means of pleasure, as is confessed by the natural desire which every mind feels of increasing its ideas. Ignorance is mere privation, by which nothing can be produced; it is a vacuity in which the soul sits motionless and torpid for want of attraction; and, without knowing why, we always rejoice when we learn, and grieve when we forget. I am therefore inclined to conclude that if nothing counteracts the natural consequence of learning, we grow more happy as our minds take a wider range.

"In enumerating the particular comforts of life, we shall find many advantages on the side of the Europeans. They cure wounds and diseases with which we languish and perish. We suffer inclemencies of weather which they can obviate. They have engines for the despatch of many laborious works, which we must perform by manual industry. There is such communication between distant places that one friend can hardly be said to be absent from another. Their policy removes all public inconveniences; they have roads cut through their mountains, and bridges laid upon their rivers. And, if we descend to the privacies of life, their habitations are more commodious, and their possessions are more secure."

"They are surely happy," said the prince, "who have all these conveniencies, of which I envy none so much as the facility with which separated friends interchange their thoughts."

"The Europeans," answered Imlac, "are less unhappy than we, but they are not happy. Human life is everywhere a state in which much is to be endured, and little to be enjoyed."

Chapter 12. The Story of Imlac Continued

"I am not yet willing," said the prince, "to suppose that happiness is so parsimoniously distributed to mortals; nor can believe but that, if I had the choice of life, I should be able to fill every day with pleasure. I would injure no man, and should provoke no resentment: I would relieve every distress, and should enjoy the benedictions of gratitude. I would choose my friends among the wise, and my wife among the virtuous;

and therefore should be in no danger from treachery, or unkindness. My children should, by my care, be learned and pious, and would repay to my age what their childhood had received. What would dare to molest him who might call on every side to thousands enriched by his bounty, or assisted by his power? And why should not life glide quietly away in the soft reciprocation of protection and reverence? All this may be done without the help of European refinements, which appear by their effects to be rather specious than useful. Let us leave them and pursue our journey."

"From Palestine," said Imlac, "I passed through many regions of Asia; in the more civilized kingdoms as a trader, and among the barbarians of the mountains as a pilgrim. At last I began to long for my native country, that I might repose after my travels, and fatigues, in the places where I had spent my earliest years, and gladden my old companions with the recital of my adventures. Often did I figure to myself those, with whom I had sported away the gay hours of dawning life sitting round me in its evening, wondering at my tales, and listening to my counsels.

"When this thought had taken possession of my mind, I considered every moment as wasted which did not bring me nearer to Abyssinia. I hastened into Egypt, and, notwithstanding my impatience, was detained ten months in the contemplation of its ancient magnificence, and in enquiries after the remains of its ancient learning. I found in Cairo a mixture of all nations; some brought thither by the love of knowledge, some by the hope of gain, and many by the desire of living after their own manner without observation, and of lying hid in the obscurity of multitudes: for, in a city, populous as Cairo, it is possible to obtain at the same time the gratifications of society, and the secrecy of solitude.

"From Cairo I traveled to Suez, and embarked on the red sea, passing along the coast till I arrived at the port from which I had departed twenty years before. Here I joined myself to a caravan and re-entered my native country.

"I now expected the caresses of my kinsmen, and the congratulations of my friends, and was not without hope that my father, whatever value he had set upon riches, would own with gladness and pride a son who was able to add to the felicity and honor of the nation. But I was soon convinced that my thoughts were vain. My father had been dead fourteen years, having divided his wealth among my brothers, who were removed to some other provinces. Of my companions the greater part was in the grave, of the rest some could with difficulty remember me, and some considered me as one corrupted by foreign manners.

"A man used to vicissitudes is not easily dejected. I forgot, after a time, my disappointment, and endeavored to recommend myself to the nobles of the kingdom: they admitted me to their tables, heard my story, and dismissed me. I opened a school, and was prohibited to teach. I then resolved to sit down in the quiet of domestic life, and addressed a lady that was fond of my conversation, but rejected my suit, because my father was a merchant.

"Wearied at last with solicitation and repulses, I resolved to hide myself for ever from the world, and depend no longer on the opinion or caprice of others. I waited for the time when the gate of the *happy valley* should open, that I might bid farewell to hope and fear: the day came; my performance was distinguished with favor, and I resigned myself with joy to perpetual confinement."

"Hast thou here found happiness at last?" said Rasselas. "Tell me without reserve; art thou content with thy condition? or, dost thou wish to be again wandering and inquiring? All the inhabitants of this valley celebrate their lot, and, at the annual visit of the emperor, invite others to partake of their felicity."

"Great prince," said Imlac, "I shall speak the truth: I know not one of all your attendants who does not lament the hour when he entered this retreat. I am less unhappy than the rest, because I have a mind replete with images, which I can vary and combine at pleasure. I can amuse my solitude by the renovation of the knowledge which begins to fade from my memory, and by recollection of the accidents of my past life. Yet all this ends in the sorrowful consideration, that my acquirements are now useless, and that none of my pleasures can be again enjoyed. The rest, whose minds have no impression but of the present moment, are either corroded by malignant passions, or sit stupid in the gloom of perpetual vacancy."

"What passions can infest those," said the prince, "who have no trials? We are in a place where impotence precludes malice, and where all envy is repressed by community[6] of enjoyments."

"There may be community," said Imlac, "of material possessions, but there can never be community of love or of esteem. It must happen that one will please more than another; he that knows himself despised will always be envious; and still more envious and malevolent, if he is condemned to live in the presence of those who despise him. The invitations, by which they allure others to a state which they feel to be wretched, proceed from the natural malignity of hopeless misery. They are weary of themselves, and of each other, and expect to find relief in new companions. They envy the liberty which their folly has forfeited, and would gladly see all mankind imprisoned like themselves.

"From this crime, however, I am wholly free. No man can say that he is wretched by my persuasion. I look with pity on the crowds who are annually soliciting admission to captivity, and wish that it were lawful for me to warn them of their danger."

"My dear Imlac," said the prince, "I will open to thee my whole heart. I have long meditated an escape from the happy valley. I have examined the mountains on every side, but find myself insuperably barred: teach me the way to break my prison; thou shalt be the companion of my flight, the guide of my rambles, the partner of my fortune, and my sole director in the *choice of life.*"

6. Joint possession.

"Sir," answered the poet, "your escape will be difficult, and, perhaps, you may soon repent your curiosity. The world, which you figure to yourself smooth and quiet as the lake in the valley, you will find a sea foaming with tempests, and boiling with whirlpools: you will be sometimes overwhelmed by the waves of violence, and sometimes dashed against the rocks of treachery. Amidst wrongs and frauds, competitions and anxieties, you will wish a thousand times for these seats of quiet, and willingly quit hope to be free from fear."

"Do not seek to deter me from my purpose," said the prince: "I am impatient to see what thou hast seen; and, since thou art thyself weary of the valley, it is evident, that thy former state was better than this. Whatever be the consequence of my experiment, I am resolved to judge with my own eyes of the various conditions of men, and then to make deliberately my *choice of life*."

"I am afraid," said Imlac, "you are hindered by stronger restraints than my persuasions; yet, if your determination is fixed, I do not counsel you to despair. Few things are impossible to diligence and skill."

Chapter 13. Rasselas Discovers the Means of Escape

The prince now dismissed his favorite to rest, but the narrative of wonders and novelties filled his mind with perturbation. He revolved all that he had heard, and prepared innumerable questions for the morning.

Much of his uneasiness was now removed. He had a friend to whom he could impart his thoughts, and whose experience could assist him in his designs. His heart was no longer condemned to swell with silent vexation. He thought that even the *happy valley* might be endured with such a companion, and that, if they could range the world together, he should have nothing further to desire.

In a few days the water was discharged, and the ground dried. The prince and Imlac then walked out together to converse without the notice of the rest. The prince, whose thoughts were always on the wing, as he passed by the gate, said, with a countenance of sorrow, "Why art thou so strong, and why is man so weak?"

"Man is not weak" answered his companion; "knowledge is more than equivalent to force. The master of mechanics laughs at strength. I can burst the gate, but cannot do it secretly. Some other expedient must be tried."

As they were walking on the side of the mountain, they observed that the conies,[7] which the rain had driven from their burrows, had taken shelter among the bushes, and formed holes behind them, tending upwards in an oblique line. "It has been the opinion of antiquity," said Imlac, "that human reason borrowed many arts from the instinct of animals; let us, therefore, not think ourselves degraded by learning from

7. Rabbits.

the coney. We may escape by piercing the mountain in the same direction. We will begin where the summit hangs over the middle part, and labor upward till we shall issue out beyond the prominence."

The eyes of the prince, when he heard this proposal, sparkled with joy. The execution was easy, and the success certain.

No time was now lost. They hastened early in the morning to choose a place proper for their mine. They clambered with great fatigue among crags and brambles, and returned without having discovered any part that favored their design. The second and the third day were spent in the same manner, and with the same frustration. But, on the fourth, they found a small cavern, concealed by a thicket, where they resolved to make their experiment.

Imlac procured instruments proper to hew stone and remove earth, and they fell to their work on the next day with more eagerness than vigor. They were presently exhausted by their efforts, and sat down to pant upon the grass. The prince, for a moment, appeared to be discouraged. "Sir," said his companion, "practice will enable us to continue our labor for a longer time; mark, however, how far we have advanced, and you will find that our toil will some time have an end. Great works are performed, not by strength, but perseverance: yonder palace was raised by single stones, yet you see its height and spaciousness. He that shall walk with vigor three hours a day will pass in seven years a space equal to the circumference of the globe."

They returned to their work day after day, and, in a short time, found a fissure in the rock, which enabled them to pass far with very little obstruction. This Rasselas considered as a good omen. "Do not disturb your mind," said Imlac, "with other hopes or fears than reason may suggest: if you are pleased with prognostics of good, you will be terrified likewise with tokens of evil, and your whole life will be a prey to superstition. Whatever facilitates our work is more than an omen, it is a cause of success. This is one of those pleasing surprises which often happen to active resolution. Many things difficult to design prove easy to performance."

Chapter 14. Rasselas and Imlac Receive an Unexpected Visit

They had now wrought their way to the middle, and solaced their toil with the approach of liberty, when the prince, coming down to refresh himself with air, found his sister Nekayah standing before the mouth of the cavity. He started and stood confused, afraid to tell his design, and yet hopeless to conceal it. A few moments determined him to repose on her fidelity, and secure her secrecy by a declaration without reserve.

"Do not imagine," said the princess, "that I came hither as a spy: I had long observed from my window, that you and Imlac directed your walk every day towards the same point, but I did not suppose you had any better reason for the preference than a cooler shade, or more fragrant bank; nor followed you with any other design than to partake of your conversation. Since then not suspicion but fondness has detected you, let me not lose the advantage of my discovery. I am equally weary of confinement with yourself, and not less desirous of knowing what is done or suffered in the world. Permit me to fly with you from this tasteless tranquility, which will yet grow more loathsome when you have left me. You may deny me to accompany you, but cannot hinder me from following."

The prince, who loved Nekayah above his other sisters, had no inclination to refuse her request, and grieved that he had lost an opportunity of showing his confidence by a voluntary communication. It was therefore agreed that she should leave the valley with them; and that, in the mean time, she should watch, lest any other straggler should, by chance or curiosity, follow them to the mountain.

At length their labor was at an end; they saw light beyond the prominence, and, issuing to the top of the mountain, beheld the Nile, yet a narrow current, wandering beneath them.

The prince looked round with rapture, anticipated all the pleasures of travel, and in thought was already transported beyond his father's dominions. Imlac, though very joyful at his escape, had less expectation of pleasure in the world, which he had before tried, and of which he had been weary.

Rasselas was so much delighted with a wider horizon, that he could not soon be persuaded to return into the valley. He informed his sister that the way was open, and that nothing now remained but to prepare for their departure.

Chapter 15. The Prince and Princess Leave the Valley, and See Many Wonders

The prince and princess had jewels sufficient to make them rich whenever they came into a place of commerce, which, by Imlac's direction, they hid in their clothes, and, on the night of the next full moon, all left the valley. The princess was followed only by a single favorite, who did not know whither she was going.

They clambered through the cavity, and began to go down on the other side. The princess and her maid turned their eyes towards every part, and, seeing nothing to bound their prospect, considered themselves as in danger of being lost in a dreary vacuity. They stopped and trembled. "I am almost afraid," said the princess, "to begin a journey of which I cannot perceive an end, and to venture into this immense plain where I may be approached on every side by men whom I never saw." The prince felt nearly the same emotions, though he thought it more manly to conceal them.

Imlac smiled at their terrors, and encouraged them to proceed; but the princess continued irresolute till she had been imperceptibly drawn forward too far to return.

In the morning they found some shepherds in the field, who set milk and fruits before them. The princess wondered that she did not see a palace ready for her reception, and a table spread with delicacies; but, being faint and hungry, she drank the milk and ate the fruits, and thought them of a higher flavor than the products of the valley.

They traveled forward by easy journeys, being all unaccustomed to toil or difficulty, and knowing, that though they might be missed, they could not be pursued. In a few days they came into a more populous region, where Imlac was diverted with the admiration which his companions expressed at the diversity of manners, stations and employments.

Their dress was such as might not bring upon them the suspicion of having any thing to conceal, yet the prince, wherever he came, expected to be obeyed, and the princess was frighted, because those that came into her presence did not prostrate themselves before her. Imlac was forced to observe them with great vigilance, lest they should betray their rank by their unusual behavior, and detained them several weeks in the first village to accustom them to the sight of common mortals.

By degrees the royal wanderers were taught to understand that they had for a time laid aside their dignity, and were to expect only such regard as liberality and courtesy could procure. And Imlac, having, by many admonitions, prepared them to endure the tumults of a port, and the ruggedness of the commercial race, brought them down to the seacoast.

The prince and his sister, to whom every thing was new, were gratified equally at all places, and therefore remained for some months at the port without any inclination to pass further. Imlac was content with their stay, because he did not think it safe to expose them, unpracticed in the world, to the hazards of a foreign country.

At last he began to fear lest they should be discovered, and proposed to fix a day for their departure. They had no pretensions to judge for themselves, and referred the whole scheme to his direction. He therefore took passage in a ship to Suez; and, when the time came, with great difficulty prevailed on the princess to enter the vessel. They had a quick and prosperous voyage, and from Suez traveled by land to Cairo.

Chapter 16. They Enter Cairo, and Find Every Man Happy

As they approached the city, which filled the strangers with astonishment, "This," said Imlac to the prince, "is the place where travelers and merchants assemble from all the corners of the earth. You will here find men of every character and every occupation. Commerce is here honorable. I will act as a merchant, and you shall live as strangers, who have no other end of travel than curiosity. It will soon be observed that we are rich; our reputation will procure us access to all whom we shall desire to know; you will see all the conditions of humanity, and enable yourself at leisure to make your *choice of life*."

They now entered the town, stunned by the noise, and offended by the crowds. Instruction had not yet so prevailed over habit, but that they wondered to see themselves pass undistinguished along the street, and met by the lowest of the people without reverence or notice. The princess could not at first bear the thought of being leveled with the vulgar,[8] and for some days continued in her chamber, where she was served by her favorite, Pekuah, as in the palace of the valley.

Imlac, who understood traffic,[9] sold part of the jewels the next day, and hired a house, which he adorned with such magnificence that he was immediately considered as a merchant of great wealth. His politeness attracted many acquaintance, and his generosity made him courted by many dependents. His table was crowded by men of every nation, who all admired his knowledge, and solicited his favor. His companions, not being able to mix in the conversation, could make no discovery of their ignorance or surprise, and were gradually initiated in the world as they gained knowledge of the language.

The prince had, by frequent lectures, been taught the use and nature of money; but the ladies could not for a long time comprehend what the merchants did with small pieces of gold and silver, or why things of so little use should be received as equivalent to the necessaries of life.

They studied the language two years, while Imlac was preparing to set before them the various ranks and conditions of mankind. He grew acquainted with all who had anything uncommon in their fortune or conduct. He frequented the voluptuous and the frugal, the idle and the busy, the merchants and the men of learning.

The prince being now able to converse with fluency, and having learned the caution necessary to be observed in his intercourse with strangers, began to accompany Imlac to places of resort, and to enter into all assemblies, that he might make his *choice of life.*

For some time he thought choice needless, because all appeared to him equally happy. Wherever he went he met gaiety and kindness, and heard the song of joy or the laugh of carelessness. He began to believe that the world overflowed with universal plenty, and that nothing was withheld either from want or merit; that every hand showered liberality, and every heart melted with benevolence: "And who then," says he, "will be suffered to be wretched?"

Imlac permitted the pleasing delusion, and was unwilling to crush the hope of inexperience, till one day, having sat awhile silent, "I know not," said the prince, "what can be the reason that I am more unhappy than any of our friends. I see them perpetually and unalterably cheerful, but feel my own mind restless and uneasy. I am unsatisfied with those pleasures which I seem most to court; I live in the crowds of jollity, not so much to enjoy company as to shun myself, and am only loud and merry to conceal my sadness."

"Every man," said Imlac, "may, by examining his own mind, guess what passes in the minds of others; when you feel that your own gaiety

8. Ordinary people.   9. Commerce.

is counterfeit, it may justly lead you to suspect that of your companions not to be sincere. Envy is commonly reciprocal. We are long before we are convinced that happiness is never to be found, and each believes it possessed by others, to keep alive the hope of obtaining it for himself. In the assembly where you passed the last night, there appeared such sprightliness of air, and volatility of fancy, as might have suited beings of an higher order, formed to inhabit serener regions, inaccessible to care or sorrow; yet, believe me, prince, there was not one who did not dread the moment when solitude should deliver him to the tyranny of reflection."

"This," said the prince, "may be true of others, since it is true of me; yet, whatever be the general infelicity of man, one condition is more happy than another, and wisdom surely directs us to take the least evil in the *choice of life.*"

"The causes of good and evil," answered Imlac, "are so various and uncertain, so often entangled with each other, so diversified by various relations, and so much subject to accidents which cannot be foreseen, that he who would fix his condition upon incontestable reasons of preference must live and die inquiring and deliberating."

"But, surely," said Rasselas, "the wise men, to whom we listen with reverence and wonder, chose that mode of life for themselves which they thought most likely to make them happy."

"Very few," said the poet, "live by choice. Every man is placed in his present condition by causes which acted without his foresight, and with which he did not always willingly cooperate; and therefore you will rarely meet one who does not think the lot of his neighbor better than his own."

"I am pleased to think," said the prince, "that my birth has given me at least one advantage over others, by enabling me to determine for myself. I have here the world before me. I will review it at leisure; surely happiness is somewhere to be found."

Chapter 17. The Prince Associates with Young Men of Spirit and Gaiety

Rasselas rose next day, and resolved to begin his experiments upon life. "Youth," cried he, "is the time of gladness: I will join myself to the young men, whose only business is to gratify their desires, and whose time is all spent in a succession of enjoyments."

To such societies he was readily admitted, but a few days brought him back weary and disgusted. Their mirth was without images,[1] their laughter without motive; their pleasures were gross and sensual, in which the mind had no part; their conduct was at once wild and mean; they laughed at order and at law, but the frown of power dejected, and the eye of wisdom abashed them.

---

1. Ideas.

The prince soon concluded, that he should never be happy in a course of life of which he was ashamed. He thought it unsuitable to a reasonable being to act without a plan, and to be sad or cheerful only by chance. "Happiness," said he, "must be something solid and permanent, without fear and without uncertainty."

But his young companions had gained so much of his regard by their frankness and courtesy, that he could not leave them without warning and remonstrance. "My friends," said he, "I have seriously considered our manners and our prospects, and find that we have mistaken our own interest. The first years of man must make provision for the last. He that never thinks never can be wise. Perpetual levity must end in ignorance; and intemperance, though it may fire the spirits for an hour, will make life short or miserable. Let us consider that youth is of no long duration, and that in maturer age, when the enchantments of fancy shall cease, and phantoms of delight dance no more about us, we shall have no comforts but the esteem of wise men, and the means of doing good. Let us, therefore, stop, while to stop is in our power: let us live as men who are sometime to grow old, and to whom it will be the most dreadful of all evils not to count their past years but by follies, and to be reminded of their former luxuriance of health only by the maladies which riot has produced."

They stared a while in silence one upon another, and, at last, drove him away by a general chorus of continued laughter.

The consciousness that his sentiments were just, and his intentions kind, was scarcely sufficient to support him against the horror of derision. But he recovered his tranquillity, and pursued his search.

Chapter 18. The Prince Finds a Wise and Happy Man

As he was one day walking in the street, he saw a spacious building which all were, by the open doors, invited to enter: he followed the stream of people, and found it a hall or school of declamation, in which professors read lectures to their auditory. He fixed his eye upon a sage raised above the rest, who discoursed with great energy on the government of the passions. His look was venerable, his action graceful, his pronunciation clear, and his diction elegant. He showed with great strength of sentiment and variety of illustration that human nature is degraded and debased, when the lower faculties predominate over the higher; that when fancy, the parent of passion, usurps the dominion of the mind, nothing ensues but the natural effect of unlawful government, perturbation, and confusion; that she betrays the fortresses of the intellect to rebels, and excites her children to sedition against reason, their lawful sovereign. He compared reason to the sun, of which the light is constant, uniform and lasting; and fancy to a meteor, of bright but transitory luster, irregular in its motion, and delusive in its direction.

He then communicated the various precepts given from time to time for the conquest of passion, and displayed the happiness of those who had obtained the important victory, after which man is no longer the slave of fear, nor the fool of hope; is no more emaciated by envy, inflamed by anger, emasculated by tenderness, or depressed by grief; but walks on calmly through the tumults or the privacies of life, as the sun pursues alike his course through the calm or the stormy sky.

He enumerated many examples of heroes immovable by pain or pleasure, who looked with indifference on those modes or accidents to which the vulgar give the names of good and evil. He exhorted his hearers to lay aside their prejudices, and arm themselves against the shafts of malice or misfortune, by invulnerable patience; concluding that this state only was happiness, and that this happiness was in everyone's power.

Rasselas listened to him with the veneration due to the instructions of a superior being, and, waiting for him at the door, humbly implored the liberty of visiting so great a master of true wisdom. The lecturer hesitated a moment, when Rasselas put a purse of gold into his hand, which he received with a mixture of joy and wonder.

"I have found," said the prince at his return to Imlac, "a man who can teach all that is necessary to be known; who, from the unshaken throne of rational fortitude, looks down on the scenes of life changing beneath him. He speaks, and attention watches his lips. He reasons, and conviction closes his periods. This man shall be my future guide; I will learn his doctrines, and imitate his life."

"Be not too hasty," said Imlac, "to trust or to admire the teachers of morality: they discourse like angels, but they live like men."

Rasselas, who could not conceive how any man could reason so forcibly without feeling the cogency of his own arguments, paid his visit in a few days, and was denied admission. He had now learned the power of money, and made his way by a piece of gold to the inner apartment, where he found the philosopher in a room half darkened, with his eyes misty and his face pale. "Sir," said he, "you are come at a time when all human friendship is useless; what I suffer cannot be remedied, what I have lost cannot be supplied. My daughter, my only daughter, from whose tenderness I expected all the comforts of my age, died last night of a fever. My views, my purposes, my hopes are at an end; I am now a lonely being, disunited from society."

"Sir," said the prince, "mortality is an event by which a wise man can never be surprised; we know that death is always near, and it should therefore always be expected." "Young man," answered the philosopher, "you speak like one that has never felt the pangs of separation." "Have you then forgot the precepts," said Rasselas, "which you so powerfully enforced? Has wisdom no strength to arm the heart against calamity? Consider that external things are naturally variable, but truth and reason are always the same." "What comfort," said the mourner, "can truth and reason afford me? Of what effect are they now, but to tell me that my daughter will not be restored?"

The prince, whose humanity would not suffer him to insult misery with reproof, went away, convinced of the emptiness of rhetorical sound, and the inefficacy of polished periods and studied sentences.[2]

Chapter 19. A Glimpse of Pastoral Life

He was still eager upon the same inquiry; and having heard of a hermit that lived near the lowest cataract of the Nile, and filled the whole country with the fame of his sanctity, resolved to visit his retreat, and inquire whether that felicity which public life could not afford was to be found in solitude; and whether a man whose age and virtue made him venerable could teach any peculiar art of shunning evils, or enduring them.

Imlac and the princess agreed to accompany him, and, after the necessary preparations, they began their journey. Their way lay through fields, where shepherds tended their flocks and the lambs were playing upon the pasture. "This," said the poet, "is the life which has been often celebrated for its innocence and quiet; let us pass the heat of the day among the shepherds' tents, and know whether all our searches are not to terminate in pastoral simplicity."

The proposal pleased them, and they induced the shepherds, by small presents and familiar questions, to tell their opinion of their own state. They were so rude and ignorant, so little able to compare the good with the evil of the occupation, and so indistinct in their narratives and descriptions, that very little could be learned from them. But it was evident that their hearts were cankered with discontent; that they considered themselves as condemned to labor for the luxury of the rich, and looked up with stupid malevolence toward those that were placed above them.

The princess pronounced with vehemence that she would never suffer these envious savages to be her companions, and that she should not soon be desirous of seeing any more specimens of rustic happiness; but could not believe that all the accounts of primeval pleasures were fabulous, and was yet in doubt whether life had anything that could be justly preferred to the placid gratifications of fields and woods. She hoped that the time would come, when, with a few virtuous and elegant companions, she could gather flowers planted by her own hand, fondle the lambs of her own ewe, and listen, without care, among brooks and breezes, to one of her maidens reading in the shade.

Chapter 20. The Danger of Prosperity

On the next day they continued their journey, till the heat compelled them to look round for shelter. At a small distance they saw a thick wood, which they no sooner entered than they perceived that they were

---

2. Maxims or moral axioms; "periods": complete sentences.

approaching the habitations of men. The shrubs were diligently cut away to open walks where the shades were darkest; the boughs of opposite trees were artificially interwoven; seats of flowery turf were raised in vacant spaces, and a rivulet, that wantoned along the side of a winding path, had its banks sometimes opened into small basins, and its stream sometimes obstructed by little mounds of stone heaped together to increase its murmurs.

They passed slowly through the wood, delighted with such unexpected accommodations, and entertained each other with conjecturing what, or who, he could be, that, in those rude and unfrequented regions, had leisure and art for such harmless luxury.

As they advanced, they heard the sound of music, and saw youths and virgins dancing in the grove; and, going still further, beheld a stately palace built upon a hill surrounded with woods. The laws of eastern hospitality allowed them to enter, and the master welcomed them like a man liberal and wealthy.

He was skilful enough in appearances soon to discern that they were no common guests, and spread his table with magnificence. The eloquence of Imlac caught his attention, and the lofty courtesy of the princess excited his respect. When they offered to depart he entreated their stay, and was the next day still more unwilling to dismiss them than before. They were easily persuaded to stop, and civility grew up in time to freedom and confidence.

The prince now saw all the domestics cheerful, and all the face of nature smiling round the place, and could not forbear to hope that he should find here what he was seeking; but when he was congratulating the master upon his possessions, he answered with a sigh, "My condition has indeed the appearance of happiness, but appearances are delusive. My prosperity puts my life in danger; the Bassa of Egypt is my enemy, incensed only by my wealth and popularity. I have been hitherto protected against him by the princes of the country; but, as the favor of the great is uncertain, I know not how soon my defenders may be persuaded to share the plunder with the Bassa. I have sent my treasures into a distant country, and, upon the first alarm, am prepared to follow them. Then will my enemies riot in my mansion, and enjoy the gardens which I have planted."

They all joined in lamenting his danger, and deprecating his exile; and the princess was so much disturbed with the tumult of grief and indignation, that she retired to her apartment. They continued with their kind inviter a few days longer, and then went forward to find the hermit.

Chapter 21. The Happiness of Solitude. The Hermit's History

They came on the third day, by the direction of the peasants, to the hermit's cell: it was a cavern in the side of a mountain, over-shadowed with palm-trees; at such a distance from the cataract, that nothing more was heard than a gentle uniform murmur, such as composed the mind to pensive meditation, especially when it was assisted by the wind whistling among the branches. The first rude essay of nature had been so much improved by human labor, that the cave contained several apartments, appropriated to different uses, and often afforded lodging to travelers, whom darkness or tempests happened to overtake.

The hermit sat on a bench at the door, to enjoy the coolness of the evening. On one side lay a book with pens and papers, on the other mechanical instruments of various kinds. As they approached him unregarded, the princess observed that he had not the countenance of a man that had found, or could teach, the way to happiness.

They saluted him with great respect, which he repaid like a man not unaccustomed to the forms of courts. "My children," said he, "if you have lost your way, you shall be willingly supplied with such conveniencies for the night as this cavern will afford. I have all that nature requires, and you will not expect delicacies in a hermit's cell."

They thanked him, and, entering, were pleased with the neatness and regularity of the place. The hermit set flesh and wine before them, though he fed only upon fruits and water. His discourse was cheerful without levity, and pious without enthusiasm.[3] He soon gained the esteem of his guests, and the princess repented of her hasty censure.

At last Imlac began thus: "I do not now wonder that your reputation is so far extended; we have heard at Cairo of your wisdom, and came hither to implore your direction for this young man and maiden in the *choice of life.*"

"To him that lives well," answered the hermit, "every form of life is good; nor can I give any other rule for choice, than to remove from all apparent evil."

"He will remove most certainly from evil," said the prince, "who shall devote himself to that solitude which you have recommended by your example."

"I have indeed lived fifteen years in solitude," said the hermit, "but have no desire that my example should gain any imitators. In my youth I professed arms, and was raised by degrees to the highest military rank. I have traversed wide countries at the head of my troops, and seen many battles and sieges. At last, being disgusted by the preferment of a younger officer, and feeling that my vigor was beginning to decay, I resolved to close my life in peace, having found the world full of snares, discord, and misery. I had once escaped from the pursuit of the enemy by the shelter of this cavern, and therefore chose it for my final residence. I employed artificers to form it into chambers, and stored it with all that I was likely to want.

"For some time after my retreat, I rejoiced like a tempest-beaten sailor at his entrance into the harbor, being delighted with the sudden change of the noise and hurry of war, to stillness and repose. When the pleasure of novelty went away, I employed my hours in examining the plants

---

3. "A vain belief of private revelation; a vain confidence of divine favor or communication" (Johnson's *Dictionary*).

which grow in the valley, and the minerals which I collected from the rocks. But that inquiry is now grown tasteless and irksome. I have been for some time unsettled and distracted: my mind is disturbed with a thousand perplexities of doubt, and vanities of imagination, which hourly prevail upon me, because I have no opportunities of relaxation or diversion. I am sometimes ashamed to think that I could not secure myself from vice, but by retiring from the exercise of virtue, and begin to suspect that I was rather impelled by resentment, than led by devotion, into solitude. My fancy riots in scenes of folly, and I lament that I have lost so much, and have gained so little. In solitude, if I escape the example of bad men, I want likewise the counsel and conversation of the good. I have been long comparing the evils with the advantages of society, and resolve to return into the world tomorrow. The life of a solitary man will be certainly miserable, but not certainly devout."

They heard his resolution with surprise, but, after a short pause, offered to conduct him to Cairo. He dug up a considerable treasure which he had hid among the rocks, and accompanied them to the city, on which, as he approached it, he gazed with rapture.

Chapter 22. *The Happiness of a Life Led According to Nature*

Rasselas went often to an assembly of learned men, who met at stated times to unbend their minds and compare their opinions. Their manners were somewhat coarse, but their conversation was instructive, and their disputations acute, though sometimes too violent, and often continued till neither controvertist remembered upon what question they began. Some faults were almost general among them; everyone was desirous to dictate to the rest, and everyone was pleased to hear the genius or knowledge of another depreciated.

In this assembly Rasselas was relating his interview with the hermit, and the wonder with which he heard him censure a course of life which he had so deliberately chosen, and so laudably followed. The sentiments of the hearers were various. Some were of opinion that the folly of his choice had been justly punished by condemnation to perpetual perseverance. One of the youngest among them, with great vehemence, pronounced him an hypocrite. Some talked of the right of society to the labor of individuals, and considered retirement as a desertion of duty. Others readily allowed that there was a time when the claims of the public were satisfied, and when a man might properly sequester himself, to review his life and purify his heart.

One, who appeared more affected with the narrative than the rest, thought it likely that the hermit would in a few years go back to his retreat, and perhaps, if shame did not restrain, or death intercept him, return once more from his retreat into the world. "For the hope of happiness," said he, "is so strongly impressed that the longest experience is not able to efface it. Of the present state, whatever it be, we feel and are forced to confess the misery; yet when the same state is again at a distance, imagination paints it as desirable. But the time will surely come when desire will be no longer our torment, and no man shall be wretched but by his own fault."

"This," said a philosopher who had heard him with tokens of great impatience, "is the present condition of a wise man. The time is already come when none are wretched but by their own fault. Nothing is more idle than to inquire after happiness, which nature has kindly placed within our reach. The way to be happy is to live according to nature, in obedience to that universal and unalterable law with which every heart is originally impressed; which is not written on it by precept, but engraven by destiny, not instilled by education, but infused at our nativity. He that lives according to nature will suffer nothing from the delusions of hope, or importunities of desire; he will receive and reject with equability of temper, and act or suffer as the reason of things shall alternately prescribe. Other men may amuse themselves with subtle definitions, or intricate ratiocination. Let them learn to be wise by easier means; let them observe the hind of the forest, and the linnet of the grove; let them consider the life of animals, whose motions are regulated by instinct; they obey their guide, and are happy. Let us therefore, at length, cease to dispute, and learn to live; throw away the encumbrance of precepts, which they who utter them with so much pride and pomp do not understand, and carry with us this simple and intelligible maxim, that deviation from nature is deviation from happiness."

When he had spoken, he looked round him with a placid air, and enjoyed the consciousness of his own beneficence. "Sir," said the prince with great modesty, "as I, like all the rest of mankind, am desirous of felicity, my closest attention has been fixed upon your discourse. I doubt not the truth of a position which a man so learned has so confidently advanced. Let me only know what it is to live according to nature."

"When I find young men so humble and so docile," said the philosopher, "I can deny them no information which my studies have enabled me to afford. To live according to nature, is to act always with due regard to the fitness arising from the relations and qualities of causes and effects; to concur with the great and unchangeable scheme of universal felicity; to co-operate with the general disposition and tendency of the present system of things."

The prince soon found that this was one of the sages whom he should understand less as he heard him longer. He therefore bowed and was silent; and the philosopher, supposing him satisfied, and the rest vanquished, rose up and departed with the air of a man that had co-operated with the present system.

Chapter 23. The Prince and his Sister Divide between Them the Work of Observation

Rasselas returned home full of reflections, doubtful how to direct his future steps. Of the way to happiness he found the learned and simple equally ignorant; but, as he was yet young, he flattered himself that he had time remaining for more experiments, and further inquiries. He communicated to Imlac his observations and his doubts, but was answered by him with new doubts, and remarks that gave him no comfort. He therefore discoursed more frequently and freely with his sister, who had yet the same hope with himself, and always assisted him to give some reason why, though he had been hitherto frustrated, he might succeed at last.

"We have hitherto," said she, "known but little of the world: we have never yet been either great or mean. In our own country, though we had royalty, we had no power, and in this we have not yet seen the private recesses of domestic peace. Imlac favors not our search, lest we should in time find him mistaken. We will divide the task between us: you shall try what is to be found in the splendor of courts, and I will range the shades of humbler life. Perhaps command and authority may be the supreme blessings, as they afford most opportunities of doing good: or, perhaps, what this world can give may be found in the modest habitations of middle fortune; too low for great designs, and too high for penury and distress."

Chapter 24. The Prince Examines the Happiness of High Stations

Rasselas applauded the design, and appeared next day with a splendid retinue at the court of the Bassa. He was soon distinguished for his magnificence, and admitted, as a prince whose curiosity had brought him from distant countries, to an intimacy with the great officers, and frequent conversation with the Bassa himself.

He was at first inclined to believe, that the man must be pleased with his own condition, whom all approached with reverence, and heard with obedience, and who had the power to extend his edicts to a whole kingdom. "There can be no pleasure," said he, "equal to that of feeling at once the joy of thousands all made happy by wise administration. Yet, since, by the law of subordination, this sublime delight can be in one nation but the lot of one, it is surely reasonable to think that there is some satisfaction more popular[4] and accessible, and that millions can hardly be subjected to the will of a single man, only to fill his particular breast with incommunicable content."

These thoughts were often in his mind, and he found no solution of the difficulty. But as presents and civilities gained him more familiarity, he found that almost every man who stood high in employment hated all the rest, and was hated by them, and that their lives were a continual succession of plots and detections, stratagems and escapes, faction and treachery. Many of those, who surrounded the Bassa, were sent only to watch and report his conduct; every tongue was muttering censure and every eye was searching for a fault.

4. Common.

At last the letters of revocation arrived, the Bassa was carried in chains to Constantinople, and his name was mentioned no more.

"What are we now to think of the prerogatives of power," said Rasselas to his sister; "is it without any efficacy to good? or, is the subordinate degree only dangerous, and the supreme safe and glorious? Is the Sultan the only happy man in his dominions? or, is the Sultan himself subject to the torments of suspicion, and the dread of enemies?"

In a short time the second Bassa was deposed. The Sultan, that had advanced him, was murdered by the Janisaries,[5] and his successor had other views and different favorites.

Chapter 25. The Princess Pursues Her Inquiry with More Diligence than Success

The princess, in the mean time, insinuated herself into many families; for there are few doors, through which liberality, joined with good humor, cannot find its way. The daughters of many houses were airy[6] and cheerful, but Nekayah had been too long accustomed to the conversation of Imlac and her brother to be much pleased with childish levity and prattle which had no meaning. She found their thoughts narrow, their wishes low, and their merriment often artificial. Their pleasures, poor as they were, could not be preserved pure, but were embittered by petty competitions and worthless emulation. They were always jealous of the beauty of each other; of a quality to which solicitude can add nothing, and from which detraction can take nothing away. Many were in love with triflers like themselves, and many fancied that they were in love when in truth they were only idle. Their affection was seldom fixed on sense or virtue, and therefore seldom ended but in vexation. Their grief, however, like their joy, was transient; everything floated in their mind unconnected with the past or future, so that one desire easily gave way to another, as a second stone cast into the water effaces and confounds the circles of the first.

With these girls she played as with inoffensive animals, and found them proud of her countenance,[7] and weary of her company.

But her purpose was to examine more deeply, and her affability easily persuaded the hearts that were swelling with sorrow to discharge their secrets in her ear: and those whom hope flattered, or prosperity delighted, often courted her to partake their pleasures.

The princess and her brother commonly met in the evening in a private summer-house on the bank of the Nile, and related to each other the occurrences of the day. As they were sitting together, the princess cast her eyes upon the river that flowed before her. "Answer," said she, "great father of waters, thou that rollest thy floods through eighty nations, to the invocations of the daughter of thy native king. Tell me if thou

5. Guards of the Turkish ruler.
6. "Gay; sprightly; full of mirth" (Johnson's *Dic-*
tionary).
7. Patronage, favor.

waterest, through all thy course, a single habitation from which thou dost not hear the murmurs of complaint?"

"You are then," said Rasselas, "not more successful in private houses than I have been in courts." "I have, since the last partition of our provinces,"[8] said the princess, "enabled myself to enter familiarly into many families, where there was the fairest show of prosperity and peace, and know not one house that is not haunted by some fury that destroys its quiet.

"I did not seek ease among the poor, because I concluded that there it could not be found. But I saw many poor whom I had supposed to live in affluence. Poverty has, in large cities, very different appearances: it is often concealed in splendor, and often in extravagance. It is the care of a very great part of mankind to conceal their indigence from the rest: they support themselves by temporary expedients, and every day is lost in contriving for the morrow.

"This, however, was an evil, which, though frequent, I saw with less pain, because I could relieve it. Yet some have refused my bounties; more offended with my quickness to detect their wants, than pleased with my readiness to succor them: and others, whose exigencies compelled them to admit my kindness, have never been able to forgive their benefactress. Many, however, have been sincerely grateful without the ostentation of gratitude, or the hope of other favors."

Chapter 26. The Princess Continues Her Remarks upon Private Life

Nekayah, perceiving her brother's attention fixed, proceeded in her narrative.

"In families where there is or is not poverty, there is commonly discord. If a kingdom be, as Imlac tells us, a great family, a family likewise is a little kingdom, torn with factions and exposed to revolutions. An unpracticed observer expects the love of parents and children to be constant and equal; but this kindness seldom continues beyond the years of infancy: in a short time the children become rivals to their parents. Benefits are allayed[9] by reproaches, and gratitude debased by envy.

"Parents and children seldom act in concert; each child endeavors to appropriate the esteem or fondness of the parents, and the parents, with yet less temptation, betray each other to their children. Thus, some place their confidence in the father, and some in the mother, and by degrees the house is filled with artifices and feuds.

"The opinions of children and parents, of the young and the old, are naturally opposite, by the contrary effects of hope and despondence, of expectation and experience, without crime or folly on either side. The colors of life in youth and age appear different, as the face of nature in

---

8. Division of our responsibilities.
9. To allay is "to joint anything to another, so as

to abate its predominant qualities" (Johnson's *Dictionary*).

spring and winter. And how can children credit the assertions of parents, which their own eyes show them to be false?

"Few parents act in such a manner as much to enforce their maxims by the credit of their lives. The old man trusts wholly to slow contrivance and gradual progression; the youth expects to force his way by genius, vigor, and precipitance. The old man pays regard to riches, and the youth reverences virtue. The old man deifies prudence; the youth commits himself to magnanimity and chance. The young man, who intends no ill, believes that none is intended, and therefore acts with openness and candor; but his father, having suffered the injuries of fraud, is impelled to suspect, and too often allured to practice it. Age looks with anger on the temerity of youth, and youth with contempt on the scrupulosity[1] of age. Thus parents and children, for the greatest part, live on to love less and less; and, if those whom nature has thus closely united are the torments of each other, where shall we look for tenderness and consolation?"

"Surely," said the prince, "you must have been unfortunate in your choice of acquaintance: I am unwilling to believe that the most tender of all relations is thus impeded in its effects by natural necessity."

"Domestic discord," answered she, "is not inevitably and fatally necessary, but yet is not easily avoided. We seldom see that a whole family is virtuous; the good and evil cannot well agree, and the evil can yet less agree with one another. Even the virtuous fall sometimes to variance, when their virtues are of different kinds, and tending to extremes. In general, those parents have most reverence who most deserve it; for he that lives well cannot be despised.

"Many other evils infest private life. Some are the slaves of servants whom they have trusted with their affairs. Some are kept in continual anxiety to the caprice of rich relations, whom they cannot please, and dare not offend. Some husbands are imperious, and some wives perverse; and, as it is always more easy to do evil than good, though the wisdom or virtue of one can very rarely make many happy, the folly or vice of one may often make many miserable."

"If such be the general effect of marriage," said the prince, "I shall for the future think it dangerous to connect my interest with that of another, lest I should be unhappy by my partner's fault."

"I have met," said the princess, "with many who live single for that reason; but I never found that their prudence ought to raise envy. They dream away their time without friendship, without fondness, and are driven to rid themselves of the day, for which they have no use, by childish amusements, or vicious delights. They act as beings under the constant sense of some known inferiority that fills their minds with rancor, and their tongues with censure. They are peevish at home, and malevolent abroad; and, as the outlaws of human nature, make it their business and their pleasure to disturb that society which debars them

1. "Fear of acting in any manner" (Johnson's *Dictionary*).

from its privileges. To live without feeling or exciting sympathy, to be fortunate without adding to the felicity of others, or afflicted without tasting the balm of pity, is a state more gloomy than solitude; it is not retreat but exclusion from mankind. Marriage has many pains, but celibacy has no pleasures."

"What then is to be done?" said Rasselas; "the more we inquire, the less we can resolve. Surely he is most likely to please himself that has no other inclination to regard."

Chapter 27. Disquisition upon Greatness

The conversation had a short pause. The prince, having considered his sister's observations, told her, that she had surveyed life with prejudice, and supposed misery where she did not find it. "Your narrative," says he, "throws yet a darker gloom upon the prospects of futurity: the predictions of Imlac were but faint sketches of the evils painted by Nekayah. I have been lately convinced that quiet is not the daughter of grandeur, or of power: that her presence is not to be bought by wealth, nor enforced by conquest. It is evident, that as any man acts in a wider compass, he must be more exposed to opposition from enmity or miscarriage from chance; whoever has many to please or to govern, must use the ministry of many agents, some of whom will be wicked, and some ignorant; by some he will be misled, and by others betrayed. If he gratifies one he will offend another: those that are not favored will think themselves injured; and, since favors can be conferred but upon few, the greater number will be always discontented.'

"The discontent," said the princess, "which is thus unreasonable, I hope that I shall always have spirit to despise, and you, power to repress."

"Discontent," answered Rasselas, "will not always be without reason under the most just or vigilant administration of public affairs. None, however attentive, can always discover that merit which indigence or faction may happen to obscure; and none, however powerful, can always reward it. Yet, he that sees inferior desert[2] advanced above him, will naturally impute that preference to partiality or caprice; and, indeed, it can scarcely be hoped that any man, however magnanimous by nature, or exalted by condition, will be able to persist for ever in fixed and inexorable justice of distribution: he will sometimes indulge his own affections, and sometimes those of his favorites; he will permit some to please him who can never serve him; he will discover in those whom he loves qualities which in reality they do not possess; and to those, from whom he receives pleasure, he will in his turn endeavor to give it. Thus will recommendations sometimes prevail which were purchased by money, or by the more destructive bribery of flattery and servility.

"He that has much to do will do something wrong, and of that wrong must suffer the consequences; and, if it were possible that he should always act rightly, yet when such numbers are to judge of his conduct,

2. Merit; one deserving reward.

the bad will censure and obstruct him by malevolence, and the good sometimes by mistake.

"The highest stations cannot therefore hope to be the abodes of happiness, which I would willingly believe to have fled from thrones and palaces to seats of humble privacy and placid obscurity. For what can hinder the satisfaction, or intercept the expectations, of him whose abilities are adequate to his employments, who sees with his own eyes the whole circuit of his influence, who chooses by his own knowledge all whom he trusts, and whom none are tempted to deceive by hope or fear? Surely he has nothing to do but to love and to be loved, to be virtuous and to be happy."

"Whether perfect happiness would be procured by perfect goodness," said Nekayah, "this world will never afford an opportunity of deciding. But this, at least, may be maintained, that we do not always find visible happiness in proportion to visible virtue. All natural and almost all political evils, are incident alike to the bad and good: they are confounded in the misery of a famine, and not much distinguished in the fury of a faction; they sink together in a tempest, and are driven together from their country by invaders. All that virtue can afford is quietness of conscience, a steady prospect of a happier state; this may enable us to endure calamity with patience; but remember that patience must suppose pain."

Chapter 28. Rasselas and Nekayah Continue Their Conversation

"Dear princess," said Rasselas, "you fall into the common errors of exaggeratory declamation, by producing, in a familiar disquisition,[3] examples of national calamities, and scenes of extensive misery, which are found in books rather than in the world, and which, as they are horrid, are ordained to be rare. Let us not imagine evils which we do not feel, nor injure life by misrepresentations. I cannot bear that querulous eloquence which threatens every city with a siege like that of Jerusalem,[4] that makes famine attend on every flight of locusts, and suspends pestilence on the wing of every blast that issues from the south.

"On necessary and inevitable evils, which overwhelm kingdoms at once, all disputation is vain: when they happen they must be endured. But it is evident, that these bursts of universal distress are more dreaded than felt: thousands and ten thousands flourish in youth, and wither in age, without the knowledge of any other than domestic evils, and share the same pleasures and vexations whether their kings are mild or cruel, whether the armies of their country pursue their enemies, or retreat before them. While courts are disturbed with intestine[5] competitions, and ambassadors are negotiating in foreign countries, the smith still plies his anvil, and the husbandman drives his plow forward; the necessaries of life are required and obtained, and the successive business of the seasons continues to make its wonted revolutions.

3. Family discussion of a question.
4. In 70 A.D. the Romans, under Titus, besieged
and destroyed Jerusalem.
5. Internal, domestic.

"Let us cease to consider what, perhaps, may never happen, and what, when it shall happen, will laugh at human speculation. We will not endeavor to modify the motions of the elements, or to fix the destiny of kingdoms. It is our business to consider what beings like us may perform; each laboring for his own happiness, by promoting within his circle, however narrow, the happiness of others.

"Marriage is evidently the dictate of nature; men and women were made to be companions of each other, and therefore I cannot be persuaded but that marriage is one of the means of happiness."

"I know not," said the princess, "whether marriage be more than one of the innumerable modes of human misery. When I see and reckon the various forms of connubial infelicity, the unexpected causes of lasting discord, the diversities of temper, the oppositions of opinion, the rude collisons of contrary desire where both are urged by violent impulses, the obstinate contests of disagreeing virtues, where both are supported by consciousness of good intention, I am sometimes disposed to think with the severer casuists of most nations, that marriage is rather permitted than approved, and that none, but by the instigation of a passion too much indulged, entangle themselves with indissoluble compacts."

"You seem to forget," replied Rasselas, "that you have, even now, represented celibacy as less happy than marriage. Both conditions may be bad, but they cannot both be worst. Thus it happens when wrong opinions are entertained, that they mutually destroy each other, and leave the mind open to truth."

"I did not expect," answered the princess, "to hear that imputed to falsehood which is the consequence only of frailty. To the mind, as to the eye, it is difficult to compare with exactness objects vast in their extent, and various in their parts. Where we see or conceive the whole at once we readily note the discriminations and decide the preference: but of two systems, of which neither can be surveyed by any human being in its full compass of magnitude and multiplicity of complication, where is the wonder, that judging of the whole by parts, I am alternately affected by one and the other as either presses on my memory or fancy? We differ from ourselves just as we differ from each other, when we see only part of the question, as in the multifarious relations of politics and morality: but when we perceive the whole at once, as in numerical computations, all agree in one judgment, and none ever varies his opinion."

"Let us not add," said the prince, "to the other evils of life, the bitterness of controversy, nor endeavor to vie with each other in subtleties of argument. We are employed in a search, of which both are equally to enjoy the success, or suffer by the miscarriage. It is therefore fit that we assist each other. You surely conclude too hastily from the infelicity of marriage against its institution; will not the misery of life prove equally that life cannot be the gift of heaven? The world must be peopled by marriage, or peopled without it."

"How the world is to be peopled," returned Nekayah, "is not my care, and needs not be yours. I see no danger that the present generation should omit to leave successors behind them: we are not now inquiring for the world, but for ourselves."

Chapter 29. The Debate on Marriage Continued

"The good of the whole," says Rasselas, "is the same with the good of all its parts. If marriage be best for mankind it must be evidently best for individuals, or a permanent and necessary duty must be the cause of evil, and some must be inevitably sacrificed to the convenience of others. In the estimate which you have made of the two states, it appears that the incommodities of a single life are, in a great measure, necessary and certain, but those of the conjugal state accidental and avoidable.

"I cannot forbear to flatter myself that prudence and benevolence will make marriage happy. The general folly of mankind is the cause of general complaint. What can be expected but disappointment and repentance from a choice made in the immaturity of youth, in the ardor of desire, without judgment, without foresight, without inquiry after conformity of opinions, similarity of manners, rectitude of judgment, or purity of sentiment.

"Such is the common process of marriage. A youth and maiden meeting by chance, or brought together by artifice, exchange glances, reciprocate civilities, go home, and dream of one another. Having little to divert attention, or diversify thought, they find themselves uneasy when they are apart, and therefore conclude that they shall be happy together. They marry, and discover what nothing but voluntary blindness had before concealed; they wear out life in altercations, and charge nature with cruelty.

"From those early marriages proceeds likewise the rivalry of parents and children: the son is eager to enjoy the world before the father is willing to forsake it, and there is hardly room at once for two generations. The daughter begins to bloom before the mother can be content to fade, and neither can forbear to wish for the absence of the other.

"Surely all these evils may be avoided by that deliberation and delay which prudence prescribes to irrevocable choice. In the variety and jollity of youthful pleasures life may be well enough supported without the help of a partner. Longer time will increase experience, and wider views will allow better opportunities of inquiry and selection: one advantage, as least, will be certain; the parents will be visibly older than their children."

"What reason cannot collect," said Nekayah, "and what experiment has not yet taught, can be known only from the report of others. I have been told that late marriages are not eminently happy. This is a question too important to be neglected, and I have often proposed it to those, whose accuracy of remark, and comprehensiveness of knowledge, made their suffrages[6] worthy of regard. They have generally determined that it

6. Opinions.

is dangerous for a man and woman to suspend their fate upon each other, at a time when opinions are fixed, and habits are established; when friendships have been contracted on both sides, when life has been planned into method, and the mind has long enjoyed the contemplation of its own prospects.

"It is scarcely possible that two traveling through the world under the conduct of chance should have been both directed to the same path, and it will not often happen that either will quit the track which custom has made pleasing. When the desultory levity of youth has settled into regularity, it is soon succeeded by pride ashamed to yield, or obstinacy delighting to contend. And even though mutual esteem produces mutual desire to please, time itself, as it modifies unchangeably the external mien, determines likewise the direction of the passions, and gives an inflexible rigidity to the manners. Long customs are not easily broken: he that attempts to change the course of his own life very often labors in vain; and how shall we do that for others which we are seldom able to do for ourselves?"

"But surely," interposed the prince, "you suppose the chief motive of choice forgotten or neglected. Whenever I shall seek a wife, it shall be my first question, whether she be willing to be led by reason?"

"Thus it is," said Nekayah, "that philosophers are deceived. There are a thousand familiar[6A] disputes which reason never can decide; questions that elude investigation, and make logic ridiculous; cases where something must be done, and where little can be said. Consider the state of mankind, and inquire how few can be supposed to act upon any occasions, whether small or great, with all the reasons of action present to their minds. Wretched would be the pair above all names of wretchedness, who should be doomed to adjust by reason every morning all the minute detail of a domestic day.

"Those who marry at an advanced age will probably escape the encroachments of their children; but, in diminution of this advantage, they will be likely to leave them, ignorant and helpless, to a guardian's mercy: or, if that should not happen, they must at least go out of the world before they see those whom they love best either wise or great.

"From their children, if they have less to fear, they have less also to hope, and they lose, without equivalent, the joys of early love, and the convenience of uniting with manners pliant and minds susceptible of new impressions, which might wear away their dissimilitudes by long cohabitation, as soft bodies, by continual attrition, conform their surfaces to each other.

"I believe it will be found that those who marry late are best pleased with their children, and those who marry early with their partners."

"The union of these two affections," said Rasselas, "would produce all that could be wished. Perhaps there is a time when marriage might unite them, a time neither too early for the father, nor too late for the husband."

"Every hour," answered the princess, "confirms my prejudice in favor

6A. Domestic.

of the position so often uttered by the mouth of Imlac, 'That nature sets her gifts on the right hand and on the left.' Those conditions, which flatter hope and attract desire, are so constituted that, as we approach one, we recede from another. There are goods so opposed that we cannot seize both, but, by too much prudence, may pass between them at too great a distance to reach either. This is often the fate of long consideration; he does nothing who endeavors to do more than is allowed to humanity. Flatter not yourself with contrarieties of pleasure. Of the blessings set before you make your choice, and be content. No man can taste the fruits of autumn, while he is delighting his scent with the flowers of the spring: no man can, at the same time, fill his cup from the source and from the mouth of the Nile."

Chapter 30. Imlac Enters, and Changes the Conversation

Here Imlac entered, and interrupted them. "Imlac," said Rasselas, "I have been taking from the princess the dismal history of private life, and am almost discouraged from further search."

"It seems to me," said Imlac, "that while you are making the choice of life, you neglect to live. You wander about a single city, which, however large and diversified, can now afford few novelties, and forget that you are in a country, famous among the earliest monarchies for the power and wisdom of its inhabitants; a country where the sciences first dawned that illuminate the world, and beyond which the arts cannot be traced of civil society or domestic life.

"The old Egyptians have left behind them monuments of industry and power before which all European magnificence is confessed to fade away. The ruins of their architecture are the schools of modern builders, and from the wonders which time has spared we may conjecture, though uncertainly, what it has destroyed."

"My curiosity," said Rasselas, "does not very strongly lead me to survey piles of stone, or mounds of earth; my business is with man. I came hither not to measure fragments of temples, or trace choked aqueducts, but to look upon the various scenes of the present world."

"The things that are now before us," said the princess, "require attention, and deserve it. What have I to do with the heroes or the monuments of ancient times? with times which never can return, and heroes, whose form of life was different from all that the present condition of mankind requires or allows."

"To know anything," returned the poet, "we must know its effects; to see men we must see their works, that we may learn what reason has dictated, or passion has incited, and find what are the most powerful motives of action. To judge rightly of the present we must oppose it to the past; for all judgment is comparative, and of the future nothing can be known. The truth is, that no mind is much employed upon the present: recollection and anticipation fill up almost all our moments. Our passions are joy and grief, love and hatred, hope and fear. Of joy and grief the past is the object, and the future of hope and fear; even love and hatred respect the past, for the cause must have been before the effect.

"The present state of things is the consequence of the former, and it is natural to inquire what were the sources of the good that we enjoy, or of the evil that we suffer. If we act only for ourselves, to neglect the study of history is not prudent: if we are entrusted with the care of others, it is not just. Ignorance, when it is voluntary, is criminal; and he may properly be charged with evil who refused to learn how he might prevent it.

"There is no part of history so generally useful as that which relates the progress of the human mind, the gradual improvement of reason, the successive advances of science, the vicissitudes of learning and ignorance, which are the light and darkness of thinking beings, the extinction and resuscitation of arts, and all the revolutions of the intellectual world. If accounts of battles and invasions are peculiarly the business of princes, the useful or elegant arts are not to be neglected; those who have kingdoms to govern, have understandings to cultivate.

"Example is always more efficacious than precept. A soldier is formed in war, and a painter must copy pictures. In this, contemplative life has the advantage: great actions are seldom seen, but the labors of art are always at hand for those who desire to know what art has been able to perform.

"When the eye or the imagination is struck with any uncommon work the next transition of an active mind is to the means by which it was performed. Here begins the true use of such contemplation; we enlarge our comprehension by new ideas, and perhaps recover some art lost to mankind, or learn what is less perfectly known in our own country. At least we compare our own with former times, and either rejoice at our improvements, or, what is the first motion towards good, discover our defects."

"I am willing," said the prince, "to see all that can deserve my search."

"And I," said the princess, "shall rejoice to learn something of the manners of antiquity."

"The most pompous monument of Egyptian greatness, and one of the most bulky works of manual industry," said Imlac, "are the pyramids; fabrics[7] raised before the time of history, and of which the earliest narratives afford us only uncertain traditions. Of these the greatest is still standing, very little injured by time."

"Let us visit them tomorrow," said Nekayah. "I have often heard of the Pyramids, and shall not rest, till I have seen them within and without with my own eyes."

Chapter 31. They Visit the Pyramids

The resolution being thus taken, they set out the next day. They laid tents upon their camels, being resolved to stay among the pyramids till

7. Buildings.

their curiosity was fully satisfied. They traveled gently, turned aside to everything remarkable, stopped from time to time and conversed with the inhabitants, and observed the various appearances of towns ruined and inhabited, of wild and cultivated nature.

When they came to the great pyramid, they were astonished at the extent of the base, and the height of the top. Imlac explained to them the principles upon which the pyramidal form was chosen for a fabric intended to coextend its duration with that of the world; he showed that its gradual diminution gave it such stability as defeated all the common attacks of the elements, and could scarcely be overthrown by earthquakes themselves, the least resistible of natural violence. A concussion that should shatter the pyramid would threaten the dissolution of the continent.

They measured all its dimensions, and pitched their tents at its foot. Next day they prepared to enter its interior apartments, and having hired the common guides, climbed up to the first passage, when the favorite of the princess, looking into the cavity, stepped back and trembled. "Pekuah," said the princess, "of what art thou afraid?" "Of the narrow entrance," answered the lady, "and of the dreadful gloom. I dare not enter a place which must surely be inhabited by unquiet souls. The original possessors of these dreadful vaults will start up before us, and perhaps shut us in forever." She spoke, and threw her arms round the neck of her mistress.

"If all your fear be of apparitions," said the prince, "I will promise you safety. There is no danger from the dead; he that is once buried will be seen no more."

"That the dead are seen no more," said Imlac, "I will not undertake to maintain, against the concurrent and unvaried testimony of all ages, and of all nations. There is no people, rude or learned, among whom apparitions of the dead are not related and believed. This opinion, which perhaps prevails as far as human nature is diffused, could become universal only by its truth; those that never heard of one another would not have agreed in a tale which nothing but experience can make credible. That it is doubted by single cavilers can very little weaken the general evidence; and some who deny it with their tongues confess it by their fears.

"Yet I do not mean to add new terrors to those which have already seized upon Pekuah. There can be no reason why specters should haunt the pyramid more than other places, or why they should have power or will to hurt innocence and purity. Our entrance is no violation of their privileges; we can take nothing from them, how then can we offend them?"

"My dear Pekuah," said the princess, "I will always go before you, and Imlac shall follow you. Remember that you are the companion of the princess of Abyssinia."

"If the princess is pleased that her servant should die," returned the lady, "let her command some death less dreadful than enclosure in this horrid cavern. You know I dare not disobey you; I must go if you command me, but if I once enter, I never shall come back."

The princess saw that her fear was too strong for expostulation or reproof, and, embracing her, told her that she should stay in the tent till their return. Pekuah was yet not satisfied, but entreated the princess not to pursue so dreadful a purpose as that of entering the recesses of the pyramid. "Though I cannot teach courage," said Nekayah, "I must not learn cowardice, nor leave at last undone what I came hither only to do."

Chapter 32. They Enter the Pyramid

Pekuah descended to the tents, and the rest entered the pyramid. They passed through the galleries, surveyed the vaults of marble, and examined the chest in which the body of the founder is supposed to have been reposited. They then sat down in one of the most spacious chambers to rest a while before they attempted to return.

"We have now," said Imlac, "gratified our minds with an exact view of the greatest work of man, except the wall of China.

"Of the wall it is very easy to assign the motive. It secured a wealthy and timorous nation from the incursions of barbarians, whose unskillfulness in arts made it easier for them to supply their wants by rapine than by industry, and who from time to time poured in upon the habitations of peaceful commerce, as vultures descend upon domestic fowl. Their celerity and fierceness made the wall necessary, and their ignorance made it efficacious.

"But for the pyramids, no reason has ever been given adequate to the cost and labor of the work. The narrowness of the chambers proves that it could afford no retreat from enemies, and treasures might have been reposited at far less expense with equal security. It seems to have been erected only in compliance with that hunger of imagination which preys incessantly upon life, and must be always appeased by some employment. Those who have already all that they can enjoy must enlarge their desires. He that has built for use till use is supplied, must begin to build for vanity, and extend his plan to the utmost power of human performance, that he may not be soon reduced to form another wish.

"I consider this mighty structure as a monument of the insufficiency of human enjoyments. A king, whose power is unlimited, and whose treasures surmount all real and imaginary wants, is compelled to solace, by the erection of a pyramid, the satiety of dominion and tastelessness of pleasures, and to amuse the tediousness of declining life by seeing thousands laboring without end, and one stone, for no purpose, laid upon another. Whoever thou art, that, not content with a moderate condition, imaginest happiness in royal magnificence, and dreamest that command or riches can feed the appetite of novelty with perpetual gratifications, survey the pyramids, and confess thy folly!"

Chapter 33. The Princess Meets with an Unexpected Misfortune

They rose up, and returned through the cavity at which they had entered, and the princess prepared for her favorite a long narrative of dark labyrinths, and costly rooms, and of the different impressions which the varieties of the way had made upon her. But when they came to their train, they found every one silent and dejected: the men discovered[8] shame and fear in their countenances, and the women were weeping in the tents.

What had happened they did not try to conjecture, but immediately inquired. "You had scarcely entered into the pyramid," said one of the attendants, "when a troop of Arabs rushed upon us: we were too few to resist them, and too slow to escape. They were about to search the tents, set us on our camels, and drive us along before them, when the approach of some Turkish horsemen put them to flight; but they seized the lady Pekuah with her two maids, and carried them away: the Turks are now pursuing them by our instigation, but I fear they will not be able to overtake them."

The princess was overpowered with surprise and grief. Rasselas, in the first heat of his resentment, ordered his servants to follow him, and prepared to pursue the robbers with his saber in his hand. "Sir," said Imlac, "what can you hope from violence or valor? the Arabs are mounted on horses trained to battle and retreat; we have only beasts of burden. By leaving our present station we may lose the princess, but cannot hope to regain Pekuah."

In a short time the Turks returned, having not been able to reach the enemy. The princess burst out into new lamentations, and Rasselas could scarcely forbear to reproach them with cowardice; but Imlac was of opinion, that the escape of the Arabs was no addition to their misfortune, for, perhaps, they would have killed their captives rather than have resigned them.

Chapter 34. They Return to Cairo without Pekuah

There was nothing to be hoped from longer stay. They returned to Cairo repenting of their curiosity, censuring the negligence of the government, lamenting their own rashness which had neglected to procure a guard, imagining many expedients by which the loss of Pekuah might have been prevented, and resolving to do something for her recovery, though none could find any thing proper to be done.

Nekayah retired to her chamber, where her women attempted to comfort her, by telling her that all had their troubles, and that lady Pekuah had enjoyed much happiness in the world for a long time, and might reasonably expect a change of fortune. They hoped that some good would

8. Revealed, betrayed; "train": retinue.

befall her wheresoever she was, and that their mistress would find another friend who might supply her place.

The princess made them no answer, and they continued the form of condolence, not much grieved in their hearts that the favorite was lost.

Next day the prince presented to the Bassa a memorial[9] of the wrong which he had suffered, and a petition for redress. The Bassa threatened to punish the robbers, but did not attempt to catch them, nor, indeed, could any account or description be given by which he might direct the pursuit.

It soon appeared that nothing would be done by authority. Governors, being accustomed to hear of more crimes than they can punish, and more wrongs than they can redress, set themselves at ease by indiscriminate negligence, and presently forget the request when they lose sight of the petitioner.

Imlac then endeavored to gain some intelligence by private agents. He found many who pretended to an exact knowledge of all the haunts of the Arabs, and to regular correspondence with their chiefs, and who readily undertook the recovery of Pekuah. Of these, some were furnished with money for their journey, and came back no more; some were liberally paid for accounts which a few days discovered to be false. But the princess would not suffer any means, however improbable, to be left untried. While she was doing something she kept her hope alive. As one expedient failed, another was suggested; when one messenger returned unsuccessful, another was dispatched to a different quarter.

Two months had now passed, and of Pekuah nothing had been heard; the hopes which they had endeavored to raise in each other grew more languid, and the princess, when she saw nothing more to be tried, sunk down inconsolable in hopeless dejection. A thousand times she reproached herself with the easy compliance by which she permitted her favorite to stay behind her. "Had not my fondness," said she, "lessened my authority, Pekuah had not dared to talk of her terrors. She ought to have feared me more than specters. A severe look would have overpowered her; a peremptory command would have compelled obedience. Why did foolish indulgence prevail upon me? Why did I not speak and refuse to hear?"

"Great princess," said Imlac, "do not reproach yourself for your virtue, or consider that as blameable by which evil has accidentally been caused. Your tenderness for the timidity of Pekuah was generous and kind. When we act according to our duty, we commit the event to him by whose laws our actions are governed, and who will suffer none to be finally punished for obedience. When, in prospect of some good, whether natural or moral, we break the rules prescribed us, we withdraw from the direction of superior wisdom, and take all consequences upon ourselves. Man cannot so far know the connection of causes and events, as that he may venture to do wrong in order to do right. When we pursue

9. Statement of facts.

our end by lawful means, we may always console our miscarriage by the hope of future recompense. When we consult only our own policy, and attempt to find a nearer way to good, by overleaping the settled boundaries of right and wrong, we cannot be happy even by success, because we cannot escape the consciousness of our fault; but, if we miscarry, the disappointment is irremediably embittered. How comfortless is the sorrow of him, who feels at once the pangs of guilt, and the vexation of calamity which guilt has brought upon him?

"Consider, princess, what would have been your condition, if the lady Pekuah had entreated to accompany you, and, being compelled to stay in the tents, had been carried away; or how would you have borne the thought, if you had forced her into the pyramid, and she had died before you in agonies of terror."

"Had either happened," said Nekayah, "I could not have endured life till now: I should have been tortured to madness by the remembrance of such cruelty, or must have pined away in abhorrence of myself."

"This at least," said Imlac, "is the present reward of virtuous conduct, that no unlucky consequence can oblige us to repent it."

Chapter 35. The Princess Languishes for Want of Pekuah

Nekayah, being thus reconciled to herself, found that no evil is insupportable but that which is accompanied with consciousness of wrong. She was, from that time, delivered from the violence of tempestuous sorrow, and sunk into silent pensiveness and gloomy tranquillity. She sat from morning to evening recollecting all that had been done or said by her Pekuah, treasured up with care every trifle on which Pekuah had set an accidental value, and which might recall to mind any little incident or careless conversation. The sentiments of her, whom she now expected to see no more, were treasured in her memory as rules of life, and she deliberated to no other end than to conjecture on any occasion what would have been the opinion and counsel of Pekuah.

The women, by whom she was attended, knew nothing of her real condition, and therefore she could not talk to them but with caution and reserve. She began to remit[1] her curiosity, having no great care to collect notions which she had no convenience of uttering. Rasselas endeavored first to comfort and afterwards to divert her; he hired musicians, to whom she seemed to listen, but did not hear them, and procured masters to instruct her in various arts, whose lectures, when they visited her again, were again to be repeated. She had lost her taste of pleasure and her ambition of excellence. And her mind, though forced into short excursions, always recurred to the image of her friend.

Imlac was every morning earnestly enjoined to renew his inquiries, and was asked every night whether he had yet heard of Pekuah, till not being able to return the princess the answer that she desired, he was less and less willing to come into her presence. She observed his backwardness, and commanded him to attend her. "You are not," said she, "to

1. To lay aside.

confound impatience with resentment, or to suppose that I charge you with negligence, because I repine at your unsuccessfulness. I do not much wonder at your absence; I know that the unhappy are never pleasing, and that all naturally avoid the contagion of misery. To hear complaints is wearisome alike to the wretched and the happy; for who would cloud by adventitious grief the short gleams of gaiety which life allows us? or who, that is struggling under his own evils, will add to them the miseries of another?

"The time is at hand, when none shall be disturbed any longer by the sighs of Nekayah: my search after happiness is now at an end. I am resolved to retire from the world with all its flatteries and deceits, and will hide myself in solitude, without any other care than to compose my thoughts, and regulate my hours by a constant succession of innocent occupations, till, with a mind purified from all earthly desires, I shall enter into that state, to which all are hastening, and in which I hope again to enjoy the friendship of Pekuah."

"Do not entangle your mind," said Imlac, "by irrevocable determinations, nor increase the burden of life by a voluntary accumulation of misery: the weariness of retirement will continue or increase when the loss of Pekuah is forgotten. That you have been deprived of one pleasure is no very good reason for rejection of the rest."

"Since Pekuah was taken from me," said the princess, "I have no pleasure to reject or to retain. She that has no one to love or trust has little to hope. She wants the radical principle of happiness. We may, perhaps, allow that what satisfaction this world can afford, must arise from the conjunction of wealth, knowledge and goodness: wealth is nothing but as it is bestowed, and knowledge nothing but as it is communicated: they must therefore be imparted to others, and to whom could I now delight to impart them? Goodness affords the only comfort which can be enjoyed without a partner, and goodness may be practised in retirement."

"How far solitude may admit goodness, or advance it, I shall not," replied Imlac, "dispute at present. Remember the confession of the pious hermit. You will wish to return into the world, when the image of your companion has left your thoughts." "That time," said Nekayah, "will never come. The generous frankness, the modest obsequiousness,[1] and the faithful secrecy of my dear Pekuah, will always be more missed, as I shall live longer to see vice and folly."

"The state of a mind oppressed with a sudden calamity," said Imlac, "is like that of the fabulous inhabitants of the new created earth, who, when the first night came upon them, supposed that day never would return. When the clouds of sorrow gather over us, we see nothing beyond them, nor can imagine how they will be dispelled: yet a new day succeeded to the night, and sorrow is never long without a dawn of ease. But they who restrain themselves from receiving comfort, do as the sav-

1. Obedience.

ages would have done, had they put out their eyes when it was dark. Our minds, like our bodies, are in continual flux; something is hourly lost, and something acquired. To lose much at once is inconvenient to either, but while the vital powers remain uninjured, nature will find the means of reparation. Distance has the same effect on the mind as on the eye, and while we glide along the stream of time, whatever we leave behind us is always lessening, and that which we approach increasing in magnitude. Do not suffer life to stagnate; it will grow muddy for want of motion: commit yourself again to the current of the world; Pekuah will vanish by degrees; you will meet in your way some other favorite, or learn to diffuse yourself in general conversation."

"At least," said the prince, "do not despair before all remedies have been tried: the inquiry after the unfortunate lady is still continued, and shall be carried on with yet greater diligence, on condition that you will promise to wait a year for the event, without any unalterable resolution."

Nekayah thought this a reasonable demand, and made the promise to her brother, who had been advised by Imlac to require it. Imlac had, indeed, no great hope of regaining Pekuah, but he supposed, that if he could secure the interval of a year, the princess would be then in no danger of a cloister.

Chapter 36. Pekuah Is Still Remembered. The Progress of Sorrow

Nekayah, seeing that nothing was omitted for the recovery of her favorite, and having, by her promise, set her intention of retirement at a distance, began imperceptibly to return to common cares and common pleasures. She rejoiced without her own consent at the suspension of her sorrows, and sometimes caught herself with indignation in the act of turning away her mind from the remembrance of her, whom yet she resolved never to forget.

She then appointed a certain hour of the day for meditation on the merits and fondness of Pekuah, and for some weeks retired constantly at the time fixed, and returned with her eyes swollen and her countenance clouded. By degrees she grew less scrupulous, and suffered any important and pressing avocation to delay the tribute of daily tears. She then yielded to less occasions; sometimes forgot what she was indeed afraid to remember, and, at last, wholly released herself from the duty of periodical affliction.

Her real love of Pekuah was yet not diminished. A thousand occurrences brought her back to memory, and a thousand wants, which nothing but the confidence of friendship can supply, made her frequently regretted. She, therefore, solicited Imlac never to desist from inquiry, and to leave no art of intelligence untried, that, at least, she might have the comfort of knowing that she did not suffer by negligence or sluggishness. "Yet what," said she, "is to be expected from our pursuit of happiness, when we find the state of life to be such, that happiness itself is the cause of misery? Why should we endeavor to attain that, of which the possession cannot be secured? I shall henceforward fear to yield my heart to excellence, however bright, or to fondness, however tender, lest I should lose again what I have lost in Pekuah."

Chapter 37. The Princess Hears News of Pekuah

In seven months, one of the messengers, who had been sent away upon the day when the promise was drawn from the princess, returned, after many unsuccessful rambles, from the borders of Nubia, with an account that Pekuah was in the hands of an Arab chief, who possessed a castle or fortress on the extremity of Egypt. The Arab, whose revenue was plunder, was willing to restore her, with her two attendants, for two hundred ounces of gold.

The price was no subject of debate. The princess was in ecstasies when she heard that her favorite was alive, and might so cheaply be ransomed. She could not think of delaying for a moment Pekuah's happiness or her own, but entreated her brother to send back the messenger with the sum required. Imlac, being consulted, was not very confident of the veracity of the relator, and was still more doubtful of the Arab's faith, who might, if he were too liberally trusted, detain at once the money and the captives. He thought it dangerous to put themselves in the power of the Arab, by going into his district, and could not expect that the rover[2] would so much expose himself as to come into the lower country, where he might be seized by the forces of the Bassa.

It is difficult to negotiate where neither will trust. But Imlac, after some deliberation, directed the messenger to propose that Pekuah should be conducted by ten horsemen to the monastery of St. Anthony, which is situated in the deserts of Upper Egypt, where she should be met by the same number, and her ransom should be paid.

That no time might be lost, as they expected that the proposal would not be refused, they immediately began their journey to the monastery; and, when they arrived, Imlac went forward with the former messenger to the Arab's fortress. Rasselas was desirous to go with them, but neither his sister nor Imlac would consent. The Arab, according to the custom of his nation, observed the laws of hospitality with great exactness to those who put themselves into his power, and, in a few days, brought Pekuah with her maids, by easy journeys, to their place appointed, where receiving the stipulated price, he restored her with great respect to liberty and her friends, and undertook to conduct them back toward Cairo beyond all danger of robbery or violence.

The princess and her favorite embraced each other with transport too violent to be expressed, and went out together to pour the tears of tenderness in secret, and exchange professions of kindness and gratitude. After a few hours they returned into the refectory of the convent, where,

2. Robber.

in the presence of the prior and his brethren, the prince required of Pekuah the history of her adventures.

Chapter 38. The Adventures of the Lady Pekuah

"At what time, and in what manner, I was forced away," said Pekuah, "your servants have told you. The suddenness of the event struck me with surprise, and I was at first rather stupified than agitated with any passion of either fear or sorrow. My confusion was increased by the speed and tumult of our flight while we were followed by the Turks, who, as it seemed, soon despaired to overtake us, or were afraid of those whom they made a show of menacing.

"When the Arabs saw themselves out of danger they slackened their course, and, as I was less harassed by external violence, I began to feel more uneasiness in my mind. After some time we stopped near a spring shaded with trees in a pleasant meadow, where we were set upon the ground, and offered such refreshments as our masters were partaking. I was suffered to sit with my maids apart from the rest, and none attempted to comfort or insult us. Here I first began to feel the full weight of my misery. The girls sat weeping in silence, and from time to time looked on me for succor. I knew not to what condition we were doomed, nor could conjecture where would be the place of our captivity, or whence to draw any hope of deliverance. I was in the hands of robbers and savages, and had no reason to suppose that their pity was more than their justice, or that they would forbear the gratification of any ardor of desire, or caprice of cruelty. I, however, kissed my maids, and endeavored to pacify them by remarking, that we were yet treated with decency, and that, since we were now carried beyond pursuit, there was no danger of violence to our lives.

"When we were to be set again on horseback, my maids clung round me, and refused to be parted, but I commanded them not to irritate those who had us in their power. We traveled the remaining part of the day through an unfrequented and pathless country, and came by moonlight to the side of a hill, where the rest of the troop was stationed. Their tents were pitched, and their fires kindled, and our chief was welcomed as a man much beloved by his dependents.

"We were received into a large tent, where we found women who had attended their husbands in the expedition. They set before us the supper which they had provided, and I eat it rather to encourage my maids than to comply with any appetite of my own. When the meat was taken away they spread the carpets for repose. I was weary, and hoped to find in sleep that remission of distress which nature seldom denies. Ordering myself therefore to be undressed, I observed that the women looked very earnestly upon me, not expecting, I suppose, to see me so submissively attended. When my upper vest was taken off, they were apparently struck with the splendor of my clothes, and one of them timorously laid her hand upon the embroidery. She then went out, and, in a short time, came back with another woman, who seemed to be of higher rank, and greater authority. She did, at her entrance, the usual act of reverence, and, taking me by the hand, placed me in a smaller tent, spread with finer carpets, where I spent the night quietly with my maids.

"In the morning, as I was sitting on the grass, the chief of the troop came towards me: I rose up to receive him, and he bowed with great respect. 'Illustrious lady,' said he, 'my fortune is better than I had presumed to hope; I am told by my women that I have a princess in my camp.' 'Sir,' answered I, 'your women have deceived themselves and you; I am not a princess, but an unhappy stranger who intended soon to have left this country, in which I am now to be imprisoned for ever.' 'Whoever, or whencesoever, you are,' returned the Arab, 'your dress, and that of your servants, show your rank to be high, and your wealth to be great. Why should you, who can so easily procure your ransom, think yourself in danger of perpetual captivity? The purpose of my incursions is to increase my riches, or more properly to gather tribute. The sons of Ishmael[3] are the natural and hereditary lords of this part of the continent, which is usurped by late invaders, and low-born tryants, from whom we are compelled to take by the sword what is denied to justice. The violence of war admits no distinction; the lance that is lifted at guilt and power will sometimes fall on innocence and gentleness.'

" 'How little,' said I, 'did I expect that yesterday it should have fallen upon me.'

" 'Misfortunes,' answered the Arab, 'should always be expected. If the eye of hostility could learn reverence or pity, excellence like yours had been exempt from injury. But the angels of affliction spread their toils alike for the virtuous and the wicked, for the mighty and the mean. Do not be disconsolate; I am not one of the lawless and cruel rovers of the desert; I know the rules of civil[4] life: I will fix your ransom, give a passport to your messenger, and perform my stipulation with nice punctuality.'

"You will easily believe that I was pleased with his courtesy; and finding that his predominant passion was desire of money, I began now to think my danger less, for I knew that no sum would be thought too great for the release of Pekuah. I told him that he should have no reason to charge me with ingratitude, if I was used with kindness, and that any ransom, which could be expected for a maid of common rank, would be paid, but that he must not persist to rate me as a princess. He said, he would consider what he should demand, and then, smiling, bowed and retired.

"Soon after the women came about me, each contending to be more officious[5] than the other, and my maids themselves were served with reverence. We traveled onward by short journeys. On the fourth day the

---

3. Arabs, who claim descent from Ishmael, a son of Abraham.
4. Civilized. "Nice punctuality": scrupulous

exactness.
5. Ready to serve.

chief told me, that my ransom must be two hundred ounces of gold, which I not only promised him, but told him, that I would add fifty more, if I and my maids were honorably treated.

"I never knew the power of gold before. From that time I was the leader of the troop. The march of every day was longer or shorter as I commanded, and the tents were pitched where I chose to rest. We now had camels and other conveniencies for travel, my own women were always at my side, and I amused myself with observing the manners of the vagrant nations,[6] and with viewing remains of ancient edifices with which these deserted countries appear to have been, in some distant age, lavishly embellished.

"The chief of the band was a man far from illiterate: he was able to travel by the stars or the compass, and had marked in his erratic expeditions such places as are most worthy the notice of a passenger.[7] He observed to me, that buildings are always best preserved in places little frequented, and difficult of access: for, when once a country declines from its primitive splendor, the more inhabitants are left, the quicker ruin will be made. Walls supply stones more easily than quarries, and palaces and temples will be demolished to make stables of granite, and cottages of porphyry.

Chapter 39. The Adventures of Pekuah Continued

"We wandered about in this manner for some weeks, whether, as our chief pretended, for my gratification, or, as I rather suspected, for some convenience of his own. I endeavored to appear contented where sullenness and resentment would have been of no use, and that endeavor conduced much to the calmness of my mind; but my heart was always with Nekayah, and the troubles of the night much overbalanced the amusements of the day. My women, who threw all their cares upon their mistress, set their minds at ease from the time when they saw me treated with respect, and gave themselves up to the incidental alleviations of our fatigue without solicitude or sorrow. I was pleased with their pleasure, and animated with their confidence. My condition had lost much of its terror, since I found that the Arab ranged the country merely to get riches. Avarice is an uniform and tractable vice: other intellectual distempers are different in different constitutions of mind; that which sooths the pride of one will offend the pride of another; but to the favor of the covetous there is a ready way, bring money and nothing is denied.

"At last we came to the dwelling of our chief, a strong and spacious house built with stone in an island of the Nile, which lies, as I was told, under the tropic. 'Lady,' said the Arab, 'you shall rest after your journey a few weeks in this place, where you are to consider yourself as sovereign. My occupation is war: I have therefore chosen this obscure residence, from which I can issue unexpected, and to which I can retire

6. Nomads.   7. Traveler.

unpursued. You may now repose in security: here are few pleasures, but here is no danger.' He then led me into the inner apartments, and seating me on the richest couch, bowed to the ground. His women, who considered me as a rival, looked on me with malignity; but being soon informed that I was a great lady detained only for my ransom, they began to vie with each other in obsequiousness and reverence.

"Being again comforted with new assurances of speedy liberty, I was for some days diverted from impatience by the novelty of the place. The turrets overlooked the country to a great distance, and afforded a view of many windings of the stream. In the day I wandered from one place to another as the course of the sun varied the splendor of the prospect, and saw many things which I had never seen before. The crocodiles and river-horses[8] are common in this unpeopled region, and I often looked upon them with terror, though I knew that they could not hurt me. For some time I expected to see mermaids and tritons, which, as Imlac has told me, the European travelers have stationed in the Nile, but no such beings ever appeared, and the Arab, when I inquired after them, laughed at my credulity.

"At night the Arab always attended me to a tower set apart for celestial observations, where he endeavored to teach me the names and courses of the stars. I had no great inclination to this study, but an appearance of attention was necessary to please my instructor, who valued himself for his skill, and, in a little while, I found some employment requisite to beguile the tediousness of time, which was to be passed always amidst the same objects. I was weary of looking in the morning on things from which I had turned away weary in the evening: I therefore was at last willing to observe the stars rather than do nothing, but could not always compose my thoughts, and was very often thinking on Nekayah when others imagined me contemplating the sky. Soon after the Arab went upon another expedition, and then my only pleasure was to talk with my maids about the accident by which we were carried away, and the happiness that we should all enjoy at the end of our captivity."

"There were women in your Arab's fortress," said the princess, "why did you not make them your companions, enjoy their conversation, and partake their diversions? In a place where they found business or amusement, why should you alone sit corroded with idle melancholy? or why could not you bear for a few months that condition to which they were condemned for life?"

"The diversions of the women," answered Pekuah, "were only childish play, by which the mind accustomed to stronger operations could not be kept busy. I could do all which they delighted in doing by powers merely sensitive,[9] while my intellectual faculties were flown to Cairo. They ran from room to room as a bird hops from wire to wire in his cage. They danced for the sake of motion, as lambs frisk in a meadow. One sometimes pretended to be hurt that the rest might be alarmed, or

8. Hippopotamuses.
9. "Having sense or perception, but not reason" (Johnson's *Dictionary*).

hid herself that another might seek her. Part of their time passed in watching the progress of light bodies that floated on the river, and part in marking the various forms into which clouds broke in the sky.

"Their business was only needlework, in which I and my maids sometimes helped them; but you know that the mind will easily straggle from the fingers, nor will you suspect that captivity and absence from Nekayah could receive solace from silken flowers.

"Nor was much satisfaction to be hoped from their conversation: for of what could they be expected to talk? They had seen nothing; for they had lived from early youth in that narrow spot: of what they had not seen they could have no knowledge, for they could not read. They had no ideas but of the few things that were within their view, and had hardly names for anything but their clothes and their food. As I bore a superior character, I was often called to terminate their quarrels, which I decided as equitably as I could. If it could have amused me to hear the complaints of each against the rest, I might have been often detained by long stories, but the motives of their animosity were so small that I could not listen without intercepting the tale."

"How," said Rasselas, "can the Arab, whom you represented as a man of more than common accomplishments, take any pleasure in his seraglio, when it is filled only with women like these. Are they exquisitely beautiful?"

"They do not," said Pekuah, "want that unaffecting and ignoble beauty which may subsist without spriteliness or sublimity, without energy of thought or dignity of virtue. But to a man like the Arab such beauty was only a flower casually plucked and carelessly thrown away. Whatever pleasures he might find among them, they were not those of friendship or society. When they were playing about him he looked on them with inattentive superiority: when they vied for his regard he sometimes turned away disgusted. As they had no knowledge, their talk could take nothing from the tediousness of life: as they had no choice, their fondness, or appearance of fondness, excited in him neither pride nor gratitude; he was not exalted in his own esteem by the smiles of a woman who saw no other man, nor was much obliged by that regard, of which he could never know the sincerity, and which he might often perceive to be exerted not so much to delight him as to pain a rival. That which he gave, and they received, as love, was only a careless distribution of superfluous time, such love as man can bestow upon that which he despises, such as has neither hope nor fear, neither joy nor sorrow."

"You have reason, lady, to think yourself happy," said Imlac, "that you have been thus easily dismissed. How could a mind, hungry for knowledge, be willing, in an intellectual famine, to lose such a banquet as Pekuah's conversation?"

"I am inclined to believe," answered Pekuah, "that he was for some time in suspense; for, notwithstanding his promise, whenever I proposed to dispatch a messenger to Cairo, he found some excuse for delay. While I was detained in his house he made many incursions into the neighboring countries, and, perhaps, he would have refused to discharge me, had his plunder been equal to his wishes. He returned always courteous, related his adventures, delighted to hear my observations, and endeavored to advance my acquaintance with the stars. When I importuned him to send away my letters, he soothed me with professions of honor and sincerity; and, when I could be no longer decently denied, put his troop again in motion, and left me to govern in his absence. I was much afflicted by this studied procrastination, and was sometimes afraid that I should be forgotten; that you would leave Cairo, and I must end my days in an island of the Nile.

"I grew at last hopeless and dejected, and cared so little to entertain him, that he for a while more frequently talked with my maids. That he should fall in love with them, or with me, might have been equally fatal, and I was not much pleased with the growing friendship. My anxiety was not long; for, as I recovered some degree of cheerfulness, he returned to me, and I could not forbear to despise my former uneasiness.

"He still delayed to send for my ransom, and would, perhaps, never have determined, had not your agent found his way to him. The gold, which he would not fetch, he could not reject when it was offered. He hastened to prepare for our journey hither, like a man delivered from the pain of an intestine conflict. I took leave of my companions in the house, who dismissed me with cold indifference."

Nekayah, having heard her favorite's relation, rose and embraced her, and Rasselas gave her an hundred ounces of gold, which she presented to the Arab for the fifty that were promised.

Chapter 40. The History of a Man of Learning

They returned to Cairo, and were so well pleased at finding themselves together, that none of them went much abroad. The prince began to love learning, and one day declared to Imlac, that he intended to devote himself to science,[1] and pass the rest of his days in literary solitude.

"Before you make your final choice," answered Imlac, "you ought to examine its hazards, and converse with some of those who are grown old in the company of themselves. I have just left the observatory of one of the most learned astronomers in the world, who has spent forty years in unwearied attention to the motions and appearances of the celestial bodies, and has drawn out his soul in endless calculations. He admits a few friends once a month to hear his deductions and enjoy his discoveries. I was introduced as a man of knowledge worthy of his notice. Men of various ideas and fluent conversation are commonly welcome to those whose thoughts have been long fixed upon a single point, and who find the images of other things stealing away. I delighted him with my remarks,

1. Knowledge.

he smiled at the narrative of my travels, and was glad to forget the constellations, and descend for a moment into the lower world.

"On the next day of vacation I renewed my visit, and was so fortunate
as to please him again. He relaxed from that time the severity of his rule,
and permitted me to enter at my own choice. I found him always busy,
and always glad to be relieved. As each knew much which the other was
desirous of learning, we exchanged our notions with great delight. I
perceived that I had every day more of his confidence, and always found
new cause of admiration in the profundity of his mind. His comprehension is vast, his memory capacious and retentive, his discourse is
methodical, and his expression clear.

"His integrity and benevolence are equal to his learning. His deepest
researches and most favorite studies are willingly interrupted for any
opportunity of doing good by his counsel or his riches. To his closest
retreat, at his most busy moments, all are admitted that want his assistance: 'For though I exclude idleness and pleasure, I will never,' says
he, 'bar my doors against charity. To man is permitted the contemplation of the skies, but the practice of virtue is commanded.' "

"Surely," said the princess, "this man is happy."

"I visited him," said Imlac, "with more and more frequency, and was
every time more enamored of his conversation: he was sublime without
haughtiness, courteous without formality, and communicative without
ostentation. I was at first, great princess, of your opinion, thought him
the happiest of mankind, and often congratulated him on the blessing
that he enjoyed. He seemed to hear nothing with indifference but the
praises of his condition, to which he always returned a general answer,
and diverted the conversation to some other topic.

"Amidst this willingness to be pleased, and labor to please, I had quickly
reason to imagine that some painful sentiment pressed upon his mind.
He often looked up earnestly towards the sun, and let his voice fall in
the midst of his discourse. He would sometimes, when we were alone,
gaze upon me in silence with the air of a man who longed to speak what
he was yet resolved to suppress. He would often send for me with vehement injunctions of haste, though, when I came to him, he had nothing
extraordinary to say. And sometimes, when I was leaving him, he would
call me back, pause a few moments and then dismiss me.

Chapter 41. The Astronomer Discovers the Cause of his Uneasiness

"At last the time came when the secret burst his reserve. We were
sitting together last night in the turret of his house, watching the emer-
sion of a satellite of Jupiter. A sudden tempest clouded the sky, and
disappointed our observation. We sat a while silent in the dark, and then
he addressed himself to me in these words: 'Imlac, I have long considered thy friendship as the greatest blessing of my life. Integrity without
knowledge is weak and useless, and knowledge without integrity is dan-

gerous and dreadful. I have found in thee all the qualities requisite for trust, benevolence, experience, and fortitude. I have long discharged an office which I must soon quit at the call of nature, and shall rejoice in the hour of imbecility[2] and pain to devolve it upon thee.'

"I thought myself honored by this testimony, and protested that whatever could conduce to his happiness would add likewise to mine.

" 'Hear, Imlac, what thou wilt not without difficulty credit. I have possessed for five years the regulation of weather, and the distribution of the seasons: the sun has listened to my dictates, and passed from tropic to tropic by my direction; the clouds, at my call, have poured their waters, and the Nile has overflowed at my command; I have restrained the rage of the dog-star, and mitigated the fervors of the crab.[3] The winds alone, of all the elemental powers, have hitherto refused my authority, and multitudes have perished by equinoctial tempests which I found myself unable to prohibit or restrain. I have administered this great office with exact justice, and made to the different nations of the earth an impartial dividend of rain and sunshine. What must have been the misery of half the globe, if I had limited the clouds to particular regions, or confined the sun to either side of the equator?' "

Chapter 42. The Opinion of the Astronomer Is Explained and Justified

"I suppose he discovered in me, through the obscurity of the room, some tokens of amazement and doubt, for, after a short pause, he proceeded thus:

" 'Not to be easily credited will neither surprise nor offend me; for I am, probably, the first of human beings to whom this trust has been imparted. Nor do I know whether to deem this distinction a reward or punishment; since I have possessed it I have been far less happy than before, and nothing but the consciousness of good intention could have enabled me to support the weariness of unremitted vigilance.'

" 'How long, Sir, said I, has this great office been in your hands?'

" 'About ten years ago,' said he, 'my daily observations of the changes of the sky led me to consider, whether, if I had the power of the seasons, I could confer greater plenty upon the inhabitants of the earth. This contemplation fastened on my mind, and I sat days and nights in imaginary dominion, pouring upon this country and that the showers of fertility, and seconding every fall of rain with a due proportion of sunshine. I had yet only the will to do good, and did not imagine that I should ever have the power.

" 'One day as I was looking on the fields withering with heat, I felt in my mind a sudden wish that I could send rain on the southern mountains, and raise the Nile to an inundation. In the hurry of my imagination I commanded rain to fall, and, by comparing the time of my

---

2. Feebleness.
3. Fourth sign of the Zodiac (Cancer). Sirius, "the

dog-star," was supposed to cause the heat ("dog-days") of summer.

command, with that of the inundation, I found that the clouds had listened to my lips.'

" 'Might not some other cause,' said I, 'produce this concurrence? the Nile does not always rise on the same day.'

" 'Do not believe,' said he with impatience, 'that such objections could escape me: I reasoned long against my own conviction, and labored against truth with the utmost obstinacy. I sometimes suspected myself of madness, and should not have dared to impart this secret but to a man like you, capable of distinguishing the wonderful from the impossible, and the incredible from the false.'

" 'Why, Sir,' said I, 'do you call that incredible, which you know, or think you know, to be true?'

" 'Because,' said he, 'I cannot prove it by any external evidence; and I know too well the laws of demonstration to think that my conviction ought to influence another, who cannot, like me, be conscious of its force. I therefore shall not attempt to gain credit by disputation. It is sufficient that I feel this power, that I have long possessed, and every day exerted it. But the life of man is short, the infirmities of age increase upon me, and the time will soon come when the regulator of the year must mingle with the dust. The care of appointing a successor has long disturbed me; the night and the day have been spent in comparisons of all the characters which have come to my knowledge, and I have yet found none so worthy as thyself.

Chapter 43. *The Astronomer Leaves Imlac His Directions*

" 'Hear therefore, what I shall impart, with attention, such as the welfare of a world requires. If the task of a king be considered as difficult, who has the care only of a few millions, to whom he cannot do much good or harm, what must be the anxiety of him, on whom depends the action of the elements, and the great gifts of light and heat!—Hear me therefore with attention.

" 'I have diligently considered the position of the earth and sun, and formed innumerable schemes in which I changed their situation. I have sometimes turned aside the axis of the earth, and sometimes varied the ecliptic of the sun: but I have found it impossible to make a disposition by which the world may be advantaged; what one region gains, another loses by any imaginable alteration, even without considering the distant parts of the solar system with which we are unacquainted. Do not, therefore, in thy administration of the year, indulge thy pride by innovation; do not please thyself with thinking that thou canst make thyself renowned to all future ages, by disordering the seasons. The memory of mischief is no desirable fame. Much less will it become thee to let kindness or interest prevail. Never rob other countries of rain to pour it on thine own. For us the Nile is sufficient.'

"I promised that when I possessed the power, I would use it with inflexible integrity, and he dismissed me, pressing my hand. 'My heart,' said he, 'will be now at rest, and my benevolence will no more destroy my quiet: I have found a man of wisdom and virtue, to whom I can cheerfully bequeath the inheritance of the sun.' "

The prince heard this narration with very serious regard, but the princess smiled, and Pekuah convulsed herself with laughter. "Ladies," said Imlac, "to mock the heaviest of human afflictions is neither charitable nor wise. Few can attain this man's knowledge, and few practice his virtues; but all may suffer his calamity. Of the uncertainties of our present state, the most dreadful and alarming is the uncertain continuance of reason."

The princess was recollected, and the favorite was abashed. Rasselas, more deeply affected, inquired of Imlac, whether he thought such maladies of the mind frequent, and how they were contracted.

Chapter 44. The Dangerous Prevalence[4] of Imagination

"Disorders of intellect," answered Imlac, "happen much more often than superficial observers will easily believe. Perhaps, if we speak with rigorous exactness, no human mind is in its right state. There is no man whose imagination does not sometimes predominate over his reason, who can regulate his attention wholly by his will, and whose ideas will come and go at his command. No man will be found in whose mind airy notions do not sometimes tyrannize, and force him to hope or fear beyond the limits of sober probability. All power of fancy over reason is a degree of insanity; but while this power is such as we can control and repress, it is not visible to others, nor considered as any depravation of the mental faculties; it is not pronounced madness but when it comes ungovernable, and apparently influences speech or action.

"To indulge the power of fiction, and send imagination out upon the wing, is often the sport of those who delight too much in silent speculation. When we are alone we are not always busy; the labor of excogitation is too violent to last long; the ardor of inquiry will sometimes give way to idleness or satiety. He who has nothing external that can divert him must find pleasure in his own thoughts, and must conceive himself what he is not; for who is pleased with what he is? He then expatiates in boundless futurity, and culls from all imaginable conditions that which for the present moment he should most desire, amuses his desires with impossible enjoyments, and confers upon his pride unattainable dominion. The mind dances from scene to scene, unites all pleasures in all combinations, and riots in delights which nature and fortune, with all their bounty, cannot bestow.

"In time, some particular train of ideas fixes the attention; all other intellectual gratifications are rejected; the mind, in weariness or leisure, recurs constantly to the favorite conception, and feasts on the luscious falsehood, whenever she is offended with the bitterness of truth. By degrees

4. Predominance.

the reign of fancy is confirmed; she grows first imperious, and in time despotic. Then fictions begin to operate as realities, false opinions fasten upon the mind, and life passes in dreams of rapture or of anguish.

"This, sir, is one of the dangers of solitude, which the hermit has confessed not always to promote goodness, and the astronomer's misery has proved to be not always propitious to wisdom."

"I will no more," said the favorite, "imagine myself the queen of Abyssinia. I have often spent the hours which the princess gave to my own disposal, in adjusting ceremonies and regulating the court; I have repressed the pride of the powerful, and granted the petitions of the poor; I have built new palaces in more happy situations, planted groves upon the tops of mountains, and have exulted in the beneficence of royalty, till, when the princess entered, I had almost forgotten to bow down before her."

"And I," said the princess, "will not allow myself any more to play the shepherdess in my waking dreams. I have often soothed my thoughts with the quiet and innocence of pastoral employments, till I have in my chamber heard the winds whistle, and the sheep bleat; sometimes freed the lamb entangled in the thicket, and sometimes with my crook encountered the wolf. I have a dress like that of the village maids, which I put on to help my imagination, and a pipe on which I play softly, and suppose myself followed by my flocks."

"I will confess," said the prince, "an indulgence of fantastic delight more dangerous than yours. I have frequently endeavored to image the possibility of a perfect government, by which all wrong should be restrained, all vice reformed, and all the subjects preserved in tranquility and innocence. This thought produced innumerable schemes of reformation, and dictated many useful regulations and salutary edicts. This has been the sport, and sometimes the labor, of my solitude; and I start, when I think with how little anguish I once supposed the death of my father and my brothers."

"Such," says Imlac, "are the effects of visionary schemes; when we first form them, we know them to be absurd, but familiarize them by degrees, and in time lose sight of their folly."

Chapter 45. They Discourse with an Old Man

The evening was now far past, and they rose to return home. As they walked along the bank of the Nile, delighted with the beams of the moon quivering on the water, they saw at a small distance an old man, whom the prince had often heard in the assembly of the sages. "Yonder," said he, "is one whose years have calmed his passions, but not clouded his reason. Let us close the disquisitions of the night by inquiring what are his sentiments of his own state, that we may know whether youth alone is to struggle with vexation, and whether any better hope remains for the latter part of life."

Here the sage approached and saluted them. They invited him to join their walk, and prattled a while, as acquaintance that had unexpectedly met one another. The old man was cheerful and talkative, and the way seemed short in his company. He was pleased to find himself not disregarded, accompanied them to their house, and, at the prince's request, entered with them. They placed him in the seat of honor, and set wine and conserves before him.

"Sir," said the princess, "an evening walk must give to a man of learning like you pleasures which ignorance and youth can hardly conceive. You know the qualities and the causes of all that you behold, the laws by which the river flows, the periods in which the planets perform their revolutions. Everything must supply you with contemplation, and renew the consciousness of your own dignity."

"Lady," answered he, "let the gay and the vigorous expect pleasure in their excursions; it is enough that age can obtain ease. To me the world has lost its novelty; I look round, and see what I remember to have seen in happier days. I rest against a tree, and consider that in the same shade I once disputed upon the annual overflow of the Nile with a friend who is now silent in the grave. I cast my eyes upward, fix them on the changing moon, and think with pain on the vicissitudes of life. I have ceased to take much delight in physical truth; for what have I to do with those things which I am soon to leave?"

"You may at least recreate[5] yourself," said Imlac, "with the recollection of an honorable and useful life, and enjoy the praise which all agree to give you."

"Praise," said the sage with a sigh, "is to an old man an empty sound. I have neither mother to be delighted with the reputation of her son, nor wife to partake the honors of her husband. I have outlived my friends and my rivals. Nothing is now of much importance; for I cannot extend my interest beyond myself. Youth is delighted with applause, because it is considered as the earnest of some future good, and because the prospect of life is far extended; but to me, who am now declining to decrepitude, there is little to be feared from the malevolence of men, and yet less to be hoped from their affection or esteem. Something they may yet take away, but they can give me nothing. Riches would now be useless, and high employment would be pain. My retrospect of life recalls to my view many opportunities of good neglected, much time squandered upon trifles, and more lost in idleness and vacancy. I leave many great designs unattempted, and many great attempts unfinished. My mind is burthened with no heavy crime, and therefore I compose myself to tranquility; endeavor to abstract my thoughts from hopes and cares which, though reason knows them to be vain, still try to keep their old possession of the heart; expect,[6] with serene humility, that hour which nature cannot long delay; and hope to possess, in a better state, that happiness which here I could not find, and that virtue which here I have not attained."

5. Refresh.   6. Await.

He arose and went away, leaving his audience not much elated with the hope of long life. The prince consoled himself with remarking that it was not reasonable to be disappointed by this account; for age had never been considered as the season of felicity, and if it was possible to be easy in decline and weakness, it was likely that the days of vigor and alacrity might be happy; that the noon of life might be bright, if the evening could be calm.

The princess suspected that age was querulous and malignant, and delighted to repress the expectations of those who had newly entered the world. She had seen the possessors of estates look with envy on their heirs, and known many who enjoy pleasure no longer than they can confine it to themselves.

Pekuah conjectured that the man was older than he appeared, and was willing to impute his complaints to delirious dejection; or else supposed that he had been unfortunate, and was therefore discontented. "For nothing," said she, "is more common than to call our own condition the condition of life."

Imlac, who had no desire to see them depressed, smiled at the comforts which they could so readily procure to themselves, and remembered that, at the same age, he was equally confident of unmingled prosperity, and equally fertile of consolatory expedients. He forebore to force upon them unwelcome knowledge, which time itself would too soon impress. The princess and her lady retired; the madness of the astronomer hung upon their minds, and they desired Imlac to enter upon his office, and delay next morning the rising of the sun.

Chapter 46. The Princess and Pekuah Visit the Astronomer

The princess and Pekuah, having talked in private of Imlac's astronomer, thought his character at once so amiable and so strange, that they could not be satisfied without a nearer knowledge, and Imlac was requested to find the means of bringing them together.

This was somewhat difficult; the philosopher had never received any visits from women, though he lived in a city that had in it many Europeans who followed the manners of their own countries, and many from other parts of the world that lived there with European liberty. The ladies would not be refused, and several schemes were proposed for the accomplishment of their design. It was proposed to introduce them as strangers in distress, to whom the sage was always accessible; but, after some deliberation, it appeared, that by this artifice, no acquaintance could be formed, for their conversation would be short, and they could not decently importune him often. "This," said Rasselas, "is true; but I have yet a stronger objection against the misrepresentation of your state. I have always considered it as treason against the great republic of human nature, to make any man's virtues the means of deceiving him, whether on great or little occasions. All imposture weakens confidence and chills benevolence. When the sage finds that you are not what you seemed, he will feel the resentment natural to a man who, conscious of great abilities, discovers that he has been tricked by understandings meaner than his own, and, perhaps, the distrust, which he can never afterwards wholly lay aside, may stop the voice of counsel, and close the hand of charity; and where will you find the power of restoring his benefactions to mankind, or his peace to himself?"

To this no reply was attempted, and Imlac began to hope that their curiosity would subside; but next day Pekuah told him, she had now found an honest pretense for a visit to the astronomer, for she would solicit permission to continue under him the studies in which she had been initiated by the Arab, and the princess might go with her either as a fellow-student, or because a woman could not decently come alone. "I am afraid," said Imlac, "that he will be soon weary of your company: men advanced far in knowledge do not love to repeat the elements of their art, and I am not certain, that even of the elements, as he will deliver them connected with inferences, and mingled with reflections, you are a very capable auditress." "That," said Pekuah, "must be my care: I ask of you only to take me thither. My knowledge is, perhaps, more than you imagine it, and by concurring always with his opinions I shall make him think it greater than it is."

The astronomer, in pursuance of this resolution, was told, that a foreign lady, traveling in search of knowledge, had heard of his reputation, and was desirous to become his scholar. The uncommonness of the proposal raised at once his surprise and curiosity, and when, after a short deliberation, he consented to admit her, he could not stay without impatience till the next day.

The ladies dressed themselves magnificently, and were attended by Imlac to the astronomer, who was pleased to see himself approached with respect by persons of so splendid an appearance. In the exchange of the first civilities he was timorous and bashful; but when the talk became regular, he recollected his powers, and justified the character which Imlac had given. Inquiring of Pekuah what could have turned her inclination towards astronomy, he received from her a history of her adventure at the pyramid, and of the time passed in the Arab's island. She told her tale with ease and elegance, and her conversation took possession of his heart. The discourse was then turned to astronomy: Pekuah displayed what she knew: he looked upon her as a prodigy of genius, and entreated her not to desist from a study which she had so happily begun.

They came again and again, and were every time more welcome than before. The sage endeavored to amuse them, that they might prolong their visits, for he found his thoughts grow brighter in their company; the clouds of solicitude vanished by degrees, as he forced himself to entertain them, and he grieved when he was left at their departure to his old employment of regulating the seasons.

The princess and her favorite had now watched his lips for several months, and could not catch a single word from which they could judge whether he continued, or not, in the opinion of his preternatural com-mission. They often contrived to bring him to an open declaration, but he easily eluded all their attacks, and on which side soever they pressed him escaped from them to some other topic.

As their familiarity increased they invited him often to the house of Imlac, where they distinguished him by extraordinary respect. He began gradually to delight in sublunary pleasures. He came early and departed late; labored to recommend himself by assiduity and compliance; excited their curiosity after new arts, that they might still want his assistance; and when they made any excursion of pleasure or inquiry, entreated to attend them.

By long experience of his integrity and wisdom, the prince and his sister were convinced that he might be trusted without danger; and lest he should draw any false hopes from the civilities which he received, discovered to him their condition, with the motives of their journey, and required his opinion on the choice of life.

"Of the various conditions which the world spreads before you, which you shall prefer," said the sage, "I am not able to instruct you. I can only tell that I have chosen wrong. I have passed my time in study without experience; in the attainment of sciences which can, for the most part, be but remotely useful to mankind. I have purchased knowl-edge at the expense of all the common comforts of life: I have missed the endearing elegance of female friendship, and the happy commerce of domestic tenderness. If I have obtained any prerogatives above other students, they have been accompanied with fear, disquiet, and scrupu-losity; but even of these prerogatives, whatever they were, I have, since my thoughts have been diversified by more intercourse with the world, begun to question the reality. When I have been for a few days lost in pleasing dissipation, I am always tempted to think that my inquiries have ended in error, and that I have suffered much, and suffered it in vain."

Imlac was delighted to find that the sage's understanding was breaking through its mists, and resolved to detain him from the planets till he should forget his task of ruling them, and reason should recover its orig-inal influence.

From this time the astronomer was received into familiar friendship, and partook of all their projects and pleasures: his respect kept him atten-tive, and the activity of Rasselas did not leave much time unengaged. Something was always to be done; the day was spent in making obser-vations which furnished talk for the evening, and the evening was closed with a scheme for the morrow.

The sage confessed to Imlac, that since he had mingled in the gay tumults of life, and divided his hours by a succession of amusements, he found the conviction of his authority over the skies fade gradually from his mind, and began to trust less to an opinion which he never could prove to others, and which he now found subject to variation from causes in which reason had no part. "If I am accidentally left alone for a few hours," said he, "my inveterate persuasion rushes upon my soul, and my thoughts are chained down by some irresistible violence, but they are soon disentangled by the prince's conversation, and instantaneously released at the entrance of Pekuah. I am like a man habitually afraid of specters, who is set at ease by a lamp, and wonders at the dread which harassed him in the dark, yet, if his lamp be extinguished, feels again the terrors which he knows that when it is light he shall feel no more. But I am sometimes afraid lest I indulge my quiet by criminal negligence, and voluntarily forget the great charge with which I am intrusted. If I favor myself in a known error, or am determined by my own ease in a doubtful question of this importance, how dreadful is my crime!"

"No disease of the imagination," answered Imlac, "is so difficult of cure, as that which is complicated with the dread of guilt: fancy and conscience then act interchangeably upon us, and so often shift their places, that the illusions of one are not distinguished from the dictates of the other. If fancy presents images not moral or religious, the mind drives them away when they give it pain, but when melancholic notions take the form of duty, they lay hold on the faculties without opposition, because we are afraid to exclude or banish them. For this reason the superstitious are often melancholy, and the melancholy almost always superstitious.

"But do not let the suggestions of timidity overpower your better reason: the danger of neglect can be but as the probability of the obligation, which, when you consider it with freedom, you find very little, and that little growing every day less. Open your heart to the influence of the light, which, from time to time, breaks in upon you: when scruples importune you, which you in your lucid moments know to be vain, do not stand to parley, but fly to business or to Pekuah, and keep this thought always prevalent, that you are only one atom of the mass of humanity, and have neither such virtue nor vice, as that you should be singled out for supernatural favors or afflictions."

Chapter 47. The Prince Enters, and Brings a New Topic

"All this," said the astronomer, "I have often thought, but my reason has been so long subjugated by an uncontrollable and overwhelming idea, that it durst not confide in its own decisions. I now see how fatally I betrayed my quiet, by suffering chimeras to prey upon me in secret; but melancholy shrinks from communication, and I never found a man before, to whom I could impart my troubles, though I had been certain of relief. I rejoice to find my own sentiments confirmed by yours, who are not easily deceived, and can have no motive or purpose to deceive. I hope that time and variety will dissipate the gloom that has so long surrounded me, and the latter part of my days will be spent in peace."

"Your learning and virtue," said Imlac, "may justly give you hopes."

Rasselas then entered with the princess and Pekuah, and inquired whether they had contrived any new diversion for the next day. "Such," said Nekayah, "is the state of life, that none are happy but by the anticipation of change: the change itself is nothing; when we have made it, the next wish is to change again. The world is not yet exhausted; let me see something tomorrow which I never saw before."

"Variety," said Rasselas, "is so necessary to content, that even the happy valley disgusted me by the recurrence of its luxuries; yet I could not forbear to reproach myself with impatience, when I saw the monks of St. Anthony support without complaint, a life, not of uniform delight, but uniform hardship."

"Those men," answered Imlac, "are less wretched in their silent convent than the Abyssinian princes in their prison of pleasure. Whatever is done by the monks is incited by an adequate and reasonable motive. Their labor supplies them with necessaries; it therefore cannot be omitted, and is certainly rewarded. Their devotion prepares them for another state, and reminds them of its approach, while it fits them for it. Their time is regularly distributed; one duty succeeds another, so that they are not left open to the distraction of unguided choice, nor lost in the shades of listless inactivity. There is a certain task to be performed at an appropriated hour; and their toils are cheerful, because they consider them as acts of piety, by which they are always advancing towards endless felicity."

"Do you think," said Nekayah, "that the monastic rule is a more holy and less imperfect state than any other? May not he equally hope for future happiness who converses openly with mankind, who succors the distressed by his charity, instructs the ignorant by his learning, and contributes by his industry to the general system of life; even though he should omit some of the mortifications which are practiced in the cloister, and allow himself such harmless delights as his condition may place within his reach?"

"This," said Imlac, "is a question which has long divided the wise, and perplexed the good. I am afraid to decide on either part. He that lives well in the world is better than he that lives well in a monastery. But perhaps everyone is not able to stem the temptations of public life; and if he cannot conquer, he may properly retreat. Some have little power to do good, and have likewise little strength to resist evil. Many are weary of their conflicts with adversity, and are willing to eject those passions which have long busied them in vain. And many are dismissed by age and diseases from the more laborious duties of society. In monasteries the weak and timorous may be happily sheltered, the weary may repose, and the penitent may meditate. Those retreats of prayer and contemplation have something so congenial to the mind of man, that, perhaps, there is scarcely one that does not purpose to close his life in pious abstraction with a few associates serious as himself."

"Such," said Pekuah, "has often been my wish, and I have heard the princess declare, that she should not willingly die in a crowd."

"The liberty of using harmless pleasures," proceeded Imlac, "will not be disputed; but it is still to be examined what pleasures are harmless.

The evil of any pleasure that Nekayah can image is not in the act itself, but in its consequences. Pleasure, in itself harmless, may become mischievous, by endearing to us a state which we know to be transient and probatory,[7] and withdrawing our thoughts from that, of which every hour brings us nearer to the beginning, and of which no length of time will bring us to the end. Mortification is not virtuous in itself, nor has any other use, but that it disengages us from the allurements of sense. In the state of future perfection, to which we all aspire, there will be pleasure without danger, and security without restraint."

The princess was silent, and Rasselas, turning to the astronomer, asked him, whether he could not delay her retreat, by showing her something which she had not seen before.

"Your curiosity," said the sage, "has been so general, and your pursuit of knowledge so vigorous, that novelties are not now very easily to be found: but what you can no longer procure from the living may be given by the dead. Among the wonders of this country are the catacombs, or the ancient repositories, in which the bodies of the earliest generations were lodged, and where, by the virtue of the gums which embalmed them, they yet remain without corruption."

"I know not," said Rasselas, "what pleasure the sight of the catacombs can afford; but, since nothing else is offered, I am resolved to view them, and shall place this with many other things which I have done, because I would do something."

They hired a guard of horsemen, and the next day visited the catacombs. When they were about to descend into the sepulchral caves, "Pekuah," said the princess, "we are now again invading the habitations of the dead; I know that you will stay behind; let me find you safe when I return." "No, I will not be left," answered Pekuah; "I will go down between you and the prince."

They then all descended, and roved with wonder through the labyrinth of subterraneous passages, where the bodies were laid in rows on either side.

Chapter 48. Imlac Discourses on the Nature of the Soul

"What reason," said the prince, "can be given, why the Egyptians should thus expensively preserve those carcasses which some nations consume with fire, others lay to mingle with the earth, and all agree to remove from their sight, as soon as decent rites can be performed?"

"The original of ancient customs," said Imlac, "is commonly unknown; for the practice often continues when the cause has ceased; and concerning superstitious ceremonies it is vain to conjecture; for what reason did not dictate reason cannot explain. I have long believed that the practice of embalming arose only from tenderness to the remains of relations or

---

7. Serving as a trial or test.

friends, and to this opinion I am more inclined, because it seems impossible that this care should have been general: had all the dead been embalmed, their repositories must in time have been more spacious than the dwellings of the living. I suppose only the rich or honorable were secured from corruption, and the rest left to the course of nature.

"But it is commonly supposed that the Egyptians believed the soul to live as long as the body continued undissolved, and therefore tried this method of eluding death."

"Could the wise Egyptians," said Nekayah, "think so grossly of the soul? If the soul could once survive its separation, what could it afterwards receive or suffer from the body?"

"The Egyptians would doubtless think erroneously," said the astronomer, "in the darkness of heathenism, and the first dawn of philosophy. The nature of the soul is still disputed amidst all our opportunities of clearer knowledge: some yet say, that it may be material, who, nevertheless, believe it to be immortal."

"Some," answered Imlac, "have indeed said that the soul is material, but I can scarcely believe that any man has thought it, who knew how to think; for all the conclusions of reason enforce the immateriality of mind, and all the notices of sense and investigations of science concur to prove the unconsciousness of matter.

"It was never supposed that cogitation is inherent in matter, or that every particle is a thinking being. Yet if any part of matter be devoid of thought, what part can we suppose to think? Matter can differ from matter only in form, density, bulk, motion, and direction of motion: to which of these, however varied or combined, can consciousness be annexed? To be round or square, to be solid or fluid, to be great or little, to be moved slowly or swiftly one way or another, are modes of material existence, all equally alien from the nature of cogitation. If matter be once without thought, it can only be made to think by some new modification, but all the modifications which it can admit are equally unconnected with cogitative powers."

"But the materialists," said the astronomer, "urge that matter may have qualities with which we are unacquainted."

"He who will determine," returned Imlac, "against that which he knows, because there may be something which he knows not; he that can set hypothetical possibility against acknowledged certainty, is not to be admitted among reasonable beings. All that we know of matter is, that matter is inert, senseless and lifeless; and if this conviction cannot be opposed but by referring us to something that we know not, we have all the evidence that human intellect can admit. If that which is known may be overruled by that which is unknown, no being, not omniscient, can arrive at certainty."

"Yet let us not," said the astronomer, "too arrogantly limit the Creator's power."

"It is no limitation of omnipotence," replied the poet, "to suppose that one thing is not consistent with another, that the same proposition cannot be at once true and false, that the same number cannot be even and odd, that cogitation cannot be conferred on that which is created incapable of cogitation."

"I know not," said Nekayah, "any great use of this question. Does that immateriality, which, in my opinion, you have sufficiently proved, necessarily include eternal duration?"

"Of immateriality," said Imlac, "our ideas are negative, and therefore obscure. Immateriality seems to imply a natural power of perpetual duration as a consequence of exemption from all causes of decay: whatever perishes, is destroyed by the solution of its contexture,[8] and separation of its parts; nor can we conceive how that which has no parts, and therefore admits no solution, can be naturally corrupted or impaired."

"I know not," said Rasselas, "how to conceive anything without extension: what is extended must have parts, and you allow, that whatever has parts may be destroyed."

"Consider your own conceptions," replied Imlac, "and the difficulty will be less. You will find substance without extension. An ideal form is no less real than material bulk: yet an ideal form has no extension. It is no less certain, when you think on a pyramid, that your mind possesses the idea of a pyramid, than that the pyramid itself is standing. What space does the idea of a pyramid occupy more than the idea of a grain of corn? or how can either idea suffer laceration? As is the effect such is the cause; as thought is, such is the power that thinks; a power impassive and indiscerptible."[9]

"But the Being," said Nekayah, "whom I fear to name, the Being which made the soul, can destroy it."

"He, surely, can destroy it," answered Imlac, "since, however unperishable, it receives from a superior nature its power of duration. That it will not perish by any inherent cause of decay, or principle of corruption, may be shown by philosophy; but philosophy can tell no more. That it will not be annihilated by him that made it, we must humbly learn from higher authority."

The whole assembly stood a while silent and collected. "Let us return," said Rasselas, "from this scene of mortality. How gloomy would be these mansions of the dead to him who did not know that he shall never die; that what now acts shall continue its agency, and what now thinks shall think on for ever. Those that lie here stretched before us, the wise and the powerful of ancient times, warn us to remember the shortness of our present state: they were, perhaps, snatched away while they were busy, like us, in the choice of life."

"To me," said the princess, "the choice of life is become less important; I hope hereafter to think only on the choice of eternity."

They then hastened out of the caverns, and, under the protection of their guard, returned to Cairo.

---

8. Dissolution of its structure.   9. Not to be separated.

Chapter 49. The Conclusion, in Which Nothing Is Concluded

It was now the time of the inundation of the Nile: a few days after their visit to the catacombs, the river began to rise.

They were confined to their house. The whole region being under water gave them no invitation to any excursions, and being well supplied with materials for talk, they diverted themselves with comparisons of the different forms of life which they had observed, and with various schemes of happiness which each of them had formed.

Pekuah was never so much charmed with any place as the convent of St. Anthony, where the Arab restored her to the princess, and wished only to fill it with pious maidens, and to be made prioress of the order; she was weary of expectation and disgust,[1] and would gladly be fixed in some unvariable state.

The princess thought that, of all sublunary things, knowledge was the best: she desired first to learn all sciences, and then purposed to found a college of learned women, in which she would preside, that, by conversing with the old and educating the young, she might divide her time between the acquisition and communication of wisdom, and raise up for the next age models of prudence, and patterns of piety.

The prince desired a little kingdom, in which he might administer justice in his own person, and see all the parts of government with his own eyes; but he could never fix the limits of his dominion, and was always adding to the number of his subjects.

Imlac and the astronomer were contented to be driven along the stream of life, without directing their course to any particular port.

Of these wishes that they had formed, they well knew that none could be obtained. They deliberated a while what was to be done, and resolved, when the inundation should cease, to return to Abyssinia.[2]

1759

[A Brief to Free a Slave][1]

It must be agreed that in most ages many countries have had part of their inhabitants in a state of slavery; yet it may be doubted whether slavery can ever be supposed the natural condition of man. It is impossible not to conceive that men in their original state were equal; and very

1. Aversion.
2. Probably not, as is often suggested, to the Happy Valley, which the travelers earlier fled as a prison. Presumably the travelers return, with whatever wisdom they have gained, but also with their cherished illusions, to share the common destiny of mankind.
1. Johnson detested slavery and the owners of slaves. Once, "in company with some very grave men at Oxford, his toast was, 'Here's to the next insurrection of the Negroes in the West Indies'";

and in his pamphlet *Taxation No Tyranny* (1775) he put the American rebels down with a devastating question: "how is it that we hear the loudest yelps for liberty among the drivers of Negroes?" Though slavery had been abolished in England in 1772, serfdom still existed in Scotland; and the British remained heavily involved in the slave trade. In 1777 a Negro slave, Joseph Knight, sued for freedom from the Scottish master he had escaped. On his behalf Johnson dictated this argument to Boswell.

difficult to imagine how one would be subjected to another but by violent compulsion. An individual may, indeed, forfeit his liberty by a crime; but he cannot by that crime forfeit the liberty of his children. What is true of a criminal seems true likewise of a captive. A man may accept life from a conquering enemy on condition of perpetual servitude; but it is very doubtful whether he can entail[2] that servitude on his descendants; for no man can stipulate without commission for another. The condition which he himself accepts, his son or grandson perhaps would have rejected. If we should admit, what perhaps may with more reason be denied, that there are certain relations between man and man which may make slavery necessary and just,[3] yet it can never be proved that he who is now suing for his freedom ever stood in any of those relations. He is certainly subject by no law, but that of violence, to his present master,[4] who pretends no claim to his obedience, but that he bought him from a merchant of slaves, whose right to sell him never was examined. It is said that, according to the constitutions of Jamaica, he was legally enslaved; these constitutions are merely positive;[5] and apparently injurious to the rights of mankind, because whoever is exposed to sale is condemned to slavery without appeal; by whatever fraud or violence he might have been originally brought into the merchant's power. In our own time princes have been sold, by wretches to whose care they were entrusted, that they might have an European education; but when once they were brought to a market in the plantations, little would avail either their dignity or their wrongs. The laws of Jamaica afford a Negro no redress. His color is considered as a sufficient testimony against him. It is to be lamented that moral right should ever give way to political convenience. But if temptations of interest are sometimes too strong for human virtue, let us at least retain a virtue where there is no temptation to quit it. In the present case there is apparent right on one side, and no convenience on the other. Inhabitants of this island can neither gain riches nor power by taking away the liberty of any part of the human species. The sum of the argument is this:—No man is by nature the property of another: The defendant is, therefore, by nature free: The rights of nature must be some way forfeited before they can be justly taken away: That the defendant has by any act forfeited the rights of nature we require to be proved; and if no proof of such forfeiture can be given, we doubt not but the justice of the court will declare him free.[6]

1777   1792

---

2. Settle unalterably.
3. Boswell, who strongly disagreed with Johnson's "prejudice" against slavery, argued that "To abolish a *status*, which in all ages GOD has sanctioned, and man has continued, would not only be *robbery* to an innumerable class of our fellow subjects;

but it would be extreme cruelty to the African savages."
4. Knight had been kidnapped as a child.
5. Arbitrarily instituted (opposed to *natural* laws).
6. Knight was set free by the Scottish court. The British slave trade was not abolished until 1807.

Rambler No. 4

[On Fiction]

Saturday, March 31, 1750

Simul et jucunda et idonea dicere vitae.
—HORACE, *Art of Poetry*, 334
And join both profit and delight in one.
—CREECH

The works of fiction with which the present generation seems more particularly delighted are such as exhibit life in its true state, diversified only by accidents that daily happen in the world, and influenced by passions and qualities which are really to be found in conversing with mankind.

This kind of writing may be termed, not improperly, the comedy of romance, and is to be conducted nearly by the rules of comic poetry. Its province is to bring about natural events by easy means, and to keep up curiosity without the help of wonder: it is therefore precluded from the machines[1] and expedients of the heroic romance, and can neither employ giants to snatch away a lady from the nuptial rites, nor knights to bring her back from captivity; it can neither bewilder its personages in deserts, nor lodge them in imaginary castles.

I remember a remark made by Scaliger upon Pontanus,[2] that all his writings are filled with the same images; and that if you take from him his lilies and his roses, his satyrs and his dryads, he will have nothing left that can be called poetry. In like manner, almost all the fictions of the last age will vanish if you deprive them of a hermit and a wood, a battle and a shipwreck.

Why this wild strain of imagination found reception so long in polite and learned ages, it is not easy to conceive; but we cannot wonder that while readers could be procured, the authors were willing to continue it; for when a man had by practice gained some fluency of language, he had no further care than to retire to his closet, let loose his invention, and heat his mind with incredibilities; a book was thus produced without fear of criticism, without the toil of study, without knowledge of nature, or acquaintance with life.

The task of our present writers is very different; it requires, together with that learning which is to be gained from books, that experience which can never be attained by solitary diligence, but must arise from general converse and accurate observation of the living world. Their performances have, as Horace expresses it, *plus oneris quanto veniae minus*,[3] little indulgence, and therefore more difficulty. They are engaged

1. The technical term in neoclassical critical theory for the supernatural agents who intervene in human affairs in epic and tragedy.
2. Julius Caesar Scaliger (1484–1558) critized the

Latin poems of the Italian poet Jovianus Pontanus (1426–1503).
3. *Epistles* 2.1.170.

in portraits of which everyone knows the original, and can detect any deviation from exactness of resemblance. Other writings are safe, except from the malice of learning, but these are in danger from every common reader; as the slipper ill executed was censured by a shoemaker who happened to stop in his way at the Venus of Apelles.[4]

But the fear of not being approved as just copiers of human manners is not the most important concern that an author of this sort ought to have before him. These books are written chiefly to the young, the ignorant, and the idle, to whom they serve as lectures of conduct, and introductions into life. They are the entertainment of minds unfurnished with ideas, and therefore easily susceptible of impressions; not fixed by principles, and therefore easily following the current of fancy; not informed by experience, and consequently open to every false suggestion and partial account.

That the highest degree of reverence should be paid to youth, and that nothing indecent should be suffered to approach their eyes or ears, are precepts extorted by sense and virtue from an ancient writer by no means eminent for chastity of thought.[5] The same kind, though not the same degree, of caution, is required in everything which is laid before them, to secure them from unjust prejudices, perverse opinions, and incongruous combinations of images.

In the romances formerly written, every transaction and sentiment was so remote from all that passes among men that the reader was in very little danger of making any applications to himself; the virtues and crimes were equally beyond his sphere of activity; and he amused himself with heroes and with traitors, deliverers and persecutors, as with beings of another species, whose actions were regulated upon motives of their own, and who had neither faults nor excellencies in common with himself.

But when an adventurer is leveled with the rest of the world, and acts in such scenes of the universal drama as may be the lot of any other man, young spectators fix their eyes upon him with closer attention, and hope, by observing his behavior and success, to regulate their own practices when they shall be engaged in the like part.

For this reason these familiar histories may perhaps be made of greater use than the solemnities of professed morality, and convey the knowledge of vice and virtue with more efficacy than axioms and definitions. But if the power of example is so great as to take possession of the memory by a kind of violence, and produce effects almost without the intervention of the will, care ought to be taken that when the choice is unrestrained, the best examples only should be exhibited; and that which is likely to operate so strongly should not be mischievous or uncertain in its effects.

---

4. According to Pliny the Younger (*Naturalis Historia* 35.85), the Greek painter Apelles of Kos (4th century B.C.) corrected the drawing of a sandal after hearing a shoemaker criticize it as faulty, but when the flattered artisan dared to find fault with the drawing of a leg, the artist bade him "stick to his last."

5. Juvenal, *Satires* 14.1–58.

The chief advantage which these fictions have over real life is that their authors are at liberty, though not to invent, yet to select objects, and to cull from the mass of mankind those individuals upon which the attention ought most to be employed; as a diamond, though it cannot be made, may be polished by art, and placed in such situation as to display that luster which before was buried among common stones.

It is justly considered as the greatest excellency of art to imitate nature; but it is necessary to distinguish those parts of nature which are most proper for imitation: greater care is still required in representing life, which is so often discolored by passion or deformed by wickedness. If the world be promiscuously described, I cannot see of what use it can be to read the account; or why it may not be as safe to turn the eye immediately upon mankind as upon a mirror which shows all that presents itself without discrimination.

It is therefore not a sufficient vindication of a character that it is drawn as it appears; for many characters ought never to be drawn: nor of a narrative that the train of events is agreeable to observation and experience; for that observation which is called knowledge of the world will be found much more frequently to make men cunning than good. The purpose of these writings is surely not only to show mankind, but to provide that they may be seen hereafter with less hazard; to teach the means of avoiding the snares which are laid by Treachery for Innocence, without infusing any wish for that superiority with which the betrayer flatters his vanity; to give the power of counteracting fraud without the temptation to practice it; to initiate youth by mock encounters in the art of necessary defense, and to increase prudence without impairing virtue.

Many writers, for the sake of following nature, so mingle good and bad qualities in their principal personages that they are both equally conspicuous; and as we accompany them through their adventures with delight, and are led by degrees to interest ourselves in their favor, we lose the abhorrence of their faults because they do not hinder our pleasure, or perhaps regard them with some kindness for being united with so much merit.

There have been men indeed splendidly wicked, whose endowments threw a brightness on their crimes, and whom scarce any villainy made perfectly detestable because they never could be wholly divested of their excellencies; but such have been in all ages the great corrupters of the world, and their resemblance ought no more to be preserved than the art of murdering without pain.

Some have advanced, without due attention to the consequence of this notion, that certain virtues have their correspondent faults, and therefore that to exhibit either apart is to deviate from probability. Thus men are observed by Swift to be "grateful in the same degree as they are resentful." This principle, with others of the same kind, supposes man to act from a brute impulse, and pursue a certain degree of inclination without any choice of the object; for, otherwise, though it should be allowed that gratitude and resentment arise from the same constitution of the passions, it follows not that they will be equally indulged when reason is consulted; yet, unless that consequence be admitted, this sagacious maxim becomes an empty sound, without any relation to practice or to life.

Nor is it evident that even the first motions to these effects are always in the same proportion. For pride, which produces quickness of resentment, will obstruct gratitude by unwillingness to admit that inferiority which obligation implies; and it is very unlikely that he who cannot think he receives a favor will acknowledge or repay it.

It is of the utmost importance to mankind that positions of this tendency should be laid open and confuted; for while men consider good and evil as springing from the same root, they will spare the one for the sake of the other, and in judging, if not of others at least of themselves, will be apt to estimate their virtues by their vices. To this fatal error all those will contribute who confound the colors of right and wrong, and, instead of helping to settle their boundaries, mix them with so much art that no common mind is able to disunite them.

In narratives where historical veracity has no place, I cannot discover why there should not be exhibited the most perfect idea of virtue; of virtue not angelical, nor above probability (for what we cannot credit, we shall never imitate), but the highest and purest that humanity can reach, which, exercised in such trials as the various revolutions of things shall bring upon it, may, by conquering some calamities and enduring others, teach us what we may hope, and what we can perform. Vice (for vice is necessary to be shown) should always disgust; nor should the graces of gaiety, nor the dignity of courage, be so united with it as to reconcile it to the mind. Wherever it appears, it should raise hatred by the malignity of its practices, and contempt by the meanness of its stratagems: for while it is supported by either parts or spirit, it will be seldom heartily abhorred. The Roman tyrant was content to be hated if he was but feared;[6] and there are thousands of the readers of romances willing to be thought wicked if they may be allowed to be wits. It is therefore to be steadily inculcated that virtue is the highest proof of understanding, and the only solid basis of greatness; and that vice is the natural consequence of narrow thoughts; that it begins in mistake, and ends in ignominy.

6. The Emperor Tiberius. See Suetonius's *Lives of the Caesars.*

Rambler No. 60

[Biography]

Saturday, October 13, 1750

—*Quid sit pulchrum, quid turpe, quid utile, quid non,*
Plenius ac melius Chrysippo et Crantore dicit.
——HORACE, *Epistles,* 1.2. 3–4

> Whose works the beautiful and base contain,
> Of vice and virtue more instructive rules,
> Than all the sober sages of the schools.
> ——FRANCIS

All joy or sorrow for the happiness or calamities of others is produced by an act of the imagination, that realizes the event, however fictitious, or approximates it, however remote, by placing us, for a time, in the condition of him whose fortune we contemplate; so that we feel, while the deception lasts, whatever motions would be excited by the same good or evil happening to ourselves.

Our passions are therefore more strongly moved, in proportion as we can more readily adopt the pains or pleasure proposed to our minds, by recognizing them as once our own, or considering them as naturally incident to our state of life. It is not easy for the most artful writer to give us an interest in happiness or misery, which we think ourselves never likely to feel, and with which we have never yet been made acquainted. Histories of the downfall of kingdoms, and revolutions of empires, are read with great tranquility; the imperial tragedy pleases common auditors only by its pomp of ornament, and grandeur of ideas; and the man whose faculties have been engrossed by business, and whose heart never fluttered but at the rise or fall of stocks, wonders how the attention can be seized, or the affections agitated, by a tale of love.

Those parallel circumstances, and kindred images to which we readily conform our minds, are, above all other writings, to be found in narratives of the lives of particular persons; and therefore no species of writing seems more worthy of cultivation than biography, since none can be more delightful or more useful, none can more certainly enchain the heart by irresistible interest, or more widely diffuse instruction to every diversity of condition.

The general and rapid narratives of history, which involve a thousand fortunes in the business of a day, and complicate innumerable incidents in one great transaction, afford few lessons applicable to private life, which derives its comforts and its wretchedness from the right or wrong management of things, which nothing but their frequency makes considerable, *Parva si non fiunt quotidie,* says Pliny,[1] and which can have

---

1. Pliny the Younger, *Epistles* 3.1. Johnson translates the phrase in the preceding clause.

no place in those relations which never descend below the consultation of senates, the motions of armies, and the schemes of conspirators.

I have often thought that there has rarely passed a life of which a judicious and faithful narrative would not be useful. For, not only every man has in the mighty mass of the world great numbers in the same condition with himself, to whom his mistakes and miscarriages, escapes and expedients, would be of immediate and apparent use; but there is such an uniformity in the state of man, considered apart from adventitious and separable decorations and disguises, that there is scarce any possibility of good or ill, but is common to humankind. A great part of the time of those who are placed at the greatest distance by fortune, or by temper, must unavoidably pass in the same manner; and though, when the claims of nature are satisfied, caprice, and vanity, and accident, begin to produce discriminations and peculiarities, yet the eye is not very heedful or quick, which cannot discover the same causes still[2] terminating their influence in the same effects, though sometimes accelerated, sometimes retarded, or perplexed by multiplied combinations. We are all prompted by the same motives, all deceived by the same fallacies, all animated by hope, obstructed by danger, entangled by desire, and seduced by pleasure.

It is frequently objected to relations of particular lives, that they are not distinguished by any striking or wonderful vicissitudes. The scholar who passed his life among his books, the merchant who conducted only his own affairs, the priest whose sphere of action was not extended beyond that of his duty, are considered as no proper objects of public regard, however they might have excelled in their several stations, whatever might have been their learning, integrity, and piety. But this notion arises from false measures of excellence and dignity, and must be eradicated by considering, that in the esteem of uncorrupted reason, what is of most use is of most value.

It is, indeed, not improper to take honest advantages of prejudice, and to gain attention by a celebrated name; but the business of the biographer is often to pass slightly over those performances and incidents, which produce vulgar greatness, to lead the thoughts into domestic privacies, and display the minute details of daily life, where exterior appendages are cast aside, and men excel each other only by prudence and by virtue. The account of Thuanus[3] is, with great propriety, said by its author to have been written, that it might lay open to posterity the private and familiar character of that man, *cujus ingenium et candorem ex ipsius scriptis sunt olim semper miraturi*, whose candor and genius will to the end of time be by his writings preserved in admiration.

There are many invisible circumstances which, whether we read as inquirers after natural or moral knowledge, whether we intend to enlarge our science, or increase our virtue, are more important than public

2. Always

3. Jacques-Auguste de Thou (1553–1617), an important French historian, of whom Nicholas

Rigault wrote a brief biography, a sentence of which Johnson quotes and translates below.

occurrences. Thus Sallust, the great master of nature, has not forgot, in his account of Catiline,[4] to remark that *his walk was now quick, and again slow*, as an indication of a mind revolving something with violent commotion. Thus the story of Melancthon[5] affords a striking lecture on the value of time, by informing us that when he made an appointment, he expected not only the hour, but the minute to be fixed, that the day might not run out in the idleness of suspense; and all the plans and enterprises of De Witt are now of less importance to the world, than that part of his personal character, which represents him as careful of his health, and negligent of his life.[6]

But biography has often been allotted to writers who seem very little acquainted with the nature of their task, or very negligent about the performance. They rarely afford any other account than might be collected from public papers, but imagine themselves writing a life when they exhibit a chronological series of actions or preferments; and so little regard the manners or behavior of their heroes, that more knowledge may be gained of a man's real character, by a short conversation with one of his servants, than from a formal and studied narrative, begun with his pedigree, and ended with his funeral.

If now and then they condescend to inform the world of particular facts, they are not always so happy as to select the most important. I know not well what advantage posterity can receive from the only circumstance by which Tickell has distinguished Addison from the rest of mankind, the irregularity of his pulse:[7] nor can I think myself overpaid for the time spent in reading the life of Malherbe, by being enabled to relate, after the learned biographer,[8] that Malherbe had two predominant opinions; one, that the looseness of a single woman might destroy all her boast of ancient descent; the other, that the French beggars made use very improperly and barbarously of the phrase *noble gentleman*, because either word included the sense of both.

There are, indeed, some natural reasons why these narratives are often written by such as were not likely to give much instruction or delight, and why most accounts of particular persons are barren and useless. If a life be delayed till interest and envy are at an end, we may hope for impartiality, but must expect little intelligence; for the incidents which give excellence to biography are of a volatile and evanescent kind, such as soon escape the memory, and are rarely transmitted by tradition. We know how few can portray a living acquaintance, except by his most prominent and observable particularities, and the grosser features of his mind; and it may be easily imagined how much of this little knowledge may be lost in imparting it, and how soon a succession of copies will lose all resemblance of the original.

4. Sallust, a Roman historian of the first century B.C., wrote an account of Catiline's conspiracy against the Roman state.
5. Camerarius wrote a life of Melancthon, a German theologian of the 16th century.
6. Sir William Temple, characterizing the Dutch statesman John De Witt.
7. From Thomas Tickell's preface to Addision's *Works* (1721).
8. The life of the French poet François de Malherbe (1555–1628) was written by Honorat de Racan.

If the biographer writes from personal knowledge, and makes haste to gratify the public curiosity, there is danger lest his interest, his fear, his gratitude, or his tenderness, overpower his fidelity, and tempt him to conceal, if not to invent. There are many who think it an act of piety to hide the faults or failings of their friends, even when they can no longer suffer by their detection; we therefore see whole ranks of characters adorned with uniform panegyric, and not to be known from one another, but by extrinsic and casual circumstances. "Let me remember," says Hale, "when I find myself inclined to pity a criminal, that there is likewise a pity due to the country."[9] If we owe regard to the memory of the dead, there is yet more respect to be paid to knowledge, to virtue, and to truth.

A Dictionary of the English Language   Before Johnson no standard dictionary of the English language existed. The want had troubled speakers of English for some time, both because Italian and French academies had produced major dictionaries of their own tongues, and because, in the absence of any authority, English seemed likely to change utterly from one generation to another. Many eighteenth-century authors feared that their own language would soon become obsolete: as Pope wrote in *An Essay on Criticism*,

> Our sons their fathers' failing language see,
> And such as Chaucer is shall Dryden be.

A dictionary could help retard such change; and commercially it would be a book that everyone would need to buy. In 1746 a group of London publishers commissioned Johnson, still an unknown author, to undertake the project. He hoped to finish it in three years; it took him nine. But the quantity and quality of work he accomplished, aided only by six part-time assistants, made him famous as "Dictionary Johnson." The *Dictionary* remained a standard reference book for one hundred years.

Johnson's achievement is notable in three respects: its size (40,000 words); the wealth of illustrative quotations; and the excellence of the definitions. No earlier English dictionary rivaled the scope of Johnson's two large folio volumes. About 114,000 quotations, gathered from the best English writers from Sidney to the eighteenth century, exemplify the usage of words as well as their meanings. Above all it was the definitions, however, which established the authority of Johnson's *Dictionary*. A small selection is only too likely to concentrate on a few amusing or notorious definitions; but the great majority are full, clear, and totally free from eccentricity. Indeed, many of them are still repeated in modern dictionaries. Language, Johnson knew, cannot be fixed once and for all; many of the words he defines have radically changed meaning since the eighteenth century. Yet Johnson did more than any man of his time to preserve the ideal of a standard English.

9. From Gilbert Burnet's *Life and Death of Sir Matthew Hale* (1682).

From A Dictionary of the English Language

From *Preface*

* * *

A large work is difficult because it is large, even though all its parts might singly be performed with facility; where there are many things to be done, each must be allowed its share of time and labor, in the proportion only which it bears to the whole; nor can it be expected that the stones which form the dome of a temple should be squared and polished like the diamond of a ring.

Of the event of this work, for which, having labored it with so much application, I cannot but have some degree of parental fondness, it is natural to form conjectures. Those who have been persuaded to think well of my design will require that it should fix our language, and put a stop to those alterations which time and chance have hitherto been suffered to make in it without opposition. With this consequence I will confess that I flattered myself for a while;[1] but now begin to fear that I have indulged expectation which neither reason nor experience can justify. When we see men grow old and die at a certain time one after another, from century to century, we laugh at the elixir that promises to prolong life to a thousand years; and with equal justice may the lexicographer be derided, who being able to produce no example of a nation that has preserved their words and phrases from mutability, shall imagine that his dictionary can embalm his language and secure it from corruption and decay, that it is in his power to change sublunary nature, or clear the world at once from folly, vanity, and affectation.

With this hope, however, academies have been instituted, to guard the avenues of their languages, to retain fugitives, and repulse intruders; but their vigilance and activity have hitherto been vain; sounds are too volatile and subtle for legal restraints; to enchain syllables, and to lash the wind, are equally the undertakings of pride, unwilling to measure its desires by its strength. The French language has visibly changed under the inspection of the academy;[2] the style of Amelot's translation of father Paul is observed by Le Courayer to be *un peu passé*;[3] and no Italian will maintain that the diction of any modern writer is not perceptibly different from that of Boccace, Machiavel, or Caro.[4]

Total and sudden transformations of a language seldom happen; con-

1. Johnson's *Plan* (1747) had called for "a dictionary by which the pronunciation of our language may be fixed, and its attainment facilitated; by which its purity may be preserved, its use ascertained, and its duration lengthened."
2. The French academy, founded to purify the French language, had produced a dictionary in 1694; but revisions were necessary within a few years.

3. "A bit old-fashioned." Le Courayer's translation (1736) of Father Paolo Sarpi's *History of the Council of Trent* superseded Amelot's (1683).
4. Like Boccaccio (1313–1375) and Machiavelli (1469–1527), Annibale Caro (1507–1566) was a classic Italian stylist whose work had preceded the dictionary published in 1612 by the Italian academy

quests and migrations are now very rare: but there are other causes of change, which, though slow in their operation, and invisible in their progress, are perhaps as much superior to human resistance as the revolutions of the sky, or intumescence[5] of the tide. Commerce, however necessary, however lucrative, as it depraves the manners, corrupts the language; they that have frequent intercourse with strangers, to whom they endeavor to accommodate themselves, must in time learn a mingled dialect, like the jargon which serves the traffickers[6] on the Mediterranean and Indian coasts. This will not always be confined to the exchange, the warehouse, or the port, but will be communicated by degrees to other ranks of the people, and be at last incorporated with the current speech.

There are likewise internal causes equally forcible. The language most likely to continue long without alteration would be that of a nation raised a little, and but a little, above barbarity, secluded from strangers, and totally employed in procuring the conveniencies of life; either without books, or, like some of the Mahometan countries, with very few: men thus busied and unlearned, having only such words as common use requires, would perhaps long continue to express the same notions by the same signs. But no such constancy can be expected in a people polished by arts, and classed by subordination, where one part of the community is sustained and accommodated by the labor of the other. Those who have much leisure to think, will always be enlarging the stock of ideas, and every increase of knowledge, whether real or fancied, will produce new words, or combinations of words. When the mind is unchained from necessity, it will range after convenience; when it is left at large in the fields of speculation, it will shift opinions; as any custom is disused, the words that expressed it must perish with it; as any opinion grows popular, it will innovate speech in the same proportion as it alters practice.

As by the cultivation of various sciences, a language is amplified, it will be more furnished with words deflected from their original sense; the geometrician will talk of a courtier's zenith, or the eccentric virtue of a wild hero, and the physician of sanguine expectations and phlegmatic delays.[7] Copiousness of speech will give opportunities to capricious choice, by which some words will be preferred, and others degraded; vicissitudes of fashion will enforce the use of new, or extend the signification of known terms. The tropes[8] of poetry will make hourly encroachments, and the metaphorical will become the current sense: pronunciation will be varied by levity or ignorance, and the pen must at length comply with the tongue; illiterate writers will at one time or other, by public infatuation, rise into renown, who, not knowing the original import of words, will use them with colloquial licentiousness, confound distinc-

---

5. Swelling.
6. Traders.
7. "Zenith" (the point of the sky directly overhead) and "eccentric" (deviating from the center) were originally astronomical and geometrical terms;

"sanguine" and "phlegmatic" once referred only to the physiological predominance of blood or phlegm.
8. "A change of a word from its original signification" (Johnson's *Dictionary*).

tion, and forget propriety. As politeness increases, some expressions will be considered as too gross and vulgar for the delicate, others as too formal and ceremonious for the gay and airy; new phrases are therefore adopted, which must, for the same reasons, be in time dismissed. Swift, in his petty treatise on the English language,[9] allows that new words must sometimes be introduced, but proposes that none should be suffered to become obsolete. But what makes a word obsolete, more than general agreement to forbear it? and how shall it be continued, when it conveys an offensive idea, or recalled again in the mouths of mankind, when it has once by disuse become unfamiliar, and by unfamiliarity unpleasing.

There is another cause of alteration more prevalent than any other, which yet in the present state of the world cannot be obviated. A mixture of two languages will produce a third distinct from both, and they will always be mixed, where the chief part of education, and the most conspicuous accomplishment, is skill in ancient or in foreign tongues. He that has long cultivated another language, will find its words and combinations crowd upon his memory; and haste and negligence, refinement and affectation, will obtrude borrowed terms and exotic expressions.

The great pest of speech is frequency of translation. No book was every turned from one language into another, without imparting something of its native idiom; this is the most mischievous and comprehensive innovation; single words may enter by thousands, and the fabric of the tongue continue the same, but new phraseology changes much at once; it alters not the single stones of the building, but the order[1] of the columns. If an academy should be established for the cultivation of our style, which I, who can never wish to see dependence multiplied, hope the spirit of English liberty will hinder or destroy, let them, instead of compiling grammars and dictionaries, endeavor with all their influence to stop the license of translators, whose idleness and ignorance, if it be suffered to proceed, will reduce us to babble a dialect of France.

If the changes that we fear be thus irresistible, what remains but to acquiesce with silence, as in the other insurmountable distresses of humanity? It remains that we retard what we cannot repel, that we palliate what we cannot cure. Life may be lengthened by care, though death cannot be ultimately defeated: tongues, like governments, have a natural tendency to degeneration; we have long preserved our constitution, let us make some struggles for our language.

In hope of giving longevity to that which its own nature forbids to be immortal, I have devoted this book, the labor of years, to the honor of my country, that we may no longer yield the palm of philology without a contest to the nations of the continent. The chief glory of every people arises from its authors: whether I shall add anything by my own writings to the reputation of English literature, must be left to time. Much of my

---

9. A *Proposal for Correcting, Improving, and Ascertaining the English Tongue* (1712). "Petty": little.

1. Architectural mode (Doric, etc.), which determines the style and proportions of columns.

life has been lost under the pressures of disease; much has been trifled away; and much has always been spent in provision for the day that was passing over me; but I shall not think my employment useless or ignoble, if by my assistance foreign nations, and distant ages, gain access to the propagators of knowledge, and understand the teachers of truth; if my labors afford light to the repositories of science, and add celebrity to Bacon, to Hooker, to Milton, and to Boyle.[2]

When I am animated by this wish, I look with pleasure on my book, however defective; and deliver it to the world with the spirit of a man that has endeavored well. That it will immediately become popular I have not promised to myself: a few wild blunders and risible absurdities, from which no work of such multiplicity was ever free, may for a time furnish folly with laughter, and harden ignorance in contempt; but useful diligence will at last prevail, and there never can be wanting some who distinguish desert;[3] who will consider that no dictionary of a living tongue ever can be perfect, since while it is hastening to publication, some words are budding, and some falling away; that a whole life cannot be spent upon syntax and etymology, and that even a whole life would not be sufficient; that he, whose design includes whatever language can express, must often speak of what he does not understand; that a writer will sometimes be hurried by eagerness to the end, and sometimes faint with weariness under a task, which Scaliger compares to the labors of the anvil and the mine;[4] that what is obvious is not always known, and what is known is not always present; that sudden fits of inadvertency will surprise vigilance, slight avocations[5] will reduce attention, and casual eclipses of the mind will darken learning; and that the writer shall often in vain trace his memory at the moment of need, for that which yesterday he knew with intuitive readiness, and which will come uncalled into his thoughts tomorrow.

In this work, when it shall be found that much is omitted, let it not be forgotten that much likewise is performed; and though no book was ever spared out of tenderness to the author, and the world is little solicitous to know whence proceeded the faults of that which it condemns; yet it may gratify curiosity to inform it, that the *English Dictionary* was written with little assistance of the learned, and without any patronage of the great;[6] not in the soft obscurities of retirement, or under the shelter of academic bowers, but amidst inconvenience and distraction, in sickness and in sorrow: and it may repress the triumph of malignant criticism to observe, that if our language is not here fully displayed, I have only failed in an attempt which no human powers have hitherto completed. If the lexicons of ancient tongues, now immutably fixed, and comprised

2. Richard Hooker wrote *The Laws of Ecclesiastical Polity* (1594–97), a famous defense of the Church of England. Robert Boyle (1627–1691) was a leading physicist and chemist. "Science": knowledge.
3. Merit.
4. Joseph Justus Scaliger (1540–1609), a great scholar and lexicographer, wrote Latin verses suggesting that criminals should be condemned to lexicography.
5. Whatever calls one aside.
6. See Johnson's letter to Lord Chesterfield below, in Boswell's *Life of Johnson*.

in a few volumes, be yet, after the toil of successive ages, inadequate and delusive; if the aggregated knowledge and cooperating diligence of the Italian academicians did not secure them from the censure of Beni;[7] if the embodied critics of France, when fifty years had been spent upon their work, were obliged to change its economy,[8] and give their second edition another form, I may surely be contented without the praise of perfection, which, if I could obtain, in this gloom of solitude, what would it avail me? I have protracted my work till most of those whom I wished to please have sunk into the grave,[9] and success and miscarriage are empty sounds: I therefore dismiss it with frigid tranquility, having little to fear or hope from censure or from praise.

[Some Definitions: A Small Anthology][1]

ANTHO′LOGY. *n.*

1. A collection of flowers.

To CANT. *v.*

   To talk in the jargon of particular professions, or in any kind of formal affected language, or with a peculiar and studied tone of voice.

   Men *cant* endlessly about *materia forma*; and hunt chimeras by rules
   of art, or dress up ignorance in words of bulk or sound, which may stop
   up the mouth of inquiry.—*Glanville's Scepsis Scientifica.*

ENTHU′SIASM. *n.*

1. A vain belief of private revelation; a vain confidence of divine favor or communication.

   Enthusiasm is founded neither on reason nor divine revelation, but
   rises from the conceits of a warmed or overweening brain.—*Locke.*

GE′NIUS. *n.*

1. The protecting or ruling power of men, places, or things.

   And as I awake, sweet music breathe,
   Sent by some spirit to mortals good,
   Or th' unseen *genius* of the wood.—*Milton.*

2. A man endowed with superior faculties.

3. Mental power or faculties.

4. Disposition of nature by which anyone is qualified for some peculiar employment.

5. Nature; disposition.

IMA′GINATION. *n.*

1. Fancy; the power of forming ideal pictures; the power of representing things absent to one's self or others.

2. Conception; image in the mind; idea.

3. Contrivance; scheme.

LEXICO′GRAPHER. *n.*

   A writer of dictionaries; a harmless drudge, that busies himself in tracing the original, and detailing the signification of words.

---

7. Paolo Beni's *L'Anticrusca* (1612) violently attacked the first edition of the *Vocabolario* (the Italian dictionary).
8. Organization.
9. Johnson's wife had died three years earlier.
1. Johnson's definitions include etymologies and illustrative quotations, some of which are omitted in this selection.

MELANCHO'LY. *n.*

1. A disease, supposed to proceed from a redundance of black bile.
2. A kind of madness, in which the mind is always fixed on one object.
3. A gloomy, pensive, discontented temper.

NA'TURE. *n.*

1. An imaginary being supposed to preside over the material and animal world.

> Thou, *nature*, art my goddess; to thy law
> My services are bound.—*Shakespeare.*

2. The native state or properties of anything, by which it is discriminated from others.
3. The constitution of an animated body.
4. Disposition of mind; temper.
5. The regular course of things.
6. The compass of natural existence.
7. Natural affection, or reverence; native sensations.
8. The state or operation of the material world.
9. Sort; species.
10. Sentiments or images adapted to nature, or comformable to truth and reality.
11. Physics; the science which teaches the qualities of things.

> *Nature* and *nature's* laws lay hid in night,
> God said, Let Newton be, and all was light.—*Pope.*

NE'TWORK. *n.*

Anything reticulated or decussated, at equal distances, with interstices between the intersections.

OATS. *n.*

A grain, which in England is generally given to horses, but in Scotland supports the people.

PA'STERN. *n.*

1. The knee of an horse.[2]

PA'TRON. *n.*

1. One who countenances, supports, or protects. Commonly a wretch who supports with insolence, and is paid with flattery.

PE'NSION. *n.*

An allowance made to anyone without an equivalent. In England it is generally understood to mean pay given to a state hireling for treason to his country.[3]

SA'TIRE. *n.*

A poem in which wickedness or folly is censured. Proper *satire* is distinguished, by the generality of the reflections, from a *lampoon*, which

---

2. "A lady once asked him how he came to define *Pastern* the *knee* of a horse: instead of making an elaborate defense, as she expected, he at once answered, 'Ignorance, Madam, pure ignorance' " (Boswell).

3. In 1762 Johnson was awarded a pension, but he did not revise the definition in later editions.

is aimed against a particular person; but they are too frequently confounded.

TO'RY. *n.*

One who adheres to the ancient constitution of the state, and the apostolical hierarchy of the church of England, opposed to a whig.

> The knight is more a *tory* in the country than the town, because it more advances his interest.—*Addison.*

WHIG. *n.*

2. The name of a faction.

> Whoever has a true value for church and state, should avoid the extremes of *whig* for the sake of the former, and the extremes of tory on the account of the latter.—*Swift.*

WIT. *n.*

1. The powers of the mind; the mental faculties; the intellects. This is the original signification.
2. Imagination; quickness of fancy.
3. Sentiments produced by quickness of fancy.
4. A man of fancy.
5. A man of genius.
6. Sense; judgment.
7. In the plural. Sound mind; intellect not crazed.
8. Contrivance; strategem; power of expedients.

1755

From The Preface to Shakespeare[1]

[*Shakespeare's Excellence. General Nature*]

That praises are without reason lavished on the dead, and that the honors due only to excellence are paid to antiquity, is a complaint likely to be always continued by those who, being able to add nothing to truth, hope for eminence from the heresies of paradox; or those who, being forced by disappointment upon consolatory expedients, are willing to hope from posterity what the present age refuses, and flatter themselves

---

1. This, the finest piece of Shakespeare criticism in the 18th century, is the culmination of a critical tradition that began with Nicholas Rowe's edition of the plays in 1709 (indeed with Dryden's critical remarks on Shakespeare) and that was continued by subsequent editors, notably Pope, Lewis Theobald, and William Warburton. Johnson's topics are in the main the conventional ones of 18th-century Shakespeare criticism: Shakespeare as the poet of nature, not of learning; as the creator of memorable characters; as a poet who supremely expresses and evokes the passions. Johnson follows his tradition in weighing Shakespeare's poetic virtues against his faults and finding that the virtues out-

weigh the faults. No one has praised Shakespeare more nobly and generously. The *Preface* is most original when Johnson attacks and dismisses the long-standing reverence in critical theory for the unities of time and place. By appealing to the experience of the playgoer, he demonstrates that, thanks to the imagination of the spectator, the playwright need not contain his action within a period of twenty-four hours or restrict it to one place throughout the drama.

Johnson's edition of Shakespeare also contained footnotes and brief introductions to each of the plays. We reprint here the introductory headnote to the two *Henry IV* plays.

that the regard which is yet denied by envy will be at last bestowed by time.

Antiquity, like every other quality that attracts the notice of mankind, has undoubtedly votaries that reverence it not from reason but from prejudice. Some seem to admire indiscriminately whatever has been long preserved, without considering that time has sometimes cooperated with chance; all perhaps are more willing to honor past than present excellence; and the mind contemplates genius through the shades of age, as the eye surveys the sun through artificial opacity. The great contention of criticism is to find the faults of the moderns and the beauties of the ancients. While an author is yet living we estimate his powers by his worst performance; and when he is dead we rate them by his best.

To works, however, of which the excellence is not absolute and definite, but gradual and comparative; to works not raised upon principles demonstrative and scientific, but appealing wholly to observation and experience, no other test can be applied than length of duration and continuance of esteem. What mankind have long possessed they have often examined and compared; and if they persist to value the possession, it is because frequent comparisons have confirmed opinion in its favor. As among the works of nature no man can properly call a river deep or a mountain high, without the knowledge of many mountains and many rivers; so in the productions of genius, nothing can be styled excellent till it has been compared with other works of the same kind. Demonstration[2] immediately displays its power and has nothing to hope or fear from the flux of years; but works tentative and experimental must be estimated by their proportion to the general and collective ability of man, as it is discovered in a long succession of endeavors. Of the first building that was raised, it might be with certainty determined that it was round or square, but whether it was spacious or lofty must have been referred to time. The Pythagorean scale of numbers[3] was at once discovered to be perfect; but the poems of Homer we yet know not to transcend the common limits of human intelligence, but by remarking that nation after nation, and century after century, has been able to do little more than transpose his incidents, new name his characters, and paraphrase his sentiments.

The reverence due to writings that have long subsisted arises, therefore, not from any credulous confidence in the superior wisdom of past ages, or gloomy persuasion of the degeneracy of mankind, but is the consequence of acknowledged and indubitable positions, that what has been longest known has been most considered, and what is most considered is best understood.

The poet of whose works I have undertaken the revision may now begin to assume the dignity of an ancient and claim the privilege of established fame and prescriptive veneration. He has long outlived his

---

2. "The highest degree of deducible or argumental evidence" (Johnson's *Dictionary*).

3. Pythagoras discovered the ratios that determine the principal intervals of the musical scale.

century, the term commonly fixed as the test of literary merit.[4] Whatever advantages he might once derive from personal allusions, local customs, or temporary opinions, have for many years been lost; and every
topic of merriment or motive of sorrow which the modes of artificial life
afforded him now only obscure the scenes which they once illuminated.
The effects of favor and competition are at an end; the tradition of his
friendships and his enmities has perished; his works support no opinion
with arguments nor supply any faction with invectives; they can neither
indulge vanity nor gratify malignity; but are read without any other reason than the desire of pleasure, and are therefore praised only as pleasure
is obtained; yet, thus unassisted by interest or passion, they have passed
through variations of taste and changes of manners, and, as they devolved
from one generation to another, have received new honors at every
transmission.

But because human judgment, though it be gradually gaining upon
certainty, never becomes infallible, and approbation, though long continued, may yet be only the approbation of prejudice or fashion, it is
proper to inquire by what peculiarities of excellence Shakespeare has
gained and kept the favor of his countrymen.

Nothing can please many, and please long, but just representations of
general nature. Particular manners can be known to few, and therefore
few only can judge how nearly they are copied. The irregular combinations of fanciful invention may delight awhile by that novelty of which
the common satiety of life sends us all in quest; but the pleasures of
sudden wonder are soon exhausted, and the mind can only repose on
the stability of truth.

Shakespeare is, above all writers, at least above all modern writers,
the poet of nature, the poet that holds up to his readers a faithful mirror
of manners and of life. His characters are not modified by the customs
of particular places, unpracticed by the rest of the world; by the peculiarities of studies or professions, which can operate but upon small
numbers; or by the accidents of transient fashions or temporary opinions:
they are the genuine progeny of common humanity, such as the world
will always supply and observation will always find. His persons act and
speak by the influence of those general passions and principles by which
all minds are agitated and the whole system of life is continued in motion.
In the writings of other poets a character is too often an individual: in
those of Shakespeare it is commonly a species.

It is from this wide extension of design that so much instruction is
derived. It is this which fills the plays of Shakespeare with practical axioms
and domestic wisdom. It was said of Euripides[5] that every verse was a
precept; and it may be said of Shakespeare that from his works may be
collected a system of civil and economical prudence. Yet his real power
is not shown in the splendor of particular passages, but by the progress

4. Horace, *Epistles* 2.1.39.
5. The Greek tragic poet (ca. 480–406 B.C.). The observation is Cicero's.

of his fable and the tenor of his dialogue; and he that tries to recommend him by select quotations will succeed like the pedant in Hierocles[6] who, when he offered his house to sale, carried a brick in his pocket as a specimen.

It will not easily be imagined how much Shakespeare excels in accommodating his sentiments to real life but by comparing him with other authors. It was observed of the ancient schools of declamation that the more diligently they were frequented, the more was the student disqualified for the world, because he found nothing there which he should ever meet in any other place. The same remark may be applied to every stage but that of Shakespeare. The theater, when it is under any other direction, is peopled by such characters as were never seen, conversing in a language which was never heard, upon topics which will never arise in the commerce of mankind. But the dialogue of this author is often so evidently determined by the incident which produces it, and is pursued with so much ease and simplicity, that it seems scarcely to claim the merit of fiction, but to have been gleaned by diligent selection out of common conversation and common occurrences.

Upon every other stage the universal agent is love, by whose power all good and evil is distributed and every action quickened or retarded. To bring a lover, a lady, and a rival into the fable; to entangle them in contradictory obligations, perplex them with oppositions of interest, and harass them with violence of desires inconsistent with each other; to make them meet in rapture, and part in agony; to fill their mouths with hyperbolical joy and outrageous sorrow; to distress them as nothing human ever was distressed; to deliver them as nothing human ever was delivered, is the business of a modern dramatist. For this, probability is violated, life is misrepresented, and language is depraved. But love is only one of many passions; and as it has no great influence upon the sum of life, it has little operation in the dramas of a poet who caught his ideas from the living world and exhibited only what he saw before him. He knew that any other passion, as it was regular or exorbitant, was a cause of happiness or calamity.

Characters thus ample and general were not easily discriminated and preserved; yet perhaps no poet ever kept his personages more distinct from each other. I will not say with Pope that every speech may be assigned to the proper speaker,[7] because many speeches there are which have nothing characteristical; but perhaps though some may be equally adapted to every person, it will be difficult to find that any can be properly transferred from the present possessor to another claimant. The choice is right when there is reason for choice.

Other dramatists can only gain attention by hyperbolical or aggravated characters, by fabulous and unexampled excellence or depravity, as the writers of barbarous romances invigorated the reader by a giant and a dwarf; and he that should form his expectations of human affairs from

---

6. Hierocles of Alexandria, a Greek philosopher of the 5th century A.D.

7. In the preface to his edition of Shakespeare's plays (1725).

the play or from the tale would be equally deceived. Shakespeare has no heroes; his scenes are occupied only by men, who act and speak as the reader thinks that he should himself have spoken or acted on the same occasion; even where the agency is supernatural, the dialogue is level with life. Other writers disguise the most natural passions and most frequent incidents so that he who contemplates them in the book will not know them in the world: Shakespeare approximates[8] the remote, and familiarizes the wonderful; the event which he represents will not happen, but, if it were possible, its effects would probably be such as he has assigned; and it may be said that he has not only shown human nature as it acts in real exigencies, but as it would be found in trials to which it cannot be exposed.

This therefore is the praise of Shakespeare, that his drama is the mirror of life; that he who has mazed his imagination in following the phantoms which other writers raise up before him, may here be cured of his delirious ecstasies by reading human sentiments in human language, by scenes from which a hermit may estimate the transactions of the world, and a confessor predict the progress of the passions.

[*Shakespeare's Faults. The Three Dramatic Unities*]

Shakespeare with his excellencies has likewise faults, and faults sufficient to obscure and overwhelm any other merit. I shall show them in the proportion in which they appear to me, without envious malignity or superstitious veneration. No question can be more innocently discussed than a dead poet's pretensions to renown; and little regard is due to that bigotry which sets candor[1] higher than truth.

His first defect is that to which may be imputed most of the evil in books or in men. He sacrifices virtue to convenience, and is so much more careful to please than to instruct that he seems to write without any moral purpose. From his writings indeed a system of social duty may be selected, for he that thinks reasonably must think morally, but his precepts and axioms drop casually from him; he makes no just distribution of good or evil, nor is always careful to show in the virtuous a disapprobation of the wicked; he carries his persons indifferently through right and wrong, and at the close dismisses them without further care, and leaves their examples to operate by chance. This fault the barbarity of his age cannot extenuate; for it is always a writer's duty to make the world better, and justice is a virtue independent on time or place.

The plots are often so loosely formed that a very slight consideration may improve them, and so carelessly pursued that he seems not always fully to comprehend his own design. He omits opportunities of instructing or delighting which the train of his story seems to force upon him, and apparently rejects those exhibitions which would be more affecting for the sake of those which are more easy.

8. Brings near.   1. Kindness.

It may be observed that in many of his plays the latter part is evidently neglected. When he found himself near the end of his work, and in view of his reward, he shortened the labor to snatch the profit. He therefore remits his efforts where he should most vigorously exert them, and his catastrophe is improbably produced or imperfectly represented.

He had no regard to distinction of time or place, but gives to one age or nation, without scruple, the customs, institutions, and opinions of another, at the expense not only of likelihood but of possibility. These faults Pope has endeavored, with more zeal than judgment, to transfer to his imagined interpolators. We need not wonder to find Hector quoting Aristotle, when we see the loves of Theseus and Hippolyta combined with the Gothic mythology of fairies.[2] Shakespeare, indeed, was not the only violator of chronology, for in the same age Sidney, who wanted not the advantages of learning, has, in his *Arcadia*, confounded the pastoral with the feudal times, the days of innocence, quiet, and security with those of turbulence, violence, and adventure.

In his comic scenes he is seldom very successful when he engages his characters in reciprocations of smartness and contests of sarcasm; their jests are commonly gross, and their pleasantry licentious; neither his gentlemen nor his ladies have much delicacy, nor are sufficiently distinguished from his clowns by any appearance of refined manners. Whether he represented the real conversation of his time is not easy to determine: the reign of Elizabeth is commonly supposed to have been a time of stateliness, formality, and reserve; yet perhaps the relaxations of that severity were not very elegant. There must, however, have been always some modes of gaiety preferable to others, and a writer ought to choose the best.

In tragedy his performance seems constantly to be worse as his labor is more. The effusions of passion, which exigence forces out, are for the most part striking and energetic; but whenever he solicits his invention, or strains his faculties, the offspring of his throes is tumor,[3] meanness, tediousness, and obscurity.

In narration he affects a disproportionate pomp of diction and a wearisome train of circumlocution, and tells the incident imperfectly in many words which might have been more plainly delivered in few. Narration in dramatic poetry is naturally tedious, as it is unanimated and inactive, and obstructs the progress of the action; it should therefore always be rapid and enlivened by frequent interruption. Shakespeare found it an encumbrance, and instead of lightening it by brevity, endeavored to recommend it by dignity and splendor.

His declamations or set speeches are commonly cold and weak, for his power was the power of nature; when he endeavored, like other tragic writers, to catch opportunities of amplification and, instead of inquiring what the occasion demanded, to show how much his stores of knowl-

---

2. In *Troilus and Cressida*, 2.2.166, and in *Midsummer Night's Dream*, respectively.

3. Inflated grandeur, false magnificence.

edge could supply, he seldom escapes without the pity or resentment of his reader.

It is incident to him to be now and then entangled with an unwieldy sentiment which he cannot well express, and will not reject; he struggles with it awhile, and, if it continues stubborn, comprises it in words such as occur, and leaves it to be disentangled and evolved by those who have more leisure to bestow upon it.

Not that always where the language is intricate the thought is subtle, or the image always great where the line is bulky; the equality of words to things is very often neglected, and trivial sentiments and vulgar[4] ideas disappoint the attention, to which they are recommended by sonorous epithets and swelling figures.

But the admirers of this great poet have most reason to complain when he approaches nearest to his highest excellence, and seems fully resolved to sink them in dejection and mollify them with tender emotions by the fall of greatness, the danger of innocence, or the crosses of love. What he does best, he soon ceases to do. He is not long soft and pathetic without some idle conceit or contemptible equivocation. He no sooner begins to move than he counteracts himself; and terror and pity, as they are rising in the mind, are checked and blasted by sudden frigidity.

A quibble[5] is to Shakespeare what luminous vapors are to the traveler: he follows it at all adventures; it is sure to lead him out of his way, and sure to engulf him in the mire. It has some malignant power over his mind, and its fascinations are irresistible. Whatever be the dignity or profundity of his disquisitions, whether he be enlarging knowledge or exalting affection, whether he be amusing[6] attention with incidents, or enchaining it in suspense, let but a quibble spring up before him, and he leaves his work unfinished. A quibble is the golden apple for which he will always turn aside from his career[7] or stoop from his elevation. A quibble, poor and barren as it is, gave him such delight that he was content to purchase it by the sacrifice of reason, propriety, and truth. A quibble was to him the fatal Cleopatra for which he lost the world, and was content to lose it.

It will be thought strange that in enumerating the defects of this writer, I have not yet mentioned his neglect of the unities; his violation of those laws which have been instituted and established by the joint authority of poets and critics.

For his other deviations from the art of writing, I resign him to critical justice without making any other demand in his favor than that which must be indulged to all human excellence: that his virtues be rated with his failings. But from the censure which this irregularity may bring upon

4. "Mean; low; being of the common rate" (Johnson's *Dictionary*).
5. Pun.
6. "To entertain with tranquility; to fill with thoughts that engage the mind, without distracting it" (Johnson's *Dictionary*).

7. In Greek legend Atalanta refused to marry any man who could not defeat her in a foot race. Hippomenes won her by dropping, as he ran, three of the golden apples of the Hesperides, which she paused to pick up.

him I shall, with due reverence to that learning which I must oppose, adventure to try how I can defend him.

His histories, being neither tragedies nor comedies, are not subject to any of their laws; nothing more is necessary to all the praise which they expect than that the changes of action be so prepared as to be understood; that the incidents be various and affecting, and the characters consistent, natural, and distinct. No other unity is intended, and therefore none is to be sought.

In his other works he has well enough preserved the unity of action. He has not, indeed, an intrigue regularly perplexed and regularly unraveled: he does not endeavor to hide his design only to discover it, for this is seldom the order of real events, and Shakespare is the poet of nature: but his plan has commonly what Aristotle requires,[8] a beginning, a middle, and an end; one event is concatenated with another, and the conclusion follows by easy consequence. There are, perhaps, some incidents that might be spared, as in other poets there is much talk that only fills up time upon the stage; but the general system makes gradual advances, and the end of the play is the end of expectation.

To the unities of time and place he has shown no regard; and perhaps a nearer view of the principles on which they stand will diminish their value and withdraw from them the veneration which, from the time of Corneille,[9] they have very generally received, by discovering that they have given more trouble to the poet than pleasure to the auditor.

The necessity of observing the unities of time and place arises from the supposed necessity of making the drama credible. The critics hold it impossible that an action of months or years can be possibly believed to pass in three hours; or that the spectator can suppose himself to sit in the theater while ambassadors go and return between distant kings, while armies are levied and towns besieged, while an exile wanders and returns, or till he whom they saw courting his mistress shall lament the untimely fall of his son. The mind revolts from evident falsehood, and fiction loses its force when it departs from the resemblance of reality.

From the narrow limitation of time necessarily arises the contraction of place. The spectator who knows that he saw the first act at Alexandria cannot suppose that he sees the next at Rome, at a distance to which not the dragons of Medea could, in so short a time, have transported him; he knows with certainty that he has not changed his place; and he knows that place cannot change itself, that what was a house cannot become a plain, that what was Thebes can never be Persepolis.

Such is the triumphant language with which a critic exults over the misery of an irregular poet, and exults commonly with resistance or reply. It is time, therefore, to tell him by the authority of Shakespeare that he assumes, as an unquestionable principle, a position which, while his breath is forming it into words, his understanding pronounces to be false. It is false that any representation is mistaken for reality; that any

8. *Poetics* 7.
9. Pierre Corneille (1606–1684), the French playwright, discussed the unities in his *Discours des trois unités* (1660).

dramatic fable in its materiality was ever credible or, for a single moment, was ever credited.

The objection arising from the impossibility of passing the first hour at Alexandria and the next at Rome supposes that when the play opens the spectator really imagines himself at Alexandria, and believes that his walk to the theater has been a voyage to Egypt, and that he lives in the days of Antony and Cleopatra. Surely he that imagines this may imagine more. He that can take the stage at one time for the palace of the Ptolemies may take it in half an hour for the promontory of Actium. Delusion, if delusion be admitted, has no certain limitation; if the spectator can be once persuaded that his old acquaintances are Alexander and Caesar, that a room illuminated with candles is the plain of Pharsalia or the bank of Granicus, he is in a state of elevation above the reach of reason or of truth, and from the heights of empyrean poetry may despise the circumscriptions of terrestrial nature. There is no reason why a mind thus wandering in ecstasy should count the clock, or why an hour should not be a century in that calenture[1] of the brain that can make the stage a field.

The truth is that the spectators are always in their senses, and know, from the first act to the last, that the stage is only a stage, and that the players are only players. They came to hear a certain number of lines recited with just gesture and elegant modulation. The lines relate to some action, and an action must be in some place; but the different actions that complete a story may be in places very remote from each other; and where is the absurdity of allowing that space to represent first Athens, and then Sicily, which was always known to be neither Sicily nor Athens but a modern theater?

By supposition, as place is introduced, time may be extended; the time required by the fable elapses, for the most part, between the acts; for, of so much of the action as is represented, the real and poetical duration is the same. If, in the first act, preparations for war against Mithridates are represented to be made in Rome, the event of the war may, without absurdity, be represented, in the catastrophe, as happening in Pontus; we know that there is neither war nor preparation for war; we know that we are neither in Rome nor Pontus, that neither Mithridates nor Lucullus are before us. The drama exhibits successive imitations of successive actions; and why may not the second imitation represent an action that happened years after the first, if it be so connected with it that nothing but time can be supposed to intervene? Time is, of all modes of existence, most obsequious[2] to the imagination; a lapse of years is as easily conceived as a passage of hours. In contemplation we easily contract the time of real actions, and therefore willingly permit it to be contracted when we only see their imitation.

It will be asked how the drama moves if it is not credited. It is credited with all the credit due to a drama. It is credited, whenever it moves, as

1. A delirium produced by tropical heat, which causes sailors to leap into the sea under the delu-

sion that it is a green field.
2. "Obedient; compliant" (Johnson's *Dictionary*).

a just picture of a real original; as representing to the auditor what he would himself feel if he were to do or suffer what is there feigned to be suffered or to be done. The reflection that strikes the heart is not that the evils before us are real evils, but that they are evils to which we ourselves may be exposed. If there be any fallacy, it is not that we fancy the players, but that we fancy ourselves, unhappy for a moment; but we rather lament the possibility than suppose the presence of misery, as a mother weeps over her babe when she remembers that death may take it from her. The delight of tragedy proceeds from our consciousness of fiction; if we thought murders and treasons real, they would please no more.

Imitations produce pain or pleasure, not because they are mistaken for realities, but because they bring realities to mind. When the imagination is recreated by a painted landscape, the trees are not supposed capable to give us shade or the fountains coolness; but we consider how we should be pleased with such fountains playing beside us and such woods waving over us. We are agitated in reading the history of *Henry the Fifth*; yet no man takes his book for the field of Agincourt. A dramatic exhibition is a book recited with concomitants that increase or diminish its effect. Familiar comedy is often more powerful on the theater than in the page; imperial tragedy is always less. The humor of Petruchio may be heightened by grimace; but what voice or what gesture can hope to add dignity or force to the soliloquy of Cato?[3]

A play read affects the mind like a play acted. It is therefore evident that the action is not supposed to be real; and it follows that between the acts a longer or shorter time may be allowed to pass, and that no more account of space or duration is to be taken by the auditor of a drama than by the reader of a narrative, before whom may pass in an hour the life of a hero or the revolutions of an empire.

Whether Shakespeare knew the unities and rejected them by design or deviated from them by happy ignorance, it is, I think, impossible to decide and useless to inquire. We may reasonably suppose that, when he rose to notice, he did not want[4] the counsels and admonitions of scholars and critics, and that he at last deliberately persisted in a practice which he might have begun by chance. As nothing is essential to the fable but unity of action, and as the unities of time and place arise evidently from false assumptions, and, by circumscribing the extent of the drama, lessen its variety, I cannot think it much to be lamented that they were not known by him, or not observed: nor, if such another poet could arise, should I very vehemently reproach him that his first act passed at Venice and his next in Cyprus.[5] Such violations of rules merely positive become the comprehensive genius of Shakespeare, and such censures are suitable to the minute and slender criticism of Voltaire.

3. Petruchio is the hero of Shakespeare's comedy *The Taming of the Shrew*. In Addison's tragedy *Cato* (5.1), the hero soliloquizes on immortality shortly before committing suicide.
4. Lack.
5. As is the case in *Othello*.

Non usque adeo permiscuit imis
Longus summa dies, ut non, si voce Metelli
Serventur leges, malint a Caesare tolli.[6]

Yet when I speak thus slightly of dramatic rules, I cannot but recollect how much wit and learning may be produced against me; before such authorities I am afraid to stand: not that I think the present question one of those that are to be decided by mere authority, but because it is to be suspected that these precepts have not been so easily received but for better reasons than I have yet been able to find. The result of my inquiries, in which it would be ludicrous to boast of impartiality, is that the unities of time and place are not essential to a just drama, that though they may sometimes conduce to pleasure, they are always to be sacrificed to the nobler beauties of variety and instruction; and that a play written with nice observation of critical rules is to be contemplated as an elaborate curiosity, as the product of superfluous and ostentatious art, by which is shown rather what is possible than what is necessary.

He that without diminution of any other excellence shall preserve all the unities unbroken deserves the like applause with the architect who shall display all the orders of architecture in a citadel without any deduction for its strength; but the principal beauty of a citadel is to exclude the enemy, and the greatest graces of a play are to copy nature and instruct life. * * *

[Henry IV]

None of Shakespeare's plays are more read than the first and second parts of *Henry the fourth*. Perhaps no author has ever in two plays afforded so much delight. The great events are interesting, for the fate of kingdoms depends upon them; the slighter occurrences are diverting, and, except one or two, sufficiently probable; the incidents are multiplied with wonderful fertility of invention, and the characters diversified with the utmost nicety of discernment, and the profoundest skill in the nature of man.

The prince, who is the hero both of the comic and tragic part, is a young man of great abilities and violent passions, whose sentiments are right, though his actions are wrong; whose virtues are obscured by negligence, and whose understanding is dissipated by levity. In his idle hours he is rather loose than wicked, and when the occasion forces out his latent qualities, he is great without effort, and brave without tumult. The trifler is roused into a hero, and the hero again reposes in the trifler. This character is great, original, and just.[7]

Percy is a rugged soldier, choleric, and quarrelsome, and has only the soldier's virtues, generosity and courage.

6. Lucan, *Pharsalia* 3.138–40: "The course of time has not wrought such confusion that the laws would not rather be trampled on by Caesar than saved by Metellus."
7. Exact.

But Falstaff, unimitated, unimitable Falstaff, how shall I describe thee? Thou compound of sense and vice; of sense which may be admired but not esteemed, of vice which may be despised, but hardly detested. Falstaff is a character loaded with faults, and with those faults which naturally produce contempt. He is a thief, and a glutton, a coward, and a boaster, always ready to cheat the weak, and prey upon the poor; to terrify the timorous and insult the defenseless. At once obsequious and malignant, he satirizes in their absence those whom he lives by flattering. He is familiar with the prince only as an agent of vice, but of this familiarity he is so proud as not only to be supercilious and haughty with common men, but to think his interest of importance to the duke of Lancaster. Yet the man thus corrupt, thus despicable, makes himself necessary to the prince that despises him, by the most pleasing of all qualities, perpetual gaiety, by an unfailing power of exciting laughter, which is the more freely indulged, as his wit is not of the splendid or ambitious kind, but consists in easy escapes and sallies of levity, which make sport but raise no envy. It must be observed that he is stained with no enormous or sanguinary crimes, so that his licentiousness is not so offensive but that it may be borne for his mirth.

The moral to be drawn from this representation is that no man is more dangerous than he that with a will to corrupt, hath the power to please; and that neither wit nor honesty ought to think themselves safe with such a companion when they see Henry seduced by Falstaff.

From LIVES OF THE POETS

From Cowley[1]

[Metaphysical Wit]

Wit, like all other things subject by their nature to the choice of man, has its changes and fashions, and at different times takes different forms. About the beginning of the seventeenth century appeared a race of writers that may be termed the metaphysical poets,[2] of whom in a criticism on the works of Cowley it is not improper to give some account.

The metaphysical poets were men of learning, and to show their learning was their whole endeavor; but, unluckily resolving to show it in rhyme, instead of writing poetry they only wrote verses, and very often such verses as stood the trial of the finger better than of the ear; for the

---

1. Abraham Cowley (1618–1667) was much admired during the middle of the 17th century. His reputation began to decline before 1700, but he was remembered as a writer of false wit, especially in his love poems *The Mistress*.
2. Presumably Johnson took this now common designation from a hint in Dryden's *Discourse*

Concerning the Original and Progress of Satire, 1693. Dryden condemned Donne because "he affects the metaphysics . . . and perplexes the minds of the fair sex with nice speculations of philosophy, when he should engage their hearts, and entertain them with the softnesses of love" (*Essays*, ed. W. P. Ker, 2.19).

modulation was so imperfect that they were only found to be verses by counting the syllables.

If the father of criticism[3] has rightly denominated poetry *tekhnē mimē-tikè, an imitative art,* these writers will without great wrong lose their right to the name of poets, for they cannot be said to have imitated anything: they neither copied nature nor life; neither painted the forms of matter nor represented the operations of intellect.

Those however who deny them to be poets allow them to be wits. Dryden confesses of himself and his contemporaries that they fall below Donne in it, but maintains that they surpass him in poetry.[4]

If wit be well described by Pope as being "that which has been often thought, but was never before so well expressed,"[5] they certainly never attained nor ever sought it, for they endeavored to be singular in their thoughts, and were careless of their diction. But Pope's account of wit is undoubtedly erroneous; he depresses it below its natural dignity, and reduces it from strength of thought to happiness of language.

If by a more noble and more adequate conception that be considered as wit which is at once natural and new, that which though not obvious is, upon its first production, acknowledged to be just; if it be that which he that never found it, wonders how he missed; to wit of this kind the metaphysical poets have seldom risen. Their thoughts are often new, but seldom natural; they are not obvious, but neither are they just;[6] and the reader, far from wondering that he missed them, wonders more frequently by what perverseness of industry they were ever found.

But wit, abstracted from its effects upon the hearer, may be more rigorously and philosophically considered as a kind of *discordia concors;*[7] a combination of dissimilar images, or discovery of occult resemblances in things apparently unlike. Of wit, thus defined, they have more than enough. The most heterogeneous ideas are yoked by violence together; nature and art are ransacked for illustrations, comparisons, and allusions; their learning instructs, and their subtlety surprises; but the reader commonly thinks his improvement dearly bought, and, though he sometimes admires, is seldom pleased.

From this account of their compositions it will be readily inferred that they were not successful in representing or moving the affections. As they were wholly employed on something unexpected and surprising, they had no regard to that uniformity of sentiment which enables us to conceive and to excite the pains and the pleasure of other minds: they never inquired what on any occasion they should have said or done, but wrote rather as beholders than partakers of human nature; as beings looking upon good and evil, impassive and at leisure; as Epicurean deities making remarks on the actions of men and the vicissitudes of life, without interest and without emotion. Their courtship was void of fondness

3. Aristotle in his *Poetics.*
4. *Discourse . . . of Satire* (Ker 2.102).
5. *Essay on Criticism,* lines 297–98.
6. Exact, proper.
7. Literally, "a harmonious discord." Johnson is

himself being witty in using this phrase, a familiar philosophical concept denoting the general harmony of God's creation despite its manifold and often contradictory particulars.

and their lamentation of sorrow. Their wish was only to say what they hoped had been never said before.

Nor was the sublime more within their reach than the pathetic; for they never attempted that comprehension and expanse of thought which at once fills the whole mind, and of which the first effect is sudden astonishment, and the second rational admiration. Sublimity is produced by aggregation, and littleness by dispersion. Great thoughts are always general, and consist in positions not limited by exceptions, and in descriptions not descending to minuteness. It is with great propriety that subtlety, which in its original import means exility[8] of particles, is taken in its metaphorical meaning for nicety of distinction. Those writers who lay on the watch for novelty could have little hope of greatness; for great things cannot have escaped former observation. Their attempts were always analytic: they broke every image into fragments, and could no more represent by their slender conceits and labored particularities the prospects of nature or the scenes of life, than he who dissects a sunbeam with a prism can exhibit the wide effulgence of a summer noon.

What they wanted however of the sublime they endeavored to supply by hyperbole;[9] their amplification had no limits: they left not only reason but fancy behind them, and produced combinations of confused magnificence that not only could not be credited, but could not be imagined.

Yet great labor directed by great abilities is never wholly lost: if they frequently threw away their wit upon false conceits, they likewise sometimes struck out unexpected truth: if their conceits were farfetched, they were often worth the carriage.[1] To write on their plan it was at least necessary to read and think. No man could be born a metaphysical poet, nor assume the dignity of a writer by descriptions copied from descriptions, by imitations borrowed from imitations, by traditional imagery and hereditary similes, by readiness of rhyme and volubility of syllables.

1779

From Milton[1]

[Lycidas]

One of the poems on which much praise has been bestowed is *Lycidas*; of which the diction is harsh,[2] the rhymes uncertain, and the num-

8. Thinness.
9. An image heightened beyond reality (see Johnson's *Dictionary*).
1. In the *Life of Addison*, Johnson wrote: "A simile may be compared to lines converging at a point, and is more excellent as the lines approach from greater distance . . ."
1. Johnson's treatment of Milton as man and poet gave great offense to many ardent Miltonians in his own day and damaged his reputation as a critic

in the following century. He did not admire Milton's character, and he detested his politics and religion. But no one has praised *Paradise Lost* more handsomely. Especially offensive in the 19th century was his attack on *Lycidas*. Johnson disliked modern pastorals, recognizing that the tradition had been worn threadbare. His views on the genre may be read in *Ramblers* 36 and 37.
2. This notorious word does not mean "unmelodious," but "strained, forced, affected, or labored."

bers unpleasing. What beauty there is, we must therefore seek in the sentiments and images. It is not to be considered as the effusion of real passion; for passion runs not after remote allusions and obscure opinions. Passion plucks no berries from the myrtle and ivy, nor calls upon Arethuse and Mincius, nor tells of "rough satyrs and fauns with cloven heel." Where there is leisure for fiction there is little grief.

In this poem there is no nature, for there is no truth; there is no art, for there is nothing new. Its form is that of a pastoral, easy, vulgar, and therefore disgusting:[3] whatever images it can supply are long ago exhausted; and its inherent improbability always forces dissatisfaction on the mind. When Cowley tells of Hervey that they studied together, it is easy to suppose how much he must miss the companion of his labors and the partner of his discoveries;[4] but what image of tenderness can be excited by these lines!

> We drove afield, and both together heard
> What time the grayfly winds her sultry horn,
> Battening our flocks with the fresh dews of night.

We know that they never drove afield, and that they had no flocks to batten; and though it be allowed that the representation may be allegorical, the true meaning is so uncertain and remote that it is never sought because it cannot be known when it is found.

Among the flocks and copses and flowers appear the heathen deities, Jove and Phoebus, Neptune and Aeolus, with a long train of mythological imagery, such as a college easily supplies. Nothing can less display knowledge or less exercise invention than to tell how a shepherd has lost his companion and must now feed his flocks alone, without any judge of his skill in piping; and how one god asks another god what is become of Lycidas, and how neither god can tell. He who thus grieves will excite no sympathy; he who thus praises will confer no honor.

This poem has yet a grosser fault. With these trifling fictions are mingled the most awful and sacred truths, such as ought never to be polluted with such irreverent combinations. The shepherd likewise is now a feeder of sheep, and afterwards an ecclesiastical pastor, a superintendent of a Christian flock. Such equivocations are always unskillful; but here they are indecent,[5] and at least approach to impiety, of which, however, I believe the writer not to have been conscious.

Such is the power of reputation justly acquired that its blaze drives away the eye from nice examination. Surely no man could have fancied that he read *Lycidas* with pleasure had he not known its author.

[L'Allegro, Il Penseroso]

Of the two pieces, *L'Allegro* and *Il Penseroso*, I believe opinion is uniform; every man that reads them, reads them with pleasure. The

---

3. I.e., displeasing ("disgusting") because its stale conventionality made it "vulgar" by putting it within the reach of the many.

4. Cowley's *On the Death of Mr. William Hervey* (1656).

5. Unbecoming, lacking in decorum.

author's design is not, what Theobald[1] has remarked, merely to show how objects derived their colors from the mind, by representing the operation of the same things upon the gay and the melancholy temper, or upon the same man as he is differently disposed; but rather how, among the successive variety of appearances, every disposition of mind takes hold on those by which it may be gratified.

The *cheerful* man hears the lark in the morning; the *pensive* man hears the nightingale in the evening. The *cheerful* man sees the cock strut, and hears the horn and hounds echo in the wood; then walks "not unseen" to observe the glory of the rising sun or listen to the singing milkmaid, and view the labors of the plowman and the mower; then casts his eyes about him over scenes of smiling plenty, and looks up to the distant tower, the residence of some fair inhabitant: thus he pursues rural gaiety through a day of labor or of play, and delights himself at night with the fanciful narratives of superstitious ignorance.

The *pensive* man at one time walks "unseen" to muse at midnight, and at another hears the sullen curfew. If the weather drives him home he sits in a room lighted only by "glowing embers"; or by a lonely lamp outwatches the North Star to discover the habitation of separate souls, and varies the shades of meditation by contemplating the magnificent or pathetic scenes of tragic and epic poetry. When the morning comes, a morning gloomy with rain and wind, he walks into the dark trackless woods, falls asleep by some murmuring water, and with melancholy enthusiasm expects some dream of prognostication or some music played by aerial performers.

Both Mirth and Melancholy are solitary, silent inhabitants of the breast that neither receive nor transmit communication: no mention is therefore made of a philosophical friend or a pleasant companion. The seriousness does not arise from any participation of calamity, nor the gaiety from the pleasures of the bottle.

The man of *cheerfulness* having exhausted the country tries what "towered cities" will afford, and mingles with scenes of splendor, gay assemblies, and nuptial festivities; but he mingles a mere spectator as, when the learned comedies of Jonson or the wild dramas of Shakespeare are exhibited, he attends the theater.

The *pensive* man never loses himself in crowds, but walks the cloister or frequents the cathedral. Milton probably had not yet forsaken the Church.

Both his characters delight in music; but he seems to think that cheerful notes would have obtained from Pluto a complete dismission of Eurydice, of whom solemn sounds only procured a conditional release.

For the old age of Cheerfulness he makes no provision; but Melancholy he conducts with great dignity to the close of life. His Cheerfulness is without levity, and his Pensiveness without asperity.

---

1. Lewis Theobald (1688–1744), the editor of Shakespeare and the enemy of Pope.

Through these two poems the images are properly selected and nicely distinguished, but the colors of the diction seem not sufficiently discriminated. I know not whether the characters are kept sufficiently apart. No mirth can, indeed, be found in his melancholy; but I am afraid that I always meet some melancholy in his mirth. They are two noble efforts of imagination.

[Paradise Lost]

Those little pieces may be dispatched without much anxiety; a greater work calls for greater care. I am now to examine *Paradise Lost*, a poem which, considered with respect to design, may claim the first place, and with respect to performance the second, among the productions of the human mind.

By the general consent of critics the first praise of genius is due to the writer of an epic poem, as it requires an assemblage of all the powers which are singly sufficient for other compositions. Poetry is the art of uniting pleasure with truth, by calling imagination to the help of reason. Epic poetry undertakes to teach the most important truths by the most pleasing precepts, and therefore relates some great event in the most affecting manner. History must supply the writer with the rudiments of narration, which he must improve and exalt by a nobler art, must animate by dramatic energy, and diversify by retrospection and anticipation; morality must teach him the exact bounds and different shades of vice and virtue; from policy and the practice of life he has to learn the discriminations of character and the tendency of the passions, either single or combined; and physiology must supply him with illustrations and images. To put these materials to poetical use is required an imagination capable of painting nature and realizing fiction. Nor is he yet a poet till he has attained the whole extension of his language, distinguished all the delicacies of phrase, and all the colors of words, and learned to adjust their different sounds to all the varieties of metrical modulation.

Bossu is of opinion that the poet's first work is to find a *moral*, which his fable is afterwards to illustrate and establish.[1] This seems to have been the process only of Milton: the moral of other poems is incidental and consequent; in Milton's only it is essential and intrinsic. His purpose was the most useful and the most arduous: "to vindicate the ways of God to man"; to show the reasonableness of religion, and the necessity of obedience to the Divine Law.

To convey this moral there must be a *fable*, a narration artfully constructed, so as to excite curiosity and surprise expectation. In this part of his work Milton must be confessed to have equaled every other poet. He has involved in his account of the Fall of Man the events which preceded, and those that were to follow it: he has interwoven the whole

---

1. Père le Bossu wrote a treatise on the epic poem, *Traité du Poëme Épique*, 1675, much admired during the late 17th and early 18th centuries.

system of theology with such propriety that every part appears to be necessary, and scarcely any recital is wished shorter for the sake of quickening the progress of the main action.

The subject of an epic poem is naturally an event of great importance. That of Milton is not the destruction of a city, the conduct of a colony, or the foundation of an empire. His subject is the fate of worlds, the revolutions of heaven and of earth; rebellion against the Supreme King raised by the highest order of created beings; the overthrow of their host and the punishment of their crime; the creation of a new race of reasonable creatures; their original happiness and innocence, their forfeiture of immortality, and their restoration to hope and peace.

Great events can be hastened or retarded only by persons of elevated dignity. Before the greatness displayed in Milton's poem all other greatness shrinks away. The weakest of his agents are the highest and noblest of human beings, the original parents of mankind; with whose actions the elements consented; on whose rectitude or deviation of will depended the state of terrestrial nature and the condition of all the future inhabitants of the globe.

Of the other agents in the poem, the chief are such as it is irreverence to name on slight occasions. The rest were lower powers;

> of which the least could wield
> Those elements, and arm him with the force
> Of all their regions;[2]

powers which only the control of Omnipotence restrains from laying creation waste, and filling the vast expanse of space with ruin and confusion. To display the motives and actions of beings thus superior, so far as human reason can examine them or human imagination represent them, is the task which this mighty poet has undertaken and performed.

In the examination of epic poems much speculation is commonly employed upon the *characters*. The characters in the *Paradise Lost* which admit of examination are those of angels and of man; of angels good and evil, of man in his innocent and sinful state.

Among the angels the virtue of Raphael is mild and placid, of easy condescension and free communication; that of Michael is regal and lofty, and, as may seem, attentive to the dignity of his own nature. Abdiel and Gabriel appear occasionally, and act as every incident requires; the solitary fidelity of Abdiel is very amiably painted.[3]

Of the evil angels the characters are more diversified. To Satan, as Addison observes, such sentiments are given as suit "the most exalted and most depraved being."[4] Milton has been censured by Clarke for the impiety which sometimes breaks from Satan's mouth. For there are thoughts, as he justly remarks, which no observation of character can justify, because no good man would willingly permit them to pass, however transiently, through his own mind.[5] To make Satan speak as a rebel,

2. *Paradise Lost* 6.221.
3. *Paradise Lost* 5.803 ff.
4. *Spectator* 303.
5. John Clarke, *Essay upon Study*, 1731.

without any such expressions as might taint the reader's imagination, was indeed one of the great difficulties in Milton's undertaking, and I cannot but think that he has extricated himself with great happiness. There is in Satan's speeches little that can give pain to a pious ear. The language of rebellion cannot be the same with that of obedience. The malignity of Satan foams in haughtiness and obstinacy; but his expressions are commonly general, and no otherwise offensive than as they are wicked.

The other chiefs of the celestial rebellion are very judiciously discriminated in the first and second books; and the ferocious character of Moloch appears, both in the battle and the council, with exact consistency.

To Adam and Eve are given during their innocence such sentiments as innocence can generate and utter. Their love is pure benevolence and mutual veneration; their repasts are without luxury and their diligence without toil. Their addresses to their Maker have little more than the voice of admiration and gratitude. Fruition left them nothing to ask, and Innocence left them nothing to fear.

But with guilt enter distrust and discord, mutual accusation, and stubborn self-defense; they regard each other with alienated minds, and dread their Creator as the avenger of their transgression. At last they seek shelter in his mercy, soften to repentance, and melt in supplication. Both before and after the Fall the superiority of Adam is diligently sustained.

Of the *probable* and the *marvelous*,[6] two parts of a vulgar epic poem which immerge the critic in deep consideration, the *Paradise Lost* requires little to be said. It contains the history of a miracle, of Creation and Redemption; it displays the power and the mercy of the Supreme Being: the probable therefore is marvelous, and the marvelous is probable. The substance of the narrative is truth; and as truth allows no choice, it is, like necessity, superior to rule. To the accidental or adventitious parts, as to every thing human, some slight exceptions may be made. But the main fabric is immovably supported.

It is justly remarked by Addison[7] that this poem has, by the nature of its subject, the advantage above all others, that it is universally and perpetually interesting. All mankind will, through all ages, bear the same relation to Adam and to Eve, and must partake of that good and evil which extend to themselves.

Of the *machinery*, so called from *theòs apò mēkhanēs*[8] by which is meant the occasional interposition of supernatural power, another fertile topic of critical remarks, here is no room to speak, because every thing is done under the immediate and visible direction of Heaven; but the rule is so far observed that no part of the action could have been accomplished by any other means.

Of *episodes*[9] I think there are only two, contained in Raphael's rela-

---

6. Actions in an epic poem which are wonderful because they exceed the probable.
7. *Spectator* 273.
8. Aristotle, *Poetics* 15.10. "Deus ex machina," the intervention of supernatural powers into the affairs of men.
9. Incidental but related narratives within an epic poem. Johnson is citing *Paradise Lost* 5.577 ff. and 11.334 ff.

tion of the war in heaven and Michael's prophetic account of the changes to happen in this world. Both are closely connected with the great action; one was necessary to Adam as a warning, the other as a consolation.

To the completeness or *integrity* of the design nothing can be objected; it has distinctly and clearly what Aristotle requires, a beginning, a middle, and an end. There is perhaps no poem of the same length from which so little can be taken without apparent mutilation. Here are no funeral games, nor is there any long description of a shield. The short digressions at the beginning of the third, seventh, and ninth books might doubtless be spared; but superfluities so beautiful who would take away? or who does not wish that the author of the *Iliad* had gratified succeeding ages with a little knowledge of himself? Perhaps no passages are more frequently or more attentively read than those extrinsic paragraphs; and since the end of poetry is pleasure, that cannot be unpoetical with which all are pleased.

The questions, whether the action of the poem be strictly *one*,[1] whether the poem can be properly termed *heroic*, and who is the hero, are raised by such readers as draw their principles of judgment rather from books than from reason. Milton, though he entitled *Paradise Lost* only a "poem," yet calls it himself "heroic song."[2] Dryden, petulantly and indecently, denies the heroism of Adam because he was overcome; but there is no reason why the hero should not be unfortunate except established practice, since success and virtue do not go necessarily together. Cato is the hero of Lucan, but Lucan's authority will not be suffered by Quintilian to decide. However, if success be necessary, Adam's deceiver was at last crushed; Adam was restored to his Maker's favor, and therefore may securely resume his human rank.

After the scheme and fabric of the poem must be considered its component parts, the sentiments, and the diction.

The *sentiments*, as expressive of manners or appropriated to characters, are for the greater part unexceptionably just. Splendid passages containing lessons of morality or precepts of prudence occur seldom. Such is the original formation of this poem that as it admits no human manners till the Fall, it can give little assistance to human conduct. Its end is to raise the thoughts above sublunary cares or pleasures. Yet the praise of that fortitude, with which Abdiel maintained his singularity of virtue against the scorn of multitudes, may be accommodated to all times; and Raphael's reproof of Adam's curiosity after the planetary motions, with the answer returned by Adam, may be confidently opposed to any rule of life which any poet has delivered.[3]

The thoughts which are occasionally called forth in the progress are such as could only be produced by an imagination in the highest degree fervid and active, to which materials were supplied by incessant study and unlimited curiosity. The heat of Milton's mind might be said to

---

1. I.e., a single action dealing with a single character.

2. *Paradise Lost* 9.25.
3. *Paradise Lost* 8.65 ff.

sublimate his learning, to throw off into his work the spirit of science, unmingled with its grosser parts.

He had considered creation in its whole extent, and his descriptions are therefore learned. He had accustomed his imagination to unrestrained indulgence, and his conceptions therefore were extensive. The characteristic quality of his poem is sublimity. He sometimes descends to the elegant, but his element is the great. He can occasionally invest himself with grace; but his natural port is gigantic loftiness. He can please when pleasure is required; but it is his peculiar power to astonish.

He seems to have been well acquainted with his own genius, and to know what it was that Nature had bestowed upon him more bountifully than upon others; the power of displaying the vast, illuminating the splendid, enforcing the awful, darkening the gloomy, and aggravating the dreadful: he therefore chose a subject on which too much could not be said, on which he might tire his fancy without the censure of extravagance.

*　*　*

The defects and faults of *Paradise Lost*, for faults and defects every work of man must have, it is the business of impartial criticism to discover. As in displaying the excellence of Milton I have not made long quotations, because of selecting beauties there had been no end, I shall in the same general manner mention that which seems to deserve censure; for what Englishman can take delight in transcribing passages, which, if they lessen the reputation of Milton, diminish in some degree the honor of our country?

*　*　*

The plan of *Paradise Lost* has this inconvenience, that it comprises neither human actions nor human manners. The man and woman who act and suffer are in a state which no other man or woman can ever know. The reader finds no transaction in which he can be engaged, beholds no condition in which he can by any effort of imagination place himself; he has, therefore, little natural curiosity or sympathy.

We all, indeed, feel the effects of Adam's disobedience; we all sin like Adam, and like him must all bewail our offenses; we have restless and insidious enemies in the fallen angels, and in the blessed spirits we have guardians and friends; in the Redemption of mankind we hope to be included: in the description of heaven and hell we are surely interested, as we are all to reside hereafter either in the regions of horror or of bliss.

But these truths are too important to be new: they have been taught to our infancy; they have mingled with our solitary thoughts and familiar conversation, and are habitually interwoven with the whole texture of life. Being therefore not new they raise no unaccustomed emotion in the mind: what we knew before, we cannot learn; what is not unexpected, cannot surprise.

Of the ideas suggested by these awful scenes, from some we recede with reverence, except when stated hours require their association; and from others we shrink with horror, or admit them only as salutary in-flictions, as counterpoises to our interests and passions. Such images rather obstruct the career of fancy than incite it.

Pleasure and terror are indeed the genuine sources of poetry; but poet-ical pleasure must be such as human imagination can at least conceive, and poetical terror such as human strength and fortitude may combat. The good and evil of Eternity are too ponderous for the wings of wit; the mind sinks under them in passive helplessness, content with calm belief and humble adoration.

Known truths however may take a different appearance, and be con-veyed to the mind by a new train of intermediate images. This Milton has undertaken, and performed with pregnancy and vigor of mind pecu-liar to himself. Whoever considers the few radical positions which the Scriptures afforded him will wonder by what energetic operation he expanded them to such extent and ramified them to so much variety, restrained as he was by religious reverence from licentiousness of fiction.

Here is a full display of the united force of study and genius; of a great accumulation of materials, with judgment to digest and fancy to com-bine them: Milton was able to select from nature or from story, from ancient fable or from modern science, whatever could illustrate or adorn his thoughts. An accumulation of knowledge impregnated his mind, fermented by study and exalted by imagination.

* * *

But original deficience cannot be supplied. The want of human inter-est is always felt. *Paradise Lost* is one of the books which the reader admires and lays down, and forgets to take up again. None ever wished it longer than it is. Its perusal is a duty rather than a pleasure. We read Milton for instruction, retire harassed and overburdened, and look else-where for recreation; we desert our master, and seek for companions.

* * *

Dryden remarks that Milton has some flats among his elevations.[4] This is only to say that all the parts are not equal. In every work one part must be for the sake of others; a palace must have passages, a poem must have transitions. It is no more to be required that wit should always be blazing than that the sun should always stand at noon. In a great work there is a vicissitude[5] of luminous and opaque parts, as there is in the world a succession of day and night. Milton, when he has expatiated in the sky, may be allowed sometimes to revisit earth; for what other author ever soared so high or sustained his flight so long?

* * *

4. Preface to *Sylvae*; see Essays (ed. W. P. Ker), I. 268.
5. Change.

The highest praise of genius is original invention. Milton cannot be said to have contrived the structure of an epic poem, and therefore owes reverence to that vigor and amplitude of mind to which all generations must be indebted for the art of poetical narration, for the texture of the fable, the variation of incidents, the interposition of dialogue, and all the stratagems that surprise and enchain attention. But of all the borrowers from Homer Milton is perhaps the least indebted. He was naturally a thinker for himself, confident of his own abilities and disdainful of help or hindrance; he did not refuse admission to the thoughts or images of his predecessors, but he did not seek them. From his contemporaries he neither courted nor received support; there is in his writings nothing by which the pride of other authors might be gratified or favor gained, no exchange of praise or solicitation of support. His great works were performed under discountenance and in blindness, but difficulties vanished at his touch; he was born for whatever is arduous; and his work is not the greatest of heroic poems, only because it is not the first.

1779

From Pope

[*Pope's Intellectual Character. Pope and Dryden Compared*]

Of his intellectual character, the constituent and fundamental principle was good sense, a prompt and intuitive perception of consonance and propriety. He saw immediately, of his own conceptions, what was to be chosen, and what to be rejected; and, in the works of others, what was to be shunned, and what was to be copied.

But good sense alone is a sedate and quiescent quality, which manages its possessions well, but does not increase them; it collects few materials for its own operations, and preserves safety, but never gains supremacy. Pope had likewise genius; a mind active, ambitious, and adventurous, always investigating, always aspiring; in its widest searches still longing to go forward, in its highest flights still wishing to be higher; always imagining something greater than it knows, always endeavoring more than it can do.

To assist these powers, he is said to have had great strength and exactness of memory. That which he had heard or read was not easily lost; and he had before him not only what his own meditation suggested, but what he had found in other writers that might be accommodated to his present purpose.

These benefits of nature he improved by incessant and unwearied diligence; he had recourse to every source of intelligence, and lost no opportunity of information; he consulted the living as well as the dead; he read his compositions to his friends, and was never content with mediocrity when excellence could be attained. He considered poetry as the business of his life, and however he might seem to lament his occupation, he followed it with constancy: to make verses was his first labor, and to mend them was his last.

From his attention to poetry he was never diverted. If conversation offered anything that could be improved, he committed it to paper; if a thought, or perhaps an expression more happy than was common, rose to his mind, he was careful to write it; an independent distich was preserved for an opportunity of insertion, and some little fragments have been found containing lines, or parts of lines, to be wrought upon at some other time.

He was one of those few whose labor is their pleasure; he was never elevated to negligence, nor wearied to impatience; he never passed a fault unamended by indifference, nor quitted it by despair. He labored his works first to gain reputation, and afterwards to keep it.

Of composition there are different methods. Some employ at once memory and invention, and, with little intermediate use of the pen, form and polish large masses by continued meditation, and write their productions only when, in their own opinion, they have completed them. It is related of Virgil[1] that his custom was to pour out a great number of verses in the morning, and pass the day in retrenching exuberances and correcting inaccuracies. The method of Pope, as may be collected from his translation, was to write his first thoughts in his first words, and gradually to amplify, decorate, rectify, and refine them.

With such faculties and such dispositions, he excelled every other writer in *poetical prudence*; he wrote in such a manner as might expose him to few hazards. He used almost always the same fabric of verse; and, indeed, by those few essays which he made of any other, he did not enlarge his reputation. Of this uniformity the certain consequence was readiness and dexterity. By perpetual practice, language had in his mind a systematical arrangement; having always the same use for words, he had words so selected and combined as to be ready at his call. This increase of facility he confessed himself to have perceived in the progress of his translation.

But what was yet of more importance, his effusions were always voluntary, and his subjects chosen by himself. His independence secured him from drudging at a task, and laboring upon a barren topic: he never exchanged praise for money, nor opened a shop of condolence or congratulation. His poems, therefore, were scarce ever temporary. He suffered coronations and royal marriages to pass without a song, and derived no opportunities from recent events, nor any popularity from the accidental disposition of his readers. He was never reduced to the necessity of soliciting the sun to shine upon a birthday, of calling the Graces and Virtues to a wedding, or of saying what multitudes have said before him. When he could produce nothing new, he was at liberty to be silent.

His publications were for the same reason never hasty. He is said to

---

1. By Suetonius in his brief life of the poet.

have sent nothing to the press till it had lain two years under his inspection: it is at least certain that he ventured nothing without nice examination. He suffered the tumult of imagination to subside, and the novelties
of invention to grow familiar. He knew that the mind is always enamored of its own productions, and did not trust his first fondness. He
consulted his friends, and listened with great willingness to criticism;
and, what was of more importance, he consulted himself, and let nothing pass against his own judgment.

He professed to have learned his poetry from Dryden, whom, whenever an opportunity was presented, he praised through his whole life
with unvaried liberality; and perhaps his character may receive some
illustration, if he be compared with his master.

Integrity of understanding and nicety of discernment were not allotted
in a less proportion to Dryden than to Pope. The rectitude of Dryden's
mind was sufficiently shown by the dismission of his poetical prejudices,
and the rejection of unnatural thoughts and rugged numbers. But Dryden never desired to apply all the judgment that he had. He wrote, and
professed to write, merely for the people; and when he pleased others,
he contented himself. He spent no time in struggles to rouse latent powers; he never attempted to make that better which was already good, nor
often to mend what he must have known to be faulty. He wrote, as he
tells us, with very little consideration; when occasion or necessity called
upon him, he poured out what the present moment happened to supply,
and, when once it had passed the press, ejected it from his mind; for
when he had no pecuniary interest, he had no further solicitude.

Pope was not content to satisfy; he desired to excel, and therefore
always endeavored to do his best: he did not court the candor, but dared
the judgment of his reader, and, expecting no indulgence from others,
he showed none to himself. He examined lines and words with minute
and punctilious observation, and retouched every part with indefatigable
diligence, till he had left nothing to be forgiven.

For this reason he kept his pieces very long in his hands, while he
considered and reconsidered them. The only poems which can be supposed to have been written with such regard to the times as might hasten
their publication were the two satires of *Thirty-Eight*; of which Dodsley[2]
told me that they were brought to him by the author, that they might be
fairly copied. "Almost every line," he said, "was then written twice over;
I gave him a clean transcript, which he sent some time afterwards to me
for the press, with almost every line written twice over a second time."

His declaration, that his care for his works ceased at their publication,
was not strictly true. His parental attention never abandoned them; what
he found amiss in the first edition, he silently corrected in those that
followed. He appears to have revised the *Iliad*, and freed it from some
of its imperfections; and the *Essay on Criticism* received many improve-

---

2. Robert Dodsley, the publisher.

ments after its first appearance. It will seldom be found that he altered without adding clearness, elegance, or vigor. Pope had perhaps the judgment of Dryden; but Dryden certainly wanted the diligence of Pope.

In acquired knowledge, the superiority must be allowed to Dryden, whose education was more scholastic, and who before he became an author had been allowed more time for study, with better means of information. His mind has a larger range, and he collects his images and illustrations from a more extensive circumference of science. Dryden knew more of man in his general nature, and Pope in his local manners. The notions of Dryden were formed by comprehensive speculation, and those of Pope by minute attention. There is more dignity in the knowledge of Dryden, and more certainty in that of Pope.

Poetry was not the sole praise of either; for both excelled likewise in prose; but Pope did not borrow his prose from his predecessor. The style of Dryden is capricious and varied, that of Pope is cautious and uniform; Dryden obeys the motions of his own mind, Pope constrains his mind to his own rules of composition; Dryden is sometimes vehement and rapid; Pope is always smooth, uniform, and gentle. Dryden's page is a natural field, rising into inequalities, and diversified by the varied exuberance of abundant vegetation; Pope's is a velvet lawn, shaven by the scythe, and leveled by the roller.

Of genius, that power which constitutes a poet; that quality without which judgment is cold and knowledge is inert; that energy which collects, combines, amplifies, and animates; the superiority must, with some hesitation, be allowed to Dryden. It is not to be inferred that of this poetical vigor Pope had only a little, because Dryden had more; for every other writer since Milton must give place to Pope; and even of Dryden it must be said that if he has brighter paragraphs, he has not better poems. Dryden's performances were always hasty, either excited by some external occasion, or extorted by domestic necessity; he composed without consideration, and published without correction. What his mind could supply at call, or gather in one excursion, was all that he sought, and all that he gave. The dilatory caution of Pope enabled him to condense his sentiments, to multiply his images, and to accumulate all that study might produce, or chance might supply. If the flights of Dryden therefore are higher, Pope continues longer on the wing. If of Dryden's fire the blaze is brighter, of Pope's the heat is more regular and constant. Dryden often surpasses expectation, and Pope never falls below it. Dryden is read with frequent astonishment, and Pope with perpetual delight.

This parallel will, I hope, when it is well considered, be found just; and if the reader should suspect me, as I suspect myself, of some partial fondness for the memory of Dryden, let him not too hastily condemn me; for meditation and inquiry may, perhaps, show him the reasonableness of my determination.

1781

JAMES BOSWELL

1740–1795

1763: Meets Samuel Johnson.
1768: Account of Corsica.
1773: Tour of the Highlands and the Hebrides with Johnson.
1791: *Life of Samuel Johnson.*

The discovery within this century of a vast number of James Boswell's personal papers (formerly believed to have been destroyed by his literary executors) has made it possible to know the author of the *Life of Samuel Johnson* better, perhaps, than we can know any other person, dead or living. His published letters and journals have made modern readers aware of the serious and absurd, the charming and repellent sides of his character. By the time he met Johnson, when he was only twenty-three, he had already trained himself to listen, to observe, and to remember until he found time to set it all down in writing. Only very rarely, it seems, did he ever take notes of conversations while they were in progress, which might have inhibited the speakers. His unusual memory, his instinctive sense of the characteristic, and his disciplined art enabled him in privacy to re-create and vividly preserve the many "scenes" which distinguish his journals as they do the *Life*.

Boswell was the elder son of Alexander Boswell of Auchinleck (pronounced *Aff-léck*) in Ayreshire, a judge who, by virtue of his high office, bore the courtesy title of Lord Auchinleck. As a member of an ancient family and heir to its large estate, Boswell was in the technical sense of the term a gentleman, with entrée into the best circles of Edinburgh and London. By temperament he was unstable, prone to melancholy, given to romantic excesses of feeling, and thoroughly sensual. After attending the Universities of Edinburgh and Glasgow, and studying law in Utrecht in Holland, he made the grand tour of Germany, Italy, and France, passing through Switzerland where he met and succeeded in captivating the two foremost French men of letters, Rousseau and Voltaire. He visited the beleaguered hero of Corsica, General Pasquale de Paoli, who was leading his people in their revolt against Genoa, and who seemed to European liberals to embody all the civic and military virtues of Republican Rome. Upon returning to England Boswell wrote *An Account of Corsica* (1768), which included the journal of his visit to Paoli. It was promptly translated into Dutch, German, French, and Italian, and its young author found himself with a modest European reputation.

By 1769, Boswell was established in what was to prove a successful law practice in Edinburgh and had married his cousin, Margaret Montgomerie. But he kept his ties to London and Johnson. In 1773 he persuaded Johnson to join him in a tour of the Highlands and the Hebrides. Almost every aspect of the adventure should have made it impossible, or at least unpleasant. Johnson, far from young and after years of sedentary city living, found himself astride a horse in wild country or in open boats in autumn weather. As a devout Anglican, he was an outspoken enemy of the Presbyterian Church, the national church of Scotland. As a lover of London, he could not be expected to care for the primitive, unpopulated life of the Highlands. More-over, for many years he had half-jestingly, half-seriously, made the Scots as a nation the butt of his satiric wit. But such were Boswell's social tact and Johnson's vigor and curiosity that the tour was a great success. Johnson's *Journey to the Western Isles of Scotland* (1775) is a thoughtful account of the way that people live in the Hebrides (though some Scots were offended). Boswell's *Journal of a Tour to the Hebrides* (1785), a preliminary study for the *Life*, is a lively and entertaining diary, kept throughout the journey and approved, at least in part, by Johnson himself.

In 1788, four years after Johnson's death, Boswell abandoned his Scottish practice, moved to London, was admitted to the English bar (but never actually practiced), and, often depressed and drunken, began the *Life*. For-tunately he had the help and encouragement of the distinguished literary scholar Edmond Malone, without whose guidance he might never have finished his task.

A lesser craftsman might have been overwhelmed by the very abundance of material that Boswell had to deal with: his own journals, all of Johnson's letters that he could find, his voluminous writings, and every scrap of infor-mation that his friends would furnish—all of which had to be collected, verified, and somehow reduced to unity. The *Life* is a record not of Johnson alone but of literary England during the last half of the century. But Boswell wrote with his eye on the object, and that object was Samuel Johnson, to whom every detail in the book is relevant, toward whom such eminent per-sons as Sir Joshua Reynolds, Edmund Burke, Oliver Goldsmith, Lord Ches-terfield—even the king himself—always face. Individual episodes are designed to reveal the great protagonist in a variety of aspects, and the world that Boswell created and populated is sustained by the vitality of his hero.

Boswell's gift is not only narrative: it is also dramatic. He himself was a good deal of an actor and a superb mimic, with a flair for detecting the characteristic gesture, word, tone, or trait. In reading the journals and the *Life* one often feels that their author is a gifted theatrical improviser, creating dramatic "scenes" (the word is a favorite of his) with living people, and playing simultaneously the roles of contriver of the dialogue, director of the plot, actor in the scene, and applauding audience—for Boswell kept an eye on his own performance. The quintessence of Boswell as both a social genius and a literary artist (the two complemented each other) is to be found in his description of his visit to Voltaire: "I placed myself by him. I touched the keys in unison with his imagination. I wish you had heard the music."

Although the Johnson who has become a part of our heritage is largely Boswell's Johnson, there was much in his life about which Boswell had no first-hand knowledge. When Boswell met him, Johnson was fifty-four, a widower, already established as "Dictionary" Johnson and the author of the *Rambler*, pensioned by the Crown and consequently no longer compelled to earn his living. Boswell knew nothing at first hand of the long, difficult, and heroic years during which Johnson made his way up from obscurity to eminence through difficulties that it is painful to imagine. Hence the *Life* is the portrait of a sage. Its chief glory is conversation: the talk of a man who has experienced broadly, read widely, observed and reflected on his obser-vations, whose ideas are constantly brought to the test of experience, and whose experience is habitually transmuted into ideas. The book is as large as life and as human as its central character.

From Boswell on the Grand Tour

[*Boswell Interviews Voltaire*[1]]

And whence do I now write to you, my friend?[2] From the château of Monsieur de Voltaire. I had a letter for him from a Swiss colonel at The Hague. I came hither Monday and was presented to him. He received me with dignity and that air of a man who has been much in the world which a Frenchman acquires in perfection. I saw him for about half an hour before dinner. He was not in spirits. Yet he gave me some brilliant sallies. He did not dine with us, and I was obliged to post away immediately after dinner, because the gates of Geneva shut before five and Ferney is a good hour from town. I was by no means satisfied to have been so little time with the monarch of French literature. A happy scheme sprung up in my adventurous mind. Madame Denis, the niece of Monsieur de Voltaire, had been extremely good to me. She is fond of our language. I wrote her a letter in English begging her interest to obtain for me the privilege of lodging a night under the roof of Monsieur de Voltaire, who, in opposition to our sun, rises in the evening. I was in the finest humor and my letter was full of wit. I told her, "I am a hardy and a vigorous Scot. You may mount me to the highest and coldest garret. I shall not even refuse to sleep upon two chairs in the bedchamber of your maid. I saw her pass through the room where we sat before dinner." I sent my letter on Tuesday by an express. It was shown to Monsieur de Voltaire, who with his own hand wrote this answer in the character of Madame Denis: "You will do us much honor and pleasure. We have few beds. But you will (*shall*) not sleep on two chairs. My uncle, though very sick, hath guessed at your merit. I know it better; for I have seen you longer." * * *

I returned yesterday to this enchanted castle. The magician appeared a very little before dinner. But in the evening he came into the drawing room in great spirits. I placed myself by him. I touched the keys in unison with his imagination. I wish you had heard the music. He was all brilliance. He gave me continued flashes of wit. I got him to speak English, which he does in a degree that made me now and then start up and cry. "Upon my soul this is astonishing!" When he talked our language he was animated with the soul of a Briton. He had bold flights. He had humor. He had an extravagance; he had a forcible oddity of style that the most comical of our *dramatis personae* could not have exceeded.

1. Voltaire was the name assumed by François Marie Arouet (1694–1778), the most famous French writer of his generation. Playwright, poet, satirist, philosopher, enemy of the church, and irrepressible ironist, after a stormy career he was living in splendor at his chateau at Ferney near the border of Switzerland and France, just outside Geneva. His housekeeper and mistress was his niece Marie-Louise Denis. He and Jean-Jacques Rousseau, whom Boswell had just visited and whose avowed disciple he had become, were deadly enemies.
2. This passage is taken from a letter, dated Dec. 28, 1764, written to Boswell's closest friend, a young clergyman named William Temple.

He swore bloodily, as was the fashion when he was in England.[3] He hummed a ballad; he repeated nonsense. Then he talked of our Constitution with a noble enthusiasm. I was proud to hear this from the mouth of an illustrious Frenchman. At last we came upon religion. Then did he rage. The company went to supper. Monsieur de Voltaire and I remained in the drawing room with a great Bible before us; and if ever two mortal men disputed with vehemence, we did. Yes, upon that occasion he was one individual and I another. For a certain portion of time there was a fair opposition between Voltaire and Boswell. The daring bursts of his ridicule confounded my understanding. He stood like an orator of ancient Rome. Tully[4] was never more agitated than he was. He went too far. His aged frame trembled beneath him. He cried, "Oh, I am very sick; my head turns round," and he let himself gently fall upon an easy chair. He recovered. I resumed our conversation, but changed the tone. I talked to him serious and earnest. I demanded of him an honest confession of his real sentiments. He gave it me with candor and with a mild eloquence which touched my heart. I did not believe him capable of thinking in the manner that he declared to me was "from the bottom of his heart." He expressed his veneration—his love—of the Supreme Being, and his entire resignation to the will of Him who is Allwise. He expressed his desire to resemble the Author of Goodness by being good himself. His sentiments go no farther. He does not inflame his mind with grand hopes of the immortality of the soul. He says it may be, but he knows nothing of it. And his mind is in perfect tranquility. I was moved; I was sorry. I doubted his sincerity. I called to him with emotion, "Are you sincere? are you really sincere?" He answered "Before God, I am." Then with the fire of him whose tragedies have so often shone on the theater of Paris, he said, "I suffer much. But I suffer with patience and resignation; not as a Christian—but as a man."

Temple, was not this an interesting scene? Would a journey from Scotland to Ferney have been too much to obtain such a remarkable interview? * * *

1764   1928

From The Life of Samuel Johnson, LL.D.

[*Plan of the* Life]

* * * Had Dr. Johnson written his own life, in conformity with the opinion which he has given, that every man's life may be best written by himself;[1] had he employed in the preservation of his own history, that

---

3. In 1726, in order to avoid imprisonment because of a quarrel with a nobleman, Voltaire had gone into exile in England, where he remained for three years, meeting many distinguished English writers and statesmen and learning to admire the British Constitution and the English principle of religious toleration. His *Lettres philosophiques sur les Anglais* (1734) expressed his admiration of English institutions and is an indirect criticism of France.
4. Marcus Tullius Cicero.
1. *Idler* 84.

clearness of narration and elegance of language in which he has embalmed so many eminent persons, the world would probably have had the most perfect example of biography that was ever exhibited. But although he at different times, in a desultory manner, committed to writing many particulars of the progress of his mind and fortunes, he never had persevering diligence enough to form them into a regular composition. Of these memorials a few have been preserved; but the greater part was consigned by him to the flames, a few days before his death.

As I had the honor and happiness of enjoying his friendship for upwards of twenty years; as I had the scheme of writing his life constantly in view; as he was well apprised of this circumstance, and from time to time obligingly satisfied my inquiries, by communicating to me the incidents of his early years; as I acquired a facility in recollecting, and was very assiduous in recording, his conversation, of which the extraordinary vigor and vivacity constituted one of the first features of his character; and as I have spared no pains in obtaining materials concerning him, from every quarter where I could discover that they were to be found, and have been favored with the most liberal communications by his friends; I flatter myself that few biographers have entered upon such a work as this with more advantages; independent of literary abilities, in which I am not vain enough to compare myself with some great names who have gone before me in this kind of writing. * * *

Instead of melting down my materials into one mass, and constantly speaking in my own person, by which I might have appeared to have more merit in the execution of the work, I have resolved to adopt and enlarge upon the excellent plan of Mr. Mason, in his *Memoirs of Gray*.[2] Wherever narrative is necessary to explain, connect, and supply, I furnish it to the best of my abilities; but in the chronological series of Johnson's life, which I trace as distinctly as I can, year by year, I produce, wherever it is in my power, his own minutes, letters, or conversation, being convinced that this mode is more lively, and will make my readers better acquainted with him than even most of those were who actually knew him, but could know him only partially; whereas there is here an accumulation of intelligence from various points, by which his character is more fully understood and illustrated.

Indeed I cannot conceive a more perfect mode of writing any man's life than not only relating all the most important events of it in their order, but interweaving what he privately wrote, and said, and thought; by which mankind are enabled as it were to see him live, and to "live o'er each scene"[3] with him, as he actually advanced through the several stages of his life. Had his other friends been as diligent and ardent as I was, he might have been almost entirely preserved. As it is, I will venture to say that he will be seen in this work more completely than any man who has ever yet lived.

And he will be seen as he really was; for I profess to write, not his

2. William Mason, poet and dramatist, published his life of Thomas Gray in 1774.   3. Pope's Prologue to Addison's *Cato*, line 4.

panegyric, which must be all praise, but his Life; which, great and good as he was, must not be supposed to be entirely perfect. To be as he was, is indeed subject of panegyric enough to any man in this state of being; but in every picture there should be shade as well as light, and when I delineate him without reserve, I do what he himself recommended, both by his precept and his example. * * *

I am fully aware of the objections which may be made to the minuteness on some occasions of my detail of Johnson's conversation, and how happily it is adapted for the petty exercise of ridicule, by men of superficial understanding and ludicrous fancy; but I remain firm and confident in my opinion, that minute particulars are frequently characteristic, and always amusing, when they relate to a distinguished man. I am therefore exceedingly unwilling that anything, however slight, which my illustrious friend thought it worth his while to express, with any degree of point, should perish. * * *

Of one thing I am certain, that considering how highly the small portion which we have of the table-talk and other anecdotes of our celebrated writers is valued, and how earnestly it is regretted that we have not more, I am justified in preserving rather too many of Johnson's sayings, than too few; especially as from the diversity of dispositions it cannot be known with certainty beforehand, whether what may seem trifling to some, and perhaps to the collector himself, may not be most agreeable to many; and the greater number that an author can please in any degree, the more pleasure does there arise to a benevolent mind. * * *

[Johnson's Early Years. Marriage and London]

[1709] Samuel Johnson was born at Lichfield, in Staffordshire, on the 18th of September, N.S.,[4] 1709; and his initiation into the Christian Church was not delayed; for his baptism is recorded, in the register of St. Mary's parish in that city, to have been performed on the day of his birth. His father is there styled *Gentleman*, a circumstance of which an ignorant panegyrist has praised him for not being proud; when the truth is, that the appellation of Gentleman, though now lost in the indiscriminate assumption of *Esquire*, was commonly taken by those who could not boast of gentility. His father was Michael Johnson, a native of Derbyshire, of obscure extraction, who settled in Lichfield as a bookseller and stationer. His mother was Sarah Ford, descended of an ancient race of substantial yeomanry in Warwickshire. They were well advanced in years when they married, and never had more than two children, both sons; Samuel, their first-born, who lived to be the illustrious character whose various excellence I am to endeavor to record, and Nathanael, who died in his twenty-fifth year.

---

4. New Style. In 1752 Great Britain adopted the Gregorian Calendar, introduced in 1582 by Pope Gregory XIII, to correct the accumulated inaccuracies of Julius Caesar's calendar, which had been in use since 46 B.C. By 1752 the error amounted to eleven days. Dates before Sept. 2, 1752, must therefore be corrected by adding eleven days or by using the Julian date, followed by "O.S." (Old Style).

Mr. Michael Johnson was a man of a large and robust body, and of a strong and active mind; yet, as in the most solid rocks veins of unsound substance are often discovered, there was in him a mixture of that disease, the nature of which eludes the most minute inquiry, though the effects are well known to be a weariness of life, an unconcern about those things which agitate the greater part of mankind, and a general sensation of gloomy wretchedness. From him then his son inherited, with some other qualities, "a vile melancholy," which in his too strong expression of any disturbance of the mind, "made him mad all his life, at least not sober." Michael was, however, forced by the narrowness of his circumstances to be very diligent in business, not only in his shop, but by occasionally resorting to several towns in the neighborhood, some of which were at a considerable distance from Lichfield. At that time booksellers' shops in the provincial towns of England were very rare, so that there was not one even in Birmingham, in which town old Mr. Johnson used to open a shop every market day. He was a pretty good Latin scholar, and a citizen so creditable as to be made one of the magistrates of Lichfield; and, being a man of good sense, and skill in his trade, he acquired a reasonable share of wealth, of which however he afterwards lost the greatest part, by engaging unsuccessfully in a manufacture of parchment. He was a zealous highchurch man and royalist, and retained his attachment to the unfortunate house of Stuart, though he reconciled himself, by casuistical arguments of expediency and necessity, to take the oaths imposed by the prevailing power. * * *

Johnson's mother was a woman of distinguished understanding. I asked his old schoolfellow, Mr. Hector,[5] surgeon of Birmingham, if she was not vain of her son. He said, "She had too much good sense to be vain, but she knew her son's value." Her piety was not inferior to her understanding; and to her must be ascribed those early impressions of religion upon the mind of her son, from which the world afterwards derived so much benefit. He told me that he remembered distinctly having had the first notice of Heaven, "a place to which good people went," and hell, "a place to which bad people went," communicated to him by her, when a little child in bed with her; and that it might be the better fixed in his memory, she sent him to repeat it to Thomas Jackson, their man-servant; he not being in the way, this was not done; but there was no occasion for any artificial aid for its preservation. * * *

[1728] That a man in Mr. Michael Johnson's circumstances should think of sending his son to the expensive University of Oxford, at his own charge, seems very improbable. The subject was too delicate to question Johnson upon. But I have been assured by Dr. Taylor[6] that the scheme never would have taken place had not a gentleman of Shropshire, one of his schoolfellows, spontaneously undertaken to support him at Oxford, in the character of his companion; though, in fact, he never received any assistance whatever from that gentleman.

5. Edmund Hector, a lifelong friend of Johnson's.
6. A well-to-do clergyman, who had been Johnson's school fellow in Lichfield.

He, however, went to Oxford, and was entered a Commoner of Pembroke College on the 31st of October, 1728, being then in his nineteenth year.

The Reverend Dr. Adams,[7] who afterwards presided over Pembroke College with universal esteem, told me he was present, and gave me some account of what passed on the night of Johnson's arrival at Oxford. On that evening, his father, who had anxiously accompanied him, found means to have him introduced to Mr. Jorden, who was to be his tutor. * * *

His father seemed very full of the merits of his son, and told the company he was a good scholar, and a poet, and wrote Latin verses. His figure and manner appeared strange to them; but he behaved modestly and sat silent, till upon something which occurred in the course of conversation, he suddenly struck in and quoted Macrobius; and thus he gave the first impression of that more extensive reading in which he had indulged himself.

His tutor, Mr. Jorden, fellow of Pembroke, was not, it seems, a man of such abilities as we should conceive requisite for the instructor of Samuel Johnson, who gave me the following account of him. "He was a very worthy man, but a heavy man, and I did not profit much by his instructions. Indeed, I did not attend him much. The first day after I came to college I waited upon him, and then stayed away four. On the sixth, Mr. Jorden asked me why I had not attended. I answered I had been sliding in Christ Church meadow. And this I said with as much *nonchalance* as I am now talking to you. I had no notion that I was wrong or irreverent to my tutor." BOSWELL: "That, Sir, was great fortitude of mind." JOHNSON: "No, Sir; stark insensibility." * * *

[1729] The "morbid melancholy," which was lurking in his constitution, and to which we may ascribe those particularities and that aversion to regular life, which, at a very early period, marked his character, gathered such strength in his twentieth year as to afflict him in a dreadful manner. While he was at Lichfield, in the college vacation of the year 1729, he felt himself overwhelmed with an horrible hypochondria, with perpetual irritation, fretfulness, and impatience; and with a dejection, gloom, and despair, which made existence misery. From this dismal malady he never afterwards was perfectly relieved; and all his labors, and all his enjoyments, were but temporary interruptions of its baleful influence. He told Mr. Paradise[8] that he was sometimes so languid and inefficient that he could not distinguish the hour upon the town-clock. * * *

To Johnson, whose supreme enjoyment was the exercise of his reason, the disturbance or obscuration of that faculty was the evil most to be dreaded. Insanity, therefore, was the object of his most dismal apprehension; and he fancied himself seized by it, or approaching to it, at the very time when he was giving proofs of a more than ordinary soundness and vigor of judgment. That his own diseased imagination should have

---

7. The Rev. William Adams, D.D., elected Master of Pembroke in 1775.

8. John Paradise, a member of the Essex Head Club, which Johnson founded in 1783.

so far deceived him, is strange; but it is stranger still that some of his friends should have given credit to his groundless opinion, when they had such undoubted proofs that it was totally fallacious; though it is by no means surprising that those who wish to depreciate him should, since his death, have laid hold of this circumstance, and insisted upon it with very unfair aggravation. * * *

Dr. Adams told me that Johnson, while he was at Pembroke College, "was caressed and loved by all about him, was a gay and frolicsome fellow, and passed there the happiest part of his life." But this is a striking proof of the fallacy of appearances, and how little any of us know of the real internal state even of those whom we see most frequently; for the truth is, that he was then depressed by poverty, and irritated by disease. When I mentioned to him this account as given me by Dr. Adams, he said, "Ah, Sir, I was mad and violent. It was bitterness which they mistook for frolic. I was miserably poor, and I thought to fight my way by my literature and my wit; so I disregarded all power and all authority." * * *

[1734] In a man whom religious education has secured from licentious indulgences, the passion of love, when once it has seized him, is exceedingly strong; being unimpaired by dissipation, and totally concentrated in one object. This was experienced by Johnson, when he became the fervent admirer of Mrs. Porter, after her first husband's death. Miss Porter told me that when he was first introduced to her mother, his appearance was very forbidding: he was then lean and lank, so that his immense structure of bones was hideously striking to the eye, and the scars of the scrofula were deeply visible. He also wore his hair,[9] which was straight and stiff, and separated behind: and he often had, seemingly, convulsive starts and odd gesticulations, which tended to excite at once surprise and ridicule. Mrs. Porter was so much engaged by his conversation that she overlooked all these external disadvantages, and said to her daughter, "This is the most sensible man that I ever saw in my life."

[1735] Though Mrs. Porter was double the age of Johnson, and her person and manner, as described to me by the late Mr. Garrick,[1] were by no means pleasing to others, she must have had a superiority of understanding and talents, as she certainly inspired him with a more than ordinary passion; and she having signified her willingness to accept of his hand, he went to Lichfield to ask his mother's consent to the marriage, which he could not but be conscious was a very imprudent scheme, both on account of their disparity of years and her want of fortune. But Mrs. Johnson knew too well the ardor of her son's temper, and was too tender a parent to oppose his inclinations.

I know not for what reason the marriage ceremony was not performed at Birmingham; but a resolution was taken that it should be at Derby, for which place the bride and bridegroom set out on horseback, I sup-

9. I.e., he wore no wig.
1. David Garrick (1717–1779), the most famous actor of his day. In 1736 he was one of Johnson's three pupils in an unsuccessful school at Edial.

pose in very good humor. But though Mr. Topham Beauclerk[2] used archly to mention Johnson's having told him, with much gravity, "Sir, it was a love marriage on both sides," I have had from my illustrious friend the following curious account of their journey to church upon the nuptial morn:

9th July: "Sir, she had read the old romances, and had got into her head the fantastical notion that a woman of spirit should use her lover like a dog. So, Sir, at first she told me that I rode too fast, and she could not keep up with me; and, when I rode a little slower, she passed me, and complained that I lagged behind. I was not to be made the slave of caprice; and I resolved to begin as I meant to end. I therefore pushed on briskly, till I was fairly out of her sight. The road lay between two hedges, so I was sure she could not miss it; and I contrived that she should soon come up with me. When she did, I observed her to be in tears." * * *

[1737] Johnson now thought of trying his fortune in London, the great field of genius and exertion, where talents of every kind have the fullest scope and the highest encouragement. It is a memorable circumstance that his pupil David Garrick went thither at the same time, with intention to complete his education, and follow the profession of the law, from which he was soon diverted by his decided preference for the stage.[3] * * *

[1744] * * * He produced one work this year, fully sufficient to maintain the high reputation which he had acquired. This was *The Life of Richard Savage*;[4] a man of whom it is difficult to speak impartially without wondering that he was for some time the intimate companion of Johnson; for his character was marked by profligacy, insolence, and ingratitude: yet, as he undoubtedly had a warm and vigorous, though unregulated mind, had seen life in all its varieties, and been much in the company of the statesmen and wits of his time, he could communicate to Johnson an abundant supply of such materials as his philosophical curiosity most eagerly desired; and as Savage's misfortunes and misconduct had reduced him to the lowest state of wretchedness as a writer for bread, his visits to St. John's Gate[5] naturally brought Johnson and him together.

It is melancholy to reflect that Johnson and Savage were sometimes in such extreme indigence that they could not pay for a lodging; so that they have wandered together whole nights in the streets. Yet in these

2. Topham Beauclerk, a descendant of Charles II and the actress Nell Gwynn. He was brilliant and dissolute.

3. Johnson had hoped to complete his tragedy *Irene* and to get it produced, but this was not accomplished until Garrick staged it in 1749. Meanwhile Johnson struggled against poverty, at first as a writer and translator for Edward Cave's *Gentleman's Magazine*. He gradually won recognition, but was never financially secure until he was pensioned in 1762. Garrick succeeded in the theater much more rapidly than did Johnson in literature.

4. Richard Savage, poet, courted and gained

notoriety by claiming to be the illegitimate son of Earl Rivers and the countess of Macclesfield, whose husband had divorced her because of her unfaithfulness with Rivers. Savage publicized his claim and persecuted his alleged mother. Johnson and many others believed Savage's story and resented what they considered the lady's inhumanity. Savage was a gifted man, but he lived in poverty as a hack writer, though he was long assisted by Pope and others. He died in a debtor's prison in Bristol in 1743.

5. Where Cave published the *Gentleman's Magazine*.

almost incredible scenes of distress, we may suppose that Savage mentioned many of the anecdotes with which Johnson afterwards enriched the life of his unhappy companion, and those of other poets.

He told Sir Joshua Reynolds that one night in particular, when Savage and he walked round St. James's Square for want of a lodging, they were not at all depressed by their situation; but in high spirits and brimful of patriotism, traversed the square for several hours, inveighed against the minister, and "resolved they would *stand by their country*." * * *

[1752] That there should be a suspension of his literary labors during a part of the year 1752[6] will not seem strange when it is considered that soon after closing his *Rambler*, he suffered a loss which, there can be no doubt, affected him with the deepest distress. For on the 17th of March, O.S., his wife died. * * *

The following very solemn and affecting prayer was found, after Dr. Johnson's decease, by his servant, Mr. Francis Barber, who delivered it to my worthy friend the Reverend Mr. Strahan, Vicar of Islington, who at my earnest request has obligingly favored me with a copy of it, which he and I compared with the original:

"April 26, 1752, being after 12 at night of the 25th.

"O Lord! Governor of heaven and earth, in whose hands are embodied and departed spirits, if thou hast ordained the souls of the dead to minister to the living, and appointed my departed wife to have care of me, grant that I may enjoy the good effects of her attention and ministration, whether exercised by appearance, impulses, dreams or in any other manner agreeable to thy government. Forgive my presumption, enlighten my ignorance, and however meaner agents are employed, grant me the blessed influences of thy holy Spirit, through Jesus Christ our Lord. Amen." * * *

One night when Beauclerk and Langton[7] had supped at a tavern in London, and sat till about three in the morning, it came into their heads to go and knock up Johnson, and see if they could prevail on him to join them in a ramble. They rapped violently at the door of his chambers in the Temple,[8] till at last he appeared in his shirt, with his little black wig on the top of his head, instead of a nightcap, and a poker in his hand, imagining, probably, that some ruffians were coming to attack him. When he discovered who they were, and was told their errand, he smiled, and with great good humor agreed to their proposal: "What, is it you, you dogs! I'll have a frisk with you." He was soon dressed, and they sallied forth together into Covent Garden, where the greengrocers and fruiterers

6. Johnson's important works written before the publication of the *Dictionary* are the poems *London* (1738) and *The Vanity of Human Wishes* (1749), the *Life of Savage* (1744), and the essays which made up his periodical *The Rambler* (1750–52).

7. Bennet Langton. As a boy he so much admired the *Rambler* that he sought Johnson's acquaintance. They became lifelong friends.

8. Since Johnson lived in Inner Temple Lane between 1760 and 1765, the "frisk" could not have taken place in the year of his wife's death, where Boswell, for his own convenience, placed it.

were beginning to arrange their hampers, just come in from the country. Johnson made some attempts to help them; but the honest gardeners stared so at his figure and manner and odd interference, that he soon saw his services were not relished. They then repaired to one of the neighboring taverns, and made a bowl of that liquor called *Bishop*,[9] which Johnson had always liked; while in joyous contempt of sleep, from which he had been roused, he repeated the festive lines,

> Short, O short then be thy reign,
> And give us to the world again![1]

They did not stay long, but walked down to the Thames, took a boat, and rowed to Billingsgate. Beauclerk and Johnson were so well pleased with their amusement that they resolved to persevere in dissipation for the rest of the day: but Langton deserted them, being engaged to breakfast with some young ladies. Johnson scolded him for "leaving his social friends, to go and sit with a set of wretched *un-idea'd* girls." Garrick being told of this ramble, said to him smartly, "I heard of your frolic t' other night. You'll be in the *Chronicle*." Upon which Johnson afterwards observed, "*He* durst not do such a thing. His *wife* would not *let* him!" * * *

[*The Letter to Chesterfield*]

[1754] Lord Chesterfield,[2] to whom Johnson had paid the high compliment of addressing to his Lordship the *Plan* of his *Dictionary*, had behaved to him in such a manner as to excite his contempt and indignation. The world has been for many years amused with a story confidently told, and as confidently repeated with additional circumstances, that a sudden disgust was taken by Johnson upon occasion of his having been one day kept long in waiting in his Lordship's antechamber, for which the reason assigned was that he had company with him; and that at last, when the door opened, out walked Colley Cibber;[3] and that Johnson was so violently provoked when he found for whom he had been so long excluded, that he went away in a passion, and never would return. I remember having mentioned this story to George Lord Lyttelton, who told me he was very intimate with Lord Chesterfield; and holding it as a well-known truth, defended Lord Chesterfield, by saying, that Cibber, who had been introduced familiarly by the back stairs, had probably not been there above ten minutes. It may seem strange even to entertain a doubt concerning a story so long and so widely current, and thus implicitly adopted, if not sanctioned, by the authority which I have mentioned; but Johnson himself assured me that there was not the least

9. A drink made of wine, sugar, and either lemon or orange.
1. Misquoted from Lansdowne's *Drinking Song to Sleep*.
2. Philip Dormer Stanhope, Earl of Chesterfield (1694–1773), statesman, wit, man of fashion. His *Letters*, written for the guidance of his natural son, are famous for their worldly good sense and for

their expression of the ideal of an 18th-century gentleman.
3. Colley Cibber (1671–1757), playwright, comic actor, and (after 1730) poet laureate. A fine actor but a very bad poet. Cibber was a constant object of ridicule by the wits of the town. Pope made him King of the Dunces in the *Dunciad* of 1743.

foundation for it. He told me that there never was any particular incident which produced a quarrel between Lord Chesterfield and him; but that his Lordship's continued neglect was the reason why he resolved to have no connection with him. When the *Dictionary* was upon the eve of publication, Lord Chesterfield, who, it is said, had flattered himself with expectations that Johnson would dedicate the work to him, attempted, in a courtly manner, to soothe, and insinuate himself with the sage, conscious, as it should seem, of the cold indifference with which he had treated its learned author; and further attempted to conciliate him, by writing two papers in *The World*, in recommendation of the work; and it must be confessed that they contain some studied compliments, so finely turned, that if there had been no previous offense, it is probable that Johnson would have been highly delighted. Praise, in general, was pleasing to him; but by praise from a man of rank and elegant accomplishments, he was peculiarly gratified. * * *

This courtly device failed of its effect. Johnson, who thought that "all was false and hollow,"[4] despised the honeyed words, and was even indignant that Lord Chesterfield should, for a moment, imagine that he could be dupe of such an artifice. His expression to me concerning Lord Chesterfield, upon this occasion, was, "Sir, after making great professions, he had, for many years, taken no notice of me; but when my *Dictionary* was coming out, he fell a-scribbling in *The World* about it. Upon which, I wrote him a letter expressed in civil terms, but such as might show him that I did not mind what he said or wrote, and that I had done with him."

This is that celebrated letter of which so much has been said, and about which curiosity has been so long excited, without being gratified. I for many years solicited Johnson to favor me with a copy of it, that so excellent a composition might not be lost to posterity. He delayed from time to time to give it me; till at last in 1781, when we were on a visit at Mr. Dilly's,[5] at Southill in Bedfordshire, he was pleased to dictate it to me from memory. He afterwards found among his papers a copy of it, which he had dictated to Mr. Baretti,[6] with its title and corrections, in his own handwriting. This he gave to Mr. Langton; adding that if it were to come into print, he wished it to be from that copy. By Mr. Langton's kindness, I am enabled to enrich my work with a perfect transcript of what the world has so eagerly desired to see.

TO THE RIGHT HONORABLE THE EARL OF CHESTERFIELD

February 7, 1755

MY LORD,

I have been lately informed, by the proprietor of *The World*, that two papers, in which my Dictionary is recommended to the public,

4. *Paradise Lost* 2.112.
5. Southill was the country home of Charles and Edward Dilly, publishers. The firm published all of Boswell's serious works and shared in the pub-

lication of Johnson's *Lives of the Poets* (1779–81).
6. Giuseppe Baretti, an Italian writer and lexicographer whom Johnson introduced into his circle.

were written by your Lordship. To be so distinguished, is an honor, which, being very little accustomed to favors from the great, I know not well how to receive, or in what terms to acknowledge.

When, upon some slight encouragement, I first visited your Lordship, I was overpowered, like the rest of mankind, by the enchantment of your address; and could not forbear to wish that I might boast myself *Le vainqueur du vainqueur de la terre*[7]—that I might obtain that regard for which I saw the world contending; but I found my attendance so little encouraged that neither pride nor modesty would suffer me to continue it. When I had once addressed your Lordship in public, I had exhausted all the art of pleasing which a retired and uncourtly scholar can possess. I had done all that I could; and no man is well pleased to have his all neglected, be it ever so little.

Seven years, my Lord, have now passed since I waited in your outward rooms, or was repulsed from your door; during which time I have been pushing on my work through difficulties of which it is useless to complain, and have brought it, at last, to the verge of publication, without one act of assistance, one word of encouragement, or one smile of favor. Such treatment I did not expect, for I never had a patron before.

The shepherd in Virgil grew at last acquainted with Love, and found him a native of the rocks.[8]

Is not a patron, my Lord, one who looks with unconcern on a man struggling for life in the water, and, when he has reached ground, encumbers him with help? The notice which you have been pleased to take of my labors, had it been early, had been kind; but it has been delayed till I am indifferent, and cannot enjoy it; till I am solitary, and cannot impart it; till I am known, and do not want it. I hope it is no very cynical asperity not to confess obligations where no benefit has been received, or to be unwilling that the public should consider me as owing that to a patron which Providence has enabled me to do for myself.

Having carried on my work thus far with so little obligation to any favorer of learning, I shall not be disappointed though I should conclude it, if less be possible, with less; for I have been long wakened from that dream of hope in which I once boasted myself with so much exultation, my Lord, your Lordship's most humble, most obedient servant,

SAM. JOHNSON.

"While this was the talk of the town," says Dr. Adams, in a letter to me, "I happened to visit Dr. Warburton,[9] who finding that I was acquainted with Johnson, desired me earnestly to carry his compliments

7. "The conqueror of the conqueror of the earth." From the first line of Scudéry's epic *Alaric* (1654).
8. *Eclogues* 8.44.

9. William Warburton, bishop of Gloucester, friend and literary executor of Pope, editor of Pope and Shakespeare, theological controversialist.

to him, and to tell him that he honored him for his manly behavior in rejecting these condescensions of Lord Chesterfield, and for resenting the treatment he had received from him, with a proper spirit. Johnson was visibly pleased with this compliment, for he had always a high opinion of Warburton. Indeed, the force of mind which appeared in this letter was congenial with that which Warburton himself amply possessed."

There is a curious minute circumstance which struck me, in comparing the various editions of Johnson's imitations of Juvenal. In the tenth satire, one of the couplets upon the vanity of wishes even for literary distinction stood thus:

> Yet think what ills the scholar's life assail,
> Pride, envy, want, the *garret*, and the jail.

But after experiencing the uneasiness which Lord Chesterfield's fallacious patronage made him feel, he dismissed the word *garret* from the sad group, and in all the subsequent editions the line stands

> Pride, envy, want, the *patron*, and the jail.

[1762] The accession of George the Third to the throne of these kingdoms[1] opened a new and brighter prospect to men of literary merit, who had been honored with no mark of royal favor in the preceding reign. His present Majesty's education in this country, as well as his taste and beneficence, prompted him to be the patron of science and the arts; and early this year Johnson, having been represented to him as a very learned and good man, without any certain provision, his Majesty was pleased to grant him a pension of three hundred pounds a year. The Earl of Bute,[2] who was then Prime Minister, had the honor to announce this instance of his Sovereign's bounty, concerning which many and various stories, all equally erroneous, have been propagated: maliciously representing it as a political bribe to Johnson, to desert his avowed principles, and become the tool of a government which he held to be founded in usurpation. I have taken care to have it in my power to refute them from the most authentic information. Lord Bute told me that Mr. Wedderburne, now Lord Loughborough, was the person who first mentioned this subject to him. Lord Loughborough told me that the pension was granted to Johnson solely as the reward of his literary merit, without any stipulation whatever, or even tacit understanding that he should write for administration. His Lordship added that he was confident the political tracts which Johnson afterwards did write, as they were entirely consonant with his own opinions, would have been written by him though no pension had been granted to him.[3] * * *

1. In 1760.
2. An intimate friend of George III's mother, he early gained an ascendancy over the young prince and was largely responsible for the king's autocratic views. He was hated in England both as a favorite and as a Scot.

3. Johnson's few political pamphlets in the 1770s invariably supported the policies of the Crown. The best-known is his answer to the American colonies, *Taxation No Tyranny* (1775). His dislike of the Americans was in large part due to the fact they owned slaves.

[A *Memorable Year: Boswell Meets Johnson*]

[*1763*] This is to me a memorable year; for in it I had the happiness to obtain the acquaintance of that extraordinary man whose memoirs I am now writing; an acquaintance which I shall ever esteem as one of the most fortunate circumstances in my life. * * *

Mr. Thomas Davies the actor, who then kept a bookseller's shop in Russel Street, Covent Garden, told me that Johnson was very much his friend, and came frequently to his house, where he more than once invited me to meet him; but by some unlucky accident or other he was prevented from coming to us. * * *

At last, on Monday the 16th of May, when I was sitting in Mr. Davies's back parlor, after having drunk tea with him and Mrs. Davies, Johnson unexpectedly came into the shop; and Mr. Davies having perceived him through the glass door in the room in which we were sitting, advancing towards us—he announced his awful approach to me, somewhat in the manner of an actor in the part of Horatio, when he addresses Hamlet on the appearance of his father's ghost, "Look, my Lord, it comes." I found that I had a very perfect idea of Johnson's figure, from the portrait of him painted by Sir Joshua Reynolds soon after he had published his *Dictionary*, in the attitude of sitting in his easy chair in deep meditation, which was the first picture his friend did for him, which Sir Joshua very kindly presented to me, and from which an engraving has been made for this work. Mr. Davies mentioned my name, and respectfully introduced me to him. I was much agitated; and recollecting his prejudice against the Scotch, of which I had heard much, I said to Davies, "Don't tell where I come from."—"From Scotland," cried Davies roguishly. "Mr. Johnson," said I, "I do indeed come from Scotland, but I cannot help it." I am willing to flatter myself that I meant this as light pleasantry to soothe and conciliate him, and not as an humiliating abasement at the expense of my country. But however that might be, this speech was somewhat unlucky; for with that quickness of wit for which he was so remarkable, he seized the expression "come from Scotland," which I used in the sense of being of that country; and, as if I had said that I had come away from it, or left it, retorted, "That, Sir, I find, is what a very great many of your countrymen cannot help." This stroke stunned me a good deal; and when we had sat down, I felt myself not a little embarrassed, and apprehensive of what might come next. He then addressed himself to Davies: "What do you think of Garrick? He has refused me an order for the play for Miss Williams,[4] because he knows the house will be full, and that an order would be worth three shillings." Eager to take any opening to get into conversation with him, I ventured to say, "O Sir, I cannot think Mr. Garrick would grudge such a trifle to you." "Sir," said he, with a stern look, "I have known David Garrick longer

---

4. Mrs. Anna Williams (1706–1783), a blind poet and friend of Mrs. Johnson. She continued to live in Johnson's house after his wife's death, and habitually sat up to make tea for him whenever he came home.

than you have done: and I know no right you have to talk to me on the subject." Perhaps I deserved this check; for it was rather presumptuous in me, an entire stranger, to express any doubt of the justice of his animadversion upon his old acquaintance and pupil. I now felt myself much mortified, and began to think that the hope which I had long indulged of obtaining his acquaintance was blasted. And, in truth, had not my ardor been uncommonly strong, and my resolution uncommonly persevering, so rough a reception might have deterred me forever from making any further attempts. Fortunately, however, I remained upon the field not wholly discomfited. * * *

I was highly pleased with the extraordinary vigor of his conversation, and regretted that I was drawn away from it by an engagement at another place. I had, for a part of the evening, been left alone with him, and had ventured to make an observation now and then, which he received very civilly; so that I was satisfied that though there was a roughness in his manner, there was no ill nature in his disposition. Davies followed me to the door, and when I complained to him a little of the hard blows which the great man had given me, he kindly took upon him to console me by saying, "Don't be uneasy. I can see he likes you very well."

A few days afterwards I called on Davies, and asked him if he thought I might take the liberty of waiting on Mr. Johnson at his chambers in the Temple. He said I certainly might, and that Mr. Johnson would take it as a compliment. So upon Tuesday the 24th of May, after having been enlivened by the witty sallies of Messieurs Thornton, Wilkes, Churchill, and Lloyd,[5] with whom I had passed the morning, I boldly repaired to Johnson. His chambers were on the first floor of No. 1, Inner Temple Lane, and I entered them with an impression given me by the Reverend Dr. Blair,[6] of Edinburgh, who had been introduced to him not long before, and described his having "found the giant in his den"; an expression, which, when I came to be pretty well acquainted with Johnson, I repeated to him, and he was diverted at this picturesque account of himself. Dr. Blair had been presented to him by Dr. James Fordyce.[7] At this time the controversy concerning the pieces published by Mr. James Macpherson, as translations of *Ossian*, was at its height.[8] Johnson had all along denied their authenticity; and, what was still more provoking to their admirers, maintained that they had no merit. The subject having been introduced by Dr. Fordyce, Dr. Blair, relying on the internal evidence of their antiquity, asked Dr. Johnson whether he thought any man of a modern age could have written such poems? Johnson replied, "Yes, Sir, many men, many women, and many children."

5. Bonnell Thornton, journalist; Charles Churchill, satirist; Robert Lloyd, poet and essayist. For Wilkes see a later episode. The four were bound together by a common love of wit and dissipation. Boswell enjoyed their company in 1763.

6. The Rev. Hugh Blair (1718–1800), Scottish divine and professor of Rhetoric and Belles Lettres at the University of Edinburgh.

7. A Scottish preacher.

8. Macpherson had imposed on most of his contemporaries, Scottish and English, by convincing them of the genuineness of prose poems which he had concocted but which he claimed to have translated from the original Gaelic of Ossian, a blind epic poet of the 3rd century. The vogue of the poems both in Europe and in America was enormous.

Johnson, at this time, did not know that Dr. Blair had just published a dissertation, not only defending their authenticity, but seriously ranking them with the poems of Homer and Virgil; and when he was afterwards informed of this circumstance, he expressed some displeasure at Dr. Fordyce's having suggested the topic, and said, "I am not sorry that they got thus much for their pains. Sir, it was like leading one to talk of a book when the author is concealed behind the door."

He received me very courteously; but, it must be confessed that his apartment, and furniture, and morning dress, were sufficiently uncouth. His brown suit of clothes looked very rusty; he had on a little old shriveled unpowdered wig, which was too small for his head; his shirt neck and knees of his breeches were loose; his black worsted stockings ill drawn up; and he had a pair of unbuckled shoes by way of slippers. But all these slovenly particularities were forgotten the moment that he began to talk. Some gentlemen, whom I do not recollect, were sitting with him; and when they went away, I also rose; but he said to me, "Nay, don't go." "Sir," said I, "I am afraid that I intrude upon you. It is benevolent to allow me to sit and hear you." He seemed pleased with this compliment, which I sincerely paid him, and answered, "Sir, I am obliged to any man who visits me." I have preserved the following short minute of what passed this day:

"Madness frequently discovers itself merely by unnecessary deviation from the usual modes of the world. My poor friend Smart showed the disturbance of his mind by falling upon his knees, and saying his prayers in the street, or in any other unusual place. Now although, rationally speaking, it is greater madness not to pray at all than to pray as Smart did, I am afraid there are so many who do not pray, that their understanding is not called in question."

Concerning this unfortunate poet, Christopher Smart, who was confined in a madhouse, he had, at another time, the following conversation with Dr. Burney:[9] BURNEY. "How does poor Smart do, Sir; is he likely to recover?" JOHNSON. "It seems as if his mind had ceased to struggle with the disease; for he grows fat upon it." BURNEY. "Perhaps, Sir, that may be from want of exercise." JOHNSON. "No, Sir; he has partly as much exercise as he used to have, for he digs in the garden. Indeed, before his confinement, he used for exercise to walk to the ale house; but he was *carried* back again. I did not think he ought to be shut up. His infirmities were not noxious to society. He insisted on people praying with him; and I'd as lief pray with Kit Smart as anyone else. Another charge was that he did not love clean linen; and I have no passion for it."—Johnson continued. "Mankind have a great aversion to intellectual labor; but even supposing knowledge to be easily attainable, more people would be content to be ignorant than would take even a little trouble to acquire it."

9. Dr. Charles Burney (1726–1814), historian of music and father of the novelist and diarist Fanny Burney, whom Johnson knew and loved in his old age.

Talking of Garrick, he said, "He is the first man in the world for sprightly conversation."

When I rose a second time he again pressed me to stay, which I did. * * *

[Goldsmith. Sundry Opinions. Johnson Meets His King]

As Dr. Oliver Goldsmith will frequently appear in this narrative, I shall endeavor to make my readers in some degree acquainted with his singular character. He was a native of Ireland, and a contemporary with Mr. Burke[1] at Trinity College, Dublin, but did not then give much promise of future celebrity. He, however, observed to Mr. Malone,[2] that "though he made no great figure in mathematics, which was a study in much repute there, he could turn an ode of Horace into English better than any of them." He afterwards studied physic at Edinburgh, and upon the Continent; and I have been informed, was enabled to pursue his travels on foot, partly by demanding at universities to enter the lists as a disputant, by which, according to the custom of many of them, he was entitled to the premium of a crown, when luckily for him his challenge was not accepted; so that, as I once observed to Dr. Johnson, he *disputed* his passage through Europe. He then came to England, and was employed successively in the capacities of an usher[3] to an academy, a corrector of the press, a reviewer, and a writer for a newspaper. He had sagacity enough to cultivate assiduously the acquaintance of Johnson, and his faculties were gradually enlarged by the contemplation of such a model. To me and many others it appeared that he studiously copied the manner of Johnson, though, indeed, upon a smaller scale.

At this time I think he had published nothing with his name, though it was pretty generally known that *one Dr. Goldsmith* was the author of *An Enquiry into the Present State of Polite Learning in Europe*, and of *The Citizen of the World*, a series of letters supposed to be written from London by a Chinese. No man had the art of displaying, with more advantage as a writer, whatever literary acquisitions he made. *"Nihil quod tetigit non ornavit."*[4] His mind resembled a fertile, but thin soil. There was a quick, but not a strong vegetation, of whatever chanced to be thrown upon it. No deep root could be struck. The oak of the forest did not grow there; but the elegant shrubbery and the fragrant parterre[5] appeared in gay succession. It has been generally circulated and believed that he was a mere fool in conversation; but, in truth, this has been greatly exaggerated. He had, no doubt, a more than common share of that hurry of ideas which we often find in his countrymen, and which

---

1. Edmund Burke (1729–1797), statesman, orator, and political philosopher.
2. Edmond Malone (1741–1812), distinguished editor and literary scholar. He helped Boswell in the writing and publication of the *Life*.
3. An assistant teacher; then a disagreeable and

ill-paid job.
4. "He touched nothing that he did not adorn." From Johnson's epitaph for Goldsmith's monument in Westminster Abbey.
5. A flower garden with beds laid out in patterns.

sometimes produces a laughable confusion in expressing them. He was very much what the French call *un étourdi*,[6] and from vanity and an eager desire of being conspicuous wherever he was, he frequently talked carelessly without knowledge of the subject, or even without thought. His person was short, his countenance coarse and vulgar, his deportment that of a scholar awkwardly affecting the easy gentleman. Those who were in any way distinguished, excited envy in him to so ridiculous an excess that the instances of it are hardly credible. When accompanying two beautiful young ladies with their mother on a tour in France, he was seriously angry that more attention was paid to them than to him; and once at the exhibition of the *Fantoccini* in London, when those who sat next him observed with what dexterity a puppet was made to toss a pike, he could not bear that it should have such praise, and exclaimed with some warmth, "Pshaw! I can do it better myself."[7] * * *

I had as my guests this evening at the Mitre Tavern, Dr. Johnson, Dr. Goldsmith, Mr. Thomas Davies, Mr. Eccles, an Irish gentleman, for whose agreeable company I was obliged to Mr. Davies, and the Reverend Mr. John Ogilvie,[8] who was desirous of being in company with my illustrious friend, while I, in my turn, was proud to have the honor of showing one of my countrymen upon what easy terms Johnson permitted me to live with him. * * *

Mr. Ogilvie was unlucky enough to choose for the topic of his conversation the praises of his native country. He began with saying that there was very rich land round Edinburgh. Goldsmith, who had studied physic there, contradicted this, very untruly, with a sneering laugh. Disconcerted a little by this, Mr. Ogilvie then took new ground, where, I suppose, he thought himself perfectly safe; for he observed that Scotland had a great many noble wild prospects. JOHNSON. "I believe, Sir, you have a great many. Norway, too, has noble wild prospects; and Lapland is remarkable for prodigious noble wild prospects. But, Sir, let me tell you, the noblest prospect which a Scotchman ever sees, is the highroad that leads him to England!" This unexpected and pointed sally produced a roar of applause. After all, however, those who admire the rude grandeur of nature cannot deny it to Caledonia. * * *

At night Mr. Johnson and I supped in a private room at the Turk's Head Coffeehouse, in the Strand. "I encourage this house," said he, "for the mistress of it is a good civil woman, and has not much business.

"Sir, I love the acquaintance of young people; because, in the first place, I don't like to think myself growing old. In the next place, young acquaintances must last longest, if they do last; and then, Sir, young men have more virtue than old men: they have more generous sentiments in every respect. I love the young dogs of this age: they have more wit and humor and knowledge of life than we had; but then the dogs are not so good scholars. Sir, in my early years I read very hard. It is a sad

6. One who acts without thought.
7. It is difficult to believe that Boswell did not recognize that Goldsmith was joking. Indeed, his entire characterization of Goldsmith is not without malice and distortion.
8. An eminent Scottish divine.

reflection, but a true one, that I knew almost as much at eighteen as I do now. My judgment, to be sure, was not so good; but I had all the facts. I remember very well, when I was at Oxford, an old gentleman said to me, 'Young man, ply your book diligently now, and acquire a stock of knowledge; for when years come upon you, you will find that poring upon books will be but an irksome task.' " * * *

He again insisted on the duty of maintaining subordination of rank. "Sir, I would no more deprive a nobleman of his respect than of his money. I consider myself as acting a part in the great system of society, and I do to others as I would have them to do to me. I would behave to a nobleman as I should expect he would behave to me, were I a nobleman and he Sam. Johnson. Sir, there is one Mrs. Macaulay[9] in this town, a great republican. One day when I was at her house, I put on a very grave countenance, and said to her, 'Madam, I am now become a convert to your way of thinking. I am convinced that all mankind are upon an equal footing; and to give you an unquestionable proof, Madam, that I am in earnest, here is a very sensible, civil, well-behaved fellow citizen, your footman; I desire that he may be allowed to sit down and dine with us.' I thus, Sir, showed her the absurdity of the leveling doctrine. She has never liked me since. Sir, your levelers wish to level *down* as far as themselves; but they cannot bear leveling *up* to themselves. They would all have some people under them; why not then have some people above them?" * * *

At supper this night he talked of good eating with uncommon satisfaction. "Some people," he said, "have a foolish way of not minding, or pretending not to mind, what they eat. For my part, I mind my belly very studiously, and very carefully; for I look upon it that he who does not mind his belly will hardly mind anything else." He now appeared to me *Jean Bull philosophe*,[1] and he was, for the moment, not only serious but vehement. Yet I have heard him, upon other occasions, talk with great contempt of people who were anxious to gratify their palates; and the 206th number of his *Rambler* is a masterly essay against gulosity.[2] His practice, indeed, I must acknowledge, may be considered as casting the balance of his different opinions upon this subject; for I never knew any man who relished good eating more than he did. When at table, he was totally absorbed in the business of the moment; his looks seemed riveted to his plate; nor would he, unless when in very high company, say one word, or even pay the least attention to what was said by others, till he had satisfied his appetite, which was so fierce, and indulged with such intenseness, that while in the act of eating, the veins of his forehead swelled, and generally a strong perspiration was visible. To those whose sensations were delicate, this could not but be disgusting; and it was doubtless not very suitable to the character of a philosopher, who should be distinguished by self-command. But it must be owned that Johnson,

9. Mrs. Catharine Macaulay, at this time much in the public eye as a female historian and a propounder of libertarian and egalitarian ideas.

1. I.e., John Bull (the typical hard-headed Englishman) in the role of philosopher.
2. Greediness.

though he could be rigidly *abstemious*, was not a *temperate* man either in eating or drinking. He could refrain, but he could not use moderately. He told me that he had fasted two days without inconvenience, and that he had never been hungry but once. They who beheld with wonder how much he eat upon all occasions when his dinner was to his taste, could not easily conceive what he must have meant by hunger; and not only was he remarkable for the extraordinary quantity which he eat, but he was, or affected to be, a man of very nice discernment in the science of cookery. * * *

[*1767*] In February, 1767, there happened one of the most remarkable incidents of Johnson's life, which gratified his monarchical enthusiasm, and which he loved to relate with all its circumstances, when requested by his friends. This was his being honored by a private conversation with his Majesty, in the library at the Queen's house. He had frequently visited those splendid rooms and noble collection of books, which he used to say was more numerous and curious than he supposed any person could have made in the time which the King had employed. Mr. Barnard, the librarian, took care that he should have every accommodation that could contribute to his ease and convenience, while indulging his literary taste in that place; so that he had here a very agreeable resource at leisure hours.

His Majesty having been informed of his occasional visits, was pleased to signify a desire that he should be told when Dr. Johnson came next to the library. Accordingly, the next time that Johnson did come, as soon as he was fairly engaged with a book, on which, while he sat by the fire, he seemed quite intent, Mr. Barnard stole round to the apartment where the King was, and, in obedience to his Majesty's commands, mentioned that Dr. Johnson was then in the library. His Majesty said he was at leisure, and would go to him; upon which Mr. Barnard took one of the candles that stood on the King's table, and lighted his Majesty through a suite of rooms, till they came to a private door into the library, of which his Majesty had the key. Being entered, Mr. Barnard stepped forward hastily to Dr. Johnson, who was still in a profound study, and whispered him, "Sir, here is the King." Johnson started up, and stood still. His Majesty approached him, and at once was courteously easy.

His Majesty began by observing that he understood he came sometimes to the library; and then mentioning his having heard that the Doctor had been lately at Oxford, asked him if he was not fond of going thither. To which Johnson answered that he was indeed fond of going to Oxford sometimes, but was likewise glad to come back again. The King then asked him what they were doing at Oxford. Johnson answered, he could not much commend their diligence, but that in some respects they were mended, for they had put their press under better regulations, and were at that time printing Polybius. He was then asked whether there were better libraries at Oxford or Cambridge. He answered, he believed the Bodleian was larger than any they had at Cambridge; at the same time adding, "I hope, whether we have more books or not than they have at Cambridge, we shall make as good use of them as they do." Being asked whether All Souls or Christ Church library was the largest, he answered, "All Souls library is the largest we have, except the Bodleian." "Aye," said the King, "that is the public library."

His Majesty inquired if he was then writing anything. He answered, he was not, for he had pretty well told the world what he knew, and must now read to acquire more knowledge. The King, as it should seem with a view to urge him to rely on his own stores as an original writer, and to continue his labors, then said "I do not think you borrow much from anybody." Johnson said he thought he had already done his part as a writer. "I should have thought so too," said the King, "if you had not written so well."—Johnson observed to me, upon this, that "No man could have paid a handsomer compliment; and it was fit for a king to pay. It was decisive." When asked by another friend, at Sir Joshua Reynolds's, whether he made any reply to this high compliment, he answered, "No, Sir. When the King had said it, it was to be so. It was not for me to bandy civilities with my sovereign." Perhaps no man who had spent his whole life in courts could have shown a more nice and dignified sense of true politeness than Johnson did in this instance. * * *

[Fear of Death]

[1769] When we were alone, I introduced the subject of death, and endeavored to maintain that the fear of it might be got over. I told him that David Hume said to me, he was no more uneasy to think he should *not be* after this life, than that he *had not been* before he began to exist. JOHNSON. "Sir, if he really thinks so, his perceptions are disturbed; he is mad: if he does not think so, he lies. He may tell you, he holds his finger in the flame of a candle, without feeling pain; would you believe him? When he dies, he at least gives up all he has." BOSWELL. "Foote,[3] Sir, told me, that when he was very ill he was not afraid to die." JOHNSON. "It is not true, Sir. Hold a pistol to Foote's breast, or to Hume's breast, and threaten to kill them, and you'll see how they behave." BOSWELL. "But may we not fortify our minds for the approach of death?" Here I am sensible I was in the wrong, to bring before his view what he ever looked upon with horror; for although when in a celestial frame, in his *Vanity of Human Wishes*, he has supposed death to be "kind Nature's signal for retreat," from this stage of being to "a happier seat," his thoughts upon this awful change were in general full of dismal apprehensions. His mind resembled the vast amphitheater, the Colosseum at Rome. In the center stood his judgment, which, like a mighty gladiator, combated those apprehensions that, like the wild beasts of the arena, were all around in cells, ready to be let out upon him. After a conflict, he drives them back into their dens; but not killing them, they were still assailing him.

3. Samuel Foote, actor and dramatist, famous for his wit and his skill in mimicry.

To my question, whether we might not fortify our minds for the approach of death, he answered, in a passion, "No, Sir, let it alone. It matters not how a man dies, but how he lives. The act of dying is not of importance, it lasts so short a time." He added (with an earnest look), "A man knows it must be so, and submits. It will do him no good to whine."

I attempted to continue the conversation. He was so provoked that he said, "Give us no more of this"; and was thrown into such a state of agitation that he expressed himself in a way that alarmed and distressed me; showed an impatience that I should leave him, and when I was going away, called to me sternly, "Don't let us meet tomorrow." * * *

[*Ossian. "Talking for Victory"*]

MR. BOSWELL TO DR. JOHNSON

Edinburgh, Feb. 2, 1775.

* * * As to Macpherson, I am anxious to have from yourself a full and pointed account of what has passed between you and him. It is confidently told here that before your book[4] came out he sent to you, to let you know that he understood you meant to deny the authenticity of Ossian's poems; that the originals were in his possession; that you might have inspection of them, and might take the evidence of people skilled in the Erse language; and that he hoped, after this fair offer, you would not be so uncandid as to assert that he had refused reasonable proof. That you paid no regard to his message, but published your strong attack upon him; and then he wrote a letter to you, in such terms as he thought suited to one who had not acted as a man of veracity. * * *

What words were used by Mr. Macpherson in his letter to the venerable sage, I have never heard; but they are generally said to have been of a nature very different from the language of literary contest. Dr. Johnson's answer appeared in the newspapers of the day, and has since been frequently republished; but not with perfect accuracy. I give it as dictated to me by himself, written down in his presence, and authenticated by a note in his own handwriting, *"This, I think, is a true copy."*

MR. JAMES MACPHERSON,

I received your foolish and impudent letter. Any violence offered me I shall do my best to repel; and what I cannot do for myself, the law shall do for me. I hope I shall never be deterred from detecting what I think a cheat, by the menaces of a ruffian.

What would you have me retract? I thought your book an imposture; I think it an imposture still. For this opinion I have given my reasons to the public, which I here dare you to refute. Your rage I

4. Johnson's *Journey to the Western Islands* (1775), in which he had publicly expressed his views on the Ossianic poems.

defy. Your abilities, since your Homer, are not so formidable; and what I hear of your morals inclines me to pay regard not to what you shall say, but to what you shall prove. You may print this if you will.

SAM. JOHNSON.

Mr. Macpherson little knew the character of Dr. Johnson if he supposed that he could be easily intimidated; for no man was ever more remarkable for personal courage. He had, indeed, an awful dread of death, or rather, "of something after death"; and what rational man, who seriously thinks of quitting all that he has ever known, and going into a new and unknown state of being, can be without that dread? But his fear was from reflection; his courage natural. His fear, in that one instance, was the result of philosophical and religious consideration. He feared death, but he feared nothing else, not even what might occasion death. Many instances of his resolution may be mentioned. One day, at Mr. Beauclerk's house in the country, when two large dogs were fighting, he went up to them, and beat them till they separated; and at another time, when told of the danger there was that a gun might burst if charged with many balls, he put in six or seven, and fired it off against a wall. Mr. Langton told me that when they were swimming together near Oxford, he cautioned Dr. Johnson against a pool which was reckoned particularly dangerous; upon which Johnson directly swam into it. He told me himself that one night he was attacked in the street by four men, to whom he would not yield, but kept them all at bay, till the watch came up, and carried both him and them to the roundhouse. In the playhouse at Lichfield, as Mr. Garrick informed me, Johnson having for a moment quitted a chair which was placed for him between the side-scenes, a gentleman took possession of it, and when Johnson on his return civilly demanded his seat, rudely refused to give it up; upon which Johnson laid hold of it, and tossed him and the chair into the pit. Foote, who so successfully revived the old comedy, by exhibiting living characters, had resolved to imitate Johnson on the stage, expecting great profits from his ridicule of so celebrated a man. Johnson being informed of his intention, and being at dinner at Mr. Thomas Davies's the bookseller, from whom I had the story, he asked Mr. Davies what was the common price of an oak stick; and being answered six-pence, "Why then, Sir," said he, "give me leave to send your servant to purchase me a shilling one. I'll have a double quantity; for I am told Foote means to *take me off*, as he calls it, and I am determined the fellow shall not do it with impunity." Davies took care to acquaint Foote of this, which effectually checked the wantonness of the mimic. Mr. Macpherson's menaces made Johnson provide himself with the same implement of defense; and had he been attacked, I have no doubt that, old as he was, he would have made his corporal prowess be felt as much as his intellectual. * * *

[1776] I mentioned a new gaming club, of which Mr. Beauclerk had given me an account, where the members played to a desperate extent.

JOHNSON. "Depend upon it, Sir, this is mere talk. *Who* is ruined by gaming? You will not find six instances in an age. There is a strange rout made about deep play: whereas you have many more people ruined by adventurous trade, and yet we do not hear such an outcry against it." THRALE.[5] "There may be few people absolutely ruined by deep play; but very many are much hurt in their circumstances by it." JOHNSON. "Yes, Sir, and so are very many by other kinds of expense." I had heard him talk once before in the same manner; and at Oxford he said, he wished he had learnt to play at cards. The truth, however, is that he loved to display his ingenuity in argument; and therefore would sometimes in conversation maintain opinions which he was sensible were wrong, but in supporting which, his reasoning and wit would be most conspicuous. He would begin thus: "Why, Sir, as to the good or evil of card playing ——" "Now," said Garrick, "he is thinking which side he shall take." He appeared to have a pleasure in contradiction, especially when any opinion whatever was delivered with an air of confidence; so that there was hardly any topic, if not one of the great truths of religion and morality, that he might not have been incited to argue, either for or against. Lord Elibank[6] had the highest admiration of his powers. He once observed to me, "Whatever opinion Johnson maintains, I will not say that he convinces me; but he never fails to show me that he has good reasons for it." I have heard Johnson pay his Lordship this high compliment: "I never was in Lord Elibank's company without learning something." * * *

[*Dinner with Wilkes*]

My worthy booksellers and friends, Messieurs Dilly in the Poultry, at whose hospitable and well-covered table I have seen a greater number of literary men than at any other, except that of Sir Joshua Reynolds, had invited me to meet Mr. Wilkes[7] and some more gentlemen on Wednesday, May 15. "Pray," said I, "let us have Dr. Johnson."—"What, with Mr. Wilkes? not for the world," said Mr. Edward Dilly, "Dr. Johnson would never forgive me."—"Come," said I, "if you'll let me negotiate for you, I will be answerable that all shall go well." DILLY. "Nay, if you will take it upon you, I am sure I shall be very happy to see them both here."

Notwithstanding the high veneration which I entertained for Dr.

5. Johnson met Henry Thrale, the wealthy brewer, and his charming wife Hester in 1765. Thereafter he was domesticated as much as he wished to be at their house at Streatham near London. There he enjoyed the good things of life, as well as the companionship of Mrs. Thrale and her children. Thrale died in 1781. His widow's marriage to Gabriel Piozzi, an Italian musician, in 1784, caused Johnson to quarrel with her and darkened the last months of his life.

6. Prominent in Scottish literary circles. Johnson, who admired him, had visited him on his tour of Scotland with Boswell in 1773.

7. John Wilkes (1727–1797) was obnoxious to the

Christian and Tory Johnson in every way. He was profane and dissolute, and his personal life was a public scandal; for over a decade he had been notorious as a courageous, resourceful, and finally victorious opponent of the arbitrary and tyrannical policies of the king and his ministers, and had been the envenomed critic of Lord Bute, to whom Johnson owed his pension. When Johnson met him he had totally defeated his enemies, had served as lord mayor, and was again a Member of Parliament, a post from which he had been expelled and driven into exile as an outlaw in 1764. Boswell had found Wilkes a gay and congenial companion in Italy in 1764.

Johnson, I was sensible that he was sometimes a little actuated by the spirit of contradiction, and by means of that I hoped I should gain my point. I was persuaded that if I had come upon him with a direct proposal, "Sir, will you dine in company with Jack Wilkes?" he would have flown into a passion, and would probably have answered, "Dine with Jack Wilkes, Sir! I'd as soon dine with Jack Ketch."[8] I therefore, while we were sitting quietly by ourselves at his house in an evening, took occasion to open my plan thus: "Mr. Dilly, Sir, sends his respectful compliments to you, and would be happy if you would do him the honor to dine with him on Wednesday next along with me, as I must soon go to Scotland." JOHNSON. "Sir, I am obliged to Mr. Dilly. I will wait upon him——" BOSWELL. "Provided, Sir, I suppose, that the company which he is to have, is agreeable to you." JOHNSON. "What do you mean, Sir? What do you take me for? Do you think I am so ignorant of the world as to imagine that I am to prescribe to a gentleman what company he is to have at his table?" BOSWELL. "I beg your pardon, Sir, for wishing to prevent you from meeting people whom you might not like. Perhaps he may have some of what he calls his patriotic[9] friends with him." JOHNSON. "Well, Sir, and what then? What care *I* for his *patriotic friends?* Poh!" BOSWELL. "I should not be surprised to find Jack Wilkes there." JOHNSON. "And if Jack Wilkes *should* be there, what is that to *me*, Sir? My dear friend, let us have no more of this. I am sorry to be angry with you; but really it is treating me strangely to talk to me as if I could not meet any company whatever, occasionally." BOSWELL. "Pray forgive me, Sir: I meant well. But you shall meet whoever comes, for me." Thus I secured him, and told Dilly that he would find him very well pleased to be one of his guests on the day appointed.

Upon the much-expected Wednesday, I called on him about half an hour before dinner, as I often did when we were to dine out together, to see that he was ready in time, and to accompany him. I found him buffeting his books, as upon a former occasion, covered with dust, and making no preparation for going abroad. "How is this, Sir?" said I. "Don't you recollect that you are to dine at Mr. Dilly's?" JOHNSON. "Sir, I did not think of going to Dilly's: it went out of my head. I have ordered dinner at home with Mrs. Williams." BOSWELL. "But, my dear Sir, you know you were engaged to Mr. Dilly, and I told him so. He will expect you, and will be much disappointed if you don't come." JOHNSON. "You must talk to Mrs. Williams about this."

Here was a sad dilemma. I feared that what I was so confident I had secured would yet be frustrated. He had accustomed himself to show Mrs. Williams such a degree of humane attention as frequently imposed some restraint upon him; and I knew that if she should be obstinate, he would not stir. I hastened downstairs to the blind lady's room, and told

8. After the public hangman, Jack Ketch, died in 1686, his name became the common designation of all those who filled that office.
9. In Tory circles the word had come to be used ironically of those who opposed the government.

The "patriots" considered themselves the defenders of the ancient liberties of the English. They included the partisans of both Wilkes and of the American colonists.

her I was in great uneasiness, for Dr. Johnson had engaged to me to dine this day at Mr. Dilly's, but that he had told me he had forgotten his engagement, and had ordered dinner at home. "Yes, Sir," said she, pretty peevishly, "Dr. Johnson is to dine at home."—"Madam," said I, "his respect for you is such that I know he will not leave you unless you absolutely desire it. But as you have so much of his company, I hope you will be good enough to forego it for a day; as Mr. Dilly is a very worthy man, has frequently had agreeable parties at his house for Dr. Johnson, and will be vexed if the Doctor neglects him today. And then, Madam, be pleased to consider my situation; I carried the message, and I assured Mr. Dilly that Dr. Johnson was to come, and no doubt he has made a dinner, and invited a company, and boasted of the honor he expected to have. I shall be quite disgraced if the Doctor is not there." She gradually softened to my solicitations, which were certainly as earnest as most entreaties to ladies upon any occasion, and was graciously pleased to empower me to tell Dr. Johnson that all things considered, she thought he should certainly go. I flew back to him, still in dust, and careless of what should be the event, "indifferent in his choice to go or stay";[1] but as soon as I had announced to him Mrs. Williams' consent, he roared, "Frank, a clean shirt," and was very soon dressed. When I had him fairly seated in a hackney coach with me, I exulted as much as a fortune hunter who has got an heiress into a post chaise with him to set out for Gretna Green.[2]

When we entered Mr. Dilly's drawing room, he found himself in the midst of a company he did not know. I kept myself snug and silent, watching how he would conduct himself. I observed him whispering to Mr. Dilly, "Who is that gentleman, Sir?"—"Mr. Arthur Lee."—JOHNSON. "Too, too, too" (under his breath), which was one of his habitual mutterings. Mr. Arthur Lee could not but be very obnoxious to Johnson, for he was not only a *patriot* but an *American*.[3] He was afterwards minister from the United States at the court of Madrid. "And who is the gentleman in lace?"—"Mr. Wilkes, Sir." This information confounded him still more; he had some difficulty to restrain himself, and taking up a book, sat down upon a window seat and read, or at least kept his eye upon it intently for some time, till he composed himself. His feelings, I dare say, were awkward enough. But he no doubt recollected his having rated me for supposing that he could be at all disconcerted by any company, and he, therefore, resolutely set himself to behave quite as an easy man of the world, who could adapt himself at once to the disposition and manners of those whom he might chance to meet.

The cheering sound of "Dinner is upon the table," dissolved his rev-

---

1. Addison's *Cato* 5.1.40. Boswell cleverly adapts to his own purpose Cato's words, "Indifferent in his choice to sleep or die."
2. A village just across the Scottish border where runaway couples were married by the local innkeeper or the blacksmith.
3. Johnson was extremely hostile to the rebelling American colonists. On one occasion he said: "I am willing to love all mankind, except an American." Lee had been educated in England and Scotland, and had recently been admitted to the English bar. He had been a loyal supporter of Wilkes.

erie, and we *all* sat down without any symptom of ill humor. There
were present, beside Mr. Wilkes, and Mr. Arthur Lee, who was an old
companion of mine when he studied physic at Edinburgh, Mr. (now Sir
John) Miller, Dr. Lettsom, and Mr. Slater the druggist. Mr. Wilkes
placed himself next to Dr. Johnson, and behaved to him with so much
attention and politeness that he gained upon him insensibly. No man
eat more heartily than Johnson, or loved better what was nice and delicate. Mr. Wilkes was very assiduous in helping him to some fine veal.
"Pray give me leave, Sir—It is better here—A little of the brown—Some
fat, Sir—A little of the stuffing—Some gravy—Let me have the pleasure
of giving you some butter—Allow me to recommend a squeeze of this
orange—or the lemon, perhaps, may have more zest."—"Sir, Sir, I am
obliged to you, Sir," cried Johnson, bowing, and turning his head to
him with a look for some time of "surly virtue," but, in a short while,
of complacency.

Foote being mentioned, Johnson said, "He is not a good mimic."
One of the company added, "A merry Andrew, a buffoon." JOHNSON.
"But he has wit too, and is not deficient in ideas, or in fertility and
variety of imagery, and not empty of reading; he has knowledge enough
to fill up his part. One species of wit he has in an eminent degree, that
of escape. You drive him into a corner with both hands; but he's gone,
Sir, when you think you have got him—like an animal that jumps over
your head. Then he has a great range for wit; he never lets truth stand
between him and a jest, and he is sometimes mighty coarse. Garrick is
under many restraints from which Foote is free." WILKES. "Garrick's wit
is more like Lord Chesterfield's." JOHNSON. "The first time I was in
company with Foote was at Fitzherbert's. Having no good opinion of
the fellow, I was resolved not to be pleased; and it is very difficult to
please a man against his will. I went on eating my dinner pretty sullenly,
affecting not to mind him. But the dog was so very comical, that I was
obliged to lay down my knife and fork, throw myself back upon my
chair, and fairly laugh it out. No, Sir, he was irresistible. He upon one
occasion experienced, in an extraordinary degree, the efficacy of his powers
of entertaining. Amongst the many and various modes which he tried of
getting money, he became a partner with a small-beer[4] brewer, and he
has to have a share of the profits for procuring customers amongst his
numerous acquaintance. Fitzherbert was one who took his small beer;
but it was so bad that the servants resolved not to drink it. They were at
some loss how to notify their resolution, being afraid of offending their
master, who they knew liked Foote much as a companion. At last they
fixed upon a little black boy, who was rather a favorite, to be their deputy, and deliver their remonstrance; and having invested him with the
whole authority of the kitchen, he was to inform Mr. Fitzherbert, in all
their names, upon a certain day, that they would drink Foote's small
beer no longer. On that day Foote happened to dine at Fitzherbert's,

---

4. Weak beer, served in the servants' hall.

and this boy served at table; he was so delighted with Foote's stories, and merriment, and grimace, that when he went downstairs, he told them, 'This is the finest man I have ever seen. I will not deliver your message. I will drink his small beer.'"

Somebody observed that Garrick could not have done this. WILKES. "Garrick would have made the small beer still smaller. He is now leaving the stage; but he will play *Scrub*[5] all his life." I knew that Johnson would let nobody attack Garrick but himself, as Garrick once said to me, and I had heard him praise his liberality; so to bring out his commendation of his celebrated pupil, I said, loudly, "I have heard Garrick is liberal." JOHNSON. "Yes, Sir, I know that Garrick has given away more money than any man in England that I am acquainted with, and that not from ostentatious views. Garrick was very poor when he began life; so when he came to have money, he probably was very unskillful in giving away, and saved when he should not. But Garrick began to be liberal as soon as he could; and I am of opinion, the reputation of avarice which he has had, has been very lucky for him, and prevented his having many enemies. You despise a man for avarice, but do not hate him. Garrick might have been much better attacked for living with more splendor than is suitable to a player: if they had had the wit to have assaulted him in that quarter, they might have galled him more. But they have kept clamoring about his avarice, which has rescued him from much obloquy and envy."

Talking of the great difficulty of obtaining authentic information for biography, Johnson told us, "When I was a young fellow I wanted to write the *Life of Dryden*, and in order to get materials, I applied to the only two persons then alive who had seen him; these were old Swinney,[6] and old Cibber. Swinney's information was no more than this, that at Will's Coffeehouse Dryden had a particular chair for himself, which was set by the fire in winter, and was then called his winter chair; and that it was carried out for him to the balcony in summer, and was then called his summer chair. Cibber could tell no more but that he remembered him a decent old man, arbiter of critical disputes at Will's. You are to consider that Cibber was then at a great distance from Dryden, had perhaps one leg only in the room, and durst not draw in the other." BOSWELL. "Yet Cibber was a man of observation?" JOHNSON. "I think not." BOSWELL. "You will allow his *Apology* to be well done." JOHNSON. "Very well done, to be sure, Sir. That book is a striking proof of the justice of Pope's remark:

> Each might his several province well command,
> Would all but stoop to what they understand."[7]

BOSWELL. "And his plays are good." JOHNSON. "Yes; but that was his trade; *l'esprit du corps*: he had been all his life among players and play

---

5. The servant of Squire Sullen in George Farquhar's *Beaux' Stratagem:* a favorite role of Garrick's.

6. Owen Mac Swinney, a playwright.
7. *Essay on Criticism* 1.66–67.

writers. I wondered that he had so little to say in conversation, for he had kept the best company, and learnt all that can be got by the ear. He abused Pindar to me, and then showed me an ode of his own, with an absurd couplet, making a linnet soar on an eagle's wing. I told him that when the ancients made a simile, they always made it like something real."

Mr. Wilkes remarked that "among all the bold flights of Shakespeare's imagination, the boldest was making Birnam Wood march to Dunsinane;[8] creating a wood where there never was a shrub; a wood in Scotland! ha! ha! ha!" And he also observed, that "the clannish slavery of the Highlands of Scotland was the single exception to Milton's remark of 'The mountain nymph, sweet Liberty,'[9] being worshiped in all hilly countries."—"When I was at Inverary," said he, "on a visit to my old friend, Archibald, Duke of Argyle, his dependents congratulated me on being such a favorite of his Grace. I said, 'It is then, gentlemen, truly lucky for me; for if I had displeased the Duke, and he had wished it, there is not a Campbell among you but would have been ready to bring John Wilkes's head to him in a charger. It would have been only

Off with his head! So much for Aylesbury.'[1]

I was then member for Aylesbury." * * *

Mr. Arthur Lee mentioned some Scotch who had taken possession of a barren part of America, and wondered why they should choose it. JOHNSON. "Why, Sir, all barrenness is comparative. The *Scotch* would not know it to be barren." BOSWELL. "Come, come, he is flattering the English. You have now been in Scotland, Sir, and say if you did not see meat and drink enough there." JOHNSON. "Why yes, Sir; meat and drink enough to give the inhabitants sufficient strength to run away from home." All these quick and lively sallies were said sportively, quite in jest, and with a smile, which showed that he meant only wit. Upon this topic he and Mr. Wilkes could perfectly assimilate; here was a bond of union between them, and I was conscious that as both of them had visited Caledonia, both were fully satisfied of the strange narrow ignorance of those who imagine that it is a land of famine. But they amused themselves with persevering in the old jokes. When I claimed a superiority for Scotland over England in one respect, that no man can be arrested there for a debt merely because another swears it against him; but there must first be the judgment of a court of law ascertaining its justice; and that a seizure of the person, before judgment is obtained, can take place only if his creditor should swear that he is about to fly from the country, or, as it is technically expressed, is *in meditatione fugae*: WILKES. "That, I should think, may be safely sworn of all the Scotch nation." JOHNSON (to Mr. Wilkes). "You must know, Sir, I lately took my friend Boswell and showed him genuine civilized life in an English provincial town. I

---

8. *Macbeth* 5.5. 30–52.
9. *L'Allegro*, line 36.
1. "Off with his head! So much for Buckingham."

A line in Cibber's version of Shakespeare's *Richard III*.

turned him loose at Lichfield, my native city, that he might see for once real civility: for you know he lives among savages in Scotland, and among rakes in London." WILKES. "Except when he is with grave, sober, decent people like you and me." JOHNSON (smiling). "And we ashamed of him."

They were quite frank and easy. Johnson told the story of his asking Mrs. Macaulay to allow her footman to sit down with them, to prove the ridiculousness of the argument for the equality of mankind; and he said to me afterwards, with a nod of satisfaction, "You saw Mr. Wilkes acquiesced." * * *

This record, though by no means so perfect as I could wish, will serve to give a notion of a very curious interview, which was not only pleasing at the time, but had the agreeable and benignant effect of reconciling any animosity and sweetening any acidity, which in the various bustle of political contest, had been produced in the minds of two men, who, though widely different, had so many things in common—classical learning, modern literature, wit, and humor, and ready repartee—that it would have been much to be regretted if they had been forever at a distance from each other.

Mr. Burke gave me much credit for this successful "negotiation"; and pleasantly said that there was nothing to equal it in the whole history of the *Corps Diplomatique.* * * *

[Dread of Solitude]

[*1777*] I talked to him of misery being "the doom of man" in this life, as displayed in his *Vanity of Human Wishes.* Yet I observed that things were done upon the supposition of happiness; grand houses were built, fine gardens were made, splendid places of public amusement were contrived, and crowded with company. JOHNSON. "Alas, Sir, these are all only struggles for happiness. When I first entered Ranelagh,[2] it gave an expansion and gay sensation to my mind, such as I never experienced anywhere else. But, as Xerxes wept when he viewed his immense army, and considered that not one of that great multitude would be alive a hundred years afterwards, so it went to my heart to consider that there was not one in all that brilliant circle that was not afraid to go home and think; but that the thoughts of each individual there, would be distressing when alone." * * *

["A Bottom of Good Sense." Bet Flint. "Clear Your Mind of Cant"]

[*1781*] Talking of a very respectable author, he told us a curious circumstance in his life, which was that he had married a printer's devil.[3] REYNOLDS. "A printer's devil, Sir! Why, I thought a printer's devil was a creature with a black face and in rags." JOHNSON. "Yes, Sir. But I

2. Pleasure gardens in Chelsea, where concerts were held, fireworks displayed, food and drink sold. 3. Apprentice in a print shop.

suppose, he had her face washed, and put clean clothes on her." Then looking very serious, and very earnest: "And she did not disgrace him; the woman had a bottom of good sense." The word *bottom* thus introduced was so ludicrous when contrasted with his gravity, that most of us could not forbear tittering and laughing; though I recollect that the Bishop of Killaloe kept his countenance with perfect steadiness, while Miss Hannah More[4] slyly hid her face behind a lady's back who sat on the same settee with her. His pride could not bear that any expression of his should excite ridicule, when he did not intend it; he therefore resolved to assume and exercise despotic power, glanced sternly around, and called out in a strong tone, "Where's the merriment?" Then collecting himself, and looking awful, to make us feel how he could impose restraint, and as it were searching his mind for a still more ludicrous word, he slowly pronounced, "I say the *woman* was *fundamentally* sensible"; as if he had said, "hear this now, and laugh if you dare." We all sat composed as at a funeral. * * *

He gave us an entertaining account of Bet Flint, a woman of the town, who, with some eccentric talents and much effrontery, forced herself upon his acquaintance. "Bet," said he, "wrote her own Life in verse, which she brought to me, wishing that I would furnish her with a Preface to it" (laughing). "I used to say of her that she was generally slut and drunkard; occasionally, whore and thief. She had, however, genteel lodgings, a spinnet on which she played, and a boy that walked before her chair. Poor Bet was taken up on a charge of stealing a counterpane, and tried at the Old Bailey. Chief Justice ———, who loved a wench, summed up favorably, and she was acquitted. After which Bet said, with a gay and satisfied air, 'Now that the counterpane is *my own*, I shall make a petticoat of it.' " * * *

[1783] I have no minute of any interview with Johnson till Thursday, May 15, when I find what follows: BOSWELL. "I wish much to be in Parliament, Sir." JOHNSON. "Why, Sir, unless you come resolved to support any administration, you would be the worse for being in Parliament, because you would be obliged to live more expensively." BOSWELL. "Perhaps, Sir, I should be the less happy for being in Parliament. I never would sell my vote, and I should be vexed if things went wrong." JOHNSON. "That's cant,[5] Sir. It would not vex you more in the house than in the gallery: public affairs vex no man." BOSWELL. "Have not they vexed yourself a little, Sir? Have not you been vexed by all the turbulence of this reign, and by that absurd vote of the House of Commons, 'That the influence of the Crown has increased, is increasing, and ought to be diminished?' " JOHNSON. "Sir, I have never slept an hour less, nor eat an ounce less meat. I would have knocked the factious dogs on the head, to be sure; but I was not *vexed*." BOSWELL. "I declare, Sir, upon my honor, I did imagine I was vexed, and took a pride in it; but it *was*,

---

4. Hannah More (1745–1833), blue-stocking and religious writer, one of the promoters of the Sunday School movement.

5. "A whining pretension to goodness in formal and affected terms" (Johnson's *Dictionary*).

perhaps, cant; for I own I neither ate less, nor slept less." JOHNSON. "My dear friend, clear your *mind* of cant. You may *talk* as other people do: you may say to a man, 'Sir, I am your most humble servant.' You are *not* his most humble servant. You may say, 'These are bad times; it is a melancholy thing to be reserved to such times.' You don't mind the times. You tell a man, 'I am sorry you had such bad weather the last day of your journey, and were so much wet.' You don't care sixpence whether he is wet or dry. You may *talk* in this manner; it is a mode of talking in society: but don't *think* foolishly." * * *

[*Johnson Prepares for Death*]

My anxious apprehensions at parting with him this year proved to be but too well founded; for not long afterwards he had a dreadful stroke of the palsy, of which there are very full and accurate accounts in letters written by himself, to show with what composure of mind, and resignation to the Divine Will, his steady piety enabled him to behave. * * * Two days after he wrote thus to Mrs. Thrale:

"On Monday, the 16th, I sat for my picture, and walked a considerable way with little inconvenience. In the afternoon and evening I felt myself light and easy, and began to plan schemes of life. Thus I went to bed, and in a short time waked and sat up, as has been long my custom, when I felt a confusion and indistinctness in my head, which lasted, I suppose, about half a minute. I was alarmed, and prayed God that however he might afflict my body, he would spare my understanding. This prayer, that I might try the integrity of my faculties, I made in Latin verse. The lines were not very good, but I knew them not to be very good: I made them easily, and concluded myself to be unimpaired in my faculties.

"Soon after I perceived that I had suffered a paralytic stroke, and that my speech was taken from me. I had no pain, and so little dejection in this dreadful state, that I wondered at my own apathy, and considered that perhaps death itself, when it should come, would excite less horror than seems now to attend it.

"In order to rouse the vocal organs, I took two drams. Wine has been celebrated for the production of eloquence. I put myself into violent motion, and I think repeated it; but all was vain. I then went to bed and strange as it may seem, I think slept. When I saw light, it was time to contrive what I should do. Though God stopped my speech, he left me my hand; I enjoyed a mercy which was not granted to my dear friend Lawrence,[6] who now perhaps overlooks me as I am writing, and rejoices that I have what he wanted. My first note was necessarily to my servant, who came in talking, and

6. Dr. Thomas Lawrence, president of the Royal College of Physicians and Johnson's own doctor, had died paralyzed shortly before this was written.

could not immediately comprehend why he should read what I put into his hands.

"I then wrote a card to Mr. Allen,[7] that I might have a discreet friend at hand, to act as occasion should require. In penning this note, I had some difficulty; my hand, I knew not how nor why, made wrong letters. I then wrote to Dr. Taylor to come to me, and bring Dr. Heberden; and I sent to Dr. Brocklesby, who is my neighbor.[8] My physicians are very friendly, and give me great hopes; but you may imagine my situation. I have so far recovered my vocal powers as to repeat the Lord's Prayer with no very imperfect articulation. My memory, I hope, yet remains as it was; but such an attack produces solicitude for the safety of every faculty." * * *

[1784] To Mr. Henry White, a young clergyman, with whom he now formed an intimacy, so as to talk to him with great freedom, he mentioned that he could not in general accuse himself of having been an undutiful son. "Once, indeed," said he, "I was disobedient; I refused to attend my father to Uttoxeter market. Pride was the source of that refusal, and the remembrance of it was painful. A few years ago, I desired to atone for this fault; I went to Uttoxeter in very bad weather, and stood for a considerable time bareheaded in the rain, on the spot where my father's stall used to stand. In contrition I stood, and I hope the penance was expiatory."

"I told him," says Miss Seward,[9] "in one of my latest visits to him, of a wonderful learned pig, which I had seen at Nottingham; and which did all that we have observed exhibited by dogs and horses. The subject amused him. 'Then,' said he, 'the pigs are a race unjustly calumniated. *Pig* has, it seems, not been wanting to *man*, but *man* to *pig*. We do not allow *time* for his education, we kill him at a year old.' Mr. Henry White, who was present, observed that if this instance had happened in or before Pope's time, he would not have been justified in instancing the swine as the lowest degree of groveling instinct.[1] Dr. Johnson seemed pleased with the observation, while the person who made it proceeded to remark that great torture must have been employed, ere the indocility of the animal could have been subdued. 'Certainly,' said the Doctor; 'but,' turning to me, 'how old is your pig?' I told him, three years old. 'Then,' said he, 'the pig has no cause to complain; he would have been killed the first year if he had not been *educated*, and protracted existence is a good recompense for very considerable degrees of torture.' "

[Johnson Faces Death]

As Johnson had now very faint hopes of recovery, and as Mrs. Thrale was no longer devoted to him, it might have been supposed that he

7. Edmund Allen, a printer, Johnson's landlord and neighbor.
8. These two physicians attended Johnson on his deathbed.
9. Anna Seward, "the Swan of Lichfield," a poet.
1. *Essay on Man* 1.221.

would naturally have chosen to remain in the comfortable house of his beloved wife's daughter,[2] and end his life where he began it. But there was in him an animated and lofty spirit, and however complicated diseases might depress ordinary mortals, all who saw him, beheld and acknowledged the *invictum animum Catonis*.[3] Such was his intellectual ardor even at this time that he said to one friend, "Sir, I look upon every day to be lost, in which I do not make a new acquaintance"; and to another, when talking of his illness, "I will be conquered; I will not capitulate." And such was his love of London, so high a relish had he of its magnificent extent, and variety of intellectual entertainment, that he languished when absent from it, his mind having become quite luxurious from the long habit of enjoying the metropolis; and, therefore, although at Lichfield, surrounded with friends, who loved and revered him, and for whom he had a very sincere affection, he still found that such conversation as London affords, could be found nowhere else. These feelings, joined, probably, to some flattering hopes of aid from the eminent physicians and surgeons in London, who kindly and generously attended him without accepting fees, made him resolve to return to the capital. * * * Death had always been to him an object of terror; so that, though by no means happy, he still clung to life with an eagerness at which many have wondered. At any time when he was ill, he was very much pleased to be told that he looked better. An ingenious member of the Eumelian Club[4] informs me that upon one occasion when he said to him that he saw health returning to his cheek, Johnson seized him by the hand and exclaimed, "Sir, you are one of the kindest friends I ever had." * * *

Dr. Heberden, Dr. Brocklesby, Dr. Warren, and Dr. Butter, physicians, generously attended him, without accepting any fees, as did Mr. Cruikshank, surgeon; and all that could be done from professional skill and ability was tried, to prolong a life so truly valuable. He himself, indeed, having, on account of his very bad constitution, been perpetually applying himself to medical inquiries, united his own efforts with those of the gentlemen who attended him; and imagining that the dropsical collection of water which oppressed him might be drawn off by making incisions in his body, he, with his usual resolute defiance of pain, cut deep, when he thought that his surgeon had done it too tenderly.

About eight or ten days before his death, when Dr. Brocklesby paid him his morning visit, he seemed very low and desponding, and said, "I have been as a dying man all night." He then emphatically broke out in the words of Shakespeare:

> "Canst thou not minister to a mind diseased;
> Pluck from the memory a rooted sorrow,
> Raze out the written troubles of the brain,

2. Lucy Porter.
3. "The unconquered soul of Cato." An adaptation of a phrase in Horace's *Odes* 2.1.24.
4. A club to which Boswell and Reynolds belonged.

> And with some sweet oblivious antidote
> Cleanse the stuffed bosom of that perilous stuff
> Which weighs upon the heart?"

To which Dr. Brocklesby readily answered, from the same great poet:

> "Therein the patient
> Must minister to himself."[5]

Johnson expressed himself much satisfied with the application. * * *

Amidst the melancholy clouds which hung over the dying Johnson, his characteristical manner showed itself on different occasions.

When Dr. Warren, in the usual style, hoped that he was better; his answer was, "No, Sir; you cannot conceive with what acceleration I advance towards death."

A man whom he had never seen before was employed one night to sit up with him. Being asked next morning how he liked his attendant, his answer was, "Not at all, Sir: the fellow's an idiot; he is as awkward as a turnspit[6] when first put into the wheel, and as sleepy as a dormouse."

Mr. Windham[7] having placed a pillow conveniently to support him, he thanked him for his kindness, and said, "That will do—all that a pillow can do." * * *

Johnson, with that native fortitude, which, amidst all his bodily distress and mental sufferings, never forsook him, asked Dr. Brocklesby, as a man in whom he had confidence, to tell him plainly whether he could recover. "Give me," said he, "a direct answer." The Doctor having first asked him if he could bear the whole truth, which way soever it might lead, and being answered that he could, declared that, in his opinion, he could not recover without a miracle. "Then," said Johnson, "I will take no more physic, not even my opiates; for I have prayed that I may render up my soul to God unclouded." In this resolution he persevered, and, at the same time, used only the weakest kinds of sustenance. Being pressed by Mr. Windham to take somewhat more generous nourishment, lest too low a diet should have the very effect which he dreaded, by debilitating his mind, he said, "I will take anything but inebriating sustenance."

The Reverend Mr. Strahan,[8] who was the son of his friend, and had been always one of his great favorites, had, during his last illness, the satisfaction of contributing to soothe and comfort him. That gentleman's house, at Islington, of which he is Vicar, afforded Johnson, occasionally and easily, an agreeable change of place and fresh air; and he attended also upon him in town in the discharge of the sacred offices of his profession.

Mr. Strahan has given me the agreeable assurance that, after being in

5. *Macbeth* 5.3.40–46.
6. A dog kept to turn the roasting-spit by running within a tread-wheel connected to it (*NED*).
7. William Windham, one of Johnson's younger

friends, later a Member of Parliament.
8. The Rev. George Strahan (pronounced *Strawn*), who later published Johnson's *Prayers and Meditations*.

much agitation, Johnson became quite composed, and continued so till his death.

Dr. Brocklesby, who will not be suspected of fanaticism, obliged me with the following account:

> "For some time before his death, all his fears were calmed and absorbed by the prevalence of his faith, and his trust in the merits and *propitiation* of Jesus Christ." * * *

Johnson having thus in his mind the true Christian scheme, at once rational and consolatory, uniting justice and mercy in the Divinity, with the improvement of human nature, previous to his receiving the Holy Sacrament in his apartment, composed and fervently uttered this prayer:

> "Almighty and most merciful Father, I am now as to human eyes, it seems, about to commemorate, for the last time, the death of thy Son Jesus Christ, our Saviour and Redeemer. Grant, O Lord, that my whole hope and confidence may be in his merits, and thy mercy; enforce and accept my imperfect repentance; make this commemoration available to the confirmation of my faith, the establishment of my hope, and the enlargement of my charity; and make the death of thy Son Jesus Christ effectual to my redemption. Have mercy upon me, and pardon the multitude of my offenses. Bless my friends; have mercy upon all men. Support me, by thy Holy Spirit, in the days of weakness, and at the hour of death; and receive me, at my death, to everlasting happiness, for the sake of Jesus Christ. Amen."

Having * * * made his will on the 8th and 9th of December, and settled all his worldly affairs, he languished till Monday, the 13th of that month, when he expired, about seven o'clock in the evening, with so little apparent pain that his attendants hardly perceived when his dissolution took place. * * *

1791

The Poetry of Sensibility

JAMES THOMSON
1700–1748

Perhaps it is significant that Thomson, the first and most popular nature poet of the century, did not see London until he was twenty-five years old. He grew up in the picturesque border country of Roxboroughshire in Scotland and came to London in 1725, bringing with him, in addition to a memory well stored with images of the external world, the earliest version of his descriptive poem *Winter* in 405 lines of blank verse. Published in 1726, it soon became popular. Thomson went on to publish *Summer* (1727), *Spring* (1728), and *Autumn* in the first collected edition of *The Seasons* (1730), to which he added the *Hymn to the Seasons*. During the next sixteen years, because of constant revisions and additions, the poem grew in length to 5,541 lines. The continued popularity of *The Seasons* is easily demonstrated: between 1730 and 1800 it was printed fifty times; and it continued in favor with readers well into the Romantic period. His last poem, *The Castle of Indolence* (1748), is a witty imitation of Spenser.

The Seasons set the fashion for the poetry of natural description. Generations of readers learned to look at the external world through Thomson's eyes and with the emotions which he had taught them to feel. The *eye* dominates the literature of external nature during the eighteenth century as the *imagination* was to do in the poetry of Wordsworth. And Thomson amazed his readers by his capacity to see: the general effects of light and cloud and foliage or the particular image of a leaf tossed in the gale or the slender feet of a robin or the delicate film of ice at the edge of a brook. He tries to view each season from every perspective, as it might be perceived by a bird in the sky or by the tiniest insect, by God or a painter or Newton (whom Thomson commemorated in a popular ode). As the poem grew, it became an *omnium gatherum* of contemporary ideas and interests: natural history; ideas about the nature of man and society, primitive and civilized; the conception of created nature as a source of religious experience, as an object of religious veneration, as a continuing revelation of the Deity himself.

From The Seasons

From *Autumn*

[EVENING AND NIGHT][1]

The western sun withdraws the shortened day;
And humid evening, gliding o'er the sky,
In her chill progress, to the ground condensed
The vapors throws. Where creeping waters ooze,   1085
Where marshes stagnate, and where rivers wind,
Cluster the rolling fogs, and swim along
The dusky-mantled lawn. Meanwhile the moon,
Full-orbed and breaking through the scattered clouds,
Shows her broad visage in the crimsoned east.   1090
Turned to the sun direct, her spotted disk
(Where mountains rise, umbrageous dales descend,
And caverns deep, as optic tube[2] descries)
A smaller earth, gives all his blaze again,
Void of its flame, and sheds a softer day.   1095
Now through the passing cloud she seems to stoop,
Now up the pure cerulean rides sublime.
Wide the pale deluge[3] floats, and streaming mild
O'er the skied[4] mountain to the shadowy vale,
While rocks and floods reflect the quivering gleam,   1100
The whole air whitens with a boundless tide
Of silver radiance trembling round the world.

 But when, half blotted from the sky, her light
Fainting, permits the starry fires to burn
With keener luster through the depth of heaven;   1105
Or quite extinct her deadened orb appears,
And scarce appears, of sickly beamless white;
Oft in this season, silent from the north
A blaze of meteors[5] shoots—ensweeping first
The lower skies, they all at once converge   1110
High to the crown[6] of heaven, and, all at once
Relapsing quick, as quickly reascend,
And mix and thwart,[7] extinguish and renew,
All ether coursing[8] in a maze of light.

 From look to look, contagious through the crowd,   1115
The panic runs, and into wondrous shapes

---

1. This passage, like many in *The Seasons*, went through extensive revisions. The opening lines on the harvest moon shining through fog (1082–1102) originally belonged to *Winter*; the descriptions of the aurora borealis (1108–37) and wildfire (1150–64) first appeared in *Summer*. Scientific and visionary, divine and human perspectives are contrasted; and join together in an intricate harmony.
2. Telescope. Observation of the moon had revealed shadows ("umbrageous dales"), hence an irregular surface.
3. I.e., the moonlight.
4. I.e., seeming to touch the sky.
5. Not meteors as we think of them, but the aurora borealis or Northern Lights (multicolored, streaming pulses of light in the upper atmosphere).
6. The corona or central ring of the aurora.
7. Cross.
8. Running through all the upper sky.

The appearance throws—armies in meet[9] array,
Thronged with aerial spears and steeds of fire;
Till, the long lines of full-extended war
In bleeding fight commixed, the sanguine flood   1120
Rolls a broad slaughter o'er the plains of heaven.
As thus they scan the visionary scene,
On all sides swells the superstitious din,
Incontinent; and busy frenzy talks
Of blood and battle; cities overturned,   1125
And late at night in swallowing earthquake sunk,
Or hideous wrapped in fierce ascending flame;
Of sallow famine, inundation, storm;
Of pestilence, and every great distress;
Empires subversed,[1] when ruling fate has struck   1130
The unalterable hour; even nature's self
Is deemed to totter on the brink of time.
Not so the man of philosophic eye
And inspect sage:[2] the waving brightness he
Curious surveys, inquisitive to know   1135
The causes and materials, yet unfixed,[3]
Of this appearance beautiful and new.

   Now black and deep the night begins to fall,
A shade immense! Sunk in the quenching gloom,
Magnificent and vast, are heaven and earth.   1140
Order confounded lies, all beauty void,
Distinction lost, and gay variety
One universal blot—such the fair power
Of light to kindle and create the whole.
Drear is the state of the benighted wretch   1145
Who then bewildered wanders through the dark
Full of pale fancies and chimeras[4] huge;
Nor visited by one directive ray
From cottage streaming or from airy hall.
Perhaps, impatient as he stumbles on,   1150
Struck from the root of slimy rushes, blue
The wildfire[5] scatters round, or, gathered, trails
A length of flame deceitful o'er the moss;
Whither decoyed by the fantastic blaze,
Now lost and now renewed, he sinks absorbed,   1155
Rider and horse, amid the miry gulf—
While still, from day to day, his pining wife
And plaintive children his return await,
In wild conjecture lost. At other times,
Sent by the better genius of the night,   1160

Innoxious,[6] gleaming on the horse's mane,
The meteor sits, and shows the narrow path
That winding leads through pits of death, or else
Instructs him how to take the dangerous ford.

The lengthened night elapsed, the morning shines　　　1165
Serene, in all her dewy beauty bright,
Unfolding fair the last autumnal day.
And now the mounting sun dispels the fog;
The rigid hoarfrost melts before his beam;
And, hung on every spray, on every blade　　　1170
Of grass, the myriad dewdrops twinkle round.

　　　　　　　　　　　　　　　　　1730

Ode: Rule, Britannia[1]

1

When *Britain* first, at heaven's command,
　　Arose from out the azure main;[2]
This was the charter of the land,
　　And guardian angels sung *this* strain:
　　　　"Rule, *Britannia*, rule the waves;　　　5
　　　　Britons never will be slaves."

2

The nations, not so blest as thee,
　　Must, in their turns, to tyrants fall:
While thou shalt flourish great and free,
　　The dread and envy of them all.　　　10
　　　　"Rule," etc.

3

Still more majestic shalt thou rise,
　　More dreadful, from each foreign stroke:
As the loud blast that tears the skies,
　　Serves but to root thy native oak.　　　15
　　　　"Rule," etc.

4

Thee haughty tyrants ne'er shall tame:
　　All their attempts to bend thee down,
Will but arouse thy generous flame;
　　But work their woe, and thy renown.　　　20
　　　　"Rule," etc.

5

To thee belongs the rural reign;
　　Thy cities shall with commerce shine:

---

6. Harmless. "The meteor" is the *ignis lambens* or St. Elmo's Fire, a halo of light that shines on the tips of certain objects during electrical storms.
1. This famous patriotic song, set to music by Thomas Arne, was composed for *Alfred* (1740), a masque in honor of the Prince of Wales. It was originally sung by an actor dressed as an ancient bard, accompanied by a British harp.
2. The open ocean.

All thine shall be the subject main,
　　And every shore it circles thine.   25
　　　　"Rule," etc.

6

The Muses, still[3] with freedom found,
　　Shall to thy happy coast repair:
Blest isle! with matchless beauty crowned,
　　And manly hearts to guard the fair.   30
　　　　"Rule, *Britannia*, rule the waves;
　　　　Britons never will be slaves."

1740   1745–46

3. Always.

THOMAS GRAY
1716–1771

The man who wrote the English poem best known and most loved by those whom Johnson called "the common reader" was oddly enough a scholarly recluse who lived the quiet life of a university professor in the stagnant atmosphere of mid-eighteenth-century Cambridge, where toward the end of his life he held the professorship of modern history without feeling called upon to give a single lecture. He was educated at Eton College, where he made his first intimate friends—Richard West, Thomas Ashton, and Horace Walpole, the son of the prime minister. After a little over four years at Cambridge he left without a degree in order to make the grand tour of France and Italy as the guest of his friend Walpole. The death of West in 1742 was a depressing event for Gray, who, having quarreled with Walpole, felt keenly the loss of this gifted and congenial friend. The Eton *Ode* and possibly some of the stanzas of the *Elegy Written in a Country Churchyard* are associated with memories of West.

After 1742 Gray returned to Cambridge, pursuing his studies and indulging his tastes. He was learned in the classics and modern literatures as well as history, and his curiosity led him to explore the then little-known fields of pre-Elizabethan poetry and old Welsh and Norse literature. He seldom left Cambridge except to read in the newly opened British Museum or to go in the summer to the Lake District or to Scotland in search of the sublime and beautiful in nature. He wrote little, for he worked slowly and carefully, fastidiously seeking perfection of form and phrase. His early poetry is a carefully impersonal expression of his own somewhat melancholy temperament: the solitary, brooding speaker of the Eton *Ode* and the *Elegy* is a dramatic projection of Gray himself. The later poems—the two grandiloquent Pindaric odes, *The Progress of Poesy* and *The Bard* (1757), and the translations from Welsh and Norse poetry—are accomplished literary exercises. The living Gray is to be sought in his correspondence, where his genial humor, shy affection, and wide intellectual interests are revealed in some of the most delightful letters of an age that made letter writing into an art.

Though Gray never knew Collins and had no association with the Wartons in the 1740s, he shared their interests and many of their tastes, especially their fondness for Spenser and the early Milton. The melancholy of Collins' *Ode to Evening* is that of the opening stanzas of the *Elegy*, and in both poems mood and landscape mutually sustain each other. Gray joined his contemporaries in the search for a new style, at once intimate and prophetic. Yet he wrote often in a highly artificial diction and a distorted word order (see the first four stanzas of the Eton *Ode*, for example), for he held that "the language of the age is never the language of poetry," a heresy that earned him the harsh criticism of Wordsworth in his Preface to *Lyrical Ballads*.

The *Elegy* stands alone in Gray's work: it is his one poem that belongs to world literature. It speaks to our common humanity through an art so subtle that one can know the poem for many years before becoming aware of its scores of echoes from other poems, its complex organization, and its balance of Latinate phrases with living English speech. If to express the universal is to be classic, then the *Elegy* is one of our true classics. Samuel Johnson, no friend of Gray's poetry in general, long ago said the final word on this aspect of the poem:

> The Churchyard abounds with images which find a mirror in every mind, and with sentiments to which every bosom returns an echo. The four stanzas beginning "Yet even these bones" are to me original: I have never seen the notions in any other place; yet he that reads them here, persuades himself that he has always felt them. Had Gray written often thus, it had been vain to blame, and useless to praise him.

Ode on a Distant Prospect of Eton College

Anthrōpos ikanē prophasis eis tò dustukheīn.[1]

MENANDER

Ye distant spires, ye antique towers,
    That crown the watery glade,
Where grateful Science[2] still adores
    Her Henry's holy shade;[3]
And ye, that from the stately brow   5
Of Windsor's heights the expanse below
    Of grove, of lawn, of mead survey,
Whose turf, whose shade, whose flowers among
Wanders the hoary Thames along
    His silver-winding way.   10

Ah happy hills, ah pleasing shade,
    Ah fields beloved in vain,
Where once my careless childhood strayed,

---

1. "I am a man: sufficient reason for being miserable."
2. Learning.
3. Henry VI founded Eton in 1440.

A stranger yet to pain!
I feel the gales, that from ye blow,   15
A momentary bliss bestow,
    As waving fresh their gladsome wing,
My weary soul they seem to soothe,
And, redolent of joy and youth,
    To breathe a second spring.   20

Say, Father Thames, for thou hast seen
    Full many a sprightly race
Disporting on thy margent green
    The paths of pleasure trace,
Who foremost now delight to cleave   25
With pliant arm thy glassy wave?
    The captive linnet which enthrall?[4]
What idle progeny succeed[5]
To chase the rolling circle's speed,
    Or urge the flying ball?   30

While some on earnest business bent
    Their murmuring labors ply
'Gainst graver hours, that bring constraint
    To sweeten liberty:
Some bold adventurers disdain   35
The limits of their little reign,
    And unknown regions dare descry:
Still as they run they look behind,
They hear a voice in every wind,
    And snatch a fearful joy.   40

Gay hope is theirs by fancy fed,
    Less pleasing when possessed;
The tear forgot as soon as shed,
    The sunshine of the breast:
Theirs buxom health of rosy hue,   45
Wild wit, invention ever new,
    And lively cheer of vigor born;
The thoughtless day, the easy night,
The spirits pure, the slumbers light,
    That fly the approach of morn.   50

Alas, regardless of their doom,
    The little victims play!
No sense have they of ills to come,
    Nor care beyond today.
Yet see how all around 'em wait   55
The ministers of human fate,

4. Make prisoner.
5. I.e., follow in succession Gray's generation; "rolling circle": a hoop.

And black Misfortune's baleful train!
Ah, show them where in ambush stand
To seize their prey the murderous band!
   Ah, tell them they are men!   60

These shall the fury Passions tear,
   The vultures of the mind,
Disdainful Anger, pallid Fear,
   And Shame that skulks behind;
Or pining Love shall waste their youth,   65
Or Jealousy with rankling tooth,
   That inly gnaws the secret heart,
And Envy wan, and faded Care,
Grim-visaged comfortless Despair,
   And Sorrow's piercing dart.   70

Ambition this shall tempt to rise,
   Then whirl the wretch from high,
To bitter Scorn a sacrifice,
   And grinning Infamy.
The stings of Falsehood those shall try,   75
And hard Unkindness' altered eye,
   That mocks the tear it forced to flow;
And keen Remorse with blood defiled,
And moody Madness laughing wild
   Amid severest woe.   80

Lo, in the vale of years beneath
   A grisly troop are seen,
The painful family of Death,
   More hideous than their queen:
This racks the joints, this fires the veins,   85
That every laboring sinew strains,
   Those in the deeper vitals rage:
Lo, Poverty, to fill the band,
That numbs the soul with icy hand,
   And slow-consuming Age.   90

To each his sufferings: all are men,
   Condemned alike to groan;
The tender for another's pain,
   The unfeeling for his own.
Yet ah! why should they know their fate?   95
Since sorrow never comes too late,
   And happiness too swiftly flies.
Thought would destroy their paradise.
No more; where ignorance is bliss,
   'Tis folly to be wise.   100

1742   1747

Ode on the Death of a Favorite Cat[1]

Drowned in a Tub of Goldfishes

'Twas on a lofty vase's side,
Where China's gayest art had dyed
   The azure flowers that blow;[2]
Demurest of the tabby kind,
The pensive Selima reclined,   5
   Gazed on the lake below.

Her conscious tail her joy declared;
The fair round face, the snowy beard,
   The velvet of her paws,
Her coat, that with the tortoise vies,   10
Her ears of jet, and emerald eyes,
   She saw; and purred applause.

Still had she gazed; but 'midst the tide
Two angel forms were seen to glide,
   The genii of the stream: 15
Their scaly armor's Tyrian[3] hue
Through richest purple to the view
   Betrayed a golden gleam.

The hapless nymph with wonder saw:
A whisker first and then a claw,   20
   With many an ardent wish,
She stretched in vain to reach the prize.
What female heart can gold despise?
   What cat's averse to fish?

Presumptuous maid! with looks intent   25
Again she stretched, again she bent,
   Nor knew the gulf between.
(Malignant Fate sat by and smiled)
The slippery verge her feet beguiled,
   She tumbled headlong in.   30

Eight times emerging from the flood
She mewed to every watery god,
   Some speedy aid to send.
No dolphin came, no nereid[4] stirred:
Nor cruel Tom, nor Susan heard.   35
   A favorite has no friend!

1. Selima, one of Horace Walpole's cats, had
recently drowned in a china cistern. Gray wrote
this memorial at Walpole's request.
2. Bloom.

3. Purple.
4. Sea nymph. "Tom" and "Susan" are servants'
names.

From hence, ye beauties, undeceived,
Know, one false step is ne'er retrieved,
　　And be with caution bold.
Not all that tempts your wandering eyes　　　　40
And heedless hearts is lawful prize;
　　Nor all that glisters gold.

1747　　　　　　　　　　　　　　　　　　　1748

Elegy Written in a Country Churchyard

The curfew tolls the knell of parting day,
　　The lowing herd wind slowly o'er the lea,
The plowman homeward plods his weary way,
　　And leaves the world to darkness and to me.

Now fades the glimmering landscape on the sight,　　　5
　　And all the air a solemn stillness holds,
Save where the beetle wheels his droning flight,
　　And drowsy tinklings lull the distant folds;

Save that from yonder ivy-mantled tower
　　The moping owl does to the moon complain　　　10
Of such, as wandering near her secret bower,
　　Molest her ancient solitary reign.

Beneath those rugged elms, that yew tree's shade,
　　Where heaves the turf in many a moldering heap,
Each in his narrow cell forever laid,　　　　　　　15
　　The rude[1] forefathers of the hamlet sleep.

The breezy call of incense-breathing Morn,
　　The swallow twittering from the straw-built shed,
The cock's shrill clarion, or the echoing horn,[2]
　　No more shall rouse them from their lowly bed.　　　20

For them no more the blazing hearth shall burn,
　　Or busy housewife ply her evening care;
No children run to lisp their sire's return,
　　Or climb his knees the envied kiss to share.

Oft did the harvest to their sickle yield,　　　　　25
　　Their furrow oft the stubborn glebe[3] has broke;
How jocund did they drive their team afield!
　　How bowed the woods beneath their sturdy stroke!

1. Untaught.　　　　　　　　　　　　3. Soil, turf.
2. The hunter's horn.

Let not Ambition mock their useful toil,
    Their homely joys, and destiny obscure;   30
Nor Grandeur hear with a disdainful smile
    The short and simple annals of the poor.

The boast of heraldry,[4] the pomp of power,
    And all that beauty, all that wealth e'er gave,
Awaits alike the inevitable hour.   35
    The paths of glory lead but to the grave.

Nor you, ye proud, impute to these the fault,
    If Memory o'er their tomb no trophies[5] raise,
Where through the long-drawn aisle and fretted[6] vault
    The pealing anthem swells the note of praise.   40

Can storied urn[7] or animated bust
    Back to its mansion call the fleeting breath?
Can Honor's voice provoke[8] the silent dust,
    Or Flattery soothe the dull cold ear of Death?

Perhaps in this neglected spot is laid   45
    Some heart once pregnant with celestial fire;
Hands that the rod of empire might have swayed,
    Or waked to ecstasy the living lyre.

But Knowledge to their eyes her ample page
    Rich with the spoils of time did ne'er unroll;   50
Chill Penury repressed their noble rage,
    And froze the genial current of the soul.

Full many a gem of purest ray serene,
    The dark unfathomed caves of ocean bear:
Full many a flower is born to blush unseen,   55
    And waste its sweetness on the desert air.

Some village Hampden,[9] that with dauntless breast
    The little tyrant of his fields withstood;
Some mute inglorious Milton here may rest,
    Some Cromwell guiltless of his country's blood.   60

The applause of listening senates to command,
    The threats of pain and ruin to despise,

---

4. Noble birth.
5. An ornamental or symbolic group of figures depicting the achievements of the dead man.
6. Decorated with intersecting lines in relief.
7. A funeral urn with an epitaph inscribed on it; "animated": lifelike.
8. Call forth.

9. John Hampden (1594–1643), who, both as a private citizen and as a Member of Parliament, zealously defended the rights of the people against the autocratic policies of Charles I. A gallant soldier, he was mortally wounded in a skirmish near Oxford.

To scatter plenty o'er a smiling land,
     And read their history in a nation's eyes,

Their lot forbade: nor circumscribed alone   65
     Their growing virtues, but their crimes confined;
Forbade to wade through slaughter to a throne,
     And shut the gates of mercy on mankind,

The struggling pangs of conscious truth to hide,
     To quench the blushes of ingenuous shame,   70
Or heap the shrine of Luxury and Pride
     With incense kindled at the Muse's flame.

Far from the madding crowd's ignoble strife,
     Their sober wishes never learned to stray;
Along the cool sequestered vale of life   75
     They kept the noiseless tenor of their way.

Yet even these bones from insult to protect
     Some frail memorial still erected nigh,
With uncouth rhymes and shapeless sculpture decked,[1]
     Implores the passing tribute of a sigh.   80

Their name, their years, spelt by the unlettered Muse,
     The place of fame and elegy supply:
And many a holy text around she strews,
     That teach the rustic moralist to die.

For who to dumb Forgetfulness a prey,   85
     This pleasing anxious being e'er resigned,
Left the warm precincts of the cheerful day,
     Nor cast one longing lingering look behind?

On some fond breast the parting soul relies,
     Some pious drops the closing eye requires;   90
Even from the tomb the voice of Nature cries,
     Even in our ashes live their wonted fires.

For thee, who mindful of the unhonored dead
     Dost in these lines their artless tale relate;
If chance, by lonely contemplation led,   95
     Some kindred spirit shall inquire thy fate,

Haply some hoary-headed swain may say,
     "Oft have we seen him at the peep of dawn
Brushing with hasty steps the dews away
     To meet the sun upon the upland lawn.   100

1. Cf. "the storied urn or animated bust" dedicated inside the church to "the proud" (line 41).

"There at the foot of yonder nodding beech
    That wreathes its old fantastic roots so high,
His listless length at noontide would he stretch,
    And pore upon the brook that babbles by.

"Hard by yon wood, now smiling as in scorn,   105
    Muttering his wayward fancies he would rove,
Now drooping, woeful wan, like one forlorn,
    Or crazed with care, or crossed in hopeless love.

"One morn I missed him on the customed hill,
    Along the heath and near his favorite tree;   110
Another came; nor yet beside the rill,
    Nor up the lawn, nor at the wood was he;

"The next with dirges due in sad array
    Slow through the churchway path we saw him borne.
Approach and read (for thou canst read) the lay,   115
    Graved on the stone beneath yon aged thorn."

The Epitaph

Here rests his head upon the lap of Earth
    A youth to Fortune and to Fame unknown.
Fair Science[2] frowned not on his humble birth,
    And Melancholy marked him for her own.   120

Large was his bounty, and his soul sincere,
    Heaven did a recompense as largely send:
He gave to Misery all he had, a tear,
    He gained from Heaven ('twas all he wished) a friend.

No farther seek his merits to disclose,   125
    Or draw his frailties from their dread abode
(There they alike in trembling hope repose),
    The bosom of his Father and his God.

ca. 1742–50   1751

2. Learning.

WILLIAM COLLINS

1721–1759

William Collins was born at Chichester and was educated at Winchester
and Oxford. Coming up to London from the university, he tried to establish
himself as an author, but he was given rather to planning than to writing

books. He came to know Samuel Johnson, who later remembered him affectionately as a man of learning who "loved fairies, genii, giants, and monsters" and who "delighted to rove through the meanders of enchantment." In 1746 Collins published his *Odes on Several Descriptive and Allegorical Subjects*, his part in an undertaking, with his friend Joseph Warton, to create a new poetry, more lyrical and fanciful than that of Pope's generation. Collins's *Odes* are addressed to personified abstractions (Fear, Pity, the Passions), which are imagined as vivid presences that overwhelm the poet as he calls them to life. In form these poems represent a new version of the "great" or Cowleian ode (see notes to Jonson's *Ode to Cary and Morison* and to Dryden's *Anne Killigrew*); Collins returns to Pindar's regularity of structure. But the originality of the *Odes* lies in their intensity of vision, which risks obscurity in quest of the sublime.

Because of this obscurity the volume was not much liked. Inheriting some money, the poet traveled for a while, but fits of depression gradually deepened into total debility. He spent his last years in Chichester, forgotten by all but a small circle of loyal friends. As the century progressed he gained in reputation. The Romantics admired his poems and felt akin to him as they did to Thomas Chatterton and Robert Burns. The *Ode to Evening*, which combines a chaste and cool classicism with a delicate feeling for landscape and mood, is one of the delightful poems of the century.

Ode Written in the Beginning of the Year 1746

How sleep the brave[1] who sink to rest
By all their country's wishes blest!
When Spring, with dewy fingers cold,
Returns to deck their hallowed mold,
She there shall dress a sweeter sod　　　　　　　　5
Than Fancy's feet have ever trod.

By fairy hands their knell is rung,
By forms unseen their dirge is sung;
There Honor comes, a pilgrim gray,
To bless the turf that wraps their clay,　　　　　　10
And Freedom shall awhile repair,
To dwell a weeping hermit there!

1746

Ode on the Poetical Character[1]

Strophe

As once, if not with light regard,
I read aright that gifted bard

---

1. Collins is presumably thinking of those who lost their lives defending England in 1745, when the Scotch Jacobites, led by Bonnie Prince Charlie,

penetrated to within 127 miles of London.
1. This ode, long held in comparative disregard, has more recently been elevated in critical esti-

(Him whose school above the rest
His loveliest Elfin Queen has blest),[2]
One, only one, unrivaled fair,   5
Might hope the magic girdle wear,
At solemn tourney hung on high,
The wish of each love-darting eye;[3]
Lo! to each other nymph in turn applied,
    As if, in air unseen, some hovering hand,   10
Some chaste and angel-friend to virgin-fame,
    With whispered spell had burst the starting band,
It left unblest her loathed dishonored side;
    Happier, hopeless fair, if never
    Her baffled hand with vain endeavor   15
Had touched that fatal zone to her denied!
Young Fancy thus, to me divinest name,
    To whom, prepared and bathed in Heaven
    The cest of amplest power is given:
    To few the godlike gift assigns,   20
    To gird their blest, prophetic loins,
And gaze her visions wild, and feel unmixed her flame!

Epode

The band, as fairy legends say,
Was wove on that creating day,
When He,[4] who called with thought to birth   25
Yon tented sky, this laughing earth,
And dressed with springs, and forests tall,
And poured the main engirting all,
Long by the loved Enthusiast[5] wooed,
Himself in some diviner mood,   30
Retiring, sate with her alone,
And placed her on his sapphire throne;
The whiles, the vaulted shrine around,
Seraphic wires were heard to sound,

mation, for it is now seen as an early, dramatic engagement with one of the central concerns of the Romantic Age—the origin and role of the creative imagination and, indeed, of the poet himself. "It is an allegory," A. S. P. Woodhouse tells us, "whose subject is the *creative imagination* and the poet's passionate desire for its power."

In the strophe an analogy is drawn between the *cestus* or girdle of Venus, which only the chaste can wear, and the cest of Fancy, or the creative imagination. In the epode the action of the creation of the world is presented as an act of the divine imagination.

What is especially new, such critics as Harold Bloom and Northrop Frye suggest, is Collins's implication, in the epode, that "a poet is born from the quasi-sexual union of God and imagination," or Fancy (lines 30–40). Such a reading animates

the personifications in a way that we do not encounter again until the work of William Blake. The poet's creative act is divine, analogous to the creation of the world, and he is born of the divine act.

In the antistrophe, Milton is regarded as the type of poet true enough to wear the girdle of Fancy. Collins pictures himself pursuing the "guiding steps" (line 71) of Milton, as of Spenser (in the strophe)—both poet-prophets. He retreats from the elegant school of Waller (and, by implication, that of Pope, as well)—"In vain" (line 72), however, for he lives in an age of sensibility.

2. Edmund Spenser.
3. *Faerie Queene* 4.5 tells of the contest of many beautiful ladies for the girdle of Venus.
4. God, on the day of creation.
5. I.e., Fancy.

Now sublimest triumph swelling,   35
Now on love and mercy dwelling;
And she, from out the veiling cloud,
Breathed her magic notes aloud:
And thou, thou rich-haired Youth of Morn,[6]
And all thy subject life was born!   40
The dangerous Passions kept aloof,
Far from the sainted growing woof:
But near it sate ecstatic Wonder,
Listening the deep applauding thunder:
And Truth, in sunny vest arrayed,   45
By whose the tarsel's[7] eyes were made;
All the shadowy tribes of Mind,
In braided dance their murmurs joined,
And all the bright uncounted Powers
Who feed on Heaven's ambrosial flowers.   50
Where is the bard, whose soul can now
Its high presuming hopes avow?
Where he who thinks, with rapture blind,
This hallow'd work[8] for him designed?

Antistrophe

High on some cliff, to Heaven up-piled,   55
Of rude access, of prospect wild,
Where, tangled round the jealous steep,
Strange shades o'erbrow the valleys deep,
And holy Genii guard the rock,
Its glooms embrown, its springs unlock,   60
While on its rich ambitious head,
An Eden, like his[9] own, lies spread:
I view that oak, the fancied glades among,
By which as Milton lay, his evening ear,
From many a cloud that dropped ethereal dew,   65
Nigh sphered in Heaven its native strains could hear:
On which that ancient trump he reached was hung;
    Thither oft, his glory greeting,
    From Waller's[1] myrtle shades retreating,
With many a vow from Hope's aspiring tongue,   70
My trembling feet his guiding steps pursue;
    In vain—such bliss to one alone,[2]
    Of all the sons of soul was known,
    And Heaven, and Fancy, kindred powers,

---

6. Apollo, god of the sun and of poetry, associated
with the poet himself.
7. The falcon's.
8. The girdle of Fancy.
9. Milton's.

1. Edmund Waller (1606–1687). The myrtle is the
symbol of love poetry, Waller's poetry is thought
of as trivial compared to Milton's grandeur.
2. Milton.

Have now o'erturned the inspiring bowers,   75
Or curtained close such scene from every future view.

1746

Ode to Evening[1]

If aught of oaten stop, or pastoral song,
May hope, chaste Eve, to soothe thy modest ear,
   Like thy own solemn springs,
   Thy springs and dying gales,
O nymph reserved, while now the bright-haired sun   5
Sits in yon western tent, whose cloudy skirts,
   With brede[2] ethereal wove,
   O'erhang his wavy bed:
Now air is hushed, save where the weak-eyed bat,
With short shrill shrieks flits by on leathern wing,   10
   Or where the beetle winds
   His small but sullen horn,
As oft he rises 'midst the twilight path,
Against the pilgrim borne in heedless hum:
   Now teach me, maid composed,   15
   To breathe some softened strain,
Whose numbers, stealing through thy darkening vale,
May not unseemly with its stillness suit,
   As, musing slow, I hail
   Thy genial loved return!   20
For when thy folding-star[3] arising shows
His paly circlet, at his warning lamp
   The fragrant Hours, and elves
   Who slept in flowers the day,
And many a nymph who wreaths her brows with sedge,   25
And sheds the freshening dew, and, lovelier still,
   The pensive Pleasures sweet,
   Prepare thy shadowy car.
Then lead, calm vot'ress, where some sheety lake
Cheers the lone heath, or some time-hallowed pile   30
   Or upland fallows gray
   Reflect its last cool gleam.
But when chill blustering winds, or driving rain,
Forbid my willing feet, be mine the hut
   That from the mountain's side   35
   Views wilds, and swelling floods,

---

1. Collins borrowed the metrical structure and the rhymeless lines of this ode from Milton's translation of Horace, *Odes* 1.5 (1673). The text printed here is based on the revised version, published in Dodsley's *Miscellany* (1748).
2. Embroidery.
3. The evening star, which signals the hour for herding the sheep into the sheepfold.

And hamlets brown, and dim-discovered spires,
And hears their simple bell, and marks o'er all
    Thy dewy fingers draw
    The gradual dusky veil.   40
While Spring shall pour his showers, as oft he wont,
And bathe thy breathing tresses, meekest Eve;
    While Summer loves to sport
    Beneath thy lingering light;
While sallow Autumn fills thy lap with leaves;   45
Or Winter, yelling through the troublous air,
    Affrights thy shrinking train,
    And rudely rends thy robes;
So long, sure-found beneath the sylvan shed,
Shall Fancy, Friendship, Science, rose-lipped Health,   50
    Thy gentlest influence own,
    And hymn thy favorite name!

1746, 1748

Ode on the Death of Mr. Thomson[1]

1

In yonder grave a Druid[2] lies
    Where slowly winds the stealing wave!
The year's best sweets shall duteous rise
    To deck its poet's sylvan grave![3]

2

In yon deep bed of whispering reeds   5
    His airy harp[4] shall now be laid,
That he, whose heart in sorrow bleeds,
    May love through life the soothing shade.

3

Then maids and youths shall linger here,
    And while its sounds at distance swell,   10
Shall sadly seem in pity's ear
    To hear the woodland pilgrim's knell.

4

Remembrance oft shall haunt the shore
    When Thames in summer wreaths is dressed,
And oft suspend the dashing oar   15
    To bid his gentle spirit rest!

1. James Thomson died in 1748 and was buried in the parish church of Richmond, a village on the Thames near London. Collins memorializes the poet, who was his friend, both by imagining a visit to his grave and by filling his own verses with reminiscences of Thomson's poetry.
2. I.e., Thomson himself. The Druids, an order of priests in ancient Britain, had been idealized by

Thomson as poet-philosophers of nature. Druidic circles like Stonehenge remain standing in England; and Collins's Ode itself might be said to have a circular form (the same beginning and ending).
3. The year pays tribute to Thomson because he wrote The Seasons.
4. Thomson had helped to popularize the Aeolian harp, which is played by the wind.

5

And oft as ease and health retire
    To breezy lawn or forest deep,
The friend shall view yon whitening spire,[5]
    And mid the varied landscape weep.   20

6

But thou, who own'st that earthy bed,
    Ah! what will every dirge avail?
Or tears, which love and pity shed
    That mourn beneath the gliding sail!

7

Yet lives there one, whose heedless eye   25
    Shall scorn thy pale shrine glimmering near?
With him, sweet bard, may fancy die,
    And joy desert the blooming year.

8

But thou, lorn stream, whose sullen tide
    No sedge-crowned sisters[6] now attend,   30
Now waft me from the green hill's side,
    Whose cold turf hides the buried friend!

9

And see, the fairy valleys fade,
    Dun night has veiled the solemn view!
—Yet once again, dear parted shade,   35
    Meek nature's child, again adieu!

10

The genial meads,[7] assigned to bless
    Thy life, shall mourn thy early doom,
Their hinds[8] and shepherd girls shall dress
    With simple hands thy rural tomb.   40

11

Long, long, thy stone and pointed[9] clay
    Shall melt the musing Briton's eyes,
"O! vales and wild woods," shall he say,
    "In yonder grave your Druid lies!"

1749

---

5. Richmond Church, seen from the water.   7. Fostering meadows.
6. Naiads or river nymphs, supposed to have   8. Peasants.
deserted the Thames since Thomson's death.   9. I.e., pointed out to visitors.

CHRISTOPHER SMART

1722–1771

In 1756 Christopher Smart, who had won prizes at Pembroke College,
Cambridge, as a scholar and poet, and was known in London as a wit and

bon vivant, was seized by religious mania: "a preternatural excitement to prayer," according to Mrs. Thrale, "which he held it as a duty not to control or repress." If Smart had been content to pray in private, his life might have ended as happily as it began; but unfortunately for him, he insisted on kneeling down in the streets, in parks, in assembly rooms. He became a public nuisance, and the public took its revenge. For most of the next seven years Smart was confined, first in St. Luke's hospital, then in a private madhouse. Here, severed from his wife, his children, and his friends, he began to write a bold new sort of poetry: vivid, concise, abrupt, syntactically daring. Few of his contemporaries noticed it. After Smart's release from the madhouse (1763) he fell into debt—he had always been profligate—and his *Translation of the Psalms of David* (1765) and *Hymns for the Amusement of Children* (1770) were almost completely ignored. He died, forgotten, in a debtor's prison. But in the nineteenth century his reputation revived, and since the publication of *Jubilate Agno* in 1939 his poems have become newly famous.

The work of Smart's great period (1759–1765) resembles nothing else in English. Its sources lie partly in the classics, especially Horace (whom Smart translated both in verse and prose), but far more in the Old Testament. Above all, the spirit that informs the poetry is praise and celebration, an intense vision of the divine presence shining through ordinary life. Smart believed that the world had been called into being solely to pay homage to its Maker; the function of man, and the poet most of all, was to be "minister of praise at large," to provide a voice of prayer for the whole creation. Thus the hero of his masterpiece, *A Song to David* (1763), is not only King but Psalmist of Israel, the inspired man and poet, possessed by the spirit of the Lord, who orders and blesses everything that exists. Such poets, like the first Creator, strive to construct a microcosm in which every element—word, image, and number—fits into one grand design. The stanzas of *A Song to David* are organized in groups of three and seven (divine numbers), and separate stanzas are devoted to each of David's twelve virtues, the seven days of creation, the ten commandments, the four seasons, the five senses, and finally, in a mighty climax, the five degrees in which David excelled. To critics who accused the poem of incoherence, Smart properly replied that its chief fault, if any, was "the *exact* REGULARITY and METHOD with which it is conducted." At its best, however, the poem transports its reader into that state of adoration "Where ask is have, where seek is find, / Where knock is open wide," a state of true prayer that acknowledges no division between desire and its fulfillment or God and his worshipper.

From Jubilate Agno[1]

[*My Cat Jeoffry*]

For I will consider my Cat Jeoffry.
For he is the servant of the Living God duly and daily serving him.

1. *Jubilate Agno* (*Rejoice in the Lamb*), written a few lines at a time during Smart's confinement in a madhouse from 1759 to 1763, is (1) a record of his daily life and thoughts; (2) the notebook of a scholar, crammed with puns and obscure learning, which sets out elaborate correspondences between the world of the Bible and modern England; (3) a personal Testament or book of worship, antiphonally arranged in lines beginning alternately with *Let* and *For*, which seeks to join the material and spiritual universes in one unending prayer. It has also come to be recognized, since

For at the first glance of the glory of God in the East[2] he worships in his
    way.

For is this done by wreathing his body seven times round with elegant
    quickness.

For then he leaps up to catch the musk, wch is the blessing of God upon
    his prayer.   5

For he rolls upon prank[3] to work it in.

For having done duty and received blessing he begins to consider him-
    self.

For this he performs in ten degrees.

For first he looks upon his fore-paws to see if they are clean.

For secondly he kicks up behind to clear away there.   10

For thirdly he works it upon stretch with the fore-paws extended.

For fourthly he sharpens his paws by wood.

For fifthly he washes himself.

For Sixthly he rolls upon wash.

For Seventhly he fleas himself, that he may not be interrupted upon the
    beat.   15

For Eighthly he rubs himself against a post.

For Ninthly he looks up for his instructions.

For Tenthly he goes in quest of food.

For having consider'd God and himself he will consider his neighbor.

For if he meets another cat he will kiss her in kindness.   20

For when he takes his prey he plays with it to give it a chance.

For one mouse in seven escapes by his dallying.

For when his day's work is done his business more properly begins.

For he keeps the Lord's watch in the night against the adversary.

For he counteracts the powers of darkness by his electrical skin & glaring
    eyes.   25

For he counteracts the Devil, who is death, by brisking about the life.

For in his morning orisons he loves the sun and the sun loves him.

For he is of the tribe of Tiger.

For the Cherub Cat is a term of the Angel Tiger.[4]

For he has the subtlety and hissing of a serpent, which in goodness he
    suppresses.   30

For he will not do destruction if he is well-fed, neither will he spit with-
    out provocation.

For he purrs in thankfulness, when God tells him he's a good Cat.

For he is an instrument for the children to learn benevolence upon.

For every house is incomplete without him & a blessing is lacking in
    the spirit.

For the Lord commanded Moses concerning the cats at the departure of
    the Children of Israel from Egypt.[5]   35

first published in 1939 by W. F. Stead, as a poem—
a poem unique in English for its ecstatic sense of
the presence of the Divine Spirit. The most famous
passage describes Smart's cat Jeoffry, his only companion during the years of confinement: "For I am
possessed of a cat, surpassing in beauty, from whom
I take occasion to bless Almighty God." At once a
real cat, lovingly observed in all its frisks, and visible evidence of the providential plan, Jeoffry celebrates the Maker, as all things do, in his very being.

2. The sunrise.

3. Prankishly.

4. As a cherub is a small angel, so a cat is a small
tiger.

5. No cats are mentioned in the Bible.

For every family had one cat at least in the bag.

For the English Cats are the best in Europe.

For he is the cleanest in the use of his fore-paws of any quadrupede.

For the dexterity of his defence is an instance of the love of God to him
    exceedingly.

For he is the quickest to his mark of any creature.   40

For he is tenacious of his point.

For he is a mixture of gravity and waggery.

For he knows that God is his Saviour.

For there is nothing sweeter than his peace when at rest.

For there is nothing brisker than his life when in motion.   45

For he is of the Lord's poor and so indeed·is he called by benevolence
    perpetually—Poor Jeoffry! poor Jeoffry! the rat has bit thy throat.

For I bless the name of the Lord Jesus that Jeoffry is better.

For the divine spirit comes about his body to sustain it in complete cat.

For his tongue is exceeding pure so that it has in purity what it wants in
    music.

For he is docile and can learn certain things.   50

For he can set up with gravity which is patience upon approbation.

For he can fetch and carry, which is patience in employment.

For he can jump over a stick which is patience upon proof positive.

For he can spraggle upon waggle[6] at the word of command.

For he can jump from an eminence into his master's bosom.   55

For he can catch the cork and toss it again.

For he is hated by the hypocrite and miser.

For the former is afraid of detection.

For the latter refuses the charge.

For he camels his back to bear the first notion of business.   60

For he is good to think on, if a man would express himself neatly.

For he made a great figure in Egypt for his signal services.

For he killed the Icneumon-rat very pernicious by land.[7]

For his ears are so acute that they sting again.

For from this proceeds the passing quickness of his attention.   65

For by stroking of him I have found out electricity.

For I perceived God's light about him both wax and fire.

For the Electrical fire is the spiritual substance, which God sends from
    heaven to sustain the bodies both of man and beast.

For God has blessed him in the variety of his movements.   70

For, though he cannot fly, he is an excellent clamberer.

For his motions upon the face of the earth are more than any other
    quadrupede.

For he can tread to all the measures upon the music.

For he can swim for life.

For he can creep.   75

1759–63   1939

6. He can sprawl when his master waggles a finger
or stick.

7. The Ichneumon, which resembles a weasel, was
venerated and domesticated by the ancient Egyptians.

A Song to David[1]

David the son of Jesse said, and the man who was raised up on high,
the anointed of the God of Jacob, and the sweet psalmist of Israel, said,
"The Spirit of the Lord spake by me, and His Word was in my tongue."
—2 SAMUEL 23.1,2

1

O Thou, that sit'st upon a throne,
With harp of high majestic tone,   [*Invocation*]
    To praise the King of kings;
And voice of heaven-ascending swell,
Which, while its deeper notes excel,   5
    Clear, as a clarion, rings:

2

To bless each valley, grove and coast,
And charm the cherubs to the post
    Of gratitude in throngs;
To keep the days on Zion's mount,   10
And send the year to his account,
    With dances and with songs:

3

O Servant of God's holiest charge,
The minister of praise at large,
    Which thou may'st now receive;   15
From thy blessed mansion hail and hear,
From topmost eminence appear
    To this the wreath I weave.[2]

4

Great, valiant, pious, good, and clean,   [*The excellence and
Sublime, contemplative, serene,   luster of David's char-*   20
    Strong, constant, pleasant, wise!   *acter in twelve points
Bright effluence of exceeding grace;   *of view;*]
Best man!—the swiftness and the race,
    The peril, and the prize!

5

Great—from the luster of his crown,   [*proved from the his-*   25
From Samuel's horn[3] and God's renown,   *tory of his life*]
    Which is the people's voice;
For all the host from rear to van,
Applauded and embraced the man—
    The man of God's own choice.   30

---

1. For the first edition of the poem, Smart supplied a summary of the argument, here reprinted as a running series of marginal glosses.
2. David, a king among men, and now an angel in heaven, serves the King of kings by praising him with music, which keeps the world below in tune;

Smart, in turn, sings the praises of David, the poet's intermediary with God.
3. "Then Samuel took the horn of oil, and anointed him in the midst of his brethren: and the spirit of the Lord came upon David from that day forward" (1 Samuel 16.13).

6

Valiant—the word, and up he rose—
The fight—he triumphed o'er the foes,
        Whom God's just laws abhor;
And armed in gallant faith he took
Against the boaster,[4] from the brook,   35
        The weapons of the war.

7

Pious—magnificent and grand;
'Twas he the famous temple planned:
        (The seraph in his soul)[5]
Foremost to give the Lord his dues,   40
Foremost to bless the welcome news,
        And foremost to condole.

8

Good—from Jehudah's genuine vein,
From God's best nature good in grain,[6]
        His aspect and his heart;   45
To pity, to forgive, to save,
Witness En-gedi's conscious cave,
        And Shimei's blunted dart.[7]

9

Clean—if perpetual prayer be pure,
And love, which could itself inure   50
        To fasting and to fear—
Clean in his gestures, hands, and feet,
To smite the lyre, the dance complete,
        To play the sword and spear.

10

Sublime—invention ever young,   55
Of vast conception, towering tongue
        To God the external theme;
Notes from yon exaltations caught,
Unrivaled royalty of thought,
        O'er meaner strains supreme.   60

11

Contemplative—on God to fix
His musings, and above the six
        The sabbath-day he blessed;
'Twas then his thoughts self-conquest pruned,
And heavenly melancholy tuned,   65
        To bless and bear the rest.

12

Serene—to sow the seeds of peace,
Remembering, when he watched the fleece,

---

4. Goliath, whom David slew with a stone from
the brook.
5. According to 1 Chronicles 28, David's plan for
the Temple in Jerusalem was directly inspired by
the Lord's "seraph" within him.
6. In background and substance; Judah, David's

tribe, was the tribe of kings.
7. In a cave in En-gedi, David spared Saul, who
had wanted to kill him (1 Samuel 24); though Shimei threw stones and curses at him, David later
refused to take his life (2 Samuel 16, 19).

How sweetly Kidron purled[8]—
To further knowledge, silence vice,
    And plant perpetual paradise   70
When God had calmed the world.

13

Strong—in the Lord, who could defy
Satan, and all his powers that lie   75
    In sempiternal night;
And hell, and horror, and despair
Were as the lion and the bear[9]
    To his undaunted might.

14

Constant—in love to God The Truth,
Age, manhood, infancy, and youth—   80
    To Jonathan his friend
Constant, beyond the verge of death;
And Ziba, and Mephibosheth,
    His endless fame attend.[1]

15

Pleasant—and various as the year;   85
Man, soul, and angel, without peer,
    Priest, champion, sage and boy;
In armor, or in ephod[2] clad,
His pomp, his piety was glad;
    Majestic was his joy.   90

16

Wise—in recovery from his fall,
Whence rose his eminence o'er all,
    Of all the most reviled;
The light of Israel in his ways,
Wise are his precepts, prayer and praise,   95
    And counsel to his child.[3]

17

His muse, bright angel of his verse,
Gives balm for all the thorns that pierce,   *[He consecrates his*
    For all the pangs that rage;   *genius for consolation*
Blessed light, still gaining on the gloom,   *and edification]*   100
The more than Michal of his bloom,
    The Abishag of his age.[4]

18

He sung of God—the mighty source   *[The subjects he made*
Of all things—the stupendous force   *choice of—the*
    On which all strength depends;   *Supreme Being;]*   105

8. As a young man, David kept his father's sheep near Kidron, a brook that borders the district of Jerusalem; later, fleeing his own son Absalom, he crossed Kidron into the wilderness.

9. As a shepherd, David slew a lion and a bear with the help of the Lord, as later he slew Goliath (1 Samuel 17).

1. Jonathan's son Mephibosheth was restored to Saul's land by David, and was attended by Saul's servant Ziba.

2. Vestment of a Hebrew priest.

3. The Proverbs and Psalms were supposed to be intended by David for his son Solomon.

4. More than Michal, his first wife, or Abishag, who ministered to him in old age, David's consolation is his muse, which gives balm for his sorrow as the Holy Spirit for Christ's.

From whose right arm, beneath whose eyes,
All period, power, and enterprise
　　　Commences, reigns, and ends.

19

Angels—their ministry and meed,　　　　　　　　　　　　*[angels;]*　　110
Which to and fro with blessings speed,
　　　Or with their citterns[5] wait;
Where Michael with his millions[6] bows,
Where dwells the seraph and his spouse,
　　　The cherub and her mate.

20

Of man—the semblance and effect　　　　　　　　　*[men of renown;]*　　115
Of God and Love—the Saint elect
　　　For infinite applause—
To rule the land, and briny broad,
To be laborious in his laud,
　　　And heroes in his cause.

　　　　　　　120

21

The world—the clustering spheres he made,　　　*[the works of nature*
The glorious light, the soothing shade,　　　　　　　*in all directions,*
　　　Dale, champain, grove, and hill;　　　　　*either particularly or*
The multitudinous abyss,　　　　　　　　　　　*collectively considered]*
Where secrecy remains in bliss,　　　　　　　　　　　　　　　125
　　　And wisdom hides her skill.

22

Trees, plants, and flowers—of virtuous[7] root;
Gem yielding blossom, yielding fruit,
　　　Choice gums and precious balm;
Bless ye the nosegay in the vale,　　　　　　　　　　　　　　130
And with the sweeteners of the gale
　　　Enrich the thankful psalm.

23

Of fowl—e'en every beak and wing
Which cheer the winter, hail the spring,
　　　That live in peace or prey;　　　　　　　　　　　　　135
They that make music, or that mock,
The quail, the brave domestic cock,
　　　The raven, swan, and jay.

24

Of fishes—every size and shape,
Which nature frames of light escape,　　　　　　　　　　　140
　　　Devouring man to shun:
The shells are in the wealthy deep,

---

5. Zither or lute.
6. God's legions, commanded by the archangel Michael.
7. Potent, medicinal; "Gem": bud.

The shoals[8] upon the surface leap,
    And love the glancing sun.
        25

Of beasts—the beaver plods his task;   145
While the sleek tigers roll and bask,
    Nor yet the shades arouse;
Her cave the mining coney[9] scoops;
Where o'er the mead the mountain stoops,
    The kids exult and browse.   150
        26

Of gems—their virtue and their price,
Which hid in earth from man's device,
    Their darts of luster sheathe;
The jasper of the master's stamp,[1]
The topaz blazing like a lamp   155
    Among the mines beneath.
        27

Blessed was the tenderness he felt   *[He obtains power*
When to his graceful harp he knelt,   *over infernal spirits,]*
    And did for audience call;
When Satan with his hand he quelled,   160
And in serene suspense he held
    The frantic throes of Saul.[2]
        28

His furious foes no more maligned   *[and the malignity of*
As he such melody divined,   *his enemies;]*
    And sense and soul detained;   165
Now striking strong, now soothing soft,
He sent the godly sounds aloft,
    Or in delight refrained.
        29

When up to heaven his thoughts he piled,   *[wins the heart of*
From fervent lips fair Michal smiled,   *Michal]*   170
    As blush to blush she stood;
And chose herself the queen, and gave
Her utmost from her heart, "so brave,
    And plays his hymns so good."[3]
        30

The pillars of the Lord are seven,   *[Shows that the pillars*   175
Which stand from earth to topmost heaven;   *of knowledge are the*
    His wisdom drew the plan;   *monuments of God's*
His Word accomplished the design,   *works in the first*
                                                     week]

---

8. Schools of fish.
9. Rabbit.
1. Jasper is used to make seals or signets of authority; hid in earth, it signifies no authority but God's.
2. When Saul was oppressed by an evil spirit, David

cured him by playing on the harp (1 Samuel 16).
3. Though intended by her father Saul to be a
"snare" to David, Michal fell in love with him, as
her speech (invented by Smart) indicates.

From brightest gem to deepest mine,
   From CHRIST enthroned to man.[4]   180

31

Alpha, the cause of causes, first
In station, fountain, whence the burst
   Of light, and blaze of day;
Whence bold attempt, and brave advance,
Have motion, life, and ordinance,   185
   And heaven itself its stay.[5]

32

Gamma supports the glorious arch
On which angelic legions march,
   And is with sapphires paved;
Thence the fleet clouds are sent adrift,   190
And thence the painted folds, that lift
   The crimson veil, are waved.[6]

33

Eta with living sculpture breathes,
With verdant carvings, flowery wreathes
   Of never-wasting bloom: 195
In strong relief his goodly base
All instruments of labor grace,
   The trowel, spade, and loom.

34

Next Theta stands to the Supreme—
Who formed, in number, sign,[7] and scheme,   200
   The illustrious lights that are;
And one addressed[8] his saffron robe,
And one, clad in a silver globe,
   Held rule with every star.

35

Iota's tuned to choral hymns   205
Of those that fly, while he that swims
   In thankful safety lurks;
And foot, and chapitre,[9] and niche,
The various histories enrich
   Of God's recorded works.   210

36

Sigma presents the social droves,
With him that solitary roves,
   And man of all the chief;

---

4. The seven pillars of the house of wisdom, referred to in Proverbs, are associated by the Masons with the building of the first Temple, erected by Solomon in Jerusalem according to divine order. Smart believed that both Proverbs and the Temple had been planned by David. In the following seven stanzas, each pillar is conflated with one of the days of Creation and with a Greek letter that represents one of the names of God. The implicit suggestion is that David, the greatest of poets and leaders, resembles the Creator, who called the universe into being with a Word.

5. Support. On the first day God called forth light.

6. The firmament, created on the second day, is compared to the oracle of the Temple, which holds the ark of the covenant.

7. Constellation.

8. Put on. The sun, with the moon and stars, was created on the fourth day.

9. Capital of a pillar. The abundance of fish and fowl, created on the fifth day, is compared to the rich decorations of the Temple (1 Kings 7).

Fair on whose face, and stately frame,
Did God impress his hallowed name,
    For ocular belief.

37

OMEGA! GREATEST and the BEST,
Stands sacred to the day of rest,
    For gratitude and thought;
Which blessed the world upon his pole,
And gave the universe his goal,
    And closed the infernal draught.[1]

38

O DAVID, scholar of the Lord!
Such is thy science, whence reward
    And infinite degree;[2]
O strength, O sweetness, lasting ripe!
God's harp thy symbol, and thy type[3]
    The lion and the bee!

39

There is but one who ne'er rebelled,
But One by passion unimpelled,
    By pleasure unenticed;
He from himself his semblance sent,
Grand object of his own content,
And saw the God in CHRIST.

[An exercise upon the decalogue]

40

"Tell them, I am," JEHOVA said
To Moses; while earth heard in dread,
    And smitten to the heart,
At once above, beneath, around,
All Nature, without voice or sound,
    Replied, "O Lord, THOU ART."

41

Thou art—to give and to confirm,
For each his talent and his term;
    All flesh thy bounties share:
Thou shalt not call thy brother fool;
The porches[4] of the Christian school
    Are meekness, peace, and prayer.

42

Open, and naked of offense,
Man's made of mercy, soul, and sense;
    God armed the snail and wilk;[5]
Be good to him that pulls thy plough;

1. The completed structure of the house of God (the world) shuts out the currents of Hell.
2. Elevation, rank.
3. Emblem. Theologically, a type is something in the Old Testament that prefigures some Christian truth. The lion and the bee, emblemizing the union of strength with sweetness (Judges 14), prefigure David; and David himself prefigures Christ, though, as the next stanza explains, no man can equal Him, since God is His own type. Stanzas 38 and 49 frame a ten-string "harp," the center of the poem, in which each of the ten commandments is interpreted according to the new Law of Christ's teachings.
4. Porticos where ancient philosophers debated.
5. Shellfish (the whelk).

Due food and care, due rest, allow
    For her that yields thee milk.

43

Rise up before the hoary head,
And God's benign commandment dread,
    Which says thou shalt not die;   255
"Not as I will, but as thou wilt,"[6]
Prayed He whose conscience knew no guilt;
    With whose blessed pattern vie.

44

Use all thy passions!—love is thine,
And joy, and jealousy[7] divine,   260
    Thine hope's eternal fort,
And care thy leisure to disturb,
With fear concupiscence to curb,
    And rapture to transport.

45

Act simply, as occasion asks;   265
Put mellow wine in seasoned casks;
    Till not with ass and bull:
Remember thy baptismal bond;
Keep from commixtures foul and fond,
    Nor work thy flax with wool.   270

46

Distribute: pay the Lord his tithe,
And make the widow's heart-strings blithe;
    Resort with those that weep:
As you from all and each expect,
For all and each thy love direct,   275
    And render as you reap.

47

The slander and its bearer spurn,
And propagating praise sojourn
    To make thy welcome last;
Turn from old Adam to the New;[8]   280
By hope futurity pursue;
    Look upwards to the past.

48

Control thine eye, salute success,
Honor the wiser, happier bless,
    And for thy neighbor feel;   285
Grutch not of mammon and his leaven,[9]
Work emulation up to heaven
    By knowledge and by zeal.

---

6. Matthew 26.39. Christ exemplifies the fifth commandment by submitting to his Father's will.
7. Devotion.
8. Christ. As elsewhere in this section, Smart interprets the commandment positively, less as a warning against bearing false witness than as encouragement to bear witness to truth.
9. Do not begrudge the wealthy man his rise.

49

O DAVID, highest in the list
Of worthies, on God's ways insist,   290
      The genuine word repeat.[1]
Vain are the documents of men,
And vain the flourish of the pen
      That keeps the fool's conceit.

50

Praise above all—for praise prevails;   [*The transcendent vir-*   295
Heap up the measure, load the scales,   *tue of praise and ado-*
      And good to goodness add: *ration*]
The generous soul her Saviour aids,
But peevish obloquy degrades;
      The Lord is great and glad.   300

51

For ADORATION all the ranks
Of angels yield eternal thanks,
      And DAVID in the midst;
With God's good poor, which, last and least
In man's esteem, thou to thy feast,   305
      O blessed bride-groom, bidst.

52

For ADORATION seasons change,   [*An exercise upon the*
And order, truth, and beauty range,   *seasons, and the right*
      Adjust, attract, and fill: *use of them*]
The grass the polyanthus checks;[2]   310
And polished porphyry reflects,
      By the descending rill.

53

Rich almonds color to the prime
For ADORATION; tendrils climb,
      And fruit-trees pledge their gems;   315
And Ivis[3] with her gorgeous vest
Builds for her eggs her cunning nest,
      And bell-flowers bow their stems.

54

With vinous syrup cedars spout;
From rocks pure honey gushing out,   320
      For ADORATION springs:
All scenes of painting crowd the map
Of nature; to the mermaid's pap
      The scalèd infant clings.

55

The spotted ounce and playsome cubs   325
Run rustling 'mongst the flowering shrubs,
      And lizards feed[4] the moss;

1. "Psalm 119" [Smart's note].   3. "Humming-bird" [Smart's note].
2. Checkers.   4. Eat; "ounce": lynx.

For ADORATION beasts embark,[5]
While waves upholding halcyon's ark
    No longer roar and toss.

56

While Israel sits beneath his fig,[6]
With coral root and amber sprig
    The weaned adventurer sports;
Where to the palm the jasmin cleaves,
For ADORATION 'mong the leaves
    The gale his peace reports.

57

Increasing days their reign exalt,
Nor in the pink and mottled vault
    The opposing spirits tilt;[7]
And, by the coasting reader spied,
The silverlings and crusions[8] glide
    For ADORATION gilt.

58

For ADORATION ripening canes
And cocoa's purest milk detains
    The western pilgrim's staff;
Where rain in clasping boughs inclosed,
And vines with oranges disposed,
    Embower the social laugh.

59

Now labor his reward receives,
For ADORATION counts his sheaves
    To peace, her bounteous prince;
The nectarine his strong tint imbibes,
And apples of ten thousand tribes,
    And quick[9] peculiar quince.

60

The wealthy crops of whitening rice,
'Mongst thyine[1] woods and groves of spice,
    For ADORATION grow;
And, marshalled in the fencèd land,
The peaches and pomegranates stand,
    Where wild carnations blow.

61

The laurels with the winter strive;
The crocus burnishes alive
    Upon the snow-clad earth:
For ADORATION myrtles stay

330

335

340

345

350

355

360

---

5. "There is a large quadruped that preys upon fish, and provides himself with a piece of timber for that purpose, with which he is very handy" [Smart's note]; "Halcyon's ark": the kingfisher's nest was supposed to calm the sea by floating on it.
6. According to Micah 4.4, "they shall sit every man under his vine and his fig tree; and none shall make them afraid"; "weaned adventurer": a child. As spring turns into summer, so mankind shall mature into peace.
7. Clouds clash together.
8. Tarpon and carp; "coasting": floating in a boat.
9. Pungent.
1. Sweet.

To keep the garden from dismay,   365
    And bless the sight from dearth.
        62
The pheasant shows his pompous neck;
And ermine, jealous of a speck[2]
    With fear eludes offense:
The sable, with his glossy pride,   370
For ADORATION is descried,
    Where frosts the wave condense.
        63
The cheerful holly, pensive yew,
And holy thorn,[3] their trim renew;
    The squirrel hoards his nuts: 375
All creatures batten o'er their stores,
And careful nature all her doors
    For ADORATION shuts.
        64
For ADORATION, DAVID's psalms
Lift up the heart to deeds of alms;   380
    And he, who kneels and chants,
Prevails his passions to control,
Finds meat and medicine to the soul,
    Which for translation[4] pants.
        65
For ADORATION, beyond match,   *[An exercise upon the*   385
The scholar[5] bulfinch aims to catch   *senses, and how to*
    The soft flute's ivory touch;   *subdue them]*
And careless on the hazel spray,
The daring redbreast keeps at bay
    The damsel's greedy clutch.   390
        66
For ADORATION, in the skies,
The Lord's philosopher espies
    The Dog, the Ram, and Rose;
The planet's ring, Orion's sword;
Nor is his greatness less adored   395
    In the vile worm that glows.
        67
For ADORATION on the strings[6]
The western breezes work their wings,
    The captive ear to sooth—
Hark! 'tis a voice—how still, and small[7]—   400
That makes the cataracts to fall,
    Or bids the sea be smooth.

---

2. Suspicious of distant things.
3. Hawthorn.
4. Transference to heaven.
5. Imitative (the bullfinch can learn a tune).

6. "Aeolian harp" [Smart's note], played by the wind.
7. In 1 Kings 19.11–12, the Lord does not speak in the wind but in "a still small voice."

68

For ADORATION, incense comes
From bezoar,[8] and Arabian gums;
    And from the civet's fur.
But as for prayer, or ere it faints,
Far better is the breath of saints
    Than galbanum and myrrh.[9]

69

For ADORATION from the down
Of damasins[1] to the anana's crown,
    God sends to tempt the taste;   410
And while the luscious zest invites
The sense, that in the scene delights,
    Commands desire be chaste.

70

For ADORATION, all the paths
Of grace are open, all the baths   415
    Of purity refresh;
And all the rays of glory beam
To deck the man of God's esteem,
    Who triumphs o'er the flesh.   420

71

For ADORATION, in the dome
Of Christ the sparrows find an home,
    And on his olives perch:
The swallow also dwells with thee,
O man of God's humility,
    Within his Saviour CHURCH.   425

72

Sweet is the dew that falls betimes,
And drops upon the leafy limes;   *[An amplification in*
    Sweet Hermon's fragrant air:[2]   *five degrees,]*
Sweet is the lily's silver bell,
And sweet the wakeful tapers smell   430
    That watch for early prayer.

73

Sweet the young nurse with love intense,
Which smiles o'er sleeping innocence;
    Sweet when the lost arrive: 435
Sweet the musician's ardor beats,
While his vague mind's in quest of sweets,
    The choicest flowers to hive.

74

Sweeter in all the strains of love,
The language of thy turtle dove,   440

---

8. A medicinal lump that forms in the stomachs
of some animals; "civet": civet cat.
9. Gum resins used in incense.
1. Damson plums; "anana's crown": pineapple's

tuft.
2. The dew of Hermon, a mountain in Syria, is
associated with Zion's dew in Psalm 133.

Paired to thy swelling chord;
Sweeter with every grace endued,
The glory of thy gratitude,
    Respired unto the Lord.

75

Strong is the horse upon his speed;   445
Strong in pursuit the rapid glede,[3]
    Which makes at once his game:
Strong the tall ostrich on the ground;
Strong through the turbulent profound
    Shoots xiphias[4] to his aim.   450

76

Strong is the lion—like a coal
His eyeball—like a bastion's mole[5]
    His chest against the foes:
Strong the gier-eagle[6] on his sail,
Strong against tide, the enormous whale   455
    Emerges, as he goes.

77

But stronger still, in earth and air,
And in the sea, the man of prayer;
    And far beneath the tide;
And in the seat to faith assigned,   460
Where ask is have, where seek is find,
    Where knock is open wide.

78

Beauteous the fleet before the gale;
Beauteous the multitudes in mail,
    Ranked arms and crested heads: 465
Beauteous the garden's umbrage mild,
Walk, water, meditated wild,[7]
    And all the bloomy beds.

79

Beauteous the moon full on the lawn;
And beauteous, when the veil's withdrawn,   470
    The virgin to her spouse:
Beauteous the temple decked and filled,
When to the heaven of heavens they build
    Their heart-directed vows.

80

Beauteous, yea beauteous more than these,   475
The shepherd king upon his knees,
    For his momentous trust;
With wish of infinite conceit,[8]
For man, beast, mute, the small and great,
    And prostrate dust to dust.   480

---

3. Hawk.   6. Vulture.
4. "The sword-fish" [Smart's note].   7. Artificial wild place within a garden or park.
5. Fortified wall.   8. Conception; "mute": fish.

81

Precious the bounteous widow's mite;
And precious, for extreme delight,
    The largess from the churl:[9]
Precious the ruby's blushing blaze,
And alba's[1] blest imperial rays,   485
    And pure cerulean pearl.

82

Precious the penitential tear;
And precious is the sigh sincere,
    Acceptable to God:
And precious are the winning flowers,   490
In gladsome Israel's feast of bowers,[2]
    Bound on the hallowed sod.

83

More precious that diviner part
Of David, even the Lord's own heart,
    Great, beautiful, and new: 495
In all things where it was intent,
In all extremes, in each event,
    Proof[3]—answering true to true.

84

Glorious the sun in mid career;
Glorious the assembled fires appear;   500
    Glorious the comet's train:
Glorious the trumpet and alarm;
Glorious the almighty stretched-out arm;
    Glorious the enraptured main:

85

Glorious the northern lights astream;   505
Glorious the song, when God's the theme;
    Glorious the thunder's roar:
Glorious hosanna from the den;
Glorious the catholic amen;
    Glorious the martyr's gore: 510

86

Glorious—more glorious is the crown
Of Him, that brought salvation down
    By meekness, called thy Son;
Thou that stupendous truth believed,
And now the matchless deed's achieved,   515
    DETERMINED, DARED, and DONE.

*[which is wrought up
to this conclusion,
That the best poet
which ever lived was
thought worthy of the
highest honor which
possibly can be con-
ceived, as the Saviour
of the World was
ascribed to his house,
and called his son in
the body.]*

1763

9. "Samuel 25:18" [Smart's note]. Against the will
of Nabal, a churlish rich man, his wife Abigail
gave largess to David.
1. "Revelation 2:17" [Smart's note]; a white stone,
given to the church triumphant.

2. The Feast of Tabernacles, or Succoth, ordained
five days after the day of atonement, in thanksgiving for deliverance from Egypt.
3. Meeting the test.

OLIVER GOLDSMITH
ca. 1730–1774

Goldsmith was born in Ireland, the son of an Anglican clergyman whose geniality he inherited and whose improvidence he imitated. He was early disfigured by smallpox and grew up ugly of face, ungraceful of figure, and in his early years apparently stupid and certainly idle. Nonetheless, he was sent to Trinity College, Dublin, as a sizar—i.e., a student who did menial jobs for well-to-do undergraduates—and there he took his A.B. in 1749. After several false starts in choosing a career, he was sent by a generous uncle to study medicine at the University of Edinburgh. Instead of taking a degree, he wandered for a while on the Continent, visiting Holland, France, Italy, and Switzerland. A much romanticized account of this journey can be read in the story of George Primrose in Goldsmith's novel, *The Vicar of Wakefield* (1766). He returned to England in 1756 with a mysteriously acquired M.D. and tried in vain to support himself as a physician among the poor in the Borough of Southwark. After serving for a while as an usher in a school, he drifted into the profession of hack writer for Ralph Griffiths, the proprietor of the *Monthly Review*, and later worked for and with the benevolent publisher Edward Newbery. He first attracted attention by a short book, *An Inquiry into the Present State of Polite Learning in Europe* (1759), in which he traced what he considered to be the decline of the fine arts in mideighteenth-century Europe to the lack of enlightened patronage and to the malign influence of criticism and scholarship. Soon he became a famous author and an intimate of the brilliant circle around Johnson. He earned by his writings very large sums indeed, but his habitual extravagance and generosity kept him always in debt, no matter how ample his income. He died owing the then prodigious sum (for a man whose only source of income was writing) of £2,000.

The variety and excellence of Goldsmith's work are astonishing. His easy and pleasant prose style, his abundant humor, his shrewd observations of character and scene have made his essays constantly popular. His great gift for the comedy of character and situation enabled him to achieve in his two plays, *The Good-Natured Man* (1768) and *She Stoops to Conquer* (1773), a sort of hearty and mirthful comedy—unspoiled by the fashionable sentimentality of the moment—that is unique in the century. His two important poems, *The Traveler, or A Prospect of Society* (1764) and *The Deserted Village*, are distinguished for the unforced grace of their couplets and for an air of simplicity that is far from simple to achieve.

The Deserted Village[1]

Sweet Auburn! loveliest village of the plain,
Where health and plenty cheered the laboring swain,

---

1. *The Deserted Village* is an idealization of English rural life, mingled with poignant memories of the poet's own youth in Lissoy, Ireland. Goldsmith was seriously concerned about the effects of the agricultural revolution then in progress which was being hastened by Enclosure Acts. Either for the sake of

Where smiling spring its earliest visit paid,
And parting summer's lingering blooms delayed:
Dear lovely bowers of innocence and ease,   5
Seats of my youth, when every sport could please,
How often have I loitered o'er thy green,
Where humble happiness endeared each scene;
How often have I paused on every charm,
The sheltered cot, the cultivated farm,   10
The never-failing brook, the busy mill,
The decent church that topped the neighboring hill,
The hawthorn bush, with seats beneath the shade,
For talking age and whispering lovers made;
How often have I blessed the coming day,   15
When toil remitting lent its turn to play,
And all the village train, from labor free,
Led up their sports beneath the spreading tree,
While many a pastime circled in the shade,
The young contending as the old surveyed;   20
And many a gambol frolicked o'er the ground,
And sleights of art and feats of strength went round;
And still as each repeated pleasure tired,
Succeeding sports the mirthful band inspired;
The dancing pair that simply sought renown,   25
By holding out to tire each other down;
The swain mistrustless of his smutted face,
While secret laughter tittered round the place;
The bashful virgin's sidelong looks of love,
The matron's glance that would those looks reprove: 30
These were thy charms, sweet village! sports like these,
With sweet succession, taught even toil to please;
These round thy bowers their cheerful influence shed,
These were thy charms—But all these charms are fled.

    Sweet smiling village, loveliest of the lawn,   35
Thy sports are fled, and all thy charms withdrawn;
Amidst thy bowers the tyrant's hand is seen,
And desolation saddens all thy green:
One only master grasps the whole domain,
And half a tillage stints thy smiling plain;   40
No more thy glassy brook reflects the day,
But choked with sedges, works its weedy way;

more profitable farming or to create vast private parks and landscape gardens, arable land was being "enclosed"—i.e., taken out of the hands of small proprietors—thus displacing yeoman farmers who, like their ancestors, had lived for generations in small villages, grazing their cattle on common land and raising food on small holdings. The only alternative available to many such people was to seek employment in the city or to migrate to America. Goldsmith certainly exaggerates the effects of the enclosures, nor are his diatribes against the debilitating influence of luxury borne out by history; Waterloo and the glories of the 19th century lay ahead for England. In the poem Goldsmith opposes "luxury" (the increase of wealth, the growth of cities, the costly country estates of great noblemen and wealthy merchants) to "rural virtue" (the old agrarian economy which supported a sturdy population of independent peasants). His poem is thus at once a nostalgic lament for a doomed way of life and a denunciation of what he regarded as the corrupting, destructive force of new wealth.

Along thy glades, a solitary guest,
The hollow-sounding bittern guards its nest;
Amidst thy desert walks the lapwing flies,   45
And tires their echoes with unvaried cries.
Sunk are thy bowers, in shapeless ruin all,
And the long grass o'ertops the moldering wall,
And, trembling, shrinking from the spoiler's hand,
Far, far away thy children leave the land.   50
    Ill fares the land, to hastening ills a prey,
Where wealth accumulates, and men decay;
Princes and lords may flourish, or may fade;
A breath can make them, as a breath has made;
But a bold peasantry, their country's pride.   55
When once destroyed, can never be supplied.
    A time there was, ere England's griefs began,
When every rood of ground maintained its man;
For him light labor spread her wholesome store,
Just gave what life required, but gave no more: 60
His best companions, innocence and health;
And his best riches, ignorance of wealth.
    But times are altered; Trade's unfeeling train
Usurp the land and dispossess the swain;
Along the lawn, where scattered hamlets rose,   65
Unwieldy wealth, and cumbrous pomp repose;
And every want to opulence allied,
And every pang that folly pays to pride.
These gentle hours that plenty bade to bloom,
Those calm desires that asked but little room,   70
Those healthful sports that graced the peaceful scene,
Lived in each look, and brightened all the green;
These far departing seek a kinder shore,
And rural mirth and manners are no more.
    Sweet Auburn! parent of the blissful hour,   75
Thy glades forlorn confess the tyrant's power.
Here, as I take my solitary rounds,
Amidst thy tangling walks, and ruined grounds,
And, many a year elapsed, return to view
Where once the cottage stood, the hawthorn grew,   80
Remembrance wakes with all her busy train,
Swells at my breast, and turns the past to pain.
    In all my wanderings round this world of care,
In all my griefs—and God has given my share—
I still had hopes my latest hours to crown,   85
Amidst these humble bowers to lay me down;
To husband out life's taper at the close,
And keep the flame from wasting by repose.
I still had hopes, for pride attends us still,
Amidst the swains to show my book-learned skill,   90
Around my fire an evening group to draw,

And tell of all I felt, and all I saw;
And, as an hare whom hounds and horns pursue,
Pants to the place from whence at first she flew,
I still had hopes, my long vexations past,   95
Here to return—and die at home at last.
    O blest retirement, friend to life's decline,
Retreats from care that never must be mine,
How happy he who crowns in shades like these,
A youth of labor with an age of ease;   100
Who quits a world where strong temptations try,
And, since 'tis hard to combat, learns to fly!
For him no wretches, born to work and weep,
Explore the mine, or tempt the dangerous deep;
No surly porter stands in guilty state   105
To spurn imploring famine from the gate;
But on he moves to meet his latter end,
Angels around befriending virtue's friend;
Bends to the grave with unperceived decay,
While Resignation gently slopes the way;   110
And, all his prospects brightening to the last,
His Heaven commences ere the world be passed!
    Sweet was the sound when oft at evening's close,
Up yonder hill the village murmur rose;
There, as I passed with careless steps and slow,   115
The mingling notes came softened from below;
The swain responsive as the milkmaid sung,
The sober herd that lowed to meet their young,
The noisy geese that gabbled o'er the pool,
The playful children just let loose from school;   120
The watchdog's voice that bayed the whispering wind,
And the loud laugh that spoke the vacant[2] mind;
These all in sweet confusion sought the shade,
And filled each pause the nightingale had made.
But now the sounds of population fail,   125
No cheerful murmurs fluctuate in the gale,
No busy steps the grass-grown footway tread,
For all the bloomy flush of life is fled.
All but yon widowed, solitary thing
That feebly bends beside the plashy spring;   130
She, wretched matron, forced, in age, for bread,
To strip the brook with mantling cresses spread,
To pick her wintry faggot from the thorn,
To seek her nightly shed, and weep till morn;
She only left of all the harmless train,   135
The sad historian of the pensive plain.
    Near yonder copse, where once the garden smiled,
And still where many a garden flower grows wild,

2. Idle.

There, where a few torn shrubs the place disclose,
The village preacher's modest mansion rose.   140
A man he was, to all the country dear,
And passing rich with forty pounds a year;
Remote from towns he ran his godly race,
Nor e'er had changed, nor wished to change his place;
Unpracticed he to fawn, or seek for power,   145
By doctrines fashioned to the varying hour;
Far other aims his heart had learned to prize,
More skilled to raise the wretched than to rise.
His house was known to all the vagrant train,
He chid their wanderings, but relieved their pain;   150
The long-remembered beggar was his guest,
Whose beard descending swept his aged breast;
The ruined spendthrift, now no longer proud,
Claimed kindred there, and had his claims allowed;
The broken soldier, kindly bade to stay,   155
Sate by his fire, and talked the night away;
Wept o'er his wounds, or tales of sorrow done,
Shouldered his crutch, and showed how fields were won.
Pleased with his guests, the good man learned to glow,
And quite forgot their vices in their woe;   160
Careless their merits, or their faults to scan,
His pity gave ere charity began.
    Thus to relieve the wretched was his pride,
And even his failings leaned to Virtue's side;
But in his duty prompt at every call,   165
He watched and wept, he prayed and felt, for all.
And, as a bird each fond endearment tries,
To tempt its new-fledged offspring to the skies,
He tried each art, reproved each dull delay,
Allured to brighter worlds, and led the way.   170
    Beside the bed where parting life was laid,
And sorrow, guilt, and pain, by turns dismayed,
The reverend champion stood. At his control,
Despair and anguish fled the struggling soul;
Comfort came down the trembling wretch to raise,   175
And his last faltering accents whispered praise.
    At church, with meek and unaffected grace,
His looks adorned the venerable place;
Truth from his lips prevailed with double sway,
And fools, who came to scoff, remained to pray.   180
The service past, around the pious man,
With steady zeal each honest rustic ran;
Even children followed with endearing wile,
And plucked his gown, to share the good man's smile.
His ready smile a parent's warmth expressed,   185
Their welfare pleased him, and their cares distressed;
To them his heart, his love, his griefs were given,

But all his serious thoughts had rest in Heaven.
As some tall cliff that lifts its awful form,
Swells from the vale, and midway leaves the storm,   190
Though round its breast the rolling clouds are spread,
Eternal sunshine settles on its head.
    Beside yon straggling fence that skirts the way,
With blossomed furze unprofitably gay,
There, in his noisy mansion, skilled to rule,   195
The village master taught his little school;
A man severe he was, and stern to view,
I knew him well, and every truant knew;
Well had the boding tremblers learned to trace
The day's disasters in his morning face;   200
Full well they laughed with counterfeited glee,
At all his jokes, for many a joke had he;
Full well the busy whisper circling round,
Conveyed the dismal tidings when he frowned;
Yet he was kind, or if severe in aught,   205
The love he bore to learning was in fault;[3]
The village all declared how much he knew;
'Twas certain he could write, and cipher too;
Lands he could measure, terms[4] and tides presage,
And even the story ran that he could gauge.[5]   210
In arguing too, the parson owned his skill,
For even though vanquished, he could argue still;
While words of learned length, and thundering sound,
Amazed the gazing rustics ranged around;
And still they gazed, and still the wonder grew,   215
That one small head could carry all he knew.
    But past is all his fame. The very spot
Where many a time he triumphed, is forgot.
Near yonder thorn, that lifts its head on high,
Where once the signpost caught the passing eye,   220
Low lies that house where nut-brown draughts inspired,
Where graybeard Mirth and smiling Toil retired,
Where village statesmen talked with looks profound,
And news much older than their ale went round.
Imagination fondly stoops to trace   225
The parlor splendors of that festive place:
The whitewashed wall, the nicely sanded floor,
The varnished clock that clicked behind the door;
The chest contrived a double debt to pay,
A bed by night, a chest of drawers by day;   230
The pictures placed for ornament and use,

---

3. Since the *l* was silent, "fault" and "aught"
rhymed perfectly.
4. Dates on which rent, wages, etc., were due and

tenancy began or ended; "tides": feasts and seasons
in the church year.
5. Measure the content of casks and other vessels.

The twelve good rules,[6] the royal game of goose;
The hearth, except when winter chilled the day,
With aspen boughs, and flowers, and fennel gay,
While broken teacups, wisely kept for show,   235
Ranged o'er the chimney, glistened in a row.
   Vain transitory splendors! Could not all
Reprieve the tottering mansion from its fall!
Obscure it sinks, nor shall it more impart
An hour's importance to the poor man's heart;   240
Thither no more the peasant shall repair
To sweet oblivion of his daily care;
No more the farmer's news, the barber's tale,
No more the woodman's ballad shall prevail;
No more the smith his dusky brow shall clear,   245
Relax his ponderous strength, and lean to hear;
The host himself no longer shall be found
Careful to see the mantling bliss[7] go round;
Nor the coy maid, half willing to be pressed,
Shall kiss the cup to pass it to the rest.   250
   Yes! let the rich deride, the proud disdain,
These simple blessings of the lowly train,
To me more dear, congenial to my heart,
One native charm, than all the gloss of art;
Spontaneous joys, where nature has its play,   255
The soul adopts, and owns their first-born sway;
Lightly they frolic o'er the vacant mind,
Unenvied, unmolested, unconfined.
But the long pomp, the midnight masquerade,
With all the freaks of wanton wealth arrayed,   260
In these, ere triflers half their wish obtain,
The toiling pleasure sickens into pain;
And, even while fashion's brightest arts decoy,
The heart distrusting asks if this be joy.
   Ye friends to truth, ye statesmen, who survey   265
The rich man's joys increase, the poor's decay,
'Tis yours to judge how wide the limits stand
Between a splendid and an happy land.
Proud swells the tide with loads of freighted ore,
And shouting Folly hails them from her shore;   270
Hoards, even beyond the miser's wish abound,
And rich men flock from all the world around.
Yet count our gains. This wealth is but a name
That leaves our useful products still the same.
Not so the loss. The man of wealth and pride,   275

---

6. "The twelve good rules" of conduct, attributed to Charles I, were printed in a broadside that was often seen on the walls of taverns; "goose" was a game in which counters were moved on a board according to the throw of the dice.

7. Foaming bliss, i.e., foaming ale.

Takes up a space that many poor supplied;
Space for his lake, his park's extended bounds,
Space for his horses, equipage, and hounds;
The robe that wraps his limbs in silken sloth
Has robbed the neighboring fields of half their growth;   280
His seat, where solitary sports are seen,
Indignant spurns the cottage from the green;
Around the world each needful product flies,
For all the luxuries the world supplies.
While thus the land adorned for pleasure, all   285
In barren splendor feebly waits the fall.
    As some fair female unadorned and plain,
Secure to please while youth confirms her reign,
Slights every borrowed charm that dress supplies,
Nor shares with art the triumph of her eyes: 290
But when those charms are past, for charms are frail,
When time advances, and when lovers fail,
She then shines forth, solicitous to bless,
In all the glaring impotence of dress:
Thus fares the land, by luxury betrayed;   295
In nature's simplest charms at first arrayed;
But verging to decline, its splendors rise,
Its vistas strike, its palaces surprise;
While scourged by famine from the smiling land,
The mournful peasant leads his humble band;   300
And while he sinks without one arm to save,
The country blooms—a garden, and a grave.
    Where then, ah where, shall Poverty reside,
To 'scape the pressure of contiguous Pride?
If to some common's fenceless limits strayed,   305
He drives his flock to pick the scanty blade,
Those fenceless fields the sons of wealth divide,
And even the bare-worn common is denied.
    If to the city sped—What waits him there?
To see profusion that he must not share;   310
To see ten thousand baneful arts combined
To pamper luxury, and thin mankind;
To see those joys the sons of pleasure know,
Extorted from his fellow creature's woe.
Here, while the courtier glitters in brocade,   315
There the pale artist[8] plies the sickly trade;
Here, while the proud their long-drawn pomps display,
There the black gibbet glooms beside the way.
The dome where Pleasure holds her midnight reign,
Here, richly decked, admits the gorgeous train;   320
Tumultuous grandeur crowds the blazing square,
The rattling chariots clash, the torches glare.

8. Artisan.

Sure scenes like these no troubles e'er annoy!
Sure these denote one universal joy!
Are these thy serious thoughts?—Ah, turn thine eyes   325
Where the poor houseless shivering female lies.
She once, perhaps, in village plenty blest,
Has wept at tales of innocence distressed;
Her modest looks the cottage might adorn,
Sweet as the primrose peeps beneath the thorn;   330
Now lost to all; her friends, her virtue fled,
Near her betrayer's door she lays her head,
And pinched with cold, and shrinking from the shower,
With heavy heart deplores that luckless hour,
When idly first, ambitious of the town,   335
She left her wheel and robes of country brown.
     Do thine, sweet Auburn, thine, the loveliest train,
Do thy fair tribes participate her pain?
Even now, perhaps, by cold and hunger led,
At proud men's doors they ask a little bread!   340
     Ah, no. To distant climes, a dreary scene,
Where half the convex world intrudes between,
Through torrid tracts with fainting steps they go,
Where wild Altama[9] murmurs to their woe.
Far different there from all that charmed before,   345
The various terrors of that horrid shore;
Those blazing suns that dart a downward ray,
And fiercely shed intolerable day;
Those matted woods where birds forget to sing,
But silent bats in drowsy clusters cling,   350
Those poisonous fields with rank luxuriance crowned,
Where the dark scorpion gathers death around;
Where at each step the stranger fears to wake
The rattling terrors of the vengeful snake;
Where crouching tigers wait their hapless prey,[1]   355
And savage men, more murderous still than they;
While oft in whirls the mad tornado flies,
Mingling the ravaged landscape with the skies.
Far different these from every former scene,
The cooling brook, the grassy vested green,   360
The breezy covert of the warbling grove,
That only sheltered thefts of harmless love.
     Good Heaven! what sorrows gloomed that parting day,
That called them from their native walks away;
When the poor exiles, every pleasure past,   365
Hung round their bowers, and fondly looked their last,
And took a long farewell, and wished in vain
For seats like these beyond the western main;
And shuddering still to face the distant deep,

9. The Altamaha River in Georgia.   1. Not the Asiatic tiger, but the puma.

Returned and wept, and still returned to weep.   370
The good old sire, the first prepared to go
To new-found worlds, and wept for other's woe.
But for himself, in conscious virtue brave,
He only wished for worlds beyond the grave.
His lovely daughter, lovelier in her tears,   375
The fond companion of his helpless years,
Silent went next, neglectful of her charms,
And left a lover's for a father's arms.
With louder plaints the mother spoke her woes,
And blessed the cot where every pleasure rose;   380
And kissed her thoughtless babes with many a tear,
And clasped them close in sorrow doubly dear;
Whilst her fond husband strove to lend relief
In all the silent manliness of grief.
    O luxury! Thou cursed by Heaven's decree,   385
How ill exchanged are things like these for thee!
How do thy portions, with insidious joy,
Diffuse their pleasures only to destroy!
Kingdoms, by thee, to sickly greatness grown,
Boast of a florid vigor not their own.   390
At every draught more large and large they grow,
A bloated mass of rank unwieldy woe;
Till sapped their strength, and every part unsound,
Down, down they sink, and spread a ruin round.
    Even now the devastation is begun,   395
And half the business of destruction done;
Even now, methinks, as pondering here I stand,
I see the rural Virtues leave the land.
Down where yon anchoring vessel spreads the sail,
That idly waiting flaps with every gale,   400
Downward they move, a melancholy band,
Pass from the shore, and darken all the strand.
Contented Toil, and hospitable Care,
And kind connubial Tenderness are there;
And Piety, with wishes placed above,   405
And steady Loyalty, and faithful Love:
And thou, sweet Poetry, thou loveliest maid,
Still first to fly where sensual joys invade;
Unfit in these degenerate times of shame,
To catch the heart, or strike for honest fame;   410
Dear charming Nymph, neglected and decried,
My shame in crowds, my solitary pride;
Thou source of all my bliss, and all my woe,
That found'st me poor at first, and keep'st me so;
Thou guide by which the nobler arts excel,   415
Thou nurse of every virtue, fare thee well.
Farewell, and O! where'er thy voice be tried

On Torno's cliffs, or Pambamarca's side,[2]
Whether where equinoctial fervors glow,
Or winter wraps the polar world in snow,   420
Still let thy voice, prevailing over time,
Redress the rigors of the inclement clime;
Aid slighted truth, with thy persuasive strain
Teach erring man to spurn the rage of gain;
Teach him that states of native strength possessed,   425
Though very poor, may still be very blest;
That Trade's proud empire hastes to swift decay,
As ocean sweeps the labored mole[3] away;
While self-dependent power can time defy,
As rocks resist the billows and the sky.[4]   430

                                                           1770

2. The river Torne in Sweden falls into the Gulf   3. The laboriously built breakwater.
of Bothnia; Pambamarca is a mountain in Ecua-   4. Johnson composed the last four lines of the
dor.   poem.

GEORGE CRABBE
1754–1832

Crabbe belongs to the early nineteenth rather than to the eighteenth century, but his first successful poem is very much a part of the literature of our period. Born to poverty in a small, decayed Suffolk seaport, Aldeburgh, he was apprenticed to a surgeon, but found it impossible to earn a living by practicing in his native village. In 1780 he went to London, and succeeded neither in finding a patron nor in securing literary employment, until, reduced to desperate straits, he sent an appeal to Edmund Burke, who recognized his merit and gave him timely help. Through Burke's influence *The Library* was published; Samuel Johnson agreed to correct *The Village*; and Crabbe was ordained a minister in the Anglican Church. His appointment as chaplain to the duke of Rutland enabled him to marry the woman to whom he had long been engaged.

After 1785 he published nothing until 1807, when *The Parish Register* appeared. It was followed by *The Borough* (1810), *Tales* (1812), and *Tales of the Hall* (1819). In these poems, which won the admiration of Wordsworth, Scott, and Byron, Crabbe continued his vein of realism and developed his great gift for narrative and characterization. *The Village* was widely read and admired despite its sometimes flat and often stilted language. But its unrelieved realism and gloomy darkness of tone set it sharply apart from conventional poems on rural life during the century. Indeed, it is an angry, a scornful reply to the sentimental cult of rural simplicity, innocence, and happiness. It glances at the unrealities of the pastoral convention and, somewhat more systematically, it answers Goldsmith's charming idealization of villagers and their life in *The Deserted Village*. Crabbe knew the degrading effect of hopeless poverty, he had observed rural vice, he knew the gulf that sometimes separated the landed gentry from their laboring tenants. Out of recollections of Aldeburgh and the neighboring seacoast he fashioned a setting for his poem in which a niggardly nature seems the only proper background for the penury of the men who inhabit it. The accuracy of the details created a poetry of the ugly and the barren which is at variance with the long tradition of natural description from Thomson to Cowper.

From The Village

Book 1

```
   The village life, and every care that reigns
O'er youthful peasants and declining swains;
What labor yields, and what, that labor past,
Age, in its hour of languor, finds at last;
What form the real picture of the poor,                     5
Demand a song—the Muse can give no more.
   Fled are those times when, in harmonious strains,
The rustic poet praised his native plains.
No shepherds now, in smooth altérnate verse,
Their country's beauty or their nymphs' rehearse;           10
Yet still for these we frame the tender strain,
Still in our lays fond Corydons¹ complain,
And shepherds' boys their amorous pains reveal,
The only pains, alas! they never feel.
   On Mincio's² banks, in Caesar's bounteous reign,         15
If Tityrus found the Golden Age again,
Must sleepy bards the flattering dream prolong,
Mechanic echoes of the Mantuan song?
From Truth and Nature shall we widely stray,
Where Virgil, not where Fancy, leads the way?               20
   Yes, thus the Muses sing of happy swains,
Because the Muses never knew their pains.
They boast their peasants' pipes; but peasants now
Resign their pipes and plod behind the plow;
And few, amid the rural tribe, have time                    25
To number syllables, and play with rhyme;
Save honest Duck,³ what son of verse could share
The poet's rapture, and the peasant's care?
Or the great labors of the field degrade,
With the new peril of a poorer trade?                       30
   From this chief cause these idle praises spring,
That themes so easy few forbear to sing;
```

---

1. "Corydon" is a stock name for a shepherd in pastorals, used by both Theocritus and Virgil.
2. Virgil was born near Mantua, in Italy, not far from the river Mincius. Tityrus is one of the speakers in Virgil's *Eclogues* 1.

3. Stephen Duck (1705–1756), the "Thresher Poet," was a self-educated agricultural laborer whose verses attracted attention and finally won him the patronage of Queen Caroline.

For no deep thought the trifling subjects ask:
To sing of shepherds is an easy task.
The happy youth assumes the common strain,   35
A nymph his mistress, and himself a swain;
With no sad scenes he clouds his tuneful prayer,
But all, to look like her, is painted fair.
   I grant indeed that fields and flocks have charms
For him that grazes or for him that farms;   40
But when amid such pleasing scenes I trace
The poor laborious natives of the place,
And see the midday sun, with fervid ray,
On their bare heads and dewy temples play;
While some, with feebler heads and fainter hearts,   45
Deplore their fortune, yet sustain their parts:
Then shall I dare these real ills to hide
In tinsel trappings of poetic pride?
   No; cast by Fortune on a frowning coast,
Which neither groves nor happy valleys boast;   50
Where other cares than those the Muse relates,
And other shepherds dwell with other mates;
By such examples taught, I paint the cot,
As Truth will paint it, and as bards will not:
Nor you, ye poor, of lettered scorn complain,   55
To you the smoothest song is smooth in vain;
O'ercome by labor, and bowed down by time,
Feel you the barren flattery of a rhyme?
Can poets soothe you, when you pine for bread,
By winding myrtles round your ruined shed?   60
Can their light tales your weighty griefs o'erpower,
Or glad with airy mirth the toilsome hour?
   Lo! where the heath, with withering brake grown o'er,
Lends the light turf that warms the neighboring poor;
From thence a length of burning sand appears,   65
Where the thin harvest waves its withered ears;
Rank weeds, that every art and care defy,
Reign o'er the land, and rob the blighted rye:
There thistles stretch their prickly arms afar,
And to the ragged infant threaten war;   70
There poppies, nodding, mock the hope of toil;
There the blue bugloss paints the sterile soil;
Hardy and high, above the slender sheaf,
The slimy mallow waves her silky leaf;
O'er the young shoot the charlock throws a shade,   75
And clasping tares cling round the sickly blade;
With mingled tints the rocky coasts abound,
And a sad splendor vainly shines around.
So looks the nymph whom wretched arts adorn,
Betrayed by man, then left for man to scorn;   80
Whose cheek in vain assumes the mimic rose,

While her sad eyes the troubled breast disclose;
Whose outward splendor is but folly's dress,
Exposing most, when most it gilds distress.

    Here joyless roam a wild amphibious race,   85
With sullen woe displayed in every face;
Who far from civil arts and social fly,
And scowl at strangers with suspicious eye.

    Here too the lawless merchant of the main
Draws from his plow the intoxicated swain;   90
Want only claimed the labor of the day,
But vice now steals his nightly rest away.

    Where are the swains, who, daily labor done,
With rural games played down the setting sun;
Who struck with matchless force the bounding ball,   95
Or made the ponderous quoit obliquely fall;
While some huge Ajax, terrible and strong,
Engaged some artful stripling of the throng,
And fell beneath him, foiled, while far around
Hoarse triumph rose, and rocks returned the sound?   100
Where now are these?—Beneath yon cliff they stand,
To show the freighted pinnace where to land;[4]
To load the ready steed with guilty haste;
To fly in terror o'er the pathless waste;
Or, when detected in their straggling course,   105
To foil their foes by cunning or by force;
Or, yielding part (which equal knaves demand),
To gain a lawless passport through the land.

    Here, wandering long amid these frowning fields,
I sought the simple life that Nature yields;   110
Rapine and Wrong and Fear usurped her place,
And a bold, artful, surly, savage race;
Who, only skilled to take the finny tribe,
The yearly dinner, or septennial bribe,[5]
Wait on the shore, and, as the waves run high,   115
On the tossed vessel bend their eager eye,
Which to their coast directs its venturous way;
Theirs, or the ocean's, miserable prey.

    As on their neighboring beach yon swallows stand,
And wait for favoring winds to leave the land,   120
While still for flight the ready wing is spread:
So waited I the favoring hour, and fled;
Fled from these shores where guilt and famine reign,
And cried, "Ah! hapless they who still remain;
Who still remain to hear the ocean roar,   125
Whose greedy waves devour the lessening shore;
Till some fierce tide, with more imperious sway,
Sweeps the low hut and all it holds away;

---

4. Crabbe refers to smuggling.
5. Paid to electors by candidates for election to Parliament. Since Parliaments must be elected at least every seven years, the bribes are "septennial."

When the sad tenant weeps from door to door,
And begs a poor protection from the poor!"   130
   But these are scenes where Nature's niggard hand
Gave a spare portion to the famished land;
Hers is the fault, if here mankind complain
Of fruitless toil and labor spent in vain.
But yet in other scenes, more fair in view,   135
Where Plenty smiles—alas! she smiles for few—
And those who taste not, yet behold her store,
Are as the slaves that dig the golden ore,
The wealth around them makes them doubly poor.
   Or will you deem them amply paid in health,   140
Labor's fair child, that languishes with wealth?
Go, then! and see them rising with the sun,
Through a long course of daily toil to run;
See them beneath the dog star's raging heat,
When the knees tremble and the temples beat;   145
Behold them, leaning on their scythes, look o'er
The labor past, and toils to come explore;
See them alternate suns and showers engage,
And hoard up aches and anguish for their age;
Through fens and marshy moors their steps pursue,   150
When their warm pores imbibe the evening dew;
Then own that labor may as fatal be
To these thy slaves, as thine excess to thee.
   Amid this tribe too oft a manly pride
Strives in strong toil the fainting heart to hide;   155
There may you see the youth of slender frame
Contend, with weakness, weariness, and shame;
Yet, urged along, and proudly loath to yield,
He strives to join his fellows of the field;
Till long-contending nature droops at last,   160
Declining health rejects his poor repast,
His cheerless spouse the coming danger sees,
And mutual murmurs urge the slow disease.
   Yet grant them health, 'tis not for us to tell,
Though the head droops not, that the heart is well;   165
Or will you praise that homely, healthy fare,
Plenteous and plain, that happy peasants share?
Oh! trifle not with wants you cannot feel,
Nor mock the misery of a stinted meal,
Homely, not wholesome; plain, not plenteous; such   170
As you who praise would never deign to touch.
   Ye gentle souls, whom dream of rural ease,
Whom the smooth stream and smoother sonnet please;
Go! if the peaceful cot your praises share,
Go, look within, and ask if peace be there: 175
If peace be his—that drooping weary sire,
Or theirs, that offspring round their feeble fire;

Or hers, that matron pale, whose trembling hand
Turns on the wretched hearth the expiring brand!
    Nor yet can Time itself obtain for these 180
Life's latest comforts, due respect and ease:
For yonder see that hoary swain, whose age
Can with no cares except his own engage;
Who, propped on that rude staff, looks up to see
The bare arms broken from the withering tree, 185
On which, a boy, he climbed the loftiest bough,
Then his first joy, but his sad emblem now.
    He once was chief in all the rustic trade;
His steady hand the straightest furrow made;
Full many a prize he won, and still is proud 190
To find the triumphs of his youth allowed.
A transient pleasure sparkles in his eyes;
He hears and smiles, then thinks again and sighs;
For now he journeys to his grave in pain;
The rich disdain him, nay, the poor disdain; 185
Altérnate masters now their slave command,
Urge the weak efforts of his feeble hand;
And, when his age attempts its task in vain,
With ruthless taunts, of lazy poor complain.
    Oft may you see him, when he tends the sheep, 200
His winter charge, beneath the hillock weep;
Oft hear him murmur to the winds that blow
O'er his white locks and bury them in snow,
When, roused by rage and muttering in the morn
He mends the broken hedge with icy thorn: 205
    "Why do I live, when I desire to be
At once from life and life's long labor free?
Like leaves in spring, the young are blown away,
Without the sorrows of a slow decay;
I, like yon withered leaf, remain behind, 210
Nipped by the frost, and shivering in the wind;
There it abides till younger buds come on,
As I, now all my fellow swains are gone;
Then, from the rising generation thrust,
It falls, like me, unnoticed to the dust. 215
    "These fruitful fields, these numerous flocks I see,
Are others' gain, but killing cares to me:
To me the children of my youth are lords,
Cool in their looks, but hasty in their words:
Wants of their own demand their care; and who 220
Feels his own want and succors others too?
A lonely, wretched man, in pain I go,
None need my help, and none relieve my woe;
Then let my bones beneath the turf be laid,
And men forget the wretch they would not aid!" 225
    Thus groan the old, till, by disease oppressed,

They taste a final woe, and then they rest.
　Theirs is yon house that holds the parish poor,
Whose walls of mud scarce bear the broken door;
There, where the putrid vapors, flagging, play,　　　　　230
And the dull wheel hums doleful through the day—
There children dwell, who know no parents' care;
Parents, who know no children's love, dwell there!
Heartbroken matrons on their joyless bed,
Forsaken wives, and mothers never wed;　　　　　235
Dejected widows with unheeded tears,
And crippled age with more than childhood fears;
The lame, the blind, and, far the happiest they!
The moping idiot and the madman gay.
Here too the sick their final doom receive,　　　　　240
Here brought, amid the scenes of grief, to grieve,
Where the loud groans from some sad chamber flow,
Mixed with the clamors of the crowd below;
Here, sorrowing, they each kindred sorrow scan,
And the cold charities of man to man:　　　　　245
Whose laws indeed for ruined age provide,
And strong compulsion plucks the scrap from pride;
But still that scrap is bought with many a sigh,
And pride embitters what it can't deny.
　Say ye, oppressed by some fantastic woes,　　　　　250
Some jarring nerve that baffles your repose;
Who press the downy couch, while slaves advance
With timid eye to read the distant glance;
Who with sad prayers the weary doctor tease,
To name the nameless ever-new disease;　　　　　255
Who with mock patience dire complaints endure,
Which real pain, and that alone, can cure—
How would ye bear in real pain to lie,
Despised, neglected, left alone to die?
How would ye bear to draw your latest breath,　　　　　260
Where all that's wretched paves the way for death?
　Such is that room which one rude beam divides,
And naked rafters form the sloping sides;
Where the vile bands that bind the thatch are seen,
And lath and mud are all that lie between,　　　　　265
Save one dull pane, that, coarsely patched, gives way
To the rude tempest, yet excludes the day.
Here, on a matted flock, with dust o'erspread,
The drooping wretch reclines his languid head;
For him no hand the cordial cup applies,　　　　　270
Or wipes the tear that stagnates in his eyes;
No friends with soft discourse his pain beguile,
Or promise hope till sickness wears a smile.
　But soon a loud and hasty summons calls,
Shakes the thin roof, and echoes round the walls.　　　　　275

Anon, a figure enters, quaintly neat,
All pride and business, bustle and conceit;
With looks unaltered by these scenes of woe,
With speed that, entering, speaks his haste to go,
He bids the gazing throng around him fly,   280
And carries fate and physic in his eye:
A potent quack, long versed in human ills,
Who first insults the victim whom he kills;
Whose murderous hand a drowsy Bench protect,[6]
And whose most tender mercy is neglect.   285
    Paid by the parish for attendance here,
He wears contempt upon his sapient sneer;
In haste he seeks the bed where Misery lies,
Impatience marked in his averted eyes;
And, some habitual queries hurried o'er,   290
Without reply, he rushes on the door.
His drooping patient, long inured to pain,
And long unheeded, knows remonstrance vain;
He ceases now the feeble help to crave
Of man; and silent sinks into the grave.   295
    But ere his death some pious doubts arise,
Some simple fears, which "bold bad" men despise:
Fain would he ask the parish priest to prove
His title certain to the joys above;
For this he sends the murmuring nurse, who calls   300
The holy stranger to these dismal walls;
And doth not he, the pious man, appear,
He, "passing rich with forty pounds a year"?[7]
Ah! no; a shepherd of a different stock:
And far unlike him, feeds this little flock: 305
A jovial youth, who thinks his Sunday's task
As much as God or man can fairly ask;
The rest he gives to loves and labors light,
To fields the morning, and to feasts the night;
None better skilled the noisy pack to guide,   310
To urge their chase, to cheer them or to chide;
A sportsman keen, he shoots through half the day,
And, skilled at whist, devotes the night to play.
Then, while such honors bloom around his head,
Shall he sit sadly by the sick man's bed,   315
To raise the hope he feels not, or with zeal
To combat fears that e'en the pious feel?
    Now once again the gloomy scene explore,
Less gloomy now; the bitter hour is o'er,
The man of many sorrows sighs no more.—   320
Up yonder hill, behold how sadly slow

---

6. Crabbe, who had practiced medicine among the poor of Aldeborough, well knew the indifference of the local magistrates ("the drowsy Bench") to the incompetence and callousness of the physician hired by the parish to attend its paupers.
7. Cf. Goldsmith's *Deserted Village*, line 142.

The bier moves winding from the vale below;
There lie the happy dead, from trouble free,
And the glad parish pays the frugal fee.
No more, O Death! thy victim starts to hear 325
Churchwarden stern, or kingly overseer;
No more the farmer claims his humble bow,
Thou art his lord, the best of tyrants thou!
     Now to the church behold the mourners come,
Sedately torpid and devoutly dumb; 330
The village children now their games suspend,
To see the bier that bears their ancient friend:
For he was one in all their idle sport,
And like a monarch ruled their little court;
The pliant bow he formed, the flying ball, 335
The bat, the wicket, were his labors all;
Him now they follow to his grave, and stand
Silent and sad, and gazing, hand in hand;
While bending low, their eager eyes explore
The mingled relics of the parish poor. 340
The bell tolls late, the moping owl flies round,
Fear marks the flight and magnifies the sound;
The busy priest, detained by weightier care,
Defers his duty till the day of prayer;
And, waiting long, the crowd retire distressed, 345
To think a poor man's bones should lie unblessed.

1780–83   1783

WILLIAM COWPER
1731–1800

There are no saner poems in the language than Cowper's, yet they were written by a man who was periodically insane and who, for forty years, lived day to day with the possibility of madness. One form that his madness took was a conviction that he was damned for having committed the unforgivable sin, the "sin against the Holy Ghost." When he recovered from his first attack, in which he had attempted suicide, he was persuaded by his physician that this conviction was a delusion, and he embraced the doctor's own hopeful Evangelical creed, an inner assurance of divine mercy. From then on, a refugee from life, he found shelter first, in 1765, in the pious family of the Evangelical clergyman, Morley Unwin, and after Unwin's death, with Mrs. Unwin, who gave him exactly the sort of loving shelter that he needed. They were never separated until her death in 1796, by which time Cowper had experienced his final attack of madness. The move of Mary Unwin and Cowper from Huntington to Olney (pronounced *Own-y*) in 1765 brought the couple under the influence of the strenuous and fervent Evangelical clergyman John Newton. With him Cowper wrote the famous *Olney Hymns*, still familiar to Methodists and other Nonconformists. But here a second attack of madness, in 1773, not only frustrated his planned marriage to Mrs. Unwin, but left him for the rest of his life with the assurance that he had been cast out by God and was inevitably damned. He never again attended services, and the main purpose of his life thereafter was to divert his mind by every possible innocent device from the numb despair that was his lot in life. He gardened, he kept pets, he walked, he wrote letters (some of the best of the century), he conversed, he read—and he wrote poetry. When it was published, it brought him a measure of fame that his modest nature could never have hoped for.

Cowper's major work is *The Task* (1785), undertaken at the bidding— hence the title—of the lively and charming Lady Austen, who, when he complained that he had no subject, directed him to write about the sofa in his parlor. It began with a mock-heroic account of the development of the sofa from a simple stool, but it grew into a long meditative poem of over five thousand lines in delicately modulated blank verse. The poet describes in his murmuring voice his small world of country, village, garden, and parlor, and from time to time he glances toward the great world to condemn cities and worldliness, war and slavery, luxury and corruption. The tone is muted, the sensibility delicate, the language on the whole precise and clear, the technique masterful. Cowper expresses the interests and taste of his age. He does not strive to be great; yet his contemporaries recognized their own concerns in his pious and humorous musings. It is still agreeable to take up his poems from time to time, and to allow his gentle talk to re-create for us the serenity and simplicity of life in an English village just before the French Revolution announced a new era.

From The Task

From *Book 1*

[A LANDSCAPE DESCRIBED. RURAL SOUNDS]

Thou[1] knowest my praise of nature most sincere,   150
And that my raptures are not conjured up
To serve occasions of poetic pomp,
But genuine, and art partner of them all.
How oft upon yon eminence our pace
Has slackened to a pause, and we have borne   155
The ruffling wind, scarce conscious that it blew,
While admiration, feeding at the eye,
And still unsated, dwelt upon the scene.
Thence with what pleasure have we just discerned
The distant plow slow moving, and beside   160
His laboring team, that swerved not from the track,
The sturdy swain diminished to a boy!
Here Ouse,[2] slow winding through a level plain
Of spacious meads with cattle sprinkled o'er,

1. Mary Unwin.
2. The village of Olney, where Cowper and Mary Unwin were living, is situated on the river Ouse.

Conducts the eye along its sinuous course   165
Delighted. There, fast rooted in their bank,
Stand, never overlooked, our favorite elms,
That screen the herdsman's solitary hut;
While far beyond, and overthwart the stream
That, as with molten glass, inlays the vale,   170
The sloping land recedes into the clouds;
Displaying on its varied side the grace
Of hedgerow beauties numberless, square tower,
Tall spire, from which the sound of cheerful bells
Just undulates upon the listening ear,   175
Groves, heaths, and smoking villages, remote.
Scenes must be beautiful, which, daily viewed,
Please daily, and whose novelty survives
Long knowledge and the scrutiny of years—
Praise justly due to those that I describe.   180
    Nor rural sights alone, but rural sounds,
Exhilarate the spirit, and restore
The tone of languid Nature. Mighty winds,
That sweep the skirt of some far-spreading wood
Of ancient growth, make music not unlike   185
The dash of ocean on his winding shore,
And lull the spirit while they fill the mind;
Unnumbered branches waving in the blast,
And all their leaves fast fluttering, all at once.
Nor less composure waits upon the roar   190
Of distant floods, or on the softer voice
Of neighboring fountain, or of rills that slip
Through the cleft rock, and, chiming as they fall
Upon loose pebbles, lose themselves at length
In matted grass, that with a livelier green   195
Betrays the secret of their silent course.
Nature inanimate employs sweet sounds,
But animated nature sweeter still,
To soothe and satisfy the human ear.
Ten thousand warblers cheer the day, and one   200
The livelong night: nor these alone, whose notes
Nice-fingered art must emulate in vain,
But cawing rooks, and kites that swim sublime
In still repeated circles, screaming loud,
The jay, the pie, and even the boding owl   205
That hails the rising moon, have charms for me.
Sounds inharmonious in themselves and harsh,
Yet heard in scenes where peace forever reigns,
And only there, please highly for their sake.

[CRAZY KATE]

    There often wanders one, whom better days
Saw better clad, in cloak of satin trimmed   .   535

With lace, and hat with splendid ribband bound.
A servingmaid was she, and fell in love
With one who left her, went to sea, and died.
Her fancy followed him through foaming waves
To distant shores; and she would sit and weep   540
At what a sailor suffers; fancy, too,
Delusive most where warmest wishes are,
Would oft anticipate his glad return,
And dream of transports she was not to know.
She heard the doleful tidings of his death—   545
And never smiled again! And now she roams
The dreary waste; there spends the livelong day,
And there, unless when charity forbids,
The livelong night. A tattered apron hides,
Worn as a cloak, and hardly hides, a gown   550
More tattered still; and both but ill conceal
A bosom heaved with never-ceasing sighs.
She begs an idle pin of all she meets,
And hoards them in her sleeve; but needful food,
Though pressed with hunger oft, or comelier clothes,   555
Though pinched with cold, asks never.—Kate is crazed!

From *Book* 3

[THE STRICKEN DEER]

I was a stricken deer, that left the herd
Long since; with many an arrow deep infixed
My panting side was charged, when I withdrew   110
To seek a tranquil death in distant shades.
There was I found by one who had himself
Been hurt by the archers. In his side he bore,
And in his hands and feet, the cruel scars.
With gentle force soliciting[3] the darts,   115
He drew them forth, and healed, and bade me live.
Since then, with few associates, in remote
And silent woods I wander, far from those
My former partners of the peopled scene;
With few associates, and not wishing more.   120
Here much I ruminate, as much I may,
With other views of men and manners now
Than once, and others of a life to come.
I see that all are wanderers, gone astray
Each in his own delusions; they are lost   125
In chase of fancied happiness, still wooed
And never won. Dream after dream ensues;
And still they dream that they shall still succeed.

---

3. "To endeavor to draw out by the use of gentle force" (*NED*).

And still are disappointed. Rings the world
With the vain stir. I sum up half mankind   130
And add two-thirds of the remaining half,
And find the total of their hopes and fears
Dreams, empty dreams.

From *Book* 4

[THE WINTER EVENING: A BROWN STUDY]

    Come evening once again, season of peace,
Return sweet evening, and continue long!
Methinks I see thee in the streaky west,   245
With matron-step slow-moving, while the night
Treads on thy sweeping train; one hand employed
In letting fall the curtain of repose
On bird and beast, the other charged for man
With sweet oblivion of the cares of day;   250
Not sumptuously adorned, nor needing aid
Like homely featured night, of clustering gems;
A star or two just twinkling on thy brow
Suffices thee; save that the moon is thine
No less than hers, not worn indeed on high   255
With ostentatious pageantry, but set
With modest grandeur in thy purple zone,[4]
Resplendent less, but of an ampler round.[5]
Come then and thou shalt find thy votary calm,
Or make me so. Composure is thy gift.   260
And whether I devote thy gentle hours
To books, to music, or the poet's toil,
To weaving nets for bird-alluring fruit;
Or twining silken threads round ivory reels
When they command whom man was born to please;[6]   265
I slight thee not, but make thee welcome still.
    Just when our drawing rooms begin to blaze
With lights by clear reflection multiplied
From many a mirror, in which he of Gath,
Goliath,[7] might have seen his giant bulk   270
Whole without stooping, towering crest and all,
My pleasures too begin. But me perhaps
The glowing hearth may satisfy awhile
With faint illumination that uplifts
The shadow to the ceiling, there by fits   275
Dancing uncouthly to the quivering flame.
Not undelightful is an hour to me

4. Encircling band. Evening is seen both as a personified goddess, whose "zone" is her royal belt, and as a natural phenomenon, where the "zone" is a stripe of color in the sky.
5. The moon looks larger at evening, when just over the horizon, than at night, when it is higher and brighter.
6. I.e., women.
7. Goliath, the giant of Gath slain by David (1 Samuel 17.19–51).

So spent in parlor twilight; such a gloom
Suits well the thoughtful or unthinking mind,
The mind contemplative, with some new theme   280
Pregnant, or indisposed alike to all.
Laugh ye, who boast your more mercurial powers
That never feel a stupor, know no pause,
Nor need one. I am conscious,[8] and confess,
Fearless, a soul that does not always think.   285
Me oft has fancy ludicrous and wild
Soothed with a waking dream of houses, towers,
Trees, churches, and strange visages expressed
In the red cinders, while with poring eye
I gazed, myself creating what I saw.   290
Nor less amused have I quiescent watched
The sooty films that play upon the bars,[9]
Pendulous and foreboding, in the view
Of superstition prophesying still,
Though still deceived, some stranger's near approach.[1]   295
'Tis thus the understanding takes repose
In indolent vacuity of thought,
And sleeps and is refreshed. Meanwhile the face
Conceals the mood lethargic with a mask
Of deep deliberation, as[2] the man   300
Were tasked to his full strength, absorbed and lost.
Thus oft reclined at ease, I lose an hour
At evening, till at length the freezing blast
That sweeps the bolted shutter, summons home
The recollected powers, and snapping short   305
The glassy threads with which the fancy weaves
Her brittle toys, restores me to myself.
How calm is my recess, and how the frost,
Raging abroad, and the rough wind, endear
The silence and the warmth enjoyed within.   310
I saw the woods and fields at close of day,
A variegated show; the meadows green,
Though faded; and the lands where lately waved
The golden harvest, of a mellow brown,
Upturned so lately by the forceful share.[3]   315
I saw far off the weedy fallows[4] smile
With verdure not unprofitable, grazed
By flocks fast feeding and selecting each
His favorite herb; while all the leafless groves
That skirt the horizon wore a sable hue,   320
Scarce noticed in the kindred dusk of eve.
Tomorrow brings a change, a total change!

---

8. Conscious of.
9. The grate of a fireplace.
1. The piece of soot that often flaps on the bars of a grate was called a "stranger," and supposed to portend an unexpected visitor. Lines 272–310 may be compared with Coleridge's *Frost at Midnight*.
2. As if.
3. Plowshare.
4. Plowed but unseeded land.

Which even now, though silently performed
And slowly, and by most unfelt, the face
Of universal nature undergoes.   325
Fast falls a fleecy shower. The downy flakes,
Descending and with never-ceasing lapse,[5]
Softly alighting upon all below,
Assimilate all objects. Earth receives
Gladly the thickening mantle, and the green   330
And tender blade that feared the chilling blast,
Escapes unhurt beneath so warm a veil.

1785

The Castaway

Obscurest night involved the sky,
   The Atlantic billows roared,
When such a destined wretch as I,
   Washed headlong from on board,
Of friends, of hope, of all bereft,   5
His floating home forever left.

No braver chief[1] could Albion boast
   Than he with whom he went,
Nor ever ship left Albion's coast,
   With warmer wishes sent.   10
He loved them both, but both in vain,
Nor him beheld, nor her again.

Not long beneath the whelming brine,
   Expert to swim, he lay;
Nor soon he felt his strength decline,   15
   Or courage die away;
But waged with death a lasting strife,
Supported by despair of life.

He shouted; nor his friends had failed
   To check the vessel's course,   20
But so the furious blast prevailed,
   That, pitiless perforce,
They left their outcast mate behind,
And scudded still before the wind.

Some succor yet they could afford;   25
   And, such as storms allow,

---

5. Gentle downward glide.
1. George, Lord Anson (1697–1762), in whose
Voyage (1748), Cowper, years before writing this
poem, had read the story of the sailor washed overboard in a storm.

The cask, the coop, the floated cord,
    Delayed not to bestow.
But he (they knew) nor ship, nor shore,
Whate'er they gave, should visit more.   30

Nor, cruel as it seemed, could he
    Their haste himself condemn,
Aware that flight, in such a sea,
    Alone could rescue them;
Yet bitter felt it still to die   35
Deserted, and his friends so nigh.

He long survives, who lives an hour
    In ocean, self-upheld;
And so long he, with unspent power,
    His destiny repelled;   40
And ever, as the minutes flew,
Entreated help, or cried, "Adieu!"

At length, his transient respite past,
    His comrades, who before
Had heard his voice in every blast,   45
    Could catch the sound no more.
For then, by toil subdued, he drank
The stifling wave, and then he sank.

No poet wept him; but the page
    Of narrative sincere,   50
That tells his name, his worth, his age,
    Is wet with Anson's tear.
And tears by bards or heroes shed
Alike immortalize the dead.

I therefore purpose not, or dream,
    Descanting on his fate,   55
To give the melancholy theme
    A more enduring date:
But misery still delights to trace
Its semblance in another's case.   60

No voice divine the storm allayed,
    No light propitious shone,
When, snatched from all effectual aid,
    We perished, each alone;
But I beneath a rougher sea,   65
And whelmed in deeper gulfs than he.

Poems in Process

Poets in all ages have claimed that their poems were not willed but were inspired, whether by a muse, by divine visitation, or by sudden emergence from the author's unconscious mind. But as the poet Richard Aldington has remarked, "genius is not enough; one must also work." The working manuscripts of the greatest writers show that, however involuntary the origin of a poem, vision was usually followed by laborious revision before the work achieved the seeming inevitability of its final form.

Milton is the first major English author for whom we possess drafts of poems indubitably written in his own hand; the excerpt from his manuscript of *Lycidas* shows him altering and expanding his initial efforts. It is no surprise to find Pope, one of the most meticulous of craftsmen, working and reworking his drafts, and radically enlarging *The Rape of the Lock* even after the success which attended its first printed version. But the recently discovered manuscript of Samuel Johnson's greatest poem, *The Vanity of Human Wishes*, is a surprise, for it shows that this neoclassic writer who, in his critical theory, regarded poetry as primarily an art of achieving preconceived ends by tested means, in fact composed with even greater speed and assurance than the Romantic Byron, who liked to represent himself to his readers as dashing off his verses with casual and unreflecting ease. In the manuscript of Gray's *Elegy Written in a Country Churchyard* we find that the poet, by late afterthought, converted a relatively simple elegiac meditation into a longer and much more complex apologia for his chosen way of life. In all these selections we look on as each poet, no matter how rapidly he achieves a result he is willing to let stand, carries on his inevitably tentative efforts to meet the multiple requirements of meaning, syntax, meter, sound pattern, and the constraints imposed by his chosen stanza. And because these are all very good poets, the seeming conflict between the necessities of significance and form results not in the distortion but in the perfection of the poetic statement.

Our transcriptions from the poets' drafts attempt to reproduce, as accurately as the change from script to print will allow, the appearance of the manuscript page. A poet's first attempt at a line or phrase is reproduced in larger type, his revisions in smaller type. The line numbers which are used to identify an excerpt are those of the final form of the complete poem, as reprinted in this anthology. The marginal numbers beside the extract from *The Vanity of Human Wishes* are Johnson's own additions.

SELECTED BIBLIOGRAPHY

Autograph Poetry in the English Language, 2 vols., 1973, compiled by P. J. Croft, reproduces and transcribes one or more pages of manuscript in the poet's own hand, from the 14th century to the present time; volume 1 includes many of the poets represented in this volume of *The Norton Anthology of English Literature*, from John Skelton to George Crabbe. Books which discuss the process of poetic composition and revision, with examples from manuscripts and printed versions, are: Charles D. Abbott, ed., *Poets at Work*, 1948; Phyllis Bartlett, *Poems in Process*, 1951; A. F. Scott, *The Poet's Craft*, 1957. In *Word for Word: A Study of Authors' Alterations*, 1965, Wallace Hildick analyzes the composition of prose fiction, as well as poems. George Sherburn has a revealing study of "Pope at Work" in *Essays on the Eighteenth Century Presented to David Nichol Smith*, 1945.

JOHN MILTON
From Lycidas[1]

[Lines 1–14][2]

yet once more O ye laurells and once more

ye myrtl's browne wth Ivie never sere

I come to pluck yor berries harsh and crude

~~before the mellowing yeare~~ and wth forc't fingers rude

~~and crop yor young~~ shatter yor leaves before y^e mellowing yeare

bitter constraint, and sad occasion deare

compells me to disturbe yor season due

for ~~young~~ Lycidas is dead, dead ere his prime

young Lycidas and hath not left his peere

who would $\wedge$^not sing for Lycidas he well knew

himselfe to sing & build the loftie rime

he must not flote upon his watrie beare

unwept, and welter to the parching wind

without the meed of some melodious teare

[Lines 56–63]

ay mee I fondly dreame

~~had yee~~ bin there, ~~for~~ what could that have don?

~~what could the golden hayrd Calliope~~

for her inchaunting son

~~when shee beheld   (the gods farre sighted bee)~~

~~his goarie scalpe rowle downe the Thracian lee~~

whome universal nature might lament

~~and heaven and hel deplore~~

~~when his divine head downe~~

the streame was sent

downe the Swift Hebrus to the Lesbian shore.

[THE THIRD AND FOLLOWING LINES ARE REWRITTEN ON A SEPARATE PAGE]

what could the muse her selfe that Orpheus bore

the muse her selfe for her inchanting son

~~for her inchanting son~~

1. Transcribed from a manuscript of 50 pages in the library of Trinity College, Cambridge. Among the poems written in Milton's own hand are *Lycidas*, *Comus*, seven sonnets, and several other short poems. The manuscript has been photographically reproduced, with printed transcriptions, by W. Aldis Wright, *Facsimile of the Manuscript of Milton's Minor Poems* (Cambridge, England, 1899).
2. This draft is written on a separate page of the manuscript, which also contains drafts of the passages, "What could the muse her selfe" and "Bring the rathe primrose," transcribed below.

whome universal nature ~~might~~ did lament
when by the rout that made the hideous roare
goarie his ~~divine~~ gorie visage down the streame was sent
downe the swift Hebrus to ye Lesbian shoare.

[Lines 132–53]

Returne Alpheus the dred voice is past
   that shrunk thy streams, returne Sicilian Muse
   and call the vales and bid them hither cast
   thire bells, and flowrets of a thousand hues
   yee vallies low where the mild wispers use

of shades, and wanton winds, and goshing brooks   ✱
                                                     ✱ sparely
on whose fresh lap the swart starre sparely looks   ~~faintly~~

✱ ~~bring~~ hither all yor quaint enamel'd eyes   ✱ throw
   that on the greene terfe suck the honied showrs

and purple all the ground wth vernal flowrs

                    ———— Bring the rathe &c.[3]
to strew the laureat herse where Lycid' lies
for so to interpose a little ease
              ✱ fraile
let our ~~sad~~ thoughts dally wth false surmise   ✱ fraile

[LINES 142–50 ARE DRAFTED ON A SEPARATE PAGE, AS FOLLOWS]

Bring the rathe primrose that unwedded dies
~~collu~~ colouring the pale cheeke of uninjoyd love
and that sad floure that strove
to write his owne woes on the vermeil graine

next adde Narcissus y^t still weeps in vaine
the woodbine and ye pancie freak't wth jet
the glowing violet
the cowslip wan that hangs his pensive head
and every bud that sorrows liverie weares

let Daffadillies fill thire cups with teares
bid Amaranthus all his beautie shed
to strew the laureat herse &c.

Bring the rathe primrose that forsaken dies
the tufted crowtoe and pale Gessamin
                    ye
the white pinke, and pansie freakt wth jet
the glowing violet

─────────────────────

3. I.e., Milton plans to insert here the passage that follows.

the muske rose and ~~the garish columbine~~ the well-attired woodbine

wth cowslips wan that hang the pensive head

and every flower that sad escutcheon ~~beares~~ weare ✱ imbroidrie ~~beares~~ weares

2 ~~let~~ & daffadillies fill thire cups wth teares
1 bid Amaranthus all his beauties shed
to strew &c.

ALEXANDER POPE
From The Rape of the Lock[1]

[*1712 Version: Canto 1, Lines 1–24*]

WHAT dire Offence from Am'rous Causes springs,
    What mighty Quarrels rise from Trivial Things,
    I sing—This Verse to *C—l,* Muse! is due;
This, ev'n *Belinda* may vouchsafe to view:
Slight is the Subject, but not so the Praise,
If she inspire, and He approve my Lays.
    Say what strange Motive, Goddess! cou'd compel
A well-bred *Lord* t'assault a gentle *Belle?*
Oh say what stranger Cause, yet unexplor'd,
Cou'd make a gentle *Belle* reject a *Lord?*
And dwells such Rage in *softest Bosoms* then?
And lodge such daring Souls in *Little Men?*
    Sol thro' white Curtains did his Beams display,
And op'd those Eyes which brighter shine than they;
Shock just had giv'n himself the rowzing Shake,
And Nymphs prepar'd their *Chocolate* to take;
Thrice the wrought Slipper knock'd against the Ground,
And striking Watches the tenth Hour resound.
Belinda rose, and 'midst attending Dames
Launch'd on the Bosom of the silver *Thames:*
A Train of well-drest Youths around her shone,
And ev'ry Eye was fix'd on her alone;
On her white Breast a sparking *Cross* she wore,
Which *Jews* might kiss, and Infidels adore.

[*Revised Version: Canto 1, Lines 1–22*]

WHAT dire Offence from am'rous Causes springs,
    What mighty Contests rise from trivial Things,
    I sing—This Verse to *Caryll,* Muse! is due;

1. The first version of *The Rape of the Lock,* published 1712, consisted of two cantos and a total of
334 lines. Two years later, in 1714, Pope published an enlarged version of five cantos and 794
lines, in which he added the supernatural

"machinery" of the Sylphs and Gnomes as well as
a number of mock-epic episodes. The excerpts
reprinted here show how Pope revised and expanded
passages which he retained from the first version
of the poem. The revised version includes changes

This, ev'n *Belinda* may vouchsafe to view:
Slight is the Subject, but not so the Praise,
If She inspire, and He approve my Lays.
    Say what strange Motive, Goddess! cou'd compel
A well-bred *Lord* t'assault a gentle *Belle?*
Oh say what stranger Cause, yet unexplor'd,
Cou'd make a gentle *Belle* reject a *Lord?*
In Tasks so bold, can Little Men engage,
And in soft Bosoms dwells such mighty Rage?
    Sol thro' white Curtains shot a tim'rous Ray,
And op'd those Eyes that must eclipse the Day;
Now Lapdogs give themselves the rowzing Shake,
And sleepless Lovers, just at Twelve, awake:
Thrice rung the Bell, the Slipper knock'd the Ground,
And the press'd Watch return'd a silver Sound.
Belinda still her downy Pillow prest,
Her Guardian *Sylph* prolong'd the balmy Rest.
'Twas he had summon'd to her silent Bed
The Morning-Dream that hover'd o'er her Head.

[*Revised Version: Canto 2, Lines 1–8*]

Not with more Glories, in th' Etherial Plain,
    The Sun first rises o'er the purpled Main,
    Than issuing forth, the Rival of his Beams
Launch'd on the Bosom of the Silver *Thames*.
Fair Nymphs, and well-drest Youths around her shone,
But ev'ry Eye was fix'd on her alone.
On her white Breast a sparkling *Cross* she wore,
Which *Jews* might kiss, and Infidels adore.

From An Essay on Man[2]

[*From the First Manuscript*]

                    we ourselves
1. Learn ~~then thyself~~, not God presume to scan,
            But
        ~~And~~ know, the Study of Mankind is <u>Man.</u>
    Plac'd on this <u>Isthmus</u> of a Middle State,
    A Being <u>darkly wise</u>, & <u>rudely great</u>.
    With too much <u>knowledge</u> for the <u>Sceptic</u> side,
    And too much <u>Weakness</u> for a <u>Stoic's</u> Pride,

that Pope added in later editions of the enlarged
text of 1714.
2. Two of Pope's holograph manuscripts of *An
Essay on Man* have survived. The earlier one is at
the Pierpont Morgan Library in New York. The

second one, at the Houghton Library, Harvard,
was evidently intended as a fair copy for printing;
but Pope, who was an inveterate reviser, introduced some last-minute improvements. The passage transcribed here from each of these manuscripts

He hangs between, uncertain where to rest;
Whether to deem himself a <u>God</u> or <u>Beast</u>;
Whether his <u>Mind</u> or <u>Body</u> to prefer,
Born but to <u>die</u>, & reas'ning but to <u>err</u>;
Alike in <u>Ignorance,</u> (~~that~~ ^his^ Reason such)
Whether he thinks too <u>little</u> or too <u>much</u>:
Chaos of <u>Thought</u> & <u>Passion</u>, all confus'd,
Still by <u>himself</u> abus'd & dis-abus'd:
Created half to <u>rise</u>, & half to <u>fall</u>;
Great <u>Lord</u> of all things, yet a <u>prey</u> to all;
Sole <u>Judge</u> of <u>Truth</u>, in endless <u>Error</u> hurl'd;
The <u>Glory</u>, <u>Jest</u>, and <u>Riddle</u> of the World.

[*From the Second Manuscript*][3]

~~Incipit I~~ ^Know^
~~Incipit III~~ ~~Learn~~ we ourselves, not God presume to scan,
The only Science ^Convinc'd,^
~~But know,~~ the Study of Mankind is <u>Man</u>;
[Plac'd on this Isthmus of a Middle <u>State</u>,
A Being darkly wise, and rudely great;
With too much Knowledge for the Sceptic side,
^With^
~~And~~ too much Weakness for a Stoic's Pride,
^in doubt to act or^
He hangs between, ~~uncertain where to~~ rest,
^Part of^
Whether ~~To~~ deem himself a ^᠎^God or Beast;
^In doubt^
Whether his Mind, or Body to prefer.
~~This born~~   ~~that~~
Born but to die, and reas'ning but to err;
Alike in Ignorance, his Reason such,
^Whether he thinks^   ^or too much.^
~~Who thinks~~ too little, ~~or who thinks too much:~~
Chaos of Thought and Passion, all confus'd,
Still by himself abus'd and dis-abus'd:
Created half to rise, and half to fall;
Great Lord of all things, yet a prey to all;
Sole Judge of Truth, in endless error hurl'd;
The Glory, Jest, and Riddle of the World!

is Pope's famed description of man's "middle state" in the great chain of being; in the published version, it opens Epistle 2, lines 1–18.

3. In this version of the manuscript, Pope inserted some marginal glosses. In the right-hand margin (next to the line beginning "Learn we ourselves . . ."), he wrote: "Of Man, as an Individual," while next to the line beginning "Plac'd on this Isthmus . . .," he wrote "His Middle Nature." And in the left-hand margin, a little below the line beginning "With too much knowledge . . .," he wrote "His Powers, and Imperfections."

SAMUEL JOHNSON

Johnson told Boswell in 1766 that when composing verses "I have generally had them in my mind, perhaps fifty at a time, walking up and down in my room; and then I have written them down, and often, from laziness, have written only half lines. . . . I remember I wrote a hundred lines of *The Vanity of Human Wishes* in a day." When the first manuscript draft of this poem turned up in the 1940s among Boswell's papers at Malahide Castle, it supported Johnson's account, for it had been written and corrected in haste, with only sparse punctuation; while the second half of each line had been filled out, obviously from memory, at some time after the writing of the first half, in a darker ink. In the transcriptions from this manuscript (which is in the collection of Mary Hyde, Somerville, New Jersey), the half-lines and emendations that Johnson added to his initial draft are printed in boldface type.

The draft was written on the right-hand pages of a small homemade pocket book; some words in the added half-line, impinging on the right margin of the page, had to be completed above or below the line. The two added lines, "See Nations slowly wise . . . the tardy Bust," were written on the blank left-hand page, at the place where they were to be inserted. The numeration of every tenth line was added by Johnson in the manuscript, and incorporates these two additional lines.

Johnson published the poem in 1749 and revised it for a second publication in 1755, when it achieved the final form printed in the selections from Johnson, above. It was in 1755 that Johnson introduced his most famous emendation when, after his disillusionment with Lord Chesterfield as literary patron, he substituted in line 162 the word "patron" for "garret": "Toil, envy, want, the patron, and the jail."

From The Vanity of Human Wishes

[Lines 135–64]

When first the College Rolls **receive his nam**[e]
The young Enthusiast **quits his ease for fame**

    Quick fires his breast
~~Each act betrays~~ **the fever of renown**
Caught from **the strong Contagion of the Gown**
On his banks he waves, from noise withdrawn
140 In sober state **th' imaginary Lawn**
O'er Bodley's Dome **his future Labours spread**
And Bacon's Mansion **trembles o'er his head.**
Are these thy views, **proceed illustrious Youth**
And Virtue guard **thee to the throne of Trut**[h]
Yet should th~~y fate~~ **Soul indulge the gen'rous**
                      Heat

Till Captive Science yields her last Retreat
Should Reason guide thee with her brightest Ray
And pour on misty Doubt resistless day
Should no false kindness lure to loose delight
150 Nor Praise relax, nor difficulty fright
Should tempting Novelty thy cell refrain
                           vain
And Sloth's bland opiates shed their fumes in
sShould Beuty blunt on fops her fatal dart
Nor claim the triumph of a letter'd heart
~~S Nor~~ Should no Disease thy torpid veins invade
Nor Melancholys Spectres haunt thy Shade

         hope
Yet ~~dream~~ not Life from Grief or Danger free,
Nor think the doom of Man revers'd for thee
Deign   passing to
~~Turn~~ on the world ~~awhile~~ turn thine eyes
160 And pause awhile from Learning to be wise
There mark what ill the Scholar's life assail

See Nations slowly wise, and meanly just,
To buried merit raise the tardy Bust.

             the
Toil envy Want ~~a~~ Garret and the Jayl
Dreams
If ~~Hope~~ yet flatter once again attend
Hear Lydiats life and Galileo's End.

THOMAS GRAY

There are three manuscript versions of the *Elegy* in Gray's handwriting; the one reproduced here in part is the earliest of these, preserved at Eton College, England; Gray entitled it "Stanzas wrote in a Country Church-Yard."

It is evident that Gray originally intended to conclude his poem at the end of the fifth stanza transcribed below. At some later time he bracketed off the last four stanzas, introduced a transitional stanza which incorporated the last two lines of the original conclusion, and then went on to write a new and much enlarged conclusion to the poem, which includes the closing "Epitaph." A comparison with the final version of the *Elegy*, above, will show that the author deleted some of these added stanzas, and also made a number of verbal changes, in his published texts of the poem.

From Elegy Written in a Country Churchyard

[*Lines 69–128*]

The struggleing Pangs of conscious Truth to hide,
To quench the Blushes of ingenuous Shame,

And at the Shrine of Luxury & Pride
With   by
~~Burn~~ Incense hallowd in the Muse's Flame.
    kindled at

The thoughtless World to Majesty may bow
Exalt the brave, & idolize Success
But more to Innocence their Safety owe
Than Power & Genius e'er conspired to bless

And thou, who mindful of the unhonour'd Dead
                eir
Dost in these notes thy artless Tale relate
By Night & lonely Contemplation led
To linger in the gloomy Walks of Fate

Hark how the sacred Calm, that broods around
Bids ev'ry fierce tumultuous Passion cease
In still small Accents whisp'ring from the Ground
A grateful Earnest of eternal Peace

No more with Reason & thyself at Strife
Give anxious Cares & endless Wishes room
But thro' the cool sequester'd Vale of Life
Pursue the silent Tenour of thy Doom.

        Far from the madding Crowd's ignoble Strife;
        Their sober Wishes never knew to stray:
        Along the cool sequester'd Vale of Life
                    noiseless
        They kept the silent Tenour of their Way.

Yet even these Bones from Insult to protect
Some frail Memorial still erected nigh
With
~~In~~ uncouth Rhime, & shapeless Sculpture deckt
Implores the passing Tribute of a Sigh.

Their Name, their Years, spelt by th' unletter'd Muse
The Place of Fame, & Epitaph supply,
And many a holy Text around she strews
That teach the rustic Moralist to die.

For who to dumb Forgetfulness a Prey
This pleasing anxious Being e'er resign'd;
Left the warm Precincts of the chearful Day,
Nor cast one longing lingring Look behind?

On some fond Breast the parting Soul relies,
Some pious Drops the closing Eye requires:

Even from the Tomb the Voice of Nature cries,
And buried Ashes glow with social Fires
   For Thee, who mindful &c: as above.[1]

If chance that e'er some pensive Spirit more,
By sympathetic Musings here delay'd,
With vain, tho' kind, Enquiry shall explore
Thy once-loved Haunt, this long-deserted Shade.

Haply some hoary-headed Swain shall say,[2]
Oft have we seen him at the Peep of Dawn
With hasty Footsteps brush the Dews away
On the high Brow of yonder hanging Lawn
Him have we seen the Green-wood Side along,
While o'er the Heath we hied, our Labours done,
Oft as the Woodlark piped her farewell Song
With whistful Eyes pursue the setting Sun.

                spreading   nodding
Oft at the Foot of yonder hoary Beech
That wreathes its old fantastic Roots so high
His listless Length at Noontide would he stretch,
And pore upon the Brook that babbles by.

   With Gestures quaint now smileing as in Scorn,
            wayward fancies   ~~loved~~ would he
   Mutt'ring his fond Conceits he ~~wont to~~ rove:
     drooping,
   Now woeful wan, ~~he droop'd,~~ as one forlorn
   Or crazed with Care, or cross'd in hopeless Love.

     One Morn we miss'd him on th' accustom'd Hill,
      Along the   near
     By the Heath-~~side~~, & at his fav'rite Tree.
     Another came, nor yet beside the Rill,
            by
     Nor up the Lawn, nor at the Wood was he.

   ~~There scatter'd oft, the earliest~~
     The next with Dirges meet in sad Array
      by
     Slow thro the Church-way Path we saw him born
     Approach & read, for thou can'st read the Lay
      Graved carved   yon
     Wrote on the Stone beneath that ancient Thorn

                          Year
     There scatter'd oft the earliest of yᵉ ~~Spring~~
              showers of
     By Hands unseen are frequent Vi'lets found
      Redbreast
     The Robin loves to build & warble there,
     And little Footsteps lightly print the Ground.

---

1. I.e., Gray indicates that the second bracketed stanza, above, is to be inserted here, except that the opening "And thou" is to be altered to "For Thee."
2. At this point in the manuscript Gray ceases to leave a space between the stanzas. The first edition of 1751, at Gray's request, was printed without any spaces between the stanzas; the spaces were, however, introduced in later editions printed during Gray's lifetime.

Here rests his Head upon the Lap of Earth[3]
A Youth to Fortune & to Fame unknown
Fair Science frown'd not on his humble Birth
And Melancholy mark'd him for her own

Large was his Bounty & his Heart sincere;
Heaven did a Recompence as largely send.
He gave to Mis'ry all he had, a Tear.
He gain'd from Heav'n, 'twas all he wish'd, a Friend

No farther seek his Merits to disclose,
              think
Nor seek to draw them from their dread Abode
(His Frailties there in trembling Hope repose)
The Bosom of his Father & his God.

3. These last three stanzas (which Gray in the first edition of 1751 labeled "The Epitaph") are written in the right-hand margin, with the page turned crosswise.

Selected Bibliographies

The Selected Bibliographies incorporate a list of Suggested General Readings on English literature, followed by bibliographies for each of the periods in this volume. For ease of reference, the authors within each period are arranged in alphabetical order. Entries for certain classes of writings (e.g., "Songs and Poems of the Sixteenth Century") are listed alphabetically among the authors. Such entries include cross-reference to the bibliographies of individual authors within these classes.

SUGGESTED GENERAL READINGS

Histories of England and of English Literature

George Macaulay Trevelyan's *History of England*, rev., 1945, is an excellent survey in one volume; for detailed studies of single periods, see *The Oxford History of England*, 15 vols., 1934 ff., by a variety of historians. Designed especially as a background for students of literature is Robert M. Adams, *The Land and Literature of England: A Historical Account*, 1983. For single books in the comprehensive 12-volume *Oxford History of English Literature*, ed. F. P. Wilson and Bonamy Dobrée, 1945 ff., see the listings below. *The New Pelican Guide to English Literature*, ed. Boris Ford, is available in a sequence of paperbacks, 1982 following. Useful one-volume histories are Albert C. Baugh and others, *A Literary History of England*, rev., 1967; Hardin Craig and others, *A History of English Literature*, 1950; and (less densely factual, and more a running literary appreciation) David Daiches, *A Critical History of English Literature*, 2 vols., rev., 1970. *Annals of English Literature, 1475–1950*, rev., 1961, lists important publications year by year, together with the significant literary events in each year. Ellen Moers, *Literary Women*, 1976, is a history of the circumstances, interinfluences, and distinctive features of literature written by women; the editorial materials in Sandra M. Gilbert and Susan Gubar, *The Norton Anthology of Literature by Women*, 1985, constitute a concise history and set of biographies of women authors since the Middle Ages.

Drama

Allardyce Nicoll, *British Drama*, rev., 1962, and *A History of English Drama, 1660–1900*, 6 vols., rev., 1952–59; Richard Courtney, *Outline History of British Drama*, 1982.

The Novel

The most detailed, although somewhat pedestrian, history is Ernest A. Baker's *History of the English Novel*, 10 vols., 1924–39. Among the short histories are Walter A. Raleigh, *The English Novel*, rev., 1911, which stops at Walter Scott; and, more up-to-date, Arnold Kettle, *An Introduction to the English Novel*, 2 vols., 1951–53; Walter Allen, *The English Novel*, 1954; Ian Watt, *The Rise of the Novel*, 1957; and Lionel Stevenson, *The English Novel*, 1960.

Poetry

W. J. Courthope, *A History of English Poetry*, 6 vols., 1895–1910, and H. J. C. Grierson and J. C. Smith, *A Critical History of English Poetry*, rev., 1947. In addition, Douglas Bush's two books, *Mythology and the Renaissance Tradition in English Poetry*, 1932, and *Mythology and the Romantic Tradition in English Poetry*, 1937, constitute an excellent account, from their special perspective, of English poetry from the 16th century through T. S. Eliot; see also Bush's *English Poetry: The Main Currents from Chaucer to the Present*, rev., 1965. Another book that ranges from the Middle Ages through the 18th century is E. M. W. Tillyard, *The English Epic and Its Background*, 1954.

Literary Criticism

George Saintsbury, *A History of English Criticism*, 1911, is still referred to. More recent histories of English criticism are M. H. Abrams, *The Mirror and the Lamp: Romantic Theory and the Critical Tradition*, 1953; W. K. Wimsatt, Jr., and Cleanth Brooks, *Literary Criticism: A Short History*, 1957; George Watson, *The Literary Critics*, 1962; René Wellek, *A History of Modern Criticism: 1750–1950*, 1955 ff., of which four of the projected five volumes have been published; and Frank Lentricchia, *After the New Criticism*, 1980. René Wellek and Austin Warren, *Theory of Literature*, rev., 1970, is a useful introduction to the variety of scholarly and critical approaches up to the time of its publication. Convenient introductions to structuralist, poststructuralist, and other recent theories are Jonathan Culler, *Structuralist Poetics*, 1975, and *On Deconstruction*, 1982. Among recent collections of feminist criticism are Lee Edwards and Arlyn Diamond, eds., *Authority of Experience*, 1977, and Mary Jacobus, ed., *Women Writing and Writing about Women*, 1979.

Reference Works

The New Cambridge Bibliography of English Literature, ed. George Watson, 1969–77, lists all the books of the major and many minor British authors, together with a large selection from biographical, scholarly, and critical works written about these authors. Literary biographies and critical books published since that time can be found in the *MLA International Bibliography*; for separate periods, see listings below. F. W. Bateson, ed., *A Guide to English Literature*, rev., 1976, is a selected list of editions, and of scholarly and critical treatments, of important English writers; for poetry only see A. E. Dyson, ed., *English Poetry: Select Bibliographical Guides*, 1971. *Poetry Explication*, rev. Joseph M. Kuntz, 1962, lists close analyses of English poems, old and recent, and I. F. Bell and Donald Baird, *The English Novel, 1578–1956*, 1958, pro-

vides a useful list of 20th-century criticisms of fiction. Further bibliographical aids are described in Richard D. Altick and Andrew Wright, *Selective Bibliography for the Study of English and American Literature*, rev., 1979; Arthur G. Kennedy, *A Concise Bibliography for Students of English*, rev., 1972; and Margaret C. Patterson, *Literary Research Guide*, rev., 1983.

For compact biographies of English authors, see the multivolumed *Dictionary of National Biography*, ed. Leslie Stephen and Sidney Lee in 1885–1900, with supplements that carry the work to 1960; condensed biographies will be found in the *Concise Dictionary of National Biography*, part 1 (1953) and part 2 (1961). Handy reference books of authors, works, and various literary terms and allusions are *The Oxford Companion to English Literature*, ed. Margaret Drabble, rev., 1985; *The Reader's Companion to World Literature*, ed. Calvin S. Brown, 1956; *The Oxford Companion to the Theatre*, Phyllis Hartnoll, rev., 1967; *Dictionary of World Literature*, ed. Joseph T. Shipley, rev., 1953; and *Encyclopedia of Poetry and Poetics*, ed. Alex Preminger and others, rev., 1974. Low-priced handbooks that define and illustrate literary concepts and terms are: M. H. Abrams, *A Glossary of Literary Terms*, rev., 1981; W. F. Thrall and Addison Hibbard, *A Handbook to Literature*, rev. C. Hugh Holman, rev., 1980. On the Greek and Roman background, see *The Oxford Classical Dictionary*, rev., 1970, and G. M. Kirkwood, *A Short Guide to Classical Mythology*, 1959.

Albert C. Baugh, *A History of the English Language*, rev., 1978 with Thomas W. Cable, will be found helpful, as will various treatments of English meters and stanza forms, such as: R. M. Alden, *English Verse*, 1903; Karl Shapiro and Robert Beum, *A Prosody Handbook*, 1965; Paul Fussell, Jr., *Poetic Meter and Poetic Form*, rev., 1979; *The Structure of Verse: Modern Essays in Prosody*, ed. Harvey Gross, 1966; and Derek Attridge, *Rhythms of English Poetry*, 1982.

Intellectual History and Criticism

Students interested in intellectual history as a background for English literature will profit from Arthur T. Lovejoy, *The Great Chain of Being*, 1936, and *Essays in the History of Ideas*, 1948; Marjorie Nicolson, *The Breaking of the Circle*, 1950, *Science and Imagination*, 1956, and *Mountain Gloom and*

Mountain Glory, 1959; Basil Willey, *The Seventeenth Century Background*, 1934, *The Eighteenth Century Background*, 1940, and *Nineteenth Century Studies*, 1949; and M. H. Abrams, *Natural Supernaturalism: Tradition and Revolution in Romantic Literature*, 1971. In addition, the following is a selection of books in literary history and criticism that have been notably influential in shaping modern approaches to English literature and literary forms: Erich Auerbach, *Mimesis: The Representation of Reality in Western Literature*, 1953; Maud Bodkin, *Archetypal Patterns in Poetry*, 1934; Cleanth Brooks, *The Well Wrought Urn*, 1947; Ronald Crane, *The Languages of Criticism and the Structure of Poetry*, 1953; *The Idea of the Humanities*, 2 vols., 1967, and, as editor, *Critics and Criticism, Ancient and Modern*, 1952; T. S. Eliot, *Selected Essays*, 3rd ed., 1951, and *On Poetry and Poets*, 1957; William Empson, *Seven Types of Ambiguity*, 3rd ed., 1953; William K. Wimsatt, *The Verbal Icon*, 1954; Francis Fergusson, *The Idea of a Theater*, 1949; Northrop Frye, *Anatomy of Criticism*, 1957; Henry James, *The Art of the Novel: Critical Prefaces*, 1934; F. R. Leavis, *Revaluation*, 1936, and *The Great Tradition* (i.e., in the novel), 1948; C. S. Lewis, *The Allegory of Love*, rev., 1938; Percy Lubbock, *The Craft of Fiction*, 1926; I. A. Richards, *Principles of Literary Criticism*, rev., 1934, and *Practical Criticism*, 1930; Caroline Spurgeon, *Shakespeare's Imagery*, 1935; Lionel Trilling, *The Liberal Imagination*, 1950, and *The Opposing Self*, 1955; Edmund Wilson, *Axel's Castle: A Study in the Imaginative Literature of 1870–1930*, 1936, and *The Wound and the Bow*, 1941; Wayne C. Booth, *The Rhetoric of Fiction*, 1961, and *A Rhetoric of Irony*, 1974; W. J. Bate, *The Burden of the Past and the English Poet*, 1970; and Harold Bloom, *The Anxiety of Influence*, 1973.

THE MIDDLE AGES

Scholarship during this era may be conveniently divided between the Old and Middle English periods. A reference book for the whole era is the *Dictionary of the Middle Ages* by Joseph Strayer *et al.*, still in progress.

The Old English Period

The reader who wishes to acquire historical background for the literature of the period will profit greatly from Dorothy Whitelock's concise study, *The Beginnings of English Society*, 1952. The most detailed history is F. M. Stenton's authoritative *Anglo-Saxon England*, 3rd ed., 1971. Also highly informative are P. Hunter Blair's *An Introduction to Anglo-Saxon England*, 1956, and *Roman Britain and Early England, 55 B.C.–A.D. 871*, 1963. The classic study of the culture of the primitive Germanic peoples is H. M. Chadwick's *The Heroic Age*, 1912. For those who wish to sample basic historical documents of the period, there are available the translations by G. N. Garmonsway of *The Anglo-Saxon Chronicle*, 1953, and by L. Sherley-Price of Bede's *Ecclesiastical History*, published under the title *A History of the English Church and People*, rev. R. E. Latham, 1968.

All the surviving poetry in Old English is contained in the six volumes edited by G. P. Krapp and E. V. K. Dobbie, *The Anglo-Saxon Poetic Records*, 1931–53, but the absence of glossaries makes this edition difficult for nonspecialists. Excellent texts of the shorter poems translated in this anthology are contained in J. C. Pope's *Seven Old English Poems*, 1966. The standard text of *Beowulf and the Fight at Finnsburg* is F. Klaeber's 3rd ed., 1950; C. L. Wrenn's edition, *Beowulf, with the Finnsburg Fragment*, rev. W. F. Bolton, 1973, is very useful; H. D. Chickering, Jr., has made a dual-language edition with extensive commentary. Modern English translations of many of the Old English poems have been published under various titles by C. W. Kennedy and Michael Alexander. The senior editor's translation is the text included in *Beowulf*, A Norton Critical Edition, ed. Joseph F. Tuso, 1975.

Good critical discussion of Old English literature will be found in volume 1 of the *Cambridge History of English Literature*; in Kemp Malone's section of *A Literary History of England*, ed. A. C. Baugh, rev., 1967; in S. B. Greenfield's *A Critical History of Old English Literature*, 1965, and his *The Interpretation of Old English Poems*, 1972; in C. L. Wrenn, *A Study of Old English Literature*, 1966; and in D. A. Pearsall, *Old and Middle English Poetry*,

1977. Important critical articles have been collected by R. P. Creed, *Old English Poetry*, 1967, J. B. Bessinger and S. J. Kahrl, *Essential Articles for the Study of Old English Poetry*, 1968, and Martin Stevens and Jerome Mandel, *Old English Literature*, 1968. General introductions designed primarily for students are T. A. Shippey, *Old English Verse*, 1972, B. C. Raw, *The Art and Background of Old English Poetry*, 1978, and Michael Alexander, *Old English Literature*, 1983.

The best critical essay on *Beowulf* remains J. R. R. Tolkien's Gollancz lecture, *Beowulf, the Monsters, and the Critics*, 1937 (see Nicholson and Fry, below). The most exhaustive scholarly discussion is R. W. Chambers's *Beowulf: An Introduction to the Study of the Poem*, 3rd ed., with a supplement by C. L. Wrenn, 1959. W. W. Lawrence's *Beowulf and the Epic Tradition*, 1928, is still of value. Works by Dorothy Whitelock, *The Audience of Beowulf*, 1951; A. C. Brodeur, *The Art of Beowulf*, 1959; Kenneth Sisam, *The Structure of Beowulf*, 1965; and E. B. Irving, *A Reading of Beowulf*, 1968, and *Introduction to Beowulf*, 1969, mingle fine general criticism with some highly specialized discussion. Useful collections of essays on *Beowulf*, including Tolkien's lecture, have been made by L. E. Nicholson, *An Anthology of Beowulf Criticism*, 1963, and D. K. Fry, *The Beowulf Poet*, 1968.

The Middle English Period

Good and fairly compact accounts of the history of England between the Norman Conquest and the end of the Middle Ages are contained in the two volumes by Christopher Brooke, *From Alfred to Henry III, 871–1272*, 1961, and George Holmes, *The Later Middle Ages, 1272–1485*, 1962; see also May McKisack, *The Fourteenth Century, 1307–99*, 1959, and D. M. Stenton, *English Society in the Early Middle Ages (1066–1307)*, 1951, and A. R. Myers, *England in the Late Middle Ages*, 1952. Interesting illustrations of life in the Middle Ages, especially in the later centuries, will be found in three books by G. G. Coulton: *Chaucer and His England*, 1908, *The Medieval Scene*, 1930, *Medieval Panorama*, 1938; in Eileen Power's *Medieval People*, 1924; in Edith Rickert's *Chaucer's World*, 1948; in volume 1 of G. M. Trevelyan's *Illustrated English Social History*,

Chaucer's England and the Early Tudors, 1949; see also the picture books listed under Chaucer below. The spirit of the 15th and late 14th century is brilliantly discussed by J. Huizinga, *The Waning of the Middle Ages*, 1924. F. R. H. Du Boulay gives an interpretation of the age that complements and qualifies Huizinga in *An Age of Ambition*, 1970.

For general discussions of Middle English literature including Chaucer, see volume 2 of the *Cambridge History of English Literature*, A. C. Baugh's section of *A Literary History of England*, edited by Baugh, rev., 1967, D. A. Pearsall, *Old and Middle English Poetry*, 1977, J. A. Burrow, *Middle English Literature and Its Background*, 1982; *Medieval Literature: Chaucer and the Alliterative Tradition* (vol. 1 of the *New Pelican Guide to English Literature*), ed. Boris Ford, 1982; and D. S. Brewer, *English Gothic Literature*, 1983. W. P. Ker's *English Literature: Medieval*, 1912, is still provocative. D. M. Zesmer's *Guide to English Literature from Beowulf through Chaucer and Medieval Drama*, 1961, is a most useful survey; C. S. Lewis, *The Discarded Image*, 1964, is very popular; W. L. Renwick and H. Orton, *The Beginnings of English Literature to Skelton*, 3rd ed., 1966, is a good survey with bibliographical notes; also useful is H. S. Bennett, *Chaucer and the Fifteenth Century*, 1947. Edward Vasta's collection of essays by various scholars, *Middle English Survey: Critical Essays*, 1965, will offer stimulation to students of *Piers Plowman*, *Sir Gawain and the Green Knight*, the drama, and the ballads. J. A. Burrow, *Ricardian Poetry: Chaucer, Gower, Langland and the Gawain Poet*, 1971, is extremely interesting on the authors in his title and their period. Chapters 6–10 of Erich Auerbach's *Mimesis: The Representation of Reality in Western Literature*, translated by W. R. Trask, 1953, while dealing with none of the works included in this anthology, shed much light on the spirit of medieval literature. For the Middle English language, see Helge Kökeritz's *A Guide to Chaucer's Pronunciation*, 1954; Samuel Moore's *Historical Outlines of English Sounds and Inflections*, rev. A. H. Marckwardt, 1951; John W. Clark's *Early English*, 1957, 1967; and David Burnley's *A Guide to Chaucer's Language*, 1983.

For general discussion of non-Chaucerian Middle English literature, see R. M.

Wilson, *Early Middle English Literature*, 1939, and E. K. Chambers, *English Literature at the Close of the Middle Ages*, 1954, which between them thoroughly cover the beginning and the end of the period. George Kane's *Middle English Literature*, 1951, has good chapters on the romances, the religious lyrics, and *Piers Plowman*, and A. L. Kellogg, *Chaucer, Langland, Arthur*, 1972, treats his selected topics provocatively. A. C. Spearing's *Medieval Dream-Poetry*, 1976, is a fine treatment of the genre. A broad sampling of non-Chaucerian literature in translation is offered by *Medieval English Verse*, ed. R. S. Loomis and R. Willard, 1948.

The standard bibliography is A *Manual of the Writings in Middle English, 1050–1500*, six vols., 1967–80, ed. J. B. Severs, A. E. Hartung, *et al.*, which is based on and supersedes the *Manual* of J. E. Wells, 1916, with 9 supplements through 1945.

Geoffrey Chaucer

The standard edition of Chaucer's writing is F. N. Robinson's *The Complete Works of Chaucer*, 2nd ed., 1957 (a 3rd ed. by various hands is in preparation). The senior editor's anthology of Chaucer's poetry, 2nd ed., 1975, from which are taken the selections printed here, is helpful to the nonspecialist, as are A. C. Baugh's *Chaucer's Major Poetry*, 1963, and John H. Fisher's *The Complete Poetry and Prose of Geoffrey Chaucer*, 1977. Vivid presentations of Chaucer in the background of 14th-century England are found in Marchette Chute's *Geoffrey Chaucer of England*, 1946, and D. S. Brewer's *Chaucer and His World*, 1978, which is beautifully illustrated. Pictorial companions to Chaucer's works, especially the *Canterbury Tales*, include R. S. Loomis, *A Mirror of Chaucer's World*, 1965, Maurice Hussey, *Chaucer's World*, 1967, Ian Serraillier, *Chaucer and His World*, 1968, and Roger Hart, *English Life in Chaucer's Day*, 1973. John Gardner's *The Life and Times of Chaucer*, 1977, is a fictionalized biography, fairly lively but unsubstantial. The raw material for Chaucer's biography is contained in *Chaucer Life-Records*, edited by M. M. Crow and C. C. Olson, 1966. For succinct accounts of the sources and literary background of Chaucer's works see R. D. French's A *Chaucer Handbook*, 2nd ed., 1947; reproductions of many of the known sources of the *Canterbury Tales* are contained in the scholarly

compendium *Sources and Analogues of Chaucer's Canterbury Tales*, edited by W. F. Bryan and Germaine Dempster, 1941, 1958. Useful literary materials are collected in R. P. Miller's *Chaucer: Sources and Backgrounds*, 1977. Muriel Bowden, A *Commentary on the General Prologue to the Canterbury Tales*, 1948, provides a wealth of background information on the individual Canterbury pilgrims; see also J. M. Manly's *Some New Light on Chaucer*, 1926, and Jill Mann's *Chaucer and Medieval Estates Satire*, 1973. Various aspects of Chaucer's work are treated by a number of scholars in *Chaucer and Chaucerians*, edited by D. S. Brewer, 1966; *Geoffrey Chaucer (Writers and Their Background)*, also edited by Brewer, 1974; *Companion to Chaucer Studies*, edited by Beryl Rowland, rev., 1979; and *Chaucer's Mind and Art*, edited by A. C. Cawley, 1969. For literary criticism, the following contain stimulating discussions: H. S. Bennett, *Chaucer and the Fifteenth Century*, 1947; D. S. Brewer, *Chaucer*, 3rd ed., 1973; B. H. Bronson, *In Search of Chaucer*, 1960; Robert B. Burlin, *Chaucerian Fiction*, 1977; G. K. Chesterton, *Chaucer*, 1932; Nevill Coghill, *The Poet Chaucer*, 1949, and *Geoffrey Chaucer*, 1956; H. S. Corsa, *Chaucer, Poet of Mirth and Morality*, 1964; W. C. Curry, *Chaucer and the Medieval Sciences*, rev., 1960; Alfred David, *The Strumpet Muse*, 1976; E. T. Donaldson, *Speaking of Chaucer*, 1970, 1983; Peter Elbow, *Oppositions in Chaucer*, 1975; D. R. Howard, *The Idea of the Canterbury Tales*, 1976; Maurice Hussey, A. C. Spearing, and James Winny, *An Introduction to Chaucer*, 1965; S. S. Hussey, *Chaucer: An Introduction*, 1971; George Kane, *Chaucer*, 1984; P. M. Kean, *Chaucer and the Making of English Poetry*, 2 vols., 1972; G. L. Kittredge, *Chaucer and His Poetry*, 1915; Traugott Lawler, *The One and the Many in the Canterbury Tales*, 1980; W. W. Lawrence, *Chaucer and the Canterbury Tales*, 1950; John Lawlor, *Chaucer*, 1968; J. L. Lowes, *Geoffrey Chaucer and the Development of His Genius*, 1934; R. M. Lumiansky, *Of Sondry Folk*, 1955; Charles Muscatine, *Chaucer and the French Tradition*, 1957; H. R. Patch, *On Rereading Chaucer*, 1939; R. O Payne, *The Key of Remembrance*, 1963; Raymond Preston, *Chaucer*, 1952; R. K. Root, *The Poetry of Chaucer*, 2nd ed., 1972; T. W. Ross, *Chaucer's Bawdy*, 1972; P. G. Ruggiers, *The*

Art of the Canterbury Tales, 1965. D. W. Robertson's *A Preface to Chaucer*, 1962, is a most learned, stimulating, doctrinaire, and controversial introduction to the reading of Chaucer. V. A. Kolve's *Chaucer and the Imagery of Narrative*, 1984, relates the first five of the *Canterbury Tales* to medieval art. The following are collections of critical essays by various writers: *Discussions of the Canterbury Tales*, edited by C. J. Owen, 1961; *Chaucer Criticism: The Canterbury Tales*, edited by R. J. Schoeck and J. Taylor, 1960; *Chaucer: Modern Essays in Criticism*, edited by E. C. Wagenknecht, 1959; *Geoffrey Chaucer: A Critical Anthology*, 1969, edited by J. A. Burrow; and *Geoffrey Chaucer (Contemporary Studies in Literature)*, edited by G. D. Economou, 1975. See also the prefatory remarks on Chaucer's poems in Robinson's edition and the senior editor's commentary in his anthology.

Perhaps the most reliable glossary is that edited by Norman Davis, *et al.*, 1979. The standard bibliographies are E. P. Hammond, *Chaucer: A Bibliographical Manual*, 1908; D. D. Griffith, *Bibliography of Chaucer*, 1955; W. R. Crawford, *Bibliography of Chaucer 1954–63*, 1967; L. Y. Baird, *A Bibliography of Chaucer 1964–1973*, 1977; and A. C. Baugh, *Chaucer*, 1968, 1977. See also Caroline Spurgeon's *Five Hundred Years of Chaucer Criticism and Allusion, 1357–1900*, 1925.

Everyman

See entries under **The Second Shepherds' Play**.

Margery Kempe

The standard Middle English text of *The Book of Margery Kempe* is that of S. B. Meech and H. E. Allen, 1940; a modernization has been made by W. Butler-Bowden, 1936. An excellent biographical, historical, and critical study is C. W. Atkinson's *Mystic and Pilgrim: the Book and the World of Margery Kempe*.

Sir Thomas Malory

The Winchester manuscript of Malory's *Morte Darthur*, with full commentary and valuable discussion, is given in Eugène Vinaver's *The Works of Sir Thomas Malory*, 3 vols., 2nd ed., 1967; the one-volume edition, 2nd ed., Oxford, 1970, contains the text only. The Caxton version is most readily available in *Caxton's Malory*, edited by

J. W. Spisak, 1983. Vinaver's *Malory*, 1929, surveys Malory's life and career. A number of critical problems in Malory's work, especially its unity, are discussed in three collections of essays by various scholars: *Essays on Malory*, edited by J. A. W. Bennett, 1963, *Malory's Originality*, edited by R. M. Lumianski, 1964, and *Studies in Malory*, edited by J. W. Spisak, 1985. Two excellent studies of the work are those by L. D. Benson, *Malory's Morte Darthur*, 1976, and Mark Lambert, *Malory: Style and Vision in Le Morte Darthur*, 1975. In *The Ill-Framed Knight*, 1966, William Matthews challenges the traditional identification of the author of the *Morte Darthur* with that knight-prisoner, the details of whose stormy career have been unearthed by scholars interested in the book.

A most valuable summary of the Arthurian literary background is R. S. Loomis's *The Development of Arthurian Romance*, 1963.

Middle English Lyrics

The best selections of Middle English lyrics are *Early English Lyrics*, edited by E. K. Chambers and F. Sidgwick, 1921; *Medieval English Lyrics: A Critical Anthology*, edited by R. T. Davies, 1963; *Middle English Lyrics*, A Norton Critical Edition, ed. M. S. Luria and R. L. Hoffman, 1974; *The Oxford Book of Medieval English Verse*, ed. Celia and Kenneth Sisam, 1970; *English Lyrics before 1500*, ed. Theodore Silverstein, 1971; modernized and semimodernized selections appear in M. R. Adamson's *A Treasury of Middle English Verse*, 1930, and in R. D. Stevick's *One Hundred Middle English Poems*, 1964. For criticism see A. K. Moore, *The Secular Lyric in Middle English*, 1951, Kane's chapter in *Middle English Literature*, Stephen Manning, *Wisdom and Number*, 1962, and Rosemary Woolf, *The English Religious Lyric in the Middle Ages*, 1968.

Piers Plowman

The most handy edition of *Piers Plowman* is W. W. Skeat's *The Vision of William Concerning Piers the Plowman . . .* , 2 vols., 1886, which gives all three versions. The most scholarly edition of the A text is that edited by George Kane, 1960, and of the B text that by Kane and E. T. Donaldson, 1975. J. A. W. Bennett's edition of the first eight passus of the B text, 1972, is very useful, as is D. A. Pearsall's edition of the C text, 1978. There are modern translations by H. W. Wells, *The Vision of Piers Plowman*, 1935; by Nevill Coghill (selections only), *Visions from Piers Plowman*, 1949; and by Margaret Williams, *Piers the Plowman*, 1972. A literal prose translation is J. F. Goodridge's *Langland: Piers the Ploughman*, rev., 1966. The best general account of the poem is in chapters 4–5 of R. W. Chambers's *Man's Unconquerable Mind*, 1939; see also Kane's chapter in *Middle English Literature*. Recent studies by Elizabeth Salter, *Piers Plowman: An Introduction*, 1962, and John Lawlor, *Piers Plowman: An Essay in Criticism*, 1962, are most useful to the beginner, as are chapters on the poem in the works by Howard and Spearing mentioned below under **Sir Gawain and the Green Knight**. Collections of critical essays have been made by Edward Vasta, *Interpretations of Piers Plowman*, 1968; R. J. Blanch, *Style and Symbolism in Piers Plowman*, 1969; and S. S. Hussey, *Piers Plowman: Critical Approaches*, 1969. Useful background material has been collected by Jeanne Krochalis and Edward Peters in *The World of Piers Plowman*, 1975.

Popular Ballads

The great ballad collection is that of F. J. Child, *The English and Scottish Popular Ballads*, 1882, more available in the somewhat abridged edition by H. C. Sargent and G. L. Kittredge, 1904. Selections will be found in *The Faber Book of Ballads*, edited by M. J. C. Hodgart, 1965, and *The Oxford Book of Ballads*, ed. James Kinsley, 1969. For general discussion, see F. B. Gummere, *The Popular Ballads*, 1907; G. H. Gerould, *The Ballad of Tradition*, 1932; W. J. Entwistle, *European Balladry*, 1939; and M. J. C. Hodgart, *The Ballads*, 1950.

The Second Shepherds' Play; The York Play of the Crucifixion; Everyman

The classic work on the medieval drama is E. K. Chambers's *The Medieval Stage*, 1905. More recent are Hardin Craig's exhaustive *English Religious Drama of the Middle Ages*, 1955, and O. B. Hardison's fine study, *Christian Rite and Christian Drama in the*

Middle Ages, 1965. For good discussions of the Middle English mystery cycles, see V. A. Kolve's *The Play Called Corpus Christi*, 1966, and Rosemary Woolf's *The English Mystery Plays*, 1972. Good selections of Middle English plays are presented by J. Q. Adams, *Chief Pre-Shakespearean Dramas*, 1924, by A. C. Cawley, *Everyman and Medieval Miracle Plays*, 1960, by D. M. Berington, *Medieval Drama*, 1975, and by Peter Happé, *The English Mystery Plays*, 1975. Cawley's *The Wakefield Pageants in the Towneley Cycle*, 1958, has a discussion of the work of the "Wakefield Master" whose hand is seen in the *Second Shepherds' Play*. A collection of critical essays has been made by Jerome Taylor and A. H. Nelson in *Medieval English Drama*, 1972.

Sir Gawain and the Green Knight

The standard Middle English text of the poem is that of J. R. R. Tolkien and E. V. Gordon, 1925 (revised by Norman Davis, 1967). Perhaps easier to use are the editions by R. A. Waldron, 1970, rev. for *The Poems of the Pearl Manuscript*, 1978, and J. A. Burrow, 1972. Good discussion of various aspects of the poem appear in Marie Borroff's *Sir Gawain and the Green Knight: A Stylistic and Metrical Study*, 1962; L. D. Benson, *Art and Tradition in Sir Gawain and the Green Knight*, 1965 (especially good on the sources); and J. A. Burrow, *A Reading of Sir Gawain and the Green Knight*, 1965. Interesting chapters on the poem are contributed by A. C. Spearing in *Criticism and Medieval Poetry*, 2nd ed., 1972, and *The Gawain Poet*, 1971, and D. R. Howard in *The Three Temptations: Medieval Man in Search of the World*, 1966. There are three collections of critical essays on the poet: R. J. Blanch's *Sir Gawain and Pearl*, 1966; Denton Fox's *Twentieth-Century Interpretations of Sir Gawain and the Green Knight*, 1968; and D. R. Howard and C. K. Zacher's *Critical Studies of Sir Gawain and the Green Knight*.

The York Play of the Crucifixion

See entries under **The Second Shepherds' Play**.

THE SIXTEENTH CENTURY

Some general books on the history of the period are: J. B. Black, *The Reign of Elizabeth, 1558–1603*, 2nd ed., 1959; G. R. Elton, *England Under the Tudors*, 1955;

J. H. Hexter, *Reappraisals in History*, 1961; Joel Hurstfield, *The Elizabethan Nation*, 1964, and *Freedom, Corruption, and Government in Elizabethan England*, 1973; J. E. Neale, *Queen Elizabeth I*, 1933; Conrad Russell, *The Crisis of Parliaments: English History, 1509–1660*, 1971. Political theory in the period is surveyed in J. W. Allen, *A History of Political Thought in the Sixteenth Century*, 3rd ed., 1957; Quentin Skinner, *The Foundations of Modern Political Thought*, 2 vols., 1978. Exploration and military history are treated in J. A. Williamson, *The Age of Drake*, 4th ed., 1960; and G. Mattingly, *The Armada*, 1959. For church history and religion, see P. Collinson, *The Elizabethan Puritan Movement*, 1967; Horton Davies, *Worship and Theology in England from Cranmer to Hooker, 1534–1603*, 1970; W. Haller, *The Rise of Puritanism*, 1938; and J. F. H. New, *Anglican and Puritan: The Basis of Their Opposition, 1558–1640*, 1964.

Important works for social and economic history are: Muriel St. Clare Byrne, ed., *The Lisle Letters*, 1981; G. N. Clark, *The Wealth of England, 1496–1760*, 1946; Peter Laslett, *The World We Have Lost*, 3rd. ed., 1984; Lawrence Stone, *The Crisis of the Aristocracy, 1558–1641*, 1965, and *The Family, Sex, and Marriage in England, 1500–1800*, 1977; R. H. Tawney, *Religion and the Rise of Capitalism*, 1926; and *The Agrarian Problem in the Sixteenth Century*, 1967; Louis B. Wright, *Middle Class Culture in Elizabethan England*, 1935, rpt. 1965. The institution of patronage and courtiership, with special reference to literature, is analyzed in Guy Fitch Lytle and Stephen Orgel, eds., *Patronage in the Renaissance*, 1981; and David Javitch, *Poetry and Courtliness in Renaissance England*, 1976. On the situation of women in Renaissance England, see Pearl Hogrefe, *Tudor Women: Commoners and Queens* 1975 and *Women of Action in Tudor England: Nine Biographical Sketches* 1977; Ruth Kelso, *Doctrine for the Lady of the Renaissance*, rpt., 1978; Retha M. Warnicke, *Women of the English Renaissance and Reformation*, 1983.

Various aspects of Renaissance thought are treated in: Jacob Burckhardt, *The Civilization of the Renaissance*, rev. 1944; Douglas Bush, *The Renaissance and English Humanism*, 1939; Ernst Cassirer et al. eds., *The Renaissance Philosophy of Man*, 1948;

Hiram Haydn, *The Counter-Renaissance*, 1950; Paul O. Kristeller, *Renaissance Thought*, 2 vols., 1961; Erwin Panofsky, *Renaissance and Renascences in Western Art*, 2 vol., 1960; Isabel Rivers, *Classical and Christian Ideas in English Renaissance Poetry*, 1979; E. M. W. Tillyard, *The Elizabethan World Picture*, 1943; Keith Thomas, *Religion and the Decline of Magic*, 1971. Renaissance science, old and new, is discussed in A. R. Hall, *The Scientific Revolution, 1500–1800*, rev., 1966; P. Kocher, *Science and Religion in Elizabethan England*, 1953; Wayne Shumaker, *The Occult Sciences in the Renaissance*, 1972; A. Wolf, *A History of Science, Technology, and Philosophy in the 16th and 17th Centuries*, 1959.

Education in the period is the subject of Kenneth Charlton, *Education in Renaissance England*, 1965; and Thomas W. Baldwin, *William Shakespere's Small Latine and Lesse Greeke*, 2 vols., 1944. On logic and rhetoric see W. S. Howell, *Logic and Rhetoric in England, 1500–1700*, 1956; Sister Miriam Joseph, *Rhetoric in Shakespeare's Time*, 1962; and Frances Yates, *The Art of Memory*, 1966. On publishing and the book trade, see H. S. Bennett, *English Books and Readers, 1475–1557*, 1952, and *English Books and Readers, 1558–1603*, 1965; Elizabeth L. Eisenstein, *The Printing Press as an Agent of Change*, 2 vols., 1979; and E. H. Miller, *The Professional Writer in Elizabethan England*, 1959.

Some books pertaining to art, architecture, and culture are: E. Auerbach, *Tudor Artists*, 1954; H. C. Baker and W. G. Constable, *English Painting of the Sixteenth and Seventeenth Centuries*, 1930; J. Buxton, *Elizabethan Taste*, 1963; Mark Girouard, *Life in the English Country House*, 1978; Roy Strong, *The English Icon: Elizabethan and Jacobean Portraiture*, 1969; Marcus Whiffin, *An Introduction to Elizabethan and Jacobean Architecture*, 1952. Renaissance iconology and emblem books often illuminate literary imagery; important studies are Rosemary Freeman, *English Emblem Books*, 1948; Erwin Panofsky, *Studies in Iconology*, 1939; Jean Seznec, *The Survival of the Pagan Gods*, trans. B. F. Sessions, 1963; Edgar Wind, *Pagan Mysteries in the Renaissance*, rev., 1968. Wylie Sypher, *Four Stages of Renaissance Style*, 1955, treats stylistic analogues between literature and the visual arts.

For Tudor music and musicians and their

association with lyric poetry in the period, see M. C. Boyd, *Elizabethan Music and Music Criticism*, 1940; E. H. Fellowes, *English Madrigal Verse*, rev., 1967; G. L. Finney, *Musical Backgrounds for English Literature*, 1962; John Stevens, *Music and Poetry in the Early Tudor Court*, 1961; W. L. Woodfill, *Musicians in English Society from Elizabeth to Charles I*, 1953. Important studies of music's symbolic and structural relation to poetry include John Hollander, *The Untuning of the Sky: Ideas of Music in English Poetry, 1500–1700*, 1961; and Paula Johnson, *Form and Transformation in Music and Poetry of the English Renaissance*, 1975.

Anthologies of Elizabethan literary criticism are G. G. Smith, *Elizabethan Critical Essays*, 2 vols., 1904; and O. B. Hardison, Jr., *English Literary Criticism: The Renaissance*, 1963. Important studies of Renaissance literary theory and criticism are: Don C. Allen, *Mysteriously Meant: The Rediscovery of Pagan Symbolism and Allegorical Interpretation in the Renaissance*, 1970; Baxter Hathaway, *Marvels and Commonplaces: Renaissance Literary Criticism*, 1968; M. W. Ferguson, *Trials of Desire: Renaissance Defenses of Poetry*, 1983; S. K. Heninger, *Touches of Sweet Harmony: Pythagorean Cosmology and Renaissance Poetics*, 1974; Lawrence Manley, *Convention*, 1970; Rosemond Tuve, *Elizabethan and Metaphysical Imagery*, 1947.

On the vernacular versions of the Bible, see A. C. Partridge, *English Biblical Translation*, 1973; and David Daiches, *The King James Version of the English Bible*, 1968. John E. Booty has edited the 1559 *Book of Common Prayer*, 1976, with a very useful introduction.

Major studies of the stage and drama are David Bevington, *From "Mankind" to Marlowe*, 1962, and *Tudor Drama and Politics*, 1968; F. T. Bowers, *Elizabethan Revenge Tragedy, 1578–1642*, 1940; M. D. Bradbrook, *Themes and Conventions of Elizabethan Tragedy*, 1935, and *The Growth and Structure of Elizabethan Comedy*, 1955; E. K. Chambers, *The Elizabethan Stage*, 4 vols., 1923; Ann Cook, *The Privileged Playgoers of Shakespeare's London, 1576–1642*, 1981; A. C. Dessen, *Elizabethan Drama and the Viewer's Eye*, 1977; Madeleine Doran, *Endeavors of Art*, 1954; C. Walter Hodges, *The Globe Restored*, 1973; Glynne Wick-

ham, *Early English Stages, 1300–1660*, 3 vols., 1959–81.

Some distinguished theoretical and historical studies of Renaissance literature include: Douglas Bush, *Mythology and the Renaissance Tradition in English Poetry*, rev., 1963; Rosalie Colie, *The Resources of Kind: Genre-Theory in the Renaissance*, 1973; Maurice Evans, *English Poetry in the Sixteenth Century*, rev., 1967; Stephen Greenblatt, *Renaissance Self-Fashioning*, 1980; Thomas M. Greene, *The Light in Troy: Imitation and Discovery in Renaissance Poetry*, 1982; C. S. Lewis, *English Literature in the Sixteenth Century, Excluding Drama*, 1954 (with extensive bibliography). Important studies of particular Renaissance genres and kinds include: Lily B. Campbell, *Divine Poetry and Drama in Sixteenth-Century England*, 1959; Helen Cooper, *Pastoral: Medieval to Romance*, 1977; Anne Ferry, *The "Inward" Language: Sonnets of Wyatt, Sidney, Shakespeare, and Donne*, 1983; Alvin Kernan, *The Cankered Muse: Satire of the English Renaissance*, 1959; J. W. Lever, *The Elizabethan Love Sonnet*, 1956; Janel Mueller, *The Native Tongue and the Word: Developments in English Prose Style, 1380–1580*, 1984; Patricia Parker, *Inescapable Romance*, 1979; Douglas L. Peterson, *The English Lyric from Wyatt to Donne*, 1966.

Valuable collections of critical essays are edited by Paul Alpers, *Elizabethan Poetry: Modern Essays in Criticism*, 1967; J. R. Brown and B. Harris, *Elizabethan Poetry*, 1960; and Maynard Mack and George Lord, *Poetic Traditions of the English Renaissance*, 1982. A useful reference tool is James E. Ruoff, *Handbook of Elizabethan and Stuart Literature*, 1975. The Goldentree bibliography for the period, John L. Lievsay, *The Sixteenth Century: Skelton Through Hooker*, 1968, is a handy, basic reference; the journal *Studies in English Literature*, contains an annual review of scholarship in the Renaissance.

Anonymous Lyrics

Notable Renaissance collections include: *The Phoenix Nest* (1593), ed. Hyder E. Rollins, 1931; and *England's Helicon* (1600), ed. Hyder E. Rollins, 2 vols., 1935.

Roger Ascham

The Whole Works of Roger Ascham, ed. J. A. Giles, 3 vols., 1864–65, rpt. 1965, remains standard, although it omits some theological works and letters. The standard edition of *The Scholemaster* is John E. B. Mayor's annotated edition, 1863, rpt., 1967. An important biographical and critical study is Lawrence V. Ryan, *Roger Ascham*, 1963. "Recent Studies in Ascham" are surveyed in *English Literary Renaissance*, 10 (1980), 300–310.

Thomas Campion

The standard edition is Percival Vivian, *Campion's Works*, 1907, rpt. 1960, including a biography. Campion's English works, with a selection from his Latin poetry, were edited by Walter R. Davis, 1967. Important studies include: Muriel T. Eldridge, *Thomas Campion: His Poetry and Music*, 1977; Miles M. Kastendieck, *England's Musical Poet*, rpt. 1963; E. Lowbury, T. Salter, and A. Young, *Thomas Campion, Poet, Composer, Physician*, 1970; Stephen Ratcliffe, *Campion: On Song*, 1981; and John Hollander, "The Case of Campion," in *Vision and Resonance: Two Senses of Poetic Form*, 1975, pp. 71–90. "Recent Studies" are surveyed in *English Literary Renaissance*, 4 (1974), 404–411.

Samuel Daniel

The only complete edition is the *Complete Works in Verse and Prose*, ed. A. B. Grosart, 5 vols., 1885–96, rpt., 1963. A. C. Sprague has edited *Poems and A Defense of Rhyme*, 1930. Some useful studies of Daniel's life and works are: Joan Rees, *Samuel Daniel, A Critical and Biographical Study*, 1964; Cecil Seronsy, *Samuel Daniel*, 1967; and Andrew F. Marotti, " 'Love is not love': Elizabethan Sonnet Sequences and the Social Order," *ELH* 49 (1982), 396–428.

Michael Drayton

The standard edition is by J. W. Hebel, 5 vols., 1931–41; a useful selected edition is by John Buxton, 1953. The standard biography is B. H. Newdigate, *Michael Drayton and His Circle*, 1941. Critical studies include J. A. Berthelot, *Michael Drayton*, 1967; and R. F. Hardin, *Michael Drayton and the Passing of Elizabethan England*, 1973.

Queen Elizabeth I

Leicester Bradner, ed., *The Poems of Queen Elizabeth I*, 1964, prints several poems and verse translations certainly or probably ascribed to Elizabeth; her partial translation of Petrarch's *Triumph of Eternity* is in Ruth Hughey's edition (2 vols.) of the *Arundel Harington Manuscript*, 1960; her partial translations of Boethius, Plutarch, and Horace's "De Arte Poetica" were edited by Caroline Pemberton, 1889, rpt. 1973; her prose translation of Queen Margaret of Navarre's poem, *The Mirror of the Sinful Soul*, was edited by P. W. Ames, 1897; Adam Fox and J. P. Hodges edited and translated her Latin prayers, 1970; and 21 of her speeches are printed in George P. Rice, Jr., *The Public Speaking of Queen Elizabeth: Selections from Her Official Addresses*, 1951, rpt. 1966. The standard biography remains J. E. Neale, *Queen Elizabeth I*, 1934, rpt. 1967; her significance as symbol is treated by Roy Strong, *The Cult of Elizabeth: Elizabethan Portraiture and Pagentry*, 1977. *English Literary Renaissance* 14 (1984), 409–425, surveys recent studies pertaining to Elizabeth and other women writers of the period.

John Foxe

There is no standard edition of Foxe's collected works. The most useful modern edition of *The Acts and Monuments* is in 8 volumes, ed. Stephen R. Cattley, 1837–41, rpt., 1965. Foxe's two Latin comedies were edited and translated by J. H. Smith, 1973. The best account of his life is in J. F. Mozley's *John Foxe and His Book*, 1940, rpt., 1970. An indispensable work on Foxe's significance is William Haller, *The Elect Nation: The Meaning and Relevance of Foxe's Book of Martyrs*, 1963. Also important are: John N. King, *English Reformation Literature: The Tudor Origins of the Protestant Tradition*, 1982; V. Olson, *John Foxe and the Elizabethan Church*, 1973; and Helen C. White, *Tudor Books of Saints and Martyrs*, 1963. A survey of recent studies is in *English Literary Renaissance*, 11 (1981), 224–232.

George Gascoigne

John W. Cunliffe edited the *Complete Works*, 2 vols., 1907–10. The standard edition of his poems, *A Hundreth Sundrie Flowres*, is by C. T. Prouty, 1942, as is the authoritative study of his life and works, *George Gascoigne, Elizabethan Courtier, Soldier, and Poet*, 1942 rpt., 1966. Ivor Winters promoted a reevaluation of Gascoigne's lyric poetry in "The 16th Century

Lyric in England," rpt. in P. Alpers, *Elizabethan Poetry*, 1967. Walter Davis analyzes his prose fiction, *Master F. J.*, in *Idea and Act in Elizabethan Fiction*, 1969. Recent studies are surveyed in *English Literary Renaissance*, 3 (1973), 322–327.

Fulke Greville

Most of Greville's literary works are in *The Poems and Dramas of Fulke Greville, First Lord Brooke*, ed. Geoffrey Bullough, 2 vols., 1939, rpt., 1945; G. A. Wilkes edited the other philosophical poems, *The Remains, Being Poems of Monarchy and Religion*, 1965; Nowell Smith edited his *Life of Sir Philip Sidney*, 1906. The major biography is by Ronald A. Rebholz, 1971. Important critical studies are: Morris Croll, *The Works of Fulke Greville*, 1903; Joan Rees, *Critical Biography*, 1971; Richard Waswo, *The Fatal Mirror: Themes and Techniques in the Poetry of Fulke Greville*, 1972. *English Literary Renaissance*, 2 (1972), 376–382, contains a review of recent studies.

Richard Hakluyt

The major modern edition of his collection, *The Principal Navigations, Voyages, Traffics, and Discoveries* (1598–1600)— which includes John Lane's letter—is the 12-volume, Glasgow, 1903–5 edition. See George B. Parks, *Richard Hakluyt and the English Voyages*, 1928.

Mary (Sidney) Herbert, Countess of Pembroke

J. C. A. Rathmell edited *The Psalms of Sir Philip Sidney and the Countess of Pembroke*, 1963; G. F. Waller edited her occasional poems, other psalm versions, and the translation of Petrarch's *Triumph of Death*, 1977; her verse translation of Garnier's play, *Marc-Antoine*, is in Geoffrey Bullough's *Narrative and Dramatic Sources of Shakespeare*, vol. 5, 1964, and Diane Bornstein edited her translation of Philippe de Mornay's *Discourse of Life and Death*, 1983. An important study is G. F. Waller, *Mary Sidney, Countess of Pembroke: A Critical Study of Her Writings and Literary Milieu* (1979). *English Literary Renaissance*, 14 (1984), 426–437, surveys recent studies.

Sir Thomas Hoby

Hoby's *Book of the Courtier* was published with an introduction by Walter Raleigh, 1900; his diary, *The Booke of the Travaile*

and Lief of Me, was edited by E. Powell, 1902. The qualities of Hoby's prose are discussed in F. O. Matthiessen, *Translation, An Elizabethan Art*, 1931. Castiglione's original, *Il Cortegiano*, was edited by V. Cian in 1929, and received a splendid modern translation by C. S. Singleton in 1959. The significance of the work is discussed in Robert W. Hanning and David Rosand, eds., *Castiglione: The Ideal and the Real in Renaissance Culture*, 1983; and Wayne A. Rebhorn, *Courtly Performances*, 1978.

Richard Hooker

Hooker's *Works* are now coming out in a Folger Library edition, 1977—; the first three volumes include the *Laws*, edited by G. Edelen and W. Speed Hill, 1977–81. Biographical works include the early *Life* by Isaac Walton (1665); and *The Judicious Marriage of Mr. Hooker and the Birth of "The Laws of Ecclesiastical Polity,"* by C. J. Sisson, 1940. Some important studies are: E. T. Davies, *The Political Ideas of Richard Hooker*, 1946; P. Munz, *The Place of Hooker in the History of Thought*, 1952; and W. Speed Hill, ed., *Studies in Richard Hooker*, 1972.

Aemilia Lanyer

The edition of her *Salve Deus Rex Judaeorum* by A. L. Rowse (1978) supplies some important biographical facts, but identifies her (on highly questionable evidence) as Shakespeare's Dark Lady. The only critical study to date is Barbara K. Lewalski, "Of God and Good Women: The Poems of Aemilia Lanyer," in *Silent But for the Word: Tudor Women as Patrons, Translators, and Writers of Religious Works*, ed. Margaret Hannay, 1985.

Christopher Marlowe

Fredson Bowers has edited the *Complete Works* in 2 vols., 1973; also important is C. F. Tucker Brooke's edition, 1910, rpt. 1966. Roma Gill has a useful edition of *Dr Faustus* (1965); and W. W. Greg edited parallel texts of the two versions in 1950. Stephen Orgel edited *The Complete Poems and Translations of Christopher Marlowe*, 1971. For Marlowe's biography, see Leslie Hotson, *The Death of Christopher Marlowe*, 1925; John Bakeless, *The Tragicall History of Christopher Marlowe*, 1942; and Mark Eccles, *Christopher Marlowe in London*, 1934 rpt. 1967. Valuable critical studies include: Douglas Cole, *Suffering and Evil in the Plays of Christopher Marlowe*, 1962; John P. Cutts, *The Left Hand of God*, 1973; W. L. Godshalk, *The Marlovian World Picture*, 1974; J. D. Jump, ed., *Marlowe: Dr. Faustus, A Casebook*, 1969; Clifford Leech, ed., *Marlowe: A Collection of Critical Essays*, 1965; Harry Levin, *The Overreacher*, 1952; and Wilbur Sanders, *The Dramatist and the Received Idea*, 1968. For *Hero and Leander*, the facsimile of the first edition (1972) has an important introduction and textual commentary by Louis L. Martz; on the genre, see Elizabeth S. Donno, *Elizabethan Minor Epics*, 1963, and Clark Hulse, *Metamorphic Verse: The Elizabethan Minor Epic*, 1981. "Recent Studies in Marlowe" are surveyed in *ELH*, 7 (1977), 382–399.

Sir Thomas More

The standard edition is the great *Yale Edition of the Complete Works of St. Thomas More* (1965—). Volume 4, *Utopia*, is edited by E. L. Surtz and J. H. Hexter, and Hexter's introduction provides a brilliant, balanced, and highly readable interpretation. Robert M. Adams edited *Utopia* for the Norton Critical Editions, 1975, which contains an earlier version of the translation used in this anthology as well as a range of background readings and contemporary interpretations. R. W. Chambers's biography, *Thomas More*, 1935, is standard, but its humanist emphasis is challenged by the focus on statecraft and polemics in Richard Marius's *Thomas More: A Biography*, 1984. *Utopia* has attracted a wide variety of interpretations, among them: R. A. Ames, *Citizen Thomas More and his Utopia*, 1949; J. H. Hexter, *More's "Utopia": The Biography of an Idea*, 1952; Robbin S. Johnson, *More's Utopia: Ideal and Illusion*, 1969; George M. Logan, *The Meaning of More's Utopia*, 1983; E. L. Surtz, *The Praise of Pleasure: Philosophy, Education, and Communism in More's Utopia*, 1957. *ELR*, 9 (1979), 442–458, contains a bibliography of recent studies.

Thomas Nashe

The standard edition, in 5 vols., is edited by R. W. McKerrow, rev., F. P. Wilson, 1958. There are selected editions by Stanley Wells, 1965, and J. B. Steane, 1972. Useful critical studies are: G. R. Hibbard, *Thomas Nashe, A Critical Introduction*, 1962; and Jonathan V. Crewe, *Unredeemed Rhetoric: Thomas Nashe and the Scandal of Authorship*, 1982. *English Literary Renaissance*, 11 (1981), 344–350, has a review of recent studies.

Sir Walter Raleigh

The standard edition of the poems is by A. M. C. Latham, rev., 1950; a useful edition is Gerard Hammond, ed., *Selected Writings*, 1984. Noteworthy studies include: Stephen Greenblatt, *Sir Walter Ralegh*, 1973; W. F. Oakeshott, *The Queen and the Poet*, 1960; E. A. Strathmann, *Sir Walter Ralegh, A Study in Elizabethan Skepticism*, 1951.

William Shakespeare

Major editions of *1 Henry IV* are the *Variorum*, edited by S. B. Hemingway, 1936, with a supplement by G. B. Evans, 1956; the *New Arden*, edited by A. R. Humphries, 1960; and *The Riverside Shakespeare*, ed. G. B. Evans, 1974. For criticism see the Norton Critical Edition, ed. J. L. Sanderson, rev. 1969; *Henry IV Parts I and II: A Casebook*, ed. G. K. Hunter, 1970; Robert Ornstein, *A Kingdom for a Stage: The Achievement of Shakespeare's History Plays*, 1972; M. M. Reese, *The Cease of Majesty: A Study of Shakespeare's History Plays*, 1961; Irving Ribner, *The English History Play in the Age of Shakespeare*, rev., 1965; E. M. W. Tillyard, *Shakespeare's History Plays*, 1944; John Dover Wilson, *The Fortunes of Falstaff*, 1944.

Stephen Booth has edited the sonnets, including a facsimile of the first edition, with a modernized text on facing pages and an elaborate commentary, 1977; Hyder Rollins's *Variorum* edition, 2 vols., 1944, presents an exhaustive summary of the many commentaries and problems associated with these poems; another useful edition is by W. G. Ingram and T. Redpath, 1965. There are many paperback editions. Significant criticism includes Stephen Booth, *An Essay on Shakespeare's Sonnets*, 1969; G. Wilson Knight, *The Mutual Flame*, 1955, rpt., 1962; and Hallett Smith, *The Tension of the Lyre: Poetry in Shakespeare's Sonnets*, 1981. Important critical essays are collected in *The Riddle of Shakespeare's Sonnets*, ed. Edward Hubler, 1962; *The Sonnets: A Casebook*, ed. Peter Jones, 1977; *New Essays on Shakespeare's Sonnets*, ed. Hilton Landry, 1976; and *Discussions of Shakespeare's Sonnets*, ed.

Barbara Herrnstein Smith, 1964. *Shakespeare Survey* 15, 1962, is largely devoted to Shakespeare's songs, sonnets, and other poems.

The standard study of the life and works is E. K. Chambers, *William Shakespeare: A Study of Facts and Problems*, 2 vols., 1930. S. Schoenbaum's important biographical research is recorded in *William Shakespeare: A Documentary Life*, 1975, and *A Compact Documentary Life*, 1977. Some very useful aids to scholarship are: Geoffrey Bullough, *Narrative and Dramatic Sources of Shakespeare*, 8 vols., 1957–75; Kenneth Muir and S. Schoenbaum, eds., *A New Companion to Shakespeare Studies*, 1971, in which many fields of Shakespeare studies are surveyed by various authorities; and M. M. Reese's handbook, *Shakespeare: His World and His Work*, rev., 1980.

Sir Philip Sidney

The definitive edition of Sidney's poetry is by William Ringler, 1962. Jean Robertson edited the *Old Arcadia*, 1973; Carl Dennis prepared a facsimile edition of the incomplete *New Arcadia* (1590), 1970; Maurice Evans edited *The Countess of Pembroke's Arcadia* (the 1593 composite version) in 1977. *The Defence of Poesy* is included in the *Miscellaneous Prose* edited by K. Duncan-Jones and J. Van Dorsten, 1973; in individual editions by Geoffrey Shepherd (1965) and J. Van Dorsten (1966), among others; and in collections of criticism. The earliest biography was by Fulke Greville, 1652; important modern studies of the life and works are: John Buxton, *Sir Philip Sidney and the English Renaissance*, 1954, rpt., 1964; A. C. Hamilton, *Sir Philip Sidney: A Study of His Life and Works*, 1977; Roger Howell, *Sir Philip Sidney: The Shepherd Knight*, 1968; and James M. Osborn, *Young Philip Sidney*, 1972. Some important critical studies include: Walter R. Davis and Richard Lanham. *Sidney's Arcadia*, 1965; David Kalstone, *Sidney's Poetry: Contexts and Interpretations*, 1965; Jon S. Lawry, *Sidney's Two Arcadias: Pattern and Proceeding*, 1972; Neil L. Rudenstine, *Sidney's Poetic Development*, 1967; Andrew Weiner, *Sir Philip Sidney and the Poetics of Protestantism*, 1978. *English Literary Renaissance*, 2 (1972), 148–164, and 8(1978), 212–233 provide a review of recent studies.

John Skelton

The complete edition is Alexander Dyce, *Poetical Works*, 2 vols., 1843, rpt., 1965; other important editions are *Complete Poems*, ed., Philip Henderson, rev., 1948; *Poems of Skelton*, ed. R. S. Kinsman, 1969; *The Complete English Poems*, ed. John Scattergood, 1973. Biographical studies include Maurice Pollet, *John Skelton*, 1962; and H. L. R. Edwards, *Skelton: The Life and Times of an Early Tudor Poet*, 1949. Noteworthy critical studies are by Stanley Fish, *John Skelton's Poetry*, 1965, and Arthur R. Heiserman, *Skelton and Satire*, 1961. *English Literary Renaissance*, 1 (1971), 89–96, contains a useful resume of scholarship.

Robert Southwell

The standard edition of the English poetry is *The Poems of Robert Southwell, S. J.*, by James H. McDonald and Nancy Pollard Brown, 1967, which also includes a biographical account. Some valuable studies are by P. Janelle, *Robert Southwell the Writer*, 1935; Louis L. Martz, in *The Poetry of Meditation*, rev., 1962; and Helen C. White in *Tudor Books of Saints and Martyrs*, 1963. *English Literary Renaissance*, 2 (1983), 221–227, contains a review of recent studies.

Edmund Spenser

The major scholarly edition is *The Works of Edmund Spenser, a Variorum Edition*, ed. Edwin A. Greenlaw et al., 10 vols., 1932–49. Also important are A. C. Hamilton's annotated edition of *The Faerie Queene*, 1977; and the selection of poetry and criticism in the Norton Critical Edition edited by Hugh Maclean, rev., 1982. The chief biography is *The Life of Edmund Spenser* by Alexander Judson, 1945. Important critical studies include: Paul J. Alpers, *The Poetry of The Faerie Queene*, 1967; Graham Hough, *A Preface to "The Faerie Queene,"* 1962; C. S. Lewis, *The Allegory of Love*, 1936; Isabel MacCaffrey, *Spenser's Allegory: The Anatomy of Imagination*, 1975; William Nelson, *The Poetry of Edmund Spenser*, 1963; James Nohrnberg, *The Analogy of the Faerie Queene*, 1976; T. P. Roche, Jr., *The Kindly Flame* (on books 3 and 4), 1964; Mark Rose, *Spenser's Art: A Companion to Book I of The Faerie Queene*, 1975; Rosemond Tuve, *Allegorical Imagery*, 1966; Kathleen Williams, *Spenser's World of Glass*, 1966. A helpful selection of criticism is provided in A. C. Hamilton, ed., *Essential Articles for the Study of Edmund Spenser*, 1972. A guide to recent work is provided in Waldo F. McNeir and Foster Provost, *Edmund Spenser: An Annotated Bibliography*, 1975.

Henry Howard, Earl of Surrey

The standard edition is by Frederick M. Padelford, 1928, rpt., 1966; Emrys Jones's edition, 1964, has a good introductory essay on style, themes, and influences. *Tottel's Miscellany* is edited by Hyder E. Rolllins, rev., 1965. There is a biography by E. R. Casady, *Henry Howard, Earl of Surrey*, 1938. Noteworthy among the few critical studies are Walter R. Davis, "Contexts in Surrey's Poetry," *ELR*, 4 (1974), 40–55; Ants Oras, "Surrey's Technique of Phonetic Echoes," *JEGP*, 50 (1951), 289–308; and Patricia Thomson, "The First English Petrarchans," *HLQ*, 22 (1958/59), 85–105. A review of recent studies appears in *English Literary Renaissance*, 2 (1971), 188–191.

Lady Mary Wroth

The Countess of Montgomery's Urania was first published in 1621; a 145-page manuscript continuation in the Newberry Library is as yet unpublished. Josephine A. Roberts edited *The Poems of Lady Mary Wroth*, 1983, including the sonnet sequence *Pamphilia to Amphilanthus* and the poems from *Urania*. Wroth's unpublished play, *Love's Victorie*, is at the Huntington Library. Studies include May Nelson Paulissen, *The Love Sonnets of Lady Mary Wroth: A Critical Introduction*, 1982; and Carolyn R. Swift, "Feminine Identity in Lady Mary Wroth's Romance *Urania*," *ELR* 14, 328–346.

Sir Thomas Wyatt

The best edition is Richard C. Harrier, *The Canon of Sir Thomas Wyatt's Poetry*, 1975; others are by J. Daalder, 1975; Kenneth Muir and Patricia Thomson, 1969; and R. A. Rebholz, 1978. *Tottel's Miscellany* is edited by Hyder E. Rollins, rev., 1965. Letters and life records are included in Kenneth Muir's biography, *Life and Letters of Sir Thomas Wyatt*, 1963. Patricia Thomson treats both life and works in *Sir Thomas Wyatt and his Background*, 1965. Critical studies include E. K. Chambers, *Sir Thomas Wyatt and Some Collected Studies*, 1933; Raymond Southall, *The Courtly Maker*, 1964; and E. M. W. Tillyard, *The Poetry of Sir Thomas Wyatt*, rpt., 1949. A review of recent studies appears in *English Literary Renaissance*, 1 (1971), 178–188.

THE EARLY SEVENTEENTH CENTURY

The best single-volume general history of England in the 17th century is by Christopher Hill, *The Century of Revolution*, rev. 1966. Differing views of the same events are offered by Godfrey Davies, *The Early Stuarts*, 2nd ed., 1959; by G. M. Trevelyan, *England Under the Stuarts*, 8th ed., 1919; and by Barry Coward, *The Stuart Age*, 1980. A close account of the crucial English revolution and civil wars will be found in two volumes by C. V. Wedgwood, *The King's Peace, 1637–41*, 1955, and *The King's War, 1641–42*, 1958. More recent studies of these events include Lawrence Stone, *The Crisis of the Aristocracy, 1558–1641*, 1965, and Austin Woolrych, *Commonwealth to Protectorate*, 1982. Christopher Hill's *The World Turned Upside Down*, 1972, studies the radical fringe in the revolution. Monuments of the older scholarship are David Masson's *Life of John Milton: Narrated in Connexion with the . . . History of His Time*, in 8 vols.,

1859–96, and Samuel Rawson Gardiner's *History of the Civil Wars*, covering the period of 1603–60 in 17 vols., 1863–1903. Both contain far more than the beginning student will want to know, but both make impressively clear how much there is to be known.

Seventeenth-century English history comes perilously close to being a self-contained subject; before getting absorbed into it, students should frame their pictures by finding out in a broad way what was happening at the same time on the European continent. Among many books serving this end are two wide-ranging but not overwhelming volumes both published in 1971: *A Modern History of Europe* by Eugen Weber, and the *Norton History of Modern Europe* under the general editorship of Felix Gilbert.

A very influential essay on the Protestant ethic and the spirit of capitalism by the German sociologist Max Weber was published in 1904 and 1905, then reworked, translated, popularized, and after major modifications incorporated in a most eloquent book by R. H. Tawney, *Religion and the Rise of Capitalism*, 1926. The thesis that Protestant ideas, notably the doctrine of the religious calling or vocation, were engines in the hands of an aspiring capitalist class, has been much disputed, with H. R. Trevor-Roper leading the attack. In the course of the controversy, many points were scored on both sides; but most recent historians have been concerned less with "interpretations" of the 17th century as a whole than with exploring limited districts, actions, or spots of time. County or city histories, the membership of particular parliaments or political factions, the ties uniting family groups, the interests that entered into specific decisions—these are frequent themes of modern histories. Such close histories are often vivid and exciting, but they presuppose some sort of intellectual framework into which the details can be fitted. It is good to acquire such a framework early on; it is very good indeed to keep it under constant critical scrutiny.

Specialized historical studies of particular interest to the literary student are to be found on every hand. In 1937, L. C. Knights, studying *Drama and Society in the Age of Jonson*, linked the literature of the early century to the social stresses of the age. Peter Burke, in *The Renaissance Sense of the Past*, 1969, and Ricardo Quinones, in *The Renaissance Discovery of Time*, 1972, help one to recognize and appreciate important differences in basic attitude between the Middle Ages and the Renaissance, and between the Renaissance and ourselves. Two volumes by Elizabeth Eisenstein on *The Printing Press as an Agent of Change*, 1979, are particularly relevant to the literature of the 16th and 17th centuries; while a still larger view is taken by Peter Laslett in *The World We Have Lost*, 3rd ed., 1984. To imagine life in a pre-industrial society is hard for a modern reader; Laslett's book helps. See also Keith Wrightson, *English Society, 1580-1680*, 1982, and Lawrence Stone's massive study of *The Family, Sex, and Marriage in England 1500-1800*, 1977. David Underdown, *Pride's Purge*, 1971, and J. P. Kenyon, *The Popish Plot*, 1972, though ostensibly about single episodes in the history of the century, cast much light on the period as a whole. Studying the development of a scientific point of view in the early

17th century is an important project, but an enormous and complicated one, because the new approach had to disentangle itself, not only from the conventional assumptions of the age, but from lingering presences of astrology, alchemy, cabalistic lore, hermetic teachings, natural magic, and the superstitions of witchcraft. The image of a universe bound together by strains of occult sympathy and moral analogy had been inherited from the Middle Ages, and was widely accepted at the start of the century; the scheme is described, perhaps too simply, in E. M. W. Tillyard's concise and very influential study, *The Elizabethan World Picture*, 1943; useful complications can be introduced by referring to C. S. Lewis's brilliantly polemic *The Discarded Image*, 1964; and a collection of relevant documents is assembled in James Winny's *The Frame of Order*, 1957. See also S. K. Heninger, Jr., *The Cosmographical Glass: Renaissance Diagrams of the Universe*, 1977. Basil Willey's *The Seventeenth Century Background*, 1934, does not entirely escape the temptation to see 17th-century conflicts in 19th-century terms, but is useful in setting up an intellectual scaffold. In *The Temple of the Mind*, 1969, John R. Mulder emphasizes the extent to which school curricula, academic practices, and elementary catechisms shaped the thinking of the early century, leaving many marks on the poetry of Milton, Herbert, and Donne. The beginnings of the Royal Society of London for Improving Natural Knowledge have been many times studied, most recently by Dorothy Stimson in *Scientists and Amateurs*, 1948, and by Sir H. Hartley in *The Royal Society: Its Origins and Founders*, 1960.

But the conventional wisdom of the age was entwined with more mysterious and sometimes superstitious strains of thought, conveniently designated occult. These are deep and murky waters, best approached through a somewhat sceptical survey like Wayne Shumaker's *The Occult Sciences in the Renaissance*, 1972. The bibliography of this book will suggest much further reading. Frances Yates and her colleague at the Warburg Institute, David P. Walker, have explored many of the complexities of hermetic thought, she in a brilliant and sometimes questioned series of books, the first of which was *Giordano Bruno*, 1964, he in a study of *Spiritual and Demonic Magic*, 1958. Among the opinionated proselytizers, to be taken with a grain or more of salt, are authors like A. E. Waite and Montague Summers.

A useful and hard-headed study by Keith Thomas on *Religion and the Decline of Magic*, 1971, may provide congenial entry into the vast areas surveyed by the eight volumes of Lynn Thorndike's *History of Magic and Experimental Science*, 1923–58. From the philosophical point of view, E. A. Burtt's *Metaphysical Foundations of Modern Physical Science*, rev., 1932, is still reliable and informative; while an important sidelight is contributed by Christopher Hill in *The Intellectual Origins of the English Revolution*, 1965. Hugh Kearney, in *Science and Change 1500–1700*, 1971, and Allen Debus, in *Man and Nature in the Renaissance*, 1978, offer concise overviews of the Scientific Revolution. But perhaps the most direct way to approach this Protean subject of emergent science is through the lives and works of individual scientists: Gilbert (magnetism), Napier and Wallis (mathematics), Bacon (theory), Harvey (physiology), and of course Newton, the universal genius. Important as they are, abstract ideas about the growth of a secular scientific attitude should be supplemented by some sense of what an early capitalist economy amounted to and how it functioned; an old but still useful book on the subject is that of G. Unwin, *Industrial Organization in the 16th and 17th Centuries*, 1904.

General literary histories of the age include Douglas Bush, *English Literature in the Earlier 17th Century*, rev., 1962, which is vol. 5 of the *Oxford History of English Literature*; also a shorter, less bibliographical introduction by C. V. Wedgwood, *Seventeenth-Century English Literature*, 1950. But the great variety of 17th-century literature does not lend itself so well to formal history as to assemblages of essays clustering around a theme or themes. Older but still informative collections are those of H. J. C. Grierson, *Cross Currents in English Literature of the 17th Century*, 1929, and L. C. Knights, *Explorations*, 1946. More recent is Rosemond Tuve, *Essays: Spenser, Herbert, Milton*, 1970. Above all, those 17th-century essays of T. S. Eliot, which wrought a palpable revolution in modern thinking, not only about the 17th century but about poetry as such, merit thoughtful reading; they are not hard to pick out of his *Selected Essays* (any edition after 1951 will have most of them).

Rosemond Tuve in *Elizabethan and Metaphysical Imagery*, 1947, and Ruth Wallerstein in *Studies in Seventeenth Century Poetic*, 1950, probed the relation between critical theory and poetic practice. An elderly but unreplaced collection includes major critical documents of the age: J. E. Spingarn, *Critical Essays of the Seventeenth Century*, 1908–9.

Anthologies of women's writing that include 17th-century women have been edited by Joan Goulianos, *"by a Woman writ": Literature from Six Centuries by and about Women*, 1973; Mary R. Mahl and Helene Koon, *The Female Spectator: English Women Writers Before 1800*, 1977; Betty Travitsky, *The Paradise of Women: Writings by Englishwomen of the Renaissance*, 1981; and Sandra M. Gilbert and Susan Gubar, *The Norton Anthology of Literature by Women*, 1985. A reader who wants to go adventuring in the byways of literature will be grateful to George Saintsbury, who collected in three volumes the *Minor Poets of the Caroline Period*, 1905–21. A large selection of Elizabethan and Jacobean plays has recently been made available at moderate price, and with competently edited texts, in three series: The New Mermaids, The Revels Plays, and Regents Renaissance Drama.

A spate of books on the metaphysical poets appeared during the 1930s, of which the best are Joan Bennett's *Five* (originally *Four*) *Metaphysical Poets*, 1934; Helen C. White's *The Metaphysical Poets*, 1936; and J. B. Leishman's book of the same title, 1934. Louis L. Martz, in *The Poetry of Meditation*, 1954, discussed a traditional mode of thought as it influenced the metaphysicals, illustrated it with an anthology, *The Meditative Poem*, 1963, and continued the same line of investigation in *The Paradise Within*, 1964. Barbara K. Lewalski explored the relation between theology and poetry in *Protestant Poetics and the Seventeenth-Century Religious Lyric*, 1979. Earl Miner wrote on *The Metaphysical Mode from Donne to Cowley*, 1969—and went on to study *The Cavalier Mode from Jonson to Cotton*, 1971, and *The Restoration Mode from Milton to Dryden*, 1974. Continental perspectives on English authors of the 17th century are supplied by two important books of Mario Praz: *Studies in Seventeenth-Century Imagery*, 1939, and *The Flaming Heart*, 1958. Marjorie Nicolson's *The Breaking of the Circle*, 2nd ed., 1960, deals with the impact of developing scientific thought, largely on Donne, as her earlier *Newton*

Demands the Muse, 1946, carries the same theme into the later century. Harry Levin studies a single, but often central, theme in *The Myth of the Golden Age in the Renaissance*, 1969; his book could well be read in conjunction with that of A. Bartlett Giamatti on *The Earthly Paradise and the Renaissance Epic*, 1969. Rosalie Colie studied in *Paradoxia Epidemica*, 1966, Renaissance applications of a single literary device; and the student of classic myth in 17th-century poetry will find Douglas Bush's *Mythology and the Renaissance Tradition in English Poetry*, 1932, an indispensable directive.

Until 1969, *Studies in Philology* published an annual bibliography of Renaissance and 17th-century studies; after that date, the appropriate section of the MLA bibliography should be consulted. *Studies in English Literature* annually surveys new books in the area.

Francis Bacon

No individual can afford to, or probably wants to, own *The Complete Works of Bacon* (English and Latin), in 14 volumes edited by Spedding, Ellis, and Heath, 1857–74; but for the whole thing that's the place to look. A good deal handier is the limited selection edited by R. F. Jones, 1937; it includes the essays and a modest quantum of the philosophic writing. There is a good recent edition of *The Advancement of Learning* and *The New Atlantis* by Arthur Johnson, 1974, and another of book 1 of the *Advancement* by William Armstrong, 1975. Two relatively modern biographies are those of Mary Sturt, 1932, and Charles Williams, 1933. On Bacon's impeachment, see Jonathan L. Marwil, *The Trials of Counsel: Francis Bacon in 1621*, 1976. Anthony Quinton, *Francis Bacon*, 1980, provides a useful introduction to the man and his work. Christopher Hill's *Intellectual Origins of the English Revolution*, noted above, argues the existence of a popular and vernacular scientific tradition that lent substance to Bacon's magisterial scientific dicta. A recent trend in discussion of Bacon is to discount his intellectual stature and to emphasize his powers as a persuasive, imaginative writer. Instances of this trend are Brian Vickers, *Francis Bacon and Renaissance Prose*, 1968, and Lisa Jardine, *Francis Bacon, Discovery and the Art of Discourse*, 1974.

Especially in the late 19th century, an immense amount of nonsense was written setting forth alleged cryptographic evidence for Bacon's authorship of Shakespeare's plays, Spenser's poetry, and various other literary works. William F. and Elizabeth S. Friedman, in *The Shakespearean Ciphers Examined*, 1957, subject all these theories to scrupulous technical examination, and dismiss them all as worthless. It would be pleasant if this closed the matter, but that is doubtless too much to hope.

See also **Prose of the Early Seventeenth Century.**

Sir Thomas Browne

A handy annotated *Religio Medici* was published in 1963 by James Winny, and there is a handsome *Religio Medici and Other Works* edited by L. C. Martin, 1964. Norman Endicott edited *The Prose of Sir Thomas Browne* in 1967, and C. A. Patrides edited *Sir Thomas Brown: The Major Works* in 1977. Robin Robbins has edited and annotated copiously the already copious *Pseudodoxia Epidemica*, 1981: a snapper-up of unconsidered trifles will find here his Elysium. Beautiful but expensive is the 6-volume *Works of Sir Thomas Browne*, ed. Geoffrey L. Keynes, 1928–31. Recent studies are those of Joan Bennett and F. L. Huntley, both 1962; also about Browne is Leonard Nathanson's *The Strategy of Truth*, 1967, and a collection of studies edited by C. A. Patrides, 1982. A classic account of the backgrounds of skepticism and fideism is Louis Bredvold's *The Intellectual Milieu of John Dryden*, 1934; though mainly about Dryden, it is extremely useful in relating Browne to his intellectual heritage.

See also **Prose of the Early Seventeenth Century.**

Robert Burton

Holbrook Jackson prepared, in 1932, a handy edition of the complete *Anatomy of Melancholy*; it has paraphrases or translations of the Latin and Greek quotations, a glossary of obsolete words, and for unobtrusive authenticity Burton's magnificent footnotes in their original languages at the back of the several Partitions.

For melancholy as such, the standard modern work, as much a classic in our day as Burton's was in his, is *Saturn and Melancholy*, 1964, by Raymond Klibansky, Erwin Panofsky, and Fritz Saxl. Less formidable are three studies: *The Psychiatry of Robert Burton*, 1944, by Bergen Evans with professional assistance; *The Anatomy of*

Robert Burton's England, 1952, by W. R. Mueller, which describes the social background; and Lawrence Babb's *Sanity in Bedlam*, 1959, a general introduction to the *Anatomy*.

See also **Prose of the Early Seventeenth Century.**

Thomas Carew

The edition by Rhodes Dunlap, 1949, includes all of the poems, Carew's single masque, and a useful note on the musical settings that his poetry attracted. A study of the evolution of the Stuart love lyric (Hugh Richmond, *The School of Love*, 1964) devotes considerable attention to Carew.

See also **Poetic Modes of the Early Seventeenth Century.**

Edward Hyde, Earl of Clarendon

As befits the man who founded the Clarendon Press, the earl's works have always been well printed. The 1888 edition of the *History* includes fresh readings and previously suppressed passages. The *Autobiography* was first printed in 1759, and in 1911 a *Life* in two volumes by Sir Henry Craik supplemented it. For background Keith Feiling, *A History of the Tory Party*, 1924, is indispensable; a relatively recent study is Brian Wormald, *Clarendon: Politics, History, and Religion*, 1951.

See also **Prose of the Early Seventeenth Century.**

Abraham Cowley

Cowley's English writings were edited in two volumes by A. R. Waller, 1905–6, but not since; his *Essays and Other Prose Writings* were reprinted by A. B. Gough in 1915. There is a biography by A. H. Nethercot, *Abraham Cowley, the Muses' Hannibal*, 1931, and an appreciation by R. B. Hinman, *Abraham Cowley's World of Order*, 1960. David Trotter has written a comprehensive account of *The Poetry of Abraham Cowley*, 1979.

See also **Poetic Modes of the Early Seventeenth Century.**

Richard Crashaw

The standard edition is that prepared by L. C. Martin, 1927. An early misjudgment of Crashaw's work was his inclusion in a 1930 wiseacre anthology of the worst English poetry, *The Stuffed Owl*, ed. D. B. Wyndham Lewis. (Though not to be taken with utmost solemnity, anthologies of bad poetry are often useful in developing an indepen-dent critical taste.) Two books which, with Martin's edition, reversed the accepted view of Crashaw, are Ruth Wallerstein, *Richard Crashaw: A Study in Style and Poetic Development*, 1935, and Austin Warren, *Richard Crashaw: A Study in Baroque Sensibility*, 1939. Influential ideas about Crashaw are to be found in Wylie Sypher, *Four Stages of Renaissance Style*, 1955, and in Mario Praz, *The Flaming Heart*, 1958. Robert Peterson, in *The Art of Ecstasy: Teresa, Bernini, and Crashaw*, 1970, explores in close detail Crashaw's most characteristic style and its continental analogues.

Sir John Denham

A modern edition of Denham's *Poetical Works* is that of T. H. Banks, 1928; Brian O'Hehir wrote a life of the poet under the title *Harmony from Discords*, 1968, and followed it in 1969 with a study of *Cooper's Hill* including a critical edition of the poem under the title *Expans'd Hieroglyphics*.

See also **Poetic Modes of the Early Seventeenth Century.**

John Donne

For nearly 50 years the accepted edition of Donne's poems was that in two volumes edited by Sir Herbert J. C. Grierson, 1912. In 1952 Dame Helen Gardner re-edited the *Divine Poems*, rev., 1978, and in 1965 a volume containing *The Elegies and The Songs and Sonnets*. In 1967, W. Milgate added to this series the *Satires, Epigrams, and Verse Letters*, and in 1978 the *Epithalamions, Anniversaries, and Epicedes*. These new editions alter the text of some poems in some particulars on the basis of new manuscript evidence, and offer to redate many of them. It is by no means clear that the text is always improved by the new readings, or that the new datings will stand up. One can only say that many questions remain open. Under the editorship of G. R. Potter and Evelyn Simpson, a new edition of Donne's *Sermons* has been issued in 10 vols., 1953–62; Anthony Raspa edited the *Devotions Upon Emergent Occasions* in 1975. Among several handy, handsome popular editions of Donne's poetry, we note the *Songs and Sonets*, ed. Theodore Redpath, 1956, rev., 1983; *John Donne's Poetry*, ed. A. L. Clements for Norton Critical Editions, 1966; and two editions of *The Complete English Poems*: one by A. J. Smith, 1971, and the other by C. A. Patrides, 1985.

Though recognized as inadequate in many

ways, Sir Edmund Gosse's *Life and Letters of John Donne*, 1899, held sway for a long time as the best available biography. It has now been replaced by R. C. Bald's *John Donne, a Life*, 1970, which the author regrettably did not live to finish, and by John Carey, *John Donne, Life, Mind, and Art*, 1981. Carey presents a rough, vigorous, and challenging view of Donne; his book could well be read in counterpoint with Izaak Walton's much blander, much more "establishment" pastel.

Two major studies that dedicate long sections to the poetry of Donne are Rosemond Tuve's influential *Elizabethan and Metaphysical Imagery*, 1947, and Robert Ellrodt's *L'inspiration personnelle et l'ésprit du temps chez les poètes métaphysiques anglais* (1960). Pierre Legouis's pioneering *Donne the Craftsman*, 1928, paved the way for close studies by J. B. Leishman, 1951, Clay Hunt, 1954, Arnold Stein, 1962, Wilbur Sanders, 1971, and Murray Roston, 1974. Donne's poetry is also treated in Barbara K. Lewalski's *Protestant Poetics and the Seventeenth-Century Religious Lyric*, 1979, and in Terry G. Sherwood's *Fulfilling the Circle: A Study of John Donne's Thought*, 1984. Hardly any of Donne's poems has not been the subject of several articles at least; but Cleanth Brooks's *The Well Wrought Urn*, 1947, contains in its discussion of *The Canonization* one of the most influential poetic explications of modern criticism. Collections of critical essays by several hands have been assembled by Helen Gardner and Frank Kermode, both 1962, and by A. J. Smith, 1972, who also edited *John Donne: The Critical Heritage*, 1975. Donne's interest in antiquated lore can be explored in an early study by Mary Ramsay, *Les doctrines mediévales chez Donne*, 2nd ed., 1924, his complementary awareness of scientific change in Marjorie Nicolson, *The Breaking of the Circle*, 2nd ed., 1960. Joan Webber has studied Donne's prose style in *Contrary Music*, 1963.

The standard bibliography of Donne, first published by Geoffrey Keynes in 1914, went into its 4th ed. in 1973; and there are annotated bibliographies of modern criticism by John R. Roberts—one for the period 1912–67, published 1973, and another for 1968–78, published 1982.

Lady Anne Halkett

The *Memoirs* of Lady Anne Halkett were edited by John Loftis in 1979. Under the title of *The Weaker Vessel*, 1984, Antonia Fraser has studied at great length and in fascinating detail the position of women in 17th-century England, with particular emphasis on the redefinition of roles brought about by the civil wars.

See also **Prose of the Early Seventeenth Century.**

George Herbert

An admirable edition of the *Works* is that of F. E. Hutchinson, rev., 1945; C. A. Patrides has produced a compact edition of *The English Poems*, 1974. A series of books on Herbert began appearing in the 1950s, among which may be mentioned Rosemond Tuve's *A Reading of George Herbert*, 1952, like all her work, learned and acute. Margaret Bottrall's introductory appreciation, *George Herbert*, appeared in the same year, 1954, as J. H. Summers' seminal *George Herbert, His Religion and Art*. Recent studies include those of Arnold Stein, *George Herbert's Lyrics*, 1968; Helen Vendler, *The Poetry of George Herbert*, 1975; Stanley Fish, *The Living Temple*, 1978, along with a chapter in his *Self-Consuming Artifacts*, 1972; and Richard Strier, *Love Known*, 1983. A new *Life of George Herbert*, fuller than any previous one, is that of Amy M. Charles, 1977. Particularly valuable for its extensive annotated bibliographies is Mario A. Di Cesare, *George Herbert and the 17th-Century Religious Poets*, a Norton Critical Edition, 1978. John R. Roberts has prepared an annotated bibliography of modern (1905–74) criticism of Herbert, 1978, and C. A. Patrides has edited *George Herbert: The Critical Heritage*, 1983.

Robert Herrick

A thorough and careful edition is the *Poetical Works*, ed. L. C. Martin, 1956; J. Max Patrick has also produced an edition of the *Complete Poetry*, 1963. F. W. Moorman wrote a full-length study, *Robert Herrick*, 1910; G. W. Scott, writing under the same title, 1974, has little of value on the poetry, but vivid and copious documentation of the social background. Robert Deming's critical study, *Ceremony and Art: Robert Herrick's Poetry*, also appeared in 1974, and a volume of essays, edited by Roger B. Rollin and J. Max Patrick, was published in 1978. Marchette Chute, joining Herrick with George Herbert, described them as *Two Gentle Men*, 1959. There is an interesting novel about Herrick by Rose Macaulay, *The Shadow Flies*, 1932.

Thomas Hobbes

The classic edition of Hobbes, old-fashioned and weighty, is that by Sir William Molesworth: the *English Works* in 11 vols., the *Opera Philosophica* in 5, 1839–45. For most occasions a student of literature will be contented with C. P. MacPherson's Penguin edition of the *Leviathan*, 1968. There is a delightful 17th-century biographical sketch by John Aubrey (among his *Brief Lives*), and a recent intellectual biography by Miriam M. Reik, under the title *The Golden Lands of Thomas Hobbes*, 1977. A useful study of the philosopher's literary theory is that of C. D. Thorpe, *The Aesthetic Theory of Thomas Hobbes*, 1940; and Michael Oakeshott's perceptive introduction to a 1946 edition of the *Leviathan* does much to orient Hobbes in the framework of the modern world. In *The Hunting of Leviathan*, 1962, S. I. Mintz recounts the many and often amusing 17th-century reactions to Hobbes's thought.

See also **Prose of the Early Seventeenth Century**.

Ben Jonson

"Monumental" is the word for the edition of Jonson's works by C. H. Herford and Percy and Evelyn Simpson, published by the Clarendon Press in 11 vols., 1925–52. This edition is meticulous in reproducing the old spellings and recording the variants; typographically it is a constant delight. But to find one's way around in it takes some practice. The Yale edition of Ben Jonson provides a good modernized and annotated version of the major plays (one play to a volume); so does the paperback series known as The New Mermaids. Handy editions of the verse are those of W. B. Hunter, *The Complete Poetry of Ben Jonson*, 1963, Ian Donaldson, and George Parfitt, both 1975; Stephen Orgel has edited the *Complete Masques*, 1969.

Because Jonson's work falls into several distinct categories, general introductory accounts of the whole man are few. G. Gregory Smith did a biography for the English Men of Letters series, 1919, and a more recent popular introduction, graceful, dexterous, and perceptive, is that of J. B. Bamborough, 1970. Useful recent studies of the plays are those of E. B. Partridge, *The Broken Compass*, 1958; G. B. Jackson, *Vision and Judgment in Ben Jonson's Drama*, 1968; *The World Upside Down*, 1970, by Ian Donaldson; and *Ben Jonson, His Vision*

and His Art by Alexander Leggatt, 1981. G. B. Johnston (1945), Wesley Trimpi (1962), and Richard S. Peterson (1981) have written good accounts of Jonson's poetry. Students not rich enough to own *Inigo Jones: The Theatre of the Stuart Court* by Stephen Orgel and Roy Strong, 1973, will want to consult it in the library for the particular delight of the drawings and designs.

In 1963, Jonas Barish edited a collection of critical essays on Jonson, and another appeared ten years later in *Studies in the Literary Imagination #6*. In 1938, S. A. Tannenbaum published a *Concise Bibliography* of Jonson, and in 1947 added to it a supplement—which was itself supplemented in 1974 by D. Heyward Brock and James M. Welsh, *Ben Jonson: A Quadricentennial Bibliography, 1947–1972*. There are also two Reference Guides: one to *The Plays of Ben Jonson*, by Walter D. Lehrman, Delores J. Sarafinski, and Elizabeth Savage, 1980, and the other to *The Nondramatic Works of Ben Jonson*, by David C. Judkins, 1982. D. Heyward Brock, *A Ben Jonson Companion*, 1983, is a kind of Jonson encyclopedia, complete with bibliography.

Henry King

Essentially the author of a single poem, Henry King has not been much studied. The standard edition of his *Poems* is by Margaret Crum, 1965. There is a critical biography by Ronald Berman, *Henry King and the 17th Century*, 1964.

See also **Poetic Modes of the Early Seventeenth Century**.

John Lilburne

The turbulent, truculent activities of John Lilburne may be traced through William Haller's two fine volumes, *Tracts on Liberty in the Puritan Revolution*, 1934. In 1947, M. A. Gibb produced the first biography, *John Lilburne the Leveller*; a second, by Pauline Gregg, appeared in 1961, under the title *Free-born John*.

See also **Prose of the Early Seventeenth Century**.

John Locke

P. H. Nidditch's edition of the *Essay Concerning Human Understanding*, 1975, forms part of the ongoing Clarendon Edition of the *Works of John Locke*. A good background for reading Locke, and the English philosophers in general, can be picked up from a general survey of European thought,

2564 SELECTED BIBLIOGRAPHIES

such as J. H. Randall, Jr.'s *Making of the Modern Mind*, 1926. Another sort of context is provided by G. P. Gooch and Harold Laski, *English Democratic Ideas in the 17th Century*, 1927. Under the title *Understanding Locke*, 1983, John J. Jenkins has written a terse, lucid anatomy of Locke's thought, balancing sympathetic exposition with strenuously argued criticism. Carl Becker's book on *The Declaration of Independence*, 1922, gives a good idea of Locke's influence on that document; and Kenneth Maclean studied, amusingly, rev., 1962, *John Locke and the English Literature of the 18th Century*.

Richard Lovelace

C. H. Wilkinson edited the *Poems* for the Oxford English Poets series, 1925. Commentary can be found in M. Weidhorn, *Richard Lovelace*, 1970, and Earl Miner, *The Cavalier Mode from Jonson to Cotton*, 1971.

See also **Poetic Modes of the Early Seventeenth Century.**

Andrew Marvell

The tercentenary of Marvell's birth in 1921 produced a volume of essays in tribute to a then-neglected author, among them a highly influential piece by T. S. Eliot. Since then the tide of critical commentary has risen to a flood. The accepted edition is now the two-volume *Poems and Letters*, ed. H. M. Margoliouth, 1927, 1952, and a 3rd ed., revised by Pierre Legouis and E. E. Duncan-Jones, 1971. There are also handy editions of the *Complete Poetry* by George de F. Lord, 1968, and Elizabeth Story Donno, 1972. Frank Kermode's edition of *Selected Poems*, 1967, is excellent. A good general introduction is that of M. C. Bradbrook and M. G. Lloyd Thomas (1940); or see John Dixon Hunt's profusely illustrated *Andrew Marvell: His Life and Writings* (1978). Ruth Wallerstein's *Studies in 17th-Century Poetic* (1950) are knotty and hard to read; the Marvell to whom they point is not a suave and playful ironist, but a complex and serious metaphysician. Whether he gains or loses by the change is up to the reader. H. E. Toliver, *Marvell's Ironic Vision*, 1965, and J. B. Leishman, *The Art of Marvell's Poetry*, 1966, were literary in their interests; John Wallace, in *Destiny His Choice*, 1968, focused on Marvell's intricate political attitudes. The pastoral poetry was studied by Patrick Cullen in *Spenser, Marvell, and Renaissance Pastoral*, as well as by Donald Friedman in *Marvell's Pastoral Art*, both

1970. Two general studies appeared in the same year under the titles *My Echoing Song*, by Rosalie Colie, and *The Resolved Soul*, by Anne Berthoff. Two more studies of Marvell's public poetry are Annabel M. Patterson, *Marvell and the Civic Crown*, 1978, and Warren L. Chernaik, *The Poet's Time*, 1983. Collections of critical essays on Marvell have been edited by George de F. Lord, 1968, John Carey, Michael Wilding, both 1969, Kenneth Friedenreich, 1977, C. A. Patrides, 1978, R. L. Brett, 1979, and Arthur Pollard, 1980. E. S. Donno edited *Andrew Marvell: The Critical Heritage*, 1978, and there is a Reference Guide by Dan S. Collins, 1981.

John Milton

Despite occasional editorial eccentricities, the 18-volume Columbia Milton, a complete edition of the poetry and prose with a 2-volume index, 1931–38, is widely accepted; controversy continues over details, however, and anyone interested may consult Harris Fletcher's 4-volume facsimile of the *Poetical Works*, 1943–48, Helen Darbishire's re-editing for Oxford English Texts of the poetry, 1952–55, and the 8-volume Yale edition of the *Prose Works*, 1953–82. For most purposes the student will want to use Merritt Hughes's *Complete Poems and Major Prose*, 1957, or the *Poems*, ed. John Carey and Alastair Fowler, 1968. The notes of both editions are weighty, penetrating, and perhaps a bit depressing for the beginner; used with discretion, they may help but not overwhelm. Douglas Bush's edition of *The Complete Poetical Works*, 1965, comes in at about half the weight of Carey and Fowler. An edition of *Paradise Lost* with deliberately modest annotation has been done by Scott Elledge for the Norton Critical Editions, 1975; Christopher Ricks's Penguin edition, 1968, includes *Paradise Regained* as well. A multivolume variorum commentary began appearing in 1970.

As a life to be read, the old vacuum-cleaner biography by David Masson (noted above) has been replaced by W. R. Parker's 2-volume survey, 1968; and Christopher Hill has written a masterful account of *Milton and the English Revolution*, 1977. Sir Walter Raleigh's *Milton*, 1900, (Sir Walter was no relation) is an old introductory study, crisp, clear, and still disputed—a good sign of intellectual vitality. Every decade or so brings another book on *Paradise Lost* and the modern reader—who has, of course, become a little more modern in the interim. Thomas Wheeler's book under that title, 1974, is sensible, lucid, and short; it may well prove useful even beyond its allotted ten-year span. Another lively introduction that has proved its permanent value is C. S. Lewis's *Preface to Paradise Lost*, 1942; it is one-sided, in giving little weight to Milton's Puritanism, but stimulating nonetheless. Its bias may be corrected by reading in A. J. A. Waldock, *Paradise Lost and Its Critics*, 1947; Joseph Summers, *The Muse's Method*, 1962; Anne Ferry, *Milton's Epic Voice*, 1963; and Helen Gardner, *A Reading of Paradise Lost*, 1965. Guidebooks like Marjorie Nicolson's *John Milton: A Reader's Guide to His Poetry*, 1963, and Lois Potter's *Preface to Milton*, 1971, can provide a general orientation. But perhaps the best advice that can be given is just to jump in and flounder around, trying out the various critical approaches on one's own individual sense of the poetry. Milton's God is a traditional stumbling-block for readers of *Paradise Lost*; William Empson has written a tough, tightly argued book on the subject, which puts the case very strongly indeed, rev., 1965. Starting from such a center, one's reading can spread widely. Another such focal book is Stanley Fish's *Surprised by Sin*, 1967, which invites the reader to inspect and criticize his own responses to the developing action of *Paradise Lost*: this is never an unfruitful activity. Or again, one might take as a focus of interest the reaction against Milton initiated in the 1920s by T. S. Eliot and F. R. Leavis—along with the various defensive gambits developed by supporters in books such as *Paradise Lost in Our Time*, 1945, by Douglas Bush. Other suggestive books on *Paradise Lost* are Isabel G. MacCaffrey, *Paradise Lost as "Myth"*, 1959; Northrop Frye, *The Return of Eden*, 1965; John M. Steadman, *Milton and the Renaissance Hero*, 1967; G. K. Hunter, *Paradise Lost*; and Robert Crosman, *Reading Paradise Lost*, 1980. For an entirely different approach to Milton's epics, see Roland M. Frye, *Milton's Imagery and the Visual Arts*, 1978. B. Rajan studies Milton's major poetry in *The Lofty Rhyme*, 1970. Mary Ann Radzinowicz, *Toward Samson Agonistes: The Growth of Milton's Mind*, 1978, and Louis L. Martz, *Poet of Exile*, 1980, chart Milton's poetic development.

Different approaches to Milton can also be sampled in collections of critical essays edited by A. E. Barker, 1965, Louis L. Martz, 1966, A. P. Fiore, 1967, R. D. Emma and J. T. Shawcross, 1967, C. A. Patrides, 1968, Alan Rudrum, 1968, B. Rajan, 1969, and Thomas Kranidas, 1969; and there's an impressive collection of *Critical Essays on Milton from ELH*, also 1969. John T. Shawcross has edited two volumes of *Milton: The Critical Heritage*, 1970, 1972. But specialized and limited studies, though too many to be listed here in full, probably provide the readiest access to the enormous and complicated topic of Milton. There are, for example, several collections of studies bearing on *Lycidas*, including those of C. A. Patrides, 1961, and Scott Elledge, 1966, which might lead toward J. R. Knott's study of pastoralism in *Paradise Lost: Milton's Pastoral Vision*, 1971. Robert Bridges's time-tested account of *Milton's Prosody*, rev., 1921, might lead one to two relatively modest reading enterprises: *The Sonnets of Milton* by John S. Smart, 1921, and *The Italian Element in Milton's Verse* by F. T. Prince, 1954. Continuing on the theme of stylistics, one could read Theodore Banks on *Milton's Imagery*, 1950, Christopher Ricks on *Milton's Grand Style*, 1963, and Rosemond Tuve's characteristically incisive little book titled *Images and Themes in Five Poems by Milton*, 1957. An interest in theology might lead one through Maurice Kelley's *This Great Argument*, 1941, to Malcolm M. Ross, *Poetry and Dogma*, 1954, and beyond into such vexed questions as Milton's relation to the hexameral tradition or the extent of his acquaintance with rabbinical lore— topics which have bibliographies of their own. One might start with *Comus*, and Angus Fletcher's ingenious study, *The Transcendental Masque*, 1971, and then move out to investigate other masques, or to consider more intensively Milton's feelings about love, marriage, and chastity, as in articles by A. S. P. Woodhouse, *University of Toronto Quarterly*, 11 (1941–42) and William and Malleville Haller in *Huntington Library Quarterly*, 5 (1942).

For the older and inevitably less interesting matter of Miltonic study, there is ample bibliographical help, in a basic *Reference Guide* by D. H. Stevens, 1930, with supplements by Harris Fletcher, 1931, and Calvin Huckabay, 1969. More recently, there is a concise *Milton*, rev. 1979, by James H. Hanford and William A. McQueen, for the Goldentree Bibliographies. But the current terrifying spate of books and articles on Milton may leave the bibliographers in the lurch.

Sir Isaac Newton

Much new work continues to be done on Newton. For the two hundredth anniversary of his death the History of Science Society published (1928) a sheaf of papers on his work and influence. The *Correspondence* in 7 volumes edited by various hands appeared between 1959 and 1977; Newton's papers on optics and other branches of science are collected in *Isaac Newton's Papers & Letters on Natural Philosophy*, ed. Bernard Cohen, 2nd ed., 1978. Richard S. Westfall's biography, *Never at Rest*, 1980, is a majestic and often demanding account, not only of his personal life but of his intellectual activities.

Dorothy Osborne

The letters of Dorothy Osborne, like the autobiography of Lady Anne Halkett, lay long in obscurity; first brought to light in 1888, they were definitively edited in 1928 by G. C. Moore Smith.

See also **Prose of the Early Seventeenth Century.**

Poetic Modes of the Early Seventeenth Century

From plays, masques, songbooks, manuscripts, and broadsides, several pleasant and accessible anthologies of early 17th-century lyrics have been assembled by Norman Ault, 1928, 1950; by R. G. Howarth, 1931; and by H. J. C. Grierson with Geoffrey Bullough, 1934. Selections from the metaphysical poets have been prepared by H. J. C. Grierson, 1921, and Helen Gardner, 1957; from *Ben Jonson and the Cavalier Poets* by Hugh Maclean, in a Norton Critical Edition, 1974. The always-admirable series of Oxford English Texts includes the poems of Carew, Crashaw, Donne, Herbert, Herrick, Lovelace, Marvell, Milton, Suckling, Traherne, and Vaughan; these have generally been the preferred texts referred to in the individual author-bibliographies. Lesser-known but no less interesting items of 17th-century poetry can often be picked up by an adventurous searcher in reprint form—for instance, the *Poetical Works* of Giles and Phineas Fletcher, ed. F. S. Boas, 1908–9; Henry More's philosophical poems, ed. Geoffrey Bullough, 1931; and just about any of the many worthies and poets edited during the late 19th century by Dr. A. B. Grosart.

Criticism and commentary on 17th-century verse abounds; every new book one reads suggests at least three others that one ought to read, and no preprogrammed bibliography equals in value the one independently compiled by moving from book to book as one's curiosity directs. Still, we may recommend among major contributions to be investigated the following fairly recent books. They are listed in order of publication, without other implications of priority. R. L. Sharp, *From Donne to Dryden*, 1940; Rosemary Freeman, *English Emblem Books*, 1948; Odette de Mourgues, *Metaphysical, Baroque, and Précieux Poetry*, 1953; Geoffrey Walton, *Metaphysical to Augustan*, 1955; Earl Wasserman, *The Subtler Language*, 1959; George Williamson, *17th Century Contexts*, 1961; F. J. Warnke, *European Metaphysical Poetry*, 1961; Lowry Nelson, Jr., *Baroque Lyric Poetry*, 1961; John Hollander, *The Untuning of the Sky, Ideas of Music in English Poetry 1500–1700*, 1961; W. B. Piper, *The Heroic Couplet*, 1969; Jerome Mazzaro, *Transformations in the English Renaissance Lyric*, 1970; Joseph Summers, *The Heirs of Donne and Jonson*, 1970; and Earl Miner's three books on 17th-century poetic modes (see the first section of the bibliography). There is also a new collection of studies edited by Claude J. Summers and Ted-Larry Petworth, *Classic and Cavalier: Essays on Jonson and the Sons of Ben*, 1982.

See also entries on **Thomas Carew, Abraham Cowley, Sir John Denham, Henry King, Richard Lovelace, Sir John Suckling, Thomas Traherne,** and **Edmund Waller.**

Prose of the Early Seventeenth Century

Much basic work on the prose of the early 17th century was done by Morris Croll in a series of articles on Ciceronian and anti-Ciceronian styles in the later Renaissance: these were collected posthumously in a volume titled *Style, Rhetoric, and Rhythm*, 1966. R. F. Jones in *Ancients and Moderns*, 1936, urged the importance of the new science and the Royal Society in the development of a plain style. But there were other considerations, such as the need of Puritan preachers, pamphleteers, and propagandists to make themselves understood in the great war of words brilliantly described by William Haller in his *Rise of Puritanism*, 1938. Writers of "characters," biographies, and histories found it increasingly desirable to adopt a plain, colloquial style; the birth of periodical journalism imposed simplicity of expression, and no doubt of thought too. The ease, polish, and chaffing humor of "gentlemanly" conversation contributed to the ideal of a natural and unpretentious style. The development of English prose thus becomes an aspect of social history.

For the early century, George Williamson's *The Senecan Amble*, 1951, deals with an important variety of plain prose. For the later century, D. J. Milburn, *The Age of Wit*, 1966, and G. R. Cragg, *From Puritanism to the Age of Reason*, 1950, may be useful. Taking an intractable subject a piece at a time, W. F. Mitchell has documented in *English Pulpit Oratory from Andrewes to Tillotson*, 1932, the growing predominance of the plain style; E. N. S. Thompson has analyzed in *The 17th-Century English Essay*, 1926, a particular mode of informal discourse; and Donald Stauffer, describing *English Biography Before 1700*, 1930, has set forth some new strategies of psychological understanding and prose representation. Similarly, Martha Ornstein in *The Role of Scientific Societies in the 17th Century*, 3rd ed., 1938, and Jacob Bronowski in *Science and Human Values*, 1956, outline fundamental changes of attitude, such as could not have failed to have repercussions on prose expression. Acute self-consciousness is also a prevalent 17th-century attitude: in *The Eloquent "I,"* 1968, Joan Webber explores its manifestations in eight prose writers of the period. An influential recent book is Stanley Fish, *Self-Consuming Artifacts: The Experience of 17th-Century Literature*, 1972; Fish has also edited a collection of essays— starting with Croll—on 17th-century prose, 1971.

See also entries on **Francis Bacon, Sir Thomas Browne, Robert Burton, Edward Hyde, Earl of Clarendon, Lady Anne Halkett, Thomas Hobbes, John Lilburne, Dorothy Osborne** and **Izaak Walton.**

Sir John Suckling

The plays of Suckling have been edited by L. A. Beaurline, the nondramatic works by Thomas Clayton, both volumes appearing in 1971. A particularly interesting article on the poetry, by F. O. Henderson, will be found in *ELH*, 4 (1937), 274–298.

See also **Poetic Modes of the Early Seventeenth Century.**

Thomas Traherne

Traherne's writings, edited in two volumes by H. M. Margoliouth, appeared among the Oxford English Texts in 1958. Recent studies include those of K. W. Salter, 1964, A. L. Clements, 1969, and S. N. Stewart, 1970.

See also **Poetic Modes of the Early Seventeenth Century.**

Henry Vaughan

The *Works* of Henry Vaughan were edited by L. C. Martin, rev., 1957, and there are editions of the *Complete Poetry* by French Fogle, 1964, and Alan Rudrum, 1976. In 1947 F. E. Hutchinson wrote the standard biography. Elizabeth Holmes opened up the topic of *Henry Vaughan and the Hermetic Philosophy*, 1932, and since then there has been much discussion, not only of occult influences, but of the contrasts between Vaughan's earlier secular poetry and his later, so-called mystical verses. Critical studies include E. C. Pettet's seminal *Of Paradise and Light*, 1960, James D. Simmonds' *Masques of God*, 1972, and Thomas O. Calhoun's *Henry Vaughan: The Achievement of Silex Scintillans*, 1981. The *Unfolding Vision* by Jonathan Post, 1982, offers a firm, comprehensive overview; it is the best general study to date.

Edmund Waller

Though not edited recently, Waller has been a good deal studied; A. W. Alison, in *Toward an Augustan Poetic*, 1962, and W. L. Chernaik, in *The Poetry of Limitation*, 1968, emphasize the poet's contribution. Also of interest is an essay by George Williamson, "The Rhetorical Pattern of Neo-Classical Wit," in *17th Century Contexts*, noted above under **Poetic Modes of the Early Seventeenth Century.**

Izaak Walton

A handy, handsome *Compleat Walton* was edited by Geoffrey Keynes in 1929; it includes the *Angler* and all the lives. By itself, the idyllic *Complete Angler* has been for many years one of the classics for the fine-binding trade. No full-length independent biography of Walton has yet been published. A major study of Walton's own activities as a biographer—he smoothed, he polished, he expanded, he made edifying— is David Novarr's *The Making of Walton's Lives*, 1958.

See also **Prose of the Early Seventeenth Century.**

John Webster

The reputation of Webster, and particularly of *The Duchess of Malfi*, became a subject of active dispute in the late 19th century, with Swinburne taking a very high position, William Archer a relatively low one. These essays with many others have been reprinted in *John Webster: A Critical Anthology*, eds., G. K. and S. K. Hunter, 1969. There are also collections of essays edited by Norman Rabkin, 1968, and R. V. Holdsworth, 1975, and a volume in the Critical Heritage series edited by Don D. Moore, 1981. Robert Dent traced *John Webster's Borrowings*, 1960. There are book-length studies of *The Duch-*

ess *of Malfi* by Gunnar Boklund, 1962, Clifford Leech, 1963, and Joyce Peterson, 1978. Webster also figures in Fredson Bowers' *Elizabethan Revenge Tragedy*, 1940. F. L. Lucas edited the *Complete Works*, 1927. The Revels Plays edition of *The Duchess of Malfi*, ed. by John Russell Brown, 1964, includes much interesting material; and there is a handy new edition of Webster's *Selected Plays* by Jonathan Dollimore and Alan Sinfield, 1983. Muriel Bradbrook has written the dramatist's biography, 1980.

THE RESTORATION AND THE EIGHTEENTH CENTURY

The relevant chapters of George M. Trevelyan's *History of England*, 1926, offer a readable narrative of English history during the 18th century; J. H. Plumb, *England in the Eighteenth Century*, 1950, describes the structure of society. A fuller account is provided by J. R. Jones, *Country and Court: England, 1658–1714*, 1978; W. A. Speck, *Stability and Strife: England, 1714–1760*, 1977; and J. Steven Watson, *The Reign of George III, 1760–1815*, 1960. Studies in the social life of the period abound—among them A. S. Turberville's *English Men and Manners in the Eighteenth Century*, 1926, and as editor, *Johnson's England: An Account of the Life and Manners of His Age*, 2 vols., 1933; Dorothy Marshall's *English People in the Eighteenth Century*, 1956; George Rudé's *Hanoverian London, 1714–1808*, 1971; and Neil McKendrick's and John Brewer's *The Birth of a Consumer Society*, 1982. Three useful guides for the literary student are A. R. Humphreys's *The Augustan World: Society, Thought, and Letters in Eighteenth-Century England*, 1954; Donald Greene's *The Age of Exuberance: Backgrounds to Eighteenth-Century English Literature*, 1970; and Pat Rogers's *The Augustan Vision*, 1974.

Helpful books dealing with the intellectual background of the period are Arthur O. Lovejoy's *The Great Chain of Being*, 1936, and *Essays in the History of Ideas*, 1948; Sir Leslie Stephen's *History of English Thought in the Eighteenth Century*, 2 vols., 1876; Basil Willey's *The Eighteenth Century Background*, 1940, a study of the idea of nature; J. W. Johnson's *The Formation of Neo-Classical Thought*, 1967; and John Sitter's *Literary Loneliness in Mid-Eighteenth-Century England*, 1982. Paul Hazard's *The*

European Mind, 1680–1715, 1953, and *European Thought in the Eighteenth Century*, 1954, are translations from the French by J. L. May, rapid, readable surveys of intellectual movements on the Continent as well as in England. Peter Gay's *The Enlightenment: An Interpretation*, 2 vols., 1969, forcefully defends the philosophers of the "age of reason." Marjorie H. Nicolson's *Newton Demands the Muse: Newton's "Opticks" and the Eighteenth-Century Poets*, 1946, and *Science and the Imagination*, 1956, valuable studies of the relation between science and literature in the period, may be supplemented by William P. Jones, *The Rhetoric of Science*, 1966. Myra Reynolds's *The Learned Lady in England, 1650–1760*, 1920, is still useful. Martin Price's *To the Palace of Wisdom: Studies in Order and Energy from Dryden to Blake*, 1964, Paul Fussell's *The Rhetorical World of Augustan Humanism*, 1965, W. J. Bate's *The Burden of the Past and the English Poet*, 1970, and Jean Hagstrum's *Sex and Sensibility: Ideal and Erotic Love from Milton to Mozart*, 1980, are all thoughtful and stimulating studies that relate ideas to literary art.

Three volumes of the *Oxford History of English Literature* deal with our period in some detail: James Sutherland's *English Literature of the Late Seventeenth Century*, 1969, Bonamy Dobrée's *English Literature in the Early Eighteenth Century, 1700–1740*, 1959 and John Butt's and Geoffrey Carnall's *English Literature in the Mid-Eighteenth Century*, 1979. Briefer surveys of the literature of the age include George Sherburn's "The Restoration and Eighteenth Century" (the standard work), in A. C. Baugh, ed., *A Literary History of England*, rev. 1967; and Roger Lonsdale, ed., *Dryden to Johnson*, 1971, Vol. 4 of the Sphere History of Literature.

Among books that deal with a single literary mode, James Sutherland's *A Preface to Eighteenth-Century Poetry*, 1948, skillfully introduces a body of poetry that sometimes seems alien to modern readers, and Eric Rothstein's *Restoration and Eighteenth-Century Poetry, 1660–1800*, 1981, is a fresh, informative survey. They may be supplemented by Ian Jack's *Augustan Satire: Intention and Idiom in English Poetry 1660–1750*, 1952; Rachel Trickett's *The Honest Muse: A Study in Augustan Verse*, 1967; Margaret A. Doody's *The Daring Muse*, 1985; P. W. K. Stone, *The Art of Poetry, 1750–1820*, 1967; David Morris's *The Religious Sublime*, 1972; and Earl Miner's *The Restoration Mode from Milton to Dryden*, 1974. Allardyce Nicoll's *A History of Restoration Drama 1660–1700*, *A History of Early Eighteenth-Century Drama, 1700–1750*, and *A History of Late Eighteenth-Century Drama, 1750–1800*, rev., 1952, are standard sources of information, supplemented by *The London Stage, 1660–1800*, 11 vols., 1960–68, whose critical introductions are separately available in five paperback books; and by *The Revels History of Drama in English*, Vol. V, 1660–1750, 1976, and Vol. VI, 1750–1880, 1975. Five of the most important plays of the period, together with critical commentary and background material on theaters, staging, and audience, will be found in a Norton Critical Edition edited by Scott McMillin, *Restoration and Eighteenth-Century Comedy*, 1973. Two collections, Earl Miner, ed., *Restoration Dramatists*, 1966, and John Loftis, ed., *Restoration Drama, Modern Essays in Criticism*, 1966, provide studies by various writers; and Loftis has also analyzed *Comedy and Society from Congreve to Fielding*, 1959. Walter Graham has surveyed *English Literary Periodicals*, 1930; and Donald A. Stauffer, *English Biography before 1700*, 1930, and *The Art of Biography in Eighteenth-Century England*, 2 vols., 1941. John N. Morris, *Versions of the Self: Studies in English Autobiography from John Bunyan to John Stuart Mill*, 1966, and Howard Anderson, Philip B. Daghlian, and Irvin Ehrenpreis, eds., *The Familiar Letter in the Eighteenth Century*, 1966, provide introductions to two influential but neglected genres. Patricia Spacks's *Imagining a Self*, 1976, discusses conceptions of personal identity in many 18th-century autobiographies and novels. The novel is treated in detail in E. A. Baker's *The History of the English Novel*, vol. 3 (1930), vol. 4 (1939), vol. 5 (1934). This work should be supplemented by two excellent modern studies, Ian Watt's *The Rise of the Novel: Studies in Defoe, Richardson and Fielding*, 1957, and Alan D. McKillop's *The Early Masters of English Fiction*, 1956, which deals with Defoe, Richardson, Fielding, Smollett, and Sterne. Other aspects of fiction are discussed by Ronald Paulson, *Satire and the Novel in Eighteenth Century England*, 1967, R. F. Brissenden, *Virtue in Distress: Studies in the Novel of Sentiment from Richardson to Sade*, 1974, Lennard Davis, *Factual Fictions*, 1983, and Leopold Damrosch, *God's Plot and Man's Stories*, 1985.

Studies of critical movements in this period are numerous and tend to be rather specialized. The two standard collections of neoclassical criticism are Joel E. Spingarn's *Critical Essays of the Seventeenth Century*, Vols. II and III, 1908 (the preface is not yet outdated), and Scott Elledge's *Eighteenth-Century Critical Essays*, 2 vols., 1961. The best statement of the critical canons of the age is Ronald S. Crane's "Neo-Classical Criticism," in J. T. Shipley, ed., *A Dictionary of World Literature*, 1943. The student may also consult René Wellek, *A History of Modern Criticism 1750–1950*, 1955, Vol. I; William K. Wimsatt, Jr., and Cleanth Brooks, *Literary Criticism: A Short History*, 1957; and James Engell, *The Creative Imagination*, 1981. M. H. Abrams, *The Mirror and the Lamp*, 1953, though primarily concerned with romantic theory, has much to say that is valuable about the 18th century.

Studies that discuss the treatment of external nature in the literature of the period (a theme as important for the 18th as it was for the 19th century) include Samuel Holt Monk's *The Sublime: A Study of Critical Theories in Eighteenth-Century England*, 1935, John Arthos's *The Language of Natural Description in Eighteenth-Century Poetry*, 1949, and John Dixon Hunt's *The Figure in the Landscape: Poetry, Painting and Gardening during the Eighteenth Century*, 1977. Martin Battestin compares ideas of religious and artistic order in *The Providence of Wit*, 1974. B. Sprague Allen's *Tides of English Taste 1619–1800*, 2 vols., 1937, on architecture, gardening, and decoration, and Sir Kenneth Clark's *The Gothic Revival*, 2nd ed., 1950, on architecture, are not irrelevant to literature. Jean Hagstrum has studied *The Sister Arts*, 1958, and Lawrence Lipking, *The Ordering of the Arts in Eighteenth-Century England*, 1970. In addition, many of the best essays on 18th-century topics have appeared in collections dedicated to a single scholar: for instance, for Frederick A. Pottle, *From Sensibility to Romanticism*, edited by F. W. Hilles and Harold Bloom, 1965; and for Samuel H. Monk, *Studies in Criticism and Aesthetics, 1660–1800*, edited by Howard Anderson and John S. Shea, 1967. James L. Clifford has collected a number of essays of various writers on the period in *Eighteenth-Century English Literature: Modern Essays in Criticism*, 1959. *Studies in English Literature* devotes its summer issue to the Restoration and Eighteenth Century and includes an article reviewing important work on the period published in the preceding year.

Finally, for further and elaborate bibliographies of 18th-century studies, the student may be referred to the bibliography of English literature, 1600–1800, that has appeared annually since 1926 in *Philological Quarterly*, and, since 1976, in yearly volumes, *The Eighteenth Century: A Current Bibliography*.

Joseph Addison and Sir Richard Steele

There is no scholarly edition of the collected works; the Bohn edition of Addison, 6 vols., 1854–56, rev. and enl., 1869–73, is available in libraries. *Letters* were edited by Walter Graham, 1941. *The Spectator* in five volumes was published by Donald F. Bond, 1965. This is the definitive edition. John Stephens has edited *The Guardian*, 1982. The authoritative biography of Addison is by Peter Smithers, 1968. Edward and Lillian Bloom survey Addison's ideas of society in *Joseph Addison's Sociable Animal*, 1971. Of lives of Steele, George A. Aitken's, 2 vols, 1889; and Calhoun Winton's *Captain Steele: The Early Career of Richard Steele*, 1964, and *Sir Richard Steele, M.P.: The Later Career*, 1970, are the best. Richard Dammers' *Richard Steele*, 1982, is an introductory guide. Rae Blanchard has edited Steele's *Correspondence*, 1941; *Tracts and Pamphlets*, 1944; *Occasional Verse*, 1952; and also other lesser works. The *Plays* have been edited by Shirley Kenny, 1971. Walter Graham's *English Literary Periodi-*

cals, 1930, may be consulted on both the *Tatler* and the *Spectator*. *The Tatler*, ed., G. A. Aitken, 4 vols, 1898–99, is the best modern edition of that work. Richmond P. Bond has analyzed *The Tatler: The Making of a Literary Journal*, 1971.

Mary Astell

There is no scholarly edition of any of the works, but *A Serious Proposal to the Ladies* and *Some Reflections upon Marriage* are available in modern reprints. A forthcoming biography by Ruth Perry will supersede Florence M. Smith's pioneering *Mary Astell*, 1912. Hilda L. Smith's *Reason's Disciples*, 1982, includes a good section on Astell.

James Boswell

A vast amount has been written about Boswell, much now outmoded by the discovery within the 20th century of Boswell's private papers. Frederick A. Pottle's *James Boswell, The Earlier Years, 1740–1769*, 1966, and Frank Brady's *James Boswell, The Later Years, 1769–1795*, 1984, are the two halves of the standard biography, judicious and well-informed. C. B. Tinker's lively *Young Boswell*, 1922, is useful, as is Mary Hyde's *The Impossible Friendship: Boswell and Mrs. Thrale*, 1972. Pottle's *The Literary Career of James Boswell*, 1929, was the first attempt to establish the canon of Boswell's writings. The *Letters*, edited by C. B. Tinker, 2 vols., 1924, will have to be supplemented by the recently recovered correspondence, of which three volumes have been published: Ralph S. Walker, ed. *The Correspondence of James Boswell and John Johnston of Grange*, 1966; Marshall Waingrow, ed., *The Correspondence and Other Papers of James Boswell Relating to the Making of the Life of Johnson*, 1969; and Charles Fifer, ed., *The Correspondence of James Boswell with Certain Members of the Club*, 1976. *The Private Papers of James Boswell from Malahide Castle*, eds. Geoffrey Scott and F. A. Pottle, 18 vols., 1928–34, made available the first of Boswell's papers to be discovered. Volumes of the trade edition of the *Journals*, under the general editorship of F. A. Pottle, appear regularly. *The Journal of a Tour to the Hebrides* has been edited, as first published, by R. W. Chapman, 1924; and, as originally written, by Frederick A. Pottle, 1936. All these volumes include valuable introductions and notes.

A wise and sympathetic brief study of Boswell is B. H. Bronson's "Boswell's Boswell," in *Johnson and Boswell, 1944. Johnson, Boswell, and Their Circle: Essays Presented to L. F. Powell*, 1965, is a valuable collection. The best edition of the *Life* is L. F. Powell's revised and enlarged edition of the earlier edition by G. B. Hill, 6 vols., 1934–50. A good one-volume edition by R. W. Chapman and J. D. Fleeman, 1982, is available in paperback. A helpful guide through the *Life* is J. L. Smith-Dampier's *Who's Who in Boswell?*, 1935. Mention should perhaps be made of Thomas Babington Macaulay's brilliantly paradoxical, highly prejudiced, often reprinted account of Boswell in his review in 1831 of Croker's edition of the *Life of Johnson*. It blackened Boswell's reputation for nearly a century.

John Bunyan

Bunyan was a prolific writer: Part II of *The Pilgrim's Progress*, dealing with the journey of Christian's wife and children, appeared in 1684; *The Life and Death of Mr. Badman* in 1680; *The Holy War* in 1682. But these major works form only a small part of all his writings.

The standard life is John Brown's *John Bunyan: His Life, Times, and Work*, 1885, revised by Frank M. Harrison, 1928. The critical edition of *The Pilgrim's Progress* is by J. B. Wharey, 1928, revised by Roger Sharrock, 1960; Sharrock has also edited *Grace Abounding to the Chief of Sinners*, 1962, and, with James Forrest, *The Holy War*, 1980. Among interesting modern studies are George B. Harrison, *John Bunyan: A Study in Personality*, 1928; William Y. Tindall, *John Bunyan, Mechanick Preacher*, 1934; Henri A. Talon. *John Bunyan, The Man and His Work*, 1951, a translation from the French; U. Milo Kaufmann, *The Pilgrim's Progress and Traditions in Puritan Meditation*, 1966; and Monica Furlong, *Puritan's Progress*, 1975.

Samuel Butler

Materials for a full-length biography of Butler do not exist. Of editions of *Hudibras*, Zachary Grey's, 2 vols., 1744, is still useful for its illustrative notes. The best modern edition is John Wilders's, 1967. *Characters*, edited by Charles W. Daves, 1970, and *Prose Observations*, ed. Hugh de Quehen, 1979, are invaluable for studying Butler's opin-

ions; René Lamar has edited *Satires and Miscellaneous Poetry and Prose*, 1928. E. A. Richards's *Hudibras in the Burlesque Tradition*, 1937, is useful. An excellent essay on Butler is included in Ian Jack's *Augustan Satire 1660–1750*, 1952.

William Collins

The *Works* of Collins, which amount only to one slim volume, have been well edited by Richard Wendorf and Charles Ryskamp, 1979. Lonsdale's edition (see *Gray* below) has copious notes. P. L. Carver's *The Life of a Poet*, 1967, is the fullest biography. Wendorf's *William Collins and Eighteenth-Century English Poetry*, 1981, is a fine critical study.

William Congreve

Congreve's *Complete Works* have been edited by Montague Summers, 4 vols., 1923; and the *Plays* by Herbert Davis in 1967. The best biography is John C. Hodges's *William Congreve the Man*, 1941. Kathleen Lynch's *A Congreve Gallery*, 1951, contains studies of some members of Congreve's circle, including one of Henrietta, Duchess of Marlborough. Maximilian Novak's *William Congreve*, 1971, and Harold Love's *Congreve*, 1975, are both good critical introductions. Criticism of Congreve is abundant in books on Restoration drama. See, for example, Thomas H. Fujimura's *The Restoration Comedy of Wit*, 1952; Norman N. Holland's *The First Modern Comedies*, 1959; Ian Donaldson's *The World Upside Down: Comedy from Jonson to Fielding*, 1970; Harriet Hawkins's *Likenesses of Truth in Elizabethan and Restoration Drama*, 1972; and Robert Hume's *The Development of English Drama in the Late Seventeenth Century*, 1976.

William Cowper

Poems, 1748–1782 have been edited by John D. Baird and Charles Ryskamp, 1980. This is the first volume of what will be the standard edition. A convenient edition in one volume is H. S. Milford's, 4th ed., 1934. James King and Ryskamp have edited Cowper's *Letters and Prose Writings*, 4 vols., 1979–84. Maurice J. Quinlan's *William Cowper*, 1953, is the most recent scholarly biography. Charles Ryskamp's *William Cowper*, 1959, concentrates on the poet's early life. Useful critical studies include Norman Nicholson's *William Cowper*, 1951,

Morris Golden's *In Search of Stability: The Poetry of William Cowper*, 1960, and Martin Priestman's *Cowper's Task*, 1983.

George Crabbe

Crabbe's biography was written by his son, George, in 1834. It has been re-edited by E. M. Forster, 1932, and by Edmund Blunden, 1947. The *Poetical Works*, well edited by A. J. and R. M. Carlyle, were published in 1914. *New Poems*, edited by Arthur Pollard, 1960, contains hitherto unpublished poems. Howard Mills has edited *George Crabbe: Tales (1812) and Other Selected Poems*, 1967. Lilian Haddakin's *Poetry of Crabbe*, 1955; Oliver Sigworth's *Nature's Sternest Painter*, 1965; and Peter New's *George Crabbe's Poetry*, 1976, are essays in criticism.

Daniel Defoe

The best biography of Defoe is James Sutherland's *Defoe*, 1937, rev., 1950; Sutherland has also written a fine critical study, *Daniel Defoe*, 1971. The *Letters* were edited by George H. Healey, 1955. Ian Watt's *The Rise of the Novel*, 1957, contains an interesting study of Defoe's novels in relation to social and economic history. Full-length studies include John R. Moore's *Daniel Defoe: Citizen of the Modern World*, 1958; Maximilian E. Novak, *Economics and the Fiction of Daniel Defoe*, 1962, and *Defoe and the Nature of Man*, 1963; G. A. Starr, *Defoe and Casuistry*, 1971; John Richetti, *Defoe's Narratives*, 1975; and Peter Earle, *The World of Defoe*, 1976. J. R. Moore has also provided a useful *Checklist of the Writings of Daniel Defoe*, 1960.

Two of Defoe's novels are in the Norton Critical Editions series: *Moll Flanders*, edited by Edward Kelly, 1974, and *Robinson Crusoe*, edited by Michael Shinagel, 1975.

John Dryden

Charles E. Ward's *Life of John Dryden*, 1961, the standard biography, may be supplemented by the excellent sketch in George R. Noyes's edition of the *Poetical Works*, 2nd ed., 1950. Samuel Johnson's *Life of Dryden* is still worth reading. Until recently, the only edition of the *Works* has been the unsatisfactory one in 18 columns by Sir Walter Scott and George Saintsbury, 1882–93. A good scholarly edition of the *Works* has been appearing at intervals since 1956, under the general editorship first of E. N. Hooker, then H. T. Swedenberg, and lately Alan Roper. The poems have been edited by James Kinsley, 4 vols., 1958. W. P. Ker, 1900, 1926, and George Watson, 2 vols., 1962, have edited the *Essays*.

Mark Van Doren's *John Dryden: A Study of His Poetry*, 1920, remains valuable for its fresh critical responses, as do T. S. Eliot's brief studies, *Homage to John Dryden*, 1924, and *John Dryden the Poet, the Dramatist, the Critic*, 1932. Important modern criticism includes Arthur Hoffman's *John Dryden's Imagery*, 1962, Alan Roper's *Dryden's Poetic Kingdoms*, 1965, and Earl Miner's *Dryden's Poetry*, 1967. Steven Zwicker has studied *Politics and Language in Dryden's Poetry*, 1984. The standard work on Dryden's philosophical and religious ideas is Philip Harth's fine *Contexts of Dryden's Thought*, 1968. Robert Hume analyzes *Dryden's Criticism*, 1970; Edward Pechter, *Dryden's Classical Theory of Literature*, 1975; and John C. Aden, in *The Critical Opinions of John Dryden, A Dictionary*, 1963, brings together Dryden's critical ideas under convenient headings.

John Gay

The standard life is W. H. Irving's *John Gay: Favorite of the Wits*, 1940. Vinton A. Dearing and Charles Beckwith have edited Gay's *Poetry and Prose*, 2 vols., 1974; John Fuller, the *Dramatic Works*, 2 vols., 1983; and C. F. Burgess the *Letters*, 1966. Critical studies include Sven Armens, *John Gay, Social Critic*, 1954; Patricia Spacks, *John Gay*, 1965; and Adina Forsgren, *Gay: Poet "of a Lower Order,"* 2 vols., 1964, 1971.

Oliver Goldsmith

The Collected Works of Goldsmith was published by Arthur Friedman in 1966. The standard biography of Goldsmith is Ralph M. Wardle's *Oliver Goldsmith*, 1957. Sir James Prior's *Life of Oliver Goldsmith*, 2 vols., 1837, is the important biography of the last century. Kathleen C. Balderston has edited the *Collected Letters*, 1928; Austin Dobson edited the *Plays*, 1901. An important addition to the canon of Goldsmith's works was made by Ronald S. Crane in his edition of *New Essays*, 1927. The notes in Lonsdale's edition of the *Poems* (see **Gray** below) are valuable; Ricardo Quintana's *Oliver Goldsmith*, 1967, is a useful critical survey.

Thomas Gray

The poems of Gray, Collins, and Gold-smith have been edited, with informative notes, by Roger Lonsdale, 1969. The standard edition of Gray's *Works* is that of Edmund Gosse, 4 vols., rev., 1902–6; of the *Correspondence*, that of Paget Toynbee and Leonard Whibley, 3 vols., 1935; of the poems that of H. W. Starr and J. R. Hendrickson, 1966. R. W. Ketton-Cremer's *Thomas Gray*, 1955, is the most recent and the best biography. The best extended critical study is unfortunately in French: Roger Martin's *Essai sur Gray*, 1934. A more specialized study is William P. Jones's *Thomas Gray, Scholar*, 1937. James Downey and Ben Jones have edited a collection of essays on Gray, *Fearful Joy*, 1974. Frederick W. Hilles and Harold Bloom, eds., *From Sensibility to Romanticism*, 1965, contains studies of the *Elegy* by F. Brady, B. H. Bronson, and I. Jack.

Samuel Johnson

Others among Johnson's friends besides Boswell wrote of him: notably, Mrs. Hester Lynch Thrale Piozzi, whose *Anecdotes* appeared in 1786 and have been edited, along with William Shaw's *Anecdotes*, by Arthur Sherbo, 1974; Sir John Hawkins, whose *Life* was published in 1787 and reissued in 1961, edited and abridged by Bertram H. Davis; and Fanny Burney (Mme D'Arblay), from whose diary the Johnsonian passages are found most conveniently in C. B. Tinker's *Dr. Johnson and Fanny Burney*, 1911. James L. Clifford's *Young Sam Johnson*, 1955, and *Dictionary Johnson*, 1979, are thorough studies of Johnson's early and middle years that supplement Boswell's rather sketchy account of Johnson's life before their meeting in 1763. There are fine modern biographies by John Wain, 1975, and W. J. Bate, 1977. The poems were admirably edited by David Nichol Smith and E. L. McAdam, 2nd ed. rev. by J. D. Fleeman, 1974. The best collected edition of Johnson's *Works* appeared as long ago as 1825. A new Yale edition, which has been coming out irregularly since 1958, will eventually become standard. G. B. Hill's edition of *Johnsonian Miscellanies*, 2 vols., 1897, and *The Lives of the Poets*, 3 vols., 1905, both with superb notes, have recently been reprinted. R. W. Chapman's edition of the letters, 3 vols., 1952, is authoritative. There is a valuable survey and bibliography

of critical studies, rev., 1970, by J. L. Clifford and D. J. Greene.

Some interesting modern studies of Johnson are J. W. Krutch's *Samuel Johnson*, 1944; B. H. Bronson's "Johnson Agonistes," 1944 (reissued in *Johnson Agonistes and Other Essays*, 1965); W. J. Bate's *The Achievement of Samuel Johnson*, 1955; W. K. Wimsatt, Jr., *The Prose Style of Samuel Johnson*, 1941; Donald J. Greene's *The Politics of Samuel Johnson*, 1960; Arieh Sachs's *Passionate Intelligence*, 1967; Paul Fussell's *Samuel Johnson and the Life of Writing*, 1971; and Charles E. Pierce's *The Religious Life of Samuel Johnson*, 1982. Aspects of Johnson's criticism are treated in Joseph E. Brown's *The Critical Opinions of Samuel Johnson*, 1926; Jean Hagstrum's *Samuel Johnson's Literary Criticism*, 1952; Leopold Damrosch, Jr., *The Uses of Johnson's Criticism*, 1976; and William Edinger's *Samuel Johnson and Poetic Style*, 1977. E. L. McAdam's *Johnson and Boswell: A Survey of their Writings*, 1969, and D. J. Greene's *Samuel Johnson*, 1970, are brief useful guides.

Lady Mary Wortley Montagu

The standard modern biography is Robert Halsband's *The Life of Lady Mary Wortley Montagu*, 1956. Halsband has also edited *The Complete Letters*, 3 vols., 1965–67; *Selected Letters*, 1970; and with Isobel Grundy, *Essays and Poems and Simplicity, a Comedy*, 1977.

Samuel Pepys

The standard edition of *The Diary of Samuel Pepys*, edited by Robert Latham and William Matthews, 11 vols., 1970–83, includes a companion and index. Latham has also edited a good one-volume selection, *The Illustrated Pepys*, 1978. J. R. Tanner's lectures, reprinted as *Samuel Pepys and the Royal Navy*, 1920, helped call attention to the serious work of Pepys's life. The best biography is Arthur Bryant's *Samuel Pepys*, 3 vols., 1933–38.

Alexander Pope

There is no reliable complete edition of all of Pope's works. Defective though it is in many respects, the Victorian edition in 10 volumes by Elwin and Courthope, 1871–89, must still be consulted, though with caution. The excellent Twickenham Edition of the poems, 11 volumes, 1939–67, a co-operative undertaking by several scholars (under John Butt), includes valuable introductory and critical materials and notes. A convenient selection in a single volume, with selected notes, omits the translations of Homer. Only one volume of Norman Ault's edition of *The Prose Works*, 1936, was published before the editor's death.

No sound biography of Pope exists. George Sherburn's *Early Career of Alexander Pope*, 1934, corrects many misinterpretations and distortions of Pope's character and motives that mar earlier biographies, but unfortunately it does not study the poet's life beyond about 1726. Maynard Mack's elegant study, *The Garden and the City: Retirement and Politics in the Later Poetry of Pope, 1731–1743*, 1969, is the first installment of a biography that should set new standards; a second volume is forthcoming. Mack's *Collected in Himself*, 1982, includes several essays on Pope. Howard Erskine-Hill has described *The Social Milieu of Alexander Pope*, 1975. Ault's *New Light on Pope*, 1949, makes important miscellaneous contributions to Pope's biography. Sherburn's edition of the *Correspondence*, 1956, 5 vols., is standard. R. H. Griffith, *Alexander Pope: A Bibliography*, 1962, is a 2-volume listing of Pope's writings.

The best detailed critical study of the poems is Geoffrey Tillotson's *On the Poetry of Pope*, 2nd ed., 1950; and the same author's *Pope and Human Nature*, 1958, throws light on a difficult subject. David B. Morris's *Alexander Pope: The Genius of Sense*, 1984, is a good critical survey. Austin Warren's *Alexander Pope as Critic and Humanist*, 1929, though somewhat dated, is still useful. Much information is gathered up in Robert W. Rogers's *The Major Satires of Alexander Pope*, 1955. Reuben A. Brower's *Alexander Pope: The Poetry of Allusion*, 1959, is an enlightening study of Pope's lifelong habit of felicitous quotation from and adaptation of phrases, images, and ideas from earlier European poets, especially, though not exclusively, from the poets of classical antiquity. Aubrey Williams incisively analyzes *Pope's Dunciad*, 1955, and may be supplemented by John F. Sitter's *The Poetry of Pope's Dunciad* 1971. Maynard Mack, ed., *Essential Articles for the Study of Alexander Pope*, 1964, conveniently brings together a number of short studies, and, with

James Winn, Mack has edited *Pope: Recent Essays*, 1980.

Matthew Prior

The complete critical edition of Prior is *Literary Works*, edited by H. B. Wright and M. K. Spears, 2 vols., 1971. The older and less complete edition in 2 volumes by A. R. Waller, 1905, 1907, is useful. The best biography is Charles K. Eves's *Matthew Prior, Poet and Diplomatist*, 1939.

John Wilmot, Earl of Rochester

There are fine scholarly editions of Rochester's poems by David M. Vieth, 1968, and Keith Walker, 1984. Vivian de Sola Pinto's biography, *Enthusiast in Wit*, 1962, may be supplemented by John Adlard's gathering of source materials, *The Debt to Pleasure*, 1974, and Jeremy Treglown's edition of the *Letters*, 1980. Dustin Griffin's *Satires Against Man*, 1973, and David Farley-Hills' *Rochester's Poetry*, 1978, are good critical studies.

Christopher Smart

A standard edition of Smart's *Poetical Works* has reached two volumes, the first, edited by Karina Williamson of *Jubilate Agno*, 1980, the second, of *Religious Poetry 1763–1771*, edited by Marcus Walsh and Williamson, 1983. There is a good one-volume selection by R. E. Brittain, 1950. On the life, Christopher Devlin's *Poor Kit Smart*, 1961, should be supplemented by Arthur Sherbo's *Christopher Smart, Scholar of the University*, 1967; Moira Dearnley surveys *The Poetry of Christopher Smart*, 1968. Geoffrey Hartman includes interesting essays on Smart and Collins in *Beyond Formalism*, 1970, and *The Fate of Reading*, 1975.

Sir Richard Steele

See entries under **Joseph Addison and Sir Richard Steele.**

Jonathan Swift

Irvin Ehrenpreis's excellent, full-length biography, *Swift: The Man, His Works, and the Age*, consists of three volumes: *Mr. Swift and His Contemporaries*, 1962, *Dr. Swift*, 1967, and *Dean Swift*, 1983. Louis A. Landa's judicious *Swift and the Church of Ireland*, 1954, avoids the special pleading that mars many books about Swift.

The standard edition of the poems is by Sir Harold Williams, 3 vols., 1937, rev.,

1958. Pat Rogers' edition of Swift's *Complete Poems*, 1983, is reliable and less expensive. Herbert Davis's edition of the prose works in 14 volumes, published over a period of years, is now complete. Swift's *Correspondence* has been edited by Sir Harold Williams, 5 vols., 1963–65. Distinguished editions of other works are Herbert Davis's *The Drapier's Letters*, 1935; Harold Williams' *Journal to Stella*, 1948; A. C. Guthkelch and D. Nichol Smith, *A Tale of a Tub*, 2nd ed., 1958; and Frank H. Ellis, *A Discourse of the Contests and Dissentions Between the Nobles and the Commons in Athens and Rome*, 1967. For the Norton Critical Editions series, Robert A. Greenberg has edited *Gulliver's Travels*, rev., 1971, and, with W. B. Piper, *The Writings of Jonathan Swift*, 1973.

Critical studies long and short abound. The student should find especially helpful Ricardo Quintana's *The Mind and Art of Jonathan Swift*, 1936, and *Swift: an Introduction*, 1955; and Kathleen Williams's *Jonathan Swift and the Age of Compromise*, 1958. Arthur E. Case's *Four Essays on Gulliver's Travels*, 1945; Maurice Johnson's *The Sin of Wit: Jonathan Swift as a Poet*, 1950; C. J. Rawson's *Gulliver and the Gentle Reader*, 1973; and Nora Jaffe's *The Poet Swift*, 1977, are useful special studies. Most of Herbert Davis's excellent critical pieces on Swift have been brought together in *Jonathan Swift, Essays on his Satire and Other Studies*, 1964. Two good collections of essays are *Jonathan Swift: A Critical Anthology*, ed. Denis Donoghue, 1971, and *The Character of Swift's Satire*, ed. Claude Rawson, 1983.

James Thomson

The most recent biographical study of Thomson is Douglas Grant's *James Thomson, Poet of "The Seasons,"* 1951. A. D. McKillop has edited *James Thomson, Letters and Documents*, 1958, which contains much about Thomson's friends and the interests of his literary circle, and *James Thomson: The Castle of Indolence and Other Poems*, 1961. There are good notes in James Sambrook's edition of *The Seasons and The Castle of Indolence*, 1972, and Sambrook has edited a scholarly text of *The Seasons*, 1981. The most valuable study of the content of *The Seasons* is McKillop's *The Background of Thomson's Seasons*, 1942. Ralph Cohen, *The Art of Discrimination: Thomson's The Seasons and the Language of Criticism*, 1964, is a valuable work which uses responses to the poem to illustrate the development of critical theory; and Cohen has added a critical study, *The Unfolding of the Seasons*, 1970. Patricia Meyer Spacks, *The Poetry of Vision: Five Eighteenth-Century Poets*, 1966, contains a chapter on Thomson, as well as others on Collins, Gray, Smart, and Cowper.

Anne Finch, Countess of Winchilsea

Myra Reynolds added a long biographical introduction to her valuable edition of the *Poems*, 1903. Katharine M. Rogers has edited *Selected Poems*, 1979. A better edition is needed, for many manuscript poems have never been published. Ann Messenger's "Publishing without Perishing: Lady Winchilsea's *Miscellany Poems* of 1713," *Restoration*, 5:1(1981), 27–37, compares the published and unpublished poems.

British Money

Since 1971, British money has been calculated on the decimal system, with 100 pence to the pound; the pound has fluctuated from a bit more than 2 American dollars to virtual parity—whatever dollars may be worth. Before 1971, the pound consisted of 20 shillings, each containing 12 pence, thus 240 pence to the pound. In paper money the change has not been great; 1-, 5-, and 10-pound notes constitute the mass of the bills under both the old and the new systems; nowadays, in addition, 20- and 50-pound notes have been added. But in the smaller coinage the change has been considerable and the simplification remarkable. Most notable is abolition of the shilling, which goes into retirement now with the mark (worth in its day two-thirds of a pound or 13 shillings 4 pence) and the angel (once worth 10 shillings but replaced by the 10-shilling note, now in its turn abolished). The guinea, an oddity of the old currency, amounted to a pound and a shilling; though it has not been minted since 1813, quality products (a suit from a good tailor, a piece of fine silver, a rare book) are still generally priced in guineas. Colloquially, a pound used to be a quid, a shilling a bob, sixpence a tanner, a penny a copper. The common signs were £ for pound, s. for shilling, d. for a penny (from Latin *denarius*). A sum would normally be written £2.19.3, i.e., 2 pounds, 19 shillings, 3 pence. That is Bloom's budget for June 16, 1904. In new currency, it would be about £2.96d.

Old	New
1 pound note	1 pound note
10 shilling (half-pound) note	50 pence
5 shilling (crown)	
2 ½ shilling (half crown)	
2 shilling (florin)	10 pence
1 shilling	5 pence
6 pence	
3 pence	1 penny
2 pence	
1 penny	½ penny
½ penny	
¼ penny (far-thing)	

What the pound was worth at any point in history is never easy to state. In the first part of the twentieth century, 1 pound equalled about 5 American dollars; but those dollars bought more than twice what 1985 dollars will buy. The value of the pound might be definable in terms of the goods and services it would purchase; but these too vary radically with special circumstances, wars, harvests, and the like. In a loose way, it's clear that money used to be worth much more than it is now. A Saxon penny was the biggest coin in general circulation; four of them would buy a sheep. Peasants before the Black Death made 2 or 3 pence a day—an annual income of £3 or £4. At the modern ratio that would be only $5 or so per annum. However incredibly low their standard of living, however much they supplemented their cash income with produce from their own fields, that figure is impossible: the pound must have been worth much more than it is now, perhaps by a factor of several hundred. Hugh Latimer reports that in his day (the early 1500s) it was a common saying, "Oh, he's a rich man, he's worth £500." Probably he means, not fabulously, just comfortably rich; still, it's clear that the pound was a solid sum of money, equal perhaps to 400 or 500 American dollars of the year 1983.

In Jonson's *Alchemist*, Subtle tells Face that as an honest servant he had been a mere "livery-three-pound thrum"— that is, he had his uniform, food, and lodging, plus £3 a year. By cheating on household expenses, he had built up over the years, "a pretty stock, some twenty marks," about £13. Of course, the comic point of all this is the miserable sums involved in the lives of such squalid rascals. Forty pounds a year in independent income (generally rents) was the minimum requirement for a justice of the peace; it was also the sum fixed by King James at which a man could be forced to accept knighthood. It marked the threshold of gentry, and we must multiply it by 150 or 200 to get an equivalent in dollars. In 1661 that good bourgeois Samuel Pepys, just after he began working for the navy, calculated his worth at a modest £650; five years later, he was worth more than £6,000 and his annual income was about £3,000—cause for complacency. Of course, he was working for most of this income. Pepys was a rising official and would become a very important one; but he never achieved a title or even knighthood because the smell of commerce had never been washed from his money by possession of land.

On a far humbler level, Joseph Andrews (in Fielding's novel, published 1742) worked as a footman in the house of Lady Booby for £8 a year; but he got his room, board, and livery in addition, plus the occasional tip. Among the comfortable classes again, Mr. Bennet of Jane Austen's *Pride and Prejudice* (1813) enjoyed an income of £2,000 a year (but he had a family of five nonearning females to support, and the income ceased at his death). Mr. Bingley had £4,000 per year of his own, Mr. Darcy close to £10,000; and this raises us close to the rarefied atmosphere of the aristocracy. In his deepest degradation David Copperfield (of Dickens's 1850 novel) worked in the warehouse of Murdstone & Grinby for 6 or 7 shillings a week (£15 to £18 a year). Mr. Murdstone paid extra for his lodging and laundry, but even so the boy was bitterly impoverished, though he had only himself to feed. When his father died, his mother was thought to be pretty well taken care of with £105 a year, a little less than £9 per month. Only a few years later, Dorothea Brooke of *Middlemarch* (1872) is more than easy with £700 per year of her own; if she marries and has a son, he may inherit from her uncle as much as £3,000 per year in addition. That is high plutocracy for the folk of Tipton parish; one may estimate that Miss Brooke's pound is now worth between 20 and 50 American dollars of 1985 vintage. When John Davidson at the end of the century wrote of the horrors of being a clerk with a family at 30 bob a week, that stipend wouldn't work out much better than $1,500 to $3,000 of modern money. We see what he means.

Across the centuries, it's evident that money diminished in value; it's equally apparent that in every era there's been a gap between the poor and the rich. What money was worth depended heavily on which of those classes you belonged to. It also depended on where you lived. London was always very dear, and in the provinces (as is traditional everywhere) a small income went further. Finally, the value of money depended on the current rate of taxation. In the days of the Danegeld (ancestor of the modern income tax), nobody was rich except the Danes. Pitt introduced the modern income tax in 1798 as a war measure, Peel in 1842 made it a routine part of government financing; and it is one reason why an income of £10,000, though it was glorious aristocratic luxury for Mr. Fitzwilliam Darcy and his Elizabeth, does not today represent much more than solid middle-class comfort. For now, in addition to being heavily taxed, it's worth only a bit more than the same number of current dollars.

Adapted from *The Land and Literature of England: A Historical Account,* by Robert M. Adams (New York: Norton, 1983).

The British Baronage

The English monarchy is hereditary, passing from father to elder son, to daughters in order of seniority if there is no son, to a brother if there are no children, and in default of direct descendants to collateral lines (cousins, nephews, nieces) in order of closeness. There have been breaks in the order of succession (1066, 1399, 1688), but so far as possible the usurpers always tried to paper over the break with a legitimate, i.e., a hereditary claim. When a queen succeeds to the throne and takes a husband, he does not become king unless he is in the line of blood succession; rather, he is named prince consort, as Albert was to Victoria and Philip is to Queen Elizabeth II. He may father kings, but is not one himself.

The original Saxon nobles were the king's thanes, ealdormen, or earls, who in return for booty, gifts, or landed estates provided the king with military service and counsel. William the Conqueror, arriving from France where feudalism was fully developed, added largely to this group. Archbishops and bishops, abbots and priors, who frequently held their land from the king though they might hold their office from the pope, served as counselors and very often in secular offices as well, as royal administrators. In addition, as the king distributed the lands of his new kingdom, he also distributed dignities to men who became known collectively as "the baronage." "Baron" in its root meaning signifies simply "man," and barons were the king's men. As the title was common, a distinction was early made between greater and lesser barons, the former gradually assuming loftier and more impressive titles. The king, no longer duke of Normandy, created the first English duke in 1337. "Marquess" or "marquis" was created in 1385 and "viscount" in 1440 (the former pronounced "markwis," the latter "vyekount"); though it's the oldest title of all, an "earl" now comes, in order of dignity and precedence, between a marquess and a viscount; only "baronets," created first in 1611, rank below barons in the scale of hereditary nobility.

Kings and queens are addressed as "Your Majesty," princes and princesses as "Your Highness," the other hereditary nobility as "My Lord" or "Your Lordship." When a commoner is created a peer (always by the monarch), he may select his own title; thus Disraeli became earl of Beaconsfield after the district where his house stood; modest Clement Attlee, prime minister from 1945 to 1951, became simply Earl Attlee. Byron was the sixth baron of that line, by birth; Tennyson was created first Baron Tennyson. Peerages (other than the recently created Life Peerages) descend by primogeniture; they are given to a man with right of succession, they are not incidental to tenure of land—though when a man is given a peerage, he is sometimes given a pension or an estate to sustain the dignity. On the other hand, the children, even of a duke, are commoners unless they are specifically granted some other title or inherit their father's title from him. (Sons may enjoy the courtesy title "the Honorable," as daughters are referred to as "Lady" So and

The king and queen	(These are all of the royal line.)
Prince and princess	
Duke and duchess	(These may or may not be of the
Marquess and marchioness	royal line, but are ordinarily
Earl and countess	remote from the succession.)
Viscount and viscountess	
Baron and baroness	
Baronet and lady	

So; but these carry no social rank.) A peerage can be forfeited by act of attainder, as for example when a lord is convicted of treason; and, when forfeited, or lapsed for lack of a successor, can be bestowed on another family. Thus Robert Cecil was made in 1605 first earl of Salisbury in the third creation, the first creation dating from 1149, the second from 1337, the title having been in abeyance since 1539.

Scottish peers sat in the Parliament of Scotland, as English peers did in the Parliament of England till at the Act of Union (1707) Scots peers were granted 16 seats in the English House of Lords, to be filled by election. Similarly, Irish peers, when the Irish Parliament was abolished in 1801, were granted the right to elect 28 of their number to the House of Lords in Westminister. (Now that Eire is a separate nation, of course, this no longer applies.) For a genealogical guide through the tangled thickets of the aristocracy, see the classic compilation of Sir John Burke, known for brevity's sake as *Burke's Peerage*. The same author's *Landed Gentry* is popularly known in county society as "the stud book."

Below the hereditary peerage the chief title of honor is knight. Knighthood is not hereditary; it is generally a reward for services rendered. Though the word itself comes from Anglo-Saxon *cniht*, there seems to be some doubt whether knighthood amounted to much before the arrival of the Normans. The feudal system required military service as a condition of land tenure, and a man who came to serve his king at the head of an army of tenants required a title of authority and badges of identity—hence the title of knighthood and the coat of arms. During the Crusades, when men were far removed from their land (or had even sold it in order to go on crusade), more elaborate forms of fealty sprang up which soon expanded into the orders of knighthood. The Templars, Hospitallers, Knights of the Teutonic Order, Knights of Malta, and Knights of the Golden Fleece were but a few of these companionships; their similarity to the monastic and itinerant orders of friars was often remarked.

Gradually, with the rise of centralized government and the decline of feudal tenures, military knighthood became obsolete, and the rank largely honorific—sometimes it even degenerated into a scheme of the royal government for making money. For hundreds of years after its establishment in the fourteenth century, the Order of the Garter was the only English order of knighthood, an exclusive courtly companionship. Then, during the late seventeenth, eighteenth, and nineteenth centuries, a number of additional orders were created—the Thistle, Saint Patrick, the Bath, Saint Michael and Saint George, plus a number of special Victorian and Indian orders. They retain the terminology, ceremony, and dignity of knighthood, but the military implications are all vestigial.

Knights are addressed using their first names, as "Sir John"; their wives are "Lady Eleanor"; their children are commoners. The female equivalent of a knight bears the title of "Dame." The Order of Merit, instituted by Edward VII, is an exclusive and very honorable order. The Distinguished Service Order and the Victoria Cross—DSO and VC—are high awards for military heroism, the VC the very highest. The OBE (Order of the British Empire) is awarded for services to the empire, either at home or abroad, by persons of either gender. It is but one of many special medals awarded for outstanding accomplishment in one form or another.

Adapted from *The Land and Literature of England: A Historical Account*, by Robert M. Adams (New York: Norton, 1983).

Religious Sects in England

Religious distinctions and denominations are important in British social history, hence deeply woven into the nation's literature. The numerous (over 300) British churches and sects divide along a scale from high to low, depending on the amount of authority they give to the church or the amount of liberty they concede to the individual conscience. At one end of the scale is the Roman Catholic Church, asserting papal infallibility, universal jurisdiction, and the supreme importance of hierarchy as guide and intercessor. For political and social reasons, Catholicism struck deep roots in Ireland but was the object of prolonged, bitter hatred on the part of Protestants from the Reformation through the nineteenth century. The Established English (Anglican) Episcopal Church has been the official national church since the sixteenth century; it enjoys the support (once direct and exclusive, now indirect and peripheral) of the national government. Its creed is defined by Thirty-Nine Articles, but these are intentionally vague, so there are numerous ways of adhering to the Church of England. Roughly and intermittently, the chief classes of Anglicans have been known as High Church (with its highest portion calling itself Anglo-Catholic); Broad Church or Latitudinarian (when they get so broad that they admit anyone believing in God, they may be known as Deists, or some may leave the church altogether and be known as Unitarians); and Low Church, whose adherents may stay in the English church and yet come close to shaking hands with Presbyterians or Methodists. These various groups may be arranged, from the High down to the Low Church, in direct relation to the amount of ritual each prefers and in the degree of authority conceded to the upper clergy—and in inverse relation to the importance ascribed to a saving faith directly infused by God into an individual conscience.

All English Protestants who decline to subscribe to the English established church are classed as Dissenters or Nonconformists; for a time in the sixteenth and seventeenth centuries, they were also known as Puritans. (Nowadays, though Puritanism has less distinct theological meaning, it marks a distinct character type; because of his passionate emphasis on individual conscience and moral economy, George Bernard Shaw was a prototypical Puritan.) The Presbyterians model their church government on that established by John Calvin in the Swiss city of Geneva. It has no bishops, and therefore is more democratic for the clergy; but it gains energy by associating lay elders with clergymen in matters of social discipline, and tends to be strict with the ungodly. From its first reformation the Scottish Kirk was fixed on the Presbyterian model. During the civil wars of the seventeenth century, a great many sects sprang up on the left wing of the Presbyterians, most of them touched by Calvinism but some rebelling against it; a few of these still survive. The Independents became our modern Congregationalists; the Quakers are still Quakers, as Baptists are still Baptists, though multiply divided.

But many of the sects flourished and perished within the space of a few years. Among these now vanished groups were the Shakers (though a few groups still exist in America), the Seekers, the Ranters, the Anabaptists, the Muggletonians, the Fifth Monarchy Men, the Family of Love, the Sweet Singers of Israel, and many others, forgotten by all except scholars. During the eighteenth and nineteenth centuries, new sects arose, supplanting old ones; the Methodists, under John and Charles Wesley, became numerous and important, taking root particularly in Wales. (The three "subject" nationalities, Ireland, Scotland, and Wales, thus turned three different ways to avoid the Anglican church.) With the passage of time a small number of Swedenborgians sprang up, followers of the Swedish mystic Emanuel Swedenborg—to be followed by the Plymouth Brethren, Christian Scientists, Jehovah's Witnesses, and countless other nineteenth-century groups. All these sects constantly grow, shrink, split, and occasionally disappear as they succeed or fail in attracting new converts.

Within the various churches and sects, independent of them all but amazingly persistent, there has always survived a stream of esoteric or hermetic thought—a belief in occult powers, and sometimes in magic as well, exemplified by the pseudo-sciences of astrology and alchemy but taking many other forms. From the mythical Egyptian seer Hermes Trismegistus through Paracelsus, Cornelius Agrippa, Giordano Bruno, Jakob Boehme, the society of Rosicrucians, and a hundred other shadowy figures, the line can be traced to William Blake and William Butler Yeats, who both in their different ways brought hermetic Protestantism close to its ultimate goal, a mystic church of one single man, poised within his own mind-elaborated cosmos.

Poetic Forms and Literary Terminology

Verse is generally distinguished from prose as a more compressed and more regularly rhythmic form of statement. This approximate truth underlines the importance of **meter** in poetry, as the means by which rhythm is measured and described.

In the classical languages, meter was established on a **quantitative** basis, by the regular alternation of long and short syllables (that is, syllables classified according to the time taken to pronounce them). Outside of a few experiments (and the songs of Thomas Campion), this system has never proved congenial to English, which distinguishes, instead, between **stressed** and **unstressed**, or accented and unaccented syllables. Two varieties of accented stress may be distinguished. On the one hand, there is the natural stress pattern of words themselves; *syllable* is accented on the first syllable, *deplorable* on the second, and so on. Then there is the sort of stress which indicates rhetorical emphasis. If the sentence "You went to Greece?" is given a pronounced accent on the last word, it implies "Greece (of all places)?" If the accent falls on the first word, it implies "you (of all people)?" The meter of poetry—that is, its rhythm—is ordinarily built up out of a regular recurrence of accents, whether established as **word accents** or **rhetorical accents**; once started in the reader's mind, it has (like all rhythm) a persistent effect of its own.

The unit which is repeated to give steady rhythm to a poem is called a **poetic foot**; in English it usually consists of accented and unaccented syllables in one of five fairly simple patterns:

The **iambic foot** (or **iamb**) consists of an unstressed followed by a stressed syllable, as in *unìte, repeàt,* or *insìst.* Most English verse falls naturally into the iambic pattern.

The **trochaic foot** (**trochee**) inverts this order; it is a stressed followed by an unstressed syllable—for example, *ùnit, rèaper,* or *ìnstant.*

The **anapestic foot** (**anapest**) consists of two unstressed syllables followed by a stressed syllable, as in *intercède, disarrànged,* or *Cameròon.*

The **dactylic foot** (**dactyl**) consists of a stressed syllable followed by two unstressed syllables, as in *Wàshington, Ècuador,* or *àpplejack.*

The **spondaic foot** (**spondee**) consists of two successive stressed syllables, as in *heartbreak, headline,* or *Kashmir.*

In all the examples above, word accent and the quality of the metrical foot coincide exactly. But the metrical foot may well consist of several words, or, on the other hand, one word may well consist of several metrical feet. *Phòtolithògraphy* consists of two excellent dactyls in a single word; *dàrk and with spòts on it*, though it consists of six words rather than one, is also two dactyls—not quite such good ones. When we read a piece of poetry with the intention of discovering its underlying metrical pattern, we are said to scan it—that is, we go through it line by line, indicating by conventional signs which are the accented and which the unaccented syllables within the feet (the ictus ` generally designates accented, the mora ˘ unaccented syllables). We also count the number of feet in each line, or, more properly, **verse**— since a single poetic line is generally called a "verse." Verse lengths are conventionally described in terms derived from the Greek:

Monometer: one foot (of rare occurrence)
Dimeter: two feet (also rare)
Trimeter: three feet
Tetrameter: four feet
Pentameter: five feet
Hexameter: six feet (six iambic feet make an **Alexandrine**)
Heptameter: seven feet (also rare)

Samuel Johnson's little parody of simpleminded poets would thus be scanned this way:

> Ĭ pùt m̆y hàt ŭpòn m̆y hèad
> Ånd wàlked ĭntò th̆e Strànd,
> Ånd thère Ĭ mèt ănòth̆er man
> Wh̆òse hàt w̆as ĭn h̆is hànd.

The poem is iambic in rhythm, alternating tetrameter and trimeter in verse length. The fact that it scans so nicely is, however, no proof that it is good poetry. Quite the contrary. Many of poetry's most subtle effects are achieved by establishing an underlying rhythm and then varying it by means of a whole series of devices, some dramatic and expressive, others designed simply to lend variety and interest to the verse. A well-known sonnet of Shakespeare's (116) begins,

> Let me not to the marriage of true minds
> Admit impediments. Love is not love
> Which alters when it alteration finds,
> Or bends with the remover to remove.

It is perfectly possible, if one crushes all one's sensitivities, to read the first line of this poem as mechanical iambic pentameter:

> Lĕt mè nŏt tò th̆e màrrĭàge òf trŭe mìnds.

But of course nobody ever reads it that way, except to make a point; read with normal English accent and some sense of what it is saying, the line would probably form a pattern something like this:

> Lèt m̆e nŏt tŏ th̆e màrrĭàge ŏf trùe mìnds,

which is neither pentameter nor in any way iambic. The second line is a little more iambic, but, read for expression, falls just as far short of pentameter:

Ădmìt ĭmpèdĭmeñts. Lòve ĭs nŏt lòve.

Only in the third and fourth lines of the sonnet do we get verses which read as well as scan like five iambic feet.

The fact is that perfectly regular metrical verse is easy to write and dull to read. Among the devices in common use for varying too regular a pattern are, for instance, the insertion of a trochaic foot among iambics, especially at the opening of a line, where the soft first syllable of the iambic foot often needs stiffening (see line 1 above); the more or less free addition of extra unaccented syllables; and the use of **caesura,** or strong grammatical pause within a line (conventionally indicated, in scanning, by the sign ‖). The second line of the sonnet above is a good example of caesura:

Admit impediments. ‖ Love is not love.

The strength of the caesura, and its placing in the line, may be varied to produce striking variations of effect. More broadly, the whole relation between the poem's sound- and rhythm-patterns and its pattern as a sequence of assertions (phrases, clauses, sentences) may be manipulated by the poet. Sometimes his statements fit neatly within the lines, so that each line ends with a strong mark of punctuation; they are then known as **end-stopped lines.** Sometimes the sense flows over the ends of the lines, creating **run-on lines;** this process is also known, from the French, as **enjambment** (literally, "straddling").

End-stopped lines (Marlowe, *Hero and Leander,* lines 45–48):

> So lovely fair was Hero, Venus' nun,
> As Nature wept, thinking she was undone,
> Because she took more from her than she left
> And of such wondrous beauty her bereft.

Run-on lines (Keats, *Endymion* 1.89–93):

> Full in the middle of this pleasantness
> There stood a marble altar, with a tress
> Of flowers budded newly; and the dew
> Had taken fairy fantasies to strew
> Daisies upon the sacred sward, . . .

Following the example of such poets as Blake, Rimbaud, and Whitman, many poets of the twentieth century have undertaken to write what is called **free verse**—that is, verse which has neither a fixed metrical foot, nor (consequently) a fixed number of feet in its lines, but which depends for its rhythm on a pattern of cadences, or the rise and fall of the voice in utterance. All freedom in art is of course relative; free verse, with its special aptitude for metrical variety and nervous, colloquial phrasing—its total responsiveness, in other words, to its subject matter—has so successfully established itself that it is now widely recognized as a new and rather demanding form of artistic discipline.

SENSE AND SOUND

The very words of which poetic lines—whether free or traditional—are composed cause them to have different sounds and produce different effects. Polysyllables, being pronounced fast, often cause a line to move swiftly; monosyllables, especially when heavy and requiring distinct accents, may cause it to move heavily, as in Milton's famous line (*Paradise Lost* 2.621):

> Rocks, caves, lakes, fens, bogs, dens, and shades of death.

Poetic assertions are often dramatized and reinforced by means of **alliteration**—that is, the use of several nearby words or stressed syllables beginning with the same consonant. When Shakespeare writes (*Sonnet 64*),

> Ruin hath taught me thus to ruminate
> That Time will come and take my love away,

the rich, round, vague echoes of the first line contrast most effectively with the sharp anxiety and directness of the alliterative *t*'s in the second. When Dryden starts *Absalom and Achitophel* with that wicked couplet,

> In pious times, ere priestcraft did begin,
> Before polygamy was made a sin,

the satiric undercutting is strongly reinforced by the triple alliteration which links "*p*ious" with "*p*riestcraft" and "*p*olygamy."

Assonance, or repetition of the same or similar vowel sounds within a passage (usually in accented syllables), also serves to enrich it, as in two lines from Keats's *Ode on Melancholy:*

> For shade to shade will come too drowsily,
> And drown the wakeful anguish of the soul.

It is clear that the round, hollow tones of "drowsily," repeated in "drown" and darkening to the full *o*-sound of "soul," have much to do with the effect of the passage. A related device is **consonance,** or the repetition of a pattern of consonants with changes in the intervening vowels—for example: *linger, longer, languor; rider, reader, raider, ruder.*

Direct verbal imitation of natural sounds (known as **onomatopoeia**) has been much attempted, from Virgil's galloping horse—

> *Quadrupedante putrem sonitu quatit ungula campum—*

to Tennyson's account, in *The Princess*, of

> The moan of doves in immemorial elms,
> And murmuring of innumerable bees.

Often ingeniously exploited as a side effect, onomatopoeia is essentially a trick, with about the same value in poetry as it has in music.

Rhyme consists of a repetition of accented sounds in words, usually those falling at the end of verse lines. If the rhyme sound is the very last syllable of the line (*rebound, sound*), the rhyme is called **masculine;** if the accented syllable is followed by an unaccented syllable (*hounding, bounding*), the rhyme is called **feminine.** Rhymes amounting to three or more syllables, like forced rhymes, generally have a comic effect in English, and have been freely used for this purpose, e.g., by Byron (*intellectual, henpecked-you-all*). Rhymes occurring within a single line are called **internal;** for instance, the Mother Goose rhyme, "Mary, Mary, quite contrary," or from Coleridge's *Ancient Mariner* ("We were the first that ever burst / Into that silent sea"). **Eye rhymes** are words used as rhymes which look alike but actually sound different (for example, *alone, done; remove, love*); **off rhymes** (sometimes called **partial, imperfect,** or **slant rhymes**) are occasionally the result of pressing exigencies or lack of skill, but are also, at times, used deliberately by modern poets for special effects. For instance, a poem by Wilfred Owen (*Strange Meeting*) contains such "rhymes" as *years / yours* or *tigress / progress.* Owen called these pairings "pararhymes;" they are varieties of assonance.

Blank verse is unrhymed iambic pentameter; until the recent advent of free verse, it was the only unrhymed measure to achieve general popularity in English. First used by the earl of Surrey, blank verse was during the sixteenth century largely dramatic in character; *Paradise Lost* was one of the first nondramatic poems in English to use it. But Milton's authority and his success were so great that during the eighteenth and nineteenth centuries blank verse came to be used for a great variety of discursive, descriptive, and philosophical poems—besides remaining the standard metrical form for epics. Thomson's *Seasons,* Cowper's *Task,* Wordsworth's *Prelude,* and Tennyson's *Idylls of the King* were all written in blank verse.

A **stanza** is a recurring unit of a poem, consisting of a number of verses. Certain poems (for example, Dryden's *Alexander's Feast*) have stanzas comprising a variable number of verses, of varying lengths. Others are more regular, hence easier to describe.

The simplest form of stanza is the **couplet;** it is two lines rhyming together. A single couplet considered in isolation is sometimes called a **distich;** when it expresses a complete thought, ending with a terminal mark of punctuation, it is called a **closed couplet.** The development of very regular end-stopped couplets in the mid-seventeenth century, their use in so-called heroic tragedies, and their consequent acquisition of the name **heroic couplets** are described in the introduction to The Early Seventeenth Century, volume 1. The heroic couplet was the principal form of English neoclassical style.

Another traditional and challenging form of couplet is the **tetrameter,** or **four-beat couplet.** All rhymed couplets are hard to manage without monotony; and since, in addition, a four-beat line is hard to divide by caesura without splitting it into two tick-tock dimeters, tetrameter couplets have posed a perpetual challenge to poets, and still provide an admirable finger-exercise for aspiring versifiers. A model of tetrameter couplets managed with marvelous variety, complexity, and expressiveness is Marvell's *To His Coy Mistress:*

> Thou by the Indian Ganges' side
> Shouldst rubies find; I by the tide

Of Humber would complain. I would
Love you ten years before the flood,
And you should, if you please, refuse
Till the conversion of the Jews.

English has not done much with rhymes grouped in threes, but has borrowed from Italian the form known as **terza rima,** in which Dante composed his *Divine Comedy.* This form consists of linked groups of three rhymes according to the following pattern: *aba bcb cdc ded,* etc. Shelley's *Ode to the West Wind* is composed in stanzas of *terza rima,* the poem as a whole ending with a couplet.

Quatrains are stanzas of four lines; the lines usually rhyme alternately, *abab,* or in the second and fourth lines, *abcb.* When they alternate tetrameter and trimeter lines, as in Johnson's little poem about men in hats (above), or as in *Sir Patrick Spens,* they are called **ballad stanza.** Dryden's *Annus Mirabilis* and Gray's *Elegy Written in a Country Churchyard* are in **heroic quatrains;** these rhyme alternately, and employ five-stress iambic verse throughout. Tennyson used for *In Memoriam* a tetrameter quatrain rhymed *abba,* and FitzGerald translated *The Rubáiyát of Omar Khayyám* into a pentameter quatrain rhymed *aaba;* but these forms have not been very generally adopted.

Chaucer's *Troilus and Criseyde* is an early example in English of **rime royal,** a seven-line iambic pentameter stanza consisting essentially of a quatrain dovetailed onto two couplets, according to the rhyme scheme *ababbcc* (the fourth line serves both as the final line of the quatrain and the first line of the first couplet). Closely akin to rime royal, but differentiated by an extra *a*-rhyme between the two *b*-rhymes, is **ottava rima,** that is, an eight-line stanza rhyming *abababcc.* As its name suggests, ottava rima is of Italian origin; it was first used in English by Wyatt. Its final couplet, being less prepared for than in rime royal, and usually set off as a separate verbal unit, has a special witty snap to it, for which Byron found good use in *Don Juan.*

The longest and most intricate stanza generally used for narrative purposes in English is that devised by Edmund Spenser for *The Faerie Queene.* The **Spenserian stanza** has nine lines rhyming *ababbcbcc;* the first eight lines are pentameter, the last line an Alexandrine. Slow-moving, intricate of pattern, and demanding in its rhyme scheme (the *b*-sound recurs four times, the *c*-sound three), the Spenserian stanza has nonetheless appealed widely to poets seeking a rich and complicated metrical form. Keats's *Eve of St. Agnes* and Shelley's *Adonais* are brilliantly successful nineteenth-century examples of its use.

The **sonnet,** originally a stanza of Italian origin which has developed into an independent lyric form, is usually defined nowadays as fourteen lines of iambic pentameter. None of the elements in this definition is absolute and in earlier centuries there were sonnets in hexameters (the first of Sidney's *Astrophil and Stella*), and sonnets of as many as twenty lines (Milton's *On the New Forcers of Conscience*). Most, however, come close to the definition. The different varieties—Petrarchan, Shakespearean, and Spenserian— are described in the introduction to the sixteenth-century section, 1.413. Most Elizabethan sonnets dealt with courtly love; and some poets, like Sidney, Spenser, and Shakespeare, imitated Petrarch in grouping together their sonnets dealing with a particular lady or situation. A neutral word for these gatherings is **sonnet sequences;** whether or not they tell a story is a matter of long-standing dispute. Since Elizabethan times, the sonnet has been applied to a wide range of subject matters—religious, political, satiric, moral and philosophic.

In blank verse or irregularly rhymed verse, where stanzaic divisions do not exist or are indistinct, the poetry sometimes falls into **verse paragraphs,** which are in effect divisions of sense like prose paragraphs. This division can be clearly seen in Milton's *Lycidas* or Spenser's *Epithalamion.* In the latter poem, it is reinforced by **a refrain,** which is simply a line repeated at the end of each stanza. Ballads also customarily have refrains; for example, the refrain of *Lord Randall* is

> mother, make my bed soon,
> For I'm weary wi' hunting, and fain wald lie down.

FIGURATIVE LANGUAGE

The act of bringing words together into rich and vigorous poetic lines is complex and demanding, chiefly because so many variables require control. There is the "thought" of the lines, their verbal texture, their emotional resonance, the developing perspective of the reader—all these to be managed at once. One of the poet's chief resources toward this end is figurative language. Here, as in matters of meter, one may distinguish a great variety of devices, some of which we use in everyday speech without special awareness of their names and natures. When we say someone eats "like a horse" or "like a bird," we are using a **simile,** that is, a comparison marked out by a specific word of likening—"like" or "as." When we omit the word of comparison but imply a likeness—as in the sentence, "That hog has guzzled all the champagne"—we are making use of **metaphor.** The **epic simile,** frequent in epic poetry, is an extended simile in which the thing compared is described as an object in its own right, beyond its point of likeness with the main subject. Milton starts to compare Satan to Leviathan, but concludes his simile with the story of a sailor who moored his ship by mistake, one night, to a whale (*Paradise Lost* 1.200–208). Metaphors and similes have been complexly but usefully distinguished according to their special effects; they may be, for instance, violent, comic, degrading, decorative, or ennobling.

When we speak of "forty head of cattle" or ask someone to "lend a hand" with a job, we are using **synecdoche,** a figure which substitutes the part for the whole. When we speak of a statement coming "from the White House," or a man much interested in "the turf," we are using **metonymy,** or the substitution of one term for another with which it is closely associated. **Antithesis** is a device for placing opposing ideas in grammatical parallel, as, for example, in the following passage from Pope's *Rape of the Lock* (5.25–30), where there are more examples of antithesis than there are lines:

> But since, alas! frail beauty must decay,
> Curled or uncurled, since locks will turn to gray;
> Since painted, or not painted, all shall fade,
> And she who scorns a man must die a maid;
> What then remains but well our power to use,
> And keep good humor still whate'er we lose?

Irony is a verbal device which implies an attitude quite different from (and often opposite to) that which is literally expressed. When Eliot writes, in *Whispers of Immortality*, that "Grishkin is nice," the adjective is carefully chosen to let an ironic grimace of distaste appear. And when Donne "proves," in *The Canonization*, that he and his mistress are going to found a new religion of love, he seems to be inviting us to take a subtly ironic attitude toward religion as well as love.

Because it is easy to see through, **hyperbole**, or willful exaggeration, is a favorite device of irony—which is not to say that it may not be "serious" as well. When she hears that a young man is "dying for love" of her, a sensible girl does not accept this statement literally, but it may convey a serious meaning to her nonetheless. The **pun**, or play on words (known to the learned, sometimes, as **paronomasia**), may also be serious or comic in intent; witness, for example, the famous series of puns in Donne's *Hymn to God the Father*. **Oxymoron** is a figure of flat contradiction—for instance, Milton's famous description of hell as containing "darkness visible" (*Paradise Lost* 1.63). A **paradox** is a statement which seems absurd but turns out to have rational meaning after all, usually in some unexpected sense; Donne speaks of fear being great courage and high valor (*Satire* 3, line 16), and turns out to mean that fear of God is greater courage than any earthly bravery. A **conceit** is a far-fetched and ingenious comparison. Writing in the fourteenth century, the Italian poet Francis Petrarch popularized a great number of conceits handy for use in love poetry, and readily adapted by his English imitators. Wyatt, for example, is using **Petrarchan conceits** when he compares love to a warrior, or the lover's state to that of a storm-tossed ship; and a hundred other sonneteers developed the themes of the lady's stony heart, incendiary glances, and so forth. On the other hand, the **metaphysical conceit** was a more intellectualized, many-leveled comparison, giving a strong sense of the poet's ingenuity in overcoming obstacles—for instance, Donne's comparison of separated lovers to the legs of a compass (A *Valediction: Forbidding Mourning*) or Herbert's comparison of devotion to a pulley, in the poem of that name.

Images are often described as "mental pictures"; it is more accurate to say that they are verbal representations of something capable of being visualized; some readers form such mental pictures, and respond to them, more than others. Images not only convey what things look like, but direct us, by their pattern of associated and involved feelings, in our reactions to what is being represented. Indeed, there may be such a weight of meaning or feeling behind the image that the verbal picture itself becomes transparent and its "meaning" becomes primary. Abstract ideas can get attached to specific images—water, snake, bird, sun, worm, lion, whatever—in a multitude of ways, of which the reader need sometimes only be reminded. Of course the poet can also be arbitrary about it, letting his reader know simply that Redcrosse "stands for" Holiness and Archimago "stands for" Hypocrisy. If that's as far as it goes, we have a primitive variety of **allegory**. But the relation between the tenor of the image (its abstract meaning) and the vehicle (the concrete picture) can be much more indefinite and insubstantial. If the poet mentions a peacock, he may or may not intend his reader to think of immortality, because the unfolding of the peacock's tail and the opening of its "eyes" has traditionally suggested the rebirth of the soul after death. If that is the way the image works, then it is a **symbol**. Or again, if the poet mentions a fish, he may well intend the reader to think of Christ. This isn't because of any similarity between the fish and Christ; the identification depends on a mildly esoteric bit of information, that the Greek word for fish, *ichthys*, forms an anagram of the Greek words for "Jesus Christ, Son of God, Savior." When the connection between tenor and vehicle is arbitrary, or involves the elements of a puzzle, the image may be referred to as an **emblem**. In the sixteenth and seventeenth centuries, emblems often took the form of puzzling little drawings, the meaning of which was explained in appended verses: for an example see the emblem prefixed to Crashaw's poem *To the Countess of Denbigh* (1.1361).

Personification is the attribution of human qualities to an inanimate object (for example, the Sea) or an abstract concept (Freedom); a special variety of it is called (in a term of John Ruskin's invention) the **pathetic fallacy**. When we speak of leaves "dancing" or a lake "smiling," we attribute human traits to nonhuman objects. Ruskin thought this was false and therefore "morbid"; modern criticism tends to view the practice as artistically and morally neutral. A more formal and abstract variety of personification is **allegory**, in which a narrative (such as *Pilgrim's Progress*) is constructed by representing general concepts (Faithfulness, Sin, Despair) as persons. A **fable** (like *The Nun's Priest's Tale*) represents beasts behaving like humans; a **parable** is a brief story, or simply an observation, with strong moral application; and an **exemplum** is a story told to illustrate a point in a sermon. A special series of devices, nearly obsolete today, used to be available to poets who could count on readers trained in the classics. These were the devices of **classical epithet** and **allusion**. In their simplest form, the classic myths used to provide a repertoire of agreeable stage properties, and a convenient shorthand for expressing emotional attitudes. Picturesque creatures like centaurs, satyrs, and sphinxes, heroes and heroines like Hector and Helen, and the whole pantheon of Olympic deities could be used to make ready reference to a great many aspects of human nature. One does not have to explain the problems of a man who is "cleaning the Augean stables"; if he is afflicted with an "Achilles' heel," or is assailing "Hydra-headed difficulties," his state is clear. These epithets, or descriptive phrases, making reference to mythological stories, suggest in a phrase situations that would normally require cumbersome explanations. Conceivably other mythologies might have served the same end in analogous ways. But because they could be taken for granted as the common possession of all educated readers, the classic myths entered into English literature as early as Chaucer, and are only now passing away as a viable system of allusions. In poets like Spenser and Milton, classical allusion becomes a kind of enormously learned game, in which the poet seeks to make his points as indirectly as possible. For instance, Spenser writes in the *Epithalamion*, lines 328–29:

> Lyke as when Jove with fayre Alcmena lay,
> When he begot the great Tirynthian groome.

The mere mention of Alcmena in the first line suggests, to the knowing reader, Hercules; Spenser's problem in the second line is to find a way of referring to him which is neither redundant nor heavy-handed. "Tirynthian" reminds us of his long connection with the city of Tiryns, stretching our minds (as it were) across his whole career; and "groome" compresses references to a man-child, a servant, and a bridegroom, all of which apply to different aspects of Hercules' history. Thus, far from simply avoiding redundancy, Spenser has enriched the whole texture of his verse, thought, and feeling by his gift for precise classical epithet.

SCHOOLS

Within the broad periods it is customary to group in **schools** writers who show common stylistic traits or thematic concerns. Whether they considered themselves a group doesn't much matter. None of the **Romantic poets** knew they were being romantic, although Hazlitt, Shelley, and other writers of the time recognized shared features that they called "the spirit of the age." The followers of Spenser are known as **Spenserians**; they knew they liked Spenser, but didn't realize that made them a group. **Cavalier** poets are set decisively apart from **Metaphysical** poets, though pretty surely none of the two-dozen-odd men involved knew that was what they were. And so with the **Gothic novelists,** and the so-called **Graveyard School** of the eighteenth century, so with the modern surrealists. These schools are generally grouped, defined, and named by scholars and critics after the event. Use of a common form or subject matter constitutes a more superficial similarity than use of a common style, common techniques, or common philosophical backgrounds. But literary history, being nothing if not pragmatic, makes use of all sorts of common denominators.

Intellectual affinities have led some writers to be classified under the names of the philosophical schools of Greece and Rome. These are chiefly the **Epicureans,** who specify that the aim of life and the source of value is pleasure; the **Stoics,** who emphasize stern virtue and the dignified endurance of what cannot be avoided; and the **Skeptics,** who doubt that anything can be known for sure. These categories are useful as capsule descriptions, but they aren't very tidy, as they overlap one another and cut across other categories. Dryden is an author strongly tinged with **skepticism,** but many of his poems suggest an unabashed **epicureanism.** *The Vanity of Human Wishes,* by Samuel Johnson, is the classic poem in English of **stoic** philosophy, but it also expresses a particularly strong coloring of **Christian humanism.**

Plato and **Aristotle,** as they summarized contrasting attitudes toward existence, are often used to define the outlook of writers. Both were prolific writers of enormous range and complexity, but in literary contexts their names most often define attitudes toward reality. Aristotle tended to find reality, not exclusively but primarily, in concrete and particular substances, which he brilliantly categorized and generalized. Plato tended to place reality in abstract ideal forms, of which the concrete things we experience in daily life are but partial and shadowy manifestations. During the Middle Ages, many Dominican friars, of whom St. Thomas Aquinas is best known, tended to be **Aristotelian** in their assumptions and in the structure of their logic; St. Bonaventura, among the Franciscans, was more strongly tinged with a **Platonism** that he derived largely from Saint Augustine. During the Renaissance Spenser, and during the Romantic period Shelley, were **Platonists** or **Neo-Platonists.** (A Neo-Platonist is a Platonist diluted with other worldviews—perhaps Pythagorean mysticism, perhaps Christian theology, perhaps Aristotelian thought itself. In a narrower sense, the term is applied to philosophers writing in the tradition of Plotinus [3rd century A.D.], who held that all things in the world, spiritual and material, "emanate," or flow out, from the "Absolute," or the "One"—the single source of all truth, goodness, and beauty.) **Aristotelianism,** as it is more commonsensical, had faded by Spenser's time to the common teaching of the schools, and by Shelley's time to the practical, pragmatic materialism of everyday life.

TERMS OF ART

The following section groups together various sets of frequently used and closely related literary terms in an effort to discriminate and define them.

Allegory, Symbol, Emblem, Type. Allegory is an extended metaphorical narrative in which a figure (say, Spenser's Redcrosse Knight) stands for a specific quality (Holiness). A **symbol** may have several different meanings, which typically grow out of its relation to other symbols, as in the twenty-odd poems of Yeats which allude to the rose. An **emblem,** in the sixteenth and seventeenth centuries, was an enigmatic picture with a motto and an explanatory verse attached. In modern usage, an emblem is a visible object representing an abstract quality, as a dove is the emblem of peace. A **type** is a historical figure who prefigures another and later figure as (in some Christian interpretations) Moses in liberating the children of Israel was thought to prefigure Christ in freeing men from Satan.

Baroque and **Mannerist** are terms imported into literary study from the history of art, and applied by analogy. Michelangelo is a **baroque** artist; he holds great masses in powerful dynamic tension, his style is heavily ornamented and restless. In these respects he is sometimes compared with Milton. El Greco is a **mannerist,** whose gaunt and distorted figures often seem to be laboring under great spiritual stress, whose light seems to be focused in spots against a dark background. He has been compared to Donne. Analogies of this sort are occasionally suggestive, but they must be carefully handled to avoid degenerating into parallels which are forced and nominal rather than substantial.

Bathos. See **Pathos, Bathos, and the Sublime.**

Burlesque and **Mock Heroic** differ in that the former makes its subject mean and absurd by directly cutting it down, the latter makes its subject ludicrous by inflating it. In Pope's mock-heroic *Dunciad,* the figure of Dulness (Colley Cibber) is given inappropriately heroic dimensions; in Butler's burlesque *Hudibras,* the knightly hero is characterized by low and vulgar attributes, and persistently engages in inappropriately low behavior. Burlesque contributed to the development of the English novel; and during the nineteenth century, when formal drama tended to be stagy and melodramatic, a vigorous burlesque stage flourished in England, making fun of the classics. See **Imitation and Parody.**

Classic and **Neo-Classic.** See **Gothic, Classic, Neo-Classic.**

Convention and **Tradition. Conventions** are agreed-upon artistic procedures peculiar to an art form. None of Shakespeare's contemporaries spoke blank verse in everyday life, but characters in his plays do, and the audience accepts it—as the audience at an opera accepts that characters will sing arias to express their feelings, something that few of us do in everyday life. A **tradition** is a particular way of viewing or representing things; it generally includes a great many conventions. Often thought of as a dead weight to be overcome by "originality," tradition (since an important essay by T. S. Eliot) is now more often recognized as an active energy, working to enrich an art form that makes knowing use of it by playing variations on it.

Didactic poetry teaches a lesson, generally practical. The eighteenth century, for example, produced didactic poetry on the wool trade, field sports, health practices, and the sexuality of plants.

Dramatic irony and **Dramatic monologue** are quite different devices. In **dramatic irony** a stage character says something which has one meaning for him and for the onstage person he is addressing, but quite another for the audience. The **dramatic monologue** is a poetic form associated with Robert Browning and discussed in the introduction to that poet's work (2.1229); it presents a character as revealed unintentionally by his own words.

Eclogue. See **Pastorals.**

Emblem. See **Allegory, Symbol, Emblem, Type.**

Eulogy and **Elegy.** The **eulogy** is a work of praise, in prose or poetry, for a person either very distinguished or recently dead; an **elegy** is a poem of lamentation for the dead. In Greek and Latin poetry, elegies were poems written in alternating pentameters and hexameters, called elegiac meter. They could deal with a broad variety of topics, and English elegies also tended to be discursive poems on meditative themes. Donne, following his Roman predecessors, wrote some elegies that are jocose, even bawdy.

Euphemism and **Euphuism. Euphemism,** or "fine speech" is a verbal device for avoiding an unpleasant concept or expression, as when, instead of saying a person "died," we say he "passed away." Euphues was the hero of a prose romance (published 1579–80) by John Lyly; his adventures are recounted in a mannered style full of puns, alliteration, and antithetical "points." Under the name of **Euphuism** this courtly style enjoyed a brief vogue.

Fancy and **Imagination.** The distinction between these two mental powers greatly exercised the early Romantic poets. **Fancy** (a word directly derived by contraction from "fantasy") was defined by Coleridge as essentially the power of combining several known properties into new combinations; **imagination,** on the other hand, was the faculty of using those known properties to create a whole that is entirely new.

Folios, Quartos, etc. are terms used to define the size of book pages. To make a **folio,** a sheet of paper (14″ x 20″ or larger) is folded just once (producing thereby four pages); **quartos** are folded twice (producing eight pages). Shakespeare's plays were first printed in quartos (often in several different editions) but when they were collected together, in 1623, they appeared as the First Folio.

Genre, Decorum. A **genre** is an established literary form, such as stage comedy, the picaresque novel, the epic, the sonnet. Being of a certain genre predisposes a work to represent certain characters and events and to seek certain effects. Its success in achieving these effects and avoiding incongruous ones can thus be judged; and this is one sort of **decorum** (fittingness), the decorum of genre. Satire was once considered a low, popular form, for which only low, popular speech was decorous (fitting). There are also decorums of character, of occasion, of rhetorical mode, etc.

Gothic, Classic, Neo-Classic. Gothic and **Classic** distinguish styles and tendencies in art and literature. **Gothic** implies vital, primitive, but irregular work, with the qualities of the barbarian North. **Classic** implies lucid, rational, and idealized work, as in the sunlit Southern civilizations of Greece and Rome. For Pope and his contemporaries "Gothic" was generally a word of contempt; for Ruskin, in the nineteenth century, it was a term of highest praise. "Gothic" novels, written in the period of transition between these two attitudes, and taking full advantage of dark medieval settings, were shockers and thrillers of the late eighteenth and early nineteenth centuries. **Neo-classicism** describes work which, while keeping one eye on a classical original, modifies it to comment on modern conditions: a literary example is Doctor Samuel Johnson's *Vanity of Human Wishes*, based on Juvenal's *Tenth Satire.*

Heroic poems, heroic couplets. Because they concentrate on the figure of a typical hero (Achilles, Aeneas), epic poems were frequently called "**heroic.**" Trying to transfer epic grandeur to the stage, playwrights of the Restoration period generally achieved only grandiosity; but the stately couplets in which they made their characters speak became known as **heroic couplets.**

Humor. See **Wit and Humor.**

Humors and **Temperaments** are psychological terms used by Renaissance writers. The four basic humors of every constitution were the **choleric** (bile), the **sanguine** (blood), the **phlegmatic** (phlegm), and the **melancholy** (black bile). A man's **temperament** was determined by the mixture of these humors, the way in which they were "tempered." When a particular humor predominated, it pushed the character in that direction: choler = anger; sanguine = geniality; phlegm = cold torpor; and melancholy = gloomy self-absorption.

Imagination. See **Fancy** and **Imagination.**

Imitation and **Parody** are devices by which a literary work assumes an attitude toward its own predecessor. **Imitation** involves not simply copying, but transposing the different features of the earlier work into modern particulars, while retaining the same pattern and the same approximate tonal level. **Parody** generally lowers the level of its original; it is a device of ridicule, though sometimes of self-ridicule. When Joyce parodies ancient Irish legend (as in the "Cyclops" chapter of *Ulysses*), there is no separating ridicule of the past from contempt for the present. See also **Burlesque.**

Irony, Sarcasm. Irony and **sarcasm,** though both are ways of saying one thing and meaning another, go about the job differently. **Sarcasm** is broader and more deliberate in its reversal of meanings; **irony** may be, and in literature generally is, very fine. The patriarch Job is bitterly **sarcastic** when he replies to his comforters (12.2) "No doubt but ye are the people, and wisdom shall die with you." On the other hand, Jane Austen, in the first sentence of *Pride and Prejudice* overstates her case just enough to make it drily **ironic** when she writes, "It is a truth universally acknowledged, that a single man in possession of a good fortune, must be in want of a wife."

Legend. See **Myth and Legend.**

Logic. See **Rhetoric and Logic.**

Masque. For a discussion of the English **masque,** see the introduction to Jonson's *Pleasure Reconciled to Virtue* (1.1232).

Myth and **Legend** are stories that incorporate themselves into the instinctual thinking of humanity. **Myths** are narratives which purport to account, in supernatural terms, for why the world is as it is, why people act as they do. Myths often spring up to explain rituals, the original meanings of which have been forgotten; or they may be folk tales based on popular nightmares or fantasies. An ordinary or even inferior tale may take on mythic dimensions—witness Mary Wollstonecraft Shelley's *Frankenstein* or the wooden volumes of Horatio Alger, Jr. A **legend** is any old and popularly repeated story; the word usually implies, in addition, that the story is false. But a proper myth hardly pretends to be historically true—it is a flowering of the mind into narrative. Three great bodies of mythical material are the Celtic, the Norse or Germanic, and the classical fables. A body of associated myths is **a mythology;** a student and collector of myths is **a mythographer.**

Naturalism. See **Realism and Naturalism.**

Neo-Classic. See **Gothic, Classic, Neo-Classic.**

Novel. See **Romance, Novel.**

Ode. See the discussions of English odes in the headnote to Jonson's *Ode to Cary and Morison* (1.1221), and Dryden's *Ode to the Memory of Mrs. Anne Killigrew* (1.1825).

Pastorals (from the Latin word for "shepherd," *pastor*) are poems set in idealized, often artificial, rural surroundings. They are sometimes called **eclogues.** Though low on the social scale and limited in his interests, the shepherd can be made to comment indirectly on large social issues. Virgil's shepherds regularly do so, and John Gay, by transferring his scene (in *The Beggar's Opera*) from the rural fields to Newgate prison, was able to make his whores and highwaymen reflect sardonically on the national politics of his day. Alice, the heroine of *Alice in Wonderland* has been seen, very perceptively, as a pastoral figure. Clearly, the concept is very adaptable. **Pastoral elegies** (like *Lycidas* by Milton, *Adonais* by Shelley, and *Thyrsis* by Matthew Arnold) have been particulary successful, perhaps because a somber theme adds weight to a basically artificial form.

Pathos, Bathos, and the Sublime. Pathos is the feeling of sympathy—pity or sorrow particularly—aroused by a literary work; the word comes from the Greek term for "suffering." **Bathos,** a comic parallel from the Greek word for "deep," describes the anticlimax that comes when an author, striving for elevation, trips and falls on his face. The idea of loftiness as the most desirable of literary qualities goes back to the late-classical rhetorician Longinus, who wrote a treatise *On the Sublime*. An early publication by Edmund Burke distinguishes the **sublime** (with its mixture of pain and danger) from the merely beautiful.

Quarto. See **Folios, Quartos.**

Realism and Naturalism are both terms used to describe fiction which aims at minute fidelity to actual existence. **Realism** connotes an attempt to give the illusion of ordinary life, in which unexceptional people undergo everyday experiences. **Naturalism** is associated with the example of Émile Zola and the thesis that a novel should present a "slice of life," a cross-section of actual existence; the emphasis is usually on man's instinctual nature, especially the sexual and acquisitive instincts. This type flourished during the late nineteenth and early twentieth centuries. Harold Biffen, a character in George Gissing's novel *New Grub Street*, is devoting his life to a work of "absolute realism in the sphere of the ignobly decent"—and this can epitomize realism. A work of naturalism, on the other hand, might be said to devote itself to the ignobly indecent.

Rhetoric and Logic. During the Renaissance, **rhetoric,** which is the art of persuading an audience, assumed fresh importance by contrast with the

logic traditionally used by scholastic philosophers. Cicero particularly exemplified the "open hand" of rhetoric as opposed to the "closed fist" of Aristotelian logic. Though mostly fought out in terms of Latin style, the controversy had its effect on an evolving ideal of English prose. Sidney's *Defense of Poesy* and Milton's *Areopagitica* are both structured along the lines of a classical oration. During the Renaissance, "figures of rhetoric," often culled from textbooks and anthologies, comprised the substance of many schoolboy themes, and then carried over into mature works of literary art, such as (most spectacularly) the euphuistic romances of John Lyly: see **Euphemism, Euphuism.**

Romance, Novel. Medieval **romances** are narratives of adventure, following a hero through the successive episodes of a quest toward his chosen or appointed goal. **Novels** are more or less realistic studies of social relationships, more tightly structured than romances, less given to the fabulous, and dealing generally with the middle strata of society. But these distinctions were far from airtight to begin with, and with the years have grown steadily vaguer. Is Kafka's *The Castle* a novel or a romance? It is always called the former, it looks much more like the latter, and it is actually more like an extended parable.

Sarcasm. See **Irony, Sarcasm.**

Satire comes from the Latin word for medley, *satura*; the impression that it has to do with the word "satyr" is a popular delusion. Under **satire** are included all the many literary ways for diminishing a subject by making it laughable or contemptible. For a discussion of the backgrounds of English satire, see the introduction to Donne's *Satire 3* (1.1085).

Sensibility, as used in literary discussion, does not mean "sensitivity," but the entire complex of thoughts, feelings, and suppositions characteristic of an individual or an age. T. S. Eliot, borrowing the concept from Rémy de Gourmont, said the seventeenth century did not have, as people have had since, a sensibility divided between the world of rational thought and that of feeling. But this idea has not proved very applicable to studies of particular authors or periods.

Style in a minimal sense is the way anyone uses language; thus each of us possesses (for better or worse) an individual style. In the better sense of language endowed with point and force, language of special distinction which accomplishes its ends swiftly and clearly, it has been described by Swift as "proper words in proper places"—a definition on which there is no improving.

Sublime. See **Pathos, Bathos, and the Sublime.**

Symbol. See **Allegory, Symbol, Emblem, Type.**

Tradition. See **Convention and Tradition.**

Type. See **Allegory, Symbol, Emblem, Type.**

Wit and Humor. Wit is one of those words too useful ever to be exactly defined. As employed during the seventeenth and eighteenth centuries, it might mean general intelligence or the ability to say something funny, wisdom or ability, prudence, fantasy, vivacity of speech, quickness of repartee, a good command of sexual innuendo, and many other things including the current meaning of a verbal thrust or dig. **Humor** is a gentler, less intellectual quality; it is tinged with the feeling of "good humor," which is geniality.

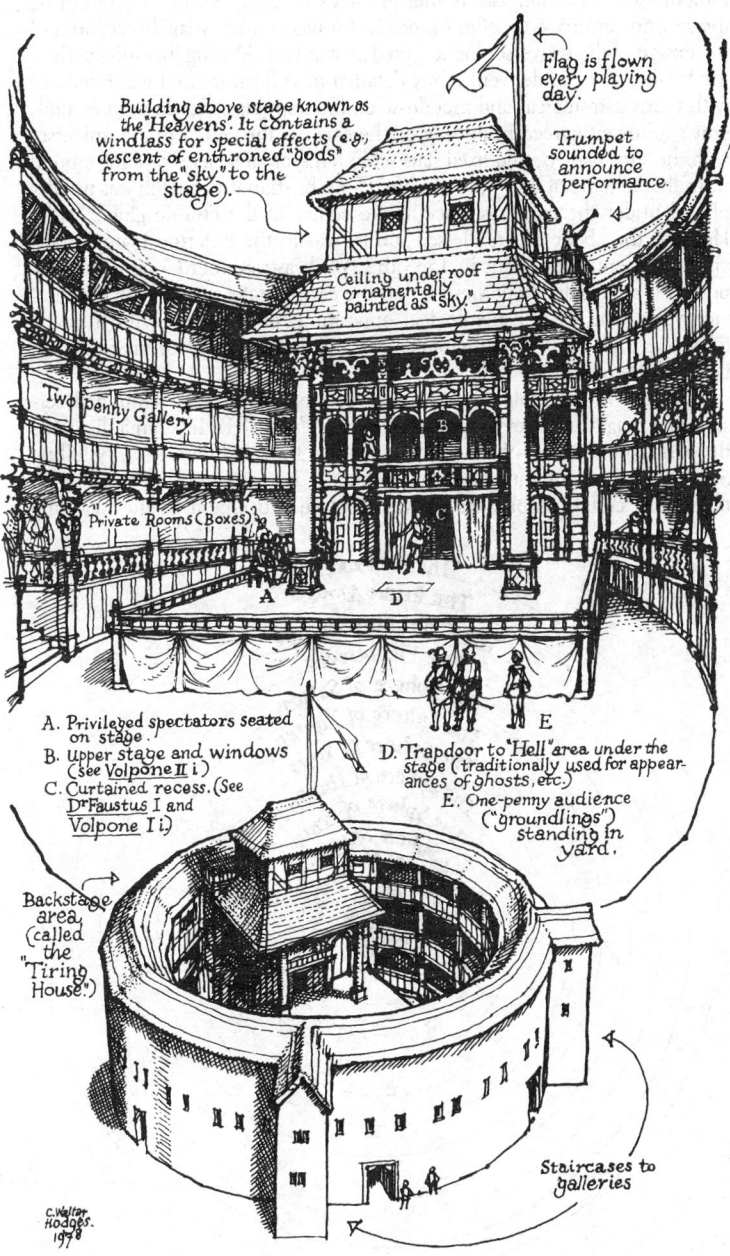

Flag is flown every playing day.

Trumpet sounded to announce performance.

Building above stage known as the "Heavens". It contains a windlass for special effects (e.g. descent of enthroned "gods" from the "sky" to the stage).

Ceiling under roof ornamentally painted as "sky."

Two penny Gallery

Private Rooms (Boxes)

A. Privileged spectators seated on stage.
B. Upper stage and windows (see *Volpone* II i.)
C. Curtained recess. (See *Dr Faustus* I and *Volpone* I i.)
D. Trapdoor to "Hell" area under the stage (traditionally used for appearances of ghosts, etc.)
E. One-penny audience ("groundlings") standing in yard.

Backstage area (called the "Tiring House.")

Staircases to galleries

C. Walter Hodges. 1958

Ptolemy was a Roman astronomer of Greek descent, born in Egypt during the second century A.D.; after his death, for nearly 1500 years his account of the design of the universe was accepted as standard. During that long period, the basic pattern underwent many detailed modifications and was fitted out with many astrological and pseudo-scientific trappings. But in essence Ptolemy's followers agreed in portraying the earth as the center of the universe, with the sun, planets, and fixed stars set in transparent spheres orbiting around it. In this scheme of things, as modified for Christian usage, Hell was usually placed under the earth's surface at the center of the cosmic globe, while Heaven, the abode of the blessed spirits, was in the outermost, uppermost circle, the empyrean. But in 1543 the Polish astronomer Copernicus proposed an alternative hypothesis—that the earth rotates around the sun, not vice versa; and despite theological opposition, observations with the new telescope and careful mathematical calculations insured ultimate acceptance of the new view.

The map of the Ptolemaic universe represented here is a simplified version of a diagram in Peter Apian's *Cosmography* (1584). In such a diagram, the Firmament is the sphere which contained the fixed stars; the Crystalline Sphere, which contained no heavenly bodies, is a late innovation, included to explain certain anomalies in the observed movement of the heavenly

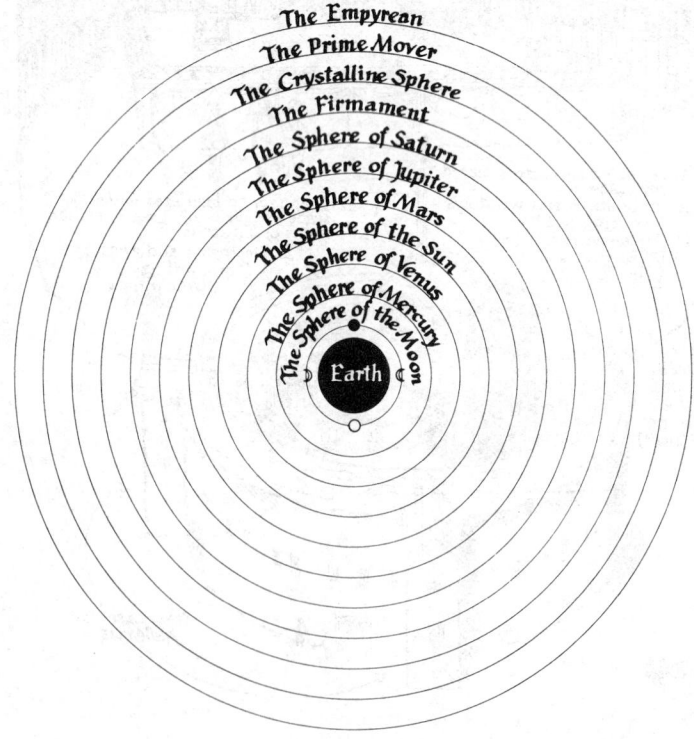

The Empyrean
The Prime Mover
The Crystalline Sphere
The Firmament
The Sphere of Saturn
The Sphere of Jupiter
The Sphere of Mars
The Sphere of the Sun
The Sphere of Venus
The Sphere of Mercury
The Sphere of the Moon
Earth

bodies; and the Prime Mover is the sphere which, itself put into motion by God, imparts rotation around the earth to all the other spheres.

Milton, writing in mid-seventeenth century, made use of two universes. The Copernican universe, though he alludes to it, was too large, formless, and unfamiliar to serve as the setting for the war between Heaven and Hell in *Paradise Lost*. He therefore adopted as his setting the Ptolemaic cosmos, but placed Heaven well outside this smaller earth-centered universe, Hell far beneath it, and assigned the vast middle space to Chaos.

PERMISSIONS ACKNOWLEDGMENTS

Bell & Hyman. Samuel Pepys: from *The Diary of Samuel Pepys*, transcribed and edited by Robert Latham and William Matthews. Reprinted by permission.

Eton College. Thomas Gray: from the manuscript of "Elegy Written in a Country Churchyard," transcribed by permission of the Provost and the Fellows of Eton College.

Granada Publishing Ltd. Christopher Smart: "My Cat Jeoffry" from *Jubilate Agno*. Reprinted by permission.

Isobel Grundy: Lady Mary Wortley Montagu: from *Essays and Poems by Lady Mary Wortley Montagu*, edited by Robert Halsband and Isobel Grundy. Copyright © 1977. Reprinted by permission.

William Heinemann Ltd. James Boswell: from *Boswell on the Grand Tour: Germany and Switzerland*, 1764, edited by Frederick A. Pottle. Reprinted by permission.

Houghton Library. Alexander Pope: from the manuscript of *An Essay on Man*, transcribed by permission of the Houghton Library.

Hyde Collection. Samuel Johnson: from the manuscript of *The Vanity of Human Wishes*, transcribed by permission of the Hyde Collection, Somerville, New Jersey.

McGraw-Hill. James Boswell: from *Boswell on the Grand Tour: Germany and Switzerland*, 1764, edited by Frederick A. Pottle. © 1928, 1953 by Yale University. Reprinted by permission.

W. W. Norton & Company, Inc. *Beowulf: Beowulf, A New Prose Translation* by E. Talbot Donaldson. Reprinted by permission of W. W. Norton & Company, Inc. Copyright © 1966 by W. W. Norton & Company, Inc. *Sir Gawain and the Green Knight: Sir Gawain and the Green Knight, A New Verse Translation* by Marie Borroff. Reprinted by permission of W. W. Norton & Company, Inc. Copyright © 1967 by W. W. Norton & Company, Inc.

Oxford University Press. Sir Philip Sidney: from *The Poems of Sir Philip Sidney*, edited by William A. Ringler, Jr. (1962): © Oxford University Press, 1962. From *Miscellaneous Prose of Sir Philip Sidney*, edited by Katherine Duncan-Jones and Jan Van Dorsten (1973): © Oxford University Press, 1973. Thomas Traherne: "Wonder" and "On Leaping over the Moon," from *Centuries, Poems, and Thanksgivings*, edited by H. M. Margoliouth (1958): © Oxford University Press, 1958. Reprinted by permission.

Penguin Books Ltd. Sir Philip Sidney: from Maurice Evans, ed., *The Countess of Pembroke's Arcadia*, published 1977. Reprinted by permission.

Pierpont Morgan Library. Alexander Pope: from the manuscript of *An Essay on Man*, transcribed by permission.

Scott, Foresman and Company. Geoffrey Chaucer: from *Chaucer's Poetry: An Anthology for the Modern Reader*, translated and edited by E. T. Donaldson. Copyright © 1975, 1958 by Scott, Foresman and Company. Reprinted by permission.

Trinity College. John Milton: from the manuscript of *Lycidas*, transcribed by permission of the Master and Fellows of Trinity College, Cambridge.

University Press of New England. Queen Elizabeth I: reprinted from *The Poems of Queen Elizabeth I*, edited by Leicester Bradner, by permission of University Press of New England. Copyright 1964 by Brown University.

Index